COMMITTEES IN THE
U.S. CONGRESS
1993-2010

COMMITTEES IN THE
U.S. CONGRESS
1993-2010

GARRISON NELSON

University of Vermont

CHARLES STEWART III

Massachusetts Institute of Technology

CQ PRESS

A Division of SAGE
Washington, D.C.

CQ Press
2300 N Street, NW, Suite 800
Washington, DC 20037

Phone: 202-729-1900; toll-free, 1-866-4CQ-PRESS (1-866-427-7737)

Web: www.cqpress.com

Cover design: El Jefe
Composition: C&M Digitals (P) Ltd.

⊗ The paper used in this publication exceeds the requirements of the American National Standard for Information Sciences—Permanence of Paper for Printed Library Materials, ANSI Z39.48-1992.

Printed and bound in the United States of America

14 13 12 11 10   1 2 3 4 5

ISBN: 978-1-60426-605-4
ISSN: In process

COMMITTEES IN THE U.S. CONGRESS
1993-2010

PART I:
Committee Backgrounds, Jurisdictions, and Member Rosters

PART II:
Members of Congress and Their Committee Assignments

Garrison Nelson
Charles Stewart III

ABBREVIATED TABLE OF CONTENTS

Detailed Table of Contents

Part IA: Senate Standing Committees
1993-2011

Part IB: Senate Select and Special Committees 1993-2011

Part IC: House Standing Committees
1993-2011

Part ID: House Select and Special Committees
1993-2011

Part IE: Joint Committees of the Congress
1993-2011

Part II: Members of Congress and Their Committee Assignments
1993-2010

Acknowledgments

This volume is the latest in a seven-volume set documenting all of the assignments to committees in the U.S. Congress from the First Congress in 1789 until the present. The project is an outgrowth of more than a generation of research on leadership recruitment and selection in the U.S. House of Representatives.

In conversations with House leaders, it became clear that the committee assignment process was an important signaling device to members of the House who were assessing their future careers. The decision of members to remain in the House and patiently accrue seniority rather than seek their state's governorship or a seat in the U.S. Senate was clearly related to positive signals that these future leaders received early in their careers from the existing House power structure.

The favorable committee assignments given to these talented members of the House was a way of letting them know that they had a future in the House and that the leadership was well aware of their abilities.

Three very important members of the House graciously shared their observations about the importance of committee assignments in shaping their leadership careers. John W. McCormack (D-Mass.), who served as Speaker of the House from 1962 through 1970, recounted how he was urged by Speaker John Nance Garner (D-Tex.) to run for a seat on the Ways and Means Committee in only his third year in the House. McCormack was elected by the Democratic Caucus for this seat in 1931, and it served as his base in advancing his leadership career.

McCormack's career as leader spanned thirty-one years from 1940 through 1970 in which he served as Speaker, floor leader and whip—the longest House leadership career in American history. It was the sponsorship of Representative McCormack by Speaker Garner that created the "Austin-Boston Connection," which dominated the leadership of the House from 1937 to 1989 and is documented in Anthony Champagne, Douglas B. Harris, James Riddlesperger Jr., and Garrison Nelson, *The Austin-Boston Connection: Five Decades of House Democratic Leadership, 1937-1989* (College Station: Texas A+M University Press, 2009).

Wilbur Mills (D-Ark.) told of his conversations with Speaker Sam Rayburn (D-Tex.) about efforts in Arkansas to get him to run for the U.S. Senate in 1944. According to Mills, Speaker Rayburn told him that "Wilbur, as long as you are on Ways and Means, there is no point in running for the Senate." Mills heeded Rayburn's advice and remained in the House and by 1956, at the age of 46, he became Chair of Ways and Means and served until 1974 when an unfortunate incident ended his distinguished career as the leader of that powerful committee.

Richard Bolling (D-Mo.) shared his conversations with Speaker Rayburn about the respective merits of serving on the Ways and Means Committee and the Rules Committee. It was Dick Bolling who clarified the linkage between one's committee assignments and ability to shape the legislative agenda. Bolling chaired the House Rules Committee from 1979 to 1983 and also chaired the Select Committee on Committees in 1973. Bolling's extraordinary grasp of congressional history and his enjoyable tolerance of intellectuals played a major role in opening the House to a generation of congressional scholars.

These were among the giants of the House.

A project of this scale needs talented personnel for it to succeed. I was fortunate to have access to an eager and extraordinarily capable set of undergraduates at the University of Vermont to assist me in this project. Many students participated in this effort as it stretched through the years and their efforts have been acknowledged in the previous volumes. University of Vermont students who assisted in this latest volume include Jeffrey Auger, Claire Eaton, Kat Nopper, Larry Sandage, and Matthew Sleeman.

Preparing this reference book also required the cooperation of a number of people in the congressional community. I was delighted by the assistance extended to me by the staffs of U.S. senator Patrick J. Leahy and that of former U.S. senator and U.S. representative James M. Jeffords. These staffs gave me the names of people on Capitol Hill who assisted me in tracking down hard-to-locate pieces of information.

The countless assistants on the Hill who filled in gaps in the book are impossible, to identify but I hope that the publication of this book will lighten their research burdens.

The Government Division of the Congressional Research Service in the Library of Congress contains the single greatest collection of talented congressional scholars assembled anywhere. Many of my original contacts in CRS have moved on and their contributions have been previously noted, but the incomparable Judy Schneider and Carol Hardy-Vincent have continued to be major sources of information. The encouragement of CRS over the years has been immense and greatly appreciated.

Other people who have been readily available for my questions include Richard A. Baker and Donald A. Ritchie of the Senate Historical Office; Nancy Kerwin of the Senate Library; Fred Buettler, the House's Deputy Historian; and Matthew Wasniewski of the House's Office of History and Preservation.

The late dean of congressional research on the Hill, Floyd M. "Doc" Riddick, the Senate's Parliamentarian Emeritus, was an invaluable source of information and encouragement.

There have been a number of academic supporters of the project who have not wavered over the years in their belief that this was an important use of my time when I often concluded otherwise. Included here would be my fellow toilers in the legislative fields: David Brady, Joe Cooper, Dick Fenno, Ron Hedlund, Sam Kernell, Nelson Polsby, David Mayhew, Sam Patterson, Robert Peabody, and John C. Wahlke.

Professors Charles Stewart III of M.I.T. and David Canon of the University of Wisconsin-Madison took the barely edited raw data that I had assembled for the first seventy-nine Congresses from 1789 to 1946, and produced a remarkably well-organized four-volume set for CQ Press, which was published in 2002. Professor Stewart and his associates at M.I.T. have continued to update and improve the modern committee assignment data, building off the dataset I had begun, which ran until 1993. It is this updated dataset that was the starting point for the listings contained in this current work. My gratitude for these two talented scholars and their skilled assistants goes beyond words.

Two departed colleagues inspired me throughout: Raul Hilberg, of the University of Vermont, who convinced me that big books could be produced at small universities; and Jack L. Walker of the University of Michigan, the quintessential realist, who made me understand that the only way to improve a political system was to understand fully how it operates.

A project of this magnitude takes its toll on one's good health and good humor. Having others tolerate you when both health and humor are in short supply requires a level of forbearance not always found in academic departments. For this reason, my colleagues in the Political Science Department at the University of Vermont are deserving of special mention. My children Shyla and Ethan were in grammar school when this project was conceived and now that they have grown into wonderful adults and made me a grandfather four times over, with Emily, Sophia, Addison, and Chase brightening my life, they may at last understand what impelled Dad to commit himself to this effort.

—Garrison Nelson
Burlington, Vermont
June, 2010

Preface

Politics and the Congressional Committee System

The U.S. Congress has the most powerful standing committee system in the world. Congress wields the most influence, spends the most money, and impacts the legislative agendas and relative success of the presidential occupants of the White House—arguably the most powerful political leaders on the planet—and it does so through the operations of its standing committee system.

Finding the locus of legislative power in the Congress has been a constant pursuit of the members of Congress itself and of generations of outside observers, be they journalists or academics. It has been true from the First Congress, as noted in the diary of Pennsylvania's U.S. senator William Maclay, who complained about President George Washington and Vice President John Adams challenging the institutional authority of the Senate, up to the present day, when some House members lament the expansive role of House Speaker Nancy Pelosi in imposing her agenda upon a reluctant membership. While presidential prerogatives can create external legislative pressure upon Congress, most locational assessments focus upon the institution's internal dynamics.

The reason is simple: power flows unevenly throughout each chamber of Congress from the elected party leaders to the committee chairs to the members themselves acting individually, as they may in the Senate, or collectively through issue-defined caucuses, as they often do in the House. And power points vary by issue and by Congress. Hence, the pursuit for locational authority is a never-ending one. This has been true for the more than two centuries since the First Congress assembled in New York City in March 1789.

Of all the locational assessments of legislative power, none have been more often quoted than those of the twenty-eight year-old Woodrow Wilson, whose Johns Hopkins doctoral dissertation was published as *Congressional Government* in 1885.

> . . . it is not far from the truth to say that Congress in session is Congress on public exhibition, whilst Congress in its committees is Congress at work.

> I know not how better to describe our form of government in a single phrase than by calling it a government by the chairmen of the Standing Committees of Congress.

Wilson, who chose not to travel the forty miles from Baltimore to Washington while he prepared his dissertation, identified the one key figure in the U.S. House by stating that "all are subordinate to the chairman of the Committee on Appropriations." Perhaps had Wilson spent any time in D.C., he might have learned that chairing House Appropriations at that time was Democratic protectionist Samuel J. Randall of Pennsylvania, who had already spent five-plus years as Speaker (1875-1881) and was able to transfer his power from the Speaker's chair to the Appropriations Committee. Wilson might also have noted that the first chair of Appropriations, Thaddeus Stevens of Pennsylvania, was the key architect of President Andrew Johnson's 1868 impeachment. Also, while Wilson was completing his research, James A. Garfield of Ohio, the committee's ranking member, was elected president in 1880, and James G. Blaine of Maine, a former senior member of Appropriations, was nominated in 1884. Regardless of Wilson's unique nineteenth-century perspective, it is safe to say that his statements about committee power had an enormous impact upon academic assessments of Congress in the post-World War II era of congressional scholarship.

Democratic Factionalism: Setting the Stage

For two generations between 1930 and 1994, the Democratic Party had two competing factions—the presidential Democrats and the congressional Democrats—and the committees of the U.S. Congress often became their battleground. The presidential Democrats shaped by President Franklin D. Roosevelt and his New Deal dominated the presidential nomination process while the congressional Democrats focused upon gaining and holding control of the two chambers of Congress. This was particularly true of the House of Representatives, where Democrats held a party majority in thirty of the thirty-two Congresses from 1930 to 1994, including one remarkable forty-year run from 1955 to 1994—the 84th to the 103rd Congresses. While the two Democratic factions shared the same party label, their demographic composition and their philosophical propensities differed.

The presidential Democrats were based in the big cities of the large states heavy with the electoral votes necessary for presidential victories in the Electoral College—New York, Chicago, Detroit, Philadelphia, and Boston. They were religiously and ethnically diverse—Catholics, Jews, immigrants, and later, blacks and Latinos. Philosophically, they were supportive of government involvement in the economic sector and distrustful of market-based solutions to pressing public needs. Growing out of the earlier Progressive Era, the presidential Democrats were generally characterized as liberal, and they saw federal government involvement as a way to ameliorate the societal tensions caused by the inequities that existed between the various social groups that comprised their Northern political majorities.

Their intra-party rivals, the congressional Democrats, were primarily Southern and retained their loyalty to the Democratic Party as an echo of their political home in the aftermath of the Civil War. It was the South that provided a post-Civil War political haven for Democrats. The eleven states of the Confederacy sent Democrat-only delegations to the House of Representatives for almost a full century. And their political allies in the Border States of Maryland, Kentucky, Missouri, and Oklahoma sent Democrat-dominant delegations to the House for almost as long. Demographically, they were a relatively homogeneous group of white, native-born, rural and small town Protestants. Coming from an economically depressed part of the nation that had had been devastated by the Civil War, they also saw federal government economic involvement as a positive factor in their restoration. While the Southern Democrats' economic agenda dove-tailed with that of the presidential Democrats, the lingering impact of deep racial tensions growing out of pre-Civil War slavery and post-Civil War segregation made the alliance between the two sectors of the Democratic Party tenuous. They generally opposed the anti-discrimination social agenda of the northern presidential Democrats.

However, both factions needed one another. Presidential Democrats needed the 120-plus electoral votes of the South as a base to add to their urban majorities in order to win the White House, while the congressional Democrats needed the presidential initiatives and legislative majorities engendered by their Northern allies to gain federal economic relief, generally in the form of defense appropriations targeted for Southern military bases. It was a valuable but combustible alliance.

From 1930 to 1994, it was the congressional committee system and the seniority rules that provided the links to keep the Democratic alliance intact. Most of the Southern and big city Democrats came from one-party, safe congressional districts that enabled them to obtain the seniority that guaranteed them leadership posts on the committees.

Congressional Republicans and the Conservative Coalition

The Congressional Republicans from the Northeast and the Middle West were more demographically similar—overwhelmingly native-born, white, and Protestant—and more philosophically united. With the West relatively small and Republican gains in the South yet to be achieved, these were the two regions that contended for Republican supremacy. The tensions between their big city internationalist Eastern wing—its small presidential faction—and their rural and small town isolationist Midwestern wing—its larger congressional faction—played out in international issues. However, the two wings seldom disagreed over the Republican domestic agenda of market-based policy solutions with balanced budgets, lower taxes, and less government involvement in the private sector. Although the northern Republicans were demographically similar to the southern Democrats, the political descendants of "the party of Lincoln" chose not to subscribe to the long-standing southern social agenda of racial segregation.

While the Republicans only organized the House twice in those sixty-four years—the 80th (1947-1949) and the 83rd (1953-1955) Congresses, they had a much greater legislative impact as a consequence of their philosophical alliance with many Southern Democrats. Generally known as the Conservative Coalition, Republicans and Southern Democrats controlled the congressional agenda for most of the years following President Franklin D. Roosevelt's ill-fated plan to "pack" the Supreme Court in 1937 and his ensuing efforts to "purge" conservative Democrats in the 1938 congressional

elections. While the Conservative Coalition held philosophical control of the congressional agenda, the Southern Democrats remained loyal to the party's leaders and kept the Democrats in procedural control of the House. Democratic dominance of the U.S. Congress had become a constant of American political life.

The key to this ambiguous mix of Democratic procedural control but conservative agenda control was the Democratic political hegemony in the South. With Democratic voting majorities back home and a rigidly enforced seniority system in Washington, conservative Southern Democrats were rewarded with power on congressional committees and were not punished for their challenges to the liberal and urban-based legislative agendas of Democratic presidents Franklin Roosevelt, Harry Truman, John F. Kennedy, and Lyndon B. Johnson. The House committees were often at the center of this conflict.

The 1946 Legislative Reorganization Act

From the first Congress in 1789 through the end of the 79th Congress in 1947, the standing committee system of the Congress grew dramatically, and on occasion, underwent revisions. However, these revisions were most often confined to one of the two chambers. No coordinated bicameral effort to upgrade and streamline the committee system took place before 1946.

It was during World War II that congressional leaders realized that their cumbersome committee system could not provide sufficient oversight of the expanding federal bureaucracy that had mushroomed during the New Deal years and the prosecution of the war effort. Dr. George B. Galloway, the staff director of the Joint Committee on the Organization of Congress in 1946, wrote in his book, *Congress at the Crossroads*, (New York, 1946):

Congress as an institution is heavily handicapped in many ways in performing its modern functions. Of all its handicaps the rising tide of legislative and other business is undoubtedly the basic obstacle. The business of Congress—once relatively limited in scope, small in volume, and simple in nature—has now become almost unlimited in subject matter, enormous in amount, and exceedingly complex in character. (p. 49)

The need was for a streamlined committee system and the Legislative Reorganization Act of 1946 (Public Law 79-601) was the solution. The Joint Committee on the Organization of Congress, led by U.S. senator Robert M. LaFollette Jr. (Prog-Wisc.) and U.S. representative A.S. Mike Monroney (D-Okla.) succeeded in having Congress pass this extraordinary reformation of its cluttered committee system.

By the time of the 1946 act, the number of House committees stood at forty-eight, following the addition of the Select Committee on Small Business and the highly controversial Committee on Un-American Activities. With the passage of the Act, the number was shrunk to nineteen. Six committees, four dealing with elections, were abolished outright. The new committee on House Administration took over the elections function as well as the legislative jurisdictions of six other committees. Six committees were also folded into the new committee on Public Lands (later called the Committee on Interior and Insular Affairs, and presently renamed the Committee on Natural Resources).

Committee consolidation occurred on both sides of the Capitol as the thirty-three standing committees of the Senate were halved by the Reorganization Act and it was left with fifteen committees. The Claims Committee was abolished and the new committee of Rules and Administration picked up the jurisdictions of six small committees while the two committees of Interstate and Foreign Commerce and Interior and Insular Affairs acquired the jurisdictions of five and four committees respectively.

Fears that many senior members would be upset about the disappearance of their committee chairmanships through consolidation were rendered moot by the stunning victory of the Republicans in the 1946 congressional elections. All of the Democratic chairs lost their posts through the party shift and were in no position to resist the changes. This fact eased the transition to the new committee structure. For the most part, the 1946 Reorganization Act created the parameters of the congressional committee system that remains in place today, over six decades later.

Two Party Control Eras: 1947-1995 and 1995-2011

The first party control era of the modern Congress, 1947-1995, represented a continuation of Democratic Party control of the Congress that dated back to 1931 in the House of Representatives and 1933 in the Senate. Democrats organized the House in forty-two of those forty-six years (91.3%) and they organized the Senate in thirty-six of those years (78.3%). There was one six-year period, 1981-1987, following the victory of President Ronald Reagan, when Republicans organized the Senate while Democrats maintained partisan control of the House. Divided government had become the norm following World War II. Republican presidents Dwight Eisenhower, Richard M. Nixon, Gerald Ford, Ronald Reagan, and George H.W. Bush faced Democratic majorities in the House for twenty-six of their twenty-eight years in office (92.9%) and in the Senate for twenty years (71.4%). Only Democratic President Harry Truman had to face a Republican Congress and that lasted only two years, 1947-1949.

The latest era, 1995-2011, has been a period of Republican domination and it represents the longest period of Republican control of the Congress since the 1920s. Republicans gained control of both houses in the 1994 mid-term election, often referred to as the Republican Revolution. They were able to control the House for twelve consecutive years, from 1995 until the mid-term election of 2006 and the Democrats' return to power.

The most dramatic shift in party control occurred in June, 2001, when Vermont's U.S. senator James M. Jeffords, the most liberal Senate Republican, tired of battling with the increasingly conservative agenda of the Senate Republicans and the administration of President George W. Bush, became an Independent and agreed to caucus with the Senate Democrats. Because the Senate had convened in January, 2001 with a 50-50 split, a "power-sharing" arrangement was agreed to, with majority status determined by the party of the vice president who as President of the Senate had the

authority to break ties. From January 3 to January 20, 2001 with Vice President Al Gore presiding, the Democrats were ostensibly the majority, but when Richard B. Cheney was sworn in on January 20, 2001, the Republicans became the majority. Each committee had an equal number of Republicans and Democrats and staffs were equally comprised as well. The arrangement was to last until one of the parties gained a numeric majority. The Jeffords switch ended the arrangement and Democrats became the Senate majority from June 6, 2001, until Republicans regained a Senate majority in the 2002 mid-term election.

Divided government continued to be the norm as Democratic president Bill Clinton faced a Republican Congress for six of his eight years in office, 1995-2001; while Republican George W. Bush faced a Democratic Senate for nineteen months in 2001-2003 and a Democratic Congress in his last two years in office, 2007-2009. Democratic President Barack Obama opened his administration with the Democratic 111th Congress, 2009-2011. Of the eighteen years covered in this volume, united party government between the president and both houses of Congress existed for only 8.5 years (47.2%).

Committee Changes, 1947-1995

Senate Standing Committees: The U.S. Senate functioned without legislative standing committees for the first twenty eight years of its existence (1789-1816). Its relatively small size and its reliance upon floor speeches had made a standing committee system unnecessary. But once standing committees were created they were seldom abolished and by 1914, the Senate had seventy-four committees. The committee system of the Senate was in danger of outnumbering the membership, which then stood at ninety-six. Many of these committees had ceased to function legislatively and were primarily a source of prestige and staff for their chairs.

Change came to the Senate more emphatically than it did to the House. Forty-one standing committees were abolished in 1921. Virtually all were "sinecure" committees whose impact upon the Senate's legislative business was minimal. The Legislative Reorganization Act of 1946 reduced the remaining thirty-three committees to fifteen.

Following the Reorganization Act, the Senate committees remained relatively stable with only three additions—the Committee on Aeronautics and Space Exploration in 1958, the Veteran's Affairs Committee in 1970, and the Budget Committee in 1974 as an outgrowth of the Budgeting and Impoundment Control Act.

By 1975, with committee memberships growing larger, it became clear that further reform was necessary. Senator Adlai E. Stevenson III (D-Ill.) chaired the Temporary Select Committee to Study the Senate Committee System committee, which folded the District of Columbia and Post Office and Civil Service Committees into the newly reconstituted Governmental Affairs Committee. The Aeronautics and Space Exploration Committee, once chaired by Lyndon Johnson, was absorbed by Commerce under its new designation, the Committee on Commerce, Science and Transportation. Six of the twelve committee name changes that occurred in the Senate between 1947 and 1994 took place during the 1977 reorganization. Following the recommendations of the committee, the Senate reduced its committees (standing, joint, and special) from 31 to 24, and its sub-committees from 174 to 118. As a result, the average number of total assignments per senator dropped from eighteen in the 94th Congress to eleven in the 95th. However, the size changes did not last and the 234 Senate standing committee assignments in 1977 grew to 306 by the 103rd Congress (1993-1995).

By the close of the 103rd Congress in 1994, the Senate retained its fifteen standing committees and had only added Small Business from its long-time select status in 1981. Four other Senate select committees had become "permanent"—Special Aging, Select Ethics, Select Intelligence, and Indian Affairs—and were named concurrently with the standing committees and functioned similarly, with the exception that they could not introduce legislation. But even here there was an exception in that Select Intelligence had been granted that authority.

The Senate went through more political change than the House in the post-1946 era due to the Republican victory of 1980 and the election of Ronald Reagan as president. Republicans controlled the Senate for six years, 1981-1987, until Democrats regained control in the 1986 election and held it for the next eight years, 1987-1995. In spite of the two party shifts, the Senate's sixteen standing and four long-term select committees remained as they were in the aftermath of the 1977 reorganization.

While this has not been the case over the past thirty years, the Senate historically has shown a greater propensity to revamp its committee system than has the House. One major reason for this is due to the lesser role that committees play in the Senate relative to the House. With unlimited debate and no Rules Committee to restrict amendments, the Senate has been able to conduct more of its legislative business on the floor than has the House. As a result, Senate careers are not as dependent upon committee assignments as House careers are. This lowers the stakes involved in any alteration in committee jurisdictions and makes reform easier to accomplish.

Senate Select and Special Committees: The Senate named forty select and special committees in the 1947-1994 era, many of which were used to promote the presidential candidacies of senators. Among senators with presidential aspirations who made use of these committees to increase their public profiles were Democrats John Sparkman of Alabama, Estes Kefauver of Tennessee, Lyndon B. Johnson of Texas, John F. Kennedy of Massachusetts, Hubert H. Humphrey of Minnesota, George S. McGovern of South Dakota, Frank Church of Idaho, Walter Mondale of Minnesota, and John F. Kerry of Massachusetts, and Republicans Robert J. Dole of Kansas, Dan Quayle of Indiana, and John S. McCain of Arizona. Apart from Sparkman's Select Small Business Committee, the committees led by those senators were temporary ones. Of the forty select and special committees named in those years, only four would be designated as "permanent"—Aging, Ethics, Indian Affairs, and Intelligence.

House Standing Committees: Changes in the committees of the House were infrequent between 1947 and 1994. The successful launching of earth orbiting satellites by the Soviet Union caused anxiety in Congress as well as the nation, and in 1958, the House Committee on Science and Astronautics was created. A payroll scandal concerning Adam Clayton Powell (D-N.Y.), the chair of the Education and Labor Committee, led to the creation of the House Committee on Standards of Official Conduct in 1967.

Although the House passed another Legislative Reorganization Act in 1970, the committees were not directly affected. But in 1973, the House Select Committee on Committees, chaired by Representative Richard Bolling (D-Mo.), was able to bring about some reform in the committee system. The two major changes were to abolish the House Committee on Internal Security (the successor to Un-American Activities) and to make the Select Committee on Small Business a standing one. Some jurisdictional shifting occurred, but the hopes of revamping the committees that long-time House reformers had sought failed to materialize.

It was in response to President Richard Nixon's expansion of executive power that led the Congress to enact the most important committee system change between 1946 and 1994. This was the Budget and Impoundment Control Act of 1974, which was intended to limit the president's authority to withhold funds appropriated by Congress for programs and projects that the President opposed. This act created the Budget committees in both the House and Senate. These committees quickly emerged as centers of institutional power.

Another reform movement to alter the House committee system occurred in 1979 with the Select Committee on Committees chaired by Rep. Jerry Patterson (D-Cal.). Its major impact was to consolidate overlapping energy jurisdictions within the renamed Committee on Energy and Commerce. Standing committee name changes were relatively infrequent in the 1947-1994 era, with only eleven recorded during that forty-eight-year period.

For the almost fifty years between 1947 and 1994, with Democrats holding the House for all but four of those years, the House functioned with the standing committee system that it created in the 1946 Reorganization Act. Apart from the net addition of three committees, what changes occurred took place in the growing number of committee assignments for each of the standing committees and the large number of subcommittees. From the First Session in 1947 through the Second Session in 1992 the number of assigned places on House standing committees grew from 493 to 850—a 72% increase—and the number of House subcommittees grew from 87 to 137—a 57% increase.

House Select and Special Committees: The House named forty-six select and special committees in the 1947-1994 period, especially during the 1970s when fourteen new ones were named between 1973 and 1979. Five of them acquired the status of quasi-standing committees: Aging; Children, Youth, and Families; Intelligence; Hunger; and Narcotics Abuse and Control, but four were terminated at the start of business in 1993 at the opening of the 103rd Congress. Only the Permanent Select Intelligence Committee survived.

Joint Committees: Joint committees have varied in their structures and jurisdictions. It was the hope of the 1946 Legislative Reorganization Act that joint committees would increase intercameral cooperation and reduce duplication. In both the 81st and 82nd Congresses (1949-1953) twelve joint committees were named. Over the next thirty years, twenty-five joint committees were named. By the 1970s, joint committees lost favor with the membership and gradually disappeared. The Senate's smaller membership gave it a heavier burden than the House in staffing these committees, and it initiated most of the joint committee terminations, either by not naming members to the panels or by actually legislating them out of existence.

Following the Senate Committee Reorganization Amendments of 1977 in the 95th Congress, only four joint committees were left in operation: Library, Printing, Taxation, and the Joint Economic Committee. The Joint Committee on the Library and the Joint Committee on Printing, which had existed in some form since the nineteenth century, were staffed by members of the House Administration Committee and the Senate Rules and Administration Committee. The Joint Committee on Taxation, created in 1926, was staffed by the five senior most members of the House Ways and Means Committee and the five senior most members of the Senate Finance Committee. The Joint Economic Committee was the only joint committee with membership independent of the standing committees. These four committees have achieved the continuity of standing committees.

Since 1975 only three temporary joint committees were appointed: Bicentennial Arrangements (1975-1977), Deficit Reduction (1987-1989), and the Joint Committee on Congressional Organization (1992-1993), which was named in the closing days of 1992, and none since.

Post-1995 Committee Changes

Senate Standing Committees: The Republican Revolution of 1994 gave Republicans party control of the Senate from 1995 until 2001. The 2000 election created an evenly divided Senate with fifty Republicans and fifty Democrats. That led to the implementation of a unique power-sharing arrangement to accommodate the even split among the senators that ended in June 2001, when Vermont's liberal Republican senator James M. Jeffords became an independent and caucused with the Democrats, giving them control of the Senate for the next nineteen months. Buoyed by President George W. Bush's post-9/11 popularity, Republicans were able to regain control of the Senate in the 2002 mid-term election. Over the next eight years, party control of the Senate has been evenly divided with Republicans holding the Senate for four years, 2003-2007, and the Democrats for four years, 2007-2011.

The Senate's sixteen standing and four permanent select committees remained intact with the names of three committees changed. Labor and Human Resources, originally known as Labor and Public Welfare, became Health, Education, Labor, and Pensions (HELP) in 1999, and Small Business was renamed Small Business and Entrepreneurship in 2001. The September 11, 2001, terrorist attacks on New York City and Washington, D.C., led the Senate to expand the jurisdiction of the Governmental Affairs Committee and to rename it as the Committee on Homeland Security and Governmental Affairs in 2004. This differed from the House's response, which was to create a new standing committee.

Political change did not lead to Senate committee change. Apart from the renaming of the afore-mentioned three committees, the Senate committee system remained intact. But the inexorable growth of standing committee assignments continued, with 344 seats assigned in the 111th Congress (2009-2011)—an increase of 38 from the 306 assigned in 1995 (12.4%) and an increase of 108 from the 242 standing assignments in 1977 (42.1%) at the time of the last major Senate committee reform.

Senate Select and Special Committees: During this most recent era, 1993-2010, the four permanent select committees of Special Aging, Ethics, Indian Affairs, and Intelligence have remained intact, and only two temporary special committees were created: one investigating accusations concerning President Bill Clinton and First Lady Hillary Rodham Clinton and their involvement in the Whitewater Development Corporation, and a committee to investigate the likely repercussions of the year 2000 changeover on computer software. This was a clear contrast from the earlier era.

House Standing Committees: A gain of fifty-plus seats in the 1994 mid-term election gave Republicans control of the House for the first time since 1954. While party change did not bring committee change to the Senate, the same cannot be said for the House. Led by the creative and controversial Speaker of the House, Newton L. Gingrich (R-Ga.), the Republicans implemented a far-ranging restructuring of the House standing committee system. Three long-term standing committees—District of Columbia, Post Office and Civil Service, and Merchant Marine and Fisheries were terminated and their jurisdictions were reassigned. This left the House with nineteen committees—the same number that remained following the 1946 Reorganization. While the number may have reverted to the earliest days of the modern Congress, Speaker Gingrich wished to indicate that a new era had dawned by renaming ten of the nineteen committees.

Unlike the Senate, Republican control of the House remained in place for the next twelve years—six with Democratic president Bill Clinton, 1995-2001 and six with Republican president George W. Bush, 2001-2007. While Republican control remained intact, Gingrich's service as speaker ended in 1999 after only four years, following the House Select Ethics Committee fining him $300,000 in 1997 for misleading the House's Standards and Conduct Committee during an investigation into the activities of his GOPAC organization. Following the abrupt resignation of Gingrich's presumed successor, Appropriations Chair Robert Livingston (R-La.) early in 1999, J. Dennis Hastert (R-Ill.) became Speaker and held that post for the next eight years of Republican control.

House committee jurisdictions were reorganized in 1995 along with multiple committee name changes. In the past eighteen years, there have been twenty-two name changes—ten in 1995 alone as House Speaker Newt Gingrich sought to create dramatic distance between the Republican 104th Congress and the twenty-three mostly Democratic Congresses that preceded it. Gingrich's departure in 1999 and Democratic resumption of House control in 2007 has led to seven of the prior committee names returning—Armed Services, Education and Labor, Energy and Commerce, Foreign Affairs, House Administration, Natural Resources, and Science and Technology. The only Gingrich-era name change currently in use is that of the Transportation and Infrastructure Committee.

Only one new standing committee was created during this period—the Committee on Homeland Security that was created in response to the September 11, 2001, terrorist attacks. It began its existence as a nine-member select committee in 2002, grew to fifty members in 2003, and became a standing committee in 2005, a status it continues to hold.

The 103rd Congress (1993-1995), the last pre-Gingrich Democratic one, had 870 member assignments and the 104th Congress (1995-1997) had only 772— a net shrinkage of ninety-eight seats and a percentage drop of 11.3 percent. Most of the shrinkage was due to the loss of eighty-one seats on the three terminated committees. Among the other seventeen seats lost were eleven seats from two internal committees—House Administration and Standards of Official Conduct.

But as noted earlier with the Senate, assignment growth resumed and there are 840 assignments in the 111th Congress—a modest growth of sixty-eight since 1995 (8.9%), much of which is attributable to the new thirty-three-member Committee on Homeland Security. There are now four House committees with at last sixty members—Appropriations, Armed Services, Financial Services, and Transportation and Infrastructure—with the latter two exceeding seventy members, the largest standing committees in the history of the Congress.

House Select and Special Committees: While Permanent Select Intelligence remained intact and Homeland Security became a standing committee, only five new select committees were created during these eight Congresses, a continuation of the practices of the early 1990s. Two deserve special notice. The Select Bipartisan Committee to Investigate the Preparation for and Response to Hurricane Katrina was named in 2005 in response to the devastation wreaked on New Orleans by Hurricane Katrina. No prior congressional committee had ever been called "bipartisan" and House Democrats suspected that the committee would "whitewash" President George W. Bush's response to the crisis, and none agreed to serve on the committee in spite of its title. As anticipated, most of the blame was laid upon the Democratic governor of Louisiana Kathleen Blanco and the Democratic mayor of New Orleans Ray Nagin for insufficient preparation. The other select committee, Energy Independence and Global Warming, first named in 2007 and renewed in 2009, has the earmarks of a select committee that may one day become a standing one.

Joint Committees: In spite of efforts to eliminate the Joint Committees on the Library and Printing, both survived, but the only new joint committee named since 1992 was the Temporary Joint Committee on Congressional Organization and it was terminated in 1993. So the Joint Committees on the Library, Printing, Taxation and the Joint Economic Committee remain in place.

Committee Assignments

The Senate: The assignment of members to Senate committees differs from that of the House because of the continuity principle within that chamber. The Senate is a continuing body and its members hold their assignments for as long as they wish. When vacancies occur, the assignments are referred to each party's committee on committees. As described by Congressional Research Service's Judy Schneider:

> Senate Republicans primarily use a Committee on Committees for this purpose, although the Republican leader nominates senators for assignment to some standing committees. Senate Democrats use a Steering and Coordination Committee to nominate Democrats for assignment to all standing committees. The

processes these panels use are distinct. Republicans rely on a seniority formula to make nominations, while Democrats make nominations on a seat-by-seat basis, considering a variety of factors.

Generally speaking, the assignment of members to Senate committees is not as contested as those of the House, for the simple reason that the Senate relies less upon its committees than does the House. Due to the importance of floor debate, a Senator need not be a member of the reporting committee to have a material impact upon the legislative outcome of a bill.

The less intense atmosphere of the Senate regarding committee assignments made it possible for Democratic Leader Lyndon Johnson to institute the "Johnson Rule" in 1953. Under this "rule", all Democratic senators were to have one major committee assignment (i.e., Finance, Appropriations, Foreign Relations, etc.) before any senator was assigned to a second major committee. This rule strengthened Johnson's influence among junior members.

Conflict within the Senate regarding chairmanships is less intense. With twenty regularly-appointed standing and select committees and sixty-eight subcommittees, virtually every majority member gets to chair a committee or a subcommittee while almost every minority member gets to serve as a ranking member on at least one committee or subcommittee. With less at stake, no Senate committee chairs have been deposed since the Legislative Reorganization Act was passed.

The House of Representatives: Methods of selection of members for the House standing committees have varied over the years. The original House committees were elected by the membership, but almost immediately, it became clear that it was far easier to have the Speaker make the committee assignments. This arrangement of Speaker-appointed committees lasted from 1790 until 1910, when the revolt against Speaker Joseph G. Cannon (R-Ill.) stripped that power from the office.

Democrats: From 1911 through 1974, the Democratic members of the Ways and Means Committee served as the Democratic Committee on Committees and made assignments for their party. This gave the ranking Democratic member on the Ways and Means Committee power comparable to the floor leader. Democratic members of Ways and Means could not, however, fill their own vacancies. This had to be done by election in the House Democratic Caucus. The major advantage of the system was that it removed arbitrary power from the Speaker, but its major disadvantage was that it created another power base among House Democrats and further blurred the lines between committee power and party power.

When Ways and Means Chair Wilbur D. Mills (D-Ark.) was caught in an embarrassing scandal in 1974, the House Democrats moved the power over committee assignments from Ways and Means to the Steering and Policy Committee, whose members were elected by the House Democratic Caucus and upon which the party's major leaders served (the Speaker, the Floor Leader, and the Democratic Whip). Speaker Thomas P. (Tip) O'Neill, Jr. (D-Mass.) who presided over the House from 1977 to 1987, used the Steering and Policy Committee to assign members to key committees whose legislative goals were more in concert with the party's national agenda. That objective continues to the present day.

Republicans: Republican House members created their own committee on committees in the wake of the Speaker's loss of power in 1910. Their committee consisted of a single member from each state with at least one Republican House member. Each member had votes weighted by the number of Republican members in the state delegation, with committee members from large states such as New York, California, Ohio, Illinois, and Pennsylvania wielding great power. Often, the most senior members of each state delegation (i.e., the "deans") served on the Committee on Committees and endeavored to get their fellow delegation members onto the most prestigious committees. In the wave of post-Watergate reform, Republicans also subjected their senior-most committee and subcommittee members to votes within the House Republican Conference, but the pre-1995 impact was minimal.

The Republican Revolution of 1995 moved the power of committee assignments into the leadership-dominated and renamed Steering Committee. Speaker Gingrich gave himself five votes on the committee and began 1995 with bypassing three senior Republicans for chairmanships. The other major alteration was to limit Republican chairs to only three consecutive terms, thus preventing them from gaining authority apart from the party leaders. The only exception was for the chairmanship of the Rules Committee. As a result of his assignment practices and the naming of task forces to get around committee jurisdictions, Gingrich greatly undermined the authority of the House committees and engaged in what Professor Barbara Sinclair of UCLA described as "unorthodox lawmaking."

Committee Chairs

Of all the congressional norms that observers find most puzzling, none engenders more opposition than the "seniority principle" that historically awarded the chairmanship of a congressional committee to the majority member with the longest continuous (i.e., unbroken) service on the committee. Complaints about senior senators often focus on their age with the clear inference that the older they become, presumably the more out-of-touch they become with the American people. Complaints about senior House members touch a different nerve. While age is often cited, it is presumed that senior House members are most likely to be elected from safe non-competitive one-party districts, whose political composition renders them ill-attuned to the diversity of viewpoints and values that comprise the nation. Beginning with the Gingrich ascendancy to the Speakership in 1995, the seniority principle has been eroded considerably in the House, first among Republicans, and now among the Democrats.

The Senate: Seniority had been an informal selection guide for Congress during much of the nineteenth century, particularly in the Senate in the years prior to the Civil War. Because there were so many Senate committees named and with most legislative business conducted during floor debate, the seniority principle did not engender much conflict.

In the post-1993 Senate, there are a number of instances when members are senior on more than one committee and they are obliged to choose which committee to chair. A recent example occurred in 2009 when Senate Agriculture Chair Thomas R. Harkin (D-Iowa), the third-ranking Democrat on the Health, Education, Labor, and Pensions (HELP) Committee, became chair when Sen. Edward M. Kennedy (D-Mass.) died in August, 2009 while second-ranking Sen. Christopher J. Dodd (D-Conn.) chose to remain as chair of Banking, Housing, and Urban Affairs. When Senator Harkin chose to chair the HELP Committee, he relinquished the chair of the Agriculture Committee to fifth-ranking senator Blanche Lambert Lincoln (D-Ark.). Each of the other senators above Lincoln chaired other committees: second-ranking Patrick J. Leahy (D-Vt.) chaired Judiciary; third-ranking Kent Conrad (D-N.D.) chaired Budget; and fourth-ranked Max Baucus (D-Mont.) chaired Finance. A recent health-related shift involved eighty-four-year-old Daniel K. Inouye (D-Hi.) replacing ninety-one-year-old Robert C. Byrd (D-W.Va.) at the helm of the Senate Appropriations Committee in 2009. These presumed "seniority violations" are noted in the case of each committee.

The House of Representatives: It was a different history in the House because of the centrality of committees in that chamber. Infamous House Speaker Joseph G. (Uncle Joe) Cannon (R-Ill.) used the power of naming committee chairs during his eight years as Speaker, 1903-1911, to push a conservative legislative agenda by removing fellow Republican chairs that he deemed as too progressive. Disaffected Progressive Republicans allied with Democrats in 1909-1910 to limit the Speaker's power by removing him from the Rules Committee, limiting his absolute power of recognition, and by eliminating his authority to name the members of House committees, thereby ending his authority over the committee chairs. In its place, the seniority principle for determining chairs became formalized. The seniority rule's major advantage was that it took much of the internal politicking out of the selection process for the committee chairmanship.

House Democrats: In the post-1946 era, complaints about seniority were most often linked to conservative southern Democratic chairs blocking civil rights legislation. The Democratic Study Group (DSG), created in 1959, with its large contingent of northern and western liberals, sought to limit the role of seniority in determining committee chairmanships. However, the only chair deposed prior to 1970 was U.S. representative Adam Clayton Powell (D-N.Y.), then the chair of the Education and Labor Committee. Powell, who was only the second African American to chair a standing committee, had become embroiled in a number of lawsuits, which limited his ability to manage the committee's business. Powell was excluded from House membership in March 1967. The Supreme Court ruled in June 1969 that he was entitled to his seat, but the chairmanship of Education and Labor remained with Carl Perkins (D-Ky.).

The greatest challenge to the seniority rule in naming House chairs occurred in 1971-1973 with a series of reforms known as the Subcommittee Bill of Rights, which was adopted by the Democratic Caucus. Under the new rules, committee chairs could be voted on by the Caucus and subcommittee chairs were to stand for election by the party members of their committees. The most dramatic impact of this change occurred in 1975 when the influx of the newly elected liberal "Watergate babies" led to the defeat of three long-time standing committee chairs: W.R. Poage (D-Tex.) on Agriculture; F. Edward Hebert (D-La.) on Armed Services; and Wright Patman (D-Tex.) on Banking and Currency. Since then, other Democratic committee chairs who lost their posts included C. Melvin Price (D-Ill.) on Armed Services at the beginning of 1985; and

Frank Annunzio (D-Ill.) on House Administration; and Glenn M. Anderson (D-Cal.) on Public Works and Transportation, at the end of 1990. In 1994, Daniel Rostenkowski (D-Ill.) was indicted in the House Post Office scandal and caucus rules required that he had to step aside as chair of Ways and Means. A similar fate would befall Ways and Means Chair Charles Rangel (D-N.Y.) in 2010. Rangel had defeated Adam Clayton Powell in the 1970 primary.

A voluntary displacement occurred in the 102nd Congress that continued into the 103rd when William H. Natcher (D-Ky.) was elected chair of Appropriations due to the ill health of its long-time chair Jamie L. Whitten (D-Miss.). A semi-official shift occurred in 1998 when the Committee on Banking and Financial Services received a resolution that "the powers and duties conferred upon the ranking minority members by House rules shall be exercised by the next senior member until otherwise ordered by the House." This was intended to give second-ranking John J. LaFalce (D-N.Y.) authority to displace the ailing ranking member Henry B. Gonzalez (D-Tex.).

With the Democrats' return to power in 2007, the only deposed chair was Energy and Commerce's John Dingell (D-Mich.), an eighty-two-year-old member serving in his record-breaking fifty-third year in the House, who lost a caucus vote to sixty-nine-year-old second-ranking member Henry Waxman (D-Cal.) in 2009.

House Republicans: With the forty year gap, 1955-1994, between their House majorities, the House Republicans of the 104th Congress were unencumbered by traditional (and Democratic) norms of committee chairmanship selection. In 1995, new House Speaker Gingrich chose second-ranking Thomas Bliley (R-Va.) to chair Commerce; second-ranking Henry Hyde (R-Ill.) to chair Judiciary; and fifth-ranking Robert Livingston (R-La.) to chair Appropriations. Carlos J. Moorhead (R-Cal.) was the ranking member bypassed by both Bliley and Hyde, and he retired in 1996. A voluntary displacement occurred in that Congress when James H. Quillen (R-Tenn.) was named "Chair Emeritus" and stepped aside to allow Gerald B.H. Solomon (R-N.Y.) to become chair of the Rules Committee.

One of the more unusual moves was for Speaker Gingrich to urge the retired Robert F. Smith (R-Ore.) to return to the House in 1997 to become chair of the Agriculture Committee over Larry E. Combest (R-Tex.) in the 105th. Smith retired again, and Combest would chair the committee in the 106th and 107th Congresses (1999-2003) but was replaced as chair by third-ranking Robert W. Goodlatte (R-Va.) in the 108th Congress, and he then resigned. A similar move occurred in 1983 when House Republicans sought to block James M. Jeffords (R-Vt.) from becoming ranking member on Agriculture by inducing Edward Madigan (R-Ill.) to leave Budget and outrank Jeffords. As the only House Republican to vote against President Reagan's 1981 tax cut, Jeffords had become a marked man in the House. Twenty years later, as a member of the Senate in 2001, Jeffords would wreak further havoc on the congressional Republicans.

In the 107th Congress (2001-2003), the House Republicans' three-term limit on chairmanships led to new chairs for Armed Services, Financial Services, International Relations, Education and the Workforce, House Administration, Judiciary, Resources, Transportation and Infrastructure, Veterans Affairs, and Ways and Means. While some like Ways and Means Chair William A. Archer (R-Tex.), retired, others moved to chair different committees. William M. Thomas (R-Cal.) left the chair of House Administration to replace Archer. Donald E. Young (R-Alas.) moved from chairing Natural Resources to chairing Transportation and Infrastructure, even though most of his relevant seniority had been accrued on the defunct Merchant Marine and Fisheries Committee. F. James Sensenbrenner, Jr. (R-Wisc.), who was scheduled for his third term as chair of Science, left to replace Henry Hyde (R-Ill.) as chair of Judiciary when Hyde moved to chair International Relations, replacing Benjamin A. Gilman (R-N.Y.), who had reached his six-year limit. After serving as chair of the Republican Conference, 1995-1999, John A. Boehner (R-Ohio), the third-ranking member, became chair of Education and the Workforce in the 107th Congress. It was clearly an exercise in "musical chairs."

The largest leap was that of Michael G. Oxley (R-Ohio), the third-ranking member of Energy and Commerce, who was named chair of Financial Services in 2001, without having ever been named to the panel and leapfrogging twenty-seven members of the committee who had served on it.

The pace of change slowed in the later Congresses, but it was new chairs Thomas Davis III (R-Va.) of the Government Reform Committee in the 108th Congress and Charles J. (Jerry) Lewis (R-Cal.) of Appropriations in the 109th Congress replacing three-termers. The only House committee exempted from this directive is the House Rules Committee, which has seen David T. Dreier (R-Cal.) serve as its chair for eight years, 1999-2007, and its ranking member for the last four years, 2007-2010.

The three-term limit for chairs was eliminated from the rules when Democrats regained control of the House in 2007.

Committee Membership and Political Ambition

The changes in the congressional committee system wrought by the 1946 Reorganization Act and the subsequent alterations that have sought to keep the U.S. Congress abreast of fast-moving developments in the past two decades, 1993-2010, are the focus of this work. How the committees were created, how they changed over time, and the contemporary issues that they confront today constitute the background of each committee chapter.

It is the membership of the committees that often determines the power of each panel as they compete for power within their respective chambers. For talented and ambitious politicians a career in the Congress provides them with the power, prestige, and visibility that they will need to further their dreams of full engagement in the nation's political process. This is especially true of the House of Representatives, which has been regarded as a major stepping-stone to the fulfillment of those personal dreams.

In the past thirty years, five politicians who later demonstrated presidential ambitions first sought membership in the House to launch their national political careers—Bill Clinton of Arkansas, Joe Lieberman of Connecticut, George W. Bush of Texas, John F. Kerry of Massachusetts, and Barack Obama of Illinois. Each of the five failed to be elected to the House. These five may have wished to emulate the presidential success of three House members of a previous generation—John F. Kennedy of Massachusetts, Lyndon B.

Johnson of Texas, and Richard M. Nixon of California—who were able to move through the House into the Senate and on to the White House itself.

The congressional committees upon which those three served gave their careers the direction that they needed to gain the nation's highest offices. For Richard Nixon, it was the House Committee on Un-American Activities and the investigation of White House foreign policy aide Alger Hiss that provided him with national visibility and brought him to the attention of Republican leaders. For John Kennedy, it was his aggressive investigation of labor union corruption while on the Senate's Labor and Public Welfare Committee and his willingness to challenge a key Democratic constituency that demonstrated his fitness for the presidency. For Lyndon Johnson, his long-time membership on both the House and Senate Armed Services Committees and his chairmanship of Aeronautical and Space Sciences indicated his readiness to lead the nation at the peak of Cold War tension.

Members choose the congressional committees that will further both their personal and their political goals. While some may see Congress as a stepping-stone, most members seem to regard service in the U.S. Congress as the ultimate goal and culmination of their aspirations. The committees that they choose to sit on often reveal what it was that these American public officials truly seek as their political lives take shape. For those members whose goal is to simply serve the people of their districts, the committees provide ample opportunity to "bring home the bacon" in the form of congressional appropriations to build the roads, bridges, and dams to enhance the economic well-being of their constituents. For others whose focus is upon lifting legal restrictions from those of the nation's citizens who have been barred from full participation in the political process, the committees provide that opportunity as well. While other members see in the congressional committees an opportunity to reset the national agenda and to challenge White House initiatives that they fear will move the nation off-course. The goals may vary but the committees provide opportunities for members to attain them. The congressional committees are yet another vantage point from which to understand the dimensions of a public career, and that is the reason why this set of volumes was initially designed more than thirty years ago.

Comparing the Committees

In analyzing the membership of the committees, key statistical indicators will be used. Membership size of each committee over time is an indication of their relative attractiveness; the mean seniority of the members—years in the Senate and terms in the House—is an indicator of their ability to hold onto their members, a measure that is further augmented by examining the retention rates of the committees from one Congress to the next.

Further examination of each committee's members will reveal who were the key leaders of the committee—the chairs and the ranking minority members. The political career aspirations of the committee members will be explored to see if the committees varied in the number of members serving on the committee who either sought power within the chamber as floor leaders or whips, or power outside the chamber as candidates for the presidency and vice presidency as in

the case of the U.S. Senate or as successful candidates for the Senate or state governorships as in the case of the U.S. House of Representatives.

The next section of each committee's chapter will present the listings of the formal jurisdictional areas. Jurisdictional listings for the House will include those for the 80th Congress (1947-1949), the first post-Reorganization Congress; the 94th Congress (1975-1977), the first to be governed by the early reform efforts; the 103rd Congress (1993-1995), the last Democratic-organized Congress of the twentieth century, and the 111th Congress (2009-2011), the present Congress, which will reflect the changes wrought by the Republican revolution, 1995-2007 and the Democratic restoration, starting in 2007. In the Senate, jurisdictions will be included for the 80th Congress (1947-1949), the first post-Reorganization Congress; the 95th Congress (1977-1979), the first Congress under the rules of the 1977 Committee Reform amendments; the 103rd Congress (1993-1995), the last Democratic Congress of the twentieth century, and the present 111th Congress (2009-2011) .

Each committee's functioning subcommittees are listed after the jurisdictions, but before the full and complete listings of each committee's membership from 1993 to 2010. In the 107th Congress, there are two separate Senate committee listings as a consequence of the departure of U.S. senator James M. Jeffords of Vermont from the Republican Party in 2001 to serve as an Independent and to caucus with the Democrats.

The rosters for each committee contain the full names, parties and states of each member presented in the order listed in the official documents, the *Congressional Record* and the *Congressional Directory.* In addition, each member's service in the chamber—by term for the House and by year for the Senate—and on the committee is listed. Should members serve on the committee at different intervals, there will be designations to indicate which period of service is listed in that Congress. Changes within each Congress are noted as members may have died, resigned the chamber, or moved to different committees within them. Special note is also made of members who have moved from the committee at the end of the Congress either due to their departures from the chamber: retirement, reelection or renomination defeat, or election or appointment to other offices or movement to other committees within the chamber.

Overview

The committee system of the U.S. Congress is one of the great contributions of the American system of government. Within the congressional committees, partisanship can be submerged as members come to grips with problems of common interest. The committees often act in united ways when they present their proposals to their full chambers. They often serve as a counter to the partisan spirit which otherwise pervades the Capitol.

The American congressional committees, with their power to investigate the executive branch through the oversight function and their control of executive spending through the appropriations process, have been successful in providing a further check and balance in the American political constellation that the Founding Fathers may not have foreseen. However, it is clearly in keeping with their wishes.

Two hundred and twenty years have passed since 1789 when Congress first opened its doors to conduct the nation's legislative business and from the very start, committees were used to guarantee that legislative proposals would receive full and careful assessment before they would be brought to the floor of their respective chambers. The influence of the congressional committees may vary between eras, but they will continue in place to address the nation's needs.

Bibliographical Essay

Backgrounds: For each of the essays on the committees in the U.S. Congress that have functioned since 1993 included in this volume, the Backgrounds section contains the organizational histories, membership information concerning changes in size and majority-minority ratios, the names of committee leaders—chairs and ranking members; party leaders; and other notables who may have served on the committee. Given the prominence of the modern-era Senate in presidential nominating politics, each of the Senate background sections contains material on the presidential aspirations of committee members. Regarding notables, committee members with Cabinet experience and who had been governors were given special attention.

In putting these essays together, extensive use was made of the public documents prepared by the various staffs of the House and Senate Historical Offices, the National Archives and Records Administration, the Government Division in the Library of Congress's Congressional Research Service (CRS), and the official documents of the committees themselves. Augmenting these official sources were the careful and objective analyses by the staff of *Congressional Quarterly* and those of the political scientists and historians who have devoted their careers to understanding and explaining the committee system in the U.S. Congress, the world's most important legislative body.

Committee Jurisdictions: Throughout this third book on the post-1947 Modern Congress, the official congressional sources—the *Senate Manual* and the *House Manual*—have been used to document the committee jurisdictions that were in place during the various Congresses covered during the 1947-2010 era. Jurisdictional change is an intriguing topic and a worthwhile examination of how these changes engender conflict may be found in David C. King, *Turf Wars: How Congressional Committees Claim Jurisdiction* (Cambridge, Mass.: John F. Kennedy School of Government, Harvard University, 1997).

Committee Overviews: Two classic nineteenth-century books that provide a starting point for any over time assessment of congressional committees are Woodrow Wilson's well-known *Congressional Government: A Study in American Politics* (Boston: Houghton, Mifflin, 1885); and the less well-known but equally valuable book by Lauros G. McConachie, *Congressional Committees: A Study of the Origins and Development* of *Our National and Local Legislative Methods* (New York: Thomas Y. Crowell, 1898).

Two books by congressional staff members with major academic credentials captured the congressional committee system during its major periods of transition. George B. Galloway's *Congress at the Crossroads* (New York: Thomas Y. Crowell, 1946) dealt with the committee system at the time of the Legislative Reorganization Act of 1946. It was during the 1970s that the committee system underwent another major transformation and that time is well-presented in Roger H. Davidson and Walter J. Oleszek, *Congress Against Itself* (Bloomington: Indiana University Press, 1977). Scott E. Adler's insightful *Why Congressional Reforms Fail: Reelection and the House Committee System* (Chicago: University of Chicago Press, 2002) is a sobering look at why so many ambitious reform efforts had left the House committees relatively unchanged for years.

Recent books that place committee reform into the wider framework of institutional change in Congress are Eric Schickler's ambitious *Disjointed Pluralism: Institutional Innovation and the Development of the U.S. Congress* (Princeton, N.J.: Princeton University Press, 2001) that probes four separate congressional eras from 1890 to 1989 to demonstrate that the different eras produced differing power configurations of party leaders and the committees; Julian E. Zelizer's *On Capitol Hill: The Struggle to Reform Congress and Its Consequences. 1948-2000* (New York: Cambridge University Press, 2004) documents the decline of the committee domination of the congressional agenda; and Stephen S. Smith's recent *Party Influence in Congress* (New York: Cambridge University Press, 2007) illuminates the resurgence of party influence on legislative behavior in both the House and the Senate. The continuing work of David W. Rohde and John H. Aldrich on "conditional party government" promises to yield even further insights as to how shifting power configurations will determine the legislative direction of the 21st century

Earlier descriptive institutional work by academic researchers on the committee system during the time when they held greater sway may be found in George Goodwin Jr., *The Little Legislatures: The Committees of Congress* (Amherst: University of Massachusetts Press, 1970); Barbara Hinckley, *The Seniority System in Congress* (Bloomington: Indiana University Press, 1971); and William L. Morrow, *Congressional Committees* (New York: Charles Scribner's Sons, 1969). A valuable compilation of essays on congressional committees written during the 1970s reorganizations of the committees may be found in Norman J. Ornstein, "Changing Congress: The Committee System," in *The Annals of the American Academy of Political and Social Science,* Vol. 411 (January 1974).

To date, the best contemporary overview of the committee system may be found in: Stephen S. Smith and Christopher J. Deering, *Committees in Congress* (Washington, D.C.: Congressional Quarterly, 1984), which is now in its third edition (1997). A fascinating analysis of the declining role of committees during the era of the Republican Revolution may be found in Barbara Sinclair, *Unorthodox Lawmaking: New Legislative Processes in the U.S. Congress*, 3rd ed. (Washington, D.C.: CQ Press, 2007).

In recent years, congressional scholars addressed the competition for power between the committees and the parties, as may be seen in Forrest Maltzman's *Competing Principles: Committees, Parties, and the Organization of Congress* (Ann Arbor: University of Michigan Press, 1998). This has been especially true of analysts of power in the House. Two scholars who stress the role of parties as "legislative cartels" making use of committees to control the congressional agenda are Gary W. Cox and Mathew D. McCubbins in *Legislative Leviathan: Party Government in the House* (Berkeley and Los Angeles: University of California Press, 1993); and *Setting the Agenda: Responsible Party Government in the U.S. House of Representatives* (New York: Cambridge University Press, 2005).

Committee Reference Works: A valuable starting point for committee histories are the two volumes prepared by the staff of the National Archives: Charles E. Schamel, et al., *Guide to the Records of the United States House of Representatives, 1789-1989* (Washington, D.C., 1989) and Robert W. Corren, et al., *Guide to the Records of the United States Senate, 1789-1989* (Washington, D.C., 1989).

The six previous volumes in this series provide a complete collection of the many thousands of member assignments to the standing, select, and special committees of the U.S. Senate and the U.S. House of Representatives: Garrison Nelson with Clark H. Bensen, *Committees in the U.S. Congress, 1947-1992*, Vol. 1, *Committee Jurisdictions and Member Rosters* (Washington, D.C., Congressional Quarterly, 1993); Garrison Nelson with Clark H. Bensen, and Mary T. Mitchell, *Committees in the U.S. Congress, 1947-1992*, Vol. 2, *Committee Histories and Member Assignments* (Washington, D.C.: Congressional Quarterly, 1994); David T. Canon, Garrison Nelson, and Charles Stewart III, *Committees in the U.S. Congress, 1789-1946*, 4 vols. (Washington, D.C.: Congressional Quarterly, 2002), Vol. 1, *House Standing Committees, 1789-1946*; Vol. 2, *Senate Standing Committees,1807-1946*; Vol. 3, *Members, 1789-1946* and Vol. 4, *Select Committees, 1789-1946.*

General Reference Works: Useful essays may be found in Donald C. Bacon, Roger H. Davidson, and Morton Keller, eds., *The Encyclopedia of the United States Congress* (New York: Simon and Schuster, 1995), 4 vols.; Joel H. Silbey, ed., *Encyclopedia of the American Legislative System* (New York: Charles Scribner's Sons, 1994), 3 vols.; Congressional Quarterly, *Guide to Congress*, 6th edition, 2 vols. (Washington, D.C.: Congressional Quarterly, Inc., 2007); and Paul J. Quirk and Sarah A. Binder, eds., *Institutions of American Democracy: The Legislative Branch* (New York: Oxford University Press, 2008).

Senate Standing Committee Official Histories: A number of committees have had valuable histories prepared for them by members of the Congressional Research Service and have been issued as committee prints and published by the Government Printing Office in Washington, D.C. Among those used for the Senate committee histories section of this volume and their years of publication include the following committee histories: *The United States Senate Committee on Agriculture, Nutrition, and Forestry, 1825-1998: Members, Jurisdiction and History,* Senate Document 105-24, 105th Congress, 2nd session (1998); Committee on Appropriations, *Committee on Appropriations, 141st Anniversary, 1867-2008,* Senate Document 110-14, 110th Congress, 2nd session (2008), this is the fifth history of the committee; Committee on Banking and Currency, *Committee on Banking and Currency, 50th Anniversary, 1913-1963,* Senate Document 88-15, 88th Congress, 1st Session (1963); *Committee on the Budget, 1974-2006,* Senate Document 109-24, 109th Congress, 2nd session (2006); Committee on Commerce, *History, Membership and Jurisdiction of the Senate Committee on Commerce, 1816-1966,* Senate Document 89-100, 89th Congress, 2nd session (1978); Committee on Commerce, Science, and Transportation, *A Brief History of the Senate Committee on Commerce, Science, and Transportation and Its Activities Since 1947,* S. Doc. 95-93, 95th Congress, 2nd session

(1978); Committee on Energy and Natural Resources, *History of the Committee on Energy and Natural Resources, 1816-1988,* Senate Document 100-46, 100th Congress, 2nd session (1988); Committee on Finance, *History of the Committee on Finance,* Senate Document 97-5, 97th Congress, 1st session (1981); this is the fourth history since 1976; Committee on Foreign Relations, *Committee on Foreign Relations, Millennium Edition, 1816-2000,* Senate Document 105-28, 105th Congress, 2nd session (1998); Committee on Government Operations, *Committee on Government Operations, United States Senate, 50th Anniversary, 1921-1971,* Senate Document 92-32, 92nd Congress, 1st session (1971); Committee on the Judiciary, *History of the Committee on the Judiciary, 1816-1981,* Senate Document 97-18, 97th Congress, 1st session (1982), the fifth history of the committee; Committee on Labor and Public Welfare, *History of the Committee on Labor and Human Resources, 1869-1979,* Senate Document 96-71, 96th Congress, 2nd session (1980), the committee's second history following *Committee on Labor and Public Welfare, United States Senate, 100th Anniversary, 1869-1969,* Senate Document 90-108, 90th Congress, 2nd session (1968); Environment and Public Works Committee, *History of the Committee on Environment and Public Works,* Senate Document 100-45, 100th Congress, 2nd session (1988); Committee on Rules and Administration, *History of the Committee on Rules and Administration,* United States Senate, Senate Document 96-27, 96th Congress, 1st session (1980); and the Committee on Veterans' Affairs, *Legislative and Oversight Activities during the 101st Congress by the Senate Committee on Veterans' Affairs,* S.Rept. 102-34 (1992).

House Standing Committee Official Histories: Official committee histories utilized in the House portion of the book include: Committee on Agriculture, *United States House of Representatives Committee on Agriculture, 150th Anniversary,* H.Doc. 91-350, 91st Congress, 2nd Session (1970); Committee on Appropriations, *A History of the Committee on Appropriations, House of Representatives,* H.Doc. 77-299, 77th Congress, 1st Session (1941); Committee on Foreign Affairs, *Survey of Activities, 92nd Congress: 105th Anniversary Issue,* House Committee Print (1973); Committee on Government Operations, *Activities of the House Committee on Government Operations, 97th Congress, First and Second Sessions,* H.Rept. 97-994, 97th Congress. 2nd Session (1982); Committee on House Administration, *Report on the Activities of the Committee on House Administration of the House of Representatives during the 102nd Congress,* H.Rept. 102-1083, 102nd Congress, 2nd Session (1992); Committee on Interstate and Foreign Commerce, *180 Years of Service: A Brief History of the Committee on Interstate and Foreign Commerce, U.S. House of Representatives,* House Committee Print, 94th Congress, 1st Session (1975); Committee on the Judiciary, *History of the Committee on the Judiciary of the House of Representatives,* H.Doc. 80-366, 80th Congress, 1st Session (1947, updated 1972 and 1982); Carol Hardy-Vincent, *History of the House Committee on Merchant Marine and Fisheries,* U.S. House of Representatives, Committee Doc., 101st Congress, 2nd Session (1990); Public Works Committee, *1883 to Present: Structure and Function of the Committee on Public Works, U.S. House of Representatives,* House Committee Print 93-48, 93rd Congress, 2nd Session (1982). Committee on Resources, *Historical Information of the Committee on Resources and Its Predecessor Committees,*

1807-2002: Preparation for a Bicentennial, House Committee Print, 107-G. 107th Congress, 2nd Session (2002); Committee on Rules, *A History of the Committee on Rules, 1st to 97th Congress, 1789-1981*, House Committee Print, 97th Congress, 2nd Session (1983); U.S. Representative Ken Hechler's monograph, *Toward the Endless Frontier: History of the Committee on Science and Technology, 1959-1979*, House Committee Print (1980); Committee on Small Business, *A History and Accomplishments of the Permanent Select Committee on Small Business, House of Representatives, 77th to 92nd Congress, 1941-1972*, H.Doc. 93-197, 93rd Congress, 2nd Session (1974); Committee on Veterans' Affairs, *History of House Committees Considering Veterans' Legislation*, House Print, 98-3, 98th Congress, 1st Session, 1983); and the Committee on Ways and Means, *The Committee on Ways and Means: A Bicentennial History, 1789-1989*, H.Doc.100-244, 100th Congress, 2nd Session (1988).

Select and Special Committees: A useful starting point is Walter L. Stubbs, comp., *Congressional Committees, 1789-1982: A Checklist* (Westport, Conn.: Greenwood Press, 1985). This book provides a list of most of the committees named arranged by keyword with a chronological list in the appendices. However, there are significant omissions from the Stubbs compilation. Therefore, the previously cited work by Canon, Nelson, and Stewart, *Committees in the U.S. Congress, 1789-1946*, should be consulted for a more complete census of congressional committees before 1946, especially for information about the special and select committees that dominated congressional organization for the first half-century of the republic. The Congressional Research Service worked with the first Select House Committee on Committees (1973-1975) chaired by Richard W. Bolling (D-Mo.), and it prepared an excellent report for the House Rules Committee entitled, "Guidelines for the Establishment of Select Committees" (1977, rev. ed. 1983). This report provides a solid framework for understanding the select committees of the House. Senate select and special committees and joint committees have not been as closely studied and the histories of those committees in this book were modeled after the Bolling Committee's work. It was Dick Bolling's two books, *House Out of Order* (New York: Dutton, 1965) and *Power in the House: A History of the Leadership in the House of Representatives* (New York: Dutton, 1968) that provided much of the intellectual thrust for committee reform.

The Nader Project Histories: In the 1970s Ralph Nader's Study of Congress Project published a number of "reformist" studies of the committees which provide valuable information at a time of committee transition. Among them were: David Price, *The Commerce Committees: A Study of the House and Senate Commerce Committees* (New York: Grossman Publishers, 1975); Mark Nadel, dir., *The Environment Committees: A Study of the House and Senate Interior, Agriculture and Science Committees* (New York: Grossman Publishers, 1975); Lester M. Salamon, dir., *The Money Committees: A Study of the House and Senate Banking and Currency Committees* (New York: Grossman Publishers, 1975); Peter H. Schuck, dir., *The Judiciary Committees: A Study of the House and Senate Judiciary Committees* (New York: Grossman Publishers, 1975); Ted Siff and Alan Weil, dirs., *Ruling Congress: A Study of How the House and Senate Rules Govern the Legislative Process* (New York: Grossman Publishers, 1975); and Richard Spohn and Charles McCollum, dirs., *The Revenue Committees: A Study of the House Ways and Means and Senate Finance Committees and the House and Senate Appropriations Committees* (New York: Grossman Publishers, 1975).

Archival Based Research: Archival-based researchers on committee histories should start with Joseph Cooper, *The Origins of Standing Committees and the Development of the Modern House* (Houston: Rice University Press, 1970). Cooper traces the development of the contemporary committees from their historical antecedents. The Senate's committees have been traced in George L. Robinson's doctoral dissertation, "The Development of the Senate Committee System" (Ph.D. dissertation, New York University, 1955).

Interview Based Research: Interviewing committee members became the hallmark of the research conducted by Richard F. Fenno, Jr. in his *The Power of the Purse: Appropriations Politics in Congress* (Boston: Little, Brown and Co., 1966) and *Congressmen in Committees* (Boston: Little, Brown and Co., 1973). Two books using the Fenno model on the Ways and Means Committee are John F. Manley, *The Politics of Finance: The House Committee on Ways and Means* (Boston: Little, Brown and Co., 1970), and Randall Strahan, *The New Ways and Means: Reform and Change in a Congressional Committee* (Chapel Hill: University of North Carolina Press, 1990).

Two academic researchers who moved into the Congress itself as members are David Price (D-N.C.) and Stephen Horn (R-Cal.). Their books on committees apparently did not dissuade them from the worth of congressional service. Price's committee books are: *Who Makes the Laws?: Creativity and Power in Senate Committees* (Cambridge, Mass.: Schenkman Publishing Co., 1972) and *The Commerce Committees: A Study of the House and Senate Commerce Committees*. Horn's book contrasts the Senate Appropriations Committee with its House counterpart in *Unused Power: The Work of the Senate Committee on Appropriations* (Washington, D.C.: The Brookings Institution, 1970).

Single Committee Books: Senate: Bernard Asbell, *The Senate Nobody Knows* (Garden City, N.Y.: Doubleday, 1978); Eleanor E. Dennison, *The Senate Foreign Relations Committee* (Palo Alto, Cal.: Stanford University Press, 1942); David N. Farnsworth, *The Senate Committee on Foreign Relations: A Study of the Decision-Making Process* (Urbana: University of Illinois Press, 1961). House: Walter Goodman, *The Committee: The Extraordinary Career of the House Committee on Un-American Activities* (New York: Farrar, Straus, and Giroux, 1968); Thomas A. Henderson, *Congressional Oversight of Executive Agencies: A Study of the House Committee on Government Operations* (Gainesville: University of Florida Press, 1970); Lewis J. Lapham, *Party Leadership and the House Committee on Rules* (New York: Garland Publishing, 1988); James A. Robinson, *The House Rules Committee* (Indianapolis, Ind.: Bobbs-Merrill, 1963); Albert C.F. Westphal, *The House Committee on Foreign Affairs* (New York: Columbia University Press, 1942). The House Appropriations Committee continues to fascinate students of Congress, as may be seen in Richard Munson's critical journalistic book, *The Cardinals of Capitol Hill: The Men and Women Who Control Government Spending* (New York: Grove Press, 1993); and in the more analytical book by D. Roderick Kiewiet and Mathew D. McCubbins, *The Logic of Delegation: Congressional Parties and the Appropriations Process* (Chicago: University of Chicago Press, 1991).

Biographical Research: Biographical assessment of committee leadership was pioneered in Manley's *The Politics of Finance* (1973) that treated its long-time chair Wilbur D. Mills (D-Ark.) in some detail. A work on Mills' role in expanding the reach of federal power is presented in Julian E. Zelizer, *Taxing America: Wilbur D. Mills, Congress, and the State, 1945-1975* (New York: Cambridge University Press, 1998). Mills' best-known successor is covered in Richard E. Cohen, *Rostenkowski: The Pursuit of Power and the End of the Old Politics* (Chicago: Ivan R. Dee, 1999) and James L. Merriner, *Mr. Chairman: Power in Dan Rostenkowski's America* (Carbondale, Ill.: Southern Illinois University Press, 1999). Leader-focused books on the House Rules Committee include Spark M. Matsunaga and Ping Chen, *Rulemakers of the House* (Urbana: University of Illinois Press, 1976); and Bruce J. Dierenfield, *Keeper of the Rules; Congressman Howard W. Smith of Virginia* (Charlottesville, Va.: The University Press of Virginia, 1987).

A leader-based model which others should emulate can be found in Andree E. Reeves, *Congressional Committee Chairmen: Three Who Made an Evolution* (Lexington, Ky.: University of Kentucky Press, 1993). This book examines the House Education and Labor Committee as it sought to deal with a large legislative agenda during the chairmanships of three very dissimilar people: Graham Barden (D-N.C.), Adam Clayton Powell Jr. (D-N.Y.), and Carl D. Perkins (D-Ky.).

A Senate book with a multi-committee focus on leaders is C. Lawrence Evans, *Leadership in Committee: A Comparative Analysis of Leadership Behavior in the U.S. Senate* (Ann Arbor: University of Michigan, 2001).

Analytical Research: A very sophisticated mathematical rendering of committee assignment choices may be found in Kenneth A. Shepsle, *The Giant Jigsaw Puzzle: Democratic Committee Assignments in the Modern House* (Chicago: University of Chicago Press, 1978). Following up on Shepsle's work is the valuable Scott A. Frisch and Sean Q. Kelly book, *Committee Assignment Politics in the U.S. House of Representatives* (Norman: University of Oklahoma Press, 2006).

Another analytical treatment which assesses differences in House committee performance through cluster-bloc roll call analysis is Joseph K. Unekis and Leroy N. Rieselbach, *Congressional Committee Politics: Continuity and Change* (New York: Praeger Special Studies, 1984). See also Glenn R. Parker and Suzanne L. Parker, *Factions in House Committees* (Knoxville: University of Tennessee Press, 1985) that attempts to probe intra-committee politics and John R. Baughman's *Common Ground: Committee Politics in the U.S. House of Representatives* (Stanford, Cal.: Stanford University Press, 2006).

Policy Based Research Works: Agriculture Policy: William P. Browne, *Cultivating Congress: Constituents, Issues, and Interests in Agricultural Policymaking* (Lawrence: University Press of Kansas, 1995). **Campaign Finance:** Robert L. Peabody, Jeffrey M. Berry, William G. Frasure, and Jerry Goldman, *To Enact a Law: Congress and Campaign Financing* (New York: Praeger, 1972). **Budget and Economic Policy:** Aaron Wildavsky, *Politics of the Budgetary Process*, 4th ed. (Boston: Little, Brown, 1964); Allen Schick, ed., *Making*

Economic Policy in Congress (Washington, D.C.: American Enterprise Institute, 1983); and Irene S. Rubin, *The Politics of Public Budgeting: Getting and Spending, Borrowing and Balancing*, 5th ed. (Washington, D.C.: CQ Press, 2006). **Civil Rights:** Daniel M. Berman, *A Bill Becomes a Law: The Civil Rights Act of 1960* (New York: Macmillan, 1962). **Defense Policy:** Barry M. Blechman, *The Politics of National Security: Congress and U.S. Defense Policy* (New York: Oxford University Press, 1990); and Randall B. Ripley and James M. Lindsay, eds., *Congress Resurgent: Foreign and Defense Policy on Capitol Hill* (Ann Arbor: University of Michigan Press, 1993). **Education Policy:** Eugene Eidenburg and Roy D. Morey, *An Act of Congress: The Legislative Process and the Making of Education Policy* (New York: W.W. Norton, 1969). **Environment Policy:** Gary Bryner, *Blue Skies, Green Politics: The Clean Air Act of 1990* (Washington, D.C.: CQ Press, 1993); and Richard E. Cohen, *Washington at Work: Back Rooms and Clean Air*, 2nd ed. (Needham Heights, Mass.: Allyn and Bacon, 1995). **Foreign Policy:** Holbert Carroll, *The House of Representatives and Foreign Affairs*, rev. ed. (Boston: Little, Brown, 1966); Cecil V. Crabb and Pat M. Holt, *Invitation to Struggle: Congress, the President and Foreign Policy* (Washington, D.C.: Congressional Quarterly, 1980); Charles W. Whalen, Jr., *The House and Foreign Policy: The Irony of Congressional Reform* (Chapel Hill: University of North Carolina Press, 1982); David R. Kepley, *The Collapse of the Middle Way: Senate Republicans and the Bipartisan Foreign Policy, 1948-1952* (New York: Greenwood Press, 1988); and Stephen A. Weissman, *A Culture of Deference: Congress's Failure of Leadership in Foreign Policy* (New York: Basic Books, 1995). **Intelligence Policy:** Loch K. Johnson, *A Season of Inquiry: The Senate Intelligence Committee Investigation* (Lexington: University of Kentucky Press, 1985); and David M. Barrett, *The C.I.A. and Congress: The Untold Story* (Lawrence: University Press of Kansas, 2005). **Labor Policy:** Eric Redman, *The Dance of Legislation* (New York: Simon and Schuster, 1973). **Public Works:** John A. Ferejohn, *Pork Barrel Politics: Rivers and Harbors Legislation, 1947-1968* (Stanford, Cal.: Stanford University Press, 1974); T.R. Reid, *Congressional Odyssey: The Saga of a Senate Bill* (San Francisco: W.H. Freeman, 1980); and Diana Evans, *Greasing the Wheels: Using Pork Barrel Projects to Build Majority Coalitions in Congress* (New York: Cambridge University Press, 2004); **Taxation and Spending:** Lucius Wilmerding, Jr., *The Spending Power: A History of the Efforts of Congress to Control Expenditures* (Hampden, Conn.: Archon Books, 1971 reprint of 1943 original); Allen Schick, *Congress and Money: Budgeting, Spending, and Taxing* (Washington, DC: Urban Institute, 1980); and Timothy J. Conlan, Margaret T. Wrightson, and David R. Beam, *Taxing Choices: The Politics of Tax Reform* (Washington, D.C.: CQ Press, 1989).

As should be obvious, the outpouring of published research on the committee system of the U.S. Congress is a testament to their centrality in the understanding of the American legislative process. Congressional committees may be less powerful today than in the not-too-distant past, but the "disjointed pluralism" of American political power configurations may return them once again to preeminence.

Introduction to the 1993-2010 Volume

Part I: Committee Backgrounds, Jurisdictions, and Member Rosters

This latest volume presents congressional committee assignment listings from January 3, 1993, the opening of the 103rd Congress until May 31, 2010, during the second session of the 111th Congress. It is a continuation of the first two volumes in the series, which were published in 1993 and 1994, *Committees in the U.S. Congress: Committee Jurisdictions and Member Rosters* (CQ Press, 1993) and *Committees in the U.S. Congress: Committee Histories and Member Assignments* (CQ Press, 1994). The initial volumes used the Legislative Reorganization Act of 1946 as the demarcation point of the modern Congress. This present volume covering the years from 1993 to 2010 deals with an era of major party control shifts and transformative change in the congressional committee system.

Committee Types and Jurisdictions

The U.S. Congress functions with a division of legislative labor. To make that division work, most committees are given legislative jurisdiction over specific items within the national agenda—defense, foreign policy, banking, energy, transportation, and housing, etc. Each committee is responsible for a specific area. Other committees cover a broader range of issues, such as the House and Senate Appropriations Committees, which determine federal spending priorities, and the tax-writing House Ways and Means Committee and Senate Finance Committee, which govern revenue policy. A third set of committees deals with the internal functioning of each chamber; these include the Rules, House Administration, and Standards of Official Conduct Committees in the House and the Rules and Administration Committee in the Senate.

Standing Committees:

The standing committees of the Congress are continuing entities, and do not have to be re-created at the beginning of each new Congress. The powers of the standing committees of the Congress have been institutionalized with their legislative responsibilities outlined in the respective Rules of each chamber. Within each chamber, there are further distinctions between the standing committees that relate to the eligibility of whom may serve on them. These are discussed in the opening chapters for each chamber.

Standing Committee Jurisdictions: For the Senate, the document containing the committee jurisdictions is the *Authority and Rules of Senate Committees* and the jurisdictions are presented in Rule XXV. Senate jurisdictional listings in this part of the volume include: the 80th Congress (1947-1949), the first Congress following the Legislative Reorganization Act;

the 95th Congress (1977-1979), the Congress following the Senate's 1977 committee reorganization; the 103rd Congress, the last preRevolution Democratic Congress; and the 111th Congress (2009-2011), the most recent Congress.

For the House of Representatives, the relevant document delineating those responsibilities is the *Rules of the House of Representatives* and the jurisdictions are presented in Rule X. The House jurisdictional listings in this part of the volume include: the 80th Congress (1947-1949), the first Congress following the Legislative Reorganization Act; the 103rd Congress (1993-1995), the last Democratic Congress prior to the Republican Revolution; the 104th Congress (1995-1997), the first Congress following the Republican restructuring of the committees; and the 111th Congress (2009-2011), the last Congress included in this volume.

Below is an example of a jurisdictional statement from the House Standing Committee on Agriculture for the 111th Congress:

From the *Rules of the House of Representatives* (as revised to June 16, 2009, H.Doc. 110-162):

[Rule X.1.(a)] Committee on Agriculture

1. Adulteration of seeds, insect pests, and protection of birds and animals in forest reserves.
2. Agriculture generally.
3. Agricultural and industrial chemistry.
4. Agricultural colleges and experiment stations.
5. Agricultural economics and research.
6. Agricultural education extension services
7. Agricultural production, marketing and stabilization of prices of agricultural products, and commodities (not including distribution outside of the United States).
8. Animal industry and diseases of animals.
9. Commodity exchanges.
10. Crop insurance and soil conservation.
11. Dairy industry.
12. Entomology and plant quarantine.
13. Extension of farm credit and farm security.
14. Inspection of livestock, and poultry, and meat products, and seafood and seafood products.
15. Forestry in general and forest reserves other than those created from the public domain.
16. Human nutrition and home economics.
17. Plant industry, soils, and agricultural engineering.
18. Rural electrification.
19. Rural development
20. Water conservation related to activities of the Department of Agriculture.

Select and Special Committees:

Select and special committees are created for the purpose of investigation and reporting to their respective chambers. Historically, there were distinctions between the select and special committees, but the intent of both terms was to indicate their temporary nature. In the modern Congress, the distinction between selects and specials has disappeared. The "select" designation is the preferred one. These committees are not authorized to introduce legislation and they generally are terminated with the filing of their investigative reports. However, the investigative reports which they file with their respective chambers are used as guides for the standing committees to report legislation. The jurisdictional responsibilities of the select and special committees are delineated in the establishing resolutions. Unlike other select and special committees, the Permanent Select Committees on Intelligence in both the House and the Senate are authorized to report legislation to their respective chambers.

In recent years, the Congress has adopted the concept of designating some select committees as "permanent." Included are those on Aging, Intelligence, Ethics and Indian Affairs in the Senate and Intelligence in the House. The jurisdictions of these permanent select committees have become part of the rules of their respective chambers, and therefore are not re-created at the beginning of each Congress. The post-1946 precedents for permanent select committees were the Small Business committees in each chamber. Although listed as a House select committee, Small Business was appointed every Congress from 1947 until it became a standing committee in 1975.

Similarly, the Senate Committee on Small Business, which also began as a select committee in 1950, became a Standing Committee in 1981. The membership of those select committees had been named at the same time as the standing committees.

Select Committee Jurisdictions: For most of the Senate select and special committees, only the jurisdiction contained in the establishing resolution is included. In addition, for those select committees which no longer exist, the date of termination of the committee is cited, as well as the authority by which the committee was terminated. Wherever possible, the date and number of the committee's final report is also noted.

The Senate select committees that are designated "permanent" include the jurisdiction contained in the establishing resolution and the jurisdiction in effect for the 111th Congress. In some cases, there will be a note indicating that the jurisdiction has not changed since the select committee's establishment. Below is an example of a jurisdictional excerpt from the House Select Committee on Energy Independence and Global Warming that was first created in 2007:

Jurisdiction from House Resolution 202, Section 4 (c), March 8, 2007

The select committee shall not have legislative jurisdiction and shall have no authority to take legislative action on any bill or resolution. Its sole authority shall be to investigate study, make findings, and develop recommendations on policies, strategies, technologies and other innovations, intended to reduce the dependence of the United States on foreign sources of energy and achieve substantial and permanent reductions in emissions and other activities that contribute to climate change and global warming.

Joint Committees: Joint Committees are distinguished by the fact that each chamber provides an equal number of members to serve on them. Once hailed as a major reform in 1946, only four joint committees survive: Library, Printing, Taxation, and Economic. Since 1993, no new ones have been added and none has been eliminated.

Joint Committee Jurisdictions: Because the four regularly-appointed joint committees have attained standing status, their jurisdictions are listed in both chamber's compilations of rules. Below is the jurisdiction assigned to the Joint Committee on Taxation that consists of ten members the five senior-most members of Senate Finance and House Ways and Means.

Jurisdiction, 110th Congress, 2007-2009

From Chapter 92. – POWERS AND DUTIES OF THE JOINT COMMITTEE– *Senate Manual* for the 110th Congress, Senate Document 110-1 (2008)., p. 964

It shall be the duty of the Joint Committee—

(1) Investigation—
   (A) Operation and effects of law.—To investigate the operation and effects of the Federal system of internal revenue taxes;
   (B) Administration.—To investigate the administration of such taxes by the Internal Revenue Service or any executive department, establishment, or agency charged with their administration; and
   (C) Other investigations.—To make such other investigations in respect of such system of taxes as the Joint Committee may deem necessary.
(2) Simplification of law.—
   (A) Investigation of methods.—To investigate measures and methods for the simplification of such taxes, particularly the income tax; and
   (B) Publication of proposals.—To publish, from time to time, for public examination and analysis, proposed measures and methods for the simplification of such taxes.
(3) Reports.—
   (A) To report, from time to time, to the Committee on Finance and the Committee on Ways and Means, and, in its discretion, to the Senate or the House of Representatives, or both, the results of its investigations, together with such recommendations as it may deem advisable.

Names of Subcommittees

Because subcommittees play such an important role in the functioning of the congressional committees, the names of the subcommittees that functioned in the past nine Congresses are included. Subcommittee names are less permanent than those of the full committees and they are generally announced a few weeks after the full committees have been named. Among the factors that influence subcommittee name changes are new policy areas, party control shifts, or the arrival of a new full committee chair who wishes to refocus the committee's activities.

The subcommittee names listed here come from official congressional documents, most notably, the *Congressional Directory,* which was published by the U.S. Government

Printing Office twice each session in the 80th Congress (1947-1949), then once each session from the 81st Congress (1949) through the 95th Congress (1978), and biannually since the 96th Congress (1979-1991). These listings were checked against the daily publication, the *Congressional Record*. Further confirmation of these listings was made by cross-referencing with non-governmental sources such as Congressional Quarterly's biennial listing of "Committee and Subcommittee Assignments" (Washington, D.C.: Congressional Quarterly Inc., 1951-date).

Membership on the Committees

This part of the volume is devoted to membership rosters of the committees which have existed during the nine Congresses from January 3, 1993, through May 31, 2010. The standing committees are listed alphabetically by the committee's current name with the member listings presented chronologically. A special note should be made of the 107th Senate. Because of the Jeffords defection that led to the majority Republicans becoming the minority and the minority Democrats becoming the majority, there are two listings for that Congress in the section on Senate sections of the book. The select and special committees are presented in the order of the dates of their creation

Membership lists contained in this book were developed from official congressional documents, most notably, the daily publication, *Congressional Record*. Since the *Congressional Directory* is now only published during second sessions of Congress, it often omits first session assignment changes. These listings were checked against the annual *Journals* published by each chamber of Congress. Further confirmation of these listings was made by cross-referencing Congressional Quarterly's biennial listing of "Committee and Subcommittee Assignments" (Washington, D.C.: Congressional Quarterly Inc., 1951-date), the year-end lists of committee and subcommittee assignments prepared by the *U.S. Code Congressional and Administrative News* (St. Paul, Minn.: West Publishing Co., 1947-date), and with regularly updated online lists provided by the Secretary of the Senate and the Clerk of the House of Representatives. A recent innovation that has eased the tracking of committee assignment changes is the Library of Congress' data retrieval system THOMAS.

Roster Contents

Each Membership Roster contains a complete history of an individual committee for a given Congress. Please refer to the sample membership roster while reading the following guide. The sequence of presentation of the committee membership rosters is:

IA. Standing Committees of the U.S. Senate
IB. Select and Special Committees of the U.S. Senate
IC. Standing Committees of the U.S. House of Representatives
ID. Select and Special Committees of the U.S. House of Representatives
IE. Joint Committees of the U.S. Congress

Committee Name and Congress: Each committee section is self-contained. Committee names are included in every individual congressional roster. The committee name

appearing on each roster is the one in place at the time of the appointment of members to the committee for that Congress. Changes in the committee's name are noted both in the jurisdiction section at the front of each committee's listing, as well as in the roster of the Congress in which the change occurred.

Service Dates of Senior Senate Members: The first set of the dates listed, **Service Dates of Committee Chair** refers to the original chair of the committee. The first date is the date on which the chair is named and the second date is the ending date of that chair's service. If the original Chair ceases to serve as Chair or leaves that committee before the end of that Congress, the service dates of the succeeding Chair will be listed as well. Congressional documents indicate the date on which a new Chair was selected. The abbreviations **Ch1** and **Ch2** are used to represent the first committee Chair and the second committee Chair. Two cases in which members may serve as chair but are not full replacements are the **ChA** designation used to indicate an Acting Chair and the **ChT** designation for Temporary Chairs. During the period in the 107th Congress from January 3 to January 20, 2001, when Democratic vice president Al Gore presided over the Senate, the Democrats were the majority party under the "power-sharing" arrangement that had been worked out to handle the fifty-fifty Senate party split. Their chairmanships listed during that time were temporary ones.

Service Dates of Senate Members: As a continuing body, service on a Senate committee does not terminate with the adjournment of a Congress. For Senate standing committees, **Service Dates of Majority Members** indicate the dates of service from the initial appointment of the majority party members to the committee through the appointment of new members to the committee in the subsequent Congress. As above, **Service Dates of Minority Members** indicate the dates of service from the initial appointment of the minority party members to the committee through the appointment of new members to the committee in the subsequent Congress.

Majority and Minority Status: Majority parties organize each Congress and a common practice has been to select the committee's majority party members earlier than the minority party ones. Party control of the Senate has changed four times over the past eight Congresses from 1993 through 2010. The first Congress in this volume—the 103rd (1993-1995)—was organized by the Democrats. Republicans replaced the Democrats as the Senate's majority party in the 1994 election and organized the Senate in the next three Congresses, the 104th (1995-1997), the 105th (1997-1999) and the 106th Congress (1999-2001). The 107th Congress (2001-2003) with its fifty-fifty split in the Senate led to the "power sharing" agreement that determined majority status on the basis of the party affiliation of the Vice President serving as President of the Senate, has been described earlier. On January 20, 2001, Republican Richard B. Cheney became Vice President and Republicans assumed majority status in the Senate. That arrangement ended with the June 6, 2001, defection of Vermont's James M. Jeffords from the Republican Party to serve as an Independent but caucusing with the Democrats, giving that party control of the Senate for the remaining nineteen months of the 107th Congress.

Republicans regained control of the Senate in the 108th Congress (2003-2005) and retained control in the 109th Congress (2005-2007). In the 2006 mid-term election, Democrats were able to parlay dissatisfaction with the administration of President George W. Bush to win a Senate majority for the 110th Congress (2007-2009) and to hold it in the 111th Congress (2009-2011).

Third party members have been rare in the Senate. In recent Congresses, Jeffords sat as an independent from June 2001 until his retirement in 2007. Jeffords was replaced by U.S. representative Bernard Sanders of Vermont who had served as an Independent in the House from 1991 to 2007. A special case involves U.S. senator Joseph I. Lieberman of Connecticut, the 2000 Democratic nominee for vice president. Lieberman was defeated in the 2008 Democratic Senate primary but ran as an independent in the general election and was reelected. He is designated as an Independent Democrat (IDem). Both Sanders and Lieberman caucus with the Democrats and have received their committee assignments from that party. Because Lieberman had endorsed Republican senator John S. McCain's presidential bid in 2008, there was sentiment to deny him the chairmanship of the Homeland Security and Governmental Affairs Committee. However, Senate Democrats wishing to provide a "filibuster proof" sixty-vote majority allowed Lieberman to retain his chair.

Another unusual case also involved a New Englander. Republican U.S. senator Robert Smith of New Hampshire informally left the Republican Party in July, 1999 to flirt with a presidential nomination from the U.S. Taxpayers Party. Smith never formally left the Republicans and returned in October in time to become chair of Environment and Public Works upon the death of Sen. John Chafee (R-R.I.).

Senate Select and Special Committees: Service dates for Senate select and special committees are dated from the time of the appointment of Members to the committee by the President of the Senate or the President *pro tempore*. The select and special committee members serve through the termination date of the committee either by resolution or by the submission of the committee's final report. For some select and special committees that continue for more than one Congress, there is no listing in the *Senate Journal* or the *Congressional Record* of the full complement of committee members after the first Congress in which they are named. This means that the committee members continued their service into the subsequent Congress. In these cases, the ending service date is listed as "Continued." When new members are named to continuing committees, the date on which they are named is used as the starting "service date" for that Congress. This will be indicated in the "Notes" for that roster. If no new members are named to a continuing committee, January 3 will be used as the starting "Service Date."

Because the full listings are seldom published in the *Congressional Record* or the *Senate Journal,* the list of members for each Congress were rechecked with the *Congressional Directory,* published committee reports, and THOMAS.

Chairs are generally those members chosen first by the majority party. Select and special committees are often comprised of members from different standing committees and therefore, are not as bound by strict adherence to seniority rules in selecting their chairs. In some cases, the chair will be chosen at the committee's first organizational meeting and will not be listed in the *Congressional Record* or the *Senate Journal.* The *Congressional Directory* or the committee's final report was used to determine the chair of these committees during their terms of service.

In recent years, the senior minority member on some of the Senate's select committees, such as Intelligence, has been designated as Vice Chair (**VCh**) rather than as "Ranking Minority Member" (**RM**). The Vice Chair is able to preside over the committee in the absence of the chair. This enhances the power of the committee's minority and presumably increases the bipartisanship of the select committee.

Service Dates of Senior House Members: The first set of the dates listed, **Service Dates of Committee Chair** refers to the original chair of the committee. The first date is the date on which the chair is named and the second date is the ending date of that chair's service. If the original Chair ceases to serve as Chair or leaves that committee before the end of that Congress, the service dates of the succeeding Chair will be listed as well. Congressional documents indicate the date on which a new Chair was selected. The abbreviations **Ch1** and **Ch2** are used to represent the first committee Chair and the second committee Chair. Two cases in which a member may serve as chair but are not full replacements are the **ChA** designation used to indicate an Acting Chair and the **ChT** designation for Temporary Chairs. When Democratic Caucus rules obliged Charles Rangel (D-N.Y.) to surrender his chairmanship of the Ways and Means Committee in 2010, second-ranking Fortney (Pete) Stark (D-Cal.) became ChT for one day and then was succeeded by third-ranking Sander Levin (D-Mich.) as ChA.

In recent years, there have been a number of occasions in the House when Ranking Minority Members were named the same day as the committee chairs but well in advance of the naming of the other minority members. These are indicated as **Service Dates of Ranking Member.**

Service Dates of House Members: The House of Representatives is not a continuing body and the service of committee members ends with the termination of each Congress. Since the ratification of the 20th Amendment to the Constitution in 1933, the termination of the Congresses is at noon on January 3 of odd numbered years. For House standing committees, **Service Dates of Majority Members** indicate the dates of service from the initial selection of the majority party members to the committee through the termination of the Congress. **Service Dates of Minority Members** indicate the dates of service from the initial selection of the minority party members to the committee through the termination of the Congress.

In some Congresses, the House did not make all of its committee assignments on the same day, nor did all members of each committee get named. Members named at a later date are included in the roster, but their dates of assignment are found under the heading **Vacancies Filled.**

Majority and Minority Status: As in the Senate, majority parties organize each Congress and the practice has been to select the majority party members earlier than the minority party ones. Party control of the House has changed only twice over the past nine Congresses from 1993 through 2010. The first Congress in this volume—the 103rd (1993-1995) —was organized by the Democrats. The Republican Revolution of 1994 gave the Republicans control of the House for the next six Congresses—the 104th through the 109th (1995-2007). Democrats regained control of the House in the 2006 midterm election and have organized the last two Congresses—the 110th and the 111th (2007-1201).

House Select and Special Committees: Service dates on House select and special committees are dated from the time of the appointment of Members to the committee by the Speaker of the House or floor leaders acting in his stead. The select and special committee members serve through the termination date of the committee as determined either by House resolution or by the submission of the committee's final report. For those select and special committees that continue for more than one Congress, the January 3 termination date for each Congress is used. Chairs are generally those members chosen first by the majority party. As in the Senate, select and special committees are often comprised of members from different standing committees and therefore, are not bound by strict adherence to the seniority rule in selecting their chairs. In some cases, the chair will be chosen at the committee's first organizational meeting and will not be listed in the *Congressional Record* or the *House Journal*. The *Congressional Directory* or the committee's final report was used to determine the chair of these committees during their terms of service.

Joint Committees: Because Joint Committees are composed of members of both chambers, the "Service Dates" are separated by chamber. Only rarely are the majority and minority members of each chamber named on different dates. Service dates of House members are listed first because they have specific termination dates, i.e., the closing date of that Congress.

As with Senate select and special committees, Senate members on joint committees are often not fully listed in the *Senate Journal* or the *Congressional Record* after the first Congress in which they are named. No full listing of the committee generally means that the committee members have continued their service into the subsequent Congress. In these cases, the ending "Service Date" is listed as "Continued." When new members are named to continuing committees, the date on which they are named is used as the starting "Service Date" for that Congress. This will be indicated in the "Notes" for that roster. If no new members are named, January 3 is used as the starting "Service Date." The full list of Senate members for each Congress has been checked with the *Congressional Directory* and when possible with committee reports.

One unusual practice of the joint committees is to shift senior titles between the chambers. For example, the Joint Committee on Taxation is comprised of the five senior most members—three majority and two minority—of House Ways and Means and Senate Finance. Because Section 7 of Article I of the Constitution requires that "All bills for raising Revenue shall originate in the House of Representatives; but the Senate may propose or concur with Amendments as on other Bills." it is the senior majority member of Ways and Means who always serves as chair during the first session and the ranking Senate member who serves as chair during the second session. The Joint Library and Printing Committees have an even more unique arrangement with the ranking House member serving as chair **(CVc)** and the ranking Senate member serving as vice chair **(VcC)**. The order is reversed in the second session and the two committees alternate the practice.

Rank

Each roster lists the committee membership in order of their ranking as indicated by the *Congressional Record* at the time of appointment. Changes in the ranking after the initial appointments are made are not reflected in the list, but are explained in the "Notes". Exceptions to this rule are rankings on some Select, Special, and Joint committees, where discrepancies between the *Congressional Record* and the committees' own reports are resolved in favor of the committee's reports. In the case of some Joint Committees, no chair or ranking minority member was identified in the *Congressional Directory*.

The following is a list of abbreviations used in the **Rank** columns:

Chr	First and only Chair of the committee during that Congress.
Ch1	First Chair of more than one Chair during that Congress.
Ch2	Second Chair of more than one Chair during that Congress.
Ch3	Third Chair of more than two Chairs during that Congress.
ChA	Acting Chair for part or all of that Congress
ChT	Temporary Chair for part or all of that Congress
CoCh	Co-Chair during that Congress.
RM	First and only Ranking Minority Member during that Congress.
RM1	First Ranking Minority Member of more than one Ranking Minority Member during that Congress.
RM2	Second Ranking Minority Member of more than one Ranking Minority Member during that Congress.
RM3	Third Ranking Minority Member of more than two Ranking Minority Members during that Congress
VCh	Vice Chair during that Congress.
VCh1	First Vice Chair of more than one Vice Chair during that Congress.
VCh2	Second Vice Chair of more than one Vice Chair during that Congress.
CVc	Chair for 1st Session of that Congress, Vice Chair for 2nd Session of that Congress.
VcC	Vice Chair for 1st Session of that Congress, Chair for 2nd Session of that Congress.
Del	Delegate to Congress (from Alaska and Hawaii before their admission to the Union, or from the District of Columbia, Virgin Islands, Guam, American Samoa, or the Northern Marina Islands), not counted in the committee size or party ratio unless otherwise noted.
RsC	Resident Commissioner (from Puerto Rico), not counted in the committee size or party ratio unless otherwise noted.

Name of Member

In most cases, this book uses the formal name of each member in order to correspond with the on-line *Biographical Directory of the United States American Congress 1774-2010* (Washington, D.C.: Government Printing Office). Informal names such as Bob or Bill are generally not used, even if that is how the member is best known. For those members who are best known by their middle name, e.g., U.S. senator J. Strom Thurmond (R-S.C.) and C. Trent Lott (R-Miss.) we have generally used an initial to abbreviate the first name.

In some cases, nicknames appear in parentheses, for example, George W. (Buddy) Darden (D-Ga.) and Randall (Duke) Cunningham (R-Cal.). In the case of women members who have married after being elected, they are listed twice but their assignments are located under their most recent name, for example, Mary Bono Mack (R-Cal.), Stephanie Herseth Sandlin (D-S.D.), and Cathy McMorris Rodgers (R-Mich.)

Party of Member

The party affiliation of each committee member at the time of appointment is listed. The following is a list of abbreviations used in the Party column:

Dem = Democratic Party
DFL = Democratic Farmer Labor Party (Minnesota)
Ind = Independent
NPr = New Progressive (Puerto Rico)
Rep = Republican Party
PpD = Popular Democrat (Puerto Rico)
IDem = Independent Democrat

State

The state, territory, or federal district from which each member of the committee is elected is listed. Under the State column the following designations have been used:

Ala. = Alabama
Alas. = Alaska
AmS = American Samoa
Ariz. = Arizona
Ark. = Arkansas
Cal. = California
Colo. = Colorado
Conn. = Connecticut
D.C. = District of Columbia
Del. = Delaware
Fla. = Florida
Ga. = Georgia
Guam = Guam
Hi. = Hawaii
Ida. = Idaho
Ill. = Illinois
Ind. = Indiana
Iowa = Iowa
Kans. = Kansas
Ky. = Kentucky
La. = Louisiana
Mass. = Massachusetts
Md. = Maryland
Me. = Maine
Mich. = Michigan
Minn. = Minnesota
Miss. = Mississippi
Mo. = Missouri
Mont. = Montana
Neb. = Nebraska
Nev. = Nevada
N.C. = North Carolina
N.D. = North Dakota

N.J. = New Jersey
N.H. = New Hampshire
N.M. = New Mexico
N.Y. = New York
N.M.I. = Northern Mariana Islands
Ohio = Ohio
Okla. = Oklahoma
Ore. = Oregon
Penn. = Pennsylvania
P.R. = Puerto Rico
R.I. = Rhode Island
S.C. = South Carolina
S.D. = South Dakota
Tenn. = Tennessee
Tex. = Texas
Utah = Utah
Va. = Virginia
V.I. = Virgin Islands
Vt. = Vermont
W.Va. = West Virginia
Wash. = Washington
Wisc. = Wisconsin
Wyo. = Wyoming

Years in: Senate/Comm.

Because the Senate is a continuous body, seniority is measured by the number of consecutive years served. Seniority in the Senate begins to accrue when a senator is sworn or appointed by a governor to fill a vacancy. Seniority on the committee begins to accrue from the date of initial naming to that committee. In the following example, taken from the Senate Agriculture, Nutrition, and Forestry Committee for the 108th Congress (2003-2005), James M. Talent (R-Mo.) who began as a Senator on January 3, 2003, is in his first year in the Senate and in his first year on the committee, which was appointed on January 14, 2003.

AGRICULTURE, NUTRITION, AND FORESTRY/108th Congress

				Years in:	
Rank	Name	Party	State	Senate	Comm.
9th	Talent, James M.	Rep	Mo.	1	1

The next example is taken from the same committee in the 109th Congress (2005-2007), which was appointed on January 6, 2005. Talent's third year of service in the Senate began on January 3, 2005, before his reappointment to this committee; hence, there is a "3" under the column Years in: Senate. Talent's third year of service on the committee began on January 14, 2005, after the appointment of members to this committee for the 109th Congress. As of January 6, 2005, the day members are appointed to the committee for the 109th Congress, Talent is still in his second year of service on the committee; hence, there is a "2" under the column Years in: Comm. Had Talent been reappointed to the committee after January 14, 2005, there would be a "3" under that column.

AGRICULTURE, NUTRITION, AND FORESTRY/109th Congress

Rank	Name	Party	State	Years in: Senate	Comm.
6th	Talent, James M.	Rep	Mo.	3	2

If a member departs from either chamber and subsequently returns to that same chamber, their previous service is included in the Years in: Senate or Terms in: House column. However, if a member returns to the committee, he or she is not credited for prior committee service.

Terms in: House/Comm.

Representatives are elected to two-year terms, which begin at noon on January 3 of each odd numbered year. Thus, seniority in the House is measured in consecutive terms of service. In the example of David R. Obey (D-Wisc.), the ranking member on House Appropriations in the 106th Congress (1999-2001), the 16 under the **Terms in: House** column indicates that Obey has served for sixteen consecutive terms in the House. Similarly the 16 under the **Terms in: Comm.** indicates that Obey has served sixteen consecutive terms on the Committee. Representative Obey in this example has been on the Appropriations Committee continuously since his first term in the House.

APPROPRIATIONS/106th Congress

Rank	Name	Party	State	Terms in: House	Comm.
RM	Obey, David R.	Dem	Wisc.	16	16

In some cases, House members are elected in special elections after the adjournment of a Congress. A member so elected is given seniority credit for that Congress, even though he or she was not sworn as a member of that Congress. For example, Robert E. Andrews (D-N.J.) was elected on November 6, 1990 both to fill the balance of James J. Florio's (D-N.J.) term in the 101st Congress and to his own term in the 102nd Congress.

The following example is taken from the House Education and Labor Committee in the 103rd Congress:

EDUCATION AND LABOR/103rd Congress

Rank	Name	Party	State	Terms in: House	Comm.
13th	Andrews, Robert E.	Dem	N.J.	3	2

Representative Andrews is listed as having served 3 terms in the House. He was credited for service in both the 101st Congress and the 102nd Congress.

*Period of Service on the Committee

In previous times a member would forfeit whatever seniority he or she had accrued when they left a committee. Therefore, if the member was reassigned to the same committee, former service was generally not counted, and he or she began accruing seniority as a new member. When a member serves more than one non-consecutive period of service on the same committee, that fact is marked by the member's name with an asterisk (*).

The number accompanying the asterisk indicates which period of service the member is serving during that particular Congress. On the sample roster, House Armed Services in the 109th Congress (2005-2007) there is a *1 next to Representative Howard P. (Buck) McKeon's (R-Cal.) name. This indicates that McKeon is in his first of more than one period of service on this committee. McKeon left Armed Services to chair Education and the Workforce in 2006 but rejoined Armed Services in the 110th Congress with his ranking unaffected by his departure. In the most recent 1993-2010 period, continuous seniority rules were less rigidly enforced. Many members, but not all, could (and did) leave committees and return with no discernible rankling impact upon their seniority.

ARMED SERVICES/109th Congress

Rank	Name	Party	State	Terms in: House	Comm.
8th	McKeon, Howard P. (Buck)	Rep	Cal.	7	*1 6

ARMED SERVICES/110th Congress

Rank	Name	Party	State	Terms in: House	Comm.
6th	McKeon, Howard P. (Buck)	Rep	Cal.	8	*2 1

On the sample roster, there is a *2 next to Robert E. Andrews's "Terms in: Comm." column, indicating that he served on the committee previously, and then left. He was in his second period of service on the committee in the 109th Congress. Andrews served on Armed Services in the 106th-108th Congresses until his departure in 2003 to serve on Select Homeland Security and he returned to Armed Services in 2005.

In extremely rare cases, a member will serve on the same committee for three separate periods. The third period of service is indicated by a *3. Sen. Charles E. Grassley (R-Iowa) served on the Senate Agriculture, Nutrition, and Forestry Committee three separate times.

Representatives occasionally serve on a committee in a temporary capacity, filling a vacancy until a permanent replacement is named. Temporary members are indicated in the text by a *T. Members do not accrue seniority while serving in a temporary capacity; therefore, temporary service is not reflected under the "Terms in: Comm." column.

Notes

The "Notes" contain information explaining unusual circumstances concerning ranking and committee size.

Chair and Ranking Minority Member:

Generally, the Chair of a committee is the majority member with the longest continuous service on that committee. Similarly, the Ranking Minority Member is the minority member with the longest continuous service on that committee. All other members are ranked in order of their seniority. There are however, many exceptions to this rule, and for the Standing committees, these exceptions are explained in the "Notes".

In the following example from the Senate Committee on Agriculture, Nutrition, and Forestry for the 109th Congress, Chair Saxby Chambliss (R-Ga.) with two years of service on the committee is ranked above Richard G. Lugar (R-Ind.), with twenty-eight years of service on the committee is ranked second; W. Thad Cochran (R-Miss.) with 26 years of service is ranked third; A. Mitchell (Mitch) McConnell (R-Ky.) with twenty years of service is ranked fourth; and C. Patrick Roberts (R-Kans.) with eight years is ranked fifth. The "Notes" indicate that Lugar was chair of the Foreign Relations Committee during the 109th Congress; Cochran was chair of Appropriations; McConnell was Senate Majority Leader; and Roberts was chair of Select Intelligence. None of them chose to chair Agriculture, Nutrition and Forestry.

AGRICULTURE, NUTRITION AND FORESTRY/109th Congress

				Years in:	
Rank	Name	Party	State	Senate	Comm.
Chr	Chambliss, Saxby	Rep	Ga.	3	2
2nd	Lugar, Richard G.	Rep	Ind.	29	28
3rd	Cochran, W. Thad	Rep	Miss.	27	26
3rd	Conrad, Kent	Dem	N.D.	19	19
3rd	Cochran, W. Thad	Rep	Miss.	27	26
4th	McConnell, A. Mitchell (Mitch)	Rep	Ky.	21	20
5th	Roberts, C. Patrick	Rep	Kans.	9	8

Ratio Changes:

Changes in the ratio of majority members to minority members are also explained, wherever possible, in the "Notes". Usually these changes in ratio are due to overall gains by one party or the other in special elections or, in the case of the Senate, by gubernatorial appointments. Before the 95th Congress, a Senate Resolution was necessary in order to change a Senate committee's size. The date of each such Resolution is noted. After the 95th Congress, the date used to indicate size and ratio changes is that of the appointment of additional members (see below under Additions).

Similarly, the House abandoned the practice of separate resolutions altering committee size following the 1974 committee reform amendments.

Delegates and Resident Commissioners:

Territorial Delegates from Alaska (until 1959), and Hawaii (until 1959), the District of Columbia, the Virgin Islands, Guam, and American Samoa and the Resident Commissioner from Puerto Rico were not allowed to accrue seniority nor were they included in the committee's party ratio until the 93rd Congress (1973-1975). These changing conditions of their membership are included in the "Notes." If the Delegate or Resident Commissioner is assigned on a different day than the other members of the committee, this is noted as well. In the 111th Congress, a Delegate from the Northern Mariana Islands was added to the House.

Party Switching and Third Party Members:

In addition, the seniority status and affect on the party ratio of a committee member who changes parties in the middle of a Congress, or who does not caucus with either the Democratic or Republican Party is explained in the "Notes" as well. As political polarization has increased in recent years, the number of members switching political parties after their initial elections has increased as well. At the point of their departures, the party that originally appointed them will vacate their assignments on the impacted committees.

Senate: Between 1947 and 1992, only three U.S. senators switched parties: Republican **Wayne Morse of Oregon,** became an Independent in 1952 and a Democrat in 1955; Democrat J. **Strom Thurmond** of South Carolina became a Republican in 1964; and Democrat **Harry Flood Byrd, Jr.** of Virginia became an Independent in 1970 but continued to caucus with the Democrats.

Since 1993, four U.S. senators switched parties: Democrats **Richard C. Shelby** of Alabama and **Ben Nighthorse Campbell** of Colorado became Republicans in the 104th Congress after the Republican takeover. The most dramatic switch took place in 2001 when Republican **James M. Jeffords** of Vermont became an Independent caucusing with the Democrats. That switch changed party control of the Senate for nineteen months in the 107th Congress. Republican **Arlen Specter** of Pennsylvania became a Democrat in 2009.

Although **Joseph I. Lieberman** of Connecticut became an Independent Democrat in 2006, after losing the Democratic primary that year, he continued to caucus with the Democrats. Republican **Robert C. Smith** of New Hampshire became an Independent for a few months in 1999 but returned to the party when a chairmanship became available.

House: Twelve representatives switched parties in the 1947-92 era. Eight Democrats became Republicans: **Albert W. Watson** of South Carolina in 1965; **John Jarman** of Oklahoma in 1975; **Eugene V. Atkinson** of Pennsylvania in 1961; **Robert Stump** of Arizona in 1983, **W. Phil Gramm** of Texas in 1983; **Andrew Ireland** of Florida in 1984; **Bill Grant** of Florida in 1989; and **Tommy Robinson** of Arkansas in 1989.

Only four Republicans became Democrats: **Vincent J. Dellay** of New Jersey in 1958; **Ogden R. Reid** of New York in 1972; **Donald W. Reigle** of Michigan in 1973; and **Peter A. Peyser** of New York in 1976. The Democratic switchers were from the North while most of the Republican switchers came the Sunbelt states.

Both Representatives Riegle and Gramm were elected to the Senate after their party switches.

In 1995 alone, five southern Democratic representatives became Republicans: **J. Nathan Deal** of Georgia, **Gregory H. Laughlin** of Texas, **Michael Parker** of Mississippi, and Louisianans **James A. Hayes** and **W. J. (Billy) Tauzin.** The pace of conversion continued as southern Democrats **Virgil H. Goode, Jr.** of Virginia, who served as an Independent in 2000, became a Republican in 2002; as did **Rodney Alexander** of Louisiana in 2004; **Ralph M. Hall** of Texas in 2004; and **Parker Griffith** of Alabama in 2009. **Wes Watkins** of Oklahoma, who served in the House as a Democrat (1977-91) returned as a Republican in 1997. After losing renomination in 2000, Democrat **Matthew G. Martinez** of California became a Republican but lost again in the general election.

Jo Ann Emerson of Missouri, widow of Republican Bill Emerson sat as an Independent following her 1996 special election but then was seated as a Republican in 1997.

While ten Democrats became Republicans, the only Republican to become a Democrat was **Michael P. Forbes** of New York in 1999.

The Jeffords Switch of 2001:

No event caused as much change in the history of the modern Congress as did the decision of Vermont's U.S. senator James M. Jeffords to leave the Republican Party and to declare as an Independent and to caucus with the Democrats. See Garrison Nelson, "Jim Jeffords's Long Goodbye," an op-ed article for *The New York Times* (May 25, 2001), p. 23.

Because the 2000 election had led to a 50-50 split in the Senate, a "power sharing" arrangement was worked out with majority status to be determined by the party affiliation of the Vice President (i.e., the President of the Senate). Democrat Al Gore presided over the Senate from Jan. 3, 2001 until Jan. 20, 2001 when he was succeeded by Republican Richard B. Cheney. The arrangement led to each party having the same number of seats on all Senate committees and an equal number of staff assistants on each committee. The arrangement was to remain in place until one party gained a numeric edge over the other.

On May 25, 2001, Jeffords announced his decision at a Vermont press conference. This changed the party split in the Senate to fifty Democrats, forty-nine Republicans and one Independent, but whose decision to caucus with the Democrat gave the Democrats majority standing. On June 6, the change was confirmed in the *Congressional Record* and the changes began to take place but it was not until July 10 that all of the new committee assignments had been made with Democrats gaining one additional seat on each Senate seat to give them majority control.

The impact of the Jeffords switches are noted in the Member Assignments section of Part 2 with a plus sign (**+**) . For most senators who shifted between majority and minority status, their rankings were unaffected. This may be seen in the case of the Energy and Natural Resources Committee with U.S. senators Daniel K. Akaka (D-Hi.) and Pete V. Domenici (R-N.M.) changing their status but not their ranks.

ENERGY AND NATURAL RESOURCES/107th Congress

Daniel K. Akaka (D-Hi.)

Cong.	Ranking	Years in: Senate	Comm.	Date of Assignment
107th	Min-2nd	11	11	Jan. 25, 2001
+107th	Maj-2nd	12	12	June 6, 2001

Pete V. Domenici (R-N.M.)

Cong.	Ranking	Years in: Senate	Comm.	Date of Assignment
107th	Maj-2nd	29	24	Jan. 25, 2001
+107th	Min-2nd	29	25	June 6, 2001

Democrats who served on committees that Jeffords switched to—Finance, Environment and Public Works, Veterans' Affairs and Special Aging—were dropped down a rank while Republicans on those same committees were moved up a rank.

VETERANS' AFFAIRS/107th Congress

Daniel K. Akaka (D-Hi.)

Cong.	Ranking	Years in: Senate	Comm.	Date of Assignment
107th	Min-3rd	11	11	Jan. 25, 2001
+107th	Maj-4th	12	12	July 10, 2001

Ben Nighthorse Campbell (R-Colo.)

Cong.	Ranking	Years in: Senate	Comm.	Date of Assignment
107th	Maj-5th	9	*2 6	Jan. 25, 2001
+107th	Min-4th	9	*2 7	July 10, 2001

Ranking Changes:

Occasionally, the original ranking of members as reported in the *Congressional Record* is changed later in that Congress, and the new ranking is reported in the *Congressional Record*. These changes are reported in the "Notes". For the Select, Special and Joint committees of both chambers, changes made in ranking after the original appointment are not always reported in the *House Journal, Senate Journal* or the *Congressional Record*, but are reflected in the membership listing of the committees' reports. As a rule, standing committee rosters are checked with the *Congressional Record*; select, special and joint committees are checked with committee reports wherever possible.

Seniority from Abolished Committees:

After the Committee System Reorganization Amendments of 1977, several Senate standing committees were consolidated. Many members of committees that were abolished—District of Columbia, Post Office and Civil Service, Aeronautical and Space Sciences—were reassigned to successor committees with their seniority intact. Therefore, their previous service on the abolished committee is included under the "Years in: Comm." column, and explained in the "Notes".

A similar circumstance occurred in the House following the 1995 reorganization when three committees were terminated—District of Columbia, Merchant Marine and Fisheries, and Post Office and Civil Service. Members who were reassigned to successor committees had their prior seniority acknowledged. Therefore, their previous service on the abolished committee is included under the "Terms in: Comm." column, and explained in the "Notes".

House Budget Committee:

Representatives who serve on the House Budget committee are allowed to take a leave of absence from the other committees to which they have been named without forfeiting their seniority. When they return to active service on these committees after having served on the Budget Committee, their absence and seniority status are explained in the Notes.

Vacancies Filled

Committee assignments are made at the beginning of each new Congress. Vacancies on the committees due to the departures of members from the previous Congress, or due to a committee size increase or ratio change are usually filled at this time. Sometimes, vacancies remain after the original assignment of members, and are filled at a later date. Majority vacancies that are filled after the date noted by "Service Dates of Majority Members" and minority vacancies that are filled after the date noted by "Service Dates of Minority Members" are listed in the roster *and* are noted under the heading Vacancies Filled. The majority or minority status of the member filling the vacancy, the rank of the seat being filled, his or her last name, and the date of assignment are listed under this heading.

Additions

When the ratio of Democrats to Republicans in the entire chamber changes in the middle of a Congress due to special elections, gubernatorial appointments, unfilled vacancies created by departing members, or a change in the party affiliation of a member, the agreed upon ratio of Democrats to Republicans on a committee may change as well. This results in either the forced departure of a member, or more commonly, to the addition of one or more new committee members. A member added under such circumstances is listed under the heading "Addition." Wherever possible, the reason for his or her addition is explained in the Notes. Unlike members filling existing vacancies, members added to a committee due to a size increase do not appear in the roster of committee members, therefore more information about that member is included. The rank to which they are assigned, their full name, party affiliation, state represented and the date on which they were assigned to the committee are included under the heading Addition.

Changes

All members who leave the committee before the January 3 termination date of the Congress, as well as the members who replace them (if they do so before January 3 of that Congress), are listed under the heading "Changes." The full name of the member, his or her party affiliation, state represented and date of departure or assignment is listed. For departing members, the reason for their departure is noted. Common reasons for departure include death, resignation, and appointment to another office. For replacement members, the member whose seat they are filling is noted.

The House and the Senate have differing procedures regarding notification of departures. In the House, a letter is sent by the resigning member to the Speaker indicating his or her departure from the committee. Generally the date that the letter is published in the *House Journal* or *Congressional Record* is the one used for the departure. Occasionally, a member will indicate an effective date of departure different from the date the letter is published, in which case both dates are noted. In the Senate, the departure officially takes place when the replacement member is named to the committee.

Chair changes: When the chair of a committee changes during a Congress, the name of the original chair, his or her party affiliation, state represented, the date of departure or cessation of duties as chair, and reason for departure or cessation is noted under the sub-heading Chair. Also listed are the name of his or her successor and the date of their succession. The date of succession used corresponds to the date

of passage of the appropriate Resolution, as reported in the official documents. When House Foreign Affairs Committee Chair Thomas P. Lantos (D-Cal.) died on Feb. 11, 2008, he was succeeded by second-ranking Howard Berman (D-Cal.) on March 11, 2008. Berman's assignments on Foreign Affairs for the 110th Congress in Part II are listed twice—the date of the initial assignment and the date of the chairmanship, as denoted by =.

FOREIGN AFFAIRS/110th Congress

Cong.	Ranking	Terms in: Senate	Comm.	Date of Assignment
110th	Maj-2nd	13	13	Jan. 12, 2007
=110th	Maj-Ch2	13	13	Mar. 11, 2008

Ranking Minority Member changes: No resolution is required for the succession of Ranking Minority Members. Therefore, when the original Ranking Minority Member of a committee departs a committee or ceases to serve in this capacity during a Congress, it is assumed that the succeeding Ranking Minority Member takes over from his or her predecessor on the date of the predecessor's departure as Ranking Minority Member.

Departures

Under this heading are listed all members who served on the committee until the end of the Congress, but who do not return to the committee at the beginning of the subsequent Congress. There are two categories of departures: Departures from the House or Senate and Departures from Committee.

Departures from the Chamber: Departures from the respective chamber of Congress can occur for a number of reasons.

Electoral factors play the major role in ending congressional committee careers. A number of departures from the chamber are due to a member's failure to be re-nominated in the state or district primary of his or her party ("Defeated for Renomination") or the failure to be reelected ("Defeated for Reelection"). In some Senate cases, a member appointed by a governor to fill a portion of the unexpired term of a departed Senator may fail to win election to fill the balance of the term ("Defeated in Special Election"). Also, a temporary assignee will resign the office once a successor had been elected, as in the case of Paul G. Kirk (D-Mass.), who was temporally appointed to fill the vacancy of the late U.S. senator Edward M. Kennedy in 2009. Kirk stepped aside in 2010 after Scott Brown (R-Mass.) won the special election.

"Died in office" refers to members who died during their congressional service. "Resigned and retired" refers to those members who leave the Congress to resume private life and retire from politics. In some cases, the resignation was due to illness which impeded the member from carrying out official duties. In other cases, there may have been legal difficulties which made the member's continued service problematical. "Resigned ..." for other offices refers to members who leave their congressional chamber to contest for another office or to accept appointment to another office. In these cases, an effort has been made to identify the office sought, if it was an elective post, or the office selected for, if it was an appointive post. House members frequently contest for Senate seats which accounts for a substantial number of departures from that chamber. Those who are successful are identified as "Elected to U.S. Senate." Those who are not are listed as "Lost Election to U.S. Senate" or "Lost Nomination for U.S. Senate" if they failed to survive their party's primary election.

Some House members from large states will leave the House for state-wide offices such as governor or state attorney general as a way of broadening their constituencies in hopes of obtaining later election to the Senate. In the pre-1993 era, a small group of members returned home for municipal offices, such as mayor. Included here would be Representatives John V. Lindsay (R-N.Y.) and Edward I. Koch (D-N.Y.), both of whom left the House to be elected Mayor of New York City. Since 1993, that route from the Congress has not been taken.

Senators seldom leave the Senate for state or local elective office. However, three post-1993 U.S. senators left to become governors: Republicans Dirk Kempthorne of Idaho in 1999 and Frank Murkowski of Alaska in 2002, and Democrat Jon S. Corzine of New Jersey in 2006.

Judgeships, both federal and state, often prove alluring to members of Congress who desire to remain in public life but wish to avoid the risks of reelection.

Senators are more likely to leave the chamber to accept appointment to the Cabinet or an ambassadorship.

A few members have run for president and had to relinquish their congressional seats as a consequence. Sen. Robert J. Dole (R-Kans.) and Rep. Richard A. Gephardt (D-Mo.) fall into this category. Most contemporary U.S. senators who seek the White House do so in the years that they are not up for reelection.

Leaving the Congress to accept employment in the private sector is relatively rare. However, it happened most recently when Rep. Robert Wexler (D-Fla.) left the House in 2010 to become President of the Center for Middle East Peace and Economic Cooperation.

Departures from the Committee: Departures from the committee refer to those cases where a Member retains his or her seat in the Congress but leaves the committee assignment. The most common reason for committee departures is assignment to another committee. In these cases, the committee to which the member has been assigned is identified.

Other reasons for committee departures include election to a major party leadership post, such as Speaker, floor leader, or whip. In other cases, the departure may be due to assuming the chairmanship or ranking minority slot on another committee.

In some cases, members leave a committee without a new assignment or leadership role. This generally occurs when election results change the number of seats available to a party on the committee or because a member chooses to focus his or her energy on fewer committee assignments.

The information under the Departures heading is listed in three columns: the first lists the reason for departure, the second lists the full name, state represented and party affiliation of all departing majority members, and the third lists the full name, state represented and party affiliation of all departing minority members.

On the sample roster of the House Armed Services Committee for the 109th Congress, under the "Departures from the House" heading, the Democratic victory in 2006 led to Republicans Wayne C. (Curt) Weldon of Pennsylvania, John N. Hostettler of Indiana, Jim Ryun of Kansas, Jeb Bradley of New Hampshire, and Robert Simmons of Connecticut were defeated for reelection and John H. (Joe) Schwarz of Michigan was defeated for re-nomination and thus did not return to the House or the committee in the 110th Congress. Also, Republican Joel M. Hefley of Colorado and Democrat Lane A. Evans of Illinois retired from the House.

Under the "Departures from Committee" heading, the consequence of the Democrats regaining the House is clear with four Armed Services Democrats moving up the committee prestige ladder to Ways and Means, Appropriations and Energy and Commerce.

All members of the committee in the example (including all members added to the committee or filling vacancies) not reported to have departed the committee either during the Congress under Changes, or at the end of the Congress under Departures will appear in the committee's roster for the next Congress. This makes it possible to follow the committee's membership from one Congress to the next and see exactly which members were serving at any given time.

ARMED SERVICES/109th Congress

Service Dates of Committee Chair: Jan. 6, 2005-Jan. 3, 2007
Service Dates of Majority Members: Jan. 26, 2005-Jan. 3, 2007
Service Dates of Minority Members: Jan. 26, 2005-Jan. 3, 2007
Roster Filled: Majority with 34 members, Jan. 26, 2005; Minority with 28 members, Jan. 26, 2005.

				Majority Terms in:						**Minority** Terms in:	
Rank	Name	Party	State	House	Comm.	Rank	Name	Party	State	House	Comm.
Chr	Hunter, Duncan L.	Rep	Cal.	13	13	RM	Skelton, Isaac N. (Ike)	Dem	Mo.	15	13
2nd	Weldon, Wayne C. (Curt)	Rep	Penn.	10	10	2nd	Spratt, John M. Jr.	Dem	S.C.	12	12
3rd	Hefley, Joel M.	Rep	Colo.	10	9	3rd	Ortiz, Solomon P.	Dem	Tex.	12	12
4th	Saxton, H. James	Rep	N.J.	12	8	4th	Evans, Lane A.	Dem	Ill.	12	10
5th	McHugh, John M.	Rep	N.Y.	7	7	5th	Taylor, G. Eugene (Gene)	Dem	Miss.	9	9
6th	Everett, R. Terry	Rep	Ala.	7	7	6th	Abercrombie, Neil	Dem	Hi.	9	*2 8
7th	Bartlett, Roscoe G.	Rep	Md.	7	7	7th	Meehan, Martin T.	Dem	Mass.	7	7
8th	McKeon, Howard P. (Buck)	Rep	Cal.	7	*1 6	8th	Reyes, Silvestre	Dem	Tex.	5	5
9th	Thornberry, William M. (Mac)	Rep	Tex.	6	6	9th	Snyder, Victor F.	Dem	Ark.	5	5
10th	Hostettler, John N.	Rep	Ind.	6	6	10th	Smith, Adam	Dem	Wash.	5	5

11th	Jones, Walter B. Jr.	Rep	N.C.	6	6		11th	Sanchez, Loretta	Dem	Cal.	5		5
12th	Ryun, Jim	Rep	Kans.	6	5		12th	McIntyre, Mike	Dem	N.C.	5		5
13th	Gibbons, James A.	Rep	Nev.	5	5		13th	Tauscher, Ellen O.	Dem	Cal.	5		5
14th	Hayes, Robert (Robin)	Rep	N.C.	4	4		14th	Brady, Robert A.	Dem	Penn.	5		5
15th	Calvert, Ken	Rep	Cal.	7	3		15th	Andrews, Robert E.	Dem	N.J.	9	*2	1
16th	Simmons, Robert	Rep	Conn.	3	3		16th	Davis, Susan A.	Dem	Cal.	3		3
17th	Davis, Jo Ann	Rep	Va.	3	3		17th	Langevin, James R.	Dem	R.I.	3	*1	3
18th	Akin, W. Todd	Rep	Mo.	3	3		18th	Israel, Steve	Dem	N.Y.	3		2
19th	Forbes, J. Randy	Rep	Va.	3	3		19th	Larsen, Richard R. (Rick)	Dem	Wash.	3		3
20th	Miller, Jefferson B.	Rep	Fla.	3	3		20th	Cooper, James H.S.	Dem	Tenn.	8		2
21st	Wilson, Addison G. (Joe)	Rep	S.C.	3	3		21st	Marshall, Jim	Dem	Ga.	2		2
22nd	LoBiondo, Frank A.	Rep	N.J.	6	2		22nd	Meek, Kendrick B.	Dem	Fla.	2	*1	2
23rd	Bradley, Jeb	Rep	N.H.	2	2		23rd	Bordallo, Madeleine Z.	Dem	Guam	2		2
24th	Turner, Michael R.	Rep	Ohio	2	2		24th	Ryan, Timothy J.	Dem	Ohio	2		2
25th	Kline, John	Rep	Minn.	2	2		25th	Udall, Mark	Dem	Colo.	4		1
26th	Miller, Candice S.	Rep	Mich.	2	2		26th	Butterfield, George K. Jr.	Dem	N.C.	2		1
27th	Rogers, Mike D.	Rep	Ala.	2	2		27th	McKinney, Cynthia A.	Dem	Ga.	6	*2	1
28th	Franks, Trent	Rep	Ariz.	2	2		28th	Boren, Daniel D.	Dem	Okla.	1	*1	1
29th	Shuster, William	Rep	Penn.	3	*1 1								
30th	Drake, Thelma D.	Rep	Va.	1	1								
31st	Schwarz, John J.H. (Joe)	Rep	Mich.	1	1								
32nd	McMorris, Cathy	Rep	Wash.	1	1								
33rd	Conaway, K. Michael	Rep	Tex.	1	1								
34th	Davis, Geoffrey C.	Rep	Ky.	1	1								

*1: Member's first period of service on the committee.
*2: Member's second period of service on committee

Note: Teritorial Delegate Madeleine Z. Bordallo (D-Guam) was allowed to accrue committee seniority but was not included in the party ratio.

Changes:

Majority:

McKeon, Howard P. (Buck)	Rep Cal.	June 29, 2006 Resigned committee; elected Chair of Education and the Workforce
Bilbray, Brian P.	Rep Cal.	June 29, 2006 Replaced McKeon
Gibbons, James A.	Rep Nev.	Dec. 31, 2006 Resigned the House; elected Governor of Nevada

Departures from the House:

	Majority			Minority		
Defeated for Re-election	Weldon, Wayne C. (Curt)	Rep	Penn.	None		
	Hostettler, John N.	Rep	Ind.			
	Ryun, Jim	Rep	Kans.			
	Bradley, Jeb	Rep	N.H.			
	Simmons, Robert	Rep	Conn.			
Defeated for Re-nomination	Schwarz, John J.H. (Joe)	Rep	Mich.	None		
Retired	Hefley, Joel M.	Rep	Colo.	Evans, Lane A.	Dem	Ill.

Departures from Committee:

Moved to Appropriations	None			Israel, Steve	Dem	N.Y.
				Ryan, Timothy J.	Dem	Ohio
Moved to Energy and Commerce	None			Butterfield, George K. Jr.	Dem	N.C.
Moved to Natural Resources	Shuster, William	Rep	Penn.	None		
Moved to Science and Technology	Bilbray, Brian P.	Rep	Cal.	None		
Moved to Ways and Means	None			Meek, Kendrick B.	Dem	Fla.

Part II: Members of Congress and Their Committee Assignments

Introduction to Part II

The second part of the volume provides lists of the committee assignments of the individual members. It is relatively self-explanatory. Presented below is the congressional committee history of long-time U.S. senator Daniel K. Akaka of Hawaii who has served in both the House and the Senate.

Under Akaka's name are listed: **Dates:** Senator Akaka's birth date; **House:** the dates of his service in the U.S. House; **Left the House:** the reason for his departure from the House. In his case, he was appointed to the U.S. Senate; **Senate:** the dates of his service in the U.S. Senate. He is listed as still "Serving in the 111th Congress." Since Akaka became a U.S. senator during a Congress rather than at the start of one, a note was added to explain the circumstances of his becoming a U.S. senator. In his case, it was due to his appointment to fill the vacancy caused by the death of U.S. senator Spark M. Matsunaga. Both the date of the appointment and the date of the seating of Senator Akaka are included. Because Akaka was already seated in the U.S. House, the dates were identical. More often than not, there is a gap between the two dates. Because he was seated while Congress was in session, Senator Akaka received committee assignments. Members who are appointed to the Senate or are sworn as members of the House after an adjournment receive credit for service but are not assigned to committees.

The order of committees is determined by the date of the member being named to them. Standing committees are listed first in each chamber, followed by select and special committees, and then by joint committees. If a committee name has been changed during the member's service, the date of the name change is used and the Congresses in which the committee functioned under that name are identified. In the pre-1993 Congress, Senator Akaka served on three standing committees and two select ones. In the Senate, he has served on five standing committees and two select committees. The committee listings indicate the **Dates** of service on each committee and the reasons for **Departure** from them. Each period of separate service on a committee is explained. The notations used in this part of the book are identical to those described in Part I.

Each Congress in which a member served on the committee is listed with their ranks noted. **Maj-3rd** would be a third-ranking majority member while **Min-3rd** would be a third-ranked minority member. **MjA** is a Majority Addition while **MnA** is a Minority Addition. The number following the additions is an indication that the committee has been enlarged to accommodate additional members. **MjR-1st** would be the first Majority Replacement while **MnR-1st** would be the first Minority Replacement. The chairmanship and ranking member notations are listed in the Introduction to Part I.

Members who switch parties during their congressional service are listed by their most recent identification and the dates of their service under the differing party affiliations are noted.

Special note should be made of the dual listings for senators who served in the 107th Congress (2001-2003). This was the Congress affected by the party switch of Vermont's James M. Jeffords. The first listing is the assignment prior to the Jeffords switch and the second listing is the assignment after the Jeffords switch and is designated with a **+ sign.**

Leadership posts are listed after the committee assignments. The only leadership posts included in this volume are the Senate President *pro tempore*, the Senate Majority and Minority Floor Leaders, and the Senate Majority and Minority Whips; and the Speaker of the House, the House Majority and Minority Floor Leaders, and the House Majority and Minority Whips. The notes included for them indicate the dates of their elections and the number of votes that were cast for them.

Daniel K. Akaka (D-Hai.)

Dates: Sep. 11, 1924
House: Jan. 3, 1977-May 16, 1990
Left the House: Resigned; appointed to U.S. Senate
Senate: May 16, 1990-date
Serving in the 111th Congress

S: Akaka was appointed to the 101st Congress, May 16, 1990, to fill the vacancy caused by the death of Spark M. Matsunaga (D-Hai.) and was subsequently elected. He was seated on May 16, 1990, and was assigned to committees.

HOUSE STANDING COMMITTEES

1st AGRICULTURE
Dates: Jan. 19, 1977-Jan. 3, 1981
Departure: Moved to Appropriations

2nd MERCHANT MARINE AND FISHERIES
Dates: Jan. 19, 1977-Jan. 3, 1981
Departure: Moved to Appropriations

3rd APPROPRIATIONS
Dates: Jan. 28, 1981-May 16, 1990
Departure: Resigned the House; appointed U.S. Senator

HOUSE SELECT COMMITTEES

1st SELECT POPULATION
Dates: Oct. 14, 1977-Dec. 29, 1978
Termination: House Report 1842 (95-2) filed

2nd SELECT NARCOTICS ABUSE AND CONTROL (Temporary)
1st Dates: Mar. 16, 1978-Jan. 3, 1979
1st Departure: Left committee; no new assignment
2nd Dates: Feb. 25, 1981-May 16, 1990
2nd Departure: Resigned the House; appointed U.S. Senator

SENATE STANDING COMMITTEES

1st ENERGY AND NATURAL RESOURCES
Dates: May 16, 1990-Jan. 21, 2009
Departure: Left committee; no new assignment

Cong.	Ranking	Years in: Senate	Comm.	Date of Assignment
103rd	Maj-6th	3	3	Jan. 7, 1993
104th	Min-6th	5	5	Jan. 4, 1995
105th	Min-4th	7	7	Jan. 9, 1997
106th	Min-2nd	9	9	Jan. 7, 1999
107th	Min-2nd	11	11	Jan. 25, 2001
+107th	Maj-2nd	12	12	June 6, 2001
108th	Min-2nd	13	13	Jan. 15, 2003
109th	Min-2nd	15	15	Jan. 6, 2005
110th	Maj-2nd	17	17	Jan. 12, 2007

2nd GOVERNMENTAL AFFAIRS renamed Oct. 9, 2004
HOMELAND SECURITY AND GOVERNMENTAL AFFAIRS
Dates: May 16, 1990-date
Departure: Still serving in the 111th Congress

Cong.	Ranking	Years in: Senate	Comm.	Date of Assignment
103rd	Maj-7th	3	3	Jan. 7, 1993
104th	Min-6th	5	5	Jan. 4, 1995
105th	Min-4th	7	7	Jan. 9, 1997
106th	Min-3rd	9	9	Jan. 7, 1999
107th	Min-3rd	11	11	Jan. 25, 2001
+107th	Maj-3rd	12	12	June 6, 2001
108th	Min-3rd	13	13	Jan. 15, 2003
109th	Min-3rd	15	15	Jan. 6, 2005
110th	Maj-3rd	17	17	Jan. 12, 2007
111th	Maj-3rd	19	19	Jan. 21, 2009

3rd VETERANS' AFFAIRS
Dates: May 16, 1990-date
Departure: Still serving in the 111th Congress

Cong.	Ranking	Years in: Senate	Comm.	Date of Assignment
103rd	Maj-5th	3	3	Jan. 21, 1993
104th	Min-3rd	5	5	Jan. 6, 1995
105th	Min-3rd	7	7	Jan. 9, 1997
106th	Min-3rd	9	9	Jan. 7, 1999
107th	Min-3rd	11	11	Jan. 25, 2001
+107th	Maj-4th	12	12	July 10, 2001

Cong.	Ranking	Years in: Senate	Comm.	Date of Assignment
108th	Min-4th	13	13	Jan. 15, 2003
109th	Min-RM	15	15	Jan. 6, 2005
110th	Maj-Chr	17	17	Jan 12, 2007
111th	Maj-Chr	19	19	Jan. 21, 2009

4th ARMED SERVICES
Dates: Jan. 25, 2001-date
Departure: Still serving in the 111th Congress

Cong.	Ranking	Years in: Senate	Comm.	Date of Assignment
107th	Min-8th	11	1	Jan. 25, 2001
+107th	Maj-8th	12	1	June 6, 2001
108th	Min-6th	13	2	Jan. 15, 2003
109th	Min-6th	15	4	Jan. 6, 2005
110th	Maj-6th	17	6	Jan. 12, 2007
111th	Maj-6th	19	8	Jan. 21, 2009

5th BANKING, HOUSING AND URBAN AFFAIRS
1st Dates: July 10, 2001-Jan. 14, 2003
1st Departure: Left committee; no new assignment
2nd Dates: Jan. 12, 2007-date
2nd Departure: Still serving in the 111th Congress

Cong.	Ranking	Years in: Senate	Comm.	Date of Assignment
+107th	MjA-11th	11	*1 1	July 10, 2001
110th	Maj-8th	17	*2 1	Jan. 12, 2007
111th	Maj-7th	19	*2 3	Jan. 21, 2009

SENATE SELECT AND SPECIAL COMMITTEES

1st INDIAN AFFAIRS
INDIAN AFFAIRS (Permanent)
Dates: Feb. 5, 1991-date
Departure: Still serving in the 111th Congress

Cong.	Ranking	Years in: Senate	Comm.	Date of Assignment
103rd	Maj-6th	3	2	Jan. 5, 1993
104th	Min-5th	5	4	Jan. 9, 1995
105th	Min-4th	7	6	Jan. 9, 1997
106th	Min-4th	9	8	Jan. 7, 1999
107th	Min-4th	11	10	Jan. 25, 2001
+107th	Maj-4th	12	11	June 6, 2001
108th	Min-4th	13	12	Jan. 15, 2003
109th	Min-4th	15	14	Jan. 6, 2005
110th	Maj-4th	17	16	Jan. 12, 2007
111th	Maj-4th	19	18	Jan. 21, 2009

2nd SELECT ETHICS (Permanent)
Dates: Jan. 25, 2001-Jan. 18, 2006
Departure: Resigned committee; no new assignment

Cong.	Ranking	Years in: Senate	Comm.	Date of Assignment
107th	Min-2nd	11	1	Jan. 25, 2001
+107th	Maj-2nd	12	1	June 6, 2001
108th	Min-2nd	13	2	Jan. 15, 2003
109th	Min-2nd	15	4	Jan. 6, 2005

Part I

A. Standing Committees of the Senate

Backgrounds, Jurisdictions, and Rosters
1993-2011

Senate Standing Committees
1993-2011

Committees of the Senate: A Brief History

From its opening session in March 1789 until the closing months of the 14th Congress in December 1816, the U.S. Senate functioned without legislative standing committees. This contrasted with the House of Representatives, which already developed a standing committee system and selection procedures for its members that would be in place for a century. The House was clearly the lead congressional chamber as the new nation struggled to draft legislation in a changing world. The Senate's relatively small size and its reliance upon floor speeches apparently made a standing committee system seem unnecessary. For the most part, the Senate utilized a system of naming hundreds of ad hoc select and special committees to handle each floor vote coming before the chamber.

By 1816, the Senate had grown from twenty-six members to thirty-six and on the verge of statehood were the four territories of Indiana, Illinois, Mississippi, and Alabama. As the Senate faced further expansion, the need for a standing committee system became more urgent. On December 10, 1816, led by Senator James Barbour of Virginia, an anti-Democrat and States Righter, the Senate created its first eleven legislative standing committees to augment its existing housekeeping ones. Many had names similar to those already operating in the House, such as Claims, Commerce and Manufactures; Foreign Affairs; the Judiciary; Military Affairs; the Militia, Naval Affairs; Pensions; Post Offices and Post Roads; and Ways and Means. The only amendment was to change the name of Ways and Means to Finance. Eight days later on December 18, 1816, a new committee on the District of Columbia was added to the roster. While Senator Barbour was revamping the Senate's committees, his younger brother Philip P. Barbour had begun a career in the House of Representatives that would eventually lead to his election as Speaker of the House in 1821 and later to be named to the U.S. Supreme Court by President Andrew Jackson in 1836.

Each of the original Senate standing committees had five members with the majority Jeffersonian Republicans holding three seats and the minority Federalists two. The membership of each committee was determined by balloting of the Senate. By 1823 with the diminished Federalists almost missing from the chamber and led once again by Sen. James Barbour, the Senate agreed to let the presiding officer of the Senate select committee members. While this procedure was identical to that adopted by the House in 1790 when the Speaker was empowered to select committee members, no distinction was made between which Senate presiding officer would make the selections. Was it to be the president of the Senate, the vice president who was not an elected member of the chamber, or the Senate president *pro tempore*? Vice President John C. Calhoun's 1826 appointments were so prejudicial that the Senate returned to balloting for committee members, but the process continued to be muddled with opposition to Jackson's vice president Martin Van Buren fueling further discontent. By 1846, the Senate's internal party organizations had gained

control over the composition of the committees, and as service in the Senate lengthened, the prospect of using continuous seniority on committees to determine chairmanships became more appealing by limiting conflict over the choice.

As the nation moved west and expanded in size, Senate committees grew steadily in number with very few abolished. However, the Senate's committees never gained the prominence that the House committees did. Woodrow Wilson, whose insightful observation on the powerful House committees in his 1885 classic *Congressional Government* is the most quoted assessment of the late nineteenth century Congress, had this to say about the Senate committees:

> The [Senate] Committee system ... makes all the prizes of leadership small, and nowhere gathers power into a few hands. (142)
> Men who have acquired all their habits in the matter of dealing with legislative measures in the House of Representatives, where committee work is everything and public discussion nothing but "talking to the nation," find themselves still mere declaimers when they get into the Senate, where no previous question utters its interrupting voice from the tongues of tyrannical committeemen and where, consequently, talk is free to all. (145)

By 1911, the Senate was poised to accept the political consequences of the Seventeenth Amendment that would make its members subject to the votes of the citizens and not the state legislatures. The Senate now had seventy-one committees for its ninety-two members. The senators of the 61st Senate (1909-1911) served in 700 places on seventy-one separate committees—an average of 7.6 places per senator. There were already more Senate committees than majority members to chair them and their growth was perilously close to outnumbering the membership itself. Many of these committees seldom met and existed only for the purpose of providing a clerk and office space for their chairs. The Senate's Committee on Transportation Routes to the Seaboard that existed for forty-nine years (1872-1921) yet apparently never met is the legendary example of this practice.

Change came to the Senate more emphatically than it did to the House. Forty-one standing committees were abolished in 1921. Virtually all were so-called sinecure committees whose impact upon the Senate's legislative business was minimal. Thus, by the convening of the 79th Congress in 1945 the Senate was not as heavily encumbered by its committee system as was the House.

The Legislative Reorganization Act of 1946 (P.L. 79-601) reduced the Senate's thirty-three committees to fifteen, with Rules and Administration picking up the jurisdictions of six committees. Public Lands picked up five; while Interstate and Foreign Commerce collected four. Each committee was to be limited to thirteen members, with only the Appropriations Committee allotted twenty-one seats. This lasted until 1953, when pressure from junior members led to the increase of assigned seats to fifteen. However, the Senate's even split in that 83rd Congress between its forty-eight Republicans, forty-seven Democrats, and the unaffiliated Wayne Morse of Oregon made internal organization difficult. The resulting confusion opened the way for Wisconsin Republican Joe McCarthy to parlay his chairmanship of the relatively minor Government Operations Committee into a national headline-hunting crusade against communists, real and imagined.

When Democrats regained control of the Senate in the 1954 election, Sen. Lyndon B. Johnson (Dem-Texas) became Majority Floor Leader and he instituted the "Johnson rule" that opened up major committees to junior senators by limiting a second major committee assignment to a senior senator until each junior member received at least one major assignment. While this move was presumed to strengthen Johnson's presidential aspirations, it also lessened junior-senior tensions among the Senate's Democrats.

Besides reducing the number of standing committees the other major consequence of the Legislative Reorganization Act was to bring some stability to the committee system by making it difficult to create new standing committees. Over the next thirty years, only three new standing committees were added to the Senate roster—the Committee on Aeronautical and Space Sciences in 1958 as the Senate's response to the orbiting of Soviet satellites, Veteran's Affairs in 1970, and the Budget Committee in 1974 as an outgrowth of the Congressional Budget and Impoundment Control Act (P.L. 93-44). That act sought to limit President Richard Nixon's efforts to "impound" money that Congress had appropriated. While standing committee membership remained relatively stable, the number of select and special committees grew rapidly and membership on those committees and the standing committee subcommittees increased dramatically. By 1975, it became clear that further reform was necessary.

Sen. Adlai E. Stevenson III (Dem-Ill.) chaired the committee that reorganized the Senate's system in 1977. Following the recommendations of the Temporary Select Committee to Study the Senate Committee System, as contained in Senate Resolution 95-4, the Senate reduced its committees (standing, joint, and special) from 31 to 24; and its subcommittees from 174 to 118. As a result, the average number of assignments per senator dropped from 18 in the 94th Congress to 11 in the 95th.

Three standing committees were eliminated as the functions of the District of Columbia Committee and Post Office and Civil Service were folded into the newly reconstituted Governmental Affairs Committee. Both of these committees had encountered difficulty in getting senators to serve on them and their departure from the chamber was not greatly lamented. The Aeronautical and Space Sciences Committee, the only standing committee ever chaired by Lyndon B. Johnson (Dem-Tex.) and once filled with the Senate's senior members, had fallen on hard times as appropriations for the space program dried up in the 1970s. This committee was absorbed by Commerce under its new designation, the Committee on Commerce, Science and Transportation.

In spite of these efforts, Senate committee membership continued to carry less weight than House committee membership. Phil Gramm of Texas, who served first as a Democrat in the House and later as a Republican in the Senate, made the following observation in Ross K. Baker's book, *House and Senate*:

I have been a little bit surprised at the Senate in that the committees are less important over here. First of all, subcommittees are almost meaningless over here. The committees are small enough that all the work is done in full committee. And a subcommittee chairmanship is of relatively little value.

And quite frankly, Senate committees don't do a whole lot. At least not in my two years here. Much of the work is done on the floor. (59-60)

Because the Senate's standing committees play a lesser role than those of the House, the Senate has shown a greater propensity to revamp its committee system than has the House. With barely limited floor debate and no Rules Committee to restrict amendments, the Senate has been able to conduct more of its legislative business on the floor than has the House. This lowers the stakes involved in any alteration in committee jurisdictions and makes reform easier to accomplish.

As a result, Senate careers are not as dependent upon committee assignments as House careers are. As Richard Fenno, the dean of congressional scholars, points out:

Senate committees are important as arenas in which decisions are made. But they are not especially important as sources of individual member influence—not when compared to House committees. That is, a Senator's committee membership adds far less to his total potential for influence inside his chamber than a Representative's committee membership adds to his potential for influence in his chamber. (*Congressmen in Committees*, 1973, 147)

In spite of these observations, the Senate continues to name sixteen standing committees and its one hundred members continue to seek membership on them.

Committees of the Senate, 1993-2011

The Political Context: The Senate's centrality in American politics received a renewed boost in 2008 when both major party presidential nominees, Republican John S. McCain of Arizona and Democrat Barack Obama of Illinois, were sitting senators for the first time in history. As members of the 111th Congress watched on January 20, 2009, two U.S. senators from the 110th Congress who had served together on the Senate Foreign Relations Committee were sworn in—Barack Obama as president and Joseph R. Biden Jr. of Delaware as vice president. Only once before had two sitting U.S. senators been elected president and vice president—John F. Kennedy of Massachusetts and Lyndon B. Johnson of Texas in 1960. Unlike Obama and Biden, they never shared a committee assignment, but in 1956, Senator Johnson relinquished the chair of the Select Committee on the Senate Reception Room to Kennedy. In that post, Kennedy got the opportunity to name the five greatest U.S. senators and to further burnish his credentials for the 1960 presidential nomination.

During the eighteen years covered in these volumes, the U.S. Senate experienced a remarkable level of interparty competition leading to four shifts in party control in 1994, 2001, 2002, and 2006. Divided government was the norm. The Senate convened with a party majority different from that of the president in nine and one-half years of this period (52.7%) with Republicans controlling the Senate for six years during Democratic president Bill Clinton's administration

(1995-2001) and Democrats controlling the Senate for three and one half years of Republican president George W. Bush's administration (2001-2003 and 2007-2009).

In the forty-six years between 1947 and 1993, only three U.S. senators changed their party affiliations. The first was Wayne L. Morse of Oregon, who left the triumphant Republican Party on the eve of its 1952 takeover of the 83rd Congress and would lose his major committee assignments as a consequence. Morse would serve as an Independent until 1956 when he joined the Democratic Party. South Carolina's J. Strom Thurmond left the Democratic Party in 1964 to support the Republican presidential candidacy of fellow conservative U.S. senator Barry M. Goldwater of Arizona. The third switcher was Harry Flood Byrd Jr. of Virginia, whose defeat in the 1970 Democratic primary led him to run and be elected as an Independent; Byrd chose to remain in the Democratic caucus.

Over the past sixteen years, the rate of senatorial party switching has increased. Since 1994, five U.S. senators changed their party affiliations: Richard Shelby of Alabama and Ben Nighthorse Campbell of Colorado left the Democratic Party for the Republicans in the 104th Congress; Jim Jeffords of Vermont left the Republicans in 2001 to become an Independent, thereby returning control of the Senate to the Democrats for eighteen months; Joseph I. Lieberman of Connecticut, the 2000 Democratic nominee for vice president, who was elected as an Independent Democrat in 2006 with Republican votes after losing the Democratic primary of that year; and Pennsylvania's Arlen Specter joined the Democratic party in 2009 after twenty-eight years of serving in the Senate as a Republican. Also, Vermont's voters sent Bernie Sanders to the Senate in 2006, ostensibly as a political independent but philosophically a socialist. Both Senators Sanders and Lieberman presently caucus with the Senate Democrats.

Presented below are the party splits in the Senate for the nine Congresses since 1993. Special note is taken of the impact of specific party shifts caused by the changes in affiliation occurring through special elections and appointments.

Party Representation in the U.S. Senate and the Impact of Changes, 1993-2011

Congress	Years	Democrats	Republicans	Independents
103rd	1993-1995	57	43	0
1993 Hutchison (R-Tex.) won special election over Krueger (D-Tex.)				
		56	44	0
104th	1995-1997	48	52	0
1995 Shelby (D-Ala.) and Campbell (D-Colo.) switched to Republican Party				
1996 Wyden (D-Ore.) replaced Packwood (R-Ore.)				
		47	53	0
105th	1997-1999	45	55	0
106th	1999-2001	45	55	0
2000 Miller (D-Ga.) replaced Coverdell (R-Ga.)				
		46	54	
107th	2001-2003	50	50	0
2001 Jeffords (R-Vt.) switched to Independent				
2002 Wellstone (DFL-Minn.) replaced by Barkley (I-Minn.)				
		49	49	2
108th	2003-2005	48	51	1
109th	2005-2007	44	55	1
110th	2007-2009	49	49	2
111th	2009-2011	56	41	2
2009 Specter (R-Penn.) switched to Democratic Party				
2009 Franken (DFL-Minn.) won recount over Coleman (R-Minn.)				
2010 Brown (R-Mass.) replaced Kennedy (D-Mass.)				
		57	41	2

With party control of the Senate shifting back and forth between the two major parties, every special election or party switch has had a political impact upon the functioning of the Senate. The Senate's smaller size means that any party shift leads to a ratio adjustment on a number of the committees. This happened when Texas Republican Kay Bailey Hutchison defeated Democratic appointee U.S. senator Robert Krueger in 1993; in 1996 when Democratic U.S. representative Ronald L. Wyden of Oregon won the special election to replace the resigned Republican, U.S. senator Robert Packwood; and in 2000 when Georgia Democratic ex-governor Zell Miller was appointed to fill the seat of the deceased Republican U.S. senator Paul Coverdell. However, when Independent Dean Barkley of Minnesota was named to replace the deceased U.S. senator Paul Wellstone in November, 2002, he was sworn but not seated on committees.

The 2000 election provided the most dramatic illustration of this when the Senate convened in January of 2001 with fifty Republican senators and fifty Democratic senators. With no discernible majority party to organize the Senate, the two parties agreed to a "power-sharing" arrangement whereby the "majority" party would be determined by the party affiliation of the vice president but that each party would receive the same number of seats on each committee and have an equal number of committee staffers. The arrangement would end when one of the parties would gain a numeric edge over the other. Between January 3 and January 20, 2001, with Democratic vice president Albert Gore Jr. presiding over the Senate, the Democrats were the "majority" and when Republican vice president Richard B. Cheney succeeded Gore on January 20, the Republicans were the "majority." This ended in May when Vermont Republican U.S. senator Jim Jeffords, first elected in 1988, chose to leave the Republican Party and to be seated as an Independent and to caucus with the Democrats. Senator Jeffords had long been at odds with the southern and western tilt of the Senate's Reaganite Republicans and his departure was not surprising (Garrison Nelson, "Jim Jeffords's Long Goodbye," *New York Times*, May 25, 2001). His switch at this point in time shifted control of the Senate to the Democrats. However, what difficulty the Jeffords switch meant for President George W. Bush's legislative agenda was ended in the patriotic "rally around the flag" that took place after the September 11, 2001, terrorist attacks on New York City and Washington, D.C.

The next most dramatic shift occurred in 2010, after Senate Democrats had gained a sixty-vote majority in 2009 with the aid of Independents Sanders of Vermont and Lieberman of Connecticut and augmented by the party switch of Arlen Specter of Pennsylvania in April and the recount victory of Al Franken in Minnesota. Prior to 1975, the Senate required a two-thirds vote of senators "present and voting" to impose cloture on a filibuster. Those were in the days of lengthy speeches and late night quorum calls. But in 1975, Rule XXII was amended so that three-fifths of the Senate—generally sixty senators—could end a filibuster. In today's Senate, a filibuster occurs when the leader of a minority faction informs the majority leader that the minority has at least the forty-one votes necessary to control debate and stop an unwanted vote on legislation. No speeches and no late-night roll calls occur but the impact is the same. The Democrats of the 111th Congress finally obtained the 60th vote when Senator Franken was seated in July after the Minnesota recount. However, the August 2009 death of Sen. Edward M. Kennedy (Dem-Mass.) put their tally at fifty-nine, and the January 2010 special election of Republican Scott P. Brown

to fill the Massachusetts seat gave Senate Republicans the forty-one votes they needed to block implementation of President Obama's legislative agenda.

Consequently, the Senate floor has become less hospitable and the Senate has been obliged to rely more upon its committees to produce legislation that will enable bills to pass and the nation's business to be served.

The Committee Context: The sixteen standing committees that opened the 103rd Congress in 1993 remain in place. No new committees have been added, but change has occurred in the names of three committees and the growth of member assignments. On January 21, 1999, at the start of the 106th Congress and during the chairmanship of Senator Jeffords, Labor and Human Resources became the Committee on Health, Education, Labor, and Pensions (HELP). Two years later on June 29, 2001, the Small Business committee was renamed the Committee on Small Business and Entrepreneurship. In the wake of the September 11, 2001, terrorist attacks on the nation, the Committee on Governmental Affairs was renamed the Committee on Homeland Security and Governmental Affairs on October 8, 2004. While their names were changed, the legislative jurisdictions of these three committees, as well as those of the thirteen other Senate committees that were not renamed, remained intact. The jurisdictions established by the 1977 reorganization of the Senate committees have been little altered over the past three decades.

Regarding size, fourteen of the sixteen standing committees increased their membership during these nine Congresses. The two exceptions were Small Business and Foreign Relations, a powerful committee that has been impacted by other changes regarding its relative prestige. The 103rd Congress had 301 assigned places in its Senate standing committees while the 111th Congress has 344—a net gain of 43 seats and a percentage increase of 14.3 percent. Whether this will foretell another restructuring of the Senate committee system remains to be seen.

Since the 1977 reorganization, an internal ranking system of the committees was put in place. There are three categories intended to make the assignment process more equitable. The classifications are listed below:

"A" Committees
Agriculture, Nutrition, and Forestry
Appropriations
Armed Services
Banking, Housing and Urban Affairs
Commerce, Science, and Transportation
Energy and Natural Resources
Environment and Public Works
Finance
Foreign Relations
Health, Education, Labor and Pensions
Homeland Security and Governmental Affairs
Judiciary
Select Intelligence

"B" Committees
Budget
Rules and Administration
Small Business and Entrepreneurship
Veterans Affairs
Special Aging
Joint Economic

"C" Committees
Select Ethics
Indian Affairs
Joint Taxation
Joint Library
Joint Printing

According to the Congressional Research Service's Judy Schneider,

The restrictions [on committee membership] are intended to treat Senators equitably in the assignment process.

Essentially, each Senator is limited to service on two of the "A" committees, and one of the "B" committees. Service on "C" committees is unrestricted. (Schneider, *Committee Assignment Process in the U.S. Senate: Democratic and Republican Party Procedures*," November 3, 2006, CRS-4)

In spite of those efforts, there are discernible differences between the committees that may be seen in the three variables comparing the Senate standing committees relative to one another. The three variables are committee size, mean seniority of the members who served within each of the nine Congresses, and the mean retention rate of members who served in the previous Congress and continued to serve in the subsequent one.

Senate Standing Committees: Comparative Statistics

Ranks of Committee	Mean Size	Mean Seniority	Mean Retention Rate
1st	28.7 Appropriations	17.80 Rules+Admin.	98.22 Finance
2nd	23.1 Armed Services	16.91 Appropriations	97.75 Rules+Admin.
3rd	22.6 Budget	15.07 Finance	94.91 Appropriations
4th	22.1 Comm, Sci+Trans	14.48 Judiciary	94.19 Comm, Sci+Trans
5th	21.4 Energy+Nat Res.	12.48 Agriculture, N+F	91.62 Budget
6th	20.6 Finance	12.29 HSGA	89.84 Judiciary
7th	20.1 BHUA	12.17 Armed Services	89.02 Veterans Affairs
8th	19.8 Agriculture, N+F	12.07 Comm, Sci+Trans	88.35 Small Bsn+Entprn
9th	19.4 HELP	11.84 Budget	88.23 Agriculture+N+F
10th	19.1 Small Bsn+Entprn.	10.68 HELP	87.09 Armed Services
11th	18.9 Foreign Relations	10.58 Foreign Relations	86.70 BHUA
12th	18.4 Judiciary	10.42 Veterans Affairs	86.16 HELP
13th	18.3 Environment+PW	9.99 Environment+PW	83.60 Energy+Nat. Res.
14th	17.6 Rules+Admin.	9.84 Energy+Nat. Res.	82.64 Foreign Relations
15th	16.1 HSGA	9.19 Small Bsn+Entprn	81.49 HSGA
16th	13.7 Veterans Affairs	8.37 BHUA	81.46 Environment+PW

Abbreviation Guide:
  Agriculture, N+F = Agriculture, Nutrition, and Forestry;
  BHUA = Banking, Housing, and Urban Affairs;
  Comm. Sci+Trans = Communication, Science and Transportation;
  Energy+Nat Res = Energy and Natural Resources;
  Environment+PW = Environment and Public Works
  HELP = Health, Education, Labor, and Pensions
  HSGA = Homeland Security and Urban Affairs
  Rules+Admin = Rules and Administration
  Small Bsn+Entprn = Small Business and Entrepreneurship

No abbreviations: Appropriations, Armed Services, Budget, Finance, Foreign Relations, Judiciary, Veterans' Affairs

There is a large range in the relative sizes of the committees with Appropriations retaining its historic place as the Senate's largest committee with an average of 28.7 members while Veterans' Affairs, one of the newer standing committees, is in sixteenth place with an average of 13.7 members. The fastest growing committee in recent years was Armed Services which grew from twenty to twenty-six in these nine Congresses. During the Jeffords-impacted 107th Congress, tie-breaking seats were added to all of the committees after the shift and most of those size adjustments have remained in place.

That the Finance and Appropriations committees rank near the top of the mean seniority and retention rate is no surprise. Both are "A" committees and have produced Senate notables for generations. Their being joined by the Rules and Administration Committee may be accounted for by its status as the "B" committee most preferred by Senate floor leaders and Whips. Twenty-one of the Senate's thirty-six (58.3%) post-1947 floor leaders and Whips served on Rules and Administration of which twelve were Republicans and nine were Democrats. Perhaps the most striking information contained in this table is the relatively low ranking of the Foreign Relations Committee, one that is regularly referred to as part of the Senate's "big three" along with Finance and Appropriations. Ranked at eleventh in mean seniority and at fourteenth in retention rate, it would appear that membership on Foreign Relations may have lost its luster for senators. But the Foreign Relations Committee appears to continue its appeal for those U.S. senators who seek the White House. Eleven of the Senate's twenty-three presidential and vice presidential nominees since 1947 have served on Foreign Relations. And the recent electoral triumphs of two of the committee's alumni—Barack Obama and Joe Biden—will continue to provide the committee with presidential aspirants if not long-serving members of the Senate.

In the next section of the book, each of the Senate's sixteen standing committees will be presented with backgrounds on their organizational history, membership characteristics, and notable members; jurisdictional listings over the years with a list of subcommittee names from 1993 to 2010; and full committee rosters covering the nine Congresses from the 103rd to the 111th, with the 107th Congress listed twice with both the committee rosters named prior to the Jeffords shift in 2001 and the rosters named after that shift.

Senate Standing Committees
1993-2011

Agriculture, Nutrition, and Forestry

Senate Committee on Agriculture, Nutrition, and Forestry, 103rd-111th Congresses (1993-2011)

BACKGROUND

Organizational History: The Senate's first standing committee on Agriculture dates from December 9, 1825, when Sen. William Findley (DR-Penn.) convinced the Senate that since both commerce and manufactures were represented by separate standing committees in the Senate, and that it was only right that agriculture's interests be protected as well. Findley was named the committee's first chair and its initial membership was set at five.

In the 35th Congress in 1857, the standing Committee on Agriculture was abolished as part of an efficiency move to reduce the number of standing committees. Six years later in 1863, in the midst of the Civil War, the committee was reestablished, the year following the creation of the Department of Agriculture in the executive branch.

The *Guide to the Records of the United States Senate at the National Archives, 1789-1989,* lists as Agriculture, Nutrition, and Forestry's predecessor committees, the Committee on Forest Reservations and the Protection of Game 1896-1921, and that committee's predecessor select committees: the Select Committee on Forest Reservations in California, established July 28, 1892, and that select committee's successor, the Select Committee on Forest Reservations, established March 15, 1893.

As the Nation moved westward and inhabited more forested areas, the committee's name was changed to the standing Committee on Agriculture and Forestry in February 1884 during the 48th Congress. This was the title by which it was known for most of the next century until 1977. As a consequence of the Committee System Reorganization Amendments of 1977 (S.Res. 95-4), the Agriculture and Forestry Committee was given the jurisdiction formerly held by the Senate Select Committee on Nutrition and Human Needs that had been created and chaired by Sen. George S. McGovern (Dem-S.D.). The name of the committee was then changed to the Committee on Agriculture, Nutrition and Forestry. This broadened the committee's mandate into social services in light of the "rural renaissance" of the 1960s and 1970s that had led to the migration of urban expatriates back to small towns and rural communities in search of simpler lifestyles.

The committee's original jurisdiction that was mostly focused on agricultural commodities was augmented to cover legislation and matters relating to the inspection of all agricultural products, not just livestock and meat products; agricultural commodities; pests and pesticide; rural development and watersheds; as well as rural electrification. The committee also became responsible for new jurisdictional areas such as human nutrition, food stamp programs, and food from fresh waters.

Key pieces of committee-drafted legislation in recent years included the Federal Improvement and Reform Act of 1996 (P.L. 104-127) that restructured long-standing federal farm subsidy policy in efforts to permit larger agribusiness firms more flexibility in choosing which commodities to grow. This act known by its backers as "the Freedom to Farm Act" was later altered, following the 2001 Jeffords switch by the Farm Security and Rural Investment Act of 2002 (P.L. 107-171) reestablishing federal price support programs and encouraging smaller farmers to practice more conservation.

Membership: In the Legislative Reorganization Act of 1946, the Senate Committee on Agriculture and Forestry was assigned thirteen seats, but the committee continued to grow, first reaching its present peak of twenty-one members in the aftermath of the Jim Jeffords defection in the 107th Congress (2001-2003). There are twenty-one members on the Agriculture, Nutrition, and Forestry Committee in the 111th Congress: twelve Democrats and nine Republicans. Since 1993, it has had an average size of 19.8—eighth place among the sixteen Senate committees. The mean seniority of its members is 12.48 years, for sixth place. Since 1993, its rate of maintaining members from one Congress to the next is 88.2 percent placing it ninth among the sixteen standing committees.

Eighteen senators moved from Agriculture, Nutrition, and Forestry during these nine Congresses, while five moved to the committee, resulting in a net loss of thirteen. While it lost four members to Environment and Public Works, it also picked up three from that committee as Republican Craig Thomas of Wyoming moved back and forth between the two committees. Two of its 2001 departing members assumed the chairs of other committees: Charles Grassley (Rep-Iowa) left to chair Finance and Larry Craig (Rep-Ida.) became chair of Select Aging.

Committee Leaders: Sen. Arthur Capper (Rep-Kans.) was the Agriculture and Forestry Committee's first modern-era chair, serving from 1947 until his retirement from the Senate in 1949. Capper was followed by Elmer Thomas (Dem-Okla.), the first post-reorganization Democratic chair. Thomas served from 1949 until his departure from the Senate in 1951, after his defeat in a 1950 senatorial primary.

In 1951, Allen J. Ellender (Dem-La.) became chair of the committee for the first time. He chaired the committee in nine Congresses including one period of eight Congresses in a row (1955-1971). Ellender stepped aside as chair of Agriculture and Forestry in 1971 to succeed Richard B. Russell (Dem-Ga.) as the chair of the Appropriations Committee. George D.

Aiken (Rep-Vt.) interrupted Ellender's service as chair in the 83rd Congress. Aiken was the only Republican chair of the committee from 1949, until the election of 1980 gave Republicans control of the Senate.

When Ellender stepped aside as chair in 1971, he was succeeded by Herman E. Talmadge (Dem-Ga.). Talmadge chaired the committee for ten years until his departure in 1981, following his defeat for re-election in 1980. Talmadge was succeeded by Jesse Helms (Rep-N.C.), the committee's first Republican chair since 1955. Following the loss of the Senate to the Democrats in the 1986 election, Helms was succeeded in the chair by Vermont's Patrick J. Leahy. Leahy's chairmanship lasted for eight years (1987-1995). With Republicans regaining the Senate in 1994, Richard G. Lugar (Rep-Ind.) became chair and held the seat until 2001, when the defection of Vermont's James Jeffords from the Republican Party to Independent status gave control of the Senate to the Democrats for the balance of the 107th Congress. When Republicans regained the Senate in the 2002 election, Lugar left the top post to take over the Foreign Relations Committee. He was replaced by W. Thad Cochran (Rep-Miss.) in 2003, who left two years later to chair Appropriations. Cochran's successor was Saxby Chambliss (Rep-Ga.), who became chair in 2005 in only his third year in the Senate. Iowa's Thomas R. Harkin, who had been the senior Democrat on the committee since 1997, became chair in 2007 when Democrats took the Senate back in 2006. Harkin's chairmanship lasted until September 9, 2009, when he succeeded the late Edward M. Kennedy (Dem-Mass.) as chair of Health, Education, Labor, and Pensions. The committee's first woman chair, Blanche Lambert Lincoln (Dem-Ark.), replaced Harkin as chair for the balance of the 111th Congress.

The first ranking minority member of the Agriculture and Forestry Committee in the modern era was Elmer Thomas of Oklahoma (1947-1949). When the Democrats regained the Senate in 1949, George D. Aiken became the committee's ranking minority member. He served in this capacity for ten of the eleven Congresses between 1949 and 1971. The interruption occurred in 1953 when Ellender and Aiken swapped posts as a result of the Republican victory for the 83rd Congress. Aiken stepped aside in 1971 to become the ranking minority member on the Foreign Relations Committee.

Six different ranking minority members of the committee served in an eight-Congress span between 1971 and 1987: Jack R. Miller (Rep-Iowa, 1971-1973); Carl T. Curtis (Rep-Neb., 1973-1975); Robert J. Dole (Rep-Kans., 1975-1979); Jesse A. Helms (Rep-N.C., 1979-1981); Walter D. Huddleston (Dem-Ky., 1981-1985); and Edward Zorinsky (Dem-Neb., 1985-1987). Miller's stint as ranking minority member ended with his defeat for re-election in 1972. Senators Curtis and Dole both left the ranking minority slot on Agriculture for the same one on the Finance Committee.

When Helms became chair in 1981, Walter Huddleston who had been the sixth-ranking Democrat in the 95th Congress and the third-ranking one in the 96th found himself as his party's senior most member after only eight years on the committee. Huddleston's defeat in 1984 brought Patrick Leahy into the senior minority slot. In 1985, Leahy served as Vice Chair of the Select Committee on Intelligence and relinquished the ranking member position on the committee to Edward Zorinsky. In 1987, Richard Lugar lost a bitter battle to Helms in the Republican caucus for ranking minority member on Foreign Relations and took the ranking slot on Agriculture after Helms relinquished it

for Foreign Relations. Lugar held the ranking slot for the next eight years (1987-1995) until he became chair in 1995. Leahy who had been chair became ranking minority member in 1995 for just two years, until he took the same slot on Judiciary. He was succeeded by Harkin who held the ranking position throughout the remaining ten years of the Republicans' domination of the Senate (1997-2007). Saxby Chambliss became ranking minority member in 2007 and has held it in both the 110th and 111th Congresses (2007-2011)

Party Leaders: Hubert Humphrey, who served as his party's Whip for four years (1961-1965), was one of six elected party leaders to serve on Agriculture. Other Democratic leaders included Scott Lucas of Illinois, the Democratic floor leader in 1951-1953, Earle C. Clements of Kentucky, Democratic Whip (1953-1955), and Thomas S. Daschle (Dem-S.D.), floor leader from 1995 to 2005. While Humphrey left the leadership for the vice presidency, Senators Lucas, Clements, and Daschle were defeated for re-election. The only two Republican leaders from the committee were Dole who led the GOP from 1985 until his resignation from the Senate to pursue the presidency in 1996 and the present Republican Leader Mitch McConnell of Kentucky who began his leadership career as Whip in 2003 and became floor leader in 2007.

Presidential Aspirations: Four presidential nominees served on the modern-era Agriculture committee: three Democrats—Hubert Humphrey of Minnesota, the 1968 nominee; George S. McGovern of South Dakota, the 1972 nominee; and Walter F. Mondale of Minnesota, the 1984 nominee; and one Republican—Robert Dole of Kansas in 1996. Senators Humphrey, Mondale, and Dole had each been nominated for vice president, with Humphrey and Mondale winning in 1964 and 1976, respectively, while Dole who served on the committee with Mondale lost in 1976. Three senators actively involved in the Vietnam-era debates—Humphrey, McGovern, and 1968 presidential challenger Eugene McCarthy (DFL-Minn.)—were members of the committee.

Other Notables: Four members of the committee served in the Cabinet, two of whom served as Secretaries of Agriculture prior to their Senate service: Clinton Anderson (Dem-N.M.) served as President Truman's Secretary of Agriculture (1945-1949) before he joined the Senate in 1949 and recently-elected Mike Johanns (Rep-Neb.) served as President George W. Bush's Agriculture Secretary. Another former Cabinet member serving on Agriculture, Nutrition and Forestry was Elizabeth Dole (Rep-N.C.), who was Secretary of Transportation under President Reagan and Secretary of Labor under President George H.W. Bush. Kenneth Salazar (Dem-Colo.), President Obama's Secretary of the Interior, is also an alumnus of the committee.

Selected References

Balaam, David N., "Agriculture, Nutrition, and Forestry Committee, Senate," in Donald C. Bacon, Roger H. Davidson, and Morton Keller, eds., *The Encyclopedia of the United States Congress* (New York: Simon & Schuster, 1995), I: 35-38.

Boynton, G. Robert, "Ideas and Actions: A Cognitive Model of the Senate Agriculture Committee," *Political Behavior*, 12 (June, 1990), 181-213.

Boynton, G. Robert, "The Senate Agriculture Committee Produces a Homeostat," *Policy Sciences*, 22 (March, 1989), 51-80.

Browne, William P., *Cultivating Congress: Constituents, Issues, and Interests in Agricultural Policymaking* (Lawrence: University Press of Kansas, 1995).

Browne, William P., *Private Interests, Public Policy, and American Agriculture* (Lawrence: University Press of Kansas, 1988).

Coren, Robert W., et al., "Records of the Committee on Agriculture and Forestry and Related Committees, 1825-1968," *Guide to the Records of the United States Senate at the National Archives: 1789-1989 Bicentennial Edition* (Washington, D.C.: National Archives and Records Administration, 1989), 21-26.

Engeke, Joanne, et al., "The House Agriculture Committee and the Senate Agriculture and Forestry Committee," in the Ralph Nader Congress Project, *The Environment Committees A Study of the House and Senate Interior, Agriculture, and Science Committees* (New York: Grossman, 1975), 145-280.

Hansen, John Mark, *Gaining Access: Congress and the Farm Lobby*, 1919-1981 (Chicago: University of Chicago Press, 1991).

Peters, John, "The 1981 Farm Bill," in Don F. Hadwiger and Ross B. Talbot, eds., *Food Policy and Farm Programs* (New York: Academy of Political Science, 1982), 157-170.

Porter, Laurellen, "Congress and Agricultural Policy," in Don F. Hadwiger and William P. Browne, eds., *The New Politics of Food* (Lexington, Mass.: Lexington Books, 1978), 15-22.

U.S. Senate, Committee on Agriculture and Forestry, *A Brief History of the Committee on Agriculture and Forestry, United States Senate, and Landmark Agricultural Legislation, 1825-1970*, Senate Document 91-107, 91st Congress, 2nd session (1970).

U.S. Senate, Committee on Agriculture and Forestry, *A Brief History of the Committee on Agriculture and Forestry, United States Senate, and Landmark Agricultural Legislation, 1825-1986*, Senate Print 99-213, 99th Congress, 2nd session (1986).

U.S. Senate, *The United States Senate Committee on Agriculture, Nutrition, and Forestry, 1825-1998: Members, Jurisdiction and History*, Senate Document 105-24, 105th Congress, 2nd session (1998).

U.S. Senate, Select Committee on Nutrition and Human Needs, *Legislative History of the Select Committee on Nutrition and Human Needs*, Senate Committee Print, 94th Congress, 2nd session (October, 1976). The committee was reorganized into the Senate Committee on Agriculture, Nutrition, and Forestry in 1977.

RESPONSIBILITIES, JURISDICTIONAL CHANGES, AND SUBCOMMITTEES

AGRICULTURE AND FORESTRY

Jurisdiction, 80th Congress (1947-49)

Established by the Legislative Reorganization Act of 1946:

[Section 102.(1)(a)]

(1) **Committee on Agriculture and Forestry**, to consist of thirteen Senators, to which committee shall be referred all proposed legislation, messages, petitions, memorials, and other matters relating to the following subjects:

    (1) Agriculture generally

    (2) Inspection of livestock and meat products

    (3) Animal industry and diseases of animals

    (4) Adulteration of seeds, insect pests, and protection of birds and animals in forest reserves

    (5) Agricultural colleges and experiment stations

    (6) Forestry in general, and forest reserves other than those created from the public domain

    (7) Agricultural economics and research

    (8) Agricultural and industrial chemistry

    (9) Dairy industry

    (10) Entomology and plant quarantine

    (11) Human nutrition and home economics

    (12) Plant industry, soils, and agricultural engineering

    (13) Agricultural educational extension services

    (14) Extension of farm credit and farm security

    (15) Rural electrification

    (16) Agricultural production and marketing and stabilization of prices of agricultural products

    (17) Crop insurance and soil conservation

AGRICULTURE, NUTRITION, AND FORESTRY

Reorganization, 1977

The Committee was reorganized as the Standing Committee on Agriculture, Nutrition, and Forestry following the passage of Senate Resolution 4, the Committee System Reorganization Amendments of 1977, February 4, 1977.

Post-Reorganization Jurisdiction, 1977

[Section 1.(a)(1)]

(1) **Committee on Agriculture, Nutrition, and Forestry**, to which committee shall be referred all proposed legislation, messages, petitions, memorials, and other matters relating primarily to the following subjects:

- (1) Agriculture and agricultural commodities
- (2) Inspection of livestock, meat, and agricultural products
- (3) Animal industry and disease
- (4) Pests and pesticides
- (5) Agricultural extension services and experiment stations
- (6) Forestry and forest reserves and wilderness areas other than those created from the public domain
- (7) Agricultural economics and research
- (8) Home economics
- (9) Plant industry, soils, and agricultural engineering
- (10) Farm credit and farm security
- (11) Rural development, rural electrification, and watersheds
- (12) Agricultural production, marketing, and stabilization of prices
- (13) Crop insurance and soil conservation
- (14) Human nutrition
- (15) School nutrition programs
- (16) Food stamp programs
- (17) Food from fresh waters

(2) Such committee shall also study and review, on a comprehensive basis, matters relating to food, nutrition, and hunger, both in the United States and in foreign countries, and rural affairs, and report thereon from time to time.

Jurisdiction, 103rd Congress (1993-94)

From the *Standing Rules of the Senate* in the *Senate Manual*, 103rd Congress, 1st Session, S. Doc. 103-1:

[Rule XXV. (1)(a)]

(1) **Committee on Agriculture, Nutrition, and Forestry**, to which committee shall be referred all proposed legislation, messages, petitions, memorials, and other matters relating primarily to the following subjects:

- (1) Agricultural economics and research
- (2) Agricultural extension services and experiment stations
- (3) Agricultural production, marketing, and stabilization of prices
- (4) Agriculture and agricultural commodities
- (5) Animal industry and diseases
- (6) Crop insurance and soil conservation
- (7) Farm credit and farm security
- (8) Food from fresh waters
- (9) Food stamp programs
- (10) Forestry, and forest reserves and wilderness areas other than those created from the public domain
- (11) Home economics
- (12) Human nutrition
- (13) Inspection of livestock, meat, and agricultural products
- (14) Pests and pesticides
- (15) Plant industry, soils, and agricultural engineering
- (16) Rural development, rural electrification, and watersheds
- (17) School nutrition programs

(2) Such committee shall also study and review, on a comprehensive basis, matters relating to food, nutrition, and hunger, both in the United States and in foreign countries, and rural affairs, and report thereon from time to time

Jurisdiction, 111th Congress (2009-10)

From *Authority and Rules of Senate Committees, 2009-2010*, Sen. Doc. 111-3, pursuant to S.Res, 166, June 2, 2009.

[Rule XXV (a)(1)]

(1) **Committee on Agriculture, Nutrition, and Forestry** to which committee shall be referred all proposed legislation, messages, petitions, memorials, and other matters relating primarily to the following subjects:

- (1) Agricultural economics and research
- (2) Agricultural extension services and experiment stations
- (3) Agricultural production, marketing, and stabilization of prices
- (4) Agriculture and agricultural commodities

   (5) Animal industry and diseases
   (6) Crop insurance and soil conservation
   (7) Farm credit and farm security
   (8) Food from fresh waters
   (9) Food stamp programs
 (10) Forestry, and forest reserves and wilderness areas other than those created from the public domain
 (11) Home economics
 (12) Human nutrition
 (13) Inspection of livestock, meat, and agricultural products
 (14) Pests and pesticides
 (15) Plant industry, soils, and agricultural engineering
 (16) Rural development, rural electrification, and watersheds
 (17) School nutrition programs

(2) Such committee shall also study and review, on a comprehensive basis, matters relating to food, nutrition, and hunger, both in the United States and in foreign countries, and rural affairs, and report thereon from time to time.

NAMES OF SUBCOMMITTEES

Committee on Agriculture, Nutrition, and Forestry, 103rd-111th Congresses

Agricultural Credit, 103
Agricultural Production and Stabilization of Prices, 103
Agricultural Research, Conservation, Forestry, and General Legislation, 103
Domestic and Foreign Marketing, Inspection, and Plant, and Animal Health, 110, 111
Domestic and Foreign Marketing and Product Promotion, 103
Energy, Science, and Technology, 110, 111
Forestry, Conservation, and Rural Revitalization, 104, 105, 106, 107, 108, 109
Hunger, Nutrition, and Family Farms, 111
Marketing, Inspection, and Product Promotion, 104, 105, 106, 107, 108, 109
Nutrition and Food Assistance, Sustainable and Organic Agriculture, and General Legislation, 110
Nutrition and Investigations, 103
Production, Income Protection, and Price Support, 110, 111
Production and Price Competitiveness, 104, 105, 106, 107, 108, 109
Research, Nutrition, and General Legislation, 104, 105, 106, 107, 108, 109
Rural Development and Rural Electrification, 103
Rural Revitalization, Conservation, Forestry, and Credit Jurisdiction, 110
Rural Revitalization, Conservation, Forestry, and Credit, 111

MEMBERSHIP ROSTERS, 103rd-111th Congresses, 1993-2010

AGRICULTURE, NUTRITION, AND FORESTRY / 103rd Congress

Service Dates of Committee Chair: Jan. 7, 1993-Jan. 11, 1995

Service Dates of Majority Members: Jan. 7, 1993-Jan. 4, 1995

Service Dates of Minority Members: Jan. 7, 1993-Jan. 4, 1995

Majority

Rank Name	Party	State	Years in: Senate	Years in: Comm.
Chr Leahy, Patrick J.	Dem	Vt.	19	18
2nd Pryor, David H.	Dem	Ark.	15	14
3rd Boren, David L.	Dem	Okla.	15	14
4th Heflin, Howell T.	Dem	Ala.	15	13
5th Harkin, Thomas R.	Dem	Iowa	9	8
6th Conrad, Kent	Dem	N.D.	7	7
7th Daschle, Thomas A.	Dem	S.D.	7	7
8th Baucus, Max S.	Dem	Mont.	15	4
9th Kerrey, J. Robert	Dem	Neb.	5	4
10th Feingold, Russell D.	Dem	Wisc.	1	1

Minority

Rank Name	Party	State	Years in: Senate	Years in: Comm.
RM Lugar, Richard G.	Rep	Ind.	17	16
2nd Dole, Robert J.	Rep	Kans.	25	24
3rd Helms, Jesse A.	Rep	N.C.	21	20
4th Cochran, W. Thad	Rep	Miss.	15	14
5th McConnell, A. Mitchell (Mitch)	Rep	Ky.	9	8
6th Craig, Larry E.	Rep	Ida.	3	2
7th Coverdell, Paul	Rep	Ga.	1	1
8th Grassley, Charles E.	Rep	Iowa	13	*1 2

*1: Member's first period of service on the committee.

Note: Rankings on this committee for the following members were affected by other chamber service: Robert J. Dole (Rep-Kans.), Senate Minority Leader; Jesse A. Helms (Rep-N.C.), Ranking Minority Member, Foreign Relations; and Charles E. Grassley (Rep-Iowa) served on three other standing committees in this Congress and was obliged by Republican Conference rules to waive his seniority.

Changes:

Majority:

Boren, David L.	Dem	Okla.	Nov. 15, 1994	Resigned the Senate; became president of the University of Oklahoma

Departures from Committee:	Majority			Minority		
Moved to Judiciary	Feingold, Russell D.	Dem	Wisc.	None		
Moved to Governmental Affairs	None			Grassley, Charles E.	Rep	Iowa

AGRICULTURE, NUTRITION, AND FORESTRY / 104th Congress

Service Dates of Committee Chair: Jan. 11, 1995-Jan. 9, 1997

Service Dates of Majority Members: Jan. 4, 1995-Jan. 9, 1997

Service Dates of Minority Members: Jan. 4, 1995-Jan. 9, 1997

			Majority						Minority		
				Years in:						Years in:	
Rank Name	Party	State	Senate	Comm.		Rank Name	Party	State	Senate	Comm.	
Chr Lugar, Richard G.	Rep	Ind.	19	18		RM Leahy, Patrick J.	Dem	Vt.	21	20	
2nd Dole, Robert J.	Rep	Kans.	27	26		2nd Pryor, David H.	Dem	Ark.	17	16	
3rd Helms, Jesse A.	Rep	N.C.	23	22		3rd Heflin, Howell T.	Dem	Ala.	17	14	
4th Cochran, W. Thad	Rep	Miss.	17	16		4th Harkin, Thomas R.	Dem	Iowa	11	10	
5th McConnell, A. Mitchell (Mitch)	Rep	Ky.	11	10		5th Conrad, Kent	Dem	N.D.	9	8	
6th Craig, Larry E.	Rep	Ida.	5	4		6th Daschle, Thomas A.	Dem	S.D.	9	8	
7th Coverdell, Paul	Rep	Ga.	3	2		7th Baucus, Max S.	Dem	Mont.	17	6	
8th Santorum, Richard J. (Rick)	Rep	Penn.	1	*1 1		8th Kerrey, J. Robert	Dem	Neb.	7	6	
9th Warner, John	Rep	Va.	17	1							

*1: Member's first period of service on the committee.

Note: Rankings on this committee for the following members were affected by other chamber service: Robert J. Dole (Rep-Kans.), Senate Majority Leader; and Jesse A. Helms (Rep-N.C.), Chair, Foreign Relations.

Additions:

Majority:

10th Campbell, Ben Nighthorse	Rep	Colo.	Mar. 24, 1995 Had switched to Republican party

Changes:

Majority:

Campbell, Ben Nighthorse	Rep	Colo.	Oct. 12, 1995 Left the committee; moved to Appropriations.
Grassley, Charles E.	Rep	Iowa	Oct. 12, 1995 Replaced Campbell.
Dole, Robert J.	Rep	Kans.	June 11, 1996 Resigned the Senate; campaigned for the presidency.
Gramm, W. Phil	Rep	Tex.	June 20, 1996 Replaced Dole.

Departures from the Senate:	Majority			Minority		
Retired	None			Pryor, David H.	Dem	Ark.
				Heflin, Howell T.	Dem	Ala.

Departures from Committee:

Moved to Labor and Human Resources and returned to Special Aging	Warner, John	Rep	Va.	None		

AGRICULTURE, NUTRITION, AND FORESTRY / 105th Congress

Service Dates of Committee Chair: Jan. 9, 1997-Jan. 7, 1999

Service Dates of Majority Members: Jan. 9, 1997-Jan. 7, 1999

Service Dates of Minority Members: Jan. 9, 1997-Jan. 7, 1999

			Majority						Minority		
				Years in:						Years in:	
Rank Name	Party	State	Senate	Comm.		Rank Name	Party	State	Senate	Comm.	
Chr Lugar, Richard G.	Rep	Ind.	21	20		RM Harkin, Thomas R.	Dem	Iowa	13	12	
2nd Helms, Jesse A.	Rep	N.C.	25	24		2nd Leahy, Patrick J.	Dem	Vt.	23	22	

3rd Cochran, W. Thad	Rep	Miss.	19	18		3rd Conrad, Kent	Dem	N.D.	11	11
4th McConnell, A. Mitchell (Mitch)	Rep	Ky.	13	12		4th Daschle, Thomas A.	Dem	S.D.	11	11
5th Coverdell, Paul	Rep	Ga.	5	5		5th Baucus, Max S.	Dem	Mont.	19	8
6th Santorum, Richard J. (Rick)	Rep	Penn.	3	*1 3		6th Kerrey, J. Robert	Dem	Neb.	9	8
7th Roberts, C. Patrick	Rep	Kans.	1	1		7th Landrieu, Mary L.	Dem	La.	1	1
8th Grassley, Charles E.	Rep	Iowa	17	*2 2		8th Johnson, Timothy P.	Dem	S.D.	1	1
9th Gramm, W. Phil	Rep	Tex.	13	1						
10th Craig, Larry E.	Rep	Ida.	7	6						

*1: Member's first period of service on the committee.
*2: Member's second period of service on the committee.

Note: Rankings on this committee for the following members were affected by other chamber service: Jesse A. Helms (Rep-N.C.), Chair, Foreign Relations; and Patrick J. Leahy (Dem-Vt.), Ranking Minority Member, Judiciary.

Departures from Committee:	**Majority**			**Minority**		
Became Chair of Banking, Housing, and Urban Affairs	Gramm, W. Phil	Rep	Tex.	None		
Moved to Armed Services	None			Landrieu, Mary L.	Dem	La.

AGRICULTURE, NUTRITION, AND FORESTRY / 106th Congress

Service Dates of Committee Chair: Jan. 7, 1999-Jan. 3, 2001

Service Dates of Majority Members: Jan. 7, 1999-Jan. 25, 2001

Service Dates of Minority Members: Jan. 7, 1999-Jan. 25, 2001

Majority						**Minority**				
			Years in:						**Years in:**	
Rank Name	Party	State	Senate	Comm.		Rank Name	Party	State	Senate	Comm.
Chr Lugar, Richard G.	Rep	Ind.	23	22		RM Harkin, Thomas R.	Dem	Iowa	15	14
2nd Helms, Jesse A.	Rep	N.C.	27	26		2nd Leahy, Patrick J.	Dem	Vt.	25	24
3rd Cochran, W. Thad	Rep	Miss.	21	20		3rd Conrad, Kent	Dem	N.D.	13	13
4th McConnell, A. Mitchell (Mitch)	Rep	Ky.	15	14		4th Daschle, Thomas A.	Dem	S.D.	13	13
5th Coverdell, Paul	Rep	Ga.	7	7		5th Baucus, Max S.	Dem	Mont.	21	10
6th Roberts, C. Patrick	Rep	Kans.	3	2		6th Kerrey, J. Robert	Dem	Neb.	11	10
7th Fitzgerald, Peter G.	Rep	Ill.	1	1		7th Johnson, Timothy P.	Dem	S.D.	3	2
8th Grassley, Charles E.	Rep	Iowa	19	*2 4		8th Lincoln, Blanche Lambert	Dem	Ark.	1	1
9th Craig, Larry E.	Rep	Ida.	9	8						
10th Santorum, Richard J. (Rick)	Rep	Penn.	5	*1 5						

*1: Member's first period of service on the committee.
*2: Member's second period of service on the committee.

Note: Rankings on this committee for the following members were affected by other chamber service: Jesse A. Helms (Rep-N.C.), Chair, Foreign Relations; and Patrick J. Leahy (Dem-Vt.), Ranking Minority Member, Judiciary.

Additions:

Majority:

11th Voinovich, George V.	Rep	Ohio	Dec. 6, 2000

Minority:

9th Miller, Zell B.	Dem	Ga.	Sept. 12, 2000

Changes:

Majority:

Coverdell, Paul	Rep	Ga.	July 18, 2000 Died in office.
Smith, Gordon H.	Rep	Ore.	Sept. 12, 2000 Replaced Coverdell.

Departures from the Senate:	**Majority**			**Minority**		
Retired	None			Kerrey, J. Robert	Dem	Neb.

Departures from Committee:						
Became Chair of Finance	Grassley, Charles E.	Rep	Iowa	None		
Became Chair of Special Aging	Craig, Larry E.	Rep	Ida.			
Moved to Appropriations and Select Indian Affairs	None			Johnson, Timothy P.	Dem	S.D.
Moved to Joint Printing	Santorum, Richard J. (Rick)	Rep	Penn.			
Moved to Commerce, Science, and Transportation	Smith, Gordon H.	Rep	Ore.	None		

AGRICULTURE, NUTRITION, AND FORESTRY / 107th Congress, Pre-Jeffords Shift

Service Dates of Committee Chair: ChT: Jan. 3, 2001-Jan. 25, 2001 Harkin (Dem-Iowa)

Ch1: Jan. 25, 2001-June 6, 2001 Lugar (Rep-Ind.)

Service Dates of Majority Members: Jan. 25, 2001-June 6, 2001

Service Dates of Minority Members: Jan. 25, 2001-June 6, 2001

Majority					Minority				
			Years in:					Years in:	
Rank Name	Party	State	Senate	Comm.	Rank Name	Party	State	Senate	Comm.
Ch1 Lugar, Richard G.	Rep	Ind.	25	24	RM1 Harkin, Thomas R.	Dem	Iowa	17	16
2nd Helms, Jesse A.	Rep	N.C.	29	29	2nd Leahy, Patrick J.	Dem	Vt.	27	27
3rd Cochran, W. Thad	Rep	Miss.	23	23	3rd Conrad, Kent	Dem	N.D.	15	15
4th McConnell, A. Mitchell (Mitch)	Rep	Ky.	17	16	4th Daschle, Thomas A.	Dem	S.D.	15	15
5th Roberts, C. Patrick	Rep	Kans.	5	5	5th Baucus, Max S.	Dem	Mont.	23	12
6th Fitzgerald, Peter G.	Rep	Ill.	3	3	6th Lincoln, Blanche Lambert	Dem	Ark.	3	3
7th Thomas, Craig L.	Rep	Wyo.	7	*1 1	7th Miller, Zell B.	Dem	Ga.	1	1
8th Allard, A. Wayne	Rep	Colo.	5	1	8th Stabenow, Deborah Ann	Dem	Mich.	1	1
9th Hutchinson, Y. Timothy	Rep	Ark.	5	1	9th Nelson, E. Benjamin	Dem	Neb.	1	1
10th Crapo, Michael D.	Rep	Ida.	3	1	10th Dayton, Mark	DFL	Minn.	1	1

*1: Member's first period of service on the committee.

Note 1: Rankings on this committee for the following members were affected by other chamber service: Jesse A. Helms (Rep-N.C.), Chair, Foreign Relations; and Patrick J. Leahy (Dem-Vt.), Ranking Minority Member, Judiciary.

Note 2: The committee majority in the 2001 Senate power-sharing arrangement was determined by the party of the vice president. Democrat Al Gore Jr. served from Jan. 3, 2001, to Jan. 20, 2001, and was succeeded by Republican Richard B. Cheney on Jan. 20, 2001. When Senator Jeffords of Vermont left the Republican Party, effective June 6, 2001, to become an Independent, Democrats regained the majority for the remainder of the 107th Congress.

AGRICULTURE, NUTRITION, AND FORESTRY / 107th Congress, Post-Jeffords Shift

Service Dates of Committee Chair: June 6, 2001-Jan. 14, 2003

Service Dates of Majority Members: June 6, 2001-Jan. 14, 2003

Service Dates of Minority Members: June 6, 2001-Jan. 15, 2003

Majority					Minority				
			Years in:					Years in:	
Rank Name	Party	State	Senate	Comm.	Rank Name	Party	State	Senate	Comm.
Ch2 Harkin, Thomas R.	Dem	Iowa	17	17	RM2 Lugar, Richard G.	Rep	Ind.	25	25
2nd Leahy, Patrick J.	Dem	Vt.	27	27	2nd Helms, Jesse A.	Rep	N.C.	29	29
3rd Conrad, Kent	Dem	N.D.	15	15	3rd Cochran, W. Thad	Rep	Miss.	23	23
4th Daschle, Thomas A.	Dem	S.D.	15	15	4th McConnell, A. Mitchell (Mitch)	Rep	Ky.	17	17
5th Baucus, Max S.	Dem	Mont.	23	13	5th Roberts, C. Patrick	Rep	Kans.	5	5
6th Lincoln, Blanche Lambert	Dem	Ark.	3	3	6th Fitzgerald, Peter G.	Rep	Ill.	3	3
7th Miller, Zell B.	Dem	Ga.	1	1	7th Thomas, Craig L.	Rep	Wyo.	7	*1 1
8th Stabenow, Deborah Ann	Dem	Mich.	1	1	8th Allard, A. Wayne	Rep	Colo.	5	1
9th Nelson, E. Benjamin	Dem	Neb.	1	1	9th Hutchinson, Y. Timothy	Rep	Ark.	5	1
10th Dayton, Mark	DFL	Minn.	1	1	10th Crapo, Michael D.	Rep	Ida.	3	1
11th Wellstone, Paul D.	DFL	Minn.	11	1					

*1: Member's first period of service on the committee.

Note: Rankings on this committee for the following members were affected by other chamber service: Patrick J. Leahy (Dem-Vt.), Chair, Judiciary; and Jesse A. Helms (Rep-N.C.), Chair, Ranking Minority Member, Foreign Relations.

Additions:
   Majority:
      11th Wellstone, Paul D.   DFL   Minn.   July 10, 2001

Changes:
   Majority:
      Wellstone, Paul D.   DFL   Minn.   Oct. 25, 2002 Died in office.

Departures from the Senate:	Majority			Minority		
Defeated for Re-election	None			Hutchinson, Y. Timothy	Rep	Ark.
Retired	None			Helms, Jesse A.	Rep	N.C.

Departures from Committee:

Returned to Environment and Public Works	None		
Moved to Environment and Public Works	None		

Thomas, Craig L.	Rep	Wyo.
Allard, A. Wayne	Rep	Colo.

AGRICULTURE, NUTRITION, AND FORESTRY / 108th Congress

Service Dates of Committee Chair: Jan. 14, 2003-Jan. 6, 2005

Service Dates of Majority Members: Jan. 14, 2003-Jan. 6, 2005

Service Dates of Minority Members: Jan. 15, 2003-Jan. 6, 2005

Majority					Minority				
			Years in:					Years in:	
Rank Name	Party	State	Senate	Comm.	Rank Name	Party	State	Senate	Comm.
Chr Cochran, W. Thad	Rep	Miss.	25	24	RM Harkin, Thomas R.	Dem	Iowa	19	18
2nd Lugar, Richard G.	Rep	Ind.	27	26	2nd Leahy, Patrick J.	Dem	Vt.	29	28
3rd McConnell, A. Mitchell (Mitch)	Rep	Ky.	19	18	3rd Conrad, Kent	Dem	N.D.	17	17
4th Roberts, C. Patrick	Rep	Kans.	7	7	4th Daschle, Thomas A.	Dem	S.D.	17	17
5th Fitzgerald, Peter G.	Rep	Ill.	5	5	5th Baucus, Max S.	Dem	Mont.	25	14
6th Chambliss, Saxby	Rep	Ga.	1	1	6th Lincoln, Blanche Lambert	Dem	Ark.	5	5
7th Coleman, Norman	Rep	Minn.	1	1	7th Miller, Zell B.	Dem	Ga.	3	3
8th Crapo, Michael D.	Rep	Ida.	5	2	8th Stabenow, Deborah Ann	Dem	Mich.	3	2
9th Talent, James M.	Rep	Mo.	1	1	9th Nelson, E. Benjamin	Dem	Neb.	3	2
10th Dole, Elizabeth Hanford	Rep	N.C.	1	1	10th Dayton, Mark	DFL	Minn.	3	2
11th Grassley, Charles E.	Rep	Iowa	23	*3 1					

*3: Member's third period of service on the committee.

Note: Rankings on this committee for the following members were affected by other chamber service: Richard G. Lugar (Rep-Ind.) Chair, Foreign Relations; and Patrick J. Leahy (Dem-Vt.), Ranking Minority Member, Judiciary.

Departures from the Senate:	Majority			Minority		
Defeated for Re-election	None			Daschle, Thomas A.	Dem	S.D.
Retired	Fitzgerald, Peter G.	Rep	Ill.	Miller, Zell B.	Dem	Ga.

Departures from Committee:					
No new assignment	Dole, Elizabeth Hanford	Rep	N.C.	None	

AGRICULTURE, NUTRITION, AND FORESTRY / 109th Congress

Service Dates of Committee Chair: Jan. 6, 2005-Jan. 12, 2007

Service Dates of Majority Members: Jan. 6, 2005-Jan. 12, 2007

Service Dates of Minority Members: Jan. 6, 2005-Jan. 12, 2007

Majority					Minority				
			Years in:					Years in:	
Rank Name	Party	State	Senate	Comm.	Rank Name	Party	State	Senate	Comm.
Chr Chambliss, Saxby	Rep	Ga.	3	2	RM Harkin, Thomas R.	Dem	Iowa	21	20
2nd Lugar, Richard G.	Rep	Ind.	29	28	2nd Leahy, Patrick J.	Dem	Vt.	31	30
3rd Cochran, W. Thad	Rep	Miss.	27	26	3rd Conrad, Kent	Dem	N.D.	19	19
4th McConnell, A. Mitchell (Mitch)	Rep	Ky.	21	20	4th Baucus, Max S.	Dem	Mont.	27	16
5th Roberts, C. Patrick	Rep	Kans.	9	8	5th Lincoln, Blanche Lambert	Dem	Ark.	7	6
6th Talent, James M.	Rep	Mo.	3	2	6th Stabenow, Deborah Ann	Dem	Mich.	5	4
7th Thomas, Craig L.	Rep	Wyo.	11	*2 1	7th Nelson, E. Benjamin	Dem	Neb.	5	4
8th Santorum. Richard J.	Rep	Penn.	11	*2 1	8th Dayton, Mark	DFL	Minn.	5	4
9th Coleman, Norman	Rep	Minn.	3	2	9th Salazar, Kenneth L.	Dem	Colo.	1	1
10th Crapo, Michael D.	Rep	Ida.	7	4					
11th Grassley, Charles E.	Rep	Iowa	25	*3 2					

*2: Member's second period of service on the committee.

*3: Member's third period of service on the committee.

Note: Rankings on this committee for the following members were affected by other chamber service: Richard G. Lugar (Rep-Ind.) Chair, Foreign Relations; Thad Cochran (Rep-Miss.) Chair, Appropriations; Mitch McConnell, Majority Leader; C. Patrick Roberts, Chair, Select Intelligence, and Patrick J. Leahy (Dem-Vt.), Ranking Minority Member, Judiciary.

Departures from the Senate:	Majority			Minority		
Defeated for Re-election	Talent, James M.	Rep	Mo.	None		
	Santorum, Richard J. (Rick)	Rep	Penn.			
Retired	None			Dayton, Mark	DFL	Minn.

Departures from Committee:					
Returned to Environment and Public Works	Thomas, Craig L.	Rep	Wyo.	None	

AGRICULTURE, NUTRITION, AND FORESTRY / 110th Congress

Service Dates of Committee Chair: Jan. 12, 2001-Jan. 21, 2009

Service Dates of Majority Members: Jan. 12, 2001-Jan. 21, 2009

Service Dates of Minority Members: Jan. 12, 2001-Jan. 21, 2009

Majority			Years in:		Minority			Years in:	
Rank Name	Party	State	Senate	Comm.	Rank Name	Party	State	Senate	Comm.
Chr Harkin, Thomas R.	Dem	Iowa	23	22	RM Chambliss, Saxby	Rep	Ga.	5	4
2nd Leahy, Patrick J.	Dem	Vt.	33	32	2nd Lugar, Richard G.	Rep	Ind.	31	30
3rd Conrad, Kent	Dem	N.D.	21	21	3rd Cochran, W. Thad	Rep	Miss.	29	28
4th Baucus, Max S.	Dem	Mont.	29	18	4th McConnell, A. Mitchell (Mitch)	Rep	Ky.	23	22
5th Lincoln, Blanche Lambert	Dem	Ark.	9	9	5th Roberts, C. Patrick	Rep	Kans.	11	11
6th Stabenow, Deborah Ann	Dem	Mich.	7	6	6th Graham, Lindsey O.	Rep	S.C.	5	1
7th Nelson, E. Benjamin	Dem	Neb.	7	6	7th Coleman, Norman	Rep	Minn.	5	4
8th Salazar, Kenneth L.	Dem	Colo.	3	3	8th Crapo, Michael D.	Rep	Ida.	9	6
9th Brown, Sherrod	Dem	Ohio	1	1	9th Thune, John	Rep	S.D.	3	1
10th Casey, Robert P. Jr.	Dem	Penn.	1	1	10th Grassley, Charles E.	Rep	Iowa	27	*3 4
11th Klobuchar, Amy	DFL	Minn.	1	1					

*3: Member's third period of service on the committee.

Note: Rankings on this committee for the following members were affected by other chamber service: Patrick J. Leahy (Dem-Vt.), Chair, Judiciary; Richard G. Lugar (Rep-Ind.) Ranking Minority Member, Foreign Relations; Thad Cochran (Rep-Miss.) Ranking Minority Member, Appropriations; and Mitch McConnell, Minority Leader.

Departures from the Senate:	Majority	Minority		
Defeated for Re-election	None	Coleman, Norman	Rep	Minn.

Departures from Committee:				
Moved to Homeland Security and				
Governmental Affairs and Special Aging	None	Graham, Lindsey O.	Rep	S.C.
Returned to Environment and Public Works	None	Crapo, Michael D.	Rep	Ida.

Note: Kenneth L. Salazar (Dem-Colo.) resigned the Senate on Jan. 20, 2009; named Secretary of the Interior

AGRICULTURE, NUTRITION, AND FORESTRY / 111th Congress

Service Dates of Committee Chair: Ch1: Jan. 21, 2009-Sept. 9, 2009, Harkin (Dem-Iowa)

Ch2: Sept. 9, 2009- Lincoln (Dem-Ark.)

Service Dates of Majority Members: Jan. 21, 2009-

Service Dates of Minority Members: Jan. 21, 2009-

Majority			Years in:		Minority			Years in:	
Rank Name	Party	State	Senate	Comm.	Rank Name	Party	State	Senate	Comm.
Ch1 Harkin, Thomas R.	Dem	Iowa	25	24	RM Chambliss, Saxby	Rep	Ga.	7	7
2nd Leahy, Patrick J.	Dem	Vt.	35	34	2nd Lugar, Richard G.	Rep	Ind.	33	32
3rd Conrad, Kent	Dem	N.D.	23	23	3rd Cochran, W. Thad	Rep	Miss.	31	30
4th Baucus, Max S.	Dem	Mont.	31	20	4th McConnell, A. Mitchell (Mitch)	Rep	Ky.	25	24
5th Ch2 Lincoln, Blanche Lambert	Dem	Ark.	11	11	5th Roberts, C. Patrick	Rep	Kans.	13	13
6th Stabenow, Deborah Ann	Dem	Mich.	9	8	6th Johanns, Mike	Rep	Neb.	1	1
7th Nelson, E. Benjamin	Dem	Neb.	9	8	7th Grassley, Charles E.	Rep	Iowa	29	*3 7
8th Brown, Sherrod	Dem	Ohio	3	3	8th Thune, John	Rep	S.D.	5	3
9th Casey, Robert P. Jr.	Dem	Penn.	3	3	9th Cornyn, John	Rep	Tex.	7	1

10th Klobuchar, Amy	DFL	Minn.	3	3	
11th Bennet, Michael F.	Dem	Colo.	1	1	*3: Member's third period of service on the committee.
12th Gillibrand, Kirsten E.	Dem	N.Y.	1	1	

Note: Initial rankings on this committee for the following members were affected by other chamber service: Patrick J. Leahy (Dem-Vt.), Chair, Judiciary; Richard G. Lugar (Rep-Ind.) Ranking Minority Member, Foreign Relations; Thad Cochran (Rep-Miss.) Ranking Minority Member, Appropriations; and Mitch McConnell, Minority Leader. Fifth-ranked Lincoln replaced Harkin as chair because 3rd-ranked Kent Conrad (Dem-N.D.) was Chair of Budget and 4th-ranked Max Baucus (Dem-Mont.) was Chair of Finance.

Filled Vacancies:
  Majority:
    11th and 12th seats by Bennet and Gillibrand on Jan. 27, 2009
  Minority:
    9th seat by Cornyn on July 21, 2009

Changes:
  Chair:

Harkin, Thomas R.	Dem	Iowa	Sept. 9, 2009 Relinquished chairmanship to succeed Kennedy on Health, Education, Labor and Pensions
Lincoln, Blanche Lambert	Dem	Ark.	Sept. 9, 2009 Succeeded Harkin as Chair

Note: The disputed election in Minnesota between Democrat Al Franken and incumbent Republican Norman Coleman led both parties to hold seats open pending the outcome of the recount.

Appropriations

Senate Committee on Appropriations, 103rd-111th Congresses (1993-2011)

BACKGROUND

Organizational History: In the modern Congress, following World War II, the Appropriations Committee was the largest in the Senate and one of its most important. It remains the largest of the Senate's standing committees, but it traditionally has had a role of lesser significance than its House counterpart.

The Senate had developed appropriations procedures long before a separate Appropriations Committee was created in 1867. In the earliest Congresses, conflict over fiscal matters erupted between Secretary of the Treasury Alexander Hamilton (Fed-N.Y.) and Albert Gallatin (DR-Penn.). Hamilton saw himself in the British mold as the nation's "Chancellor of the Exchequer" and took relatively little heed of congressional wishes. Gallatin challenged Hamilton in the House and following Hamilton's resignation from Treasury in 1795, he was able to establish a Ways and Means Committee to review taxing and spending measures. Gallatin would later exercise his fiscal acumen as Secretary of the Treasury for both Presidents Thomas Jefferson and James Madison.

In the early Senate, the appropriating function was carried out by select committees which were used to review spending proposals. The appropriating and taxation functions in the Senate became part of the standing committee structure with the establishment of the Senate Finance Committee in December, 1816. And prior to 1867, both revenue and appropriations bills were handled by the Senate Finance Committee. This circumstance was identical to that in the House involving the Ways and Means Committee prior to 1865. However, the enormous financial burdens of the Civil War led both chambers of Congress to divide the revenue-raising responsibility of taxes and tariffs from the spending authority. This was accomplished in both Houses through the creation of separate committees on appropriations.

As recounted in the 1973 report of Ralph Nader's Congress Project, *The Revenue Committees* directed by Richard Spohn and Charles McCollum:

> The costs during the Civil War made those expenditures [the Mexican War] seem like chicken feed, however. By 1865, expenditures went past the billion dollar mark for the first time and the interest on the national debt rocketed to $100 million per year. The Ways and Means and Finance committees were overworked to the point that, during the Civil War, Abraham Lincoln all but ignored the appropriations process and simply spent monies as he saw fit. There was almost no congressional opposition to this in a time of crisis but—even after Congress moved to reassert its authority in 1865—one major point had been made: the two congressional committees entrusted with both taxation and appropriations simply could no longer handle the burden. (220-221)

The leading Senate spokesman for the separation was Henry B. Anthony (Rep-R.I.), and it was accepted by the Senate on March 6, 1867. Sen. Lot M. Morrill (Rep-Maine), who chaired the District of Columbia Committee, became the first chair of Senate Appropriations a day later on March 7, 1867. None of the committee's initial seven members had served on the Finance Committee in the preceding session of the Congress.

The House moved jurisdictional authority away from the Appropriations Committee in the 1880's to limit the power of then-Chair and former Speaker Samuel J. Randall (Dem-Penn.). The Senate followed suit in the 1890's but the motivation for the move seemed more regional than personal. Virginia Senator John W. Daniel, a Democrat argued, "There is not a single Senator from the Maryland line to the Rio Grande upon the Appropriations Committee. There is not a single Senator from a cotton State . . . upon the Committee on Appropriations."

According to Stephen Horn's *Unused Power: The Work of the Senate Committee on Appropriations* (Washington, 1970), the effort to limit the jurisdiction of the Appropriations Committee was led by freshman senator Fred T. Dubois (Rep-Ida.) and his supporters who attacked the Committee on Appropriations for ignoring the recommendations of the legislative committees. A single committee, they argued, simply could not give adequate consideration to fourteen appropriations bills. The legislative committees might even become fiscally conservative if they were granted the responsibility to appropriate funds. A higher level of interest in budget matters would be elicited from all senators, and it would be a convenience for witnesses to deal with only one committee rather than divide their efforts between a legislative and an appropriations committee. These were the rational arguments, but a more basic motive for the Dubois resolution was voiced by a southern senator who hailed the attempt "to change the distribution of power in the Senate, to emancipate the Senate from the monopolistic dominance of about 20 men here who compose the two leading committees, those of Appropriations and Finance. . . . There is too much power lodged in one committee."

After these changes in 1899, matters handled by the committee such as appropriations for rivers and harbors, agriculture, the Army, the Military Academy, Indians, the Navy, pensions, and Post Offices were referred to their respective legislative committees. Following this rule change, the Senate Appropriations Committee retained control of only deficiency, diplomatic and consular, District of Columbia, fortifications, legislative, and sundry civil appropriation bills. In July 1919, the Senate moved appropriations for the diplomatic and consular services to the Committee on Foreign Relations.

In the book, *The Revenue Committees*, it is contended that

> The end result [of giving appropriations measures to legislative committees] was chaos, which the Senate also managed to achieve by 1899. With committees handling both the substantive legislation and the appropriations of most agencies, the bureaucrats moved to exploit the

situation, building up more than cordial relations with the committees charged with overseeing their operations. . . . No committee took notice of what the others did, and agencies were free to submit their budgets directly to the Congress with no presidential overview. To top it off, Appropriations still maintained control over deficiency requests of all agencies. Throughout the better part of a thirty-year period neither the executive nor the legislative branch had any real control over the budget. (222)

It was the Budget and Accounting Act of June 10, 1921, that gave the Senate Appropriations Committee its enormous influence within that body. The Budget and Accounting Act created the Bureau of the Budget within the executive branch as a means of centralizing authority over the budget. The Congress responded accordingly by establishing the General Accounting Office, its auditing arm, and by moving appropriations bills from the subject matter committees to the Appropriations Committee. In addition, chairs of the subject matter committees (e.g., agriculture, army, navy, post offices, etc.) were made *ex officio* members of Appropriations. This combination of moves led to the enhancement of the legislative power and authority of the various subcommittees of the Appropriations Committee by giving these senior members control over both legislation and spending within their respective subject areas.

The *Guide to the Records of the United States Senate at the National Archives, 1789-1989* points out that:

Although the Legislative Reorganization Act of 1946 specified for the first time committee jurisdiction and permitted employment of a professional committee staff, the rules of the Senate with respect to appropriation bills remained largely unchanged until 1950. In that year, all appropriations were consolidated into a single bill, but, owing to its complexity and magnitude, the process was not repeated. A more permanent post-World War II change increased the use of the authorization process by legislative committees and enhanced fiscal controls over executive agencies by defining an upper limit to an agency's or program's appropriation.

Initially, under the Legislative Reorganization Act of 1946, a legislative budget was tried and found wanting. During the first two months of each session, Congress was to establish an expenditure ceiling for the ensuing fiscal year that would limit the appropriations approved later in the session. In 1950, an omnibus appropriation bill that consolidated all of the subcommittee bills was tried and abandoned. Sporadically since 1952, legislation to establish a joint committee on the budget has repeatedly been approved by the Senate, only to die in the House of Representatives.

The jurisdictional adjustments that were made to the Appropriations Committee in the Reorganization Amendments of 1977 (S.Res. 95-4) remain in place today. Despite anxiety that the 1974 creation of the Senate Budget Committee would strip Appropriations of its power and relative internal prestige does not appear to have occurred. The two leading Democrats on the Appropriations Committee in the 111th Congress—Chair Daniel K. Inouye (Dem-Hai.) and former chair Robert C. Byrd (Dem-W.Va.) began their congressional service as House members during the Eisenhower Administration. President Obama is the eleventh president with whom they have served and their combined length of service in Congress is 110 years.

Membership: The growth of the Appropriations Committee's power also led to an increase in its membership, and by the time of the Reorganization Act, with twenty-one members it was clearly the largest committee in the Senate. That has continued in recent Congresses, and in the 111th Congress, it became the first Senate standing committee to have thirty members. Since 1993, its average size of 28.7 members ranks it first and easily the Senate's largest. In addition, the Appropriations Committee has a seniority average of 16.91 years, ranking it second, and its 94.9 percent interCongress retention rate ranks it third behind Rules and Administration and Finance.

The Appropriations Committee gained twenty-two members during these nine Congresses while eleven moved to other committees, resulting in a net gain of eleven. Seven of the departing members moved to Finance and two to Foreign Relations, while Democrat Harry Reid of Nevada left the committee when he became Majority Leader in 2007.

Committee Leaders: Senator H. Styles Bridges (Rep-N.H.) was the Appropriations Committee's first modern-era chair (1947-1949). He also chaired the committee in the 83rd Congress (1953-1955). Serving as chair of Appropriations between Bridges's two tours of duty was Kenneth D. McKellar (Dem-Tenn.), who held the chair from 1949 until 1953, when he left the Senate following his defeat in the 1952 Democratic primary by Al Gore.

In 1955, Carl Hayden (Dem-Ariz.) became chair of Appropriations and served in that post until his retirement in 1969, at which time Hayden had become the longest-serving member of Congress in American history with fifteen years in the House and almost forty-two in the Senate. Hayden was succeeded by Richard B. Russell (Dem-Ga.) who served as chair from 1969 until his death on January 21, 1971. Russell's successor, Allen J. Ellender (Dem-La.), also died in office during his first term as chair of Appropriations. Russell had left the chair of Armed Services to take over the Appropriations Committee while Ellender had surrendered his chairmanship of Agriculture and Forestry for that honor.

Senator McKellar was the committee's first post-1947 ranking minority member. H. Styles Bridges, the Republican chair in the 80th and 83rd Congresses, served as its ranking minority member in the six other Congresses which convened between 1947 until his death in 1961. Bridges was succeeded in this post by his fellow New Englander, Leverett Saltonstall (Rep-Mass.), who served until his retirement in 1967. North Dakota's Milton R. Young served as the committee's ranking minority member for the next seven Congresses (1967-1981) until his retirement.

Following Ellender's death, John McClellan (Dem-Ark.) gave up his chairmanship of the Government Operations Committee to chair Appropriations. McClellan served from 1972 until his death on November 28, 1977. McClellan's successor was Warren G. Magnuson (Dem-Wash.), who was chair of the Commerce Committee. Magnuson was the fourth consecutive chair of Appropriations to relinquish the chairmanship of another committee for the privilege of chairing Appropriations, an indisputable mark of its importance in the Senate. However, Magnuson did not suffer the fate of his three immediate predecessors. He left the chairmanship via his defeat for re-election in 1980.

When the Republicans gained control of the Senate in 1981, Mark O. Hatfield (Rep-Ore.) assumed the chair and held it for three Congresses (1981-1987). John C. Stennis

(Dem-Miss.), the "dean" of the Senate and the president *pro tempore* became chair in 1987 upon the Democratic recapture of the Senate. Following Stennis's retirement from the Senate in 1989, Robert C. Byrd (Dem-W.Va.) retired as Senate Majority Leader to succeed Stennis as both Senate president *pro tempore* and chair of the Appropriations Committee, posts which continued until 1995. Republican gains in 1994 moved Byrd to the ranking minority post for twelve years (1995-2007), but he resumed the chair in 2007. In 2009, after twenty years as the senior Democrat on Appropriations, ninety-one year-old Senator Byrd relinquished the chair to Hawaii's Daniel K. Inouye, who was eighty-four at the start of the 111th Congress.

During the six-Congress sequence when Republicans controlled the Senate, there were three different chairs—Mark Hatfield who resumed the chair for two years (1995-1997); Theodore F. Stevens of Alaska (1997-2001, 2003-2005); and W. Thad Cochran of Mississippi (2005-2007). Stevens and Byrd flipped senior posts during the aftermath of the Jeffords defection in 2001.

Republican control of the Senate in 1981 led to William Proxmire (Dem-Wisc.) assuming the ranking minority slot. Senator Stennis, who chose to serve as ranking minority member on Armed Services in the 97th Congress (1981-1983) exercised his seniority rights and became the committee's ranking Democrat for the next two Congresses (1983-1987).

Following the Democratic recapture of the Senate in 1986, Mark Hatfield became the ranking minority member from 1987 to 1995, when the Republicans resumed control of the Senate. Once again, Robert Byrd became ranking minority member for all but eighteen months of the twelve-year Republican hegemony from 1995 to 2007. Since 2007, Thad Cochran of Mississippi has held the ranking minority slot on Appropriations.

Party Leaders: Because of the committee's high level of prestige, its ranks have been filled with prominent members of the modern era Senate. Of the thirty-six floor leaders and party Whips since 1947, seventeen had served on the Appropriations Committee. Among the Democrats, there have been four floor leaders: Lyndon B. Johnson (Dem-Tex.), Mike Mansfield (Dem-Mont.), Robert C. Byrd (Dem-W.Va.), and Harry Reid (Dem-Nev.); and three Whips: Earle C. Clements (Dem-Ky.), Hubert H. Humphrey (DFL-Minn.), and Richard Durbin (Dem-Ill.). Johnson, Mansfield, Byrd, and Reid all apprenticed for the floor leadership by serving in the Whip post. Both Democratic leaders in the 111th Congress, Reid and Durbin, are presently serving on Appropriations.

Senate Republicans have made greater use of the Appropriations Committee as a source of their leaders—five floor leaders: Kenneth Wherry (Rep-Neb.), H. Styles Bridges (Rep-N.H.), William Knowland (Rep-Cal.), Everett M. Dirksen (Rep-Ill.), and Mitch McConnell (Rep-Ky.); and five Whips: Leverett Saltonstall (Rep-Mass.), Thomas Kuchel (Rep-Cal.), Theodore Stevens (Rep-Alas.), Don Nickles (Rep-Okla.), and Jon Kyl (Rep-Ariz.). Wherry, Dirksen, and McConnell began their leadership careers as Whips before their elections as floor leaders. With both Republican leaders, McConnell and Kyl, presently serving on the committee alongside both Democratic leaders, Reid and Durbin, there can be little doubt that Appropriations is the powerhouse committee of the 111th Congress.

Presidential Aspirations: The Senate Appropriations Committee appears to be more a source of "inside" power, as none of its members were directly nominated for president and only four members were nominated for vice president. All were Democrats: Estes Kefauver (Dem-Tenn.) on the Adlai Stevenson ticket of 1956; Lyndon Johnson on the Kennedy ticket of 1960; Hubert Humphrey (DFL-Minn.) on the Johnson ticket in 1964; and Thomas Eagleton (Dem-Mo.), the initial nominee on the McGovern ticket of 1972.

Other Notables: Two noteworthy members of the Appropriations Committee were Joseph R. McCarthy (Rep-Wisc.) and Mike Monroney (Dem-Okla.). In the 82nd Congress (1951-1953), Senator McCarthy, the Senate's controversial leader of anti-communist investigations, had the unusual distinction of serving on the committee twice during the same Congress as special elections tipped the narrow party ratio on the committee back and forth. Senator Monroney's contributions to the committee system of the Congress are enormous. As the House author of the Legislative Reorganization Act of 1946, it was his legislation which ushered in the modern era.

Two former Cabinet members served on Appropriations—Brock Adams (Dem-Wash.) who was President Carter's Secretary of Transportation, and Lamar Alexander (Rep-Tenn.) who served under President George H.W. Bush as Secretary of Education. Pennsylvania Republican senator Richard Schweiker, who was floated as a vice presidential nominee by California governor Ronald Reagan during his 1976 nomination challenge to President Ford, was named by President Reagan to be his Secretary of Health and Human Services in 1981.

Selected References

Coren, Robert W., et al., "Records of the Committee on Appropriations, 1867-1968," *Guide to the Records of the United States Senate at the National Archives: 1789-1989 Bicentennial Edition* (Washington, D.C.: National Archives and Records Administration, 1989), 29-33.

Fenno, Richard F., Jr., *The Power of the Purse: Appropriations Politics in Congress* (Boston: Little, Brown, 1966).

Horn, Stephen, *Unused Power: The Work of the Senate Committee on Appropriations,* 2 vols. (Washington, D.C.: Brookings Institution, 1970),

Meier, Kenneth J. and Gary W. Copeland, "Interest Groups and Public Policy," *Social Science Quarterly*, 64 (September, 1983), 641-646.

Munson, Richard, *The Cardinals of Capitol Hill: The Men and Women Who Control Government Spending* (New York: Grove Press, 1993).

Schick, Allen, *Congress and Money: Budgeting, Spending and Taxing* (Washington, D.C.: The Urban Institute, 1980).

Schick, Allen, "The Three-Ring Budget Process: The Appropriations, Tax and Budget Committees in Congress," in Thomas Mann and Norman J. Ornstein, eds., *The New Congress* (Washington, D.C.: American Enterprise Institute, 1981), 288-328.

Spohn, Richard and Charles McCollum, dirs., "The House and Senate Appropriations Committees," in the Ralph Nader Congress Project, *The Revenue Committees: A Study of the House Ways and Means and Senate Finance Committee and the House and Senate Appropriations Committees* (New York: Grossman, 1975), 217-260.

Stewart, Charles, *Budget Reform Politics: The Design of the Appropriations Process, 1865-1921* (Cambridge, U.K.: Cambridge University Press, 1989).

U.S. Senate, Committee on Appropriations, Committee on Appropriations, *141st Anniversary, 1867-2008,* Senate Document

110-14, 110th Congress, 2nd session (2008). This is the fifth history of the committee. Earlier editions included: the 100th Anniversary, 1867-1967, Senate Document 90-21, 90th Congress, 1st session (1967); the *126th Anniversary, 1867-1993*, Senate Document 103-17, 103rd Congress, 1st session (1993); the *135th Anniversary, 1867-2002*, Senate Document 107-13, 107th Congress, 2nd session (2002); and the *138th Anniversary, 1867-2005*, Senate Document 109-5, 109th Congress, 1st session (2005).

White, Joseph, "Appropriations Committee, Senate," in Donald C. Bacon, Roger H. Davidson, and Morton Keller, eds., *The Encyclopedia of the United States Congress* (New York: Simon & Schuster, 1995), I: 78-82.

White, Joseph, "Decision Making in the in the Appropriations Subcommittees on Defense and Foreign Operations," in Randall B. Ripley and James M. Lindsay, eds., *Congress Resurgent: Foreign and Defense Policy on Capitol Hill* (Ann Arbor: University of Michigan Press, 1993), 183-206.

Yarwood, Dean L., "Oversight of Presidential Funds by Appropriations Committees: Learning from the Watergate Crisis," *Administration and Society*, 13 (November, 1981), 299-346.

RESPONSIBILITIES, JURISDICTIONAL CHANGES, AND SUBCOMMITTEES

APPROPRIATIONS

Jurisdiction, 80th Congress (1947-49)

Established by the Legislative Reorganization Act of 1946:

[Section 102.(1)(b)]

(1) Committee on Appropriations, to consist of twenty-one Senators, to which committee shall be referred all proposed legislation, messages, petitions, memorials, and other matters relating to the following subjects:

   (1) Appropriation of the revenue for the support of the Government.

[Section 139.]

   (a) No general appropriation bill shall be considered in either House unless, prior to the consideration of such bill, printed committee hearings and reports on such bill have been available for at least three calendar days for the Members of the House in which such bill is to be considered.

   (b) The Committees on Appropriations of the two Houses are authorized and directed, acting jointly, to develop a standard appropriation classification schedule which will clearly define in concise and uniform accounts the subtotals of appropriations asked for by agencies in the executive branch of the Government. That part of the printed hearings containing each such agency's request for appropriations shall be preceded by such a schedule.

   (c) No general appropriation bill or amendment thereto shall be received or considered in either House if it contains a provision reappropriating unexpended balances of appropriations; except that this provision shall not apply to appropriations in continuation of appropriations for public works on which work has commenced.

   (d) The Appropriations Committees of both Houses are authorized and directed to make a study of

   (1) existing permanent appropriations with a view to limiting the number of permanent appropriations and to recommend to their respective Houses what permanent appropriations, if any, should be discontinued; and

   (2) the disposition of funds resulting from the sale of Government property or services by all departments and agencies in the executive branch of the Government with a view to recommending to their respective Houses a uniform system of control with respect to such funds.

Post-Reorganization Jurisdiction, 1977

From Committee System Reorganization Amendments of 1977, S.Res. 95-4, *Senate Journal*, Feb. 4, 1977:

[XXV Section 101.(b)]

(1) Committee on Appropriations, to which committee shall be referred all proposed legislation, messages, petitions, memorials, and other matters relating to the following subjects:

   (1) Except as provided in subparagraph (e) [Committee on the Budget] appropriation of the revenue for the support of the Government.

   (2) Rescission of appropriations contained in appropriation Acts (referred to in section 105 of title 1, United States Code).

   (3) The amount of new spending authority described in section 401(c)(2) (A) and (B) of the Congressional Budget Act of 1974 provided in bills and resolutions referred to the committee under section 401 (b)(2) of the Act but subject to the provisions of section 401 (b)(3) of that Act.).

   (4) New advance spending authority described in section 401(c)(2) (C) of the Congressional Budget Act of 1974 provided in bills and resolutions referred to the committee under section 401(b)(2) of that Act (but subject to the provisions of section 401(b)(3) of that Act).

Jurisdiction, 103rd Congress (1993-94)

From the *Standing Rules of the Senate* in the *Senate Manual*, 103rd Congress, 1st Session, S. Doc. 103-1:

[Rule XXV. (1)(b)]

(1) **Committee on Appropriations**, to which committee shall be referred all proposed legislation, messages, petitions, memorials, and other matters relating to the following subjects:

(1) Appropriation of the revenue for the support of the Government, except as provided in subparagraph (e). [Committee on the Budget]

(2) Rescission of appropriations contained in appropriation Acts (referred to in section 105 of title 1, United States Code).

(3) The amount of new spending authority described in section 401(c)(2) (A) and (B) of the Congressional Budget Act of 1974 which is to be effective for a fiscal year.

(4) New spending authority described in section 401(c)(2) (C) of the Congressional Budget Act of 1974 provided in bills and resolutions referred to the committee under section 401(b)(2) of that Act (but subject to the provisions of section 401(b)(3) of the Act).

Jurisdiction, 111th Congress (2009-10)

From *Authority and Rules of Senate Committees, 2009-2010*, Sen. Doc. 111-3, pursuant to S.Res, 166, June 2, 2009.

[Rule XXV. (1)(b)]

(1) **Committee on Appropriations**, to which committee shall be referred all proposed legislation, messages, petitions, memorials, and other matters relating to the following subjects:

(1) Appropriation of the revenue for the support of the Government, except as provided in subparagraph (e).

(2) Rescission of appropriations contained in appropriation Acts (referred to in section 105 of title 1, United States Code).

(3) The amount of new spending authority described in section 401(c)(2) (A) and (B) of the Congressional Budget Act of 1974 which is to be effective for a fiscal year.

(4) New spending authority described in section 401(c)(2)(C) of the Congressional Budget Act of 1974 provided in bills and resolutions referred to the committee under section 401(b)(2) of that Act (but subject to the provisions of section 401(b)(3) of that Act).

NAMES OF SUBCOMMITTEES

Committee on Appropriations, 103rd-111th Congresses

Agriculture, Rural Development, and Related Agencies, 103, 104, 105, 106, 107, 108, 109
Agriculture, Rural Development, Food and Drug Administration, and Related Agencies, 110, 111
Commerce, Justice, State, and the Judiciary, 103, 104, 105, 106, 107, 108
Commerce, Justice, Science, and Related Agencies, 109, 110, 111
Defense, 103, 104, 105, 106, 107, 108, 109, 110
District of Columbia, 103, 104, 105, 106, 107, 108, 109
Energy and Water Development, 103, 104, 105, 106, 107, 108, 110, 111
Energy, Water, and Related Agencies, 109
Foreign Operations, 103, 104, 105, 106, 107, 108
Interior and Related Agencies, 103, 104, 109
Interior, 105, 106, 107, 108
Interior, Environment, and Related Agencies, 110, 111
Labor, Health and Human Services, and Education, 103, 104, 105, 106, 107, 108
Labor, Health and Human Services, and Education, and Related Agencies, 109, 110, 111
Legislative Branch, 103, 104, 105, 106, 107, 108, 109, 110, 111
Military Construction, 103, 104, 105, 106, 107, 108
Military Construction, Veterans' Affairs, and Related Agencies, 109, 110, 111
Transportation and Related Agencies, 103
Transportation, 104, 105, 106, 107
Transportation/Treasury and General Government, 108
Transportation, Treasury, the Judiciary, HUD, and Related Agencies, 109
Transportation, Housing and Urban Development, and Related Agencies, 110, 111
Treasury, Postal Service, and General Government, 103, 104
Treasury and General Government, 105, 106, 107
VA-HUD-Independent Agencies, 103, 104, 105, 106, 107, 108
Homeland Security, 108, 109, 110, 111
Financial Services and General Government, 110, 111
State, Foreign Operations, and Related Programs, 110, 111

MEMBERSHIP ROSTERS, 103rd-111th Congresses, 1993-2010

APPROPRIATIONS / 103rd Congress

Service Dates of Committee Chair: Jan. 7, 1993-Jan. 11, 1995

Service Dates of Majority Members: Jan. 7, 1993-Jan. 4, 1995

Service Dates of Minority Members: Jan. 7, 1993-Jan. 4, 1995

Majority

Rank Name	Party	State	Years in: Senate	Comm.
Chr Byrd, Robert C.	Dem	W.Va.	35	34
2nd Inouye, Daniel K.	Dem	Hawaii	31	22
3rd Hollings, Ernest F.	Dem	S.C.	27	22
4th Johnston, J. Bennett Jr.	Dem	La.	21	18
5th Leahy, Patrick J.	Dem	Vt.	19	16
6th Sasser, James R.	Dem	Tenn.	17	16
7th DeConcini, Dennis W.	Dem	Ariz.	17	16
8th Bumpers, Dale	Dem	Ark.	19	15
9th Lautenberg, Frank R.	Dem	N.J.	11	*1 8
10th Harkin, Thomas R.	Dem	Iowa	9	8
11th Mikulski, Barbara A.	Dem	Md.	7	7
12th Reid, Harry M.	Dem	Nev.	7	7
13th Kerrey, J. Robert	Dem	Neb.	5	4
14th Kohl, Herbert H.	Dem	Wisc.	5	1
15th Murray, Patty	Dem	Wash.	1	1
16th Feinstein, Dianne	Dem	Cal.	1	*1 1

Minority

Rank Name	Party	State	Years in: Senate	Comm.
RM Hatfield, Mark O.	Rep	Ore.	27	21
2nd Stevens, Theodore F.	Rep	Alas.	25	21
3rd Cochran, W. Thad	Rep	Miss.	15	13
4th D'Amato, Alfonse M.	Rep	N.Y.	13	13
5th Specter, Arlen	Rep	Penn.	13	13
6th Domenici, Pete V.	Rep	N.M.	21	11
7th Nickles, Donald L.	Rep	Okla.	13	7
8th Gramm, W. Phil	Rep	Tex.	9	4
9th Bond, Christopher S. (Kit)	Rep	Mo.	7	2
10th Gorton, T. Slade III	Rep	Wash.	11	2
11th McConnell, A. Mitchell (Mitch)	Rep	Ky.	9	1
12th Mack, Connie III	Rep	Fla.	5	1
13th Burns, Conrad	Rep	Mont.	5	1

*1: Member's first period of service on the committee.

Departures from the Senate:

	Majority			Minority
Defeated for Re-election	Sasser, James R.	Dem	Tenn.	None
Retired	DeConcini, Dennis W.	Dem	Ariz.	None

Departures from Committee:

	Majority			Minority		
Moved to Foreign Relations	Feinstein, Dianne	Dem	Cal.	None		
Moved to Finance	None			D'Amato, Alfonse M.	Rep	N.Y.
				Nickles, Donald L.	Rep	Okla.
Moved to Rules and Administration	None			Nickles, Donald L.	Rep	Okla.

APPROPRIATIONS / 104th Congress

Service Dates of Committee Chair: Jan. 11, 1995-Jan. 9, 1997

Service Dates of Majority Members: Jan. 4, 1995-Jan. 9, 1997

Service Dates of Minority Members: Jan. 4, 1995-Jan. 9, 1997

Majority

Rank Name	Party	State	Years in: Senate	Comm.
Chr Hatfield, Mark O.	Rep	Ore.	29	23
2nd Stevens, Theodore F.	Rep	Alas.	27	23
3rd Cochran, W. Thad	Rep	Miss.	17	14
4th Specter, Arlen	Rep	Penn.	15	14
5th Domenici, Pete V.	Rep	N.M.	23	13
6th Gramm, W. Phil	Rep	Tex.	11	6
7th Bond, Christopher S. (Kit)	Rep	Mo.	9	4
8th Gorton, T. Slade III	Rep	Wash.	13	4
9th McConnell, A. Mitchell (Mitch)	Rep	Ky.	11	2
10th Mack, Connie III	Rep	Fla.	7	2
11th Burns, Conrad	Rep	Mont.	7	2
12th Shelby, Richard C.	Rep	Ala.	9	1
13th Jeffords, James M.	Rep	Vt.	7	1
14th Gregg, Judd A.	Rep	N.H.	3	1
15th Bennett, Robert F.	Rep	Utah	3	1

Minority

Rank Name	Party	State	Years in: Senate	Comm.
RM Byrd, Robert C.	Dem	W.Va.	37	36
2nd Inouye, Daniel K.	Dem	Hawaii	33	24
3rd Hollings, Ernest F.	Dem	S.C.	29	24
4th Johnston, J. Bennett Jr.	Dem	La.	23	20
5th Patrick J. Leahy	Dem	Vt.	21	18
6th Bumpers, Dale	Dem	Ark.	21	17
7th Lautenberg, Frank R.	Dem	N.J.	13	*1 10
8th Harkin, Thomas R.	Dem	Iowa	11	10
9th Mikulski, Barbara A.	Dem	Md.	9	8
10th Reid, Harry M.	Dem	Nev.	9	8
11th Kerrey, J. Robert	Dem	Neb.	7	6
12th Kohl, Herbert H.	Dem	Wisc.	7	2
13th Murray, Patty	Dem	Wash.	3	2

*1: Member's first period of service on the committee.

Changes:

Majority:

Gramm, W. Phil	Rep	Tex.	Oct. 12, 1995 Left the committee; moved to Finance.
Campbell, Ben Nighthorse	Rep	Colo.	Oct. 12, 1995 Replaced Gramm.

Departures from the Senate:	**Majority**			**Minority**		
Retired	Hatfield, Mark O.	Rep	Ore.	Johnston, J. Bennett Jr.	Dem	La.

Departures from Committee:						
Moved to Finance	Mack, Connie III	Rep	Fla.	Kerrey, J. Robert	Dem	Neb.
	Jeffords, James M.	Rep	Vt.			

APPROPRIATIONS / 105th Congress

Service Dates of Committee Chair: Jan. 9, 1997-Jan. 7, 1999

Service Dates of Majority Members: Jan. 9, 1997-Jan. 7, 1999

Service Dates of Minority Members: Jan. 9, 1997-Jan. 7, 1999

Majority					Minority				
			Years in:					**Years in:**	
Rank Name	Party	State	Senate	Comm.	Rank Name	Party	State	Senate	Comm.
Chr Stevens, Theodore F.	Rep	Alas.	29	25	RM Byrd, Robert C.	Dem	W.Va.	39	38
2nd Cochran, W. Thad	Rep	Miss.	19	17	2nd Inouye, Daniel K.	Dem	Hai.	35	26
3th Specter, Arlen	Rep	Penn.	17	17	3rd Hollings, Ernest F.	Dem	S.C.	31	26
4th Domenici, Pete V.	Rep	N.M.	25	15	4th Leahy, Patrick J.	Dem	Vt.	23	20
5th Bond, Christopher S. (Kit)	Rep	Mo.	11	6	5th Bumpers, Dale	Dem	Ark.	23	19
6th Gorton, T. Slade III	Rep	Wash.	15	6	6th Lautenberg, Frank R.	Dem	N.J.	15	*1 12
7th McConnell, A. Mitchell (Mitch)	Rep	Ky.	13	5	7th Harkin, Thomas R.	Dem	Iowa	13	12
8th Burns, Conrad	Rep	Mont.	9	5	8th Mikulski, Barbara A.	Dem	Md.	11	11
9th Shelby, Richard C.	Rep	Ala.	11	3	9th Reid, Harry M.	Dem	Nev.	11	11
10th Gregg, Judd A.	Rep	N.H.	5	3	10th Kohl, Herbert H.	Dem	Wisc.	9	5
11th Bennett, Robert F.	Rep	Utah	5	3	11th Murray, Patty	Dem	Wash.	5	5
12th Campbell, Ben Nighthorse	Rep	Colo.	5	2	12th Dorgan, Byron L.	Dem	N.D.	5	1
13th Craig, Larry E.	Rep	Idaho	7	1	13th Boxer, Barbara	Dem	Cal.	5	1
14th Faircloth, D.M. (Lauch)	Rep	N.C.	5	1					
15th Hutchison, Kay Bailey	Rep	Tex.	4	1	*1: Member's first period of service on the committee.				

Departures from the Senate:	**Majority**			**Minority**		
Defeated for Re-election	Faircloth, D.M. (Lauch)	Rep	N.C.	None		
Retired	None			Bumpers, Dale	Dem	Ark.

Departures from Committee:						
Moved to Foreign Relations	None			Boxer, Barbara	Dem	Cal.

APPROPRIATIONS / 106th Congress

Service Dates of Committee Chair: Jan. 7, 1999-Jan. 3, 2001

Service Dates of Majority Members: Jan. 7, 1999-Jan. 25, 2001

Service Dates of Minority Members: Jan. 7, 1999-Jan. 25, 2001

Majority					Minority				
			Years in:					**Years in:**	
Rank Name	Party	State	Senate	Comm.	Rank Name	Party	State	Senate	Comm.
Chr Stevens, Theodore F.	Rep	Alas.	31	27	RM Byrd, Robert C.	Dem	W.Va.	41	40
2nd Cochran, W. Thad	Rep	Miss.	21	19	2nd Inouye, Daniel K.	Dem	Hai.	37	28
3th Specter, Arlen	Rep	Penn.	19	19	3rd Hollings, Ernest F.	Dem	S.C.	33	28
4th Domenici, Pete V.	Rep	N.M.	27	17	4th Leahy, Patrick J.	Dem	Vt.	25	22
5th Bond, Christopher S. (Kit)	Rep	Mo.	13	8	5th Lautenberg, Frank R.	Dem	N.J.	17	*1 14
6th Gorton, T. Slade III	Rep	Wash.	17	8	6th Harkin, Thomas R.	Dem	Iowa	15	14
7th McConnell, A. Mitchell (Mitch)	Rep	Ky.	15	7	7th Mikulski, Barbara A.	Dem	Md.	13	13
8th Burns, Conrad	Rep	Mont.	11	7	8th Reid, Harry M.	Dem	Nev.	13	13
9th Shelby, Richard C.	Rep	Ala.	13	5	9th Kohl, Herbert H.	Dem	Wisc.	11	7
10th Gregg, Judd A.	Rep	N.H.	7	5	10th Murray, Patty	Dem	Wash.	7	7
11th Bennett, Robert F.	Rep	Utah	7	5	11th Dorgan, Byron L.	Dem	N.D.	7	2

12th Campbell, Ben Nighthorse	Rep	Colo.	7	4
13th Craig, Larry E.	Rep	Ida.	9	2
14th Hutchison, Kay Bailey	Rep	Tex.	6	2
15th Kyl, Jon L.	Rep	Ariz.	5	1

12th Feinstein, Dianne	Dem	Cal.	7	*2 1
13th Durbin, Richard J.	Dem	Ill.	3	1

*1: Member's first period of service on the committee.

*2: Member's second period of service on the committee.

Departures from the Senate:	**Majority**			**Minority**		
Defeated for Re-election	Gorton, T. Slade III	Rep	Wash.	None		
Retired	None			Lautenberg, Frank R.	Dem	N.J.

Departures from Committee:					
Returned to Energy and Natural Resources and moved to Finance	Kyl, Jon L.	Rep	Ariz.	None	

APPROPRIATIONS / 107th Congress, Pre-Jeffords switch

Service Dates of Committee Chair: ChT: Jan. 3, 2001-Jan. 25, 2001 Byrd (Dem-W.Va.)

Ch1: Jan. 25, 2001-June 6, 2001 Stevens (Rep-Tex.)

Service Dates of Majority Members: Jan. 25, 2001-June 6, 2001

Service Dates of Minority Members: Jan. 25, 2001-June 6, 2001

Majority					**Minority**				
			Years in:					**Years in:**	
Rank Name	**Party**	**State**	**Senate**	**Comm.**	**Rank Name**	**Party**	**State**	**Senate**	**Comm.**
Ch1 Stevens, Theodore F.	Rep	Alas.	33	29	RM1 Byrd, Robert C.	Dem	W.Va.	43	43
2nd Cochran, W. Thad	Rep	Miss.	23	21	2nd Inouye, Daniel K.	Dem	Hai.	39	30
3th Domenici, Pete V.	Rep	N.M.	29	19	3th Hollings, Ernest F.	Dem	S.C.	35	30
4th Specter, Arlen	Rep	Penn.	21	21	4th Leahy, Patrick J.	Dem	Vt.	27	24
5th Bond, Christopher S. (Kit)	Rep	Mo.	15	10	5th Harkin, Thomas R.	Dem	Iowa	17	16
6th McConnell, A. Mitchell (Mitch)	Rep	Ky.	17	9	6th Mikulski, Barbara A.	Dem	Md.	15	15
7th Burns, Conrad	Rep	Mont.	13	9	7th Reid, Harry M.	Dem	Nev.	15	15
8th Shelby, Richard C.	Rep	Ala.	15	7	8th Kohl, Herbert H.	Dem	Wisc.	13	9
9th Gregg, Judd A.	Rep	N.H.	9	7	9th Murray, Patty	Dem	Wash.	9	9
10th Bennett, Robert F.	Rep	Utah	9	7	10th Dorgan, Byron L.	Dem	N.D.	9	5
11th Campbell, Ben Nighthorse	Rep	Colo.	9	6	11th Feinstein, Dianne	Dem	Cal.	9	*2 3
12th Craig, Larry E.	Rep	Ida.	11	5	12th Durbin, Richard J.	Dem	Ill.	5	3
13th Hutchison, Kay Bailey	Rep	Tex.	8	5	13th Johnson, Timothy P.	Dem	S.D.	5	1
14th DeWine, Michael	Rep	Ohio	7	1	14th Landrieu, Mary L.	Dem	La.	5	1

*2: Member's second period of service on the committee.

Note: The committee majority in the 2001 Senate power-sharing arrangement was determined by party of the vice president. Democrat Al Gore Jr. served from Jan. 3, 2001, to Jan. 20, 2001, and was succeeded by Republican Richard B. Cheney on Jan. 20, 2001. When Senator Jeffords of Vermont left the Republican Party, effective June 6, 2001, to become an Independent, Democrats regained the majority for the remainder of the 107th Congress.

APPROPRIATIONS / 107th Congress, Post-Jeffords switch

Service Dates of Committee Chair: June 6, 2001-Jan. 14, 2003

Service Dates of Majority Members: June 6, 2001-Jan. 14, 2003

Service Dates of Minority Members: June 6, 2001-Jan. 15, 2003

Majority					**Minority**				
			Years in:					**Years in:**	
Rank Name	**Party**	**State**	**Senate**	**Comm.**	**Rank Name**	**Party**	**State**	**Senate**	**Comm.**
Ch2 Byrd, Robert C.	Dem	W.Va.	43	43	RM2 Stevens, Theodore F.	Rep	Alas.	33	30
2nd Inouye, Daniel K.	Dem	Hai.	39	31	2nd Cochran, W. Thad	Rep	Miss.	23	21
3rd Hollings, Ernest F.	Dem	S.C.	35	31	3rd Domenici, Pete V.	Rep	N.M.	29	19
4th Leahy, Patrick J.	Dem	Vt.	27	25	4th Specter, Arlen	Rep	Penn.	21	21
5th Harkin, Thomas R.	Dem	Iowa	17	17	5th Bond, Christopher S. (Kit)	Rep	Mo.	15	11
6th Mikulski, Barbara A.	Dem	Md.	15	15	6th McConnell, A. Mitchell (Mitch)	Rep	Ky.	17	9
7th Reid, Harry M.	Dem	Nev.	15	15	7th Burns, Conrad	Rep	Mont.	13	9
8th Kohl, Herbert H.	Dem	Wisc.	13	9	8th Shelby, Richard C.	Rep	Ala.	15	7
9th Murray, Patty	Dem	Wash.	9	9	9th Gregg, Judd A.	Rep	N.H.	9	7
10th Dorgan, Byron L.	Dem	N.D.	9	5	10th Bennett, Robert F.	Rep	Utah	9	7

11th Feinstein, Dianne	Dem	Cal.	9	*2 3		11th Campbell, Ben Nighthorse	Rep	Colo.	9	6
12th Durbin, Richard J.	Dem	Ill.	5	3		12th Craig, Larry E.	Rep	Ida.	11	5
13th Johnson, Timothy P.	Dem	S.D.	5	1		13th Hutchison, Kay Bailey	Rep	Tex.	9	5
14th Landrieu, Mary L.	Dem	La.	5	1		14th DeWine, Michael	Rep	Ohio	7	1
15th Reed, John F.	Dem	R.I	5	*1 1						

*1: Member's first period of service on the committee.

*2: Member's second period of service on the committee.

Additions:

  Majority:

  15th Reed, John F.   Dem   R.I.   July 10, 2001

Departures from Committee: **Majority**   **Minority**

  No new assignment   Reed, John F.   Dem   R.I.   None

APPROPRIATIONS / 108th Congress

Service Dates of Committee Chair: Jan. 14, 2003-Jan. 6, 2005

Service Dates of Majority Members: Jan. 14, 2003-Jan. 6, 2005

Service Dates of Minority Members: Jan. 15, 2003-Jan. 6, 2005

Majority			Years in:		Minority			Years in:	
Rank Name	Party	State	Senate	Comm.	Rank Name	Party	State	Senate	Comm.
Chr Stevens, Theodore F.	Rep	Alas.	35	31	RM Byrd, Robert C.	Dem	W.Va.	45	45
2nd Cochran, W. Thad	Rep	Miss.	25	23	2nd Inouye, Daniel K.	Dem	Hai.	41	32
3th Specter, Arlen	Rep	Penn.	23	23	3rd Hollings, Ernest F.	Dem	S.C.	37	32
4th Domenici, Pete V.	Rep	N.M.	31	21	4th Leahy, Patrick J.	Dem	Vt.	29	26
5th Bond, Christopher S. (Kit)	Rep	Mo.	17	12	5th Harkin, Thomas R.	Dem	Iowa	19	18
6th McConnell, A. Mitchell (Mitch)	Rep	Ky.	19	11	6th Mikulski, Barbara A.	Dem	Md.	17	17
7th Burns, Conrad	Rep	Mont.	15	11	7th Reid, Harry M.	Dem	Nev.	17	17
8th Shelby, Richard C.	Rep	Ala.	17	9	8th Kohl, Herbert H.	Dem	Wisc.	15	11
9th Gregg, Judd A.	Rep	N.H.	11	9	9th Murray, Patty	Dem	Wash.	11	11
10th Bennett, Robert F.	Rep	Utah	11	9	10th Dorgan, Byron L.	Dem	N.D.	11	7
11th Campbell, Ben Nighthorse	Rep	Colo.	11	8	11th Feinstein, Dianne	Dem	Cal.	11	*2 5
12th Craig, Larry E.	Rep	Ida.	13	7	12th Durbin, Richard J.	Dem	Ill.	7	5
13th Hutchison, Kay Bailey	Rep	Tex.	10	7	13th Johnson, Timothy P.	Dem	S.D.	7	2
14th DeWine, Michael	Rep	Ohio	9	2	14th Landrieu, Mary L.	Dem	La.	7	2
15th Brownback, Sam D.	Rep	Kans.	7	1					

*2: Member's second period of service on the committee.

Departures from the Senate: **Majority**   **Minority**

  Retired   Campbell, Ben Nighthorse   Rep   Colo.   Hollings, Ernest F.   Dem   S.C.

APPROPRIATIONS / 109th Congress

Service Dates of Committee Chair: Jan. 6, 2005-Jan. 12, 2007

Service Dates of Majority Members: Jan. 6, 2005-Jan. 12, 2007

Service Dates of Minority Members: Jan. 6, 2005-Jan. 12, 2007

Majority			Years in:		Minority			Years in:	
Rank Name	Party	State	Senate	Comm.	Rank Name	Party	State	Senate	Comm.
Chr Cochran, W. Thad	Rep	Miss.	27	25	RM Byrd, Robert C.	Dem	W.Va.	47	46
2nd Stevens, Theodore F.	Rep	Alas.	37	33	2nd Inouye, Daniel K.	Dem	Hai.	43	34
3th Specter, Arlen	Rep	Penn.	25	25	3rd Leahy, Patrick J.	Dem	Vt.	31	28
4th Domenici, Pete V.	Rep	N.M.	33	23	4th Harkin, Thomas R.	Dem	Iowa	21	20
5th Bond, Christopher S. (Kit)	Rep	Mo.	19	14	5th Mikulski, Barbara A.	Dem	Md.	19	19
6th McConnell, A. Mitchell (Mitch)	Rep	Ky.	21	12	6th Reid, Harry M.	Dem	Nev.	19	19
7th Burns, Conrad	Rep	Mont.	17	12	7th Kohl, Herbert H.	Dem	Wisc.	17	12
8th Shelby, Richard C.	Rep	Ala.	19	11	8th Murray, Patty	Dem	Wash.	13	12
9th Gregg, Judd A.	Rep	N.H.	13	11	9th Dorgan, Byron L.	Dem	N.D.	13	8
10th Bennett, Robert F.	Rep	Utah	13	11	10th Feinstein, Dianne	Dem	Cal.	13	*2 6

Rank Name	Party	State	Senate	Comm.
11th Craig, Larry E.	Rep	Ida.	15	8
12th Hutchison, Kay Bailey	Rep	Tex.	12	8
13th DeWine, Michael	Rep	Ohio	11	4
14th Brownback, Sam D.	Rep	Kans.	9	3
15th Allard, A. Wayne	Rep	Colo.	9	1

Rank Name	Party	State	Senate	Comm.
11th Durbin, Richard J.	Dem	Ill.	9	6
12th Johnson, Timothy P.	Dem	S.D.	9	4
13th Landrieu, Mary L.	Dem	La.	9	4

*2: Member's second period of service on the committee.

Departures from the Senate:

	Majority			Minority		
Defeated for Re-election	Burns, Conrad	Rep	Mont.	None		
	DeWine, Michael	Rep	Ohio			

Departures from Committee:

Moved to Rules and Administration; and elected Majority Leader	None			Reid, Harry M.	Dem	Nev

APPROPRIATIONS / 110th Congress

Service Dates of Committee Chair: Jan. 12, 2007-Jan. 21, 2009

Service Dates of Majority Members: Jan. 12, 2007-Jan. 21, 2009

Service Dates of Minority Members: Jan. 12, 2007-Jan. 21, 2009

Majority

Rank Name	Party	State	Senate	Comm.
Chr Byrd, Robert C.	Dem	W.Va.	49	48
2nd Inouye, Daniel K.	Dem	Hai.	45	36
3rd Leahy, Patrick J.	Dem	Vt.	33	30
4th Harkin, Thomas R.	Dem	Iowa	23	22
5th Mikulski, Barbara A.	Dem	Md.	21	21
6th Kohl, Herbert H.	Dem	Wisc.	19	15
7th Murray, Patty	Dem	Wash.	15	15
8th Dorgan, Byron L.	Dem	N.D.	15	11
9th Feinstein, Dianne	Dem	Cal.	15	*2 9
10th Durbin, Richard J.	Dem	Ill.	11	9
11th Johnson, Timothy P.	Dem	S.D.	11	6
12th Landrieu, Mary L.	Dem	La	11	6
13th Reed, John F.	Dem	R.I.	11	*2 1
14th Lautenburg, Frank R.	Dem	N.J.	23	*2 1
15th Nelson, E. Benjamin	Dem	Neb.	7	1

Minority

Rank Name	Party	State	Senate	Comm.
RM Cochran, W. Thad	Rep	Miss.	29	27
2nd Stevens, Theodore F.	Rep	Alas.	39	35
3rd Specter, Arlen	Rep	Penn.	27	27
4th Domenici, Pete V.	Rep	N.M.	35	25
5th Bond, Christopher S. (Kit)	Rep	Mo.	21	16
6th McConnell, A. Mitchell (Mitch)	Rep	Ky.	23	15
7th Shelby, Richard C.	Rep	Ala.	21	13
8th Gregg, Judd A.	Rep	N.H.	15	13
9th Bennett, Robert F.	Rep	Utah	15	13
10th Craig, Larry E.	Rep	Ida.	17	11
11th Hutchison, Kay Bailey	Rep	Tex.	14	11
12th Brownback, Sam D.	Rep	Kans.	11	5
13th Allard, A. Wayne	Rep	Colo.	11	3
14th Alexander, Lamar	Rep	Tenn.	5	1

*2: Member's second period of service on the committee.

Departures from the Senate:

	Majority	Minority		
Defeated for Re-election	None	Stevens, Theodore F.	Rep	Alas.
Retired	None	Domenici, Pete V.	Rep	N.M.
		Craig, Larry E.	Rep	Ida.
		Allard, A. Wayne	Rep	Colo.

APPROPRIATIONS / 111th Congress

Service Dates of Committee Chair: Jan. 21, 2009-

Service Dates of Majority Members: Jan. 21, 2009-

Service Dates of Minority Members: Jan. 21, 2009-

Majority

Rank Name	Party	State	Senate	Comm.
Chr Inouye, Daniel K.	Dem	Hai.	47	38
2nd Byrd, Robert C.	Dem	W.Va.	51	51
3rd Leahy, Patrick J.	Dem	Vt.	35	32
4th Harkin, Thomas R.	Dem	Iowa	25	24
5th Mikulski, Barbara A.	Dem	Md.	23	23
6th Kohl, Herbert H.	Dem	Wisc.	21	17
7th Murray, Patty	Dem	Wash.	17	17
8th Dorgan, Byron	Dem	N.D.	17	13
9th Feinstein, Dianne	Dem	Cal.	17	*2 11

Minority

Rank Name	Party	State	Senate	Comm.
RM Cochran, W. Thad	Rep	Miss.	31	29
2nd Specter, Arlen	Rep	Penn.	29	29
3rd Bond, Christopher S. (Kit)	Rep	Mo.	23	18
4th McConnell, A. Mitchell (Mitch)	Rep	Ky.	25	17
5th Shelby, Richard C.	Rep	Ala.	23	15
6th Gregg, Judd A.	Rep	N.H.	17	15
7th Bennett, Robert F.	Rep	Utah	17	15
8th Hutchison, Kay Bailey	Rep	Tex.	16	13
9th Brownback, Sam D.	Rep	Kans.	13	7

10th Durbin, Richard J.	Dem	Ill.	13	11
11th Johnson, Timothy P.	Dem	S.D.	13	8
12th Landrieu, Mary L.	Dem	La	13	8
13th Reed, John F.	Dem	R.I.	13	*2 3
14th Lautenburg, Frank R.	Dem	N.J.	25	*2 3
15th Nelson, E. Benjamin	Dem	Neb.	9	3
16th Pryor, Mark	Dem	Ariz.	7	1
17th Tester, Jon	Dem	Mont.	3	1

10th Alexander, Lamar	Rep	Tenn.	7	3
11th Collins, Susan M.	Rep	Me.	13	1
12th Voinovich, George V.	Rep	Ohio	11	1
13th Murkowski, Lisa	Rep	Alas.	7	1

*2: Member's second period of service on the committee.

Additions:
  Majority:

18th Specter, Arlen	Dem	Penn.	May 5, 2009

Changes:
  Minority:

Specter, Arlen	Rep	Penn.	May 5, 2009 Switched from the Republican Party to the Democratic Party and was placed in the 18th Majority slot with his seniority to be determined at a later date.

Armed Services

Senate Committee on Armed Services, 103rd-111th Congresses (1993-2011)

BACKGROUND

Organizational History: The Senate Committee on Armed Services was created by the Legislative Reorganization Act of 1946 from the standing committees on Military Affairs and Naval Affairs. Both of the predecessor committees were among the eleven original standing committees of the Senate created on December 10, 1816. These committees were adopted by the Senate pursuant to a resolution introduced by Sen. James Barbour, an Anti-Democrat States Righter from Virginia.

Each of the two original committees had only five members in 1816. Sen. John Williams (DR-Tenn.) was the first chair of Military Affairs while Sen. Charles Tait (DR-Ga.) was the first chair of Naval Affairs. Apart from the incorporation within Military Affairs of the jurisdiction of the Committee on the Militia in December 16, 1857, the committees changed relatively little prior to the 1946 Legislative Reorganization Act. The *Guide to the Records of the National Archives* includes the Committee on Coast Defenses (1885-1921) which was "responsible for a segment of national defense" as a predecessor committee (35). The only other changes occurred in their size. By 1946, each committee had a membership of eighteen members.

In accordance with the National Security Act of 1947 (P.L. 80-235, 61 Stat. 496), the Department of War was named the Department of the Army and along with the Department of the Navy was absorbed into the National Military Establishment (NME) with a Secretary of Defense as NME's senior presiding official. On August 10, 1949, the NME was renamed the Department of Defense.

The reorganization of the Defense Department had major implications for the Executive Branch. It led to a downgrading of the Department of War, which was primarily focused on the Army and the Department of the Navy from Cabinet-level posts to sub-cabinet ones and the separation of the Air Force from the Army and its upgrading to a sub-cabinet post. The Armed Services Committee reflected those changes in its jurisdiction.

The 1977 Senate Committee Reorganization Amendments (S.Res. 95-4) led to the relocation of the aeronautical and space activities peculiar to or primarily associated with the development of weapons systems or military operations from the former standing Committee on Aeronautical and Space Sciences that had existed from 1958 to the Armed Services Committee. Also included in this transfer were matters related to national security aspects of nuclear energy.

Only half of the areas the committee was originally specifically given jurisdiction over remained listed as under its authority: strategic and critical materials necessary for the common defense; the selective service system; pay, promotion, retirement, and other benefits and privileges of members of the Armed Forces with the addition of the overseas education of civilian and military dependents; common defense in general; the Department of the Navy; and matters pertaining to the Panama Canal.

Since the 1977 Reorganization, the committee's jurisdictional responsibilities have remained intact. But that fact understates the committee's contemporary responsibilities. Although the Senate's Foreign Relations Committee has jurisdiction over formal declarations of war, it is the Armed Services committees in each chamber that have the prime responsibility for maintaining the nation's military readiness. As wars—both large and small—loom in the international arena, it is the Armed Services Committee that continues to prepare the U.S. military for those crises.

In recent times, the Senate Armed Services Committee has also had to become involved in social issues as the controversial "don't ask, don't tell" policy regarding gays in the military which has sprung to the fore and the committee members have been obliged to address this issue.

Membership: The Legislative Reorganization Act of 1946 reduced the membership from a combined total of thirty-six on the two committees to one of thirteen. It has grown slowly since Armed Services first hit the twenty-member mark in the 100th Congress (1987-1989) and hovered close to that amount until its recent membership peaks of twenty-five in the 110th Congress (2007-2009) and twenty-six in the 111th (2009-2011). Since 1993, the committee's average size was 23.1, placing it second among the sixteen standing committees. Its mean seniority per Congress is 12.17 years ranking it seventh and its mean inter-Congress retention rate is 87.1 percent, placing it tenth, just below the median.

During the past nine Congresses, Armed Services has gained twelve members and lost eighteen for a net loss of six members. Half of its gains came from the Environment and Public Works and Foreign Relations Committees with three joiners each. Ten departing members, clearly the largest contingent, moved to the Finance Committee, including Trent Lott (Rep-Miss.) in 1995 who had also been elected Majority Whip.

One of the more unusual developments in recent years has been the movement to the Armed Services Committee of senior senators later in the careers. Senators John H. Glenn of Ohio and Daniel K. Akaka of Hawaii joined the committee in their eleventh years in the Senate; Edward M. Kennedy in his twenty-first year; and former majority leader Robert C. Byrd (Dem-W.Va.) in his thirty-first year. The only Republican to emulate these Democrats was Malcolm C. Wallop (Rep-Wyo.) who joined Armed Services in his thirteenth year.

Committee Leaders: Senator J. Chandler Gurney (Rep-S.D.), who had served on the Military Affairs Committee in the preceding Congress, was the first chair of the Armed Services Committee (1947-1949). He was followed by Millard E. Tydings (Dem-Md.), who served as chair from 1949 until 1951. Tydings was defeated for re-election in 1950 by John Marshall Butler. Tydings's defeat was attributed to the active and controversial intervention of Sen. Joseph R. McCarthy (Rep-Wisc.), who contended that Tydings was responsible for Communist subversion and lapses in national security.

After Tydings's loss, Richard B. Russell (Dem-Ga.) became chair of the Senate Armed Services Committee in 1951. Russell chaired the committee for eight of the next nine Congresses (1951-1953 and 1955-1969). He was interrupted in 1953-1955 by the Republican victory in the election of 1952, as Leverett Saltonstall (Rep-Mass.) became chair.

Russell left the chairmanship of Armed Services in 1969 to become chair of Appropriations. He was succeeded by John C. Stennis (Dem-Miss.), who held the chair for twelve years (1969-1981). Stennis relinquished the chair in 1981 to Sen. John G. Tower (Rep-Tex.), as the Republicans regained control of the Senate for the first time in twenty-six years.

Both Tydings and Russell served as ranking minority members in the 80th and 83rd Congresses, respectively. The senior Republican on Armed Services, H. Styles Bridges of New Hampshire, was also the senior Republican on Appropriations for most of the 1940s and 1950s. In the 81st and 82nd Congresses (1949-1953), Bridges served simultaneously as the ranking minority member on both committees. However in the 84th through the 87th Congresses (1955-1961), Bridges would step aside shortly after the assignments were announced and turn the ranking minority slot on Armed Services over to Saltonstall. Following Bridges's death in 1961, Saltonstall also became the ranking minority member on Appropriations. Saltonstall chose to remain in the ranking slot on both committees and served simultaneously as the ranking minority member on both the Armed Forces and Appropriations Committees from November, 1961 until his retirement from the Senate in 1967.

Senator Margaret Chase Smith (Rep-Me.) followed Saltonstall and served as ranking minority member on Armed Services from 1967 until her defeat for re-election in 1972. Mrs. Smith was succeeded by J. Strom Thurmond (Rep-S.C.), whose service in the Senate was begun as a Democrat (1954-1956 and 1956-1964). Thurmond became a Republican during the Johnson-Goldwater presidential contest of 1964. The Senate Republicans honored his previous seniority in the Senate, and he was thus able to become the ranking minority member on Armed Services after only eight years as a Republican member of the committee. Thurmond left the ranking minority slot on Armed Services in 1977 to become the ranking minority member on the Judiciary Committee.

Thurmond's successor was John G. Tower (Rep-Tex.). Tower served as ranking minority member until 1981 when the Republican victory in the 1980 Senate elections propelled him into the chairmanship of the committee. He chaired the committee in the 97th and 98th Congresses (1981-1985). In 1989, Tower suffered an indignity when his appointment to be Secretary of Defense by President George H.W. Bush was rejected both by the Armed Services Committee and by the Senate itself. After Tower retired in 1985 to enter private life, Barry M. Goldwater (Rep-Ariz.) became chair and held the post until the Democrats recaptured the Senate in the 1986 election.

John Stennis, the committee's long-term chair, became ranking minority member for the first time in 1981. He left that post to become ranking minority member of Appropriations in 1983 and was succeeded by Henry M. Jackson (Dem-Wash.). Jackson died on September 1, 1983, and was succeeded as ranking minority member by Samuel A. Nunn (Dem-Ga.). Nunn's great-uncle was the legendary Carl Vinson, the "swamp fox" who chaired the House Armed Services Committee for fourteen years (1949-1953 and 1955-1965). Nunn continued as ranking minority member until 1987, when he assumed the chair of the committee as a result of Democratic gains in 1986 and held the post until 1994 and the Republican recapture of the Senate. Nunn served for two more years as ranking minority member until his retirement in 1997. Nunn was succeeded by Carl M. Levin (Dem-Mich.), who has served as the committee's senior Democrat from 1997 to the present.

John W. Warner (Rep-Va.) served as ranking minority member from the 1987 Democratic takeover of the Senate until he gained the chair in 1995. Warner held the chair for all but the eighteen-month Jeffords hiatus during the twelve years from 1995 to 2007. When the Democrats recaptured the Senate in 2006 and with his own retirement pending, Warner relinquished the senior Republican slot on the committee to John S. McCain of Arizona in 2007.

Party Leaders: Each party selected four members of the committee to lead them in the post-1947 Senate. Among them were the two contending floor leaders of the Eisenhower era—Lyndon B. Johnson (Dem-Tex.) and William F. Knowland (Rep-Cal.). Two Democratic Whips who served in succession came from Armed Services: Russell B. Long of Louisiana, Whip from 1965 to 1969, when he was defeated by Edward M. Kennedy of Massachusetts, Whip from 1969 to 1971, when he was defeated by Robert C. Byrd of West Virginia, who served as Whip until 1977 when he was elected majority floor leader. Both Russell Long and Ted Kennedy began their service in the Senate at the Constitutional minimum age of thirty.

Presidential Aspirations: While only two Armed Services members succeeded in being nominated for president, the committee has been a hotbed of presidential aspirants. In addition to Democratic vice presidential nominees Johnson, Kefauver, Bentsen, Gore, and Lieberman, other contenders included W. Stuart Symington (Dem-Mo.), Henry M. Jackson (Dem-Wash.), Edward M. Kennedy (Dem-Mass.), Gary W. Hart (Dem-Colo.), and John H. Glenn Jr. (Dem-Ohio).

It was from this post that John McCain sought and obtained the 2008 Republican nomination for president, following in the footsteps of fellow Arizona Republican Barry M. Goldwater who used the committee as his launch pad for the 1964 presidential nomination. While neither Goldwater nor McCain succeeded, J. Danforth Quayle (Rep-Ind.), who served on the committee, was nominated and elected vice president with George H.W. Bush in 1988. While no Democratic presidential nominees were chosen from the committee, five vice presidential nominees were: C. Estes Kefauver of Tennessee on the Stevenson ticket in 1956; Lyndon B. Johnson of Texas on the Kennedy ticket in 1960; Lloyd M. Bentsen Jr. of Texas on the Dukakis ticket in 1988; Albert Gore Jr. of Tennessee on the Clinton ticket in 1992; and Joseph I. Lieberman of Connecticut on the Gore ticket in 2000. Johnson and Gore succeeded in winning the vice presidency while Kefauver, Bentsen, and Lieberman did not.

Other Notables: Two other noteworthy members of the committee were Sen. Prescott Bush (Rep-Conn.), founder of the Bush presidential dynasty of Presidents George H.W. Bush (1989-1993) and George W. Bush (2001-2009), and the irrepressible Wayne Morse of Oregon. In 1953, Morse left the Republican Party and sat in the Senate as an Independent. He was stripped of his assignment to the Armed Services Committee by the Republicans. In a motion on the floor, Morse appealed to the entire Senate for a return to Armed Services. His appeal was rebuffed by a substantial margin when he received only seven votes of eighty-eight cast for the final slot on the committee. Morse continued in the Senate for another sixteen years, fourteen of them as a Democrat, but he never served again on Armed Services.

The committee also witnessed the notable father-son team of Harry Flood Byrd (Dem-Va.) and Harry Flood Byrd Jr. (Dem/Ind.-Va.). The case of the Byrds is quite unusual because the son not only filled his father's seat in the Senate, he also was assigned to fill his father's vacancy on Armed Services. Members of the Armed Services Committee have had a great deal of Cabinet experience. Sen. Elizabeth Dole (Rep-N.C.) served as Secretary of Transportation under President Reagan and as Secretary of Labor under President Ford before her 2002 election to the Senate. This was also the case with Sen. Mel Martinez (Rep-Fla.), who served as President George W. Bush's Secretary of Housing and Urban Development before his 2004 election. Seven committee members joined the Cabinet after their service in the Senate: 1982 appointee Nicholas Brady (Rep-N.J.), who served as Secretary of the Treasury under George H.W. Bush, as did his successor Lloyd M. Bentsen Jr. (Dem-Tex.), who held the same post under President Clinton. Others in that category would include William Saxbe (Rep-Ohio), President Nixon's fourth and final Attorney General; Richard Schweiker (Rep-Penn.), President Reagan's Secretary of Health and Human Services; William Cohen (Rep-Maine), President Clinton's Secretary of Defense in his second term; Dirk Kempthorne (Rep-Ida.), President George W. Bush's Secretary of the Interior; and Senator Hillary Rodham Clinton (Dem-N.Y.) who is serving as Secretary of State under President Obama.

Only one of the post-1993 members of the Armed Services Committee left it to return home to serve as governor of his state—Republican Dirk Kempthorne of Idaho, who was elected governor in 1998 and returned to Washington in 2006 as Secretary of the Interior.

Selected References

Blechman, Barry M., *The Politics of National Security: Congress and U.S. Defense Policy* (New York: Oxford University Press, 1990).

Coren, Robert W., et al., "Records of the Committee on Armed Services and Its Predecessors, 1816-1968," *Guide to the Records of the United States Senate at the National Archives: 1789-1989 Bicentennial Edition* (Washington, D.C.: National Archives and Records Administration, 1989), 35-45.

Deering, Christopher J., "Armed Services Committee, Senate," in Donald C. Bacon, Roger H. Davidson, and Morton Keller, eds., *The Encyclopedia of the United States Congress* (New York: Simon & Schuster, 1995), I: 93-96.

Deering, Christopher J., "Decision Making in the Armed Services Committees," in Randall B. Ripley and James M. Lindsay, eds., *Congress Resurgent: Foreign and Defense Policy on Capitol Hill* (Ann Arbor: University of Michigan Press, 1993), 155-182.

Gist, John R., "The Impact of Annual Authorizations on Military Appropriations in the U.S. Congress," *Legislative Studies Quarterly*, 8 (August, 1981), 439-454.

Ray, Bruce A., "The Responsiveness of the U.S. Congressional Armed Services Committees to Their Parent Bodies," *Legislative Studies Quarterly*, 5 (Nov., 1980), 501-515

RESPONSIBILITIES, JURISDICTIONAL CHANGES, AND SUBCOMMITTEES

Armed Services

Jurisdiction, 80th Congress (1947-49)

Established by the Legislative Reorganization Act of 1946:

[Section 102. (1)(c)]

(1) **Committee on Armed Services**, to consist of thirteen Senators, to which committee shall be referred all proposed legislation, messages, petitions, memorials, and other matters relating to the following subjects:

    (1) Common defense generally
    (2) The War Department and the Military Establishment generally
    (3) The Navy Department and the Naval Establishment generally
    (4) Soldiers' and sailors' homes
    (5) Pay, promotion, retirement, and other benefits and privileges of members of the armed forces
    (6) Selective service
    (7) Size and composition of the Army and Navy
    (8) Forts, arsenals, military reservations, and navy yards
    (9) Ammunition depots
    (10) Maintenance and operation of the Panama Canal, including the administration, sanitation, and government of the Canal Zone
    (11) Conservation, development, and use of naval petroleum and oil shale reserves
    (12) Strategic and critical materials necessary for the common defense

Post-Reorganization Jurisdiction, 1977

From Committee System Reorganization Amendments of 1977, S.Res. 95-4, *Senate Journal*, Feb. 4, 1977:

[XXV. Section 101. 1.(c)]

(1) **Committee on Armed Services,** to which committee shall be referred all proposed legislation, messages, petitions, memorials, and other matters relating to the following subjects:

   (1) The Common defense
   (2) Department of Defense, the Department of the Army, the Department of the Navy, and the Department of the Air Force, generally
   (3) Pay, promotion, retirement, and other benefits and privileges of members of the Armed Forces, including overseas education of civilian and military dependents
   (4) Military research and development
   (5) Selective service system
   (6) Strategic and critical materials necessary for the common defense
   (7) Aeronautical and space activities peculiar to or primarily associated with the development of weapons systems or military operations
   (8) Maintenance and operation of the Panama Canal, including administration, sanitation, and government of the Canal Zone
   (9) National security aspects of nuclear energy
   (10) Naval petroleum reserves, except those in Alaska

(2) Such committee shall also study and review, on a comprehensive basis, matters relating to the common defense policy of the United States, and report thereon from time to time.

Jurisdiction, 103rd Congress (1993-94)

From the *Standing Rules of the Senate* in the *Senate Manual*, 103rd Congress, 1st Session, S. Doc. 103-1:

[Rule XXV.(1)(c)]

(1) **Committee on Armed Services,** to which committee shall be referred all proposed legislation, messages, petitions, memorials, and other matters relating to the following subjects:

   (1) Aeronautical and space activities peculiar to or primarily associated with the development of weapons systems or military operations
   (2) Common defense
   (3) Department of Defense, the Department of the Army, the Department of the Navy, and the Department of the Air Force, generally
   (4) Maintenance and operation of the Panama Canal, including administration, sanitation, and government of the Canal Zone
   (5) Military research and development
   (6) National security aspects of nuclear energy
   (7) Naval petroleum reserves, except those in Alaska
   (8) Pay, promotion, retirement, and other benefits and privileges of members of the Armed Forces, including overseas education of civilian and military dependents
   (9) Selective service system
   (10) Strategic and critical materials necessary for the common defense

(2) Such committee shall also study and review, on a comprehensive basis, matters relating to the common defense policy of the United States, and report thereon from time to time.

Jurisdiction, 111th Congress (2009-10)

From *Authority and Rules of Senate Committees, 2009-2010*, Sen. Doc. 111-3, pursuant to S.Res, 166, June 2, 2009.

[Rule XXV (c)(1)]

(1) **Committee on Armed Services,** to which committee shall be referred all proposed legislation, messages, petitions, memorials, and other matters relating to the following subjects:

   (1) Aeronautical and space activities peculiar to or primarily associated with the development of weapons systems or military operations
   (2) Common defense
   (3) Department of Defense, the Department of the Army, the Department of the Navy, and the Department of the Air Force, generally
   (4) Maintenance and operation of the Panama Canal, including administration, sanitation, and government of the Canal Zone
   (5) Military research and development
   (6) National security aspects of nuclear energy
   (7) Naval petroleum reserves, except those in Alaska
   (8) Pay, promotion, retirement, and other benefits and privileges of members of the Armed Forces, including overseas education of civilian and military dependents

(9) Selective service system

(10) Strategic and critical materials necessary for the common defense

(2) Such committee shall also study and review, on a comprehensive basis, matters relating to the common defense policy of the United States, and report thereon from time to time.

NAMES OF SUBCOMMITTEES

Committee on Armed Services, 103rd-111th Congresses

Acquisition and Technology, 104, 105
Airland Forces, 104, 105
Airland, 106, 107, 108, 109, 110, 111
Coalition Defense and Reinforcing Forces, 103
Defense Technology, Acquisition, and Industrial Base, 103
Emerging Threats and Capabilities, 106, 107, 108, 109, 110, 111
Force Requirements and Personnel, 103
Military Readiness and Defense Infrastructure, 103
Nuclear Deterrence, Arms Control, and Defense Intelligence, 103
Personnel, 104, 105, 106, 107, 108, 109, 110, 111
Readiness, 104, 105
Readiness and Management Support, 106, 107, 108, 109, 110, 111
Regional Defense and Contingency Forces, 103
Seapower, 104, 105, 108, 109, 110, 111
Strategic, 106, 107
Strategic Forces, 104, 105, 108, 109, 110, 111

MEMBERSHIP ROSTERS, 103rd-111th Congresses, 1993-2010

ARMED SERVICES / 103rd Congress

Service Dates of Committee Chair: Jan. 7, 1993-Jan. 11, 1995

Service Dates of Majority Members: Jan. 7, 1993-Jan. 4, 1995

Service Dates of Minority Members: Jan. 7, 1993-Jan. 4, 1995

Majority

Rank Name	Party	State	Years in: Senate	Comm.
Chr Nunn, Samuel A.	Dem	Ga.	21	21
2nd Exon, J. James	Dem	Neb.	15	14
3rd Levin, Carl M.	Dem	Mich.	15	14
4th Kennedy, Edward M.	Dem	Mass.	31	11
5th Bingaman, J.F. (Jeff)	Dem	N.M.	11	*1 11
6th Glenn, John H. Jr.	Dem	Ohio	19	8
7th Shelby, Richard C.	Dem	Ala.	7	7
8th Byrd, Robert C.	Dem	W.Va.	35	*2 4
9th Graham, D. Robert	Dem	Fla.	7	1
10th Robb, Charles S.	Dem	Va.	5	1
11th Lieberman, Joseph I.	Dem	Conn.	5	1

Minority

Rank Name	Party	State	Years in: Senate	Comm.
RM Thurmond, J. Strom	Rep	S.C.	38	*2 29
2nd Warner, John W.	Rep	Va.	15	14
3rd Cohen, William S.	Rep	Me.	15	14
4th McCain, John S. III	Rep	Ariz.	7	7
5th Lott, C. Trent	Rep	Miss.	5	4
6th Coats, Daniel R.	Rep	Ind.	5	4
7th Smith, Robert C.	Rep	N.H.	3	2
8th Kempthorne, Dirk	Rep	Ida.	1	1
9th Faircloth, D.M. (Lauch)	Rep	N.C.	1	1

*1: Member's first period of service on the committee.
*2: Member's second period of service on the committee.

Note: Thurmond served previously on this committee as a Democrat, 1959-1964

Additions:
  Majority:
    12th Bryan, Richard H.   Dem   Nev.   July 15, 1993
  Minority:
    10th Hutchison, Kay Bailey   Rep   Tex.   July 1, 1993

Departures from Committee:	Majority			Minority		
Moved to Appropriations and Select Intelligence	Shelby, Richard C.	Dem	Ala.	None		
Moved to Finance	Graham, D. Robert	Dem	Fla.	None		
No new assignment	None			Faircloth, D.M. (Lauch)	Rep	N.C.

ARMED SERVICES / 104th Congress

Service Dates of Committee Chair: Jan. 11, 1995-Jan. 9, 1997

Service Dates of Majority Members: Jan. 4, 1995-Jan. 9, 1997

Service Dates of Minority Members: Jan. 4, 1995-Jan. 9, 1997

Majority

Rank Name	Party	State	Senate	Comm.
Chr Thurmond, J. Strom	Rep	S.C.	40	*2 31
2nd Warner, John W.	Rep	Va.	17	16
3rd Cohen, William S.	Rep	Me.	17	16
4th McCain, John S. III	Rep	Ariz.	9	8
5th Lott, C. Trent	Rep	Miss.	7	6
6th Coats, Daniel R.	Rep	Ind.	7	6
7th Smith, Robert C.	Rep	N.H.	5	4
8th Kempthorne, Dirk	Rep	Ida.	3	2
9th Hutchison, Kay Bailey	Rep	Tex.	2	2
10th Inhofe, James M.	Rep	Okla.	1	1
11th Santorum, Richard J. (Rick)	Rep	Penn.	1	1

Minority

Rank Name	Party	State	Senate	Comm.
RM Nunn, Samuel A.	Dem	Ga.	23	23
2nd Exon, J. James	Dem	Neb.	17	16
3rd Levin, Carl M.	Dem	Mich.	17	16
4th Kennedy, Edward M.	Dem	Mass.	33	13
5th Bingaman, J.F. (Jeff)	Dem	N.M.	13	*1 13
6th Glenn, John H. Jr.	Dem	Ohio	21	10
7th Byrd, Robert C.	Dem	W.Va.	37	*2 6
8th Robb, Charles S.	Dem	Va.	7	2
9th Lieberman, Joseph I.	Dem	Conn.	7	2
10th Bryan, Richard H.	Dem	Nev.	7	2

*1: Member's first period of service on the committee.

*2: Member's second period of service on the committee.

Note: Thurmond served previously on this committee as a Democrat, 1959-1964

Changes:

Majority:

Lott, C. Trent	Rep Miss.	June 20, 1996 Left the committee; elected Majority Leader and moved to Finance and Rules and Administration.
Frahm, Sheila	Rep Kans.	June 20, 1996 Replaced Lott.
Frahm, Sheila	Rep Kans.	Nov. 5, 1996 Resigned the Senate; defeated for nomination.

Departures from the Senate:	**Majority**			**Minority**		
Retired	Cohen, William S.	Rep	Me.	Nunn, Samuel A.	Dem	Ga.
				Exon, J. James	Dem	Neb.

Departures from Committee:						
Moved to Rules and Administration and Appropriations	Hutchison, Kay Bailey	Rep	Tex.		None	
Moved to Finance	None			Bryan, Richard H.	Dem	Nev.

ARMED SERVICES / 105th Congress

Service Dates of Committee Chair: Jan. 9, 1997-Jan. 7, 1999

Service Dates of Majority Members: Jan. 9, 1997-Jan. 7, 1999

Service Dates of Minority Members: Jan. 9, 1997-Jan. 7, 1999

Majority

Rank Name	Party	State	Senate	Comm.
Chr Thurmond, J. Strom	Rep	S.C.	42	*2 33
2nd Warner, John W.	Rep	Va.	19	18
3rd McCain, John S. III	Rep	Ariz.	11	11
4th Coats, Daniel R.	Rep	Ind.	9	8
5th Smith, Robert C.	Rep	N.H.	7	6
6th Kempthorne, Dirk	Rep	Ida.	5	5
7th Inhofe, James M.	Rep	Okla.	3	3
8th Santorum, Richard J. (Rick)	Rep	Penn.	3	3
9th Snowe, Olympia J.B.	Rep	Me.	3	1
10th Roberts, C. Patrick	Rep	Kans.	1	1

Minority

Rank Name	Party	State	Senate	Comm.
RM Levin, Carl M.	Dem	Mich.	19	18
2nd Kennedy, Edward M.	Dem	Mass.	35	15
3rd Bingaman, J.F. (Jeff)	Dem	N.M.	15	*1 15
4th Glenn, John H. Jr.	Dem	Ohio	23	12
5th Byrd, Robert C.	Dem	W.Va.	39	*2 8
6th Robb, Charles S.	Dem	Va.	9	5
7th Lieberman, Joseph I.	Dem	Conn.	9	5
8th Cleland, J. Maxwell (Max)	Dem	Ga.	1	1

*1: Member's first period of service on the committee.

*2: Member's second period of service on the committee.

Note: Thurmond served previously on this committee as a Democrat, 1959-1964

Departures from the Senate:	Majority			Minority		
Elected Governor	Kempthorne, Dirk	Rep	Ida.	None		
Retired	Coats, Daniel R.	Rep	Ind.	Glenn, John H. Jr.	Dem	Ohio

ARMED SERVICES / 106th Congress

Service Dates of Committee Chair: Jan. 7, 1999-Jan. 3, 2001

Service Dates of Majority Members: Jan. 7, 1999-Jan. 25, 2001

Service Dates of Minority Members: Jan. 7, 1999-Jan. 25, 2001

				Years in:							Years in:	
Rank Name (Majority)		**Party**	**State**	**Senate**	**Comm.**	**Rank Name** (Minority)		**Party**	**State**	**Senate**	**Comm.**	
Chr Warner, John W.		Rep	Va.	21	20	RM Levin, Carl M.		Dem	Mich.	21	20	
2nd Thurmond, J. Strom		Rep	S.C.	44	*2 35	2nd Kennedy, Edward M.		Dem	Mass.	37	17	
3rd McCain, John S. III		Rep	Ariz.	13	13	3rd Bingaman, J.F. (Jeff)		Dem	N.M.	17	*1 17	
4th Smith, Robert C.		Rep	N.H.	9	8	4th Byrd, Robert C.		Dem	W.Va.	41	*2 10	
5th Inhofe, James M.		Rep	Okla.	5	5	5th Robb, Charles S.		Dem	Va.	11	7	
6th Santorum, Richard J. (Rick)		Rep	Penn.	5	5	6th Lieberman, Joseph I.		Dem	Conn.	11	7	
7th Snowe, Olympia J.B.		Rep	Me.	5	2	7th Cleland, J. Maxwell (Max)		Dem	Ga.	3	2	
8th Roberts, C. Patrick		Rep	Kans.	3	2	8th Landrieu, Mary L.		Dem	La.	3	1	
9th Allard, A. Wayne		Rep	Colo.	3	1	9th Reed, John F.		Dem	R.I.	3	1	
10th Hutchinson, Y. Timothy		Rep	Ark.	3	1							
11th Sessions, Jefferson B. III		Rep	Ala.	3	1							

*1: Member's first period of service on the committee.

*2: Member's second period of service on the committee.

Note: Thurmond served previously on this committee as a Democrat, 1959-1964

Departures from the Senate:	Majority			Minority		
Defeated for Re-election	None			Robb, Charles S.	Dem	Va.
Departures from Committee:						
Moved to Finance	Snowe, Olympia J.B.	Rep	Me.	Bingaman, J.F. (Jeff)	Dem	N.M.

ARMED SERVICES / 107th Congress, Pre-Jeffords switch

Service Dates of Committee Chair: ChT: Jan. 3, 2001-Jan. 25, 2001 Levin (Dem-Mich.)

            Ch1: Jan. 25, 2001-June 6, 2001 Warner (Rep-Va.)

Service Dates of Majority Members: Jan. 25, 2001-June 6, 2001

Service Dates of Minority Members: Jan. 25, 2001-June 6, 2001

				Years in:							Years in:	
Rank Name (Majority)		**Party**	**State**	**Senate**	**Comm.**	**Rank Name** (Minority)		**Party**	**State**	**Senate**	**Comm.**	
Ch1 Warner, John W.		Rep	Va.	23	23	RM1 Levin, Carl M.		Dem	Mich.	23	23	
2nd Thurmond, J. Strom		Rep	S.C.	46	*2 37	2nd Kennedy, Edward M.		Dem	Mass.	39	19	
3rd McCain, John S. III		Rep	Ariz.	15	15	3rd Byrd, Robert C.		Dem	W.Va.	43	*2 12	
4th Smith, Robert C.		Rep	N.H.	11	10	4th Lieberman, Joseph I.		Dem	Conn.	13	9	
5th Inhofe, James M.		Rep	Okla.	7	7	5th Cleland, J. Maxwell (Max)		Dem	Ga.	5	5	
6th Santorum, Richard J. (Rick)		Rep	Penn.	7	7	6th Landrieu, Mary L.		Dem	La.	5	3	
7th Roberts, C. Patrick		Rep	Kans.	5	5	7th Reed, John F.		Dem	R.I.	5	3	
8th Allard, A. Wayne		Rep	Colo.	5	3	8th Akaka, Daniel K.		Dem	Hai.	11	1	
9th Hutchinson, Y. Timothy		Rep	Ark.	5	3	9th Nelson, C. William (Bill)		Dem	Fla.	1	1	
10th Sessions, Jefferson B. III		Rep	Ala.	5	3	10th Nelson, E. Benjamin		Dem	Neb.	1	1	
11th Collins, Susan M.		Rep	Me.	5	1	11th Carnahan, Jean		Dem	Mo.	1	1	
12th Bunning, James P.D.		Rep	Ky.	3	1	12th Dayton, Mark		DFL	Minn.	1	1	

*2: Member's second period of service on the committee.

Note 1: Thurmond served previously on this committee as a Democrat, 1959-1964

Note: 2 The committee majority in the 2001 Senate power-sharing arrangement was determined by party of the vice president. Democrat Al Gore Jr. served from Jan. 3, 2001, to Jan. 20, 2001, and was succeeded by Republican Richard B. Cheney on Jan. 20, 2001. When Senator Jeffords of Vermont left the Republican Party, effective June 6, 2001, to become an Independent, Democrats regained the majority for the remainder of the 107th Congress.

ARMED SERVICES / 107th Congress, Post-Jeffords switch

Service Dates of Committee Chair: June 6, 2001-Jan. 14, 2003

Service Dates of Majority Members: June 6, 2001-Jan. 14, 2003

Service Dates of Minority Members: June 6, 2001-Jan. 15, 2003

	Majority						**Minority**				
				Years in:						**Years in:**	
Rank Name		**Party**	**State**	**Senate**	**Comm.**	**Rank Name**		**Party**	**State**	**Senate**	**Comm.**
Ch2 Levin, Carl M.		Dem	Mich.	23	23	RM2 Warner, John W.		Rep	Va.	23	23
2nd Kennedy, Edward M.		Dem	Mass.	39	19	2nd Thurmond, J. Strom		Rep	S.C.	46	*2 37
3rd Byrd, Robert C.		Dem	W.Va.	43	*2 13	3rd McCain, John S. III		Rep	Ariz.	15	15
4th Lieberman, Joseph I.		Dem	Conn.	13	9	4th Smith, Robert C.		Rep	N.H.	11	11
5th Cleland, J. Maxwell (Max)		Dem	Ga.	5	5	5th Inhofe, James M.		Rep	Okla.	7	7
6th Landrieu, Mary L.		Dem	La.	5	3	6th Santorum, Richard J. (Rick)		Rep	Penn.	7	7
7th Reed, John F.		Dem	R.I.	5	3	7th Roberts, C. Patrick		Rep	Kans.	5	5
8th Akaka, Daniel K.		Dem	Hai.	12	1	8th Allard, A. Wayne		Rep	Colo.	5	3
9th Nelson, C. William (Bill)		Dem	Fla.	1	1	9th Hutchinson, Y. Timothy		Rep	Ark.	5	3
10th Nelson, E. Benjamin		Dem	Neb.	1	1	10th Sessions, Jefferson B. III		Rep	Ala.	5	3
11th Carnahan, Jean		Dem	Mo.	1	1	11th Collins, Susan M.		Rep	Me.	5	1
12th Dayton, Mark		DFL	Minn.	1	1	12th Bunning, James P.D.		Rep	Ky.	3	1
13th Bingaman, J.F. (Jeff)		Dem	N.M.	19	*2 1						

*2: Member's second period of service on the committee.

Note: Thurmond served previously on this committee as a Democrat, 1959-1964

Additions:

Majority:

13th Bingaman, J.F. (Jeff)	Dem	N.M.	July 10, 2001	

Changes:

Majority:

Carnahan, Jean	Dem	Mo.	Nov. 25, 2002 Resigned the Senate; defeated in special election by James M. Talent (Rep-Mo.)

Departures from the Senate:

	Majority				**Minority**		
Defeated for Re-election	Cleland, J. Maxwell (Max)	Dem	Ga.		Hutchinson, Y. Timothy	Rep	Ark.
Defeated for Re-nomination	None				Smith, Robert C.	Rep	N.H.
Retired	None				Thurmond, J. Strom	Rep	S.C.

Departures from Committee:

Moved to Finance	None				Santorum, Richard J. (Rick)	Rep	Penn.
					Bunning, James P.D.	Rep	Ky.
Moved to Budget, Energy and Natural Resources, and Veterans' Affairs	None				Bunning, James P.D.	Rep	Ky.
No new assignment	Landrieu, Mary L.	Dem	La.		None		
	Bingaman, J.F. (Jeff)	Dem	N.M.				

ARMED SERVICES / 108th Congress

Service Dates of Committee Chair: Jan. 14, 2003-Jan. 6, 2005

Service Dates of Majority Members: Jan. 14, 2003-Jan. 6, 2005

Service Dates of Minority Members: Jan. 15, 2003-Jan. 6, 2005

	Majority						**Minority**				
				Years in:						**Years in:**	
Rank Name		**Party**	**State**	**Senate**	**Comm.**	**Rank Name**		**Party**	**State**	**Senate**	**Comm.**
Chr Warner, John W.		Rep	Va.	25	24	RM Levin, Carl M.		Dem	Mich.	25	24
2nd McCain, John S. III		Rep	Ariz.	17	17	2nd Kennedy, Edward M.		Dem	Mass.	41	21
3rd Inhofe, James M.		Rep	Okla.	9	9	3rd Byrd, Robert C.		Dem	W.Va.	45	*2 14
4th Roberts, C. Patrick		Rep	Kans.	7	7	4th Lieberman, Joseph I.		Dem	Conn.	15	11
5th Allard, A. Wayne		Rep	Colo.	7	5	5th Reed, John F.		Dem	R.I.	7	5
6th Sessions, Jefferson B. III		Rep	Ala.	7	5	6th Akaka, Daniel K.		Dem	Hai.	13	2
7th Collins, Susan M.		Rep	Me.	7	2	7th Nelson, C. William (Bill)		Dem	Fla.	3	2
8th Ensign, John E.		Rep	Nev.	3	1	8th Nelson, E. Benjamin		Dem	Neb.	3	2
9th Talent, James M.		Rep	Mo.	1	1	9th Dayton, Mark		Dem	Minn.	3	2

Rank Name	Party	State	Senate	Comm.		Rank Name	Party	State	Senate	Comm.
10th Chambliss, Saxby	Rep	Ga.	1	1		10th Bayh, B. Evans	Dem	Ind.	5	1
11th Graham, Lindsey O.	Rep	S.C.	1	1		11th Clinton, Hillary Rodham	Dem	N.Y.	3	1
12th Dole, Elizabeth Hanford	Rep	N.C.	1	1		12th Pryor, Mark	Dem	Ark.	1	*1 1
13th Cornyn, John	Rep	Tex.	1	1						

*1: Member's first period of service on the committee.
*2: Member's second period of service on the committee.

Departures from Committee:	Majority			Minority		
Moved to Appropriations	Allard, A. Wayne	Rep	Colo.	None		
Moved to Commerce, Science, and Transportation and Select Ethics	None			Pryor, Mark	Dem	Ark.

ARMED SERVICES / 109th Congress

Service Dates of Committee Chair: Jan. 6, 2005-Jan. 12, 2007

Service Dates of Majority Members: Jan. 6, 2005-Jan. 12, 2007

Service Dates of Minority Members: Jan. 6, 2005-Jan. 12, 2007

Majority						Minority				
			Years in:						Years in:	
Rank Name	Party	State	Senate	Comm.		Rank Name	Party	State	Senate	Comm.
Chr Warner, John W.	Rep	Va.	27	26		RM Levin, Carl M.	Dem	Mich.	27	26
2nd McCain, John S. III	Rep	Ariz.	19	19		2nd Kennedy, Edward M.	Dem	Mass.	43	23
3rd Inhofe, James M.	Rep	Okla.	11	11		3rd Byrd, Robert C.	Dem	W.Va.	47	*2 16
4th Roberts, C. Patrick	Rep	Kans.	9	8		4th Lieberman, Joseph I.	Dem	Conn.	17	12
5th Sessions, Jefferson B. III	Rep	Ala.	9	6		5th Reed, John F.	Dem	R.I	9	6
6th Collins, Susan M.	Rep	Me.	9	4		6th Akaka, Daniel K.	Dem	Hai.	15	4
7th Ensign, John E.	Rep	Nev.	5	2		7th Nelson, C. William (Bill)	Dem	Fla.	5	4
8th Talent, James M.	Rep	Mo.	3	2		8th Nelson, E. Benjamin	Dem	Neb.	5	4
9th Chambliss, Saxby	Rep	Ga.	3	2		9th Dayton, Mark	DFL	Minn.	5	4
10th Graham, Lindsey O.	Rep	S.C.	3	2		10th Bayh, B. Evans	Dem	Ind.	7	2
11th Dole, Elizabeth Hanford	Rep	N.C.	3	2		11th Clinton, Hillary Rodham	Dem	N.Y.	5	2
12th Cornyn, John	Rep	Tex.	3	2						
13th Thune, John	Rep	S.D.	1	1						

*2: Member's second period of service on the committee.

Departures from the Senate:	Majority			Minority		
Defeated for Re-election	Talent, James M.	Rep	Mo.	None		
Retired	None			Dayton, Mark	DFL	Minn.

Departures from Committee:						
Moved to Finance	Roberts, C. Patrick	Rep	Kans.	None		

ARMED SERVICES / 110th Congress

Service Dates of Committee Chair: Jan. 12, 2007-Jan. 21, 2009

Service Dates of Majority Members: Jan. 12, 2007-Jan. 21, 2009

Service Dates of Minority Members: Jan. 12, 2007-Jan. 21, 2009

Majority						Minority				
			Years in:						Years in:	
Rank Name	Party	State	Senate	Comm.		Rank Name	Party	State	Senate	Comm.
Chr Levin, Carl M.	Dem	Mich.	29	28		RM McCain, John S. III	Rep	Ariz.	21	21
2nd Kennedy, Edward M.	Dem	Mass.	45	25		2nd Warner, John W.	Rep	Va.	29	28
3rd Byrd, Robert C.	Dem	W.Va.	49	*2 18		3rd Inhofe, James M.	Rep	Okla.	13	13
4th Lieberman, Joseph I.	IDem	Conn.	19	15		4th Sessions, Jefferson B. III	Rep	Ala.	11	9
5th Reed, John F.	Dem	R.I.	11	9		5th Collins, Susan M.	Rep	Me.	11	6
6th Akaka, Daniel K.	Dem	Hai.	17	6		6th Ensign, John E.	Rep	Nev.	7	4
7th Nelson, C. William (Bill)	Dem	Fla.	7	6		7th Chambliss, Saxby	Rep	Ga.	5	4
8th Nelson, E. Benjamin	Dem	Neb.	7	6		8th Graham, Lindsey O.	Rep	S.C.	5	4
9th Bayh, B. Evans	Dem	Ind.	9	4		9th Dole, Elizabeth Hanford	Rep	N.C.	5	4
10th Clinton, Hillary Rodham	Dem	N.Y.	7	4		10th Cornyn, John	Rep	Tex.	5	4
11th Pryor, Mark	Dem	Ark.	5	*2 1		11th Thune, John	Rep	S.D.	3	3
12th Webb, James	Dem	Va.	1	1		12th Martinez, Melquiades R. (Mel)	Rep	Fla.	3	1
13th McCaskill, Claire	Dem	Mo.	1	1						

*2: Member's second period of service on the committee.

Changes:

Minority:

Ensign, John E.	Rep	Nev.	July 17, 2007 Left the committee; moved to Finance	
Corker, Robert	Rep	Tenn.	July 17, 2007 Replaced Ensign.	
Corker, Robert	Rep	Tenn.	Jan. 24, 2008 Left the committee; moved to Banking, Housing, and Urban Affairs.	
Wicker, Roger F.	Rep	Miss.	Jan. 24, 2008 Replaced Corker.	

Departures from the Senate:	**Majority**			**Minority**		
Defeated for Re-election	None			Dole, Elizabeth Hanford	Rep	N.C.
Retired	None			Warner, John W.	Rep	Va.

Departures from Committee:						
Moved to Appropriations	Pryor, Mark	Dem	Ark.	None		
Moved to Finance	None			Cornyn, John	Rep	Tex.

Note: Hillary Rodham Clinton (Dem-N.Y.) resigned the Senate on Jan. 21, 2009; named Secretary of State.

ARMED SERVICES / 111th Congress

Service Dates of Committee Chair: Jan. 21, 2009-

Service Dates of Majority Members: Jan. 21, 2009-

Service Dates of Minority Members: Jan. 21, 2009-

Majority					**Minority**				
			Years in:					**Years in:**	
Rank Name	**Party**	**State**	**Senate**	**Comm.**	**Rank Name**	**Party**	**State**	**Senate**	**Comm.**
Chr Levin, Carl M.	Dem	Mich.	31	30	RM McCain, John S. III	Rep	Ariz.	23	23
2nd Kennedy, Edward M.	Dem	Mass.	47	27	2nd Inhofe, James M.	Rep	Okla.	15	15
3rd Byrd, Robert C.	Dem	W.Va.	51	*2 20	3rd Sessions, Jefferson B. III	Rep	Ala.	13	11
4th Lieberman, Joseph I.	IDem	Conn.	21	17	4th Chambliss, Saxby	Rep	Ga.	7	7
5th Reed, John F.	Dem	R.I.	13	11	5th Graham, Lindsey O.	Rep	S.C.	7	7
6th Akaka, Daniel K.	Dem	Hai.	19	8	6th Thune, John	Rep	S.D.	5	5
7th Nelson, C. William (Bill)	Dem	Fla.	9	8	7th Martinez, Melquiades R. (Mel)	Rep	Fla.	5	3
8th Nelson, E. Benjamin	Dem	Neb.	9	8	8th Wicker, Roger F.	Rep	Miss.	2	1
9th Bayh, B. Evans	Dem	Ind.	11	7	9th Burr, Richard M.	Rep	N.C.	5	1
10th Webb, James	Dem	Va.	3	3	10th Vitter, David	Rep	La.	5	1
11th McCaskill, Claire	Dem	Mo.	3	3	11th Collins, Susan M.	Rep	Me.	13	8
12th Udall, Mark	Dem	Colo.	1	1					
13th Hagan, Kay R.	Dem	N.C.	1	1	*2: Member's second period of service on the committee.				
14th Begich, Mark	Dem	Alas.	1	1					
15th Burris, Roland W.	Dem	Ill.	1	1					

Changes:

Majority:

Kennedy, Edward M.	Dem	Mass.	Aug. 25, 2009 Died in office
Kirk, Paul G. Jr.	Dem	Mass.	Sept. 29, 2009 Replaced Kennedy
Kirk, Paul G. Jr.	Dem	Mass.	Feb. 4, 2010 Temporary term expired; successor elected

Minority:

Martinez, Melquiades R. (Mel)	Rep	Fla.	Sept. 22, 2009 Resigned the Senate
LeMieux, George S.	Rep	Fla.	Sept. 22, 2009 Replaced Martinez, ranked following Wicker
Brown, Scott P.	Rep	Mass.	Mar. 2, 2001 Minority addition; ranked 9th after LeMieux

Banking, Housing, and Urban Affairs

Senate Committee on Banking, Housing, and Urban Affairs, 103rd-111th Congresses (1993-2011)

BACKGROUND

Organizational History: Watching over the nation's banking industry is the chief responsibility of the Senate's Banking, Housing, and Urban Affairs Committee. It is responsible for legislation dealing with regulation of the U.S. financial system. Although the panel has jurisdiction over housing and urban issues, its agenda has been dominated from the 1980s to the present with the savings and loan industry bailouts earlier and banking regulations. The continuing financial crisis of recent years has placed the Senate Banking Committee at the center of much of the debate.

The Senate Committee on Banking, Housing, and Urban Affairs was originally the Committee on Banking and Currency and derived its jurisdiction over banking and currency legislation from the Senate Finance Committee. The Banking and Currency Committee's existence dates from March 15, 1913, making it the youngest of the Senate standing committees to survive the Legislative Reorganization Act of 1946 (Public Law 79-601).

Twelve members served on the committee during its initial appearance in the 63rd Congress. The committee's first chair was Sen. Robert L. Owen (Dem-Okla.) whose mother was of Cherokee descent. Senator Owen gained the post due to his role as a major sponsor of the Owen-Glass Federal Reserve Act of 1913 (38 Stat. 251-275).

The Senate had earlier committees dealing with banking matters. As reported in the *Guide to the Records of the United States Senate at the National Archives, 1789-1989,*

> On several occasions before the 63d Congress, the Senate had appointed select committees to consider specific measures relating to banking and currency matters. One such select committee . . . is the Select Committee on the Memorial of the President, Directors, and Company of the Bank of the United States (22d Cong.), which was appointed in 1832 to consider the bank's request for renewal of its charter. Other select committees on banking activities . . . are the Select Committee on Banks in the District of Columbia (35th Cong.) and the Select Committee on National Banks (53d- 60th Congresses).

The Committee on Banking and Currency became the Committee on Banking, Housing, and Urban Affairs with the passage of the Legislative Reorganization Act of 1970 (Public Law 91-510), in part to reflect the 1965 establishment of the Cabinet-level Department of Housing and Urban Development in the Johnson Administration. The House followed suit in 1975 by renaming its committee on Banking and Currency to Banking, Currency, and Housing in the 94th Congress and renaming it again to Banking, Finance, and Urban Affairs in the 95th Congress (1977-1979). Although the House removed "Banking and Urban Affairs" from its committee's name to become the House Committee on Financial Services in 1997, the Senate committee's name and jurisdiction have remained unchanged since the 1977 Reorganization.

With financial troubles emanating from subprime home mortgage loans and continued uncertainty surrounding the government's two major housing funding agencies, Fannie Mae (Federal National Mortgage Association) and Freddie Mac (Federal Home Loan Mortgage Corporation), the Senate Banking Committee has faced a great deal of unwanted attention in recent years.

Membership: In the 80th Congress, the Banking and Currency committee had thirteen members. Its size did not vary greatly in the early post-Reorganization Congresses. It was in 1989 that the renamed Banking, Housing, and Urban Affairs Committee first reached twenty-one members, but it was not until the present 111th Congress, with its twenty-three members, that the committee exceeded that number. Its average size is 20.1—seventh largest among the sixteen standing committees and its members had an overall seniority mean of 8.37 years, the lowest average among the Senate committees. With regard to its membership retention rate, the Senate Committee on Banking, Housing, and Urban Affairs has a rate of 86.7 percent, ranking it in eleventh place of the sixteen standing committees in the last nine Congresses.

Only five members of the Senate Banking Committee left other committees to join Banking, the most notable being Phil Gramm (Rep-Texas) who left Agriculture, Nutrition, and Forestry to assume the chairmanship of the committee in 1999. Eighteen Banking Committee members left the committee, including five who took no new assignments. Four departing members each joined the Finance and Health, Education, Labor, and Pensions (HELP) committees.

Committee Leaders: Sen. Charles W. Tobey (Rep-N.H.) served as the committee's first modern-era chair. He was followed by Burnett R. Maybank (Dem-S.C.) whose continuous service on the committee had been broken. Maybank became chair in 1949, the third continuous year of his second period of service on the committee. Three other members of the committee had longer continuous service on Banking and Currency than Maybank; however, Maybank's cumulative seniority was outranked only by Sen. Robert F. Wagner (Dem-N.Y.), whose ill health prevented him from chairing the committee. Maybank chaired the committee for four years (1949-1953).

Senator Tobey left Banking and Currency in the 83rd Congress for the chairmanship of Interstate and Foreign Commerce. He was succeeded by Homer Capehart (Rep-Ind.) who held the chair in 1953-1955. When the Democrats regained the Senate, J. William Fulbright (Dem-Ark.) became chair and he served from 1955 until February 6, 1959, when he relinquished the chair of Banking and Currency for the chair of Foreign Relations. He was succeeded by A. Willis Robertson (Dem-Va.), who served from 1959 until his defeat in the 1966 Senate primary by William Spong.

Sen. John J. Sparkman (Dem-Ala.), the 1952 Democratic vice presidential candidate with Governor Adlai E. Stevenson, became chair in 1967 and served for eight years. In the middle of Sparkman's tenure, the committee was renamed Banking, Housing, and Urban Affairs. Sparkman left the chairmanship to succeed J. William Fulbright (Dem-Ark.) as chair of the Foreign Relations Committee in 1975. Sparkman's successor, William Proxmire (Dem-Wisc.), served for six years as chair (1975-1981) until the Republican takeover of the Senate in 1981, when Jake Garn of Utah chaired the committee during the Republican-controlled 97th-99th Congresses (1981-1987).

Senator Wagner was the committee's first modern-era ranking minority member (1947-1949). He was followed in 1949 by Senator Tobey, who left the committee in 1951. Tobey was succeeded by Homer Capehart, who served as ranking minority member of Banking and Currency for five Congresses (1951-1953 and 1955-1963). Capehart's service in this capacity was ended by his defeat in the 1962 general election by Birch Bayh (Dem-Ind.). Maybank served as ranking minority member in the 83rd Congress from 1953 until his death on September 1, 1954. Fulbright succeeded Maybank as Banking and Currency's ranking minority member for the duration of that Congress.

In 1963, Wallace F. Bennett (Rep-Utah) became the ranking minority member on the committee. He served until 1971 when he left that slot to become the ranking minority member on the Finance Committee. Bennett's successor was John G. Tower (Rep-Tex.), who served from 1971 until February 22, 1977, when he became the ranking minority member on Armed Services. Tower's successor, the Senate's first popularly elected African-American, Edward W. Brooke (Rep-Mass.), served only until 1979. He was defeated in the 1978 general election by Paul Tsongas. Brooke was followed by Garn as ranking member and served in that post in four Congresses (1979-1981 and 1987-1993) until his retirement from the Senate in 1993.

In the 97th Congress in 1981, Harrison A. Williams Jr. (Dem-N.J.), the former chair of the Labor and Human Resources Committee, was named ranking minority member of Banking, Housing, and Urban Affairs. Williams was the only senator caught in the Justice Department's "Abscam" sting operation, and he resigned the Senate on March 11, 1982. He was succeeded for the balance of the 97th Congress by Donald W. Riegle (Dem-Mich.). Senator Proxmire, the committee's chair in the 94th-96th Congresses (1975-1981), opted for the ranking minority slot on the Appropriations Committee for the 97th Congress. Proxmire returned to his senior status on the committee in 1983 and served as ranking minority member in the 98th and 99th Congresses (1983-1987) and as chair in the 100th (1987-1989). Upon Proxmire's retirement in 1989, Riegle assumed the chair, which he held through 1995 and his retirement. Riegle was followed as the Democrats' senior member by Paul Sarbanes (Dem-Md.) serving both as ranking minority member (1995-2001 and 2003-2006) and as chair during the Jeffords defection (2001-2003) for the next twelve years until his retirement in 2006. It would be Connecticut's Christopher Dodd who would chair Banking, Housing, and Urban Affairs in the Democratic-controlled 110th and 111th Congresses (2007-2011).

The Republican takeover in 1995 led to Alfonse M. D'Amato (Rep-N.Y.) moving from the ranking minority slot that he held in the 103rd Congress (1993-1995) to the chairmanship, a post that he held until his re-election defeat in 1998. D'Amato was succeeded by W. Phil Gramm of Texas, whose congressional career was marked by the authorship of two landmark bills—the Gramm-Latta Omnibus Reconciliation Act of 1981 implementing Reagan-era tax cuts, and the Gramm-Rudman-Hollings Balanced Budget and Emergency Deficit Control Act of 1985 (Public Law 99-177). Gramm served as chair from 1997 to 2001 when the Jeffords defection moved him into the ranking minority slot. He resigned his Senate seat on November 30, 2002, and Richard C. Shelby of Alabama succeeded him. Both Gramm and Shelby had initially been elected to Congress as Democrats but both defected to the Republican Party: Gramm in 1983 during his House service and Shelby in 1995 following the Senate victory of the Republicans. The Democratic recapture of the Senate in 2006 led Shelby to assume the post of ranking minority member in the 110th and 111th Congresses.

Party Leaders: The Banking Committee has not been a major source of floor leaders or party Whips. Only three committee alumni held either post: Russell Long of Louisiana, who served as Whip from 1965 to 1969 and Alan Cranston of California, the Democratic Whip from 1977 until 1991. Committee alumnus Robert C. Byrd of West Virginia, who was Whip from 1971 until 1977 and Floor Leader from 1977 to 1989, left the committee in 1961. On the Republican side, there have been only two Banking members to hold key posts—Everett McK. Dirksen of Illinois, who began as Whip in 1957 and served as floor leader from 1959 until his death in 1969, and William Frist of Tennessee, who served as floor leader from 2003 until his retirement in 2006. It was early in the Senate career of Dirksen that he was witness to the Senate's toughest intramural conflict of the early 1950s, involving fellow Banking Committee members Sen. Joseph R. McCarthy (Rep-Wisc.) and Sen. Ralph Flanders (Rep-Vt.), who tangled publicly over McCarthy's investigatory practices.

Presidential Aspirations: While Gramm unsuccessfully sought the Republican presidential nomination in 1996, the only Republican nominee with Banking Committee service was Arizona's 1964 nominee Barry Goldwater, who served on the committee during his freshman term (1953-1955). It would seem that Banking Committee Democrats have been more successful with John Kerry of Massachusetts receiving the presidential nomination in 2004 and five others named as vice presidential contenders: John Sparkman of Alabama on the 1952 Stevenson ticket, Edmund S. Muskie of Maine on the 1968 Humphrey ticket, Walter Mondale of Minnesota on the 1976 Carter ticket, John Edwards of North Carolina on the 2004 Kerry ticket, and Joseph R. Biden on the 2008 Obama ticket. Senators Mondale, Edwards, and Biden had left the committee before their nominations.

Other Notables: Six Senate Banking Committee members served in the Cabinet with three recent Republican senators elected to the Senate after serving in the Cabinet: Elizabeth Dole of North Carolina, who was Reagan's Secretary of Transportation and George H.W. Bush's Secretary of Labor prior to her 2002 election, and two of President George W. Bush's Cabinet members, Mel Martinez of Florida who served as Secretary of Housing and Urban Development before his 2004 election and Mike Johanns of Nebraska as Secretary of Agriculture before his 2008 election. Two other Republicans joined the Cabinet after Senate service: Bill Brock of Tennessee, named as Secretary of Labor by President Reagan after his Senate defeat in 1976, and Nicholas Brady, a 1982 appointee from New Jersey named as Secretary of Treasury by President George H.W. Bush. The lone Senate Banking Committee Democrat with modern-day Cabinet experience was Edmund S. Muskie of Maine, who left the Senate to become Secretary of State for President Jimmy Carter in 1980. Muskie replaced Cyrus Vance, who left the administration four days after his advice was ignored in the planning of Carter's ill-fated effort to rescue American hostages held at the embassy in Tehran, Iran.

The only post-1993 Banking Committee member to serve as governor after leaving the Senate was Democrat Jon S. Corzine, who left the Senate in 2006 after being elected governor of New Jersey but was defeated after a single term in 2009.

Selected References

Bibby, John F. and Roger H. Davidson, "The Congressional Committee: The Politics of the Senate Committee on Banking, Housing and Urban Affairs," in Bibby and Davidson, *Studies in the Legislative Process*, 2nd ed. (Hinsdale, Ill.: Dryden Press, 1972), 183-206.

Coren, Robert W., et al., "Records of the Committee on Banking and Currency, 1913-1968," *Guide to the Records of the United States Senate at the National Archives: 1789-1989 Bicentennial Edition* (Washington, D.C.: National Archives and Records Administration, 1989), 47-51.

Grier, Kevin B., "Congressional Influence on U.S. Monetary Policy: An Empirical Test," *Journal of Monetary Economics*, 28 (October, 1991), 201-220.

Huitt, Ralph K., "The Congressional Committee: A Case Study," *American Political Science Review*, 48 (June, 1954), 340-365.

Salamon, Lester M., dir., *The Money Committees: A Study of the House Banking and Currency Committee and the Senate Banking, Housing and Urban Affairs Committee* in the Ralph Nader Congress Project (New York: Grossman, 1975).

Schroedel, Jean Reith, "Banking, Housing, and Urban Affairs Committee, Senate," in Donald C. Bacon, Roger H. Davidson, and Morton Keller, eds., *The Encyclopedia of the United States Congress* (New York: Simon & Schuster, 1995), I: 140-142.

U.S. Senate, Committee on Banking and Currency, *Committee on Banking and Currency, 50th Anniversary, 1913-1963*, Senate Document 88-15, 88th Congress, 1st Session (1963).

RESPONSIBILITIES, JURISDICTIONAL CHANGES, AND SUBCOMMITTEES

BANKING AND CURRENCY

Jurisdiction, 80th Congress (1947-49)
Established by the Legislative Reorganization Act of 1946:

[Section 102.(1)(d)]

(1) **Committee on Banking and Currency**, to consist of thirteen Senators, to which committee shall be referred all proposed legislation, messages, petitions, memorials, and other matters relating to the following subjects:

    (1) Banking and currency generally

    (2) Financial aid to commerce and industry, other than matters relating to such aid which are specifically assigned to other committees under this rule

    (3) Deposit insurance

    (4) Public and private housing

    (5) Federal Reserve System

    (6) Gold and silver, including the coinage thereof

    (7) Issuance of notes and redemption thereof

    (8) Valuation and revaluation of the dollar

    (9) Control of prices of commodities, rents, or services

Committee Renamed

BANKING, HOUSING, AND URBAN AFFAIRS

Banking and Currency was renamed the Committee on Banking, Housing, and Urban Affairs on October 26, 1970.

Post-Reorganization Jurisdiction, 1977

From Committee System Reorganization Amendments of 1977, S.Res. 95-4, *Senate Journal*, Feb. 4, 1977:

[XXV. Section 101. 1.(d)]

(1) **Committee on Banking, Housing, and Urban Affairs**, to which committee shall be referred all proposed legislation, messages, petitions, memorials, and other matters relating to the following subjects:

    (1) Banks, banking, and financial institutions

    (2) Financial aid to commerce and industry

   (3) Deposit insurance
   (4) Public and private housing (including veterans' housing)
   (5) Federal monetary policy, including Federal Reserve System
   (6) Money and credit, including currency and coinage
   (7) Issuance and redemption of notes
   (8) Control of prices of commodities, rents, and services
   (9) Urban development and urban mass transit
   (10) Economic stabilization and defense production
   (11) Export controls
   (12) Export and foreign trade promotion
   (13) Nursing home construction
   (14) Renegotiation of Government contracts

(2) Such committee shall also study and review, on a comprehensive basis, matters relating to international economic policy as it affects United States monetary affairs, credit, and financial institutions; economic growth, urban affairs, and credit, and report thereon from time to time.

Jurisdiction, 103rd Congress (1993-94)

From the *Standing Rules of the Senate* in the *Senate Manual*, 103rd Congress, 1st Session, S. Doc. 103-1:

[Rule XXV.(1)(d)]

(1) **Committee on Banking, Housing, and Urban Affairs**, to which committee shall be referred all proposed legislation, messages, petitions, memorials, and other matters relating to the following subjects:

   (1) Banks, banking, and financial institutions
   (2) Control of prices of commodities, rents, and services
   (3) Deposit insurance
   (4) Economic stabilization and defense production
   (5) Export and foreign trade promotion
   (6) Export controls
   (7) Federal monetary policy, including Federal Reserve System
   (8) Financial aid to commerce and industry
   (9) Issuance and redemption of notes
   (10) Money and credit, including currency and coinage
   (11) Nursing home construction
   (12) Public and private housing (including veterans' housing)
   (13) Renegotiation of Government contracts
   (14) Urban development and urban mass transit

(2) Such committee shall also study and review, on a comprehensive basis, matters relating to international economic policy as it affects United States monetary affairs, credit, and financial institutions; economic growth, urban affairs, and credit, and report thereon from time to time.

Jurisdiction, 111th Congress (2009-10)

From *Authority and Rules of Senate Committees, 2009-2010*, Sen. Doc. 111-3, pursuant to S.Res, 166, June 2, 2009.

(1) **Committee on Banking, Housing, and Urban Affairs**, to which committee shall be referred all proposed legislation, messages, petitions, memorials, and other matters relating to the following subjects:

   (1) Banks, banking, and financial institutions
   (2) Control of prices of commodities, rents, and services
   (3) Deposit insurance
   (4) Economic stabilization and defense production
   (5) Export and foreign trade promotion
   (6) Export controls
   (7) Federal monetary policy, including Federal Reserve System
   (8) Financial aid to commerce and industry
   (9) Issuance and redemption of notes
   (10) Money and credit, including currency and coinage
   (11) Nursing home construction
   (12) Public and private housing (including veterans' housing)
   (13) Renegotiation of Government contracts
   (14) Urban development and urban mass transit

(2) Such committee shall also study and review, on a comprehensive basis, matters relating to international economic policy as it affects United States monetary affairs, credit, and financial institutions; economic growth, urban affairs, and credit, and report thereon from time to time.

NAMES OF SUBCOMMITTEES

Committee on Banking, Housing, and Urban Affairs, 103rd-111th Congresses

Economic Policy, 106, 107, 108, 109, 110, 111
Economic Stabilization and Rural Development, 103
Financial Institutions, 106, 107, 108, 109, 110, 111
Financial Institutions and Regulatory Relief, 104, 105
Financial Services and Technology, 105
Housing and Transportation, 106, 107, 108, 109
Housing and Urban Affairs, 103
Housing Opportunity and Community Development, 104, 105
Housing, Transportation, and Community Development, 110, 111
HUD Oversight and Structure, 104 only
International Finance, 104, 105
International Finance and Monetary Policy, 103
International Trade and Finance, 106, 107, 108, 109
Securities, 103, 104, 105, 106
Securities and Investment, 107, 108, 109
Securities, Insurance, and Investment, 110, 111
Security and International Trade and Finance, 110, 111

MEMBERSHIP ROSTERS, 103rd-111th Congresses, 1993-2010

BANKING, HOUSING, AND URBAN AFFAIRS / 103rd Congress

Service Dates of Committee Chair: Jan. 7, 1993-Jan. 11, 1995

Service Dates of Majority Members: Jan. 7, 1993-Jan. 4, 1995

Service Dates of Minority Members: Jan. 7, 1993-Jan. 4, 1995

Majority

Rank Name	Party	State	Senate	Comm.
Chr Riegle, Donald W. Jr.	Dem	Mich.	17	16
2nd Sarbanes, Paul S.	Dem	Md.	17	16
3rd Dodd, Christopher J.	Dem	Conn.	13	13
4th Sasser, James R.	Dem	Tenn.	17	11
5th Shelby, Richard C.	Dem	Ala.	7	7
6th Kerry, John F.	Dem	Mass.	9	4
7th Bryan, Richard H.	Dem	Nev.	5	4
8th Boxer, Barbara	Dem	Cal.	1	1
9th Campbell, Ben Nighthorse	Dem	Colo.	1	1
10th Moseley Braun, Carol	Dem	Ill.	1	1
11th Murray, Patty	Dem	Wash.	1	1

Minority

Rank Name	Party	State	Senate	Comm.
RM D'Amato, Alfonse M.	Rep	N.Y.	13	13
2nd Gramm, W. Phil	Rep	Tex.	9	8
3rd Bond, Christopher S. (Kit)	Rep	Mo.	7	7
4th Mack, Connie III	Rep	Fla.	5	4
5th Faircloth, D.M. (Lauch)	Rep	N.C.	1	1
6th Bennett, Robert F.	Rep	Utah	1	1
7th Roth, William V. Jr.	Rep	Del.	23	*2 4
8th Domenici, Pete V.	Rep	N.M.	21	*1 2

*1: Member's first period of service on the committee.
*2: Member's second period of service on the committee.

Note: Ranking on this committee for the following member was affected by other chamber service: William V. Roth Jr. (Rep-Del.), Ranking Minority Member, Governmental Affairs.

Departures from the Senate:

	Majority			Minority
Defeated for Re-election	Sasser, James R.	Dem	Tenn.	None
Retired	Riegle, Donald W. Jr.	Dem	Mich.	None

Departures from Committee:

Moved to Joint Taxation		None		Roth, William V. Jr.	Rep	Del.
No new assignment	Campbell, Ben Nighthorse	Dem	Colo	Domenici, Pete V.	Rep	N.M.

BANKING, HOUSING, AND URBAN AFFAIRS / 104th Congress

Service Dates of Committee Chair: Jan. 11, 1995-Jan. 9, 1997

Service Dates of Majority Members: Jan. 4, 1995-Jan. 9, 1997

Service Dates of Minority Members: Jan. 4, 1995-Jan. 9, 1997

Majority					Minority				
			Years in:					**Years in:**	
Rank Name	**Party**	**State**	**Senate**	**Comm.**	**Rank Name**	**Party**	**State**	**Senate**	**Comm.**
Chr D'Amato, Alfonse M.	Rep	N.Y.	15	14	RM Sarbanes, Paul S.	Dem	Md.	19	18
2nd Gramm, W. Phil	Rep	Tex.	11	10	2nd Dodd, Christopher J.	Dem	Conn.	15	14
3rd Shelby, Richard C.	Rep	Ala.	9	8	3rd Kerry, John F.	Dem	Mass.	11	6
4th Bond, Christopher S. (Kit)	Rep	Mo.	9	8	4th Bryan, Richard H.	Dem	Nev.	7	6
5th Mack, Connie III	Rep	Fla.	7	6	5th Boxer, Barbara	Dem	Cal.	3	2
6th Faircloth, D.M. (Lauch)	Rep	N.C.	3	2	6th Moseley Braun, Carol	Dem	Ill.	3	2
7th Bennett, Robert F.	Rep	Utah	3	2	7th Murray, Patty	Dem	Wash.	3	2
8th Grams, Rod	Rep	Minn.	1	1					
9th Frist, William H.	Rep	Tenn.	1	1					

Note: Shelby was a member of Banking in the 103rd as a Democrat and changed party affiliation on Nov. 9, 1994, to be effective in the 104th Congress.

Changes:

Majority:

Frist, William H.	Rep	Tenn.	Oct. 12, 1995 Left the committee; moved to Commerce, Science, and Transportation.
Domenici, Pete V.	Rep	N.M.	Oct. 12, 1995 Replaced Frist.
Domenici, Pete V.	Rep	N.M.	June 20, 1996 Left the committee; moved to Governmental Affairs.
Frahm, Sheila	Rep	Kans.	June 20, 1996 Replaced Domenici.
Frahm, Sheila	Rep	Kans.	Nov. 5, 1996 Resigned the Senate; defeated for nomination.

Departures from Committee:	**Majority**			**Minority**		
Moved to Labor and Human Resources, Veterans' Affairs, and Select Ethics	None			Murray, Patty	Dem	Wash.
No new assignment	Bond, Christopher S. (Kit)	Rep	Mo.	None		

BANKING, HOUSING, AND URBAN AFFAIRS / 105th Congress

Service Dates of Committee Chair: Jan. 9, 1997-Jan. 7, 1999

Service Dates of Majority Members: Jan. 9, 1997-Jan. 7, 1999

Service Dates of Minority Members: Jan. 9, 1997-Jan. 7, 1999

Majority					Minority				
			Years in:					**Years in:**	
Rank Name	**Party**	**State**	**Senate**	**Comm.**	**Rank Name**	**Party**	**State**	**Senate**	**Comm.**
Chr D'Amato, Alfonse M.	Rep	N.Y.	17	17	RM Sarbanes, Paul S.	Dem	Md.	21	20
2nd Gramm, W. Phil	Rep	Tex.	13	12	2nd Dodd, Christopher J.	Dem	Conn.	17	17
3rd Shelby, Richard C.	Rep	Ala.	11	11	3rd Kerry, John F.	Dem	Mass.	13	8
4th Mack, Connie III	Rep	Fla.	9	8	4th Bryan, Richard H.	Dem	Nev.	9	8
5th Faircloth, D.M. (Lauch)	Rep	N.C.	5	5	5th Boxer, Barbara	Dem	Cal.	5	5
6th Bennett, Robert F.	Rep	Utah	5	5	6th Moseley Braun, Carol	Dem	Ill.	5	5
7th Grams, Rod	Rep	Minn.	3	3	7th Johnson, Timothy P.	Dem	S.D.	1	1
8th Allard, A. Wayne	Rep	Colo.	1	1	8th Reed, John F.	Dem	R.I.	1	1
9th Enzi, Michael B.	Rep	Wyo.	1	1					
10th Hagel, Charles T. (Chuck)	Rep	Neb.	1	1					

Note: The original S. Res. 16 of Jan. 4, 1995, has Campbell in the 5th slot but the later version of S. Res. 16 placed Bryan in the 4th slot and does not list Campbell on the committee.

Departures from the Senate:	**Majority**			**Minority**		
Defeated for Re-election	D'Amato, Alfonse M.	Rep	N.Y.	Moseley Braun, Carol	Dem	Ill.
	Faircloth, D.M. (Lauch)	Rep	N.C.			

Departures from Committee:	**Majority**			**Minority**		
Moved to Foreign Relations	None			Boxer, Barbara	Dem	Cal.

BANKING, HOUSING, AND URBAN AFFAIRS / 106th Congress

Service Dates of Committee Chair: Jan. 7, 1999-Jan. 3, 2001

Service Dates of Majority Members: Jan. 7, 1999-Jan. 25, 2001

Service Dates of Minority Members: Jan. 7, 1999-Jan. 25, 2001

Majority					Minority				
			Years in:					Years in:	
Rank Name	Party	State	Senate	Comm.	Rank Name	Party	State	Senate	Comm.
Chr Gramm, W. Phil	Rep	Tex.	15	14	RM Sarbanes, Paul S.	Dem	Md.	23	22
2nd Shelby, Richard C.	Rep	Ala.	13	13	2nd Dodd, Christopher J.	Dem	Conn.	19	19
3rd Mack, Connie III	Rep	Fla.	11	10	3rd Kerry, John F.	Dem	Mass.	15	10
4th Bennett, Robert F.	Rep	Utah	7	7	4th Bryan, Richard H.	Dem	Nev.	11	10
5th Grams, Rod	Rep	Minn.	5	5	5th Johnson, Timothy P.	Dem	S.D.	3	2
6th Allard, A. Wayne	Rep	Colo.	3	2	6th Reed, John F.	Dem	R.I.	3	2
7th Enzi, Michael B.	Rep	Wyo.	3	2	7th Schumer, Charles E.	Dem	N.Y.	1	1
8th Hagel, Charles T. (Chuck)	Rep	Neb.	3	2	8th Bayh, B. Evans	Dem	Ind.	1	1
9th Santorum, Richard J. (Rick)	Rep	Penn.	5	1	9th Edwards, John	Dem	N.C.	1	1
10th Bunning, James P.D.	Rep	Ky.	1	1					
11th Crapo, Michael D.	Rep	Ida.	1	1					

Additions:
  Majority:

12th Nickles, Donald L.	Rep	Okla.	Dec. 6, 2000	

  Minority:

10th Miller, Zell B.	Dem	Ga.	Sept. 12, 2000	

Departures from the Senate:	Majority			Minority		
Defeated for Re-election	Grams, Rod	Rep	Minn.	None		
Retired	Mack, Connie III	Rep	Fla.	Bryan, Richard H.	Dem	Nev.

Departures from Committee:						
Moved to Finance	None			Kerry, John F.	Dem	Mass.
Moved to Commerce, Science, and, Transportation Health, Education, Labor, and Pensions, and Select Intelligence	None			Edwards, John	Dem	N.C.
No new assignment	Nickles, Donald L.	Rep	Okla.	None		

BANKING, HOUSING, AND URBAN AFFAIRS / 107th Congress, Pre-Jeffords switch

Service Dates of Committee Chair: ChT: Jan. 3, 2001-Jan. 25, 2001 Sarbanes (Dem-Md.)

Ch1: Jan. 25, 2001-June 6, 2001 Gramm (Rep-Tex.)

Service Dates of Majority Members: Jan. 25, 2001-June 6, 2001

Service Dates of Minority Members: Jan. 25, 2001-June 6, 2001

Majority					Minority				
			Years in:					Years in:	
Rank Name	Party	State	Senate	Comm.	Rank Name	Party	State	Senate	Comm.
Ch1 Gramm, W. Phil	Rep	Tex.	17	16	RM1 Sarbanes, Paul S.	Dem	Md.	25	24
2nd Shelby, Richard C.	Rep	Ala.	15	15	2nd Dodd, Christopher J.	Dem	Conn.	21	21
3rd Bennett, Robert F.	Rep	Utah	9	9	3rd Johnson, Timothy P.	Dem	S.D.	5	5
4th Allard, A. Wayne	Rep	Colo.	5	5	4th Reed, John F.	Dem	R.I.	5	5
5th Enzi, Michael B.	Rep	Wyo.	5	5	5th Schumer, Charles E.	Dem	N.Y.	3	3
6th Hagel, Charles T. (Chuck)	Rep	Neb.	5	5	6th Bayh, B. Evans	Dem	Ind.	3	3
7th Santorum, Richard J. (Rick)	Rep	Penn.	7	3	7th Miller, Zell B.	Dem	Ga.	1	1
8th Bunning, James P.D.	Rep	Ky.	3	3	8th Carper, Thomas R.	Dem	Del.	1	1
9th Crapo, Michael D.	Rep	Ida.	3	3	9th Stabenow, Deborah Ann	Dem	Mich.	1	1
10th Ensign, John E.	Rep	Nev.	1	1	10th Corzine, Jon S.	Dem	N.J.	1	1

Note: The committee majority in the 2001 Senate power-sharing arrangement was determined by the party of the vice president. Democrat Al Gore Jr. served from Jan. 3, 2001, to Jan. 20, 2001, and was succeeded by Republican Richard B. Cheney on Jan. 20, 2001. When Senator Jeffords of Vermont left the Republican Party, effective June 6, 2001, to become an Independent, Democrats regained the majority for the remainder of the 107th Congress.

BANKING, HOUSING, AND URBAN AFFAIRS / 107th Congress, Post-Jeffords switch

Service Dates of Committee Chair: June 6, 2001-Jan. 14, 2003

Service Dates of Majority Members: June 6, 2001-Jan. 14, 2003

Service Dates of Minority Members: June 6, 2001-Jan. 15, 2003

Majority					Minority				
			Years in:					**Years in:**	
Rank Name	Party	State	Senate	Comm.	Rank Name	Party	State	Senate	Comm.
Ch2 Sarbanes, Paul S.	Dem	Md.	25	25	RM2 Gramm, W. Phil	Rep	Tex.	17	17
2nd Dodd, Christopher J.	Dem	Conn.	21	21	2nd Shelby, Richard C.	Rep	Ala.	15	15
3rd Johnson, Timothy P.	Dem	S.D.	5	5	3rd Bennett, Robert F.	Rep	Utah	9	9
4th Reed, John F.	Dem	R.I.	5	5	4th Allard, A. Wayne	Rep	Colo.	5	5
5th Schumer, Charles E.	Dem	N.Y.	3	3	5th Enzi, Michael B.	Rep	Wyo.	5	5
6th Bayh, B. Evans	Dem	Ind.	3	3	6th Hagel, Charles T. (Chuck)	Rep	Neb.	5	5
7th Miller, Zell B.	Dem	Ga.	1	1	7th Santorum, Richard J. (Rick)	Rep	Penn.	7	3
8th Carper, Thomas R.	Dem	Del.	1	1	8th Bunning, James P.D.	Rep	Ky.	3	3
9th Stabenow, Deborah Ann	Dem	Mich.	1	1	9th Crapo, Michael D.	Rep	Ida.	3	3
10th Corzine, Jon S.	Dem	N.J.	1	1	10th Ensign, John E.	Rep	Nev.	1	1
11th Akaka, Daniel K.	Dem	Hai.	11	*1 1					

*1: Member's first period of service on the committee

Additions:
  Majority:

11th Akaka, Daniel K.	Dem	Hai.	July 10, 2001

Changes:
  Minority:

Gramm, W. Phil	Rep	Tex.	Nov. 30, 2002 Resigned the Senate and retired.

Departures from Committee:	Majority				Minority		
Moved to Armed Services, Budget, Health, Education, Labor, and Pensions, and Veterans' Affairs	None				Ensign, John E.	Rep	Nev.
No new assignment	Akaka, Daniel K.	Dem	Hai.		None		

BANKING, HOUSING, AND URBAN AFFAIRS / 108th Congress

Service Dates of Committee Chair: Jan. 14, 2003-Jan. 3, 2005

Service Dates of Majority Members: Jan. 14, 2003-Jan. 3, 2005

Service Dates of Minority Members: Jan. 15, 2003-Jan. 3, 2005

Majority					Minority				
			Years in:					**Years in:**	
Rank Name	Party	State	Senate	Comm.	Rank Name	Party	State	Senate	Comm.
Chr Shelby, Richard C.	Rep	Ala.	17	17	RM Sarbanes, Paul S.	Dem	Md.	27	26
2nd Bennett, Robert F.	Rep	Utah	11	11	2nd Dodd, Christopher J.	Dem	Conn.	23	23
3rd Allard, A. Wayne	Rep	Colo.	7	7	3rd Johnson, Timothy P.	Dem	S.D.	7	7
4th Enzi, Michael B.	Rep	Wyo.	7	7	4th Reed, John F.	Dem	R.I.	7	7
5th Hagel, Charles T. (Chuck)	Rep	Neb.	7	7	5th Schumer, Charles E.	Dem	N.Y.	5	5
6th Santorum, Richard J. (Rick)	Rep	Penn.	9	5	6th Bayh, B. Evans	Dem	Ind.	5	5
7th Bunning, James P.D.	Rep	Ky.	5	5	7th Miller, Zell B.	Dem	Ga.	3	3
8th Crapo, Michael D.	Rep	Ida.	5	5	8th Carper, Thomas R.	Dem	Del.	3	2
9th Sununu, John E.	Rep	N.H.	1	1	9th Stabenow, Deborah Ann	Dem	Mich.	3	2
10th Dole, Elizabeth Hanford	Rep	N.C.	1	1	10th Corzine, Jon S.	Dem	N.J.	3	2
11th Chafee, Lincoln D.	Rep	R.I.	4	1					

Departures from the Senate:	Majority				Minority		
Retired	None				Miller, Zell B.	Dem	Ga.

Departures from Committee:							
Moved to Homeland Security and Governmental Affairs	Chafee, Lincoln D.		Rep	R.I.	None		

BANKING, HOUSING, AND URBAN AFFAIRS / 109th Congress

Service Dates of Committee Chair: Jan. 6, 2005-Jan. 12, 2007

Service Dates of Majority Members: Jan. 6, 2005-Jan. 12, 2007

Service Dates of Minority Members: Jan. 6, 2005-Jan. 12, 2007

Majority

Rank Name	Party	State	Years in: Senate	Comm.
Chr Shelby, Richard C.	Rep	Ala.	19	19
2nd Bennett, Robert F.	Rep	Utah	13	12
3rd Allard, A. Wayne	Rep	Colo.	9	8
4th Enzi, Michael B.	Rep	Wyo.	9	8
5th Hagel, Charles T. (Chuck)	Rep	Neb.	9	8
6th Santorum, Richard J. (Rick)	Rep	Penn.	11	6
7th Bunning, James P.D.	Reo	Ky.	7	6
8th Crapo, Michael D.	Rep	Ida.	7	6
9th Sununu, John E.	Rep	N.H.	3	2
10th Dole, Elizabeth Hanford	Rep	N.C.	3	2
11th Martinez, Melquiades R. (Mel)	Rep	Fla.	1	1

Minority

Rank Name	Party	State	Years in: Senate	Comm.
RM Sarbanes, Paul S.	Dem	Md.	29	28
2nd Dodd, Christopher J.	Dem	Conn.	25	25
3rd Johnson, Timothy P.	Dem	S.D.	9	8
4th Reed, John F.	Dem	R.I.	9	8
5th Schumer, Charles E.	Dem	N.Y.	7	6
6th Bayh, B. Evans	Dem	Ind.	7	6
7th Carper, Thomas R.	Dem	Del.	5	4
8th Stabenow, Deborah Ann	Dem	Mich.	5	4
9th Corzine, Jon S.	Dem	N.J.	5	4

Changes:

Minority:

Corzine, Jon S.	Dem	N.J.	Jan. 17, 2006 Resigned the Senate; elected governor of New Jersey
Menendez, Robert	Dem	N.J.	Jan. 18, 2006 Replaced Corzine

Departures from the Senate:

	Majority			Minority		
Defeated for Re-election	Santorum, Richard J. (Rick)	Rep	Penn.	None		
Retired	None			Sarbanes, Paul S.	Dem	Md.

Departures from Committee:

		Minority		
Moved to Finance	None	Stabenow, Deborah Ann	Dem	Mich.

BANKING, HOUSING, AND URBAN AFFAIRS / 110th Congress

Service Dates of Committee Chair: Jan. 12, 2007-Jan. 21, 2009

Service Dates of Majority Members: Jan. 12, 2007-Jan. 21, 2009

Service Dates of Minority Members: Jan. 12, 2007-Jan. 21, 2009

Majority

Rank Name	Party	State	Years in: Senate	Comm.
Chr Dodd, Christopher J.	Dem	Conn.	27	27
2nd Johnson, Timothy P.	Dem	S.D.	11	11
3rd Reed, John F.	Dem	R.I.	11	11
4th Schumer, Charles E.	Dem	N.Y.	9	9
5th Bayh, B. Evans	Dem	Ind.	9	9
6th Carper, Thomas R.	Dem	Del.	7	6
7th Menendez, Robert	Dem	N.J.	1	1
8th Akaka, Daniel K.	Dem	Hai.	17	*2 1
9th Brown, Sherrod	Dem	Ohio	1	1
10th Casey, Robert P. Jr.	Dem	Penn.	1	1
11th Tester, Jon	Dem	Mont.	1	1

Minority

Rank Name	Party	State	Years in: Senate	Comm.
RM Shelby, Richard C.	Rep	Ala.	21	21
2nd Bennett, Robert F.	Rep	Utah	15	15
3rd Allard, A. Wayne	Rep	Colo.	11	11
4th Enzi, Michael B.	Rep	Wyo.	11	11
5th Hagel, Charles T. (Chuck)	Rep	Neb.	11	11
6th Bunning, James P.D.	Rep	Ky.	9	9
7th Crapo, Michael D.	Rep	Ida.	9	9
8th Sununu, John E.	Rep	N.H.	5	4
9th Dole, Elizabeth Hanford	Rep	N.C.	5	4
10th Martinez, Melquiades R. (Mel)	Rep	Fla.	3	3

*2: Member's second period of service on the committee.

Changes:

Minority:

Sununu, John E.	Rep	N.H.	Jan. 24, 2008 Left the committee; moved to Finance.
Corker, Robert	Rep	Tenn.	Jan. 24, 2008 Replaced Sununu.

Departures from the Senate:

	Majority			Minority		
Defeated for Re-election	None			Dole, Elizabeth Hanford	Rep	N.C.
				Sununu, John E.	Rep	N.H.
Retired	None			Allard, A. Wayne	Rep	Colo.
				Hagel, Charles T. (Chuck)	Rep	Neb.

Departures from Committee:

	Majority			Minority		
Moved to Finance	Carper, Thomas R.	Dem	Del.	Enzi, Michael B.	Rep	Wyo.
Moved to Health, Education, Labor and Pensions	Casey, Robert P. Jr.	Dem	Penn.	None		

BANKING, HOUSING, AND URBAN AFFAIRS / 111th Congress

Service Dates of Committee Chair: Jan. 21, 2009-

Service Dates of Majority Members: Jan. 21, 2009-

Service Dates of Minority Members: Jan. 21, 2009-

Majority

Rank Name	Party	State	Years in: Senate	Comm.
Chr Dodd, Christopher J.	Dem	Conn.	29	29
2nd Johnson, Timothy P.	Dem	S.D.	13	13
3rd Reed, John F.	Dem	R.I.	13	13
4th Schumer, Charles E.	Dem	N.Y.	11	11
5th Bayh, B. Evans	Dem	Ind.	11	11
6th Menendez, Robert	Dem	N.J.	4	4
7th Akaka, Daniel K.	Dem	Hai.	19	*2 3
8th Brown, Sherrod	Dem	Ohio	3	3
9th Tester, Jon	Dem	Mont.	3	3
10th Kohl, Herbert H.	Dem	Wisc.	21	1
11th Warner, Mark R.	Dem	Va.	1	1
12th Merkley, Jeff	Dem	Ore.	1	1
13th Bennet, Michael F.	Dem	Colo.	1	1

Minority

Rank Name	Party	State	Years in: Senate	Comm.
RM Shelby, Richard C.	Rep	Ala.	23	23
2nd Bennett, Robert F.	Rep	Utah	17	17
3rd Bunning, James P.D.	Rep	Ky.	11	11
4th Crapo, Michael D.	Rep	Ida.	11	11
5th Martinez, Melquiades R. (Mel)	Rep	Fla.	5	5
6th Corker, Robert	Rep	Tenn.	3	1
7th DeMint, James W.	Rep	S.C.	5	1
8th Vitter, David	Rep	La.	5	1
9th Johanns, Mike	Rep	Neb.	1	1
10th Hutchison, Kay Bailey	Rep	Tex.	16	1

*2: Member's second period of service on the committee.

Filled Vacancy:

Majority:

13th seat by Michael F. Bennet on Jan. 27, 2009

Changes:

Minority:

Martinez, Melquiades R. (Mel)	Rep	Fla.	Sept. 22, 2009 Resigned the Senate
Gregg, Judd A.	Rep	N.H.	Sept. 22, 2009 Replaced Martinez

Budget

Senate Committee on the Budget, 103rd-111th Congresses (1993-2011)

BACKGROUND

Organizational History: The Senate Committee on the Budget was an outgrowth of the Congressional Budget and Impoundment Control Act of 1974, (Public Law 93-344) and it dates from July 12, 1974. The Act was a response to conflicts between Republican president Richard M. Nixon over the spending practices of the Democratically-controlled Congress. In 1973, following his massive forty-nine state landslide, President Nixon attempted to reduce the federal budget by "impounding" (i.e., not spending) money, which Congress had appropriated for highway programs. By the end of the session, both chambers had approved legislation to limit the president's impoundment authority.

The Budget Committee was given the duties of reporting matters under Titles III and IV of the Congressional Budget Act; of studying the effect on budget outlays of existing and proposed legislation and reporting the results of these studies to the Senate; and also of requesting and evaluating studies of tax expenditures, devising methods of coordinating these expenditures, policies, and programs with direct budget outlays, and reporting the results of these studies to the Senate. Those duties were reaffirmed in the 1977 Committee Reorganization Amendments (S.Res. 95-4) and remain in place today.

Although there was some anxiety that the Budget Committee would undermine the power and prestige of Senate Appropriations, that does not appear to have occurred. Sen. Edmund Muskie of Maine, the Democrats' 1968 vice presidential nominee and the early front-running challenger to President Nixon's 1972 re-election was its first chair. He had served earlier on Banking and Currency, and at the time, was the second-ranking member on Public Works. He surrendered no assignment to become Budget chair in 1974. Five members of Senate Appropriations were among Budget's original fifteen members including Appropriation's second-ranking Democrat, Warren Magnuson of Washington State, and its two senior-most Republicans, Milton H. Young of North Dakota and Roman L. Hruska of Nebraska. This overlap in membership limited any potential turf conflicts between the two committees.

The latest budget submitted by President Barack Obama to the 111th Congress is the largest ever and Obama is the eighth president to have to wrestle with the Senate Budget Committee to move his agenda through Congress.

Membership: Unlike its House counterpart, the Senate Budget Committee does not have restrictive rules concerning the institutional locations of its members nor does it have the same restrictions governing length of service on the committee. Its most distinctive early feature was its rapid growth. It grew from fifteen members in the 93rd Congress to a peak of twenty-four in the 100th Congress (1987-1989), at which time it had become the second largest standing committee in the Senate. Since 2001, its size has stabilized between twenty-two

to twenty-three members and its mean size of 22.6 members places it third behind Appropriations and Armed Services. It is the largest of the four Senate standing committees to function without subcommittees.

The mean seniority of its members is 11.84 years, placing it ninth and its mean inter-Congress retention rate of 91.6 places it fifth among the sixteen standing committees. Since 1993, Budget has gained five members and lost fifteen for a net loss of ten members. Six of the departing members joined select committees, including four who moved to the Select Committee on Intelligence. Both the Finance and Rules and Administration committees acquired four members each from Budget, including both recent Republican majority floor leaders, Trent Lott (Rep-Miss.) and Bill Frist (Rep-Tenn.)

Committee Leaders: Edmund S. Muskie (Dem-Me.) was the committee's first chair and served from 1974 until his appointment in 1980 as Secretary of State in the Cabinet of President Jimmy Carter. He was succeeded by Ernest F. Hollings (Dem-S.C.) in 1980, who served until the Republican takeover of the Senate in 1980. New Mexico's Peter V. Domenici chaired the committee from 1981 to 1987 during those three Republican Senates. With Democrats regaining the Senate in 1986, Domenici was followed by Lawton M. Chiles Jr. of Florida, who retired in 1988 and would later be elected governor of Florida in 1994. Chiles was succeeded by James Sasser of Tennessee, who chaired Budget from 1989 until his re-election defeat in 1994.

Senator Domenici of New Mexico returned to chair Budget in 1995 and held that post until the Jeffords defection in June 2001 when Domenici became ranking minority member for the second time. Domenici served as the committee's senior Republican for twenty-two years. When he relinquished the chairmanship of Budget in 2003 to assume the chairmanship of Energy and Natural Resources, he was succeeded by Donald L. Nickles of Oklahoma, who chaired the committee until his retirement in 2004. Judd Gregg of New Hampshire held the chair in the 109th Congress (2005-2007) until the Democrats regained power. Kent Conrad of North Dakota has chaired the committee in the past two Congresses (2007-2011).

The first ranking minority member of Budget was Peter H. Dominick of Colorado, who served from 1974 until his defeat for re-election later that year by Gary W. Hart (Dem-Colo.). Dominick was followed by Henry Bellmon of Oklahoma who served as ranking minority member until his retirement in 1980.

The first Democratic ranking member on Budget was Ernest F. Hollings of South Carolina who served only in the 97th Congress and left to hold that same post on Commerce, Science, and Transportation in 1983. Lawton Chiles succeeded Hollings and became chair in 1987. After Pete Domenici's eight years as ranking minority member (1987-1995) ended with the Republican resumption of power, Democrats J. James Exon of Nebraska (1995-1997) and Frank R. Lautenberg of

New Jersey (1997-2001) served as ranking members until their respective retirements. In 2001, Kent Conrad became the senior Democrat on the committee and he flipped seats with Domenici during the Jeffords defection, and again following the Republican restoration in 2003. For the past two Congresses (2007-2011), New Hampshire Republican Judd Gregg has been the committee's ranking minority member.

Party Leaders: Among the five floor leaders with Budget Committee service were two Democrats—Robert C. Byrd of West Virginia, 1977-1989, who was succeeded by George Mitchell of Maine, 1989-1995; and three consecutive Republican leaders—Bob Dole, 1987-1996; C. Trent Lott of Mississippi, 1996-2003; and William Frist of Tennessee, 2003-2007. While both Byrd and Lott served as Whips before becoming floor leaders, two other Budget members served only as Whips—Democrat Alan Cranston of California from 1977 to 1991 and Republican Don Nickles of Oklahoma from 1996-2003.

Presidential Aspirations: While Ed Muskie's 1968 vice presidential nomination preceded the Budget Committee's creation, there have been four Budget alumni who received two presidential nominations—Democrat Walter F. Mondale (DFL-Minn.) in 1984 and Republican Robert J. Dole (Rep-Kans.) in 1996 and six vice presidential nominations—two each for Democrat Mondale in 1976 and 1980 and Republican J. Danforth Quayle of Indiana in 1988 and 1992, as well as single nominations for Bob Dole in 1976 with Gerald Ford and Joseph R. Biden in 2008 with Barack Obama.

Other Notables: Maine's Ed Muskie was the first Budget Committee alumnus to be named to the Cabinet when he was appointed by President Carter to be Secretary of State in 1980 following the abrupt resignation of Cyrus Vance. Sen. Hillary Rodham Clinton of New York joined the Cabinet of President Barack Obama in 2009 as Secretary of State, apparently putting aside feelings of disappointment after her defeat by Obama for the 2008 Democratic presidential nomination. Budget Committee member Republican Spencer Abraham of Michigan joined the Cabinet of President George W. Bush as Transportation Secretary in 2001 following his re-election defeat in 2000. Former Tennessee Republican governor Lamar Alexander who served as Secretary of Education for President George H.W. Bush served on the Senate Budget Committee in the109th Congress (2005-2007).

Only one post-1993 Budget Committee member left the Senate to serve as governor—Democrat Jon S. Corzine of New Jersey who was elected in 2005 and defeated after a single term in 2009.

Selected References

Ellwood, John W. and James A. Thurber, "The New Congressional Budget Process: The Hows and Whys of House Senate Differences," in Lawrence C. Dodd and Bruce I. Oppenheimer, eds., *Congress Reconsidered* (New York: Praeger, 1977), 163-192.

Rubin, Irene S., *The Politics of Public Budgeting: Getting and Spending, Borrowing and Balancing*, 5th ed. (Washington, D.C.: CQ Press, 2006).

Schick, Allen, *Congress and Money: Budgeting, Spending and Taxing* (Washington, D.C.: The Urban Institute, 1980).

Schick, Allen, "The Three-Ring Budget Process: The Appropriations, Tax and Budget Committees in Congress," in Thomas Mann and Norman J. Ornstein, eds., *The New Congress* (Washington, D.C.: American Enterprise Institute, 1981), 288-328.

Thurber, James A., "Budget Committee, Senate," in Donald C. Bacon, Roger H. Davidson, and Morton Keller, eds., *The Encyclopedia of the United States Congress* (New York: Simon & Schuster, 1995), I: 211-212.

Thurber, James A., "New Rules for an Old Game: Zero-Sum Budgeting in the Postreform Congress," in Roger H. Davidson, ed., *The Postreform Congress* (New York: St. Martin's Press, 1992), 257-278.

Thurber, James A. and Samantha L. Durst, "The 1990 Budget Enforcement Act: Zero-Sum Budgeting and the Decline of Government Accountability," in Lawrence C. Dodd and Bruce I. Oppenheimer, eds., *Congress Reconsidered*, 5th ed. (Washington, D.C.: CQ Press. 1993), 375-400.

U.S. Senate, *Committee on the Budget, 1974-2006,* Senate Document 109-24, 109th Congress, 2nd session (2006).

RESPONSIBILITIES AND JURISDICTIONAL CHANGES

Creation of Committee, 1974

The Senate Committee on the Budget and its original jurisdiction were established by Public Law 93-344, the Congressional Budget and Impoundment Control Act of 1974, 93rd Congress, Second Session, July 12, 1974 (88 *Statutes* 297, 301):

Jurisdiction, 1974

Jurisdiction established by Public Law 93-344, the Congressional Budget and Impoundment Control Act of 1974, 93rd Congress, Second Session, July 12, 1974 (88 *Statutes* 297, 301):

[Section 102.(a)(2)]

Such committee shall have the duty—

    (A) to report the matters required to be reported by it under titles III and IV of the Congressional Budget Act of 1974;

    (B) to make continuing studies of the effect on budget outlays of relevant existing and proposed legislation and to report the results of such studies to the Senate on a recurring basis;

    (C) to request and evaluate continuing studies of tax expenditures, to devise methods of coordinating tax expenditures, policies, and programs with direct budget outlays, and to report the results of such studies to the Senate on a recurring basis; and

    (D) to review, on a continuing basis, the conduct by the Congressional Budget Office of its functions and duties.

Post-Reorganization Jurisdiction, 1977

From Committee System Reorganization Amendments of 1977, S.Res. 95-4, *Senate Journal*, Feb. 4, 1977:

[XXV.Section 101. 1.(e)]

(1) **Committee on the Budget**, to which committee shall be referred all concurrent resolutions on the budget (as defined in section 3(a)(4) of the Congressional Budget Act of 1974) and all other matters required to be referred to that committee under titles III and IV of that Act, and messages, petitions, memorials, and other matters relating thereto.

(2) Such committee shall have the duty—

    (A) to report the matters required to be reported by it under titles III and IV of the Congressional Budget Act of 1974;

    (B) to make continuing studies of the effect on budget outlays of relevant existing and proposed legislation and to report the results of such studies to the Senate on a recurring basis;

    (C) to request and evaluate continuing studies of tax expenditures, to devise methods of coordinating tax expenditures, policies, and programs with direct budget outlays, and to report the results of such studies to the Senate on a recurring basis; and

    (D) to review, on a continuing basis, the conduct by the Congressional Budget Office of its functions and duties.

Jurisdiction, 103rd Congress (1993-94)

From the *Standing Rules of the Senate* in the *Senate Manual*, 103rd Congress, 1st Session, S. Doc. 103-1:

[Rule XXV.(1)(e)]

(1) **Committee on the Budget**, to which committee shall be referred all concurrent resolutions on the budget (as defined in section 3(a)(4) of the Congressional Budget Act of 1974) and all other matters required to be referred to that committee under titles III and IV of that Act, and messages, petitions, memorials, and other matters relating thereto.

(2) Such committee shall have the duty—

    (A) to report the matters required to be reported by it under titles III and IV of the Congressional Budget Act of 1974;

    (B) to make continuing studies of the effect on budget outlays of relevant existing and proposed legislation and to report the results of such studies to the Senate on a recurring basis;

    (C) to request and evaluate continuing studies of tax expenditures, to devise methods of coordinating tax expenditures, policies, and programs with direct budget outlays, and to report the results of such studies to the Senate on a recurring basis; and

    (D) to review, on a continuing basis, the conduct by the Congressional Budget Office of its functions and duties.

Jurisdiction, 111th Congress (2009-10)

From *Authority and Rules of Senate Committees, 2009-2010*, Sen. Doc. 111-3, pursuant to S.Res, 166, June 2, 2009.

[Rule XXV.(1)(e)]

(1) **Committee on the Budget**, to which committee shall be referred all concurrent resolutions on the budget (as defined in section 3(a)(4) of the Congressional Budget Act of 1974) and all other matters required to be referred to that committee under titles III and IV of that Act, and messages, petitions, memorials, and other matters relating thereto.

(2) Such committee shall have the duty

    (A) to report the matters required to be reported by it under titles III and IV of the Congressional Budget Act of 1974;

    (B) to make continuing studies of the effect on budget outlays of relevant existing and proposed legislation and to report the results of such studies to the Senate on a recurring basis;

    (C) to request and evaluate continuing studies of tax expenditures, to devise methods of coordinating tax expenditures, policies, and programs with direct budget outlays, and to report the results of such studies to the Senate on a recurring basis; and

    (D) to review, on a continuing basis, the conduct by the Congressional Budget Office of its functions and duties.

Committee on the Budget — No Subcommittees, 103rd-111th Congresses

MEMBERSHIP ROSTERS, 103rd-111th Congresses, 1993-2010

BUDGET / 103rd Congress

Service Dates of Committee Chair: Jan. 21, 1993-Jan. 6, 1995

Service Dates of Majority Members: Jan. 21, 1993-Jan. 6, 1995

Service Dates of Minority Members: Jan. 21, 1993-Jan. 6, 1995

	Majority						Minority				
				Years in:						Years in:	
Rank Name		Party	State	Senate	Comm.	Rank Name		Party	State	Senate	Comm.
Chr Sasser, James R.		Dem	Tenn.	17	16	RM Domenici, Pete V.		Rep	N.M.	21	18
2nd Hollings, Ernest F.		Dem	S.C.	27	19	2nd Grassley, Charles E.		Rep	Iowa	13	13
3rd Johnston, J. Bennett Jr.		Dem	La.	21	16	3rd Nickles, Donald L.		Rep	Okla.	13	7
4th Riegle, Donald W. Jr.		Dem	Mich.	17	14	4th Gramm, W. Phil		Rep	Tex.	9	5
5th Exon, J. James		Dem	Neb.	15	14	5th Bond, Christopher S. (Kit)		Rep	Mo.	7	4
6th Lautenberg, Frank R.		Dem	N.J.	11	*1 9	6th Lott, C. Trent		Rep	Miss.	5	2
7th Simon, Paul M.		Dem	Ill.	9	7	7th Brown, G. Hanks (Hank)		Rep	Colo.	3	2
8th Conrad, Kent		Dem	N.D.	7	7	8th Gorton, T. Slade III		Rep	Wash.	11	*2 1
9th Dodd, Christopher J.		Dem	Conn.	13	7	9th Gregg, Judd A.		Rep	N.H.	1	1
10th Sarbanes, Paul S.		Dem	Md.	17	1						
11th Boxer, Barbara		Dem	Cal.	1	1	*1: Member's first period of service on the committee.					
12th Murray, Patty		Dem	Wash.	1	1	*2: Member's second period of service on the committee.					

Note: Rankings on this committee for the following members were affected by other chamber service: Ernest F. Hollings (Dem-S.C.), Chair, Commerce, Science, and Transportation; and J. Bennett Johnston, Jr. (Dem-La.), Chair, Energy and Natural Resources.

Departures from the Senate:	Majority				Minority
Defeated for Re-election	Sasser, James R.	Dem	Tenn.		None
Retired	Riegle, Donald W. Jr.	Dem	Mich.		None

BUDGET / 104th Congress

Service Dates of Committee Chair: Jan. 6, 1995-Jan. 9, 1997

Service Dates of Majority Members: Jan. 6, 1995-Jan. 9, 1997

Service Dates of Minority Members: Jan. 6, 1995-Jan. 9, 1997

	Majority						Minority				
				Years in:						Years in:	
Rank Name		Party	State	Senate	Comm.	Rank Name		Party	State	Senate	Comm.
Chr Domenici, Pete V.		Rep	N.M.	23	20	RM Exon, J. James		Dem	Neb.	17	16
2nd Grassley, Charles E.		Rep	Iowa	15	15	2nd Hollings, Ernest F.		Dem	S.C.	29	21
3rd Nickles, Donald L.		Rep	Okla.	15	9	3rd Johnston, J. Bennett Jr.		Dem	La.	23	18
4th Gramm, W. Phil		Rep	Tex.	11	7	4th Lautenberg, Frank R.		Dem	N.J.	13	*1 10
5th Bond, Christopher S. (Kit)		Rep	Mo.	9	6	5th Simon, Paul M.		Dem	Ill.	11	9
6th Lott, C. Trent		Rep	Miss.	7	4	6th Conrad, Kent		Dem	N.D.	9	9
7th Brown, G. Hanks (Hank)		Rep	Colo.	5	4	7th Dodd, Christopher J.		Dem	Conn.	15	9
8th Gorton, T. Slade III		Rep	Wash.	13	*2 2	8th Sarbanes, Paul S.		Dem	Md.	19	2
9th Gregg, Judd A.		Rep	N.H.	3	2	9th Boxer, Barbara		Dem	Cal.	3	2
10th Snowe, Olympia J.B.		Rep	Me.	1	1	10th Murray, Patty		Dem	Wash.	3	2
11th Abraham, Spencer		Rep	Mich.	1	1						
12th Frist, William H.		Rep	Tenn.	1	1	*1: Member's first period of service on the committee.					
						*2: Member's second period of service on the committee.					

Note: Rankings on this committee for the following members were affected by other chamber service: Ernest F. Hollings (Dem-S.C.), Ranking Minority Member, Commerce, Science, and Transportation; and J. Bennett Johnston, Jr. (Dem-La.), Ranking Minority Member, Energy and Natural Resources.

Additions:
Majority:

13th Grams, Rod	Rep Minn.	Mar. 29, 1996

Minority:

11th Wyden, Ronald L.	Dem Ore.	Mar. 29, 1996

Changes:
Majority:

Lott, C. Trent	Rep	Miss.	June 20, 1996 Left the committee; moved to Finance and Rules and Administration; elected Majority Leader
Mack, Connie III	Rep	Fla.	June 20, 1996 Replaced Lott.

Departures from the Senate:	Majority				Minority		
Retired	Brown, G. Hanks (Hank)	Rep	Colo.		Exon, J. James	Dem	Neb.
					Johnston, J. Bennett Jr.	Dem	La.
					Simon, Paul M.	Dem	Ill.

Departures from Committee:						
No new assignment	None			Dodd, Christopher J.	Dem	Conn.

BUDGET / 105th Congress

Service Dates of Committee Chair: Jan. 9, 1997-Jan. 7, 1999

Service Dates of Majority Members: Jan. 9, 1997-Jan. 7, 1999

Service Dates of Minority Members: Jan. 9, 1997-Jan. 7, 1999

| | | | Years in: | | | | | | Years in: | |
Rank Name	Party	State	Senate	Comm.	Rank Name	Party	State	Senate	Comm.
Majority					**Minority**				
Chr Domenici, Pete V.	Rep	N.M.	25	22	RM Lautenberg, Frank R.	Dem	N.J.	15	*1 12
2nd Grassley, Charles E.	Rep	Iowa	17	17	2nd Hollings, Ernest F.	Dem	S.C.	31	23
3rd Nickles, Donald L.	Rep	Okla.	17	11	3rd Conrad, Kent	Dem	N.D.	11	11
4th Gramm, W. Phil	Rep	Tex.	13	9	4th Sarbanes, Paul S.	Dem	Md.	21	4
5th Bond, Christopher S. (Kit)	Rep	Mo.	11	8	5th Boxer, Barbara	Dem	Cal.	5	4
6th Gorton, T. Slade III	Rep	Wash.	15	*2 4	6th Murray, Patty	Dem	Wash.	5	4
7th Gregg, Judd A.	Rep	N.H.	5	4	7th Wyden, Ronald L.	Dem	Ore.	2	1
8th Snowe, Olympia J.B.	Rep	Me.	3	3	8th Feingold, Russell D.	Dem	Wisc.	5	1
9th Abraham, Spencer	Rep	Mich.	3	3	9th Johnson, Timothy P.	Dem	S.D.	1	1
10th Frist, William H.	Rep	Tenn.	3	3	10th Durbin, Richard J.	Dem	Ill.	1	1
11th Grams, Rod	Rep	Minn.	3	1					
12th Smith, Gordon H.	Rep	Ore.	1	1					

*1: Member's first period of service on the committee.

*2: Member's second period of service on the committee.

Note: Ranking on this committee for the following member was affected by other chamber service: Ernest F. Hollings (Dem-S.C.), Ranking Minority Member, Commerce, Science, and Transportation.

Filled Vacancy:

Gregg (Rep-N.H.) was unlisted on Jan. 7, 1999 but returned to Budget on Jan. 14, 1999.

BUDGET / 106th Congress

Service Dates of Committee Chair: Jan. 7, 1999-Jan. 3, 2001

Service Dates of Majority Members: Jan. 7, 1999-Jan. 25, 2001

Service Dates of Minority Members: Jan. 7, 1999-Jan. 25, 2001

| | | | Years in: | | | | | | Years in: | |
Rank Name	Party	State	Senate	Comm.	Rank Name	Party	State	Senate	Comm.
Majority					**Minority**				
Chr Domenici, Pete V.	Rep	N.M.	27	24	RM Lautenberg, Frank R.	Dem	N.J.	17	*1 14
2nd Grassley, Charles E.	Rep	Iowa	19	19	2nd Hollings, Ernest F.	Dem	S.C.	33	25
3rd Nickles, Donald L.	Rep	Okla.	19	13	3rd Conrad, Kent	Dem	N.D.	13	13
4th Gramm, W. Phil	Rep	Tex.	15	10	4th Sarbanes, Paul S.	Dem	Md.	23	6
5th Bond, Christopher S. (Kit)	Rep	Mo.	13	10	5th Boxer, Barbara	Dem	Cal.	7	6
6th Gorton, T. Slade III	Rep	Wash.	17	*2 6	6th Murray, Patty	Dem	Wash.	7	6
7th Gregg, Judd A.	Rep	N.H.	7	6	7th Wyden, Ronald L.	Dem	Ore.	4	3
8th Snowe, Olympia J.B.	Rep	Me.	5	5	8th Feingold, Russell D.	Dem	Wisc.	7	2
9th Abraham, Spencer	Rep	Mich.	5	5	9th Johnson, Timothy P.	Dem	S.D.	3	2
10th Frist, William H.	Rep	Tenn.	5	5	10th Durbin, Richard J.	Dem	Ill.	3	2
11th Grams, Rod	Rep	Minn.	5	3					
12th Smith, Gordon H.	Rep	Ore.	3	2					

*1: Member's first period of service on the committee.

*2: Member's second period of service on the committee.

Note: Ranking on this committee for the following member was affected by other chamber service: Ernest F. Hollings (Dem-S.C.), Ranking Minority Member, Commerce, Science, and Transportation.

Departures from the Senate:	Majority			Minority		
Defeated for Re-election	Gorton, T. Slade III	Rep	Wash.	None		
	Abraham, Spencer	Rep	Mich.			
	Grams, Rod	Rep	Minn.			
Retired	None			Lautenberg, Frank R.	Dem	N.J.
Departures from Committee:						
Moved to Commerce, Science, and Transportation	None			Boxer, Barbara	Dem	Cal.
Returned to Judiciary and moved to Select Intelligence	None			Durbin, Richard J.	Dem	Ill.

BUDGET / 107th Congress, Pre-Jeffords switch

Service Dates of Committee Chair: ChT: Jan. 3, 2001-Jan. 25, 2001 Conrad (Dem-N.D.)

Ch1: Jan. 25, 2001-June 6, 2001 Domenici (Rep-N.M.)

Service Dates of Majority Members: Jan. 25, 2001-June 6, 2001

Service Dates of Minority Members: Jan. 25, 2001-June 6, 2001

			Years in:					Years in:	
Majority					**Minority**				
Rank Name	**Party**	**State**	**Senate**	**Comm.**	**Rank Name**	**Party**	**State**	**Senate**	**Comm.**
Ch1 Domenici, Pete V.	Rep	N.M.	29	27	RM1 Conrad, Kent	Dem	N.D.	15	15
2nd Grassley, Charles E.	Rep	Iowa	21	21	2nd Hollings, Ernest F.	Dem	S.C.	35	27
3rd Nickles, Donald L.	Rep	Okla.	21	15	3rd Sarbanes, Paul S.	Dem	Md.	25	9
4th Gramm, W. Phil	Rep	Tex.	17	12	4th Murray, Patty	Dem	Wash.	9	9
5th Bond, Christopher S. (Kit)	Rep	Mo.	15	12	5th Wyden, Ronald L.	Dem	Ore.	6	5
6th Gregg, Judd A.	Rep	N.H.	9	9	6th Feingold, Russell D.	Dem	Wisc.	9	5
7th Snowe, Olympia J.B.	Rep	Me.	7	7	7th Johnson, Timothy P.	Dem	S.D.	5	5
8th Frist, William H.	Rep	Tenn.	7	7	8th Byrd, Robert C.	Dem	W.Va.	43	1
9th Smith, Gordon H.	Rep	Ore.	5	5	9th Nelson, C. William (Bill)	Dem	Fla.	1	1
10th Allard, A. Wayne	Rep	Colo.	5	1	10th Stabenow, Deborah Ann	Dem	Mich.	1	1
11th Hagel, Charles T. (Chuck)	Rep	Neb.	5	1	11th Clinton, Hillary Rodham	Dem	N.Y.	1	1

Note 1: Ranking on this committee for the following member was affected by other chamber service: Ernest F. Hollings (Dem-S.C.) Ranking Minority Member, Commerce, Science, and Transportation.

Note 2: The committee majority in the 2001 Senate power-sharing arrangement was determined by the party of the vice president. Democrat Al Gore Jr. served from Jan. 3, 2001, to Jan. 20, 2001, and was succeeded by Republican Richard B. Cheney on Jan. 20, 2001. When Senator Jeffords of Vermont left the Republican Party, effective June 6, 2001, to become an Independent, Democrats regained the majority for the remainder of the 107th Congress.

BUDGET / 107th Congress. Post-Jeffords switch

Service Dates of Committee Chair: June 6, 2001-Jan. 14, 2003

Service Dates of Majority Members: June 6, 2001-Jan. 14, 2003

Service Dates of Minority Members: June 6, 2001-Jan. 15, 2003

			Years in:					Years in:	
Majority					**Minority**				
Rank Name	**Party**	**State**	**Senate**	**Comm.**	**Rank Name**	**Party**	**State**	**Senate**	**Comm.**
Ch2 Conrad, Kent	Dem	N.D.	15	15	RM2 Domenici, Pete V.	Rep	N.M.	29	27
2nd Hollings, Ernest F.	Dem	S.C.	35	27	2nd Grassley, Charles E.	Rep	Iowa	21	21
3rd Sarbanes, Paul S.	Dem	Md.	25	9	3rd Nickles, Donald L.	Rep	Okla.	21	15
4th Murray, Patty	Dem	Wash.	9	9	4th Gramm, W. Phil	Rep	Tex.	17	13
5th Wyden, Ronald L.	Dem	Ore.	6	6	5th Bond, Christopher S. (Kit)	Rep	Mo.	15	13
6th Feingold, Russell D.	Dem	Wisc.	9	5	6th Gregg, Judd A.	Rep	N.H.	9	9
7th Johnson, Timothy P.	Dem	S.D.	5	5	7th Snowe, Olympia J.B.	Rep	Me.	7	7
8th Byrd, Robert C.	Dem	W.Va.	43	1	8th Frist, William H.	Rep	Tenn.	7	7
9th Nelson, C. William (Bill)	Dem	Fla.	1	1	9th Smith, Gordon H.	Rep	Ore.	5	5
10th Stabenow, Deborah Ann	Dem	Mich.	1	1	10th Allard, A. Wayne	Rep	Colo.	5	1
11th Clinton, Hillary Rodham	Dem	N.Y.	1	1	11th Hagel, Charles T. (Chuck)	Rep	Neb.	5	1
12th Corzine, Jon S.	Dem	N.J.	1	1					

Note: Ranking on this committee for the following member was affected by other chamber service: Ernest F. Hollings (Dem-S.C.), Chair, Commerce, Science, and Transportation.

Additions:
  Majority:

12th Corzine, Jon S.	Dem	N.J.	July 10, 2001	

Changes:
  Minority:

Gramm, W. Phil	Rep	Tex.	Nov. 30, 2002 Resigned the Senate and retired.	

Departures from Committee:

Majority		
Moved to Armed Services	Clinton, Hillary Rodham	Dem N.Y.
Moved to Select Intelligence	None	

Minority		
Bond, Christopher S. (Kit)	Rep	Mo.
Snowe, Olympia J.B.	Rep	Me.
Hagel, Charles T. (Chuck)	Rep	Neb.

Moved to Finance	None		Frist, William H.	Rep	Tenn.
			Smith, Gordon H.	Rep	Ore.
Moved to Rules and Administration	None		Frist, William H.	Rep	Tenn.
			Smith, Gordon H.	Rep	Ore.
Moved to Select Indian Affairs and Joint Printing	None		Smith, Gordon H.	Rep	Ore.

BUDGET / 108th Congress

Service Dates of Committee Chair: Jan. 14, 2003-Jan. 3, 2005

Service Dates of Majority Members: Jan. 14, 2003-Jan. 3, 2005

Service Dates of Minority Members: Jan. 15, 2003-Jan. 3, 2005

| Majority | | | Years in: | | Minority | | | Years in: | |
Rank Name	Party	State	Senate	Comm.	Rank Name	Party	State	Senate	Comm.
Chr Nickles, Donald L.	Rep	Okla.	23	17	RM Conrad, Kent	Dem	N.D.	17	17
2nd Domenici, Pete V.	Rep	N.M.	31	28	2nd Hollings, Ernest F.	Dem	S.C.	37	29
3rd Grassley, Charles E.	Rep	Iowa	23	23	3rd Sarbanes, Paul S.	Dem	Md.	27	10
4th Gregg, Judd A.	Rep	N.H.	11	10	4th Murray, Patty	Dem	Wash.	11	10
5th Allard, A. Wayne	Rep	Colo.	7	2	5th Wyden, Ronald L.	Dem	Ore.	8	7
6th Burns, Conrad	Rep	Mont.	15	1	6th Feingold, Russell D.	Dem	Wisc.	11	7
7th Enzi, Michael B.	Rep	Wyo.	7	1	7th Johnson, Timothy P.	Dem	S.D.	7	7
8th Sessions, Jefferson B. III	Rep	Ala.	7	1	8th Byrd, Robert C.	Dem	W.V.	45	2
9th Bunning, James P.D.	Rep	Ky.	5	1	9th Nelson, C. William (Bill)	Dem	Fla.	3	2
10th Crapo, Michael D.	Rep	Ida.	5	1	10th Stabenow, Deborah Ann	Dem	Mich.	3	2
11th Ensign, John E.	Rep	Nev.	3	1	11th Corzine, Jon S.	Dem	N.J.	3	2
12th Cornyn, John	Rep	Tex.	1	1					

Note: Rankings on this committee for the following members were affected by other chamber service: Pete V. Domenici, (Rep-N.M.), Chair, Energy and Natural Resources; and Ernest F. Hollings (Dem-S.C.), Ranking Minority Member, Commerce, Science, and Transportation.

Departures from the Senate:	**Majority**			**Minority**		
Retired	Nickles, Donald L.	Rep	Okla.	Hollings, Ernest F.	Dem	S.C.
Departures from Committee:						
Returned to Special Aging	Burns, Conrad	Rep	Mont.	None		

BUDGET / 109th Congress

Service Dates of Committee Chair: Jan. 6, 2005-Jan. 12, 2007

Service Dates of Majority Members: Jan. 6, 2005-Jan. 12, 2007

Service Dates of Minority Members: Jan. 6, 2005-Jan. 12, 2007

| Majority | | | Years in: | | Minority | | | Years in: | |
Rank Name	Party	State	Senate	Comm.	Rank Name	Party	State	Senate	Comm.
Chr Gregg, Judd A.	Rep	N.H.	13	12	RM Conrad, Kent	Dem	N.D.	19	19
2nd Domenici, Pete V.	Rep	N.M.	33	30	2nd Sarbanes, Paul S.	Dem	Md.	29	12
3rd Grassley, Charles E.	Rep	Iowa	25	25	3rd Murray, Patty	Dem	Wash.	13	12
4th Allard, A. Wayne	Rep	Colo.	9	4	4th Wyden, Ronald L.	Dem	Ore.	10	9
5th Enzi, Michael B.	Rep	Wyo.	9	2	5th Feingold, Russell D.	Dem	Wisc.	13	8
6th Sessions, Jefferson B. III	Rep	Ala.	9	2	6th Johnson, Timothy P.	Dem	S.D.	9	8
7th Bunning, James P.D.	Rep	Ky.	7	2	7th Byrd, Robert C.	Dem	W.Va.	47	4
8th Crapo, Michael D.	Rep	Ida.	7	2	8th Nelson, C. William (Bill)	Dem	Fla.	5	4
9th Ensign, John E.	Rep	Nev.	5	2	9th Stabenow, Deborah Ann	Dem	Mich.	5	4
10th Cornyn, John	Rep	Tex.	3	2	10th Corzine, Jon S.	Dem	N.J.	5	4
11th Alexander, Lamar	Rep	Tenn.	3	1					
12th Graham, Lindsey O.	Rep	S.C.	3	1					

Note: Ranking on this committee for the following member was affected by other chamber service: Pete V. Domenici, (Rep-N.M.), Chair, Energy and Natural Resources.

Changes:

Minority:

| Corzine, Jon S. | Dem N.J. | Jan. 17, 2006 Resigned the Senate; elected Governor of New Jersey. |
| Menendez, Robert | Dem N.J. | Jan. 18, 2006 Replaced Corzine. |

Departures from the Senate:	Majority			Minority		
Retired	None			Sarbanes, Paul S.	Dem	Md.

Departures from Committee:						
Moved to Appropriations, Environment and Public Works, and Rules and Administration	Alexander, Lamar	Rep	Tenn.	None		
No new assignment	None			Johnson, Timothy P.	Dem	S.D.

BUDGET / 110th Congress

Service Dates of Committee Chair: Jan. 12, 2007-Jan. 21, 2009

Service Dates of Majority Members: Jan. 12, 2007-Jan. 21, 2009

Service Dates of Minority Members: Jan. 12, 2007-Jan. 21, 2009

Majority			Years in:		Minority			Years in:	
Rank Name	**Party**	**State**	**Senate**	**Comm.**	**Rank Name**	**Party**	**State**	**Senate**	**Comm.**
Chr Conrad, Kent	Dem	N.D.	21	21	RM Gregg, Judd A.	Rep	N.H.	15	14
2nd Murray, Patty	Dem	Wash.	15	14	2nd Domenici, Pete V.	Rep	N.M.	35	32
3rd Wyden, Ronald L.	Dem	Ore.	12	11	3rd Grassley, Charles E.	Rep	Iowa	27	27
4rd Feingold, Russell D.	Dem	Wisc.	15	11	4th Allard, A. Wayne	Rep	Colo.	11	6
5th Byrd, Robert C.	Dem	W.Va.	49	6	5th Enzi, Michael B.	Rep	Wyo.	11	4
6th Nelson, C. William (Bill)	Dem	Fla.	7	6	6th Sessions, Jefferson B. III	Rep	Ala.	11	4
7th Stabenow, Deborah Ann	Dem	Mich.	7	6	7th Bunning, James P.D.	Rep	Ky.	9	4
8th Menendez, Robert	Dem	N.J.	1	1	8th Crapo, Michael D.	Rep	Ida.	9	4
9th Cardin, Benjamin L.	Dem	Md.	1	1	9th Ensign John E.	Rep	Nev.	7	4
10th Lautenberg, Frank R.	Dem	N.J.	23	*2 1	10th Cornyn, John	Rep	Tex.	5	4
11th Sanders, Bernard	Ind	Vt.	1	1	11th Graham, Lindsey O.	Rep	S.C.	5	3
12th Whitehouse, Sheldon	Dem	R.I.	1	1					

*2: Member's second period of service on the committee.

Note: Ranking on this committee for the following member was affected by other chamber service: Pete V. Domenici, (Rep-N.M.), Ranking Minority Member, Energy and Natural Resources.

Departures from the Senate:	Majority			Minority		
Retired	None			Domenici, Pete V.	Rep	N.M.
				Allard, A. Wayne	Rep	Colo.

Departures from Committee:						
No new assignment	Lautenberg, Frank R.	Dem	N.J.	None		

BUDGET / 111th Congress

Service Dates of Committee Chair: Jan. 21, 2009-

Service Dates of Majority Members: Jan. 21, 2009-

Service Dates of Minority Members: Jan. 21, 2009-

Majority			Years in:		Minority			Years in:	
Rank Name	**Party**	**State**	**Senate**	**Comm.**	**Rank Name**	**Party**	**State**	**Senate**	**Comm.**
Chr Conrad, Kent	Dem	N.D.	23	23	RM Gregg, Judd A.	Rep	N.H.	17	17
2nd Murray, Patty	Dem	Wash.	17	17	2nd Grassley, Charles E.	Rep	Iowa	29	29
3rd Wyden, Ronald L.	Dem	Ore.	14	13	3rd Enzi, Michael	Rep	Wyo.	13	7
4th Feingold, Russell D.	Dem	Wisc.	17	13	4th Sessions, Jefferson B. III	Rep	Ala.	13	7
5th Byrd, Robert C.	Dem	W.Va.	51	8	5th Bunning, James P.D.	Rep	Ky.	11	7
6th Nelson, C. William (Bill)	Dem	Fla.	9	8	6th Crapo, Michael D.	Rep	Ida.	11	7
7th Stabenow, Deborah Ann	Dem	Mich.	9	8	7th Ensign, John E.	Rep	Nev.	9	7
8th Menendez, Robert	Dem	N.J.	4	4	8th Cornyn, John	Rep	Tex.	7	7
9th Cardin, Benjamin L.	Dem	Md.	3	3	9th Graham, Lindsey O.	Rep	S.C.	7	5
10th Sanders, Bernard	Ind	Vt.	3	3	10th Alexander, Lamar	Rep	Tenn.	7	1
11th Whitehouse, Sheldon	Dem	R.I.	3	3					
12th Warner, Mark R.	Dem	Va.	1	1					
13th Merkley, Jeff	Dem	Ore.	1	1					

Note: Ranking on this committee for the following member was affected by other chamber service: Charles E. Grassley (Rep-Iowa), Ranking Minority Member, Finance.

Commerce, Science and Transportation

Senate Committee on Commerce, Science and Transportation, 103rd-111th Congresses (1993-2011)

BACKGROUND

Organizational History: The Senate Committee on Commerce, Science and Transportation has been through a number of transformations. Its original predecessor was the Committee on Commerce and Manufactures, one of the Senate's original eleven standing committees, following adoption of a resolution proposed by Virginia's James Barbour on December 10, 1816. William Hunter (Fed-R.I.) was the first chair of the committee.

The commerce and manufacturing elements of the committee conflicted over tariff-related issues and on December 7, 1825, it was split into separate committees—the Committee on Commerce and the Committee on Manufactures. Sen. James Lloyd (Fed-Mass.) became the first chair of Commerce while Mahlon Dickerson (DR-N.J.) became the first chair of Manufactures. Each of the committees developed their own jurisdictional interests and constituencies, with the Commerce Committee being the more active and important of the two, focusing largely on river and harbor improvements.

While continuity was difficult to establish in the antebellum Senate, the committee was regularly named after the Civil War. As reported in the *Guide to the Records of the United States Senate*:

> Under the Senate rules at the time, committees did not continue from one Congress to the next, but rather were reconstituted at the beginning of the first session of each Congress. From the beginning of the 34th Congress in 1855 until February 10, 1864, in the 2d session of the 38th Congress, there was no Committee on Manufactures. Thereafter, the committee met in each Congress until the Legislative Reorganization Act of 1946 . . . The Commerce Committee met during every Congress through the 79th Congress (1945-46) . . .

According to the committee's 1978 report, *A Brief History of the Senate Committee on Commerce, Science, and Transportation and Its Activities Since 1947,* "The Commerce Committee and the Committee on Manufactures existed separately for the next 140 years (until the Reorganization Act of 1946), although no Committee on Manufactures was elected between 1857 and 1864." (5)

Two other predecessor standing committees were the Committee on Interstate Commerce established on December 12, 1887, and the Committee on Interoceanic Canals, established December 15, 1899. The Committee on Interstate Commerce succeeded a select committee that had been appointed in 1885. The Select Committee To Investigate Interstate Commerce, also known as the Cullom Committee after its chair Shelby Cullom (Rep-Ill.), was established on March 17, 1885. According to the *Guide,* "During the 49th Congress, the select committee reported at least two bills, S. 1093 and S. 1532, the latter enacted as the Interstate Commerce Act of 1887."

In the Committee's official 150th year history:

> Senator Cullom became its first chair. . . , piloting out of the committee and through the Senate the landmark Interstate Commerce Act of 1887. . . . When the trust-busting movement reached its peak following Theodore Roosevelt's vigorous attacks on big business in the . . . campaign of 1902, the Committee on Interstate Commerce entered one of its busiest periods. In 1903 the committee approved two major bills designed to check the powers of the trusts. The first of these, the Expediting Act, gave preference to Federal suits brought under the Interstate Commerce Act and the Sherman Anti-Trust Act. The second was the Elkins Anti-Rebate Act, drafted to clarify the law and eliminate one of the worst practices of the railroads. (5)

The Committee on Interoceanic Canals held the major legislative responsibility for the acquisition, construction and oversight of the Panama Canal. Several smaller committees (often beginning as select committees)—concerning railroads, fisheries, interoceanic canals, waterway transportation and river improvements, industrial expositions, and standards, weights, and measures—originally were established to deal with particular legislative matters, but survived in order to provide clerical support to their chair. Many of these minor "shadow" committees were abolished in 1921 in the first wave of committee reform.

Most notable among these departed committees was Transportation Routes to the Seaboard. As noted in George H. Haynes's classic *The Senate of the United States* (Boston, 1938): "In 1917 the Committee on Transportation Routes to the Seaboard—which was said not to have had a meeting in thirty-eight years—numbered in its membership Senators of the grade of McCumber, Lodge, Sheppard, and Martin." (I, .283n)

The Legislative Reorganization Act of 1946 (Public Law 79-601) further consolidated the committees by creating a single Committee on Interstate and Foreign Commerce which inherited the responsibilities of four former committees—Commerce, Interoceanic Canals, Interstate Commerce, and Manufactures—except for a few jurisdictional areas that were assigned to other committees, such as flood control and improvement of rivers and harbors, which were assigned to the Committee on Public Works.

In 1977, the next major reorganization of the committee system, authorized by S. Res. 4, 95th Cong., led to the creation of the Committee on Commerce, Science and Transportation, which acquired jurisdiction over nonmilitary aspects of the space program from the abolished Committee on Aeronautical and Space Sciences, and relinquished jurisdiction over river and harbor improvements to the Committee on Environment and Public Works.

While its jurisdiction has remained unchanged since the 1977 reorganization, innovations in communication and transportation have pressured the committee to frequently address the issues of deregulation of transportation policy and the telecommunication industry. In the 104th Congress, the long-standing Interstate Commerce Commission was officially terminated (Public Law 104-50) and the committee played a major role in drafting the far-reaching Telecommunications Act of 1996 (Public Law 104-104) that opened up long distance telephone lines to regional Bell companies to increase competition and to lower costs.

In recent times, the safety issue of "driving while distracted" has come before the Commerce Committee as the use of cell phones in automobiles and the practice of "texting" while driving has led to a growing number of fatal accidents.

Membership: Like most of the post-reorganization Senate standing committees, its initial incarnation, the Interstate and Foreign Commerce Committee, had only thirteen members. It grew steadily, and as of today, Commerce, Science and Transportation has a relatively high committee size mean of 22.11 members, placing it fourth behind the Appropriations, Armed Services, and Budget committees. Its peak membership total of twenty-five members was recently achieved in the present 111th Congress (2009-2011). Since 1993, its members' average seniority is 12.07 years—eighth place overall and close to the Senate mean, while its mean inter-Congress retention rate of 94.2 percent places it fourth behind Finance, Rules and Administration, and Appropriations.

In terms of gaining and losing members, Commerce, Science and Transportation has been a net gainer, with seventeen members gained and only nine lost, for an overall net gain of eight. Apart from the Judiciary Committee that lost three members to Commerce, none of the other Senate committees have lost more than two. William H. Frist (Rep-Tenn.) left the committee in 2003 after his election as Majority Leader and two others moved to Finance, but there has been no pattern in the committee locations of the handful of Commerce departing members.

Committee Leaders: The first post-war chair of the Interstate and Foreign Commerce Committee was Wallace H. White Jr. (Rep-Me.), who was also the Majority Floor Leader in that Congress (1947-1949). Its first post-reorganization ranking minority member was Edwin C. Johnson of Colorado, who was also the first Democrat to chair the committee in the 81st and 82nd Congresses (1949-1953), while New Hampshire Republican Charles W. Tobey served as ranking minority member in those Congresses (1949-1953). Tobey chaired the committee in the 83rd Congress for only a few months (Jan. 13-July 24, 1953) before his death that summer. Tobey was succeeded by John W. Bricker (Rep-Ohio), who had been governor of Ohio during 1939-1945 and was Thomas E. Dewey's vice presidential running-mate in 1944.

Democrats gained control of the Senate in 1954 and held it for thirteen consecutive Congresses (1955-1981). The chairs during that period were Warren G. Magnuson (Dem-Wash.), who served from 1955 until 1978, when he became chair of the Appropriations Committee. Magnuson remained on the Commerce Committee but was succeeded as chair by Howard W. Cannon (Dem-Nev.), who served from 1978 until the Republican takeover in 1980.

Former chair Bricker became ranking minority member in the 84th and 85th Congresses (1955-1959) until his defeat for re-election in 1958. Andrew F. Schoeppel (Rep-Kans.) succeeded Bricker as ranking minority member and served in that capacity from 1959 until his death in January, 1962. Schoeppel was followed by John Marshall Butler (Rep-Md.), who held that slot through the balance of that year until his retirement.

The longest-serving ranking minority member of the Commerce Committee was Norris Cotton (Rep-N.H.) who held that post from the 88th through the 93rd Congress (1963-1974). Cotton retired in December of 1974, but was temporarily appointed to the Senate and the committee for a few weeks in August and September 1975, owing to the highly contested Durkin-Wyman Senate contest of 1974. James B. Pearson (Rep-Kans.) held the ranking minority post during the 94th and 95th Congresses (1975-1979) until his retirement. He was succeeded by Oregon's Robert W. Packwood for the 96th Congress (1979-81).

With Republicans gaining the Senate in the 1980 election, former chair Cannon served as ranking minority member in the 97th Congress until his re-election defeat in 1982 and Bob Packwood was elevated to chair the committee in the 97th and 98th Congresses (1981-1985), until he became chair of the Finance Committee in 1985 and was succeeded as chair by John C. Danforth (Rep-Mo.).

South Carolina's former Democratic governor Ernest F. "Fritz" Hollings succeeded Cannon as ranking minority member in 1983 and served as the committee's senior Democrat until his retirement twenty-two years later—nine and one-half years as chair (1987-1995 and 2001-2003) and twelve and one-half years as ranking minority member (1983-1987, 1995-2001, and 2003-2005). Senator Danforth served with Hollings as the Commerce Committee's ranking minority member from 1987 through 1995 and his retirement from the Senate.

Republican gains in 1994 gave the chairmanship of the committee to South Dakota's Larry Pressler who lost his re-election in 1996. Pressler was replaced as chair by John S. McCain of Arizona, who served from 1997 through 2005, both before and after the Jeffords defection. In 2005, McCain became chair of Indian Affairs and lessened his committee work to pursue the 2008 Republican presidential nomination. Succeeding McCain as the committee's senior Republican was long-serving Theodore F. Stevens of Alaska, who served as chair in the 109th Congress (2005-2007) and ranking minority member in the 110th (2007-2009) until his re-election defeat in 2008.

Sen. Daniel K. Inouye of Hawaii followed Hollings as the committee's senior Democrat serving as ranking minority member in the 109th Congress and as chair in the 110th. Inouye yielded the chairmanship of Commerce to John D. Rockefeller IV in 2009 when Inouye became chair of Appropriations.

Party Leaders: Republican Senate leaders who served on the committee include five floor leaders—Wallace H. White Jr. of Maine (1947-1949), Hugh D. Scott Jr. of Pennsylvania (1969-1977), Howard W. Baker Jr. of Tennessee (1977-1985), Trent Lott of Mississippi (1996-2003), and William Frist of Tennessee (2003-2007); and four Whips: Scott (1969), Robert P. Griffin of Michigan (1969-1977), Theodore F. Stevens of Alaska (1977-1985), and Lott (1995-1996).

Most of the Democratic leaders who served on the Commerce committee held their posts early in the post-1947 era: Francis J. Myers of Pennsylvania, the Democratic Whip, 1949-1951; Ernest W. McFarland of Arizona who served as Majority

Floor Leader, 1951-1953, until his defeat by Barry Goldwater. McFarland was succeeded as Floor Leader by Lyndon B. Johnson of Texas, who served as his Whip (1951-1953) and was to lead the Senate Democrats from 1953 until his election as vice president in 1960. Johnson's Whip Earle C. Clements of Kentucky served from 1953 to 1957 and his re-election defeat. The two Commerce Committee Democrats who held leadership posts in the past half-century were both Whips—Russell B. Long of Louisiana in the 89th and 90th Congresses (1965-1969) and Wendell Ford of Kentucky who served from 1991 to 1999. Johnson and Ford also served on the Aeronautical and Space Sciences Committee that was folded into the Commerce Committee making in 1977.

Presidential Aspirations: Although the committee is not considered to be one of the Senate's top-tier panels, its membership has been quite distinguished. Seven members of the committee received presidential and vice presidential nominations, while sixteen of the thirty-six senators who held key post-1947 leadership posts spent time on the Commerce Committee, and one of its predecessors, the Aeronautical and Space Sciences Committee, included Lyndon Johnson, who was that committee's first chair in 1958.

Presidential politicians among Commerce Committee members include: J. Strom Thurmond of South Carolina, who began his lengthy career in the Senate on this committee after having run unsuccessfully as the States Rights candidate for president in 1948. While John F. Kerry of Massachusetts was the only Democrat to receive a presidential nomination while serving on the committee, four other Democrats received vice presidential selections: Estes Kefauver of Tennessee in 1956; Lyndon Johnson of Texas in 1960; Al Gore Jr. of Tennessee in 1992; and John Edwards of North Carolina in 2004. Walter Mondale, who served on Aeronautics, was the fifth vice presidential nominee and the third successful one who passed through Commerce and its predecessors. Among the Republican presidential nominees, only Arizona's Barry Goldwater in 1964 and John McCain in 2008 saw service on Commerce, but Goldwater's service occurred after his election defeat.

Other Notables: Senate Commerce Committee members with prior Cabinet experience include Brock Adams (Dem-Wash.), President Carter's Secretary of Transportation, and two of President George W. Bush's Cabinet appointees—Mel Martinez (Rep-Fla.), his Secretary of Housing and Urban Development who retired from the Senate in 2009, and Mike Johanns (Rep-Neb.), his second Secretary of Agriculture, who joined the Senate in 2009. Election defeats in 2000 led to George W. Bush Cabinet appointments for former senators Spencer Abraham (Rep-Mich.) as Secretary of Transportation and John Ashcroft (Rep-Mo.) as Attorney General. Lloyd Bentsen (Dem-Texas), President Clinton's Secretary of the Treasury, was the only Democratic senator to leave Commerce for the Cabinet.

The short-lived Senate Committee on Aeronautical and Space Sciences that was folded into Commerce in the 1977 reorganization had two alumni with Cabinet experience. Democrat Clinton Anderson of New Mexico, President Truman's Secretary of Agriculture, was a charter member of the committee in 1958 and served as its chair for ten years. William Saxbe (Rep-Ohio), who was named to the Nixon cabinet as Attorney General in its closing months, was a one-time member of Aeronautical and Space Sciences.

Two of the senators most responsible for restructuring the Senate committee system served on the Commerce Committee: A.S. Mike Monroney (Dem-Okla.), the House coauthor of the Legislative Reorganization Act of 1946, which established the modern Congress's committee system, and Adlai E. Stevenson III (Dem-Ill.), whose 1976-1977 Temporary Select Committee on the Senate Committee System revised the names and jurisdictions of the present committees.

Selected References

Coren, Robert W., et al., "Records of the Committee on Commerce and Related Committees, 1816-1968," *Guide to the Records of the United States Senate at the National Archives: 1789-1989 Bicentennial Edition* (Washington, D.C.: National Archives and Records Administration, 1989), 61-84.

Evans, C. Lawrence, *Leadership in Committee: A Comparative Analysis of Leadership Behavior in the U.S. Senate* (Ann Arbor: University of Michigan Press, 2001).

Jahnige, Thomas P., "Congressional Committee System and the Oversight Process: Congress and NASA," *Western Political Quarterly*, 21 (June, 1968), 227-239.

McKissick, Gary and Richard L. Hall, "Commerce, Science, and Transportation Committee, Senate," in Donald C. Bacon, Roger H. Davidson, and Morton Keller, eds., *The Encyclopedia of the United States Congress* (New York: Simon & Schuster, 1995), I: 400-404.

Nadel, Mark, et al., "The House Science and Astronautics Committee and the Senate Aeronautical and Space Science Committee," in the Ralph Nader Congress Project, *The Environment Committees A Study of the House and Senate Interior, Agriculture, and Science Committees* (New York: Grossman, 1975), 281-357.

Peabody, Robert L., Jeffrey M. Berry, William G. Frasure, and Jerry Goldman, *To Enact a Law: Congress and Campaign Financing* (New York: Praeger, 1972).

Price, David E., dir., *The Commerce Committees: A Study of the House and Senate Commerce Committees* in the Ralph Nader Congress Project (New York: Grossman, 1975).

Price, David E., *Who Makes the Laws? Creativity and Power in Senate Committees* (Cambridge. Mass.: Schenkman, 1972).

Ripley, Randall B., "Congress Champions Aid to Airports, 1958-1969," in Frederic N. Cleaveland and Associates, *Congress and Urban Problems: A Casebook on the Legislative Process* (Washington, D.C.: the Brookings Institution, 1969), 20-71.

U.S. Senate, Committee on Aeronautical and Space Sciences, *Committee on Aeronautical and Space Sciences, United States Senate, 1958-1976*, Senate Committee Print, 94th Congress, 2nd session (1976). This was an update of the Tenth Anniversary report published in 1968 as Senate Document 90-116, 90th Congress, 2nd session. The committee was reorganized into the Committee on Commerce, Science, and Transportation in 1977.

U.S. Senate, Committee on Commerce, *History, Membership and Jurisdiction of the Senate Committee on Commerce, 1816-1966*, Senate Document 89-100, 89th Congress, 2nd session (1978).

U.S. Senate, Committee on Commerce, Science, and Transportation, *A Brief History of the Senate Committee on Commerce, Science, and Transportation and Its Activities Since 1947*, S. Doc. 95-93, 95th Congress, 2nd session (1978).

RESPONSIBILITIES, JURISDICTIONAL CHANGES, AND SUBCOMMITTEES

INTERSTATE AND FOREIGN COMMERCE

Jurisdiction, 80th Congress (1947-49)

Established by the Legislative Reorganization Act of 1946:

[Section 102.(1)(j)]

(1) **Committee on Interstate and Foreign Commerce**, to consist of thirteen Senators, to which committee shall be referred all proposed legislation, messages, petitions, memorials, and other matters relating to the following subjects:

   (1) Interstate and foreign commerce generally
   (2) Regulation of interstate railroads, buses, trucks, and pipe lines
   (3) Communication by telephone, telegraph, radio, and television
   (4) Civil aeronautics
   (5) Merchant marine generally
   (6) Registering and licensing of vessels and small boats
   (7) Navigation and the laws relating thereto, including pilotage
   (8) Rules and international arrangements to prevent collisions at sea
   (9) Merchant marine officers and seamen
   (10) Measures relating to the regulation of common carriers by water and to the inspection of merchant marine vessels, lights and signals, life-saving equipment, and fire protection on such vessels
   (11) Coast and Geodetic Survey
   (12) The Coast Guard, including lifesaving service, lighthouses, lightships, and ocean derelicts
   (13) The United States Coast Guard and Merchant Marine Academies
   (14) Weather Bureau
   (15) Except as provided in paragraph (c) [Committee on Armed Services], the Panama Canal and interoceanic canals generally
   (16) Inland waterways
   (17) Fisheries and wildlife, including research, restoration, refuges, and conservation
   (18) Bureau of Standards including standardization of weights and measures and the metric system

Committee Renamed, 1961

Interstate and Foreign Commerce was renamed the Committee on Commerce on April 13, 1961.

Committee Reorganized, 1977

COMMERCE, SCIENCE, AND TRANSPORTATION

The Committee was reorganized as the Standing Committee on Commerce, Science, and Transportation following the passage of Senate Resolution 4, the Committee System Reorganization Amendments of 1977, February 4, 1977.

Reorganized Jurisdiction, 1977

From Senate Resolution 4, the Committee System Reorganization Amendments of 1977, February 4, 1977:

[Section (f)(1)]

(1) **Committee on Commerce, Science, and Transportation**, to which committee shall be referred all proposed legislation, messages, petitions, memorials, and other matters relating to the following subjects:

   (1) Interstate commerce
   (2) Transportation
   (3) Regulation of interstate common carriers, including railroads, buses, trucks, vessels, pipelines, and civil aviation
   (4) Merchant marine and navigation
   (5) Marine and ocean navigation, safety, and transportation, including navigational aspects of deepwater ports
   (6) Coast Guard
   (7) Inland waterways, except construction
   (8) Communications
   (9) Regulation of consumer products and services, including testing related to toxic substances, other than pesticides, and except for credit, financial services, and housing
   (10) Except as provided in paragraph (c), [Committee on Armed Services] the Panama Canal and interoceanic canals generally

(11) Standards and measurement
(12) Highway safety
(13) Science, engineering, and technology research and development and policy
(14) Nonmilitary aeronautical and space sciences
(15) Transportation and commerce aspects of Outer Continental and Shelf lands
(16) Marine fisheries
(17) Coastal zone management
(18) Oceans, weather, and atmospheric activities
(19) Sports

(2) Such committee shall also study and review, on a comprehensive basis, all matters relating to science and technology, oceans policy, transportation, communications, and consumer affairs, and report thereon from time to time.

Jurisdiction, 103rd Congress (1993-94)

From the *Standing Rules of the Senate* in the *Senate Manual*, 103rd Congress, 1st Session, S. Doc. 103-1:

[Rule XXV (1)(f)]

(1) **Committee on Commerce, Science, and Transportation**, to which committee shall be referred all proposed legislation, messages, petitions, memorials, and other matters relating to the following subjects:

(1) Coast Guard
(2) Coastal zone management
(3) Communications
(4) Highway safety
(5) Inland waterways, except construction
(6) Interstate commerce
(7) Marine and ocean navigation, safety, and transportation, including navigational aspects of deepwater ports
(8) Marine fisheries
(9) Merchant marine and navigation
(10) Nonmilitary aeronautical and space sciences
(11) Oceans, weather, and atmospheric activities
(12) Panama Canal and interoceanic canals generally, except as provided in subparagraph (c) [Committee on Armed Services]
(13) Regulation of consumer products and services, including testing related to toxic substances, other than pesticides, and except for credit, financial services, and housing
(14) Regulation of interstate common carriers, including railroads, buses, trucks, vessels, pipelines, and civil aviation
(15) Science, engineering, and technology research and development and policy
(16) Sports
(17) Standards and measurement
(18) Transportation
(19) Transportation and commerce aspects of Outer Continental Shelf lands

(2) Such committee shall also study and review, on a comprehensive basis, all matters relating to science and technology, oceans policy, transportation, communications, and consumer affairs, and report thereon from time to time.

Jurisdiction, 111th Congress (2009-10)

From *Authority and Rules of Senate Committees, 2009-2010*, Sen. Doc. 111-3, pursuant to S.Res, 166, June 2, 2009.

[Rule XXV (1)(f)]

(1) **Committee on Commerce, Science, and Transportation**, to which committee shall be referred all proposed legislation, messages, petitions, memorials, and other matters relating to the following subjects:

(1) Coast Guard
(2) Coastal zone management
(3) Communications
(4) Highway safety
(5) Inland waterways, except construction
(6) Interstate commerce
(7) Marine and ocean navigation, safety, and transportation, including navigational aspects of deepwater ports
(8) Marine fisheries
(9) Merchant marine and navigation
(10) Nonmilitary aeronautical and space sciences
(11) Oceans, weather, and atmospheric activities
(12) Panama Canal and inter-oceanic canals generally, except as provided in subparagraph (c)
(13) Regulation of consumer products and services, including testing related to toxic substances, other than pesticides, and except for credit, financial services, and housing

(14)   Regulation of interstate common carriers, including railroads, buses, trucks, vessels, pipelines, and civil aviation
(15)   Science, engineering, and technology research and development and policy
(16)   Sports
(17)   Standards and measurement
(18)   Transportation
(19)   Transportation and commerce aspects of Outer Continental Shelf lands

(2)   Such committee shall also study and review, on a comprehensive basis, all matters relating to science and technology, oceans policy, transportation, communications, and consumer affairs, and report thereon from time to time.

NAMES OF SUBCOMMITTEES

Committee on Commerce, Science, and Transportation, 103rd -111th Congresses

Aviation, 103, 104, 105, 106, 107, 108, 109
Aviation Operations, Safety and Security, 110, 111
Communications, 103, 104,105, 106, 107, 108
Communications, Technology, and the Internet, 111
Competition, Foreign Commerce, and Infrastructure, 108
Competitiveness, Innovation, and Export Promotion, 111
Consumer, 103
Consumer Affairs, Foreign Commerce and Tourism, 104, 105, 106, 107
Consumer Affairs and Product Safety, 108
Consumer Affairs, Product Safety, and Insurance, 109
Consumer Affairs, Insurance and Automotive Safety, 110
Consumer Protection, Product Safety, and Insurance, 111
Disaster Prevention and Prediction, 109
Fisheries and the Coast Guard, 109
Foreign Commerce and Tourism, 103
Global Climate Change and Impacts, 109
Interstate Commerce, Trade, and Tourism, 110
Manufacturing and Competitiveness, 105, 106
Merchant Marine, 103
National Ocean Policy Study Group, 103
National Ocean Policy Study, 110
Oceans and Fisheries, 104, 105, 106
Oceans, Atmosphere and Fisheries, 107
Oceans, Fisheries and the Coast Guard, 108
Oceans, Atmosphere, Fisheries, and the Coast Guard, 110, 111
Science, Technology, and Space, 103, 104, 105, 106, 107, 108
Science and Space, 109, 111
Science, Technology, and Innovation, 110
Space, Aeronautics, and Related Agencies, 110
Surface Transportation, 103
Surface Transportation and Merchant Marine, 104, 105, 106, 107, 108, 109, 111
Surface Transportation and Merchant Marine, Infrastructure, Safety, and Security, 110
Technology Innovation and Competitiveness, 109
Trade, Tourism, and Economic Development, 109

MEMBERSHIP ROSTERS, 103rd-111th Congresses, 1993-2010

COMMERCE, SCIENCE AND TRANSPORTATION / 103rd Congress

Service Dates of Committee Chair: Jan. 7, 1993-Jan. 11, 1995

Service Dates of Majority Members: Jan. 7, 1993-Jan. 4, 1995

Service Dates of Minority Members: Jan. 7, 1993-Jan. 4, 1995

Majority					Minority				
			Years in:					Years in:	
Rank Name	Party	State	Senate	Comm.	Rank Name	Party	State	Senate	Comm.
Chr Hollings, Ernest F.	Dem	S.C.	27	26	RM Danforth, John C.	Rep	Mo.	17	16
2nd Inouye, Daniel K.	Dem	Hai.	31	24	2nd Packwood, Robert W.	Rep	Ore.	25	16

			Senate	Comm.					Senate	Comm.
3rd Ford, Wendell H.	Dem	Ky.	19	18	3rd Pressler, Larry L.	Rep	S.D.	15	14
4th Exon, J. James	Dem	Neb.	15	14	4th Stevens, Theodore F.	Rep	Alas.	25	*2 13
5th Rockefeller, John D. IV	Dem	W.Va.	9	8	5th McCain, John S. III	Rep	Ariz.	7	7
6th Bentsen, Lloyd M. Jr.	Dem	Tex.	23	7	6th Burns, Conrad	Rep	Mont.	5	4
7th Kerry, John F.	Dem	Mass.	9	7	7th Gorton, T. Slade III	Rep	Wash.	11	*2 4
8th Breaux, John B.	Dem	La.	7	7	8th Lott, C. Trent	Rep	Miss.	5	4
9th Bryan, Richard H.	Dem	Nev.	5	4	9th Gregg, Judd A.	Rep	N.H.	1	1
10th Robb, Charles S.	Dem	Va.	5	4					
11th Dorgan, Byron L.	Dem	N.D	1	1	*2: Member's second period of service on the committee.				

Note 1: Ranking on the committee for the following member was affected by other chamber service: Robert W. Packwood (Rep-Ore.), Ranking Minority Member, Finance.

Note 2: Although Krueger was listed as being on the committee on Jan. 7, 1993, he was not formally named until Jan. 21, 1993, following Bentsen's resignation to become Secretary of Treasury.

Changes:
  Majority:

Bentsen, Lloyd M. Jr.	Dem	Tex.	Jan. 20, 1993 Resigned the Senate; appointed Secretary of the Treasury.
Krueger, Robert C.	Dem	Tex.	Jan. 21, 1993 Replaced Bentsen.
Krueger, Robert C.	Dem	Tex.	June 14, 1993 Resigned the Senate; defeated in special election by Kay Bailey Hutchison (Rep-Tex.)
Mathews, Harlan	Dem	Tenn.	July 15, 1993 Replaced Krueger.
Mathews, Harlan	Dem	Tenn.	Dec. 1, 1994 Resigned the Senate; replaced by special election winner Fred D. Thompson (Rep-Tenn.)

  Minority:

Gregg, Judd A.	Rep	N.H.	July 1, 1993 Moved to Foreign Relations.
Hutchison, Kay Bailey	Rep	Tex.	July 1, 1993 Replaced Gregg.

Departures from the Senate:	**Majority**			**Minority**		
Retired	None			Danforth, John C.	Rep	Mo.

Departures from Committee:					
Moved to Select Intelligence	Robb, Charles S.	Dem	Va.	None	

COMMERCE, SCIENCE AND TRANSPORTATION / 104th Congress

Service Dates of Committee Chair: Jan. 11, 1995-Jan. 9, 1997

Service Dates of Majority Members: Jan. 4, 1995-Jan. 9, 1997

Service Dates of Minority Members: Jan. 4, 1995-Jan. 9, 1997

	Majority						Minority				
				Years in:						**Years in:**	
Rank Name	**Party**	**State**	**Senate**	**Comm.**		**Rank Name**	**Party**	**State**	**Senate**	**Comm.**
Chr Pressler, Larry L.	Rep	S.D.	17	16		RM Hollings, Ernest F.	Dem	S.C.	29	28
2nd Packwood, Robert W.	Rep	Ore.	27	18		2nd Inouye, Daniel K.	Dem	Hai.	33	26
3rd Stevens, Theodore F.	Rep	Alas.	27	*2 14		3rd Ford, Wendell H.	Dem	Ky.	21	20
4th McCain, John S. III	Rep	Ariz.	9	8		4th Exon, J. James	Dem	Neb.	17	16
5th Burns, Conrad	Rep	Mont.	7	6		5th Rockefeller, John D. IV	Dem	W.Va.	11	10
6th Gorton, T. Slade III	Rep	Wash.	13	*2 6		6th Kerry, John F.	Dem	Mass.	11	8
7th Lott, C. Trent	Rep	Miss.	7	6		7th Breaux, John B.	Dem	La.	9	8
8th Hutchison, Kay Bailey	Rep	Tex.	2	2		8th Bryan, Richard H.	Dem	Nev.	7	6
9th Snowe, Olympia J.B.	Rep	Me.	1	1		9th Dorgan, Byron L.	Dem	N.D	3	2
10th Ashcroft, John D.	Rep	Mo.	1	1						

*2: Member's second period of service on the committee.

Note: Ranking on the committee for the following member was affected by other chamber service: Robert W. Packwood (Rep-Ore.), Chair, Finance.

Additions:
  Majority:

11th Abraham, Spencer	Rep	Mich.	Mar. 29, 1996

  Minority:

10th Wyden, Ronald L.	Dem	Ore.	Mar. 29, 1996

Changes:
  Majority:

Packwood, Robert W.	Rep	Ore.	Oct. 1, 1995 Resigned the Senate and retired.
Frist, William H.	Rep	Tenn.	Oct. 12, 1995 Replaced Packwood.

Departures from the Senate:	**Majority**			**Minority**		
Defeated for Re-election	Pressler, Larry L.	Rep	S.D.	None		
Retired	None			Exon, J. James	Dem	Neb.

COMMERCE, SCIENCE AND TRANSPORTATION / 105th Congress

Service Dates of Committee Chair: Jan. 9, 1997-Jan. 7, 1999

Service Dates of Majority Members: Jan. 9, 1997-Jan. 7, 1999

Service Dates of Minority Members: Jan. 9, 1997-Jan. 7, 1999

Majority						Minority				
			Years in:						**Years in:**	
Rank Name	**Party**	**State**	**Senate**	**Comm.**		**Rank Name**	**Party**	**State**	**Senate**	**Comm.**
Chr McCain, John S. III	Rep	Ariz.	11	11		RM Hollings, Ernest F.	Dem	S.C.	31	30
2nd Stevens, Theodore F.	Rep	Alas.	29	*2 17		2nd Inouye, Daniel K.	Dem	Hai.	35	28
3rd Burns, Conrad	Rep	Mont.	9	8		3rd Ford, Wendell H.	Dem	Ky.	23	22
4th Gorton, T. Slade III	Rep	Wash.	15	*2 8		4th Rockefeller, John D. IV	Dem	W.Va.	13	12
5th Lott, C. Trent	Rep	Miss.	9	8		5th Kerry, John F.	Dem	Mass.	13	11
6th Hutchison, Kay Bailey	Rep	Tex.	4	4		6th Breaux, John B.	Dem	La.	11	11
7th Snowe, Olympia J.B.	Rep	Me.	3	3		7th Bryan, Richard H.	Dem	Nev.	9	8
8th Ashcroft, John D.	Rep	Mo.	3	3		8th Dorgan, Byron L.	Dem	N.D	5	5
9th Frist, William H.	Rep	Tenn.	3	2		9th Wyden, Ronald L.	Dem	Ore.	2	1
10th Abraham, Spencer	Rep	Mich.	3	1						
11th Brownback, Sam D.	Rep	Kans.	1	*1 1						

*1: Member's first period of service on the committee.

*2: Member's second period of service on the committee.

Note: Ranking on the committee for the following member was affected by other chamber service: Theodore F. Stevens (Rep-Alas.), Chair, Appropriations.

Departures from the Senate:	**Majority**			**Minority**		
Retired	None			Ford, Wendell H.	Dem	Ky.

COMMERCE, SCIENCE AND TRANSPORTATION / 106th Congress

Service Dates of Committee Chair: Jan. 7, 1999-Jan. 3, 2001

Service Dates of Majority Members: Jan. 7, 1999-Jan. 25, 2001

Service Dates of Minority Members: Jan. 7, 1999-Jan. 25, 2001

Majority						Minority				
			Years in:						**Years in:**	
Rank Name	**Party**	**State**	**Senate**	**Comm.**		**Rank Name**	**Party**	**State**	**Senate**	**Comm.**
Chr McCain, John S. III	Rep	Ariz.	13	13		RM Hollings, Ernest F.	Dem	S.C.	33	32
2nd Stevens, Theodore F.	Rep	Alas.	31	*2 19		2nd Inouye, Daniel K.	Dem	Hai.	37	30
3rd Burns, Conrad	Rep	Mont.	11	10		3rd Rockefeller, John D. IV	Dem	W.Va.	15	14
4th Gorton, T. Slade III	Rep	Wash.	17	*2 10		4th Kerry, John F.	Dem	Mass.	15	13
5th Lott, C. Trent	Rep	Miss.	11	10		5th Breaux, John B.	Dem	La.	13	13
6th Hutchison, Kay Bailey	Rep	Tex.	6	6		6th Bryan, Richard H.	Dem	Nev.	11	10
7th Snowe, Olympia J.B.	Rep	Me.	5	5		7th Dorgan, Byron L.	Dem	N.D	7	7
8th Ashcroft, John D.	Rep	Mo.	5	5		8th Wyden, Ronald L.	Dem	Ore.	4	3
9th Frist, William H.	Rep	Tenn.	5	4		9th Cleland, J. Maxwell (Max)	Dem	Ga.	3	1
10th Abraham, Spencer	Rep	Mich.	5	3						
11th Brownback, Sam D.	Rep	Kans.	3	*1 2						

*1: Member's first period of service on the committee.

*2: Member's second period of service on the committee.

Note: Ranking on the committee for the following member was affected by other chamber service: Theodore F. Stevens (Rep-Alas.), Chair, Appropriations.

Departures from the Senate:	**Majority**			**Minority**		
Defeated for Re-election	Gorton, T. Slade III	Rep	Wash.	None		
	Ashcroft, John D.	Rep	Mo.			
	Abraham, Spencer	Rep	Mich.			
Retired	None			Bryan, Richard H.	Dem	Nev.
Departures from Committee:						
Elected Majority Leader	Frist, William H.	Rep	Tenn.	None		

COMMERCE, SCIENCE AND TRANSPORTATION / 107th Congress, Pre-Jeffords switch

Service Dates of Committee Chair: ChT: Jan. 3, 2001-Jan. 25, 2001 Hollings (Dem-S.C.)

Ch1: Jan. 25, 2001-June 6, 2001 McCain (Rep-Ariz.)

Service Dates of Majority Members: Jan. 25, 2001-June 6, 2001

Service Dates of Minority Members: Jan. 25, 2001-June 6, 2001

				Majority							Minority	
				Years in:							Years in:	
Rank Name	Party	State	Senate	Comm.		Rank Name	Party	State	Senate	Comm.
Ch1 McCain, John S. III	Rep	Ariz.	15	15		RM1 Hollings, Ernest F.	Dem	S.C.	35	35
2nd Stevens, Theodore F.	Rep	Alas.	33	*2 21		2nd Inouye, Daniel K.	Dem	Hai.	39	33
3rd Burns, Conrad	Rep	Mont.	13	12		3rd Rockefeller, John D. IV	Dem	W.Va.	17	16
4th Lott, C. Trent	Rep	Miss.	13	12		4th Kerry, John F.	Dem	Mass.	17	15
5th Hutchison, Kay Bailey	Rep	Tex.	8	8		5th Breaux, John B.	Dem	La.	15	15
6th Snowe, Olympia J.B.	Rep	Me.	7	7		6th Dorgan, Byron L.	Dem	N.D	9	9
7th Brownback, Sam D.	Rep	Kans.	5	*1 5		7th Wyden, Ronald L.	Dem	Ore.	6	5
8th Smith, Gordon H.	Rep	Ore.	5	1		8th Cleland, J. Maxwell (Max)	Dem	Ga.	5	3
9th Fitzgerald, Peter G.	Rep	Ill.	3	1		9th Boxer, Barbara	Dem	Cal.	9	1
10th Ensign, John E.	Rep	Nev.	1	1		10th Edwards, John	Dem	N.C.	3	1
11th Allen, George F.	Rep	Va.	1	1		11th Carnahan, Jean	Dem	Mo.	1	1

*1: Member's first period of service on the committee.

*2: Member's second period of service on the committee.

Note 1: Ranking on the committee for the following member was affected by other chamber service: Theodore F. Stevens (Rep-Alas.), Chair, Appropriations.

Note 2: The committee majority in the 2001 Senate power-sharing arrangement was determined by the party of the vice president. Democrat Al Gore Jr. served from Jan. 3, 2001, to Jan. 20, 2001, and was succeeded by Republican Richard B. Cheney on Jan. 20, 2001. When Senator Jeffords of Vermont left the Republican Party, effective June 6, 2001, to become an Independent, Democrats regained the majority for the remainder of the 107th Congress.

COMMERCE, SCIENCE AND TRANSPORTATION / 107th Congress, Post-Jeffords switch

Service Dates of Committee Chair: June 6, 2001-Jan. 14, 2003

Service Dates of Majority Members: June 6, 2001-Jan. 14, 2003

Service Dates of Minority Members: June 6, 2001-Jan. 15, 2003

				Majority							Minority	
				Years in:							Years in:	
Rank Name	Party	State	Senate	Comm.		Rank Name	Party	State	Senate	Comm.
Ch2 Hollings, Ernest F.	Dem	S.C.	35	35		RM2 McCain, John S. III	Rep	Ariz.	15	15
2nd Inouye, Daniel K.	Dem	Hai.	39	33		2nd Stevens, Theodore F.	Rep	Alas.	33	*2 21
3rd Rockefeller, John D. IV	Dem	W.Va.	17	17		3rd Burns, Conrad	Rep	Mont.	13	13
4th Kerry, John F.	Dem	Mass.	17	15		4th Lott, C. Trent	Rep	Miss.	13	13
5th Breaux, John B.	Dem	La.	15	15		5th Hutchison, Kay Bailey	Rep	Tex.	9	8
6th Dorgan, Byron L.	Dem	N.D	9	9		6th Snowe, Olympia J.B.	Rep	Me.	7	7
7th Wyden, Ronald L.	Dem	Ore.	6	6		7th Brownback, Sam D.	Rep	Kans.	5	*1 5
8th Cleland, J. Maxwell (Max)	Dem	Ga.	5	3		8th Smith, Gordon H.	Rep	Ore.	5	1
9th Boxer, Barbara	Dem	Cal.	9	1		9th Fitzgerald, Peter G.	Rep	Ill.	3	1
10th Edwards, John	Dem	N.C.	3	1		10th Ensign, John E.	Rep	Nev.	1	1
11th Carnahan, Jean	Dem	Mo.	1	1		11th Allen, George F.	Rep	Va.	1	1
12th Nelson, C. William (Bill)	Dem	Fla.	1	1						

*1: Member's first period of service on the committee.

*2: Member's second period of service on the committee.

Note: Ranking on the committee for the following member was affected by other chamber service: Theodore F. Stevens (Rep-Alas.), Ranking Minority Member, Appropriations.

Additions:

  Majority:

    12th Nelson, C. William (Bill) Dem Fla.   July 10, 2001

Changes:

  Majority:

    Carnahan, Jean Dem Mo.   Nov. 25, 2002 Resigned the Senate; defeated in special election by James M. Talent (Rep-Mo.).

Departures from the Senate:	**Majority**			**Minority**
Defeated for Re-election	Cleland, J. Maxwell (Max)	Dem	Ga.	None

Departures from Committee:				
No new assignment	Edwards, John	Dem	N.C.	None

COMMERCE, SCIENCE AND TRANSPORTATION / 108th Congress

Service Dates of Committee Chair: Jan. 14, 2003-Jan. 6, 2005

Service Dates of Majority Members: Jan. 14, 2003-Jan. 6, 2005

Service Dates of Minority Members: Jan. 15, 2003-Jan. 6, 2005

Majority					Minority				
			Years in:					**Years in:**	
Rank Name	Party	State	Senate	Comm.	Rank Name	Party	State	Senate	Comm.
Chr McCain, John S. III	Rep	Ariz.	17	17	RM Hollings, Ernest F.	Dem	S.C.	37	37
2nd Stevens, Theodore F.	Rep	Alas.	35	*2 23	2nd Inouye, Daniel K.	Dem	Hai.	41	35
3rd Burns, Conrad	Rep	Mont.	15	14	3rd Rockefeller, John D. IV	Dem	W.Va.	19	18
4th Lott, C. Trent	Rep	Miss.	15	14	4th Kerry, John F.	Dem	Mass.	19	17
5th Hutchison, Kay Bailey	Rep	Tex.	10	10	5th Breaux, John B.	Dem	La.	17	17
6th Snowe, Olympia J.B.	Rep	Me.	9	9	6th Dorgan, Byron L.	Dem	N.D	11	11
7th Brownback, Sam D.	Rep	Kans.	7	*1 7	7th Wyden, Ronald L.	Dem	Ore.	8	7
8th Smith, Gordon H.	Rep	Ore.	7	2	8th Boxer, Barbara	Dem	Cal.	11	2
9th Fitzgerald, Peter G.	Rep	Ill.	5	2	9th Nelson, C. William (Bill)	Dem	Fla.	3	2
10th Ensign, John E.	Rep	Nev.	3	2	10th Cantwell, Maria E.	Dem	Wash.	3	1
11th Allen, George F.	Rep	Va.	3	2	11th Lautenberg, Frank R.	Dem	N.J.	19	*2 1
12th Sununu, John E.	Rep	N.H.	1	1					

*1: Member's first period of service on the committee.

*2: Member's second period of service on the committee.

Note: Ranking on the committee for the following member was affected by other chamber service: Theodore F. Stevens (Rep-Alas.), Ranking Minority Member, Appropriations.

Departures from the Senate:	**Majority**			**Minority**		
Retired	Fitzgerald, Peter G.	Rep	Ill.	Hollings, Ernest F.	Dem	S.C.
				Breaux, John B.	Dem	La.

Departures from Committee:						
Returned to Judiciary	Brownback, Sam D.	Rep	Kans.	None		
Moved to Finance	None			Wyden, Ronald L.	Dem	Ore.

COMMERCE, SCIENCE AND TRANSPORTATION / 109th Congress

Service Dates of Committee Chair: Jan. 6, 2005-Jan. 12, 2007

Service Dates of Majority Members: Jan. 6, 2005-Jan. 12, 2007

Service Dates of Minority Members: Jan. 6, 2005-Jan. 12, 2007

Majority					Minority				
			Years in:					**Years in:**	
Rank Name	Party	State	Senate	Comm.	Rank Name	Party	State	Senate	Comm.
Chr Stevens, Theodore F.	Rep	Alas.	37	*2 25	RM Inouye, Daniel K.	Dem	Hai.	43	36
2nd McCain, John S. III	Rep	Ariz.	19	19	2nd Rockefeller, John D. IV	Dem	W.Va.	21	20
3rd Burns, Conrad	Rep	Mont.	17	16	3rd Kerry, John F.	Dem	Mass.	21	19
4th Lott, C. Trent	Rep	Miss.	17	16	4th Dorgan, Byron L.	Dem	N.D	13	12
5th Hutchison, Kay Bailey	Rep	Tex.	12	12	5th Boxer, Barbara	Dem	Cal.	13	4
6th Snowe, Olympia J.B.	Rep	Me.	11	11	6th Nelson, C. William (Bill)	Dem	Fla.	5	4
7th Smith, Gordon H.	Rep	Ore.	9	4	7th Cantwell, Maria E.	Dem	Wash.	5	2
8th Ensign, John E.	Rep	Nev.	5	4	8th Lautenberg, Frank R.	Dem	N.J.	21	*2 2
9th Allen, George F.	Rep	Va.	5	4	9th Nelson, E. Benjamin	Dem	Neb.	5	1
10th Sununu, John E.	Rep	N.H.	3	2	10th Pryor, Mark	Dem	Ark.	3	1
11th DeMint, James W.	Rep	S.C.	1	1					
12th Vitter, David	Rep	La.	1	1					

*2: Member's second period of service on the committee.

Departures from the Senate:	**Majority**			**Minority**		
Defeated for Re-election	Burns, Conrad	Rep	Mont.	None		
	Allen, George F.	Rep	Va.			

Departures from Committee:						
Moved to Appropriations	None			Nelson, E. Benjamin	Dem	Neb.

COMMERCE, SCIENCE AND TRANSPORTATION / 110th Congress

Service Dates of Committee Chair: Jan. 12, 2007-Jan. 21, 2009

Service Dates of Majority Members: Jan. 12, 2007-Jan. 21, 2009

Service Dates of Minority Members: Jan. 12, 2007-Jan. 21, 2009

Majority Rank Name	Party	State	Years in: Senate	Years in: Comm.	Minority Rank Name	Party	State	Years in: Senate	Years in: Comm.
Chr Inouye, Daniel K.	Dem	Hai.	45	38	RM Stevens, Theodore F.	Rep	Alas.	39	*2 27
2nd Rockefeller, John D. IV	Dem	W.Va.	23	22	2nd McCain, John S. III	Rep	Ariz.	21	21
3rd Kerry, John F.	Dem	Mass.	23	21	3rd Lott, C. Trent	Rep	Miss.	19	18
4th Dorgan, Byron L.	Dem	N.D	15	15	4th Hutchison, Kay Bailey	Rep	Tex.	14	14
5th Boxer, Barbara	Dem	Cal.	15	6	5th Snowe, Olympia J.B.	Rep	Me.	13	13
6th Nelson, C. William (Bill)	Dem	Fla.	7	6	6th Smith, Gordon H.	Rep	Ore.	11	6
7th Cantwell, Maria E.	Dem	Wash.	7	4	7th Ensign, John E.	Rep	Nev.	7	6
8th Lautenberg, Frank R.	Dem	N.J.	23	*2 4	8th Sununu, John E.	Rep	N.H.	5	4
9th Pryor, Mark	Dem	Ark.	5	3	9th DeMint, James W.	Rep	S.C.	3	3
10th Carper, Thomas R.	Dem	Del.	7	1	10th Vitter, David	Rep	La	3	3
11th McCaskill, Claire	Dem	Mo.	1	1	11th Thune, John	Rep	S.D.	3	1
12th Klobuchar, Amy	DFL	Minn.	1	1					

*2: Member's second period of service on the committee.

Changes:

Minority:

Lott, C. Trent	Rep	Miss.	Dec. 18, 2007 Resigned the Senate and retired.
Wicker, Roger F.	Rep	Miss.	Jan. 24, 2008 Replaced Lott.

Departures from the Senate:

	Majority		Minority		
Defeated for Re-election	None		Stevens, Theodore F.	Rep	Alas.
			Smith, Gordon H.	Rep	Ore.
			Sununu, John E.	Rep	N.H.

Departures from Committee:

	Majority			Minority		
Moved to Finance	Carper, Thomas R.	Dem	Del.	None		
Moved to Energy and Natural Resources and returned to Homeland Security and Governmental Affairs	None			McCain, John S. III	Rep	Ariz.

COMMERCE, SCIENCE AND TRANSPORTATION / 111th Congress

Service Dates of Committee Chair: Jan. 21, 2009-

Service Dates of Majority Members: Jan. 21, 2009-

Service Dates of Minority Members: Jan. 21, 2009-

Majority Rank Name	Party	State	Years in: Senate	Years in: Comm.	Minority Rank Name	Party	State	Years in: Senate	Years in: Comm.
Chr Rockefeller, John D. IV	Dem	W.Va.	25	24	RM Hutchison, Kay Bailey	Rep	Tex.	16	16
2nd Inouye, Daniel K.	Dem	Hai.	47	41	2nd Snowe, Olympia J.B.	Rep	Me.	15	15
3rd Kerry, John F.	Dem	Mass.	25	23	3rd Ensign, John E.	Rep	Nev.	9	8
4th Dorgan, Byron L.	Dem	N.D	17	17	4th DeMint, James W.	Rep	S.C.	5	5
5th Boxer, Barbara	Dem	Cal.	17	8	5th Thune, John	Rep	S.D.	5	3
6th Nelson, C. William (Bill)	Dem	Fla.	9	8	6th Wicker, Roger F.	Rep	Miss.	2	1
7th Cantwell, Maria E.	Dem	Wash.	9	7	7th Isakson, Johnny	Rep	Ga.	5	1
8th Lautenberg, Frank	Dem	N.J.	25	*2 7	8th Vitter, David	Rep	La	5	5
9th Pryor, Mark	Dem	Ark.	7	5	9th Brownback, Sam D.	Rep	Kans.	13	*2 1
10th McCaskill, Claire	Dem	Mo.	3	3	10th Martinez, Melquiades R. (Mel)	Rep	Fla.	5	1
11th Klobuchar, Amy	DFL	Minn.	3	3	11th Johanns, Mike	Rep	Neb.	1	1
12th Udall, Thomas	Dem	N.M.	1	1					
13th Warner, Mark R.	Dem	Va.	1	1					
14th Begich, Mark	Dem	Alas.	1	1					

*2: Member's second period of service on the committee.

Changes:

Minority:

Martinez, Melquiades R. (Mel)	Rep	Fla.	Sept. 22, 2009 Resigned the Senate
LeMieux, George S.	Rep	Fla.	Sept. 22, 2009 Replaced Martinez, ranked following Wicker

Energy and Natural Resources

Senate Committee on Energy and Natural Resources, 103rd-111th Congresses (1993-2011)

BACKGROUND

Organizational History: The Senate Committee on Energy and Natural Resources is operating under its third title since the Legislative Reorganization Act of 1946 (79-601). Under that act, its initial name of Public Lands indicated that the committee was built on the jurisdictional base of the Senate Public Lands and Surveys Committee to which was added the jurisdiction of four other standing committees—Indian Affairs, Mines and Mining, Territorial and Insular Affairs, and Irrigation and Reclamation. However, it soon became clear that this name was insufficiently inclusive to comprise all of its myriad responsibilities and the committee was renamed Interior and Insular Affairs on January 28, 1948, as the House had earlier.

Public Lands was the original name of the committee at the time of its creation in the Senate resolution of December 10, 1816, as one of the Senate's original standing committees. Senator Jeremiah Morrow (DR-Ohio) was the committee's first chair during the 15th Congress, its first full one in operation.

As the nation expanded westward, Congress became ever more involved legislatively with the development of the land and its resources. In the years immediately prior to the establishment of the Senate standing committees, the Senate had organized select committees on the Territories of Louisiana, Florida, Illinois, and Missouri. By 1816, the General Land Office was busy selling land to settlers in these territories.

The *Guide to the Records of the United States Senate* notes that: "One historian has determined that by 1838 Congress had enacted 375 laws dealing with the public domain, and had considered and either reported adversely or simply ignored many more proposed bills."

Development of the railroads occupied the committee in the post-Civil War Congresses, but awareness of the needs of conservation led to the inclusion of the national parks system and national resources, including energy and timber, under the committee's jurisdiction in the late nineteenth century and the first half of the twentieth century. In the 1921 reorganization of Senate committees, Public Lands acquired the jurisdiction of the Committee on the Geological Survey, and it was renamed the Committee on Public Lands and Surveys.

Another of its predecessor committees was Indian Affairs, established by a Senate resolution introduced by Walter Leake (DR-Miss.) on January 3, 1820, with Leake as its first chair. Both before and after the creation of the standing committee on Indian Affairs, select and special committees were appointed in the Senate to deal with these matters, including the Select Committee on the Extinguishment of Indian Title to Certain Lands, which existed for approximately two weeks in 1818 (15th Cong.) and the Select Committee on Indian Depredations which ran from 1889 to 1893, and eventually sat as a standing committee until the 1921 reorganization.

Indian Affairs became a subcommittee of the Interior and Insular Affairs Committee until the Committee System Reorganization Amendments of 1977, when it was recreated as the Select Committee on Indian Affairs. In 1993, the "Select" designation was dropped.

The Senate Committee on Territories was established on March 28, 1844, on a Senate resolution Arthur P. Bagby (Dem-Ala.) introduced in the midst of the heated debate over Oregon and the United States' dispute with Great Britain. The committee's first chair was George Evans (Whig-Me.) and Bagby served as its senior minority member. The committee's function shifted as the various territories became states. The committee, reorganized as the Committee on Territories and Insular Possessions, was established on April 18, 1921, with the adoption of S. Res. 43, 67th Cong., with Harry S. New (Rep-Ind.) as its chair. This reform eliminated many standing and select committees, including the Committee on the Pacific Islands, Puerto Rico, and the Virgin Islands, and the Committee on the Philippines. On June 17, 1929, the Senate approved S. Res. 55, 71st Cong., which changed the name to the Committee on Territories and Insular Affairs, with Hiram Bingham (Rep-Conn.) as its chair. This was its title until the committee was absorbed into the Interior and Insular Affairs Committee in the 80th Congress.

A fourth predecessor was the Committee on Mines and Mining, which was established on December 6, 1865, by the Senate resolution establishing the standing committees of the Senate for the 39th Congress, with John Conness (UnRep-Cal.) as its chair. It oversaw the regulation of mines and mining operations but mineral rights on public lands remained with the Public Lands Committee.

The fifth of the major predecessors was the Committee on Irrigation and Reclamation of Arid Lands which was established on December 16, 1891, with Francis E. Warren (Rep-Wyo.) as its chair. It succeeded a select committee which had been created two years earlier for the purpose of determining how best to irrigate arid lands. The committee's name was shortened to Committee on Irrigation and Reclamation in 1921. And in the 1946 Reorganization, it was absorbed by Interior and Insular Affairs (previously known as Public Lands). A minor predecessor committee was the Committee on the Conservation of National Resources, which was established by Senate resolution on March 21, 1909, with Joseph M. Dixon (Rep-Mont.) as its first chair. It supported the protection of water, timber, and coal lands, but it was terminated in 1921 by S. Res. 43, 67th Congress.

The complexity of the reorganization of this committee was due to the merger of five separate standing committees with long histories and powerful constituencies. The organization of the five standing subcommittees of the Interior and Insular Affairs Committees paralleled closely the committees that were merged into the Committee on Public Lands by the Legislative Reorganization Act of 1946. An ambitious effort of Chair

Joseph O'Mahoney (Dem-Wyo.) to eliminate subcommittees at the committee meeting of January 12, 1949, failed and the surviving subcommittees continued to maintain much of their pre-1947 jurisdiction.

Once created the Public Lands Committee and its successors remained almost exclusively under the control of western state senators, particularly those from the Mountain states where the federal government remains as the region's largest land-holder. Following the lead of the House, the committee was renamed the Committee on Interior and Insular Affairs on January 28, 1948, and held that name until the 1977 reorganization.

The admission of Alaska to the Union on January 3, 1959, and Hawaii on August 24, 1959, removed them from the Interior Committee's jurisdiction. Also, the creation of the standing Committee on Veterans' Affairs in 1970 moved jurisdiction over military parks and battlefields and national cemeteries to the Veterans Committee from the Interior Committee.

By 1977, the energy crisis had been a part of American life for some years, and Sen. Henry M. Jackson (Dem-Wash.), the committee's leading member, wished to have the committee more directly focused upon energy issues and natural resources. The committee became a major player in allocation decisions regarding mineral and oil exploration. This was what led to the committee's renaming as Energy and Natural Resources in Senate Resolution 4, the Committee System Reorganization Amendments of 1977, February 4, 1977 [Section (g)(1)]. Perhaps one of the strongest contrasts between the ways in which the Senate and the House dealt with energy matters was that the Senate placed its energy jurisdiction into a committee dominated by "producer" states while the House lodged its energy responsibilities in a "consumer" committee, that of Energy and Commerce.

While the initial energy crisis appears to have abated, energy issues continue to appear on the national agenda. Legislation known as "cap and trade" regarding fuel emissions that increase the dangers of the "greenhouse effect" has been a major focal point of the Energy and Natural Resources Committee in recent years. It has emerged as the Senate's lead committee in the efforts to slow the progress of global warming.

Membership: Although the Energy and Natural Resources committee's average membership size of 21.5 members places it fifth among the sixteen committees, other indicators of the committee's relative appeal are less positive. The mean seniority of its members is only 9.84 years placing it fourteenth and its mean inter-Congress retention rate of 83.6 percent ranks only thirteenth among the Senate's standing committees.

Membership movement on and off the Energy and Natural Resources Committee has been relatively high with ten senators joining the committee and twenty-four departing it—a net loss of fourteen. The Committee on Health, Education, Labor, and Pensions (HELP) provided Energy with three of its former members. Among the twenty-four departing members, six of the departing members left for no other assignment, while Appropriations with five and Finance with three, appear to be the major destinations of former Energy committee members.

One curious feature of the regional composition of the committee has been its lack of appeal to senators from the northeast. Paul Tsongas (Dem-Mass.) and Jim Jeffords (Rep/Ind.-Vt.) were the only New Englanders to serve on the committee between 1947 and 2007. Over that sixty-year period, only four New Yorkers served on the committee: Herbert H.

Lehman (Dem-N.Y.) who left in his third year; James F. Buckley (Con.-N.Y.), who left after two years; Daniel Patrick Moynihan (Dem-N.Y.), who left after a month; and Kenneth B. Keating (Rep-N.Y.), who left after thirteen days. Their total service is less than one-third of that accrued by New Jersey Democrat William W. Bradley, who served on the Energy Committee from his arrival in the Senate in 1979 until his retirement in 1996.

Committee Leaders: The first modern-era chair of Public Lands was Republican Hugh A. Butler of Nebraska who served as chair in the 80th Congress (1947-1949) and as ranking minority member in the two Democratic Congresses after the committee was renamed Interior and Insular Affairs (1949-1953). Carl A. Hatch (Dem-N.M.), the author of the 1939 Hatch Act, which limited the political activities of government employees, served as ranking minority member in the 80th Congress, and then declined to run for a second full term and left the Senate in 1949 shortly before his appointment to the federal bench. Joseph C. O'Mahoney (Dem-Wyo.) was the first Democratic chair of the Interior and Insular Affairs Committee in the 81st and 82nd Congresses (1949-1953) until his defeat for re-election in 1952.

With the 1952 election tilting the Senate toward the Republicans, Hugh Butler resumed the chair in 1953 and served until his death on July 1, 1954. He was succeeded by Guy Cordon (Rep-Ore.), who served out the balance of the 83rd Congress. Cordon was defeated for re-election in 1954. James E. Murray (Dem-Mont.) was ranking minority member in the 83rd Congress. He became chair in 1955 and held the post until his retirement from the Senate in 1961.

Turnover in the senior ranks was high. Eugene D. Millikin (Rep-Colo.), the ranking minority member of Finance, served one term (1955-1957) as ranking minority member of Interior and then retired. Millikin was succeeded as ranking minority member by George W. Malone (Rep-Nev.) in the 85th Congress (1957-1959), who lost his 1958 re-election bid. In the 86th and 87th Congresses, Henry C. Dworshak (Rep-Ida.) served as ranking minority member until his death July 23, 1962. Sen. Clinton P. Anderson (Dem-N.M.), who was President Harry Truman's Secretary of Agriculture (1945-1949), served as committee chair in the 87th Congress. Anderson ceded his position to Henry M. Jackson (Dem-Wash.) after being named chair of the Aeronautical and Space Sciences Committee in 1963.

Jackson stabilized the chairmanship by remaining as chair from the 88th through the 96th Congresses (1963-1981) and was the leading proponent of the 1977 name change from Interior and Insular Affairs to Energy and Natural Resources. When the Republicans gained the Senate in 1981, Jackson served as ranking minority member but left that position in 1983 to become ranking minority member on the Armed Services Committee, where he was serving at the time of his death on September 1, 1983.

Thomas H. Kuchel (Rep-Cal), the Republican Whip, succeeded Dworshak and served as ranking minority member from the 87th through the 90th Congresses (1962-1969) until his defeat for renomination in the 1968 California primary by Superintendent of Schools Max Rafferty. Kuchel was succeeded by Gordon L. Allott (Rep-Colo.), who served as ranking minority member in the 91st and 92nd Congresses (1969-1973) until his defeat for re-election in 1972. He was followed by Paul J. Fannin (Rep-Ariz.) who served as ranking minority member in the 93rd and 94th Congresses (1973-1977) until his retirement from the Senate.

Clifford P. Hansen of Wyoming was the first ranking minority member of the renamed Energy and Natural Resources Committee in the 95th Congress. Hansen resigned the Senate at the end of 1978. In 1979, Mark O. Hatfield (Rep-Ore.) served as the fifth ranking minority member during the long committee chairmanship of Henry Jackson. When the Republicans gained control of the Senate in the 1980 election, Hatfield, the Energy Committee's senior majority member, moved to chair the powerful Senate Appropriations Committee and ceded the chair to James A. McClure (Rep-Ida.). McClure served as chair in the 97th through 99th Congresses (1981-1987). Upon the resumption of Democratic control in 1987, McClure served as ranking minority member in the 100th and 101st Congresses (1987-1991), after which he retired from the Senate.

Jackson's successor as senior Democrat was J. Bennett Johnston Jr. (Dem.-La.) who served as ranking minority member in the 98th and 99th Congresses (1983-1987) and became the Energy Committee's chair in the 100th through the 103rd Congresses (1987-1995) and as ranking member in the 104th (1995-1997). From 1991 to 1995, Republican Malcolm Wallop of Wyoming served as the committee's ranking minority member until his retirement. Alaska's Frank Murkowski became chair of the committee when Republicans organized the Senate in 1995 and served as its ranking Republican until he resigned the Senate on December 2, 2002, to become governor of Alaska. After twenty-two years of service as the senior Republican on Budget, Pete Domenici of New Mexico assumed the chairmanship in 2003 and held the post until 2007 and the Democrats recapture of the Senate. Serving for one last term as ranking minority member, Domenici retired in 2008.

With Johnston's retirement in 1996, Democrat Dale Bumpers of Arkansas became ranking member and served from 1997 until his retirement in 1998. Jeff Bingaman of New Mexico became the senior Democrat on Energy and Natural Resources in 1999, serving as ranking member (1999-2001 and 2003-2007) and as chair (2001-2003 and 2007-2011). With both senior members of the committee elected from New Mexico, the Energy Committee's regional tilt toward the west is obvious.

Party Leaders: Energy Committee alumni have been more successful in obtaining leadership posts. Four Democratic leaders served on the committee. One served as floor leader—Ernest W. McFarland of Arizona (1951-53); and three as Whips—Earle C. Clements of Kentucky in 1953-1957; Russell B. Long of Louisiana in 1965-1969; and Wendell Ford of Kentucky in 1991-1999. Also, Carl Hayden, the Senate's long-time president *pro tempore* (1957-1969) who had been Arizona's first elected representative returned to the committee in 1963, during his 36th year in the Senate. Hayden had served for twenty years on one of the predecessor committees, Territories and Insular Affairs (1927-1947).

While Democratic leaders among the committee's alumni may have served longer, there were more Republican leaders who had served on Energy and Natural Resources and its predecessors. The first Republican leader with experience on the committee was floor leader Everett McK. Dirksen of Illinois, who served on ten separate standing committees during his years in the Senate. Serving with Dirksen as Whip from 1959 to 1969 was Thomas H. Kuchel of California, the committee's ranking member from 1962 to 1969. Republican Whips Ted Stevens of Alaska (1977-1985) and Don Nickles of Oklahoma (1996-2003), who each served on eight different committees,

were alumni of the Energy Committee as were both Trent Lott and Mitch McConnell, who began their leadership careers as Whips in 1995 and 2003, respectively, before serving as floor leaders in the subsequent Congresses.

Presidential Aspirations: Because the committee has been so dominated by one region, it has not been a major source of presidential aspirants. The three presidential nominees who served on the committee were the Arizona Republican twosome of Barry M. Goldwater, the 1964 nominee, and John S. McCain III, the 2008 nominee. Neither was successful, nor was the only Democratic alumnus of the committee to be nominated for president, George S. McGovern of South Dakota in 1972. Three of its members who failed to be nominated were Henry M. (Scoop) Jackson (Dem-Wash.) in 1972 and 1976, Frank F. Church (Dem-Ida.) in 1976, and Paul E. Tsongas (Dem-Mass.) in 1992.

Other Notables: Of the four modern-era members of the committee with Cabinet experience, three served prior to their Senate elections. Democrat Clinton Anderson of New Mexico as President Harry Truman's Secretary of Agriculture; Republican Lamar Alexander of Tennessee as President George H.W. Bush's Secretary of Education; and Republican Mel Martinez of Florida as President George W. Bush's Secretary of Housing and Urban Development. Democrat Kenneth Salazar of Colorado left the Senate and its Energy Committee in 2009 to become President Barack Obama's Secretary of the Interior.

Unique notable career moves were made by post-1993 Energy Committee alumni Republican Frank Murkowski of Alaska, who left the Senate to become governor in 2002 and Democrat Jon S. Corzine of New Jersey, who followed the same path in 2006. Both were out of office after a single term, with Murkowski losing his renomination bid to Sarah Palin in 2006 and Corzine losing his re-election bid to Chris Christie in 2009.

Selected References

Boesl, Mary Etta, "Energy and Natural Resources Committee, Senate," in Donald C. Bacon, Roger H. Davidson, and Morton Keller, eds., *The Encyclopedia of the United States Congress* (New York: Simon & Schuster, 1995), I: 752-754.

Coren, Robert W., et al., "Records of the Committee on Interior and Insular Affairs and Predecessor Committees, 1816-1968," *Guide to the Records of the United States Senate at the National Archives: 1789-1989 Bicentennial Edition* (Washington, D.C.: National Archives and Records Administration, 1989), 125-140.

Kriz, Margaret, "The Power Broker," *National Journal*, 24 (1992), 494-499.

Magida, Arthur J., "The House and Senate Interior and Insular Affairs Committees," in the Ralph Nader Congress Project, *The Environment Committees A Study of the House and Senate Interior, Agriculture, and Science Committees* (New York: Grossman, 1975), 1-141.

U.S. Senate, Committee on Energy and Natural Resources, *History of the Committee on Energy and Natural Resources, 1816-1988*, Senate Document 100-46, 100th Congress, 2nd session (1988).

U.S. Senate, Committee on Interior and Insular Affairs, *Committee's History, Jurisdiction, and Summary and Accomplishments During the 87th, 88th, 89th, 90th and 91st Congresses*, 92nd Congress, 1st Session (1971).

RESPONSIBILITIES, JURISDICTIONAL CHANGES, AND SUBCOMMITTEES

PUBLIC LANDS

Jurisdiction, 80th Congress (1947-49)

Established by the Legislative Reorganization Act of 1946:

[Section 102.(1)(m)]

(1) **Committee on Public Lands,** to consist of thirteen Senators, to which committee shall be referred all proposed legislation, messages, petitions, memorials, and other matters relating to the following subjects:

    (1) Public lands generally, including entry, easements, and grazing thereon

    (2) Mineral resources of the public lands

    (3) Forfeiture of land grants and alien ownership, including alien ownership of mineral lands

    (4) Forest reserves and national parks created from the public domain

    (5) Military parks and battlefields, and national cemeteries

    (6) Preservation of prehistoric ruins and objects of interest on the public domain

    (7) Measures relating generally to Hawaii, Alaska, and the insular possessions of the United States, except those affecting their revenue and appropriations

    (8) Irrigation and reclamation, including water supply for reclamation projects, and easements of public lands for irrigation projects

    (9) Interstate compacts relating to apportionment of waters for irrigation purposes

    (10) Mining interests generally

    (11) Mineral land laws and claims and entries thereunder

    (12) Geological survey

    (13) Mining schools and experimental stations

    (14) Petroleum conservation and conservation of the radium supply in the United States

    (15) Relations of the United States with the Indians and the Indian tribes

    (16) Measures relating to the care, education, and management of Indians, including the care and allotment of Indian lands and general and special measures relating to claims which are paid out of Indian funds

Committee Renamed, 1948

Public Lands was renamed the Committee on Interior and Insular Affairs on January 28, 1948.

ENERGY AND NATURAL RESOURCES

Reorganization, 1977

Interior and Insular Affairs was reorganized as the Standing Committee on Energy and Natural Resources following the passage of Senate Resolution 4, the Committee System Reorganization Amendments of 1977, February 4, 1977.

Reorganized Jurisdiction, 1977

From Senate Resolution 4, the Committee System Reorganization Amendments of 1977, February 4, 1977:

[Section (g)(1)]

(1) **Committee on Energy and Natural Resources**, to which committee shall be referred all proposed legislation, messages, petitions, memorials, and other matters relating to the following subjects:

    (1) Energy policy

    (2) Energy regulation and conservation

    (3) Energy research and development

    (4) Solar energy systems

    (5) Nonmilitary development of nuclear energy

    (6) Naval petroleum reserves in Alaska

    (7) Oil and gas production and distribution

    (8) Extraction of minerals from oceans and Outer Continental Shelf lands

    (9) Energy related aspects of deepwater ports

    (10) Hydroelectric power, irrigation, and reclamation

    (11) Coal production, distribution, and utilization

    (12) Public lands and forests, including farming and grazing thereon, and mineral extraction therefrom

    (13) National parks, recreation areas, wilderness areas, wild and scenic rivers, historical sites, military parks and battlefields on the public domain, and preservation of prehistoric ruins and objects of interest

   (14) Mining, mineral lands, mining claims, and mineral conservation
   (15) Mining education and research
   (16) Territorial possessions of the United States, including trusteeships

(2) Such committee shall also study and review, on a comprehensive basis, matters relating to energy and resources development, and report thereon from time to time.

Jurisdiction, 103rd Congress (1993-94)

From the *Standing Rules of the Senate* in the *Senate Manual*, 103rd Congress, 1st Session, S. Doc. 103-1:

[Rule XXV.(1)(g)]

(1) **Committee on Energy and Natural Resources**, to which committee shall be referred all proposed legislation, messages, petitions, memorials, and other matters relating to the following subjects:

   (1) Coal production, distribution, and utilization
   (2) Energy policy
   (3) Energy regulation and conservation
   (4) Energy related aspects of deepwater ports
   (5) Energy research and development
   (6) Extraction of minerals from oceans and Outer Continental Shelf lands
   (7) Hydroelectric power, irrigation, and reclamation
   (8) Mining education and research
   (9) Mining, mineral lands, mining claims, and mineral conservation
   (10) National parks, recreation areas, wilderness areas, wild and scenic rivers, historical sites, military parks and battlefields, and on the public domain, preservation of prehistoric ruins and objects of interest
   (11) Naval petroleum reserves in Alaska
   (12) Nonmilitary development of nuclear energy
   (13) Oil and gas production and distribution
   (14) Public lands and forests, including farming and grazing thereon, and mineral extraction therefrom
   (15) Solar energy systems
   (16) Territorial possessions of the United States, including trusteeships

(2) Such committee shall also study and review, on a comprehensive basis, matters relating to energy and resources development, and report thereon from time to time.

Jurisdiction, 111th Congress (2009-10)

From *Authority and Rules of Senate Committees, 2009-2010*, Sen. Doc. 111-3, pursuant to S.Res, 166, June 2, 2009.

[Rule XXV.(1)(g)]

(1) **Committee on Energy and Natural Resources**, to which committee shall be referred all proposed legislation, messages, petitions, memorials, and other matters relating to the following subjects:

   (1) Coal production, distribution, and utilization
   (2) Energy policy
   (3) Energy regulation and conservation
   (4) Energy related aspects of deepwater ports
   (5) Energy research and development
   (6) Extraction of minerals from oceans and Outer Continental Shelf lands
   (7) Hydroelectric power, irrigation, and reclamation
   (8) Mining education and research
   (9) Mining, mineral lands, mining claims, and mineral conservation
   (10) National parks, recreation areas, wilderness areas, wild and scenic rivers, historical sites, military parks and battlefields, and on the public domain, preservation of prehistoric ruins and objects of interest
   (11) Naval petroleum reserves in Alaska
   (12) Nonmilitary development of nuclear energy
   (13) Oil and gas production and distribution
   (14) Public lands and forests, including farming and grazing thereon, and mineral extraction therefrom
   (15) Solar energy systems
   (16) Territorial possessions of the United States, including trusteeships

(2) Such committee shall also study and review, on a comprehensive basis, matters relating to energy and resources development, and report thereon from time to time.

NAMES OF SUBCOMMITTEES

Committee on Energy and Natural Resources, 103rd -111th Congresses

Energy, 107, 108, 109, 110, 111
Energy Research and Development, 103, 104
Energy, Research, Development, Production, and Regulation, 105, 106
Energy Production and Regulation, 104
Forests and Public Land Management, 104, 105, 106
Mineral Resources Development and Production, 103
National Parks, Historic Preservation, and Recreation, 105, 106
National Parks, 107, 108, 109, 110, 111
Oversight and Investigations, 104
Parks, Historic Preservation, and Recreation, 104
Public Lands, National Parks and Forests, 103
Public Lands and Forests, 107, 108, 109, 110, 111
Renewable Energy, Energy Efficiency, and Competitiveness, 103
Water and Power, 103, 105, 106, 107, 108, 109, 110, 111

MEMBERSHIP ROSTERS, 103rd-111th Congresses, 1993-2010

ENERGY AND NATURAL RESOURCES / 103rd Congress

Service Dates of Committee Chair: Jan. 7, 1993-Jan. 11, 1995

Service Dates of Majority Members: Jan. 7, 1993-Jan. 5, 1995

Service Dates of Minority Members: Jan. 7, 1993-Jan. 4, 1995

Majority

Rank Name	Party	State	Years in: Senate	Comm.
Chr Johnston, J. Bennett Jr.	Dem	La.	21	21
2nd Bumpers, Dale	Dem	Ark.	19	19
3rd Ford, Wendell H.	Dem	Ky.	19	16
4th Bradley, William W.	Dem	N.J.	15	14
5th Bingaman, J.F. (Jeff)	Dem	N.M.	11	8
6th Akaka, Daniel K.	Dem	Hai.	3	3
7th Shelby, Richard C.	Dem	Ala.	7	*1 2
8th Wellstone, Paul D.	DFL	Minn.	3	2
9th Campbell, Ben Nighthorse	Dem	Colo.	1	*1 1
10th Mathews, Harlan	Dem	Tenn.	1	1
11th Krueger, Robert C.	Dem	Tex.	1	1

Minority

Rank Name	Party	State	Years in: Senate	Comm.
RM Wallop, Malcolm	Rep	Wyo.	17	14
2nd Hatfield, Mark O.	Rep	Ore.	27	26
3rd Domenici, Pete V.	Rep	N.M.	21	16
4th Murkowski, Frank H.	Rep	Alas.	13	13
5th Nickles, Donald L.	Rep	Okla.	13	13
6th Craig, Larry E.	Rep	Ida.	3	2
7th Bennett, Robert F.	Rep	Utah	1	1
8th Specter, Arlen	Rep	Penn.	13	1
9th Lott, C. Trent	Rep	Miss.	5	1

*1: Member's first period of service on the committee.

Note 1: Rankings on this committee for the following members were affected by other chamber service: Mark O. Hatfield (Rep-Ore.), Ranking Minority Member, Appropriations; and Pete V. Domenici (Rep-N.M.), Ranking Minority Member, Budget.

Note 2: Although Krueger was listed as being on the committee on Jan. 7, 1993, he was not formally named until Jan. 21, 1993, when he replaced Conrad who had left the committee to replace Bentsen on Finance.

Changes:

Majority:

Conrad, Kent	Dem	N.D.	Jan. 21, 1993 Left the committee; moved to Finance.
Krueger, Robert C.	Dem	Tex.	Jan. 21, 1993 Replaced Conrad.
Krueger, Robert C.	Dem	Tex.	June 14, 1993 Resigned the Senate; defeated in special election by Kay Bailey Hutchison (Rep-Tex.).
Dorgan, Byron L.	Dem	N.D.	July 15, 1993 Replaced Krueger.
Mathews, Harlan	Dem	Tenn.	Dec. 1, 1994 Resigned the Senate; replaced by special election winner Fred D. Thompson (Rep-Tenn.).

Departures from the Senate:	Majority			Minority		
Retired	None			Wallop, Malcolm	Rep	Wyo.

Departures from Committee:						
Elected Majority Whip	None			Lott, C. Trent	Rep	Miss.
Moved to Appropriations	Shelby, Richard C.	Dem	Ala.	Bennett, Robert F.	Rep	Utah
Moved to Select Intelligence	Shelby, Richard C.	Dem	Ala.	Specter, Arlen	Rep	Penn.
No new assignment	Dorgan, Byron L.	Dem	N.D.	None		

ENERGY AND NATURAL RESOURCES / 104th Congress

Service Dates of Committee Chair: Jan. 11, 1995-Jan. 9, 1997

Service Dates of Majority Members: Jan. 5, 1995-Jan. 9, 1997

Service Dates of Minority Members: Jan. 4, 1995-Jan. 9, 1997

Majority

			Years in:	
Rank Name	Party	State	Senate	Comm.
Chr Murkowski, Frank H.	Rep	Alas.	15	15
2nd Hatfield, Mark O.	Rep	Ore.	29	28
3rd Domenici, Pete V.	Rep	N.M.	23	18
4th Nickles, Donald L.	Rep	Okla.	15	15
5th Craig, Larry E.	Rep	Ida.	5	4
6th Thomas, Craig L.	Rep	Wyo.	1	1
7th Kyl, Jon L.	Rep	Ariz.	1	*1 1
8th Grams, Rod	Rep	Minn.	1	1
9th Jeffords, James M.	Rep	Vt.	7	1
10th Burns, Conrad	Rep	Mont.	7	*2 1

Minority

			Years in:	
Rank Name	Party	State	Senate	Comm.
RM Johnston, J. Bennett Jr.	Dem	La.	23	23
2nd Bumpers, Dale	Dem	Ark.	21	21
3rd Ford, Wendell H.	Dem	Ky.	21	18
4th Bradley, William W.	Dem	N.J.	17	16
5th Bingaman, J.F. (Jeff)	Dem	N.M.	13	10
6th Akaka, Daniel K.	Dem	Hai.	5	5
7th Wellstone, Paul D.	DFL	Minn.	5	4
8th Campbell, Ben Nighthorse	Dem	Colo.	3	*1 2

*1: Member's first period of service on the committee.

*2: Member's second period of service on the committee.

Note: 1: Rankings on this committee for the following members were affected by other chamber service: Mark O. Hatfield (Rep-Ore.), Chair, Appropriations; and Pete V. Domenici (Rep-N.M.), Chair, Budget.

Note 2: Campbell switched to the Republican Party on Mar. 4, 1995, and was seated 6th on the majority side on Mar. 24, 1995, shifting the party ratio from 10-8 to 11-7. To replace Campbell, Democrats named Howell T. Heflin (Dem-Ala.) on Mar. 28, 1995, who had served on the committee previously. Byron L. Dorgan (Dem-N.D.) was also added on Mar. 28, 1995, to restore an appropriate ratio of 11-9.

Changes:

Minority:

Campbell, Ben Nighthorse	Dem	Colo.	Mar. 3, 1995 Seat as minority Democrat vacated; returned as a majority Republican addition on Mar. 24, 1995 ranking 6th.
Heflin, Howell T.	Dem	Ala.	Mar. 28, 1995 Replaced Campbell.
Dorgan, Byron L.	Dem	N.D.	Mar. 28, 1995 Added in 9th minority slot

Departures from the Senate:

	Majority			Minority		
Retired	Hatfield, Mark O.	Rep	Ore.	Johnston, J. Bennett Jr.	Dem	La.
				Bradley, William W.	Dem	N.J.
				Heflin, Howell T.	Dem	Ala.

Departures from Committee:

Moved to Finance	Jeffords, James M.	Rep	Vt.	None		
Moved to Foreign Relations	None			Wellstone, Paul D.	DFL	Minn.

ENERGY AND NATURAL RESOURCES / 105th Congress

Service Dates of Committee Chair: Jan. 9, 1997-Jan. 7, 1999

Service Dates of Majority Members: Jan. 9, 1997-Jan. 7, 1999

Service Dates of Minority Members: Jan. 9, 1997-Jan. 7, 1999

Majority

			Years in:	
Rank Name	Party	State	Senate	Comm.
Chr Murkowski, Frank H.	Rep	Alas.	17	17
2nd Domenici, Pete V.	Rep	N.M.	25	20
3rd Nickles, Donald L.	Rep	Okla.	17	17
4th Craig, Larry E.	Rep	Ida.	7	6
5th Campbell, Ben Nighthorse	Rep	Colo.	5	*2 2
6th Thomas, Craig L.	Rep	Wyo.	3	3
7th Kyl, Jon L.	Rep	Ariz.	3	*1 3
8th Grams, Rod	Rep	Minn.	3	3
9th Smith, Gordon H.	Rep	Ore.	1	1
10th Gorton, T. Slade III	Rep	Wash.	15	1
11th Burns, Conrad	Rep	Mont.	9	*2 3

Minority

			Years in:	
Rank Name	Party	State	Senate	Comm.
RM Bumpers, Dale	Dem	Ark.	23	23
2nd Ford, Wendell H.	Dem	Ky.	23	20
3rd Bingaman, J.F. (Jeff)	Dem	N.M.	15	12
4th Akaka, Daniel K.	Dem	Hai.	7	7
5th Dorgan, Byron L.	Dem	N.D.	5	*2 2
6th Graham, D. Robert	Dem	Fla.	11	1
7th Wyden, Ronald L.	Dem	Ore.	2	1
8th Johnson, Timothy P.	Dem	S.D.	1	1
9th Landrieu, Mary L.	Dem	La.	1	1

*1: Member's first period of service on the committee.

*2: Member's second period of service on the committee.

Note: Ranking on this committee for the following members was affected by other chamber service: Pete V. Domenici (Rep-N.M.), Chair, Budget.

Departures from the Senate:	Majority			Minority		
Retired	None			Bumpers, Dale	Dem	Ark.
				Ford, Wendell H.	Dem	Ky.

Departures from Committee:					
Moved to Appropriations and Special Year 2000 Technology Problem	Kyl, Jon L.	Rep	Ariz.	None	
No new assignment	Grams, Rod	Rep	Minn.	None	

ENERGY AND NATURAL RESOURCES / 106th Congress

Service Dates of Committee Chair: Jan. 7, 1999-Jan. 3, 2001

Service Dates of Majority Members: Jan. 7, 1999-Jan. 25, 2001

Service Dates of Minority Members: Jan. 7, 1999-Jan. 25, 2001

Majority			Years in:		Minority			Years in:	
Rank Name	Party	State	Senate	Comm.	Rank Name	Party	State	Senate	Comm.
Chr Murkowski, Frank H.	Rep	Alas.	19	19	RM Bingaman, J.F. (Jeff)	Dem	N.M.	17	14
2nd Domenici, Pete V.	Rep	N.M.	27	22	2nd Akaka, Daniel K.	Dem	Hai.	9	9
3rd Nickles, Donald L.	Rep	Okla.	19	19	3rd Dorgan, Byron L.	Dem	N.D.	7	*2 4
4th Craig, Larry E.	Rep	Ida.	9	8	4th Graham, D. Robert	Dem	Fla.	13	2
5th Campbell, Ben Nighthorse	Rep	Colo.	7	*2 4	5th Wyden, Ronald L.	Dem	Ore.	4	2
6th Thomas, Craig L.	Rep	Wyo.	5	5	6th Johnson, Timothy P.	Dem	S.D.	3	2
7th Smith, Gordon H.	Rep	Ore.	3	2	7th Landrieu, Mary L.	Dem	La.	3	2
8th Bunning, James P.D.	Rep	Ky.	1	*1 1	8th Bayh, B. Evans	Dem	Ind.	1	*1 1
9th Fitzgerald, Peter G.	Rep	Ill.	1	1	9th Lincoln, Blanche Lambert	Dem	Ark.	1	*1 1
10th Gorton, T. Slade III	Rep	Wash.	17	2					
11th Burns, Conrad	Rep	Mont.	11	*2 5					

*1: Member's first period of service on the committee.

*2: Member's second period of service on the committee.

Note: Ranking on this committee for the following members was affected by other chamber service: Pete V. Domenici (Rep-N.M.), Chair, Budget.

Departures from the Senate:	Majority			Minority		
Defeated for Re-election	Gorton, T. Slade III	Rep	Wash.	None		

Departures from Committee:						
Moved to Armed Services	Bunning, James P.D.	Rep	Ky.	None		
Moved to Commerce, Science, Transportation, and Special Aging	Fitzgerald, Peter G.	Rep	Ill.	None		
Moved to Finance and Select Ethics	None			Lincoln, Blanche Lambert	Dem	Ark.

ENERGY AND NATURAL RESOURCES / 107th Congress, Pre-Jeffords switch

Service Dates of Committee Chair: ChT: Jan. 3, 2001-Jan. 25, 2001 Bingaman (Dem-N.M.)

Ch1: Jan. 25, 2001-June 6, 2001 Murkowski (Rep-Alas.)

Service Dates of Majority Members: Jan. 25, 2001-June 6, 2001

Service Dates of Minority Members: Jan. 25, 2001-June 6, 2001

Majority			Years in:		Minority			Years in:	
Rank Name	Party	State	Senate	Comm.	Rank Name	Party	State	Senate	Comm.
Ch1 Murkowski, Frank H.	Rep	Alas.	21	21	RM1 Bingaman, J.F. (Jeff)	Dem	N.M.	19	16
2nd Domenici, Pete V.	Rep	N.M.	29	24	2nd Akaka, Daniel K.	Dem	Hai.	11	11
3rd Nickles, Donald L.	Rep	Okla.	21	21	3rd Dorgan, Byron L.	Dem	N.D.	9	*2 6
4th Craig, Larry E.	Rep	Ida.	11	10	4th Graham, D. Robert	Dem	Fla.	15	5
5th Campbell, Ben Nighthorse	Rep	Colo.	9	*2 6	5th Wyden, Ronald L.	Dem	Ore.	6	5
6th Thomas, Craig L.	Rep	Wyo.	7	7	6th Johnson, Timothy P.	Dem	S.D.	5	5
7th Shelby, Richard C.	Rep	Ala.	15	*2 1	7th Landrieu, Mary L.	Dem	La.	5	5
8th Burns, Conrad	Rep	Mont.	13	*2 7	8th Bayh, B. Evans	Dem	Ind.	3	*1 3
9th Kyl, Jon L.	Rep	Ariz.	7	*2 1	9th Feinstein, Dianne	Dem	Cal.	9	1

10th Hagel, Charles T. (Chuck)	Rep	Neb.	5	1		10th Schumer, Charles E.	Dem	N.Y.	3	1
11th Smith, Gordon H.	Rep	Ore.	5	5		11th Cantwell, Maria E.	Dem	Wash.	1	1

*1: Member's first period of service on the committee.
*2: Member's second period of service on the committee.

Note 1: Ranking on this committee for the following members was affected by other chamber service: Pete V. Domenici (Rep-N.M.), Chair, Budget.

Note 2: The committee majority in the 2001 Senate power-sharing arrangement was determined by the party of the vice president. Democrat Al Gore Jr. served from Jan. 3, 2001, to Jan. 20, 2001, and was succeeded by Republican Richard B. Cheney on Jan. 20, 2001. When Senator Jeffords of Vermont left the Republican Party, effective June 6, 2001, to become an Independent, Democrats regained the majority for the remainder of the 107th Congress.

ENERGY AND NATURAL RESOURCES / 107th Congress, Post-Jeffords switch

Service Dates of Committee Chair: June 6, 2001-Jan. 15, 2003
Service Dates of Majority Members: June 6, 2001-Jan. 15, 2003
Service Dates of Minority Members: June 6, 2001-Jan. 15, 2003

Majority						Minority				
			Years in:						Years in:	
Rank Name	Party	State	Senate	Comm.		Rank Name	Party	State	Senate	Comm.
Ch2 Bingaman, J.F. (Jeff)	Dem	N.M.	19	17		RM2 Murkowski, Frank H.	Rep	Alas.	21	21
2nd Akaka, Daniel K.	Dem	Hai.	12	12		2nd Domenici, Pete V.	Rep	N.M.	29	25
3rd Dorgan, Byron L.	Dem	N.D.	9	*2 7		3rd Nickles, Donald L.	Rep	Okla.	21	21
4th Graham, D. Robert	Dem	Fla.	15	5		4th Craig, Larry E.	Rep	Ida.	11	11
5th Wyden, Ronald L.	Dem	Ore.	6	5		5th Campbell, Ben Nighthorse	Rep	Colo.	9	*2 7
6th Johnson, Timothy P.	Dem	S.D.	5	5		6th Thomas, Craig L.	Rep	Wyo.	7	7
7th Landrieu, Mary L.	Dem	La.	5	5		7th Shelby, Richard C.	Rep	Ala.	15	*2 1
8th Bayh, B. Evans	Dem	Ind.	3	*1 3		8th Burns, Conrad	Rep	Mont.	13	*2 7
9th Feinstein, Dianne	Dem	Cal.	9	1		9th Kyl, Jon L.	Rep	Ariz.	7	*2 1
10th Schumer, Charles E.	Dem	N.Y.	3	1		10th Hagel, Charles T. (Chuck)	Rep	Neb.	5	1
11th Cantwell, Maria E.	Dem	Wash.	1	1		11th Smith, Gordon H.	Rep	Ore.	5	5
12th Carper, Thomas R.	Dem	Del.	1	1						

*1: Member's first period of service on the committee.
*2: Member's second period of service on the committee.

Note: Ranking on this committee for the following members was affected by other chamber service: Pete V. Domenici (Rep-N.M.), Ranking Minority Member, Budget.

Additions:
  Majority:

12th Carper, Thomas R.	Dem	Del.	July 10, 2001

Changes:
  Minority:

Murkowski, Frank H.	Dem	Alas.	Dec. 2, 2002 Resigned the Senate; elected Governor of Alaska.

Departures from Committee:

	Majority				Minority		
Moved to Governmental Affairs	None				Shelby, Richard C.	Rep	Ala.
Moved to Select Intelligence	None				Hagel, Charles T. (Chuck)	Rep	Neb.
No new assignment	Carper, Thomas R.	Dem	Del.		None		

ENERGY AND NATURAL RESOURCES / 108th Congress

Service Dates of Committee Chair: Jan. 15, 2003-Jan. 6, 2005
Service Dates of Majority Members: Jan. 15, 2003-Jan. 6, 2005
Service Dates of Minority Members: Jan. 15, 2003-Jan. 6, 2005

Majority						Minority				
			Years in:						Years in:	
Rank Name	Party	State	Senate	Comm.		Rank Name	Party	State	Senate	Comm.
Chr Domenici, Pete V.	Rep	N.M.	31	26		RM Bingaman, J.F. (Jeff)	Dem	N.M.	21	18
2nd Nickles, Donald L.	Rep	Okla.	23	23		2nd Akaka, Daniel K.	Dem	Hai.	13	13
3rd Craig, Larry E.	Rep	Ida.	13	12		3rd Dorgan, Byron L.	Dem	N.D.	11	*2 8
4th Campbell, Ben Nighthorse	Rep	Colo.	11	*2 8		4th Graham, D. Robert	Dem	Fla.	17	7
5th Thomas, Craig L.	Rep	Wyo.	9	9		5th Wyden, Ronald L.	Dem	Ore.	8	7
6th Alexander, Lamar	Rep	Tenn.	1	1		6th Johnson, Timothy P.	Dem	S.D.	7	7

7th Murkowski, Lisa	Rep	Alas.	1	1
8th Talent, James M.	Rep	Mo.	1	1
9th Burns, Conrad	Rep	Mont.	15	*2 9
10th Smith, Gordon H.	Rep	Ore.	7	7
11th Bunning, James P.D.	Rep	Ky.	5	*2 1
12th Kyl, Jon L.	Rep	Ariz.	9	*2 2

7th Landrieu, Mary L.	Dem	La.	7	7
8th Bayh, B. Evans	Dem	Ind.	5	*1 5
9th Feinstein, Dianne	Dem	Cal.	11	2
10th Schumer, Charles E.	Dem	N.Y.	5	2
11th Cantwell, Maria E.	Dem	Wash.	3	2

*1: Member's first period of service on the committee.
*2: Member's second period of service on the committee.

Departures from the Senate:	Majority			Minority		
Retired	Nickles, Donald L.	Rep	Okla.	Graham, D. Robert	Dem	Fla.
	Campbell, Ben Nighthorse	Rep	Colo.			

Departures from Committee:						
Moved to Finance	None			Schumer, Charles E.	Dem	N.Y.
No new assignment	Kyl, Jon L.	Rep	Ariz.	Bayh, B. Evans	Dem	Ind.

ENERGY AND NATURAL RESOURCES / 109th Congress

Service Dates of Committee Chair: Jan. 6, 2005-Jan. 12, 2007

Service Dates of Majority Members: Jan. 6, 2005-Jan. 12, 2007

Service Dates of Minority Members: Jan. 6, 2005-Jan. 12, 2007

Majority			Years in:		Minority			Years in:	
Rank Name	Party	State	Senate	Comm.	Rank Name	Party	State	Senate	Comm.
Chr Domenici, Pete V.	Rep	N.M.	33	28	RM Bingaman, J.F. (Jeff)	Dem	N.M.	23	20
2nd Craig, Larry E.	Rep	Ida.	15	14	2nd Akaka, Daniel K.	Dem	Hai.	15	15
3rd Thomas, Craig L.	Rep	Wyo.	11	11	3rd Dorgan, Byron L.	Dem	N.D.	13	*2 10
4th Alexander, Lamar	Rep	Tenn.	3	2	4th Wyden, Ronald L.	Dem	Ore.	10	8
5th Murkowski, Lisa	Rep	Alas.	3	2	5th Johnson, Timothy P.	Dem	S.D.	9	8
6th Burr, Richard M.	Rep	N.C.	1	1	6th Landrieu, Mary L.	Dem	La.	9	8
7th Martinez, Melquiades R. (Mel)	Rep	Fla.	1	1	7th Feinstein, Dianne	Dem	Cal.	13	4
8th Talent, James M.	Rep	Mo.	3	2	8th Cantwell, Maria E.	Dem	Wash.	5	4
9th Burns, Conrad	Rep	Mont.	17	*2 11	9th Corzine, Jon S.	Dem	N.J.	5	1
10th Allen, George F.	Rep	Va.	5	1	10th Salazar, Kenneth L.	Dem	Colo.	1	1
11th Smith, Gordon H.	Rep	Ore.	9	8					
12th Bunning, James P.D.	Rep	Ky.	7	*2 2	*2: Member's second period of service on the committee.				

Changes:

Minority:

Corzine, Jon S.	Dem	N.J.	Jan. 17, 2006 Resigned the Senate; elected Governor of New Jersey.
Menendez, Robert	Dem	N.J.	Jan. 18, 2006 Replaced Corzine.

Departures from the Senate:	Majority			Minority
Defeated for Re-election	Talent, James M,	Rep	Mo.	None
	Burns, Conrad	Rep	Mont.	
	Allen, George F.	Rep	Va.	

Departures from Committee:						
Became Chair of Rules and Administration; moved to Joint Library and Joint Printing	None			Feinstein, Dianne	Dem	Cal.
Moved to Appropriations, Environment and Public Works, and Rules and Administration	Alexander, Lamar	Rep	Tenn.	None		

ENERGY AND NATURAL RESOURCES / 110th Congress

Service Dates of Committee Chair: Jan. 12, 2007-Jan. 21, 2009

Service Dates of Majority Members: Jan. 12, 2007-Jan. 21, 2009

Service Dates of Minority Members: Jan. 12, 2007-Jan. 21, 2009

Majority					Minority				
			Years in:					**Years in:**	
Rank Name	**Party**	**State**	**Senate**	**Comm.**	**Rank Name**	**Party**	**State**	**Senate**	**Comm.**
Chr Bingaman, J.F. (Jeff)	Dem	N.M.	25	22	RM Domenici, Pete V.	Rep	N.M.	35	30
2nd Akaka, Daniel K.	Dem	Hai.	17	17	2nd Craig, Larry E.	Rep	Ida.	17	16
3rd Dorgan, Byron L.	Dem	N.D.	15	*2 12	3rd Thomas, Craig L.	Rep	Wyo.	13	13
4th Wyden, Ronald L.	Dem	Ore.	12	11	4th Murkowski, Lisa	Rep	Ala.s.	5	4
5th Johnson, Timothy P.	Dem	S.D.	11	11	5th Burr, Richard M.	Rep	N.C.	3	3
6th Landrieu, Mary L.	Dem	La.	11	11	6th DeMint, James W.	Rep	S.C.	3	1
7th Cantwell, Maria E.	Dem	Wash.	7	6	7th Corker, Robert	Rep	Tenn.	1	1
8th Salazar, Kenneth L.	Dem	Colo.	3	3	8th Sessions, Jefferson B. III	Rep	Ala.	11	1
9th Menendez, Robert	Dem	N.J.	1	1	9th Smith, Gordon H.	Rep	Ore.	11	11
10th Lincoln, Blanche Lambert	Dem	Ark.	9	*2 1	10th Bunning, James P.D.	Rep	Ky.	9	*2 4
11th Sanders, Bernard	Ind	Vt.	1	1	11th Martinez, Melquiades R. (Mel)	Rep	Fla.	3	3
12th Tester, Jon	Dem	Mont.	1	1					

*2: Member's second period of service on the committee.

Changes:

Minority:

Thomas, Craig L.	Rep	Wyo.		June 4, 2007 Died in office.
Barrasso, John A.	Rep	Wyo.		July 10, 2007 Replaced Thomas; ranked following Corker.

Departures from the Senate:	**Majority**			**Minority**		
Defeated for Re-election	None			Smith, Gordon H.	Rep	Ore.
Retired	None			Domenici, Pete V.	Rep	N.M.
				Craig, Larry E.	Rep	Ida.

Departures from Committee:						
Moved to Appropriations	Tester, Jon	Dem	Mont.	None		
Moved to Banking, Housing, and Urban Affairs	None			DeMint, James W.	Rep	S.C.
Moved to Commerce, Science, and Transportation	None			Martinez, Melquiades R. (Mel)	Rep	Fla.
No new assignment	Akaka, Daniel K.	Dem	Hai.	None		

Note: Kenneth L. Salazar (Dem-Colo.) resigned the Senate Jan. 20, 2009; named Secretary of the Interior

---

ENERGY AND NATURAL RESOURCES / 111th Congress

Service Dates of Committee Chair: Jan. 21, 2009-

Service Dates of Majority Members: Jan. 21, 2009-

Service Dates of Minority Members: Jan. 21, 2009-

Majority					Minority				
			Years in:					**Years in:**	
Rank Name	**Party**	**State**	**Senate**	**Comm.**	**Rank Name**	**Party**	**State**	**Senate**	**Comm.**
Chr Bingaman, J.F. (Jeff)	Dem	N.M.	27	24	RM Murkowski, Lisa	Rep	Alas.	7	7
2nd Dorgan, Byron L.	Dem	N.D.	17	*2 14	2nd Burr, Richard M.	Rep	N.C.	5	5
3rd Wyden, Ronald L.	Dem	Ore.	14	13	3rd Barrasso, John A.	Rep	Wyo.	2	2
4th Johnson, Timothy P.	Dem	S.D.	13	13	4th Brownback, Sam D.	Rep	Kans.	13	1
5th Landrieu, Mary L.	Dem	La.	13	13	5th Risch, James	Rep	Ida.	1	1
6th Cantwell, Maria E.	Dem	Wash.	9	8	6th McCain, John S. III	Rep	Ariz.	23	1
7th Menendez, Robert	Dem	N.J.	4	4	7th Bennett, Robert F.	Rep	Utah	17	1
8th Lincoln, Blanche Lambert	Dem	Ark.	11	*2 3	8th Bunning, James P.D.	Rep	Ky.	11	*2 7
9th Sanders, Bernard	Ind	Vt.	3	3	9th Sessions, Jefferson B. III	Rep	Ala.	13	2
10th Bayh, B. Evans	Dem	Ind.	11	*2 1	10th Corker, Robert	Rep	Tenn.	3	3
11th Stabenow, Deborah Ann	Dem	Mich.	9	1					
12th Udall, Mark	Dem	Colo.	1	1					
13th Shaheen, Jeanne	Dem	N.H.	1	1					

*2: Member's second period of service on the committee.

Environment and Public Works

Senate Committee on Environment and Public Works, 103rd-111th Congresses (1993-2011)

BACKGROUND

Organizational History: The Senate Committee on Environment and Public Works grew out of the Committee on Public Works, which was established on January 2, 1947, by the Legislative Reorganization Act of 1946. The Public Works Committee inherited the legislative duties of the Committee on Public Buildings and Grounds, some jurisdictional areas of the Committee on Commerce and the highways responsibility of the former committee on Post Offices and Post Roads.

The committee's initial predecessor, Roads and Canals, was established as a standing committee on February 8, 1820, following approval of a motion of William A. Trimble of Ohio. Rufus King (Fed-N.Y.) was appointed chair. The Committee on Public Buildings and Grounds began as a joint committee in the 25th Congress and was replaced with a standing committee on December 6, 1838. Its major mission in the nineteenth century was to improve and expand the Capitol Building and its grounds and to oversee the construction of federal office buildings, courthouses, and post offices throughout the United States.

With the creation of the Public Works Committee in 1946, jurisdiction of the original Public Buildings and Grounds Committee was augmented with responsibilities formerly handled by the Committee on Commerce. Among these were: flood control and improvement of rivers and harbors, public works for the benefit of navigation, bridges, dams, water power projects, and prevention of oil and other pollution of navigable waters. It also received jurisdiction from the Committee on Post Offices and Post Roads over the construction and maintenance of Federal highways.

The growth of environmental awareness and the impact of industrial pollution upon the lives of Americans led the committee to undergo yet another change in its focus. The Public Works Committee was reorganized as the Committee on Environment and Public Works following the passage of Senate Resolution 4, the Committee System Reorganization Amendments of 1977.

Although the committee's jurisdiction was extended to cover regional economic development, the bulk of its new responsibilities were derived from environmental issues. It now became responsible for legislation and matters pertaining to environmental policy in general; environmental research and development; ocean dumping; fisheries and wildlife; the environmental aspects of Outer Continental Shelf lands; solid waste disposal and recycling; environmental effects of toxic substances, excluding pesticides; water resources; environmental aspects of deepwater ports; air and noise pollution; and nonmilitary environmental regulation and control of nuclear energy.

The decade of the 1970's was the heyday of the committee, a time when landmark environmental laws were passed and federal money still flowed freely for the public works activities that it championed. In recent times, the committee has not fared as well. In spite of its "pork barrel" opportunities for supplying roads, bridges, and dams back home, the Environment and Public Works Committee has not been a very large Senate committee, unlike its House counterpart, the mammoth Transportation and Infrastructure Committee

Membership: The Public Works Committee had thirteen members in its initial Congress, the 80th, and its renamed successor, Environment and Public Works, hit a peak membership of nineteen in the aftermath of the Jeffords switch in 2001 and held at that number in the 111th Congress (2009-2011). Since 1993, its average size of 18.3 members places it in thirteenth place among the Senate's sixteen standing committees. The committee's mean seniority for its members is 9.99 years, placing it thirteenth as well, and its mean inter-Congress retention rate of 81.46 percent places it in last place, just below Homeland Security and Governmental Affairs.

Other evidence of the Environment Committee's difficulty in retaining members is the fact that it has lost twenty-five members since 1993, while gaining only five, for a net loss of twenty, the highest net loss of any of the Senate's standing committees. Wyoming Republican Craig Thomas who moved back and forth between Agriculture, Nutrition, and Forestry and Environment and Public Works accounted for two of its twenty-four departures and two of its five gains, and A. Wayne Allard (Rep-Colo.) accounted for one gain from Agriculture and two departures—to Armed Services in 1999 and Appropriations in 2005. With four members each, the Finance and HELP committees were the major destinations of Environment Committee departing members, with three each moving to Armed Services and Homeland Security and Governmental Affairs, including Senator Barack Obama (Dem-Ill.)

The committee also witnessed the second notable father-son team of John H. Chafee (Rep-R.I.) and Lincoln D. Chafee (Rep-R.I.) who resembled the Byrds of Virginia, when the son not only filled his father's seat in the Senate, but also was assigned to fill his father's vacancy on Environment and Public Works.

Committee Leaders: W. Chapman Revercomb (Rep-W. Va.) was the first post-reorganization chair having served on one its predecessor committees, Public Buildings and Grounds. His service ended with his defeat in 1948. Dennis Chavez of New Mexico, who had served as ranking minority member in the 80th Congress after the 1948 death of Louisiana's John H. Overton, was the committee's first Democratic chair. Chavez chaired the committee in six of seven Congresses between 1949 and his death in 1962. Chavez was succeeded by Patrick V. McNamara of Michigan, who held the chair from 1963 until his death in 1966. It was then that Jennings Randolph from the coal-mining state of West Virginia began his almost nineteen years as the committee's senior Democrat, serving as chair from 1966 to 1981 and as ranking minority member from 1981 to 1985 when he retired.

While Republican Harry Cain of Washington State served as ranking member in the Democratic 81st and 82nd Congresses (1949-1953), it was Edward Martin of Pennsylvania who got to serve as chair in the Republican-controlled 83rd Congress (1953-1955). Martin served as ranking member from 1955 to 1959 when he retired and was succeeded by Francis H. Case of South Dakota, whose service as ranking member from 1959 ended with his death in 1962. Case was followed by John Sherman Cooper of Kentucky, who had returned to the committee in 1959 after an earlier defeat and would serve as the committee's senior Republican from 1962 until his retirement in 1972. Howard Baker of Tennessee succeeded Cooper in 1973 and served as ranking member for four years until his election as Minority Leader in 1977. That year, the committee was renamed Environment and Public Works and environmentally conscious Robert T. Stafford of Vermont became its ranking member and would become chair in 1981 when the Republicans gained the Senate in 1980 after a twenty-six year lapse.

Stafford held the senior Republican rank for twelve years as chair from 1981 through 1987 and ranking member again in 1987 through 1989 and his retirement. Although Stafford spent eight years serving alongside Jennings Randolph, his Democratic counterpart, he spent two years with Lloyd M. Bentsen of Texas as ranking member for just the 99th Congress (1985-1987), when Bentsen left the committee to move to Commerce, Science and Transportation.

Bentsen's departure and the return of Democratic control enabled Quentin N. Burdick of North Dakota to gain the chairmanship and he served from 1987 until his death in 1992. Daniel Patrick Moynihan (Dem-N.Y.) held the post for just a few months between Burdick's death in September 1992 and his departure to chair Finance in January 1993. Stafford's retirement in 1988 led John H. Chafee, another New England environmentalist, to become the committee's senior Republican for the next eleven years until his death in 1999, serving as ranking member for six years (1989-1995) and as chair for five years (1995-1999).

Max S. Baucus (Dem-Mont.) followed Moynihan and held the senior Democratic rank for the next eight years (1993-2001), the first two as chair and the next six as ranking minority member (1995-2001). Baucus became ranking member on Finance in January 2001 and relinquished his senior role on the Environment Committee to Harry M. Reid of Nevada, who would then cede the post six months later to Vermont's James M. Jeffords, whose June 2001 decision to leave the Republican Party to become an independent shifted control of the Senate to the Democrats. Jeffords had served on the committee earlier in his Senate career as a Republican (1989-1993) and would serve in the senior Democratic slot as an Independent who caucused with the Democrats until his 2006 retirement. He surrendered his chairmanship of the Senate Committee on Health, Education, Labor, and Pensions when he declared his independence and was able to extract the chairmanship of Environment and Public Works from a grateful Democratic Caucus.

When John Chafee died in October, 1999, New Hampshire's Robert C. Smith replaced him as chair. Smith had dropped out of the Republican Party for a few months earlier that year but returned when he realized that he was next-in-line to succeed Chafee as chair. Smith's renomination defeat to John Sununu ended his Senate career in 2002. Smith was succeeded as chair by James M. Inhofe of Oklahoma,

who has held the senior Republican rank for the past eight years—four as chair (2003-2007) and four as ranking minority member (2007-2011). Succeeding Jeffords in the senior Democratic rank was Barbara Boxer of California, who has chaired the committee for the last four years (2007-2011).

Party Leaders: Democrats have relied less on this committee as a training ground for their leaders as only three Democratic leaders served on the committee—Earle C. Clements of Kentucky, the Democratic Whip in 1953-1957 and two contemporary floor leaders—George S. Mitchell of Maine, the Democratic floor leader from 1989 to 1995, and Harry Reid of Nevada, the current Democratic leader who served as Whip in 1999-2005 and became floor leader following Thomas Daschle of South Dakota's defeat in 2004.

Four Republicans who served on the Environment Committee and its Public Works predecessor served as floor leaders and four as party Whips. Among the leaders were: Hugh D. Scott Jr. of Pennsylvania who led the Senate Republicans from 1969 to 1977; Howard W. Baker Jr. of Tennessee who succeeded Scott in 1977 and served as leader until 1985, when he was succeeded by Bob Dole of Kansas who served as leader from 1985 until he resigned in 1996 to pursue yet again his presidential aspirations. The present Republican floor leader Mitch McConnell of Kentucky is the fourth alumnus of the committee to lead the Senate Republicans. While both Scott and McConnell served apprenticeships as Republican Whips before becoming floor leaders, four other former members of the Environment Committee served only as Whips—Thomas H. Kuchel of California (1959-1969); Robert P. Griffin of Michigan (1969-1977); Theodore F. Stevens of Alaska (1977-1985) and Alan Simpson of Wyoming (1985-1995). Among the seven former leaders, five retired—Scott, Baker, Griffin, Dole, and Simpson, while Kuchel lost his renomination in 1968 and Stevens lost his bid for re-election in 2008.

Presidential Aspirations: Eight senators who served on the Environment Committee and its predecessors have been nominated for either president or vice president. Seven were Democrats but the only presidential nominee among them was Barack Obama, who was nominated and elected in 2008. The other six Democrats were vice presidential nominees—John Sparkman of Alabama on the 1952 Stevenson ticket; Edmund Muskie of Maine on the 1968 Humphrey ticket; Thomas Eagleton, the short-lived vice presidential nominee on the McGovern ticket in 1972; Lloyd M. Bentsen of Texas on the 1988 Dukakis ticket; Joseph I. Lieberman of Connecticut on the 2000 Gore ticket; and Joseph R. Biden of Delaware, who successfully joined Obama on the 2008 ticket. Only the Obama-Biden pairing was successful and it is clear that they share an environmentalist commitment even though Biden's service on the committee was a fleeting one three decades earlier.

The only Republican alumnus of the committee to be nominated was Robert J. Dole of Kansas, an unsuccessful vice presidential nominee in 1976 and presidential one in 1996.

Other Notables: Three Democratic alumni of the Environment and Public Works Committee left to join the Cabinet and each received a prominent post: Edmund Muskie of Maine was President Jimmy Carter's second Secretary of State; Lloyd Bentsen of Texas was President Bill Clinton's first Secretary of the Treasury; and Hillary Rodham Clinton was named in 2009 to be President Barack Obama's Secretary of State. The only present-day senator on the Environment Committee with Cabinet experience is Lamar Alexander (Rep-Tenn.), who served as Secretary of Education under President George H.W. Bush.

Three post-1993 members of the committee left the Senate to become governors of their states—Republicans Dirk Kempthorne of Idaho in 1999 and Frank Murkowski of Alaska in 2002 and Democrat Jon S. Corzine of New Jersey in 2006. While Murkowski lost his renomination bid to Sarah Palin in 2006 and Corzine lost his re-election bid to Chris Christie in 2009, Kempthorne was re-elected and returned to Washington as President George W. Bush's second Secretary of the Interior in 2006.

Selected References

Asbell, Bernard, *The Senate Nobody Knows* (Garden City, N.Y.: Doubleday, 1978)

Bryner, Gary, *Blue Skies, Green Politics: The Clean Air Act of 1990* (Washington, D.C.: CQ Press, 1993)

Cohen, Richard E., *Washington at Work: Back Rooms and Clean Air*, 2nd ed. (Needham Heights, Mass.: Allyn and Bacon, 1995).

Coren, Robert W., et al., "Records of the Committee on Public Works and Related Committees, 1820-1968," *Guide to the Records of the United States Senate at the National Archives: 1789-1989 Bicentennial Edition* (Washington, D.C.: National Archives and Records Administration, 1989), 185-189.

Evans, C. Lawrence, *Leadership in Committee: A Comparative Analysis of Leadership Behavior in* the *U.S. Senate* (Ann Arbor: University of Michigan, 2001).

Melnick, R. Shep, "Environment and Public Works Committee, Senate," in Donald C. Bacon, Roger H. Davidson, and Morton Keller, eds., *The Encyclopedia of the United States Congress* (New York: Simon & Schuster, 1995), I: 770-771.

Reid, T.R., *Congressional Odyssey: The Saga of a Senate Bill* (San Francisco: W.H. Freeman, 1980).

U.S. Senate, Environment and Public Works Committee, *History of the Committee on Environment and Public Works,* Senate Document 100-45, 100th Congress, 2nd session (1988).

RESPONSIBILITIES, JURISDICTIONAL CHANGES, AND SUBCOMMITTEES

PUBLIC WORKS

Jurisdiction, 80th Congress (1947-49)

Established by the Legislative Reorganization Act of 1946:

[Section 102.(1)(n)]

(1) The **Committee on Public Works**, to consist of thirteen Senators, to which committee shall be referred all proposed legislation, messages, petitions, memorials and other matters relating to the following subjects:

  (1) Flood control and improvement of rivers and harbors
  (2) Public works for the benefit of navigation, and bridges and dams (other than international bridges and dams)
  (3) Water power
  (4) Oil and other pollution of navigable waters
  (5) Public buildings and occupied or improved grounds of the United States generally
  (6) Measures relating to the purchase of sites and construction of post offices, customhouses, Federal courthouses, and Government buildings within the District of Columbia
  (7) Measures relating to the Capitol building and the Senate and House Office Buildings
  (8) Measures relating to the construction or reconstruction, maintenance, and care of the buildings and grounds of the Botanic Gardens, the Library of Congress, and the Smithsonian Institution
  (9) Public reservations and parks within the District of Columbia, including Rock Creek Park and the Zoological Park
  (10) Measures relating to the construction or maintenance of roads and post roads

Committee Reorganization, 1977

The Senate Committee on Public Works was reorganized as the Committee on Environment and Public Works following the passage of Senate Resolution 4, the Committee System Reorganization Amendments of 1977, February 4, 1977.

ENVIRONMENT AND PUBLIC WORKS

Reorganized Jurisdiction, 1977

From Senate Resolution 4, the Committee System Reorganization Amendments of 1977, February 4, 1977:

[Rule XXV.(1)(h)]

(1) **Committee on Environment and Public Works**, to which committee shall be referred all proposed legislation, messages, petitions, memorials, and other matters relating to the following subjects:

  (1) Environmental Policy
  (2) Environmental research and development
  (3) Ocean dumping

    (4) Fisheries and wildlife

    (5) Environmental aspects of Outer Continental Shelf lands

    (6) Solid waste disposal and recycling

    (7) Environmental effects of toxic substances, other than pesticides

    (8) Water resources

    (9) Flood control and improvements of rivers and harbors, including environmental aspects of deepwater ports

  (10) Public works, bridges, and dams

  (11) Water pollution

  (12) Air pollution

  (13) Noise pollution

  (14) Nonmilitary environmental regulation and control of nuclear energy

  (15) Regional economic development

  (16) Construction and maintenance of highways

  (17) Public buildings and improved grounds of the United States generally, including Federal buildings in the District of Columbia

(2) Such committee shall also study and review, on a comprehensive basis, matters relating to environmental protection and resource utilization and conservation, and report thereon from time to time.

Jurisdiction, 103rd Congress (1993-94)

From the *Standing Rules of the Senate* in the *Senate Manual*, 103rd Congress, 1st Session, S. Doc. 103-1:

[Rule XXV.(1)(h)]

(1) **Committee on Environment and Public Works**, to which committee shall be referred all proposed legislation, messages, petitions, memorials, and other matters relating to the following subjects:

    (1) Air Pollution

    (2) Construction and maintenance of highways

    (3) Environmental aspects of Outer Continental Shelf lands

    (4) Environmental effects of toxic substances, other than pesticides

    (5) Environmental policy

    (6) Environmental research and development

    (7) Fisheries and wildlife

    (8) Flood control and improvements of rivers and harbors, including environmental aspects of deepwater ports

    (9) Noise pollution

  (10) Nonmilitary environmental regulation and control of nuclear energy

  (11) Ocean dumping

  (12) Public buildings and improved grounds of the United States generally, including Federal buildings in the District of Columbia

  (13) Public works, bridges, and dams

  (14) Regional economic development

  (15) Solid waste disposal and recycling

  (16) Water pollution

  (17) Water resources

(2) Such committee shall also study and review, on a comprehensive basis, matters relating to environmental protection and resource utilization and conservation, and report thereon from time to time.

Jurisdiction, 111th Congress (2009-10)

From *Authority and Rules of Senate Committees, 2009-2010*, Sen. Doc. 111-3, pursuant to S.Res, 166, June 2, 2009.

[Rule XXV.(1)(h)]

(1) **Committee on Environment and Public Works**, to which committee shall be referred all proposed legislation, messages, petitions, memorials, and other matters relating to the following subjects:

    (1) Air pollution

    (2) Construction and maintenance of highways

    (3) Environmental aspects of Outer Continental Shelf lands

    (4) Environmental effects of toxic substances, other than pesticides

    (5) Environmental policy

    (6) Environmental research and development

    (7) Fisheries and wildlife

    (8) Flood control and improvements of rivers and harbors, including environmental aspects of deepwater ports

    (9) Noise pollution

  (10) Nonmilitary environmental regulation and control of nuclear energy

(11)   Ocean dumping
(12)   Public buildings and improved grounds of the United States generally, including Federal buildings in the District of Columbia
(13)   Public works, bridges, and dams
(14)   Regional economic development
(15)   Solid waste disposal and recycling
(16)   Water pollution
(17)   Water resources

(2) Such committee shall also study and review, on a comprehensive basis, matters relating to environmental protection and resource utilization and conservation, and report thereon from time to time.

NAMES OF SUBCOMMITTEES

Committee on Environment and Public Works, 103rd -111th Congreses

Children's Health, 111
Clean Air and Nuclear Regulation, 103
Clean Air, Wetlands, Private Property, and Nuclear Safety, 104, 105, 106
Clean Air, Wetlands, and Climate Change, 107, 108
Clean Air, Climate Change, and Nuclear Safety, 109
Clean Air and Nuclear Safety, 110, 111
Clean Water, Fisheries and Wildlife, 103
Drinking Water, Fisheries and Wildlife, 104, 105
Fisheries, Wildlife, and Drinking Water, 106
Fisheries, Wildlife, and Water, 107, 108, 109
Green Jobs and the Economy, 111
Oversight, 111
Private Sector and Consumer Solutions to Global Warming and Wildlife Protection, 110
Public Sector Solutions to Global Warming, Oversight, and Children Health Protection, 110
Superfund, Recycling and Solid Waste Management, 103
Superfund, Waste Control, and Risk Assessment, 104, 105, 106
Superfund, Toxics, Risk, and Waste Management, 107
Superfund and Waste Management, 108, 109
Superfund and Environmental Health, 110
Superfund, Toxics, and Environmental Health, 111
Toxic Substances, Research and Development, 103
Transportation and Infrastructure, 104, 105, 106, 108, 109, 110, 111
Transportation, Infrastructure, and Nuclear Energy, 107
Transportation Safety, Infrastructure Security, and Water Quality, 110
Water and Wildlife, 111
Water Resources, Transportation, Public Buildings and Economic Development, 103

MEMBERSHIP ROSTERS, 103rd-111th Congresses, 1993-2010

ENVIRONMENT AND PUBLIC WORKS / 103rd Congress

Service Dates of Committee Chair: Ch1 Jan. 7, 1993-Jan. 21, 1993 Moynihan, (D-N.Y.)

Ch2 Jan. 21, 1993-Jan. 5, 1995 Baucus, (D-Mont.)

Service Dates of Majority Members: Jan. 7, 1993-Jan. 5, 1995

Service Dates of Minority Members: Jan. 7, 1993-Jan. 4, 1995

Majority						Minority				
			Years in:						Years in:	
Rank Name	Party	State	Senate	Comm.		Rank Name	Party	State	Senate	Comm.
Ch1 Moynihan, Daniel Patrick	Dem	N.Y.	17	16		RM Chafee, John H.	Rep	R.I.	17	16
2nd Mitchell, George J.	Dem	Me.	13	13		2nd Simpson, Alan K.	Rep	Wyo.	15	14
Ch2 3rd Baucus, Max S.	Dem	Mont.	15	13		3rd Durenberger, David F.	Rep	Minn.	15	11
4th Lautenberg, Frank R.	Dem	N.J.	11	*1 9		4th Warner, John W.	Rep	Va.	15	7
5th Reid, Harry M.	Dem	Nev.	7	7		5th Smith, Robert C.	Rep	N.H.	3	2
6th Graham, D. Robert	Dem	Fla.	7	7		6th Faircloth, D.M. (Lauch)	Rep	N.C.	1	1

7th Lieberman, Joseph I.	Dem	Conn.	5	4		7th Kempthorne, Dirk	Rep	Ida.	1	1
8th Metzenbaum, Howard M.	Dem	Ohio	19	3						
9th Wofford, Harris	Dem	Penn.	2	2		*1: Member's first period of service on the committee.				
10th Boxer, Barbara	Dem	Cal.	1	1						

Changes:

Chairs:

Ch1 Moynihan, Daniel Patrick   Dem   N.Y.   Jan. 21, 1993 Relinquished Chair having become Chair of Finance on when Bentsen resigned to become Secretary of Treasury.

Ch2 Baucus, Max S.   Dem   Mont.   Jan. 21, 1993 Succeeded Moynihan as Chair.

Departures from the Senate:	**Majority**				**Minority**		
Defeated for Re-election	Wofford, Harris	Dem	Penn.		None		
Retired	Mitchell, George J.	Dem	Me.		Durenberger, David F.	Rep	Minn.
	Metzenbaum Howard M.	Dem	Ohio				

Departures from Committee:							
Moved to Finance	None				Simpson, Alan K.	Rep	Wyo.

ENVIRONMENT AND PUBLIC WORKS / 104th Congress

Service Dates of Committee Chair: Jan. 5, 1995-Jan. 9, 1997

Service Dates of Majority Members: Jan. 5, 1995-Jan. 9, 1997

Service Dates of Minority Members: Jan. 4, 1995-Jan. 9, 1997

Majority					Minority				
			Years in:					**Years in:**	
Rank Name	**Party**	**State**	**Senate**	**Comm.**	**Rank Name**	**Party**	**State**	**Senate**	**Comm.**
Chr Chafee, John H.	Rep	R.I.	19	18	RM Baucus, Max S.	Dem	Mont.	17	14
2nd Warner, John W.	Rep	Va.	17	8	2nd Moynihan, Daniel Patrick	Dem	N.Y.	19	18
3rd Smith, Robert C.	Rep	N.H.	5	4	3rd Lautenberg, Frank R.	Dem	N.J.	13	*1 10
4th Faircloth, D.M. (Lauch)	Rep	N.C.	3	2	4th Reid, Harry M.	Dem	Nev.	9	8
5th Kempthorne, Dirk	Rep	Ida.	3	2	5th Graham, D. Robert	Dem	Fla.	9	8
6th Inhofe, James M.	Rep	Okla.	1	1	6th Lieberman, Joseph I.	Dem	Conn.	7	6
7th Thomas, Craig L.	Rep	Wyo.	1	*1 1	7th Boxer, Barbara	Dem	Cal.	3	2
8th McConnell, A. Mitchell (Mitch)	Rep	Ky.	11	1	*1: Member's first period of service on the committee.				
9th Bond, Christopher S. (Kit)	Rep	Mo.	9	1					

Note: Ranking on this committee for the following member was affected by other chamber service: Daniel Patrick Moynihan (Dem-N.Y.), Ranking Minority Member, Finance.

Additions:

Majority:

10th Bennett, Robert F.   Rep   Utah   Mar. 29, 1996

Minority:

8th Wyden, Ronald L.   Dem   Ore.   Mar. 29, 1996

Departures from Committee:	**Majority**				**Minority**	
Moved to Appropriations and Small Business	Faircloth, D.M. (Lauch)	N.C.	Rep		None	
Moved to Labor and Human Resources and Joint Printing	McConnell, A. Mitchell (Mitch)	Ky.	Rep		None	
No new assignment	Bennett, Robert F.	Utah	Rep		None	

ENVIRONMENT AND PUBLIC WORKS / 105th Congress

Service Dates of Committee Chair: Jan. 9, 1997-Jan. 7, 1999

Service Dates of Majority Members: Jan. 9, 1997-Jan. 7, 1999

Service Dates of Minority Members: Jan. 9, 1997-Jan. 7, 1999

Majority					Minority				
			Years in:					**Years in:**	
Rank Name	**Party**	**State**	**Senate**	**Comm.**	**Rank Name**	**Party**	**State**	**Senate**	**Comm.**
Chr Chafee, John H.	Rep	R.I.	21	20	RM Baucus, Max S.	Dem	Mont.	19	17
2nd Warner, John W.	Rep	Va.	19	11	2nd Moynihan, Daniel Patrick	Dem	N.Y.	21	20

3rd Smith, Robert C.	Rep	N.H.	7	6
4th Kempthorne, Dirk	Rep	Ida.	5	5
5th Inhofe, James M.	Rep	Okla.	3	3
6th Thomas, Craig L.	Rep	Wyo.	3	*1 3
7th Bond, Christopher S. (Kit)	Rep	Mo.	11	3
8th Hutchinson, Y. Timothy	Rep	Ark.	1	1
9th Allard, A. Wayne	Rep	Colo.	1	*1 1
10th Sessions, Jefferson B. III	Rep	Ala.	1	1

3rd Lautenberg, Frank R.	Dem	N.J.	15	*1 13
4th Reid, Harry M.	Dem	Nev.	11	11
5th Graham, D. Robert	Dem	Fla.	11	11
6th Lieberman, Joseph I.	Dem	Conn.	9	8
7th Boxer, Barbara	Dem	Cal.	5	5
8th Wyden, Ronald L.	Dem	Ore.	2	1

*1: Member's first period of service on the committee.

Note: Ranking on this committee for the following member was affected by other chamber service: Daniel P. Moynihan (Dem-N.Y.), Ranking Minority Member, Finance.

Departures from the Senate:	Majority			Minority
Elected Governor	Kempthorne, Dirk	Rep	Ida.	None

Departures from Committee:				
Moved to Armed Services	Hutchinson, Y. Timothy	Rep	Ark.	None
	Allard, A. Wayne	Rep	Colo.	
	Sessions, Jefferson B. III	Rep	Ala.	
Moved to Special Committee on Aging	Hutchinson, Y. Timothy	Rep	Ark.	None
Moved to Labor and Human Resources	Sessions, Jefferson B. III	Rep	Ala.	None

ENVIRONMENT AND PUBLIC WORKS / 106th Congress

Service Dates of Committee Chair: Ch1 Jan. 7, 1999-Oct. 24, 1999 Chafee (Rep-R.I.)

Ch2 Nov. 9, 1999-Jan. 3, 2001 Smith (Rep-N.H.)

Service Dates of Majority Members: Jan. 7, 1999-Jan. 25, 2001

Service Dates of Minority Members: Jan. 7, 1999-Jan. 25, 2001

			Majority						Minority	
				Years in:						Years in:	
Rank Name	Party	State	Senate	Comm.		Rank Name	Party	State	Senate	Comm.
Ch1 Chafee, John H.	Rep	R.I.	23	22		RM Baucus, Max S.	Dem	Mont.	21	19
2nd Warner, John W.	Rep	Va.	21	13		2nd Moynihan, Daniel Patrick	Dem	N.Y.	23	22
Ch2 3rd Smith, Robert C.	Rep	N.H.	9	8		3rd Lautenberg, Frank R.	Dem	N.J.	17	*1 15
4th Inhofe, James M.	Rep	Okla.	5	5		4th Reid, Harry M.	Dem	Nev.	13	13
5th Thomas, Craig L.	Rep	Wyo.	5	*1 5		5th Graham, D. Robert	Dem	Fla.	13	13
6th Bond, Christopher S. (Kit)	Rep	Mo.	13	5		6th Lieberman, Joseph I.	Dem	Conn.	11	10
7th Voinovich, George V.	Rep	Ohio	1	1		7th Boxer, Barbara	Dem	Cal.	7	7
8th Crapo, Michael D.	Rep	Ida.	1	*1 1		8th Wyden, Ronald L.	Dem	Ore.	4	3
9th Bennett, Robert F.	Rep	Utah	7	*2 1						
10th Hutchison, Kay Bailey	Rep	Tex.	6	1						

*1: Member's first period of service on the committee.
*2: Member's second period of service on the committee.

Note: Imtilal ranking on this committee for the following member was affected by other chamber service: Daniel P. Moynihan (Dem-N.Y.), Ranking Minority Member, Finance. Third-ranked Smith became chair because 2nd-ranked John W. Warner (Rep-Va.), Chair of Armed Services.

Changes:
Chairs:

Ch1 Chafee, John H.	Rep	R.I.	Oct. 24, 1999 Died in office.
Ch2 Smith, Robert C.	Rep	N.H.	Nov. 9, 1999 Succeeded John H. Chafee (Rep-R.I.) as Chair.

Majority:

Chafee, John H.	Rep	R.I.	Oct. 24, 1999 Died in office.
Chafee, Lincoln D.	Rep	R.I.	Nov. 9, 1999 Replaced John H. Chafee (Rep-R.I.).

Departures from the Senate:	Majority			Minority		
Retired	None			Moynihan, Daniel Patrick	Dem	N.Y.
				Lautenberg, Frank R.	Dem	N.J.

Departures from Committee:				
Moved to Agriculture, Nutrition, and Forestry, Finance, and Select Ethics	Thomas, Craig L.	Rep	Wyo.	None
Returned to Governmental Affairs	Bennett, Robert F.	Rep	Utah	None
No new assignment	Hutchison, Kay Bailey	Rep	Tex.	None

ENVIRONMENT AND PUBLIC WORKS / 107th Congress, Pre-Jeffords switch

Service Dates of Committee Chair: ChT: Jan. 3, 2001-Jan. 25, 2001 Reid (Dem-Nev.)

Ch1: Jan. 25, 2001-June 6, 2001 Smith (Rep-N.H.)

Service Dates of Majority Members: Jan. 25, 2001-June 6, 2001

Service Dates of Minority Members: Jan. 25, 2001-June 6, 2001

Majority					Minority				
			Years in:					**Years in:**	
Rank Name	**Party**	**State**	**Senate**	**Comm.**	**Rank Name**	**Party**	**State**	**Senate**	**Comm.**
Ch1 Smith, Robert C.	Rep	N.H.	11	10	RM1 Reid, Harry M.	Dem	Nev.	15	15
2nd Warner, John W.	Rep	Va.	23	15	2nd Baucus, Max S.	Dem	Mont.	23	21
3rd Inhofe, James M.	Rep	Okla.	7	7	3rd Graham, D. Robert	Dem	Fla.	15	15
4th Bond, Christopher S. (Kit)	Rep	Mo.	15	7	4th Lieberman, Joseph I.	Dem	Conn.	13	12
5th Voinovich, George V.	Rep	Ohio	3	3	5th Boxer, Barbara	Dem	Cal.	9	9
6th Crapo, Michael D.	Rep	Ida.	3	*1 3	6th Wyden, Ronald L.	Dem	Ore.	6	5
7th Chafee, Lincoln D.	Rep	R.I.	2	2	7th Carper, Thomas R.	Dem	Del.	1	1
8th Specter, Arlen	Rep	Penn.	21	*1 1	8th Clinton, Hillary Rodham	Dem	N.Y.	1	1
9th Campbell, Ben Nighthorse	Rep	Colo.	9	1	9th Corzine Jon S.	Dem	N.J.	1	1

*1: Member's first period of service on the committee.

Note 1: Rankings on this committee for the following member were affected by other chamber service: John W. Warner (Rep-Va.), Chair, Armed Services; and Max S. Baucus (Dem-Mont.), Ranking Minority Member, Finance.

Note 2: The committee majority in the 2001 Senate power-sharing arrangement was determined by the party of the vice president. Democrat Al Gore Jr. served from Jan. 3, 2001, to Jan. 20, 2001, and was succeeded by Republican Richard B. Cheney on Jan. 20, 2001. When Senator Jeffords of Vermont left the Republican Party, effective June 6, 2001, to become an Independent, Democrats regained the majority for the remainder of the 107th Congress.

ENVIRONMENT AND PUBLIC WORKS / 107th Congress, Post-Jeffords switch

Service Dates of Committee Chair: Ch2 June 6, 2001-July 10, 2001 Reid (Dem-Nev.)

Ch3: July 10, 2001-Jan. 14, 2003 Jeffords (Ind-Vt.)

Service Dates of Majority Members: June 6, 2001-Jan. 14, 2003

Service Dates of Minority Members: June 6, 2001-Jan. 15, 2003

Majority					Minority				
			Years in:					**Years in:**	
Rank Name	**Party**	**State**	**Senate**	**Comm.**	**Rank Name**	**Party**	**State**	**Senate**	**Comm.**
Ch3 Jeffords, James M.	Ind.	Vt.	13	*2 1	RM2 Smith, Robert C.	Rep	N.H.	11	11
2nd Ch2 Reid, Harry M.	Dem	Nev.	15	15	2nd Warner, John W.	Rep	Va.	23	15
3rd Baucus, Max S.	Dem	Mont.	23	21	3rd Inhofe, James M.	Rep	Okla.	7	7
4th Graham, D. Robert	Dem	Fla.	15	15	4th Bond, Christopher S. (Kit)	Rep	Mo.	15	7
5th Lieberman, Joseph I.	Dem	Conn.	13	13	5th Voinovich, George V.	Rep	Ohio	3	3
6th Boxer, Barbara	Dem	Cal.	9	9	6th Crapo, Michael D.	Rep	Ida.	3	*1 3
7th Wyden, Ronald L.	Dem	Ore.	6	6	7th Chafee, Lincoln D.	Rep	R.I.	2	2
8th Carper, Thomas R.	Dem	Del.	1	1	8th Specter, Arlen	Rep	Penn.	21	*1 1
9th Clinton, Hillary Rodham	Dem	N.Y.	1	1	9th Campbell, Ben Nighthorse	Rep	Colo.	9	1
10th Corzine Jon S.	Dem	N.J.	1	1					

*1: Member's first period of service on the committee.

Note 1: As part of the Jeffords shift from Republican to Independent, he was named chiar, replacing Harry M. Reid (Dem-Nev.). Rankings on this committee for the following members were affected by other chamber service: John W. Warner (Rep-Va.), Ranking Member, Armed Services; and Max S. Baucus (Dem-Mont.), Chair, Finance.

Note 2: All Democratic members were re-ranked on July 10, 2001; no change in Republican ranks after June 6, 2001.

Additions:
  Majority:

Ch3 Jeffords, James M.	Ind.	Vt.	July 10, 2001

Changes:
  Chairs:

Ch2 Reid, Harry M.	Dem	Nev.	July 10, 2001 Stepped aside as Chair to open slot for Jeffords.
Ch3 Jeffords, James M.	Ind	Vt.	July 10, 2001 Succeeded Reid as Chair.

Departures from the Senate:	Majority			Minority		
Defeated for Re-nomination	None			Smith, Robert C.	Rep	N.H.
Departures from Committee:						
Moved to Foreign Relations	Corzine, Jon S.	Dem	N.J.	None		
Returned to Homeland Security and Governmental Affairs	None			Specter, Arlen	Rep	Penn.
No new assignment	None			Campbell, Ben Nighthorse	Rep	Colo.

ENVIRONMENT AND PUBLIC WORKS / 108th Congress

Service Dates of Committee Chair: Jan. 14, 2003-Jan. 6, 2005

Service Dates of Majority Members: Jan. 14, 2003-Jan. 6, 2005

Service Dates of Minority Members: Jan. 15, 2003-Jan. 6, 2005

	Majority						Minority				
				Years in:						Years in:	
Rank Name	Party	State	Senate	Comm.		Rank Name	Party	State	Senate	Comm.
Chr Inhofe, James M.	Rep	Okla.	9	9		RM Jeffords, James M.	Ind	Vt.	15	*2 2
2nd Warner, John W.	Rep	Va.	25	17		2nd Baucus, Max S.	Dem	Mont.	25	23
3rd Bond, Christopher S. (Kit)	Rep	Mo.	17	9		3rd Reid, Harry M.	Dem	Nev.	17	17
4th Voinovich, George V.	Rep	Ohio	5	5		4th Graham, D. Robert	Dem	Fla.	17	17
5th Crapo, Michael D.	Rep	Ida.	5	*1 5		5th Lieberman, Joseph I.	Dem	Conn.	15	14
6th Chafee, Lincoln D.	Rep	R.I.	4	4		6th Boxer, Barbara	Dem	Cal.	11	11
7th Cornyn, John	Rep	Tex.	1	1		7th Wyden, Ronald L.	Dem	Ore.	8	7
8th Murkowski, Lisa	Rep	Alas.	1	1		8th Carper, Thomas R.	Dem	Del.	3	2
9th Thomas, Craig L.	Rep	Wyo.	9	*2 1		9th Clinton, Hillary Rodham	Dem	NY	3	2
10th Allard, A. Wayne	Rep	Colo.	7	*2 1						

*1: Member's first period of service on the committee.

*2: Member's second period of service on the committee.

Note: Rankings on this committee for the following members were affected by other chamber service: John W. Warner (Rep-Va.), Chair, Armed Services; and Max S. Baucus (Dem-Mont.), Ranking Minority Member, Finance. James M. Jeffords (Ind.-Vt.) became Ranking Minority Member as a result of his 2001 arrangement to switch his party affiliation from Republican to Independent.

Departures from the Senate:	Majority			Minority		
Retired	None			Graham, D. Robert	Dem	Fla.
Departures from Committee:						
Elected Minority Leader	None			Reid, Harry M.	Dem	Nev.
Moved to Finance	Crapo, Michael D.	Rep	Ida.	Wyden, Ronald L.	Dem	Ore.
Moved to Indian Affairs	Crapo, Michael D.	Rep	Ida.	None		
Moved to Small Business and Entrepreneurship and Joint Economic	Cornyn, John	Rep	Tex.	None		
Returned to Agriculture, Nutrition, and Forestry	Thomas, Craig L.	Rep	Wyo.	None		
Moved to Appropriations	Allard, A. Wayne	Rep	Colo.	None		

ENVIRONMENT AND PUBLIC WORKS / 109th Congress

Service Dates of Committee Chair: Jan. 6, 2005-Jan. 12, 2007

Service Dates of Majority Members: Jan. 6, 2005-Jan. 12, 2007

Service Dates of Minority Members: Jan. 6, 2005-Jan. 12, 2007

	Majority						Minority				
				Years in:						Years in:	
Rank Name	Party	State	Senate	Comm.		Rank Name	Party	State	Senate	Comm.
Chr Inhofe, James M.	Rep	Okla.	11	11		RM Jeffords, James M.	Ind	Vt.	17	*2 4
2nd Warner, John W.	Rep	Va.	27	19		2nd Baucus, Max S.	Dem	Mont.	27	25
3rd Bond, Christopher S. (Kit)	Rep	Mo.	19	11		3rd Lieberman, Joseph I.	Dem	Conn.	17	16
4th Voinovich, George V.	Rep	Ohio	7	6		4th Boxer, Barbara	Dem	Cal.	13	12
5th Chafee, Lincoln D.	Rep	R.I.	6	6		5th Carper, Thomas R.	Dem	Del.	5	4
6th Murkowski, Lisa	Rep	Alas.	3	2		6th Clinton, Hillary Rodham	Dem	NY	5	4
7th Thune, John	Rep	S.D.	1	1		7th Lautenberg, Frank R.	Dem	N.J.	21	*2 1

8th DeMint, James W.	Rep	S.C.	1	1		8th Obama, Barack	Dem	Ill.	1	1
9th Isakson, Johnny	Rep	Ga.	1	1						
10th Vitter, David	Rep	La.	1	1		*2: Member's second period of service on the committee.				

Note: Rankings on this committee for the following members were affected by other chamber service: John W. Warner (Rep-Va.), Chair, Armed Services; and Max S. Baucus (Dem-Mont.), Ranking Minority Member, Finance. James M. Jeffords (Ind.-Vt.) became Ranking Minority Member as a result of his 2001 arrangement to switch his party affiliation from Republican to Independent.

Departures from the Senate:	Majority				Minority		
Defeated for Re-election	Chafee, Lincoln D.	Rep	R.I.		None		
Retired	None				Jeffords, James M.	Ind	Vt.

Departures from Committee:							
Moved to Health, Education, Labor, and Pensions	Murkowski, Lisa	Rep	Alas.		Obama, Barack	Dem	Ill.
Moved to Agriculture, Nutrition, and Forestry, and Commerce, Science, and Transportation	Thune, John	Rep	S.D.		None		
Moved to Foreign Relations and Energy and Natural Resources	DeMint, James W.	Rep	S.C.		None		
Moved to Homeland Security and Governmental Affairs	None				Obama, Barack	Dem	Ill.

ENVIRONMENT AND PUBLIC WORKS / 110th Congress

Service Dates of Committee Chair: Jan. 12, 2007-Jan. 21, 2009

Service Dates of Majority Members: Jan. 12, 2007-Jan. 21, 2009

Service Dates of Minority Members: Jan. 12, 2007-Jan. 21, 2009

			Majority						Minority	
			Years in:						Years in:	
Rank Name	Party	State	Senate	Comm.		Rank Name	Party	State	Senate	Comm.
Chr Boxer, Barbara	Dem	Cal.	15	15		RM Inhofe, James M.	Rep	Okla.	13	13
2nd Baucus, Max S.	Dem	Mont.	29	27		2nd Warner, John W.	Rep	Va.	29	21
3rd Lieberman, Joseph I.	IDem	Conn.	19	18		3rd Voinovich, George V.	Rep	Ohio	9	9
4rd Carper, Thomas R.	Dem	Del.	7	6		4th Isakson, Johnny	Rep	Ga.	3	3
5th Clinton, Hillary Rodham	Dem	NY	7	6		5th Vitter, David	Rep	La.	3	3
6th Lautenberg, Frank R.	Dem	N.J.	23	*2 3		6th Craig, Larry E.	Rep	Ida.	17	1
7th Cardin, Benjamin L.	Dem	Md.	1	1		7th Alexander, Lamar	Rep	Tenn.	5	1
8th Sanders, Bernard	Ind	Vt.	1	1		8th Thomas, Craig L.	Rep	Wyo.	13	*3 1
9th Klobuchar, Amy	DFL	Minn.	1	1		9th Bond, Christopher S. (Kit)	Rep	Mo.	21	13
10th Whitehouse, Sheldon	Dem	R.I.	1	1						

*2: Member's second period of service on the committee.

*3: Member's third period of service on the committee.

Note: Rankings on this committee for the following members were affected by other chamber service: Max S. Baucus (Dem-Mont.), Chair, Finance; Joseph I. Lieberman (IDem-Ct.), Chair Homeland Security and Governmental Affairs; John W. Warner (Rep-Va.), Ranking Minority Member, Armed Services; and Christopher S. (Kit) Bond (Rep-Mo.), Vice Chair, Select Intelligence.

Changes:

Minority:

Thomas, Craig L.	Rep	Wyo.	June 4, 2007 Died in office.
Barrasso, John A.	Rep	Wyo.	July 10, 2007 Replaced Thomas; ranked following Vitter.

Departures from the Senate:	Majority				Minority		
Retired	None				Warner, John W.	Rep	Va.
					Craig, Larry E.	Rep	Ida.

Departures from Committee:							
Moved to Commerce, Science, and Transportation	None				Isakson, Johnny	Rep	Ga.
No new assignment	Lieberman, Joseph I.	Dem	Conn.		None		

Note: Hillary Rodham Clinton (Dem-N.Y.) resigned the Senate on Jan. 21, 2009; named Secretary of State.

ENVIRONMENT AND PUBLIC WORKS / 111th Congress

Service Dates of Committee Chair: Jan. 21, 2009-
Service Dates of Majority Members: Jan. 21, 2009-
Service Dates of Minority Members: Jan. 21, 2009-

Majority			Years in:		Minority			Years in:	
Rank Name	Party	State	Senate	Comm.	Rank Name	Party	State	Senate	Comm.
Chr Boxer, Barbara	Dem	Cal.	17	17	RM Inhofe, James M.	Rep	Okla.	15	15
2nd Baucus, Max S.	Dem	Mont.	31	29	2nd Voinovich, George V.	Rep	Ohio	11	11
3rd Carper, Thomas R.	Dem	Del.	9	8	3rd Vitter, David	Rep	La.	5	5
4rd Lautenberg, Frank R.	Dem	N.J.	25	*2 5	4th Barrasso, John A.	Rep	Wyo.	2	2
5th Cardin, Benjamin L.	Dem	Md.	3	3	5th Specter, Arlen	Rep	Penn.	29	*2 1
6th Sanders, Bernard	Ind	Vt.	3	3	6th Crapo, Michael D.	Rep	Ida.	11	*2 1
7th Klobuchar, Amy	DFL	Minn.	3	3	7th Bond, Christopher S. (Kit)	Rep	Mo.	23	15
8th Whitehouse, Sheldon	Dem	R.I.	3	3	8th Alexander, Lamar	Rep	Tenn.	7	3
9th Udall, Thomas	Dem	N.M.	1	1					
10th Merkley, Jeff	Dem	Ore.	1	1	*2: Member's second period of service on the committee.				
11th Gillibrand, Kirsten E.	Dem	N.Y.	1	1					

Note: Rankings on this committee for the following members were affected by other chamber service: Max S. Baucus (Dem-Mont.), Chair, Finance and Christopher S. (Kit) Bond (Rep-Mo.), Vice Chair, Select Intelligence.

Filled vacancy:
  Majority:
      11th seat filled by Gillibrand on Jan. 27, 2009

Additions:
  Majority:
      12th Specter, Arlen   Dem   Penn.   May, 5, 2009

Changes:
  Minority:
      Specter, Arlen   Rep   Penn.   May 5, 2009 Switched from the Republican Party to the Democratic Party; assigned to the
                                                            12th Majority slot with his seniority to be determined at a later date.

Finance

Senate Committee on Finance, 103rd-111th Congresses (1993-2011)

BACKGROUND

Organizational History: The Senate established its initial standing committees on December 10, 1816, on a resolution by Senator James Barbour (DR-Va.). One of them was the Committee on Finance intended to parallel the powerful House Committee on Ways and Means. In fact, Ways and Means was its initial name until it was changed later that day. Its immediate predecessor, the Select Committee on Finance and on Uniform National Currency, was established to consider the parts of President James Madison's message of December 5, 1815, concerning finance and currency matters. The select committee was chaired by Senator George W. Campbell (DR-Tenn.) who had chaired Ways and Means while in the House. The select committee handled both the Tariff of 1816 and the creation of the Second Bank of the United States. Campbell was the first chair of the standing committee.

Up through the end of the Civil War, the Senate Finance Committee handled legislative matters relating to the collection of revenue through customs duties and taxes; regulation of customs collection and ports of entry; banking, currency, and the national debt; and appropriation bills until the Reconstruction.

In 1867, following the House's lead, appropriations matters were delegated to a new standing Committee on Appropriations. The ratification of the Sixteenth Amendment in 1913 expanded the taxing authority of the Congress and the Finance Committee's role grew. It was at that point that it shifted banking and currency items to the newly created Banking and Currency Committee.

World War I also impacted the Finance Committee by changing the nature of veterans' compensation with the creation of the war risk insurance program in 1917. This represented a shift away from pensions as gratuities to benefits—such as low-cost government insurance—as compensation. After World War II, the committee handled the Servicemen's Readjustment Act of 1944, the "GI Bill of Rights," which provided education benefits, unemployment assistance, vocational training, housing and business loan guarantees, and other benefits.

Because the Finance Committee was responsible for veterans programs from 1917 to 1947, another of the original standing committees of the Senate, the Committee on Pensions which was established in 1816, gradually became unnecessary. For 130 years, the Pensions Committee dealt with the pensions for veterans of the Revolutionary War and the War of 1812 and their widows and orphans. It also proposed private acts for those pensioners whose payments had been denied. And as part of the Legislative Reorganization Act of 1946, the Committee on Pensions was abolished.

The Finance Committee continued to have jurisdiction over income and excise taxes, Social Security and related programs, funding aspects of welfare and related social services, unemployment compensation, and reciprocal trade and tariff legislation. In President Lyndon Johnson's "Great Society" program of the 1960s, the committee's role was expanded to include health care programs under the Social Security Act and those financed by a special tax or trust fund.

From 1947 to 1971, matters relating to veteran's compensation and veterans measures generally were referred to the Committee on Finance, while matters relating to the vocational rehabilitation, education, medical care, civil relief, and civilian readjustment of veterans were referred to the Committee on Labor and Public Welfare. The 1970 Legislative Reorganization Act moved jurisdiction over all veterans matters to the Committee on Veterans Affairs, effective with the 92nd Congress (1971-1973).

The committee's most significant power rested in its continuing jurisdiction over income and excise taxes, Social Security and related programs, welfare and related programs, unemployment compensation, and tariff and trade legislation. The panel is one of the most heavily lobbied in Congress because of these powers and assignment to the committee is keenly sought by senators.

Because the Constitution says revenue bills must originate in the House, the Ways and Means Committee has taken the lead on most tax bills. Ways and Means usually operates under strict rules to shepherd its proposals safely through the House without major amendments. The Senate Finance Committee operates very differently; committee members' special wishes are accommodated, and other senators are allowed much latitude to add amendments on the floor.

In recent Congresses, the Finance Committee has emerged as "first among equals" among the major "A"-level committees. The committee's preeminence in the continuing debate over the scope and breadth of health care legislation, as well as the obvious need to find revenues to fund those far-reaching reforms have given it a central place in any serious discussion of domestic policy.

Membership: The Finance Committee had thirteen members in the 80th Congress, and stabilized its present membership of twenty-one in the 97th Congress (1981-1983). Since 1993, the average membership size of Finance is 20.6 senators, placing it sixth between the Banking and Energy committees. Its mean seniority of 15.07 years places Finance third behind Rules and Administration and Appropriations. However, its retention rate of 98.2 percent is the highest of all sixteen committees, with only two members departing the committee for other responsibilities—Tom Daschle (Dem-S.D.) who left to assume the post of Democratic floor leader in 1995 and Larry Craig (Rep-Ida.), who became Chair of Special Aging in 2003.

The preeminence of the Senate Finance Committee is dramatically demonstrated by examining the on/off patterns of intercommittee transfers. Since 1993, forty-two senators have moved to Finance from other committees while only two have departed—a net gain of forty, accounting for 58.8 percent (40/68) of the net gains recorded by the Senate committees. Senate Finance received most of its gainers from three committees—Armed Services (10), Foreign Relations (8), and Appropriations (7).

Committee Leaders: Eugene D. Millikin (Rep-Colo.) held the chair of the Finance Committee in the first two Republican Senates of the modern era—the 80th (1947-1949) and the 83rd (1953-1955). During the first four Congresses of the era, Milliken and Democrat Walter F. George of Georgia traded chairmanships and ranking member slots. While Millikin retained his senior rank on the committee in the 84th Congress (1955-1957), Walter George left Finance to chair Foreign Relations. He was succeeded by the ultra-conservative Harry Flood Byrd Sr. (Dem-Va.) from 1955 through his 1965 retirement, one of the only two Democrats to hold the chairmanship of the committee from 1955 through 1981. The other was Russell B. Long of Louisiana, who led the committee for fifteen years after Byrd's resignation until 1981 and the capture of the Senate by Republicans. Long served an additional six years as its ranking minority member until his retirement in 1986. Long's twenty-one years as the senior Democrat on Finance is the second longest senior rank tenure on any committee in the modern Senate.

The ranking minority members during the Byrd-Long era included Edward Martin of Pennsylvania for two years (1957-1959) who was followed by "the watchdog of the Treasury" John J. Williams of Delaware, who served as ranking member from 1959 until his resignation in 1970. Williams's successor, Wallace F. Bennett of Utah, served until his 1974 resignation. Carl T. Curtis of Nebraska followed Bennett and served as ranking member until his retirement in 1978.

It was then that Robert J. Dole of Kansas became the senior Republican on Finance, first as its ranking member in 1979-1981, then as chair for four years until he began his career as Majority Leader in 1985. Robert W. Packwood of Oregon succeeded Dole as chair in 1985 and was its senior Republican until September, 1995, when scandal obliged him to relinquish his chairmanship to William V. Roth Jr. of Delaware. Three weeks later Packwood resigned the Senate. Roth served as chair until he was defeated for re-election in 2000.

Following Russell Long's retirement, the Finance Committee Democrats were led by Lloyd M. Bentsen of Texas, who chaired the committee from 1987 until his resignation in 1993 to become Secretary of the Treasury under President Bill Clinton. Bentsen's resignation opened the chairmanship of the committee to Daniel Patrick Moynihan of New York, who assumed the chair in 1993 and would become the committee's ranking minority member for six years (1995-2001) following the Republican takeover of the Senate in 1995.

Since 2001, Charles Grassley of Iowa and Max Baucus of Montana have swapped leadership roles on the committee: Grassley as chair (2001 and 2003-2007) and Baucus as chair (2001-2003 and 2007-2011) and each serving as ranking minority member when the other chaired the committee.

Party Leaders: Republicans have selected nine of their nineteen post-1947 floor leaders and Whips from Finance Committee members while Democrats have chosen seven of their seventeen. Five Republican floor leaders served on Finance: Robert A. Taft, 1953-1954; Everett McK. Dirksen of Illinois, 1959-1969; and included a run of twenty consecutive years from 1987 to 2007, with Bob Dole of Kansas, 1987-1996;

Trent Lott of Mississippi, 1996-2003; and Bill Frist of Tennessee, 2003-2007. Finance alumni produced six Whips, two of whom, Dirksen and Lott, became floor leaders; while four others peaked at Whip: Robert P. Griffin of Michigan, 1969-1977; Alan Simpson of Wyoming, 1985-1995; Don Nickles of Oklahoma, 1996-2003; and the present Republican Whip Jon Kyl of Arizona who has served since 2007.

Of the seven Finance Committee members who have led the Democrats, five were floor leaders: Alben Barkley, 1937-1949; Scott Lucas of Illinois, 1949-1951; Lyndon Johnson, 1953-1961; George J. Mitchell of Maine, 1989-1995; and Thomas A. Daschle of South Dakota, 1995-2005. While Lucas and Johnson began their leadership careers as Whip, Francis Myers of Pennsylvania, 1949-1951; and Russell Long of Louisiana, 1965-1969, never attained the floor leadership post. One contrast between Democratic leaders with Finance Committee experience is that three of the seven lost their re-election bids—Lucas, Myers, and Daschle—while none of the Republican leaders did.

Presidential Aspirations: Despite the relative prestige of the Finance Committee, it has not been a major Senate launch pad for the presidency. Only six Finance Committee members have been nominated: two for president—Republican Robert J. Dole of Kansas in 1996 and Democrat John F. Kerry of Massachusetts in 2004. The other nominations were for vice president—Alben Barkley of Kentucky on the Truman ticket in 1948; Lyndon Johnson of Texas on the Kennedy ticket in 1960; Walter Mondale of Minnesota on the Carter ticket in 1976 and 1980; and Lloyd M. Bentsen of Texas on the Dukakis ticket in 1988. While neither presidential nominee was successful, three of the Democratic vice presidential nominees were elected—Barkley, Johnson, and Mondale. Dole, the lone Finance Republican to be nominated for president, was named first as a vice presidential candidate on the Ford ticket in 1976. While both Democrats Lyndon Johnson and Walter Mondale were nominated for president, each was chosen after serving as vice president and not from the Senate. And no one with Finance Committee service had more presidential frustration than Ohio's Robert A. Taft, son of President and Chief Justice William Howard Taft, who was thwarted in his efforts to be nominated in 1940, 1948, and 1952.

Other Notables: The only modern-era Finance Committee Democrats to be elected to the Senate after their Cabinet service were New Mexico's Clinton Anderson, President Truman's Secretary of Agriculture, and Connecticut's Abraham Ribicoff, President Kennedy's Secretary of Health, Education, and Welfare. One-time Democratic National Chair J. Howard McGrath of Rhode Island left the Senate's Finance Committee to become Attorney General in the Truman Administration. Similar Democratic moves from the Senate Finance Committee occurred in 1993 when Lloyd M. Bentsen of Texas, the committee's chair, became Secretary of the Treasury under President Clinton and in 2009 when Kenneth Salazar of Colorado left Finance to become President Obama's Secretary of the Interior.

The only post-1947 Finance Committee alumnus to move to the Cabinet was Tennessee's William Brock, who served as President Reagan's second Secretary of Labor. However, Brock had already left the Senate as a result of his 1976 defeat to James Sasser (Dem-Tenn.). And the only post-1993 Finance Committee member to return home as governor was Republican Frank Murkowski of Alaska in 2002, who would lose his re-nomination bid to Sarah Palin in 2006.

Selected References

Bradley, John P., "Shaping Administrative Policy with the Aid of Congressional Oversight: The Senate Finance Committee and Medicare," *Western Political Quarterly*, 33 (December, 1980), 492-501.

Conlan, Timothy J., "Finance Committee, Senate," in Donald C. Bacon, Roger H. Davidson, and Morton Keller, eds., *The Encyclopedia of the United States Congress* (New York: Simon & Schuster, 1995), I: 837-840.

Conlan, Timothy J., Margaret T. Wrightson, and David R. Beam, *Taxing Choices: The Politics of Tax Reform* (Washington, D.C.: CQ Press, 1989).

Coren, Robert W., et al., "Records of the Committee on Finance and Related Records, 1816-1968," *Guide to the Records of the United States Senate at the National Archives: 1789-1989 Bicentennial Edition* (Washington, D.C.: National Archives and Records Administration, 1989), 95-103.

Nathan, Richard P. and Susannah E. Calkins, "The Story of Revenue Sharing," in Robert L. Peabody, ed., *Cases in American Politics* (New York: Praeger, 1976), 11-43.

Price, David E., *Who Makes the Laws? Creativity and Power in Senate Committees* (Cambridge. Mass.: Schenkman, 1972).

Rudder, Catherine E., "Fiscal Responsibility, Fairness, and the Revenue Committees," in Lawrence C. Dodd and Bruce

I. Oppenheimer, eds., *Congress Reconsidered*, 4th ed. (Washington. D.C.: CQ Press, 1989), 225-244.

Rudder, Catherine E., "Fiscal Responsibility and the Revenue Committees," in Lawrence C. Dodd and Bruce I. Oppenheimer, eds., *Congress Reconsidered*, 3rd ed. (Washington. D.C.: CQ Press, 1985), 211-222.

Schick, Allen, *Congress and Money: Budgeting, Spending and Taxing* (Washington, D.C.: The Urban Institute, 1980).

Schick, Allen, "The Three-Ring Budget Process: The Appropriations, Tax and Budget Committees in Congress," in Thomas Mann and Norman J. Ornstein, eds., *The New Congress* (Washington, D.C.: American Enterprise Institute, 1981), 288-328.

Spohn, Richard and Charles McCollum, dirs., "The House Ways and Means and Senate Finance Committees," in the Ralph Nader Congress Project, *The Revenue Committees: A Study of the House Ways and Means and Senate Finance Committee and the House and Senate Appropriations Committees* (New York: Grossman, 1975), 1-213.

U.S. Senate, Committee on Finance, *History of the Committee on Finance*, Senate Document 97-5, 97th Congress, 1st session (1981). This is the fourth history since 1976: 1) Senate Document 9-57, 91st Congress, 2nd session (1970); 2) Senate Document 95-27, 95th Congress, 1st session (1977); and 3) *Addendum to the History of the Committee on Finance*, Senate Print 96-2, 96th Congress, 1st session (1979).

RESPONSIBILITIES, JURISDICTIONAL CHANGES, AND SUBCOMMITTEES

FINANCE

Jurisdiction, 80th Congress (1947-49)

Established by the Legislative Reorganization Act of 1946:

[Section 102.(1)(h)]

(1) **Committee on Finance**, to consist of thirteen Senators, to which committee shall be referred all proposed legislation, messages, petitions, memorials, and other matters relating to the following subjects:

    (1) Revenue measures generally
    (2) The bonded debt of the United States
    (3) The deposit of public moneys
    (4) Customs, collection districts, and ports of entry and delivery
    (5) Reciprocal trade agreements
    (6) Transportation of dutiable goods
    (7) Revenue measures relating to the insular possessions
    (8) Tariffs and import quotas, and matters related thereto
    (9) National social security
    (10) Veterans' measures generally
    (11) Pensions of all the wars of the United States, general and special
    (12) Life insurance issued by the Government on account of service in the armed forces
    (13) Compensation of veterans

Post-Reorganization Jurisdiction, 1977

From Committee System Reorganization Amendments of 1977, S.Res. 95-4, *Senate Journal*, Feb. 4, 1977:

[Section 101. 1.(i)]

(1) **Committee on Finance**, to which committee shall be referred all proposed legislation, messages, petitions, memorials, and other matters relating to the following subjects:

   (1) Except as provided in the Congressional Budget Act of 1974, revenue measures generally
   (2) Except as provided in the Congressional Budget Act of 1974, the bonded debt of the United States
   (3) Deposit of public moneys
   (4) Customs, collection districts, and ports of entry and delivery
   (5) Reciprocal trade agreements
   (6) Transportation of dutiable goods
   (7) Revenue measures relating to the insular possessions
   (8) Tariffs and import quotas, and matters related thereto
   (9) National social security
   (10) General revenue sharing
   (11) Health programs under the Social Security Act and health programs financed by a specific tax or trust fund

Jurisdiction, 103rd Congress (1993-94)

From the *Standing Rules of the Senate* in the *Senate Manual*, 103rd Congress, 1st Session, S. Doc. 103-1:

[Rule XXV (1)(i)]

(1) **Committee on Finance**, to which committee shall be referred all proposed legislation, messages, petitions, memorials, and other matters relating to the following subjects:

   (1) Bonded debt of the United States, except as provided in the Congressional Budget Act of 1974
   (2) Customs, collection districts, and ports of entry and delivery
   (3) Deposit of public moneys
   (4) General revenue sharing
   (5) Health programs under the Social Security Act and health programs financed by a specific tax or trust fund
   (6) National social security
   (7) Reciprocal trade agreements
   (8) Revenue measures generally, except as provided in the Congressional Budget Act of 1974
   (9) Revenue measures relating to the insular possessions
   (10) Tariffs and import quotas, and matters related thereto
   (11) Transportation of dutiable goods

Jurisdiction, 111th Congress (2009-10)

From *Authority and Rules of Senate Committees, 2009-2010*, Sen. Doc. 111-3, pursuant to S.Res, 166, June 2, 2009.

[Rule XXV (1)(i)]

(1) **Committee on Finance**, to which committee shall be referred all proposed legislation, messages, petitions, memorials, and other matters relating to the following subjects:

   (1) Bonded debt of the United States, except as provided in the Congressional Budget Act of 1974
   (2) Customs, collection districts, and ports of entry and delivery
   (3) Deposit of public moneys
   (4) General revenue sharing
   (5) Health programs under the Social Security Act and health programs financed by a specific tax or trust fund
   (6) National social security
   (7) Reciprocal trade agreements
   (8) Revenue measures generally, except as provided in the Congressional Budget Act of 1974
   (9) Revenue measures relating to the insular possessions
   (10) Tariffs and import quotas, and matters related thereto
   (11) Transportation of dutiable goods

NAMES OF SUBCOMMITTEES

Committee on Finance, 103rd -111th Congresses

Deficits, Debt Management and Long-Term Economic Growth, 103
Energy and Agricultural Taxation, 103

MEMBERSHIP ROSTERS, 103rd-111th Congresses, 1993-2010

FINANCE / 103rd Congress

Service Dates of Committee Chair: Ch1 Jan. 7, 1993-Jan. 21, 1993 Bentsen (Dem-Tex.)

Ch2 Jan. 21, 1993-Jan. 11, 1995 Moynihan (Dem-N.Y.)

Service Dates of Majority Members: Jan. 7, 1993-Jan. 4, 1995

Service Dates of Minority Members: Jan. 7, 1993-Jan. 4, 1995

Majority

Rank Name	Party	State	Years in: Senate	Years in: Comm.
Ch1 Bentsen, Lloyd M. Jr.	Dem	Tex.	23	21
Ch2 Moynihan, Daniel Patrick	Dem	N.Y.	17	16
3rd Baucus, Max S.	Dem	Mont.	15	14
4th Boren, David L.	Dem	Okla.	15	14
5th Bradley, William W.	Dem	N.J.	15	14
6th Mitchell, George J.	Dem	Me.	13	13
7th Pryor, David H.	Dem	Ark.	15	11
8th Riegle, Donald W. Jr.	Dem	Mich.	17	7
9th Rockefeller, John D. IV	Dem	W.Va.	9	7
10th Daschle, Thomas A.	Dem	S.D.	7	*1 7
11th Breaux, John B.	Dem	La.	7	3

Minority

Rank Name	Party	State	Years in: Senate	Years in: Comm.
RM Packwood, Robert W.	Rep	Ore.	25	20
2nd Dole, Robert J.	Rep	Kans.	25	20
3rd Roth, William V. Jr.	Rep	Del.	23	20
4th Danforth, John C.	Rep	Mo.	17	16
5th Chafee, John H.	Rep	R.I.	17	14
6th Durenberger, David F.	Rep	Minn.	15	14
7th Grassley, Charles E.	Rep	Iowa	13	*2 2
8th Hatch, Orrin G.	Rep	Utah	17	2
9th Wallop, Malcolm	Rep	Wyo.	17	*2 1

*1: Member's first period of service on the committee.
*2: Member's second period of service on the committee.

Note: Ranking on this committee for the following member was affected by other chamber service: Robert J. Dole (Rep-Kans.), Senate Minority Leader.

Changes:
Chair:

Ch1 Bentsen, Lloyd M. Jr.	Dem	Tex.	Jan. 20, 1993 Resigned the Senate; appointed Secretary of the Treasury.
Ch2 Moynihan, Daniel Patrick	Dem	N.Y.	Jan. 21, 1993 Succeeded Bentsen as Chair.

Majority:

Bentsen, Lloyd M. Jr.	Dem	Tex.	Jan. 21, 1993 Resigned the Senate; appointed Secretary of the Treasury.
Conrad, Kent	Dem	N.D.	Jan. 21, 1993 Replaced Bentsen.
Boren, David L.	Dem	Okla.	Nov. 15, 1994 Resigned the Senate; became president of the University of Oklahoma.

Departures from the Senate:

	Majority				Minority		
Retired	Mitchell, George J.	Dem	Me.		Danforth, John C.	Rep	Mo.
	Riegle, Donald W. Jr.	Dem	Mich.		Durenberger, David F.	Rep	Minn.
					Wallop, Malcolm	Rep	Wyo.

Departures from Committee:

Elected Minority Leader	Daschle, Thomas A.	Dem	S.D.	None	

FINANCE / 104th Congress

Service Dates of Committee Chair: Ch1: Jan. 11, 1995-Sep. 8, 1995 Packwood (Rep-Ore.)

Ch2: Sep. 12, 1995-Jan. 9, 1997 Roth (Rep-Del.)

Service Dates of Majority Members: Jan. 4, 1995-Jan. 9, 1997

Service Dates of Minority Members: Jan. 4, 1995-Jan. 9, 1997

Majority					Minority				
			Years in:					Years in:	
Rank Name	Party	State	Senate	Comm.	Rank Name	Party	State	Senate	Comm.
Ch1 Packwood, Robert W.	Rep	Ore.	27	22	RM Moynihan, Daniel Patrick	Dem	N.Y.	19	18
2nd Dole, Robert J.	Rep	Kans.	27	22	2nd Baucus, Max S.	Dem	Mont.	17	16
Ch2 3rd Roth, William V. Jr.	Rep	Del.	25	22	3rd Bradley, William W.	Dem	N.J.	17	16
4th Chafee, John H.	Rep	R.I.	19	16	4th Pryor, David H.	Dem	Ark.	17	13
5th Grassley, Charles E.	Rep	Iowa	15	*2 4	5th Rockefeller, John D. IV	Dem	W.Va.	11	8
6th Hatch, Orrin G.	Rep	Utah	19	4	6th Breaux, John B.	Dem	La.	9	5
7th Simpson, Alan K.	Rep	Wyo.	17	1	7th Conrad, Kent	Dem	N.D.	9	2
8th Pressler, Larry L.	Rep	S.D.	17	1	8th Graham, D. Robert	Dem	Fla.	9	1
9th D'Amato, Alfonse M.	Rep	N.Y.	15	1	9th Moseley Braun, Carol	Dem	Ill.	3	1
10th Murkowski, Frank H.	Rep	Alas.	15	1					
11th Nickles, Donald L.	Rep	Okla.	15	1	*2: Member's second period of service on the committee.				

Note: Ranking on this committee for the following member was affected by other chamber service: Robert J. Dole (Rep-Kans.), Senate Majority Leader.

Changes:
Chair:

Ch1 Packwood, Robert W.	Rep	Ore.	Sep. 8, 1995 Relinquished chairmanship.
Ch2 Roth, William V. Jr.	Rep	Del.	Sep. 12, 1995 Succeeded Packwood as Chair.

Majority:

Packwood, Robert W.	Rep	Ore.	Oct. 1, 1995 Resigned the Senate and retired.
Gramm, W. Philip	Rep	Tex.	Oct. 12, 1995 Replaced Packwood.
Dole, Robert J.	Rep	Kans.	June 11, 1996 Resigned the Senate to run for president.
Lott, C. Trent	Rep	Miss.	June 20, 1996 Replaced Dole.

Departures from the Senate:	Majority			Minority		
Defeated for Re-election	Pressler, Larry L.	Rep	S.D.	None		
Retired	Simpson, Alan K.	Rep	Wyo.	Bradley, William W.	Dem	N.J.
				Pryor, David H.	Dem	Ark.

FINANCE / 105th Congress

Service Dates of Committee Chair: Jan. 9, 1997-Jan. 7, 1999

Service Dates of Majority Members: Jan. 9, 1997-Jan. 7, 1999

Service Dates of Minority Members: Jan. 9, 1997-Jan. 7, 1999

Majority					Minority				
			Years in:					Years in:	
Rank Name	Party	State	Senate	Comm.	Rank Name	Party	State	Senate	Comm.
Chr Roth, William V. Jr.	Rep	Del.	27	24	RM Moynihan, Daniel Patrick	Dem	N.Y.	21	20
2nd Chafee, John H.	Rep	R.I.	21	18	2nd Baucus, Max S.	Dem	Mont.	19	18
3rd Grassley, Charles E.	Rep	Iowa	17	*2 6	3rd Rockefeller, John D. IV	Dem	W.Va.	13	11
4th Hatch, Orrin G.	Rep	Utah	21	6	4th Breaux, John B.	Dem	La.	11	7
5th D'Amato, Alfonse M.	Rep	N.Y.	17	3	5th Conrad, Kent	Dem	N.D.	11	4
6th Murkowski, Frank H.	Rep	Alas.	17	2	6th Graham, D. Robert	Dem	Fla.	11	3
7th Nickles, Donald L.	Rep	Okla.	17	3	7th Moseley Braun, Carol	Dem	Ill.	5	3
8th Gramm, W. Philip	Rep	Tex.	13	2	8th Bryan, Richard H.	Dem	Nev.	9	1
9th Lott, C. Trent	Rep	Miss.	9	1	9th Kerrey, J. Robert	Dem	Neb.	9	1
10th Jeffords, James M.	Rep	Vt.	9	*1 1	*1: Member's first period of service on the committee.				
11th Mack, Connie III	Rep	Fla.	9	1	*2: Member's second period of service on the committee.				

Note: Ranking on this committee for the following member was affected by other chamber service: Robert J. Dole (Rep-Kans.), Senate Majority Leader.

Departures from the Senate:	Majority			Minority		
Defeated for Re-election	D'Amato, Alfonse M.	Rep	N.Y.	Moseley Braun, Carol	Dem	Ill.

FINANCE / 106th Congress

Service Dates of Committee Chair: Jan. 7, 1999-Jan. 3, 2001

Service Dates of Majority Members: Jan. 7, 1999-Jan. 25, 2001

Service Dates of Minority Members: Jan. 7, 1999-Jan. 25, 2001

Majority

Rank Name	Party	State	Senate	Comm.
Chr Roth, William V. Jr.	Rep	Del.	29	26
2nd Chafee, John H.	Rep	R.I.	23	20
3rd Grassley, Charles E.	Rep	Iowa	19	*2 8
4th Hatch, Orrin G.	Rep	Utah	23	8
5th Murkowski, Frank H.	Rep	Alas.	19	5
6th Nickles, Donald L.	Rep	Okla.	19	5
7th Gramm, W. Phil	Rep	Tex.	15	4
8th Lott, C. Trent	Rep	Miss.	11	2
9th Jeffords, James M.	Rep	Vt.	11	*1 2
10th Mack, Connie III	Rep	Fla.	11	2
11th Thompson, Fred D.	Rep	Tenn.	5	1

Minority

Rank Name	Party	State	Senate	Comm.
RM Moynihan, Daniel Patrick	Dem	N.Y.	23	22
2nd Baucus, Max S.	Dem	Mont.	21	20
3rd Rockefeller, John D. IV	Dem	W.Va.	15	13
4th Breaux, John B.	Dem	La.	13	9
5th Conrad, Kent	Dem	N.D.	13	6
6th Graham, D. Robert	Dem	Fla.	13	5
7th Bryan, Richard H.	Dem	Nev.	11	2
8th Kerrey, J. Robert	Dem	Neb.	11	2
9th Robb, Charles S.	Dem	Va.	11	1

*1: Member's first period of service on the committee.

*2: Member's second period of service on the committee.

Changes:

Majority:

Chafee, John H.	Rep R.I.	Oct. 24, 1999 Died in office.
Coverdell, Paul	Rep Ga.	Nov. 9, 1999 Replaced Chafee.
Coverdell, Paul	Rep Ga.	July 18, 2000 Died in office.
Craig, Larry E.	Rep Ida.	Sept. 12, 2000 Replaced Coverdell.

Departures from the Senate:

	Majority			**Minority**		
Defeated for Re-election	Roth, William V. Jr.	Rep	Del.	Robb, Charles S.	Dem	Va.
Retired	Mack, Connie III	Rep	Fla.	Moynihan, Daniel Patrick	Dem	N.Y.
				Bryan, Richard H.	Dem	Nev.
				Kerrey, J. Robert	Dem	Neb.

Departures from Committee:

Became Chair of Special Aging	Craig, Larry E.	Rep	Ida.	None

FINANCE / 107th Congress, Pre-Jeffords switch

Service Dates of Committee Chair: ChT: Jan. 3, 2001-Jan. 25, 2001 Baucus (Dem-Mont.)

Ch1: Jan. 25, 2001-June 6, 2001 Grassley (Rep-Iowa)

Service Dates of Majority Members: Jan. 25, 2001-June 6, 2001

Service Dates of Minority Members: Jan. 25, 2001-June 6, 2001

Majority

Rank Name	Party	State	Senate	Comm.
Ch1 Grassley, Charles E.	Rep	Iowa	21	*2 10
2nd Hatch, Orrin G.	Rep	Utah	25	10
3rd Murkowski, Frank H.	Rep	Alas.	21	7
4th Nickles, Donald L.	Rep	Okla.	21	7
5th Gramm, W. Philip	Rep	Tex.	17	6
6th Lott, C. Trent	Rep	Miss.	13	5
7th Jeffords, James M.	Rep	Vt.	13	*1 5
8th Thompson, Fred	Rep	Tenn.	7	3
9th Snowe, Olympia J.B.	Rep	Me.	7	1
10th Kyl, Jon L.	Rep	Ariz.	7	1

Minority

Rank Name	Party	State	Senate	Comm.
RM1 Baucus, Max S.	Dem	Mont.	23	23
2nd Rockefeller, John D. IV	Dem	W.Va.	17	15
3rd Daschle, Thomas A.	Dem	S.D.	15	*2 1
4th Breaux, John B.	Dem	La.	15	11
5th Conrad, Kent	Dem	N.D.	15	9
6th Graham, D. Robert	Dem	Fla.	15	7
7th Bingaman, J.F. (Jeff)	Dem	N.M	19	1
8th Kerry, John F.	Dem	Mass.	17	1
9th Torricelli, Robert G.	Dem	N.J.	5	1
10th Lincoln, Blanche Lambert	Dem	Ark.	3	1

*1: Member's first period of service on the committee.

*2: Member's second period of service on the committee.

Note: The committee majority in the 2001 Senate power-sharing arrangement was determined by the party of the vice president. Democrat Al Gore Jr. served from Jan. 3, 2001, to Jan. 20, 2001, and was succeeded by Republican Richard B. Cheney on Jan. 20, 2001. When Senator Jeffords of Vermont left the Republican Party, effective June 6, 2001, to become an Independent, Democrats regained the majority for the remainder of the 107th Congress.

FINANCE / 107th Congress, Post-Jeffords switch

Service Dates of Committee Chair:: June 6, 2001-Jan. 14, 2003

Service Dates of Majority Members: June 6, 2001-Jan. 14, 2003

Service Dates of Minority Members: June 6, 2001-Jan. 15, 2003

Majority

Rank Name	Party	State	Years in: Senate	Years in: Comm.
Ch2 Baucus, Max S.	Dem	Mont.	23	23
2nd Rockefeller, John D. IV	Dem	W.Va.	17	15
3rd Daschle, Thomas A.	Dem	S.D.	15	*2 1
4th Breaux, John B.	Dem	La.	15	12
5th Conrad, Kent	Dem	N.D.	15	9
6th Graham, D. Robert	Dem	Fla.	15	7
7th Jeffords, James M.	Ind.	Vt.	13	*2 1
8th Bingaman, J.F. (Jeff)	Dem	N.M	19	1
9th Kerry, John F.	Dem	Mass.	17	1
10th Torricelli, Robert G.	Dem	N.J.	5	1
11th Lincoln, Blanche Lambert	Dem	Ark.	3	1

Minority

Rank Name	Party	State	Years in: Senate	Years in: Comm.
RM2 Grassley, Charles E.	Rep	Iowa	21	*2 11
2nd Hatch, Orrin G.	Rep	Utah	25	10
3rd Murkowski, Frank H.	Rep	Alas.	21	7
4th Nickles, Donald L.	Rep	Okla.	21	7
5th Gramm, W. Philip	Rep	Tex.	17	6
6th Lott, C. Trent	Rep	Miss.	13	5
7th Thompson, Fred D.	Rep	Tenn.	7	3
8th Snowe, Olympia J.B.	Rep	Me.	7	1
9th Kyl, Jon L.	Rep	Ariz.	7	1
10th Thomas, Craig L.	Rep	Wyo.	7	1

*2: Member's second period of service on the committee.

Note: Democratic members from 7th through 11th and Republican members from 7th through 9th were re-ranked on July 10, 2001

Additions:

Majority:

7th Jeffords, James M.	Ind.	Vt.	July 10, 2001

Changes:

Minority:

Jeffords, James M.	Ind	Vt.	June 6, 2001 Seat vacated as a Republican; renamed an addition as an Independent to rank 7th among the majority Democrats.
Thomas, Craig L.	Rep	Wyo.	July 10, 2001 Replaced Jeffords Gramm, W. Philip Rep Tex. Nov. 30, 2002 Resigned the Senate; retired
Murkowski, Frank H.	Rep	Alas.	Dec. 2, 2002 Resigned the Senate; elected Governor of Alaska.
Gramm, W. Philip	Rep	Miss.	Nov. 30, 2002 Resigned and retired

Departures from the Senate:

	Majority				Minority		
Retired	Torricelli, Robert G.	Dem	N.J.		Thompson, Fred D.	Rep	Tenn.

FINANCE / 108th Congress

Service Dates of Committee Chair: Jan. 14, 2003-Jan. 6, 2005

Service Dates of Majority Members: Jan. 14, 2003-Jan. 6, 2005

Service Dates of Minority Members: Jan. 15, 2003-Jan. 6, 2005

Majority

Rank Name	Party	State	Years in: Senate	Years in: Comm.
Chr Grassley, Charles E.	Rep	Iowa	23	*2 12
2nd Hatch, Orrin G.	Rep	Utah	27	12
3rd Nickles, Donald L.	Rep	Okla.	23	9
4th Lott, C. Trent	Rep	Miss.	15	7
5th Snowe, Olympia J.B.	Rep	Me.	9	2
6th Kyl, Jon L.	Rep	Ariz.	9	2
7th Thomas, Craig L.	Rep	Wyo.	9	2
8th Santorum, Richard J. (Rick)	Rep	Penn.	9	1
9th Frist, William H.	Rep	Tenn.	9	1
10th Smith, Gordon H.	Rep	Ore.	7	1
11th Bunning, James P.D.	Rep	Ky.	5	1

Minority

Rank Name	Party	State	Years in: Senate	Years in: Comm.
RM Baucus, Max S.	Dem	Mont.	25	24
2nd Rockefeller, John D. IV	Dem	W.Va.	19	17
3rd Daschle, Thomas A.	Dem	S.D.	17	*2 2
4th Breaux, John B.	Dem	La.	17	13
5th Conrad, Kent	Dem	N.D.	17	10
6th Graham, D. Robert	Dem	Fla.	17	9
7th Jeffords, James M.	Ind	Vt	15	*2 2
8th Bingaman, J.F. (Jeff)	Dem	N.M.	21	2
9th Kerry, John F.	Dem	Mass.	19	2
10th Lincoln, Blanche Lambert	Dem	Ark.	5	2

*2: Member's second period of service on the committee.

Departures from the Senate:

	Majority			Minority		
Defeated for Re-election	None			Daschle, Thomas A.	Dem	S.D.
Retired	Nickles, Donald L.	Rep	Okla.	Breaux, John B.	Dem	La.
				Graham, D. Robert	Dem	Fla.

FINANCE / 109th Congress

Service Dates of Committee Chair: Jan. 6, 2005-Jan. 12, 2007

Service Dates of Majority Members: Jan. 6, 2005-Jan. 12, 2007

Service Dates of Minority Members: Jan. 6, 2005-Jan. 12, 2007

Majority					**Minority**				
			Years in:					**Years in:**	
Rank Name	**Party**	**State**	**Senate**	**Comm.**	**Rank Name**	**Party**	**State**	**Senate**	**Comm.**
Chr Grassley, Charles E.	Rep	Iowa	25	*2 14	RM Baucus, Max S.	Dem	Mont.	27	26
2nd Hatch, Orrin G.	Rep	Utah	29	14	2nd Rockefeller, John D. IV	Dem	W.Va.	21	19
3rd Lott, C. Trent	Rep	Miss.	17	9	3rd Conrad, Kent	Dem	N.D.	19	12
4th Snowe, Olympia J.B.	Rep	Me.	11	4	4th Jeffords, James M.	Ind	Vt	17	*2 4
5th Kyl, Jon L.	Rep	Ariz.	11	4	5th Bingaman, J.F. (Jeff)	Dem	N.M.	23	4
6th Thomas, Craig L.	Rep	Wyo.	11	4	6th Kerry, John F.	Dem	Mass.	21	4
7th Santorum, Richard J. (Rick)	Rep	Penn.	11	2	7th Lincoln, Blanche Lambert	Dem	Ark.	7	4
8th Frist, William H.	Rep	Tenn.	11	2	8th Wyden, Ronald L.	Dem	Ore.	10	1
9th Smith, Gordon H.	Rep	Ore.	9	2	9th Schumer, Charles E.	Dem	N.Y.	7	1
10th Bunning, James P.D.	Rep	Ky.	7	2					
11th Crapo, Michael D.	Rep	Ida.	7	1					

*2: Member's second period of service on the committee.

Departures from the Senate:

	Majority			**Minority**	
Defeated for Re-election	Santorum, Richard J. (Rick)	Rep	Penn.		None
Retired	Frist, William H.	Rep	Tenn.	Jeffords, James M.	Ind Vt.

FINANCE / 110th Congress

Service Dates of Committee Chair: Jan. 12, 2007-Jan. 21, 2009

Service Dates of Majority Members: Jan. 12, 2007-Jan. 21, 2009

Service Dates of Minority Members: Jan. 12, 2007-Jan. 21, 2009

Majority					**Minority**				
			Years in:					**Years in:**	
Rank Name	**Party**	**State**	**Senate**	**Comm.**	**Rank Name**	**Party**	**State**	**Senate**	**Comm.**
Chr Baucus, Max S.	Dem	Mont.	29	28	RM Grassley, Charles E.	Rep	Iowa	27	*2 16
2nd Rockefeller, John D. IV	Dem	W.Va.	23	21	2nd Hatch, Orrin G.	Rep	Utah	31	16
3rd Conrad, Kent	Dem	N.D.	21	14	3rd Lott, C. Trent	Rep	Miss.	19	11
4th Bingaman, J.F. (Jeff)	Dem	N.M	25	6	4th Snowe, Olympia J.B.	Rep	Me.	13	6
5th Kerry, John F.	Dem	Mass.	23	6	5th Kyl, Jon L.	Rep	Ariz.	13	6
6th Lincoln, Blanche Lambert	Dem	Ark.	9	6	6th Thomas, Craig L.	Rep	Wyo.	13	6
7th Wyden, Ronald L.	Dem	Ore.	12	3	7th Smith, Gordon H.	Rep	Ore.	11	4
8th Schumer, Charles E.	Dem	N.Y.	9	3	8th Bunning, James P.D.	Rep	Ky.	9	4
9th Stabenow, Deborah Ann.	Dem	Mich.	7	1	9th Crapo, Michael D.	Rep	Ida.	9	3
10th Cantwell, Maria E.	Dem	Wash.	7	1	10th Roberts, C. Patrick	Rep	Kans.	11	1
11th Salazar, Kenneth L.	Dem	Colo.	3	1					

*2: Member's second period of service on the committee.

Changes:

Minority:

Thomas, Craig L.	Rep	Wyo.	June 4, 2007 Died in office.
Ensign, John E.	Rep	Nev.	July 10, 2007 Replaced Thomas.
Lott, C. Trent	Rep	Miss.	Dec. 18, 2007 Resigned the Senate and retired.
Sununu, John E.	Rep	N.H.	Jan. 24, 2008 Replaced Lott.

Departures from the Senate:

	Majority	**Minority**		
Defeated for Re-election	None	Smith, Gordon H.	Rep	Ore.
		Sununu, John E.	Rep	N.H.

Note: Kenneth L. Salazar (Dem-Colo) resigned the Senate on Jan. 20, 2009; named Secretary of the Interior

FINANCE / 111th Congress

Service Dates of Committee Chair: Jan. 21, 2009-
Service Dates of Majority Members: Jan. 21, 2009-
Service Dates of Minority Members: Jan. 21, 2009-

Majority

Rank Name	Party	State	Years in: Senate	Years in: Comm.
Chr Baucus, Max S.	Dem	Mont.	31	30
2nd Rockefeller, John D. IV	Dem	W.Va.	25	23
3rd Conrad, Kent	Dem	N.D.	23	17
4th Bingaman, J.F. (Jeff)	Dem	N.M	27	8
5th Kerry, John F.	Dem	Mass.	25	8
6th Lincoln, Blanche Lambert	Dem	Ark.	11	8
7th Wyden, Ronald L.	Dem	Ore.	14	5
8th Schumer, Charles E.	Dem	N.Y.	11	5
9th Stabenow, Deborah Ann	Dem	Mich.	9	3
10th Cantwell, Maria E.	Dem	Wash.	9	3
11th Nelson, C. William (Bill)	Dem	Fla.	9	1
12th Menendez, Robert	Dem	N.J.	4	1
13th Carper, Thomas R.	Dem	Del.	9	1

Minority

Rank Name	Party	State	Years in: Senate	Years in: Comm.
RM Grassley, Charles E.	Rep	Iowa	29	*2 18
2nd Hatch, Orrin G.	Rep	Utah	33	18
3rd Snowe, Olympia J.B.	Rep	Me.	15	8
4th Kyl, Jon L.	Rep	Ariz.	15	8
5th Bunning, James P.D.	Rep	Ky.	11	7
6th Crapo, Michael D.	Rep	Ida.	11	5
7th Roberts, C. Patrick	Rep	Kans.	13	3
8th Ensign, John E.	Rep	Nev.	9	2
9th Enzi, Michael B.	Rep	Wyo.	13	1
10th Cornyn, John	Rep	Tex.	7	1

*2: Member's second period of service on the committee.

Foreign Relations

Senate Committee on Foreign Relations, 103rd-111th Congresses (1993-2011)

BACKGROUND

Organizational History: The Committee on Foreign Relations was established on December 10, 1816, as one of the original eleven standing committees. Senator James Barbour of Virginia, the author of the motion creating the committees, was its initial chair. A new nation had to invent a foreign policy during its first quarter century under the Constitution and the Senate was to play a major role in shaping that policy. Prior to 1816, treaties and ambassadorial nominations were generally dealt with by select committees.

It was the War of 1812 which solidified the new nation's place in the world and increased the business of the Senate, especially the consideration of nominations and national defense needs arising from the War, which necessitated a stable institutional locus for foreign policy.

Throughout the nineteenth century, the Foreign Relations Committee was an important, but not the preeminent, Senate committee. By the end of the century, the Spanish-American War of 1898 and the growth of American territorial expansion in the Pacific and the Caribbean had set the stage for a greater American role in the world. This was confirmed dramatically by our late but fateful entry into World War I, an event which expanded the visibility and power of the committee.

The bitter conflict in 1919 between President Woodrow Wilson and Henry Cabot Lodge (Rep-Mass.), the chair of Foreign Relations, disrupted the president's post-war plans for the League of Nations. The conflict also contributed much to the nation's isolationism in the years between the two world wars as typified by its chairs, William E. Borah (Rep-Ida.,1924-1933) and Key Pittman (Dem-Utah, 1933-1940).

A new world awaited the United States in 1945, and the 1946 Reorganization Act sought to give the Foreign Relations Committee a clear role in the post-war era. The committee's jurisdiction expanded to meet the requirements of the dominant role of the United States in world affairs and of the growing interest in international issues, such as nuclear weapons and disarmament, trade, international energy and investment, international organization, security agreements, foreign aid, and the world environment.

The next major crisis between the White House and the Foreign Relations Committee occurred as a consequence of the undeclared war in Vietnam. In 1965, Foreign Relations chair Senator J. William Fulbright (Dem-Ark.) was the first major congressional figure to challenge the objectives of American policy in Southeast Asia. It was the hearings conducted by the Foreign Relations Committee, which legitimized the anti-war protest of the 1960s and 1970s, earning Fulbright and fellow anti-war senators on the committee the enmity of Presidents Johnson and Nixon. Since 1973, the committee has had the responsibility of monitoring many executive agreements between the United States and foreign governments that are often used instead of formal treaties.

The Fulbright-era Foreign Relations Committee expanded its oversight role to cover executive agencies and foreign policy. Its jurisdiction now extends over the annual authorization bills for and programs of all foreign relations agencies except the Central Intelligence Agency. Since 1968, the committee's oversight of executive agreements with foreign governments and the commitment of U.S. armed forces to a potential combat situation have been extended by the Case Act (Public Law 92-403) and the War Powers Resolution (Public Law 93-148), respectively.

Included in the 1992 jurisdiction contained in the *Standing Rules of the Senate* are the following areas, which were not present in 1946: foreign economic, military, technical, and humanitarian assistance; international aspects of nuclear energy, including nuclear transfer policy; international law as it relates to foreign policy; national security and international aspects of trusteeships of the United States; and oceans and international environmental and scientific affairs as they relate to foreign policy.

Although traditionally one of the most prestigious committees, Foreign Relations had lost much of its power and influence by the 1980s. It no longer occupied the vital role in foreign policy decision-making that it had in previous decades. One factor in this change was the general decline in the foreign policy authority of Congress. As power shifted from Congress to the executive branch, the committee lost its role in many key international issues. The unpopularity of foreign aid programs also handicapped the committee. Another factor was the increasing partisan division on the committee. By the late 1980s the committee was deeply divided between mostly liberal Democrats and a group of very conservative Republicans. Debates on important issues, such as war in Central America and nuclear arms control, were marked by bitter arguments between the two factions.

Although the Senate grants the power to declare war to the Foreign Relations Committee, the last formal declarations of war occurred on June 5, 1942, when war was declared on Nazi allies Bulgaria, Hungary, and Romania. Since then the increasing use of "authorizations of military force" have been used by presidents to justify the military presence of American troops in foreign lands and the Senate has more often than not been presented with a foreign policy *fait accompli.*

Membership: Like most of the post-Reorganization committees, Foreign Relations opened the 80th Congress with thirteen members. Its membership reached nineteen by the 89th Congress (1965-1967) but it was reduced to fifteen in 1969, when Majority Leader Michael J. Mansfield (Dem-Mont.) feared that more conservative newly-elected senators would dilute the committees anti-Vietnam war stance. Since 1993, it appears as if the committees preeminence among the Senate's sixteen standing committees has slipped. Its mean size of 18.9 members placed it eleventh. That was not surprising. What is surprising is that the committee's mean seniority of 10.58 years ranked it eleventh and its inter-Congress mean retention rate of 82.6 percent lodged Foreign Relations in fourteenth place, only outranking Homeland Security and Governmental Affairs and Environment and Public Works.

As expected, the Senate Foreign Relations has been a recent net loser of members, gaining only seven, while losing twenty-four for a net loss of seventeen, the second-highest net loss among the sixteen standing committees, edging out only the Environment and Public Works Committee.

Committee Leaders: Republican Arthur H. Vandenberg of Michigan was the first post-war chair of the Foreign Relations Committee and Democrat Thomas T. Connally of Texas was its ranking minority member. Vandenberg and Connally swapped roles in the 81st and 82nd Congresses (1949-1953). When Vandenberg died in 1951, during the 82nd Congress he was succeeded by Alexander Wiley of Wisconsin, who became chair in 1953 when Republicans regained control of the Senate. When Connally retired in 1952, Walter F. George left his senior rank on Finance in 1953 to become the senior Democrat on Foreign Relations, which led to his becoming chair in 1955. George was succeeded as chair by the venerable Theodore Francis Green of Rhode Island, who had an ancestor who served in the Continental Congress. Green was eighty-nine when he began service in 1957, and two years later, he was induced to step down as chair on February 6,1959 at the age of ninety-one. Green's advanced age and the continuing Cold War crisis led Majority Leader Lyndon B. Johnson to urge that Green relinquish the chair of this critical committee to Fulbright.

Wiley served as the senior Republican until his re-election defeat in 1962. Iowa's Bourke B. Hickenlooper succeeded Wiley and was its ranking Republican until his retirement in 1968. At that point, he succeeded by the "wise old owl" of Vermont, George D. Aiken, who retired from the Senate in 1974.

While senior Republicans changed, Fulbright continued to chair Foreign Relations from 1959 until 1975, throughout the Vietnam War, and was often at odds with President Lyndon Johnson, who felt that Fulbright had been ungrateful to him for Johnson's role in first gaining him the chairmanship of this prestigious panel from Teddy Green. Fulbright was defeated for renomination in 1974 by Arkansas governor Dale Bumpers. Part of the Fulbright legacy was his hiring of a young Georgetown University student Bill Clinton as an intern.

John J. Sparkman (Dem-Ala.) became chair in 1975 after Fulbright's defeat and held it until his own retirement in 1978. Frank F. Church (Dem-Ida.) succeeded Sparkman and held the chair until his defeat in 1980. A beneficiary of the Republican victory in 1980, Charles H. Percy (Rep-Ill.) chaired the committee from 1981 until his 1984 re-election defeat. Similar fates befell the two Republican ranking minority members who followed Aiken, with Clifford P. Case of New Jersey and Jacob K. Javits of New York both losing primaries in 1978 and 1980, respectively. Senior ranks on the Foreign Relations Committee require a lot of attention to international events and, with few constituency benefits, those senior members have difficulty translating their "Hill-style" prestige into "home-style" security, making them vulnerable to electoral defeat.

Percy was replaced as chair by Richard G. Lugar (Rep-Ind.), who gained the post in 1985 when North Carolina's tobacco growers obliged the more senior Jesse Helms to remain as chair of Agriculture, Nutrition and Forestry. Rhode Island's patrician Democrat Claiborne deB. Pell, who like fellow Rhode Islander Green, had congressional ancestors dating back to the John Adams administration, served as the committee's senior Democrat for sixteen years—as ranking minority member (1981-1987 and 1995-1997) and as its chair from 1987 to 1995—until his retirement in 1996.

In 1987, Jesse Helms defeated Lugar in the Republican Conference for the ranking position on Foreign Relations and Lugar took over Helms's slot as the ranking Republican on Agriculture, Nutrition and Forestry. Helms was the senior Republican for the next sixteen years—six-plus as chair (1995-2001) and nine-plus as ranking minority member (1987-1995, 2001-2003) and served until his retirement in 2002. Lugar resumed the chairmanship of Foreign Relations in 2003 and held it until 2007 when Democrats regained Senate control. He has served as ranking minority member in the past two Congresses (2007-2011).

Succeeding Pell was Delaware's Joseph R. Biden Jr., who held the senior Democratic slot as ranking minority member (1997-2001 and 2003-2007) and as chair (2001-2003 and 2007-2009) until his election as vice president in 2008. John F. Kerry of Massachusetts, the Democratic presidential nominee in 2004, presently chairs Foreign Relations.

Party Leaders: Eight Republican leaders served on Foreign Relations, while only five of the committee's Democrats did. Among the eight Republicans were seven floor leaders: Wallace H. White of Maine, 1947-1948, who first came to Washington as a clerk for his grandfather; Senator William P. Frye who served as Senate president *pro tempore* from 1895 to 1911; Robert A. Taft, 1953-1954; William F. Knowland, 1954-1959; Hugh D. Scott of Pennsylvania, 1969-1977; Howard Baker Jr. of Tennessee, 1977-1985; Bill Frist of Tennessee, 2003-2007; and the current Republican leader since 2007, Mitch McConnell of Kentucky. While both Scott and McConnell served as Republican Whips prior to becoming floor leader, the only Republican leader who only served as Whip was Robert P. Griffin of Michigan, 1969-1977.

The five Democratic party leaders who served on Foreign Relations were two floor leaders—Alben Barkley of Kentucky, 1937-1949 and Mike Mansfield of Montana, 1961-1977; and three Whips, Hubert Humphrey of Minnesota, 1961-1965 who followed Mansfield's 1957-1961 stint as LBJ's Whip; Russell Long of Louisiana who succeeded Humphrey, 1965-1969; and Alan Cranston of California, 1977-1991.

Presidential Aspirations: The 2008 election of President Obama and Vice President Biden reveals a valuable point about the Foreign Relations Committee's role as a presidential springboard. Eleven of the Senate's twenty-three presidential and vice presidential nominees since 1947 have served on Foreign Relations. While it may increase one's electoral vulnerability back home, membership on the committee is seen as a way of establishing foreign policy *bona fides* for an aspiring presidential candidate. This is particularly true of Democratic contenders. Five Democratic presidential nominees served on Foreign Relations—John F. Kennedy of Massachusetts, the 1960 nominee; Hubert H. Humphrey of Minnesota, the 1968 nominee; George S. McGovern of South Dakota, the 1972 nominee; John F. Kerry, the 2004 nominee; and Barack Obama of Illinois, the 2008 nominee. While Kennedy and Obama succeeded to the presidency, Humphrey's career peaked at vice president. In addition to Humphrey's vice presidential nomination in 1964 on Lyndon Johnson's ticket, other Foreign Relations Democrats receiving vice presidential nods include Alben Barkley of Kentucky, who ran with President Truman in 1948; John Sparkman of Alabama, who ran with Stevenson in 1952; Edmund Muskie of Maine, who ran with Humphrey in 1968; and Thomas Eagleton of Missouri, McGovern's ill-fated first choice in 1972. The three winners were Barkley, Humphrey, and Biden.

So common is it that at least one if not more Democratic members of Foreign Relations contend for the presidency that it is hard to recall a presidential year when one did not. Among the committee's non-nominated Democratic contenders were: Albert Gore Sr. of Tennessee, Stuart Symington of Missouri, Wayne Morse of Oregon, Eugene McCarthy of Minnesota, Frank Church of Idaho, John Glenn of Ohio, Alan Cranston of California, Paul Simon of Illinois, Terry Sanford of North Carolina, Paul Tsongas of Massachusetts, and Christopher Dodd of Connecticut.

Senate Republicans receive fewer nominations than Senate Democrats—only six Republicans to seventeen Democrats—and the only Foreign Relations Republican nominated was Henry Cabot Lodge of Massachusetts in 1960 as Richard Nixon's running-mate. Lodge's Senate career had ended in 1952 with a defeat to John F. Kennedy, who would top the ticket that would leave Lodge once again on the losing side. However, that lack of success has not stopped other Republicans on the committee from contending for the White House—Robert A. Taft of Ohio, William F. Knowland of California, Howard Baker of Tennessee, and Larry Pressler of South Dakota. As in the case of the nominees, Democratic aspirants outnumber Republican ones.

Other Notables: Given the high level of interest demonstrated by Foreign Relations Committee members in the executive branch, it is surprising that only one member of the committee voluntarily left to serve in the Cabinet—Edmund Muskie of Maine who served less than a year as President Jimmy Carter's Secretary of State in 1980, following Cyrus Vance's unexpectedly angry resignation from that post over the failed hostage rescue mission in Tehran. Committee member John Ashcroft of Missouri became Attorney General after his Senate defeat in 2000. Three modern-era committee members had prior Cabinet service: two Republicans—Lamar Alexander of Tennessee, President George H.W. Bush's Secretary of Education and Mel Martinez of Florida, President George W. Bush's Secretary of Housing and Urban Development—and one Democrat, Brock Adams of Washington, who was Secretary of Transportation under President Carter.

Two post-1993 Foreign Relations Committee members left the Senate to return home as governors—Republican Frank Murkowski of Alaska in 2002 and Democrat Jon S. Corzine of New Jersey in 2006. Neither would be re-elected. Murkowski lost his renomination bid to Sarah Palin in 2006 and Corzine lost his re-election bid to Chris Christie in 2009.

Selected References

Coren, Robert W., et al., "Records of the Committee on Foreign Relations, 1816-1968," *Guide to the Records of the United States Senate at the National Archives: 1789-1989 Bicentennial Edition* (Washington, D.C.: National Archives and Records Administration, 1989), 105-115.

Crabb, Cecil V. and Pat M. Holt, *Invitation to Struggle: Congress, the President and Foreign Policy* (Washington, D.C.: Congressional Quarterly, 1980).

Dennison, Eleanor E., *The Senate Foreign Relations Committee* (Palo Alto, Cal.: Stanford University Press, 1942).

Gould, James W., "The Origins of the Senate Committee on Foreign Relations," *Western Political Quarterly*, 12 (1959), 670-682.

Farnsworth, David, *The Senate Committee on Foreign Relations* (Urbana: University of Illinois Press, 1961).

Holt, Pat M., "Foreign Relations Committee, Senate," in Donald C. Bacon, Roger H. Davidson, and Morton Keller, eds., *The Encyclopedia of the United States Congress* (New York: Simon & Schuster, 1995), I: 876-880.

Kepley, David R., *The Collapse of the Middle Way: Senate Republicans and the Bipartisan Foreign Policy, 1948-1952* (New York: Greenwood Press, 1988).

McCormick, James M., "Decision Making in the Foreign Affairs and Foreign Relations Committees," in Randall B. Ripley and James M. Lindsay, eds., *Congress Resurgent: Foreign and Defense Policy on Capitol Hill* (Ann Arbor: University of Michigan Press, 1993), 115-154.

Sparkman, U.S. Senator John J., "The Role of the Senate in Determining Foreign Policy," in Nathaniel Stone Preston, ed., *The Senate Institution* (New York: Van Nostrand Reinhold Co., 1969), 31-39.

U.S. Senate, Committee on Foreign Relations, *Committee on Foreign Relations, Millennium Edition, 1816-2000*, Senate Document 105-28, 105th Congress, 2nd session (1998). This is the third committee history since 1976: 1) the *160th Anniversary, 1816-1976*, Senate Document 94-265, 04th Congress, 2nd session (1976); and 2) the *170th Anniversary, 1816-1986*, Senate Document 99-21, 99th Congress, 2nd session (1986).

U.S. Senate, Committee on Foreign Relations, *The Senate Role in Foreign Affairs Appointments*, Committee Print, 97th Congress, 2nd session (1982).

RESPONSIBILITIES, JURISDICTIONAL CHANGES, AND SUBCOMMITTEES

FOREIGN RELATIONS

Jurisdiction, 80th Congress (1947-49)

Established by the Legislative Reorganization Act of 1946:

[Section 102.(1)(i)]

(1) **Committee on Foreign Relations**, to consist of thirteen Senators, to which committee shall be referred all proposed legislation, messages, petitions, memorials, and other matters relating to the following subjects:

    (1) Relations of the United States with foreign nations generally

    (2) Treaties

(3) Establishment of boundary lines between the United States and foreign nations
(4) Protection of American citizens abroad and expatriation
(5) Neutrality
(6) International conferences and congresses
(7) The American National Red Cross
(8) Intervention abroad and declarations of war
(9) Measures relating to the diplomatic service
(10) Acquisition of land and buildings for embassies and legations in foreign countries
(11) Measures to foster commercial intercourse with foreign nations and to safeguard American business interests abroad
(12) United Nations Organization and international financial and monetary organizations
(13) Foreign loans

Post-Reorganization Jurisdiction, 1977

From Committee System Reorganization Amendments of 1977, S.Res. 95-4, *Senate Journal*, Feb. 4, 1977:

[XXV.Section 101. 1.(j)]

(1) **Committee on Foreign Relations**, to which committee shall be referred all proposed legislation, messages, petitions, memorials, and other matters relating to the following subjects:

(1) Relations of the United States with foreign nations generally
(2) Treaties and executive agreements, except reciprocal trade agreements
(3) Boundaries of the United States
(4) Protection of United States citizens abroad and expatriation
(5) Intervention abroad and declarations of war
(6) Foreign economic, military, technical, and humanitarian assistance
(7) United Nations and its affiliated organizations
(8) International conferences and congresses
(9) Diplomatic service.
(10) International law as it relates to foreign policy
(11) Oceans and international environmental and scientific affairs as they relate to foreign policy
(12) International activities of the American National Red Cross and the International Committee of the Red Cross
(13) International aspects of nuclear energy, including nuclear transfer policy
(14) Foreign loans
(15) Measures to foster commercial intercourse with foreign nations and to safeguard American business interests abroad
(16) The World Bank group, the regional development banks, and other international organizations established primarily for development assistance purposes
(17) The International Monetary Fund and other international organizations established primarily for international monetary purposes (except that, at the request of the Committee on Banking, Housing, and Urban Affairs, any proposed legislation relating to such subjects reported by the Committee on Foreign Relations shall be referred to the Committee on Banking, Housing, and Urban Affairs)
(18) Acquisition of land and buildings for embassies and legations in foreign countries
(19) National security and international aspects of trusteeships of the United States

(2) Such committee shall also study and review, on a comprehensive basis, matters relating to the national security policy, foreign policy, and international economic policy as it relates to foreign policy of the United States, and matters relating to food, hunger, and nutrition in foreign countries, and report thereon from time to time.

Jurisdiction, 103rd Congress (1993-94)

From the *Standing Rules of the Senate* in the *Senate Manual*, 103rd Congress, 1st Session, S. Doc. 103-1:

[Rule XXV.(1)(j)]

(1) **Committee on Foreign Relations**, to which committee shall be referred all proposed legislation, messages, petitions, memorials, and other matters relating to the following subjects:

(1) Acquisition of land and buildings for embassies and legations in foreign countries
(2) Boundaries of the United States
(3) Diplomatic service
(4) Foreign economic, military, technical, and humanitarian assistance
(5) Foreign loans
(6) International activities of the American National Red Cross and the International Committee of the Red Cross
(7) International aspects of nuclear energy, including nuclear transfer policy
(8) International conferences and congresses

(9)   International law as it relates to foreign policy

(10)   International Monetary Fund and other international organizations established primarily for international monetary purposes (except that, at the request of the Committee on Banking, Housing, and Urban Affairs, any proposed legislation relating to such subjects reported by the Committee on Foreign Relations shall be referred to the Committee on Banking, Housing, and Urban Affairs)

(11)   Intervention abroad and declarations of war

(12)   Measures to foster commercial intercourse with foreign nations and to safeguard American business interests abroad

(13)   National security and international aspects of trusteeships of the United States

(14)   Oceans and international environmental and scientific affairs as they relate to foreign policy

(15)   Protection of United States citizens abroad and expatriation

(16)   Relations of the United States with foreign nations generally

(17)   Treaties and executive agreements, except reciprocal trade agreements

(18)   United Nations and its affiliated organizations

(19)   World Bank group, the regional development banks, and other international organizations established primarily for development assistance purposes

(2)   Such committee shall also study and review, on a comprehensive basis, matters relating to the national security policy, foreign policy, and international economic policy as it relates to foreign policy of the United States, and matters relating to food, hunger, and nutrition in foreign countries, and report thereon from time to time.

Jurisdiction, 111th Congress (2009-10)

From *Authority and Rules of Senate Committees, 2009-2010*, Sen. Doc. 111-3, pursuant to S.Res, 166, June 2, 2009.

[Rule XXV.(1)(j)]

(1)   **Committee on Foreign Relations**, to which committee shall be referred all proposed legislation, messages, petitions, memorials, and other matters relating to the following subjects:

(1)   Acquisition of land and buildings for embassies and legations in foreign countries

(2)   Boundaries of the United States

(3)   Diplomatic service

(4)   Foreign economic, military, technical, and humanitarian assistance

(5)   Foreign loans

(6)   International activities of the American National Red Cross and the International Committee of the Red Cross

(7)   International aspects of nuclear energy, including nuclear transfer policy

(8)   International conferences and congresses

(9)   International law as it relates to foreign policy

(10)   International Monetary Fund and other international organizations established primarily for international monetary purposes (except that, at the request of the Committee on Banking, Housing, and Urban Affairs, any proposed legislation relating to such subjects reported by the Committee on Foreign Relations shall be referred to the Committee on Banking, Housing, and Urban Affairs)

(11)   Intervention abroad and declarations of war

(12)   Measures to foster commercial intercourse with foreign nations and to safeguard American business interests abroad

(13)   National security and international aspects of trusteeships of the United States

(14)   Oceans and international environmental and scientific affairs as they relate to foreign policy

(15)   Protection of United States citizens abroad and expatriation

(16)   Relations of the United States with foreign nations generally

(17)   Treaties and executive agreements, except reciprocal trade agreements

(18)   United Nations and its affiliated organizations

(19)   World Bank group, the regional development banks, and other international organizations established primarily for development assistance purposes

(2)   Such committee shall also study and review, on a comprehensive basis, matters relating to the national security policy, foreign policy, and international economic policy as it relates to foreign policy of the United States, and matters relating to food, hunger, and nutrition in foreign countries, and report thereon from time to time.

NAMES OF SUBCOMMITTEES

Committee on Foreign Relations, 103rd -111th Congresses

African Affairs, 103, 104, 105, 106, 107, 108, 109, 110, 111
Central Asia and South Caucuses, 107 only
East Asian and Pacific Affairs, 103, 104, 105, 106, 107, 108, 109, 110, 111

European Affairs, 103, 104, 105, 106, 107, 108, 109, 110, 111
International Development and Foreign Assistance, Economic Affairs and International Environmental Protection, 110, 111
International Economic Policy, Trade, Oceans and Environment, 103
International Economic Policy, Export and Trade Promotion, 104, 105, 106, 107, 108, 109
International Operations, 104, 105, 106
International Operations and Terrorism, 107, 108, 109
International Operations and Organizations, Democracy and Human Rights, 110
International Operations and Organizations, Human Rights, Democracy, and Global Women Issues, 111
Near Eastern and South Asian Affairs, 103, 104, 105, 106, 107, 108, 109
Near Eastern, South and Central Asian Affairs, 110, 111
Terrorism, Narcotics and International Operations, 103
Western Hemisphere and Peace Corps Affairs, 103, 104
Western Hemisphere, Peace Corps, Narcotics, and Terrorism, 105, 106
Western Hemisphere, Peace Corps, and Narcotics Affairs, 107, 108, 109, 110, 111

MEMBERSHIP ROSTERS, 103rd-111th Congresses, 1993-2010

FOREIGN RELATIONS / 103rd Congress

Service Dates of Committee Chair: Jan. 7, 1993-Jan. 5, 1995

Service Dates of Majority Members: Jan. 7, 1993-Jan. 5, 1995

Service Dates of Minority Members: Jan. 7, 1993-Jan. 4, 1995

Majority						Minority				
			Years in:						Years in:	
Rank Name	Party	State	Senate	Comm.		Rank Name	Party	State	Senate	Comm.
Chr Pell, Claiborne D.	Dem	R.I.	33	28		RM Helms, Jesse A.	Rep	N.C.	21	14
2nd Biden, Joseph R. Jr.	Dem	Del.	21	18		2nd Lugar, Richard G.	Rep	Ind.	17	14
3rd Sarbanes, Paul S.	Dem	Md.	17	16		3rd Kassebaum, Nancy Landon	Rep	Kans.	15	13
4th Dodd, Christopher J.	Dem	Conn.	13	13		4th Pressler, Larry L.	Rep	S.D.	15	13
5th Kerry, John F.	Dem	Mass.	9	8		5th Murkowski, Frank H.	Rep	Alas.	13	11
6th Simon, Paul M.	Dem	Ill.	9	7		6th Brown, G. Hanks (Hank)	Rep	Colo.	3	2
7th Moynihan, Daniel Patrick	Dem	N.Y.	17	7		7th Jeffords, James M.	Rep	Vt.	5	3
8th Robb, Charles S.	Dem	Va.	5	4		8th Coverdell, Paul	Rep	Ga.	1	1
9th Wofford, Harris	Dem	Penn.	2	2		9th Gregg, Judd A.	Rep	N.H.	1	1
10th Feingold, Russell D.	Dem	Wisc.	1	1						
11th Mathews, Harlan	Dem	Tenn.	1	1						

Note: A party ratio change occurred when Kay Bailey Hutchison (Rep-Tex.) replaced Robert G. Krieger (Dem-Tex.) in a special election.

Additions:
   Minority:

9th Gregg, Judd A.	Rep	N.H.	July 1, 1993

Changes:
   Majority:

Mathews, Harlan	Dem	Tenn.	Dec. 1, 1994 Resigned the Senate and retired; replaced by special election winner Fred D. Thompson (Rep-Tenn.).

Departures from the Senate:	**Majority**			**Minority**		
Defeated for Re-election	Wofford, Harris	Dem	Penn.	None		

Departures from Committee:						
Became Chair of Commerce, Science, and Transportation	None			Pressler, Larry L.	Rep	S.D.
Moved to Finance	None			Pressler, Larry L.	Rep	S.D.
				Murkowski, Frank H.	Rep	Alas.
Moved to Appropriations				Gregg, Judd A.	Rep	N.H.
				Jeffords, James M.	Rep	Vt.
Moved to Energy and Natural Resources	None			Jeffords, James M.	Rep	Vt.
No new assignment	Simon, Paul M.	Dem	Ill.			
	Moynihan, Daniel Patrick	Dem	N.Y.			

FOREIGN RELATIONS / 104th Congress

Service Dates of Committee Chair: Jan. 5, 1995-Jan. 9, 1997

Service Dates of Majority Members: Jan. 5, 1995-Jan. 9, 1997

Service Dates of Minority Members: Jan. 4, 1995-Jan. 9, 1997

Majority					Minority				
			Years in:					Years in:	
Rank Name	Party	State	Senate	Comm.	Rank Name	Party	State	Senate	Comm.
Chr Helms, Jesse A.	Rep	N.C.	23	16	RM Pell, Claiborne D.	Dem	R.I.	35	30
2nd Lugar, Richard G.	Rep	Ind.	19	16	2nd Biden, Joseph R. Jr.	Dem	Del.	23	20
3rd Kassebaum, Nancy Landon	Rep	Kans.	17	15	3rd Sarbanes, Paul S.	Dem	Md.	19	18
4th Brown, G. Hanks (Hank)	Rep	Colo.	5	4	4th Dodd, Christopher J.	Dem	Conn.	15	14
5th Coverdell, Paul	Rep	Ga.	3	2	5th Kerry, John F.	Dem	Mass.	11	10
6th Snowe, Olympia J.B.	Rep	Me.	1	1	6th Robb, Charles S.	Dem	Va.	7	6
7th Thompson, Fred D.	Rep	Tenn.	1	1	7th Feingold, Russell D.	Dem	Wisc.	3	2
8th Thomas, Craig L.	Rep	Wyo.	1	1	8th Feinstein, Dianne	Dem	Cal.	3	1
9th Grams, Rod	Rep	Minn.	1	1					
10th Ashcroft, John D.	Rep	Mo.	1	1					

Departures from the Senate:		Majority				Minority		
Retired		Kassebaum, Nancy Landon	Rep	Kans.		Pell, Claiborne D.	Dem	R.I.
		Brown, G. Hanks (Hank)	Rep	Colo.				

Departures from Committee:						
Became Chair of Governmental Affairs	Thompson, Fred D.	Rep	Tenn.	None	
Moved to Armed Services	Snowe, Olympia J.B.	Rep	Me.	None	

FOREIGN RELATIONS / 105th Congress

Service Dates of Committee Chair: Jan. 9, 1997-Jan. 7, 1999

Service Dates of Majority Members: Jan. 9, 1997-Jan. 7, 1999

Service Dates of Minority Members: Jan. 9, 1997-Jan. 7, 1999

Majority					Minority				
			Years in:					Years in:	
Rank Name	Party	State	Senate	Comm.	Rank Name	Party	State	Senate	Comm.
Chr Helms, Jesse A.	Rep	N.C.	25	18	RM Biden, Joseph R. Jr.	Dem	Del.	25	22
2nd Lugar, Richard G.	Rep	Ind.	21	18	2nd Sarbanes, Paul S.	Dem	Md.	21	20
3rd Coverdell, Paul	Rep	Ga.	5	5	3rd Dodd, Christopher J.	Dem	Conn.	17	17
4th Hagel, Charles T. (Chuck)	Rep	Neb.	1	1	4th Kerry, John F.	Dem	Mass.	13	12
5th Smith, Gordon H.	Rep	Ore.	1	1	5th Robb, Charles S.	Dem	Va.	9	8
6th Thomas, Craig L.	Rep	Wyo.	3	3	6th Feingold, Russell D.	Dem	Wisc.	5	5
7th Ashcroft, John D.	Rep	Mo.	3	3	7th Feinstein, Dianne	Dem	Cal.	5	3
8th Grams, Rod	Rep	Minn.	3	3	8th Wellstone, Paul D.	DFL	Minn.	7	1
9th Frist, William H.	Rep	Tenn.	3	1					
10th Brownback, Sam D.	Rep	Kans.	1	1					

Departures from Committee:	Majority				Minority		
Moved to Finance	None				Robb, Charles S.	Dem	Va.
Returned to Appropriations	None				Feinstein, Dianne	Dem	Cal.

FOREIGN RELATIONS / 106th Congress

Service Dates of Committee Chair: Jan. 7, 1999-Jan. 3, 2001

Service Dates of Majority Members: Jan. 7, 1999-Jan. 25, 2001

Service Dates of Minority Members: Jan. 7, 1999-Jan. 25, 2001

Majority					Minority				
			Years in:					Years in:	
Rank Name	Party	State	Senate	Comm.	Rank Name	Party	State	Senate	Comm.
Chr Helms, Jesse A.	Rep	N.C.	27	20	RM Biden, Joseph R. Jr.	Dem	Del.	27	24
2nd Lugar, Richard G.	Rep	Ind.	23	20	2nd Sarbanes, Paul S.	Dem	Md.	23	22

3rd Coverdell, Paul	Rep	Ga.	7	7
4th Hagel, Charles T. (Chuck)	Rep	Neb.	3	2
5th Smith, Gordon H.	Rep	Ore.	3	2
6th Grams, Rod	Rep	Minn.	5	5
7th Brownback, Sam D.	Rep	Kans.	3	2
8th Thomas, Craig L.	Rep	Wyo.	5	5
9th Ashcroft, John D.	Rep	Mo.	5	5
10th Frist, William H.	Rep	Tenn.	5	2

3rd Dodd, Christopher J.	Dem	Conn.	19	19
4th Kerry, John F.	Dem	Mass.	15	14
5th Feingold, Russell D.	Dem	Wisc.	7	7
6th Wellstone, Paul D.	Dem	Minn.	9	2
7th Boxer, Barbara	Dem	Cal.	7	1
8th Torricelli, Robert G.	Dem	N.J.	3	1

Changes:
Majority:

Coverdell, Paul	Rep	Ga.	Nov. 9, 1999 Left the committee; moved to Finance.
Chafee, Lincoln D.	Rep	R.I.	Nov. 9, 1999 Replaced Coverdell.

Departures from the Senate:

	Majority			**Minority**
Defeated for Re-election	Grams, Rod	Rep	Minn.	None
	Ashcroft, John D.	Rep	Mo.	

FOREIGN RELATIONS / 107th Congress, Pre-Jeffords switch

Service Dates of Committee Chair: ChT: Jan. 3, 2001-Jan. 25, 2001 Biden (Dem-Del.)

Ch1: Jan. 25, 2001-June 6, 2001 Helms (Rep-N.C.)

Service Dates of Majority Members: Jan. 25, 2001-June 6, 2001

Service Dates of Minority Members: Jan. 25, 2001-June 6, 2001

Majority			Years in:		**Minority**			Years in:	
Rank Name	Party	State	Senate	Comm.	Rank Name	Party	State	Senate	Comm.
Ch1 Helms, Jesse A.	Rep	N.C.	29	23	RM1 Biden, Joseph R. Jr.	Dem	Del.	29	27
2nd Lugar, Richard G.	Rep	Ind.	25	23	2nd Sarbanes, Paul S.	Dem	Md.	25	24
3rd Hagel, Charles T. (Chuck)	Rep	Neb.	5	5	3rd Dodd, Christopher J.	Dem	Conn.	21	21
4th Smith, Gordon H.	Rep	Ore.	5	5	4th Kerry, John F.	Dem	Mass.	17	16
5th Thomas, Craig L.	Rep	Wyo.	7	7	5th Feingold, Russell D.	Dem	Wisc.	9	9
6th Frist, William H.	Rep	Tenn.	7	5	6th Wellstone, Paul D.	DFL	Minn.	11	5
7th Chafee, Lincoln D.	Rep	R.I.	2	2	7th Boxer, Barbara	Dem	Cal.	9	3
8th Allen, George F.	Rep	Va.	1	1	8th Torricelli, Robert G.	Dem	N.J.	5	3
9th Brownback, Sam D.	Rep	Kans.	5	5	9th Nelson, C. William (Bill)	Dem	Fla.	1	1

Note: The committee majority in the 2001 Senate power-sharing arrangement was determined by the party of the vice president. Democrat Al Gore Jr. served from Jan. 3, 2001, to Jan. 20, 2001, and was succeeded by Republican Richard B. Cheney on Jan. 20, 2001. When Senator Jeffords of Vermont left the Republican Party, effective June 6, 2001, to become an Independent, Democrats regained the majority for the remainder of the 107th Congress.

FOREIGN RELATIONS / 107th Congress, Post-Jeffords switch

Service Dates of Committee Chair: June 6, 2001-Jan. 14, 2003

Service Dates of Majority Members: June 6, 2001-Jan. 14, 2003

Service Dates of Minority Members: June 6, 2001-Jan. 15, 2003

Majority			Years in:		**Minority**			Years in:	
Rank Name	Party	State	Senate	Comm.	Rank Name	Party	State	Senate	Comm.
Ch2 Biden, Joseph R. Jr.	Dem	Del.	29	27	RM2 Helms, Jesse A.	Rep	N.C.	29	23
2nd Sarbanes, Paul S.	Dem	Md.	25	25	2nd Lugar, Richard G.	Rep	Ind.	25	23
3rd Dodd, Christopher J.	Dem	Conn.	21	21	3rd Hagel, Charles T. (Chuck)	Rep	Neb.	5	5
4th Kerry, John F.	Dem	Mass.	17	17	4th Smith, Gordon H.	Rep	Ore.	5	5
5th Feingold, Russell D.	Dem	Wisc.	9	9	5th Thomas, Craig L.	Rep	Wyo.	7	7
6th Wellstone, Paul D.	DFL	Minn.	11	5	6th Frist, William H.	Rep	Tenn.	7	5
7th Boxer, Barbara	Dem	Cal.	9	3	7th Chafee, Lincoln D.	Rep	R.I.	2	2
8th Torricelli, Robert G.	Dem	N.J.	5	3	8th Allen, George F.	Rep	Va.	1	1
9th Nelson, C. William (Bill)	Dem	Fla.	1	1	9th Brownback, Sam D.	Rep	Kans.	5	5
10th Rockefeller, John D. IV	Dem	W. Va.	17	1					

Additions:
Majority:

10th Rockefeller IV, John D.	Dem	W. Va.	July 10, 2001

Changes:
Majority:

Wellstone, Paul D.	DFL	Minn.	Oct. 25, 2002 Died in office.

Minority:

Thomas, Craig L.	Rep	Wyo.	July 10, 2001 Left the committee; moved to Finance to fill Jeffords' vacancy.
Enzi, Michael B.	Rep	Wyo.	July 10, 2001 Replaced Thomas.

Departures from the Senate:	**Majority**				**Minority**		
Retired	Torricelli, Robert G.	Dem	N.J.		Helms, Jesse A.	Rep	N.C.

Departures from Committee:							
Moved to Finance	None				Smith, Gordon H.	Rep	Ore.
					Frist, William H.	Rep	Tenn.
Moved to Indian Affairs, Rules and Administration, and Joint Printing			None		Smith, Gordon H.	Rep	Ore.

FOREIGN RELATIONS / 108th Congress

Service Dates of Committee Chair: Jan. 14, 2003-Jan. 6, 2005

Service Dates of Majority Members: Jan. 14, 2003-Jan. 6, 2005

Service Dates of Minority Members: Jan. 15, 2003-Jan. 6, 2005

Majority			Years in:		Minority			Years in:	
Rank Name	Party	State	Senate	Comm.	Rank Name	Party	State	Senate	Comm.
Chr Lugar, Richard G.	Rep	Ind.	27	24	RM Biden, Joseph R. Jr.	Dem	Del.	31	28
2nd Hagel, Charles T. (Chuck)	Rep	Neb.	7	7	2nd Sarbanes, Paul S.	Dem	Md.	27	26
3rd Chafee, Lincoln D.	Rep	R.I.	4	4	3rd Dodd, Christopher J.	Dem	Conn.	23	23
4th Allen, George F.	Rep	Va.	3	2	4th Kerry, John F.	Dem	Mass.	19	18
5th Brownback, Sam D.	Rep	Kans.	7	7	5th Feingold, Russell D.	Dem	Wisc.	11	11
6th Enzi, Michael B.	Rep	Wyo.	7	2	6th Boxer, Barbara	Dem	Cal.	11	5
7th Voinovich, George V.	Rep	Ohio	5	1	7th Nelson, C. William (Bill)	Dem	Fla.	3	2
8th Alexander, Lamar	Rep	Tenn.	1	1	8th Rockefeller, John D. IV	Dem	W.Va.	19	2
9th Coleman, Norman	Rep	Minn.	1	1	9th Corzine, Jon S.	Dem	N.J.	3	1
10th Sununu, John E.	Rep	N.H.	1	1					

Departures from Committee:	**Majority**				**Minority**		
Returned to Judiciary	Brownback, Sam D.	Rep	Kans.		None		
Moved to Energy and Natural Resources and Select Intelligence	None				Corzine, Jon S.	Dem	N.J.
No new assignment	Enzi, Michael B.	Rep	Wyo.		Rockefeller, John D. IV	Dem	W.Va.

FOREIGN RELATIONS / 109th Congress

Service Dates of Committee Chair: Jan. 6, 2005-Jan. 12, 2007

Service Dates of Majority Members: Jan. 6, 2005-Jan. 12, 2007

Service Dates of Minority Members: Jan. 6, 2005-Jan. 12, 2007

Majority			Years in:		Minority			Years in:	
Rank Name	Party	State	Senate	Comm.	Rank Name	Party	State	Senate	Comm.
Chr Lugar, Richard G.	Rep	Ind.	29	26	RM Biden, Joseph R. Jr.	Dem	Del.	33	30
2nd Hagel, Charles T. (Chuck)	Rep	Neb.	9	8	2nd Sarbanes, Paul S.	Dem	Md.	29	28
3rd Chafee, Lincoln D.	Rep	R.I.	6	6	3rd Dodd, Christopher J.	Dem	Conn.	25	25
4th Allen, George F.	Rep	Va.	5	4	4th Kerry, John F.	Dem	Mass.	21	20
5th Coleman, Norman	Rep	Minn.	3	2	5th Feingold, Russell D.	Dem	Wisc.	13	12
6th Voinovich, George V.	Rep	Ohio	7	2	6th Boxer, Barbara	Dem	Cal.	13	6
7th Alexander, Lamar	Rep	Tenn	3	2	7th Nelson, C. William (Bill)	Dem	Fla.	5	4
8th Sununu, John E.	Rep	N.H.	3	2	8th Obama, Barack	Dem	Ill.	1	1
9th Murkowski, Lisa	Rep	Alas.	3	1					
10th Martinez, Melquiades R. (Mel)	Rep	Fla.	1	1					

Departures from the Senate:	**Majority**				**Minority**		
Defeated for Re-election	Chafee, Lincoln D.	Rep	R.I.		None		
	Allen, George F.	Rep	Va.				
Retired	None				Sarbanes, Paul S.	Dem	Md.

Departures from Committee:							
Moved to Appropriations, Environment and Public Works, and Rules and Administration	Alexander, Lamar	Rep	Tenn.		None		
Moved to Armed Services	Martinez, Melquiades R. (Mel)	Rep	Fla.		None		

FOREIGN RELATIONS / 110th Congress

Service Dates of Committee Chair: Jan. 12, 2007-Jan. 21, 2009

Service Dates of Majority Members: Jan. 12, 2007-Jan. 21, 2009

Service Dates of Minority Members: Jan. 12, 2007-Jan. 21, 2009

Majority					Minority				
			Years in:					Years in:	
Rank Name	Party	State	Senate	Comm.	Rank Name	Party	State	Senate	Comm.
Chr Biden, Joseph R. Jr.	Dem	Del.	35	32	RM Lugar, Richard G.	Rep	Ind.	31	28
2nd Dodd, Christopher J.	Dem	Conn.	27	27	2nd Hagel, Charles T. (Chuck)	Rep	Neb.	11	11
3rd Kerry, John F.	Dem	Mass.	23	22	3rd Coleman, Norman	Rep	Minn.	5	4
4th Feingold, Russell D.	Dem	Wisc.	15	15	4th Corker, Robert	Rep	Tenn.	1	1
5th Boxer, Barbara	Dem	Cal.	15	9	5th Sununu, John E.	Rep	N.H.	5	4
6th Nelson, C. William (Bill)	Dem	Fla.	7	6	6th Voinovich, George V.	Rep	Ohio	9	4
7th Obama, Barack	Dem	Ill.	3	3	7th Murkowski, Lisa	Rep	Alas.	5	3
8th Menendez, Robert	Dem	N.J.	1	1	8th DeMint, James W.	Rep	S.C.	3	1
9th Cardin, Benjamin L.	Dem	Md.	1	1	9th Isakson, Johnny	Rep	Ga.	3	1
10th Casey, Robert P. Jr.	Dem	Penn.	1	1	10th Vitter, David	Rep	La.	3	1
11th Webb, James	Dem	Va.	1	1					

Changes:

Majority:

Obama, Barack	Dem	Ill.		Nov. 16, 2008 Resigned the Senate; elected President.

Departures from the Senate:	Majority			Minority		
Elected Vice President	Biden, Joseph R. Jr.	Dem	Del.	None		
Defeated for Re-election	None			Coleman, Norman	Rep	Minn.
				Sununu, John E.	Rep	N.H.
Retired		None		Hagel, Charles T. (Chuck)	Rep	Neb.

Departures from Committee:						
Moved to Finance	Nelson, C. William (Bill)	Dem	Fla.	None		
Moved to Appropriations	None			Voinovich, George V.	Rep	Ohio
				Murkowski, Lisa	Rep	Alas.
Moved to Armed Services and Banking, Housing, and Urban Affairs	None			Vitter, David	Rep	La.

FOREIGN RELATIONS / 111th Congress

Service Dates of Committee Chair: Jan. 21, 2009-

Service Dates of Majority Members: Jan. 21, 2009-

Service Dates of Minority Members: Jan. 21, 2009-

Majority					Minority				
			Years in:					Years in:	
Rank Name	Party	State	Senate	Comm.	Rank Name	Party	State	Senate	Comm.
Chr Kerry, John F.	Dem	Mass.	25	24	RM Lugar, Richard G.	Rep	Ind.	33	30
2nd Dodd, Christopher J.	Dem	Conn.	29	29	2nd Corker, Robert	Rep	Tenn.	3	3
3rd Feingold, Russell D.	Dem	Wisc.	17	17	3rd Isakson, Johnny	Rep	Ga.	5	3
4th Boxer, Barbara	Dem	Cal.	17	11	4th Risch, James	Rep	Ida.	1	1
5th Menendez, Robert	Dem	N.J.	4	3	5th DeMint, James W.	Rep	S.C.	5	3
6th Cardin, Benjamin L.	Dem	Md.	3	3	6th Barrasso, John A.	Rep	Wyo.	2	1
7th Casey, Robert P. Jr.	Dem	Penn.	3	3	7th Wicker, Roger F.	Rep	Miss.	2	1
8th Webb, James	Dem	Va.	3	3	8th Inhofe, James M.	Rep	Okla.	15	1
9th Shaheen, Jeanne	Dem	N.H.	1	1					
10th Kaufman, Edward E.	Dem	Del.	1	1					
11th Gillibrand, Kirsten E.	Dem	N.Y.	1	1					

Filled vacancy:

Majority:

11th seat by Gillibrand on Jan. 27, 2009.

Minority:

8th seat by Inhofe on July 21, 2009.

Note: The disputed election in Minnesota between Democrat Al Franken and incumbent Republican Norman Coleman led both parties to hold seats open pending the outcome of the recount.

Health, Education, Labor and Pensions

Senate Committee on Labor and Human Resources, 103rd-105th
Congresses (1993-1999)

Senate Committee on Health, Education, Labor and Pensions
106th-111th Congresses (1999-2011)

BACKGROUND

Organizational History: Under the 1946 Reorganization Act, the Senate Committee on Education and Labor was renamed the Committee on Labor and Public Welfare. Its name was changed to the Committee on Human Resources in the 95th Congress (1977-1979) and then again to Labor and Human Resources in 1979. Its name was changed again at the start of the 107th Congress in 2001 to Health, Education, Labor, and Pensions, giving the committee the acronym, HELP.

Its original predecessor was the Committee on Education, established on January 28, 1869, on a motion introduced by Justin S. Morrill (Rep-Vt.), the author of the Morrill Land-Grant Act. Its first chair was Charles W. Drake (Rep-Mo.). The committee was renamed the Committee on Education and Labor on February 14, 1870, due in part to the growing number of petitions and memorials received by the Senate after the 1868 enactment of the first eight-hour workday law.

The passage in 1935 of the National Labor Relations Act followed shortly by the Walsh-Healey Public Contracts Act of 1936 and the Fair Labor Standards Act of 1938 gave the Education and Labor Committee renewed respect. The committee's responsibilities expanded in World War II, as it investigated the lack of physical fitness of potential draftees and oversaw passage of nurse training legislation. Responsibility for the Public Health Service was moved in 1944 from Commerce to Education and Labor.

Its most notable legislative achievement in the last pre-reorganization Congress was the passage of the Hospital Survey and Construction (Hill-Burton) Act of 1946, which modernized and enlarged the nation's hospital system. Its most notable achievement in the first post-reorganization Congress was the Taft-Hartley Act of 1947 which limited the power of labor unions to call strikes. The sympathy of the committee's Democrats to labor issues led the Senate to add mine safety legislation to its agenda in 1949.

Unlike the House, the Senate committee reformers of 1946 initially failed to establish a separate standing committee on veterans. The consequence was to give the Labor and Public Welfare Committee jurisdiction over veterans' vocational rehabilitation and education, medical treatment and hospitals, civil relief, and readjustment to civilian life. These veterans-related functions were moved to the newly established Veterans Affairs Committee in 1970 under provisions of the Legislative Reorganization Act of 1970 (Public Law 91-510).

Another legislative eruption from the committee occurred during President Lyndon B. Johnson's Great Society programs of the 1960s. It was a time in which the committee reported much of the health, education, and manpower legislation of the War on Poverty, most notably, the Economic Opportunity Act of 1964. By the end of the Johnson Administration in 1969, the committee's jurisdiction was extended into many other fields as the Federal Government established programs to support the aging, the arts and humanities, biomedical research and development, equal employment opportunity, and student loans, and to regulate occupational safety and health and private pension plans.

The creation of the standing Committee on Veterans Affairs in 1970 moved the veterans-related items—veterans' medical care, treatment, and hospitals; civil relief of soldiers and sailors; and readjustment of servicemen to civil life—from the Labor and Public Welfare Committee.

With the passage of Senate Resolution 4, the 1977 Committee System Reorganization Amendments, the committee was renamed the Committee on Human Resources, but this change was short-lived. Pressure from organized labor unions led the committee to reinsert "Labor" back into its title and the committee was renamed as the Committee on Labor and Human Resources on March 7, 1979 (S. Res. 30, 96th Cong.).

Historically, this committee has been seen as the Senate's most liberal one and with liberal leaders such as Edward M. Kennedy of Massachusetts, Jim Jeffords of Vermont, and Tom Harkin of Iowa directing the committee, it would be difficult to challenge that depiction.

Membership: The original Labor and Public Welfare Committee had thirteen members in the 80th Congress. Its renamed successor, Labor and Human Resources, reached a peak of eighteen members in the 98th Congresses (1983-1985) but was reduced to sixteen in 1985 and stood at seventeen in the 102nd Congress (1991-1993). During the last nine Congresses, the Committee on Health, Education, Labor, and Pensions has averaged 19.4 members, placing it in ninth among the sixteen standing committees. Its mean seniority of 10.68 years for its members places it tenth while its 86.16 percent mean retention rate produced a twelfth-place ranking.

Inter-committee transfers affected twenty-nine of the post-1993 senators who served on Labor and Human Resources and its successor Health, Education, Labor, and Pensions. The committee gained eleven members from other committees and lost eighteen, for a net loss of seven. Five of the departing members left the committee to become chairs elsewhere—Orrin Hatch (Rep-Utah) to chair Judiciary in 1995; J. Strom Thurmond (Rep-S.C) to chair Armed Services in 1995; John W. Warner (Rep-Va.), replacing Thurmond as chair of Armed Services in 1999; Mitch McConnell (Rep-Ky.) to chair Rules and Administration in 1999; and Susan Collins (Rep-Me.) to chair Governmental Affairs in 2003. Of the committee's eleven gains, four came from Banking, Housing, and Urban Affairs and Environment and Public Works, including Barack Obama (Dem-Ill.), and three total from Governmental Affairs and its successor, Homeland Security and Governmental Affairs.

Committee Leaders: The first chair of the reorganized Senate Committee on Labor and Public Welfare was Robert A. Taft (Rep-Ohio), author of the Taft-Hartley Act. Taft served as ranking minority member in the following two Democratic Congresses (1949-53) but relinquished the chairmanship to H. Alexander Smith of New Jersey when the GOP regained the Senate and he was chosen Majority Floor Leader in 1953. Elbert D. Thomas of Utah was its first ranking minority member in the 80th Congress (1947-1949) and its first Democratic chair in the 81st (1949-1951), but was defeated for re-election in 1950. James E. Murray of Montana succeeded Thomas as chair in 1951 and as ranking minority member in 1953-1955, until he relinquished his senior rank to J. Lister Hill of Alabama in 1955 when he became chair of Interior and Insular Affairs.

Lister Hill's service as chair began in 1955 and he would serve as the Labor Committee chair for the next fourteen years until his retirement in 1968. H. Alexander Smith was ranking minority member in the first four years of his chairmanship until his retirement in 1958. Smith's successor was Barry M. Goldwater, the leading Senate spokesman for conservatism. Goldwater served as ranking minority member until his defeat as the 1964 Republican presidential nominee. Jacob K. Javits of New York, an archetypal moderate-liberal "Rockefeller Republican," succeeded Goldwater in 1965 and served as the Labor committee's ranking minority member until he became ranking member on Foreign Relations in 1979. Javits's immediate successor as ranking member was Richard Schweiker of Pennsylvania, who left the Senate in 1981 and was named Secretary of Health and Human Services in the Reagan administration.

Hill's immediate successor as chair in 1969 was Ralph W. Yarbrough of Texas, who lost his renomination battle to Lloyd Bentsen in 1970. Succeeding Yarbrough was New Jersey's Harrison (Pete) Williams, who held the chair until 1980 and the loss of his chairmanship due to his involvement as the only senator caught in the FBI-sponsored "Abscam" sting operation.

Following Harrison as the committee's senior Democrat was the legendary Edward M. Kennedy of Massachusetts, whose almost twenty-nine years of senior service—twelve-plus years as chair (1987-1995, 2001-2003, and 2007-2009) and sixteen-plus years as ranking minority member (1981-1987, 1995-2001, 2003-2007)—ended with his death in August, 2009. This committee had become a Kennedy legacy since both of his older brothers, John F. Kennedy of Massachusetts and Robert F. Kennedy of New York, had served on it as well, with both Robert and Ted Kennedy serving conterminously on it in 1965-1968 until Robert's assassination.

Republican Orrin Hatch of Utah, then only in his fifth year, became chair in 1981 when Vermont's Robert Stafford became chair of Environment and Public Works. Hatch served as the committee's senior Republican for the next twelve years—six as chair, 1981-1987, and six as ranking minority member, 1987-1993. He stepped aside in 1993 to become ranking member on Judiciary and was succeeded by Nancy Landon Kassebaum of Kansas. She became chair in

the 104th Congress when Republicans regained control of the Senate, but retired in 1996 after two years as chair.

Kassebaum was succeeded as chair by Vermont Republican James M. Jeffords, who became suspect in Republican eyes for being the only House Republican to vote against President Reagan's 1981 tax cut and one of two Senate Republicans to vote against the confirmation of Clarence Thomas's appointment to the Supreme Court. In spite of growing ideological tension in the Senate, Jeffords and Kennedy worked closely together on the committee for the next four-plus years and they convinced the Senate to rename it as the Committee on Health, Education, Labor, and Pensions (HELP) in 1999.

Jeffords was one of five Republicans to vote against both articles of impeachment against President Bill Clinton in 1999 and was becoming more disenchanted with the hardening conservatism of the Senate Republicans. While the outcome of the 2000 presidential election was determined by a 5-4 majority in the Supreme Court in favor of Texas governor George W. Bush, the same closeness—fifty Republicans and fifty Democrats—in the Senate led to an unusual power-sharing arrangement. Party control of the Senate would be determined by the party of the vice president. From January 3, 2001 to January 20, 2001, Vice President Al Gore Jr. gave party control to the Democrats and with the swearing-in of Vice President Richard B. Cheney, the Republicans would be the majority party. Each party would have the same number of seats on each Senate committee and the same number of staff members, but the Republicans would hold the chairs while the Democrats would be the ranking minority members on each committee. However, the moment that one of the parties gained a fifty-first seat, the power-sharing arrangement would end.

Conflicts over President George W. Bush's budget and spending priorities finally led Jeffords to abandon his lifelong commitment to the Republican Party. In May 2001 he declared that he would leave the Republican Party to become an independent and would caucus with the Democrats. This became official on June 6, 2001, and gave the Democrats the numeric edge and ended the power-sharing. It took until July 10 to sort out the changes, but when it was over, Jeffords left the HELP Committee to return to chair Environment and Public Works, where he had served earlier, and Ted Kennedy resumed his chairmanship of the committee. Replacing Jeffords as the senior Republican was Judd A. Gregg of New Hampshire.

When Republicans regained control of the Senate in 2003, Gregg became chair and Kennedy became ranking minority member. Gregg relinquished the chairmanship of HELP in 2005 to chair the Budget Committee and was succeeded by Michael B. Enzi of Wyoming. The Democrats' return to power in 2007 restored Kennedy to the chair and moved Enzi to the ranking minority slot. With Kennedy's death in August, 2009, Thomas R. Harkin of Iowa left the chairmanship of Agriculture, Nutrition, and Forestry to succeed him.

Party Leaders: Senate Republicans have sought more leaders from Labor Committee members than the Democrats have. Four Republican floor leaders—Robert A. Taft of Ohio, 1953-1954, Everett McK. Dirksen of Illinois, 1959-1969, William Frist of Tennessee, 2003-2007, and the current leader since 2007, Mitch McConnell of Kentucky—have served on the committee in one of its many incarnations. In addition to Dirksen and McConnell who began their leadership careers as Whips, two other Republican Whips were veterans of the committee—Robert P. Griffin of Michigan, 1969-1977, and Donald Nickles of Oklahoma, 1996-2003.

Senate Republican reliance upon the committee's members contrasts with the Democrats who named none of the committee's members to serve as floor leader and only three as Whip; two short-termers, Hubert Humphrey of Minnesota, 1961-1965; Edward Kennedy of Massachusetts, 1969-1971; and Alan Cranston of California, who served the longest, from 1977 to 1991.

Presidential Aspirations: Although the committee is not a top-tier one in Senate prestige, ten members who have served on it have received nine presidential and eight vice presidential nominations. President Richard Nixon of California accounted for three presidential nominations (1960, 1968, and 1972) and two vice presidential ones (1952 and 1956). The other Republican veterans of the committee to be nominated were Barry M. Goldwater of Arizona, the party's presidential nominee in 1964, and J. Danforth Quayle of Indiana, who was elected vice president in 1988 and lost in 1992. The only two Democrats from the committee to be nominated and elected president were John F. Kennedy of Massachusetts in 1960 and Barack Obama in 2008. While both Minnesota Democrats Hubert H. Humphrey and Walter Mondale were elected vice president in 1964 and 1976, respectively, both failed in their respective 1968 and 1984 presidential quests. The two other nominated but non-elected committee members were Thomas Eagleton of Missouri and his month-long vice presidential candidacy in 1972 and John F. Kerry for president in 2004.

Other presidential aspirants include the three Kennedy brothers, for whom this is the only committee upon which all three brothers served—John F. (Dem-Mass.) from 1953 until his election as president in 1960; Edward M. (Dem-Mass.) from 1963 until his death in 2009; and Robert F. (Dem-N.Y.) from 1965 until his assassination in 1968. It was a source of great amusement for thirty-two-year-old Teddy that he outranked the thirty-eight-year-old Bobby on the committee.

Other Notables: Five Senate veterans of service on this committee have been named to the Cabinet, with the most prominent being Hillary Rodham Clinton (Dem-N.Y.) who was named Secretary of State by her 2008 nomination rival, President Barack Obama in 2009. William Saxbe (Rep-Ohio) left the committee to become President Nixon's Attorney General in 1974, after then–Attorney General Elliott Richardson resigned during the Watergate-linked "Saturday Night Massacre" of October 1973. Richard S. Schweiker (Rep-Penn.) had already retired from the Senate in 1981, when he was named President Reagan's Secretary of Health and Human Services. Two Republican senators who lost in 2000 were named to the Cabinet by President George W. Bush in 2001—Spencer Abraham of Michigan as Secretary of Transportation and John Ashcroft of Missouri as Attorney General.

Selected References

Auerbach, Jerald, "The La Follette Committee and the C.I.O.," *Wisconsin Magazine of History*, 48 (Winter, 1964), 3-20.

Coren, Robert W., et al., "Records of the Committee on Labor and Public Welfare and Related Committees, 1869-1968," *Guide to the Records of the United States Senate at the National Archives: 1789-1989 Bicentennial Edition* (Washington, D.C.: National Archives and Records Administration, 1989), 167-173.

Eidenburg, Eugene and Roy D. Morey, *An Act of Congress: The Legislative Process and the Making of Education Policy*, (New York: W.W. Norton, 1969).

Evans, C. Lawrence, "Influence in Congressional Committees: Participation, Manipulation, and Anticipation," in Christopher J. Deering, ed., *Congressional Politics* (Homewood, Ill.: The Dorsey Press, 1989), 155-175.

Evans, C. Lawrence, *Leadership in Committee: A Comparative Analysis of Leadership Behavior in the U.S. Senate* (Ann Arbor: University of Michigan, 2001).

Price, David E., *Who Makes the Laws? Creativity and Power in Senate Committees* (Cambridge. Mass.: Schenkman, 1972).

Redman, Eric, *The Dance of Legislation* (New York: Simon and Schuster, 1973).

Reeves, Andree E., "Labor and Human Resources Committee, Senate," in Donald C. Bacon, Roger H. Davidson, and Morton Keller, eds., *The Encyclopedia of the United States Congress* (New York: Simon & Schuster, 1995), I: 1237-1240.

U.S. Senate, Committee on Labor and Public Welfare, *History of the Committee on Labor and Human Resources, 1869-1979*, Senate Document 96-71, 96th Congress, 2nd session (1980). This is the committee's 2nd history following *Committee on Labor and Public Welfare, United States Senate, 100th Anniversary, 1869-1969*, Senate Document 90-108, 90th Congress, 2nd session (1968).

RESPONSIBILITIES, JURISDICTIONAL CHANGES, AND SUBCOMMITTEES

LABOR AND PUBLIC WELFARE

Jurisdiction, 80th Congress (1947-49)

Established by the Legislative Reorganization Act of 1946:

[Section 102.(1)(l)

(1) **Committee on Labor and Public Welfare**, to consist of thirteen Senators, to which committee shall be referred all proposed legislation, messages, petitions, memorials, and other matters relating to the following subjects:

    (1) Measures relating to education, labor, or public welfare generally

    (2) Mediation and arbitration of labor disputes

    (3) Wages and hours of labor

(4) Convict labor and the entry of goods made by convicts into interstate commerce
(5) Regulation or prevention of importation of foreign laborers under contract
(6) Child labor
(7) Labor statistics
(8) Labor standards
(9) School-lunch program
(10) Vocational rehabilitation
(11) Railroad labor and railroad retirement and unemployment, except revenue measures relating thereto
(12) United States Employees' Compensation Commission
(13) Columbia Institution for the Deaf, Dumb, and Blind; Howard University; Freedmen's Hospital; and Saint Elizabeth's Hospital
(14) Public health and quarantine
(15) Welfare of miners
(16) Vocational rehabilitation and education of veterans
(17) Veterans' hospitals, medical care and treatment of veterans
(18) Soldiers' and sailors' civil relief
(19) Readjustment of servicemen to civil life

HUMAN RESOURCES

Reorganization, 1977

The Labor and Public Welfare Committee was reorganized as the Standing Committee on Human Resources following the passage of Senate Resolution 4, the Committee System Reorganization Amendments of 1977, February 4, 1977.

Reorganized Jurisdiction, 1977

Jurisdiction contained in Senate Resolution 4, the Committee System Reorganization Amendments of 1977, February 4, 1977.

[Rule XXV.(1)(l)]

(1) **Committee on Human Resources**, to which committee shall be referred all proposed legislation, messages, petitions, memorials, and other matters relating to the following subjects:

(1) Measures relating to education, labor, health, and public welfare
(2) Labor standards and labor statistics
(3) Wages and hours of labor
(4) Child labor
(5) Mediation and arbitration of labor disputes
(6) Convict labor and the entry of goods made by convicts into interstate commerce
(7) Regulation of foreign laborers
(8) Handicapped individuals
(9) Equal employment opportunity
(10) Occupational safety and health, including the welfare of miners
(11) Private pension plans
(12) Aging
(13) Railway labor and retirement
(14) Public health
(15) Arts and humanities
(16) Gallaudet College, Howard University, and Saint Elizabeth's Hospital
(17) Biomedical research and development
(18) Student loans
(19) Agricultural colleges
(20) Domestic activities of the American National Red Cross

(2) Such committee shall also study and review, on a comprehensive basis, matters relating to health, education and training, and public welfare, and report thereon from time to time.

Committee Renamed

Human Resources was renamed the Committee on Labor and Human Resources on March 7, 1979.

LABOR AND HUMAN RESOURCES

Jurisdiction, 103rd Congress (1993-94)

From the *Standing Rules of the Senate* in the *Senate Manual*, 103rd Congress, 1st Session, S. Doc. 103-1:

[Rule XXV (1)(m)]

(1) **Committee on Labor and Human Resources**, to which committee shall be referred all proposed legislation, messages, petitions, memorials, and other matters relating to the following subjects:

   (1) Measures relating to education, labor, health, and public welfare
   (2) Aging
   (3) Agricultural colleges
   (4) Arts and humanities
   (5) Biomedical research and development
   (6) Child labor
   (7) Convict labor and the entry of goods made by convicts into interstate commerce
   (8) Domestic activities of the American National Red Cross
   (9) Equal employment opportunity
  (10) Gallaudet College, Howard University, and Saint Elizabeth's Hospital
  (11) Handicapped individuals
  (12) Labor standards and labor statistics
  (13) Mediation and arbitration of labor disputes
  (14) Occupational safety and health, including the welfare of miners
  (15) Private pension plans
  (16) Public health
  (17) Railway labor and retirement
  (18) Regulation of foreign laborers
  (19) Student loans
  (20) Wages and hours of labor

(2) Such committee shall also study and review, on a comprehensive basis, matters relating to health, education and training, and public welfare, and report thereon from time to time.

Committee Renamed

HEALTH, EDICATION, LABOR, AND PENSIONS (HELP)

Labor and Human Resources was renamed the Committee on Health, Education, Labor, and Pensions (HELP) on Jan. 21, 1999.

Jurisdiction, 111th Congress (2009-10)

From *Authority and Rules of Senate Committees, 2009-2010*, Sen. Doc. 111-3, pursuant to S.Res, 166, June 2, 2009.

[Rule XXV (1)(m)]

(1) **Committee on Health, Education, Labor and Pensions**, to which committee shall be referred all proposed legislation, messages, petitions, memorials, and other matters relating to the following subjects:

   (1) Measures relating to education, labor, health, and public welfare
   (2) Aging
   (3) Agricultural colleges
   (4) Arts and humanities
   (5) Biomedical research and development
   (6) Child labor
   (7) Convict labor and the entry of goods made by convicts into interstate commerce
   (8) Domestic activities of the American National Red Cross
   (9) Equal employment opportunity
  (10) Gallaudet College, Howard University, and Saint Elizabeth's Hospital
  (11) Individuals with disabilities
  (12) Labor standards and labor statistics
  (13) Mediation and arbitration of labor disputes
  (14) Occupational safety and health, including the welfare of miners
  (15) Private pension plans
  (16) Public health
  (17) Railway labor and retirement
  (18) Regulation of foreign laborers
  (19) Student loans
  (20) Wages and hours of labor

(2) Such committee shall also study and review, on a comprehensive basis, matters relating to health, education and training, and public welfare, and report thereon from time to time.

NAMES OF SUBCOMMITTEES

Committee on Labor and Human Resources, 103rd -106th Congresses

Aging, 103, 104, 105, 106
Children and Families, 104, 105, 106
Children, Family, Drugs and Alcoholism, 103
Disability Policy, 103, 104
Education, Arts, and Humanities, 103, 104
Employment and Productivity, 103
Employment and Training, 105
Employment, Safety, and Training, 106
Labor, 103
Public Health and Safety, 105
Public Health, 106

Committee on Health, Education, Labor, and Pensions, 107th-111th Congresses

Aging, 107, 108
Bioterrorism and Public Health Preparedness, 109
Children and Families, 107, 108, 110, 111
Education and Early Childhood Development, 109
Employment, Safety, and Training, 107, 108
Employment and Workplace Safety, 109, 110, 111
Public Health, 107
Retirement and Aging, 110, 111
Retirement Security and Aging, 109
Substance Abuse and Mental Health Services, 108

MEMBERSHIP ROSTERS, 103rd-111th Congresses, 1993-2010

LABOR AND HUMAN RESOURCES / 103rd Congress

Service Dates of Committee Chair: Jan. 7, 1993-Jan. 4, 1995

Service Dates of Majority Members: Jan. 7, 1993-Jan. 4, 1995

Service Dates of Minority Members: Jan. 7, 1993-Jan. 4, 1995

Majority

Rank Name	Party	State	Senate	Comm.
Chr Kennedy, Edward M.	Dem	Mass.	31	30
2nd Pell, Claiborne D.	Dem	R.I.	33	32
3rd Metzenbaum, Howard M.	Dem	Ohio	19	14
4th Dodd, Christopher J.	Dem	Conn.	13	10
5th Simon, Paul M.	Dem	Ill.	9	8
6th Harkin, Thomas R.	Dem	Iowa	9	7
7th Mikulski, Barbara A.	Dem	Md.	7	7
8th Bingaman, J.F. (Jeff)	Dem	N.M.	11	*1 3
9th Wellstone, Paul D.	DFL	Minn.	3	2
10th Wofford, Harris	Dem	Penn.	2	1

Minority

Rank Name	Party	State	Senate	Comm.
RM Kassebaum, Nancy Landon	Rep	Kans.	15	4
2nd Jeffords, James M.	Rep	Vt.	5	*1 4
3rd Coats, Daniel R.	Rep	Ind.	5	4
4th Gregg, Judd A.	Rep	N.H.	1	1
5th Thurmond, J. Strom	Rep	S.C.	38	*2 9
6th Hatch, Orrin G.	Rep	Utah	17	*1 16
7th Durenberger, David F.	Rep	Minn.	15	4

*1: Member's first period of service on the committee.
*2: Member's second period of service on the committee.

Note: Rankings on this committee for the following members were affected by other chamber service: Claiborne D. Pell (Dem-R.I.), Chair, Foreign Relations; J. Strom Thurmond (Rep-S.C.), Ranking Minority Member, Armed Services; Orrin G. Hatch (Rep-Utah), Ranking Minority Member, Judiciary.

Departures from the Senate:	Majority			Minority		
Defeated for Re-election	Wofford, Harris	Dem	Penn.	None		
Retired	Metzenbaum, Howard M.	Dem	Ohio	Durenberger, David F.	Rep	Minn.

Departures from Committee:						
Became Chair of Judiciary		None		Hatch, Orrin G.	Rep	Utah
Became Chair of Armed Services		None		Thurmond, J. Strom	Rep	S.C.
Moved to Select Indian Affairs		None		Hatch, Orrin G.	Rep	Utah
No new assignment	Bingaman, J.F. (Jeff)	Dem	N.M.	None		

LABOR AND HUMAN RESOURCES / 104th Congress

Service Dates of Committee Chair: Jan. 4, 1995-Jan. 9, 1997

Service Dates of Majority Members: Jan. 4, 1995-Jan. 9, 1997

Service Dates of Minority Members: Jan. 4, 1995-Jan. 9, 1997

Majority

Rank Name	Party	State	Years in: Senate	Years in: Comm.
Chr Kassebaum, Nancy Landon	Rep	Kans.	17	6
2nd Jeffords, James M.	Rep	Vt.	7	*1 6
3rd Coats, Daniel R.	Rep	Ind.	7	6
4th Gregg, Judd A.	Rep	N.H.	3	2
5th Frist, William H.	Rep	Tenn	1	1
6th DeWine, Michael	Rep	Ohio	1	*1 1
7th Ashcroft, John D.	Rep	Mo.	1	1
8th Abraham, Spencer	Rep	Mich.	1	1
9th Gorton, T. Slade III	Rep	Wash.	13	1

Minority

Rank Name	Party	State	Years in: Senate	Years in: Comm.
RM Kennedy, Edward M.	Dem	Mass.	33	32
2nd Pell, Claiborne D.	Dem	R.I.	35	34
3rd Dodd, Christopher J.	Dem	Conn.	15	12
4th Simon, Paul M.	Dem	Ill.	11	10
5th Harkin, Thomas R.	Dem	Iowa	11	8
6th Mikulski, Barbara A.	Dem	Md.	9	8
7th Wellstone, Paul D.	DFL	Minn.	5	4

*1: Member's first period of service on the committee.

Note: Rankings on this committee for the following members were affected by other chamber service: Claiborne D. Pell (Dem-R.I.), Chair, Foreign Relations.

Changes:

Majority:

Abraham, Spencer	Rep	Mich.	Apr. 16, 1996 Left committee; moved to Commerce, Science, and Transportation.
Faircloth, D.M. (Lauch)	Rep	N.C.	Apr. 16, 1996 Replaced Abraham.

Departures from the Senate:

	Majority			Minority		
Retired	Kassebaum, Nancy Landon	Rep	Kans.	Pell, Claiborne D.	Dem	R.I.
				Simon, Paul M.	Dem	Ill.

Departures from Committee:

Moved to Judiciary	Ashcroft, John D.	Rep	Mo.	None
Moved to Appropriations and Small Business	Faircloth, D.M. (Lauch)	Rep	N.C.	None
Moved to Energy and Natural Resources	Gorton, T. Slade III	Rep	Wash.	None

LABOR AND HUMAN RESOURCES / 105th Congress

Service Dates of Committee Chair: Jan. 9, 1997-Jan. 7, 1999

Service Dates of Majority Members: Jan. 9, 1997-Jan. 7, 1999

Service Dates of Minority Members: Jan. 9, 1997-Jan. 7, 1999

Majority

Rank Name	Party	State	Years in: Senate	Years in: Comm.
Chr Jeffords, James M.	Rep	Vt.	9	*1 8
2nd Coats, Daniel R.	Rep	Ind.	9	8
3rd Gregg, Judd A.	Rep	N.H.	5	5
4th Frist, William H.	Rep	Tenn.	3	3
5th DeWine, Michael	Rep	Ohio	3	*1 3
6th Enzi, Michael B.	Rep	Wyo.	1	1
7th Hutchinson, Y. Timothy	Rep	Ark.	1	1
8th Collins, Susan M.	Rep	Me.	1	1
9th Warner, John W.	Rep	Va.	19	*1 1
10th McConnell, A. Mitchell (Mitch)	Rep	Ky.	13	1

Minority

Rank Name	Party	State	Years in: Senate	Years in: Comm.
RM Kennedy, Edward M.	Dem	Mass.	35	34
2nd Dodd, Christopher J.	Dem	Conn.	17	14
3rd Harkin, Thomas R.	Dem	Iowa	13	11
4th Mikulski, Barbara A.	Dem	Md.	11	11
5th Bingaman, J.F. (Jeff)	Dem	N.M.	15	*2 1
6th Wellstone, Paul D.	DFL	Minn.	7	6
7th Murray, Patty	Dem	Wash.	5	1
8th Reed, John F.	Dem	R.I.	1	1

*1: Member's first period of service on the committee.

*2: Member's second period of service on the committee.

Departures from the Senate:

	Majority			Minority
Retired	Coats, Daniel R.	Rep	Ind.	None

Departures from Committee:

Became Chair of Rules and Administration	McConnell, A. Mitchell (Mitch)	Rep	Ky.	None
Became Chair of Armed Services	Warner, John W.	Rep	Va.	None
Moved to Joint Library	McConnell, A. Mitchell (Mitch)	Rep	Ky.	None

HEALTH, EDUCATION, LABOR AND PENSIONS / 106th Congress

* The Senate Committee on Labor and Human Resources was renamed as the Committee on HEALTH, EDUCATION, LABOR AND PENSIONS on Jan. 21, 1999, by S. Res. 28.

Service Dates of Committee Chair: Jan. 7, 1999-Jan. 3, 2001

Service Dates of Majority Members: Jan. 7, 1999-Jan. 25, 2001

Service Dates of Minority Members: Jan. 7, 1999-Jan. 25, 2001

			Majority						Minority		
				Years in:						Years in:	
Rank Name	Party	State	Senate	Comm.		Rank Name	Party	State	Senate	Comm.	
Chr Jeffords, James M.	Rep	Vt.	11	10		RM Kennedy, Edward M.	Dem	Mass.	37	36	
2nd Gregg, Judd A.	Rep	N.H.	7	7		2nd Dodd, Christopher J.	Dem	Conn.	19	16	
3rd Frist, William H.	Rep	Tenn.	5	5		3rd Harkin, Thomas R.	Dem	Iowa	15	13	
4th DeWine, Michael	Rep	Ohio	5	*1 5		4th Mikulski, Barbara A.	Dem	Md.	13	13	
5th Enzi, Michael B.	Rep	Wyo.	3	2		5th Bingaman, J.F. (Jeff)	Dem	N.M.	17	*2 2	
6th Hutchinson, Y. Timothy	Rep	Ark.	3	2		6th Wellstone, Paul D.	DFL	Minn.	9	8	
7th Collins, Susan M.	Rep	Me.	3	2		7th Murray, Patty	Dem	Wash.	7	2	
8th Brownback, Sam D.	Rep	Kans.	3	1		8th Reed, John F.	Dem	R.I.	3	2	
9th Hagel, Charles T. (Chuck)	Rep	Neb.	3	1							
10th Sessions, Jefferson B. III	Rep	Ala.	3	1							

*1: Member's first period of service on the committee.

*2: Member's second period of service on the committee.

Departures from Committee:	Majority			Minority
Moved to Appropriations	DeWine, Michael	Rep	Ohio	None
Moved to Judiciary	Brownback, Sam D.	Rep	Kans.	None
Moved to Budget and Energy and Natural Resources	Hagel, Charles T. (Chuck)	Rep	Neb.	None

HEALTH, EDUCATION, LABOR AND PENSIONS / 107th Congress, Pre-Jeffords switch

Service Dates of Committee Chair: ChT: Jan. 3, 2001-Jan. 25, 2001 Kennedy (Dem-Mass.)

Ch1: Jan. 25, 2001-June 6, 2001 Jeffords (Rep-Vt.)

Service Dates of Majority Members: Jan. 25, 2001-June 6, 2001

Service Dates of Minority Members: Jan. 25, 2001-June 6, 2001

			Majority						Minority		
				Years in:						Years in:	
Rank Name	Party	State	Senate	Comm.		Rank Name	Party	State	Senate	Comm.	
Ch1 Jeffords, James M.	Rep	Vt.	13	*1 12		RM1 Kennedy, Edward M.	Dem	Mass.	39	38	
2nd Gregg, Judd A.	Rep	N.H.	9	9		2nd Dodd, Christopher J.	Dem	Conn.	21	18	
3rd Frist, William H.	Rep	Tenn.	7	7		3rd Harkin, Thomas R.	Dem	Iowa	17	15	
4th Enzi, Michael B.	Rep	Wyo.	5	5		4th Mikulski, Barbara A.	Dem	Md.	15	15	
5th Hutchinson, Y. Timothy	Rep	Ark.	5	5		5th Bingaman, J.F. (Jeff)	Dem	N.M.	19	*2 5	
6th Warner, John W.	Rep	Va.	23	*2 1		6th Wellstone, Paul D.	DFL	Minn.	11	10	
7th Bond, Christopher S. (Kit)	Rep	Mo.	15	1		7th Murray, Patty	Dem	Wash.	9	5	
8th Roberts, C. Patrick	Rep	Kans.	5	1		8th Reed, John F.	Dem	R.I.	5	5	
9th Collins, Susan M.	Rep	Me.	5	5		9th Edwards, John	Dem	N.C.	3	1	
10th Sessions, Jefferson B. III	Rep	Ala.	5	3		10th Clinton, Hillary Rodham	Dem	N.Y.	1	1	

*1: Member's first period of service on the committee.

*2: Member's second period of service on the committee.

Note: The committee majority in the 2001 Senate power-sharing arrangement was determined by the party of the vice president. Democrat Al Gore Jr. served from Jan. 3, 2001, to Jan. 20, 2001, and was succeeded by Republican Richard B. Cheney on Jan. 20, 2001. When Senator Jeffords of Vermont left the Republican Party, effective June 6, 2001, to become an Independent, Democrats regained the majority for the remainder of the 107th Congress.

HEALTH, EDUCATION, LABOR AND PENSIONS / 107th Congress, Post-Jeffords switch

Service Dates of Committee Chair: June 6, 2001-Jan. 15, 2003

Service Dates of Majority Members: June 6, 2001-Jan. 15, 2003; Majority members were re-ranked on July 10, 2001

Service Dates of Minority Members: June 6, 2001-Jan. 15, 2003

Majority						Minority					
			Years in:						**Years in:**		
Rank Name	**Party**	**State**	**Senate**	**Comm.**		**Rank Name**	**Party**	**State**	**Senate**	**Comm.**	
Ch2 Kennedy, Edward M.	Dem	Mass.	39	39		RM2 Gregg, Judd A.	Rep	N.H.	9	9	
2nd Dodd, Christopher J.	Dem	Conn.	21	19		2nd Frist, William H.	Rep	Tenn.	7	7	
3rd Harkin, Thomas R.	Dem	Iowa	17	15		3rd Enzi, Michael B.	Rep	Wyo.	5	5	
4th Mikulski, Barbara A.	Dem	Md.	15	15		4th Hutchinson, Y. Timothy	Rep	Ark.	5	5	
5th Jeffords, James M.	Ind.	Vt.	13	*2 1		5th Warner, John W.	Rep	Va.	23	*2 1	
6th Bingaman, J.F. (Jeff)	Dem	N.M.	19	*2 5		6th Bond, Christopher S. (Kit)	Rep	Mo.	15	1	
7th Wellstone, Paul D.	DFL	Minn.	11	11		7th Roberts, C. Patrick	Rep	Kans.	5	1	
8th Murray, Patty	Dem	Wash.	9	5		8th Collins, Susan M.	Rep	Me.	5	5	
9th Reed, John F.	Dem	R.I.	5	5		9th Sessions, Jefferson B. III	Rep	Ala.	5	3	
10th Edwards, John	Dem	N.C.	3	1		10th DeWine, Michael	Rep	Ohio	7	*2 1	
11th Clinton, Hillary Rodham	Dem	N.Y.	1	1							

*2: Member's second period of service on the committee.

Note: Democratic members from 5th through 11th and Republican members from 1st through 9th were re-ranked on July 10, 2001

Additions:
  Majority:

5th Jeffords, James M.	Ind.	Vt.	July 10, 2001

Changes:
  Ranking Member:

RM2 Gregg, Judd A.	Rep	N.H.	June 6, 2001 Succeeded Jeffords as senior Republican on the committee

  Majority:

Wellstone, Paul D.	DFL	Minn.	Oct. 25, 2002 Died in office.

  Minority:

Jeffords, James M.	Rep	Vt.	June 6, 2001 Seat as Republican vacated; remained on committee as a majority addition ranking 5th among Democrats.
DeWine, Michael	Rep	Ohio	July 10, 2001 Replaced Jeffords.

Departures from the Senate:

	Majority				**Minority**		
Defeated for Re-election	None				Hutchinson, Y. Timothy	Rep	Ark.

Departures from Committee:

	Majority				**Minority**		
Became Chair of Governmental Affairs	None				Collins, Susan M.	Rep	Me.
Moved to Joint Economic Committee	None				Collins, Susan M.	Rep	Me.

HEALTH, EDUCATION, LABOR AND PENSIONS / 108th Congress

Service Dates of Committee Chair: Jan. 15, 2003-Jan. 6, 2005

Service Dates of Majority Members: Jan. 15, 2003-Jan. 6, 2005

Service Dates of Minority Members: Jan. 15, 2003-Jan. 6, 2005

Majority						Minority					
			Years in:						**Years in:**		
Rank Name	**Party**	**State**	**Senate**	**Comm.**		**Rank Name**	**Party**	**State**	**Senate**	**Comm.**	
Chr Gregg, Judd A.	Rep	N.H.	11	11		RM Kennedy, Edward M.	Dem	Mass.	41	40	
2nd Frist, William H.	Rep	Tenn.	9	9		2nd Dodd, Christopher J.	Dem	Conn.	23	20	
3rd Enzi, Michael B.	Rep	Wyo.	7	7		3rd Harkin, Thomas R.	Dem	Iowa	19	17	
4th Alexander, Lamar	Rep	Tenn.	1	1		4th Mikulski, Barbara A.	Dem	Md.	17	17	
5th Bond, Christopher S. (Kit)	Rep	Mo.	17	2		5th Jeffords, James M.	Ind	Vt.	15	*2 2	
6th DeWine, Michael	Rep	Ohio	9	*2 2		6th Bingaman, J.F. (Jeff)	Dem	N.M.	21	*2 7	
7th Roberts, C. Patrick	Rep	Kans.	7	2		7th Murray, Patty	Dem	Wash.	11	7	
8th Sessions, Jefferson B. III	Rep	Ala	7	5		8th Reed, John F.	Dem	R.I.	7	7	
9th Ensign, John E.	Rep	Nev.	3	1		9th Edwards, John	Dem	N.C.	5	2	
10th Graham, Lindsey O.	Rep	S.C.	1	1		10th Clinton, Hillary Rodham	Dem	N.Y.	3	2	
11th Warner, John W.	Rep	Va.	25	*2 2							

*2: Member's second period of service on the committee.

Departures from the Senate:

	Majority				**Minority**		
Retired; lost vice presidential election	None				Edwards, John	Dem	N.C.

Departures from Committee:

	Majority				**Minority**	
Moved to Budget	Graham, Lindsey O.	Rep	S.C.		None	
Moved to Homeland Security and Governmental Affairs	Warner, John W.	Rep	Va.		None	
No new assignment	Bond, Christopher S. (Kit)	Rep	Mo.		None	

HEALTH, EDUCATION, LABOR AND PENSIONS / 109th Congress

Service Dates of Committee Chair: Jan. 6, 2005-Jan. 12, 2007

Service Dates of Majority Members: Jan. 6, 2005-Jan. 12, 2007

Service Dates of Minority Members: Jan. 6, 2005-Jan. 12, 2007

Majority						Minority					
				Years in:						Years in:	
Rank Name	Party	State	Senate	Comm.		Rank Name	Party	State	Senate	Comm.	
Chr Enzi, Michael B.	Rep	Wyo.	9	8		RM Kennedy, Edward M.	Dem	Mass.	43	42	
2nd Gregg, Judd A.	Rep	N.H.	13	12		2nd Dodd, Christopher J.	Dem	Conn.	25	22	
3rd Frist, William H.	Rep	Tenn.	11	11		3rd Harkin, Thomas R.	Dem	Iowa	21	19	
4th Alexander, Lamar	Rep	Tenn.	3	2		4th Mikulski, Barbara A.	Dem	Md.	19	19	
5th Burr, Richard M.	Rep	N.C.	1	1		5th Jeffords, James M.	Ind	Vt.	17	*2 4	
6th Isakson, Johnny	Rep	Ga.	1	1		6th Bingaman, J.F. (Jeff)	Dem	N.M.	23	*2 8	
7th DeWine, Michael	Rep	Ohio	11	*2 4		7th Murray, Patty	Dem	Wash.	13	8	
8th Ensign, John E.	Rep	Nev.	5	2		8th Reed, John F.	Dem	R.I.	9	8	
9th Hatch, Orrin G.	Rep	Utah	29	*2 1		9th Clinton, Hillary Rodham	Dem	N.Y.	5	4	
10th Sessions, Jefferson B. III	Rep	Ala.	9	6							
11th Roberts, C. Patrick	Rep	Kans.	9	4		*2: Member's second period of service on the committee.					

Note: Rankings on this committee for the following members were affected by other chamber service: Judd A. Gregg (Rep-N.H.) Chair, Budget; and William H. Frist (Rep-Tenn.), Majority Leader.

Departures from the Senate:	Majority			Minority		
Defeated for Re-election	DeWine, Michael	Rep	Ohio	None		
Retired	Frist, William H.	Rep	Tenn.	Jeffords, James M.	Ind	Vt.

Departures from Committee:						
Moved to Energy and Natural Resources	Sessions, Jefferson B. III	Rep	Ala.			
No new assignment	Ensign, John E.	Rep	Nev.	None		

HEALTH, EDUCATION, LABOR AND PENSIONS / 110th Congress

Service Dates of Committee Chair: Jan. 12, 2007-Jan. 21, 2009

Service Dates of Majority Members: Jan. 12, 2007-Jan. 21, 2009

Service Dates of Minority Members: Jan. 12, 2007-Jan. 21, 2009

Majority						Minority					
				Years in:						Years in:	
Rank Name	Party	State	Senate	Comm.		Rank Name	Party	State	Senate	Comm.	
Chr Kennedy, Edward M.	Dem	Mass.	45	44		RM Enzi, Michael B.	Rep	Wyo.	11	11	
2nd Dodd, Christopher J.	Dem	Conn.	27	24		2nd Gregg, Judd A.	Rep	N.H.	15	15	
3rd Harkin, Thomas R.	Dem	Iowa	23	21		3rd Alexander, Lamar	Rep	Tenn.	5	4	
4th Mikulski, Barbara A.	Dem	Md.	21	21		4th Burr, Richard M.	Rep	N.C.	3	3	
5th Bingaman, J.F. (Jeff)	Dem	N.M.	25	*2 11		5th Isakson, Johnny	Rep	Ga.	3	3	
6th Murray, Patty	Dem	Wash.	15	11		6th Murkowski, Lisa	Rep	Alas.	5	1	
7th Reed, John F.	Dem	R.I.	11	11		7th Hatch, Orrin G.	Rep	Utah	31	*2 3	
8th Clinton, Hillary Rodham	Dem	N.Y.	7	6		8th Roberts, C. Patrick	Rep	Kans.	11	6	
9th Obama, Barack	Dem	Ill.	3	1		9th Allard, A. Wayne	Rep	Colo.	11	1	
10th Sanders, Bernard	Ind	Vt.	1	1		10th Coburn, Thomas A.	Rep	Okla.	3	1	
11th Brown, Sherrod	Dem	Ohio	1	1							

*2: Member's second period of service on the committee.

Note: Ranking on this committee for the following member was affected by other chamber service: Judd A. Gregg (Rep-N.H.) Ranking Minority Member, Budget.

Changes:
Majority:

Obama, Barack	Dem	Ill.		Nov. 16, 2008 Resigned the Senate; elected President.

Departures from the Senate:	Majority		Minority		
Retired			Allard, A. Wayne	Rep	Colo.

Note: Hillary Rodham Clinton (Dem-N.Y.) resigned the Senate on Jan. 21, 2009; named Secretary of State.

HEALTH, EDUCATION, LABOR AND PENSIONS / 111th Congress

Service Dates of Committee Chair: Ch1: Jan. 21, 2009-Aug. 25, 2009, Kennedy (Dem-Mass.)

Ch2: Sept. 9, 2009- Harkin (Dem-Iowa)

Service Dates of Majority Members: Jan. 21, 2009-

Service Dates of Minority Members: Jan. 21, 2009-

			Majority							Minority		
				Years in:							**Years in:**	
Rank Name	**Party**	**State**	**Senate**	**Comm.**		**Rank Name**	**Party**	**State**	**Senate**	**Comm.**
Ch1 Kennedy, Edward M.	Dem	Mass.	47	46		RM Enzi, Michael B.	Rep	Wyo.	13	13
2nd Dodd, Christopher J.	Dem	Conn.	29	26		2nd Gregg, Judd A.	Rep	N.H.	17	17
3rd Ch2 Harkin, Thomas R.	Dem	Iowa	25	23		3rd Alexander, Lamar	Rep	Tenn.	7	7
4th Mikulski, Barbara A.	Dem	Md.	23	23		4th Burr, Richard M.	Rep	N.C.	5	5
5th Bingaman, J.F. (Jeff)	Dem	N.M.	27	*2 13		5th Isakson, Johnny	Rep	Ga.	5	5
6th Murray, Patty	Dem	Wash.	17	13		6th McCain, John S. III	Rep	Ariz.	23	1
7th Reed, John F.	Dem	R.I.	13	13		7th Hatch, Orrin G.	Rep	Utah	33	*2 5
8th Sanders, Bernard	Ind	Vt.	3	3		8th Murkowski, Lisa	Rep	Alas.	7	3
9th Brown, Sherrod	Dem	Ohio	3	3		9th Coburn, Thomas A.	Rep	Okla.	5	3
10th Casey, Robert P. Jr.	Dem	Penn.	3	1		10th Roberts, C. Patrick	Rep	Kans.	13	8
11th Hagan, Kay R.	Dem	N.C.	1	1						
12th Merkley, Jeff	Dem	Ore.	1	1		*2: Member's second period of service on the committee.				
13th Whitehouse, Sheldon	Dem	R.I.	3	*T 1						

Note: Initial ranking on this committee for the following member was affected by other chamber service: Judd A. Gregg (Rep-N.H.) Ranking Minority Member, Budget. Third-ranking Thomas R. Harkin (Dem-Iowa) became chair replacing Edward M. Kennedy (Dem-Mass.) because 2nd-ranked Christopher J. Dodd (Dem-Conn.) was Chair of Banking, Housing, and Urban Affairs.

Filled Vacancy:
 Majority:
  13th seat by Whitehouse as a temporary assignment on May 5, 2009.

Changes:
 Chair:

Kennedy, Edward M.	Dem	Mass.	Aug. 25, 2009 Died in office
Harkin, Thomas R.	Dem	Iowa	Sept. 9, 2009 Suceeded Kennedy as Chair

 Majority:

Whitehouse, Sheldon	Dem.	R.I.	July 15, 2009 Left committee to open seat for Franken
Franken, Al	DFL	Minn.	July 15, 2009 Replaced Whitehouse
Kennedy, Edward M.	Dem	Mass.	Aug. 25, 2009 Died in office
Bennet, Michael F.	Dem	Colo.	Sept. 29, 2009 Replaced Kennedy

Homeland Security and Governmental Affairs

Senate Committee on Governmental Affairs, 103rd-108th Congresses (1993-2005)

Senate Committee on Homeland Security and Governmental Affairs, 109th-111th Congresses (2005-2011)

BACKGROUND

Organizational History: Long before the committee was renamed Homeland Security and Governmental Affairs, the Senate Committee on Governmental Affairs was charged with overseeing how the federal government operates. It has the authority to probe almost every cranny of the bureaucracy. Although it is rarely responsible for major legislation, the committee's oversight role is so broad that aggressive senators can use a seat on the panel to pursue almost any matter that interests them. The committee has been somewhat of a residual committee. During its various incarnations it has inherited the jurisdictions of more than a dozen standing, select, and special committees.

Its earliest predecessor was the Senate Committee on Retrenchment, established in 1842. Its most direct predecessor was the Committee on Organization, Conduct, and Expenditures in the Executive Departments (1899), first chaired by Louis E. McComas (Rep-Md.). On April 18, 1921, the Senate approved S. Res. 43, 67th Cong., which eliminated approximately forty standing and select committees. All of the separate Expenditures committees were consolidated into the Committee on Expenditures in the Executive Departments, which existed for over thirty years and continued intact through the Legislative Reorganization Act of 1946.

With the passage of S. Res. 280, 82nd Cong. on March 3, 1952, the committee was renamed the Committee on Government Operations, and in the next two decades it established itself as the primary investigative body of the Senate. Most notably, it was the committee's Permanent Subcommittee on Investigations (PSI) which led the charge through its broad mandate to investigate inefficiency, mismanagement, and corruption in Government.

For one Congress, the 83rd (1953-1955), the Government Operations Committee and its Permanent Subcommittee on Investigations were both chaired by Senator Joseph R. McCarthy (Rep-Wisc.) who used the committees to set the political agenda of the Republican Party. Senator McCarthy's anti-communist crusade extended into all reaches of the government, the armed forces, defense-related industries, universities and colleges, the mass media, and the entertainment industry. Careers were ruined and the "scare tactics" of the senator gave rise to the term "McCarthyism."

From 1955 until 1973, John L. McClellan (Dem-Ark.) chaired the PSI. McClellan continued some of McCarthy's anti-communist investigations, but he also investigated business activities and alleged improper activities by Eisenhower Administration appointees and political associates. In the 85th Congress (1957), the PSI's investigation of labor unions led the Senate to appoint the Select Committee on Improper Activities in the Labor or Management Field, which gave public prominence to John F. Kennedy (Dem-Mass.), and his brother, the PSI's lead counsel, Robert F. Kennedy. Government financial scandals and labor racketeering occupied the PSI's interest in the 1960s and 1970s as the anti-communist fervor of the McCarthyite era waned.

In 1977, the next major reorganization of the committee system, authorized by S. Res. 4, 95th Cong., led to the renaming of the Government Operations Committee as the Committee on Governmental Affairs, which in turn received control over the jurisdictional remains of the District of Columbia and Post Office and Civil Service Committees.

With complaints that the federal government has become too large and unresponsive, each of the most recent presidents has sought to redesign the government. The most ambitious effort undertaken in recent years took place in the Clinton Administration, led by Vice President Al Gore Jr. and his "Reinventing Government" (REGO) project. With the Governmental Affairs Committee playing a prominent role, Congress passed the Government Performance and Results Act (P.L. 103-62) requiring agencies to prepare strategic plans and assess results. Although not as far-reaching as hoped, the Act continues to provide performance goals for federal agencies that congressional oversight committees like Governmental Affairs may use to hold them accountable.

Membership: Expenditures in the Executive Departments, the predecessor to Governmental Affairs, opened the 80th Congress with thirteen members. Its membership dropped to nine in the 86th and 87th Congresses (1957-1961); reached a peak of nineteen by the 98th Congress (1983-1985); and resumed its original size of thirteen in 1985. Although its average size increased to 16.1 members in the last nine Congresses (1993-2011), it still ranks fifteenth among the sixteen standing committees. Since 1993, there is an anomaly between its mean seniority of 12.29 years for its members, ranking it sixth while its mean inter-Congress rate of 81.49 percent placed the committee in fifteenth place, a fraction of a percentage point ahead of the sixteenth-ranked committee, Environment and Public Works.

Thirty members of Governmental Affairs and its successor Homeland Security and Governmental Affairs were involved in on/off transfers with other committees. The committee gained twelve members—including three from Environment and Public Works and two each from Agriculture, Nutrition, and Forestry; Banking, Housing, and Urban Affairs; and HELP, and lost eighteen—three each to Appropriations and HELP, as well as two each to Agriculture, Nutrition and Forestry and Commerce, Science and Transportation, for a net loss of six. Four chairs moved off the committee: John S. McCain III (Rep-Ariz.) to chair Commerce, Science and Transportation in 1997; Robert C. Smith (Rep-N.H.) to chair Select Ethics in

1997; Thad Cochran (Rep-Miss.) to chair Agriculture, Nutrition and Forestry in 2003; and Arlen Specter (Rep-Penn.) to chair Judiciary in 2007. Illinois Democrat Richard J. Durbin left the committee after being elected Minority Whip in 2005.

Committee Leaders: George D. Aiken (Rep-Vt.) served as the chair of Expenditures in the Executive Departments in the 80th Congress (1947-1949), with John L. McClellan (Dem-Ark.) serving as its ranking minority member in the 80th Congress. McClellan became chair in the two subsequent Congresses (1949-1953), when its name was changed to the Committee on Government Operations in 1952. Aiken left the committee to become the senior Republican on Agriculture and Forestry and was replaced by the controversial Joseph R. McCarthy of Wisconsin. McClellan and McCarthy held the two senior committee ranks from 1953 until McCarthy's death in May, 1957. Although McCarthy was censured by the Senate for blatant misuse of the committee's investigatory authority in the 1954 Army-McCarthy hearings, he was allowed to remain as the committee's senior Republican until his death.

McClellan chaired the committee from 1955 to 1972, when he succeeded Allen J. Ellender (Dem-La.) as chair of Appropriations. McClellan's twenty-six years as the committee's senior Democrat (1947-1972) represent the longest period of committee senior service in the modern Senate. During his service as chair, McClellan served most often with Karl E. Mundt of South Dakota, who succeeded McCarthy in 1957, and served as its ranking minority member until the Senate removed him from the post on February 23, 1971, due to his having suffered a debilitating stroke.

Mundt was succeeded as ranking member by Charles H. Percy of Illinois and McClellan was succeeded as chair by Samuel J. Ervin of North Carolina. It was during Ervin's chairmanship of the committee from 1972 to 1974 that the "Watergate crisis" erupted. It was as chair of this committee that Senator Ervin was chosen to lead the Senate Select Committee on Presidential Campaign Activities in 1973 that would hold dramatic televised hearings investigating financial and tactical abuses in President Nixon's 1972 re-election campaign. It made Ervin a national celebrity but he chose to resign and retire from public life in 1974. However, the select committee so undermined the Nixon presidency that Nixon was obliged to resign in August, 1974, after the House Judiciary Committee passed three articles of impeachment.

Although he was not a member of the select committee, Percy served as the standing committee's ranking minority member from 1972 until 1981, when he became chair of the Foreign Relations Committee. Ervin was succeeded in 1975 by Abraham A. Ribicoff of Connecticut, who would serve as chair until his retirement in 1980. Ribicoff presided over the committee during its major reorganization in 1977 and its renaming as the Committee on Governmental Affairs.

The Reagan landslide of 1980 gave control of the Senate to the Republicans and William V. Roth of Delaware became the committee's first Republican chair since Joe McCarthy in 1954. Roth chaired the committee until 1987 and the Democratic recapture of the Senate. He served as its ranking minority member from 1987 until 1994 and resumed the chairmanship in 1995 once Republicans returned to power. Later that year, he relinquished the chair to Theodore F. Stevens of Alaska when Roth was named to replace Robert Packwood of Oregon as chair of the Finance Committee.

Thomas Eagleton of Missouri served as ranking minority member during Roth's chairmanship until he retired in 1986. Democratic control brought John H. Glenn of Ohio into the chairmanship and he served as chair from 1987 to 1995 and as ranking minority member from 1995 until his retirement in 1998. For eight months in 1982, Glenn and Harrison H. Schmitt (Rep-N.M.) the Senate's only two astronauts served together on the committee.

In 1997, with Roth chairing Finance and Ted Stevens chairing Appropriations, the chairmanship of Governmental Affairs went to Tennessee's Fred D. Thompson, then only in his third year in the Senate. Thompson was no stranger to Washington, for he had been the minority counsel to Howard W. Baker Jr., the senior Republican on the "Watergate committee" in 1973. Thompson served as the committee's senior Republican until he retired in 2002. Thompson was succeeded by Susan M. Collins of Maine, who chaired the committee from 2003 to 2007. Collins followed in the footsteps of her fellow Mainer, Margaret Chase Smith, the first woman to win four successive Senate elections and who had served on the committee and its predecessors for all twenty-four of her years in the Senate, 1949-1973.

Following Glenn's 1998 retirement, Joseph I. Lieberman became the committee's senior Democrat serving as ranking minority member in 1999-2001 up to the Jeffords defection and as chair during the subsequent eighteen months. Republicans regained the Senate in 2002 and Lieberman resumed the post of ranking minority member. The September 11, 2001, terrorist attacks on New York City and Washington, D.C. heightened tension in Congress and broadened the mandate of the committee enough so that it was renamed Homeland Security and Governmental Affairs. The change would also impact the self-perception of some of its key members, most notably Joe Lieberman.

Lieberman who ran for vice president with Vice President Al Gore Jr. in 2000 would seek the presidency for himself in 2004. The 2000 election defeat of Gore-Lieberman to Bush-Cheney was tightly-contested, while Lieberman's 2004 primary campaign never got off the ground. Lieberman became disenchanted with his fellow Democrats and they became disenchanted with him. After losing the 2006 Democratic primary in Connecticut, Lieberman ran as an Independent Democrat, and with a sizeable number of Republican votes, he was able to gain re-election. Although the 2006 victory of the Senate Democrats placed him once again in the chairmanship of Governmental Affairs, he chose to address the 2008 Republican National Convention praising John McCain and denouncing Barack Obama's candidacy. He also campaigned in Maine that year for Susan Collins, who holds the senior Republican rank on the committee.

When the 111th Congress convened in 2009, it was clear that the majority Democrats would need at least sixty votes if they were to head off unified Republican filibusters intended to slow Obama's legislative agenda. To hold onto as many votes as possible, the Senate Democrats agreed not to remove Lieberman from the chairmanship of Governmental Affairs in exchange for his agreeing to join the Democrats on procedural votes to limit filibusters.

Party Leadership: If experience was counted on two of the committees that were folded into Governmental Affairs in 1977—District of Columbia and Post Office and Civil

Service—then Democrats have selected six leaders with experience on the committee. Democratic Whip Earle Clements of Kentucky served on both the District and Post Office Committees during his service as Whip, 1953-1957; Mike Mansfield of Montana served on the District Committee during his Whip service, 1957-1961; and Whips Hubert Humphrey of Minnesota, 1961-1965, and Russell Long of Louisiana, 1965-1969, served on both the Post Office and Government Operations committees. Mansfield would also serve as floor leader from 1961 to 1977. Only two Democratic leaders have had Governmental Affairs experience in the past thirty years—floor leader George Mitchell of Maine, 1989-1995; and the present Democratic Whip from 2005, Richard Durbin of Illinois, now that it is known as Homeland Security and Governmental Affairs.

Senate Republicans also named six members of the committee to their leadership posts. Everett McK. Dirksen who led the Republicans from 1959 until his death in 1969 served on all three committees—District of Columbia, Post Office and Civil Service, and Government Operations prior to being elected Whip in 1955. Dirksen chaired the House's District Committee in the 80th Congress (1947-1949), when freshman John F. Kennedy of Massachusetts served reluctantly on the committee. Dirksen's son-in-law, Howard W. Baker, Jr. of Tennessee, who led the Senate GOP from 1977 to 1985, was the only other alumnus of the committee to be floor leader. Bob Dole of Kansas, who led Senate Republicans from 1985 until he resigned in 1996 to pursue the presidency, served for only eight months on Post Office in 1975, a little more than a year before the committee would be reorganized into Governmental Affairs. The other three Republican leaders to have served on the committee were named as Whips: Robert Griffin of Michigan, 1969-1977; Ted Stevens of Alaska, 1977-1985 and Don Nickles of Oklahoma, 1996-2003.

Presidential Aspirations: Richard Nixon of California, the 1960, 1968, and 1972 nominee and John McCain of Arizona, the 2008 nominee, were the only two Republican alumni of the committee to be nominated for president. Nixon and Bob Dole, the 1996 nominee served on two of the predecessor committees—District of Columbia and Post Office and Civil Service Committees—but their service was short-lived.

The Democrats have relied more heavily upon alumni of the Senate Government Committee for their nominees. Eight committee Democrats were successful in obtaining nominations, including four for president — John F. Kennedy of Massachusetts in 1960; Hubert H. Humphrey of Minnesota in 1968; Al Gore Jr. of Tennessee in 2000; and Barack Obama of Illinois in 2008. Both Humphrey and Gore were first nominated and elected vice president in 1964 and 1992 respectively before their unsuccessful presidential nominations, while committee alumni Ed Muskie of Maine in 1968; Thomas Eagleton of Missouri in 1972; Joe Lieberman in 2000; and John Edwards in 2004 received vice presidential selections that were also unsuccessful. While Government committee experience may help Democrats to be nominated, it is not an apparent stepping-stone to the White House.

Other Notables: Among the eight senators who served on Homeland Security and Governmental Affairs and its two predecessors whose jurisdictions were absorbed in 1977—the committees on the District of Columbia and Post Office and Civil Service—only one served in the Cabinet before serving on the committee: Connecticut Democrat Abraham Ribicoff who was President Kennedy's Secretary of Health, Education, and Welfare. The seven others who served in the Cabinet after their Senate service included five Republicans. They were: John Foster Dulles of New York, a 1948 appointee who served on both the District and Post Office Committees and became President Eisenhower's first Secretary of State in 1953; Fred Seaton of Nebraska, a 1951 appointee who also served on both the District and Post Office Committees and became Eisenhower's second Secretary of the Interior in 1956; William Saxbe of Ohio, who resigned to become President Nixon's fourth and final Attorney General in 1974, eight months before the president's resignation; William Brock of Tennessee who was named Secretary of Labor by President Reagan in 1981 after his Senate defeat; and William S. Cohen of Maine a Republican who had retired from the Senate but returned to government service as Secretary of Defense in Democrat Bill Clinton's administration in 1997.

The only two Democrats in this category were Democrat J. Howard McGrath of Rhode Island, a member of the District Committee, who resigned the Senate in 1949 to become President Truman's Attorney General and Maine's Edmund Muskie, a long-time Government Committee member, who resigned the Senate in 1980 to become President Carter's second Secretary of State.

Selected References

Coren, Robert W., et al., "Records of the Committee on the District of Columbia, 1816-1968," *Guide to the Records of the United States Senate at the National Archives: 1789-1989 Bicentennial Edition* (Washington, D.C.: National Archives and Records Administration, 1989), 87-93.

Coren, Robert W., et al., "Records of the Committee on Government Operations and Related Committees, 1842-1968," *Guide to the Records of the United States Senate at the National Archives: 1789-1989 Bicentennial Edition* (Washington, D.C.: National Archives and Records Administration, 1989), 117-122.

Coren, Robert W., et al., "Records of the Committee on Post Office and Civil Service and Predecessor Committees, 1816-1968," *Guide to the Records of the United States Senate at the National Archives: 1789-1989 Bicentennial Edition* (Washington, D.C.: National Archives and Records Administration, 1989), 175-182.

Gilmour, Robert S., "Governmental Affairs Committee, Senate," in Donald C. Bacon, Roger H. Davidson, and Morton Keller, eds., *The Encyclopedia of the United States Congress* (New York: Simon & Schuster, 1995), I: 917-920.

Malbin, Michael J., *Unelected Representatives: Congressional Staff and the Future of Representative Government* (New York: Basic Books, 1989), Chapter 4, "Shepherding a Bill through the Senate: The Sunset Bill."

U.S. Senate, Committee on Government Operations, *Committee on Government Operations, United States Senate, 50th Anniversary, 1921-1971*, Senate Document 92-32, 92nd Congress, 1st session (1971).

Wilmerding, Locus, Jr., *The Spending Power: A History of the Efforts of Congress to Control Expenditures* (Hampden, Conn.: Archon Books, 1971 reprint of 1943 original).

RESPONSIBILITIES, JURISDICTIONAL CHANGES, AND SUBCOMMITTEES

EXPENDITURES IN THE EXECUTIVE DEPARTMENTS

Jurisdiction, 80th Congress (1947-49)

Established by the Legislative Reorganization Act of 1946:

[Section 102.(1)(g)]

(1) **Committee on Expenditures in the Executive Departments**, to consist of thirteen Senators, to which committee shall be referred all proposed legislation, messages, petitions, memorials, and other matters relating to the following subjects:

    (A) Budget and accounting measures, other than appropriations.
    (B) Reorganizations in the executive branch of the Government.

(2) Such committee shall have the duty of:

    (A) receiving and examining reports of the Comptroller General of the United States and of submitting such recommendations to the Senate as it deems necessary or desirable in connection with the subject matter of such reports;
    (B) studying the operation of Government activities at all levels with a view to determining its economy and efficiency;
    (C) evaluating the effects of laws enacted to reorganize the legislative and executive branches of the Government;
    (D) studying intergovernmental relationships between the United States and the States and municipalities, and between the United States and international organizations of which the United States is a member.

Committee Renamed, 1952

Expenditures in the Executive Departments was renamed the Committee on Government Operations on March 2, 1952.

GOVERNMENTAL AFFAIRS

Committee Reorganized, 1977

The Senate Committee on Government Operations was reorganized as the Committee on Governmental Affairs following the passage of Senate Resolution 4, the Committee System Reorganization Amendments of 1977, February 4, 1977.

Reorganized Jurisdiction, 1977

From Senate Resolution 4, the Committee System Reorganization Amendments of 1977, February 4, 1977:

[Section (k)(1)]

(1) **Committee on Government Affairs**, to which committee shall be referred all proposed legislation, messages, petitions, memorials, and other matters relating to the following subjects:

    (1) Except as provided in the Congressional Budget Act of 1974, budget and accounting measures, other than appropriations.
    (2) Organization and reorganization of the executive branch of the Government.
    (3) Intergovernmental relations.
    (4) Government information.
    (5) Municipal affairs of the District of Columbia, except appropriations therefor.
    (6) Federal Civil Service.
    (7) Status of officers and employees of the United States, including their classification, compensation, and benefits.
    (8) Postal service.
    (9) Census and collection of statistics, including economic and social statistics.
    (10) Archives of the United States.
    (11) Organization and management of United States nuclear export policy.
    (12) Congressional organization, except for any part of the matter that amends the rules or orders of the Senate.

(2) Such committee shall have the duty of:

    (A) receiving and examining reports of the Comptroller General of the United States, and of submitting such recommendations to the Senate as it deems necessary or desirable in connection with the subject matter of such reports;
    (B) studying the efficiency, economy, and effectiveness of all agencies and departments of the government;
    (C) evaluating the effects of laws enacted to reorganize the legislative and executive branches of the government;
    (D) studying the intergovernmental relationships between the United States and the States and municipalities, and between the United States and international organizations of which the United States is a member.

Jurisdiction, 103rd Congress (1993-94)

From the *Standing Rules of the Senate* in the *Senate Manual*, 103rd Congress, 1st Session, S. Doc. 103-1:

[Rule XXV.(1)(k)]

(1) **Committee on Governmental Affairs**, to which committee shall be referred all proposed legislation, messages, petitions, memorials, and other matters relating to the following subjects:

    (1) Archives of the United States.

    (2) Budget and accounting measures, other than appropriations, except as provided in the Congressional Budget Act of 1974.

    (3) Census and collection of statistics, including economic and social statistics.

    (4) Congressional organization, except for any part of the matter that amends the rules or orders of the Senate.

    (5) Federal Civil Service.

    (6) Government information.

    (7) Intergovernmental relations.

    (8) Municipal affairs of the District of Columbia, except appropriations therefor.

    (9) Organization and management of United States nuclear export policy.

    (10) Organization and reorganization of the executive branch of the Government.

    (11) Postal Service.

    (12) Status of officers and employees of the United States, including their classification, compensation, and benefits.

(2) Such committee shall have the duty of:

    (A) receiving and examining reports of the Comptroller General of the United States and of submitting such recommendations to the Senate as it deems necessary or desirable in connection with the subject matter of such reports;

    (B) studying the efficiency, economy, and effectiveness of all agencies and departments of the Government;

    (C) evaluating the effects of laws enacted to reorganize the legislative and executive branches of the Government; and

    (D) studying the intergovernmental relationships between the United States and the States and municipalities, and between the United States and international organizations of which the United States is a member.

Committee Renamed, 2004

Governmental Affairs was renamed the Senate Committee on Homeland Security and Government Operations on October 8, 2004.

HOMELAND SECURITY AND GOVERNMENTAL AFFAIRS

Jurisdiction, 111th Congress (2009-10)

From *Authority and Rules of Senate Committees, 2009-2010*, Sen. Doc. 111-3, pursuant to S. Res, 166, June 2, 2009.

[Rule XXV.(1)(k)]

(1) **Committee on Homeland Security and Governmental Affairs**, to which committee shall be referred all proposed legislation, messages, petitions, memorials, and other matters relating to the following subjects:

    (1) Archives of the United States.

    (2) Budget and accounting measures, other than appropriations, except as provided in the Congressional Budget Act of 1974.

    (3) Census and collection of statistics, including economic and social statistics.

    (4) Congressional organization, except for any part of the matter that amends the rules or orders of the Senate.

    (5) Federal Civil Service.

    (6) Government information.

    (7) Intergovernmental relations.

    (8) Municipal affairs of the District of Columbia, except appropriations therefor.

    (9) Organization and management of United States nuclear export policy.

    (10) Organization and reorganization of the executive branch of the Government.

    (11) Postal Service.

    (12) Status of officers and employees of the United States, including their classification, compensation, and benefits.

(2) Such committee shall have the duty of:

    (A) receiving and examining reports of the Comptroller General of the United States and of submitting such recommendations to the Senate as it deems necessary or desirable in connection with the subject matter of such reports;

    (B) studying the efficiency, economy, and effectiveness of all agencies and departments of the Government;

    (C) evaluating the effects of laws enacted to reorganize the legislative and executive branches of the Government; and

    (D) studying the intergovernmental relationships between the United States and the States and municipalities, and between the United States and international organizations of which the United States is a member.

NAMES OF SUBCOMMITTEES

Committee on Governmental Affairs, 103rd-108th Congresses

Federal Services, Post Office, and Civil Service, 103
Financial Management, the Budget, and International Security, 108
General Services, Federalism, and the District of Columbia, 103
International Security, Proliferation, and Federal Services, 105, 106, 107
Oversight of Government Management, 103
Oversight of Government Management and the District of Columbia, 104
Oversight of Government Management, Restructuring, and District of Columbia, 105, 106, 107
Oversight of Government Management, the Federal Workforce, and District of Columbia, 108
Permanent Subcommittee on Investigations, 103, 104, 105, 106, 107, 108
Post Office and Civil Service, 104
Regulation and Government Information, 103

Committee on Homeland Security and Governmental Affairs, 109th -111th Congresses

Contracting Oversight (ad hoc), 111
Disaster Recovery (ad hoc), 111
Federal Financial Management, Government Information, and International Security, 109
Federal Financial Management, Government Information, Federal Services, and International Security, 110, 111
Oversight of Government Management, the Federal Workforce, and District of Columbia,109, 110, 111
Permanent Subcommittee on Investigations, 109, 110, 111
State, Local, and Private Sector Preparedness Integration (ad hoc), 111

MEMBERSHIP ROSTERS, 103rd-111th Congresses, 1993-2010

GOVERNMENTAL AFFAIRS / 103rd Congress

Service Dates of Committee Chair: Jan. 7, 1993-Jan. 5, 1995

Service Dates of Majority Members: Jan. 7, 1993-Jan. 5, 1995

Service Dates of Minority Members: Jan. 7, 1993-Jan. 5, 1995

Majority			Years in:		Minority			Years in:	
Rank Name	Party	State	Senate	Comm.	Rank Name	Party	State	Senate	Comm.
Chr Glenn, John H. Jr.	Dem	Ohio	19	18	RM Roth, William V. Jr.	Rep	Del.	23	*1 22
2nd Nunn, Samuel A.	Dem	Ga.	21	21	2nd Stevens, Theodore F.	Rep	Alas.	25	*2 16
3rd Levin, Carl M.	Dem	Mich.	15	14	3rd Cohen, William S.	Rep	Me.	15	14
4th Sasser, James R.	Dem	Tenn.	17	*2 7	4th Cochran, W. Thad	Rep	Miss.	15	*2 1
5th Pryor, David H.	Dem	Ark.	15	*3 7	5th McCain, John S. III	Rep	Ariz.	7	*1 1
6th Lieberman, Joseph I.	Dem	Conn.	5	4	6th Bennett, Robert F.	Rep	Utah	1	*1 1
7th Akaka, Daniel K.	Dem	Hai.	3	3					
8th Dorgan, Byron L.	Dem	N.D.	1	1					

*1: Member's first period of service on the committee.
*2: Member's second period of service on the committee.
*3: Member's third period of service on the committee.

Notes: "Years in committee" for Glenn include his continuous service on the District of Columbia Committee. "Years in committee" for Stevens include his continuous service on the Post Office and Civil Service Committee. Rankings on this committee for the following members were affected by other chamber service: Samuel A. Nunn (Dem-Ga.), Chair, Armed Services; and Theodore F. Stevens (Rep-Alas.), Ranking Minority Member, Rules and Administration.

Vacancies Filled:
   Minority:
      6th seat filled by Bennett on Sept. 30, 1993

Departures from the Senate:	Majority			Minority
Defeated for Re-election	Sasser, James R.	Dem	Tenn.	None

Departures from the Cmmittee:

Moved to Appropriations	None	Bennett, Robert F.	Rep	Utah

GOVERNMENTAL AFFAIRS / 104th Congress

Service Dates of Committee Chair: Ch1: Jan. 5, 1995-Sep. 12, 1995, Roth (Rep-Del.)

Ch2: Sep. 12, 1995-Jan. 9, 1997, Stevens (Rep-Alas.)

Service Dates of Majority Members: Jan. 5, 1995-Jan. 9, 1997

Service Dates of Minority Members: Jan. 4, 1995-Jan. 9, 1997

			Majority						Minority		
				Years in:						Years in:	
Rank Name	Party	State	Senate	Comm.		Rank Name	Party	State	Senate	Comm.
Ch1 Roth, William V. Jr.	Rep	Del.	25	*1 24		RM Glenn, John H. Jr.	Dem	Ohio	21	20
Ch2 Stevens, Theodore F.	Rep	Alas.	27	*2 18		2nd Nunn, Samuel A.	Dem	Ga.	23	23
3rd Cohen, William S.	Rep	Me.	17	16		3rd Levin, Carl M.	Dem	Mich.	17	16
4th Thompson, Fred D.	Rep	Tenn.	1	1		4th Pryor, David H.	Dem	Ark.	17	*3 8
5th Cochran, W. Thad	Rep	Miss.	17	*2 2		5th Lieberman, Joseph I.	Dem	Conn.	7	6
6th Grassley, Charles E.	Rep	Iowa	15	1		6th Akaka, Daniel K.	Dem	Hai.	5	5
7th McCain, John S. III	Rep	Ariz.	9	*1 2		7th Dorgan, Byron L.	Dem	N.D.	3	2
8th Smith, Robert C.	Rep	N.H.	5	1						

*1: Member's first period of service on the committee.

*2: Member's second period of service on the committee.

*3: Member's third period of service on the committee.

Notes: "Years in committee" for Glenn include his continuous service on the District of Columbia Committee. "Years in committee" for Stevens include his continuous service on the Post Office and Civil Service Committee. Rankings on this committee for the following members were affected by other chamber service: Theodore F. Stevens (Rep-Alas.), Chair, Rules and Administration and Samuel A. Nunn (Dem-Ga.), Ranking Minority Member, Armed Services.

Changes:

Chairs:

Ch1 Roth, William V. Jr.	Rep	Del.	Sep. 12, 1995 Relinquished chair to succeed Packwood as Chair of Finance.
Ch2 Stevens, Theodore F.	Rep	Alas.	Sep. 12, 1995 Succeeded Roth as Chair.

Majority:

Grassley, Charles E.	Rep	Iowa	Oct. 12, 1995 Left committee; moved to Agriculture, Nutrition and Forestry.
Brown, G. Hanks (Hank)	Rep	Colo.	Oct. 12, 1995 Replaced Grassley.
Brown, G. Hanks (Hank)	Rep	Colo.	June 20, 1996 Left committee; no new assignment.
Domenici, Pete V.	Rep	N.M.	June 20, 1996 Replaced Brown.

Departures from the Senate:	**Majority**				**Minority**		
Retired	Cohen, William S.	Rep	Me.		Nunn, Samuel A.	Dem	Ga.
					Pryor, David H.	Dem	Ark.

Departures from Committee:							
Became Chair of Commerce, Science, and Transportation	McCain, John S. III	Rep	Ariz.		None		
Became Chair of Select Ethics	Smith, Robert C.	Rep	N.H.		None		
Moved to Agriculture and Joint Committee on Taxation	Grassley, Charles E.	Rep	Iowa		None		
Moved to Appropriations	None				Dorgan, Byron L.	Dem	N.D.

GOVERNMENTAL AFFAIRS / 105th Congress

Service Dates of Committee Chair: Jan. 9, 1997-Jan. 7, 1999

Service Dates of Majority Members: Jan. 9, 1997-Jan. 7, 1999

Service Dates of Minority Members: Jan. 9, 1997-Jan. 7, 1999

			Majority						Minority		
				Years in:						Years in:	
Rank Name	Party	State	Senate	Comm.		Rank Name	Party	State	Senate	Comm.
Chr Thompson, Fred D.	Rep	Tenn.	3	3		RM Glenn, John H. Jr.	Dem	Ohio	23	22
2nd Roth, William V. Jr.	Rep	Del	27	*1 26		2nd Levin, Carl M.	Dem	Mich.	19	18

3rd Stevens, Theodore F.	Rep	Alas.	29	*2 20
4th Collins, Susan M.	Rep	Me.	1	1
5th Brownback, Sam D.	Rep	Kans.	1	1
6th Domenici, Pete V.	Rep	N.M.	25	*1 1
7th Cochran, W. Thad	Rep	Miss.	19	*2 5
8th Nickles, Donald L.	Rep	Okla.	17	1
9th Specter, Arlen	Rep	Penn.	17	*1 1

3rd Lieberman, Joseph I.	Dem	Conn.	9	8
4th Akaka, Daniel K.	Dem	Hai.	7	7
5th Durbin, Richard J.	Dem	Ill.	1	1
6th Torricelli, Robert G.	Dem	N.J	1	1
7th Cleland, J. Maxwell (Max)	Dem	Ga.	1	1

*1: Member's first period of service on the committee.
*2: Member's second period of service on the committee.

Notes: "Years in committee" for Glenn include his continuous service on the District of Columbia Committee. "Years in committee" for Stevens include his continuous service on the Post Office and Civil Service Committee. Rankings on this committee for the following members were affected by other chamber service: William V. Roth (Rep-Del.), Chair of Finance; and Theodore F. Stevens (Rep-Alas.), Chair of Appropriations.

Changes:

Majority:

Roth, William V. Jr.	Rep	Del.	May 21, 1997 Left committee for duration of campaign finance investigation, returned Mar. 4, 1998 (S. Res. 191)
Stevens, Theodore F.	Rep	Alas.	May 21, 1997 Left committee for duration of campaign finance investigation, returned Mar. 4, 1998 (S. Res. 191)
Smith, Robert C.	Rep	N.H.	May 21, 1997 Replaced Roth for duration of campaign finance investigation
Bennett, Robert F.	Rep	Utah	May 21, 1997 Replaced Stevens for duration of campaign finance investigation
Smith, Robert C.	Rep	N.H.	Mar. 4, 1998 Left committee to make room for Roth's return
Bennett, Robert F.	Rep	Utah	Mar. 4, 1998 Left committee to make room for Stevens' return
Roth, William V. Jr.	Rep	Del.	Mar. 4, 1998 Returned to replace Smith with original rank
Stevens, Theodore F.	Rep	Alas.	Mar. 4, 1998 Returned to replace Bennett with original rank

Departures from the Senate:

	Majority				Minority		
Retired	None				Glenn, John H. Jr.		Dem	Ohio

Departures from Committee:

					Minority
Moved to Labor and Human Resources	Brownback, Sam D.	Rep	Kans.	None
Moved to Joint Printing	Nickles, Donald L.	Rep	Okla.	None

GOVERNMENTAL AFFAIRS / 106th Congress

Service Dates of Committee Chair: Jan. 7, 1999-Jan. 3, 2001

Service Dates of Majority Members: Jan. 7, 1999-Jan. 25, 2001

Service Dates of Minority Members: Jan. 7, 1999-Jan. 25, 2001

Majority					Minority				
			Years in:					Years in:	
Rank Name	Party	State	Senate	Comm.	Rank Name	Party	State	Senate	Comm.
Chr Thompson, Fred D.	Rep	Tenn.	5	5	RM Lieberman, Joseph I.	Dem	Conn.	11	10
2nd Roth, William V. Jr.	Rep	Del.	29	*2 2	2nd Levin, Carl M.	Dem	Mich.	21	20
3rd Stevens, Theodore F.	Rep	Alas.	31	*3 1	3rd Akaka, Daniel K.	Dem	Hai.	9	9
4th Collins, Susan M.	Rep	Me.	3	2	4th Durbin, Richard J.	Dem	Ill.	3	2
5th Voinovich, George V.	Rep	Ohio	1	1	5th Torricelli, Robert G.	Dem	N.J.	3	2
6th Domenici, Pete V.	Rep	N.M.	27	*1 3	6th Cleland, J. Maxwell (Max)	Dem	Ga.	3	2
7th Cochran, W. Thad	Rep	Miss.	21	*2 7	7th Edwards, John	Dem	N.C.	1	1
8th Specter, Arlen	Rep	Penn.	19	*1 2					
9th Gregg, Judd A.	Rep	N.H.	7	1					

*1: Member's first period of service on the committee.
*2: Member's second period of service on the committee.
*3: Member's third period of service on the committee.

Note: Ranking on this committee for the following member was affected by other chamber service: Carl M. Levin (Dem-Mich.), Ranking Minority Member on Armed Services.

Departures from the Senate:

	Majority				Minority
Defeated for Re-election	Roth, William V. Jr.	Rep	Del.		None

Departures from Committee:

					Minority
Moved to Environment and Public Works	Specter, Arlen	Rep	Penn.		None
Moved to Commerce, Science, and Transportation, Health, Education, Labor and Pensions, and Select Intelligence	None				Edwards, John	Dem	N.C.

GOVERNMENTAL AFFAIRS / 107th Congress, Pre-Jeffords switch

Service Dates of Committee Chair: ChT: Jan. 3, 2001-Jan. 25, 2001 Lieberman (Dem-Conn.)

Ch1: Jan. 25, 2001-June 6, 2001 Thompson (Rep-Tenn.)

Service Dates of Majority Members: Jan. 25, 2001-June 6, 2001

Service Dates of Minority Members: Jan. 25, 2001-June 6, 2001

Majority						Minority				
			Years in:						Years in:	
Rank Name	Party	State	Senate	Comm.		Rank Name	Party	State	Senate	Comm.
Ch1 Thompson, Fred D.	Rep	Tenn.	7	7		RM1 Lieberman, Joseph I.	Dem	Conn.	13	12
2nd Stevens, Theodore F.	Rep	Alas.	33	*3 3		2nd Levin, Carl M.	Dem	Mich.	23	23
3rd Collins, Susan M.	Rep	Me.	5	5		3rd Akaka, Daniel K.	Dem	Hai.	11	11
4th Voinovich, George V.	Rep	Ohio	3	3		4th Durbin, Richard K.	Dem	Ill.	5	5
5th Domenici, Pete V.	Rep	N.M.	29	*1 5		5th Torricelli, Robert G.	Dem	N.J.	5	5
6th Cochran, W. Thad	Rep	Miss.	23	*2 9		6th Cleland, J. Maxwell (Max)	Dem	Ga.	5	5
7th Gregg, Judd A.	Rep	N.H.	9	3		7th Carper, Thomas R.	Dem	Del.	1	1
8th Bennett, Robert F.	Rep	Utah	9	*3 1		8th Carnahan, Jean	Dem	Mo.	1	1

*1: Member's first period of service on the committee.
*2: Member's second period of service on the committee.
*3: Member's third period of service on the committee.

Note 1: The committee majority in the 2001 Senate power-sharing arrangement was determined by the party of the vice president. Democrat Al Gore, Jr. served from Jan. 3, 2001 to Jan. 20, 2001, and was succeeded by Republican Richard B. Cheney on Jan. 20, 2001. When Senator Jeffords of Vermont left the Republican Party, effective June 6, 2001 to become an Independent, Democrats regained the majority for the remainder of the 107th Congress.

Note 2: Ranking on this committee for the following member was affected by other chamber service: Carl M. Levin (Dem-Mich.), Ranking Minority Member on Armed Services.

GOVERNMENTAL AFFAIRS / 107th Congress, Post-Jeffords switch

Service Dates of Committee Chair: June 6, 2001-Jan. 14, 2003

Service Dates of Majority Members: June 6, 2001-Jan. 14, 2003

Service Dates of Minority Members: June 6, 2001-Jan. 15, 2003

Majority						Minority				
			Years in:						Years in:	
Rank Name	Party	State	Senate	Comm.		Rank Name	Party	State	Senate	Comm.
Ch2 Lieberman, Joseph I.	Dem	Conn.	13	13		RM2 Thompson, Fred	Rep	Tenn.	7	7
2nd Levin, Carl M.	Dem	Mich.	23	23		2nd Stevens, Theodore F.	Rep	Alas.	33	*3 4
3rd Akaka, Daniel K.	Dem	Hai.	12	12		3rd Collins, Susan M.	Rep	Me.	5	5
4th Durbin, Richard K.	Dem	Ill.	5	5		4th Voinovich, George V.	Rep	Ohio	3	3
5th Torricelli, Robert G.	Dem	N.J.	5	5		5th Domenici, Pete V.	Rep	N.M.	29	*1 5
6th Cleland, J. Maxwell (Max)	Dem	Ga.	5	5		6th Cochran, W. Thad	Rep	Miss.	23	*2 9
7th Carper, Thomas R.	Dem	Del.	1	1		7th Gregg, Judd A.	Rep	N.H.	9	3
8th Carnahan, Jean	Dem	Mo.	1	1		8th Bennett, Robert F.	Rep	Utah	9	*3 1
9th Dayton, Mark	DFL	Minn.	1	1						

*1: Member's first period of service on the committee.
*2: Member's second period of service on the committee.
*3: Member's third period of service on the committee.

Note: Ranking on this committee for the following member was affected by other chamber service: Carl M. Levin (Dem-Mich.), Chair of Armed Services.

Additions:
Majority:

9th Dayton, Mark	DFL	Minn.	July 10, 2001

Changes:
Majority:

Carnahan, Jean	Dem	Mo.	Nov. 25, 2002 Resigned the Senate; defeated in special election by James M. Talent (Rep-Mo.)

Minority:

Gregg, Judd A.	Rep	N.H.	July 10, 2001 Left the committee; became Ranking Member on Health, Education, Labor, and Pensions after Jeffords vacated his seat
Fitzgerald, Peter G.	Rep	Ill.	July 10, 2001 Replaced Gregg

Departures from the Senate:	Majority			Minority		
Defeated for Re-election	Cleland, J. Maxwell (Max)	Dem	Ga.	None		
Retired	Torricelli, Robert G.	Dem	N.J.	Thompson, Fred D.	Rep	Tenn.

Departures from Committee:						
Became Chair of Agriculture, Nutrition, and Forestry	None			Cochran, W. Thad	Rep	Miss.
No new assignment	None			Domenici, Pete V.	Rep	N.M.

GOVERNMENTAL AFFAIRS / 108th Congress

* The Senate Committee on Governmental Affairs was renamed as the Committee on HOMELAND SECURITY AND GOVERNMENTAL AFFAIRS on Oct. 9, 2004 by S. Res. 445.

Service Dates of Committee Chair: Jan. 14, 2003-Jan. 6, 2005

Service Dates of Majority Members: Jan. 14, 2003-Jan. 6, 2005

Service Dates of Minority Members: Jan. 15, 2003-Jan. 6, 2005

Majority			Years in:		Minority			Years in:	
Rank Name	Party	State	Senate	Comm.	Rank Name	Party	State	Senate	Comm.
Chr Collins, Susan M.	Rep	Me.	7	7	RM Lieberman, Joseph I.	Dem	Conn.	15	14
2nd Stevens, Theodore F.	Rep	Alas.	35	*3 5	2nd Levin, Carl M.	Dem	Mich.	25	24
3rd Voinovich, George V.	Rep	Ohio	5	5	3rd Akaka, Daniel K.	Dem	Hai.	13	13
4th Coleman, Norman	Rep	Minn.	1	1	4th Durbin, Richard J.	Dem	Ill.	7	7
5th Specter, Arlen	Rep	Penn.	23	*2 1	5th Carper, Thomas R.	Dem	Del.	3	2
6th Bennett, Robert F.	Rep	Utah	11	*3 3	6th Dayton, Mark	DFL	Minn.	3	2
7th Fitzgerald, Peter G.	Rep	Ill.	5	2	7th Lautenberg, Frank R.	Dem	N.J.	19	1
8th Sununu, John E.	Rep	N.H.	1	*1 1	8th Pryor, Mark	Dem	Ark	1	1
9th Shelby, Richard C.	Rep	Ala.	17	1					

*1: Member's first period of service on the committee.
*2: Member's second period of service on the committee.
*3: Member's third period of service on the committee.

Note: Ranking on this committee for the following member was affected by other chamber service: Carl M. Levin (Dem-Mich.), Ranking Minority Member on Armed Services.

Departures from the Senate:	Majority			Minority		
Retired	Fitzgerald, Peter G.	Rep	Ill.	None		

Departures from Committee:						
Became Chair of Judiciary	Specter, Arlen	Rep	Penn.	None		
Elected Minority Whip	None			Durbin, Richard J.	Dem	Ill.
No new assignment	Sununu, John E.	Rep	N.H.	None		
	Shelby, Richard C.	Rep	Ala.			

HOMELAND SECURITY AND GOVERNMENTAL AFFAIRS / 109th Congress

Service Dates of Committee Chair: Jan. 6, 2005-Jan. 12, 2007

Service Dates of Majority Members: Jan. 6, 2005-Jan. 12, 2007

Service Dates of Minority Members: Jan. 6, 2005-Jan. 12, 2007

Majority			Years in:		Minority			Years in:	
Rank Name	Party	State	Senate	Comm.	Rank Name	Party	State	Senate	Comm.
Chr Collins, Susan M.	Rep	Me.	9	8	RM Lieberman, Joseph I.	Dem	Conn.	17	16
2nd Stevens, Theodore F.	Rep	Alas.	37	*3 7	2nd Levin, Carl M.	Dem	Mich.	27	26
3rd Voinovich, George V.	Rep	Ohio	7	6	3rd Akaka, Daniel K.	Dem	Hai.	15	15
4th Coleman, Norman	Rep	Minn.	3	2	4th Carper, Thomas R.	Dem	Del.	5	4
5th Coburn, Thomas A.	Rep	Okla.	1	1	5th Dayton, Mark	DFL	Minn.	5	4
6th Chafee, Lincoln D.	Rep	R.I.	6	1	6th Lautenberg, Frank R.	Dem	N.J.	21	2
7th Bennett, Robert F.	Rep	Utah	13	*3 5	7th Pryor, Mark	Dem	Ark.	3	2
8th Domenici, Pete V.	Rep	N.M.	33	*2 1					
9th Warner, John W.	Rep	Va.	27	1					

*2: Member's second period of service on the committee.
*3: Member's third period of service on the committee.

Note: Ranking on this committee for the following member was affected by other chamber service: Carl M. Levin (Dem-Mich.), Ranking Minority Member on Armed Services.

Departures from the Senate:	Majority			Minority		
Defeated for Re-election	Chafee, Lincoln D.	Rep	R.I.	None		
Retired	None			Dayton, Mark	DFL	Minn.
Departures from Committee:						
Moved to Joint Library and Joint Printing	Bennett, Robert F.	Rep	Utah	None		
Returned to Appropriations and Budget	None			Lautenberg, Frank R.	Dem	N.J.

HOMELAND SECURITY AND GOVERNMENTAL AFFAIRS / 110th Congress

Service Dates of Committee Chair: Jan. 12, 2007-Jan. 21, 2009

Service Dates of Majority Members: Jan. 12, 2007-Jan. 21, 2009

Service Dates of Minority Members: Jan. 12, 2007-Jan. 21, 2009

	Majority						Minority				
				Years in:						Years in:	
Rank Name	Party	State	Senate	Comm.		Rank Name	Party	State	Senate	Comm.	
Chr Lieberman, Joseph I.	IDem	Conn.	19	18		RM Collins, Susan M.	Rep	Me.	11	11	
2nd Levin, Carl M.	Dem	Mich.	29	28		2nd Stevens, Theodore F.	Rep	Alas.	39	*3 9	
3rd Akaka, Daniel K.	Dem	Hai.	17	17		3rd Voinovich, George V.	Rep	Ohio	9	9	
4th Carper, Thomas R.	Dem	Del.	7	6		4th Coleman, Norman	Rep	Minn.	5	4	
5th Pryor, Mark	Dem	Ark.	5	4		5th Coburn, Thomas A.	Rep	Okla.	3	3	
6th Landrieu, Mary L.	Dem	La.	11	1		6th Domenici, Pete V.	Rep	N.M.	35	*2 3	
7th Obama, Barack	Dem	Ill.	3	1		7th Warner, John W.	Rep	Va.	29	3	
8th McCaskill, Claire	Dem	Mo.	1	1		8th Sununu, John E.	Rep	N.H.	5	*2 1	
9th Tester, Jon	Dem	Mont.	1	1							

*2: Member's second period of service on the committee.

*3: Member's third period of service on the committee.

Note: Ranking on this committee for the following member was affected by other chamber service: Carl M. Levin (Dem-Mich.), Chair of Armed Services.

Changes:
  Majority:

Obama, Barack	Dem Ill.	Nov. 16, 2008 Resigned the Senate; elected President

Departures from the Senate:	Majority			Minority		
Defeated for Re-election	None			Stevens, Theodore F.	Rep	Alas.
				Coleman, Norman	Rep	Minn.
				Sununu, John E.	Rep	N.H.
Retired	None			Warner, John W.	Rep	Va.
				Domenici, Pete V.	Rep	N.M.

HOMELAND SECURITY AND GOVERNMENTAL AFFAIRS / 111th Congress

Service Dates of Committee Chair: Jan. 21, 2009-

Service Dates of Majority Members: Jan. 21, 2009-

Service Dates of Minority Members: Jan. 21, 2009-

	Majority						Minority				
				Years in:						Years in:	
Rank Name	Party	State	Senate	Comm.		Rank Name	Party	State	Senate	Comm.	
Chr Lieberman, Joseph I.	IDem	Conn.	21	20		RM Collins, Susan M.	Rep	Me.	13	13	
2nd Levin, Carl M.	Dem	Mich.	31	30		2nd Coburn, Thomas A.	Rep	Okla.	5	5	
3rd Akaka, Daniel K.	Dem	Hai.	19	19		3rd McCain, John S. III	Rep	Ariz.	23	*2 1	
4th Carper, Thomas R.	Dem	Del.	9	8		4th Voinovich, George V.	Rep	Ohio	11	11	
5th Pryor, Mark	Dem	Ark.	7	7		5th Ensign, John E.	Rep	Nev.	9	1	
6th Landrieu, Mary L.	Dem	La.	13	3		6th Graham, Lindsey O.	Rep	S.C.	7	1	
7th McCaskill, Claire	Dem	Mo.	3	3		7th Bennett, Robert F.	Rep	Utah	17	*4 1	
8th Tester, Jon	Dem	Mont.	3	3							
9th Burris, Roland W.	Dem	Ill.	1	1							
10th Bennet, Michael F.	Dem	Colo.	1	1							

*2: Member's second period of service on the committee.

*4: Member's fourth period of service on the committee.

Note 1: Ranking on this committee for the following member was affected by other chamber service: Carl M. Levin (Dem-Mich.), Chair of Armed Services.

Note 2: The disputed election in Minnesota between Democrat Al Franken and incumbent Republican Norman Coleman led both parties to hold seats open pending the outcome of the recount.

Filled vacancy:
  Majority:
    10th seat by Michael F. Bennet (Dem-Colo.) on Jan. 27, 2009
  Minority:
    7th seat by Robert F. Bennett (Rep-Utah) on July 21, 2009

Changes:
  Majority:

Bennet, Michael F.	Dem	Colo.	Sept. 29, 2009 Left committee; moved to Health, Education, Labor and Pensions
Kirk, Paul G. Jr.	Dem	Mass.	Sept. 29, 2009 Replaced Bennet
Kirk, Paul G. Jr.	Dem	Mass.	Feb. 4, 2010 Temporary term expired; successor elected

  Minority:

Brown, Scott P.	Rep	Mass.	Mar. 2, 2010 Minority addition; ranked 3rd after Coburn

Judiciary

Senate Committee on the Judiciary, 103rd-111th Congresses (1993-2011)

BACKGROUND

Organizational History: The Senate Committee on the Judiciary is one of the original standing committees authorized on December 10, 1816. Throughout its history the Judiciary Committee has seen its jurisdiction expand and contract. Changing laws would lead to the emergence of new legislative concerns and the expansion of the committee's jurisdiction. As these matters developed more nuances and spawned their own constituencies, they would be moved from the Judiciary Committee into new committees more directly focused on these issues. Some of the items that have remained within the committee's purview are those concerning the courts, law enforcement, and judicial administration.

However, other functions have moved from the Judiciary Committee and returned to it. Of the latter-day Judiciary Committee's predecessors, perhaps the most important was the Senate Committee on Immigration established on December 12, 1889, on a motion introduced by Orville H. Platt (Rep-Conn.). This committee was created in response to the great waves of southern European and Asian immigration to the United States in the late nineteenth century.

With the passage of the Legislative Reorganization Act of 1946, (Public Law 79-601), the functions of the Committee on Immigration were transferred to the Judiciary Committee. Since then, immigration matters have been referred to its various subcommittees on immigration and naturalization and refugee policy. The Judiciary Committee has relied heavily upon its subcommittees. The subcommittees on Immigration and Naturalization and Patents, Copyrights and Trademarks replaced pre-1947 standing committees. The other subcommittees had less tradition but soon proliferated until the 93rd and 94th Congresses (1973-1977) when the Judiciary Committee had seventeen standing and special subcommittees to handle its workload.

The two key constitutional issues of the 1950s and 1960s were legal restrictions on civil liberties and the expansion of civil rights legislation. Both of these issues were often enmeshed with Cold War concerns involving domestic Communists, and the Judiciary Committee often found itself in the middle of them. A key player in these debates was the Judiciary Committee's Special Subcommittee to Investigate the Administration of the Internal Security Act and Other Internal Security Laws, which existed from 1951 to 1977. It was best-known as the Senate Internal Security Subcommittee (SISS), and it was authorized to study and investigate the administration, operation and enforcement of the Internal Security Act of 1950 (Public Law 81-831, also known as the McCarran Act) and other laws relating to espionage, sabotage, and the protection of the internal security of the United States and the extent, nature, and effects of subversive activities in the United States "including, but not limited to, espionage, sabotage, and infiltration of persons who are or may be under the domination of the foreign government or organization controlling the world Communist movement or any movement seeking to overthrow the Government of the United States by force and violence."

The subcommittee soon acquired the reputation of the Senate version of the House's Un-American Activities Committee (HUAC). Pat A. McCarran (Dem-Nev.), the author of the McCarran Act, was its first chair and did much to set the subcommittee's aggressive agenda. When the Republicans gained control of the Senate in 1952, William E. Jenner (Rep-Ind.) became chair of the SISS. He was followed by James O. Eastland (Dem-Miss.) who became chair in 1955, a position he held until the subcommittee was abolished in the 1977 Senate reorganization. Its critics had come to believe that the SISS was being used by Eastland, an opponent of racial integration, to thwart civil rights legislation by linking civil rights activism to communist-inspired plots and thereby discrediting the movement. An effort to revive the committee's interest in these matters was led by Jeremiah Denton (Rep-Ala.) with the subcommittee on Security and Terrorism, but this subcommittee began and ended with Senator Denton's lone term in the Senate (1981-1987).

In recent years, the Judiciary Committee has been less aggressive legislatively, but it continues to occupy center stage in American politics through its use of televised hearings to examine the credentials of nominees for the U.S. Supreme Court. Supreme Court confirmation hearings concerning the failed nomination of Federal Judge Robert Bork in 1987 and the 1991 successful nomination of Federal Judge Clarence Thomas held the nation's attention for weeks, with much public focus on the committee. While two of President Bill Clinton nominees, Ruth Bader Ginsburg (96-3) and Steven Breyer (87-9) were confirmed easily, testy confirmation battles over President George W. Bush's appointees, John Roberts (78-22) and Samuel Alito (58-42) and President Barack Obama's choice of Sonia Sotomayor (68-31) have once again placed the committee and the Supreme Court confirmation process in the public eye.

Apart from the three Supreme Court confirmations, the most contentious battles inside the committee have come over the confirmation of lower court federal judges as the Bush-Cheney Administration relied heavily upon the recommendations of the conservative Federalist Society rather than the more mainstream American Bar Association as the ultimate screener of judicial quality. With divided government the norm in the past eighteen years, both Democratic president Clinton and Republican president George W. Bush found their lower court nominees held up over ideological disagreements when their party opponents had control of the Judiciary Committee.

Membership: The Judiciary Committee had thirteen members in the 80th Congress. Its early membership reached eighteen in the 97th-99th Congresses (1981-1987) but was reduced to fourteen in 1987. However, following the Jeffords shift in 2001, the committee grew to nineteen and has remained at that number ever since. It remains a relatively small committee, with an average 1993-2011 membership of 18.4 senators—twelfth place among the sixteen standing committees. It ranks relatively high in both mean seniority—14.49 years—fourth place behind only Rules and Administration, Appropriations, and Finance—and in sixth place with an inter-Congress retention rate of 89.8 percent.

Since 1993, seven members joined Judiciary and fifteen left it—a net loss of eight. Judiciary's largest gain was three members from Health, Education, Labor, and Pensions. Four of its departing members left to chair other committees—Larry L. Pressler (Rep-S.D.) to chair Commerce, Science and Transportation in 1995; William S. Cohen (Rep-Me.) to chair Special Aging in 1995; Larry Craig (Rep-Ida.) to chair Veterans' Affairs in 2005; and Saxby Chambliss (Rep-Ga.) to chair Agriculture, Nutrition and Forestry in 2005 also. Mitch McConnell left the committee in 2003 after he was elected Majority Whip. Regarding its losses to other standing committees—four departed Judiciary for Finance; three for Commerce, Science and Transportation, and two to Appropriations.

Committee Leaders: Republican Alexander Wiley of Wisconsin chaired Judiciary in the first post-reorganization Congress (1947-1949) with Nevada Democrat Patrick J. McCarran serving as ranking minority member. Both had served on the committee for extended periods prior to the reorganization. McCarran became its first post-1947 Democratic chair in the 81st and 82nd Congresses, with Wiley serving as ranking member. Republican gains in 1952 led to Wiley relinquishing his senior Republican post to become chair of Foreign Relations. He was replaced by William Langer in the 83rd Congress, but returned as the senior Republican in 1955 and served in that post until his 1962 defeat for re-election.

Pat McCarran died in September, 1954 and he was replaced as the committee's senior Democrat by Harley M. Kilgore of West Virginia. The Democratic recapture of the Senate in November 1954 gave Kilgore the chairmanship of the committee, but his death in February 1956 led to staunch segregationist James O. Eastland of Mississippi assuming the chair, a post that he would hold for more than twenty-two consecutive years until his resignation from the Senate in December, 1978.

During Eastland's lengthy chairmanship of Judiciary, he would serve with several Republican ranking minority members—Alexander Wiley until 1963; Everett McK. Dirksen of Illinois, from 1963 until his death in 1969; Roman L. Hruska of Nebraska from 1969 until his resignation in 1976. J. Strom Thurmond of South Carolina, a like-minded Southern senator, became the Judiciary Committee's senior Republican in 1977. Thurmond remained in that rank until 1993. Orrin Hatch served as Judiciary's chair for six years (1981-1987) and as its ranking minority member for ten years (1977-1981 and 1987-1993).

When Eastland retired, the Judiciary Committee would next be chaired by Edward M. Kennedy of Massachusetts, arguably the most effective Senate liberal of the past half-century. Although Kennedy only chaired the committee in the 96th Congress (1979-1981), the transformation of the committee's agenda was dramatic. During the six years from 1981 to 1987, after Reagan-era Republicans gained control of the Senate in 1980, Kennedy relinquished the senior Democratic rank to Joseph R. Biden of Delaware so that he could become the senior Democrat on Labor and Human Resources, a post he would hold until his death in August, 2009. Biden served as the senior Democrat on Judiciary until 1997 with eight years as chair (1987-1995) and eight as ranking member (1981-1987 and 1995-1997). Biden relinquished his senior rank on Judiciary to become ranking minority member on Foreign Relations in 1997. Biden was succeeded by Patrick J. Leahy of Vermont, who has served as Judiciary's senior Democrat for the last fourteen years—five-plus years as chair (2001-2003 and 2007-2011) and eight-plus years as ranking minority member (1997-2001 and 2003-2007).

Party Leaders: Twelve Judiciary Committee members were chosen to lead their respective Senate parties—eight Republicans and four Democrats. Five Republican members of Judiciary were elected floor leader. Four were elected in succession over a thirty-eight-year period: Everett McK. Dirksen of Illinois, 1959-1969, who was succeeded by Hugh D. Scott of Pennsylvania, 1969-1977, who was succeeded by Dirksen's son-in-law Howard W. Baker, Jr. of Tennessee, 1977-1985, and who was followed by Bob Dole of Kansas, 1985-1996. The present Republican floor leader (2007-2011), Mitch McConnell of Kentucky is the fifth Republican floor leader with Judiciary Committee experience. While Dirksen, Scott, and McConnell apprenticed as Whips prior to being elected floor leader, three other Republicans served only as Whips —Robert Griffin of Michigan, 1969-1977, the party Whip under Scott; Alan Simpson of Wyoming, 1985-1995, the Whip under Dole; and Jon Kyl of Arizona who succeeded McConnell as Whip in 2007 and continues to serve in the 111th Congress.

Of the four Democrats to hold leadership posts, only Bob Byrd of West Virginia served as floor leader serving from 1977 to 1989 after he had served for six years as Whip, 1971-1977. The others served only as Whips—Earl Clements of Kentucky, 1953-1957, Ted Kennedy of Massachusetts, 1969-1971 who lost his post to Byrd, and the present Democratic Whip since 2005, Richard Durbin of Illinois.

Presidential Aspirations: The Judiciary Committee has not provided many presidential or vice presidential nominees to the nation. Joe Biden's 2008 election as vice president made him the only Senate Judiciary Committee alumnus to be nominated and elected. Democrats Estes Kefauver of Tennessee and John Edwards of North Carolina were nominated for vice president in 1956 and 2004, but neither was elected. Nor was Judiciary member Bob Dole of Kansas, whose vice presidential bid in 1976 and presidential one in 1996 were unsuccessful.

Other Notables: During the post-1947 era, no senator joined the Judiciary Committee after previous Cabinet service. Four former senators joined the Cabinet after their service in the Senate had ended. Only Democrat J. Howard McGrath of Rhode Island resigned the Senate to join the Cabinet when he left in 1949 to become President Truman's Attorney General. Maine Republican William S. Cohen joined the Cabinet of Democratic President Bill Clinton in 1997 shortly after his Senate retirement. Two Judiciary Committee Republicans who had lost their re-election bids were named in 2001 to President George W. Bush's Cabinet—Spencer Abraham of Michigan as Secretary of Transportation and John Ashcroft of Missouri as Attorney General.

Selected References

Berman, Daniel M., *A Bill Becomes a Law: The Civil Rights Act of 1960* (New York: Macmillan, 1962).

Coren, Robert W., et al., "Records of the Committee on the Judiciary and Related Committees, 1816-1968," *Guide to the Records of the United States Senate at the National Archives: 1789-1989 Bicentennial Edition* (Washington,

D.C.: National Archives and Records Administration, 1989), 143-165.

Evans, C. Lawrence., "Judiciary Committee, Senate," in Donald C. Bacon, Roger H. Davidson, and Morton Keller, eds., *The Encyclopedia of the United States Congress* (New York: Simon & Schuster, 1995), I: 1200-1204.

Evans, C. Lawrence, *Leadership in Committee: A Comparative Analysis of Leadership Behavior in the U.S. Senate* (Ann Arbor: University of Michigan, 2001).

Farrelly, David G., "The Senate Judiciary Committee: Qualifications of Members," *American Political Science Review*, 37 (June, 1943), 469-475.

Nunn, Sam, "The Impact of the Senate Permanent Subcommittee on Investigations on Federal Policy," *Georgia Law Review*, 21 (1986), 17-56.

Schuck, Peter H., *The Judiciary Committees: A Study of the House and Senate Judiciary Committees* in the Ralph Nader Congress Project (New York: Grossman, 1975).

Thorpe, James A., "The Appearance of Supreme Court Nominees before the Senate Judiciary Committee," *Journal of Public Law*, 18 (1969), 371-402.

U.S. Senate, Committee on the Judiciary, *History of the Committee on the Judiciary, 1816-1981*, Senate Document 97-18, 97th Congress, 1st session (1982). This is the fifth history of the committee: 1) *History of the Committee on the Judiciary together with Chairmen and Members Assigned Thereto 1816-1962*, Senate Committee Print, 87th Congress, 2nd session (1962); 2) *History of the Committee on the Judiciary together with Chairmen and Members Assigned Thereto 1816-1966*, Senate Committee Print, 89th Congress, 2nd session (1966); 3) *History of the Committee on the Judiciary United States Senate*, Senate Document 90-78, 90th Congress, 2nd session (1968); and 4) *History of the Committee on the Judiciary, 1816-1976,* Senate Document 97-19, 97th Congress, 2nd session (1976).

RESPONSIBILITIES, JURISDICTIONAL CHANGES, AND SUBCOMMITTEES

JUDICIARY

Jurisdiction, 80th Congress (1947-49)

Established by the Legislative Reorganization Act of 1946:

[Section 102.(1)(k)]

(1) **Committee on the Judiciary**, to consist of thirteen Senators, to which committee shall be referred all proposed legislation, messages, petitions, memorials, and other matters relating to the following subjects:

(1) Judicial proceedings, civil and criminal, generally.
(2) Constitutional amendments.
(3) Federal courts and judges.
(4) Local courts in the Territories and possessions.
(5) Revision and codification of the statutes of the United States.
(6) National penitentiaries.
(7) Protection of trade and commerce against unlawful restraints and monopolies.
(8) Holidays and celebrations.
(9) Bankruptcy, mutiny, espionage, and counterfeiting.
(10) State and Territorial boundary lines.
(11) Meetings of Congress, attendance of Members, and their acceptance of incompatible offices.
(12) Civil liberties.
(13) Patents, copyrights, and trade-marks.
(14) Patent Office.
(15) Immigration and naturalization.
(16) Apportionment of Representatives.
(17) Measures relating to claims against the United States.
(18) Interstate compacts generally.

Post-Reorganization Jurisdiction, 1977

From Committee System Reorganization Amendments of 1977, S. Res. 95-4, *Senate Journal*, Feb. 4, 1977:

[XXV. Section 101. 1.(m)]

(1) **Committee on the Judiciary**, to which committee shall be referred all proposed legislation, messages, petitions, memorials, and other matters relating to the following subjects:

(1) Judicial proceedings, civil and criminal, generally.
(2) Constitutional amendments.

    (3) Federal courts and judges.
    (4) Local courts in the territories and possessions.
    (5) Revision and codification of the statutes of the United States.
    (6) National penitentiaries.
    (7) Protection of trade and commerce against unlawful restraints and monopolies.
    (8) Holidays and celebrations.
    (9) Bankruptcy, mutiny, espionage, and counterfeiting.
  (10) State and territorial boundary lines.
  (11) Civil liberties.
  (12) Patents, copyrights, and trademarks.
  (13) Patent Office.
  (14) Immigration and naturalization.
  (15) Apportionment of Representatives.
  (16) Measures relating to claims against the United States.
  (17) Interstate compacts generally.
  (18) Government information.

Jurisdiction, 103rd Congress (1993-94)

From the *Standing Rules of the Senate* in the *Senate Manual*, 103rd Congress, 1st Session, S. Doc. 103-1:

[Rule XXV.(1)(l)]

(1) **Committee on the Judiciary**, to which committee shall be referred all proposed legislation, messages, petitions, memorials, and other matters relating to the following subjects:

    (1) Apportionment of Representatives.
    (2) Bankruptcy, mutiny, espionage, and counterfeiting.
    (3) Civil liberties.
    (4) Constitutional amendments.
    (5) Federal courts and judges.
    (6) Government information.
    (7) Holidays and celebrations.
    (8) Immigration and naturalization.
    (9) Interstate compacts generally.
  (10) Judicial proceedings, civil and criminal, generally.
  (11) Local courts in the territories and possessions.
  (12) Measures relating to claims against the United States.
  (13) National penitentiaries.
  (14) Patent Office.
  (15) Patents, copyrights, and trademarks.
  (16) Protection of trade and commerce against unlawful restraints and monopolies.
  (17) Revision and codification of the statutes of the United States.
  (18) State and territorial boundary lines.

Jurisdiction, 111th Congress (2009-10)

From *Authority and Rules of Senate Committees, 2009-2010*, Sen. Doc. 111-3, pursuant to S. Res, 166, June 2, 2009.

[Rule XXV.(1)(l)]

(1) **Committee on the Judiciary**, to which committee shall be referred all proposed legislation, messages, petitions, memorials, and other matters relating to the following subjects:

    (1) Apportionment of Representatives.
    (2) Bankruptcy, mutiny, espionage, and counterfeiting.
    (3) Civil liberties.
    (4) Constitutional amendments.
    (5) Federal courts and judges.
    (6) Government information.
    (7) Holidays and celebrations.
    (8) Immigration and naturalization.
    (9) Interstate compacts generally.
  (10) Judicial proceedings, civil and criminal, generally.
  (11) Local courts in the territories and possessions.
  (12) Measures relating to claims against the United States.
  (13) National penitentiaries.

(14) Patent Office.
(15) Patents, copyrights, and trademarks.
(16) Protection of trade and commerce against unlawful restraints and monopolies.
(17) Revision and codification of the statutes of the United States.
(18) State and territorial boundary lines.

NAMES OF SUBCOMMITTEES

Committee on the Judiciary, 103rd -111th Congresses

Administrative Oversight and the Courts, 104, 105, 106, 107, 108, 109, 110, 111
Antitrust, Business Rights, and Competition, 104, 105, 106
Antitrust, Competition, and Business and Consumer Rights, 107
Antitrust, Competition Policy, and Consumer Rights, 108, 109, 110, 111
Antitrust, Monopolies and Business Rights, 103
Constitution, 103, 107, 110, 111
Constitution, Federalism, and Property Rights, 104, 105, 108, 109
Corrections and Rehabilitation, 109
Courts and Administrative Practice, 103
Crime and Drugs, 107, 109, 110, 111
Crime, Corrections, and Victims' Rights, 108
Criminal Justice Oversight, 106
Human Rights and the Law, 110, 111
Immigration and Refugee Affairs, 103
Immigration, 104, 105, 106, 107
Immigration, Border Security, and Citizenship, 108, 109
Immigration, Refugees, and Border Security, 110, 111
Intellectual Property, 109
Juvenile Justice, 103
Patents, Copyrights and Trademarks, 103
Technology and the Law, 103
Technology, Terrorism, and Government Information, 105, 106, 107
Terrorism, Technology, and Government Information, 104
Terrorism, Technology, and Homeland Security, 108, 109, 110
Terrorism and Homeland Security, 111
Youth Violence, 104, 105, 106

MEMBERSHIP ROSTERS, 103rd-111th Congresses, 1993-2010

JUDICIARY / 103rd Congress

Service Dates of Committee Chair: Jan. 7, 1993-Jan. 4, 1995

Service Dates of Majority Members: Jan. 7, 1993-Jan. 4, 1995

Service Dates of Minority Members: Jan. 7, 1993-Jan. 4, 1995

Majority					Minority				
			Years in:					Years in:	
Rank Name	Party	State	Senate	Comm.	Rank Name	Party	State	Senate	Comm.
Chr Biden, Joseph R. Jr.	Dem	Del.	21	16	RM Hatch, Orrin G.	Rep	Utah	17	16
2nd Kennedy, Edward M.	Dem	Mass.	31	30	2nd Thurmond, J. Strom	Rep	S.C.	38	26
3rd Metzenbaum, Howard M.	Dem	Ohio	19	16	3rd Simpson, Alan K.	Rep	Wyo.	15	14
4th DeConcini, Dennis W.	Dem	Ariz.	17	16	4th Grassley, Charles E.	Rep	Iowa	13	13
5th Leahy, Patrick J.	Dem	Vt.	19	14	5th Specter, Arlen	Rep	Penn.	13	13
6th Heflin, Howell T.	Dem	Ala.	15	14	6th Brown, G. Hanks (Hank)	Rep	Colo.	3	2
7th Simon, Paul M.	Dem	Ill.	9	8	7th Cohen, William S.	Rep	Me.	15	1
8th Kohl, Herbert H.	Dem	Wisc.	5	4	8th Pressler, Larry L.	Rep	S.D.	15	1
9th Feinstein, Dianne	Dem	Cal.	1	1					
10th Moseley Braun, Carol	Dem	Ill.	1	1					

Note: Rankings on this committee for the following members were affected by other chamber service: Edward M. Kennedy (Dem-Mass.), Chair, Labor and Human Resources; J. Strom Thurmond (Rep-S.C.), Ranking Minority Member, Armed Services.

Departures from the Senate:	Majority			Minority		
Retired	Metzenbaum, Howard M.	Dem	Ohio	None		
	DeConcini, Dennis W.	Dem	Ariz.			

Departures from Committee:						
Became Chair of Commerce, Science, and Transportation	None			Pressler, Larry L.	Rep	S.D.
Became Chair of Special Aging	None			Cohen, William S.	Rep	Me.
Moved to Finance	Moseley Braun, Carol	Dem	Ill.	Pressler, Larry L.	Rep	S.D.
Moved to Special Committee on Aging	Moseley Braun, Carol	Dem	Ill.	None		
Returned to Select Intelligence	None			Cohen, William S.	Rep	Me.

JUDICIARY / 104th Congress

Service Dates of Committee Chair: Jan. 4, 1995-Jan. 9, 1997

Service Dates of Majority Members: Jan. 4, 1995-Jan. 9, 1997

Service Dates of Minority Members: Jan. 4, 1995-Jan. 9, 1997

Majority			Years in:		Minority			Years in:	
Rank Name	Party	State	Senate	Comm.	Rank Name	Party	State	Senate	Comm.
Chr Hatch, Orrin G.	Rep	Utah	19	18	RM Biden, Joseph R. Jr.	Dem	Del.	23	18
2nd Thurmond, J. Strom	Rep	S.C.	40	28	2nd Kennedy, Edward M.	Dem	Mass.	33	32
3rd Simpson, Alan K.	Rep	Wyo.	17	16	3rd Leahy, Patrick J.	Dem	Vt.	21	16
4th Grassley, Charles E.	Rep	Iowa	15	14	4th Heflin, Howell T.	Dem	Ala.	17	16
5th Specter, Arlen	Rep	Penn.	15	14	5th Simon, Paul M.	Dem	Ill.	11	10
6th Brown, G. Hanks (Hank)	Rep	Colo.	5	4	6th Kohl, Herbert H.	Dem	Wisc.	7	6
7th Thompson, Fred D.	Rep	Tenn.	1	1	7th Feinstein, Dianne	Dem	Cal.	3	2
8th Kyl, Jon L.	Rep	Ariz.	1	1	8th Feingold, Russell D.	Dem	Wisc.	3	1
9th DeWine, Michael	Rep	Ohio	1	1					
10th Abraham, Spencer	Rep	Mich.	1	1					

Note: Rankings on this committee for the following members were affected by other chamber service: J. Strom Thurmond (Rep-S.C.), Chair Armed Services and Edward M. Kennedy (Dem-Mass.), Ranking Minority Member, Labor and Human Resources.

Departures from the Senate:	Majority			Minority		
Retired	Simpson, Alan K.	Rep	Wyo.	Heflin, Howell T.	Dem	Ala.
	Brown, G. Hanks (Hank)	Rep	Colo.	Simon, Paul M.	Dem	Ill

JUDICIARY / 105th Congress

Service Dates of Committee Chair: Jan. 9, 1997-Jan. 7, 1999

Service Dates of Majority Members: Jan. 9, 1997-Jan. 7, 1999

Service Dates of Minority Members: Jan. 9, 1997-Jan. 7, 1999

Majority			Years in:		Minority			Years in:	
Rank Name	Party	State	Senate	Comm.	Rank Name	Party	State	Senate	Comm.
Chr Hatch, Orrin G.	Rep	Utah	21	20	RM Leahy, Patrick J.	Dem	Vt.	23	18
2nd Thurmond, J. Strom	Rep	S.C.	42	30	2nd Kennedy, Edward M.	Dem	Mass.	35	34
3rd Grassley, Charles E.	Rep	Iowa	17	17	3rd Biden, Joseph R. Jr.	Dem	Del.	25	20
4th Specter, Arlen	Rep	Penn.	17	17	4th Kohl, Herbert H.	Dem	Wisc.	9	8
5th Thompson, Fred D.	Rep	Tenn.	3	3	5th Feinstein, Dianne	Dem	Cal.	5	5
6th Kyl, Jon L.	Rep	Ariz.	3	3	6th Feingold, Russell D.	Dem	Wisc.	5	3
7th DeWine, Michael	Rep	Ohio	3	3	7th Durbin, Richard J.	Dem	Ill.	1	*1 1
8th Ashcroft, John D.	Rep	Mo.	3	1	8th Torricelli, Robert G.	Dem	N.J.	1	1
9th Abraham, Spencer	Rep	Mich.	3	3					
10th Sessions, Jefferson B. III	Rep	Ala.	1	1	*1: Member's first period of service on the committee.				

Note: Rankings on this committee for the following members were affected by other chamber service: J. Strom Thurmond (Rep-S.C.), Chair Armed Services; Edward M. Kennedy (Dem-Mass.), Ranking Minority Member, Labor and Human Resources; and Joseph R. Biden, Jr. (Dem-Del.) Ranking Minority Member, Foreign Relations.

Departures from Committee:	Majority			Minority		
Moved to Finance	Thompson, Fred D.	Rep	Tenn.	None		
Moved to Appropriations and Select Ethics	None			Durbin, Richard J.	Dem	Ill.

JUDICIARY / 106th Congress

Service Dates of Committee Chair: Jan. 7, 1999-Jan. 3, 2001

Service Dates of Majority Members: Jan. 7, 1999-Jan. 25, 2001

Service Dates of Minority Members: Jan. 7, 1999-Jan. 25, 2001

	Majority							Minority				
				Years in:						Years in:	
Rank	Name	Party	State	Senate	Comm.		Rank	Name	Party	State	Senate	Comm.
Chr	Hatch, Orrin G.	Rep	Utah	23	22		RM	Leahy, Patrick J.	Dem	Vt.	25	20
2nd	Thurmond, J. Strom	Rep	S.C.	44	32		2nd	Kennedy, Edward M.	Dem	Mass.	37	36
3rd	Grassley, Charles E.	Rep	Iowa	19	19		3rd	Biden, Joseph R. Jr.	Dem	Del.	27	22
4th	Specter, Arlen	Rep	Penn.	19	19		4th	Kohl, Herbert H.	Dem	Wisc.	11	10
5th	Kyl, Jon L.	Rep	Ariz.	5	5		5th	Feinstein, Dianne	Dem	Cal.	7	7
6th	DeWine, Michael	Rep	Ohio	5	5		6th	Feingold, Russell D.	Dem	Wisc.	7	5
7th	Ashcroft, John D.	Rep	Mo.	5	2		7th	Torricelli, Robert G.	Dem	N.J.	3	2
8th	Abraham, Spencer	Rep	Mich.	5	5		8th	Schumer, Charles E.	Dem	N.Y.	1	1
9th	Sessions, Jefferson B. III	Rep	Ala.	3	2							
10th	Smith, Robert C.	Rep	N.H.	9	1							

Note: Rankings on this committee for the following members were affected by other chamber service: J. Strom Thurmond (Rep-S.C.), Chair Armed Services; Edward M. Kennedy (Dem-Mass.), Ranking Minority Member, Labor and Human Resources; and Joseph R. Biden, Jr. (Dem-Del.) Ranking Minority Member, Foreign Relations.

Departures from the Senate:	Majority			Minority		
Defeated for Re-election	Ashcroft, John	Rep	Mo.	None		
	Abraham, Spencer	Rep	Mich.			

Departures from Committee:						
Moved to Finance	None			Torricelli, Robert G.	Dem	N.J.
No new assignment	Smith, Robert C.	Rep	N.H.	None		

JUDICIARY / 107th Congress, Pre-Jeffords switch

Service Dates of Committee Chair: ChT: Jan. 3, 2001-Jan. 25, 2001 Leahy (Dem-Vt.)

Ch1: Jan. 25, 2001-June 6, 2001 Hatch (Rep-Utah)

Service Dates of Majority Members: Jan. 25, 2001-June 6, 2001

Service Dates of Minority Members: Jan. 25, 2001-June 6, 2001

	Majority							Minority				
				Years in:						Years in:	
Rank	Name	Party	State	Senate	Comm.		Rank	Name	Party	State	Senate	Comm.
Ch1	Hatch, Orrin G.	Rep	Utah	25	24		RM1	Leahy, Patrick J.	Dem	Vt.	27	23
2nd	Thurmond, J. Strom	Rep	S.C.	46	35		2nd	Kennedy, Edward M.	Dem	Mass.	39	38
3rd	Grassley, Charles E.	Rep	Iowa	21	21		3rd	Biden, Joseph R. Jr.	Dem	Del.	29	24
4th	Specter, Arlen	Rep	Penn.	21	21		4th	Kohl, Herbert H.	Dem	Wisc.	13	12
5th	Kyl, Jon L.	Rep	Ariz.	7	7		5th	Feinstein, Dianne	Dem	Cal.	9	9
6th	DeWine, Michael	Rep	Ohio	7	7		6th	Feingold, Russell D.	Dem	Wisc.	9	7
7th	Sessions, Jefferson B. III	Rep	Ala.	5	5		7th	Schumer, Charles E.	Dem	N.Y.	3	3
8th	Brownback, Sam D.	Rep	Kans.	5	*1 1		8th	Durbin, Richard J.	Dem	Ill.	5	*2 1
9th	McConnell, A. Mitchell (Mitch)	Rep	Ky.	17	1		9th	Cantwell, Maria E.	Dem	Wash.	1	1

*1: Member's first period of service on the committee.

*2: Member's second period of service on the committee.

Note 1: Rankings on this committee for the following members were affected by other chamber service: J. Strom Thurmond (Rep-S.C.), Chair Armed Services; Edward M. Kennedy (Dem-Mass.), Ranking Minority Member, Labor and Human Resources; and Joseph R. Biden, Jr. (Dem-Del.) Ranking Minority Member, Foreign Relations.

Note 2: The committee majority in the 2001 Senate power-sharing arrangement was determined by the party of the vice president. Democrat Al Gore, Jr. served from Jan. 3, 2001 to Jan. 20, 2001 and was succeeded by Republican Richard B. Cheney on Jan. 20, 2001. When Senator Jeffords of Vermont left the Republican Party, effective June 6, 2001 to become an Independent, Democrats regained the majority for the remainder of the 107th Congress.

JUDICIARY / 107th Congress, Post-Jeffords switch

Service Dates of Committee Chair: June 6, 2001-Jan. 14, 2003

Service Dates of Majority Members: June 6, 2001-Jan. 14, 2003

Service Dates of Minority Members: June 6, 2001-Jan. 15, 2003

| | | | Majority | | | | | | | Minority | | |
| | | | | Years in: | | | | | | | Years in: | |
Rank Name	Party	State	Senate	Comm.		Rank Name	Party	State	Senate	Comm.
Ch2 Leahy, Patrick J.	Dem	Vt.	27	23		RM2 Hatch, Orrin G.	Rep	Utah	25	25
2nd Kennedy, Edward M.	Dem	Mass.	39	39		2nd Thurmond, J. Strom	Rep	S.C.	46	35
3rd Biden, Joseph R. Jr.	Dem	Del.	29	25		3rd Grassley, Charles E.	Rep	Iowa	21	21
4th Kohl, Herbert H.	Dem	Wisc.	13	13		4th Specter, Arlen	Rep	Penn.	21	21
5th Feinstein, Dianne	Dem	Cal.	9	9		5th Kyl, Jon L.	Rep	Ariz.	7	7
6th Feingold, Russell D.	Dem	Wisc.	9	7		6th DeWine, Michael	Rep	Ohio	7	7
7th Schumer, Charles E.	Dem	N.Y.	3	3		7th Sessions, Jefferson B. III	Rep	Ala.	5	5
8th Durbin, Richard J.	Dem	Ill.	5	*2 1		8th Brownback, Sam D.	Rep	Kans.	5	*1 1
9th Cantwell, Maria E.	Dem	Wash.	1	1		9th McConnell, A. Mitchell (Mitch)	Rep	Ky.	17	1
10th Edwards, John	Dem	N.C.	3	1						

*1: Member's first period of service on the committee.

*2: Member's second period of service on the committee.

Note: Rankings on this committee for the following members were affected by other chamber service: Edward M. Kennedy (Dem-Mass.), Chair of Labor and Human Resources; Joseph R. Biden, Jr. (Dem-Del.), Chair of Foreign Relations; and J. Strom Thurmond (Rep-S.C.), Ranking Minority Member, Armed Services.

Additions:
  Majority:

10th Edwards, John	Dem	N.C.	July 10, 2001	

Departures from the Senate:

	Majority					Minority		
Retired	None					Thurmond, J. Strom	Rep	S.C.

Departures from Committee:

	Majority					Minority		
Moved to Commerce, Science and Transportation	Cantwell, Maria E.		Dem	Wash.				
Moved to Appropriations	None					Brownback, Sam D.	Rep	Kans.
Elected Majority Whip	None					McConnell, A. Mitchell (Mitch)	Rep	Ky.

JUDICIARY / 108th Congress

Service Dates of Committee Chair: Jan. 14, 2003-Jan. 6, 2005

Service Dates of Majority Members: Jan. 14, 2003-Jan. 6, 2005

Service Dates of Minority Members: Jan. 15, 2003-Jan. 6, 2005

| | | | Majority | | | | | | | Minority | | |
| | | | | Years in: | | | | | | | Years in: | |
Rank Name	Party	State	Senate	Comm.		Rank Name	Party	State	Senate	Comm.
Chr Hatch, Orrin G.	Rep	Utah	27	26		RM Leahy, Patrick J.	Dem	Vt.	29	24
2nd Grassley, Charles E.	Rep	Iowa	23	23		2nd Kennedy, Edward M.	Dem	Mass.	41	40
3rd Specter, Arlen	Rep	Penn.	23	23		3rd Biden, Joseph R. Jr.	Dem	Del.	31	26
4th Kyl, Jon L.	Rep	Ariz.	9	9		4th Kohl, Herbert H.	Dem	Wisc.	15	14
5th DeWine, Michael	Rep	Ohio	9	9		5th Feinstein, Dianne	Dem	Cal.	11	11
6th Sessions, Jefferson B. III	Rep	Ala.	7	7		6th Feingold, Russell D.	Dem	Wisc.	11	9
7th Graham, Lindsey O.	Rep	S.C.	1	1		7th Schumer, Charles E.	Dem	N.Y.	5	5
8th Craig, Larry E.	Rep	Ida.	13	1		8th Durbin, Richard J.	Dem	Ill.	7	*2 2
9th Chambliss, Saxby	Rep	Ga.	1	1		9th Edwards, John	Dem	N.C.	5	2
10th Cornyn, John	Rep	Tex.	1	1						

*2: Member's second period of service on the committee.

Note: Rankings on this committee for the following members were affected by other chamber service: Edward M. Kennedy (Dem-Mass.), Ranking Minority Member, Labor and Human Resources; and Joseph R. Biden, Jr. (Dem-Del.) Ranking Minority Member, Foreign Relations.

Departures from the Senate:	Majority			Minority		
Retired; lost vice presidential election	None			Edwards, John	Dem	N.C.

Departures from Committee:	Majority			Minority
Became Chair of Veterans' Affairs	Craig, Larry E.	Rep	Ida.	None
Became Chair of Agriculture, Nutrition and Forestry	Chambliss, Saxby	Rep	Ga.	

JUDICIARY / 109th Congress

Service Dates of Committee Chair: Jan. 6, 2005-Jan. 12, 2007

Service Dates of Majority Members: Jan. 6, 2005-Jan. 12, 2007

Service Dates of Minority Members: Jan. 6, 2005-Jan. 12, 2007

Majority			Years in:		Minority			Years in:	
Rank Name	Party	State	Senate	Comm.	Rank Name	Party	State	Senate	Comm.
Chr Specter, Arlen	Rep	Penn.	25	25	RM Leahy, Patrick J.	Dem	Vt.	31	26
2nd Hatch, Orrin G.	Rep	Utah	29	28	2nd Kennedy, Edward M.	Dem	Mass.	43	42
3rd Grassley, Charles E.	Rep	Iowa	25	25	3rd Biden, Joseph R. Jr.	Dem	Del.	33	28
4th Kyl, Jon L.	Rep	Ariz.	11	11	4th Kohl, Herbert H.	Dem	Wisc.	17	16
5th DeWine, Michael	Rep	Ohio	11	11	5th Feinstein, Dianne	Dem	Cal.	13	12
6th Sessions, Jefferson B. III	Rep	Ala.	9	8	6th Feingold, Russell	Dem	Wisc.	13	11
7th Graham, Lindsey O.	Rep	S.C.	3	2	7th Schumer, Charles E.	Dem	N.Y.	7	6
8th Cornyn, John	Rep	Tex.	3	2	8th Durbin, Richard J.	Dem	Ill.	9	*2 4
9th Brownback, Sam D.	Rep	Kans.	9	*2 1					
10th Coburn, Thomas A.	Rep	Okla.	1	1	*2: Member's second period of service on the committee.				

Note: After six terms as Chair, Orrin G. Hatch (Rep-Utah) relinquished the chairmanship to Arlen Specter (Rep-Penn.) Rankings on this committee for the following members were affected by other chamber service: Edward M. Kennedy (Dem-Mass.), Ranking Minority Member, Health, Education, Labor, and Pensions; and Joseph R. Biden, Jr. (Dem-Del.) Ranking Minority Member, Foreign Relations.

Departures from the Senate:	Majority			Minority
Defeated for Re-election	DeWine, Michael	Rep	Ohio	None

JUDICIARY / 110th Congress

Service Dates of Committee Chair: Jan. 12, 2007-Jan. 21, 2009

Service Dates of Majority Members: Jan. 12, 2007-Jan. 21, 2009

Service Dates of Minority Members: Jan. 12, 2007-Jan. 21, 2009

Majority			Years in:		Minority			Years in:	
Rank Name	Party	State	Senate	Comm.	Rank Name	Party	State	Senate	Comm.
Chr Leahy, Patrick J.	Dem	Vt.	33	28	RM Specter, Arlen	Rep	Penn.	27	27
2nd Kennedy, Edward M.	Dem	Mass.	45	44	2nd Hatch, Orrin G.	Rep	Utah	31	30
3rd Biden, Joseph R. Jr.	Dem	Del.	35	30	3rd Grassley, Charles E.	Rep	Iowa	27	27
4th Kohl, Herbert H.	Dem	Wisc.	19	18	4th Kyl, Jon L.	Rep	Ariz.	13	13
5th Feinstein, Dianne	Dem	Cal.	15	15	5th Sessions, Jefferson B. III	Rep	Ala.	11	11
6th Feingold, Russell D.	Dem	Wisc.	15	13	6th Graham, Lindsey O.	Rep	S.C.	5	4
7th Schumer, Charles E.	Dem	N.Y.	9	9	7th Cornyn, John	Rep	Tex.	5	4
8th Durbin, Richard J.	Dem	Ill.	11	*2 6	8th Brownback, Sam D.	Rep	Kans.	11	*2 3
9th Cardin, Benjamin L.	Dem	Md.	1	1	9th Coburn, Thomas A.	Rep	Okla.	3	3
10th Whitehouse, Sheldon	Dem	R.I.	1	1	*2: Member's second period of service on the committee.				

Note: Rankings on this committee for the following members were affected by other chamber service: Edward M. Kennedy (Dem-Mass.), Chair, Health, Education, Labor, and Pensions; Joseph R. Biden, Jr. (Dem-Del.) Chair, Foreign Relations; and Orrin G. Hatch (Rep-Utah) relinquished the Ranking Minority Member slot to Arlen Specter (Rep-Penn.).

Departures from the Senate:	Majority			Minority
Elected Vice President	Biden, Joseph R. Jr.	Dem	Del.	None

Departures from Committee:

Returned to Commerce, Science and Transportation; and moved to Energy and Natural Resources and Special Aging	Brownback, Sam D.	Rep	Kans.
No new assignment	Kennedy, Edward M.	Dem	Mass.

JUDICIARY / 111th Congress

Service Dates of Committee Chair: Jan. 21, 2009-

Service Dates of Majority Members: Jan. 21, 2009-

Service Dates of Minority Members: Jan. 21, 2009-

Majority

			Years in:	
Rank Name	Party	State	Senate	Comm.
Chr Leahy, Patrick J.	Dem	Vt.	35	30
2nd Kohl, Herbert H.	Dem	Wisc.	21	20
3rd Feinstein, Dianne	Dem	Cal.	17	17
4th Feingold, Russell D.	Dem	Wisc.	17	15
5th Schumer, Charles E.	Dem	N.Y.	11	11
6th Durbin, Richard J.	Dem	Ill.	13	*2 8
7th Cardin, Benjamin L.	Dem	Md.	3	3
8th Whitehouse, Sheldon	Dem	R.I.	3	3
9th Wyden, Ronald L.	Dem	Ore.	14	1
10th Klobuchar, Amy	DFL	Minn.	3	1
11th Kaufman, Edward E.	Dem	Del.	1	1

Minority

			Years in:	
Rank Name	Party	State	Senate	Comm.
RM1 Specter, Arlen	Rep	Penn.	29	29
2nd Hatch, Orrin G.	Rep	Utah	33	32
3rd Grassley, Charles E.	Rep	Iowa	29	29
4th Kyl, Jon L.	Rep	Ariz.	15	15
RM2 5th Sessions, Jefferson B. III	Rep	Ala.	13	13
6th Graham, Lindsey O.	Rep	S.C.	7	7
7th Cornyn, John	Rep	Tex.	7	7
8th Coburn, Thomas A.	Rep	Okla.	5	5

*2: Member's second period of service on the committee.

Note: Initial ranking on this committee for the following member when Orrin G. Hatch (Rep-Utah) relinquished the Ranking Minority Member slot to Arlen Specter (Rep-Penn.).

Additions:

Majority:

12th Specter, Arlen	Dem	Penn.	May 5, 2009

Changes:

Ranking Member:

RM1 Specter, Arlen	Rep	Penn.	May 5, 2009 Switched from the Republican Party to the Democratic Party
RM2 Sessions, Jefferson B. III	Rep	Ala.	May 5, 2009 Succeeded Specter as Ranking Member

Majority:

Wyden, Ronald L.	Dem	Ore.	July 7, 2009 Left committee to open seat for Franken
Franken, Al	DFL	Minn	July 7, 2009 Replaced Wyden; ranked following Specter

Minority:

Specter, Arlen	Rep	Penn.	May 5, 2009 Switched from the Republican Party to the Democratic Party and was assigned the 12th majority slot with his seniority to be determined at a later date

Rules and Administration

Senate Committee on Rules and Administration, 103rd-111th Congresses (1993-2011)

BACKGROUND

Organizational History: The 1946 Reorganization Act created the Senate Committee on Rules and Administration to consolidate the responsibilities of the standing Senate Committees on Enrolled Bills, Audit and Control of the Contingent Expenses of the Senate, Library, Printing, Privileges and Elections, and Rules.

From the start of the nation, the Senate made use of committees to handle its internal business. The first of these was the Joint Committee on Enrolled Bills, established on July 27, 1789, to make sure that bills were correctly worded before they were sent to the president to be signed into law. The Senate maintained the files of the joint committee. In 1947, the Committee's function of formal examination of bills, amendments and joint resolutions was moved to Rules and Administration and by S. Res. 55, 80th Cong., the function of enrollment of bills was moved again to the Office of the Secretary of the Senate.

The Senate's key internal oversight committee was the Committee to Audit and Control the Contingent Expenses of the Senate which was established on November 4, 1807, on a motion of John Quincy Adams (Fed-Mass.). Other predecessor committees included: the separate Senate Committee on the Library (1876); the Committee on Printing (1841); the Committee on Privileges and Elections (1871); and the Committee on Rules (1874).

Since 1947, the Senate Committee on Rules and Administration has performed primarily "housekeeping" chores. It is therefore more akin to the Committee on House Administration than it is to the House Rules Committee. The Senate's tradition of unlimited debate would be in conflict with the functioning of a time-limiting committee such as House Rules, which not only contains debate but limits the degree to which bills may be amended on the floor.

Two responsibilities assigned to the Committee on Rules and Administration in the 1977 reorganization were: "(2) Such committee shall also—(A) make a continuing study of the organization and operation of the Congress of the United States and shall recommend improvements in such organization and operation with a view toward strengthening the Congress, simplifying its operations, improving its relationships with other branches of the United States Government, and enabling it better to meet its responsibilities under the constitution of the United States; and (B) identify any court proceeding or action which, in the opinion of the Committee, is of vital interest to the Congress as a constitutionally established institution of the Federal Government and call such proceeding or action to the attention of the Senate."

The Senate as an institutionally conservative body seldom changes its rules. However, as the battle over President George W. Bush's lower court nominations for the federal bench heated up in 2005, there was a movement afoot to alter the Senate's filibuster rules to permit Vice President Dick Cheney to exercise a "nuclear option" through a simple majority point of order to deny the minority Democrats the opportunity to filibuster the Bush judicial nominees. A bipartisan "Gang of 14"—seven Democrats (three of whom served on Rules and Administration) and seven Republicans intervened—to move many of the Bush nominees through and to maintain the super-majority sixty-member requirement to obtain cloture on filibusters.

Membership: The original Rules and Administration Committee had thirteen members in the 80th Congress. It dropped to nine members in 1953 and reached its present peak of sixteen members in the 100th Congress (1987-1989). It remains relatively small with an average post-1993 membership size of 17.6 senators—fourteenth place—outranking only Homeland Security and Governmental Affairs and Veterans' Affairs. As a category "B" committee, one can be a member of Rules and Administration without surrendering service on more substantive panels. It has become the B committee of choice for the Senate's party leaders and as a result, it ranks at the top of the committee list in terms of mean seniority at 17.80 years per member and second only to Finance in terms of inter-Congress retention rates at 97.8 percent.

With only fifteen senators moving between Rules and Administration and other committees, it has the lowest number of on/off movements of the standing committees. Twelve members moved to Rules and Administration and three departed it. Apart from Budget, another B committee that provided the Rules Committee with four gainers, it acquired two members each from Appropriations, Armed Services, Energy and Natural Resources, and Foreign Relations. Its only three departing members are, John Warner, Chair of Armed Services, returned to Select Intelligence; Gordon Smith (Rep-Ore.) moved to chair Special Aging in 2005; while Democratic Majority Leader Harry Reid (Dem-Nev.) left Rules in 2009 for no other assignment.

Committee Leaders: The first post-reorganization chair of Rules and Administration was Republican C. Wayland Brooks of Illinois while Carl Hayden of Arizona was the committee's ranking minority member. Brooks was defeated for re-election in 1948 but Hayden continued as the committee's senior Democrat in the following three Congresses—two as chair (1949-1953) and one again as ranking member (1953-1955). Brooks was succeeded by Republican floor leader Kenneth S. Wherry of Nebraska who served as ranking member until his death in 1951. Wherry was replaced by Henry Cabot Lodge Jr. of Massachusetts who held that slot until his defeat by John F. Kennedy in the 1952 election. Lodge, a senior adviser to the successful 1952 presidential campaign of Dwight D. Eisenhower was apparently too preoccupied with presidential politics.

Eisenhower's victory in 1952 gave Republicans a narrow edge in the Senate and William E. Jenner of Indiana, another

McCarthy-like anti-communist, became the committee chair in 1953 and its ranking member in 1955. Jenner left Rules to become ranking member on Finance in 1957. Succeeding Jenner as ranking minority member in 1957 was Carl T. Curtis of Nebraska, who would hold that senior slot for the next fourteen years until he left the committee in 1971.

When Democrats resumed control of the Senate in 1955, Rhode Island's Theodore F. Green became chair after Hayden relinquished his senior rank to become chair of Finance. Green left the Rules chair to become chair of Foreign Relations in 1957 and was followed by Thomas C. Hennings of Missouri who served as chair until his death in 1960. Majority Leader Mike Mansfield of Montana chaired the committee only in the 87th Congress (1961-1963) until he moved to Appropriations. B. Everett Jordan of North Carolina succeeded Mansfield in 1963 and held the chair for the next ten years until his defeat for renomination in 1972. Jordan was the committee's longest-serving chair.

The committee's overall lack of prestige has contributed to the relative high turnover of senior members. Three Republicans served as ranking member in the 92nd Congress—Winston L. Prouty of Vermont, who held the post until his death in September, 1971; Ted Stevens of Alaska, who served for five months before moving to Appropriations; and newcomer Marlow W. Cook of Kentucky, who finished up the Congress in 1972. Cook lost his 1974 re-election bid.

Democrat Howard W. Cannon of Nevada became chair in 1973 and served until 1979 when he left to chair Commerce, Science and Transportation and was succeeded by Claiborne deB. Pell of Rhode Island, who served out the remainder of that year and chaired Rules in the following 96th Congress (1979-1981) until the Reagan-era Republicans gained control of the Senate in 1980. Although Oregon's Mark O. Hatfield had served as ranking member from 1975 to 1981, he relinquished his senior rank to chair Appropriations in 1981.

Since Rules and Administration is not one of the chamber's more prestigious committees, turnover in the senior posts tends to be relatively high as chairs and ranking minority members leave the Senate Rules Committee for more prominent assignments. After the Republicans captured the Senate in the 1980 election, every senior Republican in the 97th Congress was elevated to a committee chairmanship with the lone exception of moderate liberal Charles McC. Mathias Jr. (Rep-Md.). In a very unusual move for the modern Congress, Mathias became chair of Rules and Administration, a committee upon which he had never previously served. He chaired the committee for the next three Congresses (1981-1987) until his retirement from the Senate. Ted Stevens of Alaska, who served in a senior role on four Senate standing committees became ranking member on Rules in 1987 and served until 1995. Stevens chaired Rules for a brief time in 1995 when he became chair of Governmental Affairs. He was succeeded by Virginia's John W. Warner who served from 1995 to 1999 when he then became chair of Armed Services, replacing J. Strom Thurmond. During the next four Congresses, 1999-2007, two Republicans who had held both the floor leadership and Whip posts would serve as the senior Republicans on Rules—Mitch McConnell of Kentucky as chair, 1999-2001 and ranking member, 2001-2003; and C. Trent Lott of Mississippi as chair 2003-2007.

In 1981, Wendell H. Ford of Kentucky began his service as ranking minority member and would eventually become the Senate Rules committee's longest serving senior Democrat with eight years as chair, 1987 to 1995 and eight years as ranking member, 1981-1987 and 1995-1997. Ford was succeeded by Connecticut's Christopher J. Dodd who served as both ranking minority member (1997-2001 and 2003-2007) and as chair (2001-2003) over the next ten years until he became chair of Commerce, Science and Transportation in 2007.

Democratic success in the 2006 election gave the chairmanship of Senate Rules to Dianne Feinstein of California in 2007. When she relinquished her post in 2009 to chair the Senate Intelligence Committee, she was succeeded by Charles E. Schumer of New York. Assuming the ranking minority post in the last two Congresses was Robert F. Bennett of Utah (2007-2011).

Party Leadership: Twenty-one of the Senate's thirty-six (58.3%) floor leaders and Whips served on Rules and Administration of which twelve were Republicans and nine were Democrats. Among the twelve Republicans were all five of their floor leaders who had also served as Whips: Kenneth S. Wherry of Nebraska, Everett McK. Dirksen of Illinois, Hugh D. Scott of Pennsylvania, C. Trent Lott of Mississippi, and Mitch McConnell of Kentucky. Apart from Lott, each had served on Rules and Administration before their elections as Whips. Two of the three Rules Committee Republicans who served only as Whips—Ted Stevens of Alaska and Don Nickles of Oklahoma—had served on the committee prior to their elections. Only Michigan's Bob Griffin, Hugh Scott's Whip from 1968 to 1977 did not. Thus, six of the eight Republican Whips who served on Rules had prior service on the committee at the time of their selection. This was true also of the Republican floor leaders with William Knowland of California and Bob Dole of Kansas joining Wherry, Dirksen, Scott, and McConnell with service on the Rules Committee prior to their elections as leaders. Eight of the twelve Republican floor leaders and eight of their thirteen Whips had prior committee service. In addition to Lott and Griffin, Republican floor leaders Howard W. Baker Jr. and Bill Frist joined the committee after they were elected leaders.

This pattern is similar to the nine Rules Committee Democrats who held leadership posts. Two of the three Rules Committee Democrats elected both as Whip and floor leader—Mike Mansfield of Montana and Robert C. Byrd of West Virginia—served on the committee prior to their leadership elections. Harry Reid of Nevada, the present Democratic leader who held both posts, joined Rules in 2007 after he was selected as floor leader in 2004. Democratic Whips Francis Myers of Pennsylvania, Earle Clements of Kentucky, Russell Long of Louisiana, Wendell Ford of Kentucky, and Richard Durbin of Illinois each had previous service on Rules with Myers, Clements, Ford, and Durbin, having served on the committee during their time as Whips. Tom Daschle of South Dakota who led the Democrats until his 2004 defeat joined the Rules Committee shortly after his election as leader. In summation, Senate leaders and Whips often serve earlier on the Rules Committee and apart from a few exceptions, they do not join the committee after their elections.

Presidential Aspirations: While the Rules and Administration Committee may produce a disproportionate share of Senate party leaders, senators who seek the presidency have generally avoided service on the committee. Only two Republican aspirants served on Rules—Henry Cabot Lodge Jr. of Massachusetts, Richard Nixon's 1960 ticket-mate and Bob Dole of Kansas who lost for vice president with Gerald Ford in 1976 and in 1996 with his own presidential campaign. The only Democratic aspirant from the committee was Al Gore Jr. of Tennessee, who was elected as vice president with Arkansas governor Bill Clinton in 1992 and ran for president in 2000.

Other Notables: Only three modern-era Cabinet members have seen service on Rules and Administration. Brock Adams (Dem-Wash.) served as President Carter's Secretary of Transportation and Lamar Alexander (Rep-Tenn.) served as President George W. Bush's Secretary of Education before each joined the Senate. The only Senate Rules Committee member to become a Cabinet member after leaving the Senate was Richard S. Schweiker (Rep-Penn.), who served as President Reagan's first Secretary of Health and Human Services.

Selected References

Boesl, Mary Etta, "Rules and Administration Committee, Senate," in Donald C. Bacon, Roger H. Davidson, and Morton Keller, eds., *The Encyclopedia of the United States Congress* (New York: Simon & Schuster, 1995), I: 1742-1744.

Butler, Anne M. and Wendy Wolff, *United States Senate: Election, Expulsion and Censure Cases, 1793-1990*, Senate Document 103-33, 103rd Congress, 1st session (1995).

Coren, Robert W., et al., "Records of the Committee on Rules and Administration and Related Committees, 1789-1968," *Guide to the Records of the United States Senate at the National Archives: 1789-1989 Bicentennial Edition* (Washington, D.C.: National Archives and Records Administration, 1989), 191-201.

Siff, Ted and Alan Weil, dirs., *Ruling Congress: How the House and Senate Rules Govern the Legislative Process*, in the Ralph Nader Congress Project (New York: Grossman, 1975).

U.S. Senate, Committee on Rules and Administration, *History of the Committee on Rules and Administration, United States Senate*, Senate Document 96-27, 96th Congress, 1st session (1980).

RESPONSIBILITIES AND JURISDICTIONAL CHANGES

RULES AND ADMINISTRATION

Jurisdiction, 80th Congress (1947-49)

Established by the Legislative Reorganization Act of 1946:

[Section 102.(1)(o)]

(1) **Committee on Rules and Administration**, to consist of thirteen Senators, to which committee shall be referred all proposed legislation, messages, petitions, memorials, and other matters relating to the following subjects:

    (A) Matters relating to the payment of money out of the contingent fund of the Senate or creating a charge upon the same; except that any resolution relating to substantive matter within the jurisdiction of any other standing committee of the Senate shall be first referred to such committee.

    (B) Except as provided in paragraph (n) 8, [Committee on Public Works], matters relating to the Library of Congress and the Senate Library; statuary and pictures; acceptance or purchase of works of art for the Capitol; the Botanic Gardens; management of the Library of Congress; purchase of books and manuscripts; erection of monuments to the memory of individuals.

    (C) Except as provided in paragraph (n) 8, matters relating to the Smithsonian Institution and the incorporation of similar institutions.

    (D) Matters relating to the election of the President, Vice President, or Members of Congress; corrupt practices; contested elections; credentials and qualifications; Federal elections generally; Presidential succession.

    (E) Matters relating to parliamentary rules; floor and gallery rules; Senate Restaurant; administration of the Senate Office Building and of the Senate Wing of the Capitol; assignment of office space; and services to the Senate.

    (F) Matters relating to printing and correction of the Congressional Record.

(2) Such committee shall also have the duty of examining all bills, amendments, and joint resolutions after passage by the Senate; and, in cooperation with the Committee on House Administration of the House of Representatives, of examining all bills and joint resolutions which shall have passed both Houses, to see that the same are correctly enrolled; and when signed by the Speaker of the House and the President of the Senate, shall forthwith present the same, when they shall have originated in the Senate, to the President of the United States in person, and report the fact and date of such presentation to the Senate. Such committee shall also have the duty of assigning office space in the Senate Wing of the Capitol and in the Senate Office Building.

Jurisdiction, 1977

Jurisdiction as contained in Senate Resolution 4, the Committee System Reorganization Amendments of 1977, February 4, 1977:

[Rule XXV.(1)(n)]

(1) **Committee on Rules and Administration**, to which committee shall be referred all proposed legislation, messages, petitions, memorials, and other matters relating to the following subjects:

    (1) Meetings of the Congress and attendance of Members.

    (2) Federal elections generally, including the election of the President, Vice President, and Members of the Congress.

    (3) Credentials and qualifications of Members of the Senate, contested elections, and acceptance of incompatible offices.

    (4) Presidential succession.

    (5) Corrupt practices.

    (6) The United States Capitol and congressional office buildings, the Library of Congress, the Smithsonian Institution (and the incorporation of similar institutions), and the Botanic Gardens.

    (7) The Government Printing Office, and the printing and correction of the Congressional Record.

    (8) The Senate Library and statuary, art, and pictures in the Capitol and Senate Office Buildings.

    (9) Purchase of books and manuscripts and erection of monuments to the memory of individuals.

    (10) Payment of money out of the contingent fund of the Senate or creating a charge upon the same (except that any resolution relating to substantive matter within the jurisdiction of any other standing committee of the Senate shall be first referred to such committee).

    (11) Congressional organization relative to rules and procedures, and Senate rules and regulations, including floor and gallery rules.

    (12) Administration of the Senate Office Buildings and the Senate wing of the Capitol, including the assignment of office space.

    (13) Services to the Senate, including the Senate restaurant.

(2) Such committee shall also—

    (A) make a continuing study of the organization and operation of the congress of the United States and shall recommend improvements in such organization and operation with a view toward strengthening the Congress, simplifying its operations, improving its relationships with other branches of the United States Government, and enabling it better to meet its responsibilities under the constitution of the United States; and

    (B) identify any court proceeding or action which, in the opinion of the Committee, is of vital interest to the Congress as a constitutionally established institution of the Federal Government and call such proceeding or action to the attention of the Senate.

Jurisdiction, 103rd Congress (1993-94)

From the *Standing Rules of the Senate* in the *Senate Manual*, 103rd Congress, 1st Session, S. Doc. 103-1:

[Rule XXV.(1)(n)]

(1) **Committee on Rules and Administration**, to which committee shall be referred all proposed legislation, messages, petitions, memorials, and other matters relating to the following subjects:

    (1) Administration of the Senate Office Buildings and the Senate wing of the Capitol, including the assignment of office space.

    (2) Congressional organization relative to rules and procedures, and Senate rules and regulations, including floor and gallery rules.

    (3) Corrupt practices.

    (4) Credential and qualifications of Members of the Senate, contested elections, and acceptance of incompatible offices.

    (5) Federal elections generally, including the election of the President, Vice President, and Members of the Congress.

    (6) Government Printing Office, and the printing and correction of the Congressional Record, as well as those matters provided for under rule XI.

    (7) Meetings of the Congress and attendance of Members.

    (8) Payment of money out of the contingent fund of the Senate or creating a charge upon the same (except that any resolution relating to substantive matter within the jurisdiction of any other standing committee of the Senate shall be first referred to such committee).

    (9) Presidential succession.

    (10) Purchase of books and manuscripts and erection of monuments to the memory of individuals.

    (11) Senate Library and statuary, art, and pictures in the Capitol and Senate Office Buildings.

    (12) Services to the Senate, including the Senate restaurant.

    (13) United States Capitol and congressional office buildings, the Library of Congress, the Smithsonian Institution (and the incorporation of similar institutions), and the Botanic Gardens.

(2) Such committee shall also:

    (A) make a continuing study of the organization and operation of the Congress of the United States and shall recommend improvements in such organization and operation with a view towards strengthening the Congress, simplifying its operations, improving its relationships with other branches of the United States Government, and enabling it better to meet its responsibilities under the Constitution of the United States; and,

(B) identify any court proceeding or action which, in the opinion of the Committee, is of vital interest to the Congress as a constitutionally established institution of the Federal Government and call such proceeding or action to the attention of the Senate.

Jurisdiction, 111th Congress (2009-10)

From *Authority and Rules of Senate Committees, 2009-2010*, Sen. Doc. 111-3, pursuant to S. Res, 166, June 2, 2009.

[Rule XXV.(1)(n)]

(1) **Committee on Rules and Administration**, to which committee shall be referred all proposed legislation, messages, petitions, memorials, and other matters relating to the following subjects:

(1) Administration of the Senate Office Buildings and the Senate wing of the Capitol, including the assignment of office space.
(2) Congressional organization relative to rules and procedures, and Senate rules and regulations, including floor and gallery rules.
(3) Corrupt practices.
(4) Credentials and qualifications of Members of the Senate, contested elections, and acceptance of incompatible offices.
(5) Federal elections generally, including the election of the President, Vice President, and Members of the Congress.
(6) Government Printing Office, and the printing and correction of the Congressional Record, as well as those matters provided for under rule XI.
(7) Meetings of the Congress and attendance of Members.
(8) Payment of money out of the contingent fund of the Senate or creating a charge upon the same (except that any resolution relating to substantive matter within the jurisdiction of any other standing committee of the Senate shall be first referred to such committee).
(9) Presidential succession.
(10) Purchase of books and manuscripts and erection of monuments to the memory of individuals.
(11) Senate Library and statuary, art, and pictures in the Capitol and Senate Office Buildings.
(12) Services to the Senate, including the Senate restaurant.
(13) United States Capitol and congressional office buildings, the Library of Congress, the Smithsonian Institution (and the incorporation of similar institutions), and the Botanic Gardens.

(2) Such committee shall also:

(A) make a continuing study of the organization and operation of the Congress of the United States and shall recommend improvements in such organization and operation with a view toward strengthening the Congress, simplifying its operations, improving its relationships with other branches of the United States Government, and enabling it better to meet its responsibilities under the Constitution of the United States;
(B) identify any court proceeding or action which, in the opinion of the Committee, is of vital interest to the Congress as a constitutionally established institution of the Federal Government and call such proceeding or action to the attention of the Senate; and develop, implement, and update as necessary a strategy planning process and a strategic plan for the functional and technical infrastructure support of the Senate and provide oversight over plans developed by Senate officers and others in accordance with the strategic planning process.

Committee on Rules and Administration—No Subcommittees, 103rd-111th Congresses

MEMBERSHIP ROSTERS, 103rd-111th Congresses, 1993-2010

RULES AND ADMINISTRATION / 103rd Congress

Service Dates of Committee Chair: Jan. 21, 1993-Jan. 6, 1995

Service Dates of Majority Members: Jan. 21, 1993-Jan. 6, 1995

Service Dates of Minority Members: Jan. 21, 1993-Jan. 6, 1995

			Majority						Minority	
				Years in:						**Years in:**	
Rank Name	**Party**	**State**	**Senate**	**Comm.**	**Rank Name**	**Party**	**State**	**Senate**	**Comm.**
Chr Ford, Wendell H.	Dem	Ky.	19	15	RM Stevens, Theodore F.	Rep	Alas.	25	*2 8
2nd Pell, Claiborne D.	Dem	R.I.	33	33	2nd Hatfield, Mark O.	Rep	Ore.	27	21

3rd Byrd, Robert C.	Dem	W.Va.	35	30	
4th Inouye, Daniel K.	Dem	Hai.	31	11	
5th DeConcini, Dennis W.	Dem	Ariz.	17	*2 11	
6th Moynihan, Daniel Patrick	Dem	N.Y.	17	7	
7th Dodd, Christopher J.	Dem	Conn.	13	7	
8th Feinstein, Dianne	Dem	Cal.	1	1	
9th Mathews, Harlan	Dem.	Tenn.	1	1	

3rd Helms, Jesse A.	Rep	N.C.	21	13
4th Warner, John W.	Rep	Va.	15	*2 2
5th Dole, Robert J.	Rep	Kans.	25	13
6th McConnell, A. Mitchell (Mitch)	Rep	Ky.	9	4
7th Cochran, W. Thad	Rep	Miss.	15	1

*2: Member's second period of service on the committee.

Notes: Rankings on this committee for the following members were affected by other chamber service: Claiborne D. Pell (Dem-R.I.), Chair, Foreign Relations; and Robert C. Byrd (Dem-W.Va.), Chair, Appropriations; Mark O. Hatfield (Rep-Ore.), Ranking Minority Member, Appropriations; Jesse A. Helms (Rep-N.C.), Ranking Minority Member, Foreign Relations; and Robert J. Dole, Senate Minority Leader. John W. Warner (Rep-Va.) returned to the committee after serving on the Special Committee on Aging, and was credited by the Republican Conference with his previous seniority and ranked 4th.

Changes:
  Majority:

Mathews, Harlan	Dem	Tenn.	Dec. 1, 1994 Resigned the Senate; replaced by special election winner Fred D. Thompson (Rep-Tenn.)

Departures from the Senate:

Majority			Minority
Retired	DeConcini, Dennis W.	Dem Ariz.	None

RULES AND ADMINISTRATION / 104th Congress

RULES AND ADMINISTRATION / 104th Congress

Service Dates of Committee Chair: Ch1: Jan. 6, 1995-Sep. 12, 1995, Stevens (Rep-Alas.)

Ch2: Sep. 12, 1995-Jan. 9, 1997, Warner (Rep-Va.)

Service Dates of Majority Members: Jan. 6, 1995-Jan. 9, 1997

Service Dates of Minority Members: Jan. 6, 1995-Jan. 9, 1997

Majority			**Years in:**		**Minority**			**Years in:**	
Rank Name	Party	State	Senate	Comm.	Rank Name	Party	State	Senate	Comm.
Ch1 Stevens, Theodore F.	Rep	Alas.	27	*2 10	RM Ford, Wendell H.	Dem	Ky.	21	17
2nd Hatfield, Mark O.	Rep	Ore.	29	22	2nd Pell, Claiborne D.	Dem	R.I.	35	34
3rd Helms, Jesse A.	Rep	N.C.	23	15	3rd Byrd, Robert C.	Dem	W.Va.	37	32
4th Chr2 Warner, John W.	Rep	Va.	17	*2 4	4th Inouye, Daniel K.	Dem	Hai.	33	13
5th Dole, Robert J.	Rep	Kans.	27	15	5th Moynihan, Daniel Patrick	Dem	N.Y.	19	9
6th McConnell, A. Mitchell (Mitch)	Rep	Ky.	11	6	6th Dodd, Christopher J.	Dem	Conn.	15	9
7th Cochran, W. Thad	Rep	Miss.	17	2	7th Feinstein, Dianne	Dem	Cal.	3	2
8th Santorum, Richard J. (Rick)	Rep	Penn.	1	1					
9th Nickles, Donald L.	Rep	Okla.	15	1					

*2: Member's second period of service on the committee.

Notes: Rankings on this committee for the following members were affected by other chamber service: Mark O. Hatfield (Rep-Ore.), Chair, Appropriations; Jesse A. Helms (Rep-N.C.), Chair, Foreign Relations; and Robert J. Dole (Rep-Kans.), Senate Majority Leader; Claiborne D. Pell (Dem-R.I.), Ranking Minority Member, Foreign Relations; and Robert C. Byrd (Dem-W.Va.), Ranking Minority Member, Appropriations. John W. Warner (Rep-Va.) was credited by the Republican Conference with his previous seniority and ranked 4th.

Changes:
  Chair:

Ch1 Stevens, Theodore F.	Rep	Alas.	Sep. 12, 1995 Relinquished chair to serve as Chair of Governmental Affairs
Ch2 Warner, John W.	Rep	Va.	Sep. 12, 1995 Succeeded Stevens as Chair

  Majority:

Dole, Robert J.	Rep	Kans.	June 11, 1996 Resigned the Senate to run for president
Lott, C. Trent	Rep	Miss.	June 20, 1996 Replaced Dole

Departures from the Senate:

	Majority			Minority	
Retired	Hatfield, Mark O.	Rep Ore.		Pell, Claiborne D.	Dem R.I.

RULES AND ADMINISTRATION / 105th Congress

Service Dates of Committee Chair: Jan. 9, 1997-Jan. 7, 1999

Service Dates of Majority Members: Jan. 9, 1997-Jan. 7, 1999

Service Dates of Minority Members: Jan. 9, 1997-Jan. 7, 1999

Majority				
			Years in:	
Rank Name	Party	State	Senate	Comm.
Chr Warner, John W.	Rep	Va.	19	*2 6
2nd Helms, Jesse A.	Rep	N.C.	25	17
3rd Stevens, Theodore F.	Rep	Alas.	29	*2 12
4th McConnell, A. Mitchell (Mitch)	Rep	Ky.	13	8
5th Cochran, W. Thad	Rep	Miss.	19	4
6th Santorum, Richard J. (Rick)	Rep	Penn.	3	3
7th Nickles, Donald L.	Rep	Okla.	17	2
8th Lott, C. Trent	Rep	Miss.	9	1
9th Hutchison, Kay Bailey	Rep	Tex.	4	1

Minority				
			Years in:	
Rank Name	Party	State	Senate	Comm.
RM Ford, Wendell H.	Dem	Ky.	23	19
2nd Byrd, Robert C.	Dem	W.Va.	39	34
3rd Inouye, Daniel K.	Dem	Hai.	35	15
4th Moynihan, Daniel Patrick	Dem	N.Y.	21	11
5th Dodd, Christopher J.	Dem	Conn.	17	11
6th Feinstein, Dianne	Dem	Cal.	5	4
7th Torricelli, Robert G.	Dem	N.J.	1	1

*2: Member's second period of service on the committee.

Notes: Rankings on this committee for the following members were affected by other chamber service: Jesse A. Helms (Rep-N.C.), Chair, Foreign Relations; Theodore F. Stevens (Rep-Alas.), Chair, Appropriations; and Robert C. Byrd (Dem-W.Va.), Ranking Minority Member, Appropriations.

Departures from the Senate:	Majority		Minority		
Retired	None		Ford, Wendell H.	Dem	Ky.

RULES AND ADMINISTRATION / 106th Congress

Service Dates of Committee Chair: Jan. 7, 1999-Jan. 3, 2001

Service Dates of Majority Members: Jan. 7, 1999-Jan. 25, 2001

Service Dates of Minority Members: Jan. 7, 1999-Jan. 25, 2001

Majority				
			Years in:	
Rank Name	Party	State	Senate	Comm.
Chr McConnell, A. Mitchell (Mitch)	Rep	Ky.	15	10
2nd Helms, Jesse A.	Rep	N.C.	27	19
3rd Stevens, Theodore F.	Rep	Alas.	31	*2 14
4th Warner, John W.	Rep	Va.	21	*2 8
5th Cochran, W. Thad	Rep	Miss.	21	6
6th Santorum, Richard J. (Rick)	Rep	Penn.	5	5
7th Nickles, Donald L.	Rep	Okla.	19	5
8th Lott, C. Trent	Rep	Miss.	11	2
9th Hutchison, Kay Bailey	Rep	Tex.	6	2

Minority				
			Years in:	
Rank Name	Party	State	Senate	Comm.
RM Dodd, Christopher J.	Dem	Conn.	19	13
2nd Byrd, Robert C.	Dem	W.Va.	41	36
3rd Inouye, Daniel K.	Dem	Hai.	37	17
4th Moynihan, Daniel Patrick	Dem	N.Y.	23	13
5th Feinstein, Dianne	Dem	Cal.	7	6
6th Torricelli, Robert G.	Dem	N.J.	3	2
7th Schumer, Charles E.	Dem	N.Y.	1	1

*2: Member's second period of service on the committee.

Notes: Rankings on this committee for the following members were affected by other chamber service: Jesse A. Helms (Rep-N.C.), Chair, Foreign Relations; Theodore F. Stevens (Rep-Alas.), Chair, Appropriations; Robert C. Byrd (Dem-W.Va.), Ranking Minority Member, Appropriations; and Daniel K. Inouye (Dem-Hai.), Ranking Minority Member, Select Indian Affairs.

Departures from the Senate:	Majority		Minority		
Retired	None		Moynihan, Daniel Patrick	Dem	N.Y.

RULES AND ADMINISTRATION / 107th Congress, Pre-Jeffords switch

Service Dates of Committee Chair: ChT: Jan. 3, 2001-Jan. 25, 2001 Dodd (Dem-Conn.)

Ch1: Jan. 25, 2001-June 6, 2001 McConnell (Rep-Ky.)

Service Dates of Majority Members: Jan. 25, 2001-June 6, 2001

Service Dates of Majority Members: Jan. 25, 2001-June 6, 2001

Majority				
			Years in:	
Rank Name	Party	State	Senate	Comm.
Ch1 McConnell, A. Mitchell (Mitch)	Rep	Ky.	17	12
2nd Warner, John W.	Rep	Va.	23	*2 10
3rd Helms, Jesse A.	Rep	N.C.	29	21
4th Stevens, Theodore F.	Rep	Alas.	33	*2 16
5th Cochran, W. Thad	Rep	Miss.	23	9
6th Santorum, Richard J. (Rick)	Rep	Penn.	7	7
7th Nickles, Donald L.	Rep	Okla.	21	7

Minority				
			Years in:	
Rank Name	Party	State	Senate	Comm.
RM1 Dodd, Christopher J.	Dem	Conn.	21	15
2nd Byrd, Robert C.	Dem	W.Va.	43	38
3rd Inouye, Daniel K.	Dem	Hai.	39	19
4th Feinstein, Dianne	Dem	Cal.	9	9
5th Torricelli, Robert G.	Dem	N.J.	5	5
6th Schumer, Charles E.	Dem	N.Y.	3	3
7th Breaux, John B.	Dem	La.	15	1

| 8th Lott, C. Trent | Rep | Miss. | 13 | 5 | 8th Daschle, Thomas A. | Dem | S.D. | 15 | 1 |
| 9th Hutchison, Kay Bailey | Rep | Tex. | 8 | 5 | 9th Dayton, Mark | DFL | Minn. | 1 | 1 |

*2: Member's second period of service on the committee.

Note 1: The committee majority in the 2001 Senate power-sharing arrangement was determined by the party of the vice president. Democrat Al Gore, Jr. served from Jan. 3, 2001 to Jan. 20, 2001 and was succeeded by Republican Richard B. Cheney on Jan. 20, 2001. When Senator Jeffords of Vermont left the Republican Party, effective June 6, 2001 to become an Independent, Democrats regained the majority for the remainder of the 107th Congress.

Note 2: Rankings on this committee for the following members were affected by other chamber service: Jesse A. Helms (Rep-N.C.), Chair, Foreign Relations; Theodore F. Stevens (Rep-Alas.), Chair, Appropriations; Robert C. Byrd (Dem-W.Va.), Ranking Minority Member, Appropriations; and Daniel K. Inouye (Dem-Hai.), Ranking Minority Member, Select Indian Affairs.

RULES AND ADMINISTRATION / 107th Congress, Post-Jeffords switch

Service Dates of Committee Chair: June 6, 2001-Jan. 14, 2003

Service Dates of Majority Members: June 6, 2001-Jan. 14, 2003

Service Dates of Minority Members: June 6, 2001-Jan. 15, 2003

Majority					Minority				
			Years in:					Years in:	
Rank Name	Party	State	Senate	Comm.	Rank Name	Party	State	Senate	Comm.
Ch2 Dodd, Christopher J.	Dem	Conn.	21	15	RM2 McConnell, A. Mitchell (Mitch)	Rep	Ky.	17	13
2nd Byrd, Robert C.	Dem	W.Va.	43	39	2nd Warner, John W.	Rep	Va.	23	*2 11
3rd Inouye, Daniel K.	Dem	Hai.	39	20	3rd Helms, Jesse A.	Rep	N.C.	29	21
4th Feinstein, Dianne	Dem	Cal.	9	9	4th Stevens, Theodore F.	Rep	Alas.	33	*2 17
5th Torricelli, Robert G.	Dem	N.J.	5	5	5th Cochran, W. Thad	Rep	Miss.	23	9
6th Schumer, Charles E.	Dem	N.Y.	3	3	6th Santorum, Richard J. (Rick)	Rep	Penn.	7	7
7th Breaux, John B.	Dem	La.	15	1	7th Nickles, Donald L.	Rep	Okla.	21	7
8th Daschle, Thomas A.	Dem	S.D.	15	1	8th Lott, C. Trent	Rep	Miss.	13	5
9th Dayton, Mark	DFL	Minn.	1	1	9th Hutchison, Kay Bailey	Rep	Tex.	9	5
10th Durbin, Richard J.	Dem	Ill.	5	1					

*2: Member's second period of service on the committee.

Note:: Rankings on this committee for the following members were affected by other chamber service: Robert C. Byrd (Dem-W.Va.), Chair, Appropriations; and Daniel K. Inouye (Dem-Hai.), Chair, Select Indian Affairs; Jesse A. Helms (Rep-N.C.), Ranking Minority Member, Foreign Relations; and Theodore F. Stevens (Rep-Alas.), Ranking Minority Member, Appropriations.

Additions:
Majority:

| 10th Durbin, Richard J. | Dem | Ill. | July 10, 2001 |

Departures from the Senate: | **Majority** | | | **Minority** | | |
| Retired | Torricelli, Robert G. | Dem | N.J. | Helms, Jesse A. | Rep | N.C. |

Departures from Committee:
| Returned to Select Intelligence | None | | | Warner, John W. | Rep | Va. |

RULES AND ADMINISTRATION / 108th Congress

Service Dates of Committee Chair: Jan. 14, 2003-Jan. 6, 2005

Service Dates of Majority Members: Jan. 14, 2003-Jan. 6, 2005

Service Dates of Minority Members: Jan. 15, 2003-Jan. 6, 2005

Majority					Minority				
			Years in:					Years in:	
Rank Name	Party	State	Senate	Comm.	Rank Name	Party	State	Senate	Comm.
Chr Lott, C. Trent	Rep	Miss.	15	7	RM Dodd, Christopher J.	Dem	Conn.	23	17
2nd Stevens, Theodore F.	Rep	Alas.	35	*2 18	2nd Byrd, Robert C.	Dem	W.Va.	45	40
3rd McConnell, A. Mitchell (Mitch)	Rep	Ky.	19	14	3rd Inouye, Daniel K.	Dem	Hai.	41	21
4th Cochran, W. Thad	Rep	Miss.	25	10	4th Feinstein, Dianne	Dem	Cal.	11	10
5th Santorum, Richard J. (Rick)	Rep	Penn.	9	9	5th Schumer, Charles E.	Dem	N.Y.	5	5
6th Nickles, Donald L.	Rep	Okla.	23	9	6th Breaux, John B.	Dem	La.	17	2
7th Hutchison, Kay Bailey	Rep	Tex.	10	7	7th Daschle, Thomas A.	Dem	S.D.	17	2
8th Frist, William H.	Rep	Tenn.	9	1	8th Dayton, Mark	DFL	Minn.	3	2
9th Smith, Gordon H.	Rep	Ore.	7	1	9th Durbin, Richard J.	Dem	Ill.	7	2
10th Chambliss, Saxby	Rep	Ga.	1	1					

*2: Member's second period of service on the committee.

Note: Rankings on this committee for the following members were affected by other chamber service: Theodore F. Stevens (Rep-Alas.), Chair, Appropriations; A. Mitchell McConnell (Rep-Ky.); Senate Majority Whip; W. Thad Cochran (Rep-Miss.), Chair, Agriculture, Nutrition, and Forestry; Robert C. Byrd (Dem-W.Va.), Ranking Minority Member, Appropriations; and Daniel K. Inouye (Dem-Hai.), Ranking Minority Member, Select Indian Affairs;

Departures from the Senate:	Majority			Minority		
Defeated for Re-election	None			Daschle, Thomas A.	Dem	S.D.
Retired	Nickles, Donald L.	Rep	Okla.	Breaux, John B.	Dem	La.

Departures from Committee:						
Became Chair of Special Aging	Smith, Gordon H.	Rep	Ore.	None		

RULES AND ADMINISTRATION / 109th Congress

Service Dates of Committee Chair: Jan. 6, 2005-Jan. 12, 2007

Service Dates of Majority Members: Jan. 6, 2005-Jan. 12, 2007

Service Dates of Minority Members: Jan. 6, 2005-Jan. 12, 2007

			Years in:						Years in:	
Majority					**Minority**					
Rank Name	**Party**	**State**	**Senate**	**Comm.**	**Rank Name**	**Party**	**State**	**Senate**	**Comm.**	
Chr Lott, C. Trent	Rep	Miss.	17	9	RM Dodd, Christopher J.	Dem	Conn.	25	19	
2nd Stevens, Theodore F.	Rep	Alas.	37	*2 20	2nd Byrd, Robert C.	Dem	W.Va.	47	42	
3rd McConnell, A. Mitchell (Mitch)	Rep	Ky.	21	16	3rd Inouye, Daniel K.	Dem	Hai.	43	23	
4th Cochran, W. Thad	Rep	Miss.	27	12	4th Feinstein, Dianne	Dem	Cal.	13	12	
5th Santorum, Richard J. (Rick)	Rep	Penn.	11	11	5th Schumer, Charles E.	Dem	N.Y.	7	6	
6th Frist, William H.	Rep	Tenn.	11	2	6th Dayton, Mark	DFL	Minn.	5	4	
7th Chambliss, Saxby	Rep	Ga.	3	2	7th Durbin, Richard J.	Dem	Ill.	9	4	
8th Hutchison, Kay Bailey	Rep	Tex.	12	8	8th Nelson, E. Benjamin	Dem	Neb.	5	1	
9th Bennett, Robert F.	Rep	Utah	13	1						
10th Hagel, Charles T. (Chuck)	Rep	Neb.	9	1	*2: Member's second period of service on the committee.					

Note: Rankings on this committee for the following members were affected by other chamber service: Theodore F. Stevens (Rep-Alas.), Chair, Commerce, Science, and Transportation; A. Mitchell McConnell (Rep-Ky.); Senate Majority Whip; W. Thad Cochran (Rep-Miss.), Chair, Appropriations; Robert C. Byrd (Dem-W.Va.), Ranking Minority Member, Appropriations; and Daniel K. Inouye (Dem-Hai.), Ranking Minority Member, Commerce, Science, and Transportation.

Departures from the Senate:	Majority			Minority		
Defeated for Re-election	Santorum, Richard J. (Rick)	Rep	Penn.	None		
Retired	Frist, William H.	Rep	Tenn.	Dayton, Mark	DFL	Minn.

RULES AND ADMINISTRATION / 110th Congress

Service Dates of Committee Chair: Jan. 12, 2007-Jan. 21, 2009

Service Dates of Majority Members: Jan. 12, 2007-Jan. 21, 2009

Service Dates of Minority Members: Jan. 12, 2007-Jan. 21, 2009

			Years in:						Years in:	
Majority					**Minority**					
Rank Name	**Party**	**State**	**Senate**	**Comm.**	**Rank Name**	**Party**	**State**	**Senate**	**Comm.**	
Chr Feinstein, Dianne	Dem	Cal.	15	14	RM Bennett, Robert F.	Rep	Utah	15	3	
2nd Dodd, Christopher J.	Dem	Conn.	27	21	2nd Stevens, Theodore F.	Rep	Alas.	39	*2 22	
3rd Byrd, Robert C.	Dem	W.Va.	49	44	3rd McConnell, A. Mitchell (Mitch)	Rep	Ky.	23	18	
4th Inouye, Daniel K.	Dem	Hai.	45	25	4th Cochran, W. Thad	Rep	Miss.	29	14	
5th Schumer, Charles E.	Dem	N.Y.	9	9	5th Lott, C. Trent	Rep	Miss.	19	11	
6th Durbin, Richard J.	Dem	Ill.	11	6	6th Chambliss, Saxby	Rep	Ga.	5	4	
7th Nelson, E. Benjamin	Dem	Neb.	7	3	7th Hutchison, Kay Bailey	Rep	Tex.	14	11	
8th Reid, Harry M.	Dem	Nev.	21	1	8th Hagel, Charles T. (Chuck)	Rep	Neb.	11	3	
9th Murray, Patty	Dem	Wash.	15	1	9th Alexander, Lamar	Rep	Tenn.	5	1	
10th Pryor, Mark	Dem	Ark.	5	1						

*2: Member's second period of service on the committee.

Note: Rankings on this committee for the following members were affected by other chamber service: Christopher J. Dodd (Dem-Conn.), Chair, Banking, Housing, and Urban Affairs; Robert C. Byrd (Dem-W.Va.), Chair, Appropriations; Daniel K. Inouye (Dem-Hai.), Chair, Commerce, Science, and Transportation; Theodore F. Stevens (Rep-Alas.), Ranking Minority Member, Commerce, Science, and Transportation; A. Mitchell McConnell (Rep-Ky.); Senate Minority Leader; W. Thad Cochran (Rep-Miss.), Ranking Minority Member, Appropriations; and C. Trent Lott (Rep-Miss.), Senate Minority Whip.

Changes:

Majority:

Lott, C. Trent	Rep	Miss.	Dec. 18, 2007 Resigned the Senate and retired
Ensign, John E.	Rep	Nev.	Jan. 24, 2008 Replaced Lott

Departures from the Senate:	**Majority**			**Minority**		
Defeated for Re-election	None			Stevens, Theodore F.	Rep	Alas.
Retired	None			Hagel, Charles T. (Chuck)	Rep	Neb.

Departures from Committee					
No new assignment	Reid, Harry M.	Dem	Nev.	None	

RULES AND ADMINISTRATION / 111th Congress

Service Dates of Committee Chair: Jan. 21, 2009-

Service Dates of Majority Members: Jan. 21, 2009-

Service Dates of Minority Members: Jan. 21, 2009-

			Majority						Minority		
				Years in:						**Years in:**	
Rank Name	**Party**	**State**	**Senate**	**Comm.**		**Rank Name**	**Party**	**State**	**Senate**	**Comm.**	
Chr Schumer, Charles E.	Dem	N.Y.	11	11		RM Bennett, Robert F.	Rep	Utah	17	5	
2nd Feinstein, Dianne	Dem	Cal.	17	17		2nd McConnell, A. Mitchell (Mitch)	Rep	Ky.	25	20	
3rd Dodd, Christopher J.	Dem	Conn.	29	23		3rd Cochran, W. Thad	Rep	Miss.	31	17	
4th Byrd, Robert C.	Dem	W.Va.	51	46		4th Chambliss, Saxby	Rep	Ga.	7	7	
5th Inouye, Daniel K.	Dem	Hai.	47	27		5th Hutchison, Kay Bailey	Rep	Tex.	16	13	
6th Durbin, Richard J.	Dem	Ill.	13	8		6th Alexander, Lamar	Rep	Tenn.	7	3	
7th Nelson, E. Benjamin	Dem	Neb.	9	5		7th Roberts, C. Patrick	Rep	Kans.	13	1	
8th Murray, Patty	Dem	Wash.	17	3		8th Ensign, John E.	Rep	Nev.	9	2	
9th Pryor, Mark	Dem	Ark.	7	3							
10th Warner, Mark R.	Dem	Va.	1	1							
11th Udall, Thomas	Dem	N.M.	1	1							

Note 1: Rankings on this committee for the following members were affected by other chamber service: Dianne Feinstein (Dem-Cal.), Chair, Select Intelligence; Christopher J. Dodd (Dem-Conn.), Chair, Banking, Housing, and Urban Affairs; Daniel K. Inouye (Dem-Hai.), Chair, Appropriations; A. Mitchell McConnell (Rep-Ky.); Senate Minority Leader; and W. Thad Cochran (Rep-Miss.), Ranking Minority Member, Appropriations.

Note 2: The majority membership on Rules and Administration was reordered by S. Res. 343 on November 6, 2009: Senators Schumer, Byrd, Inouye, Dodd, Feinstein, Durbin, Nelson of Nebraska, Murray, Pryor, Udall of New Mexico, and Warner.

Small Business and Entrepreneurship

Senate Committee on Small Business, 103rd-107th Congresses (1993-2001)

Senate Committee on Small Business and Entrepreneurship, 107th-111th Congresses (2001-2011)

BACKGROUND

Organizational History The modern-era Senate treated the Small Business Committee with ambivalence. The Select Committee on Small Business was the first of the "permanent" select committees, and its creation was controversial. The Special Committee to Study Problems of American Small Business, a select committee, had been established in 1940. When the Legislative Reorganization Act of 1946 did not provide for a standing committee on small business in the Senate, the select committee was allowed to continue. Nevertheless, the Committee on Banking and Currency established a Subcommittee on Small Business in January 1947. The select committee and the subcommittee existed simultaneously until 1949, when the select committee was not reauthorized by the full Senate.

In 1950, the Senate created the Select Committee on Small Business to examine issues concerning American small business, but it was denied authority to consider or report legislation. The absence of legislative authority avoided jurisdictional conflicts with established standing committees, such as Commerce, Banking and Currency, and Finance, while providing a continuing forum where America's small businesses could be assured a hearing. It conducted many studies; sometimes held seminars or clinics to help small businesses learn about securing government contracts; and issued numerous publications explaining such issues as procurement practices of federal agencies, tax depreciation allowances, the impact of imports, food marketing, and the emergence of shopping centers.

After existing for most of the post-war years as a regularly-appointed select committee, Small Business was elevated to standing committee status on March 25, 1981, during the 97th Congress, the first Congress of the Reagan Administration. On June 29, 2001, shortly after the Jeffords's switch gave control of the Senate to the Democrats, newly-named chair, John F. Kerry (Dem-Mass.) changed the name of the committee to the Committee on Small Business and Entrepreneurship.

Members of Congress regularly extol the virtues of small businesses, and by adding "entrepreneurship" to the committee's title, it would seem that the Small Business and Entrepreneurship Committee would play a larger role in the making of domestic economic policy. That does not appear to be the case and the committee has not functioned as a major player in efforts to revive the economy.

Membership: As a standing committee, Small Business opened with seventeen members in the 97th Congress (1981-1983) and in 1993 it expanded to twenty-two members. It moved under twenty in the 105th Congress (1995-1997) and it has remained close to that number with an average size of 19.11 senators, ranking it tenth among the sixteen standing committees. While presently-named Small Business and Entrepreneurship ranks near the bottom in terms of mean seniority at 9.19 years—fifteenth place—it has a mid-level eighth place retention rate of 88.4 percent.

Only two members of other committees moved to Small Business from other committees—Lauch Faircloth (Rep-N.C.) from Environment and Public Works and Labor and Human Resources in 1997 and John Cornyn (Rep-Tex.) from Environment and Public Works in 2005, and then left the committee to become ranking Member on Select Ethics in 2007. Two Small Business members left to chair other committees—John Chafee (Rep-R.I.) to chair Environment and Public Works in 1995 and John W. Warner to chair Armed Services in 1999. Five members left Small Business for no other assignments while it lost three to Finance and two to Appropriations.

Committee Leaders: With Reagan-era Republicans recapturing the Senate in 1980, Lowell P. Weicker Jr. of Connecticut would become the first chair of the standing Senate Committee on Small Business from the 97th through the 99th Congresses (1981-1987) while Sam Nunn of Georgia was the standing committee's first ranking minority member. Nunn relinquished that post to become ranking member on Armed Services and was succeeded by Dale Bumpers of Arkansas, who became ranking minority member in the 99th Congress (1985-1987) and chair in 1997 when Democrats regained control of the Senate and Weicker became ranking member. Weicker would lose re-election in 1988 to Joseph I. Lieberman.

Bumpers remained as chair of the standing Small Business Committee until the Republicans returned to power in the 1994 election. He served one last term as ranking minority member (1995-1997) and relinquished the slot to John F. Kerry of Massachusetts when he assumed the ranking member position on Energy and Natural Resources in 1997. Kerry served as the committee's senior Democrat from 1997 to 2009 when he replaced Vice President Joseph R. Biden of Delaware as chair of Foreign Relations. Mary Landrieu of Louisiana succeeded Kerry as the committee's chair in 2009.

On the Republican side, succeeding Weicker as the committee's senior Republican and ranking minority member in the 101st Congress (1989-1991) was Rudolph Boschwitz of Minnesota, who lost his re-election bid in 1990 and was in turn followed by Robert W. Kasten Jr. of Wisconsin in the 102nd Congress (1991-93), who lost his re-election in 1992, and then by Larry L. Pressler of South Dakota in 1993. Pressler served one term as ranking member until he became chair of Commerce. Science and Transportation in 1995 and was defeated as well in 1996. Pressler's successor in 1995 was Christopher S. (Kit) Bond of Missouri, the fifth consecutive senior Republican on the committee in five Congresses. Bond's service as Small Business's senior Republican lasted for eight years—six-plus years as chair (1995-2001) and one-plus year as ranking member (2001-2003). The committee's renaming to become the Committee on Small Business and Entrepreneurship took place in June, 2001, the same month that Jim Jeffords's defection from the Republican Party also occurred. Following Bond as senior Republican was Olympia J.B. Snowe of Maine, who has served as chair in two Congresses (2003-2007) and as ranking member in the last (2007-2011).

Party Leadership: In the thirty-four post-reorganization years from 1947 to 1981, when Small Business was a long-standing select committee, eleven Senate floor leaders and Whips had seen service on the committee. Eight were Republicans, including four floor leaders Kenneth S. Wherry of Nebraska, 1949-1951; Hugh D. Scott of Pennsylvania, 1969-1977; Howard W. Baker Jr. of Tennessee, 1977-1985; and Bob Dole of Kansas, 1985-1996; and four party Whips—Leverett Saltonstall of Massachusetts, 1949-1957; Thomas Kuchel of California, 1959-1969; Ted Stevens of Alaska, 1977-1985; and Don Nickles of Oklahoma, 1996-2003. Senate Democrats were less likely to select leaders from Select Small Business. Only one floor leader—Ernest W. McFarland of Arizona, 1951-1953—and only two party Whips—Hubert H. Humphrey of Minnesota, 1961-1965, and Russell B. Long of Louisiana, 1965-1969—came from the committee.

In the thirty years since Small Business became a standing committee, its role as a leadership feeder diminished dramatically with no Democratic floor leaders or Whips chosen from the committee and only two Republicans selected who served on the standing committee—floor leaders C. Trent Lott of Mississippi, 1996-2003 and Bill Frist of Tennessee, 2003-2007.

Presidential Aspirations: As in the case of party leaders, the Small Business Committee was more successful in producing presidential and vice presidential nominees when it was a select committee than as a standing one. The five Select Small Business alumni receiving presidential nominations were Democrats John F. Kennedy of Massachusetts in 1960, Hubert H. Humphrey and Walter F. Mondale of Minnesota in 1968 and 1984, respectively, and Republicans Barry M. Goldwater of Arizona in 1964 and Bob Dole of Kansas in 1996. Two of the Select Committee's vice presidential nominees were elected—Humphrey in 1964 and Mondale in 1976

while two others were not—Democrat John J. Sparkman in 1952 and Bob Dole of Kansas in 1976.

Since Small Business became a standing committee of the Senate in 1981, only four presidential and vice presidential nominees emerged from the committee. Three were Democrats—Joe Lieberman of Connecticut, Al Gore's 2000 running-mate, and both ends of the Democrats 2004 ticket—John Kerry of Massachusetts and John Edwards of North Carolina—and one was a long-ago Republican, Barry M. Goldwater of Arizona. To date presidential success has eluded alumni of the Small Business Committee.

Other Notables: In keeping with the low profile of Small Business Committee members, only two former Cabinet secretaries have served on the committee and both were Republicans—Elizabeth Dole (Rep-N.C.) who was President Reagan's Secretary of Transportation and George H.W. Bush's Secretary of Labor and Lamar Alexander (Rep-Tenn.), who served with Mrs. Dole in the George H.W. Bush administration as Secretary of Education. One Republican member had a different route. Dirk Kempthorne of Idaho left Small Business to serve as governor, 1999-2006, and returned to Washington in 2006 as President George W. Bush's second Secretary of the Interior.

Selected References

Boesl, Mary Etta, "Small Business Committee, Senate," in Donald C. Bacon, Roger H. Davidson, and Morton Keller, eds., *The Encyclopedia of the United States Congress* (New York: Simon & Schuster, 1995), I: 1831-1833.

Coren, Robert W., et al., "Records of Select Committees, 1947-68 (80th-90th Congresses): Select Committee on Small Business (February 20, 1950)," *Guide to the Records of the United States Senate at the National Archives: 1789-1989 Bicentennial Edition* (Washington, D.C.: National Archives and Records Administration, 1989), 218-219.

Malbin, Michael J., *Unelected Representatives: Congressional Staff and the Future of Representative Government* (New York: Basic Books, 1989).

Vinyard, Dale, "The Congressional Committees on Small Business: Patterns of Legislative Committee-Executive Agency Relations," *Western Political Quarterly*, 21 (September, 1968), 391-399.

RESPONSIBILITIES, JURISDICTIONAL CHANGES, AND SUBCOMMITTEES

SMALL BUSINESS

Committee Reorganized, 1981

Senate Select Committee on Small Business was reorganized as the Standing Committee on Small Business, S. Res. 101, March 25, 1981.

Reorganized Jurisdiction, 1981

From Senate Resolution 101, March 25, 1981:

[Section 3, Rule XXV.(1)(o)]

(1)   **Committee on Small Business**, to which committee shall be referred all proposed legislation, messages, petitions, memorials, and other matters relating to the Small Business Administration.

(2) Any proposed legislation reported by such committee which relates to matters other than the functions of the Small Business Administration shall, at the request of the chairman of any standing committee having jurisdiction over the subject matter extraneous to the functions of the Small Business Administration, be considered and reported by such standing committee prior to its consideration by the Senate; and likewise measures reported by other committees directly relating to the Small Business Administration shall, at the request of the chairman of the Committee on Small Business, be referred to the Committee on Small Business for its consideration of any portions of the measure dealing with the Small Business Administration, and be reported by this committee prior to its consideration by the Senate.

(3) Such committee shall also study and survey by means of research and investigation all problems of American small business enterprises, and report thereon from time to time.

Jurisdiction, 103rd Congress (1993-94)

From the *Standing Rules of the Senate* in the *Senate Manual*, 103rd Congress, 1st Session, S. Doc. 103-1:

[Rule XXV (1)(o)]

(1) **Committee on Small Business**, to which committee shall be referred all proposed legislation, messages, petitions, memorials, and other matters relating to the Small Business Administration.

(2) Any proposed legislation reported by such committee which relates to matters other than the functions of the Small Business Administration shall, at the request of the chairman of any standing committee having jurisdiction over the subject matter extraneous to the functions of the Small Business Administration, be considered and reported by such standing committee prior to its consideration by the Senate; and likewise measures reported by other committees directly relating to the Small Business Administration shall, at the request of the chairman of the Committee on Small Business, be referred to the Committee on Small Business for its consideration of any portions of the measure dealing with the Small Business Administration, and be reported by this committee prior to its consideration by the Senate.

(3) Such committee shall also study and survey by means of research and investigation all problems of American small business enterprises, and report thereon from time to time.

Committee Renamed, 2001

Small Business was renamed the Committee on Small Business and Entrepreneurship on June 29, 2001.

Jurisdiction, 111th Congress (2009-10)

From *Authority and Rules of Senate Committees, 2009-2010*, Sen. Doc. 111-3, pursuant to S. Res, 166, June 2, 2009.

[Rule XXV (1)(o)]

(1) **Committee on Small Business and Entrepeneurship,** to which committee shall be referred all proposed legislation, messages, petitions, memorials, and other matters relating to the Small Business Administration.

(2) Any proposed legislation reported by such committee which relates to matters other than the functions of the Small Business Administration shall, at the request of the chairman of any standing committee having jurisdiction over the subject matter extraneous to the functions of the Small Business Administration, be considered and reported by such standing committee prior to its consideration by the Senate; and likewise measures reported by other committees directly relating to the Small Business Administration shall, at the request of the chairman of the Committee on Small Business, be referred to the Committee on Small Business for its consideration of any portions of the measure dealing with the Small Business Administration, and be reported by this committee prior to its consideration by the Senate.

(3) Such committee shall also study and survey by means of research and investigation all problems of American small business enterprises, and report thereon from time to time.

NAMES OF SUBCOMMITTEES

Committee on Small Business, 103rd Only

Competitiveness, Capital Formation and Economic Opportunity, 103
Export Expansion and Agricultural Development, 103
Government Contracting and Paperwork Reduction, 103
Innovation, Manufacturing and Technology, 103
Rural Economy and Family Farming, 103
Urban and Minority-Owned Business Development, 103

Committee on Small Business — No Subcommittees, 104, 105, 106, 107, 108, 109, 110, 111

MEMBERSHIP ROSTERS, 103rd-111th Congresses, 1993-2010

SMALL BUSINESS / 103rd Congress

Service Dates of Committee Chair: Jan. 21, 1993-Jan. 6, 1995

Service Dates of Majority Members: Jan. 21, 1993-Jan. 6, 1995

Service Dates of Minority Members: Jan. 21, 1993-Jan. 6, 1995

Majority			Years in:		Minority			Years in:	
Rank Name	Party	State	Senate	Comm.	Rank Name	Party	State	Senate	Comm.
Chr Bumpers, Dale	Dem	Ark.	19	15	RM Pressler, Larry L.	Rep	S.D.	15	*2 11
2nd Nunn, Samuel A.	Dem	Ga.	21	21	2nd Wallop, Malcolm	Rep	Wyo.	17	7
3rd Levin, Carl M.	Dem	Mich.	15	14	3rd Bond, Christopher S. (Kit)	Rep	Mo.	7	7
4th Harkin, Thomas R.	Dem	Iowa	9	8	4th Burns, Conrad	Rep	Mont.	5	4
5th Kerry, John F.	Dem	Mass.	9	8	5th Mack, Connie III	Rep	Fla.	5	2
6th Lieberman, Joseph I.	Dem	Conn.	5	4	6th Coverdell, Paul	Rep	Ga.	1	1
7th Wellstone, Paul D.	DFL	Minn.	3	2	7th Kempthorne, Dirk	Rep	Ida.	1	1
8th Wofford, Harris	Dem	Penn.	2	2	8th Bennett, Robert F.	Rep	Utah	1	1
9th Heflin, Howell T.	Dem	Ala.	15	1	9th Chafee, John H.	Rep	R.I.	17	1
10th Lautenberg, Frank R.	Dem	N.J.	11	1	10th Hutchison, Kay Bailey	Rep	Tex.	1	1
11th Kohl, Herbert H.	Dem	Wisc.	5	1					
12th Moseley Braun, Carol	Dem	Ill.	1	1	*2: Member's second period of service on the committee.				

Note: "Years in committee" include members' continuous service on the Select Committee on Small Business. Ranking on this committee for the following member was affected by other chamber service: Samuel A. Nunn (Dem-Ga.), Chair, Armed Services.

Additions:
  Minority:
      10th Hutchison, Kay Bailey   Rep   Tex.   July 1, 1993

Departures from the Senate:	Majority			Minority		
Defeated for Re-election	Wofford, Harris	Dem	Penn.	None		
Retired	None			Wallop, Malcolm	Rep	Wyo.

Departures from Committee:						
Became Chair of Environment and Public Works	None			Chafee, John H.	Rep	R.I.
Moved to Finance and Special Aging	Moseley Braun, Carol	Dem	Ill.	None		
No new assignment	Kohl, Herbert H.	Dem	Wisc.	None		

SMALL BUSINESS / 104th Congress

Service Dates of Committee Chair: Jan. 6, 1995-Jan. 9, 1997

Service Dates of Majority Members: Jan. 6, 1995-Jan. 9, 1997

Service Dates of Minority Members: Jan. 6, 1995-Jan. 9, 1997

Majority			Years in:		Minority			Years in:	
Rank Name	Party	State	Senate	Comm.	Rank Name	Party	State	Senate	Comm.
Chr Bond, Christopher S. (Kit)	Rep	Mo.	9	9	RM Bumpers, Dale	Dem	Ark.	21	17
2nd Pressler, Larry L.	Rep	S.D.	17	*2 13	2nd Nunn, Samuel A.	Dem	Ga.	23	23
3rd Burns, Conrad	Rep	Mont.	7	6	3rd Levin, Carl M.	Dem	Mich.	17	16
4th Mack, Connie III	Rep	Fla.	7	4	4th Harkin, Thomas R.	Dem	Iowa	11	10
5th Coverdell, Paul	Rep	Ga.	3	2	5th Kerry, John F.	Dem	Mass.	11	10
6th Kempthorne, Dirk	Rep	Ida.	3	2	6th Lieberman, Joseph I.	Dem	Conn.	7	6
7th Bennett, Robert F.	Rep	Utah	3	2	7th Wellstone, Paul D.	DFL	Minn.	5	4
8th Hutchison, Kay Bailey	Rep	Tex.	2	2	8th Heflin, Howell T.	Dem	Ala.	17	2
9th Warner, John W.	Rep	Va.	17	1	9th Lautenberg, Frank R.	Dem	N.J.	13	2
10th Frist, William H.	Rep	Tenn.	1	1					
11th Snowe, Olympia J.B.	Rep	Me.	1	1	*2: Member's second period of service on the committee.				

Note: "Years in committee" include members' continuous service on the Select Committee on Small Business. Ranking on this committee for the following members were affected by other chamber service: Larry L. Pressler (Rep-S.D.), Chair, Commerce, Science and Transportation; and Samuel A. Nunn (Dem-Ga.), Ranking Minority Member, Armed Services.

Vacancies Filled:
  Majority:
    11th seat filled by Snowe on Jan. 17, 1995

Departures from the Senate:	Majority			Minority		
Defeated for Re-election	Pressler, Larry L.	Rep	S.D.	None		
Retired	None			Nunn, Samuel A.	Dem	Ga.
				Heflin, Howell T.	Dem	Ala.

Departures from Committee:						
Moved to Finance	Mack, Connie III	Rep	Fla.	None		
Moved to Appropriations and Rules and Administration	Hutchison, Kay Bailey	Rep	Tex.	None		
Moved to Select Intelligence	None			Lautenberg, Frank R.	Dem	N.J.

SMALL BUSINESS / 105th Congress

Service Dates of Committee Chair: Jan. 9, 1997-Jan. 7, 1999

Service Dates of Majority Members: Jan. 9, 1997-Jan. 7, 1999

Service Dates of Minority Members: Jan. 9, 1997-Jan. 7, 1999

Majority			Years in:		Minority			Years in:	
Rank Name	Party	State	Senate	Comm.	Rank Name	Party	State	Senate	Comm.
Chr Bond, Christopher S. (Kit)	Rep	Mo.	11	11	RM Kerry, John F.	Dem	Mass.	13	12
2nd Burns, Conrad	Rep	Mont.	9	8	2nd Bumpers, Dale	Dem	Ark.	23	19
3rd Coverdell, Paul	Rep	Ga.	5	4	3rd Levin, Carl M.	Dem	Mich.	19	18
4th Kempthorne, Dirk	Rep	Ida.	5	4	4th Harkin, Thomas R.	Dem	Iowa	13	12
5th Bennett, Robert F.	Rep	Utah	5	4	5th Lieberman, Joseph I.	Dem	Conn.	9	8
6th Warner, John W.	Rep	Va.	19	3	6th Wellstone, Paul D.	DFL	Minn.	7	6
7th Frist, William H.	Rep	Tenn.	3	3	7th Cleland, J. Maxwell (Max)	Dem	Ga.	1	1
8th Snowe, Olympia J.B.	Rep	Me.	3	2	8th Landrieu, Mary L.	Dem	La.	1	1
9th Faircloth, D.M. (Lauch)	Rep	N.C	5	1					
10th Enzi, Michael B.	Rep	Wyo.	1	1					

Note: "Years in committee" include members' continuous service on the Select Committee on Small Business. Ranking on this committee for the following members were affected by other chamber service: Dale Bumpers (Dem-Ark.), Ranking Minority Member; Energy and Natural Resources; and Carl M. Levin (Dem-Mich.), Ranking Minority Member, Armed Services.

Departures from the Senate:	Majority			Minority		
Elected Governor	Kempthorne, Dirk	Rep	Ida.	None		
Defeated for Re-election	Faircloth, D.M. (Lauch)	Rep	N.C.	None		
Retired	None			Bumpers, Dale	Dem	Ark.

Departures from Committee:						
Became Chair of Armed Services	Warner, John W.	Rep	Va.			
No new assignment	Frist, William H.	Rep	Tenn.	None		

SMALL BUSINESS / 106th Congress

Service Dates of Committee Chair: Jan. 7, 1999-Jan. 3, 2001

Service Dates of Majority Members: Jan. 7, 1999-Jan. 25, 2001

Service Dates of Minority Members: Jan. 7, 1999-Jan. 25, 2001

Majority			Years in:		Minority			Years in:	
Rank Name	Party	State	Senate	Comm.	Rank Name	Party	State	Senate	Comm.
Chr Bond, Christopher S. (Kit)	Rep	Mo.	13	13	RM Kerry, John F.	Dem	Mass.	15	14
2nd Burns, Conrad	Rep	Mont.	11	10	2nd Levin, Carl M.	Dem	Mich.	21	20

3rd Coverdell, Paul	Rep	Ga.	7	6	3rd Harkin, Thomas R.	Dem	Iowa	15	14
4th Bennett, Robert F.	Rep	Utah	7	6	4th Lieberman, Joseph I.	Dem	Conn.	11	10
5th Snowe, Olympia J.B.	Rep	Me.	5	4	5th Wellstone, Paul D.	DFL	Minn.	9	8
6th Enzi, Michael B.	Rep	Wyo.	3	2	6th Cleland, J. Maxwell (Max)	Dem	Ga.	3	2
7th Fitzgerald, Peter G.	Rep	Ill.	1	1	7th Landrieu, Mary L.	Dem	La.	3	2
8th Crapo, Michael D.	Rep	Ida.	1	1	8th Edwards, John	Dem	N.C.	1	1
9th Voinovich, George V.	Rep	Ohio	1	1					
10th Abraham, Spencer	Rep	Mich.	5	1					

Note: "Years in committee" include members' continuous service on the Select Committee on Small Business. Ranking on this committee for the following member was affected by other chamber service: Carl M. Levin (Dem-Mich.), Ranking Minority Member, Armed Services.

Changes:
Majority:

Coverdell, Paul	Rep	Ga.	July 18, 2000 Died in office

Departures from the Senate:	**Majority**			**Minority**
Defeated for Re-election	Abraham, Spencer	Rep	Mich.	None

Departures from Committee:				
No new assignment	Voinovich, George V.	Rep	Ohio	None

SMALL BUSINESS / 107th Congress, Pre-Jeffords switch

* The Senate Committee on Small Business was renamed as the Committee on SMALL BUSINESS AND ENTREPRENEURSHIP on June 29, 2001 by S. Res. 123.

Service Dates of Committee Chair: ChT: Jan. 3, 2001-Jan. 25, 2001 Kerry (Dem-Mass.)

Ch1: Jan. 25, 2001-June 6, 2001 Bond (Rep-Mo.)

Service Dates of Majority Members: Jan. 25, 2001-June 6, 2001

Service Dates of Minority Members: Jan. 25, 2001-June 6, 2001

Majority			**Years in:**		**Minority**			**Years in:**	
Rank Name	Party	State	Senate	Comm.	Rank Name	Party	State	Senate	Comm.
Ch1 Bond, Christopher S. (Kit)	Rep	Mo.	15	15	RM1 Kerry, John F.	Dem	Mass.	17	16
2nd Burns, Conrad	Rep	Mont.	13	12	2nd Levin, Carl M.	Dem	Mich.	23	23
3rd Bennett, Robert F.	Rep	Utah	9	9	3rd Harkin, Thomas R.	Dem	Iowa	17	16
4th Snowe, Olympia J.B.	Rep	Me.	7	7	4th Lieberman, Joseph I.	Dem	Conn.	13	12
5th Enzi, Michael B.	Rep	Wyo.	5	5	5th Wellstone, Paul D.	DFL	Minn.	11	10
6th Fitzgerald, Peter G.	Rep	Ill.	3	3	6th Cleland, J. Maxwell (Max)	Dem	Ga.	5	5
7th Crapo, Michael D.	Rep	Ida.	3	3	7th Landrieu, Mary L.	Dem	La.	5	5
8th Allen, George F.	Rep	Va.	1	1	8th Edwards, John	Dem	N.C.	3	3
9th Ensign, John E.	Rep	Nev.	1	1	9th Cantwell, Maria E.	Dem	Wash.	1	1

Note 1: The committee majority in the 2001 Senate power-sharing arrangement was determined by the party of the vice president. Democrat Al Gore, Jr. served from Jan. 3, 2001 to Jan. 20, 2001 and was succeeded by Republican Richard B. Cheney on Jan. 20, 2001. When Senator Jeffords of Vermont left the Republican Party, effective June 6, 2001 to become an Independent, Democrats regained the majority for the remainder of the 107th Congress.

Note 2: "Years in committee" include members' continuous service on the Select Committee on Small Business. Ranking on this committee for the following member was affected by other chamber service: Carl M. Levin (Dem-Mich.), Ranking Minority Member, Armed Services.

SMALL BUSINESS AND ENTREPRENEURSHIP / 107th Congress, Post-Jeffords switch

Service Dates of Committee Chair: June 6, 2001-Jan. 14, 2003

Service Dates of Majority Members: June 6, 2001-Jan. 14, 2003

Service Dates of Minority Members: June 6, 2001-Jan. 15, 2003

Majority			**Years in:**		**Minority**			**Years in:**	
Rank Name	Party	State	Senate	Comm.	Rank Name	Party	State	Senate	Comm.
Ch2 Kerry, John F.	Dem	Mass.	17	17	RM2 Bond, Christopher S. (Kit)	Rep	Mo.	15	15
2nd Levin, Carl M.	Dem	Mich.	23	23	2nd Burns, Conrad	Rep	Mont.	13	13
3rd Harkin, Thomas R.	Dem	Iowa	17	17	3rd Bennett, Robert F.	Rep	Utah	9	9
4th Lieberman, Joseph I.	Dem	Conn.	13	13	4th Snowe, Olympia J.B.	Rep	Me.	7	7
5th Wellstone, Paul D.	DFL	Minn.	11	11	5th Enzi, Michael B.	Rep	Wyo.	5	5

6th Cleland, J. Maxwell (Max)	Dem	Ga.	5	5
7th Landrieu, Mary L.	Dem	La.	5	5
8th Edwards, John	Dem	N.C.	3	3
9th Cantwell, Maria E.	Dem	Wash.	1	1
10th Carnahan, Jean	Dem	Mo.	1	1

6th Fitzgerald, Peter G.	Rep	Ill.	3	3
7th Crapo, Michael D.	Rep	Ida.	3	3
8th Allen, George F.	Rep	Va.	1	1
9th Ensign, John E.	Rep	Nev.	1	1

Note: "Years in committee" include members' continuous service on the Select Committee on Small Business. Ranking on this committee for the following member was affected by other chamber service: Carl M. Levin (Dem-Mich.), Chair, Armed Services.

Additions:
   Majority:

10th Carnahan, Jean	Dem	Mo.	July 10, 2001

Changes:
   Majority:

Wellstone, Paul D.	DFL	Minn.	Oct. 25, 2002 Died in office
Carnahan, Jean	Dem	Mo.	Nov. 25, 2002 Resigned the Senate; defeated in special election by James M. Talent (Rep-Mo.)

Departures from the Senate:	**Majority**			**Minority**
Defeated for Re-election	Cleland, J. Maxwell (Max)	Dem	Ga.	None

SMALL BUSINESS AND ENTREPRENEURSHIP / 108th Congress

Service Dates of Committee Chair: Jan. 14, 2003-Jan. 6, 2005

Service Dates of Majority Members: Jan. 14, 2003-Jan. 6, 2005

Service Dates of Minority Members: Jan. 15, 2003-Jan. 6, 2005

Majority			**Years in:**		**Minority**			**Years in:**	
Rank Name	Party	State	Senate	Comm.	Rank Name	Party	State	Senate	Comm.
Chr Snowe, Olympia J.B.	Rep	Me.	9	8	RM Kerry, John F.	Dem	Mass.	19	18
2nd Bond, Christopher S. (Kit)	Rep	Mo.	17	17	2nd Levin, Carl M.	Dem	Mich.	25	24
3rd Burns, Conrad	Rep	Mont.	15	14	3rd Harkin, Thomas R.	Dem	Iowa	19	18
4th Bennett, Robert F.	Rep	Utah	11	10	4th Lieberman, Joseph I.	Dem	Conn.	15	14
5th Enzi, Michael B.	Rep	Wyo.	7	7	5th Landrieu, Mary L.	Dem	La.	7	7
6th Fitzgerald, Peter G.	Rep	Ill.	5	5	6th Edwards, John	Dem	N.C.	5	5
7th Crapo, Michael D.	Rep	Ida.	5	5	7th Cantwell, Maria E.	Dem	Wash.	3	2
8th Allen, George F.	Rep	Va.	3	2	8th Bayh, B. Evans	Dem	Ind.	5	1
9th Ensign, John E.	Rep	Nev.	3	2	9th Pryor, Mark	Dem	Ark.	1	1
10th Coleman, Norman	Rep	Minn.	1	1					

Note: "Years in committee" include members' continuous service on the Select Committee on Small Business. Ranking on this committee for the following members were affected by other chamber service: Robert F. Bennett (Rep-Utah), Chair, Joint Economic Committee; and Carl M. Levin (Dem-Mich.), Ranking Minority Member, Armed Services.

Departures from the Senate:	**Majority**			**Minority**		
Retired	Fitzgerald, Peter G.	Rep	Ill.			
Retired; lost vice presidential election	None			Edwards, John	Dem	N.C.

Departures from Committee:					
Moved to Rules and Administration	Bennett, Robert F.	Rep	Utah	None	
Moved to Finance and Select Indian Affairs	Crapo, Michael D.	Rep	Ida.	None	
No new assignment	Ensign, John E.	Rep	Nev.	None	

SMALL BUSINESS AND ENTRPRENEURSHIP / 109th Congress

Service Dates of Committee Chair: Jan. 6, 2005-Jan. 12, 2007

Service Dates of Majority Members: Jan. 6, 2005-Jan. 12, 2007

Service Dates of Minority Members: Jan. 6, 2005-Jan. 12, 2007

Majority			**Years in:**		**Minority**			**Years in:**	
Rank Name	Party	State	Senate	Comm.	Rank Name	Party	State	Senate	Comm.
Chr Snowe, Olympia J.B.	Rep	Me.	11	10	RM Kerry, John F.	Dem	Mass.	21	20

2nd Bond, Christopher S. (Kit)	Rep	Mo.	19	19		2nd Levin, Carl M.	Dem	Mich.	27	26
3rd Burns, Conrad	Rep	Mont.	17	16		3rd Harkin, Thomas R.	Dem	Iowa	21	20
4th Allen, George F.	Rep	Va.	5	4		4th Lieberman, Joseph I.	Dem	Conn.	17	16
5th Coleman, Norman	Rep	Minn.	3	2		5th Landrieu, Mary L.	Dem	La.	9	8
6th Thune, John	Rep	S.D.	1	1		6th Cantwell, Maria E.	Dem	Wash.	5	4
7th Isakson, Johnny	Rep	Ga.	1	1		7th Bayh, B. Evans	Dem	Ind.	7	2
8th Vitter, David	Rep	La.	1	1		8th Pryor, Mark	Dem	Ark.	3	2
9th Enzi, Michael B.	Rep	Wyo.	9	8						
10th Cornyn, John	Rep	Tex.	3	1						

Note: "Years in committee" include members' continuous service on the Select Committee on Small Business. Ranking on this committee for the following member was affected by other chamber service: Carl M. Levin (Dem-Mich.), Ranking Minority Member, Armed Services.

Departures from the Senate:	**Majority**			**Minority**
Defeated for Re-election	Burns, Conrad	Rep	Mont.	None
	Allen, George F.	Rep	Va.	

Departures from Committee:				
Moved to Select Ethics as Ranking Member	Cornyn, John	Rep	Tex.	None

SMALL BUSINESS AND ENTREPRENEURSHIP / 110th Congress

Service Dates of Committee Chair: Jan. 12, 2007-Jan. 21, 2009

Service Dates of Majority Members: Jan. 12, 2007-Jan. 21, 2009

Service Dates of Minority Members: Jan. 12, 2007-Jan. 21, 2009

Majority						**Minority**				
			Years in:						**Years in:**	
Rank Name	**Party**	**State**	**Senate**	**Comm.**		**Rank Name**	**Party**	**State**	**Senate**	**Comm.**
Chr Kerry, John F.	Dem	Mass.	23	22		RM Snowe, Olympia J.B.	Rep	Me.	13	12
2nd Levin, Carl M.	Dem	Mich.	29	28		2nd Bond, Christopher S. (Kit)	Rep	Mo.	21	21
3rd Harkin, Thomas R.	Dem	Iowa	23	22		3rd Coleman, Norman	Rep	Minn.	5	4
4th Lieberman, Joseph I.	IDem	Conn.	19	18		4th Vitter, David	Rep	La.	3	3
5th Landrieu, Mary L.	Dem	La.	11	11		5th Dole, Elizabeth Hanford	Rep	N.C.	5	1
6th Cantwell, Maria E.	Dem	Wash.	7	6		6th Thune, John	Rep	S.D.	3	3
7th Bayh, B. Evans	Dem	Ind.	9	4		7th Corker, Robert	Rep	Tenn.	1	1
8th Pryor, Mark	Dem	Ark.	5	4		8th Enzi, Michael B.	Rep	Wyo.	11	11
9th Cardin, Benjamin L.	Dem	Md.	1	1		9th Isakson, Johnny	Rep	Ga.	3	3
10th Tester, Jon	Dem	Mont.	1	1						

Note: "Years in committee" include members' continuous service on the Select Committee on Small Business. Ranking on this committee for the following members were affected by other chamber service: Carl M. Levin (Dem-Mich.), Chair, Armed Services; and Christopher S. (Kit) Bond (Rep-Mo.), Vice Chair, Select Intelligence.

Departures from the Senate:	**Majority**			**Minority**		
Defeated for Re-election	None			Coleman, Norman	Rep	Minn.
				Dole, Elizabeth Hanford	Rep	N.C.

Departures from Committee:						
Moved to Appropriations	Tester, Jon	Dem	Mont.	None		
Moved to Commerce, Science, and Transportation	None			Isakson, Johnny	Rep	Ga.
No new assignment	None			Corker, Robert	Rep	Tenn.

SMALL BUSINESS AND ENTREPENEURSHIP / 111th Congress

Service Dates of Committee Chair: Jan. 21, 2009-

Service Dates of Majority Members: Jan. 21, 2009-

Service Dates of Minority Members: Jan. 21, 2009-

	Majority						Minority			
				Years in:						Years in:
Rank Name	Party	State	Senate	Comm.		Rank Name	Party	State	Senate	Comm.
Chr Landrieu, Mary L.	Dem	La.	13	13		RM Snowe, Olympia J.B.	Rep	Me.	15	15
2nd Kerry, John F.	Dem	Mass.	25	24		2nd Bond, Christopher S. (Kit)	Rep	Mo.	23	23
3rd Levin, Carl M.	Dem	Mich.	31	30		3rd Vitter, David	Rep	La.	5	5
4th Harkin, Thomas R.	Dem	Iowa	25	24		4th Thune, John	Rep	S.D.	5	5
5th Lieberman, Joseph I.	IDem	Conn.	21	20		5th Enzi, Michael B.	Rep	Wyo.	13	13
6th Cantwell, Maria E.	Dem	Wash.	9	8		6th Isakson, Johnny	Rep	Ga.	5	5
7th Bayh, B. Evans	Dem	Ind.	11	7		7th Wicker, Roger F.	Rep	Miss.	2	1
8th Pryor, Mark	Dem	Ark.	7	7		8th Risch, James	Rep	Ida.	1	1
9th Cardin, Benjamin L.	Dem	Md.	3	3						
10th Hagan, Kay R.	Dem	N.C.	1	1						
11th Shaheen, Jeanne	Dem	N.H.	1	1						

Note 1: "Years in committee" include members' continuous service on the Select Committee on Small Business. Ranking on this committee for the following members were affected by other chamber service: John F. Kerry (Dem-Mass.), Chair, Foreign Relations; Carl M. Levin (Dem-Mich.), Chair, Armed Services; Thomas R. Harkin (Dem-Iowa), Chair, Agriculture, Nutrition, and Forestry; and Christopher S. (Kit) Bond (Rep-Mo.), Vice Chair, Select Intelligence.

Note 2: The disputed election in Minnesota between Democrat Al Franken and incumbent Republican Norman Coleman led both parties to hold seats open pending the outcome of the recount.

Note 3: The order of Senators Shaheen and Hagan were reversed in S. Pub. 111-15, December 17, 2009.

Filled Vacancy:
  Minority:
    8th seat by Risch on July 21, 2009

Veterans' Affairs

Senate Committee on Veterans' Affairs, 103rd-111th Congresses (1993-2011)

BACKGROUND

Organizational History: The Veterans' Affairs Committee was created in 1970 to transfer responsibilities for veterans from the Finance and Labor committees to a single panel. From 1947 to 1970, matters relating to veterans compensation and veterans generally were referred to the Committee on Finance, while matters relating to the vocational rehabilitation, education, medical care, civil relief, and civilian readjustment of veterans were referred to the Committee on Labor and Public Welfare.

Congressional legislation affecting veterans changed over the years. For the members of the armed forces and their families in the nation's early wars—the Revolutionary War, the War of 1812, the Mexican War, the Civil War, and the Spanish-American War—the response of the federal government had been essentially financial. This was clearly the legislative mission of the Senate Committee on Pensions which was created as one of the Senate's original standing committees in 1816 and continued until its termination in the Legislative Reorganization Act of 1946.

During World War I the nature of the congressional response to veterans' needs changed towards a more diversified set of programs. A war risk insurance program, which was referred to the Senate Finance Committee, changed the consideration of veterans' benefits in the Senate. The Finance Committee was the Senate standing committee most responsible for veterans programs from 1917 to 1947. After World War II, the Finance Committee handled the Servicemen's Readjustment Act of 1944, the "GI Bill of Rights," which extended to servicemen and their families, a number of benefits including unemployment assistance, education, vocational training, housing and business loan guarantees, as well as the traditional medical and pension benefits of previous times. Many experts believe this law was one of the most important elements in the expansion of the middle class following World War II.

It was the Legislative Reorganization Act of 1970 (P.L. 91-510) that led to the creation of the Senate Committee on Veterans' Affairs and removed this jurisdiction from that of the Finance Committee. It continues to be focused on the issues of employment, education, housing, and medical care for the nation's servicemen. Since 1945 and the end of World War II, the American military has been engaged in multiple foreign wars. Fourteen million of the 23.2 million American veterans alive in 2009 served after World War II in Korea, Vietnam, Iraq, Afghanistan, and in a host of other military engagements. It has become the role of the Veterans' Affairs Committee to be the congressional spokesmen for these millions of the nation's servicemen and women.

Membership: The Veterans Affairs Committee had only nine members in its initial Congress, the 92nd (1971-1973). It first reached its present peak of fifteen members in 2001 in the aftermath of the Jeffords switch and continues to maintain that size. The Veterans Committee has remained the Senate's smallest standing committee with its average post-1993 size of 13.7 members lodging it in sixteenth place. Like Budget, Rules and Administration, and Small Business and Entrepreneurship, the Senate Veterans' committee functions without subcommittees. Its mean seniority of 10.42 years moved it to the twelfth rank and its 89.8 percent mean retention rate elevated the committee on that dimension to seventh place among the Senate's sixteen standing committees.

Since 1993, only four members left other committees to move to Veterans' affairs. Larry Craig (Rep-Ida.) left Judiciary to assume the chair of Veterans Affairs in the 109th Congress (2005-2007), while two others—Patty Murray (Dem-Wash.) and John Ensign (Rep-Nev.) left the Banking Committee to gain reassignments to other committees including Veterans Affairs. Among the ten departing members from Veterans' Affairs was Tom Daschle (Dem-S.D.), who left the committee upon his election as Minority Leader in 1995. Other departing members moved to Commerce, Science, and Transportation (2) and Rules and Administration (2).

Committee Leaders: R. Vance Hartke (Dem-Ind.), a senior member of the Finance Committee's Veterans' Legislation subcommittee, was the original chair of the Veterans' Affairs Committee and served from 1971 to 1977. J. Strom Thurmond of South Carolina was the committee's first ranking minority member in 1971 but stepped aside to become ranking member on Armed Services in 1973. Thurmond was succeeded by Clifford P. Hansen of Wyoming who served as its senior Republican from 1973 until 1977, when he became ranking minority member on Energy and Natural Resources in 1977. That was the year that Alan Cranston of California would begin service as chair, eventually becoming the committee's longest serving senior Democrat. Cranston served as chair of the committee in the 95th and 96th Congresses (1977-1981); then as ranking minority member in the 97th-99th Congresses (1981-1987); and then again as chair from 1987 until his retirement from the Senate in 1992, marking a total of sixteen years as the committee's senior Democrat.

In the 95th Congress (1977-1979), all three Republican members—Hansen, Thurmond, and Robert Stafford of Vermont—served as ranking minority member as the 1977 reorganization sorted itself out. Alan K. Simpson of Wyoming became ranking member in 1979 and chair in 1981-1985 until he stepped aside to serve as Republican Whip in 1985. Frank H. Murkowski of Alaska succeeded Simpson as chair in 1985 and served as ranking minority member from 1987 to 1991 and again from 1993-1995, when he was replaced by Arlen Specter of Pennsylvania during Murkowski's service as vice chair of Select Intelligence. Simpson returned as chair in 1995 and served until his retirement in 1996.

Democrat John D. (Jay) Rockefeller, IV of West Virginia succeeded Cranston as chair of Veterans' Affairs in 1993 and served as its senior Democrat until 2003, both before and after the Jeffords defection. In 2003, D. Robert Graham became ranking minority member and served one term in that post before being replaced by Hawaii's Daniel K. Akaka in 2005, who became chair of the committee for the last two Congresses (2007-2011).

Specter resumed the chairmanship of Veterans' Affairs in 1997 and held it until the 2001 Jeffords defection and regained it in 2003 until he left the post to become chair of Judiciary in 2005. At that point, Larry Craig of Idaho succeeded him as chair, and Craig served as ranking member until 2008 when a scandal led to his being replaced by Richard Burr of North Carolina, who remains in the 111th Congress as the ranking minority member on Veterans' Affairs.

Party Leadership: As might be expected from one of the Senate's newer and smaller standing committees, service on Veterans' Affairs has not played a major role in the careers of most Senate floor leaders and Whips. The only Democratic floor leaders to have served on the committee were George J. Mitchell of Maine, 1989-1995, and Thomas A. Daschle of South Dakota, 1995-2005, and the only committee Democrat to be party Whip was Cranston, who held that post from 1977 to 1991. The only two Republican leaders to have served on the committee served as Whips—Ted Stevens of Alaska, 1977-1985, and Alan Simpson of Wyoming, 1985-1995.

Presidential Aspirations: Veterans' Affairs has not been much of a presidential launch pad either with only President Barack Obama, a non-veteran, serving on it. That the Senate's best-known military veterans who were nominated recently— Bob Dole of Kansas, John F. Kerry of Massachusetts, and John S. McCain of Arizona—did not serve on the committee indicates that they saw other Senate panels as preparing them better for their presidential candidacies than Veterans' Affairs.

Other Notables: Apart from William Saxbe (Rep-Ohio), who served on the Senate Veterans' Affairs Committee prior to becoming President Nixon's Attorney General in 1974, the only other senator on the committee to move to the Cabinet is President Obama's Secretary of the Interior, Kenneth L. Salazar (Dem-Colo.), while the only committee member with prior Cabinet experience was former G.W. Bush Secretary of Agriculture and newly-elected senator Mike Johanns (Rep-Neb.).

The only post-1993 member of Veterans' Affairs to leave the Senate to return home to serve as governor was Frank Murkowski of Alaska, who served from 2002 to 2006 until his renomination defeat by Sarah Palin, who would succeed him as governor and then become the Republican vice presidential nominee with John McCain of Arizona in 2008.

Selected References

Boesl, Mary Etta, "Veterans' Affairs Committee, Senate," in Donald C. Bacon, Roger H. Davidson, and Morton Keller, eds., *The Encyclopedia of the United States Congress* (New York: Simon & Schuster, 1995), I: 2035-2037.

Coren, Robert W., et al., *Guide to the Records of the United States Senate at the National Archives: 1789-1989 Bicentennial Edition* (Washington, D.C.: National Archives and Records Administration, 1989), 95-96, 168, and 260.

Keller, Bill, "How a Unique Lobby Force Protects Over $21 Billion in Vast Veterans' Programs," *CQ Weekly Report*, 138 (June 14, 1980), 1527-1639.

U.S. Senate, Committee on Veterans' Affairs, *Legislative and Oversight Activities during the 101st Congress by the Senate Committee on Veterans' Affairs*, S.Rept. 102-34 (1992).

RESPONSIBILITIES AND JURISDICTIONAL CHANGES

VETERANS' AFFAIRS

Creation of Committee, 1970

The Senate Committee on Veterans Affairs was established in Public Law 91-510, the Legislative Reorganization Act of 1970, 9lst Congress, Second Session, October 26, 1970 (84 *Statutes* 1140, 1164):

Jurisdiction, 1970

Jurisdiction established in Public Law 91-510, the Legislative Reorganization Act of 1970, 9lst Congress, Second Session, October 26, 1970 (84 *Statutes* 1140, 1164):

[Section 131(q)]

(1) **Committee on Veterans' Affairs**, to which committee shall be referred all proposed legislation, messages, petitions, memorials, and other matters relating to the following subjects:

   (1) Veterans' measures generally.
   (2) Pensions of all wars of the United States, general and special.
   (3) Life insurance issued by the Government on account of service in the armed forces.
   (4) Compensation of veterans.
   (5) Vocational rehabilitation and education of veterans.
   (6) Veterans' hospitals, medical care and treatment of veterans.
   (7) Soldiers' and sailors' civil relief.

    (8) Readjustment of servicemen to civil life.
    (9) National cemeteries; and

(6) by striking out in subparagraph (k) (relating to the Committee on Interior and Insular Affairs) the following item—

    (5) Military parks and battlefields, and national cemeteries and inserting in lieu thereof—
    (5) Military parks and battlefields.

Post-Reorganization Jurisdiction, 1977

From Committee System Reorganization Amendments of 1977, S. Res. 95-4, *Senate Journal*, Feb. 4, 1977:

[XXV. Section 101. 1.(o)]

(1) **Committee on Veterans' Affairs**, to which committee shall be referred all proposed legislation, messages, petitions, memorials, and other matters relating to the following subjects:

    (1) Veterans' measures generally.
    (2) Pensions of all wars of the United States, general and special.
    (3) Life insurance issued by the Government on account of service in the Armed Forces.
    (4) Compensation of veterans.
    (5) Vocational rehabilitation and education of veterans.
    (6) Veterans' hospitals, medical care and treatment of veterans.
    (7) Soldiers' and sailors' civil relief.
    (8) Readjustment of servicemen to civil life.
    (9) National cemeteries.

Jurisdiction, 103rd Congress (1993-94)

From the *Standing Rules of the Senate* in the *Senate Manual*, 103rd Congress, 1st Session, S. Doc. 103-1:

[Rule XXV.(1)(p)]

(1) **Committee on Veterans' Affairs**, to which committee shall be referred all proposed legislation, messages, petitions, memorials, and other matters relating to the following subjects:

    (1) Compensation of veterans.
    (2) Life insurance issued by the Government on account of service in the Armed Forces.
    (3) National cemeteries.
    (4) Pensions of all wars of the United States, general and special.
    (5) Readjustment of servicemen to civil life.
    (6) Soldiers' and sailors' civil relief.
    (7) Veterans' hospitals, medical care and treatment of veterans.
    (8) Veterans' measures generally.
    (9) Vocational rehabilitation and education of veterans.

Jurisdiction, 111th Congress (2009-10)

From *Authority and Rules of Senate Committees, 2009-2010*, Sen. Doc. 111-3, pursuant to S. Res, 166, June 2, 2009.

[Rule XXV.(1)(p)]

(1) **Committee on Veterans' Affairs**, to which committee shall be referred all proposed legislation, messages, petitions, memorials, and other matters relating to the following subjects:

    (1) Compensation of veterans.
    (2) Life insurance issued by the Government on account of service in the Armed Forces.
    (3) National cemeteries.
    (4) Pensions of all wars of the United States, general and special.
    (5) Readjustment of servicemen to civil life.
    (6) Soldiers' and sailors' civil relief.
    (7) Veterans' hospitals, medical care and treatment of veterans.
    (8) Veterans' measures generally.
    (9) Vocational rehabilitation and education of veterans.

Committee on Veterans' Affairs—No Subcommittees, 103rd-111th Congresses

MEMBERSHIP ROSTERS, 103rd-111th Congresses, 1993-2010

VETERANS' AFFAIRS / 103rd Congress

Service Dates of Committee Chair: Jan. 21, 1993-Jan. 6, 1995

Service Dates of Majority Members: Jan. 21, 1993-Jan. 6, 1995

Service Dates of Minority Members: Jan. 21, 1993-Jan. 6, 1995

	Majority						Minority				
				Years in:						Years in:	
Rank Name	Party	State	Senate	Comm.		Rank Name	Party	State	Senate	Comm.	
Chr Rockefeller, John D. IV	Dem	W.Va.	9	8		RM Murkowski, Frank H.	Rep	Alas.	13	12	
2nd DeConcini, Dennis W.	Dem	Ariz.	17	13		2nd Specter, Arlen	Rep	Penn.	13	13	
3rd Mitchell, George J.	Dem	Me.	13	13		3rd Simpson, Alan K.	Rep	Wyo.	15	14	
4th Graham, D. Robert	Dem	Fla.	7	7		4th Thurmond, J. Strom	Rep	S.C.	38	22	
5th Akaka, Daniel K.	Dem	Hai.	3	3		5th Jeffords, James M.	Rep	Vt.	5	*1 4	
6th Daschle, Thomas A.	Dem	S.D.	7	2							
7th Campbell, Ben Nighthorse	Dem	Colo.	1	*1 1		*1: Member's first period of service on the committee.					

Note: Rankings on this committee for the following members were affected by other chamber service: Dennis DeConcini (Dem-Ariz.), Chair, Select Intelligence; George J. Mitchell (Dem-Me.), Senate Majority Leader; Alan K. Simpson (Rep-Wyo.), Senate Minority Whip; and J. Strom Thurmond (Rep-S.C.), Ranking Minority Member, Armed Services.

Departures from the Senate:	**Majority**			**Minority**
Retired	DeConcini, Dennis W.	Dem	Ariz.	None
	Mitchell, George J.	Dem	Me.	

Departures from Committee:				
Elected Minority Leader	Daschle, Thomas A.	Dem	S.D.	None

VETERANS' AFFAIRS / 104th Congress

Service Dates of Committee Chair: Jan. 6, 1995-Jan. 9, 1997

Service Dates of Majority Members: Jan. 6, 1995-Jan. 9, 1997

Service Dates of Minority Members: Jan. 6, 1995-Jan. 9, 1997

	Majority						Minority				
				Years in:						Years in:	
Rank Name	Party	State	Senate	Comm.		Rank Name	Party	State	Senate	Comm.	
Chr Simpson, Alan K.	Rep	Wyo.	17	16		RM Rockefeller, John D. IV	Dem	W.Va.	11	10	
2nd Murkowski, Frank H.	Rep	Alas.	15	14		2nd Graham, D. Robert	Dem	Fla.	9	8	
3rd Specter, Arlen	Rep	Penn.	15	15		3rd Akaka, Daniel K.	Dem	Hai.	5	5	
4th Thurmond, J. Strom	Rep	S.C.	40	24		4th Campbell, Ben Nighthorse	Dem	Colo.	3	*1 2	
5th Jeffords, James M.	Rep	Vt.	7	*1 6		5th Dorgan, Byron L.	Dem	N.D.	3	1	
6th Craig, Larry E.	Rep	Ida.	5	1							
7th Brown, G. Hanks (Hank)	Rep	Colo.	5	1		*1: Member's first period of service on the committee.					

Note: Ranking on this committee for the following member was affected by other chamber service: J. Strom Thurmond (Rep-S.C.), Chair, Armed Services.

Changes:

Majority:

Brown, G. Hanks (Hank)	Rep	Colo.	Mar. 24, 1995 Left committee to open seat for Campbell; no new assignment
Campbell, Ben Nighthorse	Rep	Colo.	Mar. 24, 1995 Replaced Brown; ranked following Jeffords

Minority:

Campbell, Ben Nighthorse	Dem	Colo.	Mar. 28, 1995 Seat as Democrat vacated; returned to committee as Republican
Wellstone, Paul D.	DFL	Minn.	Mar. 28, 1995 Replaced Campbell
Dorgan, Byron	Dem	N.D.	Dec. 29, 1995 Left committee; became Ranking Member on Select Ethics
Murray, Patty	Dem	Wash.	Dec. 29, 1995 Replaced Dorgan

Departures from the Senate:	**Majority**			**Minority**
Retired	Simpson, Alan K.	Rep	Wyo.	None

VETERANS' AFFAIRS / 105th Congress

Service Dates of Committee Chair: Jan. 9, 1997-Jan. 7, 1999

Service Dates of Majority Members: Jan. 9, 1997-Jan. 7, 1999

Service Dates of Minority Members: Jan. 9, 1997-Jan. 7, 1999

Majority			Years in:		Minority			Years in:	
Rank Name	Party	State	Senate	Comm.	Rank Name	Party	State	Senate	Comm.
Chr Specter, Arlen	Rep	Penn.	17	17	RM Rockefeller, John D. IV	Dem	W.Va.	13	12
2nd Murkowski, Frank H.	Rep	Alas.	17	16	2nd Graham, D. Robert	Dem	Fla.	11	11
3rd Thurmond, J. Strom	Rep	S.C.	42	26	3rd Akaka, Daniel K.	Dem	Hai.	7	7
4th Jeffords, James M.	Rep	Vt.	9	*1 8	4th Wellstone, Paul D.	DFL	Minn.	7	2
5th Campbell, Ben Nighthorse	Rep	Colo.	5	*2 2	5th Murray, Patty D.	Dem	Wash.	5	1
6th Craig, Larry E.	Rep	Ida.	7	3					
7th Hutchinson, Y. Timothy	Rep	Ark.	1	1					

*1: Member's first period of service on the committee.

*2: Member's second period of service on the committee.

Note: Ranking on this committee for the following member was affected by other chamber service: J. Strom Thurmond (Rep-S.C.), Chair, Armed Services.

VETERANS' AFFAIRS / 106th Congress

Service Dates of Committee Chair: Jan. 7, 1999-Jan. 3, 2001

Service Dates of Majority Members: Jan. 7, 1999-Jan. 25, 2001

Service Dates of Minority Members: Jan. 7, 1999-Jan. 25, 2001

Majority			Years in:		Minority			Years in:	
Rank Name	Party	State	Senate	Comm.	Rank Name	Party	State	Senate	Comm.
Chr Specter, Arlen	Rep	Penn.	19	19	RM Rockefeller, John D. IV	Dem	W.Va.	15	14
2nd Murkowski, Frank H.	Rep	Alas.	19	18	2nd Graham, D. Robert	Dem	Fla.	13	13
3rd Thurmond, J. Strom	Rep	S.C.	44	28	3rd Akaka, Daniel K.	Dem	Hai.	9	9
4th Jeffords, James M.	Rep	Vt.	11	*1 10	4th Wellstone, Paul D.	DFL	Minn.	9	4
5th Campbell, Ben Nighthorse	Rep	Colo.	7	*2 4	5th Murray, Patty D.	Dem	Wash.	7	2
6th Craig, Larry E.	Rep	Ida.	9	5	6th Miller, Zell B.	Dem	Ga.	1	1
7th Hutchinson, Y. Timothy	Rep	Ark.	3	2					

*1: Member's first period of service on the committee.

*2: Member's second period of service on the committee.

Note: Ranking on this committee for the following member was affected by other chamber service: J. Strom Thurmond (Rep-S.C.), Chair, Armed Services.

Additions:

Minority:

6th Miller, Zell B.	Dem	Ga.	Sept. 12, 2000

VETERANS' AFFAIRS / 107th Congress, Pre-Jeffords switch

Service Dates of Committee Chair: ChT: Jan. 3, 2001-Jan. 25, 2001 Rockefeller (Dem-W.Va.)

Ch1: Jan. 25, 2001-June 6, 2001 Specter (Rep-Penn.)

Service Dates of Majority Members: Jan. 25, 2001-June 6, 2001

Service Dates of Majority Members: Jan. 25, 2001-June 6, 2001

Majority			Years in:		Minority			Years in:	
Rank Name	Party	State	Senate	Comm.	Rank Name	Party	State	Senate	Comm.
Ch1 Specter, Arlen	Rep	Penn.	21	21	RM1 Rockefeller, John D. IV	Dem	W.Va.	17	16
2nd Murkowski, Frank H.	Rep	Alas.	21	20	2nd Graham, D. Robert	Dem	Fla.	15	15
3rd Thurmond, J. Strom	Rep	S.C.	46	30	3rd Akaka, Daniel K.	Dem	Hai.	11	11
4th Jeffords, James M.	Rep	Vt.	13	*1 12	4th Wellstone, Paul D.	DFL	Minn.	11	6
5th Campbell, Ben Nighthorse	Rep	Colo.	9	*2 6	5th Murray, Patty D.	Dem	Wash.	9	5

| 6th Craig, Larry E. | Rep | Ida. | 11 | 7 | 6th Miller, Zell B. | Dem | Ga. | 1 | 1 |
| 7th Hutchinson, Y. Timothy | Rep | Ark. | 5 | 5 | 7th Nelson, E. Benjamin | Dem | Neb. | 1 | 1 |

*1: Member's first period of service on the committee.
*2: Member's second period of service on the committee.

Note 1: The committee majority in the 2001 Senate power-sharing arrangement was determined by the party of the vice president. Democrat Al Gore, Jr. served from Jan. 3, 2001 to Jan. 20, 2001 and was succeeded by Republican Richard B. Cheney on Jan. 20, 2001. When Senator Jeffords of Vermont left the Republican Party, effective June 6, 2001 to become an Independent, Democrats regained the majority for the remainder of the 107th Congress.

Note 2: Ranking on this committee for the following member was affected by other chamber service: J. Strom Thurmond (Rep-S.C.), Chair, Armed Services.

VETERANS' AFFAIRS / 107th Congress, Post-Jeffords switch

Service Dates of Committee Chair: June 6, 2001-Jan. 14, 2003
Service Dates of Majority Members: June 6, 2001-Jan. 14, 2003
Service Dates of Minority Members: June 6, 2001-Jan. 15, 2003

Majority					**Minority**				
			Years in:					Years in:	
Rank Name	Party	State	Senate	Comm.	Rank Name	Party	State	Senate	Comm.
Ch2 Rockefeller, John D. IV	Dem	W.Va.	17	17	RM2 Specter, Arlen	Rep	Penn.	21	21
2nd Graham, D. Robert	Dem	Fla.	15	15	2nd Murkowski, Frank H.	Rep	Alas.	21	21
3rd Jeffords, James M.	Ind.	Vt.	13	*2 1	3rd Thurmond, J. Strom	Rep	S.C.	46	31
4th Akaka, Daniel K.	Dem	Hai.	12	12	4th Campbell, Ben Nighthorse	Rep	Colo.	9	*2 7
5th Wellstone, Paul D.	DFL	Minn.	11	7	5th Craig, Larry E.	Rep	Ida.	11	7
6th Murray, Patty	Dem	Wash.	9	5	6th Hutchinson, Y. Timothy	Rep	Ark.	5	5
7th Miller, Zell B.	Dem	Ga.	1	1	7th Hutchison, Kay Bailey	Rep	Tex.	9	1
8th Nelson, E. Benjamin	Dem	Neb.	1	1					

*2: Member's second period of service on the committee.

Note 1: Democratic members from 3rd through 8th and Republican members from 4th through 6th were reranked July 10, 2001.

Note 2: Ranking on this committee for the following member was affected by other chamber service: J. Strom Thurmond (Rep-S.C.), Ranking Minority Member, Armed Services.

Additions:
  Majority:
    3rd Jeffords, James M.   Ind.   Vt.   July 10, 2001
  Minority;
    7th Hutchison, Kay Bailey   Rep   Tex.   July 25, 2001

Changes:
  Majority:
    Wellstone, Paul D.   DFL   Minn.   Oct. 25, 2002 Died in office
  Minority:
    Jeffords, James M.   Rep   Vt.   June 6, 2001 Seat as a Republican vacated; switched to Independent, remained on committee ranked as 3rd Democrat following Graham

    Hutchison, Kay Bailey   Rep   Tex.   July 25, 2001 Replaced Jeffords
    Murkowski, Frank H.   Rep   Alas.   Dec. 2, 2002 Resigned the Senate; elected Governor

Departures from the Senate:	**Majority**			**Minority**		
Defeated for Re-election	None			Hutchinson, Y. Timothy	Rep	Ark.
Retired	None			Thurmond, J. Strom	Rep	S.C.

VETERANS' AFFAIRS / 108th Congress

Service Dates of Committee Chair: Jan. 14, 2003-Jan. 6, 2005
Service Dates of Majority Members: Jan. 14, 2003-Jan. 6, 2005
Service Dates of Minority Members: Jan. 15, 2003-Jan. 6, 2005

Majority					**Minority**				
			Years in:					Years in:	
Rank Name	Party	State	Senate	Comm.	Rank Name	Party	State	Senate	Comm.
Chr Specter, Arlen	Rep	Penn.	23	23	RM Graham, D. Robert	Dem	Fla.	17	17
2nd Campbell, Ben Nighthorse	Rep	Colo.	11	*2 8	2nd Rockefeller, John D. IV	Dem	W.Va.	19	18

3rd Craig, Larry E.	Rep	Ida.	13	9	
4th Hutchison, Kay Bailey	Rep	Tex.	10	2	
5th Bunning, James P.D.	Rep	Ky.	5	1	
6th Ensign, John E.	Rep	Nev.	3	1	
7th Graham, Lindsey O.	Rep	S.C.	1	1	
8th Murkowski, Lisa	Rep	Alas.	1	1	

3rd Jeffords, James M.	Ind	Vt.	15	*2 2
4th Akaka, Daniel K.	Dem	Hai.	13	13
5th Murray, Patty	Dem	Wash.	11	7
6th Miller, Zell B.	Dem	Ga.	3	3
7th Nelson, E. Benjamin	Dem	Neb.	3	2

*2: Member's second period of service on the committee.

Note: Ranking on this committee for the following member was affected by other chamber service: John D. Rockefeller, IV (Dem-W.Va.), Vice Chair, Select Intelligence.

Departures from the Senate:	Majority			Minority		
Retired	Campbell, Ben Nighthorse	Rep	Colo.	Graham, D. Robert	Dem	Fla.
				Miller, Zell B.	Dem	Ga.

Departures from Committee:						
Moved to Foreign Relations	Murkowski, Lisa	Rep	Alas.	None		
Moved to Commerce, Science, and Transportation and Rules and Administration	None			Nelson, E. Benjamin	Dem	Neb.
No new assignment	Bunning, James P.D.	Rep	Ky.			

VETERANS' AFFAIRS / 109th Congress

Service Dates of Committee Chair: Jan. 6, 2005-Jan. 12, 2007

Service Dates of Majority Members: Jan. 6, 2005-Jan. 12, 2007

Service Dates of Minority Members: Jan. 6, 2005-Jan. 12, 2007

Majority					**Minority**				
			Years in:					Years in:	
Rank Name	Party	State	Senate	Comm.	Rank Name	Party	State	Senate	Comm.
Chr Craig, Larry E.	Rep	Ida.	15	11	RM Akaka, Daniel K.	Dem	Hai.	15	15
2nd Specter, Arlen	Rep	Penn.	25	25	2nd Rockefeller, John D. IV	Dem	W.Va.	21	20
3rd Hutchison, Kay Bailey	Rep	Tex.	12	4	3rd Jeffords, James M.	Ind	Vt.	17	*2 4
4th Graham, Lindsey O.	Rep	S.C.	3	2	4th Murray, Patty	Dem	Wash.	13	8
5th Burr, Richard M.	Rep	N.C.	1	1	5th Obama, Barack	Dem	Ill.	1	1
6th Ensign, John E.	Rep	Nev.	5	2	6th Salazar, Kenneth L.	Dem	Colo.	1	1
7th Thune, John	Rep	S.D.	1	1					
8th Isakson, Johnny	Rep	Ga.	1	1	*2: Member's second period of service on the committee.				

Note: Rankings on this committee for the following members were affected by other chamber service: Arlen Specter (Rep-Penn.), Chair, Judiciary; and John D. Rockefeller, IV (Dem-W.Va.), Vice Chair, Select Intelligence.

Departures from the Senate:	Majority			Minority		
Retired	None			Jeffords, James M.	Ind	Vt.

Departures from Committee:						
Moved to Agriculture, Nutrition, and Forestry and Commerce, Science, and Transportation	Thune, John	Rep	S.D.	None		
Moved to Finance	None			Salazar, Kenneth L.	Dem	Colo.

VETERANS' AFFAIRS / 110th Congress

Service Dates of Committee Chair: Jan. 12, 2007-Jan. 21, 2009

Service Dates of Majority Members: Jan. 12, 2007-Jan. 21, 2009

Service Dates of Minority Members: Jan. 12, 2007-Jan. 21, 2009

Majority					**Minority**				
			Years in:					Years in:	
Rank Name	Party	State	Senate	Comm.	Rank Name	Party	State	Senate	Comm.
Chr Akaka, Daniel K.	Dem	Hai.	17	17	RM Craig, Larry E.	Rep	Ida.	17	13
2nd Rockefeller, John D. IV	Dem	W.Va.	23	22	2nd Specter, Arlen	Rep	Penn.	27	27
3rd Murray, Patty	Dem	Wash.	15	11	3rd Burr, Richard M.	Rep	N.C.	3	3

4th Obama, Barack	Dem	Ill.	3	3		4th Isakson, Johnny	Rep	Ga.	3	3
5th Sanders, Bernard	Ind	Vt.	1	1		5th Graham, Lindsey O.	Rep	S.C.	5	4
6th Brown, Sherrod	Dem	Ohio	1	1		6th Hutchison, Kay Bailey	Rep	Tex.	14	6
7th Webb, James	Dem	Va.	1	1		7th Ensign, John E.	Rep	Nev.	7	4
8th Tester, Jon	Dem	Mont.	1	1						

Note: Rankings on this committee for the following members were affected by other chamber service: John D. Rockefeller, IV (Dem-W.Va.), Chair, Select Intelligence; and Arlen Specter (Rep-Penn.), Ranking Minority Member, Judiciary.

Changes:
  Majority:

Obama, Barack	Dem	Ill.	Nov. 16, 2008 Resigned the Senate; elected President

Minority:

Ensign, John	Rep	Nev.	Jan. 24, 2008 Left committee; moved to Rules and Administration
Wicker, Roger F.	Rep	Miss.	Jan. 24, 2008 Replaced Ensign

Departures from the Senate: **Majority**   **Minority**

Retired	None		Craig, Larry E.	Rep	Ida.

Departures from Committee:

Moved to Banking, Housing, and Urban Affairs	None		Hutchison, Kay Bailey	Rep	Tex.

VETERANS' AFFAIRS / 111th Congress

Service Dates of Committee Chair: Jan. 21, 2009-

Service Dates of Majority Members: Jan. 21, 2009-

Service Dates of Minority Members: Jan. 21, 2009-

Majority						**Minority**				
			Years in:						**Years in:**	
Rank Name	**Party**	**State**	**Senate**	**Comm.**		**Rank Name**	**Party**	**State**	**Senate**	**Comm.**
Chr Akaka, Daniel K.	Dem	Hai.	19	19		RM Burr, Richard M.	Rep	N.C.	5	5
2nd Rockefeller, John D. IV	Dem	W.Va.	25	24		2nd Specter, Arlen	Rep	Penn.	29	29
3rd Murray, Patty	Dem	Wash.	17	13		3rd Isakson, Johnny	Rep	Ga.	5	5
4th Sanders, Bernard	Ind	Vt.	3	3		4th Wicker, Roger F.	Rep	Miss.	2	1
5th Brown, Sherrod	Dem	Ohio	3	3		5th Johanns, Mike	Rep	Neb.	1	1
6th Webb, James	Dem	Va.	3	3		6th Graham, Lindsey O.	Rep	S.C.	7	7
7th Tester, Jon	Dem	Mont.	3	3						
8th Begich, Mark	Dem	Alas.	1	1						
9th Burris, Roland W.	Dem	Ill.	1	1						

Note: Rankings on this committee for the following members were affected by other chamber service: John D. Rockefeller, IV (Dem-W.Va.), Chair, Commerce, Science, and Transportation; and Arlen Specter (Rep-Penn.), Ranking Minority Member, Judiciary.

Additions:
  Majority:

10th Specter, Arlen	Dem	Penn.	May 5, 2009

Changes:
  Minority:

Specter, Arlen	Rep	Penn.	May 5, 2009 Switched from the Republican Party to the Democratic Party and was assigned 10th majority slot with his seniority to be determined at a later date
Brown, Scott P.	Rep	Mass.	Mar. 2, 2010 Minority addition; ranked 5th after Johanns

Part I

B. Select and Special Committees of the Senate

Backgrounds, Jurisdictions, and Rosters
1993-2011

Senate Select and Special Committees
1993-2011

Select and special committees have been in existence since the First Congress. The first House select committee was named on April 2, 1789, to prepare the "Standing Rules and Orders" of the chamber. Its initial fourteen members included such notables as Roger Sherman of Connecticut, James Madison of Virginia, and Elbridge Gerry of Massachusetts. The House's second order of business was to name a select committee "To Bring in a Bill Regulating the Taking of the Constitutional Oath" on April 6, 1789. On that same day, the Senate's first select committee was named "To Prepare the Certificates of Election of the President and the Vice President and to Prepare Letters to George Washington and John Adams." It was a four-member committee with two future Supreme Court justices serving on it—William Paterson of New Jersey and Oliver Ellsworth of Connecticut. Thanks to its select committees, Congress was open for business twenty-four days before President George Washington took the oath of office on April 30, 1789.

Unlike the standing committees of each chamber, whose existence continues from Congress to Congress and whose jurisdictional authority is codified in the formal Rules of each chamber, select and special committees are created for the purpose of gathering information in a specific subject area and reporting the information back to the standing committees for legislative action. Select committees possess the advantage of being chosen from the membership of more than one standing committee and enabling them to address issues that might fall between the jurisdictional cracks of the standing committees. Select committees have been given "oversight" responsibility in their investigative roles, but most often they do not have legislative authority to report legislation. Recent exceptions have been made for the Select Committees on Intelligence in each chamber to have that ability.

Originally, the difference between select and special committees was that select committees were chosen by the chamber's presiding officer, while special committees were selected by the parties and the floor leaders. Over the years, this distinction has become blurred. Now the practice seems to be to use the term "select" for committees that are likely to be renewed by the subsequent Congress, while the term "special" appears to be used for committees that are unlikely to survive the close of business of the Congress in which they are appointed. This distinction gave rise to the recent designations of "permanent select committees" and "temporary select committees."

From 1789 to 1816 the Senate conducted all of its business through select committees, mostly in three-member panels. In the first thirteen Congresses, 1789-1815, the Senate named an average of 164.7 committees per Congress, topping two hundred committees in the 11th-13th Congresses (1809-1815) and peaking at 250 in the 12th Congress (1811-1813). With Speaker of the House Henry Clay (DR-Ky.) leading a vibrant chamber across the Capitol and the Senate engaged in seemingly endless rounds of committee selection,

the Senate finally established a roster of standing committees in 1815, during the 14th Congress.

However, the Senate's establishment of a standing committee system slowed but did not end its propensity to create select and special committees. From the 16th to the 36th Congress, 1817-1861, the average number of Senate select and special committees dropped to 13.3 per Congress with only four of these committees created in the 28th (1843-1845) and 34th Congress (1855-1857).

As secessionist sentiment grew throughout the South and with President-elect Abraham Lincoln's inauguration less than a week away, the Senate of the 36th Congress named its tenth and final select committee, on February 27, 1861, to respond to the "Communication from the Convention of the Twenty-one States of the Confederacy." The committee was terminated the following day. With seven states already gone from the Union and Jefferson Davis named as president of the Confederacy, little was to be accomplished and the nation's bloodiest conflict would soon begin.

During the Civil War and Reconstruction in the 37th to 44th Congresses (1861-1877), the Senate named an average of only 10.25 select and special committees per Congress. Then the Senate's tendency to create these committees reappeared and the next three Congresses—the 45th-47th (1877-1883) saw an average of 24.3 select and special committees named. A counter trend appeared with the Senate's increase in the naming of standing committees and the number of select and special committees declined. By 1883, the Senate shifted to the naming of select and special committees with some degree of congressional continuity, akin to the modern era's use of permanent select committees. The Select Committees on the Construction of the Nicaraguan Canal, the Condition of the Potomac River and Woman Suffrage, were each named to the next eight Congresses, 1883-1899 with the Nicaraguan Canal committee becoming the standing committee on Interoceanic Canals in 1899. The Potomac River and Woman Suffrage committees were named for an additional ten years, 1899-1909, until Woman Suffrage became a standing committee in 1909.

The first decades of the twentieth century saw the Senate continuing to name a handful of select and special committees each Congress, but at a modest pace with its more commonly named ones becoming standing committees, such as Standards, Weights, and Measures (1909), Industrial Expositions (1909), and Relations with the Five Civilized Tribes of Indians (1909). Many of the standing committees that grew out of the selects and specials did not survive the Senate's committee reorganization in 1921.

In the 1940s, with another world war engulfing the nation, the Senate named three select committees that would have later impact. The Senate Select Committee to Investigate Problems of American Small Business, 1940-1946 would eventually become the Senate's Standing Committee on Small Business and Entrepreneurship while the Select

Committee to Investigate Problems Related to the Development, Use, and Control of Atomic Energy, 1945-1946 would be folded into the Joint Committee on Atomic Energy. However, it was the Senate's Committee to Investigate Contracts under the National Defense Program, 1941-1948 that would have the most profound impact upon American politics. U.S. senator Harry S. Truman, then beginning his second term in the Senate, was named chair of this investigating committee. It quickly became known as the "Truman Committee" and the committee's actions in support of President Franklin D. Roosevelt's war efforts were compared favorably to those of Sen. Benjamin F. Wade's (Rep-Ohio) Joint Committee on the Conduct of the War that was seen as hectoring President Abraham Lincoln during the early years of the Civil War. It is said that Confederate commander Robert E. Lee described Wade's Joint Committee as providing him with two divisions during the Civil War.

The "Truman Committee" brought Senator Truman a great deal of positive public notice, and when many Democrats feared that President Roosevelt's failing health would lead to the mystical Vice President Henry A. Wallace becoming president, the cities and the South rallied behind Truman and gained him the vice presidential nomination over Wallace on the second ballot at the 1944 convention. FDR's death in April 1945, three months after his fourth inauguration, placed Truman in the White House, and as potential rival, U.S. senator Carl Hayden (Dem-Ariz.) noted; a "garden variety" senator had just become president of the United States, a fact accomplished by a Senate select committee.

The Senate's 1946 reorganization of its standing committees made select committees an attractive alternative to deal with short-term legislative matters. The post-reorganization Senate continued to make wider use of these committees than does the House, and many of them have been used as launching pads for the presidential ambitions of their chairs.

Examples of the attention-gathering and nomination-producing power of the Senate select and special committees are numerous, especially among Democratic contenders. Harry Truman (Dem-Mo.), the 1944 vice presidential nominee, chaired the Select Committee on the National Defense Program; John Sparkman (Dem-Ala.), the 1952 vice presidential nominee, chaired the Select Committee on Small Business; Estes Kefauver (Dem-Tenn.), the 1956 vice presidential nominee, chaired the Select Committee on Organized Crime in Interstate Commerce; John F. Kennedy (Dem-Mass.), the 1960 presidential nominee, chaired the Select Committee on the Senate Reception Room; Lyndon B. Johnson (Dem-Tex.), the 1960 vice presidential nominee, chaired the Select Committee on Astronautics and Space Exploration; Hubert H. Humphrey Jr. (DFL-Minn.), the 1964 vice presidential nominee, chaired the Special Committee on Disarmament; Eugene J. McCarthy (DFL-Minn.), a 1968 contender, chaired the Select Committee on Unemployment Problems; George McGovern (Dem-S.D.),

the 1972 presidential nominee, chaired the Select Committee on Nutrition and Human Needs; Walter Mondale (DFL-Minn.), the 1976 vice presidential nominee, chaired the Select Committee on Equal Education Opportunity; and Frank Church (Dem-Ida.), a 1976 contender, chaired the Select Committee on Intelligence Activities.

Among Republican contenders, the Senate Select Committee on Presidential Campaign Activities ("Watergate") fueled the presidential ambitions of both Howard H. Baker, Jr. (Rep-Tenn.), its ranking member, and its minority counsel (and future senator), Fred Thompson (Rep-Tenn.), who would seek Republican presidential nominations in 1980 and 2008, respectively. Robert J. Dole (Rep-Kans.), who was defeated for vice president in 1976 and for president in 1996, sought to broaden his base by chairing the Select Committee on Security and Cooperation in Europe (1983-1985). J. Danforth Quayle (Rep-Ind.), the 1988 Republican vice presidential nominee, chaired the second Select Committee to Study the Senate Committee System in 1984. Most recently, Vietnam War veterans John F. Kerry (Dem-Mass.), the 2004 Democratic presidential nominee, and John S. McCain (Rep-Ariz.), the 2008 Republican presidential nominee, were the two most prominent members of the Temporary Senate Select Committee on POW/MIA Affairs, in 1991-1993.

All sixteen senators listed were serious contenders for their party's presidential and vice presidential nominations. Twelve of them received nineteen nominations—ten for vice president and nine for president. While only three of them became president—Truman, Kennedy, and Johnson—all made use of these select and special committees as platforms to further their careers beyond the Senate. In Senate parlance, these were "show horse" committees, unlike the "work horse" standing committees.

Most of these select and special committees had short lives. In spite of this, many had a great impact on the nation. Sen. Estes Kefauver's Special Committee to Investigate Organized Crime in Interstate Commerce, 1950-1951, held the first nationally televised set of congressional committee hearings and demonstrated the power of television to shape the public's awareness of how the Senate worked. Later publicly televised Senate hearings, such as those in the 1954 Army-McCarthy hearings, would be less positively received. Sen. Sam Ervin's (Dem-N.C.) Select Committee on Presidential Campaign Activities, 1973-1974, unraveled the Watergate scandal and led to the resignation of President Nixon. Interestingly, the two Senate select committees that focused most directly on presidential misadventures—Sam Ervin's Watergate committee and the Senate Select Committee to Investigate Secret Military Assistance to Iran and the Nicaraguan Opposition ("Iran-Contra") chaired by Daniel K. Inouye (Dem-Hai.) in 1987 yielded no serious presidential contenders apart from Howard Baker's abortive run in 1980.

SENATE SELECT COMMITTEES AND PRESIDENTIAL POLITICS

Committee Name	Leader	Nomination/Election Outcome
National Defense Program, 1941-1948	Chair Harry Truman (Dem-Mo.)	Elected vice president in 1944
Small Business, 1950-1981	Chair John Sparkman (Dem-Ala.)	Nominated for vice president in 1952
Organized Crime in Interstate Commerce, 1950-1951	Chair Estes Kefauver (Dem-Tenn.)	Nominated for vice president in 1956
Senate Reception Room, 1955-1957	Chair John F. Kennedy (Dem-Mass.)	Elected president in 1960

Space and Astronautics, 1958-1959	Chair Lyndon B. Johnson (Dem-Tex.)	Elected vice president in 1960
Disarmament, 1955-1958	Chair Hubert Humphrey (DFL-Minn.)	Elected vice president in 1964
Unemployment Problems, 1959-1960	Chair Eugene McCarthy (DFL-Minn.)	Contender in 1968
Nutrition and Human Needs, 1968-1977	Chair George McGovern (Dem-S.D.)	Nominated for president in 1972
Equal Education Opportunity, 1970-1972	Chair Walter Mondale (DFL-Minn.)	Elected vice president in 1976
Government Operations with Respect to Intelligence Activities,1975-1976	Chair Frank Church (Dem-Ida.)	Contender in 1976
Presidential Campaign Activities (Watergate), 1973-1974	RM Howard Baker, Jr. (Rep-Tenn.)	Contender in 1980
Presidential Campaign Activities (Watergate), 1973-1974	Counsel Fred Thompson (Rep-Tenn.)	Contender in 2008
Senate Committee System, 1984	Chair J. Danforth Quayle (Rep-Ind.)	Elected vice president in 1988
Security and Cooperation In Europe, 1983-1985	Chair Robert Dole (Rep-Kans.)	Nominated for vice president in 1976 Nominated for president in 1996
POW/MIA Affairs, 1991-1993	Chair John F. Kerry (Dem-Mass.)	Nominated for president in 2004
POW/MIA Affairs, 1991-1993	Min-2nd John McCain (Rep-Ariz.)	Nominated for president in 2008

The Senate continues to make regular use of select and special committees to conduct its business. Four of these committees have acquired quasi-standing status—the Special Committee on Aging from 1961 and the Select Committees on Ethics (1964), Intelligence (1976), and Indian Affairs (1977). The Senate's Committee Reform Amendments of 1977 designated Aging, Ethics, and Intelligence as "permanent select committees," with Indian Affairs receiving that designation in 1984.

Since 1993, only two Senate select committees have been created—the Special Committee to Investigate the Whitewater Development Corporation and Related Matters named in 1995 to investigate allegations that President Bill Clinton and his wife (and future U.S. senator and Secretary of State) Hillary Rodham Clinton had profited unduly from pre-presidential land speculation deals in Arkansas. The committee was short-lived, and it gained insufficient public attention to aid the future presidential aspirations of majority Republican William J. Frist of Tennessee or the four minority Democrats—John F. Kerry of Massachusetts, Christopher J. Dodd of Connecticut, and Carole Moseley Braun and Paul M. Simon of Illinois. Similarly, the Special Committee on the Year 2000 Technology Problem named in 1998 to examine what catastrophes might occur to electronic equipment when the next millennium began in the year 2000 was also short-lived and spawned no presidential contenders.

The present-day Senate seems content to manage its legislative business through its sixteen standing and four permanent select committees and its historic tendency to name multiple select and special committees is of an era long ago consigned to history.

Senate Select and Special Committees 1993-2011

Special Aging

Senate Special Committee on Aging, 103rd-111th Congresses (1993-2011)

BACKGROUND

Organizational History: The Senate Special Committee on Aging was created on February 13, 1961, upon the request of the Labor and Public Welfare's subcommittee on Problems of the Aged and Aging. While there had been interest in such a committee for some time, it was pushed heavily in the 86th Congress (1959-1961) by two members of the subcommittee, Sen. Patrick V. McNamara (Dem-Mich.), a senior member of Labor and Public Welfare, who would be the first chair of Special Aging, and John F. Kennedy (Dem-Mass.), then on the cusp of his successful presidential candidacy. It was they who contended that it had been overwhelmed by amassing "a wealth of information on the subject which is unmatched anywhere," and suggested a coordinated review of the information it had collected, and further study into the problems associated with aging by a special committee devoting itself full-time to the issues.

The Senate's liberal Democrats hoped that the Special Committee would enable them to implement a federal health care plan for the elderly by maneuvering around the opposition of conservative Democrat Harry Flood Byrd of Virginia, who chaired the tax-writing Finance Committee. It succeeded and the committee's research contributed to the passage of the Older Americans Act of 1965 (P.L. 89-73) and the Social Security Amendments of 1965 (Medicare and Medicaid) (P.L. 89-97).

In March 1974 a resolution was introduced to make the special committee a "permanent" one, so that there would not be a need for recreating the committee each year. That effort failed, and during the Senate's committee reorganization meetings in 1976, an effort was made to abolish the committee but it survived albeit with only nine members—its lowest total. It was at that point that Special Aging eliminated its subcommittees, but it was not until the Senate Reorganization Act of 1977, however, that the special committee was given the status of a permanent select committee.

On the House side of the Capitol, it would require a number of efforts to establish a comparable committee on aging. Despite many attempts, it would be almost fourteen years later, in October 1974, before the House of Representatives would establish a counterpart in the House Select Aging Committee. That committee was terminated in 1993 after less than twenty years of existence, while the Senate's Permanent Special Committee on Aging continues to influence legislation for the elderly and the disabled who came under the committee's purview with the passage of the Social Security Amendments of 1972 (P.L. 92-603) that created the Supplemental Security Income (SSI) Program to consolidate existing federal programs for those who are disabled but ineligible for Social Security Disability Insurance.

Over the past four decades, Democratic presidents since Lyndon Johnson have tried to expand health care protections for all Americans based on the Medicare model. President Bill Clinton came close in the 103rd Congress (1993-1995), but his health care reform bill never came out of committee. Democrats on the Senate Special Aging Committee in the 111th Congress were among the leaders in dealing with the public attention that has led to great anxiety among American seniors that their Medicare payments might be adversely impacted by President Obama's recently-passed health care legislation.

Membership: The committee created by Senate Resolution 33 stipulated a membership size of nine and the original members were appointed by Vice President Lyndon Johnson on February 20, 1961. A month later, on March 22, Senate Resolution 111 increased the size substantially to twenty-one members, with a ratio of fourteen Democrats and seven Republicans. The additional twelve members made the special committee second in size only to the Appropriations Committee.

The membership size was changed again on February 17, 1967 (S. Res 20), reducing the number of majority members by one. On January 4, 1973, the size was changed back to twenty-one with a ratio of twelve and nine (S. Res 11), only to be increased again on January 18, 1973, to thirteen and nine (S. Res 20). The committee was increased to fourteen and nine by Senate Resolution 258 on September 19, 1975.

At the time the committee was reorganized in 1977 as a permanent special committee, its size was dramatically reduced to its original size of nine members, with a ratio of six Democrats to three Republicans. At the beginning of the 96th Congress, the size was set at six Democrats and four Republicans, but was increased to seven Democrats and five Republicans by Senate Resolution 101 on March 13, 1979. The committee increased two more times (S. Res 24 on January 19, 1981, and S. Res 338 on February 9, 1984) before settling on the ratio of ten majority and nine minority members for the 98th-101st Congresses (1983-1991). The special committee had eleven Democrats and ten Republicans in the 102nd and 103rd Congresses (1991-1995). The Republican takeover in 1995 dropped the committee's size to nineteen initially in the 104th, but two later additions returned it to twenty-one. It had only eighteen members in the 105th (1997-1999), and at the start of the 106th Congresses (1999-2001), but two late additions brought it back to twenty. In the evenly divided 107th Congress, the committee started with twenty members—ten Democrats and ten Republican—but when Jim Jeffords of Vermont left the Republican Party to become an Independent and was a member of the committee, a twenty-first seat was added to make the committee ratio eleven to ten. It remained at twenty-one in both the 108th and 110th Congresses, but dropped to twenty in the 109th (2005-2007). The Aging Committee opened the 111th Congress, with twenty members and a party ratio of eleven majority to nine minority members. One seat was left vacant owing to the highly contested election in Minnesota between Republican U.S. senator Norm Coleman and his Democratic challenger, Al Franken. With Franken victorious in the recount and another committee member switching from the Republican to the Democratic Party in 2009—Arlen Specter of Pennsylvania—the Aging Committee in the 111th Congress presently has a thirteen to eight party ratio.

With an average of 20.44 members per Congress in the last nine Congresses, 1993-2011, Special Aging is the largest of the non-standing committees in the Senate and it would rank seventh in size among the standing committees. The Special Aging Committee's interCongress retention rate of 84.78 percent is the second-highest among the non-standing committees—behind the 90.99 percent of Indian Affairs—and it would place Aging in the thirteenth slot among the standing committees. While its mean seniority of 9.06 years is the highest among the selects and specials, it would only outrank the sixteenth-place Banking Committee if included among the standing committees. One unusual recent development has been the assignment of very senior members to the committee. In 2003, Theodore F. Stevens (Rep-Alas.) joined the committee in his thirty-fifth year in the Senate and Orrin G. Hatch (Rep-Utah) returned to it in his twenty-seventh Senate year; and in 2007, Arlen Specter (Rep-Penn.) returned to Special Aging in his twenty-seventh year in the Senate.

Committee Leaders: Senator Patrick V. McNamara (Dem-Mich.) was the Senate Aging Committee's first chair. When he assumed the chairmanship of the standing committee on Public Works at the beginning of the 88th Congress, he handed over the top job on Aging to George A. Smathers (Dem-Fla.). Smathers served as chair from 1963 to 1967. Smathers' successor, Harrison A. Williams (Dem-N.J.), served until 1971, when he stepped down to become chair of the standing committee on Labor and Public Welfare. Frank Church (Dem-Ida.) chaired the committee from 1971 until 1979, when he became chair of the Senate Committee on Foreign Relations. Church was succeeded by Lawton Chiles (Dem-Fla.) in 1979.

Minority Leader Everett M. Dirksen of Illinois served as the committee's first ranking minority member. He served in that capacity until his death on September 7, 1969. Winston L. Prouty (Rep-Vt.) took over the position until his death on September 10, 1971. Prouty was succeeded by Hiram L. Fong (Rep-Hai.), who served as ranking minority member from 1971 until his retirement from the Senate in 1977. Pete Domenici (Rep-N.M.) succeeded Fong, serving in the top minority rank in both the 95th and 96th Congresses (1977-1981).

When Republicans gained the Senate majority in 1981, Chiles became ranking minority member and the chair went to John Heinz (Rep-Penn.), the first Republican chair of the special committee. Heinz remained chair until the Democrats regained control of the Senate in 1987, at which time John Melcher (Dem-Mont.) became the chair. When Melcher was defeated for reelection in 1988, David Pryor (Dem-Ark.) succeeded him as chair for the 101st-103rd Congresses (1989-1995).

With the Republican victory in the 1980 elections, Domenici became chair of the Senate Budget Committee, and let the chair of Aging go to John Heinz (Rep-Penn.). Chiles became ranking minority member in the 97th Congress, the first Democratic senator to serve in that capacity. Chiles left that post to John Glenn (Dem-Ohio) in the 98th Congress, to take over as ranking minority member of Budget. Glenn remained the ranking minority member through the 99th Congress. With the Republicans back in the minority in the 100th Congress, John Heinz (Rep-Penn.) was their ranking minority member and remained so until his death on April 4, 1991, when he was succeeded by William S. Cohen (Rep-Me.).

The Republican takeover of the Senate in 1995 led to Senators Cohen and Pryor switching places on Special Aging, with Cohen becoming chair and Pryor becoming ranking member. Both retired in 1996 and Charles E. Grassley (Rep-Iowa) succeeded Cohen as chair and John B. Breaux (Dem-La.) succeeded Pryor as ranking member. They served in those respective roles until 2001, when Grassley left to become chair of Finance. The evenly-divided 107th Congress opened with Larry E. Craig (Rep-Ida.) as chair, with Breaux continuing as ranking member. The Jeffords switch in June, 2001, led to a swap of the top posts between Craig and Breaux. The Republican restoration in the 108th Congress led Senators Craig and Breaux to resume their earlier posts. Breaux retired in 2005 and Craig stepped aside from the chairmanship opening the way for Gordon H. Smith (Rep-Ore.) to become the committee's chair in 2005 and Herbert H. Kohl (Dem-Wisc.) to become its ranking member.

With Democrats regaining the Senate in the 2006 election, Kohl became chair in 2007 and continues to hold that post. Smith became ranking member in 2007, but his defeat for re-election in 2008 led to Melquiades R. (Mel) Martinez of Florida becoming ranking minority member, a post Martinez held until his resignation in September, 2009. His resignation led to Robert Corker (Rep-Tenn.) assuming the post of ranking member for the remainder of the 111th Congress, the third occupant of that slot in three years.

Party Leaders: Five Senate leaders served on Aging—two Democrats and three Republicans. The two Democrats were Edward M. Kennedy (Dem-Mass.), who was a one Congress Democratic whip (1969-1971) and Harry M. Reid (Dem-Nev.), the party's present Majority Floor Leader. Everett McK. Dirksen, who began his leadership career as Republican Whip in 1957 and served as Minority Leader from 1959 until his death in 1969, was the only Republican floor leader with service on the Special Aging Committee. The two other Republican Party leaders to serve on the committee were both Whips—Alan K. Simpson of Wyoming and Donald Nickles of Oklahoma.

Presidential Aspirations: Three of the Democratic members of the Special Aging Committee received vice presidential nominations—Edmund S. Muskie (Dem-Me.) on the 1968 Humphrey ticket; Thomas Eagleton (Dem-Mo.), the initial nominee on the ill-fated 1972 McGovern ticket; and Walter F. Mondale (DFL-Minn.) on the successful 1976 Carter ticket. Both of the Republican presidential nominees who served on the committee came from Arizona, a major destination of "Frostbelt" retirees—Barry M. Goldwater in 1964 and John

S. McCain in 2008. Other presidential hopefuls who failed to gain the nomination were Frank M. Church (Dem-Ida.) in 1976; John H. Glenn (Dem-Ohio) in 1984; William W. Bradley (Dem-N.J.) in 2000; D. Robert Graham (Dem-Fla.) in 2004; and Hillary Rodham Clinton (Dem-N.Y.) in 2008.

Other Notables: Prescott S. Bush (Rep-Conn.), father of George H.W. Bush, the nation's 41st president, and grandfather of George W. Bush, the nation's 43rd president, was on the original roster of the Special Aging Committee. Seven Cabinet members who were alumni of the committee include Republicans William B. Saxbe of Ohio, President Nixon's fourth and final Attorney General; Lamar Alexander of Tennessee, President George H.W. Bush's Secretary of Education; and Mel Martinez, President George H.W. Bush's Secretary of Housing and Urban Development. The other four Cabinet members who served on the committee were two senators from Maine, Democrat Edmund S. Muskie, President Carter's second Secretary of State and Republican William S. Cohen, President Clinton's third Secretary of Defense; and two of President Obama's Cabinet members—Hillary Rodham Clinton of New York, the Secretary of State, and Kenneth L. Salazar of Colorado, the Secretary of the Interior. Sen. Elizabeth H. Dole of North Carolina served on the committee after her Cabinet stints as President Reagan's Secretary of Transportation and George H.W. Bush's Secretary of Labor.

Two Aging Committee members who left the Senate to run for governor were Republican Pete Wilson of California and Democrat Lawton M. Chiles, Jr. of Florida. Also serving on Special Aging from 1971 to 1977 were the nation's first Chinese-descended Senator, Hiram L. Fong (Rep-Hai.) and the first popularly-elected African-American senator, Edward W. Brooke (Rep-Mass.).

Selected References

Halamandaris, Val J., "Aging Committee, Senate Special," in Donald C. Bacon, Roger H. Davidson, and Morton Keller, eds., *The Encyclopedia of the United States Congress* (New York: Simon & Schuster, 1995), I: 17-18.

Halamandaris, Val J., *Profiles in Caring: Advocates for the Elderly.*

Moss, Frank E. and Val J. Halamandaris, *Too Old, Too Sick, Too Bad: Nursing Homes in America* (Germantown. Md.: Aspen Systems, 1977).

U.S. Senate, Committee on Labor and Public Welfare, Subcommittee on the Problems of the Aged and the Aging, *The Aged and Aging in the United States: A National Problem*, 86th Congress, 2nd Session, 1960 (S. Report 86-1121).

RESPONSIBILITIES AND JURISDICTIONAL CHANGES

SPECIAL AGING

Jurisdiction, 1961

From Senate Resolution 33, 87th Congress, First Session, February 13, 1961:

[Section 2]

It shall be the duty of such committee to make a full and complete study and investigation of any and all matters pertaining to problems of older people, including but not limited to, problems of maintaining health, of assuring adequate income, of finding employment, of engaging in productive and rewarding activity, of securing proper housing, and when necessary, care or assistance. No proposed legislation shall be referred to such committee, and such committee shall not have power to report by bill or otherwise have legislative jurisdiction.

PERMANENT SPECIAL AGING

Reorganization, 1977

By authority of Senate Resolution 4, the Committee Systems Reorganization Amendments of 1977, 95th Congress, First Session, the committee became the Permanent Select Committee on Aging.

Jurisdiction, 1977

From Senate Resolution 4, the Committee System Reorganization Amendments of 1977, 95th Congress, First Session, February 4, 1977:

[Section 104]

(b.1)   It shall be the duty of the special committee to conduct a continuing study of any and all matters pertaining to problems and opportunities of older people, including, but not limited to, problems and opportunities of maintaining health, of assuring adequate income, of finding employment, of engaging in productive and rewarding activity, of securing proper housing, and, when necessary, of obtaining care or assistance. No proposed legislation shall be referred to such committee, and such committee shall not have power to report by bill, or otherwise have legislative jurisdiction.

(d)   All records and papers of the temporary special committee on Aging, established by Senate Resolution 33, 87th Congress, are transferred to the Special Committee.

Jurisdiction, 1992

From *Authority and Rules of Senate Committees*, Senate Document 102-6, printed under the authority of Senate Resolution 58 (102-1), agreed to March 13, 1991:

[Section 104]

(b.1)   It shall be the duty of the special committee to conduct a continuing study of any and all matters pertaining to problems and opportunities of older people, including, but not limited to, problems and opportunities of maintaining health, of assuring adequate income, of finding employment, of engaging in productive and rewarding activity, of securing proper housing, and, when necessary, of obtaining care or assistance. No proposed legislation shall be referred to such committee, and such committee shall not have power to report by bill, or otherwise have legislative jurisdiction.

Jurisdiction, 2009-2011

From *Authority and Rules of Senate Committees, 2009-2011*, Sen. Doc. 111-3, pursuant to S. Res, 166, June 2, 2009.

[Section 104]

(b.1)   It shall be the duty of the special committee to conduct a continuing study of any and all matters pertaining to problems and opportunities of older people, including, but not limited to, problems and opportunities of maintaining health, of assuring adequate income, of finding employment, of engaging in productive and rewarding activity, of securing proper housing, and, when necessary, of obtaining care or assistance. No proposed legislation shall be referred to such committee, and such committee shall not have power to report by bill, or otherwise have legislative jurisdiction.

MEMBERSHIP ROSTERS, 103rd-111th Congresses, 1993-2011

SPECIAL AGING / 103rd Congress

Service Dates of Committee Chair: Jan. 21, 1993-Jan. 11, 1995

Service Dates of Majority Members: Jan. 21, 1993-Jan. 11, 1995

Service Dates of Minority Members: Jan. 21, 1993-Jan. 6, 1995

Majority					Minority				
			Years in:					Years in:	
Rank Name	Party	State	Senate	Comm.	Rank Name	Party	State	Senate	Comm.
Chr Pryor, David H.	Dem	Ark.	15	14	RM Cohen, William S.	Rep	Me.	15	14
2nd Glenn, John H. Jr.	Dem	Ohio	19	16	2nd Pressler, Larry L.	Rep	S.D.	15	13
3rd Bradley, William W.	Dem	N.J.	15	14	3rd Grassley, Charles E.	Rep	Iowa	13	13
4th Johnston, J. Bennett Jr.	Dem	La.	21	9	4th Simpson, Alan K.	Rep	Wyo.	15	7
5th Breaux, John B.	Dem	La.	7	7	5th Jeffords, James M.	Rep	Vt.	5	*1 3
6th Shelby, Richard C.	Dem	Ala.	7	7	6th McCain, John S. III	Rep	Ariz.	7	2
7th Reid, Harry M.	Dem	Nev.	7	7	7th Durenberger, David F.	Rep	Minn.	15	*3 3
8th Graham, D. Robert	Dem	Fla.	7	4	8th Craig, Larry E.	Rep	Ida.	3	2
9th Kohl, Herbert H.	Dem	Wisc.	5	4	9th Burns, Conrad	Rep	Mont.	5	*1 2
10th Feingold, Russell D.	Dem	Wisc.	1	1	10th Specter, Arlen	Rep	Penn.	13	*1 2
11th Krueger, Robert C.	Dem	Tex.	1	1					

*1: Member's first period of service on the committee.

*3: Member's third period of service on the committee.

Changes:

Majority:

Krueger, Robert C.	Dem	Tex.	June 14, 1993 Resigned the Senate; defeated in special election by Kay Bailey Hutchison (Rep-Tex.)

Departures from the Senate:

	Majority		Minority		
Retired	None		Durenberger, David F.	Rep	Minn.

Departures from Committee:

	Majority			Minority		
Moved to Finance	Graham, D. Robert	Dem	Fla.	None		
Returned to Select Intelligence as Chair	None			Specter, Arlen	Rep	Penn.
Became Chair of Select Indian Affairs	None			McCain, John S. III	Rep	Ariz.

SPECIAL AGING / 104th Congress

Service Dates of Committee Chair: Jan. 11, 1995-Jan. 9, 1997

Service Dates of Majority Members: Jan. 11, 1995-Jan. 9, 1997

Service Dates of Minority Members: Jan. 6, 1995-Jan. 9, 1997

Majority						Minority				
			Years in:						Years in:	
Rank Name	Party	State	Senate	Comm.		Rank Name	Party	State	Senate	Comm.
Chr Cohen, William S.	Rep	Me.	17	16		RM Pryor, David H.	Dem	Ark.	17	16
2nd Pressler, Larry L.	Rep	S.D.	17	15		2nd Glenn, John H. Jr.	Dem	Ohio	21	18
3rd Grassley, Charles E.	Rep	Iowa	15	14		3rd Bradley, William W.	Dem	N.J.	17	16
4th Simpson, Alan K.	Rep	Wyo.	17	9		4th Johnston, J. Bennett Jr.	Dem	La.	23	11
5th Jeffords, James M.	Rep	Vt.	7	*1 4		5th Breaux, John B.	Dem	La.	9	9
6th Craig, Larry E.	Rep	Ida.	5	4		6th Reid, Harry M.	Dem	Nev.	9	9
7th Burns, Conrad	Rep	Mont.	7	*1 4		7th Kohl, Herbert H.	Dem	Wisc.	7	6
8th Shelby, Richard C.	Rep	Ala.	9	9		8th Feingold, Russell D.	Dem	Wisc.	3	2
9th Santorum, Richard J. (Rick)	Rep	Penn.	1	1		9th Moseley Braun, Carol	Dem	Ill.	3	1
10th Thompson, Fred D.	Rep	Tenn.	1	1						

*1: Member's first period of service on the committee.

Note: Shelby was a member of Special Aging in the 103rd as a Democrat and changed party affiliation on Nov. 9, 1994 to be effective in the 104th Congress.

Additions:
   Majority:
      11th Warner, John W.   Rep   Va.   Mar. 29, 1996
   Minority:
      10th Wyden, Ronald L.   Dem   Ore.   Mar. 29, 1996

Departures from the Senate:	**Majority**			**Minority**		
Defeated for Re-election	Pressler, Larry L.	Rep	S.D.	None		
Retired	Cohen, William S.	Rep	Me.	Pryor, David H.	Dem	Ark.
	Simpson, Alan K.	Rep	Wyo.	Bradley, William W.	Dem	N.J.
				Johnston, J. Bennett Jr.	Dem	La.

Departures from Committee:					
Became Chair of Governmental Affairs	Thompson, Fred D.	Rep	Tenn.	None	

SPECIAL AGING / 105th Congress

Service Dates of Committee Chair: Jan. 9, 1997-Jan. 7, 1999

Service Dates of Majority Members: Jan. 9, 1997-Jan. 7, 1999

Service Dates of Minority Members: Jan. 9, 1997-Jan. 7, 1999

Majority						Minority				
			Years in:						Years in:	
Rank Name	Party	State	Senate	Comm.		Rank Name	Party	State	Senate	Comm.
Chr Grassley, Charles E.	Rep	Iowa	17	17		RM Breaux, John B.	Dem	La.	11	11
2nd Jeffords, James M.	Rep	Vt.	9	*1 6		2nd Glenn, John H. Jr.	Dem	Ohio	23	20
3rd Craig, Larry E.	Rep	Ida.	7	6		3rd Reid, Harry M.	Dem	Nev.	11	11
4th Burns, Conrad	Rep	Mont.	9	*1 6		4th Kohl, Herbert H.	Dem	Wisc.	9	8
5th Shelby, Richard C.	Rep	Ala.	11	11		5th Feingold, Russell D.	Dem	Wisc.	5	4
6th Santorum, Richard J. (Rick)	Rep	Penn.	3	2		6th Moseley Braun, Carol	Dem	Ill.	5	3
7th Warner, John W.	Rep	Va.	19	*2 1		7th Wyden, Ronald L.	Dem	Ore.	2	1
8th Hagel, Charles T. (Chuck)	Rep	Neb.	1	*1 1		8th Reed, John F.	Dem	R.I.	1	1
9th Collins, Susan M.	Rep	Me.	1	1						
10th Enzi, Michael B.	Rep	Wyo.	1	1						

*1: Member's first period of service on the committee.
*2: Member's second period of service on the committee.

Departures from the Senate:	**Majority**		**Minority**		
Defeated for Re-election	None		Moseley Braun, Carol	Dem	Ill.
Retired	None		Glenn, John H. Jr.	Dem	Ohio

Departures from Committee:					
Became Chair of Armed Services	Warner, John W.	Rep	Va.	None	

SPECIAL AGING / 106th Congress

Service Dates of Committee Chair: Jan. 7, 1999-Jan. 3, 2001

Service Dates of Majority Members: Jan. 7, 1999-Jan. 25, 2001

Service Dates of Minority Members: Jan. 7, 1999-Jan. 25, 2001

			Years in:						Years in:	
Majority						**Minority**				
Rank Name	**Party**	**State**	**Senate**	**Comm.**		**Rank Name**	**Party**	**State**	**Senate**	**Comm.**
Chr Grassley, Charles E.	Rep	Iowa	19	19		RM Breaux, John B.	Dem	La.	13	13
2nd Jeffords, James M.	Rep	Vt.	11	*1 8		2nd Reid, Harry M.	Dem	Nev.	13	13
3rd Craig, Larry E.	Rep	Ida.	9	8		3rd Kohl, Herbert H.	Dem	Wisc.	11	10
4th Burns, Conrad	Rep	Mont.	11	*1 8		4th Feingold, Russell D.	Dem	Wisc.	7	6
5th Shelby, Richard C.	Rep	Ala.	13	13		5th Wyden, Ronald L.	Dem	Ore.	4	3
6th Santorum, Richard J. (Rick)	Rep	Penn.	5	4		6th Reed, John F.	Dem	R.I.	3	2
7th Hagel, Charles T. (Chuck)	Rep	Neb.	3	*1 2		7th Bayh, B. Evans	Dem	Ind.	1	1
8th Collins, Susan M.	Rep	Me.	3	2		8th Lincoln, Blanche Lambert	Dem	Ark.	1	1
9th Enzi, Michael B.	Rep	Wyo.	3	2						
10th Bunning, James P.D.	Rep	Ky.	1	1		*1: Member's first period of service on the committee.				

Additions:
  Majority:
    11th Hutchinson, Y. Timothy   Rep   Ark.   Jan. 14, 1999
  Minority:
    9th Bryan, Richard H.   Dem   Nev.   Mar. 2, 1999

Departures from the Senate:	**Majority**			**Minority**		
Retired	None			Bryan, Richard H.	Dem	Nev.

Departures from Committee:	**Majority**			**Minority**		
Became Chair of Finance	Grassley, Charles E.	Rep	Iowa	None		
Moved to Budget and Energy and Natural Resources	Hagel, Charles T. (Chuck)	Rep	Neb.	None		
Moved to Armed Services	Bunning, James P.D.	Rep	Ky.	None		
Moved to Joint Economic	None			Reed, John F.	Dem	R.I.

SPECIAL AGING / 107th Congress, Pre-Jeffords switch

Service Dates of Committee Chair: ChT: Jan. 3, 2001-Jan. 25, 2001 Breaux (Dem-La.)

Ch1: Jan. 25, 2001-June 6, 2001 Craig (Rep-Ida.)

Service Dates of Majority Members: Jan. 25, 2001-June 6, 2001

Service Dates of Minority Members: Jan. 25, 2001-June 6, 2001

			Years in:						Years in:	
Majority						**Minority**				
Rank Name	**Party**	**State**	**Senate**	**Comm.**		**Rank Name**	**Party**	**State**	**Senate**	**Comm.**
Ch1 Craig, Larry E.	Rep	Ida.	11	10		RM1 Breaux, John B.	Dem	La.	15	15
2nd Jeffords, James M.	Rep	Vt.	13	*1 11		2nd Reid, Harry M.	Dem	Nev.	15	15
3rd Burns, Conrad	Rep	Mont.	13	*1 10		3rd Kohl, Herbert H.	Dem	Wisc.	13	12
4th Shelby, Richard C.	Rep	Ala.	15	15		4th Feingold, Russell D.	Dem	Wisc.	9	9
5th Santorum, Richard J. (Rick)	Rep	Penn.	7	7		5th Wyden, Ronald L.	Dem	Ore.	6	5
6th Collins, Susan M.	Rep	Me.	5	5		6th Bayh, B. Evans	Dem	Ind.	3	3
7th Enzi, Michael B.	Rep	Wyo.	5	5		7th Lincoln, Blanche Lambert	Dem	Ark.	3	3
8th Hutchinson, Y. Timothy	Rep	Ark.	5	3		8th Carper, Thomas R.	Dem	Del.	1	1
9th Fitzgerald, Peter G.	Rep	Ill.	3	*1 1		9th Stabenow, Deborah Ann	Dem	Mich.	1	1
10th Ensign, John E.	Rep	Nev.	1	1		10th Carnahan, Jean	Dem	Mo.	1	1

*1: Member's first period of service on the committee.

Note: The committee majority in the 2001 Senate power-sharing arrangement was determined by the party of the vice president. Democrat Al Gore, Jr. served from Jan. 3, 2001 to Jan. 20, 2001 and was succeeded by Republican Richard B. Cheney on Jan. 20, 2001. When Senator Jeffords of Vermont left the Republican Party, effective June 6, 2001 to become an Independent, Democrats regained the majority for the remainder of the 107th Congress.

SPECIAL AGING / 107th Congress, Post-Jeffords switch

Service Dates of Committee Chair: June 6, 2001-Jan. 14, 2003

Service Dates of Majority Members: June 6, 2001-Jan. 14, 2003 Majority members were re-ranked on July 10, 2001

Service Dates of Minority Members: July 24, 2001-Jan. 15, 2003

Majority						Minority				
			Years in:						Years in:	
Rank Name	Party	State	Senate	Comm.		Rank Name	Party	State	Senate	Comm.
Ch2 Breaux, John B.	Dem	La.	15	15		RM2 Craig, Larry E.	Rep	Ida.	11	11
2nd Reid, Harry M.	Dem	Nev.	15	15		2nd Burns, Conrad	Rep	Mont.	13	*1 11
3rd Kohl, Herbert H.	Dem	Wisc.	13	13		3rd Shelby, Richard C.	Rep	Ala.	15	15
4th Jeffords, James M.	Ind	Vt.	13	*2 1		4th Santorum, Richard J. (Rick)	Rep	Penn.	7	7
5th Feingold, Russell D.	Dem	Wisc.	9	9		5th Collins, Susan M.	Rep	Me.	5	5
6th Wyden, Ronald L.	Dem	Ore.	6	6		6th Enzi, Michael B.	Rep	Wyo.	5	5
7th Bayh, B. Evans	Dem	Ind.	3	3		7th Hutchinson, Y. Timothy	Rep	Ark.	6	4
8th Lincoln, Blanche Lambert	Dem	Ark.	3	3		8th Fitzgerald, Peter G.	Rep	Ill.	3	3
9th Carper, Thomas R.	Dem	Del.	1	1		9th Ensign, John E.	Rep	Nev.	1	1
10th Stabenow, Deborah Ann	Dem	Mich.	1	1		10th Hagel, Charles T. (Chuck)	Rep	Neb.	6	*1 1
11th Carnahan, Jean	Dem	Mo.	1	1						

*1: Member's first period of service on the committee.

*2: Member's second period of service on the committee.

Note: Democratic members from 4th through 11th were re-ranked on July 10, 2001 and Republican members from 2nd through 10th were re-ranked on July 24, 2001.

Additions:

Majority:

4th Jeffords, James M.	Ind	Vt.	July 10, 2001

Changes:

Majority:

Carnahan, Jean	Dem	Mo.	Nov, 25, 2002 Resigned the Senate; lost special election to James M. Talent (Rep-Mo.)

Minority:

Jeffords, James M.	Rep	Vt.	June 6, 2001 Seat as a Republican vacated; switched to Independent, remained on committee ranked 4th with Democrat majority
Hagel, Charles T. (Chuck)	Rep	Neb.	July 24, 2001 Replaced Jeffords
Fitzgerald, Peter G.	Rep	Ill.	Apr. 30, 2002 Left committee; no new assignment
Smith, Gordon H.	Rep	Ore.	Apr. 30, 2002 Replaced Fitzgerald

Departures from the Senate:	**Majority**			**Minority**		
Defeated for Re-election	None			Hutchinson, Y. Timothy	Rep	Ark.

Departures from Committee:	**Majority**			**Minority**		
Moved to Budget	None			Burns, Conrad	Rep	Mont.
				Ensign, John E.	Rep	Nev.
Moved to Armed Services, Health, Education, Labor, and Pensions, and Veterans' Affairs	None			Ensign, John E.	Rep	Nev.
Moved to Select Intelligence	None			Hagel, Charles T. (Chuck)	Rep	Neb.

SPECIAL AGING / 108th Congress

Service Dates of Committee Chair: Jan. 14, 2003-Jan. 6, 2005

Service Dates of Majority Members: Jan. 14, 2003-Jan. 6, 2005

Service Dates of Minority Members: Jan. 15, 2003-Jan. 6, 2005

Majority						Minority				
			Years in:						Years in:	
Rank Name	Party	State	Senate	Comm.		Rank Name	Party	State	Senate	Comm.
Chr Craig, Larry E.	Rep	Ida.	13	12		RM Breaux, John B.	Dem	La.	17	17
2nd Shelby, Richard C.	Rep	Ala.	17	17		2nd Reid, Harry M.	Dem	Nev.	17	17
3rd Collins, Susan M.	Rep	Me.	7	7		3rd Kohl, Herbert H.	Dem	Wisc.	15	14
4th Enzi, Michael B.	Rep	Wyo.	7	7		4th Jeffords, James M.	Ind	Vt.	15	*2 2
5th Smith, Gordon H.	Rep	Ore.	7	1		5th Feingold, Russell D.	Dem	Wisc.	11	10
6th Talent, James M.	Rep	Mo.	1	1		6th Wyden, Ronald L.	Dem	Ore.	8	7
7th Fitzgerald, Peter G.	Rep	Ill.	5	*2 1		7th Lincoln, Blanche Lambert	Dem	Ark.	5	5

8th Hatch, Orrin G.	Rep	Utah	27	*1 1		8th Bayh, B. Evans	Dem	Ind.	5	5
9th Dole, Elizabeth Hanford	Rep	N.C.	1	1		9th Carper, Thomas R.	Dem	Del.	3	2
10th Stevens, Theodore F.	Rep	Alas.	35	1		10th Stabenow, Deborah Ann	Dem	Mich.	3	2
11th Santorum, Richard J. (Rick)	Rep	Penn.	9	9						

*2: Member's second period of service on the committee.

Departures from the Senate: Majority, Minority

	Majority			Minority		
Retired	Fitzgerald, Peter G.	Rep	Ill.	Breaux, John B.	Dem	La.

Departures from Committee:

	Majority			Minority		
Elected Minority Leader	None			Reid, Harry M.	Dem	Nev.
Returned to Health, Education, Labor, and Pensions	Hatch, Orrin G.	Rep	Utah	None		
No new assignment	Enzi, Michael B.	Rep	Wyo.	Stabenow, Deborah Ann	Dem	Mich.
	Stevens, Theodore F.	Rep	Alas.			

SPECIAL AGING / 109th Congress

Service Dates of Committee Chair: Jan. 6, 2005-Jan. 12, 2007

Service Dates of Majority Members: Jan. 6, 2005-Jan. 12, 2007

Service Dates of Minority Members: Jan. 6, 2005-Jan. 12, 2007

			Majority	Years in:					Minority	Years in:	
Rank Name	Party	State	Senate	Comm.		Rank Name	Party	State	Senate	Comm.
Chr Smith, Gordon H.	Rep	Ore.	9	3		RM Kohl, Herbert H.	Dem	Wisc.	17	16
2nd Shelby, Richard C.	Rep	Ala.	19	19		2nd Jeffords, James M.	Ind	Vt.	17	*2 4
3rd Collins, Susan M.	Rep	Me.	9	8		3rd Feingold, Russell D.	Dem	Wisc.	13	12
4th Talent, James M.	Rep	Mo.	3	2		4th Wyden, Ronald L.	Dem	Ore.	10	9
5th Dole, Elizabeth Hanford	Rep	N.C.	3	2		5th Lincoln, Blanche Lambert	Dem	Ark.	7	6
6th Martinez, Melquiades R. (Mel)	Rep	Fla.	1	1		6th Bayh, B. Evans	Dem	Ind.	7	6
7th Craig, Larry E.	Rep	Ida.	15	14		7th Carper, Thomas R.	Dem	Del.	5	4
8th Santorum, Richard J. (Rick)	Rep	Penn.	11	10		8th Nelson, C. William (Bill)	Dem	Fla.	5	1
9th Burns, Conrad	Rep	Mont.	17	*2 1		9th Clinton, Hillary Rodham	Dem	N.Y.	5	1
10th Alexander, Lamar	Rep	Tenn.	3	1						
11th DeMint, James W.	Rep	S.C.	1	1						

*2: Member's second period of service on the committee.

Changes:

Minority:

Feingold, Russell D.	Dem	Wisc.	Jan. 18, 2006 Left committee; moved to Select Intelligence
Salazar, Kenneth L.	Dem	Colo.	Jan. 18, 2006 Replaced Feingold

Departures from the Senate:

	Majority			Minority		
Defeated for Re-election	Talent, James M.	Rep	Mo.	None		
	Santorum, Richard J. (Rick)	Rep	Penn.			
	Burns, Conrad	Rep	Mont.			
Retired	None			Jeffords, James M.	Ind	Vt.

Departures from Committee:

	Majority			Minority		
Moved to Appropriations, Environment and Public Works, and Rules and Administration	Alexander, Lamar	Rep	Tenn.	None		
Moved to Foreign Relations	DeMint, James W.	Rep	S.C.	None		

SPECIAL AGING / 110th Congress

Service Dates of Committee Chair: Jan. 12, 2007-Jan. 21, 2009

Service Dates of Majority Members: Jan. 12, 2007-Jan. 21, 2009

Service Dates of Minority Members: Jan. 12, 2007-Jan. 21, 2009

			Majority	Years in:					Minority	Years in:	
Rank Name	Party	State	Senate	Comm.		Rank Name	Party	State	Senate	Comm.
Chr Kohl, Herbert H.	Dem	Wisc.	19	18		RM Smith, Gordon H.	Rep	Ore.	11	5
2nd Wyden, Ronald L.	Dem	Ore.	12	11		2nd Shelby, Richard C.	Rep	Ala.	21	21

3rd Lincoln, Blanche Lambert	Dem	Ark.	9	9
4th Bayh, B. Evans	Dem	Ind.	9	9
5th Carper, Thomas R.	Dem	Del.	7	6
6th Nelson, C. William (Bill)	Dem	Fla.	7	3
7th Clinton, Hillary Rodham	Dem	N.Y.	7	3
8th Salazar, Kenneth L.	Dem	Colo.	3	1
9th Casey, Robert P. Jr.	Dem	Penn.	1	1
10th McCaskill, Claire	Dem	Mo.	1	1
11th Whitehouse, Sheldon	Dem	R.I.	1	1

3rd Collins, Susan M.	Rep	Me.	11	11
4th Martinez, Melquiades R. (Mel)	Rep	Fla.	3	3
5th Craig, Larry E.	Rep	Ida.	17	16
6th Dole, Elizabeth Hanford	Rep	N.C.	5	4
7th Coleman, Norman	Rep	Minn.	5	1
8th Vitter, David	Rep	La.	3	1
9th Corker, Robert	Rep	Tenn.	1	1
10th Specter, Arlen	Rep	Penn.	27	*2 1

*2: Member's second period of service on the committee.

Departures from the Senate:	Majority			Minority		
Defeated for Re-election	None			Smith, Gordon H.	Rep	Ore.
				Dole, Elizabeth Hanford	Rep	N.C.
				Coleman, Norman	Rep	Minn.
Retired	None			Craig, Larry E.	Rep	Ida.

Departures from Committee:						
Moved to Finance	Carper, Thomas R.	Dem	Del.	None		
Moved to Armed Services and Banking, Housing, and Urban Affairs	None			Vitter, David	Rep	La.

Note: Hillary Rodham Clinton (Dem-N.Y.) resigned the Senate on Jan. 21, 2009; named Secretary of State. Kenneth L. Salazar (Dem-Colo) resigned the Senate on Jan. 20, 2009; named Secretary of the Interior.

SPECIAL AGING / 111th Congress

Service Dates of Committee Chair: Jan. 21, 2009-

Service Dates of Majority Members: Jan. 21, 2009-

Service Dates of Minority Members: Jan. 21, 2009-

Majority

Rank Name	Party	State	Years in: Senate	Years in: Comm.
Chr Kohl, Herbert H.	Dem	Wisc.	21	20
2nd Wyden, Ronald L.	Dem	Ore.	14	13
3rd Lincoln, Blanche Lambert	Dem	Ark.	11	11
4th Bayh, B. Evans	Dem	Ind.	11	11
5th Nelson, C. William (Bill)	Dem	Fla.	9	5
6th Casey, Robert P. Jr.	Dem	Penn.	3	3
7th McCaskill, Claire	Dem	Mo.	3	3
8th Whitehouse, Sheldon	Dem	R.I.	3	3
9th Udall, Mark	Dem	Colo.	1	1
10th Bennet, Michael F.	Dem	Colo.	1	1
11th Gillibrand, Kirsten E.	Dem	N.Y.	1	1

Minority

Rank Name	Party	State	Years in: Senate	Years in: Comm.
RM1 Martinez, Melquiades R. (Mel)	Rep	Fla.	5	5
2nd Shelby, Richard C.	Rep	Ala.	23	23
3rd Collins, Susan M.	Rep	Me.	13	13
4th Specter, Arlen	Rep	Penn.	29	*2 3
5th RM2 Corker, Robert	Rep	Tenn.	3	3
6th Hatch, Orrin G.	Rep	Utah	31	*2 1
7th Brownback, Sam D.	Rep	Kans.	13	1
8th Graham, Lindsey O.	Rep	S.C.	7	1
9th Chambliss, Saxby	Rep	Ga.	7	1

*2: Member's second period of service on the committee.

Filled Vacancies:

  Majority:
    10th and 11th seats by Bennet and Gillibrand on Jan. 27, 2009
  Minority:
    9th seat by Chambliss on July 21, 2009

Additions:

  Majority:

12th Specter, Arlen	Dem	Penn	May 5, 2009
13th Franken, Al	DFL	Minn	July 7, 2009

Changes:

  Minority:

Specter, Arlen	Rep	Penn.	May 5, 2009 Switched from the Republican Party to the Democratic Party and was placed in the 12th Majority slot with his seniority to be determined at a later date
Martinez, Melquiades R. (Mel)	Rep	Fla.	Sept. 22, 2009 Resigned the Senate
Corker, Robert	Rep	Tenn.	Sept. 22, 2009 Succeeded Martinez as Ranking Member
LeMieux, George S.	Rep	Fla.	Sept. 22, 2009 Replaced Martinez, ranked following Hatch

Select Ethics

Senate Permanent Select Committee on Ethics, 103rd-111th Congresses (1993-2011)

BACKGROUND

Organizational History: No less a source than the United States Constitution confers on each House of Congress the power to punish and expel its Members. Article I provides that: "Each House may determine the Rules of its Proceedings, punish its Members for disorderly Behavior, and, with the Concurrence of two thirds, expel a Member."

As in the case of any institution where power and money flow freely, scandal is bound to arise. The Senate's first foray into the financial misconduct of one of its members led to the expulsion of U.S. senator William Blount of Tennessee in 1797. A land speculator, Blount's financial difficulties led him to concoct an invasion of Spanish Florida and Louisiana with frontiersmen aided by Creek and Cherokee Indians to secure those lands and transfer them to Great Britain. When the plot was revealed, he was impeached by the House and the Senate voted to expel him, but no Senate trial occurred since he had already been expelled.

During the years prior to the 1913 passage of the Seventeenth Amendment, the senators were selected by the state legislatures. Consequently, allegations of vote buying in the legislatures led to a number of senators being challenged for their seats, including Marcus A. Hanna (Rep-Ohio), the mastermind of William McKinley's 1896 presidential victory. The passage of the amendment lessened the frequency of these charges, but it did not end the accusations of vote buying, as was clear in the 1918 Michigan contest between the two industrialists Democrat Henry Ford and Republican Truman H. Newberry.

In the post-reorganization Senate, two select committees were named in 1956 to investigate bribery charges against lobbyists. The first was created on February 6, 1956, and focused on a natural gas lobbyist's efforts to bribe Sen. Francis Case (Rep-S.D.) while the second committee was formed on February 22, 1956, and broadened the investigation and called for the improvement and modernization of the Federal Corrupt Practices Act of 1925 (P.L. 68-506), the Hatch Act of 1939 (P.L. 76-252), and the Federal Regulation of Lobbying Act of 1946 (P.L. 79-601). Both committees have an equal number of Democrats and Republicans on them, a practice that would be continued in the creation of subsequent ethics committees.

The triggering event for the creation of a regularly appointed Senate Ethics Committee involved Bobby Baker, the Secretary to the Senate Majority and a protégé of newly-installed President Lyndon Johnson. Baker resigned his job in the Senate at the end of 1963 in order to avoid answering questions regarding his finances and issues of conflict of interest. Shortly thereafter, Baker and other Senate staff became the subject of a highly controversial and partisan investigation by the Senate Rules Committee. Concluding its business in March over the vehement objections of committee Republicans, a report was issued that, while accusing Baker of "gross

improprieties," fell short of a full-scale indictment. Republicans called the investigation a "whitewash." Under pressure, the investigation of Baker was resumed, but partisan politics continued to dominate.

B. Everett Jordan (Dem-N.C.), chair of the Rules and Administration committee, introduced Senate Resolution 338 on July 1, 1964. As originally introduced, this resolution gave Jordan's committee the jurisdiction "to investigate every alleged violation of the rules of the Senate, and to make appropriate findings of fact and conclusions with respect thereto after according to any individual concerned due notice and opportunity for hearing." Not satisfied with Rules and Administration's handling of the Bobby Baker case, John Sherman Cooper (Rep-Ky.), one of the three minority members of the Rules and Administration committee, introduced an amendment to Jordan's resolution. It proposed the creation of a six-member select committee made up of equal numbers of Democrats and Republicans named by the vice president and responsible for investigating allegations of rules violations and recommending appropriate disciplinary action. Cooper's amendment passed the Senate by a vote of 61 to 19 on July 24, 1964.

It took a year to name the membership of the Select Committee on Standards and Conduct. John C. Stennis (Dem-Miss.), who had voted against its creation, was nonetheless chosen to chair the six-member committee. Wallace F. Bennett (Rep-Utah) served as the committee's initial ranking minority member.

The committee's first major investigation involved charges of campaign fund misuse and double-billing for travel by Thomas J. Dodd (Dem-Conn.). Dodd's censure on both counts was recommended by the committee, but the Senate agreed only to the first on June 23, 1967 by a vote of 92-5. In the following year, the Senate created its first formal Code of Conduct, which would be later amended in 1977.

After the passage of the Senate Committee Reorganization Amendments of 1977 (Sen. Res. 4) the committee was renamed the Senate Permanent Select Committee on Ethics and its six members—three majority and three minority—were to be chosen by the full Senate, at the beginning of each Congress, as with the standing committees.

Although it was the House whose members were more implicated in the "Abscam" scandal of 1979-1980, in which FBI agents dressed as oil-rich Arab sheiks tried to bribe members of Congress, one senator, Harrison A. (Pete) Williams (Dem-N.J.) was caught in the web, convicted in 1980, and chose to resign in 1982 shortly before the Senate was about to vote on his expulsion from that body.

The committee was especially burdened in the 101st Congress (1989-1991) by charges against five senators known as "the Keating Five"—John H. Glenn Jr. (Dem-Ohio), Alan Cranston (Dem-Cal.), Donald W. Riegle (Dem-Mich.), Dennis DeConcini (Dem-Ariz.), and John McCain (Rep-Ariz.). They had been identified as having had financial dealings with

Charles Keating, the owner of a failed savings and loan operation. During the 102nd Congress, on August 2, 1991, Senate Resolution 169 provided that members of the select committee for the 101st Congress would continue their inquiry into an investigation of the "Keating Five." All other business of the committee would be handled by the members named to the committee for the 102nd Congress. David Pryor (Dem-Ark.), who had left the committee in May of 1991, rejoined the committee investigation of the "Keating Five" on September 10, 1991. According to S. Res. 169, Jeff Bingaman (Dem-N.M.), who had replaced Pryor in May, was not to be involved with the "Keating Five" investigation. The committee's report on the matter was filed on November 20, 1991. Only Cranston was censured for his relationship with Keating.

The most serious misconduct issue of the post-1993 Senate that came before the Ethics Committee involved U.S. senator Robert W. Packwood (Rep-Ore.), whose Senate career ended with his resignation on September 7, 1995, after twenty-nine women reported unwanted sexual advances by Packwood. Most were reported by lobbyists and former staffers. The Ethics Committee unanimously recommended his expulsion from the Senate, but his resignation forestalled that effort.

Sen. Larry Craig (Rep-Ida.) was admonished by the Senate Ethics Committee on February 13, 2008, after he had been arrested for allegedly soliciting sex from an undercover policeman in a Minneapolis airport. His "improper conduct" reflected "discreditably" on the United States Senate. Furthermore, the committee criticized Craig for using campaign funds to cover his legal fees in the solicitation case, a violation of the **Senate Code of Ethics**. Craig retired from the Senate in 2009.

Unlike the House, where financial misdeeds appear to be more common, the only serious post-1993 Senate financial scandal implicated one-time Senate President **pro tem** Theodore Stevens (Rep-Alas.), who was convicted on seven counts of bribery and tax evasion on October 27, 2008, just prior to the 2008 election. He lost his re-election bid, but President Obama's new Attorney General Eric Holder dismissed the charges when he learned that the Justice Department had illegally withheld evidence from defense counsel.

Membership: The original Senate Select Committee on Standards and Conduct had six members—three majority and three minority members with the senior minority member designated as vice chair named on July 9, 1965. This was its size and party ratio during the twelve years that it existed, prior to the passage of the 1977 Committee Reform Amendments.

After the passage of the Committee Systems Reorganization Amendments of 1977, the members were to be chosen by the full Senate, at the beginning of each Congress, as with the standing committees. New provisions were added stipulating that no member could serve for more than three continuous Congresses (a rule that appeared to be seldom enforced), and that as much as possible, membership should be made up of equal parts first-term, second-term, and third- or higher-term Senators.

None of the six members of Select Standards and Conduct was named to the new Select Ethics Committee. The new slate of members assigned to the Select Ethics named in February of 1977 was headed by Adlai E. Stevenson III (Dem-Ill.) as chair, and Harrison Schmitt (Rep-N.M.), in his first year as a senator, as vice chair. The committee's size and party ratio has remained constant at three majority members

and three minority members throughout its history as both the Select Committee on Standards and Conduct and the Permanent Select Committee on Ethics.

Committee Leaders: The first chair of the Senate Select Committee on Standards and Conduct in the 89th Congress (1965-1967) was John C. Stennis (Dem-Miss.) and the committee's first vice chair was Wallace F. Bennett (Rep-Utah). Both Senators Stennis and Bennett remained in their respective roles from 1965 to 1974. Stennis, who had become chair of Armed Services in 1969, stepped aside as chair in 1974 and was replaced by Howard W. Cannon (Dem-Nev.), who would remain in that post until the 1977 reorganization. Bennett resigned the Senate on December 20, 1974, and was succeeded as vice chair by Carl T. Curtis (Rep-Neb.).

Senators Stevenson and Schmitt left the committee on October 31, 1979, and were replaced by Howell T. Heflin (Dem-Ala.) and Malcolm Wallop (Rep-Wyo.), respectively. With the Republican Senate victory in 1980, Wallop became chair and Heflin became vice chair in the 97th Congress (1981-1983). Wallop left the committee in 1983 and was replaced as chair by Theodore F. Stevens (Rep-Alas.), who left in 1985 for the Rules and Administration Committee. Stevens was replaced by Warren B. Rudman (Rep-N.H.).

Heflin served as vice chair from 1979 to 1987 and became chair of Select Ethics, when the Democrats regained control of the Senate in 1986. Rudman became vice chair in 1987 and he and Heflin had to preside over the difficult "Keating Five" investigation. While Heflin remained on the committee through the committee's November 20, 1991, final report on the "Keating Five," Rudman continued on as vice chair through the end of the 102nd Congress (1991-1993) and his retirement from the Senate.

Richard H. Bryan (Dem-Nev.) and A. Mitchell (Mitch) McConnell (Rep-Ky.) became the new chair and vice chair respectively of Select Ethics in 1993 and swapped those titles when the Senate Republicans took power in the 104th Congress (1995-1997). Bryan left the committee in January 1996 and was succeeded as vice chair by Byron L. Dorgan (Dem-N.D.). In 1997, McConnell left Ethics for Labor and Human Resources while Dorgan moved to the Appropriations Committee.

In 1997, Robert C. Smith (Rep-N.H.) became the committee's new chair and Harry M. Reid (Dem-Nev.) its new vice chair. Smith stepped aside as chair in November 1999, when he replaced the late John H. Chafee (Rep-R.I.) as chair of the Environment and Public Works Committee. Smith was replaced as chair by C. Patrick Roberts (Rep-Kans.)

Senators Roberts and Reid would be the two senior members of Select Ethics during the confusing set of events in the evenly-divided 107th Congress. Because majority status in the Senate was determined by the party identity of the vice president, Reid was chair and Roberts was vice chair from January 3 to January 20, 2001, when Democrat Albert Gore, Jr. was vice president, and then had their roles reversed when Republican Richard B. Cheney was sworn as vice president on January 20, 2001. Reid and Roberts would resume their earlier roles when Vermont's James M. Jeffords left the Republican Party in June, 2001 to become an Independent and returned control of the Senate to the Democrats.

The Republican victory in the 2002 congressional elections gave them control of the 108th Congress and Roberts stepped aside for George V. Voinovich (Rep-Ohio), who then became chair and served in that post until he left the committee in 2007. Reid served on Select Ethics until 2005 and his election as Minority Floor Leader. Reid was succeeded by Timothy P. Johnson (Dem-S.D.).

With Democrats regaining control of the Senate in the 2006 election, Johnson was slated to become chair of Select Ethics but a debilitating stroke, from which he would recover, led the Senate to choose Barbara Boxer (Dem-Cal.) to become Acting Chair from January 12, 2007, until March 31, 2008, when the "Acting" designation was removed. Senator Boxer continued as chair in the 111th Congress (2009-2011). John Cornyn (Rep-Tex.) became vice chair in the 110th Congress until his departure in 2009 for the Finance Committee. Cornyn's successor in the 111th Congress (2009-2011) was Johnny Isakson (Rep-Ga.).

Party Leaders: As an internal affairs committee, it is not surprising that so many of its members would assume leadership posts within the Senate. Seven leaders served on Select Ethics, four of whom were Democrats—Democratic floor leader Thomas A. Daschle (Dem-S.D.) and party whip Russell B. Long (Dem-La.), and both of the present Democratic leaders, Harry M. Reid (Dem-Nev.) and Democratic Whip Richard J. Durbin. The three Republican leaders who saw service on Ethics were former whip Theodore F. Stevens (Rep-Alas.) and C. Trent Lott (Rep-Miss.) and A. Mitchell (Mitch) McConnell (Rep-Ky.), both of whom served as both party floor leader and whip.

Presidential Aspirations: Ethics is not a committee that has drawn the interest of presidential hopefuls. Thomas F. Eagleton (Dem-Mo.), the short-lived vice presidential nominee on George S. McGovern's disastrous 1972 Democratic ticket served on the committee, as did Eugene J. McCarthy (DFL-Minn.), who challenged President Lyndon B. Johnson's renomination in 1968.

Other Notables: Former governor of Connecticut and President John F. Kennedy's first Secretary of Health, Education, and Welfare, Abraham A. Ribicoff, served on Ethics. as did John G. Tower (Rep-Tex.), who was appointed Secretary of Defense by President George H. W. Bush in 1989,

only to be defeated for confirmation. Tower's service on Ethics was interrupted in February 28, 1978, by allegations of his involvement in the "Koreagate" bribery scandal of lobbyist Tongsun Park. The charges against Tower were quickly dismissed and he resumed service on Ethics only to leave the committee for Rules and Administration in 1979. Kenneth L. Salazar, who served on Ethics in the 110th Congress (2007-2009), was named Secretary of the Interior by President Barack Obama in 2009.

Selected References

Amer, Mildred, *The Senate Select Committee on Ethics: A Brief History of Its Evolution and Jurisdiction,* Congressional Research Service, The Library of Congress (March 17, 1993).

Amer, Mildred, *History of Congressional Ethics Enforcement*, Congressional Research Service, The Library of Congress (February 18, 1993).

Baker, Richard A. *Representation and Responsibility, Exploring Legislative Ethics, The History of Congressional Ethics* (New York, Plenum Press, 1985).

Butler, Anne M. and Wendy Wolf, *United States Senate Election, Expulsion and Censure Cases 1793–1990* (Washington, D.C.: U.S. Senate Historical Office, 1995).

Davidson, Michael, Morgan J. Frankel and Claire M. Sylvia, *Two periods—1787 to 1873 and 1951 to 1977—In the Development of Legal and Ethical Constraints on the Conduct of Members of the Senate, With Particular Emphasis on Conflicts of Interest and Unwritten Standards of Conduct*, (March 1991).

Douglas, Paul, *Ethics in Government* (Cambridge: Harvard University Press, 1952).

Maskell, Jack, *Expulsion and Censure Actions Taken by the Full Senate Against Members*, Congressional Research Service, The Library of Congress (October 3, 1990, revised September 17, 1993).

RESPONSIBILITIES AND JURISDICTIONAL CHANGES

STANDARDS AND CONDUCT

Jurisdiction, 1964

From Senate Resolution 338, as amended, 88th Congress, Second Session, July 24, 1964

[Section 2]

(a) It shall be the duty of the select committee to:

    (1) receive complaints and investigate allegations of improper conduct which may reflect upon the Senate, violations of law, and violations of rules and regulations of the Senate, relating to the conduct of individuals in the performance of their duties as Members of the Senate, or as officers or employees of the Senate, and to make appropriate findings of fact and conclusions with respect thereto;

    (2) recommend to the Senate by report or resolution by a majority vote of the full committee disciplinary action to be taken with respect to such violations which the select committee shall determine, after according to the individuals concerned due notice and opportunity for hearing, to have occurred;

    (3) recommend to the Senate, by report or resolution, such additional rules or regulations as the select committee shall determine to be necessary or desirable to insure proper standards of conduct by Members of the Senate, and by officers or employees of the Senate, in the performance of their duties and the discharge of their responsibilities; and

    (4) report violations by a majority vote of the full committee of any law to the proper Federal and State authorities.

(b) The Select Committee from time to time shall transmit to the Senate its recommendation as to any legislative measures which it may consider to be necessary for the effective discharge of its duties.

SELECT ETHICS (Permanent)

By authority of Senate Resolution 4, the Committee Systems Reorganization Amendments of 1977, 95th Congress, First Session, the committee became the Permanent Select Committee on Ethics on February 4, 1977.

Jurisdiction, 102nd Congress (1991-1993)

From *Authority and Rules of Senate Committees*, Senate Document 102-6, printed under the authority of Senate Resolution 58 (102-1), agreed to March 13, 1991:

[Section 2 (a)]

It shall be the duty of the Select Committee to—

    (1) receive complaints and investigate allegations of improper conduct which may reflect upon the Senate, violations of law, violations of the Senate Code of official Conduct and violations of rules and regulations of the Senate, relating to the conduct of individuals in the performance of their duties as Members of the Senate, or as officers or employees of the Senate, and to make appropriate findings of fact and conclusions with respect thereto;

    (2) recommend to the Senate by report or resolution by a majority vote of the full committee disciplinary action (including, but not limited to, in the case of a Member: censure, expulsion, or recommendation to the appropriate party conference regarding such Member's seniority or positions of responsibility; and in the case of an officer or employee: suspension or dismissal) to be taken with respect to such violations which the Select Committee shall determine, after according to the individuals concerned due notice and opportunity for hearing to have occurred.

    (3) recommend to the Senate, by report or resolution, such additional rules or regulations as the Select Committee shall determine to be necessary or desirable to insure proper standards of conduct by Members of the Senate, and by officers or employees of the Senate, in the performance of their duties and the discharge of their responsibilities; and

    (4) report violations by a majority vote of the full committee of any law to the proper Federal and State authorities.

SELECT ETHICS (Permanent)
Jurisdiction, 111th Congress (2009-2011)

From *Authority and Rules of Senate Committees, 2009-2011*, Sen. Doc. 111-3, pursuant to S. Res, 166, June 2, 2009.

[Section 2 (a)]

It shall be the duty of the Select Committee to—

    (1) receive complaints and investigate allegations of improper conduct which may reflect upon the Senate, violations of law, violations of the Senate Code of official Conduct and violations of rules and regulations of the Senate, relating to the conduct of individuals in the performance of their duties as Members of the Senate, or as officers or employees of the Senate, and to make appropriate findings of fact and conclusions with respect thereto;

(2) (A) recommend to the Senate by report or resolution by a majority vote of the full committee disciplinary action taken with respect to such violations which the select committee shall determine, after according to the individual concerned due notice and opportunity for a hearing to have occurred;

   (B) pursuant to subparagraph (A) recommend discipline, including—

   (i) in the case of a Member, a recommendation to the Senate for expulsion, censure, payment of restitution, recommendation to a Member's party conference regarding such Member's seniority or positions of responsibility, or a combination of these; and

   (ii) in the case of an officer or employee, dismissal, suspension, payment of restitution, or a combination of these;

(3) subject to the provisions of subsection (e), by a unanimous vote of 6 members, order that a Member, officer, or employee be reprimanded or pay restitution, or both, if the Select Committee determines, after according to the Member, officer, or employee due notice and opportunity for a hearing that misconduct occurred warranting discipline less serious than discipline by the full Senate;

(4) in the circumstances described in subsection(d)(3) issue a public or private letter of admonition to a Member, officer, or employee, which shall not be subject to appeal to the Senate;

(5) recommend to the Senate, by report or resolution, such additional rules or regulations as the Select Committee shall determine to be necessary or desirable to insure proper standards of conduct by Members of the Senate, and by officers or employees of the Senate, in the performance of their duties and the discharge of their responsibilities;

(6) by a majority vote of the full committee, report violations of any law, including the provision of false information to the Select Committee to the proper Federal and State authorities; and

(7) develop and implement programs and designed to educate Members, officers, and employees about the laws, rules, regulations, and standards applicable to such individuals in the performance of their duties.

MEMBERSHIP ROSTERS, 103rd-111th Congresses, 1993-2011

SELECT ETHICS / 103rd Congress

Service Dates of Committee Chair: Jan. 26, 1993-Jan. 11, 1995

Service Dates of Majority Members: Jan. 26, 1993-Jan. 11, 1995

Service Dates of Minority Members: Jan. 26, 1993-Jan. 11, 1995

			Majority						Minority	
			Years in:						**Years in:**	
Rank Name	**Party**	**State**	**Senate**	**Comm.**		**Rank Name**	**Party**	**State**	**Senate**	**Comm.**
Chr Bryan, Richard H.	Dem	Nev.	5	2		VCh McConnell, A. Mitchell (Mitch)	Rep	Ky.	9	1
2nd Mikulski, Barbara A.	Dem	Md.	7	1		2nd Stevens, Theodore F.	Rep	Alas.	25	*2 1
3rd Daschle, Thomas A.	Dem	S.D.	7	1		3rd Smith, Robert C.	Rep	N.H.	3	1

*2: Member's second period of service on the committee.

Changes:
   Minority:

Stevens, Theodore F.	Rep	Alas.	May 19, 1993 Left committee; no new assignment	
Craig, Larry E.	Rep	Ida.	May 19, 1993 Replaced Stevens	

Departures from Committee:	**Majority**			**Minority**
Elected Minority Leader	Daschle, Thomas A.	Dem	S.D.	None

SELECT ETHICS / 104th Congress

Service Dates of Committee Chair: Jan. 11, 1995-Jan. 9, 1997

Service Dates of Majority Members: Jan. 11, 1995-Jan. 9, 1997

Service Dates of Minority Members: Jan. 11, 1995-Jan. 9, 1997

			Majority						Minority	
			Years in:						**Years in:**	
Rank Name	**Party**	**State**	**Senate**	**Comm.**		**Rank Name**	**Party**	**State**	**Senate**	**Comm.**
Chr McConnell, A. Mitchell (Mitch)	Rep	Ky.	11	2		VC1 Bryan, Richard H.	Dem	Nev.	7	4
2nd Smith, Robert C.	Rep	N.H.	5	2		2nd Mikulski, Barbara A.	Dem	Md.	9	2
3rd Craig, Larry E.	Rep	Ida.	5	2		VCh2 3rd Dorgan, Byron L.	Dem	N.D.	3	1

Changes:

Vice Chair:

VC1 Bryan, Richard H.	Dem	Nev.	Jan. 23, 1996 Left committee; no new assignment
VC2 Dorgan, Byron L.	Dem	N.D.	Jan. 23, 1996 Succeeded Bryan as Vice Chair

Minority:

Bryan, Richard H.	Dem	Nev.	Jan. 23, 1996 Left committee; no new assignment
Mikulski, Barbara A.	Dem	Md.	Jan. 23, 1996 Left committee; no new assignment
Reid, Harry M.	Dem	Nev.	Jan. 23, 1996 Replaced Bryan
Murray, Patty	Dem	Wash.	Jan. 23, 1996 Replaced Mikulski

Departures from Committee:

	Majority			Minority		
Moved to Labor and Human Resources and Joint Printing	McConnell, A. Mitchell (Mitch)	Rep	Ky.	None		
Moved to Appropriations	Craig, Larry E.	Rep	Ida.	Dorgan, Byron L.	Dem	N.D.

SELECT ETHICS / 105th Congress

Service Dates of Committee Chair: Jan. 9, 1997-Jan. 7, 1999

Service Dates of Majority Members: Jan. 9, 1997-Jan. 7, 1999

Service Dates of Minority Members: Jan. 9, 1997-Jan. 7, 1999

Majority			Years in:		Minority			Years in:	
Rank Name	Party	State	Senate	Comm.	Rank Name	Party	State	Senate	Comm.
Chr Smith, Robert C.	Rep	N.H.	7	4	VCh Reid, Harry M.	Dem	Nev.	11	1
2nd Roberts, C. Patrick	Rep	Kans.	1	1	2nd Murray, Patty	Dem	Wash.	5	1
3rd Sessions, Jefferson B. III	Rep	Ala.	1	1	3rd Conrad, Kent	Dem	N.D.	11	1

Departures from Committee:

	Majority			Minority		
Moved to Armed Services and Labor and Human Resources	Sessions, Jefferson B. III	Rep	Ala.	None		
No new assignment	None			Murray, Patty	Dem	Wash.

SELECT ETHICS / 106th Congress

Service Dates of Committee Chair: Ch1: Jan. 7, 1999-Nov. 9, 1999, Smith (Rep-N.H.)

Ch2: Nov. 9, 1999-Jan. 3, 2001, Roberts (Rep-Kans.)

Service Dates of Majority Members: Jan. 7, 1999-Jan. 25, 2001

Service Dates of Minority Members: Jan. 7, 1999-Jan. 25, 2001

Majority			Years in:		Minority			Years in:	
Rank Name	Party	State	Senate	Comm.	Rank Name	Party	State	Senate	Comm.
Ch1 Smith, Robert C.	Rep	N.H.	9	6	VCh Reid, Harry M.	Dem	Nev.	13	2
Ch2 Roberts, C. Patrick	Rep	Kans.	3	2	2nd Conrad, Kent	Dem	N.D.	13	3
3rd Voinovich, George V.	Rep	Ohio	1	1	3rd Durbin, Richard J.	Dem	Ill.	3	1

Changes:

Chair:

Ch1 Smith, Robert C.	Rep	N.H.	Nov. 9, 1999 Re-ranked behind Roberts; became Chair of Environment and Public Works
Ch2 Roberts, C. Patrick	Rep	Kans.	Nov. 9, 1999 Succeeded Smith as Chair

Departures from Committee:

	Majority			Minority		
Became Ranking Member on Budget	None			Conrad, Kent	Dem	N.D.
Moved to Judiciary and Select Intelligence	None			Durbin, Richard J.	Dem	Ill.
No new assignment	Smith, Robert C.	Rep	N.H.			

SELECT ETHICS / 107th Congress, Pre-Jeffords switch

Service Dates of Committee Chair: ChT: Jan. 3, 2001-Jan. 25, 2001 Reid (Dem-Nev.)

Ch1: Jan. 25, 2001-June 6, 2001 Roberts (Rep-Kans.)

Service Dates of Majority Members: Jan. 25, 2001-June 6, 2001

Service Dates of Minority Members: Jan. 25, 2001-June 6, 2001

| | | | Majority | | | | | | Minority | | |
Rank Name	Party	State	Senate	Comm.		Rank Name	Party	State	Senate	Comm.
Ch1 Roberts, C. Patrick	Rep	Kans.	5	5		VC1 Reid, Harry M.	Dem	Nev.	15	5
2nd Voinovich, George V.	Rep	Ohio	3	3		2nd Akaka, Daniel K.	Dem	Hai.	11	1
3rd Thomas, Craig L.	Rep	Wyo.	7	1		3rd Lincoln, Blanche Lambert	Dem	Ark.	3	1

Note: The committee majority in the 2001 Senate power-sharing arrangement was determined by the party of the vice president. Democrat Al Gore, Jr. served from Jan. 3, 2001 to Jan. 20, 2001 and was succeeded by Republican Richard B. Cheney on Jan. 20, 2001. When Senator Jeffords of Vermont left the Republican Party, effective June 6, 2001 to become an Independent, Democrats regained the majority for the remainder of the 107th Congress.

SELECT ETHICS / 107th Congress, Post-Jeffords switch

Service Dates of Committee Chair: June 6, 2001-Jan. 14, 2003

Service Dates of Majority Members: June 6, 2001-Jan. 14, 2003

Service Dates of Minority Members: June 6, 2001-Jan. 15, 2003

| | | | Majority | | | | | | Minority | | |
Rank Name	Party	State	Senate	Comm.		Rank Name	Party	State	Senate	Comm.
Ch2 Reid, Harry M.	Dem	Nev.	15	5		VC2 Roberts, C. Patrick	Rep	Kans.	5	5
2nd Akaka, Daniel K.	Dem	Hai.	12	1		2nd Voinovich, George V.	Rep	Ohio	3	3
3rd Lincoln, Blanche Lambert	Dem	Ark.	3	1		3rd Thomas, Craig L.	Rep	Wyo.	7	1

SELECT ETHICS / 108th Congress

Service Dates of Committee Chair: Jan. 14, 2003-Jan. 6, 2005

Service Dates of Majority Members: Jan. 14, 2003-Jan. 6, 2005

Service Dates of Minority Members: Jan. 14, 2003-Jan. 6, 2005

| | | | Majority | | | | | | Minority | | |
Rank Name	Party	State	Senate	Comm.		Rank Name	Party	State	Senate	Comm.
Chr Voinovich, George V.	Rep	Ohio	5	5		VCh Reid, Harry M.	Dem	Nev.	17	7
2nd Roberts, C. Patrick	Rep	Kans.	7	7		2nd Akaka, Daniel K.	Dem	Hai.	13	2
3rd Thomas, Craig L.	Rep	Wyo.	9	2		3rd Lincoln, Blanche Lambert	Dem	Ark.	5	2

Departures from Committee:	Majority				Minority			
Elected Minority Leader	None				Reid, Harry M.	Dem	Nev.	
No new assignment	None				Lincoln, Blanche Lambert	Dem	Ark.	

SELECT ETHICS / 109th Congress

Service Dates of Committee Chair: Jan. 6, 2005-Jan. 12, 2007

Service Dates of Majority Members: Jan. 6, 2005-Jan. 12, 2007

Service Dates of Minority Members: Jan. 6, 2005-Jan. 12, 2007

| | | | Majority | | | | | | Minority | | |
Rank Name	Party	State	Senate	Comm.		Rank Name	Party	State	Senate	Comm.
Chr Voinovich, George V.	Rep	Ohio	7	6		VCh Johnson, Timothy P.	Dem	S.D.	9	1
2nd Roberts, C. Patrick	Rep	Kans.	9	8		2nd Akaka, Daniel K.	Dem	Hai.	15	4
3rd Thomas, Craig L.	Rep	Wyo.	11	4		3rd Pryor, Mark	Dem	Ark.	3	1

Changes:

Minority:

Akaka, Daniel K.	Dem	Hai.	Jan. 18, 2006 Left committee; no new assignment
Salazar, Kenneth L.	Dem	Colo.	Jan. 18, 2006 Replaced Akaka

Departures from Committee:

	Majority			**Minority**
No new assignment	Voinovich, George V.	Rep	Ohio	None

SELECT ETHICS / 110th Congress

Service Dates of Committee Chair: Jan. 12, 2007-Jan. 21, 2009

Service Dates of Majority Members: Jan. 12, 2007-Jan. 21, 2009

Service Dates of Minority Members: Jan. 12, 2007-Jan. 21, 2009

Majority					**Minority**				
			Years in:					Years in:	
Rank Name	Party	State	Senate	Comm.	Rank Name	Party	State	Senate	Comm.
Ch1 Johnson, Timothy P.	Dem	S.D.	11	3	VCh Cornyn, John	Rep	Tex.	5	1
ChA Boxer, Barbara	Dem	Cal.	15	1	2nd Roberts, C. Patrick	Rep	Kans.	11	11
3rd Pryor, Mark	Dem	Ark.	5	3	3rd Thomas, Craig L.	Rep	Wyo.	13	6
4th Salazar, Kenneth L.	Dem	Colo.	3	1					

Changes:

Majority:

Johnson, Timothy P.	Dem	S.D.	Jan. 12, 2007 Due to Senator Johnson's incapacity, Senator Barbara Boxer (Dem-Cal.) was named as Acting Chair. A further modification was made on Mar. 31, 2008 when the "Acting" designation was removed.

Minority:

Thomas, Craig L.	Rep	Wyo.	June 4, 2007 Died in office
Isakson, Johnny	Rep	Ga.	June 13, 2007 Replaced Thomas

Departures from Committee:

	Majority			**Minority**		
Moved to Finance	None			Cornyn, John	Rep	Tex.
No new assignment	Johnson, Timothy P.	Dem	S.D.	None		

Note: Kenneth L Salazar (Dem-Colo.) resigned the Senate; Jan. 20, 2009; appointed Secretary of the Interior.

SELECT ETHICS / 111th Congress

Service Dates of Committee Chair: Jan. 21, 2009-

Service Dates of Majority Members: Jan. 21, 2009-

Service Dates of Minority Members: Jan. 21, 2009-

Majority					**Minority**				
			Years in:					Years in:	
Rank Name	Party	State	Senate	Comm.	Rank Name	Party	State	Senate	Comm.
Chr Boxer, Barbara	Dem	Cal.	17	3	VCh Isakson, Johnny	Rep	Ga.	5	2
2nd Pryor, Mark	Dem	Ark.	7	5	2nd Roberts, C. Patrick	Rep	Kans.	13	13
3rd Brown, Sherrod	Dem	Ohio	3	1	3rd Risch, James	Rep	Ida.	1	1

Indian Affairs

Senate Committee on Indian Affairs, 103rd-111th Congresses (1993-2011)

BACKGROUND

Organizational History: The Senate's first committee dealing with Indian Affairs was created following a resolution introduced by Sen. Walter Leake (DR-Miss.) on January 3, 1820. It was a standing committee and had been preceded by the Select Committee on the Extinguishment of Indian Title to Certain Lands (1818). The best-known select committees dealing with Indian-related matters were the Select Committee on Relations with the Five Civilized Tribes of Indians, a select committee from 1887 to 1909 and a standing committee from 1909 to 1921; and the Select Committee on Indian Depredations, a select committee from 1889 to 1893 that became a standing committee in 1893. Both committees were abolished in 1921.

From 1907 to 1913, both native American senators served on the standing Committee on Indian Affairs—Republican Charles Curtis of Kansas, whose mother was three-quarters' Native American, of ethnic Kaw, Osage, and Pottawatomie ancestry, spent his childhood living with his maternal grandparents on their Kaw reservation and Democrat Robert L. Owen of Oklahoma, the son of a Cherokee-descended mother. Owen had been a federal agent for the Five Civilized Tribes—the Cherokee, the Chickasaw, the Choctaw, the Creek, and the Seminole tribes. While Owen would retire from the Senate in 1925, Curtis would be chosen Senate Majority Floor Leader that year and then be elected as Herbert Hoover's vice presidential running-mate in 1928. He remains the nation's only native American vice president.

The standing committee on Indian Affairs was regularly named from 1820 until the 1946 Reorganization Act when it was folded into the Public Lands Committee. That committee was renamed Interior and Insular Affairs in 1948; and again as Energy and Natural Resources in 1977, its present designation.

Until the creation of the Select Committee on Indian Affairs in 1977, the only congressional committee wholly committed to Indian issues was the Joint Committee on Navaho-Hopi Indian Administration created in 1950 that was generally populated by members from Arizona and New Mexico. The committee seldom met, no chairs or ranking members were regularly identified, and it was terminated in 1973.

In the opening days of the 95th Congress (1977-1979), the Senate was busy considering Senate Resolution 4, which was to implement the most significant overhaul in the Senate's committee structure since the Legislative Reorganization Act of 1946. A product of the Select Committee on Committees, Senate Resolution 4 was referred to the Rules and Administration Committee, where it underwent significant changes. One of these changes involved the proposed creation of a select committee on Indian Affairs to operate during the 95th Congress only. The Rules committee report on S. Res 4 indicates that the primary impetus for the new committee was the

imminent completion of a study by the American Indian Policy Review Commission (comprised of members of both houses of Congress, as well as representatives from American Indian tribes) recommending various changes in Federal law relating to Native Americans.

Insisting that the select committee would be abolished at the end of 1978, the Rules Committee wanted a single committee to review all proposed legislation stemming from the Commission's analysis, and report back to the Senate its own recommendations. Without such a committee, legislation would be reviewed by as many as five Senate subcommittees with jurisdiction over Indian affairs. The measure was accepted by the Senate and included in the Reorganization Amendments of 1977, which passed February 4, 1977.

It became clear as the 95th Congress progressed, that there was a continuing need for concentrated oversight of Indian affairs. The committee was regularly extended until the Senate voted to give the select committee permanent status when it agreed to Senate Resolution 127 (98-2) on June 6, 1984. Two previous attempts to make the select committee permanent had been rejected.

Its major organizational changes occurred in the early 1990s, when its membership was increased from eight to sixteen in 1991, then to eighteen in 1993, and "Select" was removed from its title. However, in the last eight issues of the **Congressional Directory** it was only listed among the standing committees in the 103rd and 108th Congresses, but it was listed in the section devoted to Senate Select and Special Committees in the 104th-107th and 109th and 110th Congresses.

As contained in the *Senate Manual:*

The Committee was established as the Select Committee on Indian Affairs. Section 25 of S. Res. 71, 103d Cong., 1st Sess., redesignated it as the Committee on Indian Affairs.

(a)(1) There is established a Select Committee on Indian Affairs (hereafter in this section referred to as the "select committee") which shall consist of [eighteen] Members, [ten] to be appointed by the President of the Senate, upon the recommendation of the majority leader, from among Members of the majority party and [eight] to be appointed by the President of the Senate, upon the recommendation of the minority leader, from among the Members of the minority party. The select committee shall select a Chairman from among its Members.

Since 1993, the major focus of the committee has been the Indian Health Care Improvement Reauthorization and Extension Act. Authored by the chair of the Indian Affairs Committee, Byron L. Dorgan (Dem-N.D.), who will retire at the end of 2010, the bill strengthens and improves health care for 1.9 million American Indians and Native Alaskans. It was approved in 2010 as part of President Obama's overall health care bill. The Jack Abramoff scandal that targeted Indian gaming casinos as major revenue sources grazed the committee, but none of its members were implicated,

Membership: The party ratio on this committee began at 3:2 for the 95th and 96th Congresses (1977-1981). It grew to seven in the 97th and 98th Congresses (1981-1985) and to nine in the 99th (1985-1987), then to eight in the 100th and 101st Congresses (1987-1991). Its membership doubled in 1991 to sixteen members with a majority-minority ratio of 9:7. It peaked at seventeen in the 103rd and 104th Congresses (1993-1997). Since then the committee's size has varied between fifteen and fourteen. Since 1993, it has averaged 14.5 members over the last nine Congresses. Its mean seniority of 13.08 years and its mean retention rate of 91.0 percent are the highest among the Senate's regularly appointed select committees. Were it to be included among the standing committees, Indian Affairs would rank fifth in mean seniority and sixth in its mean interCongress retention rate.

Committee Leaders: The initial Select Committee on Indian Affairs named on February 11, 1977, was led by James G. Abourezk (Dem-S.D.) as chair and Dewey F. Bartlett (Rep-Okla.) as ranking minority member in the 95th Congress. Both Abourezk and Bartlett retired in 1979 and were succeeded as chair by John Melcher (Dem-Mont.) and William L. Armstrong (Rep-Colo.) as ranking member respectively.

The Republican takeover of the Senate in the wake of Ronald Reagan's 1980 victory placed William S. Cohen (Rep-Me.) in the post of chair while Melcher became the committee's ranking member for the next three Congresses, 1981-1987. Cohen left Indian Affairs for the Intelligence Committee and Mark Andrews (Rep-N.D.) replaced him as chair. Andrews was defeated in 1986 when Democrats regained control of the Senate.

With Democrats once again organizing the Senate, Daniel K. Inouye (Dem-Alas.) who joined the committee in 1979 became its senior Democrat for the first time in 1987. He would serve as chair from 1987 to 1995 and from July, 2001 to 2003 and as vice chair from 1995 to July, 2001 and again from 2003 to 2005. After eighteen years as the committee's senior Democrat, Inouye stepped aside for Byron L Dorgan (Dem-N.D.) who served in that capacity from 2005 until 2011—two years as vice chair, 2005-2007, and four years as chair, 2007-2011, until his retirement from the Senate.

When the Democrats regained the Senate in 1987, Daniel J. Evans (Rep-Wash.) became the committee's vice chair and served until his 1989 retirement. At that time, John S. McCain (Rep-Ariz.) became the committee's senior Republican, serving as vice chair from 1987 to 1995 and as chair from 1995 to 1997.

Following the Republican takeover of the Senate in 1995, Ben Nighthorse Campbell of Colorado, who was originally elected to the Senate as a Democrat, changed his party affiliation to Republican and a seat on Indian Affairs was vacated for him. Campbell is of Cheyenne descent on his father's side

and he became chair of Indian Affairs in 1997 and served as the committee's senior Republican as chair and vice chair until his retirement in 2005. McCain resumed the chair in the 109th Congress (2005-2007) but stepped aside in 2007 as Craig L. Thomas (Rep-Wyo.) became vice chair in the Democratic-dominated 110th Congress. Thomas' death in June 2007, led to Lisa Murkowski (Rep-Alas.) becoming vice chair for the remainder of the 110th Congress. Her father, Frank H. Murkowski, had served on the committee from 1983 until his resignation in 2002 after his election as Governor of Alaska. In 2009, Ms. Murkowski stepped aside and John A. Barrasso (Rep-Wyo.) who was elected to fill the Thomas vacancy, became vice chair in the 111th Congress (2009-2011).

Party Leaders: Because of the regional nature of the committee's focus, the only Senate party leaders to have served on Indian Affairs came from states with large Native American populations. They include Democratic leaders—Thomas A. Daschle of South Dakota, 1995-2005, and Harry M. Reid of Nevada who served as Daschle's whip, 1999-2005, and is now Democratic floor leader, 2005-date. The only Republican leader with Indian Affairs service was Donald L. Nickles of Oklahoma, who became Republican whip in June, 1996 when Majority Leader Robert J. Dole (Rep-Kans.) left the Senate to contest for the presidency and was succeeded as leader by Republican Whip C. Trent Lott (Rep-Miss.). Nickles served as whip under Lott from 1996 until 2003 and under William H. Frist (Rep-Tenn.), who succeeded Lott as leader in 2003. Nickles served under Frist until his own retirement in 2005.

Presidential Aspirations: None of the Democratic members on Indian Affairs made it to the presidential sweepstakes but both of the Arizona Republican senators who were nominated for president—Barry M. Goldwater, the 1964 nominee, and John S. McCain, the 2008 nominee, were long-time members of the Indian Affairs Committee.

Other Notables: Cabinet experience among Indian Affairs Committee members has been limited to William S. Cohen, President Bill Clinton's third Secretary of Defense, and Mike Johanns (Rep-Neb.), President George W. Bush's Secretary of Agriculture, 2005-2007, a post he assumed after serving as Governor of Nebraska, from 1999 to 2005. Two Republican governors served on Indian Affairs in its first Congress, 1977-1979—Dewey F. Bartlett of Oklahoma and Mark O. Hatfield of Oregon, while one recent member, Frank H. Murkowski, left the committee and the Senate in 2002 to become governor of Alaska.

Selected References

Bee, Robert L., *The Politics of American Indian Policy* (Cambridge, Mass.: Schenckman Publishing, 1982).

Henriksson, Markku, *The Indian on Capitol Hill: Indian Legislation and the American Congress, 1862-1907* (Helsinki: Societas Historica Finlandie, 1988).

Tyler, S. Lyman, *A History of Indian Policy* (Washington, D.C.: U.S. Department of Interior, Bureau of Indian Affairs, 1973).

RESPONSIBILITIES AND JURISDICTIONAL CHANGES

SELECT INDIAN AFFAIRS

Jurisdiction, 1977

From Senate Resolution 4, 95th Congress, First Session, February 4, 1977:

[Section 105.(b)(2)]

It shall be the duty of the select committee to conduct a study of any and all matters pertaining to problems and opportunities of Indians, including but not limited to, Indian land management and trust responsibilities, Indian education, health, special services, and loan programs, and Indian claims against the United States.

SELECT INDIAN AFFAIRS (Permanent)

Reorganization, 1984

The Select Committee was made a Permanent Select Committee by authority of Senate Resolution 127 (98-2) agreed to June 6, 1984.

Jurisdiction, 102nd Congress (1991-1993)

From *Authority and Rules of Senate Committees*, Senate Document 102-6, printed under the authority of Senate Resolution 58 (102-1), agreed to March 13, 1991:

[Section 2]

It shall be the duty of the select committee to conduct a study of any and all matters pertaining to problems and opportunities of Indians, including but not limited to, Indian land management and trust responsibilities, Indian education, health, special services, and loan programs, and Indian claims against the United States.

INDIAN AFFAIRS

The Committee was established as the Select Committee on Indian Affairs. Section 25 of S. Res. 71, 103d Cong., 1st Sess., redesignates it as the Committee on Indian Affairs.

Jurisdiction, 111th Congress (2009-2011)

From *Authority and Rules of Senate Committees, 2009-2011*, Sen. Doc. 111-3, pursuant to S. Res, 166, June 2, 2009.

(2) It shall be the duty of the select committee to conduct a study of any and all matters pertaining to problems and opportunities of Indians, including but not limited to, Indian land management and trust responsibilities, Indian education, health, special services, and loan programs, and Indian claims against the United States.

MEMBERSHIP ROSTERS, 103rd-111th Congresses, 1993-2011

INDIAN AFFAIRS / 103rd Congress

Service Dates of Committee Chair: Jan. 5, 1993-Jan. 11, 1995

Service Dates of Majority Members: Jan. 5, 1993-Jan. 11, 1995

Service Dates of Minority Members: Jan. 5, 1993-Jan. 9, 1995

Majority					Minority				
			Years in:					Years in:	
Rank Name	Party	State	Senate	Comm.	Rank Name	Party	State	Senate	Comm.
Chr Inouye, Daniel K.	Dem	Hai.	31	14	VCh McCain, John S. III	Rep	Ariz.	7	6
2nd DeConcini, Dennis W.	Dem	Ariz.	17	14	2nd Murkowski, Frank H.	Rep	Alas.	13	11
3rd Daschle, Thomas A.	Dem	S.D.	7	6	3rd Cochran, W. Thad	Rep	Miss.	15	4
4th Reid, Harry M.	Dem	Nev.	7	4	4th Gorton, T. Slade III	Rep	Wash.	11	*2 4
5th Simon, Paul M.	Dem	Ill.	9	2	5th Domenici, Pete V.	Rep	N.M.	21	2
6th Akaka, Daniel K.	Dem	Hai.	3	2	6th Kassebaum, Nancy Landon	Rep	Kans.	15	2
7th Wellstone, Paul D.	DFL	Minn.	3	2	7th Nickles, Donald L.	Rep	Okla.	13	2

| 8th Dorgan, Byron, L. | Dem | N.D. | 1 | 1 |
| 9th Campbell, Ben Nighthorse | Dem | Colo. | 1 | *1 1 |

| 8th Hatfield, Mark O. | Rep | Ore. | 27 | *2 1 |

*2: Member's second period of service on the committee.

Vacancies Filled:
  Majority:
    8th and 9th seats filled by Dorgan and Campbell on Jan. 21, 1993
  Minority:
    8th seat filled by Hatfield on Feb. 2, 1993

Departures from the Senate:	**Majority**			**Minority**		
Retired	DeConcini, Dennis W.	Dem	Ariz.	None		

Departures from Committee:						
Became Chair of Appropriations	None			Hatfield, Mark O.	Rep	Ore.
Elected Minority Leader	Daschle, Thomas A.	Dem	S.D.	None		
Moved to Joint Library and Joint Printing	None			Cochran, W. Thad	Rep	Miss.

INDIAN AFFAIRS / 104th Congress

Service Dates of Committee Chair: Jan. 11, 1995-Jan. 9, 1997

Service Dates of Majority Members: Jan. 11, 1995-Jan. 9, 1997

Service Dates of Minority Members: Jan. 9, 1995-Jan. 9, 1997

Majority			**Years in:**		**Minority**			**Years in:**	
Rank Name	**Party**	**State**	**Senate**	**Comm.**	**Rank Name**	**Party**	**State**	**Senate**	**Comm.**
Chr McCain, John S. III	Rep	Ariz.	9	9	VCh Inouye, Daniel K.	Dem	Hai.	33	16
2nd Murkowski, Frank H.	Rep	Alas.	15	13	2nd Conrad, Kent	Dem	N.D.	9	*2 1
3rd Gorton, T. Slade III	Rep	Wash.	13	*2 6	3rd Reid, Harry M.	Dem	Nev.	9	6
4th Domenici, Pete V.	Rep	N.M.	23	4	4th Simon, Paul M.	Dem	Ill.	11	4
5th Kassebaum, Nancy Landon	Rep	Kans.	17	4	5th Akaka, Daniel K.	Dem	Hai.	5	4
6th Nickles, Donald L.	Rep	Okla.	15	4	6th Wellstone, Paul D.	DFL	Minn.	5	4
7th Thomas, Craig L.	Rep	Wyo.	1	1	7th Dorgan, Byron, L.	Dem	N.D.	3	2
8th Hatch, Orrin G.	Rep	Utah	19	1	8th Campbell, Ben Nighthorse	Dem	Colo.	3	*1 2
9th Coverdell, Paul	Rep	Ga.	3	1					

*1: Member's first period of service on the committee.

*2: Member's second period of service on the committee.

Changes:
  Majority:

| Coverdell, Paul | Rep | Ga. | Mar. 24, 1995 Left committee to open seat for Campbell |
| Campbell, Ben Nighthorse | Rep | Colo. | Mar. 24, 1995 Replaced Coverdell |

  Minority:

| Campbell, Ben Nighthorse | Rep | Colo. | Mar. 3, 1995 Seat as a Democrat vacated; remained on committee as a Republican ranking after Nickles |

Departures from the Senate:	**Majority**			**Minority**		
Retired	Kassebaum, Nancy Landon	Rep	Kans.	Simon, Paul M.	Dem	Ill.

Departures from Committee:						
Moved to Governmental Affairs	Nickles, Donald L.	Rep	Okla.	None		

INDIAN AFFAIRS / 105th Congress

Service Dates of Committee Chair: Jan. 9, 1997-Jan. 7, 1999

Service Dates of Majority Members: Jan. 9, 1997-Jan. 7, 1999

Service Dates of Minority Members: Jan. 9, 1997-Jan. 7, 1999

Majority			**Years in:**		**Minority**			**Years in:**	
Rank Name	**Party**	**State**	**Senate**	**Comm.**	**Rank Name**	**Party**	**State**	**Senate**	**Comm.**
Chr Campbell, Ben Nighthorse	Rep	Colo.	5	*2 2	VCh Inouye, Daniel K.	Dem	Hai.	35	18
2nd Murkowski, Frank H.	Rep	Alas.	17	15	2nd Conrad, Kent	Dem	N.D.	11	*2 3
3rd McCain, John S. III	Rep	Ariz.	11	11	3rd Reid, Harry M.	Dem	Nev.	11	8

Rank Name	Party	State	Senate	Comm.
4th Gorton, T. Slade III	Rep	Wash.	15	*2 8
5th Domenici, Pete V.	Rep	N.M.	25	6
6th Thomas, Craig L.	Rep	Wyo.	3	2
7th Hatch, Orrin G.	Rep	Utah	21	2
8th Inhofe, James M.	Rep	Okla.	3	1

Rank Name	Party	State	Senate	Comm.
4th Akaka, Daniel K.	Dem	Hai.	7	6
5th Wellstone, Paul D.	DFL	Minn.	7	6
6th Dorgan, Byron, L.	Dem	N.D.	5	4

*2: Member's second period of service on the committee.

INDIAN AFFAIRS / 106th Congress

Service Dates of Committee Chair: Jan. 7, 1999-Jan. 3, 2001

Service Dates of Majority Members: Jan. 7, 1999-Jan. 25, 2001

Service Dates of Minority Members: Jan. 7, 1999-Jan. 25, 2001

Majority

Rank Name	Party	State	Senate	Comm.
Chr Campbell, Ben Nighthorse	Rep	Colo.	7	*2 4
2nd Murkowski, Frank H.	Rep	Alas.	19	17
3rd McCain, John S. III	Rep	Ariz.	13	13
4th Gorton, T. Slade III	Rep	Wash.	17	*2 10
5th Domenici, Pete V.	Rep	N.M.	27	8
6th Thomas, Craig L.	Rep	Wyo.	5	4
7th Hatch, Orrin G.	Rep	Utah	23	4
8th Inhofe, James M.	Rep	Okla.	5	3

Minority

Rank Name	Party	State	Senate	Comm.
VCh Inouye, Daniel K.	Dem	Hai.	37	20
2nd Conrad, Kent	Dem	N.D.	13	*2 4
3rd Reid, Harry M.	Dem	Nev.	13	10
4th Akaka, Daniel K.	Dem	Hai.	9	8
5th Wellstone, Paul D.	DFL	Minn.	9	8
6th Dorgan, Byron, L.	Dem	N.D.	7	6

*2: Member's second period of service on the committee.

INDIAN AFFAIRS / 107th Congress, Pre-Jeffords switch

Service Dates of Committee Chair: ChT: Jan. 3, 2001-Jan. 25, 2001 Inouye (Dem-Hai.)

Ch1: Jan. 25, 2001-June 6, 2001 Campbell (Rep-Colo.)

Service Dates of Majority Members: Jan. 25, 2001-June 6, 2001

Service Dates of Minority Members: Jan. 25, 2001-June 6, 2001

Majority

Rank Name	Party	State	Senate	Comm.
Ch1 Campbell, Ben Nighthorse	Rep	Colo.	9	*2 6
2nd Murkowski, Frank H.	Rep	Alas.	21	19
3rd McCain, John S. III	Rep	Ariz.	15	15
4th Domenici, Pete V.	Rep	N.M.	29	10
5th Thomas, Craig L.	Rep	Wyo.	7	7
6th Hatch, Orrin G.	Rep	Utah	25	7
7th Inhofe, James M.	Rep	Okla.	7	5

Minority

Rank Name	Party	State	Senate	Comm.
VC1 Inouye, Daniel K.	Dem	Hai.	39	23
2nd Conrad, Kent	Dem	N.D.	15	*2 7
3rd Reid, Harry M.	Dem	Nev.	15	12
4th Akaka, Daniel K.	Dem	Hai.	11	10
5th Wellstone, Paul D.	DFL	Minn.	11	10
6th Dorgan, Byron, L.	Dem	N.D.	9	9
7th Johnson, Timothy P.	Dem	S.D.	5	1

*2: Member's second period of service on the committee.

Note: The committee majority in the 2001 Senate power-sharing arrangement was determined by the party of the vice president. Democrat Al Gore, Jr. served from Jan. 3, 2001 to Jan. 20, 2001 and was succeeded by Republican Richard B. Cheney on Jan. 20, 2001. When Senator Jeffords of Vermont left the Republican Party, effective June 6, 2001 to become an Independent, Democrats regained the majority for the remainder of the 107th Congress.

INDIAN AFFAIRS / 107th Congress, Post-Jeffords switch

Service Dates of Committee Chair: June 6, 2001-Jan. 14, 2003

Service Dates of Majority Members: June 6, 2001-Jan. 14, 2003

Service Dates of Minority Members: June 6, 2001-Jan. 15, 2003

Majority

Rank Name	Party	State	Senate	Comm.
Ch2 Inouye, Daniel K.	Dem	Hai.	39	23
2nd Conrad, Kent	Dem	N.D.	15	*2 7
3rd Reid, Harry M.	Dem	Nev.	15	13
4th Akaka, Daniel K.	Dem	Hai.	12	11

Minority

Rank Name	Party	State	Senate	Comm.
VC2 Campbell, Ben Nighthorse	Rep	Colo.	9	*2 7
2nd Murkowski, Frank H.	Rep	Alas.	21	19
3rd McCain, John S. III	Rep	Ariz.	15	15
4th Domenici, Pete V.	Rep	N.M.	29	11

5th Wellstone, Paul D.	DFL	Minn.	11	11
6th Dorgan, Byron, L.	Dem	N.D.	9	9
7th Johnson, Timothy P.	Dem	S.D.	5	1
8th Cantwell, Maria E.	Dem	Wash.	1	1

5th Thomas, Craig L.	Rep	Wyo.	7	7
6th Hatch, Orrin G.	Rep	Utah	25	7
7th Inhofe, James M.	Rep	Okla.	7	5

*2: Member's second period of service on the committee.

Additions:
Majority:

8th Cantwell, Maria E.	Dem	Wash.	July 10, 2001

Changes:
Majority:

Wellstone, Paul D.	DFL	Minn.	Oct. 25, 2002 Died in office

Minority:

Murkowski, Frank H.	Rep	Alas.	Dec. 2, 2002 Resigned the Senate; elected Governor of Alaska

INDIAN AFFAIRS / 108th Congress

Service Dates of Committee Chair: Jan. 14, 2003-Jan. 6, 2005

Service Dates of Majority Members: Jan. 14, 2003-Jan. 6, 2005

Service Dates of Minority Members: Jan. 15, 2003-Jan. 6, 2005

Majority

			Years in:	
Rank Name	Party	State	Senate	Comm.
Chr Campbell, Ben Nighthorse	Rep	Colo.	11	*2 8
2nd McCain, John S. III	Rep	Ariz.	17	17
3rd Domenici, Pete V.	Rep	N.M.	31	12
4th Thomas, Craig L.	Rep	Wyo.	9	9
5th Hatch, Orrin G.	Rep	Utah	27	9
6th Inhofe, James M.	Rep	Okla.	9	7
7th Smith, Gordon H.	Rep	Ore.	7	1
8th Murkowski, Lisa	Rep	Alas.	1	1

Minority

			Years in:	
Rank Name	Party	State	Senate	Comm.
VCh Inouye, Daniel K.	Dem	Hai.	41	24
2nd Conrad, Kent	Dem	N.D.	17	*2 9
3rd Reid, Harry M.	Dem	Nev.	17	14
4th Akaka, Daniel K.	Dem	Hai.	13	12
5th Dorgan, Byron, L.	Dem	N.D.	11	10
6th Johnson, Timothy P.	Dem	S.D.	7	2
7th Cantwell, Maria E.	Dem	Wash.	3	2

*2: Member's second period of service on the committee.

Departures from the Senate:	**Majority**			**Minority**		
Retired	Campbell, Ben Nighthorse	Rep	Colo.	None		

Departures from Committee:						
Returned to Health, Education, Labor and Pensions	Hatch, Orrin G.	Rep	Utah	None		
Elected Minority Leader	None			Reid, Harry M.	Dem	Nev.
No new assignment	Inhofe, James M.	Rep	Okla.	None		

INDIAN AFFAIRS / 109th Congress

Service Dates of Committee Chair: Jan. 6, 2005-Jan. 12, 2007

Service Dates of Majority Members: Jan. 6, 2005-Jan. 12, 2007

Service Dates of Minority Members: Jan. 6, 2005-Jan. 12, 2007

Majority

			Years in:	
Rank Name	Party	State	Senate	Comm.
Chr McCain, John S. III	Rep	Ariz.	19	19
2nd Thomas, Craig L.	Rep	Wyo.	11	10
3rd Murkowski, Lisa	Rep	Alas.	3	2
4th Coburn, Thomas A.	Rep	Okla.	1	1
5th Domenici, Pete V.	Rep	N.M.	33	14
6th Smith, Gordon H.	Rep	Ore.	9	2
7th Crapo, Michael D.	Rep	Ida.	7	*1 1
8th Burr, Richard M.	Rep	N.C.	1	1

Minority

			Years in:	
Rank Name	Party	State	Senate	Comm.
VCh Dorgan, Byron, L.	Dem	N.D.	13	12
2nd Inouye, Daniel K.	Dem	Hai.	43	26
3rd Conrad, Kent	Dem	N.D.	19	*2 10
4th Akaka, Daniel K.	Dem	Hai.	15	14
5th Johnson, Timothy P.	Dem	S.D.	9	4
6th Cantwell, Maria E.	Dem	Wash.	5	4

*1: Member's first period of service on the committee.
*2: Member's second period of service on the committee.

Departures from Committee:	Majority			Minority
No new assignment	Crapo, Michael D.	Rep	Ida.	None

INDIAN AFFAIRS / 110th Congress

Service Dates of Committee Chair: Jan. 12, 2007-Jan. 21, 2009

Service Dates of Majority Members: Jan. 12, 2007-Jan. 21, 2009

Service Dates of Minority Members: Jan. 12, 2007-Jan. 21, 2009

Majority

Rank Name	Party	State	Years in: Senate	Comm.
Chr Dorgan, Byron, L.	Dem	N.D.	15	14
2nd Inouye, Daniel K.	Dem	Hai.	45	28
3rd Conrad, Kent	Dem	N.D.	21	*2 13
4th Akaka, Daniel K.	Dem	Hai.	17	16
5th Johnson, Timothy P.	Dem	S.D.	11	6
6th Cantwell, Maria E.	Dem	Wash.	7	6
7th McCaskill, Claire	Dem	Mo.	1	1
8th Tester, Jon	Dem	Mont.	1	1

Minority

Rank Name	Party	State	Years in: Senate	Comm.
VC1 Thomas, Craig L.	Rep	Wyo.	13	13
2nd McCain, John S. III	Rep	Ariz.	21	21
3rd VC2 Murkowski, Lisa	Rep	Alas.	5	4
4th Coburn, Thomas A.	Rep	Okla.	3	3
5th Domenici, Pete V.	Rep	N.M.	35	16
6th Smith, Gordon H.	Rep	Ore.	11	4
7th Burr, Richard M.	Rep	N.C.	3	3

*2: Member's second period of service on the committee.

Changes:
Minority:

	Party	State	
RM1 Thomas, Craig L.	Rep	Wyo.	June 4, 2007 Died in office
RM2 Murkowski, Lisa	Rep	Alas.	July 10, 2007 Appointed vice chair
Barrasso, John A.	Rep	Wyo.	July 10, 2007 Replaced Thomas; ranked following Coburn

Departures from the Senate:	Majority		Minority		
Defeated for Re-election	None		Smith, Gordon H.	Rep	Ore.
Retired	None		Domenici, Pete V.	Rep	N.M.

Departures from Committee:					
Became Ranking Member on Veterans' Affairs	None		Burr, Richard M.	Rep	N.C.
No new assignment	McCaskill, Claire	Dem	Mo.		

INDIAN AFFAIRS / 111th Congress

Service Dates of Committee Chair: Jan. 21, 2009-

Service Dates of Majority Members: Jan. 21, 2009-

Service Dates of Minority Members: Jan. 21, 2009-

Majority

Rank Name	Party	State	Years in: Senate	Comm.
Chr Dorgan, Byron L.	Dem	N.D.	17	16
2nd Inouye, Daniel K.	Dem	Hai.	47	30
3rd Conrad, Kent	Dem	N.D.	23	*2 15
4th Akaka, Daniel K.	Dem	Hai.	19	18
5th Johnson, Timothy P.	Dem	S.D.	13	8
6th Cantwell, Maria E.	Dem	Wash.	9	8
7th Tester, Jon	Dem	Mont.	3	3
8th Udall, Thomas	Dem	N.M.	1	1
9th Franken, Al	DFL	Minn.	1	1

Minority

Rank Name	Party	State	Years in: Senate	Comm.
VCh Barrasso, John A.	Rep	Wyo.	2	2
2nd McCain, John S. III	Rep	Ariz.	23	23
3rd Murkowski, Lisa	Rep	Alas.	7	7
4th Coburn, Thomas A.	Rep	Okla.	5	5
5th Crapo, Michael D.	Rep	Ida.	11	*2 1
6th Johanns, Mike	Rep	Neb.	1	1

*2: Member's second period of service on the committee.

Filled Vacancy:
Majority:

9th seat by Franken on July 7, 2009

Note: The disputed election in Minnesota between Democrat Al Franken and incumbent Republican Norman Coleman led both parties to hold seats open pending the outcome of the recount.

Select Intelligence

Senate Permanent Select Committee on Intelligence, 103rd-111th Congresses (1993-2011)

BACKGROUND

Organizational History: In the wake of the congressional Watergate investigations of 1973-1974, public mistrust of government institutions was running high. Further independent investigations by the media into operations by the Central Intelligence Agency and the Federal Bureau of Investigation turned up abundant evidence of disturbing disrespect for law and constitutional rights to free association, free speech, and privacy throughout the Vietnam War era.

These independent investigations revealed that the FBI had a long-standing program with the acronym, COINTELPRO—Counter Intelligence Program—that was a series of covert, and often illegal, projects conducted by the agency aimed at investigating and disrupting dissident political organizations within the United States. This program dated back to the 1950s.

In the case of the CIA, a 1974 investigation revealed that the agency had covertly interfered in the internal affairs of Chile, and had successfully worked to overthrow the popularly elected government of President Salvador Allende, resulting in his assassination. Furthermore, it was reported by the *New York Times* that the CIA had coordinated a massive undercover surveillance of United States citizens and organizations involved in legal activities to end the war in Vietnam, or otherwise active in social change movements. This was not only in direct violation of the CIA's charter, but was blatantly illegal and unconstitutional.

In January of 1975, CIA director William Colby admitted CIA wrongdoing in a report to the Senate Appropriations subcommittee on Intelligence Operations. Two weeks later, on January 27, 1975, the Senate passed Senate Resolution 21 by a vote of 82 to 4, creating a select committee to investigate the intelligence activities of the United States. It was to be the first thorough Congressional study of the CIA, FBI, and other government intelligence agencies since the passage of the National Security Act in 1947. Despite the introduction of almost 200 proposals over the years calling for the creation of an oversight committee, none had made it past the powerful Armed Services or Appropriations committees, each of which had subcommittees with nominal oversight responsibilities.

Majority Leader Mike Mansfield (Dem-Mont.) and Minority Leader Hugh Scott (Rep-Penn.) selected the eleven members of this committee on January 27, 1975. The ratio was six Democrats and five Republicans. Frank Church (Dem-Ida.) was chosen committee chair, while John G. Tower (Rep-Tex.) was ranking minority member. No changes occurred in the committee's membership.

The select committee was extended by Senate Resolution 377 (94-2) and terminated by its authority on May 31, 1976. The select committee's final report, Senate Report 755 (94-2), was filed on April 26, 1976. In its two-volume final report, the so-called Church committee examined both domestic intelligence and foreign and military intelligence operations.

Harshly critical of the excesses of the intelligence community, the select committee also held the legislative branch responsible for ineffective oversight and control. The final report warned, "if intelligence agencies continue to operate under a structure in which executive power is not effectively checked and examined—then we will have neither quality intelligence, nor a society which is free at home and respected abroad."

The explosive disclosures of the Select Committee to Study Government Operations with Respect to Intelligence Activities resulted in a bill proposing the establishment of a permanent standing committee to oversee intelligence matters that was referred to the Senate committee on Government Operations. The bill was authored by Frank Church (Dem-Ida.), chair of the temporary select committee.

At the time of the hearings, there were no fewer than eight congressional committees with access to intelligence information and there was general agreement among the intelligence community and the Senators that a single, focused committee was preferable. There was disagreement, however, over the authority to be given to this new committee. Some members of the Senate wished to give the Senate veto power over presidentially instigated covert operations. The intelligence community and many members of the Senate, including Frank Church, saw this as a usurpation of the president's constitutional right to conduct foreign policy as he saw fit. John Tower (Rep-Tex.), the vice chair of the predecessor intelligence committee in the 94th Congress, and senior member of the Armed Services committee, opposed the creation of a new committee altogether.

What emerged from the Government Operations committee on March 1, 1976, was Senate Resolution 400, submitted along with Senate Report 675. The unanimous report recommended the establishment of a new standing committee with the power to set the budgets of the intelligence agencies and to report legislation regarding foreign and domestic activities. This was not the version of the resolution that would eventually pass the Senate however.

Senate Resolution 400 was referred to both the Judiciary and the Rules and Administration committees. Not wanting to be deprived of its power to oversee the Justice Department, which included the FBI, the Judiciary committee approved an amended version of the resolution. The Rules committee also heard objections from representatives of the Armed Services committee, who feared losing authority over the CIA and Defense Department intelligence. On April 29, 1976, the Rules and Administration committee reported a thoroughly altered Senate Resolution 400, the result of a substitute amendment authored by Rules chair Howard W. Cannon (Dem-Nev.). The newly worked proposal called for a select committee to continue the work of the so-called "Church Committee." The jurisdictions of the standing committees would hardly be affected.

The final version was passed by a vote of 72-22 on May 19, 1976. It included recommendations that the president confer with Congress before undertaking covert operations, but did not give Congress legally binding veto power. With the controversy of the Pentagon Papers still fresh in mind, the Senate bill did stipulate that after notification of the president, and upon the recommendation of a majority of members of the select committee, the full Senate could vote to release the classified information.

On May 20, 1976, the initial appointments of the Select Committee on Intelligence were made on the recommendations of Sen. Mike Mansfield (Dem-Mont.), the Majority Leader, and Sen. Hugh D. Scott (Rep-Penn.), the Minority Leader. Eight members, equally divided between the Democrats and the Republicans, were chosen from the four standing committees of Appropriations, Armed Services, Foreign Relations, and the Judiciary. Seven at large members were also selected. Senate Resolution 400 stipulated that the majority and minority leaders of the Senate shall be *ex officio* members of the committee but shall have no vote in the committee and shall not be counted for purpose of determining a quorum.

The establishing resolution further stipulated that no senator remain on the committee for more than eight years of continuous service, and that as far as practicable, at least one third of the committee be comprised of members who did not serve on the committee in the previous Congress. The intent was to prevent the fostering of long-time members whose objectivity regarding intelligence matters might be compromised. It was at this time on October 25, 1978, that the Foreign Intelligence Surveillance Act—FISA (P.L. 95-511) was passed creating a special court to hear executive branch requests for warrants to wiretap individuals.

Apart from the term "select" in its title, the committee functions as a standing committee with the authority to report legislation and is named at the same time as are the standing committees. That is not the case with the other select and special committees. However, the spending authority on intelligence matters is controlled by the Subcommittee on Intelligence of Senate Appropriations.

In the past decade, the Senate Intelligence Committee's most controversial move was to issue the *Report of the Select Committee on Intelligence on the U.S. Intelligence Community's Prewar Intelligence Assessments on Iraq* concerning the U.S. intelligence community's assessments of Iraq during the time leading up to the U.S. invasion of Iraq. Released on July 9, 2004, the report identified numerous failures in the intelligence-gathering and analysis process that led to the creation of materials by President George W. Bush's administration that misled both government policymakers and the American public.

Although the Committee's Republicans and Democrats agreed on the report's major conclusions and unanimously endorsed its findings, they disagreed on the impact that statements on Iraq by senior members of the Bush administration had on the intelligence process. The second phase of the investigation, addressing the way senior policymakers used the intelligence, was published on May 25, 2007 in the *Report of the Select Committee on Intelligence on Prewar Intelligence Assessments about Postwar Iraq.*

Portions of the phase II report not released at that time include the review of public statements by U.S. government leaders prior to the war, with special emphasis on the activities of Douglas Feith and the Pentagon's Office of Special Plans in their *Report on Intelligence Activities Relating to Iraq Conducted by the Policy Counterterrorism Evaluation Group and the Office of Special Plans within the Office of the Under Secretary of Defense for Policy.*

Contemporary debate continues with applications of the USA Patriot Act of 2001 (P.L. 107-56, 115 Stat. 272), passed after the September 11, 2001, terrorist attacks on New York City and the Pentagon and the use of warrantless wiretapping by the Bush Administration in apparent violation of the FISA.

Membership: The original size of the committee was fifteen members and its initial party ratio was 8:7. Five of the original fifteen members had served on the Senate Select Committee to Study Governmental Operations with Respect to Intelligence Activities. With the lone exception of the 95th Congress (1977-1979) when it expanded to seventeen, with two additional at large members and a party ratio of 9:8, the Intelligence Committee maintained its fifteen-member size until 1993. The committee once again expanded to seventeen from 1993 to 1997, then to nineteen in the 105th Congress (1997-1999); returning to seventeen from 1999 to 2007 when it returned to its original size of fifteen. However, the Intelligence Committee regularly has places for *ex officio* members such as the majority and minority floor leaders and the chair and ranking member of the Senate Armed Services Committee.

In spite of its eight-year term limitation, Select Intelligence has a mean interCongress retention rate of 83.62 and a mean seniority of 12.96 years. While its retention rate would place it twelfth among the standing committees, its high seniority mean would place it in the fifth slot.

Committee Leaders: Daniel K. Inouye (Dem-Hai.) was chosen as the select committee's first chair and Clifford P. Case (Rep-N.J.) was its original vice chair. On January 27, 1978 Birch Bayh (Dem-Ind.) won the caucus election to succeed Inouye. He in turn was succeeded in the 97th Congress by Barry M. Goldwater (Rep-Ariz.), who took over when the Republicans won a majority in the Senate in the 1980 Reagan victory. Goldwater was succeeded by fellow Republican David Durenberger of Minnesota in 1985. Democratic gains in the 1986 election returned them to control of the Senate and David L. Boren (Dem-Okla.) took over as chair in the 100th Congress and remained in that position through the 102nd Congress, 1987 to 1993. Dennis DeConcini (Dem-Ariz.) chaired the committee in the 103rd Congress until his retirement in 1995.

The Republican takeover of the Senate in 1995 placed Arlen Specter of Pennsylvania in the chair for the 104th Congress (1995-1997) until he departed for the Government Affairs Committee. Richard C. Shelby of Alabama, who had left the Democratic party in 1995, served as the committee's chair from 1997 until the Jeffords switch in 2001, when Shelby became vice chair. The restoration of Republican power in the 2002 election placed C. Patrick Roberts of Kansas in the chair, an office he held from 2003 to 2007. With Democrats regaining the Senate in the 2006 election, John D. (Jay) Rockefeller IV of West Virginia became chair in the 110th Congress (2007-2009). When Rockefeller stepped aside to chair the Committee on Commerce, Science and Transportation, Dianne Feinstein of California became chair in the 111th Congress (2009-2011).

Clifford P. Case (Rep-N.J.), the committee's original vice chair, was replaced in 1977 by Senator Goldwater. Daniel Patrick Moynihan (Dem-N.Y.) became vice chair in the 97th

Congress and served in that post from 1981, until he left the committee in 1985. Patrick J. Leahy (Dem-Vt.) was vice chair in the 99th Congress (1985-1987). When the Republicans once again became the minority party in the 100th Congress, Leahy became chair of Agriculture, Nutrition and Forestry and William S. Cohen (Rep-Me.) took over as vice chair of the committee in January 1987. He was succeeded in the 102nd Congress by Frank H. Murkowski (Rep-Alas.). Murkowski's departure led to John W. Warner becoming vice chair for 1993-1995.

With Democrats once again a minority in the 104th Congress (1995-1997), J. Robert Kerrey (Dem-Neb.) became vice chair, a post he held from 1995 until both he and Michael DeWine (Rep-Ohio) were obliged to leave the committee per order of Senate Resolution 232, passed on November 10, 1999 (effective January 6, 2000). Kerrey was succeeded by Richard H. Bryan (Dem-Nev.) who served out the balance of the 106th Congress until his 2001 retirement.

During the evenly-divided Senate of the 107th Congress (2001-2003), D. Robert Graham (Dem-Fla.) served as chair temporarily from January 3 to January 25, 2001, until the power-sharing agreement between the Democrats and Republicans was negotiated. He served as vice chair until June 6, 2001, when the switch of James M. Jeffords of Vermont from the Republican Party to serve as an Independent but to caucus with the Democrats, made the Democrats the new Senate majority. Graham then became chair and Richard Shelby became vice chair. Both left the committee following the Republican restoration to majority status in the 2002 election, with Shelby becoming chair of Banking, Housing and Urban Affairs and Graham leaving Intelligence for no new assignment.

John D. (Jay) Rockefeller IV (Dem-W.Va.) succeeded Graham as vice chair and served from 2003 to 2007 when Democratic victories in 2006 gave him the chairmanship of the committee. Republican Christopher S. (Kit) Bond of Missouri became Select Intelligence's new vice chair in 2007 and held it until his retirement in 2011.

Party Leaders: The Senate Intelligence Committee is the most visible of the Senate's four regularly appointed select committees and it has been a semi-draw for Senate floor leaders. Among the four Republican party leaders who served on the committee were Howard Baker, Jr. of Tennessee, floor leader from 1977 to 1983; C. Trent Lott of Mississippi, party whip, 1995-1996, floor leader, 1996-2003, and whip again, 2007-2008; A. Mitchell (Mitch) McConnell of Kentucky, party whip, 2003-2007, and the present floor leader, 2007-date, and Jon L. Kyl of Arizona, the present Republican party whip, 2007-date.

George S. Mitchell of Maine was the only Democratic floor leader to serve on Select Intelligence and the only two Democratic whips with service on Intelligence were Alan Cranston of California and the present whip, Richard J. Durbin of Illinois.

Presidential Aspirations: Given the importance of the Senate Select Intelligence Committee in the area of national security, it is not surprising to see many presidential hopefuls serving on the committee. This is especially true of Democrats starting with its initial chair, Frank S. Church of Idaho, who made a late bid to challenge Jimmy Carter, the ex-governor of Georgia for the 1976 presidential nomination. Walter F. Mondale (DFL-Minn.), who was the Democrats' presidential

nominee in 1984, and John F. Kerry of Massachusetts, the 2004 nominee, were the only two committee members to receive presidential nominations.

Five committee Democrats received vice presidential nominations, of whom two were elected—Walter F. Mondale of Minnesota under Carter and Joseph R. Biden, Jr. of Delaware, who is President Barack Obama's vice president. The three others were Thomas Eagleton (Dem-Mo.), the short-lived nominee on Sen. George McGovern's disastrous 1972 ticket; Lloyd Bentsen (Dem-Tex.), on Massachusetts governor Michael S. Dukakis' 1988 ticket; and John Edwards (Dem-N.C.), on John Kerry's 2004 ticket.

Barry M. Goldwater (Rep-Ariz.) was the only committee member to receive a Republican nomination—the 1964 Republican presidential nomination—but that occurred twelve years before his service on Intelligence from 1976 to 1985. This was also true of J. Strom Thurmond of South Carolina, the 1948 Dixiecrat nominee for president, who left the Democrats in 1964 to support Goldwater's candidacy and whose service on Select Intelligence began twenty-eight years after his presidential candidacy. The only Republican committee members with presidential aspirations were Howard H. Baker Jr. of Tennessee and Richard G. Lugar of Indiana. Both failed to be nominated.

Intelligence Committee Democrats have not been shy about pursuing presidential nominations. Among the nine committee Democrats whose names were tossed into the presidential ring but failed to be nominated include: Birch E. Bayh of Indiana, Gary W. Hart of Colorado, Henry M. Jackson of Washington State, Joseph R. Biden, Jr. of Delaware, Lloyd M. Bentsen Jr. of Texas, Bill Bradley of New Jersey, D. Robert Graham of Florida, J. Robert Kerrey of Nebraska, and John Edwards of North Carolina. It appears as if Select Intelligence was a rival of the Senate Foreign Relations Committee as a presidential springboard.

Other Notables: It appears that the Select Intelligence Committee has not been a source of Cabinet appointments. Committee members Lloyd M. Bentsen (Dem-Tex.), President Bill Clinton's first Secretary of the Treasury and William S. Cohen (Rep-Me.), Clinton's third Secretary of Defense are the only two Cabinet members to be alumni of the committee. The only committee member to leave the Senate and return home to be elected governor was Frank Murkowski of Alaska, whose gubernatorial career was ended in 2006 when he was defeated for renomination by Sarah Palin.

Selected References

Johnson, Loch K., *A Season of Inquiry: The Senate Intelligence Investigation* (Lexington, University Press of Kentucky, 1985).

Lowenthal, Mark M., *Intelligence: From Secrets to Policy*, 2nd ed. (Washington, D.C.: CQ Press, 2003).

Smith, Frank J., Jr., *Congress Oversees the United States Intelligence Community, 1947-1994*, 2nd ed. (Knoxville: University of Tennessee Press, 1994).

U.S. Senate Select Committee on Intelligence, *Legislative Oversight of Intelligence Activities: The U.S. Experience, 103rd Congress*, 2nd Session, Senate Print, 103-88 (Washington, D.C.: U.S. Government Printing Office, 1994).

RESPONSIBILITIES AND JURISDICTIONAL CHANGES

Jurisdiction, 1976

From Senate Resolution 400, 94th Congress, Second Session, May 19, 1976:

[Section 1]

Resolved, That it is the purpose of this resolution to establish a new select committee of the Senate, to be known as the Select Committee on Intelligence, to oversee and make continuing studies of the intelligence activities and programs of the United States Government, and to submit to the Senate appropriate proposals for legislation and report to the Senate concerning such intelligence activities and programs. In carrying out this purpose, the Select Committee on Intelligence shall make every effort to assure that the appropriate departments and agencies of the United States provide informed and timely intelligence necessary for the executive and legislative branches to make sound decisions affecting the security and vital interests of the Nation. It is further the purpose of this resolution to provide vigilant legislative oversight over the intelligence activities of the United States to assure that such activities are in conformity with the Constitution and laws of the United States.

[Section 13a]

The select committee shall make a study with respect to the following matters, taking into consideration with respect to each such matter, all relevant aspects of the effectiveness of planning, gathering, use, security, and dissemination of intelligence:

(1) the quality of the analytical capabilities of United States foreign intelligence agencies and means for integrating more closely analytical intelligence and policy formulation;

(2) the extent and nature of the authority of the departments and agencies of the executive branch to engage in intelligence activities and the desirability of developing charters for each intelligence agency or department;

(3) the organization of intelligence activities in the executive branch to maximize the effectiveness of the conduct, oversight, and accountability of intelligence activities; to reduce duplication or overlap; and to improve the morale of the personnel of the foreign intelligence agencies;

(4) the conduct of covert and clandestine activities and the procedures by which Congress is informed of such activities;

(5) the desirability of changing any law, Senate rule or procedure, or any Executive order, rule, or regulation to improve the protection of intelligence secrets and provide for disclosure of information for which there is no compelling reason for secrecy;

(6) the desirability of establishing a standing committee of the Senate on intelligence activities;

(7) the desirability of establishing a joint committee of the Senate and the House of Representatives on intelligence activities in lieu of having separate committees in each House of Congress, or of establishing procedures under which separate committees on intelligence activities of the two Houses of Congress would receive joint briefings from the intelligence agencies and coordinate their policies with respect to the safeguarding of sensitive intelligence information;

(8) the authorization of funds for the intelligence activities of the Government and whether disclosure of any of the amounts of such funds is in the public interest; and

(9) the development of a uniform set of definitions for terms to be used in policies or guidelines which may be adopted by the executive or legislative branches to govern, clarify, and strengthen the operation of intelligence activities.

Jurisdiction, 102nd Congress (1991-93)

From *Authority and Rules of Senate Committees*, Senate Document 102-6, printed under the authority of Senate Resolution 58 (102-1), agreed to March 13, 1991:

[Section 3. (a)]

There shall be referred to the select committee all proposed legislation, messages, petitions, memorials, and other matters relating to the following:

(1) The Central Intelligence Agency and the Director of Central Intelligence.

(2) Intelligence activities of all other departments and agencies of the government, including, but not limited to, the intelligence activities of the Defense Intelligence Agency, the National Security Agency, and other agencies of the Department of Defense; the Department of State; the Department of Justice; and the Department of the Treasury.

(3) The organization or reorganization of any department or agency of the Government to the extent that the organization or reorganization relates to a function or activity involving intelligence activities.

(4) Authorizations for appropriations, both direct and indirect, for the following:

  (A) The Central Intelligence Agency and Director of Central Intelligence.

  (B) The Defense Intelligence Agency.

  (C) The National Security Agency.

(D) The intelligence activities of other agencies and subdivisions of the Department of Defense.

(E) The intelligence activities of the Department of State.

(F) The intelligence activities of the Federal Bureau of Investigation, including all activities of the Intelligence Division.

(G) Any department, agency, or subdivision which is the successor to any agency named in clause (A), (B), or (C); and the activities of any department, agency, or subdivision which is the successor to any department, agency, bureau, or subdivision named in clause (D), (E), or (F) to the extent that the activities of such successor department, agency, or subdivision are activities described in clause (D), (E), or (F).

Jurisdiction, 111th Congress (2009-2011)

From *Authority and Rules of Senate Committees, 2009-2011,* Sen. Doc. 111-3, pursuant to S. Res, 166, June 2, 2009.

[Section 3. (a)]

There shall be referred to the select committee all proposed legislation, messages, petitions, memorials, and other matters relating to the following:

(1) The Office of the Director of National Intelligence and the Director of National Intelligence.

(2) The Central Intelligence Agency and the Director of the Central Intelligence Agency.

(3) Intelligence activities of all other departments and agencies of the government, including, but not limited to, the intelligence activities of the Defense Intelligence Agency, the National Security Agency, and other agencies of the Department of Defense; the Department of State; the Department of Justice; and the Department of the Treasury.

(4) The organization or reorganization of any department or agency of the Government to the extent that the organization or reorganization relates to a function or activity involving intelligence activities.

(5) Authorizations for appropriations, both direct and indirect, for the following:

(A) The Office of the Director of National Intelligence and the Director of National Intelligence.

(B) The Central Intelligence Agency and the Director of Central Intelligence.

(C) The Defense Intelligence Agency.

(D) The National Security Agency.

(E) The intelligence activities of other agencies and subdivisions of the Department of Defense.

(F) The intelligence activities of the Department of State.

(G) The intelligence activities of the Federal Bureau of Investigation, including all activities of the Intelligence Division.

(H) Any department, agency, or subdivision which is the successor to any agency named in clause (A), (B), (C), or (D); and the activities of any department, agency, or subdivision which is the successor to any department, agency, bureau, or subdivision named in clause (D), (E), or (F) to the extent that the activities of such successor department, agency, or subdivision are activities described in clause (E), (F), or (G).

MEMBERSHIP ROSTERS, 103rd-111th Congresses, 1993-2011

SELECT INTELLIGENCE / 103rd Congress

Service Dates of Committee Chair: Jan. 27, 1993-Jan. 6, 1995

Service Dates of Majority Members: Jan. 27, 1993-Jan. 6, 1995

Service Dates of Minority Members: Jan. 27, 1993-Jan. 6, 1995

Majority					Minority				
			Years in:					Years in:	
Rank Name	Party	State	Senate	Comm.	Rank Name	Party	State	Senate	Comm.
Chr DeConcini, Dennis W.	Dem	Ariz.	17	6	VCh Warner, John W.	Rep	Va.	15	*1 6
2nd Metzenbaum, Howard M.	Dem	Ohio	19	6	2nd D'Amato, Alfonse M.	Rep	N.Y.	13	4
3rd Glenn, John H. Jr.	Dem	Ohio	19	4	3rd Danforth, John C.	Rep	Mo.	17	4
4th Kerrey, J. Robert	Dem	Neb.	5	2	4th Gorton, T. Slade III	Rep	Wash.	11	2
5th Bryan, Richard H.	Dem	Nev.	5	1	5th Chafee, John H.	Rep	R.I.	17	*2 2
6th Graham, D. Robert	Dem	Fla.	7	1	6th Stevens, Theodore F.	Rep	Alas.	25	1
7th Kerry, John F.	Dem	Mass.	9	1	7th Lugar, Richard G.	Rep	Ind.	17	*2 1
8th Baucus, Max S.	Dem	Mont.	15	1	8th Wallop, Malcolm	Rep	Wyo.	17	*2 1
9th Johnston, J. Bennett Jr.	Dem	La.	21	1					

*1: Member's first period of service on the committee.

*2: Member's second period of service on the committee.

Note: *Ex officio* members: Majority and Minority Leaders, George Mitchell (Dem-Me.) and Bob Dole (Rep-Kans.) respectively.

Departures from the Senate:	Majority			Minority		
Retired	DeConcini, Dennis W.	Dem	Ariz.	Danforth, John C.	Rep	Mo.
	Metzenbaum, Howard M.	Dem	Ohio	Wallop, Malcolm	Rep	Wyo.

Departures from Committee:						
Became Chair of Environment and Public Works	None			Chafee, John H.	Rep	R.I.
Became Chair of Rules and Administration	None			Stevens, Theodore F.	Rep	Alas.
Moved to Agriculture, Nutrition, and Forestry and Small Business	None			Warner, John W.	Rep	Va.
Moved to Finance	None			D'Amato, Alfonse M.	Rep	N.Y.
Moved to Labor and Human Resources	None			Gorton, T. Slade III	Rep	Wash.

SELECT INTELLIGENCE / 104th Congress

Service Dates of Committee Chair: Jan. 6, 1995-Jan. 9, 1997

Service Dates of Majority Members: Jan. 6, 1995-Jan. 9, 1997

Service Dates of Minority Members: Jan. 6, 1995-Jan. 9, 1997

Majority					**Minority**				
			Years in:					Years in:	
Rank Name	Party	State	Senate	Comm.	Rank Name	Party	State	Senate	Comm.
Chr Specter, Arlen	Rep	Penn.	15	*2 1	VCh Kerrey, J. Robert	Dem	Neb.	7	3
2nd Lugar, Richard G.	Rep	Ind.	19	*2 2	2nd Glenn, John H. Jr.	Dem	Ohio	21	6
3rd Shelby, Richard C.	Rep	Ala.	9	1	3rd Bryan, Richard H.	Dem	Nev.	7	2
4th DeWine, Michael	Rep	Ohio	1	*1 1	4th Graham, D. Robert	Dem	Fla.	9	2
5th Kyl, Jon L.	Rep	Ariz.	1	1	5th Kerry, John F.	Dem	Mass.	11	2
6th Inhofe, James M.	Rep	Okla.	1	1	6th Baucus, Max S.	Dem	Mont.	17	2
7th Hutchison, Kay Bailey	Rep	Tex.	2	1	7th Johnston, J. Bennett Jr.	Dem	La.	23	2
8th Mack, Connie III	Rep	Fla.	7	1	8th Robb, Charles S.	Dem	Va.	7	1
9th Cohen, William S.	Rep	Me.	17	*2 1					

*1: Member's first period of service on the committee.

*2: Member's second period of service on the committee.

Note: *Ex officio* members: Majority and Minority Leaders, Robert J. Dole (Rep-Kans.) who was succeeded by C. Trent Lott (Rep-Miss.) and Thomas A. Daschle (Dem-S.D.) respectively.

Departures from the Senate:	Majority			Minority		
Retired	Cohen, William S.	Rep	Me.	Johnston, J. Bennett Jr.	Dem	La.

Departures from Committee:						
Moved to Governmental Affairs	Specter, Arlen	Rep	Penn.	None		
Moved to Appropriations and Rules and Administration	Hutchison, Kay Bailey	Rep	Tex.	None		
Moved to Finance	Mack, Connie III	Rep	Fla.	None		

SELECT INTELLIGENCE / 105th Congress

Service Dates of Committee Chair: Jan. 9, 1997-Jan. 7, 1999

Service Dates of Majority Members: Jan. 9, 1997-Jan. 7, 1999

Service Dates of Minority Members: Jan. 9, 1997-Jan. 7, 1999

Majority					**Minority**				
			Years in:					Years in:	
Rank Name	Party	State	Senate	Comm.	Rank Name	Party	State	Senate	Comm.
Chr Shelby, Richard C.	Rep	Ala.	11	3	VCh Kerrey, J. Robert	Dem	Neb.	9	5
2nd Chafee, John H.	Rep	R.I.	21	*3 1	2nd Glenn, John H. Jr.	Dem	Ohio	23	8
3rd Lugar, Richard G.	Rep	Ind.	21	*2 4	3rd Bryan, Richard H.	Dem	Nev.	9	4
4th DeWine, Michael	Rep	Ohio	3	*1 3	4th Graham, D. Robert	Dem	Fla.	11	4
5th Kyl, Jon L.	Rep	Ariz.	3	3	5th Kerry, John F.	Dem	Mass.	13	4
6th Inhofe, James M.	Rep	Okla.	3	3	6th Baucus, Max S.	Dem	Mont.	19	4
7th Hatch, Orrin G.	Rep	Utah	21	*2 1	7th Robb, Charles S.	Dem	Va.	9	3
8th Roberts, C. Patrick	Rep	Kans.	1	1	8th Lautenberg, Frank R.	Dem	N.J.	15	1

| 9th Allard, A. Wayne | Rep | Colo. | 1 | 1 |
| 10th Coats, Daniel R. | Rep | Ind. | 9 | 1 |

| 9th Levin, Carl M. | Dem | Mich. | 19 | 1 |

*1: Member's first period of service on the committee.
*2: Member's second period of service on the committee.
*3: Member's third period of service on the committee.

Note: *Ex officio* members: Majority and Minority Leaders, C. Trent Lott (Rep-Miss.) and Thomas A. Daschle (Dem-S.D.) respectively.

Departures from the Senate: | **Majority** | | | **Minority** | |
| Retired | Coats, Daniel R. | Rep | Ind. | Glenn, John H. Jr. | Dem | Ohio |

SELECT INTELLIGENCE / 106th Congress

Service Dates of Committee Chair: Jan. 7, 1999-Jan. 3, 2001

Service Dates of Majority Members: Jan. 7, 1999-Jan. 25, 2001

Service Dates of Minority Members: Jan. 7, 1999-Jan. 25, 2001

| | | | **Majority** | Years in: | | | | | **Minority** | Years in: | |
Rank Name	Party	State	Senate	Comm.		Rank Name	Party	State	Senate	Comm.
Chr Shelby, Richard C.	Rep	Ala.	13	5		VC1 Kerrey, J. Robert	Dem	Neb.	11	7
2nd Chafee, John H.	Rep	R.I.	23	*3 2		VC2 Bryan, Richard H.	Dem	Nev.	11	6
3rd Lugar, Richard G.	Rep	Ind.	23	*2 6		3rd Graham, D. Robert	Dem	Fla.	13	6
4th DeWine, Michael	Rep	Ohio	5	*1 5		4th Kerry, John F.	Dem	Mass.	15	6
5th Kyl, Jon L.	Rep	Ariz.	5	5		5th Baucus, Max S.	Dem	Mont.	21	6
6th Inhofe, James M.	Rep	Okla.	5	5		6th Robb, Charles S.	Dem	Va.	11	5
7th Hatch, Orrin G.	Rep	Utah	23	*2 2		7th Lautenberg, Frank R.	Dem	N.J.	17	2
8th Roberts, C. Patrick	Rep	Kans.	3	2		8th Levin, Carl M.	Dem	Mich.	21	2
9th Allard, A. Wayne	Rep	Colo.	3	2						

*1: Member's first period of service on the committee.
*2: Member's second period of service on the committee.
*3: Member's third period of service on the committee.

Note: *Ex officio* members: Majority and Minority Leaders, C. Trent Lott (Rep-Miss.) and Thomas A. Daschle (Dem-S.D.) respectively.

Changes:

Majority:

Chafee, John H.	Rep	R.I.	Oct. 24, 1999 Died in office
Mack, Connie III	Rep	Fla.	Nov. 9, 1999 Replaced Chafee
DeWine, Michael	Rep	Ohio	Nov. 10, 1999 Removed from the committee by S. Res. 232, effective Jan. 6, 2000

Minority:

| VC1 Kerrey, J. Robert | Dem | Neb. | Nov. 10, 1999 Removed from the committee by S. Res. 232, effective Jan. 6, 2000 |
| VC2 Bryan, Richard H. | Dem | Nev. | Nov. 10, 1999 Succeeded Kerrey as Vice Chair |

Departures from the Senate: | **Majority** | | | **Minority** | |
Defeated for Re-election	None			Robb, Charles S.	Dem	Va.
Retired	Mack, Connie III	Rep	Fla.	Kerrey, J. Robert	Dem	Neb.
				Bryan, Richard H.	Dem	Nev.
				Lautenberg, Frank R.	Dem	N.J.

Departures from Committee:
Moved to Agriculture, Nutrition, and Forestry and Budget	Allard, A. Wayne	Rep	Colo.	None		
Moved to Finance	None			Kerry, John F.	Dem	Mass.
No new assignment	None			Baucus, Max S.	Dem	Mont.

SELECT INTELLIGENCE / 107th Congress, Pre-Jeffords switch

Service Dates of Committee Chair: ChT: Jan. 3, 2001-Jan. 25, 2001 Graham (Dem-Fla.)

Ch1: Jan. 25, 2001-June 6, 2001 Shelby (Rep-Ala.)

Service Dates of Majority Members: Jan. 25, 2001-June 6, 2001

Service Dates of Minority Members: Jan. 25, 2001-June 6, 2001

	Majority						Minority			
				Years in:						**Years in:**
Rank Name	**Party**	**State**	**Senate**	**Comm.**		**Rank Name**	**Party**	**State**	**Senate**	**Comm.**
Ch1 Shelby, Richard C.	Rep	Ala.	15	7		VCh1 Graham, D. Robert	Dem	Fla.	15	8
2nd Kyl, Jon L.	Rep	Ariz.	7	7		2nd Levin, Carl M.	Dem	Mich.	23	5
3rd Inhofe, James M.	Rep	Okla.	7	7		3rd Rockefeller, John D. IV	Dem	W.Va.	17	1
4th Hatch, Orrin G.	Rep	Utah	25	*2 5		4th Feinstein, Dianne	Dem	Cal.	9	1
5th Roberts, C. Patrick	Rep	Kans.	5	5		5th Wyden, Ronald L.	Dem	Ore.	6	1
6th DeWine, Michael	Rep	Ohio	7	*2 1		6th Durbin, Richard J.	Dem	Ill.	5	1
7th Thompson, Fred D.	Rep	Tenn.	7	1		7th Bayh, B. Evans	Dem	Ind.	3	1
8th Lugar, Richard G.	Rep	Ind.	25	*2 8		8th Edwards, John	Dem	N.C.	3	1

*2: Member's second period of service on the committee.

Note 1: *Ex officio* members: Majority and Minority Leaders, C. Trent Lott (Rep-Miss.) and Thomas A. Daschle (Dem-S.D.) respectively.

Note 2: The committee majority in the 2001 Senate power-sharing arrangement was determined by the party of the vice president. Democrat Al Gore, Jr. served from Jan. 3, 2001 to Jan. 20, 2001 and was succeeded by Republican Richard B. Cheney on Jan. 20, 2001. When Senator Jeffords of Vermont left the Republican Party, effective June 6, 2001 to become an Independent, Democrats regained the majority for the remainder of the 107th Congress.

SELECT INTELLIGENCE / 107th Congress, Post-Jeffords switch

Service Dates of Committee Chair: June 6, 2001-Jan. 14, 2003

Service Dates of Majority Members: June 6, 2001-Jan. 14, 2003

Service Dates of Minority Members: June 6, 2001-Jan. 15, 2003

	Majority						Minority			
				Years in:						**Years in:**
Rank Name	**Party**	**State**	**Senate**	**Comm.**		**Rank Name**	**Party**	**State**	**Senate**	**Comm.**
Ch2 Graham, D. Robert	Dem	Fla.	15	9		VCh2 Shelby, Richard C.	Rep	Ala.	15	7
2nd Levin, Carl M.	Dem	Mich.	23	5		2nd Kyl, Jon L.	Rep	Ariz.	7	7
3rd Rockefeller, John D. IV	Dem	W.Va.	17	1		3rd Inhofe, James M.	Rep	Okla.	7	7
4th Feinstein, Dianne	Dem	Cal.	9	1		4th Hatch, Orrin G.	Rep	Utah	25	*2 5
5th Wyden, Ronald L.	Dem	Ore.	6	1		5th Roberts, C. Patrick	Rep	Kans.	5	5
6th Durbin, Richard J.	Dem	Ill.	5	1		6th DeWine, Michael	Rep	Ohio	7	*2 1
7th Bayh, B. Evans	Dem	Ind.	3	1		7th Thompson, Fred D.	Rep	Tenn.	7	1
8th Edwards, John	Dem	N.C.	3	1		8th Lugar, Richard G.	Rep	Ind.	25	*2 9
9th Mikulski, Barbara A.	Dem	Md.	15	1						

*2: Member's second period of service on the committee.

Note: *Ex officio* members: Majority and Minority Leaders, Thomas A. Daschle (Dem-S.D.) and C. Trent Lott (Rep-Miss.) respectively.

Additions:
  Majority:
    9th Mikulski, Barbara A.   Dem   Md.   July 10, 2001

Departures from the Senate:	**Majority**			**Minority**		
Retired	None			Thompson, Fred D.	Rep	Tenn.

Departures from Committee:						
Became Chair of Banking, Housing, and Urban Affairs	None			Shelby, Richard C.	Rep	Ala.
Became Chair of Environment and Public Works	None			Inhofe, James M.	Rep	Okla.
Became Chair of Foreign Relations	None			Lugar, Richard G.	Rep	Ind.
Moved to Governmental Affairs	None			Shelby, Richard C.	Rep	Ala.
No new assignment	Graham, D. Robert	Dem	Fla.	Kyl, Jon L.	Rep	Ariz.

SELECT INTELLIGENCE / 108th Congress

Service Dates of Committee Chair: Jan. 14, 2003-Jan. 6, 2005

Service Dates of Majority Members: Jan. 14, 2003-Jan. 6, 2005

Service Dates of Minority Members: Jan. 15, 2003-Jan. 6, 2005

Majority			Years in:		Minority			Years in:	
Rank Name	Party	State	Senate	Comm.	Rank Name	Party	State	Senate	Comm.
Chr Roberts, C. Patrick	Rep	Kans.	7	7	VCh Rockefeller, John D. IV	Dem	W.Va.	19	2
2nd Hatch, Orrin G.	Rep	Utah	27	*2 7	2nd Levin, Carl M.	Dem	Mich.	25	7
3rd DeWine, Michael	Rep	Ohio	9	*2 2	3rd Feinstein, Dianne	Dem	Cal.	11	2
4th Bond, Christopher S. (Kit)	Rep	Mo.	17	1	4th Wyden, Ronald L.	Dem	Ore.	8	2
5th Lott, C. Trent	Rep	Miss.	15	1	5th Durbin, Richard J.	Dem	Ill.	7	2
6th Snowe, Olympia J.B.	Rep	Me.	9	1	6th Bayh, B. Evans	Dem	Ind.	5	2
7th Hagel, Charles T. (Chuck)	Rep	Neb.	7	1	7th Edwards, John	Dem	N.C.	5	2
8th Chambliss, Saxby	Rep	Ga.	1	1	8th Mikulski, Barbara A.	Dem	Md.	17	2
9th Warner, John W.	Rep	Va.	25	*2 1					

*2: Member's second period of service on the committee.

Note: *Ex officio* members: Majority and Minority Leaders, William H. Frist (Rep-Tenn.) and Thomas A. Daschle (Dem-S.D.) respectively.

Departures from the Senate:	Majority			Minority		
Retired; lost vice presidential election	None			Edwards, John	Dem	N.C.

Departures from Committee:						
Elected Minority Whip	None			Durbin, Richard J.	Dem	Ill.

SELECT INTELLIGENCE / 109th Congress

Service Dates of Committee Chair: Jan. 6, 2005-Jan. 12, 2007

Service Dates of Majority Members: Jan. 6, 2005-Jan. 12, 2007

Service Dates of Minority Members: Jan. 6, 2005-Jan. 12, 2007

Majority			Years in:		Minority			Years in:	
Rank Name	Party	State	Senate	Comm.	Rank Name	Party	State	Senate	Comm.
Chr Roberts, C. Patrick	Rep	Kans.	9	8	VCh Rockefeller, John D. IV	Dem	W.Va.	21	4
2nd Hatch, Orrin G.	Rep	Utah	29	*2 8	2nd Levin, Carl M.	Dem	Mich.	27	8
3rd DeWine, Michael	Rep	Ohio	11	*2 4	3rd Feinstein, Dianne	Dem	Cal.	13	4
4th Bond, Christopher S. (Kit)	Rep	Mo.	19	2	4th Wyden, Ronald L.	Dem	Ore.	10	4
5th Lott, C. Trent	Rep	Miss.	17	2	5th Bayh, B. Evans	Dem	Ind.	7	4
6th Snowe, Olympia J.B.	Rep	Me.	11	2	6th Mikulski, Barbara A.	Dem	Md.	19	4
7th Hagel, Charles T. (Chuck)	Rep	Neb.	9	2	7th Corzine, Jon S.	Dem	N.J.	5	1
8th Chambliss, Saxby	Rep	Ga.	3	2					
9th Warner, John W.	Rep	Va.	27	*2 2					

*2: Member's second period of service on the committee.

Note: *Ex officio* members: Majority and Minority Leaders, William H. Frist (Rep-Tenn.) and Harry M. Reid (Dem-Nev.) respectively; Chairman on Armed Services, John W. Warner.

Changes:

Minority:				
Corzine, Jon S.	Dem	N.J.	Jan. 17, 2006 Resigned the Senate; elected governor of N.J.	
Feingold, Russell D.	Dem	Wisc.	Jan. 18, 2006 Replaced Corzine	

Departures from the Senate:	Majority			Minority
Defeated for Re-election	DeWine, Michael	Rep	Ohio	None

Departures from Committee:				
Moved to Finance	Roberts, C. Patrick	Rep	Kans.	None
Elected Minority Whip	Lott, C. Trent	Rep	Miss.	None

SELECT INTELLIGENCE / 110th Congress

Service Dates of Committee Chair: Jan. 12, 2007-Jan. 21, 2009

Service Dates of Majority Members: Jan. 12, 2007-Jan. 21, 2009

Service Dates of Minority Members: Jan. 12, 2007-Jan. 21, 2009

Majority						Minority					
				Years in:						Years in:	
Rank Name	Party	State	Senate	Comm.		Rank Name	Party	State	Senate	Comm.	
Chr Rockefeller, John D. IV	Dem	W.Va.	23	6		VCh Bond, Christopher S. (Kit)	Rep	Mo.	21	4	
2nd Feinstein, Dianne	Dem	Cal.	15	6		2nd Warner, John W.	Rep	Va.	29	*2 4	
3rd Wyden, Ronald L.	Dem	Ore.	12	6		3rd Hagel, Charles T. (Chuck)	Rep	Neb.	11	4	
4th Bayh, B. Evans	Dem	Ind.	9	6		4th Chambliss, Saxby	Rep	Ga.	5	4	
5th Mikulski, Barbara A.	Dem	Md.	21	6		5th Hatch, Orrin G.	Rep	Utah	31	*2 11	
6th Feingold, Russell D.	Dem	Wisc.	15	1		6th Snowe, Olympia J.B.	Rep	Me.	13	4	
7th Nelson, C. William (Bill)	Dem	Fla.	7	1		7th Burr, Richard M.	Rep	N.C.	3	1	
8th Whitehouse, Sheldon	Dem	R.I.	1	1							

*2: Member's second period of service on the committee.

Note: *Ex officio* members: Majority and Minority Leaders, Harry M. Reid (Dem-Nev.) and A. Mitchell McConnell (Rep-Ky.) respectively; Chairman and Ranking Member on Armed Services, Carl M. Levin (Dem-Mich.) and John S. McCain III (Rep-Ariz.) respectively.

Departures from the Senate:	Majority	Minority		
Retired	None	Warner, John W.	Rep	Va.
		Hagel, Charles T. (Chuck)	Rep	Neb.

SELECT INTELLIGENCE / 111th Congress

Service Dates of Committee Chair: Jan. 21, 2009-

Service Dates of Majority Members: Jan. 21, 2009-

Service Dates of Minority Members: Jan. 21, 2009-

Majority						Minority					
				Years in:						Years in:	
Rank Name	Party	State	Senate	Comm.		Rank Name	Party	State	Senate	Comm.	
Chr Feinstein, Dianne	Dem	Cal.	17	8		VCh Bond, Christopher S. (Kit)	Rep	Mo.	23	7	
2nd Rockefeller, John D. IV	Dem	W.Va.	25	8		2nd Hatch, Orrin G.	Rep	Utah	33	*2 13	
3rd Wyden, Ronald L.	Dem	Ore.	14	8		3rd Snowe, Olympia J.B.	Rep	Me.	15	7	
4th Bayh, B. Evans	Dem	Ind.	11	8		4th Chambliss, Saxby	Rep	Ga.	7	7	
5th Mikulski, Barbara A.	Dem	Md.	23	8		5th Burr, Richard M.	Rep	N.C.	5	3	
6th Feingold, Russell D.	Dem	Wisc.	17	4		6th Coburn, Thomas A.	Rep	Okla.	5	1	
7th Nelson, C. William (Bill)	Dem	Fla.	9	3		7th Risch, James	Rep	Ida.	1	1	
8th Whitehouse, Sheldon	Dem	R.I.	3	3							

*2: Member's second period of service on the committee.

Note: *Ex officio* members: Majority and Minority Leaders, Harry M. Reid (Dem-Nev.) and A. Mitchell McConnell (Rep-Ky.) respectively; Chairman and Ranking Member on Armed Services, Carl M. Levin (Dem-Mich.) and John S. McCain III (Rep-Ariz.) respectively.

Special Committee to Investigate Whitewater Development Corporation and Related Matters

104th Congress (1995-1996)

BACKGROUND

Organizational History: During his term in office as governor of Arkansas and before his election to the presidency in 1992, Bill Clinton and his wife, First Lady Hillary Rodham Clinton, were involved in a speculative real estate venture, known as the Whitewater Development Corporation. Their associates were family friends Jim and Susan McDougal. The Clintons invested heavily in the corporation in the 1970s and 1980s, but the business failed.

It was when Clinton became president in 1993 that allegations of financial misdeeds surfaced, when it was alleged that Governor Clinton had pressured David Hale of Madison Guaranty to loan money to Susan McDougal. Hale's checkered history of looting corporations that he had created and the fact that he was under federal indictment made him a less than credible source of the allegations. However, the Republican takeover of the Senate in 1994 had placed Republicans hostile to Clinton in control of the Senate Committee on Banking, Housing and Urban Affairs.

The Senate Banking Committee then created the Special Committee to Investigate the Whitewater Development Corporation and Related Matters with S. Res. 120, and the committee was named on July 20, 1995.

The committee met for eleven months and took a great deal of testimony while a parallel investigation was conducted by the Securities and Exchange Commission. It was the SEC investigation that had the most impact, in that it led to convictions against the McDougals for their role in the Whitewater project and to the prosecution of Jim Guy Tucker, who had succeeded Clinton as governor of Arkansas. Tucker was convicted and jailed, while Susan McDougal was convicted of contempt of court for refusing to answer questions concerning Whitewater and was imprisoned for eighteen months. She was later pardoned by President Clinton.

The Clintons were never prosecuted for their role in the Whitewater matter, as there was insufficient evidence to implicate them in the land fraud. However, the Justice Department of Attorney General Janet Reno named a special prosecutor, Robert Fiske, to investigate the matter. To avoid the appearance of political impropriety, Fiske was succeeded by Kenneth Starr, who was named special prosecutor by a three-member panel of federal judges. It would be Starr's continuing investigations of President Clinton that would lead to his 1998 impeachment by the House following revelations of his lying to a grand jury regarding his inappropriate relationship with Monica Lewinsky, a White House intern,

Membership: The resolution creating the committee stipulated that "The special committee shall consist of— (A) the members of the Committee on Banking, Housing, and Urban Affairs; and (B) the chairman and ranking member of the Committee on the Judiciary, or their designees from the Committee on the Judiciary." With sixteen members from Banking and the two senior members of Judiciary this brought the number of senators on the committee to eighteen, with a 10-8 majority-minority split. The two senior members of the Judiciary Committee named were Chair Orrin G. Hatch (Rep-Utah) and Ranking Member Paul M. Simon (Dem-Ill.).

W. Phil Gramm (Rep-Tex.), the second-ranking member of the Banking Committee chose not to serve on the special committee and he was replaced by Frank H. Murkowski (Rep-Alas.). The only membership change occurred on October 12, 1995, when Majority Leader William H. Frist left the Banking Committee to move to Commerce, Science and Transportation and was replaced on the special committee by Pete V. Domenici (Rep-N.M.).

Committee Leaders: The creating resolution named Alfonse M. D'Amato (Rep-N.Y.) the chair of the Committee on Banking, Housing and Urban Affairs as the chair of the special committee Paul S. Sarbanes, the ranking member of the Committee on Banking, Housing and Urban Affairs as the ranking member of the special committee.

Selected References

U.S. Senate, Special Committee to Investigate Whitewater Development Corporation and Related Matters, *Investigation of Whitewater Development Corporation and Related Matters*, Final Report, Senate Report 104-280, June 17, 1996.

JURISDICTION

Jurisdiction, 1995

From Senate Resolution 120, 104th Congress

SECTION 1. ESTABLISHMENT OF SPECIAL COMMITTEE.

(a) ESTABLISHMENT- There is established a special committee administered by the Committee on Banking, Housing, and Urban Affairs to be known as the 'Special Committee to Investigate Whitewater Development Corporation and Related Matters' (hereafter in this resolution referred to as the 'special committee').

(b) PURPOSES- The purposes of the special committee are—

    (1) to conduct an investigation and public hearings into, and study of, whether improper conduct occurred regarding the way in which White House officials handled documents in the office of White House Deputy Counsel Vincent Foster following his death;

    (2) to conduct an investigation and public hearings into, and study of, the following matters developed during, or arising out of, the investigation and public hearings concluded by the Committee on Banking, Housing, and Urban Affairs prior to the adoption of this resolution—

        (A) whether any person has improperly handled confidential Resolution Trust Corporation (hereafter in this resolution referred to as the 'RTC') information relating to Madison Guaranty Savings and Loan Association or Whitewater Development Corporation, including whether any person has improperly communicated such information to individuals referenced therein;

        (B) whether the White House has engaged in improper contacts with any other agency or department in the Government with regard to confidential RTC information relating to Madison Guaranty Savings and Loan Association or Whitewater Development Corporation;

        (C) whether the Department of Justice has improperly handled RTC criminal referrals relating to Madison Guaranty Savings and Loan Association or Whitewater Development Corporation;

        (D) whether RTC employees have been improperly importuned, prevented, restrained, or deterred in conducting investigations or making enforcement recommendations relating to Madison Guaranty Savings and Loan Association or Whitewater Development Corporation; and

        (E) whether the report issued by the Office of Government Ethics on July 31, 1994, or related transcripts of deposition testimony—

            (i) were improperly released to White House officials or others prior to their testimony before the Committee on Banking, Housing, and Urban Affairs pursuant to Senate Resolution 229 (103d Congress); or

            (ii) were used to communicate to White House officials or to others confidential RTC information relating to Madison Guaranty Savings and Loan Association or Whitewater Development Corporation;

    (3) to conduct an investigation and public hearings into, and study of, all matters that have any tendency to reveal the full facts about—

        (A) the operations, solvency, and regulation of Madison Guaranty Savings and Loan Association, and any subsidiary, affiliate, or other entity owned or controlled by Madison Guaranty Savings and Loan Association;

        (B) the activities, investments, and tax liability of Whitewater Development Corporation and, as related to Whitewater Development Corporation, of its officers, directors, and shareholders;

        (C) the policies and practices of the RTC and the Federal banking agencies (as that term is defined in section 3 of the Federal Deposit Insurance Act) regarding the legal representation of such agencies with respect to Madison Guaranty Savings and Loan Association;

        (D) the handling by the RTC, the Office of Thrift Supervision, the Federal Deposit Insurance Corporation, and the Federal Savings and Loan Insurance Corporation of civil or administrative actions against parties regarding Madison Guaranty Savings and Loan Association;

        (E) the sources of funding and the lending practices of Capital Management Services, Inc., and its supervision and regulation by the Small Business Administration, including any alleged diversion of funds to Whitewater Development Corporation;

        (F) the bond underwriting contracts between Arkansas Development Finance Authority and Lasater & Company; and

        (G) the lending activities of Perry County Bank, Perryville, Arkansas, in connection with the 1990 Arkansas gubernatorial election;

    (4) to make such findings of fact as are warranted and appropriate;

    (5) to make such recommendations, including recommendations for legislative, administrative, or other actions, as the special committee may determine to be necessary or desirable; and

    (6) to fulfill the constitutional oversight and informational functions of the Congress with respect to the matters described in this section.

MEMBERSHIP ROSTER, 104th Congress, 1995-1996

SPECIAL COMMITTEE TO INVESTIGATE WHITEWATER DEVELOPMENT CORPORATION AND RELATED MATTERS / 104th Congress

Service Dates of Committee Chair: July 20, 1995-June 17, 1996

Service Dates of Majority Members: July 20, 1995-June 17, 1996

Service Dates of Minority Members: July 20, 1995-June 17, 1996

Majority					Minority				
			Terms in:					Terms in:	
Rank Name	Party	State	House	Comm.	Rank Name	Party	State	House	Comm.
Chr D'Amato, Alfonse M.	Rep	N.Y.	15	1	RM Sarbanes, Paul S.	Dem	Md.	19	1
2nd Shelby, Richard C.	Rep	Ala.	9	1	2nd Dodd, Christopher J.	Dem	Conn.	15	1
3rd Bond, Christopher S. (Kit)	Rep	Mo.	9	1	3rd Kerry, John F.	Dem	Mass.	11	1
4th Mack, Connie III	Rep	Fla.	7	1	4th Bryan, Richard H.	Dem	Nev.	7	1
5th Faircloth, D.M. (Lauch)	Rep	N.C.	3	1	5th Boxer, Barbara	Dem	Cal.	3	1
6th Bennett, Robert F.	Rep	Utah	3	1	6th Moseley Braun, Carol	Dem	Ill.	3	1
7th Grams, Rod	Rep	Minn.	1	1	7th Murray, Patty	Dem	Wash.	3	1
8th Frist, William H.	Rep	Tenn.	1	1	8th Simon, Paul M.	Dem	Ill.	11	1
9th Hatch, Orrin G.	Rep	Utah	19	1					
10th Murkowski, Frank H.	Rep	Alas.	15	1					

Changes:

Majority:

Frist, William H.	Rep	Tenn.	Oct. 12, 1995 Left committee; moved to Commerce, Science, and Transportation
Domenici, Pete V.	Rep	N.M.	Oct. 12, 1995 Replaced Frist; ranked immediately following Grams

Special Committee on the Year 2000 Technology Problem
105th-106th Congresses (1998-2000)

BACKGROUND

Organizational History: With the millennial year of 2000, or Y2K as it was popularly known, fast approaching, anxiety levels were raised concerning how computers in both the private and public sectors would adjust to the digital reality of this new era. Anxiety levels were high enough to impel the Senate to name a special committee to address the likely consequences of this change and to dispel many of the doomsday scenarios about how the computers in the United States and throughout the world would be able to cope with what was feared to be an extraordinarily troublesome circumstance.

The Special Committee on the Year 2000 Technology Problem was established on April 2, 1998, and its chair, Senator Robert F. Bennett (Rep-Utah), was named by Majority Leader C. Trent Lott (Rep-Miss.) on April 3, 1998.

In its February 24, 1999, Executive Statement, the Special Committee submitted a balanced assessment, contending that, "The true extent of Y2K failures will match neither the most optimistic nor the most apocalyptic predictions. Rather, Y2K problems will hit sporadically, based on geography, size of organization, and level of preparedness, and will cause more inconveniences than tragedies."

Shortly after the Special Committee submitted that report, Republicans on the Commerce, Science, and Transportation Committee led by Senator McCain (Rep-Ariz.) reported out a bill entitled the Year 2000 Fairness and Responsibility Act (S. 461), by a vote of 10-7. It sought to put legislation in place that would limit the expected eruption of lawsuits related to Y2K issues. With anxiety levels rising and many people unconvinced by the soothing words of the special committee, the pace of lawsuits filed increased steadily and a number were resolved with million-dollar-plus settlements.

Even before the Special Committee submitted its summary report to the Senate, Republicans on the Commerce, Science and Transportation Committee led by Senator John S. McCain (Rep-Ariz.), introduced S. 96 on January 19, 1999, to be known as the Y2K Act, "To regulate commerce between and among the several States by providing for the orderly resolution of disputes arising out of computer-based problems related to processing data that includes a 2-digit expression of the year's date." The vote came out of the Commerce Committee, with all eleven Republicans favoring passage and all nine Democrats opposed. The key issue at stake was the limit on liability to $250,000 in damages. The bill was seen as a battle ground between the high-tech firms fearful of lawsuits and the trial lawyers who were opposed to the $250,000 maximum cap on liability. Both groups had been supportive of President Clinton in his 1992 and 1996 election bids, but with Republicans controlling Congress, the high-tech firms had the upper hand.

On March 26, 1999, the Senate Judiciary Committee approved "The Year 2000 Fairness and Responsibility Act," by a vote of ten to seven, with the latest of several Congressional proposals aimed at restricting lawsuits related to the Year 2000 problem. The Act was cosponsored by Senators Orrin G. Hatch (Rep-Utah), Chair of the Senate Judiciary Committee, and Dianne Feinstein (Dem-Cal.), and was embraced by industry associations, high-tech and insurance companies, and small businesses. All of the Judiciary Committee's Democrat members, with the exception of Feinstein, voted against the measure, signaling the possibility of a larger partisan conflict.

After fending off amendments and cloture votes, S. 96 finally passed the Senate by a 62 to 37 vote on June 15, 1999. Republicans split 50 to 4 for the bill while Democrats split 12 to 33 against it. The legislation was a narrower version of a bill that already passed in the House of Representatives. The bill now moved to a House-Senate conference before the final version was sent to President Clinton, who threatened to veto it if consumer protections were left out. Under the Y2K liability bill, punitive damages were capped and plaintiffs were required to wait ninety days before filing a lawsuit to allow the offending company the opportunity to fix the problem.

President Clinton signed the compromise legislation into law on July 20 as Public Law 106-37. The new law limited the liability of companies that do not adequately address issues resulting from the Year 2000 computer problem. As agreed to, the act's purpose was to:

(1) establish uniform legal standards that give all businesses and users of technology products reasonable incentives to solve year 2000 computer date-change problems before they develop; (2) encourage continued remediation and testing efforts to solve such problems by providers, suppliers, customers, and other contracting partners; (3) encourage private and public parties alike to resolve disputes relating to year 2000 computer date-change problems by alternative dispute mechanisms in order to avoid costly and time-consuming litigation, to initiate those mechanisms as early as possible, and to encourage the prompt identification and correction of such problems, and; (4) lessen the burdens on interstate commerce by discouraging insubstantial lawsuits while preserving the ability of individuals and businesses that have suffered real injury to obtain complete relief.

After the Select Committee had filed its Final Report, the Senate passed S. Res. 264 on Feb. 29. 2000, "Congratulating and thanking Chairman Robert F. Bennett and Vice Chairman Christopher J. Dodd for their tremendous leadership, poise, and dedication in leading the special committee on the year 2000 technology problem and commending the members of the Committee for their fine work."

Membership: In the resolution creating the committee, it was stated that, "The special committee shall consist of

7 members of the Senate— (A) 4 of whom shall be appointed by the President pro tempore of the Senate from the majority party of the Senate upon the recommendation of the Majority Leader of the Senate; and (B) 3 of whom shall be appointed by the President pro tempore of the Senate from the minority party of the Senate upon the recommendation of the Minority Leader of the Senate. The chairman and ranking minority member of the Appropriations Committee shall be appointed ex-officio members."

The original seven members of the committee came from fourteen of the Senate's sixteen standing committees—with only Agriculture, Nutrition and Forestry and Commerce, Science and Transportation excluded. When Susan Collins (Rep-Me.) was replaced by Richard G. Lugar (Rep-Ind.), the chair of Agriculture, only the Commerce committee was excluded from the special committee, even though it was the one with the major role in drafting the legislation.

Committee Leaders: According to the S. Res. 208, "The chairman of the special committee shall be selected by the Majority Leader of the Senate and the vice chairman of the special committee shall be selected by the Minority Leader of the Senate. The vice chairman shall discharge such responsibilities as the special committee or the chairman may assign."

Senator Robert Bennett (Rep-Utah) chaired the committee throughout its existence with Christopher J. Dodd (Dem-Conn.) as vice chair.

Selected References

U.S. Senate, Special Committee on the Year 2000 Technology Problem, *Investigating the Impact of the Year 2000 Problem*, Committee Summary, Feb. 24, 1999.

U.S. Senate, Special Committee on the Year 2000 Technology Problem, *Investigating the Year 2000 Problem: The 100 Day Report*, Committee Summary, Senate Print 106-31, Sept. 22, 1999.

U.S. Senate, Special Committee on the Year 2000 Technology Problem, *Y2K Aftermath-Crisis Averted,* Final Committee Report, Senate Print 106-42, Feb. 29, 2000.

JURISDICTION

Jurisdiction, 1998

From Senate Resolution 208, 105th Congress, April 2, 1998

SECTION 1. ESTABLISHMENT OF THE SPECIAL COMMITTEE.

(a) ESTABLISHMENT- There is established a special committee of the Senate to be known as the Special Committee on the Year 2000 Technology Problem (hereafter in this resolution referred to as the 'special committee').

(b) PURPOSE- The purpose of the special committee is—

(1) to study the impact of the year 2000 technology problem on the Executive and Judicial Branches of the Federal Government, State governments, and private sector operations in the United States and abroad;

(2) to make such findings of fact as are warranted and appropriate; and

(3) to make such recommendations, including recommendations for new legislation and amendments to existing laws and any administrative or other actions, as the special committee may determine to be necessary or desirable.

No proposed legislation shall be referred to the special committee, and the committee shall not have power to report by bill, or otherwise have legislative jurisdiction.

MEMBERSHIP ROSTERS, 105th-106th Congress, 1998-2000

SPECIAL COMMITTEE ON THE YEAR 2000 TECHNOLOGY PROBLEM / 105th Congress

Service Dates of Committee Chair: Apr. 3, 1998-Continued

Service Dates of Committee Vice Chair: Apr. 23, 1998-Continued

Service Dates of Majority Members: Apr. 28, 1998-Continued

Service Dates of Minority Members: Apr. 23, 1998-Continued

Majority					Minority				
			Years in:					Years in:	
Rank Name	Party	State	Senate	Comm.	Rank Name	Party	State	Senate	Comm.
Chr Bennett, Robert F.	Rep	Utah	6	1	VCh Dodd, Christopher J.	Dem	Conn.	18	1
2nd Kyl, Jon L.	Rep	Ariz.	4	1	2nd Moynihan, Daniel Patrick	Dem	N.Y.	22	1

3rd Smith, Gordon H.	Rep	Ore.	2	1
4th Collins, Susan M.	Rep	Me.	2	1
ExO Stevens, Theodore F.	Rep	Alas.	40	1

3rd Bingaman, J.F. (Jeff)	Dem	N.M.	16	1
ExO Byrd, Robert C.	Dem	W.Va.	40	1

Note: *Ex officio* members named Apr. 28, 1998 were Senators Stevens and Byrd, Chair and Ranking Member respectively of Senate Appropriations.

SPECIAL COMMITTEE ON THE YEAR 2000 TECHNOLOGY PROBLEM / 106th Congress

Service Dates of Committee Chair: Continued-Feb. 29, 2000

Service Dates of Committee Vice Chair: Continued-Feb. 29, 2000

Service Dates of Majority Members: Continued-Feb. 29, 2000

Service Dates of Minority Members: Continued-Feb. 29, 2000

Majority

Rank Name	Party	State	Years in: Senate	Comm.
Chr Bennett, Robert F.	Rep	Utah	7	1
2nd Kyl, Jon L.	Rep	Ariz.	5	1
3rd Smith, Gordon H.	Rep	Ore.	3	1
4th Collins, Susan M.	Rep	Me.	3	1
ExO Stevens, Theodore F.	Rep	Alas.	41	1

Minority

Rank Name	Party	State	Years in: Senate	Comm.
VCh Dodd, Christopher J.	Dem	Conn.	19	1
2nd Moynihan, Daniel Patrick	Dem	N.Y.	23	1
3rd Bingaman, J.F. (Jeff)	Dem	N.M.	17	1
ExO Byrd, Robert C.	Dem	W.Va.	41	1

Changes:

Majority:

Collins, Susan M.	Rep	Me.	June 30, 1999 Left committee; no new assignment
Lugar, Richard G.	Rep	Ind.	June 30, 1999 Replaced Collins

Part I

C. Standing Committees of the House of Representatives

Backgrounds, Jurisdictions, and Rosters
1993-2011

House Standing Committees
1993-2011

From the 1946 Reorganization to the Republican Revolution and Its Aftermath
Committee Changes in the House, 1947-1974

From 1947 to 1974, changes in the party control of the House were almost non-existent. After losing control of the House in the 1946 mid-term election, the Democrats regained control of the House of Representatives in the 1948 election. And apart from narrowly losing the House in 1952 during the Dwight Eisenhower landslide, they were in almost total party control of the House. In the forty-six years from 1949 to 1995, congressional Democrats had a party majority in the House for 44 of those years—95.7 percent of the time. From the 1954 election to the 1994 congressional election, Democrats organized the House for twenty consecutive Congresses—the longest one party control of any elected federal institution in American history. However, party control was not the same as philosophical control, for many of the southern Democrats who agreed to organize the House with fellow Democrats holding major leadership posts would often vote with the Republicans to block the liberal legislation emanating from other Democrats from the north and the west.

The early party continuity of the post-1946 era mirrored the continuity of the committee system.

Nineteen committees survived the 1946 Reorganization Act and by 1974 and the Committee Reform Amendments of that year, only two new standing committees had been added in almost thirty years. This was quite a contrast from the prior century when House committees proliferated every decade and were seldom terminated.

It was the successful launching of earth-orbiting satellites by the Soviet Union in 1957 that caused grave anxiety in Congress as well as throughout the nation that led to the 1958 creation of the House Committee on Science and Astronautics. Created initially as a select committee, it was the first new standing committee added to the House roster since the Reorganization. The second new standing committee grew out of a payroll scandal in the House concerning Adam Clayton Powell (Dem-N.Y.), the controversial chair of the Education and Labor Committee. It led to the creation of the House Committee on Standards of Official Conduct in 1967.

This was a time when inviolable seniority rules virtually guaranteed that the House committees would be chaired by long-time safe-seat conservative southerners and the occasional city machine northern Democrat. This was an era when the "Austin-Boston Connection" of Sam Rayburn of Texas, John McCormack of Massachusetts, and Carl Albert of Oklahoma held the speakership of the House for all but four of the twenty-eight years between 1947 and 1974. Moderate conservative Republican Joe Martin of Massachusetts, a close friend of both Rayburn and McCormack and Carl Albert of Oklahoma, a Rayburn protégé, held the speaker's chair for the other eight years. It was a time when partisan conflict was kept in check by this alliance but it was also a time when

committee chairs ruled the chamber. Not all of the committee chairs were autocratic but those who were autocrats gained power and were protected by the seniority system.

Kennedy-style Democrats, mostly liberal, well-educated, and representing northern and western suburban districts, chafed at the long-time Roosevelt-era alliance of the South and the big cities from non-competitive House seats that had gained and held power in the House through the operation of the seniority system. In 1970, 79 year-old House Speaker John W. McCormack (Dem-Mass.), who had served as a House leader for thirty-one years, mostly with the legendary Sam Rayburn of Texas as Speaker, retired. McCormack was an embodiment of the South-big city alliance and his retirement opened the door for the passage of the Legislative Reorganization Act of 1970 (P.L. 91-510). That act focused more on floor procedure and staff expansion and left the committees relatively untouched but the pace of reform would quicken.

The Democratic Caucus created the Committee on Organization, Study and Review, led by Julia Butler Hansen (Dem-Wash.) in 1971. It limited the number of subcommittee chairmanships that could be held; removed the seniority requirement for chairmanships; and allowed members to request secret ballots for votes on chairs. The passage of the Subcommittee Bill of Rights in 1973 further limited the power of the standing committee chairs but the number, names, and jurisdictions of the House committees remained in place.

The Limited Reforms of 1974 and 1980

In 1973, the House Select Committee on Committees, chaired by Richard W. Bolling (Dem-Mo.), a founder of the liberal Democratic Study Group, was able to bring about some alteration in the House committee system. With support from House Speaker Carl Albert (Dem-Okla.) and Majority Leader Thomas P. "Tip" O'Neill, Jr. (Dem-Mass.) the Bolling committee had hoped for ambitious changes. Issued as the Committee Reform Amendments of 1974, the Bolling Committee's reforms were somewhat limited. Fearing a further loss of their power, a number of the House chairs blocked many of Bolling's proposals and the results were relatively modest—the termination of the long-discredited House Committee on Internal Security (the successor to Un-American Activities) and elevating the long-serving Select Committee on Small Business to a standing one.

The 93rd Congress (1973-1975) convened with the White House of President Richard Nixon facing congressional scrutiny due to the 1972 "Watergate affair" that implicated a number of White House operatives in efforts to gain Nixon's re-election through a combination of break-ins and illegal pay-offs. Led initially in the Senate with its 1973 Select Committee to Investigate Presidential Campaign Activities, the House followed suit with impeachment proceedings against President Nixon in the Judiciary Committee that would produce three charges and lead to his August 9, 1974, resignation.

Growing opposition to the White House's expansion of executive power led the Congress to counter with the enactment of two far-ranging pieces of legislation. The first was the War Powers Act of 1973 (P.L. 93-148) that limited executive authority in placing U.S. troops in combat and the Congressional Budget and Impoundment Control Act of 1974 (P.L. 93-344) that limited the president's authority to withhold funds appropriated by Congress for programs and projects which the President opposed. While subsequent presidents have chosen to challenge the constitutionality of the War Powers Act and to ignore its provisions, the Congressional Budget Act continues to play a major role in fiscal legislation. It was this act that created the Budget committees in both the House and Senate.

The arrival of more than seventy Democratic freshmen following the 1974 election and their designation as "Watergate babies" led to a major power shift in the House as three long-serving oligarchic committee chairs were voted out of their posts by the Democratic Caucus—Agriculture Chair W. R. Poage (Dem-Texas), Armed Services Chair F. Edward Hebert (Dem-La.), and Banking and Currency Chair Wright Patman (Dem-Texas). The lessening of the security held by the chairs enhanced the power of the Albert-O'Neill leadership team. By 1974, further member pressure led the Democratic leadership to remove the power of committee appointments from the Democratic members of the Ways and Means Committee that had gained authority in the aftermath of the 1909-1910 overthrow of autocratic House Speaker Joseph G. Cannon (Rep-Ill.). Wilbur Mills (Dem-Ark.), the long-time chair of Ways and Means had become increasingly erratic in the wake of his forlorn 1972 presidential bid and the leadership capitalized on this opportunity by creating the Democratic Steering and Policy Committee in 1974 to serve as the "committee on committees" with the Speaker serving as chair.

With Speaker Carl Albert's retirement, "Tip" O'Neill, a protégé of John McCormack, became Speaker of the House in 1977. During O'Neill's ten years as Speaker (1977-1987), he created a number of select committees in the House whose members were appointed by the Steering and Policy Committee that he chaired. O'Neill, who had never chaired a standing committee, saw the expansion of the select committees as a way to reward the junior members by letting them gain chairmanships of the subcommittees of the new select committees. O'Neill's alliance with the junior members combined with the growing authority of the Caucus diminished further the power of the House chairs.

Another less ambitious committee reform movement occurred in 1979-1981 with the Select Committee on Committees chaired by Representative Jerry Patterson (Dem-Cal.). As the 1970s energy crisis became more acute with gas lines lengthening and tempers shortening, sentiment grew to provide the House with more authority to deal with the crisis. The initial effort made by Speaker O'Neill was to create a Select Committee on Energy in 1977. A later consequence was to consolidate the many overlapping energy jurisdictions within the Committee on Commerce. That committee had long been regarded as having a broad legislative mandate and chaired by veteran lawmaker John Dingell (Dem-Mich.), the reconfigured and renamed Committee on Energy and Commerce gained even further stature among the House's committees. However, other jurisdictional reforms failed to gain acceptance.

Speaker O'Neill was followed in 1987 in the Speaker's chair by Majority Leader James C. Wright (Dem-Texas), whose financial indiscretions led him to resign the speakership and his own House seat in June, 1989. Wright's departure ended the five decade-long control of the House Democrats by the "Austin-Boston connection" from Texas and Massachusetts. Wright was succeeded by Majority Leader Thomas Foley (Dem-Wash.), who had been chair of the House Agriculture Committee and the first former committee chair to hold the speakership since the legendary Sam Rayburn left the Interstate and Foreign Commerce Committee in 1937 to become majority leader. Under Foley, the standing committee chairs enjoyed resurgent authority, most notably, the triumvirate of Joe Moakley (Dem-Mass.) of Rules, John Dingell (Dem-Mich.) of Energy and Commerce, and Dan Rostenkowski (Dem-Ill.) of Ways and Means.

With Speaker Foley's acquiescence, the 103rd Congress (1993-1995) ended the legislative life of four of the surviving select House committees—Aging (established in 1974), Narcotics Abuse and Control (1976), Children, Youth and Families (1983), and Hunger (1984). Between them, these four select committees had provided 171 committee slots, and their termination led to the loss of power positions among many junior members. Only the Permanent Select Committee on Intelligence was retained.

Although newly-elected Democratic President Bill Clinton had a very high rate of legislative success with the Democratic 103rd Congress, its accomplishments were overshadowed by the check-kiting practices of many House members as they regularly overdrew their personal accounts at the House bank. Sometimes characterized as "rubbergate," the House Bank scandal confirmed suspicions that the forty-year reign of Democrats in the House, 1955-1995, had made their members complacent and corrupt.

An era would end.

The Republican Revolution and Its Committee Aftermath, 1995-2007

The Political Context: Congressional scandals in the House Bank and in its post office combined with President Clinton's diminished popularity opened the door to Republican capture of the U.S. Congress. The Republicans had gained earlier control of the Senate in the wake of Ronald Reagan's 1980 election and had held it for six years (1981-1987). In that election, Republicans had gained an even-split of the twenty-two Senators from the South, but Republican control of the House had been a goal that had eluded them for the forty years since 1954.

Gaining control of the House for the Republicans was the goal of House Minority Whip Newt Gingrich (Rep-Ga.) who had gained the leadership of the House Republicans in 1994 by shouldering long-time Minority Leader Robert Michel (Rep-Ill.) into retirement. Working with pollsters and like-minded conservatives, Gingrich and his allies Dick Armey (Rep-Texas) and Robert Walker (Rep-Penn.) crafted a list of propositions and legislative policy goals with wonderful sounding names such as the American Dream Restoration Act and the Personal Responsibility Act to produce a "Contract with America" that would be fulfilled once Republicans gained control of the House of Representatives. Virtually all of the Republican House candidates in 1994 signed onto the Contract. Leading Democrats scoffed at the proposals calling it the "Contract ON America," but they underestimated voter anger and when the polls closed, Republicans had gained their first House victory since 1952 and the largest since 1946.

The 1994 congressional elections gave control of the House to the Republican Party for the first time since the 83rd Congress (1953-1955) was elected in the Dwight D. Eisenhower landslide of 1952. Among the Democratic electoral casualties were House Speaker Foley, the first speaker voted out of office since Pennsylvania's Galusha Grow in 1862, Ways and Means Chair Rostenkowski, and Judiciary Committee Chair Jack Brooks (Dem-Texas). No Republican incumbents in elections for the House, the Senate, or governor lost their seats in that election. It was described as a "tsunami."

A key aspect of the victory was that for the first time ever, Republicans had gained an edge among House seats elected from the South. In part, some of this was due to the creation of "majority-minority" districts by "packing" minorities into House districts where they would have a majority of voters. This was a policy pushed by the Democratic members of the Congressional Black Caucus who hoped to increase the numbers of black and Latino members. Although it led to a near doubling of the number of Democratic black and Latino members, it had the unintended consequence of making the adjacent districts whiter ("bleached") and more amenable to conservative Republican overtures and more than twenty southern districts affected by this demographic shift moved into the Republican column.

How party control of the House shifted from the Democrats in 1994 to a twelve-year Republican regime, 1995-2007, and then back to Democratic control in the 2006 congressional elections is presented in the following table.

PARTY REPRESENTATION IN THE U.S. HOUSE, 1993-2011

Congress	Years	Democrats	Republicans	Independents
103rd	1993-1995	258	176	1
104th	1995-1997	204	230	1
Special election victories and party switches				
		198	234	2
105th	1997-1999	206	228	1
106th	1999-2001	211	223	1
107th	2001-2003	209	222	1
108th	2003-2005	205	229	1
109th	2005-2007	201	232	1
110th	2007-2009	233	202	0
111th	2009-2010	256	178	0

Note: Vacancies account for the House seats not totaling the allotted 435 number.

The fifty-four seat gain by the Republicans in the 1994 congressional elections was the latest of the thirteen fifty-seat shifts since the opening of the 20th century. However, it was only the third shift of that magnitude since the 1948 election landslide gained Democrats 75 seats, reversing the outcome of the 55 seats gained in the 1946 Republican landslide. Since the 1946 and 1948 contests, only three congressional elections in the past six decades have seen seat swings of a fifty-plus magnitude—the recession-impacted 1958 congressional election with 54 seats gained by the Democrats; the "Watergate" election of 1974 with its Democratic gain of 52 seats; and the 1994 "Contract with America" election.

Republican gains in 1994 were augmented by the defections of five conservative southern House Democrats to the Republican Party in 1995 creating a Republican margin of 36

seats over the Democrats. That margin—the highest since the 80th Congress (1947-1949)—shrunk in both the 1996 and 1998 elections until it was only twelve seats. It was the narrowing of the seat margin in 1998 that led a number of Republicans to urge the brilliant but controversial Speaker of the House Newt Gingrich to relinquish the speakership as he had become a lightning rod for criticism of their congressional performance. Gingrich went even further and resigned the House as well as departing the speakership.

Gingrich's departure opened the speakership for Robert Livingston (Rep-La.), the chair of the always powerful House Appropriations Committee, but revelations of Livingston's previous marital indiscretions—similar to those surrounding Democrat President Bill Clinton—ended that bid. Livingston also resigned from the House a short time after Gingrich did. Republicans led by the tough-minded and often abrasive Majority Whip Tom DeLay (Rep-Texas) chose J. Dennis Hastert (Rep-Ill.) to serve as Speaker. Hastert's pleasant Midwestern mien was a contrast with that of the hard-charging DeLay, whose nickname on the Hill was "the Hammer."

The extraordinary closeness of the 2000 presidential election between Democratic vice president Al Gore, Jr. and Texas governor George W. Bush manifested itself in the Senate results as well with a 50-50 split in that chamber. The House results in 2000 were similar to those in 1998, so the House was able to avoid the confusion that roiled both the presidency and the Senate. Newly-elected President George W. Bush lost party control of the Senate when Vermont's moderate liberal James M. Jeffords left the Republicans in June 2001 to become an Independent and to caucus with the Democrats, giving them control of that body. The terrorist attacks of September 11, 2001, on the World Trade Towers in New York City and the Pentagon in Arlington, Virginia, led to Americans rallying around President Bush and the political impact of the Jeffords defection was dissipated. The rally continued into the 2002 congressional elections. With President Bush's success that year, he became the first president since Franklin D. Roosevelt in 1934 to increase his party's House seat margin in a mid-term contest.

Helped by Majority Leader Tom DeLay's mid-decade redrawing of the Texas congressional districts and President Bush's coattails in 2004, House Republicans were able to push their seat margin over the Democrats to 31 seats. But events in 2005 would lead to the slow and inexorable decline of President Bush's popularity. The administration's bungled response to the devastation of New Orleans and the Gulf caused by Hurricanes Katrina and Rita and the continuing military quagmires in Iraq and Afghanistan led to the diminishing popularity of the Republican brand.

In 2006, the House Democrats took advantage of the opening and picked up 32 seats and regained control of the House for the first time since the 103rd Congress (1993-1995). The 53 percent presidential victory of Senator Barack Obama (Dem-Ill.) in the 2008 election provided coattails long enough to enable Democrats to pick up an additional 23 House seats and to increase the Democratic margin over the Republicans to 78 seats (256 to 178). The Democrats had restored their control of the House but would it last?

The Committee Context: The 104th Congress convened in January, 1995 with seventy-three Republican first-time members who were committed to implementing the conservative provisions of the "Contract with America" that Gingrich and his allies had crafted. The first order of business was to address the public accountability issues that had surfaced in the House Bank scandal of the previous Democratic 103rd Congress. The next order was to reform House procedure and to restructure the House's committee system.

By 1995, the House standing committee system had remained relatively intact since the 1946 Reorganization Act and had only been slightly modified by the subsequent reforms. Apart from the addition of three standing committees—Space and Astronautics, Standards of Official Conduct, and Budget—and the termination of Internal Security, the major changes that occurred in that forty-eight-year period took place in the growing number of committee assignments for each of the standing committees and the expansion of sub-committees. From 1947 through 1992, the number of assigned places on House standing committees had grown from 484 to 848—a 75 percent increase—and the number of House subcommittees grew from 89 in 1947 to 137 in 1992—a 54 percent increase.

Gingrich's leadership team of Majority Leader Dick Armey (Rep-Texas) and Majority Whip Tom DeLay (Rep-Texas) would change the game. The first step of the Gingrich team was to abolish three less well-regarded standing committees—District of Columbia, Merchant Marine and Fisheries, and Post Office and Civil Service. Members had been increasingly reluctant to serve on them and two had shrunken in size. The Senate had previously abolished their District of Columbia and Post Office and Civil Service Committees in 1977 and it never had a stand-alone Merchant Marine committee.

As stated in the "Changes in Committee System" of January 4, 1995

Sec. 202. (a) **The Committees and Their Jurisdiction:** Clause 1 of rule X of the Rules of the House of Representatives is amended to read as follows:

(b) Any reference in the rules of the House at the end of the One Hundred Third Congress to the following standing committees of the House: the Committee on Armed Services; the Committee on the District of Columbia; the Committee on Education and Labor; the Committee on Energy and Commerce; the Committee on Foreign Affairs; the Committee on Government Operations; the Committee on House Administration; the Committee on Natural Resources; and the Committee on Science, Space and Technology; shall be amended to be a reference to the following standing committees of the House, respectively: the Committee on National Security; the Committee on Government Reform and Oversight; the Committee on Economic and Educational Opportunities; the Committee on Commerce; the Committee on International Relations; the Committee on Government Reform and Oversight; the Committee on House Oversight; the Committee on Resources; and the Committee on Science.

Nineteen standing committees remained, equal to the number that emerged from the original Legislative Reorganization Act forty-eight years earlier. The new Republican majority quickly put their own unique stamp on the remaining nineteen standing committees by renaming ten of them, as an apparent signal to the nation that a new congressional order had been established in the House. Among the name changes implemented in 1995 were: 1) Armed Services became National Security; 2) Education and Labor was renamed Economic and Educational Opportunities in 1995 and renamed again as Education and the Workforce in 1997; 3) Energy and Commerce which gained that name in 1981 had been known as Interstate and Foreign Commerce in the 1946 Act now became Commerce; 4)

Banking, Finance, and Urban Affairs, which had already been renamed from Banking, Currency, and Housing in 1977 after being known originally as Banking and Currency (1947-1975) now became the Committee on Banking and Financial Services in 1995 and just Financial Services in 1999; 5) Foreign Affairs once again became International Relations, a name it had held earlier (1975-1979); 6) Government Operations, originally known as Expenditures in the Executive Departments in the 1946 Reorganization and renamed in 1952, became Government Reform and Oversight; 7) House Administration became House Oversight; 8) Natural Resources, which had just been renamed in 1993, was originally known as Public Lands from 1947 to 1951 and as Interior and Insular Affairs from 1951 to 1993, and now became Resources, its fourth post-1946 identity; 9) Science, Space and Technology, known as Science and Astronautics (1958-1975) and Science and Technology (1975-1987) became Science; and 10) Public Works and Transportation became Transportation and Infrastructure.

Unsurprisingly, the five committees that had survived the 1946 Reorganization with their names intact retained their names and most of their jurisdictional responsibilities in the post-1995 era—Agriculture, Appropriations, Judiciary, Rules, and Ways and Means—as did Veterans' Affairs, which was a creation of the 1946 Act. The three newer committees that were spared renaming were Budget, Small Business, and Standards of Official Conduct.

Another key feature of the Gingrich regime was to select committee chairs that were in accord with the Speaker's "Contract with America" agenda regardless of their relative seniority. Non senior-most chairs were named in three committees—Commerce, Judiciary, and Appropriations. In the cases of Commerce and Judiciary, the second-ranking Republicans—Thomas Bliley of Virginia and Henry Hyde of Illinois—were placed ahead of the senior-most Republicans as chairs. It was on the Appropriations Committee that the boldest step was taken by elevating fifth-ranked Robert Livingston of Louisiana to the chairmanship of this powerhouse committee.

A further benefit of loosening seniority requirements was that Gingrich was able to induce five Southern Democrats to became Republicans—Nathan Deal of Georgia, Greg Laughlin of Texas, Mike Parker of Mississippi, and Billy Tauzin and Jimmy Hayes of Louisiana in 1995, and to reward them with attractive committee assignments and to reorder their seniority on those committees. Four other Southern Democrats would follow in subsequent years—Virgil Goode of Virginia in 2000, Rodney Alexander of Louisiana in 2004, Ralph Hall of Texas in 2005 and Parker Griffith of Alabama in 2009. Two other post-1993 party switchers differed from the nine southern Democrats: California Democrat Matthew (Marty) Martinez became a Republican in 2000 following his defeat in a primary by Linda Sanchez (Dem-Cal.) and New York Republican Michael P. Forbes became a Democrat in 1999 but would lose that party's 2000 primary.

Only one new standing committee was added to the lineup during the twelve-year Republican hegemony and that was the Committee on Homeland Security. The committee was created in response to the September 11, 2001, terrorist attacks on New York City and the Pentagon. It was first designated as a select committee in the 107th Congress with nine members named on June 19, 2002. Among the original members were Republicans Majority Leader Dick Armey of Texas and Majority Whip Tom DeLay of Texas and Democratic Minority Whip Nancy Pelosi of California. The select committee grew to fifty members in the

108th Congress and became the twentieth standing committee of the contemporary House in the 109th Congress (2005-2007) with a membership of thirty-four members. The House's decision to create a new committee varied with that of the Senate which chose to add similar jurisdictional responsibilities to its already existing Committee on Governmental Affairs and to rename the committee accordingly as the Senate Committee on Homeland Security and Governmental Affairs.

The Republican takeover continued the House's three-fold categorization of the committees with "exclusive" committees, those where membership is presumed to be confined to one committee; "non-exclusive" committees where membership is less constrained; and "exempt" committees where service on those committees has no discernible impact upon the service on the exclusive and non-exclusive committees. The categorization of the committees and their assignment availability are similar but not identical for the two congressional parties, as may be seen in the following table prepared by Judy Schneider of the Congressional Research Service. Committee names have been updated.

CATEGORIES OF HOUSE COMMITTEES

Category	Democrats	Republicans
Exclusive	Appropriations Rules Ways and Means Energy and Commerce (for post-104th members and subsequent ones.) Financial Services (for post-109th members and subsequent ones.)	Appropriations Rules Ways and Means Energy and Commerce
Non-Exclusive	Agriculture Armed Services Budget Education and Labor* Energy and Commerce (for pre-104th Congress members) Financial Services (for pre-109th Congress Members) Foreign Affairs* Homeland Security House Administration Judiciary Natural Resources* Oversight and Government Reform* Science and Technology* Small Business Transportation and Infrastructure Veterans' Affairs	Agriculture Armed Services Budget Education and Labor* Financial Services Foreign Affairs* Homeland Security House Adminstration Judiciary Natural Resources* Oversight and Government Reform* Science and Technology* Small Business Transportation and Infrastructure Veterans' Affairs
Exempt	Standards of Official Conduct Select Energy Independence and Global Warming Permanent Select Intelligence (Treated as exempt)	Standards of Official Conduct Select Energy Independence and Global Warming Permanent Select Intelligence

Source: Adapted and updated from Judy Schneider, "House Committees: Categories and Rules for Committee Assignments," (Congressional Research Service, 2005), 98-151, p. CRS-3.

*Names of committees have been updated for the 111th Congress.

The Democratic restoration of control of the House had relatively minimal impact upon the committee system. No standing committees were abolished and no new ones were created. Two new select committees were created but only the Select Committee on Energy Independence and Global Warming appears to have any staying power. No efforts were made to resurrect the defunct committees on the District of Columbia, Merchant Marine and Fisheries, or Post Office and Civil Service.

Committee jurisdictions remained virtually intact while all but one of the Gingrich-era name changes was revoked. In the 110th Congress (2007-2009), the first of the Democratic restoration, the Committees of Education and the Workforce and International Relations resumed their previous names of Education and Labor and Foreign Affairs respectively. Resources became Natural Resources as it had been in 1993-1995 while Science resumed the name Science and Technology, which had been its designation from 1975 to 1987. Earlier name changes created by Gingrich reverted to pre-Gingrich ones after he left the House in 1999. House Oversight resumed the name of House Administration in 1999; Commerce resumed the name of Energy and Commerce in 2001; and National Security became Armed Services again in 2005. The Gingrich-era renaming of Banking, Finance and Urban Affairs to be the Committee on Banking and Financial Services became simply Financial Services in 2001 while the 1995 renaming of Government Operations to become Government Reform and Oversight was reversed in 2007 to become the Committee on Oversight and Government Reform. The only Gingrich-era committee name to survive intact was the Committee on Transportation and Infrastructure, the sole remaining evidence of the Gingrich presence.

The nine committee names unaffected by the Republican Revolution were also unaffected by the Democratic Restoration—Agriculture, Appropriations, Budget, Judiciary, Rules, Small Business, Standards of Official Conduct, Veterans' Affairs, and Ways and Means.

A statistical portrait of the House's nineteen standing committees reveals some unexpected developments that have contributed to how the House has functioned over the past eighteen years. Three comparative statistics—1) mean size of the committee; 2) mean term seniority of the members on the committee; and 3) the overall inter-Congress retention rate of the members—are presented and ranked in the following table.

The most noteworthy aspect of the size measurements listed here is the replacement of the Appropriations Committee at the top of the list by both the Transportation and Infrastructure and the Financial Services Committees. Appropriations emerged from the 1946 Reorganization as the House's largest standing committee and it held that designation until 1993, when Transportation and Infrastructure passed it in size, and then again in 2001, when Financial Services passed it and moved the Appropriations Committee into third place. Appropriations continues to hold its relative prestige prominence by topping the list with the mean seniority of its members and its second-place ranking to Ways and Means with its very high membership retention rate.

HOUSE STANDING COMMITTEES: COMPARATIVE STATISTICS, 1993-2011

Ranks of Committee	Mean Size	Mean Seniority	Mean Retention Rate
1st	72.7 Trans. + Infrastructure	7.43 Appropriations	98.50 Ways and Means
2nd	64.0 Financial Services	6.98 Ways and Means	97.74 Appropriations
3rd	62.7 Appropriations	6.39 Rules	97.04 Energy + Commerce
4th	59.7 Armed Services	6.16 Energy + Commerce	92.08 Judiciary
5th	53.8 Energy + Commerce	5.72 Judiciary	90.27 Armed Services
6th	49.2 Natural Resources	5.64 Foreign Affairs	87.83 Foreign Affairs
7th	48.9 Agriculture	5.50 House Administration	87.23 Trans. + Infrastructure
8th	48.1 Foreign Affairs	5.28 Natural Resources	86.94 Financial Services
9th	47.8 Science + Technology	5.23 Education and Labor	Tie 85.89 Education and Labor
10th	47.3 Education and Labor	5.20 Standards of Conduct	Tie 85.89 Agriculture
11th	43.7 Oversight/Govt. Reform	4.73 Oversight/Govt. Reform	85.57 Rules
12th	41.6 Budget	4.63 Armed Services	85.39 Natural Resources
13th	40.0 Ways and Means	4.52 Trans. + Infrastructure	82.35 Veterans' Affairs
14th	37.6 Judiciary	4.36 Budget	80.45 Oversight/Govt. Reform
15th	36.2 Small Business	4.35 Financial Services	78.31 Science + Technology
16th	30.9 Veterans' Affairs	4.30 Veterans' Affairs	67.82 Budget
17th	13.0 Rules	4.16 Science + Technology	66.67 Small Business
18th	Tie 10.4 House Administration	3.46 Agriculture	61.73 House Administration
19th	Tie 10.4 Standards of Conduct	2.87 Small Business	57.50 Standards of Conduct

Note: Owing to its recent creation, Homeland Security was not included in these lists.

Regarding relative seniority, it is not surprising to see the House's traditional "big three" of the Appropriations, Ways and Means, and Rules Committees topping the list. Energy and Commerce's emergence as a relative power source among the committees is attested to by its fourth-place showing in mean member seniority and its third place in the rate of its inter-Congress membership retention. What is surprising is to see the Rules Committee lodged in eleventh place among the nineteen continuing committees on the membership-retention dimension. In recent years, the prestigious and powerful Rules Committee has had a relatively large number of first-term members seated on the committee. Only two first termers were assigned to the House Rules Committee between 1947 and 1995 but since then seven first termers have been named to the committee—five in the last two Congresses alone (2007-2011). They apparently serve a term on Rules and then move elsewhere. This recent practice is one that would have baffled both two of the most powerful Speakers in House history—Thomas B. (Czar) Reed of Maine and Sam Rayburn of Texas.

In earlier times, junior members would be socialized into deferential House mores by assignment to minor committees with only tangential benefits for their constituents. Once they had demonstrated their electoral survival skills then they would be moved to more attractive committee locations. Typical of earlier days would be to assign an urban member like John McCormack of Boston to the Territories Committee before moving him to Ways and Means three years later, or like Shirley Chisholm (Dem-N.Y.), the first African-American woman to serve in the House who represented Brooklyn and was initially assigned to the Agriculture Committee, until her public protest ended that plan and she was relocated immediately to Veterans' Affairs, then to Education and Labor, and ultimately to Rules. John F. Kennedy was initially assigned to the District of Columbia Committee in 1947 but never displayed the appropriate deference to the House leadership and remained on that ill-regarded committee for six years, longer than any other Massachusetts member.

The relative low ranking of the Budget and Standards of Official Conduct Committees on the rate of membership retention is because they have membership stipulations that limit the length of time that members may serve on them. Service on Standards of Official Conduct is limited to three Congresses during any five successive Congresses (Rule X: 5) and Budget Committee members are limited to no more than four Congresses in any six successive Congresses (Rule X: 5 (a)(2)(B) and as Schneider notes, "Democratic Caucus rules limit members to no more than three Congresses in any five" ("House Committees," p. 2).

Other membership changes that have appeared in recent years also follow from the relaxation of rigid seniority requirements. One is the increasing frequency of members returning to serve on committees that they had departed earlier. In the 103rd Congress (1993-1995), there were twenty instances of members in their second period of service on any of the nineteen standing committees covered in this book and one instance of a member in a third period of service. By the 111th Congress (2009-2011), the number of members returning for a second period of service grew to sixty-four and the number of members in their third period of service was six.

The second consequence of these changes has been a relaxing of the "exclusivity" rules that limited members of presumably exclusive committees like Ways and Means, Appropriations, and Rules from serving simultaneously on non-exclusive committees. In the 103rd Congress twenty-three of the thirty-six Ways and Means Committee members (63.9%) served only on it or on the Joint Committee on Taxation, which consists of the three senior majority and the two senior minority members of Ways and Means. Five Ways and Means members served on Budget as required by House rules and six others served on "exempt" committees such as Standards of Official Conduct, Permanent Select Intelligence, or the joint committees. Only seven served on non-exclusive standing committees—four on House Administration and three on the District of Columbia, the two committees at the bottom of the committee pecking order.

In the 111th Congress (2009-2011), twenty-two of forty members served only on Ways and Means or the exempt committees. Eight served simultaneously on Budget while ten served on non-exclusive committees—Foreign Affairs (3); Oversight and Government Reform (2); and one each on Agriculture, Homeland Security, House Administration, Judiciary, and Natural Resources. Similar relaxations of the exclusivity rule may be seen in the Appropriations Committee of the 111th Congress which has ten members serving on non-exclusive committees—Science and Technology (3), Judiciary (2), Oversight and Government Reform (2), and one each on Foreign Affairs, Natural Resources, and Veterans' Affairs.

A majority of the thirteen members of the presumably exclusive Rules Committee in the 111th Congress serves concurrently on other standing committees. Six serve on the non-exclusive committees of Agriculture, Armed Services, Budget, Education and Labor, Financial Services, and Transportation and Infrastructure. And one current member of Rules, Doris Matsui (Dem-Cal.) presently serves on another presumably exclusive committee—Energy and Commerce.

Clearly, the provisions in the House rules that permit members to receive permission from their respective caucuses to serve simultaneously on exclusive and non-exclusive committees are more in evidence today than in previous Congresses.

The standing committee system of the House dates from April 13, 1789, seventeen days before the inauguration of President George Washington in New York City. It has moved from an era of powdered wigs and horse-drawn carriages when communication took many days to a time when trans-Atlantic travel takes a few hours and communication is instantaneous. The committee system has outlasted a brutal civil war, two world wars, a lengthy cold war, the atomic and hydrogen bombs, four presidential assassinations, congressional scandals aplenty, and most importantly, the rise of the United States from a far-flung collection of thirteen states scattered along the Atlantic Seaboard with three million people to be the world's preeminent nation with more than 300 million people filling nearly half a continent. The House's standing committee system has survived all of these changes because it continues to do what its creators more than two centuries ago hoped it would do—provide a forum for the people's will to be expressed; to tax and spend the public monies appropriately, and to oversee and control the executive branch.

House Standing Committees 1993-2011

Agriculture

House Committee on Agriculture, 103rd-111th Congresses (1993-2011)

BACKGROUND

Organizational History: The House of Representatives has had a standing committee dealing with agricultural issues since December 14, 1795 when the House voted to create the Committee of Commerce, Manufactures, and Agriculture. In the 16th Congress, both the Manufactures and Agriculture Committees were created as separate entities. The official date for the creation of a distinct Committee on Agriculture was May 3, 1820.

In the debate creating the original committee the House champion of the new panel, Rep. Lewis Williams of South Carolina, described his view of the need in words that reverberate down to the latest Congress:

"[H]ow happens it ... that the agricultural, the great and leading substantial interest in this country, has no committees—no organized tribunal in this House to hear and determine on their grievances? If the commercial or manufacturing interests are affected, the cry resounds throughout the country; remonstrances flow in upon us; they are referred to committees appointed for the purpose of guarding them, and adequate remedies are provided. But ... when agriculture is oppressed, and makes complaint, what tribunal is in this House to hear and determine on the grievances?"

The 1880 reorganization of the House committees gave the Committee on Agriculture jurisdiction over issues relating to forestry and it was given oversight of the U.S. Department of Agriculture's appropriations. It lost this power in 1920 when the Appropriations Committee assumed jurisdiction of all appropriation measures.

Since its inception, the chief responsibility of the House Agriculture Committee is oversight of the federal government's many programs of financial support and assistance to farmers. In the years since the New Deal and the ill-fated Agricultural Adjustment Act of 1933, the federal government has become increasingly involved in using financial price supports to encourage farmers to adjust their production to prevailing market forces. Through a variety of mechanisms the federal programs determine the minimum prices farmers receive for their crops with the goal of providing some protection against wide swings in market prices for farm products.

In the 85th Congress (1957-1959), the House Agriculture Committee had eighteen subcommittees in an elaborate system arrayed along specific commodity lines with cotton, sugar, corn, wheat, tobacco, dairy and poultry, and livestock among the commodities with their own subcommittees. In recent years, the number of subcommittees has stabilized at six and their responsibilities are now broader. Issues of conservation and environmental pollution have led the committee to address the use of agricultural pesticides. The awareness that the number of full-time farmers in rural America has declined as a consequence of the growth of major agribusiness corporations and that most residents of rural America are not farmers has led to a commitment on the part of the committee to address rural development issues. All of the recent jurisdictional listings for the committee include "rural development" on the list. The federal food stamp program, which helps low-income people buy food, falls within the committee's jurisdiction. One additional food product that has been added to the list of Agriculture Committee jurisdictional commodities is seafood, which was assigned to Agriculture after the 1995 dismemberment of the Merchant Marine and Fisheries Committee.

The committee's most ambitious international effort was the Agricultural Trade Development Assistance Act of July 10, 1954, known initially as Public Law 480 and renamed in 1961 by President John F. Kennedy as the Food for Peace Program. While the program is administered by the U.S. Agency for International Development, the Agriculture Committee retains oversight over aspects of the program and its oversight was reauthorized by the Federal Agriculture Improvement and Reform Act of 1996 (P.L. 104-127), sometimes referred to as the "Freedom to Farm" or FAIR bill.

Membership: Committee members, who mostly represent heavily rural areas, are the leading advocates in the House for the interests of farms. Historically, most of its Democrats come from the South and most of its Republicans come from the Midwest. There are few members from big cities or industrial areas. Individually they are not great in numbers, but through the operation of the long-established "farm coalition" they have had much success. The coalition is essential because no single crop is important everywhere in the nation. But long ago committee members learned to join together in a common front for all farm products. Since the mid-1960s they have found allies in urban members, often Democrats, who are interested in the food stamp program, which by the 1990s was one of the federal government's biggest cash transfer programs. It is of immense importance to House members from big cities, who otherwise had little interest in farm programs. By including generous funding for food stamps in farm legislation, Agriculture Committee members were able to win the support of many liberal, urban Democrats for farm programs.

In the years between 1947 and 1992, the Agriculture Committee varied in size from twenty-seven members in the 80th and 81st Congresses (1947-1951) to forty-six in the 95th (1977-1979). Its membership stabilized at forty-five from 1989 to 1992. Since 1993, its first fifty-member Congress was the 103rd (1993-1995) when five additional members were placed on the committee after the initial appointments. It reached a peak of fifty-one members in three subsequent Congresses (1999-2005). Then it declined again and since 2005, the committee's membership has remained at forty-six. Its mean size since 1993 of 48.89 placed it seventh among the nineteen regularly appointed House committees and its mean seniority of 3.46 terms per member placed it in eighteenth place, outranking only Small Business. In spite of the low seniority numbers, the Agriculture Committee had a mean inter-Congress retention rate of 85.89 percent, placing it in a two-way tie for ninth with the Education and Labor Committee.

Committee Leaders: The first post-Reorganization chair was Clifford R. Hope (Rep-Kans.) who had been the Agriculture Committee's senior Republican since 1937 and would chair the committee in both the Republican 80th and 83rd Congresses. Its first post-1946 ranking minority member was John W. Flannagan, Jr. (Dem-Va.) who had chaired the committee from 1944 to 1947. He retired in 1949 with Harold D. Cooley (Dem-N.C.) becoming its senior Democrat who chaired the committee for eight of the nine Congresses between 1949 and 1967. Five Republican ranking members served with Cooley. Hope served as ranking member in the Democratic Congresses until his 1957 retirement. Minnesota's August H. Andresen followed Hope but died in 1958 and was succeeded by William S. Hill (Rep-Colo.) who retired in 1959. Charles B. Hoeven (Rep-Iowa) became ranking member in 1959 and served until his retirement in 1965. Paul B. Dague (Rep-Penn.) succeeded Hoeven and retired in 1967.

Cooley's re-election defeat in 1966 election gave the chair to W.R. Poage (Dem-Tex.). Poage served with two Republican ranking members—Page H. Belcher of Oklahoma, from 1967 until his 1973 retirement, Charles M. Teague of California, from 1973 until his death in 1974, and William C. Wampler of Virginia from 1974 until his 1982 defeat. Following Wampler's defeat, House Republicans moved Edward R. Madigan of Illinois back to Agriculture from the Budget Committee to outrank Vermont's second-ranking James M. Jeffords, who had become a pariah among Republicans for being the only House Republican to vote against President Ronald Reagan's 1981 tax cut. Madigan would leave the House in 1991 to become Secretary of Agriculture under President George H.W. Bush. Madigan's successor E. Thomas Coleman (Rep-Mo.) served out the remainder of the 102nd Congress until his 1992 re-election defeat.

W.R. Poage served as chair of Agriculture until his 1974 defeat in the Democratic Caucus for the 94th Congress in one of the first instances in which a committee chair was deposed by the Caucus. Poage lost to second-ranking Thomas S. Foley (Dem-Wash.), a six-term member. Foley held the chair until 1981 when he became Majority Whip in the Democratic leadership on his way to becoming House Speaker in 1989. His successor was E. (Kika) de la Garza (Dem-Tex.) who held the chair from 1981 to 1995 and served as ranking member until his 1997 retirement. Fellow Texan Charles Stenholm, a leader of the Conservative Democratic Forum—"the boll weevils"—succeeded de la Garza and served as ranking member until his election defeat in 2004. Stenholm's successor was Collin C. Peterson (DFL-Minn.), who became ranking member in 2005 and chair of Agriculture in 2007, where he still presides.

Kansas Republican Pat Roberts became ranking minority member in 1993, and in 1995 the committee's first Republican chair since fellow Kansan Clifford Hope held that post forty years earlier. Roberts left the House in 1997 following his election to the U.S. Senate. In an unusual development, Roberts was replaced as chair by Robert F. Smith of Oregon who had retired in 1995 but was induced to return to the House and to serve as chair of Agriculture in the 105th Congress (1997-1999). Smith's successor as chair was Larry Combest (Rep-Tex.) who stepped aside as chair in 2003 for Robert W. Goodlatte (Rep-Va.) who served as chair of Agriculture from 2003 to 2007 and as ranking member until 2009, when he stepped aside for Paul D. Lucas (Rep-Okla.).

Party Leaders: Although not considered to be a traditional major committee in the House, the Agriculture Committee has provided the Democrats with two long-serving leaders—Carl Albert of Oklahoma who became Democratic Whip in 1955; Majority Leader in 1962; and succeeded John W. McCormack as Speaker of the House from 1971 until his retirement in 1977, and Thomas S. Foley, who became Whip from 1981 to 1987; Majority Leader from 1987 to 1989; and who succeeded James C. Wright as Speaker of the House in 1989 and served until his re-election defeat in 1994. Another Agriculture Committee alumnus serving in the party leadership was Anthony L. Coelho of California who served as Democratic Whip from 1981 until his resignation in 1989.

Among Republicans, John Boehner (Rep-Ohio) the present Minority Leader is an Agriculture Committee alumnus as is former Whip Roy Blunt (Rep-Mo.) who Boehner defeated for the leadership post.

Notable Members: Two modern-era presidential nominees served on the House Agriculture Committee—George S. McGovern of South Dakota, the Democratic presidential nominee in 1972 and Robert J. Dole of Kansas, the Republican vice presidential nominee in 1976 and their presidential nominee in 1996. The first modern-era House Agriculture Committee member to serve in a presidential cabinet was Clinton B. Anderson of New Mexico who served as Secretary of Agriculture under President Harry Truman. Since then, three recent Presidents, Jimmy Carter, George H.W. Bush and Bill Clinton, selected four Secretaries of Agriculture with Agriculture Committee experience, with Bob Bergland (DFL-Minn.) serving under Carter; Edward R. Madigan (Rep-Ill.) under George H.W. Bush and Mike Espy (Dem-Miss.) and Dan Glickman (Dem-Kans.) under Clinton. Other Cabinet members with House Agriculture service include Melvin Laird (Rep-Wisc.), President Nixon's Secretary of Defense; Thomas Kleppe (Rep-N.D.), President Ford's Secretary of the Interior; Margaret Heckler (Rep-Mass.), President Reagan's second Secretary of Health and Human Services; and Ray LaHood (Rep-Ill.), President Obama's Secretary of Transportation.

Post-1947, twenty-eight former House Agriculture Committee members served in the Senate: eighteen Democrats—Delegate E.L. (Bob) Bartlett of Alaska, Daniel K. Inouye, Spark M. Matsunaga, and Daniel K. Akaka all of Hawaii, George S. McGovern, Thomas Daschle, and Timothy P. Johnson all of South Dakota, Eugene J. McCarthy of Minnesota, Ross Bass of Tennessee, Thomas R. Harkin of Iowa, Ben Nighthorse Campbell and Mark Udall of Colorado, Byron L. Dorgan of North Dakota, Richard J. Durbin of Illinois, John Melcher of Montana, Deborah A. Stabenow of Michigan, Blanche Lambert Lincoln of Arkansas, and Kirsten E Gillibrand of New York.

Ten Republican senators served on House Agriculture—Robert J. Dole and C. Patrick Roberts of Kansas, Norris Cotton of New Hampshire, Steven Symms and Michael D. Crapo of Idaho, Charles Grassley of Iowa, James M. Jeffords of Vermont, A. Wayne Allard of Colorado, John R. Thune of South Dakota, and Saxby Chambliss of Georgia.

In addition, six former Agriculture committee members went on to become governors: two Democrats—Arthur A. Link of North Dakota and John Baldacci of Maine; and four Republicans—Albert H. Quie of Minnesota, Charles Thone of Nebraska, Ernest L. Fletcher of Kentucky, and Robert Riley of Alabama. South Dakota Republican Governor William J. Janklow reversed the path as a four-term governor whose subsequent career on Agriculture ended with a vehicular manslaughter charge a year after being elected to the House.

Selected References

Carter, John J., "A Constituency Committee under Pressure," *Southeastern Political Review,* 18 (Fall, 1990), 47-60.

Cochrane, Willard W. and Mary E. Ryan, *American Farm Policy: 1948-1973* (Minneapolis: University of Minnesota Press, 1976).

Engeke, Joanne, et al., "The House Agriculture Committee and the Senate Agriculture and Forestry Committee," in the Ralph Nader Congress Project, *The Environment Committees A Study of the House and Senate Interior, Agriculture, and Science Committees* (New York: Grossman, 1975), 145-280.

Lyons, Michael S. and Marcia Whicker Taylor, "Farm Politics in Transition: The House Agriculture Committee," *Agricultural History,* 55 (1981), 128-146.

Jones, Charles O., "Representation in Congress: The Case of the House Agriculture Committee," *American Political Science Review,* 55 (June, 1961), 358-367.

Ornstein, Norman J. and David W. Rohde, "Shifting Forces, Changing Rules, and Political Outcomes: The Impact of Congressional Change on Four House Committees," in Robert L. Peabody and Nelson W. Polsby, eds., *New Perspectives on the House of Representatives,* 3rd ed. (Chicago: Rand McNally, 1977), 186-269.

Panning, William, "The Structural Approach to the Identification of Voting Blocs: The Case of the House Agriculture Committee," *Political Methodology* 8 (1982), 61-85.

Peters, John, "The 1977 Farm Bill: Coalitions in Congress," in Don F. Hadwiger and William P. Browne, eds., *The New Politics of Food* (Lexington, Mass.: Lexington Books, 1978), 23-55.

Saloutos, Theodore, *The American Farmer and the New Deal* (Ames: Iowa State University Press, 1982).

Schamel, Charles E. et al., "Records of the Agriculture Committee," *Guide to the Records of the United States House of Representatives at the National Archives: 1789-1989 Bicentennial Edition* (Washington, D.C.: National Archives and Records Administration,1989), 23-29.

Talbot, Ross B. and Don F. Hadwiger, *The Policy Process in American Agriculture* (San Francisco: Chandler, 1968).

U.S. House of Representatives, Committee on Agriculture, *United States House of Representatives Committee on Agriculture, 150th Anniversary,* H.Doc. 91-350, 91st Congress, 2nd Session (1970).

Wright, John R., "Contributions, Lobbying, and Committee Voting in the U.S. House of Representatives," *American Political Science Review,* 84 (June, 1990), 417-438.

RESPONSIBILITIES, JURISDICTIONAL CHANGES, AND SUBCOMMITTEES

AGRICULTURE

Jurisdiction, 80th Congress (1947-1949)

Established by the Reorganization Act of 1946

Established by the Legislative Reorganization Act of 1946:

[Section 121.(1)(a)] Committee on Agriculture
   (1) Agriculture generally.
   (2) Inspection of livestock and meat products.
   (3) Animal industry and diseases of animals.
   (4) Adulteration of seeds, insect pests, and protection of birds and animals in forest reserves.
   (5) Agricultural colleges and experiment stations.
   (6) Forestry in general, and forest reserves other than those created from the public domain.
   (7) Agricultural economics and research.
   (8) Agricultural and industrial chemistry.
   (9) Dairy industry.
   (10) Entomology and plant quarantine.
   (11) Human nutrition and home economics.
   (12) Plant industry, soils, and agricultural engineering.
   (13) Agricultural educational extension services.
   (14) Extension of farm credit and farm security.
   (15) Rural electrification.

(16) Agricultural production and marketing and stabilization of prices of agricultural products.
(17) Crop insurance and soil conservation.

Jurisdiction, 103rd Congress (1993-1995)

From the Rules of the House of Representatives, 103rd Congress (House Document 102-405)

[Rule X. 1. (a)] Committee on Agriculture
(1)   Adulteration of seeds, insect pests, and protection of birds and animals in forest reserves.
(2)   Agriculture generally.
(3)   Agricultural and industrial chemistry.
(4)   Agricultural colleges and experiment stations.
(5)   Agricultural economics and research.
(6)   Agricultural education extension services.
(7)   Agricultural production and marketing and stabilization of prices of agricultural products, and commodities (not including distribution outside of the United States).
(8)   Animal industry and diseases of animals.
(9)   Crop insurance and soil conservation.
(10) Dairy industry.
(11) Entomology and plant quarantine.
(12) Extension of farm credit and farm security.
(13) Forestry in general, and forest reserves other than those created from the public domain.
(14) Human nutrition and home economics.
(15) Inspection of livestock and meat products.
(16) Plant industry, soils, and agricultural engineering.
(17) Rural electrification.
(18) Commodities exchanges.
(19) Rural development.

Jurisdiction, 104th Congress (1995-1997) Changes in Committee System

From H. Res. 6, Section 202 (a), the Committees and Their Jurisdiction, January 4, 1995

[Rule X. 1. (a)] Committee on Agriculture
(1)   Adulteration of seeds, insect pests, and protection of birds and animals in forest reserves.
(2)   Agriculture generally.
(3)   Agricultural and industrial chemistry.
(4)   Agricultural colleges and experiment stations.
(5)   Agricultural economics and research.
(6)   Agricultural education extension services.
(7)   Agricultural production and marketing and stabilization of prices of agricultural products, and commodities (not including distribution outside of the United States).
(8)   Animal industry and diseases of animals.
(9)   Commodities exchanges.
(10) Crop insurance and soil conservation.
(11) Dairy industry.
(12) Entomology and plant quarantine.
(13) Extension of farm credit and farm security.
(14) Inspection of livestock, and poultry, and meat products, and seafood and seafood products.
(15) Forestry in general, and forest reserves other than those created from the public domain.
(16) Human nutrition and home economics.
(17) Plant industry, soils, and agricultural engineering.
(18) Rural electrification.
(19) Rural development.
(20) Water conservation related to activities of the Department of Agriculture.

Jurisdiction, 111th Congress (2009-2011)

From the Rules of the House of Representatives (as revised to June 16, 2009, H.Doc. 110-162):

[Rule X.1.(a)] Committee on Agriculture
(1)   Adulteration of seeds, insect pests, and protection of birds and animals in forest reserves.
(2)   Agriculture generally.

(3) Agricultural and industrial chemistry.
(4) Agricultural colleges and experiment stations.
(5) Agricultural economics and research.
(6) Agricultural education extension services.
(7) Agricultural production, marketing and stabilization of prices of agricultural products, and commodities (not including distribution outside of the United States).
(8) Animal industry and diseases of animals.
(9) Commodity exchanges.
(10) Crop insurance and soil conservation.
(11) Dairy industry.
(12) Entomology and plant quarantine.
(13) Extension of farm credit and farm security.
(14) Inspection of livestock, and poultry, and meat products, and seafood and seafood products.
(15) Forestry in general and forest reserves other than those created from the public domain.
(16) Human nutrition and home economics.
(17) Plant industry, soils, and agricultural engineering.
(18) Rural electrification.
(19) Rural development.
(20) Water conservation related to activities of the Department of Agriculture.

NAMES OF AGRICULTURE SUBCOMMITTEES FROM THE *CONGRESSIONAL DIRECTORY*

Conservation, Credit, Rural Development and Research, 107, 108, 109
Conservation, Credit, Energy, and Research, 110, 111
Department Operations and Nutrition, 103
Department Operations, Nutrition and Foreign Agriculture, 104, 105
Department Operations, Oversight, Nutrition, and Forestry, 106, 107, 108, 110, 111
Department Operations, Oversight, Dairy, Nutrition, and Forestry, 109
Environment, Credit and Rural Development, 103
Foreign Agriculture and Hunger, 103
Forestry, Resource Conservation and Research, 105
General Farm Commodities. 103, 104, 105
General Farm Commodities, Resource Conservation and Credit, 106
General Farm Commodities and Risk Management, 107, 108, 109, 110, 111
Horticulture and Organic Agriculture, 110, 111
Livestock, 103
Livestock and Horticulture, 106, 107, 108, 109
Livestock, Dairy and Poultry, 104, 105, 110, 111
Resource Conservation, Research, and Forestry, 104
Risk Management and Specialty Crops, 104, 105
Risk Management, Research and Specialty Crops, 106
Rural Development, Biotechnology, Specialty Crops, and Foreign Agriculture, 111
Specialty Crops and Natural Resources, 103
Specialty Crops and Foreign Agriculture Programs, 107, 109
Specialty Crops and Foreign Agriculture, 108
Specialty Crops, Rural Development and Foreign Agriculture, 110

MEMBERSHIP ROSTERS, 103rd-111th Congresses, 1993-2011

AGRICULTURE / 103rd Congress

Service Dates of Committee Chair: Jan. 5, 1993-Jan. 3, 1995

Service Dates of Majority Members: Jan. 5, 1993-Jan. 3, 1995

Service Dates of Minority Members: Jan. 5, 1993-Jan. 3, 1995

Roster Filled: Majority with 27 members, Jan. 5, 1993; Minority with 18 members, Jan. 5, 1993.

Majority

Rank Name	Party	State	Terms in: House	Terms in: Comm.
Chr de la Garza, E. (Kika)	Dem	Tex.	15	15
2nd Brown, George E. Jr.	Dem	Cal.	15	11
3rd Rose, Charles G. III	Dem	N.C.	11	11
4th English, Glenn L. Jr.	Dem	Okla.	10	10
5th Panetta, Leon E.	Dem	Cal.	9	9
6th Glickman, Daniel R.	Dem	Kans.	9	9
7th Stenholm, Charles W.	Dem	Tex.	8	8
8th Volkmer, Harold L.	Dem	Mo.	9	*2 7
9th Penny, Timothy J.	DFL	Minn.	6	6
10th Johnson, Timothy P.	Dem	S.D.	4	4
11th Espy, A. Michael	Dem	Miss.	4	4
12th Sarpalius, William	Dem	Tex.	3	3
13th Long, Jill L.	Dem	Ill.	3	3
14th Condit, Gary A.	Dem	Cal.	3	3
15th Peterson, Collin C.	DFL	Minn.	2	2
16th Dooley, Calvin M.	Dem	Cal.	2	2
17th Clayton, Eva M.	Dem	N.C.	2	1
18th Minge, David B.	DFL	Minn.	1	1
19th Hilliard, Earl F.	Dem	Ala.	1	1
20th Inslee, Jay R.	Dem	Wash.	1	1
21st Barlow, Thomas J.	Dem	Ky.	1	1
22nd Pomeroy, Earl R. III	Dem	N.D.	1	*1 1
23rd Holden, T. Timothy	Dem	Penn.	1	1
24th McKinney, Cynthia A.	Dem	Ga.	1	1
25th Baesler, H. Scott (Scotty)	Dem	Ky.	1	1
26th Thurman, Karen L.	Dem	Fla.	1	1
27th Bishop, Sanford D. Jr.	Dem	Ga.	1	1

Minority

Rank Name	Party	State	Terms in: House	Terms in: Comm.
RM Roberts, C. Patrick	Rep	Kans.	7	7
2nd Emerson, N. William	Rep	Mo.	7	7
3rd Gunderson, Steven C.	Rep	Wisc.	7	7
4th Lewis, Thomas F.	Rep	Fla.	6	5
5th Smith, Robert F.	Rep	Ore.	6	*1 5
6th Combest, Larry E.	Rep	Tex.	5	5
7th Camp, David L.	Rep	Mich.	2	2
8th Allard, A. Wayne	Rep	Colo.	2	2
9th Barrett, William E.	Rep	Neb.	2	2
10th Nussle, James A.	Rep	Iowa	2	2
11th Boehner, John A.	Rep	Ohio	2	2
12th Ewing, Thomas W.	Rep	Ill.	2	2
13th Doolittle, John T.	Rep	Cal.	2	1
14th Kingston, Jack	Rep	Ga.	1	1
15th Goodlatte, Robert W.	Rep	Va.	1	1
16th Dickey, Jay W. Jr.	Rep	Ark.	1	1
17th Pombo, Richard W.	Rep	Cal.	1	1
18th Canady, Charles T.	Rep	Fla.	1	1

*1: Member's first period of service on the committee.
*2: Member's second period of service on the committee.

Additions:

Majority:

28th Thompson, Bennie	Dem	Miss.	Apr. 29, 1993
29th Farr, Sam	Dem	Cal.	June 23, 1993

Minority:

19th Everett, R. Terry	Rep	Ala.	May 27, 1993
20th Lucas, Frank D.	Rep	Okla.	May 24, 1994
21st Lewis, Ron	Rep	Ky.	June 15, 1994

Changes:

Majority:

Panetta, Leon E.	Dem	Cal.	Jan. 21, 1993 Resigned the House; appointed Director, Office of Management and Budget
Espy, A. Michael	Dem	Miss.	Jan. 22, 1993 Resigned the House; appointed Secretary of Agriculture
Williams, J. Patrick	Dem	Mont.	Feb. 4, 1993 Replaced Panetta
Lambert, Blanche	Dem	Ark.	Feb. 4, 1993 Replaced Espy
English, Glenn L. Jr.	Dem	Okla.	Jan. 7, 1994 Resigned the House; became CEO of National Rural Electric Cooperative Association

Minority:

Camp, David L.	Rep	Mich.	Feb. 4, 1993 Resigned committee; moved to Ways and Means
Smith, Nick H.	Rep	Mich.	May 27, 1993 Replaced Camp

Departures from the House:

	Majority			Minority		
Defeated for Re-election	Glickman, Daniel R.	Dem	Kans.	None		
	Sarpalius, William	Dem	Tex.			
	Long, Jill L.	Dem	Ind.			
	Inslee, Jay R.	Dem	Wash.			
	Barlow, Thomas J.	Dem	Ky.			
Retired	Penny, Timothy J.	Dem	Minn.	Lewis, Thomas F.	Rep	Fla.
				Smith, Robert F.	Rep	Ore.

Departures from Committee:

	Majority			Minority		
Moved to Appropriations	None			Kingston, Jack	Rep	Ga.
				Dickey, Jay W. Jr.	Rep	Ark.
Moved to Budget	None			Nussle, James A.	Rep	Iowa
Moved to Economic and Educational Opportunities	Williams, J. Patrick	Dem	Mont.	None		
Moved to Ways and Means	None			Nussle, James A.	Rep	Iowa
No new assignment	Lambert, Blanche	Dem	Ark.			

AGRICULTURE / 104th Congress

Service Dates of Committee Chair: Jan. 4, 1995-Jan. 3, 1997

Service Dates of Majority Members: Jan. 4, 1995-Jan. 3, 1997

Service Dates of Minority Members: Jan. 4, 1995-Jan. 3, 1997

Roster Filled: Majority with 27 members, Jan. 4, 1995; Minority with 22 members, Jan. 4, 1995.

	Majority						Minority				
				Terms in:						Terms in:	
Rank Name	Party	State	House	Comm.		Rank Name	Party	State	House	Comm.	
Chr Roberts, C. Patrick	Rep	Kans.	8	8		RM de la Garza, E. (Kika)	Dem	Tex.	16	16	
2nd Emerson, N. William	Rep	Mo.	8	8		2nd Brown, George E. Jr.	Dem	Cal.	16	12	
3rd Gunderson, Steven C.	Rep	Wisc.	8	8		3rd Rose, Charles G. III	Dem	N.C.	12	12	
4th Combest, Larry E.	Rep	Tex.	6	6		4th Stenholm, Charles W.	Dem	Tex.	9	9	
5th Allard, A. Wayne	Rep	Colo.	3	3		5th Volkmer, Harold L.	Dem	Mo.	10	*2 8	
6th Barrett, William E.	Rep	Neb.	3	3		6th Johnson, Timothy P.	Dem	S.D.	5	5	
7th Boehner, John A.	Rep	Ohio	3	3		7th Condit, Gary A.	Dem	Cal.	4	4	
8th Ewing, Thomas W.	Rep	Ill.	3	3		8th Peterson, Collin C.	DFL	Minn.	3	3	
9th Doolittle, John T.	Rep	Cal.	3	2		9th Dooley, Calvin M.	Dem	Cal.	3	3	
10th Goodlatte, Robert W.	Rep	Va.	2	2		10th Clayton, Eva M.	Dem	N.C.	3	2	
11th Pombo, Richard W.	Rep	Cal.	2	2		11th Minge, David B.	DFL	Minn.	2	2	
12th Canady, Charles T.	Rep	Fla.	2	2		12th Hilliard, Earl F.	Dem	Ala.	2	2	
13th Smith, Nick H.	Rep	Mich.	2	2		13th Pomeroy, Earl R. III	Dem	N.D.	2	*1 2	
14th Everett, R. Terry	Rep	Ala.	2	2		14th Holden, T. Timothy	Dem	Penn.	2	2	
15th Lucas, Frank D.	Rep	Okla.	2	2		15th McKinney, Cynthia A.	Dem	Ga.	2	2	
16th Lewis, Ron	Rep	Ky.	2	2		16th Baesler, H. Scott (Scotty)	Dem	Ky.	2	2	
17th Baker, Richard H.	Rep	La.	5	1		17th Thurman, Karen L.	Dem	Fla.	2	2	
18th Crapo, Michael D.	Rep	Ida.	2	1		18th Bishop, Sanford D. Jr.	Dem	Ga.	2	2	
19th Calvert, Ken	Rep	Cal.	2	*1 1		19th Thompson, Bennie	Dem	Miss.	2	2	
20th Chenoweth, Helen P.	Rep	Ida.	1	1		20th Farr, Sam	Dem	Cal.	2	2	
21st Hostettler, John N.	Rep	Ind.	1	1		21st Pastor, Edward L.	Dem	Ariz.	3	1	
22nd Bryant, Ed	Rep	Tenn.	1	1		22nd Baldacci, John E.	Dem	Me.	1	1	
23rd Latham, Thomas	Rep	Iowa	1	1							
24th Cooley, Wes	Rep	Ore.	1	1		*1: Member's first period of service on the committee.					
25th Foley, Mark A.	Rep	Fla.	1	1		*2: Member's second period of service on the committee.					
26th Chambliss, Saxby	Rep	Ga.	1	1							
27th LaHood, Ray H.	Rep	Ill.	1	1							

Changes:

Majority:

Emerson, N. William	Rep	Mo.	June 22, 1996 Died in office
Funderburk, David	Rep	N.C.	Aug. 2, 1996 Replaced Emerson

Minority:

McKinney, Cynthia A.	Dem	Ga.	Feb. 28, 1996 Resigned committee; moved to Banking and Financial Services

Departures from the House:

	Majority			Minority		
Elected to U.S. Senate	Roberts, C. Patrick	Rep	Kans.	Johnson, Timothy P.	Dem	S.D.
	Allard, A. Wayne	Rep	Colo.			
Defeated for Re-election	Funderburk, David	Rep	N.C.	Volkmer, Harold L.	Dem	Mo.
Retired	Gunderson, Steven C.	Rep	Wisc.	de la Garza, E. (Kika)	Dem	Tex.
	Cooley, Wes	Rep	Ore.	Rose, Charles G. III	Dem	N.C.

Departures from Committee:

	Majority			Minority		
Moved to Appropriations	Latham, Thomas	Rep	Iowa	None		
Returned to Appropriations	None			Pastor, Edward L.	Dem	Ariz.
Moved to Resources	Crapo, Michael D.	Rep	Ida.	None		
Moved to Transportation and Infrastructure	Baker, Richard H.	Rep	La.	None		
Moved to Ways and Means	None			Thurman, Karen L.	Dem	Fla.
No new assignment	Calvert, Ken	Rep	Cal.	None		

AGRICULTURE / 105th Congress

Service Dates of Committee Chair: Jan. 7, 1997-Jan. 3, 1999

Service Dates of Majority Members: Jan. 7, 1997-Jan. 3, 1999

Service Dates of Minority Members: Jan. 7, 1997-Jan. 3, 1999

Roster Filled: Majority with 27 members, Jan. 7, 1997; Minority with 23 members, Feb. 5, 1997.

Majority						Minority				
			Terms in:						**Terms in:**	
Rank Name	Party	State	House	Comm.		Rank Name	Party	State	House	Comm.
Chr Smith, Robert F.	Rep	Ore.	7	*2 1		RM Stenholm, Charles W.	Dem	Tex.	10	10
2nd Combest, Larry E.	Rep	Tex.	7	7		2nd Brown, George E. Jr.	Dem	Cal.	17	13
3rd Barrett, William E.	Rep	Neb.	4	4		3rd Condit, Gary A.	Dem	Cal.	5	5
4th Boehner, John A.	Rep	Ohio	4	4		4th Peterson, Collin C.	DFL	Minn.	4	4
5th Ewing, Thomas W.	Rep	Ill.	4	4		5th Dooley, Calvin M.	Dem	Cal.	4	4
6th Doolittle, John T.	Rep	Cal.	4	3		6th Clayton, Eva M.	Dem	N.C.	4	3
7th Goodlatte, Robert W.	Rep	Va.	3	3		7th Minge, David B.	DFL	Minn.	3	3
8th Pombo, Richard W.	Rep	Cal.	3	3		8th Hilliard, Earl F.	Dem	Ala.	3	3
9th Canady, Charles T.	Rep	Fla.	3	3		9th Pomeroy, Earl R. III	Dem	N.D.	3	*1 3
10th Smith, Nick H.	Rep	Mich.	3	3		10th Holden, T. Timothy	Dem	Penn.	3	3
11th Everett, R. Terry	Rep	Ala.	3	3		11th Baesler, H. Scott (Scotty)	Dem	Ky.	3	3
12th Lucas, Frank D.	Rep	Okla.	3	3		12th Bishop, Sanford D. Jr.	Dem	Ga.	3	3
13th Lewis, Ron	Rep	Ky.	3	3		13th Thompson, Bennie	Dem	Miss.	3	3
14th Chenoweth, Helen P.	Rep	Ida.	2	2		14th Farr, Sam	Dem	Cal.	3	3
15th Hostettler, John N.	Rep	Ind.	2	2		15th Baldacci, John E.	Dem	Me.	2	2
16th Bryant, Ed	Rep	Tenn.	2	2		16th Berry, R. Marion	Dem	Ark.	1	1
17th Foley, Mark A.	Rep	Fla.	2	2		17th Goode, Virgil H. Jr.	Dem	Va.	1	1
18th Chambliss, Saxby	Rep	Ga.	2	2		18th McIntyre, Mike	Dem	N.C.	1	1
19th LaHood, Ray H.	Rep	Ill.	2	2		19th Stabenow, Deborah Ann	Dem	Mich.	1	1
20th Emerson, Jo Ann	Rep	Mo.	2	1		20th Etheridge, Bobby R.	Dem	N.C.	1	1
21st Moran, Jerry	Rep	Ka.	1	1		21st John, Christopher	Dem	La.	1	1
22nd Blunt, Roy	Rep	Mo.	1	1		22nd Johnson, Jay W.	Dem	Wisc.	1	1
23rd Pickering, Charles W. (Chip) Jr.	Rep	Miss.	1	*1 1		23rd Boswell, Leonard L.	Dem	Iowa	1	*1 1
24th Schaffer, Robert W.	Rep	Colo.	1	1						
25th Thune, John R.	Rep	S.D.	1	1		*1: Member's first period of service on the committee.				
26th Jenkins, William L.	Rep	Tenn.	1	1		*2: Member's second period of service on the committee.				
27th Cooksey, John	Rep	La.	1	1						

Notes: Smith served on the Committee on Agriculture from 1983 to 1995 when he retired. He returned to the House and was named as Chair of the Committee on Agriculture in the 105th Congress and retired again in 1998.

Vacancies Filled:
  Minority:

22nd Johnson, Jay W.	Dem	Wisc.	Feb 5, 1997
23rd Boswell, Leonard L.	Dem	Iowa	Feb 5, 1997

Departures from the House:

	Majority				**Minority**		
Defeated for Re-election	None				Johnson, Jay W.	Dem	Wisc.
Lost Election to U.S. Senate	None				Baesler, H. Scott (Scotty)	Dem	Ky.
Retired	Smith, Robert F.	Rep	Ore.		None		

Departures from Committee:

Moved to Appropriations	Emerson, Jo Ann	Rep	Mo.		Farr, Sam	Dem	Cal.
Moved to Commerce	Bryant, Ed	Rep	Tex.		None		
	Pickering, Charles W. (Chip) Jr.	Rep	Miss.				
	Blunt, Roy	Rep	Mo.				
Moved to Government Reform	Doolittle, John T.	Rep	Cal.		None		
Moved to Transportation and Infrastructure	Doolittle, John T.	Rep	Cal.		None		
Moved to Ways and Means	Lewis, Ron	Rep	Ky.		None		
	Foley, Mark A.	Rep	Fla.				

AGRICULTURE / 106th Congress

Service Dates of Committee Chair: Jan. 6, 1999-Jan. 3, 2001

Service Dates of Majority Members: Jan. 6, 1999-Jan. 3, 2001

Service Dates of Minority Members: Jan. 6, 1999-Jan. 3, 2001

Roster Filled: Majority with 27 members, Jan. 6, 1999; Minority with 24 members, Jan. 19, 1999.

Majority						Minority				
			Terms in:						**Terms in:**	
Rank Name	Party	State	House	Comm.		Rank Name	Party	State	House	Comm.
Chr Combest, Larry E.	Rep	Tex.	8	8		RM Stenholm, Charles W.	Dem	Tex.	11	11
2nd Barrett, William E.	Rep	Neb.	5	5		2nd Brown, George E. Jr.	Dem	Cal.	18	14

3rd Boehner, John A.	Rep	Ohio	5	5	
4th Ewing, Thomas W.	Rep	Ill.	5	5	
5th Goodlatte, Robert W.	Rep	Va.	4	4	
6th Pombo, Richard W.	Rep	Cal.	4	4	
7th Canady, Charles T.	Rep	Fla.	4	4	
8th Smith, Nick H.	Rep	Mich.	4	4	
9th Everett, R. Terry	Rep	Ala.	4	4	
10th Lucas, Frank D.	Rep	Okla.	4	4	
11th Chenoweth, Helen P.	Rep	Ida.	3	3	
12th Hostettler, John N.	Rep	Ind.	3	3	
13th Chambliss, Saxby	Rep	Ga.	3	3	
14th LaHood, Ray H.	Rep	Ill.	3	3	
15th Moran, Jerry	Rep	Ka.	2	2	
16th Schaffer, Robert W.	Rep	Colo.	2	2	
17th Thune, John R.	Rep	S.D.	2	2	
18th Jenkins, William L.	Rep	Tenn.	2	2	
19th Cooksey, John	Rep	La.	2	2	
20th Calvert, Ken	Rep	Cal.	4	*2 1	
21st Gutknecht, Gilbert W.	Rep	Minn.	3	1	
22nd Riley, Robert	Rep	Ala.	2	1	
23rd Walden, Greg	Rep	Ore.	1	1	
24th Simpson, Michael K.	Rep	Ida.	1	1	
25th Ose, Doug	Rep	Cal.	1	1	
26th Hayes, Robert (Robin)	Rep	N.C.	1	1	
27th Fletcher, Ernest L.	Rep	Ky.	1	1	

3rd Condit, Gary A.	Dem	Cal.	6	6	
4th Peterson, Collin C.	DFL	Minn.	5	5	
5th Dooley, Calvin M.	Dem	Cal.	5	5	
6th Clayton, Eva M.	Dem	N.C.	5	4	
7th Minge, David B.	DFL	Minn.	4	4	
8th Hilliard, Earl F.	Dem	Ala.	4	4	
9th Pomeroy, Earl R. III	Dem	N.D.	4	*1 4	
10th Holden, T. Timothy	Dem	Penn.	4	4	
11th Bishop, Sanford D. Jr.	Dem	Ga.	4	4	
12th Thompson, Bennie	Dem	Miss.	4	4	
13th Baldacci, John E.	Dem	Me.	3	3	
14th Berry, R. Marion	Dem	Ark.	2	2	
15th Goode, Virgil H. Jr.	Dem	Va.	2	2	
16th McIntyre, Mike	Dem	N.C.	2	2	
17th Stabenow, Deborah Ann	Dem	Mich.	2	2	
18th Etheridge, Bobby R.	Dem	N.C.	2	2	
19th John, Christopher	Dem	La.	2	2	
20th Boswell, Leonard L.	Dem	Iowa	2	*1 2	
21st Phelps, David D.	Dem	Ill.	1	1	
22nd Lucas, Ken	Dem	Ky.	1	*1 1	
23rd Thompson, Michael	Dem	Cal.	1	1	
24th Hill, Baron P.	Dem	Ind.	1	1	

*1: Member's first period of service on the committee.
*2: Member's second period of service on the committee.

Filled Vacancy:

Minority: Hill, Baron P.	Dem	Ind.	Jan. 19, 1999

Changes:

Minority:

Brown, George E. Jr.	Dem	Cal.	July 15, 1999 Died in office
Baca, Joe	Dem	Cal.	Nov. 18, 1999 Replaced Brown
Goode, Virgil H. Jr.	Dem	Va.	Feb. 1, 2000 Service on committee as a Democrat vacated; moved to Appropriations as an Independent Majority member

Departures from the House:

	Majority			Minority		
Elected to U.S. Senate	None			Stabenow, Deborah Ann	Dem	Mich.
Defeated for Re-election	None			Minge, David B.	DFL	Minn.
Retired	Barrett, William E.	Rep	Neb.	None		
	Ewing, Thomas W.	Rep	Ill.			
	Canady, Charles T.	Rep	Fla.			
	Chenoweth, Helen P.	Rep	Ida.			

Departures from Committee:

Moved to Appropriations	LaHood, Ray H.	Rep	Ill.	None		
Moved to Armed Services	Calvert, Ken	Rep	Cal.	None		
Moved to Energy and Commerce	Walden, Greg	Rep	Ore.	None		
Moved to Judiciary	Hostettler, John N.	Rep	Ida.	None		
Moved to Ways and Means	None			Pomeroy, Earl R. III	Dem	N.D.

AGRICULTURE / 107th Congress

Service Dates of Committee Chair: Jan. 6, 2001-Jan. 3, 2003

Service Dates of Majority Members: Jan. 6, 2001-Jan. 3, 2003

Service Dates of Minority Members: Jan. 31, 2001-Jan. 3, 2003

Roster Filled: Majority with 27 members, Jan. 6, 2001; Minority with 24 members, Mar. 14, 2001.

	Majority			Terms in:			Minority			Terms in:	
Rank Name	Party	State	House	Comm.		Rank Name	Party	State	House	Comm.	
Chr Combest, Larry E.	Rep	Tex.	9	9		RM Stenholm, Charles W.	Dem	Tex.	12	12	
2nd Boehner, John A.	Rep	Ohio	6	6		2nd Condit, Gary A.	Dem	Cal.	7	7	
3rd Goodlatte, Robert W.	Rep	Va.	5	5		3rd Peterson, Collin C.	DFL	Minn.	6	6	
4th Pombo, Richard W.	Rep	Cal.	5	5		4th Dooley, Calvin M.	Dem	Cal.	6	6	
5th Smith, Nick H.	Rep	Mich.	5	5		5th Clayton, Eva M.	Dem	N.C.	6	5	
6th Everett, R. Terry	Rep	Ala.	5	5		6th Hilliard, Earl F.	Dem	Ala.	5	5	
7th Lucas, Frank D.	Rep	Okla.	5	5		7th Holden, T. Timothy	Dem	Penn.	5	5	

8th Chambliss, Saxby	Rep	Ga.	4	4		8th Bishop, Sanford D. Jr.	Dem	Ga.	5	5		
9th Moran, Jerry	Rep	Ka.	3	3		9th Thompson, Bennie	Dem	Miss.	5	5		
10th Schaffer, Robert W.	Rep	Colo.	3	3		10th Baldacci, John E.	Dem	Me.	4	4		
11th Thune, John R.	Rep	S.D.	3	3		11th Berry, R. Marion	Dem	Ark.	3	3		
12th Jenkins, William L.	Rep	Tenn.	3	3		12th McIntyre, Mike	Dem	N.C.	3	3		
13th Cooksey, John	Rep	La.	3	3		13th Etheridge, Bobby R.	Dem	N.C.	3	3		
14th Gutknecht, Gilbert W.	Rep	Minn.	4	2		14th John, Christopher	Dem	La.	3	3		
15th Riley, Robert	Rep	Ala.	3	2		15th Boswell, Leonard L.	Dem	Iowa	3	*1 3		
16th Simpson, Michael K.	Rep	Ida.	2	2		16th Phelps, David D.	Dem	Ill.	2	2		
17th Ose, Doug	Rep	Cal.	2	2		17th Thompson, Michael	Dem	Cal.	2	2		
18th Hayes, Robert (Robin)	Rep	N.C.	2	2		18th Hill, Baron P.	Dem	Ind.	2	2		
19th Fletcher, Ernest L.	Rep	Ky.	2	2		19th Baca, Joe	Dem	Cal.	2	2		
20th Pickering, Charles W. (Chip) Jr.	Rep	Miss.	3	*2 1		20th Ross, Michael A.	Dem	Ark.	1	1		
21st Johnson, Timothy V.	Rep	Ill.	1	1		21st Acevedo-Vilá, Aníbal	Dem	P.R.	1	1		
22nd Osborne, Thomas	Rep	Neb.	1	1		22nd Lucas, Ken	Dem	Ky.	2	*1 2		
23rd Pence, Mike	Rep	Ind.	1	1		23rd Kind, Ron	Dem	Wisc.	3	1		
24th Rehberg, Dennis	Rep	Mont.	1	1		24th Shows, C. Ronald	Dem	Miss.	2	1		
25th Graves, Samuel B.	Rep	Mo.	1	1								
26th Putnam, Adam H. Jr.	Rep	Fla.	1	1								
27th Kennedy, Mark	Rep	Minn.	1	1								

*1: Member's first period of service on the committee.

*2: Member's second period of service on the committee.

Notes: Lucas returned to the committee on March 14, 2001 and was listed after Acevedo-Vilá yet was ranked immediately after Phelps and ranked immediately after Acevido-Vilá, followed by Shows. Acevedo-Vila was allowed to accrue committee seniority but was not included in the party ratio.

Filled Vacancies:

Minority:

20th and 21st seats by Ross and Acevedo-Vilá on Feb. 8, 2001

22nd, 23rd, and 24th seats by Lucas, Kind, and Shows on Mar. 14, 2001

Changes:

Majority:

Fletcher, Ernest L.	Rep	Ky.	Mar. 20, 2002 Resigned committee; moved to Energy and Commerce
Gekas, George W.	Rep	Penn.	July 26, 2002 Replaced Fletcher

Minority:

John, Christopher	Dem	La.	Feb. 8, 2001 Resigned committee; moved to Energy and Commerce
Larsen, Richard R. (Rick)	Dem	Wash.	Feb. 8, 2001 Replaced John

Departures from the House:

	Majority				Minority		
Elected to U.S. Senate	Chambliss, Saxby	Rep	Ga.		None		
Elected Governor	Riley, Robert	Rep	Ala.		Baldacci, John E.	Dem	Me.
Defeated for Re-election	Gekas, George W.	Rep	Penn.		Phelps, David D.	Dem	Ill.
					Shows, C. Ronald	Dem	Miss.
Defeated for Re-nomination	None				Condit, Gary A.	Dem	Cal.
					Hilliard, Earl F.	Dem	Ala.
Lost Election to U.S. Senate	Thune, John R.	Rep	S.D.		None		
Lost Nomination to U.S. Senate	Cooksey, John	Rep	La.				
Retired	Schaffer, Robert W.	Rep	Colo.		Clayton, Eva M.	Dem	N.C.

Departures from Committee:

	Majority				Minority		
Moved to Appropriations	Simpson, Michael K.	Rep	Ida.		Bishop, Sanford D. Jr.	Dem	Ga.
					Berry, R. Marion	Dem	Ark.
Moved to Budget	None				Kind, Ron	Dem	Wisc.
Moved to Financial Services	Kennedy, Mark	Rep	Minn.		None		
No new assignment	None				John, Christopher	Dem	La.

AGRICULTURE / 108th Congress

Service Dates of Committee Chair: Jan. 8, 2003-Jan. 3, 2005

Service Dates of Majority Members: Jan. 28, 2003-Jan. 3, 2005

Service Dates of Ranking Member: Jan. 8, 2003-Jan. 3, 2005

Service Dates of Minority Members: Jan. 28, 2003-Jan. 3, 2005

Roster Filled: Majority with 27 members, Jan. 28, 2003; Minority with 24 members, Feb. 13, 2003.

Majority					**Minority**				
			Terms in:					**Terms in:**	
Rank Name	Party	State	House	Comm.	Rank Name	Party	State	House	Comm.
Chr Goodlatte, Robert W.	Rep	Va.	6	6	RM Stenholm, Charles W.	Dem	Tex.	13	13
2nd Combest, Larry E.	Rep	Tex.	10	10	2nd Peterson, Collin C.	DFL	Minn.	7	7

3rd Boehner, John A.	Rep	Ohio	7	7		3rd Dooley, Calvin M.	Dem	Cal.	7	7
4th Pombo, Richard W.	Rep	Cal.	6	6		4th Holden, T. Timothy	Dem	Penn.	6	6
5th Smith, Nick H.	Rep	Mich.	6	6		5th Thompson, Bennie	Dem	Miss.	6	6
6th Everett, R. Terry	Rep	Ala.	6	6		6th McIntyre, Mike	Dem	N.C.	4	4
7th Lucas, Frank D.	Rep	Okla.	6	6		7th Etheridge, Bobby R.	Dem	N.C.	4	4
8th Moran, Jerry	Rep	Ka.	4	4		8th Boswell, Leonard L.	Dem	Iowa	4	*1 4
9th Jenkins, William L.	Rep	Tenn.	4	4		9th Lucas, Ken	Dem	Ky.	3	*1 3
10th Gutknecht, Gilbert W.	Rep	Minn.	5	3		10th Hill, Baron P.	Dem	Ind.	3	3
11th Ose, Doug	Rep	Cal.	3	3		11th Baca, Joe	Dem	Cal.	3	3
12th Hayes, Robert (Robin)	Rep	N.C.	3	3		12th Larsen, Richard R. (Rick)	Dem	Wash.	2	*1 2
13th Pickering, Charles W. (Chip) Jr.	Rep	Miss.	4	*2 2		13th Ross, Michael A.	Dem	Ark.	2	2
14th Johnson, Timothy V.	Rep	Ill.	2	2		14th Acevedo-Vilá, Aníbal	Dem	P.R.	2	2
15th Osborne, Thomas	Rep	Neb.	2	2		15th Case, Ed	Dem	Hai.	2	1
16th Pence, Mike	Rep	Ind.	2	2		16th Alexander, Rodney	Dem	La.	1	1
17th Rehberg, Dennis	Rep	Mont.	2	2		17th Ballance, Frank W. Jr.	Dem	N.C.	1	1
18th Graves, Samuel B.	Rep	Mo.	2	2		18th Cardoza, Dennis A.	Dem	Cal.	1	1
19th Putnam, Adam H. Jr.	Rep	Fla.	2	2		19th Scott, David	Dem	Ga.	1	1
20th Janklow, William J.	Rep	S.D.	1	1		20th Marshall, Jim	Dem	Ga.	1	1
21st Burns, Max	Rep	Ga.	1	1		21st Pomeroy, Earl R. III	Dem	N.D.	6	*2 1
22nd Bonner, Josiah R. Jr.	Rep	Ala.	1	1		22nd Thompson, Michael	Dem	Cal.	3	3
23rd Rogers, Mike D.	Rep	Ala.	1	1		23rd Udall, Mark	Dem	Colo.	3	1
24th King, Steve	Rep	Iowa	1	1		24th Davis, Lincoln	Dem	Tenn.	1	1
25th Chocola, Chris	Rep	Ind.	1	1						
26th Musgrave, Marilyn N.	Rep	Colo.	1	1						
27th Nunes, Devin	Rep	Cal.	1	1						

*1: Member's first period of service on the committee.

*2: Member's second period of service on the committee.

Notes: Resident Commissuionert Anibal Acevedo-Vila (Dem-P.R.) was allowed to accrue committee seniority but was not included in the party ratio.

Filled Vacancies:

Minority:

16th through 20th seats by Alexander, Ballance, Cardoza, Scott, and Marshall on Feb. 5, 2003

21st through 24th seats by Pomeroy, Thompson, Udall, and Davis, on Feb. 13, 2003

Changes:

Majority:

Combest, Larry E.	Rep	Tex.	May 31, 2003 Resigned the House and retired
Neugebauer, Randy	Rep	Tex.	June 19, 2003 Replaced Combest
Janklow, William J.	Rep	S.D.	Jan. 20, 2004 Resigned the House and retired
Putnam, Adam H. Jr.	Rep	Fla.	Sept. 28, 2004 Resigned committee; moved to Rules

Minority:

Boswell, Leonard L.	Dem	Iowa	Feb. 5, 2003 Resigned committee; returned on Feb. 13, 2003, ranked 20th
Larsen, Richard R. (Rick)	Dem	Wash.	Feb. 5, 2003 Resigned committee; moved to Armed Services; returned on Feb. 13, 2003
Case, Ed	Dem	Hai.	Feb. 5, 2003 Replaced Boswell
Lucas, Ken	Dem	Ky.	Feb. 12, 2003 Resigned committee; moved to Select Homeland Security
Lucas, Ken	Dem	Ky.	Feb. 26, 2003 Filled own vacancy
Lucas, Ken	Dem	Ky.	Mar. 30, 2004 Resigned from Agriculture again; no new assignment
Chandler, A.B. (Ben)	Dem	Ky.	Mar. 31, 2004 Replaced Lucas
Thompson, Michael	Dem	Cal.	June 3, 2004 Resigned committee to open seat for Herseth; no new assignment
Herseth, Stephanie	Dem	S.D.	June 3, 2004 Replaced M. Thompson, ranked after Marshall
Ballance, Frank W. Jr.	Dem	N.C.	June 11, 2004 Resigned the House due to health issues
Herseth, Stephanie	Dem	S.D.	June 14, 2004 Reranked following Chandler
Butterfield, George K. Jr.	Dem	N.C.	July 22, 2004 Replaced Ballance
Alexander, Rodney	Dem	La.	Aug. 9, 2004 Service on committee as a Democrat vacated; returned as a Republican on Sept. 9, 2004

Departures from the House:

	Majority			Minority		
Elected Governor	None			Acevedo-Vilá, Aníbal	Dem	P.R.
Defeated for Re-election	Burns, Max	Rep	Ga.	Stenholm, Charles W.	Dem	Tex.
				Hill, Baron P.	Dem	Ind.
Retired	Smith, Nick H.	Rep	Mich.	Dooley, Calvin M.	Dem	Cal.
	Ose, Doug	Rep	Cal.	Lucas, Ken	Dem	Ky.

Departures from Committee:

	Majority			Minority		
Moved to Appropriations	Rehberg, Dennis	Rep	Mont.	Alexander, Rodney	Dem	La.
Moved to Armed Services	None			Udall, Mark	Dem	Colo.
Moved to Energy and Commerce	None			Ross, Michael A.	Dem	Ark.
Moved to Ways and Means	Chocola, Chris	Rep	Ind.	None		
No new assignment	Pickering, Charles W. (Chip) Jr.	Rep	Miss.	None		

AGRICULTURE / 109th Congress

Service Dates of Committee Chair: Jan. 6, 2005-Jan. 3, 2007

Service Dates of Majority Members: Jan. 26, 2005-Jan. 3, 2007

Service Dates of Minority Members: Jan. 26, 2005-Jan. 3, 2007

Roster Filled: Majority with 25 members, Jan. 26, 2005; Minority with 21 members, Feb. 2, 2005.

Majority					Minority				
			Terms in:					**Terms in:**	
Rank Name	**Party**	**State**	**House**	**Comm.**	**Rank Name**	**Party**	**State**	**House**	**Comm.**
Chr Goodlatte, Robert W.	Rep	Va.	7	7	RM Peterson, Collin C.	DFL	Minn.	8	8
2nd Boehner, John A.	Rep	Ohio	8	8	2nd Holden, T. Timothy	Dem	Penn.	7	7
3rd Pombo, Richard W.	Rep	Cal.	7	7	3rd Thompson, Bennie	Dem	Miss.	7	7
4th Everett, R. Terry	Rep	Ala.	7	7	4th McIntyre, Mike	Dem	N.C.	5	5
5th Lucas, Frank D.	Rep	Okla.	7	7	5th Etheridge, Bobby R.	Dem	N.C.	5	5
6th Moran, Jerry	Rep	Ka.	5	5	6th Baca, Joe	Dem	Cal.	4	4
7th Jenkins, William L.	Rep	Tenn.	5	5	7th Case, Ed	Dem	Hai.	3	2
8th Gutknecht, Gilbert W.	Rep	Minn.	6	4	8th Cardoza, Dennis A.	Dem	Cal.	2	2
9th Hayes, Robert (Robin)	Rep	N.C.	4	4	9th Scott, David	Dem	Ga.	2	2
10th Johnson, Timothy V.	Rep	Ill.	3	3	10th Marshall, Jim	Dem	Ga.	2	2
11th Osborne, Thomas	Rep	Neb.	3	3	11th Herseth, Stephanie	Dem	S.D.	2	2
12th Pence, Mike	Rep	Ind.	3	3	12th Butterfield, George K. Jr.	Dem	N.C.	2	2
13th Graves, Samuel B.	Rep	Mo.	3	3	13th Cuellar, Henry	Dem	Tex.	1	1
14th Bonner, Josiah R. Jr.	Rep	Ala.	2	2	14th Melancon, Charles J.	Dem	La.	1	1
15th Rogers, Mike D.	Rep	Ala.	2	2	15th Costa, Jim	Dem	Cal.	1	1
16th King, Steve	Rep	Iowa	2	2	16th Salazar, John T.	Dem	Colo.	1	1
17th Musgrave, Marilyn N.	Rep	Colo.	2	2	17th Barrow, John	Dem	Ga.	1	1
18th Nunes, Devin	Rep	Cal.	2	2	18th Pomeroy, Earl R. III	Dem	N.D.	7	*2 2
19th Neugebauer, Randy	Rep	Tex.	2	2	19th Boswell, Leonard L.	Dem	Iowa	5	*2 2
20th Boustany, Charles W. Jr.	Rep	La.	1	1	20th Larsen, Richard R. (Rick)	Dem	Wash.	3	*2 2
21st Schwarz, John J.H.	Rep	Mich.	1	1	21st Davis, Lincoln	Dem	Tenn.	2	2
22nd Kuhl, John R. (Randy) Jr.	Rep	N.Y.	1	1					
23rd Foxx, Virginia A.	Rep	N.C.	1	1					
24th Conaway, K. Michael	Rep	Tex.	1	1					
25th Fortenberry, Jeff	Rep	Neb.	1	1					

*2: Member's second period of service on the committee.

Filled Vacancies:

Minority:

Pomeroy, Earl R. III	Dem	N.D.	Feb. 2, 2005
Boswell, Leonard L.	Dem	Iowa	Feb. 2, 2005
Larsen, Richard R. (Rick)	Dem	Wash.	Feb. 2, 2005
Davis, Lincoln	Dem	Tenn.	Feb. 2, 2005

Changes:

Majority:

Nunes, Devin	Rep	Cal.	May 5, 2005 Resigned committee; moved to Ways and Means
Schmidt, Jean	Rep	Ohio	Sept. 15, 2005 Replaced Nunes
Boehner, John A.	Rep	Ohio	Feb. 6, 2006 Resigned committee; elected House Majority Leader Feb. 3, 2006
Sodrel, Michael E.	Rep	Ind.	Mar. 9, 2006 Replaced Boehner

Minority:

Thompson, Bennie	Dem	Miss.	Feb. 1, 2005 Resigned committee; moved to Homeland Security as Ranking Minority Member
Chandler, A.B. (Ben)	Dem	Ky.	Feb. 2, 2005 Replaced Thompson

Departures from the House:

	Majority			**Minority**		
Defeated for Re-election	Pombo, Richard W.	Rep	Cal.	None		
	Gutknecht, Gilbert W.	Rep	Minn.			
	Sodrel, Michael E.	Rep	Ind.			
Defeated for Re-nomination	Schwarz, John J.H.	Rep	Mich.	None		
Lost Nomination for Governor	Osborne, Thomas	Rep	Neb.	None		
Lost Nomination to U.S. Senate	None			Case, Ed	Dem	Hai.
Retired	Jenkins, William L.	Rep	Tenn.	None		

Departures from Committee:

	Majority			**Minority**		
Moved to Appropriations	None			Chandler, A.B. (Ben)	Dem	Ky.
Moved to Energy and Commerce	None			Butterfield, George K. Jr.	Dem	N.C.
				Melancon, Charles J.	Dem	La.
Moved to Science and Technology	None			Chandler, A.B. (Ben)	Dem	Ky.
Moved to Small Business	None			Larsen, Richard R. (Rick)	Dem	Wash.
No new assignment	Pence, Mike	Rep	Ind.	None		

AGRICULTURE / 110th Congress

Service Dates of Committee Chair: Jan. 4, 2007-Jan. 3, 2009

Service Dates of Majority Members: Jan. 12, 2007-Jan. 3, 2009

Service Dates of Minority Members: Jan. 10, 2007-Jan. 3, 2009

Roster Filled: Majority with 25 members, Jan. 12, 2007; Minority with 21 members, Jan. 10, 2007.

			Majority						**Minority**	
			Terms in:						Terms in:	
Rank Name	Party	State	House	Comm.		Rank Name	Party	State	House	Comm.
Chr Peterson, Collin C.	DFL	Minn.	9	9		RM Goodlatte, Robert W.	Rep	Va.	8	8
2nd Holden, T. Timothy	Dem	Penn.	8	8		2nd Everett, R. Terry	Rep	Ala.	8	8
3rd McIntyre, Mike	Dem	N.C.	6	6		3rd Lucas, Frank D.	Rep	Okla.	8	8
4th Etheridge, Bobby R.	Dem	N.C.	6	6		4th Moran, Jerry	Rep	Ka.	6	6
5th Boswell, Leonard L.	Dem	Iowa	6	*2 3		5th Hayes, Robert (Robin)	Rep	N.C.	5	5
6th Baca, Joe	Dem	Cal.	5	5		6th Johnson, Timothy V.	Rep	Ill.	4	4
7th Cardoza, Dennis A.	Dem	Cal.	3	3		7th Graves, Samuel B.	Rep	Mo.	4	4
8th Scott, David	Dem	Ga.	3	3		8th Bonner, Josiah R. Jr.	Rep	Ala.	3	3
9th Marshall, Jim	Dem	Ga.	3	3		9th Rogers, Mike D.	Rep	Ala.	3	3
10th Herseth, Stephanie	Dem	S.D.	3	3		10th King, Steve	Rep	Iowa	3	3
11th Cuellar, Henry	Dem	Tex.	2	2		11th Musgrave, Marilyn N.	Rep	Colo.	3	3
12th Costa, Jim	Dem	Cal.	2	2		12th Neugebauer, Randy	Rep	Tex.	3	3
13th Salazar, John T.	Dem	Colo.	2	2		13th Boustany, Charles W. Jr.	Rep	La.	2	2
14th Ellsworth, Brad	Dem	Ind.	1	1		14th Kuhl, John R. (Randy) Jr.	Rep	N.Y.	2	2
15th Boyda, Nancy	Dem	Kans.	1	1		15th Foxx, Virginia A.	Rep	N.C.	2	2
16th Space, Zachary T.	Dem	Ohio	1	1		16th Conaway, K. Michael	Rep	Tex.	2	2
17th Walz, Timothy J.	DFL	Minn.	1	1		17th Fortenberry, Jeff	Rep	Neb.	2	2
18th Gillibrand, Kirsten E.	Dem	N.Y.	1	1		18th Schmidt, Jean	Rep	Ohio	2	2
19th Kagen, Steven L.	Dem	Wisc.	1	1		19th Smith, Adrian	Rep	Neb.	1	1
20th Pomeroy, Earl R. III	Dem	N.D.	8	*2 3		20th McCarthy, Kevin	Rep	Cal.	1	1
21st Davis, Lincoln	Dem	Tenn.	3	3		21st Walberg, Tim	Rep	Mich.	1	1
22nd Barrow, John	Dem	Ga.	2	2						
23rd Lampson, Nicholas V.	Dem	Tex.	5	1		*2: Member's second period of service on the committee.				
24th Donnelly, Joe	Dem	Ind.	1	1						
25th Mahoney, Tim	Dem	Fla.	1	1						

Changes:

Majority:

Davis, Lincoln	Dem	Tenn.	June 5, 2008 Resigned committee; no new assignment
Childers, Travis W.	Dem	Miss.	June 10, 2008 Replaced L. Davis

Minority:

McCarthy, Kevin	Rep	Cal.	Oct. 2, 2007 Resigned committee; moved to Financial Services
Latta, Robert E.	Rep	Ohio	Dec. 18, 2007 Replaced McCarthy
Bonner, Josiah R. Jr.	Rep	Ala.	Feb. 25, 2008 Resigned committee; moved to Appropriations

Departures from the House:

	Majority			**Minority**		
Defeated for Re-election	Boyda, Nancy	Dem	Kans.	Hayes, Robert (Robin)	Rep	N.C.
	Lampson, Nicholas V.	Dem	Tex.	Musgrave, Marilyn N.	Rep	Colo.
	Mahoney, Tim	Dem	Fla.	Kuhl, John R. (Randy) Jr.	Rep	N.Y.
				Walberg, Tim	Rep	Mich.
Retired	None			Everett, R. Terry	Rep	Ala.

Departures from Committee

Moved to Appropriations	Salazar, John T.	Dem	Colo.	None		
Moved to Energy and Commerce	Space, Zachary T.	Dem	Ohio	None		
Moved to Select Energy Independence and Global Warming	Salazar, John T.	Dem	Colo.	None		
Moved to Ways and Means	Etheridge, Bobby R.	Dem	N.C.	Boustany, Charles W. Jr.	Rep	La.
No new assignment	Barrow, John	Dem	Ga.	None		
	Donnelly, Joe	Dem	Ind.			

AGRICULTURE / 111th Congress

Service Dates of Committee Chair: Jan. 6, 2009-Jan. 3, 2011

Service Dates of Majority Members: Jan. 21, 2009-Jan. 3, 2011

Service Dates of Minority Members: Jan. 9, 2009-Jan. 3, 2011

Roster Filled: Majority with 28 members, Jan. 21, 2009; Minority with 18 members, Feb. 4, 2009

	Majority			Terms in:	
Rank Name	Party	State	House	Comm.	
Chr Peterson, Collin C.	DFL	Minn.	10	10	
2nd Holden, T. Timothy	Dem	Penn.	9	9	
3rd McIntyre, Mike	Dem	N.C.	7	7	
4th Boswell, Leonard L.	Dem	Iowa	7	*2 4	
5th Baca, Joe	Dem	Cal.	6	6	
6th Cardoza, Dennis A.	Dem	Cal.	4	4	
7th Scott, David	Dem	Ga.	4	4	
8th Marshall, Jim	Dem	Ga.	4	4	
9th Herseth Sandlin, Stephanie	Dem	S.D.	4	4	
10th Cuellar, Henry	Dem	Tex.	3	3	
11th Costa, Jim	Dem	Cal.	3	3	
12th Ellsworth, Brad	Dem	Ind.	2	2	
13th Walz, Timothy J.	DFL	Minn.	2	2	
14th Gillibrand, Kirsten E.	Dem	N.Y.	2	2	
15th Kagen, Steven L.	Dem	Wisc.	2	2	
16th Schrader, Kurt	Dem	Ore.	1	1	
17th Halvorson, Deborah L.	Dem	Ill.	1	1	
18th Dahlkemper, Kathleen A.	Dem	Penn.	1	1	
19th Massa, Eric J. J.	Dem	N.Y.	1	1	
20th Bright, Bobby Neal Sr.	Dem	Ala.	1	1	
21st Markey, Betsy	Dem	Colo.	1	1	
22nd Kratovil, Frank M.	Dem	Md.	1	1	
23rd Schauer, Mark H.	Dem	Mich.	1	1	
24th Kisssell, Larry	Dem	N.C.	1	1	
25th Boccieri, John A.	Dem	Ohio	1	1	
26th Pomeroy, Earl R. III	Dem	N.D.	9	*2 4	
27th Childers, Travis W.	Dem	Miss.	2	2	
28th Minnick, Walt	Dem	Ida.	1	1	

	Minority			Terms in:	
Rank Name	Party	State	House	Comm.	
RM Lucas, Frank D.	Rep	Okla.	9	9	
2nd Goodlatte, Robert W.	Rep	Va.	9	9	
3rd Moran, Jerry	Rep	Ka.	7	7	
4th Johnson, Timothy V.	Rep	Ill.	5	5	
5th Graves, Samuel B.	Rep	Mo.	5	5	
6th Rogers, Mike	Rep	Ala.	5	4	
7th King, Steve	Rep	Iowa	4	4	
8th Neugebauer, Randy	Rep	Tex.	4	4	
9th Foxx, Virginia A.	Rep	N.C.	3	3	
10th Conaway, K. Michael	Rep	Tex.	3	3	
11th Fortenberry, Jeff	Rep	Neb.	3	3	
12th Schmidt, Jean	Rep	Ohio	3	3	
13th Smith, Adrian	Rep	Neb.	2	2	
14th Latta, Robert E.	Rep	Ohio	2	2	
15th Roe, David P. (Phil)	Rep	Tenn.	1	1	
16th Luetkemeyer, Blaine	Rep	Mo.	1	1	
17th Thompson, Glenn	Rep	Penn.	1	1	

*2: Member's second period of service on the committee.

Additions:

Minority:

18th Lummis, Cynthia M.	Rep	Wyo.	Feb 4, 2009

Changes:

Majority:

Gillibrand, Kirsten E.	Dem	N.Y.	Jan. 26, 2009 Resigned House; appointed to the Senate
Murphy, Scott	Dem	N.Y.	Apr. 30, 2009 Replaced Gillibrand; ranked following Boccieri
Massa, Eric J. J.	Dem	N.Y	Mar. 8, 2010 Resigned the House due to ethics issues
Owens, William L.	Dem	N.Y.	Replaced Massa

Minority

Foxx, Virginia A.	Rep	N.C.	Jan. 15, 2009 Resigned committee; had moved to Rules
Cassidy, Bill	Rep	La.	Jan. 22, 2009 Replaced Foxx, ranked following Thompson
Latta, Robert E.	Rep.	Ohio	Mar. 25, 2010 Resigned committee; moved to Energy and Commerce

Appropriations

House Committee on Appropriations, 103rd-111th Congresses (1993-2011)

BACKGROUND

Organizational History: By custom, all spending bills begin in the House of Representatives. The job of the Appropriations Committee is to write the first versions of the regular appropriation bills each year, as well as any emergency funding measures that may be required. The full committee looks to its subcommittees to make most of the important decisions. The recommendations of these thirteen annual spending bills are generally accepted by the full committee without much change. The legendary power of the thirteen Appropriations subcommittee chairs has led them to be referred to as "the College of Cardinals."

The House Committee on Appropriations was created on March 2, 1865. With the enormous costs of the Civil War increasing the burden on the Ways and Means Committee, the House carved three new committees out of Ways and Means. The Appropriations Committee was the most important of the three; the two others created were Banking and Currency and Pacific Railroads. While the Ways and Means Committee kept its power over revenue legislation, the oversight function that accompanies each congressional allocation of funds fell within the domain of the new Appropriations Committee. The importance of the new committee can be attested to by the fact that Thaddeus Stevens (Rep-Penn.), the chair of Ways and Means during the 37th and 38th Congresses (1861-1865), left that position to become the first chair of Appropriations. The leading Democrat sponsoring this change was Samuel S. "Sunset" Cox; of Ohio (he later represented New York). During his chairmanship of Appropriations, Stevens was the floor leader in the effort to impeach President Andrew Johnson. Two of Stevens' Appropriations Committee protégés—James A. Garfield (Rep-Ohio) and James G. Blaine (Rep-Maine)—would receive Republican presidential nominations in 1880 and 1884 respectively.

Stevens' decision, and the active role of the chairmen who followed him, led Woodrow Wilson to conclude in his book Congressional Government (1883) that "all House chairmen are subordinate to the chairman of the Committee on Appropriations." Shortly after Wilson's book appeared, opposition to Chairman Samuel J. Randall's (Dem-Penn.) tight-fisted exercise of power and to his high tariff policies led to the first major diminution in the legislative authority of the Appropriations Committee when House members voted to take away the panel's jurisdiction over several government programs, including defense, river and harbor projects, agriculture, and the Post Office. By 1885 the committee had lost control over half the federal budget.

But dispersal of spending power to several different committees frustrated efforts to establish control over government budget policy. To centralize spending power, the House on July 1, 1920, restored to the Appropriations Committee the exclusive right to approve appropriations bills.

Appropriations Committee members gained power and independence in the modern-era Congress as they often won re-election year after year. Their long years of service and the seniority system placed them in positions of power as chairs of the committee and key subcommittees, where they became politically entrenched. They were thus able to pursue their own goals with little interference from the House leadership.

Some of this began to change in the 1970s as reforms forced open the traditionally closed subcommittee hearings and the rigid seniority system buckled. In 1975 the majority Democrats emphasized the importance of appropriations subcommittees by requiring that the chairs of those panels, like the chairs of full committees, be elected by a secret vote of all House Democrats. With the threat of being voted out hanging over their heads, most chairs became more responsive to the needs and interests of other House members, including the elected party leadership. A second rules change barred a member from serving on more than two subcommittees, thereby blocking senior members from monopolizing the most important positions.

It is the linkage of the oversight function with the authorization and appropriation of Federal government monies that has made the Appropriations Committee a congressional powerhouse and continues to do so today. According to the House Manual (2008):

The authority to conduct studies and examinations of the organization and operation of executive departments and agencies was first given to this committee on February 11, 1943; continued by resolution of January 9, 1945; and incorporated into permanent law in section 202(b) of the Legislative Reorganization Act of 1946 (60 Stat. 812). This authority was first made part of the standing rules on January 3, 1953, and is now listed as a special oversight responsibility of the committee in clause 3 of rule X, effective January 3, 1975 (formerly clause 2(b)(3) of rule X) (H. Res. 988, 93d Cong., Oct. 8, 1974).

The Congressional Budget and Impoundment Control Act of 1974 (P.L. 93-344) which created the Congressional Budget Office and the House and Senate Budget Committees could have diminished the authority of House Appropriations, but with the House mandating that five members each from Appropriations and Ways and Means had to be seated on the Budget Committee, this potential "turf war" was averted.

The most recent evidence of the continuing importance of the House Appropriations Committee is the recent change creating a new Select Intelligence Oversight Panel on Appropriations (H. Res. 35, 110th Congress.) As described in a September 18, 2008, report issued by the Congressional Research Service [with emphasis added]:

A recent change in the House places three members of the Intelligence Committee on a new Select Intelligence Oversight Panel on the Appropriations Committee (H. Res. 35). The new panel, which appears unprecedented in the history of Congress, is to study and make recommendations to relevant appropriations subcommittees. This includes the Defense Appropriations Subcommittee, which continues to prepare the annual intelligence community budget, as part of the classified annex to the bill making appropriations for the Department of Defense. (Frederick M. Kaiser, Congressional Oversight of Intelligence: Current Structure and Alternatives, p. CRS-3.

As evidenced in this latest augmentation of its legislative authority, the House Appropriations Committee remains today as it has for more than a century, a powerhouse committee upon which membership is greatly sought and seldom relinquished.

Membership: By 1939, the Appropriations Committee had forty members and it retained that size until the Legislative Reorganization Act. For most of the post-1946 Congresses, the House Appropriations Committee was the largest standing committee in Congress and one of the most powerful as well. The committee continued to grow until it reached fifty members in the 82nd Congress (1951-1953) and it became the first standing committee with sixty members in 1993. However, it was in the 103rd Congress (1993-1995) that the Public Works and Transportation Committee (now Transportation and Infrastructure) would surpass Appropriations as the largest House committee, as would the Financial Services Committee in 2001.

In the 109th and 110th Congresses (2005-2009), Appropriations peaked at sixty-six seats—a modest increase over the sixty in the 103rd Congress. However, in the 111th Congress (2009-2011), it dropped back down to sixty, while both Transportation and Infrastructure and Financial Services have exceeded the seventy-member mark and the Armed Services Committee, with sixty-two members, has pushed Appropriations into fourth place in membership size. Its mean member size of 62.67 during the past nine Congresses, 1993-2011, placed it in third place behind the Transportation and Financial Services committees. The mean seniority of its members within the last nine Congresses is 7.43 terms, placing Appropriations at the top of the committee mean seniority list well ahead of both Ways and Means (6.98 terms) and Rules (6.39 terms). Unsurprisingly, its mean inter-Congress retention rate is 97.74 percent—second place behind Ways and Means (98.50%).

Although Appropriations is no longer the House's largest committee, assignments to Appropriations remain highly desirable since its members continue to play a crucial role in the annual process by which Congress determines funding levels for government agencies and programs.

Committee Leaders: Leadership of the Appropriations Committee has been in the hands of just a few members of Congress throughout the post-1947 modern era period. Most of these were conservative Democrats who took a limited view of the government's role in society, although that philosophy did little to halt the escalation of federal spending. The first modern era Republican chair was John Taber from upstate New York, who served as chair in both the 80th and 83rd Congresses. Taber first became the committee's senior Republican in 1933

and remained in that post until his 1963 retirement, when he was succeeded by Ben F. Jensen (Rep-Iowa) who lost in the 1964 Democratic landslide.

The dominant Democratic chair was Clarence Cannon (Dem-Mo.) who first became chair in September 1941 and chaired the committee for nineteen of the twenty-three years between 1941 and his death in 1964. Cannon's service on Capitol Hill began when he served as an assistant to House Speaker James B. "Champ" Clark (Dem-Mo.) who had presided over the House from 1911 to 1919 during most of the Wilson Administration. It is Clarence Cannon's compilation of House Precedents that continues as a procedural reference today. Cannon was succeeded by George H. Mahon (Dem-Tex.), who served from 1964 until his retirement from the House in 1979.

During Mahon's time as chair, Frank T. Bow (Rep-Ohio) served as ranking member from 1965 until his death in 1972 and Elford A. Cederberg (Rep-Mich.) succeeded Bow and served until his 1978 election defeat.

The next ranking member was Silvio O. Conte (Rep-Mass.), a fellow Boston College alum of Democrats (and Washington roommates) Speaker O'Neill and high ranking majority member Edward P. Boland (Dem-Mass.).

Conte's death in 1991 resulted in Joseph M. McDade becoming ranking minority member.

Mahon's successor was Jamie L. Whitten (Dem-Miss.) who became chair in 1979 and remained in the position until 1993. Whitten's fifty-four year career in the House (1941-1995) had been the longest in congressional history. However, declining health had in effect removed Whitten from leadership of the panel for some time. Whitten turned over many duties as chair to William H. Natcher (Dem-Ky.) in a letter dated June 9, 1992. Natcher served less than a full Congress as the committee's official chair. His death on March 29, 1994, ended his forty-year House career, in which he distinguished himself by voting on 18,401 consecutive roll calls.

The subsequent Democratic Caucus election in 1994 resulted in a victory for the fifth-ranking member, the younger and more liberal David Obey (Dem-Wisc.), as chair. Obey served as the committee's ranking minority member during the Republican-controlled 104th-109th Congresses (1995-2007) and resumed the chair of Appropriations in 2007 and still holds that post.

Much as the Democrats had done, the Republicans elevated Robert L. Livingston (Rep-La.), the fifth-ranking Republican on the committee to be chair in 1995. Livingston's prominence was recognized in 1998 when it was declared that he would be the next Republican nominee for Speaker of the House following Newt Gingrich's announced retirement. However, long-forgotten romantic entanglements of Livingston resurfaced while Republicans were preparing challenges to President Bill Clinton's continuance in office for similar extra-marital behavior and Livingston stepped aside as the speakership nominee and then shortly afterwards, resigned from the House. C.W. "Bill" Young of Florida succeeded Livingston as chair in 1999 and served as the Republican chair for a maximum of three terms and stepped aside for Charles "Jerry" Lewis of California, to become chair in 2005. Lewis presently serves as the ranking minority member on Appropriations.

Party Leaders: While the Ways and Means Committee historically has been the most common source of floor leaders for the House Democrats, the Appropriations Committee has been a major source of leadership talent for the House Republicans. Three consecutive Republican floor leaders—Gerald R. Ford Jr. (Rep-Mich., 1965-1973), John J. Rhodes Jr. (Rep-Ariz., 1973-1981), and Robert H. Michel (Rep-Ill., 1981-1995) were serving on Appropriations at the time of their selections. Each had been a protégé of John Taber. More recent Appropriations Committee Republican leaders would include Thomas DeLay (Rep-Texas) who became whip in 1995 and Majority Leader in 1999. Recent Republican Whip Roy Blunt (Rep-Mo.) served for a few months on Appropriations, but it was not a primary assignment. And had Robert Livingston's past indiscretions not resurfaced in 1998, he would have been the first Appropriations Committee alumnus to become Speaker of the House since Joseph W. Byrns (Dem-Tenn.) in 1935-1936 and the first Republican Appropriations alumnus since the legendary "Uncle Joe" Cannon (Rep-Ill.) ruled the House with an iron fist during most of his eight years as Speaker, 1903-1911.

While the present Democratic leadership team of House Speaker Nancy Pelosi of California, Majority Leader Steny Hoyer of Maryland, and Majority Whip James Clyburn of South Carolina all served together on Appropriations, the only prior Democratic Party leaders to emerge from Appropriations were John McCall (Dem-Cal.) and William L. Gray III (Dem-Penn.), who served as whips.

Notable Members: President Gerald Ford is the most prominent former member of House Appropriations along with 1996 Republican vice presidential nominee Jack Kemp of New York. The only Cabinet members to come from Appropriations were Melvin Laird (Rep-Wisc.) who became Richard Nixon's first Secretary of Defense in 1969 and Ray LaHood (Rep-Ill.), President Barack Obama's Secretary of Transportation in 2009.

Since 1947, twenty U.S. senators had served earlier on House Appropriations: twelve Democrats—Albert Gore, Sr. of Tennessee. Henry M. Jackson of Washington State, Joseph Montoya and Thomas Udall of New Mexico, David H. Pryor of Arkansas, William Hathaway of Maine, Max Baucus of Minnesota, Mark Andrews of North Dakota, Donald W. Riegle of Michigan, Daniel K. Akaka of Hawaii, and Richard J. Durbin of Illinois; and nine Republicans—Everett McK. Dirksen of Illinois, Francis H. Case of South Dakota, Norris Cotton, Louis Wyman and John E. Sununu all of New Hampshire, Roman L. Hruska of Nebraska, William L. Armstrong of Colorado, David Vitter of Louisiana, and Roger F. Wicker of Mississippi.

Only three modern-era members left Appropriations to become governor: two Democrats Foster Furcolo of Massachusetts, a John McCormack protégé, who left the House to be elected state treasurer in 1952 and David Pryor of Arkansas; and one Republican Carroll A. Campbell of South Carolina. Fred G. Aandahl of North Dakota left the governorship for a House seat but lost his Senate bid. Pryor succeeded in moving from the state house to the Senate while Furcolo failed in his senatorial effort. Four of the nation's largest cities have chosen mayors with Appropriations Committee experience—Ed Koch of New York City, John Shelley of San Francisco, William Boner of Nashville, and Thomas D'Alesandro of Baltimore, whose daughter Nancy Pelosi, the Speaker of the House is a fellow alumnus of the Appropriations Committee.

Selected References

Aldrich, John H. and David W. Rohde, "The Republican Revolution and the House Appropriations Committee," *Journal of Politics,* 62 (Feb., 2000), 1-33.

Fenno, Richard F., Jr., *Congressmen in Committees* (Boston: Little, Brown, 1973).

Fenno, Richard F., Jr., "House Appropriations Committee as a Political System: The Problem of Integrations", *American Political Science Review.* 56 (June, 1962), 310-324.

Fenno, Richard F., Jr., *The Power of the Purse: Appropriations Politics in Congress* (Boston: Little, Brown, 1966).

Kiewiet, D. Roderick and Matthew D. McCubbins, *The Logic of Delegation: Congressional Parties and the Appropriations Process* (Chicago: University of Chicago Press, 1991).

LeLoup, Lance T., "Appropriations Politics in Congress: The House Appropriations Committee and the Executive Agencies," *Public Budgeting and Finance,* 4 (Winter, 1984), 79-98.

Meier, Kenneth J. and Gary W. Copeland, "Interest Groups and Public Policy," *Social Science Quarterly,* 64 (September, 1983), 641-646.

Munson, Richard, *The Cardinals of Capitol Hill: The Men and Women Who Control Government Spending* (New York: Grove Press, 1993).

Savage, James D., "Saints and Cardinals in Appropriations Committees and the Fight Against Distributive Politics," *Legislative Studies Quarterly,* 16 (August, 1991), 329-348.

Schamel, Charles E. et al., "Records of the Appropriations Committee," *Guide to the Records of the United States House of Representatives at the National Archives: 1789-1989 Bicentennial Edition* (Washington, D.C.: National Archives and Records Administration,1989), 31-37.

Schick, Allen, *Congress and Money: Budgeting, Spending, and Taxing* (Washington, DC: Urban Institute, 1980).

Schick, Allen, "The Three-Ring Budget Process: The Appropriations, Tax and Budget Committees in Congress," in Thomas Mann and Norman J. Ornstein, eds., *The New Congress* (Washington, D.C.: American Enterprise Institute, 1981), 288-328.

Spohn, Richard and Charles McCollum, dirs., "The House and Senate Appropriations Committees," in the Ralph Nader Congress Project, *The Revenue Committees: A Study of the House Ways and Means and Senate Finance Committee and the House and Senate Appropriations Committees* (New York: Grossman, 1975), 217-260.

Stewart, Charles, *Budget Reform Politics: The Design of the Appropriations Process,* 1865-1921 (Cambridge, U.K.: Cambridge University Press, 1989).

U.S. House of Representatives, Committee on Appropriations, *A History of the Committee on Appropriations, House of Representatives,* H. Doc. 77-299, 77th Congress, 1st Session (1941).

White, Joseph, "Decision Making in the Appropriations Subcommittees on Defense and Foreign Operations," in Randall B. Ripley and James M. Lindsay, eds., *Congress Resurgent: Foreign and Defense Policy on Capitol Hill* (Ann Arbor: University of Michigan Press, 1993), 183-206.

Wildavsky, Aaron, *Politics of the Budgetary Process,* 4th ed. (Boston: Little, Brown, 1964).

Yarwood, Dean L., "Oversight of Presidential Funds by Appropriations Committees: Learning from the Watergate Crisis," *Administration and Society,* 13 (November, 1981), 299-346.

RESPONSIBILITIES, JURISDICTIONAL CHANGES, AND SUBCOMMITTEES

APPROPRIATIONS

Jurisdiction, 80th Congress (1947-1949)

Established by the Legislative Reorganization Act of 1946:

[Section 121.(1)(b)] Committee on Appropriations

(1) Appropriation of the revenue for the support of the Government.

[Sec. 139]

(a) No general appropriation bill shall be considered in either House unless, prior to the consideration of such bill, printed committee hearings and reports on such bill have been available for at least three calendar days for the Members of the House in which such bill is to be considered.

(b) The Committees on Appropriations of the two Houses are authorized and directed, acting jointly; to develop a standard appropriation classification schedule which will clearly define in concise and uniform accounts the subtotals of appropriations asked for by agencies in the executive branch of the Government. That part of the printed hearings containing each such agency's request for appropriations shall be preceded by such a schedule.

(c) No general appropriation bill or amendment thereto shall be received or considered in either House if it contains a provision reappropriating unexpended balances of appropriations; except that this provision shall not apply to appropriations in continuation of appropriations for public works on which work has commenced.

(d) The Appropriations Committees of both Houses are authorized and directed to make a study of (1) existing permanent appropriations with a view to limiting the number of permanent appropriations and to recommend to their respective Houses what permanent appropriations, if any, should be discontinued; and (2) the disposition of funds resulting from the sale of Government property or services by all departments and agencies in the executive branch of the Government with a view to recommending to their respective Houses a uniform system of control with respect to such funds.

Jurisdiction, 103rd Congress (1993-1995)

From the Rules of the House of Representatives, 103rd Congress (House Document 102-405)

[Rule X. 1. (b)] Committee on Appropriations

(1) Appropriation of the revenue for the support of the Government.
(2) Rescissions of appropriations contained in appropriation Acts.
(3) Transfers of unexpended balances.
(4) The amount of new spending authority (as described in the Congressional Budget Act of 1974) which is to be effective for a fiscal year, including bills and resolutions (reported by other committees) which provide new spending authority and are referred to the committee under clause 4(a). The committee shall include separate headings for "Rescissions" and "Transfers of Unexpended Balances" in any bill or resolution as reported from the committee under its jurisdiction specified in subparagraph (2) or (3), with all proposed rescissions and proposed transfers listed therein; and shall include a separate section with respect to such rescissions or transfers in the accompanying committee report. In addition to its jurisdiction under the preceding provisions of this paragraph, the committee shall have the fiscal oversight function provided for in clause 2(b)(3) and the budget hearing function provided for in clause 4(a).

Additional functions of the Committee in Appropriations [Rule X. 4.(a)(1)]

(A) The Committee on Appropriations shall, within thirty days after the transmittal of the Budget to the Congress each year, hold hearings on the Budget as a whole with particular reference to—

(i) the basic recommendations and budgetary policies of the President in the presentation of the Budget; and
(ii) the fiscal, financial, and economic assumptions used as bases in arriving at total estimated expenditures and receipts.

(B) In holding hearings pursuant to subdivision (A), the committee shall receive testimony from the Secretary of the Treasury, the Director of the Office of Management and Budget, the Chairman of the Council of Economic Advisers, and such other persons as the committee may desire.

[Rule X. 4.(a)(2)]

Whenever any bill or resolution which provides new spending authority described in section 401(c) (2) (C) of the Congressional Budget Act of 1974 is reported by a committee of the House and the amount of new budget authority which will be required for the fiscal year involved if such bill or resolution is enacted as so reported exceeds the appropriate allocation of new budget authority reported as described in clause 4(h) in connection with the most recently agreed to concurrent resolution on the budget for such fiscal year, such bill or resolution shall then be referred to the Committee on Appropriations with instructions to report it, with the committee's recommendations and (if the committee deems it desirable) with an amendment limiting the total amount of new spending authority provided in the bill or resolution, within 15 calendar days (not counting any day on which the House is not in session) beginning with the day following the day on which it is so referred. If the Committee on Appropriations fails to report the bill or resolution within such 15-day period, the committee shall be automatically discharged from further consideration of the bill or resolution and the bill or resolution shall be placed on the appropriate calendar.

[Rule 4.(a)(3)]

In addition, the Committee on Appropriations shall study on a continuing basis those provisions of law which (on the first day of the first fiscal year for which the congressional budget process is effective) provide spending authority or permanent budget authority, and shall report to the House from time to time its recommendations for terminating or modifying such provisions.

Jurisdiction, 104th Congress (1995-1997) Changes in Committee System

From H. Res. 6, Section 202 (a), the Committees and Their Jurisdiction, January 4, 1995

[Rule X. 1. (b)] Committee on Appropriations
(1) Appropriation of the revenue for the support of the Government.
(2) Rescissions of appropriations contained in appropriation Acts.
(3) Transfers of unexpended balances.
(4) The amount of new spending authority (as described in the Congressional Budget Act of 1974) which is to be effective for a fiscal year, including bills and resolutions (reported by other committees) which provide new spending authority and are referred to the committee under clause 4(a). The committee shall include separate headings for 'Rescissions' and 'Transfers of Unexpended Balances' in any bill or resolution as reported from the committee under its jurisdiction specified in subparagraph (2) or (3), with all proposed rescissions and proposed transfers listed therein; and shall include a separate section with respect to such rescissions or transfers in the accompanying committee report. In addition to its jurisdiction under the preceding provisions of this paragraph, the committee shall have the fiscal oversight function provided for in clause 2(b)(3)and the budget hearing function provided for in clause 4(a).

[Rule X.3.] General Oversight Responsibilities
(3) The Committee on Appropriations shall conduct such studies and examinations of the organization and operation of executive departments and other executive agencies (including any agency the majority of the stock of which is owned by the Government of the United States) as it may deem necessary to assist it in the determination of matters within its jurisdiction.

[Rule X.4.] Additional Functions of Committees

(a)(1)(A) The Committee on Appropriations shall, within thirty days after the transmittal of the Budget to the Congress each year, hold hearings on the Budget as a whole with particular reference to—

   (i) the basic recommendations and budgetary policies of the President in the presentation of the Budget; and
   (ii) the fiscal, financial, and economic assumptions used as bases in arriving at total estimated expenditures and receipts.

   (B) In holding hearings pursuant to subdivision (A), the committee shall receive testimony from the Secretary of the Treasury, the Director of the Office of Management and Budget, the Chairman of the Council of Economic Advisers, and such other persons as the committee may desire.
   (C) Sec. 694b. Procedure for Budget Hearings pursuant to subdivision (A), or any part thereof, shall be held in open session, except when the committee, in open session and with a quorum present, determines by rollcall vote that the testimony to be taken at that hearing on that day may be related to a matter of national security: Provided, however, That the committee may by the same procedure close one subsequent day of hearing. A transcript of all such hearings shall be printed and a copy thereof furnished to each Member, Delegate, and the Resident Commissioner from Puerto Rico.
   (D) Hearings pursuant to subdivision (A), or any part thereof, may be held before joint meetings of the committee and the Committee on Appropriations of the Senate in accordance with such procedures as the two committees jointly may determine.

   (3) In addition, the Committee on Appropriations shall study on a continuing basis those provisions of law which (on the first day of the first fiscal year for which the congressional budget process is effective) provide spending authority or permanent budget authority and shall report to the House from time to time its recommendations for terminating or modifying such provisions.

Jurisdiction, 111th Congress (2009-2011)

From the Rules of the House of Representatives (as revised to June 16, 2009, H. Doc. 110-162):

[Rule X.1.(b)] Committee on Appropriations

(1) Appropriation of the revenue for the support of the Government.

(2) Rescissions of appropriations contained in appropriation Acts.

(3) Transfers of unexpended balances.

(4) Bills and joint resolutions reported by other committees that provide new entitlement authority as defined in section 3(9) of the Congressional Budget Act of 1974 and referred to the committee under clause 4(a)(2).

[Rule X.3. (a)] Special Oversight Functions

The Committee on Appropriations shall conduct such studies and examinations of the organization and operation of executive departments and other executive agencies (including an agency the majority of the stock which is owned by the United States) as it considers necessary to assist in the determination of matters within its jurisdiction.

[Rule X.4.(a)(1)(A)] Additional Functions of the Committee on Appropriations:

(A) The Committee on Appropriations shall, within 30 days after the transmittal of the Budget to the Congress each year, hold hearings on the Budget as a whole with particular reference to—

   (i) the basic recommendations and budgetary policies of the President in the presentation of the Budget; and

   (ii) the fiscal, financial, and economic assumptions used as bases in arriving at total estimated expenditures and receipts.

(B) In holding hearings under subdivision (A), the committee shall receive testimony from the Secretary of the Treasury, the Director of the Office of Management and Budget, the Chairman of the Council of Economic Advisers, and such other persons as the committee may desire.

[Rule X.4.(a)(3)]

In addition, the Committee on Appropriations shall study on a continuing basis those provisions of law that (on the first day of the first fiscal year for which the congressional budget process is effective) provide spending authority or permanent budget authority, and shall report to the House from time to time its recommendations for terminating or modifying such provisions.

[Rule X.5. (a)(5)(A)] Select Intelligence Oversight Panel

(A) There is established a Select Intelligence Oversight Panel of the Committee on Appropriations (hereinafter in this paragraph referred to as "select panel"). The select panel shall be composed of not more than 13 Members, Delegates, or the Resident Commissioner appointed by the Speaker, of whom not more than eight may be from the same political party. The select panel shall include the chair and ranking minority member of the Committee on Appropriations, the chair and ranking minority member of its Subcommittee on Defense, six additional members of the Committee on Appropriations, and three members of the Permanent Select Committee on Intelligence.

(B) The Speaker shall designate one member of the select panel as its chair and one member as its ranking minority member.

(C) Each member on the select panel shall be treated as though a member of the Committee on Appropriations for purposes of the select panel.

(D) The select panel shall review and study on a continuing basis budget requests for and execution of intelligence activities; make recommendations to relevant subcommittees of the Committee on Appropriations; and, on an annual basis, prepare a report to the Defense Subcommittee of the Committee on Appropriations containing budgetary and oversight observations and recommendations for use by such subcommittee in preparation of the classified annex to the bill making appropriations for the Department of Defense.

(E) Rule XI shall apply to the select panel in the same manner as a subcommittee (except for clause 2(m)(1)(B) of that rule).

(F) A subpoena of the Committee on Appropriations or its Subcommittee on Defense may specify terms of return to the select panel.

NAMES OF APPROPRIATIONS SUBCOMMITTEES FROM THE *CONGRESSIONAL DIRECTORY*

Agriculture, Rural Development and Related Agencies, 103
Agriculture, Rural Development, Food and Drug Administration, and Related Agencies, 104, 105, 106, 107, 108, 109, 110, 111
Commerce, Justice, Science and Related Agencies, 110, 111
Commerce, Justice, State, and Judiciary, 103, 104, 105, 106, 107, 108
Defense, 103, 106, 107, 108, 109, 110, 111
National Security, 104, 105
District of Columbia, 103, 104, 105, 106, 107, 108
Energy and Water Development, 103, 104, 105, 106, 107, 108, 110, 111
Energy and Water Development, and Related Agencies, 109
Financial Services and General Government, 111
Foreign Operations, 103
Foreign Operations, Export Financing, and Related Programs, 104, 105, 106, 107, 108, 109
Homeland Security, 109, 110, 111
Interior, 103, 104, 105, 106, 107, 108
Interior, Environment, and Related Agencies, 109, 110, 111

Labor, Health and Human Services, and Education, 103, 104, 105, 106, 107, 108
Labor, Health and Human Services, Education and Related Agencies, 109, 110, 111
Legislative, 105
Legislative Branch, 103, 104, 106, 107, 108, 110, 111
Military Construction, 103, 104, 105, 106, 107, 108
Military Quality of Life and Veterans Affairs, and Related Agencies, 109
Military Construction, Veterans' Affairs, and Related Agencies, 110, 111
Science, the Departments of State, Justice, and Commerce, and Related Agencies, 109
Select Intelligence Oversight Panel, 110, 111
State, Foreign Operations, and Related Programs, 110, 111
Transportation, 103, 104, 105, 106, 107
Transportation, Treasury, and Independent Agencies, 108
Transportation, Treasury, HUD, the Judiciary, District of Columbia, and Related Agencies, 109
Transportation, Housing and Urban Development, and Related Agencies, 110, 111
Treasury, Postal Service and General Government, 103, 104, 105, 106, 107
Veterans Affairs, Housing and Urban Development, and Independent Agencies, 103, 104, 105, 106, 107, 108

MEMBERSHIP ROSTERS, 103rd-111th Congresses, 1993-2011

APPROPRIATIONS / 103rd Congress

Service Dates of Committee Chair: Ch1 Jan. 5, 1993-Mar. 29, 1994 Natcher (Dem-Ky.)

Ch2 Apr. 12, 1994-Jan. 3, 1995 Obey (Dem-Wisc.)

Service Dates of Majority Members: Jan. 5, 1993-Jan. 3, 1995

Service Dates of Minority Members: Jan. 5, 1993-Jan. 3, 1995

Roster Filled: Majority with 37 members, Jan. 5, 1993; Minority with 23 members, Jan. 5, 1993.

			Terms in:						Terms in:	
Majority						**Minority**				
Rank Name	**Party**	**State**	**House**	**Comm.**		**Rank Name**	**Party**	**State**	**House**	**Comm.**
Ch1 Natcher, William H.	Dem	Ky.	21	20		RM1 McDade, Joseph M.	Rep	Penn.	16	15
2nd Whitten, Jamie L.	Dem	Miss.	27	26		2nd Myers, John T.	Rep	Ind.	14	12
3rd Smith, Neal E.	Dem	Iowa	18	17		3rd Young, C.W. Bill	Rep	Fla.	12	11
4th Yates, Sidney R.	Dem	Ill.	22	*2 15		4th Regula, Ralph S.	Rep	Ohio	11	10
5th Ch2 Obey, David R.	Dem	Wisc.	13	13		5th Livingston, Robert L. Jr.	Rep	La.	9	7
6th Stokes, Louis	Dem	Ohio	13	12		6th Lewis, Charles J. (Jerry)	Rep	Cal.	8	7
7th Bevill, Tom	Dem	Ala.	14	12		7th Porter, John Edward	Rep	Ill.	8	7
8th Murtha, John P. Jr.	Dem	Penn.	11	10		8th Rogers, Harold D.	Rep	Ky.	7	6
9th Wilson, Charles	Dem	Tex.	11	10		9th Skeen, Joseph R.	Rep	N.M.	7	5
10th Dicks, Norman D.	Dem	Wash.	9	9		10th Wolf, Frank R.	Rep	Va.	7	5
11th Sabo, Martin Olav	DFL	Minn.	8	8		11th DeLay, Thomas D.	Rep	Tex.	5	*1 4
12th Dixon, Julian C.	Dem	Cal.	8	8		12th Kolbe, James T.	Rep	Ariz.	5	4
13th Fazio, Victor H.	Dem	Cal.	8	8		13th Gallo, Dean A.	Rep	N.J.	5	3
14th Hefner, W. G. (Bill)	Dem	N.C.	10	8		14th Vucanovich, Barbara F.	Rep	Nev.	6	2
15th Hoyer, Steny H.	Dem	Md.	7	7		15th Lightfoot, Jim Ross	Rep	Iowa	5	1
16th Carr, M. Robert	Dem	Mich.	9	6		16th Packard, Ronald C.	Rep	Cal.	6	1
17th Durbin, Richard J.	Dem	Ill.	6	5		17th Callahan, H.L. (Sonny)	Rep	Ala.	5	1
18th Coleman, Ronald D.	Dem	Tex.	6	5		18th Bentley, Helen Delich	Rep	Md.	5	1
19th Mollohan, Alan B.	Dem	W.Va.	6	5		19th Walsh, James T.	Rep	N.Y.	3	1
20th Chapman, Jim	Dem	Tex.	5	3		20th Taylor, Charles H.	Rep	N.C.	2	1
21st Kaptur, Marcia C. (Marcy)	Dem	Ohio	6	3		21st Hobson, David L.	Rep	Ohio	2	1
22nd Skaggs, David E.	Dem	Colo.	4	2		22nd Istook, Ernest Jim Jr.	Rep	Okla.	1	1
23rd Price, David E.	Dem	N.C.	4	*1 2		23rd Bonilla, Henry	Rep	Tex.	1	1
24th Pelosi, Nancy	Dem	Cal.	4	2						
25th Visclosky, Peter J.	Dem	Ind.	5	2		*1: Member's first period of service on the committee.				
26th Foglietta, Thomas M.	Dem	Penn.	7	1		*2: Member's second period of service on the committee.				
27th Torres, Esteban Edward	Dem	Cal.	6	1						
28th Darden, George W. (Buddy)	Dem	Ga.	6	1						
29th Lowey, Nita M.	Dem	N.Y.	3	1						
30th Thornton, Raymond H. Jr.	Dem	Ark.	5	1						
31st Serrano, Jose E.	Dem	N.Y.	3	*1 1						
32nd DeLauro, Rosa L.	Dem	Conn.	2	*1 1						

33rd Moran, James P. Jr.	Dem	Va.	2	*1 1
34th Peterson, Douglas B. (Pete)	Dem	Fla.	2	1
35th Olver, John W.	Dem	Mass.	2	*1 1
36th Pastor, Edward L.	Dem	Ariz.	2	*1 1
37th Meek, Carrie P.	Dem	Fla.	1	*1 1

Note: Due to the ill health of Jamie L. Whitten (Dem-Miss.), William H. Natcher (Dem-Ky.) was elected Chair of the Committee, duties that he assumed during the 102nd Congress.

Changes:

Majority:

| Ch1 Natcher, William H. | Dem | Ky. | Mar. 29, 1994 Died in office |
| Ch2 Obey, David R. | Dem | Wisc. | Apr. 12, 1994 Elected Chair |

Minority:

| Gallo, Dean A. | Rep | N.J. | Nov. 6, 1994 Died in office |

Departures from the House:	Majority			Minority		
Defeated for Re-election	Smith, Neal E.	Dem	Iowa	None		
	Price, David E.	Dem	N.C.			
	Darden, George W. (Buddy)	Dem	Ga.			
Lost Election to U.S. Senate	Carr, M. Robert	Dem	Mich.	None		
Lost Nomination for Governor	None			Bentley, Helen Delich	Rep	Md.
Retired	Whitten, Jamie L.	Dem	Miss.	None		

Departures from Committee:					
Moved to Agriculture	Pastor, Edward L.	Dem	Ariz.	None	
Moved to Budget	Olver, John W.	Dem	Mass.	None	
	Meek, Carrie P.	Dem	Fla.		
Moved to Government Reform and Oversight	Moran, James P. Jr.	Dem	Va.	None	
	Meek, Carrie P.	Dem	Fla.		
Moved to House Oversight	Pastor, Edward L.	Dem	Ariz.	None	
Moved to International Relations	Moran, James P.	Dem	Va.	None	
Moved to National Security	DeLauro, Rosa L.	Dem	Conn.	None	
	Peterson, Douglas B. (Pete)	Dem	Fla.		
Returned to Science	Olver, John W.	Dem	Mass.	None	
Moved to Small Business	Peterson, Douglas B. (Pete)	Dem	Fla.	None	

APPROPRIATIONS / 104th Congress

Service Dates of Committee Chair: Jan. 4, 1995-Jan. 3, 1997

Service Dates of Majority Members: Jan. 4, 1995-Jan. 3, 1997

Service Dates of Minority Members: Jan. 4, 1995-Jan. 3, 1997

Roster Filled: Majority with 32 members, Jan. 4, 1995; Minority with 24 members, Jan. 4, 1995.

	Majority			Terms in:			Minority			Terms in:	
Rank Name		Party	State	House	Comm.	Rank Name		Party	State	House	Comm.
Chr Livingston, Robert L. Jr.		Rep	La.	10	8	RM Obey, David R.		Dem	Wisc.	14	14
2nd McDade, Joseph M.		Rep	Penn.	17	16	2nd Yates, Sidney R.		Dem	Ill.	23	*2 16
3rd Myers, John T.		Rep	Ind.	15	13	3rd Stokes, Louis		Dem	Ohio	14	13
4th Young, C.W. Bill		Rep	Fla.	13	12	4th Bevill, Tom		Dem	Ala.	15	13
5th Regula, Ralph S.		Rep	Ohio	12	11	5th Murtha, John P. Jr.		Dem	Penn.	12	11
6th Lewis, Charles J. (Jerry)		Rep	Cal.	9	8	6th Wilson, Charles		Dem	Tex.	12	11
7th Porter, John Edward		Rep	Ill.	9	8	7th Dicks, Norman D.		Dem	Wash.	10	10
8th Rogers, Harold D.		Rep	Ky.	8	7	8th Sabo, Martin Olav		DFL	Minn.	9	9
9th Skeen, Joseph R.		Rep	N.M.	8	6	9th Dixon, Julian C.		Dem	Cal.	9	9
10th Wolf, Frank R.		Rep	Va.	8	6	10th Fazio, Victor H.		Dem	Cal.	9	9
11th DeLay, Thomas D.		Rep	Tex.	6	*1 5	11th Hefner, W. G. (Bill)		Dem	N.C.	11	9
12th Kolbe, James T.		Rep	Ariz.	6	5	12th Hoyer, Steny H.		Dem	Md.	8	8
13th Vucanovich, Barbara F.		Rep	Nev.	7	3	13th Durbin, Richard J.		Dem	Ill.	7	6
14th Lightfoot, Jim Ross		Rep	Iowa	6	2	14th Coleman, Ronald D.		Dem	Tex.	7	6
15th Packard, Ronald C.		Rep	Cal.	7	2	15th Mollohan, Alan B.		Dem	W.Va.	7	6
16th Callahan, H.L. (Sonny)		Rep	Ala.	6	2	16th Chapman, Jim		Dem	Tex.	6	4
17th Walsh, James T.		Rep	N.Y.	4	2	17th Kaptur, Marcia C. (Marcy)		Dem	Ohio	7	4
18th Taylor, Charles H.		Rep	N.C.	3	2	18th Skaggs, David E.		Dem	Colo.	5	3
19th Hobson, David L.		Rep	Ohio	3	2	19th Pelosi, Nancy		Dem	Cal.	5	3
20th Istook, Ernest Jim Jr.		Rep	Okla.	2	2	20th Visclosky, Peter J.		Dem	Ind.	6	3

21st Bonilla, Henry	Rep	Tex.	2	2	
22nd Knollenberg, Joseph	Rep	Mich.	2	1	
23rd Miller, Daniel	Rep	Fla.	2	1	
24th Dickey, Jay W. Jr.	Rep	Ark.	2	1	
25th Kingston, Jack	Rep	Ga.	2	1	
26th Riggs, Frank D.	Rep	Cal.	2	1	
27th Frelinghuysen, Rodney P.	Rep	N.J.	1	1	
28th Wicker, Roger F.	Rep	Miss.	1	1	
29th Forbes, Michael P.	Rep	N.Y.	1	1	
30th Nethercutt, George R. Jr.	Rep	Wash.	1	1	
31st Bunn, Jim	Rep	Ore.	1	1	
32nd Neumann, Mark W.	Rep	Wisc.	1	1	

21st Foglietta, Thomas M.	Dem	Penn.	8	2	
22nd Torres, Esteban Edward	Dem	Cal.	7	2	
23rd Lowey, Nita M.	Dem	N.Y.	4	2	
24th Thornton, Raymond H. Jr.	Dem	Ark.	6	2	

*1: Member's first period of service on the committee

*2: Member's second period of service on the committee.

Additions:
Majority:

Parker, Michael	Rep	Miss.	Mar. 14, 1996 Parker's service as a Democrat vacated on Nov. 10, 1995, was added to committee as a Republican and ranked following Riggs

Minority:

Serrano, Jose E.	Dem	N.Y.	Mar. 14, 1996

Changes:
Minority:

Wilson, Charles	Dem	Tex.	Oct. 8, 1996 Resigned the House and retired
Thornton, Raymond H. Jr.	Dem	Ark.	Jan 1, 1997 Resigned the House; elected to Arkansas State Supreme Court

Departures from the House:

	Majority			Minority		
Elected to U.S. Senate	None			Durbin, Richard J.	Dem	Ill.
Defeated for Re-election	Bunn, Jim	Rep	Ore.	None		
Defeated for Senate Nomination	None			Chapman, Jim	Dem	Tex.
Lost Election to U.S. Senate	Lightfoot, Jim Ross	Rep	Iowa	None		
Retired	Myers, John T.	Rep	Ind.	Bevill, Tom	Dem	Ala.
	Vucanovich, Barbara F.	Rep	Nev.	Coleman, Ronald D.	Dem	Tex.

Departures from Committee:

Returned to Transportation and Infrastructure	Riggs, Frank D.	Rep	Cal.	None	

APPROPRIATIONS / 105th Congress

Service Dates of Committee Chair: Jan. 7, 1997-Jan. 3, 1999

Service Dates of Majority Members: Jan. 7, 1997-Jan. 3, 1999

Service Dates of Minority Members: Jan. 7, 1997-Jan. 3, 1999

Roster Filled: Majority with 34 members, Jan. 7, 1997; Minority with 26 members, Jan. 7, 1997.

Majority			Terms in:		Minority			Terms in:	
Rank Name	Party	State	House	Comm.	Rank Name	Party	State	House	Comm.
Chr Livingston, Robert L. Jr.	Rep	La.	11	9	RM Obey, David R.	Dem	Wisc.	15	15
2nd McDade, Joseph M.	Rep	Penn.	18	17	2nd Yates, Sidney R.	Dem	Ill.	24	*2 17
3rd Young, C.W. Bill	Rep	Fla.	14	13	3rd Stokes, Louis	Dem	Ohio	15	14
4th Regula, Ralph S.	Rep	Ohio	13	12	4th Murtha, John P. Jr.	Dem	Penn.	13	12
5th Lewis, Charles J. (Jerry)	Rep	Cal.	10	9	5th Dicks, Norman D.	Dem	Wash.	11	11
6th Porter, John Edward	Rep	Ill.	10	9	6th Sabo, Martin Olav	DFL	Minn.	10	10
7th Rogers, Harold D.	Rep	Ky.	9	8	7th Dixon, Julian C.	Dem	Cal.	10	10
8th Skeen, Joseph R.	Rep	N.M.	9	7	8th Fazio, Victor H.	Dem	Cal.	10	10
9th Wolf, Frank R.	Rep	Va.	9	7	9th Hefner, W. G. (Bill)	Dem	N.C.	12	10
10th DeLay, Thomas D.	Rep	Tex.	7	*1 6	10th Hoyer, Steny H.	Dem	Md.	9	9
11th Kolbe, James T.	Rep	Ariz.	7	6	11th Mollohan, Alan B.	Dem	W.Va.	8	7
12th Packard, Ronald C.	Rep	Cal.	8	3	12th Kaptur, Marcia C. (Marcy)	Dem	Ohio	8	5
13th Callahan, H.L. (Sonny)	Rep	Ala.	7	3	13th Skaggs, David E.	Dem	Colo.	6	4
14th Walsh, James T.	Rep	N.Y.	5	3	14th Pelosi, Nancy	Dem	Cal.	6	4
15th Taylor, Charles H.	Rep	N.C.	4	3	15th Visclosky, Peter J.	Dem	Ind.	7	4
16th Hobson, David L.	Rep	Ohio	4	3	16th Foglietta, Thomas M.	Dem	Penn.	9	3
17th Istook, Ernest Jim Jr.	Rep	Okla.	3	3	17th Torres, Esteban Edward	Dem	Cal.	8	3
18th Bonilla, Henry	Rep	Tex.	3	3	18th Lowey, Nita M.	Dem	N.Y.	5	3
19th Knollenberg, Joseph	Rep	Mich.	3	2	19th Serrano, Jose E.	Dem	N.Y.	5	*2 2
20th Miller, Daniel	Rep	Fla.	3	2	20th DeLauro, Rosa L.	Dem	Conn.	4	*2 1
21st Dickey, Jay W. Jr.	Rep	Ark.	3	2	21st Moran, James P. Jr.	Dem	Va.	4	*2 1

22nd Kingston, Jack	Rep	Ga.	3	2		22nd Olver, John W.	Dem	Mass.	4	*2 1
23rd Parker, Michael	Rep	Miss.	5	2		23rd Pastor, Edward L.	Dem	Ariz.	4	*2 1
24th Frelinghuysen, Rodney P.	Rep	N.J.	2	2		24th Meek, Carrie P.	Dem	Fla.	3	*2 1
25th Wicker, Roger F.	Rep	Miss.	2	2		25th Price, David E.	Dem	N.C.	5	*2 1
26th Forbes, Michael P.	Rep	N.Y.	2	2		26th Edwards, T. Chester (Chet)	Dem	Tex.	4	1
27th Nethercutt, George R. Jr.	Rep	Wash.	2	2						
28th Neumann, Mark W.	Rep	Wisc.	2	2		*1: Member's first period of service on the committee.				
29th Cunningham, Randall (Duke)	Rep	Cal.	4	1		*2: Member's second period of service on the committee.				
30th Tiahrt, Todd	Rep	Kans.	2	1						
31st Wamp, Zachary P.	Rep	Tenn.	2	1						
32nd Latham, Thomas	Rep	Iowa	2	1						
33rd Northup, Anne M.	Rep	Ky.	1	1						
34th Aderholt, Robert	Rep	Ala.	1	1						

Changes:

Minority:

Foglietta, Thomas M.	Dem	Penn.	Nov. 11, 1997 Resigned the House; appointed Ambassador to Italy
Cramer, Robert E. (Bud) Jr.	Dem	Ala.	Nov. 13, 1997 Replaced Foglietta

Departures from the House:

	Majority			**Minority**		
Lost Election to U.S. Senate	Neumann, Mark W.	Rep	Wisc.	None		
Retired	McDade, Joseph M.	Rep	Penn.	Yates, Sidney R.	Dem	Ill.
	Parker, Michael	Rep	Miss.	Stokes, Louis	Dem	Ohio
				Fazio, Victor H.	Dem	Cal.
				Hefner, W.G. (Bill)	Dem	N.C.
				Skaggs, David E.	Dem	Colo.
				Torres, Esteban Edward	Dem	Cal.

Departures from the Committee:

No new assignment	Livingston, Robert L. Jr.	Rep	La.	None	

APPROPRIATIONS / 106th Congress

Service Dates of Committee Chair: Jan. 6, 1999-Jan. 3, 2001

Service Dates of Majority Members: Jan. 6, 1999-Jan. 3, 2001

Service Dates of Minority Members: Jan. 6, 1999-Jan. 3, 2001

Roster Filled: Majority with 34 members, Jan. 6, 1999; Minority with 27 members, Jan. 6, 1999.

	Majority						**Minority**				
				Terms in:						**Terms in:**	
Rank Name	Party	State	House	Comm.		Rank Name	Party	State	House	Comm.
Chr Young, C.W. Bill	Rep	Fla.	15	14		RM Obey, David R.	Dem	Wisc.	16	16
2nd Regula, Ralph S.	Rep	Ohio	14	13		2nd Murtha, John P. Jr.	Dem	Penn.	14	13
3rd Lewis, Charles J. (Jerry)	Rep	Cal.	11	10		3rd Dicks, Norman D.	Dem	Wash.	12	12
4th Porter, John Edward	Rep	Ill.	11	10		4th Sabo, Martin Olav	DFL	Minn.	11	11
5th Rogers, Harold D.	Rep	Ky.	10	9		5th Dixon, Julian C.	Dem	Cal.	11	11
6th Skeen, Joseph R.	Rep	N.M.	10	8		6th Hoyer, Steny H.	Dem	Md.	10	10
7th Wolf, Frank R.	Rep	Va.	10	8		7th Mollohan, Alan B.	Dem	W.Va.	9	8
8th DeLay, Thomas D.	Rep	Tex.	8	*1 7		8th Kaptur, Marcia C. (Marcy)	Dem	Ohio	9	6
9th Kolbe, James T.	Rep	Ariz.	8	7		9th Pelosi, Nancy	Dem	Cal.	7	5
10th Packard, Ronald C.	Rep	Cal.	9	4		10th Visclosky, Peter J.	Dem	Ind.	8	5
11th Callahan, H.L. (Sonny)	Rep	Ala.	8	4		11th Lowey, Nita M.	Dem	N.Y.	6	4
12th Walsh, James T.	Rep	N.Y.	6	4		12th Serrano, Jose E.	Dem	N.Y.	6	*2 3
13th Taylor, Charles H.	Rep	N.C.	5	4		13th DeLauro, Rosa L.	Dem	Conn.	5	*2 2
14th Hobson, David L.	Rep	Ohio	5	4		14th Moran, James P. Jr.	Dem	Va.	5	*2 2
15th Istook, Ernest Jim Jr.	Rep	Okla.	4	4		15th Olver, John W.	Dem	Mass.	5	*2 2
16th Bonilla, Henry	Rep	Tex.	4	4		16th Pastor, Edward L.	Dem	Ariz.	5	*2 2
17th Knollenberg, Joseph	Rep	Mich.	4	3		17th Meek, Carrie P.	Dem	Fla.	4	*2 2
18th Miller, Daniel	Rep	Fla.	4	3		18th Price, David E.	Dem	N.C.	6	*2 2
19th Dickey, Jay W. Jr.	Rep	Ark.	4	3		19th Edwards, T. Chester (Chet)	Dem	Tex.	5	2
20th Kingston, Jack	Rep	Ga.	4	3		20th Cramer, Robert E. (Bud) Jr.	Dem	Ala.	5	2
21st Frelinghuysen, Rodney P.	Rep	N.J.	3	3		21st Clyburn, James E.	Dem	S.C.	4	*1 1
22nd Wicker, Roger F.	Rep	Miss.	3	3		22nd Hinchey, Maurice D.	Dem	N.Y.	4	1
23rd Forbes, Michael P.	Rep	N.Y.	3	3		23rd Roybal-Allard, Lucille	Dem	Cal.	4	1
24th Nethercutt, George R. Jr.	Rep	Wash.	3	3		24th Farr, Sam	Dem	Cal.	4	1
25th Cunningham, Randall (Duke)	Rep	Cal.	5	2		25th Jackson, Jesse L. Jr.	Dem	Ill.	3	1
26th Tiahrt, Todd	Rep	Kans.	3	2		26th Kilpatrick, Carolyn C.	Dem	Mich.	2	1

Rank Name	Party	State		
27th Wamp, Zachary P.	Rep	Tenn.	3	2
28th Latham, Thomas	Rep	Iowa	3	2
29th Northup, Anne M.	Rep	Ky.	2	2
30th Aderholt, Robert	Rep	Ala.	2	2
31st Emerson, Jo Ann	Rep	Mo.	3	1
32nd Sununu, John E.	Rep	N.H.	2	1
33rd Granger, Kay	Rep	Tex.	2	1
34th Peterson, John E.	Rep	Penn.	2	1
35th Blunt, Roy	Rep	Mo.	2	1

27th Boyd, F. Allen Jr.	Dem	Fla.	2	1

Third Party:

1st Goode, Virgil H. Jr.	Ind	Va.	2	1

*1: Member's first period of service on the committee.
*2: Member's second period of service on the committee.

Note: Livingston, who had chaired Appropriations Committee in the 104th and 105th Congresses, announced his resignation effective March 1, 1999, and was not reappointed to Appropriations.

Changes:

Majority:

Forbes, Michael P.	Rep	N.Y.	Aug. 5, 1999 Service on committee as a Republican was vacated; became a Democrat
Blunt, Roy	Rep	Mo.	July 19, 1999 Replaced Forbes
Blunt, Roy	Rep	Mo.	Feb. 1, 2000 Resigned committee to open seat for Goode; no new assignment
Goode, Virgil H. Jr.	Ind	Va.	Feb. 1, 2000 Assigned to Appropriations by Republicans as an Independent

Minority:

Clyburn, James E.	Dem	S.C.	Aug. 5, 1999 Resigned committee to open seat for Forbes; no new assignment
Forbes, Michael P.	Dem	N.Y.	Aug. 5, 1999 Returned as a Democrat replacing Clyburn, ranked following Price
Dixon, Julian C.	Dem	Cal.	Dec. 8, 2000 Died in office

Departures from the House:	Majority			Minority		
Defeated for Re-election	Dickey, Jay W. Jr.	Rep	Ark.	None		
Defeated for Nomination	None			Forbes, Michael P.	Dem	N.Y.
Retired	Porter, John Edward	Rep	Ill.	None		
	Packard, Ronald C.	Rep	Cal.			

APPROPRIATIONS / 107th Congress

Service Dates of Committee Chair: Jan. 6, 2001-Jan. 3, 2003

Service Dates of Majority Members: Jan. 6, 2001-Jan. 3, 2003

Service Dates of Minority Members: Jan. 31, 2001-Jan. 3, 2003

Roster Filled: Majority with 35 members, Jan. 6, 2001; Minority with 29 members, Feb. 8, 2001.

	Majority			Terms in:			Minority			Terms in:	
Rank Name		Party	State	House	Comm.	Rank Name		Party	State	House	Comm.
Chr Young, C.W. Bill		Rep	Fla.	16	15	RM Obey, David R.		Dem	Wisc.	17	17
2nd Regula, Ralph S.		Rep	Ohio	15	14	2nd Murtha, John P. Jr.		Dem	Penn.	15	14
3rd Lewis, Charles J. (Jerry)		Rep	Cal.	12	11	3rd Dicks, Norman D.		Dem	Wash.	13	13
4th Rogers, Harold D.		Rep	Ky.	11	10	4th Sabo, Martin Olav		DFL	Minn.	12	12
5th Skeen, Joseph R.		Rep	N.M.	11	9	5th Hoyer, Steny H.		Dem	Md.	11	11
6th Wolf, Frank R.		Rep	Va.	11	9	6th Mollohan, Alan B.		Dem	W.Va.	10	9
7th DeLay, Thomas D.		Rep	Tex.	9	*1 8	7th Kaptur, Marcia C. (Marcy)		Dem	Ohio	10	7
8th Kolbe, James T.		Rep	Ariz.	9	8	8th Pelosi, Nancy		Dem	Cal.	8	6
9th Callahan, H.L. (Sonny)		Rep	Ala.	9	5	9th Visclosky, Peter J.		Dem	Ind.	9	6
10th Walsh, James T.		Rep	N.Y.	7	5	10th Lowey, Nita M.		Dem	N.Y.	7	5
11th Taylor, Charles H.		Rep	N.C.	6	5	11th Serrano, Jose E.		Dem	N.Y.	7	*2 4
12th Hobson, David L.		Rep	Ohio	6	5	12th DeLauro, Rosa L.		Dem	Conn.	6	*2 3
13th Istook, Ernest Jim Jr.		Rep	Okla.	5	5	13th Moran, James P. Jr.		Dem	Va.	6	*2 3
14th Bonilla, Henry		Rep	Tex.	5	5	14th Olver, John W.		Dem	Mass.	6	*2 3
15th Knollenberg, Joseph		Rep	Mich.	5	4	15th Pastor, Edward L.		Dem	Ariz.	6	*2 3
16th Miller, Daniel		Rep	Fla.	5	4	16th Meek, Carrie P.		Dem	Fla.	5	*2 3
17th Kingston, Jack		Rep	Ga.	5	4	17th Price, David E.		Dem	N.C.	7	*2 3
18th Frelinghuysen, Rodney P.		Rep	N.J.	4	4	18th Edwards, T. Chester (Chet)		Dem	Tex.	6	3
19th Wicker, Roger F.		Rep	Miss.	4	4	19th Cramer, Robert E. (Bud) Jr.		Dem	Ala.	6	3
20th Nethercutt, George R. Jr.		Rep	Wash.	4	4	20th Kennedy, Patrick J.		Dem	R.I.	4	1
21st Cunningham, Randall (Duke)		Rep	Cal.	6	3	21st Clyburn, James E.		Dem	S.C.	5	*2 1
22nd Tiahrt, Todd		Rep	Kans.	4	3	22nd Hinchey, Maurice D.		Dem	N.Y.	5	2
23rd Wamp, Zachary P.		Rep	Tenn.	4	3	23rd Roybal-Allard, Lucille		Dem	Cal.	5	2
24th Latham, Thomas		Rep	Iowa	4	3	24th Farr, Sam		Dem	Cal.	5	2
25th Northup, Anne M.		Rep	Ky.	3	3	25th Jackson, Jesse L. Jr.		Dem	Ill.	4	2
26th Aderholt, Robert		Rep	Ala.	3	3	26th Kilpatrick, Carolyn C.		Dem	Mich.	3	2
27th Emerson, Jo Ann		Rep	Mo.	4	2	27th Boyd, F. Allen Jr.		Dem	Fla.	3	2
28th Sununu, John E.		Rep	N.H.	3	2	28th Fattah, Chaka		Dem	Penn.	4	1
29th Granger, Kay		Rep	Tex.	3	2	29th Rothman, Steven R.		Dem	N.J.	3	1

				Terms in:	
30th Peterson, John E.	Rep	Penn.	3	2	
31st Doolittle, John T.	Rep	Cal.	6	1	
32nd LaHood, Ray H.	Rep	Ill.	4	1	
33rd Sweeney, John E.	Rep	N.Y.	2	1	
34th Vitter, David	Rep	La.	2	1	
35th Goode, Virgil H. Jr.	Rep	Va.	3	2	

Third Party:

1st Goode, Virgil H. Jr.	Ind.	Va.	3	2	

*1: Member's first period of service on the committee.

*2: Member's second period of service on the committee.

Filled Vacancies:

Minority:

28th and 29th seats filled by Fattah and Rothman on Feb. 8, 2001

Additions:

Majority:

36th Sherwood, Don	Rep	Penn.	Mar. 7, 2001

Changes:

Majority:

Goode, Virgil H. Jr.	Ind.	Va.	Aug. 1, 2002 Formally joined Republican Party; had already been assigned by Republicans as an Independent

Departures from the House:

	Majority			Minority		
Elected to U.S. Senate	Sununu, John E.	Rep	N.H.	None		
Retired	Skeen, Joseph R.	Rep	N.M.	Meek, Carrie P.	Dem	Fla.
	Callahan, H.L. (Sonny)	Rep	Ala.			
	Miller, Daniel	Rep	Fla.			

Departures from Committee:

	Majority			Minority		
Elected Minority Leader	None			Pelosi, Nancy	Dem	Cal.
Elected Majority Leader	DeLay, Thomas D.	Rep	Tex.	None		

APPROPRIATIONS / 108th Congress

Service Dates of Committee Chair: Jan. 8, 2003-Jan. 3, 2005

Service Dates of Majority Members: Jan. 28, 2003-Jan. 3, 2005

Service Dates of Ranking Member: Jan. 8, 2003-Jan. 3, 2005

Service Dates of Minority Members: Jan. 28, 2003-Jan. 3, 2005

Roster Filled: Majority with 36 members, Jan. 28, 2003; Minority with 29 members, Jan. 28, 2003.

Majority			Terms in:		Minority			Terms in:	
Rank Name	Party	State	House	Comm.	Rank Name	Party	State	House	Comm.
Chr Young, C.W. Bill	Rep	Fla.	17	16	RM Obey, David R.	Dem	Wisc.	18	18
2nd Regula, Ralph S.	Rep	Ohio	16	15	2nd Murtha, John P. Jr.	Dem	Penn.	16	15
3rd Lewis, Charles J. (Jerry)	Rep	Cal.	13	12	3rd Dicks, Norman D.	Dem	Wash.	14	14
4th Rogers, Harold D.	Rep	Ky.	12	11	4th Sabo, Martin Olav	DFL	Minn.	13	13
5th Wolf, Frank R.	Rep	Va.	12	10	5th Hoyer, Steny H.	Dem	Md.	12	12
6th Kolbe, James T.	Rep	Ariz.	10	9	6th Mollohan, Alan B.	Dem	W.Va.	11	10
7th Walsh, James T.	Rep	N.Y.	8	6	7th Kaptur, Marcia C. (Marcy)	Dem	Ohio	11	8
8th Taylor, Charles H.	Rep	N.C.	7	6	8th Visclosky, Peter J.	Dem	Ind.	10	7
9th Hobson, David L.	Rep	Ohio	7	6	9th Lowey, Nita M.	Dem	N.Y.	8	6
10th Istook, Ernest Jim Jr.	Rep	Okla.	6	6	10th Serrano, Jose E.	Dem	N.Y.	8	*2 5
11th Bonilla, Henry	Rep	Tex.	6	6	11th DeLauro, Rosa L.	Dem	Conn.	7	*2 4
12th Knollenberg, Joseph	Rep	Mich.	6	5	12th Moran, James P. Jr.	Dem	Va.	7	*2 4
13th Kingston, Jack	Rep	Ga.	6	5	13th Olver, John W.	Dem	Mass.	7	*2 4
14th Frelinghuysen, Rodney P.	Rep	N.J.	5	5	14th Pastor, Edward L.	Dem	Ariz.	7	*2 4
15th Wicker, Roger F.	Rep	Miss.	5	5	15th Price, David E.	Dem	N.C.	8	*2 4
16th Nethercutt, George R. Jr.	Rep	Wash.	5	5	16th Edwards, T. Chester (Chet)	Dem	Tex.	7	4
17th Cunningham, Randall (Duke)	Rep	Cal.	7	4	17th Cramer, Robert E. (Bud) Jr.	Dem	Ala.	7	4
18th Tiahrt, Todd	Rep	Kans.	5	4	18th Kennedy, Patrick J.	Dem	R.I.	5	2
19th Wamp, Zachary P.	Rep	Tenn.	5	4	19th Clyburn, James E.	Dem	S.C.	6	*2 2
20th Latham, Thomas	Rep	Iowa	5	4	20th Hinchey, Maurice D.	Dem	N.Y.	6	3
21st Northup, Anne M.	Rep	Ky.	4	4	21st Roybal-Allard, Lucille	Dem	Cal.	6	3
22nd Aderholt, Robert	Rep	Ala.	4	4	22nd Farr, Sam	Dem	Cal.	6	3
23rd Emerson, Jo Ann	Rep	Mo.	5	3	23rd Jackson, Jesse L. Jr.	Dem	Ill.	5	3
24th Granger, Kay	Rep	Tex.	4	3	24th Kilpatrick, Carolyn C.	Dem	Mich.	4	3
25th Peterson, John E.	Rep	Penn.	4	3	25th Boyd, F. Allen Jr.	Dem	Fla.	4	3
26th Goode, Virgil H. Jr.	Rep	Va.	4	3	26th Fattah, Chaka	Dem	Penn.	5	2
27th Doolittle, John T.	Rep	Cal.	7	2	27th Rothman, Steven R.	Dem	N.J.	4	2

28th LaHood, Ray H.	Rep	Ill.	5	2
29th Sweeney, John E.	Rep	N.Y.	3	2
30th Vitter, David	Rep	La.	3	2
31st Sherwood, Don	Rep	Penn.	3	2
32nd Weldon, David J.	Rep	Fla.	5	1
33rd Simpson, Michael K.	Rep	Ida.	3	1
34th Culberson, John	Rep	Tex.	2	1
35th Kirk, Mark S.	Rep	Ill.	2	1
36th Crenshaw, Ander	Rep	Fla.	2	1

| 28th Bishop, Sanford D. Jr. | Dem | Ga. | 6 | 1 |
| 29th Berry, R. Marion | Dem | Ark. | 4 | 1 |

*2: Member's second period of service on the committee.

Departures from the House:

	Majority			Minority
Elected to U.S. Senate	Vitter, David	Rep	La.	None
Lost Election to U.S. Senate	Nethercutt, George R. Jr.	Rep	Wash.	None

APPROPRIATIONS / 109th Congress

Service Dates of Committee Chair: Jan. 6, 2005-Jan. 3, 2007

Service Dates of Majority Members: Jan. 6, 2005-Jan. 3, 2007

Service Dates of Minority Members: Jan. 26, 2005-Jan. 3, 2007

Roster Filled: Majority with 37 members, Jan. 6, 2005; Minority with 29 members, Jan. 26, 2005.

Majority			Terms in:		Minority			Terms in:	
Rank Name	Party	State	House	Comm.	Rank Name	Party	State	House	Comm.
Chr Lewis, Charles J. (Jerry)	Rep	Cal.	14	13	RM Obey, David R.	Dem	Wisc.	19	19
2nd Young, C.W. Bill	Rep	Fla.	18	17	2nd Murtha, John P. Jr.	Dem	Penn.	17	16
3rd Regula, Ralph S.	Rep	Ohio	17	16	3rd Dicks, Norman D.	Dem	Wash.	15	15
4th Rogers, Harold D.	Rep	Ky.	13	12	4th Sabo, Martin Olav	DFL	Minn.	14	14
5th Wolf, Frank R.	Rep	Va.	13	11	5th Hoyer, Steny H.	Dem	Md.	13	13
6th Kolbe, James T.	Rep	Ariz.	11	10	6th Mollohan, Alan B.	Dem	W.Va.	12	11
7th Walsh, James T.	Rep	N.Y.	9	7	7th Kaptur, Marcia C. (Marcy)	Dem	Ohio	12	9
8th Taylor, Charles H.	Rep	N.C.	8	7	8th Visclosky, Peter J.	Dem	Ind.	11	8
9th Hobson, David L.	Rep	Ohio	8	7	9th Lowey, Nita M.	Dem	N.Y.	9	7
10th Istook, Ernest Jim Jr.	Rep	Okla.	7	7	10th Serrano, Jose E.	Dem	N.Y.	9	*2 6
11th Bonilla, Henry	Rep	Tex.	7	7	11th DeLauro, Rosa L.	Dem	Conn.	8	*2 5
12th Knollenberg, Joseph	Rep	Mich.	7	6	12th Moran, James P. Jr.	Dem	Va.	8	*2 5
13th Kingston, Jack	Rep	Ga.	7	6	13th Olver, John W.	Dem	Mass.	8	*2 5
14th Frelinghuysen, Rodney P.	Rep	N.J.	6	6	14th Pastor, Edward L.	Dem	Ariz.	8	*2 5
15th Wicker, Roger F.	Rep	Miss.	6	6	15th Price, David E.	Dem	N.C.	9	*2 5
16th Cunningham, Randall (Duke)	Rep	Cal.	8	5	16th Edwards, T. Chester (Chet)	Dem	Tex.	8	5
17th Tiahrt, Todd	Rep	Kans.	6	5	17th Cramer, Robert E. (Bud) Jr.	Dem	Ala.	8	5
18th Wamp, Zachary P.	Rep	Tenn.	6	5	18th Kennedy, Patrick J.	Dem	R.I.	6	3
19th Latham, Thomas	Rep	Iowa	6	5	19th Clyburn, James E.	Dem	S.C.	7	*2 3
20th Northup, Anne M.	Rep	Ky.	5	5	20th Hinchey, Maurice D.	Dem	N.Y.	7	4
21st Aderholt, Robert	Rep	Ala.	5	5	21st Roybal-Allard, Lucille	Dem	Cal.	7	4
22nd Emerson, Jo Ann	Rep	Mo.	6	4	22nd Farr, Sam	Dem	Cal.	7	4
23rd Granger, Kay	Rep	Tex.	5	4	23rd Jackson, Jesse L. Jr.	Dem	Ill.	6	4
24th Peterson, John E.	Rep	Penn.	5	4	24th Kilpatrick, Carolyn C.	Dem	Mich.	5	4
25th Goode, Virgil H. Jr.	Rep	Va.	5	4	25th Boyd, F. Allen Jr.	Dem	Fla.	5	4
26th Doolittle, John T.	Rep	Cal.	8	3	26th Fattah, Chaka	Dem	Penn.	6	3
27th LaHood, Ray H.	Rep	Ill.	6	3	27th Rothman, Steven R.	Dem	N.J.	5	3
28th Sweeney, John E.	Rep	N.Y.	4	3	28th Bishop, Sanford D. Jr.	Dem	Ga.	7	2
29th Sherwood, Don	Rep	Penn.	4	3	29th Berry, R. Marion	Dem	Ark.	5	2
30th Weldon, David J.	Rep	Fla.	6	2					
31st Simpson, Michael K.	Rep	Ida.	4	2					
32nd Culberson, John	Rep	Tex.	3	2					
33rd Kirk, Mark S.	Rep	Ill.	3	2					
34th Crenshaw, Ander	Rep	Fla.	3	2					
35th Rehberg, Dennis	Rep	Mont.	3	1					
36th Carter, John R.	Rep	Tex.	2	1					
37th Alexander, Rodney	Rep	La.	2	1					

*2: Member's second period of service on the committee.

Changes:

Majority:

Cunningham, Randall (Duke)	Rep	Cal.	Dec. 1, 2005 Resigned the House due to ethics issues
DeLay, Thomas D.	Rep	Tex.	Feb. 8, 2006 Returned to committee, replacing Cunningham, ranked after Wolf
DeLay, Thomas D.	Rep	Tex.	June 9, 2006 Resigned the House due to ethics issues

Departures from the House:	Majority			Minority		
Defeated for Re-election	Taylor, Charles H.	Rep	N.C.	None		
	Bonilla, Henry	Rep	Tex.			
	Northup, Anne M.	Rep	Ky.			
	Sweeney, John E.	Rep	N.Y.			
	Sherwood, Don	Rep	Penn.			
Lost Nomination for Governor	Istook, Ernest Jim Jr.	Rep	La.	None		
Retired	Kolbe, James T.	Rep	Ariz.	Sabo, Martin Olav	DFL	Minn.

Departures from Committee:	Majority			Minority		
Elected Majority Leader	None			Hoyer, Steny H.	Dem	Md.
Elected Majority Whip	None			Clyburn, James E.	Dem	S.C.

APPROPRIATIONS / 110th Congress

Service Dates of Committee Chair: Jan. 4, 2007-Jan. 3, 2009

Service Dates of Majority Members: Jan. 4, 2007-Jan. 3, 2009

Service Dates of Minority Members: Jan. 4, 2007-Jan. 3, 2009

Roster Filled: Majority with 37 members, Jan. 4, 2007; Minority with 29 members, Jan. 4, 2007.

	Majority						**Minority**				
				Terms in:						**Terms in:**	
Rank Name	Party	State	House	Comm.		Rank Name	Party	State	House	Comm.	
Chr Obey, David R.	Dem	Wisc.	20	20		RM Lewis, Charles J. (Jerry)	Rep	Cal.	15	14	
2nd Murtha, John P. Jr.	Dem	Penn.	18	17		2nd Young, C.W. Bill	Rep	Fla.	19	18	
3rd Dicks, Norman D.	Dem	Wash.	16	16		3rd Regula, Ralph S.	Rep	Ohio	18	17	
4th Mollohan, Alan B.	Dem	W.Va.	13	12		4th Rogers, Harold D.	Rep	Ky.	14	13	
5th Kaptur, Marcia C. (Marcy)	Dem	Ohio	13	10		5th Wolf, Frank R.	Rep	Va.	14	12	
6th Visclosky, Peter J.	Dem	Ind.	12	9		6th Walsh, James T.	Rep	N.Y.	10	8	
7th Lowey, Nita M.	Dem	N.Y.	10	8		7th Hobson, David L.	Rep	Ohio	9	8	
8th Serrano, Jose E.	Dem	N.Y.	10	*2 7		8th Knollenberg, Joseph	Rep	Mich.	8	7	
9th DeLauro, Rosa L.	Dem	Conn.	9	*2 6		9th Kingston, Jack	Rep	Ga.	8	7	
10th Moran, James P. Jr.	Dem	Va.	9	*2 6		10th Frelinghuysen, Rodney P.	Rep	N.J.	7	7	
11th Olver, John W.	Dem	Mass.	9	*2 6		11th Wicker, Roger F.	Rep	Miss.	7	7	
12th Pastor, Edward L.	Dem	Ariz.	9	*2 6		12th Tiahrt, Todd	Rep	Kans.	7	6	
13th Price, David E.	Dem	N.C.	10	*2 6		13th Wamp, Zachary P.	Rep	Tenn.	7	6	
14th Edwards, T. Chester (Chet)	Dem	Tex.	9	6		14th Latham, Thomas	Rep	Iowa	7	6	
15th Cramer, Robert E. (Bud) Jr.	Dem	Ala.	9	6		15th Aderholt, Robert	Rep	Ala.	6	6	
16th Kennedy, Patrick J.	Dem	R.I.	7	4		16th Emerson, Jo Ann	Rep	Mo.	7	5	
17th Hinchey, Maurice D.	Dem	N.Y.	8	5		17th Granger, Kay	Rep	Tex.	6	5	
18th Roybal-Allard, Lucille	Dem	Cal.	8	5		18th Peterson, John E.	Rep	Penn.	6	5	
19th Farr, Sam	Dem	Cal.	8	5		19th Goode, Virgil H. Jr.	Rep	Va.	6	5	
20th Jackson, Jesse L. Jr.	Dem	Ill.	7	5		20th Doolittle, John T.	Rep	Cal.	9	4	
21st Kilpatrick, Carolyn C.	Dem	Mich.	6	5		21st LaHood, Ray H.	Rep	Ill.	7	4	
22nd Boyd, F. Allen Jr.	Dem	Fla.	6	5		22nd Weldon, David J.	Rep	Fla.	7	3	
23rd Fattah, Chaka	Dem	Penn.	7	4		23rd Simpson, Michael K.	Rep	Ida.	5	3	
24th Rothman, Steven R.	Dem	N.J.	6	4		24th Culberson, John	Rep	Tex.	4	3	
25th Bishop, Sanford D. Jr.	Dem	Ga.	8	3		25th Kirk, Mark S.	Rep	Ill.	4	3	
26th Berry, R. Marion	Dem	Ark.	6	3		26th Crenshaw, Ander	Rep	Fla.	4	3	
27th Lee, Barbara	Dem	Cal.	6	1		27th Rehberg, Dennis	Rep	Mont.	4	2	
28th Udall, Thomas	Dem	N.M.	5	1		28th Carter, John R.	Rep	Tex.	3	2	
29th Schiff, Adam B.	Dem	Cal.	4	1		29th Alexander, Rodney	Rep	La.	3	2	
30th Honda, Michael M.	Dem	Cal.	4	1							
31st McCollum, Betty	DFL	Minn.	4	1		*2: Member's second period of service on the committee.					
32nd Israel, Steve	Dem	N.Y.	4	1							
33rd Ryan, Timothy J.	Dem	Ohio	3	1							
34th Ruppersberger, C.A. (Dutch)	Dem	Md.	3	1							
35th Chandler, A.B. (Ben)	Dem	Ky.	3	1							
36th Wasserman Schultz, Debbie	Dem	Fla.	2	1							
37th Rodriguez, Ciro D.	Dem	Tex.	5	1							

Changes:

   Minority:

Doolittle, John T.	Rep	Cal.	April 20, 2007 Resigned temporarily from Appropriations due to ethics issues
Calvert, Ken	Rep	Cal.	May 10, 2007 Replaced Doolittle
Wicker, Roger F.	Rep	Miss.	Dec. 31, 2007 Resigned the House; appointed to U.S. Senate
Bonner, Josiah R. Jr.	Rep	Ala.	Feb. 26, 2008 Replaced Wicker

Departures from the House:	Majority			Minority		
Elected to the U.S. Senate	Udall, Thomas	Dem	N.M.	None		
Defeated for Re-election	None			Knollenberg, Joseph	Rep	Mich.
				Goode, Virgil H. Jr.	Rep	Va.
Retired	Cramer, Robert E. (Bud) Jr.	Dem	Ala.	Walsh, James T.	Rep	N.Y.
				Hobson, David L.	Rep	Ohio
				Peterson, John E.	Rep	Penn.
				Doolittle, John T.	Rep	Cal.
				LaHood, Ray H.	Rep	Ill.
				Weldon, David J.	Rep	Fla.
				Regula, Ralph S.	Rep	Ohio

APPROPRIATIONS / 111th Congress

Service Dates of Committee Chair: Jan. 6, 2009-Jan. 3, 2011

Service Dates of Majority Members: Jan. 7, 2009-Jan. 3, 2011

Service Dates of Minority Members: Jan. 9, 2009-Jan. 3, 2011

Roster Filled: Majority with 37 members, Jan. 7, 2009; Minority with 23 members, Jan. 9, 2009

Majority					Minority				
			Terms in:					Terms in:	
Rank Name	Party	State	House	Comm.	Rank Name	Party	State	House	Comm.
Chr Obey, David R.	Dem	Wisc.	21	21	RM Lewis, Charles J. (Jerry)	Rep	Cal.	16	15
2nd Murtha, John P. Jr.	Dem	Penn.	19	18	2nd Young, C.W. Bill	Rep	Fla.	20	19
3rd Dicks, Norman D.	Dem	Wash.	17	17	3rd Rogers, Harold D.	Rep	Ky.	15	14
4th Mollohan, Alan B.	Dem	W.Va.	14	13	4th Wolf, Frank R.	Rep	Va.	15	13
5th Kaptur, Marcia C. (Marcy)	Dem	Ohio	14	11	5th Kingston, Jack	Rep	Ga.	9	8
6th Visclosky, Peter J.	Dem	Ind.	13	10	6th Frelinghuysen, Rodney P.	Rep	N.J.	8	8
7th Lowey, Nita M.	Dem	N.Y.	11	9	7th Tiahrt, Todd	Rep	Kans.	8	7
8th Serrano, Jose E.	Dem	N.Y.	11	*2 8	8th Wamp, Zachary P.	Rep	Tenn.	8	7
9th DeLauro, Rosa L.	Dem	Conn.	10	*2 7	9th Latham, Thomas	Rep	Iowa	8	7
10th Moran, James P. Jr.	Dem	Va.	10	*2 7	10th Aderholt, Robert	Rep	Ala.	7	7
11th Olver, John W.	Dem	Mass.	10	*2 7	11th Emerson, Jo Ann	Rep	Mo.	8	6
12th Pastor, Edward L.	Dem	Ariz.	10	*2 7	12th Granger, Kay	Rep	Tex.	7	6
13th Price, David E.	Dem	N.C.	11	*2 7	13th Simpson, Michael K.	Rep	Ida.	6	4
14th Edwards, T. Chester (Chet)	Dem	Tex.	10	7	14th Culberson, John	Rep	Tex.	5	4
15th Kennedy, Patrick J.	Dem	R.I.	8	5	15th Kirk, Mark S.	Rep	Ill.	5	4
16th Hinchey, Maurice D.	Dem	N.Y.	9	6	16th Crenshaw, Ander	Rep	Fla.	5	4
17th Roybal-Allard, Lucille	Dem	Cal.	9	6	17th Rehberg, Dennis	Rep	Mont.	5	3
18th Farr, Sam	Dem	Cal.	9	6	18th Carter, John R.	Rep	Tex.	4	3
19th Jackson, Jesse L. Jr.	Dem	Ill.	8	6	19th Alexander, Rodney	Rep	La.	4	3
20th Kilpatrick, Carolyn C.	Dem	Mich.	7	6	20th Calvert, Ken	Rep	Cal.	9	2
21st Boyd, F. Allen Jr.	Dem	Fla.	7	6	21st Bonner, Josiah R. Jr.	Rep	Ala.	4	2
22nd Fattah, Chaka	Dem	Penn.	8	5	22nd LaTourette, Steven C.	Rep	Ohio	8	1
23rd Rothman, Steven R.	Dem	N.J.	7	5	23rd Cole, Tom	Rep	Okla.	4	1
24th Bishop, Sanford D. Jr.	Dem	Ga.	9	4					
25th Berry, R. Marion	Dem	Ark.	7	4	*2: Member's second period of service on the committee.				
26th Lee, Barbara	Dem	Cal.	7	2					
27th Schiff, Adam B.	Dem	Cal.	5	2					
28th Honda, Michael M.	Dem	Cal.	5	2					
29th McCollum, Betty	DFL	Minn.	5	2					
30th Israel, Steve	Dem	N.Y.	5	2					
31st Ryan, Timothy J.	Dem	Ohio	4	2					
32nd Ruppersberger, C.A. (Dutch)	Dem	Md.	4	2					
33rd Chandler, A.B. (Ben)	Dem	Ky.	4	2					
34th Wasserman Schultz, Debbie	Dem	Fla.	3	2					
35th Rodriguez, Ciro D.	Dem	Tex.	6	2					
36th Davis, Lincoln	Dem	Tenn.	4	1					
37th Salazar, John T.	Dem	Colo.	3	1					

Changes:
Majority:

Murtha, John P. Jr.	Dem	Penn.	Feb. 8, 2010 Died in office
Murphy, Patrick J.	Dem	Penn.	Replaced Murtha

Armed Services

House Committee on Armed Services, 103rd Congress (1993-1995)

House Committee on National Security, 104th-108th Congresses (1995-2005)

House Committee on Armed Services, 109th-111th Congresses (2005-2011)

BACKGROUND

Organizational History: The Committee on Armed Services was created by the Legislative Reorganization Act of 1946 from the House Committees on Military Affairs and Naval Affairs. Both predecessor committees were established by the Select Committee on Rules on March 13, 1822. Another of the predecessors was the Committee on the Militia which existed from 1835 until its absorption by Military Affairs in 1911. Both Naval Affairs and Military Affairs were beneficiaries of the 1885 resolution, which took jurisdiction away from the Appropriations Committee. However, in 1920, control over military and naval appropriations was returned to the Appropriations Committee.

As established in the 1946 Legislative Reorganization Act, the Armed Services Committee was responsible for measures related to the common defense of the United States and the War and Navy Departments and the Military and Naval Establishment. The committee was also given jurisdiction over matters related to armed services personnel, including the size and composition of the Army and Navy; the selective service; pay, promotion, retirement, and other benefits for the armed forces; and soldiers' and sailors' homes. The third and final component of the committee's responsibilities covered matters related to defense resources.

The National Security Act of 1947 (P.L. 80-253, 61 Statutes 495) replaced the separate Cabinet-level Departments of War and the Navy with the National Defense Establishment, to be headed by a Secretary of Defense with subcabinet status for the Departments of the Army, the Navy, and the Air Force that had been separated from the Army. This act also created the National Security Council and the Central Intelligence Agency.

The Armed Services Committee retained responsibility for this department and its jurisdictional authority over the department was clearly established in 1953 (House Manual, 2008). The legislative authority of the committee was augmented by its gaining jurisdiction over military applications of nuclear energy following the 1977 abolition of the Joint Committee on Atomic Energy. The committee has also been granted special oversight functions to review and study international arms control and disarmament and the education of military dependents.

With the Republican takeover of the House on January 4, 1995, the Armed Services Committee was renamed the Committee on National Security for two Congresses (1995-1999) and then resumed its name as Armed Services on January 6, 1999. During that time, the termination of the Committee on the Merchant Marine and Fisheries in 1995 led the committee to gain jurisdiction over: 1) interoceanic canals generally, including measures relating to the maintenance, operation, and administration of interoceanic canals; 2) 'the Merchant

Marine Academy, and State Maritime Academies; and 3) national security aspects of the merchant marine, including financial assistance for the construction and operation of vessels, the maintenance of the U.S. shipbuilding and ship repair industrial base, cabotage, cargo preference, and merchant marine officers and seamen as these matters relate to national security.

The continuing military involvement of American armed forces in various trouble spots around the world places the House Armed Services Committee in the center of public debates about the appropriate force levels and combat readiness of American troops. Social issues have also appeared on the committee's agenda. In 1993 Congress passed the "don't ask, don't tell" policy regarding the enlistment of gay service people (P.L.103-160). That policy led to the discharge of 13,000 enlisted personnel since 1993 but it has come into serious question with officials in the Obama Administration who are seeking to remove it. The Armed Services Committee now finds itself in the midst of an ideological battlefield far removed from the wartime preparedness issues that have defined its agenda for most of its existence.

Membership: For much of the post-World War II period the committee was dominated by Democrats from the South where most of the military bases had sprouted during and after World War II. Armed Services grew from thirty-three members in the 80th Congress to fifty-four in the 102nd Congress. The Armed Services Committee had its first sixty-member Congress in the 106th Congress (1997-1999) and in the last three Congresses (2005-2011); its membership has stabilized at sixty-two.

In the nine Congresses between 1993 and 2011, Armed Services ranked high in mean size per Congress—fourth place with 59.67 members—but middling in mean member seniority per Congress—twelfth place with an average 4.63 terms per member. Its mean inter-Congress retention rate in these years has been relatively high—90.27 percent—fifth place among the nineteen committees that functioned throughout these Congresses.

Committee Leaders: The first post-Reorganization Republican chair of Armed Services was Walter G. Andrews (Rep-N.Y.) who had been the ranking member on Military Affairs from 1937 to 1947. He would retire in 1949. Carl Vinson (Dem-Ga.), the first Democrat to chair Armed Services, became the senior Democrat on Naval Affairs in 1923 and would chair the committee throughout the Franklin D. Roosevelt Administration. After the Reorganization, Vinson chaired the committee for eight of the next nine Congresses (1949-1965), interrupted by the only other Congress (the 83rd, 1953-1955) in which Republicans had a majority and Dewey Short (Rep-Mo.) served as chair. Vinson retired in

1965, at which time he had served for more than fifty years (1914-1965), the first House member to have served for half a century. Vinson's grand-nephew, Sam Nunn (Dem-Ga.), chaired the Senate Armed Services Committee from 1987 until his retirement in 1995.

In addition to Andrews and Short, other Republicans who served with Vinson did so as ranking minority members. Long-time House Minority Whip Leslie C. Arends (Rep-Ill.) held this role after Short's 1956 defeat and served until Republican Conference rules obliged him to relinquish the post to William H. Bates (Rep-Mass.) in 1967. Bates would serve as ranking member until his death in 1969, when Arends resumed the senior ranking slot that he held until 1973 and the convening of his last Congress. His successor William H. Bray (Rep-Ind.) failed to be re-elected in 1974.

Vinson's chairmanship passed to L. Mendel Rivers (Dem-S.C.), who died on December 28, 1970. His campaign slogan "Rivers delivers" was based on his ability to funnel military appropriations into his Columbia, South Carolina, district. Rivers was succeeded for a few days by lame-duck Phillip J. Philbin (Dem-Mass.) who lost his 1970 renomination bid. In 1971, F. Edward Hebert (Dem-La.) became chair and served for two Congresses until his 1975 defeat (133-152) in the Democratic Caucus by C. Melvin Price (Dem-Ill.). Hebert was one of the three House chairs demoted by 1974's class of insurgent "Watergate babies." Observers of the committee long noted that this dominance by Southerners resulted in billions of military expenditures being poured into the districts and the states they represented during the Cold War period that followed World War II.

Price's rise, however, was the beginning of a significant transition in the committee's leadership. He lost the job as chair in the 99th Congress by a secret ballot vote (118-121) of the Democratic Caucus, Jan. 4, 1985, as younger and more liberal party members sought more active participation in military decisions. Price, who remained on the committee until his death April 22, 1988, had suffered from advancing age and illness. Republican ranking members serving with Price were Robert C. Wilson (Rep-Cal.), who retired from the House in 1981, and William L. Dickinson (Rep-Ala.), who followed Wilson and also served with Aspin until his own retirement in 1993.

Further change occurred when Price was ousted in the 99th Congress by seventh-ranking Les Aspin (Dem-Wisc.), a widely respected authority on military matters. Although generally sympathetic to the armed forces and one of Defense Secretary Robert S. McNamara's "whiz kids," Aspin often was a sharp critic of the military and challenged many of the traditional assumptions of the military establishment. He held the position through the 102nd Congress until his appointment as Secretary of Defense by President Bill Clinton in 1993.

The movement away from the old Southern dominance continued when Ronald V. Dellums (Dem-Cal.), one of the most liberal members of Congress, became chair in 1993. Dellums, a prominent member of the Congressional Black Caucus, had first been elected to Congress due to his opposition to the Vietnam War, and he fiercely opposed every ensuing U.S. military intervention right through the 1991 Persian Gulf conflict with Iraq. Throughout the 1980s, he continually argued for deep defense spending cuts to divert more funds to domestic spending programs. But by the time of Dellums' accession the political and military landscape had changed.

The Soviet Union had collapsed and huge federal budget deficits had already set defense spending on a downward slide. Dellums served as ranking member until his retirement in February, 1998. Dellums was succeeded by "Ike" Skelton (Dem-Mo.) who has been the committee's senior Democrat since 1998, with eight-plus years as ranking member and the last four as chair, 2007-2011.

Floyd D. Spence (Rep-S.C.) succeeded Dickinson in 1993 and when Republicans organized the House in 1993, he became the first Republican chair of Armed Services since Dewey Short in the 83rd Congress (1953-1955). Under Republican Conference rules, Spence served as chair until 2001, when he relinquished the chair to Robert Stump (Rep-Ariz.) who had been one of the earlier party switchers from Democrat to Republican. Stump's retirement in 2003 opened the chair to Duncan L. Hunter (Rep-Cal.) who served as chair, 2003-2007, and as ranking member, 2007-2009. Hunter's successor, John M. McHugh (Rep-N.Y.), resigned the House in 2009 to become President Barack Obama's Secretary of the Army.

Party Leaders: While no modern-era Speakers served on Armed Services, Leslie Arends (Rep-Ill.), the Republican party's longest serving whip who had served on the predecessor Military Affairs Committee, served on Armed Services for twenty-eight years, 1947-1975, often as ranking member, and former Republican Minority Leader Charles A. Halleck (Rep-Ind.) served on the committee in his last Congress (1967-1969) after he had lost his post to Gerald Ford (Rep-Mich.) in 1965.

Notable Members: The most prominent member with post-1947 service on Armed Services would be President Lyndon B. Johnson of Texas, who had served on the predecessor Naval Affairs Committee with its chair Carl Vinson. John J. Sparkman (Dem-Ala.), the Democrats' 1952 vice presidential nominee with Adlai Stevenson, served on the other predecessor committee, Military Affairs, during his service as House Democratic Whip. Les Aspin (Dem-Wisc.) left the chair of Armed Services to become President Bill Clinton's first Secretary of Defense in 1993. Two junior members of Armed Services named to the Cabinet were Richard Schweiker (Rep-Penn.), named President Reagan's first Secretary of Health and Human Services in 1981, and Lynn Martin (Rep-Ill.), Secretary of Labor under President George H.W. Bush.

Nineteen modern-era Senators served on the House Armed Services Committee, eighteen before they moved to the Senate and one after his Senate career ended—Democrat Alton A. Lennon of North Carolina.

The six Democrats among the eighteen were Lyndon B. Johnson of Texas, Delegate E.L. (Bob) Bartlett of Alaska, Daniel Brewster of Maryland, Barbara Boxer of California, Mark Udall of Colorado, and Kirsten E Gillibrand of New York.

Among the twelve Republicans were Margaret Chase Smith of Maine, J. Glenn Beall, Jr., of Maryland, William L. Armstrong of Colorado, Richard Schweiker of Pennsylvania, Robert T. Stafford of Vermont, Paul S. Trible of Virginia, Robert C. Smith of New Hampshire, Jon Kyl of Arizona, James M. Talent of Missouri, James M. Inhofe of Oklahoma, Saxby Chambliss of Georgia, and Lindsey O. Graham of South Carolina.

Five modern-era governors with prior Armed Services experience include four Republicans—John G. Rowland of Connecticut, David Treen of Louisiana, Robert Riley of South Carolina, and James A. Gibbons of Nevada, as well as Democrat Rod Blagojevich of Illinois, who would leave the committee for a short-lived and tumultuous gubernatorial career. Vermont Republican Robert T. Stafford and Maine Democratic Governor Joseph E. Brennan were among the handful of small-state governors who served in the House after leaving the governorship. While Stafford moved on to the Senate, Brennan tried to regain the governorship after four years as a junior House member, but his effort fell short.

Selected References

Blechman, Barry M., *The Politics of National Security: Congress and U.S. Defense Policy* (New York: Oxford University Press, 1990).

Deering, Christopher J., "Decision Making in the Armed Services Committees," in Randall B. Ripley and James M. Lindsay, eds., *Congress Resurgent: Foreign and Defense Policy on Capitol Hill* (Ann Arbor: University of Michigan Press, 1993), 155-182.

Entin, Kenneth, "Information Exchange in Congress: The Case of the House Armed Services Committee," *Western Political Quarterly,* 26 (Sept., 1973), 427-439.

Gist, John R., "The Impact of Annual Authorizations on Military Appropriations in the U.S. Congress," *Legislative Studies Quarterly,* 8 (August, 1981), 439-454.

Goss, Carol F., "Military Committee Membership and Defense-Related Benefits in the House of Representatives," *Western Political Quarterly,* 25 (June, 1972), 215-233.

Kambrod, Matthew R., *Lobbying for Defense: An Insider's View* (Annapolis, Md.: Naval Institute Press, 2007).

Ray, Bruce A., "Military Committee Membership in the House of Representatives and the Allocation of Defense Department Outlays," *Western Political Quarterly,* 34 (June, 1981), 222-234.

Ray, Bruce A., "The Responsiveness of the U.S. Congressional Armed Services Committees to Their Parent Bodies," *Legislative Studies Quarterly,* 5 (Nov., 1980), 501-515

Schamel, Charles E. et al., "Records of the Armed Services Committee and Its Predecessors," *Guide to the Records of the United States House of Representatives at the National Archives: 1789-1989 Bicentennial Edition* (Washington, D.C.: National Archives and Records Administration,1989), 39-61.

RESPONSIBILITIES, JURISDICTIONAL CHANGES, AND SUBCOMMITTEES

Jurisdiction, 80th Congress (1947-1949)

Established by the Legislative Reorganization Act of 1946:

[Section 121.(1)(c)]

Committee on Armed Services

(1) Common defense generally
(2) The War Department and the Military Establishment generally
(3) The Navy Department and the Naval Establishment generally
(4) Soldiers' and sailors' homes
(5) Pay, promotion, retirement, and other benefits and privileges of members of the armed forces
(6) Selective service
(7) Size and composition of the Army and Navy
(8) Forts, arsenals, military reservations, and navy yards
(9) Ammunition depots
(10) Conservation, development, and use of naval petroleum and oil shale reserves
(11) Strategic and critical materials necessary for the common defense
(12) Scientific research and development in support of the armed services

Jurisdiction, 103rd Congress (1993-1995)

From the Rules of the House of Representatives, 103rd Congress (House Document 102-405)

[Rule X.1.(c)]

Committee on Armed Services

(1) Common defense generally
(2) The Department of Defense generally, including the Departments of the Army, Navy and Air Force generally
(3) Ammunition depots; forts; arsenals; Army, Navy, and Air Force reservations and establishments
(4) Conservation, development, and use of naval petroleum and oil shale reserves
(5) Pay, promotion, retirement, and other benefits and privileges of members of the armed forces
(6) Scientific research and development in support of the armed services
(7) Selective service
(8) Size and composition of the Army, Navy, and Air Force
(9) Soldiers' and sailors' homes

(10) Strategic and critical materials necessary for the common defense

(11) Military applications of nuclear energy

In addition to its legislative jurisdiction under the preceding provisions of this paragraph (and its general oversight function under clause 2(b)(1)), the committee shall have the special oversight function provided for in clause 3(a) with respect to international arms control and disarmament, and military dependents education.

[Rule X.3.(a)]

The Committee on Armed Services shall have the function of reviewing and studying, on a continuing basis, all laws, programs, and Government activities dealing with or involving international arms control and disarmament and the education of military dependents in schools.

NATIONAL SECURITY

Armed Services was renamed the Committee on National Security on January 4, 1995.

Jurisdiction, 104th Congress (1995-1997) Changes in Committee System

From H. Res. 6, Section 202 (a), the Committees and Their Jurisdiction, January 4, 1995

[Rule X.1(k)] Committee on National Security
(1) Ammunition depots; forts; arsenals; Army, Navy, and Air Force reservations and establishments
(2) Common defense generally
(3) Conservation, development, and use of naval petroleum and oil shale reserves
(4) The Department of Defense generally, including the Departments of the Army, Navy, and Air Force generally
(5) Interoceanic canals generally, including measures relating to the maintenance, operation, and administration of interoceanic canals
(6) Merchant Marine Academy, and State Maritime Academies
(7) Military applications of nuclear energy
(8) Tactical intelligence and intelligence related activities of the Department of the Defense
(9) National security aspects of merchant marine, including financial assistance for the construction and operation of vessels, the maintenance of the U.S. shipbuilding and ship repair industrial base, cabotage, cargo preference and merchant marine officers and seamen as these matters relate to the national security
(10) Pay, promotion, retirement, and other benefits and privileges of members of the armed forces
(11) Scientific research and development in support of the armed services
(12) Selective service
(13) Size and composition of the Army, Navy, Marine Corps, and Air Force
(14) Soldiers' and sailors' homes
(15) Strategic and critical materials necessary for the common defense

In addition to its legislative jurisdiction under the preceding provisions of this paragraph (and its general oversight function under clause 2(b)(1)), the committee shall have the special oversight function provided for in clause 3(a) with respect to international arms control and disarmament, and military dependents.

[Rule X.3.(b)] Special oversight functions

The Committee on National Security shall review and study on a continuing basis laws, programs, and Government activities relating to international arms control and disarmament and the education of military dependents in schools.

ARMED SERVICES

National Security was redesignated the Committee on Armed Services on January 6, 1999.

Jurisdiction, 111th Congress (2009-2011)

From the Rules of the House of Representatives (as revised to June 16, 2009, H.Doc. 110-162):

[Rule X.1.(c)]Committee on Armed Services
(1) Ammunition depots; forts; arsenals; and Army, Navy, and Air Force reservations and establishments
(2) Common defense generally
(3) Conservation, development, and use of naval petroleum and oil shale reserves
(4) The Department of Defense generally, including the Departments of the Army, Navy, and Air Force generally
(5) Interoceanic canals generally, including measures relating to the maintenance, operation, and administration of interoceanic canals
(6) Merchant Marine Academy and state Maritime Academies
(7) Military applications of nuclear energy

(8) Tactical intelligence and intelligence-related activities of the Department of Defense

(9) National security aspects of merchant marine, including financial assistance for the construction and operation of vessels, maintenance of the U.S. shipbuilding and ship repair industrial base, cabotage, cargo preference, and merchant marine officers and seamen as these matters relate to the national security

(10) Pay, promotion, retirement, and other benefits and privileges of members of the armed forces

(11) Scientific research and development in support of the armed services

(12) Selective service

(13) Size and composition of the Army, Navy, Marine Corps, and Air Force

(14) Soldiers' and sailors' homes

(15) Strategic and critical materials necessary for the common defense

[Rule X.3.(b)] Special oversight functions

The Committee on Armed Services shall review and study on a continuing basis laws, programs, and Government activities relating to international arms control and disarmament and the education of military dependents in schools.

NAMES OF ARMED SERVICES SUBCOMMITTEES FROM THE *CONGRESSIONAL DIRECTORY*

Armed Services, 103rd Congress
Military Acquisition, 103 Military Forces and Personnel, 103
Military Installations and Facilities, 103 Oversight and Investigations, 103
Readiness, 103 Research and Technology, 103
National Security, 104th-108th Congresses
Military Installations, 104 Military Installations and Facilities, 105, 106, 107
Military Personnel, 104, 105, 106, 107 Military Procurement, 104, 105, 106, 107
Military Readiness, 104, 105, 106, 107 Military Research and Development, 104, 105, 106, 107
Projection Forces, 108 Readiness, 108
Strategic Forces, 108 Tactical Land and Air Forces, 108
Terrorism, Unconventional Threats and Capabilities, 108 Total Force, 108
Special Oversight Panel on Morale, Welfare, and Recreation, 105
Special Oversight Panel on the Merchant Marine, 105
Armed Services, 109th and 111th Congresses
Air and Land Forces, 110, 111 Military Personnel, 109, 110
Oversight and Investigations, 110, 111 Projection Forces, 109
Readiness, 109, 110, 111 Seapower and Expeditionary Forces, 110, 111
Strategic Forces, 109, 110, 111 Tactical Air and land Forces, 109
Terrorism and Unconventional Threats, 110 Terrorism, Unconventional Threats and Capabilities, 109, 111

MEMBERSHIP ROSTERS, 103rd-111th Congresses, 1993-2011

ARMED SERVICES / 103rd Congress

Service Dates of Committee Chair: Ch1 Jan. 5, 1993-Jan. 20, 1993 Aspin (Dem-Wisc.)

Ch2 Jan. 27, 1993-Jan. 3, 1995 Dellums (Dem-Cal.)

Service Dates of Majority Members: Jan. 5, 1993-Jan. 3, 1995

Service Dates of Minority Members: Jan. 5, 1993-Jan. 3, 1995

Roster Filled: Majority with 34 members, Jan. 27, 1993; Minority with 22 members, Jan. 5, 1993

Majority					Minority				
			Terms in:					Terms in:	
Rank Name	Party	State	House	Comm.	Rank Name	Party	State	House	Comm.
Ch1 Aspin, Les	Dem	Wisc.	12	12	RM Spence, Floyd D.	Rep	S.C.	12	12
2nd Montgomery, G.V. (Sonny)	Dem	Miss.	14	12	2nd Stump, Robert L.	Rep	Ariz.	9	*2 6
Ch2 3rd Dellums, Ronald V.	Dem	Cal.	12	11	3rd Hunter, Duncan L.	Rep	Cal.	7	7
4th Schroeder, Patricia S.	Dem	Colo.	11	11	4th Kasich, John R.	Rep	Ohio	6	6
5th Hutto, Earl D.	Dem	Fla.	8	8	5th Bateman, Herbert H.	Rep	Va.	6	5
6th Skelton, Isaac N. (Ike)	Dem	Mo.	9	7	6th Hansen, James V.	Rep	Utah	7	5
7th McCurdy, David K.	Dem	Okla.	7	7	7th Weldon, Wayne C. (Curt)	Rep	Penn.	4	4
8th Lloyd, Marilyn L.	Dem	Tenn.	10	7	8th Kyl, Jon L.	Rep	Ariz.	4	4
9th Sisisky, Norman	Dem	Va.	6	6	9th Ravenel, Arthur A. Jr.	Rep	S.C.	4	4
10th Spratt, John M. Jr.	Dem	S.C.	6	6	10th Dornan, Robert K.	Rep	Cal.	8	3

11th McCloskey, Francis X.	Dem	Ind.	6	6		11th Hefley, Joel M.	Rep	Colo.	4	3
12th Ortiz, Solomon P.	Dem	Tex.	6	6		12th Machtley, Ronald K.	Rep	R.I.	3	3
13th Hochbrueckner, George J.	Dem	N.Y.	4	4		13th Saxton, H. James	Rep	N.J.	6	2
14th Pickett, Owen B.	Dem	Va.	4	4		14th Cunningham, Randall (Duke)	Rep	Cal.	2	2
15th Lancaster, H. Martin	Dem	N.C.	4	4		15th Inhofe, James, M.	Rep	Okla.	4	1
16th Evans, Lane A.	Dem	Ill.	6	4		16th Buyer, Stephen E.	Rep	Ind.	1	1
17th Bilbray, James H.	Dem	Nev.	4	3		17th Torkildson, Peter G.	Rep	Mass.	1	1
18th Tanner, John S.	Dem	Tenn.	3	3		18th Fowler, Tillie K.	Rep	Fla.	1	1
19th Browder, J. Glen	Dem	Ala.	3	3		19th McHugh, John M.	Rep	N.Y.	1	1
20th Taylor, G. Eugene (Gene)	Dem	Miss.	3	3		20th Talent, James M.	Rep	Miss.	1	1
21st Abercrombie, Neil	Dem	Hai.	3	*2 2		21st Everett, R. Terry	Rep	Ala.	1	1
22nd Andrews, Thomas H.	Dem	Me.	2	2		22nd Bartlett, Roscoe G.	Rep	Md.	1	1
23rd Edwards, T. Chester (Chet)	Dem	Tex.	2	2						
24th Johnson, C. Donald Jr.	Dem	Ga.	1	1						
25th Tejeda, Frank M.	Dem	Tex.	1	1						
26th Mann, David S.	Dem	Ohio	1	1						
27th Stupak, Bart T.	Dem	Mich.	1	1						
28th Meehan, Martin T.	Dem	Mass.	1	1						
29th Underwood, Robert A.	Dem	Guam	1	1						
30th Harman, Jane L.	Dem	Cal.	1	1						
31st McHale, Paul F. Jr.	Dem	Penn.	1	1						
32nd Geren, Preston M. (Pete)	Dem	Tex.	3	1						
33rd Furse, Elizabeth	Dem	Ore.	1	1						
34th Farr, Sam	Dem	Cal.	1	1						

*2: Member's second period of service on the committee.

Notes: Ranking on this committee for the following member was affected by other chamber service: G.V. (Sonny) Montgomery (Dem-Miss.), Chair, Veterans' Affairs. Territorial Delegate Robert A. Underwood (Dem-Guam) was allowed to accrue committee seniority but was not included in the party ratio.

Vacancies Filled:
   Majority:
      32nd and 33rd seats by Geren and Furse on Jan. 27, 1993; 34th seat filled by Farr on July 21, 1993

Changes:
   Majority:

Aspin, Les	Dem	Wisc.	Jan. 20, 1993 Resigned the House; appointed Secretary of Defense
Holden, T. Timothy	Dem	Penn.	Jan. 21, 1993 Replaced Aspin
Dellums, Ronald V.	Dem	Cal.	Jan. 27, 1993 Succeeded Aspin as Chair

   Minority:

Inhofe, James M.	Rep	Okla.	Nov. 15, 1994 Resigned the House; elected to the U.S. Senate.

Departures from the House:	**Majority**			**Minority**		
Elected to U.S. Senate	None			Kyl, Jon L.	Rep	Ariz.
Lost Election to U.S. Senate	McCurdy, David K.	Dem	La.	None		
	Andrews, Thomas H.	Dem	Me.			
Lost Nomination for Governor	None			Ravenel, Arthur A. Jr.	Rep	S.C.
				Machtley, Ronald K.	Rep	R.I.
Defeated for Re-election	McCloskey, Francis X.	Dem	Ind.	None		
	Hochbrueckner, George J.	Dem	N.Y.			
	Lancaster, H. Martin	Dem	N.C.			
	Bilbray, James H.	Dem	Nev.			
	Johnson, C. Donald Jr.	Dem	Ga.			
	Mann, David S.	Dem	Ohio			
Retired	Hutto, Earl D.	Dem	Fla.	None		
	Lloyd, Marilyn L.	Dem	Tenn.			

Departures from Committee:						
Moved to Commerce	Stupak, Bart T.	Dem	Mich.	None		
	Furse, Elizabeth	Dem	Ore.			
No new assignment	Holden, T. Timothy	Dem	Penn.			
	Farr, Sam	Dem	Cal			

NATIONAL SECURITY / 104th Congress

Service Dates of Committee Chair: Jan. 4, 1995-Jan. 3, 1997

Service Dates of Majority Members: Jan. 4, 1995-Jan. 3, 1997

Service Dates of Minority Members: Jan. 4, 1995-Jan. 3, 1997

Roster Filled: Majority with 30 members, Jan. 4, 1995; Minority with 25 members, Jan. 4, 1995

	Majority						Minority				
				Terms in:						**Terms in:**	
Rank Name		Party	State	House	Comm.	Rank Name		Party	State	House	Comm.
Chr Spence, Floyd D.		Rep	S.C.	13	13	RM Dellums, Ronald V.		Dem	Cal.	13	12
2nd Stump, Robert L.		Rep	Ariz.	10	*2 7	2nd Montgomery, G.V. (Sonny)		Dem	Miss.	15	13
3rd Hunter, Duncan L.		Rep	Cal.	8	8	3rd Schroeder, Patricia S.		Dem	Colo.	12	12
4th Kasich, John R.		Rep	Ohio	7	7	4th Skelton, Isaac N. (Ike)		Dem	Mo.	10	8
5th Bateman, Herbert H.		Rep	Va.	7	6	5th Sisisky, Norman		Dem	Va.	7	7
6th Hansen, James V.		Rep	Utah	8	6	6th Spratt, John M. Jr.		Dem	S.C.	7	7
7th Weldon, Wayne C. (Curt)		Rep	Penn.	5	5	7th Ortiz, Solomon P.		Dem	Tex.	7	7
8th Dornan, Robert K.		Rep	Cal.	9	4	8th Pickett, Owen B.		Dem	Va.	5	5
9th Hefley, Joel M.		Rep	Colo.	5	4	9th Evans, Lane A.		Dem	Ill.	7	5
10th Saxton, H. James		Rep	N.J.	7	3	10th Tanner, John S.		Dem	Tenn.	4	4
11th Cunningham, Randall (Duke)		Rep	Cal.	3	3	11th Browder, J. Glen		Dem	Ala.	4	4
12th Buyer, Stephen E.		Rep	Ind.	2	2	12th Taylor, G. Eugene (Gene)		Dem	Miss.	4	4
13th Torkildson, Peter G.		Rep	Mass.	2	2	13th Abercrombie, Neil		Dem	Hai.	4	3
14th Fowler, Tillie K.		Rep	Fla.	2	2	14th Edwards, T. Chester (Chet)		Dem	Tex.	3	3
15th McHugh, John M.		Rep	N.Y.	2	2	15th Tejeda, Frank M.		Dem	Tex.	2	2
16th Talent, James M.		Rep	Miss.	2	2	16th Meehan, Martin T.		Dem	Mass.	2	2
17th Everett, R. Terry		Rep	Ala.	2	2	17th Underwood, Robert A.		Dem	Guam	2	2
18th Bartlett, Roscoe G.		Rep	Md.	2	2	18th Harman, Jane L.		Dem	Cal.	2	2
19th McKeon, Howard P. (Buck)		Rep	Cal.	2	*1 1	19th McHale, Paul F. Jr.		Dem	Penn.	2	2
20th Lewis, Ron		Rep	Ky.	2	1	20th Geren, Preston M. (Pete)		Dem	Tex.	4	2
21st Watts, Julius C. Jr.		Rep	Okla.	1	1	21st Peterson, Douglas B. (Pete)		Dem	Fla.	3	1
22nd Thornberry, William M. (Mac)		Rep	Tex.	1	1	22nd Jefferson, William J.		Dem	La.	3	1
23rd Hostettler, John N.		Rep	Ind.	1	1	23rd DeLauro, Rosa L.		Dem	Conn.	2	1
24th Chambliss, Saxby		Rep	Ga.	1	1	24th Ward, Michael D.		Dem	Ky.	1	1
25th Hilleary, Van		Rep	Tenn.	1	1	25th Kennedy, Patrick J.		Dem	R.I.	1	1
26th Scarborough, C. Joseph		Rep	Fla.	1	1						
27th Jones, Walter B. Jr.		Rep	N.C.	1	1						
28th Longley, James B. Jr.		Rep	Me.	1	1						
29th Tiahrt, Todd		Rep	Kans.	1	1						
30th Hastings, Richard (Doc)		Rep	Wash.	1	1						

*1: Member's first period of service on the committee.
*2: Member's second period of service on the committee.

Notes: Ranking on this committee for the following member was affected by other chamber service: G.V. (Sonny) Montgomery (Dem-Miss.), Ranking Member, Veterans' Affairs. Territorial Delegate Robert A. Underwood (Dem-Guam) was allowed to accrue committee seniority but was not included in the party ratio.

Changes:
    None reported in this Congress

Departures from the House:	Majority			Minority		
Appointed U.S. Ambassador to Vietnam	None			Peterson, Douglas B. (Pete)	Dem	Fla.
Defeated for Re-election	Dornan, Robert K.	Rep	Cal.	Ward, Michael D.	Dem	Ky.
	Torkildson, Peter G.	Rep	Mass.			
	Longley, James B. Jr.	Rep	Me.			
Lost Nomination to U.S. Senate	None			Browder, J. Glen	Dem	Ala.
Retired	None			Montgomery, G.V. (Sonny)	Dem	Miss.
				Schroeder, Patricia S.	Dem	Colo.
				Geren, Preston M. (Pete)	Dem	Tex.

Departures from Committee:						
Moved to Appropriations	Cunningham, Randall (Duke)	Rep	Cal.	Edwards, T. Chester (Chet)	Dem	Tex.
	Tiahrt, Todd	Rep	Kans.			
Returned to Appropriations	None			DeLauro, Rosa L.	Dem	Conn.
Moved to Rules	Hastings, Richard (Doc)	Rep	Wash.			
Moved to Ways and Means	None			Tanner, John S.	Dem	Tenn.
Returned to Ways and Means	None			Jefferson, William J.	Dem	La.

NATIONAL SECURITY / 105th Congress

Service Dates of Committee Chair: Jan. 7, 1997-Jan. 3, 1999

Service Dates of Majority Members: Jan. 7, 1997-Jan. 3, 1999

Service Dates of Minority Members: Jan. 7, 1997-Jan. 3, 1999

Roster Filled: Majority with 30 members, Jan. 7, 1997; Minority with 25 members, Feb. 5, 1997

Majority					Minority				
			Terms in:					**Terms in:**	
Rank Name	Party	State	House	Comm.	Rank Name	Party	State	House	Comm.
Chr Spence, Floyd D.	Rep	S.C.	14	14	RM1 Dellums, Ronald V.	Dem	Cal.	14	13
2nd Stump, Robert L.	Rep	Ariz.	11	*2 8	RM2 Skelton, Isaac N. (Ike)	Dem	Mo.	11	9
3rd Hunter, Duncan L.	Rep	Cal.	9	9	3rd Sisisky, Norman	Dem	Va.	8	8
4th Kasich, John R.	Rep	Ohio	8	8	4th Spratt, John M. Jr.	Dem	S.C.	8	8
5th Bateman, Herbert H.	Rep	Va.	8	7	5th Ortiz, Solomon P.	Dem	Tex.	8	8
6th Hansen, James V.	Rep	Utah	9	7	6th Pickett, Owen B.	Dem	Va.	6	6
7th Weldon, Wayne C. (Curt)	Rep	Penn.	6	6	7th Evans, Lane A.	Dem	Ill.	8	6
8th Hefley, Joel M.	Rep	Colo.	6	5	8th Taylor, G. Eugene (Gene)	Dem	Miss.	5	5
9th Saxton, H. James	Rep	N.J.	8	4	9th Abercrombie, Neil	Dem	Hai.	5	4
10th Buyer, Stephen E.	Rep	Ind.	3	3	10th Tejeda, Frank M.	Dem	Tex.	3	3
11th Fowler, Tillie K.	Rep	Fla.	3	3	11th Meehan, Martin T.	Dem	Mass.	3	3
12th McHugh, John M.	Rep	N.Y.	3	3	12th Underwood, Robert A.	Dem	Guam	3	3
13th Talent, James M.	Rep	Miss.	3	3	13th Harman, Jane L.	Dem	Cal.	3	3
14th Everett, R. Terry	Rep	Ala.	3	3	14th McHale, Paul F. Jr.	Dem	Penn.	3	3
15th Bartlett, Roscoe G.	Rep	Md.	3	3	15th Kennedy, Patrick J.	Dem	R.I.	2	2
16th McKeon, Howard P. (Buck)	Rep	Cal.	3	*1 2	16th Blagojevich, Rod R.	Dem	Ill.	1	1
17th Lewis, Ron	Rep	Ky.	3	2	17th Reyes, Silvestre	Dem	Tex.	1	1
18th Watts, Julius C. Jr.	Rep	Okla.	2	2	18th Allen, Thomas H.	Dem	Me.	1	1
19th Thornberry, William M. (Mac)	Rep	Tex.	2	2	19th Snyder, Victor F.	Dem	Ark.	1	1
20th Hostettler, John N.	Rep	Ind.	2	2	20th Turner, Jim	Dem	Tex.	1	1
21st Chambliss, Saxby	Rep	Ga.	2	2	21st Boyd, F. Allen Jr.	Dem	Fla.	1	1
22nd Hilleary, Van	Rep	Tenn.	2	2	22nd Smith, Adam	Dem	Wash.	1	1
23rd Scarborough, C. Joseph	Rep	Fla.	2	2	23rd Sanchez, Loretta	Dem	Cal.	1	1
24th Jones, Walter B. Jr.	Rep	N.C.	2	2	24th Maloney, James H.	Dem	Conn.	1	1
25th Graham, Lindsey O.	Rep	S.C.	2	1	25th McIntyre, Mike	Dem	N.C.	1	1
26th Bono, Sonny	Rep	Cal.	2	1					
27th Ryun, Jim	Rep	Kans.	2	1	*1: Member's first period of service on the committee.				
28th Pappas, Michael J.	Rep	N.J.	1	1	*2: Member's second period of service on the committee.				
29th Riley, Robert	Rep	Ala.	1	1					
30th Gibbons, James A.	Rep	Nev.	1	1					

Note: Territorial Delegate Robert A. Underwood (Dem-Guam) was allowed to accrue committee seniority but was not included in the party ratio.

Filled Vacancies:
　Minority:
　　23rd, 24th, and 25th seats by Sanchez, Maloney, and McIntyre on Feb. 5, 1997.

Additions:
　Majority:

31st Redmond, William T.	Rep	N.M.	July 23, 1997
32nd Bono, Mary	Rep	Cal.	May 13, 1998

　Minority:

26th McKinney, Cynthia A.	Dem	Ga.	July 31, 1997
27th Tauscher, Ellen O.	Dem	Cal.	June 24, 1998

Changes:
　Majority:

Bono, Sonny	Rep	Cal.	Jan. 5, 1998 Died in office
Granger, Kay	Rep	Tex.	Feb. 11, 1998 Replaced Sonny Bono

　Minority:

Tejeda, Frank M.	Dem	Tex.	Jan. 30, 1997 Died in office
Rodriguez, Ciro D.	Dem	Tex.	Apr. 17, 1997 Replaced Tejeda
Dellums, Ronald V.	Dem	Cal.	Feb. 6, 1998 Resigned the House
Skelton, Isaac N. (Ike)	Dem	Mo.	Feb. 6, 1998 Succeeded Dellums as Ranking Member
Brady, Robert A.	Dem	Penn.	June 24, 1998 Replaced Dellums

Departures from the House:

	Majority			Minority		
Lost Nomination for Governor	None			Harman, Jane L.	Dem	Cal.
Defeated for Re-election	Pappas, Michael J.	Rep	N.J.	None		
	Redmond, William T.	Rep	N.M.			
Retired	None			McHale, Paul F. Jr.	Dem	Penn.

Departures from Committee:

Moved to Ways and Means	Lewis, Ron	Rep	Ky.	None		
Moved to Appropriations	Granger, Kay	Rep	Tex.	Boyd, F. Allen Jr.	Dem	Fla.

ARMED SERVICES / 106th Congress

Service Dates of Committee Chair: Jan. 6, 1999-Jan. 3, 2001

Service Dates of Majority Members: Jan. 6, 1999-Jan. 3, 2001

Service Dates of Minority Members: Jan. 6, 1999-Jan. 3, 2001

Roster Filled: Majority with 32 members, Jan. 6, 1999; Minority with 28 members, Jan. 19, 1999.

	Majority			Terms in:			Minority			Terms in:	
Rank Name		Party	State	House	Comm.	Rank Name		Party	State	House	Comm.
Chr	Spence, Floyd D.	Rep	S.C.	15	15	RM	Skelton, Isaac N. (Ike)	Dem	Mo.	12	10
2nd	Stump, Robert L.	Rep	Ariz.	12	*2 9	2nd	Sisisky, Norman	Dem	Va.	9	9
3rd	Hunter, Duncan L.	Rep	Cal.	10	10	3rd	Spratt, John M. Jr.	Dem	S.C.	9	9
4th	Kasich, John R.	Rep	Ohio	9	9	4th	Ortiz, Solomon P.	Dem	Tex.	9	9
5th	Bateman, Herbert H.	Rep	Va.	9	8	5th	Pickett, Owen B.	Dem	Va.	7	7
6th	Hansen, James V.	Rep	Utah	10	8	6th	Evans, Lane A.	Dem	Ill.	9	7
7th	Weldon, Wayne C. (Curt)	Rep	Penn.	7	7	7th	Taylor, G. Eugene (Gene)	Dem	Miss.	6	6
8th	Hefley, Joel M.	Rep	Colo.	7	6	8th	Abercrombie, Neil	Dem	Hai.	6	5
9th	Saxton, H. James	Rep	N.J.	9	5	9th	Meehan, Martin T.	Dem	Mass.	4	4
10th	Buyer, Stephen E.	Rep	Ind.	4	4	10th	Underwood, Robert A.	Dem	Guam	4	4
11th	Fowler, Tillie K.	Rep	Fla.	4	4	11th	Kennedy, Patrick J.	Dem	R.I.	3	3
12th	McHugh, John M.	Rep	N.Y.	4	4	12th	Blagojevich, Rod R.	Dem	Ill.	2	2
13th	Talent, James M.	Rep	Miss.	4	4	13th	Reyes, Silvestre	Dem	Tex.	2	2
14th	Everett, R. Terry	Rep	Ala.	4	4	14th	Allen, Thomas H.	Dem	Me.	2	2
15th	Bartlett, Roscoe G.	Rep	Md.	4	4	15th	Snyder, Victor F.	Dem	Ark.	2	2
16th	McKeon, Howard P. (Buck)	Rep	Cal.	4	*1 3	16th	Turner, Jim	Dem	Tex.	2	2
17th	Watts, Julius C. Jr.	Rep	Okla.	3	3	17th	Smith, Adam	Dem	Wash.	2	2
18th	Thornberry, William M. (Mac)	Rep	Tex.	3	3	18th	Sanchez, Loretta	Dem	Cal.	2	2
19th	Hostettler, John N.	Rep	Ind.	3	3	19th	Maloney, James H.	Dem	Conn.	2	2
20th	Chambliss, Saxby	Rep	Ga.	3	3	20th	McIntyre, Mike	Dem	N.C.	2	2
21st	Hilleary, Van	Rep	Tenn.	3	3	21st	Rodriguez, Ciro D.	Dem	Tex.	2	2
22nd	Scarborough, C. Joseph	Rep	Fla.	3	3	22nd	McKinney, Cynthia A.	Dem	Ga.	4	*1 2
23rd	Jones, Walter B. Jr.	Rep	N.C.	3	3	23rd	Tauscher, Ellen O.	Dem	Cal.	2	2
24th	Graham, Lindsey O.	Rep	S.C.	3	2	24th	Brady, Robert A.	Dem	Penn.	2	2
25th	Ryun, Jim	Rep	Kans.	3	2	25th	Andrews, Robert E.	Dem	N.J.	6	*1 1
26th	Riley, Robert	Rep	Ala.	2	2	26th	Hill, Baron P.	Dem	Ind.	1	1
27th	Gibbons, James A.	Rep	Nev.	2	2	27th	Thompson, Michael	Dem	Cal.	1	1
28th	Bono, Mary	Rep	Cal.	2	2	28th	Larson, John B.	Dem	Conn.	1	1
29th	Pitts, Joseph R.	Rep	Penn.	2	1						
30th	Hayes, Robert (Robin)	Rep	N.C.	1	1						
31st	Kuykendall, Steven T.	Rep	Cal.	1	1						
32nd	Sherwood, Don	Rep	Penn.	1	1						

*1: Member's first period of service on the committee.

*2: Member's second period of service on the committee.

Note: Territorial Delegate Robert A. Underwood (Dem-Guam) was allowed to accrue committee seniority but was not included in the party ratio.

Filled Vacancies:
  Minority:
      28th seat by Larson on Jan. 19, 1999

Changes:
  Majority:

Bateman, Herbert H.	Rep	Va.	Sept. 11, 2000 Died in office
Wilson, Heather A.	Rep	N.M.	Oct. 3, 2000 Replaced Bateman

Departures from the House:

	Majority			Minority		
Lost Election for Governor	Talent, James M.	Rep	Miss.	None		
Defeated for Re-election	Kuykendall, Steven T.	Rep	Cal.	None		
Retired	Kasich, John R.	Rep	Ohio	Pickett, Owen B.	Dem	Va.
	Fowler, Tillie K.	Rep	Fla.			

Departures from Committee:

	Majority			Minority		
Moved to Energy and Commerce	Buyer, Stephen E.	Rep	Ind.	None		
	Bono, Mary	Rep	Cal.			
	Pitts, Joseph R.	Rep	Penn.			
Moved to International Relations	Pitts, Joseph R.	Rep	Penn.			
Moved to Appropriations	None			Kennedy, Patrick J.	Dem	R.I.

ARMED SERVICES / 107th Congress

Service Dates of Committee Chair: Jan. 6, 2001-Jan. 3, 2003

Service Dates of Majority Members: Jan. 6, 2001-Jan. 3, 2003

Service Dates of Ranking Member: Jan. 8, 2001.-Jan. 3, 2003

Service Dates of Minority Members: Jan. 31, 2001-Jan. 3, 2003

Roster Filled: Majority with 28 members, June 28, 2001; Minority with 24 members, Jan. 31, 2001

			Majority Terms in:					Minority Terms in:	
Rank Name	Party	State	House	Comm.	Rank Name	Party	State	House	Comm.
Chr Stump, Robert L.	Rep	Ariz.	13	*2 10	RM Skelton, Isaac N. (Ike)	Dem	Mo.	13	11
2nd Spence, Floyd D.	Rep	S.C.	16	16	2nd Sisisky, Norman	Dem	Va.	10	10
3rd Hunter, Duncan L.	Rep	Cal.	11	11	3rd Spratt, John M. Jr.	Dem	S.C.	10	10
4th Hansen, James V.	Rep	Utah	11	9	4th Ortiz, Solomon P.	Dem	Tex.	10	10
5th Weldon, Wayne C. (Curt)	Rep	Penn.	8	8	5th Evans, Lane A.	Dem	Ill.	10	8
6th Hefley, Joel M.	Rep	Colo.	8	7	6th Taylor, G. Eugene (Gene)	Dem	Miss.	7	7
7th Saxton, H. James	Rep	N.J.	10	6	7th Abercrombie, Neil	Dem	Hai.	7	6
8th McHugh, John M.	Rep	N.Y.	5	5	8th Meehan, Martin T.	Dem	Mass.	5	5
9th Everett, R. Terry	Rep	Ala.	5	5	9th Underwood, Robert A.	Dem	Guam	5	5
10th Bartlett, Roscoe G.	Rep	Md.	5	5	10th Blagojevich, Rod R.	Dem	Ill.	3	3
11th McKeon, Howard P. (Buck)	Rep	Cal.	5	*1 4	11th Reyes, Silvestre	Dem	Tex.	3	3
12th Watts, Julius C. Jr.	Rep	Okla.	4	4	12th Allen, Thomas H.	Dem	Me.	3	3
13th Thornberry, William M. (Mac)	Rep	Tex.	4	4	13th Snyder, Victor F.	Dem	Ark.	3	3
14th Hostettler, John N.	Rep	Ind.	4	4	14th Turner, Jim	Dem	Tex.	3	3
15th Chambliss, Saxby	Rep	Ga.	4	4	15th Smith, Adam	Dem	Wash.	3	3
16th Hilleary, Van	Rep	Tenn.	4	4	16th Sanchez, Loretta	Dem	Cal.	3	3
17th Scarborough, C. Joseph	Rep	Fla.	4	4	17th Maloney, James H.	Dem	Conn.	3	3
18th Jones, Walter B. Jr.	Rep	N.C.	4	4	18th McIntyre, Mike	Dem	N.C.	3	3
19th Graham, Lindsey O.	Rep	S.C.	4	3	19th Rodriguez, Ciro D.	Dem	Tex.	3	3
20th Ryun, Jim	Rep	Kans.	4	3	20th McKinney, Cynthia A.	Dem	Ga.	5	*1 3
21st Riley, Robert	Rep	Ala.	3	3	21st Tauscher, Ellen O.	Dem	Cal.	3	3
22nd Gibbons, James A.	Rep	Nev.	3	3	22nd Brady, Robert A.	Dem	Penn.	3	3
23rd Hayes, Robert (Robin)	Rep	N.C.	2	2	23rd Andrews, Robert E.	Dem	N.J.	7	*1 2
24th Sherwood, Don	Rep	Penn.	2	2	24th Hill, Baron P.	Dem	Ind.	2	2
25th Wilson, Heather A.	Rep	N.M.	3	2	25th Thompson, Michael	Dem	Cal.	2	2
26th Calvert, Ken	Rep	Cal.	5	1	26th Larson, John B.	Dem	Conn.	2	2
27th Simmons, Robert	Rep	Conn.	1	1	27th Davis, Susan A.	Dem	Cal.	1	1
28th Crenshaw, Ander	Rep	Fla.	1	1	28th Langevin, James R.	Dem	R.I.	1	*1 1
29th Kirk, Mark S.	Rep	Ill.	1	1					
30th Davis, Jo Ann	Rep	Va.	1	1					
31st Schrock, Edward	Rep	Va.	1	1					
32nd Akin, W. Todd	Rep	Mo.	1	1					

*1: Member's first period of service on the committee.

*2: Member's second period of service on the committee.

Note: Territorial Delegate Robert A. Underwood (Dem-Guam) was allowed to accrue committee seniority but was not included in the party ratio.

Changes:

Majority:

Sherwood, Don	Rep	Penn.	Mar. 7, 2001 Resigned committee; moved to Appropriations
Forbes, J. Randy	Rep	Va.	June 28, 2001 Replaced Sherwood
Spence, Floyd D.	Rep	S.C.	Aug. 16, 2001 Died in office
Scarborough, C. Joseph	Rep	Fla.	Sept. 6, 2001 Resigned the House
Miller, Jefferson B.	Rep	Fla.	Nov. 8, 2001 Replaced Spence
Wilson, Addison G. (Joe)	Rep	S.C.	Jan. 19, 2002 Replaced Scarborough

Minority:

Sisisky, Norman	Dem	Va.	Mar. 29, 2001 Died in office.
Larsen, Richard R. (Rick)	Dem	Wash.	July 25, 2001 Replaced Sisisky.

Departures from the House:

	Majority			Minority		
Elected Governor	Riley, Robert	Rep	Ala.	Blagojevich, Rod R.	Dem	Ill.
Elected to U.S. Senate	Chambliss, Saxby	Rep	Ga.	None		
	Graham, Lindsey O.	Rep	S.C.			
Defeated for Re-election	None			Maloney, James H.	Dem	Conn.
Defeated for Re-nomination	None			McKinney, Cynthia A.	Dem	Ga.
Lost Election for Governor	Hilleary, Van	Rep	Tenn.	Underwood, Robert A.	Dem	Guam
Retired	Stump, Robert L.	Rep	Ariz.	None		
	Hansen, James V.	Rep	Utah			
	Watts, Julius C. Jr.	Rep	La.			

Departures from Committee:

Moved to Appropriations	Crenshaw, Ander	Rep	Fla.	None
	Kirk, Mark S.	Rep	Ill.	
Moved to Budget	None			Thompson, Michael	Dem	Cal.
Moved to Energy and Commerce	None			Allen, Thomas H.	Dem	Me.
Moved to Transportation and Infrastructure	None			Thompson, Michael	Dem	Cal.

ARMED SERVICES / 108th Congress

Service Dates of Committee Chair: Jan. 8, 2003-Jan. 3, 2005

Service Dates of Majority Members: Jan. 28, 2003-Jan. 3, 2005

Service Dates of Ranking Member: Jan. 8, 2003-Jan. 3, 2005

Service Dates of Minority Members: Jan. 28, 2003-Jan. 3, 2005

Roster Filled: Majority with 33 members, Jan. 28, 2003; Minority with 28 members, Feb. 5, 2003

Majority			Terms in:		Minority			Terms in:	
Rank Name	Party	State	House	Comm.	Rank Name	Party	State	House	Comm.
Chr Hunter, Duncan L.	Rep	Cal.	12	12	RM Skelton, Isaac N. (Ike)	Dem	Mo.	14	12
2nd Weldon, Wayne C. (Curt)	Rep	Penn.	9	9	2nd Spratt, John M. Jr.	Dem	S.C.	11	11
3rd Hefley, Joel M.	Rep	Colo.	9	8	3rd Ortiz, Solomon P.	Dem	Tex.	11	11
4th Saxton, H. James	Rep	N.J.	11	7	4th Evans, Lane A.	Dem	Ill.	11	9
5th McHugh, John M.	Rep	N.Y.	6	6	5th Taylor, G. Eugene (Gene)	Dem	Miss.	8	8
6th Everett, R. Terry	Rep	Ala.	6	6	6th Abercrombie, Neil	Dem	Hai.	8	*2 7
7th Bartlett, Roscoe G.	Rep	Md.	6	6	7th Meehan, Martin T.	Dem	Mass.	6	6
8th McKeon, Howard P. (Buck)	Rep	Cal.	6	*1 5	8th Reyes, Silvestre	Dem	Tex.	4	4
9th Thornberry, William M. (Mac)	Rep	Tex.	5	5	9th Snyder, Victor F.	Dem	Ark.	4	4
10th Hostettler, John N.	Rep	Ind.	5	5	10th Turner, Jim	Dem	Tex.	4	4
11th Jones, Walter B. Jr.	Rep	N.C.	5	5	11th Smith, Adam	Dem	Wash.	4	4
12th Ryun, Jim	Rep	Kans.	5	4	12th Sanchez, Loretta	Dem	Cal.	4	4
13th Gibbons, James A.	Rep	Nev.	4	4	13th McIntyre, Mike	Dem	N.C.	4	4
14th Hayes, Robert (Robin)	Rep	N.C.	3	3	14th Rodriguez, Ciro D.	Dem	Tex.	4	4
15th Wilson, Heather A.	Rep	N.M.	4	3	15th Tauscher, Ellen O.	Dem	Cal.	4	4
16th Calvert, Ken	Rep	Cal.	6	2	16th Brady, Robert A.	Dem	Penn.	4	4
17th Simmons, Robert	Rep	Conn.	2	2	17th Andrews, Robert E.	Dem	N.J.	8	*1 3
18th Davis, Jo Ann	Rep	Va.	2	2	18th Hill, Baron P.	Dem	Ind.	3	3
19th Schrock, Edward	Rep	Va.	2	2	19th Larson, John B.	Dem	Conn.	3	3
20th Akin, W. Todd	Rep	Mo.	2	2	20th Davis, Susan A.	Dem	Cal.	2	2
21st Forbes, J. Randy	Rep	Va.	2	2	21st Langevin, James R.	Dem	R.I.	2	*1 2
22nd Miller, Jefferson B.	Rep	Fla.	2	2	22nd Israel, Steve	Dem	N.Y.	2	1
23rd Wilson, Addison G. (Joe)	Rep	S.C.	2	2	23rd Larsen, Richard R. (Rick)	Dem	Wash.	2	2
24th LoBiondo, Frank A.	Rep	N.J.	5	1	24th Cooper, James H.S.	Dem	Tenn.	7	1
25th Cole, Tom	Rep	Okla.	1	*1 1	25th Marshall, Jim	Dem	Ga.	1	1
26th Bradley, Jeb	Rep	N.H.	1	1	26th Meek, Kendrick B.	Dem	Fla.	1	*1 1
27th Bishop, Robert	Rep	Utah	1	*1 1	27th Bordallo, Madeleine Z.	Dem	Guam	1	1
28th Turner, Michael R.	Rep	Ohio	1	1	28th Alexander, Rodney	Dem	La.	1	1
29th Kline, John	Rep	Minn.	1	1					
30th Miller, Candice S.	Rep	Mich.	1	1					
31st Gingrey, Phil	Rep	Ga.	1	*1 1					
32nd Rogers, Mike D.	Rep	Ala.	1	1					
33rd Franks, Trent	Rep	Ariz.	1	1					

*1: Member's first period of service on the committee.

*2: Member's second period of service on the committee.

Note: Teritorial Delegate Madeleine Z. Bordallo (Dem-Guam) was allowed to accrue committee seniority but was not included in the party ratio.

Filled Vacancies:
Minority:
22nd, 23rd, 24th, 25th, 26th, 27th, and 28th seats filled by Israel, Larsen, Cooper, Marshall, Meek, Bordallo, and Alexander on Feb. 5, 2003

Changes:
Minority:

Andrews, Robert E.	Dem	N.J.	Feb. 12, 2003 Resigned committee; moved to Select Homeland Security
Ruppersberger, C.A. (Dutch)	Dem	Md.	Mar. 5, 2003 Replaced Andrews
Ruppersberger, C.A. (Dutch)	Dem	Md.	Mar. 5, 2003 Leave of absence from committee for existing service on Government Reform and Select Intelligence

Ryan, Timothy J.	Dem	Ohio	Mar. 5, 2003 Replaced Ruppersberger
Alexander, Rodney	Dem	La.	Sept. 7, 2004 Service on committee as a Democrat vacated; moved to Transportation and Infrastructure as a Republican
Stenholm, Charles W.	Dem	Tex.	Sept. 8, 2004 Replaced Alexander

Departures from the House:	**Majority**				**Minority**			
Defeated for Re-election	None				Hill, Baron P.		Dem	Ind.
					Stenholm, Charles W.		Dem	Tex.
Defeated for Re-nomination	None				Rodriguez, Ciro D.		Dem	Tex.
Retired	Schrock, Edward		Rep	Va.	Turner, Jim		Dem	Tex.
Departures from Committee:								
Moved to Permanent Select								
Intelligence	Wilson, Heather A.		Rep	N.M.	None			
Moved to Rules	Cole, Tom		Rep	La.	None			
	Bishop, Robert		Rep	Utah				
	Gingrey, Phil		Rep	Ga.				
Moved to Standards of Official Conduct	Cole, Tom		Rep	La.	None			
Moved to Ways and Means	None				Larson, John B.		Dem	Conn.

ARMED SERVICES / 109th Congress

Service Dates of Committee Chair: Jan. 6, 2005-Jan. 3, 2007

Service Dates of Majority Members: Jan. 26, 2005-Jan. 3, 2007

Service Dates of Minority Members: Jan. 26, 2005-Jan. 3, 2007

Roster Filled: Majority with 34 members, Jan. 26, 2005; Minority with 28 members, Jan. 26, 2005

Majority					**Minority**				
			Terms in:					Terms in:	
Rank Name	Party	State	House	Comm.	Rank Name	Party	State	House	Comm.
Chr Hunter, Duncan L.	Rep	Cal.	13	13	RM Skelton, Isaac N. (Ike)	Dem	Mo.	15	13
2nd Weldon, Wayne C. (Curt)	Rep	Penn.	10	10	2nd Spratt, John M. Jr.	Dem	S.C.	12	12
3rd Hefley, Joel M.	Rep	Colo.	10	9	3rd Ortiz, Solomon P.	Dem	Tex.	12	12
4th Saxton, H. James	Rep	N.J.	12	8	4th Evans, Lane A.	Dem	Ill.	12	10
5th McHugh, John M.	Rep	N.Y.	7	7	5th Taylor, G. Eugene (Gene)	Dem	Miss.	9	9
6th Everett, R. Terry	Rep	Ala.	7	7	6th Abercrombie, Neil	Dem	Hai.	9	*2 8
7th Bartlett, Roscoe G.	Rep	Md.	7	7	7th Meehan, Martin T.	Dem	Mass.	7	7
8th McKeon, Howard P. (Buck)	Rep	Cal.	7	*1 6	8th Reyes, Silvestre	Dem	Tex.	5	5
9th Thornberry, William M. (Mac)	Rep	Tex.	6	6	9th Snyder, Victor F.	Dem	Ark.	5	5
10th Hostettler, John N.	Rep	Ind.	6	6	10th Smith, Adam	Dem	Wash.	5	5
11th Jones, Walter B. Jr.	Rep	N.C.	6	6	11th Sanchez, Loretta	Dem	Cal.	5	5
12th Ryun, Jim	Rep	Kans.	6	5	12th McIntyre, Mike	Dem	N.C.	5	5
13th Gibbons, James A.	Rep	Nev.	5	5	13th Tauscher, Ellen O.	Dem	Cal.	5	5
14th Hayes, Robert (Robin)	Rep	N.C.	4	4	14th Brady, Robert A.	Dem	Penn.	5	5
15th Calvert, Ken	Rep	Cal.	7	3	15th Andrews, Robert E.	Dem	N.J.	9	*2 1
16th Simmons, Robert	Rep	Conn.	3	3	16th Davis, Susan A.	Dem	Cal.	3	3
17th Davis, Jo Ann	Rep	Va.	3	3	17th Langevin, James R.	Dem	R.I.	3	*1 3
18th Akin, W. Todd	Rep	Mo.	3	3	18th Israel, Steve	Dem	N.Y.	3	2
19th Forbes, J. Randy	Rep	Va.	3	3	19th Larsen, Richard R. (Rick)	Dem	Wash.	3	3
20th Miller, Jefferson B.	Rep	Fla.	3	3	20th Cooper, James H.S.	Dem	Tenn.	8	2
21st Wilson, Addison G. (Joe)	Rep	S.C.	3	3	21st Marshall, Jim	Dem	Ga.	2	2
22nd LoBiondo, Frank A.	Rep	N.J.	6	2	22nd Meek, Kendrick B.	Dem	Fla.	2	*1 2
23rd Bradley, Jeb	Rep	N.H.	2	2	23rd Bordallo, Madeleine Z.	Dem	Guam	2	2
24th Turner, Michael R.	Rep	Ohio	2	2	24th Ryan, Timothy J.	Dem	Ohio	2	2
25th Kline, John	Rep	Minn.	2	2	25th Udall, Mark	Dem	Colo.	4	1
26th Miller, Candice S.	Rep	Mich.	2	2	26th Butterfield, George K. Jr.	Dem	N.C.	2	1
27th Rogers, Mike D.	Rep	Ala.	2	2	27th McKinney, Cynthia A.	Dem	Ga.	6	*2 1
28th Franks, Trent	Rep	Ariz.	2	2	28th Boren, Daniel D.	Dem	Okla.	1	*1 1
29th Shuster, William	Rep	Penn.	3	*1 1					
30th Drake, Thelma D.	Rep	Va.	1	1	*1: Member's first period of service on the committee.				
31st Schwarz, John J.H. (Joe)	Rep	Mich.	1	1	*2: Member's second period of service on the committee				
32nd McMorris, Cathy	Rep	Wash.	1	1					
33rd Conaway, K. Michael	Rep	Tex.	1	1					
34th Davis, Geoffrey C.	Rep	Ky.	1	1					

Note: Teritorial Delegate Madeleine Z. Bordallo (Dem-Guam) was allowed to accrue committee seniority but was not included in the party ratio.

Changes:

Majority:

McKeon, Howard P. (Buck)	Rep	Cal.	June 29, 2006 Resigned committee; elected Chair of Education and the Workforce
Bilbray, Brian P.	Rep	Cal.	June 29, 2006 Replaced McKeon
Gibbons, James A.	Rep	Nev.	Dec. 31, 2006 Resigned the House; elected Governor of Nevada

Departures from the House:

	Majority			**Minority**		
Defeated for Re-election	Weldon, Wayne C. (Curt)	Rep	Penn.	None		
	Hostettler, John N.	Rep	Ind.			
	Ryun, Jim	Rep	Kans.			
	Bradley, Jeb	Rep	N.H.			
	Simmons, Robert	Rep	Conn.			
Defeated for Re-nomination	Schwarz, John J.H. (Joe)	Rep	Mich.	None		
Retired	Hefley, Joel M.	Rep	Colo.	Evans, Lane A.	Dem	Ill.

Departures from Committee:

	Majority			**Minority**		
Moved to Appropriations	None			Israel, Steve	Dem	N.Y.
				Ryan, Timothy J.	Dem	Ohio
Moved to Energy and Commerce	None			Butterfield, George K. Jr.	Dem	N.C.
Moved to Natural Resources	Shuster, William	Rep	Penn.	None		
Moved to Science and Technology	Bilbray, Brian P.	Rep	Cal.	None		
Moved to Ways and Means	None			Meek, Kendrick B.	Dem	Fla.

ARMED SERVICES / 110th Congress

Service Dates of Committee Chair: Jan. 4, 2007-Jan. 3, 2009

Service Dates of Majority Members: Jan. 10, 2007-Jan. 3, 2009

Service Dates of Minority Members: Jan. 10, 2007-Jan. 3, 2009

Roster Filled: Majority with 34 members, Jan. 12, 2007; Minority with 28 members, Jan. 10, 2007

	Majority						**Minority**				
				Terms in:						**Terms in:**	
Rank Name	Party	State	House	Comm.		Rank Name	Party	State	House	Comm.	
Chr Skelton, Isaac N. (Ike)	Dem	Mo.	16	14		RM Hunter, Duncan L.	Rep	Cal.	14	14	
2nd Spratt, John M. Jr.	Dem	S.C.	13	13		2nd Saxton, H. James	Rep	N.J.	13	9	
3rd Ortiz, Solomon P.	Dem	Tex.	13	13		3rd McHugh, John M.	Rep	N.Y.	8	8	
4th Taylor, G. Eugene (Gene)	Dem	Miss.	10	10		4th Everett, R. Terry	Rep	Ala.	8	8	
5th Abercrombie, Neil	Dem	Hai.	10	*2 9		5th Bartlett, Roscoe G.	Rep	Md.	8	8	
6th Meehan, Martin T.	Dem	Mass.	8	8		6th McKeon, Howard P. (Buck)	Rep	Cal.	8	*2 1	
7th Reyes, Silvestre	Dem	Tex.	6	6		7th Thornberry, William M. (Mac)	Rep	Tex.	7	7	
8th Snyder, Victor F.	Dem	Ark.	6	6		8th Jones, Walter B. Jr.	Rep	N.C.	7	7	
9th Smith, Adam	Dem	Wash.	6	6		9th Hayes, Robert (Robin)	Rep	N.C.	5	5	
10th Sanchez, Loretta	Dem	Cal.	6	6		10th Calvert, Ken	Rep	Cal.	8	4	
11th McIntyre, Mike	Dem	N.C.	6	6		11th Davis, Jo Ann	Rep	Va.	4	4	
12th Tauscher, Ellen O.	Dem	Cal.	6	6		12th Akin, W. Todd	Rep	Mo.	4	4	
13th Brady, Robert A.	Dem	Penn.	6	6		13th Forbes, J. Randy	Rep	Va.	4	4	
14th Andrews, Robert E.	Dem	N.J.	10	*2 2		14th Miller, Jefferson B.	Rep	Fla.	4	4	
15th Davis, Susan A.	Dem	Cal.	4	4		15th Wilson, Addison G. (Joe)	Rep	S.C.	4	4	
16th Langevin, James R.	Dem	R.I.	4	*1 4		16th LoBiondo, Frank A.	Rep	N.J.	7	3	
17th Larsen, Richard R. (Rick)	Dem	Wash.	4	4		17th Cole, Tom	Rep	Okla.	3	*2 1	
18th Cooper, James H.S.	Dem	Tenn.	9	3		18th Bishop, Robert	Rep	Utah	3	*2 1	
19th Marshall, Jim	Dem	Ga.	3	3		19th Turner, Michael R.	Rep	Ohio	3	3	
20th Bordallo, Madeleine Z.	Dem	Guam	3	3		20th Kline, John	Rep	Minn.	3	3	
21st Udall, Mark	Dem	Colo.	5	2		21st Miller, Candice S.	Rep	Mich.	3	3	
22nd Boren, Daniel D.	Dem	Okla.	2	*1 2		22nd Gingrey, Phil	Rep	Ga.	3	*2 1	
23rd Ellsworth, Brad	Dem	Ind.	1	1		23rd Rogers, Mike D.	Rep	Ala.	3	3	
24th Boyda, Nancy	Dem	Kans.	1	1		24th Franks, Trent	Rep	Ariz.	3	3	
25th Murphy, Patrick J.	Dem	Penn.	1	1		25th Drake, Thelma D.	Rep	Va.	2	2	
26th Johnson, Hank	Dem	Ga.	1	1		26th McMorris Rodgers, Cathy	Rep	Wash.	2	2	
27th Shea-Porter, Carol	Dem	N.H.	1	1		27th Conaway, K. Michael	Rep	Tex.	2	2	
28th Courtney, Joe	Dem	Conn.	1	1		28th Davis, Geoffrey C.	Rep	Ky.	2	2	
29th Loebsack, Dave	Dem	Iowa	1	1							
30th Gillibrand, Kirsten E.	Dem	N.Y.	1	1		*1: Member's first period of service on the committee.					
31st Sestak, Joe	Dem	Penn.	1	1		*2: Member's second period of service on the committee.					

32nd Giffords, Gabrielle	Dem	Ariz.	1	1
33rd Castor, Kathy	Dem	Fla.	1	1
34th Cummings, Elijah E.	Dem	Md.	7	1

Note: Teritorial Delegate Madeleine Z. Bordallo (Dem-Guam) was allowed to accrue committee seniority but was not included in the party ratio.

Filled Vacancies:

Majority

34th seat by Cummings on Jan. 12, 2007

Changes:

Majority:

Langevin, James R.	Dem	R.I.	Jan. 18, 2007 Leave of absence from committee; moved to Permanent Select Intelligence
Meek, Kendrick B.	Dem	Fla.	Jan 18, 2007 Replaced Langevin
Meehan, Martin T.	Dem	Mass.	July 1, 2007 Resigned the House; appointed Chancellor of University of Massachusetts at Lowell
Langevin, James R.	Dem	R.I.	Sept. 20, 2007 Replaced Meehan
Langevin, James R.	Dem	R.I.	Oct. 31, 2007 Resigned committee; remained on Permanent Select Intelligence
Tsongas, Nicola (Niki)	Dem	Mass.	Nov. 1, 2007 Replaced Langevin; ranked after Giffords

Minority:

Calvert, Ken	Rep	Cal.	May 10, 2007 Resigned committee; moved to Appropriations; letter of May 14, 2007
Shuster, William	Rep	Penn	May 10, 2007 Replaced Calvert, ranked behind Franks
Davis, Jo Ann	Rep	Va.	Oct. 6, 2007 Died in office
Lamborn, Doug	Rep	Colo.	Oct. 10, 2007 Replaced Davis
Miller, Candice S.	Rep	Mich.	Mar. 10, 2008 Resigned committee; moved to Homeland Security
Wittman, Robert J.	Rep	Va.	Mar. 11, 2008 Replaced Miller

Departures from the House:	**Majority**			**Minority**		
Elected to the U.S. Senate	Udall, Mark	Dem	Colo.	None		
Defeated for Re-election	Boyda, Nancy	Dem	Kans.	Hayes, Robert (Robin)	Rep	N.C.
				Drake, Thelma D.	Rep	Va.
Retired	None			Hunter, Duncan L.	Rep	Cal.
				Saxton, H. James	Rep	N.J.
				Everett, R. Terry	Rep	Ala.

Departures from Committee:						
Moved to Appropriations	None			Cole, Tom	Rep	Okla.
Moved to Energy and Commerce	Castor, Kathy	Dem	Fla	Gingrey, Phil	Rep	Ga.
Moved to Standards of Official Conduct	Castor, Kathy	Dem	Fla.	None		
Moved to Ways and Means	None			Davis, Geoffrey C.	Rep	Ky.
No new assignment	Cummings, Elijah E.	Dem	Md.	None		
	Meek, Kendrick B.	Dem	Fla.			

ARMED SERVICES / 111th Congress

Service Dates of Committee Chair: Jan. 6, 2009-Jan. 3, 2011

Service Dates of Majority Members: Jan. 7, 2009-Jan. 3, 2011

Service Dates of Minority Members: Jan. 9, 2009-Jan. 3, 2011

Roster Filled: Majority with 37 members, Jan. 7, 2009; Minority with 25 members, Jan. 9, 2009

Majority			**Terms in:**		**Minority**			**Terms in:**	
Rank Name	Party	State	House	Comm.	Rank Name	Party	State	House	Comm.
Chr Skelton, Isaac N. (Ike)	Dem	Mo.	17	15	RM1 McHugh, John M.	Rep	N.Y.	9	9
2nd Spratt, John M. Jr.	Dem	S.C.	14	14	2nd Bartlett, Roscoe G.	Rep	Md.	9	9
3rd Ortiz, Solomon P.	Dem	Tex.	14	14	RM2 3rd McKeon, Howard P. (Buck)	Rep	Cal.	9	*2 2
4th Taylor, G. Eugene (Gene)	Dem	Miss.	11	11	4th Thornberry, William M. (Mac)	Rep	Tex.	8	8
5th Abercrombie, Neil	Dem	Hai.	11	*2 10	5th Jones, Walter B. Jr.	Rep	N.C.	8	8
6th Reyes, Silvestre	Dem	Tex.	7	7	6th Akin, W. Todd	Rep	Mo.	5	5
7th Snyder, Victor F.	Dem	Ark.	7	7	7th Forbes, J. Randy	Rep	Va.	5	5
8th Smith, Adam	Dem	Wash.	7	7	8th Miller, Jefferson B.	Rep	Fla.	5	5
9th Sanchez, Loretta	Dem	Cal.	7	7	9th Wilson, Addison G. (Joe)	Rep	S.C.	5	5
10th McIntyre, Mike	Dem	N.C.	7	7	10th LoBiondo, Frank A.	Rep	N.J.	8	4
11th Tauscher, Ellen O.	Dem	Cal.	7	7	11th Bishop, Robert	Rep	Utah	4	*2 2
12th Brady, Robert A.	Dem	Penn.	7	7	12th Turner, Michael R.	Rep	Ohio	4	4

13th Andrews, Robert E.	Dem	N.J.	11	*2 3
14th Davis, Susan A.	Dem	Cal.	5	5
15th Langevin, James R.	Dem	R.I.	5	*3 1
16th Larsen, Richard R. (Rick)	Dem	Wash.	5	5
17th Cooper, James H.S.	Dem	Tenn.	10	4
18th Marshall, Jim	Dem	Ga.	4	4
19th Bordallo, Madeleine Z.	Dem	Guam	4	4
20th Boren, Daniel D.	Dem	Okla.	3	*1 3
21st Ellsworth, Brad	Dem	Ind.	2	2
22nd Murphy, Patrick J.	Dem	Penn.	2	2
23rd Johnson, Hank	Dem	Ga.	2	2
24th Shea-Porter, Carol	Dem	N.H.	2	2
25th Courtney, Joe	Dem	Conn.	2	2
26th Loebsack, Dave	Dem	Iowa	2	2
27th Gillibrand, Kirsten E.	Dem	N.Y.	2	2
28th Sestak, Joe	Dem	Penn.	2	2
29th Giffords, Gabrielle	Dem	Ariz.	2	2
30th Tsongas, Nicola (Niki)	Dem	Mass.	2	2
31st Nye, Glenn C. III	Dem	Va.	1	1
32nd Pingree, Chellie	Dem	Me.	1	1
33rd Kissell, Larry	Dem	N.C.	1	1
34th Heinrich, Martin	Dem	NM	1	1
35th Kravotil, Frank J.	Dem	Md.	1	1
36th Massa, Eric J. J.	Dem	N.Y.	1	1
37th Bright, Bobby Neal Sr.	Dem	Ala.	1	1

13th Kline, John	Rep	Minn.	4	4
14th Rogers, Mike	Rep	Ala.	5	4
15th Franks, Trent	Rep	Ariz.	4	4
16th Shuster, William	Rep	Penn.	5	*2 2
17th McMorris Rodgers, Cathy	Rep	Wash.	3	3
18th Conaway, K. Michael	Rep	Tex.	3	3
19th Lamborn, Doug	Rep	Colo.	2	2
20th Wittman, Robert J.	Rep	Va.	2	2
21st Fallin, Mary	Rep	Okla.	2	1
22nd Hunter, Duncan D.	Rep	Cal.	1	1
23rd Fleming, John	Rep	La.	1	1
24th Coffman, Michael	Rep	Colo.	1	1
25th Rooney, Thomas J.	Rep	Fla.	1	1

*1: Member's first period of service on the committee.
*2: Member's second period of service on the committee.
*3: Member's third period of service on the committee.

Note: Teritorial Delegate Madeleine Z. Bordallo (Dem-Guam) was allowed to accrue committee seniority but was not included in the party ratio.

Changes:

Majority

Gillibrand, Kirsten E.	Dem	N.Y.	Jan. 26, 2009 Resigned House; appointed to the Senate
Boren, Daniel D.	Dem	Okla.	Feb. 5, 2009 Leave of absence; moved to Select Intelligence; returned on Apr. 30, 2009 without seniority intact
Murphy, Scott	Dem	N.Y.	Apr. 30, 2009 Replaced Gillibrand, ranked following Bright
Tauscher, Ellen O.	Dem	Cal	June 26, 2009 Resigned the House; appointed to State Department
Owens, William L.	Dem	N.Y.	Nov. 19, 2009 Replaced Tauscher, ranked following Scott Murphy
Abercrombie, Neil	Dem	Hai	Feb. 28, 2010 Resigned the House and retired
Massa, Eric J.J.	Dem	N.Y.	Mar. 8, 2010 Resigned the House due to ethics issues
Abercrombie, Neil	Dem	Hai	Feb. 28, 2010 Resigned the House to run for Governor
Massa, Eric J.J.	Dem	N.Y.	Mar. 8, 2010 Resigned the House due to ethics issues
Murphy, Patrick J.	Dem	Penn.	May 5, 2010 Resigned committee; moved to Appropriations
Garamendi, John J.	Dem	Cal.	May 6, 2010 Replaced Abercrombie; ranked following Owens
Boswell. Leonard L.	Dem	Iowa	May 6, 2010 Replaced Massa, ranked following Garamendi
Johnson, Hank	Dem	Ga.	May 6, 2010 Replaced Murphy; reranked following Boren

Minority

RM1 McHugh, John M.	Rep	N.Y.	June 3, 2009 Resigned committee; nominated as Secretary of Army
McKeon, Howard P. (Buck)	Rep	Cal.	June 16, 2009 Replaced McHugh as Ranking Member
Platts, Todd R.	Rep	Penn	June 16, 2009 Replaced McHugh

Budget

House Committee on the Budget, 103rd-111th Congresses (1993-2011)

BACKGROUND

Organizational History: The House Budget Committee was created by the Congressional Budget and Impoundment Control Act of 1974 (P.L. 93-344) and dates from July 12, 1974. It was in response to President Richard Nixon's expansion of executive power that led the Congress to enact the most important committee system change since 1946. The Congressional Budget and Impoundment Control Act was intended to limit the president's authority to withhold funds appropriated by Congress for programs and projects which the president opposed. Coming as it did near the close of the Nixon presidency, this act may be seen as the domestic analog of the War Powers Resolution of 1973 (P.L. 93-148) that sought to constrain the war-making powers of the president. This Congressional Budget Act created the Budget committees in both the House and Senate. Each of these committees has emerged as centers of institutional power.

Of all the House committees, it is the one most concerned with broad questions about the overall shape of federal spending and taxation. It has responsibility for ensuring that the House complies with the budget planning process created by the 1974 law. Like its Senate counterpart, the House panel does not have authority to directly approve substantive legislation or spending bills. Instead its task is to set out guidelines and goals for bills approved by other committees. To do that it has two main duties. One is to propose an annual budget resolution, which establishes targets for total federal spending and revenue, and the amounts that can be spent on broad categories of federal programs, such as defense or welfare. The other duty is to try to make the whole House and the other committees comply with those spending targets.

The committee also is the first one to examine the president's budget each year, which can influence the tenor of the budget debate for the whole year. The committee also may prepare instructions, included in the annual budget resolution, that require other committees to cut programs to meet budget targets.

During the mid-1980s, two key pieces of legislation were passed affecting the federal budget—the Gramm-Rudman-Hollings Balanced Budget and Emergency Deficit Control Act of 1985 (P.L. 99-177) and the Budget and Emergency Deficit Control Reaffirmation Act of 1987 (P.L. 100-119). Both acts were generally referred to as "Gramm-Rudman," with U.S. Senator W. Phil Gramm (Rep-Texas) generally credited as the major architect of both pieces of legislation. Gramm, who would chair the Senate's Budget Committee, was an alumnus of the House Budget Committee, 1981-1985.

In the decades since its creation, however, the committee did not become a major player in the budgeting process. It lost much of its power to shape budget policy when, in 1990, Congress and President George H.W. Bush negotiated the Budget Enforcement Act, a portion of the Omnibus Budget Reconciliation Act of 1990 (P.L. 101-508). This was a deficit reduction agreement—$500 billion over five years—that set spending limits, defined pay-as-you-go rules for mandatory spending, and allowed the deficit to keep growing. In effect, it stripped the committee—at least temporarily—of its power to make decisions about the budget. Even before the 1990 agreement, however, the committee had become a relatively weak player in the budget process. One reason was the House rule that most members could not serve more than six consecutive years, limiting the opportunity to build up experience and knowledge of budget issues. The Senate Budget Committee has no such limit. Another problem was the deep partisan divisions between Democratic and Republican members that prevented them from agreeing on most issues.

According to the House Manual (2008), the Republican-controlled 104th Congress (1995-1997)

. . . expand[ed] the limited legislative jurisdiction of the committee by: (1) adding other measures setting forth appropriate levels of budget totals to subparagraph (2) (now subparagraph (1)); (2) granting the committee jurisdiction over the congressional budget process generally in a new subparagraph (3) (now subparagraph (2)); and (3) granting the committee jurisdiction over special controls over the Federal budget in a new subparagraph (4) (now subparagraph (3)), including receiving from the former Committee on Government Operations (now Oversight and Government Reform) jurisdiction over budgetary treatment of off-budget Federal agencies and measures providing exemption from sequestration orders issued under the Balanced Budget and Emergency Deficit Control Act (sec. 202(a), H. Res. 6, Jan. 4, 1995).

And in recent Congresses, "This committee has primary jurisdiction, and the Committee on Ways and Means has additional jurisdiction, over a bill taking Social Security trust funds off budget (Dec. 15, 2000). This committee has primary jurisdiction, and the Committee on Rules has additional jurisdiction, over a bill amending the Budget Act to establish new legislative points of order and directing that the president include a specified matter with his budget (Feb. 13, 2001).

Membership: Its original membership was set at twenty-three and was expanded to thirty-seven by 1991. This committee has the most distinctive membership rules of any standing committee in the House. Ten members are selected from Appropriations and Ways and Means with each committee providing five members. They are to serve with one member of the majority leadership and one member of the minority leadership. The others are to be selected from the rest of the House membership. "All selections of Members to serve on the committee shall be made without regard to seniority." In addition, according to the House Manual for the 105th Congress (1997) none of the non-leadership members "shall serve as a member of the Committee on the Budget during more than four Congresses in any period of six successive Congresses." As a result, the committee has a low membership retention rate.

For most of the post-1993 Congresses, Budget had forty-three seats but in the last three Congresses, 2005-2011, the membership has been reduced to thirty-nine. Its overall mean membership size of 41.56 per Congress placed it in 12th place among the nineteen regularly appointed committees and its relatively low mean seniority of 4.36 terms per member—14th place—may be explained by the rules constraining membership continuity on the committee. Further evidence of these constraining rules may be found in the committee's low 16th place inter-Congress retention rate of 67.82 percent. Only the low prestige House Administration (61.73%) and Small Business Committees (66.67%) rank lower. The tiny Standards of Official Conduct Committee also has a lower retention rate of 57.50 percent but with only ten members, any departure will have a major statistical impact.

Committee Leaders: The first chair of the House Budget Committee was Al Ullman (Dem-Ore.) who left to chair Ways and Means in 1975. Chairmanship turnover has been high with seven chairs between 1974 and 1993. Included would be Brock Adams (Dem-Wash.), 1975-1977; Robert N. Giaimo (Dem-Conn.), 1977-1981; James R. Jones (Dem-Okla.), 1981-1985; William H. Gray III (Dem-Penn.), 1985-1989; Leon Panetta (Dem-Cal.), 1989-1993; and Martin Olav Sabo (DFL-Minn.), 1993-1995. Republican ranking minority members lasted longer—John J. Rhodes (Rep-Ariz.), 1974-1975; Delbert L. Latta (Rep-Ohio), 1975-1989; William E. Frenzel (Rep-Minn.), 1989-1991; and Willis D. Gradison (Rep-Ohio), 1991-1993.

During the post-1993 Congresses, John Kasich (Rep-Ohio) served as the senior Republican for eight years as ranking minority member, 1993-1995, and as chair, 1995-2001, until his retirement to explore a presidential nomination. He was succeeded by James Nussle (Rep-Iowa) who held the chair from 2001 until his defeat for a Senate seat in 2006. On the Democratic side, Martin Olav Sabo became chair in 1993 when Panetta resigned the House and served as ranking minority member for two years when Republicans captured the House. Sabo was succeeded in 1997 by John M. Spratt Jr. (Dem-S.C.) who has been the committee's senior Democrat for the past fourteen years—ten as ranking member, 1997-2007, and the last four as chair, 2007-2011. Serving with Spratt as the committee's present ranking member is Paul D. Ryan (Rep-Wisc.) who gained that rank in 2007.

Party Leaders: Budget Committee membership is a requirement of House leadership. However, Richard Gephardt (Dem-Mo.) and William H. Gray III (Dem-Penn.) who were elected Majority Leader and Majority Whip in 1989 respectively, served on Budget before they assumed their leadership posts. This was also true of Robert Michel (Rep-Ill.) who served on Budget before becoming Minority Whip in 1975 and Richard K. Armey (Rep-Texas) who served before becoming Majority Leader in 1995.

Notable Members: While no presidential candidates emerged from Budget, two vice presidential candidates did—Geraldine Ferraro (Dem-N.Y.), a Tip O'Neill protégé and the first woman ever named on a vice presidential ticket when she ran with Walter Mondale in 1984, and Jack Kemp (Rep-N.Y) who ran with Robert J. Dole in 1996. Six Cabinet members served on Budget—Brock Adams (Dem-Wash.) who left the

chair of Budget to become President Jimmy Carter's Secretary of Transportation in 1977; Lynn Martin (Rep-Ill.), Secretary of Labor under President George H.W. Bush; Les Aspin (Dem-Wisc.) and Mike Espy (Dem-Miss.) President Clinton's first Secretaries of Defense and Agriculture; Norman Mineta (Dem-Cal.) the first Asian-American Cabinet member who served as Bill Clinton's Secretary of Commerce and George W. Bush's Secretary of Transportation, and most recently, Ray LaHood (Rep-Ill.) President Obama's Secretary of Transportation. Two other notables would include Leon E. Panetta (Dem-Cal.) who left in 1993 to become Director of the Office of Management and Budget in the Clinton Administration and is now President Obama's Director of Central Intelligence. Also Willis D. Gradison Jr. (Rep-Ohio) who left his ranking minority post in 1993 to head the Health Insurance Association of America, the small insurers' most effective lobby against federal health care reform.

Since its creation in the 93rd Congress, twenty-two members of Budget have been elected to the U.S. Senate, fourteen Republicans—Hank Brown and A. Wayne Allard of Colorado, Paul S. Trible of Virginia, W. Phil Gramm of Texas, James T. Broyhill of North Carolina, Connie Mack III of Florida, Olympia J.B. Snowe of Maine, Richard J. (Rick) Santorum of Pennsylvania, Sam D. Brownback of Kansas, James P.D. Bunning of Kentucky, John Sununu of New Hampshire, Saxby Chambliss of Georgia, Roger F. Wicker of Mississippi, and David Vitter of Louisiana. The seven Democrats were Timothy E. Wirth of Colorado, Paul M. Simon and Richard J. Durbin of Illinois, Barbara Boxer of California, Brock Adams of Washington State, C.W. (Bill) Nelson of Florida, Charles E. Schumer of New York, and Benjamin L. Cardin of Maryland.

Six governors have emerged from the House Budget Committee: three Republicans—James G. Martin of North Carolina, Ernest L. Fletcher of Kentucky, and Robert L. Ehrlich of Maryland; and three Democrats—Kenneth H. (Buddy) MacKay of Florida, Michael E. Lowry of Washington State, and Robert E. Wise of West Virginia.

Selected References

Ellwood, John W. and James A. Thurber, "The New Congressional Budget Process: The Hows and Whys of House Senate Differences," in Lawrence C. Dodd and Bruce I. Oppenheimer, eds., *Congress Reconsidered* (New York: Praeger, 1977), 163-192.

Milyo, Jeffrey, "Electoral and Financial Effects of Changes in Committee Power: The Gramm-Rudman-Hollings Budget Reform, the Tax Reform Act of 1986, and the Money Committees in the House," *Journal of Law and Economics,* 40 (April, 1997), 93-112.

Schick, Allen, ed., *Making Economic Policy in Congress* (Washington, D.C.: American Enterprise Institute, 1983).

Schick, Allen, "The Three-Ring Budget Process: The Appropriations, Tax and Budget Committees in Congress," in Thomas Mann and Norman J. Ornstein, eds., *The New Congress* (Washington, D.C.: American Enterprise Institute, 1981), 288-328.

Schick, Allen, Robert Keith, and Edward Davis, *Manual on the Federal Budget Process, Congressional Research Service, Library of Congress* (Dec. 24, 1991).

RESPONSIBILITIES AND JURISDICTIONAL CHANGES

Jurisdiction, 93rd Congress (1973-1975)

Established by Public Law 93-344, the Congressional Budget and Impoundment Control Act of 1974, 93rd Congress, Second Session, July 12, 1974 (88 Statutes 297, 300):

[Section 101.(c)]

(c) Rule X.1. of the Rules of the House of Representatives is amended by redesignating clauses 5 through 33 as clauses 6 through 34, respectively, and by inserting after clause 4 the following new clause:

Committee on the Budget

(a) All concurrent resolutions on the budget (as defined in section 3(a)(4)of the Congressional Budget Act of 1974) and other matters required to be referred to the committee under titles III and IV of that Act.

(b) The committee shall have the duty—

    (1) to report the matters required to be reported by it under titles III and IV of the Congressional Budget Act of 1974;

    (2) to make continuing studies of the effect on budget outlays of relevant existing and proposed legislation and to report the results of such studies to the House on a recurring basis;

    (3) to request and evaluate continuing studies of tax expenditures, to devise methods of coordinating tax expenditures, policies, and programs with direct budget outlays, and to report the results of such studies to the House on a recurring basis; and

    (4) to review, on a continuing basis, the conduct by the Congressional Budget Office of its functions and duties.

Jurisdiction, 103rd Congress (1993-1995)

From the Rules of the House of Representatives, 103rd Congress (House Document 102-405)

[Rule X.1.(e)(2)] Committee on the Budget

All concurrent resolutions on the budget (as defined in section 3(a) (4) of the Congressional Budget Act of 1974) and other matters required to be referred to the committee under titles III and IV of that Act.

[Rule X.1.(e)(3)]

The committee shall have the duty—

(A) to report the matters required to be reported by it under titles III and IV of the Congressional Budget Act of 1974;

(B) to make continuing studies of the effect on budget outlays of relevant existing and proposed legislation and to report the results of such studies to the House on a recurring basis;

(C) to request and evaluate continuing studies of tax expenditures, to devise methods of coordinating tax expenditures, policies, and programs with direct budget outlays, and to report the results of such studies to the House on a recurring basis; and

(D) to review, on a continuing basis, the conduct by the Congressional Budget Office of its functions and duties.

[Rule X.3.(b)]

The Committee on the Budget shall have the function of—

    (1) making continuing studies of the effect on budget outlays of relevant existing and proposed legislation, and reporting the results of such studies to the House on a recurring basis; and

    (2) requesting and evaluating continuing studies of tax expenditures, devising methods of coordinating tax expenditures, policies, and programs with direct budget outlays, and reporting the results of such studies to the House on a recurring basis.

[Rule X.4.(b)]

The Committee on the Budget shall have the duty—

    (1) to review on a continuing basis the conduct by the Congressional Budget Office of its functions and duties;

    (2) to hold hearings, and receive testimony from Members of Congress and such appropriate representatives of Federal departments and agencies, the general public, and national organizations as it deems desirable, in developing the first concurrent resolution on the budget for each fiscal year;

    (3) to make all reports required of it by the Congressional Budget Act of 1974, including the reporting of reconciliation bills and resolutions when so required;

    (4) to study on a continuing basis those provisions of law which exempt Federal agencies or any of their activities or outlays from inclusion in the Budget of the United States Government, and to report to the House from time to time its recommendations for terminating or modifying such provisions; and

    (5) to study on a continuing basis proposals designed to improve and facilitate methods of congressional budget-making, and to report to the House from time to time the results of such study together with its recommendations.

Relevant provisions of the Congressional Budget and Impoundment Control Act of 1974:

[Section 3.(a)]

The term "concurrent resolution on the budget" means—

(A) a concurrent resolution setting forth the congressional budget for the United States Government for a fiscal year as provided in section 301;

(B) a concurrent resolution reaffirming or revising the congressional budget for the United States Government for a fiscal year as provided in section 310; and

(C) any other concurrent resolution revising the congressional budget for the United States Government for a fiscal year as described in section 304.

Jurisdiction, 104th Congress (1995-1997) Changes in Committee System

From H. Res. 6, Section 202 (a), the Committees and Their Jurisdiction, January 4, 1995

[Rule X.1.(d)] (1) Committee on the Budget, consisting of the following Members:

(A) Members who are members of other standing committees, including five Members who are members of the Committee on Appropriations, and five Members who are members of the Committee on Ways and Means;

(B) one Member from the leadership of the majority party; and

(C) one Member from the leadership of the minority party.

(1) No Member other than a representative from the leadership of a party may serve as a member of the Committee on the Budget during more than four Congresses in any period of six successive Congresses (disregarding for this purpose any service performed as a member of such committee for less than a full session in any Congress), except that an incumbent chairman or ranking minority member having served on the committee for four Congresses and having served as chairman or ranking minority member of the committee for not more than one Congress shall be eligible for reelection to the committee as chairman or ranking minority member for one additional Congress.

(2) All concurrent resolutions on the budget (as defined in section 3 of the Congressional Budget Act of 1974), other matters required to be referred to the committee under titles III and IV of that Act, and other measures setting forth appropriate levels of budget totals for the United States Government.

(3) Measures relating to the congressional budget process, generally.

(4) Measures relating to the establishment, extension, and enforcement of special controls over the Federal budget, including the budgetary treatment of off-budget Federal agencies and measures providing exemption from reduction under any order issued under part C of the Balanced Budget and Emergency Deficit Control Act of 1985.

(5) The committee shall have the duty—

(A) to report the matters required to be reported by it under titles III and IV of the Congressional Budget Act of 1974;

(B) to make continuing studies of the effect on budget outlays of relevant existing and proposed legislation and to report the results of such studies to the House on a recurring basis;

(C) to request and evaluate continuing studies of tax expenditures; to devise methods of coordinating tax expenditures, policies, and programs with direct budget outlays, and to report the results of such studies to the House on a recurring basis; and

(D) to review, on a continuing basis, the conduct by the Congressional Budget Office of its functions and duties.

(c) The chairman of the Committee on the Budget, when elected, may revise (within the appropriate levels established in House Concurrent Resolution 218 of the One Hundred Third Congress) allocations of budget outlays, new budget authority, and entitlement authority among committees of the House in the One Hundred Fourth Congress to reflect changes in jurisdiction under clause 1 of rule X. He shall publish the revised allocations in the Congressional Record. Once published, the revised allocations shall be effective in the House as though made pursuant to sections 302(a) and 602(a) of the Congressional Budget Act of 1974.

[Rule X.3.(b)] Special Oversight Functions

(b) The Committee on the Budget shall have the function of—

(1) making continuing studies of the effect on budget outlays of relevant existing and proposed legislation, and reporting the results of such studies to the House on a recurring basis; and

(2) requesting and evaluating continuing studies of tax expenditures, devising methods of coordinating tax expenditures, policies, and programs with direct budget outlays, and reporting the results of such studies to the House on a recurring basis.

Jurisdiction, 111th Congress (2009-2011)

From the Rules of the House of Representatives (as revised to June 16, 2009, H.Doc. 110-162):

[Rule X.1.(d)] Committee on the Budget

(1) Concurrent resolutions on the budget (as defined in section 3(4) of the Congressional Budget Act of 1974), other matters required to be referred to the committee under titles III and IV of that Act, and other measures setting forth appropriate levels of budget totals for the United States Government.

(2) Budget process generally.

(3) Establishment, extension, and enforcement of special controls over the Federal budget, including the budgetary treatment of off-budget Federal agencies and measures providing exemption from reduction under any order issued under part C of the Balanced Budget and Emergency Deficit Control Act of 1985.

[Rule X.3.(c)] Special Oversight Function

The Committee on the Budget shall study on a continuing basis the effect on budget outlays of relevant existing and proposed legislation and report the results of such studies to the House on a recurring basis.

[Rule X.4.(b)] Additional Functions

The Committee on the Budget shall—

(1) review on a continuing basis the conduct by the Congressional Budget Office of its functions and duties;

(2) hold hearings, and receive testimony from Members, Senators, Delegates, the Resident Commissioner, and such appropriate representatives of Federal departments and agencies, the general public, and national organizations as it considers desirable in developing concurrent resolutions on the budget for each fiscal year;

(3) make all reports required of it by the Congressional Budget Act of 1974;

(4) study on a continuing basis those provisions of law that exempt Federal agencies or any of their activities or outlays from inclusion in the Budget of the United States Government, and report to the House from time to time its recommendations for terminating or modifying such provisions; and

(5) study on a continuing basis proposals designed to improve and facilitate the congressional budget process, and report to the House from time to time the results of such studies, together with its recommendations; and

(6) request and evaluate continuing studies of tax expenditures, devise methods of coordinating tax expenditures, policies, and programs with direct budget outlays, and report the results of such studies to the House on a recurring basis.

NAMES OF BUDGET SUBCOMMITTEES FROM THE *CONGRESSIONAL DIRECTORY*

No Subcommittees, 103 but Task Forces

104, 105, 106, 107, 108, 109, 110, 111

MEMBERSHIP ROSTERS, 103rd-111th Congresses, 1993-2011

BUDGET / 103rd Congress

Service Dates of Committee Chair: Ch1 Jan. 5, 1993-Jan. 21, 1993, Panetta (Dem-Cal.)

Ch2 Jan. 25, 1993-Jan. 3, 1995, Sabo (DFL-Minn.)

Service Dates of Majority Members: Jan. 5, 1993-Jan. 3, 1995

Service Dates of Minority Members: Jan. 5, 1993-Jan. 3, 1995

Roster Filled: Majority with 26 members on Jan. 5, 1993; Minority with 17 members on Jan. 26, 1993

			Majority	Terms in:					Minority	Terms in:	
Rank Name	Party	State	House	Comm.		Rank Name	Party	State	House	Comm.	
Ch1 Panetta, Leon E.	Dem	Cal.	9	3		RM Kasich, John R.	Rep	Ohio	6	3	
2nd Gephardt, Richard A.	Dem	Mo.	9	*2 3		2nd McMillan, J. Alex	Rep	N.C.	5	2	
3rd Kildee, Dale E.	Dem	Mich.	9	3		3rd Kolbe, James T.	Rep	Ariz.	5	2	
4th Beilenson, Anthony C.	Dem	Cal.	9	3		4th Shays, Christopher H.	Rep	Conn.	4	*1 2	
5th Ch2 Sabo, Martin Olav	DFL	Minn.	8	3		5th Snowe, Olympia J.B.	Rep	Me.	8	1	
6th Berman, Howard L.	Dem	Cal.	6	3		6th Herger, Walter W.	Rep	Cal	4	1	
7th Wise, Robert E. Jr.	Dem	W.Va.	6	3		7th Bunning, James P.D.	Rep	Ky.	4	1	
8th Bryant, John W.	Dem	Tex.	6	3		8th Smith, Lamar S.	Rep	Tex.	4	1	
9th Spratt, John M. Jr.	Dem	S.C.	6	*1 3		9th Cox, C. Christopher	Rep	Cal.	3	1	
10th Stenholm, Charles W.	Dem	Tex.	8	2		10th Allard, A. Wayne	Rep	Colo.	2	1	
11th Frank, Barney	Dem	Mass.	7	2		11th Hobson, David L.	Rep	Ohio	2	1	

12th Cooper, James H.S.	Dem	Tenn.	6	*1 2	
13th Slaughter, Louise Macintosh	Dem	N.Y.	4	2	
14th Parker, Michael	Dem	Miss.	3	*1 2	
15th Coyne, William J.	Dem	Penn.	7	1	
16th Kennelly, Barbara B.	Dem	Conn.	7	1	
17th Andrews, Michael A.	Dem	Tex.	6	1	
18th Mollohan, Alan B.	Dem	W. Va.	6	1	
19th Gordon, Barton J.	Dem	Tenn.	5	1	
20th Price, David E.	Dem	N.C.	4	*1 1	
21st Costello, Jerry F.	Dem	Ill.	4	1	
22nd Johnston, Harry A. II	Dem	Fla.	3	1	
23rd Mink, Patsy T.	Dem	Hai.	9	*2 1	
24th Orton, William	Dem	Utah	2	1	
25th Blackwell, Lucien E.	Dem	Penn.	2	1	
26th Pomeroy, Earl R. III	Dem	N.D.	1	1	

12th Miller, Daniel	Rep	Fla.	2	1
13th Lazio, Enrico A. (Rick)	Rep	N.Y.	1	1
14th Franks, Robert D.	Rep	N.J.	1	1
15th Smith, Nick H.	Rep	Mich.	1	1
16th Inglis, Robert D.	Rep	S.C.	1	1
17th Hoke, Martin R.	Rep	Ohio	1	1

*1: Member's first period of service on the committee.

*2: Member's second period of service on the committee.

Note: Due to the nature of rotating membership on the Budget committee, the Democratic Caucus does not necessarily use committee seniority to determine rank. When in the majority, the Democratic Caucus reserves the second rank for the House Majority Leader.

Vacancies Filled:
   Minority:
      6th, 7th, and 11th seats by Herger, Bunning, and Hobson on Jan. 26, 1993

Changes:
   Chair:

Ch1 Panetta, Leon E.	Dem	Cal.	Jan. 21, 1993 Resigned the House; appointed Director, Office of Management and Budget
Ch2 Sabo, Martin Olav	DFL	Minn.	Jan. 25, 1993 Succeeded Panetta as Chair

   Majority:

Panetta, Leon E.	Dem	Cal.	Jan. 21, 1993 Resigned the House; appointed Director, Office of Management and Budget
Spratt, John M. Jr.	Dem	S.C.	Feb. 17, 1993 Resigned committee; returned to Government Operations
Browder, J. Glen	Dem	Ala.	March 3, 1993 Replaced Panetta
Woolsey, Lynn C.	Dem	Cal.	March 3, 1993 Replaced Spratt

Departures from the House:	**Majority**			**Minority**		
Elected to U.S. Senate	None			Snowe, Olympia J.B.	Rep	Me.
Lost Election to U.S. Senate	Cooper, James H.S.	Dem	Tenn.	None		
Lost Nomination to U.S. Senate	Andrews, Michael A.	Dem	Tex.	None		
Defeated for Re-nomination	Blackwell, Lucien E.	Dem	Penn.	None		
Defeated for Re-election	Price, David E.	Dem	N.C.	None		
Retired	None			McMillan, J. Alex	Rep	N.C.

Departures from Committee:						
Elected Minority Leader	Gephardt, Richard A.	Dem	Mo.	None		
Moved to Commerce	Gordon, Barton J.	Dem	Tenn.	Cox, C. Christopher	Rep	Cal.
Returned to Government Reform and Oversight	Wise, Robert E. Jr.	Dem	W.Va.	None		
Returned to Resources	Kildee, Dale E.	Dem	Mich.	None		
No new assignment	Beilenson, Anthony C.	Dem	Cal.	None		
	Berman, Howard L.	Dem	Cal.			
	Bryant, John W.	Dem	Tex.			
	Frank, Barney	Dem	Mass.			
	Kennelly, Barbara B.	Dem	Conn.			

BUDGET / 104th Congress

Service Dates of Committee Chair: Jan. 4, 1995-Jan. 3, 1997

Service Dates of Majority Members: Jan. 4, 1995-Jan. 3, 1997

Service Dates of Minority Members: Jan. 4, 1995-Jan. 3, 1997

Roster Filled: Majority with 24 members on Jan. 4, 1995; Minority with 18 members on Jan. 4, 1995

	Majority						**Minority**				
				Terms in:						**Terms in:**	
Rank Name		**Party**	**State**	**House**	**Comm.**	**Rank Name**		**Party**	**State**	**House**	**Comm.**
Chr Kasich, John R.		Rep	Ohio	7	4	RM Sabo, Martin Olav		DFL	Minn.	9	4
2nd Hobson, David L.		Rep	Ohio	3	2	2nd Stenholm, Charles W.		Dem	Tex.	9	3

3rd Walker, Robert S.	Rep	Penn.	10	1		3rd Slaughter, Louise Macintosh	Dem	N.Y.	5		3
4th Kolbe, James T.	Rep	Ariz.	6	3		4th Parker, Michael	Dem	Miss.	4	*1	3
5th Shays, Christopher H.	Rep	Conn.	5	*1 3		5th Coyne, William J.	Dem	Penn.	8		2
6th Herger, Walter W.	Rep	Cal	5	2		6th Mollohan, Alan B.	Dem	W. Va.	7		2
7th Bunning, James P.D.	Rep	Ky.	5	2		7th Costello, Jerry F.	Dem	Ill.	5		2
8th Smith, Lamar S.	Rep	Tex.	5	2		8th Johnston, Harry A. II	Dem	Fla.	4		2
9th Allard, A. Wayne	Rep	Colo.	3	2		9th Mink, Patsy T.	Dem	Hai.	10	*2	2
10th Miller, Daniel	Rep	Fla.	3	2		10th Orton, William	Dem	Utah	3		2
11th Lazio, Enrico A. (Rick)	Rep	N.Y.	2	2		11th Pomeroy, Earl R. III	Dem	N.D.	2		2
12th Franks, Robert D.	Rep	N.J.	2	2		12th Browder, J. Glen	Dem	Ala.	4		2
13th Smith, Nick H.	Rep	Mich.	2	2		13th Woolsey, Lynn C.	Dem	Cal.	2		2
14th Inglis, Robert D.	Rep	S.C.	2	2		14th Olver, John W.	Dem	Mass.	3		1
15th Hoke, Martin R.	Rep	Ohio	2	2		15th Roybal-Allard, Lucille	Dem	Cal.	2		1
16th Molinari, Susan	Rep	N.Y.	4	1		16th Meek, Carrie P.	Dem	Fla.	2		1
17th Nussle, James A.	Rep	Iowa	3	1		17th Rivers, Lynn N.	Dem	Mich.	1		1
18th Hoekstra, Peter	Rep	Mich.	2	*1 1		18th Doggett, Lloyd A. II	Dem	Tex.	1	*1	1
19th Largent, Steve	Rep	Okla.	2	1							
20th Myrick, Sue	Rep	N.C.	1	1							
21st Brownback, Sam D.	Rep	Kans.	1	1							
22nd Shadegg, John B.	Rep	Ariz.	1	1							
23rd Radanovich, George P.	Rep	Cal.	1	1							
24th Bass, Charles F.	Rep	N.H.	1	1							

*1: Member's first period of service on the committee.

*2: Member's first period of service on the committee.

Changes:
Majority:

Hoekstra, Peter	Rep	Mich.	Feb. 1, 1996 Resigned committee; no new assignment
Neumann, Mark W.	Rep	Wisc.	Feb. 1, 1996 Replaced Hoekstra
Brownback, Sam D.	Rep	Kans.	Nov. 7, 1996 Resigned the House; elected to U.S. Senate

Minority:

Parker, Michael	Dem	Miss.	Nov. 15, 1995 Service on committee as a Democrat vacated; moved to Appropriations as a Republican on Mar. 14, 1996
Levin, Sander M.	Dem	Mich.	April 22, 1996 Replaced Parker
Johnston, Harry A. II.	Dem	Fla.	April 25, 1996 Resigned committee; no new assignment
Thompson, Bennie	Dem	Miss.	April 22, 1996 Replaced Johnston

Departures from the House:

	Majority			Minority		
Elected to U.S. Senate	Allard, A. Wayne	Rep	Colo.	None		
Lost Nomination to U.S. Senate	None			Browder, J. Glen	Dem	Ala.
Defeated for Re-election	Hoke, Martin R.	Rep	Ohio	Orton, William	Dem	Utah
Retired	Walker, Robert S.	Rep	Penn.	None		

Departures from Committee:

	Majority			Minority		
Returned to Appropriations	None			Olver, John W.	Dem	Mass.
				Meek, Carrie P.	Dem	Fla.
Moved to Commerce	Lazio, Enrico A. (Rick)	Rep	N.Y.	None		
	Largent, Steve	Rep	La.			
Moved to Rules	Myrick, Sue	Rep	N.C.	None		
No new assignment	Kolbe, James T.	Rep	Ariz.	Sabo, Martin Olav	DFL	Minn.
				Stenholm, Charles W.	Dem	Tex.
				Coyne, William J.	Dem	Penn.
				Levin, Sander M.	Dem	Mich.

BUDGET / 105th Congress

Service Dates of Committee Chair: Jan. 7, 1997-Jan 3, 1999

Service Dates of Majority Members: Jan. 7, 1997-Jan. 3, 1999

Service Dates of Minority Members: Jan. 7, 1997-Jan. 3, 1999

Roster Filled: Majority with 24 members on Jan. 7, 1997; Minority with 19 members on Mar. 6, 1997

	Majority			Terms in:			Minority			Terms in:	
Rank Name	Party	State	House	Comm.		Rank Name	Party	State	House	Comm.	
Chr Kasich, John R.	Rep	Ohio	8	5		RM Spratt, John M. Jr.	Dem	S.C.	8	*2 1	
2nd Hobson, David L.	Rep	Ohio	4	3		2nd Slaughter, Louise Macintosh	Dem	N.Y.	6	*2 4	

3rd Shays, Christopher H.	Rep	Conn.	6	*1 4
4th Herger, Walter W.	Rep	Cal	6	3
5th Bunning, James P.D.	Rep	Ky.	6	3
6th Smith, Lamar S.	Rep	Tex.	6	3
7th Miller, Daniel	Rep	Fla.	4	3
8th Franks, Robert D.	Rep	N.J.	3	3
9th Smith, Nick H.	Rep	Mich.	3	3
10th Inglis, Robert D.	Rep	S.C.	3	3
11th Molinari, Susan	Rep	N.Y.	5	2
12th Nussle, James A.	Rep	Iowa	4	2
13th Hoekstra, Peter	Rep	Mich.	3	*2 1
14th Shadegg, John B.	Rep	Ariz.	2	*2 2
15th Radanovich, George P.	Rep	Cal.	2	2
16th Bass, Charles F.	Rep	N.H.	2	2
17th Neumann, Mark W.	Rep	Wisc.	2	2
18th Parker, Michael	Rep	Miss.	5	*2 1
19th Ehrlich, Robert L. Jr.	Rep	Md.	2	1
20th Gutknecht, Gilbert W.	Rep	Minn.	2	1
21st Hilleary, Van	Rep	Tenn.	2	1
22nd Granger, Kay	Rep	Tex.	1	*1 1
23rd Sununu, John E.	Rep	N.H.	1	1
24th Pitts, Joseph R.	Rep	Penn.	1	1

3rd Mollohan, Alan B.	Dem	W. Va.	8	3
4th Costello, Jerry F.	Dem	Ill.	6	3
5th Mink, Patsy T.	Dem	Hai.	11	*2 3
6th Pomeroy, Earl R. III	Dem	N.D.	3	3
7th Woolsey, Lynn C.	Dem	Cal.	3	3
8th Roybal-Allard, Lucille	Dem	Cal.	3	2
9th Rivers, Lynn N.	Dem	Mich.	2	2
10th Doggett, Lloyd A. II	Dem	Tex.	2	*1 2
11th Thompson, Bennie	Dem	Miss.	3	2
12th Cardin, Benjamin L.	Dem	Md.	6	1
13th Baesler, H. Scott (Scotty)	Dem	Ky.	3	1
14th Minge, David B.	DFL	Minn.	3	1
15th Bentsen, Kenneth E. Jr.	Dem	Tex.	2	1
16th Davis, Jim	Dem	Fla.	1	1
17th Sherman, Brad	Dem	Cal.	1	1
18th Weygand, Robert A.	Dem	R.I.	1	1
19th McDermott, James A.	Dem	Wash.	5	1

*1: Member's first period of service on the committee.
*2: Member's second period of service on the committee.

Filled Vacancy:
  Minority:
    19th seat filled by McDermott on Mar. 6, 1997

Changes:
  Majority:
    Molinari, Susan   Rep   N.Y.   Aug. 2, 1997 Resigned the House to work for CBS News
  Minority:
    Slaughter, Louise Macintosh   Dem   N.Y.   Feb. 5, 1997 Resigned committee; had returned to Rules
    Clayton, Eva M.   Dem   N.C.   Feb. 5, 1997 Replaced Slaughter
    Sherman, Brad   Dem   Cal.   Sept. 5, 1997 Resigned committee; moved to Banking and Financial Services
    Price, David E.   Dem   N.C.   Nov. 13, 1997 Replaced Sherman; service postponed until Jan. 1998 to permit a full years on the Budget Committee

Departures from the House:

	Majority			Minority		
Elected to U.S. Senate	Bunning, James P.D.	Rep	Ky.	None		
Lost Election to U.S. Senate	Inglis, Robert D.	Rep	S.C.	Baesler, H. Scott (Scotty)	Dem	Ky.
	Neumann, Mark W.	Rep	Wisc.			
Retired	Parker, Michael	Rep	Miss.	None		

Departures from Committee:

	Majority			Minority		
Moved to Appropriations	Granger, Kay	Rep	Tex.	Roybal-Allard, Lucille	Dem	Ca
Moved to Commerce	Shadegg, John B.	Rep	Ariz.	None		
	Erlich, Robert L. Jr.	Rep	Md.			
Returned to Government Reform	None			Mink, Patsy T.	Dem	Hai.
Moved to International Relations	None			Pomeroy, Earl R. III	Dem	N.D.
Returned to Science	Smith, Lamar S.	Rep	Tex.	Woolsey, Lynn C.	Dem	Cal.
	None			Costello, Jerry F.	Dem	Ill.
Moved to Ways and Means	None			Doggett, Lloyd A. II	Dem	Tex.
No new assignment	Hobson, David L.	Rep	Ohio	Mollohan, Alan B.	Dem	W.Va.
				Cardin, Benjamin L.	Dem	Md.

BUDGET / 106th Congress

Service Dates of Committee Chair: Jan. 6, 1999-Jan. 3, 2001

Service Dates of Majority Members: Jan. 6, 1999-Jan. 3, 2001

Service Dates of Minority Members: Jan. 6, 1999-Jan. 3, 2001

Roster Filled: Majority with 24 members on Jan. 19, 1999; Minority with 19 members on Jan. 6, 1999

Majority					Minority				
			Terms in:					**Terms in:**	
Rank Name	**Party**	**State**	**House**	**Comm.**	**Rank Name**	**Party**	**State**	**House**	**Comm.**
Chr Kasich, John R.	Rep	Ohio	9	6	RM Spratt, John M. Jr.	Dem	S.C.	9	*2 2
2nd Chambliss, Saxby	Rep	Ga.	3	1	2nd McDermott, James A.	Dem	Wash.	6	2

Rank Name	Party	State	House	Comm.
3rd Shays, Christopher H.	Rep	Conn.	7	*1 5
4th Herger, Walter W.	Rep	Cal	7	4
5th Miller, Daniel	Rep	Fla.	5	4
6th Franks, Robert D.	Rep	N.J.	4	4
7th Smith, Nick H.	Rep	Mich.	4	4
8th Nussle, James A.	Rep	Iowa	5	3
9th Hoekstra, Peter	Rep	Mich.	4	*2 2
10th Radanovich, George P.	Rep	Cal.	3	3
11th Bass, Charles F.	Rep	N.H.	3	3
12th Gutknecht, Gilbert W.	Rep	Minn.	3	2
13th Hilleary, Van	Rep	Tenn.	3	2
14th Sununu, John E.	Rep	N.H.	2	2
15th Pitts, Joseph R.	Rep	Penn.	2	2
16th Knollenberg, Joseph	Rep	Mich.	4	1
17th Thornberry, William M. (Mac)	Rep	Tex.	3	1
18th Ryun, Jim	Rep	Kans.	3	1
19th Wamp, Zachary P.	Rep	Tenn.	3	1
20th Green, Mark	Rep	Wisc.	1	1
21st Fletcher, Ernest L.	Rep	Ky.	1	1
22nd Miller, Gary G.	Rep	Cal.	1	1
23rd Ryan, Paul D.	Rep	Wisc.	1	*1 1
24th Toomey, Patrick J.	Rep	Penn.	1	1

Rank Name	Party	State	House	Comm.
3rd Rivers, Lynn N.	Dem	Mich.	3	3
4th Thompson, Bennie	Dem	Miss.	4	3
5th Minge, David B.	DFL	Minn.	4	2
6th Bentsen, Kenneth E. Jr.	Dem	Tex.	3	2
7th Davis, Jim	Dem	Fla.	2	2
8th Weygand, Robert A.	Dem	R.I.	2	2
9th Clayton, Eva M.	Dem	N.C.	5	2
10th Price, David E.	Dem	N.C.	6	*2 2
11th Markey, Edward J.	Dem	Mass.	13	1
12th Kleczka, Gerald D.	Dem	Wisc.	9	1
13th Clement, Robert N.	Dem	Tenn.	7	1
14th Moran, James P. Jr.	Dem	Va.	5	1
15th Hooley, Darlene	Dem	Ore.	2	*1 1
16th Lucas, Ken	Dem	Ky.	1	1
17th Holt, Rush D.	Dem	N.J.	1	1
18th Hoeffel, Joseph M.	Dem	Penn.	1	1
19th Baldwin, Tammy	Dem	Wisc.	1	1

*1: Member's first period of service on the committee.
*2: Member's second period of service on the committee.

Filled Vacancies:

Wamp on Jan. 19, 1999, ranked 19th to follow Ryun

Changes:

Majority:

Miller, Daniel	Rep	Fla.	Jan. 19, 1999 Resigned committee; no new assignment
Collins, Michael A. (Mac)	Rep	Ga.	Jan. 19, 1999 Replaced Miller

Departures from the House:

	Majority			Minority		
Lost Election to U.S. Senate	None			Weygand, Robert A.	Dem	R.I.
Lost Nomination to U.S. Senate	Franks, Robert D.	Rep	N.J.	None		
Defeated for Re-election	None			Minge, David B.	DFL	Minn.
Retired	Kasich, John R.	Rep	Ohio	None		

Departures from Committee:

Moved to Education and the Workforce	None			Rivers, Lynn N.	Dem	Mich.
Moved to Energy and Commerce	Radanovich, George P.	Rep	Cal.	None		
	Pitts, Joseph R.	Rep	Penn.			
Moved to Financial Services	Shays, Christopher H.	Rep	Conn.	Lucas, Ken	Dem	Ky.
Moved to International Relations	Smith, Nick H.	Rep	Mich.	None		
	Pitts, Joseph R.	Rep	Penn.			
Moved to Judiciary	Green, Mark	Rep	Wisc.	None		
Moved to Permanent Select Intelligence	Chambliss, Saxby	Rep	Ga.	None		
Returned to Science	Shays, Christopher H.	Rep	Conn.	None		
Moved to Ways and Means	Ryan, Paul D.	Rep	Wisc.	None		
No new assignment	Herger, Walter W.	Rep	Cal.	None		

BUDGET / 107th Congress

Service Dates of Committee Chair: Jan. 6, 2001-Jan. 3, 2003

Service Dates of Majority Members: Jan. 6, 2001-Jan. 3, 2003

Service Dates of Minority Members: Jan. 31, 2001-Jan. 3, 2003

Roster Filled: Majority with 24 members on Mar. 7, 2001; Minority with 19 members on Feb. 8, 2001

Majority					**Minority**				
			Terms in:					**Terms in:**	
Rank Name	Party	State	House	Comm.	Rank Name	Party	State	House	Comm.
Chr Nussle, James A.	Rep	Iowa	6	4	RM Spratt, John M. Jr.	Dem	S.C.	10	*2 3
2nd Sununu, John E.	Rep	N.H.	3	3	2nd McDermott, James A.	Dem	Wash.	7	3
3rd Hoekstra, Peter	Rep	Mich.	5	*2 3	3rd Thompson, Bennie	Dem	Miss.	5	4
4th Bass, Charles F.	Rep	N.H.	4	4	4th Bentsen, Kenneth E. Jr.	Dem	Tex.	4	3
5th Gutknecht, Gilbert W.	Rep	Minn.	4	3	5th Davis, Jim	Dem	Fla.	3	3
6th Hilleary, Van	Rep	Tenn.	4	3	6th Clayton, Eva M.	Dem	N.C.	6	3
7th Knollenberg, Joseph	Rep	Mich.	5	2	7th Price, David E.	Dem	N.C.	7	*2 3

8th Thornberry, William M. (Mac)	Rep	Tex.	4	2		8th Markey, Edward J.	Dem	Mass.	14	2
9th Ryun, Jim	Rep	Kans.	4	2		9th Kleczka, Gerald D.	Dem	Wisc.	10	2
10th Collins, Michael A. (Mac)	Rep	Ga.	5	2		10th Clement, Robert N.	Dem	Tenn.	8	2
11th Wamp, Zachary P.	Rep	Tenn.	4	2		11th Moran, James P. Jr.	Dem	Va.	6	2
12th Fletcher, Ernest L.	Rep	Ky.	2	2		12th Hooley, Darlene	Dem	Ore.	3	*1 2
13th Miller, Gary G.	Rep	Ky.	2	2		13th Holt, Rush D.	Dem	N.J.	2	2
14th Toomey, Patrick J.	Rep	Penn.	2	2		14th Hoeffel, Joseph M.	Dem	Penn.	2	2
15th Watkins, Wesley W.	Rep	Okla.	10	1		15th Baldwin, Tammy	Dem	Wisc.	2	2
16th Hastings, Richard (Doc)	Rep	Wash.	4	1		16th McCarthy, Carolyn	Dem	N.Y.	3	1
17th Portman, Robert J.	Rep	Ohio	5	1		17th Moore, Dennis	Dem	Kans.	2	1
18th Schrock, Edward	Rep	Va.	1	1		18th Capuano, Michael E.	Dem	Mass.	2	1
19th Culberson, John	Rep	Tex.	1	1		19th Honda, Michael M.	Dem	Cal.	1	1
20th Brown, Henry E. Jr.	Rep	S.C.	1	1						
21st Crenshaw, Ander	Rep	Fla.	1	1						
22nd Putnam, Adam H. Jr.	Rep	Fla.	1	1						
23rd Kirk, Mark S.	Rep	Ill.	1	1						
24th Granger, Kay	Rep	Tex.	3	*2 1						

*1: Member's first period of service on the committee.

*2: Member's second period of service on the committee.

Vacancies Filled:

Majority:

23rd seat filled by Kirk on Feb. 8, 2001, 24th seat filled by Granger, who ranks after LaHood, on Mar. 7, 2001

Minority:

16th through 19th seats filled by McCarthy, Moore, Capuano, and Honda on Feb. 8, 2001

Changes:

Majority:

Sununu, John E.	Rep	N.H.	Jan. 20, 2001 Re-ranked to follow after Nussle as Vice Chair
Knollenberg, Joseph	Rep	Mich.	Mar. 7, 2001 Resigned committee; no new assignment
Wamp, Zachary P.	Rep	Tenn.	Mar. 7, 2001 Resigned committee; no new assignment
Doolittle, John T.	Rep	Cal.	Mar. 7, 2001 Replaced Knollenberg, ranked after Hastings
LaHood, Ray H.	Rep	Ill.	Mar. 7, 2001 Replaced Wamp, ranked after Portman
Fletcher, Ernest L.	Rep	Ky.	Mar. 20, 2002 Resigned committee; moved to Energy and Commerce

Minority:

Markey, Edward J.	Dem	Mass.	Resigned from Budget
Matheson, James D.	Dem	Utah	Mar. 14, 2001 Replaced Markey
Capuano, Michael E.	Dem	Mass.	July 8, 2002 Resigned committee; moved to Transportation and Infrastructure; vacancy left unfilled

Departures from the House:

	Majority			Minority		
Elected to U.S. Senate	Sununu, John E.	Rep	N.H.	None		
Lost Election to U.S. Senate	None			Clement, Robert N.	Dem	Tenn.
Lost Nomination to U.S. Senate	None			Bentsen, Kenneth E. Jr.	Dem	Tex.
Lost Election for Governor	Hilleary, Van	Rep	Tenn.	None		
Retired	Watkins, Wesley W.	Rep	Okla.	Clayton, Eva M.	Dem	N.C.

Departures from Committee:

Moved to Appropriations	Culberson, John	Rep	Tex.	None		
	Kirk, Mark S.	Rep	Ill.			
Moved to Energy and Commerce	None			Davis, Jim	Dem	Fla.
Moved to Financial Services	None			McCarthy, Carolyn	Dem	N.Y.
				Matheson, James D.	Dem	Utah
Moved to Select Homeland Security	Granger, Kay	Rep	Tex.	Thompson, Bennie	Dem	Miss.
Moved to Select Intelligence	Collins, Michael A. (Mac)	Rep	Ga.	Holt, Rush D.	Dem	N.J.
Moved to Transportation and Infrastructure	None			Hoeffel, Joseph M.	Dem	Penn.
Returned to Transportation and Infrastructure	Hoekstra, Peter	Rep	Mich.	None		
	Miller, Gary G.	Rep	Ky.			
No new assignment	Bass, Charles F.	Rep	N.H.	McDermott, James A.	Dem	Wash.
	Doolittle, John T.	Rep	Cal.	Price, David E.	Dem	N.C.
	LaHood, Ray H.	Rep	Ill.	Kleczka, Gerald D.	Dem	Wisc.
				Honda, Michael M.	Dem	Cal.

BUDGET / 108th Congress

Service Dates of Committee Chair: Jan. 8, 2003-Jan. 3, 2005

Service Dates of Majority Members: Jan. 28, 2003-Jan. 3, 2005

Service Dates of Ranking Member: Jan. 8, 2003-Jan. 3, 2005

Service Dates of Minority Members: Jan. 28, 2003-Jan. 3, 2005

Roster Filled: Majority with 24 members on Feb. 11, 2003; Minority with 19 members on Feb. 5, 2003

Majority					Minority				
			Terms in:					**Terms in:**	
Rank Name	Party	State	House	Comm.	Rank Name	Party	State	House	Comm.
Chr Nussle, James A.	Rep	Iowa	7	5	RM Spratt, John M. Jr.	Dem	S.C.	11	*2 4
VCh 2nd Shays, Christopher H.	Rep	Conn.	9	*2 1	2nd Moran, James P. Jr.	Dem	Va.	7	3
3rd Gutknecht, Gilbert W.	Rep	Minn.	5	4	3rd Hooley, Darlene	Dem	Ore.	4	*1 3
4th Thornberry, William M. (Mac)	Rep	Tex.	5	3	4th Baldwin, Tammy	Dem	Wisc.	3	3
5th Ryun, Jim	Rep	Kans.	5	3	5th Moore, Dennis	Dem	Kans.	3	2
6th Toomey, Patrick J.	Rep	Penn.	3	3	6th Lewis, John R.	Dem	Ga.	9	1
7th Hastings, Richard (Doc)	Rep	Wash.	5	2	7th Neal, Richard E.	Dem	Mass.	8	1
8th Portman, Robert J.	Rep	Ohio	6	2	8th DeLauro, Rosa L.	Dem	Conn.	7	1
9th Schrock, Edward	Rep	Va.	2	2	9th Edwards, T. Chester (Chet)	Dem	Tex.	7	1
10th Brown, Henry E. Jr.	Rep	S.C.	2	2	10th Scott, Robert C.	Dem	Va.	6	*1 1
11th Crenshaw, Ander	Rep	Fla.	2	2	11th Ford, Harold E. Jr.	Dem	Tenn.	4	1
12th Putnam, Adam H. Jr.	Rep	Fla.	2	2	12th Capps, Lois	Dem	Cal.	4	1
13th Wicker, Roger F.	Rep	Miss.	5	1	13th Thompson, Michael	Dem	Cal.	3	1
14th Hulshof, Kenny	Rep	Mo.	4	1	14th Baird, Brian	Dem	Wash.	3	1
15th Tancredo, Thomas G.	Rep	Colo.	3	1	15th Cooper, James H.S.	Dem	Tenn.	7	*2 1
16th Vitter, David	Rep	La.	3	1	16th Meek, Kendrick B.	Dem	Fla.	1	1
17th Bonner, Josiah (Jo) R. Jr.	Rep	Ala.	1	1	17th Emanuel, Rahm	Dem	Ill.	1	1
18th Franks, Trent	Rep	Ariz.	1	1	18th Davis, Artur	Dem	Ala.	1	1
19th Garrett, Scott	Rep	N.J.	1	1	19th Majette, Denise L.	Dem	Ga.	1	1
20th Barrett, J. Gresham	Rep	S.C.	1	1					
21st McCotter, Thaddeus	Rep	Mich.	1	1	*1: Member's first period of service on the committee.				
22nd Diaz-Balart, Mario	Rep	Fla.	1	1	*2: Member's second period of service on the committee.				
23rd Hensarling, Jeb	Rep	Tex.	1	1					
24th Brown-Waite, Virginia	Rep	Fla.	1	1					

Vacancies Filled:

Majority:

8th seat filled by Portman, 11th seat filled by Crenshaw, 13th and 14th seats filled by Wicker and Hulshof, 16th seat filled by Vitter on Jan.31, 2003. 2nd seat filled by Shays as Vice Chairman, and 24th seat filled by Brown-Waite on Feb. 11, 2003

Minority:

19th seat filled by Majette on Feb. 5, 2003

Changes:

Majority:

Minority:

Meek, Kendrick B.	Dem	Fla.	Feb. 12, 2003 Leave of absence from committee; moved to Select Homeland Security
Kind, Ron	Dem	Wisc.	Feb. 26, 2003 Replaced Meek

Departures from the House:

	Majority			Minority		
Elected to U.S. Senate	Vitter, David	Rep	La.	None		
Lost Election to U.S. Senate	None			Majette, Denise L.	Dem	Ga.
Lost Nomination to U.S. Senate	Toomey, Patrick J.	Rep	Penn.	None		
Retired	Schrock, Edward	Rep	Va.	None		

Departures from Committee:

Became Chair on Standards of Official Conduct	Hastings, Richard (Doc)	Rep	Wash.	None		
Returned to Education and the Workforce	None			Scott, Robert C.	Dem	Va.
Moved to Energy and Commerce	None			Baldwin, Tammy	Dem	Wisc.
Moved to Government Reform	Brown-Waite, Virginia	Rep	Fla.			
Returned to Government Reform	Gutknecht, Gilbert W.	Rep	Minn.	None		
Moved to Judiciary	Franks, Trent	Rep	Ariz.	None		
Moved to Permanent Select Intelligence	Thornberry, William M. (Mac)	Rep	Tex.	None		
Moved to Resources	Brown, Henry E. Jr.	Rep	S.C.	None		
Returned to Science	None			Hooley, Darlene	Dem	Ore.
Moved to Ways and Means	None			Thompson, Michael	Dem	Cal.
				Emanuel, Rahm	Dem	Ill.
No new assignment	Tancredo, Thomas G.	Rep	Colo.	Moran, James P. Jr.	Dem	Va.
	Shays, Christopher H.	Rep	Conn.	Lewis, John R.	Dem	Ga.

BUDGET / 109th Congress

Service Dates of Committee Chair: Jan. 6, 2005-Jan. 3, 2007

Service Dates of Majority Members: Jan. 26, 2005-Jan. 3, 2007

Service Dates of Minority Members: Jan. 26, 2005-Jan. 3, 2007

Roster Filled: Majority with 21 members on Feb. 8, 2005; Minority with 17 members on Feb. 9, 2005

Majority

Rank Name	Party	State	Terms in: House	Terms in: Comm.
Chr Nussle, James A.	Rep	Iowa	8	6
2nd Portman, Robert J.	Rep	Ohio	7	3
3rd Ryun, Jim	Rep	Kans.	6	4
4th Crenshaw, Ander	Rep	Fla.	3	3
5th Putnam, Adam H. Jr.	Rep	Fla.	3	3
6th Wicker, Roger F.	Rep	Miss.	6	2
7th Hulshof, Kenny	Rep	Mo.	5	2
8th Bonner, Josiah (Jo) R. Jr.	Rep	Ala.	2	2
9th Garrett, Scott	Rep	N.J.	2	2
10th Barrett, J. Gresham	Rep	S.C.	2	2
11th McCotter, Thaddeus	Rep	Mich.	2	2
12th Diaz-Balart, Mario	Rep	Fla.	2	2
13th Hensarling, Jeb	Rep	Tex.	2	2
14th Ros-Lehtinen, Ileana	Rep	Fla.	9	1
15th Lungren, Daniel E.	Rep	Cal.	6	1
16th Sessions, Pete	Rep	Tex.	5	1
17th Ryan, Paul D.	Rep	Wisc.	4	*2 1
18th Simpson, Michael K.	Rep	Idaho	4	1
19th Bradley, Jeb	Rep	N.H.	2	1
20th McHenry, Patrick T.	Rep	N.C.	1	1
21st Mack, Connie IV	Rep	Fla.	1	1
22nd Conaway, K. Michael	Rep	Tex.	1	1

Minority

Rank Name	Party	State	Terms in: House	Terms in: Comm.
RM Spratt, John M. Jr.	Dem	S.C.	12	*2 5
2nd Moore, Dennis	Dem	Kans.	4	3
3rd Neal, Richard E.	Dem	Mass.	9	2
4th DeLauro, Rosa L.	Dem	Conn.	8	2
5th Edwards, T. Chester (Chet)	Dem	Tex.	8	2
6th Ford, Harold E. Jr.	Dem	Tenn.	5	2
7th Capps, Lois	Dem	Cal.	5	2
8th Baird, Brian	Dem	Wash.	4	2
9th Cooper, James H.S.	Dem	Tenn.	8	*2 2
10th Davis, Artur	Dem	Ala.	2	2
11th Jefferson, William J.	Dem	La.	8	1
12th Allen, Thomas H.	Dem	Me.	5	1
13th Case, Ed	Dem	Hai.	2	1
14th McKinney, Cynthia A.	Dem	Ga.	6	1
15th Cuellar, Henry	Dem	Tex.	1	1
16th Kind, Ron	Dem	Wisc.	5	2
17th Schwartz, Allyson Y.	Dem	Penn.	1	1

*2: Member's second period of service on the committee.

Vacancies Filled:

Majority:

4th seat filled by Crenshaw, 6th seat filled by Wicker, 14th seat filled by Ros-Lehtinen on Feb. 2, 2005; 18th seat filled by Simpson on Feb. 8, 2005

Minority:

16th seat filled by Kind on Feb. 2, 2005; 17th seat filled by Schwartz on Feb. 9, 2003

Changes:

Majority:

Portman, Robert J.	Rep	Ohio	April 29, 2005 Resigned the House; appointed U.S. Trade Representative
Chocola, Chris	Rep	Ind.	May 17, 2005 Replaced Portman
Ros-Lehtinen, Ileana	Rep	Fla.	Feb. 8, 2006 Resigned committee; no new assignment
Campbell, John	Rep	Cal.	Feb. 8, 2006 Replaced Ros-Lehtinen

Note: Congressional Record lists a Sep. 28, 2004, letter of resignation from Adam H. Putnam Jr., but he remained on the committee in the 109th Congress

Departures from the House:

	Majority			Minority		
Lost Election to U.S. Senate	None			Ford, Harold E. Jr.	Dem	Tenn.
Lost Nomination to U.S. Senate	None			Case, Ed	Dem	Hai.
Lost Election for Governor	Nussle, James A.	Rep	Iowa	None		
Defeated for Re-nomination	None			McKinney, Cynthia A.	Dem	Ga.
Defeated for Re-election	Ryun, Jim	Rep	Kans.	None		
	Bradley, Jeb	Rep	N.H.			
	Chocola, Chris	Rep	Ind.			

Departures from Committee:

	Majority			Minority		
Moved to Financial Services	Putnam, Adam H. Jr.	Rep	Fla.	None		
Moved to Judiciary	None			Davis, Artur	Dem	Ala.
Moved to Homeland Security	None			Cuellar, Henry	Dem	Tex.
Moved to Small Business	None			Jefferson, William J.	Dem	La.

		Cuellar, Henry	Dem	Tex.
Moved to Ways and Means	None	Davis, Artur	Dem	Ala.
		Kind, Ron	Dem	Wisc.
No new assignment	Crenshaw, Ander	Rep	Fla.	Neal, Richard E.	Dem	Mass.
	Wicker, Roger F.	Rep	Miss.
	Hulshof, Kenny	Rep	Mo.
	Sessions, Pete	Rep	Tex.

BUDGET / 110th Congress

Service Dates of Committee Chair: Jan. 4, 2007-Jan. 3, 2009

Service Dates of Majority Members: Jan. 18, 2007-Jan. 3, 2001

Service Dates of Minority Members: Jan. 18, 2007-Jan. 3, 2009

Roster Filled: Majority with 22 members on Jan. 18, 2007; Minority with 17 members on Jan. 18, 2007

Majority

			Terms in:	
Rank Name	Party	State	House	Comm.
Chr Spratt, John M. Jr.	Dem	S.C.	13	*2 6
2nd DeLauro, Rosa L.	Dem	Conn.	9	3
3rd Edwards, T. Chester (Chet)	Dem	Tex.	9	3
4th Capps, Lois	Dem	Cal.	6	3
5th Cooper, James H.S.	Dem	Tenn.	9	*2 3
6th Allen, Thomas H.	Dem	Me.	6	2
7th Schwartz, Allyson Y.	Dem	Penn.	2	2
8th Kaptur, Marcia C. (Marcy)	Dem	Ohio	13	*2 1
9th Becerra, Xavier	Dem	Cal.	8	1
10th Doggett, Lloyd A. II	Dem	Tex.	7	*2 1
11th Blumenauer, Earl	Dem	Ore.	7	1
12th Berry, R. Marion	Dem	Ark.	6	1
13th Boyd, F. Allen Jr.	Dem	Fla.	6	1
14th McGovern, James P.	Dem	Mass.	6	1
15th Sutton, Betty	Dem	Ohio	1	1
16th Andrews, Robert E.	Dem	N.J.	10	1
17th Scott, Robert C.	Dem	Va.	8	*2 1
18th Etheridge, Bobby R.	Dem	N.C.	6	1
19th Hooley, Darlene	Dem	Ore.	6	*2 1
20th Baird, Brian	Dem	Wash.	5	3
21st Moore, Dennis	Dem	Kans.	5	4
22nd Bishop, Timothy H.	Dem	N.Y.	3	1

Minority

			Terms in:	
Rank Name	Party	State	House	Comm.
RM Ryan, Paul D.	Rep	Wisc.	5	*2 2
2nd Bonner, Josiah (Jo) R. Jr.	Rep	Ala.	3	3
3rd Garrett, Scott	Rep	N.J.	3	3
4th Barrett, J. Gresham	Rep	S.C.	3	3
5th McCotter, Thaddeus	Rep	Mich.	3	3
6th Diaz-Balart, Mario	Rep	Fla.	3	3
7th Hensarling, Jeb	Rep	Tex.	3	3
8th Lungren, Daniel E.	Rep	Cal.	7	2
9th Simpson, Michael K.	Rep	Idaho	5	2
10th McHenry, Patrick T.	Rep	N.C.	2	2
11th Mack, Connie IV	Rep	Fla.	2	2
12th Conaway, K. Michael	Rep	Tex.	2	2
13th Campbell, John	Rep	Cal.	2	2
14th Tiberi, Patrick	Rep	Ohio	4	1
15th Porter, Jon C.	Rep	Nev.	3	1
16th Alexander, Rodney	Rep	La.	3	1
17th Smith, Adrian	Rep	Neb.	1	1

*2: Member's second period of service on the committee.

Changes:

Majority:

Capps, Lois	Dem	Cal.	Feb. 15, 2007 Resigned committee; no new assignment
Moore, Gwendolynne S.	Dem	Wisc.	Mar. 19, 2007 Replaced Capps
Sutton, Betty	Dem	Ohio	July 12, 2007 Resigned committee; moved to Judiciary
Tsongas, Nicola (Niki)	Dem	Mass.	Nov. 1, 2007 Replaced Sutton

Minority:

McCotter, Thaddeus	Rep	Mich.	May 15, 2007 Resigned committee; moved to Financial Services
Jordan, Jim	Rep	Ohio	Feb. 26, 2008 Replaced McCotter

Departures from the House:

	Majority			**Minority**		
Defeated for Re-election	None			Porter, Jon C.	Rep	Nev.
Lost Election to U.S. Senate	Allen, Thomas H.	Dem	Me.	None		
Retired	Hooley, Darlene	Dem	Ore.	None		

Departures from Committee:

Became RM on Standards of Official Conduct	None			Bonner, Josiah (Jo) R. Jr.	Rep	Ala.
No new assignment	Cooper, James H.S.	Dem	Tenn.	Barrett, J. Gresham	Rep	S.C.
	Baird, Brian	Dem	Wash.	Tiberi, Patrick	Rep	Ohio
	Moore, Dennis	Dem	Kans.	Smith, Adrian	Rep	Neb.

BUDGET / 111th Congress

Service Dates of Committee Chair: Jan. 6, 2009-Jan. 3, 2011

Service Dates of Majority Members: Jan. 21, 2009-Jan. 3, 2011

Service Dates of Minority Members: Jan. 9, 2009-Jan. 3, 2011

Roster Filled: Majority with 24 members, Jan. 21, 2009; Minority with 15 members, Jan. 9, 2009

Majority

Rank Name	Party	State	House	Comm.
Chr Spratt, John M. Jr.	Dem	S.C.	14	*2 7
2nd Schwartz, Allyson Y.	Dem	Penn.	3	3
3rd Kaptur, Marcia C. (Marcy)	Dem	Ohio	14	*2 2
4th Becerra, Xavier	Dem	Cal.	9	2
5th Doggett, Lloyd A. II	Dem	Tex.	8	*2 2
6th Blumenauer, Earl	Dem	Ore.	8	2
7th Berry, R. Marion	Dem	Ark.	7	2
8th Boyd, F. Allen Jr.	Dem	Fla.	7	2
9th McGovern, James P.	Dem	Mass.	7	2
10th Tsongas, Nicola (Niki)	Dem	Mass.	2	2
11th Etheridge, Bobby R.	Dem	N.C.	7	2
12th McCollum, Betty	DFL	Minn.	5	1
13th Melancon, Charles J.	Dem	La.	3	1
14th Yarmuth, John A.	Dem	Ky.	2	1
15th Andrews, Robert E.	Dem	N.J.	11	2
16th Delauro, Rosa L.	Dem	Conn.	10	4
17th Edwards, T. Chester (Chet)	Dem	Tex.	10	4
18th Scott, Robert C.	Dem	Va.	9	*2 2
19th Langevin, James R.	Dem	R.I.	5	1
20th Larsen, Richard R. (Rick)	Dem	Wash.	5	1
21st Bishop, Timothy H.	Dem	N.Y.	4	2
22nd Moore, Gwendolynne S.	Dem	Wisc.	3	2
23rd Connolly, Gerald E.	Dem	Va.	1	1
24th Schrader, Kurt	Dem	Ore.	1	1

Minority

Rank Name	Party	State	House	Comm.
RM Ryan, Paul D.	Rep	Wisc.	6	*2 3
2nd Garrett, Scott	Rep	N.J.	4	4
3rd Diaz-Balart, Mario	Rep	Fla.	4	4
4th Hensarling, Jeb	Rep	Tex.	4	4
5th Lungren, Daniel E.	Rep	Cal.	8	3
6th Simpson, Michael K.	Rep	Ida.	6	3
7th McHenry, Patrick T.	Rep	N.C.	3	3
8th Mack, Connie IV	Rep	Fla.	3	3
9th Conaway, K. Michael	Rep	Tex.	3	3
10th Campbell, John	Rep	Cal.	3	3
11th Alexander, Rodney	Rep	La.	4	2
12th Jordan, Jim	Rep	Ohio	2	2
13th Nunes, Devin	Rep	Cal.	4	1
14th Lummis, Cynthia M.	Rep	Wyo.	1	1
15th Austria, Steve	Rep	Ohio	1	1

*2: Member's second period of service on the committee.

Changes:

Majority

Melancon, Charles J.	Dem	La.	Mar. 3, 2010 Resigned committee; no new assignment
Moore, Dennis	Dem	Kans.	Mar. 10, 2010 Replaced Melancon

Minority

Lungren, Daniel E.	Rep	Cal.	Jan. 16, 2009 Resigned committee; became Ranking Member on House Administration
Alexander, Rodney	Rep	La.	Jan. 21, 2009 Resigned committee; no new assignment
Aderholt, Robert	Rep	Ala.	Jan. 22, 2009 Replaced Lungren, ranked after Nunes
Harper, Gregg	Rep	Miss.	Jan. 22, 2009 Replaced Alexander
Conaway, K. Michael	Rep	Tex.	Jan. 26, 2009 Resigned committee; moved to Select Intelligence
Latta, Robert E.	Rep	Ohio	Mar. 24, 2009 Replaced Conaway
Latta, Robert E.	Rep	Ohio	Mar. 25, 2010 Resigned committee; moved to Energy and Commerce

District of Columbia

House Committee on the District of Columbia, 103rd Congress (1993-1995)

BACKGROUND

Organizational History: The House District Committee was created on January 27, 1808, in a motion introduced by Rep. Philip B. Key (Fed.-Md.), the uncle of Francis Scott Key, the author of "The Star-Spangled Banner." Its name and jurisdiction remained relatively unchanged for almost 190 years.

The District Committee declined steadily in the 1970s as it became less relevant in the House. The committee had overseen the municipal affairs of Washington, D.C., including such very local matters as public health and safety, sales of intoxicating liquor, the municipal code, and St. Elizabeth's Hospital, over which it gained jurisdictional control in 1975 from the Education and Labor Committee. Much of the committee's work was sharply curtailed after "home rule" advocates convinced Congress to grant the District of Columbia limited self-government in 1973. Although its last set of majority members were committed to the passage of a constitutional amendment to make the District the nation's fifty-first state, the committee itself passed into history at the start of the Republican-controlled 104th Congress in 1995.

Its demise as a standing committee of the House was announced in "Changes in Committee System," from H. Res. 6, Section 202 (a), the Committees and Their Jurisdiction, January 4, 1995.

(d) In clause 8 of rule XXIV, strike 'the Committee on the District of Columbia' through the end of the sentence and insert: 'the Committee on Government Reform and Oversight, be set apart for the consideration of such business relating to the District of Columbia as may be presented by said committee.'

Although the District committee's functions were relocated to the renamed Committee on Government Reform and Oversight, only one of its ten continuing members moved to that committee while seven of its continuing members received no new assignment in the 104th Congress.

Membership: The original size of the District of Columbia Committee was seven. The committee grew steadily but not dramatically. By the time of the 1946 Reorganization Act, it had twenty-five members. The committee remained at this size until 1975 when it was reduced to twenty-four. Its size dropped to fourteen in 1979 and by 1981, its size stabilized at twelve representatives. In the 103rd Congress (1993-1995), its last one, the committee had shrunk to eleven members. The District of Columbia Committee faced the steepest membership drop among standing committees during the modern era.

The committee was generally used to locate new members whose re-election prospects were marginal. At a glance, the members who seemed to want assignment to the committee were from the Maryland and Northern Virginia suburbs of Washington whose constituents had employment in the District. Because of the racial composition of the District, Southern Democrats with segregationist pasts would also seek membership on the committee and maintained tight control over the

finances of the District. That would change with the establishment of home rule for the District in 1973. At that time, the District Committee became more sympathetic to the wishes of the District's overwhelming African-American population. This led to more African-American members seeking assignment to the committee as conservative southerners began to leave the committee.

Committee Leaders: The first post-reorganization chair of the District of Columbia Committee was Everett McKinley Dirksen (Rep-Ill.), who had been its ranking Republican since 1935, but chaired the committee only in the 80th Congress and then retired because of eye problems. Four years later, Dirksen would return to Congress as a U.S. senator. For many years before "home rule" was granted in 1973, southern conservatives dominated the committee, maintaining strict financial control of the District and segregating its predominantly black population. This was especially true of John L. McMillan (Dem-S.C.) who chaired the District committee in twelve of the fourteen Congresses from 1946 to 1973, a tenure that tied for the longest chairmanship tenure recorded for any of the House standing committees of the modern Congress. Under his leadership, the committee regularly blocked a succession of bills to grant self-government to D.C. residents.

While McMillan remained as chair, a number of Republicans served as ranking member including Sidney E. Simpson (Rep-Ill.) who served as ranking member with one stint as chair in the 83rd Congress until his death in 1958. James C. Auchincloss (Rep-N.J.) followed Simpson in 1959, relinquishing the chair in 1963 to Joel T. Broyhill (Rep-Va.) and then resuming the post in 1964 when Broyhill moved to Ways and Means.

Auchincloss' retirement in 1965 moved Ancher Nelsen (Rep-Minn.) into the ranking member slot where he served until his 1974 resignation from the House.

The panel's composition changed dramatically following the 1972 elections. McMillan was defeated for renomination and five other southern Democrats on the committee either lost their bids for re-election or retired. In 1973, the new chair was Charles C. Diggs Jr. (Dem-Mich.), the first African-American to chair the panel. That year the committee finally approved a home rule bill, a compromise version of which later became law. Gilbert Gude (Rep-Md.) was the first ranking member to serve with Diggs and upon his retirement in 1975, he was succeeded by Stewart B. McKinney (Rep-Conn.), who held the ranking member slot until his death in 1987 when Stanford E. Parris (Rep-Va.) replaced him. Thomas J. Bliley (Dem-Va.) became its next (and last) ranking member upon Parris's 1990 defeat.

Upon Diggs' resignation from the chair in 1979 owing to legal and ethical difficulties, Ronald V. Dellums (Dem-Cal.) became chair. Dellums held the post until 1993 when he became chair of Armed Services upon the resignation of Les Aspin (Dem-Wisc.). Fortney H. (Pete) Stark (Dem-Cal.) succeeded Dellums as chair and served until the committee's termination at the end of the 103rd Congress.

Notable Members: As the House's least well-regarded committee, notable Members tended to be few. One curious irony of the committee's history was that in the 80th Congress (1947-1949), its chair was Everett McKinley Dirksen (Rep-Ill.) who would later serve as Senate Minority Leader during the 1961-1963 presidency of John F. Kennedy (Dem-Mass.) and who spent six years serving on the District committee (1947-1953), largely due to his feud with long-time House leader John McCormack (Dem-Mass.). The only party leader with service on the District Committee was Majority Whip William L. Gray III of Philadelphia, the House's first elected African-American leader, and the only Cabinet members with experience on the committee were Brock Adams (Dem-Wash.), Jimmy Carter's Secretary of Transportation; Lynn M. Martin (Rep-Ill.), George H.W. Bush's Secretary of Labor; and Les Aspin (Dem-Wisc.), Bill Clinton's Secretary of Defense.

Only six House members served on the District committee prior to their Senate careers: two Democrats—John F. Kennedy and Brock Adams and four Republicans—Dirksen, Steven D. Symms of Idaho, and two Marylanders: J. Glenn Beall Sr. and Charles McC. Mathias Jr. One ex-senator served on the post-1947 committee after losing his Senate seat—Republican James W. Wadsworth Jr. of New York.

Only five governors served on the District committee, of whom the best-known was Democrat John Bell Williams of Mississippi, who was removed from the Democratic Caucus in 1965 for backing Barry Goldwater's 1964 presidential election bid. Other Democrats included Arthur A. Link of North Dakota, Ray Blanton of Tennessee, and James J. Florio of New Jersey. The lone Republican governor with service on the committee, Vernon W. Thompson of Wisconsin, did so after he left the state house.

Selected References

Bullock, Charles S. III, "Freshman Committee Assignments and Re-election in the United States House of Representatives," *American Political Science Review*, 66 (September, 1972), 996-1007.

Harris, Charles W., "Federal and Local Interests in the Nation's Capitol," *Public Budgeting and Finance,* 9 (1989), 66-82.

Schamel, Charles E. et al., "Records of the District of Columbia Committee," *Guide to the Records of the United States House of Representatives at the National Archives: 1789-1989 Bicentennial Edition* (Washington, D.C.: National Archives and Records Administration,1989), 111-122.

Weaver, R. Kent and Charles W. Harris, "Who's in Charge Here: Congress and the Nation's Capital," *The Brookings Review,* 7 (1989), 39-45.

RESPONSIBILITIES, JURISDICTIONAL CHANGES, AND SUBCOMMITTEES

Jurisdiction, 80th Congress (1947-1949)

Established by the Legislative Reorganization Act of 1946:

[Section 121.(1)(f)] Committee on the District of Columbia
(1) All measures relating to the municipal affairs of the District of Columbia in general, other than appropriations therefor, including—
(2) Public health and safety, sanitation, and quarantine regulations.
(3) Regulation of sale of intoxicating liquors.
(4) Adulteration of food and drugs.
(5) Taxes and tax sales.
(6) Insurance, executors, administrators, wills, and divorce.
(7) Municipal and juvenile courts.
(8) Incorporation and organization of societies.
(9) Municipal code and amendments to the criminal and corporation laws.

Jurisdiction, 103rd Congress (1993-1995)

From the Rules of the House of Representatives, 103rd Congress (House Document 102-405)

[Rule X.1.(f)] Committee on the District of Columbia
(1) All measures relating to the municipal affairs of the District of Columbia in general, other than appropriations therefor, including—
(2) Adulteration of foods and drugs.
(3) Incorporation and organization of societies.
(4) Insurance, executors, administrators, wills, and divorce.
(5) Municipal code and amendments to the criminal and corporation laws.
(6) Municipal and juvenile courts.
(7) Public health and safety, sanitation, and quarantine regulations.
(8) Regulation of sale of intoxicating liquors.
(9) Taxes and tax sales.
(10) Saint Elizabeth's Hospital.

NAMES OF DISTRICT OF COLUMBIA SUBCOMMITTEES FROM THE *CONGRESSIONAL DIRECTORY*

Fiscal Affairs and Health, 103

Government Operations and Metropolitan Affairs, 103

Judiciary and Education, 103

MEMBERSHIP ROSTER, 103rd Congress, 1993-1995

DISTRICT OF COLUMBIA / 103rd Congress

Service Dates of Committee Chair: Jan. 27, 1993-Jan. 3, 1995

Service Dates of Majority Members: Feb. 18, 1993-Jan. 3, 1995

Service Dates of Minority Members: Jan. 5, 1993-Jan. 3, 1995

Roster Filled: Majority with 7 of 8 seats filled, Feb. 18, 1993; Minority with 4 of 6 seats filled, Feb. 4, 1993

Majority

Rank Name	Party	State	Terms in: House	Terms in: Comm.
Chr Stark, Fortney H. (Pete)	Dem	Cal.	11	*2 9
2nd Wheat, Alan D.	Dem	Mo.	6	5
3rd McDermott, James A.	Dem	Wash.	3	4
4th Norton, Eleanor Holmes	Dem	D.C.	2	2
5th Levin, Sander M.	Dem	Mich.	6	2
6th Lewis, John R.	Dem	Ga.	4	1
7th Jefferson, William J.	Dem	La.	2	1

Minority

Rank Name	Party	State	Terms in: House	Terms in: Comm.
RM Bliley, Thomas J. Jr.	Rep	Va.	7	7
2nd Rohrabacher, Dana	Rep	Cal.	3	3
3rd Saxton, H. James	Rep	N.J.	6	1
4th Ballenger, Cass	Rep	N.C.	5	1

*2: Member's second period of service on the committee.

Note: Delegate Eleanor Holmes Norton (Dem-D.C.) was allowed to accrue committee seniority, but not included in the party ratio.

Vacancies Filled:
  Minority:
    4th seat by Ballenger on Feb. 4, 1993

Changes:
  Majority:

Levin, Sander M.	Dem	Mich.	Feb. 22, 1993 Resigned committee; no new assignment
Dellums, Ronald V.	Dem	Cal.	Apr. 22, 1993 Replaced Levin; ranked 2nd

Departures from the House:

	Majority			Minority
Lost Election to U.S. Senate	Wheat, Alan D.	Dem	Mo.	None

Departures from Committee:

	Majority			Minority		
Moved to Government Reform and Oversight	Norton, Eleanor Holmes	D.C. Dem		None		
Moved to House Oversight	Jefferson, William J.	Dem	La.	None		
Moved to National Security	Jefferson, William J.	Dem	La.	None		
Moved to Resources	None			Saxton, H. James	Rep	N.J.
No new assignment	Stark, Fortney H. (Pete)	Dem	Cal.	Bliley, Thomas J. Jr.	Rep	Va.
	McDermott, James A.	Dem	Wash.	Rohrabacher, Dana	Rep	Cal.
	Lewis, John R.	Dem	Ga.	Ballenger, Cass	Rep	N.C.
	Dellums, Ronald V.	Dem	Cal.			

Education and Labor

House Committee on Education and Labor, 103rd Congress (1993-1995)

Committee on Economic and Educational Opportunities, 104th Congress (1995-1997)

Committee on Education and the Workforce, 105th-109th Congresses (1997-2007)

Committee on Education and Labor, 110th-111th Congresses (2007-2011)

BACKGROUND

Organizational History: The House first established a standing committee on Education and Labor on March 21, 1867, in the 40th Congress on motion H.J. Res. 83 presented by Rep. (and later president) James A. Garfield (Rep-Ohio). Its initial chair was Jehu Baker (Rep-Ill.). In December, 1883, the Labor Committee was made a separate entity by H.J. Res. 154 in the 48th Congress with James H. Hopkins (Dem-Penn.) as its initial chair. This division of two committees continued for the next sixty-three years until the reuniting of the panels in the 1946 Legislative Reorganization Act.

The Education and Labor committee is responsible for many of the programs established by the federal government to attack poverty and other social problems. Its jurisdiction includes federal spending for education and job training, as well as a wide range of efforts to aid children, the poor, and the disabled.

With this mandate, it had its greatest successes during the presidency of Lyndon B. Johnson in the 1960's, when Johnson was pushing his Great Society legislative program. Among key pieces of legislation that occurred at that time were the Economic Opportunity Act of 1964 (P.L. 88-452; 78 Stat. 508), the Elementary and Secondary Education Act of 1965 (P.L. 89-10, 79 Stat. 27) that for the first time provided federal financial support for locally controlled elementary and secondary education; the Higher Education Act of 1965 (P.L. 89-329, 70 Stat. 1219), and the Fair Labor Standards Act Amendments of 1966 (P.L. 89-601, 80 Stat. 830). In later years the committee greatly expanded financial aid to college students, oversaw in-school food programs for children, set up programs for health and safety in the workplace, and banned discrimination against the disabled.

It is a committee whose Democrats have historically been social liberals and supporters of organized labor while its Republicans have been resistant to these pressures. This can be expected in view of the committee's jurisdiction over the mediation and arbitration of labor disputes, wages and hours legislation, labor statistics and standards, convict labor, the welfare of miners, and vocational rehabilitation. However, its influence in the House diminished greatly as budget restrictions in the 1980s and 1990s and a conservative political climate in the nation limited opportunities to pass new legislation in the mold of the 1960s.

The Republican takeover in 1995 led to the committee being renamed Economic and Educational Opportunities in tune with Speaker Newt Gingrich's concept of an "opportunity society." That title lasted only a single Congress, and in 1997,

the committee was renamed the Committee on Education and the Workforce. It was the Democratic restoration of 2007 that led the committee to resume its prior designation as the Committee on Education and Labor.

The most controversial educational policy to move through Congress in recent years was the well-supported No Child Left Behind Act of 2001 (NCLB). Initiated by the administration of President George W. Bush, the act intended to emphasize the testing of schoolchildren on regular intervals in various subject matters with a primary focus on math and reading skills. It was hoped that regular testing and the ranking of schools on their relative success would increase the accountability of the schools to the parents of those children. In spite of relatively evenly divided congressional parties in the 107th Congress (2001-2003), the bill was easily passed in the House 384 to 45 and was passed overwhelmingly in the Senate 91 to 3. It was seen by the George W. Bush Administration as its greatest legislative achievement.

However, problems regarding the implementation of NCLB and the severity of its financial punishments on school districts seen as lagging behind in these performance indicators has led many educators to urge a major overhaul of the program. In the 111th Congress, the Obama Administration has asked the House's Education and Labor Committee to hammer out a legislative policy that will maintain some of the key testing requirements for accountability while lessening the financial penalties levied against school districts whose scores have yet to meet the standards.

Membership: There were nine members on the original Education and Labor Committee in 1867. By 1946 there were twenty-one members on each of the two committees. Only fourteen holdovers were among the twenty-five members on the first post-reorganization Education and Labor Committee, seven from Labor, four from Education, and three members who served on both committees. The committee had its first thirty-member Congress in 1955 and its first forty-member Congress in 1991. In the 108th Congress (2003-2005), the committee reached fifty members but dropped to forty-nine in the last three Congresses (2005-2011).

In the nine Congresses from 1993 to 2011, the committee's mean membership size of 47.33 located Education and Labor in ninth place among the nineteen continuing committees, and the committee's mean seniority of 5.35 terms for its members by Congress lodged it in eighth place. Its inter-Congress member retention rate also places it in the middle ranks with its 85.89 percent rate placing it in a two-way tie for ninth place with the Agriculture Committee.

Committee Leaders: Education and Labor's first modern-era Republican chair in the 80th Congress was Fred A. Hartley (Rep-W.Va.), a long-serving member of the Labor Committee and the coauthor of the Taft-Hartley Labor-Management Relations Act (P.L. 80-101) which limited organized labor's ability to strike. He retired in 1949 and was succeeded as the committee's senior Republican by Samuel K. McConnell (Rep-Penn.) who would hold that designation until his resignation in 1957. McConnell would be the committee's chair in the 83rd Congress (1953-1955), the last Republican Congress for the next forty years. Following McConnell would be a number of short term ranking members including Ralph W. Gwinn (Rep-N.Y.), 1957-1959; Carroll D. Kearns (Rep-Penn.), 1959-1963; Peter H.B. Frelinghuysen (Rep-N.J.), 1963-1965; and William H. Ayres (Rep-Ohio), 1965-1971.

Among the Democrats, John Lesinski (Dem-Mich.) also came from the Labor Committee and served as the senior Democrat and as chair of the committee until his death in 1950. Lesinski was followed by conservative Democrat Graham A. Barden (Dem-N.C.), the last chair of the stand-alone Education Committee who chaired Education and Labor. Barden chaired the committee for nine of the next eleven years until his retirement in 1961.

Succeeding Barden in 1961 was the committee's most famous chair, the flamboyant and controversial New York City Democrat, the Reverend Adam Clayton Powell Jr. Powell lost a libel suit in New York and was accused of placing one of his wives on the committee's payroll even though she was in Puerto Rico. Powell was stripped of his chairmanship of the committee by action of the Democratic Caucus in 1967. His legal troubles continued to mount and he was excluded from the House pursuant to H.Res 278 on February 20, 1967. Powell sued the House and the Supreme Court ruled that Congress could not deny a seat to an elected individual who met the requirements stipulated in the Constitution in *Powell v. McCormack,* 395 U.S. 486 (1969). Powell was seated in 1969 but was not returned to his chairmanship and was defeated for re-nomination in 1970 by Charles Rangel (Dem-N.Y.)

Carl D. Perkins (Dem-Ky.) first became chair upon the demotion of Powell and served in that post until his death on August 3, 1984. Serving with Perkins as ranking members were three Republicans: Albert H. Quie (Rep-Minn.), 1971-1979; John M. Ashbrook (Rep-Ohio), 1979-1982; and John N. Erlenborn (Rep-Ill.), 1982-1985. Perkins was replaced in 1984 by Augustus P. Hawkins (Dem-Cal.), the committee's second African-American chair who resigned the chairmanship of House Administration. Hawkins was coauthor of the ill-fated Humphrey-Hawkins bill of the mid-1970s and Hawkins chaired Education and Labor until his retirement in 1991. Serving with Hawkins as ranking member was James M. Jeffords (Rep-Vt.), 1985-1989, who was elected to the Senate, and William F. Goodling (Rep-Penn.), the senior Republican on the committee from 1989 until his retirement in 2001.

While William D. Ford (Dem-Mich) only chaired the committee in the 103rd Congress (1993-1995), Goodling, the committee's first Republican chair in forty years, got to chair the committee for two of its name changes in three Congresses, 1995-2001. John H. Boehner (Rep-Ohio) succeeded Goodling in 2001 and chaired the committee until 2006 and his election as Majority Leader. William L. Clay Sr. (Dem-Mo.) served as ranking member during Goodling's chairmanship until 2001 and was replaced by George Miller (Dem-Cal.). Miller became

chair in 2007 and remains in that post while Boehner's successor Howard P. (Buck) McKeon (Rep-Cal.) left to become ranking member on Armed Services in 2009. Succeeding McKeon as ranking member was John Kline (Rep-Minn.), the committee's tenth-ranked Republican.

Party Leaders: Five party leaders served on the Education Committee during their House careers including Speaker of the House Carl Albert (Dem-Okla.), Majority Leaders Richard K. Armey (Rep-Texas) and John Boehner (Rep-Ohio), Minority Leader John Rhodes (Rep-Ariz.), and Majority Whip John Brademas (Dem-Ind.).

Notable Members: Five members of Education and Labor received modern-era major party presidential and vice presidential nominations, including two junior members who served together in the 80th and 81st Congresses, 1947-1951—John F. Kennedy (Dem-Mass.) and Richard M. Nixon (Rep-Cal.)—who would face one another in the twentieth century's closest presidential contest. While both men would be elected president, that was not the case for the three others with committee experience. George S. McGovern (Dem-S.D.), the Democrats' 1972 presidential nominee; Jack Kemp (Rep-N.Y.), the Republicans' 1996 vice presidential nominee; and John S. McCain III (Rep-Ariz.), the Republicans' 2008 presidential nominee, would all be unsuccessful. Stewart Udall (Dem-Ariz.) who served as Secretary of the Interior in both the Kennedy and Johnson Administrations, Bill Richardson (Dem-N.M.), Bill Clinton's third Secretary of Energy, and Hilda L. Solis, Barack Obama's Secretary of Labor, were the only three alumni of the committee to serve in the Cabinet.

Twenty-one post-1947 members—six Democrats and fifteen Republicans of the House Education Committee served prior to their elections to the U.S. Senate and one served in the House after leaving the Senate—Democrat Hugh B. Mitchell of Washington State. The six House Democrats were John F. Kennedy of Massachusetts, Lee Metcalf of Montana, George S. McGovern of South Dakota, William Hathaway of Maine, Paul M. Simon of Illinois, and John F. Reed of Rhode Island.

The thirteen elected Republicans were Richard M. Nixon of California, Charles E. Potter of Michigan, Thruston B. Morton of Kentucky, Edward J. Gurney of Florida, Lindsey O. Graham and James W. DeMint of South Carolina, Robert A. Taft Jr. of Ohio, Larry L. Pressler of South Dakota, Larry E. Craig of Idaho, James M. Jeffords of Vermont, Y. Timothy Hutchinson of Arkansas, James M. Talent of Missouri, and Johnny Isakson of Georgia.

Two Republican members of the Education and Labor committee were appointed to the Senate and both replaced Democrats. Robert P. Griffin of Michigan replaced the deceased Patrick V. McNamara in 1966 while Charles E. Goodell of New York was appointed in 1968 to fill the seat of the martyred Robert F. Kennedy (Dem-N.Y.), brother of President John F. Kennedy and former Attorney General. Griffin was elected in his own right; Goodell was not. He lost a three-way contest in 1970 to Independent James Buckley, brother of long-time conservative editor William F. Buckley. Goodell's son Roger is presently the Commissioner of the National Football League.

The nine governors with prior Education Committee service include five Democrats—Ella T. Grasso of Connecticut, the first woman elected to the office without a preceding family member, Hugh L. Carey of New York, Bill Richardson of New Mexico, Ted Strickland of Ohio, and Robert E. Wise of

West Virginia; and four Republicans—Ernest L. Fletcher of Kentucky, Albert H. Quie of Minnesota, John R. McKernan of Maine, and Bobby Jindal of Louisiana. Education committee member Republican Michael N. Castle of Delaware is one of a number of small-state governors elected to the U.S. House after leaving the governorship.

Selected References

Eidenburg, Eugene and Roy D. Morey, *An Act of Congress: The Legislative Process and the Making of Education Policy,* (New York: W.W. Norton, 1969).

Feig, Douglas G., "Partisanship and Integration in Two House Committees: Ways and Means and Education and Labor," *Western Political Quarterly,* 34 (September, 1981), 426-437.

Fenno, Richard F. Jr., *Congressmen in Committees* (Boston: Little, Brown, 1973).

Fenno, Richard F. Jr. "The House Committee on Education and Labor," in Frank J. Munger and Richard F. Fenno Jr., *National Politics and Federal Aid to Education* (Syracuse, N.Y.: Syracuse University Press, 1962), 109-124.

Hall, Richard F., "Participation and Purpose in Committee Decision-Making," *American Political Science Review,* 81 (1987), 105-121.

Parker, Glenn R. and Suzanne L. Parker, *Factions in House Committees* (Knoxville: University of Tennessee Press, 1985).

Price, H. Douglas, "Schools, Scholarships, and Congressmen: The Kennedy Aid-to-Education Program," in Alan F. Westin, ed., *The Centers of Power: 3 Cases in American National Government* (New York: Harcourt, Brace, and World, 1964), 53-105.

Reeves, Andre E., *Congressional Committee Chairmen: Three Who Made an Evolution* (Lexington: University of Kentucky Press, 1993).

Schamel, Charles E. et al., "Records of the Committees on Education and Labor," *Guide to the Records of the United States House of Representatives at the National Archives: 1789-1989 Bicentennial Edition* (Washington, D.C.: National Archives and Records Administration,1989), 123-132.

Unekis, Joseph K. and Leroy N. Rieselbach, *Congressional Committee Politics: Continuity and Change* (New York: Praeger, 1984).

RESPONSIBILITIES, JURISDICTIONAL CHANGES, AND SUBCOMMITTEES

EDUCATION AND LABOR

Jurisdiction, 80th Congress (1947-1949)

Established by the Legislative Reorganization Act of 1946:

[Section 121.(1)(g)] Committee on Education and Labor
  (1) Measures relating to education or labor generally.
  (2) Mediation and arbitration of labor disputes.
  (3) Wages and hours of labor.
  (4) Convict labor and the entry of goods made by convicts into interstate commerce.
  (5) Regulation or prevention of importation of foreign laborers under contract.
  (6) Child labor.
  (7) Labor statistics.
  (8) Labor standards.
  (9) School-lunch program.
  (10) Vocational rehabilitation.
  (11) United States Employees' Compensation Commission.
  (12) Columbia Institution for the Deaf, Dumb, and Blind; Howard University; Freedmen's Hospital; and Saint Elizabeth's Hospital.
  (13) Welfare of miners.

EDUCATION AND LABOR

Jurisdiction, 103rd Congress (1993-1995)

From the Rules of the House of Representatives, 103rd Congress (House Document 102-405)

[Rule X. 1. (g)] Committee on Education and Labor
  (1) Measures relating to education or labor generally.
  (2) Child labor.
  (3) Columbia Institution for the Deaf, Dumb, and Blind; Howard University; Freedmen's Hospital.
  (4) Convict labor and the entry of goods made by convicts into interstate commerce.
  (5) Labor standards.
  (6) Labor statistics.

(7) Mediation and arbitration of labor disputes.
(8) Regulation or prevention of importation of foreign laborers under contract.
(9) Food programs for children in schools.
(10) United States Employees' Compensation Commission.
(11) Vocational rehabilitation.
(12) Wages and hours of labor.
(13) Welfare of miners.
(14) Work incentive programs.

In addition to its legislative jurisdiction under the preceding provisions of this paragraph (and its general oversight function under clause 2(b)(1)), the committee shall have the special oversight function provided for in clause 3(c) with respect to domestic educational programs and institutions, and programs of student assistance, which are within the jurisdiction of other committees.

[Rule X. 3.(c)] Special Oversight

The Committee on Education and Labor shall have the function of reviewing, studying, and coordinating, on a continuing basis, all laws, programs, and Government activities dealing with or involving domestic educational programs and institutions, and programs of student assistance, which are within the jurisdiction of other committees.

ECONOMIC AND EDUCATIONAL OPPORTUNITIES

Education and Labor was renamed the Committee on Economic and Educational Opportunities on January 4, 1995.

Jurisdiction, 104th Congress (1995-1997) Changes in Committee System

From H. Res. 6, Section 202 (a), the Committees and Their Jurisdiction, January 4, 1995.

[Rule X.1. (f)] Committee on Economic and Educational Opportunities.
(1) Child labor.
(2) Columbia Institution for the Deaf, Dumb, and Blind; Howard University; Freedmen's Hospital.
(3) Convict labor and the entry of goods made by convicts into interstate commerce.
(4) Food programs for children in schools.
(5) Labor standards and statistics.
(6) Measures relating to education or labor generally.
(7) Mediation and arbitration of labor disputes.
(8) Regulation or prevention of importation of foreign laborers under contract.
(9) United States Employees' Compensation Commission.
(10) Vocational rehabilitation.
(11) Wages and hours of labor.
(12) Welfare of miners.
(13) Work incentive programs.

In addition to its legislative jurisdiction under the preceding provisions of this paragraph (and its general oversight function under clause 2(b)(1)), the committee shall have the special oversight function provided for in clause 3(c) with respect to domestic educational programs and institutions, and programs of student assistance, which are within the jurisdiction of other committees.

EDUCATION AND THE WORKFORCE

Economic and Educational Opportunities was renamed the Committee on Education and the Workforce on January 7, 1997.

EDUCATION AND LABOR

Education and the Workforce was redesignated the Committee on Education and Labor on January 4, 2007.

Jurisdiction, 111th Congress (2009-2011)

From the Rules of the House of Representatives (as revised to June 16, 2009, H.Doc. 110-162):

[Rule X.1.(e)] Committee on Education and Labor
(1) Child labor.
(2) Gallaudet University and Howard University and Hospital.

(3) Convict labor and the entry of goods made by convicts into interstate commerce.
(4) Food programs for children in schools.
(5) Labor standards and statistics.
(6) Education or labor generally.
(7) Mediation and arbitration of labor disputes.
(8) Regulation or prevention of importation of foreign laborers under contract.
(9) Workers' compensation.
(10) Vocational rehabilitation.
(11) Wages and hours of labor.
(12) Welfare of miners.
(13) Work incentive programs.

[Rule X.3.(d)] Special Oversight Function

The Committee on Education and Labor shall review, study, and coordinate on a continuing basis laws, programs, and Government activities relating to domestic educational programs and institutions and programs of student assistance within the jurisdiction of other committees.

NAMES OF EDUCATION AND LABOR SUBCOMMITTEES FROM THE *CONGRESSIONAL DIRECTORY*

Education and Labor, 103rd Congress
Elementary, Secondary and Vocational Education, 103 Human Resources, 103
Labor-Management Issues, 103 Labor Standards, Occupational Health and Safety, 103
Postsecondary Education and Training, 103 Select Education and Civil Rights, 103

Economic and Educational Opportunities, 104th Congress
Early Childhood, Youth and Families, 104 Employer-Employee Relations, 104
Oversight and Investigations, 104 Postsecondary Education, Training, and Life-Long Learning, 104
Workforce Protections, 104

Education and the Workforce, 105th-109th Congresses
Early Childhood, Youth and Families, 105, 106 Education Reform, 107, 108, 109
Employer-Employee Relations, 105, 106, 107, 108, 109 Oversight and Investigations, 105, 106
Postsecondary Education, Training, and Life-Long Learning, 105, 106
Workforce Protections, 105, 106, 107, 108, 109 Select Education, 107, 108. 109
21st Century Competitiveness, 107, 108, 109

Education and Labor, 110th-111th Congresses
Early Childhood, Elementary and Secondary Education, 110, 111
Health, Employment, Labor, and Pensions, 110, 111
Healthy Families, 110
Healthy Families and Communities, 111
Higher Education, Lifelong Learning, and Competitiveness, 110, 111
Workforce Protections, 110, 111

MEMBERSHIP ROSTERS, 103rd-111th Congresses, 1993-2011

EDUCATION AND LABOR / 103rd Congress

Service Dates of Committee Chair: Jan. 5, 1993-Jan. 3, 1995

Service Dates of Majority Members: Jan. 5, 1993-Jan. 3, 1995

Service Dates of Minority Members: Jan. 5, 1993-Jan. 3, 1995

Roster Filled: Majority with 28 members, Apr. 22, 1993; Minority with 15 members, Jan. 5, 1993

| | Majority | | | | | | Minority | | | | |
| | | | | Terms in: | | | | | | Terms in: | |
Rank Name	Party	State	House	Comm.		Rank Name	Party	State	House	Comm.	
Chr Ford, William D.	Dem	Mich.	15	15		RM Goodling, William F.	Rep	Penn.	10	10	
2nd Clay, William L. Sr.	Dem	Mo.	13	13		2nd Petri, Thomas E.	Rep	Wisc.	8	8	
3rd Miller, George	Dem	Cal.	10	*2 3		3rd Roukema, Margaret S.	Rep	N.J.	7	7	
4th Murphy, Austin J.	Dem	Penn.	9	9		4th Gunderson, Steven C.	Rep	Wisc.	7	7	

5th Kildee, Dale E.	Dem	Mich.	9	9
6th Williams, J. Patrick	Dem	Mont.	8	8
7th Martinez, Matthew G.	Dem	Cal.	7	7
8th Owens, Major R.	Dem	N.Y.	6	6
9th Sawyer, Thomas C.	Dem	Ohio	4	4
10th Payne, Donald M.	Dem	N.J.	3	3
11th Unsoeld, Jolene	Dem	Wash.	3	3
12th Mink, Patsy T.	Dem	Hai.	9	*2 3
13th Andrews, Robert E.	Dem	N.J.	3	2
14th Reed, John F.	Dem	R.I.	2	2
15th Roemer, Timothy J.	Dem	Ind.	2	2
16th Engel, Eliot L.	Dem	N.Y.	3	1
17th Becerra, Xavier	Dem	Cal.	1	1
18th Scott, Robert C.	Dem	Va.	1	*1 1
19th Green, R. Eugene (Gene)	Dem	Tex.	1	1
20th Woolsey, Lynn C.	Dem	Cal.	1	1
21st Romero-Barceló, Carlos A.	Dem	P.R.	1	1
22nd Klink, Ronald	Dem	Penn.	1	1
23rd English, Karan	Dem	Ariz.	1	1
24th Strickland, Ted	Dem	Ohio	1	1
25th de Lugo, Ron	Dem	V.I.	10	2
26th Faleomavaega, Eni F.H.	Dem	Am.S.	3	1
27th Baesler, H. Scott (Scotty)	Dem	Ky.	1	1
28th Underwood, Robert A.	Dem	Guam	1	1

5th Armey, Richard K.	Rep	Tex.	5	5
6th Fawell, Harris W.	Rep	Ill.	5	5
7th Henry, Paul B.	Rep	Mich.	5	5
8th Ballenger, Cass	Rep	N.C.	4	4
9th Molinari, Susan	Rep	N.Y.	3	2
10th Barrett, William E.	Rep	Neb.	2	2
11th Boehner, John A.	Rep	Ohio	2	*1 2
12th Cunningham, Randall (Duke)	Rep	Cal.	2	2
13th Hoekstra, Peter	Rep	Mich.	1	*1 1
14th McKeon, Howard P. (Buck)	Rep	Cal.	1	1
15th Miller, Daniel	Rep	Fla.	1	1

*1: Member's first period of service on the committee.

*2: Member's second period of service on the committee.

Notes: Territorial Delegates Ron de Lugo (Dem-V.I.), Eni F.H. Faleomavaega (Dem-Am.S.), Robert A. Underwood (Dem-Guam) and Resident Commissioner Carlos A. Romero-Barceló (Dem-P.R) were allowed to accrue committee seniority but were not included in the party ratio.

Vacancies Filled:

Majority:

25th through 27th seats by de Lugo, Faleomavaega, and Baesler on Jan. 21, 1993. 28th seat by Underwood on Apr. 22, 1993.

Changes:

Majority:

Henry, Paul B.	Rep	Mich.	July 31, 1993 Died in office
Castle, Michael N.	Rep	Del.	Oct. 4, 1993 Replaced Henry

Departures from the House:	**Majority**			**Minority**		
Defeated for Re-election	Unsoeld, Jolene	Dem	Wash.	None		
	English, Karan	Dem	Ariz.			
	Strickland, Ted	Dem	Ohio			
Retired	Ford, William D.	Dem	Mich.	None		
	Murphy, Austin J.	Dem	Penn.			
	de Lugo, Ron	Dem	V.I.			

Departures from Committee:						
Elected Majority Leader	None			Armey, Richard K.	Rep	Tex.
Became Chair of Republican Conference	None			Boehner, John A.	Rep	Ohio
Moved to Appropriations	None			Miller, Daniel	Rep	Fla.
Moved to Budget	None			Molinari, Susan	Rep	N.Y.
Moved to Commerce	Klink, Ronald	Dem	Penn.	None		
No new assignment	Faleomavaega, Eni F.H.	Dem	Am.S.	None		
	Baesler, H. Scott (Scotty)	Dem	Ky.			
	Underwood, Robert A.	Dem	Guam			

ECONOMIC AND EDUCATIONAL OPPORTUNITIES / 104th Congress

Service Dates of Committee Chair: Jan. 4, 1995-Jan. 3, 1997

Service Dates of Majority Members: Jan. 4, 1995-Jan. 3, 1997

Service Dates of Minority Members: Jan. 4, 1995-Jan. 3, 1997

Roster Filled: Majority with 24 members, Jan. 4, 1995; Minority with 19 members, Jan. 4, 1995

Majority					**Minority**				
			Terms in:					**Terms in:**	
Rank Name	Party	State	House	Comm.	Rank Name	Party	State	House	Comm.
Chr Goodling, William F.	Rep	Penn.	11	11	RM Clay, William L. Sr.	Dem	Mo.	14	14
2nd Petri, Thomas E.	Rep	Wisc.	9	9	2nd Miller, George	Dem	Cal.	11	*2 4
3rd Roukema, Margaret S.	Rep	N.J.	8	8	3rd Kildee, Dale E.	Dem	Mich.	10	10

4th Gunderson, Steven C.	Rep	Wisc.	8	8
5th Fawell, Harris W.	Rep	Ill.	6	6
6th Ballenger, Cass	Rep	N.C.	5	5
7th Barrett, William E.	Rep	Neb.	3	3
8th Cunningham, Randall (Duke)	Rep	Cal.	3	3
9th Hoekstra, Peter	Rep	Mich.	2	*1 2
10th McKeon, Howard P. (Buck)	Rep	Cal.	2	2
11th Castle, Michael N.	Rep	Del.	2	2
12th Meyers, Jan	Rep	Kans.	6	1
13th Johnson, Sam	Rep	Tex.	3	1
14th Talent, James M.	Rep	Mo.	2	1
15th Greenwood, James C.	Rep	Penn.	2	1
16th Hutchinson, Y. Timothy	Rep	Ark.	2	1
17th Knollenberg, Joseph	Rep	Mich.	2	1
18th Riggs, Frank D.	Rep	Cal.	2	1
19th Graham, Lindsey O.	Rep	S.C.	1	1
20th Weldon, David J.	Rep	Fla.	1	1
21st Funderburk, David	Rep	N.C.	1	1
22nd Souder, Mark E.	Rep	Ind.	1	*1 1
23rd McIntosh, David M.	Rep	Ind.	1	1
24th Norwood, Charles W. Jr.	Rep	Ga.	1	1

4th Williams, J. Patrick	Dem	Mont.	9	9
5th Martinez, Matthew G.	Dem	Cal.	8	8
6th Owens, Major R.	Dem	N.Y.	7	7
7th Sawyer, Thomas C.	Dem	Ohio	5	5
8th Payne, Donald M.	Dem	N.J.	4	4
9th Mink, Patsy T.	Dem	Hai.	10	*2 4
10th Andrews, Robert E.	Dem	N.J.	4	3
11th Reed, John F.	Dem	R.I.	3	3
12th Roemer, Timothy J.	Dem	Ind.	3	3
13th Engel, Eliot L.	Dem	N.Y.	4	2
14th Becerra, Xavier	Dem	Cal.	2	2
15th Scott, Robert C.	Dem	Va.	2	*1 2
16th Green, R. Eugene (Gene)	Dem	Tex.	2	2
17th Woolsey, Lynn C.	Dem	Cal.	2	2
18th Romero-Barceló, Carlos A.	Dem	P.R.	2	2
19th Reynolds, Mel	Dem	Ill.	2	1

*1: Member's first period of service on the committee.

*2: Member's second period of service on the committee.

Notes: Resident Commissioner Carlos A. Romero-Barceló (Dem-P.R) was allowed to accrue committee seniority but was not included in the party ratio.

Changes:
  Minority:

Reynolds, Mel	Dem	Ill.	Oct. 1, 1995 Resigned the House and retired
Fattah, Chaka	Dem	Penn.	Oct. 11, 1995 Replaced Reynolds
Engel, Eliot L.	Dem	N.Y.	April 22, 1996 Resigned committee; moved to Commerce
Blumenauer, Earl	Dem	Ore.	June 5, 1996 Replaced Engel

Departures from the House:

	Majority			Minority		
Elected to U.S. Senate	Hutchinson, Y. Timothy	Rep	Ark.	Reed, John F.	Dem	R.I.
Defeated for Re-election	Funderburk, David	Rep	N.C.			
Retired	Gunderson, Steven C.	Rep	Wisc.	Williams, J. Patrick	Dem	Mont.
	Meyers, Jan	Rep	Kans.			

Departures from Committee:

Moved to Appropriations	Cunningham, Randall (Duke)	Rep	Cal.	None		
Moved to Banking and Financial Services	Weldon, David J.	Rep	Fla.	None		
Moved to Commerce	None			Sawyer, Thomas C.	Dem	Ohio
				Green, R. Eugene (Gene)	Dem	Tex.
Moved to Ways and Means	None			Becerra, Xavier	Dem	Cal.

EDUCATION AND THE WORKFORCE / 105th Congress

Service Dates of Committee Chair: Jan. 7, 1997-Jan. 3, 1999

Service Dates of Majority Members: Jan. 7, 1997-Jan. 3, 1999

Service Dates of Minority Members: Jan. 7, 1997-Jan. 3, 1999

Roster Filled: Majority with 25 members, Jan. 21, 1997; Minority with 20 members, Jan. 7, 1997

			Majority						**Minority**	
			Terms in:						**Terms in:**	
Rank Name	**Party**	**State**	**House**	**Comm.**		**Rank Name**	**Party**	**State**	**House**	**Comm.**
Chr Goodling, William F.	Rep	Penn.	12	12		RM Clay, William L. Sr.	Dem	Mo.	15	15
2nd Petri, Thomas E.	Rep	Wisc.	10	10		2nd Miller, George	Dem	Cal.	12	*2 5
3rd Roukema, Margaret S.	Rep	N.J.	9	9		3rd Kildee, Dale E.	Dem	Mich.	11	11
4th Fawell, Harris W.	Rep	Ill.	7	7		4th Martinez, Matthew G.	Dem	Cal.	9	9
5th Ballenger, Cass	Rep	N.C.	6	6		5th Owens, Major R.	Dem	N.Y.	8	8
6th Barrett, William E.	Rep	Neb.	4	4		6th Payne, Donald M.	Dem	N.J.	5	5
7th Hoekstra, Peter	Rep	Mich.	3	*1 3		7th Mink, Patsy T.	Dem	Hai.	11	*2 5
8th McKeon, Howard P. (Buck)	Rep	Cal.	3	3		8th Andrews, Robert E.	Dem	N.J.	5	4
9th Castle, Michael N.	Rep	Del.	3	3		9th Roemer, Timothy J.	Dem	Ind.	4	4
10th Johnson, Sam	Rep	Tex.	4	2		10th Scott, Robert C.	Dem	Va.	3	*1 3
11th Talent, James M.	Rep	Mo.	3	2		11th Woolsey, Lynn C.	Dem	Cal.	3	3

12th Greenwood, James C.	Rep	Penn.	3	2	
13th Knollenberg, Joseph	Rep	Mich.	3	2	
14th Riggs, Frank D.	Rep	Cal.	3	2	
15th Graham, Lindsey O.	Rep	S.C.	2	2	
16th Souder, Mark E.	Rep	Ind.	2	*1 2	
17th McIntosh, David M.	Rep	Ind.	2	2	
18th Norwood, Charles W. Jr.	Rep	Ga.	2	2	
19th Paul, Ronald E.	Rep	Tex.	5	1	
20th Schaffer, Robert W.	Rep	Colo.	1	1	
21st Peterson, John E.	Rep	Penn.	1	1	
22nd Upton, Frederick S.	Rep	Mich.	6	1	
23rd Deal, J. Nathan	Rep	Ga.	3	1	
24th Hilleary, Van	Rep	Tenn.	2	1	
25th Scarborough, C. Joseph	Rep	Fla.	2	1	

12th Romero-Barceló, Carlos A.	Dem	P.R.	3	3
13th Fattah, Chaka	Dem	Penn.	2	2
14th Blumenauer, Earl	Dem	Ore.	2	2
15th Hinojosa, Rubén	Dem	Tex.	1	1
16th McCarthy, Carolyn	Dem	N.Y.	1	1
17th Tierney, John F.	Dem	Mass.	1	1
18th Kind, Ron	Dem	Wisc.	1	1
19th Sanchez, Loretta	Dem	Cal.	1	1
20th Ford, Harold E. Jr.	Dem	Tenn.	1	1

*1: Member's first period of service on the committee.
*2: Member's second period of service on the committee.

Notes: Resident Commissioner Carlos A. Romero-Barceló (Dem-P.R) was allowed to accrue committee seniority but was not included in the party ratio.

Vacancies Filled:
Majority:
22nd through 25th seats filled by Upton, Deal, Hilleary, and Scarborough on Jan. 21, 1997

Changes:
Majority:

Schaffer, Robert W.	Rep	Colo.	Jan. 21, 1997 Switched ranks with Peterson
Peterson, John E.	Rep	Penn.	Jan. 21, 1997 Switched ranks with Schaffer
Scarborough, C. Joseph	Rep	Fla.	May 6, 1998 Leave of absence from committee.; no new assignment
Parker, Michael	Rep	Miss.	May 13, 1998 Replaced Scarborough

Minority:

Blumenauer, Earl	Dem	Ore.	Mar. 5, 1997 Resigned committee; moved to Transportation and Infrastructure
Kucinich, Dennis	Dem	Ohio	Mar. 6, 1997 Replaced Blumenauer

Departures from the House:	**Majority**			**Minority**
Retired	Fawell, Harris W.	Rep	Ill.	None
	Riggs, Frank D.	Rep	Cal.	
	Parker, Michael	Rep	Miss.	

Departures from Committee:				
Moved to Appropriations	Peterson, John E.	Rep	Penn.	None
Moved to Budget	Knollenberg, Joseph	Rep	Mich.	None

EDUCATION AND THE WORKFORCE / 106th Congress

Service Dates of Committee Chair: Jan. 6, 1999-Jan 3, 2001

Service Dates of Majority Members: Jan. 6, 1999-Jan. 3, 2001

Service Dates of Minority Members: Jan. 6, 1999-Jan. 3, 2001

Roster Filled: Majority with 27 members, Mar. 2, 1999; Minority with 22 members, Jan. 6, 1999

Majority			Terms in:		Minority			Terms in:	
Rank Name	Party	State	House	Comm.	Rank Name	Party	State	House	Comm.
Chr Goodling, William F.	Rep	Penn.	13	13	RM Clay, William L. Sr.	Dem	Mo.	16	16
2nd Petri, Thomas E.	Rep	Wisc.	11	11	2nd Miller, George	Dem	Cal.	13	*2 6
3rd Roukema, Margaret S.	Rep	N.J.	10	10	3rd Kildee, Dale E.	Dem	Mich.	12	12
4th Ballenger, Cass	Rep	N.C.	7	7	4th Martinez, Matthew G.	Dem	Cal.	10	10
5th Barrett, William E.	Rep	Neb.	5	5	5th Owens, Major R.	Dem	N.Y.	9	9
6th Boehner, John A.	Rep	Ohio	5	*2 1	6th Payne, Donald M.	Dem	N.J.	6	6
7th Hoekstra, Peter	Rep	Mich.	4	*1 4	7th Mink, Patsy T.	Dem	Hai.	12	*2 6
8th McKeon, Howard P. (Buck)	Rep	Cal.	4	4	8th Andrews, Robert E.	Dem	N.J.	6	5
9th Castle, Michael N.	Rep	Del.	4	4	9th Roemer, Timothy J.	Dem	Ind.	5	5
10th Johnson, Sam	Rep	Tex.	5	3	10th Scott, Robert C.	Dem	Va.	4	*1 4
11th Talent, James M.	Rep	Mo.	4	3	11th Woolsey, Lynn C.	Dem	Cal.	4	4
12th Greenwood, James C.	Rep	Penn.	4	3	12th Romero-Barceló, Carlos A.	Dem	P.R.	4	4
13th Graham, Lindsey O.	Rep	S.C.	3	3	13th Fattah, Chaka	Dem	Penn.	3	3
14th Souder, Mark E.	Rep	Ind.	3	*1 3	14th Hinojosa, Rubén	Dem	Tex.	2	2
15th McIntosh, David M.	Rep	Ind.	3	3	15th McCarthy, Carolyn	Dem	N.Y.	2	2
16th Norwood, Charles W. Jr.	Rep	Ga.	3	3	16th Tierney, John F.	Dem	Mass.	2	2
17th Paul, Ronald E.	Rep	Tex.	6	2	17th Kind, Ron	Dem	Wisc.	2	2
18th Schaffer, Robert W.	Rep	Colo.	2	2	18th Sanchez, Loretta	Dem	Cal.	2	2

19th Upton, Frederick S.	Rep	Mich.	7	2		19th Ford, Harold E. Jr.	Dem	Tenn.	2	2
20th Deal, J. Nathan	Rep	Ga.	4	2		20th Kucinich, Dennis	Dem	Ohio	2	2
21st Hilleary, Van	Rep	Tenn.	3	2		21st Wu, David	Dem	Ore.	1	1
22nd Ehlers, Vernon J.	Rep	Mich.	4	1		22nd Holt, Rush D.	Dem	N.J.	1	1
23rd Salmon, Matthew J.	Rep	Ariz.	3	1						
24th Tancredo, Thomas G.	Rep	Colo.	1	1		*1: Member's first period of service on the committee.				
25th Fletcher, Ernest L.	Rep	Ky.	1	1		*2: Member's second period of service on the committee.				
26th DeMint, James W.	Rep	S.C.	1	1						
27th Isakson, Johnny	Rep	Ga.	1	1						

Notes: Resident Commissioner Carlos A. Romero-Barceló (Dem-P.R.) was allowed to accrue committee seniority but was not included in the party ratio.

Vacancies Filled:

   Majority:

   27th seat filled by Isakson on Mar. 2, 1999

Changes:

   Minority:

Martinez, Matthew G.	Dem	Cal.	July 27, 2000 Lost re-nomination; service on committee as a Democrat was vacated; moved to Transportation and Infrastructure as a Republican

Departures from the House:

	Majority			Minority		
Lost Election for Governor	Talent, James M.	Rep	Mo.	None		
	McIntosh, David M.	Rep	Ind.			
Defeated for Re-election	None			Romero-Barceló, Carlos A.	Dem	P.R.
Defeated for Re-nomination	None			Martinez, Matthew G.	Dem	Cal.
Retired	Goodling, William F.	Rep	Penn.	Clay, William L. Sr.	Dem	Mo.
	Barrett, William E.	Rep	Neb.			
	Salmon, Matthew J.	Rep	Ariz.			

Departures from Committee:

Moved to International Relations	Paul, Ronald E.	Rep	Tex.	None	
No new assignment	Deal, J. Nathan	Rep	Ga.	None	

EDUCATION AND THE WORKFORCE / 107th Congress

Service Dates of Committee Chair: Jan. 6, 2001-Jan. 3, 2003

Service Dates of Majority Members: Jan. 6, 2001-Jan. 3, 2003

Service Dates of Minority Members: Jan. 31, 2001-Jan. 3, 2003

Roster Filled: Majority with 27 members, Mar. 7, 2001; Minority with 22 members, Jan. 31, 2001

	Majority						Minority				
				Terms in:						**Terms in:**	
Rank Name		**Party**	**State**	**House**	**Comm.**	**Rank Name**		**Party**	**State**	**House**	**Comm.**
Chr Boehner, John A.		Rep	Ohio	6	*2 2	RM Miller, George		Dem	Cal.	14	*2 7
2nd Petri, Thomas E.		Rep	Wisc.	12	12	2nd Kildee, Dale E.		Dem	Mich.	13	13
3rd Roukema, Margaret S.		Rep	N.J.	11	11	3rd Owens, Major R.		Dem	N.Y.	10	10
4th Ballenger, Cass		Rep	N.C.	8	8	4th Payne, Donald M.		Dem	N.J.	7	7
5th Hoekstra, Peter		Rep	Mich.	5	*1 5	5th Mink, Patsy T.		Dem	Hai.	13	*2 7
6th McKeon, Howard P. (Buck)		Rep	Cal.	5	5	6th Andrews, Robert E.		Dem	N.J.	7	6
7th Castle, Michael N.		Rep	Del.	5	5	7th Roemer, Timothy J.		Dem	Ind.	6	6
8th Johnson, Sam		Rep	Tex.	6	4	8th Scott, Robert C.		Dem	Va.	5	*1 5
9th Greenwood, James C.		Rep	Penn.	5	4	9th Woolsey, Lynn C.		Dem	Cal.	5	5
10th Graham, Lindsey O.		Rep	S.C.	4	4	10th Rivers, Lynn N.		Dem	Mich.	4	1
11th Souder, Mark E.		Rep	Ind.	4	*1 4	11th Fattah, Chaka		Dem	Penn.	4	4
12th Norwood, Charles W. Jr.		Rep	Ga.	4	4	12th Hinojosa, Rubén		Dem	Tex.	3	3
13th Schaffer, Robert W.		Rep	Colo.	3	3	13th McCarthy, Carolyn		Dem	N.Y.	3	3
14th Upton, Frederick S.		Rep	Mich.	8	3	14th Tierney, John F.		Dem	Mass.	3	3
15th Hilleary, Van		Rep	Tenn.	4	3	15th Kind, Ron		Dem	Wisc.	3	3
16th Ehlers, Vernon J.		Rep	Mich.	5	2	16th Sanchez, Loretta		Dem	Cal.	3	3
17th Tancredo, Thomas G.		Rep	Colo.	2	2	17th Ford, Harold E. Jr.		Dem	Tenn.	3	3
18th Fletcher, Ernest L.		Rep	Ky.	2	2	18th Kucinich, Dennis		Dem	Ohio	3	3
19th DeMint, James W.		Rep	S.C.	2	2	19th Wu, David		Dem	Ore.	2	2
20th Isakson, Johnny		Rep	Ga.	2	2	20th Holt, Rush D.		Dem	N.J.	2	2
21st Biggert, Judith B.		Rep	Ill.	2	1	21st McCollum, Betty		DFL	Minn.	1	1
22nd Platts, Todd R.		Rep	Penn.	1	1	22nd Solis, Hilda L.		Dem	Cal.	1	1

23rd Tiberi, Patrick	Rep	Ohio	1	1
24th Keller, Richard (Ric)	Rep	Fla.	1	1
25th Osborne, Thomas	Rep	Neb.	1	1
26th Culberson, John	Rep	Tex.	1	1
27th Goodlatte, Robert W.	Rep	Va.	5	1

*1: Member's first period of service on the committee.
*2: Member's second period of service on the committee.

Vacancies Filled:

Majority:

27th seat filled by Goodlatte on Mar. 7, 2001

Changes:

Majority:

| Fletcher, Ernest L. | Rep | Ky. | Mar. 20, 2002 Resigned committee; moved to Energy and Commerce |
| Wilson, Addison G. (Joe) | Rep | S.C. | Apr. 18, 2002 Replaced Fletcher |

Minority:

Fattah, Chaka	Dem	Penn.	Feb. 7, 2001 Resigned committee; moved to Appropriations
Davis, Susan A.	Dem	Cal.	Feb. 8, 2001 Replaced Fattah, ranked following Holt
Mink, Patsy T.	Dem	Hai.	Sept. 28, 2002 Died in office

Departures from the House:	Majority			Minority		
Elected to U.S. Senate	Graham, Lindsey O.	Rep	S.C.	None		
Lost Election for Governor	Hilleary, Van	Rep	Tenn.	None		
Defeated for Re-nomination	None			Rivers, Lynn N.	Dem	Mich.
Retired	Roukema, Margaret S.	Rep	N.J.	Roemer, Timothy J.	Dem	Ind.
	Schaffer, Robert W.	Rep	Colo.			

Departures from Committee:						
Moved to Appropriations	Culberson, John	Rep	Tex.	None		
Moved to Budget	Tancredo, Thomas G.	Rep	Colo.	Scott, Robert C.	Dem	Va.
				Ford, Harold E. Jr.	Dem	Tenn.
Moved to Energy and Commerce	None			Solis, Hilda L.	Dem	Cal.
Moved to Select Homeland Security	Goodlatte, Robert W.	Rep	Va.	None		

EDUCATION AND THE WORKFORCE / 108th Congress

Service Dates of Committee Chair: Jan. 8, 2003-Jan. 3, 2005

Service Dates of Majority Members: Jan. 28, 2003-Jan. 3, 2005

Service Dates of Ranking Member: Jan. 8, 2003-Jan. 3, 2005

Service Dates of Minority Members: Jan. 28, 2003-Jan. 3, 2005

Roster Filled: Majority with 27 members, Feb. 11, 2003; Minority with 22 members, Feb. 13, 2003

Majority			Terms in:		**Minority**			Terms in:	
Rank Name	Party	State	House	Comm.	Rank Name	Party	State	House	Comm.
Chr Boehner, John A.	Rep	Ohio	7	*2 3	RM Miller, George	Dem	Cal.	15	*2 8
2nd Petri, Thomas E.	Rep	Wisc.	13	13	2nd Kildee, Dale E.	Dem	Mich.	14	14
3rd Ballenger, Cass	Rep	N.C.	9	9	3rd Owens, Major R.	Dem	N.Y.	11	11
4th Hoekstra, Peter	Rep	Mich.	6	*1 6	4th Payne, Donald M.	Dem	N.J.	8	8
5th McKeon, Howard P. (Buck)	Rep	Cal.	6	6	5th Andrews, Robert E.	Dem	N.J.	8	7
6th Castle, Michael N.	Rep	Del.	6	6	6th Woolsey, Lynn C.	Dem	Cal.	6	6
7th Johnson, Sam	Rep	Tex.	7	5	7th Hinojosa, Rubén	Dem	Tex.	4	4
8th Greenwood, James C.	Rep	Penn.	6	5	8th McCarthy, Carolyn	Dem	N.Y.	4	4
9th Souder, Mark E.	Rep	Ind.	5	*1 5	9th Tierney, John F.	Dem	Mass.	4	4
10th Norwood, Charles W. Jr.	Rep	Ga.	5	5	10th Kind, Ron	Dem	Wisc.	4	4
11th Upton, Frederick S.	Rep	Mich.	9	4	11th Sanchez, Loretta	Dem	Cal.	4	4
12th Ehlers, Vernon J.	Rep	Mich.	6	3	12th Kucinich, Dennis	Dem	Ohio	4	4
13th DeMint, James W.	Rep	S.C.	3	3	13th Wu, David	Dem	Ore.	3	3
14th Isakson, Johnny	Rep	Ga.	3	3	14th Holt, Rush D.	Dem	N.J.	3	3
15th Biggert, Judith B.	Rep	Ill.	3	2	15th Davis, Susan A.	Dem	Cal.	2	2
16th Platts, Todd R.	Rep	Penn.	2	2	16th McCollum, Betty	DFL	Minn.	2	2
17th Tiberi, Patrick	Rep	Ohio	2	2	17th Davis, Danny K.	Dem	Ill.	4	1
18th Keller, Richard (Ric)	Rep	Fla.	2	2	18th Case, Ed	Dem	Hai.	1	1
19th Osborne, Thomas	Rep	Neb.	2	2	19th Grijalva, Raúl M.	Dem	Ariz.	1	1
20th Wilson, Addison G. (Joe)	Rep	S.C.	2	2	20th Majette, Denise L.	Dem	Ga.	1	1
21st Cole, Tom	Rep	Okla.	1	1	21st Van Hollen, Christopher	Dem	Md.	1	1
22nd Porter, Jon C.	Rep	Nev.	1	1	22nd Ryan, Timothy J.	Dem	Ohio	1	1
23rd Kline, John	Rep	Minn.	1	1	23rd Bishop, Timothy H.	Dem	N.Y.	1	1

24th Carter, John R.	Rep	Tex.	1	1	
25th Musgrave, Marilyn N.	Rep	Colo.	1	1	*1: Member's first period of service on the committee.
26th Blackburn, Marsha	Rep	Tenn.	1	1	*2: Member's second period of service on the committee.
27th Gingrey, Phil	Rep	Ga.	1	1	

Vacancies Filled:

Majority:

27th seat filled by Gingrey on Feb. 11, 2003

Minority:

18th through 22nd seats filled by Case, Grijalva, Majette, Van Hollen, and Ryan, respectively, on Feb. 5, 2003;

23rd seat filled by Bishop on Mar. 5, 2003

Changes:

Majority:

Souder, Mark E.	Rep	Ind.	Feb. 11, 2003 Resigned committee; moved to Select Homeland Security
Burns, Max	Rep	Ga.	Feb. 12, 2003 Replaced Souder

Minority:

Sanchez, Loretta	Dem	Cal.	Feb. 12, 2003 Leave of absence from committee; moved to Select Homeland Security
Davis, Danny K.	Dem	Ill.	Feb. 13, 2003 Replaced Sanchez; ranked after McCollum

Departures from the House:

	Majority			Minority		
Elected to U.S. Senate	DeMint, James W.	Rep	S.C.	None		
	Isakson, Johnny	Rep	Ga.			
Lost Election to U.S. Senate	None			Majette, Denise L.	Dem	Ga.
Defeated for Re-election	Burns, Max	Rep	Ga.	None		
Retired	Ballenger, Cass	Rep	N.C.	None		
	Greenwood, James C.	Rep	Penn.			

Departures from Committee:

Became Chair of Select Intelligence	Hoekstra, Peter	Rep	Mich.			
Moved to Rules	Cole, Tom	Rep	La.	None		
	Gingrey, Phil	Rep	Ga.			
Moved to Appropriations	Carter, John R.	Rep	Tex.	None		
Moved to Budget	None			Case, Ed	Dem	Hai.
Moved to Energy and Commerce	Blackburn, Marsha	Rep	Tenn.	None		
Moved to Standards of Official Conduct	Cole, Tom	Rep	Okla	None		
No new assignment	Upton, Frederick S.	Rep	Mich.	None		

EDUCATION AND THE WORKFORCE / 109th Congress

Service Dates of Committee Chair: Ch1 Jan. 6, 2005-Feb. 6, 2006 Boehner (Rep-Ohio)

Ch2 Feb. 15, 2006-Jan. 3, 2007 McKeon (Rep-Cal.)

Service Dates of Majority Members: Jan. 26, 2005-Jan. 3, 2007

Service Dates of Minority Members: Jan. 26, 2005-Jan. 3, 2007

Roster Filled: Majority with 27 members, Feb. 2, 2005; Minority with 22 members, Jan. 26, 2005

Majority			Terms in:		Minority			Terms in:	
Rank Name	Party	State	House	Comm.	Rank Name	Party	State	House	Comm.
Ch1 Boehner, John A.	Rep	Ohio	8	*2 4	RM Miller, George	Dem	Cal.	16	*2 9
2nd Petri, Thomas E.	Rep	Wisc.	14	14	2nd Kildee, Dale E.	Dem	Mich.	15	15
Ch2 McKeon, Howard P. (Buck)	Rep	Cal.	7	7	3rd Owens, Major R.	Dem	N.Y.	12	12
4th Castle, Michael N.	Rep	Del.	7	7	4th Payne, Donald M.	Dem	N.J.	9	9
5th Johnson, Sam	Rep	Tex.	8	6	5th Andrews, Robert E.	Dem	N.J.	9	8
6th Souder, Mark E.	Rep	Ind.	6	*2 1	6th Scott, Robert C.	Dem	Va.	7	*2 1
7th Norwood, Charles W. Jr.	Rep	Ga.	6	6	7th Woolsey, Lynn C.	Dem	Cal.	7	7
8th Ehlers, Vernon J.	Rep	Mich.	7	4	8th Hinojosa, Rubén	Dem	Tex.	5	5
9th Biggert, Judith B.	Rep	Ill.	4	3	9th McCarthy, Carolyn	Dem	N.Y.	5	5
10th Platts, Todd R.	Rep	Penn.	3	3	10th Tierney, John F.	Dem	Mass.	5	5
11th Tiberi, Patrick	Rep	Ohio	3	3	11th Kind, Ron	Dem	Wisc.	5	5
12th Keller, Richard (Ric)	Rep	Fla.	3	3	12th Kucinich, Dennis	Dem	Ohio	5	5
13th Osborne, Thomas	Rep	Neb.	3	3	13th Wu, David	Dem	Ore.	4	4
14th Wilson, Addison G. (Joe)	Rep	S.C.	3	3	14th Holt, Rush D.	Dem	N.J.	4	4
15th Porter, Jon C.	Rep	Nev.	2	2	15th Davis, Susan A.	Dem	Cal.	3	3
16th Kline, John	Rep	Minn.	2	2	16th McCollum, Betty	DFL	Minn.	3	3
17th Musgrave, Marilyn N.	Rep	Colo.	2	2	17th Davis, Danny K.	Dem	Ill.	5	2

18th Inglis, Robert D.	Rep	S.C.	4	1	
19th McMorris, Cathy	Rep	Wash.	1	1	
20th Marchant, Kenny	Rep	Tex.	1	1	
21st Price, Tom	Rep	Ga.	1	1	
22nd Fortuño, Luis G.	Rep	P.R.	1	1	
23rd Jindal, Bobby	Rep	La.	1	1	
24th Boustany, Charles W. Jr.	Rep	La.	1	1	
25th Foxx, Virginia A.	Rep	N.C.	1	1	
26th Drake, Thelma D.	Rep	Va.	1	1	
27th Kuhl, John R. (Randy) Jr.	Rep	N.Y.	1	1	

18th Grijalva, Raúl M.	Dem	Ariz.	2	2
19th Van Hollen, Christopher	Dem	Md.	2	2
20th Ryan, Timothy J.	Dem	Ohio	2	2
21st Bishop, Timothy H.	Dem	N.Y.	2	2
22nd Barrow, John	Dem	Ga.	1	1

*2: Member's second period of service on the committee.

Vacancies Filled:

Majority:

6th seat filled by Souder who returned on Feb. 2, 2005, to rank immediately after Johnson

Changes:

Majority:

Boehner, John A.	Rep	Ohio	Feb. 6, 2006 Resigned as Chair; elected Majority Floor Leader
McKeon, Howard P. (Buck)	Rep	Cal.	Feb. 15, 2006 Named Chair of Education and the Workforce

Seat vacancy remained as of Dec. 8, 2006 according to Congressional Record.

Minority:

Barrow, John	Dem	Ga.	Feb. 15, 2006 Resigned committee; moved to Transportation and Infrastructure; vacancy remained

Departures from the House:

	Majority			Minority		
Lost Nomination for Governor	Osborne, Thomas	Rep	Neb.	None		
Retired	None			Owens, Major R.	Dem	N.Y.

Departures from Committee:

	Majority			Minority		
Moved to Appropriations	None			McCollum, Betty	Dem	Minn.
				Ryan, Timothy J.	Dem	Ohio
Moved to Budget	Tiberi, Patrick	Rep	Ohio	None		
	Porter, Jon C.	Rep	Nev.			
Returned to Oversight and Government Reform	None			McCollum, Betty	Dem	Minn.
Moved to Transportation and Infrastructure	Drake, Thelma D.	Rep	Va.	None		
Moved to Ways and Means	Tiberi, Patrick	Rep	Ohio	Kind, Ron	Dem	Wisc.
	Porter, Jon C.	Rep	Nev.	Van Hollen, Christopher	Dem	Md.
No new assignment	Jindal, Bobby	Rep	La.	None		
	Johnson, Sam	Rep	Tex.			
	Musgrave, Marilyn N.	Rep	Colo.			
	Norwood, Charles W. Jr.	Rep	Ga.			

EDUCATION AND LABOR / 110th Congress

Service Dates of Committee Chair: Jan. 4, 2007-Jan. 3, 2009

Service Dates of Majority Members: Jan. 10, 2007-Jan. 3, 2009

Service Dates of Minority Members: Jan. 10, 2007-Jan. 3, 2009

Roster Filled: Majority with 27 members, Jan. 10, 2007; Minority with 22 members, Mar. 12, 2007

	Majority			Terms in:			Minority			Terms in:	
Rank Name		**Party**	**State**	**House**	**Comm.**	**Rank Name**		**Party**	**State**	**House**	**Comm.**
Chr Miller, George		Dem	Cal.	17	*2 10	RM McKeon, Howard P. (Buck)		Rep	Cal.	8	8
2nd Kildee, Dale E.		Dem	Mich.	16	16	2nd Petri, Thomas E.		Rep	Wisc.	15	15
3rd Payne, Donald M.		Dem	N.J.	10	10	3rd Hoekstra, Peter		Rep	Mich.	8	*2 1
4th Andrews, Robert E.		Dem	N.J.	10	9	4th Castle, Michael N.		Rep	Del.	8	8
5th Scott, Robert C.		Dem	Va.	8	*2 2	5th Souder, Mark E.		Rep	Ind.	7	*2 2
6th Woolsey, Lynn C.		Dem	Cal.	8	8	6th Ehlers, Vernon J.		Rep	Mich.	8	5
7th Hinojosa, Rubén		Dem	Tex.	6	6	7th Biggert, Judith B.		Rep	Ill.	5	4
8th McCarthy, Carolyn		Dem	N.Y.	6	6	8th Platts, Todd R.		Rep	Penn.	4	4
9th Tierney, John F.		Dem	Mass.	6	6	9th Keller, Richard (Ric)		Rep	Fla.	4	4
10th Kucinich, Dennis		Dem	Ohio	6	6	10th Wilson, Addison G. (Joe)		Rep	S.C.	4	4
11th Wu, David		Dem	Ore.	5	5	11th Kline, John		Rep	Minn.	3	3

12th Holt, Rush D.	Dem	N.J.	5	5		12th Inglis, Robert D.	Rep	S.C.	5	2
13th Davis, Susan A.	Dem	Cal.	4	4		13th McMorris Rodgers, Cathy	Rep	Wash.	2	2
14th Davis, Danny K.	Dem	Ill.	6	3		14th Marchant, Kenny	Rep	Tex.	2	2
15th Grijalva, Raúl M.	Dem	Ariz.	3	3		15th Price, Tom	Rep	Ga.	2	2
16th Bishop, Timothy H.	Dem	N.Y.	3	3		16th Fortuño, Luis G.	Rep	P.R.	2	2
17th Sánchez, Linda T.	Dem	Cal.	3	1		17th Boustany, Charles W. Jr.	Rep	La.	2	2
18th Sarbanes, John	Dem	Md.	1	1		18th Foxx, Virginia A.	Rep	N.C.	2	2
19th Sestak, Joe	Dem	Penn.	1	1		19th Kuhl, John R. (Randy) Jr.	Rep	N.Y.	2	2
20th Loebsack, Dave	Dem	Iowa	1	1		20th Bishop, Robert	Rep	Utah	3	1
21st Hirono, Mazie K.	Dem	Hai.	1	1		21st Davis, David	Rep	Tenn.	1	1
22nd Altmire, Jason	Dem	Penn.	1	1		22nd Walberg, Tim	Rep	Mich.	1	1
23rd Yarmuth, John A.	Dem	Ky.	1	1						
24th Hare, Phil	Dem	Ill.	1	1		*2: Member's second period of service on the committee.				
25th Clarke, Yvette D.	Dem	N.Y.	1	1						
26th Courtney, Joe	Dem	Conn.	1	1						
27th Shea-Porter, Carol	Dem	N.H.	1	1						

Changes:

Minority:

Inglis, Robert D.	Rep	S.C.	Mar. 9, 2007 Resigned committee; no new assignment
Heller, Dean	Rep	Nev.	Mar. 12, 2007 Replaced Inglis
Heller, Dean	Rep	Nev.	Feb. 25, 2008 Resigned committee; moved to Financial Services

Departures from the House:	**Majority**			**Minority**		
Elected Governor	None			Fortuño, Luis G.	Rep	P.R.
Defeated for Re-election	None			Keller, Richard (Ric)	Rep	Fla.
				Kuhl, John R. (Randy) Jr.	Rep	N.Y.
				Walberg, Tim	Rep	Mich.
Defeated for Re-nomination	None			Davis, David	Rep	Tenn.

Departures from Committee:						
Moved to Budget	Yarmuth, John A.	Dem	Ky.	None		
Moved to Energy and Commerce	Sarbanes, John	Dem	Md.	None		
Moved to Ways and Means	Davis, Danny K.	Dem	Ill.	Boustany, Charles W. Jr.	Rep	La.
	Sanchez, Linda T.	Dem	Cal.			
	Yarmuth, John A.	Dem	Ky.			
No new assignment	None			Marchant, Kenny	Rep	Tex.

EDUCATION AND LABOR / 111th Congress

Service Dates of Committee Chair: Jan. 6, 2009-Jan. 3, 2011

Service Dates of Majority Members: Jan. 21, 2009-Jan. 3, 2011

Service Dates of Minority Members: Jan. 9, 2009-Jan. 3, 2011

Roster Filled: Majority with 30 members, July 16, 2009; Minority with 19 members, Jan. 9, 2009

Majority			**Terms in:**		**Minority**			**Terms in:**	
Rank Name	**Party**	**State**	**House**	**Comm.**	**Rank Name**	**Party**	**State**	**House**	**Comm.**
Chr Miller, George	Dem	Cal.	18	*2 11	RM1 McKeon, Howard P. (Buck)	Rep	Cal.	9	9
2nd Kildee, Dale E.	Dem	Mich.	17	17	2nd Petri, Thomas E.	Rep	Wisc.	16	16
3rd Payne, Donald M.	Dem	N.J.	11	11	3rd Hoekstra, Peter	Rep	Mich.	9	*2 2
4th Andrews, Robert E.	Dem	N.J.	11	10	4th Castle, Michael N.	Rep	Del.	9	9
5th Scott, Robert C.	Dem	Va.	9	*2 3	5th Souder, Mark E.	Rep	Ind.	8	*2 3
6th Woolsey, Lynn C.	Dem	Cal.	9	9	6th Ehlers, Vernon J.	Rep	Mich.	9	6
7th Hinojosa, Rubén	Dem	Tex.	7	7	7th Biggert, Judith B.	Rep	Ill.	6	5
8th McCarthy, Carolyn	Dem	N.Y.	7	7	8th Platts, Todd R.	Rep	Penn.	5	5
9th Tierney, John F.	Dem	Mass.	7	7	9th Wilson, Addison G. (Joe)	Rep	S.C.	5	5
10th Kucinich, Dennis	Dem	Ohio	7	7	10th RM2 Kline, John	Rep	Minn.	4	4
11th Wu, David	Dem	Ore.	6	6	11th McMorris Rodgers, Cathy	Rep	Wash.	3	3
12th Holt, Rush D.	Dem	N.J.	6	6	12th Price, Tom	Rep	Ga.	3	3
13th Davis, Susan A.	Dem	Cal.	5	5	13th Foxx, Virginia A.	Rep	N.C.	3	3
14th Grijalva, Raúl M.	Dem	Ariz.	4	4	14th Bishop, Robert	Rep	Utah	4	2
15th Bishop, Timothy H.	Dem	N.Y.	4	4	15th Guthrie, Brett	Rep	Ky.	1	1
16th Sestak, Joe	Dem	Penn.	2	2	16th Cassidy, Bill	Rep	La.	1	1
17th Loebsack, Dave	Dem	Iowa	2	2	17th McClintock, Thomas	Rep	Cal.	1	1
18th Hirono, Mazie K.	Dem	Hai.	2	2	18th Hunter, Duncan D.	Rep	Cal.	1	1

19th Altmire, Jason	Dem	Penn.	2	2
20th Hare, Phil	Dem	Ill.	2	2
21st Clarke, Yvette D.	Dem	N.Y.	2	2
22nd Courtney, Joe	Dem	Conn.	2	2
23rd Shea-Porter, Carol	Dem	N.H.	2	2
24th Fudge, Marcia L.	Dem	Ohio	2	1
25th Polis, Jared	Dem	Colo.	1	1
26th Tonko, Paul	Dem	N.Y.	1	1
27th Pierluisi, Pedro R.	Dem	P.R.	1	1
28th Sablan, Gregorio Kilili	Dem	N.M.I.	1	1
29th Titus, Alice (Dina)	Dem	Nev.	1	1
30th Chu, Judy	Dem	Cal.	1	1

| 19th Roe, David P. (Phil) | Rep | Tenn. | 1 | 1 |

*2: Member's second period of service on the committee.

Note: Teritorial Delegate Gregorio Kilili Sablan (Dem-Northern Mariana Islands) and Resident Commissioner Pedro R. Pierluisi (Dem-P.R.) were allowed to accrue committee seniority but were not included in the party ratio.

Filled Vacancy:

Majority:

30th seat by Judy Chu (Dem-Cal.) on July 16, 2009

Changes:

Minority

Foxx, Virginia A.	Rep	N.C.	Jan. 15, 2009 Resigned committee; moved to Rules
Thompson, Glenn	Rep	Penn.	Feb. 4, 2009 Replaced Foxx
RM1 McKeon, Howard P. (Buck)	Rep	Cal.	June 16, 2009 Replaced McHugh as Ranking Member on Armed Services
RM2 Kline, John	Rep	Minn	June 25, 2009 Succeeded McKeon as Ranking Member

Energy and Commerce

House Committee on Energy and Commerce, 103rd Congress (1993-1995)

House Committee on Commerce, 104th-106th Congresses (1995-2001)

House Committee on Energy and Commerce, 107th-111th Congresses (2001-2011)

BACKGROUND

Organizational History: The newly renamed Energy and Commerce Committee is the continuation of the House standing committee with the longest service representing a substantive interest. The first committee dealing with commercial matters was the Committee on Commerce, Manufactures, and Agriculture, created on December 14, 1795, on a motion introduced by Hugh Williamson (Fed.-N.C.). In 1819, the Manufactures Committee was created and in 1820, the Agriculture Committee was created, leaving Commerce to stand alone as the name of the committee.

According to Article I, Section 8, Clause 3 of the Constitution, "[The Congress shall have power] to regulate Commerce with foreign Nations, and among the several States, and with the Indian tribes." Known generally as the "commerce clause," this has provided the committee with sufficient legislative elasticity to create the nation's first major regulatory agency, the Interstate Commerce Commission in 1887 to regulate the railroads. In 1895, the Committee on Commerce became the Committee on Interstate and Foreign Commerce and it held this name until 1981, when it was renamed the Committee on Energy and Commerce.

Because of the legislative elasticity of the "commerce clause," the Commerce Committee has often been used by progressive presidents to expand federal power. Sam Rayburn (Dem-Tex.) who would serve as Speaker of the House for seventeen years was chair of the Interstate and Foreign Commerce Committee during President Franklin D. Roosevelt's New Deal. Rayburn was responsible for the successful floor management of the Federal Securities Act of 1933 (P.L. 73-22; 48 Stat. 74), the Securities Exchange Act of 1934 (P.L. 73-291; 48 Stat. 881), and the Public Utility Holding Company Act of 1935 (P.L. 74-333; 49 Stat. 803). The first two acts addressed the Wall Street speculation that led to the 1929 stock market crash while the Public Utility Holding Act enhanced the regulatory authority of the Federal Power Commission and the Federal Trade Commission over the interstate transmission of gas and electricity.

The committees visibility increased in the 1950s as it investigated several scandals including rigged television quiz shows and "payola" or payoffs given by the record industry to radio disc jockeys in exchange for air time. One of the long running debates in the committee was over energy pricing, with top Democrats resisting deregulation of oil and natural gas well into the 1970s. In that decade, the panel's jurisdiction shifted as responsibility for most forms of transportation, except railroads, a special interest of then chair Harley O. Staggers (Dem-W.Va.), were shifted to Public Works, and

Transportation and Commerce picked up health issues from the Ways and Means Committee.

The committee's power continued to grow and late in 1974, a short-lived effort was made to rename it the Committee on Commerce and Health, but it resumed the Interstate and Foreign Commerce designation at the opening of the 94th Congress in 1975. However, it was clear that the committee intended to expand its jurisdiction. The 1974 termination of the Joint Committee on Atomic Energy gave the committee authority over nuclear energy as well as non-nuclear energy. Further jurisdictional opportunities arose during the energy crisis of the 1970s. That crisis led to the creation of the forty-member House Select Committee on Energy (Ad Hoc) chaired by Thomas L. Ashley (Dem-Ohio) in 1977-1978, who was not a member of Commerce. It was the second Select Committee on Committees chaired by Jerry Patterson (Dem-Cal.) in 1979-1980, that urged the House to find a central locus for the burgeoning number of energy issues confronting the nation. In 1977, the Senate had already lodged energy issues in its western and producer-dominated Energy and Natural Resources Committee. In 1980, the House chose to locate energy issues in a more urban and consumer-oriented committee. Commerce was renamed Energy and Commerce Committee and John D. Dingell Jr. (Dem-Mich.) would become its chair for the first time in 1981.

As a result, the committee gained jurisdiction over national energy policy, conservation, technology, resources, information, and interstate energy compacts, as well as the management of the Department of Energy and the Federal Energy Regulatory Commission. The committee's authority over energy also extends to matters related to power: generation and marketing; interstate transmission; ratemaking; and siting of generation facilities. Other matters related to commerce that the Committee retains responsibility for include inland waterways, railroads, interstate and foreign communications, securities and exchanges, and public health and quarantine. The committee has also assumed responsibility for consumer affairs and protection, travel and tourism, and health and health facilities.

With its sweeping jurisdiction and long history of colorful personalities, the committee has been a hot spot and center of controversy for decades. In the modern era, topics such as auto emissions, oil industry pricing, and regulation of cable television have produced dramatic legislative and lobbying efforts at both the subcommittee and full committee levels. Lobbyists give special attention to this committee whose legislative actions affect the interests of many industries and environmental, medical, and consumer groups. Its jurisdiction includes energy, health, communication, consumer safety, the stock market, part of the transportation industry, and numerous regulatory agencies.

The committee's jurisdiction over air pollution and health led to one of the renowned continuing battles in Congress, in which long-time chair, John Dingell, its senior Democrat since 1981, was pitted against Henry Waxman (Dem-Cal.). Dingell, generally an economic liberal, also represented a major auto manufacturing district and sided with the auto industry against strict engine emission controls. Waxman, representing a mostly liberal and affluent constituency in smog-choked Los Angeles, fought for tougher pollution control. His power base was as chair of the Subcommittee on Health and Environment. A 1989 compromise contributed to the enactment of the Clean Air Act Amendments of 1990 (P.L. 100-549).

Following the Republican takeover in 1995, Energy was dropped from the committee's title and efforts were made to rein in its jurisdictional expansiveness. Two years after Newt Gingrich left the speakership, the committee resumed the name of Energy and Commerce in 2001 and has retained it ever since.

When John Dingell headed the committee's Oversight and Investigations Subcommittee, he focused on allegations of government wrongdoing, particularly misuse of government funds. Aided by a team of eager investigators, he targeted waste and corruption in defense contracting, fraud in government financed scientific research, and the misuse of federal grants by private universities. This also brought him elbow to elbow with Waxman, who was the senior Democrat on Government Reform for most of the years after the 1995 Republican takeover and was that committee's chair in the 110th Congress (2007-2009). Finally, in November 2008, Waxman had the votes in the Democratic Caucus to defeat Dingell 137 to 122 for the chairmanship of Energy and Commerce.

With the issue of global warming raising serious questions about the role of fossil fuel consumption in that highly contentious issue, the House's Committee on Energy and Commerce will continue to remain as a major public policy battleground.

Membership: While its mission grew, the committee's size increased from the 1946 Reorganization Act's low of twenty-seven in the 80th Congress (1947-1949) to forty-four in the 103rd Congress (1993-1995). In the nine Congresses from 1993 to 2011, the committee has grown by fifteen members and presently has a membership of fifty-nine, its highest total ever. The committee's mean membership size of 53.4 for the last nine Congresses placed it fifth among the nineteen continuing committees.

Its importance has grown to such a degree that House Republicans now consider Energy and Commerce to be an "exclusive" assignment. along with Appropriations, Rules, and Ways and Means, thus limiting their members to this assignment only. As proof of its new-found prominence, the committee's mean seniority ranking of 6.18 member terms per Congress, placed it fourth, just behind the rankings of the House's traditional "big three" committees. Higher still is Energy and Commerce's third-place ranking on the inter-Congress member retention rate—97.04 percent—behind only the Ways and Means (98.50%) and Appropriations Committees (97.74%).

Committee Leaders: For a committee of its great importance and the high seniority of its members, the Energy and Commerce Committee has had relatively few senior leaders. Charles A. Wolverton (Rep-N.J.) was Interstate and Foreign Commerce's first post-reorganization chair and he served as

its senior Republican until his retirement in 1959, also chairing the committee in the 83rd Congress (1953-1955). The first senior Democrat was Clarence Lea (Dem-Cal.) who retired in 1949, with Robert Crosser (Dem-Ohio) succeeding him and chairing the committee in the 81st and 82nd Congresses (1949-1953). Crosser's renomination defeat in 1954 created a vacancy filled by J. Percy Priest (Dem-Tenn.), who resigned as Democratic Whip to assume the chair of the committee. Priest's death in 1956 led the chair to be filled by Oren Harris (Dem-Ark.) from 1957 until his appointment as a federal judge in 1966, and then by Harley Staggers (Dem-W.Va.), who chaired the committee from 1966 until his retirement in 1981. Succeeding Harris was John D. Dingell Jr. (Dem-Mich.) whose service on the committee began as a thirty-year-old in 1957 and who would serve as its senior Democrat for the next twenty-eight years until 2009. Dingell's service is the longest committee senior service in modern House history—sixteen years as chair, 1981-1995 and 2007-2009; and twelve years as ranking member, 1995-2007. This ended in 2009 when long-time second-ranking Henry Waxman (Dem-Cal.) was able to wrest the chairmanship from the eighty-two-year-old Dingell.

While the Democrats had only three senior members in the fifty-two years from 1957 to 2009, Republican seniors, all of whom served as ranking minority members, had a higher turnover history—John B. Bennett (Rep-Mich.), 1959-1964; William L. Springer (Rep-Ill.), 1964-1973; Samuel L. Devine (Rep-Ohio), 1973-1979; James T. Broyhill (Rep-N.C.), 1979-1986; Norman F. Lent (Rep-N.Y.), 1986-1993; and Carlos J. Moorhead (Rep-Cal.), 1993-1995. The Republican victory in 1994 enabled second-ranking Thomas J. Bliley (Rep-Va.) to gain the chairmanship, bypassing Moorhead. Bliley served the three chairmanship terms permitted by the Republican Conference and retired in 2001. He was followed by W.J. (Billy) Tauzin (Rep-La.). who had moved from the Democratic side of the committee to the Republican one in 1995 with his seniority intact. Tauzin chaired the committee until 2004 when he stepped aside in his last year for Joe L. Barton (Rep-Tex.), who would chair the committee from 2004 through 2007 and is presently its ranking minority member.

Party Leaders: Sam Rayburn (Dem-Tex.), the longest serving Speaker of the House, left the chair of Interstate and Foreign Commerce in 1937 to become Majority Leader and begin his storied career as an elected House leader. It had been his only committee assignment. The only other modern-era Democratic leader to serve on the committee was J. Percy Priest (Dem-Tenn.), the Democratic Whip from 1951 to 1955, who left the leadership to chair Interstate and Foreign Commerce. House Republican leaders with service on the committee include J. Dennis Hastert (Rep-Ill.) who served as Speaker of the House for eight years, 1999-2007; C. Trent Lott (Rep-Miss.) who served as Minority Whip from 1981 until his 1989 election to the Senate; and Roy Blunt (Rep-Mo.), Republican Whip from 2003-2007. After Hastert's fourth term as Speaker ended in 2007, he returned to the committee and then retired a year later.

Notable Members: Only two House Commerce committee members received modern-era presidential and vice presidential nominations—Alben W. Barkley (Dem-Ky.), Harry Truman's 1948 running-mate, and Albert Gore Jr. (Dem-Tenn.) who ran successfully for vice president with Bill Clinton in 1992 and 1996 and was narrowly defeated by Texas governor George W. Bush in Gore's own presidential bid in 2000. Four Cabinet appointments received by Commerce members were given to Brock Adams (Dem-Wash.), Jimmy Carter's Secretary of Transportation; Edward R. Madigan (Rep-Ill.), George H.W. Bush's second Secretary of Agriculture; William B. Richardson (Dem-N.M.), Bill Clinton's third Secretary of Energy; and Hilda L. Solis (Dem-Cal.), Barack Obama's Secretary of Labor.

Twenty-two Commerce members moved to the U.S. Senate: twelve Democrats—Alben W. Barkley, Virgil M. Chapman, and Thomas S. Underwood of Kentucky; Albert A. Gore Jr. of Tennessee; Barbara A. Mikulski of Maryland; Richard C. Shelby of Alabama; Robert C. Krueger of Texas; Brock Adams of Washington; Timothy E. Wirth of Colorado; Ronald L. Wyden of Oregon; Blanche Lambert Lincoln of Arkansas; and Sherrod Brown of Ohio; and ten Republicans: Hugh D. Scott and H. John Heinz III of Pennsylvania, Peter H. Dominick of Colorado, James T. Broyhill of North Carolina, W. Phil Gramm of Texas, C. Trent Lott of Mississippi, Daniel R. Coats of Indiana, Richard M. Burr of North Carolina, Michael D. Crapo of Idaho, and Thomas A. Coburn of Oklahoma.

The Energy and Commerce Committee and its previous incarnations are linked to twelve governors. Eleven committee members were elected governors after serving on the committee: seven Democrats—John Bell Williams of Mississippi, James J. Florio of New Jersey, Bill Richardson of New Mexico, John Gilligan and Ted Strickland of Ohio, Ray Blanton of Tennessee, and Thomas B. Stanley of Virginia; and four Republicans—William H. Avery of Kansas, Robert L. Ehrlich of Maryland, Ernest L. Fletcher of Kentucky, and C.L. "Butch" Otter of Idaho. Vernon W. Thomson of Wisconsin served on Commerce after he had left the governorship.

Selected References

Cohen, Richard E., *Washington at Work: Back Rooms and Clean Air,* 2nd ed. (Needham Heights, Mass.: Allyn and Bacon, 1995).

Hall, Richard L., *Participation in Congress* (New Haven. Conn.: Yale University Press, 1995)

Hall, Richard L. and C. Lawrence Evans, "The Power of Subcommittees," *Journal of Politics,* 52 (1990), 335-355.

King, David C., "The Nature of Congressional Committee Jurisdictions," *American Political Science Review*, 88 (March, 1994), 48-62.

King, David C., *Turf Wars: How Congressional Committees Claim Jurisdiction* (Cambridge, Mass.: J.F. Kennedy School, Harvard University, 1997).

Ornstein, Norman J. and David W. Rohde, "Shifting Forces, Changing Rules, and Political Outcomes: The Impact of Congressional Change on Four House Committees," in Robert L. Peabody and Nelson W. Polsby, eds., *New Perspectives on the House of Representatives,* 3rd ed. (Chicago:" Rand McNally, 1977), 186-269.

Peabody, Robert L., Jeffrey M. Berry, William G. Frasure, and Jerry Goldman, To *Enact a Law: Congress and Campaign Financing* (New York: Praeger, 1972).

Price, David E., dir., *The Commerce Committees: A Study of the House and Senate Commerce Committees in the Ralph Nader Congress Project* (New York: Grossman, 1975).

Schamel, Charles E. et al., "Records of the Commerce Committees," *Guide to the Records of the United States House of Representatives at the National Archives: 1789-1989 Bicentennial Edition* (Washington, D.C.: National Archives and Records Administration,1989), 93-110.

U.S. House of Representatives, Committee on Interstate and Foreign Commerce, *Historical Data Regarding the Creation and Jurisdiction of the Committee on Interstate and Foreign Commerce,* House of Representatives, House Committee Print, 92nd Congress, 1st Session (1971).

U.S. House of Representatives, Committee on Interstate and Foreign Commerce, *180 Years of Service: A Brief History of the Committee on Interstate and Foreign Commerce,* U.S. House of Representatives, House Committee Print, 94th Congress, 1st Session (1975).

Whiteman, David, "The Fate of Policy Analysis in Congressional Decision Making: Three Types of Use in Committees," *Western Political Quarterly*, 38 (June, 1985), 294-311.

RESPONSIBILITIES, JURISDICTIONAL CHANGES, AND SUBCOMMITTEES

INTERSTATE AND FOREIGN COMMERCE

Jurisdiction, 80th Congress (1947-1949)

Established by the Legislative Reorganization Act of 1946:

[Section 121.(1)(k)] Committee on Interstate and Foreign Commerce
  (1) Interstate and foreign commerce generally.
  (2) Regulation of interstate and foreign transportation, except transportation by water not subject to the jurisdiction of the Interstate Commerce Commission.
  (3) Regulation of interstate and foreign communications.
  (4) Civil aeronautics.
  (5) Weather bureau.
  (6) Interstate oil compacts; and petroleum and natural gas, except on the public lands.
  (7) Securities and exchanges.
  (8) Regulation of interstate transmission of power, except the installation of connections between Government water power projects.

(9) Railroad labor and railroad retirement and unemployment, except revenue measures relating thereto.
(10) Public health and quarantine.
(11) Inland waterways.
(12) Bureau of Standards, standardization of weights and measures, and the metric system.

ENERGY AND COMMERCE

Interstate and Foreign Commerce was renamed the Committee on Energy and Commerce on March 25, 1980, effective January 3, 1981.

Jurisdiction, 103rd Congress (1993-1995)

From the Rules of the House of Representatives, 103rd Congress (House Document 102-405)

[Rule X.1.(h)] Committee on Energy and Commerce

(1) Interstate and foreign commerce, generally.
(2) National energy policy generally.
(3) Measures relating to the exploration, production, storage, supply, marketing, pricing, and regulation of energy resources, including all fossils, fuels, solar energy, and other unconventional or renewable energy resources.
(4) Measures relating to the conservation of energy resources.
(5) Measures relating to the commercial application of energy technology.
(6) Measures relating to energy information generally.
(7) Measures relating to

   (A) the generation and marketing of power (except by federally chartered or Federal regional power marketing authorities,
   (B) the reliability and interstate transmission of, and ratemaking for, all power, and
   (C) the siting of generation facilities; except the installation of interconnections between Government waterpower projects.

(8) Interstate energy compacts.
(9) Measures relating to general management of the Department of Energy, and the management and all functions of the Federal Energy Regulatory Commission.
(10) Inland waterways.
(11) Railroads, including railroad labor, railroad retirement and unemployment, except revenue measures related thereto.
(12) Regulations of interstate and foreign communications.
(13) Securities and exchanges.
(14) Consumer affairs and consumer protection.
(15) Travel and tourism.
(16) Public health and quarantine.
(17) Health and health facilities, except health care supported by payroll deductions.
(18) Biomedical research and development.

Such committee shall have the same jurisdiction with respect to regulation of nuclear facilities and of use of nuclear energy as it has with respect to regulation of non-nuclear facilities and of use of non-nuclear energy.

In addition to its legislative jurisdiction under the preceding provisions of this paragraph (and its general oversight functions under clause 2(b)(1)), such committee shall have the special oversight functions provided for in clause (3)(h) with respect to all laws, programs, and Government activities affecting nuclear and other energy.

[Rule X.3.(h)] Additional Functions

The Committee on Energy and Commerce shall have the function of reviewing and studying on a continuing basis, all laws, programs and government activities relating to nuclear and other energy matters.

COMMERCE

Energy and Commerce was renamed the Committee on Commerce on January 4, 1995.

Jurisdiction, 104th Congress (1995-1997) Changes in Committee System

From H. Res. 6, Section 202 (a), the Committees and Their Jurisdiction, January 4, 1995

[Rule X.1.(e)] Committee on Commerce

(1) Biomedical research and development.
(2) Consumer affairs and consumer protection.

(3) Health and health facilities, except health care supported by payroll deductions.

(4) Interstate energy compacts.

(5) Interstate and foreign commerce generally.

(6) Measures relating to the exploration, production, storage, supply, marketing, pricing, and regulation of energy resources, including all fossil fuels, solar energy, and other unconventional or renewable energy resources.

(7) Measures relating to the conservation of energy resources.

(8) Measures relating to energy information generally.

(9) Measures relating to (A) the generation and marketing of power (except by federally chartered or Federal regional power marketing authorities), (B) the reliability and interstate transmission of, and ratemaking for, all power, and (C) the siting of generation facilities; except the installation of interconnections between Government waterpower projects.

(10) Measures relating to general management of the Department of Energy, and the management and all functions of the Federal Energy Regulatory Commission.

(11) National energy policy generally.

(12) Public health and quarantine.

(13) Regulation of the domestic nuclear energy industry, including regulation of research and development reactors and nuclear regulatory research.

(14) Regulation of interstate and foreign communications.

(15) Securities and exchanges.

(16) Travel and tourism. The committee shall have the same jurisdiction with respect to regulation of nuclear facilities and of use of nuclear energy as it has with respect to regulation of non-nuclear facilities and of use of non-nuclear energy. In addition to its legislative jurisdiction under the preceding provisions of this paragraph (and its general oversight functions under clause 2(b)(1)), such committee shall have the special oversight functions provided for in clause (3)(h) with respect to all laws, programs, and Government activities affecting nuclear and other energy, and nonmilitary nuclear energy and research and development including the disposal of nuclear waste.

ENERGY AND COMMERCE

Commerce was redesignated the Committee on Energy and Commerce on January 3, 2001.

Jurisdiction, 111th Congress (2009-2011)

From the Rules of the House of Representatives (as revised to June 16, 2009, H.Doc. 110-162):

[Rule X.1.(f)] Committee on Energy and Commerce

(1) Biomedical research and development.

(2) Consumer affairs and consumer protection.

(3) Health and health facilities (except health care supported by payroll deductions).

(4) Interstate energy compacts.

(5) Interstate and foreign commerce generally.

(6) Exploration, production, storage, supply, marketing, pricing, and regulation of energy resources, including all fossil fuels, solar energy, and other unconventional or renewable energy resources.

(7) Conservation of energy resources.

(8) Energy information generally.

(9) The generation and marketing of power (except by federally chartered or Federal regional power marketing authorities); reliability and interstate transmission of, and ratemaking for, all power; and siting of generation facilities (except the installation of interconnections between Government waterpower projects).

(10) General management of the Department of Energy and management and all functions of the Federal Energy Regulatory Commission.

(11) National energy policy generally.

(12) Public health and quarantine.

(13) Regulation of the domestic nuclear energy industry, including regulation of research and development reactors and nuclear regulatory research.

(14) Regulation of interstate and foreign communications.

(15) Travel and tourism.

(16) The committee shall have the same jurisdiction with respect to regulation of nuclear facilities and of use of nuclear energy as it has with respect to regulation of non-nuclear facilities and of use of non-nuclear energy.

[Rule X.3.(e)] Special Oversight Function

The Committee on Energy and Commerce shall review and study on a continuing basis laws, programs, and Government activities relating to nuclear and other energy and nonmilitary nuclear energy research and development including the disposal of nuclear waste.

NAMES OF ENERGY AND COMMERCE SUBCOMMITTEES FROM THE *CONGRESSIONAL DIRECTORY*

Energy and Commerce, 103rd Congress

Commerce, Consumer Protection, and Competitiveness, 103
Energy and Power, 103
Health and Environment, 103 Telecommunications and Finance, 103
Transportation and Hazardous Materials, 103 Oversight and Investigations, 103

Commerce, 104th-106th Congresses

Commerce, Trade and Hazardous Materials, 104 Energy and Power, 104, 105, 106
Finance and Hazardous Materials, 105, 106 Health and Environment, 104, 105, 106
Oversight and Investigations, 104, 105, 106 Telecommunications and Finance, 104
Telecommunications, Trade, and Consumer Protection, 105, 106

Energy and Commerce, 107th-111th Congresses

Commerce, Trade, and Consumer Protection, 107, 108, 109, 110, 111
Energy and Air Quality, 107, 108, 109, 110
Energy and Environment, 111
Environment and Hazardous Materials, 107, 108, 109, 110
Health, 107, 108, 109, 110, 111
Oversight and Investigations, 107, 108, 109, 110, 111
Telecommunications and the Internet, 107, 108, 109, 110
Communications, Technology, and the Internet, 111

MEMBERSHIP ROSTERS, 103rd-111th Congresses, 1993-2011

ENERGY AND COMMERCE / 103rd Congress

Service Dates of Committee Chair: Jan. 5, 1993-Jan. 3, 1995

Service Dates of Majority Members: Jan. 5, 1993-Jan. 3, 1995

Service Dates of Minority Members: Jan. 5, 1993-Jan. 3, 1995

Roster Filled: Majority with 27 members, Jan. 5, 1993; Minority with 17 members, Jan. 5, 1993

Majority

Rank Name	Party	State	Terms in: House	Terms in: Comm.
Chr Dingell, John D. Jr.	Dem	Mich.	20	19
2nd Waxman, Henry A.	Dem	Cal.	10	10
3rd Sharp, Philip R.	Dem	Ind.	10	10
4th Markey, Edward J.	Dem	Mass.	10	9
5th Swift, Allan B.	Dem	Wash.	8	8
6th Collins, Cardiss	Dem	Ill.	11	*1 7
7th Synar, Michael L.	Dem	Okla.	8	7
8th Tauzin, W.J. (Billy)	Dem	La.	8	*1 7
9th Wyden, Ronald L.	Dem	Ore.	7	7
10th Hall, Ralph M.	Dem	Tex.	7	*1 7
11th Richardson, William B.	Dem	N.M.	6	*1 6
12th Slattery, James C.	Dem	Kans.	6	6
13th Bryant, John W.	Dem	Tex.	6	6
14th Boucher, Frederick C.	Dem	Va.	6	4
15th Cooper, James H.S.	Dem	Tenn.	6	4
16th Rowland, J. Roy	Dem	Ga.	6	3
17th Manton, Thomas J.	Dem	N.Y.	5	3
18th Towns, Edolphus	Dem	N.Y.	6	3
19th Studds, Gerry E.	Dem	Mass.	11	2
20th Lehman, Richard H.	Dem	Cal.	6	2

Minority

Rank Name	Party	State	Terms in: House	Terms in: Comm.
RM Moorhead, Carlos J.	Rep	Cal.	11	10
2nd Bliley, Thomas J. Jr.	Rep	Va.	7	7
3rd Fields, Jack M. Jr.	Rep	Tex.	7	6
4th Oxley, Michael G.	Rep	Ohio	7	6
5th Bilirakis, Michael	Rep	Fla.	6	5
6th Schaefer, Daniel L.	Rep	Colo.	6	5
7th Barton, Joe L.	Rep	Tex.	5	4
8th McMillan, J. Alex	Rep	N.C.	5	3
9th Hastert, J. Dennis	Rep	Ill.	4	*1 2
10th Upton, Frederick S.	Rep	Mich.	4	2
11th Stearns, Clifford B.	Rep	Fla.	3	1
12th Paxon, L. William	Rep	N.Y.	3	1
13th Gillmor, Paul E.	Rep	Ohio	3	*1 1
14th Klug, Scott L.	Rep	Wisc.	2	1
15th Franks, Gary A.	Rep	Conn.	2	1
16th Greenwood, James C.	Rep	Penn.	1	1
17th Crapo, Michael D.	Rep	Ida.	1	1

*1: Member's first period of service on the committee.

21st Pallone, Frank Jr.	Dem	N.J.	4	*1 1	
22nd Washington, Craig A.	Dem	Tex.	3	1	
23rd Schenk, Lynn	Dem	Cal.	1	1	
24th Brown, Sherrod	Dem	Ohio	1	1	
25th Kreidler, Myron B. (Mike)	Dem	Penn.	1	1	
26th Margolies-Mezvinsky, Marjorie	Dem	Penn.	1	1	
27th Lambert, Blanche	Dem	Ark.	1	1	

Departures from the House:	**Majority**			**Minority**		
Lost Election to U.S. Senate	Cooper, James H.S.	Dem	Tenn.	None		
Lost Election for Governor	Slattery, James C.	Dem	Kans.	None		
Defeated for Re-nomination	Synar, Michael L.	Dem	La.	None		
	Washington, Craig A.	Dem	Tex.			
Defeated for Re-election	Lehman, Richard H.	Dem	Cal.	None		
	Schenk, Lynn	Dem	Cal.			
	Kreidler, Myron B. (Mike)	Dem	Penn.			
	Margolies-Mezvinsky, Marjorie	Dem	Penn.			
Retired	Sharp, Philip R.	Dem	Ind.	McMillan, J. Alex	Rep	N.C.
	Swift, Allan B.	Dem	Wash.			
	Rowland, J. Roy	Dem	Ga.			

Departures from Committee:					
No new assignment	Collins, Cardiss	Dem	Ill.	None	
	Richardson, William B.	Dem	N.M.		
	Lambert, Blanche	Dem	Ark.		

COMMERCE / 104th Congress

Service Dates of Committee Chair: Jan. 4, 1995-Jan. 3, 1997

Service Dates of Majority Members: Jan. 4, 1995-Jan. 3, 1997

Service Dates of Minority Members: Jan. 4, 1995-Jan. 3, 1997

Roster Filled: Majority with 25 members, Jan. 4, 1995; Minority with 21 members, Jan. 4, 1995

Majority					**Minority**				
			Terms in:					Terms in:	
Rank Name	Party	State	House	Comm.	Rank Name	Party	State	House	Comm.
Chr Bliley, Thomas J. Jr.	Rep	Va.	8	8	RM Dingell, John D. Jr.	Dem	Mich.	21	20
2nd Moorhead, Carlos J.	Rep	Cal.	12	11	2nd Waxman, Henry A.	Dem	Cal.	11	11
3rd Fields, Jack M. Jr.	Rep	Tex.	8	7	3rd Markey, Edward J.	Dem	Mass.	11	10
4th Oxley, Michael G.	Rep	Ohio	8	7	4th Tauzin, W.J. (Billy)	Dem	La.	9	*1 8
5th Bilirakis, Michael	Rep	Fla.	7	6	5th Wyden, Ronald L.	Dem	Ore.	8	8
6th Schaefer, Daniel L.	Rep	Colo.	7	6	6th Hall, Ralph M.	Dem	Tex.	8	*1 8
7th Barton, Joe L.	Rep	Tex.	6	5	7th Bryant, John W.	Dem	Tex.	7	7
8th Hastert, J. Dennis	Rep	Ill.	5	*1 3	8th Boucher, Frederick C.	Dem	Va.	7	5
9th Upton, Frederick S.	Rep	Mich.	5	3	9th Manton, Thomas J.	Dem	N.Y.	6	4
10th Stearns, Clifford B.	Rep	Fla.	4	2	10th Towns, Edolphus	Dem	N.Y.	7	4
11th Paxon, L. William	Rep	N.Y.	4	2	11th Studds, Gerry E.	Dem	Mass.	12	3
12th Gillmor, Paul E.	Rep	Ohio	4	*1 2	12th Pallone, Frank Jr.	Dem	N.J.	5	*1 2
13th Klug, Scott L.	Rep	Wisc.	3	2	13th Brown, Sherrod	Dem	Ohio	2	2
14th Franks, Gary A.	Rep	Conn.	3	2	14th Lincoln, Blanche Lambert	Dem	Ark.	2	2
15th Greenwood, James C.	Rep	Penn.	2	2	15th Gordon, Barton J.	Dem	Tenn.	6	1
16th Crapo, Michael D.	Rep	Ida.	2	2	16th Furse, Elizabeth	Dem	Ore.	2	1
17th Cox, C. Christopher	Rep	Cal.	4	1	17th Deutsch, Peter R.	Dem	Fla.	2	1
18th Burr, Richard M.	Rep	N.C.	1	1	18th Rush, Bobby L.	Dem	Ill.	2	1
19th Bilbray, Brian P.	Rep	Cal.	1	1	19th Eshoo, Anna G.	Dem	Cal.	2	1
20th Whitfield, W. Edward	Rep	Ky.	1	1	20th Klink, Ronald	Dem	Penn.	2	1
21st Ganske, Greg	Rep	Iowa	1	1	21st Stupak, Bart T.	Dem	Mich.	2	1
22nd Frisa, Daniel	Rep	N.Y.	1	1					
23rd Norwood, Charles W. Jr.	Rep	Ga.	1	1	*1: Member's first period of service on the committee.				
24th White, Richard A.	Rep	Wash.	1	1					
25th Coburn, Thomas A.	Rep	Okla.	1	1					

Additions:

Majority:

Deal, J. Nathan	Rep	Ga.	May 25, 1995 Left the Democratic Party and was ranked after Cox
Tauzin, W.J. (Billy)	Rep	La.	Sept. 12, 1995 Left the Democratic Party; returned as a Republican and ranked after Moorhead

Minority:

Richardson, William B.	Dem	N.M.	Sept. 27, 1995 Ranked immediately after Hall

Changes:
Minority:

Tauzin, W.J. (Billy)	Dem	La.	Sep. 6, 1995 Service on committee as a Democrat was vacated; returned to Commerce as a Republican on Sept. 12, 1995
Collins, Cardiss	Dem	Ill.	Sep. 27, 1995 Replaced Tauzin
Wyden, Ronald L.	Dem	Ore.	Feb. 5, 1996 Resigned the House; elected to U.S. Senate
Engel, Eliot L.	Dem	N.Y.	Apr. 22, 1996 Replaced Wyden

Departures from the House:

	Majority			Minority		
Lost Nomination to U.S. Senate	None			Bryant, John W.	Dem	Tex.
Defeated for Re-election	Franks, Gary A.	Rep	Conn.	None		
	Frisa, Daniel	Rep	N.Y.			
Retired	Moorhead, Carlos J.	Rep	Cal.	Studds, Gerry E.	Dem	Mass.
	Fields, Jack M. Jr.	Rep	Tex.	Lincoln, Blanche Lambert	Dem	Ark.
				Collins, Cardiss	Dem	Ill.

Departures from Committee:

	Majority			Minority		
No new assignment	None			Pallone, Frank Jr.	Dem	N.J.

COMMERCE / 105th Congress

Service Dates of Committee Chair: Jan. 7, 1997-Jan. 3, 1999

Service Dates of Majority Members: Jan. 7, 1997-Jan. 3, 1999

Service Dates of Minority Members: Jan. 7, 1997-Jan. 3, 1999

Roster Filled: Majority with 28 members, Jan. 7, 1997; Minority with 23 members, Jan. 21, 1997

	Majority			Terms in:			Minority			Terms in:	
Rank Name		Party	State	House	Comm.	Rank Name		Party	State	House	Comm.
Chr Bliley, Thomas J. Jr.		Rep	Va.	9	9	RM Dingell, John D. Jr.		Dem	Mich.	22	21
2nd Tauzin, W.J. (Billy)		Rep	La.	10	*2 2	2nd Waxman, Henry A.		Dem	Cal.	12	12
3rd Oxley, Michael G.		Rep	Ohio	9	8	3rd Markey, Edward J.		Dem	Mass.	12	11
4th Bilirakis, Michael		Rep	Fla.	8	7	4th Hall, Ralph M.		Dem	Tex.	9	*1 9
5th Schaefer, Daniel L.		Rep	Colo.	8	7	5th Richardson, William B.		Dem	N.M.	8	*2 2
6th Barton, Joe L.		Rep	Tex.	7	6	6th Boucher, Frederick C.		Dem	Va.	8	6
7th Hastert, J. Dennis		Rep	Ill.	6	*1 4	7th Manton, Thomas J.		Dem	N.Y.	7	5
8th Upton, Frederick S.		Rep	Mich.	6	4	8th Towns, Edolphus		Dem	N.Y.	8	5
9th Stearns, Clifford B.		Rep	Fla.	5	3	9th Brown, Sherrod		Dem	Ohio	3	3
10th Paxon, L. William		Rep	N.Y.	5	3	10th Gordon, Barton J.		Dem	Tenn.	7	2
11th Gillmor, Paul E.		Rep	Ohio	5	*1 3	11th Furse, Elizabeth		Dem	Ore.	3	2
12th Klug, Scott L.		Rep	Wisc.	4	3	12th Deutsch, Peter R.		Dem	Fla.	3	2
13th Greenwood, James C.		Rep	Penn.	3	3	13th Rush, Bobby L.		Dem	Ill.	3	2
14th Crapo, Michael D.		Rep	Ida.	3	3	14th Eshoo, Anna G.		Dem	Cal.	3	2
15th Cox, C. Christopher		Rep	Cal.	5	2	15th Klink, Ronald		Dem	Penn.	3	2
16th Deal, J. Nathan		Rep	Ga.	3	2	16th Stupak, Bart T.		Dem	Mich.	3	2
17th Largent, Steve		Rep	Okla.	3	1	17th Engel, Eliot L.		Dem	N.Y.	5	2
18th Burr, Richard M.		Rep	N.C.	2	2	18th Wynn, Albert R.		Dem	Md.	3	1
19th Bilbray, Brian P.		Rep	Cal.	2	2	19th Green, R. Eugene (Gene)		Dem	Tex.	3	1
20th Whitfield, W. Edward		Rep	Ky.	2	2	20th McCarthy, Karen		Dem	Mo.	2	1
21st Ganske, Greg		Rep	Iowa	2	2	21st Strickland, Ted		Dem	Ohio	2	1
22nd Norwood, Charles W. Jr.		Rep	Ga.	2	2	22nd DeGette, Diana		Dem	Colo.	1	1
23rd White, Richard A.		Rep	Wash.	2	2	23rd Sawyer, Thomas C.		Dem	Ohio	6	1
24th Coburn, Thomas A.		Rep	Okla.	2	2						
25th Lazio, Enrico A. (Rick)		Rep	N.Y.	3	1						
26th Cubin, Barbara		Rep	Wy.	2	1						
27th Rogan, James E.		Rep	Cal.	1	1						
28th Shimkus, John M.		Rep	Ill.	1	1						

*1: Member's first period of service on the committee.
*2: Member's second period of service on the committee.

Note: Sawyer re-ranked on Jan. 21, 1997, moved from 23rd seat to 18th seat to follow immediately after Engel.

Additions:
Majority:

29th Wilson, Heather A.	Rep	N.M.	Aug. 3, 1998

Changes:

Minority:

Richardson, William B.	Dem	N.M.	Feb. 13, 1997 Resigned the House; appointed U.S. Ambassador to the United Nations	
Pallone, Frank Jr.	Dem	N.J.	Feb. 13, 1997 Returned to committee, replacing Richardson; ranked following Towns	

Departures from the House:	Majority			Minority		
Elected to U.S. Senate	Crapo, Michael D.	Rep	Ida.	None		
Defeated for Re-election	White, Richard A.	Rep	Wash.	None		
Retired	Schaefer, Daniel L.	Rep	Colo.	Manton, Thomas J.	Dem	N.Y.
	Paxon, L. William	Rep	N.Y.	Furse, Elizabeth	Dem	Ore.
	Klug, Scott L.	Rep	Wisc.			

Departures from Committee:	Majority			Minority
Elected Speaker of the House	Hastert, J. Dennis	Rep	Ill.	None

COMMERCE / 106th Congress

Service Dates of Committee Chair: Jan. 6, 1999-Jan. 3, 2001

Service Dates of Majority Members: Jan. 6, 1999-Jan. 3, 2001

Service Dates of Minority Members: Jan. 6, 1999-Jan. 3, 2001

Roster Filled: Majority with 29 members, Jan. 6, 1999; Minority with 24 members, Jan. 6, 1999

	Majority					Minority				
				Terms in:					**Terms in:**	
Rank Name	**Party**	**State**	**House**	**Comm.**		**Rank Name**	**Party**	**State**	**House**	**Comm.**
Chr Bliley, Thomas J. Jr.	Rep	Va.	10	10		RM Dingell, John D. Jr.	Dem	Mich.	23	22
2nd Tauzin, W.J. (Billy)	Rep	La.	11	*2 3		2nd Waxman, Henry A.	Dem	Cal.	13	13
3rd Oxley, Michael G.	Rep	Ohio	10	9		3rd Markey, Edward J.	Dem	Mass.	13	12
4th Bilirakis, Michael	Rep	Fla.	9	8		4th Hall, Ralph M.	Dem	Tex.	10	*1 10
5th Barton, Joe L.	Rep	Tex.	8	7		5th Boucher, Frederick C.	Dem	Va.	9	7
6th Upton, Frederick S.	Rep	Mich.	7	5		6th Towns, Edolphus	Dem	N.Y.	9	6
7th Stearns, Clifford B.	Rep	Fla.	6	4		7th Pallone, Frank Jr.	Dem	N.J.	7	*2 2
8th Gillmor, Paul E.	Rep	Ohio	6	*1 4		8th Brown, Sherrod	Dem	Ohio	4	4
9th Greenwood, James C.	Rep	Penn.	4	4		9th Gordon, Barton J.	Dem	Tenn.	8	3
10th Cox, C. Christopher	Rep	Cal.	6	3		10th Deutsch, Peter R.	Dem	Fla.	4	3
11th Deal, J. Nathan	Rep	Ga.	4	3		11th Rush, Bobby L.	Dem	Ill.	4	3
12th Largent, Steve	Rep	Okla.	4	2		12th Eshoo, Anna G.	Dem	Cal.	4	3
13th Burr, Richard M.	Rep	N.C.	3	3		13th Klink, Ronald	Dem	Penn.	4	3
14th Bilbray, Brian P.	Rep	Cal.	3	3		14th Stupak, Bart T.	Dem	Mich.	4	3
15th Whitfield, W. Edward	Rep	Ky.	3	3		15th Engel, Eliot L.	Dem	N.Y.	6	3
16th Ganske, Greg	Rep	Iowa	3	3		16th Sawyer, Thomas C.	Dem	Ohio	7	2
17th Norwood, Charles W. Jr.	Rep	Ga.	3	3		17th Wynn, Albert R.	Dem	Md.	4	2
18th Coburn, Thomas A.	Rep	Okla.	3	3		18th Green, R. Eugene (Gene)	Dem	Tex.	4	2
19th Lazio, Enrico A. (Rick)	Rep	N.Y.	4	2		19th McCarthy, Karen	Dem	Mo.	3	2
20th Cubin, Barbara	Rep	Wy.	3	2		20th Strickland, Ted	Dem	Ohio	3	2
21st Rogan, James E.	Rep	Cal.	2	2		21st DeGette, Diana	Dem	Colo.	2	2
22nd Shimkus, John M.	Rep	Ill.	2	2		22nd Barrett, Thomas M.	Dem	Wisc.	4	1
23rd Wilson, Heather A.	Rep	N.M.	2	2		23rd Luther, William P.	DFL	Minn.	3	1
24th Shadegg, John B.	Rep	Ariz.	3	1		24th Capps, Lois	Dem	Cal.	2	1
25th Pickering, Charles W. (Chip) Jr.	Rep	Miss.	2	1						
26th Fossella, Vito J.	Rep	N.Y.	2	1		*1: Member's first period of service on the committee.				
27th Blunt, Roy	Rep	Mo.	2	*1 1		*2: Member's second period of service on the committee.				
28th Bryant, Ed	Rep	Tenn.	3	1						
29th Ehrlich, Robert L. Jr.	Rep	Md.	3	1						

Departures from the House:	Majority			Minority		
Lost Election to U.S. Senate	Lazio, Enrico A. (Rick)	Rep	N.Y.	Klink, Ronald	Dem	Penn.
Defeated for Re-election	Bilbray, Brian P.	Rep	Cal.	None		
	Rogan, James E.	Rep	Cal.			
Retired	Bliley, Thomas J. Jr.	Rep	Va.	None		
	Coburn, Thomas A.	Rep	Okla.			

Departures from Committee:				
Moved to Financial Services as Chair	Oxley, Michael G.	Rep	Ohio	None

ENERGY AND COMMERCE / 107th Congress

Service Dates of Committee Chair: Jan. 6, 2001-Jan. 3, 2003

Service Dates of Majority Members: Jan. 6, 2001-Jan. 3, 2003

Service Dates of Minority Members: Jan. 31, 2001-Jan. 3, 2003

Roster Filled: Majority with 31 members, Feb. 8, 2001; Minority with 26 members, Feb. 8, 2001

	Majority			Terms in:			Minority			Terms in:	
Rank Name		Party	State	House	Comm.	Rank Name		Party	State	House	Comm.
Chr Tauzin, W.J. (Billy)		Rep	La.	12	*2 4	RM Dingell, John D. Jr.		Dem	Mich.	24	23
2nd Bilirakis, Michael		Rep	Fla.	10	9	2nd Waxman, Henry A.		Dem	Cal.	14	14
3rd Barton, Joe L.		Rep	Tex.	9	8	3rd Markey, Edward J.		Dem	Mass.	14	13
4th Upton, Frederick S.		Rep	Mich.	8	6	4th Hall, Ralph M.		Dem	Tex.	11	*1 11
5th Stearns, Clifford B.		Rep	Fla.	7	5	5th Boucher, Frederick C.		Dem	Va.	10	8
6th Gillmor, Paul E.		Rep	Ohio	7	*1 5	6th Towns, Edolphus		Dem	N.Y.	10	7
7th Greenwood, James C.		Rep	Penn.	5	5	7th Pallone, Frank Jr.		Dem	N.J.	8	*2 3
8th Cox, C. Christopher		Rep	Cal.	7	4	8th Brown, Sherrod		Dem	Ohio	5	5
9th Deal, J. Nathan		Rep	Ga.	5	4	9th Gordon, Barton J.		Dem	Tenn.	9	4
10th Largent, Steve		Rep	Okla.	5	3	10th Deutsch, Peter R.		Dem	Fla.	5	4
11th Burr, Richard M.		Rep	N.C.	4	4	11th Rush, Bobby L.		Dem	Ill.	5	4
12th Whitfield, W. Edward		Rep	Ky.	4	4	12th Eshoo, Anna G.		Dem	Cal.	5	4
13th Ganske, Greg		Rep	Iowa	4	4	13th Stupak, Bart T.		Dem	Mich.	5	4
14th Norwood, Charles W. Jr.		Rep	Ga.	4	4	14th Engel, Eliot L.		Dem	N.Y.	7	4
15th Cubin, Barbara		Rep	Wy.	4	3	15th Sawyer, Thomas C.		Dem	Ohio	8	3
16th Shimkus, John M.		Rep	Ill.	3	3	16th Wynn, Albert R.		Dem	Md.	5	3
17th Wilson, Heather A.		Rep	N.M.	3	3	17th Green, R. Eugene (Gene)		Dem	Tex.	5	3
18th Shadegg, John B.		Rep	Ariz.	4	2	18th McCarthy, Karen		Dem	Mo.	4	3
19th Pickering, Charles W. (Chip) Jr.		Rep	Miss.	3	2	19th Strickland, Ted		Dem	Ohio	4	3
20th Fossella, Vito J.		Rep	N.Y.	3	2	20th DeGette, Diana		Dem	Colo.	3	3
21st Blunt, Roy		Rep	Mo.	3	*1 2	21st Barrett, Thomas M.		Dem	Wisc.	5	2
22nd Davis, Thomas M. III		Rep	Va.	4	1	22nd Luther, William P.		DFL	Minn.	4	2
23rd Bryant, Ed		Rep	Tenn.	4	2	23rd Capps, Lois		Dem	Cal.	3	2
24th Ehrlich, Robert L. Jr.		Rep	Md.	4	2	24th Doyle, Michael F.		Dem	Penn.	4	1
25th Buyer, Stephen E.		Rep	Ind.	5	1	25th John, Christopher		Dem	La.	3	1
26th Radanovich, George P.		Rep	Cal.	4	1	26th Harman, Jane L.		Dem	Cal.	4	*1 1
27th Bass, Charles F.		Rep	N.H.	4	1						
28th Pitts, Joseph R.		Rep	Penn.	3	1						
29th Bono, Mary		Rep	Cal.	3	1						
30th Walden, Greg		Rep	Ore.	2	1						
31st Terry, Lee R.		Rep	Neb.	2	1						

*1: Member's first period of service on the committee.

*2: Member's second period of service on the committee.

Vacancies Filled:

  Majority:

    27th seat filled by Bass on Feb. 8, 2001

  Minority:

    24th through 26th seats filled by Doyle, John, and Harman on Feb. 8, 2001

Changes:

  Majority:

Largent, Steve	Rep	Okla.	Feb. 15, 2002 Resigned the House; lost for Governor
Fletcher, Ernest L.	Rep	Ky.	Mar. 20, 2002 Replaced Largent

Departures from the House:	**Majority**			**Minority**		
Elected Governor	Ehrlich, Robert L. Jr.	Rep	Md.	None		
Lost Nomination to U.S. Senate	Bryant, Ed	Rep	Tenn.	None		
Lost Election to U.S. Senate	Ganske, Greg	Rep	Iowa	None		
Lost Election for Governor	None			Barrett, Thomas M.	Dem	Wisc.
Defeated for Re-nomination	None			Sawyer, Thomas C.	Dem	Ohio
Defeated for Re-election	None			Luther, William P.	Dem	Minn.

Departures from Committee:						
Became Chair of Government Reform	Davis, Thomas M. III	Rep	Va.	None		
Became RM on Permanent Select Intelligence	None			Harman, Jane L.	Dem	Cal.

ENERGY AND COMMERCE / 108th Congress

Service Dates of Committee Chair: Ch1 Jan. 8, 2003-Feb. 16, 2004 Tauzin (Rep-La.)

Ch2 Feb. 26, 2004-Jan. 3, 2005 Barton (Rep-Tex.)

Service Dates of Majority Members: Jan. 28, 2003-Jan. 3, 2005

Service Dates of Ranking Member: Jan. 8, 2003-Jan. 3, 2005

Service Dates of Minority Members: Jan. 28, 2003-Jan. 3, 2005

Roster Filled: Majority with 31 members, Jan. 28, 2003; Minority with 26 members, Jan. 28, 2003

	Majority			Terms in:			Minority			Terms in:	
Rank Name		Party	State	House	Comm.	Rank Name		Party	State	House	Comm.
Ch1 Tauzin, W.J. (Billy)		Rep	La.	13	*2 5	RM Dingell, John D. Jr.		Dem	Mich.	25	24
2nd Bilirakis, Michael		Rep	Fla.	11	10	2nd Waxman, Henry A.		Dem	Cal.	15	15
3rd Ch2 Barton, Joe L.		Rep	Tex.	10	9	3rd Markey, Edward J.		Dem	Mass.	15	14
4th Upton, Frederick S.		Rep	Mich.	9	7	4th Hall, Ralph M.		Dem	Tex.	12	*1 12
5th Stearns, Clifford B.		Rep	Fla.	8	6	5th Boucher, Frederick C.		Dem	Va.	11	9
6th Gillmor, Paul E.		Rep	Ohio	8	*1 6	6th Towns, Edolphus		Dem	N.Y.	11	8
7th Greenwood, James C.		Rep	Penn.	6	6	7th Pallone, Frank Jr.		Dem	N.J.	9	*2 4
8th Cox, C. Christopher		Rep	Cal.	8	5	8th Brown, Sherrod		Dem	Ohio	6	6
9th Deal, J. Nathan		Rep	Ga.	6	5	9th Gordon, Barton J.		Dem	Tenn.	10	5
10th Burr, Richard M.		Rep	N.C.	5	5	10th Deutsch, Peter R.		Dem	Fla.	6	5
11th Whitfield, W. Edward		Rep	Ky.	5	5	11th Rush, Bobby L.		Dem	Ill.	6	5
12th Norwood, Charles W. Jr.		Rep	Ga.	5	5	12th Eshoo, Anna G.		Dem	Cal.	6	5
13th Cubin, Barbara		Rep	Wy.	5	4	13th Stupak, Bart T.		Dem	Mich.	6	5
14th Shimkus, John M.		Rep	Ill.	4	4	14th Engel, Eliot L.		Dem	N.Y.	8	5
15th Wilson, Heather A.		Rep	N.M.	4	4	15th Wynn, Albert R.		Dem	Md.	6	4
16th Shadegg, John B.		Rep	Ariz.	5	3	16th Green, R. Eugene (Gene)		Dem	Tex.	6	4
17th Pickering, Charles W. (Chip) Jr.		Rep	Miss.	4	3	17th McCarthy, Karen		Dem	Mo.	5	4
18th Fossella, Vito J.		Rep	N.Y.	4	3	18th Strickland, Ted		Dem	Ohio	5	4
19th Blunt, Roy		Rep	Mo.	4	*1 3	19th DeGette, Diana		Dem	Colo.	4	4
20th Buyer, Stephen E.		Rep	Ind.	6	2	20th Capps, Lois		Dem	Cal.	4	3
21st Radanovich, George P.		Rep	Cal.	5	2	21st Doyle, Michael F.		Dem	Penn.	5	2
22nd Bass, Charles F.		Rep	N.H.	5	2	22nd John, Christopher		Dem	La.	4	2
23rd Pitts, Joseph R.		Rep	Penn.	4	2	23rd Allen, Thomas H.		Dem	Me.	4	1
24th Bono, Mary		Rep	Cal.	4	2	24th Davis, Jim		Dem	Fla.	4	1
25th Walden, Greg		Rep	Ore.	3	2	25th Schakowsky, Janice D.		Dem	Ill.	3	1
26th Terry, Lee R.		Rep	Neb.	3	2	26th Solis, Hilda L.		Dem	Cal.	2	1
27th Fletcher, Ernest L.		Rep	Ky.	3	2						
28th Ferguson, Michael		Rep	N.J.	2	1						
29th Rogers, Mike		Rep	Mich.	2	1						
30th Issa, Darrell E.		Rep	Cal.	2	1						
31st Otter, C.L. (Butch)		Rep	Ida.	2	1						

*1: Member's first period of service on the committee

*2: Member's second period of service on the committee.

Changes:

Majority:

Fletcher, Ernest L.	Rep	Ky.	Dec. 8, 2003 Resigned the House; elected Governor of Kentucky
Hall, Ralph M.	Rep	Tex.	Jan. 28, 2004 Returned to committee as a Republican; replacing Fletcher and ranked 3rd
Blunt, Roy	Rep	Mo.	Jan. 28, 2004 Resigned committee; moved to International Relations
Sullivan, John	Rep	Okla.	Jan. 28, 2004 Replaced Blunt
Tauzin, W.J. (Billy)	Rep	La.	Feb. 16, 2004 Resigned as chair of Energy and Commerce; ranked following Barton
Barton, Joe L.	Rep	Tex.	Feb. 26, 2004 Named Chair of Energy and Commerce

Minority:

Hall, Ralph M.	Dem	Tex.	Jan. 5, 2005 Service on committee as a Democrat was vacated; returned as a Republican on Jan. 28, 2004.
Gonzalez, Charles A.	Dem	Tex.	Jan. 21, 2004 Replaced Hall

Departures from the House:

	Majority			Minority		
Elected to U.S. Senate	Burr, Richard M.	Rep	N.C.	None		
Lost Nomination to U.S. Senate	None			Deutsch, Peter R.	Dem	Fla.
Lost Election to U.S. Senate	None			John, Christopher	Dem	La.
Retired	Tauzin, W.J. (Billy)	Rep	La.	McCarthy, Karen	Dem	Mo.
	Greenwood, James C.	Rep	Penn.			

Departures from Committee:

	Majority			Minority
Moved to Government Reform	Issa, Darrell E.	Rep	Cal.	None
Returned to International Relations	Issa, Darrell E.	Rep	Cal.	None

Returned to Judiciary	Issa, Darrell E.	Rep	Cal.	None
No new assignment	Cox, C. Christopher	Rep	Cal.	None

ENERGY AND COMMERCE / 109th Congress

Service Dates of Committee Chair: Jan. 6, 2005-Jan. 3, 2007

Service Dates of Majority Members: Jan. 6, 2005-Jan. 3, 2007

Service Dates of Minority Members: Jan. 26, 2005-Jan. 3, 2007

Roster Filled: Majority with 31 members, Jan. 26, 2005; Minority with 26 members, Jan. 26, 2005

Majority

			Terms in:	
Rank Name	Party	State	House	Comm.
Chr Barton, Joe L.	Rep	Tex.	11	10
2nd Hall, Ralph M.	Rep	Tex.	13	*2 2
3rd Bilirakis, Michael	Rep	Fla.	12	11
4th Upton, Frederick S.	Rep	Mich.	10	8
5th Stearns, Clifford B.	Rep	Fla.	9	7
6th Gillmor, Paul E.	Rep	Ohio	9	*1 7
7th Deal, J. Nathan	Rep	Ga.	7	6
8th Whitfield, W. Edward	Rep	Ky.	6	6
9th Norwood, Charles W. Jr.	Rep	Ga.	6	6
10th Cubin, Barbara	Rep	Wy.	6	5
11th Shimkus, John M.	Rep	Ill.	5	5
12th Wilson, Heather A.	Rep	N.M.	5	5
13th Shadegg, John B.	Rep	Ariz.	6	4
14th Pickering, Charles W. (Chip) Jr.	Rep	Miss.	5	4
15th Fossella, Vito J.	Rep	N.Y.	5	4
16th Blunt, Roy	Rep	Mo.	5	*2 1
17th Buyer, Stephen E.	Rep	Ind.	7	3
18th Radanovich, George P.	Rep	Cal.	6	3
19th Bass, Charles F.	Rep	N.H.	6	3
20th Pitts, Joseph R.	Rep	Penn.	5	3
21st Bono, Mary	Rep	Cal.	5	3
22nd Walden, Greg	Rep	Ore.	4	3
23rd Terry, Lee R.	Rep	Neb.	4	3
24th Ferguson, Michael	Rep	N.J.	3	2
25th Rogers, Mike	Rep	Mich.	3	2
26th Otter, C.L. (Butch)	Rep	Ida.	3	2
27th Myrick, Sue	Rep	N.C.	6	1
28th Sullivan, John	Rep	Okla.	3	2
29th Murphy, Timothy	Rep	Penn.	2	1
30th Burgess, Michael C.	Rep	Tex.	2	1
31st Blackburn, Marsha	Rep	Tenn.	2	*1 1

Minority

			Terms in:	
Rank Name	Party	State	House	Comm.
RM Dingell, John D. Jr.	Dem	Mich.	26	25
2nd Waxman, Henry A.	Dem	Cal.	16	16
3rd Markey, Edward J.	Dem	Mass.	16	15
4th Boucher, Frederick C.	Dem	Va.	12	10
5th Towns, Edolphus	Dem	N.Y.	12	9
6th Pallone, Frank Jr.	Dem	N.J.	10	*2 5
7th Brown, Sherrod	Dem	Ohio	7	7
8th Gordon, Barton J.	Dem	Tenn.	11	6
9th Rush, Bobby L.	Dem	Ill.	7	6
10th Eshoo, Anna G.	Dem	Cal.	7	6
11th Stupak, Bart T.	Dem	Mich.	7	6
12th Engel, Eliot L.	Dem	N.Y.	9	6
13th Wynn, Albert R.	Dem	Md.	7	5
14th Green, R. Eugene (Gene)	Dem	Tex.	7	5
15th Strickland, Ted	Dem	Ohio	6	5
16th DeGette, Diana	Dem	Colo.	5	5
17th Capps, Lois	Dem	Cal.	5	4
18th Doyle, Michael F.	Dem	Penn.	6	3
19th Allen, Thomas H.	Dem	Me.	5	2
20th Davis, Jim	Dem	Fla.	5	2
21st Schakowsky, Janice D.	Dem	Ill.	4	2
22nd Solis, Hilda L.	Dem	Cal.	3	2
23rd Gonzalez, Charles A.	Dem	Tex.	4	2
24th Inslee, Jay R.	Dem	Wash.	5	1
25th Baldwin, Tammy	Dem	Wisc.	4	1
26th Ross, Michael A.	Dem	Ariz.	3	1

*1: Member's first period of service on the committee.

*2: Member's second period of service on the committee.

Vacancies Filled:

  Majority:

   9th seat filled by Norwood and the 13th seat filled by Shadegg on Jan. 26, 2005

Changes:

  Majority:

Blunt, Roy	Rep	Mo.	Oct. 26, 2005 Temporarily resigned committee to serve as Interim Majority Leader
Barrett, J. Gresham	Rep	S.C.	Oct. 26, 2005 Replaced Blunt
Barrett, J. Gresham	Rep	S.C.	Feb. 7, 2006 Resigned committee to open seat for Blunt
Blunt, Roy	Rep	Mo.	Feb. 8, 2006 Replaced Barrett; resumed rank following Fossella

Departures from the House:

	Majority			Minority		
Elected to U.S. Senate	None			Brown, Sherrod	Dem	Ohio
Elected Governor	Otter, C.L. (Butch)	Rep	Ida.	Strickland, Ted	Dem	Ohio
Lost Election for Governor	None			Davis, Jim	Dem	Fla.
Defeated for Re-election	Bass, Charles F.	Rep	N.H.	None		
Retired	Bilirakis, Michael	Rep	Fla.	None		

Departures from Committee:

Elected Republican Whip	Blunt, Roy	Rep	Mo.	None
Moved to Financial Services	Blackburn, Marsha	Rep	Tenn.	
Moved to Homeland Security	Blackburn, Marsha	Rep	Tenn.	
No new assignment	Gillmor, Paul E.	Rep	Ohio	

ENERGY AND COMMERCE / 110th Congress

Service Dates of Committee Chair: Jan. 4, 2007-Jan. 3, 2009
Service Dates of Majority Members: Jan. 4, 2007-Jan.3 , 2009
Service Dates of Minority Members: Jan. 10, 2007-Jan. 3, 2009
Roster Filled: Majority with 31 members, Jan. 4, 2007; Minority with 26 members, Jan. 10, 2007

Majority

Rank Name	Party	State	House	Comm.
Chr Dingell, John D. Jr.	Dem	Mich.	27	26
2nd Waxman, Henry A.	Dem	Cal.	17	17
3rd Markey, Edward J.	Dem	Mass.	17	16
4th Boucher, Frederick C.	Dem	Va.	13	11
5th Towns, Edolphus	Dem	N.Y.	13	10
6th Pallone, Frank Jr.	Dem	N.J.	11	*2 6
7th Gordon, Barton J.	Dem	Tenn.	12	7
8th Rush, Bobby L.	Dem	Ill.	8	7
9th Eshoo, Anna G.	Dem	Cal.	8	7
10th Stupak, Bart T.	Dem	Mich.	8	7
11th Engel, Eliot L.	Dem	N.Y.	10	7
12th Wynn, Albert R.	Dem	Md.	8	6
13th Green, R. Eugene (Gene)	Dem	Tex.	8	6
14th DeGette, Diana	Dem	Colo.	6	6
15th Capps, Lois	Dem	Cal.	6	5
16th Doyle, Michael F.	Dem	Penn.	7	4
17th Harman, Jane L.	Dem	Cal.	7	*2 1
18th Allen, Thomas H.	Dem	Me.	6	3
19th Schakowsky, Janice D.	Dem	Ill.	5	3
20th Solis, Hilda L.	Dem	Cal.	4	3
21st Gonzalez, Charles A.	Dem	Tex.	5	3
22nd Inslee, Jay R.	Dem	Wash.	6	2
23rd Baldwin, Tammy	Dem	Wisc.	5	2
24th Ross, Michael A.	Dem	Ark.	4	2
25th Hooley, Darlene	Dem	Ore.	6	1
26th Weiner, Anthony D.	Dem	N.Y.	5	1
27th Matheson, James D.	Dem	Utah	4	1
28th Butterfield, George K. Jr.	Dem	N.C.	3	1
29th Melancon, Charles J.	Dem	La.	2	1
30th Barrow, John	Dem	Ga.	2	1
31st Hill, Baron P.	Dem	Ind.	4	1

Minority

Rank Name	Party	State	House	Comm.
RM Barton, Joe L.	Rep	Tex.	12	11
2nd Hall, Ralph M.	Rep	Tex.	14	*2 3
3rd Hastert, J. Dennis	Rep	Ill.	11	*2 1
4th Upton, Frederick S.	Rep	Mich.	11	9
5th Stearns, Clifford B.	Rep	Fla.	10	8
6th Deal, J. Nathan	Rep	Ga.	8	7
7th Whitfield, W. Edward	Rep	Ky.	7	7
8th Norwood, Charles W. Jr.	Rep	Ga.	7	7
9th Cubin, Barbara	Rep	Wy.	7	6
10th Shimkus, John M.	Rep	Ill.	6	6
11th Wilson, Heather A.	Rep	N.M.	6	6
12th Shadegg, John B.	Rep	Ariz.	7	5
13th Pickering, Charles W. (Chip) Jr.	Rep	Miss.	6	5
14th Fossella, Vito J.	Rep	N.Y.	6	5
15th Buyer, Stephen E.	Rep	Ind.	8	4
16th Radanovich, George P.	Rep	Cal.	7	4
17th Pitts, Joseph R.	Rep	Penn.	6	4
18th Bono, Mary	Rep	Cal.	6	4
19th Walden, Greg	Rep	Ore.	5	4
20th Terry, Lee R.	Rep	Neb.	5	4
21st Ferguson, Michael	Rep	N.J.	4	3
22nd Rogers, Mike	Rep	Mich.	4	3
23rd Myrick, Sue	Rep	N.C.	7	2
24th Sullivan, John	Rep	Okla.	4	3
25th Murphy, Timothy	Rep	Penn.	3	2
26th Burgess, Michael C.	Rep	Tex.	3	2

*2: Member's second period of service on the committee.

Changes:

Majority:

Wynn, Albert R.	Dem	Md.	Apr. 9, 2008 Resigned the House; defeated for re-nomination
Matsui, Doris O.	Dem	Cal.	June 10, 2008 Replaced Wynn

Minority:

Norwood, Charles W. Jr.	Rep	Ga.	Feb. 13, 2007 Died in office
Blackburn, Marsha	Rep	Tenn.	Mar. 12, 2007 Replaced Norwood
Sullivan, John	Rep	Okla.	June 19, 2007 Temporary leave of absence
Gillmor, Paul E.	Rep	Ohio	June 19, 2007 Replaced Sullivan during Sullivan's temporary leave of absence; ranked after Stearns
Sullivan, John	Rep	Okla.	June 27, 2007 Returned from temporary leave of absence, ranked after Myrick
Gillmor, Paul E.	Rep	Ohio	June 28, 2007 Resigned from Energy and Commerce, Sullivan having returned from temporary leave of absence; no new assignment
Hastert, J. Dennis	Rep	Ill.	Nov. 26, 2007 Resigned the House and retired
Blunt, Roy	Rep	Mo.	Dec. 18, 2007 Replaced Hastert; ranked immediately following Fossella

Departures from the House:

	Majority			**Minority**		
Lost Election to U.S. Senate	Allen, Thomas H.	Dem	Me.	None		
Lost Nomination to U.S. Senate	None			Wilson, Heather A.	Rep	N.M.
Retired	Hooley, Darlene	Dem	Ore.	Cubin, Barbara	Rep	Wyo.
				Pickering, Charles W. (Chip) Jr.	Rep	Miss.
				Fossella, Vito J.	Rep	N.Y.
				Ferguson, Michael	Rep	N.J.

Departures from Committee:

Became Chair of Oversight and Government Reform	Towns, Edolphus	Dem N.Y.	None

Note: Hilda L. Solis (Dem-Cal.) who served on the committee in the 110th was unassigned in the 111th, and resigned the House on Feb. 24, 2009, appointed Secretary of Labor.

ENERGY AND COMMERCE / 111th Congress

Service Dates of Committee Chair: Jan. 6, 2009-Jan. 3, 2011

Service Dates of Majority Members: Jan. 7, 2009-Jan. 3, 2011

Service Dates of Minority Members: Jan. 9, 2009-Jan. 3, 2011

Roster Filled: Majority with 26 members, Jan. 7, 2009; Minority with 23 members, Jan. 22, 2009

Majority					Minority				
Rank Name	Party	State	House	Comm.	Rank Name	Party	State	House	Comm.
Chr Waxman, Henry A.	Dem	Cal.	18	18	RM Barton, Joe L.	Rep	Tex.	13	12
2nd Dingell, John D. Jr.	Dem	Mich.	28	27	2nd Hall, Ralph M.	Rep	Tex.	15	*2 4
3rd Markey, Edward J.	Dem	Mass.	18	17	3rd Upton, Frederick S.	Rep	Mich.	12	10
4th Boucher, Frederick C.	Dem	Va.	14	12	4th Stearns, Clifford B.	Rep	Fla.	11	9
5th Pallone, Frank Jr.	Dem	N.J.	12	*2 7	5th Deal, J. Nathan	Rep	Ga.	9	8
6th Gordon, Barton J.	Dem	Tenn.	13	8	6th Whitfield, W. Edward	Rep	Ky.	8	8
7th Rush, Bobby L.	Dem	Ill.	9	8	7th Shimkus, John M.	Rep	Ill.	7	7
8th Eshoo, Anna G.	Dem	Cal.	9	8	8th Shadegg, John B.	Rep	Ariz.	8	6
9th Stupak, Bart T.	Dem	Mich.	9	8	9th Blunt, Roy	Rep	Mo.	7	*3 2
10th Engel, Eliot L.	Dem	N.Y.	11	8	10th Buyer, Stephen E.	Rep	Ind.	9	5
11th Green, R. Eugene (Gene)	Dem	Tex.	9	7	11th Radanovich, George P.	Rep	Cal.	8	5
12th DeGette, Diana	Dem	Colo.	7	7	12th Pitts, Joseph R.	Rep	Penn.	7	5
13th Capps, Lois	Dem	Cal.	7	6	13th Bono Mack, Mary	Rep	Cal.	7	5
14th Doyle, Michael F.	Dem	Penn.	8	5	14th Walden, Greg	Rep	Ore.	6	5
15th Harman, Jane L.	Dem	Cal.	8	*2 2	15th Terry, Lee R.	Rep	Neb.	6	5
16th Schakowsky, Janice D.	Dem	Ill.	6	4	16th Rogers, Mike	Rep	Mich.	5	4
17th Gonzalez, Charles A.	Dem	Tex.	6	4	17th Myrick, Sue	Rep	N.C.	8	3
18th Inslee, Jay R.	Dem	Wash.	7	3	18th Sullivan, John	Rep	Okla.	5	4
19th Baldwin, Tammy	Dem	Wisc.	6	3	19th Murphy, Timothy	Rep	Penn.	4	3
20th Ross, Michael A.	Dem	Ark.	5	3	20th Burgess, Michael C.	Rep	Tex.	4	3
21st Weiner, Anthony D.	Dem	N.Y.	6	2	21st Blackburn, Marsha	Rep	Tenn.	4	*2 2
22nd Matheson, James D.	Dem	Utah	5	2	22nd Gingrey, Phil	Rep	Ga.	4	1
23rd Butterfield, George K. Jr.	Dem	N.C.	4	2	23rd Scalise, Steve	Rep	La.	2	1
24th Melancon, Charles J.	Dem	La.	3	2					
25th Barrow, John	Dem	Ga.	3	2					
26th Hill, Baron P.	Dem	Ind.	5	2					
27th Matsui, Doris O.	Dem	Cal.	3	2					
28th Christensen, Donna M.C.	Dem	V.I.	7	1					
29th Castor, Kathy	Dem	Fla.	2	1					
30th Sarbanes, John	Dem	Md.	2	1					
31st Murphy, Patrick J.	Dem	Penn.	2	1					
32nd Space, Zachary T.	Dem	Ohio	2	1					
33rd McNerney, Jerry	Dem	Cal.	2	1					
34th Sutton, Betty	Dem	Ohio	2	1					
35th Braley, Bruce L.	Dem	Iowa	2	1					
36th Welch, Peter	Dem	Vt.	2	1					

*2: Member's second period of service on the committee.

Note: Territorial Delegate Donna M.C. Christensen, Donna (Dem-V.I.) was allowed to accrue committee seniority but was not included in the party ratio.

Filled Vacancy:
  Minority:
    23rd seat filled by Scalise on Jan. 22, 2009

Changes:
  Minority:

Walden, Greg	Rep	Ore.	Feb. 23, 2010 Stepped aside for Griffith; no new assignment named to Republican leadership
Griffith, Parker	Rep	Ala	Feb. 23, 2010 Replaced Walden
Deal, J. Nathan	Rep	Ga.	Mar. 21, 2010 Resigned to run for Governor
Latta, Robert E.	Rep	Ohio	Mar. 25, 2010 Replaced Deal

Financial Services

House Committee on Banking, Finance and Urban Affairs, 103rd Congress (1993-1995)

House Committee on Banking and Financial Services, 104th-106th Congresses (1995-2001)

House Committee on Financial Services, 107th-111th Congresses (2001-2011)

BACKGROUND

Organizational History: The original name of the committee was Banking and Currency and it dates from March 2, 1865. Like the Appropriations Committee, it was created from the Ways and Means Committee during the Civil War. The sponsor of the legislation was Samuel S. (Sunset) Cox of New York, one of the few remaining Democrats in the 38th Congress (1863-1865). The committee's first chair was Theodore M. Pomeroy (Rep-N.Y.) who would serve as Speaker of the House for a single day, March 3, 1869, when Speaker Schuyler Colfax of Ohio resigned to become Ulysses S. Grant's first vice president. Its junior-most member in that initial Congress was Samuel J. Randall (Dem-Penn.), who would later serve as Speaker (1875-1881) and would be the chair of Appropriations in 1883 when Woodrow Wilson decreed in Congressional Government that "all are subordinate to the Chairman of Appropriations."

The committee's jurisdiction and form remained relatively unchanged from 1880 through 1946. In the 1946 Reorganization Act, Banking and Currency was given most of the jurisdiction formerly accorded to the Committee on Coinage, Weights, and Measures, a committee that had existed since January 24, 1864, predating Banking by a year. Beginning in 1971, the committee expanded its scope. Functions carried out by the Select Small Business Committee were to be gradually transferred to Banking, most notably, the oversight of tax-exempt foundations and charitable trusts, on the advice of Wright Patman (Dem-Texas), who had chaired both committees. However, the Committee Reform Amendments of 1974 elevated Small Business from a select committee to a standing committee and that effort slowed. But according to the House Manual (2008), those 1974 amendments gave the Banking committee:

> jurisdiction over Federal monetary policy, money and credit, urban development, economic stabilization, defense production, and renegotiation (the latter matter formerly within the jurisdiction of the Committee on Ways and Means), international finance, and international financial and monetary organizations (formerly within the jurisdiction of the Committee on Foreign Affairs).

It was those amendments that led to the renaming of the committee as Banking, Currency, and Housing in the 94th Congress (1975-1977), but this was also the Congress in which Wright Patman would lose the chairmanship to Henry Reuss (Dem-Wisc.). In 1977, the Committee's name was changed again to the Committee on Banking, Finance and Urban Affairs. This brought the committee's name and jurisdiction more in line with the Senate's standing committee on Banking, Housing and Urban Affairs.

The committee is responsible for regulation of the complex U.S. financial system and focuses primarily on the rapidly changing financial world. In the 1990s it spent relatively little time on the urban problems that dominated its agenda in the 1960s. In the 1980s and the following decades, the committee was faced with adjusting the rules that govern the financial system in response to the now global world of finance. The committee deals with a wide range of authorizing legislation, from the Export-Import Bank to rehabilitation of rental housing, and it shares responsibility for international trade. In the late 1980s and early 1990s, troubles in the savings and loan industry dominated its agenda as hundreds of savings and loan institutions went bankrupt under the weight of bad loans, recession, and a collapsed real estate market. Multibillion dollar bailouts financed by taxpayers were required.

Following the Republican takeover in the 104th Congress (1995-1997), the committee's name was changed to Banking and Financial Services, and in 2001 the name was changed once again to be simply Financial Services. That name change was accompanied by its gaining jurisdiction over securities and exchanges from the Committee on Energy and Commerce and jurisdiction over insurance generally.

Although the committee still has jurisdiction over bills providing consolidation of grant-in-aid programs for urban development, its major focus has been on the nation's financial sector, including public credit, issues of notes, and state taxation and redemption, propositions to maintain the parity of the money of the United States, the issue of silver certificates as currency, national banks and current deposits of public money, the incorporation of an international bank, as well as subjects relating to the Freedman's Bank, the Federal Reserve System, Farm Loan Act, home loan bills, stabilization of the dollar, War Finance Corporation, and Federal Reserve bank building.

Led by its present chair, the colorful Barney Frank (Dem-Mass.), the Financial Services Committee has made use of its large membership expansion to address the serious fiscal issues left in the wake of the Wall Street meltdown of 2007-2008 and to hold the Securities and Exchanges Commission accountable for many of the nation's recent fiscal woes.

Membership: The original size of the Banking committee in 1865 was nine, but it had grown to seventeen by 1898. In

1933, the Banking and Currency Committee's size was set at twenty-five and that number remained in place until 1947. The committee then known as Banking, Finance and Urban Affairs reached the fifty-member mark for the first time in 1989. With four members added in 1998, the Banking and Financial Affairs Committee reached sixty and by the 107th Congress in 2001, the committee now known as Financial Services, numbered seventy-one members—a growth of twenty seats since 1993. As a result of its recent growth, Financial Services had a mean membership size of sixty-four, 11 in the most recent nine Congresses edging out the Appropriations Committee (62.11) for second place and ranked only behind Transportation and Infrastructure among the nineteen standing committees active throughout the years from 1993 to 2011.

However, as often happens to congressional committees experiencing rapid growth, the large influx of junior members led to a drop in the level of mean seniority per member. As a result, Financial Affairs has a mean term seniority of 4.38 per member, ranking it in fourteenth place and in the lower third tier of the House committees. The committee's mean inter-Congress retention rate of 86.94 percent lodged it in eighth place among the nineteen continuing House committees of this era.

Committee Leaders: Since 1947, the leadership of the committee has been relatively stable. Only four members chaired the committee between 1947 and 1981. The first post-reorganization chair was Jesse P. Wolcott (Rep-Mich.) who had first become its senior Republican in 1937 and would hold that designation until his retirement in 1957. Brent Spence (Dem-Ky.) became the senior Democrat and chair in 1943, and apart from the two Republican 80th and 83rd Congresses, served as chair until his retirement in 1963. Serving with Spence as ranking members were Henry O. Talle (Rep-Iowa), 1957-1959, and Clarence E. Kilburn (Rep-N.Y.), 1959-1963.

Succeeding Spence as chair in 1963 was the committee's most prominent chair, Wright Patman (Dem-Tex.), a long-time Sam Rayburn protégé and a consummate populist, who led the committee from 1963 to 1975. Patman used the position as a pulpit to attack Federal Reserve Board restraints on credit. He ran the committee with a tight control until 1975, when at age 81, his ability to hold the fractious panel in line had diminished. He was one of three chairs ousted that year by the Democratic Caucus after a loosening of seniority rules. William B. Widnall (Rep-N.J.) served as ranking member for most of Patman's chairmanship until his own defeat for re-election in 1974.

Patman was replaced by the committee's fourth-ranking member, Henry S. Reuss (Dem-Wisc.), who chaired the committee until 1981 with a more academic interest in both banking and urban affairs. Widnall was succeeded first by Albert W. Johnson (Rep-Penn.), 1975-1977; and then by J. William Stanton (Rep-Ohio), 1977-1983. As chair, Reuss suffered some embarrassing floor defeats, a result many observers attributed to weak political skills. He was replaced by Fernand J. St Germain (Dem-R.I.), who served until defeated for re-election in 1988. St Germain was criticized for close financial ties with the banking and housing industries, but was absolved by the House Ethics Committee in 1987 of allegations that he had grown rich through abuse of his office. Succeeding Stanton and serving through the St Germain chairmanship as ranking member was Chalmers P. Wylie (Rep-Ohio), 1983-1993.

St Germain was followed by another Democratic populist out of Texas, Henry B. Gonzalez, who sought to focus more attention on housing issues. Democrat Gonzalez chaired the committee until the Republican takeover in 1994. He was unfortunate enough to be in the job when a political storm broke over what became known as the Whitewater affair. This involved charges that Democratic president Clinton and his wife, Hillary, during Clinton's years in Arkansas as governor, had been involved in a web of business and political relationships that involved the abuse of office. The Clintons consistently denied wrongdoing but under the glare of unrelenting media attention and political pressure from Capitol Hill, particularly from Republicans, investigations were continuing in mid-1994. One of those was a set of hearings by the Banking Committee that were run in a manner by Gonzalez that Republicans contended amounted to a "cover-up" of the Whitewater events.

The Republican takeover moved Gonzalez to the ranking member slot in 1995 and his failing health led to the passage of H. Res. 369, Feb. 25, 1998: Committee on Banking and Financial Services: "That the powers and duties conferred upon the ranking minority members by House rules shall be exercised by the next senior member until otherwise ordered by the House." This made John J. LaFalce (Dem-N.Y.) the de facto ranking member. Gonzalez's retirement made LaFalce the ranking member for the next two Congresses, 1999-2003. Moderate Republican James A.S. Leach of Iowa became the first Republican chair in forty years and held it for three Congresses, 1995-2001 until he relinquished the post to Michael G. Oxley (Rep-Ohio) who became chair in 2001. Oxley had never served on the committee prior to becoming chair and had moved over from his third-ranking slot on Energy and Commerce. Oxley retired in 2006 as Republicans were about to lose the House and was succeeded by Spencer Bachus (Rep-Ala.), who has served as ranking member since 2007.

Another in the list of strong chairs of the committee is Barney Frank (Dem-Mass.), who became the senior Democrat in 2003 and its chair in 2007. Frank has had the lead role in the House on the banking and housing crisis that befell the nation in the closing years of the President George W. Bush administration.

Party Leaders: The first modern-era leader to have served on the committee when it was known as Banking and Currency was T. Hale Boggs (Dem-La.) who became Democratic Whip in 1962 and was elected Majority Leader in 1971. Boggs, who had served on the committee prior to the reorganization, left it in 1949 for Ways and Means. In 1972, Boggs's plane disappeared and was never found while he campaigned in Alaska for freshman member Nicholas J. Begich (Dem-Alas.). In its newer and larger incarnations, the committee, now known as Financial Services, has played a more prominent role in House leadership selection with recent service from Speaker Nancy Pelosi (Dem-Cal.), Majority Leaders Richard K. Armey (Rep-Tex.) and Steny Hoyer (Dem-Md.), and Minority Whip Eric Cantor (Rep-Va.). Although he was never elected leader, one-time committee member Richard W. Bolling (Dem-Mo.) contested twice for the majority leadership in 1962 and 1977.

Notable Members: Although the committee has yet to produce any major party presidential or vice presidential nominees, five Cabinet members saw service on it: Joseph W. Barr (Dem-Ind.), who served as Secretary of the Treasury in the last month of Lyndon Johnson's presidency; two Reagan appointees, Margaret M. Heckler (Rep-Mass.), his second Secretary of Health and Human Services, and William E. Brock III (Rep-Tenn.), his second Secretary of Labor; Edward J. Derwinski (Rep-Ill.), who was named by President George H.W. Bush to be the nation's first Secretary of Veterans' Affairs; and Thomas J. Ridge (Rep-Penn.), who was named by President George W. Bush to be the first Secretary of Homeland Security.

Fifteen members of the committee moved to the U.S. Senate: seven Democrats—A.S. Mike Monroney of Oklahoma, the House coauthor of the Legislative Reorganization Act of 1946; Eugene J. McCarthy of Minnesota, the first anti-war challenger to President Johnson's 1968 re-nomination; Daniel K. Inouye of Hawaii, that state's first representative; Paul E. Tsongas of Massachusetts, who ran unsuccessfully for the 1992 Democratic nomination; Charles E. Schumer of New York; C. William (Bill) Nelson of Florida; and Thomas R. Carper of Delaware; and seven Republicans—J. Glenn Beall Jr. of Maryland, William E. Brock III of Tennessee, Robert A. Taft Jr. of Ohio, Charles E. Grassley of Iowa, James P.D. Bunning of Kentucky, Rod Grams of Minnesota, and Craig L. Thomas of Wyoming; and the committee's lone Independent, Bernard Sanders of Vermont. Democrats Hugh B. Mitchell of Washington State and Claude D. Pepper of Florida reversed direction and were named to Banking and Currency after serving in the Senate.

Much like Commerce, the House's committee dealing with financial issues was linked to twelve governorships. Eleven governors were alumni of the committee: five Democrats—Hugh L. Carey of New York, James J. Blanchard of Michigan, Charles G. (Buddy) Roemer of Louisiana, Michael E. Lowry of Washington State, and Thomas R. Carper of Delaware; and six Republicans—William G. Stratton of Illinois, Carroll A. Campbell of South Carolina, Robert L. Ehrlich of Maryland, William W. Scranton and Thomas J. Ridge of Pennsylvania, and Robert Riley of Alabama. Delaware's Republican governor Michael N. Castle left the governorship for the U.S. House. Other committee notables include Edward I. Koch (Dem-N.Y.), the mayor of New York City, and Andrew J. Young (Dem-Ga.), the mayor of Atlanta.

Selected References

Bennett, Randall W. and Christine Loucks, "Savings and Loan and Finance Industry PAC Contributions to Incumbent Members of the House Banking Committee," *Public Choice,* 79 (April, 1994), 83-104.

Grier, Kevin B., "Congressional Influence on U.S. Monetary Policy: An Empirical Test," *Journal of Monetary Economics,* 39 (October, 1991), 201-220.

Grier, Kevin B, "Congressional Oversight Committee Influence on U.S. Monetary Policy Revisited," *Journal of Monetary Economics,* 44 (December, 1996), 571-580.

Kroszner, Randall S. and Thomas Stratmann, "Interest-Group Competition and the Organization of Congress: Theory and Evidence from Financial Services' Political Action Committees," *American Economic Review,* 88 (December, 1988), 1163-1187.

Krutz, Glen S., "New Issues, New Members: Committee Composition and the Transformation of Issue Agendas on the House Banking and Public Works Committees," in Frank R. Baumgartner and Bryan D. Jones, eds., *Policy Dynamics* (Chicago: University of Chicago Press, 2002).

Owens, John E., "Extreme Advocacy Leadership in the Pre-Reform House: Wright Patman and the House Banking and Currency Committee," *British Journal of Political Science,* 15 (April, 1985), 187-205.

Salamon, Lester M., dir., *The Money Committees: A Study of the House Banking and Currency Committee and the Senate Banking, Housing and Urban Affairs Committee in the Ralph Nader Congress Project* (New York: Grossman, 1975).

Schamel, Charles E. et al., "Records of the Banking and Currency Committee," *Guide to the Records of the United States House of Representatives at the National Archives: 1789-1989 Bicentennial Edition* (Washington, D.C.: National Archives and Records Administration,1989), 63-72.

Schroedel, Jean Reith, "Campaign Contributions and Legislative Outcomes," *Western Political Quarterly,* 39 (September, 1986), 371-389.

RESPONSIBILITIES, JURISDICTIONAL CHANGES, AND SUBCOMMITTEES

BANKING AND CURRENCY, 1947

Jurisdiction, 80th Congress (1947-1949)

Established by the Legislative Reorganization Act of 1946:

[Section 121.(1)(d)] Committee on Banking and Currency

(1) Banking and currency generally.

(2) Financial aid to commerce and industry, other than matters relating to such aid which are specifically assigned to other committees under this rule.

(3) Deposit insurance.

(4) Public and private housing.

(5) Federal Reserve System.

(6) Gold and silver, including the coinage thereof.

(7) Issuance of notes and redemption thereof.

(8) Valuation and revaluation of the dollar.

(9) Control of prices of commodities, rents, or services.

BANKING, CURRENCY AND HOUSING

Banking and Currency was renamed the Committee on Banking, Currency and Housing on January 3, 1975.

BANKING, FINANCE AND URBAN AFFAIRS

Banking, Currency and Housing was renamed the Committee on Banking, Finance and Urban Affairs on January 4, 1977.

Jurisdiction, 103rd Congress (1993-1995)

From the Rules of the House of Representatives, 103rd Congress (House Document 102-405)

[Rule X.1.(d)] Committee on Banking, Finance and Urban Affairs
   (1) Banks and banking, including deposit insurance and Federal monetary policy.
   (2) Money and credit, including currency and the issuance of notes and redemption thereof; gold and silver, including the coinage thereof; valuation and revaluation of the dollar.
   (3) Urban development.
   (4) Public and private housing.
   (5) Economic stabilization, defense production, renegotiation, and control of the price of commodities, rents, and services.
   (6) International finance.
   (7) Financial aid to commerce and industry (other than transportation).
   (8) International Financial and Monetary organizations.

BANKING AND FINANCIAL SERVICES

Banking, Finance and Urban Affairs was renamed the Committee on Banking and Financial
Services on January 4, 1995.

Jurisdiction, 104th Congress (1995-1997) Changes in Committee System

From H. Res. 6, Section 202 (a), the Committees and Their Jurisdiction, January 4, 1995

[Rule X.1.(c)] Committee on Banking and Financial Services
   (1) Banks and banking, including deposit insurance and Federal monetary policy.
   (2) Bank capital markets activities generally.
   (3) Depository institution securities activities generally, including the activities of any affiliates, except for functional regulation under applicable securities laws, not involving safety and soundness.
   (4) Economic stabilization, defense production, renegotiation, and control of the price of commodities, rents, and services.
   (5) Financial aid to commerce and industry (other than transportation).
   (6) International finance.
   (7) International financial and monetary organizations.
   (8) Money and credit, including currency and the issuance of notes and redemption thereof; gold and silver, including the coinage thereof; valuation and revaluation of the dollar.
   (9) Public and private housing.
  (10) Urban development.

FINANCIAL SERVICES

Banking and Financial Services was renamed the Committee on Financial Services on January 3, 2001.

Jurisdiction, 111th Congress (2009-2011)

From the Rules of the House of Representatives (as revised to June 16, 2009, H.Doc. 110-162):

[Rule X.1.(g)] Committee on Financial Services
   (1) Banks and banking, including deposit insurance and Federal monetary policy.
   (2) Economic stabilization, defense production, renegotiation, and control of the price of commodities, rents, and services.
   (3) Financial aid to commerce and industry (other than transportation).
   (4) Insurance generally.
   (5) International finance.
   (6) International financial and monetary organizations.

(7) Money and credit, including currency and the issuance of notes and redemption thereof; gold and silver, including the coinage thereof; valuation and revaluation of the dollar.
(8) Public and private housing.
(9) Securities and exchanges.
(10) Urban development.

NAMES OF FINANCIAL SERVICES SUBCOMMITTEES FROM THE *CONGRESSIONAL DIRECTORY*

Banking, Finance and Urban Affairs, 103rd Congress

Consumer Credit and Finance, 103
Economic Growth and Credit Formation, 103
Financial Institutions: Supervision, Regulation, and Deposit Insurance, 103
General Oversight, Investigations and the Resolution of Failed Financial Institutions, 103
Housing and Community Development, 103
International Development, Finance, Trade, and Monetary Policy, 103

Banking and Financial Services, 104th-106th Congresses

Capital Markets, Insurance, and Government-Sponsored Enterprises, 104
Capital Markets, Securities, and Government-Sponsored Enterprises, 105, 106
Domestic and International Monetary Policy, 104, 105, 106
Financial Institutions and Consumer Credit, 104, 105, 106
General Oversight and Investigations, 104, 105, 106
Housing and Community Opportunity, 104, 105, 106

Financial Services, 107th-111th Congresses

Capital Markets, Insurance, and Government-Sponsored Enterprises, 107, 108, 109, 110, 111
Domestic Monetary Policy, Technology and Economic Growth, 107
Domestic and Monetary Policy and Technology, 111
Domestic and International Monetary Policy, Trade, and Technology, 108, 109, 110
Financial Institutions and Consumer Credit, 107, 108, 109, 110, 111
Housing and Community Opportunity, 107, 108, 109, 110, 111
International Monetary Policy and Trade, 107, 111
Oversight and Investigations, 107, 108, 109, 110, 111

MEMBERSHIP ROSTERS, 103rd-111th Congresses, 1993-2011

BANKING, FINANCE AND URBAN AFFAIRS / 103rd Congress

Service Dates of Committee Chair: Jan. 5, 1993-Jan. 3, 1995

Service Dates of Majority Members: Jan. 5, 1993-Jan. 3, 1995

Service Dates of Minority Members: Jan. 5, 1993-Jan. 3, 1995

Roster Filled: Majority with 30 members on Jan. 21, 1993; Minority with 20 members on Jan. 5, 1993; Third party filled on Feb. 18, 1993

	Majority			Terms in:			Minority			Terms in:	
Rank Name		Party	State	House	Comm.	Rank Name		Party	State	House	Comm.
Chr Gonzalez, Henry B.		Dem	Tex.	17	17	RM Leach, James A.S.		Rep	Iowa	9	9
2nd Neal, Stephen L.		Dem	N.C.	10	10	2nd McCollum, Ira W. (Bill) Jr.		Rep	Fla.	7	7
3rd LaFalce, John J.		Dem	N.Y.	10	10	3rd Roukema, Margaret S.		Rep	N.J.	7	7
4th Vento, Bruce F.		DFL	Minn.	9	9	4th Bereuter, Douglas K.		Rep	Neb.	8	7
5th Schumer, Charles E.		Dem	N.Y.	7	7	5th Ridge, Thomas J.		Rep	Penn.	6	6
6th Frank, Barney		Dem	Mass.	7	7	6th Roth, Tobias A.		Rep	Wisc.	8	5
7th Kanjorski, Paul E.		Dem	Penn.	5	5	7th McCandless, Alfred A.		Rep	Cal.	6	5
8th Kennedy, Joseph P. II		Dem	Mass.	4	4	8th Baker, Richard H.		Rep	La.	4	3
9th Flake, Floyd H.		Dem	N.Y.	4	4	9th Nussle, James A.		Rep	Iowa	2	2
10th Mfume, Kweisi		Dem	Md.	4	4	10th Thomas, Craig L.		Rep	Wyo.	3	2
11th Waters, Maxine		Dem	Cal.	2	2	11th Johnson, Sam		Rep	Tex.	2	2

12th LaRocco, Larry	Dem	Ida.	2	2		12th Pryce, Deborah D.	Rep	Ohio	1	*1 1
13th Orton, William	Dem	Utah	2	2		13th Linder, John E.	Rep	Ga.	1	1
14th Bacchus, James	Dem	Fla.	2	2		14th Knollenberg, Joseph	Rep	Mich.	1	1
15th Klein, Herbert C.	Dem	N.J.	1	1		15th Lazio, Enrico A. (Rick)	Rep	N.Y.	1	1
16th Maloney, Carolyn B.	Dem	N.Y.	1	1		16th Grams, Rod	Rep	Minn.	1	1
17th Deutsch, Peter R.	Dem	Fla.	1	1		17th Bachus, Spencer T.	Rep	Ala.	1	1
18th Gutierrez, Luis V.	Dem	Ill.	1	1		18th Huffington, Michael	Rep	Cal.	1	1
19th Rush, Bobby L.	Dem	Ill.	1	1		19th Castle, Michael N.	Rep	Del.	1	1
20th Roybal-Allard, Lucille	Dem	Cal.	1	1		20th King, Peter T.	Rep	N.Y.	1	*1 1
21st Barrett, Thomas M.	Dem	Wisc.	1	1						
22nd Furse, Elizabeth	Dem	Ore.	1	1		**Third Party:**				
23rd Velázquez, Nydia M.	Dem	N.Y.	1	1		1st Sanders, Bernard	Ind	Vt.	2	2
24th Wynn, Albert R.	Dem	Md.	1	1						
25th Fields, Cleo	Dem	La.	1	1		*1: Member's first period of service on the committee.				
26th Watt, Melvin L.	Dem	N.C.	1	1						
27th Hinchey, Maurice D.	Dem	N.Y.	1	1						
28th Dooley, Calvin M.	Dem	Cal.	2	1						
29th Klink, Ronald	Dem	Penn.	1	1						
30th Fingerhut, Eric D.	Dem	Ohio	1	1						

Note: Bernard Sanders (Ind-Vt.) was re-elected to the 103rd Congress as an Independent. He was assigned to the committee by the Democratic Caucus during the 102nd Congress, but not allowed to accrue seniority, nor was he included in the committee's party ratio. His assignment to the Committee for the 103rd Congress commenced Feb. 18, 1993.

Vacancies Filled:
  Majority:
    28th through 30th seats by Dooley, Klink, and Fingerhut on Jan. 21, 1993

Departures from the House:

	Majority			Minority		
Elected to U.S. Senate	None			Grams, Rod	Rep	Minn.
				Thomas, Craig L.	Rep	Wyo.
				Ridge, Thomas J.	Rep	Penn.
Elected Governor	None			Huffington, Michael	Rep	Cal.
Lost Election to U.S. Senate	None			None		
Defeated for Re-election	LaRocco, Larry	Dem	Ida.	None		
	Klein, Herbert C.	Dem	N.J.			
	Fingerhut, Eric D.	Dem	Ohio			
Retired	Neal, Stephen L.	Dem	N.C.	McCandless, Alfred A.	Rep	Cal.
	Bacchus, James	Dem	Fla.			

Departures from Committee:

	Majority			Minority		
Moved to Appropriations	None			Knollenberg, Joseph	Rep	Mich.
Moved to Budget	None			Nussle, James A.	Rep	Iowa
Moved to Commerce	Deutsch, Peter R.	Dem	Fla.	None		
	Rush, Bobby L.	Dem	Ill.			
	Furse, Elizabeth	Dem	Ore.			
	Klink, Ronald	Dem	Penn.			
Moved to Economic and	None			Johnson, Sam	Rep	Tex.
Educational Opportunities				Knollenberg, Joseph	Rep	Mich.
Moved to Rules	None			Pryce, Deborah D.	Rep	Ohio
				Linder, John E.	Rep	Ga.
Moved to Ways and Means	None			Nussle, James A.,	Rep	Iowa
				Johnson, Sam	Rep	Tex.
No new assignment	Dooley, Calvin M.	Dem	Cal.	None		

BANKING AND FINANCIAL SERVICES / 104th Congress

Service Dates of Committee Chair: Jan. 4, 1995-Jan. 3, 1997

Service Dates of Majority Members: Jan. 4, 1995-Jan. 3, 1997

Service Dates of Minority Members: Jan. 4, 1995-Jan. 3, 1997

Roster Filled: Majority with 27 members on Jan. 4, 1995; Minority with 22 members on Jan. 5, 1993; Third party filled on Jan. 9, 1993

Majority					Minority				
			Terms in:					**Terms in:**	
Rank Name	**Party**	**State**	**House**	**Comm.**	**Rank Name**	**Party**	**State**	**House**	**Comm.**
Chr Leach, James A.S.	Rep	Iowa	10	10	RM Gonzalez, Henry B.	Dem	Tex.	18	18
2nd McCollum, Ira W. (Bill) Jr.	Rep	Fla.	8	8	2nd LaFalce, John J.	Dem	N.Y.	11	11
3rd Roukema, Margaret S.	Rep	N.J.	8	8	3rd Vento, Bruce F.	DFL	Minn.	10	10

4th Bereuter, Douglas K.	Rep	Neb.	9	8		4th Schumer, Charles E.	Dem	N.Y.	8	8		
5th Roth, Tobias A.	Rep	Wisc.	9	6		5th Frank, Barney	Dem	Mass.	8	8		
6th Baker, Richard H.	Rep	La.	5	4		6th Kanjorski, Paul E.	Dem	Penn.	6	6		
7th Lazio, Enrico A. (Rick)	Rep	N.Y.	2	2		7th Kennedy, Joseph P. II	Dem	Mass.	5	5		
8th Bachus, Spencer T.	Rep	Ala.	2	2		8th Flake, Floyd H.	Dem	N.Y.	5	5		
9th Castle, Michael N.	Rep	Del.	2	2		9th Mfume, Kweisi	Dem	Md.	5	5		
10th King, Peter T.	Rep	N.Y.	2	*1 2		10th Waters, Maxine	Dem	Cal.	3	3		
11th Royce, Edward R.	Rep	Cal.	2	1		11th Orton, William	Dem	Utah	3	3		
12th Lucas, Frank D.	Rep	Okla.	2	1		12th Maloney, Carolyn B.	Dem	N.Y.	2	2		
13th Weller, Gerald C.	Rep	Ill.	1	1		13th Gutierrez, Luis V.	Dem	Ill.	2	2		
14th Hayworth, John D. Jr.	Rep	Ariz.	1	1		14th Roybal-Allard, Lucille	Dem	Cal.	2	2		
15th Metcalf, Jack	Rep	Wash.	1	1		15th Barrett, Thomas M.	Dem	Wisc.	2	2		
16th Bono, Sonny	Rep	Cal.	1	1		16th Velázquez, Nydia M.	Dem	N.Y.	2	2		
17th Ney, Robert W.	Rep	Ohio	1	1		17th Wynn, Albert R.	Dem	Md.	2	2		
18th Ehrlich, Robert L. Jr.	Rep	Md.	1	1		18th Fields, Cleo	Dem	La.	2	2		
19th Barr, Bob	Rep	Ga.	1	1		19th Watt, Melvin L.	Dem	N.C.	2	2		
20th Chrysler, Dick	Rep	Mich.	1	1		20th Hinchey, Maurice D.	Dem	N.Y.	2	2		
21st Cremeans, Frank A.	Rep	Ohio	1	1		21st Ackerman, Gary L.	Dem	N.Y.	7	*2 1		
22nd Fox, Jon D.	Rep	Penn.	1	1		22nd Bentsen, Kenneth E. Jr.	Dem	Tex.	1	1		
23rd Heineman, Fred	Rep	N.C.	1	1								
24th Stockman, Steve	Rep	Tex.	1	1		**Third Party:**						
25th LoBiondo, Frank A.	Rep	N.J.	1	1		1st Sanders, Bernard	Ind	Vt.	3	3		
26th Watts, Julius C. Jr.	Rep	Okla.	1	1								
27th Kelly, Sue W.	Rep	N.Y.	1	1								

*1: Member's first period of service on the committee.

*2: Member's second period of service on the committee.

Additions:

  Majority:

    28th seat by Thomas J. Campbell (Rep-Cal.) on Dec. 27, 1995, to rank immediately after King

  Minority:

    23rd seat by Jesse L. Jackson Jr. (Dem-Ill.) on Jan. 5, 1996

Changes:

  Minority:

Mfume, Kweisi	Dem	Md.	Feb. 18, 1996 Resigned the House; became head of NAACP
McKinney, Cynthia A.	Dem	Ga.	Feb. 28, 1996 Replaced Mfume

Departures from the House:

	Majority			**Minority**		
Defeated for Re-election	Chrysler, Dick	Rep	Mich.	Orton, William	Dem	Utah
	Cremeans, Frank A.	Rep	Ohio			
	Heineman, Fred	Rep	N.C.			
	Stockman, Steve	Rep	Tex.			
Retired	Roth, Tobias A.	Rep	Wisc.	Fields, Cleo	Dem	La.

Departures from Committee:

Moved to Commerce	None			Wynn, Albert R.	Dem	Md.
Moved to National Security	Bono, Sonny	Rep	Cal.	None		
Moved to Ways and Means	Weller, Gerald C.	Rep	Ill.	None		
	Hayworth, John D. Jr.	Rep	Ariz.			

BANKING AND FINANCIAL SERVICES / 105th Congress

Service Dates of Committee Chair: Jan. 7, 1997-Jan. 3, 1999

Service Dates of Majority Members: Jan. 7, 1997-Jan. 3, 1999

Service Dates of Minority Members: Jan. 7, 1997-Jan. 3, 1999

Roster Filled: Majority with 30 members on April 16, 1997; Minority with 25 members on April 16, 1997;

Third party filled on Jan. 7, 1997.

Majority			Terms in:			**Minority**			Terms in:	
Rank Name	Party	State	House	Comm.		Rank Name	Party	State	House	Comm.
Chr Leach, James A.S.	Rep	Iowa	11	11		RM1 Gonzalez, Henry B.	Dem	Tex.	19	19
2nd McCollum, Ira W. (Bill) Jr.	Rep	Fla.	9	9		RM2 LaFalce, John J.	Dem	N.Y.	12	12

3rd Roukema, Margaret S.	Rep	N.J.	9		9	3rd Vento, Bruce F.	DFL	Minn.	11		11
4th Bereuter, Douglas K.	Rep	Neb.	10		9	4th Schumer, Charles E.	Dem	N.Y.	9		9
5th Baker, Richard H.	Rep	La.	6		5	5th Frank, Barney	Dem	Mass.	9		9
6th Lazio, Enrico A. (Rick)	Rep	N.Y.	3		3	6th Kanjorski, Paul E.	Dem	Penn.	7		7
7th Bachus, Spencer T.	Rep	Ala.	3		3	7th Kennedy, Joseph P. II	Dem	Mass.	6		6
8th Castle, Michael N.	Rep	Del.	3		3	8th Flake, Floyd H.	Dem	N.Y.	6		6
9th King, Peter T.	Rep	N.Y.	3	*1	3	9th Waters, Maxine	Dem	Cal.	4		4
10th Campbell, Thomas J.	Rep	Cal.	4	*2	2	10th Maloney, Carolyn B.	Dem	N.Y.	3		3
11th Royce, Edward R.	Rep	Cal.	3		2	11th Gutierrez, Luis V.	Dem	Ill.	3		3
12th Lucas, Frank D.	Rep	Okla.	3		2	12th Roybal-Allard, Lucille	Dem	Cal.	3		3
13th Metcalf, Jack	Rep	Wash.	2		2	13th Barrett, Thomas M.	Dem	Wisc.	3		3
14th Ney, Robert W.	Rep	Ohio	2		2	14th Velázquez, Nydia M.	Dem	N.Y.	3		3
15th Ehrlich, Robert L. Jr.	Rep	Md.	2		2	15th Watt, Melvin L.	Dem	N.C.	3		3
16th Barr, Bob	Rep	Ga.	2		2	16th Hinchey, Maurice D.	Dem	N.Y.	3		3
17th Fox, Jon D.	Rep	Penn.	2		2	17th Ackerman, Gary L.	Dem	N.Y.	8	*2	2
18th LoBiondo, Frank A.	Rep	N.J.	2		2	18th Bentsen, Kenneth E. Jr.	Dem	Tex.	2		2
19th Watts, Julius C. Jr.	Rep	Okla.	2		2	19th Jackson, Jesse L. Jr.	Dem	Ill.	2		2
20th Kelly, Sue W.	Rep	N.Y.	2		2	20th McKinney, Cynthia A.	Dem	Ga.	3		2
21st Paul, Ronald E.	Rep	Tex.	5	*3	1	21st Kilpatrick, Carolyn C.	Dem	Mich.	1		1
22nd Weldon, David J.	Rep	Fla.	2		1	22nd Maloney, James H.	Dem	Conn.	1		1
23rd Ryun, Jim	Rep	Kans.	2		1	23rd Hooley, Darlene	Dem	Ore.	1		1
24th Cook, Merrill	Rep	Utah	1		1	24th Carson, Julia M.	Dem	Ind.	1		1
25th Snowbarger, Vincent K.	Rep	Kans.	1		1	25th Torres, Esteban Edward	Dem	Cal.	8		1
26th Riley, Robert	Rep	AL	1		1						
27th Hill, Rick	Rep	Mont.	1		1	**Third Party:**					
28th Sessions, Pete	Rep	Tex.	1		1	Sanders, Bernard	Ind	Vt.	4		4
29th LaTourette, Steven C.	Rep	Ohio	2		1						
30th Jones, Walter B. Jr.	Rep	N.C.	2		1						

*1: Member's first period of service on the committee.

*2: Member's second period of service on the committee.

*3 Member's third period of service on committee.

Note:

Gonzalez, Henry B.	Dem	Tex.	Feb. 25, 1998	Replaced as Ranking Member; ranked 2nd
LaFalce, John J.	Dem	N.Y.	Feb. 25, 1998	Replaced Gonzalez as Ranking Member

H. Res. 369, Feb. 25, 1998: Committee on Banking and Financial Services: "That the powers and duties conferred upon the ranking minority members by House rules shall be exercised by the next senior member until otherwise ordered by the House."

Vacancies Filled:

Majority:

29th seat by LaTourette on Jan. 21, 1997

30th seat by Jones on April 16, 1997

Minority:

25th seat by Torres on April 16, 1997

Additions:

Majority:

31st Redmond, William T.	Rep	N.M.	July 23, 1997
32nd Fossella, Vito J.	Rep	N.Y.	Nov. 12, 1997

Minority:

26th Sherman, Brad	Dem	Cal.	Sept. 5, 1997
27th Meeks, Gregory W.	Dem	N.Y.	Feb. 5, 1998
28th Goode, Virgil H. Jr.	Dem	Va.	June 24, 1998

Changes:

Majority:

LoBiondo, Frank A.	Rep	N.J.	Feb. 25, 1997 Resigned committee; moved to Transportation and Infrastructure
Watts, Julius C. Jr.	Rep	Okla.	Feb. 27, 1997 Resigned committee; moved to Transportation and Infrastructure
Manzullo, Donald A.	Rep	Ill.	April 16, 1997 Replaced LoBiondo
Foley, Mark A.	Rep	Fla.	April 16, 1997 Replaced Julius C. Watts Jr

Minority:

McKinney, Cynthia A.	Dem	Ga.	July 31, 1997 Resigned committee; moved to National Security
Weygand, Robert A.	Dem	R.I.	July 31, 1997 Replaced McKinney
Flake, Floyd H.	Dem	N.Y.	Nov. 17, 1997 Resigned the House and retired
Sandlin, Max A.	Dem	Tex.	Feb. 5, 1998 Replaced Flake
Torres, Esteban Edward	Dem	Cal.	Apr. 29, 1998 Resigned committee; no new assignment
Lee, Barbara	Dem	Cal.	Apr. 29, 1998 Replaced Torres

Departures from the House:

	Majority			**Minority**		
Elected to U.S. Senate	None			Schumer, Charles E.	Dem	N.Y.
Defeated for Re-election	Fox, Jon D.	Rep	Penn.	None		

	Snowbarger, Vincent K.	Rep	Kans.				
	Redmond, William T.	Rep	N.M.				
Retired	None			Gonzalez, Henry B.	Dem	Tex.	
				Kennedy, Joseph P. II.	Dem	Mass.	

Departures from Committee:

Moved to Appropriations	None			Roybal-Allard, Lucille	Dem	Cal.	
				Hinchey, Maurice D.	Dem	N.Y.	
				Jackson, Jesse L. Jr.	Dem	Ill.	
				Kilpatrick, Carolyn C.	Dem	Mich.	
Moved to Commerce	Ehrlich, Robert L. Jr.	Rep	Md.	Barrett, Thomas M.	Dem	Wisc.	
	Fossella, Vito J.	Rep	N.Y.				
Moved to Rules	Sessions, Pete	Rep	Tex.	None			
Moved to Ways and Means	Foley, Mark A.	Rep	Fla.	None			

BANKING AND FINANCIAL SERVICES / 106th Congress

Service Dates of Committee Chair: Jan. 6, 1999-Jan. 3, 2001

Service Dates of Majority Members: Jan. 6, 1999-Jan. 3, 2001

Service Dates of Minority Members: Jan. 6, 1999-Jan. 3, 2001

Roster Filled: Majority with 32 members on Jan. 6, 1999; Minority with 27 members on Jan. 6, 1999; Third party filled on Jan. 6, 1999

Majority

Rank Name	Party	State	House	Comm.
Chr Leach, James A.S.	Rep	Iowa	12	12
2nd McCollum, Ira W. (Bill) Jr.	Rep	Fla.	10	10
3rd Roukema, Margaret S.	Rep	N.J.	10	10
4th Bereuter, Douglas K.	Rep	Neb.	11	10
5th Baker, Richard H.	Rep	La.	7	6
6th Lazio, Enrico A. (Rick)	Rep	N.Y.	4	4
7th Bachus, Spencer T.	Rep	Ala.	4	4
8th Castle, Michael N.	Rep	Del.	4	4
9th King, Peter T.	Rep	N.Y.	4	*1 4
10th Campbell, Thomas J.	Rep	Cal.	5	*2 3
11th Royce, Edward R.	Rep	Cal.	4	3
12th Lucas, Frank D.	Rep	Okla.	4	3
13th Metcalf, Jack	Rep	Wash.	3	3
14th Ney, Robert W.	Rep	Ohio	3	3
15th Barr, Bob	Rep	Ga.	3	3
16th Kelly, Sue W.	Rep	N.Y.	3	3
17th Paul, Ronald E.	Rep	Tex.	6	*3 2
18th Weldon, David J.	Rep	Fla.	3	2
19th Ryun, Jim	Rep	Kans.	3	2
20th Cook, Merrill	Rep	Utah	2	2
21st Riley, Robert	Rep	Ala.	2	2
22nd Hill, Rick	Rep	Mont.	2	2
23rd LaTourette, Steven C.	Rep	Ohio	3	2
24th Manzullo, Donald A.	Rep	Ill.	4	2
25th Jones, Walter B. Jr.	Rep	N.C.	3	2
26th Ryan, Paul D.	Rep	Wisc.	1	1
27th Ose, Doug	Rep	Cal.	1	1
28th Sweeney, John E.	Rep	N.Y.	1	1
29th Biggert, Judith B.	Rep	Ill.	1	1
30th Terry, Lee R.	Rep	Neb.	1	1
31st Green, Mark	Rep	Wisc.	1	1
32nd Toomey, Patrick J.	Rep	Penn.	1	1

Minority

Rank Name	Party	State	House	Comm.
RM LaFalce, John J.	Dem	N.Y.	13	13
2nd Vento, Bruce F.	DFL	Minn.	12	12
3rd Frank, Barney	Dem	Mass.	10	10
4th Kanjorski, Paul E.	Dem	Penn.	8	8
5th Waters, Maxine	Dem	Cal.	5	5
6th Maloney, Carolyn B.	Dem	N.Y.	4	4
7th Gutierrez, Luis V.	Dem	Ill.	4	4
8th Velázquez, Nydia M.	Dem	N.Y.	4	4
9th Watt, Melvin L.	Dem	N.C.	4	4
10th Ackerman, Gary L.	Dem	N.Y.	9	*2 3
11th Bentsen, Kenneth E. Jr.	Dem	Tex.	3	3
12th Maloney, James H.	Dem	Conn.	2	2
13th Hooley, Darlene	Dem	Ore.	2	2
14th Carson, Julia M.	Dem	Ind.	2	2
15th Weygand, Robert A.	Dem	R.I.	2	2
16th Sherman, Brad	Dem	Cal.	2	2
17th Sandlin, Max A.	Dem	Tex.	2	2
18th Meeks, Gregory W.	Dem	N.Y.	2	2
19th Lee, Barbara	Dem	Cal.	2	*1 2
20th Goode, Virgil H. Jr.	Dem	Va.	2	2
21st Mascara, Frank R.	Dem	Penn.	3	1
22nd Inslee, Jay R.	Dem	Wash.	2	1
23rd Schakowsky, Janice D.	Dem	Ill.	1	1
24th Moore, Dennis	Dem	Kans.	1	1
25th Gonzalez, Charles A.	Dem	Tex.	1	1
26th Jones, Stephanie Tubbs	Dem	Ohio	1	1
27th Capuano, Michael E.	Dem	Mass.	1	1

Third Party:

1st Sanders, Bernard	Ind	Vt.	5	5

*1: Member's first period of service on the committee.

*2: Member's second period of service on the committee.

*3: Member's third period of service on committee.

Note: Ackerman resigned Banking and Financial Services on Aug. 8, 1999, to accommodate Forbes' party switch. Forbes replaced Ackerman, who returned on Nov. 2, 1999, to replace Lee.

Changes:

  Minority:

Ackerman, Gary L.	Dem	N.Y.	Aug. 5, 1999 Resigned committee to open seat for Forbes; returned Nov. 2, 1999
Forbes, Michael P.	Dem	N.Y.	Aug. 5, 1999 Replaced Ackerman

Lee, Barbara	Dem	Cal.	Nov. 1, 1999 Resigned committee; returned on Feb. 1, 2000
Ackerman, Gary L.	Dem	N.Y.	Nov. 2, 1999 Replaced Lee
Lee, Barbara	Dem	Cal.	Feb. 1, 2000 Replaced Goode
Goode, Virgil H. Jr.	Dem	Va.	Feb. 1, 2000 Service on committee vacated as a Democrat; moved to Appropriations as an Independent majority member on Feb. 2, 2000
Vento, Bruce F.	DFL	Minn.	Oct. 10, 2000 Died in office

Departures from the House:	Majority			Minority		
Lost Election to U.S. Senate	Lazio, Enrico A. (Rick)	Rep	N.Y.	Weygand, Robert A.	Dem	R.I.
	McCollum, Ira W. (Bill) Jr.	Rep	Fla.	None		
	Campbell, Thomas J.	Rep	Cal.			
Defeated for Re-nomination	Cook, Merrill	Rep	Utah	Forbes, Michael P.	Dem	N.Y.
Retired	Metcalf, Jack	Rep	Wash.	None		
	Hill, Rick	Rep	Mont.			

Departures from Committee:						
Moved to Appropriations	Sweeney, John E.	Rep	N.Y.	None		
Moved to Energy and Commerce	Terry, Lee R.	Rep	Neb.	None		
Moved to Ways and Means	Ryan, Paul D.	Rep	Wisc.	None		

FINANCIAL SERVICES / 107th Congress

Service Dates of Committee Chair: Jan. 6, 2001-Jan. 3, 2003

Service Dates of Majority Members: Jan. 6, 2001-Jan. 3, 2003

Service Dates of Minority Members: Jan. 31, 2001-Jan. 3, 2003

Roster Filled: Majority with 37 members on Jan. 6, 2001; Minority with 32 members on Feb. 8, 2001;

Third party filled on Feb. 13, 2001

Majority					Minority				
			Terms in:					**Terms in:**	
Rank Name	Party	State	House	Comm.	Rank Name	Party	State	House	Comm.
Chr Oxley, Michael G.	Rep	Ohio	11	1	RM LaFalce, John J.	Dem	N.Y.	14	14
2nd Leach, James A.S.	Rep	Iowa	13	13	2nd Frank, Barney	Dem	Mass.	11	11
3rd Roukema, Margaret S.	Rep	N.J.	11	11	3rd Kanjorski, Paul E.	Dem	Penn.	9	9
4th Bereuter, Douglas K.	Rep	Neb.	12	11	4th Waters, Maxine	Dem	Cal.	6	6
5th Baker, Richard H.	Rep	La.	8	7	5th Maloney, Carolyn B.	Dem	N.Y.	5	5
6th Bachus, Spencer T.	Rep	Ala.	5	5	6th Gutierrez, Luis V.	Dem	Ill.	5	5
7th Castle, Michael N.	Rep	Del.	5	5	7th Velázquez, Nydia M.	Dem	N.Y.	5	5
8th King, Peter T.	Rep	N.Y.	5	*1 5	8th Watt, Melvin L.	Dem	N.C.	5	5
9th Royce, Edward R.	Rep	Cal.	5	4	9th Ackerman, Gary L.	Dem	N.Y.	10	*3 2
10th Lucas, Frank D.	Rep	Okla.	5	4	10th Bentsen, Kenneth E. Jr.	Dem	Tex.	4	4
11th Ney, Robert W.	Rep	Ohio	4	4	11th Maloney, James H.	Dem	Conn.	3	3
12th Barr, Bob	Rep	Ga.	4	4	12th Hooley, Darlene	Dem	Ore.	3	3
13th Kelly, Sue W.	Rep	N.Y.	4	4	13th Carson, Julia M.	Dem	Ind.	3	3
14th Paul, Ronald E.	Rep	Tex.	7	*3 3	14th Sherman, Brad	Dem	Cal.	3	3
15th Gillmor, Paul E.	Rep	Ohio	7	*2 1	15th Sandlin, Max A.	Dem	Tex.	3	3
16th Cox, C. Christopher	Rep	Cal.	7	1	16th Meeks, Gregory W.	Dem	N.Y.	3	3
17th Weldon, David J.	Rep	Fla.	4	3	17th Lee, Barbara	Dem	Cal.	3	*2 2
18th Ryun, Jim	Rep	Kans.	4	3	18th Mascara, Frank R.	Dem	Penn.	4	2
19th Riley, Robert	Rep	Alas.	3	3	19th Inslee, Jay R.	Dem	Wash.	3	2
20th LaTourette, Steven C.	Rep	Ohio	4	3	20th Schakowsky, Janice D.	Dem	Ill.	2	2
21st Manzullo, Donald A.	Rep	Ill.	5	3	21st Moore, Dennis	Dem	Kans.	2	2
22nd Jones, Walter B. Jr.	Rep	N.C.	4	3	22nd Gonzalez, Charles A.	Dem	Tex.	2	2
23rd Ose, Doug	Rep	Cal.	2	2	23rd Jones, Stephanie Tubbs	Dem	Ohio	2	2
24th Biggert, Judith B.	Rep	Ill.	2	2	24th Capuano, Michael E.	Dem	Mass.	2	2
25th Green, Mark	Rep	Wisc.	2	2	25th Ford, Harold E. Jr.	Dem	Tenn.	3	1
26th Toomey, Patrick J.	Rep	Penn.	2	2	26th Hinojosa, Rubén	Dem	Tex.	3	1
27th Shays, Christopher H.	Rep	Conn.	8	1	27th Lucas, Ken	Dem	Ky.	2	1
28th Shadegg, John B.	Rep	Ariz.	4	1	28th Shows, C. Ronald	Dem	Miss.	2	1
29th Fossella, Vito J.	Rep	N.Y.	3	*2 1	29th Crowley, Joseph	Dem	N.Y.	2	1
30th Miller, Gary G.	Rep	Cal.	2	1	30th Clay, William L. Jr.	Dem	Mo.	1	1
31st Cantor, Eric I.	Rep	Va.	1	1	31st Israel, Steve	Dem	N.Y.	1	1
32nd Grucci, Felix J. Jr.	Rep	N.Y.	1	1	32nd Ross, Michael A.	Dem	Ark.	1	1
33rd Hart, Melissa	Rep	Penn.	1	1					
34th Capito, Shelley Moore	Rep	W.Va.	1	*1 1	**Third Party:**				
35th Ferguson, Michael	Rep	N.J.	1	1	1st Sanders, Bernard	Ind	Vt.	6	6
36th Rogers, Mike	Rep	Mich.	1	1					

37th Tiberi, Patrick	Rep	Ohio	1	1	*1: Member's first period of service on the committee.
					*2: Member's second period of service on the committee.
					*3: Member's third period of service on committee.

Note: Committee minority was expanded Feb. 8, 2001, 25th through 32nd seats filled with Ford, Hinojosa, Lucas, Shows, Crowlwy, Clay, Israel, and Ross.

Departures from the House:	Majority			Minority		
Elected Governor	Riley, Robert	Rep	Ala.	None		
Lost Election to U.S. Senate	None			Bentsen, Kenneth E. Jr.	Dem	Tex.
Defeated for Re-nomination	Barr, Bob	Rep	Ga.	Mascara, Frank R.	Dem	Penn.
Defeated for Re-election	Grucci, Felix J. Jr.	Rep	N.Y.	Maloney, James H.	Dem	Conn.
				Shows, C. Ronald	Dem	Miss.
Retired	Roukema, Margaret S.	Rep	N.J.	LaFalce, John J.	Dem	N.Y.
Departures from Committee:						
Moved to Chair Select Homeland Security	Cox, C. Christopher	Rep	Cal.	None		
Moved to Appropriations	Weldon, David J.	Rep	Fla.	None		
Moved to Energy and Commerce	Ferguson, Michael	Rep	N.J.	Schakowsky, Janice D.	Dem	Ill.
	Rogers, Mike	Rep	Mich.			
Moved to Ways and Means	Cantor, Eric I.	Rep	Va.	Sandlin, Max A.	Dem	Tex.
				Jones, Stephanie Tubbs	Dem	Ohio

FINANCIAL SERVICES / 108th Congress

Service Dates of Committee Chair: Jan. 8, 2003-Jan. 3, 2005

Service Dates of Majority Members: Jan. 28, 2003-Jan. 3, 2005

Service Dates of Ranking Member: Jan. 8, 2003-Jan. 3, 2005

Service Dates of Minority Members: Jan. 28, 2003-Jan. 3, 2005

Roster Filled: Majority with 37 members on Jan. 28, 2003; Minority with 32 members on Feb. 5, 2003; Third party filled on Jan. 28, 2003 (and 3/5?).

Majority					Minority				
			Terms in:					**Terms in:**	
Rank Name	Party	State	House	Comm.	Rank Name	Party	State	House	Comm.
Chr Oxley, Michael G.	Rep	Ohio	12	2	RM Frank, Barney	Dem	Mass.	12	12
2nd Leach, James A.S.	Rep	Iowa	14	14	2nd Kanjorski, Paul E.	Dem	Penn.	10	10
3rd Bereuter, Douglas K.	Rep	Neb.	13	12	3rd Waters, Maxine	Dem	Cal.	7	7
4th Baker, Richard H.	Rep	La.	9	8	4th Sanders, Bernard	Ind	Vt.	7	7
5th Bachus, Spencer T.	Rep	Ala.	6	6	5th Maloney, Carolyn B.	Dem	N.Y.	6	6
6th Castle, Michael N.	Rep	Del.	6	6	6th Gutierrez, Luis V.	Dem	Ill.	6	6
7th King, Peter T.	Rep	N.Y.	6	*1 6	7th Velázquez, Nydia M.	Dem	N.Y.	6	6
8th Royce, Edward R.	Rep	Cal.	6	5	8th Watt, Melvin L.	Dem	N.C.	6	6
9th Lucas, Frank D.	Rep	Okla.	6	5	9th Ackerman, Gary L.	Dem	N.Y.	11	*3 3
10th Ney, Robert W.	Rep	Ohio	5	5	10th Hooley, Darlene	Dem	Ore.	4	4
11th Kelly, Sue W.	Rep	N.Y.	5	5	11th Carson, Julia M.	Dem	Ind.	4	4
12th Paul, Ronald E.	Rep	Tex.	8	*3 4	12th Sherman, Brad	Dem	Cal.	4	4
13th Gillmor, Paul E.	Rep	Ohio	8	*2 2	13th Meeks, Gregory W.	Dem	N.Y.	4	4
14th Ryun, Jim	Rep	Kans.	5	4	14th Lee, Barbara	Dem	Cal.	4	*2 3
15th LaTourette, Steven C.	Rep	Ohio	5	4	15th Inslee, Jay R.	Dem	Wash.	4	3
16th Manzullo, Donald A.	Rep	Ill.	6	4	16th Moore, Dennis	Dem	Kans.	3	3
17th Jones, Walter B. Jr.	Rep	N.C.	5	4	17th Gonzalez, Charles A.	Dem	Tex.	3	3
18th Ose, Doug	Rep	Cal.	3	3	18th Capuano, Michael E.	Dem	Mass.	3	3
19th Biggert, Judith B.	Rep	Ill.	3	3	19th Ford, Harold E. Jr.	Dem	Tenn.	4	2
20th Green, Mark	Rep	Wisc.	3	3	20th Hinojosa, Rubén	Dem	Tex.	4	2
21st Toomey, Patrick J.	Rep	Penn.	3	3	21st Lucas, Ken	Dem	Ky.	3	2
22nd Shays, Christopher H.	Rep	Conn.	9	2	22nd Crowley, Joseph	Dem	N.Y.	3	2
23rd Shadegg, John B.	Rep	Ariz.	5	2	23rd Clay, William L. Jr.	Dem	Mo.	2	2
24th Fossella, Vito J.	Rep	N.Y.	4	*2 2	24th Israel, Steve	Dem	N.Y.	2	2
25th Miller, Gary G.	Rep	Cal.	3	2	25th Ross, Michael A.	Dem	Ark.	2	2
26th Hart, Melissa	Rep	Penn.	2	2	26th McCarthy, Carolyn	Dem	N.Y.	4	1
27th Capito, Shelley Moore	Rep	W.Va.	2	*1 2	27th Baca, Joe	Dem	Cal.	3	1
28th Tiberi, Patrick	Rep	Ohio	2	2	28th Matheson, James D.	Dem	Utah	2	1
29th Kennedy, Mark	Rep	Minn.	2	1	29th Lynch, Stephen F.	Dem	Mass.	2	1
30th Feeney, Tom	Rep	Fla.	1	1	30th Davis, Lincoln	Dem	Tenn.	1	*1 1
31st Hensarling, Jeb	Rep	Tex.	1	1	31st Miller, Brad	Dem	N.C.	1	1
32nd Garrett, Scott	Rep	N.J.	1	1	32nd Emanuel, Rahm	Dem	Ill.	1	1
33rd Murphy, Timothy	Rep	Penn.	1	1	33rd Scott, David	Dem	Ga.	1	1
34th Brown-Waite, Virginia	Rep	Fla.	1	1					

35th Barret, Gresham	Rep	S.C.	1	1		
36th Harris, Katherine	Rep	Fla.	1	1		
37th Renzi, Rick	Rep	Ariz.	1	1		

Third Party:

1st Sanders, Bernard	Ind	Vt.	7	7

*1. Member's first period of service on committee
*2: Member's second period of service on committee
*3: Member's third period of service on committee

Notes: Independent Sanders accrued seniority and was ranked 4th on the committee. Emanuel moved to rank 32nd following Miller on Feb. 5, 2003.

Changes:

Majority:

Bereuter, Douglas K.	Rep	Neb.	Aug. 31, 2004 Resigned and retired
Gerlach, Jim	Rep	Penn.	Sept. 23, 2004 Replaced Bereuter

Minority:

Davis, Lincoln	Dem	Tenn.	Feb. 5, 2003 Resigned committee due to clerical error; had been assigned to Transportation and Infrastructure on Jan. 28, 2003, and to Agriculture on Feb. 13, 2003
Davis, Artur	Dem	Ala.	Feb. 5, 2003 Replaced Lincoln Davis
Gonzalez, Charles A.	Dem	Tex.	Jan. 20, 2004 Resigned committee; moved to Energy and Commerce
Bell, Chris	Dem	Tex.	Jan. 28, 2004 Replaced Gonzalez

Departures from the House:

	Majority			Minority		
Defeated for Re-nomination	None			Bell, Chris	Dem	Tex.
Lost Nomination to U.S. Senate	Toomey, Patrick J.	Rep	Penn.	None		
Retired	Ose, Doug	Rep	Cal.	Lucas, Ken	Dem	Ky.

Departures from Committee:

Moved to Energy and Commerce	Murphy, Timothy	Rep	Penn.	Inslee, Jay R.	Dem	Wash.
				Ross, Michael A.	Dem	Ark.
Moved to Rules	Capito, Shelley Moore	Rep	W.Va.	None		
Moved to Standards of Official Conduct	Hart, Melissa	Rep	Penn.	None		
Moved to Ways and Means	Hart, Melissa	Rep	Penn.	Emanuel, Rahm	Dem	Ill.
No new assignment	Green, Mark	Rep	Wisc.			
	Shadegg, John B.	Rep	Ariz.			

FINANCIAL SERVICES / 109th Congress

Service Dates of Committee Chair: Jan. 6, 2005-Jan. 3, 2007

Service Dates of Majority Members: Jan. 26, 2005-Jan. 3, 2007

Service Dates of Minority Members: Jan. 26, 2005-Jan. 3, 2007

Roster Filled: Majority with 37 members on Feb. 2, 2005; Minority with 32 members on Jan. 26, 2005; Third party filled on Jan. 26, 2005

	Majority					Minority				
				Terms in:					**Terms in:**	
Rank Name	Party	State	House	Comm.		Rank Name	Party	State	House	Comm.
Chr Oxley, Michael G.	Rep	Ohio	13	3		RM Frank, Barney	Dem	Mass.	13	13
2nd Leach, James A.S.	Rep	Iowa	15	15		2nd Kanjorski, Paul E.	Dem	Penn.	11	11
3rd Baker, Richard H.	Rep	La.	10	9		3rd Waters, Maxine	Dem	Cal.	8	8
4th Pryce, Deborah D.	Rep	Ohio	7	*2 1		4th Sanders, Bernard	Ind	Vt	8	8
5th Bachus, Spencer T.	Rep	Ala.	7	7		5th Maloney, Carolyn B.	Dem	N.Y.	7	7
6th Castle, Michael N.	Rep	Del.	7	7		6th Gutierrez, Luis V.	Dem	Ill.	7	7
7th King, Peter T.	Rep	N.Y.	7	*1 7		7th Velázquez, Nydia M.	Dem	N.Y.	7	7
8th Royce, Edward R.	Rep	Cal.	7	6		8th Watt, Melvin L.	Dem	NC.	7	7
9th Lucas, Frank D.	Rep	Okla.	7	6		9th Ackerman, Gary L.	Dem	N.Y.	12	*3 4
10th Ney, Robert W.	Rep	Ohio	6	6		10th Hooley, Darlene	Dem	Ore.	5	5
11th Kelly, Sue W.	Rep	N.Y.	6	6		11th Carson, Julia M.	Dem	Ind.	5	5
12th Paul, Ronald E.	Rep	Tex.	9	*3 5		12th Sherman, Brad	Dem	Cal.	5	5
13th Gillmor, Paul E.	Rep	Ohio	9	*2 3		13th Meeks, Gregory W.	Dem	N.Y.	5	5
14th Ryun, Jim	Rep	Kans.	6	5		14th Lee, Barbara	Dem	Cal.	5	*2 4
15th LaTourette, Steven C.	Rep	Ohio	6	5		15th Moore, Dennis	Dem	Kans.	4	4
16th Manzullo, Donald A.	Rep	Ill.	7	5		16th Capuano, Michael E.	Dem	Mass.	4	4
17th Jones, Walter B. Jr.	Rep	N.C.	6	5		17th Ford, Harold E. Jr.	Dem	Tenn.	5	3
18th Biggert, Judith B.	Rep	Ill.	4	4		18th Hinojosa, Rubén	Dem	Tex.	5	3
19th Shays, Christopher H.	Rep	Conn.	10	3		19th Crowley, Joseph	Dem	N.Y.	4	3
20th Fossella, Vito J.	Rep	N.Y.	5	*2 3		20th Clay, William L. Jr.	Dem	Mo.	3	3
21st Miller, Gary G.	Rep	Cal.	4	3		21st Israel, Steve	Dem	N.Y.	3	3
22nd Tiberi, Patrick	Rep	Ohio	3	3		22nd McCarthy, Carolyn	Dem	N.Y.	5	2
23rd Kennedy, Mark	Rep	Minn.	3	2		23rd Baca, Joe	Dem	Cal.	4	2
24th Feeney, Tom	Rep	Fla.	2	2		24th Matheson, James D.	Dem	Utah	3	2

Rank Name	Party	State		
25th Hensarling, Jeb	Rep	Tex.	2	2
26th Garrett, Scott	Rep	N.J.	2	2
27th Brown-Waite, Virginia	Rep	Fla.	2	2
28th Barret, Gresham	Rep	S.C.	2	2
29th Harris, Katherine	Rep	Fla.	2	2
30th Renzi, Rick	Rep	Ariz.	2	2
31st Gerlach, Jim	Rep	Penn.	2	2
32nd Pearce, Stevan	Rep	N.M.	2	1
33rd Neugebauer, Randy	Rep	Tex.	2	1
34th Price, Tom	Rep	Ga.	1	1
35th Fitzpatrick, Michael G.	Rep	Penn.	1	1
36th Davis, Geoffrey C.	Rep	Ky.	1	1
37th McHenry, Patrick T.	Rep	N.C.	1	1

Rank Name	Party	State		
25th Lynch, Stephen F.	Dem	Mass.	3	2
26th Miller, Brad	Dem	N.C.	2	2
27th Scott, David	Dem	Ga.	2	2
28th Davis, Artur	Dem	Ala.	2	2
29th Green, Al	Dem	Tex.	1	1
30th Cleaver, Emanuel II	Dem	Mo.	1	1
31st Bean, Melissa L.	Dem	Ill.	1	1
32nd Wasserman Schultz, Debbie	Dem	Fla.	1	1
33rd Moore, Gwendolynne S.	Dem	Wisc.	1	1

*2: Member's second period of service on the committee.

*3: Member's third period of service on committee.

Filled Vacancies:

32nd seat filled by Pearce on Feb. 2, 2005

Changes:

Majority:

King, Peter T.	Rep	N.Y.	Feb. 8, 2006 Resigned committee; had become Chair on Homeland Security
Campbell, John	Rep	Cal.	Feb. 8, 2006 Replaced King
Ney, Robert W.	Rep	Ohio	Nov. 3, 2006 Resigned the House due to ethics issues

Departures from the House:

	Majority				Minority		
Elected to U.S. Senate	None				Sanders, Bernard	Ind.	Vt.
Lost Election to U.S. Senate	Kennedy, Mark	Rep	Minn.		Ford, Harold E. Jr.	Dem	Tenn.
	Harris, Katherine	Rep	Fla.				
Defeated for Re-election	Leach, James A.S.	Rep	Iowa		None		
	Kelly, Sue W.	Rep	N.Y.				
	Ryun, Jim	Rep	Kans.				
	Fitzpatrick, Michael G.	Rep	Penn.				
Retired	Oxley, Michael G.	Rep	Ohio		None		

Departures from Committee:

	Majority				Minority		
Moved to Appropriations	None				Lee, Barbara	Dem	Cal.
					Israel, Steve	Dem	N.Y.
					Wasserman Schultz, Debbie	Dem	Fla.
Moved to Budget	Tiberi, Patrick	Rep	Ohio		Hooley, Darlene	Dem	Ore.
Moved to Energy and Commerce	None				Hooley, Darlene	Dem	Ore.
					Matheson, James D.	Dem	Utah
Moved to Judiciary	None				Davis, Artur	Dem	Ala.
Moved to Ways and Means	Tiberi, Patrick	Rep	Ohio		Crowley, Joseph	Dem	N.Y.
					Davis, Artur	Dem	Ala.
No new assignment	Fossella, Vito J.	Rep	N.Y.		None		

FINANCIAL SERVICES / 110th Congress

Service Dates of Committee Chair: Jan. 4, 2007-Jan. 3, 2009

Service Dates of Majority Members: Jan. 12, 2007-Jan. 3, 2009

Service Dates of Minority Members: Jan. 10, 2007-Jan. 3, 2009

Roster Filled: Majority with 37 members on Jan. 23, 2007; Minority with 33 members on Jan. 10, 2007

	Majority					**Minority**				
				Terms in:						**Terms in:**
Rank Name	Party	State	House	Comm.		Rank Name	Party	State	House	Comm.
Chr Frank, Barney	Dem	Mass.	14	14		RM Bachus, Spencer T.	Rep	Ala.	8	8
2nd Kanjorski, Paul E.	Dem	Penn.	12	12		2nd Baker, Richard H.	Rep	La.	11	10
3rd Waters, Maxine	Dem	Cal.	9	9		3rd Pryce, Deborah D.	Rep	Ohio	8	*2 2
4th Maloney, Carolyn B.	Dem	N.Y.	8	8		4th Castle, Michael N.	Rep	Del.	8	8
5th Gutierrez, Luis V.	Dem	Ill.	8	8		5th King, Peter T.	Rep	N.Y.	8	*2 1
6th Velázquez, Nydia M.	Dem	N.Y.	8	8		6th Royce, Edward R.	Rep	Cal.	8	7
7th Watt, Melvin L.	Dem	N.C.	8	8		7th Lucas, Frank D.	Rep	Okla.	8	7
8th Ackerman, Gary L.	Dem	N.Y.	13	*3 5		8th Paul, Ronald E.	Rep	Tex.	10	*3 6
9th Carson, Julia M.	Dem	Ind.	6	6		9th Gillmor, Paul E.	Rep	Ohio	10	*2 4

10th Sherman, Brad	Dem	Cal.	6	6		10th LaTourette, Steven C.	Rep	Ohio	7	6
11th Meeks, Gregory W.	Dem	N.Y.	6	6		11th Manzullo, Donald A.	Rep	Ill.	8	6
12th Moore, Dennis	Dem	Kans.	5	5		12th Jones, Walter B. Jr.	Rep	N.C.	7	6
13th Capuano, Michael E.	Dem	Mass.	5	5		13th Biggert, Judith B.	Rep	Ill.	5	5
14th Hinojosa, Rubén	Dem	Tex.	6	4		14th Shays, Christopher H.	Rep	Conn.	11	4
15th Clay, William L. Jr.	Dem	Mo.	4	*2 4		15th Miller, Gary G.	Rep	Cal.	5	4
16th McCarthy, Carolyn	Dem	N.Y.	6	3		16th Capito, Shelley Moore	Rep	W.Va.	4	*2 1
17th Baca, Joe	Dem	Cal.	5	3		17th Feeney, Tom	Rep	Fla.	3	3
18th Lynch, Stephen F.	Dem	Mass.	4	3		18th Hensarling, Jeb	Rep	Tex.	3	3
19th Miller, Brad	Dem	N.C.	3	3		19th Garrett, Scott	Rep	N.J.	3	3
20th Scott, David	Dem	Ga.	3	3		20th Brown-Waite, Virginia	Rep	Fla.	3	3
21st Green, Al	Dem	Tex.	2	2		21st Barrett, J. Gresham	Rep	S.C.	3	3
22nd Cleaver, Emanuel II	Dem	Mo.	2	2		22nd Renzi, Rick	Rep	Ariz.	3	3
23rd Bean, Melissa L.	Dem	Ill.	2	2		23rd Gerlach, Jim	Rep	Penn.	3	3
24th Moore, Gwendolynne S.	Dem	Wisc.	2	2		24th Pearce, Stevan	Rep	N.M.	3	2
25th Davis, Lincoln	Dem	Tenn.	3	*2 1		25th Neugebauer, Randy	Rep	Tex.	3	2
26th Sires, Albio	Dem	N.J.	1	1		26th Price, Tom	Rep	Ga.	2	2
27th Hodes, Paul W.	Dem	N.H.	1	1		27th Davis, Geoffrey C.	Rep	Ky.	2	2
28th Ellison, Keith	DFL	Minn.	1	1		28th McHenry, Patrick T.	Rep	N.C.	2	2
29th Klein, Ron	Dem	Fla.	1	1		29th Campbell, John	Rep	Cal.	2	2
30th Mahoney, Tim	Dem	Fla.	1	1		30th Putnam, Adam H. Jr.	Rep	Fla.	4	1
31st Wilson, Charles A.	Dem	Ohio	1	1		31st Blackburn, Marsha	Rep	Tenn.	3	1
32nd Perlmutter, Ed	Dem	Colo.	1	1		32nd Bachmann, Michele	Rep	Minn.	1	1
33rd Murphy, Christopher S.	Dem	Conn.	1	1		33rd Roskam, Peter	Rep	Ill.	1	1
34th Donnelly, Joe	Dem	Ind.	1	1						
35th Wexler, Robert	Dem	Fla.	6	1						
36th Marshall, Jim	Dem	Ga.	3	1						
37th Boren, Daniel D.	Dem	Okla.	1	1						

*2: Member's second period of service on the committee.
*3: Member's third period of service on committee.

Filled Vacancies:

Majority:

37th seat by Boren on Jan. 18, 2007, and 35th seat by Wexler on Jan. 23, 2007

Changes:

Majority:

Carson, Julia M.	Dem	Ind.	Dec. 15, 2007 Died in office
Sires, Albio	Dem	N.J.	Mar. 11, 2008 Resigned committee; moved to Transportation and Infrastructure
Foster, Bill	Dem	Ill.	Apr. 1, 2008 Replaced Julia Carson
Carson, André	Dem	Ind.	Apr. 1, 2008 Replaced Sires
Wexler, Robert	Dem	Fla.	June 6, 2008 Resigned committee; no new assignment
Boren, Daniel D.	Dem	Okla.	June 6, 2008 Resigned committee; no new assignment, exceeded majority ratio
Marshall, Jim	Dem	Ga.	June 10, 2008 Resigned committee; no new assignment
Speier, K. Jacqueline	Dem	Cal.	June 10, 2008 Replaced Wexler
Cazayoux, Donald J. Jr.	Dem	La.	June 10, 2008 Replaced Boren
Childers, Travis W.	Dem	Miss.	June 10, 2008 Replaced Marshall

Minority:

Blackburn, Marsha	Rep	Tenn.	Mar. 9, 2007 Resigned committee; returned to Energy and Commerce
Marchant, Kenny	Rep	Tex.	Mar. 12, 2007 Replaced Blackburn
Renzi, Rick	Rep	Ariz.	Apr. 24, 2007 Resigned committee due to ethics issues
McCotter, Thaddeus	Rep	Mich.	May 10, 2007 Replaced Renzi
Gillmor, Paul E.	Rep	Ohio	Sep. 5, 2007 Died in office
McCarthy, Kevin	Rep	Cal.	Oct. 2, 2007 Replaced Gillmor
Baker, Richard H.	Rep	La.	Feb. 2, 2008 Resigned the House and retired
Heller, Dean	Rep	Nev.	Feb. 26, 2008 Replaced Baker

Departures from the House:

	Majority			**Minority**		
Lost Election to U.S. Senate	None			Pearce, Stevan	Rep	N.M.
Defeated for Re-election	Mahoney, Tim	Dem	Fla.	Shays, Christopher H.	Rep	Conn.
	Cazayoux, Donald J. Jr.	Dem	La.	Feeney, Tom	Rep	Fla.
Retired	None			Pryce, Deborah D.	Rep	Ohio

Departures from Committee:

Moved to Appropriations	Davis, Lincoln	Dem	Tenn.	LaTourette, Steven C.	Rep	Ohio.
Moved to Energy and Commerce	Murphy, Christopher S.	Dem	Conn.	None		
Returned to Science and Technology	Davis, Lincoln	Dem	Tenn.	None		
Moved to Ways and Means	None			Heller, Dean	Rep	Nev.
				Brown Waite, Virginia	Rep	Fla.
				Davis, Geoffrey C.	Rep	Ky.
				Roskam, Peter	Rep	Ill.

FINANCIAL SERVICES / 111th Congress

Service Dates of Committee Chair: Jan. 6, 2009-Jan. 3, 2011

Service Dates of Majority Members: Jan. 7, 2009-Jan. 3, 2011

Service Dates of Minority Members: Jan. 9, 2009-Jan. 3, 2011

Roster Filled: Majority with 42 members, Jan. 7, 2009; Minority with 29 members, Jan. 9, 2009

Majority

Rank Name	Party	State	Terms in: House	Terms in: Comm.
Chr Frank, Barney	Dem	Mass.	15	15
2nd Kanjorski, Paul E.	Dem	Penn.	13	13
3rd Waters, Maxine	Dem	Cal.	10	10
4th Maloney, Carolyn B.	Dem	N.Y.	9	9
5th Gutierrez, Luis V.	Dem	Ill.	9	9
6th Velázquez, Nydia M.	Dem	N.Y.	9	9
7th Watt, Melvin L.	Dem	N.C.	9	9
8th Ackerman, Gary L.	Dem	N.Y.	14	*3 6
9th Sherman, Brad	Dem	Cal.	7	7
10th Meeks, Gregory W.	Dem	N.Y.	7	7
11th Moore, Dennis	Dem	Kans.	6	6
12th Capuano, Michael E.	Dem	Mass.	6	6
13th Hinojosa, Rubén	Dem	Tex.	7	5
14th Clay, William L. Jr.	Dem	Mo.	5	*2 5
15th McCarthy, Carolyn	Dem	N.Y.	7	4
16th Baca, Joe	Dem	Cal.	6	4
17th Lynch, Stephen F.	Dem	Mass.	5	4
18th Miller, Brad	Dem	N.C.	4	4
19th Scott, David	Dem	Ga.	4	4
20th Green, Al	Dem	Tex.	3	3
21st Cleaver, Emanuel II	Dem	Mo.	3	3
22nd Bean, Melissa L.	Dem	Ill.	3	3
23rd Moore, Gwendolynne S.	Dem	Wisc.	3	3
24th Hodes, Paul W.	Dem	N.H.	2	2
25th Ellison, Keith	DFL	Minn.	2	2
26th Klein, Ron	Dem	Fla.	2	2
27th Wilson, Charles A.	Dem	Ohio	2	2
28th Perlmutter, Ed	Dem	Colo.	2	2
29th Donnelly, Joe	Dem	Ind.	2	2
30th Foster, Bill	Dem	Ill.	2	2
31st Carson, André	Dem	Ind.	2	2
32nd Speier, K. Jacqueline	Dem	Cal.	2	2
33rd Childers, Travis W.	Dem	Miss.	2	2
34th Minnick, Walt	Dem	Ida.	1	1
35th Adler, John H.	Dem	N.J.	1	1
36th Kilroy, Mary Jo	Dem	Ohio	1	1
37th Dreihaus, Steve	Dem	Ohio	1	1
38th Kosmas, Suzanne M.	Dem	Fla.	1	1
39th Grayson, Alan	Dem	Fla.	1	1
40th Himes, James A.	Dem	Conn.	1	1
41st Peters, Gary	Dem	Mich.	1	1
42nd Maffei, Daniel B.	Dem	N.Y.	1	1

Minority

Rank Name	Party	State	Terms in: House	Terms in: Comm.
RM Bachus, Spencer T.	Rep	Ala.	9	9
2nd Castle, Michael N.	Rep	Del.	9	9
3rd King, Peter T.	Rep	N.Y.	9	*2 2
4th Royce, Edward R.	Rep	Cal.	9	8
5th Lucas, Frank D.	Rep	Okla.	9	8
6th Paul, Ronald E.	Rep	Tex.	11	*3 7
7th Manzullo, Donald A.	Rep	Ill.	9	7
8th Jones, Walter B. Jr.	Rep	N.C.	8	7
9th Biggert, Judith B.	Rep	Ill.	6	6
10th Miller, Gary G.	Rep	Cal.	6	5
11th Capito, Shelley Moore	Rep	W.Va.	5	*2 2
12th Hensarling, Jeb	Rep	Tex.	4	4
13th Garrett, Scott	Rep	N.J.	4	4
14th Barrett, J. Gresham	Rep	S.C.	4	4
15th Gerlach, Jim	Rep	Penn.	4	4
16th Neugebauer, Randy	Rep	Tex.	4	3
17th Price, Tom	Rep	Ga.	3	3
18th McHenry, Patrick T.	Rep	N.C.	3	3
19th Campbell, John	Rep	Cal.	3	3
20th Putnam, Adam H. Jr.	Rep	Fla.	5	2
21st Bachmann, Michele	Rep	Minn.	2	2
22nd Marchant, Kenny	Rep	Tex.	2	2
23rd McCotter, Thaddeus	Rep	Mich.	4	2
24th McCarthy, Kevin	Rep	Cal.	2	2
25th Posey, Bill	Rep	Fla.	1	1
26th Jenkins, Lynn	Rep	Kans.	1	1
27th Lee, Christopher J.	Rep	N.Y.	1	1
28th Paulsen, Erik	Rep	Minn.	1	1
29th Lance, Leonard	Rep	N.J.	1	1

*2: Member's second period of service on the committee.

*3: Member's third period of service on committee.

Foreign Affairs

House Committee on Foreign Affairs, 103rd Congresses (1993-1995)

House Committee on International Relations, 104th-109th Congresses (1995-2007)

House Committee on Foreign Affairs, 110th-111th Congresses (2007-2011)

BACKGROUND

Organizational History: The House first created a Select Committee on Foreign Affairs on October 29, 1807, at the behest of John Dawson, a Virginia Jeffersonian, but the standing committee dates from March 13, 1822, along with the other standing committees on Military Affairs and Naval Affairs. Jonathan Russell of Massachusetts was the standing committee's first chair.

Although created early in the history of the nation, the panel has traditionally been overshadowed by its Senate counterpart—the Foreign Relations Committee. To a great extent, this reflects the relative foreign policy roles of the House and Senate as reflected in the Constitution. Since the Constitution gives the Senate exclusive control over international treaties and ambassadorial nominations, the Senate panel often is at the center of debate over major international issues, while the House panel is not.

From 1885 to 1920, the committee gained power to report appropriations after the House took much of that authority from the Appropriations Committee but in 1920, Appropriations regained that authority and the Foreign Affairs Committee was diminished. Because the House has much less authority in foreign affairs, the House Foreign Affairs Committee has less authority as well. This natural limitation has been exacerbated in modern times by the executive branch's grasp of much greater power in foreign affairs and by the expansion of authority by other committees with interests in foreign policy, especially the Armed Services Committee.

The committee's name was changed to International Relations in 1975 and the Committee Reform Amendments of 1974 gave the committee jurisdiction over international economic policy and export controls, international commodity agreements, trading with the enemy, and international education, while it lost jurisdiction over international financial and monetary organizations and international fishing agreements. It also acquired control over the nonproliferation of nuclear technology and exports from the defunct Joint Committee on Atomic Energy.

The original name of Foreign Affairs was restored in 1979. The Republican takeover of the House in 1995 led to its renaming once again as the Committee on International Relations, but the Democrats' regaining control of the House in 2007 led to the committee resuming its historic identity as Foreign Affairs.

It has broad responsibility for legislation dealing with the relations of the United States with other countries, including those dealing with American citizens abroad and expatriation. The most important legislative topics that fall under its jurisdiction are foreign aid programs, which provide economic assistance to poor and developing countries, and military equipment and training for U.S. allies around the world. Despite its seemingly significant responsibilities including jurisdiction over communications from the president notifying the House, consistent with the War Powers Resolution, of the deployment abroad of U.S. armed forces to participate in an embargo against another nation (Nov. 4, 1993), the panel has had relatively little overall impact on the direction of U.S. foreign policy.

Membership: The Foreign Affairs Committee's size at the time of the 1946 Reorganization Act was twenty-five, a number which had been in force since 1933. By 1993, the committee's membership was forty-five and after shrinking to forty-two in 1995 and growing back to forty-seven in 1997, its membership reached fifty in the 109th and 110th Congresses (2005-2009) but returned to forty-seven members in the 111th Congress (2009-2011). The committee's mean membership size over the last nine Congresses of 47.66 members placed it in eighth place among the nineteen committees, while its mean member seniority of 5.68 terms located it in sixty place and among the top third of the House committees. Ironically, this would give the House Foreign Affairs Committee a higher recent chamber ranking on this dimension than its better-known counterpart, the Senate Foreign Relations Committee across the Capitol. Its 87.83 percent inter-Congress member retention rate ranked it sixth among the nineteen continuing House committees.

Committee Leaders: The chairs of the Foreign Affairs committee have been less prominent than some of its members. Six different chairs presided between 1947 and 1959. The first post-reorganization chair was Charles A. Eaton (Rep-N.J.), the committee's senior Republican since 1943. Eaton chaired only the 80th Congress. In the other Republican Congress, the 83rd, Robert B. Chiperfield (Rep-Ill.) chaired the committee. The best known of the early chairs was Sol Bloom (Dem-N.Y.), who first became chair in 1939, and apart from the Republican 80th Congress, was chair until his death in 1949. Bloom's successor was John Kee (Dem-W. Va.), who served until his death in 1951, when he was succeeded by James P. Richards (Dem-S.C.) until Richard's 1957 appointment as a senior adviser for the Middle East in the Eisenhower administration. Richard's successor, Thomas S. Gordon (Dem-Ill.) served only one term, 1957-1959, while Chiperfield, the Republican senior member, served in that role from 1953 to 1963.

In 1957, Thomas E. "Doc" Morgan (Dem-Penn.) took over the committee and presided until 1977, the committee's longest chairmanship stint. It was during Morgan's chairmanship that President Nixon sought to use the House's Foreign Affairs

Committee with its larger and more "hawkish" membership to counter the Senate's smaller and more "dovish" Foreign Relations Committee during the heated congressional debates during the Vietnam War. In addition to Chiperfield, Morgan served with five other ranking members—Frances P. Bolton (Rep-Ohio), 1963-1969; E. Ross Adair (Rep-Ind.), 1969-1971; William S. Mailliard (Rep-Cal.), 1971-1974; Peter H.B. Frelinghuysen (Rep-N.J.), 1974-1975; and William S. Broomfield (Rep-Mich.), 1975-1993.

Morgan was succeeded by Clement J. Zablocki (Dem-Wisc.), 1977-1983, Dante B. Fascell (Dem-Fla.), 1984-1993 and Lee H. Hamilton (Dem-Ind.), who chaired the committee in the 103rd Congress (1993-1995) and served as its ranking member until his retirement in 2001. After eighteen years as the committee's senior Republican, Broomfield retired in 1993 and was succeeded by Benjamin A. Gilman (Rep-N.Y.), who would become the committee's first Republican chair in forty years. Gilman chaired the committee for the next three Congresses, 1995-2001, and stepped aside to let Henry J. Hyde (Rep-Ill.), the former chair of Judiciary chair the committee for the subsequent three Congresses, 2001-2007. Hyde's retirement in 2007 and the Democrats' return to power led to Cuban-born Ileana Ros-Lehtinen (Rep-Fla.) becoming the Foreign Affairs Committee's ranking member.

Lee Hamilton's immediate successor as Democratic ranking member in 1999 was Samuel Gejdenson (Dem-Conn.) whose re-election defeat in 2000 opened the way for Holocaust survivor Tom Lantos (Dem-Cal.), whose eight years as senior Democrat included two as chair, 2007-2008 until his death led to the succession of Howard L. Berman (Dem-Cal.), the committee's present chair.

Party Leaders: Unlike the Senate Foreign Relations Committee, House Foreign Affairs has not been a springboard to the floor leadership. Former House Speaker Joseph W. Martin Jr. (Rep-Mass.) served on the committee after he was ousted from the post of Minority Leader in 1959 and since then the only other party leaders have been three whips: Democrat William Gray III of Pennsylvania and the last two Republican Whips, Roy Blunt of Missouri and Eric L. Cantor of Virginia.

Notable Members: The only two alumni of the House Foreign Affairs Committee to be nominated for major offices were J. Danforth Quayle (Rep-Ind.), who was elected vice president in 1988 with George H.W. Bush and defeated with him in 1992, and John S. McCain III (Rep-Ariz.), the unsuccessful 2008 Republican nominee for president. The only committee members named to the Cabinet were Christian A. Herter (Rep-Mass.), who left the committee after his election as governor of Massachusetts and returned to serve as President Eisenhower's second Secretary of State, 1959-61, replacing the deceased John Foster Dulles; Abraham A. Ribicoff, who left the governorship of Connecticut to become President Kennedy's first Secretary of Health, Education, and Welfare in 1961; and Edward J. Derwinski (Rep-Ill.), named by President George H.W. Bush as the nation's first Secretary of Veterans' Affairs in 1989.

The committee's major appeal is as a springboard to the U.S. Senate. Twenty-nine post-1947 Foreign Affairs Committee members have been elected to the Senate. Among them are fifteen Democrats—George A. Smathers of Florida; Michael J. Mansfield of Montana; Abraham A. Ribicoff and Thomas J. Dodd of Connecticut; Robert C. Byrd of West Virginia; Harrison A. Williams, Robert J. Torricelli, and Robert Menendez of New Jersey; John V. Tunney of California; John C. Culver of Iowa; Donald W. Riegle of Michigan; Harry M. Reid of Nevada;

Charles E. Schumer of New York; Marie E. Cantwell of Washington State; and Sherrod Brown of Ohio. Both John Culver and John Tunney roomed with Sen. Ted Kennedy of Massachusetts—Culver at Harvard during Kennedy's undergraduate years and Tunney at the University of Virginia Law School. Not surprisingly, Mansfield, Byrd, and Reid became Senate majority leaders.

The fourteen Republican alumni of Foreign Affairs/International Relations who moved to the Senate were Karl E. Mundt of South Dakota, Jacob K. Javits of New York, Winston L. Prouty of Vermont, William V. Roth Jr. of Delaware, Robert A. Taft Jr. and Michael DeWine of Ohio, Wyche Fowler Jr. of Georgia, J. Danforth Quayle of Indiana, John S. McCain III of Arizona, Connie Mack III of Florida, Olympia J.B. Snowe of Maine, Richard M. Burr of North Carolina, Sam D. Brownback of Kansas, and Lindsey O. Graham of South Carolina.

In addition to former governors Herter and Ribicoff who also served in the Cabinet, four other Foreign Affairs members were governors—Republicans John Davis Lodge of Connecticut, grandson of Senate Majority Leader Henry Cabot Lodge of Massachusetts and brother of Senator Henry Cabot Lodge Jr. (Rep-Mass.); Pierre S. du Pont IV of Delaware; and Marshall C. (Mark) Sanford of South Carolina, and Democrat Kenneth H. (Buddy) MacKay of Florida. Three former governors who were elected to the House and served on Foreign Affairs were Democrat Chester B. Bowles of Connecticut and Republicans Vernon W. Thomson of Wisconsin and the ill-fated William J. Janklow of South Dakota, whose House career ended after a year due to a conviction of vehicular manslaughter.

Former committee members and Democrats James P. Richards of South Carolina and Chester B. Bowles of Connecticut served as foreign policy advisers to President Eisenhower while John Davis Lodge served as Ambassador to Spain, Bowles was named Ambassador to India, and Mike Mansfield was named Ambassador to Japan.

Selected References

Carroll, Holbert, *The House of Representatives and Foreign Policy*, rev. ed. (Boston: Little, Brown, 1966).

Crabb, Cecil V. and Pat M. Holt, *Invitation to Struggle: Congress, the President and Foreign Policy* (Washington, D.C.: Congressional Quarterly, 1980).

Fenno, Richard F., Jr., *Congressmen in Committees* (Boston: Little, Brown, 1973).

Galey, Margaret E., "Congress, Foreign Policy and Human Rights: Ten Years after Helsinki," *Human Rights Quarterly*, 7 (August, 1985), 334-372.

Kaiser, Fred M., "Oversight of Foreign Policy: The U.S. Committee on International Relations," *Legislative Studies Quarterly*, 2 (1977), 255-279.

McCormick, James M., "The Changing Role of the House Foreign Affairs Committee in 1970s and 1980s," *Congress and the Presidency*, 12 (Spring, 1985), 1-20.

McCormick, James M., "Decision Making in the Foreign Affairs and Foreign Relations Committees," in Randall B. Ripley and James M. Lindsay, eds., *Congress Resurgent: Foreign and Defense Policy on Capitol Hill* (Ann Arbor: University of Michigan Press, 1993), 115-154.

McCubbins, Mathew D. and Thomas Schwartz, "Congressional Oversight Overlooked: Police Patrols versus Fire Alarms," *American Journal of Political Science*, 28 (1984), 165-179.

Ornstein, Norman J. and David W. Rohde, "Shifting Forces, Changing Rules, and Political Outcomes: The Impact of Congressional Change on Four House Committees," in Robert L. Peabody and Nelson W. Polsby, eds., *New Perspectives on the House of Representatives,* 3rd ed. (Chicago: Rand McNally, 1977), 186-269.

Schamel, Charles E. et al., "Records of the Foreign Affairs Committee," *Guide to the Records of the United States House of Representatives at the National Archives: 1789-1989 Bicentennial Edition* (Washington, D.C.: National Archives and Records Administration,1989), 133-145.

U.S. House of Representatives, Committee on Foreign Affairs, *Survey of Activities, 92nd Congress: 105th Anniversary Issue,* House Committee Print (1973).

Weissman, Stephen A., *A Culture of Deference: Congress's Failure of Leadership in Foreign Policy* (New York: Basic Books, 1995).

Westphal, Albert C.F., *The House Committee on Foreign Affairs* (New York: Columbia University Press, 1942).

Whalen, Charles W., Jr. The House and Foreign Policy: The Irony of Congressional Reform (Chapel Hill: University of North Carolina Press, 1982).

RESPONSIBILITIES, JURISDICTIONAL CHANGES, AND SUBCOMMITTEES

FOREIGN AFFAIRS

Jurisdiction, 80th Congress (1947-1949)

Established by the Legislative Reorganization Act of 1946:

[Section 121.(1)(i)] Committee on Foreign Affairs
(1) Relations of the United States with foreign nations generally.
(2) Establishment of boundary lines between the United States and foreign nations.
(3) Protection of American citizens abroad and expatriation.
(4) Neutrality.
(5) International conferences and congresses.
(6) The American National Red Cross.
(7) Intervention abroad and declarations of war.
(8) Measures relating to the diplomatic service.
(9) Acquisition of land and buildings for embassies and legations in foreign countries.
(10) Measures to foster commercial intercourse with foreign nations and to safeguard American business interests abroad.
(11) United Nations Organization and international financial and monetary organizations.
(12) Foreign loans.

INTERNATIONAL RELATIONS

Foreign Affairs was renamed the Committee on International Relations on March 19, 1975.

FOREIGN AFFAIRS

International Relations was redesignated the Committee on Foreign Affairs on February 5, 1979.

Jurisdiction, 103rd Congress (1993-1995)

From the Rules of the House of Representatives, 103rd Congress (House Document 102-405)

[Rule X.1.(i)] Committee on Foreign Affairs
(1) Relations of the United States with foreign nations generally.
(2) Acquisition of land and buildings for embassies and legations in foreign countries.
(3) Establishment of boundary lines between the United States and foreign nations.
(4) Foreign loans.
(5) International conferences and congresses.
(6) Intervention abroad and declarations of war.
(7) Measures relating to the diplomatic service.
(8) Measures to foster commercial intercourse with foreign nations and to safeguard American business interests abroad.
(9) Neutrality.
(10) Protection of American citizens abroad and expatriation.
(11) The American National Red Cross.
(12) United Nations Organizations.
(13) Measures relating to international economic policy.

(14) Export controls, including nonproliferation of nuclear technology and nuclear hardware.
(15) International commodity agreements (other than those involving sugar), including all agreements for cooperation in the export of nuclear technology and nuclear hardware.
(16) Trading with the enemy.
(17) International education.

In addition to its legislative jurisdiction under the preceding provisions of this paragraph (and its general oversight function under clause 2(b)(1)), the committee shall have the special oversight functions provided for in clause 3(d) with respect to customs administration, intelligence activities relating to foreign policy, international financial and monetary organizations, and international fishing agreements.

[Rule X.3.(d)] Additional Functions

The Committee on Foreign Affairs shall have the function of reviewing and studying, on a continuing basis, all laws, programs, and Government activities dealing with or involving customs administration, intelligence activities relating to foreign policy, international financial and monetary organizations, and international fishing agreements.

INTERNATIONAL RELATIONS

Foreign Affairs was renamed the Committee on International Relations on January 4, 1995.

Jurisdiction, 104th Congress (1995-1997) Changes in Committee System

From H. Res. 6, Section 202 (a), the Committees and Their Jurisdiction, January 4, 1995

[Rule X.1.(i)] Committee on International Relations.
(1) Relations of the United States with foreign nations generally.
(2) Acquisition of land and buildings for embassies and legations in foreign countries.
(3) Establishment of boundary lines between the United States and foreign nations.
(4) Export controls, including nonproliferation of nuclear technology and nuclear hardware.
(5) Foreign loans.
(6) International commodity agreements (other than those involving sugar), including all agreements for cooperation in the export of nuclear technology and nuclear hardware.
(7) International conferences and congresses.
(8) International education.
(9) Intervention abroad and declarations of war.
(10) Measures relating to the diplomatic service.
(11) Measures to foster commercial intercourse with foreign nations and to safeguard American business interests abroad.
(12) Measures relating to international economic policy.
(13) Neutrality.
(14) Protection of American citizens abroad and expatriation.
(15) The American National Red Cross.
(16) Trading with the enemy.
(17) United Nations organizations.

In addition to its legislative jurisdiction under the preceding provisions of this paragraph (and its general oversight function under clause 2(b)(1)), the committee shall have the special oversight functions provided for in clause 3(d) with respect to customs administration, intelligence activities relating to foreign policy, international financial and monetary organizations, and international fishing agreements.

FOREIGN AFFAIRS

International Relations was redesignated the Committee on Foreign Affairs on January 4, 2007.

Jurisdiction, 111th Congress (2009-2011)

From the Rules of the House of Representatives (as revised to June 16, 2009, H.Doc. 110-162):

[Rule X.1.(h)] Committee on Foreign Affairs
(1) Relations of the United States with foreign nations generally.
(2) Acquisition of land and buildings for embassies and legations in foreign countries.
(3) Establishment of boundary lines between the United States and foreign nations.
(4) Export controls, including nonproliferation of nuclear technology and nuclear hardware.
(5) Foreign loans.
(6) International commodity agreements (other than those involving sugar), including all agreements for cooperation in the export of nuclear technology and nuclear hardware.

(7) International conferences and congresses.

(8) International education.

(9) Intervention abroad and declarations of war.

(10) Diplomatic service.

(11) Measures to foster commercial intercourse with foreign nations and to safeguard American business interests abroad.

(12) International economic policy.

(13) Neutrality.

(14) Protection of American citizens abroad and expatriation.

(15) The American National Red Cross.

(16) Trading with the enemy.

(17) United Nations organizations.

[Rule X.3.(f)] Special Oversight Function

The Committee on Foreign Affairs shall review and study on a continuing basis laws, programs, and Government activities relating to customs administration, intelligence activities relating to foreign policy, international financial and monetary organizations, and international fishing agreements.

NAMES OF FOREIGN AFFAIRS SUBCOMMITTEES FROM THE *CONGRESSIONAL DIRECTORY*

Foreign Affairs, 103rd Congress

Africa, 103
Asia and the Pacific, 103
Economic Policy, Trade, and the Environment, 103
Europe and the Middle East, 103
International Operations, 103
International Security, International Organizations, and Human Rights, 103
Western Hemisphere Affairs, 103

International Relations, 104th-109th Congresses

Africa, 104, 105, 106, 107, 108 Africa, Global Human Rights and International Operations, 109
Asia and the Pacific, 104, 105, 106, 107, 108, 109 Europe, 107, 108
Europe and Emerging Threats, 109 International Economic Policy and Trade, 104, 105, 106
International Operations and Human Rights, 104, 105, 106, 107
International Terrorism, Nonproliferation and Human Rights, 108
International Terrorism and Nonproliferation, 109 Middle East and South Asia, 107
Middle East and Central Asia, 108, 109 Oversight and Investigations, 109
Western Hemisphere, 104, 105, 106, 107, 108, 109

Foreign Affairs, 110th-111th Congresses

Africa and Global Health, 110, 111
Asia, the Pacific, and the Global Environment, 110, 111
Europe, 110, 111
International Organizations, Human Rights, and Oversight, 110, 111
Middle East and South Asia, 110, 111
Terrorism, Nonproliferation, and Trade, 110, 111
Western Hemisphere, 110, 111

MEMBERSHIP ROSTERS, 103rd-111th Congresses, 1993-2011

FOREIGN AFFAIRS / 103rd Congress

Service Dates of Committee Chair: Jan. 5, 1993-Jan. 3, 1995

Service Dates of Majority Members: Jan. 5, 1993-Jan. 3, 1995

Service Dates of Minority Members: Jan. 5, 1993-Jan. 3, 1995

Roster Filled: Majority with 27 members, Nov. 10, 1993; Minority with 18 members, Jan. 5, 1993

	Majority						Minority				
				Terms in:						Terms in:	
Rank Name		Party	State	House	Comm.	Rank Name		Party	State	House	Comm.
Chr Hamilton, Lee H.		Dem	Ind.	15	15	RM Gilman, Benjamin A.		Rep	N.Y.	11	11
2nd Gejdenson, Samuel		Dem	Conn.	7	7	2nd Goodling, William F.		Rep	Penn.	10	*3 6
3rd Lantos, Thomas P.		Dem	Cal.	7	7	3rd Leach, James A.S.		Rep	Iowa	9	7
4th Torricelli, Robert G.		Dem	N.J.	6	6	4th Roth, Tobias A.		Rep	Wisc.	8	7
5th Berman, Howard L.		Dem	Cal.	6	6	5th Snowe, Olympia J.B.		Rep	Me.	8	7
6th Ackerman, Gary L.		Dem	N.Y.	6	6	6th Hyde, Henry J.		Rep	Ill.	10	7
7th Johnston, Harry A. II.		Dem	Fla.	3	3	7th Bereuter, Douglas K.		Rep	Neb.	8	6
8th Engel, Eliot L.		Dem	N.Y.	3	*1 3	8th Smith, Christopher H.		Rep	N.J.	7	5
9th Faleomavaega, Eni F.H.		Dem	A.S.	3	3	9th Burton, Danny L.		Rep	Ind.	6	5
10th Oberstar, James L.		DFL	Minn.	10	1	10th Meyers, Jan		Rep	Kans.	5	4
11th Schumer, Charles E.		Dem	N.Y.	7	1	11th Gallegly, Elton W.		Rep	Cal.	4	3
12th Martinez, Matthew G.		Dem	Cal.	7	1	12th Ros-Lehtinen, Ileana		Rep	Fla.	3	3
13th Borski, Robert A.		Dem	Penn.	6	1	13th Ballenger, Cass		Rep	N.C.	5	1
14th Payne, Donald M.		Dem	N.J.	3	3	14th Rohrabacher, Dana		Rep	Cal.	3	1
15th Andrews, Robert E.		Dem	N.J.	3	1	15th Levy, David A.		Rep	N.Y.	1	1
16th Menendez, Robert		Dem	N.J.	1	1	16th Manzullo, Donald A.		Rep	Ill.	1	*1 1
17th Brown, Sherrod		Dem	Ohio	1	1	17th Diaz-Balart, Lincoln		Rep	Fla.	1	1
18th McKinney, Cynthia A.		Dem	Ga.	1	1	18th Royce, Edward R.		Rep	Cal.	1	1
19th Cantwell, Maria E.		Dem	Wash.	1	1						
20th Hastings, Alcee L.		Dem	Fla.	1	1						
21st Fingerhut, Eric D.		Dem	Ohio	1	1						
22nd Deutsch, Peter R.		Dem	Fla.	1	1						
23rd Wynn, Albert R.		Dem	Md.	1	1						
24th Edwards, William D. (Don)		Dem	Cal.	16	1						
25th McCloskey, Francis X.		Dem	Ind.	6	3						
26th Sawyer, Thomas C.		Dem	Ohio	4	2						
27th Gutierrez, Luis V.		Dem	Ill.	1	1						

*1: Member's first period of service on the committee.
*3: Member's third period of service on the committee.

Note: Territorial Delegate Eni F. H. Faleomavaega (Dem-Am.S.) was allowed to accrue committee seniority but was not included in the party ratio.

Vacancies Filled:

  Majority:

    24th through 26th seats filled by Edwards, McCloskey, and Sawyer on Jan. 21, 1993. 27th seat filled by Gutierrez on Nov. 10, 1993

Departures from the House:	Majority			Minority		
Elected to U.S. Senate	None			Snowe, Olympia J.B.	Rep	Me.
Defeated for Re-nomination	None			Levy, David A.	Rep	N.Y.
Defeated for Re-election	Cantwell, Maria E.	Dem	Wash.	None		
	Fingerhut, Eric D.	Dem	Ohio			
	McCloskey, Francis X.	Dem	Ind.			
Retired	Edwards, William D. (Don)	Dem	Cal.	None		

Departures from Committee:						
Moved to Commerce	Deutsch, Peter R.	Dem	Fla.	None		
Moved to House Oversight	None			Diaz-Balart, Lincoln	Rep	Fla.
Moved to Rules	None			Diaz-Balart, Lincoln	Rep	Fla.
No new assignment	Oberstar, James L.	DFL	Minn.	None		
	Schumer, Charles E.	Dem	N.Y.			
	Borski, Robert A.	Dem	Penn.			
	Sawyer, Thomas C.	Dem	Ohio			
	Gutierrez, Luis V.	Dem	Ill.			

INTERNATIONAL RELATIONS / 104th Congress

Service Dates of Committee Chair: Jan. 4, 1995-Jan. 3, 1997

Service Dates of Majority Members: Jan. 4, 1995-Jan. 3, 1997

Service Dates of Minority Members: Jan. 4, 1995-Jan. 3, 1997

Roster Filled: Majority with 23 members, Jan. 27, 1995; Minority with 19 members, Jan. 4, 1995;

Frazer filled the Independent seat on Jan. 27, 1995

	Majority						Minority				
				Terms in:						Terms in:	
Rank Name		Party	State	House	Comm.	Rank Name		Party	State	House	Comm.
Chr Gilman, Benjamin A.		Rep	N.Y.	12	12	RM Hamilton, Lee H.		Dem	Ind.	16	16
2nd Goodling, William F.		Rep	Penn.	11	*3 7	2nd Gejdenson, Samuel		Dem	Conn.	8	8
3rd Leach, James A.S.		Rep	Iowa	10	8	3rd Lantos, Thomas P.		Dem	Cal.	8	8
4th Roth, Tobias A.		Rep	Wisc.	9	8	4th Torricelli, Robert G.		Dem	N.J.	7	7
5th Hyde, Henry J.		Rep	Ill.	11	8	5th Berman, Howard L.		Dem	Cal.	7	7
6th Bereuter, Douglas K.		Rep	Neb.	9	7	6th Ackerman, Gary L.		Dem	N.Y.	7	7
7th Smith, Christopher H.		Rep	N.J.	8	6	7th Johnston, Harry A. II		Dem	Fla.	4	4
8th Burton, Danny L.		Rep	Ind.	7	6	8th Engel, Eliot L.		Dem	N.Y.	4	*1 4
9th Meyers, Jan		Rep	Kans.	6	5	9th Faleomavaega, Eni F.H.		Dem	A.S.	4	4
10th Gallegly, Elton W.		Rep	Cal.	5	4	10th Martinez, Matthew G.		Dem	Cal.	8	2
11th Ros-Lehtinen, Ileana		Rep	Fla.	4	4	11th Payne, Donald M.		Dem	N.J.	4	4
12th Ballenger, Cass		Rep	N.C.	6	2	12th Andrews, Robert E.		Dem	N.J.	4	2
13th Rohrabacher, Dana		Rep	Cal.	4	2	13th Menendez, Robert		Dem	N.J.	2	2
14th Manzullo, Donald A.		Rep	Ill.	2	*1 2	14th Brown, Sherrod		Dem	Ohio	2	2
15th Royce, Edward R.		Rep	Cal.	2	2	15th McKinney, Cynthia A.		Dem	Ga.	2	2
16th King, Peter T.		Rep	N.Y.	2	1	16th Hastings, Alcee L.		Dem	Fla.	2	2
17th Kim, Jay C.		Rep	Cal.	2	1	17th Wynn, Albert R.		Dem	Md.	2	2
18th Brownback, Sam D.		Rep	Kans.	1	1	18th McNulty, Michael R.		Dem	N.Y.	4	1
19th Funderburk, David		Rep	N.C.	1	1	19th Moran, James P. Jr.		Dem	Va.	3	1
20th Chabot, Steven J.		Rep	Ohio	1	1						
21st Sanford, Marshall C. (Mark) Jr.		Rep	S.C.	1	1	**Third Party:**					
22nd Salmon, Matthew J.		Rep	Ariz.	1	1	1st Frazer, Victor O.		Ind.	V.I.	1	1
23rd Houghton, Amory Jr.		Rep	N.Y.	5	*2 1						

*1: Member's first period of service on the committee.

*2: Member's second period of service on the committee.

*3: Member's third period of service on the committee.

Note: Territorial Delegates Eni F. H. Faleomavaega (Dem-Am.S.) and Victor O. Frazer (Ind.-V.I.) were allowed to accrue committee seniority but were not included in the party ratio.

Vacancies Filled:
> **Majority:**
>> 23rd seat filled by Houghton on Jan. 27, 1995

Additions:
> **Majority:**

Campbell, Thomas J.	Rep	Cal.	Dec. 27, 1995	
Fox, Jon D.	Rep	Penn.	June 25, 1996	

> **Minority:**

Danner, Patsy A. (Pat)	Dem	Mo.	Feb. 28, 1996	

Changes:
> **Majority:**

Brownback, Sam D.	Rep	Kans.	Nov. 7, 1996 Resigned the House; elected to U.S. Senate

> **Minority:**

McNulty, Michael R.	Dem	N.Y.	Jan. 24, 1996 Resigned committee; returned to Ways and Means
Rose, Charles G. III	Dem	N.C.	Feb. 28, 1996 Replaced McNulty
Engel, Eliot L.	Dem	N.Y.	Apr. 22, 1996 Resigned committee; moved to Commerce
Hilliard, Earl F.	Dem	Ala.	June 5, 1996 Replaced Engel

Departures from the House:	**Majority**			**Minority**		
Elected to U.S. Senate	Brownback, Sam D.	Rep	Kans.	Torricelli, Robert G.	Dem	N.J.
Defeated for Re-election	Funderburk, David	Rep	N.C.	Frazer, Victor O.	Ind.	V.I.
Retired	Roth, Tobias A.	Rep	Wisc.	Johnston, Harry A. II	Dem	Fla.
	Meyers, Jan	Rep	Kans.	Rose, Charles G. III	Dem	N.C.

Departures from Committee:					
Returned to Appropriations	None			Moran, James P. Jr.	Dem	Va.
Moved to Commerce	None			Wynn, Albert R.	Dem	Md.

INTERNATIONAL RELATIONS / 105th Congress

Service Dates of Committee Chair: Jan. 7, 1997-Jan. 3, 1999

Service Dates of Majority Members: Jan. 7, 1997-Jan. 3, 1999

Service Dates of Minority Members: Jan. 7, 1997-Jan. 3, 1999

Roster Filled: Majority with 26 members, Jan. 21, 1997; Minority with 21 members, Feb. 5, 1997

	Majority						Minority			
				Terms in:						**Terms in:**	
Rank Name	Party	State	House	Comm.		Rank Name	Party	State	House	Comm.
Chr Gilman, Benjamin A.	Rep	N.Y.	13	13		RM Hamilton, Lee H.	Dem	Ind.	17	17
2nd Goodling, William F.	Rep	Penn.	12	*3 8		2nd Gejdenson, Samuel	Dem	Conn.	9	9
3rd Leach, James A.S.	Rep	Iowa	11	9		3rd Lantos, Thomas P.	Dem	Cal.	9	9
4th Hyde, Henry J.	Rep	Ill.	12	9		4th Berman, Howard L.	Dem	Cal.	8	8
5th Bereuter, Douglas K.	Rep	Neb.	10	8		5th Ackerman, Gary L.	Dem	N.Y.	8	8
6th Smith, Christopher H.	Rep	N.J.	9	7		6th Faleomavaega, Eni F.H.	Dem	A.S.	5	5
7th Burton, Danny L.	Rep	Ind.	8	7		7th Martinez, Matthew G.	Dem	Cal.	9	3
8th Gallegly, Elton W.	Rep	Cal.	6	5		8th Payne, Donald M.	Dem	N.J.	5	5
9th Ros-Lehtinen, Ileana	Rep	Fla.	5	5		9th Andrews, Robert E.	Dem	N.J.	5	3
10th Ballenger, Cass	Rep	N.C.	7	3		10th Menendez, Robert	Dem	N.J.	3	3
11th Rohrabacher, Dana	Rep	Cal.	5	3		11th Brown, Sherrod	Dem	Ohio	3	3
12th Manzullo, Donald A.	Rep	Ill.	3	*1 3		12th McKinney, Cynthia A.	Dem	Ga.	3	3
13th Royce, Edward R.	Rep	Cal.	3	3		13th Hastings, Alcee L.	Dem	Fla.	3	3
14th King, Peter T.	Rep	N.Y.	3	2		14th Danner, Patsy A. (Pat)	Dem	Mo.	3	2
15th Kim, Jay C.	Rep	Cal.	3	2		15th Hilliard, Earl F.	Dem	Ala.	3	2
16th Chabot, Steven J.	Rep	Ohio	2	2		16th Capps, Walter H.	Dem	Cal.	1	1
17th Sanford, Marshall C. (Mark) Jr.	Rep	S.C.	2	2		17th Sherman, Brad	Dem	Cal.	1	1
18th Salmon, Matthew J.	Rep	Ariz.	2	2		18th Wexler, Robert	Dem	Fla.	1	1
19th Houghton, Amory J.	Rep	N.Y.	6	*2 2		19th Kucinich, Dennis	Dem	Ohio	1	1
20th Campbell, Thomas J.	Rep	Cal.	4	2		20th Rothman, Steven R.	Dem	N.J.	1	1
21st Fox, Jon D.	Rep	Penn.	2	2		21st Clement, Robert N.	Dem	Tenn.	6	1
22nd McHugh, John M.	Rep	N.Y.	3	1						
23rd Graham, Lindsey O.	Rep	S.C.	2	1		*1: Member's first period of service on the committee.				
24th Blunt, Roy	Rep	Mo.	1	*1 1		*2: Member's second period of service on the committee.				
25th Moran, Jerry	Rep	Kans.	1	1		*3: Member's third period of service on the committee.				
26th Brady, Kevin P.	Rep	Tex.	1	1						

Note: Territorial Delegate Eni F.H. Faleomavaega (Dem-Am.S.) was allowed to accrue committee seniority but was not included in the party ratio.

Vacancies Filled:
   Majority:
      26th seat filled by Brady on Jan. 21, 1997
   Minority:
      21st seat filled by Clement on Feb. 5, 1997

Additions:
   Minority:

Davis, Jim	Dem	Fla.	Apr. 17, 1997

Changes:
   Majority:

Moran, Jerry	Rep	Kans.	July 31, 1997 Resigned committee; moved to Transportation and Infrastructure
Burr, Richard M.	Rep	N.C.	May 13, 1998 Replaced Moran

   Minority:

Kucinich, Dennis	Dem	Ohio	Mar. 6, 1997 Resigned committee; moved to Education and the Workforce
Luther, William P.	DFL	Minn.	Mar. 21, 1997 Replaced Kucinich
Capps, Walter H.	Dem	Cal.	Oct. 28, 1997 Died in office
Capps, Lois	Dem	Cal.	Mar. 27, 1998 Replaced Walter H. Capps

Departures from the House:

	Majority			**Minority**		
Defeated for Re-nomination	Kim, Jay C.	Rep	Cal.	None		
Defeated for Re-election	Fox, Jon. D.	Rep	Penn.	None		
Retired	None			Hamilton, Lee H.	Dem	Ind.

Departures from Committee:

	Majority			**Minority**		
Moved to Armed Services	None			Andrews, Robert E.	Dem	N.J.
Moved to Budget	None			Clement, Robert N.	Dem	Tenn.
Moved to Commerce	Blunt, Roy	Rep	Mo.	Luther, William P.	DFL	Minn.
				Capps, Lois	Dem	Cal.
No new assignment	Graham, Lindsey O.	Rep	S.C.			

INTERNATIONAL RELATIONS / 106th Congress

Service Dates of Committee Chair: Jan. 6, 1999-Jan. 3, 2001

Service Dates of Majority Members: Jan. 6, 1999-Jan. 3, 2001

Service Dates of Minority Members: Jan. 6, 1999-Jan. 3, 2001

Roster Filled: Majority with 26 members, Jan. 6, 1999; Minority with 23 members, Jan. 19, 1999

Majority

Rank Name	Party	State	House	Comm.
Chr Gilman, Benjamin A.	Rep	N.Y.	14	14
2nd Goodling, William F.	Rep	Penn.	13	*3 9
3rd Leach, James A.S.	Rep	Iowa	12	10
4th Hyde, Henry J.	Rep	Ill.	13	10
5th Bereuter, Douglas K.	Rep	Neb.	11	9
6th Smith, Christopher H.	Rep	N.J.	10	8
7th Burton, Danny L.	Rep	Ind.	9	8
8th Gallegly, Elton W.	Rep	Cal.	7	6
9th Ros-Lehtinen, Ileana	Rep	Fla.	6	6
10th Ballenger, Cass	Rep	N.C.	8	4
11th Rohrabacher, Dana	Rep	Cal.	6	4
12th Manzullo, Donald A.	Rep	Ill.	4	*1 4
13th Royce, Edward R.	Rep	Cal.	4	4
14th King, Peter T.	Rep	N.Y.	4	3
15th Chabot, Steven J.	Rep	Ohio	3	3
16th Sanford, Marshall C. (Mark) Jr.	Rep	S.C.	3	3
17th Salmon, Matthew J.	Rep	Ariz.	3	3
18th Houghton, Amory Jr.	Rep	N.Y.	7	*2 3
19th Campbell, Thomas J.	Rep	Cal.	5	3
20th McHugh, John M.	Rep	N.Y.	4	2
21st Brady, Kevin P.	Rep	Tex.	2	2
22nd Burr, Richard M.	Rep	N.C.	3	2
23rd Gillmor, Paul E.	Rep	Ohio	6	1
24th Radanovich, George P.	Rep	Cal.	3	1
25th Cooksey, John	Rep	La.	2	1
26th Tancredo, Thomas G.	Rep	Colo.	1	1

Minority

Rank Name	Party	State	House	Comm.
RM Gejdenson, Samuel	Dem	Conn.	10	10
2nd Lantos, Thomas P.	Dem	Cal.	10	10
3rd Berman, Howard L.	Dem	Cal.	9	9
4th Ackerman, Gary L.	Dem	N.Y.	9	9
5th Faleomavaega, Eni F.H.	Dem	A.S.	6	6
6th Martinez, Matthew G.	Dem	Cal.	10	4
7th Payne, Donald M.	Dem	N.J.	6	6
8th Menendez, Robert	Dem	N.J.	4	4
9th Brown, Sherrod	Dem	Ohio	4	4
10th McKinney, Cynthia A.	Dem	Ga.	4	4
11th Hastings, Alcee L.	Dem	Fla.	4	4
12th Danner, Patsy A. (Pat)	Dem	Mo.	4	3
13th Hilliard, Earl F.	Dem	Ala.	4	3
14th Sherman, Brad	Dem	Cal.	2	2
15th Wexler, Robert	Dem	Fla.	2	2
16th Rothman, Steven R.	Dem	N.J.	2	2
17th Davis, Jim	Dem	Fla.	2	2
18th Pomeroy, Earl R. III	Dem	N.D.	4	1
19th Delahunt, William D.	Dem	Mass.	2	1
20th Meeks, Gregory W.	Dem	N.Y.	2	1
21st Lee, Barbara	Dem	Cal.	2	*1 1
22nd Crowley, Joseph	Dem	N.Y.	1	*1 1
23rd Hoeffel, Joseph M.	Dem	Penn.	1	1

*1: Member's first period of service on the committee.

*2: Member's second period of service on the committee.

*3: Member's third period of service on the committee.

Note: Territorial Delegate Eni F. H. Faleomavaega (Dem-Am.S.) was allowed to accrue committee seniority but was not included in the party ratio.

Vacancies Filled:

  Minority:

    18th through 21st seats filled by Pomeroy, Delahunt, Meeks, Lee, all to rank above Crowley on Jan. 19, 1999

Changes:

  Minority:

Martinez, Matthew G.	Dem	Cal.	July 27, 2000 Lost re-nomination; service on committee as a Democrat was vacated; moved to Transportation and Infrastructure as a Republican

Departures from the House:	Majority				Minority		
Lost Election to U.S. Senate	Campbell, Thomas J.	Rep	Cal.		None		
Defeated for Re-election	None				Gejdenson, Samuel	Dem	Conn.
Defeated for Re-nomination	None				Martinez, Matthew G.	Dem	Cal
Retired	Goodling, William F.	Rep	Penn.		Danner, Patsy A. (Pat)	Dem	Mo.
	Sanford, Marshall C. (Mark) Jr.	Rep	S.C.				
	Salmon, Matthew J.	Rep	Ariz.				

Departures from Committee:							
Became Chair on Small Business	Manzullo, Donald A.	Rep	Ill.				
Moved to Energy and Commerce	Radanovich, George P.	Rep	Cal.		None		
Moved to Financial Services	Gillmor, Paul E.	Rep	Ohio		None		
Moved to Ways and Means	Brady, Kevin P.	Rep	Tex.		Pomeroy, Earl R. III	Dem	N.D.

INTERNATIONAL RELATIONS / 107th Congress

Service Dates of Committee Chair: Jan. 6, 2001-Jan. 3, 2003

Service Dates of Majority Members: Jan. 6, 2001-Jan. 3, 2003

Service Dates of Minority Members: Jan. 31, 2001-Jan. 3, 2003

Roster Filled: Majority with 26 members, Jan. 6, 2001; Minority with 23 members, Feb. 8, 2001

Majority					Minority				
			Terms in:					**Terms in:**	
Rank Name	**Party**	**State**	**House**	**Comm.**	**Rank Name**	**Party**	**State**	**House**	**Comm.**
Chr Hyde, Henry J.	Rep	Ill.	14	11	RM Lantos, Thomas P.	Dem	Cal.	11	11
2nd Gilman, Benjamin A.	Rep	N.Y.	15	15	2nd Berman, Howard L.	Dem	Cal.	10	10
3rd Leach, James A.S.	Rep	Iowa	13	11	3rd Ackerman, Gary L.	Dem	N.Y.	10	10
4th Bereuter, Douglas K.	Rep	Neb.	12	10	4th Faleomavaega, Eni F.H.	Dem	A.S.	7	7
5th Smith, Christopher H.	Rep	N.J.	11	9	5th Payne, Donald M.	Dem	N.J.	7	7
6th Burton, Danny L.	Rep	Ind.	10	9	6th Menendez, Robert	Dem	N.J.	5	5
7th Gallegly, Elton W.	Rep	Cal.	8	7	7th Brown, Sherrod	Dem	Ohio	5	5
8th Ros-Lehtinen, Ileana	Rep	Fla.	7	7	8th McKinney, Cynthia A.	Dem	Ga.	5	5
9th Ballenger, Cass	Rep	N.C.	9	5	9th Hastings, Alcee L.	Dem	Fla.	5	5
10th Rohrabacher, Dana	Rep	Cal.	7	5	10th Hilliard, Earl F.	Dem	Ala.	5	4
11th Royce, Edward R.	Rep	Cal.	5	5	11th Sherman, Brad	Dem	Cal.	3	3
12th King, Peter T.	Rep	N.Y.	5	4	12th Wexler, Robert	Dem	Fla.	3	3
13th Chabot, Steven J.	Rep	Ohio	4	4	13th Rothman, Steven R.	Dem	N.J.	3	3
14th Houghton, Amory Jr.	Rep	N.Y.	8	*2 4	14th Davis, Jim	Dem	Fla.	3	3
15th McHugh, John M.	Rep	N.Y.	5	3	15th Delahunt, William D.	Dem	Mass.	3	2
16th Burr, Richard M.	Rep	N.C.	4	3	16th Meeks, Gregory W.	Dem	N.Y.	3	2
17th Cooksey, John	Rep	La.	3	2	17th Lee, Barbara	Dem	Cal.	3	*1 2
18th Tancredo, Thomas G.	Rep	Colo.	2	2	18th Crowley, Joseph	Dem	N.Y.	2	*1 2
19th Paul, Ronald E.	Rep	Tex.	7	1	19th Hoeffel, Joseph M.	Dem	Penn.	2	2
20th Smith, Nick H.	Rep	Mich.	5	1	20th Blumenauer, Earl	Dem	Ore.	4	1
21st Pitts, Joseph R.	Rep	Penn.	3	1	21st Berkley, Shelley	Dem	Nev.	2	1
22nd Issa, Darrell E.	Rep	Cal.	1	*1 1	22nd Napolitano, Grace F.	Dem	Cal.	2	1
23rd Cantor, Eric I.	Rep	Va.	1	1	23rd Schiff, Adam B.	Dem	Cal.	1	1
24th Flake, Jeff	Rep	Ariz.	1	1					
25th Kerns, Brian D.	Rep	Ind.	1	1	*1; Member's first period of service on the committee.				
26th Davis, Jo Ann	Rep	Va.	1	1	*2: Member's second period of service on the committee.				

Note: Territorial Delegate Eni F. H. Faleomavaega (Dem-Am.S.) was allowed to accrue committee seniority but was not included in the party ratio.

Vacancies Filled:

Minority:

20th to 23rd seats filled by Blumenauer, Berkley, Napolitano, and Schiff on Feb. 8, 2001

Changes:

Majority:

Burr, Richard M.	Rep	N.C.	Feb. 19, 2002 Resigned committee; no new assignment
Green, Mark	Rep	Wisc.	Feb. 26, 2002 Replaced Burr

Minority:

Rothman, Steven R.	Dem	N.J.	Feb. 7, 2001 Resigned committee; moved to Appropriations
Engel, Eliot L.	Dem	N.Y.	Feb. 27, 2001 Replaced Rothman, ranked after Davis
Hastings, Alcee L.	Dem	Fla.	June 19, 2001 Resigned committee; moved to Rules
Watson, Diane E.	Dem	Cal.	June 19, 2001 Replaced Hastings

Departures from the House:	**Majority**			**Minority**		
Lost Nomination to U.S. Senate	Cooksey, John	Rep	La.	None		
Defeated for Re-nomination	Kerns, Brian D.	Rep	Ind.	McKinney, Cynthia A.	Dem	Ga.
				Hilliard, Earl F.	Dem	Ala.
Retired	Gilman, Benjamin A.	Rep	N.Y.	None		

Departures from Committee:						
Moved to Energy and Commerce	Issa, Darrell E.	Rep	Cal.	Davis, Jim	Dem	Fla.
Moved to Ways and Means	Cantor, Eric I.	Rep	Va.	None		

INTERNATIONAL RELATIONS / 108th Congress

Service Dates of Committee Chair: Jan. 8, 2003-Jan. 3, 2005

Service Dates of Majority Members: Jan. 28, 2003-Jan. 3, 2005

Service Dates of Ranking Member: Jan. 8, 2003-Jan. 3, 2005

Service Dates of Minority Members: Jan. 28, 2003-Jan. 3, 2005

Roster Filled: Majority with 26 members, Jan. 28, 2003; Minority with 23 members, Feb. 5, 2003

Majority

Rank Name	Party	State	Terms in: House	Terms in: Comm.
Chr Hyde, Henry J.	Rep	Ill.	15	12
2nd Leach, James A.S.	Rep	Iowa	14	12
3rd Bereuter, Douglas K.	Rep	Neb.	13	11
4th Smith, Christopher H.	Rep	N.J.	12	10
5th Burton, Danny L.	Rep	Ind.	11	10
6th Gallegly, Elton W.	Rep	Cal.	9	8
7th Ros-Lehtinen, Ileana	Rep	Fla.	8	8
8th Ballenger, Cass	Rep	N.C.	10	6
9th Rohrabacher, Dana	Rep	Cal.	8	6
10th Royce, Edward R.	Rep	Cal.	6	6
11th King, Peter T.	Rep	N.Y.	6	5
12th Chabot, Steven J.	Rep	Ohio	5	5
13th Houghton, Amory Jr.	Rep	N.Y.	9	*2 5
14th McHugh, John M.	Rep	N.Y.	6	4
15th Tancredo, Thomas G.	Rep	Colo.	3	3
16th Paul, Ronald E.	Rep	Tex.	8	2
17th Smith, Nick H.	Rep	Mich.	6	2
18th Pitts, Joseph R.	Rep	Penn.	4	2
19th Flake, Jeff	Rep	Ariz.	2	2
20th Davis, Jo Ann	Rep	Va.	2	2
21st Green, Mark	Rep	Wisc.	3	2
22nd Weller, Gerald C.	Rep	Ill.	5	1
23rd Pence, Mike	Rep	Ind.	2	1
24th McCotter, Thaddeus	Rep	Mich.	1	1
25th Janklow, William J.	Rep	S.D.	1	1
26th Harris, Katherine	Rep	Fla.	1	1

Minority

Rank Name	Party	State	Terms in: House	Terms in: Comm.
RM Lantos, Thomas P.	Dem	Cal.	12	12
2nd Berman, Howard L.	Dem	Cal.	11	11
3rd Ackerman, Gary L.	Dem	N.Y.	11	11
4th Faleomavaega, Eni F.H.	Dem	A.S.	8	8
5th Payne, Donald M.	Dem	N.J.	8	8
6th Menendez, Robert	Dem	N.J.	6	6
7th Brown, Sherrod	Dem	Ohio	6	6
8th Sherman, Brad	Dem	Cal.	4	4
9th Wexler, Robert	Dem	Fla.	4	4
10th Engel, Eliot L.	Dem	N.Y.	8	*2 2
11th Delahunt, William D.	Dem	Mass.	4	3
12th Meeks, Gregory W.	Dem	N.Y.	4	3
13th Lee, Barbara	Dem	Cal.	4	*1 3
14th Crowley, Joseph	Dem	N.Y.	3	*1 3
15th Hoeffel, Joseph M.	Dem	Penn.	3	3
16th Blumenauer, Earl	Dem	Ore.	5	2
17th Berkley, Shelley	Dem	Nev.	3	2
18th Napolitano, Grace F.	Dem	Cal.	3	2
19th Schiff, Adam B.	Dem	Cal.	2	2
20th Watson, Diane E.	Dem	Cal.	2	2
21st Smith, Adam	Dem	Wash.	4	1
22nd McCollum, Betty	DFL	Minn.	2	1
23rd Bell, Chris	Dem	Tex.	1	1

*1: Member's first period of service on the committee.

*2: Member's second period of service on the committee.

Note: Territorial Delegate Eni F.H. Faleomavaega (Dem-Am.S.) was allowed to accrue committee seniority but was not included in the party ratio.

Vacancies Filled:
Minority:
21st through 23rd seats filled by Smith, McCollum, and Bell on Feb. 5, 2003

Changes:
Majority:

Janklow, William J.	Rep	S.D.	Jan. 20, 2004 Resigned the House due to ethics issues
Blunt, Roy	Rep	Mo.	Jan. 28, 2004 Replaced Janklow, ranked after McHugh
Bereuter, Douglas K.	Rep	Neb.	Aug. 31, 2004 Resigned the House and retired; vacancy remained

Minority:

Bell, Chris	Dem	Tex.	Mar. 25, 2004 Resigned committee; no new assignment
Chandler, A.B. (Ben)	Dem	Ky.	Mar. 31, 2004 Replaced Bell

Departures from the House:

	Majority		
Lost Election to U.S. Senate	None		
Defeated for Re-election	None		
Retired	Ballenger, Cass	Rep	N.C.
	Houghton, Amory Jr.	Rep	N.Y.
	Smith, Nick H.	Rep	Mich.

	Minority		
	Hoeffel, Joseph M.	Dem	Penn.
	Bell, Chris	Dem	Tex.
	None		

Departures from Committee:

No new assignment	Pitts, Joseph R.	Rep	Penn.
	Blunt, Roy	Rep	Mo.
None			

INTERNATIONAL RELATIONS / 109th Congress

Service Dates of Committee Chair: Jan. 6, 2005-Jan. 3, 2007

Service Dates of Majority Members: Jan. 26, 2005-Jan. 3, 2007

Service Dates of Minority Members: Jan. 26, 2005-Jan. 3, 2007

Roster Filled: Majority with 27 members, Jan. 26, 2005; Minority with 23 members, Jan. 26, 2005

Majority

Rank Name	Party	State	Terms in: House	Terms in: Comm.
Chr Hyde, Henry J.	Rep	Ill.	16	13
2nd Leach, James A.S.	Rep	Iowa	15	13
3rd Smith, Christopher H.	Rep	N.J.	13	11
4th Burton, Danny L.	Rep	Ind.	12	11
5th Gallegly, Elton W.	Rep	Cal.	10	9
6th Ros-Lehtinen, Ileana	Rep	Fla.	9	9
7th Rohrabacher, Dana	Rep	Cal.	9	7
8th Royce, Edward R.	Rep	Cal.	7	7
9th King, Peter T.	Rep	N.Y.	7	6
10th Chabot, Steven J.	Rep	Ohio	6	6
11th McHugh, John M.	Rep	N.Y.	7	5
12th Tancredo, Thomas G.	Rep	Colo.	4	4
13th Paul, Ronald E.	Rep	Tex.	9	3
14th Issa, Darrell E.	Rep	Cal.	3	*2 1
15th Flake, Jeff	Rep	Ariz.	3	3
16th Davis, Jo Ann	Rep	Va.	3	3
17th Green, Mark	Rep	Wisc.	4	3
18th Weller, Gerald C.	Rep	Ill.	6	2
19th Pence, Mike	Rep	Ind.	3	2
20th McCotter, Thaddeus	Rep	Mich.	2	2
21st Harris, Katherine	Rep	Fla.	2	2
22nd Wilson, Addison G. (Joe)	Rep	S.C.	3	1
23rd Boozman, John	Rep	Ark.	3	1
24th Mack, Connie IV	Rep	Fla.	1	1
25th Fortenberry, Jeff	Rep	Neb.	1	1
26th McCaul, Michael T.	Rep	Tex.	1	1
27th Poe, Ted	Rep	Tex.	1	1

Minority

Rank Name	Party	State	Terms in: House	Terms in: Comm.
RM Lantos, Thomas P.	Dem	Cal.	13	13
2nd Berman, Howard L.	Dem	Cal.	12	12
3rd Ackerman, Gary L.	Dem	N.Y.	12	12
4th Faleomavaega, Eni F.H.	Dem	A.S.	9	9
5th Payne, Donald M.	Dem	N.J.	9	9
6th Menendez, Robert	Dem	N.J.	7	7
7th Brown, Sherrod	Dem	Ohio	7	7
8th Sherman, Brad	Dem	Cal.	5	5
9th Wexler, Robert	Dem	Fla.	5	5
10th Engel, Eliot L.	Dem	N.Y.	9	*2 3
11th Delahunt, William D.	Dem	Mass.	5	4
12th Meeks, Gregory W.	Dem	N.Y.	5	4
13th Lee, Barbara	Dem	Cal.	5	*1 4
14th Crowley, Joseph	Dem	N.Y.	4	*1 4
15th Blumenauer, Earl	Dem	Ore.	6	3
16th Berkley, Shelley	Dem	Nev.	4	3
17th Napolitano, Grace F.	Dem	Cal.	4	3
18th Schiff, Adam B.	Dem	Cal.	3	3
19th Watson, Diane E.	Dem	Cal.	3	3
20th Smith, Adam	Dem	Wash.	5	2
21st McCollum, Betty	DFL	Minn.	3	2
22nd Chandler, A.B. (Ben)	Dem	Ky.	2	2
23rd Cardoza, Dennis A.	Dem	Cal.	2	1

*1: Member's first period of service on the committee.

*2: Member's second period of service on the committee.

Note: Territorial Delegate Eni F.H. Faleomavaega (Dem-Am.S.) was allowed to accrue committee seniority but was not included in the party ratio.

Changes:

Majority:

McHugh, John M.	Rep	N.Y.	Jan. 26, 2005 Resigned committee; moved to Permanent Select Intelligence
Barrett, J. Gresham	Rep	S.C.	Feb. 2, 2005 Replaced McHugh, ranked after Boozman

Minority:

Menendez, Robert	Dem	N.J.	Jan. 16, 2006 Resigned the House; appointed to U.S. Senate
Carnahan, Russ	Dem	Mo.	Feb. 15, 2006 Replaced Menendez

Departures from the House:

	Majority			Minority		
Elected to U.S. Senate	None			Brown, Sherrod	Dem	Ohio
Lost Election to U.S. Senate	Harris, Katherine	Rep	Fla.	None		
Lost Election for Governor	Green, Mark	Rep	Wisc.	None		
Defeated for Re-election	Leach, James A.S.	Rep	Iowa	None		
Retired	Hyde, Henry J.	Rep	Ill.	None		

Departures from Committee:

	Majority			Minority		
Moved to Appropriations	None			Lee, Barbara	Dem	Cal.
				Schiff, Adam B.	Dem	Cal.
				McCollum, Betty	Dem	Minn.
				Chandler, A.B. (Ben)	Dem	Ky.
Moved to Budget	None			Blumenauer, Earl	Dem	Ore.
Returned to Financial Services	King, Peter T.	Rep	N.Y.	None		
Returned to Oversight and Government Reform	None			McCollum, Betty	Dem	Minn.
Moved to Permanent Select Intelligence	Issa, Darrell E.	Rep	Cal.	None		
Moved to Rules	None			Cardoza, Dennis A.	Dem	Cal.
Moved to Science and Technology	None			Chandler, A.B. (Ben)	Dem	Ky.

Moved to Transportation and Infrastructure	None	
Moved to Ways and Means	None	

Napolitano, Grace F.	Dem	Cal.	
Crowley, Joseph	Dem	N.Y.	
Blumenauer, Earl	Dem	Ore.	
Berkley, Shelley	Dem	Nev.	

No new assignment	Weller, Gerald C.	Rep	Ill. None

FOREIGN AFFAIRS / 110th Congress

Service Dates of Committee Chair: Ch1 Jan. 4, 2007-Feb. 11, 2008, Lantos (Dem-Cal.)

Ch2: Mar. 11, 2008-Jan. 3, 2009, Berman (Dem-Cal.)

Service Dates of Majority Members: Jan. 12, 2007-Jan. 3, 2009

Service Dates of Minority Members: Jan. 10, 2007-Jan. 3, 2009

Roster Filled: Majority with 27 members, Apr. 19, 2007; Minority with 23 members, Jan. 18, 2007

	Majority						**Minority**				
				Terms in:						**Terms in:**	
Rank Name	**Party**	**State**	**House**	**Comm.**		**Rank Name**	**Party**	**State**	**House**	**Comm.**	
Ch1 Lantos, Thomas P.	Dem	Cal.	14	14		RM Ros-Lehtinen, Ileana	Rep	Fla.	10	10	
2nd Ch2 Berman, Howard L.	Dem	Cal.	13	13		2nd Smith, Christopher H.	Rep	N.J.	14	12	
3rd Ackerman, Gary L.	Dem	N.Y.	13	13		3rd Burton, Danny L.	Rep	Ind.	13	12	
4th Faleomavaega, Eni F.H.	Dem	A.S.	10	10		4th Gallegly, Elton W.	Rep	Cal.	11	10	
5th Payne, Donald M.	Dem	N.J.	10	10		5th Rohrabacher, Dana	Rep	Cal.	10	8	
6th Sherman, Brad	Dem	Cal.	6	6		6th Manzullo, Donald A.	Rep	Ill.	8	*2 1	
7th Wexler, Robert	Dem	Fla.	6	6		7th Royce, Edward R.	Rep	Cal.	8	8	
8th Engel, Eliot L.	Dem	N.Y.	10	*2 4		8th Chabot, Steven J.	Rep	Ohio	7	7	
9th Delahunt, William D.	Dem	Mass.	6	5		9th Tancredo, Thomas G.	Rep	Colo.	5	5	
10th Meeks, Gregory W.	Dem	N.Y.	6	5		10th Paul, Ronald E.	Rep	Tex.	10	4	
11th Watson, Diane E.	Dem	Cal.	4	4		11th Flake, Jeff	Rep	Ariz.	4	4	
12th Smith, Adam	Dem	Wash.	6	3		12th Davis, Jo Ann	Rep	Va.	4	4	
13th Carnahan, Russ	Dem	Mo.	2	2		13th Pence, Mike	Rep	Ind.	4	3	
14th Tanner, John S.	Dem	Tenn.	10	1		14th McCotter, Thaddeus	Rep	Mich.	3	3	
15th Green, R. Eugene (Gene)	Dem	Tex.	8	1		15th Wilson, Addison G. (Joe)	Rep	S.C.	4	2	
16th Woolsey, Lynn C.	Dem	Cal.	8	*1 1		16th Boozman, John	Rep	Ark.	4	2	
17th Jackson-Lee, Sheila	Dem	Tex.	7	1		17th Barrett, J. Gresham	Rep	S.C.	3	2	
18th Hinojosa, Rubén	Dem	Tex.	6	1		18th Mack, Connie IV	Rep	Fla.	2	2	
19th Crowley, Joseph	Dem	N.Y.	5	*2 1		19th Fortenberry, Jeff	Rep	Neb.	2	2	
20th Wu, David	Dem	Ore.	5	1		20th McCaul, Michael T.	Rep	Tex.	2	2	
21st Miller, Brad	Dem	N.C.	3	1		21st Poe, Ted	Rep	Tex.	2	2	
22nd Sánchez, Linda T.	Dem	Cal.	3	1		22nd Inglis, Robert D.	Rep	S.C.	5	1	
23rd Scott, David	Dem	Ga.	3	1		23rd Fortuño, Luis G.	Rep	P.R.	2	1	
24th Costa, Jim	Dem	Cal.	2	1							
25th Sires, Albio	Dem	N.J.	1	1		*1: Member's first period of service on the committee.					
26th Giffords, Gabrielle	Dem	Ariz.	1	1		*2: Member's second period of service on the committee.					
27th Klein, Ron	Dem	Fla.	1	1							

Note: Territorial Delegate Eni F.H. Faleomavaega (Dem-Am.S.) and Luis G. Fortuño (Rep-P.R.) were allowed to accrue committee seniority but were not included in the party ratio.

Vacancies Filled:
   Majority:
      15th seat filled by Green and the 19th seat filled by Crowley on Apr. 19, 2007

Changes:
   Majority:

Lantos, Thomas P.	Dem	Cal.	Feb. 11, 2008 Died in office
Lee, Barbara	Dem	Cal.	Feb. 26, 2008 Replaced Lantos
Berman, Howard L.	Dem	Cal.	Mar. 11,2008 Elected Chair of Foreign Affairs

   Minority:

Manzullo, Donald A.	Rep	Ill.	Jan. 18, 2007 Reranked to follow immediately after Rohrabacher
McCotter, Thaddeus	Rep	Mich.	May 15, 2007 Resigned committee; moved to Financial Services
Bilirakis, Gus	Rep	Fla.	May 10, 2007 Replaced McCotter
Davis, Jo Ann	Rep	Va.	Oct. 6, 2007 Died in office
Blunt, Roy	Rep	Mo.	Oct. 10, 2007 Served temporarily to replace Davis; ranked immediately following Chabot
Blunt, Roy	Rep	Mo.	Dec. 18,2007 Resigned committee to open seat for Wittman
Wittman, Robert J.	Rep	Va.	Dec. 18, 2007 Replaced Blunt
Wittman, Robert J.	Rep	Va.	Mar. 11, 2008 Resigned committee; moved to Armed Services; vacancy remained

Departures from the House:	Majority				Minority			
Elected Governor	None				Fortuño, Luis G.		Rep	P.R.
Defeated for Re-election	None				Chabot, Steven J.		Rep	Ohio
Lost Presidential Nomination	None				Tancredo, Thomas G.		Rep	Colo.

Departures from Committee:						
Moved to Ways and Means	Sanchez, Linda T.	Dem	Cal.		None	
No new assignment	Woolsey, Lynn C.	Dem	Cal.		None	
	Hinojosa, Rubén	Dem	Tex.			
	Wu, David	Dem	Ore.			

FOREIGN AFFAIRS / 111th Congress

Service Dates of Committee Chair: Jan. 6, 2009-Jan. 3, 2011

Service Dates of Majority Members: Jan. 21, 2009-Jan. 3, 2011

Service Dates of Minority Members: Jan. 9, 2009-Jan. 3, 2011

Roster Filled: Majority with 28 members, Jan. 21, 2009; Minority with 19 members, Jan. 9, 2009

	Majority						Minority				
				Terms in:						Terms in:	
Rank Name		Party	State	House	Comm.	Rank Name		Party	State	House	Comm.
Chr Berman, Howard L.		Dem	Cal.	14	14	RM Ros-Lehtinen, Ileana		Rep	Fla.	11	11
2nd Ackerman, Gary L.		Dem	N.Y.	14	14	2nd Smith, Christopher H.		Rep	N.J.	15	13
3rd Faleomavaega, Eni F.H.		Dem	A.S.	11	11	3rd Burton, Danny L.		Rep	Ind.	14	13
4th Payne, Donald M.		Dem	N.J.	11	11	4th Gallegly, Elton W.		Rep	Cal.	12	11
5th Sherman, Brad		Dem	Cal.	7	7	5th Rohrabacher, Dana		Rep	Cal.	11	9
6th Wexler, Robert		Dem	Fla.	7	7	6th Manzullo, Donald A.		Rep	Ill.	9	*2 2
7th Engel, Eliot L.		Dem	N.Y.	11	*2 5	7th Royce, Edward R.		Rep	Cal.	9	9
8th Delahunt, William D.		Dem	Mass.	7	6	8th Paul, Ronald E.		Rep	Tex.	11	5
9th Meeks, Gregory W.		Dem	N.Y.	7	6	9th Flake, Jeff		Rep	Ariz.	5	5
10th Watson, Diane E.		Dem	Cal.	5	5	10th Pence, Mike		Rep	Ind.	5	4
11th Smith, Adam		Dem	Wash.	7	4	11th Wilson, Addison G. (Joe)		Rep	S.C.	5	3
12th Carnahan, Russ		Dem	Mo.	3	3	12th Boozman, John		Rep	Ark.	5	3
13th Sires, Albio		Dem	N.J.	2	2	13th Barrett, J. Gresham		Rep	S.C.	4	3
14th Connolly, Gerald E.		Dem	Va.	1	1	14th Mack, Connie IV		Rep	Fla.	3	3
15th McMahon, Michael E.		Dem	N.Y.	1	1	15th Fortenberry, Jeff		Rep	Neb.	3	3
16th Tanner, John S.		Dem	Tenn.	11	2	16th McCaul, Michael T.		Rep	Tex.	3	3
17th Green, R. Eugene (Gene)		Dem	Tex.	9	2	17th Poe, Ted		Rep	Tex.	3	3
18th Jackson-Lee, Sheila		Dem	Tex.	8	2	18th Inglis, Robert D.		Rep	S.C.	6	2
19th Lee, Barbara		Dem	Cal.	7	*2 2	19th Bilirakis, Gus		Rep	Fla.	2	2
20th Berkley, Shelley		Dem	Nev.	6	*2 1						
21st Crowley, Joseph		Dem	N.Y.	6	*2 2						
22nd Ross, Michael A.		Dem	Ark.	5	1						
23rd Miller, Brad		Dem	N.C.	4	2						
24th Scott, David		Dem	Ga.	4	2						
25th Costa, Jim		Dem	Cal.	3	2						
26th Ellison, Keith		DFL	Minn.	2	1						
27th Giffords, Gabrielle		Dem	Ariz.	2	2						
28th Klein, Ron		Dem	Fla.	2	2						

*2: Member's second period of service on the committee.

Note: Territorial Delegate Eni F.H. Faleomavaega (Dem-Am.S.) wasallowed to accrue committee seniority but was not included in the party ratio.

Changes:

Majority

Smith, Adam	Dem	Wash.	Feb. 9, 2009 Leave of absence; moved to Select Intelligence
Woolsey, Lynn C.	Dem	Cal.	Mar. 12, 2009 Replaced Smith, ranked behind Green
Wexler, Robert	Dem	Fla.	Jan. 4, 2010 Resigned the House; named President of Center for Middle East Peace and Economic Cooperation
Deutch, Theodore E.	Dem	Fla.	May. 6, 2010 Repalced Wexler, ranked following McMahon

Homeland Security

House Select Committee on Homeland Security, 107th-108th Congresses (2002-2005)

House Committee on Homeland Security, 109th-111th Congresses (2005-2011)

BACKGROUND

Organizational History: The Committee on Homeland Security was first created as a nine-member select committee by the U.S. House of Representatives in the 107th Congress (2001-2003) on June 19, 2002, in the aftermath of the September 11, 2001, terrorist attacks on the World Trade Center in New York City and on the Pentagon in Arlington, Virginia. Its initial function was to oversee the creation of the new federal Department of Homeland Security. Among its initial members were House Majority Leader Dick Armey (Rep-Tex.), Majority Whip Tom DeLay (Rep-Tex.), and Minority Whip Nancy Pelosi (Dem-Cal.). The Select Committee was re-established with fifty members in the 108th Congress on January 7, 2003, with none of the original leaders named to it. It was designated as a standing committee of the House on January 4, 2005, the first day of the 109th Congress. It was the first standing committee created in the House since the 1974 creation of the Budget Committee and it became the House's twentieth standing committee.

The creation of Homeland Security as an initial select committee and then transforming it into a standing committee paralleled a similar crisis-related committee creation in 1958. In that year, Congress reacted to the successful launching of earth-orbiting rockets by the Soviet Union by creating the thirteen-member Select Committee on Astronautics and Space Exploration and assigning Majority Leader John W. McCormack (Dem-Mass.), Minority Leader Joseph W. Martin Jr. (Rep-Mass.), and Minority Whip Leslie C. Arends (Rep-Ill.) to senior posts on the committee. The select committee was named on March 5, 1958, and reorganized as a standing committee on July 21, 1958, four-plus months later.

In the Senate, the functions that the House Homeland Security Committee was assigned were added to the renamed Committee on Homeland Security and Governmental Affairs. Consequently, there was no standing committee equivalent of the House committee in the Senate.

In addition to its oversight of the Department of Homeland Security, the committee has been given responsibility for border and port security, customs, integration, analysis, and dissemination of homeland security information, domestic preparedness for and collective response to terrorism, and transportation security.

Membership: The members of the Select Committee on Homeland Security were first named on June 14, 2002. It was originally composed of nine members—five majority Republican and four minority Democrats. The select committee mushroomed to fifty members in the 108th Congress (2003-2005) until it became a standing committee in 2005 and its membership stabilized at thirty-four in the past three Congresses, 2005-2011, placing it fifteenth among the twenty presently constituted House standing committees and its seniority mean of 5.53 terms per member would locate it in seventh place among the twenty.

Committee Leaders: As often happens with a select committee named to address a national emergency, the original chair of Select Homeland Security in 2002 was a party leader, Majority Leader Richard K. Armey (Rep-Tex.), and its original ranking member was Minority Whip Nancy Pelosi (Dem-Cal.). This was similar to what happened in 1958 when the House Select Committee Astronautics and Space Exploration Committee convened its initial meetings with Majority Leader John W. McCormack (Dem-Mass.) and Minority Leader Joseph W. Martin Jr. (Rep-Mass.) as its original senior leaders.

The party leaders had departed in the 108th Congress as C. Christopher Cox (Rep-Cal.) became chair and Jim Turner (Dem-Tex.) became ranking member. Cox left the House in 2005 to head the Securities and Exchanges Commission and served in that role during the Wall Street financial crisis of 2007-2009. Cox was succeeded as chair by Peter T. King (Rep-N.Y) and who served as ranking member during the Democratic 110th and 111th Congresses (2007-2011). Turner's retirement in 2005 led to Bennie Thomson (Dem-Miss.) becoming the committee's senior Democrat as ranking member in the 109th Congress and as chair in the 110th and 111th Congresses (2007-2011).

Notable Members: U.S. Senate Democrats Benjamin L. Cardin of Maryland and Robert Menendez of New Jersey served on Homeland Security when it was a Select Committee but as the House's newest standing committee, most of Homeland Security's members have yet to test the waters of higher ambition, with the exceptions of two Republican Governors: James Gibbons elected governor of Nevada in 2006 and Bobby Jindal elected governor of Louisiana in 2008.

RESPONSIBILITIES, JURISDICTIONAL CHANGES, AND SUBCOMMITTEES

HOMELAND SECURITY

Jurisdiction, 111th Congress (2009-2011)

From the Rules of the House of Representatives (as revised to June 16, 2009, H.Doc. 110-162):

[Rule X.1.(i)] Committee on Homeland Security
  (1) Overall homeland security policy
  (2) Organization and administration of the Department of Homeland Security.
  (3) Functions of the Department of Homeland Security relating to the following:

  (A) Border and port security (except immigration policy and non-border enforcement).
  (B) Customs (except customs revenue).
  (C) Integration, analysis, and dissemination of homeland security information.
  (D) Domestic preparedness for and collective response to terrorism.
  (E) Research and development.
  (F) Transportation security.

Special Oversight Function [Rule X.3.(g)]

The Committee on Homeland Security shall review and study on a continuing basis all Government activities relating to homeland security, including the interaction of all departments and agencies with the Department of Homeland Security.

NAMES OF HOMELAND SECURITY SUBCOMMITTEES FROM THE *CONGRESSIONAL DIRECTORY*

Border, Maritime, and Global Counterterrorism, 111
Border, Maritime, and Global Terrorism, 110
Economic Security, Infrastructure Protection, and Cybersecurity, 109
Emergency Communications, Preparedness, and Response, 110, 111
Emergency Preparedness, Science, and Technology, 109
Emerging Threats, Cybersecurity, and Science and Technology, 110, 111
Intelligence, Information Sharing, and Terrorism Risk Assessment, 109, 110, 111
Management, Investigations, and Oversight, 109, 110, 111
Prevention of Nuclear and Biological Attack, 109
Transportation Security and Infrastructure Protection, 110, 111

MEMBERSHIP ROSTERS, 107th-111th Congresses, 2002-2011

HOUSE SELECT COMMITTEE: HOMELAND SECURITY / 107th Congress

Service Dates of Committee Chair: June 19, 2002-Jan. 3, 2003

Service Dates of Majority Members: June 19, 2002-Jan. 3, 2003

Service Dates of Minority Members: June 19, 2002-Jan. 3, 2003

			Majority Terms in:						Minority Terms in:	
Rank Name	Party	State	House	Comm.	Rank Name	Party	State	House	Comm.
Chr Armey, Richard K.	Rep	Tex.	9	1	RM Pelosi, Nancy	Dem	Cal.	8	1
2nd DeLay, Thomas D.	Rep	Tex.	9	1	2nd Frost, J. Martin III	Dem	Tex.	12	1
3rd Watts, Julius C. Jr.	Rep	Okla.	4	1	3rd Menendez, Robert	Dem	N.J.	5	1
4th Pryce, Deborah D.	Rep	Ohio	5	1	4th DeLauro, Rosa L.	Dem	Conn.	6	1
5th Portman, Robert J.	Rep	Ohio	5	1					

Departures from Committee

  None of the originally named nine members of the initial Select Committee on Homeland Securiy continued on the Select Committee
  On Homeland Security appointed in the 108th Congress.

Departures from the House:	Majority			Minority		
Retired	Armey, Richard K.	Rep	Tex.	None		
	Watts, Julius C. Jr.	Rep	Okla.			

Departures from Committee:						
Elected Majority Floor Leader	Delay, Thomas D.	Rep	Tex.	None		
Elected Minority Leader	None			Pelosi, Nancy	Dem	Cal.
Moved to Budget	None			DeLauro, Rosa L.	Dem	Conn.
No new assignment	Pryce, Deborah D.	Rep	Ohio	Menendez, Robert	Dem	N.J.
	Portman, Robert J.	Rep	Ohio	Frost, J. Martin III	Dem	Tex.

HOUSE SELECT COMMITTEE: HOMELAND SECURITY / 108th Congress

Service Dates of Committee Chair: Feb. 12, 2003-Jan. 3, 2005

Service Dates of Majority Members: Feb. 12, 2003-Jan. 3, 2005

Service Dates of Minority Members: Feb. 12, 2003-Jan. 3, 2005

Roster Filled: Majority with 27 members, Mar. 5, 2003; Minority with 23 members, Feb. 12, 2003

Majority						Minority					
				Terms in:						Terms in:	
Rank Name	Party	State	House	Comm.		Rank Name	Party	State	House	Comm.	
Chr Cox, C. Christopher	Rep	Cal.	8	1		RM Turner, Jim	Dem	Tex.	4	1	
2nd Dunn, Jennifer B.	Rep	Wash.	6	1		2nd Thompson, Bennie	Dem	Miss.	6	1	
3rd Young, C.W. Bill	Rep	Fla.	17	1		3rd Sanchez, Loretta	Dem	Cal.	4	1	
4th Young, Donald E.	Rep	Alas.	16	1		4th Markey, Edward J.	Dem	Mass.	15	1	
5th Sensenbrenner, F. James Jr.	Rep	Wisc.	13	1		5th Dicks, Norman D.	Dem	Wash.	14	1	
6th Tauzin, W.J. (Billy)	Rep	La.	13	1		6th Frank, Barney	Dem	Mass.	12	1	
7th Drier, David	Rep	Cal.	12	1		7th Harman, Jane L.	Dem	Cal.	5	1	
8th Hunter, Duncan L.	Rep	Cal.	12	1		8th Cardin, Benjamin L.	Dem	Md.	9	1	
9th Rogers, Harold D.	Rep	Ky.	12	1		9th Slaughter, Louise Macintosh	Dem	N.Y.	9	1	
10th Boehlert, Sherwood L.	Rep	N.Y.	11	1		10th DeFazio, Peter A.	Dem	Ore.	9	1	
11th Smith, Lamar S.	Rep	Tex.	9	1		11th Lowey, Nita M.	Dem	N.Y.	8	1	
12th Weldon, Wayne C. (Curt)	Rep	Penn.	9	1		12th Andrews, Robert E.	Dem	N.J.	8	1	
13th Shays, Christopher H.	Rep	Conn.	9	1		13th Norton, Eleanor Holmes	Dem	D.C.	7	1	
14th Goss, Porter J.	Rep	Fla.	8	1		14th Lofgren, Zoe	Dem	Cal.	5	1	
15th Camp, David L.	Rep	Mich.	7	1		15th McCarthy, Karen	Dem	Mo.	5	1	
16th Diaz-Balart, Lincoln	Rep	Fla.	6	1		16th Jackson-Lee, Sheila	Dem	Tex.	5	1	
17th Goodlatte, Robert W.	Rep	Va.	6	1		17th Pascrell, William J. Jr.	Dem	N.C.	4	1	
18th Istook, Ernest Jim Jr.	Rep	Okla.	6	1		18th Christensen, Donna M.C.	Dem	V.I.	4	1	
19th King, Peter T.	Rep	N.Y.	6	1		19th Etheridge, Bobby R.	Dem	N.C.	4	1	
20th Linder, John E.	Rep	Ga.	6	1		20th Gonzalez, Charles A.	Dem	Tex.	3	1	
21st Shadegg, John B.	Rep	Ariz.	5	1		21st Lucas, Ken	Dem	Ky.	3	1	
22nd Souder, Mark E.	Rep	Ind.	5	1		22nd Langevin, James R.	Dem	R.I.	2	1	
23rd Thornberry, William M. (Mac)	Rep	Tex.	5	1		23rd Meek, Kendrick B.	Dem	Fla.	1	1	
24th Gibbons, James A.	Rep	Nev.	4	1							
25th Granger, Kay	Rep	Tex.	4	1							
26th Sessions, Pete	Rep	Tex.	4	1							
27th Sweeney, John E.	Rep	N.Y.	3	1							

Note: As result of the correction of Speaker's appointment, Shays, originally ranked immediately after Boehlert, was re-ranked to follow Weldon on Mar. 5, 2003. Delegates Eleanor Holmes Norton (Dem-D.C.) and Donna M.C. Christensen (Dem-V.I.) were allowed to accrue committee seniority but were not included in the party ratio.

Changes:

Majority:

Tauzin, W.J. (Billy)	Rep	La.	Apr. 23, 2004 Resigned committee after his resignation as Chair of Energy and Commerce; no new assignment
Barton, Joe L.	Rep	Tex.	Apr. 27, 2004 Replaced Tauzin; ranked after Boehlert
Goss, Porter J.	Rep	Fla.	Sept. 23, 2004 Resigned the House; named Director of Central Intelligence Agency

Minority:

Gonzalez, Charles A.	Dem	Tex.	Jan. 20, 2004 Resigned committee; moved to Energy and Commerce; vacancy remained

Departures from the House:	Majority			Minority		
Retired	Dunn, Jennifer B.	Rep	Wash.	Turner, Jim	Dem	Tex.
				McCarthy, Karen	Dem	Mo.
				Lucas, Ken	Dem	Ky.

Departures from the Committee: Did not continue on the reorganized standing committee

Majority				Minority		
Young, C.W. Bill		Rep	Fla	Frank, Barney	Dem	Mass.
Sensenbrenner, F. James Jr.		Rep	Wisc.	Cardin, Benjamin L.	Dem	Md.
Drier, David		Rep	Cal.	Slaughter, Louise Macintosh	Dem	N.Y.
Hunter, Duncan L.		Rep	Cal.	Andrews, Robert E.	Dem	N.J.
Rogers, Harold D.		Rep	Ky.	Gonzalez, Charles A.	Dem	Tex.
Boehlert, Sherwood L.		Rep	N.Y.			
Camp, David L.		Rep	Mich.			
Diaz-Balart, Lincoln		Rep	Fla			
Goodlatte, Robert W.		Rep	Va.			
Istook, Ernest Jim Jr.		Rep	Okla			
Shadegg, John B.		Rep	Ariz.			
Thornberry, William M. (Mac)		Rep	Tex.			
Gibbons, James A.		Rep	Nev.			
Granger, Kay		Rep	Tex.			
Sessions, Pete		Rep	Tex.			
Sweeney, John E.		Rep	N.Y.			

HOMELAND SECURITY / 109th Congress

Became a House Standing Committee on Jan. 4, 2005

Became a standing committee on Jan. 4, 2005

Service Dates of Committee Chair: Ch1: Jan. 6, 2005-Aug. 2, 2005 Cox (Rep-Cal.)

Ch2: Sep. 15, 2005-Jan. 3, 2007 King (Rep-N.Y.)

Service Dates of Majority Members: Jan. 26, 2005-Jan. 3, 2007

Service Dates of Minority Members: Feb. 9, 2005-Jan. 3, 2007

Roster Filled: Majority with 19 members on Feb. 9, 2005; Minority with 15 members on Feb. 9, 2005

			Terms in:						Terms in:	
Rank Name	**Party**	**State**	**House**	**Comm.**		**Rank Name**	**Party**	**State**	**House**	**Comm.**
Ch1 Cox, C. Christopher	Rep	Cal.	9	2		RM Thompson, Bennie	Dem	Miss.	7	2
2nd Young, Donald E.	Rep	Alas.	17	2		2nd Sanchez, Loretta	Dem	Cal.	5	2
3rd Smith, Lamar S.	Rep	Tex.	10	2		3rd Markey, Edward J.	Dem	Mass.	16	2
4th Weldon, Wayne C. (Curt)	Rep	Penn.	10	2		4th Dicks, Norman D.	Dem	Wash.	15	2
5th Shays, Christopher H.	Rep	Conn.	10	2		5th Harman, Jane L.	Dem	Cal.	6	2
Ch2 6th King, Peter T.	Rep	N.Y.	7	2		6th DeFazio, Peter A.	Dem	Ore.	10	2
7th Linder, John E.	Rep	Ga.	7	2		7th Lowey, Nita M.	Dem	N.Y.	9	2
8th Souder, Mark E.	Rep	Ind.	6	2		8th Norton, Eleanor Holmes	Dem	D.C.	8	2
9th Davis, Thomas M. III	Rep	Va.	6	1		9th Lofgren, Zoe	Dem	Cal.	6	2
10th Lungren, Daniel E.	Rep	Cal.	6	1		10th Jackson-Lee, Sheila	Dem	Tex.	6	2
11th Gibbons, James A.	Rep	Nev.	5	1		11th Pascrell, William J. Jr.	Dem	N.C.	5	*1 2
12th Simmons, Robert	Rep	Conn.	3	1		12th Christensen, Donna M.C.	Dem	V.I.	5	2
13th Rogers, Mike D.	Rep	Ala.	2	1		13th Etheridge, Bobby R.	Dem	N.C.	5	2
14th Pearce, Stevan	Rep	N.M.	2	1		14th Langevin, James R.	Dem	R.I.	3	2
15th Harris, Katherine	Rep	Fla.	2	1		15th Meek, Kendrick B.	Dem	Fla.	2	2
16th Jindal, Bobby	Rep	La.	1	1						
17th Reichert, David G.	Rep	Wash.	1	1						
18th McCaul, Michael T.	Rep	Tex.	1	1						
19th Dent, Charles W.	Rep	Penn.	1	1						

*1: Member's first period of service on the committee.

Note: Delegates Eleanor Holmes Norton (Dem-D.C.) and Donna M.C. Christensen (Dem-V.I.) were allowed to accrue committee seniority but were not included in the party ratio.

Vacancies Filled:

  Majority:

    2nd through 9th seats filled by Young, Smith, Weldon, Shays, King, Linder, Souder, and Davis, as well as 11th through 15th seat filled by Gibbons, Simmons, Rogers, Pearce, and Harris on Feb. 9, 2005. Filled vacancies resulted in re-ranking of Lungren to the 10th seat, as well as Jindal, Reichert, McCaul, and Dent to the 16th through 19th seats

Changes:
  Majority:

Cox, C. Christopher	Rep	Cal.	Aug. 2, 2005 Resigned the House; appointed Chair of the Securities and Exchanges Commission
King, Peter T.	Rep	N.Y.	Sep. 15, 2005 Elected Chair of Homeland Security
Brown-Waite, Virginia	Rep	Fla.	Sep. 15, 2005 Replaced Cox
Gibbons, James A.	Rep	Nev	Dec. 31, 2006 Resigned the House; elected Governor of Nevada

Departures from the House:	**Majority**			**Minority**		
Defeated for Re-election	Weldon, Wayne C. (Curt)	Rep	Penn.	None		
	Simmons, Robert	Rep	Conn.			
Lost Election to U.S. Senate	Harris, Katherine	Rep	Fla.	None		

Departures from Committee:						
Became RM on Natural Resources	Young, Donald E.	Rep	Alas.	None		
Moved to Ways and Means	None			Pascrell, William J. Jr.	Dem	N.C.
				Meek, Kendrick B.	Dem	Fla.
No new assignment	Linder, John E.	Rep	Ga.	None		
	Pearce, Stevan	Rep	N.M.			

HOMELAND SECURITY / 110th Congress

Service Dates of Committee Chair: Jan. 4, 2007-Jan. 3, 2009

Service Dates of Majority Members: Jan. 12, 2007-Jan. 3, 2009

Service Dates of Minority Members: Jan. 10, 2007-Jan. 3, 2009

Roster Filled: Majority with 19 members on Sept. 20, 2007; Minority with 15 members on Jan. 10, 2007

	Majority						**Minority**				
				Terms in:						**Terms in:**	
Rank Name		Party	State	House	Comm.	Rank Name		Party	State	House	Comm.
Chr Thompson, Bennie		Dem	Miss.	8	3	RM King, Peter T.		Rep	N.Y.	8	3
2nd Sanchez, Loretta		Dem	Cal.	6	3	2nd Smith, Lamar S.		Rep	Tex.	11	3
3rd Markey, Edward J.		Dem	Mass.	17	3	3rd Shays, Christopher H.		Rep	Conn.	11	3
4th Dicks, Norman D.		Dem	Wash.	16	3	4th Souder, Mark E.		Rep	Ind.	7	3
5th Harman, Jane L.		Dem	Cal.	7	3	5th Davis, Thomas M. III		Rep	Va.	7	2
6th DeFazio, Peter A.		Dem	Ore.	11	3	6th Lungren, Daniel E.		Rep	Cal.	7	2
7th Lowey, Nita M.		Dem	N.Y.	10	3	7th Rogers, Mike D.		Rep	Ala.	3	2
8th Norton, Eleanor Holmes		Dem	D.C.	9	3	8th Jindal, Bobby		Rep	La.	2	2
9th Lofgren, Zoe		Dem	Cal.	7	3	9th Reichert, David G.		Rep	Wash.	2	2
10th Jackson-Lee, Sheila		Dem	Tex.	7	3	10th McCaul, Michael T.		Rep	Tex.	2	2
11th Christensen, Donna M.C.		Dem	V.I.	6	3	11th Dent, Charles W.		Rep	Penn.	2	2
12th Etheridge, Bobby R.		Dem	N.C.	6	3	12th Brown-Waite, Virginia		Rep	Fla.	3	2
13th Langevin, James R.		Dem	R.I.	4	3	13th Blackburn, Marsha		Rep	Tenn.	3	1
14th Cuellar, Henry		Dem	Tex.	2	1	14th Bilirakis, Gus		Rep	Fla.	1	1
15th Carney, Chris		Dem	Penn.	1	1	15th Davis, David		Rep	Tenn.	1	1
16th Clarke, Yvette D.		Dem	N.Y.	1	1						
17th Green, Al		Dem	Tex.	2	1	*2: Member's second period of service on the committee.					
18th Perlmutter, Ed		Dem	Colo.	1	1						
19th Pascrell, William J. Jr.		Dem	N.J.	6	*2 1						

Note: Delegates Eleanor Holmes Norton (Dem-D.C.) and Donna M.C. Christensen (Dem-V.I.) were allowed to accrue committee seniority but were not included in the party ratio.

Vacancies Filled:
  Majority:
    19th seat filled by Pascrell on Sept. 20, 2007

Changes:
  Minority:

Blackburn, Marsha	Rep	Tenn.	Mar. 9, 2007 Resigned committee; returned to Energy and Commerce
McCarthy, Kevin	Rep	Cal.	Mar. 12, 2007 Replaced Blackburn
McCarthy, Kevin	Rep	Cal.	May 10, 2007 Resigned committee; moved to Natural Resources

Broun, Paul C. Jr.	Rep	Ga.	July 25, 2007 Replaced McCarthy
Jindal, Bobby	Rep	La.	Jan. 14, 2008 Resigned the House; elected Governor of Louisiana
Miller, Candice S.	Rep	Mich.	Mar. 11, 2008 Replaced Jindal
Davis, Thomas M. III	Rep	Va.	Nov. 24, 2008 Resigned the House and retired

Departures from the House:

	Majority			Minority		
Defeated for Re-election	None			Shays, Christopher H.	Rep	Conn.
Defeated for Re-nomination	None			Davis, David	Rep	Tenn.

Departures from Committee:

Returned to Armed Services	Langevin, James R.	Dem	R.I.	None		
Moved to Budget	Langevin, James R.	Dem	R.I.	None		
Moved to Energy and Commerce	Christensen, Donna M.C.	Dem	V.I.	None		
Moved to Rules	Perlmutter, Ed	Dem	Colo.	None		
Moved to Ways and Means	Etheridge, Bobby R.	Dem	N.C.	Reichert, David G.	Rep	Wash.
				Brown-Waite, Virginia	Rep	Fla.
No new assignment	Markey, Edward J.	Dem	Mass.	None		
	Dicks, Norman D.	Dem	Wash.			
	Lowey, Nita M.	Dem	N.Y.			

HOMELAND SECURITY / 111th Congress

Service Dates of Committee Chair: Jan. 6, 2009-Jan. 3, 2011

Service Dates of Majority Members: Jan. 28, 2009-Jan. 3, 2011

Service Dates of Minority Members: Jan. 9, 2009-Jan. 3, 2011

Roster Filled: Majority with 20 members, Jan. 28, 2009; Minority with 13 members, Jan. 9, 2009

Majority					**Minority**				
			Terms in:					**Terms in:**	
Rank Name	Party	State	House	Comm.	Rank Name	Party	State	House	Comm.
Chr Thompson, Bennie	Dem	Miss.	9	4	RM King, Peter T.	Rep	N.Y.	9	4
2nd Sanchez, Loretta	Dem	Cal.	7	4	2nd Smith, Lamar S.	Rep	Tex.	12	4
3rd Harman, Jane L.	Dem	Cal.	8	4	3rd Souder, Mark E.	Rep	Ind.	8	4
4th DeFazio, Peter A.	Dem	Ore.	12	4	4th Lungren, Daniel E.	Rep	Cal.	8	3
5th Norton, Eleanor Holmes	Dem	D.C.	10	4	5th Rogers, Mike D.	Rep	Ala.	4	3
6th Lofgren, Zoe	Dem	Cal.	8	4	6th McCaul, Michael T.	Rep	Tex.	3	3
7th Jackson-Lee, Sheila	Dem	Tex.	8	4	7th Dent, Charles W.	Rep	Penn.	3	3
8th Cuellar, Henry	Dem	Tex.	3	2	8th Bilirakis, Gus	Rep	Fla.	2	2
9th Carney, Chris	Dem	Penn.	2	2	9th Broun, Paul C. Jr.	Rep	Ga.	2	2
10th Clarke, Yvette D.	Dem	N.Y.	2	2	10th Miller, Candice S.	Rep	Mich.	4	2
11th Richardson, Laura	Dem	Cal.	2	1	11th Olson, Pete	Rep	Tex.	1	1
12th Kirkpatrick, Ann	Dem	Ariz.	1	1	12th Cao, Anh (Joseph)	Rep	La.	1	1
13th Luján, Ben Ray	Dem	N.M.	1	1	13th Austria, Steve	Rep	Ohio	1	1
14th Pascrell, William J. Jr.	Dem	N.J.	7	*2 2					
15th Cleaver, Emanuel II	Dem	Mont.	3	1					
16th Green, Al	Dem	Tex.	3	2					
17th Himes, James A.	Dem	Conn.	1	1					
18th Kilroy, Mary Jo	Dem	Ohio	1	1					
19th Massa, Eric J.J.	Dem	N.Y.	1	1					
20th Titus, Alice (Dina)	Dem	Nev.	1	1					

*2: Member's second period of service on the committee.

Note: Delegate Eleanor Holmes Norton (Dem-D.C.) was allowed to accrue committee seniority but not included in the party ratio.

Addition:
Majority

Owens, William I.	Dem	N.Y.	Nov. 19, 2009 Ranked 14th following Lujan

Changes
Majority

Massa, Eric J.J.	Dem	N.Y.	Mar. 8, 2010 Resigned the House due to ethics issues
Luján, Ben Ray	Dem	N.M.	May 5, 2010 Resigned committee; moved to Natural Resources
Owens, William L.	Dem	N.Y.	May 6, 2010 Reranked following Titus

House Administration

House Committee on House Administration, 103rd Congress (1993-1995)

House Committee on House Oversight, 104th-105th Congresses (1995-1999)

House Committee on House Administration, 106th-111th Congresses (1999-2011)

BACKGROUND

Organizational History: The House Administration Committee was created by the Legislative Reorganization Act out of twelve other committees. Some of the committee's predecessors dated back to the earliest Congresses. The Elections Committee was created on April 13, 1789, as the first standing committee in Congress and Enrolled Bills, established on July 27, 1789, was the first joint committee. Another President George Washington-era committee was Claims, which was first approved as a standing committee on November 13, 1794.

Others of its predecessors had lengthy histories also: Accounts (1804); War Claims (1813, then known as Pensions and Revolutionary Claims); Library (1843); Printing (1846); Disposition of Executive Papers (1889); Election of President, Vice President and Representatives of Congress (1893); Elections No. 2 (1895); Elections No. 3 (1895); and Memorials (1929). Although, the twelve committees had a total of 113 members in the 79th Congress (1945-1947) prior to the passage of the Reorganization act, House Administration had only twenty-five after its passage.

This committee holds jurisdiction over a great many of the administrative and housekeeping details necessary for the functioning of the House of Representatives. This includes responsibility for the expenditures, appropriations, and auditing of the contingent fund. It also handles administrative details related to day-to-day functioning, such as measures related to House employees, including clerks for members and committees, and reporters of debates; travel funds; assignment of office space; printing and correction of the Congressional Record; and services to the House, such as the House Restaurant and administration of the House wing of the Capitol. The committee also holds jurisdiction over matters related to the disposition of useless executive papers; the Library of Congress and the House Library; statuary and pictures, acceptance or purchase of works of art for the Capitol; the Botanic Gardens; management of the Library of Congress; purchase of books and manuscripts; and the erection of monuments to the memory of individuals.

It also has responsibility over federal elections, including election of the president, vice president and members of Congress; corrupt practices; contested elections; campaign contributions to candidates; and credentials and qualifications. The House Administration Committee makes sure that bills, amendments, and joint resolutions passed by both Houses are correctly enrolled and, if originated in the House, that they be presented to the president. Authority over matters related to services has been expanded to also include responsibility for parking facilities. Legislative jurisdiction has also been expanded to cover measures related to compensation, retirement, and benefits for members, officers, and employees of the Congress. Among its oversight responsibilities include reporting to the Sergeant at Arms on the travel of House Members and a scheduling service to eliminate meeting and scheduling conflicts for committees and subcommittees of the House.

The 1995 Republican takeover of the House resulted in the committee being renamed House Oversight when it received the Franking Commission (aka the House Commission on Congressional Mailing Standards) from the defunct Post Office and Civil Service Committee. After the 1999 departure of House Speaker Newt Gingrich, the committee's name reverted to House Administration.

Although committee chairs usually are supreme in their own territory, the House Administration Committee has held a different view. To Administration Committee members, other committee chairs are an annual parade of supplicants, asking for money to run their committees. Individual members also must deal with the committee, depending on it for office space and allowances, and approval for various expenditures.

The House Administration Committee has had an unfortunate history with its senior leadership as three of its chairs became embroiled in scandal—Wayne L. Hays (Dem-Ohio) was implicated in the 1976 Elizabeth Ray romantic entanglement; Frank W. Thompson (Dem-N.J.) was sent to jail for his involvement in the 1980 "Abscam" episode when FBI agents dressed as Arab businessmen offered bribes to members of Congress; and Robert W. Ney (Rep-Ohio), who lost his freedom over accepting gifts and favors from disgraced lobbyist Jack Abramoff. Ironically, Hays sought a political comeback by being elected to the Ohio House of Representatives in 1978 but was defeated for re-election in 1980 by Ney.

Membership: The House Administration Committee had twenty-five members named in its initial Congress in 1947. It remained at that number for most of the next thirty-four years, 1947-1981, with a 1973-1975 peak of twenty-six. It began its downward slide in 1981 when its membership dropped to nineteen where it remained for eight years (1981-1989). Despite rebounds in the 101st Congress (1989-1991) and the 102nd Congress (1991-1993) where committee members reached twenty-one and twenty-four respectively, it returned to nineteen in 1993. In the 104th Congress renamed as House Oversight, it dropped to twelve.

While its name of House Administration was restored in 1999, its membership has remained at nine for the past seven Congresses (1997-2011). House Administration shared with the District of Columbia and Post Office and Civil Service Committees the distinction of having lost membership size since 1947. However, they were both terminated while House Administration lingers on albeit with only nine members, the smallest standing committee in the House. The committee's inter-Congress retention rate of 61.82 percent ranked it eighteenth, above only the Standards of Official Conduct Committee.

Committee Leaders: As is often the case with less prestigious committees, turnover in the senior ranks of House Administration is high. Karl M. LeCompte (Rep-Iowa) who had served on the Committee on the Election of President, Vice President and Members of Congress for six years became the first post-reorganization chair and served as the committee's senior Republican for twelve years, 1947-1959, chairing the committee again in the 83rd Congress (1953-1955). Mary T. Norton (Dem-N.J.), who had chaired Labor in the previous Congress and had been a senior member of Memorials, became the new committee's ranking member. Norton chaired the committee in the 81st Congress (1949-1951), and upon her retirement Thomas B. Stanley (Dem-Va.) became chair in the 82nd Congress (1951-1953) and its ranking minority member in 1953 until he resigned upon his election as Governor of Virginia. His successor, Omar T. Burleson (Dem-Tex.) became the committee's senior Democrat and would be its longest-serving chair, from 1955 until 1968. He left the chair of House Administration to fill the fifteenth majority vacancy on the Ways and Means Committee. This is the first non-rules induced instance of a chair leaving a standing committee for membership on another committee in the modern era.

Following LeCompte in 1959, Paul F. Schenck (Rep-Ohio) became ranking member and served until his election defeat in 1964. Schenck's successor, Glenard P. Lipscomb (Rep-Cal.) held that spot until his death in 1970 when Lipscomb was followed by Samuel L. Devine (Rep-Ohio), who served until 1973 when he became ranking member on Interstate and Foreign Commerce. Devine was succeeded by William L. Dickinson (Rep-Ala.) in 1973, and Dickinson stepped aside in 1981 to become ranking member on Armed Services. Dickinson's successor was William E. Frenzel (Rep-Minn.), who left the committee in 1989 to serve on Budget. For three months from January to April 1989, the ranking minority member on House Administration would be the irrepressible Newt L. Gingrich (Rep-Ga.) who would leave the committee to replace Minority Whip Richard B. Cheney (Rep-Wyo.). William M. Thomas (Rep-Cal.) would succeed Gingrich.

On the Democratic side, Burleson's immediate successor, Samuel N. Friedel, chaired the committee from 1968 until his renomination defeat in 1970. Following Friedel would be the House Administration Committee's most controversial chair, Wayne L. Hays (Dem-Ohio). While most of the spending requests of the committee are handled routinely, but the panel has the potential to be both difficult and powerful. Hays, who chaired the committee from 1971 to 1976, used his authority over money and office space to reward friends and punish enemies. Even petty matters, such as orders for new telephones, were reviewed to see whether the request had come from an ally, or someone who had irritated the prickly chairman. Hays's empire collapsed after revelations that he had kept a mistress on the committee payroll and he resigned from the House in 1976.

Hays's successor as chair, Frank J. Thompson Jr. (Dem-N.J.), also used his authority against those who crossed him. Thompson was indicted as part of the "Abscam" scandal,

which involved federal agents posing as oil rich Arabs trying to buy personal favors from powerful congressmen. He had to step aside as committee chair to be replaced by Acting Chair Lucien N. Nedzi (Dem-Mich.) and lost re-election in 1980. The departure of two chairmen in disgrace cost the House Administration Committee much of the influence it once had in the House and it suffered a severe budget cut in 1981 and a reduction in size. Since 1981, two other chairs have left. Augustus P. Hawkins (Dem-Cal.) departed the committee in 1984 to chair Education and Labor and in 1991, Frank Annunzio (Dem-Ill.) who followed Hawkins, was voted out as chair in 1991 (125-127) and was the sixth House chair to be demoted by the Democratic Caucus since 1975.

In the 102nd and 103rd Congresses (1991-1995), newly installed chair Charles G. Rose III (Dem-N.C.) had to deal with two of the most controversial scandals of recent times. This involved allegations of wrongdoing at the House bank, with thousands of checks being mishandled, and at the House post office, where serious allegations of drug dealing and embezzlement led to a committee investigation that was critical of how both the bank and the post office were run. These scandals contributed to the negative climate regarding House Democrats that would lead to their losing control of the House in the 1994 mid-term election.

With the new majority in 1995, William Thomas became chair of House Administration and remained in that post until he became chair of Ways and Means in 2001. His successor Robert W. Ney (Rep-Ohio), who served as chair until 2006, when yet another House Administration chair was felled by scandal. The Abramoff influence peddling scandal cost Ney the chairmanship and he resigned. Vernon J. Ehlers (Rep-Mich.) finished out Ney's term as chair and served as ranking member in the 110thCongress until he left for no new assignment. Ehlers's successor as senior Republican in the 111th Congress is Daniel E. Lungren (Rep-Cal.)

Senior Democratic turnover remained high with Victor H. Fazio (Dem-Cal.) replacing Rose in 1995; Samuel Gedjenson (Dem-Conn.) replacing him in 1997; Steny Hoyer (Dem-Md.) following Gejdenson in 1999; John B. Larson (Dem-Conn.) taking over in 2003; and Juanita Millender-McDonald (Dem-Cal.), in 2005. Millender-McDonald became chair in 2007 but her death in 2008 led to Robert A. Brady (Dem-Penn.) becoming chair, a post that he continues to hold.

Party Leaders: Ten party leaders served on House Administration, including four Speakers of the House: John W. McCormack (Dem-Mass.), Carl Albert (Dem-Okla.), Thomas S. Foley (Dem-Wash.), and Newt L. Gingrich (Rep-Ga.). Each of these had held the two penultimate posts of party whip and floor leader before becoming Speaker. In addition, three Majority Leaders: Charles A. Halleck (Rep-Ind.), John Boehner (Rep-Ohio), and Steny H. Hoyer (Dem-Md.); and three Whips: John McFall (Dem-Cal.), John Brademas (Dem-Ind.), and Anthony Coelho (Dem-Cal.) served on House Administration. Of the ten leaders, McCormack, Halleck, and Foley served on House Administration after they had attained their leadership posts, while the other seven served on the committee before they made their moves to challenge for the leadership. It is a committee where favors can be done for other members that may pave the way for leadership posts.

Notable Members: The House Administration Committee has limited appeal for those whose ambitions go beyond the House. Apart from John B. Anderson (Rep-Ill.), who ran as a third party candidate for president in 1980, no major presidential or vice presidential nominees served on the committee and only one Cabinet member served—Lynn M. Martin, George H.W. Bush's second Secretary of Labor. David A. Stockman (Rep-Mich.), President Reagan's first Director of the Office of Management and Budget and the architect of "Reaganomics," served on the committee during his only two terms in the House, 1977-1981. Leon Panetta (Dem-Cal.), President Clinton's Director of OMB and President Obama's Director of Central Intelligence, was also an alumnus of the committee.

Only six members of the committee moved to the Senate. Three were Democrats—George A. Smathers of Florida in 1951, Robert C. Byrd of West Virginia in 1959, and Benjamin L. Cardin of Maryland in 2007. Three were Republicans: Charles E. Goodell of New York, C. Patrick Roberts of Kansas, and J. Caleb Boggs of Delaware, who was the only Republican committee member to move to the Senate and to be elected governor. Two other governors—Democrat Hugh L. Carey of New York and Republican Albert H. Quie of Minnesota—also served on House Administration, as did New York City's mayor Edward I. Koch (Dem-N.Y.).

Goodell was the only appointed senator to have served on House Administration. In 1968, he was named by New York governor Nelson A. Rockefeller to fill the seat of the martyred Robert F. Kennedy (Dem-N.Y.), brother of President John F. Kennedy and former Attorney General. Goodell, a moderate Republican, lost a three-way contest in 1970 to Independent James Buckley, brother of long-time conservative editor William F. Buckley. Goodell's son Roger is presently the Commissioner of the National Football League.

Given the narrowness of House Administration's "insider" agenda, it is somewhat surprising that six alumni of the committee were elected governors of their states. Three were Democrats—John Bell Williams of South Carolina, Thomas B. Stanley of Virginia, and Hugh L. Carey of New York. And three were Republicans—J. Caleb Boggs of Delaware, Albert H. Quie of Minnesota, and Carroll A. Campbell of South Carolina.

Selected References

Schamel, Charles E. et al., "Records of the House Administration Committee and Its Predecessors," *Guide to the Records of the United States House of Representatives at the National Archives: 1789-1989 Bicentennial Edition* (Washington, D.C.: National Archives and Records Administration,1989), 165-178.

U.S. House of Representatives, Committee on House Administration, *Report on the Activities of the Committee on House Administration of the House of Representatives during the 102nd Congress,* H.Rept. 102-1083, 102nd Congress, 2nd Session (1992).

RESPONSIBILITIES, JURISDICTIONAL CHANGES, AND SUBCOMMITTEES

HOUSE ADMINSTRATION

Jurisdiction, 80th Congress (1947-1949)

Established by the Legislative Reorganization Act of 1946:

[Section 121.(1)(j)]

(1) Committee on House Administration.

   (A)   Employment of persons by the House, including clerks for Members and committees, and reporters of debates.

   (B)   Expenditure of the contingent fund of the House.

   (C)   The auditing and settling of all accounts which may be charged to the contingent fund.

   (D)   Measures relating to accounts of the House generally.

   (E)   Appropriations from the contingent fund.

   (F)   Measures relating to services to the House, including the House Restaurant and administration of the House Office Buildings and of the House wing of the Capitol.

   (G)   Measures relating to the travel of Members of the House.

   (H)   Measures relating to the assignment of office space for Members and committees.

   (I)   Measures relating to the disposition of useless executive papers.

   (J)   Except as provided in paragraph (o) 8, matters relating to the Library of Congress and the House Library; statuary and pictures; acceptance or purchase of works of art for the Capitol; the Botanic Gardens; management of the Library of Congress; purchase of books and manuscripts; erection of monuments to the memory of individuals.

   (K)   Except as provided in paragraph (o) 8, matters relating to the Smithsonian Institution and the incorporation of similar institutions.

   (L)   Matters relating to printing and correction of the Congressional Record.

   (M)   Measures relating to the election of the President, Vice President, or Members of Congress; corrupt practices; contested elections; credentials and qualifications; and Federal elections generally.

(2) Such committee shall also have the duty of—

   (A)   examining all bills, amendments, and joint resolution after passage by the House; and in cooperation with the Senate Committee on Rules and Administration, of examining all bills and joint resolutions which shall have passed both Houses, to see that they are correctly enrolled; and when signed by the Speaker of the House and the President of the Senate, shall forthwith present the same, when they shall have originated in the House, to the President of the United States in person, and report the fact and date of such presentation to the House;

(B) reporting to the Sergeant at Arms of the House the travel of Members of the House;

(C) arranging a suitable program for each day observed by the House of Representatives as a memorial day in memory of Members of the Senate and House of Representatives who have died during the preceding period, and to arrange for the publication of the proceedings thereof.

Jurisdiction, 103rd Congress (1993-1995)

From the Rules of the House of Representatives, 103rd Congress (House Document 102-405)

[Rule X.1.(k)] Committee on House Administration

(1) Appropriations from the contingent fund.

(2) Auditing and settling of all accounts which may be charged to the contingent fund.

(3) Employment of persons by the House, including clerks for Members and committees, and reporters of debates.

(4) Except as provided in clause I(p)(4)[Committee on Public Works and Transportation], matters relating to the Library of Congress and the House Library; statuary and pictures; acceptance or purchase of works of art for the Capitol; the Botanic Gardens; management of the Library of Congress; purchase of books and manuscripts; erection of monuments to the memory of individuals.

(5) Except as provided in clause I(p)(4), matters relating to the Smithsonian Institution and the incorporation of similar institutions.

(6) Expenditure of contingent fund of the House.

(7) Matters relating to printing and correction of the Congressional Record.

(8) Measures relating to accounts of the House generally.

(9) Measures relating to assignment of office space for Members and committees.

(10) Measures relating to the disposition of useless executive papers.

(11) Measures relating to the election of the President, Vice President, or Members of Congress;corrupt practices; contested elections; credentials and qualifications; and Federal elections generally.

(12) Measures relating to services to the House, including the House Restaurant, parking facilities and administration of the House Office Buildings and of the House wing of the Capitol.

(13) Measures relating to the travel of Members of the House.

(14) Measures relating to the raising, reporting and use of campaign contributions for candidates for office of Representative in the House of Representatives and of Resident Commissioner to the United States from Puerto Rico.

(15) Measures relating to the compensation, retirement and other benefits of the Members, officers, and employees of the Congress.

In addition to its legislative jurisdiction under the preceding provisions of this paragraph (and its general oversight function under clause 2(b)(1)), the committee shall have the function of performing the duties which are provided for in clause 4(d).

[Rule X.4.(d)] Additional Functions

The Committee on House Administration shall have the function of—

(1) examining all bills, amendments, and joint resolutions after passage by the House and, in cooperation with the Senate, examining all bills and joint resolutions which shall have passed both Houses to see that they are correctly enrolled, forthwith presenting those which originated in the House to the President of the United States in person after their signature by the Speaker of the House and the President of the Senate and reporting the fact and date of such presentation to the House;

(2) reporting to the Sergeant-at-Arms of the House concerning the travel of Members of the House; and

(3) providing, through the House Information Systems a scheduling service which may be used by all the committees and subcommittees of the House to eliminate, insofar as possible, any meeting and scheduling conflicts.

HOUSE OVERSIGHT

House Administration was renamed the Committee on House Oversight on January 4, 1995.

Jurisdiction, 104th Congress (1995-1997) Changes in Committee System

From H. Res. 6, Section 202 (a), the Committees and Their Jurisdiction, January 4, 1995

[Rule X.1.(h)] Committee on House Oversight.

(1) Appropriations from accounts for committee salaries and expenses (except for the Committee on Appropriations), House Information Systems, and allowances and expenses of Members, House officers and administrative offices of the House.

(2) Auditing and settling of all accounts described in subparagraph (1)

(3) Employment of persons by the House, including clerks for Members and committees, and reporters of debates.

(4) Except as provided in clause 1(q)(11), matters relating to the Library of Congress and the House Library; statuary and pictures; acceptance or purchase of works of art for the Capitol; the Botanic Gardens; management of the Library of Congress; purchase of books and manuscripts.

(5) Except as provided in clause 1(q)(11), matters relating to the Smithsonian Institution and the incorporation of similar institutions.

(6) Expenditure of accounts described in subparagraph (1)

(7) Franking Commission.

(8) Matters relating to printing and correction of the Congressional Record.

(9) Measures relating to accounts of the House generally.

(10) Measures relating to assignment of office space for Members and committees.

(11) Measures relating to the disposition of useless executive papers.

(12) Measures relating to the election of the President, Vice President, or Members of Congress; corrupt practices; contested elections; credentials and qualifications; and Federal elections generally.

(13) Measures relating to services to the House, including the House Restaurant, parking facilities and administration of the House office buildings and of the House wing of the Capitol.

(14) Measures relating to the travel of Members of the House.

(15) Measures relating to the raising, reporting and use of campaign contributions for candidates for office of Representative in the House of Representatives, of Delegate, and of Resident Commissioner to the United States from Puerto Rico.

(16) Measures relating to the compensation, retirement and other benefits of the Members, officers, and employees of the Congress.

In addition to its legislative jurisdiction under the preceding provisions of this paragraph (and its general oversight function under clause 2(b)(1)), the committee shall have the function of performing the duties which are provided for in clause 4(d).

HOUSE ADMINISTRATION

House Oversight was redesignated as the Committee on House Administration on January 6, 1999.

Jurisdiction, 111th Congress (2009-2011)

From the Rules of the House of Representatives (as revised to June 16, 2009, H.Doc. 110-162):

[Rule X.1.(j)] Committee on House Administration

(1) Appropriations from accounts for committee salaries and expenses (except for the Committee on Appropriations); House Information Resources; and allowance and expenses of Members, Delegates, the Resident (2) Commissioner, officers, and administrative offices of the House.

(3) Auditing and settling of all accounts described in subparagraph (1)

(4) Employment of persons by the House, including staff for Members, Delegates, the Resident Commissioner, and committees; and reporters of debates, subject to rule VI.

(5) Except as provided in paragraph (r)(11), the Library of Congress, including management thereof; the House Library; statuary and pictures; acceptance or purchase of works of art for the Capitol; the Botanic Garden; and purchase of books and manuscripts.

(6) The Smithsonian Institution and the incorporation of similar institutions (except as provided in paragraph (r)(11)).

(7) Expenditure of accounts described in subparagraph (1)

(8) Franking Commission.

(9) Printing and correction of the Congressional Record.

(10) Accounts of the House generally.

(11) Assignment of office space for Members, Delegates, the Resident Commissioner, and committees.

(12) Disposition of useless executive papers.

(13) Election of the President, Vice President, Members, Senators, Delegates, or the Resident Commissioner; corrupt practices; contested elections; credentials and qualifications; and Federal elections generally.

(14) Services to the House, including the House Restaurant, parking facilities, and administration of the House Office Buildings and of the House wing of the Capitol.

(15) Travel of Members, Delegates, and the Resident Commissioner.

(16) Raising, reporting, and use of campaign contributions for candidates for office of Representative, of Delegate, and of Resident Commissioner.

(17) Compensation, retirement, and other benefits of the Members, Delegates, the Resident Commissioner, officers, and employees of Congress.

[Rule X.4.(d)(1)] Additional Functions of Committee

The Committee on House Administration shall:

(A) provide policy direction for the Inspector General and oversight of the Clerk, Sergeant-at-Arms, Chief Administrative Officer, and Inspector General:

(B) have the function of accepting on behalf of the House a gift, except as otherwise provided by the law, if the gift does not involve a duty, burden, or condition, or is not made dependent upon some future performance by the House; and

(C) promulgate regulations to carry out subdivision (B)

[Rule X.4.(d)(2)]

An employing office of the House may enter into a settlement of a complaint under the Congressional Accountability Act of 1995 that provides for the payment of funds only after receiving the joint approval of the chairman and ranking minority member of the Committee on House Administration concerning the amount of such payment.

NAMES OF HOUSE ADMINISTRATION SUBCOMMITTEES FROM THE *CONGRESSIONAL DIRECTORY*

House Administration, 103rd Congress

Accounts, 103	Administrative Oversight, 103
Elections, 103	Libraries and Memorials, 103
Office Systems, 103	Personnel and Police, 103

No Subcommittees, 104th, 105th, 106th, 107th, 108th, and 109th Congresses

House Administration, 110th-111th Congresses

Capitol Security, 110, 111 Elections, 110, 111

MEMBERSHIP ROSTERS, 103rd-111th Congresses, 1993-2011

HOUSE ADMINISTRATION / 103rd Congress

Service Dates of Committee Chair: Jan. 21, 1993-Jan. 3, 1995

Service Dates of Majority Members: Jan. 21, 1993-Jan. 3, 1995

Service Dates of Minority Members: Jan. 5, 1993-Jan. 3, 1995

Roster Filled: Majority with 12 members, Jan. 21, 1993; Minority with 7 members, Feb. 4, 1993

			Majority Terms in:						Minority Terms in:	
Rank Name	**Party**	**State**	**House**	**Comm.**	**Rank Name**	**Party**	**State**	**House**	**Comm.**
Chr Rose, Charles G. III	Dem	N.C.	11	10	RM Thomas, William M.	Rep	Cal.	8	7
2nd Swift, Allan B.	Dem	Wash.	8	8	2nd Gingrich, Newton L.	Rep	Ga.	8	8
3rd Clay, William L. Sr.	Dem	Mo.	13	5	3rd Roberts, C. Patrick	Rep	Kans.	7	6
4th Gejdenson, Samuel	Dem	Conn.	7	5	4th Livingston, Robert L. Jr.	Rep	La.	9	2
5th Frost, J. Martin III	Dem	Tex.	8	3	5th Barrett, William E.	Rep	Neb.	2	2
6th Manton, Thomas J.	Dem	N.Y.	5	3	6th Boehner, John A.	Rep	Ohio	2	1
7th Hoyer, Steny H.	Dem	Md.	7	2	7th Dunn, Jennifer B.	Rep	Wash.	1	1
8th Kleczka, Gerald D.	Dem	Wisc.	6	2					
9th Kildee, Dale E.	Dem	Mich.	9	2					
10th Derrick, Butler C. Jr.	Dem	S.C.	10	1					
11th Kennelly, Barbara B.	Dem	Conn.	7	1					
12th Cardin, Benjamin L.	Dem	Md.	4	1					

Vacancies Filled:
  Minority:
        7th seat filled by Dunn on Feb. 4, 1993

Departures from the House:	**Majority**			**Minority**		
Retired	Swift, Allan B.	Dem	Wash.	None		
	Derrick, Butler C. Jr.	Dem	S.C.			

Departures from Committee:						
Elected Speaker of the House	None			Gingrich, Newton L.	Rep	Ga.

						Livingston, Robert L. Jr.	Rep	La.
Became Chair of Appropriations	None							
Became RM on Economic and Education Opportunities	Clay, William L. Sr.	Dem	Mo.			None		
Returned to Resources	Kildee, Dale E.	Dem	Mich.			None		
No new assignment	Rose, Charles G. III	Dem	N.C.			Barrett, William E.	Rep	Neb.
	Cardin, Benjamin L.	Dem	Md.					
	Frost, J. Martin III	Dem	Tex.					
	Manton, Thomas J.	Dem	N.Y.					
	Kleczka, Gerald D.	Dem	Wisc.					
	Kennelly, Barbara B.	Dem	Conn.					

HOUSE OVERSIGHT / 104th Congress

Service Dates of Committee Chair: Jan. 4, 1995-Jan. 3, 1997

Service Dates of Majority Members: Jan. 4, 1995-Jan. 3, 1997

Service Dates of Minority Members: Jan. 4, 1995-Jan. 3, 1997

Roster Filled: Majority with 7 members, Jan. 4, 1995; Minority with 5 members, Jan. 11, 1995

			Majority						Minority		
				Terms in:						Terms in:	
Rank Name	Party	State	House	Comm.		Rank Name	Party	State	House	Comm.	
Chr Thomas, William M.	Rep	Cal.	9	8		RM Fazio, Victor H.	Dem	Cal.	9	*2 1	
2nd Ehlers, Vernon J.	Rep	Mich.	2	1		2nd Gejdenson, Samuel	Dem	Conn.	8	6	
3rd Roberts, C. Patrick	Rep	Kans.	8	7		3rd Hoyer, Steny H.	Dem	Md.	8	3	
4th Boehner, John A.	Rep	Ohio	3	2		4th Jefferson, William J.	Dem	La.	3	1	
5th Dunn, Jennifer B.	Rep	Wash.	2	2		5th Pastor, Edward L.	Dem	Ariz.	3	1	
6th Diaz-Balart, Lincoln	Rep	Fla.	2	1							
7th Ney, Robert W.	Rep	Ohio	1	1		*2: Member's second period of service on the committee.					

	Majority				Minority			
Departures from the House:								
Elected to U.S. Senate	Roberts, C. Patrick	Rep	Kans.		None			
Departures from Committee:								
Returned to Appropriations	None				Pastor, Edward L.	Dem	Ariz.	
Returned to Ways and Means	None				Jefferson, William J.	Dem	La.	
No new assignment	Dunn, Jennifer B.	Rep	Wash.		Fazio, Victor H.	Dem	Cal.	
	Diaz-Balart, Lincoln	Rep	Fla.					

HOUSE OVERSIGHT / 105th Congress

Service Dates of Committee Chair: Jan. 7, 1997-Jan. 3, 1999

Service Dates of Majority Members: Jan. 7, 1997-Jan. 3, 1999

Service Dates of Minority Members: Feb. 5, 1997-Jan. 3, 1999

Roster Filled: Majority with 6 members, Apr. 30, 1997; Minority with 5 members, Feb. 5, 1997

			Majority						Minority		
				Terms in:						Terms in:	
Rank Name	Party	State	House	Comm.		Rank Name	Party	State	House	Comm.	
Chr Thomas, William M.	Rep	Cal.	10	9		RM Gejdenson, Samuel	Dem	Conn.	9	7	
2nd Boehner, John A.	Rep	Ohio	4	3		2nd Hoyer, Steny H.	Dem	Md.	9	4	
3rd Ehlers, Vernon J.	Rep	Mich.	3	2		3rd Kilpatrick, Carolyn C.	Dem	Mich.	1	1	
4th Ney, Robert W.	Rep	Ohio	2	2							
5th Granger, Kay	Rep	Tex.	1	1							
6th Mica, John L.	Rep	Fla.	3	1							

Vacancies Filled:

Majority:

6th seat filled by Mica on Apr. 30, 1997

	Majority				Minority			
Departures from Committee:								
Became RM on International Relations	None				Gejdenson, Samuel	Dem	Conn.	
Moved to Appropriations	Granger, Kay	Rep	Tex.		Kilpatrick, Carolyn C.	Dem	Mich.	

HOUSE ADMINISTRATION / 106th Congress

Service Dates of Committee Chair: Jan. 6, 1999-Jan. 3, 2001

Service Dates of Majority Members: Jan. 6, 1999-Jan. 3, 2001

Service Dates of Minority Members: Feb. 10, 1999-Jan. 3, 2001

Roster Filled: Majority with 6 members, Jan. 6, 1999; Minority with 3 members, Feb. 10, 1999

Majority			Terms in:		**Minority**			Terms in:	
Rank Name	**Party**	**State**	**House**	**Comm.**	**Rank Name**	**Party**	**State**	**House**	**Comm.**
Chr Thomas, William M.	Rep	Cal.	11	10	RM Hoyer, Steny H.	Dem	Md.	10	5
2nd Boehner, John A.	Rep	Ohio	5	4	2nd Fattah, Chaka	Dem	Penn.	3	1
3rd Ehlers, Vernon J.	Rep	Mich.	4	3	3rd Davis, Jim	Dem	Fla.	2	1
4th Ney, Robert W.	Rep	Ohio	3	3					
5th Mica, John L.	Rep	Fla.	4	2					
6th Ewing, Thomas W.	Rep	Ill.	5	1					

Changes:
Majority:

Ewing, Thomas W.	Rep	Ill.	July 27, 2000 Resigned from House Administration; no new assignment
Linder, John E.	Rep	Ga.	July 27, 2000 Replaced Ewing

Departures from Committee:	**Majority**			**Minority**
Became Chair of Education and the Workforce	Boehner, John A.	Rep	Ohio	None
Became Chair of Ways and Means	Thomas, William M.	Rep	Cal.	None

HOUSE ADMINISTRATION / 107th Congress

Service Dates of Committee Chair: Jan. 20, 2001-Jan. 3, 2003

Service Dates of Majority Members: Jan. 31, 2001-Jan. 3, 2003

Service Dates of Minority Members: Jan. 31, 2001-Jan. 3, 2003

Roster Filled: Majority with 6 members, Jan. 31, 2001; Minority with 3 members, Jan. 21, 2001

Majority			Terms in:		**Minority**			Terms in:	
Rank Name	**Party**	**State**	**House**	**Comm.**	**Rank Name**	**Party**	**State**	**House**	**Comm.**
Chr Ney, Robert W.	Rep	Ohio	4	4	RM Hoyer, Steny H.	Dem	Md.	11	6
2nd Ehlers, Vernon J.	Rep	Mich.	5	4	2nd Fattah, Chaka	Dem	Penn.	4	2
3rd Mica, John L.	Rep	Fla.	5	3	3rd Davis, Jim	Dem	Fla.	3	2
4th Linder, John E.	Rep	Ga.	5	2					
5th Doolittle, John T.	Rep	Cal.	6	1					
6th Reynolds, Thomas M.	Rep	N.Y.	2	1					

Departures from Committee:	**Majority**			**Minority**		
Elected Minority Whip	None			Hoyer, Steny H.	Dem	Md.
Moved to Energy and Commerce	None			Davis, Jim	Dem	Fla.
No new assignment	None			Fattah, Chaka	Dem	Penn.

HOUSE ADMINISTRATION / 108th Congress

Service Dates of Committee Chair: Jan. 8, 2003-Jan. 3, 2005

Service Dates of Majority Members: Jan. 28, 2003-Jan. 3, 2005

Service Dates of Minority Members: Feb. 5, 2003-Jan. 3, 2005

Roster Filled: Majority with 6 members, Jan. 28, 2003; Minority with 3 members, Feb. 5, 2003

Majority			Terms in:		**Minority**			Terms in:	
Rank Name	**Party**	**State**	**House**	**Comm.**	**Rank Name**	**Party**	**State**	**House**	**Comm.**
Chr Ney, Robert W.	Rep	Ohio	5	5	RM Larson, John B.	Dem	Conn.	3	1
2nd Ehlers, Vernon J.	Rep	Mich.	6	5	2nd Millender-McDonald, Juanita	Dem	Cal.	5	1

3rd Mica, John L.	Rep	Fla.	6	4
4th Linder, John E.	Rep	Ga.	6	3
5th Doolittle, John T.	Rep	Cal.	7	2
6th Reynolds, Thomas M.	Rep	N.Y.	3	2

| 3rd Brady, Robert A. | Dem | Penn. | 4 | 1 |

Departures from Committee: Majority / Minority

| Moved to Ways and Means | Linder, John E. | Rep | Ga. | Larson, John B. | Dem | Conn. |

HOUSE ADMINISTRATION / 109th Congress

Service Dates of Committee Chair: Ch1: Jan. 6, 2005-Jan. 17, 2006, Ney (Rep-Ohio)

Ch2: Feb.1, 2006-Jan. 3, 2007, Ehlers (Rep-Mich.)

Service Dates of Majority Members: Jan. 26, 2005-Jan. 3, 2007

Service Dates of Minority Members: Jan. 26, 2005-Jan. 3, 2007

Roster Filled: Majority with 6 members, Jan. 26, 2005; Minority with 3 members, Feb. 16, 2005

Majority

Rank Name	Party	State	House	Comm.
Ch1 Ney, Robert W.	Rep	Ohio	6	6
Ch2 2nd Ehlers, Vernon J.	Rep	Mich.	7	6
3rd Mica, John L.	Rep	Fla.	7	5
4th Doolittle, John T.	Rep	Cal.	8	3
5th Reynolds, Thomas M.	Rep	N.Y.	4	3
6th Miller, Candice S.	Rep	Mich.	2	1

Minority

Rank Name	Party	State	House	Comm.
RM Millender-McDonald, Juanita	Dem	Cal.	6	2
2nd Brady, Robert A.	Dem	Penn.	5	2
3rd Lofgren, Zoe	Dem	Cal.	6	1

Vacancies Filled:
Minority:
3rd seat filled by Lofgren on Feb. 16, 2005

Changes:
Majority:

Ney, Robert W.	Rep	Ohio	Jan. 17, 2006 Resigned as Chair of committee due to ethics issues
Ehlers, Vernon J.	Rep	Mich.	Feb. 1, 2006 Elected Chair of House Administration
Ney, Robert W.	Rep	Ohio	Nov. 3, 2006 Resigned the House due to ethics issues

Departures from Committee: Majority / Minority

Became RM on Transportation and Infrastructure	Mica, John L.	Rep	Fla.	None
Moved to Select Energy Independence and Global Warming	Miller, Candice S.	Rep	Mich.	None
Moved to Transportation and Infrastructure	Miller, Candice S.	Rep	Mich.	None
No new assignment	Reynolds, Thomas M.	Rep	N.Y.	
	Doolittle, John T.	Rep	Cal.	

HOUSE ADMINISTRATION / 110th Congress

Service Dates of Committee Chair: Ch1: Jan. 4, 2007-Apr. 22, 2007 Millender-McDonald (Dem-Cal.)

Ch2: May 24, 2007-Jan. 3, 2009 Brady (Dem-Penn.)

Service Dates of Majority Members: Feb. 8, 2007-Jan. 3, 2009

Service Dates of Minority Members: Jan. 4, 2007-Jan. 3, 2009

Roster Filled: Majority with 6 members, Feb. 8, 2007; Minority with 3 members, Jan. 4, 2007

Majority

Rank Name	Party	State	House	Comm.
Ch1 Millender-McDonald, Juanita	Dem	Cal.	7	3
Ch2 2nd Brady, Robert A.	Dem	Penn.	6	3
3rd Lofgren, Zoe	Dem	Cal.	7	2
4th Capuano, Michael E.	Dem	Mass.	5	1
5th Gonzalez, Charles A.	Dem	Tex.	5	1
6th Davis, Susan A.	Dem	Cal.	4	1

Minority

Rank Name	Party	State	House	Comm.
RM Ehlers, Vernon J.	Rep	Mich.	8	7
2nd Lungren, Daniel E.	Rep	Cal.	7	1
3rd McCarthy, Kevin	Rep	Cal.	1	1

Changes:

Majority:

Millender-McDonald, Juanita	Dem	Cal.	Apr. 22, 2007 Died in office
Davis, Artur	Dem	Ala.	May 3, 2007 Replaced Millender-McDonald
Brady, Robert A.	Dem	Penn.	May 24, 2007 Elected Chair of House Administration

Departures from Committee:	**Majority**	**Minority**		
No new assignment	None	Ehlers, Vernon J.	Rep	Mich.

HOUSE ADMINISTRATION / 111th Congress

Service Dates of Committee Chair: Jan. 6, 2009-Jan. 3, 2011

Service Dates of Majority Members: Jan. 13, 2009-Jan. 3, 2011

Service Dates of Minority Members: Jan. 9, 2009-Jan. 3, 2011

Roster Filled: Majority with 6 members, Jan. 13, 2009; Minority with 3 members, Jan. 9, 2009

	Majority			**Terms in:**			**Minority**			**Terms in:**	
Rank Name		**Party**	**State**	**House**	**Comm.**	**Rank Name**		**Party**	**State**	**House**	**Comm.**
Chr Brady, Robert A.		Dem	Penn.	7	4	RM Lungren, Daniel E.		Rep	Cal.	8	2
2nd Lofgren, Zoe		Dem	Cal.	8	3	2nd McCarthy, Kevin		Rep	Cal.	2	2
3rd Capuano, Michael E.		Dem	Mass.	6	2	3rd Harper, Gregg		Rep	Miss.	1	1
4th Gonzalez, Charles A.		Dem	Tex.	6	2						
5th Davis, Susan A.		Dem	Cal.	5	2						
6th Davis, Artur		Dem	Ala.	4	2						

Judiciary

House Committee on the Judiciary, 103rd-111th Congresses (1993-2011)

BACKGROUND

Organizational History: It was on June 3, 1813, that the House Committee on the Judiciary was created pursuant to a resolution offered by John G. Jackson, a Virginia Jeffersonian, and its first chair was Charles J. Ingersoll of Pennsylvania. Ingersoll's father Jared Ingersoll was a signer of the Constitution and was the vice presidential nominee with DeWitt Clinton on the Federalist ticket of 1812 that lost to President James Madison, the Constitution's primary author and Massachusetts governor Elbridge Gerry, its most vocal non-signer. From 1813 to the present, the committee has not had its name changed, joining the House Ways and Means Committee with that unique distinction.

Unlike the Senate Judiciary Committee that has the major responsibility for the appointment of federal judges, the House Judiciary Committee has the power to remove them through the process of impeachment. The House committee brings the impeachment charges and if passed by a simple majority vote in the House the proceedings move to the Senate where an extraordinary two-thirds majority vote is necessary for removal. Before the Judiciary Committee was officially constituted, the House voted impeachments against Sen. William Blount of Tennessee in 1797 and Associate Supreme Court Justice Samuel Chase in 1805 but neither was convicted in the Senate, unlike the unfortunate federal judge John Pickering of New Hampshire, who was removed from office in 1804.

The last thirteen impeachments moved through the Judiciary Committee including those of Presidents Andrew Johnson in 1868 and William J. Clinton in 1998. Those impeachment motions were passed by the House but the Senate failed to convict in both cases. President Richard M. Nixon received three House Judiciary Committee votes for impeachment in 1974 but his resignation on August 9, 1974, stopped the proceedings from moving to the Senate. The other impeached officials were William W. Belknap, President U.S. Grant's Secretary of War and ten federal judges. Three of the judges were impeached and convicted in 1986-89. All three were removed but one. Alcee Hastings of Florida returned to public life and has been a member of the U.S. House since 1993.

The Judiciary Committee has absorbed a number of functions originally intended for other committees. The Legislative Reorganization Act of 1946 gave the House Judiciary Committee the jurisdictions originally handled by the standing committees on Patents (created in 1837), Revision of the Laws (1868), and Immigration and Naturalization (1893). In 1975, the Judiciary Committee was given the jurisdiction over internal security matters which had been the province of the Internal Security Committee and its predecessor, the highly controversial House Committee on Un-American Activities (HUAC), which dated from 1945 as a standing committee.

As contained in the current rules, Judiciary has legislative jurisdiction over civil and criminal proceedings; federal courts and judges; revision and codification of the statutes of the U.S.; claims against the U.S.; bankruptcy; mutiny; espionage; counterfeiting; and immigration and naturalization. The committee also is responsible for constitutional amendments, civil liberties, and national penitentiaries; interstate compacts as well as state and territorial boundary lines. The committee has legislative jurisdiction over matters related to presidential succession, apportionment of representatives, and meetings of Congress, attendance by members, and their acceptance of incompatible offices. The Committee has some responsibility for commerce matters, including protection of trade and commerce from monopolies and unlawful restraints; patents; copyrights; trademarks; and the Patent Office.

Throughout the turbulent decades of the 1950s and 1960s, the House Judiciary Committee led by New York City liberal Democrat Emanuel Celler and the Senate Judiciary Committee led by Mississippi segregationist Democrat James O. Eastland regularly battled over civil rights legislation. Once civil rights bills in the House got through the House Rules Committee chaired by segregationist Howard W. Smith of Virginia, they were passed on the House floor and in spite of Eastland's vocal opposition, most passed into law.

While the Senate Judiciary Committee gains public attention during Supreme Court confirmation hearings, the House Judiciary Committee has been at the center of the political storm twice during presidential impeachment hearings. In 1974, Chair Peter W. Rodino (Dem-N.J.) had to preside over the Judiciary Committee's finest moment when it conducted hearings and took testimony on the Watergate scandal which engulfed the Nixon presidency. Those hearings were handled fairly and competently. At times even eloquent constitutional discourse emanated from the committee, most notably, from Barbara C. Jordan (Dem-Tex.), a first-term member and the first female African-American ever elected from the South. These hearings contributed greatly to positive public feelings towards the House of Representatives in the months which followed. The Judiciary Committee reported favorably three of the five indictments for impeachable offenses to the full House on July 30, 1974. Ten days later, President Nixon resigned his office.

The committee also has jurisdiction over the hundreds of amendments to the Constitution that are submitted to Congress. In the case of the Twenty-fifth Amendment, the Presidential Succession and Disability Amendment, the Judiciary Committee has jurisdiction over presidential nominations to fill vacancies in the vice presidency. Twice this occurred: in 1973 when Vice President Spiro T. Agnew resigned and was replaced by House Minority leader Gerald R. Ford Jr. (Rep-Mich.) and again in 1974 following the Nixon resignation when newly sworn President Ford submitted the name of New York governor Nelson A. Rockefeller to fill the vice presidency

The 1974 Watergate hearings were almost non-partisan with many Republicans joining the Democratic majority's votes regarding President Nixon's involvement in the Watergate coverup. However, the sexual misconduct hearings of 1998 against President Bill Clinton were highly partisan as conservative Republicans led by Judiciary Chair Henry J. Hyde (Rep-Ill.) tried to remove the president from office on two narrowly framed charges. Both charges were voted down handily in the Senate. The House votes on perjury were 228 to 206 and on obstruction of justice, 221 to 212. Needing a 2/3 vote of 67 in the Senate, the first article was voted down 50 to 50 while the second was voted down 45 to 55. Thirteen Republican House Judiciary Committee members served as managers of the impeachment in the Senate in 1999, but no one on that committee emerged as particularly heroic or eloquent.

Immigration issues also come before the Judiciary Committee and the highly charged atmosphere of Democrats on one side, supporting immigration reform that will enable illegal aliens to gain some form of citizenship through amnesty provisions and Republicans on the other, vocally opposed to those provisions will once again keep the Judiciary Committee rife with contention.

Membership: There were twenty-seven members of the Judiciary Committee in the 79th Congress and twenty-seven in the 80th. The 1946 reorganization had no impact upon the committee's size even though it absorbed the functions of three standing committees which had a total of fifty-five seats between them. The committee's membership size has been relatively stable. It began the post-1947 era with twenty-seven members and peaked at thirty-eight in 1971-1975. That high water mark in prestige and effectiveness was hard to sustain and Judiciary's attractiveness waned. By 1981, the committee's size had shrunk by ten places from its 1971-1975 peaks to twenty-eight places. It grew back to thirty-five and hovered between thirty-five to thirty-seven members from 1985 to 2005 when it stabilized at forty members, its present size.

Although the Judiciary Committee's mean size of 37.6 members in the past nine Congresses only ranked it fourteenth among the nineteen continuing House committees; its relatively high mean seniority of 5.72 terms ranked it fifth and its very high retention rate of 92.08 percent was the fourth highest among the continuing House committees.

Committee Leaders: Not only has the Judiciary Committee's membership been stable, so has its leadership. Both the committee's first post-reorganization chair Earl C. Michener (Rep-Mich.) and its ranking member Emanuel Celler (Dem-N.Y.) began their senior service in 1947. While Michener would retire in 1951, Manny Celler remained as Judiciary's senior Democrat until his defeat for renomination in 1972. First serving as the committee's senior Republican during the Celler era was Chauncey W. Reed (Rep-Ill.), the committee's chair in the Republican 83rd Congress and its ranking member in the Democratic Congresses. Reed's death in 1956 led Kenneth B. Keating (Rep-N.Y.) to become ranking member, a post he held until his 1958 election to the U.S. Senate. Keating's successor, William M. McCulloch (Rep-Ohio) served as ranking member until his retirement in 1973, during which time he played a major role in providing bipartisan support for the far-reaching civil rights legislation of the 1960s.

The 93rd Congress opened in 1973 with two new senior members leading the Judiciary Committee—Chair Peter W. Rodino (Dem-N.J.) and ranking member J. Edward Hutchinson (Rep-Mich.)—during the dramatic "Watergate" crisis that would lead the committee in 1974 to vote three articles of impeachment against President Richard Nixon and to the first and only presidential resignation in American history. Hutchinson retired in 1977 and was succeeded first by Robert McClory (Rep-Ill.), 1977-1983 and then by Hamilton Fish Jr. (Rep-N.Y)—from the fourth generation of Hamilton Fishes to sit in Congress—who held the ranking slot from 1983 to 1995. Peter Rodino continued as chair until his retirement in 1989 when he was succeeded by Jack B. Brooks (Dem-Tex.) who left the chairmanship of Government Operations to chair Judiciary and served until his defeat in the 1994 Republican landslide.

As happened twice before, the 104th Congress opened in 1995 with new senior members—Chair Henry J. Hyde (Rep-Ill.) and ranking member John Conyers Jr. (Dem-Mich.), the first African-American to serve on Judiciary. Hyde chaired the committee for three Congresses, 1995-2001, until Republican Conference rules obliged him to step aside for F. James Sensenbrenner Jr. (Rep-Wisc.) who took over the committee while Hyde moved to chair International Relations. Sensenbrenner chaired his allotted three Congresses, 2001-2007 and relinquished the senior slot to Lamar S. Smith (Rep-Tex.) in 2007. With the Democrats return to power in 2007, John Conyers, who had served twelve years as ranking member became chair for the first time, a post he still holds.

Party Leaders: The House Judiciary Committee has not been a fertile source for House party leaders. No modern-era Speakers or floor leaders served on the committee and the only party whip was Republican C. Trent Lott of Mississippi, who served as whip from 1981 to 1989 before his election to the Senate.

Notable Members: None of the House Judiciary Committee alumni were nominated for president and only two were nominated for vice president—Democrat C. Estes Kefauver of Tennessee, Adlai Stevenson's running-mate in 1956, and William E. Miller of New York, who was Barry M. Goldwater's running-mate in 1964. A case could be made to include membership on the infamous HUAC (later the Committee on Internal Security), much of whose jurisdiction ended up in Judiciary. That would add Richard M. Nixon to the list, since Miller already served on both committees. The only two Cabinet members to have served on House Judiciary were both appointed by President Bill Clinton later in his administration—Dan Glickman (Dem-Kans.) as Secretary of Agriculture in 1995 and William S. Cohen (Rep-Maine) as Secretary of Defense in 1997. Although a Republican, Cohen's strong pro-impeachment stance during the Watergate hearings and his vigorous questioning of Reagan foreign policy operatives during the "Iran-Contra" hearings of the late 1980s endeared him to many Democrats.

Besides Senators Kefauver and Cohen, twenty other House Judiciary members would move to the Senate including eight Democrats—Paul S. Sarbanes and Benjamin L. Cardin of Maryland, Joseph Montoya of New Mexico, James G. Abourezk of South Dakota, Richard C. Shelby of Alabama, Christopher J. Dodd of Connecticut, Charles E. Schumer of New York, and John F. Reed of Rhode Island.

Twelve other Republicans moved through House Judiciary en route to the Senate—J. Caleb Boggs of Delaware, moderates Hugh D. Scott of Pennsylvania, Clifford P. Case of New Jersey, Kenneth B. Keating of New York, and Charles McC. Mathias Jr. of Maryland, as well as William V. Roth Jr. of Delaware, C. Trent Lott of Mississippi, George F. Allen of Virginia, Hank Brown of Colorado, Lindsey O. Graham of South Carolina, David Vitter of Louisiana, and Michael DeWine of Ohio, who detoured into the Lt. Governor's office before joining the Senate. The only post-1947 member of House Judiciary to serve in the Senate before serving in the House was John M. Robsion (Rep-Ky.).

Five Republican governors: J. Caleb Boggs of Delaware, Arch A. Moore Jr. of West Virginia, Thomas J. Meskill of Connecticut, William T. Cahill of New Jersey, and George F. Allen of Virginia, as well as Democratic Governor Edwin W. Edwards of Louisiana, saw service on House Judiciary before returning home to run for governor. The one former governor elected to the House who served on Judiciary was William M. Tuck of Virginia. Both Edwards and Tuck served on the highly controversial HUAC. Tuck served on HUAC while Edwards served on its renamed version, Internal Security.

Selected References

Fish, Hamilton Jr., "Antitrust Relief and the House Judiciary Committee," *Antitrust Bulletin*, 35 (Spring, 1990), 219-249.

Granberg, Donald, "An Analysis of the House Judiciary Committee's Recommendation to Impeach Richard Nixon," *Political Psychology*, 2 (Fall, 1980), 50-65.

Perkins, Lynette P., "Influence of Members' Goals on Their Committee Behavior: The U.S. House Judiciary Committee," *Legislative Studies Quarterly*, 5 (1980), 373-392.

Perkins, Lynette P., "Member Recruitment to a Mixed Goal Committee: The House Judiciary Committee," *Journal of Politics*, 43 (1981), 348-364.

Schamel, Charles E. et al., "Records of the Judiciary Committee and Related Committees," *Guide to the Records of the United States House of Representatives at the National Archives: 1789-1989 Bicentennial Edition* (Washington, D.C.: National Archives and Records Administration,1989), 201-218.

Schuck, Peter H., *The Judiciary Committees: A Study of the House and Senate Judiciary Committees* in the Ralph Nader Congress Project (New York: Grossman, 1975).

U.S. House of Representatives, Committee on the Judiciary, *History of the Committee on the Judiciary of the House of Representatives*, H.Doc. 80-366, 80th Congress, 1st Session (1947). Updated in the 92nd Congress, 2nd Session (1972) and the 97th Congress, 2nd Session (1982).

RESPONSIBILITIES, JURISDICTIONAL CHANGES, AND SUBCOMMITTEES

JUDICIARY

Jurisdiction, 80th Congress (1947-1949)

Established by the Legislative Reorganization Act of 1946:

[Section 121.(1)(l)] Committee on the Judiciary
  (1) Judicial proceedings, civil and criminal, generally.
  (2) Constitutional amendments.
  (3) Federal courts and judges.
  (4) Local courts in the Territories and possessions.
  (5) Revision and codification of the statutes of the United States.
  (6) National penitentiaries.
  (7) Protection of trade and commerce against unlawful restraints and monopolies.
  (8) Holidays and celebrations.
  (9) Bankruptcy, mutiny, espionage, and counterfeiting.
  (10) State and Territorial boundary lines.
  (11) Meetings of Congress, attendance of Members, and their acceptance of incompatible offices.
  (12) Civil liberties.
  (13) Patents, copyrights, and trade-marks.
  (14) Patent Office.
  (15) Immigration and naturalization.
  (16) Apportionment of Representatives.
  (17) Measures relating to claims against the United States.
  (18) Interstate compacts generally.
  (19) Presidential succession.

Jurisdiction, 103rd Congress (1993-1995)

From the *Rules of the House of Representatives, 103rd Congress* (House Document 102-405)

[Rule X.1.(m)] Committee on the Judiciary
  (1) Judicial proceedings, civil and criminal generally.
  (2) Apportionment of Representatives.
  (3) Bankruptcy, mutiny, espionage, and counterfeiting.
  (4) Civil liberties.
  (5) Constitutional amendments.
  (6) Federal courts and judges.

(7) Immigration and naturalization.
(8) Interstate compacts generally.
(9) Local courts in the Territories and possessions.
(10) Measures relating to claims against the United States.
(11) Meetings of Congress, attendance of Members and their acceptance of incompatible offices.
(12) National penitentiaries.
(13) Patent Office.
(14) Patents, copyrights, and trademarks.
(15) Presidential succession.
(16) Protection of trade and commerce against unlawful restraints and monopolies.
(17) Revision and codification of the Statutes of the United States.
(18) State and territorial boundary lines.
(19) Communist and other subversive activities affecting the internal security of the United States.

Jurisdiction, 104th Congress (1995-1997) Changes in Committee System

From H. Res. 6, Section 202 (a), the Committees and Their Jurisdiction, January 4, 1995

[Rule X.1.(j)] Committee on the Judiciary

(1) The judiciary and judicial proceedings, civil and criminal.
(2) Administrative practice and procedure.
(3) Apportionment of Representatives.
(4) Bankruptcy, mutiny, espionage, and counterfeiting.
(5) Civil liberties.
(6) Constitutional amendments.
(7) Federal courts and judges, and local courts in the Territories and possessions.
(8) Immigration and naturalization.
(9) Interstate compacts, generally.
(10) Measures relating to claims against the United States.
(11) Meetings of Congress, attendance of Members and their acceptance of incompatible offices.
(12) National penitentiaries.
(13) Patents, the Patent Office, copyrights, and trademarks.
(14) Presidential succession.
(15) Protection of trade and commerce against unlawful restraints and monopolies.
(16) Revision and codification of the Statutes of the United States.
(17) State and territorial boundaries.
(18) Subversive activities affecting the internal security of the United States.

Jurisdiction, 111th Congress (2009-2011)

From the *Rules of the House of Representatives* (as revised to June 16, 2009, H.Doc. 110-162):

[Rule X.1.(k)] Committee on the Judiciary

(1) The judiciary and judicial proceedings, civil and criminal.
(2) Administrative practice and procedure.
(3) Apportionment of Representatives.
(4) Bankruptcy, mutiny, espionage, and counterfeiting.
(5) Civil liberties.
(6) Constitutional amendments.
(7) Criminal law enforcement
(8) Federal courts and judges, and local courts in the Territories and possessions.
(9) Immigration policy and non-border enforcement
(10) Interstate compacts generally.
(11) Claims against the United States.
(12) Meetings of Congress; attendance of Members, Delegates, and the Resident Commissioner; and their acceptance of incompatible offices.
(13) National penitentiaries.
(14) Patents, the Patent and Trademark Office, copyrights, and trademarks.
(15) Presidential succession.
(16) Protection of trade and commerce against unlawful restraints and monopolies.
(17) Revision and codification of the Statutes of the United States.
(18) State and territorial boundary lines.
(19) Subversive activities affecting the internal security of the United States.

NAMES OF JUDICIARY SUBCOMMITTEES FROM THE *CONGRESSIONAL DIRECTORY*

Administrative Law and Governmental Relations, 103
Civil and Constitutional Rights, 103
Commercial and Administrative Law, 104, 105, 106, 107, 108, 109, 110, 111
[The] Constitution, 104, 105, 106, 107, 108, 109
The Constitution, Civil Rights, and Civil Liberties, 110, 111
Courts and Intellectual Property, 104, 105, 106
Courts, the Internet, and Intellectual Property, 107, 108, 109, 110
Courts and Competition Policy, 111
Crime, 104, 105, 106, 107
Crime and Criminal Justice, 103
Crime, Terrorism, and Homeland Security, 108, 109, 110, 111
Economic and Commercial Law, 103
Immigration and Claims, 104, 105, 106, 107
Immigration, Border Security and Claims, 108, 109
Immigration, Citizenship, Refugees, Border Security, and International Law, 110, 111
Intellectual Property and Judicial Administration, 103
International Law, Immigration, and Refugees, 103
Taskforce on Antitrust

MEMBERSHIP ROSTERS, 103rd-111th Congresses, 1993-2011

JUDICIARY / 103rd Congress

Service Dates of Committee Chair: Jan. 5, 1993-Jan. 3, 1995

Service Dates of Majority Members: Jan. 5, 1993-Jan. 3, 1995

Service Dates of Minority Members: Jan. 5, 1993-Jan. 3, 1995

Roster Filled: Majority with 21 members on Jan. 21, 1993; Minority with 14 members on Jan. 5, 1993

Majority

Rank Name	Party	State	House	Comm.
Chr Brooks, Jack B.	Dem	Tex.	21	20
2nd Edwards, William D. (Don)	Dem	Cal.	16	16
3rd Conyers, John Jr.	Dem	Mich.	15	15
4th Mazzoli, Romano L.	Dem	Ky.	12	10
5th Hughes, William J.	Dem	N.J.	10	10
6th Synar, Michael L.	Dem	Okla.	8	8
7th Schroeder, Patricia S.	Dem	Colo.	11	7
8th Glickman, Daniel R.	Dem	Kans.	9	8
9th Frank, Barney	Dem	Mass.	7	7
10th Schumer, Charles E.	Dem	N.Y.	7	6
11th Berman, Howard L.	Dem	Cal.	6	6
12th Boucher, Frederick C.	Dem	Va.	6	6
13th Bryant, John W.	Dem	Tex.	6	5
14th Sangmeister, George E.	Dem	Ill.	3	3
15th Washington, Craig A.	Dem	Tex.	3	3
16th Reed, John F.	Dem	R.I.	2	2
17th Nadler, Jerrold	Dem	N.Y.	2	1
18th Scott, Robert C.	Dem	Va.	1	1
19th Mann, David S.	Dem	Ohio	1	1
20th Watt, Melvin L.	Dem	N.C.	1	1
21st Becerra, Xavier	Dem	Cal.	1	1

Minority

Rank Name	Party	State	House	Comm.
RM Fish, Hamilton Jr.	Rep	N.Y.	13	13
2nd Moorhead, Carlos J.	Rep	Cal.	11	11
3rd Hyde, Henry J.	Rep	Ill.	10	10
4th Sensenbrenner, F. James Jr.	Rep	Wisc.	8	8
5th McCollum, Ira W. (Bill) Jr.	Rep	Fla.	7	7
6th Gekas, George W.	Rep	Penn.	6	6
7th Coble, Howard	Rep	N.C.	5	5
8th Smith, Lamar S.	Rep	Tex.	4	4
9th Schiff, Steven H.	Rep	N.M.	3	2
10th Ramstad, James	Rep	Minn.	2	2
11th Gallegly, Elton W.	Rep	Cal.	4	1
12th Canady, Charles T.	Rep	Fla.	1	1
13th Inglis, Robert D.	Rep	S.C.	1	*1 1
14th Goodlatte, Robert W.	Rep	Va.	1	1

*1: Member's first period of service on the committee.

Vacancies Filled:
  Majority:
    21st seat filled by Becerra on Jan. 21, 1993

Departures from the House:	Majority			Minority
Defeated for Re-nomination	Synar, Michael L.	Dem	La.	None
	Washington, Craig A.	Dem	Tex.	

Defeated for Re-election	Brooks, Jack B.	Dem	Tex.			
	Glickman, Daniel R.	Dem	Kans.			
	Mann, David S.	Dem	Ohio			
Retired	Edwards, William D. (Don)	Dem	Cal.	Fish, Hamilton Jr.	Rep	N.Y.
	Mazzoli, Romano L.	Dem	Ky.			
	Hughes, William J.	Dem	N.J.			
	Sangmeister, George E.	Dem	Ill.			

Departures from Committee:

Moved to Ways and Means	None			Ramstad, James	Rep	Minn.

JUDICIARY / 104th Congress

Service Dates of Committee Chair: Jan. 4, 1995-Jan. 3, 1997

Service Dates of Majority Members: Jan. 4, 1995-Jan. 3, 1997

Service Dates of Minority Members: Jan. 4, 1995-Jan. 3, 1997

Roster Filled: Majority with 20 members on Jan. 4, 1995; Minority with 15 members on Jan. 4, 1995

	Majority						Minority				
				Terms in:						**Terms in:**	
Rank Name	Party	State	House	Comm.		Rank Name	Party	State	House	Comm.
Chr Hyde, Henry J.	Rep	Ill.	11	11		RM Conyers, John Jr.	Dem	Mich.	16	16
2nd Moorhead, Carlos J.	Rep	Cal.	12	12		2nd Schroeder, Patricia S.	Dem	Colo.	12	8
3rd Sensenbrenner, F. James Jr.	Rep	Wisc.	9	9		3rd Frank, Barney	Dem	Mass.	8	8
4th McCollum, Ira W. (Bill) Jr.	Rep	Fla.	8	8		4th Schumer, Charles E.	Dem	N.Y.	8	7
5th Gekas, George W.	Rep	Penn.	7	7		5th Berman, Howard L.	Dem	Cal.	7	7
6th Coble, Howard	Rep	N.C.	6	6		6th Boucher, Frederick C.	Dem	Va.	7	7
7th Smith, Lamar S.	Rep	Tex.	5	5		7th Bryant, John W.	Dem	Tex.	7	6
8th Schiff, Steven H.	Rep	N.M.	4	3		8th Reed, John F.	Dem	R.I.	3	3
9th Gallegly, Elton W.	Rep	Cal.	5	2		9th Nadler, Jerrold	Dem	N.Y.	3	2
10th Canady, Charles T.	Rep	Fla.	2	2		10th Scott, Robert C.	Dem	Va.	2	2
11th Inglis, Robert D.	Rep	S.C.	2	*1 2		11th Watt, Melvin L.	Dem	N.C.	2	2
12th Goodlatte, Robert W.	Rep	Va.	2	2		12th Becerra, Xavier	Dem	Cal.	2	2
13th Buyer, Stephen E.	Rep	Ind.	2	1		13th Serrano, Jose E.	Dem	N.Y.	4	1
14th Hoke, Martin R.	Rep	Ohio	2	1		14th Lofgren, Zoe	Dem	Cal.	1	1
15th Bono, Sonny	Rep	Cal.	1	1		15th Jackson-Lee, Sheila	Dem	Tex.	1	1
16th Heineman, Fred	Rep	N.C.	1	1						
17th Bryant, Ed	Rep	Tenn.	1	*1 1		*1: Member's first period of service on the committee				
18th Chabot, Steven J.	Rep	Ohio	1	1						
19th Flanagan, Michael Patrick	Rep	Ill.	1	1						
20th Barr, Bob	Rep	Ga.	1	1						

Changes:

  Minority:

Serrano, Jose E.	Dem	N.Y.	Mar. 14, 1996 Resigned committee; returned to Appropriations
Waters, Maxine	Dem	Cal.	Apr. 25, 1996 Replaced Serrano

Departures from the House:

	Majority				Minority		
Elected to U.S. Senate	None				Reed, John F.	Dem	R.I.
Lost Nomination to U.S. Senate	None				Bryant, John W.	Dem	Tex.
Defeated for Re-election	Hoke, Martin R.	Rep	Ohio		None		
	Heineman, Fred	Rep	N.C.				
	Flanagan, Michael Patrick	Rep	Ill.				
Retired	Moorhead, Carlos J.	Rep	Cal.		Schroeder, Patricia S.	Dem	Colo.

Departures from Committee:

Moved to Ways and Means	None			Becerra, Xavier	Dem	Cal.

JUDICIARY / 105th Congress

Service Dates of Committee Chair: Jan. 7, 1997-Jan. 3, 1999

Service Dates of Majority Members: Jan. 7, 1997-Jan. 3, 1999

Service Dates of Minority Members: Jan. 7, 1997-Jan. 3, 1999

Roster Filled: Majority with 20 members on Jan. 7, 1997; Minority with 15 members on Jan. 7, 1997

Majority						Minority				
			Terms in:						**Terms in:**	
Rank Name	**Party**	**State**	**House**	**Comm.**		**Rank Name**	**Party**	**State**	**House**	**Comm.**
Chr Hyde, Henry J.	Rep	Ill.	12	12		RM Conyers, John Jr.	Dem	Mich.	17	17
2nd Sensenbrenner, F. James Jr.	Rep	Wisc.	10	10		2nd Frank, Barney	Dem	Mass.	9	9
3rd McCollum, Ira W. (Bill) Jr.	Rep	Fla.	9	9		3rd Schumer, Charles E.	Dem	N.Y.	9	8
4th Gekas, George W.	Rep	Penn.	8	8		4th Berman, Howard L.	Dem	Cal.	8	8
5th Coble, Howard	Rep	N.C.	7	7		5th Boucher, Frederick C.	Dem	Va.	8	8
6th Smith, Lamar S.	Rep	Tex.	6	6		6th Nadler, Jerrold	Dem	N.Y.	4	3
7th Schiff, Steven H.	Rep	N.M.	5	4		7th Scott, Robert C.	Dem	Va.	3	3
8th Gallegly, Elton W.	Rep	Cal.	6	3		8th Watt, Melvin L.	Dem	N.C.	3	3
9th Canady, Charles T.	Rep	Fla.	3	3		9th Lofgren, Zoe	Dem	Cal.	2	2
10th Inglis, Robert D.	Rep	S.C.	3	*1 3		10th Jackson-Lee, Sheila	Dem	Tex.	2	2
11th Goodlatte, Robert W.	Rep	Va.	3	3		11th Waters, Maxine	Dem	Cal.	4	2
12th Buyer, Stephen E.	Rep	Ind.	3	2		12th Meehan, Martin T.	Dem	Mass.	3	1
13th Bono, Sonny	Rep	Cal.	2	2		13th Delahunt, William D.	Dem	Mass.	1	1
14th Bryant, Ed	Rep	Tenn.	2	*1 2		14th Wexler, Robert	Dem	Fla.	1	1
15th Chabot, Steven J.	Rep	Ohio	2	2		15th Rothman, Steven R.	Dem	N.J.	1	1
16th Barr, Bob	Rep	Ga.	2	2						
17th Jenkins, William L.	Rep	Tenn.	1	1		*1: Member's first period of service on the committee				
18th Hutchinson, Asa	Rep	Ark.	1	1						
19th Pease, Edward A.	Rep	Ind.	1	1						
20th Cannon, Christopher B.	Rep	Utah	1	1						

Additions:
  Majority:

21st Graham, Lindsey O.	Rep	S.C.	Feb. 26, 1998	

  Minority:

16th Barrett, Thomas M.	Dem	Wisc.	Sep. 11, 1998	

Changes:
  Majority:

Bono, Sonny	Rep	Cal.	Jan. 5, 1998 Died in office	
Rogan, James E.	Rep	Cal.	Feb. 11, 1998 Replaced Bono, ranked after Cannon	
Schiff, Steven H.	Rep	N.M.	Mar. 25, 1998 Died in office	
Bono, Mary	Rep	Cal.	May 13, 1998 Replaced Schiff	

Departures from the House:

	Majority			**Minority**		
Elected to U.S. Senate	None			Schumer, Charles E.	Dem	N.Y.
Lost Election to U.S. Senate	Inglis, Robert D.	Rep	S.C.	None		

Departures from Committee:

Moved to Commerce	None		Barrett, Thomas M.	Dem	Wisc.

JUDICIARY / 106th Congress

Service Dates of Committee Chair: Jan. 6, 1999-Jan. 3, 2001

Service Dates of Majority Members: Jan. 6, 1999-Jan. 3, 2001

Service Dates of Minority Members: Jan. 6, 1999-Jan. 3, 2001

Roster Filled: Majority with 21 members on Feb. 2, 1999; Minority with 16 members on Jan. 6, 1999

Majority						Minority				
			Terms in:						**Terms in:**	
Rank Name	**Party**	**State**	**House**	**Comm.**		**Rank Name**	**Party**	**State**	**House**	**Comm.**
Chr Hyde, Henry J.	Rep	Ill.	13	13		RM Conyers, John Jr.	Dem	Mich.	18	18
2nd Sensenbrenner, F. James Jr.	Rep	Wisc.	11	11		2nd Frank, Barney	Dem	Mass.	10	10
3rd McCollum, Ira W. (Bill) Jr.	Rep	Fla.	10	10		3rd Berman, Howard L.	Dem	Cal.	9	9
4th Gekas, George W.	Rep	Penn.	9	9		4th Boucher, Frederick C.	Dem	Va.	9	9
5th Coble, Howard	Rep	N.C.	8	8		5th Nadler, Jerrold	Dem	N.Y.	5	4
6th Smith, Lamar S.	Rep	Tex.	7	7		6th Scott, Robert C.	Dem	Va.	4	4
7th Gallegly, Elton W.	Rep	Cal.	7	4		7th Watt, Melvin L.	Dem	N.C.	4	4
8th Canady, Charles T.	Rep	Fla.	4	4		8th Lofgren, Zoe	Dem	Cal.	3	3
9th Goodlatte, Robert W.	Rep	Va.	4	4		9th Jackson-Lee, Sheila	Dem	Tex.	3	3

10th Buyer, Stephen E.	Rep	Ind.	4	3	
11th Bryant, Ed	Rep	Tenn.	3	*1 3	
12th Chabot, Steven J.	Rep	Ohio	3	3	
13th Barr, Bob	Rep	Ga.	3	3	
14th Jenkins, William L.	Rep	Tenn.	2	2	
15th Hutchinson, Asa	Rep	Ark.	2	2	
16th Pease, Edward A.	Rep	Ind.	2	2	
17th Cannon, Christopher B.	Rep	Utah	2	2	
18th Rogan, James E.	Rep	Cal.	2	2	
19th Graham, Lindsey O.	Rep	S.C.	3	2	
20th Bono, Mary	Rep	Cal.	2	2	
21st Bachus, Spencer T.	Rep	Ala.	4	1	

10th Waters, Maxine	Dem	Cal.	5	3	
11th Meehan, Martin T.	Dem	Mass.	4	2	
12th Delahunt, William D.	Dem	Mass.	2	2	
13th Wexler, Robert	Dem	Fla.	2	2	
14th Rothman, Steven R.	Dem	N.J.	2	2	
15th Baldwin, Tammy	Dem	Wisc.	1	*1 1	
16th Weiner, Anthony D.	Dem	N.Y.	1	1	

*1: Member's first period of service on the committee

Vacancies Filled:
  Majority:
      21st seat filled by Bachus on Feb. 2, 1999

Changes:
  Majority:

Buyer, Stephen E.	Rep	Ind.	Feb. 25, 1999 Resigned committee and requested rescission of waiver to serve on 3 standing committees
Scarborough, C. Joseph	Rep	Fla.	Mar. 11, 1999 Replaced Buyer
Bryant, Ed	Rep	Tenn.	June 24, 1999 Resigned committee to open seat for Vitter; no new assignment
Vitter, David	Rep	La.	June 25, 1999 Replaced Bryant

Departures from the House:	**Majority**			**Minority**
Lost Election to U.S. Senate	McCollum, Ira W. (Bill) Jr.	Rep	Fla.	None
Defeated for Re-election	Rogan, James E.	Rep	Cal.	None
Retired	Canady, Charles T.	Rep	Fla.	None
	Pease, Edward A.	Rep	Ind.	

Departures from Committee:				**Minority**
Moved to Appropriations	Vitter, David	Rep	La.	None
Moved to Energy and Commerce	Bono, Mary	Rep	Cal.	

JUDICIARY / 107th Congress

Service Dates of Committee Chair: Jan. 6, 2001-Jan. 3, 2003

Service Dates of Majority Members: Jan. 6, 2001-Jan. 3, 2003

Service Dates of Minority Members: Jan. 31, 2001-Jan. 3, 2003

Roster Filled: Majority with 21 members on Jan. 6, 2001; Minority with 16 members on Jan. 31, 2001

Majority			Terms in:		**Minority**			Terms in:	
Rank Name	**Party**	**State**	**House**	**Comm.**	**Rank Name**	**Party**	**State**	**House**	**Comm.**
Chr Sensenbrenner, F. James Jr.	Rep	Wisc.	12	12	RM Conyers, John Jr.	Dem	Mich.	19	19
2nd Hyde, Henry J.	Rep	Ill.	14	14	2nd Frank, Barney	Dem	Mass.	11	11
3rd Gekas, George W.	Rep	Penn.	10	10	3rd Berman, Howard L.	Dem	Cal.	10	10
4th Coble, Howard	Rep	N.C.	9	9	4th Boucher, Frederick C.	Dem	Va.	10	10
5th Smith, Lamar S.	Rep	Tex.	8	8	5th Nadler, Jerrold	Dem	N.Y.	6	5
6th Gallegly, Elton W.	Rep	Cal.	8	5	6th Scott, Robert C.	Dem	Va.	5	5
7th Goodlatte, Robert W.	Rep	Va.	5	5	7th Watt, Melvin L.	Dem	N.C.	5	5
8th Chabot, Steven J.	Rep	Ohio	4	4	8th Lofgren, Zoe	Dem	Cal.	4	4
9th Barr, Bob	Rep	Ga.	4	4	9th Jackson-Lee, Sheila	Dem	Tex.	4	4
10th Jenkins, William L.	Rep	Tenn.	3	3	10th Waters, Maxine	Dem	Cal.	6	4
11th Hutchinson, Asa	Rep	Ark.	3	3	11th Meehan, Martin T.	Dem	Mass.	5	3
12th Cannon, Christopher B.	Rep	Utah	3	3	12th Delahunt, William D.	Dem	Mass.	3	3
13th Graham, Lindsey O.	Rep	S.C.	4	3	13th Wexler, Robert	Dem	Fla.	3	3
14th Bachus, Spencer T.	Rep	Ala.	5	2	14th Rothman, Steven R.	Dem	N.J.	3	3
15th Scarborough, C. Joseph	Rep	Fla.	4	2	15th Baldwin, Tammy	Dem	Wisc.	2	*1 2
16th Hostettler, John N.	Rep	Ind.	4	1	16th Weiner, Anthony D.	Dem	N.Y.	2	2
17th Green, Mark	Rep	Wisc.	2	1					
18th Keller, Richard (Ric)	Rep	Fla.	1	1					
19th Issa, Darrell E.	Rep	Cal.	1	*1 1					

*1: Member's first period of service on the committee.

20th Hart, Melissa A.	Rep	Penn.	1	1
21st Flake, Jeff	Rep	Ariz.	1	1

Changes:

Majority:

Hutchinson, Asa	Rep	Ark.	Aug. 6, 2001 Resigned the House; appointed Director of the Drug Enforcement Administration
Scarborough, C. Joseph	Rep	Fla.	Sept. 6, 2001 Resigned the House; to begin a media career
Bryant, Ed	Rep	Tenn.	Oct. 2, 2001 Returned to committee; replacing Hutchinson and ranked after Goodlatte
Pence, Mike	Rep	Ind.	Oct. 2, 2001 Replaced Scarborough
Bryant, Ed	Rep	Tenn.	May 16, 2002 Resigned committee; no new assignment
Forbes, J. Randy	Rep	Va.	May 16, 2002 Replaced Bryant

Minority:

Rothman, Steven R.	Dem	N.J.	Feb. 7, 2001 Resigned committee; moved to Appropriations
Schiff, Adam B.	Dem	Cal.	Feb. 8, 2001 Replaced Rothman

Departures from the House:	**Majority**			**Minority**		
Elected to U.S. Senate	Graham, Lindsey O.	Rep	S.C.	None		
Lost Election to U.S. Senate	Bryant, Ed	Rep	Tenn.	None		
Defeated for Re-nomination	Barr, Bob	Rep	Ga.	None		
Defeated for Re-election	Gekas, George W.	Rep	Penn.	None		

Departures from Committee:						
Became RM on Financial Services	None			Frank, Barney	Dem	Mass.
Moved to Energy and Commerce	Issa, Darrell E.	Rep	Cal.	None		
Moved to Select Homeland Security	None			Frank, Barney	Dem	Mass.

JUDICIARY / 108th Congress

Service Dates of Committee Chair: Jan. 8, 2003-Jan. 3, 2005

Service Dates of Majority Members: Jan. 28, 2003-Jan. 3, 2005

Service Dates of Ranking Member: Jan. 8, 2003-Jan. 3, 2005

Service Dates of Minority Members: Jan. 28, 2003-Jan. 3, 2005

Roster Filled: Majority with 21 members on Jan. 28, 2003; Minority with 16 members on Jan. 28, 2003

Majority			**Terms in:**		**Minority**			**Terms in:**	
Rank Name	**Party**	**State**	**House**	**Comm.**	**Rank Name**	**Party**	**State**	**House**	**Comm.**
Chr Sensenbrenner, F. James Jr.	Rep	Wisc.	13	13	RM Conyers, John Jr.	Dem	Mich.	20	20
2nd Hyde, Henry J.	Rep	Ill.	15	15	2nd Berman, Howard L.	Dem	Cal.	11	11
3rd Coble, Howard	Rep	N.C.	10	10	3rd Boucher, Frederick C.	Dem	Va.	11	11
4th Smith, Lamar S.	Rep	Tex.	9	9	4th Nadler, Jerrold	Dem	N.Y.	7	6
5th Gallegly, Elton W.	Rep	Cal.	9	6	5th Scott, Robert C.	Dem	Va.	6	6
6th Goodlatte, Robert W.	Rep	Va.	6	6	6th Watt, Melvin L.	Dem	N.C.	6	6
7th Chabot, Steven J.	Rep	Ohio	5	5	7th Lofgren, Zoe	Dem	Cal.	5	5
8th Jenkins, William L.	Rep	Tenn.	4	4	8th Jackson-Lee, Sheila	Dem	Tex.	5	5
9th Cannon, Christopher B.	Rep	Utah	4	4	9th Waters, Maxine	Dem	Cal.	7	5
10th Bachus, Spencer T.	Rep	Ala.	6	3	10th Meehan, Martin T.	Dem	Mass.	6	4
11th Hostettler, John N.	Rep	Ind.	5	2	11th Delahunt, William D.	Dem	Mass.	4	4
12th Green, Mark	Rep	Wisc.	3	2	12th Wexler, Robert	Dem	Fla.	4	4
13th Keller, Richard (Ric)	Rep	Fla.	2	2	13th Baldwin, Tammy	Dem	Wisc.	3	*1 3
14th Hart, Melissa A.	Rep	Penn.	2	2	14th Weiner, Anthony D.	Dem	N.Y.	3	3
15th Flake, Jeff	Rep	Ariz.	2	2	15th Schiff, Adam B.	Dem	Cal.	2	2
16th Pence, Mike	Rep	Ind.	2	2	16th Sánchez, Linda	Dem	Cal.	1	1
17th Forbes, J. Randy	Rep	Va.	2	2					
18th King, Steve	Rep	Iowa	1	1					
19th Carter, John R.	Rep	Tex.	1	1					
20th Feeney, Tom	Rep	Fla.	1	1					
21st Blackburn, Marsha	Rep	Tenn.	1	1					

*1: Member's first period of service on the committee.

Departures from the House:	**Majority**			**Minority**		
Moved to Appropriations	Carter, John R.	Rep	Tex.	None		
Moved to Energy and Commerce	Blackburn, Marsha	Rep	Tenn.	Baldwin, Tammy	Dem	Wisc.
Moved to Standards of Official Conduct	Hart, Melissa A.	Rep	Penn.	None		
Moved to Ways and Means	Hart, Melissa A.	Rep	Penn.	None		

JUDICIARY / 109th Congress

Service Dates of Committee Chair: Jan. 6, 2005-Jan. 3, 2007

Service Dates of Majority Members: Jan. 26, 2005-Jan. 3, 2007

Service Dates of Minority Members: Jan. 26, 2005-Jan. 3, 2007

Roster Filled: Majority with 23 members on Jan. 26, 2005; Minority with 17 members on Feb. 9, 2005

Majority

Rank Name	Party	State	House	Comm.
Chr Sensenbrenner, F. James Jr.	Rep	Wisc.	14	14
2nd Hyde, Henry J.	Rep	Ill.	16	16
3rd Coble, Howard	Rep	N.C.	11	11
4th Smith, Lamar S.	Rep	Tex.	10	10
5th Gallegly, Elton W.	Rep	Cal.	10	7
6th Goodlatte, Robert W.	Rep	Va.	7	7
7th Chabot, Steven J.	Rep	Ohio	6	6
8th Lungren, Daniel E.	Rep	Cal.	6	*2 1
9th Jenkins, William L.	Rep	Tenn.	5	5
10th Cannon, Christopher B.	Rep	Utah	5	5
11th Bachus, Spencer T.	Rep	Ala.	7	4
12th Inglis, Robert D.	Rep	S.C.	4	*2 1
13th Hostettler, John N.	Rep	Ind.	6	3
14th Green, Mark	Rep	Wisc.	4	3
15th Keller, Richard (Ric)	Rep	Fla.	3	3
16th Issa, Darrell E.	Rep	Cal.	3	*2 1
17th Flake, Jeff	Rep	Ariz.	3	3
18th Pence, Mike	Rep	Ind.	3	3
19th Forbes, J. Randy	Rep	Va.	3	3
20th King, Steve	Rep	Iowa	2	2
21st Feeney, Tom	Rep	Fla.	2	2
22nd Franks, Trent	Rep	Ariz.	2	1
23rd Gohmert, Louie	Rep	Tex.	1	1

Minority

Rank Name	Party	State	House	Comm.
RM Conyers, John Jr.	Dem	Mich.	21	21
2nd Berman, Howard L.	Dem	Cal.	12	12
3rd Boucher, Frederick C.	Dem	Va.	12	12
4th Nadler, Jerrold	Dem	N.Y.	8	7
5th Scott, Robert C.	Dem	Va.	7	7
6th Watt, Melvin L.	Dem	N.C.	7	7
7th Lofgren, Zoe	Dem	Cal.	6	6
8th Jackson-Lee, Sheila	Dem	Tex.	6	6
9th Waters, Maxine	Dem	Cal.	8	6
10th Meehan, Martin T.	Dem	Mass.	7	5
11th Delahunt, William D.	Dem	Mass.	5	5
12th Wexler, Robert	Dem	Fla.	5	5
13th Weiner, Anthony D.	Dem	N.Y.	4	4
14th Schiff, Adam B.	Dem	Cal.	3	3
15th Sánchez, Linda	Dem	Cal.	2	2
16th Smith, Adam	Dem	Wash.	5	1
17th Van Hollen, Christopher	Dem	Md.	2	1

*2: Member's second period of service on the committee.

Vacancies Filled:

Minority:

16th and 17th seats filled by Smith and Van Hollen on Feb. 9, 2005

Changes:

Minority:

Smith, Adam	Dem	Wash.	June 8, 2005 Resigned committee; no new assignment
Wasserman Schultz, Debbie	Dem	Fla.	June 8, 2005 Replaced Smith; ranked after Sánchez

Departures from the House:	Majority			Minority
Lost Election for Governor	Green, Mark	Rep	Wisc.	None
Defeated for Re-election	Hostettler, John N.	Rep	Ind.	None
Retired	Hyde, Henry J.	Rep	Ill.	None
	Jenkins, William L.	Rep	Tenn.	

Departures from Committee:					
Became RM on Financial Services	Bachus, Spencer T.	Rep	Ala.	None	
Moved to Foreign Affairs	Inglis, Robert D.	Rep	S.C.	None	
Moved to Ways and Means	None			Van Hollen, Christopher	Dem	Md.
No new assignment	Flake, Jeff	Rep	Ariz.	None	

JUDICIARY / 110th Congress

Service Dates of Committee Chair: Jan. 4, 2007-Jan. 3, 2009

Service Dates of Majority Members: Jan. 18, 2007-Jan. 3, 2009

Service Dates of Minority Members: Jan. 10, 2007-Jan. 3, 2009

Roster Filled: Majority with 23 members on Apr. 17, 2007; Minority with 17 members on Jan. 10, 2007

Majority					Minority				
			Terms in:					**Terms in:**	
Rank Name	Party	State	House	Comm.	Rank Name	Party	State	House	Comm.
Chr Conyers, John Jr.	Dem	Mich.	22	22	RM Smith, Lamar S.	Rep	Tex.	11	11
2nd Berman, Howard L.	Dem	Cal.	13	13	2nd Sensenbrenner, F. James Jr.	Rep	Wisc.	15	15
3rd Boucher, Frederick C.	Dem	Va.	13	13	3rd Coble, Howard	Rep	N.C.	12	12
4th Nadler, Jerrold	Dem	N.Y.	9	8	4th Gallegly, Elton W.	Rep	Cal.	11	8
5th Scott, Robert C.	Dem	Va.	8	8	5th Goodlatte, Robert W.	Rep	Va.	8	8
6th Watt, Melvin L.	Dem	N.C.	8	8	6th Chabot, Steven J.	Rep	Ohio	7	7
7th Lofgren, Zoe	Dem	Cal.	7	7	7th Lungren, Daniel E.	Rep	Cal.	7	*2 2
8th Jackson-Lee, Sheila	Dem	Tex.	7	7	8th Cannon, Christopher B.	Rep	Utah	6	6
9th Waters, Maxine	Dem	Cal.	9	7	9th Keller, Richard (Ric)	Rep	Fla.	4	4
10th Meehan, Martin T.	Dem	Mass.	8	6	10th Issa, Darrell E.	Rep	Cal.	4	*2 2
11th Delahunt, William D.	Dem	Mass.	6	6	11th Pence, Mike	Rep	Ind.	4	4
12th Wexler, Robert	Dem	Fla.	6	6	12th Forbes, J. Randy	Rep	Va.	4	4
13th Sánchez, Linda T.	Dem	Cal.	3	3	13th King, Steve	Rep	Iowa	3	3
14th Cohen, Stephen L.	Dem	Tenn.	1	1	14th Feeney, Tom	Rep	Fla.	3	3
15th Johnson, Hank	Dem	Ga.	1	1	15th Franks, Trent	Rep	Ariz.	3	2
16th Gutierrez, Luis V.	Dem	Ill.	8	1	16th Gohmert, Louie	Rep	Tex.	2	2
17th Sherman, Brad	Dem	Cal.	6	1	17th Jordan, Jim	Rep	Ohio	1	1
18th Baldwin, Tammy	Dem	Wisc.	5	*2 1					
19th Weiner, Anthony D.	Dem	N.Y.	5	5					
20th Schiff, Adam B.	Dem	Cal.	4	4					
21st Davis, Artur	Dem	Ala.	3	1					
22nd Wasserman Schultz, Debbie	Dem	Fla.	2	2					
23rd Ellison, Keith	DFL	Minn.	1	1					

*2: Member's second period of service on the committee.

Vacancies Filled:

Majority:

22nd seat filled by Wasserman Schultz on Jan. 23, 2007; 18th seat filled by Balwin on Apr. 17, 2007

Changes:

Majority

Meehan, Martin T.	Dem	Mass.	July 1, 2007 Resigned the House; appointed Chancellor of University of Massachusetts at Lowell
Sutton, Betty	Dem	Ohio	July 12, 2007 Replaced Meehan

Departures from the House:	**Majority**			**Minority**		
Defeated for Re-election	None			Chabot, Steven J.	Rep	Ohio
				Keller, Richard (Ric)	Rep	Fla.
				Feeney, Tom	Rep	Fla.
Defeated for Re-nomination	None			Cannon, Christopher B.	Rep	Utah

Departures from Committee:						
Became Chair of the Republican Conference	None			Pence, Mike	Rep	Ind.
Moved to Energy and Commerce	Sutton, Betty	Dem	Ohio	None		
Moved to Foreign Affairs	Ellison, Keith	DFL	Minn.	None		
No new assignment	Davis, Artur	Dem	Ala.	None		

JUDICIARY / 111th Congress

Service Dates of Committee Chair: Jan. 6, 2009-Jan. 3, 2011

Service Dates of Majority Members: Jan. 21, 2009-Jan. 3, 2011

Service Dates of Minority Members: Jan. 9, 2009-Jan. 3, 2011

Roster Filled: Majority with 24 members, Apr. 30, 2009; Minority with 16 members, Jan. 9, 2009

Majority					Minority				
			Terms in:					**Terms in:**	
Rank Name	Party	State	House	Comm.	Rank Name	Party	State	House	Comm.
Chr Conyers, John Jr.	Dem	Mich.	23	23	RM Smith, Lamar S.	Rep	Tex.	12	12
2nd Berman, Howard L.	Dem	Cal.	14	14	2nd Sensenbrenner, F. James Jr.	Rep	Wisc.	16	16
3rd Boucher, Frederick C.	Dem	Va.	14	14	3rd Coble, Howard	Rep	N.C.	13	13
4th Nadler, Jerrold	Dem	N.Y.	10	9	4th Gallegly, Elton W.	Rep	Cal.	12	9
5th Scott, Robert C.	Dem	Va.	9	9	5th Goodlatte, Robert W.	Rep	Va.	9	9

6th Watt, Melvin L.	Dem	N.C.	9	9		
7th Lofgren, Zoe	Dem	Cal.	8	8		
8th Jackson-Lee, Sheila	Dem	Tex.	8	8		
9th Waters, Maxine	Dem	Cal.	10	8		
10th Delahunt, William D.	Dem	Mass.	7	7		
11th Wexler, Robert	Dem	Fla.	7	7		
12th Cohen, Stephen L.	Dem	Tenn.	2	2		
13th Johnson, Hank	Dem	Ga.	2	2		
14th Pierluisi, Pedro R.	Dem	P.R.	1	1		
15th Gutierrez, Luis V.	Dem	Ill.	9	2		
16th Sherman, Brad	Dem	Cal.	7	2		
17th Baldwin, Tammy	Dem	Wisc.	6	*2 2		
18th Gonzalez, Charles A.	Dem	Tex.	6	1		
19th Weiner, Anthony D.	Dem	N.Y.	6	6		
20th Schiff, Adam B.	Dem	Cal.	5	5		
21st Sanchez, Linda T.	Dem	Cal.	4	4		
22nd Wasserman Schultz, Debbie	Dem	Fla.	3	3		
23rd Maffei, Daniel B.	Dem	N.Y.	1	1		

6th Lungren, Daniel E.	Rep	Cal.	8	*2 3
7th Issa, Darrell E.	Rep	Cal.	5	*2 3
8th Forbes, J. Randy	Rep	Va.	5	5
9th King, Steve	Rep	Iowa	4	4
10th Franks, Trent	Rep	Ariz.	4	3
11th Gohmert, Louie	Rep	Tex.	3	3
12th Jordan, Jim	Rep	Ohio	2	2
13th Poe, Ted	Rep	Tex.	3	1
14th Chaffetz, Jason	Rep	Utah	1	1
15th Rooney, Thomas J.	Rep	Fla.	1	1
16th Harper, Gregg	Rep	Miss.	1	1

*2: Member's second period of service on the committee.

Note: Resident Commissioner Pedro R. Pierluisi (Dem-P.R.) was allowed to accrue committee senioirty but was not included in the party ratio.

Additions:

Majority:

Mike Quigley (Dem-Ill.) on Apr. 30, 2009, to rank following Pierluisi

Changes

Majority

Sherman, Brad	Dem	Cal.	Oct. 14, 2009	Left the committee; no new assignment
Chu, Judy	Dem	Cal.	Oct. 15, 2009	Replaced Sherman; ranked 16th following Quigley
Wexler, Robert	Dem	Fla.	Jan. 4, 2010	Resigned the House; named President of Center for Middle East Peace and Economic Cooperation
Wasserman Schultz, Debbie	Dem	Fla.	May 5, 2010	Resigned committee; no new assignment
Deutch, Theodore E.	Dem	Fla.	May. 6, 2010	Replaced Wexler, ranked following McMahon
Polis, Jared	Dem	Colo.	May 6, 2010	Replaced Wasserman-Schultz

Merchant Marine and Fisheries

House Committee on Merchant Marine and Fisheries, 103rd Congress (1993-1995)

BACKGROUND

Organizational History: On December 21, 1887, the House created the standing Committee on Merchant Marine and Fisheries in response to a motion introduced by Nelson Dingley, Jr. (Rep-Me.). Dingley was a close political associate of House Speaker Thomas B. Reed (Rep-Me.) and would later serve as chair of Ways and Means, 1895-1899, thereby becoming House Majority Leader. Because the 50th Congress was controlled by the Democrats, Poindexter Dunn (Dem-Ark.) was named as its first chair while Dingley became its first ranking minority member. Merchant Marine and Fisheries was an outgrowth of the Select Committee on American Shipbuilding and Shipowning Interests (1883) and absorbed that committee's jurisdiction upon its creation.

In 1919, wireless telegraphy (i.e., radio) was assigned to the committee's jurisdiction and from January 4, 1932, until February 26, 1935, the committee was known as the Committee on Merchant Marine, Radio, and Fisheries. That name change was short-lived as that jurisdiction was taken over by Chairman Sam Rayburn's Interstate and Foreign Commerce Committee and "radio" was removed from the committee's title and it resumed the name of Merchant Marine and Fisheries.

The Legislative Reorganization Act of 1946 specified its jurisdiction as:

a) Merchant marine generally. b) Coast and Geodetic Survey. c) Coast Guard, including lifesaving service, lighthouses, lightships, and ocean derelicts. d) Fisheries and wildlife, including research, restoration, refuges, and conservation. e) Measures relating to the regulation of common carriers by water (except matters subject to the jurisdiction of the Interstate Commerce Commission) and to the inspection of merchant marine vessels, lights and signals, lifesaving equipment, and fire protection on such vessels. f) Merchant marine officers and seamen. g) Navigation and the laws relating thereto, including pilotage. h) Panama Canal and the maintenance and operation of the Panama Canal, including the administration, sanitation, and government of the Canal Zone; and interoceanic canals generally. i) Registering and licensing of vessels and small boats. j) Rules and international arrangements to prevent collisions at sea. k) United States Coast Guard and Merchant Marine Academies.

It was an odd mix of legislative responsibilities that made the committee a hybrid, where supporters of the shipping industry would rub shoulders with environmental activists. A primary activity of the committee was to keep in place the massive subsidies and cargo preference rules that had supported the ailing U.S. shipping industry since 1916, but the committee seldom had the clout to expand support of the industry, which has been swamped by international competition and hampered by dissension among unions, shipbuilders, and ship operators. In addition to shipping, the committee oversaw the oceans, including fishing policy, wildlife and fisheries, and the Coast Guard, its academy and state maritime schools. It held jurisdiction over the Panama Canal, and on many water-related environmental issues it shared jurisdiction with other committees.

Because of its narrow jurisdiction, advocates of congressional streamlining proposed eliminating the panel in the 1970s but were unsuccessful until the Republicans marked the committee for extinction at the opening of the 104th Congress in 1995.

Three standing committees received jurisdictional authority from the dismembering of Merchant Marine and Fisheries. The National Security Committee (now Armed Services) received jurisdiction over: interoceanic canals generally, including measures relating to the maintenance, operation, and administration of interoceanic canals (e.g., the Panama Canal); the Merchant Marine Academy, and State Maritime Academies; and national security aspects of merchant marine, including financial assistance for the construction and operation of vessels, the maintenance of the U.S. shipbuilding and ship repair industrial base, cabotage, cargo preference, and merchant marine officers and seamen as these matters relate to national security.

The Resources Committee (now Natural Resources) gained jurisdiction over fisheries and wildlife, including research, restoration, refuges, and conservation; international fishing agreements; marine affairs (including coastal zone management), except for measures relating to oil and other pollution of navigable waters; and oceanography. And the Transportation and Infrastructure Committee, which ended up with most of its dislocated members, acquired jurisdiction over the Coast Guard, including lifesaving service, lighthouses, lightships, ocean derelicts, and the Coast Guard Academy; inspection of merchant marine vessels, lights and signals, lifesaving equipment, and fire protection on such vessels; navigation and the laws relating thereto, including pilotage; registering and licensing of vessels and small boats; and rules and international arrangements to prevent collisions at sea.

Membership: In 1911, the size of the Merchant Marine and Fisheries Committee was set at twenty-one, and it remained at that figure until 1947 when it was increased to twenty-five. The committee reached its high of forty-eight members in the 103rd Congress (1993-1995) and its last. Considered a secondary committee, it attracted members from coastal and Great Lakes districts, but members seldom remained on it. The Republican takeover of the House in 1995 led to the termination of Merchant Marine and Fisheries, making it the largest standing committee ever put out of business. Twelve of its forty-eight members left the House with eight of its Democrats defeated for re-election. Thirteen others were not reassigned to new committees including Jack Fields (Rep-Texas), the committee's ranking member. The other twenty-three were scattered throughout the remaining committees, with six moving to the renamed Resources Committee, including Merchant Marine's former chair, Gerry Studds (Dem-Mass.) and four each to the renamed Commerce and Transportation and Infrastructure committees.

Committee Leaders: Eleven different members chaired the Merchant Marine Committee in the post-1947 era, two of them were "acting" chairs—Thomas L. Ashley (Dem-Ohio), who assumed the chair in 1980 following John M. Murphy's (Dem-N.Y.) indictment in the "Abscam" sting and Gerry E. Studds who assumed the chair in 1992 during the final illness of Walter B. Jones (Dem-N.C.) and held it until the committee's termination in 1995.

The first post-reorganization chair was Frederick V. Bradley (Rep-Mich.), who died in May, 1947 and was replaced by Alvin F. Weichel (Rep-Ohio) who served as the committee's senior Republican until his 1955 retirement and after his second stint as chair. Weichel's successor was Thor C. Tollefson (Rep-Wash.), who served as ranking member from 1955 until his 1964 election defeat.

Schuyler Otis Bland (Dem-Va.) was the first post-1947 ranking member and had been its senior Democrat since 1933 when the committee was then known as the Committee on Merchant Marine, Radio, and Fisheries. Bland's death in 1950 placed Edward J. Hart (Dem-N.J.) in the chair from 1950 to 1953. After one term as ranking member, Hart retired in 1955 and Herbert C. Bonner (Dem-N.C.) succeeded him and served until his death in 1965. Bonner's successor, Edward A. Garmatz (Dem-Md.) held the chair until his 1973 retirement.

Garmatz was succeeded by Leonor Kretzer Sullivan (Dem-Mo.), the first woman chair in twenty years and the first woman to chair a committee of this size in the House. She retired after two terms, 1973-1977, and was succeeded by John M. Murphy (Dem-N.Y.). Murphy's service as chair ended in 1980 during the "Abscam" bribery scandal. He was temporarily replaced by Acting Chair Thomas L. Ashley (Dem-Ohio). Both Murphy and Ashley were defeated for re-election in 1980, opening the chairmanship for Walter B. Jones (Dem-N.C.) who would chair the committee until his death in 1992. Gerry E. Studds would become acting chair in 1992 and would serve as chair until the Merchant Marine Committee was dissolved in 1995.

Turnover among Republican ranking members was very high as the lure of other committee service pulled them away from Merchant Marine. William S. Mailliard (Rep-Cal.) served for six years, 1965-1971 until he stepped aside to become ranking member on Foreign Affairs and was succeeded by Thomas M. Pelly (Rep-Wash.) and James R. Grover, Jr. (Rep-N.Y.) for one Congress each. Michigan's Philip E. Ruppe served only twice as ranking member, 1975-1979 when he retired and was succeeded by Paul N. (Pete) McCloskey (Rep-Cal.) who left this slot in 1981 to become ranking member on a Government Operations subcommittee. M.G. (Gene) Snyder (Rep-Ky.) who replaced McCloskey stepped aside in 1983 to become ranking member on Public Works and Transportation. His successor Edwin B. Forsythe (Rep-N.J.) died in 1984 and Snyder returned as ranking member for the remainder of the 98th Congress, serving as ranking member on two committees.

Snyder stepped aside again in 1985 and his next successor Norman F. Lent (Rep-N.Y.) served only one term in this post, until he too stepped aside in 1987 to become ranking member on Energy and Commerce. Lent's successor Robert W. Davis (Rep-Mich.) served from 1987 until his retirement in 1993. Davis would be succeeded by Jack Fields (Rep-Texas), the committee's last ranking member.

Party Leaders: The two best-known modern-era alumni of the low prestige House Committee on Merchant Marine and Fisheries were the Boston-area Speakers of the House—John W. McCormack and his protégé Thomas P. (Tip) O'Neill,

Jr. McCormack, then serving as Majority Leader, left the committee after one Congress (1951-1953) when Republicans regained the House and returned to his earlier post as Minority Whip. O'Neill took his place in 1953 on Merchant Marine and then left the committee in 1955 for a seat on the Rules Committee with McCormack's blessing. He would steadily rise up the "leadership ladder" as Majority Whip in 1971; Majority Leader in 1973; and ultimately becoming House Speaker in 1977, where he would serve for ten years, 1977-1987, the longest consecutive speakership career. Two other House leaders with Merchant Marine experience were C. Trent Lott of Mississippi, the Republican Whip, 1981-1989 and David Bonior of Michigan, the Democratic Whip, 1995-2002. Lott ran successfully for the Senate in 1988 while Bonior failed to be nominated in his quest to become governor of Michigan.

Notable Members: No modern-era presidential or vice presidential nominees had served on Merchant Marine and Fisheries. Only two Cabinet members had ever seen service on the committee. Republican Rogers C.B. Morton of Maryland served as Secretary of the Interior for both Presidents Nixon and Ford, 1971-1975 and would later be named by President Ford to be his Secretary of Commerce in 1975. The other was William S. Cohen (Rep-Maine), who was named as President Bill Clinton's third Secretary of Defense in 1997.

Twenty U.S. senators served on Merchant Marine. Twelve Democrats served on it before they joined the Senate—Paul S. Sarbanes and Barbara A. Mikulski of Maryland, Henry M. Jackson and Maria E. Cantwell of Washington State, Delegate E.L. (Bob) Bartlett of Alaska, Daniel K. Akaka of Hawaii, William Hathaway of Maine, John B. Breaux of Louisiana, Barbara Boxer of California, Blanche Lambert Lincoln of Arkansas, John F. Reed of Rhode Island, and Thomas R. Carper of Delaware—while Democrat Alton A. Lennon of North Carolina served on the committee after leaving the Senate.

The seven Senate Republicans who served on Merchant Marine were Charles E. Potter of Michigan, William V. Roth, Jr. of Delaware, Paul S. Trible of Virginia, C.Trent Lott of Mississippi, William S. Cohen of Maine, James M. Inhofe of Oklahoma, and James P.D. Bunning of Kentucky.

Eight governors saw service on the committee: six future governors—four Republicans—Pierre S. du Pont of Delaware, David C. Treen of Louisiana, Thomas J. Meskill of New Jersey, and John K. McKernan of Maine—and two Democrats—Michael E. Lowry of Washington State and Thomas R. Carper of Delaware. California Republican Ed Reinecke who left the committee to become lieutenant governor had his ambitions dashed in a financial scandal. The two former governors who served on Merchant Marine were Democrat Joseph E. Brennan of Maine and Republican Michael N. Castle of Delaware. Two ambassadors served on Merchant Marine—William S. Mailliard (Rep-Cal.), who was named Ambassador to the Organization of American States, and William J. Hughes (Dem-N.J.), named as Ambassador to Panama.

Selected References

Hardy-Vincent, Carol, *History of the House Committee on Merchant Marine and Fisheries*, U.S. House of Representatives, Committee Doc., 101st Congress, 2nd Session (1990).

Schamel, Charles E. et al., "Records of the Merchant Marine and Fisheries Committee," *Guide to the Records of the United States House of Representatives at the National Archives: 1789-1989 Bicentennial Edition* (Washington, D.C.: National Archives and Records Administration,1989), 219-225.

Starobin, Paul, "Merchant Marine: Too Close to Its 'Clients'?," *CQ Weekly Report*, 46 (June 11, 1988), 1559.

U.S. House of Representatives, Committee on Merchant Marine and Fisheries, *Report on the Activities of Merchant Marine and Fisheries Committee,* H. Doc. 101-1018, 101st Congress, 2nd Session (1990).

RESPONSIBILITIES, JURISDICTIONAL CHANGES, AND SUBCOMMITTEES

MERCHANT MARINE AND FISHERIES

Jurisdiction, 80th Congress (1947-1949)

Established by the Legislative Reorganization Act of 1946:

[Section 121.(1)(m)] Committee on Merchant Marine and Fisheries
 (1) Merchant marine generally.
 (2) Registering and licensing of vessels and small boats.
 (3) Navigation and the laws relating thereto, including pilotage.
 (4) Rules and international arrangements to prevent collisions at sea.
 (5) Merchant marine officers and seamen.
 (6) Measures relating to the regulation of common carriers by water (except matters subject to the jurisdiction of the Interstate Commerce Commission) and to the inspection of merchant marine vessels, lights and signals, lifesaving equipment, and fire protection on such vessels.
 (7) The Coast Guard, including lifesaving service, lighthouses, lightships, and ocean derelicts.
 (8) United States Coast Guard and Merchant Marine Academies.
 (9) Coast and Geodetic Survey.
 (10) The Panama Canal and the maintenance and operation of the Panama Canal, including the administration, sanitation, and government of the Canal Zone; and interoceanic canals generally.
 (11) Fisheries and wildlife, including research, restoration, refuges, and conservation.

Jurisdiction, 103rd Congress (1993-1995)

From the *Rules of the House of Representatives, 103rd Congress* (House Document 102-405)

[Rule X.1.(n)] Committee on Merchant Marine and Fisheries
 (1) Merchant marine generally.
 (2) Oceanography and Marine Affairs, including coastal zone management.
 (3) Coast Guard, including lifesaving service, lighthouses, lightships, and ocean derelicts.
 (4) Fisheries and wildlife, including research, restoration, refuges, and conservation.
 (5) Measures relating to the regulation of common carriers by water (except matters subject to the jurisdiction of the Interstate Commerce Commission) and to the inspection of merchant marine vessels, lights and signals, lifesaving equipment, and fire protection on such vessels.
 (6) Merchant marine officers and seamen.
 (7) Navigation and the laws relating thereto, including pilotage.
 (8) Panama Canal and the maintenance and operation of the Panama Canal, including the administration, sanitation, and government of the Canal Zone; and interoceanic canals generally.
 (9) Registering and licensing of vessels and small boats.
 (10) Rules and international arrangements to prevent collisions at sea.
 (11) United States Coast Guard and Merchant Marine Academies, and State Maritime Academies.
 (12) International fishing agreements.

NAMES OF MERCHANT MARINE AND FISHERIES SUBCOMMITTEES FROM THE *CONGRESSIONAL DIRECTORY*

Coast Guard and Navigation, 103
Environment and Natural Resources, 103
Fisheries Management, 103
Merchant Marine, 103
Oceanography, Gulf of Mexico, and Outer Continental Shelf, 103

MEMBERSHIP ROSTER, 103rd Congress, 1993-1995

MERCHANT MARINE AND FISHERIES / 103rd Congress

Service Dates of Committee Chair: Jan. 5, 1993-Jan. 3, 1995

Service Dates of Majority Members: Jan. 5, 1993-Jan. 3, 1995

Service Dates of Minority Members: Jan. 5, 1993-Jan. 3, 1995

Roster Filled: Majority with 28 members on Jan. 27, 1993; Minority with 18 members on May 27, 1993

Majority					Minority				
			Terms in:					**Terms in:**	
Rank Name	Party	State	House	Comm.	Rank Name	Party	State	House	Comm.
Chr Studds, Gerry E.	Dem	Mass.	11	11	RM Fields, Jack M. Jr.	Rep	Tex.	7	7
2nd Hughes, William J.	Dem	N.J.	10	9	2nd Young, Donald E.	Rep	Alas.	11	11
3rd Hutto, Earl D.	Dem	Fla.	8	8	3rd Bateman, Herbert H.	Rep	Va.	6	6
4th Tauzin, W. J. (Billy)	Dem	La.	8	7	4th Saxton, H. James	Rep	N.J.	6	5
5th Lipinski, William O.	Dem	Ill.	6	6	5th Coble, Howard	Rep	N.C.	5	4
6th Ortiz, Solomon P.	Dem	Tex.	6	6	6th Weldon, Wayne C. (Curt)	Rep	Penn.	4	4
7th Manton, Thomas J.	Dem	N.Y.	5	5	7th Inhofe, James M.	Rep	Okla.	4	3
8th Pickett, Owen B.	Dem	Va.	4	4	8th Ravenel, Arthur A. Jr.	Rep	S.C.	4	3
9th Hochbrueckner, George J.	Dem	N.Y.	4	4	9th Gilchrest, Wayne T.	Rep	Md.	2	2
10th Pallone, Frank Jr.	Dem	N.J.	4	3	10th Cunningham, Randall (Duke)	Rep	Cal.	2	2
11th Laughlin, Gregory H.	Dem	Tex.	3	3	11th Kingston, Jack	Rep	Ga.	1	1
12th Unsoeld, Jolene	Dem	Wash.	3	3	12th Fowler, Tillie K.	Rep	Fla.	1	1
13th Taylor, G. Eugene (Gene)	Dem	Miss.	3	3	13th Castle, Michael N.	Rep	Del.	1	1
14th Reed, John F.	Dem	R.I.	2	2	14th King, Peter T.	Rep	N.Y.	1	1
15th Lancaster, H. Martin	Dem	N.C.	4	2	15th Diaz-Balart, Lincoln	Rep	Fla.	1	1
16th Andrews, Thomas H.	Dem	Me.	2	1	16th Pombo, Richard W.	Rep	Cal.	1	1
17th Furse, Elizabeth	Dem	Ore.	1	1	17th Bentley, Helen Delich	Rep	Md.	5	*2 1
18th Schenk, Lynn	Dem	Cal.	1	1	18th Taylor, Charles H.	Rep	N.C.	1	1
19th Green, R. Eugene (Gene)	Dem	Tex.	1	1					
20th Hastings, Alcee L.	Dem	Fla.	1	1					
21st Hamburg, Daniel	Dem	Cal.	1	1					
22nd Lambert, Blanche	Dem	Ark.	1	1					
23rd Eshoo, Anna G.	Dem	Cal.	1	1					
24th Barlow, Thomas J.	Dem	Ky.	1	1					
25th Stupak, Bart T.	Dem	Mich.	1	1					
26th Cantwell, Maria E.	Dem	Wash.	1	1					
27th Deutsch, Peter R.	Dem	Fla.	1	1					
28th Ackerman, Gary L.	Dem	N.Y.	6	1					

*2: Member's second period of service on the committee.

Note: Rankings on this committee for the following member was affected by other chamber service: Donald E. Young (Rep-Alas.), Ranking Minority Member, Natural Resources.

Vacancies Filled:
Majority:
16th seat by Andrews, 26th and 27th seats by Cantwell and Deutsch on Jan. 21, 1993.
28th seat by Ackerman on Jan. 27, 1993.
Minority:
16th seat by Pombo on Feb. 4, 1993; 17th and 18th seats by Bentley and Taylor on May 27, 1993.

Additions:
Majority:

29th Thompson, Bennie	Dem	Miss.	Apr. 29, 1993

Minority:

19th Torkildsen, Peter G.	Rep	Mass.	May 27, 1993

Changes:
Minority:

Inhofe, James M.	Rep	Okla.	Nov. 15, 1994 Resigned the House; elected to U.S. Senate; vacancy remained.

Departures from the House:	Majority			Minority		
Appointed U.S. Ambassador to Panama	Hughes, William J.	Dem	N.J.	None		
Lost Nomination for Governor	None			Ravenel, Arthur A. Jr.	Rep	S.C.
				Bentley, Helen Delich	Rep	Md.

Lost Election to U.S. Senate	Andrews, Thomas H.	Dem	Me.	None		
Defeated for Re-election	Hochbrueckner, George J.	Dem	N.Y.	None		
	Lancaster, H. Martin	Dem	N.C.			
	Schenk, Lynn	Dem	Cal.			
	Hamburg, Daniel	Dem	Cal.			
	Barlow, Thomas J.	Dem	Ky.			
	Cantwell, Maria E.	Dem	Wash.			
	Unsoeld, Jolene	Dem	Wash.			
Retired	Hutto, Earl D.	Dem	Fla.	None		

Departures from Committee:

Moved to Appropriations	None			Kingston, Jack	Rep	Ga.
Returned to Banking and Financial Services	Ackerman, Gary L.	Dem	N.Y.	None		
Moved to Commerce	Furse, Elizabeth	Dem	Ore.	None		
	Eshoo, Anna G.	Dem	Cal.			
	Deutsch, Peter R.	Dem	Fla.			
	Stupak, Bart	Dem	Mich.			
Moved to Government Reform and Oversight	Taylor, G. Eugene (Gene)	Dem	Miss.	None		
Moved to House Oversight	None			Diaz-Balart, Lincoln	Rep	Fla.
Moved to International Relations	None			King, Peter T.	Rep	N.Y.
Moved to Resources	Studds, Gerry E.	Dem	Mass.	Saxton, H. James	Rep	N.J.
	Tauzin, W.J. (Billy)	Dem	La.	Gilchrest, Wayne T.	Rep	Md.
	Ortiz, Solomon P.	Dem	Tex.	Torkildsen, Peter G.	Rep	Mass.
Moved to Rules	None			Diaz-Balart, Lincoln	Rep	Fla.
Moved to Science	Hastings, Alcee L.	Dem	Fla.	Weldon, Wayne C. (Curt)	Rep	Penn.
Moved to Select Intelligence	None			Castle, Michael N.	Rep	Del.
Moved to Transportation and Infrastructure	None			Young, Donald E.	Rep	Alas.
				Bateman, Herbert H.	Rep	Va.
				Coble, Howard	Rep	N.C.
				Fowler, Tillie K.	Rep	Fla.
No new assignment	Lipinski, William O.	Dem	Ill.	Fields, Jack M. Jr.	Rep	Tex.
	Manton, Thomas J.	Dem	N.Y.	Cunningham, Randall (Duke)	Rep	Cal.
	Pickett, Owen B.	Dem	Va.	Pombo, Richard W.	Rep	Cal.
	Pallone, Frank Jr.	Dem	N.J.	Taylor, Charles H.	Rep	N.C.
	Green, R. Eugene (Gene)	Dem	Tex.			
	Laughlin, Gregory H.	Dem	Tex.			
	Reed, John F.	Dem	R.I.			
	Lambert, Blanche	Dem	Ark.			
	Thompson, Bennie	Dem	Miss.			

Natural Resources

House Committee on Natural Resources, 103rd Congress (1993-1995)

House Committee on Resources, 104th-109th Congresses (1995-2007)

House Committee on Natural Resources, 110th-111th Congresses (2007-2011)

BACKGROUND

Organizational History: For most of the post-1947 period, this committee was known as the Interior and Insular Affairs Committee. It has had several names in its long history, dating back to the earliest days of the Republic. The original name was the House Public Lands Committee and it was created on December 17, 1805, on a motion introduced by Rep. William Findley (DR-Penn.) with Andrew Gregg, a fellow Pennsylvania Jeffersonian, serving as its first chair. In the next two decades, two other committees linked to the development of the nation emerged from Public Lands: the Committee on Post Offices and Post Roads in the 10th Congress (1808) and the Committee on Territories in the 19th Congress (1825).

The Committee on Public Lands remained a distinct entity until 1947 when the Legislative Reorganization Act placed the jurisdictions of five other standing committees within it. The five additional committees and their dates of creation were Territories (1825), Mines and Mining (1865), Indian Affairs (1821), Irrigation and Reclamation (1893), and Insular Affairs (1899).

At the time of the 79th Congress (1945-1947), these six committees had a total of 128 members (excluding eight delegates), but in the post-reorganization 80th Congress there were only twenty-five members on the Public Lands Committee. In the 82nd Congress, on Feb. 2, 1951, Public Lands became the Interior and Insular Affairs Committee. That name was changed to Natural Resources at the opening of the 103rd Congress in 1993, but the Republican takeover in 1995, renamed it the Committee on Resources. With the return of Democrats to control the House in 2007, the committee resumed the name of Natural Resources.

With territorial delegates serving regularly on the committee, it was the House entity most sensitive to the creation of new states. With the Territories of Alaska and Hawaii both becoming states in 1959, their Territorial Delegates became representatives in the 86th Congress. Although the committee has more sitting delegates than any other in the House, the *House Manual* (2008) reports that

"The Committee Reform Amendments of 1974, effective January 3, 1975, gave the committee jurisdiction over parks within the District of Columbia, formerly within the jurisdiction of the Committee on Public Works and Transportation (now Transportation and Infrastructure) and it lost specific jurisdiction over Indian education and over Hawaii and Alaska, generally....

"The authority of the committee to report as privileged bills for the forfeiture of land grants to railroad and other corporations, bills preventing speculation in the public lands, bills for the preservation of the public lands for the benefit of actual and bona fide settlers, and bills for the admission of new States was eliminated in the Committee Reform Amendments of 1974, effective January 3, 1975."

While the Interior and Insular Affairs Committee faced jurisdictional shrinkage with the 1974 Reform Amendments, it was able to expand its authority in 1977 with the termination of the Joint Committee on Atomic Energy by acquiring partial authority over the domestic nuclear energy industry. Unlike the Senate that has chosen to combine energy and resource issues in its Energy and Natural Resources Committee, the House often faces jurisdictional issues by keeping the two areas in separate committees—Energy and Commerce and Natural Resources. As a result, the House will move jurisdiction from one committee to the other.

Natural Resources handled some aspects of energy policy, such as regulation of nuclear power and restrictions on strip mining of coal, but the Energy and Commerce Committee is the primary House energy panel and it is that committee that now has authority over nonmilitary nuclear energy and research and development, including disposal of nuclear waste.

The Resources Committee also gained power with the 1995 termination of the Merchant Marine and Fisheries Committee by acquiring jurisdiction over fisheries and wildlife, including research, restoration, refuges, and conservation; international fishing agreements; marine affairs (including coastal zone management), except for measures relating to oil and other pollution of navigable waters; and oceanography. In addition, the committee's responsibilities include mineral leasing on the Outer Continental Shelf and the Trans-Alaska Oil Pipeline.

The committee continues to oversee the nation's public lands, carrying out the decades-old conservationist philosophy that some land should be set aside and managed by the government for the good of all. Long-standing conflicts between preserving the land as wilderness or using it for logging, grazing, and mining often fall to this committee to resolve. Many environmental issues, such as clean air and water, lie outside its jurisdiction. Even federal lands are not entirely within its purview. It shared management of wildlife refuges with the now-defunct Merchant Marine and Fisheries Committee and oversight of forestry with the Agriculture Committee.

In one area of vital concern in the West—water projects—the committee has produced a mixed record. While the committee oversees the Bureau of Reclamation, which since 1902 has provided water in the West at subsidized rates, it sometimes finds itself at odds with environmentalists when it has pushed for the construction of dams and waterworks.

One crucial area differentiating the House Committee on Natural Resources from the Senate's Committee on Energy and Natural Resources is that Native American issues regarding relations between the United States and the various tribes are dealt with on the subcommittee level in the House committee, while in the Senate, there is a permanent select committee devoted specifically to Indian Affairs.

Membership: The Public Lands Committee opened the 80th Congress with twenty-five Representatives, two Territorial Delegates from Alaska and Hawaii and the Resident Commissioner from Puerto Rico. By 1951, now known as the Interior and Insular Affairs Committee, its membership reached thirty. The committee's first forty-member Congress was the 93rd (1973-1975) and its first fifty-member Congress was the 105th (1997-1999). Since 1995, the committee's size has varied from forty-eight to fifty-two members. Historically, legislators from the West, where most federal land is located, dominate the committee. The panel also oversees the water projects that subsidize irrigation of arid western areas and make large-scale agriculture possible. One characteristic of the committee's membership which differentiates it from the others is the number of territorial delegates who serve on it. Delegates from Alaska and Hawaii regularly served on the committee until both territories attained statehood in 1959.

In the 111th Congress, the Resident Commissioner from Puerto Rico and four Territorial Delegates from American Samoa, Guam, the Virgin Islands, and the recently added Northern Mariana Islands are seated on the committee. These delegates have been allowed to accrue committee seniority since 1973, but they are not included in the party ratios for the committees. Also, these delegates have voting rights within the committee, but they do not have voting rights on the floor.

During the past nine Congresses, 1993-2011, the Natural Resources Committee had an average membership of 49.22 members, placing it sixth among the nineteen continuing committees. Its mean seniority of 5.28 terms placed it eighth while it's mean inter-Congress retention rate of 85.39 percentplaced it twelfth.

Committee Leaders: Richard J. Welch (Rep-Cal.), the last ranking member on Insular Affairs in the 79th Congress became the first chair of Public Lands in the Reorganization era while Andrew L. Somers (Dem-N.Y.), the last chair of Mines and Mining became the new committee's first ranking member. They switched places in the Democratic-controlled 81st Congress, but both would die in 1949 within months of one another. Somers was replaced by J. Hardin Peterson (Dem-Fla.) while Welch was replaced by Fred L. Crawford (Rep-Mich.). Peterson would retire in 1951 and Crawford would be denied renomination in 1952. John R. Murdock (Dem-Ariz.) succeeded Peterson as chair but lost his 1954 re-election bid and was followed by Clair Engle (Dem-Cal.). Crawford's successor, Arthur L. Miller (Rep-Neb.) was the committee's senior Republican for six years, 1953-1959, chairing it in the 83rd Congress (1953-1955) but was defeated in 1958. Engle left the chair in 1958 to be elected U.S. senator from California, a very rare occurrence.

The next senior members, Democrat Wayne N. Aspinall of Colorado and Republican John P. Saylor, served as chair and ranking member respectively for the next fourteen years, 1959-1973. Accommodating the timber and mineral industries seemed to be Aspinall's constituency goal but during his chairmanship, the committee passed the 1964 Wilderness Act (P.L. 88-577), a landmark bill that designated 9.1 million acres as "wilderness." Aspinall lost his renomination in 1972 and Saylor died in 1973. Their successors were James A. Haley (Dem-Fla.) as chair and Craig Hosmer (Rep-Cal.) as ranking member. Hosmer resigned in 1974 and Haley retired in 1977. Hosmer's successor, Joe Skubitz (Rep-Kans.), served as ranking member until his resignation in 1978, while Haley's successor, Morris K. Udall (Dem-Ariz.), would chair the committee from 1977 until his May, 1991 resignation from the House. Udall's older brother Stewart served as Secretary of the Interior for the entirety of the Kennedy-Johnson Administrations, 1961-1969. Morris challenged Speaker John McCormack in 1969 and later for floor leader in 1971, but was unsuccessful both times. Udall was a strong advocate of protecting public lands, but was also a staunch defender of the massive Central Arizona Project, which promised to bring water to the arid cities of Tucson and Phoenix in his state.

Skubitz was succeeded initially by Don H. Clausen (Rep-Cal.) in 1979 but who stepped aside in 1981 to become ranking member on Public Works and Transportation, ceding the Interior Committee's ranking member slot to Manuel Lujan Jr. (Rep-N.M.). Lujan served for four years, 1981-1985, until he stepped aside to become ranking member on Science and Technology in 1985. Lujan's successor, Donald E. Young (Rep-Alas.), has been a committee fixture since he first became ranking member in 1985, serving in that role for twelve years, 1985-1995 and 2007-2009, and as chair for three Congresses, 1995-2001, during the committee's renaming as Natural Resources, 1993-1995, and as Resources, 1995-2007. Udall's successor, George Miller (Dem-Cal.), chaired the committee from 1991 to 1995 and served as ranking member from 1995 to 2001, when he became ranking member on Education and the Workforce.

In recent years, the committee was chaired by Republicans James V. Hansen (Rep-Utah), 2001-2003, until his retirement and Richard W. Pombo (Rep-Cal.), 2003-2007, until his 2006 defeat, and by Democrat Nick Joe Rahall II (Dem-W.Va.) since 2007. Prior to becoming chair, Rahall was the committee's ranking member from 2001 to 2007. Its present ranking member is Richard "Doc" Hastings (Rep-Wash.).

Party Leaders: The Natural Resources Committee has not been a major source of House leadership with only one Speaker, Thomas S. Foley (Dem-Wash.); one Minority Leader, John Rhodes (Rep-Ariz.); and one Republican Whip, Richard B. Cheney (Rep-Wyo.), having served on it. The one committee member who sought party leadership in the House, but was denied twice, was Morris K. Udall (Dem-Ariz.), whose unsuccessful challenge to Speaker John W. McCormack (Dem-Mass.) undermined his later bid to capture the open Majority Leader post in 1971.

Notable Members: The first vice presidential nominee with experience on the committee was Lloyd M. Bentsen, Jr. (Dem-Tex.) who served on Public Lands, its initial post-reorganization incarnation. Bentsen ran with Massachusetts governor Michael S. Dukakis in 1988. The most successful of the committee's former members would appear to be Richard B. Cheney, who was elected Republican Whip in 1989; appointed Secretary of Defense by President George H.W. Bush in 1989; and served as vice president for eight years, 2001-2009, with President George W. Bush, arguably as the most powerful vice president in American history. Another former member of the committee, John S. McCain III (Rep-Ariz.), the 2008 Republican presidential nominee, was less successful.

Bentsen, President Bill Clinton's Secretary of the Treasury, and Cheney, the elder Bush's Secretary of Defense, were two of the seven former members of the committee to be named to the Cabinet. Stewart L. Udall (Dem-Ariz.) served as Secretary of the Interior under both Presidents John Kennedy and Lyndon Johnson while Rogers C.B. Morton (Rep-Md.) served as Secretary of the Interior under both Presidents Nixon and Ford and as Ford's Secretary of Commerce. Three Latino-American former members of the committee received Cabinet appointments—Manuel Lujan (Rep-N.M.) was President George H.W. Bush's Secretary of the Interior, Bill Richardson (Dem-N.M.) was Bill Clinton's third Secretary of Energy, and Hilda L. Solis (Dem-Cal.) is President Obama's Secretary of Labor.

With so many of its members coming from small Western states and their districts comprising a large percentage of the state's population, it is not surprising that many members of this committee have been able to move from the House to the Senate. Prior to their Senate elections thirty U.S. senators served on the committee during its multiple name changes. Among them were eighteen Democrats: Clair Engle, John V. Tunney, and Barbara Boxer of California; Lee Metcalf and John Melcher of Montana; Thomas Udall of New Mexico; John A. Carroll, Ben Nighthorse Campbell, and Mark Udall of Colorado; Lloyd M. Bentsen, Jr. of Texas; Delegate E.L. (Bob) Bartlett of Alaska; Eugene J. McCarthy of Minnesota; Paul E. Tsongas of Massachusetts; Quentin N. Burdick and Mark Andrews of North Dakota; Charles E. Schumer of New York; and James G. Abourezk and Timothy P. Johnson of South Dakota. The twelve Republican committee members to move to the Senate were Frank A. Barrett and Craig L. Thomas of Wyoming; James A. McClure, Steven D. Symms, Larry E. Craig, and Michael D. Crapo of Idaho; Peter H. Dominick, Hank Brown, and A. Wayne Allard of Colorado; George H. Bender of Ohio; John S. McCain III of Arizona; and John E. Ensign of Nevada.

In addition to its heavy contribution to the Senate, the Natural Resources Committee and its predecessors served as a launch pad for five western governors—Republicans Frank A. Barrett of Wyoming, Charles H. Russell and James A. Gibbons of Nevada, and C.L. (Butch) Otter of Idaho and Democrat Bill Richardson of New Mexico; two Northeast governors—Democrats Hugh L. Carey of New York and James J. Florio of New Jersey; and two Southern governors—Republicans James G. Martin of North Carolina and Bobby Jindal of Louisiana. Republican Fred G. Aandahl of North Dakota and Democrat John E. Miles of New Mexico both served on Public Lands, the committee's first post-1947 incarnation after having been governor. Two mayors of Los Angeles—Republican C. Norris Poulson and Democrat Samuel W. Yorty—also passed through the committee en route to city hall.

Selected References

Cohen, Richard, "The New Barons," *National Journal*, 26 (1994), 940-945.

Fenno, Richard F., Jr., *Congressmen in Committees* (Boston: Little, Brown, 1973).

Magida, Arthur J., "The House and Senate Interior and Insular Affairs Committees," in the Ralph Nader Congress Project, *The Environment Committees: A Study of the House and Senate Interior, Agriculture, and Science Committees* (New York: Grossman, 1975), 1-141.

Schamel, Charles E. et al., "Records of the Committee on Interior and Insular Affairs and Its Predecessors," *Guide to the Records of the United States House of Representatives at the National Archives: 1789-1989 Bicentennial Edition* (Washington, D.C.: National Archives and Records Administration,1989), 179-199.

U.S. House of Representatives, Committee on Resources, *Historical Information of the Committee on Resources and Its Predecessor Committees, 1807-2002: Preparation for a Bicentennial*, House Committee Print, 107-G. 107th Congress, 2nd Session (2002).

RESPONSIBILITIES, JURISDICTIONAL CHANGES, AND SUBCOMMITTEES

PUBLIC LANDS

Jurisdiction, 80th Congress (1947-1949)

Established by the Legislative Reorganization Act of 1946:

[Section 121.(1)(n)] Committee on Public Lands

(1) Public lands generally, including entry, easements, and grazing thereon.

(2) Mineral resources of the public lands.

(3) Forfeiture of land grants and alien ownership, including alien ownership of mineral lands.

(4) Forest reserves and national parks created from the public domain.

(5) Military parks and battlefields, and national cemeteries.

(6) Preservation of prehistoric ruins and objects of interest on the public domain.

(7) Measures relating generally to Hawaii, Alaska, and the insular possessions of the United States, except those affecting the revenue and appropriations.

(8) Irrigation and reclamation, including water supply for reclamation projects, and easements of public lands for irrigation projects, and acquisition of private lands when necessary to complete irrigation projects.

(9) Interstate compacts relating to apportionment of waters for irrigation purposes.
(10) Mining interests generally.
(11) Mineral land laws and claims and entries thereunder.
(12) Geological survey.
(13) Mining schools and experimental stations.
(14) Petroleum conservation on the public lands and conservation of the radium supply in the United States.
(15) Relations of the United States with the Indians and the Indian tribes.
(16) Measures relating to the care, education, and management of Indians, including the care and allotment of Indian lands and general and special measures relating to claims which are paid out of Indian funds.

INTERIOR AND INSULAR AFFAIRS

Public Lands was renamed the Committee on Interior and Insular Affairs on February 2, 1951.

Jurisdiction, 103rd Congress (1993-1995)

From the *Rules of the House of Representatives, 103rd Congress* (House Document 102-405)

[Rule X.1.(I)] Committee on Interior and Insular Affairs

(1) Forest reserves and national parks created from the public domain.
(2) Forfeiture of land grants and alien ownership, including alien ownership of mineral lands.
(3) Geological Survey.
(4) Interstate compacts relating to apportionment of waters for irrigation purposes.
(5) Irrigation and reclamation, including water supply for reclamation projects, and easements of public lands for irrigation projects, and acquisition of private lands when necessary to complete irrigation projects.
(6) Measures relating to the care and management of Indians, including the care and allotment of Indian lands and general and special measures relating to claims which are paid out of Indian funds.
(7) Measures relating generally to the insular possessions of the United States, except those affecting the revenue and appropriations.
(8) Military parks and battlefields, national cemeteries administered by the Secretary of the Interior, and parks within the District of Columbia.
(9) Mineral land laws and claims and entries thereunder.
(10) Mineral resources of the public lands.
(11) Mining interests generally.
(12) Mining schools and experimental stations.
(13) Petroleum conservation on the public lands and conservation of the radium supply in the United States.
(14) Preservation of prehistoric ruins and objects of interest on the public domain.
(15) Public lands, generally, including entry, easements, and grazing thereon.
(16) Relations of the United States with the Indians and the Indian tribes.
(17) Regulation of the domestic nuclear energy industry, including regulation of research and development reactors and nuclear regulatory research.

In addition to its legislative jurisdiction under the preceding provisions of this paragraph (and its general oversight function under clause 2(b)(1)), the committee shall have the special oversight functions provided for in clause 3(e) with respect to all programs affecting Indians and nonmilitary nuclear energy and research and development including the disposal of nuclear waste.

[Rule X.3.(e)]

The Committee on Interior and Insular Affairs shall have the function of reviewing and studying, on a continuing basis, all laws, programs, and Government activities dealing with Indians and nonmilitary nuclear energy and research and development including the disposal of nuclear waste.

NATURAL RESOURCES

Interior and Insular Affairs was renamed the Committee on Natural Resources on January 5,1993.

RESOURCES

Natural Resources was renamed the Committee on Resources on January 4, 1995.

Jurisdiction, 104th Congress (1995-1997) Changes in Committee System

From H. Res. 6, Section 202 (a), the Committees and Their Jurisdiction, January 4, 1995.

[Rule X.1.(I)] Committee on Resources.

(1) Fisheries and wildlife, including research, restoration, refuges, and conservation.
(2) Forest reserves and national parks created from the public domain.
(3) Forfeiture of land grants and alien ownership, including alien ownership of mineral lands.
(4) Geological Survey.
(5) International fishing agreements.
(6) Interstate compacts relating to apportionment of waters for irrigation purposes.
(7) Irrigation and reclamation, including water supply for reclamation projects, and easements of public lands for irrigation projects, and acquisition of private lands when necessary to complete irrigation projects.
(8) Measures relating to the care and management of Indians, including the care and allotment of Indian lands and general and special measures relating to claims which are paid out of Indian funds.
(9) Measures relating generally to the insular possessions of the United States, except those affecting the revenue and appropriations.
(10) Military parks and battlefields, national cemeteries administered by the Secretary of the Interior, parks within the District of Columbia, and the erection of monuments to the memory of individuals.
(11) Mineral land laws and claims and entries thereunder.
(12) Mineral resources of the public lands.
(13) Mining interests generally.
(14) Mining schools and experimental stations.
(15) Marine affairs (including coastal zone management), except for measures relating to oil and other pollution of navigable waters.
(16) Oceanography.
(17) Petroleum conservation on the public lands and conservation of the radium supply in the United States.
(18) Preservation of prehistoric ruins and objects of interest on the public domain.
(19) Public lands generally, including entry, easements, and grazing thereon.
(20) Relations of the United States with the Indians and the Indian tribes.
(21) Trans-Alaska Oil Pipeline.

In addition to its legislative jurisdiction under the preceding provisions of this paragraph (and its general oversight function under clause 2(b)(1)), the committee shall have the special oversight functions provided for in clause 3(e) with respect to all programs affecting Indians.

NATURAL RESOURCES

Resources was redesignated the Committee on Natural Resources on January 4, 2007.

Jurisdiction, 111th Congress (2009-2011)

From the *Rules of the House of Representatives* (as revised to June 16, 2009, H.Doc. 110-162):

[Rule X.1.(I)] Committee on Natural Resources

(1) Fisheries and wildlife, including research, restoration, refuges, and conservation.
(2) Forest reserves and national parks, created from the public domain.
(3) Forfeiture of land grants and alien ownership, including alien ownership of mineral lands.
(4) Geological Survey.
(5) International fishing agreements.
(6) Interstate compacts relating to apportionment of waters for irrigation purposes.
(7) Irrigation and reclamation, including water supply for reclamation projects and easements of public lands for irrigation projects; and acquisition of private lands when necessary to complete irrigation projects.
(8) Native Americans generally, including the care and allotment of Native American lands and general and special measures relating to claims that are paid out of Native American funds.
(9) Insular possessions of the United States generally (except those affecting the revenue and appropriations).
(10) Military parks and battlefields, national cemeteries administered by the Secretary of the Interior, parks within the District of Columbia, and the erection of monuments to the memory of individuals.
(11) Mineral land laws and claims and entries thereunder.
(12) Mineral resources of public lands.
(13) Mining interests generally.
(14) Mining schools and experimental stations.
(15) Marine affairs, including coastal zone management (except for measures relating to oil and other pollution of navigable waters).
(16) Oceanography.
(17) Petroleum conservation on public lands and conservation of the radium supply in the United States.
(18) Preservation of prehistoric ruins and objects of interest on the public domain.
(19) Public lands generally, including entry, easements, and grazing thereon.

(20) Relations of the United States with Native Americans and Native American tribes.

(21) Trans-Alaska Oil Pipeline (except ratemaking).

[Rule X.3.(h)] Special Oversight Function

The Committee on Natural Resources shall review and study on a continuing basis laws, programs, and Government activities relating to Native Americans.

NAMES OF NATURAL RESOURCES SUBCOMMITTEES FROM THE *CONGRESSIONAL DIRECTORY*

Natural Resources, 103rd Congress

Energy and Mineral Resources, 103 Insular and International Affairs, 103
National Parks, Forests, and Public Lands, 103 Native American Affairs, 103
Oversight and Investigations, 103

Resources, 104th-109th Congresses

Energy and Mineral Resources, 104, 105, 106, 107, 108, 109 Fisheries, Wildlife and Oceans, 104
Fisheries Conservation, Wildlife, and Oceans, 105, 106, 107, 108, 109
Forests and Forest Health, 105, 106, 107, 108, 109 National Parks, Forests, and Lands, 104
National Parks and Public Lands, 105, 106 National Parks, Recreation, and Public Lands, 107, 108, 109
Native American and Insular Affairs, 104 Water and Power Resources, 104
Water and Power, 105, 106, 107, 108, 109

Natural Resources, 110th-111th Congresses

Energy and Mineral Resources, 110,111 Fisheries, Wildlife and Oceans, 110
Insular Affairs, 110 Insular Affairs, Oceans and Wildlife, 111
National Parks, Forests, and Public Lands, 110, 111 Water and Power, 110, 111

MEMBERSHIP ROSTERS, 103rd-111th Congresses, 1993-2011

NATURAL RESOURCES / 103rd Congress

Service Dates of Committee Chair: Jan. 5, 1993-Jan. 3, 1995

Service Dates of Majority Members: Jan. 5, 1993-Jan. 3, 1995

Service Dates of Minority Members: Jan. 5, 1993-Jan. 3, 1995

Roster Filled: Majority with 28 members, Jan. 21, 1993; Minority with 15 members, Jan. 5, 1993

Majority

Rank Name	Party	State	House	Comm.
Chr Miller, George	Dem	Cal.	10	*1 10
2nd Sharp, Philip R.	Dem	Ind.	10	9
3rd Markey, Edward J.	Dem	Mass.	10	*1 9
4th Murphy, Austin J.	Dem	Penn.	9	9
5th Rahall, Nick Joe II	Dem	W.Va.	9	9
6th Vento, Bruce F.	DFL	Minn.	9	9
7th Williams, J. Patrick	Dem	Mont.	8	*2 3
8th de Lugo, Ron	Dem	V.I.	10	*2 7
9th Gejdenson, Samuel	Dem	Conn.	7	7
10th Lehman, Richard H.	Dem	Cal.	6	6
11th Richardson, William B.	Dem	N.M.	6	6
12th DeFazio, Peter A.	Dem	Ore.	4	*1 4
13th Faleomavaega, Eni F.H.	Dem	A.Sm.	3	3
14th Johnson, Timothy P.	Dem	S.D.	4	3
15th LaRocco, Larry	Dem	Ida.	2	2
16th Abercrombie, Neil	Dem	Hai.	3	2
17th Dooley, Calvin M.	Dem	Cal.	2	2
18th Peterson, Collin C.	DFL	Minn.	2	1
19th Romero-Barceló, Carlos A.	Dem	P.R.	1	1
20th English, Karan	Dem	Ariz.	1	1

Minority

Rank Name	Party	State	House	Comm.
RM Young, Donald E.	Rep	Alas.	11	11
2nd Hansen, James V.	Rep	Utah.	7	7
3rd Vucanovich, Barbara F.	Rep	Nev.	6	6
4th Gallegly, Elton W.	Rep	Cal.	4	4
5th Smith, Robert F.	Rep	Ore.	6	*1 3
6th Thomas, Craig L.	Rep	Wyo.	3	3
7th Duncan, John J. (Jimmy) Jr.	Rep	Tenn.	4	3
8th Hefley, Joel M.	Rep	Colo.	4	2
9th Doolittle, John T.	Rep	Cal.	2	2
10th Allard, A. Wayne	Rep	Colo.	2	2
11th Baker, Richard H.	Rep	La.	4	*2 2
12th Calvert, Ken	Rep	Cal.	1	1
13th McInnis, Scott	Rep	Colo.	1	*1 1
14th Pombo, Richard W.	Rep	Cal.	1	1
15th Dickey, Jay W. Jr.	Rep	Ark.	1	1

*1: Member's first period of service on the committee.

*2: Member's second period of service on the committee.

21st Shepherd, Karen	Dem	Utah	1		1
22nd Deal, J. Nathan	Dem	Ga.	1		1
23rd Hinchey, Maurice D.	Dem	N.Y.	1	*1	1
24th Underwood, Robert A.	Dem	Guam	1		1
25th Evans, Lane A.	Dem	Ill.	6		1
26th Mink, Patsy T.	Dem	Hai.	9	*2	1
27th Barlow, Thomas J.	Dem	Ky.	1		1
28th Barrett, Thomas M.	Dem	Wisc.	1		1

Note: Territorial Delegates Ron de Lugo (Dem-V.I.), Eni F.H. Faleomavaega (Dem-A.Sm.), and Robert A. Underwood (Dem-Guam) and Resident Commissioner Carlos A. Romero-Barceló (Dem-P.R.) were allowed to accrue committee seniority but were not included in the party ratio.

Vacancies Filled:

25th through 28th seats filled by Evans, Mink, Barlow, and Barrett on Jan. 21, 1993.

Changes:

Majority:

Peterson, Collin C.	DFL	Minn.	Jan. 21, 1993 Resigned committee; no new assignment.
Berman, Howard L.	Dem	Cal.	Jan. 21, 1993 Replaced Peterson.
Berman, Howard L.	Dem	Cal.	June 18, 1993 Resigned committee; no new assignment.
Farr, Sam	Dem	Cal.	June 23, 1993 Replaced Berman, ranked after Underwood.

Departures from the House:	**Majority**			**Minority**		
Elected to U.S. Senate	None			Thomas, Craig L.	Rep	Wyo.
Defeated for Re-election	Lehman, Richard H.	Dem	Cal.			
	LaRocco, Larry	Dem	Ida.			
	English, Karan	Dem	Ariz.			
	Shepherd, Karen	Dem	Utah			
	Barlow, Thomas J.	Dem	Ky.			
Retired	Sharp, Philip R.	Dem	Ind.	Smith, Robert F.	Rep	Ore.
	de Lugo, Ron	Dem	V.I.			
	Murphy, Austin J.	Dem	Penn.			

Departures from Committee:						
Moved to Agriculture	None			Baker, Richard H.	Rep	La.
Moved to Appropriations	None			Dickey, Jay W. Jr.	Rep	Ark.
Moved to Rules	None			McInnis, Scott	Rep	Colo.
No new assignment	Markey, Edward J.	Dem	Mass.	Vucanovich, Barbara F.	Rep	Nev.
	Evans, Lane A.	Dem	Ill.			
	Mink, Patsy T.	Dem	Hai.			
	Barrett, Thomas M.	Dem	Wisc.			

RESOURCES / 104th Congress

Service Dates of Committee Chair: Jan. 4, 1995-Jan. 3, 1997

Service Dates of Majority Members: Jan. 4, 1995-Jan. 3, 1997

Service Dates of Minority Members: Jan. 9, 1995-Jan. 3, 1997

Roster Filled: Majority with 25 members, Jan. 4, 1995; Minority with 20 members, Jan. 9, 1995

Majority			Terms in:		**Minority**			Terms in:	
Rank Name	Party	State	House	Comm.	Rank Name	Party	State	House	Comm.
Chr Young, Donald E.	Rep	Alas.	12	12	RM Miller, George	Dem	Cal.	11	*1 11
2nd Hansen, James V.	Rep	Utah.	8	8	2nd Rahall, Nick Joe II	Dem	W.Va.	10	10
3rd Saxton, H. James	Rep	N.J.	7	1	3rd Vento, Bruce F.	DFL	Minn.	10	10
4th Gallegly, Elton W.	Rep	Cal.	5	5	4th Kildee, Dale E.	Dem	Mich.	10	*2 1
5th Duncan, John J. (Jimmy) Jr.	Rep	Tenn.	5	4	5th Williams, J. Patrick	Dem	Mont.	9	*2 4
6th Hefley, Joel M.	Rep	Colo.	5	3	6th Gejdenson, Samuel	Dem	Conn.	8	8
7th Doolittle, John T.	Rep	Cal.	3	3	7th Richardson, William B.	Dem	N.M.	7	7
8th Allard, A. Wayne	Rep	Colo.	3	3	8th DeFazio, Peter A.	Dem	Ore.	5	*1 5
9th Gilchrest, Wayne T.	Rep	Md.	3	1	9th Faleomavaega, Eni F.H.	Dem	A.Sm.	4	4
10th Calvert, Ken	Rep	Cal.	2	2	10th Johnson, Timothy P.	Dem	S.D.	5	4
11th Pombo, Richard W.	Rep	Cal.	2	2	11th Abercrombie, Neil	Dem	Hai.	4	3
12th Torkildsen, Peter G.	Rep	Mass.	2	1	12th Studds, Gerry E.	Dem	Mass.	12	1
13th Hayworth, John D. Jr.	Rep	Ariz.	1	*1 1	13th Tauzin, W.J. (Billy)	Dem	La.	9	*1 1
14th Cremeans, Frank A.	Rep	Ohio	1	1	14th Ortiz, Solomon P.	Dem	Tex.	7	1

15th Cubin, Barbara	Rep	Wyo.	1	1		15th Dooley, Calvin M.	Dem	Cal.	3	3
16th Cooley, Wes	Rep	Ore.	1	1		16th Romero-Barceló, Carlos A.	Dem	P.R.	2	2
17th Chenoweth, Helen P.	Rep	Ida.	1	1		17th Deal, J. Nathan	Dem	Ga.	2	2
18th Smith, Linda	Rep	Wash.	1	1		18th Hinchey, Maurice D.	Dem	N.Y.	2	*1 2
19th Radanovich, George P.	Rep	Cal.	1	1		19th Underwood, Robert A.	Dem	Guam	2	2
20th Jones, Walter B. Jr.	Rep	N.C.	1	1		20th Farr, Sam	Dem	Cal.	2	2
21st Thornberry, William M. (Mac)	Rep	Tex.	1	1						
22nd Hastings, Richard (Doc)	Rep	Wash.	1	*1 1						
23rd Metcalf, Jack	Rep	Wash.	1	1						
24th Longley, James B. Jr.	Rep	Me.	1	1						
25th Shadegg, John B.	Rep	Ariz.	1	1						

*1: Member's first period of service on the committee.
*2: Member's second period of service on the committee.

Note 1: With elements of the Committee on Merchant, Marine, and Fisheries absorbed into Resources in 1995, Saxton (Rep-N.J.) was credited with five terms of service, 1985-1995.

Note 2: Territorial Delegates Eni F.H. Faleomavaega (Dem-A.Sm.) and Robert A. Underwood (Dem-Guam) and Resident Commissioner Carlos A. Romero-Barceló (Dem-P.R.) were allowed to accrue committee seniority but were not included in the party ratio.

Additions:
  Majority:

Ensign, John E.	Rep	Nev.	May 25, 1995
Tauzin, W.J. (Billy)	Rep	La.	Sept. 12, 1995 Ranked 2nd after Young.

  Minority:

Pallone, Frank Jr.	Dem	N.J.	June 13, 1995
Kennedy, Patrick J.	Dem	R.I.	Nov. 20, 1995

Changes:
  Minority:

Deal, J. Nathan	Dem	Ga.	May 10, 1995 Service on committee as a Democrat was vacated; moved to Commerce as a Republican on May 25, 1995.
Pickett, Owen B.	Dem	Va.	June 13, 1995 Replaced Deal.
Tauzin, W.J. (Billy)	Dem	La.	Sep. 6, 1995 Service on committee as a Democrat was vacated; returned to Resources as a Republican on Sept. 12, 1995, ranked after Young.
Markey, Edward J.	Dem	Mass.	Nov. 20, 1995 Replaced Tauzin, ranked after Miller.

Departures from the House:

	Majority			**Minority**		
Elected to U.S. Senate	Allard, A. Wayne	Rep	Colo.	Johnson, Timothy P.	Dem	S.D.
Defeated for Re-election	Torkildsen, Peter G.	Rep	Mass.			
	Cremeans, Frank A.	Rep	Ohio			
	Longley, James B. Jr.	Rep	Me.			
Retired	Cooley, Wes	Rep	Ore.	Williams, J. Patrick	Dem	Mont.
				Studds, Gerry E.	Dem	Mass.

Departures from Committee:

Moved to Rules	Hastings, Richard (Doc)	Rep	Wash.	None
Moved to Transportation and Infrastructure	Metcalf, Jack	Rep	Wash.	None
Moved to Ways and Means	Hayworth, John D. Jr.	Rep	Ariz.	None

RESOURCES / 105th Congress

Service Dates of Committee Chair: Jan. 7, 1997-Jan. 3, 1999

Service Dates of Majority Members: Jan. 7, 1997-Jan. 3, 1999

Service Dates of Minority Members: Jan. 7, 1997-Jan. 3, 1999

Roster Filled: Majority with 27 members, Jan. 21, 1997; Minority with 23 members, Jan. 7, 1997

	Majority					**Minority**				
				Terms in:					**Terms in:**	
Rank Name	Party	State	House	Comm.		Rank Name	Party	State	House	Comm.
Chr Young, Donald E.	Rep	Alas.	13	13		RM Miller, George	Dem	Cal.	12	*1 12
2nd Tauzin, W.J. (Billy)	Rep	La.	10	*2 2		2nd Markey, Edward J.	Dem	Mass.	12	*2 2
3rd Hansen, James V.	Rep	Utah.	9	9		3rd Rahall, Nick Joe II	Dem	W.Va.	11	11
4th Saxton, H. James	Rep	N.J.	8	2		4th Vento, Bruce F.	DFL	Minn.	11	11
5th Gallegly, Elton W.	Rep	Cal.	6	6		5th Kildee, Dale E.	Dem	Mich.	11	*2 2
6th Duncan, John J. (Jimmy) Jr.	Rep	Tenn.	6	5		6th Gejdenson, Samuel	Dem	Conn.	9	9
7th Hefley, Joel M.	Rep	Colo.	6	4		7th Richardson, William B.	Dem	N.M.	8	8

8th Doolittle, John T.	Rep	Cal.	4	4		8th DeFazio, Peter A.	Dem	Ore.	6	*1 6		
9th Gilchrest, Wayne T.	Rep	Md.	4	2		9th Faleomavaega, Eni F.H.	Dem	A.Sm.	5	5		
10th Calvert, Ken	Rep	Cal.	3	3		10th Abercrombie, Neil	Dem	Hai.	5	4		
11th Pombo, Richard W.	Rep	Cal.	3	3		11th Ortiz, Solomon P.	Dem	Tex.	8	2		
12th Cubin, Barbara	Rep	Wyo.	2	2		12th Pickett, Owen B.	Dem	Va.	6	2		
13th Chenoweth, Helen P.	Rep	Ida.	2	2		13th Pallone, Frank Jr.	Dem	N.J.	6	2		
14th Smith, Linda	Rep	Wash.	2	2		14th Dooley, Calvin M.	Dem	Cal.	4	4		
15th Radanovich, George P.	Rep	Cal.	2	2		15th Romero-Barceló, Carlos A.	Dem	P.R.	3	3		
16th Jones, Walter B. Jr.	Rep	N.C.	2	2		16th Hinchey, Maurice D.	Dem	N.Y.	3	*1 3		
17th Thornberry, William M. (Mac)	Rep	Tex.	2	2		17th Underwood, Robert A.	Dem	Guam	3	3		
18th Shadegg, John B.	Rep	Ariz.	2	2		18th Farr, Sam	Dem	Cal.	3	3		
19th Ensign, John E.	Rep	Nev.	2	2		19th Kennedy, Patrick J.	Dem	R.I.	2	*1 2		
20th Smith, Robert F.	Rep	Ore.	7	*2 1		20th Smith, Adam	Dem	Wash.	1	1		
21st Cannon, Christopher B.	Rep	Utah	1	1		21st Delahunt, William D.	Dem	Mass.	1	1		
22nd Brady, Kevin P.	Rep	Tex.	1	1		22nd John, Christopher	Dem	La.	1	1		
23rd Peterson, John E.	Rep	Penn.	1	1		23rd Christian-Green, Donna	Dem	V.I.	1	1		
24th Hill, Rick	Rep	Mont.	1	1								
25th Schaffer, Robert W.	Rep	Colo.	1	1		*1: Member's first period of service on the committee.						
26th Gibbons, James A.	Rep	Nev.	1	1		*2: Member's second period of service on the committee.						
27th Crapo, Michael D.	Rep	Ida.	3	1								

Note: Territorial Delegates Eni F.H. Faleomavaega (Dem-A.Sm.), Robert A. Underwood (Dem-Guam), and Donna Christian-Green (Dem-V.I.) and Resident Commissioner Carlos A. Romero-Barceló (Dem-P.R.) were allowed to accrue committee seniority but were not included in the party ratio.

Vacancies Filled:
Majority:
   27th seat by Crapo on Jan. 21, 1997.

Changes:
Minority:

Gejdenson, Samuel	Dem	Conn.	Feb. 5, 1997 Resigned committee; moved to Joint Library and Joint Printing.	
Lampson, Nicholas V.	Dem	Tex.	Feb. 5, 1997 Replaced Gejdenson.	
Richardson, William B.	Dem	N.M.	Feb. 13, 1997 Resigned the House; appointed U.S. Ambassador to United Nations.	
Kind, Ron	Dem	Wisc.	Feb. 13, 1997 Replaced Richardson.	
Lampson, Nicholas V.	Dem	Tex.	Apr. 17, 1997 Resigned committee; moved to Transportation and Infrastructure.	
Doggett, Lloyd A. II	Dem	Tex.	Apr. 17, 1997 Replaced Lampson.	

Departures from the House:

	Majority			Minority
Elected to U.S. Senate	Crapo, Michael D.	Rep	Ida.	None
Lost Election to U.S. Senate	Ensign, John E.	Rep	Nev.	None
	Smith, Linda	Rep	Wash.	
Retired	Smith, Robert F.	Rep	Ore.	

Departures from Committee:

Moved to Appropriations	None			Hinchey, Maurice D.	Dem	N.Y.
				Farr, Sam	Dem	Cal.
Moved to Budget	None			Markey, Edward J.	Dem	Mass.
Moved to Commerce	Shadegg, John B.	Rep	Ariz.	None	
Moved to Ways and Means	None			Doggett, Lloyd A. II	Dem	Tex.

RESOURCES / 106th Congress

Service Dates of Committee Chair: Jan. 6, 1999-Jan. 3, 2001

Service Dates of Majority Members: Jan. 6, 1999-Jan. 3, 2001

Service Dates of Minority Members: Jan. 6, 1999-Jan. 3, 2001

Roster Filled: Majority with 28 members, Jan. 6, 1999; Minority with 25 members, June 9, 1999

Majority					Minority				
			Terms in:					**Terms in:**	
Rank Name	Party	State	House	Comm.	Rank Name	Party	State	House	Comm.
Chr Young, Donald E.	Rep	Alas.	14	14	RM Miller, George	Dem	Cal.	13	*1 13
2nd Tauzin, W.J. (Billy)	Rep	La.	11	*2 3	2nd Rahall, Nick Joe II	Dem	W.Va.	12	12
3rd Hansen, James V.	Rep	Utah	10	10	3rd Vento, Bruce F.	DFL	Minn.	12	12
4th Saxton, H. James	Rep	N.J.	9	3	4th Kildee, Dale E.	Dem	Mich.	12	*2 3
5th Gallegly, Elton W.	Rep	Cal.	7	7	5th DeFazio, Peter A.	Dem	Ore.	7	*1 7
6th Duncan, John J. (Jimmy) Jr.	Rep	Tenn.	7	6	6th Faleomavaega, Eni F.H.	Dem	A.Sm.	6	6

7th Hefley, Joel M.	Rep	Colo.	7	5	
8th Doolittle, John T.	Rep	Cal.	5	5	
9th Gilchrest, Wayne T.	Rep	Md.	5	3	
10th Calvert, Ken	Rep	Cal.	4	4	
11th Pombo, Richard W.	Rep	Cal.	4	4	
12th Cubin, Barbara	Rep	Wyo.	3	3	
13th Chenoweth, Helen P.	Rep	Ida.	3	3	
14th Radanovich, George P.	Rep	Cal.	3	3	
15th Jones, Walter B. Jr.	Rep	N.C.	3	3	
16th Thornberry, William M. (Mac)	Rep	Tex.	3	3	
17th Cannon, Christopher B.	Rep	Utah	2	2	
18th Brady, Kevin P.	Rep	Tex.	2	2	
19th Peterson, John E.	Rep	Penn.	2	2	
20th Hill, Rick	Rep	Mont.	2	2	
21st Schaffer, Robert W.	Rep	Colo.	2	2	
22nd Gibbons, James A.	Rep	Nev.	2	2	
23rd Souder, Mark E.	Rep	Ind.	3	1	
24th Walden, Greg	Rep	Ore.	1	1	
25th Sherwood, Don	Rep	Penn.	1	1	
26th Hayes, Robert (Robin)	Rep	N.C.	1	1	
27th Simpson, Michael K.	Rep	Ida.	1	1	
28th Tancredo, Thomas G.	Rep	Colo.	1	1	

7th Abercrombie, Neil	Dem	Hai.	6	5	
8th Ortiz, Solomon P.	Dem	Tex.	9	3	
9th Pickett, Owen B.	Dem	Va.	7	3	
10th Pallone, Frank Jr.	Dem	N.J.	7	3	
11th Dooley, Calvin M.	Dem	Cal.	5	5	
12th Romero-Barceló, Carlos A.	Dem	P.R.	4	4	
13th Underwood, Robert A.	Dem	Guam	4	4	
14th Kennedy, Patrick J.	Dem	R.I.	3	*1 3	
15th Smith, Adam	Dem	Wash.	2	2	
16th Delahunt, William D.	Dem	Mass.	2	2	
17th John, Christopher	Dem	La.	2	2	
18th Christensen, Donna M.C.	Dem	V.I.	2	2	
19th Kind, Ron	Dem	Wisc.	2	2	
20th Inslee, Jay R.	Dem	Wash.	2	1	
21st Napolitano, Grace F.	Dem	Cal.	1	1	
22nd Udall, Thomas	Dem	N.M.	1	1	
23rd Udall, Mark	Dem	Colo.	1	1	
24th Crowley, Joseph	Dem	N.Y.	1	1	

*1: Member's first period of service on the committee.
*2: Member's second period of service on the committee.

Note: Territorial Delegates Eni F.H. Faleomavaega (Dem-A.Sm.), Robert A. Underwood (Dem-Guam), and Donna M.C. Christensen (Dem-V.I.) and Resident Commissioner Carlos A. Romero-Barceló (Dem-P.R.) were allowed to accrue committee seniority but were not included in the party ratio.

Changes:

Minority:

Delahunt, William D.	Dem	Mass.	Feb. 24, 1999 Resigned committee; no new assignment.
Holt, Rush D.	Dem	N.J.	June 9, 1999 Replaced Delahunt.
Vento, Bruce F.	DFL	Minn.	Oct. 10, 2000 Died in office; vacancy left unfilled.

Departures from the House:

	Majority			Minority		
Defeated for Re-election	None			Romero-Barceló, Carlos A.	Dem	P.R.
Retired	Chenoweth, Helen P.	Rep	Ida.	Pickett, Owen B.	Dem	Va.
	Hill, Rick	Rep	Mont.			

Departures from Committee:

	Majority			Minority		
Became RM on Education and the Workforce	None			Miller, George	Dem	Cal.
Moved to Appropriations	Doolittle, John T.	Rep	Cal.	Kennedy, Patrick J.	Dem	R.I.
Moved to Energy and Commerce	None			John, Christopher	Dem	La.
Moved to Financial Services	None			Crowley, Joseph	Dem	N.Y.
Moved to House Administration	Doolittle, John T.	Rep	Cal.	None		

RESOURCES / 107th Congress

Service Dates of Committee Chair: Jan. 6, 2001-Jan. 3, 2003

Service Dates of Majority Members: Jan. 6, 2001-Jan. 3, 2003

Service Dates of Minority Members: Feb. 8, 2001-Jan. 3, 2003

Roster Filled: Majority with 28 members, Jan. 6, 2001; Minority with 24 members, May 2, 2001

Majority			Terms in:		Minority			Terms in:	
Rank Name	Party	State	House	Comm.	Rank Name	Party	State	House	Comm.
Chr Hansen, James V.	Rep	Utah.	11	11	RM Rahall, Nick Joe II	Dem	W.Va.	13	13
2nd Young, Donald E.	Rep	Alas.	15	15	2nd Miller, George	Dem	Cal.	14	*2 1
3rd Tauzin, W.J. (Billy)	Rep	La.	12	*2 4	3rd Markey, Edward J.	Dem	Mass.	14	*3 1
4th Saxton, H. James	Rep	N.J.	10	4	4th Kildee, Dale E.	Dem	Mich.	13	*2 4
5th Gallegly, Elton W.	Rep	Cal.	8	8	5th DeFazio, Peter A.	Dem	Ore.	8	*1 8
6th Duncan, John J. (Jimmy) Jr.	Rep	Tenn.	8	7	6th Faleomavaega, Eni F.H.	Dem	A.Sm.	7	7
7th Hefley, Joel M.	Rep	Colo.	8	6	7th Abercrombie, Neil	Dem	Hai.	7	6
8th Gilchrest, Wayne T.	Rep	Md.	6	4	8th Ortiz, Solomon P.	Dem	Tex.	10	4
9th Calvert, Ken	Rep	Cal.	5	5	9th Pallone, Frank Jr.	Dem	N.J.	8	4
10th McInnis, Scott	Rep	Colo.	5	*2 1	10th Dooley, Calvin M.	Dem	Cal.	6	6
11th Pombo, Richard W.	Rep	Cal.	5	5	11th Underwood, Robert A.	Dem	Guam	5	5

12th Cubin, Barbara	Rep	Wyo.	4	4		12th Smith, Adam	Dem	Wash.	3	3
13th Radanovich, George P.	Rep	Cal.	4	4		13th Christensen, Donna M.C.	Dem	V.I.	3	3
14th Jones, Walter B. Jr.	Rep	N.C.	4	4		14th Kind, Ron	Dem	Wisc.	3	3
15th Thornberry, William M. (Mac)	Rep	Tex.	4	4		15th Inslee, Jay R.	Dem	Wash.	3	2
16th Cannon, Christopher B.	Rep	Utah	3	3		16th Napolitano, Grace F.	Dem	Cal.	2	2
17th Brady, Kevin P.	Rep	Tex.	3	3		17th Udall, Thomas	Dem	N.M.	2	2
18th Peterson, John E.	Rep	Penn.	3	3		18th Udall, Mark	Dem	Colo.	2	2
19th Schaffer, Robert W.	Rep	Colo.	3	3		19th Holt, Rush D.	Dem	N.J.	2	*1 2
20th Gibbons, James A.	Rep	Nev.	3	3		20th McGovern, James P.	Dem	Mass.	3	1
21st Souder, Mark E.	Rep	Ind.	4	2		21st Acevedo-Vilá, Aníbal	Dem	P.R.	1	1
22nd Walden, Greg	Rep	Ore.	2	2		22nd Solis, Hilda L.	Dem	Cal.	1	*1 1
23rd Sherwood, Don	Rep	Penn.	2	2		23rd Carson, Brad	Dem	Okla.	1	1
24th Hayes, Robert (Robin)	Rep	N.C.	2	2		23rd McCollum, Betty	DFL	Minn.	1	*1 1
25th Simpson, Michael K.	Rep	Ida.	2	2						
26th Tancredo, Thomas G.	Rep	Colo.	2	2		*1: Member's first period of service on the committee.				
27th Otter, C.L. (Butch)	Rep	Ida.	1	1		*2: Member's second period of service on the committee.				
28th Osborne, Thomas	Rep	Neb.	1	1		*3: Member's third period of service on the committee.				

Note: Territorial Delegates Eni F.H. Faleomavaega (Dem-A.Sm.), Robert A. Underwood (Dem-Guam), and Donna M.C. Christensen (Dem-V.I.) and Resident Commissioner Anibal Acevedo-Vilá (Dem-P.R.) were allowed to accrue committee seniority but were not included in the party ratio.

Vacancies Filled:
  Minority:
    Miller returned on May 2, 2001, ranked after Rahall.

Changes:
  Majority:

Hayes, Robert (Robin)	Rep	N.C.	Feb. 7, 2001 Resigned committee; moved to Transportation and Infrastructure.
Brady, Kevin P.	Rep	Tex.	Feb. 8, 2001 Resigned committee; had moved to Ways and Means.
Flake, Jeff	Rep	Ariz.	Feb. 8, 2001 Replaced Hayes.
Rehberg, Dennis	Rep	Mont.	Feb. 8, 2001 Replaced Brady.
Sherwood, Don	Rep	Penn.	Mar. 7, 2001 Resigned committee; moved to Appropriations.
Hayworth, John D. Jr.	Rep	Ariz.	June 20, 2001 Replaced Sherwood.

  Minority:

McGovern, James P.	Dem	Mass.	May 7, 2002 Resigned committee; moved to Rules.
Holden, T. Timothy	Dem	Penn.	July 8, 2002 Replaced McGovern.

Departures from the House:

	Majority			Minority		
Lost Election for Governor	None			Underwood, Robert A.	Dem	Guam
Retired	Hansen, James V.	Rep	Utah	None		
	Schaffer, Robert W.	Rep	Colo.			

Departures from Committee:

	Majority			Minority		
Moved to Appropriations	Simpson, Michael K.	Rep	Ida.	None		
Moved to Energy and Commerce	Otter, C.L. (Butch)	Rep	Ida.	Solis, Hilda L.	Dem	Cal.
Moved to International Relations	None			McCollum, Betty	DFL	Minn.
Moved to Permanent Select Intelligence	None			Holt, Rush D.	Dem	N.J.
Moved to Select Homeland Security	Thornberry, William M. (Mac)	Rep	Tex.	None		
No new assignment	None			Holden, T. Timothy	Dem	Penn.

RESOURCES / 108th Congress

Service Dates of Committee Chair: Jan. 8, 2003-Jan. 3, 2005

Service Dates of Majority Members: Jan. 28, 2003-Jan. 3, 2005

Service Dates of Ranking Member: Jan. 8, 2003-Jan. 3, 2005

Service Dates of Minority Members: Jan. 28, 2003-Jan. 3, 2005

Roster Filled: Majority with 28 members, Jan. 28, 2003; Minority with 24 members, March 5, 2003

Majority			Terms in:		Minority			Terms in:	
Rank Name	Party	State	House	Comm.	Rank Name	Party	State	House	Comm.
Chr Pombo, Richard W.	Rep	Cal.	6	6	RM Rahall, Nick Joe II	Dem	W.Va.	14	14
2nd Young, Donald E.	Rep	Alas.	16	16	2nd Miller, George	Dem	Cal.	15	*2 2
3rd Tauzin, W.J. (Billy)	Rep	La.	13	*2 5	3rd Markey, Edward J.	Dem	Mass.	15	*3 2
4th Saxton, H. James	Rep	N.J.	11	5	4th Kildee, Dale E.	Dem	Mich.	14	*2 5

5th Gallegly, Elton W.	Rep	Cal.	9	9	5th DeFazio, Peter A.	Dem	Ore.	9	*1 9
6th Duncan, John J. (Jimmy) Jr.	Rep	Tenn.	**9**	8	6th Faleomavaega, Eni F.H.	Dem	A.Sm.	8	8
7th Hefley, Joel M.	Rep	Colo.	9	7	7th Abercrombie, Neil	Dem	Hai.	8	7
8th Gilchrest, Wayne T.	Rep	Md.	7	5	8th Ortiz, Solomon P.	Dem	Tex.	11	5
9th Calvert, Ken	Rep	Cal.	6	6	9th Pallone, Frank Jr.	Dem	N.J.	9	5
10th McInnis, Scott	Rep	Colo.	6	*2 2	10th Dooley, Calvin M.	Dem	Cal.	7	7
11th Cubin, Barbara	Rep	Wyo.	5	5	11th Smith, Adam	Dem	Wash.	4	4
12th Radanovich, George P.	Rep	Cal.	5	5	12th Christensen, Donna M.C.	Dem	V.I.	4	4
13th Jones, Walter B. Jr.	Rep	N.C.	5	5	13th Kind, Ron	Dem	Wisc.	4	4
14th Cannon, Christopher B.	Rep	Utah	4	4	14th Inslee, Jay R.	Dem	Wash.	4	3
15th Peterson, John E.	Rep	Penn.	4	4	15th Napolitano, Grace F.	Dem	Cal.	3	3
16th Gibbons, James A.	Rep	Nev.	4	4	16th Udall, Thomas	Dem	N.M.	3	3
17th Souder, Mark E.	Rep	Ind.	5	3	17th Udall, Mark	Dem	Colo.	3	3
18th Walden, Greg	Rep	Ore.	3	3	18th Acevedo-Vilá, Aníbal	Dem	P.R.	2	2
19th Tancredo, Thomas G.	Rep	Colo.	3	3	19th Carson, Brad	Dem	Okla.	2	2
20th Hayworth, John D. Jr.	Rep	Ariz.	5	*2 2	20th Grijalva, Raúl M.	Dem	Ariz.	1	1
21st Osborne, Thomas	Rep	Neb.	2	2	21st Cardoza, Dennis A.	Dem	Cal.	1	1
22nd Flake, Jeff	Rep	Ariz.	2	2	22nd Bordallo, Madeleine Z.	Dem	Guam	1	1
23rd Rehberg, Dennis	Rep	Mont.	2	2	23rd Hinojosa, Rubén	Dem	Tex.	4	1
24th Renzi, Rick	Rep	Ariz.	1	1	24th Rodriguez, Ciro D.	Dem	Tex.	4	1
25th Cole, Tom	Rep	Okla.	1	*1 1					
26th Pearce, Stevan	Rep	N.M.	1	1	*1: Member's first period of service on the committee.				
27th Bishop, Robert	Rep	Utah	1	*1 1	*2: Member's second period of service on the committee.				
28th Nunes, Devin	Rep	Cal.	1	1	*3: Member's third period of service on the committee.				

Note: Territorial Delegates Eni F.H. Faleomavaega (Dem-A.Sm.), Donna M.C. Christensen (Dem-V.I.), and Madeleine Z. Bordallo (Dem-Guam) and Resident Commissioner Aníbal Acevedo-Vilá (Dem-P.R.) were allowed to accrue committee seniority but were not included in the party ratio.

Vacancies Filled:

Minority:

20th, 21st, and 22nd seats filled by Grijalva, Cardoza, and Bordallo on Feb. 5, 2003.

23rd and 24th seats filled by Hinojosa and Rodriguez on Mar. 5, 2003.

Changes:

Majority:

Hefley, Joel M.	Rep	Colo.	Jan. 30, 2003 Resigned committee; no new assignment.
Putnam, Adam H. Jr.	Rep	Fla.	Apr. 29, 2003 Replaced Hefley.
Putnam, Adam H. Jr.	Rep	Fla.	June 19, 2003 Resigned committee to open seat for Neugebauer.
Neugebauer, Randy	Rep	Tex.	June 19, 2003 Replaced Putnam, ranked after Nunes.

Minority:

Miller, George	Dem	Cal.	Feb. 5, 2003 Resigned committee; no new assignment; returned on Mar. 5, 2003.
Smith, Adam	Dem	Wash.	Feb. 5, 2003 Resigned committee; moved to International Relations.
Markey, Edward J.	Dem	Mass.	Feb. 12, 2003 Leave of absence from committee; moved to Select Homeland Security; returned on Mar. 5, 2003.
DeFazio, Peter A.	Dem	Ore.	Feb. 12, 2003 Leave of absence from committee; moved to Select Homeland Security; did not return.
Baca, Joe	Dem	Cal.	Mar. 5, 2003 Replaced Smith.
McCollum, Betty	DFL	Minn.	Mar. 5, 2003 Replaced DeFazio.
McCollum, Betty	DFL	Minn.	June 14, 2004 Resigned committee; moved to Government Reform.
Herseth, Stephanie	Dem	S.D.	June 16, 2004 Replaced McCollum.

Departures from the House:	**Majority**			**Minority**		
Lost Election to U.S. Senate	None			Carson, Brad	Dem	La.
Defeated for Re-nomination	None			Rodriguez, Ciro D.	Dem	Tex.
Elected Governor	None			Acevedo-Vilá, Aníbal	Dem	P.R.
Retired	Tauzin, W.J. (Billy)	Rep	La.	Dooley, Calvin M.	Dem	Cal.
	McInnis, Scott	Rep	Colo.			

Departures from Committee:						
Moved to Appropriations	Rehberg, Dennis	Rep	Mont.	None		
Moved to Financial Services	Neugebauer, Randy	Rep	Tex.	None		
Moved to Rules	Cole, Tom	Rep	La.	None		
	Bishop, Robert	Rep	Utah			
Moved to Standards of Official Conduct	Cole, Tom	Rep	La.	None		
Moved to Transportation and Infrastructure	Osborne, Thomas	Rep	Neb.	None		
No new assignment	None			Baca, Joe	Dem	Cal.
				Hinojosa, Rubén	Dem	Tex.

RESOURCES / 109th Congress

Service Dates of Committee Chair: Jan. 6, 2005-Jan. 3, 2007

Service Dates of Majority Members: Jan. 26, 2005-Jan. 3, 2007

Service Dates of Minority Members: Jan. 26, 2005-Jan. 3, 2007

Roster Filled: Majority with 27 members, Jan. 26, 2005; Minority with 22 members, Feb. 2, 2005

Majority

Rank Name	Party	State	Terms in: House	Terms in: Comm.
Chr Pombo, Richard W.	Rep	Cal.	7	7
2nd Young, Donald E.	Rep	Alas.	17	17
3rd Saxton, H. James	Rep	N.J.	12	6
4th Gallegly, Elton W.	Rep	Cal.	10	10
5th Duncan, John J. (Jimmy) Jr.	Rep	Tenn.	10	9
6th Gilchrest, Wayne T.	Rep	Md.	8	6
7th Calvert, Ken	Rep	Cal.	7	7
8th Cubin, Barbara	Rep	Wyo.	6	6
9th Radanovich, George P.	Rep	Cal.	6	6
10th Jones, Walter B. Jr.	Rep	N.C.	6	6
11th Cannon, Christopher B.	Rep	Utah	5	5
12th Peterson, John E.	Rep	Penn.	5	5
13th Gibbons, James A.	Rep	Nev.	5	5
14th Souder, Mark E.	Rep	Ind.	6	4
15th Walden, Greg	Rep	Ore.	4	4
16th Tancredo, Thomas G.	Rep	Colo.	4	4
17th Hayworth, John D. Jr.	Rep	Ariz.	6	*2 3
18th Flake, Jeff	Rep	Ariz.	3	3
19th Renzi, Rick	Rep	Ariz.	2	2
20th Pearce, Stevan	Rep	N.M.	2	2
21st Nunes, Devin	Rep	Cal.	2	2
22nd Brown, Henry E. Jr.	Rep	S.C.	3	1
23rd Drake, Thelma D.	Rep	Va.	1	1
24th Fortuño, Luis G.	Rep	P.R.	1	1
25th McMorris, Cathy	Rep	Wash.	1	1
26th Jindal, Bobby	Rep	La.	1	1
27th Gohmert, Louie	Rep	Tex.	1	1

Minority

Rank Name	Party	State	Terms in: House	Terms in: Comm.
RM Rahall, Nick Joe II	Dem	W.Va.	15	15
2nd Kildee, Dale E.	Dem	Mich.	15	*2 6
3rd Faleomavaega, Eni F.H.	Dem	A.Sm.	9	9
4th Abercrombie, Neil	Dem	Hai.	9	8
5th Ortiz, Solomon P.	Dem	Tex.	12	6
6th Pallone, Frank Jr.	Dem	N.J.	10	6
7th Christensen, Donna M.C.	Dem	V.I.	5	5
8th Kind, Ron	Dem	Wisc.	5	5
9th Napolitano, Grace F.	Dem	Cal.	4	4
10th Udall, Thomas	Dem	N.M.	4	4
11th Grijalva, Raúl M.	Dem	Ariz.	2	2
12th Bordallo, Madeleine Z.	Dem	Guam	2	2
13th Costa, Jim	Dem	Cal.	1	1
14th Melancon, Charles J.	Dem	La.	1	1
15th Boren, Daniel D.	Dem	Okla.	1	1
16th Miller, George	Dem	Cal.	16	*3 2
17th Markey, Edward J.	Dem	Mass.	16	*4 2
18th DeFazio, Peter A.	Dem	Ore.	10	*2 1
19th Inslee, Jay R.	Dem	Wash.	5	4
20th Udall, Mark	Dem	Colo.	4	4
21st Cardoza, Dennis A.	Dem	Cal.	2	2
22nd Herseth, Stephanie	Dem	S.D.	1	2

*1: Member's first period of service on the committee.

*2: Member's second period of service on the committee.

*3: Member's third period of service on the committee.

*4: Member's fourth period of service on the committee.

Note: Territorial Delegates Eni F.H. Faleomavaega (Dem-A.Sm.), Donna M.C. Christensen (Dem-V.I.), and Madeleine Z. Bordallo (Dem-Guam) and Resident Commissioner Luis G. Fortuno (Rep-P.R.) were allowed to accrue committee seniority but were not included in the party ratio.

Vacancies Filled:

Minority:

16th through 22nd seats filled by Miller, Markey, DeFazio, Inslee, Udall of Colorado, Cardoza, and Herseth on Feb. 2, 2005.

Changes:

Majority:

Souder, Mark E.	Rep	Ind.	Feb. 2, 2005 Resigned committee; returned to Education and the Workforce.
Musgrave, Marilyn N.	Rep	Colo.	Feb. 16, 2005 Replaced Souder.
Nunes, Devin	Rep	Cal.	May 5, 2005 Resigned committee; moved to Ways and Means.
Gibbons, James A.	Rep	Nev.	Dec. 31, 2005 Resigned the House; elected Governor of Nevada.

Departures from the House:

	Majority			Minority		
Defeated for Re-election	Pombo, Richard W.	Rep	Cal.	None		
	Hayworth, John D. Jr.	Rep	Ariz.			

Departures from Committee:

	Majority			Minority		
Moved to Appropriations	None			Udall, Thomas	Dem	N.M.
Moved to Energy and Commerce	None			Melancon, Charles J.	Dem	La.
Moved to Rules	None			Cardoza, Dennis A.	Dem	Cal.
Moved to Select Energy Independence and Global Warming	Walden, Greg	Rep	Ore.	None		
Moved to Transportation and Infrastructure	Drake, Thelma D.	Rep	Va.	None		
No new assignment	Cubin, Barbara	Rep	Wyo.	None		
	Radanovich, George P.	Rep	Cal.			
	Jones, Walter B. Jr.	Rep	N.C.			
	Peterson, John E.	Rep	Penn.			
	Musgrave, Marilyn N.	Rep	Colo.			

NATURAL RESOURCES / 110th Congress

Service Dates of Committee Chair: Jan. 4, 2007-Jan. 3, 2009

Service Dates of Majority Members: Jan. 18, 2007-Jan. 3, 2009

Service Dates of Minority Members: Jan. 10, 2007-Jan. 3, 2009

Roster Filled: Majority with 27 members, Jan. 18, 2007; Minority with 22 members, Jan. 10, 2007

Majority					Minority				
			Terms in:					Terms in:	
Rank Name	Party	State	House	Comm.	Rank Name	Party	State	House	Comm.
Chr Rahall, Nick Joe II	Dem	W.Va.	16	16	RM Young, Donald E.	Rep	Alas.	18	18
2nd Kildee, Dale E.	Dem	Mich.	16	*2 7	2nd Saxton, H. James	Rep	N.J.	13	7
3rd Faleomavaega, Eni F.H.	Dem	A.Sm.	10	10	3rd Gallegly, Elton W.	Rep	Cal.	11	11
4th Abercrombie, Neil	Dem	Hai.	10	9	4th Duncan, John J. (Jimmy) Jr.	Rep	Tenn.	11	10
5th Ortiz, Solomon P.	Dem	Tex.	13	7	5th Gilchrest, Wayne T.	Rep	Md.	9	7
6th Pallone, Frank Jr.	Dem	N.J.	11	7	6th Calvert, Ken	Rep	Cal.	8	8
7th Christensen, Donna M.C.	Dem	V.I.	6	6	7th Cannon, Christopher B.	Rep	Utah	6	6
8th Napolitano, Grace F.	Dem	Cal.	5	5	8th Tancredo, Thomas G.	Rep	Colo.	5	5
9th Holt, Rush D.	Dem	N.J.	5	*2 1	9th Flake, Jeff	Rep	Ariz.	4	4
10th Grijalva, Raúl M.	Dem	Ariz.	3	3	10th Renzi, Rick	Rep	Ariz.	3	3
11th Bordallo, Madeleine Z.	Dem	Guam	3	3	11th Pearce, Stevan	Rep	N.M.	3	3
12th Costa, Jim	Dem	Cal.	2	2	12th Brown, Henry E. Jr.	Rep	S.C.	4	2
13th Boren, Daniel D.	Dem	Okla.	2	2	13th Fortuño, Luis G.	Rep	P.R.	2	2
14th Sarbanes, John	Dem	Md.	1	1	14th McMorris Rogers, Cathy	Rep	Wash.	2	2
15th Miller, George	Dem	Cal.	17	*3 3	15th Jindal, Bobby	Rep	La.	2	2
16th Markey, Edward J.	Dem	Mass.	17	*4 3	16th Gohmert, Louie	Rep	Tex.	2	2
17th DeFazio, Peter A.	Dem	Ore.	11	*2 2	17th Cole, Tom	Rep	Okla.	3	*2 1
18th Hinchey, Maurice D.	Dem	N.Y.	8	*2 1	18th Bishop, Robert	Rep	Utah	3	*2 1
19th Kennedy, Patrick J.	Dem	R.I.	7	*2 1	19th Shuster, William	Rep	Penn.	4	1
20th Kind, Ron	Dem	Wisc.	6	6	20th Heller, Dean	Rep	Nev.	1	1
21st Capps, Lois	Dem	Cal.	6	1	21st Sali, Bill	Rep	Ida.	1	1
22nd Inslee, Jay R.	Dem	Wash.	6	5	22nd Lamborn, Doug	Rep	Colo.	1	1
23rd Udall, Mark	Dem	Colo.	5	5					
24th Baca, Joe	Dem	Cal.	5	*2 1					
25th Solis, Hilda L.	Dem	Cal.	4	*2 1					
26th Herseth, Stephanie	Dem	S.D.	3	3					
27th Shuler, Heath	Dem	N.C.	1	1					

*2: Member's second period of service on the committee.

*3: Member's third period of service on the committee.

*4: Member's fourth period of service on the committee.

Note: Territorial Delegates Eni F.H. Faleomavaega (Dem-A.Sm.), Donna M.C. Christensen (Dem-V.I.), and Madeleine Z. Bordallo (Dem-Guam) and Resident Commissioner Luis G. Fortuno (Rep-P.R.) were allowed to accrue committee seniority but were not included in the party ratio.

Changes:

Minority:

Renzi, Rick	Rep	Ariz.	Apr. 24, 2007 Resigned committee due to ethics issue.
Fallin, Mary	Rep	Okla.	May 10, 2007 Replaced Renzi.
Calvert, Ken	Rep	Cal.	May 14, 2007 Resigned committee; moved to Appropriations.
McCarthy, Kevin	Rep	Ariz.	May 10, 2007 Replaced Calvert.
McCarthy, Kevin	Rep	Ariz.	Oct. 2, 2007 Resigned committee; moved to Financial Services.
Jindal, Bobby	Rep	La.	Jan. 14, 2008 Resigned the House; elected Governor of Louisiana.
Heller, Dean	Rep	Nev.	Feb. 25, 2008 Resigned committee; moved to Financial Services.
Smith, Adrian	Rep	Neb.	Feb. 26, 2008 Replaced McCarthy.
Wittman, Robert J.	Rep	Va.	Feb. 26, 2008 Replaced Jindal.
Scalise, Steve	Rep	La.	May 14, 2008 Replaced Heller.

Departures from the House:	Majority			Minority		
Elected Governor	None			Fortuño, Luis G.	Rep	P.R.
Elected to U.S. Senate	Udall, Mark	Dem	Colo.	None		
Lost Election to U.S. Senate	None			Pearce, Stevan	Rep	N.M.
Lost Presidential Nomination	None			Tancredo, Thomas G.	Rep	Colo.
Defeated for Re-election	None			Sali, Bill	Rep	Ida.
Defeated for Re-nomination	None			Gilchrest, Wayne T.	Rep	Md.
				Cannon, Christopher B.	Rep	Utah
Retired	None			Saxton, H. James	Rep	N.J.

Departures from Committee:						
Moved to Appropriations	None			Cole, Tom	Rep	Okla.
Moved to Armed Services	None			Fallin, Mary	Rep	Okla.

	Name	Party	State	Name	Party	State
Moved to Energy and Commerce	None			Scalise, Steve	Rep	La.
Moved to Oversight and Government Reform	Kennedy, Patrick J.	Dem	R.I.	None		
Moved to Transportation and Infrastructure	Ortiz, Solomon P.	Dem	Tex.	Scalise, Steve	Rep	La.
No new assignment	Shuler, Heath	Dem	N.C.	None		

Note: Hilda L. Solis (Dem-Cal.) who served on the committee in the 110th Congress was unassigned in the 111th and resigned on Feb. 24, 2009, appointed Secretary of Labor.

NATURAL RESOURCES / 111th Congress

Service Dates of Committee Chair: Jan. 6, 2009-Jan. 3, 2011

Service Dates of Majority Members: Jan. 21, 2009-Jan. 3, 2011

Service Dates of Minority Members: Jan. 9, 2009-Jan. 3, 2011

Roster Filled: Majority with 29 members, Jan. 21, 2009; Minority with 20 members, Jan. 9, 2009

Majority

			Terms in:	
Rank Name	Party	State	House	Comm.
Chr Rahall, Nick Joe II	Dem	W.Va.	17	17
2nd Kildee, Dale E.	Dem	Mich.	17	*2 8
3rd Faleomavaega, Eni F.H.	Dem	A.Sm.	11	11
4th Abercrombie, Neil	Dem	Hai.	11	10
5th Pallone, Frank Jr.	Dem	N.J.	12	8
6th Napolitano, Grace F.	Dem	Cal.	6	6
7th Holt, Rush D.	Dem	N.J.	6	*2 2
8th Grijalva, Raúl M.	Dem	Ariz.	4	4
9th Bordallo, Madeleine Z.	Dem	Guam	4	4
10th Costa, Jim	Dem	Cal.	3	3
11th Boren, Daniel D.	Dem	Okla.	3	3
12th Sablan, Gregorio Kilili	Dem	N.M.I.	1	1
13th Heinrich, Martin	Dem	N.M.	1	1
14th Miller, George	Dem	Cal.	18	*3 4
15th Markey, Edward J.	Dem	Mass.	18	*4 4
16th DeFazio, Peter A.	Dem	Ore.	12	*2 3
17th Hinchey, Maurice D.	Dem	N.Y.	9	*2 2
18th Christensen, Donna M.C.	Dem	V.I.	7	7
19th DeGette, Diana	Dem	Colo.	7	1
20th Kind, Ron	Dem	Wisc.	7	7
21st Capps, Lois	Dem	Cal.	7	2
22nd Inslee, Jay R.	Dem	Wash.	7	6
23rd Baca, Joe	Dem	Cal.	6	*2 2
24th Herseth Sandlin, Stephanie	Dem	S.D.	4	4
25th Sarbanes, John	Dem	Md.	2	2
26th Shea-Porter, Carol	Dem	N.H.	2	1
27th Tsongas, Nicola (Niki)	Dem	Mass.	2	1
28th Kratovil, Frank M.	Dem	Md.	1	1
29th Pierluisi, Pedro R.	Dem	P.R.	1	1

Minority

			Terms in:	
Rank Name	Party	State	House	Comm.
RM Hastings, Richard (Doc)	Rep	Wash.	8	*2 1
2nd Young, Donald E.	Rep	Alas.	19	19
3rd Gallegly, Elton W.	Rep	Cal.	12	12
4th Duncan, John J. (Jimmy) Jr.	Rep	Tenn.	12	11
5th Flake, Jeff	Rep	Ariz.	5	5
6th Brown, Henry E. Jr.	Rep	S.C.	5	3
7th McMorris Rogers, Cathy	Rep	Wash.	3	3
8th Gohmert, Louie	Rep	Tex.	3	3
9th Bishop, Robert	Rep	Utah	4	*2 2
10th Shuster, William	Rep	Penn.	5	2
11th Lamborn, Doug	Rep	Colo.	2	2
12th Smith, Adrian	Rep	Neb.	2	2
13th Wittman, Robert J.	Rep	Va.	2	2
14th Broun, Paul C. Jr.	Rep	Ga.	2	1
15th Fleming, John	Rep	La.	1	1
16th Coffman, Michael	Rep	Colo.	1	1
17th Chaffetz, Jason	Rep	Utah	1	1
18th Lummis, Cynthia M.	Rep	Wyo.	1	1
19th McClintock, Thomas	Rep	Cal.	1	1
20th Cassidy, Bill	Rep	La.	1	1

*2: Member's second period of service on the committee.

*3: Member's third period of service on the committee.

*4: Member's fourth period of service on the committee.

Note: Territorial Delegates Eni F.H. Faleomavaega (Dem-A.Sm.), Gregorio Kilili Sablan (Dem-Northern Mariana Islands), Donna M.C. Christensen (Dem-V.I.), and Madeleine Z. Bordallo (Dem-Guam) and Resident Commissioner Pedro R. Pierluisi (Dem-P.R.) were allowed to accrue committee seniority but were not included in the party ratio.

Changes:

Majority:

Abercrombie, Neil	Dem	Hai.	Feb. 28, 2010 Resigned the House and retired.
Luján, Ben Ray	Dem	N.M.	May 6, 2010 Replaced Abercrombie

Oversight and Government Reform

House Committee on Government Operations, 103rd Congress (1993-1995)

House Committee on Government Reform and Oversight, 104th-105th Congresses (1995-1999)

House Committee on Government Reform, 106th-109th Congresses (1999-2007)

House Committee on Oversight and Government Reform, 110th-111th Congresses (2007-2011)

BACKGROUND

Organizational History: The antecedents of the House Committee on Government Operations were the various expenditures committees created to oversee the spending practices of the executive departments. On March 30, 1816, in the 14th Congress, pursuant to a resolution introduced by Jeffersonian representative Henry St. George Tucker of Virginia, six standing committees, each with three members, were approved to oversee government expenditures. These committees were to examine expenditures in the Departments of State, Treasury, War, Navy, the Post Office, and "Upon Public Buildings." While Henry St. George Tucker would serve as chair of Expenditures on the Public Buildings in the 15th Congress (1817-1819), his similarly named cousin, George Tucker, a fellow Virginia Jeffersonian would chair the Expenditures in the War Department in the 18th Congress (1823-1825).

As the executive branch grew so did the number of expenditures committees: Interior (1860), Justice (1874), Agriculture (1889), and Commerce and Labor (1912) that would be divided into separate expenditure committees in 1914 when the departments split. In 1927, the eleven expenditures committees with seventy-four members were grouped together under the name of the House Committee on Expenditures in the Executive Departments with only twenty-one seats. William Williamson (Rep-S.D.) who had chaired Expenditures in the Interior Department became the new chair of the consolidated committee. This was the committee's name at the time of the 1946 reorganization and in 1952; the committee's name was changed to its best-known title, Government Operations.

Following the 1995 Republican takeover of the House, the committee was renamed Government Reform and Oversight. Oversight was dropped from its title in 1999 but it returned in 2007 with the Democratic restoration with the order reversed. It has been known as the Committee on Oversight and Government Reform in the past two Congresses (2007-2011).

The Committee Reform Amendments of 1974, effective January 3, 1975, assigned the committee jurisdiction over measures relating to the overall economy and efficiency of Government operations and activities, including Federal procurement, intergovernmental relationships, and general revenue sharing. (It would lose that authority to Ways and Means in the 104th Congress.)

The Government Reform Committee was the major beneficiary of the 1995 termination of the District of Columbia and Post Office and Civil Service Committees. It received most of the jurisdiction of the District Committee and from Post Office and Civil Service, it received authority over the National Archives and other functions except that relating to the Franking Commission, including the Federal civil service—including intergovernmental personnel—and the status of officers and employees of the United States, including their compensation, classification, and retirement; government management and accounting measures generally; overall economy, efficiency, and management of government operations and activities, including Federal procurement; and Postal service generally, including transportation of the mails.

The committee focuses primarily on how the federal government functions. Its sweeping jurisdiction permits an aggressive chair to pursue almost any issue of interest. But Government Operations has been mostly detail-minded, tackling such subjects as computer security and the retirement system for civil servants. The legislation handled by the committee includes proposals for government reorganization, including new agencies or departments, and intergovernmental relations. Some subcommittees have concentrated on investigations, and exposure of waste and fraud is a theme that runs through many reports. The committee has often focused on procurement—what and how the government buys from private industry. While the committee seldom makes headlines, this committee and Appropriations are the two House committees that the federal bureaucracy eyes warily.

Membership: At the time of the 1946 Legislative Reorganization Act, there were twenty-one members on the Expenditures in the Executive Departments Committee. Following the passage of that act, the committee had twenty-five authorized seats. Renamed as Government Operations, the committee grew steadily and hit its peak of fifty-two seats in the 104th Congress (1995-1997) under its new name of Government Reform and Oversight. The committee dropped to forty-four members in the next four Congresses (1997-2005) and presently has forty seats in the 111th Congress (2009-2011). Its average membership size in the last nine Congresses, 1993-2011 is 43.67—eleventh place among the nineteen continuing committees. This is the same ranking that the committee, now known as Oversight and Government Reform, achieved with its mean seniority of 4.73 terms per member. The committee's inter-Congress retention rate of 80.45 percent is relatively low, ranking it fourteenth among the House committees.

Committee Leaders: Clare E. Hoffman (Rep-Mich.) was the first modern-era chair and served as the committee's senior Republican for sixteen years (1947-1963). In 1949,

William L. Dawson (Dem-Ill.) of Chicago was the first Democrat to chair the committee and the first ever African-American to chair a standing congressional committee. Dawson and Hoffman occupied the two senior slots until 1963, when Hoffman retired. Dawson continued as the committee's chair until his death in 1970. Hoffman's successor R. Walter Riehlman (Rep-N.Y.) was defeated in 1964 and was replaced by Clarence J. Brown (Rep-Ohio), who died in 1965, and was succeeded by Florence P. Dwyer (Rep-N.J.), who held the senior Republican rank until her retirement in 1973.

Chet Holifield (Dem-Cal.) succeeded Dawson in 1970 and served until his resignation in 1974. Holifield's successor Jack B. Brooks (Dem-Texas) and Dwyer's 1973 successor Frank J. Horton (Rep-N.Y.) held the two senior slots until 1989 when Brooks left the committee to chair Judiciary. With Brooks's departure, John Conyers Jr. (Dem-Mich.) of Detroit became the Government Operations Committee's second African-American chair. Frank Horton continued as the committee's ranking member until his retirement in 1993 after having served as a House committee's ranking minority member for twenty years without ever chairing it.

Conyers continued as chair until the 1994 Republican takeover. Jack Brooks was one of the casualties of that election and Conyers moved to replace him as the senior Democrat on Judiciary. Conyers was replaced in 1995 as the committee's senior Democrat by Cardiss Collins (Dem-Ill.), the committee's third African-American senior Democrat and the first black woman to ever hold senior rank on a House committee. Horton's successor William F. Clinger Jr. (Rep-Penn.) would be the first Republican chair of the committee now known as Government Reform and Oversight since Clare Hoffman chaired it forty years earlier. Clinger and Collins both retired in 1997. Clinger's retirement brought Danny L. Burton (Rep-Ind.) into the chairmanship. Burton's speculation that Vincent Foster, Bill Clinton's legal adviser and Hillary Clinton's former law partner had been murdered and not a victim of suicide became a preoccupation of the committee during Burton's tenure as chair. Collins's successor was Henry A. Waxman (Dem-Cal.). Post-1995 Republican Conference rules limited chairs to three terms and Burton stepped aside in 2003 for Thomas M. Davis III (Rep-Va.). The House Democrats do not have such rules and Waxman continued as the committee's senior Democrat until 2009 and after ten years as ranking member, 1997-2007, and two as chair, 2007-2009, he left the committee in 2009. Waxman had been victorious over John Dingell (Rep-Mich.) in a caucus battle for the chairmanship of Energy and Commerce. Waxman's successor and present chair Edolphus Towns (Dem-N.Y.) is the fourth senior African-American Democrat on the committee now known as Oversight and Government Reform. Davis retired in 2009 and the ranking minority slot is presently held by Darrel Issa (Rep-Cal.).

Party Leaders: Following the 1946 Reorganization, the committee was known as the Committee on Expenditures in the Executive Departments, and the first leader to serve on the committee was Minority Whip John W. McCormack (Dem-Mass.). He was placed second on the committee behind ranking member Carter Manasco (Dem-Ala.), a protégé of the late Speaker William B. Bankhead (Dem-Ala.). Manasco's defeat in the Dixiecrat election of 1948 elevated William L. Dawson of Chicago into the top slot over McCormack. Dawson, as the first African-American to chair a congressional committee, needed support during these racially-troubled times and

McCormack provided it by not asserting his higher rank and by remaining on the committee in a subordinate capacity to prevent any Southern "walkouts" from the committee as had occurred at the 1948 Democratic National Convention. McCormack remained on the committee and served with Dawson until his election as Speaker in 1962. Ironically, serving on the committee in the early years of the Dawson-McCormack alliance was the aggressive liberal Richard W. Bolling (Dem-Mo.) who spent much of his time in the House plotting to overthrow McCormack.

Three other modern-era House Speakers who served on the committee were Democrats James C. Wright, Jr. of Texas and the present Speaker Nancy Pelosi of California. The only Republican Speaker with service on the committee was Speaker Pelosi's predecessor, J. Dennis Hastert of Illinois.

Other party leaders who served on Government Operations, as it was most commonly known, include Republican floor leaders Charles A. Halleck (Rep-Ind.), Robert Michel (Rep-Ill.) Richard K. Armey (Rep-Texas), and Thomas DeLay (Rep-Texas) along with present-day Republican Whip Eric L. Cantor (Rep-Va.).

Notable Members: The only presidential nominee with service on the House Government Operations Committee was Robert J. Dole (Rep-Kans.), the 1996 Republican candidate. However, one-time committee member John B. Anderson (Rep-Ill.) mounted a serious third party challenge to President Jimmy Carter and ex-California governor Ronald Reagan in 1980 and received 7 percent of the total vote. The first vice presidential nominee with experience on this committee was William E. Miller, Barry M. Goldwater's 1964 running mate. Next up was Bob Dole, President Gerald Ford's 1976 running mate. The most successful nominee with Government Operations experience was J. Danforth Quayle (Rep-Ind.) who was elected in 1988 running with Reagan's vice president George H.W. Bush, but was unsuccessful in 1992.

Only four Cabinet members served on the committee—Democrat Les Aspin (Dem-Wisc.), who was named Secretary of Defense by President Bill Clinton and Republicans Donald Rumsfeld (Rep-Ill.), Secretary of Defense under both Presidents Gerald R. Ford and George W. Bush, Richard Schweiker (Rep-Penn.) and Margaret M. Heckler (Rep-Mass.), Ronald Reagan's first two Secretaries of Health and Human Services. In 1961, President Kennedy named committee member Kathryn Granahan (Dem-Penn.) to the largely honorific post of Treasurer of the United States.

Twenty-four U.S. Senators left the House with Government Operations Committee experience. Eighteen were Republicans, five were Democrats, and one was an Independent. Among the eighteen Republicans were Richard Schweiker and H. John Heinz III of Pennsylvania, Judd Gregg and John Sununu of New Hampshire, J. Caleb Boggs of Delaware, George H. Bender of Ohio, Robert P. Griffin of Michigan, Edward J. Gurney of Florida, Robert J. Dole of Kansas, Lowell P. Weicker, Jr. of Connecticut, Robert W. Kasten, Jr. of Wisconsin, J. Danforth Quayle of Indiana, Olympia J.B. Snowe of Maine, Larry E. Craig of Idaho, Jon Kyl of Arizona, James M. Inhofe of Oklahoma, Craig L. Thomas of Wyoming, and David Vitter of Louisiana. And one Republican, James W. Wadsworth, Jr. of New York, served on the House Expenditures Committee after he lost his Senate seat.

The five Democrats to move to the Senate were Thomas J. Dodd of Connecticut, Ross Bass of Tennessee, Harrison A. Williams, Jr. of New Jersey, John C. Culver of Iowa, and

Barbara Boxer of California. Also leaving the committee for service in the Senate was Independent Bernard Sanders of Vermont.

State governors in the modern era passed through House Government Operations on their way to the state houses, the largest number of any House committee. Among them were Republicans: J. Caleb Boggs of Delaware, Charles Thone of Nebraska, Judd Gregg of New Hampshire, John R. McKernan, Jr. of Maine, Marshall C. (Mark) Sanford of South Carolina, Robert J. Ehrlich of Maryland, and C.L. (Butch) Otter of Idaho. Republican Lowell P. Weicker, Jr. was elected governor of Connecticut as a third-party candidate after his Senate re-election defeat. The three Democratic governors with committee experience were Kenneth H. (Buddy) MacKay of Florida, Robert E. Wise, Jr. of West Virginia, and Rod R. Blagojevich of Illinois. McKay's service was only twenty-three days after the death of Governor Lawton Chiles, while Blagojevich was impeached and removed from office in 2009. A thirteenth committee member who had gubernatorial experience was William H. Janklow of South Dakota, who was elected to the House in 2002 after four terms as governor, but had to resign a year later after being involved in a fatal traffic accident. And as noted in other instances, San Francisco mayor John F. Shelley (Dem-Cal.) and Chicago's first African-American mayor Harold Washington (Dem-Ill.) moved from the committee to their respective city halls.

Selected References

Cohen, Richard E., "The King of Oversight," *Government Executive* (September, 1988), 16-18.

Oleszek, Walter J., *Congressional Procedures and the Policy Process*, 6th ed. (Washington, D.C.: CQ Press, 1989).

Ornstein, Norman J. and David W. Rohde, "Shifting Forces, Changing Rules, and Political Outcomes: The Impact of Congressional Change on Four House Committees," in Robert L. Peabody and Nelson W. Polsby, eds., *New Perspectives on the House of Representatives*, 3rd ed. (Chicago: Rand McNally, 1977), 186-269.

Schamel, Charles E. et al., "Records of the Government Operations Committee and Its Predecessors," *Guide to the Records of the United States House of Representatives at the National Archives: 1789-1989 Bicentennial Edition* (Washington, D.C.: National Archives and Records Administration, 1989), 147-163.

U.S. House of Representatives, Committee on Government Operations, *Activities of the House Committee on Government Operations, 97th Congress, First and Second Sessions,* H.Rept. 97-994, 97th Congress, 2nd Session (1982), 9-12.

Wilmerding, Lucius, Jr., *The Spending Power: A History of the Efforts of Congress to Control Expenditures* (Hampden, Conn.: Archon Books, 1971 reprint of 1943 original).

RESPONSIBILITIES, JURISDICTIONAL CHANGES, AND SUBCOMMITTEES

EXPENDITURES IN THE EXECUTIVE DEPARTMENTS

Jurisdiction, 80th Congress (1947-1949)

Established by the Legislative Reorganization Act of 1946:

[Section 121.(1)(h)] Committee on Expenditures in the Executive Departments

(A) Budget and accounting measures, other than appropriations.

(B) Reorganizations in the executive branch of the Government.

[Section 121.(2)]

Such committee shall have the duty of—

(A) receiving and examining reports of the Comptroller General of the United States and of submitting such recommendations to the House as it deems necessary or desirable in connection with the subject matter of such reports;

(B) studying the operation of Government activities at all levels with a view to determining its economy and efficiency;

(C) evaluating the effects of laws enacted to reorganize the legislative and executive branches of the Government;

(D) studying intergovernmental relationships between the United States and the States and municipalities, and between the United States and international organizations of which the United States is a member.

GOVERNMENT OPERATIONS

Expenditures in the Executive Departments was renamed the Committee on Government Operations on July 3, 1952.

Jurisdiction, 103rd Congress (1993-1995)

From the *Rules of the House of Representatives, 103rd Congress* (House Document 102-405)

[Rule X.1. (j)] Committee on Government Operations
    (1) Budget and accounting measures, other than appropriations.
    (2) The overall economy and efficiency of Government operations and activities, including Federal procurement.
    (3) Reorganizations in the executive branch of the Government.
    (4) Intergovernmental relationships between the United States and the States and municipalities, and general revenue sharing.
    (5) National archives.
    (6) Measures providing for off-budget treatment of Federal agencies or programs.
    (7) Measures providing exemption from reduction under any order issued under part C of the Balanced Budget and Emergency Deficit Control Act of 1985.

In addition to its legislative jurisdiction under the preceding provisions of this paragraph (and its oversight functions under clause 2(b) (1) and (2)), the committee shall have the function of performing the activities and conducting the studies which are provided for in clause 4(c).

[Rule X.4.(c)(1)] Additional Functions

The Committee on Government Operations shall have the general function of—

(A) receiving and examining reports of the Comptroller General of the United States and of submitting such recommendations to the House as it deems necessary or desirable in connection with the subject matter of such reports;

(B) evaluating the effects of laws enacted to reorganize the legislative and executive branches of the Government; and

(C) studying intergovernmental relationships between the United States and the States and municipalities, and between the United States and international organizations of which the United States is a member.

[Rule X.4.(c)(2)]

In addition to its duties under subparagraph (1), the Committee on Government Operations may at any time conduct investigations of any matter without regard to the provisions of clause 1, 2, or 3 (or this clause) conferring jurisdiction over such matter upon another standing committee. The committee's findings and recommendations in any such investigation shall be made available to the other standing committee or committees having jurisdiction over the matter involved (and included in the report of any such other committee when required by clause 2(1)(3) of Rule XI).

GOVERNMENT REFORM AND OVERSIGHT

Government Operations was renamed the Committee on Government Reform and Oversight on January 4, 1995.

Jurisdiction, 104th Congress (1995-1997) Changes in Committee System

From H. Res. 6, Section 202 (a), the Committees and Their Jurisdiction, January 4, 1995

[Rule X.1.(g)] Committee on Government Reform and Oversight.
    (1) The Federal Civil Service, including intergovernmental personnel; the status of officers and employees of the United States, including their compensation, classification, and retirement.
    (2) Measures relating to the municipal affairs of the District of Columbia in general, other than appropriations.
    (3) Federal paperwork reduction.
    (4) Budget and accounting measures, generally.
    (5) Holidays and celebrations.
    (6) The overall economy, efficiency and management of government operations and activities, including Federal procurement.
    (7) National archives.
    (8) Population and demography generally, including the Census.
    (9) Postal service generally, including the transportation of the mails.
  (10) Public information and records.
  (11) Relationship of the Federal Government to the States and municipalities generally.
  (12) Reorganizations in the executive branch of the Government.

In addition to its legislative jurisdiction under the preceding provisions of this paragraph (and its oversight functions under clause 2(b) (1) and (2)), the committee shall have the function of performing the duties and conducting the studies which are provided for in clause 4(c).

OVERSIGHT AND GOVERNMENT REFORM

Government Reform and Oversight was renamed the Committee on Oversight and Government Reform on January 4, 2007.

Jurisdiction, 111th Congress (2009-2011)

From the *Rules of the House of Representatives* (as revised to June 16, 2009, H.Doc. 110-162):

[Rule X.1.(m)] Committee on Oversight and Government Reform

(1) Federal civil service, including intergovernmental personnel; and the status of officers and employees of the United States, including their compensation, classification, and retirement.

(2) Municipal affairs of the District of Columbia in general (other than appropriations).

(3) Federal paperwork reduction.

(4) Government management and accounting measures generally.

(5) Holidays and celebrations.

(6) Overall economy, efficiency, and management of government operations and activities, including Federal procurement.

(7) National archives.

(8) Population and demography generally, including the Census.

(9) Postal service generally, including transportation of the mails.

(10) Public information and records.

(11) Relationship of the Federal Government to the States and municipalities generally.

Reorganizations in the executive branch of the Government.

[Rule X.3.(i)] Special Oversight Function

The Committee on Oversight and Government Reform shall review and study on a continuing basis the operation of Government activities at all levels with a view to determining their economy and efficiency.

[Rule X.4.(c)(1)] Additional Functions

The Committee on Oversight and Government Reform shall—

(A) receive and examine reports of the Comptroller General of the United States and submit to the House such recommendations as it considers necessary or desirable in connection with the subject matter of the reports;

(B) evaluate the effects of laws enacted to reorganize the legislative and executive branches of the Government; and

(C) study intergovernmental relationships between the United States and the States and municipalities and between the United States and international organizations of which the United States is a member.

[Rule X.4.(c)(2)]

In addition to its duties under subparagraph (1), the Committee on Oversight and Government Reform may at any time conduct investigations of any matter without regard to clause 1, 2, 3 (or this clause) conferring jurisdiction over the matter to another standing committee. The findings and recommendations of the committee in such investigation shall be made available to any other standing committee having jurisdiction over the matter involved.

NAMES OF OVERSIGHT AND GOVERNMENT REFORM SUBCOMMITTEES FROM THE *CONGRESSIONAL DIRECTORY*

Government Operations, 103rd Congress

Commerce, Consumer and Monetary Affairs, 103
Environment, Energy and Natural Resources, 103
Information, Justice, Transportation, and Agriculture, 103
Employment, Housing, and Aviation, 103
Human Resources and Intergovernmental Relations, 103
Legislation and National Security, 103

Government Reform and Oversight, 104th-109th Congresses

Census, 106, 107
Civil Service, 104, 105, 106
Civil Service and Agency Organization, 107, 108
Criminal Justice, Drug Policy and Human Resources, 106, 107, 108, 109
District of Columbia, 104, 105, 106, 107
Energy Policy, Natural Resources, and Regulatory Affairs, 107, 108
Energy and Resources, 109
Federal Workforce and Agency Organization, 109
Federalism and the Census, 109
Government Management, Information and Technology, 104, 105, 106
Government Efficiency, Financial Management, and Intergovernmental Relations, 107
Government Efficiency and Financial Management, 108
Government Management, Finance, and Accountability, 109
Human Resources and Intergovernmental Relations, 104
Human Resources, 105
National Economic Growth, Natural Resources, and Regulatory Affairs, 104, 105, 106
National Security, International Affairs and Criminal Justice, 104, 105

MEMBERSHIP ROSTERS, 103rd-111th Congresses, 1993-2011

GOVERNMENT OPERATIONS / 103rd Congress

Service Dates of Committee Chair: Jan. 5, 1993-Jan. 3, 1995

Service Dates of Majority Members: Jan. 5, 1993-Jan. 3, 1995

Service Dates of Minority Members: Jan. 5, 1993-Jan. 3, 1995

Roster Filled: Majority with 25 members on July 21, 1993; Minority with 16 members on Jan. 5, 1993; Third Party with Sanders on Feb. 18, 1993

Majority Rank Name	Party	State	Terms in: House	Terms in: Comm.	Minority Rank Name	Party	State	Terms in: House	Terms in: Comm.
Chr Conyers, John Jr.	Dem	Mich.	15	12	RM Clinger, William F. Jr.	Rep	Penn.	8	7
2nd Collins, Cardiss	Dem	Ill.	11	11	2nd McCandless, Alfred A.	Rep	Cal.	6	6
3rd English, Glenn L. Jr.	Dem	Okla.	10	10	3rd Hastert, J. Dennis	Rep	Ill.	4	*1 4
4th Waxman, Henry A.	Dem	Cal.	10	9	4th Kyl, Jon L.	Rep	Ariz.	4	4
5th Synar, Michael L.	Dem	Okla.	8	8	5th Shays, Christopher H.	Rep	Conn.	4	4
6th Neal, Stephen L.	Dem	N.C.	10	7	6th Schiff, Steven H.	Rep	N.M.	3	3
7th Lantos, Thomas P.	Dem	Cal.	7	7	7th Cox, C. Christopher	Rep	Cal.	3	*1 3
8th Owens, Major R.	Dem	N.Y.	6	6	8th Thomas, Craig L.	Rep	Wyo.	3	3
9th Towns, Edolphus	Dem	N.Y.	6	6	9th Ros-Lehtinen, Ileana	Rep	Fla.	3	3
10th Spratt, John M. Jr.	Dem	S.C.	6	*2 1	10th Machtley, Ronald K.	Rep	R.I.	3	2
11th Condit, Gary A.	Dem	Cal.	3	3	11th Zimmer, Richard	Rep	N.J.	2	2
12th Peterson, Collin C.	DFL	Minn.	2	2	12th Zeliff, William H. Jr.	Rep	N.H.	2	2
13th Thurman, Karen L.	Dem	Fla.	1	1	13th McHugh, John M.	Rep	N.Y.	1	1
14th Woolsey, Lynn C.	Dem	Cal.	1	*1 1	14th Horn, J. Steven	Rep	Cal.	1	1
15th Rush, Bobby L.	Dem	Ill.	1	1	15th Pryce, Deborah D.	Rep	Ohio	1	1
16th Maloney, Carolyn B.	Dem	N.Y.	1	1	16th Mica, John L.	Rep	Fla.	1	1
17th Barrett, Thomas M.	Dem	Wisc.	1	1					
18th Flake, Floyd H.	Dem	N.Y.	4	1	**Third Party:**				
19th Hayes, James A.	Dem	La.	4	1	Sanders, Bernard	Ind	Vt.	2	2
20th Washington, Craig A.	Dem	Tex.	3	1					
21st Collins, Barbara-Rose	Dem	Mich.	2	1	*1: Member's first period of service on the committee.				
22nd Brown, Corrine	Dem	Fla.	1	1	*2: Member's second period of service on the committee.				
23rd Margolies-Mezvinsky, Marjorie	Dem	Penn.	1	1					
24th Green, R. Eugene (Gene)	Dem	Tex.	1	1					
25th Stupak, Bart T.	Dem	Mich.	1	1					

Note: Peterson returned to Government Operations to rank immediately following Condit (then later Spratt) on Jan. 21, 1993. Was neither a Filled Vacancy or an Addition.

Vacancies Filled:
   Majority:
      18th through 23rd seats filled by Flake, Hayes, Washington, Collins, Brown, Margolies-Mezvinsky on Feb. 4, 1993; 10th seat filled by Spratt on Feb. 18, 1993; 24th and 25th seats filled by Green and Stupak on July 14, 1993.

Additions:

Minority:

17th Portman, Robert J.	Rep	Ohio	May 26, 1993	

Changes:

Majority:

Woolsey, Lynn C. — Dem — Cal. — Jan. 21, 1993 Resigned committee; moved to Science, Space, and Technology; returned on Feb. 4, 1993, ranked after Margolies-Mezvinsky.

Payne, Donald M. — Dem — N.J. — Jan. 21, 1993 Replaced Woolsey.

English, Glenn L. Jr. — Dem — Okla. — Jan. 7, 1994 Resigned the House and retired; vacancy remained.

Minority:

Machtley, Ronald K. — Rep — R.I. — Sept. 13, 1993 Resigned committee; no new assignment.

Lucas, Frank D. — Rep — Okla. — May 25, 1994 Replaced Machtley.

Departures from the House:	Majority			Minority		
Elected to U.S. Senate	None			Kyl, Jon L.	Rep	Ariz.
				Thomas, Craig L.	Rep	Wyo.
Defeated for Re-nomination	Synar, Michael L.	Dem	La.	None		
	Washington, Craig A.	Dem	Tex.			
Defeated for Re-election	Margolies-Mezvinsky, Marjorie	Dem	Penn.	None		
Retired	Neal, Stephen L.	Dem	N.C.	McCandless, Alfred A.	Rep	Cal.

Departures from Committee:						
Became RM on Judiciary	Conyers, John Jr.	Dem	Mich.	None		
Moved to Banking and Financial Services	None			Lucas, Frank D.	Rep	La.
Moved to Commerce	Rush, Bobby L.	Dem	Ill.	Cox, C. Christopher	Rep	Cal.
	Stupak, Bart T.	Dem	Mich.			
Moved to Rules	None			Pryce, Deborah D.	Rep	Ohio
Moved to Ways and Means	None			Zimmer, Richard	Rep	N.J.
				Portman, Robert J.	Rep	Ohio
No new assignment	Flake, Floyd H.	Dem	N.Y.	Hastert, J. Dennis	Rep	Ill.
	Hayes, James A.	Dem	La.			
	Brown, Corrine	Dem	Fla.			
	Payne, Donald M.	Dem	N.J.			
	Woolsey, Lynn C.	Dem	Cal.			

GOVERNMENT REFORM AND OVERSIGHT / 104th Congress

Service Dates of Committee Chair: Jan. 4, 1995-Jan. 3, 1997

Service Dates of Majority Members: Jan. 4, 1995-Jan. 3, 1997

Service Dates of Minority Members: Jan. 9, 1995-Jan. 3, 1997

Roster Filled: Majority with 27 members on Jan. 4, 1995; Minority with 22 members on Jan. 9, 1995; Third Party with Sanders on Jan. 9, 1995

Majority			Terms in:		Minority			Terms in:	
Rank Name	Party	State	House	Comm.	Rank Name	Party	State	House	Comm.
Chr Clinger, William F. Jr.	Rep	Penn.	9	8	RM Collins, Cardiss	Dem	Ill.	12	12
2nd Gilman, Benjamin A.	Rep	N.Y.	12	1	2nd Waxman, Henry A.	Dem	Cal.	11	10
3rd Burton, Danny L.	Rep	Ind.	7	*2 1	3rd Lantos, Thomas P.	Dem	Cal.	8	8
4th Morella, Constance A.	Rep	Md.	5	1	4th Wise, Robert E. Jr.	Dem	W.Va.	7	*2 1
5th Shays, Christopher H.	Rep	Conn.	5	5	5th Owens, Major R.	Dem	N.Y.	7	7
6th Schiff, Steven H.	Rep	N.M.	4	4	6th Towns, Edolphus	Dem	N.Y.	7	7
7th Ros-Lehtinen, Ileana	Rep	Fla.	4	4	7th Spratt, John M. Jr.	Dem	S.C.	7	*2 2
8th Zeliff, William H. Jr.	Rep	N.H.	3	3	8th Slaughter, Louise Macintosh	Dem	N.Y.	5	*2 1
9th McHugh, John M.	Rep	N.Y.	2	2	9th Kanjorski, Paul E.	Dem	Penn.	6	1
10th Horn, J. Steven	Rep	Cal.	2	2	10th Condit, Gary A.	Dem	Cal.	4	4
11th Mica, John L.	Rep	Fla.	2	2	11th Peterson, Collin C.	DFL	Minn.	3	3
12th Blute, Peter I.	Rep	Mass.	2	1	12th Thurman, Karen L.	Dem	Fla.	2	2
13th Davis, Thomas M. III	Rep	Va.	1	1	13th Maloney, Carolyn B.	Dem	N.Y.	2	2
14th McIntosh, David M.	Rep	Ind.	1	1	14th Barrett, Thomas M.	Dem	Wisc.	2	2
15th Fox, Jon D.	Rep	Penn.	1	1	15th Taylor, G. Eugene (Gene)	Dem	Miss.	4	1
16th Tate, Randy J.	Rep	Wash.	1	1	16th Collins, Barbara-Rose	Dem	Mich.	3	2
17th Chrysler, Dick	Rep	Mich.	1	1	17th Norton, Eleanor Holmes	Dem	D.C.	3	*1 1
18th Gutknecht, Gilbert W.	Rep	Minn.	1	*1 1	18th Moran, James P. Jr.	Dem	Va.	3	1
19th Souder, Mark E.	Rep	Ind.	1	1	19th Green, R. Eugene (Gene)	Dem	Tex.	2	2
20th Martini, William J.	Rep	N.J.	1	1	20th Meek, Carrie P.	Dem	Fla.	2	1

21st Scarborough, C. Joseph	Rep	Fla.	1	1	
22nd Shadegg, John B.	Rep	Ariz.	1	1	
23rd Flanagan, Michael Patrick	Rep	Ill.	1	1	
24th Bass, Charles F.	Rep	N.H.	1	1	
25th LaTourette, Steven C.	Rep	Ohio	1	1	
26th Sanford, Marshall C. (Mark) Jr.	Rep	S.C.	1	1	
27th Ehrlich, Robert L. Jr.	Rep	Md.	1	1	

21st Mascara, Frank R.	Dem	Penn.	1	1
22nd Fattah, Chaka	Dem	Penn.	1	1
Third Party:				
Sanders, Bernard	Ind	Vt.	3	3

*1: Member's first period of service on the committee.

*2: Member's second period of service on the committee.

Note: With the Committee on Post Office and Civil Service absorbed into Government Reform and Oversight in 1995, Gilman (Rep-N.Y.) was credited with ten terms of service on Post Office and Civil Service, 1975-1995; Burton (Rep-Ind.) with five terms, 1985-1995; Morella (Rep-Md.) with four terms, 1987-1995; and Kanjorski (Dem-Penn.) with three terms, 1989-1995. Delegate Eleanor Holmes Norton (Dem-D.C.) was allowed to accrue committee seniority but not included in the party ratio.

Additions:

Majority:

Hastert, J. Dennis	Rep	Ill.	May 25, 1995 Ranked 4th after Burton.

Minority:

Brewster, William K.	Dem	Okla.	June 13, 1995

Changes:

Majority:

Fox, Jon D.	Rep	Penn.	June 25, 1996 Resigned committee; moved to International Relations.
Klug, Scott L.	Rep	Wisc.	July 22, 1996 Replaced Fox.

Minority:

Mascara, Frank R.	Dem	Penn.	July 11, 1995 Resigned committee; moved to Transportation and Infrastructure.
Holden, T. Timothy	Dem	Penn.	July 12, 1995 Replaced Mascara.
Taylor, G. Eugene (Gene)	Dem	Miss.	Feb. 28, 1996 Resigned committee; moved to Transportation and Infrastructure.
Cummings, Elijah E.	Dem	Md.	Apr. 25, 1996 Replaced Taylor.

Departures from the House:

	Majority			Minority		
Lost Nomination for Governor	Zeliff, William H. Jr.	Rep	N.H.	None		
Defeated for Re-nomination	None			Collins, Barbara-Rose	Dem	Mich.
Defeated for Re-election	Blute, Peter I.	Rep	Mass.	None		
	Tate, Randy J.	Rep	Wash.			
	Chrysler, Dick	Rep	Mich.			
	Martini, William J.	Rep	N.J.			
	Flanagan, Michael Patrick	Rep	Ill.			
Retired	Clinger, William F. Jr.	Rep	Penn.	Collins, Cardiss	Dem	Ill.
				Brewster, William K.	Dem	La.

Departures from Committee:

	Majority			Minority		
Returned to Appropriations	None			Moran, James P. Jr.	Dem	Va.
				Meek, Carrie P.	Dem	Fla.
Moved to Budget	Gutknecht, Gilbert W.	Rep	Minn.	None		
Returned to Budget	None			Spratt, John M. Jr.	Dem	S.C.
Moved to Commerce	None			Green, R. Eugene (Gene)	Dem	Tex.
Moved to Permanent Select Intelligence	Bass, Charles F.	Rep	N.H.	None		
Returned to Rules	None			Slaughter, Louise Macintosh	Dem	N.Y.
Moved to Transportation and Infrastructure	Bass, Charles F.	Rep	N.H.	None		
Moved to Ways and Means	None			Thurman, Karen L.	Dem	Fla.
No new assignment	Klug, Scott L.	Rep	Wisc.	None		

GOVERNMENT REFORM AND OVERSIGHT / 105th Congress

Service Dates of Committee Chair: Jan. 7, 1997-Jan. 3, 1999

Service Dates of Majority Members: Jan. 7, 1997-Jan. 3, 1999

Service Dates of Minority Members: Jan. 7, 1997-Jan. 3, 1999

Roster Filled: Majority with 24 members on Jan. 7, 1997; Minority with 19 members on Feb. 5, 1997; Third Party with Sanders on Jan. 7, 1997

Majority					Minority				
			Terms in:					Terms in:	
Rank Name	Party	State	House	Comm.	Rank Name	Party	State	House	Comm.
Chr Burton, Danny L.	Rep	Ind.	8	*2 2	RM Waxman, Henry A.	Dem	Cal.	12	11
2nd Gilman, Benjamin A.	Rep	N.Y.	13	2	2nd Lantos, Thomas P.	Dem	Cal.	9	9

3rd Hastert, J. Dennis	Rep	Ill.	6	*2 2		
4th Morella, Constance A.	Rep	Md.	6	2		
5th Shays, Christopher H.	Rep	Conn.	6	6		
6th Schiff, Steven H.	Rep	N.M.	5	5		
7th Cox, C. Christopher	Rep	Cal.	5	*2 1		
8th Ros-Lehtinen, Ileana	Rep	Fla.	5	5		
9th McHugh, John M.	Rep	N.Y.	3	3		
10th Horn, J. Steven	Rep	Cal.	3	3		
11th Mica, John L.	Rep	Fla.	3	3		
12th Davis, Thomas M. III	Rep	Va.	2	2		
13th McIntosh, David M.	Rep	Ind.	2	2		
14th Souder, Mark E.	Rep	Ind.	2	2		
15th Scarborough, C. Joseph	Rep	Fla.	2	2		
16th Shadegg, John B.	Rep	Ariz.	2	2		
17th LaTourette, Steven C.	Rep	Ohio	2	2		
18th Sanford, Marshall C. (Mark) Jr.	Rep	S.C.	2	2		
19th Ehrlich, Robert L. Jr.	Rep	Md.	2	2		
20th Sununu, John E.	Rep	N.H.	1	1		
21st Sessions, Pete	Rep	Tex.	1	1		
22nd Pappas, Michael J.	Rep	N.J.	1	1		
23rd Brady, Kevin P.	Rep	Tex.	1	1		
24th Snowbarger, Vincent K.	Rep	Kans.	1	1		

3rd Wise, Robert E. Jr.	Dem	W.Va.	8	*2 2
4th Owens, Major R.	Dem	N.Y.	8	8
5th Towns, Edolphus	Dem	N.Y.	8	8
6th Kanjorski, Paul E.	Dem	Penn.	7	2
7th Condit, Gary A.	Dem	Cal.	5	5
8th Peterson, Collin C.	DFL	Minn.	4	4
9th Maloney, Carolyn B.	Dem	N.Y.	3	3
10th Barrett, Thomas M.	Dem	Wisc.	3	3
11th Norton, Eleanor Holmes	Dem	D.C.	4	*1 2
12th Fattah, Chaka	Dem	Penn.	2	2
13th Holden, T. Timothy	Dem	Penn.	3	2
14th Cummings, Elijah E.	Dem	Md.	2	2
15th Kucinich, Dennis	Dem	Ohio	1	1
16th Blagojevich, Rod R.	Dem	Ill.	1	1
17th Tierney, John F.	Dem	Mass.	1	*1 1
18th Turner, Jim	Dem	Tex.	1	1
19th Allen, Thomas H.	Dem	Me.	1	1

Third Party:

Sanders, Bernard	Ind	Vt.	4	4

*1: Member's first period of service on the committee.
*2: Member's second period of service on the committee.

Vacancies Filled:

Minority:

17th through 19th seats filled by Tierney, Turner, and Allen on Feb. 5, 1997.

Changes:

Majority:

Brady, Kevin P.	Rep	Tex.	Feb. 5, 1997 Resigned committee; had moved to International Relations on Jan. 21, 1997.
Barr, Bob	Rep	Ga.	Jan. 21, 1997 Replaced Brady.
Ehrlich, Robert L. Jr.	Rep	Md.	Mar. 19, 1997 Leave of absence to serve on Budget; never returned.
Portman, Robert J.	Rep	Ohio	Apr. 9, 1997 Replaced Ehrlich.
Portman, Robert J.	Rep	Ohio	Nov. 14, 1997 Resigned committee; moved to subcommittee of Standards of Official Conduct.
Miller, Daniel	Rep	Fla.	Nov. 13, 1997 Replaced Portman.
Schiff, Steven H.	Rep	N.M.	Mar. 25, 1998 Died in office.
Lewis, Ron	Rep	Ky.	May 13, 1998 Replaced Schiff.

Minority:

Peterson, Collin C.	DFL	Minn.	Feb. 4, 1997 Resigned committee; no new assignment.
Davis, Danny K.	Dem	Ill.	Feb. 5, 1997 Replaced Peterson.
Holden, T. Timothy	Dem	Penn.	Apr. 17, 1997 Resigned committee; moved to Transportation and Infrastructure.
Ford, Harold E. Jr.	Dem	Tenn.	Apr. 17, 1997 Replaced Holden.

Departures from the House:

	Majority			**Minority**
Defeated for Re-election	Pappas, Michael J.	Rep	N.J.	None
	Snowbarger, Vincent K.	Rep	Kans.	

Departures from Committee:

	Majority			**Minority**		
Elected Speaker of the House	Hastert, J. Dennis	Rep	Ill.	None		
Moved to Appropriations	Sununu, John E.	Rep	N.H.	None		
Moved to Commerce	Shadegg, John B.	Rep	Ariz.	Barrett, Thomas M.	Dem	Wisc.
Moved to Rules	Sessions, Pete	Rep	Tex.	None		
Moved to Ways and Means	Lewis, Ron	Rep	Ky.	None		

GOVERNMENT REFORM / 106th Congress

Service Dates of Committee Chair: Jan. 6, 1999-Jan. 3, 2001

Service Dates of Majority Members: Jan. 6, 1999-Jan. 3, 2001

Service Dates of Minority Members: Jan. 6, 1999-Jan. 3, 2001

Roster Filled: Majority with 24 members on Feb. 2, 1999; Minority with 19 members on Jan. 6, 1999; Third Party with Sanders on Jan. 6, 1999

Majority					**Minority**				
			Terms in:					**Terms in:**	
Rank Name	Party	State	House	Comm.	Rank Name	Party	State	House	Comm.
Chr Burton, Danny L.	Rep	Ind.	9	*2 3	RM Waxman, Henry A.	Dem	Cal.	13	12
2nd Gilman, Benjamin A.	Rep	N.Y.	14	3	2nd Lantos, Thomas P.	Dem	Cal.	10	10

3rd Morella, Constance A.	Rep	Md.	7	3		3rd Wise, Robert E. Jr.	Dem	W.Va.	9	*2 3
4th Shays, Christopher H.	Rep	Conn.	7	7		4th Owens, Major R.	Dem	N.Y.	9	9
5th Cox, C. Christopher	Rep	Cal.	6	*2 2		5th Towns, Edolphus	Dem	N.Y.	9	9
6th Ros-Lehtinen, Ileana	Rep	Fla.	6	6		6th Kanjorski, Paul E.	Dem	Penn.	8	3
7th McHugh, John M.	Rep	N.Y.	4	4		7th Condit, Gary A.	Dem	Cal.	6	6
8th Horn, J. Steven	Rep	Cal.	4	4		8th Mink, Patsy T.	Dem	Hai.	12	*2 1
9th Mica, John L.	Rep	Fla.	4	4		9th Maloney, Carolyn B.	Dem	N.Y.	4	4
10th Davis, Thomas M. III	Rep	Va.	3	3		10th Norton, Eleanor Holmes	Dem	D.C.	5	*1 3
11th McIntosh, David M.	Rep	Ind.	3	3		11th Fattah, Chaka	Dem	Penn.	3	3
12th Souder, Mark E.	Rep	Ind.	3	3		12th Cummings, Elijah E.	Dem	Md.	3	3
13th Scarborough, C. Joseph	Rep	Fla.	3	3		13th Kucinich, Dennis	Dem	Ohio	2	2
14th LaTourette, Steven C.	Rep	Ohio	3	3		14th Blagojevich, Rod R.	Dem	Ill.	2	2
15th Sanford, Marshall C. (Mark) Jr.	Rep	S.C.	3	3		15th Davis, Danny K.	Dem	Ill.	2	2
16th Barr, Bob	Rep	Ga.	3	2		16th Tierney, John F.	Dem	Mass.	2	*1 2
17th Miller, Daniel	Rep	Fla.	4	2		17th Turner, Jim	Dem	Tex.	2	2
18th Hutchinson, Asa	Rep	Ark.	2	1		18th Allen, Thomas H.	Dem	Me.	2	2
19th Terry, Lee R.	Rep	Nebr.	1	1		19th Ford, Harold E. Jr.	Dem	Tenn.	2	2
20th Biggert, Judith B.	Rep	Ill.	1	1						
21st Walden, Greg	Rep	Ore.	1	1		**Third Party:**				
22nd Ose, Doug	Rep	Cal.	1	1		Sanders, Bernard	Ind	Vt.	5	5
23rd Ryan, Paul D.	Rep	Wisc.	1	1						
24th Doolittle, John T.	Rep	Cal.	5	1						

*1: Member's first period of service on the committee.

*2: Member's second period of service on the committee.

Vacancies Filled:

  Majority:

    24th seat by Doolittle on Feb. 2, 1999.

Changes:

  Majority:

Cox, C. Christopher	Rep	Cal.	Jan. 19, 1999 Resigned committee; became Chair of Select National Security Concerns with China.
Chenoweth, Helen P.	Rep	Ida.	Feb. 2, 1999 Replaced Cox.
Doolittle, John T.	Rep	Cal.	June 24, 1999 Resigned committee to open seat for Vitter; no new assignment.
Vitter, David	Rep	La.	June 25, 1999 Replaced Doolittle.

  Minority:

Condit, Gary A.	Dem	Cal.	Mar. 4, 1999 Leave of absence; moved to Permanent Select Intelligence.
Schakowsky, Janice D.	Dem	Ill.	Mar. 17, 1999 Replaced Condit.

Departures from the House:

	Majority			**Minority**		
Elected Governor	None			Wise, Robert E. Jr.	Dem	W.Va.
Lost Election for Governor	McIntosh, David M.	Rep	Ind.	None		
Retired	Sanford, Marshall C. (Mark) Jr.	Rep	S.C.	None		
	Chenoweth, Helen P.	Rep	Ida.			

Departures from Committee:

Moved to Appropriations	Vitter, David	Rep	La.	None
Moved to Education and the Workforce	Biggert, Judith B.	Rep	Ill.	None
Moved to Energy and Commerce	Terry, Lee R.	Rep	Neb.	None
	Walden, Greg	Rep	Ore.	
Moved to Standards of Official Conduct	Biggert, Judith B.	Rep	Ill.	None
Moved to Ways and Means	Ryan, Paul D.	Rep	Wisc.	None

GOVERNMENT REFORM / 107th Congress

Service Dates of Committee Chair: Jan. 6, 2001-Jan. 3, 2003

Service Dates of Majority Members: Jan. 6, 2001-Jan. 3, 2003

Service Dates of Minority Members: Jan. 31, 2001-Jan. 3, 2003

Roster Filled: Majority with 24 members on Feb. 8, 2001; Minority with 19 members on Feb. 8, 2001; Third Party with Sanders on Feb. 13, 2001

Majority					**Minority**				
			Terms in:					**Terms in:**	
Rank Name	**Party**	**State**	**House**	**Comm.**	**Rank Name**	**Party**	**State**	**House**	**Comm.**
Chr Burton, Danny L.	Rep	Ind.	10	*2 4	RM Waxman, Henry A.	Dem	Cal.	14	13
2nd Gilman, Benjamin A.	Rep	N.Y.	15	4	2nd Lantos, Thomas P.	Dem	Cal.	11	11

3rd Morella, Constance A.	Rep	Md.	8	4		3rd Owens, Major R.	Dem	N.Y.	10	10
4th Shays, Christopher H.	Rep	Conn.	8	8		4th Towns, Edolphus	Dem	N.Y.	10	10
5th Ros-Lehtinen, Ileana	Rep	Fla.	7	7		5th Kanjorski, Paul E.	Dem	Penn.	9	4
6th McHugh, John M.	Rep	N.Y.	5	5		6th Mink, Patsy T.	Dem	Hai.	13	*2 2
7th Horn, J. Steven	Rep	Cal.	5	5		7th Maloney, Carolyn B.	Dem	N.Y.	5	5
8th Mica, John L.	Rep	Fla.	5	5		8th Norton, Eleanor Holmes	Dem	D.C.	6	*1 4
9th Davis, Thomas M. III	Rep	Va.	4	4		9th Fattah, Chaka	Dem	Penn.	4	4
10th Souder, Mark E.	Rep	Ind.	4	4		10th Cummings, Elijah E.	Dem	Md.	4	4
11th Scarborough, C. Joseph	Rep	Fla.	4	4		11th Kucinich, Dennis	Dem	Ohio	3	3
12th LaTourette, Steven C.	Rep	Ohio	4	4		12th Blagojevich, Rod R.	Dem	Ill.	3	3
13th Barr, Bob	Rep	Ga.	4	3		13th Davis, Danny K.	Dem	Ill.	3	3
14th Miller, Daniel	Rep	Fla.	5	3		14th Tierney, John F.	Dem	Mass.	3	*1 3
15th Hutchinson, Asa	Rep	Ark.	3	2		15th Turner, Jim	Dem	Tex.	3	3
16th Ose, Doug	Rep	Cal.	2	2		16th Allen, Thomas H.	Dem	Me.	3	3
17th Lewis, Ron	Rep	Ky.	5	*2 1		17th Ford, Harold E. Jr.	Dem	Tenn.	3	3
18th Flake, Jeff	Rep	Ariz.	1	*1 1		18th Schakowsky, Janice D.	Dem	Ill.	2	2
19th Davis, Jo Ann	Rep	Va.	1	1		19th Clay, William L. Jr.	Dem	Mo.		
20th Platts, Todd R.	Rep	Penn.	1	1						
21st Weldon, David J.	Rep	Fla	4	1		**Third Party:**				
22nd Cannon, Christopher B.	Rep	Utah	3	1		Sanders, Bernard	Ind	Vt.	6	6
23rd Putnam, Adam H. Jr.	Rep	Fla.	1	*1 1						
24th Otter, C.L. (Butch)	Rep	Ida.	1	1						

*1: Member's first period of service on the committee.
*2: Member's second period of service on the committee.

Note 1: Majority: With the Committee on Post Office and Civil Service absorbed into Government Reform and Oversight in 1995, Gilman was credited with ten terms of service on Post Office and Civil Service, 1975-1995, Burton with five terms, 1985-1995, and Morella with four terms, 1987-1995. Delegate Eleanor Holmes Norton (Dem-D.C.) was allowed to accrue committee seniority but not included in the party ratio.

Note 2: Minority: Sanders ranked among Democrats immediately after Schakowsky.

Vacancies Filled:
  Majority:
    21st through 24th seats filled by Weldon, Cannon, Putnam, and Otter on Feb. 8, 2001.
  Minoriy:
    19th seat filled by Clay on Feb. 8, 2001.

Changes:
  Majority:

Flake, Jeff	Rep	Ariz.	Feb. 8, 2001 Resigned committee; moved to Resources.
Schrock, Edward	Rep	Va.	Feb. 8, 2001 Replaced Flake.
Scarborough, C. Joseph	Rep	Fla.	June 5, 2001 Resigned committee; resigned the House on Sept. 6, 2001.
Duncan, John J. (Jimmy) Jr.	Rep	Tenn.	June 7, 2001 Replaced Scarborough.
Hutchinson, Asa	Rep	Ark.	Aug. 6, 2001 Resigned the House; became Director of the Drug Enforcement Agency.
Sullivan, John	Rep	Okla.	May 16, 2002 Replaced Hutchinson.

  Minority:

Fattah, Chaka	Dem	Penn.	Feb. 7, 2001 Resigned committee; moved to Appropriations.
Ford, Harold E. Jr.	Dem	Tenn.	Feb. 8, 2001 Resigned committee; moved to Financial Services.
Watson, Diane E.	Dem	Cal.	June 19, 2001 Replaced Fattah.
Lynch, Stephen F.	Dem	Mass.	Nov. 7, 2001 Replaced Ford.
Mink, Patsy T.	Dem	Hai.	Sept. 28, 2002 Died in office; vacancy remained.

Departures from the House:	**Majority**			**Minority**		
Elected Governor	None			Blagojevich, Rod R.	Dem	Ill.
Defeated for Re-nomination	Barr, Bob	Rep	Ga.	None		
Defeated for Re-election	Morella, Constance A.	Rep	Md.	None		
Retired	Gilman, Benjamin A.	Rep	N.Y.	None		
	Horn, J. Steven	Rep	Cal.			
	Miller, Daniel	Rep	Fla.			

Departures from Committee:						
Moved to Appropriations	Weldon, David J.	Rep	Fla.	None		
Moved to Energy and Commerce	Otter, C.L. (Butch)	Rep	Ida.	Allen, Thomas H.	Dem	Me.
				Schakowsky, Janice D.	Dem	Ill.

GOVERNMENT REFORM / 108th Congress

Service Dates of Committee Chair: Jan. 8, 2003-Jan. 3, 2005

Service Dates of Majority Members: Jan. 28, 2003-Jan. 3, 2005

Service Dates of Ranking Member: Jan. 8, 2003-Jan. 3, 2005

Service Dates of Minority Members: Jan. 28, 2003-Jan. 3, 2005

Roster Filled: Majority with 24 members on Jan. 28, 2003; Minority with 19 members on Feb. 13, 2003; Third Party with Sanders on Mar. 5, 2005

Majority

Rank Name	Party	State	Terms in: House	Terms in: Comm.
Chr Davis, Thomas M. III	Rep	Va.	5	5
2nd Burton, Danny L.	Rep	Ind.	11	*2 5
3rd Shays, Christopher H.	Rep	Conn.	9	9
4th Ros-Lehtinen, Ileana	Rep	Fla.	8	8
5th McHugh, John M.	Rep	N.Y.	6	6
6th Mica, John L.	Rep	Fla.	6	6
7th Souder, Mark E.	Rep	Ind.	5	5
8th LaTourette, Steven C.	Rep	Ohio	5	5
9th Ose, Doug	Rep	Cal.	3	3
10th Lewis, Ron	Rep	Ky.	6	*2 2
11th Davis, Jo Ann	Rep	Va.	2	2
12th Platts, Todd R.	Rep	Penn.	2	2
13th Cannon, Christopher B.	Rep	Utah	4	2
14th Putnam, Adam H. Jr.	Rep	Fla.	2	*1 2
15th Schrock, Edward	Rep	Va.	2	2
16th Duncan, John J. (Jimmy) Jr.	Rep	Tenn.	9	2
17th Sullivan, John	Rep	Okla.	2	2
18th Deal, J. Nathan	Rep	Ga.	6	1
19th Miller, Candice S.	Rep	Mich.	1	1
20th Murphy, Timothy	Rep	Penn.	1	1
21st Turner, Michael R.	Rep	Ohio	1	1
22nd Carter, John R.	Rep	Tex.	1	1
23rd Janklow, William J.	Rep	S.D.	1	1
24th Blackburn, Marsha	Rep	Tenn.	1	1

Minority

Rank Name	Party	State	Terms in: House	Terms in: Comm.
RM Waxman, Henry A.	Dem	Cal.	15	14
2nd Lantos, Thomas P.	Dem	Cal.	12	12
3rd Owens, Major R.	Dem	N.Y.	11	11
4th Towns, Edolphus	Dem	N.Y.	11	11
5th Kanjorski, Paul E.	Dem	Penn.	10	5
6th Maloney, Carolyn B.	Dem	N.Y.	6	6
7th Norton, Eleanor Holmes	Dem	D.C.	7	*1 5
8th Cummings, Elijah E.	Dem	Md.	5	5
9th Kucinich, Dennis	Dem	Ohio	4	4
10th Davis, Danny K.	Dem	Ill.	4	4
11th Tierney, John F.	Dem	Mass.	4	*1 4
12th Turner, Jim	Dem	Tex.	4	4
13th Clay, William L. Jr.	Dem	Mo.	2	2
14th Watson, Diane E.	Dem	Cal.	2	2
15th Lynch, Stephen F.	Dem	Mass.	2	2
16th Van Hollen, Christopher	Dem	Md	1	1
17th Sánchez, Linda T.	Dem	Cal.	1	1
18th Ruppersberger, C.A. (Dutch)	Dem	Md.	1	1
19th Cooper, James H.S.	Dem	Tenn	7	*1 1

Third Party:

	Party	State	House	Comm.
Sanders, Bernard	Ind	Vt.	7	7

*1: Member's first period of service on the committee.

*2: Member's second period of service on the committee.

Note 1 Majority: With the Committee on Post Office and Civil Service absorbed into Government Reform and Oversight in 1995, Burton was credited with five terms, 1985-1995. Sanders accrued seniority among Democrats ranking immediately after Kanjorski. Delegate Eleanor Holmes Norton (Dem-D.C.) was allowed to accrue committee seniority but not included in the party ratio.

Vacancies Filled:
  Minority:
    16th, 17th, and 18th seats filled by Van Hollen, Sánchez, and Ruppersberger on Feb. 5, 2003; 19th seat filled by Cooper on Feb. 13, 2003.

Changes:
  Majority:

Janklow, William J.	Rep	S.D.	Jan. 20, 2004 Resigned the House and retired.
Sullivan, John	Rep	Okla.	Jan. 28, 2004 Resigned committee; moved to Energy and Commerce.
Tiberi, Patrick	Rep	Ohio	Mar. 10, 2004 Replaced Janklow.
Harris, Katherine	Rep	Fla.	Mar. 10, 2004 Replaced Sullivan.
Davis, Jo Ann	Rep	Va.	Aug. 10, 2004 Resigned committee; moved to Permanent Select Intelligence.
Burgess, Michael C.	Rep	Tex.	Sept. 23, 2004 Replaced Davis.
Putnam, Adam H. Jr.	Rep	Fla.	Sept. 28, 2004 Resigned committee; moved to Rules.
Cantor, Eric I.	Rep	Va.	Sept. 29, 2004 Replaced Putnam.
Cantor, Eric I.	Rep	Va.	Oct. 6, 2004 Resigned committee; no new assignment.
Putnam, Adam H. Jr.	Rep	Fla.	Oct. 7, 2004 Replaced Cantor.

  Minority:

Turner, Jim	Dem	Tex.	Feb. 5, 2003 Leave of absence; moved to Select Homeland Security as Ranking Member; never returned.
Bell, Chris	Dem	Tex.	Feb. 5, 2003 Replaced Turner.
Norton, Eleanor Holmes	Dem	D.C.	Feb. 12, 2003 Leave of absence; moved to Select Homeland Security; returned Feb. 26, 2003, ranked after Ruppersberger in the 17th slot.
Bell, Chris	Dem	Tex.	Jan. 28, 2004 Resigned committee; moved to Financial Services.
McCollum, Betty	DFL	Minn.	June 14, 2004 Replaced Bell.

Departures from the House:

				Minority
Retired		**Majority**		None
	Ose, Doug	Rep	Cal.	
	Schrock, Edward	Rep	Va.	

Departures from Committee:

				Minority
Moved to Appropriations	Carter, John R.	Rep	Tex.	None
Moved to Energy and Commerce	Murphy, Timothy	Rep	Penn.	None

No new assignment	Burgess, Michael C.	Rep	Tex.			
	Blackburn, Marsha	Rep	Tenn.			
	Lewis, Ron	Rep	Ky.	McCollum, Betty	DFL	Minn.
	Deal, J. Nathan	Rep	Ga.	Cooper, James H.S.	Dem	Tenn.
	Putnam, Adam H. Jr.	Rep	Fla.	Norton, Eleanor Holmes	Dem	D.C.
	Tiberi, Patrick	Rep	Ohio			

GOVERNMENT REFORM / 109th Congress

Service Dates of Committee Chair: Jan. 6, 2005-Jan. 3, 2007

Service Dates of Majority Members: Jan. 26, 2005-Jan. 3, 2007

Service Dates of Minority Members: Jan. 26, 2005-Jan. 3, 2007

Roster Filled: Majority with 23 members on Jan. 26, 2005; Minority with 17 members on Jan. 26, 2005; Third Party with Sanders on Jan. 26, 2005

			Terms in:					Terms in:	
Majority					**Minority**				
Rank Name	**Party**	**State**	**House**	**Comm.**	**Rank Name**	**Party**	**State**	**House**	**Comm.**
Chr Davis, Thomas M. III	Rep	Va.	6	6	RM Waxman, Henry A.	Dem	Cal.	16	15
2nd Burton, Danny L.	Rep	Ind.	12	*2 6	2nd Lantos, Thomas P.	Dem	Cal.	13	13
3rd Shays, Christopher H.	Rep	Conn.	10	10	3rd Owens, Major R.	Dem	N.Y.	12	12
4th Ros-Lehtinen, Ileana	Rep	Fla.	9	9	4th Towns, Edolphus	Dem	N.Y.	12	12
5th McHugh, John M.	Rep	N.Y.	7	7	5th Kanjorski, Paul E.	Dem	Penn.	11	6
6th Mica, John L.	Rep	Fla.	7	7	6th Maloney, Carolyn B.	Dem	N.Y.	7	7
7th Gutknecht, Gilbert W.	Rep	Minn.	6	*2 1	7th Cummings, Elijah E.	Dem	Md.	6	6
8th Souder, Mark E.	Rep	Ind.	6	6	8th Kucinich, Dennis	Dem	Ohio	5	5
9th LaTourette, Steven C.	Rep	Ohio	6	6	9th Davis, Danny K.	Dem	Ill.	5	5
10th Platts, Todd R.	Rep	Penn.	3	3	10th Tierney, John F.	Dem	Mass.	5	*1 5
11th Cannon, Christopher B.	Rep	Utah	5	3	11th Clay, William L. Jr.	Dem	Mo.	3	3
12th Duncan, John J. (Jimmy) Jr.	Rep	Tenn.	10	3	12th Watson, Diane E.	Dem	Cal.	3	3
13th Miller, Candice S.	Rep	Mich.	2	2	13th Lynch, Stephen F.	Dem	Mass.	3	3
14th Turner, Michael R.	Rep	Ohio	2	2	14th Van Hollen, Christopher	Dem	Md.	2	2
15th Harris, Katherine	Rep	Fla.	2	2	15th Sánchez, Linda T.	Dem	Cal.	2	2
16th Issa, Darrell E.	Rep	Cal.	3	1	16th Ruppersberger, C.A. (Dutch)	Dem	Md.	2	2
17th Brown-Waite, Virginia	Rep	Fla.	2	1	17th Higgins, Brian	Dem	N.Y.	1	1
18th Porter, Jon C.	Rep	Nev.	2	1					
19th Marchant, Kenny	Rep	Tex.	1	1	**Third Party:**				
20th Westmoreland, Lynn A.	Rep	Ga.	1	1	Sanders, Bernard	Ind	Vt.	8	8
21st McHenry, Patrick T.	Rep	N.C.	1	1					
22nd Dent, Charles W.	Rep	Penn.	1	1	*1: Member's first period of service on the committee.				
23rd Foxx, Virginia A.	Rep	N.C.	1	1	*2: Member's second period of service on the committee.				

Note: Sanders accrued seniority among Democrats ranking immediately after Kanjorski. Delegate Eleanor Holmes Norton (Dem-D.C.) was allowed to accrue committee seniority but not included in the party ratio.

Changes:

Majority:

Harris, Katherine	Rep	Fla.	Feb. 8, 2005 Resigned committee; moved to Homeland Security.
Brown-Waite, Virginia	Rep	Fla.	Sep. 30, 2005 Resigned committee; had moved to Homeland Security.
Schmidt, Jean	Rep	Ohio	Sept. 15, 2005 Replaced Harris.
Bilbray, Brian P.	Rep	Cal.	June 29, 2006 Replaced Brown-Waite.

Minority:

Tierney, John F.	Dem	Mass.	Feb. 1, 2005 Leave of absence; moved to Select Intelligence.
Norton, Eleanor Holmes	Dem	D.C.	Feb. 2, 2005 Replaced Tierney.

Departures from the House:

	Majority			**Minority**		
Defeated for Re-election	Gutknecht, Gilbert W.	Rep	Minn.	None		
Retired	None			Owens, Major R.	Dem	N.Y.

Departures from Committee:

	Majority			**Minority**		
Became RM on Foreign Affairs	Ros-Lehtinen, Ileana	Rep	Fla.	None		
Moved to Appropriations	None			Ruppersberger, C.A. (Dutch)	Dem	Md.
Moved to Budget	Porter, Jon C.	Rep	Nev.	None		
Moved to Education and Labor	None			Sánchez, Linda T.	Dem	Cal.
Moved to Foreign Affairs	None			Sánchez, Linda T.	Dem	Cal.
Moved to Select Energy Independence and Global Warming	Miller, Candice S.	Rep	Mich.	None		

Moved to Transportation and Infrastructure	Miller, Candice S.	Rep	Mich.	None
Moved to Ways and Means	Porter, Jon C.	Rep	Nev.	None
No new assignment	LaTourette, Steven C.	Rep	Ohio	None
	Dent, Charles W.	Rep	Penn.	
	Schmidt, Jean	Rep	Ohio	

OVERSIGHT AND GOVERNMENT REFORM / 110th Congress

Service Dates of Committee Chair: Jan. 4, 2007-Jan. 3, 2009

Service Dates of Majority Members: Jan. 12, 2007-Jan. 3, 2009

Service Dates of Minority Members: Jan. 10, 2007-Jan. 3, 2009

Roster Filled: Majority with 23 members on Jan. 12, 2007; Minority with 18 members on May 10, 2007

	Majority						**Minority**				
				Terms in:						**Terms in:**	
Rank Name		**Party**	**State**	**House**	**Comm.**	**Rank Name**		**Party**	**State**	**House**	**Comm.**
Chr Waxman, Henry A.		Dem	Cal.	17	16	RM Davis, Thomas M. III		Rep	Va.	7	7
2nd Lantos, Thomas P.		Dem	Cal.	14	14	2nd Burton, Danny L.		Rep	Ind.	13	*2 7
3rd Towns, Edolphus		Dem	N.Y.	13	13	3rd Shays, Christopher H.		Rep	Conn.	11	11
4th Kanjorski, Paul E.		Dem	Penn.	12	7	4th McHugh, John M.		Rep	N.Y.	8	8
5th Maloney, Carolyn B.		Dem	N.Y.	8	8	5th Mica, John L.		Rep	Fla.	8	8
6th Cummings, Elijah E.		Dem	Md.	7	7	6th Souder, Mark E.		Rep	Ind.	7	7
7th Kucinich, Dennis		Dem	Ohio	6	6	7th Platts, Todd R.		Rep	Penn.	4	4
8th Davis, Danny K.		Dem	Ill.	6	6	8th Cannon, Christopher B.		Rep	Utah	6	4
9th Tierney, John F.		Dem	Mass.	6	*2 1	9th Duncan, John J. (Jimmy) Jr.		Rep	Tenn.	11	4
10th Clay, William L. Jr.		Dem	Mo.	4	4	10th Turner, Michael R.		Rep	Ohio	3	3
11th Watson, Diane E.		Dem	Cal.	4	4	11th Issa, Darrell E.		Rep	Cal.	4	2
12th Lynch, Stephen F.		Dem	Mass.	4	4	12th Marchant, Kenny		Rep	Tex.	2	2
13th Higgins, Brian		Dem	N.Y.	2	2	13th Westmoreland, Lynn A.		Rep	Ga.	2	2
14th Yarmuth, John A.		Dem	Ky.	1	1	14th McHenry, Patrick T.		Rep	N.C.	2	2
15th Braley, Bruce L.		Dem	Iowa	1	1	15th Foxx, Virginia A.		Rep	N.C.	2	2
16th Norton, Eleanor Holmes		Dem	D.C.	9	*3 2	16th Bilbray, Brian P.		Rep	Cal.	5	2
17th McCollum, Betty		DFL	Minn.	4	*2 1	17th Sali, Bill		Rep	Ida.	1	1
18th Cooper, James H.S.		Dem	Tenn.	9	*2 1	18th Jordan, Jim		Rep	Ohio	1	1
19th Van Hollen, Christopher		Dem	Md.	3	3						
20th Hodes, Paul W.		Dem	N.H.	1	1	*2: Member's second period of service on the committee.					
21st Murphy, Christopher S.		Dem	Conn.	1	1	*3: Member's third period of service on the committee.					
22nd Sarbanes, John		Dem	Md.	1	1						
23rd Welch, Peter		Dem	Vt.	1	1						

Note: Delegate Eleanor Holmes Norton (Dem-D.C.) was allowed to accrue committee seniority but not included in the party ratio.

Vacancies Filled:
  Minority:
    18th seat filled by Jordan on May 10, 2007.

Changes:
  Majority:

Lantos, Thomas P.	Dem	Cal.	Feb. 10, 2008 Died in office.
Speier, K. Jacqueline	Dem	Cal.	July 15, 2008 Replaced Lantos.

  Minority:

Davis, Thomas M. III	Rep	Va.	Nov. 24, 2008 Resigned the House and retired.

Departures from the House:	**Majority**			**Minority**		
Defeated for Re-election	None			Shays, Christopher H.	Rep	Conn.
				Sali, Bill	Rep	Ida.
Defeated for Re-nomination	None			Cannon, Christopher B.	Rep	Utah

Departures from Committee:					
Became Chair on Energy and Commerce	Waxman, Henry A.	Dem	Cal.	None	
Moved to Budget	Yarmuth, John A.	Dem	Ky.	None	
	McCollum, Betty	DFL	Minn.		
Moved to Energy and Commerce	Braley, Bruce L.	Dem	Iowa	None	
	Sarbanes, John	Dem	Md.		

Moved to Ways and Means	Higgins, Brian	Dem	N.Y.	None	
	Yarmuth, John A.	Dem	Ky.		
No new assignment	None			Marchant, Kenny	Rep	Tex.

OVERSIGHT AND GOVERNMENT REFORM / 111th Congress

Service Dates of Committee Chair: Jan. 6, 2009-Jan. 3, 2011

Service Dates of Majority Members: Jan. 28, 2009-Jan. 3, 2011

Service Dates of Minority Members: Jan. 9, 2009-Jan. 3, 2011

Roster Filled: Majority with 25 members, Oct. 15, 2009; Minority with 16 members, Jan. 9, 2009

Majority			Terms in:		Minority			Terms in:	
Rank Name	Party	State	House	Comm.	Rank Name	Party	State	House	Comm.
Chr Towns, Edolphus	Dem	N.Y.	14	14	RM Issa, Darrell E.	Rep	Cal.	5	3
2nd Kanjorski, Paul E.	Dem	Penn.	13	8	2nd Burton, Danny L.	Rep	Ind.	14	*2 8
3rd Maloney, Carolyn B.	Dem	N.Y.	9	9	3rd McHugh, John M.	Rep	N.Y.	9	9
4th Cummings, Elijah E.	Dem	Md.	8	8	4th Mica, John L.	Rep	Fla.	9	9
5th Kucinich, Dennis	Dem	Ohio	7	7	5th Souder, Mark E.	Rep	Ind.	8	8
6th Tierney, John F.	Dem	Mass.	7	*2 2	6th Platts, Todd R.	Rep	Penn.	5	5
7th Clay, William L. Jr.	Dem	Mo.	5	5	7th Duncan, John J. (Jimmy) Jr.	Rep	Tenn.	12	5
8th Watson, Diane E.	Dem	Cal.	5	5	8th Turner, Michael R.	Rep	Ohio	4	4
9th Lynch, Stephen F.	Dem	Mass.	5	5	9th Westmoreland, Lynn A.	Rep	Ga.	3	3
10th Cooper, James H.S.	Dem	Tenn.	10	*2 2	10th McHenry, Patrick T.	Rep	N.C.	3	3
11th Connolly, Gerald E.	Dem	Va.	1	1	11th Foxx, Virginia A.	Rep	N.C.	3	3
12th Norton, Eleanor Holmes	Dem	D.C.	10	*3 3	12th Bilbray, Brian P.	Rep	Cal.	6	3
13th Kennedy, Patrick J.	Dem	R.I.	8	1	13th Jordan, Jim	Rep	Ohio	2	2
14th Davis, Danny K.	Dem	Ill.	7	7	14th Flake, Jeff	Rep	Ariz.	5	*2 1
15th Van Hollen, Christopher	Dem	Md.	4	4	15th Fortenberry, Jeff	Rep	Neb.	3	1
16th Cuellar, Henry	Dem	Tex.	3	1	16th Chaffetz, Jason	Rep	Utah	1	1
17th Hodes, Paul W.	Dem	N.H.	2	2					
18th Murphy, Christopher S.	Dem	Conn.	2	2	*2: Member's second period of service on the committee.				
19th Welch, Peter	Dem	Vt.	2	2	*3: Member's third period of service on the committee.				
20th Foster, Bill	Dem	Ill.	2	1					
21st Speier, K. Jacqueline	Dem	Cal.	2	2					
22nd Driehaus, Steve	Dem	Ohio	1	1					

Note: Delegate Eleanor Holmes Norton (Dem-D.C.) was allowed to accrue committee seniority but not included in the party ratio.

Additions:

  Majority:

Quigley, Mike	Dem	Ill.	Apr. 30, 2009 Ranked 12th after Connolly.
Kaptur, Marcia (Marcy) C.	Dem	Ohio	Apr. 30, 2009 Ranked 13th after Quigley.
Chu, Judy	Dem	Cal.	Oct. 15, 2009 Ranked 25th.

Changes:

  Minority:

Foxx, Virginia A.	Rep	N.C.	Jan. 15, 2009 Resigned committee; moved to Rules.
Schock, Aaron	Reo.	Ill.	Jan. 22, 2009 Replaced Foxx.
Platts, Todd R.	Rep	Penn.	June 15, 2009 Resigned committee; moved to Armed Services.
Luetkemeyer, Blaine	Rep	Mo.	Sept. 9, 2009 Replaced Platts.
McHugh, John M.	Rep	N.Y.	Sept. 21, 2009 Resigned the House; appointed Secretary of the Army.
Cao, Anh (Joseph)	Rep	La.	Oct. 7, 2009 Replaced McHugh.

Post Office and Civil Service

House Committee on Post Office and Civil Service, 103rd Congress (1993-1995)

BACKGROUND

Organizational History: The initial committee created by the House to deal with postal matters was the Committee on Post Office and Post Roads, created on November 9, 1808, on a motion by John Rhea, a Jeffersonian from Tennessee. Given its ability to distribute political patronage, the committee's first roster was very large, with seventeen original members named. Rhea was selected as its first chair and served in that role until 1815. By that time the committee's membership stood at seven, a more typical size for House committees of that era. Another predecessor was Reform in the Civil Service, that had begun legislative life as a select committee on March 12, 1865, on a motion by Thomas A. Jenckes (Rep-R.I.), who was its first chair and it became a standing committee on August 18, 1893, with its first chair, Robert E. De Forest (Dem-Conn.). The committee was renamed Civil Service on January 14, 1924, and Frederick R. Lehlbach (Rep-N.J.) who was the committee's senior Republican from 1917 to 1937 chaired the renamed committee. The third predecessor committee was Census which first appeared as the Select Committee on the Twelfth Census on June 27, 1898, with Albert J. Hopkins (Rep-Ill.) as its first chair. Hopkins remained as chair when it became the standing Committee on the Census on December 2, 1901.

At the time of the 1946 reorganization, the three committees had an allocated membership of sixty-seven that would be consolidated into twenty-five seats. The Civil Service Committee had the most impressive membership with Majority Whip Robert Ramspeck (Dem-Ga.) as its chair and included in its membership was a future Secretary of State, Christian A. Herter (Rep-Mass.) and two future U.S. senators who would become very prominent—Henry M. Jackson (Dem-Wash.) and Clifford P. Case (Rep-N.J.).

During its existence, the committee's major concern was the hiring, firing, and retiring of members of the federal bureaucracy. Although agencies and departments usually have little contact with the committee, the panel handled salary levels and major personnel questions, such as a 1978 civil service reform, a 1986 revamp of the federal retirement system, and a 1990 overhaul of the pay system for federal employees. The committee was heavily lobbied by the unions that represent federal employees. During the post-reorganization years, the committee was one of the least prominent and it survived the creation of the earlier committee reform efforts in 1974 and 1980, largely due to its support from the federal employee unions.

The Post Office responsibilities of the committee that dated back to 1808 were diminished in 1970 when the Postal Service became an independent corporation. But the committee continued to be a forum for complaints about deliveries and postal rates and it continued to influence postal operations. Companies with large postal budgets, such as those that advertise through mass mailings or send material by subscription, were a key constituency group.

However in 1995 at the start of the Republican-controlled 104th Congress, the House Committee on Post Office and Civil Service was terminated, eighteen years after the Senate's Post Office and Civil Service Committee was folded into its renamed Governmental Affairs Committee in 1977. Most of the committee's remaining jurisdictions were moved to the renamed Committee on Government Reform and Oversight. This was also the destination of five of the committee's last twenty-four members. Three of the twenty-four left the House; four others were reassigned to committees other than Government Reform and the remaining twelve—nine Democrats and three Republicans were not reassigned.

Membership: At the time of the 1946 reorganization, the reorganized committee had twenty-five members. The committee reached a small peak of twenty-eight members in the 94th Congress (1975-77) and 97th Congresses (1981-1983) but slipped back to 25 in 1985 and to twenty-three and twenty-two in subsequent Congresses. In the 102nd Congress (1991-1993), it had twenty-two members and in its last Congress, only twenty-four. Like the District of Columbia and House Administration Committees, this committee had become smaller than it was at the time of the 1946 reorganization.

With the committee's termination in 1995, twelve of its continuing twenty-one members were not given new assignments, including John T. Myers (Rep-Ind.), its last ranking member. Five members went to Government Reform and Oversight, the committee that received most of Post Office and Civil Service's jurisdictional responsibilities and William L. Clay (Dem-Mo.) moved over to become ranking member on Economic and Educational Opportunities.

Committee Leaders: Unlike the other low prestige committees, Post Office and Civil Service had a great deal of leadership stability during its first thirty years. Its first post-reorganization chair was Edward H. Rees (Rep-Kans.), the last ranking member on Civil Service, who was the senior Republican on the committee until his retirement in 1961, chairing it in both Republican Congresses, the 80th and 83rd. Its first ranking member was Thomas J. Murray (Dem-Tenn.), who had come from Post Office and Post Roads. Murray was the committee's senior Democrat from 1947 until he resigned in 1966 after being denied renomination. During those twenty years, Murray was chair for sixteen (1949-1953 and 1955-1966) and ranking member for four (1947-1949 and 1953-1955).

Rees was succeeded by Robert J. Corbett (Rep-Penn.) who served as ranking member from 1961 until his death in 1971 and was replaced by Harold R. Gross (Rep-Iowa) who served until his retirement in 1975. Murray's successor, Thaddeus J. Dulski (Dem-N.Y.), chaired the committee from 1967 until he resigned from the House in 1974. With Dulski's retirement, instability set in and the committee had three successive one-term chairs—David N. Henderson (Dem-N.C.)

who retired in 1977; Robert N.C. Nix (Dem-Penn.), who lost his renomination in 1978; and James M. Hanley (Dem-N.Y.), who retired in 1981. Continuity in the chair returned with William D. Ford (Dem-Mich.) who chaired the committee from 1981 until 1991, when he departed to chair the Education and Labor Committee. On the minority side, Gross's initial successor Edward J. Derwinski (Rep-Ill.) served from 1975 until he lost his renomination in 1982. His successor, Gene Taylor (Rep-Mo.) served from 1983 until his retirement in 1989.

The last senior members of Post Office and Civil Service were William L. Clay (Dem-Mo.), who chaired the committee from 1991 until its termination in 1995 and Benjamin A. Gilman, its ranking member from 1989 to 1993, who left to become ranking member on Foreign Affairs, and John T. Myers (Rep-Ind.) were the committee's last ranking members.

Party Leaders: Carl Albert (Dem-Okla.), who ascended the "leadership ladder" as Whip in 1955, Majority Leader in 1962, and Speaker in 1971, and Thomas S. Foley (Dem-Wash.), who followed the same path as Whip in 1981, Majority Leader in 1987; and as Speaker in 1989, were two of the post-1947 House leaders to have served on Post Office and Civil Service, although one-time Speaker John W. McCormack (Dem-Mass.) had served on Civil Service, one of its predecessor committees in 1929-1931. Three Whips—Republican C. Trent Lott (Rep-Miss.) and two Democrats J. Percy Priest (Dem-Tenn.) and Steny H. Hoyer (Dem-Md.), the present Majority Leader—passed through the Post Office and Civil Service Committee early in their House careers.

Notable Members: No member of Post Office and Civil Service was nominated for president and the only vice presidential nomination for a former committee member went to Geraldine Ferraro (Dem-N.Y.), on ex-vice president Walter Mondale's ticket in 1984 . Three Cabinet members served on Post Office, each of whom was a pioneer. Edward J. Derwinski (Rep-Ill.) was the inaugural Secretary of Veterans' Affairs when he was named by President George H.W. Bush in 1989 and Thomas J. Ridge (Rep-Penn.) was the nation's first Secretary of Homeland Security when he was named in 2003. The third Cabinet member to have served on the committee, Norman Y. Mineta (Dem-Cal.), was the Cabinet's first Asian-American. Mineta originally served as Bill Clinton's Secretary of Commerce and later as George W. Bush's Secretary of Transportation. Two lesser executive appointments were made to two women members of the committee by President Kennedy. Kathryn M. Granahan (Dem-Penn.) was appointed Treasurer of the United States and Catherine D. Norrell (Dem-Ark.) was named Deputy Assistant Secretary of State.

Fourteen former members of the committee moved on to the Senate. Eight were Democrats: Earle C. Clements of Kentucky, Eugene J. McCarthy of Minnesota, John V. Tunney of California, Spark M. Matsunaga of Hawaii, Paul M. Simon of Illinois, Thomas A. Daschle of South Dakota, Charles E. Schumer of New York, and Sherrod Brown of Ohio. Six were Republicans: Thruston B. Morton of Kentucky, James T. Broyhill of North Carolina, James A. McClure of Idaho, William L. Scott of Virginia, C. Trent Lott of Mississippi, and Connie Mack III of Florida. Four future governors served on the Post Office committee during their House careers: Democrats Earle C. Clements of Kentucky and J. Lindsay Almond of Virginia and Republicans Thomas J. Meskill of Connecticut and Thomas J. Ridge of Pennsylvania, and one prior governor, William M. Tuck of Virginia. Former Democratic senator Garrett L. Withers of Kentucky—who originally served in the Senate during 1949-1950, replacing Alben W. Barkley who had resigned to become Truman's Vice President and later replacing the deceased John A. Whitaker (Dem-Ky.) in the House—served on Post Office and Civil Service for two-plus months in 1953 prior to his own death.

Selected References

Fenno, Richard F., Jr., *Congressmen in Committees* (Boston: Little, Brown, 1973).

Schamel, Charles E. et al., "Records of the Post Office and Civil Service Committees," *Guide to the Records of the United States House of Representatives at the National Archives: 1789-1989 Bicentennial Edition* (Washington, D.C.: National Archives and Records Administration,1989), 227-235.

RESPONSIBILITIES, JURISDICTIONAL CHANGES, AND SUBCOMMITTEES

POST OFFICE AND CIVIL SERVICE

Jurisdiction, 80th Congress (1947-1949)

Established by the Legislative Reorganization Act of 1946:

[Section 121. (1) (e)] Committee on Post Office and Civil Service
    (1) The Federal civil service generally.
    (2) The status of officers and employees of the United States, including their compensation, classification, and retirement.
    (3) The postal service generally, including the railway mail service, and measures relating to ocean mail and pneumatic-tube service; but excluding post roads.
    (4) Postal-savings banks.
    (5) Census and the collection of statistics generally.
    (6) The National Archives.

Jurisdiction, 103rd Congress (1993-1995)

From the *Rules of the House of Representatives, 103rd Congress* (House Document 102-405)

[Rule X.1.(o)] Committee on Post Office and Civil Service
(1) Census and the collection of statistics generally.
(2) All Federal Civil Service, including intergovernmental personnel.
(3) Postal-savings banks.
(4) Postal service generally, including the railway mail service, and measures relating to ocean mail and pneumatic tube service; but excluding post roads.
(5) Status of officers and employees of the United States, including their compensation, classification, and retirement.
(6) Hatch Act.
(7) Holidays and celebrations.
(8) Population and demography.

NAMES OF POST OFFICE AND CIVIL SERVICE SUBCOMMITTEES FROM THE *CONGRESSIONAL DIRECTORY*

Census, Statistics, and Postal Personnel, 103 Civil Service, 103
Compensation and Employee Benefits, 103 Oversights and Investigations, 103
Postal Operations and Services, 103

MEMBERSHIP ROSTER, 103rd Congress, 1993-1995

POST OFFICE AND CIVIL SERVICE / 103rd Congress

Service Dates of Committee Chair: Jan. 21, 1993-Jan. 3, 1995

Service Dates of Majority Members: Jan. 21, 1993-Jan. 3, 1995

Service Dates of Minority Members: Jan. 5, 1993-Jan. 3, 1995

Roster Filled: Majority with 15 members on Jan. 27, 1993; Minority with 9 members on Feb. 18, 1993

Majority

Rank Name	Party	State	Terms in: House	Terms in: Comm.
Chr Clay, William L.	Dem	Mo.	13	11
2nd Schroeder, Patricia S.	Dem	Colo.	11	11
3rd McCloskey, Francis X.	Dem	Ind.	6	6
4th Ackerman, Gary L.	Dem	N.Y.	6	6
5th Sawyer, Thomas C.	Dem	Ohio	4	3
6th Kanjorski, Paul E.	Dem	Penn.	5	3
7th Norton, Eleanor Holmes	Dem	D.C.	2	2
8th Collins, Barbara-Rose	Dem	Mich.	2	2
9th Byrne, Leslie L.	Dem	Va.	1	1
10th Watt, Melvin L.	Dem	N.C.	1	1
11th Wynn, Albert R.	Dem	Md.	1	1
12th Laughlin, Gregory H.	Dem	Tex.	3	1
13th Bishop, Sanford D. Jr.	Dem	Ga.	1	1
14th Brown, Sherrod	Dem	Ohio	1	1
15th Hastings, Alcee L.	Dem	Fla.	1	1

Minority

Rank Name	Party	State	Terms in: House	Terms in: Comm.
RM Myers, John T.	Rep	Ind.	14	5
2nd Gilman, Benjamin A.	Rep	N.Y.	11	10
3rd Young, Donald E.	Rep	Alas.	11	5
4th Burton, Danny L.	Rep	Ind.	6	5
5th Morella, Constance A.	Rep	Md.	4	4
6th Ridge, Thomas J.	Rep	Penn.	6	3
7th Petri, Thomas E.	Rep	Wisc.	8	1
8th Boehlert, Sherwood L.	Rep	N.Y.	6	1
9th Saxton, H. James	Rep	N.J.	6	1

Note: Delegate Eleanor Holmes Norton (Dem-D.C.) was allowed to accrue committee seniority but not included in the party ratio.

Vacancies Filled:
   Majority:
      12th through 15th seats filled by Laughlin, Bishop, Brown, and Hastings on Jan. 27, 1993.
   Minority:
      7th through 9th seats filled by Petri, Boehlert, and Saxton on Feb. 18, 1993.

Changes:
   Minority:

Saxton, H. James	Rep	N.J.	Sept. 13, 1993 Resigned committee; no new assignment; vacancy remained.

	Majority			Minority		
Departures from the House:						
Elected Governor	None			Ridge, Thomas J.	Rep	Penn.
Defeated for Re-election	McCloskey, Francis X.	Dem	Ind.	None		
	Byrne, Leslie L.	Dem	Va.			
Departures from Committee:						
Became RM on Economic and Educational Opportunities	Clay, William L.	Dem	Mo.	None		
Returned to Banking and Financial Services	Ackerman, Gary L.	Dem	N.Y.	None		
Moved to Government Reform and Oversight	Kanjorski, Paul E.	Dem	Penn.	Gilman, Benjamin A.	Rep	N.Y.
	Norton, Eleanor Holmes	Dem	D.C.	Burton, Danny L.	Rep	Ind.
				Morella, Constance A.	Rep	Md.
Moved to Science	Hastings, Alcee L.	Dem	Fla.	None		
Moved to Transportation and Infrastructure	None			Young, Donald E.	Rep	Alas.
No new assignment	Brown, Sherrod	Dem	Ohio	Myers, John T.	Rep	Ind.
	Schroeder, Patricia S.	Dem	Colo.	Petri, Thomas E.	Rep	Wisc.
	Sawyer, Thomas C.	Dem	Ohio	Boehlert, Sherwood L.	Rep	N.Y.
	Collins, Barbara-Rose	Dem	Mich.			
	Watt, Melvin L.	Dem	N.C.			
	Wynn, Albert R.	Dem	Md.			
	Laughlin, Gregory H.	Dem	Tex.			
	Bishop, Sanford D. Jr.	Dem	Ga.			

Rules

House Committee on Rules, 103rd-111th Congresses (1993-2011)

BACKGROUND

Organizational History: The Rules Committee was first created as an eleven-member select panel in 1789, chaired by Nicholas Gilman (Fed-N.H.). Although it is one of the oldest committees in the House, its rise to power was unsteady. Once the rules were created in the First Congress (1789-1791), they were generally adopted without much debate at the opening of the new Congress. The committee's size dropped to five in 1791 and three in 1793 and 1795. However, former Speakers Frederick A.C. Muhlenberg (DR-Penn.) and Jonathan Trumbull (Fed-Conn.) chaired the Rules Committee in the House's first decade.

Between 1817 and 1827, the Select Committee on Rules was named only in the 18th Congress (1823-1825). It resumed regular operations in 1827. In 1849, the prolonged speakership battle won by Howell Cobb (Dem-Ga.) led to the committee being made a standing one, but it was reduced to the status of a select committee again in 1851. In the 35th Congress (1857-1859), Speaker James L. Orr (Dem-S.C.) designated himself as a member and the chair of the Rules Committee. Speakers named themselves chairs from that time until the aftermath of the "revolt" against Speaker Joseph G. Cannon (Rep-Ill.) in the 61st Congress (1909-1911).

Under Speaker Samuel J. Randall (Dem-Penn.), the Rules Committee once again became a standing one in 1880. Randall and his successors used the committee to control the House floor. It began issuing rules for floor debate in 1883. By 1886, the jurisdiction of the committee was expanded to allow it to fix the days for consideration of particular bills; in 1887, the House rules provided that all special orders providing for consideration of a particular bill or class of bills must pass through the Rules Committee. By 1889 the House rules defined the jurisdiction of the committee to include "all proposed action touching the rules, joint rules, and order of business." Resolutions calling for special committees and investigations also came under the committee's purview.

The power of the Rules Committee over floor business was exercised freely by such strong House Speakers as Thomas B. "Czar" Reed (Rep-Me.) and Cannon. It was the arbitrariness of Speaker Cannon and his committee assignment policy that led to the House removing the speaker from the Rules Committee and its being made independent of the leadership in 1909-1910. This was the result of an alliance between the minority Democrats led by Democratic Floor Leader, James B. (Champ) Clark (Dem-Mo.) and Progressive Republicans led by George W. Norris (Rep-Neb.).

It was another cross-party alliance that would alter the committee's dynamics in the late 1930s when a coalition of conservative southern Democrats and Republicans took control of the panel and frustrated the Democratic Party leadership for the next two decades. This was particularly true during the 1950s when its two senior Democrats, Howard W. Smith (Dem-Va.), the chair, and second-ranking William M. Colmer (Dem-Miss.) worked with the four Republicans on the committee to stymie civil rights legislation. Committee votes would often split 6-6 and legislation would be stopped.

The Democratic leadership's first effort to gain control of Rules followed the recapture of the House in 1954 when they obtained four additional majority seats on the committee. Two of the new members would play a major role in the future of the House. They were Richard W. Bolling (Dem-Mo.), the very bright and acerbic protégé of House Speaker Sam Rayburn (Dem-Tex.), and Thomas P. (Tip) O'Neill, Jr. (Dem-Mass.), the shrewd and avuncular protégé of House Majority Leader John W. McCormack (Dem-Mass.). Bolling and O'Neill were recognized as talented junior members and were assigned by the party's floor leaders to be their "eyes and ears" on the Rules Committee as they monitored the alliance between Smith and Colmer and the Republicans.

In 1961, newly elected Democratic President John F. Kennedy wanted to implement a liberal civil rights agenda. The House's leadership, Speaker Rayburn and Majority Leader McCormack, engineered a 217-212 vote to expand the membership of the Rules Committee from twelve and a 6 to 6 split to fifteen and an 8 to 7 committee majority supportive of the liberal agenda. It was Sam Rayburn's last great legislative victory. Under new Speaker McCormack, the enlargement was made permanent in 1963 and since then the Rules Committee has often been an arm of the leadership.

The centrality of the Rules Committee is unlikely to be derived from the sparse jurisdiction of the Rules Committee outlined in the 2009 *Rules of the House of Representatives*, Rule X.1.(n):

Committee on Rules

(1) The rules and joint rules (other than rules and joint rules relating to the Code of Official Conduct), and order of business of the House.
(2) Recesses and final adjournments of Congress.

Or as recounted in the *House Manual* (2008):

The jurisdiction of this committee is primarily over propositions to make or change the rules), to create committees, and to direct them to make investigations. Effective January 3, 1975, however, the authority for all committees to conduct investigations and studies was made a part of the standing rules), as was the authority to issue subpoenas (H. Res. 988, 93d Cong., Oct. 8, 1974). The Committee also reports resolutions relating to the hour of daily meeting and the days on which the House shall sit, and orders relating to the use of the galleries during the electoral count.

The battles for control of the House Rules Committee derive from its role as the "traffic cop of the House"—its most popular public depiction. However, this function is more than just directing traffic; it allows the committee to influence the substance of legislation through deciding which bills will get to the floor (and thereby bringing pressure on the originating legislative committee to draft a measure to the wishes of the Rules members) and by laying down the ground rules for floor debate through the issuance of "special rules."

As described on the Rules Committee website:

"RULE, SPECIAL. Also known as a special order, order of business resolution, or rule, a special rule is a simple resolution of the House of Representatives, usually reported by the Committee on Rules, to permit the immediate consideration of a legislative measure, notwithstanding the usual order of business, and to prescribe conditions for its debate and amendment. The authority of the Rules Committee to report special rules can be traced to 1883. Prior to that time, bills could not be considered out of their order on the calendars of the House except by unanimous consent or under a suspension of the rules, which required a two-thirds vote. Since special rules reported from the Rules Committee required only a majority vote in the House, the new practice greatly facilitated the ability of the majority leadership to depart from the regular order of business and schedule major legislation according to the majority's priorities.

These "special orders" or "rules," are used to: (1) set the amount of time for general debate, (2) make the legislation open to amendment or not, and (3) waive (or not waive) points of order. The rules may be "open rules" that permit amendments or "closed rules" that prevent them. These special orders have expedited legislative business in the increasingly complex House agenda. And in an increasingly politically polarized House, the incidence of "closed rules" emanating from the Rules Committee has increased regardless of which party has had control of the chamber.

Membership: The House Rules Committee had shrunk from fourteen members that had been in place from 1935 to 1945 to twelve on the eve of the 1946 reorganization. That would be its post-reorganization size with eight majority members and four minority ones regardless of the overall party ratio in the House. This became a problem in the 1950s when the committee's two conservative senior Southern Democrats, Howard W. Smith of Virginia and William M. Colmer of Mississippi joined with the committee's four Republicans to prevent liberal legislation from moving to the House floor by votes of 6 to 6.

In a gesture intended to help the legislative agenda of newly-elected President John Kennedy and his Vice President Lyndon Johnson, Speaker Sam Rayburn's long-time Texas protégé, Rayburn pushed an effort through the House to enlarge Rules Committee to fifteen. It was anticipated that Democratic liberals would get two of the three new seats and that legislation could be moved from the Rules Committee to the House floor by votes of 8 to 7.

From 1961 to 1975, the membership of Rules remained at fifteen with ten majority seats and five minority seats. In 1975, a sixteenth seat was added to the majority changing the ratio to 11 to five for the majority. In 1983, the committee was reduced to thirteen with nine majority seats and four minority ones. That has been the committee's size and its party ratio during the past nine Congresses, 1993-2011. As has been true since the committee was first organized, the Rules Committee party ratio is unaffected by any party ratio shifts within the House itself.

One of the anomalous aspects of the committee rankings is that the Rules Committee has a mean seniority of its members of 6.39 terms, ranking it third behind Appropriations (7.43) and Ways and Means (6.98). However, in recent years, the Rules Committee has opened its membership to a number of relatively junior members who will serve on it for a term or two and then leave the committee. Consequently, the Rules Committee has a relatively low membership retention rate of 85.87 percent—ranking it in eleventh place among the nineteen continuing committees.

Committee Leaders: The first post-reorganization chair of Rules was Leo E. Allen (Rep-Ill.) who had been the committee's ranking member in the previous Congress. He would remain as the committee's senior Republican until his retirement in 1961. The committee's two senior Democrats, Adolph J. Sabath, an immigrant from Chicago and E. Eugene "Goober" Cox (Dem-Ga.), embodied the northern immigrant-southern native mix of the post-FDR Democratic Party. They ran the Rules Committee when Democrats controlled the House in 1949-1952 and then both died seven weeks apart in 1952 on the eve of the Republican takeover of the 83rd Congress. Their deaths left the Rules Committee in the hands of two Southern segregationists, Howard W. Smith of Virginia and William M. Colmer of Mississippi.

These two men controlled the Rules Committee until Smith's renomination defeat in 1966 and Colmer's retirement in 1973. Often aided by the committee's conservative Republicans like ranking members Clarence J. Brown (Rep-Ohio), 1961-1965 and H. Allen Smith (Rep-Cal.), 1965-1973, the Smith-Colmer tandem stopped liberal legislation from getting to the floor. In 1955, Sam Rayburn protégés—moderate Democrat W. Homer Thornberry (Dem-Texas) and liberal Democrat Richard W. Bolling (Dem-Mo.) and John McCormack protégé Thomas P. (Tip) O'Neill, Jr. (Dem-Mass.)—were added to the committee, but the new assignments had less impact than hoped. In 1973, both Colmer and Smith were gone and with the Watergate case about to erupt, change would come to the Rules Committee.

With a supportive Carl Albert as Speaker, Tip O'Neill the new Majority Leader and Dick Bolling named to chair a Select Committee on Committees to reform a system that had stagnated in the quarter-century since the 1946 reorganization, change appeared on the horizon. Eighty-year-old Ray J. Madden (Dem-Ind.) became chair of Rules in 1973 for the first time and served until his 1976 renomination defeat and he was replaced in 1977 by seventy-six-year-old James J. Delaney (Dem-N.Y.), who resigned in 1978 at the end of the 95th Congress. These two old war horses embodied the complaints of younger and newer members about the demonstrable pitfalls of the seniority system. At last in 1979, sixty-two-year-old Dick Bolling became chair in his thirty-first year in the House and his twenty-fifth year on the committee. Bolling's committee reforms were less ambitious than those of the 1946 Reorganization Act and only a few were accepted. But a consequence of the Albert-O'Neill-Bolling alliance was to make the leadership of Rules responsive to the House Democrats' floor leaders. After having waited a quarter-century and twice been thwarted in floor leadership contests, a tired and disappointed Dick Bolling retired from the House in 1983, only to be replaced as chair by eighty-two-year-old Claude D. Pepper (Dem-Fla.), one of the handful of twentieth-century U.S. representatives who had first been elected to Congress as a U.S. senator.

While the Democrats saw leadership change at Rules, the Republicans did not. David T. Martin (Rep-Neb.) succeeded

H. Allen Smith as ranking member in 1973 and resigned in 1974. Tennessee's James H. Quillen followed Martin in 1975 and served as ranking member until he waived his seniority in December 1990 to become "Republican Chair Emeritus."

Pepper's death in 1989 gave the chair to Boston's John Joseph Moakley (Dem-Mass.), a protégé of O'Neill and with Gerald B.H. Solomon (Rep-N.Y.) replacing Quillen in 1991; the Rules Committee had relatively new blood at the top. Moakley and Solomon ran Rules for eight years—four with the Democrats in power, 1991-1995 and four with the Republicans in power, 1995-1999. Moakley continued as the senior Democrat until his death in 2001. Moakley's death led to J. Martin Frost III (Dem-Texas) becoming ranking member, a post he would hold until his 2004 election defeat. Frost's successor Louise McIntosh Slaughter, served one term as ranking member and became chair in 2007 when Democrats recaptured Congress and is its present chair.

Gerald Solomon was succeeded as chair of Rules by David T. Dreier in 1999. Since the Rules Committee has become an arm of the leadership, the chair is chosen by the Speaker and the Majority Leader with no input from the Steering Committee or the House Republican Conference, thus waiving the three-term requirement for Dreier, who continues today as the Rules Committee's senior Republican, logging eight years as chair and presently in his fourth year as ranking member.

Party Leaders: Four House party leaders served on Rules. Speaker Thomas P. (Tip) O'Neill, Jr. who was first appointed to the committee in 1955 became Whip in 1971, Majority Leader in 1973, and Speaker in 1977 serving for ten years in that post. Republican Minority Leader John J. Rhodes of Arizona joined the panel after serving as floor leader from 1973 to 1981. Two party whips who served on Rules were Republican C. Trent Lott of Mississippi who moved to the Senate in 1989 and Democrat David J. Bonior of Michigan who left the post in 2002 to run unsuccessfully for the Democratic gubernatorial nomination.

Notable Members: The Rules Committee is a House "insiders" committee and it does not attract members whose career goals lie beyond the House. It does not generate a great deal of publicity and as a consequence its members have not engendered much presidential notice. None of the eighteen modern-era major party presidential and vice presidential nominees who served in the House ever served on Rules. The only committee member who ran for president was John B. Anderson (Rep-Ill.), whose independent third party candidacy received 7 percent of the vote against Democratic President Jimmy Carter and Republican ex-Governor of California Ronald Reagan in the 1980 presidential contest.

The first modern-era Cabinet member to serve on Rules, Christian A. Herter (Rep-Mass.), was Eisenhower's second Secretary of State and was the only former member to be elected governor. The only other Cabinet member to serve on Rules was Lynn M. Martin, President George H.W. Bush's second Secretary of Labor. In 1977, Andrew J. Young (Dem-Ga.) left Rules to be President Carter's Ambassador to the United Nations and later would be elected mayor of Atlanta.

Only four members left Rules to serve in the Senate: two Republicans—Hugh D. Scott of Pennsylvania and C. Trent Lott of Mississippi, a Bill Colmer protégé—and two Democrats—Spark M. Matsunaga of Hawaii and Christopher J. Dodd of Connecticut. Both Scott and Lott would be elected floor leaders in the Senate. Similarly, only two Rules Committee members left the committee to return home as governor—Republicans

Herter of Massachusetts and William H. Avery of Kansas. Three members of the House Rules Committee served after being U.S. senators: Republican James W. Wadsworth, Jr. of New York and Democrats Hugh B. Mitchell of Washington State and Claude D. Pepper of Florida.

Selected References

Bach, Stanley, "The Structure of Choice in the House of Representatives: The Impact of Complex Special Rules," *Harvard Journal on Legislation*, 18 (Summer, 1981), 553-602.

Berman, Daniel M., *A Bill Becomes a Law: The Civil Rights Act of 1960* (New York: Macmillan, 1962).

Bolling, Richard, *Power in the House: A History of the Leadership in the House of Representatives* (New York: Dutton, 1968).

Cummings, Milton C., Jr. and Robert L. Peabody, "The Decision to Enlarge the Committee on Rules: An Analysis of the 1961 Vote," in Robert L. Peabody and Nelson W. Polsby, eds., *New Perspectives on the House of Representatives*, 2nd ed. (Chicago: Rand, McNally, 1969), 253-281.

Dierenfield, Bruce J., *Keeper of the Rules; Congressman Howard W. Smith of Virginia* (Charlottesville, Va.: The University Press of Virginia, 1987).

Jones, Charles O. "Joseph G. Cannon and Howard W. Smith: An Essay on the Limits of Leadership in the House of Representatives," *Journal of Politics,* 30 (August, 1968), 617-646.

Lapham, Lewis J., *Party Leadership and the House Committee on Rules* (New York: Garland Publishing, 1988).

Matsunaga, Spark M. and Ping Chen, *Rulemakers of the House* (Urbana: University of Illinois Press, 1976).

Oppenheimer, Bruce I., "The House Rules Committee: New Arm of Leadership in a Decentralized House," in Lawrence C. Dodd and Bruce I. Oppenheimer, eds., *Congress Reconsidered*, 1st ed. (Washington, DC: CQ Press, 1977), 96-116.

Oppenheimer, Bruce I., "The Changing Relationship between House Leadership and the Committee on Rules," in Frank H. Mackaman, ed., *Understanding Congressional Leadership* (Washington, D.C.: CQ Press, 1981), 207-226.

Peabody, Robert L., "The Enlarged Rules Committee," in Robert L. Peabody and Nelson W. Polsby, eds., *New Perspectives on the House of Representatives* (Chicago: Rand, McNally, 1963), 129-164.

Price, H. Douglas, "Race, Religion, and the Rules Committee: The Kennedy Aid-to-Education Bills," in Alan F. Westin, ed., *The Uses of Power: 7 Case Studies* (New York: Harcourt, Brace, and World, 1962).

Robinson, James A., *The House Rules Committee* (Indianapolis: Bobbs-Merrill, 1963).

Schamel, Charles E. et al., "Records of the Committee on Rules," *Guide to the Records of the United States House of Representatives at the National Archives: 1789-1989 Bicentennial Edition* (Washington, D.C.: National Archives and Records Administration,1989), pp. 253-259.

Siff, Ted and Alan Weil, dirs., *Ruling Congress: How the House and Senate Rules Govern the Legislative Process*, in the Ralph Nader Congress Project (New York: Grossman, 1975).

U.S. House of Representatives, Committee on Rules, *A History of the Committee on Rules, 1st to 97th Congress, 1789-1981*, House Committee Print, 97th Congress, 2nd Session (1983).

RESPONSIBILITIES, JURISDICTIONAL CHANGES, AND SUBCOMMITTEES

RULES

Jurisdiction, 80th Congress (1947-1949)

Established by the Legislative Reorganization Act of 1946:

[Section 121.(1)(p)] Committee on Rules
(1) The rules, joint rules, and order of business of the House.
(2) Recesses and final adjournments of Congress.

Jurisdiction, 103rd Congress (1993-1995)

From the *Rules of the House of Representatives, 103rd Congress* (House Document 102-405)

[Rule X.1.(q)] Committee on Rules
(1) The rules and joint rules (other than rules or joint rules relating to the Code of Official Conduct), and order of business of the House.
(2) Recesses and final adjournments of Congress.
(3) The Committee on Rules is authorized to sit and act whether or not the House is in session.

Jurisdiction, 104th Congress (1995-1997) Changes in Committee System

From H. Res. 6, Section 202 (a), the Committees and Their Jurisdiction, January 4, 1995

[Rule X.1.(m)] Committee on Rules.
(1) The rules and joint rules (other than rules or joint rules relating to the Code of Official Conduct), and order of business of the House.
(2) Recesses and final adjournments of Congress.

The Committee on Rules is authorized to sit and act whether or not the House is in session.

Jurisdiction, 111th Congress (2009-2011)

From the *Rules of the House of Representatives* (as revised to June 16, 2009, H.Doc. 110-162):

[Rule X.1.(n)] Committee on Rules
(1) Rules and joint rules (other than those relating to the Code of Official Conduct) and the order of business of the House.
(2) Recesses and final adjournments of Congress.

[Rule X.3.(j)] Special Oversight Function

The Committee on Rules shall review and study on a continuing basis the congressional budget process, and the committee shall report its findings and recommendations to the House from time to time.

NAMES OF RULES SUBCOMMITTEES FROM THE *CONGRESSIONAL DIRECTORY*

Legislative Process, 103
Legislative and Budget Process, 104, 105, 106, 107, 108, 109, 110, 111
Rules of the House, 103
Rules and the Organization of the House, 104, 105, 106, 109, 110, 111
Technology and the House, 107, 108

MEMBERSHIP ROSTERS, 103rd-111th Congresses, 1993-2011

RULES / 103rd Congress

Service Dates of Committee Chair: Jan. 5, 1993-Jan. 3, 1995

Service Dates of Majority Members: Jan. 5, 1993-Jan. 3, 1995

Service Dates of Minority Members: Jan. 5, 1993-Jan. 3, 1995

Roster Filled: Majority with 9 members on Jan. 5, 1993; Minority with 4 members on Jan. 5, 1993

	Majority					Minority				
			Terms in:						Terms in:	
Rank Name	Party	State	House	Comm.		Rank Name	Party	State	House	Comm.
Chr Moakley, John Joseph	Dem	Mass.	11	10		RM Solomon, Gerald B.H.	Rep	N.Y.	8	3
2nd Derrick, Butler C. Jr.	Dem	S.C.	10	8		2nd Quillen, James H.	Rep	Tenn.	16	15
3rd Beilenson, Anthony C.	Dem	Cal.	9	8		3rd Dreier, David T.	Rep	Cal.	7	2
4th Frost, J. Martin III	Dem	Tex.	8	8		4th Goss, Porter J.	Rep	Fla.	4	1
5th Bonior, David E.	Dem	Mich.	9	7						
6th Hall, Tony P.	Dem	Ohio	8	7						
7th Wheat, Alan D.	Dem	Mo.	6	6						
8th Gordon, Barton J.	Dem	Tenn.	5	4						
9th Slaughter, Louise Macintosh	Dem	N.Y.	4	*1 3						

*1: Member's first period of service on the committee.

Departures from the House:	Majority			Minority
Lost Election to U.S. Senate	Wheat, Alan D.	Dem	Mo.	None
Retired	Derrick, Butler C. Jr.	Dem	S.C.	None

Departures from Committee:				
Elected Minority Whip	Bonior, David E.	Dem	Mich.	None
Moved to Commerce	Gordon, Barton J.	Dem	Tenn.	None
Returned to Government Reform and Oversight	Slaughter, Louise Macintosh	Dem	N.Y.	None

RULES / 104th Congress

Service Dates of Committee Chair: Jan. 4, 1995-Jan. 3, 1997

Service Dates of Majority Members: Jan. 4, 1995-Jan. 3, 1997

Service Dates of Minority Members: Jan. 4, 1995-Jan. 3, 1997

Roster Filled: Majority with 9 members on Jan. 4, 1995; Minority with 4 members on Jan. 4, 1995

	Majority					Minority				
			Terms in:						Terms in:	
Rank Name	Party	State	House	Comm.		Rank Name	Party	State	House	Comm.
Chr Solomon, Gerald B.H.	Rep	N.Y.	9	4		RM Moakley, John Joseph	Dem	Mass.	12	11
2nd Quillen, James H.	Rep	Tenn.	17	16		2nd Beilenson, Anthony C.	Dem	Cal.	10	9
3rd Dreier, David T.	Rep	Cal.	8	3		3rd Frost, J. Martin III	Dem	Tex.	9	9
4th Goss, Porter J.	Rep	Fla.	5	2		4th Hall, Tony P.	Dem	Ohio	9	8
5th Linder, John E.	Rep	Ga.	2	1						
6th Pryce, Deborah D.	Rep	Ohio	2	1						
7th Diaz-Balart, Lincoln	Rep	Fla.	2	1						
8th McInnis, Scott	Rep	Colo.	2	1						
9th Greene, Enid	Rep	Utah	1	1						

Departures from the House:	Majority			Minority		
Retired	Quillen, James H.	Rep	Tenn.	Beilenson, Anthony C.	Dem	Cal.
	Greene, Enid	Rep	Utah			

RULES / 105th Congress

Service Dates of Committee Chair: Jan. 7, 1997-Jan. 3, 1999

Service Dates of Majority Members: Jan. 7, 1997-Jan. 3, 1999

Service Dates of Minority Members: Jan. 7, 1997-Jan. 3, 1999

Roster Filled: Majority with 9 members on Jan. 7, 1997; Minority with 4 members on Jan. 7, 1997

	Majority					Minority				
			Terms in:						Terms in:	
Rank Name	Party	State	House	Comm.		Rank Name	Party	State	House	Comm.
Chr Solomon, Gerald B.H.	Rep	N.Y.	10	5		RM Moakley, John Joseph	Dem	Mass.	13	12
2nd Dreier, David T.	Rep	Cal.	9	4		2nd Frost, J. Martin III	Dem	Tex.	10	10
3rd Goss, Porter J.	Rep	Fla.	6	3		3rd Hall, Tony P.	Dem	Ohio	10	9
4th Linder, John E.	Rep	Ga.	3	2		4th Slaughter, Louise Macintosh	Dem	N.Y.	6	*2 1
5th Pryce, Deborah D.	Rep	Ohio	3	2						
6th Diaz-Balart, Lincoln	Rep	Fla.	3	2						

*2: Member's second period of service on the committee.

7th McInnis, Scott	Rep	Colo.	3	2
8th Hastings, Richard (Doc)	Rep	Wash.	2	1
9th Myrick, Sue	Rep	N.C.	2	1

Departures from the House:		Majority						Minority
Retired		Solomon, Gerald B.H.			Rep	N.Y.		None

Departures from Committee:								
Moved to Ways and Means		McInnis, Scott			Rep	Colo.		None

RULES / 106th Congress

Service Dates of Committee Chair: Jan. 6, 1999-Jan. 3, 2001

Service Dates of Majority Members: Jan. 6, 1999-Jan. 3, 2001

Service Dates of Minority Members: Jan. 6, 1999-Jan. 3, 2001

Roster Filled: Majority with 9 members on Jan. 6, 1999; Minority with 4 members on Jan. 6, 1999

Majority					**Minority**				
			Terms in:					**Terms in:**	
Rank Name	Party	State	House	Comm.	Rank Name	Party	State	House	Comm.
Chr Dreier, David T.	Rep	Cal.	10	5	RM Moakley, John Joseph	Dem	Mass.	14	13
2nd Goss, Porter J.	Rep	Fla.	7	4	2nd Frost, J. Martin III	Dem	Tex.	11	11
3rd Linder, John E.	Rep	Ga.	4	3	3rd Hall, Tony P.	Dem	Ohio	11	10
4th Pryce, Deborah D.	Rep	Ohio	4	3	4th Slaughter, Louise Macintosh	Dem	N.Y.	7	*2 2
5th Diaz-Balart, Lincoln	Rep	Fla.	4	3					
6th Hastings, Richard (Doc)	Rep	Wash.	3	2	*2: Member's second period of service on the committee.				
7th Myrick, Sue	Rep	N.C.	3	2					
8th Sessions, Pete	Rep	Tex.	2	1					
9th Reynolds, Thomas M.	Rep	N.Y.	1	1					

RULES / 107th Congress

Service Dates of Committee Chair: Jan. 3, 2001-Jan. 3, 2003

Service Dates of Majority Members: Jan. 3, 2001-Jan. 3, 2003

Service Dates of Minority Members: Jan. 3, 2001-Jan. 3, 2003

Roster Filled: Majority with 9 members on Jan. 3, 2001; Minority with 4 members on Jan. 3, 2001

Majority					**Minority**				
			Terms in:					**Terms in:**	
Rank Name	Party	State	House	Comm.	Rank Name	Party	State	House	Comm.
Chr Dreier, David T.	Rep	Cal.	11	6	RM1 Moakley, John Joseph	Dem	Mass.	15	14
2nd Goss, Porter J.	Rep	Fla.	8	5	RM2 Frost, J. Martin III	Dem	Tex.	12	12
3rd Linder, John E.	Rep	Ga.	5	4	3rd Hall, Tony P.	Dem	Ohio	12	11
4th Pryce, Deborah D.	Rep	Ohio	5	4	4th Slaughter, Louise Macintosh	Dem	N.Y.	8	*2 3
5th Diaz-Balart, Lincoln	Rep	Fla.	5	4					
6th Hastings, Richard (Doc)	Rep	Wash.	4	3	*2: Member's second period of service on the committee.				
7th Myrick, Sue	Rep	N.C.	4	3					
8th Sessions, Pete	Rep	Tex.	3	2					
9th Reynolds, Thomas M.	Rep	N.Y.	2	2					

Changes:
  Minority:

RM1 Moakley, John Joseph	Dem	Mass.	May 28, 2001 Died in office.
RM2 Frost, J. Martin III	Dem	Tex.	May 28, 2001 Replaced Moakley as Ranking Member.
McGovern, James P.	Dem	Mass.	June 19, 2001 Replaced Moakley initially; stepped aside for Hastings.
Hastings, Alcee L.	Dem	Fla.	June 19, 2001 Replaced McGovern.
Hall, Tony P.	Dem	Ohio	May 7, 2002 Resigned committee; resigned House on Sept. 9, 2002, to become Ambassador to UN for Food and Agriculture.
McGovern, James P.	Dem	Mass.	May 7, 2002 Replaced Hall, ranked after Slaughter.

RULES / 108th Congress

Service Dates of Committee Chair: Jan. 7, 2003-Jan. 3, 2005

Service Dates of Majority Members: Jan. 7, 2003-Jan. 3, 2005

Service Dates of Minority Members: Jan. 7, 2003-Jan. 3, 2005

Roster Filled: Majority with 9 members on Jan. 7, 2003; Minority with 4 members on Jan. 7, 2003

Majority					Minority				
			Terms in:					**Terms in:**	
Rank Name	**Party**	**State**	**House**	**Comm.**	**Rank Name**	**Party**	**State**	**House**	**Comm.**
Chr Dreier, David T.	Rep	Cal.	12	7	RM Frost, J. Martin III	Dem	Tex.	13	13
2nd Goss, Porter J.	Rep	Fla.	9	6	2nd Slaughter, Louise Macintosh	Dem	N.Y.	9	*2 4
3rd Linder, John E.	Rep	Ga.	6	5	3rd McGovern, James P.	Dem	Mass.	4	2
4th Pryce, Deborah D.	Rep	Ohio	6	5	4th Hastings, Alcee L.	Dem	Fla.	6	2
5th Diaz-Balart, Lincoln	Rep	Fla.	6	5					
6th Hastings, Richard (Doc)	Rep	Wash.	5	4	*2: Member's second period of service on the committee.				
7th Myrick, Sue	Rep	N.C.	5	4					
8th Sessions, Pete	Rep	Tex.	4	3					
9th Reynolds, Thomas M.	Rep	N.Y.	3	3					

Changes:
  Majority:

Goss, Porter J.	Rep	Fla.	Sept. 23, 2004 Resigned the House; became Director of the Central Intelligence Agency.
Putnam, Adam H. Jr.	Rep	Fla.	Sept. 29, 2004 Replaced Goss.

Departures from the House:	**Majority**			**Minority**		
Defeated for Re-election	None			Frost, J. Martin III	Dem	Tex.

Departures from Committee:					
Moved to Energy and Commerce	Myrick, Sue	Rep	N.C.	None	
Returned to Financial Services	Pryce, Deborah D.	Rep	Ohio	None	
Moved to Ways and Means	Linder, John E.	Rep	Ga.	None	
	Reynolds, Thomas M.	Rep	N.Y.		

RULES / 109th Congress

Service Dates of Committee Chair: Jan. 4, 2005-Jan. 3, 2007

Service Dates of Majority Members: Jan. 4, 2005-Jan. 3, 2007

Service Dates of Ranking Member: Jan. 6, 2005-Jan. 3, 2007

Service Dates of Minority Members: Jan. 26, 2005-Jan. 3, 2007

Roster Filled: Majority with 9 members on Jan. 6, 2005; Minority with 4 members on Mar. 16, 2005

Majority					Minority				
			Terms in:					**Terms in:**	
Rank Name	**Party**	**State**	**House**	**Comm.**	**Rank Name**	**Party**	**State**	**House**	**Comm.**
Chr Dreier, David T.	Rep	Cal.	13	8	RM Slaughter, Louise Macintosh	Dem	N.Y.	10	*2 5
2nd Diaz-Balart, Lincoln	Rep	Fla.	7	6	2nd McGovern, James P.	Dem	Mass.	5	3
3rd Hastings, Richard (Doc)	Rep	Wash.	6	5	3rd Hastings, Alcee L.	Dem	Fla.	7	3
4th Sessions, Pete	Rep	Tex.	5	4	4th Matsui, Doris O.	Dem	Cal.	1	1
5th Putnam, Adam H. Jr.	Rep	Fla.	3	2					
6th Capito, Shelley Moore	Rep	W.Va.	3	1	*2: Member's second period of service on the committee.				
7th Cole, Tom	Rep	Okla.	2	1					
8th Bishop, Robert	Rep	Utah	2	1					
9th Gingrey, Phil	Rep	Ga.	2	1					

Vacancies Filled:
  Majority:
    9th seat filled by Gingrey on Jan. 6, 2005.
  Minority:
    4th seat filled by Matsui on Mar. 16, 2005.

Departures from Committee:					
Returned to Armed Services	Cole, Tom	Rep	La.	None	
	Bishop, Robert	Rep	Utah		
	Gingrey, Phil	Rep	Ga.		
Moved to Education and Labor	Bishop, Robert	Rep	Utah	None	
Moved to Financial Services	Putnam, Adam H. Jr.	Rep	Fla.	None	

Returned to Financial Services	Capito, Shelley Moore	Rep	W.Va.	None
Returned to Natural Resources	Cole, Tom	Rep	La.	None
	Bishop, Robert	Rep	Utah	
Returned to Science and Technology	Gingrey, Phil	Rep	Ga.	None

RULES / 110th Congress

Service Dates of Committee Chair: Jan. 4, 2007-Jan. 3, 2009

Service Dates of Majority Members: Jan. 12, 2007-Jan. 3, 2009

Service Dates of Minority Members: Jan. 4, 2007-Jan. 3, 2009

Roster Filled: Majority with 9 members on Jan. 12, 2007; Minority with 4 members on Jan. 4, 2007

Arcuri in the 9th majority slot was not originally listed in the *Congressional Record*.

	Majority			Terms in:			Minority			Terms in:	
Rank Name		Party	State	House	Comm.	Rank Name		Party	State	House	Comm.
Chr Slaughter, Louise Macintosh		Dem	N.Y.	11	*2 6	RM Dreier, David T.		Rep	Cal.	14	9
2nd McGovern, James P.		Dem	Mass.	6	4	2nd Diaz-Balart, Lincoln		Rep	Fla.	8	7
3rd Hastings, Alcee L.		Dem	Fla.	8	4	3rd Hastings, Richard (Doc)		Rep	Wash.	7	6
4th Matsui, Doris O.		Dem	Cal.	2	2	4th Sessions, Pete		Rep	Tex.	6	5
5th Cardoza, Dennis A.		Dem	Cal.	3	1						
6th Welch, Peter		Dem	Vt.	1	1	*2: Member's second period of service on the committee.					
7th Castor, Kathy		Dem	Fla.	1	1						
8th Arcuri, Michael A.		Dem	N.Y.	1	1						
9th Sutton, Betty		Dem	Ohio	1	1						

Departures from Committee:	Majority			Minority			
Returned to Natural Resources as RM	None			Hastings, Richard (Doc)	Rep	Wash.	

RULES / 111th Congress

Service Dates of Committee Chair: Jan. 6, 2009-Jan. 03, 2011

Service Dates of Majority Members: Jan. 6, 2009-Jan. 3, 2011

Service Dates of Minority Members: Jan. 9, 2009-Jan. 3, 2001

Roster Filled: Majority with 9 seats on Jan. 6, 2009; Minority with 4 seats on Jan. 14, 2009

	Majority			Terms in:			Minority			Terms in:	
Rank Name		Party	State	House	Comm.	Rank Name		Party	State	House	Comm.
Chr Slaughter, Louise Macintosh		Dem	N.Y.	12	*2 7	RM Dreier, David T.		Rep	Cal.	15	10
2nd McGovern, James P.		Dem	Mass.	7	5	2nd Diaz-Balart, Lincoln		Rep	Fla.	9	8
3rd Hastings, Alcee L.		Dem	Fla.	9	5	3rd Sessions, Pete		Rep	Tex.	7	6
4th Matsui, Doris O.		Dem	Cal.	3	3	4th Foxx, Virginia A.		Rep	N.C.	3	1
5th Cardoza, Dennis A.		Dem	Cal.	4	2						
6th Welch, Peter		Dem	Vt.	2	2	*2: Member's second period of service on the committee.					
7th Castor, Kathy		Dem	Fla.	2	2						
8th Arcuri, Michael A.		Dem	N.Y.	2	2						
9th Sutton, Betty		Dem	Ohio	2	2						

Filled Vacancy:

  Minority:

    4th seat filled by Foxx on Jan. 14, 2009.

Changes:

  Majority:

Welch, Peter	Dem	Vt.	Jan. 14, 2009 Resigned committee; had moved to Energy and Commerce.
Castor, Kathy	Dem	Fla.	Jan. 14, 2009 Resigned committee; had moved to Energy and Commerce.
Sutton, Betty	Dem	Ohio.	Jan. 14, 2009 Resigned committee; had moved to Energy and Commerce.
Perlmutter, Ed	Dem	Colo.	Jan. 13, 2009 Replaced Welch.
Pingree, Chellie	Dem	Me.	Jan. 13, 2009 Replaced Castor.
Polis, Jared	Dem	Colo.	Jan. 13, 2009 Replaced Sutton.

Science and Technology

Committee on Science, Space, and Technology, 103rd Congress (1993-1995)

Committee on Science, 104th-109th Congresses (1995-2007)

Committee on Science and Technology, 110th-111th Congresses (2007-2011)

BACKGROUND

Organizational History: On October 4, 1957, the Soviet Union launched Sputnik 1, an earth orbiting satellite. American reaction was intense and the rush to catch up in the race for outer space was deeply felt in the Congress. A month later, the anxiety of the American public grew greater with the successful launch of Sputnik 2 with the dog Laika inside. Congress acted quickly as both Houses created high-powered select and special committees on astronautics and space exploration. It was already prepared when the next step occurred—the 1961 earth-orbiting Vostok 1, with a live cosmonaut, Yuri Gagarin.

The House Select Committee on Astronautics and Space Exploration was created by H. Res. 496 on March 5, 1958, and was named later that day by Speaker Sam Rayburn (Dem-Tex.), with the House Majority Leader John W. McCormack (Dem-Mass.) as its chair and the House Minority Leader Joseph W. Martin Jr. (Dem-Mass.) as its ranking minority member. With this high-level bipartisan support behind it, the House was committed to making the committee a standing one, and H. Res. 580 passed on July 21, 1958, made it a standing committee, effective at the opening of the 86th Congress in January, 1959.

As the standing Committee on Science and Astronautics, it was the first standing committee in the House created since the passage of the Legislative Reorganization Act of 1946. It was renamed the Science and Technology Committee on January 3, 1975, and given additional jurisdiction over civil aviation research and development, environmental research and development, nonnuclear energy research and development, and the National Weather Service (now part of the National Oceanic and Atmospheric Administration) (H. Res. 988, 93d Cong., Oct. 8, 1974). In 1977, following the termination of the Joint Committee on Atomic Energy, the committee was given jurisdiction over nuclear research and development as well (H. Res. 5, Jan. 4, 1977).

During the later reorganizations, the House and Senate differed regarding their space committees. In 1977, the Senate chose to fold the responsibilities of its Astronautical and Space Exploration Committee into its renamed Commerce, Science, and Transportation Committee and eliminated its stand-alone quality. While the second House Select Committee on Committees of 1979-1980, chaired by Jerry Patterson (Dem-Cal.) amended the committee's jurisdiction, effective January 3, 1981, to specifically include energy demonstration projects and federally owned nonmilitary energy laboratories (H. Res. 549, Mar. 25, 1980).

Once preoccupied with space exploration, the committee in the 1980s focused on a wide array of government research and development programs, including the National Science Foundation. Energy, civil aviation, transportation, and environment were among the research topics within the committee's jurisdiction. It also reviewed overall government science policy. Within its own territory—research and space—the science panel showed more independence by the late 1980s. Members sought to keep research compatible with overall government science policy and even began to engage in critical questioning of the National Aeronautics and Space Administration. Some members, including long-time chair, George E. Brown, Jr. (Dem-Cal.), pressured NASA to shift its emphasis toward unmanned space exploration.

In the 100th Congress, the committee was redesignated as the Committee on Science, Space, and Technology (H. Res. 5, Jan. 6, 1987). In 1995, the 104th Congress was renamed as the Committee on Science and expanded its jurisdiction with marine research from the former Committee on Merchant Marine and Fisheries, and measures relating to the commercial application of energy technology from the Committee on Energy and Commerce (H. Res. 6, Jan. 4, 1995). The Democratic recapture of the House in the 110th Congress led to renaming the committee as the Committee on Science and Technology on January 4, 2007, resuming the name that the committee had from 1975 to 1987.

Membership: Twenty-five members were assigned in the Science and Astronautics Committee's initial list in 1959. For the next seven Congresses (1961-1975), its membership remained around thirty. In 1977, it reached forty and in 1991, the 102nd Congress, it first passed the fifty-member mark. The committee's membership peak of fifty-seven occurred in 1993, and then it steadily shrunk reaching a contemporary low of forty-one in 2005. In the current 111th Congress, the committee has forty-three members. As a semi-exclusive committee, legislators generally consider membership on it as a secondary committee.

The Science Committee's mean size of 47.8 members in the past nine Congresses, 1993-2011, placed it ninth among the nineteen continuing committees. However, its mean inter-Congress retention rate of 78.31 percent placed it sixteenth and its mean seniority of 4.16 terms per member placed it in seventeenth place, only ahead of Agriculture (3.46 terms) and Small Business (2.87 terms).

Committee Leaders: Since the first thirty-seven years of the committee's existence, 1958-1995, occurred during Democratic Congresses, its first six chairs were all Democrats. The standing committee's first chair was Overton Brooks (Dem-La.), a twelve-term member who had served on the select committee and was the second-ranking Democrat on Armed Services. The next chair was George P. Miller (Dem-Cal.) who chaired the committee from Brooks's death in 1961 until his own renomination defeat in 1972. During this time former Minority Leader Joseph W. Martin, Jr. (Rep-Mass.), served as ranking member until his renomination defeat in 1966. Miller was followed by Olin E. Teague (Dem-Tex.), who left the chairmanship of Veterans Affairs to chair the Science Committee from 1973 through the end of 1978. Joe Martin's successor was James G. Fulton (Rep-Penn.), who served as ranking member from 1967 until his death in 1971. Fulton was succeeded by Charles A. Mosher (Rep-Ohio) who was ranking member until his 1977 retirement who was then followed by John W. Wydler (Rep-N.Y.).

Teague's retirement led to Don Fuqua (Dem-Fla.) assuming the chair of Science in 1979, a post he would hold until his 1987 retirement. Fuqua's successor, Robert A. Roe (Dem-N.J.), who took over the committee in 1987, left to chair Public Works and Transportation in 1991. George E. Brown, Jr. (Dem-Cal.) became the committee's senior Democrat in 1991 and served for four years as chair, 1991-1995, and as ranking member for three-plus years until his death in July, 1999.

On the Republican side, senior turnover was high. Wydler's retirement in 1981 gave the ranking minority slot to Larry Winn (Rep-Kans.), who served until his retirement in 1985 to be followed by Manuel Lujan, Jr. (Rep-N.M.) who left the House in 1989 to become President George H.W. Bush's Secretary of the Interior. Lujan's successor was Robert S. Walker (Rep-Penn.), a Newt Gingrich ally who would serve as ranking member from 1989 to 1995, and in 1995 Walker became the Science Committee's first ever Republican chair and then resigned two years later in 1997. Walker's successor was F. James Sensenbrenner, Jr. (Rep-Wisc.), who chaired the committee in the next two Congresses, 1997-2001, then resigned to assume the chair of the Judiciary Committee. Sherwood L. Boehlert (Rep-N.Y.) would succeed Sensenbrenner as chair in 2001 and served until the Democrats recaptured the House in 2006.

The most intriguing committee leader is Ralph M. Hall who became the senior Democrat and ranking member upon the death of George Brown in 1999. Hall served in that capacity until January 2, 2004 when he switched parties to become a Republican. Bart L. Gordon (Dem-Tenn.) replaced him as ranking member and would serve in that role until 2007 when the Democratic recapture elevated Gordon to the chair of the renamed Science and Technology Committee, with Ralph Hall serving once again as ranking member but now as a Republican.

Party Leaders: In its initial March, 1958 incarnation as the Select Committee on Astronautics and Space Exploration, the committee was chaired by Majority Leader John W. McCormack (Dem-Mass.) along with Minority Leader Joseph W. Martin. Jr. (Rep-Mass.) and Minority Whip Leslie C. Arends (Rep-Ill.) as its top two Republicans. McCormack remained on the committee in the second majority slot and Martin remained ranking member when it became the standing committee on Science and Astronautics in 1959. Arends did not remain on the standing committee. McCormack was on the committee twice in 1961 and left it upon his 1962 election as Speaker, while Martin served as ranking member until his renomination defeat in 1966. The only other party leader to serve on Science was Carl Albert (Dem-Okla.) who served on the committee, 1963-1967, during the early years of his Majority Leadership.

Notable Members: The only former Science committee members to succeed in presidential politics were President Gerald R. Ford, Jr. (Rep-Mich.) who was appointed vice president in 1973 to succeed the disgraced vice president Spiro T. Agnew and succeeded President Richard M. Nixon on August 9, 1974, when Nixon resigned the office. The other was Democrat Albert A. Gore. Jr., who was elected twice as vice president with Bill Clinton in 1992 and 1996. Gore's lone presidential nomination in 2000 was less successful. Seven former committee members served in the Cabinet, with Donald Rumsfeld (Rep-Ill.), serving as Secretary of Defense under both Presidents Gerald R. Ford and George W. Bush; Bob Bergland (DFL-Minn.) and Brock Adams (Dem-Wash.) serving as President Jimmy Carter's Secretaries of Agriculture and Transportation respectively; Margaret M. Heckler (Rep-Mass.) as Ronald Reagan's second Secretary of Health and Human Services; Manuel Lujan (Rep-N.M.) as Secretary of the Interior under President George H.W. Bush; Daniel Glickman (Dem-Kans.) as Bill Clinton's second Secretary of Agriculture; and Norman Mineta (Dem-Cal.) the first Asian-American Cabinet member, who served as Bill Clinton's fourth Secretary of Commerce and George W. Bush's first Secretary of Transportation.

Twenty-three U.S. senators served on the House Science Committee before moving across the Capitol. Of these, fourteen were Democrats, including Lee Metcalf of Montana who served on the original Select Committee on Science and Astronautics and standing committee members Timothy Wirth and Mark Udall of Colorado, Paul M. Simon and Richard J. Durbin of Illinois, Al Gore, Jr. of Tennessee, Thomas R. Harkin of Iowa, Christopher Dodd of Connecticut, Robert C. Krueger of Texas, Brock Adams of Washington State, Harry M. Reid of Nevada, C.W. (Bill) Nelson of Florida, Robert G. Torricelli of New Jersey, and Deborah A. Stabenow of Michigan.

Nine former Science Committee members who became senators were Republicans—Judd Gregg and Robert C. Smith of New Hampshire, Edward J. Gurney of Florida, Lowell Weicker of Connecticut, Larry L. Pressler of South Dakota, Rod Grams of Minnesota, Lindsey O. Graham of South Carolina, George F. Allen of Virginia, and Thomas A. Coburn of Oklahoma. In addition to Republicans Judd Gregg of New Hampshire and George F. Allen of Virginia who were governors before becoming senators, three other committee members became governors—Republicans James G. Martin of North Carolina and Marshall (Mark) Sanford of South Carolina and Democrat James J. Blanchard of Michigan. Two committee members gained gubernatorial experience after failed Senate bids. Democrat Kenneth H. (Buddy) MacKay lost a Senate nomination in 1978 but was serving as Florida's lieutenant governor when Governor Lawton Chiles died and MacKay completed the twenty-three days left in the term. Republican Lowell P. Weicker, Jr. of Connecticut lost his Senate seat in 1988 and returned to office in 1990 as the state's governor on a third party ticket.

Selected References

Hechler, U.S. Representative Ken, *Toward the Endless Frontier: History of the Committee on Science and Technology, 1959-1979,* House Committee Print (1980).

Nadel, Mark, et al., "The House Science and Astronautics Committee and the Senate Aeronautical and Space Science Committee," in the Ralph Nader Congress Project, *The Environment Committees A Study of the House and Senate Interior, Agriculture, and Science Committees* (New York: Grossman, 1975), 281-357.

Schamel, Charles E. et al., "Records of the Science and Astronautics Committee," *Guide to the Records of the United States House of Representatives at the National Archives: 1789-1989 Bicentennial Edition* (Washington, D.C.: National Archives and Records Administration,1989), 261-265.

RESPONSIBILITIES, JURISDICTIONAL CHANGES, AND SUBCOMMITTEES

SCIENCE AND ASTRONAUTICS

Jurisdiction, 1958

Established by House Resolution 580 as amended, 85th Congress, Second Session, July 21, 1958 for the House Committee on Science and Astronautics:

[Paragraph 3.17] Committee on Science and Astronautics
 (a) Astronautical research and development, including resources, personnel, equipment, and facilities.
 (b) Bureau of Standards, standardization of weights and measures, and the metric system.
 (c) National Aeronautics and Space Administration.
 (d) National Aeronautics and Space Council.
 (e) National Science Foundation.
 (f) Outer space, including exploration and control thereof.
 (g) Science Scholarships.
 (h) Scientific research and development.

SCIENCE AND TECHNOLOGY

Science and Astronautics was renamed the Committee on Science and Technology on January 3, 1975.

SCIENCE, SPACE, AND TECHNOLOGY

Science and Technology was renamed the Committee on Science, Space, and Technology on January 6, 1987.

Jurisdiction, 103rd Congress (1993-1995)

From the *Rules of the House of Representatives, 103rd Congress* (House Document 102-405)

[Rule X.1.(r)] Committee on Science, Space, and Technology
 (1) Astronautical research and development, including resources, personnel, equipment, and facilities.
 (2) Bureau of Standards, standardization of weights and measures and the metric system.
 (3) National Aeronautics and Space Administration.
 (4) National Aeronautics and Space Council.
 (5) National Science Foundation.
 (6) Outer space, including exploration and control thereof.
 (7) Science Scholarships.
 (8) Scientific research and development, and demonstration, and projects therefor, and all federally-owned or operated nonmilitary energy laboratories.
 (9) Civil aviation research and development.
 (10) Environmental research and development.
 (11) All energy research, development, and demonstration, and projects, therefor, and all federally-owned or operated nonmilitary energy laboratories.
 (12) National Weather Service.

In addition to its legislative jurisdiction under the preceding provisions of this paragraph (and its general oversight function under clause 2(b)(1)), the committee shall have the special oversight function provided for in clause 3(f) with respect to all nonmilitary research and development.

[Rule X.3.(f)]

(f) The Committee on Science, Space, and Technology shall have the function of reviewing and studying, on a continuing basis, all laws, programs, and Government activities dealing with or involving nonmilitary research and development.

SCIENCE

Science, Space, and Technology was renamed the Committee on Science on January 4, 1995.

Jurisdiction, 104th Congress (1995-1997) Changes in Committee System

From H. Res. 6, Section 202 (a), the Committees and Their Jurisdiction, January 4, 1995

[Rule X.1.(n)] Committee on Science.

(1) All energy research, development, and demonstration, and projects therefor, and all federally owned or operated nonmilitary energy laboratories.
(2) Astronautical research and development, including resources, personnel, equipment, and facilities.
(3) Civil aviation research and development.
(4) Environmental research and development.
(5) Marine research.
(6) Measures relating to the commercial application of energy technology.
(7) National Institute of Standards and Technology, standardization of weights and measures and the metric system.
(8) National Aeronautics and Space Administration.
(9) National Space Council.
(10) National Science Foundation.
(11) National Weather Service.
(12) Outer space, including exploration and control thereof.
(13) Science Scholarships.
(14) Scientific research, development, and demonstration, and projects therefor.

In addition to its legislative jurisdiction under the preceding provisions of this paragraph (and its general oversight function under clause 2(b)(1)), the committee shall have the special oversight function provided for in clause 3(f) with respect to all nonmilitary research and development.

SCIENCE AND TECHNOLOGY

Science was redesignated the Committee on Science and Technology on January 4, 2007.

Jurisdiction, 111th Congress (2009-2011)

From the *Rules of the House of Representatives* (as revised to June 16, 2009, H.Doc. 110-162):

[Rule X.1.(o)] Committee on Science and Technology

(1) All energy research, development, and demonstration, and projects therefor, and all federally owned or operated nonmilitary energy laboratories.
(2) Astronautical research and development, including resources, personnel, equipment, and facilities.
(3) Civil aviation research and development.
(4) Environmental research and development.
(5) Marine research.
(6) Commercial application of energy technology.
(7) National Institute of Standards and Technology, standardization of weights and measures, and the metric system.
(8) National Aeronautics and Space Administration.
(9) National Space Council.
(10) National Science Foundation.
(11) National Weather Service.
(12) Outer space, including exploration and control thereof.
(13) Science scholarships.

Scientific research, development, and demonstration, and projects therefore.

[Rule X.3.(k)] Special Oversight Function

The Committee on Science and Technology shall review and study on a continuing basis laws, programs, and Government activities relating to nonmilitary research and development.

NAMES OF SCIENCE AND TECHNOLOGY SUBCOMMITTEES FROM THE *CONGRESSIONAL DIRECTORY*

Science, Space, and Technology, 103rd Congress

Energy, 103 Investigations and Oversight, 103
Science, 103 Space, 103
Technology, Environment, and Aviation, 103

Science, 104th-109th Congresses

Basic Research, 104, 105, 106 Energy and Environment, 104, 105, 106
Energy, 107, 108, 109 Environment, Technology, and Standards, 107, 108, 109
Research, 107, 108, 109 Space and Aeronautics, 104, 105, 106, 107, 108, 109
Technology, 104, 105, 106

Science and Technology, 110th-111th Congresses

Energy and Environment, 110, 111 Investigations and Oversight, 110, 111
Research and Science Education, 110, 111 Space and Aeronautics, 110, 111
Technology and Innovation, 110, 111

MEMBERSHIP ROSTERS, 103rd-111th Congresses, 1993-2011

SCIENCE, SPACE, AND TECHNOLOGY / 103rd Congress

Service Dates of Committee Chair: Jan. 5, 1993-Jan. 3, 1995

Service Dates of Majority Members: Jan. 5, 1993-Jan. 3, 1995

Service Dates of Minority Members: Jan. 5, 1993-Jan. 3, 1995

Roster Filled: Majority with 33 members on Nov. 10, 1993; Minority with 22 members on Jan. 5, 1993

Majority

Rank Name	Party	State	House	Comm.
Chr Brown, George E. Jr.	Dem	Cal.	15	*2 11
2nd Lloyd, Marilyn L.	Dem	Tenn.	10	10
3rd Glickman, Daniel R.	Dem	Kans.	9	9
4th Volkmer, Harold L.	Dem	Mo.	9	*1 8
5th Hall, Ralph M.	Dem	Tex.	7	*1 7
6th McCurdy, David K.	Dem	Okla.	7	7
7th Valentine, I.T. (Tim) Jr.	Dem	N.C.	6	6
8th Torricelli, Robert G.	Dem	N.J.	6	6
9th Boucher, Frederick C.	Dem	Va.	6	6
10th Traficant, James A. Jr.	Dem	Ohio	5	5
11th Hayes, James A.	Dem	La.	4	4
12th Tanner, John S.	Dem	Tenn.	3	3
13th Browder, J. Glen	Dem	Ala.	3	3
14th Geren, Preston M. (Pete)	Dem	Tex.	3	2
15th Bacchus, James	Dem	Fla.	2	2
16th Roemer, Timothy J.	Dem	Ind.	2	2
17th Cramer, Robert E. (Bud) Jr.	Dem	Ala.	2	2
18th Swett, Richard	Dem	N.H.	2	2
19th Barcia, James A.	Dem	Mich.	1	1
20th Klein, Herbert C.	Dem	N.J.	1	1
21st Fingerhut, Eric D.	Dem	Ohio	1	1
22nd McHale, Paul F. Jr.	Dem	Penn.	1	1
23rd Harman, Jane L.	Dem	Cal.	1	1
24th Johnson, C. Donald Jr.	Dem	Ga.	1	1
25th Coppersmith, Samuel G.	Dem	Ariz.	1	1
26th Eshoo, Anna G.	Dem	Cal.	1	1
27th Inslee, Jay R.	Dem	Wash.	1	1
28th Johnson, Eddie Bernice	Dem	Tex.	1	1
29th Minge, David B.	DFL	Minn.	1	1
30th Woolsey, Lynn C.	Dem	Cal.	1	1
31st Deal, J. Nathan	Dem	Ga.	1	1
32nd Scott, Robert C.	Dem	Va.	1	1
33rd Becerra, Xavier	Dem	Cal.	1	1

Minority

Rank Name	Party	State	House	Comm.
RM Walker, Robert S.	Rep	Penn.	9	9
2nd Sensenbrenner, F. James Jr.	Rep	Wisc.	8	*1 7
3rd Boehlert, Sherwood L.	Rep	N.Y.	6	6
4th Lewis, Thomas F.	Rep	Fla.	6	6
5th Henry, Paul B.	Rep	Mich.	5	5
6th Fawell, Harris W.	Rep	Ill.	5	5
7th Morella, Constance A.	Rep	Md.	4	4
8th Rohrabacher, Dana	Rep	Cal.	3	3
9th Schiff, Steven H.	Rep	N.M.	3	3
10th Barton, Joe L.	Rep	Tex.	5	2
11th Zimmer, Richard	Rep	N.J.	2	2
12th Johnson, Sam	Rep	Tex.	2	2
13th Calvert, Ken	Rep	Cal.	1	1
14th Hoke, Martin R.	Rep	Ohio	1	1
15th Smith, Nick H.	Rep	Mich.	1	*1 1
16th Royce, Edward R.	Rep	Cal.	1	1
17th Grams, Rod	Rep	Minn.	1	1
18th Linder, John E.	Rep	Ga.	1	1
19th Blute, Peter I.	Rep	Mass.	1	1
20th Dunn, Jennifer B.	Rep	Wash.	1	1
21st Baker, William P.	Rep	Cal.	1	1
22nd Bartlett, Roscoe G.	Rep	Md.	1	1

*1: Member's first period of service on the committee.

*2: Member's second period of service on the committee.

Note: When the vacancies for majority members were filled on Jan. 21, 1993, the new ranking for Xavier Becerra (Dem-Cal.) who had been appointed on Jan. 5, 1993, in the 23rd seat was placed below Robert C. Scott (Dem-Va.).

Vacancies Filled:
  Majority:
    30th through 32nd seats filled by Woolsey, Deal, and Scott on Jan. 21, 1993

Additions:
  Majority:

34th Barca, Peter W.	Dem	Wisc.	June 23, 1993
35th Rush, Bobby L.	Dem	Ill.	Nov. 10, 1993

Changes:

Majority:

Browder, J. Glen	Dem	Ala.	Mar. 3, 1993 Added to Budget; remained on committee.
Woolsey, Lynn C.	Dem	Cal.	Mar. 3, 1993 Added to Budget; remained on committee.
Woolsey, Lynn C.	Dem	Cal.	Feb. 10, 1994 Temporarily resigned committee to retain service on Budget.
Browder, J. Glen	Dem	Ala.	May 12, 1994 Temporarily resigned committee to retain service on Budget.
Vacancies unfilled			

Minority:

Henry, Paul B.	Rep	Mich.	July 31, 1993 Died in office.
Ehlers, Vernon J.	Rep	Mich.	Feb. 2, 1994 Replaced Henry.

Departures from the House:

	Majority			Minority		
Elected to U.S. Senate	None			Grams, Rod	Rep	Minn.
Lost Election to U.S. Senate	McCurdy, David K.	Dem	La.	None		
	Coppersmith, Samuel G.	Dem	Ariz.			
Defeated for Re-election	Glickman, Daniel R.	Dem	Kans.	None		
	Swett, Richard	Dem	N.H.			
	Klein, Herbert C.	Dem	N.J.			
	Fingerhut, Eric D.	Dem	Ohio			
	Johnson, C. Donald Jr.	Dem	Ga.			
	Inslee, Jay R.	Dem	Wash.			
	Barca, Peter W.	Dem	Wisc.			
Retired	Lloyd, Marilyn L.	Dem	Tenn.	Lewis, Thomas F.	Rep	Fla.
	Valentine, I.T. (Tim) Jr.	Dem	N.C.			
	Bacchus, James	Dem	Fla.			

Departures from Committee:

	Majority			Minority		
Moved to Banking and Financial Services	None			Royce, Edward R.	Rep	Cal.
Moved to Commerce	Eshoo, Anna G.	Dem	Cal.	None		
	Rush, Bobby L.	Dem	Ill.			
Moved to Economic and Educational Opportunities	None			Johnson, Sam	Rep	Tex.
Moved to Government Reform and Oversight	None			Blute, Peter I.	Rep	Mass.
Moved to Judiciary	None			Hoke, Martin R.	Rep	Ohio
Moved to Rules	None			Linder, John E.	Rep	Ga.
Moved to Ways and Means	None			Zimmer, Richard	Rep	N.J.
				Johnson, Sam	Rep	Tex.
				Dunn, Jennifer B.	Rep	Wash.
No new assignment	Volkmer, Harold L.	Dem	Mo.	Smith, Nick H.	Rep	Mich.
	Torricelli, Robert G.	Dem	N.J.			
	Boucher, Frederick C.	Dem	Va.			
	Scott, Robert C.	Dem	Va.			
	Becerra, Xavier	Dem	Cal.			
	Deal, J. Nathan	Dem	Ga.			

SCIENCE / 104th Congress

Service Dates of Committee Chair: Jan. 4, 1995-Jan. 3, 1997

Service Dates of Majority Members: Jan. 4, 1995-Jan. 3, 1997

Service Dates of Minority Members: Jan. 4, 1995-Jan. 3, 1997

Roster Filled: Majority with 27 members on Jan. 4, 1995; Minority with 23 members on Jan. 4, 1995

	Majority						Minority				
				Terms in:						**Terms in:**	
Rank Name	Party	State	House	Comm.		Rank Name	Party	State	House	Comm.
Chr Walker, Robert S.	Rep	Penn.	10	10		RM Brown, George E. Jr.	Dem	Cal.	16	*2 12
2nd Sensenbrenner, F. James Jr.	Rep	Wisc.	9	*1 8		2nd Hall, Ralph M.	Dem	Tex.	8	*1 8
3rd Boehlert, Sherwood L.	Rep	N.Y.	7	7		3rd Traficant, James A. Jr.	Dem	Ohio	6	6
4th Fawell, Harris W.	Rep	Ill.	6	6		4th Hayes, James A.	Dem	La.	5	5
5th Morella, Constance A.	Rep	Md.	5	5		5th Tanner, John S.	Dem	Tenn.	4	4
6th Weldon, Wayne C. (Curt)	Rep	Penn.	5	1		6th Geren, Preston M. (Pete)	Dem	Tex.	4	3
7th Rohrabacher, Dana	Rep	Cal.	4	4		7th Roemer, Timothy J.	Dem	Ind.	3	3
8th Schiff, Steven H.	Rep	N.M.	4	4		8th Cramer, Robert E. (Bud) Jr.	Dem	Ala.	3	3
9th Barton, Joe L.	Rep	Tex.	6	3		9th Barcia, James A.	Dem	Mich.	2	2
10th Calvert, Ken	Rep	Cal.	2	2		10th McHale, Paul F. Jr.	Dem	Penn.	2	2

11th Baker, William P.	Rep	Cal.	2	2
12th Bartlett, Roscoe G.	Rep	Md.	2	2
13th Ehlers, Vernon J.	Rep	Mich.	2	2
14th Wamp, Zachary P.	Rep	Tenn.	1	1
15th Weldon, David J.	Rep	Fla.	1	1
16th Graham, Lindsey O.	Rep	S.C.	1	1
17th Salmon, Matthew J.	Rep	Ariz.	1	1
18th Davis, Thomas M. III	Rep	Va.	1	1
19th Stockman, Steve	Rep	Tex.	1	1
20th Gutknecht, Gilbert W.	Rep	Minn.	1	1
21st Seastrand, Andrea	Rep	Cal.	1	1
22nd Tiahrt, Todd	Rep	Kans.	1	1
23rd Largent, Steve	Rep	Okla.	2	1
24th Hilleary, Van	Rep	Tenn.	1	1
25th Cubin, Barbara	Rep	Wyo.	1	1
26th Foley, Mark A.	Rep	Fla.	1	1
27th Myrick, Sue	Rep	N.C.	1	1

11th Harman, Jane L.	Dem	Cal.	2	2
12th Johnson, Eddie Bernice	Dem	Tex.	2	2
13th Minge, David B.	DFL	Minn.	2	2
14th Olver, John W.	Dem	Mass.	3	*2 1
15th Hastings, Alcee L.	Dem	Fla.	2	1
16th Rivers, Lynn N.	Dem	Mich.	1	1
17th McCarthy, Karen	Dem	Mo.	1	1
18th Ward, Michael D.	Dem	Ky.	1	1
19th Lofgren, Zoe	Dem	Cal.	1	*1 1
20th Doggett, Lloyd A. II	Dem	Tex.	1	1
21st Doyle, Michael F.	Dem	Penn.	1	1
22nd Jackson-Lee, Sheila	Dem	Tex.	1	*1 1
23rd Luther, William P.	DFL	Minn.	1	1

*1: Member's first period of service on the committee.
*2: Member's second period of service on the committee.

Changes:

Minority:

Geren, Preston M. (Pete)	Dem	Tex.	Nov. 20, 1995 Resigned committee; returned to Transportation and Infrastructure.
Hayes, James A.	Dem	La.	Dec. 12, 1995 Service on committee as a Democrat was vacated; moved to Ways and Means as a Republican on Jan. 25, 1995.
Volkmer, Harold L.	Dem	Mo.	Feb. 28, 1996 Replaced Geren, ranked after Brown.
Gordon, Barton J.	Dem	Tenn.	Feb. 28, 1996 Replaced Hayes, ranked after Hall.

Departures from the House:

	Majority			**Minority**		
Defeated for Re-election	Baker, William P.	Rep	Cal.	Volkmer, Harold L.	Dem	Mo.
	Stockman, Steve	Rep	Tex.	Ward, Michael D.	Dem	Ky.
	Seastrand, Andrea	Rep	Cal.			
Retired	Walker, Robert S.	Rep	Penn.	None		

Departures from Committee:

Moved to Appropriations	Wamp, Zachary P.	Rep	Tenn.	None		
	Tiahrt, Todd	Rep	Kans.			
Returned to Appropriations	None			Olver, John W.	Dem	Mass.
Moved to Budget	Hilleary, Van	Rep	Tenn.	Minge, David B.	DFL	Minn.
Moved to Commerce	Largent, Steve	Rep	La.	McCarthy, Karen	Dem	Mo.
	Cubin, Barbara	Rep	Wyo.			
Moved to Education and the Workforce	Hilleary, Van	Rep	Tenn.	None		
Moved to International Relations	Graham, Lindsey O.	Rep	S.C.	None		
Moved to National Security	Graham, Lindsey O.	Rep	S.C.	None		
Moved to Rules	Myrick, Sue	Rep	N.C.	None		
Moved to Select Intelligence	None			Harman, Jane L.	Dem	Cal.
Moved to Ways and Means	None			Tanner, John S.	Dem	Tenn.

SCIENCE / 105th Congress

Service Dates of Committee Chair: Jan. 9, 1997-Jan. 3, 1999

Service Dates of Majority Members: Jan. 21, 1997-Jan. 3, 1999

Service Dates of Ranking Member: Feb. 6, 1997-Jan. 3, 1999

Service Dates of Minority Members: Feb. 13, 1997-Jan. 3, 1999

Roster Filled: Majority with 25 members on Mar. 5, 1997; Minority with 21 members on Apr. 17, 1997

Majority					**Minority**				
			Terms in:					**Terms in:**	
Rank Name	**Party**	**State**	**House**	**Comm.**	**Rank Name**	**Party**	**State**	**House**	**Comm.**
Chr Sensenbrenner, F. James Jr.	Rep	Wisc.	10	*1 9	RM Brown, George E. Jr.	Dem	Cal.	17	*2 13
2nd Boehlert, Sherwood L.	Rep	N.Y.	8	8	2nd Hall, Ralph M.	Dem	Tex.	9	*1 9
3rd Fawell, Harris W.	Rep	Ill.	7	7	3rd Gordon, Barton J.	Dem	Tenn.	7	*2 2
4th Morella, Constance A.	Rep	Md.	6	6	4th Traficant, James A. Jr.	Dem	Ohio	7	7
5th Weldon, Wayne C. (Curt)	Rep	Penn.	6	2	5th Roemer, Timothy J.	Dem	Ind.	4	4
6th Rohrabacher, Dana	Rep	Cal.	5	5	6th Cramer, Robert E. (Bud) Jr.	Dem	Ala.	4	4
7th Schiff, Steven H.	Rep	N.M.	5	5	7th Barcia, James A.	Dem	Mich.	3	3
8th Barton, Joe L.	Rep	Tex.	7	4	8th McHale, Paul F. Jr.	Dem	Penn.	3	3
9th Calvert, Ken	Rep	Cal.	3	3	9th Johnson, Eddie Bernice	Dem	Tex.	3	3

10th Bartlett, Roscoe G.	Rep	Md.	3	3
11th Ehlers, Vernon J.	Rep	Mich.	3	3
12th Weldon, David J.	Rep	Fla.	2	2
13th Salmon, Matthew J.	Rep	Ariz.	2	2
14th Davis, Thomas M. III	Rep	Va.	2	2
15th Gutknecht, Gilbert W.	Rep	Minn.	2	2
16th Foley, Mark A.	Rep	Fla.	2	2
17th Ewing, Thomas W.	Rep	Ill.	4	1
18th Pickering, Charles W. (Chip) Jr.	Rep	Miss.	1	1
19th Cannon, Christopher B.	Rep	Utah	1	1
20th Brady, Kevin P.	Rep	Tex.	1	1
21st Cook, Merrill	Rep	Utah	1	1
22nd English, Philip S.	Rep	Penn.	2	1
23rd Nethercutt, George R. Jr.	Rep	Wash.	2	1
24th Coburn, Thomas A.	Rep	Okla.	2	1
25th Sessions, Pete	Rep	Tex.	1	1

10th Hastings, Alcee L.	Dem	Fla.	3	2
11th Rivers, Lynn N.	Dem	Mich.	2	2
12th Lofgren, Zoe	Dem	Cal.	2	*1 2
13th Doggett, Lloyd A. II	Dem	Tex.	2	2
14th Doyle, Michael F.	Dem	Penn.	2	2
15th Jackson-Lee, Sheila	Dem	Tex.	2	*1 2
16th Luther, William P.	DFL	Minn.	2	2
17th Capps, Walter H.	Dem	Cal.	1	1
18th Stabenow, Deborah Ann	Dem	Mich.	1	1
19th Etheridge, Bobby R.	Dem	N.C.	1	1
20th Lampson, Nicholas V.	Dem	Tex.	1	*1 1
21st Hooley, Darlene	Dem	Ore.	1	*1 1

*1: Member's first period of service on the committee.
*2: Member's second period of service on the committee.

Vacancies Filled:

Majority:

22nd through 25th seats filled by English, Nethercutt, Coburn, and Sessions on Mar. 5, 1997.

Changes:

Majority:

Schiff, Steven H.	Rep	N.M.	Mar. 25, 1998 Died in office.

Minority:

Doggett, Lloyd A. II	Dem	Tex.	Apr. 17, 1997 Resigned committee; moved to Resources.
Tauscher, Ellen O.	Dem	Cal.	Apr. 17, 1997 Replaced Doggett.
Capps, Walter H.	Dem	Cal.	Oct. 28, 1997 Died in office.
Cramer, Robert E. (Bud) Jr.	Dem	Ala.	Nov. 13, 1997 Resigned committee; moved to Appropriations.
Capps, Lois	Dem	Cal.	Mar. 27, 1998 Replaced Walter H. Capps.
Lee, Barbara	Dem	Cal.	Apr. 29, 1998 Replaced Cramer.
McHale, Paul F. Jr.	Dem	Penn.	Apr. 30, 1998 Resigned committee; no new assignment.
Tauscher, Ellen O.	Dem	Cal.	June 24, 1998 Resigned committee; moved to National Security.
Sherman, Brad	Dem	Cal.	Sept. 18, 1998 Replaced McHale.

Departures from the House:

	Majority			Minority
Retired	Fawell, Harris W.	Rep	Ill.	None

Departures from Committee:

	Majority			Minority		
Moved to Budget	None			Hooley, Darlene	Dem	Ore.
Moved to Education and the Workforce	Salmon, Matthew J.	Rep	Ariz.	None		
Moved to Commerce	Pickering, Charles W. (Chip) Jr.	Rep	Miss.	Luther, William P.	DFL	Minn.
				Capps, Lois	Dem	Cal.
Moved to Rules	Sessions, Pete	Rep	Tex.	None		
Moved to Ways and Means	Foley, Mark A.	Rep	Fla.	None		
No new assignment	Davis, Thomas M. III	Rep	Va.	Sherman, Brad	Dem	Cal.
	English, Philip S.	Rep	Penn.			
	Coburn, Thomas A.	Rep	Okla.			

SCIENCE / 106th Congress

Service Dates of Committee Chair: Jan. 6, 1999-Jan. 3, 2001

Service Dates of Majority Members: Jan. 6, 1999-Jan. 3, 2001

Service Dates of Minority Members: Jan. 6, 1999-Jan. 3, 2001

Roster Filled: Majority with 25 members on Feb. 2, 1999; Minority with 23 members on Jan. 19, 1999

Majority			Terms in:	
Rank Name	Party	State	House	Comm.
Chr Sensenbrenner, F. James Jr.	Rep	Wisc.	11	*1 10
2nd Boehlert, Sherwood L.	Rep	N.Y.	9	9
3rd Smith, Lamar S.	Rep	Tex.	7	*2 1
4th Morella, Constance A.	Rep	Md.	7	7
5th Weldon, Wayne C. (Curt)	Rep	Penn.	7	3
6th Rohrabacher, Dana	Rep	Cal.	6	6
7th Barton, Joe L.	Rep	Tex.	8	5

Minority			Terms in:	
Rank Name	Party	State	House	Comm.
RM Brown, George E. Jr.	Dem	Cal.	18	*2 14
2nd Hall, Ralph M.	Dem	Tex.	10	*1 10
3rd Gordon, Barton J.	Dem	Tenn.	8	*2 3
4th Traficant, James A. Jr.	Dem	Ohio	8	8
5th Costello, Jerry F.	Dem	Ill.	7	*2 1
6th Roemer, Timothy J.	Dem	Ind.	5	5
7th Barcia, James A.	Dem	Mich.	4	4

8th Calvert, Ken	Rep	Cal.	4	4		8th Johnson, Eddie Bernice	Dem	Tex.	4		4
9th Smith, Nick H.	Rep	Mich.	4	*2 1		9th Woolsey, Lynn C.	Dem	Cal.	4	*2 1
10th Bartlett, Roscoe G.	Rep	Md.	4	4		10th Hastings, Alcee L.	Dem	Fla.	4		3
11th Ehlers, Vernon J.	Rep	Mich.	4	4		11th Rivers, Lynn N.	Dem	Mich.	3		3
12th Weldon, David J.	Rep	Fla.	3	3		12th Lofgren, Zoe	Dem	Cal.	3	*1 3
13th Gutknecht, Gilbert W.	Rep	Minn.	3	3		13th Doyle, Michael F.	Dem	Penn.	3		3
14th Ewing, Thomas W.	Rep	Ill.	5	2		14th Jackson-Lee, Sheila	Dem	Tex.	3	*1 3
15th Cannon, Christopher B.	Rep	Utah	2	2		15th Stabenow, Deborah Ann	Dem	Mich.	2		2
16th Brady, Kevin P.	Rep	Tex.	2	2		16th Etheridge, Bobby R.	Dem	N.C.	2		2
17th Cook, Merrill	Rep	Utah	2	2		17th Lampson, Nicholas V.	Dem	Tex.	2	*1 2
18th Nethercutt, George R. Jr.	Rep	Wash.	3	2		18th Lee, Barbara	Dem	Cal.	2		2
19th Lucas, Frank D.	Rep	Okla.	4	1		19th Larson, John B.	Dem	Conn.	1		1
20th Green, Mark	Rep	Wisc.	1	1		20th Udall, Mark	Dem	Colo.	1		1
21st Kuykendall, Steven T.	Rep	Cal.	1	1		21st Wu, David	Dem	Ore.	1		1
22nd Miller, Gary G.	Rep	Cal.	1	1		22nd Weiner, Anthony D.	Dem	N.Y.	1		1
23rd Biggert, Judith B.	Rep	Ill.	1	1		23rd Capuano, Michael E.	Dem	Mass.	1		1
24th Sanford, Marshall C. (Mark) Jr.	Rep	S.C.	3	1							
25th Metcalf, Jack	Rep	Wash.	3	1							

*1: Member's first period of service on the committee.
*2: Member's second period of service on the committee.

Vacancies Filled:
Majority:
   24th and 25th seats filled by Sanford and Metcalf on Feb. 2, 1999.
Minority:
   22nd and 23rd seats filled by Weiner and Capuano on Jan. 19, 1999.

Changes:
Minority:

Lee, Barbara	Dem	Cal.	Feb. 3, 1999 Resigned committee; moved to International Relations.
Traficant, James A. Jr.	Dem	Ohio	Feb. 17, 1999 Leave of absence; no new assignment.
Roemer, Timothy J.	Dem	Ind.	Feb. 23, 1999 Leave of absence; had moved to Permanent Select Intelligence.
Hastings, Alcee L.	Dem	Fla.	May 19, 1999 Leave of absence; had moved to Permanent Select Intelligence.
Baird, Brian	Dem	Wash.	June 9, 1999 Replaced Lee.
Hoeffel, Joseph M.	Dem	Penn.	June 9, 1999 Replaced Traficant.
Moore, Dennis	Dem	Kans.	June 9, 1999 Replaced Roemer.
Brown, George E. Jr.	Dem	Cal.	July 15, 1999 Died in office.
Hall, Ralph M.	Dem	Tex.	July 15, 1999 Replaced Brown as Ranking Member.
Baca, Joe	Dem	Cal.	Nov. 18, 1999 Replaced Brown.

Departures from the House:	**Majority**			**Minority**		
Elected to U.S. Senate	None			Stabenow, Deborah Ann	Dem	Mich.
Defeated for Re-nomination	Cook, Merrill	Rep	Utah.	None		
Defeated for Re-election	Kuykendall, Steven T.	Rep	Cal.	None		
Retired	Ewing, Thomas W.	Rep	Ill.	None		
	Metcalf, Jack	Rep	Wash.			
	Sanford, Marshall C. (Mark) Jr.	Rep	S.C.			

Departures from Committee:						
Moved to Judiciary	Green, Mark	Rep	Wisc.	None		
Moved to Ways and Means	Brady, Kevin P.	Rep	Tex.	None		

SCIENCE / 107th Congress

Service Dates of Committee Chair: Jan. 6, 2001-Jan. 3, 2003

Service Dates of Majority Members: Jan. 6, 2001-Jan. 3, 2003

Service Dates of Minority Members: Jan. 31, 2001-Jan. 3, 2003

Roster Filled: Majority with 25 members on June 28, 2001; Minority with 22 members on May 2, 2001

Majority			**Terms in:**		**Minority**			**Terms in:**	
Rank Name	**Party**	**State**	**House**	**Comm.**	**Rank Name**	**Party**	**State**	**House**	**Comm.**
Chr Boehlert, Sherwood L.	Rep	N.Y.	10	10	RM Hall, Ralph M.	Dem	Tex.	11	*1 11
2nd Sensenbrenner, F. James Jr.	Rep	Wisc.	12	*1 11	2nd Gordon, Barton J.	Dem	Tenn.	9	*2 4
3rd Smith, Lamar S.	Rep	Tex.	8	*2 2	3rd Costello, Jerry F.	Dem	Ill.	8	*2 2
4th Morella, Constance A.	Rep	Md.	8	8	4th Barcia, James A.	Dem	Mich.	5	5

5th Weldon, Wayne C. (Curt)	Rep	Penn.	8	4		5th Johnson, Eddie Bernice	Dem	Tex.	5		5
6th Rohrabacher, Dana	Rep	Cal.	7	7		6th Woolsey, Lynn C.	Dem	Cal.	5	*2	2
7th Barton, Joe L.	Rep	Tex.	9	6		7th Rivers, Lynn N.	Dem	Mich.	4		4
8th Calvert, Ken	Rep	Cal.	5	5		8th Lofgren, Zoe	Dem	Cal.	4	*1	4
9th Smith, Nick H.	Rep	Mich.	5	*2 2		9th Doyle, Michael F.	Dem	Penn.	4		4
10th Bartlett, Roscoe G.	Rep	Md.	5	5		10th Jackson-Lee, Sheila	Dem	Tex.	4	*1	4
11th Ehlers, Vernon J.	Rep	Mich.	5	5		11th Etheridge, Bobby R.	Dem	N.C.	3		3
12th Weldon, David J.	Rep	Fla.	4	4		12th Lampson, Nicholas V.	Dem	Tex.	3	*1	3
13th Gutknecht, Gilbert W.	Rep	Minn.	4	4		13th Larson, John B.	Dem	Conn.	2		2
14th Cannon, Christopher B.	Rep	Utah	3	3		14th Udall, Mark	Dem	Colo.	2		2
15th Nethercutt, George R. Jr.	Rep	Wash.	4	3		15th Wu, David	Dem	Ore.	2		2
16th Lucas, Frank D.	Rep	Okla.	5	2		16th Weiner, Anthony D.	Dem	N.Y.	2		2
17th Miller, Gary G.	Rep	Cal.	2	2		17th Capuano, Michael E.	Dem	Mass.	2		2
18th Biggert, Judith B.	Rep	Ill.	2	2		18th Baird, Brian	Dem	Wash.	2	*1	2
19th Culberson, John	Rep	Tex.	1	1		19th Hoeffel, Joseph M.	Dem	Penn.	2		2
20th Akin, W. Todd	Rep	Mo.	1	1		20th Moore, Dennis	Dem	Kans.	2	*1	2
21st Johnson, Timothy V.	Rep	Ill.	1	1		21st Baca, Joe	Dem	Cal.	2		2
22nd Pence, Mike	Rep	Ind.	1	1		22nd Honda, Michael M.	Dem	Cal.	1		1
23rd Grucci, Felix J. Jr.	Rep	N.Y.	1	1							
24th Hart, Melissa A.	Rep	Penn.	1	1		*1: Member's first period of service on the committee.					
25th Forbes, J. Randy	Rep	Va.	1	1		*2: Member's second period of service on the committee.					

Vacancies Filled:

Majority:

  25th seat filled by Forbes on June 28, 2001.

Minority:

  22nd seat filled by Honda on May 2, 2001.

Changes:

Majority:

Sensenbrenner, F. James Jr.	Rep	Wisc.	Feb. 6, 2001 Resigned committee; became Chair of Judiciary.
Shays, Christopher H.	Rep	Conn.	Feb. 8, 2001 Replaced Sensenbrenner, ranked after Morella.
Culberson, John	Rep	Tex.	June 7, 2001 Resigned committee; moved to Transportation and Infrastructure.
Gilchrest, Wayne T.	Rep	Md.	June 7, 2001 Replaced Culberson.
Gilchrest, Wayne T.	Rep	Md.	June 12, 2001 Re-ranked after Biggert.
Pence, Mike	Rep	Ind.	May 16, 2002 Resigned committee; later moved to Judiciary.
Forbes, J. Randy	Rep	Va.	May 16, 2002 Resigned committee; moved to Judiciary; returned on July 10, 2002.
Sullivan, John	Rep	Okla.	May 16, 2002 Replaced Pence.

Minority:

Doyle, Michael F.	Dem	Penn.	Feb. 7, 2001 Resigned committee; moved to Energy and Commerce.
Capuano, Michael E.	Dem	Mass.	Feb. 7, 2001 Resigned committee; moved to Budget.
Matheson, James D.	Dem	Utah	Feb. 8, 2001 Replaced Doyle, ranked after Baca.
Israel, Steve	Dem	N.Y.	Feb. 8, 2001 Replaced Capuano, ranked after Matheson.

Departures from the House:	**Majority**			**Minority**		
Defeated for Re-nomination	None			Rivers, Lynn N.	Dem	Mich.
Defeated for Re-election	Morella, Constance A.	Rep	Md.	None		
	Grucci, Felix J. Jr.	Rep	N.Y.			
Elected State Senator	None			Barcia, James A.	Dem	Mich.

Departures from Committee:						
Moved to Appropriations	Weldon, David J.	Rep	Fla.	None		
Moved to Financial Services	None			Baca, Joe	Dem	Cal.
				Matheson, James D.	Dem	Utah
Moved to Transportation and Infrastructure	None			Hoeffel, Joseph M.	Dem	Penn.
Returned to Transportation and Infrastructure	Miller, Gary G.	Rep	Cal.	None		
No new assignment	Cannon, Christopher B.	Rep	Utah	None		

SCIENCE / 108th Congress

Service Dates of Committee Chair: Jan. 8, 2003-Jan. 3, 2005

Service Dates of Majority Members: Jan. 28, 2003-Jan. 3, 2005

Service Dates of Ranking Member: Jan. 8, 2003-Jan. 3, 2003

Service Dates of Minority Members: Jan. 28, 2003-Jan. 3, 2005

Roster Filled: Majority with 25 members on Feb. 11, 2003; Minority with 22 members on Feb. 13, 2003

	Majority						Minority			
				Terms in:						**Terms in:**
Rank Name		**Party**	**State**	**House**	**Comm.**	**Rank Name**	**Party**	**State**	**House**	**Comm.**
Chr Boehlert, Sherwood L.		Rep	N.Y.	11	11	RM Hall, Ralph M.	Dem	Tex.	12	*1 12
2nd Smith, Lamar S.		Rep	Tex.	9	*2 3	2nd Gordon, Barton J.	Dem	Tenn.	10	*2 5
3rd Shays, Christopher H.		Rep	Conn.	9	2	3rd Costello, Jerry F.	Dem	Ill.	9	*2 3
4th Weldon, Wayne C. (Curt)		Rep	Penn.	9	5	4th Johnson, Eddie Bernice	Dem	Tex.	6	6
5th Rohrabacher, Dana		Rep	Cal.	8	8	5th Woolsey, Lynn C.	Dem	Cal.	6	*2 3
6th Barton, Joe L.		Rep	Tex.	10	7	6th Lofgren, Zoe	Dem	Cal.	5	*1 5
7th Calvert, Ken		Rep	Cal.	6	6	7th Jackson-Lee, Sheila	Dem	Tex.	5	*1 5
8th Smith, Nick H.		Rep	Mich.	6	*2 3	8th Etheridge, Bobby R.	Dem	N.C.	4	4
9th Bartlett, Roscoe G.		Rep	Md.	6	6	9th Lampson, Nicholas V.	Dem	Tex.	4	*1 4
10th Ehlers, Vernon J.		Rep	Mich.	6	6	10th Larson, John B.	Dem	Conn.	3	3
11th Gutknecht, Gilbert W.		Rep	Minn.	5	5	11th Udall, Mark	Dem	Colo.	3	3
12th Nethercutt, George R. Jr.		Rep	Wash.	5	4	12th Wu, David	Dem	Ore.	3	3
13th Lucas, Frank D.		Rep	Okla.	6	3	13th Baird, Brian	Dem	Wash.	3	*1 3
14th Biggert, Judith B.		Rep	Ill.	3	3	14th Israel, Steve	Dem	N.Y.	2	2
15th Gilchrest, Wayne T.		Rep	Md.	7	*2 2	15th Honda, Michael M.	Dem	Cal.	2	2
16th Akin, W. Todd		Rep	Mo.	2	2	16th Bell, Chris	Dem	Tex.	1	1
17th Johnson, Timothy V.		Rep	Ill.	2	2	17th Bishop, Timothy H.	Dem	N.Y.	1	1
18th Hart, Melissa A.		Rep	Penn.	2	2	18th Miller, Brad	Dem	N.C.	1	1
19th Sullivan, John		Rep	Okla.	2	2	19th Davis, Lincoln	Dem	Tenn.	1	*1 1
20th Forbes, J. Randy		Rep	Va.	2	2	20th Sherman, Brad	Dem	Cal.	4	*2 1
21st Gingrey, Phil		Rep	Ga.	1	*1 1	21st Moore, Dennis	Dem	Kan.	3	*2 3
22nd Bishop, Robert		Rep	Utah	1	1	22nd Weiner, Anthony D.	Dem	N.Y.	3	3
23rd Burgess, Michael C.		Rep	Tex.	1	1					
24th Bonner, Josiah (Jo) R. Jr.		Rep	Ala.	1	1					
25th Feeney, Tom		Rep	Fla.	1	1					

*1: Member's first period of service on the committee.
*2: Member's second period of service on the committee.

Vacancies Filled:

Majority:

15th and 25th seats filled by Gilchrest and Feeney on Feb. 11, 2003.

Minority:

16th, 17th, 18th, and 19th seats filled by Bell, Bishop, Miller, and Davis on Feb. 5, 2003; 20th, 21st, and 22nd seats filled by Sherman, Moore, and Weiner on Feb. 13, 2003.

Changes:

Majority:

Shays, Christopher H.	Rep	Conn.	Feb. 12, 2003 Leave of absence; named Vice Chair of Budget.
Neugebauer, Randy	Rep	Tex.	June 19, 2003 Replaced Shays.
Sullivan, John	Rep	Okla.	Jan. 28, 2004 Resigned committee to open seat for Hall; moved to Energy and Commerce.
Hall, Ralph M.	Rep	Tex.	Jan. 28, 2004 Returned as a Republican; replaced Sullivan, ranked after Boehlert.
Barton, Joe L.	Rep	Tex.	Feb. 25, 2004 Resigned committee; became Chair of Energy and Commerce.

Minority:

Baird, Brian	Dem	Wash.	Feb. 5, 2003 Leave of absence to serve on Budget; returned on Feb. 13, 2003, in the 17th slot.
Israel, Steve	Dem	N.Y.	Feb. 5, 2003 Resigned committee; moved to Armed Services.
Etheridge, Bobby R.	Dem	N.C.	Feb. 12, 2003 Leave of absence; moved to Select Homeland Security; never returned.
Lofgren, Zoe	Dem	Cal.	Feb. 12, 2003 Leave of absence to serve on Select Homeland Security; returned on Mar. 5, 2003, in the 14th slot.
Jackson-Lee, Sheila	Dem	Tex.	Feb. 13, 2003 Leave of absence to serve on Select Homeland Security; returned on Mar. 5, 2003, in the 13th slot.
Matheson, James D.	Dem	Utah	Feb. 13, 2003 Replaced Israel.
Bishop, Timothy H.	Dem	N.Y.	Feb. 27, 2003 Resigned committee; moved to Education and the Workforce.
Cardoza, Dennis A.	Dem	Cal.	Mar. 5, 2003 Replaced Bishop, ranked after Matheson.
Hall, Ralph M.	Dem	Tex.	Jan. 5, 2004 Service on committee as a Democrat was vacated; returned as a Republican on Jan. 28, 2004.
Bell, Chris	Dem	Tex.	Jan. 28, 2004 Resigned committee; moved to Financial Services.

Departures from the House:

	Majority			**Minority**		
Lost Election to U.S. Senate	Nethercutt, George R. Jr.	Rep	Wash.	None		
Defeated for Re-election	None			Lampson, Nicholas V.	Dem	Tex.
Retired	Smith, Nick H.	Rep	Mich.	None		

Departures from Committee:

Moved to Energy and Commerce	Burgess, Michael C.	Rep	Tex.	None		
Moved to Financial Services	Neugebauer, Randy	Rep	Tex.	None		
Moved to International Relations	None			Cardoza, Dennis A.	Dem	Cal.
Moved to Rules	Gingrey, Phil	Rep	Ga.	None		
	Bishop, Robert	Rep	Utah			
Moved to Standards of Official Conduct	Hart, Melissa A.	Rep	Penn.	None		

Moved to Ways and Means	Hart, Melissa A.	Rep	Penn.	Larson, John B.	Dem	Conn.
No new assignment	None			Moore, Dennis	Dem	Kans.
				Weiner, Anthony D.	Dem	N.Y.

SCIENCE / 109th Congress

Service Dates of Committee Chair: Jan. 6, 2005-Jan. 3, 2007

Service Dates of Majority Members: Jan. 26, 2005-Jan. 3, 2007

Service Dates of Ranking Member: Jan. 6, 2005-Jan. 3, 2007

Service Dates of Minority Members: Jan. 26, 2005-Jan. 3, 2007

Roster Filled: Majority with 22 members on Jan. 26, 2005; Minority with 19 members on Feb. 2, 2005

| | **Majority** | | | | | | **Minority** | | | | |
| | | | | **Terms in:** | | | | | | **Terms in:** | |
Rank Name		Party	State	House	Comm.	Rank Name		Party	State	House	Comm.
Chr Boehlert, Sherwood L.		Rep	N.Y.	12	12	RM Gordon, Barton J.		Dem	Tenn.	11	*2 6
2nd Hall, Ralph M.		Rep	Tex.	13	*2 2	2nd Costello, Jerry F.		Dem	Ill.	10	*2 4
3rd Smith, Lamar S.		Rep	Tex.	10	*2 4	3rd Johnson, Eddie Bernice		Dem	Tex.	7	7
4th Weldon, Wayne C. (Curt)		Rep	Penn.	10	6	4th Woolsey, Lynn C.		Dem	Cal.	7	*2 4
5th Rohrabacher, Dana		Rep	Cal.	9	9	5th Hooley, Darlene		Dem	Ore.	5	*2 1
6th Calvert, Ken		Rep	Cal.	7	7	6th Udall, Mark		Dem	Colo.	4	4
7th Bartlett, Roscoe G.		Rep	Md.	7	7	7th Wu, David		Dem	Ore.	4	4
8th Ehlers, Vernon J.		Rep	Mich.	7	7	8th Honda, Michael M.		Dem	Cal.	3	3
9th Gutknecht, Gilbert W.		Rep	Minn.	6	6	9th Miller, Brad		Dem	N.C.	2	2
10th Lucas, Frank D.		Rep	Okla.	7	4	10th Davis, Lincoln		Dem	Tenn.	2	*1 2
11th Biggert, Judith B.		Rep	Ill.	4	4	11th Carnahan, Russ		Dem	Mo.	1	1
12th Gilchrest, Wayne T.		Rep	Md.	8	*2 3	12th Lipinksi, Daniel		Dem	Ill.	1	1
13th Akin, W. Todd		Rep	Mo.	3	3	13th Jackson-Lee, Sheila		Dem	Tex.	6	*2 2
14th Johnson, Timothy V.		Rep	Ill.	3	3	14th Lofgren, Zoe		Dem	Cal.	6	*2 2
15th Forbes, J. Randy		Rep	Va.	3	3	15th Sherman, Brad		Dem	Cal.	5	*2 2
16th Bonner, Josiah (Jo) R. Jr.		Rep	Ala.	2	2	16th Baird, Brian		Dem	Wash.	4	*2 2
17th Feeney, Tom		Rep	Fla.	2	2	17th Matheson, James D.		Dem	Utah	3	*2 2
18th Inglis, Robert D.		Rep	S.C.	4	1	18th Costa, Jim		Dem	Cal.	1	1
19th Reichert, David G.		Rep	Wash.	1	1	19th Green, Al		Dem	Tex.	1	1
20th Sodrel, Michael E.		Rep	Ind.	1	1						
21st Schwarz, John J.H. (Joe)		Rep	Mich.	1	1						
22nd McCaul, Michael T.		Rep	Tex.	1	1						

*1: Member's first period of service on the committee.

*2: Member's second period of service on the committee.

Note: Hall was credited with his 12 earlier terms on the committee as a Democrat, 1979-2004.

Vacancies Filled:

Minority:

5th seat and 13th through 20th seats filled by Hooley, Jackson-Lee, Lofgren, Sherman, Baird, Matheson, Costa, and Green on Feb. 2, 2005.

Additions:

Majority:

| 23rd Neugebauer, Randy | Rep | Tex. | Apr. 4, 2006 Ranked after Feeney. |
| 24th Diaz-Balart, Mario | Rep | Fla. | Apr. 4, 2006 |

Minority:

| 20th Melancon, Charles J. | Dem | La. | Feb. 2, 2005 |
| 21st Matsui, Doris O. | Dem | Cal. | May 4, 2006 |

Changes:

Minority:

| Lofgren, Zoe | Dem | Cal. | Feb. 16, 2005 Resigned committee; moved to House Administration. |
| Moore, Dennis | Dem | Kans. | June 8, 2005 Replaced Lofgren. |

Departures from the House:

	Majority			**Minority**
Defeated for Re-nomination	Schwarz, John J.H. (Joe)	Rep	Mich.	None
Defeated for Re-election	Weldon, Wayne C. (Curt)	Rep	Penn.	None
	Gutknecht, Gilbert W.	Rep	Minn.	
	Sodrel, Michael E.	Rep	Ind.	
Retired	Boehlert, Sherwood L.	Rep	N.Y.	None

Departures from Committee:

Moved to Financial Services	None			Davis, Lincoln	Dem	Tenn.
Moved to Foreign Affairs	None			Jackson-Lee, Sheila	Dem	Tex.
				Costa, Jim	Dem	Cal.
Moved to Homeland Security	None			Green, Al	Dem	Tex.
Moved to Judiciary	None			Sherman, Brad	Dem	Cal.
Moved to Transportation and Infrastructure	None			Matsui, Doris O.	Dem	Cal.
No new assignment	Gilchrest, Wayne T.	Rep	Md.	Moore, Dennis	Dem	Kans.
	Johnson, Timothy V.	Rep	Ill.			
	Forbes, J. Randy	Rep	Va.			

SCIENCE AND TECHNOLOGY / 110th Congress

Service Dates of Committee Chair: Jan. 4, 2007-Jan. 3, 2009

Service Dates of Majority Members: Jan. 18, 2007-Jan. 3, 2009

Service Dates of Ranking Member: Jan. 4, 2007-Jan. 3, 2009

Service Dates of Minority Members: Jan. 10, 2007-Jan. 3, 2009

Roster Filled: Majority with 25 members on Jan. 23, 2007; Minority with 22 members on Mar. 12, 2007

Majority					Minority				
			Terms in:					Terms in:	
Rank Name	Party	State	House	Comm.	Rank Name	Party	State	House	Comm.
Chr Gordon, Barton J.	Dem	Tenn.	12	*2 7	RM Hall, Ralph M.	Rep	Tex.	14	*2 3
2nd Costello, Jerry F.	Dem	Ill.	11	*2 5	2nd Sensenbrenner, F. James Jr.	Rep	Wisc.	15	*2 1
3rd Johnson, Eddie Bernice	Dem	Tex.	8	8	3rd Smith, Lamar S.	Rep	Tex.	11	*2 5
4th Woolsey, Lynn C.	Dem	Cal.	8	*2 5	4th Rohrabacher, Dana	Rep	Cal.	10	10
5th Udall, Mark	Dem	Colo.	5	5	5th Calvert, Ken	Rep	Cal.	8	8
6th Wu, David	Dem	Ore.	5	5	6th Bartlett, Roscoe G.	Rep	Md.	8	8
7th Baird, Brian	Dem	Wash.	5	*2 3	7th Ehlers, Vernon J.	Rep	Mich.	8	8
8th Miller, Brad	Dem	N.C.	3	3	8th Lucas, Frank D.	Rep	Okla.	8	5
9th Lipinksi, Daniel	Dem	Ill.	2	2	9th Biggert, Judith B.	Rep	Ill.	5	5
10th Lampson, Nicholas V.	Dem	Tex.	5	*2 1	10th Akin, W. Todd	Rep	Mo.	4	4
11th Giffords, Gabrielle	Dem	Ariz.	1	1	11th Bonner, Josiah (Jo) R. Jr.	Rep	Ala.	3	3
12th McNerney, Jerry	Dem	Cal.	1	1	12th Feeney, Tom	Rep	Fla.	3	3
13th Kanjorski, Paul E.	Dem	Penn.	12	*2 1	13th Neugebauer, Randy	Rep	Tex.	3	*2 2
14th Hooley, Darlene	Dem	Ore.	6	*2 2	14th Inglis, Robert D.	Rep	S.C.	5	2
15th Rothman, Steven R.	Dem	N.J.	6	1	15th Reichert, David G.	Rep	Wash.	2	2
16th Honda, Michael M.	Dem	Cal.	4	4	16th McCaul, Michael T.	Rep	Tex.	2	2
17th Matheson, James D.	Dem	Utah	4	*2 3	17th Diaz-Balart, Mario	Rep	Fla.	3	2
18th Ross, Michael A.	Dem	Ark.	4	1	18th Gingrey, Phil	Rep	Ga.	3	*2 1
19th Chandler, A.B. (Ben)	Dem	Ky.	3	1	19th Bilbray, Brian P.	Rep	Cal.	5	1
20th Carnahan, Russ	Dem	Mo.	2	2	20th Smith, Adrian	Rep	Neb.	1	1
21st Melancon, Charles J.	Dem	La.	2	2					
22nd Hill, Baron P.	Dem	Ind.	4	1					
23rd Mitchell, Harry E.	Dem	Ariz.	1	1					
24th Wilson, Charles A.	Dem	Ohio	1	1					

*2: Member's second period of service on the committee.

Additions:

Minority:

21st Latta, Robert E.	Rep	Ohio	Dec. 18, 2007
22nd Wittman, Robert J.	Rep	Va.	Dec. 18, 2007

Note: Ratio shift led to the immediate departures of Latta and Wittman on Dec. 18, 2007, the same day they had been named as additions.

Vacancies Filled:

Majority:

13th and 14th seats filled by Kanjorski and Hooley on Jan. 23, 2007.

Minority:

15th seat filled by Reichert on Mar. 12, 2007.

Changes:

Majority:

Honda, Michael M.	Dem	Cal.	Sept. 20, 2007 Resigned committee; no new assignment.
Richardson, Laura	Dem	Cal.	Sept. 20, 2007 Replaced Honda, ranked after McNerney.
Hooley, Darlene	Dem	Ore.	June 10, 2008 Resigned committee; no new assignment.
Carson, André	Dem	Ind.	June 10, 2008 Replaced Hooley.

Kanjorski, Paul E.	Dem	Penn.	July 14, 2008 Resigned committee; no new assignment.
Edwards, Donna F.	Dem	Md.	July 15, 2008 Replaced Kanjorski, ranked after Richardson.

Minority:

Calvert, Ken	Rep	Cal.	May 14, 2007 Resigned committee; moved to Appropriations.
Broun, Paul C. Jr.	Rep	Ga.	July 25, 2007 Replaced Calvert.
Latta, Robert E.	Rep	Ohio	Dec. 18,2007 Exceeded party ratio; resigned committee; moved to Agriculture.
Wittman, Robert J.	Rep	Va.	Dec. 18,2007 Exceeded party ratio; resigned committee; moved to Foreign Affairs
Bonner, Josiah (Jo) R. Jr.	Rep	Ala.	Feb. 25, 2008 Resigned committee; moved to Appropriations.

Departures from the House:

	Majority			**Minority**		
Elected to the U.S. Senate	Udall, Mark	Dem	Colo.	None		
Defeated for Re-election	Lampson, Nicholas V.	Dem	Tex.	Feeney, Tom	Rep	Fla.

Departures from Committee:

	Majority			**Minority**		
Moved to Budget	Melancon, Charles J.	Dem	La.	None		
Moved to Energy and Commerce	McNerney, Jerry	Dem	Cal.	Gingrey, Phil	Rep	Ga.
Moved to Foreign Affairs	Ross, Michael A.	Dem	Ark.	None		
Moved to Homeland Security	Richardson, Laura	Dem	Cal.	None		
Moved to Ways and Means	None			Reichert, David G.	Rep	Wash.

SCIENCE AND TECHNOLOGY / 111th Congress

Service Dates of Committee Chair: Jan. 6, 2009-Jan. 3, 2011

Service Dates of Majority Members: Jan. 21, 2009-Jan. 3, 2011

Service Dates of Ranking Member: Jan. 6, 2009-Jan. 3, 2011

Service Dates of Minority Members: Jan. 9, 2009-Jan. 3, 2011

Roster Filled: Majority with 27 members, Jan. 21, 2009; Minority with 17 members, Jan. 9, 2009

Majority					Minority				
			Terms in:					**Terms in:**	
Rank Name	Party	State	House	Comm.	Rank Name	Party	State	House	Comm.
Chr Gordon, Barton J.	Dem	Tenn.	13	*2 8	RM Hall, Ralph M.	Rep	Tex.	15	*2 4
2nd Costello, Jerry F.	Dem	Ill.	12	*2 6	2nd Sensenbrenner, F. James Jr.	Rep	Wisc.	16	*2 2
3rd Johnson, Eddie Bernice	Dem	Tex.	9	9	3rd Smith, Lamar S.	Rep	Tex.	12	*2 6
4th Woolsey, Lynn C.	Dem	Cal.	9	*2 6	4th Rohrabacher, Dana	Rep	Cal.	11	11
5th Wu, David	Dem	Ore.	6	6	5th Bartlett, Roscoe G.	Rep	Md.	9	9
6th Baird, Brian	Dem	Wash.	6	*2 4	6th Ehlers, Vernon J.	Rep	Mich.	9	9
7th Miller, Brad	Dem	N.C.	4	4	7th Lucas, Frank D.	Rep	Okla.	9	6
8th Lipinksi, Daniel	Dem	Ill.	3	3	8th Biggert, Judith B.	Rep	Ill.	6	6
9th Giffords, Gabrielle	Dem	Ariz.	2	2	9th Akin, W. Todd	Rep	Mo.	5	5
10th Edwards, Donna F.	Dem	Md.	2	2	10th Neugebauer, Randy	Rep	Tex.	4	*2 3
11th Fudge, Marcia L.	Dem	Ohio	2	1	11th Inglis, Robert D.	Rep	S.C.	6	3
12th Luján, Ben Ray	Dem	N.M.	1	1	12th McCaul, Michael T.	Rep	Tex.	3	3
13th Tonko, Paul	Dem	N.Y.	1	1	13th Diaz-Balart, Mario	Rep	Fla.	4	3
14th Griffith, Parker	Dem	Ala.	1	1	14th Bilbray, Brian P.	Rep	Cal.	6	2
15th Rothman, Steven R.	Dem	N.J.	7	2	15th Smith, Adrian	Rep	Neb.	2	2
16th Matheson, James D.	Dem	Utah	5	*2 4	16th Broun, Paul C. Jr.	Rep	Ga.	2	2
17th Davis, Lincoln	Dem	Tenn.	4	*2 1	17th Olson, Pete	Rep	Tex.	1	1
18th Chandler, A.B. (Ben)	Dem	Ky.	4	2					
19th Carnahan, Russ	Dem	Mo.	3	3	*2: Member's second period of service on the committee.				
20th Hill, Baron P.	Dem	Ind.	5	2					
21st Mitchell, Harry E.	Dem	Ariz.	2	2					
22nd Wilson, Charles A.	Dem	Ohio	2	2					
23rd Dahlkemper, Kathleen A.	Dem	Penn.	1	1					
24th Grayson, Alan	Dem	Fla.	1	1					
25th Kosmas, Suzanne M.	Dem	Fla.	1	1					
26th Peters, Gary	Dem	Mich.	1	1					

Vacancies Filled:

Minority:

15th seat by Adrian Smith on Jan. 22, 2009.

Additions:

Majority

Garamendi, John	Dem	Cal.	Nov. 19, 2009 Ranked 15th after Griffith.

Changes:

Majority

Griffith, Parker	Dem	Ala.	Dec. 22, 2009 Service on committee as a Democrat vacated.
Garamendi, John J.	Dem	Cal.	May 6, 2010 Reranked following Peters.

Small Business

House Committee on Small Business, 103rd-111th Congresses (1993-2011)

BACKGROUND

Organizational History: The first appearance of a small business committee in the House was the Select Committee to Investigate the National Defense Program and Its Relation to Small Business which came into existence on December 4, 1941. Wright Patman (Dem-Texas) was its original chair and Charles A. Halleck (Rep-Ind.) was its original ranking member. The committee was reappointed in both the 78th and 79th Congresses (1943-1947) and by the time of the 1946 Reorganization Act, it had become a fixture of the House committee system.

It was reconstituted by resolution every Congress until the 92nd, when the House Rules Committee ruled that the committee would become a "permanent" select committee on January 22, 1971 (H. Res. 5). Four years later on January 5, 1975, in keeping with the reforms urged by the first Select Committee on Committees chaired by Richard W. Bolling (Dem-Mo.), a one-time protégé of Wright Patman, the longest serving chair of Select Small Business, it became the third new standing committee added to the modern Congress's roster.

The Committee on Small Business was created with two areas of legislative jurisdiction, and one area of special oversight functions. Legislative jurisdiction was to be held over measures related to assistance and protection of small business, including financial aid. The committee was also to be responsible for measures pertaining to participation of small-business enterprises in federal procurement and government contracts. In terms of oversight functions, the committee was to study and investigate the problems of all types of small business.

According to the *House Manual* (2008):

The Committee Reform Amendments of 1974 established a standing Committee on Small Business, effective January 3, 1975, and vested it with legislative jurisdiction formerly held by the Committee on Banking and Currency (now Financial Services) (subpara. (1)) and the Committee on the Judiciary (subpara. (2)) (H. Res. 988, 93d Cong., Oct. 8, 1974). At the same time the general and special oversight functions were set forth in clause 2(b) and in former clause 3(g) (current clause 3(l)). The 104th Congress expanded the jurisdiction of the committee over assistance to and protection of small business by inserting the references to regulatory flexibility and paperwork reduction.

Although small businesses constitute a major growth area in the American economy with more than half a million company start-ups in recent years, the committee has not attracted many House members nor has it been able to retain many of those who served on it.

Membership: As the Select Committee on Small Business following the 1946 reorganization, the committee had only nine members but grew to nineteen by 1973 and its last Congress as a select committee. In the 94th Congress (1975-1977), its initial Congress as a standing committee, Small Business had almost doubled its size to thirty-seven members. It first reached the forty-member mark in 1979 and it would peak at 45 in the 103rd Congress (1993-1995). It was believed that the new Republican majority had targeted Small Business for extinction much like the committees on the District of Columbia, Merchant Marine and Fisheries, and Post Office and Civil Service. However, since the incoming chair was to be Jan Meyers of Kansas, the only woman slated to be a committee chair in that Congress, it survived. Its membership has declined steadily since 1993, dropping to thirty-five in 1997, thirty-three in 2005, and twenty-nine in 2009—its lowest membership total since it first became a standing committee thirty-four years earlier.

The mean size of the Small Business Committee over the past nine Congresses, 1993-2011 is 36.22—fifteenth-place among the nineteen continuing committees. The committee has been a "starter" committee for many junior members and as a result, its mean seniority of 2.87 terms per member is the lowest among the committees and its mean inter-Congress retention rate of 66.7 percent is seventeenth—third from the bottom—ranking only above the nine-member House Administration (61.7%) and the ten-member term-limited Standards of Official Conduct (57.5%) committees where any departure will have a much greater statistical.impact.

Committee Leaders: Joseph L. Evins (Dem-Tenn.), who first joined the committee in 1949, succeeded the legendary Wright Patman as chair of the select committee in 1963, when Patman became chair of Banking and Currency. Evins, the last chair of the select committee became the first chair of the standing Committee on Small Business in 1975 and would leave the committee in August, 1976. He was succeeded by Thomas J. Steed (Dem-Okla.) who stepped aside as chair in 1977 to head an Appropriations Committee subcommittee. Democratic Caucus rules barred Appropriations subcommittee chairs from chairing standing committees. Steed's successor, Neal Smith (Dem-Iowa), who held the chair for four years (1977-1981), also relinquished it to become chair of a subcommittee on Appropriations.

Smith's successor, Parren J. Mitchell (Dem-Md.) left the House after three terms as chair (1981-1987) to run unsuccessfully for nomination to be Lieutenant Governor of Maryland. While four different Democrats chaired Small Business from 1975 to 1987, Republicans had only two ranking members—Silvio Conte (Rep-Mass.), who became ranking member on the select committee in 1969 and continued this role on the standing committee until 1979 when he stepped aside to become ranking member on Appropriations. Joseph M. McDade (Rep-Penn.) held the ranking member post until 1991 when he succeeded Conte as ranking member on Appropriations after Conte's death. Completing that Congress was Andrew P. Ireland (Rep-Fla.), one of the first Southern Democrats to switch to the Republican party.

The most influential of the recent Small Business Committee leaders was John J. LaFalce (Dem-N.Y.) who joined the committee as a freshman member in 1975 and would become its senior Democrat in 1987 and held that rank for eleven-plus years, first as chair for eight years, 1987-1995; and three-plus as ranking member, 1995-1997 until he left to become ranking member on Banking and Financial Services. Serving as the senior Republican from 1993 to 1997 was Jan Meyers (Rep-Kans.) as ranking member in the 103rd Congress (1993-1995) and as its first woman chair in the 104th (1995-1997). Meyers's retirement led to James M. Talent (Rep-Mo.) serving as chair for four years, 1997-2001 until his unsuccessful bid to become Governor of Missouri.

LaFalce's successor as ranking member in 1999 was Democrat Nydia M. Velázquez of New York. She served as ranking member until 2007, when the Democratic recapture of the House elevated her as chair of Small Business, the second woman to hold that title and its present chair. Talent's initial successor as chair was Republican Donald A. Manzullo of Illinois, who chaired the committee until 2007 when he returned to the Foreign Affairs Committee. Steven J. Chabot (Rep-Ohio) succeeded Manzullo in 2007, but his re-election defeat in 2008 led to Samuel B. Graves (Rep-Mo.) becoming ranking member in 2009.

Party Leaders: The only House party leader to serve on Select Small Business was Republican Floor Leader Charles A. Halleck who served on its original incarnation in 1941-1944 and then again from1949 to 1953 in the two Democratic-controlled 81st and 82nd Congresses between the two Republican ones of the 80th and 83rd. Halleck would serve as Majority Leader when Republicans organized the House and Joseph W. Martin, Jr. of Massachusetts would serve as Speaker. But when Democrats organized the House, Martin would become Minority Leader and Halleck would be replaced as the number two Republican by Leslie C. Arends of Illinois, the party's longtime whip. This differed from the Rayburn-McCormack relationship when the two Democrats would serve as Speaker and Majority Leader when they controlled the House and as Minority Leader and Whip when they did not. As a result, Halleck's regular demotions fueled his animus towards Martin that led to his overthrowing him in 1959. John Boehner (Rep-Ohio), the present Republican floor leader, is the only House party leader to have served on the standing Small Business Committee.

Notable Members: No modern-era major party presidential nominee and onlty one vice presidential nominee served on Small Business as a standing committee, Vice President J. Danforth Quayle, who ran successfully with George H.W. Bush in 1988 and unsuccessfully for re-election in 1992. Two other vice presidential nominees served on the select committee—Democrat C. Estes Kefauver of Tennessee, Adlai Stevenson's 1956 running-mate, and Jack F. Kemp (Rep-N.Y.), Bob Dole's 1996 running-mate. There were a number of Cabinet members who served on House Small Business. Select committee veterans included Rogers C.B. Morton (Rep-Md.), who served under both Presidents Nixon and Ford as Secretary of the Interior and later as Ford's Commerce Secretary. Bob Bergland (DFL-Minn.) who was a member of Small Business as both a select and standing committee, served as Jimmy Carter's Secretary of Agriculture. President George H.W. Bush, a House alumnus, selected three Cabinet members who served on Select Small Business—Jack Kemp as Secretary of Housing and Urban Development, Manuel Lujan, Jr. (Rep-N.M.) as his Secretary of the Interior, and Edward J. Derwinski (Rep-Ill.) as the initial Secretary of Veterans' Affairs. A standing committee alumnus, William S. Cohen (Rep-Maine) joined Bill Clinton's Cabinet as his third Secretary of Defense after he retired from the Senate in 1997.

Twenty-three U.S. senors were former members of House Small Business. Four moved to the Senate after serving on the select committee—three Democrats who would be powerful senators—C. Estes Kefauver of Tennessee, Henry M. Jackson of Washington State, and Mike Mansfield of Montana and Republican James T. Broyhill of North Carolina. Among the nineteen U.S. senators who served on Small Business as a standing committee included five Democrats—Ronald L. Wyden of Oregon, Ben Nighthorse Campbell of Colorado, Byron L. Dorgan of North Dakota, and the two Udall cousins, Thomas of New Mexico and Mark of Colorado—and fourteen Republicans Larry L. Pressler and John R. Thune of South Dakota, J. Danforth Quayle of Indiana, William S. Cohen and Olympia J.B. Snowe of Maine, Robert C. Smith and John Sununu of New Hampshire, A. Wayne Allard of Colorado, Robert W. Kasten, Jr. of Wisconsin, Wyche Fowler of Georgia, James M. Talent of Missouri, George F. Allen of Virginia, Sam D. Brownback of Kansas, and James DeMint of South Carolina.

Republican Governor Arch A. Moore of West Virginia served on Select Small Committee while his daughter Shelley Moore Capito (Rep-W.Va.) serves on the standing version of Small Business in the 111th Congress. Two other Republican governors who served on Small Business were George F. Allen of Virginia who moved to the Senate after leaving Richmond and William H. Avery of Kansas. Three Democratic committee members were elected governor: Charles G. (Buddy) Roemer of Louisiana and present-day governors John Baldacci of Maine and Ted Strickland of Ohio.

Selected References

U.S. Congress, remarks by John J. LaFalce (Dem-N.Y.), "Small Business Accomplishments," *Congressional Record*, 100th Congress, 2nd Session (October 19, 1988), E3508-E3510.

U.S. House of Representatives, Committee on Small Business, *A History and Accomplishments of the Permanent Select Committee on Small Business, House of Representatives, 77th to 92nd Congress, 1941-1972*, H.Doc. 93-197, 93rd Congress, 2nd Session (1974).

Victor, Kirk, "Uncle Sam's Little Engine," *National Journal* (November 23, 1991), 2855-2859.

Vinyard, Dale, "The Congressional Committees on Small Business: Patterns of Legislative Committee-Executive Agency Relations," *Western Political Quarterly*, 21 (September, 1968), 391-399.

RESPONSIBILITIES, JURISDICTIONAL CHANGES, AND SUBCOMMITTEES

SMALL BUSINESS

Jurisdiction, 1974

Established by House Resolution 988, as amended, 93rd Congress, Second Session, October 8, 1974:

[Section 321]

Rule X of the Rules of the House of Representatives, as amended by the previous sections, is further amended by adding at the end thereof the following:

(t) Committee on Small Business.

(1) Assistance to and protection of small business, including financial aid.
(2) Participation of small-business enterprises in Federal procurement and Government contracts. In addition to its legislative jurisdiction under the preceding provisions of this paragraph (and its general oversight function under clause 2(b)(1)), the committee shall have the special oversight function provided for in clause 3(f) with respect to the problems of small business.

Jurisdiction, 103rd Congress (1993-1995)

From the *Rules of the House of Representatives, 103rd Congress* (House Document 102-405)

[Rule X.1.(s)] Committee on Small Business

(1) Assistance to and protection of small business, including financial aid.
(2) Participation of small-business enterprises in Federal procurement and Government contracts.

In addition to its legislative jurisdiction under the preceding provisions of this paragraph (and its general oversight function under clause 2(b)(1)), the committee shall have the special oversight function provided for in clause 3. (g) with respect to the problems of small business.

[Rule X.3.(g)]

The Committee on Small Business shall have the function of studying and investigating, on a continuing basis, the problems of all types of small business.

Jurisdiction, 104th Congress (1995-1997) Changes in Committee System

From H. Res. 6, Section 202 (a), the Committees and Their Jurisdiction, January 4, 1995

[Rule X.1.(o)] Committee on Small Business.

(1) Assistance to and protection of small business, including financial aid, regulatory flexibility and paperwork reduction.
(2) Participation of small-business enterprises in Federal procurement and Government contracts.

In addition to its legislative jurisdiction under the preceding provisions of this paragraph and (its general oversight function under clause 2(b)(1)), the committee shall have the special oversight function provided for in clause 3(g) with respect to the problems of small business.

Jurisdiction, 111th Congress (2009-2011)

From the *Rules of the House of Representatives* (as revised to June 16, 2009, H.Doc. 110-162):

[Rule X.1.(p)] Committee on Small Business

(1) Assistance to and protection of small business, including financial aid, regulatory flexibility, and paperwork reduction.
(2) Participation of small-business enterprises in Federal procurement and Government contracts.

[Rule X.3.(l)] Special Oversight Function

The Committee on Small Business shall study and investigate on a continuing basis the problems of all types of small business.

NAMES OF SMALL BUSINESS SUBCOMMITTEES FROM THE *CONGRESSIONAL DIRECTORY*

Contracting and Technology, 110, 111
Empowerment, 105, 106

Finance and Tax, 110, 111
Government Programs, 104
Government Programs and Oversight, 105, 106
Investigations and Oversight, 110, 111
Minority Enterprise, Finance, and Urban Development, 103
Procurement, Taxation, and Tourism, 103
Procurement, Exports and Business Opportunities, 104
Regulation, Business Opportunities, and Technology, 103
Regulation and Paperwork, 104
Regulatory Reform and Paperwork Reduction, 105, 106
Regulatory Reform and Oversight, 107, 108, 109
Regulations and Healthcare, 111
Regulations, Healthcare and Trade, 110
Rural Development, Entrepreneurship, and Trade, 111
Rural Enterprise, Exports, and the Environment, 103
Rural Opportunities for Small Business, 106
Rural Enterprises and Agricultural Policy, 107
Rural Enterprises, Agriculture, and Technology, 108, 109
Rural and Urban Entrepreneurship, 110
SBA Legislation and the General Economy, 103
Tax and Finance, 104
Tax, Finance, and Exports, 105, 106, 107, 108, 109
Workforce, Empowerment, and Government Programs, 107, 108, 109

MEMBERSHIP ROSTERS, 103rd-111th Congresses, 1993-2011

SMALL BUSINESS / 103rd Congress

Service Dates of Committee Chair: Jan. 5, 1993-Jan. 3, 1995

Service Dates of Majority Members: Jan. 5, 1993-Jan. 3, 1995

Service Dates of Minority Members: Jan. 5, 1993-Jan. 3, 1995

Roster Filled: Majority with 27 members, June 23, 1993; Minority with 18 members, Jan. 5, 1993

Majority

Rank Name	Party	State	House	Comm.
Chr LaFalce, John J.	Dem	N.Y.	10	10
2nd Smith, Neal E.	Dem	Iowa	18	15
3rd Skelton, Isaac N. (Ike)	Dem	Mo.	9	*1 9
4th Mazzoli, Romano L.	Dem	Ky.	12	7
5th Wyden, Ronald L.	Dem	Ore.	7	7
6th Sisisky, Norman	Dem	Va.	6	6
7th Conyers, John Jr.	Dem	Mich.	15	4
8th Bilbray, James H.	Dem	Nev.	4	4
9th Mfume, Kweisi	Dem	Md.	4	4
10th Flake, Floyd H.	Dem	N.Y.	4	4
11th Sarpalius, William	Dem	Tex.	3	3
12th Poshard, Glenn	Dem	Ill.	3	3
13th Lancaster, H. Martin	Dem	N.C.	4	4
14th Andrews, Thomas H.	Dem	Me.	2	2
15th Clayton, Eva M.	Dem	N.C.	2	1
16th Meehan, Martin T.	Dem	Mass.	1	1
17th Danner, Patsy A. (Pat)	Dem	Mo.	1	1
18th Strickland, Ted	Dem	Ohio	1	1
19th Velázquez, Nydia M.	Dem	N.Y.	1	1
20th Fields, Cleo	Dem	La.	1	1
21st Margolies-Mezvinsky, Marjorie	Dem	Penn.	1	1
22nd Tucker, Walter R.	Dem	Cal.	1	1
23rd Klink, Ronald	Dem	Penn.	1	1
24th Roybal-Allard, Lucille	Dem	Cal.	1	1

Minority

Rank Name	Party	State	House	Comm.
RM Meyers, Jan	Rep	Kans.	5	5
2nd Combest, Larry E.	Rep	Tex.	5	*1 5
3rd Baker, Richard H.	Rep	La.	4	4
4th Hefley, Joel M.	Rep	Colo.	4	4
5th Machtley, Ronald K.	Rep	R.I.	3	3
6th Ramstad, James	Rep	Minn.	2	2
7th Camp, David L.	Rep	Mich.	2	2
8th Johnson, Sam	Rep	Tex.	2	2
9th Zeliff, William H. Jr.	Rep	N.H.	2	2
10th Collins, Michael A. (Mac)	Rep	Ga.	1	1
11th McInnis, Scott	Rep	Colo.	1	1
12th Huffington, Michael	Rep	Cal.	1	1
13th Talent, James M.	Rep	Mo.	1	1
14th Knollenberg, Joseph	Rep	Mich.	1	1
15th Dickey, Jay W. Jr.	Rep	Ark.	1	1
16th Kim, Jay C.	Rep	Cal.	1	1
17th Manzullo, Donald A.	Rep	Ill.	1	1
18th Torkildsen, Peter G.	Rep	Mass.	1	1

*1: Member's first period of service on the committee.

25th Hilliard, Earl F.	Dem	Ala.	1		1
26th Waters, Maxine	Dem	Cal.	2	*1	1
27th Thompson, Bennie	Dem	Miss.	1		1

Notes: "Terms in committee" reflect members' previous service on the House Select Committee on Small Business. Ranking on this committee for the following member was affected by other chamber service: Neal Smith (Dem-Iowa), Chair, Commerce, Justice, State and the Judiciary Subcommittee of Appropriations. On Jan. 21, 1993, Tom Andrews (Dem-Maine) was ranked below H. Martin Lancaster (Dem-N.C.). Prior to Jan. 21, 1993, Andrews was ranked below Poshard.

Vacancies Filled:

Majority:

13th seat filled by Lancaster on Jan. 21, 1993; 26th seat filled by Waters on Feb. 4, 1993; 27th seat filled by Thompson on June 23, 1993.

Changes:

Minority:

Camp, David L.	Rep	Mich.	Feb. 4, 1993 Resigned committee; moved to Ways and Means.
Portman, Robert J.	Rep	Ohio	May 26, 1993 Replaced Camp.

Departures from the House:	Majority			Minority		
Lost Nomination for Governor	None			Machtley, Ronald K.	Rep	R.I.
Lost Election to U.S. Senate	Andrews, Thomas H.	Dem	Me.	Huffington, Michael	Rep	Cal.
Defeated for Re-election	Smith, Neal E.	Dem	Iowa	None		
	Bilbray, James H.	Dem	Nev.			
	Sarpalius, William	Dem	Tex.			
	Lancaster, H. Martin	Dem	N.C.			
	Strickland, Ted	Dem	Ohio			
	Margolies-Mezvinsky, Marjorie	Dem	Penn.			
Retired	Mazzoli, Romano L.	Dem	Ky.	None		

Departures from Committee:						
Became Chair of Permanent Select Intelligence	None			Combest, Larry E.	Rep	Tex.
Became RM on Judiciary	Conyers, John Jr.	Dem	Mich.	None		
Moved to Agriculture	None			Baker, Richard H.	Rep	La.
Moved to Appropriations	None			Knollenberg, Joseph	Rep	Mich.
				Dickey, Jay W. Jr.	Rep	Ark.
Moved to Budget	Roybal-Allard, Lucille	Dem	Cal.	None		
Moved to Commerce	Klink, Ronald	Dem	Penn.	None		
Moved to Economic and Educational Opportunities	None			Johnson, Sam	Rep	Tex.
				Knollenberg, Joseph	Rep	Mich.
Moved to International Relations	None			Kim, Jay C.	Rep	Cal.
Moved to Rules	None			McInnis, Scott	Rep	Colo.
Moved to Ways and Means	None			Ramstad, James	Rep	Minn.
				Johnson, Sam	Rep	Tex.
				Collins, Michael A. (Mac)	Rep	Ga.
				Portman, Robert J.	Rep	Ohio
No new assignment	Skelton, Isaac N. (Ike)	Dem	Mo.	None		
	Danner, Patsy A. (Pat)	Dem	Mo.			
	Waters, Maxine	Dem	Cal.			

SMALL BUSINESS / 104th Congress

Service Dates of Committee Chair: Jan. 4, 1995-Jan. 3, 1997

Service Dates of Majority Members: Jan. 4, 1995-Jan. 3, 1997

Service Dates of Minority Members: Jan. 4, 1995-Jan. 3, 1997

Roster Filled: Majority with 22 members, Jan. 4, 1995; Minority with 19 members, Jan. 4, 1995

			Majority						**Minority**		
				Terms in:						**Terms in:**	
Rank Name	Party	State	House	Comm.		Rank Name	Party	State	House	Comm.
Chr Meyers, Jan	Rep	Kans.	6	6		RM LaFalce, John J.	Dem	N.Y.	11	11
2nd Hefley, Joel M.	Rep	Colo.	5	5		2nd Wyden, Ronald L.	Dem	Ore.	8	8
3rd Zeliff, William H. Jr.	Rep	N.H.	3	3		3rd Sisisky, Norman	Dem	Va.	7	7
4th Talent, James M.	Rep	Mo.	2	2		4th Mfume, Kweisi	Dem	Md.	5	5
5th Manzullo, Donald A.	Rep	Ill.	2	2		5th Flake, Floyd H.	Dem	N.Y.	5	5
6th Torkildsen, Peter G.	Rep	Mass.	2	2		6th Poshard, Glenn	Dem	Ill.	4	4
7th Bartlett, Roscoe G.	Rep	Md.	2	1		7th Clayton, Eva M.	Dem	N.C.	3	2

8th Smith, Linda	Rep	Wash.	1	1		8th Meehan, Martin T.	Dem	Mass.	2	2
9th LoBiondo, Frank A.	Rep	N.J.	1	1		9th Velázquez, Nydia M.	Dem	N.Y.	2	2
10th Wamp, Zachary P.	Rep	Tenn.	1	1		10th Fields, Cleo	Dem	La.	2	2
11th Kelly, Sue W.	Rep	N.Y.	1	1		11th Tucker, Walter R.	Dem	Cal.	2	2
12th Chrysler, Dick	Rep	Mich.	1	1		12th Hilliard, Earl F.	Dem	Ala.	2	2
13th Longley, James B. Jr.	Rep	Me.	1	1		13th Peterson, Douglas B. (Pete)	Dem	Fla.	3	1
14th Jones, Walter B. Jr.	Rep	N.C.	1	1		14th Thompson, Bennie	Dem	Miss.	2	2
15th Salmon, Matthew J.	Rep	Ariz.	1	1		15th Fattah, Chaka	Dem	Penn.	1	1
16th Hilleary, Van	Rep	Tenn.	1	1		16th Bentsen, Kenneth E. Jr.	Dem	Tex.	1	1
17th Souder, Mark E.	Rep	Ind.	1	1		17th McCarthy, Karen	Dem	Mo.	1	1
18th Brownback, Sam D.	Rep	Kans.	1	1		18th Luther, William P.	DFL	Minn.	1	1
19th Chabot, Steven J.	Rep	Ohio	1	1		19th Kennedy, Patrick J.	Dem	R.I.	1	1
20th Myrick, Sue	Rep	N.C.	1	1						
21st Funderburk, David	Rep	N.C.	1	1						
22nd Metcalf, Jack	Rep	Wash.	1	1						

Note: Delegate Eleanor Holmes Norton (Dem-D.C.) was allowed to accrue committee seniority but not included in the party ratio.

Additions:
　Majority:
　　23rd LaTourette, Steven C.　Rep　Ohio　May 25, 1995
　Minority:
　　20th Baldacci, John E.　Dem　Me.　June 13, 1995

Changes:
　Majority:

Funderburk, David	Rep	N.C.	Sept. 4, 1996 Resigned committee; had moved to Agriculture Aug. 2, 1996.
Brownback, Sam D.	Rep	Kans.	Nov. 7, 1996 Resigned the House; elected to the Senate.

　Minority:

McCarthy, Karen	Dem	Mo.	June 13, 1995 Resigned committee; moved to Transportation and Infrastructure.
Skelton, Isaac N. (Ike)	Dem	Mo.	June 13, 1995 Replaced McCarthy.
Kennedy, Patrick J.	Dem	R.I.	Nov. 20, 1995 Resigned committee; moved to Resources.
Tucker, Walter R.	Dem	Cal.	Dec. 15, 1995 Resigned the House and retired.
Wyden, Ronald L.	Dem	Ore.	Feb. 5, 1996 Resigned the House; elected to the Senate.
Mfume, Kweisi	Dem	Md.	Feb. 15, 1996 Resigned the House; became head of NAACP.
Fattah, Chaka	Dem	Penn.	Mar. 5, 1996 Resigned committee; no new assignment.
Thompson, Bennie	Dem	Miss.	Apr. 22, 1996 Resigned committee; moved to Budget.
Jackson, Jesse L. Jr.	Dem	Ill.	Apr. 22, 1996 Replaced Kennedy.
Millender-McDonald, Juanita	Dem	Cal.	Apr. 22, 1996 Replaced Tucker.
Hilliard, Earl F.	Dem	Ala.	June 4, 1996 Resigned committee; moved to International Relations.
Blumenauer, Earl	Dem	Ore.	June 5, 1996 Replaced Wyden.
Becerra, Xavier	Dem	Cal.	Sept. 17, 1996 Replaced Mfume.
Clyburn, James E.	Dem	S.C.	Sept. 17, 1996 Replaced Fattah.
Norton, Eleanor Holmes	Dem	D.C.	Sept. 17, 1996 Replaced Thompson.
Waters, Maxine	Dem	Cal.	Sept. 17, 1996 Replaced Hilliard.

Departures from the House:	**Majority**			**Minority**		
Appointed U.S. Ambassador to Vietnam	None			Peterson, Douglas B. (Pete)	Dem	Fla.
Lost Nomination for Governor	Zeliff, William H. Jr.	Rep	N.H.	None		
Defeated for Re-election	Torkildsen, Peter G.	Rep	Mass.	None		
	Chrysler, Dick	Rep	Mich.			
	Longley, James B. Jr.	Rep	Me.			
Retired	Meyers, Jan	Rep	Kans.	Fields, Cleo	Dem	La.

Departures from Committee:						
Moved to Appropriations	Wamp, Zachary P.	Rep	Tenn.	None		
Moved to Banking and Financial Services	LaTourette, Steven C.	Rep	Ohio	None		
Moved to Budget	Hilleary, Van	Rep	Tenn.	Clayton, Eva M.	Dem	N.C.
				Bentsen, Kenneth E. Jr.	Dem	Tex.
Moved to Education and the Workforce	Hilleary, Van	Rep	Tenn.	None		
Moved to Judiciary	None			Meehan, Martin T.	Dem	Mass.
Moved to Rules	Myrick, Sue	Rep	N.C.	None		
Moved to Transportation and Infrastructure	Metcalf, Jack	Rep	Wash.	None		
Moved to Ways and Means	None			Becerra, Xavier	Dem	Cal.
No new assignment	Salmon, Matthew J.	Rep	Ariz.	Clyburn, James E.	Dem	S.C.
				Norton, Eleanor Holmes	Dem	D.C.
				Blumenauer, Earl	Dem	Ore.
				Waters, Maxine	Dem	Cal.

SMALL BUSINESS / 105th Congress

Service Dates of Committee Chair: Jan. 9, 1997-Jan. 3, 1999

Service Dates of Majority Members: Jan. 21, 1997-Jan. 3, 1999

Service Dates of Minority Members: Feb. 5, 1997-Jan. 3, 1999

Roster Filled: Majority with 19 members, Feb. 12, 1997; Minority with 16 members, Feb. 5, 1997

Majority					Minority				
			Terms in:					**Terms in:**	
Rank Name	Party	State	House	Comm.	Rank Name	Party	State	House	Comm.
Chr Talent, James M.	Rep	Mo.	3	3	RM1 LaFalce, John J.	Dem	N.Y.	12	12
2nd Combest, Larry E.	Rep	Tex.	7	*2 1	2nd Skelton, Isaac N. (Ike)	Dem	Mo.	11	*2 2
3rd Hefley, Joel M.	Rep	Colo.	6	6	3rd Sisisky, Norman	Dem	Va.	8	8
4th Manzullo, Donald A.	Rep	Ill.	3	3	4th Flake, Floyd H.	Dem	N.Y.	6	6
5th Bartlett, Roscoe G.	Rep	Md.	3	2	5th Poshard, Glenn	Dem	Ill.	5	5
6th Smith, Linda	Rep	Wash.	2	2	RM2 6th Velázquez, Nydia M.	Dem	N.Y.	3	3
7th LoBiondo, Frank A.	Rep	N.J.	2	2	7th Luther, William P.	DFL	Minn.	2	2
8th Kelly, Sue W.	Rep	N.Y.	2	2	8th Baldacci, John E.	Dem	Me.	2	2
9th Jones, Walter B. Jr.	Rep	N.C.	2	2	9th Jackson, Jesse L. Jr.	Dem	Ill.	2	2
10th Souder, Mark E.	Rep	Ind.	2	2	10th Millender-McDonald, Juanita	Dem	Cal.	2	2
11th Chabot, Steven J.	Rep	Ohio	2	2	11th Weygand, Robert A.	Dem	R.I.	1	1
12th Ryun, Jim	Rep	Kans.	2	1	12th Davis, Danny K.	Dem	Ill.	1	*1 1
13th Snowbarger, Vincent K.	Rep	Kans.	1	1	13th Boyd, F. Allen Jr.	Dem	Fla.	1	1
14th Pappas, Michael J.	Rep	N.J.	1	1	14th McCarthy, Carolyn	Dem	N.Y.	1	1
15th English, Philip S.	Rep	Penn.	2	1	15th Pascrell, William J. Jr.	Dem	N.J.	1	1
16th McIntosh, David M.	Rep	Ind.	2	1	16th Goode, Virgil H. Jr.	Dem	Va.	1	1
17th Emerson, Jo Ann	Rep	Mo.	2	1					
18th Hill, Rick	Rep	Mont.	1	1					
19th Sununu, John E.	Rep	N.H.	1	1					

*1: Member's first period of service on the committee.

*2: Member's second period of service on the committee.

Vacancies Filled:

> **Majority:**
>
> > 18th and 19th seats filled by Hill and Sununu on Feb. 12, 1997.
>
> **Minority:**
>
> > 11th and 12th seats filled by Weygand and Davis on Feb. 6, 1997.

Changes:

> **Majority:**

Jones, Walter B. Jr.	Rep	N.C.	Apr. 14, 1997 Resigned committee; moved to Banking and Financial Services.
Pitts, Joseph R.	Rep	Penn.	July 23, 1997 Replaced Jones.

> **Minority:**

Skelton, Isaac N. (Ike)	Dem	Mo.	Mar. 10, 1997 Resigned committee; moved to Permanent Select Intelligence.
Luther, William P.	DFL	Minn.	Mar. 13, 1997 Resigned committee; moved to International Relations.
Hinojosa, Rubén	Dem	Tex.	May 14, 1997 Replaced Skelton.
Berry, R. Marion	Dem	Ark.	May 14, 1997 Replaced Luther.
Weygand, Robert A.	Dem	R.I.	July 30, 1997 Leave of absence; moved to Banking and Financial Services.
Flake, Floyd H.	Dem	N.Y.	Nov. 17, 1997 Resigned the House and retired.
RM1 LaFalce, John J.	Dem	N.Y.	Feb. 26, 1998 Became Ranking Member on Banking and Financial Services.
RM2 Velázquez, Nydia M.	Dem	N.Y.	Feb. 26, 1998 Became Ranking Member.
Baldacci, John E.	Dem	Me.	Mar. 27, 1998 Resigned committee; moved to Transportation and Infrastructure.
Berry, R. Marion	Dem	Ark.	Mar. 30, 1998 Resigned committee; moved to Transportation and Infrastructure.
Christian-Green, Donna	Dem	V.I.	May 14, 1998 Replaced Weygand.
Goode, Virgil H. Jr.	Dem	Va.	June 24, 1998 Resigned committee; moved to Banking and Financial Services.
Brady, Robert A.	Dem	Penn.	June 24, 1998 Replaced Flake.

Departures from the House:

	Majority			Minority		
Lost Election for Governor	None			Poshard, Glenn	Dem	Ill.
Lost Election to U.S. Senate	Smith, Linda	Rep	Wash.	None		
Defeated for Re-election	Snowbarger, Vincent K.	Rep	Kans.	None		
	Pappas, Michael J.	Rep	N.J.			

Departures from Committee:

	Majority			Minority		
Moved to Appropriations	Emerson, Jo Ann	Rep	Mo.	Jackson, Jesse L. Jr.	Dem	Ill.
	Sununu, John E.	Rep	N.H.	Boyd, F. Allen Jr.	Dem	Fla.
Moved to Budget	Ryun, Jim	Rep	Kans.	None		
Moved to Resources	Souder, Mark E.	Rep	Ind.	None		
No new assignment	None			LaFalce, John J.	Dem	N.Y.

SMALL BUSINESS / 106th Congress

Service Dates of Committee Chair: Jan. 6, 1999-Jan. 3, 2001

Service Dates of Majority Members: Jan. 6, 1999-Jan. 3, 2001

Service Dates of Minority Members: Jan. 6, 1999-Jan. 3, 2001

Roster Filled: Majority with 19 members, Feb. 2, 1999; Minority with 17 members, Jan. 19, 1999

	Majority						Minority				
				Terms in:						**Terms in:**	
Rank Name	**Party**	**State**	**House**	**Comm.**		**Rank Name**	**Party**	**State**	**House**	**Comm.**	
Chr Talent, James M.	Rep	Mo.	4	4		RM Velázquez, Nydia M.	Dem	N.Y.	4	4	
2nd Combest, Larry E.	Rep	Tex.	8	*2 2		2nd Sisisky, Norman	Dem	Va.	9	9	
3rd Hefley, Joel M.	Rep	Colo.	7	7		3rd Millender-McDonald, Juanita	Dem	Cal.	3	3	
4th Manzullo, Donald A.	Rep	Ill.	4	4		4th Davis, Danny K.	Dem	Ill.	2	*1 2	
5th Bartlett, Roscoe G.	Rep	Md.	4	3		5th McCarthy, Carolyn	Dem	N.Y.	2	2	
6th LoBiondo, Frank A.	Rep	N.J.	3	3		6th Pascrell, William J. Jr.	Dem	N.J.	2	2	
7th Kelly, Sue W.	Rep	N.Y.	3	3		7th Hinojosa, Rubén	Dem	Tex.	2	2	
8th Chabot, Steven J.	Rep	Ohio	3	3		8th Christensen, Donna M.C.	Dem	V.I.	2	*1 2	
9th English, Philip S.	Rep	Penn.	3	2		9th Brady, Robert A.	Dem	Penn.	2	2	
10th McIntosh, David M.	Rep	Ind.	3	2		10th Udall, Thomas	Dem	N.M.	1	1	
11th Hill, Rick	Rep	Mont.	2	2		11th Moore, Dennis	Dem	Kans.	1	1	
12th Pitts, Joseph R.	Rep	Penn.	2	2		12th Jones, Stephanie Tubbs	Dem	Ohio	1	1	
13th Forbes, Michael P.	Rep	N.Y.	3	1		13th Gonzalez, Charles A.	Dem	Tex.	1	*1 1	
14th Sweeney, John E.	Rep	N.Y.	1	1		14th Phelps, David D.	Dem	Ill.	1	1	
15th Toomey, Patrick J.	Rep	Penn.	1	1		15th Napolitano, Grace F.	Dem	Cal.	1	1	
16th DeMint, James W.	Rep	S.C.	1	1		16th Baird, Brian	Dem	Wash.	1	1	
17th Pease, Edward A.	Rep	Ind.	2	1		17th Schakowsky, Janice D.	Dem	Ill.	1	1	
18th Thune, John R.	Rep	S.D.	2	1							
19th Bono, Mary	Rep	Cal.	2	1							

*1: Member's first period of service on the committee.

*2: Member's second period of service on the committee.

Vacancies Filled:
Majority:

17th through 19th seats filled by Pease, Thune, and Bono on Feb. 2, 1999.

Minority:

16th and 17th seats filled by Baird and Schakowsky on Jan. 19, 1999.

Changes:
Majority

Forbes, Michael P.	Rep	N.Y.	Aug. 5, 1999 Service on committee as Republican was vacated; moved to Banking and Financial Services as a Democrat.

Minority:

Sisisky, Norman	Dem	Va.	Feb. 23, 1999 Leave of absence; moved to Permanent Select Intelligence.
Schakowsky, Janice D.	Dem	Ill.	Mar. 17, 1999 Resigned committee; moved to Government Reform.
Berkley, Shelley	Dem	Nev.	May 25, 1999 Replaced Sisisky.
Udall, Mark	Dem	Colo.	May 25, 1999 Replaced Schakowsky.

Departures from the House:

	Majority			Minority		
Lost Election for Governor	Talent, James M.	Rep	Mo.	None		
	McIntosh, David M.	Rep	Ind.			
Defeated for Nomination	None			Forbes, Michael P.	Dem	N.Y.
Retired	Hill, Rick	Rep	Mont.	None		
	Pease, Edward A.	Rep	Ind.			

Departures from Committee:

Moved to Appropriations	Sweeney, John E.	Rep	N.Y.	None	
Moved to Energy and Commerce	Bono, Mary	Rep	Cal.	None	
	Pitts, Joseph R.	Rep	Penn.		
Moved to International Relations	Pitts, Joseph R.	Rep	Penn.	None	

SMALL BUSINESS / 107th Congress

Service Dates of Committee Chair: Jan. 6, 2001-Jan. 3, 2003

Service Dates of Majority Members: Jan. 6, 2001-Jan. 3, 2003

Service Dates of Minority Members: Jan. 31, 2001-Jan. 3, 2003

Roster Filled: Majority with 19 members, Feb. 28, 2001; Minority with 17 members, Jan. 31, 2001

Majority					Minority				
			Terms in:					**Terms in:**	
Rank Name	Party	State	House	Comm.	Rank Name	Party	State	House	Comm.
Chr Manzullo, Donald A.	Rep	Ill.	5	5	RM Velázquez, Nydia M.	Dem	N.Y.	5	5
2nd Combest, Larry E.	Rep	Tex.	9	*2 3	2nd Millender-McDonald, Juanita	Dem	Cal.	4	4
3rd Hefley, Joel M.	Rep	Colo.	8	8	3rd Davis, Danny K.	Dem	Ill.	3	*1 3
4th Bartlett, Roscoe G.	Rep	Md.	5	4	4th McCarthy, Carolyn	Dem	N.Y.	3	3
5th LoBiondo, Frank A.	Rep	N.J.	4	4	5th Pascrell, William J. Jr.	Dem	N.J.	3	3
6th Kelly, Sue W.	Rep	N.Y.	4	4	6th Hinojosa, Rubén	Dem	Tex.	3	3
7th Chabot, Steven J.	Rep	Ohio	4	4	7th Christensen, Donna M.C.	Dem	V.I.	3	*1 3
8th English, Philip S.	Rep	Penn.	4	3	8th Brady, Robert A.	Dem	Penn.	3	3
9th Toomey, Patrick J.	Rep	Penn.	2	2	9th Udall, Thomas	Dem	N.M.	2	2
10th DeMint, James W.	Rep	S.C.	2	2	10th Moore, Dennis	Dem	Kans.	2	2
11th Thune, John R.	Rep	S.D.	3	2	11th Jones, Stephanie Tubbs	Dem	Ohio	2	2
12th Pence, Mike	Rep	Ind.	1	1	12th Gonzalez, Charles A.	Dem	Tex.	2	*1 2
13th Ferguson, Michael	Rep	N.J.	1	1	13th Phelps, David D.	Dem	Ill.	2	2
14th Issa, Darrell E.	Rep	Cal.	1	1	14th Napolitano, Grace F.	Dem	Cal.	2	2
15th Graves, Samuel B.	Rep	Mo.	1	1	15th Baird, Brian	Dem	Wash.	2	2
16th Schrock, Edward	Rep	Va.	1	1	16th Berkley, Shelley	Dem	Nev.	2	2
17th Grucci, Felix J. Jr.	Rep	N.Y.	1	1	17th Udall, Mark	Dem	Colo.	2	2
18th Akin, W. Todd	Rep	Mo.	1	1					
19th Capito, Shelley Moore	Rep	W.Va.	1	1					

*1: Member's first period of service on the committee.

*2: Member's second period of service on the committee.

Vacancies Filled:

Majority:

19th seat filled by Capito on Feb. 28, 2001.

Changes:

Majority:

English, Philip S.	Rep	Penn.	Apr. 27, 2001 Resigned committee; moved to Joint Economic.
Shuster, William	Rep	Penn.	June 7, 2001 Replaced English.

Minority:

Berkley, Shelley	Dem	Nev.	Feb. 7, 2001 Resigned committee; moved to International Relations.
Moore, Dennis	Dem	Kans.	Feb. 7, 2001 Resigned committee; moved to Budget.
McCarthy, Carolyn	Dem	N.Y.	Feb. 12, 2001 Leave of absence; moved to Budget.
Langevin, James R.	Dem	R.I.	Feb. 8, 2001 Replaced Berkley.
Hinojosa, Rubén	Dem	Tex.	Feb. 28, 2001 Resigned committee; moved to Financial Services.
Ross, Michael A.	Dem	Ark.	Feb. 28, 2001 Replaced Moore.
Carson, Brad	Dem	Okla.	Feb. 28, 2001 Replaced McCarthy.
Acevedo-Vilá, Aníbal	Dem	P.R.	Feb. 28, 2001 Replaced Hinojosa.

Departures from the House:

	Majority			Minority		
Lost Election to U.S. Senate	Thune, John R.	Rep	S.D.	None		
Defeated for Re-election	Grucci, Felix J. Jr.	Rep	N.Y.	Phelps, David D.	Dem	Ill.

Departures from Committee:

	Majority			Minority		
Moved to Agriculture	None			Udall, Mark	Dem	Colo.
Moved to Armed Services	LoBiondo, Frank A.	Rep	N.J.	None		
Moved to Budget	None			Baird, Brian	Dem	Wash.
Moved to Energy and Commerce	Ferguson, Michael	Rep	N.J.	None		
	Issa, Darrell E.	Rep	Cal.			
Moved to International Relations	Pence, Mike	Rep	Ind.	None		
Moved to Ways and Means	None			Jones, Stephanie Tubbs	Dem	Ohio
No new assignment	Hefley, Joel M.	Rep	Colo.	Carson, Brad	Dem	Okla.
				Ross, Michael A.	Dem	Ark.

SMALL BUSINESS / 108th Congress

Service Dates of Committee Chair: Jan. 8, 2003-Jan. 3, 2005

Service Dates of Majority Members: Jan. 28, 2003-Jan. 3, 2005

Service Dates of Ranking Member: Jan. 8, 2003-Jan. 3, 2005

Service Dates of Minority Members: Jan. 28, 2003-Jan. 3, 2005

Roster Filled: Majority with 19 members, Feb. 25, 2003; Minority with 17 members, Feb. 13, 2003

Majority						Minority				
				Terms in:						Terms in:
Rank Name	Party	State	House	Comm.		Rank Name	Party	State	House	Comm.
Chr Manzullo, Donald A.	Rep	Ill.	6	6		RM Velázquez, Nydia M.	Dem	N.Y.	6	6
2nd Combest, Larry E.	Rep	Tex.	10	*2 4		2nd Millender-McDonald, Juanita	Dem	Cal.	5	5
3rd Bartlett, Roscoe G.	Rep	Md.	6	5		3rd Davis, Danny K.	Dem	Ill.	4	*1 4
4th Kelly, Sue W.	Rep	N.Y.	5	5		4th Pascrell, William J. Jr.	Dem	N.J.	4	4
5th Chabot, Steven J.	Rep	Ohio	5	5		5th Christensen, Donna M.C.	Dem	V.I.	4	*1 4
6th Toomey, Patrick J.	Rep	Penn.	3	3		6th Brady, Robert A.	Dem	Penn.	4	4
7th DeMint, James W.	Rep	S.C.	3	3		7th Udall, Thomas	Dem	N.M.	3	3
8th Graves, Samuel B.	Rep	Mo.	2	2		8th Gonzalez, Charles A.	Dem	Tex.	3	*1 3
9th Schrock, Edward	Rep	Va.	2	2		9th Langevin, James R.	Dem	R.I.	2	2
10th Akin, W. Todd	Rep	Mo.	2	2		10th Ballance, Frank W. Jr.	Dem	N.C.	1	1
11th Capito, Shelley Moore	Rep	W.Va.	2	2		11th Ryan, Timothy J.	Dem	Ohio	1	1
12th Shuster, William	Rep	Penn.	2	2		12th Napolitano, Grace F.	Dem	Cal.	3	3
13th Musgrave, Marilyn N.	Rep	Colo.	1	1		13th Acevedo-Vilá, Aníbal	Dem	P.R.	2	2
14th Franks, Trent	Rep	Ariz.	1	1		14th Case, Ed	Dem	Hai.	1	1
15th Gerlach, Jim	Rep	Penn.	1	1		15th Bordallo, Madeleine Z.	Dem	Guam	1	1
16th Bradley, Jeb	Rep	N.H.	1	1		16th Marshall, Jim	Dem	Ga.	1	1
17th Beauprez, Bob	Rep	Colo.	1	1		17th Michaud, Michael H.	Dem	Me.	1	1
18th Chocola, Chris	Rep	Ind.	1	1						
19th King, Steve	Rep	Iowa	1	1						

*1: Member's first period of service on the committee.

*2: Member's second period of service on the committee.

Note: Territorial Delegates Donna M.C. Christensen (Dem-V.I.), Madeleine Z. Bordallo (Dem-Guam), and Eni F.H. Faleomavaega (Dem-Am.S.) and Resident Commissioner Anibal Acevedo-Vilá (Dem-P.R.) were allowed to accrue committee seniority but were not included in the party ratio.

Vacancies Filled:

Majority:

18th seat filled by Chocola on Feb. 11, 2003; 19th seat filled by King on Feb. 25, 2003.

Minority:

10th and 11th seats filled by Ballance and Ryan on Feb. 5, 2003; 12th through 17th seats filled by Napolitano, Acevedo-Vilá, Case, Bordallo, Marshall, and Michaud on Feb. 13, 2003.

Changes:

Majority:

Combest, Larry E.	Rep	Tex.	May 31, 2003 Resigned the House and retired.
McCotter, Thaddeus	Rep	Mich.	June 19, 2003 Replaced Combest.

Minority:

Pascrell, William J. Jr.	Dem	N.J.	Feb. 12, 2003 Resigned committee; moved to Select Homeland Security.
Langevin, James R.	Dem	R.I.	Feb. 12, 2003 Leave of absence; moved to Select Homeland Security; never returned.
Christensen, Donna M.C.	Dem	V.I.	Feb. 12, 2003 Leave of absence; moved to Select Homeland Security; returned on Feb. 26, 2003, ranked after Ryan in the 7th slot.
Davis, Danny K.	Dem	Ill.	Feb. 12, 2003 Resigned committee; had moved to Education and the Workforce; returned on Feb. 26, 2003, ranked after Christensen in the 8th slot.
Gonzalez, Charles A.	Dem	Tex.	Feb. 12, 2003 Leave of absence; moved to Select Homeland Security; returned on Feb. 26, 2003, ranked after Davis in the 9th slot.
Majette, Denise L.	Dem	Ga.	Feb. 26, 2003 Replaced Pascrell, ranked after Bordallo in the 14th slot.
Brady, Robert A.	Dem	Penn.	Feb. 27, 2003 Leave of absence; moved to House Administration; never returned.
Ryan, Timothy J.	Dem	Ohio	Mar. 4, 2003 Resigned committee; moved to Armed Services.
Faleomavaega, Eni F.H.	Dem	A.Sm.	Mar. 5, 2003 Replaced Langevin, ranked after Ballance in the 5th slot.
Sánchez, Linda	Dem	Cal.	Mar. 5, 2003 Replaced Brady.
Miller, Brad	Dem	N.C.	Apr. 30, 2003 Replaced Ryan.
Gonzalez, Charles A.	Dem	Tex.	Jan. 20, 2004 Resigned committee; moved to Energy and Commerce.
Ballance, Frank W. Jr.	Dem	N.C.	June 11, 2004 Resigned the House and retired; health issue.
Butterfield, George K. Jr.	Dem	N.C.	July 22, 2004 Replaced Gonzalez, ranked after Udall in the 4th slot.

Departures from the House:

	Majority			Minority		
Elected to U.S. Senate	DeMint, James W.	Rep	S.C.	None		
Elected Governor	None			Acevedo-Vilá, Aníbal	Dem	P.R.
Lost Election to U.S. Senate	None			Majette, Denise L.	Dem	Ga.
Lost Nomination to U.S. Senate	Toomey, Patrick J.	Rep	Penn.	None		
Retired	Schrock, Edward	Rep	Va.	None		

Departures from Committee:

	Majority			Minority		
Moved to Armed Services	None			Butterfield, George K. Jr.	Dem	N.C.
Moved to Judiciary	Franks, Trent	Rep	Ariz.	None		

Moved to Rules	Capito, Shelley Moore	Rep	W.Va.	None		
Moved to Ways and Means	Beauprez, Bob	Rep	Colo.	None		
	Chocola, Chris	Rep	Ind.			
No new assignment	Gerlach, Jim	Rep	Penn.	Napolitano, Grace F.	Dem	Cal.
				Marshall, Jim	Dem	Ga.
				Miller, Brad	Dem	N.C.

SMALL BUSINESS / 109th Congress

Service Dates of Committee Chair: Jan. 6, 2005-Jan. 3, 2007

Service Dates of Majority Members: Jan. 26, 2005-Jan. 3, 2007

Service Dates of Ranking Member: Jan. 6, 2005-Jan. 3, 2007

Service Dates of Minority Members: Jan. 26, 2005-Jan. 3, 2007

Roster Filled: Majority with 18 members, Feb. 2, 2005; Minority with 15 members, Feb. 16, 2005

Majority					**Minority**				
			Terms in:					**Terms in:**	
Rank Name	Party	State	House	Comm.	Rank Name	Party	State	House	Comm.
Chr Manzullo, Donald A.	Rep	Ill.	7	7	RM Velázquez, Nydia M.	Dem	N.Y.	7	7
2nd Bartlett, Roscoe G.	Rep	Md.	7	6	2nd Millender-McDonald, Juanita	Dem	Cal.	6	6
3rd Kelly, Sue W.	Rep	N.Y.	6	6	3rd Udall, Thomas	Dem	N.M.	4	4
4th Chabot, Steven J.	Rep	Ohio	6	6	4th Lipinski, Daniel	Dem	Ill.	1	1
5th Graves, Samuel B.	Rep	Mo.	3	3	5th Faleomavaega, Eni F.H.	Dem	A.Sm.	9	2
6th Akin, W. Todd	Rep	Mo.	3	3	6th Christensen, Donna M.C.	Dem	V.I.	5	*2 2
7th Shuster, William	Rep	Penn.	3	3	7th Davis, Danny K.	Dem	Ill.	5	*2 2
8th Musgrave, Marilyn N.	Rep	Colo.	2	2	8th Case, Ed	Dem	Hai.	2	2
9th Bradley, Jeb	Rep	N.H.	2	2	9th Bordallo, Madeleine Z.	Dem	Guam	2	2
10th King, Steve	Rep	Iowa	2	2	10th Grijalva, Raúl M.	Dem	Ariz.	2	1
11th McCotter, Thaddeus	Rep	Mich.	2	2	11th Michaud, Michael H.	Dem	Me.	2	2
12th Keller, Richard (Ric)	Rep	Fla.	3	1	12th Sánchez, Linda	Dem	Cal.	2	2
13th Poe, Ted	Rep	Tex.	1	1	13th Barrow, John	Dem	Ga.	1	1
14th Sodrel, Michael E.	Rep	Ind.	1	1	14th Bean, Melissa L.	Dem	Ill.	1	1
15th Fortenberry, Jeff	Rep	Neb.	1	1	15th Moore, Gwendolynne S.	Dem	Wisc.	1	1
16th Fitzpatrick, Michael G.	Rep	Penn.	1	1					
17th Westmoreland, Lynn A.	Rep	Ga.	1	1					
18th Gohmert, Louie	Rep	Tex.	1	1					

*2: Member's second period of service on the committee.

Note: Territorial Delegates Donna M.C. Christensen (Dem-V.I.), Madeleine Z. Bordallo (Dem-Guam), and Eni F.H. Faleomavaega (Dem-Am.S.) were allowed to accrue committee seniority but were not included in the party ratio.

Vacancies Filled:

Majority:

7th, 9th, and 12th seats filled by Shuster, Bradley, and Keller on Feb. 2, 2005.

Minority:

5th through 14th seats filled by Faleomavaega, Christensen, Davis, Case, Bordallo, Grijalva, Michaud, Sánchez, Barrow, and Bean on Feb. 2, 2005. 15th seat filled by Moore on Feb. 16, 2005.

Departures from the House:	**Majority**			**Minority**		
Lost Nomination to U.S. Senate	None			Case, Ed	Dem	Hai.
Defeated for Re-election	Kelly, Sue W.	Rep	N.Y.	None		
	Bradley, Jeb	Rep	N.H.			
	Sodrel, Michael E.	Rep	Ind.			
	Fitzpatrick, Michael G.	Rep	Penn.			

Departures from Committee:						
Moved to Appropriations	None			Udall, Thomas	Dem	N.M.
Moved to Education and Labor	None			Sánchez, Linda	Dem	Cal.
Moved to Energy and Commerce	None			Barrow, John	Dem	Ga.
Moved to Foreign Affairs	None			Sánchez, Linda	Dem	Cal.
Returned to Foreign Affairs	Manzullo, Donald A.	Rep	Ill.	None		
No new assignment	McCotter, Thaddeus	Rep	Mich.	Faleomavaega, Eni F.H.	Dem	A.Sm
	Keller, Richard (Ric)	Rep	Fla.	Christensen, Donna M.C.	Dem	V.I.
	Poe, Ted	Rep	Tex.	Davis, Danny K.	Dem	Ill.
				Bordallo, Madeleine Z.	Dem	Guam

SMALL BUSINESS / 110th Congress

Service Dates of Committee Chair: Jan. 4, 2007-Jan. 3, 2009

Service Dates of Majority Members: Jan. 23, 2007-Jan. 3, 2009

Service Dates of Minority Members: Jan. 10, 2007-Jan. 3, 2009

Roster Filled: Majority with 18 members, Jan. 23, 2007; Minority with 15 members, Jan. 10, 2007

Majority					Minority				
			Terms in:					Terms in:	
Rank Name	Party	State	House	Comm.	Rank Name	Party	State	House	Comm.
Chr Velázquez, Nydia M.	Dem	N.Y.	8	8	RM Chabot, Steven J.	Rep	Ohio	7	7
2nd Millender-McDonald, Juanita	Dem	Cal.	7	7	2nd Bartlett, Roscoe G.	Rep	Md.	8	7
3rd Jefferson, William J.	Dem	La.	9	1	3rd Graves, Samuel B.	Rep	Mo.	4	4
4th Shuler, Heath	Dem	N.C.	1	1	4th Akin, W. Todd	Rep	Mo.	4	4
5th Gonzalez, Charles A.	Dem	Tex.	5	*3 1	5th Shuster, William	Rep	Penn.	4	4
6th Larsen, Richard R. (Rick)	Dem	Wash.	4	1	6th Musgrave, Marilyn N.	Rep	Colo.	3	3
7th Grijalva, Raúl M.	Dem	Ariz.	3	2	7th King, Steve	Rep	Iowa	3	3
8th Michaud, Michael H.	Dem	Me.	3	3	8th Fortenberry, Jeff	Rep	Neb.	2	2
9th Bean, Melissa L.	Dem	Ill.	2	2	9th Westmoreland, Lynn A.	Rep	Ga.	2	2
10th Cuellar, Henry	Dem	Tex.	2	1	10th Gohmert, Louie	Rep	Tex.	2	2
11th Lipinski, Daniel	Dem	Ill.	2	2	11th Heller, Dean	Rep	Nev.	1	1
12th Moore, Gwendolynne S.	Dem	Wisc.	2	2	12th Davis, David	Rep	Tenn.	1	1
13th Altmire, Jason	Dem	Penn.	1	1	13th Fallin, Mary	Rep	Okla.	1	1
14th Braley, Bruce L.	Dem	Iowa	1	1	14th Buchanan, Vernon G.	Rep	Fla.	1	1
15th Clarke, Yvette D.	Dem	N.Y.	1	1	15th Jordan, Jim	Rep	Ohio	1	1
16th Ellsworth, Brad	Dem	Ind.	1	1					
17th Johnson, Hank	Dem	Ga.	1	1					
18th Sestak, Joe	Dem	Penn.	1	1					

*3: Member's third period of service on the committee.

Changes:

Majority:

Millender-McDonald, Juanita	Dem	Cal.	Apr. 22, 2007 Died in office.
Jefferson, William J.	Dem	La.	June 5, 2007 Leave of absence to address legal issues.
Higgins, Brian	Dem	N.Y.	Sept. 20, 2007 Replaced Millender-McDonald.
Hirono, Mazie K.	Dem	Hai.	Sept. 20, 2007 Replaced Jefferson.

Minority:

Heller, Dean	Rep	Nev.	Feb. 25, 2008 Resigned committee; moved to Financial Services.
Jordan, Jim	Rep	Ohio	Feb. 25, 2008 Resigned committee; moved to Budget.

Departures from the House:

	Majority			Minority		
Defeated for Re-election	None			Chabot, Steven J.	Rep	Ohio
				Musgrave, Marilyn N.	Rep	Colo.
Defeated for Re-nomination	None			Davis, David	Rep	Tenn.

Departures from Committee:

	Majority			Minority		
Moved to Budget	Larsen, Richard R. (Rick)	Dem	Wash.	None		
Moved to Energy and Commerce	Braley, Bruce L.	Dem	Iowa	None		
Moved to Judiciary	Gonzalez, Charles A.	Dem	Tex.	None		
Moved to Oversight and Government Reform	Cuellar, Henry	Dem	Tex.	Fortenberry, Jeff	Rep	Neb.
Moved to Ways and Means	Higgins, Brian	Dem	N.Y.	None		
No new assignment	Grijalva, Raúl M.	Dem	Ariz.	Shuster, William	Rep	Penn.
	Johnson, Hank	Dem	Ga.			
	Hirono, Mazie K.	Dem	Hai.			

SMALL BUSINESS / 111th Congress

Service Dates of Committee Chair: Jan. 6, 2009-Jan. 3, 2011

Service Dates of Majority Members: Jan. 21, 2009-Jan. 3, 2011

Service Dates of Ranking Member: Jan. 6, 2009-Jan. 3, 2011

Service Dates of Minority Members: Jan. 9, 2009-Jan. 3, 2011

Roster Filled: Majority with 17 members, Jan. 21, 2009; Minority with 12 members, Jan. 9, 2009

| | | | Majority | | | | | | | Minority | | |

				Terms in:								Terms in:	
Rank Name	Party	State	House	Comm.		Rank Name	Party	State	House	Comm.
Chr Velázquez, Nydia M.	Dem	N.Y.	9	9		RM Graves, Samuel B.	Rep	Mo.	5	5
2nd Moore, Gwendolynne S.	Dem	Wisc.	3	3		2nd Bartlett, Roscoe G.	Rep	Md.	9	8
3rd Shuler, Heath	Dem	N.C.	2	2		3rd Akin, W. Todd	Rep	Mo.	5	5
4th Dahlkemper, Kathleen A.	Dem	Penn.	1	1		4th King, Steve	Rep	Iowa	4	4
5th Schrader, Kurt	Dem	Ore.	1	1		5th Westmoreland, Lynn A.	Rep	Ga.	3	3
6th Kirkpatrick, Ann	Dem	Ariz.	1	1		6th Gohmert, Louie	Rep	Tex.	3	3
7th Nye, Glenn C. III	Dem	Va.	1	1		7th Fallin, Mary	Rep	Okla.	2	2
8th Michaud, Michael H.	Dem	Me.	4	4		8th Buchanan, Vernon G.	Rep	Fla.	2	2
9th Bean, Melissa L.	Dem	Ill.	3	3		9th Luetkemeyer, Blaine	Rep	Mo.	1	1
10th Lipinski, Daniel	Dem	Ill.	3	3		10th Schock, Aaron	Rep	Ill.	1	1
11th Altmire, Jason	Dem	Penn.	2	2		11th Thompson, Glenn	Rep	Penn.	1	1
12th Clarke, Yvette D.	Dem	N.Y.	2	2		12th Coffman, Michael	Rep	Colo.	1	1
13th Ellsworth, Brad	Dem	Ind.	2	2						
14th Sestak, Joe	Dem	Penn.	2	2						
15th Bright, Bobby Neal Sr.	Dem	Ala.	1	1						
16th Griffith, Parker	Dem	Ala.	1	1						
17th Halvorson, Deborah L.	Dem	Ill.	1	1						

Vacancies Filled:

Minority:

12th seat filled by Coffman on Feb. 4, 2009.

Changes:

Majority

Griffith, Parker   Dem   Ala.   Dec. 22, 2009 Service on committee as a Democrat vacated.

Standards of Official Conduct

House Committee on Standards of Official Conduct, 103rd-111th Congresses (1993-2011)

BACKGROUND

Organizational History: The House Committee on Standards of Official Conduct, sometimes known as the House ethics committee, investigates representatives charged with ethical misconduct, such as misuse of campaign funds, failure to disclose personal finances, or improper acceptance of gratuities. The committee then reports to the full House and in some cases recommends punishment, such as reprimand, censure, or in rare cases, expulsion from the House.

The Standards Committee was an outgrowth of congressional concern about two major scandals that erupted in 1966: the Adam Clayton Powell, Jr. (Dem-N.Y.) case in the House and the Thomas Dodd (Dem-Conn.) case in the Senate. Representative Powell, the chair of the House Committee on Education and Labor, was accused of failing to pay a court-imposed fine resulting from a slander case and of keeping his wife on the congressional payroll for years while she lived apart from him in Puerto Rico. Senator Dodd was accused of misusing campaign funds for his own personal purposes. The initial committee to establish ethical guidelines for House members was the Select Committee on Standards and Conduct established on October 19, 1966. It filed its final report (House Report 2338, 89-2) on December 27, 1966, and the stage was set for a major battle regarding Powell who had just been re-elected to his twelfth term.

Given the civil rights tensions of the 1960s, House Speaker John W. McCormack (Dem-Mass.) was reluctant to move too vigorously against Powell, the first African-American to be elected from the Northeast. On January 10, 1967, the House created the Special Committee on the Seating of Adam Clayton Powell in the 90th Congress and its nine members were chosen by McCormack. The committee recommended that Powell not be stripped of his membership but that he would lose his seniority and would have to make restitution to the House. The full House rejected the resolution on March 1, 1967, and Powell was excluded from membership in the 90th Congress by a vote of 307 to 116. Powell would later sue the House and in a Supreme Court decision, *Powell v. McCormack*, 395 U.S. 486 (1969), he was restored to the membership but not to his chairmanship. Within six weeks of Powell's exclusion, the House created the standing Committee on Standards of Official Conduct on April 13, 1967 (H.Res. 418). It was only the second standing committee created in the House since the 1946 reorganization, following the Science and Astronautics Committee.

In the beginning the committee was given a limited mission by the House: to write the Code of Official Conduct. Approved in 1968, the Code expanded the committee's responsibility, giving it authority to enforce the new rules. But the code was couched in general terms, and financial disclosure was confined to sources, not amounts, of income. The House and Senate revised their codes in 1977, and in 1978 Congress applied ethics codes to the entire federal government.

The Standards Committee's powers have been modified according to the *House Manual* (2008) as stated below:

However, legislative jurisdiction over measures relating to financial disclosure was transferred to the Committee on Rules in the 95th Congress (H. Res. 5, Jan. 4, 1977); legislative jurisdiction over measures relating to campaign contributions for candidates for the House was transferred to House Administration, and legislative jurisdiction over measures relating to lobbying activities was removed from the committee (thereby devolving on the Committee on the Judiciary) in the 94th Congress (H. Res. 5, Jan. 14, 1975).

In the 96th Congress (1979-1981) the committee was assigned the functions designated in title I of the Ethics in Government Act of 1978 (P.L. 95-521) relating to the administration of government ethics laws as they apply to members, officers, and employees of the House (H. Res. 5, Jan. 15, 1979, 7). However, according to the *Rules of the House of Representatives*, the committee is no longer responsible for financial disclosure measures; nor is it responsible for recommending legislative action to establish or enforce standards of official conduct, although it can still make administrative recommendations on standards of official conduct. Letters of reproval or administrative actions are only to be issued or implemented as part of the report of fact and recommendations made to the House at the end of its investigation. Investigative hearings of alleged violations of standards of conduct can now be waived. The committee retains the responsibility to report violations of law to Federal or State authorities and can issue advisory opinions on conduct requested by individuals. The committee also holds functions designated in titles I and V of the Ethics in Government Act of 1978 and sections 7342, 7351, and 7353 of title 5, U.S. Code.

In an effort at further codification of the guidelines in the *House Ethics Manual* (102d Cong., 2d Sess.), the House created a new Select Committee on Ethics in 1992. In the manual, the committee incorporated its advisory opinions together with advisory opinions issued by the former Select Committee on Ethics, in its discussions of various ethical issues, including gifts, outside income, financial disclosure, staff rights and duties, official allowances and franking, casework considerations, campaign financing and practices, and involvement with official and unofficial organizations.

Although the Standards Committee was given jurisdiction over roll call procedures, the 110th Congress (2007-2009) chose to bypass the committee in favor of creating the six-member Select Committee to Investigate the Voting Irregularities of August 2, 2007, to investigate a peculiar sequence of roll call votes on a motion to recommit an Appropriations bill dealing with agriculture and rural development that would have explicitly denied benefits to illegal immigrants.

The thanklessness of the committee's task is evident in the number of House scandals that have drawn public notice. While Adam Clayton Powell may have lost his seat in the House, he was not jailed, unlike other House members who were implicated in later scandals. In the 1970s, John V. Dowdy (Dem-Tex.), Bertram Podell (Dem-N.Y.), Andrew J. Hinshaw (Rep-Cal.), James F. Hastings (Rep-N.Y.), and Charles Diggs (Dem-Mich), chair of the District of Columbia Committee spent time in prison for various financial crimes. Six members were implicated in the "Koreagate" activities of lobbyist Tongsun Park in 1976; two were acquitted; three were reprimanded, but only Richard T. Hanna (Dem-Cal.) went to prison.

The "Abscam" bribery sting of 1980 with FBI agents posing as wealthy Arab businessmen resulted in Sen. Harrison A. Williams (Dem-N.J.) and five House members—House Administration Chair Frank Thompson (Dem-N.J.), Michael (Ozzie) Myers (Dem-Penn.), Raymond Lederer (Dem-Penn.), Richard Kelly (Rep-Fla.), and John Jenrette (Dem-S.C.) all sentenced to prison. Myers was expelled from Congress in 1980, the first House member to be expelled since the Civil War. Another Abscam victim, John M. Murphy (Dem-N.Y.), chair of Merchant Marine and Fisheries, lost his seat in the 1980 election but faced no further legal penalties. Tax evasion sent Frederick Richmond (Dem-N.Y.) to prison in 1982. Later in the decade, the Reagan Administration-linked Wedtech scandal implicated representatives Robert Garcia (Dem-N.Y.) and Mario Biaggi (Dem-N.Y.), a highly decorated former New York City police officer, who ran afoul of the law and were sentenced to prison.

The financial indiscretions of House Speaker Jim Wright (Dem-Tex.) and Majority Whip Anthony L. Coelho (Dem-Cal.) led to their 1989 resignations from the House. But it was the "Rubbergate" misuse of the House Bank in 1991-1992 for kiting checks by hundreds of members that exploded into public consciousness and paved the way for the Republican takeover in 1994. The Standards Committee singled out twenty-six individuals—four of whom were indicted and convicted, but only Donald E. (Buz) Lukens (Rep-Ohio) went to jail on a separate offense. Although smaller in scale, the House Post Office money laundering and embezzlement scam of 1992 led to the imprisonment of Ways and Means Chair Daniel Rostenkowski (Dem-Ill.) and Joseph Kolter (Dem-Penn.). House Speaker Newt Gingrich (Rep-Ga.) who led the ethics charges against Jim Wright in 1989 was himself censured and fined $300,000.00 for financial improprieties in 1997 and resigned the speakership in 1999.

The Standards Committee twice reprimanded Thomas D. DeLay (Rep-Tex.) when he was Majority Whip in 1999 and again in 2004 when he was Majority Leader for his quasi-legal vote pressuring techniques. The Standards Committee was poised to admonish DeLay a third time in October, 2004 after he was indicted in Texas for money laundering. House Speaker Denny Hastert (Rep-Ill.), a DeLay ally, sought to change Republican Conference rules regarding indictments to permit DeLay to remain as Leader even after his indictment. Fellow Republicans protested the change so Hastert relented but not before he removed three Republicans from the Standards Committee and terminated the chairmanship of Joel Hefley (Rep-Colo.), who had tired of DeLay's heavy-handedness. The new chair, Richard (Doc) Hastings (Rep-Wash.) chose not to further admonish DeLay, who was now obliged to surrender his leadership post and would later resign his House seat in 2006. DeLay and four of his associates were also linked to disgraced lobbyist Jack Abramoff whose influence peddling

scandal of 2006 led to the resignation and eventual imprisonment of House Administration Chair Robert Ney (Rep-Ohio).

James Traficant (Dem-Ohio) in 2002 was the first twenty-first-century member to be convicted and expelled from the House, while William Janklow (Rep-S.D.) was the first imprisoned for vehicular manslaughter. Two other recent members who have been imprisoned due to financial improprieties are William J. Jefferson (Dem-La.) and Randall (Duke) Cunningham (Rep-Cal.).

While inappropriate romantic scandals have implicated other members and led to formal reprimands and admonishments, none has yet to face prison time for their behavior. It is financial misbehavior that troubles the committee more. In the 111th Congress, the committee has been embroiled in dealing with allegations of financial misconduct by Charles Rangel (Dem-N.Y.), the chair of the Ways and Means Committee who defeated Adam Clayton Powell's renomination in 1970. Rangel stepped aside from the chair of Ways and Means on March 3, 2010.

Membership: The House Committee on Standards of Official Conduct had twelve members in its initial Congress in 1967—six Democrats and six Republicans. It is the only modern-era standing committee with an equal number of majority and minority members. The size grew to fourteen in 1981 with the party ratio remaining evenly split at 7-7. In 1995, the committee was reduced to ten—five majority members and five minority members—and has remained so to the present.

The conditions of membership on the Standards Committee are specified in the House Manual (2008) in Rule X.5.(a)(3)(A) that:

> The Committee on Standards of Official Conduct shall be composed of 10 members, five from the majority party and five from the minority party. (B) Except as permitted by subdivision (C), a member of the Committee on Standards of Official Conduct may not serve on the committee during more than three Congresses in a period of five successive Congresses (disregarding for this purpose any service for less than a full session in a Congress). (C) A member of the Committee on Standards of Official Conduct may serve on the committee during a fourth Congress in a period of five successive Congresses only as either the chairman or the ranking minority member of the committee.

The chair is from the majority party. It is not a popular committee among members because any person on the panel is in the awkward position of passing judgment on the behavior of colleagues. As a result, the Standards Committee is often the last to be filled in recent Congresses.

With a mean membership average of 10.44 over the past nine Congresses, 1993-2011, the Standards Committee is tied with the House Administration Committee for the distinction of being the House's smallest standing committees. Its mean seniority of 5.20 terms per member ranked it tenth—the mid-point among the nineteen continuing committees. Because of the House rules limiting the length of service and the thanklessness of many of the committee's responsibilities, its inter-Congress retention rate of 57.5 percent is the lowest among the standing committees.

Committee Leaders: In the twenty-two Congresses since the Standards of Official Conduct was first named in 1967, twenty-four different members have served in its top two leadership slots—eleven Democrats and thirteen

Republicans—the highest rate of leadership turnover on any House standing committee.

The first chair of Standards was a long-time member, twelve-termer C. Melvin Price (Dem-Ill.) who served as chair for eight years (1967-1975) until he became chair of Armed Services. Since then, turnover among its leaders, chairs and ranking members has been high. Former Minority Leader Charles A. Halleck (Rep-Ind.) was the committee's first ranking member. Halleck retired after one term and was replaced as ranking member by long-time Republican Whip Leslie C. Arends in 1969, who left the committee in July, 1969 to become ranking member on Armed Services. Arends was succeeded by Jackson E. Betts (Rep-Ohio) who served until his 1973 retirement and his successor James H, Quillen (Rep-Tenn.) served as ranking member for one term, 1973-1975, and then stepped aside to become ranking member on Rules. Floyd D. Spence (Rep-S.C.) became ranking member in 1975, the fifth different ranking member to serve with chair Melvin Price.

Price's successor as chair in 1975 was John J. Flynt, Jr. (Dem-Fla.), who chaired the committee until his 1979 retirement. Flynt had to preside over the 1976 "Koreagate" hearings in which some members, including Majority Whip John J. McFall (Dem-Cal.), were accused of accepting money and trips from the government of the Republic of Korea in exchange for favorable votes to that government. Flynt's successor Charles E. Bennett (Dem-Fla.) chaired the committee for one term (1979-1981) until he left for no new assignment. Bennett confronted the 1980 "Abscam" cases, in which seven members of the House were lured into taking bribes from FBI agents posing as Arab sheiks in search of congressional influence. It seems that chairs leave after being drained by acrimonious scandals.

Bennett was succeeded by Louis Stokes (Dem-Ohio), the first African-American to chair the committee and the younger brother of Carl Stokes, mayor of Cleveland, the first African-American mayor of a major city. Stokes's first served as chair from 1981 to 1985 and again from 1991 to 1993. Julian C. Dixon (Dem-Cal.) chaired Standards during that three-Congress interval (1985-1991). After Louis Stokes resumed the chair in 1991 he was handed the largest case ever of member misconduct, the check-writing practices of the House Bank and the staff misconduct in the House Post Office. Not surprisingly, Stokes left in 1993. Serving as ranking member for most of those years was Floyd D. Spence (Rep-S.C.) who held that post from 1975 until June, 1988, when he was succeeded by John T. Myers (Rep-Ind.), who served as ranking member from 1988 to 1991. Myers was succeeded in 1991 by James V. Hansen (Rep-Utah).

In 1993, two new leaders took over the Standards Committee—James A. McDermott (Dem-Wash.) as chair, and one-time television star of The Love Boat, Frederick Grandy (Rep-Iowa), as ranking member. (Grandy left the House to run unsuccessfully for the 1994 Republican gubernatorial nomination.) The Republican victory in 1994 placed Nancy L. Johnson (Rep-Conn.) in the chairmanship and made McDermott its ranking member. Both left those posts in 1997. Johnson's successor as chair was James V. Hansen, who had been ranking member in the 102nd Congress (1991-1993). Lamar S. Smith (Rep-Texas) succeeded Hansen in 1999 and served only one term, 1999-2001, and was then succeeded by Joel Hefley (Rep-Colo.), who served as chair for two terms, 2001-2005. Hefley's successor and the fifth Republican to chair the Standards Committee in six Congresses was Richard (Doc) Hastings (Rep-Wash.).

On the Democratic side, McDermott's successor as ranking member was Howard L. Berman (Dem-Cal.). Berman would serve as ranking member from 1997 to February, 2003, when he left the committee and was replaced by Alan B. Mollohan (Dem-W.Va.) on February 25, 2003, twenty days after he was first assigned to the committee. Mollohan served until 2009. The Democrats' recapture of the House in 2006 allowed Stephanie Tubbs-Jones (Dem-Ohio) to become chair and to place McDermott in the ranking member slot. Tubbs-Jones's death in August, 2008 led to R. Eugene Green (Dem-Texas) becoming chair for the remainder of the 110th Congress.

The 111th Congress opened in 2009 with a new chair, Zoe Lofgren (Dem-Cal.), and a new ranking member, Josiah R. (Jo) Bonner (Rep-Ala.).

Party Leaders: In spite of its small size and the reluctance of many members to serve on it, four House party leaders served on the Standards of Official Conduct Committee including two future Speakers of the House—Thomas S. Foley (Dem-Wash.) and Nancy Pelosi (Dem-Cal.), the present Speaker. Republican leaders such as former floor leader Charles A. Halleck of Indiana and long-time Whip Leslie C. Arends of Illinois served on the Standards Committee early in its existence and late in their careers. Richard B. Cheney (Rep-Wyo.), who would become Whip in 1989, passed through the committee in his freshman term, 1979-1981.

Notable Members: Richard B. Cheney is the only member of Standards to be elected vice president when he ran twice and was elected twice with George W. Bush in 2000 and 2004. He is also the only former member to serve as a Cabinet member—Secretary of Defense under George H.W. Bush. Committee member Robert J. Portman (Rep-Ohio) was named twice by President George W. Bush to Cabinet-level posts—U.S. Trade Representative and Director of the Office of Management and Budget. Porter Goss (Rep-Fla.), was another former member named to a high post in the Bush II administration—that of Director of Central Intelligence.

Seven U.S. senators served on Standards. Six were Republicans—Robert T. Stafford of Vermont, Thad Cochran of Mississippi, Larry E. Craig of Idaho, Hank Brown of Colorado, James P.D. Bunning of Kentucky, and Jon Kyl of Arizona and one was a Democrat—Benjamin L. Cardin of Maryland. The only governors with committee experience were Republicans Albert H. Quie of Minnesota, who was elected governor after leaving the House, and Robert T. Stafford of Vermont, who served in the House after leaving the governorship.

One other noteworthy member was Democrat Kweisi Mfume of Maryland who left the House to become Executive Director of the National Association for the Advancement of Colored People (NAACP).

Selected References

Amer, Mildred, *The House Committee on Standards of Official Conduct: A Brief History of Its Evolution and Jurisdiction*, Congressional Research Service Report for Congress, 92-686 (1992).

Beard, Edmund and Stephen Horn, *Congressional Ethics: The View from the House* (Washington, D.C.: The Brookings Institution, 1975).

Jacobson, Gary C. and Michael A. Dimock, "Checking Out: The Effects of Bank Overdrafts on the 1992 House Elections," *American Journal of Political Science,* 38 (August, 1994), 601-624.

Thompson, Dennis F., *Ethics in Congress: From Individual to Institutional Corruption* (Washington, D.C.: The Brookings Institution, 1995).

RESPONSIBILITIES AND JURISDICTIONAL CHANGES

STANDARDS OF OFFICIAL CONDUCT

Jurisdiction, 1967

Established by House Resolution 418, 90th Congress, First Session, April 3, 1967:

[Paragraph 2, Sections (a) through (c)]

(a) Measures relating to the Code of Official Conduct.

(b) Measures relating to financial disclosure by Members, officers, and employees of the House of Representatives.

(c) The committee is authorized—

(1) to recommend to the House of Representatives, from time to time, such legislative or administrative actions as the committee may deem appropriate to establish or enforce standards of official conduct for Members, officers, and employees of the House of Representatives;

(2) to investigate, subject to paragraph (d) of this clause, any alleged violation, by a Member, officer, or employee of the House of Representatives, of the Code of Official Conduct or of any law, rule, regulation, or other standard of conduct applicable to the conduct of such Member, officer, or employee in the performance of his duties or the discharge of his responsibilities and, after notice and a hearing, shall recommend to the House of Representatives, by resolution or otherwise, such action as the committee may deem appropriate in the circumstances;

(3) to report to the appropriate Federal or State authorities, with approval of the House of Representatives, any substantial evidence of a violation, by a Member, officer, or employee of the House of Representatives, of any law applicable to the performance of his duties or the discharge of his responsibilities, which may have been disclosed in a committee investigation; and

(4) to give consideration to the request of a Member, officer, or employee of the House of Representatives, for an advisory opinion with respect to the general propriety of any current or proposed conduct of such Member, officer, or employee and, with appropriate deletions to assure the privacy of the individual concerned, to publish such opinion for the guidance of other Members, officers, and employees of the House of Representatives.

Jurisdiction, 103rd Congress (1993-1995)

From the *Rules of the House of Representatives, 103rd Congress* (House Document 102-405)

[Rule X.1.(t)] Committee on Standards of Official Conduct

(1) Measures relating to the Code of Official Conduct.

In addition to its legislative jurisdiction under the preceding provision of this paragraph (and its general oversight function under clause 2(b)(1)), the committee shall have the functions with respect to recommendations, studies, investigations, and reports which are provided for in clause 4(e), and the functions designated in titles I and V of the Ethics in Government Act of 1978 and sections 7342, 7351 and 7353 of title 5, United States Code.

[Rule X.4.(e)(1)] The Committee on Standards of Official Conduct is authorized;

(A) to recommend to the House from time to time such administrative actions as it may deem appropriate to establish or enforce standards of official conduct for Members, officers, and employees of the House, and any letter or reproval or other administrative action of the committee pursuant to an investigation under subdivision (B) shall only be issued or implemented as a part of a report required by such subdivision;

(B) to investigate, subject to subparagraph (2) of this paragraph, any alleged violation, by a Member, officer, or employee of the House, of the Code of Official Conduct or of any law, rule, regulation, or other standard of conduct applicable to the conduct of such Member, officer, or employee in the performance of his duties or the discharge of his responsibilities, and after notice and hearing (unless the right to a hearing is waived by the Member, officer, or employee), shall report to the House its findings of fact and recommendations, if any, upon the final disposition of any such investigation, and such action as the committee may deem appropriate in the circumstances;

(C) to report to the appropriate Federal or State authorities, with the approval of the House, any substantial evidence of a violation, by a Member, officer, or employee of the House, of any law applicable to the performance of his duties or the discharge of his responsibilities, which may have been disclosed in a committee investigation;

(D) to give consideration to the request of any Member, officer, or employee of the House for an advisory opinion with respect to the general propriety of any current or proposed conduct of such Member, officer, or employee and, with appropriate deletions to assure the privacy of the individual concerned, to publish such opinion for the guidance of other Members, officers, and employees of the House; and

(E) to give consideration to the request of any Member, officer, or employee of the House for a written waiver in exceptional circumstances with respect to clause 4 of rule XLIII.

Jurisdiction, 104th Congress (1995-1997) Changes in Committee System

From H. Res. 6, Section 202 (a), the Committees and Their Jurisdiction, January 4, 1995

[Rule X.1.(p)] Committee on Standards of Official Conduct.
(1) Measures relating to the Code of Official Conduct.

In addition to its legislative jurisdiction under the preceding provision of this paragraph (and its general oversight function under clause 2(b)(1)), the committee shall have the functions with respect to recommendations, studies, investigations, and reports which are provided for in clause 4(e), and the functions designated in titles I and V of the Ethics in Government Act of 1978 and sections 7342, 7351, and 7353 of title 5, United States Code.

Jurisdiction, 111th Congress (2009-2011)

From the *Rules of the House of Representatives* (as revised to June 16, 2009, H.Doc. 110-162):

[Rule X.1.(q)] Committee on Standards of Official Conduct
The Code of Official Conduct.

[Rule X.3.(a)] Additional Duties

The Committee on Standards of Official Conduct has the following functions:
(1) The committee may recommend to the House from time to time such administrative actions as it may consider appropriate to establish or enforce standards of official conduct for Members, Delegates, the Resident Commisioner, officers, and employees of the House. A letter of reproval or other administrative action of the committee pursuant to an investigation under subparagraph (2) shall only be issued or implemented as a part of a report required by such subparagraph.
(2) The committee may investigate, subject to paragraph (b), an alleged violation by a Member, Delegate, Resident Commissioner, officer, or employee of the House of the Code of Official Conduct or of a law, rule, regulation or other standard of conduct applicable to the conduct of such Member, Delegate, Resident Commissioner, officer, or employee in the performance of duties or the discharge of the responsibilities of such individual. After notice and hearing (unless the right to a hearing is waived by the Member, Delegate, Resident Commissioner, officer, or employee), the committee shall report to the House its findings of fact and recommendations, if any, for the final disposition of any such investigation and such action as the committee may consider appropriate in the circumstances.
(3) The committee may report to the appropriate Federal or State authorities, either with the approval of the House or by an affirmative vote of two-thirds of the members of the committee, any substantial evidence of a violation by a Member, Delegate, Resident Commissioner, officer, or employee of the House, of a law applicable to the performance of the duties or the discharge of the responsibilites of such individual that may have been disclosed in a committee investigation.
(4) The committee may consider the request of a Member, Delegate, Resident Commissioner, officer, or employee of the House for an advisory opinion with respect to the general propriety of any current or proposed conduct of such Member, Delegate, Resident Commissioner, officer, or employee. With appropriate deletions to ensure the privacy of the person concerned, the committee mau publish such opinion for guidance of other Members, Delegates, the Resident Commissioner, officers, and employees of the House.
(5) The committee may consider the request of any Member, Delegate, Resident Commissioner, officer, or employee of the House for a written waiver in exceptional circumstances with respect to clause 4 of rule XXIII.

NO STANDARDS OF OFFICIAL CONDUCT SUBCOMMITTEES

103, 104, 105, 106, 107, 108, 109, 110, 111

MEMBERSHIP ROSTERS, 103rd-111th Congresses, 1993-2011

STANDARDS OF OFFICIAL CONDUCT / 103rd Congress

Service Dates of Committee Chair: Feb. 4, 1993-Jan. 3, 1995

Service Dates of Majority Members: Feb. 4, 1993-Jan. 3, 1995

Service Dates of Minority Members: Jan. 5, 1993-Jan. 3, 1995

Roster Filled: Majority with 7 members, Feb. 4, 1993; Minority with 7 members, Feb. 4, 1993

Majority						Minority				
			Terms in:						Terms in:	
Rank Name	Party	State	House	Comm.		Rank Name	Party	State	House	Comm.
Chr McDermott, James A.	Dem	Wash.	3	2		RM Grandy, Frederick L.	Rep	Iowa	4	3
2nd Darden, George W. (Buddy)	Dem	Ga.	6	2		2nd Johnson, Nancy L.	Rep	Conn.	6	2
3rd Cardin, Benjamin L.	Dem	Md.	4	2		3rd Bunning, James P.D.	Rep	Ky.	4	2
4th Pelosi, Nancy	Dem	Cal.	4	2		4th Kyl, Jon L.	Rep	Ariz.	4	2
5th Mfume, Kweisi	Dem	Md.	4	2		5th Goss, Porter J.	Rep	Fla.	3	2
6th Borski, Robert A.	Dem	Penn.	6	1		6th Hobson, David L.	Rep	Ohio	2	2
7th Sawyer, Thomas C.	Dem	Ohio	4	1		7th Schiff, Steven H.	Rep	N.M.	3	1

Vacancies Filled:
  Minority:
    7th seat filled by Schiff on Feb. 4, 1993.

Departures from the House:	Majority			Minority		
Elected to U.S. Senate	None			Kyl, Jon L.	Rep	Ariz.
Lost Nomination for Governor	None			Grandy, Frederick L.	Rep	Iowa
Defeated for Re-election	Darden, George W. (Buddy)	Dem	Ga.	None		

Departures from Committee:					
No new assignment	Mfume, Kweisi	Dem	Md.	None	

STANDARDS OF OFFICIAL CONDUCT / 104th Congress

Service Dates of Committee Chair: Jan. 20, 1995-Jan. 3, 1997

Service Dates of Majority Members: Jan. 20, 1995-Jan. 3, 1997

Service Dates of Minority Members: Jan. 20, 1995-Jan. 3, 1997

Roster Filled: Majority with 5 members, Jan. 20, 1995; Minority with 5 members, Jan. 20, 1995

Majority						Minority				
			Terms in:						Terms in:	
Rank Name	Party	State	House	Comm.		Rank Name	Party	State	House	Comm.
Chr Johnson, Nancy L.	Rep	Conn.	7	3		RM McDermott, James A.	Dem	Wash.	4	3
2nd Bunning, James P.D.	Rep	Ky.	5	3		2nd Cardin, Benjamin L.	Dem	Md.	5	3
3rd Goss, Porter J.	Rep	Fla.	4	3		3rd Pelosi, Nancy	Dem	Cal.	5	3
4th Hobson, David L.	Rep	Ohio	3	3		4th Borski, Robert A.	Dem	Penn.	7	2
5th Schiff, Steven H.	Rep	N.M.	4	2		5th Sawyer, Thomas C.	Dem	Ohio	5	2

Departures from Committee:	Majority			Minority		
Moved to Budget	None			McDermott, James A.	Dem	Wash.
				Cardin, Benjamin L.	Dem	Md.
Moved to Commerce	None			Sawyer, Thomas C.	Dem	Ohio
No new assignment	Johnson, Nancy L.	Rep	Conn.	Pelosi, Nancy	Dem	Cal.
	Bunning, James P.D.	Rep	Ky.	Borski, Robert A.	Dem	Penn.
	Goss, Porter J.	Rep	Fla.			
	Hobson, David L.	Rep	Ohio			
	Schiff, Steven H.	Rep	N.M.			

STANDARDS OF OFFICIAL CONDUCT / 105th Congress

Service Dates of Committee Chair: Jan. 7, 1997-Jan. 3, 1999

Service Dates of Majority Members: Sept. 29, 1997-Jan. 3, 1999

Service Dates of Ranking Member: Feb. 10, 1997-Jan. 3, 1999

Service Dates of Minority Members: Sept. 29, 1997-Jan. 3, 1999

Roster Filled: Majority with 5 members, Sept. 29, 1997; Minority with 5 members, Sept. 29, 1997

Majority						Minority				
			Terms in:						Terms in:	
Rank Name	Party	State	House	Comm.		Rank Name	Party	State	House	Comm.
Chr Hansen, James V.	Rep	Utah	9	*2 1		RM Berman, Howard L.	Dem	Cal.	8	1
2nd Smith, Lamar S.	Rep	Tex.	6	1 1		2nd Sabo, Martin Olav	DFL	Minn.	10	1

3rd Hefley, Joel M.	Rep	Colo.	6	1	3rd Pastor, Edward L.	Dem	Ariz.	4	1
4th Goodlatte, Robert W.	Rep	Va.	3	1	4th Fattah, Chaka	Dem	Penn.	2	1
5th Knollenberg, Joseph	Rep	Mich.	3	1	5th Lofgren, Zoe	Dem	Cal.	2	1

*2: Member's second period of service on the committee.

Departures from Committee:	Majority			Minority
Moved to Veterans' Affairs	Hansen, James V.	Rep	Utah	None
No new assignment	Goodlatte, Robert W.	Rep	Va.	None

STANDARDS OF OFFICIAL CONDUCT / 106th Congress

Service Dates of Committee Chair: Jan. 6, 1999-Jan. 3, 2001

Service Dates of Majority Members: Jan. 19, 1999-Jan. 3, 2001

Service Dates of Minority Members: Jan. 6, 1999-Jan. 3, 2001

Roster Filled: Majority with 5 members, Jan. 19, 1999; Minority with 5 members, Jan. 6, 1999

Majority					Minority				
			Terms in:					Terms in:	
Rank Name	Party	State	House	Comm.	Rank Name	Party	State	House	Comm.
Chr Smith, Lamar S.	Rep	Tex.	7	*1 2	RM Berman, Howard L.	Dem	Cal.	9	2
2nd Hefley, Joel M.	Rep	Colo.	7	2	2nd Sabo, Martin Olav	DFL	Minn.	11	2
3rd Knollenberg, Joseph	Rep	Mich.	4	2	3rd Pastor, Edward L.	Dem	Ariz.	5	2
4th Camp, David L.	Rep	Mich.	5	1	4th Fattah, Chaka	Dem	Penn.	3	2
5th Portman, Robert J.	Rep	Ohio	4	1	5th Lofgren, Zoe	Dem	Cal.	3	2

*1: Member's first period of service on the committee.

Note: Rankings were reordered on Feb. 23, 1999; Portman was originally ranked 4th and Camp was 5th.

Departures from Committee:	Majority			Minority		
Moved to Appropriations	None			Fattah, Chaka	Dem	Penn.
No new assignment	Smith, Lamar S.	Rep	Tex.	None		
	Knollenberg, Joseph	Rep	Mich.			
	Camp, David L.	Rep	Mich.			

STANDARDS OF OFFICIAL CONDUCT / 107th Congress

Service Dates of Committee Chair: Jan. 20, 2001-Jan. 3, 2003

Service Dates of Majority Members: Mar. 6, 2001-Jan. 3, 2003

Service Dates of Ranking Member: Jan. 20, 2001-Jan. 3, 2003

Service Dates of Minority Members: Mar. 6, 2001-Jan. 3, 2003

Roster Filled: Majority with 5 members, Mar. 6, 2001; Minority with 5 members, Mar. 14, 2001

Majority					Minority				
			Terms in:					Terms in:	
Rank Name	Party	State	House	Comm.	Rank Name	Party	State	House	Comm.
Chr Hefley, Joel M.	Rep	Colo.	8	3	RM Berman, Howard L.	Dem	Cal.	10	3
2nd Portman, Robert J.	Rep	Ohio	5	2	2nd Sabo, Martin Olav	DFL	Minn.	12	3
3rd Hastings, Richard (Doc)	Rep	Wash.	4	1	3rd Pastor, Edward L.	Dem	Ariz.	6	3
4th Hutchinson, Asa	Rep	Ark.	3	1	4th Lofgren, Zoe	Dem	Cal.	4	3
5th Biggert, Judith B.	Rep	Ill.	2	1	5th Jones, Stephanie Tubbs	Dem	Ohio	2	*1 1

*1: Member's first period of service on the committee.

Vacancies Filled:
5th minority seat filled by Stephanie Tubbs Jones on Mar. 14, 2001.

Changes:
Majority:

Portman, Robert J.	Rep	Ohio	June 29, 2001 Resigned committee; no new assignment.
Hulshof, Kenny	Rep	Mo.	July 11, 2001 Replaced Portman.
Hutchinson, Asa	Rep	Ark.	Aug. 6, 2001 Resigned the House; appointed Director of Drug Enforcement Administration.
LaTourette, Steven C.	Rep	Ohio	Oct. 10, 2001 Replaced Hutchinson.

Minority:

Sabo, Martin Olav	DFL	Minn.	July 31, 2001 Resigned committee; no new assignment.
Green, R. Eugene (Gene)	Dem	Tex.	Aug. 1, 2001 Replaced Sabo.

Departures from Committee:	Majority		Minority		
Moved to Select Homeland Security	None		Lofgren, Zoe	Dem	Cal.
Moved to Ways and Means	None		Jones, Stephanie Tubbs	Dem	Ohio
No new assignment	None		Pastor, Edward L.	Dem	Ariz.

STANDARDS OF OFFICIAL CONDUCT / 108th Congress

Service Dates of Committee Chair: Jan. 8, 2003-Jan. 3, 2005

Service Dates of Majority Members: Feb. 11, 2003-Jan. 3, 2005

Service Dates of Ranking Member: Jan. 8, 2003-Jan. 3, 2005

Service Dates of Minority Members: Mar. 6, 2003-Jan. 3, 2005

Roster Filled: Majority with 5 members, Feb. 11, 2003; Minority with 5 members, Mar. 6, 2003

Majority			Terms in:		Minority			Terms in:	
Rank Name	Party	State	House	Comm.	Rank Name	Party	State	House	Comm.
Chr Hefley, Joel M.	Rep	Colo.	9	4	RM1 Berman, Howard L.	Dem	Cal.	11	4
2nd Hastings, Richard (Doc)	Rep	Wash.	5	2	RM2 Mollohan, Alan B.	Dem	W.Va.	11	*2 1
3rd Biggert, Judith B.	Rep	Ill.	3	2	3rd Green, R. Eugene (Gene)	Dem	Tex.	6	2
4th Hulshof, Kenny	Rep	Mo.	4	2	4th Roybal-Allard, Lucille	Dem	Cal.	6	1
5th LaTourette, Steven C.	Rep	Ohio	5	2	5th Doyle, Michael F.	Dem	Penn.	5	1

*2: Member's second period of service on the committee.

Note: Mollohan was assigned on Feb. 5, 2003.

Changes:

Minority:

Berman, Howard L.	Dem	Cal.	Feb. 25, 2003 Resigned committee; no new assignment.
Mollohan, Alan B.	Dem	W.Va.	Feb. 25, 2003 Became Ranking Member.
Jones, Stephanie Tubbs	Dem	Ohio	Mar. 6, 2003 Replaced Berman, ranked after Mollohan.

Departures from Committee:	Majority			Minority
No new assignment	Hefley, Joel M.	Rep	Colo.	None
	Hulshof, Kenny	Rep	Mo.	
	LaTourette, Steven C.	Rep	Ohio	

STANDARDS OF OFFICIAL CONDUCT / 109th Congress

Service Dates of Committee Chair: Feb. 2, 2005-Jan. 3, 2007

Service Dates of Majority Members: Feb. 2, 2005-Jan. 3, 2007

Service Dates of Ranking Member: Jan. 26, 2005-Jan. 3, 2007

Service Dates of Minority Members: Feb. 9, 2005-Jan. 3, 2007

Roster Filled: Majority with 5 members, Feb. 2, 2005; Minority with 5 members, Feb. 9, 2005

Majority			Terms in:		Minority			Terms in:	
Rank Name	Party	State	House	Comm.	Rank Name	Party	State	House	Comm.
Chr Hastings, Richard (Doc)	Rep	Wash.	6	3	RM Mollohan, Alan B.	Dem	W.Va.	12	*2 2
2nd Biggert, Judith B.	Rep	Ill.	4	3	2nd Jones, Stephanie Tubbs	Dem	Ohio	4	*2 2
3rd Smith, Lamar S.	Rep	Tex.	10	*2 1	3rd Green, R. Eugene (Gene)	Dem	Tex.	7	3
4th Hart, Melissa A.	Rep	Penn.	3	1	4th Roybal-Allard, Lucille	Dem	Cal.	7	2
5th Cole, Tom	Rep	Okla.	2	1	5th Doyle, Michael F.	Dem	Penn.	6	2

*2: Member's second period of service on the committee.

Departures from the House:	Majority			Minority
Defeated for Re-election	Hart, Melissa A.	Rep	Penn.	None

Departures from Committee:

Became RM on Judiciary	Smith, Lamar S.	Rep	Tex.	None	
Returned to Armed Services	Cole, Tom	Rep	La.	None	
Returned to Natural Resources	Cole, Tom	Rep	La.	None	
No new assignment	Biggert, Judith B.	Rep	Ill.	Mollohan, Alan B.	Dem W.Va.

STANDARDS OF OFFICIAL CONDUCT / 110th Congress

Service Dates of Committee Ch1: Jan. 4, 2007-Aug. 20, 2008 Jones (Dem-Ohio)

Ch2: Sept. 9, 2008-Jan. 3, 2009 Green (Dem-Tex.)

Service Dates of Majority Members: Feb. 8, 2007-Jan. 3, 2009

Service Dates of Ranking Member: Jan. 4, 2007-Jan. 3, 2009

Service Dates of Minority Members: Feb. 12, 2007-Jan. 3, 2009

Roster Filled: Majority with 5 members, Feb. 8, 2007; Minority with 5 members, Feb. 12, 2007

Majority			Terms in:		Minority			Terms in:	
Rank Name	Party	State	House	Comm.	Rank Name	Party	State	House	Comm.
Ch1 Jones, Stephanie Tubbs	Dem	Ohio	5	*2 3	RM Hastings, Richard (Doc)	Rep	Wash.	7	4
Ch2 Green, R. Eugene (Gene)	Dem	Tex.	8	4	2nd Bonner, Josiah (Jo) R. Jr.	Rep	Ala.	3	1
3rd Roybal-Allard, Lucille	Dem	Cal.	8	3	3rd Barrett, J. Gresham	Rep	S.C.	3	1
4th Doyle, Michael F.	Dem	Penn.	7	3	4th Kline, John	Rep	Minn.	3	1
5th Delahunt, William D.	Dem	Mass.	6	1	5th McCaul, Michael T.	Rep	Tex.	2	1

*2: Member's second period of service on the committee.

Changes:

Majority:

Jones, Stephanie Tubbs	Dem	Ohio	Aug. 20, 2008 Died in office.
Green, R. Eugene (Gene)	Dem	Tex.	Sept. 9, 2008 Elected Chair.
Scott, Robert C.	Dem	Va.	Sept. 11, 2008 Replaced Jones.

Departures from Committee:

	Majority			Minority		
Returned to Natural Resources as RM	None			Hastings, Richard (Doc)	Rep	Wash.
No new assignment	Green, R. Eugene (Gene)	Dem	Tex.	McCaul, Michael T.	Rep	Tex.
	Roybal-Allard, Lucille	Dem	Cal.			
	Doyle, Michael F.	Dem	Penn.			
	Delahunt, William D.	Dem	Mass.			
	Scott, Robert C.	Dem	Va.			

STANDARDS OF OFFICIAL CONDUCT / 111th Congress

Service Dates of Committee Chair: Jan. 22, 2009-Jan. 3, 2011

Service Dates of Majority Members: Jan. 22, 2009-Jan. 3, 2011

Service Dates of Minority Members: Jan. 9, 2009-Jan. 3, 2011

Roster Filled: Majority with 3 members, Jan. 22, 2009; Minority with 3 members, Jan. 9, 2009

Majority			Terms in:		Minority			Terms in:	
Rank Name	Party	State	House	Comm.	Rank Name	Party	State	House	Comm.
Chr Lofgren, Zoe	Dem	Cal.	8	1	RM Bonner, Josiah (Jo) R. Jr.	Rep	Ala.	4	2
2nd Chandler, A.B. (Ben)	Dem	Ky.	4	1	2nd Barrett, J. Gresham	Rep	S.C.	4	2
3rd Butterfield, George K. Jr.	Dem	N.C.	4	1	3rd Kline, John	Rep	Minn.	4	2
4th Castor, Kathy	Dem	Fla.	2	1	4th Conaway, K. Michael	Rep	Tex.	3	1
5th Welch, Peter	Dem	Vt.	2	1	5th Dent, Charles W.	Rep	Penn.	3	1

Changes:

Minority:

Kline, John	Rep	Minn.	July 14, 2009 Resigned committee; had become Ranking Member on Education and Labor.
Harper, Gregg	Rep	Miss.	July 14, 2009 Replaced Kline.
Barrett, J. Gresham	Rep	S.C.	Sept. 24, 2009 Resigned committee; no new assignment.
McCaul, Michael T.	Rep	Tex.	Sept. 24, 2009 Replaced Barrett.

Transportation and Infrastructure

House Committee on Public Works and Transportation, 103rd Congress (1993-1995)

House Committee on Transportation and Infrastructure, 104th-111th Congresses (1995-2011)

BACKGROUND

Organizational History: The first House committee with jurisdiction over transportation matters was the Committee on Roads and Canals, established in 1831 by Charles F. Mercer, an Anti-Jacksonian from Virginia. It became Railways and Canals in 1869 and was folded into the Committee on Interstate and Foreign Commerce in 1927. However, the true predecessors of the Transportation and Infrastructure Committee were the four committees of the 79th Congress that were combined to create the standing Committee on Public Works in the 80th Congress. The four committees' names and their years of creation were: Public Buildings and Grounds (1837); Rivers and Harbors (1883); Roads (1913); and Flood Control (1916). These committees, most notably Rivers and Harbors were major sources of constituency benefits, and members desirous of long House careers sought them out.

Prior to the Legislative Reorganization Act of 1946, the four committees had a combined membership of eighty-nine Representatives (and three Delegates). Following the act, the committee had only twenty-seven Representatives (and no Delegates). Because membership on the four committees had a relatively high degree of overlapping, the number of members displaced by the reorganization was less than the numbers cited might indicate.

With the Committee Reform Amendments of 1974 (H. Res. 988, 93d Cong., Oct. 8, 1974) the committee's name was changed from Public Works to Public Works and Transportation in 1975, when it gained jurisdiction over a number of transportation matters including civil aviation, water transportation, and roads. This was a consequence of the jurisdictional reshuffling following the recommendations of the first Select Committee on Committees chaired by Richard W. Bolling (Dem-Mo.).

The Republican takeover of the Congress in 1995 led to another name change as it was renamed the House Committee on Transportation and Infrastructure. It was the major recipient of the legislative jurisdiction of the Merchant Marine and Fisheries Committee that did not survive the party control change in the House. As noted in the *House Manual* (2008):

> The 104th Congress changed the name of the Committee from Public Works and Transportation to Transportation and Infrastructure and expanded its jurisdiction by: adding subparagraphs (1), (6)-(8), (12), and (15) to reflect the transfer of those matters from the former Committee on Merchant Marine and Fisheries; adding subparagraph (4) and enlarging subparagraph (20) to reflect the transfer of those matters from the Committee on Energy and Commerce; and adding subparagraph (2) and inserting the reference to inland, coastal,

and ocean waters in subparagraph (14), as clarifying consolidations of formerly fractionalized subjects (sec. 202(a), H. Res. 6, Jan. 4, 1995, p. 464). Clerical and stylistic changes were effected when the House recodified its rules in the 106th Congress. The 106th Congress also adopted a substantive amendment to this provision deleting the prohibition against including a provision for a specific road in a bill providing for another specific road or in a general road bill (H. Res. 5, Jan. 6, 1999, 47).

For more than two centuries, the federal government has spent hundreds of billions of dollars building roads, airports, dams, and subways, and the House Public Works Committee has had a say in almost all of those decisions. Even the politics of tight federal budgets in the 1980s and 1990s did not dim the panel's enthusiasm for road building and channel dredging. Although less prestigious than some of the other committees, such as Ways and Means or Appropriations, Public Works has always been popular in the modern Congress with legislators eager to show concrete evidence of their work. When the committee is choosing special projects, those located in the districts of committee members usually receive top priority. The committee also was responsible for the aviation and trucking industries, and played a key role in ending regulation of airlines in 1978 and trucking in 1980.

During most of the post-1947 Congresses, the committee most responsible for regulation of the railroads was the Interstate and Foreign Commerce Committee that had purview over the Interstate Commerce Commission (ICC), the first federal regulatory agency created. The major focus of the ICC was on railroad rates and routes. Over the past two decades, the Commerce Committee moved into the areas of energy regulation and health concerns and regulation of the railroads slipped from its jurisdiction as Congress moved towards greater deregulation, starting with the Staggers Rail Act of 1980 (P.L. 96-448).

Although the Transportation Committee had regularly named subcommittees dealing with railroads, its formal jurisdiction as contained in Rule X.1 (q) at the start of the 104th Congress (1995-1997) specifically gave the committee authority over "(13) Related transportation regulatory agencies, except (A) the Interstate Commerce Commission as it relates to railroads; (B) Federal Railroad Administration; and (C) Amtrak." Later that year, the ICC was terminated (P.L. 104-88, 109 Stat. 803). This shifted congressional involvement from rate regulation to railroad construction and maintenance, matters better suited for the Transportation and Infrastructure Committee.

With one-sixth of the total House membership serving on the Transportation and Infrastructure Committee, it could be a major House player, much like Appropriations was for years during the time when committee loyalty trumped party loyalty on that committee. However, it appears that once the Transportation and Infrastructure Committee's junior members have diverted sufficient federal monies back to their districts ensuring their electoral safety, they move on to committees with larger policy agendas.

Membership: When Public Works was created in the 1946 Reorganization Act, it absorbed the jurisdictions of four committees—Flood Control, Public Buildings and Grounds, Rivers and Harbors, and Roads—with a combined membership of ninety-two. However, there would only be twenty-seven members on its 1947 incarnation. Because of its great potential for acquiring constituency-pleasing "pork," it has grown steadily over the last sixty years. It surpassed thirty members in the 84th Congress (1955-1957); forty members in the 93rd Congress (1973-1975) and reached fifty for the first time in 1983. In the 103rd Congress (1993-1995), the committee reached sixty-five. In 1997, now known as Transportation and Infrastructure, the committee had seventy-three members, the first congressional committee to go beyond the seventy-member mark. Since 1999, the committee has leveled off at seventy-five members, easily surpassing House Appropriations, the House's long-time leader in committee size. Needless to say, its mean membership size of 72.67 in the past nine Congresses, 1993-2011, is the highest ever recorded in congressional history.

On the two measures that reflect relative institutional prestige, the results are mixed. The Transportation and Infrastructure Committee ranked seventh in its inter-Congress membership retention rate—87.23 percent—but only thirteenth (4.52 terms) among the nineteen continuing committees regarding the mean seniority of its members.

Committee Leaders: Fourteen different members have chaired the committee since 1947. Two were defeated for renomination; one for re-election; and one, Glenn M. Anderson (Dem-Cal.), was demoted by the Democratic Caucus in 1991 in favor of Robert A. Roe (Dem-N.J.). Brooklyn's Charles A. Buckley (Dem-N.Y.) was its senior Democrat for fourteen years, 1951-1965, but even he could not fend off electoral defeat. These defeats raise questions about the reputed powers of the "pork barrel."

The first chair of the post-Reorganization Committee on Public Works was George A. Dondero (Rep-Mich.), who had been the last ranking member on Rivers and Harbors and he would serve as the committee's senior Republican from 1947 until his retirement in 1957. The committee's first ranking member was Joseph J. Mansfield (Dem-Texas), who had been the last chair of Rivers and Harbors. Mansfield's death in 1947 opened the ranking member slot to William M. Whittington (Dem-Miss.), the last chair of the Flood Control Committee who chaired the committee in the 81st Congress (1949-1951), and then retired in 1951. He was be succeeded as chair by Charles A. Buckley, who had come from Public Buildings and Grounds. Buckley was the Public Works Committee's longest serving senior Democrat, with twelve years as chair (1951-1953 and 1955-1965) and two years as ranking member (1953-1955). Buckley's service ended in 1964 with a defeat for renomination.

Dondero's initial replacement as ranking Republican was J. Harry McGregor (Rep-Ohio), who died in October, 1958. McGregor's successor was James C. Auchincloss (Rep-N.J.), who served as ranking member from 1959 to 1965, when he

retired. In 1965, the new senior members were George H. Fallon (Dem-Md.) as chair and William C. Cramer (Rep-Fla.) as ranking member. They served together from 1965 to 1971, when both met electoral defeat—Fallon for renomination and Cramer for election to the Senate.

The new leaders of the committee in 1971 were John A. Blatnik (Dem-Minn.) as chair and William H. Harsha, Jr. (Rep-Ohio) as ranking member. While Blatnik would resign and retire in 1974, Harsha remained as ranking member until he retired in 1981. Blatnik's successor was Robert E. Jones (Dem-Ala.) who chaired the newly renamed Committee on Public Works and Transportation for the 94th Congress and retired in 1977. Jones's successor was Harold T. (Biz) Johnson (Dem-Cal.) who would be defeated for re-election in 1980.

Once again, a Congress would begin with two new leaders of the committee with James J. Howard (Dem-N.J.) as chair and Don H. Clausen (Rep-Cal.) as ranking member. Clausen's election defeat in 1982 allowed M.G. (Gene) Snyder (Rep-Ky.) to assume the post of the committee's ranking member and to hold it until his 1987 retirement. Howard died in March, 1988 and Glenn M. Anderson (Dem-Cal.) became the new chair. He would serve with John Paul Hammerschmidt (Rep-Ark.) as ranking member. Hammerschmidt had held his Arkansas seat by defeating ambitious young Democrats, most notably, Bill Clinton in 1974. He retired in 1993. In the meantime, Anderson's difficulties in managing the Public Works Committee led to his overthrow in the December, 1990 Democratic Caucus by an overwhelming 100 to 152 vote. The second ballot between second-ranking Robert A. Roe (Dem-N.J.) and third-ranking Norman Y. Mineta (Dem-Cal.) was won by Roe 121 to 107. Roe retired in 1993 and Mineta got to chair the committee in the 103rd Congress (1993-1995).

With the convening of the Republican-controlled 104th Congress in 1995, the committee received a new name— Transportation and Infrastructure—and a new chair, E.G. (Bud) Shuster (Rep-Penn.), who had replaced Hammerschmidt as the committee's senior Republican in the previous Congress. Mineta had become ranking member but resigned from the House in October, 1995 and was succeeded as ranking member by James L. Oberstar (DFL-Minn.). Shuster and Oberstar served as the committee's two senior leaders until 2001, when Republican Conference rules obliged Shuster to step aside after three terms as chair and let Donald E. Young (Rep-Alas.) lead the committee for the next three Congresses, 2001-2007. Obestar remained as ranking member throughout those years and when Democrats regained control of the House in 2006, Oberstar finally became chair after eleven-plus years as the committee's ranking member. Oberstar's fifteen-plus years, 1995-2010, as the committee's senior Democrat bested the fourteen years of Charles Buckley, 1951-1965. Presently serving with Oberstar as the committee's ranking member since 2007 is John L. Mica (Rep-Fla.).

Party Leaders: Because of its large size and the opportunity to help fellow members with constituency requests for roads, bridges, and dams in their districts, the Public Works Committee and its latest incarnation, the Transportation and Infrastructure Committee has been a major source of recent House leaders, outpacing Ways and Means, the long-time previous source. Three of the four Speakers of the House who served from 1987 to 2007 were former members of the committee—Democrat James C. Wright Jr. of Texas and Republicans Newt L. Gingrich of Georgia and J. Dennis Hastert of Illinois. Wright and Gingrich had also served as their party's floor leaders, as had Republican Charles A. Halleck of Indiana, who joined the committee after the 1965 loss of his post to Gerald R. Ford Jr. (Rep-Mich.), who as whip had served on the committee prior to ousting Halleck. Republican Thomas DeLay of Texas served as both Majority Whip and Majority Leader in the post-1995 Republican House. Republican Roy Blunt of Missouri is another of the committee members to have served as party Whip. Three Democratic Whips served on the committee: John J. McFall of California and David J. Bonior of Michigan, and the Democratic takeover in 2007 gave the Majority Whip post to James E. Clyburn of South Carolina, its present occupant.

Notable Members: President Gerald R. Ford, Jr. (Rep-Mich.) is the most notable alumnus of the House Public Works Committee, but the only member to be chosen by a national nominating convention was Geraldine A. Ferraro (Dem-N.Y.), Walter Mondale's 1984 running mate and the first woman on a presidential ticket. Lynn M. Martin, George H.W. Bush's second Secretary of Labor was the first of the modern-era committee members to be named to the Cabinet. She has been joined by Norman Mineta (Dem-Cal.) the first Asian-American Cabinet member who served as Bill Clinton's Secretary of Commerce and George W. Bush's Secretary of Transportation, and by Ray LaHood, President Obama's Secretary of Transportation.

Fifteen U.S. senators saw early service on the Public Works Committee: eleven were Republicans including George H. Bender of Ohio, J. Glenn Beall of Maryland, Thad Cochran of Mississippi, James Abdnor and John R. Thune of South Dakota, James M. Inhofe of Oklahoma, Larry E. Craig of Idaho, Y. Timothy Hutchinson of Arkansas, James W. DeMint of South Carolina, David Vitter of Louisiana, and Johnny Isakson of Georgia and only four Democrats—John B. Breaux of Louisiana, Benjamin L. Cardin of Maryland, Maria E. Cantwell of Washington State, and Robert Menendez of New Jersey. Seven governors had prior service on the committee: four Democrats—Edwin W. Edwards and Charles E. (Buddy) Roemer of Louisiana, Robert E. Wise Jr., of West Virginia and John Baldacci of Maine; and three Republicans—Charles Thone of Nebraska, John G. Rowland of Connecticut, and C.L. (Butch) Otter of Idaho. New Mexico Democrat John J. Dempsey served on the predecessor Public Works Committee after serving as governor.

Two committee members whose post-House service was notable include Pete Peterson (Dem-Fla.), a Vietnam War combat veteran who was named by President Bill Clinton to be the first American Ambassador to Vietnam and C. Christopher Cox (Rep-Cal.) who was named to head the Securities and Exchanges Commission by President George W. Bush and had to preside over the Wall Street meltdown of 2008.

Selected References

Cooper, Kenneth J., "The House Freshman's First Choice," *Washington Post* (January 5, 1993), A13.

Evans, Diana, "Before the Roll Call: Interest Group Lobbying and Public Policy Outcomes in House Committees," *Political Research Quarterly*, 49 (1996), 287-304.

Evans, Diana, *Greasing the Wheels: Using Pork Barrel Projects to Build Majority Coalitions in Congress* (New York: Cambridge University Press, 2004).

Evans, Diana, "Policy and Pork: The Use of Pork Barrel Projects to Build Policy Coalitions in the House of Representatives," *American Journal of Political Science*, 38 (November, 1994), 894-917.

Ferejohn, John A., *Pork Barrel Politics: Rivers and Harbors Legislation, 1947-1968* (1974).

Krutz, Glen S., "New Issues, New Members: Committee Composition and the Transformation of Issue Agendas on the House Banking and Public Works Committees," in Frank R. Baumgartner and Bryan D. Jones, eds., *Policy Dynamics* (Chicago: University of Chicago Press, 2002).

Murphy, James T., "Political Parties and the Porkbarrel: Party Conflict and Cooperation in House Public Works Decision Making," *American Political Science Review*, 68 (March, 1974), 169-195.

Parker, Glenn R. and Suzanne R. Parker, *Factions in House Committees* (Knoxville: University of Tennessee Press, 1985).

Schamel, Charles E. et al., "Records of the Public Works Committee," *Guide to the Records of the United States House of Representatives at the National Archives: 1789-1989 Bicentennial Edition* (Washington, D.C.: National Archives and Records Administration,1989), 237-251.

U.S. House of Representatives, Public Works Committee, *1883 to Present: Structure and Function of the Committee on Public Works, U.S. House of Representatives*, House Committee Print 93-48, 93rd Congress, 2nd Session (1982).

RESPONSIBILITIES, JURISDICTIONAL CHANGES, AND SUBCOMMITTEES

PUBLIC WORKS

Jurisdiction, 80th Congress (1947-1949)

Established by the Legislative Reorganization Act of 1946:

[Section 121.(1)(o)] Committee on Public Works
  (1) Flood control and improvement of rivers and harbors.
  (2) Public works for the benefit of navigation, including bridges and dams (other than international bridges and dams).
  (3) Water power.
  (4) Oil and other pollution of navigable waters.
  (5) Public buildings and occupied or improved grounds of the United States generally.

(6)   Measures relating to the purchase of sites and construction of post offices, customhouses, Federal courthouses, and Government buildings within the District of Columbia.

(7)   Measures relating to the Capitol Building and the Senate and House Office Buildings.

(8)   Measures relating to the construction or reconstruction, maintenance, and care of the buildings and grounds of the Botanic Gardens, the Library of Congress, and the Smithsonian Institution.

(9)   Public reservations and parks within the District of Columbia, including Rock Creek Park and the Zoological Park.

(10) Measures relating to the construction or maintenance of roads and post roads, other than appropriations therefore; but it shall not be in order for any bill providing general legislation in relation to roads to contain any provision for any specific road, nor for any bill in relation to a specific road to embrace a provision in relation to any other specific road.

PUBLIC WORKS AND TRANSPORTATION

Public Works was renamed the Committee on Public Works and Transportation on January 5, 1975.

Jurisdiction, 103rd Congress (1993-1995)

From the *Rules of the House of Representatives, 103rd Congress* (House Document 102-405)

[Rule X.1.(p)] Committee on Public Works and Transportation

(1)   Flood control and improvement of rivers and harbors.

(2)   Measures relating to the Capitol Building and the Senate and House Office Buildings.

(3)   Measures relating to the construction or maintenance of roads and post roads, other than appropriations therefor; but it shall not be in order for any bill providing general legislation in relation to roads to contain any provision for any specific road, nor for any bill in relation to a specific road to embrace a provision in relation to any other specific road.

(4)   Measures relating to the construction or reconstruction, maintenance, and care of the buildings and grounds of the Botanic Gardens, the Library of Congress, and the Smithsonian Institution.

(5)   Measures relating to the purchase of sites and construction of post offices, customhouses, Federal courthouses, and Government buildings within the District of Columbia.

(6)   Oil and other pollution of navigable waters.

(7)   Public buildings and occupied or improved grounds of the United States generally.

(8)   Public works for the benefit of navigation, including bridges and dams (other than international bridges and dams).

(9)   Water power.

(10) Transportation, including civil aviation except railroads, railroad labor, and pensions.

(11) Roads and the safety thereof.

(12) Water transportation subject to the jurisdiction of the Interstate Commerce Commission.

(13) Related transportation regulatory agencies, except

   (A)   the Interstate Commerce Commission as it relates to railroads;

   (B)   Federal Railroad Administration; and

   (C)   Amtrak.

TRANSPORTATION AND INFRASTRUCTURE

Public Works and Transportation was renamed the Committee on Transportation and Infrastructure on January 4, 1995.

Jurisdiction, 104th Congress (1995-1997) Changes in Committee System

From H. Res. 6, Section 202 (a), the Committees and Their Jurisdiction, January 4, 1995

[Rule X.1.(q)] Committee on Transportation and Infrastructure.

(1)   Coast Guard, including lifesaving service, lighthouses, lightships, ocean derelicts, and the Coast Guard Academy.

(2)   Federal management of emergencies and natural disasters.

(3)   Flood control and improvement of rivers and harbors.

(4)   Inland waterways.

(5)   Inspection of merchant marine vessels, lights and signals, lifesaving equipment, and fire protection on such vessels.

(6)   Navigation and the laws relating thereto, including pilotage.

(7)   Registering and licensing of vessels and small boats.

(8)   Rules and international arrangements to prevent collisions at sea.

(9)   Measures relating to the Capitol Building and the Senate and House office buildings.

(10) Measures relating to the construction or maintenance of roads and post roads, other than appropriations therefor; but it shall not be in order for any bill providing general legislation in relation to roads to contain any provision for any specific road, nor for any bill in relation to a specific road to embrace a provision in relation to any other specific road.

(11) Measures relating to the construction or reconstruction, maintenance, and care of the buildings and grounds of the Botanic Gardens, the Library of Congress, and the Smithsonian Institution.

(12) Measures relating to merchant marine, except for national security aspects of merchant marine.
(13) Measures relating to the purchase of sites and construction of post offices, customhouses, Federal courthouses, and Government buildings within the District of Columbia.
(14) Oil and other pollution of navigable waters, including inland, coastal, and ocean waters.
(15) Marine affairs (including coastal zone management) as they relate to oil and other pollution of navigable waters.
(16) Public buildings and occupied or improved grounds of the United States generally.
(17) Public works for the benefit of navigation, including bridges and dams (other than international bridges and dams).
(18) Related transportation regulatory agencies.
(19) Roads and the safety thereof.
(20) Transportation, including civil aviation, railroads, water transportation, transportation safety (except automobile safety), transportation infrastructure, transportation labor, and railroad retirement and unemployment (except revenue measures related thereto).
(21) Water power.

Jurisdiction, 111th Congress (2009-2011)

From the *Rules of the House of Representatives* (as revised to June 16, 2009, H.Doc. 110-162):

[Rule X.1.(r)] Committee on Transportation and Infrastructure
(1) Coast Guard, including lifesaving service, lighthouses, lightships, ocean derelicts, and the Coast Guard Academy.
(2) Federal management of emergencies and natural disasters.
(3) Flood control and improvement of rivers and harbors.
(4) Inland waterways.
(5) Inspection of merchant marine vessels, lights and signals, lifesaving equipment, and fire protection on such vessels.
(6) Navigation and laws relating thereto, including pilotage.
(7) Registering and licensing of vessels and small boats.
(8) Rules and international arrangements to prevent collisions at sea.
(9) The Capitol Building and the Senate and House Office Buildings.
(10) Construction or maintenance of roads and post roads (other than appropriations therefor).
(11) Construction or reconstruction, maintenance, and care of buildings and grounds of the Botanic Garden, the Library of Congress, and the Smithsonian Institution.
(12) Merchant marine (except for national security aspects thereof).
(13) Purchase of sites and construction of post offices, customhouses, Federal courthouses, and Government buildings within the District of Columbia.
(14) Oil and other pollution of navigable waters, including inland, coastal, and ocean waters.
(15) Marine affairs, including coastal zone management, as they relate to oil and other pollution of navigable waters.
(16) Public buildings and occupied or improved grounds of the United States generally.
(17) Public works for the benefit of navigation, including bridges and dams (other than international bridges and dams).
(18) Related transportation regulatory agencies (except the Transportation Security Administration).
(19) Roads and the safety thereof.
(20) Transportation, including civil aviation, railroads, water transportation, transportation safety (except automobile safety and transportation security, functions of the Department of Homeland Security), transportation infrastructure, transportation labor, and railroad retirement and unemployment (except revenue measures related thereto).
(21) Water power.

NAMES OF TRANSPORTATION AND INFRASTRUCTURE SUBCOMMITTEES FROM THE *CONGRESSIONAL DIRECTORY*

Public Works and Transportation, 103rd Congress
Aviation, 103 Economic Development, 103
Investigations and Oversight, 103 Public Buildings and Grounds, 103
Surface Transportation, 103 Water Resources and Environment, 103

Transportation and Infrastructure, 104th-111th Congresses
Aviation, 104, 105, 106, 107, 108, 109, 110, 111
Coast Guard and Maritime Transportation, 104, 105, 106, 107, 108, 109, 110, 111
Public Buildings and Economic Development, 104, 105
Economic Development, Public Buildings, Hazardous Materials, and Pipeline Transportation, 106
Economic Development, Public Buildings, and Emergency Management, 107, 108, 109, 110, 111
Highways and Transit, 107, 110, 111 Highways, Transit, and Pipelines, 108, 109
Oversight, Investigations, and Emergency Management, 106 Railroads, 104, 105, 107, 108, 109
Railroads, Pipelines, and Hazardous Materials, 110, 111 Ground Transportation, 106
Surface Transportation, 104, 105
Water Resources and Environment, 104, 105, 106, 107, 108, 109, 110, 111

MEMBERSHIP ROSTERS, 103rd-111th Congresses, 1993-2011

PUBLIC WORKS AND TRANSPORTATION / 103rd Congress

Service Dates of Committee Chair: Jan. 5, 1993-Jan. 3, 1995

Service Dates of Majority Members: Jan. 5, 1993-Jan. 3, 1995

Service Dates of Minority Members: Jan. 5, 1993-Jan. 3, 1995

Roster Filled: Majority with 39 members, Jan. 5, 1993; Minority with 24 members, Jan. 5, 1993.

Majority

Rank Name	Party	State	Terms in: House	Terms in: Comm.
Chr Mineta, Norman Y.	Dem	Cal.	10	10
2nd Oberstar, James L.	DFL	Minn.	10	10
3rd Rahall, Nick Joe II	Dem	W.Va.	9	9
4th Applegate, Douglas	Dem	Ohio	9	9
5th de Lugo, Ron	Dem	V.I.	9	7
6th Borski, Robert A.	Dem	Penn.	6	6
7th Valentine, I.T. (Tim) Jr.	Dem	N.C.	6	6
8th Lipinski, William O.	Dem	Ill.	6	6
9th Wise, Robert E. Jr.	Dem	W.Va.	6	*2 1
10th Traficant, James A. Jr.	Dem	Ohio	5	5
11th DeFazio, Peter A.	Dem	Ore.	4	4
12th Hayes, James A.	Dem	La.	4	4
13th Clement, Robert N.	Dem	Tenn.	4	4
14th Costello, Jerry F.	Dem	Ill.	4	4
15th Parker, Michael	Dem	Miss.	3	3
16th Laughlin, Gregory H.	Dem	Tex.	3	3
17th Geren, Preston M. (Pete)	Dem	Tex.	3	*1 3
18th Sangmeister, George E.	Dem	Ill.	3	3
19th Poshard, Glenn	Dem	Ill.	3	2
20th Swett, Richard	Dem	N.H.	2	2
21st Cramer, Robert E. (Bud) Jr.	Dem	Ala.	2	2
22nd Collins, Barbara-Rose	Dem	Mich.	2	2
23rd Norton, Eleanor Holmes	Dem	D.C.	2	2
24th Blackwell, Lucien E.	Dem	Penn.	2	2
25th Nadler, Jerrold	Dem	N.Y.	2	1
26th Coppersmith, Samuel G.	Dem	Ariz.	1	1
27th Byrne, Leslie L.	Dem	Va.	1	1
28th Cantwell, Maria E.	Dem	Wash.	1	1
29th Danner, Patsy A. (Pat)	Dem	Mo.	1	1
30th Shepherd, Karen	Dem	Utah	1	1
31st Menendez, Robert	Dem	N.J.	1	1
32nd Clyburn, James E.	Dem	S.C.	1	1
33rd Brown, Corrine	Dem	Fla.	1	1
34th Deal, J. Nathan	Dem	Ga.	1	1
35th Barcia, James A.	Dem	Mich.	1	1
36th Hamburg, Daniel	Dem	Cal.	1	1
37th Filner, Robert	Dem	Cal.	1	1
38th Tucker, Walter R.	Dem	Cal.	1	1
39th Johnson, Eddie Bernice	Dem	Tex.	1	1

Minority

Rank Name	Party	State	Terms in: House	Terms in: Comm.
RM Shuster, E.G. (Bud)	Rep	Penn.	11	11
2nd Clinger, William F. Jr.	Rep	Penn.	8	8
3rd Petri, Thomas E.	Rep	Wisc.	8	6
4th Boehlert, Sherwood L.	Rep	N.Y.	6	5
5th Inhofe, James M.	Rep	Okla.	4	4
6th Emerson, N. William	Rep	Mo.	7	4
7th Duncan, John J. (Jimmy) Jr.	Rep	Tenn.	4	3
8th Molinari, Susan	Rep	N.Y.	3	3
9th Zeliff, William H. Jr.	Rep	N.H.	2	2
10th Ewing, Thomas W.	Rep	Ill.	2	2
11th Gilchrest, Wayne T.	Rep	Md.	2	1
12th Dunn, Jennifer B.	Rep	Wash.	1	1
13th Hutchinson, Y. Timothy	Rep	Ark.	1	1
14th Baker, William P.	Rep	Cal.	1	1
15th Collins, Michael A. (Mac)	Rep	Ga.	1	1
16th Kim, Jay C.	Rep	Cal.	1	1
17th Levy, David A.	Rep	N.Y.	1	1
18th Horn, J. Steven	Rep	Cal.	1	1
19th Franks, Robert D.	Rep	N.J.	1	1
20th Blute, Peter I.	Rep	Mass.	1	1
21st McKeon, Howard P. (Buck)	Rep	Cal.	1	1
22nd Mica, John L.	Rep	Fla.	1	1
23rd Hoekstra, Peter	Rep	Mich.	1	*1 1
24th Quinn, John F. (Jack)	Rep	N.Y.	1	1

*1: Member's first period of service on the committee.

*2: Member's second period of service on the committee.

Note: Delegate Eleanor Holmes Norton (Dem-D.C.) was allowed to accrue committee seniority but was not included in the party ratio.

Additions:

Majority:

40th Barca, Peter W.	Dem	Wisc.	June 23, 1993

Minority:

25th Ehlers, Vernon J.	Rep	Mich.	Feb. 2, 1994

Changes:

Minority:

Inhofe, James M.	Rep	Okla.	Nov. 15, 1994 Resigned the House; elected to Senate.

Departures from the House:

	Majority			Minority		
Lost Election to U.S. Senate	Coppersmith, Samuel G.	Dem	Ariz.	None		
Defeated for Re-nomination	Blackwell, Lucien E.	Dem	Penn.	Levy, David A.	Rep	N.Y.
Defeated for Re-election	Swett, Richard	Dem	N.H.	None		

	Byrne, Leslie L.	Dem	Va.
	Cantwell, Maria E.	Dem	Wash.
	Shepherd, Karen	Dem	Utah
	Hamburg, Daniel	Dem	Cal.
	Barca, Peter W.	Dem	Wisc.
Retired	Applegate, Douglas	Dem	Ohio	None
	de Lugo, Ron	Dem	V.I.
	Valentine, I.T. (Tim) Jr.	Dem	N.C.
	Sangmeister, George E.	Dem	Ill.

Departures from Committee:

Moved to Budget	None			Hoekstra, Peter	Rep	Mich.
Moved to National Security	None			McKeon, Howard P. (Buck)	Rep	Cal.
Moved to Ways and Means	None			Dunn, Jennifer B.	Rep	Wash.
				Collins, Michael A. (Mac)	Rep	Ga.
No new assignment	Geren, Preston M. (Pete)	Dem	Tex.	None		

TRANSPORTATION AND INFRASTRUCTURE / 104th Congress

Service Dates of Committee Chair: Jan. 4, 1995-Jan. 3, 1997

Service Dates of Majority Members: Jan. 4, 1995-Jan. 3, 1997

Service Dates of Minority Members: Jan. 4, 1995-Jan. 3, 1997

Roster Filled: Majority with 33 members, Jan. 4, 1995; Minority with 28 members, Jan. 4, 1995

Majority					Minority				
			Terms in:					**Terms in:**	
Rank Name	Party	State	House	Comm.	Rank Name	Party	State	House	Comm.
Chr Shuster, E.G. (Bud)	Rep	Penn.	12	12	RM1 Mineta, Norman Y.	Dem	Cal.	11	11
2nd Young, Donald E.	Rep	Alas.	12	1	RM2 Oberstar, James L.	DFL	Minn.	11	11
3rd Clinger, William F. Jr.	Rep	Penn.	9	9	3rd Rahall, Nick Joe II	Dem	W.Va.	10	10
4th Petri, Thomas E.	Rep	Wisc.	9	7	4th Borski, Robert A.	Dem	Penn.	7	7
5th Boehlert, Sherwood L.	Rep	N.Y.	7	6	5th Lipinski, William O.	Dem	Ill.	7	7
6th Bateman, Herbert H.	Rep	Va.	7	1	6th Wise, Robert E. Jr.	Dem	W.Va.	7	*2 2
7th Emerson, N. William	Rep	Mo.	8	5	7th Traficant, James A. Jr.	Dem	Ohio	6	6
8th Coble, Howard	Rep	N.C.	6	1	8th DeFazio, Peter A.	Dem	Ore.	5	5
9th Duncan, John J. (Jimmy) Jr.	Rep	Tenn.	5	4	9th Hayes, James A.	Dem	La.	5	5
10th Molinari, Susan	Rep	N.Y.	4	4	10th Clement, Robert N.	Dem	Tenn.	5	5
11th Zeliff, William H. Jr.	Rep	N.H.	3	3	11th Costello, Jerry F.	Dem	Ill.	5	5
12th Ewing, Thomas W.	Rep	Ill.	3	3	12th Parker, Michael	Dem	Miss.	4	4
13th Gilchrest, Wayne T.	Rep	Md.	3	2	13th Laughlin, Gregory H.	Dem	Tex.	4	4
14th Hutchinson, Y. Timothy	Rep	Ark.	2	2	14th Poshard, Glenn	Dem	Ill.	4	3
15th Baker, William P.	Rep	Cal.	2	2	15th Cramer, Robert E. (Bud) Jr.	Dem	Ala.	3	3
16th Kim, Jay C.	Rep	Cal.	2	2	16th Collins, Barbara-Rose	Dem	Mich.	3	3
17th Horn, J. Steven	Rep	Cal.	2	2	17th Norton, Eleanor Holmes	Dem	D.C.	3	3
18th Franks, Robert D.	Rep	N.J.	2	2	18th Nadler, Jerrold	Dem	N.Y.	3	2
19th Blute, Peter I.	Rep	Mass.	2	2	19th Danner, Patsy A. (Pat)	Dem	Mo.	2	2
20th Mica, John L.	Rep	Fla.	2	2	20th Menendez, Robert	Dem	N.J.	2	2
21st Quinn, John F. (Jack)	Rep	N.Y.	2	2	21st Clyburn, James E.	Dem	S.C.	2	2
22nd Fowler, Tillie K.	Rep	Fla.	2	1	22nd Brown, Corrine	Dem	Fla.	2	2
23rd Ehlers, Vernon J.	Rep	Mich.	2	2	23rd Deal, J. Nathan	Dem	Ga.	2	2
24th Bachus, Spencer T.	Rep	Ala.	2	1	24th Barcia, James A.	Dem	Mich.	2	2
25th Weller, Gerald C.	Rep	Ill.	1	1	25th Filner, Robert	Dem	Cal.	2	2
26th Wamp, Zachary P.	Rep	Tenn.	1	1	26th Tucker, Walter R.	Dem	Cal.	2	2
27th Latham, Thomas	Rep	Iowa	1	1	27th Johnson, Eddie Bernice	Dem	Tex.	2	2
28th LaTourette, Steven C.	Rep	Ohio	1	1	28th Brewster, William K.	Dem	Okla.	3	*2 1
29th Seastrand, Andrea	Rep	Cal.	1	1					
30th Tate, Randy J.	Rep	Wash.	1	1					
31st Kelly, Sue W.	Rep	N.Y.	1	1					
32nd LaHood, Ray H.	Rep	Ill.	1	1					
33rd Martini, William J.	Rep	N.J.	1	1					

*2: Member's second period of service on the committee.

Note: Delegate Eleanor Holmes Norton (Dem-D.C.) was allowed to accrue committee seniority but was not included in the party ratio.

Additions:
  Majority:

34th Tiahrt, Todd	Rep	Kans.	June 25, 1996
35th Baker, Richard H.	Rep	La.	June 26, 1996

Minority:

29th Cummings, Elijah E.	Dem	Md.	Apr. 25, 1996	

Changes:

Majority:

Emerson, N. William	Rep	Mo.	June 22, 1996 Died in office.
Frisa, Daniel	Rep	N.Y.	June 25, 1996 Replaced Emerson.

Minority:

Deal, J. Nathan	Dem	Ga.	May 10, 1995 Assignment was vacated as a Democrat; moved to Commerce as a Republican on May 25, 1995.
McCarthy, Karen	Dem	Mo.	June 13, 1995 Replaced Deal.
Laughlin, Gregory H.	Dem	Tex.	June 30, 1995 Assignment was vacated as a Democrat; moved to Ways and Means as a Republican on July 10, 1995.
Mascara, Frank R.	Dem	Penn.	July 12, 1995 Replaced Laughlin.
Mineta, Norman Y.	Dem	Cal.	Oct. 10, 1995 Resigned the House and retired.
Oberstar, James L.	DFL	Minn.	Oct. 10, 1995 Succeeded Mineta as Ranking Member.
Parker, Michael	Dem	Miss.	Nov. 15, 1995 Assignment was vacated as a Democrat; moved to Appropriations as a Republican on Mar. 14, 1996.
Geren, Preston M. (Pete)	Dem	Tex.	Nov. 20, 1995 Replaced Mineta, ranked after Costello.
Hayes, James A.	Dem	La.	Dec. 12, 1995 Assignment was vacated as a Democrat; moved to Ways and Means as a Republican on Jan. 25, 1996.
Tucker, Walter R.	Dem	Cal.	Dec. 15, 1995 Resigned the House and retired; ethics issue.
Sawyer, Thomas C.	Dem	Ohio	Feb. 28, 1996 Replaced Parker.
Taylor, G. Eugene (Gene)	Dem	Miss.	Feb. 28, 1996 Replaced Hayes.
Millender-McDonald, Juanita	Dem	Cal.	Apr. 22, 1996 Replaced Tucker.

Departures from the House:

	Majority			Minority		
Elected to U.S. Senate	Hutchinson, Y. Timothy	Rep	Ark.	None		
Lost Nomination for Governor	Zeliff, William H. Jr.	Rep	N.H.	None		
Defeated for Re-nomination	None			Collins, Barbara-Rose	Dem	Mich.
Defeated for Re-election	Baker, William P.	Rep	Cal.	None		
	Blute, Peter I.	Rep	Mass.			
	Seastrand, Andrea	Rep	Cal.			
	Tate, Randy J.	Rep	Wash.			
	Martini, William J.	Rep	N.J.			
	Frisa, Daniel	Rep	N.Y.			
Retired	Clinger, William F. Jr.	Rep	Penn.	Brewster, William K.	Dem	La.
				Geren, Preston M. (Pete)	Dem	Tex.

Departures from Committee:

	Majority			Minority		
Moved to Appropriations	Wamp, Zachary P.	Rep	Tenn.	None		
	Latham, Thomas	Rep	Iowa			
	Tiahrt, Todd	Rep	Kans.			
Moved to Commerce	None			Sawyer, Thomas C.	Dem	Ohio
				McCarthy, Karen	Dem	Mo.
Moved to Ways and Means	Weller, Gerald C.	Rep	Ill.	None		

TRANSPORTATION AND INFRASTRUCTURE / 105th Congress

Service Dates of Committee Chair: Jan. 7, 1997-Jan. 3, 1999

Service Dates of Majority Members: Jan. 7, 1997-Jan. 3, 1999

Service Dates of Minority Members: Jan. 7, 1997-Jan. 3, 1999

Roster Filled: Majority with 40 members, Feb. 26, 1997; Minority with 33 members, Apr. 17, 1997

Majority			Terms in:		Minority			Terms in:	
Rank Name	Party	State	House	Comm.	Rank Name	Party	State	House	Comm.
Chr Shuster, E.G. (Bud)	Rep	Penn.	13	13	RM Oberstar, James L.	DFL	Minn.	12	12
2nd Young, Donald E.	Rep	Alas.	13	2	2nd Rahall, Nick Joe II	Dem	W.Va.	11	11
3rd Petri, Thomas E.	Rep	Wisc.	10	8	3rd Borski, Robert A.	Dem	Penn.	8	8
4th Boehlert, Sherwood L.	Rep	N.Y.	8	7	4th Lipinski, William O.	Dem	Ill.	8	8
5th Bateman, Herbert H.	Rep	Va.	8	2	5th Wise, Robert E. Jr.	Dem	W.Va.	8	*2 3
6th Coble, Howard	Rep	N.C.	7	2	6th Traficant, James A. Jr.	Dem	Ohio	7	7
7th Duncan, John J. (Jimmy) Jr.	Rep	Tenn.	6	5	7th DeFazio, Peter A.	Dem	Ore.	6	6
8th Molinari, Susan	Rep	N.Y.	5	5	8th Clement, Robert N.	Dem	Tenn.	6	6
9th Ewing, Thomas W.	Rep	Ill.	4	4	9th Costello, Jerry F.	Dem	Ill.	6	6

10th Gilchrest, Wayne T.	Rep	Md.	4	3		10th Poshard, Glenn	Dem	Ill.	5	4
11th Kim, Jay C.	Rep	Cal.	3	3		11th Cramer, Robert E. (Bud) Jr.	Dem	Ala.	4	4
12th Horn, J. Steven	Rep	Cal.	3	3		12th Norton, Eleanor Holmes	Dem	D.C.	4	4
13th Franks, Robert D.	Rep	N.J.	3	3		13th Nadler, Jerrold	Dem	N.Y.	4	3
14th Mica, John L.	Rep	Fla.	3	3		14th Danner, Patsy A. (Pat)	Dem	Mo.	3	3
15th Quinn, John F. (Jack)	Rep	N.Y.	3	3		15th Menendez, Robert	Dem	N.J.	3	3
16th Fowler, Tillie K.	Rep	Fla.	3	2		16th Clyburn, James E.	Dem	S.C.	3	3
17th Ehlers, Vernon J.	Rep	Mich.	3	3		17th Brown, Corrine	Dem	Fla.	3	3
18th Bachus, Spencer T.	Rep	Ala.	3	2		18th Barcia, James A.	Dem	Mich.	3	3
19th LaTourette, Steven C.	Rep	Ohio	2	2		19th Filner, Robert	Dem	Cal.	3	3
20th Kelly, Sue W.	Rep	N.Y.	2	2		20th Johnson, Eddie Bernice	Dem	Tex.	3	3
21st LaHood, Ray H.	Rep	Ill.	2	2		21st Mascara, Frank R.	Dem	Penn.	2	2
22nd Baker, Richard H.	Rep	La.	6	2		22nd Taylor, G. Eugene (Gene)	Dem	Miss.	5	2
23rd Riggs, Frank D.	Rep	Cal.	3	*2 1		23rd Millender-McDonald, Juanita	Dem	Cal.	2	2
24th Bass, Charles F.	Rep	N.H.	2	1		24th Cummings, Elijah E.	Dem	Md.	2	2
25th Ney, Robert W.	Rep	Ohio	2	*1 1		25th Sandlin, Max A.	Dem	Tex.	1	1
26th Metcalf, Jack	Rep	Wash.	2	1		26th Tauscher, Ellen O.	Dem	Cal.	1	1
27th Emerson, Jo Ann	Rep	Mo.	2	1		27th Pascrell, William J. Jr.	Dem	N.J.	1	1
28th Pease, Edward A.	Rep	Ind.	1	1		28th Johnson, Jay W.	Dem	Wisc.	1	1
29th Blunt, Roy	Rep	Mo.	1	1		29th Boswell, Leonard L.	Dem	Iowa	1	1
30th Pitts, Joseph R.	Rep	Penn.	1	1		30th McGovern, James P.	Dem	Mass.	1	1
31st Hutchinson, Asa	Rep	Ark.	1	1		31st Blumenauer, Earl	Dem	Ore.	2	1
32nd Cook, Merrill	Rep	Utah	1	1		32nd Holden, T. Timothy	Dem	Penn.	3	1
33rd Cooksey, John	Rep	La.	1	1		33rd Lampson, Nicholas V.	Dem	Tex.	1	*1 1
34th Thune, John R.	Rep	S.D.	1	1						
35th Pickering, Charles W. (Chip) Jr.	Rep	Miss.	1	1						
36th Granger, Kay	Rep	Tex.	1	1						
37th Fox, Jon D.	Rep	Penn.	2	1						
38th Davis, Thomas M. III	Rep	Va.	2	1						
39th LoBiondo, Frank A.	Rep	N.J.	2	1						
40th Watts, Julius C. Jr.	Rep	Okla.	2	1						

*1: Member's first period of service on the committee.

*2: Member's second period of service on the committee.

Vacancies Filled:

Majority:

37th through 40th seats filled by Davis, LoBiondo, and Watts on Feb. 26, 1997.

Minority:

31st seat filled by Blumenauer on Mar. 6, 1997; 32nd and 33rd seats filled by Holden and Lampson on Apr. 17, 1997.

Note: Delegate Eleanor Holmes Norton (Dem-D.C.) was allowed to accrue committee seniority but was not included in the party ratio.

Additions:

Majority:

41st Moran, Jerry	Rep	Kans.	Aug. 1, 1997

Minority:

34th Berry, R. Marion	Dem	Ark.	Mar. 27, 1998

Changes:

Majority:

Molinari, Susan	Rep	N.Y.	Aug. 2, 1997 Resigned the House to work for CBS News.
Fossella, Vito J.	Rep	N.Y.	Nov. 12, 1997 Replaced Molinari.

Minority:

Cramer, Robert E. (Bud) Jr.	Dem	Ala.	Nov. 7, 1997 Resigned committee; moved to Appropriations.
Baldacci, John E.	Dem	Me.	Mar. 27, 1998 Replaced Cramer.

Departures from the House:

	Majority			Minority		
Lost Election for Governor	None			Poshard, Glenn	Dem	Ill.
Defeated for Re-election	Fox, Jon D.	Rep	Penn.	Johnson, Jay W.	Dem	Wisc.
Defeated for Re-nomination	Kim, Jay C.	Rep	Cal.	None		
Retired	Riggs, Frank D.	Rep	Cal.	None		

Departures from Committee:

Moved to Appropriations	Emerson, Jo Ann	Rep	Mo.	Clyburn, James E.	Dem	S.C.
	Granger, Kay	Rep	Tex.			
Moved to Armed Services	Pitts, Joseph R.	Rep	Penn.			
Moved to Commerce	Blunt, Roy	Rep	Mo.	None		
	Pickering, Charles W. (Chip) Jr.	Rep	Miss.			
	Fossella, Vito J.	Rep	N.Y.			
No new assignment	Davis, Thomas M. III	Rep	Va.			

TRANSPORTATION AND INFRASTRUCTURE / 106th Congress

Service Dates of Committee Chair: Jan. 6, 1999-Jan. 3, 2001

Service Dates of Majority Members: Jan. 6, 1999-Jan. 3, 2001

Service Dates of Minority Members: Jan. 6, 1999-Jan. 3, 2001

Roster Filled: Majority with 41 members, Mar. 2, 1999; Minority with 34 members, Jan. 6, 1999

	Majority			Terms in:			Minority			Terms in:	
Rank Name		Party	State	House	Comm.	Rank Name		Party	State	House	Comm.
Chr Shuster, E.G. (Bud)		Rep	Penn.	14	14	RM Oberstar, James L.		DFL	Minn.	13	13
2nd Young, Donald E.		Rep	Ala.	14	3	2nd Rahall, Nick Joe II		Dem	W.Va.	12	12
3rd Petri, Thomas E.		Rep	Wisc.	11	9	3rd Borski, Robert A.		Dem	Penn.	9	9
4th Boehlert, Sherwood L.		Rep	N.Y.	9	8	4th Lipinski, William O.		Dem	Ill.	9	9
5th Bateman, Herbert H.		Rep	Va.	9	3	5th Wise, Robert E. Jr.		Dem	W.Va.	9	*2 4
6th Coble, Howard		Rep	N.C.	8	3	6th Traficant, James A. Jr.		Dem	Ohio	8	8
7th Duncan, John J. (Jimmy) Jr.		Rep	Tenn.	7	6	7th DeFazio, Peter A.		Dem	Ore.	7	7
8th Ewing, Thomas W.		Rep	Ill.	5	5	8th Clement, Robert N.		Dem	Tenn.	7	7
9th Gilchrest, Wayne T.		Rep	Md.	5	4	9th Costello, Jerry F.		Dem	Ill.	7	7
10th Horn, J. Steven		Rep	Cal.	4	4	10th Norton, Eleanor Holmes		Dem	D.C.	5	5
11th Franks, Robert D.		Rep	N.J.	4	4	11th Nadler, Jerrold		Dem	N.Y.	5	4
12th Mica, John L.		Rep	Fla.	4	4	12th Danner, Patsy A. (Pat)		Dem	Mo.	4	4
13th Quinn, John F. (Jack)		Rep	N.Y.	4	4	13th Menendez, Robert		Dem	N.J.	4	4
14th Fowler, Tillie K.		Rep	Fla.	4	3	14th Brown, Corrine		Dem	Fla.	4	4
15th Ehlers, Vernon J.		Rep	Mich.	4	4	15th Barcia, James A.		Dem	Mich.	4	4
16th Bachus, Spencer T.		Rep	Ala.	4	3	16th Filner, Robert		Dem	Cal.	4	4
17th LaTourette, Steven C.		Rep	Ohio	3	3	17th Johnson, Eddie Bernice		Dem	Tex.	4	4
18th Kelly, Sue W.		Rep	N.Y.	3	3	18th Mascara, Frank R.		Dem	Penn.	3	3
19th LaHood, Ray H.		Rep	Ill.	3	3	19th Taylor, G. Eugene (Gene)		Dem	Miss.	6	3
20th Baker, Richard H.		Rep	La.	7	3	20th Millender-McDonald, Juanita		Dem	Cal.	3	3
21st Bass, Charles F.		Rep	N.H.	3	2	21st Cummings, Elijah E.		Dem	Md.	3	3
22nd Ney, Robert W.		Rep	Ohio	3	*1 2	22nd Blumenauer, Earl		Dem	Ore.	3	2
23rd Metcalf, Jack		Rep	Wash.	3	2	23rd Sandlin, Max A.		Dem	Tex.	2	2
24th Pease, Edward A.		Rep	Ind.	2	2	24th Tauscher, Ellen O.		Dem	Cal.	2	2
25th Hutchinson, Asa		Rep	Ark.	2	2	25th Pascrell, William J. Jr.		Dem	N.J.	2	2
26th Cook, Merrill		Rep	Utah	2	2	26th Boswell, Leonard L.		Dem	Iowa	2	2
27th Cooksey, John		Rep	La.	2	2	27th McGovern, James P.		Dem	Mass.	2	2
28th Thune, John R.		Rep	S.D.	2	2	28th Holden, T. Timothy		Dem	Penn.	4	2
29th LoBiondo, Frank A.		Rep	N.J.	3	2	29th Lampson, Nicholas V.		Dem	Tex.	2	*1 2
30th Watts, Julius C. Jr.		Rep	Okla.	3	2	30th Baldacci, John E.		Dem	Me.	3	2
31st Moran, Jerry		Rep	Kans.	2	2	31st Berry, R. Marion		Dem	Ark.	2	2
32nd Doolittle, John T.		Rep	Cal.	5	1	32nd Shows, C. Ronald		Dem	Miss.	1	1
33rd Terry, Lee R.		Rep	Nebr.	1	1	33rd Baird, Brian		Dem	Wash.	1	1
34th Sherwood, Don		Rep	Penn.	1	1	34th Berkley, Shelley		Dem	Nev.	1	1
35th Miller, Gary G.		Rep	Cal.	1	*1 1						
36th Sweeney, John E.		Rep	N.Y.	1	1						
37th DeMint, James W.		Rep	S.C.	1	1						
38th Bereuter, Douglas K.		Rep	Nebr.	11	1						
39th Kuykendall, Steven T.		Rep	Cal.	1	1						
40th Simpson, Michael K.		Rep	Ida.	1	1						
41st Isakson, Johnny		Rep	Ga.	1	1						

*1: Member's first period of service on the committee.

*2: Member's second period of service on the committee.

Vacancies Filled:

Majority:

38th through 40th seats filled by Bereuter, Kuykendall, and Simpson on Feb. 2, 1999; 41st seat filled by Isakson on Mar. 2, 1999.

Changes:

Majority:

Watts, Julius C. Jr.	Rep	Okla.	June 25, 1999 Resigned to open seat for Vitter; no new assignment.
Vitter, David	Rep	La.	June 25, 1999 Replaced Watts.
Bateman, Herbert H.	Rep	Va.	Sept. 11, 2000 Died in office.
Martinez, Matthew G.	Rep	Cal.	Oct. 3, 2000 Replaced Bateman.

Departures from the House:

	Majority			Minority		
Elected Governor	None			Wise, Robert F. Jr.	Dem	W.Va.
Lost Nomination to U.S. Senate	Franks, Robert D.	Rep	N.J.	None		
Defeated for Re-nomination	Cook, Merrill	Rep	Utah	Martinez, Matthew G.	Dem	Cal.

Defeated for Re-election	Kuykendall, Steven T.	Rep	Cal.	None		
Retired	Ewing, Thomas W.	Rep	Ill.	Danner, Patsy A. (Pat)	Dem	Mo.
	Fowler, Tillie K.	Rep	Fla.			
	Metcalf, Jack	Rep	Wash.			
	Pease, Edward A.	Rep	Ind.			

Departures from Committee:

Moved to Appropriations	LaHood, Ray H.	Rep	Ill.	None		
	Doolittle, John T.	Rep	Cal.			
	Sweeney, John E.	Rep	N.Y.			
	Vitter, David	Rep	La.			
Moved to Agriculture	None			Shows, C. Ronald	Dem	Miss.
Moved to Energy and Commerce	Terry, Lee R.	Rep	Neb.	None		
Moved to Financial Services	Miller, Gary G.	Rep	Cal.	Shows, C. Ronald	Dem	Miss.
Moved to House Administration	Doolittle, John T.	Rep	Cal.	None		
Unassigned pending ethics investigation	None			Traficant, James A. Jr.	Dem	Ohio

TRANSPORTATION AND INFRASTRUCTURE / 107th Congress

Service Dates of Committee Chair: Jan. 6, 2001-Jan. 3, 2003

Service Dates of Majority Members: Jan. 6, 2001-Jan. 3, 2003

Service Dates of Minority Members: Jan. 31, 2001-Jan. 3, 2003

Roster Filled: Majority with 41 members, Feb. 8, 2001; Minority with 34 members, Jan. 31, 2001

Majority

Rank Name	Party	State	Terms in: House	Terms in: Comm.
Chr Young, Donald E.	Rep	Ala.	15	4
2nd Shuster, E.G. (Bud)	Rep	Penn.	15	15
3rd Petri, Thomas E.	Rep	Wisc.	12	10
4th Boehlert, Sherwood L.	Rep	N.Y.	10	9
5th Coble, Howard	Rep	N.C.	9	4
6th Duncan, John J. (Jimmy) Jr.	Rep	Tenn.	8	7
7th Gilchrest, Wayne T.	Rep	Md.	6	5
8th Horn, J. Steven	Rep	Cal.	5	5
9th Mica, John L.	Rep	Fla.	5	5
10th Quinn, John F. (Jack)	Rep	N.Y.	5	5
11th Ehlers, Vernon J.	Rep	Mich.	5	5
12th Bachus, Spencer T.	Rep	Ala.	5	4
13th LaTourette, Steven C.	Rep	Ohio	4	4
14th Kelly, Sue W.	Rep	N.Y.	4	4
15th Baker, Richard H.	Rep	La.	8	4
16th Bass, Charles F.	Rep	N.H.	4	3
17th Ney, Robert W.	Rep	Ohio	4	*1 3
18th Hutchinson, Asa	Rep	Ark.	3	3
19th Cooksey, John	Rep	La.	3	3
20th Thune, John R.	Rep	S.D.	3	3
21st LoBiondo, Frank A.	Rep	N.J.	4	3
22nd Moran, Jerry	Rep	Kans.	3	3
23rd Sherwood, Don	Rep	Penn.	2	2
24th DeMint, James W.	Rep	S.C.	2	2
25th Bereuter, Douglas K.	Rep	Nebr.	12	2
26th Simpson, Michael K.	Rep	Ida.	2	2
27th Isakson, Johnny	Rep	Ga.	2	2
28th Simmons, Robert	Rep	Conn.	1	1
29th Rogers, Mike	Rep	Mich.	1	1
30th Capito, Shelley Moore	Rep	W.Va.	1	*1 1
31st Kirk, Mark S.	Rep	Ill.	1	1
32nd Brown, Henry E. Jr.	Rep	S.C.	1	1
33rd Johnson, Timothy V.	Rep	Ill.	1	1
34th Kerns, Brian D.	Rep	Ind.	1	1
35th Rehberg, Dennis	Rep	Mont.	1	1
36th Platts, Todd R.	Rep	Penn.	1	1
37th Ferguson, Michael	Rep	N.J.	1	1
38th Graves, Samuel B.	Rep	Mo.	1	1
39th Otter, C.L. (Butch)	Rep	Ida.	1	1

Minority

Rank Name	Party	State	Terms in: House	Terms in: Comm.
RM Oberstar, James L.	DFL	Minn.	14	14
2nd Rahall, Nick Joe II	Dem	W.Va.	13	13
3rd Borski, Robert A.	Dem	Penn.	10	10
4th Lipinski, William O.	Dem	Ill.	10	10
5th DeFazio, Peter A.	Dem	Ore.	8	8
6th Clement, Robert N.	Dem	Tenn.	8	8
7th Costello, Jerry F.	Dem	Ill.	8	8
8th Norton, Eleanor Holmes	Dem	D.C.	6	6
9th Nadler, Jerrold	Dem	N.Y.	6	5
10th Menendez, Robert	Dem	N.J.	5	5
11th Brown, Corrine	Dem	Fla.	5	5
12th Barcia, James A.	Dem	Mich.	5	5
13th Filner, Robert	Dem	Cal.	5	5
14th Johnson, Eddie Bernice	Dem	Tex.	5	5
15th Mascara, Frank R.	Dem	Penn.	4	4
16th Taylor, G. Eugene (Gene)	Dem	Miss.	7	4
17th Millender-McDonald, Juanita	Dem	Cal.	4	4
18th Cummings, Elijah E.	Dem	Md.	4	4
19th Blumenauer, Earl	Dem	Ore.	4	3
20th Sandlin, Max A.	Dem	Tex.	3	3
21st Tauscher, Ellen O.	Dem	Cal.	3	3
22nd Pascrell, William J. Jr.	Dem	N.J.	3	3
23rd Boswell, Leonard L.	Dem	Iowa	3	3
24th McGovern, James P.	Dem	Mass.	3	3
25th Holden, T. Timothy	Dem	Penn.	5	3
26th Lampson, Nicholas V.	Dem	Tex.	3	*1 3
27th Baldacci, John E.	Dem	Me.	4	3
28th Berry, R. Marion	Dem	Ark.	3	3
29th Baird, Brian	Dem	Wash.	2	2
30th Berkley, Shelley	Dem	Nev.	2	2
31st Carson, Brad	Dem	Okla.	1	1
32nd Matheson, James D.	Dem	Utah	1	1
33rd Honda, Michael M.	Dem	Cal.	1	1
34th Larsen, Richard R. (Rick)	Dem	Wash.	1	1

*1: Member's first period of service on the committee.

| 40th Kennedy, Mark | Rep | Minn. | 1 | 1 |
| 41st Pombo, Richard W. | Rep | Cal. | 5 | 1 |

Note: Delegate Eleanor Holmes Norton (Dem-D.C.) was allowed to accrue committee seniority but was not included in the party ratio.

Vacancies Filled:
Majority:
41st seat filled by Pombo (Rep-Cal.) on Feb. 8, 2001.

Changes:
Majority:

Shuster, E.G. (Bud)	Rep	Penn.	Feb. 2, 2001 Resigned the House and retired.
Bass, Charles F.	Rep	N.H.	Feb. 7, 2001 Resigned committee; moved to Energy and Commerce.
Ney, Robert W.	Rep	Ohio	Feb. 7, 2001 Resigned committee; became Chair of House Administration.
Hayes, Robert (Robin)	Rep	N.C.	Feb. 8, 2001 Replaced E.G. (Bud) Shuster.
Sherwood, Don	Rep	Penn.	Mar. 7, 2001 Resigned committee; moved to Appropriations.
Ney, Robert W.	Rep	Ohio	June 7, 2001 Filled own vacancy, ranked after Baker.
Culberson, John	Rep	Tex.	June 7, 2001 Replaced Bass.
Shuster, William	Rep	Penn.	June 27, 2001 Replaced Sherwood.
Hutchinson, Asa	Rep	Ark.	Aug. 6, 2001 Resigned the House; appointed Director of the Drug Enforcement Administration.
Boozman, John	Rep	Ark.	Dec. 4, 2001 Replaced Hutchinson.
Cooksey, John	Rep	La.	Apr. 17, 2002 Resigned committee; no new assignment.
Sullivan, John	Rep	Okla.	Apr. 18, 2002 Replaced Cooksey.

Minority:

McGovern, James P.	Dem	Mass.	May 7, 2002 Resigned committee; moved to Rules.
Capuano, Michael E.	Dem	Mass.	July 8, 2002 Replaced McGovern.

Departures from the House:	Majority			Minority		
Elected Governor	None			Baldacci, John E.	Dem	Me.
Lost Election to U.S. Senate	Thune, John R.	Rep	S.D.	Clement, Robert N.	Dem	Tenn.
Defeated for Re-nomination	Kerns, Brian D.	Rep	Ind.	Mascara, Frank R.	Dem	Penn.
Retired	Horn, J. Steven	Rep	Cal.	Borski, Robert A.	Dem	Penn.
Elected State Senator	None			Barcia, James A.	Dem	Mich.

Departures from Committee:						
Became Chair of Resources	Pombo, Richard W.	Rep	Cal.	None		
Moved to Appropriations	Simpson, Michael K.	Rep	Ida.	Berry, R. Marion	Dem	Ark.
	Kirk, Mark S.	Rep	Ill.			
	Culberson, John	Rep	Tex.			
Moved to Energy and Commerce	Rogers, Mike	Rep	Mich.	None		
	Ferguson, Michael	Rep	N.J.			
	Otter, C.L. (Butch)	Rep	Ida.			
Moved to Ways and Means	None			Sandlin, Max A.	Dem	Tex.

TRANSPORTATION AND INFRASTRUCTURE / 108th Congress

Service Dates of Committee Chair: Jan. 8, 2003-Jan. 3, 2005

Service Dates of Majority Members: Jan. 28, 2003-Jan. 3, 2005

Service Dates of Ranking Member: Jan. 8, 2003-Jan. 3, 2005

Service Dates of Minority Members: Jan. 28, 2003-Jan. 3, 2005

Roster Filled: Majority with 41 members, Jan. 28, 2003; Minority with 34 members, Jan. 28, 2003

Majority					Minority				
			Terms in:					Terms in:	
Rank Name	Party	State	House	Comm.	Rank Name	Party	State	House	Comm.
Chr Young, Donald E.	Rep	Ala.	16	5	RM Oberstar, James L.	DFL	Minn.	15	15
2nd Petri, Thomas E.	Rep	Wisc.	13	11	2nd Rahall, Nick Joe II	Dem	W.Va.	14	14
3rd Boehlert, Sherwood L.	Rep	N.Y.	11	10	3rd Lipinski, William O.	Dem	Ill.	11	11
4th Coble, Howard	Rep	N.C.	10	5	4th DeFazio, Peter A.	Dem	Ore.	9	9
5th Duncan, John J. (Jimmy) Jr.	Rep	Tenn.	9	8	5th Costello, Jerry F.	Dem	Ill.	9	9
6th Gilchrest, Wayne T.	Rep	Md.	7	6	6th Norton, Eleanor Holmes	Dem	D.C.	7	7
7th Mica, John L.	Rep	Fla.	6	6	7th Nadler, Jerrold	Dem	N.Y.	7	6
8th Hoekstra, Peter	Rep	Mich.	6	*2 1	8th Menendez, Robert	Dem	N.J.	6	6
9th Quinn, John F. (Jack)	Rep	N.Y.	6	6	9th Brown, Corrine	Dem	Fla.	6	6
10th Ehlers, Vernon J.	Rep	Mich.	6	6	10th Filner, Robert	Dem	Cal.	6	6
11th Bachus, Spencer T.	Rep	Ala.	6	5	11th Johnson, Eddie Bernice	Dem	Tex.	6	6

Rank Name	Party	State	House	Comm.	Rank Name	Party	State	House	Comm.
12th LaTourette, Steven C.	Rep	Ohio	5	5	12th Taylor, G. Eugene (Gene)	Dem	Miss.	8	5
13th Kelly, Sue W.	Rep	N.Y.	5	5	13th Millender-McDonald, Juanita	Dem	Cal.	5	5
14th Baker, Richard H.	Rep	La.	9	5	14th Cummings, Elijah E.	Dem	Md.	5	5
15th Ney, Robert W.	Rep	Ohio	5	*2 2	15th Blumenauer, Earl	Dem	Ore.	5	4
16th LoBiondo, Frank A.	Rep	N.J.	5	4	16th Tauscher, Ellen O.	Dem	Cal.	4	4
17th Moran, Jerry	Rep	Kans.	4	4	17th Pascrell, William J. Jr.	Dem	N.J.	4	4
18th Miller, Gary G.	Rep	Cal.	3	*2 1	18th Boswell, Leonard L.	Dem	Iowa	4	4
19th DeMint, James W.	Rep	S.C.	3	3	19th Holden, T. Timothy	Dem	Penn.	6	4
20th Bereuter, Douglas K.	Rep	Nebr.	13	3	20th Lampson, Nicholas V.	Dem	Tex.	4	*1 4
21st Isakson, Johnny	Rep	Ga.	3	3	21st Baird, Brian	Dem	Wash.	3	3
22nd Hayes, Robert (Robin)	Rep	N.C.	3	2	22nd Berkley, Shelley	Dem	Nev.	3	3
23rd Simmons, Robert	Rep	Conn.	2	2	23rd Carson, Brad	Dem	Okla.	2	2
24th Capito, Shelley Moore	Rep	W.Va.	2	*1 2	24th Matheson, James D.	Dem	Utah	2	2
25th Brown, Henry E. Jr.	Rep	S.C.	2	2	25th Honda, Michael M.	Dem	Cal.	2	2
26th Johnson, Timothy V.	Rep	Ill.	2	2	26th Larsen, Richard R. (Rick)	Dem	Wash.	2	2
27th Rehberg, Dennis	Rep	Mont.	2	2	27th Capuano, Michael E.	Dem	Mass.	3	2
28th Platts, Todd R.	Rep	Penn.	2	2	28th Weiner, Anthony D.	Dem	N.Y.	3	1
29th Graves, Samuel B.	Rep	Mo.	2	2	29th Carson, Julia M.	Dem	Ind.	4	1
30th Kennedy, Mark	Rep	Minn.	2	2	30th Hoeffel, Joseph M.	Dem	Penn.	3	1
31st Shuster, William	Rep	Penn.	2	2	31st Thompson, Michael	Dem	Cal.	3	1
32nd Boozman, John	Rep	Ark.	2	2	32nd Bishop, Timothy H.	Dem	N.Y.	1	1
33rd Sullivan, John	Rep	Okla.	2	2	33rd Michaud, Michael H.	Dem	Me.	1	1
34th Chocola, Chris	Rep	Ind.	1	1	34th Davis, Lincoln	Dem	Tenn.	1	1
35th Beauprez, Bob	Rep	Colo.	1	1					
36th Burgess, Michael C.	Rep	Tex	1	1					
37th Burns, Max	Rep	Ga.	1	1					
38th Pearce, Stevan	Rep	N.M.	1	1					
39th Gerlach, Jim	Rep	Penn.	1	1					
40th Diaz-Balart, Mario	Rep	Fla.	1	1					
41st Porter, Jon C.	Rep	Nev.	1	1					

*1: Member's first period of service on the committee.

*2: Member's second period of service on the committee.

Note: Delegate Eleanor Holmes Norton (Dem-D.C.) was allowed to accrue committee seniority but was not included in the party ratio.

Changes:

Majority:

Sullivan, John	Rep	Okla.	Jan. 28, 2004 Resigned committee; moved to Energy and Commerce.
Bereuter, Douglas K.	Rep	Nebr.	Aug. 31, 2004 Resigned the House and retired.
Alexander, Rodney	Rep	La.	Sept. 9, 2004 Replaced Sullivan.

Departures from the House:	**Majority**			**Minority**		
Elected to U.S. Senate	DeMint, James W.	Rep	S.C.	None		
	Isakson, Johnny	Rep	Ga.			
Lost Election to U.S. Senate	None			Carson, Brad	Dem	La.
				Hoeffel, Joseph M.	Dem	Penn.
Defeated for Re-election	Burns, Max	Rep	Ga.	Lampson, Nicholas V.	Dem	Tex.
Retired	Quinn, John F. (Jack)	Rep	N.Y.	Lipinski, William O.	Dem	Ill.

Departures from Committee:						
Moved to Appropriations	Rehberg, Dennis	Rep	Mont.	None		
	Alexander, Rodney	Rep	La.			
Moved to Energy and Commerce	Burgess, Michael C.	Rep	Tex			
Moved to Rules	Capito, Shelley Moore	Rep	W.Va.	None		
Moved to Ways and Means	Chocola, Chris	Rep	Ind.	Thompson, Michael	Dem	Cal.
	Beauprez, Bob	Rep	Colo.			

TRANSPORTATION AND INFRASTRUCTURE / 109th Congress

Service Dates of Committee Chair: Jan. 6, 2005-Jan. 3, 2007

Service Dates of Majority Members: Jan. 26, 2005-Jan. 3, 2007

Service Dates of Minority Members: Jan. 26, 2005-Jan. 3, 2007

Roster Filled: Majority with 41 members, Jan. 26, 2005; Minority with 34 members, Jan. 26, 2005

	Majority					**Minority**			
			Terms in:					**Terms in:**	
Rank Name	Party	State	House	Comm.	Rank Name	Party	State	House	Comm.
Chr Young, Donald E.	Rep	Ala.	17	6	RM Oberstar, James L.	DFL	Minn.	16	16
2nd Petri, Thomas E.	Rep	Wisc.	14	12	2nd Rahall, Nick Joe II	Dem	W.Va.	15	15

3rd Boehlert, Sherwood L.	Rep	N.Y.	12	11
4th Coble, Howard	Rep	N.C.	11	6
5th Duncan, John J. (Jimmy) Jr.	Rep	Tenn.	10	9
6th Gilchrest, Wayne T.	Rep	Md.	8	7
7th Mica, John L.	Rep	Fla.	7	7
8th Hoekstra, Peter	Rep	Mich.	7	*2 2
9th Ehlers, Vernon J.	Rep	Mich.	7	7
10th Bachus, Spencer T.	Rep	Ala.	7	6
11th LaTourette, Steven C.	Rep	Ohio	6	6
12th Kelly, Sue W.	Rep	N.Y.	6	6
13th Baker, Richard H.	Rep	La.	10	6
14th Ney, Robert W.	Rep	Ohio	6	*2 3
15th LoBiondo, Frank A.	Rep	N.J.	6	5
16th Moran, Jerry	Rep	Kans.	5	5
17th Miller, Gary G.	Rep	Cal.	4	*2 2
18th Hayes, Robert (Robin)	Rep	N.C.	4	3
19th Simmons, Robert	Rep	Conn.	3	3
20th Brown, Henry E. Jr.	Rep	S.C.	3	3
21st Johnson, Timothy V.	Rep	Ill.	3	3
22nd Platts, Todd R.	Rep	Penn.	3	3
23rd Graves, Samuel B.	Rep	Mo.	3	3
24th Kennedy, Mark	Rep	Minn.	3	3
25th Shuster, William	Rep	Penn.	3	3
26th Boozman, John	Rep	Ark.	3	3
27th Pearce, Stevan	Rep	N.M.	2	2
28th Gerlach, Jim	Rep	Penn.	2	2
29th Diaz-Balart, Mario	Rep	Fla.	2	2
30th Porter, Jon C.	Rep	Nev.	2	2
31st Osborne, Thomas	Rep	Nebr.	3	1
32nd Marchant, Kenny	Rep	Tex.	1	1
33rd Sodrel, Michael E.	Rep	Ind.	1	1
34th Dent, Charles W.	Rep	Penn.	1	1
35th Poe, Ted	Rep	Tex.	1	1
36th Reichert, David G.	Rep	Wash.	1	1
37th Mack, Connie IV	Rep	Fla.	1	1
38th Kuhl, John R. (Randy) Jr.	Rep	N.Y.	1	1
39th Fortuño, Luis G.	Rep	P.R.	1	1
40th Westmoreland, Lynn A.	Rep	Ga.	1	1
41st Boustany, Charles W. Jr.	Rep	La.	1	1

3rd DeFazio, Peter A.	Dem	Ore.	10	10
4th Costello, Jerry F.	Dem	Ill.	10	10
5th Norton, Eleanor Holmes	Dem	D.C.	8	8
6th Nadler, Jerrold	Dem	N.Y.	8	7
7th Menendez, Robert	Dem	N.J.	7	7
8th Brown, Corrine	Dem	Fla.	7	7
9th Filner, Robert	Dem	Cal.	7	7
10th Johnson, Eddie Bernice	Dem	Tex.	7	7
11th Taylor, G. Eugene (Gene)	Dem	Miss.	9	6
12th Millender-McDonald, Juanita	Dem	Cal.	6	6
13th Cummings, Elijah E.	Dem	Md.	6	6
14th Blumenauer, Earl	Dem	Ore.	6	5
15th Tauscher, Ellen O.	Dem	Cal.	5	5
16th Pascrell, William J. Jr.	Dem	N.J.	5	5
17th Boswell, Leonard L.	Dem	Iowa	5	5
18th Holden, T. Timothy	Dem	Penn.	7	5
19th Baird, Brian	Dem	Wash.	4	4
20th Berkley, Shelley	Dem	Nev.	4	4
21st Matheson, James D.	Dem	Utah	3	3
22nd Honda, Michael M.	Dem	Cal.	3	3
23rd Larsen, Richard R. (Rick)	Dem	Wash.	3	3
24th Capuano, Michael E.	Dem	Mass.	4	3
25th Weiner, Anthony D.	Dem	N.Y.	4	2
26th Carson, Julia M.	Dem	Ind.	5	2
27th Bishop, Timothy H.	Dem	N.Y.	2	2
28th Michaud, Michael H.	Dem	Me.	2	2
29th Davis, Lincoln	Dem	Tenn.	2	2
30th Chandler, A.B. (Ben)	Dem	Ky.	2	1
31st Higgins, Brian	Dem	N.Y.	1	1
32nd Carnahan, Russ	Dem	Mo.	1	1
33rd Schwartz, Allyson Y.	Dem	Penn.	1	1
34th Salazar, John T.	Dem	Colo.	1	1

*2: Member's second period of service on the committee.

Note: Delegate Eleanor Holmes Norton (Dem-D.C.) and Resident Commissioner Luis G. Fortuño (Rep-P.R.) were allowed to accrue committee seniority but were not included in the party ratio.

Changes:

Majority:

Pearce, Stevan	Rep	N.M.	Feb. 9, 2005 Resigned committee; moved to Financial Services and Homeland Security.
Schmidt, Jean	Rep	Ohio	Sept. 15, 2005 Replaced Pearce.
Ney, Robert W.	Rep	Ohio	Nov. 3, 2006 Resigned House due to ethics issues.

Minority:

Menendez, Robert	Dem	N.J.	Jan. 16, 2006 Resigned the House; appointed to the Senate.
Barrow, John	Dem	Ga.	Feb. 15, 2006 Replaced Menendez.

Departures from the House:

	Majority			**Minority**
Lost Nomination for Governor	Osborne, Thomas	Rep	Neb.	None
Lost Election to U.S. Senate	Kennedy, Mark	Rep	Minn.	None
Defeated for Re-election	Kelly, Sue W.	Rep	N.Y.	None
	Sodrel, Michael E.	Rep	Ind.	
	Simmons, Robert	Rep	Conn.	
Retired	Boehlert, Sherwood L.	Rep	N.Y.	None

Departures from Committee:

	Majority					
Became RM on Financial Services	Bachus, Spencer T.	Rep	Ala.			
Moved to Appropriations	None			Honda, Michael M.	Dem	Cal.
				Chandler, A.B. (Ben)	Dem	Ky.
Moved to Budget	Porter, Jon C.	Rep	Nev.	Blumenauer, Earl	Dem	Ore.
Returned to Education and Labor	Hoekstra, Peter	Rep	Mich.	None		
Moved to Energy and Commerce	None			Matheson, James D.	Dem	Utah
				Weiner, Anthony D.	Dem	N.Y.
				Barrow, John	Dem	Ga.

Moved to Financial Services	None		
Moved to Foreign Affairs	Fortuño, Luis G.	Rep	P.R.
Moved to Science and Technology	None		
Moved to Ways and Means	Porter, Jon C.	Rep	Nev.

Davis, Lincoln	Dem	Tenn.
None		
Chandler, A.B. (Ben)	Dem	Ky.
Blumenauer, Earl	Dem	Ore.
Pascrell, William J. Jr.	Dem	N.J.
Berkley, Shelley	Dem	Nev.
Schwartz, Allyson Y.	Dem	Penn.

TRANSPORTATION AND INFRASTRUCTURE / 110th Congress

Service Dates of Committee Chair: Jan. 4, 2007-Jan. 3, 2009

Service Dates of Majority Members: Jan. 10, 2007-Jan. 3, 2009

Service Dates of Minority Members: Jan. 10, 2007-Jan. 3, 2009

Roster Filled: Majority with 41 members, Jan. 12, 2007; Minority with 34 members, Jan. 10, 2007

Majority

Rank Name	Party	State	Terms in: House	Terms in: Comm.
Chr Oberstar, James L.	DFL	Minn.	17	17
2nd Rahall, Nick Joe II	Dem	W.Va.	16	16
3rd DeFazio, Peter A.	Dem	Ore.	11	11
4th Costello, Jerry F.	Dem	Ill.	11	11
5th Norton, Eleanor Holmes	Dem	D.C.	9	9
6th Nadler, Jerrold	Dem	N.Y.	9	8
7th Brown, Corrine	Dem	Fla.	8	8
8th Filner, Robert	Dem	Cal.	8	8
9th Johnson, Eddie Bernice	Dem	Tex.	8	8
10th Taylor, G. Eugene (Gene)	Dem	Miss.	10	7
11th Millender-McDonald, Juanita	Dem	Cal.	7	7
12th Cummings, Elijah E.	Dem	Md.	7	7
13th Tauscher, Ellen O.	Dem	Cal.	6	6
14th Boswell, Leonard L.	Dem	Iowa	6	6
15th Holden, T. Timothy	Dem	Penn.	8	6
16th Baird, Brian	Dem	Wash.	5	5
17th Larsen, Richard R. (Rick)	Dem	Wash.	4	4
18th Capuano, Michael E.	Dem	Mass.	5	4
19th Carson, Julia M.	Dem	Ind.	6	3
20th Bishop, Timothy H.	Dem	N.Y.	3	3
21st Michaud, Michael H.	Dem	Me.	3	3
22nd Higgins, Brian	Dem	N.Y.	2	2
23rd Carnahan, Russ	Dem	Mo.	2	2
24th Salazar, John T.	Dem	Colo.	2	1
25th Napolitano, Grace F.	Dem	Cal.	5	1
26th Lipinski, Daniel	Dem	Ill.	2	1
27th Matsui, Doris O.	Dem	Cal.	2	1
28th Lampson, Nicholas V.	Dem	Tex.	5	*2 1
29th Space, Zachary T.	Dem	Ohio	1	1
30th Hirono, Mazie K.	Dem	Hai.	1	1
31st Braley, Bruce L.	Dem	Iowa	1	1
32nd Altmire, Jason	Dem	Penn.	1	1
33rd Walz, Timothy J.	DFL	Minn.	1	1
34th Shuler, Heath	Dem	N.C.	1	1
35th Arcuri, Michael A.	Dem	N.Y.	1	1
36th Mitchell, Harry E.	Dem	Ariz.	1	1
37th Carney, Chris	Dem	Penn.	1	1
38th Hall, John	Dem	N.Y.	1	1
39th Kagen, Steven L.	Dem	Wisc.	1	1
40th Cohen, Stephen L.	Dem	Tenn.	1	1
41st McNerney, Jerry	Dem	Cal.	1	1

Minority

Rank Name	Party	State	Terms in: House	Terms in: Comm.
RM Mica, John L.	Rep	Fla.	8	8
2nd Young, Donald E.	Rep	Ala.	18	7
3rd Petri, Thomas E.	Rep	Wisc.	15	13
4th Coble, Howard	Rep	N.C.	12	7
5th Duncan, John J. (Jimmy) Jr.	Rep	Tenn.	11	10
6th Gilchrest, Wayne T.	Rep	Md.	9	8
7th Ehlers, Vernon J.	Rep	Mich.	8	8
8th LaTourette, Steven C.	Rep	Ohio	7	7
9th Baker, Richard H.	Rep	La.	11	7
10th LoBiondo, Frank A.	Rep	N.J.	7	6
11th Moran, Jerry	Rep	Kans.	6	6
12th Miller, Gary G.	Rep	Cal.	5	*2 3
13th Hayes, Robert (Robin)	Rep	N.C.	5	4
14th Brown, Henry E. Jr.	Rep	S.C.	4	4
15th Johnson, Timothy V.	Rep	Ill.	4	4
16th Platts, Todd R.	Rep	Penn.	4	4
17th Graves, Samuel B.	Rep	Mo.	4	4
18th Shuster, William	Rep	Penn.	4	4
19th Boozman, John	Rep	Ark.	4	4
20th Gerlach, Jim	Rep	Penn.	3	3
21st Diaz-Balart, Mario	Rep	Fla.	3	3
22nd Marchant, Kenny	Rep	Tex.	2	2
23rd Dent, Charles W.	Rep	Penn.	2	2
24th Poe, Ted	Rep	Tex.	2	2
25th Reichert, David G.	Rep	Wash.	2	2
26th Mack, Connie IV	Rep	Fla.	2	2
27th Kuhl, John R. (Randy) Jr.	Rep	N.Y.	2	2
28th Westmoreland, Lynn A.	Rep	Ga.	2	2
29th Boustany, Charles W. Jr.	Rep	La.	2	2
30th Schmidt, Jean	Rep	Ohio	2	2
31st Miller, Candice S.	Rep	Mich.	3	1
32nd Drake, Thelma D.	Rep	Va.	2	1
33rd Fallin, Mary	Rep	Okla.	1	1
34th Buchanan, Vernon G.	Rep	Fla.	1	1

*2: Member's second period of service on the committee.

Note: Delegate Eleanor Holmes Norton (Dem-D.C.) was allowed to accrue committee seniority but not included in the party ratio.

Changes:

Majority:

Millender-McDonald, Juanita	Dem	Cal.	Apr. 22, 2007 Died in office.
Richardson, Laura	Dem	Cal.	Sept. 20, 2007 Replaced Millender-McDonald.
Carson, Julia M.	Dem	Ind.	Dec. 15, 2007 Died in office.

Sires, Albio	Dem	N.J.	Mar. 11, 2008 Replaced Carson.
Matsui, Doris O.	Dem	Cal.	June 10, 2008 Resigned committee; moved to Energy and Commerce.
Edwards, Donna F.	Dem	Md.	July, 15, 2008 Replaced Matsui.
Minority:			
Marchant, Kenny	Rep	Tex.	Mar. 9, 2007 Resigned committee; moved to Financial Services.
Capito, Shelley Moore	Rep	W.Va.	Mar. 12, 2007 Replaced Marchant, ranked after Boozman.
Baker, Richard H.	Rep	La.	Feb. 2, 2008 Resigned the House and retired
Latta, Robert E.	Rep	Ohio	Feb. 26, 2008 Replaced Baker.

Departures from the House:	**Majority**			**Minority**		
Defeated for Re-election	Lampson, Nicholas V.	Dem	Tex.	Hayes, Robert (Robin)	Rep	N.C.
				Kuhl, John R. (Randy) Jr.	Rep	N.Y.
				Drake, Thelma D.	Rep	Va.
Defeated for Re-nomination	None			Gilchrest, Wayne T.	Rep	Md.
Departures from Committee:						
Moved to Appropriations	Salazar, John T.	Dem	Colo.	LaTourette, Steven C.	Rep	Ohio
Moved to Energy and Commerce	McNerney, Jerry	Dem	Cal.	None		
	Space, Zachary T.	Dem	Ohio			
	Braley, Bruce L.	Dem	Iowa			
Moved to Judiciary	None			Poe, Ted	Rep	Tex.
Moved to Select Energy Independence and Global Warming	Salazar, John T.	Dem	Colo.	None		
Moved to Ways and Means	Higgins, Brian	Dem	N.Y.	Reichert, David G.	Rep	Wash.
				Boustany, Charles W. Jr.	Rep	La.

TRANSPORTATION AND INFRASTRUCTURE / 111th Congress

Service Dates of Committee Chair: Jan. 6, 2009-Jan. 3, 2001

Service Dates of Majority Members: Jan. 7, 2009-Jan. 3, 2011

Service Dates of Minority Members: Jan. 9, 2009-Jan. 3, 2011

Roster Filled: Majority with 45 members, Jan. 7, 2009; Minority with 30 members, Jan. 9, 2009

Majority			Terms in:		Minority			Terms in:	
Rank Name	**Party**	**State**	**House**	**Comm.**	**Rank Name**	**Party**	**State**	**House**	**Comm.**
Chr Oberstar, James L.	DFL	Minn.	18	18	RM Mica, John L.	Rep	Fla.	9	9
2nd Rahall, Nick Joe II	Dem	W.Va.	17	17	2nd Young, Donald E.	Rep	Alas.	19	8
3rd DeFazio, Peter A.	Dem	Ore.	12	12	3rd Petri, Thomas E.	Rep	Wisc.	16	14
4th Costello, Jerry F.	Dem	Ill.	12	12	4th Coble, Howard	Rep	N.C.	13	8
5th Norton, Eleanor Holmes	Dem	D.C.	10	10	5th Duncan, John J. (Jimmy) Jr.	Rep	Tenn.	12	11
6th Nadler, Jerrold	Dem	N.Y.	10	9	6th Ehlers, Vernon J.	Rep	Mich.	9	9
7th Brown, Corrine	Dem	Fla.	9	9	7th LoBiondo, Frank A.	Rep	N.J.	8	7
8th Filner, Robert	Dem	Cal.	9	9	8th Moran, Jerry	Rep	Kans.	7	7
9th Johnson, Eddie Bernice	Dem	Tex.	9	9	9th Miller, Gary G.	Rep	Cal.	6	*2 4
10th Taylor, G. Eugene (Gene)	Dem	Miss.	11	8	10th Brown, Henry E. Jr.	Rep	S.C.	5	5
11th Cummings, Elijah E.	Dem	Md.	8	8	11th Johnson, Timothy V.	Rep	Ill.	5	5
12th Tauscher, Ellen O.	Dem	Cal.	7	7	12th Platts, Todd R.	Rep	Penn.	5	5
13th Boswell, Leonard L.	Dem	Iowa	7	7	13th Graves, Samuel B.	Rep	Mo.	5	5
14th Holden, T. Timothy	Dem	Penn.	9	7	14th Shuster, William	Rep	Penn.	5	5
15th Baird, Brian	Dem	Wash.	6	6	15th Boozman, John	Rep	Ark.	5	5
16th Larsen, Richard R. (Rick)	Dem	Wash.	5	5	16th Capito, Shelley Moore	Rep	W.Va.	5	* 2 2
17th Capuano, Michael E.	Dem	Mass.	6	5	17th Gerlach, Jim	Rep	Penn.	4	4
18th Bishop, Timothy H.	Dem	N.Y.	4	4	18th Diaz-Balart, Mario	Rep	Fla.	4	4
19th Michaud, Michael H.	Dem	Me.	4	4	19th Dent, Charles W.	Rep	Penn.	3	3
20th Carnahan, Russ	Dem	Mo.	3	3	20th Mack, Connie IV	Rep	Fla.	3	3
21st Napolitano, Grace F.	Dem	Cal.	6	2	21st Westmoreland, Lynn A.	Rep	Ga.	3	3
22nd Lipinski, Daniel	Dem	Ill.	3	2	22nd Schmidt, Jean	Rep	Ohio	3	3
23rd Hirono, Mazie K.	Dem	Hai.	2	2	23rd Miller, Candice S.	Rep	Mich.	4	2
24th Altmire, Jason	Dem	Penn.	2	2	24th Fallin, Mary	Rep	Okla.	2	2
25th Walz, Timothy J.	DFL	Minn.	2	2	25th Buchanan, Vernon G.	Rep	Fla.	2	2
26th Shuler, Heath	Dem	N.C.	2	2	26th Latta, Robert E.	Rep	Ohio	2	2
27th Arcuri, Michael A.	Dem	N.Y.	2	2	27th Scalise, Steve	Rep	La.	2	1
28th Mitchell, Harry E.	Dem	Ariz.	2	2	28th Cao, Anh (Joseph)	Rep	La.	1	1
29th Carney, Chris	Dem	Penn.	2	2	29th Guthrie, Brett	Rep	Ky.	1	1
30th Hall, John	Dem	N.Y.	2	2	30th Schock, Aaron	Rep	Ill.	1	1

31st Kagen, Steven L.	Dem	Wisc.	2	2
32nd Cohen, Stephen L.	Dem	Tenn.	2	2
33rd Richardson, Laura	Dem	Cal.	2	2
34th Sires, Albio	Dem	N.J.	2	2
35th Edwards, Donna F.	Dem	Md.	2	2
36th Ortiz, Solomon P.	Dem	Tex.	14	1
37th Hare, Phil	Dem	Ill.	2	1
38th Boccieri, John A.	Dem	Ohio	1	1
39th Schauer, Mark H.	Dem	Mich.	1	1
40th Markey, Betsy	Dem	Colo.	1	1
41st Griffith, Parker	Dem	Ala.	1	1
42nd McMahon, Michael E.	Dem	N.Y.	1	1
43rd Perriello, Tom	Dem	Va.	1	1
44th Titus, Alice (Dina)	Dem	Nev.	1	1
45th Teague, Harry	Dem	N.M.	1	1

*2: Member's second period of service on the committee.

Note: Delegate Eleanor Holmes Norton (Dem-D.C.) was allowed to accrue committee seniority but not included in the party ratio.

Changes

Majority

Tauscher, Ellen O.	Dem	Cal	June 26, 2009 Resigned committee; appointed to State Department.
Garamendi, John	Dem	Cal.	Nov. 19, 2009 Replaced Tauscher.
Griffith, Parker	Dem	Ala	Dec. 22, 2009 Service on committee as a Democrat vacated.
Johnson, Hank	Dem	Ga.	May 6, 2010 Replaced Griffith.

Minority

Scalise, Steve	Rep	La.	Jan. 16, 2009 Resigned committee; moved to Energy and Commerce.
Guthrie, Brett	Rep	Ky.	Jan. 22, 2009 Re-ranked after Latta.
Olson, Pete	Rep	Tex.	Jan. 22, 2009 Replaced Scalise.
Latta, Robert E.	Rep	Ohio	Mar,. 25, 2010 Resigned committee; moved to Energy and Commerce.

Veterans' Affairs

House Committee on Veterans' Affairs, 103rd-111th Congresses (1993-2011)

BACKGROUND

Organizational History: The House Committee on Veterans Affairs was created by the Legislative Reorganization Act of 1946 from three standing committees: Pensions, Invalid Pensions, and World War Veterans Legislation. The Pensions Committees are descended from the first standing committee to deal with this topic, Pensions and Revolutionary Claims, which was created on December 22, 1813. Stevenson Archer, a Jeffersonian from Maryland and chair of the Claims Committee pushed for the creation of this new committee. According to Lauros McConachie's 1898 classic, *Congressional Committees,* that committee was divided into two committees in 1825—the Committee on Revolutionary Claims, chaired by Peter Little, a John Quincy Adams supporter from Maryland, and the Committee on Military Pensions. Military Pensions became Revolutionary Pensions in the 21st Congress (1829-1831) and in 1880; Revolutionary Pensions became the Committee on Pensions. Revolutionary Claims became the War Claims Committee in 1873 in the wake of the Civil War.

Also, in the 21st Congress, James Trezvant, a Jacksonian from Virginia and the chair of Military Pensions initiated the Invalid Pensions Committee. The Invalid Pensions Committee dated from January 10, 1831, but by the time of the 1946 reorganization, it was still primarily involved in dealing with pension claims from the Civil War. The third committee ancestor, the Committee on World War Veterans Legislation, was created on January 14, 1924, and was originally chaired by Royal C. Johnson (Rep-S.D.) with Carl Hayden (Dem-Ariz.) as its first ranking member. Hayden was Arizona's first representative in 1912 and his combined service of fifty-seven years—fifteen in the House and forty-two in the Senate—in the Congress remains today as the second longest ever in congressional history.

The primary responsibility for the various predecessor committees of Veterans' Affairs were Federal programs for veterans, ranging from health care to veterans' hospitals, education programs, and job counseling. Following World War II, the committee was especially focused on the readjustment to civil life of the millions of servicemen who had been uprooted by the war. In the modern post-1947 Congress, the committee has been dominated by conservative Southerners, who have had close ties to traditional veterans' lobbying groups.

By the late 1980s, however, the committee had begun to shift its outlook, as younger members began questioning the panel's traditional orientation. At the same time the conflict between old-line veterans' lobbying groups and those representing Vietnam veterans had declined.

The committee still remains the major point of legislative entry for the nation's major veterans' organizations—the American Legion, the Veterans of Foreign Wars, the AMVETS, Disabled American Veterans, and the Vietnam Veterans of America.

Membership: At the time of the 1946 Reorganization, the three predecessor committees—Invalid Pensions, Pensions, and World War Veterans' Legislation—had a combined membership of sixty-one members. Following the reorganization, the Veterans Affairs Committee had only twenty-seven members. Unlike other combination committees like Public Works, Veterans' Affairs would grow but at a slower rate and eventually would lose members. With the committee chaired by the cantankerous segregationist John E. Rankin (Dem-Miss.), the committee had trouble filling seats and shrunk to twenty-three in 1951. Veterans' Affairs did not regain its original size until 1975 when twenty-eight members were assigned to the committee. It surpassed thirty in 1979 and stabilized at thirty-four from 1985 to 1993, peaking at thirty-six in the 103rd Congress (1993-1995). It then began to shrink in size until 2005 when it returned to its original size of twenty-seven. In the last two Congresses, there have been twenty-nine members on Veterans' Affairs. Its 1993-2011 membership mean of 30.9 placed it in the sixteenth rank among the nineteen continuing committees.

The Veterans' Affairs Committee also ranked sixteenth among the standing committees in the mean seniority of its members with an average of 4.30 terms. The committee's mean inter-Congress membership retention rate of 82.35 percent placed it thirteenth among the nineteen continuing committees.

Committee Leaders: The first modern-era chair of Veterans' Affairs was Edith Nourse Rogers (Rep-Mass.), the last ranking member on the World War Veterans Legislation Committee. She would chair the committee in both of the Republican Congresses (1947-1949; 1953-1955) and be the committee's ranking member in the five other Congresses up to her death in 1960. Mrs. Rogers was the first woman to chair a post-reorganization committee and only the second Republican woman ever to chair a House standing committee. The first was Mae Ella Nolan (Rep-Cal.) who chaired Expenditures in the Post Office Department in the 68th Congress (1923-1925).

Serving with Mrs. Rogers as the senior Democrat on the committee was the notorious racist and anti-semite John E. Rankin of Mississippi, who had been the last chair of the World War Veterans Legislation Committee. He would chair Veterans' Affairs during the two Democratic Congresses, 1949-1953 until his defeat for renomination in 1952. Rankin's successor, Olin E. Teague (Dem-Tex.), a decorated World War II veteran, spent almost two decades as chair of the panel, 1955-1973, until he departed to chair Science and Astronautics. His strong support of the military was typical of committee members. After Mrs. Rogers's death, William H. Ayres (Rep-Ohio) would serve as ranking member, 1961-1965, until he stepped aside to become ranking member on Education and Labor. He was succeeded by E. Ross Adair (Rep-Ind.),who stepped aside in 1969 to become ranking member on Foreign Affairs. Adair's successor was Charles M. Teague (Rep-Cal.)

and the committee now had its two senior party leaders sharing the same surname for four years, 1969 to 1973. In 1973, both Teagues surrendered their senior slots on Veterans' Affairs. Olin Teague became chair of Science and Astronautics while Charles Teague became the ranking member on Agriculture.

W.J. Bryan Dorn (Dem-S.C.) became chair in 1973 but left the House after losing the 1974 South Carolina gubernatorial election. He was succeeded by Herbert Ray Roberts (Dem-Texas), who in 1962 had won Sam Rayburn's old seat. Roberts chaired the committee from 1975 until his re-election defeat in 1980. During this time, John Paul Hammerschmidt (Rep-Ark.) had served as the committee's ranking member from 1973 to 1987 when he stepped aside to become the ranking member on Public Works and Transportation. In 1974, Hammerschmidt easily dispatched an electoral challenge from a twenty-eight-year-old Bill Clinton. His first successor, Gerald B.H. Solomon (Rep-N.Y.), served as ranking member for only two years, 1987-1989, when he left Veterans' Affairs for Rules.

Succeeding Roberts as chair in 1981 was the highly visible champion of veterans, G.V. "Sonny" Montgomery (Dem-Miss.), who would chair the committee for fourteen years until 1995 and serve for another two years as its ranking member from 1995 until his retirement in 1997. Robert L. Stump (Rep-Ariz.), another early Republican switcher, became ranking member in 1989 and served in that role until the Republican takeover in 1995. Stump then became the first Republican chair of the Veterans' Affairs Committee since Edith Nourse Rogers had chaired it in 1953-1955. He served his allotted three terms, 1995-2001 and stepped aside for Christopher H. Smith (Rep-N.J.) in 2001 and then retired in 2003. Smith served only two terms, 2001-2005, then left the committee. Smith's successor Stephen E. Buyer (Rep-Ind.) became chair in 2005, and with the Democratic takeover in 2007, he now serves as ranking member on Veterans' Affairs.

Montgomery's successor in 1997 was Lane A. Evans (Dem-Ill.) who served as ranking member for ten years, 1997-2007, and was not serving when Democratic gains in 2006 would have made him chair of Veterans' Affairs. Instead Robert Filner (Dem-Cal.) became chair in 2007 and remains in that post.

Party Leaders: The Veterans' Affairs Committee has not been a major source for House leaders. To date, only two Democratic Whips served on the committee—Anthony L. Coelho of California and James E. Clyburn of South Carolina, the present Whip.

Notable Members: Service on the House Veterans' Affairs Committee has yet to result in a major party presidential or vice presidential nomination, although New Mexico Governor William B. Richardson (Dem-N.M.), Bill Clinton's third Secretary of Energy, gave it a try in 2008. Among the Cabinet members who have served on the committee are Margaret M. Heckler (Rep-Mass.), President Reagan's second Secretary of Health and Human Services; Thomas J. Ridge (Rep-Penn.), who was named by President George W. Bush to be the first Secretary of Homeland Security, and Ray LaHood (Rep-Ill.), President Obama's Secretary of Transportation.

Thirteen U.S. senators—seven Republicans and six Democrats—served on House Veterans' Affairs prior to their Senate service. Among the seven Republicans were Winston L. Prouty of Vermont, William L. Scott of Virginia, James Abdnor of South Dakota, W. Phil Gramm of Texas, Robert C. Smith of New Hampshire, Richard J. (Rick) Santorum of Pennsylvania, and Y. Timothy Hutchinson of Arkansas. The six Democrats included Timothy E. Wirth of Colorado, Thomas A. Daschle and Timothy P. Johnson of South Dakota, Richard C. Shelby of Alabama, Byron L. Dorgan of North Dakota, and Thomas Udall of New Mexico.

Eight governors moved from the committee to their respective state houses including four Democrats—Ella T. Grasso, James J. Florio of New Jersey, Ted Strickland of Ohio, and Bill Richardson of New Mexico as well as four Republicans—William H. Avery of Kansas, John G. Rowland of Connecticut, Thomas J. Ridge of Pennsylvania, and James A. Gibbons of Nevada.

In one of the more unusual pairings on the Veterans Affairs Committee, the 92nd Congress (1971-1973) contained two northern Democratic women on opposite sides of the civil rights struggle that defined the 1960s—Boston's Louise Day Hicks, the leader of that city's anti-busing movement, and New York City's Shirley A. Chisholm, the first African-American woman to serve in Congress. Their House careers diverged after this Congress. Ms. Chisholm had a long and distinguished House career while Ms. Hicks, who had inherited Speaker John McCormack's seat in 1970, was voted out in the next election. She was replaced by J. Joseph Moakley, who defeated Hicks as an independent and would become a major Tip O'Neill protégé and later chair the House Rules Committee for five-plus years.

Selected References

Keller, Bill, "How a Unique Lobby Force Protects Over $21 Billion in Vast Veterans' Programs," *CQ Weekly Report*, 138 (June 14, 1980), 1527-1639.

Schamel, Charles E. et al., "Records of the Veterans' Affairs Committees," *Guide to the Records of the United States House of Representatives at the National Archives: 1789-1989 Bicentennial Edition* (Washington, D.C.: National Archives and Records Administration,1989), 267-272.

U.S. House of Representatives, Committee on Veterans' Affairs, *History of House Committees Considering Veterans' Legislation*, House Print, 98-3, 98th Congress, 1st Session (1983).

RESPONSIBILITIES, JURISDICTIONAL CHANGES, AND SUBCOMMITTEES

VETERANS' AFFAIRS

Jurisdiction, 80th Congress (1947-1949)

Established by the Legislative Reorganization Act of 1946:

[Section 121.(1)(r)] Committee on Veterans' Affairs
(1) Veterans' measures generally.
(2) Pensions of all the wars of the United States, general and special.
(3) Life insurance issued by the Government on account of service in the armed forces.
(4) Compensation, vocational rehabilitation, and education of veterans.
(5) Veterans' hospitals, medical care, and treatment of veterans.
(6) Soldiers' and sailors' civil relief.
(7) Readjustment of servicemen to civil life.

Jurisdiction, 103rd Congress (1993-1995)

From the *Rules of the House of Representatives, 103rd Congress* (House Document 102-405)

[Rule X.1.(u)] Committee on Veterans' Affairs
(1) Veterans' measures generally.
(2) Cemeteries of the United States in which veterans of any war or conflict are or may be buried, whether in the United States or abroad, except cemeteries administered by the Secretary of the Interior.
(3) Compensation, vocational rehabilitation, and education of veterans.
(4) Life insurance issued by the Government on account of service in the Armed Forces.
(5) Pensions of all the wars of the United States, general and special.
(6) Readjustment of servicemen to civil life.
(7) Soldiers' and sailors' civil relief.
(8) Veterans' hospitals, medical care, and treatment of veterans.

Jurisdiction, 104th Congress (1995-1997) Changes in Committee System

From H. Res. 6, Section 202 (a), the Committees and Their Jurisdiction, January 4, 1995

[Rule X.1.(r)] Committee on Veterans' Affairs.
(1) Veterans' measures generally.
(2) Cemeteries of the United States in which veterans of any war or conflict are or may be buried, whether in the United States or abroad, except cemeteries administered by the Secretary of the Interior.
(3) Compensation, vocational rehabilitation, and education of veterans.
(4) Life insurance issued by the Government on account of service in the Armed Forces.
(5) Pensions of all the wars of the United States, general and special.
(6) Readjustment of servicemen to civil life.
(7) Soldiers' and sailors' civil relief.
(8) Veterans' hospitals, medical care, and treatment of veterans.

Jurisdiction, 111th Congress (2009-2011)

From the *Rules of the House of Representatives* (as revised to June 16, 2009, H.Doc. 110-162):

[Rule X.1.(s)] Committee on Veterans' Affairs
(1) Veterans' measures generally.
(2) Cemeteries of the United States in which veterans of any war or conflict are or may be buried, whether in the United States or abroad (except cemeteries administered by the Secretary of the Interior).
(3) Compensation, vocational rehabilitation, and education of veterans.
(4) Life insurance issued by the Government on account of service in the Armed Forces.
(5) Pensions of all the wars of the United States, general and special.
(6) Readjustment of service members to civil life.
(7) Service members' civil relief.
(8) Veterans' hospitals, medical care, and treatment of veterans.

NAMES OF VETERANS' AFFAIRS SUBCOMMITTEES FROM THE *CONGRESSIONAL DIRECTORY*

Benefits, 105, 106, 107, 108
Compensation, Pension, and Insurance, 103
Compensation, Pension, Insurance, and Memorial Affairs, 104
Disability Assistance and Memorial Affairs, 109, 110, 111
Education, Training, and Employment, 103
Education, Training, Employment and Housing, 104
Economic Opportunity, 109, 110, 111
Health, 105, 106, 107, 108, 109, 110, 111
Hospitals and Health Care, 103, 104
Housing and Memorial Affairs, 103
Oversight and Investigations, 103, 105, 106, 107, 108, 109, 110, 111

MEMBERSHIP ROSTERS, 103rd-111th Congresses, 1993-2011

VETERANS' AFFAIRS / 103rd Congress

Service Dates of Committee Chair: Jan. 5, 1993-Jan. 3, 1995

Service Dates of Majority Members: Jan. 5, 1993-Jan. 3, 1995

Service Dates of Minority Members: Jan. 5, 1993-Jan. 3, 1995

Roster Filled: Majority with 21 members, Jan. 5, 1993; Minority with 14 members, May 27, 1993

Majority

Rank Name	Party	State	House	Comm.
Chr Montgomery, G.V. (Sonny)	Dem	Miss.	14	13
2nd Edwards, William D. (Don)	Dem	Cal.	16	*2 13
3rd Applegate, Douglas	Dem	Ohio	9	9
4th Evans, Lane A.	Dem	Ill.	6	6
5th Penny, Timothy J.	DFL	Minn.	6	6
6th Rowland, J. Roy	Dem	Ga.	6	6
7th Slattery, James C.	Dem	Kans.	6	*2 2
8th Kennedy, Joseph P. II	Dem	Mass.	4	4
9th Sangmeister, George E.	Dem	Ill.	3	3
10th Long, Jill L.	Dem	Ind.	3	3
11th Edwards, T. Chester (Chet)	Dem	Tex.	2	2
12th Waters, Maxine	Dem	Cal.	2	2
13th Clement, Robert N.	Dem	Tenn.	4	2
14th Filner, Robert	Dem	Cal.	1	1
15th Tejeda, Frank M.	Dem	Tex.	1	1
16th Gutierrez, Luis V.	Dem	Ill.	1	1
17th Baesler, H. Scott (Scotty)	Dem	Ky.	1	1
18th Bishop, Sanford D. Jr.	Dem	Ga.	1	1
19th Clyburn, James E.	Dem	S.C.	1	1
20th Kreidler, Myron B. (Mike)	Dem	Wash.	1	1
21st Brown, Corrine	Dem	Fla.	1	1

Minority

Rank Name	Party	State	House	Comm.
RM Stump, Robert L.	Rep	Ariz.	9	*2 4
2nd Smith, Christopher H.	Rep	N.J.	7	7
3rd Burton, Danny L.	Rep	Ind.	6	*1 6
4th Bilirakis, Michael	Rep	Fla.	6	6
5th Ridge, Thomas J.	Rep	Penn.	6	5
6th Spence, Floyd D.	Rep	S.C.	12	2
7th Hutchinson, Y. Timothy	Rep	Ark.	1	1
8th Everett, R. Terry	Rep	Ala.	1	1
9th Buyer, Stephen E.	Rep	Ind.	1	1
10th Quinn, John F. (Jack)	Rep	N.Y.	1	1
11th Bachus, Spencer T.	Rep	Ala.	1	1
12th Linder, John E.	Rep	Ga.	1	1
13th Stearns, Clifford B.	Rep	Fla.	3	*2 1
14th King, Peter T.	Rep	N.Y.	1	1

*1: Member's first period of service on the committee.
*2: Member's second period of service on the committee.

Notes: Ranking on this committee for the following member was affected by other chamber service: William D. (Don) Edwards (Dem-Cal.), Chair, Civil and Constitutional Rights Subcommittee of Judiciary. Robert L. Stump (Rep-Ariz.) served previously on this committee as a Democrat.

Vacancies Filled:
　Minority:
　　13th and 14th seats filled by Stearns and King on May 27, 1993.

Additions:
　Minority:

15th Lewis, Ron	Rep	Ky.	June 15, 1994

Departures from the House:

	Majority			Minority		
Elected Governor	None			Ridge, Thomas J.	Rep	Penn.
Lost Election for Governor	Slattery, James C.	Dem	Kans.			
Defeated for Re-election	Long, Jill L.	Dem	Ind.	None		

Retired	Kreidler, Michael	Dem	Wash.	None		
	Edwards, William D. (Don)	Dem	Cal.			
	Applegate, Douglas	Dem	Ohio			
	Penny, Timothy J.	DFL	Minn.			
	Rowland, J. Roy	Dem	Ga.			
	Sangmeister, George E.	Dem	Ill.			

Departures from Committee:

Moved to Government Reform and Oversight	None			Burton, Danny L.	Rep	Ind.
Moved to International Relations	None			King, Peter T.	Rep	N.Y.
Moved to National Security	None			Lewis, Ron	Rep	Ky.
Moved to Rules	None			Linder, John E.	Rep	Ga.

VETERANS' AFFAIRS / 104th Congress

Service Dates of Committee Chair: Jan. 4, 1995-Jan. 3, 1997

Service Dates of Majority Members: Jan. 4, 1995-Jan. 3, 1997

Service Dates of Minority Members: Jan. 4, 1995-Jan. 3, 1997

Roster Filled: Majority with 18 members, Jan. 4, 1995; Minority with 15 members, Jan. 4, 1995

			Majority							Minority		
				Terms in:							**Terms in:**	
Rank Name	**Party**	**State**	**House**	**Comm.**		**Rank Name**	**Party**	**State**	**House**	**Comm.**		
Chr Stump, Robert L.	Rep	Ariz.	10	*2 5		RM Montgomery, G.V. (Sonny)	Dem	Miss.	15	14		
2nd Smith, Christopher H.	Rep	N.J.	8	8		2nd Evans, Lane A.	Dem	Ill.	7	7		
3rd Bilirakis, Michael	Rep	Fla.	7	7		3rd Kennedy, Joseph P. II	Dem	Mass.	5	5		
4th Spence, Floyd D.	Rep	S.C.	13	3		4th Edwards, T. Chester (Chet)	Dem	Tex.	3	3		
5th Hutchinson, Y. Timothy	Rep	Ark.	2	2		5th Waters, Maxine	Dem	Cal.	3	3		
6th Everett, R. Terry	Rep	Ala.	2	2		6th Clement, Robert N.	Dem	Tenn.	5	3		
7th Buyer, Stephen E.	Rep	Ind.	2	2		7th Filner, Robert	Dem	Cal.	2	2		
8th Quinn, John F. (Jack)	Rep	N.Y.	2	2		8th Tejeda, Frank M.	Dem	Tex.	2	2		
9th Bachus, Spencer T.	Rep	Ala.	2	2		9th Gutierrez, Luis V.	Dem	Ill.	2	2		
10th Stearns, Clifford B.	Rep	Fla.	4	*2 2		10th Baesler, H. Scott (Scotty)	Dem	Ky.	2	2		
11th Ney, Robert W.	Rep	Ohio	1	1		11th Bishop, Sanford D. Jr.	Dem	Ga.	2	2		
12th Fox, Jon D.	Rep	Penn.	1	1		12th Clyburn, James E.	Dem	S.C.	2	2		
13th Flanagan, Michael Patrick	Rep	Ill.	1	1		13th Brown, Corrine	Dem	Fla.	2	2		
14th Barr, Bob	Rep	Ga.	1	1		14th Doyle, Michael F.	Dem	Penn.	1	*1 1		
15th Stockman, Steve	Rep	Tex.	1	1		15th Mascara, Frank R.	Dem	Penn.	1	1		
16th Weller, Gerald C.	Rep	Ill.	1	1								
17th Hayworth, John D. Jr.	Rep	Ariz.	1	1		*1: Member's first period of service on the committee.						
18th Cooley, Wes	Rep	Ore.	1	1		*2: Member's second period of service on the committee.						

Changes:

Majority:

Stockman, Steve	Rep	Tex.	Feb. 15, 1995 Resigned committee; no new assignment.
Schaefer, Daniel L.	Rep	Colo.	Feb. 15, 1995 Replaced Stockman.

Minority:

Waters, Maxine	Dem	Cal.	Apr. 22, 1996 Resigned committee; moved to Judiciary.
Peterson, Collin C.	DFL	Minn.	Sept. 17, 1996 Replaced Waters.

Departures from the House:

	Majority			**Minority**		
Elected to U.S. Senate	Hutchinson, Y. Timothy	Rep	Ark.	None		
Defeated for Re-election	Flanagan, Michael Patrick	Rep	Ill.	None		
Retired	Cooley, Wes	Rep	Ore.	Montgomery, G.V. (Sonny)	Dem	Miss.

Departures from Committee:

Moved to Appropriations	None			Edwards, T. Chester (Chet)	Dem	Tex.
Moved to Budget	None			Baesler, H. Scott (Scotty)	Dem	Ky.
Moved to Government Reform and Oversight	Barr, Bob	Rep	Ga.	None		
Moved to International Relations	None			Clement, Robert N.	Dem	Tenn.
Moved to Transportation and Infrastructure	Ney, Robert W.	Rep	Ohio	None		
	Fox, Jon D.	Rep	Penn.			
Moved to Ways and Means	Weller, Gerald C.	Rep	Ill.	None		
No new assignment	None			Tejeda, Frank M.	Dem	Tex.

VETERANS' AFFAIRS / 105th Congress

Service Dates of Committee Chair: Jan. 9, 1997-Jan. 3, 1999

Service Dates of Majority Members: Jan. 21, 1997-Jan. 3, 1999

Service Dates of Minority Members: Feb. 6, 1997-Jan. 3, 1999

Roster Filled: Majority with 17 members, Feb. 6, 1997; Minority with 13 members, Feb. 6, 1997

Majority					Minority				
			Terms in:					Terms in:	
Rank Name	Party	State	House	Comm.	Rank Name	Party	State	House	Comm.
Chr Stump, Robert L.	Rep	Ariz.	11	*2 6	RM Evans, Lane A.	Dem	Ill.	8	8
2nd Smith, Christopher H.	Rep	N.J.	9	9	2nd Kennedy, Joseph P. II	Dem	Mass.	6	6
3rd Bilirakis, Michael	Rep	Fla.	8	8	3rd Filner, Robert	Dem	Cal.	3	3
4th Spence, Floyd D.	Rep	S.C.	14	4	4th Gutierrez, Luis V.	Dem	Ill.	3	3
5th Everett, R. Terry	Rep	Ala.	3	3	5th Bishop, Sanford D. Jr.	Dem	Ga.	3	3
6th Buyer, Stephen E.	Rep	Ind.	3	3	6th Clyburn, James E.	Dem	S.C.	3	3
7th Quinn, John F. (Jack)	Rep	N.Y.	3	3	7th Brown, Corrine	Dem	Fla.	3	3
8th Bachus, Spencer T.	Rep	Ala.	3	3	8th Doyle, Michael F.	Dem	Penn.	2	*1 2
9th Stearns, Clifford B.	Rep	Fla.	5	*2 3	9th Mascara, Frank R.	Dem	Penn.	2	2
10th Schaefer, Daniel L.	Rep	Colo.	8	2	10th Peterson, Collin C.	DFL	Minn.	4	2
11th Moran, Jerry	Rep	Kans.	1	1	11th Carson, Julia M.	Dem	Ind.	1	1
12th Cooksey, John	Rep	La.	1	1	12th Reyes, Silvestre	Dem	Tex.	1	*1 1
13th Hutchinson, Asa	Rep	Ark.	1	1	13th Snyder, Victor F.	Dem	Ark.	1	1
14th Hunter, Duncan L.	Rep	Cal.	9	1					
15th Hayworth, John D. Jr.	Rep	Ariz.	2	2	*1: Member's first period of service on the committee.				
16th Chenoweth, Helen P.	Rep	Ida.	2	1	*2: Member's second period of service on the committee.				
17th LaHood, Ray H.	Rep	Ill.	2	1					

Notes: Bob Barr (Rep-Ga.) was assigned to Veterans' Affairs but took a leave of absence before serving. His place was considered a vacancy filled by LaHood making the roster complete on Feb. 6, 1997.

Vacancies Filled:
   Majority:
      17th seat filled by LaHood on Feb. 6, 1997.

Changes:
   Majority:

Hunter, Duncan L.	Rep	Cal.	Feb. 10, 1997 Resigned committee; no new assignment.
Redmond, William T.	Rep	N.M.	July 23, 1997 Replaced Hunter.

   Minority:

Bishop, Sanford D. Jr.	Dem	Ga.	Mar. 6, 1997 Resigned committee; moved to Permanent Select Intelligence.
Rodriguez, Ciro D.	Dem	Tex.	May 14, 1997 Replaced Bishop.

Departures from the House:	**Majority**			**Minority**		
Defeated for Re-election	Redmond, William T.	Rep	N.M.	None		
Retired	Schaefer, Daniel L.	Rep	Colo.	Kennedy, Joseph P. II	Dem	Mass.

Departures from Committee:						
Moved to Appropriations	None			Clyburn, James E.	Dem	S.C.
Moved to Banking and Financial Services	None			Mascara, Frank R.	Dem	Penn.
Moved to Government Reform	Hutchinson, Asa	Rep	Ark.	None		
Moved to International Relations	Cooksey, John	Rep	La.	None		

VETERANS' AFFAIRS / 106th Congress

Service Dates of Committee Chair: Jan. 6, 1999-Jan. 3, 2001

Service Dates of Majority Members: Jan. 6, 1999-Jan. 3, 2001

Service Dates of Minority Members: Jan. 6, 1999-Jan. 3, 2001

Roster Filled: Majority with 17 members, Feb. 2, 1999; Minority with 14 members, June 9, 1999

Majority					Minority				
			Terms in:					Terms in:	
Rank Name	Party	State	House	Comm.	Rank Name	Party	State	House	Comm.
Chr Stump, Robert L.	Rep	Ariz.	12	*2 7	RM Evans, Lane A.	Dem	Ill.	9	9
2nd Smith, Christopher H.	Rep	N.J.	10	10	2nd Filner, Robert	Dem	Cal.	4	4

Rank Name	Party	State	House	Comm.		Rank Name	Party	State	House	Comm.
3rd Bilirakis, Michael	Rep	Fla.	9	9		3rd Gutierrez, Luis V.	Dem	Ill.	4	4
4th Spence, Floyd D.	Rep	S.C.	15	5		4th Brown, Corrine	Dem	Fla.	4	4
5th Everett, R. Terry	Rep	Ala.	4	4		5th Doyle, Michael F.	Dem	Penn.	3	*1 3
6th Buyer, Stephen E.	Rep	Ind.	4	4		6th Peterson, Collin C.	DFL	Minn.	5	3
7th Quinn, John F. (Jack)	Rep	N.Y.	4	4		7th Carson, Julia M.	Dem	Ind.	2	2
8th Bachus, Spencer T.	Rep	Ala.	4	4		8th Reyes, Silvestre	Dem	Tex.	2	*1 2
9th Stearns, Clifford B.	Rep	Fla.	6	*2 4		9th Snyder, Victor F.	Dem	Ark.	2	2
10th Moran, Jerry	Rep	Kans.	2	2		10th Rodriguez, Ciro D.	Dem	Tex.	2	*1 2
11th Hayworth, John D. Jr.	Rep	Ariz.	3	3		11th Shows, C. Ronald	Dem	Miss.	1	1
12th Chenoweth, Helen P.	Rep	Ida.	3	2		12th Berkley, Shelley	Dem	Nev.	1	1
13th LaHood, Ray H.	Rep	Ill.	3	2		13th Hill, Baron P.	Dem	Ind.	1	1
14th Hansen, James V.	Rep	Utah	10	1		14th Udall, Thomas	Dem	N.M.	1	1
15th McKeon, Howard P. (Buck)	Rep	Cal.	4	1						
16th Gibbons, James A.	Rep	Nev.	2	1						
17th Simpson, Michael K.	Rep	Ida.	1	1						

*1: Member's first period of service on the committee.

*2: Member's second period of service on the committee.

Vacancies Filled:

Majority:

14th through 16th seats filled by Hansen, McKeon, and Gibbons on Feb. 2, 1999.

Minority:

12th seat filled by Berkley on Feb. 2, 1999; 13th and 14th seats filled by Hill and Udall on June 9, 1999.

Changes:

Majority:

Bachus, Spencer T.	Rep	Ala.	Mar. 10, 1999 Resigned committee; moved to Judiciary.
Baker, Richard H.	Rep	La.	Mar. 11, 1999 Replaced Bachus.

Departures from the House:	**Majority**			**Minority**
Retired	Chenoweth, Helen P.	Rep	Ida.	None

Departures from Committee:				
Became Chair on Resources	Hansen, James V.	Rep	Utah	None
Moved to Appropriations	LaHood, Ray H.	Rep	Ill.	None

VETERANS' AFFAIRS / 107th Congress

Service Dates of Committee Chair: Jan. 6, 2001-Jan. 3, 2003

Service Dates of Majority Members: Jan. 6, 2001-Jan. 3, 2003

Service Dates of Minority Members: Jan. 31, 2001-Jan. 3, 2003

Roster Filled: Majority with 17 members, Feb. 8, 2001; Minority with 14 members, Jan. 31, 2001

	Majority		Terms in:				Minority		Terms in:	
Rank Name	Party	State	House	Comm.		Rank Name	Party	State	House	Comm.
Chr Smith, Christopher H.	Rep	N.J.	11	11		RM Evans, Lane A.	Dem	Ill.	10	10
2nd Stump, Robert L.	Rep	Ariz.	13	*2 8		2nd Filner, Robert	Dem	Cal.	5	5
3rd Bilirakis, Michael	Rep	Fla.	10	10		3rd Gutierrez, Luis V.	Dem	Ill.	5	5
4th Spence, Floyd D.	Rep	S.C.	16	6		4th Brown, Corrine	Dem	Fla.	5	5
5th Everett, R. Terry	Rep	Ala.	5	5		5th Doyle, Michael F.	Dem	Penn.	4	*1 4
6th Buyer, Stephen E.	Rep	Ind.	5	5		6th Peterson, Collin C.	DFL	Minn.	6	4
7th Quinn, John F. (Jack)	Rep	N.Y.	5	5		7th Carson, Julia M.	Dem	Ind.	3	3
8th Stearns, Clifford B.	Rep	Fla.	7	*2 5		8th Reyes, Silvestre	Dem	Tex.	3	*1 3
9th Moran, Jerry	Rep	Kans.	3	3		9th Snyder, Victor F.	Dem	Ark.	3	3
10th Hayworth, John D. Jr.	Rep	Ariz.	4	4		10th Rodriguez, Ciro D.	Dem	Tex.	3	*1 3
11th McKeon, Howard P. (Buck)	Rep	Cal.	5	2		11th Shows, C. Ronald	Dem	Miss.	2	2
12th Gibbons, James A.	Rep	Nev.	3	2		12th Berkley, Shelley	Dem	Nev.	2	2
13th Simpson, Michael K.	Rep	Ida.	2	2		13th Hill, Baron P.	Dem	Ind.	2	2
14th Baker, Richard H.	Rep	La.	8	2		14th Udall, Thomas	Dem	N.M.	2	2
15th Simmons, Robert	Rep	Conn.	1	1						
16th Crenshaw, Ander	Rep	Fla.	1	1						
17th Brown, Henry E. Jr.	Rep	S.C.	1	1						

*1: Member's first period of service on the committee.

*2: Member's second period of service on the committee.

Vacancies Filled:

Majority:

17th seat filled by Brown on Feb. 8, 2001.

Changes:

Majority:

Hayworth, John D. Jr.	Rep	Ariz.	June 20, 2001 Resigned committee; returned to Resources.
Spence, Floyd D.	Rep	S.C.	Aug. 16, 2001 Died in office.
Miller, Jefferson B.	Rep	Fla.	Nov. 8, 2001 Replaced Hayworth.
Boozman, John	Rep	Ark.	Dec. 4, 2001 Replaced Spence.

Minority:

Doyle, Michael F.	Dem	Penn.	Feb. 7, 2001 Resigned committee; moved to Energy and Commerce.
Peterson, Collin C.	DFL	Minn.	Apr. 26, 2001 Resigned committee; had moved to Permanent Select Intelligence on April 4, 2001.
Lynch, Stephen F.	Dem	Mass.	Nov. 7, 2001 Replaced Doyle, ranked after Rodriguez on Nov. 7, 2001; reranked on Nov. 8, 2001, after Shows.
Davis, Susan A.	Dem	Cal.	Nov. 7, 2001 Replaced Peterson, ranked after Udall.

Departures from the House:

	Majority			Minority		
Defeated for Re-election	None			Shows, C. Ronald	Dem	Miss.
Retired	Stump, Robert L.	Rep	Ariz.	None		

Departures from Committee:

Moved to Appropriations	Simpson, Michael K.	Rep	Ida.	None		
	Crenshaw, Ander	Rep	Fla.			
Moved to Financial Services	None			Lynch, Stephen F.	Dem	Mass.
Moved to Transportation and Infrastructure	None			Carson, Julia M.	Dem	Ind.
No new assignment	McKeon, Howard P. (Buck)	Rep	Cal.	Hill, Baron P.	Dem	Ind.

VETERANS' AFFAIRS / 108th Congress

Service Dates of Committee Chair: Jan. 8, 2003-Jan. 3, 2005

Service Dates of Majority Members: Jan. 28, 2003-Jan. 3, 2005

Service Dates of Ranking Member: Jan. 8, 2003-Jan. 3, 2005

Service Dates of Minority Members: Jan. 28, 2003-Jan. 3, 2005

Roster Filled: Majority with 17 members, Jan. 28, 2003; Minority with 14 members, Feb. 13, 2003

Majority					Minority				
			Terms in:					Terms in:	
Rank Name	Party	State	House	Comm.	Rank Name	Party	State	House	Comm.
Chr Smith, Christopher H.	Rep	N.J.	12	12	RM Evans, Lane A.	Dem	Ill.	11	11
2nd Bilirakis, Michael	Rep	Fla.	11	11	2nd Filner, Robert	Dem	Cal.	6	6
3rd Everett, R. Terry	Rep	Ala.	6	6	3rd Gutierrez, Luis V.	Dem	Ill.	6	6
4th Buyer, Stephen E.	Rep	Ind.	6	6	4th Brown, Corrine	Dem	Fla.	6	6
5th Quinn, John F. (Jack)	Rep	N.Y.	6	6	5th Snyder, Victor F.	Dem	Ark.	4	4
6th Stearns, Clifford B.	Rep	Fla.	8	*2 6	6th Rodriguez, Ciro D.	Dem	Tex.	4	*1 4
7th Moran, Jerry	Rep	Kans.	4	4	7th Michaud, Michael H.	Dem	Me.	1	1
8th Gibbons, James A.	Rep	Nev.	4	3	8th Hooley, Darlene	Dem	Ore.	4	1
9th Baker, Richard H.	Rep	La.	9	3	9th Reyes, Silvestre	Dem	Tex.	4	*1 4
10th Simmons, Robert	Rep	Conn.	2	2	10th Strickland, Ted	Dem	Ohio	4	1
11th Brown, Henry E. Jr.	Rep	S.C.	2	2	11th Berkley, Shelley	Dem	Nev.	3	3
12th Miller, Jefferson B.	Rep	Fla.	2	2	12th Udall, Thomas	Dem	N.M.	3	3
13th Boozman, John	Rep	Ark.	2	2	13th Davis, Susan A.	Dem	Cal.	2	2
14th Bradley, Jeb	Rep	N.H.	1	1	14th Ryan, Timothy J.	Dem	Ohio	1	1
15th Beauprez, Bob	Rep	Colo.	1	1					
16th Brown-Waite, Virginia	Rep	Fla.	1	1	*1: Member's first period of service on the committee.				
17th Renzi, Rick	Rep	Ariz.	1	1	*2: Member's second period of service on the committee.				

Vacancies Filled:

Minority:

7th seat filled by Michaud on Feb. 5, 2003; 8th through 14th seats filled by Hooley, Reyes, Strickland, Berkley, Udall, Davis, and Ryan on Feb. 13, 2003.

Changes:

Majority:

Gibbons, James A.	Rep	Nev.	Feb. 12, 2003 Resigned committee; moved to Select Homeland Security.
Murphy, Timothy	Rep	Penn.	Feb. 25, 2003 Replaced Gibbons.

Minority:

Reyes, Silvestre	Dem	Tex.	June 15, 2004 Resigned committee; no new assignment.
Herseth, Stephanie	Dem	S.D.	June 16, 2004 Replaced Reyes.

Departures from the House:	Majority			Minority		
Defeated for Re-nomination	None			Rodriguez, Ciro D.	Dem	Tex.
Retired	Quinn, John F. (Jack)	Rep	N.Y.	None		

Departures from Committee:						
Moved to Energy and Commerce	Murphy, Timothy	Rep	Penn.	None		
Moved to Ways and Means	Beauprez, Bob	Rep	Colo.	None		
No new assignment	Smith, Christopher H.	Rep	N.J.	Davis, Susan A.	Dem	Cal.
				Ryan, Timothy J.	Dem	Ohio

VETERANS' AFFAIRS / 109th Congress

Service Dates of Committee Chair: Jan. 6, 2005-Jan. 3, 2007

Service Dates of Majority Members: Jan. 26, 2005-Jan. 3, 2007

Service Dates of Ranking Member: Jan. 6, 2005-Jan. 3, 2007

Service Dates of Minority Members: Jan. 26, 2005-Jan. 3, 2007

Roster Filled: Majority with 15 members, Feb. 2, 2005; Minority with 12 members, Feb. 2, 2005

	Majority						Minority				
				Terms in:						**Terms in:**	
Rank Name		Party	State	House	Comm.	Rank Name		Party	State	House	Comm.
Chr Buyer, Stephen E.		Rep	Ind.	7	7	RM Evans, Lane A.		Dem	Ill.	12	12
2nd Bilirakis, Michael		Rep	Fla.	12	12	2nd Filner, Robert		Dem	Cal.	7	7
3rd Everett, R. Terry		Rep	Ala.	7	7	3rd Gutierrez, Luis V.		Dem	Ill.	7	7
4th Stearns, Clifford B.		Rep	Fla.	9	*2 7	4th Brown, Corrine		Dem	Fla.	7	7
5th Moran, Jerry		Rep	Kans.	5	5	5th Snyder, Victor F.		Dem	Ark.	5	5
6th Baker, Richard H.		Rep	La.	10	4	6th Michaud, Michael H.		Dem	Me.	2	2
7th Simmons, Robert		Rep	Conn.	3	3	7th Herseth, Stephanie		Dem	S.D.	2	2
8th Brown, Henry E. Jr.		Rep	S.C.	3	3	8th Strickland, Ted		Dem	Ohio	5	2
9th Miller, Jefferson B.		Rep	Fla.	3	3	9th Hooley, Darlene		Dem	Ore.	5	2
10th Boozman, John		Rep	Ark.	3	3	10th Reyes, Silvestre		Dem	Tex.	5	*2 1
11th Bradley, Jeb		Rep	N.H.	2	2	11th Berkley, Shelley		Dem	Nev.	4	4
12th Brown-Waite, Virginia		Rep	Fla.	2	2	12th Udall, Thomas		Dem	N.M.	4	4
13th Renzi, Rick		Rep	Ariz.	2	2						
14th Nunes, Devin		Rep	Cal.	2	1	*2: Member's second period of service on the committee.					
15th Turner, Michael R.		Rep	Ohio	2	1						

Vacancies Filled:
Majority:
    14th and 15th seats filled by Nunes and Turner on Feb. 2, 2005; 16th vacancy remained unfilled.
Minority:
    8th through 12th seats filled by Strickland, Hooley, Reyes, Berkley, and Udall on Feb. 2, 2005.

Addition:
Minority:

13th Salazar, John T.	Dem	Colo.	Feb. 15, 2006

Changes:
Majority:

Renzi, Rick	Rep	Ariz	Jan. 26, 2005 Resigned committee; moved to Permanent Select Intelligence.
Simmons, Robert	Rep	Conn.	Feb. 9, 2005 Resigned committee; moved to Homeland Security.
Burton, Danny L.	Rep	Ind.	Mar. 8, 2005 Replaced Renzi, ranked after Stearns.
Nunes, Devin	Rep	Cal.	May 5, 2005 Resigned committee; moved to Ways and Means.
Campbell, John	Rep	Cal.	Feb. 8, 2006 Replaced Simmons.
Bilbray, Brian P.	Rep	Cal.	June 29, 2006 Replaced Nunes.

Minority:

Higgins, Brian	Dem	N.Y.	Jan. 26, 2005 The original list with Higgins's name was corrected with his name removed.

Departures from the House:	Majority			Minority		
Elected Governor	None			Strickland, Ted	Dem	Ohio
Defeated for Re-election	Bradley, Jeb	Rep	N.H.	None		
Retired	Bilirakis, Michael	Rep	Fla.	Evans, Lane A.	Dem	Ill.

Departures from Committee:						
Became Chair of Select Intelligence				Reyes, Silvestre	Dem	Tex
Moved to Appropriations	None			Udall, Thomas	Dem	N.M.

Moved to Budget	None	Hooley, Darlene	Dem Ore.
Moved to Energy and Commerce	None	Hooley, Darlene	Dem Ore.
Moved to Judiciary	None	Gutierrez, Luis V.	Dem Ill.
No new assignment	Everett, R. Terry	Rep Ala.	

VETERANS' AFFAIRS / 110th Congress

Service Dates of Committee Chair: Jan. 4, 2007-Jan. 3, 2009

Service Dates of Majority Members: Jan. 12, 2007-Jan. 3, 2009

Service Dates of Ranking Member: Jan. 4, 2007-Jan. 3, 2009

Service Dates of Minority Members: Jan. 10, 2007-Jan. 3, 2009

Roster Filled: Majority with 16 members, Jan. 18, 2007; Minority with 13 members, Jan. 10, 2007

			Terms in:						Terms in:	
Majority					**Minority**					
Rank Name	Party	State	House	Comm.	Rank Name	Party	State	House	Comm.
Chr Filner, Robert	Dem	Cal.	8	8	RM Buyer, Stephen E.	Rep	Ind.	8	8
2nd Brown, Corrine	Dem	Fla.	8	8	2nd Stearns, Clifford B.	Rep	Fla.	10	*2 8
3rd Snyder, Victor F.	Dem	Ark.	6	6	3rd Burton, Danny L.	Rep	Ind.	13	*2 2
4th Michaud, Michael H.	Dem	Me.	3	3	4th Moran, Jerry	Rep	Kans.	6	6
5th Herseth, Stephanie	Dem	S.D.	3	3	5th Baker, Richard H.	Rep	La.	11	5
6th Mitchell, Harry E.	Dem	Ariz.	1	1	6th Brown, Henry E. Jr.	Rep	S.C.	4	4
7th Hall, John	Dem	N.Y.	1	1	7th Miller, Jefferson B.	Rep	Fla.	4	4
8th Hare, Phil	Dem	Ill.	1	1	8th Boozman, John	Rep	Ark.	4	4
9th Doyle, Michael F.	Dem	Penn.	7	*2 1	9th Brown-Waite, Virginia	Rep	Fla.	3	3
10th Berkley, Shelley	Dem	Nev.	5	5	10th Turner, Michael R.	Rep	Ohio	3	2
11th Salazar, John T.	Dem	Colo.	2	2	11th Bilbray, Brian P.	Rep	Cal.	5	2
12th Rodriguez, Ciro D.	Dem	Tex.	5	*2 1	12th Lamborn, Doug	Rep	Colo.	1	*1 1
13th Donnelly, Joe	Dem	Ind.	1	1	13th Bilirakis, Gus	Rep	Fla.	1	1
14th McNerney, Jerry	Dem	Cal.	1	1					
15th Space, Zachary T.	Dem	Ohio	1	1	*1: Member's first period of service on the committee.				
16th Walz, Timothy J.	DFL	Minn.	1	1	*2: Member's second period of service on the committee.				

Vacancies Filled:

Majority:

   10th and 16th seats filled by Berkley and Walz on Jan. 18, 2007.

Changes:

Majority:

Doyle, Michael F.	Dem	Penn.	June 10, 2008 Resigned committee to open seat for Cazayoux.
Cazayoux, Donald J. Jr.	Dem	La.	June 10, 2008 Replaced Doyle.

Minority:

Burton, Danny L.	Rep	Ind.	Mar. 12, 2007 "Removed from the Committee by the Speaker"
Buchanan, Vernon G.	Rep	Fla.	Mar. 12, 2007 Replaced Burton.
Baker, Richard H.	Rep	La.	Feb. 2, 2008 Resigned the House and retired.
Scalise, Steve	Rep	La.	May 14, 2008 Replaced Baker.

Departures from the House:

	Majority			**Minority**
Defeated for Re-election	Cazayoux, Donald J. Jr.	Dem	La.	None

Departures from Committee:

				Minority
Moved to Appropriations	Salazar, John T.	Dem	Colo.	None
Moved to Foreign Affairs	Berkley, Shelley	Dem	Nev.	None
Moved to Select Energy Independence and Global Warming	Salazar, John T.	Dem	Colo.	None
Moved to Transportation and Infrastructure	Hare, Phil	Dem	Ill.	
Moved to Ways and Means	None			Brown-Waite, Virginia Rep Fla.
No new assignment	None			Lamborn, Doug Rep Colo.

VETERANS' AFFAIRS / 111th Congress

Service Dates of Committee Chair: Jan. 6, 2009-Jan. 3, 2011

Service Dates of Majority Members: Jan. 21, 2009-Jan. 3, 2011

Service Dates of Minority Members: Jan. 9, 2009-Jan. 3, 2001

Roster filled: Majority with 18 members, Jan. 21, 2009; Minority with 11 members, Jan. 9, 2009

	Majority			Terms in:			Minority			Terms in:	
Rank Name	Party	State	House	Comm.		Rank Name	Party	State	House	Comm.
Chr Filner, Robert	Dem	Cal.	9	9		RM Buyer, Stephen E.	Rep	Ind.	9	9
2nd Brown, Corrine	Dem	Fla.	9	9		2nd Stearns, Clifford B.	Rep	Fla.	11	*2 9
3rd Snyder, Victor F.	Dem	Ark.	7	7		3rd Moran, Jerry	Rep	Kans.	7	7
4th Michaud, Michael H.	Dem	Me.	4	4		4th Brown, Henry E. Jr.	Rep	S.C.	5	5
5th Herseth Sandlin, Stephanie	Dem	S.D.	4	4		5th Miller, Jefferson B.	Rep	Fla.	5	5
6th Mitchell, Harry E.	Dem	Ariz.	2	2		6th Boozman, John	Rep	Ark.	5	5
7th Hall, John	Dem	N.Y.	2	2		7th Turner, Michael R.	Rep	Ohio	4	3
8th Halvorson, Deborah L.	Dem	Ill.	1	1		8th Bilbray, Brian P.	Rep	Cal.	6	3
9th Perriello, Tom	Dem	Va.	1	1		9th Bilirakis, Gus	Rep	Fla.	2	2
10th Teague, Harry	Dem	N.M.	1	1		10th Buchanan, Vernon G.	Rep	Fla.	2	2
11th Rodriguez, Ciro D.	Dem	Tex.	6	*2 2		11th Scalise, Steve	Rep	La.	2	2
12th Donnelly, Joe	Dem	Ind.	2	2						
13th McNerney, Jerry	Dem	Cal.	2	2		*2: Member's second period of service on the committee.				
14th Space, Zachary T.	Dem	Ohio	2	2						
15th Walz, Timothy J.	DFL	Minn.	2	2						
16th Adler, John H.	Dem	N.J.	1	1						
17th Kirkpatrick, Ann	Dem	Ariz.	1	1						
18th Nye, Glenn C. III	Dem	Va.	1	1						

Changes:

Minority:

Turner, Michael R.	Rep	Cal.	Jan. 13, 2009 Resigned committee; became Ranking Member on the Strategic Forces Subcommittee of House Armed Services.
Scalise, Steve	Rep	La.	Jan. 16, 2009 Resigned committee; moved to Energy and Commerce.
Lamborn, Doug	Rep	Colo.	Jan. 22, 2009 Replaced Turner, ranked after Bilbray.
Roe, David P. (Phil)	Rep	Tenn.	Jan. 22, 2009 Replaced Scalise.

Ways and Means

House Committee on Ways and Means, 103rd-111th Congresses (1993-2011)

BACKGROUND

Organizational History: The Committee on Ways and Means is the most storied committee in the U.S. Congress. As the Constitution stipulates in Section 7 of Article I, "All bills for raising Revenue shall originate in the House of Representatives …" The Constitution places this power in the House, and the House has placed it in the Ways and Means Committee. Initially created as a select committee in the 1st Congress, its first eleven members were named on July 24, 1789, and its chair was Thomas Fitzsimons (Fed.-Penn.). President George Washington's powerful Treasury Secretary, Alexander Hamilton, convinced the House that a committee was unnecessary and it was not renewed. However, on March 26, 1794, another fifteen-member Select Committee on Ways and Means was named, with William L. Smith (Fed.-S.C.) as its chair. Opposition to Hamilton grew in Congress, and after his departure, the committee was recreated on Dec. 21, 1795, by Albert H. Gallatin, a Jeffersonian from Pennsylvania, who was able to secure the regular appointment of a committee on Ways and Means and it was defined as a standing committee, a designation made formally in 1802. Ways and Means has become the longest serving committee in the U.S. Congress.

The Committee on Ways and Means has reported most major revenue bills since 1794, with the exception of a period between 1819 and 1833, when the Committee on Manufactures reported a number of protectionist tariff bills. The jurisdiction and duties of the committee have changed significantly over its two-century existence. In 1814, to relieve the committee of some of its duties, responsibility for numerous departments, appropriations for them, and reports on use of the money was given to a newly created Committee on Public Expenditures, originally created by Ways and Means Chair John W. Eppes of Virginia, President Thomas Jefferson's son-in-law. Tariffs historically were the major sources of income which fueled the ante-bellum federal apparatus. Until 1865 the committee reported the overwhelming majority of all regular appropriations bills, the three main exceptions being general public works, lighthouses and associated expenses, and rivers and harbors bills that were reported by the Commerce Committee. As the business of the government grew, the number of appropriations bills grew, as did the revenue work of the committee.

Prior to the Civil War, the committee was responsible for so much of the House's legislative agenda that its chairs became the *de facto* majority leaders of the House. Ten of the twenty-three pre-Civil War Speakers served on Ways and Means, and three of its chairs were elected Speaker—Langdon Cheves (DR-S.C.), James K. Polk (Dem-Tenn.), and John W. Jones (Dem-Va.). Polk was also one of the five pre-Civil War presidents who served on Ways and Means, joining James Madison (DR-Va.), Andrew Jackson (DR-Tenn.), John Tyler (Whig-Va.), and Millard Fillmore (Whig-N.Y.) in that unique assemblage.

In 1865, primarily from overload during the Civil War and the first imposition of a national income tax, portions of the committee's jurisdiction were given to three new committees—Banking and Currency, chaired by Theodore M. Pomeroy (Rep-N.Y.); Appropriations, chaired by Thaddeus Stevens (Rep-Penn.); and Pacific Railroads, chaired by Hiram Price (Rep-Iowa). While Pomeroy served as Speaker of the House for only one day, March 3, 1869, at the close of the 40th Congress, Stevens was a major political figure in the post-Civil War House. Stevens left the chairmanship of Ways and Means to become the first chair of Appropriations. In that capacity, it was Stevens who led the 1868 impeachment efforts against President Andrew Johnson. Stevens's successor at Ways and Means, Justin Morrill (Rep-Vt.), like Stevens, a fellow native Vermonter, was the author of the 1862 Morrill Land-Grant College Act that created most of the nation's state universities.

Stevens's move to Appropriations immediately elevated its stature comparable to Ways and Means. By 1880 the committee's jurisdiction included the raising of revenue and the bonded debt of the United States. Also in 1880, Speaker Samuel J. Randall (Dem-Penn.) used the formerly moribund Rules Committee as an agent of party leadership and Randall and subsequent Speakers would name senior members of Ways and Means and Appropriations as the other two majority members to serve with them on Rules.

Until the passage of the Sixteenth Amendment in 1913 that allowed the federal government to levy personal income taxes, tariffs were the government's chief source of revenue. Since tariff legislation came through Ways and Means, most of them were identified with a Ways and Means leader—the Morrill Tariff (1861), the Dawes Tariff (1872), the McKinley Tariff (1890), the Wilson-Gorman Tariff (1894), the Dingley Tariff (1897), the Payne-Aldrich Tariff (1909), and the Underwood-Simmons Tariff (1913).

Ways and Means continued to provide both parties with presidential and vice presidential candidates. Republican presidents James A. Garfield and William McKinley of Ohio and vice presidents, such as Republican Charles Curtis of Kansas and Democrat John Nance Garner of Texas were committee alumni. While Republican ex-Speaker James G. Blaine, a Stevens protégé, was nominated in 1884 and lost, two other notable committee members chosen as Speaker but who failed to convert the post into presidential nominations were Republican Thomas B. Reed of Maine in 1896 and Democrat James B. (Champ) Clark of Missouri in 1912.

In 1909-1910, when the House ousted autocratic Speaker Joseph G. Cannon (Rep-Ill.) from the Rules Committee and removed his power to assign members to committees, the Ways and Means Committee gained additional influence. The first elected House Majority Leaders were the Democratic chairs of Ways and Means—Oscar W. Underwood (Dem-Ala.), 1911-1915; and Claude Kitchin (Dem-N.C.), 1915-1919. Ways and Means was labeled as an "exclusive" committee in 1913, which prevented its members from serving simultaneously on any other committee. Democratic assignments to Ways and Means in this period had to be voted on by the full Democratic Caucus, as the Democratic members on Ways and Means became the party's "committee on committees" and assigned all of the other Democrats to committees. Also, during this time, legislation reported by Ways and Means has been granted "closed rules" on the floor to limit amendments to the committee's bills.

With former Ways and Means members John Nance Garner serving as vice president and Henry T. Rainey (Dem-Ill.) as Speaker during the Great Depression of the 1930s, the committee became the focal point of President Franklin D. Roosevelt's most ambitious reform—the Social Security Act. Because the benefits were to be provided by payroll taxes, Ways and Means had the lead responsibility in designing the legislation with senior committee members Chair Robert (Muley) Doughton (Dem-N.C.) and John W. McCormack (Dem-Mass.), who served as a Democratic Party leader for thirty-one years, 1940-1971, successfully moving the legislation through the House.

The Legislative Reorganization Act of 1946 consolidated Ways and Means's authority over customs, collection districts, and ports of entry and delivery; national social security; reciprocal trade agreements; revenue measures generally; revenue measures relating to the insular possessions; the bonded debt of the United States; the deposit of public moneys; and transportation of dutiable goods. The committee is also responsible for disbursing more than 45 percent of the federal budget. The panel approves taxes and tariffs, and it also makes rules about public assistance, Social Security, health insurance, and unemployment compensation.

In the 1970s, Ways and Means lost some power with the creation of the new Budget Committee that gained jurisdiction in 2000 over a bill establishing a rule of sequestration under the Balanced Budget and Emergency Deficit Control Act (Dec. 15, 2000). The Committee on the Budget has primary jurisdiction, and this committee has additional jurisdiction, over a bill taking Social Security trust funds off the budget (Dec. 15, 2000).

Also, the committee assignment responsibility that its Democratic members gained in 1911 was relocated to the party leadership-dominated Democratic Steering and Policy Committee in 1974. Simultaneous concerns about the increasingly erratic behavior of long-time chair Wilbur D. Mills (Dem-Ark.) led to a diminishing of the committee's power. According to the *House Manual* (2008):

> The Committee Reform Amendments of 1974, effective January 3, 1975, the committee gained legislative jurisdiction over tax exempt foundations and charitable trusts (subpara. (8)), formerly within the jurisdiction of the Committee on Banking and Currency (now Financial Services) because of their impact on the economy, while it was released from: jurisdiction over health care and facilities programs supported from general revenues to the Committee on Energy and Commerce; jurisdiction over work incentive programs to the Committee on Education and Labor; and jurisdiction over

renegotiation to the Committee on Banking, Finance and Urban Affairs (now Financial Services) (H. Res. 988, 93d Cong., Oct. 8, 1974, p. 34470). The Committee Reform Amendments also transferred jurisdiction over general revenue sharing from this committee to the Committee on Government Operations (now Oversight and Government Reform); however, revenue sharing was stricken from the jurisdictional statement of that committee in the 104th Congress (sec. 202(a), H. Res. 6, Jan. 4, 1995, p. 464).

In spite of these diminutions, the Ways and Means Committee continues to be powerful and its membership remains stable and senior. As long as Social Security and Medicare exist, Ways and Means will remain a hotbed of legislative contention.

Furthermore, the ongoing debate over health care reform initiated by former Democratic president Bill Clinton in 1993 and renewed by Democratic President Barack Obama in 2009 continues to place the House Ways and Means Committee in the national spotlight. However, the national spotlight has not been kind to some of its key leaders, as it also focused the nation's attention upon the unfortunate financial practices of its two most powerful committee chairs—Dan Rostenkowski (Dem-Ill.) in 1993-1994 and Charles Rangel (Dem-N.Y.) in 2009-2010. Rostenkowski's indiscretions led him to lose his committee chairmanship and his House seat in 1994 and to be sentenced to jail for nineteen months. To date, Rangel's financial woes have already cost him the chairmanship of the committee in 2010.

Membership: It was in the 66th Congress (1919-1921) that Ways and Means first achieved a membership of twenty-five. The common practice was to give fifteen seats to the majority and ten seats to the minority, regardless of the actual party split in the House. The 1946 Reorganization Act did not alter either the size or the majority-minority ratio. Apart from one Congress—the 68th (1923-1925)—when its membership rose slightly to twenty-six, the Ways and Means Committee had a stable membership size for sixty-six years, yet another indication of the committee's uniqueness.

In the wake of Wilbur Mills's fall from grace, the Ways and Means Committee was increased from twenty-five members in the 93rd Congress (1973-1975) to thirty-seven in the 94th Congress (1975-1977). In 1975, it had a new chair, Al Ullman (Dem-Ore.) and subcommittees for the first time in years. For most of the years after 1975, the committee had a membership in the mid to high thirties. In the 104th-106th Congresses, the committee grew slightly to thirty-nine and it passed the forty-member mark in 2001 for the first time. In the last five Congresses (2001-2011), Ways and Means has had forty-one members and an overall mean of 40.0 for the past nine Congresses, 1993-2011, and a thirteenth-place ranking.

In terms of the relative prestige rankings over the past eighteen years, the Ways and Means Committee ranked second behind Appropriations with regard to mean seniority—6.98 terms for Ways and Means members to 7.43 terms for Appropriations members—but first in mean inter-Congress retention rates—98.5 percent for Ways and Means members and 97.7 percent for Appropriations members.

Committee Leaders: From 1947 through 1957, Ways and Means had four chairs in five Congresses: Harold Knutson of Minnesota, 1947-1949 and Daniel A. Reed of New York, 1953-1955, who chaired the committee during the two Republican Congresses—the 80th and the 83rd; and Democrats Robert L. (Muley) Doughton of North Carolina, 1949-1953, and Jere Cooper of Tennessee, 1955-1957, who served as ranking members in the Republican Congresses and who chaired the committee in the other three. Although Doughton had chaired the committee from 1933 from the start of the Franklin D. Roosevelt era, neither he nor the other three ever gained the prominence of their nineteenth-century predecessors nor the notoriety of their late twentieth-century successors.

The best-known modern era chair of Ways and Means was Wilbur D. Mills (Dem-Ark.), who joined the committee in 1942 at the age of thirty-three in his second House term. Upon Jere Cooper's death in 1958, Mills became chair of Ways and Means at the relatively young age of forty-eight. He held the chair through 1974. Mills put a premium on consensus, keeping the members in closed meetings until they hashed out a bipartisan approach. An expert on the tax code, Mills was legendary for his successes on the House floor, where the united committee would resist major amendments to its tax bills. Ways and Means had no subcommittees between 1961 and 1974. This obliged the full committee to work together. Mills also benefited from a close personal relationship with John W. Byrnes (Rep-Wisc.), who served as the committee's ranking minority member from 1963 to 1973, and who succeeded Noah M. Mason (Rep-Ill.) Mason had himself become ranking member in January 1960, following the deaths of both Daniel Reed and Richard M. Simpson (Rep-Ill.) who had died in the previous eleven months. Herman T. Schneebeli (Rep-Penn.) served as ranking member for two Congresses, 1973-1977, bridging the transition between Mills and his immediate successor, Albert C. Ullman (Dem-Ore.).

Unfortunately for Mills an embarrassing personal scandal in 1974 ended his distinguished chairmanship of this committee and clouded his political reputation. With Mills gone, the committee's power was diminished. The House expanded the committee's membership from twenty-five to thirty-seven and the Democratic leadership regained control over committee assignments by moving that responsibility from Ways and Means to the leadership-controlled Steering and Policy Committee. Shortly afterwards and now larger, the committee itself reinstituted subcommittees. Al Ullman succeeded Mills as chair in 1975 and Barber B. Conable, Jr. (Rep-N.Y.) became ranking member in 1977. Ullman's seat was lost in the 1980 Reagan landslide in the West while Conable would serve in his post until his retirement in 1985.

In 1981, Ways and Means came under the sway of another strong chair, Daniel D. Rostenkowski (Dem-Ill.), who would lead the committee for fourteen years. Rostenkowski had to confront President Reagan, who felt that he had an electoral mandate to cut taxes, and in the 1980s the committee found itself wrestling with White House initiatives intended to rewrite the tax code. Rostenkowski held fast and restored much of the committee's earlier clout until he too ran into personal financial scandal. It led to criminal charges and Rostenkowski had to step aside in June 1994 at the height of the debate on President Clinton's health care reform package, which was to be the center-piece of the Clinton administration and a bill that Rostenkowski had hoped would be his lasting legacy in political life. Rostenkowski's "acting chair" replacement was Sam M. Gibbons (Dem-Fla.), who had years before thought to challenge Tip O'Neill's 1973 elevation to Majority Leader. Rostenkowski lost his seat in the 1994 Republican tsunami engineered by Newt Gingrich and the Contract with America. Gibbons survived but became the committee's new ranking member and would retire in 1996.

In 1995, William R. Archer of Texas, who replaced John J. Duncan (Rep-Tenn.) upon the latter's death in 1988 became the first Republican chair of Ways and Means since Dan Reed served in that capacity in 1954. Archer worked with the Speaker Gingrich team of his fellow Texans, Majority Leader Richard K. Armey and Majority Whip Thomas DeLay, but was not a part of their inner circle. Archer retired in 2001 and was succeeded as chair by third-ranking William M. Thomas of California who leapfrogged second-ranking Philip M. Crane (Rep-Ill.) to become chair in 2001 and served until the Republicans lost their House majority in 2006 and he retired.

Throughout this time, the senior Democrat on Ways and Means was Charles B. Rangel (Dem-N.Y.), who had first been elected to the House by defeating the legendary Adam Clayton Powell, Jr. in the 1970 Democratic primary. Rangel became chair of Ways and Means in 2007 until ethics charges led to Sander Levin (Dem-Mich.) becoming Acting Chair in 2010. The present ranking member is David L. Camp (Rep-Mich.), who followed James O. McCrery III (Rep-La.), who retired in 2009.

Party Leaders: Because the Democratic members on Ways and Means selected members for the other House committees for sixty years, 1911-1975, the chairs of Ways and Means in Democratic Congresses were *de facto* party leaders. As a result, the number of *de jure* party leaders who served on the post-1947 Ways and Means Committee is relatively low. John McCormack (Dem-Mass.) who served as a Democratic leader for twenty-four years in this era—as Whip, 1947-1949 and 1953-1955; Majority Leader, 1949-1953 and 1955-1962; and Speaker, 1962-1971—began his service on Ways and Means in 1931 in only his third year in the House. He left the committee to become Majority Leader for the first time in 1940. T. Hale Boggs of Louisiana who served as McCormack's Whip, 1962-1971, and Speaker Carl Albert's first majority leader, 1971-1973, was an alumnus of Ways and Means as was recent Minority Leader Richard W. Gephardt (Dem-Mo.). The only major Republican leader with Ways and Means experience is the current Minority Whip, Eric I. Cantor of Virginia.

Notable Members: The most notable member of Ways and Means in the post-1947 era would be President George H.W. Bush (Rep-Texas), who was placed on the committee as a rare freshman member in 1967. Bush then left the committee to run unsuccessfully for the U.S. Senate against Lloyd Bentsen (Dem-Texas) in 1970. Bush clearly benefitted from his legacy as one of the few House members whose father had been a two-term U.S. senator from Connecticut. This aura of great promise was clearly rewarded with the assignment, even if it took a while for the promise to be delivered when he became the eighth president to have served on Ways and Means.

While twelve one-time members of Ways and Means were chosen Secretary of the Treasury before 1947, post-1947 Cabinet members with Ways and Means experience seemed to be in short supply with only Democrat Clinton Anderson of New Mexico, President Truman's Secretary of Agriculture, and Republican Rogers C.B. Morton of Maryland qualifying. Morton served as Secretary of the Interior for both Presidents Nixon and Ford, 1971-1975 and would later be named by President Ford to be his Secretary of Commerce in 1975.

Fifteen post-1947 senators passed through Ways and Means as they moved down the long corridor of the Capitol from the House to the Senate. The number is below the average of the other House committees but not surprising; Wilbur Mills once remarked when he was asked if he ever thought of running for the Senate, "As Mr. Sam [Rayburn] said, 'Wilbur, as long as you are on Ways and Means, there is no point in running for the Senate.' " Seven of the fifteen were Democrats: Ross Bass of Tennessee, John A. Carroll of Colorado, Eugene J. McCarthy of Minnesota, Lee Metcalf of Montana, Stephen M. Young of Ohio, and two current senators—Benjamin L. Cardin of Maryland and Byron L. Dorgan of North Dakota.

The eight Republican senators who moved from Ways and Means include Thomas E. Martin of Iowa, Hank Brown of Colorado, Carl T. Curtis of Nebraska, Wyche Fowler of Georgia, Richard J. (Rick) Santorum of Pennsylvania, and current U.S. senators James P.D. Bunning of Kentucky, John E. Ensign of Nevada, and Judd Gregg of New Hampshire.

Judd Gregg was the only one of the five members of Ways and Means to return home to run for governor and then return to Congress as a U.S. senator. Democrat Jim Guy Tucker of Arkansas tried to pursue that route but failed to be nominated. He was elected Lieutenant Governor in 1990 and became governor when Bill Clinton ascended to the presidency, Democrat Hugh L. Carey of New York; and Republicans James G. Martin of North Carolina, and Carroll A. Campbell Jr. of South Carolina returned to their home states to complete their political careers as governor, their capstone.

Selected References

Cohen, Richard E., *Rostenkowski: The Pursuit of Power and the End of the Old Politics* (Chicago: Ivan R. Dee, 1999).

Feig, Douglas G., "Partisanship and Integration in Two House Committees: Ways and Means and Education and Labor," *Western Political Quarterly*, 34 (September, 1981), 426-437.

Fenno, Richard F., Jr., *Congressmen in Committees* (Boston: Little, Brown, 1973).

Manley, John F., "The House Committee on Ways and Means: Conflict Management in a Congressional Committee," *American Political Science Review*, 59 (December, 1965), 927-939.

Manley, John F., *The Politics of Finance: The House Committee on Ways and Means* (Boston: Little, Brown, 1970).

Manley, John F., "Wilbur Mills: A Study in Congressional Influence," *American Political Science Review*, 63 (June, 1969), 442-464.

Merriner, James L., *Mr. Chairman: Power in Dan Rostenkowski's America* (Carbondale, Ill.: Southern Illinois University Press, 1999).

Nathan, Richard P. and Susannah E. Calkins, "The Story of Revenue Sharing," in Robert L. Peabody, ed., *Cases in American Politics* (New York: Praeger, 1976), 11-43.

Rudder, Catherine E., "Committee Reform and the Revenue Process," in Lawrence C. Dodd and Bruce I. Oppenheimer, eds., *Congress Reconsidered* (New York: Praeger, 1977), 117-139.

Rudder, Catherine E., "Fiscal Responsibility, Fairness, and the Revenue Committees," in Lawrence C. Dodd and Bruce I. Oppenheimer, eds., *Congress Reconsidered*, 4th ed. (Washington. D.C.: CQ Press, 1989), 225-244.

Rudder, Catherine E., "Fiscal Responsibility and the Revenue Committees," in Lawrence C. Dodd and Bruce I. Oppenheimer, eds., *Congress Reconsidered*, 3rd ed. (Washington. D.C.: CQ Press, 1985), 211-222.

Schamel, Charles E. et al., "Records of the Ways and Means Committee," *Guide to the Records of the United States House of Representatives at the National Archives: 1789-1989 Bicentennial Edition* (Washington, D.C.: National Archives and Records Administration,1989), 273-285.

Schick, Allen, *Congress and Money: Budgeting, Spending, and Taxing* (Washington, DC: Urban Institute, 1980).

Schick, Allen, "The Three-Ring Budget Process: The Appropriations, Tax and Budget Committees in Congress," in Thomas Mann and Norman J. Ornstein, eds., *The New Congress* (Washington, D.C.: American Enterprise Institute, 1981), 288-328.

Schick, Allen, "The Ways and Means of Leading Ways and Means," *Brookings Review*, 7 (Fall, 1988), 16-23.

Spohn, Richard and Charles McCollum, dirs., "The House Ways and Means and Senate Finance Committees," in the Ralph Nader Congress Project, *The Revenue Committees: A Study of the House Ways and Means and Senate Finance Committee and the House and Senate Appropriations Committees* (New York: Grossman, 1975), 1-213.

Strahan, Randall W., "Agenda Change and Committee Politics in the Postreform House," *Legislative Studies Quarterly*, 13 (May, 1988), 177-197.

Strahan, Randall W., *New Ways and Means: Reform and Change in a Congressional Committee* (Chapel Hill: University of North Carolina Press, 1990).

U.S. House of Representatives, Committee on Ways and Means, *The Committee on Ways and Means: A Bicentennial History, 1789-1989*, H.Doc.100-244, 100th Congress, 2nd Session (1988).

Wright, John R., "Contributions, Lobbying, and Committee Voting in the U.S. House of Representatives," *American Political Science Review*, 84 (June, 1990), 417-438.

Zelizer, Julian E., *Taxing America: Wilbur D. Mills, Congress, and the State, 1945-1975* (New York: Cambridge University Press, 1998).

RESPONSIBILITIES, JURISDICTIONAL CHANGES, AND SUBCOMMITTEES

WAYS AND MEANS

Jurisdiction, 80th Congress (1947-1949)

Established by the Legislative Reorganization Act of 1946:

[Section 121.(1)(s)] Committee on Ways and Means
 (1) Revenue measures generally.
 (2) The bonded debt of the United States.
 (3) The deposit of public moneys.
 (4) Customs, collection districts, and ports of entry and delivery.
 (5) Reciprocal trade agreements.
 (6) Transportation of dutiable goods.
 (7) Revenue measures relating to the insular possessions.
 (8) National social security.

Jurisdiction, 103rd Congress (1993-1995)

From the *Rules of the House of Representatives, 103rd Congress* (House Document 102-405)

[Rule X.1.(v)] Committee on Ways and Means
 (1) Customs, collection districts, and ports of entry and delivery.
 (2) Reciprocal trade agreements.
 (3) Revenue measures generally.
 (4) Revenue measures relating to the insular possessions.
 (5) The bonded debt of the United States (subject to the last sentence of clause 4(g) of this rule).
 (6) The deposit of public moneys.
 (7) Transportation of dutiable goods.
 (8) Tax exempt foundations and charitable trusts.
 (9) National social security, except
 (A) health care and facilities programs that are supported from general revenues as opposed to payroll deductions and
 (B) work incentive programs.

[Rule X, Clause 4. (g) last sentence]

The views and estimates submitted by the Committee on Ways and Means under the preceding sentence shall include a specific recommendation, made after holding public hearings, as to the appropriate level of the public debt which should be set forth in the concurrent resolution on the budget referred to in such sentence and serve as the basis for an increase or decrease in the statutory limit on such debt under the procedures provided by Rule XLIX.

Jurisdiction, 104th Congress (1995-1997) Changes in Committee System

House Resolution 6, Section 202 (a), the Committees and Their Jurisdiction, January 4, 1995

[Rule X.1.(s)] Committee on Ways and Means.
 (1) Customs, collection districts, and ports of entry and delivery.
 (2) Reciprocal trade agreements.
 (3) Revenue measures generally.
 (4) Revenue measures relating to the insular possessions.
 (5) The bonded debt of the United States (subject to the last sentence of clause 4(g) of this rule).
 (6) The deposit of public moneys.
 (7) Transportation of dutiable goods.
 (8) Tax exempt foundations and charitable trusts.
 (9) National social security, except (A) health care and facilities programs that are supported from general revenues as opposed to payroll deductions and (B) work incentive programs.

Jurisdiction, 111th Congress (2009-2011)

From the *Rules of the House of Representatives* (as revised to June 16, 2009, H.Doc. 110-162):

[Rule X.1.(t)] Committee on Ways and Means
 (1) Customs, collection districts, and ports of entry and delivery.
 (2) Reciprocal trade agreements.

(3) Revenue measures generally.

(4) Revenue measures relating to insular possessions.

(5) Bonded debt of the United States, subject to the last sentence of clause 4(f).

(6) Deposit of public monies.

(7) Transportation of dutiable goods.

(8) Tax exempt foundations and charitable trusts.

(9) National social security (except health care and facilities programs that are supported from general revenues as opposed to payroll deductions and except work incentive programs)

Budget Act Responsibilities [Rule X.4.(f)(2)]

The views and estimates submitted by the Committee on Ways and Means under subparagraph (1) shall include a specific recommendation, made after holding public hearings, as to the appropriate level of the public debt that should be set forth in the concurrent resolution on the budget.

NAMES OF WAYS AND MEANS SUBCOMMITTEES FROM THE *CONGRESSIONAL DIRECTORY*

Health, 103, 104, 105, 106, 107, 108, 109, 110, 111
Human Resources, 103, 104, 105, 106, 107, 108, 109
Oversight, 103, 104, 105, 106, 107, 108, 109, 110, 111
Select Revenue Measures, 103, 107, 108, 109, 110, 111
Social Security, 103, 104, 105, 106, 107, 108, 109, 110, 111
Trade, 103, 104, 105, 106, 107, 108, 109, 110, 111
Income Security and Family Support, 110, 111

MEMBERSHIP ROSTERS, 103rd-111th Congresses, 1993-2011

WAYS AND MEANS / 103rd Congress

Service Dates of Committee Chair: Ch1: Jan. 5, 1993-June 8, 1995, Rostenkowski (Dem-Ill.)

Ch2: June 8, 1995-Jan. 3, 1995, Gibbons (Dem-Fla.)

Service Dates of Majority Members: Jan. 5, 1993-Jan. 3, 1995

Service Dates of Minority Members: Jan. 5, 1993-Jan. 3, 1995

Roster Filled: Majority with 24 members, Jan. 5, 1993; Minority with 14 members, Jan. 5, 1993

Majority

Rank Name	Party	State	Terms in: House	Terms in: Comm.
Ch1 Rostenkowski, Daniel D.	Dem	Ill.	18	16
ChA 2nd Gibbons, Sam M.	Dem	Fla.	16	13
3rd Pickle, J. J. (Jake)	Dem	Tex.	16	10
4th Rangel, Charles B.	Dem	N.Y.	12	10
5th Stark, Fortney H. (Pete)	Dem	Cal.	11	10
6th Jacobs, Andrew Jr.	Dem	Ind.	14	10
7th Ford, Harold E.	Dem	Tenn.	10	10
8th Matsui, Robert T.	Dem	Cal.	8	7
9th Kennelly, Barbara B.	Dem	Conn.	7	6
10th Coyne, William J.	Dem	Penn.	7	5
11th Andrews, Michael A.	Dem	Tex.	6	5
12th Levin, Sander M.	Dem	Mich.	6	4
13th Cardin, Benjamin L.	Dem	Md.	4	3
14th McDermott, James A.	Dem	Wash.	3	2
15th Kleczka, Gerald D.	Dem	Wisc.	6	1
16th Lewis, John R.	Dem	Ga.	4	1
17th Payne, Lewis F. Jr.	Dem	Va.	4	1
18th Neal, Richard E.	Dem	Mass.	3	1
19th Hoagland, Peter D.	Dem	Nebr.	3	1
20th McNulty, Michael R.	Dem	N.Y.	3	*1 1
21st Kopetski, Michael J.	Dem	Ore.	2	1
22nd Jefferson, William J.	Dem	La.	2	*1 1
23rd Brewster, William K.	Dem	Okla.	2	1
24th Reynolds, Mel	Dem	Ill.	1	1

Minority

Rank Name	Party	State	Terms in: House	Terms in: Comm.
RM Archer, William R.	Rep	Tex.	12	11
2nd Crane, Philip M.	Rep	Ill.	13	10
3rd Gradison, Willis D. Jr.	Rep	Ohio	10	9
4th Thomas, William M.	Rep	Cal.	8	6
5th Shaw, E. Clay Jr.	Rep	Fla.	7	4
6th Sundquist, Donald K.	Rep	Tenn.	6	3
7th Johnson, Nancy L.	Rep	Conn.	6	3
8th Bunning, James P.D.	Rep	Ky.	4	2
9th Grandy, Frederick L.	Rep	Iowa	4	2
10th Houghton, Amory Jr.	Rep	N.Y.	4	1
11th Herger, Walter W.	Rep	Cal.	4	1
12th McCrery, James O. III	Rep	La.	4	1
13th Hancock, Melton D.	Rep	Mo.	3	1
14th Santorum, Richard J. (Rick)	Rep	Penn.	2	1

*1: Member's first period of service on the committee.

Changes:

Majority:

Ch1 Rostenkowski, Daniel D.	Dem	Ill.	June 8, 1994 Indicted; stepped aside as Chair.
ChA Gibbons, Sam M.	Dem	Fla.	June 8, 1994 Replaced Rostenkowski as Acting Chair.

Minority:

Gradison, Willis D. Jr	Rep	Ohio	Jan. 31, 1993 Resigned the House; named President of HIAA.
Camp, David L.	Rep	Mich.	Feb. 4, 1993 Replaced Gradison.

Departures from the House:	Majority			Minority		
Elected Governor	None			Sundquist, Donald K.	Rep	Tenn.
Elected to U.S. Senate	None			Santorum, Richard J. (Rick)	Rep	Penn.
Lost Nomination for Governor	None			Grandy, Frederick L.	Rep	Iowa
Lost Nomination to U.S. Senate	Andrews, Michael A.	Dem	Tex.	None		
Defeated for Re-election	Rostenkowski, Daniel D.	Dem	Ill.	None		
	Hoagland, Peter D.	Dem	Neb.			
Retired	Pickle, J.J. (Jake)	Dem	Tex.	None		
	Kopetski, Michael J.	Dem	Ore.			

Departures from Committee:						
Moved to Economic and Educational Opportunities	Reynolds, Mel	Dem	Ill.	None		
Moved to House Oversight	Jefferson, William J.	Dem	La.	None		
Moved to International Relations	McNulty, Michael R.	Dem	N.Y.	None		
Moved to National Security	Jefferson, William J.	Dem	La.	None		
Returned to Transportation and Infrastructure	Brewster, William K.	Dem	La.	None		

WAYS AND MEANS / 104th Congress

Service Dates of Committee Chair: Jan. 4, 1995-Jan. 3, 1997

Service Dates of Majority Members: Jan. 4, 1995-Jan. 3, 1997

Service Dates of Minority Members: Jan. 4, 1995-Jan. 3, 1997

Roster Filled: Majority with 21 members, Jan. 4, 1995; Minority with 15 members, Jan. 4, 1995

	Majority			Terms in:			Minority			Terms in:	
Rank Name		Party	State	House	Comm.	Rank Name		Party	State	House	Comm.
Chr Archer, William R.		Rep	Tex.	13	12	RM Gibbons, Sam M.		Dem	Fla.	17	14
2nd Crane, Philip M.		Rep	Ill.	14	11	2nd Rangel, Charles B.		Dem	N.Y.	13	11
3rd Thomas, William M.		Rep	Cal.	9	7	3rd Stark, Fortney H. (Pete)		Dem	Cal.	12	11
4th Shaw, E. Clay Jr.		Rep	Fla.	8	5	4th Jacobs, Andrew Jr.		Dem	Ind.	15	11
5th Johnson, Nancy L.		Rep	Conn.	7	4	5th Ford, Harold E.		Dem	Tenn.	11	11
6th Bunning, James P.D.		Rep	Ky.	5	3	6th Matsui, Robert T.		Dem	Cal.	9	8
7th Houghton, Amory Jr.		Rep	N.Y.	5	2	7th Kennelly, Barbara B.		Dem	Conn.	8	7
8th Herger, Walter W.		Rep	Cal.	5	2	8th Coyne, William J.		Dem	Penn.	8	6
9th McCrery, James O. III		Rep	La.	5	2	9th Levin, Sander M.		Dem	Mich.	7	5
10th Hancock, Melton D.		Rep	Mo.	4	2	10th Cardin, Benjamin L.		Dem	Md.	5	4
11th Camp, David L.		Rep	Mich.	3	2	11th McDermott, James A.		Dem	Wash.	4	3
12th Ramstad, James		Rep	Minn.	3	1	12th Kleczka, Gerald D.		Dem	Wisc.	7	2
13th Zimmer, Richard		Rep	N.J.	3	1	13th Lewis, John R.		Dem	Ga.	5	2
14th Nussle, James A.		Rep	Iowa	3	1	14th Payne, Lewis F. Jr.		Dem	Va.	5	2
15th Johnson, Sam		Rep	Tex.	3	1	15th Neal, Richard E.		Dem	Mass.	4	2
16th Dunn, Jennifer B.		Rep	Wash.	2	1						
17th Collins, Michael A. (Mac)		Rep	Ga.	2	1						
18th Portman, Robert J.		Rep	Ohio	2	1						
19th English, Philip S.		Rep	Penn.	1	1						
20th Ensign, John E.		Rep	Nev.	1	1						
21st Christensen, Jon		Rep	Nebr.	1	1						

Additions:

Majority:

22nd Laughlin, Gregory H.	Rep	Tex.	July 10, 1995
23rd Hayes, James A.	Rep	La.	Jan. 25, 1996

Minority:

16th McNulty, Michael R.	Dem	N.Y.	Jan. 25, 1996

Departures from the House:	Majority			Minority		
Lost Nomination to U.S. Senate	Hayes, James A.	Rep	La.	None		
Lost Election to U.S. Senate	Zimmer, Richard	Rep	N.J.	None		
Defeated for Re-nomination	Laughlin, Gregory H.	Rep	Tex.	None		
Retired	Hancock, Melton D.	Rep	Mo.	Gibbons, Sam M.	Dem	Fla.
				Jacobs, Andrew Jr.	Dem	Ind.
				Ford, Harold E.	Dem	Tenn.
				Payne, Lewis F. Jr.	Dem	Va.

WAYS AND MEANS / 105th Congress

Service Dates of Committee Chair: Jan. 7, 1997-Jan. 3, 1999

Service Dates of Majority Members: Jan. 7, 1997-Jan. 3, 1999

Service Dates of Minority Members: Jan. 7, 1997-Jan. 3, 1999

Roster Filled: Majority with 23 members, Jan. 7, 1997; Minority with 16 members, Jan. 7, 1997

Majority			Terms in:		Minority			Terms in:	
Rank Name	Party	State	House	Comm.	Rank Name	Party	State	House	Comm.
Chr Archer, William R.	Rep	Tex.	14	13	RM Rangel, Charles B.	Dem	N.Y.	14	12
2nd Crane, Philip M.	Rep	Ill.	15	12	2nd Stark, Fortney H. (Pete)	Dem	Cal.	13	12
3rd Thomas, William M.	Rep	Cal.	10	8	3rd Matsui, Robert T.	Dem	Cal.	10	9
4th Shaw, E. Clay Jr.	Rep	Fla.	9	6	4th Kennelly, Barbara B.	Dem	Conn.	9	8
5th Johnson, Nancy L.	Rep	Conn.	8	5	5th Coyne, William J.	Dem	Penn.	9	7
6th Bunning, James P.D.	Rep	Ky.	6	4	6th Levin, Sander M.	Dem	Mich.	8	6
7th Houghton, Amory Jr.	Rep	N.Y.	6	3	7th Cardin, Benjamin L.	Dem	Md.	6	5
8th Herger, Walter W.	Rep	Cal.	6	3	8th McDermott, James A.	Dem	Wash.	5	4
9th McCrery, James O. III	Rep	La.	6	3	9th Kleczka, Gerald D.	Dem	Wisc.	8	3
10th Camp, David L.	Rep	Mich.	4	3	10th Lewis, John R.	Dem	Ga.	6	3
11th Ramstad, James	Rep	Minn.	4	2	11th Neal, Richard E.	Dem	Mass.	5	3
12th Nussle, James A.	Rep	Iowa	4	2	12th McNulty, Michael R.	Dem	N.Y.	5	*2 2
13th Johnson, Sam	Rep	Tex.	4	2	13th Jefferson, William J.	Dem	La.	4	*2 1
14th Dunn, Jennifer B.	Rep	Wash.	3	2	14th Tanner, John S.	Dem	Tenn.	5	1
15th Collins, Michael A. (Mac)	Rep	Ga.	3	2	15th Becerra, Xavier	Dem	Cal.	3	1
16th Portman, Robert J.	Rep	Ohio	3	2	16th Thurman, Karen L.	Dem	Fla.	3	1
17th English, Philip S.	Rep	Penn.	2	2					
18th Ensign, John E.	Rep	Nev.	2	2	*2: Member's second period of service on the committee.				
19th Christensen, Jon	Rep	Nebr.	2	2					
20th Watkins, Wesley W.	Rep	Okla.	8	1					
21st Hayworth, John D. Jr.	Rep	Ariz.	2	1					
22nd Weller, Gerald C.	Rep	Ill.	2	1					
23rd Hulshof, Kenny	Rep	Mo.	1	1					

Departures from the House:	Majority			Minority		
Elected to U.S. Senate	Bunning, James P.D.	Rep	Ky.	None		
Lost Nomination for Governor	Christensen, Jon	Rep	Neb.	None		
Lost Election for Governor	None			Kennelly, Barbara B.	Dem	Conn.
Lost Election to U.S. Senate	Ensign, John E.	Rep	Nev.			

WAYS AND MEANS / 106th Congress

Service Dates of Committee Chair: Jan. 6, 1999-Jan. 3, 2001

Service Dates of Majority Members: Jan. 6, 1999-Jan. 3, 2001

Service Dates of Minority Members: Jan. 6, 1999-Jan. 3, 2001

Roster Filled: Majority with 23 members, Jan. 6, 1999; Minority with 16 members, Jan. 6, 1999

Majority			Terms in:		Minority			Terms in:	
Rank Name	Party	State	House	Comm.	Rank Name	Party	State	House	Comm.
Chr Archer, William R.	Rep	Tex.	15	14	RM Rangel, Charles B.	Dem	N.Y.	15	13
2nd Crane, Philip M.	Rep	Ill.	16	13	2nd Stark, Fortney H. (Pete)	Dem	Cal.	14	13
3rd Thomas, William M.	Rep	Cal.	11	9	3rd Matsui, Robert T.	Dem	Cal.	11	10
4th Shaw, E. Clay Jr.	Rep	Fla.	10	7	4th Coyne, William J.	Dem	Penn.	10	8

			House	Comm.				House	Comm.
5th Johnson, Nancy L.	Rep	Conn.	9	6	5th Levin, Sander M.	Dem	Mich.	9	7
6th Houghton, Amory Jr.	Rep	N.Y.	7	4	6th Cardin, Benjamin L.	Dem	Md.	7	6
7th Herger, Walter W.	Rep	Cal.	7	4	7th McDermott, James A.	Dem	Wash.	6	5
8th McCrery, James O. III	Rep	La.	7	4	8th Kleczka, Gerald D.	Dem	Wisc.	9	4
9th Camp, David L.	Rep	Mich.	5	4	9th Lewis, John R.	Dem	Ga.	7	4
10th Ramstad, James	Rep	Minn.	5	3	10th Neal, Richard E.	Dem	Mass.	6	4
11th Nussle, James A.	Rep	Iowa	5	3	11th McNulty, Michael R.	Dem	N.Y.	6	*2 3
12th Johnson, Sam	Rep	Tex.	5	3	12th Jefferson, William J.	Dem	La.	5	*2 2
13th Dunn, Jennifer B.	Rep	Wash.	4	3	13th Tanner, John S.	Dem	Tenn.	6	2
14th Collins, Michael A. (Mac)	Rep	Ga.	4	3	14th Becerra, Xavier	Dem	Cal.	4	2
15th Portman, Robert J.	Rep	Ohio	4	3	15th Thurman, Karen L.	Dem	Fla.	4	2
16th English, Philip S.	Rep	Penn.	3	3	16th Doggett, Lloyd A. II	Dem	Tex.	3	1
17th Watkins, Wesley W.	Rep	Okla.	9	2					
18th Hayworth, John D. Jr.	Rep	Ariz.	3	2					
19th Weller, Gerald C.	Rep	Ill.	3	2					
20th Hulshof, Kenny	Rep	Mo.	2	2					
21st McInnis, Scott	Rep	Colo.	4	1					
22nd Lewis, Ron	Rep	Ky.	4	1					
23rd Foley, Mark A.	Rep	Fla.	3	1					

*2: Member's second period of service on the committee.

Departures from the House:		**Majority**				**Minority**	
Retired		Archer, William R.		Rep	Tex.	None	

WAYS AND MEANS / 107th Congress

Service Dates of Committee Chair: Jan. 6, 2001-Jan. 3, 2003

Service Dates of Majority Members: Jan. 6, 2001-Jan. 3, 2003

Service Dates of Minority Members: Jan. 31, 2001-Jan. 3, 2003

Roster Filled: Majority with 24 members, Jan. 6, 2001; Minority with 17 members, Jan. 31, 2001

Majority					**Minority**				
			Terms in:					**Terms in:**	
Rank Name	Party	State	House	Comm.	Rank Name	Party	State	House	Comm.
Chr Thomas, William M.	Rep	Cal.	12	10	RM Rangel, Charles B.	Dem	N.Y.	16	14
2nd Crane, Philip M.	Rep	Ill.	17	14	2nd Stark, Fortney H. (Pete)	Dem	Cal.	15	14
3rd Shaw, E. Clay Jr.	Rep	Fla.	11	8	3rd Matsui, Robert T.	Dem	Cal.	12	11
4th Johnson, Nancy L.	Rep	Conn.	10	7	4th Coyne, William J.	Dem	Penn.	11	9
5th Houghton, Amory Jr.	Rep	N.Y.	8	5	5th Levin, Sander M.	Dem	Mich.	10	8
6th Herger, Walter W.	Rep	Cal.	8	5	6th Cardin, Benjamin L.	Dem	Md.	8	7
7th McCrery, James O. III	Rep	La.	8	5	7th McDermott, James A.	Dem	Wash.	7	6
8th Camp, David L.	Rep	Mich.	6	5	8th Kleczka, Gerald D.	Dem	Wisc.	10	5
9th Ramstad, James	Rep	Minn.	6	4	9th Lewis, John R.	Dem	Ga.	8	5
10th Nussle, James A.	Rep	Iowa	6	4	10th Neal, Richard E.	Dem	Mass.	7	5
11th Johnson, Sam	Rep	Tex.	6	4	11th McNulty, Michael R.	Dem	N.Y.	7	*2 4
12th Dunn, Jennifer B.	Rep	Wash.	5	4	12th Jefferson, William J.	Dem	La.	6	*2 3
13th Collins, Michael A. (Mac)	Rep	Ga.	5	4	13th Tanner, John S.	Dem	Tenn.	7	3
14th Portman, Robert J.	Rep	Ohio	5	4	14th Becerra, Xavier	Dem	Cal.	5	3
15th English, Philip S.	Rep	Penn.	4	4	15th Thurman, Karen L.	Dem	Fla.	5	3
16th Watkins, Wesley W.	Rep	Okla.	10	3	16th Doggett, Lloyd A. II	Dem	Tex.	4	2
17th Hayworth, John D. Jr.	Rep	Ariz.	4	3	17th Pomeroy, Earl R. III	Dem	N.D.	5	1
18th Weller, Gerald C.	Rep	Ill.	4	3					
19th Hulshof, Kenny	Rep	Mo.	3	3					
20th McInnis, Scott	Rep	Colo.	5	2					
21st Lewis, Ron	Rep	Ky.	5	2					
22nd Foley, Mark A.	Rep	Fla.	4	2					
23rd Brady, Kevin P.	Rep	Tex.	3	1					
24th Ryan, Paul D.	Rep	Wisc.	2	1					

*2: Member's second period of service on the committee.

Departures from the House:		**Majority**				**Minority**		
Defeated for Re-election		None				Thurman, Karen L.	Dem	Fla.
Retired		Watkins, Wesley W.		Rep	La.	Coyne, William J.	Dem	Penn.

WAYS AND MEANS / 108th Congress

Service Dates of Committee Chair: Jan. 8, 2003-Jan. 3, 2005

Service Dates of Majority Members: Jan. 28, 2003-Jan. 3, 2005

Service Dates of Ranking Member: Jan. 8, 2003-Jan. 3, 2005

Service Dates of Minority Members: Jan. 28, 2003-Jan. 3, 2005

Roster Filled: Majority with 24 members, Jan. 28, 2003; Minority with 17 members, Jan. 28, 2003

Majority

Rank Name	Party	State	Terms in: House	Terms in: Comm.
Chr Thomas, William M.	Rep	Cal.	13	11
2nd Crane, Philip M.	Rep	Ill.	18	15
3rd Shaw, E. Clay Jr.	Rep	Fla.	12	9
4th Johnson, Nancy L.	Rep	Conn.	11	8
5th Houghton, Amory Jr.	Rep	N.Y.	9	6
6th Herger, Walter W.	Rep	Cal.	9	6
7th McCrery, James O. III	Rep	La.	9	6
8th Camp, David L.	Rep	Mich.	7	6
9th Ramstad, James	Rep	Minn.	7	5
10th Nussle, James A.	Rep	Iowa	7	5
11th Johnson, Sam	Rep	Tex.	7	5
12th Dunn, Jennifer B.	Rep	Wash.	6	5
13th Collins, Michael A. (Mac)	Rep	Ga.	6	5
14th Portman, Robert J.	Rep	Ohio	6	5
15th English, Philip S.	Rep	Penn.	5	5
16th Hayworth, John D. Jr.	Rep	Ariz.	5	4
17th Weller, Gerald C.	Rep	Ill.	5	4
18th Hulshof, Kenny	Rep	Mo.	4	4
19th McInnis, Scott	Rep	Colo.	6	3
20th Lewis, Ron	Rep	Ky.	6	3
21st Foley, Mark A.	Rep	Fla.	5	3
22nd Brady, Kevin P.	Rep	Tex.	4	2
23rd Ryan, Paul D.	Rep	Wisc.	3	2
24th Cantor, Eric I.	Rep	Va.	2	1

Minority

Rank Name	Party	State	Terms in: House	Terms in: Comm.
RM Rangel, Charles B.	Dem	N.Y.	17	15
2nd Stark, Fortney H. (Pete)	Dem	Cal.	16	15
3rd Matsui, Robert T.	Dem	Cal.	13	12
4th Levin, Sander M.	Dem	Mich.	11	9
5th Cardin, Benjamin L.	Dem	Md.	9	8
6th McDermott, James A.	Dem	Wash.	8	7
7th Kleczka, Gerald D.	Dem	Wisc.	11	6
8th Lewis, John R.	Dem	Ga.	9	6
9th Neal, Richard E.	Dem	Mass.	8	6
10th McNulty, Michael R.	Dem	N.Y.	8	*2 5
11th Jefferson, William J.	Dem	La.	7	*2 4
12th Tanner, John S.	Dem	Tenn.	8	4
13th Becerra, Xavier	Dem	Cal.	6	4
14th Doggett, Lloyd A. II	Dem	Tex.	5	3
15th Pomeroy, Earl R. III	Dem	N.D.	6	2
16th Sandlin, Max A.	Dem	Tex.	4	1
17th Jones, Stephanie Tubbs	Dem	Ohio	3	1

*2: Member's second period of service on the committee.

Changes:
Minority:

Matsui, Robert T.	Dem	Cal.	Jan. 1, 2005 Died in office after adjournment.

Departures from the House:

	Majority			Minority		
Lost Nomination to U.S. Senate	Collins, Michael A. (Mac)	Rep	Ga.	None		
Defeated for Re-election	Crane, Philip M.	Rep	Ill.	Sandlin, Max A.	Dem	Tex.
Retired	Houghton, Amory Jr.	Rep	N.Y.	Kleczka, Gerald D.	Dem	Wisc.
	Dunn, Jennifer B.	Rep	Wash.			
	McInnis, Scott	Rep	Colo.			

WAYS AND MEANS / 109th Congress

Service Dates of Committee Chair: Jan. 6, 2005-Jan. 3, 2007

Service Dates of Majority Members: Jan. 6, 2005-Jan. 3, 2007

Service Dates of Ranking Member: Jan. 6, 2005-Jan. 3, 2007

Service Dates of Minority Members: Jan. 26, 2005-Jan. 3, 2007

Roster Filled: Majority with 24 members, Jan. 6, 2005; Minority with 17 members, Jan. 26, 2005

Majority

Rank Name	Party	State	Terms in: House	Terms in: Comm.
Chr Thomas, William M.	Rep	Cal.	14	12
2nd Shaw, E. Clay Jr.	Rep	Fla.	13	10
3rd Johnson, Nancy L.	Rep	Conn.	12	9
4th Herger, Walter W.	Rep	Cal.	10	7
5th McCrery, James O. III	Rep	La.	10	7
6th Camp, David L.	Rep	Mich.	8	7

Minority

Rank Name	Party	State	Terms in: House	Terms in: Comm.
RM Rangel, Charles B.	Dem	N.Y.	18	16
2nd Stark, Fortney H. (Pete)	Dem	Cal.	17	16
3rd Levin, Sander M.	Dem	Mich.	12	10
4th Cardin, Benjamin L.	Dem	Md.	10	9
5th McDermott, James A.	Dem	Wash.	9	8
6th Lewis, John R.	Dem	Ga.	10	7

7th Ramstad, James	Rep	Minn.	8	6
8th Nussle, James A.	Rep	Iowa	8	6
9th Johnson, Sam	Rep	Tex.	8	6
10th Portman, Robert J.	Rep	Ohio	7	6
11th English, Philip S.	Rep	Penn.	6	6
12th Hayworth, John D. Jr.	Rep	Ariz.	6	5
13th Weller, Gerald C.	Rep	Ill.	6	5
14th Hulshof, Kenny	Rep	Mo.	5	5
15th Lewis, Ron	Rep	Ky.	7	4
16th Foley, Mark A.	Rep	Fla.	6	4
17th Brady, Kevin P.	Rep	Tex.	5	3
18th Reynolds, Thomas M.	Rep	N.Y.	4	1
19th Ryan, Paul D.	Rep	Wisc.	4	3
20th Cantor, Eric I.	Rep	Va.	3	2
21st Linder, John E.	Rep	Ga.	7	1
22nd Hart, Melissa A.	Rep	Penn.	3	1
23rd Beauprez, Bob	Rep	Colo.	2	1
24th Chocola, Chris	Rep	Ind.	2	1

7th Neal, Richard E.	Dem	Mass.	9	7
8th McNulty, Michael R.	Dem	N.Y.	9	*2 6
9th Jefferson, William J.	Dem	La.	8	*2 5
10th Tanner, John S.	Dem	Tenn.	9	5
11th Becerra, Xavier	Dem	Cal.	7	5
12th Doggett, Lloyd A. II	Dem	Tex.	6	4
13th Pomeroy, Earl R. III	Dem	N.D.	7	3
14th Jones, Stephanie Tubbs	Dem	Ohio	4	2
15th Thompson, Michael	Dem	Cal.	4	1
16th Larson, John B.	Dem	Conn.	4	1
17th Emanuel, Rahm	Dem	Ill.	2	1

*2: Member's second period of service on the committee.

Changes:

Majority:

Portman, Robert J.	Rep	Ohio	Apr. 29, 2005 Resigned the House; appointed U.S. Trade Representative.
Nunes, Devin	Rep	Cal.	May 5, 2005 Replaced Portman.
Foley, Mark A.	Rep	Fla.	Sept. 29, 2006 Resigned the House and retired; ethics issue.

Minority:

Jefferson, William J.	Dem	La.	June 16, 2006 Voted removal from committee due to ethics issue.
Davis, Artur	Dem	Ala.	Dec. 12, 2006 Replaced Jefferson on conditional appointment.

Departures from the House:

	Majority			Minority		
Elected to U.S. Senate	None			Cardin, Benjamin L.	Dem	Md.
Lost Election for Governor	Nussle, James A.	Rep	Iowa	None		
	Beauprez, Bob	Rep	Colo.			
Defeated for Re-election	Shaw, E. Clay Jr.	Rep	Fla.	None		
	Johnson, Nancy L.	Rep	Conn.			
	Hayworth, John D. Jr.	Rep	Ariz.			
	Hart, Melissa A.	Rep	Penn.			
	Chocola, Chris	Rep	Ind.			
Retired	Thomas, William M.	Rep	Cal.	None		

WAYS AND MEANS / 110th Congress

Service Dates of Committee Chair: Jan. 4, 2007-Jan. 3, 2009

Service Dates of Majority Members: Jan. 4, 2007-Jan. 3, 2009

Service Dates of Minority Members: Jan. 4, 2007-Jan. 3, 2009

Roster Filled: Majority with 24 members, Jan. 4, 2007; Minority with 17 members, Jan. 4, 2007

Majority			Terms in:		Minority			Terms in:	
Rank Name	Party	State	House	Comm.	Rank Name	Party	State	House	Comm.
Chr Rangel, Charles B.	Dem	N.Y.	19	17	RM McCrery, James O. III	Rep	La.	11	8
2nd Stark, Fortney H. (Pete)	Dem	Cal.	18	17	2nd Herger, Walter W.	Rep	Cal.	11	8
3rd Levin, Sander M.	Dem	Mich.	13	11	3rd Camp, David L.	Rep	Mich.	9	8
4th McDermott, James A.	Dem	Wash.	10	9	4th Ramstad, James	Rep	Minn.	9	7
5th Lewis, John R.	Dem	Ga.	11	8	5th Johnson, Sam	Rep	Tex.	9	7
6th Neal, Richard E.	Dem	Mass.	10	8	6th English, Philip S.	Rep	Penn.	7	7
7th McNulty, Michael R.	Dem	N.Y.	10	*2 7	7th Weller, Gerald C.	Rep	Ill.	7	6
8th Tanner, John S.	Dem	Tenn.	10	6	8th Hulshof, Kenny	Rep	Mo.	6	6
9th Becerra, Xavier	Dem	Cal.	8	6	9th Lewis, Ron	Rep	Ky.	8	5
10th Doggett, Lloyd A. II	Dem	Tex.	7	5	10th Brady, Kevin P.	Rep	Tex.	6	4
11th Pomeroy, Earl R. III	Dem	N.D.	8	4	11th Reynolds, Thomas M.	Rep	N.Y.	5	2
12th Jones, Stephanie Tubbs	Dem	Ohio	5	3	12th Ryan, Paul D.	Rep	Wisc.	5	4
13th Thompson, Michael	Dem	Cal.	5	2	13th Cantor, Eric I.	Rep	Va.	4	3
14th Larson, John B.	Dem	Conn.	5	2	14th Linder, John E.	Rep	Ga.	8	2
15th Emanuel, Rahm	Dem	Ill.	3	2	15th Nunes, Devin	Rep	Cal.	3	2
16th Blumenauer, Earl	Dem	Ore.	7	1	16th Tiberi, Patrick	Rep	Ohio	4	1

17th Kind, Ron	Dem	Wisc.	6	1		17th Porter, Jon C.		Rep	Nev.	3	1
18th Pascrell, William J. Jr.	Dem	N.J.	6	1							
19th Berkley, Shelley	Dem	Nev.	5	1		*2: Member's second period of service on the committee.					
20th Crowley, Joseph	Dem	N.Y.	5	1							
21st Van Hollen, Christopher	Dem	Md.	3	1							
22nd Meek, Kendrick B.	Dem	Fla.	3	1							
23rd Schwartz, Allyson Y.	Dem	Penn.	2	1							
24th Davis, Artur	Dem	Ala.	3	2							

Changes:
  Majority:

Jones, Stephanie Tubbs	Dem	Ohio	Aug. 20, 2008 Died in office.
Emanuel, Rahm	Dem	Ill.	Jan. 2, 2009 Resigned the House; appointed White House Chief of Staff.

Departures from the House:	**Majority**			**Minority**		
Lost Election for Governor	None			Hulshof, Kenny	Rep	Mo.
Defeated for Re-election	None			English, Philip S.	Rep	Penn.
				Porter, Jon C.	Rep	Nev.
Retired	McNulty, Michael R.	Dem	N.Y.	McCrery, James O. III	Rep	La.
				Ramstad, James	Rep	Minn.
				Weller, Gerald C.	Rep	Ill.
				Lewis, Ron	Rep	Ky.
				Reynolds, Thomas M.	Rep	N.Y.

WAYS AND MEANS / 111th Congress

Service Dates of Committee Chair: Jan. 6, 2009-Jan. 3, 2011

Service Dates of Majority Members: Jan. 7, 2009-Jan.3, 2011

Service Dates of Minority Members: Jan. 9, 2009-Jan. 3, 2011

Roster Filled: Majority with 26 members, Jan. 7, 2009; Minority with 15 members, Jan. 9, 2009

Majority					**Minority**				
			Terms in:					**Terms in:**	
Rank Name	**Party**	**State**	**House**	**Comm.**	**Rank Name**	**Party**	**State**	**House**	**Comm.**
Ch1 Rangel, Charles B.	Dem	N.Y.	20	18	RM Camp, David L.	Rep	Mich.	10	9
ChT 2nd Stark, Fortney H. (Pete)	Dem	Cal.	19	18	2nd Herger, Walter W.	Rep	Cal.	12	9
ChA 3rd Levin, Sander M.	Dem	Mich.	14	12	3rd Johnson, Sam	Rep	Tex.	10	8
4th McDermott, James A.	Dem	Wash.	11	10	4th Brady, Kevin P.	Rep	Tex.	7	5
5th Lewis, John R.	Dem	Ga.	12	9	5th Ryan, Paul D.	Rep	Wisc.	6	5
6th Neal, Richard E.	Dem	Mass.	11	9	6th Cantor, Eric I.	Rep	Va.	5	4
7th Tanner, John S.	Dem	Tenn.	11	7	7th Linder, John E.	Rep	Ga.	9	3
8th Becerra, Xavier	Dem	Cal.	9	7	8th Nunes, Devin	Rep	Cal.	4	3
9th Doggett, Lloyd A. II	Dem	Tex.	8	6	9th Tiberi, Patrick	Rep	Ohio	5	2
10th Pomeroy, Earl R. III	Dem	N.D.	9	5	10th Brown-Waite, Virginia	Rep	Fla.	4	1
11th Thompson, Michael	Dem	Cal.	6	3	11th Davis, Geoffrey C.	Rep	Ky.	3	1
12th Larson, John B.	Dem	Conn.	6	3	12th Reichert, David G.	Rep	Wash.	3	1
13th Blumenauer, Earl	Dem	Ore.	8	2	13th Boustany, Charles W. Jr.	Rep	La.	3	1
14th Kind, Ron	Dem	Wisc.	7	2	14th Heller, Dean	Rep	Nev.	2	1
15th Pascrell, William J. Jr.	Dem	N.J.	7	2	15th Roskam, Peter	Rep	Ill.	2	1
16th Berkley, Shelley	Dem	Nev.	6	2					
17th Crowley, Joseph	Dem	N.Y.	6	2					
18th Van Hollen, Christopher	Dem	Md.	4	2					
19th Meek, Kendrick B.	Dem	Fla.	4	2					
20th Schwartz, Allyson Y.	Dem	Penn.	3	2					
21st Davis, Artur	Dem	Ala.	4	3					
22nd Davis, Danny K.	Dem	Ill.	7	1					
23rd Etheridge, Bobby R.	Dem	N.C.	7	1					
24th Sanchez, Linda T.	Dem	Cal.	4	1					
25th Higgins, Brian	Dem	N.Y.	2	1					
26th Yarmuth, John A.	Dem	Ky.	2	1					

Changes:
  Majority:

Ch1 Rangel, Charles B.	Dem	N.Y.	Mar. 3, 2001 Ethics issue; stepped aside as Chair.
ChT Stark, Fortney H. (Pete)	Dem	Cal.	Mar. 3, 2010 Replaced Rangel as Temporary Chair.
ChA Levin, Sander M.	Dem	Mich.	Mar. 4, 2010 Replaced Rangel as Acting Chair.

Part I

D. Select and Special Committees of the House of Representatives

Backgrounds, Jurisdictions, and Rosters
1993-2011

House Select and Special Committees
1993-2011

House Select and Special Committees: A Brief History

On April 2, 1789, the newly-installed Congress of the United States appointed its first select committee four weeks before George Washington, the first president, was sworn in. The Select Committee on Standing Rules and Orders was an eleven-member panel that met for only twelve days.

Nicholas Gilman of New Hampshire was its chair and he was one of its four members who had served at the Constitutional Convention in 1787. His fellow Constitutional draftsmen on the committee were James Madison of Virginia, Elbridge Gerry of Massachusetts, and the inimitable Roger Sherman of Connecticut, whose "Connecticut Compromise" saved the Constitutional Convention from breaking up over the big state-small state conflict. Sherman, who signed the Constitution, and Gerry, who would not, had signed the 1776 Declaration of Independence, making them Founding Fathers of the first rank. Four of the other seven committee members had served in the Continental Congress, while the others had served in their state constitutional conventions and legislatures. They were a highly skilled set of legislators and were fully aware of how central committees would be in the effective functioning of legislative bodies. All told, the First Congress (1789-1791) named 220 select committees, mostly three-member panels focused on specific bills.

As the House became more institutionalized, the number of standing committees increased, and with greater consolidation of their jurisdictional authority, the role of the select and special committees diminished. This may be seen in the table presented below as the average number of select and special committees appointed each Congress dropped from the 170.8 appointed in the Federalist era, 1789-1801 to 148.0 in the first six Congresses of the Jeffersonian era. It was in Speaker Henry Clay's second Congress, the 13th, 1813-1815, that the number of select and special committees fell below one hundred for the first time. In the 18th Congress, 1823-1825, during Clay's last speakership, that the number of select committees dropped to fifty-seven in spite of the fact that the membership of the House was growing regularly after each decennial census. The number of members on the select and special committees grew larger, with between five and seven members regularly appointed, but the number of the committees themselves dropped steadily. In three of the six Congresses—the 31st to the 36th—elected before the Civil War, the number of select committees dropped into single digits, with only six named in the 32nd Congress, 1851-1853.

During the 48th Congress, 1883-1885, many of the select committees began to acquire some continuity and eventually became standing committees. Examples from that era include Select Reform in the Civil Service and Select Election of the President and Vice President and Representatives in Congress, when both became standing committees after

five successive Congresses as select committees between 1883 and 1893. These two committees survived intact until the Legislative Reorganization Act of 1946 when they were folded into the newly created standing committees of Post Office and Civil Service and House Administration respectively.

NUMBER AND AVERAGE OF HOUSE SELECT AND SPECIAL COMMITTEES APPOINTED, 1789-1883

Congresses	Years	Total	Average	High	Low
1st-6th	1789-1801	1025	170.8	221	117
7th-12th	1801-1813	888	148.0	189	127
13th-18th	1813-1825	510	85.0	122	56
19th-24th	1825-1837	189	31.5	41	23
25th-30th	1837-1849	186	31.0	54	18
31st-36th	1849-1861	80	13.3	23	6
37th-42nd	1861-1873	95	15.8	20	8
43rd-47th	1873-1883	55	11.0	17	6

In the years leading up to the 1946 Reorganization Act, the number of select committees had diminished, with less than a handful surviving more than a single Congress. The longest lasting of these was the Select Committee to Investigate Campaign Expenditures that was regularly named from 1928 until it was terminated by the Committee Reform Amendments of 1974. The best known of these later named committees was the Select Committee on Un-American Activities that was named in 1938 and was the only select committee to become a standing committee in the 1946 reorganization. That committee gained its initial impetus from the Select Committee to Investigate Communist Propaganda in the United States, chaired by Rep. Hamilton Fish (Rep-N.Y.), who served from 1930 to 1931. Fish would forever be known best, along with fellow representatives Joseph Martin Jr. (Rep-Mass.) and Bruce Barton (Rep-N.Y.) as President Franklin D. Roosevelt's foil, referred to in Roosevelt's oft-quoted remark of the Republican opposition triumvirate of "Martin, Barton, and Fish." The other predecessor of Un-American Activities was the 1934-1935 Select Committee to Investigate Nazi Propaganda Activities, chaired by Rep. John W. McCormack (Dem-Mass.), who would become Speaker of the House in 1962.

Historically, there were distinctions between the select and special committees depending upon the appointing officer, whether it would be the Speaker or the floor leaders, but the intent of both terms was to indicate their temporary nature. In the modern Congress, the distinction between the select and the special committees has disappeared. The "select" designation is the preferred one. These committees are not authorized to introduce legislation. However, the investigative reports which they file with their respective chambers are used as guides for the standing committees to report legislation. The jurisdictional responsibilities of the select and special committees are delineated in the establishing resolutions.

It was the intent of the authors of the 1946 Reorganization Act that the practice of naming select committees be discontinued and that, as much as possible, the reconstituted standing committees be given sole jurisdiction over legislative matters. However, the Act's elimination of many House standing committees led to the creation of a number of short-term select and special committees even though conflicts over creating select committees in the post-reorganization House were more heated than they were in the Senate. The House was reluctant to abandon the practice and seven select committees with fifty-seven members were named in the 80th Congress (1947-1949). The only select committee to be regularly appointed in the wake of that act was the Select Committee on Small Business that became a standing committee, following the passage of the Committee Reform Amendments of 1974.

Select and special committees began to proliferate again. From the 80th to the 93rd Congresses (1947-1975)—the post-reorganization and pre-reform Era—the House named an average of 5.4 select and special committees with an average of 38.0 members per Congress assigned to these committees. The range varied from a high in the 82nd Congress (1951-1953) of sixty members serving on eight select committees to a low of twenty-one members on three select committees in the 87th Congress (1961-1963). The select and special committees did not play a large role in the business of the House during those years.

The mid-1970's brought changes in the role of House select and special committees. The 1974 resignation of President Richard Nixon led the Congress to reassert its constitutional authority and to rein in the "imperial presidency." With the arrival in the House of the "Watergate class" in 1975 and the election of activist Speaker Thomas P. (Tip) O'Neill Jr. (D-Mass.) two years later, the select committees would grow in number and size during the post-reform era. O'Neill saw the select committees as a way of giving the new members some influence and prestige without upsetting the existing standing committee power structure.

In 1975, nine select committees were named with a total membership of 123. Two years later, in O'Neill's first year as speaker, there were ten select committees with 181 members. Three select committees accounted for the bulk of the increase: Intelligence, Aging, and Narcotics Abuse and Control. From the post-reform 94th Congress through the 102nd Congresses (1975-1993), the number of House select and special committees grew to an average of 6.8 per Congress, slightly more than in the pre-1975 Congresses, but the average number of House members mushroomed to 151.1 per Congress, almost four times the thirty-eight House members per Congress in the pre-reform era. The select committees on Intelligence, Aging, Children, Youth and Families, and Hunger even had their own subcommittees.

Select Aging grew past sixty members in 1985 and had sixty-eight members assigned in the 102nd Congress (1991-1993), the largest committee membership to that point in congressional history. The total House membership on select and special committees in the 102nd Congress reached 198 members. The consequence was retrenchment and in 1993, Aging and three Temporary Select Committees that had been renewed for years—Narcotics Abuse and Control (since 1976), Children, Youth and Families (since 1983) and Hunger (since 1984)—were terminated. The House Democratic Caucus ended these committees, along with the Select Committee on Aging, one that appeared to be a "letterhead committee" enabling its members to gain credit in the eyes of their elderly constituents but had relatively little policy impact. Between them, these four committees accounted for 172 assignments in the 102nd Congress.

Three powerhouse chairs—Joe Moakley (Dem-Mass.) of Rules, Dan Rostenkowski (Dem-Ill.) of Ways and Means, and John Dingell (Dem-Mich.) of Energy and Commerce led the retrenchment effort. They were supported by then-Speaker Tom Foley (Dem-Wash.), the first Speaker of the House to have been a committee chair since Sam Rayburn, who chaired Interstate and Foreign Commerce from 1931 to 1937 during the New Deal.

The only survivor among the select committees was the Permanent Select Committee on Intelligence, a designation of "permanent" that it shares with the three Senate committees of Ethics, Intelligence, and Indian Affairs, along with the Senate Special Committee on Aging. The jurisdictions of these permanent select committees became part of the rules of their respective chambers, and therefore are not recreated at the beginning of each Congress. The Permanent Select Committee on Intelligence. like the Senate's Permanent Select Intelligence Committee, is authorized to report legislation.

Only three select committees were named in the twelve years during the Republican Revolution of 1995-2007 and its control of the House. They continued the practice of limiting select and special committees. Their first select committee was the **Select Committee on Ethics** which met for two weeks in 1997 to consider a penalty for House Speaker Newt Gingrich, who admitted to submitting false documents to the House Standards and Conduct Committee regarding a course that he was teaching at a Georgia college. Despite his earlier denials, it appeared that Gingrich had used the staff of his political action committee GOPAC to prepare a course intended to provide talking points for Republicans in upcoming political campaigns and funneled the money through a tax-exempt foundation. Eight departing members of the Standards and Conduct Committee constituted the select committee and fined Gingrich $300,000 for misleading the House.

The second post-1995 select committee was the **Select Committee on U.S. National Security and Military/Commercial Concerns with the People's Republic of China** that was named in 1998 to deal with serious security breaches at nuclear weapons plants once it was revealed that crucial information regarding those weapons had been forwarded to military authorities in the People's Republic of China.

The third committee was the misnamed **Select Bipartisan Committee to Investigate the Preparation for and Response to Hurricane Katrina** of 2005-2006. The devastation of the southeast coasts of Louisiana and Mississippi caused by Hurricanes Katrina and Rita and the unfortunately slow response of President George W. Bush's administration to deal effectively with the crisis led to plummeting public approval ratings for the president in the first year of his second term. To reverse the political damage, House Speaker Denny Hastert (Rep-Ill.) was induced to create this committee to spread blame around and to limit the White House's exposure to further criticism. Naming the committee the

"Select Bipartisan Committee" was a first. None of the more than three thousand committees in the 210-year history of the Congress had ever been named "bipartisan." Suspecting that the White House was hoping to mitigate the political damage of its apparent early indifference to the plight of the mostly African-American victims of the hurricanes, the House Democrats refused to vote for the committee and to serve on it. Consequently, the "Bipartisan Committee" conducted its business with eleven Republicans and no Democrats.

With Democrats back in control of the House in the 110th Congress, two select committees were named—the **Select Committee on Energy Independence and Global Warming** and the **Select Committee to Investigate the Voting Irregularities of August 2, 2007.** While the Global Warming committee was named to address growing scientific concerns about world-wide climate change, the Voting Irregularities committee was named to resolve an especially contentious issue as Republicans believed that ten-term representative Michael McNulty (Dem-N.Y.), then presiding over the House, had used a quick gavel to defeat a Republican motion denying benefits to illegal immigrants. The committee met for a year, but the 215 to 213 vote that Republicans contended that they had in support of the motion was finally reported as a defeated motion by the vote of 212 to 216. The votes creating these last three select committees were especially contentious and divided clearly along partisan lines.

As the 111th Congress continues, it appears that the days of multiple select and special committees in the House appear to be over and the growth in the membership of the House standing committees and the accompanying growth of subcommittees within them have replaced that earlier propensity.

House Select and Special Committees 1993-2011

Permanent Select Committee on Intelligence

Permanent Select Committee on Intelligence, 103rd-111th Congresses (1993-2011)

BACKGROUND

Organizational History: With the Vietnam War winding down in late 1974 and early 1975, various journalists uncovered evidence that intelligence agencies such as the CIA and FBI were involved in questionable covert operations overseas, as well as in domestic surveillance of war protesters and other opponents of government policies here at home. These practices had been widespread throughout the late 1960s and early 1970s.

Political pressure mounted at the beginning of the 94th Congress for a House investigation. Given that the Senate had already established a select committee on January 27, 1975, a joint committee was infeasible. On the other hand, there were too many standing committees with some jurisdiction over intelligence matters to allow a study by any one of them to be comprehensive. This made a select committee the only option. Introduced by Robert N. Giaimo (Dem-Conn.), Lucien N. Nedzi (Dem-Mich.) and several other House Democrats on February 4, 1975, House Resolution 138 proposed a study by the House to be undertaken by a select committee. On February 19, 1975, the measure was passed by a vote of 286-120.

Lucien Nedzi, chair of the Special Intelligence subcommittee of Armed Services with years of experience in intelligence matters, was selected chair of the select committee. It turned out to be a controversial choice however, for it was soon revealed that Nedzi had received secret briefings in 1974 about illegal CIA operations, but had failed to inform his fellow select committee members, a situation that deeply disturbed his fellow Democrats on the committee.

These committee members attempted to remove Nedzi as chair. Nedzi then took the issue to the membership of the House at large by submitting his resignation from the committee. With support from Republicans and conservative Democrats, Nedzi was vindicated when the full House voted not to accept his resignation on June 16, 1975, by a vote of 64-290.

Speaker Carl Albert (Dem-Okla.) and Majority Leader Thomas P. (Tip) O'Neill (Dem-Mass.) recognized that the select committee could not function in its current state, and the House agreed to House Resolution 591 on July 17, 1975. The new measure abolished the Nedzi committee, and created a new Intelligence select committee with the same mandate but a different chair—Otis G. Pike (Dem-N.Y.) and three more members. This doomed an attempt, supported by House Minority Leader John J. Rhodes (Rep-Ariz.), to drop the investigation altogether.

While the Nedzi committee was marked by internal controversy, the Pike committee clashed continually with the Ford administration during the four months it investigated the CIA, the FBI, and other intelligence agencies. At issue was the right of Congress to access executive branch documents that the administration wanted kept secret. Going so far as to cite Secretary of State Henry Kissinger for contempt of Congress, the select committee, in this post-Watergate era, was determined to make the White House accountable.

On January 23, 1976, the select committee voted 9-4 to release its controversial final report, which was extremely critical of the intelligence community. President Ford objected to the report's release, as did many House members who feared its impact on national security. Under pressure from Ford, the full House voted 246 to 124 on January 29, 1976, not to release the report unless the president first approved it.

The press however, had fewer fears. With help from sources within the House, the *New York Times* released a summary of the controversial report on January 26, 1976. Two weeks later, on February 11, the *Village Voice* published 24 pages of excerpts. Outraged and embarrassed by the leak, the government launched several investigations to find the source. Daniel Schorr, then a reporter for CBS News, admitted to giving the classified report to the *Voice,* but refused to say from whom inside the government he had received it. Despite the intensive search, no one was ever caught.

"The Recommendations of the Final Report,: which did not contain classified material, was released as House Report 94-833 on February 11, 1976, the same day the *Village Voice* published its excerpts. Among the recommendations of the committee was the establishment of a permanent House committee to oversee intelligence activities.

It was nearly a year and a half after the Temporary Select Committee on Intelligence recommended the establishment of a permanent committee to oversee intelligence matters that the House considered H. Res. 658. Written by the Rules committee, the measure engendered controversy before it ever got to the House floor. Busy for the past year trying to find the inside source who leaked the earlier intelligence committee's final report to the press, the House was extremely sensitive to issues of access. Democrats generally favored more access to classified information, while Republicans, fearing damaging leaks, favored less. In addition, there was dissatisfaction on the part of Republicans, who objected to the proposed ratio of majority to minority members of 9-4. Finally, the Rules committee voted to send the resolution to the floor under a closed rule, prohibiting amendments and thereby angering many members who wished to consider changes.

Floor debate lasted a day and a half, and resulted in a partisan vote of 227-171 on July 14, 1977, to approve the creation of the permanent select committee. Compared to the similar Senate committee, the House Permanent Select Committee on Intelligence was heavily Democratic, and somewhat less empowered to obtain and release information that the executive branch considered vital to national security. Release to the public of classified materials was to be allowed only after approval of the full House. The committee was given legislative and budgetary jurisdiction over the CIA, which along with other intelligence departments, was to report regularly to the select committee.

It was during Edward Boland's (Dem-Mass.) lengthy chairmanship of the Intelligence Committee that he authored three legislative amendments between 1982 and 1984, all aimed at limiting U.S. government assistance to the rebel Contras against the leftist Sandinista government of Nicaragua. All three passed and were signed by President Ronald Reagan. The amendment outlawed U.S. assistance to the Contras for the purpose of overthrowing the Nicaraguan government, while allowing assistance for other purposes.

However, the Reagan Administration sought to get around the amendment with the elaborate "arms for hostages" deal that traded missiles to Iran, then battling Iraq, in exchange for cash that was located in Swiss bank accounts with access provided to the Contra rebels in Nicaragua. Known as the Iran-Contra Affair in 1986-1987, the deal's exposure led to a major foreign policy embarrassment for the Reagan Administration.

Membership: The ten original members of the initial Nedzi committee were appointed by Speaker Carl Albert (Dem-Okla.) on February 19, 1975, with a ratio of seven Democrats and three Republicans. Robert McClory (Rep-Ill.) was the original committee's ranking minority member. Controversy led to its premature termination and a new committee was appointed on July 17, 1975. Left off the new committee were Nedzi and Michael Harrington (Dem-Mass.), who had publicly released sensitive information relating to the CIA's covert role in the 1973 overthrow of Chile's president Salvador Allende. Otis G. Pike (Dem-N.Y.) was selected as the new committee's chair, while McClory remained ranking minority member. Three new slots were created on the Pike committee, with the resulting ratio of nine Democrats to four Republicans.

The original thirteen members of the Permanent Select Committee were appointed by Speaker Thomas P. O'Neill (Dem-Mass.) on July 27, 1977 of the nine Democrats and four Republicans, at least one member would be drawn from the committees on Appropriations, Armed Services, Foreign Affairs, and Judiciary. The Majority and Minority Leader were designated non-voting *ex officio* members of the select committee. Three of the original members, Les Aspin (Dem-Wisc.), Morgan F. Murphy (Dem-Ill.), and Robert McClory (Rep-Ill.) had served on one or both of the temporary intelligence committees of the 94th Congress.

During the Democratic control of the House, the committee grew to fourteen in the 96th-98th Congresses (1979-1985); then to sixteen in the 99th (1985-1987); to seventeen in the 100th (1987-1989) and to nineteen with a 12:7 majority-minority ratio in the 101st-103rd Congresses (1989-1995). Throughout this period and continuing today, the House's majority and minority leaders are *ex officio* members of Select Intelligence.

The Republican takeover in 1995 shrunk the committee to sixteen members, with a 9:7 ratio that remained for the 104th-106th Congresses (1995-2001). It then resumed its growth with twenty members in the 107th-108th Congresses (2001-2005) and to twenty-one in the 109th and 110th Congresses (2005-2009). Its size in the 111th Congress (2009-2011) is twenty-two, with a 13:9 majority-minority ratio.

With the creation of the Permanent Select Committee, rules concerning its membership became formalized. According to the latest *House Manual*,

11. (a)(1) There is [Permanent Select Committee on Intelligence.] established a Permanent Select Committee on Intelligence (hereafter in this clause referred to as the "select committee"). The select committee shall be composed of not more than 22 Members, Delegates, or the Resident Commissioner, of whom not more than 12 may be from the same party. The select committee shall include at least one Member, Delegate, or the Resident Commissioner from each of the following committees: (A) the Committee on Appropriations; (B) the Committee on Armed Services; (C) the Committee on Foreign Affairs; and (D) the Committee on the Judiciary.

(2) The Speaker and the Minority Leader shall be ex officio members of the select committee but shall have no vote in the select committee and may not be counted for purposes of determining a quorum thereof.

(4)(A) Except as permitted by subdivision (B), a Member, Delegate, or Resident Commissioner, other than the Speaker or the Minority Leader, may not serve as a member of the select committee during more than four Congresses in a period of six successive Congresses (disregarding for this purpose any service for less than a full session in a Congress).

(B) In the case of a Member, Delegate, or Resident Commissioner appointed to serve as the chairman or the ranking minority member of the select committee, tenure on the select committee shall not be limited.

Committee Leaders: Edward P. Boland (Dem-Mass.), a close friend of Speaker O'Neill, was the first chair of Permanent Select Intelligence, serving from July 1977 in the 95th through the 98th Congress at which time committee rules required him to step down. He was succeeded by Lee H. Hamilton (Dem-Ind.) in the 99th Congress (1985-1987), who was then succeeded by Louis Stokes (Dem-Ohio) in the 100th Congress (1987-1989). Anthony C. Beilenson (Dem-Cal.) served as chair in the 101st Congress (1989-1991), and was succeeded by Dave McCurdy (Dem-Okla.) in the 102nd Congress (1991-1993). Daniel R. Glickman (Dem-Kans.) was the committee's fifth consecutive one-term chair in the 103rd Congress (1993-1995).

The Republican takeover in the 104th Congress placed Larry E. Combest (Rep-Tex.) in the chair until he departed to chair the Agriculture Committee in 1997. Combest was succeeded by Porter J. Goss (Rep-Fla.), who chaired the committee from 1997 until he was named Director of the Central Intelligence Agency in August, 2004. Goss was succeeded by Peter Hoekstra (Rep-Mich.), who was elevated from the seventh ranking slot to become chair. Hoekstra chaired the committee through the balance of the 108th Congress and the 109th (2004-2007). He became ranking member when Democrats regained control of the House in the 110th and 111th Congresses (2007-2011).

Robert C. Wilson (Rep-Cal.), ranking Republican on Armed Services, was the permanent committee's first ranking minority member. He was succeeded at the beginning of the 96th Congress in 1979 by J. Kenneth Robinson (Rep-Va.), who served until the end of the 98th Congress in 1985. Robinson was succeeded by Robert Stump (Rep-Ariz.) who served as ranking minority member in the 99th Congress (1985-1987). Henry J. Hyde (Rep-Ill.) served in that capacity in the 100th and 101st Congresses (1987-1991). E.G. (Bud) Shuster (Rep-Penn.) was the committee's ranking minority member for the 102nd Congress (1991-1993), when he was succeeded in that post by Larry E. Combest in the 103rd Congress (1993-1995).

Democrats served in the minority in the next six Congresses with Norman D. Dicks (Dem-Wash.) as ranking member in the 104th and 105th Congresses (1995-1999), followed by Julian C. Dixon (Dem-Cal.) in the 106th until Dixon's death in December 2000. Nancy Pelosi (Dem-Cal.), who succeeded Dixon in 2001, served until her election as Democratic floor leader in 2003 at which point she remained on the committee as an *ex officio* member. Pelosi was succeeded as ranking member by Jane L. Harman (Dem-Cal.), who held that post from 2003 to 2007 when Harman returned to Energy and Commerce.

The Democratic restoration in the 2006 election placed Silvestre Reyes (Dem-Tex.) in the chair of the Permanent Select Intelligence Committee for the 110th and 111th Congresses (2007-2011).

Party Leaders: Three party leaders served on the House Intelligence Committee—Democrats David E. Bonior of Michigan, who was Democratic whip from 1991 to 2002, and Nancy Pelosi of California, who succeeded Bonior in 2002. She moved from the post of Minority Whip (2002-2003) to Minority Floor Leader (2003-2007) to Speaker of the House (2007-date). The only Republican leader with service on the committee was Roy Blunt of Missouri, who served as Republican Whip from 2002 to 2009, with a brief stint as interim Majority Leader between September 2005 and February 2, 2006, during the uncertainty caused by Majority Leader Tom DeLay's indictment in Texas.

Notable Members: As the House's most important select committee, it is not surprising that membership on Permanent Select Intelligence has been sought by many of the House's more prominent members. Arguably, the two most powerful vice presidents in American history served on the committee—Albert A. Gore, Jr. (Dem-Tenn.), who served with President Bill Clinton, and Richard B. Cheney (Rep-Wyo.), who served with President George W. Bush.

Four of President Clinton's Cabinet members—Secretary of Defense Les Aspin (Dem-Wisc.), Secretary of Commerce Norman Y. Mineta (Dem-Cal.), Secretary of Agriculture Daniel R. Glickman (Dem-Kans.), and Secretary of Energy Bill Richardson (Dem-N.M.) served on House Intelligence. Mineta also served in the Cabinet of George W. Bush as Secretary of Transportation. President Barack Obama named committee members Ray H. LaHood (Rep-Ill.) to be Secretary of Transportation, and John M. McHugh (Rep-N.Y.) to be Secretary of the Army. Mineta, LaHood, and McHugh all come from the party differing with the president. Other key administration officials with Intelligence Committee service include Porter J. Goss (Rep-Fla.), Director of the Central Intelligence Agency, and Asa Hutchinson (Rep-Ark.), Director of the Drug Enforcement Agency.

Four governors served on the committee—Republicans John G. Rowland of Connecticut, David C. Treen of Louisiana, and James A. Gibbons of Nevada, and Democrat Bill Richardson of New Mexico. The six U.S. senators with Intelligence Committee experience include: Democrats Wyche Fowler, Jr. of Georgia, John F. Reed of Rhode Island, and Robert G. Torricelli of New Jersey—and Republicans Robert W. Kasten of Wisconsin, Saxby Chambliss of Georgia, and Richard M. Burr of North Carolina. Two of the early party switchers served on Intelligence—Robert Stump of Arizona and Andrew Ireland of Florida, who both left the Democratic Party for the Republicans. Another notable member of the committee is Alcee L. Hastings (Dem-Fla.), who was elected to the House after being impeached as a federal judge.

Selected References

Elliff, John T., "Congress and the Intelligence Community," in Lawrence C. Dodd and Bruce I. Oppenheimer, eds., *Congress Reconsidered* (New York: Praeger, 1977), 193-206.

Kaiser, Frederick M. "Congress and the Intelligence Community," in Roger Davidson, ed., *The Post Reform Congress* (New York: St. Martin's Press, 1992).

Kaiser, Frederick M., "Congressional Rules and Conflict Resolution: Access to Information in the House Select Committee on Intelligence," *Congress and the Presidency*, 15 (Spring, 1988), 49-73.

Schneider, Judy, "House Select Committee on Intelligence: Leadership and Assignment Limitations," Congressional Research Service Reports and Issue Briefs (2007).

Smist, Frank J., Jr., *Congress Oversees the United States Intelligence Community, 1947-1989,* 2nd ed. (Knoxville: University of Tennessee Press, 1994).

RESPONSIBILITIES, JURISDICTIONAL CHANGES, AND SUBCOMMITTEES

Jurisdiction, 1977

From House Resolution 658, as amended, 95th Congress, First Session, July 14, 1977:

[Section 1]

There is hereby established a permanent select committee to be known as the Permanent Select Committee on Intelligence.

[Section 2a]

There shall be referred to the select committee all proposed legislation, messages, petitions, memorials, and other matters relating to the following:

(1) The Central Intelligence Agency and the Director of Central Intelligence.

(2) Intelligence and intelligence-related activities of all other departments and agencies of the Government, including, but not limited to, the intelligence and intelligence-related activities of the Defense Intelligence Agency, the National Security Agency, and other agencies of the Department of Defense; the Department of State; the Department of Justice; and the Department of the Treasury.

(3) The organization or reorganization of any department or agency of the Government to the extent that the organization or reorganization relates to a function or activity involving intelligence or intelligence-related activities.

(4) Authorizations for appropriations, both direct and indirect, for the following:

    (A) The Central Intelligence Agency and Director of Central Intelligence.

    (B) The Defense Intelligence Agency.

    (C) The National Security Agency.

    (D) The intelligence and intelligence-related activities of other agencies and subdivisions of the Department of Defense.

    (E) The intelligence and intelligence related activities of the Department of State.

    (F) The intelligence and intelligence related activities of the Federal Bureau of Investigation, including all activities of the Intelligence Division.

    (G) Any department, agency, or subdivision which is the successor to any agency named in subdivision (A), (B), or (C); and the activities of any department, agency, bureau, or subdivision named in subdivision (D), (E), or (F) to the extent that the activities of such successor department, agency, or subdivision are activities described in subdivision (D), (E), or (F).

[Section 3]

(a) The select committee, for the purposes of accountability to the House, shall make regular and periodic reports to the House on the nature and extent of the intelligence and intelligence-related activities of the various departments and agencies of the United States. Such committee shall promptly call to the attention of the House or to any other appropriate committee or committees of the House any matters requiring the attention of the House or such other committee or committees . . .

(b) The select committee shall obtain an annual report from the Director of the Central Intelligence Agency, the Secretary of Defense, the Secretary of State, and the Director of the Federal Bureau of Investigation. Such reports shall review the intelligence and intelligence-related activities of the agency or department concerned and the intelligence and intelligence-related activities of foreign countries directed at the United States or its interest. An unclassified version of each report may be made available to the public at the discretion of the select committee.

Jurisdiction, 1992

By the 102nd Congress, the jurisdiction of the Permanent Select Committee on Intelligence had not changed since its inception in 1977.

Jurisdiction, 111th Congress (2009-2011)

From the *Rules of the House of Representatives of the United States Congress*, One Hundred Eleventh Congress, House Document 110-62 (2009) Permanent Select Committee on Intelligence

11. (a)(1) There is established a Permanent Select Committee on Intelligence (hereafter in this clause referred to as the "select committee").

    (b)(1) There shall be referred to the select committee proposed legislation, messages, petitions, memorials, and other matters relating to the following:

        (A) The Central Intelligence Agency, the Director of National Intelligence, and the National Intelligence Program as defined in section 3(6) of the National Security Act of 1947.

        (B) Intelligence and intelligence-related activities of all other departments and agencies of the Government, including the tactical intelligence and intelligence-related activities of the Department of Defense.

(C) The organization or reorganization of a department or agency of the Government to the extent that the organization or reorganization relates to a function or activity involving intelligence or intelligence-related activities.

(D) Authorizations for appropriations, both direct and indirect, for the following:

(i) The Central Intelligence Agency, the Director of National Intelligence, and the National Intelligence Program as defined in section 3(6) of the National Security Act of 1947.

(ii) Intelligence and intelligence-related activities of all other departments and agencies of the Government, including the tactical intelligence and intelligence-related activities of the Department of Defense.

(iii) A department, agency, subdivision, or program that is a successor to an agency or program named or referred to in (i) or (ii).

(2) Proposed legislation initially reported by the select committee (other than provisions solely involving matters specified in subparagraph (1)(A) or subparagraph (1)(D)(i)) containing any matter otherwise within the jurisdiction of a standing committee shall be referred by the Speaker to that standing committee. Proposed legislation initially reported by another committee that contains matter within the jurisdiction of the select committee shall be referred by the Speaker to the select committee if requested by the chairman of the select committee.

(3) Nothing in this clause shall be construed as prohibiting or otherwise restricting the authority of any other committee to study and review an intelligence or intelligence-related activity to the extent that such activity directly affects a matter otherwise within the jurisdiction of that committee.

(4) Nothing in this clause shall be construed as amending, limiting, or otherwise changing the authority of a standing committee to obtain full and prompt access to the product of the intelligence and intelligence-related activities of a department or agency of the Government relevant to a matter otherwise within the jurisdiction of that committee.

(c)(1) For purposes of accountability to the House, the select committee shall make regular and periodic reports to the House on the nature and extent of the intelligence and intelligence-related activities of the various departments and agencies of the United States. The select committee shall promptly call to the attention of the House, or to any other appropriate committee, a matter requiring the attention of the House or another committee. In making such report, the select committee shall proceed in a manner consistent with paragraph (g) to protect national security.

(2) The select committee shall obtain annual reports from the Director of National Intelligence, the Director of the Central Intelligence Agency, the Secretary of Defense, the Secretary of State, and the Director of the Federal Bureau of Investigation. Such reports shall review the intelligence and intelligence-related activities of the agency or department concerned and the intelligence and intelligence-related activities of foreign countries directed at the United States or its interests. An unclassified version of each report may be made available to the public at the discretion of the select committee. Nothing herein shall be construed as requiring the public disclosure in such reports of the names of persons engaged in intelligence or intelligence-related activities for the United States or the divulging of intelligence methods employed or the sources of information on which the reports are based or the amount of funds authorized to be appropriated for intelligence and intelligence-related activities.

NAMES OF SELECT INTELLIGENCE SUBCOMMITTEES FROM THE *CONGRESSIONAL DIRECTORY*

Legislation, 103
Oversight and Evaluation, 103
Program and Budget Authorization, 103
Human Intelligence, Analysis, and Counterintelligence, 104, 105, 106, 107, 108, 109
Terrorism HUMINT, Analysis, and Counterintelligence, 110, 111
Intelligence Policy and National Security, 107, 108
Intelligence Policy, 109
Intelligence Community Management, 110, 111
Oversight, 109
Oversight and Investigations, 110, 111
Technical and Tactical Intelligence, 104, 105, 106, 107, 108, 109, 110, 111
Working Group on Terrorism and Homeland Security, 107, 108

MEMBERSHIP ROSTERS, 103rd-111th Congresses, 1993-2011

PERMANENT SELECT INTELLIGENCE / 103rd Congress

Service Dates of Committee Chair: Feb. 3, 1993-Jan. 3, 1995

Service Dates of Majority Members: Feb. 3, 1993-Jan. 3, 1995

Service Dates of Minority Members: Feb. 3, 1993-Jan. 3, 1995

Roster Filled: Majority with 12 members on Feb. 3, 1993; Minority with 7 members on Feb. 3, 1993.

Majority						Minority					
				Terms in:						**Terms in:**	
Rank Name		Party	State	House	Comm.	Rank Name		Party	State	House	Comm.
Chr Glickman, Daniel R.		Dem	Kans.	9	4	RM Combest, Larry E.		Rep	Tex.	5	3
2nd Richardson, William B.		Dem	N.M.	6	*1 4	2nd Bereuter, Douglas K.		Rep	Neb.	8	*1 3
3rd Dicks, Norman D.		Dem	Wash.	9	2	3rd Dornan, Robert K.		Rep	Cal.	8	3
4th Dixon, Julian C.		Dem	Cal.	8	1	4th Young, C.W. (Bill)		Rep	Fla.	12	*2 2
5th Torricelli, Robert G.		Dem	N.J.	6	1	5th Gekas, George W.		Rep	Penn.	6	2
6th Coleman, Ronald D.		Dem	Tex.	6	1	6th Hansen, James V.		Rep	Utah	7	1
7th Skaggs, David E.		Dem	Colo.	4	*1 1	7th Lewis, Charles J. (Jerry)		Rep	Cal.	8	1
8th Bilbray, James H.		Dem	Nev.	4	1						
9th Pelosi, Nancy		Dem	Cal.	4	1	*1: Member's first period of service on the committee					
10th Laughlin, Gregory H.		Dem	Tex.	3	1	*2: Member's second period of service on the committee.					
11th Cramer, Robert E. (Bud) Jr.		Dem	Ala.	2	*1 1						
12th Reed, John F.		Dem	R.I.	2	1						

Note: The Majority and Minority Leaders of the House are *ex officio* members of the committee, but do not vote and are not counted for purposes of determining a quorum. On Nov. 10, 1993, Glickman and Richardson were granted permission to serve throughout the remainder of the 103rd Congress even though each would be in their seventh year of continuous committee service.

Congressional Record, H9145.

Departures from the House:	Majority				Minority		
Defeated for Re-election	Glickman, Daniel R.		Dem	Kans.	None		
	Bilbray, James H.		Dem	Nev.			
Departures from Committee:							
No new assignment	Skaggs, David E.		Dem	Colo.	Bereuter, Douglas K.	Rep	Neb.
	Cramer, Robert E. (Bud) Jr.		Dem	Ala.	Gekas, George W.	Rep	Penn.
	Reed, John F.		Dem	R.I.			

PERMANENT SELECT INTELLIGENCE / 104th Congress

Service Dates of Committee Chair: Jan. 4, 1995-Jan. 3, 1997

Service Dates of Majority Members: Jan. 4, 1995-Jan. 3, 1997

Service Dates of Minority Members: Jan. 4, 1995-Jan. 3, 1997

Roster Filled: Majority with 9 members on Jan. 4, 1995; Minority with 7 members on Jan. 4, 1995.

Majority						Minority					
				Terms in:						**Terms in:**	
Rank Name		Party	State	House	Comm.	Rank Name		Party	State	House	Comm.
Chr Combest, Larry E.		Rep	Tex.	6	4	RM Dicks, Norman D.		Dem	Wash.	10	3
2nd Dornan, Robert K.		Rep	Cal.	9	4	2nd Richardson, William B.		Dem	N.M.	7	*1 5
3rd Young, C.W. Bill		Rep	Fla.	13	*2 3	3rd Dixon, Julian C.		Dem	Cal.	9	2
4th Hansen, James V.		Rep	Utah	8	2	4th Torricelli, Robert G.		Dem	N.J.	7	2
5th Lewis, Charles J. (Jerry)		Rep	Cal.	9	2	5th Coleman, Ronald D.		Dem	Tex.	7	2
6th Goss, Porter J.		Rep	Fla.	4	1	6th Pelosi, Nancy		Dem	Cal.	5	2
7th Shuster, E.G. (Bud)		Rep	Penn.	12	*2 1	7th Laughlin, Gregory H.		Dem	Tex.	4	2
8th McCollum, Ira W. (Bill) Jr.		Rep	Fla.	8	1						
9th Castle, Michael N.		Rep	Del.	2	1	*2: Member's second period of service on the committee.					

Note: The Majority and Minority Leaders of the House are *ex officio* members of the committee, but do not vote and are not counted for purposes of determining a quorum.

Changes:
Minority:

Laughlin, Gregory H.	Dem	Tex.	June 30, 1995 Service as a Democrat vacated; moved to Ways and Means as a Republican on July 10, 1995.
Skaggs, David E.	Dem	Colo.	July 12, 1995 Replaced Laughlin.
Richardson, William B.	Dem	N.M.	Sept. 17, 1996 Resigned committee; returned with permission of the House
Harman, Jane L.	Dem	Cal.	Sept. 27, 1996 Replaced Richardson.

| Coleman, Ronald D. | Dem | Tex. | Oct. 3, 1996 Resigned committee; no new assignment. |
| Richardson, William B. | Dem | N.M. | Oct. 4, 1996 Returned and replaced Coleman. |

Departures from the House:	Majority			Minority		
Elected to U.S. Senate	None			Torricelli, Robert G.	Dem	N.J.
Defeated for Re-election	Dornan, Robert K.	Rep	Cal.	None		
Retired	None			Coleman, Ronald D.	Dem	Tex.

Departures from Committee:						
Became Chair of Agriculture	Combest, Larry E.	Rep	Tex.			
Returned to Small Business	Combest, Larry E.	Rep	Tex.	None		
Moved to Standards of Official						
Conduct as Chair	Hansen, James V.	Rep	Utah	None		
No new assignment	None			Richardson, William B.	Dem	N.M.

PERMANENT SELECT INTELLIGENCE / 105th Congress

Service Dates of Committee Chair: Jan. 27, 1997-Jan. 3, 1999

Service Dates of Majority Members: Feb. 10, 1997-Jan. 3, 1999

Service Dates of Minority Members: Feb. 10, 1997-Jan. 3, 1999

Roster Filled: Majority with 9 members on Feb. 10, 1997; Minority with 7 members on Mar. 6, 1997.

			Majority						Minority	
				Terms in:						Terms in:
Rank Name	Party	State	House	Comm.		Rank Name	Party	State	House	Comm.
Chr Goss, Porter J.	Rep	Fla.	5	2		RM Dicks, Norman D.	Dem	Wash.	11	4
2nd Young, C.W. Bill	Rep	Fla.	14	*2 4		2nd Dixon, Julian C.	Dem	Cal.	10	3
3rd Lewis, Charles J. (Jerry)	Rep	Cal.	10	3		3rd Skaggs, David E.	Dem	Colo.	6	*2 2
4th Shuster, E.G. (Bud)	Rep	Penn.	13	*2 2		4th Pelosi, Nancy	Dem	Cal.	6	3
5th McCollum, Ira W. (Bill) Jr.	Rep	Fla.	9	2		5th Harman, Jane L.	Dem	Cal.	3	*1 2
6th Castle, Michael N.	Rep	Del.	3	2		6th Skelton, Isaac N. (Ike)	Dem	Mo.	11	*2 1
7th Boehlert, Sherwood L.	Rep	N.Y.	8	1		7th Bishop, Sanford D. Jr.	Dem	Ga.	3	1
8th Bass, Charles F.	Rep	N.H.	2	1						
9th Gibbons, James A.	Rep	Nev.	1	1						

*1: Member's first period of service on the committee.
*2: Member's second period of service on the committee.

Vacancies Filled:
  Minority:
    6th and 7th seats filled by Skelton and Bishop on Mar. 6, 1997.

Note: The Majority and Minority Leaders of the House are *ex officio* members of the committee, but do not vote and are not counted for purposes of determining a quorum.

Departures from the House:	Majority			Minority		
Lost Nomination for Governor	None			Harman, Jane L.	Dem	Cal.
Retired	None			Skaggs, David E.	Dem	Colo.

Departures from Committee:						
Became Chair of Appropriations	Young, C.W. Bill	Rep	Fla.	None		
No new assignment	Shuster, E.G. (Bud)	Rep	Penn.	Skelton, Isaac N. (Ike)	Dem	Mo.
				Dicks, Norman D.	Dem	Wash

PERMANENT SELECT INTELLIGENCE / 106th Congress

Service Dates of Committee Chair: Jan. 6, 1999-Jan. 3, 2001

Service Dates of Majority Members: Jan. 19, 1999-Jan. 3, 2001

Service Dates of Minority Members: Feb. 12, 1999-Jan. 3, 2001

Roster Filled: Majority with 9 members on Jan. 19, 1999; Minority with 7 members on Feb. 12, 1999.

			Majority						Minority	
				Terms in:						Terms in:
Rank Name	Party	State	House	Comm.		Rank Name	Party	State	House	Comm.
Chr Goss, Porter J.	Rep	Fla.	6	3		RM Dixon, Julian C.	Dem	Cal.	11	4
2nd Lewis, Charles J. (Jerry)	Rep	Cal.	11	4		2nd Pelosi, Nancy	Dem	Cal.	7	4

3rd McCollum, Ira W. (Bill) Jr.	Rep	Fla.	10	3		3rd Bishop, Sanford D. Jr.	Dem	Ga.	4	2	
4th Castle, Michael N.	Rep	Del.	4	3		4th Sisisky, Norman	Dem	Va.	9	1	
5th Boehlert, Sherwood L.	Rep	N.Y.	9	2		5th Condit, Gary A.	Dem	Cal.	6	1	
6th Bass, Charles F.	Rep	N.H.	3	2		6th Roemer, Timothy J.	Dem	Ind.	5	1	
7th Gibbons, James A.	Rep	Nev.	2	2		7th Hastings, Alcee L.	Dem	Fla.	4	*1 1	
8th LaHood, Ray H.	Rep	Ill	3	1							
9th Wilson, Heather A.	Rep	N.M.	2	*1 1		*1: Member's first period of service on the committee.					

Note: The Majority and Minority Leaders of the House are *ex officio* members of the committee, but do not vote and are not counted for purposes of determining a quorum.

Changes:
    Minority:

Dixon, Julian C.	Dem	Cal.	Dec. 8, 2000 Died in office.

Departures from the House:	**Majority**			**Minority**
Lost Election to U.S. Senate	McCollum, Ira W. (Bill) Jr.	Rep	Fla.	None

Departures from Committee:				**Minority**
No new assignment	Wilson, Heather A.	Rep	N.M.	None
	Lewis, Charles J. (Jerry)	Rep	Cal.	None

PERMANENT SELECT INTELLIGENCE / 107th Congress

Service Dates of Committee Chair: Jan. 6, 2001-Jan. 3, 2003

Service Dates of Majority Members: Jan. 30, 2001-Jan. 3, 2003

Service Dates of Ranking Member: Jan. 6, 2001-Jan. 3, 2003

Service Dates of Minority Members: Mar. 1, 2001-Jan. 3, 2003

Roster Filled: Majority with 11 members on Jan. 30, 2001; Minority with 9 members on Mar. 14, 2001.

Majority					**Minority**				
			Terms in:					**Terms in:**	
Rank Name	**Party**	**State**	**House**	**Comm.**	**Rank Name**	**Party**	**State**	**House**	**Comm.**
Chr Goss, Porter J.	Rep	Fla.	7	4	RM Pelosi, Nancy	Dem	Cal.	8	5
2nd Bereuter, Douglas K.	Rep	Nebr.	12	*2 1	2nd Bishop, Sanford D. Jr.	Dem	Ga.	5	3
3rd Castle, Michael N.	Rep	Del.	5	4	3rd Harman, Jane L.	Dem	Cal.	4	*2 1
4th Boehlert, Sherwood L.	Rep	N.Y.	10	3	4th Sisisky, Norman	Dem	Va.	10	2
5th Bass, Charles F.	Rep	N.H.	4	3	5th Condit, Gary A.	Dem	Cal.	7	2
6th Gibbons, James A.	Rep	Nev.	3	3	6th Roemer, Timothy J.	Dem	Ind.	6	2
7th LaHood, Ray H.	Rep	Ill	4	2	7th Hastings, Alcee L.	Dem	Fla.	5	*1 2
8th Cunningham, Randall (Duke)	Rep	Cal.	6	1	8th Reyes, Silvestre	Dem	Tex.	3	1
9th Hoekstra, Peter	Rep	Mich.	5	1	9th Boswell, Leonard L.	Dem	Iowa	3	1
10th Burr, Richard M.	Rep	N.C.	4	1					
11th Hutchinson, Asa	Rep	Ark.	3	1	*1: Member's first period of service on the committee.				
					*2: Member's second period of service on the committee				

Vacancies Filled:
    Minority:
      9th seat filled by Boswell on Mar. 14, 2001.

Note: The Majority and Minority Leaders of the House are *ex officio* members of the committee, but do not vote and are not counted for purposes of determining a quorum.

Changes:
    Majority:

Bass, Charles F.	Rep	N.H.	Feb. 7, 2001 Resigned committee; moved to Energy and Commerce.
Chambliss, Saxby	Rep	Ga.	Feb. 8, 2001 Replaced Bass; ranked immediately following Burr.
Hutchinson, Asa	Rep	Ark.	Aug. 6, 2001 Resigned the House; became Director of the Drug Enforcement Administration.
Everett, R. Terry	Rep	Ala.	Jan. 23, 2002 Replaced Hutchinson.

    Minority:

Sisisky, Norman	Dem	Va.	Mar. 29, 2001 Died in office.
Peterson, Collin C.	DFL	Minn.	Apr. 4, 2001 Replaced Sisisky.

Hastings, Alcee L.	Dem	Fla.	Apr. 11, 2002 Resigned committee; no new assignment
Cramer, Robert E. (Bud) Jr.	Dem	Ala.	Apr. 11, 2002 Replaced Hastings.

Departures from the House:

	Majority			Minority		
Elected to U.S. Senate	Chambliss, Saxby	Rep	Ga.	None		
Defeated for Re-nomination	None			Condit, Gary A.	Dem	Cal.
Retired	None			Roemer, Timothy J.	Dem	Ind.

Departures from Committee:

	Majority			Minority		
Moved to Appropriations	None			Bishop, Sanford D. Jr.	Dem	Ga.
No new assignment	Castle, Michael N.	Rep	Del.	None		

PERMANENT SELECT INTELLIGENCE / 108th Congress

Service Dates of Committee Chair: Ch1: Jan. 8, 2003-Aug. 10, 2004 (Goss)

Service Dates of Committee Chair: Ch2: Aug. 25, 2004 Jan. 3, 2005 (Hoekstra)

Service Dates of Majority Members: Jan. 8, 2003-Jan. 3, 2005

Service Dates of Minority Members: Jan. 8, 2003-Jan. 3, 2005

Roster Filled: Majority with 11 members on Feb. 11, 2003; Minority with 9 members on Jan. 8, 2003.

Majority			Terms in:		Minority			Terms in:	
Rank Name	Party	State	House	Comm.	Rank Name	Party	State	House	Comm.
Ch1 Goss, Porter J.	Rep	Fla.	8	5	RM Harman, Jane L.	Dem	Cal.	5	*2 2
2nd Bereuter, Douglas K.	Rep	Neb.	13	*2 2	2nd Hastings, Alcee L.	Dem	Fla.	6	*2 1
3rd Boehlert, Sherwood L.	Rep	N.Y.	11	4	3rd Reyes, Silvestre	Dem	Tex.	4	2
4th Gibbons, James A.	Rep	Nev.	4	4	4th Boswell, Leonard L.	Dem	Iowa	4	2
5th LaHood, Ray H.	Rep	Ill	5	3	5th Peterson, Collin C.	DFL	Minn.	7	2
6th Cunningham, Randall (Duke)	Rep	Cal.	7	2	6th Cramer, Robert E. (Bud) Jr.	Dem	Ala.	7	*2 2
Ch2 7th Hoekstra, Peter	Rep	Mich.	6	2	7th Eshoo, Anna G.	Dem	Cal.	6	1
8th Burr, Richard M.	Rep	N.C.	5	2	8th Holt, Rush D.	Dem	N.J.	3	1
9th Everett, R. Terry	Rep	Ala.	6	2	9th Ruppersberger, C.A. (Dutch)	Dem	Md.	1	1
10th Gallegly, Elton W.	Rep	Cal.	9	*1 1					
11th Collins, Michael A. (Mac)	Rep	Ga.	6	1					

*1: Member's first period of service on the committee.

*2: Member's second period of service on the committe

Vacancies Filled:

Majority:

10th and 11th seats filled by Gallegly and Collins on Feb. 11, 2003.

Note: The Majority and Minority Leaders of the House are *ex officio* members of the committee, but do not vote and are not counted for purposes of determining a quorum. Minority Leader Nancy Pelosi served on the committee as a regular member, 1993-2003.

Changes:

Majority:

Bereuter, Douglas K.	Rep	Nebr.	Aug. 9, 2004 Resigned the House and retired.
Goss, Porter J.	Rep	Fla.	Aug. 10, 2004 Leave of absence from the chairmanship.
Hoekstra, Peter	Rep	Mich.	Aug. 25, 2004 Elected Chair.
Bereuter, Douglas K.	Rep	Nebr.	Aug. 9, 2004 Resigned the House and retired.
Davis, Jo Ann	Rep	Va.	Sept. 8, 2004 Replaced Bereuter.
Goss, Porter J.	Rep	Fla.	Sept. 23, 2004 Resigned the House; became Director of the Central IntelligenceAdministration.
Thornberry, William M. (Mac)	Rep	Tex.	Sept. 28, 2004 Replaced Goss.
Boehlert, Sherwood L.	Rep	N.Y.	Sept. 29, 2004 "Removed by Speaker", health issue.
Blunt, Roy	Rep	Mo.	Sept. 29, 2004 Replaced Boehlert.
Blunt, Roy	Rep	Mo.	Nov. 16, 2004 Resigned committee; no new assignmwnt

Departures from the House:

	Majority			Minority		
Elected to U.S. Senate	Burr, Richard M.	Rep	N.C.	None		
Lost Nomination to U.S. Senate	Collins, Michael A. (Mac)	Rep	Ga.	None		

Departures from Committee:

	Majority			Minority		
Became RM on Agriculture	None			Peterson, Collin C.	DFL	Minn.
No new assignment	Gibbons, James A.	Rep	Nev.	None		

PERMANENT SELECT INTELLIGENCE / 109th Congress

Service Dates of Committee Chair: Jan. 4, 2005-Jan. 3, 2007

Service Dates of Majority Members: Jan. 26, 2005-Jan. 3, 2007

Service Dates of Ranking Member: Jan. 6, 2005-Jan. 3, 2007

Service Dates of Minority Members: Jan. 26, 2005-Jan. 3, 2007

Roster Filled: Majority with 12 members on Jan. 26, 2005; Minority with 9 members on Jan. 26, 2005.

			Terms in:					Terms in:	
Majority					**Minority**				
Rank Name	**Party**	**State**	**House**	**Comm.**	**Rank Name**	**Party**	**State**	**House**	**Comm.**
Chr Hoekstra, Peter	Rep	Mich.	7	3	RM Harman, Jane L.	Dem	Cal.	6	*2 3
2nd LaHood, Ray H.	Rep	Ill.	6	4	2nd Hastings, Alcee L.	Dem	Fla.	7	*2 2
3rd Cunningham, Randall (Duke)	Rep	Cal.	8	3	3rd Reyes, Silvestre	Dem	Tex.	5	3
4th Everett, R. Terry	Rep	Ala.	7	3	4th Boswell, Leonard L.	Dem	Iowa	5	3
5th Gallegly, Elton W.	Rep	Cal.	10	*1 2	5th Cramer, Robert E. (Bud) Jr.	Dem	Ala.	8	*2 3
6th Wilson, Heather A.	Rep	N.M.	5	*2 1	6th Eshoo, Anna G.	Dem	Cal.	7	2
7th Davis, Jo Ann	Rep	Va.	3	2	7th Holt, Rush D.	Dem	N.J.	4	2
8th Thornberry, William M. (Mac)	Rep	Tex.	6	2	8th Ruppersberger, C.A. (Dutch)	Dem	Md.	2	2
9th McHugh, John M.	Rep	N.Y.	7	1	9th Tierney, John F.	Dem	Mass.	5	1
10th Tiahrt, Todd	Rep	Kans.	6	1					
11th Rogers, Mike	Rep	Mich.	3	1	*1: Member's first period of service on the committee.				
12th Renzi, Rick	Rep	Ariz.	2	1	*2: Member's second period of service on the committee.				

Note: The Majority and Minority Leaders of the House are *ex officio* members of the committee, but do not vote and are not counted for purposes of determining a quorum.

Changes:
  Majority:
      Cunningham, Randall (Duke)   Rep   Cal.   Dec. 1, 2005 Resigned the House due to ethics issue

Departures from Committee:	**Majority**			**Minority**		
Returned to Energy and Commerce	None			Harman, Jane L.	Dem	Cal.
No new assignment	LaHood, Ray H.	Rep	Ill.	None		
	Gallegly, Elton W.	Rep	Cal.			
	Davis, Jo Ann	Rep	Va.			

PERMANENT SELECT INTELLIGENCE / 110th Congress

Dates of Committee Chair: Jan. 5, 2007-Jan. 3, 2009

Service Dates of Majority Members: Jan. 17, 2007-Jan. 3, 2009

Service Dates of Ranking Member: Jan. 5, 2007-Jan. 3, 2009

Service Dates of Minority Members: Jan. 17, 2007-Jan. 3, 2009

Roster Filled: Majority with 12 members on Jan. 17, 2007; Minority with 9 members on Jan. 17, 2007.

			Terms in:					Terms in:	
Majority					**Minority**				
Rank Name	**Party**	**State**	**House**	**Comm.**	**Rank Name**	**Party**	**State**	**House**	**Comm.**
Chr Reyes, Silvestre	Dem	Tex.	6	4	RM Hoekstra, Peter	Rep	Mich.	8	4
2nd Hastings, Alcee L.	Dem	Fla.	8	*2 3	2nd Everett, R. Terry	Rep	Ala.	8	4
3rd Boswell, Leonard L.	Dem	Iowa	6	4	3rd Wilson, Heather A.	Rep	N.M.	6	*2 2
4th Cramer, Robert E. (Bud) Jr.	Dem	Ala.	9	*2 4	4th Thornberry, William M. (Mac)	Rep	Tex.	7	3
5th Eshoo, Anna G.	Dem	Cal.	8	3	5th McHugh, John M.	Rep	N.Y.	8	2
6th Holt, Rush D.	Dem	N.J.	5	3	6th Tiahrt, Todd	Rep	Kans.	7	2
7th Ruppersberger, C.A. (Dutch)	Dem	Md.	3	3	7th Rogers, Mike	Rep	Mich.	4	2
8th Tierney, John F.	Dem	Mass.	6	2	8th Renzi, Rick	Rep	Ariz.	3	2
9th Thompson, Michael	Dem	Cal.	5	1	9th Issa, Darrell E.	Rep	Cal.	4	1
10th Schakowsky, Janice D.	Dem	Ill.	5	1					
11th Langevin, James R.	Dem	R.I.	4	1	*2: Member's second period of service on the committee.				
12th Murphy, Patrick J.	Dem	Penn.	1	1					

Note: The Majority and Minority Leaders of the House are *ex officio* members of the committee, but do not vote and are not counted for purposes of determining a quorum.

Changes:
    Majority:

Hastings, Alcee L.	Dem	Fla.	Dec. 12, 2007 Resigned committee; no new assignment.
Schiff, Adam B.	Dem	Cal.	Jan. 22, 2008 Replaced Hastings.

    Minority:

Renzi, Rick	Rep	Ariz	Apr. 20, 2007 Resigned committee due to ethics issues.
Gallegly, Elton W.	Rep	Cal.	May 1, 2007 Replaced Renzi

Departures from the House:	**Majority**			**Minority**		
Lost Nomination to U.S. Senate	None			Wilson, Heather A.	Rep	N.M.
Retired	Cramer, Robert E. (Bud) Jr.	Dem	Ala.	Everett, R. Terry	Rep	Ala.

Departures from Committee:						
Became RM on Armed Services	None			McHugh, John M.	Rep	N.Y.
Became RM on Oversight and Government Reform	None			Issa, Darrell E.	Rep	Cal.
No new assignment	Boswell, Leonard L.	Dem	Iowa	Tiahrt, Todd	Rep	Kans.

PERMANENT SELECT INTELLIGENCE / 111th Congress

Service Dates of Committee Chair: Jan. 6, 2009-Jan. 3, 2011

Service Dates of Majority Members: Feb. 4, 2009-Jan. 3, 2011

Service Dates of Ranking Member: Jan. 6, 2009-Jan. 3, 2011

Service Dates of Minority Members: Feb. 4, 2009-Jan. 3, 2011

Roster Filled:

Majority with 13 members on Feb. 4, 2009; Minority with 9 members on Feb. 4, 2009

Majority

Rank Name	Party	State	Terms in: House	Terms in: Comm.
Chr Reyes, Silvestre	Dem	Tex.	7	5
2nd Hastings, Alcee L.	Dem	Fla.	9	*3 1
3rd Eshoo, Anna G.	Dem	Cal.	9	4
4th Holt, Rush D.	Dem	N.J.	6	4
5th Ruppersberger, C.A. (Dutch)	Dem	Md.	4	4
6th Tierney, John F.	Dem	Mass.	7	3
7th Thompson, Michael	Dem	Cal.	6	2
8th Schakowsky, Janice D.	Dem	Ill.	6	2
9th Langevin, James R.	Dem	R.I.	5	2
10th Murphy, Patrick J.	Dem	Penn	2	2
11th Schiff, Adam B.	Dem	Cal.	5	2
12th Smith, Adam	Dem	Wash.	7	1
13th Boren, Daniel D.	Dem	Okla.	5	1

Minority

Rank Name	Party	State	Terms in: House	Terms in: Comm.
RM Hoekstra, Peter	Rep	Mich.	9	5
2nd Gallegly, Elton W.	Rep	Cal.	12	*2 2
3rd Thornberry, William M. (Mac)	Rep	Tex.	8	4
4th Rogers, Mike	Rep	Mich.	5	3
5th Myrick, Sue	Rep	N.C	8	1
6th Blunt, Roy	Rep	Mo.	7	*2 1
7th Miller, Jefferson B.	Rep	Fla.	5	1
8th Kline, John	Rep	Minn.	4	1
9th Conaway, K. Michael	Rep	Tex	3	1

*2: Member's second period of service on the committee.

*3: Member's third period of service on the committee.

Note 1: Rogers appointed on Jan. 15, 2009, but re-ranked with the other appointments on Feb. 4, 2009

Note 2: The Majority and Minority Leaders of the House are *ex officio* members of the committee, but do not vote and are not counted for purposes of determining a quorum.

Changes:
    Majority:

Kline, John	Rep	Minn.	June 23, 2009 Resigned committee; had become Ranking Member on Education and Labor
King, Peter	Rep	NY.	June 25, 2009 Replaced Kline

Select Committee on Ethics

105th Congress (1997)

BACKGROUND

Speaker of the House Newton L. Gingrich (Rep-Ga.), whose 1994 "Contract with America" had mobilized voters to place Republicans in charge of the U.S. House after forty years of Democratic control, had begun to overreach himself. He sought to solidify Republican gains using his GOPAC organization to develop materials for subsequent congressional campaigns. He did this under the guise of preparing material for a college course entitled, "Renewing American Civilization" that he taught at Kennesaw State College and at Reinhardt College. Gingrich had his lectures taped and disseminated through his American Opportunities Workshop and the American Citizens' Television Project. It was an expensive proposition costing approximately $1.2 million.

Speaker Gingrich tried to claim the monies expended were tax-deductible because the taped lectures were an educational and not a political project. However, since only the Gingrich lectures were disseminated and none of those of his fellow teachers, and since GOPAC staff had been involved in the preparation of the materials and were coordinating its dissemination, it was regarded as a political activity and not eligible for tax-deductibility.

Eighty-four ethics charges, most of which were leveled by House Democratic Whip David Bonior (Dem-Mich.), were filed against Speaker Gingrich during 1995 and 1996. Gingrich then compounded his difficulties by apparently dissembling before the House Standards and Conduct Committee when they sought more information about the project. Eighty-three of the eighty-four allegations were dropped. While Gingrich denied the charges over misuse of tax-exempt funds and contended that he might have been more diligent in obtaining relevant tax reporting advice; he admitted to providing inaccurate statements during the probe over the college course and agreed to pay $300,000 for the cost of the investigation. The House Ethics Committee concluded that the inaccurate information that he supplied to investigators represented "intentional or . . . reckless" disregard of House rules.

The House Select Ethics Committee was named on January 7, 1997. It consisted of eight members —four Republicans and four Democrats—with Nancy L. Johnson (Rep-Conn.) as its chair and Benjamin L. Cardin (Dem-Md.) as its ranking minority member. The eight members of the committee had originally heard the case against Gingrich and his dissembling in 1995, when they served together on Standards and Conduct, but since the 104th Congress adjourned on January 3, 1997, their service on Standards had ended and a new select committee had to be appointed in the 105th Congress to resolve the issues.

On January 21, 1997, the House accepted H. Res. 31 and adopted the report of the Select Committee on Ethics dated January 17, 1997, and then voted 395 to 28 to reprimand Gingrich for ethics violations dating back to September 1994. The House ordered Gingrich to pay a $300,000 penalty; the first time in the House's 208-year history it had disciplined a Speaker for ethical wrongdoing. The Select Committee on Ethics concluded its business with that vote on January 21, 1997.

Gingrich would continue as Speaker for the balance of the 105th Congress, but his reputation was tarnished, and rather than face a bruising battle from fellow Republicans to retain the speakership, he resigned from the House at the opening of the 106th Congress on January 3, 1999.

Selected References

U.S. House Select Committee on Ethics, *In the Matter of Representative Newt Gingrich,* 105th Congress, 1st Session, House Report, 108, January 17, 1997.

MEMBERSHIP ROSTER, 105th Congress (1997)

HOUSE SELECT ETHICS / 105th Congress

Service Dates of Committee Chair: Jan. 7, 1997-Jan. 21, 1997

Service Dates of Majority Members: Jan. 7, 1997-Jan. 21, 1997

Service Dates of Minority Members: Jan. 7, 1997-Jan. 21, 1997

Roster Filled: Majority with 4 members on Jan. 7, 1997; Minority with 4 members on Jan. 7, 1997.

Majority					Minority				
			Terms in:					Terms in:	
Rank Name	Party	State	House	Comm.	Rank Name	Party	State	House	Comm.
Chr Johnson, Nancy L	Rep	Conn.	8	1	RM Cardin, Benjamin L.	Dem	Md.	6	1
2nd Goss, Porter J.	Rep	Fla.	9	1	2nd Pelosi, Nancy	Dem	Cal.	6	1

| 3rd Schiff, Steven | Rep | N.M. | 5 | 1 | 3rd Borski, Robert A. | Dem | Penn. | 8 | 1 |
| 4th Bunning, James P.D. | Rep | Ky. | 6 | 1 | 4th Sawyer, Thomas C. | Dem | Ohio | 6 | 1 |

Changes:
  Majority:

| Bunning. James P.D. | Rep | Ky. | Jan. 9, 1997 Resigned committee; no new assignment |
| Smith, Lamar S. | Rep | Tex. | Jan. 9, 1997 Replaced Bunning |

Select Committee on U.S. National Security and Military/Commercial Concerns with the People's Republic of China

105th-106th Congresses (1998-1999)

BACKGROUND

Organizational History: In 1998, news accounts reported that Chinese operatives had engaged in espionage at American nuclear weapons facilities. The news was troubling to the House and a select committee was created on a motion introduced by Christopher Cox (Rep-Cal.) This select committee, was created on June 18, 1998, by a vote of 409-10 in the House.

Membership: The committee's official title was the Select Committee on U.S. National Security and Military/Commercial Concerns with the People's Republic of China and its nine members—five Republicans and four Democrats—were named on June 22, 1998. Its primary responsibility was to investigate whether technology or information was transferred to the People's Republic of China that may have contributed to the enhancement of the nuclear-armed intercontinental ballistic missiles or to the manufacture of weapons of mass destruction.

Committee Leaders: Cox was named chair of the committee and Norman L. Dicks (Dem-Wash.) was named its ranking Democrat. Porter J. Goss (Rep-Fla.), the chair of the Permanent Select Intelligence Committee who would later be appointed Director of the Central Intelligence Agency, was named as the committee's vice chair. Neither Cox nor Dicks served on the International Relations or National Security committees, which might have been expected to deal with this specific issue. Cox was chair of the Republican Policy Committee and a relatively senior member of the Commerce and Government Reform and Oversight Committees while Dicks was a senior member of Appropriations, serving on its National Security and Military Construction subcommittees.

The Senate had opened a July, 1997 investigation of China's role in the 1996 presidential and congressional elections led by U.S. senator Fred Thompson (Rep-Tenn.). The Senate investigation was more politically-focused on President Bill Clinton, believing that he had been too soft on human rights abuses in China, due to his political alliance with Bernard Schwarz, the chair of Loral Space and Communications Ltd. Schwarz was a major Democratic fund raiser and Loral had contracts with the Commerce Department to launch satellites from China.

The Senate's investigation had less public impact than that of the House's Cox-Dicks committee, which focused on serious national security concerns. Popularly-known as the "Cox Report," a redacted version of the report was released on May 25, 1999, and the committee's recommendations were accepted 428 to 0 by the House on June 9, 1999.

Its conclusions were contained in the opening paragraph of its three-volume report:

The People's Republic of China (PRC) has stolen classified design information on the United States' most advanced thermonuclear weapons. These thefts of nuclear secrets from our national weapons laboratories enabled the PRC to design, develop, and successfully test modern strategic nuclear weapons sooner than would otherwise have been possible. The stolen U.S. nuclear secrets give the PRC design information on thermonuclear weapons on a par with our own.

The PRC thefts from our National Laboratories began at least as early as the late 1970s. Significant secrets are known to have been stolen, from the laboratories or elsewhere, as recently as the mid-1990s. Such thefts almost certainly continue to the present. The People's Republic of China (PRC) has stolen design information on the United States' most advanced thermonuclear weapons. The Select Committee judges that the PRC's next generation of thermonuclear weapons, currently under development, will exploit elements of stolen U.S. design information. PRC penetration of our national nuclear weapons laboratories spans at least the past several decades and almost certainly continues today.

In summary, the Cox Report contained five major allegations about China and nuclear weapons: China stole design information regarding the United States seven most advanced thermonuclear weapons; these stolen secrets enabled the People's Liberation Army to accelerate its design, development and testing of its own nuclear weapons; China's next generation of nuclear weapons would contain elements of stolen U.S. design information and would be comparable in effectiveness to the weapons used by the United States; small warheads based on stolen U.S. information could be ready for deployment in 2002 also enabling China to integrate MIRV technology on its next generation of missiles; and these thefts were not isolated incidents, but rather the results of decades of intelligence operations against U.S. weapons laboratories conducted by the Ministry of State Security. In addition, the report described the illegal activity likely persisted, despite new security measures implemented as a result of the scandal.

Many of the Select Committee's recommendations were enacted into law, including the creation of a new National Nuclear Security Administration to take over the nuclear weapons security responsibilities of the United States Department of Energy. However, no person has ever been convicted of providing nuclear information to the PRC, and the one case that was brought in connection to these charges, that of Wen Ho Lee, collapsed.

The two major corporate violators named in the Cox report—Loral Space and Communications Corp. and Hughes Electronics Corp.—were later prosecuted by the federal government for violations of U.S. export control law, resulting in the two largest fines in the history of the Arms Export Control Act. Loral paid a $14 million fine in 2002, and Hughes paid a $32 million fine in 2003.

In spite of the seriousness of the charges, few sanctions were assessed against the Chinese government which called all of the Cox committee allegations "groundless." And American foreign policy continues to grant China "most favored nation" status in our trade relations.

Selected References

Johnston, Alastair Ian, W.K.H. Panofsky, Marco Di Capua, and Lewis R. Franklin, and M.M. May,ed, *The Cox Committee Report: An Assessment* Center for International Security and Cooperation (CISAC), Stanford University, December, 1999.

U.S. House of Representatives, *Final Report of the Select Committee on U.S. National Security and Military/Commercial Concerns with the People's Republic of China,* 105th Congress, 2nd Session, House Report 105-851, January 3, 1999; declassified pursuant to H. Res. 5, 106th Congress, 1st Session, May 25, 1999.

MEMBERSHIP ROSTERS, 105th-106th Congresses, 1998-1999

SELECT COMMITTEE ON U.S. NATIONAL SECURITY AND MILITARY/COMMERCIAL CONCERNS WITH THE PEOPLE'S REPUBLIC OF CHINA / 105th Congress

Service Dates of Committee Chair: June 22, 1998-Jan. 3, 1999

Service Dates of Majority Members: June 22, 1998-Jan. 3, 1999

Service Dates of Minority Members: June 22, 1998-Jan. 3, 1999

Roster Filled: Majority with 5 members, June 22, 1998; Minority with 4 members, June 22, 1998-

| | | | Majority | | | | | | Minority | |
| | | | | Terms in: | | | | | | Terms in: | |
Rank Name	Party	State	House	Comm.		Rank Name	Party	State	House	Comm.
Chr Cox, C. Christopher	Rep	Cal	5	1		RM Dicks, Norman D.	Dem	Wash.	11	1
2nd Goss, Porter J.	Rep	Fla.	5	1		2nd Spratt, John M. Jr.	Dem	S.C..	8	1
3rd Bereuter, Douglas K.	Rep	Neb.	10	1		3rd Roybal-Allard, Lucille	Dem	Cal.	3	1
4th Hansen, James V.	Rep	Utah.	9	1		4th Scott, Robert C.	Dem	Va.	3	1
5th Weldon, Wayne C. (Curt)	Rep	Penn	6	1						

SELECT COMMITTEE ON U.S. NATIONAL SECURITY AND MILITARY/COMMERCIAL CONCERNS WITH THE PEOPLE'S REPUBLIC OF CHINA / 106th Congress

Service Dates of Committee Chair: Jan. 19, 1999-Apr. 30, 1999

Service Dates of Majority Members: Jan. 19, 1999-Apr. 30, 1999

Service Dates of Minority Members: Jan. 19, 1999-Apr. 30, 1999

Roster Filled: Majority with 5 members, Jan. 19, 1999; Minority with 4 members, Jan. 19, 1999

| | | | Majority | | | | | | Minority | |
| | | | | Terms in: | | | | | | Terms in: | |
Rank Name	Party	State	House	Comm.		Rank Name	Party	State	House	Comm.
Chr Cox, C. Christopher	Rep	Cal.	6	2		RM Dicks, Norman D.	Dem	Wash.	12	2
2nd Goss, Porter J.	Rep	Fla.	6	2		2nd Spratt, John M. Jr.	Dem	S.C.	9	2
3rd Bereuter, Douglas K.	Rep	Neb.	11	2		3rd Roybal-Allard, Lucille	Dem	Cal.	4	2
4th Hansen, James V.	Rep	Utah.	10	2		4th Scott, Robert C.	Dem	Va.	4	2
5th Weldon, Wayne C. (Curt)	Rep	Penn.	7	2						

Select Bipartisan Committee to Investigate the Preparation for and Response to Hurricane Katrina

109th Congress, 2005-2006

BACKGROUND

Organizational History: Hurricane season along the Atlantic coast reaches its peak in the late summer months, and on August 29, 2005, Hurricane Katrina slammed the coast of southeast Louisiana. Most devastated by the hurricane and the subsequent flooding was the city of New Orleans. An estimated 80 percent of the city and its neighboring parishes were flooded as the city levee system failed to contain the waters of the Gulf of Mexico that crashed into the city. The number of confirmed deaths exceeded 1,800, most of which were among poor African-Americans who did not have transportation to move them from the city to safety. Damage to seacoast towns in Mississippi was also extensive, but it was the devastation of New Orleans that became the emblem of the hurricane's impact. It was the largest natural disaster in American history and its estimated cost of $81 billion dwarfed that of Hurricane Andrew's 1992 financial impact upon Florida.

The devastation became politicized when President George W. Bush was filmed as he flew over the flooded area on a return trip from his Texas ranch back to the White House without landing to witness the devastation first hand. This was seen by many as indifference to the plight of the city's large African-American population. The situation was further exacerbated by the role of Michael Brown, the Director of the Federal Emergency Management Administration (FEMA), who seemed to be poorly informed about the devastation wrought by the flooding and its impact upon the citizens of New Orleans. Brown's apparent lack of relevant qualifications for the job and President Bush's public support for him contributed to the president's slide in the public opinion polls. The political damage was extensive.

The original plan emanating from the White House was to have a joint committee investigate the Katrina catastrophe. Fearing a "whitewash," House Democratic leader Nancy Pelosi of California and Senate Democratic leader Harry Reid of Nevada urged that an independent commission be named to investigate the Katrina catastrophe. They saw the 9/11 Commission as their model for this suggestion. However, Republican leaders in both chambers rejected this suggestion and the Democratic leaders announced on September 8, 2005, that they would not name their members to these investigative committees. With the joint committee proposal scuttled, the Senate chose to use its Homeland Security and Governmental Affairs Committee to investigate the Katrina episode, while the House chose to name a separate select committee.

This committee was the first House select committee named to investigate an administration's policies since the House Select Committee to Investigate Covert Arms Transactions with Iran was created on January 7, 1987. Most commonly known along with its Senate counterpart, the Senate Select Committee on Secret Military Assistance to Iran and the Nicaraguan Opposition, as the "Iran-Contra committees," these committees were often cited as well-regarded models of low partisanship investigations. However, those committees were named before the post-1995 House became deeply polarized along party lines and engaged in what Juliet Eilperin of the *Washington Post* called "fight club politics."

Problems occurred immediately. Throughout the 200-plus year history of the Congress and its more than 3,000 committees, no committee had ever included "bipartisan" in its formal title, in spite of the fact that all committees are expected to have members from all parties represented on them. On September 15, 2005, the House of Representatives voted 222 to 193 to order the previous question and end debate on creating the committee. All 222 Republicans voted for the motion, while all 192 Democrats and Independent Bernie Sanders of Vermont voted against it. The resolution approving H. Res. 437, which created the Select Bipartisan Committee to Investigate the Preparation for and Response to Hurricane Katrina was carried 224 to 188, with Republicans splitting 217 to 1 for it and Democrats splitting 186 to 7 against it. There was no bipartisanship to be found.

The select committee's party ratio was eleven Republicans and nine Democrats and since the majority has subpoena power and the minority does not, it appeared to Nancy Pelosi that the committee was intended to "whitewash" the Bush Administration's response to Katrina and to move blame from the White House to the Democratic governor of Louisiana, Kathleen Blanco, and the Democratic mayor of New Orleans, Ray Nagin. Those suspicions were furthered when Republican debaters during the committee's creation showered praise on Mississippi's Republican governor Haley Barbour, even though Katrina's impact upon Mississippi was far less than that which devastated Louisiana and New Orleans, the largest city in that state.

Membership: The original resolution stated that "(a) The select committee shall be composed of 20 members appointed by the Speaker, of whom 9 shall be appointed after consultation with the Minority Leader. The Speaker shall designate one Member as chairman. And (b)(1) The Speaker and the Minority Leader shall be ex officio members of the select committee but shall have no vote in the select committee and may not be counted for purposes of determining a quorum."

Committee Leader: Speaker of the House J. Dennis Hastert (Rep-Ill.), a staunch supporter of President Bush's legislative agenda, named Rep. Tom Davis (Rep-Va.), the Chair of the House Government Reform Committee, to serve as the Chair of the Select Committee. Since no Democrats chose to serve on the committee, there was no ranking member.

On the title page of the Select Committee's Final Report, the eleven Republican members of the committee are listed without their party affiliations, and the names of five Democrats who chose to participate in some of the committee's hearings are listed without their party affiliations: Charlie Melancon and William J. Jefferson of Louisiana, Gene Taylor of Mississippi, Cynthia McKinney of Georgia, and Sheila Jackson-Lee of Texas. Representatives Jefferson, McKinney, and Jackson-Lee are African-Americans.

As anticipated, the report's summary issued on February 15, 2006 and entitled "A Failure of Initiative" blamed only Governor Blanco, Mayor Nagin, and former FEMA Director Michael Brown by name in their summary. The only federal official critically alluded to was the Secretary of Homeland Security, but Michael Chertoff, the DHS Secretary, was not mentioned by name. And the only statement addressed to the White House's response was: "It does not appear the President received adequate advice and counsel from a senior disaster professional." However, since most Americans believed that the deaths and devastation visited upon New Orleans were "a failure of response" rather than "a failure of initiative," the report failed to contain the political damage that the White House had hoped that the committee would provide.

When the Democrats organized the House in 2007 following their victory in the 2006 congressional elections, the Congressional Black Caucus urged Speaker Nancy Pelosi to name a new select committee on Hurricane Katrina to address the continuing problems faced by New Orleans citizens in getting the federal help they needed to rebuild their city.

Selected References

U.S. House of Representatives, Select Bipartisan Committee to Investigate the Preparation for and Response to Hurricane Katrina, *A Failure of Initiative: The Final Report of the Select Bipartisan Committee to Investigate the Preparation for and Response to Hurricane Katrina,* 109th Congress, 2nd Session, House Report 109-377, February 15, 2006.

U.S. House of Representatives, Select Bipartisan Committee to Investigate the Preparation for and Response to Hurricane Katrina, *Supplementary Report and Document Annex,* 109th Congress, 2nd Session, House Report 109-396, March 16, 2006.

JURISDICTION

From House Resolution 437, 109th Congress, 1st Session, September 15, 2005

To establish the Select Bipartisan Committee to Investigate the Preparation for and Response to Hurricane Katrina.

Resolved,

The select committee is authorized and directed to conduct a full and complete investigation and study and to report its findings to the House not later than February 15, 2006, regarding—

(1) the development, coordination, and execution by local, State, and Federal authorities of emergency response plans and other activities in preparation for Hurricane Katrina; and

(2) the local, State, and Federal government response to Hurricane Katrina.

MEMBERSHIP ROSTER, 109th Congress, 2005-2006

SELECT BIPARTISAN COMMITTEE TO INVESTIGATE THE PREPARATION FOR AND RESPONSE TO HURRICAN KATRINA / 109th Congress

Service Dates of Committee Chair: Sep. 21, 2005-Feb. 15, 2006

Service Dates of Majority Members: Sep. 21, 2005-Feb. 15, 2006

Service Dates of Minority Members: Never named

Roster Filled: Majority with 11 members on Sep. 21, 2005; Minority with 9 member slots unfilled

Majority						Minority			
			Terms in:					**Terms in:**	
Rank Name	**Party**	**State**	**House**	**Comm.**	**Rank Name**	**Party**	**State**	**House**	**Comm.**
Chr Davis, Thomas M. III	Rep	Va.	6	1					
2nd Sensenbrenner, F. James Jr.	Rep	Wisc.	14	1	None served				
3rd Rogers, Harold D.	Rep	Ky.	13	1					
4th Shays, Christopher H.	Rep	Conn.	10	1					
5th Bonilla, Henry	Rep	Tex.	7	1					
6th Buyer, Stephen	Rep	Ind	7	1					
7th Myrick, Sue	Rep	N.C.	6	1					
8th Thornberry, William M. (Mac)	Rep	Tex.	6	1					
9th Granger, Kay	Rep	Tex.	5	1					
10th Pickering, Charles W. (Chip) Jr.	Rep	Miss.	5	1					
11th Shuster, William	Rep	Penn.	3	1					

Changes:
  Majority:

Sensenbrenner, F. James Jr.	Rep	Wisc.	Sep. 23, 2005	Resigned committee; no new assignment
Miller, Jefferson B.	Rep	Fla.	Sep. 26, 2005	Replaced Sensenbrenner

Select Committee on Energy Independence and Global Warming

110th-111th Congresses (2007-2011)

BACKGROUND

Organizational History: Growing national concerns about the impact of global warming were furthered by the efforts of former vice president Albert A. Gore Jr., whose movie "An Inconvenient Truth" sparked a great deal of controversy about what was happening to the planet as a consequence of rapid industrialization and population pressures. With tsunamis in Asia leading to thousands of deaths and destruction, and the devastating flooding of the southeastern coast of Louisiana and Mississippi by Hurricanes Katrina and Rita, the Congress felt obliged to address these concerns by creating a select committee.

The committee was entitled the Select Committee on Energy Independence and Global Warming and it was created with the passage of H. Res. 202 on March 8, 2007. As has been the case in recent Congresses, the contention level between the parties resulted in highly polarized votes. The vote ordering the previous question to end debate on H.Res. 202 that called for funding the existing standing committees and the new select committee was 228 to 195, with Democrats voting 227-1 to end debate and Republicans voting 194-1 to continue it. The vote on final passage to fund the committee was less contentious, with a vote of 269 to 150, with Democrats voting 225-1 and Republicans 44-149.

In addition to the issue of global warming, the committee was created to find ways to reduce American independence on the importation of fuels from the volatile regions of the world, namely, the Middle East. As in the case of select committees, the committee would have no authority to introduce legislation but it could make recommendations to the House's standing committees for specific action. The committee's jurisdiction was:

The select committee shall not have legislative jurisdiction and shall have no authority to take legislative action on any bill or resolution. Its sole authority shall be to investigate study, make findings, and develop recommendations on policies, strategies, technologies and other innovations, intended to reduce the dependence of the United States on foreign sources of energy and achieve substantial and permanent reductions in emissions and other activities that contribute to climate change and global warming.

Membership: Speaker Nancy Pelosi (Dem-Cal.) named fifteen members to the select committee on March 9, 2007—nine majority Democrats and six minority Republicans. The committee was renamed in the 111th Congress with the same number of members—fifteen—and the same majority-minority ratio—9:6. Twelve of the fifteen members who served in the 110th Congress continued in the 111th Congress. The committee members were relatively senior, with majority members with a mean seniority of 5.2 Congresses and the minority members with a mean seniority of 6.2 terms. Its most notable member to depart was Hilda L. Solis (Dem-Cal.), who left the committee to become President Barack Obama's Secretary of Labor in 2009.

Committee Leaders: Edward J. Markey (Dem-Mass.) a seventeen-term member, was chosen as the committee's first chair, while F. James Sensenbrenner (Rep-Wisc.), a fifteen-term member, was its initial ranking minority member. Markey was a long-term member of both the Natural Resources and Energy and Commerce Committees while Sensenbrenner had chaired both the Judiciary and Science and Technology Committees.

Given national anxiety about the issue of global warming and the continuing debate over its causes and consequences, this is a select committee that may continue for some time. Although the select committee cannot introduce legislation, its members were instrumental in the House passage of H.R. 2454, The American Clean Energy and Security Act on June 29, 2009.

MEMBERSHIP ROSTERS, 110th-111th Congresses, 2007-2011

SELECT ENERGY INDEPENDENCE AND GLOBAL WARMING / 110th Congress

Service Dates of Committee Chair: Mar. 9, 2007-Jan. 3, 2009

Service Dates of Majority Members: Mar. 9, 2007-Jan. 3, 2009

Service Dates of Minority Members: Mar. 9, 2007-Jan. 3, 2009

Roster Filled: Majority with 9 members, Mar. 9, 2007; Minority with 6 members, Mar. 9, 2007

	Majority						Minority				
				Terms in:						**Terms in:**	
Rank Name	**Party**	**State**	**House**	**Comm.**		**Rank Name**	**Party**	**State**	**House**	**Comm.**	
Chr Markey, Edward J.	Dem	Mass.	17	1		RM Sensenbrenner, F. James Jr.	Rep	Wis	15	1	
2nd Blumenauer, Earl	Dem	Ore.	7	1		2nd Shadegg, John B.	Rep	Ariz.	7	1	
3rd Inslee, Jay R.	Dem	Wash.	6	1		3rd Walden, Greg	Rep	Ore.	5	1	
4th Larson, John B.	Dem	Conn.	5	1		4th Sullivan, John	Rep	Okl.	4	1	
5th Solis, Hilda L.	Dem	Cal.	4	1		5th Blackburn, Marsha	Rep	Tenn.	3	1	
6th Herseth, Stephanie	Dem	S.D.	3	1		6th Miller, Candace S.	Rep	Mich.	3	1	
7th Cleaver, Emanuel II	Dem	Mo.	2	1							
8th Hall, John	Dem	N.Y.	2	1							
9th McNerney, Jerry	Dem	Cal.	1	1							

Changes:

None recorded in this Congress

Departures from the Chamber

Note: Solis, Hilda L. (Dem-Cal.) Unassigned in the 111th, and resigned the House on Feb. 24, 2009, appointed Secretary of Labor

Departures from Committee:	**Majority**			**Minority**		
Moved to Energy and Commerce	McNerney, Jerry	Dem	Cal.	None		
No new assignment	None			Walden, Greg	Rep	Ore.

SELECT ENERGY INDEPENDENCE AND GLOBAL WARMING / 111th Congress

Service Dates of Committee Chair: Jan. 14, 2009-Jan. 3, 2011

Service Dates of Majority Members: Feb. 3, 2009-Jan. 3, 2011

Service Dates of Ranking Member: Jan. 14, 2009-Jan. 3, 2011

Service Dates of Minority Members: Feb. 3, 2009-Jan. 3, 2011

Roster Filled: Majority with 9 members, Feb. 3, 2009; Minority with 6 members, Feb. 3, 2009

	Majority						Minority				
				Terms in:						**Terms in:**	
Rank Name	**Party**	**State**	**House**	**Comm.**		**Rank Name**	**Party**	**State**	**House**	**Comm.**	
Chr Markey, Edward J.	Dem	Mass	18	2		RM Sensenbrenner, F. James Jr.	Rep	Wis	16	2	
2nd Blumenauer, Earl	Dem	Ore.	8	2		2nd Shadegg, John B.	Rep	Ariz.	8	2	
3rd Inslee, Jay R.	Dem	Wash.	7	2		3rd Sullivan, John	Rep	Okl.	5	2	
4th Larson, John B.	Dem	Conn.	6	2		4th Blackburn, Marsha	Rep	Tenn..	4	2	
5th Herseth Sandlin, Stephanie	Dem	S.D	4	2		5th Miller,. Candace S.	Rep	Mich.	4	2	
6th Cleaver, Emanuel II	Dem	Mo.	3	2		6th Capito, Shelley Moore	Rep	W.Va.	5	1	
7th Hall, John	Dem	N.Y.	3	2							
8th Salazar, John T.	Dem	Colo	3	1							
9th Speier, K. Jacqueline	Dem	Cal.	2	1							

Select Committee to Investigate the Voting Irregularities of August 2, 2007

110th Congress (2007-2008)

BACKGROUND

Organizational History: On August 2, 2007, as the House prepared to adjourn for the annual August recess, an especially contentious vote was taken on H.R. 3161, the Fiscal 2008 Agriculture Appropriations bill. Representative Jerry Lewis (Rep-Cal.) submitted a motion to recommit the bill to the Appropriations Committee with instructions that it be reported back to the House with language prohibiting any funds in the bill to be used for food stamps or housing assistance to illegal immigrants, who were adjudged to be unqualified to receive such assistance.

The original vote was 214 to 214, with a tie indicating that the motion had failed, but in a flurry of vote changes, Republicans contended that the bill had passed 215 to 213. Then a series of Democratic vote changes led to a new count of 212 to 216, meaning the bill had been defeated, with Republicans voting 198-0 for the motion and Democrats voting 216 to 14 against it. This is the vote tally reported in the official sources, the *House Journal* and the *Congressional Record*.

The question raised by Republicans focused upon the timing of the vote tally. Did Representative Michael McNulty (Dem-N.Y.), who presided over the House during the vote, call it too soon when it was 214 to 214. The public vote on the television screen recorded the Republican changes indicating that the motion had passed 215-213. McNulty was accused of letting time continue so that the Democrats could counter the Republican votes and defeat the motion, 212 to 216. A subsequent vote to reconsider the motion was called, with Democrats voting 223 to 4 to confirm the 212-216 tally, while most Republicans boycotted the vote by marching from the chamber.

Minority Leader John Boehner (Rep-Ohio) was sufficiently incensed to introduce H.Res. 611 on August 3, 2007. That resolution called for the establishment of the House Select Committee on the Voting Irregularities of August 2, 2007. It was to be a bipartisan six-member committee, with an equal number of Democrats and Republicans named and it would have subpoena power. The committee was approved unanimously by the House.

The six-member panel issued an interim report on September 27, 2007, and a final report was issued on September 25, 2008, with recommendations on voting rule changes. Its three major findings were:

FINDING 1: As is the traditional role of the Majority Leader, Mr. Hoyer urged the Chair to close the vote—after time for voting had expired and with no apparent voting activity in the well—when the majority was prevailing. Neither the Chair nor the rostrum staff was pressured to circumvent the rules and practices of the House. Nevertheless, the Chair's premature announcement of the vote led to a series of cascading errors on the rostrum, including the failure to process well cards submitted by the Minority and Majority Leaders and a failure in the EVS [Electronic Voting System], all of which further undermined many Members' confidence in the integrity of the vote. (p. 17)

FINDING 2: The Chair [Mr. McNulty] failed to observe the customary procedures and protocols for closing a vote, resulting in an inaccurate announcement and unintentionally raising concerns regarding the legitimacy of that vote. (p. 18)

FINDING 3: The new sentence of clause 2(a) of rule XX (creating the rule against holding a vote open for the sole purpose of reversing the outcome), added at the beginning of this Congress, was a major contributing factor to this perfect storm of events of August 2, 2007. As evidenced by those events, this sentence is unworkable in practice. (p. 20)

The committee urged that the new sentence be removed and called for better communication between the Majority and Minority Leaders and for better training of presiding officers.

As for Representative Michael McNulty, he retired from the House at the age of sixty-one, after a twenty-year House career, sixteen years of which were served on Ways and Means, at the end of the 110th Congress.

Membership: Six members were named to serve on the committee. Three Democrats were to be appointed by the Speaker and three Republicans by the Minority Leader. Their appointments were reported on September 5, 2007.

Committee Leaders: William Delahunt (Dem-Mass.) was named chair of the committee, while Mike Pence (Rep-Ind.) was named its ranking minority member. Both Delahunt and Pence were serving on the House Judiciary Committee at the time of their appointments and Delahunt was also then serving on Standards of Official Conduct.

Selected References

U.S. House of Representatives, Select Committee to Investigate the Voting Irregularities of August 2, 2007, *Interim Report,* 110th Congress, 1st Session, House Report 110-355, September 27, 2007.

U.S. House of Representatives, Select Committee to Investigate the Voting Irregularities of August 2, 2007, *Final Report and Summary of Activities,* 110th Congress, 2nd Session, House Report 110-885, September 25, 2008.

JURISDICTION

From House Resolution 611, 110th Congress, 1st Session, August 3, 2007

Resolved,

That—

(1) the Officers of the House of Representatives are immediately directed to preserve all records, documents, recordings, electronic transmissions, or other material, regardless of form, related to the voting irregularities of August 2, 2007;

(2) there is hereby established a select committee to investigate the voting irregularities of August 2, 2007 (hereinafter referred to as the 'select committee'). The select committee shall be comprised of 6 Members, of which 3 Members shall be appointed by the Speaker and 3 by the Minority Leader. The select committee shall—

   (A) investigate the circumstances surrounding the record vote requested by the gentleman from California (Mr. Lewis) on the motion to recommit to H.R. 3161, including the Chair's ruling over the objections of the Parliamentarian; and

   (B) make an interim report to the House not later than September 30, 2007, and a final report not later than September 15, 2008—

      (i) regarding the actions of any Members, officers, or employees of the House engaged in the disenfranchisement of Members in voting on the question; and

      (ii) recommending changes to the rules and procedures of the House of Representatives necessary to protect the voting rights of constitutionally elected Members chosen by the people of the United States of America; and

(3) the select committee shall have the same powers to obtain testimony and documents pursuant to subpoena as authorized under clause 2(m) of rule XI.

MEMBERSHIP ROSTER, 110th Congress, 2007-2008

SELECT COMMITTEE TO INVESTIGATE THE VOTING IRREGULARITIES OF AUGUST 2, 2007 / 110th Congress

Service Dates of Committee Chair: Sep. 5, 2007-Sep. 25, 2008

Service Dates of Majority Members: Sep. 5, 2007-Sep. 25, 2008

Service Dates of Minority Members: Sep. 5, 2007-Sep. 25, 2008

Roster Filled: Majority with 3 members, Sep. 5, 2007; Minority with 3 members, Sep. 5, 2007

	Majority						Minority			
				Terms in:						**Terms in:**	
Rank Name	**Party**	**State**	**House**	**Comm.**		**Rank Name**	**Party**	**State**	**House**	**Comm.**
Chr Delahunt, William D.	Dem	Mass	6	1		RM Pence, Mike	Rep	Ind.	4	1
2nd Davis, Artur	Dem	Ala.	3	1		2nd LaTourette, Steven C.	Rep	Ohio	7	1
3rd Herseth Sandlin, Stephanie	Dem	S.D	3	1		3rd Hulshof, Kenny	Rep	Mo.	6	1

Part I

E. Joint Committees of the U.S. Congress

Backgrounds, Jurisdictions, and Rosters
1993-2011

Joint Committees of the Congress
1993-2011

Joint Committees: A Brief History

Even though senators and representatives interact regularly with one another on conference committees to iron out differences in the wording of legislation, their chamber prerogatives are zealously guarded. Joint committees strain these prerogatives with their requirement that there be equal numbers of members chosen from each chamber to serve on each panel. Consequently, joint committees in the U.S. Congress have generally had limited appeal. In the checklist compiled by Walter Stubbs, *Congressional Committees, 1789-1982: A Checklist* (Westport, Conn., 1985), only nine different joint committees were named in the thirty-six Congresses from 1789 until the Civil War erupted in 1861. While the joint committees focusing on policy faded, the housekeeping functions of the joint committees on Enrolled Bills (1789), Library (1806), and Public Printing (1846) would continue after the war.

George B. Galloway, a long-time proponent of joint committees and the staff director of the Joint Committee on the Organization of Congress, which produced the 1946 Reorganization Act, contended in his *History of the House of Representatives* (New York, 1976, revised ed.) that:

> Joint committees flourished during the Civil War and the Reconstruction period when they were formed to investigate the conduct of the war, emancipation and reconstruction, retrenchment and Southern outrages, and the condition of the Indian tribes. (p. 289)

The best-known of the Civil War joint committees was Sen. Benjamin F. Wade's (Rep-Ohio) Joint Committee on the Conduct of the War, that has generally been decried as a committee more disruptive than supportive of President Abraham Lincoln's wartime effort. From the 37th to the 43rd Congresses (1861-1875), twelve new joint committees were named. However, between 1875 and 1893, the House and Senate convened with differing party majorities in six of nine Congresses and the naming of joint committees, a sign of intercameral cooperation, was a casualty of interparty conflict, with only nine new joint committees named in those nine Congresses. While the Joint Committee on Enrolled Bills would disappear in 1876, the new Joint Committee on the Disposition of Executive Papers would join the regularly named Joint Committees of Library and Printing in 1889.

With Democrats controlling both chambers in the 53rd Congress, (1893-1995), five new joint committees were named and added to the three continuing ones, which brought the number of joint committees to eight, then their highest total. With Republicans in control of Congress following the 1918 congressional election, six new joint committees were created in both the 66th and 67th Congresses (1919-1923). By the 67th Congress, the number of joint committees reached an all-time high of thirteen, with six new committees and seven

holdover ones. In the 69th Congress (1925-1927), a new continuing joint committee would be named—the Joint Committee on Internal Revenue Taxation.

Between 1927 and 1937, the pace of creating new joint committees slowed, as only four new joint committees were named. By 1935, only the four continuing joint committees of Library, Printing, Executive Papers, and Internal Revenue Taxation were named. Seven new joint committees were named during the 75th Congress (1937-1939), and added with the four continuing committees brought the number back to eleven. Ten would be the number of joint committees in the 79th Congress (1945-1947) as the Joint Committee of the Organization of Congress concluded its work on May 31, 1946, and would submit the report that would create the modern congressional committee system.

The Joint Committee on the Organization of Congress co-chaired by Sen. Robert M. LaFollette Jr. (Prog.-Wisc.) and Rep. A.S. Mike Monroney (D-Okla.), the authors of the Legislative Reorganization Act of 1946 (P.L. 79-601), fervently believed that joint committees would generate greater cooperation between the House and the Senate. It was the intent of the Act that joint committees could be made to expedite legislation, but the size inequality between the Senate and the House of Representatives would eventually undermine this long-term experiment in intercameral cooperation. One early experiment that failed was the Joint Committee on the Legislative Budget that was part of the Reorganization Act and existed on paper from 1946 to 1971 but was never fully staffed. In 1949, five senators were named, but no House members ever agreed to serve on it and it disappeared without a trace in the Legislative Reorganization Act of 1971 (P.L. 91-510).

The post-1946 joint committees varied greatly in their structures and jurisdictions. Some acted as standing committees with continuous identities, while others operated as select committees and expired after filing their reports. Between nine and twelve joint committees were named in each of the fourteen Congresses from 1947 to 1975. The number of assigned places on the joint committees exceeded 100 in thirteen of those fourteen Congresses, with an average of 111.3 members per Congress and a peak of 126 in the 80th Congress (1947-1949) and a low of 93 in the 91st Congress (1969-1971).

Joint committees with the greatest longevity were those that were staffed by specific standing committees. The Joint Committees on Library and Printing were staffed by members of the House Administration and Senate Rules and Administration Committees; Joint Taxation by House Ways and Means and Senate Finance; Immigration and Nationality by the two Judiciary Committees; Navaho-Hopi Indian Administration by the two Interior Committees; Defense Production by the two Banking and Currency Committees; and Reduction of Federal Expenditures primarily by the two Committees on Appropriations. Two joint committees, Atomic Energy and the Economic Report, were relatively large and had broader bases for their membership and arguably had a greater impact on public policy than the others named.

In the 1970's, joint committees eventually lost favor with the membership of each chamber and gradually disappeared. The Senate's smaller membership gave it a heavier burden than the House in staffing these committees and it initiated most of the joint committee terminations, either by not naming members to the panels or by actually legislating them out of existence. Following the Senate Committee Reorganization Amendments of 1977 in the 95th Congress, only four joint committees were left in operation: Library, Printing, Taxation, and the Joint Economic Committee, the only joint committee with membership independent of specific standing committees. These four committees have achieved the continuity of standing committees. By the 96th Congress (1979-1981), only 46 seats were assigned to joint committees—a drop of 73 seats from the 119 recorded in the 93rd Congress (1973-1975). Not included are the purely honorific Joint Committees on Inaugural Ceremonies that are generally staffed by the floor leaders and the chair of Senate Rules and Administration with a minimal impact upon congressional business.

Since 1975 only three temporary joint committees have been appointed: Bicentennial Arrangements, with twelve members (1975-1976), Deficit Reduction with fifty-nine members in 1987 and the twenty-four-member Ad Hoc Joint Committee on the Organization of Congress named in the closing days of 1992. Although this committee entertained thoughts of finishing off the remaining joint committees, the final four—Library, Printing, Taxation, and Economic—continue to function.

It appears that neither the Republican Revolution or the Democratic Restoration had plans to alter the relatively minimal role presently played by the joint committees.

Joint Committees of the Congress
1993-2011

Joint Library

Joint Committee on the Library of Congress, 103rd-111th Congresses (1993-2011)

BACKGROUND

Organizational History: The joint committee on the Library has been in existence since 1802 when it was determined that "the unexpended balance of any sums appropriated by Congress for the increase of the general library, together with such sums as may hereafter be appropriated to the same purpose shall be laid out under the direction of a joint committee of the Congress upon the Library," (2 Stat. 129). It was formally established on February 27, 1806, (*House Journal*, 9th Congress).

The committee is authorized to accept any work of the fine arts on behalf of Congress and designate a location in the United States Capitol for the work of art. (Pursuant to the *Revised Statutes*) This authority was expanded in 1875 to require that artwork that was not the property of the United States could not be displayed in the Capitol, and that rooms in the Capitol cannot be used as private studios for works of art without written permission of the Committee. The Architect of the Capitol has the authority to enforce this provision.

In 1897, the direct management of the Library of Congress was turned over to the Librarian of Congress, making the function of the joint committee one of oversight. In addition to the Library, the Botanic Gardens and art work acquired by Congress have become the responsibility of the committee.

On February 24, 1933, in the 72nd Congress. with the passage of H.Con.Res. 47, the Architect of the Capitol was authorized and directed to relocate within the Capitol any of the statues already received and placed in Statuary Hall, upon the approval of the Joint Committee on the Library, and to provide for the reception and location of statues received from the states. This provision was permanently enacted into law in 2000 in the legislative branch appropriations.

Rarely meeting formally, the Joint Committee on the Library operates primarily through consultation between the chair and vice chair and the administrators of the Library, who "regularly seek [the committee's] advice or concurrence prior to implementing new policies."

Membership: The joint committee is comprised of five members from the House Administration committee and five members from the Senate Rules and Administration committee. In the 84th Congress (1955-1957), a rotating system was instituted whereby the House ranking member would chair the first session and the Senate ranking member would chair the second session. The size of the committee with its five senators and five representatives has remained constant from 1947 to the present day.

Committee Leaders: Sen. C. Wayland Brooks (Rep-Ill.) was the first post-reorganization chair of the Joint Committee on the Library. Sen. Theodore Francis Green (Dem-R.I) served as chair and vice chair for ten years (1949-1953; 1955-1961), the longest senior service on the Library Committee. Green and Rep. Omar T. Burleson (Dem-Tex.) alternated the chairmanship from 1955 to 1961, when Green retired and Michael J. Mansfield (Dem-Mont.), the Senate Majority Leader, became its senior Senate Democrat. Mansfield's departure for Appropriations led B. Everett Jordan (Dem-N.C.) to become the senior Democrat alternating with Burleson from 1963 to 1968 and Burleson's resignation from the committee. Samuel N. Friedel (Dem-Md.) replaced Burleson and alternated with Jordan until his renomination defeat in 1970. Friedel was succeeded by Wayne L. Hays (Dem-Ohio) who alternated with Jordan until Jordan's defeat for renomination in 1972. In the 93rd Congress, the senior House majority member was Lucien N. Nedzi (Dem-Mich.) and the senior Senate majority member was Howard W. Cannon (Dem-Nev.). Nedzi and Cannon alternated the chair from 1973 to 1979 until Cannon became chair of Commerce, Science and Transportation and was succeeded by Claiborne deB. Pell (Dem-R.I.) in 1979.

The Republican takeover of the Senate in 1981 placed Charles McC. Mathias, Jr. (Rep-Md.) in the senior majority Senate slot on Joint Library, with Augustus F. Hawkins (Dem-Cal.) as the committee's senior representative after Nedzi's retirement in 1980. Hawkins left the committee in 1984 and was replaced by Allan B. Swift (Dem-Wash.). In 1985, Frank Annunzio (Dem-Ill.) became the committee's senior House member as Mathias now alternated with three senior Democrats during those three Congresses.

Democrats regained the Senate in 1986, and Pell resumed the senior Senator slot and alternated with Annunzio until the latter's departure from the committee in 1991. At that point, Charles G. Rose III (Dem-N.C.), the chair of House Administration, and Pell, a member of Rules and Administration, but also the chair of Foreign Relations, shared the chair in the 102nd and 103rd Congresses (1991-1995).

During the six Congresses when Republicans controlled the House, William M. Thomas of California was its senior Representative for the 104th-106th Congresses (1995-2001);

and Vernon J. Ehlers of Michigan succeeded him in 2001. Robert Ney of Ohio was the senior Republican representative on Library until the Jack Abramoff scandal obliged him to relinquish the post to Ehlers. In the Democratic-controlled 110th and 111th Congresses, Juanita Millender-McDonald of California served as the committee's ranking Democrat until her death in 2007, when she was succeeded by Robert A. Brady of Pennsylvania.

On the Senate side, the Republican takeover in 1995 placed Mark O. Hatfield of Oregon in the senior majority slot in the 104th Congress. He was succeeded by Theodore F. Stevens of Alaska for the next two Congresses, 1997-2001. The uncertainty following the 2000 election and the defection of James M. Jeffords of Vermont from the Republican Party in 2001 led the Senate to name the members of the Joint Library Committee later than normal and Democrat Christopher Dodd was named senior senator for the remainder of the 107th Congress. With Republicans regaining control of the Senate in 2003, Stevens resumed his post as senior Senate Republican on Joint Library.

In the two Democratic controlled 110th and 111th Congresses, Dianne Feinstein was the committee's senior majority senator in the 110th Congress and Charles E. Schumer of New York occupied that post in the 111th Congress.

Party Leaders: Democratic party leaders who served on Joint Library include Representatives Carl Albert of Oklahoma who moved up the leadership ladder from Whip in 1955 to Majority Leader in 1962 to Speaker of the House, 1971-1977; John Brademas of Indiana, the Democratic Whip from 1977 to 1981; and Steny H. Hoyer, Democratic Whip from 2005 to 2007 and serving as Majority Leader from 2007 to the present. Library Committee Senate Democrats who have held leadership posts include Russell B. Long of Louisiana who served as Democratic whip from 1965 to 1969; Michael J. Mansfield of Montana who served as Democratic whip from 1957 to 1961 and as Majority Leader from 1961 to 1977.

A number of Republican Senate leaders served on Joint Library including Everett McK. Dirksen of Illinois, party Whip from 1957 to 1959 and Minority Leader from 1959 to 1969; Hugh D. Scott of Pennsylvania, party Whip in 1969 and Minority Leader from 1969 to 1977; Robert P. Griffin of Michigan, party

Whip from 1969 to 1977; Howard H. Baker, Jr. of Tennessee, Republican floor leader from 1977 to 1985; Theodore F. Stevens of Alaska, party whip from 1977 to 1985; C. Trent Lott of Mississippi, who served as whip from 1995-1996 and again from 2007 to 2008, and as floor leader from 1996 to 2003 and A. Mitchell (Mitch) McConnell of Kentucky, the Republican whip, 2003-2007, and from 2007 the party's floor leader.

The only House Republican leaders to serve on Joint Library were C. Trent Lott of Mississippi, House Republican Whip from 1981 to 1989; Newt L. Gingrich of Georgia who moved from Whip, 1989-1995 to become Speaker of the House, 1995-1999; and the Republicans' present floor leader, John A. Boehner of Ohio. John Brademas of Indiana, Democratic Whip from 1997 to 1981 was the only Democratic leader to serve on Joint Library.

Other Notables: Joint Library members involved in presidential politics include Sen. Henry Cabot Lodge of Massachusetts, who was the Republican candidate for vice president on Vice President Richard M. Nixon's ticket in 1960 and Sen, J. Strom Thurmond (Rep-S.C.), who ran for president on the States Rights Party ticket in 1948.

Three members of the Library Committee served in President Ronald Reagan's administration. Sen. Richard S. Schweiker of Pennsylvania was Reagan's first Secretary of Health and Human Services and Rep. David A. Stockman was his first Director of the Office of Management and Budget. Howard Baker came out of retirement to become Reagan's chief of staff during the closing days of the administration as it was engulfed by the Iran-Contra affair.

Two other notables on the committee were Senators William Benton (Dem-Conn.) and Joseph R. McCarthy (Rep-Wisc.). Benton's 1950 re-election defeat was largely attributable to McCarthy's scurrilous attacks. It would foreshadow the era of McCarthyism.

Selected References

Boesl, Mary Etta, "Library Committee, Joint," in Donald C. Bacon, Roger H. Davidson, and Morton Keller, eds, *The Encyclopedia of the United States Congress* (New York: Simon & Schuster, 1995), 3: 1287-1288.

RESPONSIBILITIES AND JURISDICTIONAL CHANGES

Jurisdiction, 80th Congress (1947-1949)

From House Concurrent Resolution 47, 72nd Congress, Third Session, February 24, 1933:

[Section 2]

That the Architect of the Capitol, upon the approval of the joint committee on the Library, with the advice of the Commission of Fine Arts, is hereby authorized and directed to relocate within the Capitol any of the statues already received and placed in Statuary Hall, and to provide for the reception and location of the statues received hereafter from the States.

Jurisdiction, 96th Congress, 1979-1981

From the *Senate Manual* for the 96th Congress (1979):

[Title 40, Section 188]

The joint committee on the Library, whenever, in their judgment, it is expedient, are authorized to accept any work of the fine arts, on behalf of Congress, which may be offered, and to assign the same such place in the Capitol as they may deem suitable, and shall have the supervision of all works of art that may be placed in the Capitol.

From *Jefferson's Manual and the Rules of the House of Representatives of the United States* for the 96th Congress (1979):

[Section 983f]

The Committee considers proposals concerning the management and expansion of the Library of Congress, the development and maintenance of the Botanic Gardens, the receipt of gifts for the benefit of the Library, and certain matters relating to placing of statues and other works of art in the Capitol.

Jurisdiction, 102nd Congress, 1991-1993

From Paul S. Rundquist, Congressional Research Service, The Library of Congress, August 23, 1984:

"In addition to its basic mandate which dates from 1802 and continues in force, the Joint Committee on the Library is charged by statute with a number of duties involving both the Library of Congress and other components of the legislative branch . . ."

Jurisdiction, 110th Congress, 2007-2009

From the *Senate Manual* for the 110th Congress (2008):

[521 Section 166 9(i)]

The Director of the Congressional Research Service shall prepare and file with the Joint Committee on the Library at the beginning of each regular session of Congress a separate and special report covering, in summary and in detail, all phases of activity in the Congressional Research Service for the immediately preceding fiscal year.

[928 Section 2133]

The Joint Committee on the Library, whenever, in their judgment, it is expedient, are authorized to accept any work of the fine arts, on behalf of Congress, which may be offered, and to assign the same such place in the Capitol as they may deem suitable, and shall have the supervision of all works of art that may be placed in the Capitol.

MEMBERSHIP ROSTERS, 103rd-111th Congresses, 1993-2011

JOINT LIBRARY / 103rd Congress

Service Dates of Committee Chair: Continued-Jan. 3, 1995

Service Dates of House Members: Provisionally appointed; see note.

Service Dates of Senate Members: Jan. 28, 1993-Jan. 17, 1995

HOUSE

Majority Rank Name	Party	State	Terms in: House	Comm.	Minority Rank Name	Party	State	Terms in: House	Comm.
CVc Rose, Charles G. III	Dem	N.C.	10	2	1st Barrett, William E.	Rep	Neb.	2	2
2nd Frost, J. Martin III	Dem	Tex.	8	1	2nd Roberts, C. Patrick	Rep	Kans.	7	*2 2
3rd Manton, Thomas J.	Dem	N.Y.	5	2					

SENATE

Majority Rank Name	Party	State	Years in: Senate	Comm.	Minority Rank Name	Party	State	Years in: Senate	Comm.
VcC Pell, Claiborne D.	Dem	R.I.	33	*2 8	1st Hatfield, Mark O.	Rep	Ore.	27	*2 12
2nd DeConcini, Dennis	Dem	Ariz.	17	*2 6	2nd Stevens, Theodore F.	Rep	Alas.	25	6
3rd Moynihan, Daniel Patrick	Dem	N.Y.	17	6					

*2: Member's 2nd period of service on the committee.

Notes: Senate Concurrent Resolution 8, agreed to on Jan. 28,1993, stipulated that "effective for the One Hundred Third Congress, the Chairman of the Committee on Rules and Administration of the Senate may designate another member of the Committee to serve on the Joint Committee of the Congress on the Library in place of the Chairman." The Senate members were named on Jan. 28,1993. Only Charles G. Rose III (Dem-N.C.), the Chair, had been named as of Nov. 26,1993. The other House names were provided provisionally in "Players, Politics and Turf of the 103rd Congress," **Congressional Quarterly,** LI (May 1,1993), Supplement to No. 18, p. 98.

Departures from the Senate:	Majority			Minority
Retired	DeConcini, Dennis W.	Ariz.	Dem	None

Departures from the Committee:	Majority				Minority		
House							
No new assignment	Rose, Charles G. III	Dem	N.C.		Barrett, William E.	Rep	Neb
	Frost, J. Martin III	Dem	Tex.				
	Manton, Thomas J.	Dem	N.Y.				

JOINT LIBRARY / 104th Congress

Service Dates of Committee Chair: Jan. 17, 1995-Jan. 28, 1997

Service Dates of House Members: Feb. 23, 1995-Jan. 3, 1997

Service Dates of Senate Members: Jan. 17, 1995-Jan. 28, 1997

	Majority					Minority				
HOUSE				Terms in:					Terms in:	
Rank Name	**Party**	**State**	**House**	**Comm.**	**Rank Name**	**Party**	**State**	**House**	**Comm.**
VcC Thomas, William M.	Rep	Cal.	9	1	1st Fazio, Victor H.	Dem	Cal.	9	1
2nd Roberts, C. Patrick	Rep	Kans.	8	*2 3	2nd Pastor, Edward L.	Dem	Ariz.	3	1
3rd Ney, Robert W.	Rep	Ohio	1	*1 1					

	Majority					Minority				
SENATE				Years in:					Years in:	
Rank Name	**Party**	**State**	**Senate**	**Comm.**	**Rank Name**	**Party**	**State**	**Senate**	**Comm.**
CVc Hatfield, Mark O.	Rep	Ore.	29	*2 14	1st Pell, Claiborne D.	Dem	R.I.	35	*2 10
2nd Stevens, Theodore F.	Rep	Alas.	27	8	2nd Moynihan, Daniel Patrick	Dem	N.Y.	19	8
3rd Cochran, W. Thad	Rep	Miss.	17	*1 1					

*1: Member's first period of service on the committee.

*2: Member's second period of service on the committee.

Changes:

Senate Majority:

Cochran, W. Thad	Rep	Miss.	Nov. 3, 1995 "Removed from committee by S. Res. 192"
Warner, John W.	Rep	Va.	Nov. 3, 1995 Replaced Cochran

Departures from the House:	Majority			Minority
Elected to the U.S. Senate	Roberts, C. Patrick	Rep	Kans.	

Departures from the Senate:	Majority			Minority		
Retired	Hatfield, Mark O.	Rep	Ore.	Pell, Claiborne D.	Dem	R.I.

Departures from the Committee:	Majority	Minority		
House				
Returned to Appropriations		Pastor, Edward L.	Dem	Ariz.
No new assignment		Fazio, Victor H.	Dem	Cal.

JOINT LIBRARY / 105th Congress

Service Dates of Committee Chair: Mar. 6, 1997-Jan. 3, 1999

Service Dates of House Members: Mar. 6, 1997-Jan. 3, 1999

Service Dates of Senate Members: Jan. 28, 1997-Feb. 25, 1999

	Majority					Minority				
HOUSE				Terms in:					Terms in:	
Rank Name	**Party**	**State**	**House**	**Comm.**	**Rank Name**	**Party**	**State**	**House**	**Comm.**
CVc Thomas, William M.	Rep	Cal.	10	2	1st Kilpatrick, Carolyn C.	Dem	Mich.	1	1
2nd Ney, Robert W.	Rep	Ohio	2	*1 2	2nd Gejdenson, Samuel	Dem	Conn.	9	1
3rd Ehlers, Vernon J.	Rep	Mich.	3	1					

	Majority					Minority				
SENATE				Years in:					Years in:	
Rank Name	**Party**	**State**	**Senate**	**Comm.**	**Rank Name**	**Party**	**State**	**Senate**	**Comm.**
VcC Stevens, Theodore F.	Rep	Alas.	29	11	1st Moynihan, Daniel Patrick	Dem	N.Y.	21	11
2nd Warner, John W.	Rep	Va.	19	*2 2	2nd Feinstein, Dianne	Dem	Cal.	4	*1 1
3rd Cochran, W. Thad	Rep	Miss.	19	*2 1					

*1: Member's first period of service on the committee.

*2: Member's second period of service on the committee.

Departures from the Committee:	Majority			Minority		
House						
Moved to Appropriations				Kilpatrick, Carolyn C.	Dem	Mich
Became Ranking Member on International Relations				Gejdenson, Samuel	Dem	Conn
No new assignment	Ney, Robert W.	Rep	Ohio			
Senate						
Moved to Joint Printing				Feinstein, Dianne	Dem	Cal.
Became Chair of Armed Services	Warner, John W.	Rep	Va.			

JOINT LIBRARY / 106th Congress

Service Dates of Committee Chair: Feb. 25, 1999-Sep. 19, 2001

Service Dates of House Members: Mar. 2, 1999-Jan. 3, 2001

Service Dates of Senate Members: Feb. 25, 1999-Sep. 19, 2001

	Majority						**Minority**				
HOUSE				Terms in:						Terms in:	
Rank Name	Party	State	House	Comm.		Rank Name	Party	State	House	Comm.	
VcC Thomas, William M.	Rep	Cal.	11	3		1st Hoyer, Steny H.	Dem	Md.	10	1	
2nd Boehner, John A.	Rep	Ohio	5	1		2nd Davis, Jim	Dem	Fla.	2	1	
3rd Ehlers, Vernon J.	Rep	Mich.	4	2							

	Majority						**Minority**				
SENATE				Years in:						Years in:	
Rank Name	Party	State	Senate	Comm.		Rank Name	Party	State	Senate	Comm.	
CVc Stevens, Theodore F.	Rep	Alas.	31	13		1st Dodd, Christopher J.	Dem	Conn.	19	1	
2nd McConnell, A. Mitchell (Mitch)	Rep	Ky.	15	1		2nd Moynihan, Daniel Patrick	Dem	N.Y.	23	13	
3rd Cochran, W. Thad	Rep	Miss.	21	*2 3							

*2: Member's second period of service on the committee.

Departures from the Senate:	Majority			Minority		
Retired	None			Moynihan, Daniel Patrick	Dem	N.Y.

Departures from the Committee:	Majority			Minority		
House						
Became Chair of Ways and Means	Thomas, William M.	Rep	Cal.			
Became Chair of Education and the Workforce	Boehner, John A.	Rep	Ohio			
Senate						
Moved to Judiciary	McConnell, A. Mitchell (Mitch)	Rep	Ky.	None		

JOINT LIBRARY / 107th Congress

Service Dates of Committee Chair: June 5, 2001-Jan. 3, 2003

Service Dates of House Members: June 5, 2001-Jan. 3, 2003

Service Dates of Senate Members: Sep. 19, 2001-Mar. 13, 2003

	Majority						**Minority**				
HOUSE				Terms in:						Terms in:	
Rank Name	Party	State	House	Comm.		Rank Name	Party	State	House	Comm.	
CVc Ehlers, Vernon J.	Rep	Mich.	5	3		1st Hoyer, Steny H.	Dem	Md.	11	2	
2nd Ney, Robert W.	Rep	Ohio	4	*2 1		2nd Davis, Jim	Dem	Fla.	3	2	
3rd Taylor, Charles H.	Rep	N.C.	6	1							

Note: Taylor was named to the committee as Chair of the Legislative Branch subcommittee of House Appropriations.

	Majority						**Minority**				
SENATE				Years in:						Years in:	
Rank Name	Party	State	Senate	Comm.		Rank Name	Party	State	Senate	Comm.	
VcC Dodd, Christopher J.	Dem	Conn.	21	3		1st Stevens, Theodore F.	Rep	Alas.	33	15	
2nd Schumer, Charles E.	Dem	N.Y.	3	1		2nd Cochran, W. Thad	Rep	Miss.	23	*2 5	
3rd Dayton, Mark	DFL	Minn.	1	1							

*2: Member's second period of service on the committee.

Departures from the Committee:	Majority			Minority		
House						
Elected Minority Whip	None			Hoyer, Steny H.	Dem	Md.
Moved to Energy and Commerce	None			Davis, Jim	Dem	Fla.
No new assignment	Taylor, Charles H.	Rep	N.C.	None		
Senate						
No new assignment	Dayton, Mark	DFL	Minn.	None		

Note: Members of the Joint Committee on the Library were announced later in 2001 because of the different party control in the 107th Congress with the Republicans holding a majority in the House but the Senate's even 50-50 split between the parties led to the power-sharing agreement of December, 2000. Senator Jeffords's defection from the Republican Party to Independent in June, 2001 gave the Democrats control of the Senate and led to each of the Senate standing committees receiving an additional Democratic member in the July 10, 2001 renaming of standing committees. The two housekeeping committees of Joint Library and Joint Printing were both named on September 19, 2001 with the House Republicans holding a 3-2 majority on each committee while the Senate Democrats held a 3-2 majority on each committee. This arrangement ended at the conclusion of the 107th Congress on Jan. 3, 2003.

JOINT LIBRARY / 108th Congress

Service Dates of Committee Chair: Mar. 13, 2003-Mar. 4, 2005

Service Dates of House Members: Mar. 25, 2003-Jan. 3, 2005

Service Dates of Senate Members: Mar. 13, 2003-Mar. 4, 2005

HOUSE	Majority		Terms in:		Minority			Terms in:	
Rank Name	Party	State	House	Comm.	Rank Name	Party	State	House	Comm.
VcC Ehlers, Vernon J.	Rep	Mich.	6	4	1st Larson, John B.	Dem	Conn.	3	1
2nd Ney, Robert W.	Rep	Ohio	5	*2 2	2nd Millender-McDonald, Juanita	Dem	Cal.	5	1
3rd Kingston, Jack	Rep	Ga.	6	1					

Note: Kingston was named to the committee as Chair of the Legislative Branch subcommittee of House Appropriations.

SENATE	Majority		Years in:		Minority			Years in:	
Rank Name	Party	State	Senate	Comm.	Rank Name	Party	State	Senate	Comm.
CVc Stevens, Theodore F.	Rep	Alas.	35	17	1st Dodd, Christopher J.	Dem	Conn.	23	5
2nd Lott, C. Trent	Rep	Miss.	15	1	2nd Schumer, Charles E.	Dem	N.Y.	5	2
3rd Cochran, W. Thad	Rep	Miss.	25	*2 7					

*2: Member's second period of service on the committee.

Departure from the Committee						
House						
Moved to Ways and Means				Larson, John B.	Dem	Conn.
No new assignment	Kingston, Jack	Rep	Ga.			

JOINT LIBRARY / 109th Congress

Service Dates of Committee Chair: Ch1: Mar. 16, 2005-Jan. 17, 2006 (Ney)

Ch2: Feb. 1, 2006-Jan. 3, 2007 (Ehlers)

Service Dates of House Members: Mar. 16, 2005-Jan. 3, 2007

Service Dates of Senate Members: Mar. 4, 2005-Mar. 6, 2007

HOUSE	Majority		Terms in:		Minority			Terms in:	
Rank Name	Party	State	House	Comm.	Rank Name	Party	State	House	Comm.
Ch1 Ney, Robert W.	Rep	Ohio	6	*2 3	1st Millender-McDonald, Juanita	Dem	Cal.	6	2
C2Vc Ehlers, Vernon J.	Rep	Mich.	7	5	2nd Lofgren, Zoe	Dem	Cal.	6	1
3rd Miller, Candice	Rep	Mich.	2	1					

SENATE	Majority		Years in:		Minority			Years in:	
Rank Name	Party	State	Senate	Comm.	Rank Name	Party	State	Senate	Comm.
VcC Stevens, Theodore F.	Rep	Alas.	37	19	1st Dodd, Christopher J.	Dem	Conn.	25	7
2nd Cochran, W. Thad	Rep	Miss.	27	*2 9	2nd Schumer, Charles E.	Dem	N.Y.	7	4
3rd Lott, C. Trent	Rep	Miss.	17	2					

*2: Member's second period of service on the committee.

Changes

House Majority:

Ney, Robert W.	Rep	Ohio	Jan. 17, 2006 Stepped down as Chair
Ehlers, Vernon J.	Rep	Mich.	Feb. 1, 2006 Replaced Ney as Chair
Ney, Robert W.	Rep	Ohio	Nov. 3, 2006 Resigned the House

Departures from the Committee:	**Majority**			**Minority**
House				
Moved to Select Energy Independence and Global Warming and Transportation and Infrastructure	Miller, Candice	Rep	Mich.	None
Senate				
No new assignment	Cochran, W. Thad	Rep	Miss.	None
	Lott, C. Trent	Rep	Miss.	

JOINT LIBRARY / 110th Congress

Service Dates of Committee Chair: Mar. 6, 2007-Apr. 3, 2009

Service Dates of House Members: Mar. 14, 2007-Jan. 3, 2009

Service Dates of Senate Members: Mar. 6, 2007-Apr. 3, 2009

	Majority					**Minority**				
HOUSE			**Terms in:**						**Terms in:**	
Rank Name	Party	State	House	Comm.	Rank Name		Party	State	House	Comm.
Vc1 Millender-McDonald, Juanita	Dem	Cal.	7	3	1st Ehlers, Vernon J.		Rep	Mich.	8	6
2nd Lofgren. Zoe	Dem	Cal.	7	2	2nd Lungren, Daniel E.		Rep	Cal.	7	1
3rd Wasserman Schultz, Debbie	Dem	Fla.	2	1						

Note: Wasserman Shultz was named to the committee as Chair of the Legislative Branch subcommittee of House Appropriations.

	Majority					**Minority**				
SENATE			**Years in:**						**Years in:**	
Rank Name	Party	State	Senate	Comm.	Rank Name		Party	State	Senate	Comm.
CVc Feinstein, Dianne	Dem	Cal.	15	*2 1	1st Bennett, Robert F.		Rep	Utah	15	1
2nd Dodd, Christopher J.	Dem	Conn.	27	9	2nd Stevens, Theodore F.		Rep	Alas.	39	21
3rd Schumer, Charles E.	Dem	N.Y.	9	6						

*2: Member's second period of service on the committee.

Changes

House Majority:

Millender-McDonald, Juanita	Dem.	Cal.	Apr. 22, 2007 Died in office
Brady, Robert A.	Dem.	Penn	May 24, 2007 Replaced Millender-McDonald as Vice Chair

Departures from the Senate:

Defeated for re-election	Stevens, Theodore F.	Rep	Alas.

Departures from the Committee

House

No new assignment	Ehlers, Vernon J.	Rep	Mich.

Senate

Became Chair of Select Intelligence	Feinstein, Dianne	Dem	Cal.

JOINT LIBRARY / 111th Congress

Service Dates of Committee Chair: Mar. 31, 2009-Jan. 3, 2011

Service Dates of House Members: Mar. 31, 2009-Jan. 3, 2011

Service Dates of Senate Members: Apr. 3, 2009-

	Majority					**Minority**				
HOUSE			**Terms in:**						**Terms in:**	
Rank Name	Party	State	House	Comm.	Rank Name		Party	State	House	Comm.
CVc Brady, Robert A.	Dem	Penn.	7	2	1st Lungren, Daniel E.		Rep	Cal.	8	2

			Years in:							Years in:	
2nd Lofgren. Zoe	Dem	Cal.	8	3		2nd Harper, Gregg	Rep	Miss.	1	1
3rd Wasserman Schultz, Debbie	Dem	Fla.	3	2						

Note: Wasserman Schultz was named to the committee as Chair of the Legislative Branch subcommittee of House Appropriations.

	Majority						Minority				
SENATE			Years in:						Years in:		
Rank Name	**Party**	**State**	**Senate**	**Comm.**		**Rank Name**	**Party**	**State**	**Senate**	**Comm.**	
VcC Schumer, Charles E.	Dem	N.Y.	11	8		1st Bennett, Robert F.	Rep	Utah	17	3	
2nd Dodd, Christopher J.	Dem	Conn.	29	11		2nd Cochran, W. Thad	Rep	Miss.	31	*3 1	
3rd Durbin, Richard J.	Dem	Ill.	13	1							

*3: Member's third period of service on the committee.

Joint Printing

Joint Committee on Printing, 103rd-111th Congresses (1993-2011)

BACKGROUND

Organizational History: At least eight committees have dealt with printing issues since the House first named the Select Committee on Public Printing on March 12, 1812. The House later created a Select Committee on Printing on February 2, 1840; a Select Committee on Printing Laws on December 9, 1857; and a standing Committee on Printing on January 5, 1888. The Senate named a standing Committee on Printing on December 14, 1841; and two short-lived select committees on January 24, 1860—the Select Committee to Investigate Public Printing and the Select Committee to Investigate Certain Alleged Abuses with the Public Printing. However the true ancestor of the latter-day Joint Committee on Printing was the Joint Committee on Public Printing created by the act of August 3, 1846, (44 U.S.C. 101) consisting of three members each from the two houses. It contends that it is the oldest joint committee of the Congress, although has not been continuously organized as such.

The 1846 joint resolution formalized the method by which printing contracts were to be procured by Congress. The committee's mandate was reaffirmed in the Printing Act of January 12, 1895 and in the Legislative Appropriations Act of 1920. The current joint committee was created by the 1946 Legislative Reorganization Act and it absorbed the functions of the House Committee on Printing and the Senate Committee on Printing.

The committee's authority is derived from Title 44 of the *United States Code* and is responsible for ensuring compliance by federal entities to these laws and the Government Printing and Binding Regulations, and as such, it oversees the functions of the Government Printing Office and general printing procedures of the federal government.

Its major internal responsibility is to determine the style and layout of the *Congressional Record* and other Congressional documents, and to make sure printing is completed as quickly and economically as possible. The office of the Public Printer carries out the actual work of printing under the direction and guidance of the joint committee.

Membership: Like the members of the Joint Committee on the Library, those serving on the Joint Committee on Printing are selected from the House Administration and the Senate Rules and Administration committees. Three members from each chamber were chosen to serve in each Congress from the 80th through the 96th (1947-1991), at which time the size was officially increased to ten members, with five from the House and five from the Senate.

In the 91st Congress (1969-1971), a rotating system similar to the Joint Library Committee was instituted whereby the Senate ranking member would chair the first session and the House ranking member would chair the second session. The two committees would alternate chairs between congressional sessions.

Committee Leaders: Sen. William E. Jenner (Rep-Ind.) was the committee's first chair in the reorganized Congress and Rep. Karl M. LeCompte (Rep-Iowa) was its first vice chair. Jenner and LeCompte would reprise their roles in the Republican 83rd Congress (1953-1955). The venerable Carl Hayden (Dem-Ariz.) who first joined the committee in 1931 was its first post-reorganization Democratic chair in the 81st and 82nd Congresses (1949-1953). Representatives Mary T. Norton (Dem-N.J.) and Thomas B. Stanley (Dem-Va.) served with Hayden as vice chairs in the 81st and 82nd Congresses respectively. Senator Hayden and Rep. Omar T. Burleson (Dem-Tex.) served as Joint Printing's chair and vice chair for the next seven Congresses (1955-1969), when Burleson resigned the committee and Hayden retired from the Senate after serving in the Congress for a combined House and Senate total of fifty-seven years.

In 1969, Sen. B. Everett Jordan (Dem-N.C.) became chair and alternated leadership of the committee with Rep. Samuel N. Friedel (Dem-Md.). With Friedel's renomination defeat in 1970, Wayne L. Hays became the majority representative on Joint Printing in 1971 and served with Jordan until Jordan failed to receive renomination in 1972. Howard W. Cannon (Dem-Nev.) became the committee's senior senator in 1973 and alternated the chair with Hays from 1973 to 1976 and with Frank Thompson (Dem-N.J.) from 1976 to 1979. Cannon stepped aside in 1979 to become chair of Commerce, Science, and Transportation. He would be replaced by Claiborne deB. Pell (Dem-R.I.) who served as its senior senator for two years, 1979-1981. Representative Thompson's service began in 1976, but was ended in 1980 when he was implicated in the FBI's infamous "Abscam" sting operation. Augustus F. Hawkins (Dem-Cal.) succeeded him for the remainder of the 96th Congress and would serve as the senior representative on the Joint Printing Committee from 1980 to 1984 when he was succeeded by Frank Annunzio (Dem-Ill.).

With Republicans organizing the Senate from 1981 to 1987, Charles McC. Mathias of Maryland became the committee's ranking senator. Mathias and Annunzio alternated the chair between 1984 and 1987. Annunzio remained as the ranking representative until 1991, while Mathias was succeeded by Democrat Wendell H. Ford (Dem-Ky.) in 1987, when Democrats regained the Senate. Ford held the Senate majority slot until the Republican resumed control of the Senate in 1995. Annunzio's successor was Charles G. Rose III (Dem-N.C.), who shared the committee's leadership with Ford in the 102nd and 103rd Congresses (1991-1995).

The Republican takeover in 1995 led to the naming of Sen. Theodore F. Stevens of Alaska and Rep. William M. Thomas of California as the leaders of Joint Printing. Stevens left the committee later in November 1995 to chair Governmental Affairs and was replaced by John W. Warner of Virginia. Thomas and Warner served together in the 105th Congress (1997-1999) until Warner left to become chair of Armed Services. While

Thomas remained, Warner was succeeded by A. Mitchell (Mitch) McConnell of Kentucky in the 106th Congress (1999-2001). Thomas became chair of Ways and Means in 2001 and McConnell left for Judiciary.

As in the case of Joint Library, the Senate waited until the dust settled on the Jeffords defection before staffing the committee in the 107th. Mark Dayton (DFL-Minn.) was named the senior senator on the committee, while Robert W. Ney (Rep-Ohio) was its senior representative as the committee dealt with divided congressional government. Ney served in the senior House role until his resignation from the House in November 2006, following his implication in the Jack Abramoff Indian gaming scandal. Saxby Chambliss of Georgia, a first-year member, served as the senior Senate Republican on Joint Printing in the 108th (2003-2005), until he was replaced by former Majority Leader C. Trent Lott of Mississippi in the 109th Congress (2005-2007).

With Democrats regaining control of the Congress in 2007, Rep. Juanita Millender-McDonald of California became the ranking House member on Joint Printing while Sen. Dianne Feinstein of California became that chamber's ranking person on the committee. Millender-McDonald's death in April, 2007 led to Robert A. Brady of Pennsylvania becoming the committee's ranking representative. Brady continued in the 111th Congress while Senator Feinstein left to chair Permanent Select Intelligence and was replaced by Charles E. Schumer of New York as the committee's ranking senator.

Party Leaders: Given the small size of Joint Printing, a disproportionately large contingent of Senate Republican leaders have served on the committee. Among them were floor leaders William F. Knowland of California, Hugh D. Scott, Jr. of Pennsylvania, Howard H. Baker, Jr. of Tennessee, C. Trent Lott of Mississippi, and the current leader A. Mitchell (Mitch) McConnell of Kentucky; and party Whips Robert P. Griffin of Michigan, Theodore F. Stevens of Alaska, and Donald L. Nickles of Oklahoma. Senate Democratic leaders have been less inclined to serve on Joint Printing with only former floor leader Michael J. Mansfield of Montana and party Whips Earle C. Clements of Kentucky and Wendell H. Ford of

Kentucky having served on it. Both Clements and Mansfield were whips during the Senate floor leadership of Lyndon B. Johnson (Dem-Tex.).

Neither of the House parties have had large leadership contingents on Joint Printing. Only C. Trent Lott of Mississippi, who was House Republican Whip from 1981 to 1989; Newt L. Gingrich of Georgia, who was Republican whip from 1989 to 1995 and Speaker of the House from 1995 to 1999; and current Minority Leader John A. Boehner of Ohio served on Joint Printing. This is also true of the House Democrats with only current Democratic Majority Leader Steny H. Hoyer of Maryland and former party whip John Brademas of Indiana as the only two post-1947 Democratic leaders with service on the committee.

Other Notables: Sen. Albert A. Gore, Jr. (Dem-Tenn.) is the only member of Joint Printing in the modern era to be elected vice president. Sen. Carl T. Hayden (Dem-Ariz.), who served fifty-seven years in the Congress—fifteen in the House and forty-two in the Senate—served as the Senate's president *pro tempore* from 1957 until his retirement in 1969. Joint Printing members with prominent roles in presidential administrations include Howard Baker, President Ronald Reagan's last Chief of Staff; Lynn M. Martin (Rep-Ill.), President George H.W. Bush's second Secretary of Labor; and Leon E. Panetta (Dem-Cal.), who served as Director of the Office of Management and Budget in the administration of President Bill Clinton and as Director of the Central Intelligence Agency under President Barack Obama.

Selected References

Bolner, James, "The Reagan Administration Versus the Joint Committee on Printing: Constitutional Reflections," *Government Publications Review*, XII (March, 1985), 97-110.

Harold C Relyea, "Printing Committee, Joint," in Donald C. Bacon, Roger H. Davidson, and Morton Keller, eds, *The Encyclopedia of the United States Congress* (New York: Simon & Schuster, 1995), 3: 1623.

RESPONSIBILITIES AND JURISDICTIONAL CHANGES

Jurisdiction, 80th Congress, 1947-1949

From the Act entitled "An Act Providing for the public printing and binding and the distribution of public documents," 53rd Congress, Third Session, January 12, 1895 (28 *Statutes* 601-602):

[Section 2]

The joint committee on printing shall have power to adopt such measures as may be deemed necessary to remedy any neglect or delay in the execution of the public printing; and the committee shall have power to order reprinted not exceeding three hundred copies of a public bill pending before either House of Congress, when the supply shall have become exhausted, and the interests of the public service demand immediate action.

[Section 3]

The joint committee on Printing shall fix upon standards of paper for the different descriptions of public printing and binding . . .

[Section 6]

No contract for furnishing paper shall be valid until it has been approved by the joint committee on printing, if made under their direction . . .

Jurisdiction, 96th Congress, 1979-1981

From *Jefferson's Manual and Rules of the House of Representatives of the United States for the Ninety-Sixth Congress* (1979):

[Section 983h]

The Committee adopts and employs measures necessary to remedy inefficiencies or waste in the public printing, binding, and distribution of Government publications. It has control of the arrangement and style of the Congressional Record (44 U.S.C. 901-910). The joint committee on Printing is authorized and directed to provide for printing in the Daily Record the legislative program for the day, together with a list of congressional committee meetings and hearings and the place of meeting and subject matter; and to cause a brief resume of congressional activities for the previous day to be incorporated in Record, together with an index of its contents. Such data shall be prepared under the supervision of the Secretary of the Senate and the Clerk of the House of Representatives, respectively.

Jurisdiction, 102nd Congress, 1991-1993

From *Authority and Rules of Senate Committees*, Senate Document 102-6, printed under the authority of Senate Resolution 58 (102-1), agreed to March 13, 1991:

The Joint Committee on Printing may use any measures it considers necessary to remedy neglect, delay, duplication, or waste in the public printing and binding and the distribution of Government publications.

Jurisdiction, 110th, Congress, 2007-2009

From Title 44—PUBLIC PRINTING AND DOCUMENTS in the *Senate Manual* for the 110th Congress, Senate Document 110-1 (2008), p.1026.

The Joint Committee on Printing may use any measures it considers necessary to remedy neglect, delay, duplication, or waste in the public printing and binding and the distribution of Government publications.

MEMBERSHIP ROSTERS, 103rd-111th Congresses, 1993-2011

JOINT PRINTING / 103rd Congress

Service Dates of Committee Chair: Jan. 28, 1993-Jan. 3, 1995

Service Dates of House Members: Provisionally appointed; see note

Service Dates of Senate Members: Jan. 28, 1993-Jan. 17, 1995

HOUSE	Majority		Terms in:			Minority		Terms in:	
Rank Name	Party	State	House	Comm.	Rank Name	Party	State	House	Comm.
VcC Rose, Charles G. III	Dem	N.C.	10	2	1st Roberts, C. Patrick	Rep	Kans.	7	6
2nd Gejdenson, Samuel	Dem	Conn.	7	*1 2	2nd Gingrich, Newton L.	Rep	Ga.	8	*2 3
3rd Kleczka, Gerald D.	Dem	Wisc.	6	2					

SENATE	Majority		Years in:			Minority		Years in:	
Rank Name	Party	State	Senate	Comm.	Rank Name	Party	State	Senate	Comm.
CVc Ford, Wendell H.	Dem	Ky.	19	12	1st Stevens, Theodore F.	Rep	Alas.	25	8
2nd DeConcini, Dennis	Dem	Ariz.	17	8	2nd Hatfield, Mark O.	Rep	Ore.	27	*2 12
3rd Mathews, Harlan	Dem	Tenn.	1	1					

*1: Member's first period of service on the committee.
*2: Member's second period of service on the committee.

Changes:
   Senate Majority:

Mathews, Harlan	Dem	Tenn.	Dec. 1, 1994 Resigned the House; retired

Notes: Senate Concurrent Resolution 8, agreed to on Jan. 28,1993, stipulated that "effective for the One Hundred Third Congress, the Chairman of the Committee on Rules and Administration of the Senate may designate another member of the Committee to serve on the Joint Committee of the Congress on the Library in place of the Chairman." The Senate members were named on Jan. 28,1993. Only Charles G. Rose III (Dem-N.C.), the Vice Chair, had been named as of Nov. 26,1993. The other House names were provided provisionally in "Players, Politics and Turf of the 103rd Congress," **Congressional Quarterly,** LI (May 1,1993), Supplement to No. 18, p. 98.

Departures from the Senate:	**Majority**			**Minority**	
Retired	DeConcini, Dennis	Dem	Ariz.		

Departures from the Committee:	**Majority**			**Minority**	
House					
Elected Speaker of the House	None			Gingrich, Newton L.	Rep	Ga.
No new assignment	Rose, Charles G. III	Dem	N.C.	None	
	Gejdenson, Samuel	Dem	Conn.		
	Kleczka, Gerald D.	Dem	Wisc.		

JOINT PRINTING / 104th Congress

Service Dates of Committee Chair: Feb. 23, 1995-Jan. 3, 1997

Service Dates of House Members: Feb. 23, 1995-Jan. 3, 1997

Service Dates of Senate Members: Jan. 17, 1995-Jan. 28, 1995

HOUSE	Majority		Terms in:			Minority		Terms in:	
Rank Name	Party	State	House	Comm.	Rank Name	Party	State	House	Comm.
CVc Thomas, William M.	Rep	Cal.	9	1	1st Hoyer, Steny H.	Dem	Md.	8	1
2nd Roberts, C. Patrick	Rep	Kans.	8	7	2nd Jefferson, William J.	Dem	La.	2	1
3rd Ney, Robert W.	Rep	Ohio	1	1					

	Majority		Years in:			Minority		Years in:	
Rank Name	Party	State	Senate	Comm.	Rank Name	Party	State	Senate	Comm.
VcC Stevens, Theodore F.	Rep	Alas.	27	10	1st Ford, Wendell H.	Dem	Ky.	21	14
2nd Hatfield, Mark O.	Rep	Ore.	29	*2 14	2nd Inouye, Daniel K.	Dem	Hai.	33	1
3rd Cochran, W. Thad	Rep	Miss.	17	1					

*2: Member's second period of service on the committee.

Changes:
   Majority:

Stevens, Theodore F.	Rep	Alas.	Nov. 3, 1995 Removed from committee; had become chair of Governmental Affairs
Warner, John W.	Rep	Va.	Nov. 3, 1995 Replaced Stevens as Vice Chair

Departures from the House:	**Majority**			**Minority**	
Elected to U.S. Senate	Roberts, C. Patrick	Rep	Kans.	None	

Departures from the Senate:	Majority			Minority		
Retired	Hatfield, Mark O.	Rep	Ore.	None		

Departures from the Committee

House

Returned to Ways and Means	None			Jefferson, William J.	Dem	La.

JOINT PRINTING / 105th Congress

Service Dates of Committee Chair: Jan. 28, 1997-Feb. 25, 1999

Service Dates of House Members: Mar. 6, 1997-Jan. 3, 1999

Service Dates of Senate Members: Jan. 28, 1997-Feb. 25, 1999

	Majority					Minority				
HOUSE			**Terms in:**						**Terms in:**	
Rank Name	**Party**	**State**	**House**	**Comm.**		**Rank Name**	**Party**	**State**	**House**	**Comm.**
VcC Thomas, William M.	Rep	Cal.	10	2		1st Hoyer, Steny H.	Dem	Md.	9	2
2nd Ney, Robert W.	Rep	Ohio	2	2		2nd Gejdenson, Samuel	Dem	Conn.	9	*2 1
3rd Granger, Kay	Rep	Tex.	1	1						

	Majority					Minority				
SENATE			**Years in:**						**Years in:**	
Rank Name	**Party**	**State**	**Senate**	**Comm.**		**Rank Name**	**Party**	**State**	**Senate**	**Comm.**
CVc Warner, John W.	Rep	Va.	19	*2 2		1st Ford, Wendell H.	Dem	Ky.	23	16
2nd Cochran, W. Thad	Rep	Miss.	19	3		2nd Inouye, Daniel K.	Dem	Hai.	35	3
3rd McConnell, A. Mitchell (Mitch)	Rep	Ky.	13	1						

*2: Member's second period of service on the committee.

Departures from the Senate:	Majority			Minority		
Retired	None			Ford, Wendell H.	Dem	Ky.

Departures from the Committee:

House

Became Ranking Member on International Relations				Gejdenson, Samuel	Dem	Conn.
Moved to Appropriations	Granger, Kay	Rep	Tex.			

Senate

Became Chair of Armed Services	Warner, John W.	Rep	Va.	None		

JOINT PRINTING / 106th Congress

Service Dates of Committee Chair: Mar. 2,1999-Jan. 3, 2001

Service Dates of House Members: Mar. 2,1999-Jan. 3, 2001

Service Dates of Senate Members: Feb. 25,1999-Sep. 19, 2001

	Majority					Minority				
HOUSE			**Terms in:**						**Terms in:**	
Rank Name	**Party**	**State**	**House**	**Comm.**		**Rank Name**	**Party**	**State**	**House**	**Comm.**
CVc Thomas, William M.	Rep	Cal.	11	3		1st Hoyer, Steny H.	Dem	Md.	10	3
2nd Boehner, John A.	Rep	Ohio	5	1		2nd Fattah, Chaka	Dem	Penn.	3	1
3rd Ney, Robert W.	Rep	Ohio	3	3						

	Majority					Minority				
SENATE			**Years in:**						**Years in:**	
Rank Name	**Party**	**State**	**Senate**	**Comm.**		**Rank Name**	**Party**	**State**	**Senate**	**Comm.**
VcC McConnell, A. Mitchell(Mitch)	Rep	Ky.	15	3		1st Feinstein, Dianne	Dem	Cal.	7	*1 1
2nd Cochran, W. Thad	Rep	Miss.	21	5		2nd Inouye, Daniel K.	Dem	Hai.	37	5
3rd Nickles, Donald L.	Rep	Okla.	19	1						

*1: Member's first period of service on the committee.

Departures from the Committee:

House

	Majority			Minority		
Became Chair of Ways and Means	Thomas, William M.	Rep	Cal.			
Became Chair of Education and the Workforce	Boehner, John A.	Rep	Ohio			

Senate

Moved to Judiciary	McConnell, A. Mitchell (Mitch)	Rep	Ky.	None
No new assignment	Nickles, Donald L.	Rep	Okla.	

JOINT PRINTING / 107th Congress

Service Dates of Committee Chair: Sep. 19, 2001-Mar. 13, 2003

Service Dates of House Members: June 5, 2001-Jan. 3, 2003

Service Dates of Senate Members: Sep. 19, 2001-Mar. 13, 2003

			Majority							Minority		
HOUSE				**Terms in:**			**HOUSE**				**Terms in:**	
Rank Name	**Party**	**State**	**House**	**Comm.**			**Rank Name**	**Party**	**State**	**House**	**Comm.**	
VcC Ney, Robert W.	Rep	Ohio	4	4			1st Hoyer, Steny H.	Dem	Md.	11	4	
2nd Doolittle, John T.	Rep	Cal.	6	1			2nd Fattah, Chaka	Dem	Penn.	4	2	
3rd Linder, John E.	Rep	Ga.	5	1								

			Majority							Minority		
SENATE				**Years in:**			**SENATE**				**Years in:**	
Rank Name	**Party**	**State**	**Senate**	**Comm.**			**Rank Name**	**Party**	**State**	**Senate**	**Comm.**	
CVc Dayton, Mark	DFL	Minn.	1	1			1st Cochran, W. Thad	Rep	Miss.	23	7	
2nd Feinstein, Dianne	Dem	Cal.	9	*1 3			2nd Santorum, Richard J. (Rick)	Rep	Penn.	7	1	
3rd Inouye, Daniel K.	Dem	Hai.	39	7								

*1: Member's first period of service on the committee.

Note: Members of the Joint Committee on the Library were announced later in 2001 because of the different party control in the 107th Congress with the Republicans holding a majority in the House but the Senate's even 50-50 split between the parties led to the power-sharing agreement of December, 2000. Senator Jeffords's defection from the Republican Party to Independent in June, 2001 gave the Democrats control of the Senate and led to each of the Senate standing committees receiving an additional Democratic member in the July 10, 2001 renaming of standing committees. The two housekeeping committees of Joint Library and Joint Printing were both named on September 19, 2001 with the House Republicans holding a 3-2 majority on each committee while the Senate Democrats held a 3-2 majority on each committee. This arrangement ended at the conclusion of the 107th Congress on Jan. 3, 2003.

Departures from the Committee:	**Majority**			**Minority**		
House						
Elected Minority Whip	None			Hoyer, Steny H.	Dem	Md.
No new assignment	None			Fattah, Chaka	Dem	Penn.
Senate						
Moved to Finance	None			Santorum, Richard J. (Rick)	Rep	Penn.
No new assignment	Feinstein, Dianne	Dem	Cal.	None		

JOINT PRINTING / 108th Congress

Service Dates of Committee Chair: Mar. 25, 2003-Jan. 3, 2005

Service Dates of House Members: Mar. 25, 2003-Jan. 3, 2005

Service Dates of Senate Members: Mar. 13, 2003-Mar. 4, 2005

			Majority							Minority		
HOUSE				**Terms in:**			**HOUSE**				**Terms in:**	
Rank Name	**Party**	**State**	**House**	**Comm.**			**Rank Name**	**Party**	**State**	**House**	**Comm.**	
CVc Ney, Robert W.	Rep	Ohio	5	5			1st Larson, John B.	Dem	Conn.	3	1	
2nd Doolittle, John T.	Rep	Cal.	7	2			2nd Brady, Robert A.	Dem	Penn.	4	1	
3rd Linder, John E.	Rep	Ga.	6	2								

			Majority							Minority		
SENATE				**Years in:**			**SENATE**				**Years in:**	
Rank Name	**Party**	**State**	**Senate**	**Comm.**			**Rank Name**	**Party**	**State**	**Senate**	**Comm.**	
VcC Chambliss, Saxby	Rep	Ga.	1	1			1st Inouye, Daniel K.	Dem	Hai.	41	9	
2nd Cochran, W. Thad	Rep	Miss.	25	9			2nd Dayton, Mark	DFL	Minn.	3	2	
3rd Smith, Gordon H.	Rep	Ore.	7	1								

Departures from the Committee:	**Majority**			**Minority**		
House						
Moved to Ways and Means	Linder, John	Rep	Ga.	Larson, John B.	Dem	Conn.
Senate						
No new assignment	Smith, Gordon H.	Rep	Ore.	None		

JOINT PRINTING / 109th Congress

Service Dates of Committee Chair: Mar. 4, 2005-Mar. 6, 2007

Service Dates of House Members: Mar. 16, 2005-Jan. 3, 2007

Service Dates of Senate Members: Mar. 4, 2005-Mar. 6, 2007

HOUSE

	Majority						Minority			
			Terms in:						Terms in:	
Rank Name	Party	State	House	Comm.		Rank Name	Party	State	House	Comm.
VcC Ney, Robert W.	Rep	Ohio	6	6		1st Millender-McDonald, Juanita	Dem	Cal.	6	1
2nd Doolittle, John T.	Rep	Cal.	8	3		2nd Brady, Robert A.	Dem	Penn.	5	2
3rd Reynolds, Thomas M.	Rep	N.Y.	4	1						

SENATE

	Majority						Minority			
			Years in:						Years in:	
Rank Name	Party	State	Senate	Comm.		Rank Name	Party	State	Senate	Comm.
CVc Lott, C. Trent	Rep	Miss.	17	1		1st Inouye, Daniel K.	Dem	Hai.	43	11
2nd Cochran, W. Thad	Rep	Miss.	27	11		2nd Dayton, Mark	DFL	Minn.	5	4
3rd Chambliss, Saxby	Rep	Ga.	3	2						

Changes:

Resigned the House

Ney, Robert W.	Rep	Ohio	Nov. 3, 2006

Departures from the Senate:

	Majority			Minority		
Retired	None			Dayton, Mark	DFL	Minn.

Departures from the Committee:

House

				Minority
No new assignment	Doolittle, John T.	Rep	Cal.	None
	Reynolds, Thomas M.	Rep	N.Y.	

Senate

				Minority
No new assignment	Lott, C. Trent	Rep	Miss.	None
	Cochran, W. Thad	Rep	Miss.	

JOINT PRINTING / 110th Congress

Service Dates of Committee Chair: Ch1: Mar. 14, 2007-Apr. 22, 2007 (Millender-McDonald)

Ch2: May 24, 2007-Jan. 3, 2009 (Brady)

Service Dates of House Members: Mar. 14,2007-Jan. 3, 2009

Service Dates of Senate Members: Mar. 6,2007-Apr. 3, 2009

HOUSE

	Majority						Minority			
			Terms in:						Terms in:	
Rank Name	Party	State	House	Comm.		Rank Name	Party	State	House	Comm.
Ch1Millender-McDonald, Juanita	Dem	Cal.	7	2		1st Ehlers, Vernon J.	Rep	Mich.	8	1
C2Vc Brady, Robert A.	Dem	Penn.	6	3		2nd McCarthy, Kevin	Rep	Cal.	1	1
3rd Capuano, Michael E.	Dem	Mass.	5	1						

SENATE

	Majority						Minority			
			Years in:						Years in:	
Rank Name	Party	State	Senate	Comm.		Rank Name	Party	State	Senate	Comm.
VcC Feinstein, Dianne	Dem	Cal.	15	*2 1		1st Bennett, Robert F.	Rep	Utah	15	1
2nd Inouye, Daniel K.	Dem	Hai.	45	13		2nd Chambliss, Saxby	Rep	Ga.	5	5
3rd Murray, Patty	Dem	Wash.	15	1						

*2: Member's second period of service on the committee.

Changes

Millender-McDonald, Juanita	Dem	Cal.	Apr. 22, 2007 Died in office
Brady, Robert A.	Dem	Penn.	May 24, 2007 Became Chair
Davis, Susan A.	Dem	Cal.	June 12, 2007 Replaced Millender-McDonald

Departures from the Committee

House

	Majority			Minority		
No new assignment	None			Ehlers, Vernon J.	Rep	Mich.

Senate

Became Chair of Appropriations	Inouye, Daniel K.	Dem Hai.	None
Became Chair of Intelligence	Feinstein, Dianne	Dem Cal.	None

JOINT PRINTING / 111th Congress

Service Dates of Committee Chair: Apr. 3, 2009-

Service Dates of House Members: Mar. 31, 2009-Jan. 3, 2011

Service Dates of Senate Members: Apr. 3, 2009-

	Majority						Minority			
HOUSE				Terms in:					Terms in:	
Rank Name	**Party**	**State**	**House**	**Comm.**		**Rank Name**	**Party**	**State**	**House**	**Comm.**
VCh Brady, Robert A.	Dem	Penn.	7	4		1st Lungren, Daniel E.	Rep	Cal.	8	1
2nd Capuano, Michael E.	Dem	Mass.	6	2		2nd McCarthy, Kevin	Rep	Cal.	2	2
3rd Davis, Susan A.	Dem	Cal.	5	2						

	Majority						Minority			
SENATE				Years in:					Years in:	
Rank Name	**Party**	**State**	**Senate**	**Comm.**		**Rank Name**	**Party**	**State**	**Senate**	**Comm.**
Chr Schumer, Charles A.	Dem	N.Y.	11	1		1st Bennett, Robert F.	Rep	Utah	17	3
2nd Murray, Patty	Dem	Wash.	17	3		2nd Chambliss, Saxby	Rep	Ga.	7	7
3rd Udall, Thomas.	Dem	N.M.	1	1						

Joint Taxation

Joint Committee on Taxation, 103rd-111th Congresses (1993-2011)

BACKGROUND

Organizational History: When originated by the House, the Revenue Act of 1926 (P.L. 69-20) contained a relatively insignificant clause calling for a joint commission on Internal Revenue Taxation, to be comprised of five members of the House, five members of the Senate, and five private citizens to be appointed by the President. As originally proposed, the commission was to report back to the Congress within two years of its establishment the results of its findings. That portion of the bill was subsequently amended by the Senate.

Drawing on the work of the Senate's temporary Select Committee on Investigation of the Internal Revenue Bureau that had been established in 1924, the Senate called for an ongoing study by a joint committee to be made up of members of the Senate Finance and House Ways and Means committees. The committee would be responsible for keeping Congress better informed about the administration of the internal revenue laws and the operations of the Bureau. The Senate's version was adopted in conference, and included in the final bill, which was signed into law (P.L. 69-20) on February 26, 1926.

The original name of the committee was the Joint Committee on Internal Revenue Taxation and was designated as the Joint Committee on Taxation by Public Law 94-455 on October 4, 1976. Since that time, the Joint Committee on Taxation has been one of the most stable of the joint committees. Its jurisdictional mandate has changed little since its creation, surviving reorganization efforts in 1946, 1974, and 1977.

Membership: By law, the membership on this joint committee is comprised of five members from the House Ways and Means committee and five members from the Senate Finance committee, with the three senior-most majority and two senior-most minority members from each of the standing committees. Chairmanship rotates between the House and the Senate after the first session of each Congress, so that the ranking House member always serves as chair during the first session and the ranking Senate member always serves as chair during the second session.

Committee Leaders: Rep. Harold Knutson (Rep-Minn.) served as the first modern-era chair with Sen. Eugene D. Milliken (Rep-Colo.) as its first modern-era vice chair. Democratic control of the 81st and 82nd Congresses (1949-1953) placed Rep. Robert L. Doughton (Dem-N.C.) and Sen. Walter F. George (Dem-Ga.) in those ranking slots. When Republicans resumed control in the 83rd Congress, Senator Milliken resumed his post, while Rep. Daniel A. Reed (Rep-N.Y.) became its ranking House member.

Democratic representative Jere Cooper of Tennessee and Sen. Harry Flood Byrd of Virginia were named to head the Joint Taxation Committee in the 84th and 85th Congresses (1955-1959). Cooper's death on December 18, 1957 led Rep. Wilbur D. Mills of Arkansas to assume the House's leadership role on the committee. Mills, having become chair of Ways and Means, would serve in that capacity until 1975, when he stepped aside from the chair of Ways and Means as a consequence of unfortunate personal circumstances. The ranking senators on Joint Taxation during the Mills era were Harry Flood Byrd (Dem-Va.) in the 85th to the 89th Congresses; Russell B. Long (Dem-La.) in the 90th-96th Congresses (1967-1981). Rep. Albert C. Ullman (Dem-Ore.) succeeded Mills in 1975 and served until his re-election defeat in 1980.

Divided congressional government in the 97th-99th Congresses (1981-1987) led to Democratic representative Daniel D. Rostenkowski of Illinois sharing leadership of the committee with Republican senators Robert J. Dole of Kansas in the 97th Congress, Robert W. Packwood of Oregon in the 98th Congress, and William V. Roth, Jr. of Delaware in the 99th Congress. When Democrats regained control of the Senate in the 1986 election, Sen. Lloyd M. Bentsen, Jr. (Dem-Tex.) became the committee's ranking senator and served from 1987 until he resigned in 1993 to become President Bill Clinton's first Secretary of the Treasury. Bentsen was succeeded by Daniel Patrick Moynihan (Dem-N.Y.)

Dan Rostenkowski was among the Democratic casualties of the 1994 Republican revolution, losing his seat after thirty-six years in the House. Republican representative William R. Archer of Texas became the ranking House member on Joint Taxation, while Republican senator Packwood returned on the Senate side. Packwood's scandal-induced resignation in September 1995 placed Roth in the senior senator post on the committee. Archer and Roth led the committee in the 105th and 106th Congresses (1997-2001). Archer's retirement in 2000 led to his being succeeded by Rep. William M. Thomas of California, who would hold the senior House slot on the committee until 2007.

The power-sharing arrangement that was to cope with the fifty-fifty split in the Senate following the 2000 election, led Republican Charles E. Grassley of Iowa and Democrat Max Baucus of Montana to exchange the Senate leadership role on Joint Taxation in June, 2001 after the defection of Vermont's James M. Jeffords from the Republican Party to an Independent caucusing with the Democrats. When Republicans regained the Senate in 2002, Grassley became the senior senator on the committee, a post he held in both the 108th and 109th Congresses (2003-2007)

Democratic success in the 2006 election led Rep. Charles Rangel of New York and Sen. Max Baucus of Montana to become the senior leaders of the Joint Committee on Taxation in the 110th and 111th Congresses (2007-2011).

Party Leaders: As in the case of other joint committees, a number of Senate Republican leaders have served on Joint Taxation, including floor leaders Robert A. Taft of Ohio, Robert J. Dole of Kansas, and C. Trent Lott of Mississippi, and party Whip Donald L. Nickles of Oklahoma. Among House Republican leaders who served on Taxation would be Harold Knutson of Minnesota who was whip, 1919-1923, and C. Trent Lott who served as House Republican Whip from 1981 to 1989 before his election to the Senate.

Senate Majority Leader Alben W. Barkley (Dem-Ky.) served on Joint Taxation before his election in 1948 as Harry Truman's vice president. Other Senate Democratic leaders who served on Joint Taxation were Senate Democratic Whip Russell B. Long of Louisiana, 1965-1969; and Floor Leader Thomas A. Daschle of South Dakota, 1995-2005. The only House Democratic leader to serve on Joint Taxation was T. Hale Boggs of Louisiana who was Democratic Whip, 1962-1971 and Majority Leader, 1971-1972.

Other Notables: Three Senate Democrats who served on Joint Taxation also saw Cabinet service—Clinton P. Anderson of New Mexico, Secretary of Agriculture under President Harry Truman; Abraham A. Ribicoff of Connecticut, Secretary of Health, Education, and Welfare under President John F. Kennedy; and Lloyd M. Bentsen Jr. of Texas, Secretary of the Treasury under President Bill Clinton. The one member of the committee to leave it to return home as governor was Republican Frank Murkowski of Alaska.

Selected References

Mary Etta Boesl, "Taxation Committee, Joint," in Donald C. Bacon, Roger H. Davidson, and Morton Keller, eds, *The Encyclopedia of the United States Congress* (New York: Simon & Schuster, 1995), 3: 1287-1288.

RESPONSIBILITIES AND JURISDICTIONAL CHANGES

Jurisdiction, 80th Congress, 1947-1949

From Public Law 69-20, the Revenue Act of 1926, 69th Congress, First Session, February 26, 1926 (44 *Statutes* 9, 127-128) describing the joint committee on Internal Revenue Taxation:

[Section 1203. (c)]

(c) It shall be the duty of the joint committee—

(1) To investigate the operation and effects of the Federal system of internal-revenue taxes;

(2) To investigate the administration of such taxes by the Bureau of Internal Revenue or any executive department, establishment, or agency, charged with their administration;

(3) To make such other investigations in respect of such system of taxes as the joint committee may deem necessary;

(4) To investigate measures and methods for the simplification of such taxes, particularly the income tax;

(5) To publish, from time to time, for public examination and analysis, proposed measures and methods for the simplification of such taxes, and to make to the Senate and the House of Representatives, not later than December 31, 1927, a definite report thereon, together with such recommendations as it may deem advisable; and

(6) To report, from time to time, to the Committee on Finance and the Committee on Ways and Means and, in its discretion, to the Senate or the House of Representatives, or both, the results of its investigations, together with such recommendations as it may deem advisable.

JOINT TAXATION

The joint committee was renamed the joint committee on Taxation by Public Law 94-455 on October 4, 1976.

Jurisdiction, 102nd Congress, 1991-1993

From *Authority and Rules of Senate Committees* for the 102nd Congress, printed under authority of Senate Resolution 58, agreed to March 13, 1991:

[Section 477.5-477.9]

It shall be the duty of the joint committee—

(1) Investigation—

(A) Operation and effects of law.—To investigate the operation and effects of the Federal system of internal revenue taxes;

(B) Administration.—To investigate the administration of such taxes by the Internal Revenue Service or any executive department, establishment, or agency charged with their administration; and

(C) Other investigations.—To make such other investigations in respect of such system of taxes as the joint committee may deem necessary.

(2) Simplification of law.—

(A) Investigation of methods.—To investigate measures and methods for the simplification of such taxes, particularly the income tax; and

(B) Publication of proposals.—To publish, from time to time, for public examination and analysis, proposed measures and methods for the simplification of such taxes.

(3) Reports.—

    (A) To report, from time to time, to the Committee on Finance and the Committee on Ways and Means, and, in its discretion, to the Senate or the House of Representatives, or both, the results of its investigations, together with such recommendations as it may deem advisable.

Jurisdiction, 110th Congress, 2007-2009

From Chapter 92.—POWERS AND DUTIES OF THE JOINT COMMITTEE–*Senate Manual* for the 110th Congress, Senate Document 110-1 (2008)., p. 964

It shall be the duty of the Joint Committee—

(1) Investigation—

    (A) Operation and effects of law.—To investigate the operation and effects of the Federal system of internal revenue taxes;

    (B) Administration.—To investigate the administration of such taxes by the Internal Revenue Service or any executive department, establishment, or agency charged with their administration; and

    (C) Other investigations.—To make such other investigations in respect of such system of taxes as the Joint Committee may deem necessary.

(2) Simplification of law.—

    (A) Investigation of methods.—To investigate measures and methods for the simplification of such taxes, particularly the income tax; and

    (B) Publication of proposals.—To publish, from time to time, for public examination and analysis, proposed measures and methods for the simplification of such taxes.

(3) Reports.—

    (A) To report, from time to time, to the Committee on Finance and the Committee on Ways and Means, and, in its discretion, to the Senate or the House of Representatives, or both, the results of its investigations, together with such recommendations as it may deem advisable.

MEMBERSHIP ROSTERS, 103rd-111th Congresses, 1993-2011

JOINT TAXATION / 103rd Congress

Service Dates of House Members: Jan. 5,1993-Jan. 3,1995

—House list published in the *Congressional Record,* Mar. 18, 1993

Service Dates of Senate Members: Continued-Feb. 2,1995

Majority — HOUSE

Rank Name	Party	State	House	Comm.
CVc1 Rostenkowski, Daniel D.	Dem	Ill.	18	10
2nd Gibbons, Sam M.	Dem	Fla.	16	7
3rd Pickle, J. J. (Jake)	Dem	Tex.	16	7

Minority

Rank Name	Party	State	House	Comm.
1st Archer, William R.	Rep	Tex.	12	5
2nd Crane, Philip M.	Rep	Ill.	13	1

Majority — SENATE

Rank Name	Party	State	Senate	Comm.
VcC Moynihan, Daniel Patrick	Dem	N.Y.	17	7
2nd Baucus, Max	Dem	Mont.	15	3
3rd Boren, David L.	Dem	Okla.	15	1

Minority

Rank Name	Party	State	Senate	Comm.
1st Packwood, Robert W.	Rep	Ore.	25	14
2nd Dole, Robert J.	Rep	Kans.	25	14

Changes:

Majority:

Rostenkowski, Daniel D.	Dem.	Ill.	June 8, 1994 Steps down as Vice Chair
Gibbons, Sam M.	Dem.	Fla.	June 9, 1994 Replaced Rostenkowski as acting Vice Chair
Boren, David L.	Dem.	Okla.	Nov. 15, 1994 Resigned the Senate; became president of the University of Oklahoma

Note: Lloyd M. Bentsen Jr. resigned from the Senate on Jan. 20, 1993 to become Secretary of the Treasury. His resignation automatically elevated members of the Finance committee, providing the composition of the Senate Majority membership to be Moynihan, Baucus and Boren.

Departures from the House	Majority			Minority
Defeated for re-election	Rostenkowski, Daniel D.	Dem	Ill.	
	Retired Pickle, J. J. (Jake)	Dem	Tex.	

JOINT TAXATION / 104th Congress

Service Dates of House Members: Jan. 10, 1995-Jan. 3, 1997

—House list published in the *Congressional Record,* Jan. 11, 1995

Service Dates of Senate Members: Feb. 2, 1995-

HOUSE	Majority			Terms in:		Minority				Terms in:	
Rank Name		Party	State	House	Comm.	Rank Name		Party	State	House	Comm.
CVc Archer, William R.		Rep	Tex.	13	6	1st Gibbons, Sam M.		Dem	Fla.	17	8
2nd Crane, Philip M.		Rep	Ill.	14	2	2nd Rangel, Charles B.		Dem	N.Y.	13	1
3rd Thomas, William M.		Rep	Cal.	9	1						

SENATE	Majority			Years in:		Minority				Years in:	
Rank Name		Party	State	Senate	Comm.	Rank Name		Party	State	Senate	Comm.
VC1 Packwood, Robert W.		Rep	Ore.	27	16	1st Moynihan, Daniel Patrick		Dem	N.Y.	19	9
2nd Hatch. Orrin G.		Rep	Utah	27	*1 1	2nd Baucus, Max S.		Dem	Mont.	17	4
Vc2C Roth, William V. Jr.		Rep	Del.	25	*2 1						

*1: Member's first period of service on the committee.

*2: Member's second period of service on the committee.

Changes

Senate Majority

Dole, Robert J.	Rep	Kans.	Feb. 2, 1995 Resigned the committee; no new assignment
Hatch, Orrin G.	Rep	Utah	Feb. 2, 1995 Replaced Dole "for the duration of the 104th Congress only"
Packwood, Robert W.	Rep	Ore.	Sep. 8, 1995 Relinquished chairmanship on Finance
Roth, William V. Jr.	Rep	Del.	Sep. 12, 1995 Succeeded Packwood as Vice Chair
Packwood, Robert W.	Rep	Ore.	Oct. 1, 1995 Resigned the Senate and retired
Chafee, John H.	Rep	R.I.	Nov. 2, 1995 Replaced Packwood

Departures from the House	**Majority**		**Minority**		
Retired			Gibbons, Sam M.	Dem	Fla.

Departures from the Committee	**Majority**		**Minority**		
Senate					
No new assignment	Hatch, Orrin G.		Rep Utah		

JOINT TAXATION / 105th Congress

Service Dates of House Members: Feb. 5, 1997-Jan. 3, 1999

—House list published in the *Congressional Record,* Feb. 10, 1997

Service Dates of Senate Members: Continued from the 104th Congress

HOUSE	Majority			Terms in:		Minority				Terms in:	
Rank Name		Party	State	House	Comm.	Rank Name		Party	State	House	Comm.
CVc Archer, William R.		Rep	Tex.	14	7	1st Rangel, Charles B.		Dem	N.Y.	14	2
2nd Crane, Philip M.		Rep	Ill.	15	3	2nd Stark, Fortney H. (Pete)		Dem	Cal.	13	1
3rd Thomas, William M.		Rep	Cal.	10	2						

	Majority			Years in:		Minority				Years in:	
Rank Name		Party	State	Senate	Comm.	Rank Name		Party	State	Senate	Comm.
VcC Roth, William V. Jr.		Rep	Del.	27	*2 2	1st Moynihan, Daniel Patrick		Dem	N.Y.	21	11
2nd Chafee, John H.		Rep	R.I.	21	2	2nd Baucus, Max S.		Dem	Mont.	19	6
3rd Grassley, Charles E.		Rep	Iowa	17	1						

*2: Member's second period of service on the committee.

Note: After Orrin Hatch's service on the committee in the 104th Congress expired, the Senate Majority membership reverted to the three most senior members on the Finance committee.

JOINT TAXATION / 106th Congress

Service Dates of House Members: Jan. 6, 1999-Jan. 3, 2001

—House list published in the *Congressional Record,* Jan. 19, 1999

Service Dates of Senate Members: Continued from the 105th Congress

HOUSE	Majority			Terms in:		Rank Name	Minority			Terms in:	
Rank Name	Party	State	House	Comm.		Rank Name	Party	State	House	Comm.
CVc Archer, William R.	Rep	Tex.	15	8		1st Rangel, Charles B.	Dem	N.Y.	15	3
2nd Crane, Philip M.	Rep	Ill.	16	4		2nd Stark, Fortney H. (Pete)	Dem	Cal.	14	2
3rd Thomas, William M.	Rep	Cal.	11	3						

SENATE	Majority			Years in:			Minority			Years in:	
Rank Name	Party	State	Senate	Comm.		Rank Name	Party	State	Senate	Comm.
VcC Roth, William V. Jr.	Rep	Del.	29	*2 5		1st Moynihan, Daniel Patrick	Dem	N.Y.	23	13
2nd Chafee, John H.	Rep	R.I.	23	4		2nd Baucus, Max S.	Dem	Mont.	21	8
3rd Grassley, Charles E.	Rep	Iowa	19	3						

*2: Member's second period of service on the committee.

Changes:

Majority:				
Chafee, John H.	Rep	R.I.	Oct. 24,1999 Died in office
Hatch, Orrin G.	Rep	Utah	Nov. 19, 1999 Replaced Chafee

Departures from the House:	Majority			Minority		
Retired	Archer, William R.			Rep	Tex.	

Departures from the Senate:	Majority				Minority		
Defeated for Re-election	Roth, William V. Jr.	Rep	Del.		None		
Retired	None				Moynihan, Daniel Patrick	Dem	N.Y.

JOINT TAXATION / 107th Congress, Pre-Jeffords Switch

Service Dates of House Members: Feb. 7, 2001-Jan. 3, 2003

—House list published in the *Congressional Record,* Feb. 27, 2001

Service Dates of Senate Members: Feb. 28, 2001-June 6, 2001, pre-Jeffords switch

Service Dates of Senate Members: June 6, 2001-Feb. 24, 2003, post-Jeffords switch

HOUSE	Majority			Terms in:		Rank Name	Minority			Terms in:	
Rank Name	Party	State	House	Comm.		Rank Name	Party	State	House	Comm.
CVc Thomas, William M.	Rep	Cal.	12	4		1st Rangel, Charles B.	Dem	N.Y.	16	4
2nd Crane, Philip M.	Rep	Ill.	17	5		2nd Stark, Fortney H. (Pete)	Dem	Cal.	15	3
3rd Shaw, E. Clay Jr.	Rep	Fla.	11	1						

JOINT TAXATION / 107th Congress, Pre-Jeffords Switch

SENATE	Majority			Years in:			Minority			Years in:	
Rank Name	Party	State	Senate	Comm.		Rank Name	Party	State	Senate	Comm.
VC1 Grassley, Charles E.	Rep	Iowa	21	5		1st Baucus, Max S.	Dem	Mont.	23	10
2nd Hatch, Orrin G.	Rep	Utah	25	*2 2		2nd Rockefeller, John D. IV	Dem	W.Va.	17	1
3rd Murkowski, Frank H.	Rep	Alas.	21	1						

*2: Member's second period of service on the committee.

Note: The committee majority in the 2001 Senate power-sharing arrangement was determined by the party of the vice president. Democrat Al Gore, Jr. served from Jan. 3, 2001 to Jan.20, 2001 and was succeeded by Republican Richard B. Cheney on Jan. 20, 2001. When Senator Jeffords of Vermont left the Republican Party, effective June 6, 2001 to become an Independent, Democrats regained the majority for the remainder of the 107th Congress.

Departures from the Committee	Majority			Minority	
No new assignment	Murkowski, Frank H.	Rep	Alas.	None	

JOINT TAXATION / 107th Congress, Post-Jeffords Switch

	Majority					Minority				
SENATE			Years in:						Years in:	
Rank Name	Party	State	Senate	Comm.		Rank Name	Party	State	Senate	Comm.
VC2 Baucus, Max S.	Dem	Mont.	23	11		1st Grassley, Charles E.	Rep	Iowa	21	5
2nd Rockefeller, John D. IV	Dem	W.Va.	17	1		2nd Hatch, Orrin G.	Rep	Utah	27	*2 2
3rd Daschle, Thomas A.	Dem	S.D.	15	1						

*2: Member's second period of service on the committee.

Note: Once Democrats regained the majority on June 6, 2001, Murkowski (Rep-Alas.) lost his seat on the committee. The Democrats automatically filled the new seat with Daschle, who ranked third on the Finance committee.

Departures from the Committee	Majority			Minority
No new assignment	Daschle, Thomas A.	Dem	S.D.	None

JOINT TAXATION / 108th Congress

Service Dates of House Members: Jan, 29, 2003-Jan. 3, 2005

—House list published in the *Congressional Record,* Mar. 12, 2003

Service Dates of Senate Members: Feb. 24, 2003- Jan. 25, 2005

	Majority					Minority				
HOUSE			Terms in:						Terms in:	
Rank Name	Party	State	House	Comm.		Rank Name	Party	State	House	Comm.
CVc Thomas, William M.	Rep	Cal.	13	5		1st Rangel, Charles B.	Dem	N.Y.	17	5
2nd Crane, Philip M.	Rep	Ill.	18	6		2nd Stark, Fortney H. (Pete)	Dem	Cal.	16	4
3rd Shaw, E. Clay Jr.	Rep	Fla.	12	2						

	Majority					Minority				
SENATE			Years in:						Years in:	
Rank Name	Party	State	Senate	Comm.		Rank Name	Party	State	Senate	Comm.
VcC Grassley, Charles E.	Rep	Iowa	23	7		1st Baucus, Max S.	Dem	Mont.	25	12
2nd Hatch, Orrin G.	Rep	Utah	27	*2 4		2nd Rockefeller, John D. IV	Dem	W.Va.	19	2
3rd Nickles, Donald L.	Rep	Okla.	23	1						

*2: Member's second period of service on the committee.

Departures from the House:	Majority			Minority
Defeated for re-election	Crane, Philip M.	Rep	Ill.	None

Departures from the Senate:	Majority			Minority
Retired	Nickles, Donald L.	Rep	Okla.	None

JOINT TAXATION / 109th Congress

Service Dates of House Members: Feb. 7, 2005-Jan. 3, 2007

—House list published in the *Congressional Record,* Mar. 14, 2005

Service Dates of Senate Members: Jan. 25, 2005-Jan. 18, 2007

	Majority					Minority				
HOUSE			Terms in:						Terms in:	
Rank Name	Party	State	House	Comm.		Rank Name	Party	State	House	Comm.
CVc Thomas, William M.	Rep	Cal.	14	6		1st Rangel, Charles B.	Dem	N.Y.	18	6
2nd Shaw, E. Clay Jr.	Rep	Fla.	13	3		2nd Stark, Fortney H. (Pete)	Dem	Cal.	17	5
3rd Johnson, Nancy L.	Rep	Conn.	12	1						

	Majority					Minority				
SENATE			Years in:						Years in:	
Rank Name	Party	State	Senate	Comm.		Rank Name	Party	State	Senate	Comm.
VcC Grassley, Charles E.	Rep	Iowa	25	9		1st Baucus, Max S.	Dem	Mont.	27	14
2nd Hatch, Orrin G.	Rep	Utah	29	*2 6		2nd Rockefeller, John D. IV	Dem	W.Va.	21	4
3rd Lott, C. Trent	Rep	Miss.	17	1						

*2: Member's second period of service on the committee.

Departures from the House:	Majority			Minority
Defeated for re-election	Johnson, Nancy L.	Rep	Conn.	None
	Shaw, E. Clay Jr.	Rep	Fla.	
Retired	Thomas, William M.	Rep	Cal.	

Committee Departures: Senate	Majority			Minority
No new assignment	Lott, C. Trent	Rep	Miss.	None

JOINT TAXATION / 110th Congress

Service Dates of House Members: Jan. 17, 2007-Jan. 3, 2009

—House list published in the *Congressional Record,* Jan. 31, 2007

Service Dates of Senate Members: Jan. 18, 2007-Jan. 25, 2009

			Majority						Minority			
HOUSE					Terms in:		**HOUSE**					Terms in:
Rank Name	**Party**	**State**	**House**	**Comm.**			**Rank Name**	**Party**	**State**	**House**	**Comm.**
CVc Rangel, Charles B.	Dem	N.Y.	19	7		1st McCrery, James O. III	Rep	La.	11	1
2nd Stark, Fortney H. (Pete)	Dem	Cal.	18	6		2nd Herger, Wally	Rep	Cal.	11	1
3rd Levin, Sander M.	Dem	Mich.	13	1						

			Majority						Minority			
SENATE					Years in:		**SENATE**					Years in:
Rank Name	**Party**	**State**	**Senate**	**Comm.**			**Rank Name**	**Party**	**State**	**Senate**	**Comm.**
VcC Baucus, Max S.	Dem	Mont.	29	16		1st Grassley, Charles E.	Rep	Iowa	27	11
2nd Rockefeller, John D. IV	Dem	W.Va.	23	6		2nd Hatch, Orrin G.	Rep	Utah	31	*2 8
3rd Conrad, Kent	Dem	N.D.	21	1						

*2: Member's second period of service on the committee.

Departures from the House:	Majority	Minority		
Retired	None	McCrery, James O. III	Rep	La.

JOINT TAXATION / 111th Congress

Service Dates of Committee Chair:

Service Dates of House Members: Jan. 12, 2009-Jan. 3, 2011

—House list published in the *Congressional Record,* Feb. 4, 2009

Service Dates of Senate Members: Feb. 25, 2009-

			Majority						Minority			
HOUSE					Terms in:		**HOUSE**					Terms in:
Rank Name	**Party**	**State**	**House**	**Comm.**			**Rank Name**	**Party**	**State**	**House**	**Comm.**
CVc Rangel, Charles B.	Dem	N.Y.	20	8		1st Camp, David L.	Rep	Mich.	10	1
2nd Stark, Fortney H. (Pete)	Dem	Cal.	19	7		2nd Herger, Wally	Rep	Cal.	12	2
3rd Levin, Sander M.	Dem	Mich.	14	2						

			Majority						Minority			
SENATE					Years in:		**SENATE**					Years in:
Rank Name	**Party**	**State**	**Senate**	**Comm.**			**Rank Name**	**Party**	**State**	**Senate**	**Comm.**
VcC Baucus, Max S.	Dem	Mont.	31	18		1st Grassley, Charles E.	Rep	Iowa	29	13
2nd Rockefeller, John D. IV	Dem	W.Va.	25	8		2nd Hatch, Orrin G.	Rep	Utah	33	*2 10
3rd Conrad, Kent	Dem	N.D.	23	3						

*2: Member's second period of service on the committee.

Joint Economic

Joint Economic Committee, 103rd-111th Congresses (1993-2011)

BACKGROUND

Organizational History: The Employment Act of 1946 set up a new system for the Federal Government to follow regarding the formulation of the nation's economic policy. As signed February 20, 1946, the law (P.L. 79-304) stipulated that the president submit an annual Economic Report to Congress detailing the level of employment, the productive capacity, and overall purchasing power of the country. The report was to contain recommendations for legislative action to carry out the president's policies.

To help the president, a three-member Council of Economic Advisors was created, with the job of monitoring the country's economic health year-round. The statute also provided for a new joint committee on the Economic Report to study the president's recommendations and to guide the various standing committees of both chambers regarding legislative initiatives proposed by the president. Although the original bill itself was vigorously debated by Congress and President Truman, the joint committee itself was not controversial.

Unlike most of the other joint committees created at this time, the Joint Committee on the Economic Report, like the Joint Committee on Atomic Energy, was not linked to any specific set of standing committees.

On June 18, 1956, the committee's name was changed from the Joint Committee on the Economic Report to the Joint Economic Committee (JEC), with no real change in its function. Legislative changes in the budget process have impacted the joint committee since 1946; however, its general mandate continues to be to receive and review the president's annual economic report, and to make appropriate recommendations to the House and Senate.

The JEC continues to monitor closely unemployment rates and prices throughout the country and is clearly the most powerful of the joint committees of Congress.

Membership: At its inception, the committee membership numbered fourteen. It expanded to sixteen in 1959 and to its present size of twenty in 1967, with a 6:4 majority-minority ratio for the ten members named from each chamber. It was the only one of the four newer joint committees to survive the Senate's 1977 reorganization and continues to this day. The Joint Committees on Atomic Energy, Immigration and Naturalization, and Navaho-Hopi Administration did not survive the 1970s.

The chairmanship of this committee was held by the ranking Senator from the 80th through the 82nd Congresses (1947-1953), with the ranking House member serving as vice chair. Beginning in the 83rd Congress, the chairmanship rotated between the House and Senate with each successive Congress.

Committee Leaders: A number of legislative powerhouses chaired this committee including its first post-Reorganization chair, Senator Robert A. Taft (Rep-Ohio). Representative Jesse P. Wolcott (Rep-Mich.) was its first vice chair. The Democratic

81st and 82nd Congresses (1949-1953) convened with Sen. Joseph C. O'Mahoney of Wyoming and Rep. Edward J. Hart of New Jersey holding the committee's top slots. When Republicans regained the Congress in 1953, Representative Wolcott became the first House member to chair the JEC, with Ralph E. Flanders of Vermont serving as its first Senate vice chair.

The beginning of the Democratic era of congressional control in 1955 saw Sen. Paul H. Douglas of Illinois, a well-published economist, and Rep. J.W. Wright Patman of Texas sharing leadership on the JEC for five of the next six Congresses (1955-1967). Patman, who had become chair of Banking and Currency in 1963, stepped aside to let his protégé Richard W. Bolling (Dem-Mo.) serve as vice chair in the 88th Congress (1963-1965) but resumed his post when the chairmanship of the JEC returned to the House in 1965. Patman continued to occupy the senior House slot until his death on March 7, 1976, when Bolling succeeded him. Senator Douglas was defeated for re-election in 1966 and Senator William Proxmire of Wisconsin succeeded him in 1967, and would serve as the committee's ranking senator until 1975, when he stepped aside for Sen. Hubert H. Humphrey Jr. (DFL-Minn.) after Humphrey's return to the Senate from the vice presidency and his unsuccessful bid for the presidency in 1968.

Humphrey and Bolling served as the committee's top leaders from March, 1976 until Humphrey's death in January, 1978. Humphrey was succeeded as vice chair by Lloyd M. Bentsen Jr. of Texas, the committee's fifth-ranked Democrat. The Bentsen-Bolling tandem served in the 96th Congress until the Republicans captured the Senate in the 1980 Ronald Reagan victory.

Changes occurred frequently on the Joint Economic Committee in the three divided 97th-99th Congresses (1981-1987). Three different Democratic representatives served as their ranking members on JEC—Henry S. Reuss of Wisconsin in the 97th, Lee H. Hamilton of Indiana in the 98th, and David R. Obey of Wisconsin in the 99th, as well as two different Republican senators—Roger W. Jepsen of Iowa in the 97th and 98th Congresses and James Abdnor in the 99th Congress.

When Democrats regained control of the Senate in the 1986 elections, Paul S. Sarbanes of Maryland became the ranking Democrat on the JEC and Lee Hamilton resumed his post as the committee's senior House Democrat for the 100th-102nd Congresses (1987-1993). While Sarbanes continued as the senior Senate Democrat on the committee in the 103rd Congress, Hamilton stepped aside for David R. Obey in that Congress.

The Republican Revolution of 1995 placed Rep. H. James Saxton of New Jersey as the lead House Republican on the Joint Economic Committee. Unlike the well-enforced three Congress rules for standing committee chairs promulgated by the House Republican Conference, Saxton was able to serve in the senior House Republican slot on the JEC for all six of the Congresses organized by the GOP (1995-2007). The same was not true on the Senate side. Sen. William V. Roth of Delaware relinquished his senior slot to Connie Mack III of Florida early in 1995 and Mack would serve as the committee's senior Republican from 1995 until his retirement in the 106th Congress (1999-2001). It would be Republican senator Robert F. Bennett of Utah who would get caught in the party switch of Vermont's Jim Jeffords in 2001 and Democratic senator John F. Reed of Rhode Island, who would occupy the senior Senate slot following the Jeffords defection. With Republicans returning to power following the 2002 election, Bennett would resume being the senior Senate Republican on the JEC for the next 108th and 109th Congresses (2003-2007).

With Democrats returning to congressional control in the wake of the 2006 election, Sen. Charles E. Schumer (Dem-N.Y.) became the senior senator on the JEC and Rep. Carolyn B. Maloney (Dem-N.Y.) became its senior House member for the 110th and 111th Congresses (2007-2011),

Party Leaders: Among the Senate leaders who served on Joint Taxation were Senate Republican floor leader Robert A. Taft (Rep-Ohio); and Democratic Senate Whips Francis J. Myers (Dem-Penn.), Hubert H. Humphrey, Jr. (DFL-Minn.), and Edward M. Kennedy (Dem-Mass.). Two House floor leaders who served on the Taxation Committee were Democrat T. Hale Boggs of Louisiana and Republican Dick Armey of Texas.

Other Notables: As the most powerful of Congress' joint committees, it is not surprising that so many ambitious members have sought to serve on the Joint Economic Committee. Among Senate members with presidential aspirations, the JEC appears to be the domestic equivalent of the Senate Foreign Relations Committee. Although he served briefly on the JEC, John F. Kennedy (Dem-Mass.) is the only committee alumnus to be elected president. His brother Edward M. Kennedy (Dem-Mass.) served longer on JEC than anyone in congressional history, but fell short of his presidential ambitions. Other JEC members who were nominated for president, but were less successful, include Barry M. Goldwater (Rep-Ariz.) the 1964 Republican nominee; Hubert H. Humphrey, Jr. (DFL-Minn.), the 1968 Democratic nominee; George S. McGovern, the 1972 Democratic nominee; and Albert A. Gore, Jr. (Dem-Tenn.), the 2000 Democratic nominee. Both Humphrey and Gore were elected vice president in 1964 and 1992, respectively. JEC member Prescott S. Bush (Rep-Conn.) holds the unique distinction of being the father of the nation's 41st president George H.W. Bush and the grandfather of its 43rd president George W. Bush.

Other JEC members nominated for vice president who were unsuccessful were Sen. John J. Sparkman (Dem-Ala.), Illinois governor Adlai Stevenson's running mate in 1952, and Sen. Lloyd M. Bentsen Jr. (Dem-Tex.), Massachusetts governor Michael S. Dukakis's running mate in 1988. Rep. Ronald E. Paul (Rep-Tex.) was the Libertarian Party's presidential candidate in 1988.

Cabinet members who served on the JEC include Rep. Christian A. Herter (Rep-Mass.), President Dwight Eisenhower's second Secretary of State; Sen. Abraham A. Ribicoff (Dem-Conn.), President John F. Kennedy's first Secretary of Health, Education, and Welfare; Rep. Donald Rumsfeld (Rep-Ill.), who served as Secretary of Defense under both Presidents Gerald R. Ford and George W. Bush; Abraham A. Ribicoff (Dem-Conn.), Sen. Richard S. Schweiker (Rep-Penn.) and Rep. Margaret M. Heckler (Rep-Mass.) President Ronald Reagan's first and second Secretaries of Health and Human Services and Sen. William E. Brock III (Rep-Tenn.), President Ronald Reagan's second Secretary of Labor. One-time JEC member W. Stuart Symington (Dem-Mo.) served as Secretary of the Air Force under President Harry Truman.

The committee also produced a number of state governors—Republicans Christian A. Herter of Massachusetts, Pete Wilson of California, and Marshall (Mark) Sanford of South Carolina—as well as Democrats Hugh L. Carey of New York and Jon S. Corzine of New Jersey.

RESPONSIBILITIES AND JURISDICTIONAL CHANGES

JOINT ECONOMIC REPORT

Jurisdiction, 80th Congress, 1947-1949

From Public Law 79-304, the Employment Act of 1946, 79th Congress, Second Session, February 20, 1946 (60 *Statutes* 23, 25) for the joint committee on the Economic Report:

[Section 5.(b)]

(b) It shall be the function of the joint committee—

   (1) to make a continuing study of matters relating to the Economic Report;

   (2) to study means of coordinating programs in order to further the policy of this Act; and

   (3) as a guide to the several committees of the Congress dealing with legislation relating to the Economic Report, not later than May 1 of each year (beginning with the year 1947) to file a report with the Senate and the House of Representatives containing its findings and recommendations with respect to each of the main recommendations made by the President in the Economic Report, and from time to time to make such other reports and recommendations to the Senate and House of Representatives as it deems advisable.

JOINT ECONOMIC

The Committee was renamed the Joint Economic Committee on June 18, 1956 by authority of Public Law 591 (84-2).

Jurisdiction, 95th Congress, 1977-1979

From Public Law 95-523, the Full Employment and Balanced Growth Act of 1978, 95th Congress, Second Session (92 *Statutes* 1887, 1904-1905):

[Section 302]

(a) In conjunction with its review of the Economic Report, and the holding of hearings on the Economic Report under the Employment Act of 1946, the Joint Economic Committee shall review and analyze the short-term and medium-term goals set forth in the Economic Report pursuant to sections 3(a)(2) and 4(b) of the Employment Act of 1946 (as amended by sections 103 and 104 of this Act).

Jurisdiction, 102nd Congress, 1991-1993

From *Authority and Rules of Senate Committees,* Senate Document 102-6, printed under the authority of Senate Resolution 58 (102-1), agreed to March 13, 1991:

[Section 1024]

(b) It shall be the function of the joint committee—

(1) to make a continuing study of matters relating to the Economic Report;
(2) to study means of coordinating programs in order to further the policy of this chapter; and
(3) as a guide to the several committees of the Congress dealing with legislation relating to the Economic Report, not later than March 1 of each year (beginning with the year 1947) to file a report with the Senate and the House of Representatives containing its findings and recommendations with respect to each of the main recommendations made by the President in the Economic Report, and from time to time to make such other reports and recommendations to the Senate and House of Representatives as it deems advisable.

Jurisdiction, 110th Congress, 2007-2009

From the *Senate Manual* for the 110th Congress, Senate Document 110-1 (2008), pp. 864-865.

[Section 1024. Joint Economic Committee]

(b) It shall be the function of the joint committee—

(1) to make a continuing study of matters relating to the Economic Report;
(2) to study means of coordinating programs in order to further the policy of this chapter; and
(3) as a guide to the several committees of the Congress dealing with legislation relating to the Economic Report, not later than March 1 of each year (beginning with the year 1947) to file a report with the Senate and the House of Representatives containing its findings and recommendations with respect to each of the main recommendations made by the President in the Economic Report, and from time to time to make such other reports and recommendations to the Senate and House of Representatives as it deems advisable.

[Section 1025. Printing of Monthly Publication By Joint Economic Committee Entitled '"Economic Indicators" Distribution.]

The Joint Economic Committee is authorized to issue a monthly publication entitled "Economic Indicators", and a sufficient quantity shall be printed to furnish one copy to each Member of Congress; the Secretary and the Sergeant at Arms of the Senate; the Clerk, Sergeant at Arms, and Chief Administrative Officer of the House of Representatives; two copies to the libraries of the Senate and House, and the Congressional Library; seven hundred copies to the Joint Economic Committee; and the required number of copies to the Superintendent of Documents for distribution to depository libraries; and the Superintendent of Documents is authorized to have copies printed for sale to the public.

MEMBERSHIP ROSTERS, 103rd-111th Congresses, 1993-2011

JOINT ECONOMIC / 103rd Congress

Service Dates of Committee Chair: Jan. 27,1993-Jan. 3,1995

Service Dates of House Majority Members: Jan. 27,1993-Jan. 3,1995

Service Dates of House Minority Members: Feb. 16,1993-Jan. 3,1995

Service Dates of Senate Members: Jan. 21,1993-Feb. 2,1995

		Majority						Minority			
HOUSE				Terms in:						Terms in:	
Rank Name	Party	State	House	Comm.	Rank Name		Party	State	House	Comm.	
Chr Obey, David R.	Dem	Wisc.	13	6	1st Armey, Richard K.		Rep	Tex.	5	2	

Rank Name	Party	State		
2nd Hamilton, Lee H.	Dem	Ind.	15	10
3rd Stark, Fortney H. (Pete)	Dem	Cal.	11	5
4th Mfume, Kweisi	Dem	Md.	4	2
5th Wyden, Ronald L.	Dem	Ore.	7	1
6th Andrews, Michael A.	Dem	Tex.	6	1

Rank Name	Party	State		
2nd Saxton, H. James	Rep	N.J.	6	1
3rd Cox, C. Christopher	Rep	Cal.	3	1
4th Ramstad, James	Rep	Minn.	2	1

SENATE

			Majority							Minority		
				Years in:							Years in:	
Rank Name	Party	State	Senate	Comm.			Rank Name	Party	State	Senate	Comm.	
VCh Sarbanes, Paul S.	Dem	Md.	17	14			1st Roth, William V. Jr.	Rep	Del.	23	17	
2nd Kennedy, Edward M.	Dem	Mass.	31	18			2nd Mack, Connie III	Rep	Fla.	5	4	
3rd Bingaman, J.F. (Jeff)	Dem	N.M.	11	*1 6			3rd Craig, Larry E.	Rep	Ida.	3	1	
4th Bryan, Richard H.	Dem	Nev.	5	4			4th Bennett, Robert F.	Rep	Utah	1	1	
5th Robb, Charles S.	Dem	Va.	5	1								
6th Dorgan, Byron L.	Dem	N.D.	1	1								

*1: Member's first period of service on the committee.

Changes:

Senate Majority:

Bryan, Richard H.	Dem	Nev.	May 6, 1993 Named Chair of Select Ethics earlier.
Boxer, Barbara	Dem	Cal.	May 6, 1993 Replaced Bryan.

Departures from the House:

	Majority				Minority
Lost Senate nomination	Andrews, Michael A.	Dem	Tex		

Departures from the Committee:

House

	Majority				Minority		
Elected Majority Leader					Armey, Richard K.	Rep	Tex
Moved to Commerce					Cox, C. Christopher	Rep	Cal.
Moved to Ways and Means					Ramstad, James	Rep	Minn.
No new assignment	Wyden, Ronald L.	Dem	Ore.				

Senate

	Majority				Minority
Moved to Armed Services	Bryan, Richard H.	Dem	Nev.		None
Moved to Energy and Natural Resources, Veterans' Affairs, and Select Ethics	Dorgan, Byron L.	Dem	N.D.		None
No new assignment	Boxer, Barbara	Dem	Cal.		None

JOINT ECONOMIC / 104th Congress

Service Dates of Committee Chair: Ch1: Jan. 9, 1995-Feb. 2, 1995

Ch2: Feb. 2, 1995-Jan. 9, 1997

Service Dates of Committee Vice Chair: Jan. 19, 1995-Jan. 3,1997

Service Dates of House Majority and Minority Members: Jan. 19, 1995-Jan. 3,1997

Service Dates of Senate Members: Feb. 2, 1995-Jan. 9,1997

HOUSE

			Majority							Minority		
				Terms in:							Terms in:	
Rank Name	Party	State	House	Comm.			Rank Name	Party	State	House	Comm.	
VCh Saxton, H. James	Rep	N.J.	7	2			1st Stark, Fortney H. (Pete)	Dem	Cal.	12	6	
2nd Ewing, Thomas W.	Rep	Ill.	3	1			2nd Obey, David R.	Dem	Wisc.	14	7	
3rd Quinn, John F. (Jack)	Rep	N.Y.	2	1			3rd Hamilton, Lee H.	Dem	Ind.	16	11	
4th Thornberry, William (Mac)	Rep	Tex.	1	1			4th Mfume, Kweisi	Dem	Md.	5	3	
5th Manzullo, Donald A.	Rep	Ill.	2	1								
6th Sanford, Marshall (Mark)	Rep	S.C.	1	1								

SENATE

			Majority							Minority		
				Years in:							Years in:	
Rank Name	Party	State	Senate	Comm.			Rank Name	Party	State	Senate	Comm.	
Ch1 Roth, William V. Jr.	Rep	Del.	25	19			1st Bingaman, J.F. (Jeff)	Dem	N.M.	13	*1 8	
Ch2 Mack, Connie III	Rep	Fla.	7	6			2nd Sarbanes, Paul S.	Dem	Md.	19	16	
3rd Craig, Larry E.	Rep	Ida.	5	2			3rd Kennedy, Edward M.	Dem	Mass.	33	20	
4th Bennett, Robert F.	Rep	Utah	3	2			4th Robb, Charles S.	Dem	Va.	7	2	
5th Santorum, Richard J. (Rick)	Rep	Penn.	1	1								
6th Grams, Rod	Rep	Minn.	1	1								

*1: Member's first period of service on the committee.

Changes

Senate Majority:

Mack, Connie III	Rep	Fla.	Feb. 2, 1995 Reranked ahead of Roth to become Chair

House Minority:

Mfume, Kweisi	Dem	Md.	Feb. 15, 1996 Resigned the House; named head of NAACP
Obey, David R.	Dem	Wisc.	Mar, 7, 1996 Resigned the committee; no new assignment
Hinchey, Maurice D.	Dem	N.Y.	Mar 7, 1996 Replaced Mfume
Maloney, Carolyn B.	Dem	N.Y.	Mar. 7, 1996 Replaced Obey

Departures from the Committee:	Majority			Minority
House				
Moved to Science	Ewing, Thomas W.	Rep	Ill.	None
No new assignment	Quinn, John F. (Jack)	Rep	N.Y.	None
Senate				
Moved to Appropriations	Craig, Larry E.	Rep	Ida.	None
No new assignment	Santorum, Richard J. (Rick)	Rep	Penn.	None

JOINT ECONOMIC / 105th Congress

Service Dates of Committee Chair: Jan. 20, 1997-Jan. 3, 1999

Service Dates of House Majority Members: Feb. 27, 1997-Jan. 3, 1999

Service Dates of House Minority Members: Mar. 11, 1997-Jan. 3, 1999

Service Dates of Senate Members: Jan. 9,1997-Jan. 7,1999

			Majority	Terms in:					Minority	Terms in:	
HOUSE											
Rank Name	Party	State	House	Comm.		Rank Name	Party	State	House	Comm.	
Chr Saxton, H. James	Rep	N.J.	8	3		1st Stark, Fortney H. (Pete)	Dem	Cal.	13	7	
2nd Manzullo, Donald A.	Rep	Ill.	3	2		2nd Hamilton, Lee H.	Dem	Ind.	17	12	
3rd Sanford, Marshall (Mark)	Rep	S.C.	2	2		3rd Hinchey, Maurice D.	Dem	N.Y.	4	*1 2	
4th Thornberry, William (Mac)	Rep	Tex.	2	2		4th Maloney, Carolyn B.	Dem	N.Y.	3	2	
5th Doolittle, John T.	Rep	Cal.	4	1							
6th McCrery, James	Rep	La.	6	1							

			Majority	Years in:					Minority	Years in:	
SENATE											
Rank Name	Party	State	Senate	Comm.		Rank Name	Party	State	Senate	Comm.	
VCh Mack, Connie III	Rep	Fla.	9	8		1st Bingaman, J.F. (Jeff)	Dem	N.M.	15	*1 10	
2nd Roth, William V. Jr.	Rep	Del.	27	21		2nd Sarbanes, Paul S.	Dem	Md.	21	18	
3rd Bennett, Robert F.	Rep	Utah	5	4		3rd Kennedy, Edward M.	Dem	Mass.	35	22	
4th Grams, Rod	Rep	Minn.	3	3		4th Robb, Charles S.	Dem	Va.	9	4	
5th Brownback, Sam D.	Rep	Kans.	1	1							
6th Sessions, Jefferson B. III	Rep	Ala.	1	1		*1: Member's first period of service on the committee.					

Changes

House Majority:

Manzullo, Donald A.	Rep	Ill.	May 22, 1997 Resigned committee; moved to Financial Services
Ewing, Thomas W.	Rep.	Ill.	May 22, 1997 Replaced Manzullo

Departures from the House:	Majority		Minority		
Retired			Hamilton, Lee H.	Dem	Ind.

Departures from the Committee:	Majority			Minority		
House						
Moved to Budget	Thornberry, William (Mac)	Rep	Tex.	None		
Moved to Science	Ewing, Thomas W.	Rep.	Ill.			
Moved to Appropriations	None			Hinchey, Maurice	Dem	N.Y.
No new assignment	McCrery, James	Rep	La.	None		

JOINT ECONOMIC / 106th Congress

Service Dates of Committee Chair: Apr 15, 1999-Jan. 3, 2001

Service Dates of Committee Vice Chair: Feb. 3, 1999-Jan. 3, 2001

Service Dates of House Majority Members: Mar. 18, 1999-Jan. 3, 2001

Service Dates of House Minority Members: Mar. 25, 1999-Jan. 3, 2001

Service Dates of Senate Members: Jan. 7, 1999-Jan. 25, 2001

HOUSE			**Majority**						**Minority**			
				Terms in:							**Terms in:**	
Rank Name	Party	State	House	Comm.			Rank Name	Party	State	House	Comm.	
VCh Saxton, H. James	Rep	N.J.	8	4			1st Stark, Fortney H. (Pete)	Dem	Cal.	14	8	
2nd Sanford, Marshall (Mark)	Rep	S.C.	3	3			2nd Maloney, Carolyn B.	Dem	N.Y.	4	3	
3rd Doolittle, John T.	Rep	Cal.	5	2			3rd Minge, David B.	DFL	Minn.	4	1	
4th Campbell, Thomas J.	Rep	Cal.	5	1			4th Watt, Melvin L.	Dem	N.C.	2	1	
5th Pitts, Joseph R.	Rep	Penn.	2	1								
6th Ryan, Paul D.	Rep	Wisc.	1	1								

SENATE			**Majority**						**Minority**			
				Years in:							**Years in:**	
Rank Name	Party	State	Senate	Comm.			Rank Name	Party	State	Senate	Comm.	
Chr Mack, Connie III	Rep	Fla.	11	10			1st Robb, Charles S.	Dem	Va.	11	6	
2nd Roth, William V. Jr.	Rep	Del.	29	23			2nd Kennedy, Edward M.	Dem	Mass.	37	24	
3rd Bennett, Robert F.	Rep	Utah	7	6			3rd Sarbanes, Paul S.	Dem	Md.	23	20	
4th Grams, Rod	Rep	Minn.	5	4			4th Bingaman, J.F. (Jeff)	Dem	N.M.	17	*1 12	
5th Brownback, Sam D.	Rep	Kans.	3	2								
6th Sessions, Jefferson B. III	Rep	Ala.	3	2								

*1: Member's first period of service on the committee.

Departures from the House	**Majority**				**Minority**		
Defeated for Re-election	None				Minge, David B.		DFL Minn.
Lost election to U.S. Senate	Campbell, Thomas J.	Rep	Cal.		None		
Retired	Sanford, Marshall (Mark)	Rep	S.C.		None		

Departures from the Senate:	**Majority**				**Minority**		
Defeated for Re-election	Roth, William V. Jr.	Rep	Del.		Robb, Charles S.	Dem	Va.
	Grams, Rod	Rep	Minn.				
Retired	Mack, Connie III	Rep	Fla.		None		

Departures from the Committee:

House

	Majority				**Minority**		
Moved to Appropriations	Doolittle, John T.	Rep	Cal.		None		
Moved to Energy and Commerce	Pitts, Joseph R.	Rep	Penn.		None		

Senate

	Majority				**Minority**		
Moved to Finance	None				Bingaman, J.F. (Jeff)	Dem	N.M.

JOINT ECONOMIC / 107th Congress, Pre-Jeffords Switch

Service Dates of Committee Chair: Mar. 22, 2001-Jan. 3, 2003

Service Dates of Committee Vice Chair: VCT: Jan. 3,2001-Jan. 25,2001 Reed (Dem-R.I.)

VC1: Jan. 25,2001-June 6,2001 Bennett (Rep-Utah)

Service Dates of House Members: May 1, 2001-Jan. 3, 2003

Service Dates of Senate Members: Jan. 25, 2001-June 6, 2001, pre-Jeffords switch

HOUSE			**Majority**						**Minority**			
				Terms in:							**Terms in:**	
Rank Name	Party	State	House	Comm.			Rank Name	Party	State	House	Comm.	
Chr Saxton, H. James	Rep	N.J.	10	5			1st Stark, Fortney H. (Pete)	Dem	Cal.	15	9	
2nd. Ryan, Paul D.	Rep	Wisc.	2	2			2nd Maloney, Carolyn B.	Dem	N.Y.	5	4	
3rd. Smith, Lamar S.	Rep	Tex.	8	1			3rd Watt, Melvin L.	Dem	N.C.	3	2	
4th Dunn, Jennifer B.	Rep	Wash.	5	1			4th Hill, Baron P.	Dem	Ind.	2	*1 1	
5th English , Philip S.	Rep	Penn.	4	1								
6th Putnam, Adam H., Jr.	Rep	Fla.	1	1								

SENATE			**Majority**						**Minority**			
				Years in:							**Years in:**	
Rank Name	Party	State	Senate	Comm.			Rank Name	Party	State	Senate	Comm.	
VC1 Bennett, Robert F.	Rep	Utah	9	9			1st Reed, John F.	Dem	R.I.	5	1	
2nd Brownback, Sam D.	Rep	Kans.	5	5			2nd Kennedy, Edward M.	Dem	Mass.	39	27	
3rd Sessions, Jefferson B. III	Rep	Ala.	5	5			3rd Sarbanes, Paul S.	Dem	Md.	25	22	
4th Crapo, Michael D.	Rep	Ida.	3	1			4th Corzine, Jon	Dem	N.J.	1	1	
5th Chafee, Lincoln D.	Rep	R.I.	2	1								

*1: Member's first period of service on the committee.

Filled vacancy:

Hill, Baron (Dem -Ind.) on April 18, 2002

Note 1: The committee majority in the 2001 Senate power-sharing arrangement was determined by the party of the vice president. Democrat Al Gore, Jr. served from Jan. 3, 2001 to Jan. 20, 2001 and was succeeded by Republican Richard B. Cheney on Jan. 20, 2001. When Senator Jeffords of Vermont left the Republican Party, effective June 6, 2001 to become an Independent, Democrats regained the majority for the remainder of the 107th Congress.

Note 2: In the 107th Congress, the Republicans held a majority in the House but the Senate's even 50-50 split between the parties led to the power-sharing agreement of December, 2000. Four Democratic and five Republican Senate members of the Joint Economic Committee were announced on Jan. 25, 2001 while the House members were named on May 1, 2001. The four originally listed Democrats listed in order were Senators Reed, Kennedy, Sarbanes, and Corzine. S. Res. 279 ratified a 5-5 Senate on Feb. 7, 2001. Senator Bingaman who had served previously on the committee returned to Joint Economic and was listed by CQWR (April 28, 2001) as the 1st ranking Democrat. Senator Jeffords's defection from the Republican Party to Independent in June, 2001 gave the Democrats control of the Senate and led to each of the Senate standing committees receiving an additional Democratic member. Senate Democrats received one seat on Joint Economic making the party split—six majority to five minority—instead of the traditional 6 to 4 split. Senator Robert Torricelli (Dem-N.J.) was added on July 10, 2001. Since Senators Kennedy, Sarbanes, and Bingaman became chairs of standing committees, Reed was listed as chair on July 10, 2001. This arrangement ended at the conclusion of the 107th Congress on Jan. 3, 2003.

JOINT ECONOMIC / 107th Congress, Post-Jeffords Switch

Service Dates of Senate Members: June 6, 2001-Jan. 15, 2001, post-Jeffords switch

	Majority			Years in:			Minority			Years in:	
SENATE						**SENATE**					
Rank Name	**Party**	**State**	**Senate**	**Comm.**		**Rank Name**	**Party**	**State**	**Senate**	**Comm.**	
VC2 Reed, John F.	Dem	R.I.	5	1		1st Bennett, Robert F.	Rep	Utah	9	9	
2nd Kennedy, Edward M.	Dem	Mass.	39	27		2nd Brownback, Sam D.	Rep	Kans.	5	5	
3rd Sarbanes, Paul S.	Dem	Md.	25	23		3rd Sessions, Jefferson B. III	Rep	Ala.	5	5	
4th Bingaman, J.F. (Jeff)	Dem	N.M.	19	*2 1		4th Crapo, Michael D.	Rep	Ida.	3	1	
5th Corzine, Jon	Dem	N.J.	1	1		5th Chafee, Lincoln D.	Rep	R.I.	2	1	
6th Torricelli, Robert G.	Dem	N.J.	5	1							

*2: Member's second period of service on the committee.

Additions:
Majority
  Torricelli was added on July 10, 2001.

Departures from the Committee:	**Majority**			**Minority**		
House						
Moved to Select Homeland Security	Smith, Lamar S.	Rep	Tex.	None		
Senate						
Moved to Foreign Relations	Corzine, Jon	Dem	N.J.	None		
Moved to Budget	None			Crapo, Michael D.	Rep	Ida.
Moved to Banking, Housing, and Urban Affairs	None			Chafee, Lincoln D.	Rep	R.I.
No new assignment	Torricelli, Robert G.	Dem	N.J.	None		

JOINT ECONOMIC / 108th Congress

Service Dates of Committee Chair: Jan. 15, 2003-Jan. 6, 2005

Service Dates of Committee Vice Chair: Jan. 8, 2003-Jan. 3, 2005

Service Dates of House Majority Members: Feb. 25,2003-Jan. 3, 2005

Service Dates of House Minority Members: Mar. 12, 2003-Jan. 3, 2005

Service Dates of Senate Members: Jan. 15, 2003-Jan. 6,2005

	Majority			Terms in:			Minority			Terms in:	
HOUSE						**HOUSE**					
Rank Name	**Party**	**State**	**House**	**Comm.**		**Rank Name**	**Party**	**State**	**House**	**Comm.**	
VCh Saxton, H. James	Rep	N.J.	11	6		1st Stark, Fortney H. (Pete)	Dem	Cal.	16	10	
2nd Ryan, Paul D.	Rep	Wisc.	3	3		2nd Maloney, Carolyn B.	Dem	N.Y.	6	5	
3rd Dunn, Jennifer B.	Rep	Wash	6	2		3rd Watt, Melvin L.	Dem	N.C.	4	3	
4th English , Philip S.	Rep	Penn.	5	2		4th Hill, Baron P.	Dem	Ind.	3	*1 2	
5th Putnam, Adam H.	Rep	Fla.	2	2							
6th Paul, Ronald E.	Rep	Tex.	8	1							

	Majority			Years in:			Minority			Years in:	
SENATE						**SENATE**					
Rank Name	**Party**	**State**	**Senate**	**Comm.**		**Rank Name**	**Party**	**State**	**Senate**	**Comm.**	
Chr Bennett, Robert F.	Rep	Utah	11	10		1st Reed, John F.	Dem	R.I.	7	3	
2nd Brownback, Sam D.	Rep	Kans.	7	7		2nd Kennedy, Edward M.	Dem	Mass.	41	28	

3rd Sessions, Jefferson B. III	Rep	Ala.	7	7
4th Sununu, John E.	Rep	N.H.	1	1
5th Alexander, Lamar	Rep	Tenn.	1	1
6th Collins, Susan M.	Rep	Me.	7	1

3rd Sarbanes, Paul S.	Dem	Md.	27	24
4th Bingaman, J.F. (Jeff)	Dem	N.M.	21	*2 2

*1: Member's first period of service on the committee.

*2: Member's second period of service on the committee.

Departures from the House:	Majority			Minority		
Defeated for re-election				Hill, Baron P.	Dem	Ind.
Retired	Dunn, Jennifer B.	Rep	Wash.			

Departures from the Committee:	Majority			Minority		
House						
No new assignment	Putnam, Adam H.	Rep	Fla.	Stark, Fortney H. (Pete)	Dem	Cal.
				Watt, Melvin L.	Dem	N.C.
Senate						
Moved to Special Aging	Alexander, Lamar	Rep	Tenn.	None		
Became Chair of Governmental Affairs	Collins, Susan M.	Rep	Me.	None		

JOINT ECONOMIC / 109th Congress

Service Dates of Committee Chair: Jan. 20, 2005-Jan. 3, 2007

Service Dates of House Members: Mar, 3, 2005-Jan. 3, 2007

Service Dates of Senate Members: Jan. 6, 2005-Jan. 12, 2007

			Majority						Minority		
HOUSE			Terms in:			**HOUSE**			Terms in:		
Rank Name	Party	State	House	Comm.		Rank Name	Party	State	House	Comm.	
Chr Saxton, H. James	Rep	N.J.	12	7		1st Maloney, Carolyn B.	Dem	N.Y.	7	6	
2nd Ryan, Paul D.	Rep	Wisc.	4	4		2nd Hinchey, Maurice D.	Dem	N.Y	7	*2 1	
3rd English , Philip S.	Rep	Penn.	6	3		3rd Sanchez, Loretta	Dem	Cal.	5	1	
4th Paul, Ronald E.	Rep	Tex.	9	2		4th Cummings. Elijah	Dem	Md.	6	1	
5th Brady, Kevin P.	Rep	Tex.	5	1							
6th McCotter, Thaddeus G.	Rep	Mich.	2	1							

			Majority						Minority		
SENATE			Years in:			**SENATE**			Years in:		
Rank Name	Party	State	Senate	Comm.		Rank Name	Party	State	Senate	Comm.	
VCh Bennett, Robert F.	Rep	Utah	13	12		1st Reed, John F.	Dem	R.I.	9	5	
2nd Brownback, Sam D.	Rep	Kans.	9	8		2nd Kennedy, Edward M.	Dem	Mass.	43	30	
3rd Sununu, John E.	Rep	N.H.	3	2		3rd Sarbanes, Paul S.	Dem	Md.	29	26	
4th DeMint, James W.	Rep	S.C.	1	1		4th Bingaman, J.F. (Jeff)	Dem	N.M.	23	*2 4	
5th Sessions, Jefferson B. III	Rep	Ala.	9	8							
6th Cornyn, John	Rep	Tex.	3	1							

*2: Member's second period of service on the committee.

Departures from the Senate:	Majority			Minority		
Retired	None			Sarbanes, Paul S.	Dem	Md.

Departures from the Committee:	Majority			Minority		
House						
Became Ranking Member on Budget	Ryan, Paul D.	Rep	Wisc.	None		
No new assignment	McCotter, Thaddeus G.	Rep	Mich.	None		
Senate						
Moved to Energy and Natural Resources	Sessions, Jefferson B. III	Rep	Ala.	None		
Moved to Select Ethics As Ranking Member	Cornyn, John	Rep	Tex.	None		
Returned to Appropriations	None			Reed, John F.	Dem	R.I.

JOINT ECONOMIC / 110th Congress

Service Dates of Committee Chair: Jan. 12, 2007-Jan. 21, 2009

Service Dates of Committee Vice Chair: Jan. 18, 2007-Jan. 3, 2009

Service Dates of House Members: Mar. 27, 2007-Jan. 3, 2009

Service Dates of Senate Members: Jan. 12, 2007-Jan. 21, 2009

	Majority						Minority			
HOUSE				**Terms in:**					**Terms in:**	
Rank Name	**Party**	**State**	**House**	**Comm.**		**Rank Name**	**Party**	**State**	**House**	**Comm.**
VCh Maloney, Carolyn B.	Dem	N.Y.	8	7		1st Saxton, H. James	Rep	N.J.	13	8
2nd Hinchey, Maurice D.	Dem	N.Y.	8	*2 2		2nd Brady, Kevin P.	Rep	Tex.	6	2
3rd Hill, Baron P.	Dem	Ind.	4	*2 1		3rd English , Philip S.	Rep	Penn.	7	4
4th Sanchez, Loretta	Dem	Cal.	6	2		4th Paul, Ronald E.	Rep	Tex.	10	3
5th Cummings. Elijah E.	Dem	Md.	7	2						
6th Doggett, Lloyd A.	Dem	Tex.	7	1						

Note: Saxton (Rep-N.J.) was named on Jan. 22, 2007

	Majority						Minority			
SENATE				**Years in:**					**Years in:**	
Rank Name	**Party**	**State**	**Senate**	**Comm.**		**Rank Name**	**Party**	**State**	**Senate**	**Comm.**
Chr Schumer, Charles E.	Dem	N.Y.	9	1		1st Brownback, Sam D.	Rep	Kans.	11	11
2nd Kennedy, Edward M.	Dem	Mass.	45	32		2nd Sununu, John E.	Rep	N.H.	5	4
3rd Bingaman, J.F. (Jeff)	Dem	N.M.	25	*2 6		3rd DeMint, James W.	Rep	S.C.	3	3
4th Klobuchar, Amy	DFL	Minn.	1	1		4th Bennett, Robert F.	Rep	Utah	15	14
5th Casey, Robert P. Jr.	Dem	Penn.	1	1						
6th Webb, James	Dem	Va.	1	1						

*2: Member's second period of service on the committee.

Departures from the House:	Majority				Minority		
Defeated for re-election	None				English , Philip S.	Rep	Penn.
Retired	None				Saxton, H. James	Rep	N.J.
Departures from the Senate:							
Defeated for re-election	None				Sununu, John E.	Rep	N.H.
Departures from the Committee:							
House							
No new assignment	Doggett, Lloyd A.		Dem	Tex.	None		

JOINT ECONOMIC / 111th Congress

Service Dates of Committee Chair: Jan. 22, 2009-Jan. 3, 2011

Service Dates of House Members: Feb. 3, 2009-Jan. 3, 2011

Service Dates of Senate Members: Jan. 21, 2009-

	Majority						Minority			
HOUSE				**Terms in:**					**Terms in:**	
Rank Name	**Party**	**State**	**House**	**Comm.**		**Rank Name**	**Party**	**State**	**House**	**Comm.**
Chr Maloney, Carolyn B.	Dem	N.Y.	9	8		1st Brady, Kevin P.	Rep	Tex.	7	3
2nd Hinchey, Maurice D.	Dem	N.Y.	9	*2 3		2nd Paul, Ronald E.	Rep	Tex.	11	4
3rd Hill, Baron P.	Dem	Ind.	5	*2 2		3rd Burgess, Michael E.	Rep	Tex	4	1
4th Sanchez, Loretta	Dem	Cal.	7	3		4th Campbell, John	Rep	Cal.	3	1
5th Cummings. Elijah E.	Dem	Md.	8	3						
6th Snyder, Victor F.	Dem	Ark.	7	1						

Note: Brady (Rep-Tex.) was named on Jan. 22, 2009

	Majority						Minority			
SENATE				**Years in:**					**Years in:**	
Rank Name	**Party**	**State**	**Senate**	**Comm.**		**Rank Name**	**Party**	**State**	**Senate**	**Comm.**
VCh Schumer, Charles E.	Dem	N.Y.	11	3		1st Brownback, Sam D.	Rep	Kans.	13	13
2nd Kennedy, Edward M.	Dem	Mass.	47	35		2nd DeMint, James W.	Rep	S.C.	5	5
3rd Bingaman, J.F. (Jeff)	Dem	N.M.	27	*2 8		3rd Risch, James E.	Rep	Ida.	1	1
4th Klobuchar, Amy	DFL	Minn.	3	3		4th Bennett, Robert F.	Rep	Utah	17	17
5th Casey, Robert P. Jr.	Dem	Penn.	3	3						
6th Webb, James	Dem	Va.	3	3						

*2: Member's second period of service on the committee.

Changes:				
Senate Majority:				
Kennedy, Edward M.	Dem.	Mass.	Aug. 25, 2009 Died in office	
Warner, Mark	Dem.	Va.	Sept. 29, 2009 Replaced Kennedy	

Joint Organization of Congress (ad hoc)

Temporary Joint Committee on the Organization of Congress, 102nd-103rd Congresses (1992-1993)

BACKGROUND

In yet another effort to upgrade the functioning of Congress, Representatives Lee H. Hamilton (Dem-Ind.) and Willis D. Gradison (Rep-Ohio) introduced House Concurrent Resolution 192 on July 31, 1991. A similar measure was introduced in the Senate by David L. Boren (Dem-Okla.) and Pete V. Domenici (Rep-N.M.), but no action was taken until the following year.

Public disclosure of the mismanagement of several congressional services, most notably the House Bank and House Post Office, forced a reluctant leadership to take steps toward reform in the spring and summer of 1992.

The Hamilton-Gradison measure attracted 247 cosponsors in the House and fifty-seven in the Senate by the time of the vote on August 6, 1992. Although there was virtually no opposition to the measure in either chamber, it was agreed that to avoid partisan bickering, no work would be undertaken by the joint committee before the November 1992 elections. The Senate passed the measure by voice vote on July 30, while the House passed the measure by a vote of 412-4 on August 6, 1992.

The committee was given no legislative jurisdiction, and was to report to the Democratic Caucus and Republican Conference on its progress. Two final reports were submitted to each chamber in December, 1993: House Report 103-413, Vols. 1 and 2 and Senate Report 103-215, Vols. 1 and 2.

Early in 1993, the House Democratic Caucus initiated its own reforms by not reappointing four House select committees: Aging, Narcotics Abuse and Control, Children, Youth and Families and Hunger. However, the joint committee's effort to do away with the remaining four joint committees failed, as did some of its other proposals, such as biennial budgeting, subcommittee reduction, and a 12 percent congressional staff reduction. Its most notable achievement was reflected in House passage of the House Labor Law Compliance resolution on October 7, 1994, which guaranteed congressional staff member's workplace safety and anti-discrimination protections, similar to those imposed by Congress on private employers.

Membership and Leadership: A twenty-four-member committee equally divided by party and chamber was named with Representative Hamilton and Senator Boren serving as co-chairs of the joint committee while Representative Gradison and Senator Domenici served as co-vice chairs.

Among its notable members were three who would hold leadership posts: C. Trent Lott of Mississippi was the Republican House Whip from 1981 to 1989, the Republican Senate Whip in 1995-96 and 2007-08; and Republican Floor Leader from 1996 to 2003. Two Democratic Senate members of the committee to serve as leaders were Wendell H. Ford of Kentucky who was Democratic Whip from 1991 to 1999, and Harry M. Reid of Nevada, Democratic Whip from 2001 to 2005 and the present Democratic floor leader since 2005.

Selected References

Adler, E. Scott, *Why Congressional Reforms Fail: Reelection and the House Committee System* (Chicago: University of Chicago Press, 2002).

U.S. Congress, Joint Committee on the Organization of Congress, *Organization of the Congress*, 103rd Congress, 1st Session, House Report 193-413, 2 vols. and Senate Report 103-215, 2 vols.

JURISDICTION

Jurisdiction, 102nd Congress, 1992

From House Concurrent Resolution 192, 102nd Congress, Second Session, August 6, 1992:

[Section 2(a)]

In General.—The Committee shall—

   (1) make a full and complete study of the organization and operation of the Congress of the United States; and
   (2) recommend improvements in such organization and operation with a view toward strengthening the effectiveness of the Congress, simplifying its operations, improving its relationships with other branches of the United States Government, and improving the orderly consideration of legislation.

[Section 2(b)]

Focus of Study.—The study shall include an examination of—

(1) the organization and operation of each House of the Congress, including the employment of personnel by the Members and the committees of the Congress and the structure of, and the relationships between, the various standing, special, and select committees of the Congress;

(2) the relationship between the 2 Houses; and

(3) the relationship between the Congress and the Executive branch of the Government.

MEMBERSHIP ROSTERS, 102nd-103rd Congresses, 1992-1993

JOINT ORGANIZATION OF CONGRESS (Ad Hoc) / 102nd Congress

Service Dates of House Majority Members: Oct. 9,1992-Jan. 3,1993

Service Dates of House Minority Members: Sep. 14,1992-Jan. 3,1993 (appointments made Aug. 10,1992)

Service Dates of Senate Majority Members: Oct. 8,1992-Jan. 3,1993

Service Dates of Senate Minority Members: Sep. 25,1992-Jan. 3,1993

| HOUSE | Majority | | Terms in: | | | | Minority | | Terms in: | |
Rank Name	Party	State	House	Comm.	Rank Name	Party	State	House	Comm.
CoCh Hamilton, Lee H.	Dem	Ind.	14	1	VCh Gradison, Willis D. Jr.	Rep	Ohio	9	1
2nd Obey, David R.	Dem	Wisc.	13	1	2nd Walker, Robert S.	Rep	Penn.	8	1
3rd Swift, Allan B.	Dem	Wash.	8	1	3rd Solomon, Gerald B.	Rep	N.Y.	7	1
4th Gejdenson, Samuel	Dem	Conn.	6	1	4th Dreier, David	Rep	Cal.	6	1
5th Spratt, John M. Jr.	Dem	S.C.	5	1	5th Emerson, Bill	Rep	Mo.	6	1
6th Norton, Eleanor Holmes	Dem	D.C.	1	1	6th Allard, A. Wayne	Rep	Colo.	1	1

| SENATE | Majority | | Years in: | | | | Minority | | Years in: | |
Rank Name	Party	State	House	Comm.	Rank Name	Party	State	House	Comm.
CoCh Boren, David L.	Dem	Okla.	14	1	1st Domenici, Pete V.	Rep	N.M.	20	1
2nd Ford, Wendell H.	Dem	Ky.	18	1	2nd Kassebaum, Nancy Landon	Rep	Kans.	14	1
3rd Pryor, David	Dem	Ark.	14	1	3rd Lott, Trent	Rep	Miss.	4	1
4th Reid, Harry M.	Dem	Nev.	6	1	4th Stevens, Theodore F.	Rep	Alas.	24	1
5th Sarbanes, Paul S.	Dem	Md.	16	1	5th Lugar, Richard G.	Rep	Ind.	16	1
6th Sasser, James R.	Dem	Tenn.	16	1	6th Cohen, William S.	Rep	Me.	14	1

Note: House and Senate Majority and Minority leaders are *ex officio* members of the committee.

JOINT ORGANIZATION OF CONGRESS (Ad Hoc) / 103rd Congress

Service Dates of House Majority Members: Continued-Dec. 31,1993

Service Dates of House Minority Members: Jan. 5,1993-Dec. 31,1993

Service Dates of Senate Majority Members: Continued-Dec. 31,1993

Service Dates of Senate Minority Members: Continued-Dec. 31,1993

| HOUSE | Majority | | Terms in: | | | | Minority | | Terms in: | |
Rank Name	Party	State	House	Comm.	Rank Name	Party	State	House	Comm.
CoCh Hamilton, Lee H.	Dem	Ind.	15	2	CoVc1 Gradison, Willis D. Jr.	Rep	Ohio	10	2
2nd Obey, David R.	Dem	Wisc.	13	2	2nd Walker, Robert S.	Rep	Penn.	9	2
3rd Swift, Allan B.	Dem	Wash.	9	2	3rd Solomon, Gerald B.	Rep	N.Y.	8	2
4th Gejdenson, Samuel	Dem	Conn.	7	2	4th CoVc2 Dreier, David	Rep	Cal.	7	2
5th Spratt, John M. Jr.	Dem	S.C.	6	2	5th Emerson, Bill	Rep	Mo.	7	2
6th Norton, Eleanor Holmes	Dem	D.C.	2	2	6th Allard, A. Wayne	Rep	Colo.	2	2

				Majority							Minority		

SENATE			Years in:		Rank Name			Years in:	
Rank Name	Party	State	House	Comm.	Rank Name	Party	State	House	Comm.
CoCh Boren, David L.	Dem	Okla.	15	1	CoVc Domenici, Pete V.	Rep	N.M.	21	1
2nd Sasser, James R.	Dem	Tenn.	17	1	2nd Kassebaum, Nancy Landon	Rep	Kans.	15	1
3rd Ford, Wendell H.	Dem	Ky.	19	1	3rd Lott, Trent	Rep	Miss.	5	1
4th Reid, Harry M.	Dem	Nev.	7	1	4th Stevens, Theodore F.	Rep	Alas.	25	1
5th Sarbanes, Paul S.	Dem	Md.	17	1	5th Cohen, William S.	Rep	Me.	15	1
6th Pryor, David	Dem	Ark.	15	1	6th Lugar, Richard G.	Rep	Ind.	17	1

Note: House and Senate Majority and Minority leaders are *ex officio* members of the committee.

Changes:

Gradison, Willis D. Jr	Rep	Ohio	Jan. 31, 1993 Resigned and retired
Dreier, David	Rep	Cal.	Jan. 30, 1993 Replaced Gradison as Co-Vice Chair
Dunn, Jennifer	Rep	Wash.	Feb. 2, 1993 replaced Gradison

Part II

Member Assignments

1993-2010

A

Neil Abercrombie (D-Hai.)

Dates: June 26, 1938
House 1: Sept. 20, 1986-Sept. 23, 1987
Left House 1: Defeated for re-nomination in 1986
House 2: Jan. 2, 1991-Feb 28, 2010
Left House 2: Resigned to seek governorship

H1: Abercrombie was elected to the 99th Congress by special election, Sept. 20, 1986, to fill the vacancy caused by the resignation of U.S. Representative Cecil Heftel (D-Hai.) who was a candidate for Governor. Abercrombie was seated Sept. 23, 1986, and assigned to committees.

HOUSE STANDING COMMITTEES:

1st ARMED SERVICES, 102-103
NATIONAL SECURITY, 104-105
ARMED SERVICES, 106-111
1st Dates: Oct. 10, 1986-Jan. 3, 1987
1st Departure: Left the House; lost seat
2nd Dates: Jan. 24, 1991-Feb. 28, 2010
2nd Departure: Resigned the House to run for Governor

Cong.	Ranking	Terms in: House	Comm.	Date of Assignment
103rd	Maj-21st	3 *2	2	Jan. 5, 1993
104th	Min-13th	4 *2	3	Jan. 4, 1995
105th	Min-9th	5 *2	4	Jan. 7, 1997
106th	Min-8th	6 *2	5	Jan. 6, 1999
107th	Min-7th	7 *2	6	Jan. 31, 2001
108th	Min-6th	8 *2	7	Jan. 28, 2003
109th	Min-6th	9 *2	8	Jan. 26, 2005
110th	Maj-5th	10 *2	9	Jan. 10, 2007
111th	Maj-5th	11 *2	10	Jan. 7, 2009

2nd MERCHANT MARINE AND FISHERIES
Dates: Jan. 24, 1991-Oct. 9, 1991
Departure: Moved to Interior and Insular Affairs

3rd INTERIOR AND INSULAR AFFAIRS, 102
NATURAL RESOURCES, 103
RESOURCES, 104-109
NATURAL RESOURCES, 110-111
Dates: Oct. 9, 1991-Feb. 28, 2010
Departure: Resigned the House to run for Governor

Cong.	Ranking	Terms in: House	Comm.	Date of Assignment
103rd	Maj-16th	3	2	Jan. 5, 1993
104th	Min-11th	4	3	Jan. 4, 1995
105th	Min-10th	5	4	Jan. 7, 1997
106th	Min-7th	6	5	Jan. 6, 1999
107th	Min-7th	7	6	Feb. 8, 2001
108th	Min-7th	8	7	Jan. 28, 2003
109th	Min-4th	9	8	Jan. 26, 2005
110th	Maj-4th	10	9	Jan. 18, 2007
111th	Maj-4th	11	10	Jan. 21, 2009

HOUSE SELECT AND SPECIAL COMMITTEES:

1st SELECT AGING (Permanent)
Dates: Feb. 21, 1991-Jan. 3, 1993
Termination: Committee not renewed in 1993

Spencer Abraham (R-Mich.)

Dates: June 12, 1952
Senate: Jan. 3, 1995-Jan. 3, 2001
Left Senate: Defeated for re-election in 2000; appointed Secretary of Energy in 2001

SENATE STANDING COMMITTEES:

1st BUDGET
Dates: Jan. 6, 1995-Jan. 3, 2001
Departure: Left the Senate; lost re-election

Cong.	Ranking	Years in: Senate	Comm.	Date of Assignment
104th	Maj-11th	1	1	Jan. 6, 1995
105th	Maj-9th	3	3	Jan. 9, 1997
106th	Maj-9th	5	5	Jan. 7, 1999

2nd JUDICIARY
Dates: Jan. 4, 1995-Jan. 3, 2001
Departure: Left the Senate; lost re-election

Cong.	Ranking	Years in: Senate	Comm.	Date of Assignment
104th	Maj-10th	1	1	Jan. 4, 1995
105th	Maj-9th	3	3	Jan. 9, 1997
106th	Maj-8th	5	5	Jan. 7, 1999

3rd LABOR AND HUMAN RESOURCES
Dates: Jan. 4, 1995-Apr. 16, 1996
Departure: Left committee; moved to Commerce, Science and Transportation

Cong.	Ranking	Years in: Senate	Comm.	Date of Assignment
104th	Maj- 8th	1	1	Jan. 4, 1995

4th COMMERCE, SCIENCE AND TRANSPORTATION
Dates: March 29, 1996-Jan. 3, 2001
Departure: Left the Senate; lost re-election

Cong.	Ranking	Years in: Senate	Comm.	Date of Assignment
104th	MjA-11th	2	1	Mar. 29, 1996
105th	Maj-10th	3	1	Jan. 9, 1997
106th	Maj-10th	5	3	Jan. 7, 1999

5th SMALL BUSINESS
Dates: Jan. 7, 1999-Jan. 3, 2001
Departure: Left the Senate; lost re-election

Cong.	Ranking	Years in: Senate	Comm.	Date of Assignment
106th	Maj-10th	5	1	Jan. 7, 1999

Anibal Acevedo-Vila (D-P.R.)

Dates: Feb. 16, 1962
House: Jan. 3, 2001-Jan. 3, 2005
Left the House: Elected Governor in 2004

HOUSE STANDING COMMITTEES:

1st AGRICULTURE
Dates: Jan. 31, 2001-Jan. 3, 2005
Departure: Left the House; elected Governor

Cong.	Ranking	Terms in: House	Comm.	Date of Assignment
107th	Min-21st	1	1	Jan. 31, 2001
108th	Min-14th	2	2	Jan. 28, 2003

2nd RESOURCES
Dates: Feb. 8, 2001-Jan. 3, 2005
Departure: Left the House; elected Governor

Cong.	Ranking	Terms in: House	Comm.	Date of Assignment
107th	Min-21st	1	1	Feb. 8, 2001
108th	Min-18th	2	2	Jan. 28, 2003

3rd SMALL BUSINESS
Dates: Feb. 28, 2001-Jan. 3, 2005
Departure: Left the House; elected Governor

Cong.	Ranking	Terms in: House	Comm.	Date of Assignment
107th	MnR-4th	1	1	Feb. 28, 2001
108th	Min-13th	2	2	Feb. 13, 2003

Gary L. Ackerman (D-N.Y.)

Dates: Nov. 19, 1942
House: March 1, 1983-date
Serving in the 111th Congress

H: Ackerman was elected to the 98th Congress by special election, March 1, 1983, to fill the vacancy caused by the death of U.S. Representative Benjamin S. Rosenthal (D-N.Y.). Ackerman was seated March 2, 1983, and assigned to committees.

HOUSE STANDING COMMITTEES:

1st EDUCATION AND LABOR
Dates: Mar. 24, 1983-Jan. 3, 1985
Departure: Left committee; no new assignment

2nd FOREIGN AFFAIRS, 98-103
INTERNATIONAL RELATIONS, 104-109
FOREIGN AFFAIRS, 110-111
Dates: Feb. 29, 1984-date
Departure: Still serving in the 111th Congress

Cong.	Ranking	Terms in: House	Comm.	Date of Assignment
103rd	Maj-6th	6	6	Jan. 5, 1993
104th	Min-6th	7	7	Jan. 4, 1995
105th	Min-5th	8	8	Jan. 7, 1997
106th	Min-4th	9	9	Jan. 6, 1999
107th	Min-3rd	10	10	Jan. 31, 2001
108th	Min-3rd	11	11	Jan. 28, 2003
109th	Min-3rd	12	12	Jan. 26, 2005
110th	Maj-3rd	13	13	Jan. 12, 2007
111th	Maj-2nd	14	14	Jan. 21, 2009

3rd POST OFFICE AND CIVIL SERVICE
Dates: Feb. 29, 1984-Jan. 3, 1993
Departure: Committee abolished; returned to Banking and Financial Services

Cong.	Ranking	Terms in: House	Comm.	Date of Assignment
103rd	Maj-4th	6	6	Jan. 21, 1993

4th BANKING, FINANCE AND URBAN AFFAIRS, 100, 102
BANKING AND FINANCIAL SERVICES, 104-106
FINANCIAL SERVICES, 107-111
1st Dates: May 18, 1988-Jan. 3, 1989
1st Departure: Left committee; no new assignment
Temporary Dates: Jan. 24, 1991-Jan. 3, 1993
Temporary Departure: Moved to Merchant Marine and Fisheries
2nd Dates: Jan. 4, 1995-Aug. 5, 1999
2nd Departure: Resigned committee to open seat for Michael Forbes who had switched parties; returned with seniority credited
3rd Dates: Nov. 2, 1999-date
3rd Departure: Still serving in the 111th Congress

Cong.	Ranking	Terms in: House	Comm.	Date of Assignment
104th	Min-21st	7 *2	1	Jan. 4, 1995
105th	Min-17th	8 *2	2	Jan. 7, 1997
106th	Min-10th	9 *2	3	Jan. 6, 1999
106th	MnR-2nd	9 *3	1	Nov. 2, 1999
107th	Min-9th	10 *3	2	Jan. 31, 2001
108th	Min-9th	11 *3	3	Jan. 28, 2003
109th	Min-9th	12 *3	4	Jan. 26, 2005
110th	Maj-8th	13 *3	5	Jan. 12, 2007
111th	Maj-8th	14 *3	6	Jan. 7, 2009

5th PUBLIC WORKS AND TRANSPORTATION
Dates: Feb. 27, 1990-Jan. 3, 1991
Departure: Moved to Standards of Official Conduct and returned to Banking, Finance and Urban Affairs

6th STANDARDS OF OFFICIAL CONDUCT
Dates: Feb. 6, 1991-July 28, 1992
Departure: Left committee; no new assignment

7th MERCHANT MARINE AND FISHERIES
Dates: Jan. 5, 1993-Jan. 3, 1995
Departure: Committee abolished in 1995; returned to Banking and Financial Services

Cong.	Ranking	Terms in: House	Comm.	Date of Assignment
103rd	Maj-28th	6	1	Jan. 27, 1993

HOUSE SELECT AND SPECIAL COMMITTEES:

1st SELECT HUNGER (Temporary)
Dates: Jan. 21, 1987-Jan. 3, 1993
Termination: Committee not renewed in 1993

Robert Aderholt (R-Ala.)

Dates: July 22, 1965
House: Jan. 3, 1997-date
Serving in the 111th Congress

HOUSE STANDING COMMITTEES:

1st APPROPRIATIONS
Dates: Jan. 7, 1997-date
Departure: Still serving in the 111th Congress

Cong.	Ranking	Terms in: House	Comm.	Date of Assignment
105th	Maj-34th	1	1	Jan. 7, 1997
106th	Maj-30th	2	2	Jan. 6, 1999
107th	Maj-26th	3	3	Jan. 6, 2001
108th	Maj-22nd	4	4	Jan. 28, 2003
109th	Maj-21st	5	5	Jan. 6, 2005
110th	Min-15th	6	6	Jan. 4, 2007
111th	Min-10th	7	7	Jan. 9, 2009

2nd BUDGET
Dates: Jan. 22, 2009-date
Departure: Still serving in the 111th Congress

Cong.	Ranking	Terms in: House	Comm.	Date of Assignment
111th	MnR-1st	7	1	Jan. 22, 2009

John H. Adler (D-N.J.)

Dates: Aug. 23, 1959
House: Jan. 3, 2009-date
Serving in the 111th Congress

HOUSE STANDING COMMITTEES:

1st FINANCIAL SERVICES
Dates: Jan. 7, 2009-date
Departure: Still serving in the 111th Congress

Cong.	Ranking	Terms in: House	Comm.	Date of Assignment
111th	Maj-35th	1	1	Jan. 7, 2009

2nd VETERANS' AFFAIRS
Dates: Jan. 21, 2009-date
Departure: Still serving in the 111th Congress

Cong.	Ranking	Terms in: House	Comm.	Date of Assignment
111th	Maj-16th	1	1	Jan. 21, 2009

Daniel K. Akaka (D-Hai.)

Dates: Sep. 11, 1924
House: Jan. 3, 1977-May 16, 1990
Left the House: Resigned; appointed to U.S. Senate
Senate: May 16, 1990-date
Serving in the 111th Congress

S: Akaka was appointed to the 101st Congress, May 16, 1990, to fill the vacancy caused by the death of Spark M. Matsunaga (D-Hai.) and was subsequently elected. He was seated on May 16, 1990, and was assigned to committees.

HOUSE STANDING COMMITTEES:

1st AGRICULTURE
Dates: Jan. 19, 1977-Jan. 3, 1981
Departure: Moved to Appropriations

2nd MERCHANT MARINE AND FISHERIES
Dates: Jan. 19, 1977-Jan. 3, 1981
Departure: Moved to Appropriations

3rd APPROPRIATIONS
Dates: Jan. 28, 1981-May 16, 1990
Departure: Resigned the House; appointed U.S. Senator

HOUSE SELECT COMMITTEES

1st SELECT POPULATION
Dates: Oct. 14, 1977-Dec. 29, 1978
Termination: House Report 1842 (95-2) filed

2nd SELECT NARCOTICS ABUSE AND CONTROL (Temporary)
1st Dates: Mar. 16, 1978-Jan. 3, 1979
1st Departure: Left committee; no new assignment
2nd Dates: Feb. 25, 1981-May 16, 1990
2nd Departure: Resigned the House; appointed U.S. Senator

SENATE STANDING COMMITTEES:

1st ENERGY AND NATURAL RESOURCES
Dates: May 16, 1990-Jan. 21, 2009
Departure: Left committee; no new assignment

Cong.	Ranking	Years in: Senate	Comm.	Date of Assignment
103rd	Maj-6th	3	3	Jan. 7, 1993
104th	Min-6th	5	5	Jan. 4, 1995
105th	Min-4th	7	7	Jan. 9, 1997
106th	Min-2nd	9	9	Jan. 7, 1999
107th	Min-2nd	11	11	Jan. 25, 2001
+107th	Maj-2nd	12	12	June 6, 2001
108th	Min-2nd	13	13	Jan. 15, 2003
109th	Min-2nd	15	15	Jan. 6, 2005
110th	Maj-2nd	17	17	Jan. 12, 2007

2nd GOVERNMENTAL AFFAIRS renamed Oct. 9, 2004
HOMELAND SECURITY AND GOVERNMENTAL AFFAIRS
Dates: May 16, 1990-date
Departure: Still serving in the 111th Congress

Cong.	Ranking	Years in: Senate	Comm.	Date of Assignment
103rd	Maj-7th	3	3	Jan. 7, 1993
104th	Min-6th	5	5	Jan. 4, 1995
105th	Min-4th	7	7	Jan. 9, 1997
106th	Min-3rd	9	9	Jan. 7, 1999
107th	Min-3rd	11	11	Jan. 25, 2001
+107th	Maj-3rd	12	12	June 6, 2001
108th	Min-3rd	13	13	Jan. 15, 2003
109th	Min-3rd	15	15	Jan. 6, 2005
110th	Maj-3rd	17	17	Jan. 12, 2007
111th	Maj-3rd	19	19	Jan. 21, 2009

3rd VETERANS' AFFAIRS
Dates: May 16, 1990-date
Departure: Still serving in the 111th Congress

Cong.	Ranking	Years in: Senate	Comm.	Date of Assignment
103rd	Maj-5th	3	3	Jan. 21, 1993
104th	Min-3rd	5	5	Jan. 6, 1995
105th	Min-3rd	7	7	Jan. 9, 1997
106th	Min-3rd	9	9	Jan. 7, 1999
107th	Min-3rd	11	11	Jan. 25, 2001
+107th	Maj-4th	12	12	July 10, 2001
108th	Min-4th	13	13	Jan. 15, 2003
109th	Min-RM	15	15	Jan. 6, 2005
110th	Maj-Chr	17	17	Jan 12, 2007
111th	Maj-Chr	19	19	Jan. 21, 2009

4th ARMED SERVICES
Dates: Jan. 25, 2001-date
Departure: Still serving in the 111th Congress

Cong.	Ranking	Years in: Senate	Comm.	Date of Assignment
107th	Min-8th	11	1	Jan. 25, 2001
+107th	Maj-8th	12	1	June 6, 2001
108th	Min-6th	13	2	Jan. 15, 2003
109th	Min-6th	15	4	Jan. 6, 2005
110th	Maj-6th	17	6	Jan. 12, 2007
111th	Maj-6th	19	8	Jan. 21, 2009

5th BANKING, HOUSING, AND URBAN AFFAIRS
1st Dates: July 10, 2001-Jan. 14, 2003
1st Departure: Left committee; no new assignment
2nd Dates: Jan. 12, 2007-date
2nd Departure: Still serving in the 111th Congress

Cong.	Ranking	Years in: Senate	Comm.	Date of Assignment
+107th	MjA-11th	11	*1 1	July 10, 2001
110th	Maj-8th	17	*2 1	Jan. 12, 2007
111th	Maj-7th	19	*2 3	Jan. 21, 2009

SENATE SELECT AND SPECIAL COMMITTEES:

1st SELECT INDIAN AFFAIRS (Permanent), 102
INDIAN AFFAIRS (Permanent), 103-111
Dates: Feb. 5, 1991-date
Departure: Still serving in the 111th Congress

Cong.	Ranking	Years in: Senate	Comm.	Date of Assignment
103rd	Maj-6th	3	2	Jan. 5, 1993
104th	Min-5th	5	4	Jan. 9, 1995
105th	Min-4th	7	6	Jan. 9, 1997
106th	Min-4th	9	8	Jan. 7, 1999
107th	Min-4th	11	10	Jan. 25, 2001
+107th	Maj-4th	12	11	June 6, 2001
108th	Min-4th	13	12	Jan. 15, 2003
109th	Min-4th	15	14	Jan. 6, 2005
110th	Maj-4th	17	16	Jan. 12, 2007
111th	Maj-4th	19	18	Jan. 21, 2009

2nd SELECT ETHICS (Permanent)
Dates: Jan. 25, 2001-Jan. 18, 2006
Departure: Resigned committee; no new assignment

Cong.	Ranking	Years in: Senate	Comm.	Date of Assignment
107th	Min-2nd	11	1	Jan. 25, 2001
+107th	Maj-2nd	12	1	June 6, 2001
108th	Min-2nd	13	2	Jan. 15, 2003
109th	Min-2nd	15	4	Jan. 6, 2005

W. Todd Akin (R-Mo.)

Dates: July 5, 1947
House: Jan. 3, 2001-date
Serving in the 111th Congress

HOUSE STANDING COMMITTEES:

1st ARMED SERVICES
Dates: Jan. 6, 2001-date
Departure: Still serving in the 111th Congress

Cong.	Ranking	Terms in: House	Comm.	Date of Assignment
107th	Maj-32nd	1	1	Jan. 6, 2001
108th	Maj-20th	2	2	Jan. 28, 2003
109th	Maj-18th	3	3	Jan. 26, 2005
110th	Min-12th	4	4	Jan. 10, 2007
111th	Min-6th	5	5	Jan. 9, 2009

2nd SCIENCE, 107-109
SCIENCE AND TECHNOLOGY, 110-111
Dates: Jan. 6, 2001-date
Departure: Still serving in the 111th Congress

Cong.	Ranking	Terms in: House	Comm.	Date of Assignment
107th	Maj-20th	1	1	Jan. 6, 2001
108th	Maj-16th	2	2	Jan. 28, 2003
109th	Maj-13th	3	3	Jan. 26, 2005
110th	Min-10th	4	4	Jan. 10, 2007
111th	Min-9th	5	5	Jan. 9, 2009

3rd SMALL BUSINESS
Dates: Jan 6, 2001-date
Departure: Still serving in the 111th Congress

Cong.	Ranking	Terms in: House	Comm.	Date of Assignment
107th	Maj-18th	1	1	Jan. 6, 2001
108th	Maj-10th	2	2	Jan. 28, 2003
109th	Maj-6th	3	3	Jan. 26, 2005
110th	Min-4th	4	4	Jan. 10, 2007
111th	Min-3rd	5	5	Jan. 9, 2009

Lamar Alexander (R-Tenn.)

Dates: July 3, 1940
Senate: Jan. 3, 2003-date
Serving in the 111th Congress

SENATE STANDING COMMITTEES:

1st ENERGY AND NATURAL RESOURCES
Dates: Jan. 15, 2003-Jan. 12, 2007
Departure: Moved to Appropriations, Environment and Public Works, and Rules and Administration

Cong.	Ranking	Years in: Senate	Comm.	Date of Assignment
108th	Maj-6th	1	1	Jan. 15, 2003
109th	Maj-4th	3	2	Jan. 6, 2005

2nd FOREIGN RELATIONS
Dates: Jan. 15, 2003-Jan. 12, 2007

Departure: Moved to Appropriations, Environment and Public Works, and Rules and Administration

Cong.	Ranking	Years in: Senate	Comm.	Date of Assignment
108th	Maj-8th	1	1	Jan. 15, 2003
109th	Maj-7th	3	2	Jan. 6, 2005

3rd HEALTH, EDUCATION, LABOR, AND PENSIONS
Dates: Jan. 15, 2003-date
Departure: Still serving in the 111th Congress

Cong.	Ranking	Years in: Senate	Comm.	Date of Assignment
108th	Maj-4th	1	1	Jan. 15, 2003
109th	Maj-4th	3	2	Jan. 6, 2005
110th	Min-3rd	5	4	Jan. 12, 2007
111th	Min-3rd	7	7	Jan. 21, 2009

4th BUDGET
Dates: Jan. 6, 2005-Jan. 12, 2007
Departure: Moved to Appropriations, Environment and Public Works, and Rules and Administration

Cong.	Ranking	Years in: Senate	Comm.	Date of Assignment
109th	Maj-11th	3	1	Jan. 6, 2005

5th APPROPRIATIONS
Dates: Jan. 12, 2007-date
Departure: Still serving in the 111th Congress

Cong.	Ranking	Years in: Senate	Comm.	Date of Assignment
110th	Min-14th	5	1	Jan. 12, 2007
111th	Min-10th	7	3	Jan. 21, 2009

6th ENVIRONMENT AND PUBLIC WORKS
Dates: Jan. 12, 2007-date
Departure: Still serving in the 111th Congress

Cong.	Ranking	Years in: Senate	Comm.	Date of Assignment
110th	Min-7th	5	1	Jan. 12, 2007
111th	Min-8th	7	3	Jan. 21, 2009

7th RULES AND ADMINISTRATION
Dates: Jan. 12, 2007-date
Departure: Still serving in the 111th Congress

Cong.	Ranking	Years in: Senate	Comm.	Date of Assignment
110th	Min-9th	5	1	Jan. 12, 2007
111th	Min-6th	7	3	Jan. 21, 2009

SENATE SELECT AND SPECIAL COMMITTEES:

1st SPECIAL AGING (Permanent)
Dates: Jan. 6, 2005-Jan. 12, 2007
Departure: Moved to Appropriations, Environment and Public Works, and Rules and Administration

Cong.	Ranking	Years in: Senate	Comm.	Date of Assignment
109th	Maj-10th	3	1	Jan. 6, 2005

JOINT COMMITTEES:

1st JOINT ECONOMIC
Senate Dates: Jan. 15, 2003-Jan. 6, 2005
Departure: Moved to Special Aging

Cong.	Ranking	Years in: Senate	Comm.	Date of Assignment
108th	Maj-5th	1	1	Jan. 15, 2003

Rodney Alexander (R-La.)

Dates: Dec. 5, 1946
House: Jan. 3, 2003-date
Serving in the 111th Congress
Served as a Democrat: Jan. 3, 2003-Aug. 9, 2004
Served as a Republican: Aug. 9, 2004-date

HOUSE STANDING COMMITTEES:

1st ARMED SERVICES
Dates: Feb. 5, 2003-Aug. 9, 2004
Departure: Service on committee as a Minority Democrat vacated; moved to Transportation and Infrastructure as a Majority Republican.

Cong.	Ranking	Terms in: House	Comm.	Date of Assignment
108th	Min-28th	1	1	Feb. 5, 2003

2nd AGRICULTURE
1st Dates as Democrat: Feb. 5, 2003-Aug. 9, 2004
1st Departure: Service on committee as a Minority Democrat vacated; returned as a Majority Republican on Sept. 9, 2004
2nd Dates as Republican: Sep. 9, 2004-Jan. 3, 2005
Departure: Moved to Appropriations

Cong.	Ranking	Terms in: House	Comm.	Date of Assignment
108th	Min-16th	1	1	Feb. 5, 2003
108th	MjR-2nd	1	1	Sep. 9, 2004

3rd TRANSPORTATION AND INFRASTRUCTURE
Dates: Sept. 9, 2004-Jan. 3, 2005
Departure: Moved to Appropriations

Cong.	Ranking	Terms in: House	Comm.	Date of Assignment
108th	MjR-1st	1	1	Sept. 9, 2004

4th APPROPRIATIONS
Dates: Jan. 6, 2005-date
Departure: Still serving in the 111th Congress

Cong.	Ranking	Terms in: House	Comm.	Date of Assignment
109th	Maj-37th	2	1	Jan. 6, 2005
110th	Min-29th	3	2	Jan. 4, 2007
111th	Min-19th	4	3	Jan. 9, 2009

5th BUDGET
Dates: Jan. 18, 2007-Jan. 21, 2009
Departure: Resigned committee; no new assignment

Cong.	Ranking	Terms in: House	Comm.	Date of Assignment
110th	Min-16th	3	1	Jan. 18, 2007
111th	Min-11th	4	2	Jan. 9, 2009

A. Wayne Allard (R-Colo.)

Dates: Dec. 2, 1943
House: Jan. 3, 1991-Jan 3, 1997
Left the House: Elected to U.S. Senate in 1996
Senate: Jan. 3, 1997-Jan. 3, 2009
Left Senate: Left chamber; retired in 2008

HOUSE STANDING COMMITTEES:

1st AGRICULTURE
Dates: Jan. 24, 1991-Jan. 3, 1997
Departure: Left the House for the Senate

Cong.	Ranking	Terms in: House	Comm.	Date of Assignment
103rd	Min-8th	2	2	Jan. 5, 1993
104th	Maj-5th	3	3	Jan. 4, 1995

2nd INTERIOR AND INSULAR AFFAIRS, 102
NATURAL RESOURCES, 103
RESOURCES, 104
Dates: Jan. 24, 1991-Jan. 3, 1997
Departure: Left the House for the Senate

Cong.	Ranking	Terms in: House	Comm.	Date of Assignment
103rd	Min-10th	2	2	Jan. 5, 1993
104th	Maj-8th	3	3	Jan. 4, 1995

3rd SMALL BUSINESS
Dates: Jan. 24, 1991-Jan. 3, 1993
Departure: Moved to Budget

4th BUDGET
Dates: Jan. 5, 1993-Jan. 3, 1997
Departure: Left the House for the Senate

Cong.	Ranking	Terms in: House	Comm.	Date of Assignment
103rd	Min-10th	2	1	Jan. 5, 1993
104th	Maj-9th	3	2	Jan. 4, 1995

SENATE STANDING COMMITTEES:

1st BANKING, HOUSING AND URBAN AFFAIRS
Dates: Jan. 9, 1997-Jan. 3, 2009
Departure: Left the Senate; retired

Cong.	Ranking	Years in: Senate	Comm.	Date of Assignment
105th	Maj-8th	1	1	Jan. 9, 1997
106th	Maj-6th	3	2	Jan. 7, 1999
107th	Maj-4th	5	5	Jan. 25, 2001
+107th	Min-4th	5	5	June 6, 2001
108th	Maj-3rd	7	7	Jan. 15, 2003
109th	Maj-3rd	9	8	Jan. 6, 2005
110th	Min-3rd	11	11	Jan. 12, 2007

2nd ENVIRONMENT AND PUBLIC WORKS
1st Dates: Jan. 9, 1997-Jan. 7, 1999
1st Departure: Moved to Armed Services
2nd Dates: Jan. 15, 2003-Jan. 6, 2005
2nd Departure: Moved to Appropriations

Cong.	Ranking	Years in: Senate	Comm.	Date of Assignment
105th	Maj-9th	1 *1	1	Jan. 9, 1997
108th	Maj-10th	7 *2	1	Jan. 15, 2003

3rd ARMED SERVICES
Dates: Jan. 7, 1999-Jan. 6, 2005
Departure: Moved to Appropriations

Cong.	Ranking	Years in: Senate	Comm.	Date of Assignment
106th	Maj-9th	3	1	Jan. 7, 1999
107th	Maj-8th	5	3	Jan. 25, 2001
+107th	Min-8th	5	3	June 6, 2001
108th	Maj-5th	7	5	Jan. 15, 2003

4th AGRICULTURE, NUTRITION AND FORESTRY
Dates: Jan. 25, 2001-Jan. 15, 2003
Departure: Returned to Environment and Public Works

Cong.	Ranking	Years in: Senate	Comm.	Date of Assignment
107th	Maj-8th	5	1	Jan. 25, 2001
+107th	Min-8th	5	1	June 6, 2001

5th BUDGET
Dates: Jan. 25, 2001-Jan. 3, 2009
Departure: Left the Senate; retired

Cong.	Ranking	Years in: Senate	Comm.	Date of Assignment
107th	Maj-10th	5	1	Jan. 25, 2001
+107th	Min-10th	5	1	June 6, 2001
108th	Maj-5th	7	2	Jan. 15, 2003
109th	Maj-4th	9	4	Jan. 6, 2005
110th	Min-4th	11	6	Jan. 12, 2007

6th APPROPRIATIONS
Dates: Jan. 6, 2005-Jan. 3, 2009
Departure: Left the Senate; retired

Cong.	Ranking	Years in: Senate	Comm.	Date of Assignment
109th	Maj-15th	9	1	Jan. 6, 2005
110th	Min-13th	11	3	Jan. 12, 2007

7th HEALTH, EDUCATION, LABOR, AND PENSIONS
Dates: Jan. 12, 2007-Jan. 3, 2009
Departure: Left the Senate; retired

Cong.	Ranking	Years in: Senate	Comm.	Date of Assignment
110th	Min-9th	11	1	Jan. 12, 2007

SENATE SELECT AND SPECIAL COMMITTEES:

1st SELECT INTELLIGENCE (Permanent)
Dates: Jan. 9, 1997-Jan. 20, 2001
Departure: Moved to Agriculture, Nutrition, and Forestry and Budget

Cong.	Ranking	Years in: Senate	Comm.	Date of Assignment
105th	Maj-9th	1	1	Jan. 9, 1997
106th	Maj-9th	3	2	Jan. 7, 1999

JOINT COMMITTEES:

1st JOINT ORGANIZATION OF CONGRESS (Ad Hoc)
House Dates: Aug. 10, 1992-Dec. 17, 1993
Termination: House Report 103-413 filed

Cong.	Ranking	Terms in: House	Comm.	Date of Assignment
103rd	Min-6th	2	2	Jan. 5, 1993

George F. Allen (R-Va.)

Dates: Mar. 8, 1952
House: Nov. 5, 1991-Jan. 3, 1993
Left the House: Elected Governor in 1993
Senate: Jan. 3, 2001-Jan. 3, 2007
Left Senate: Defeated for re-election in 2006

H: Allen was elected to the 102nd Congress by special election, Nov. 5, 1991, to fill the vacancy caused by the resignation of D. French Slaughter (R-Va.). Allen was seated Nov. 12, 1991, and assigned to committees.

HOUSE STANDING COMMITTEES:

1st JUDICIARY
Dates: Nov. 12, 1991-Jan. 3, 1993
Departure: Left the House; elected Governor

2nd SCIENCE, SPACE AND TECHNOLOGY
Dates: Nov. 12, 1991-Jan. 3, 1993
Departure: Left the House; elected Governor

3rd SMALL BUSINESS
Dates: Nov. 12, 1991-Jan. 3, 1993
Departure: Left the House; elected Governor

SENATE STANDING COMMITTEES:

1st COMMERCE, SCIENCE AND TRANSPORTATION
Dates: Jan. 25, 2001-Jan. 3, 2007
Departure: Left the Senate; lost re-election

Cong.	Ranking	Years in: Senate	Comm.	Date of Assignment
107th	Maj-11th	1	1	Jan. 25, 2001
+107th	Min-11th	1	1	June 6, 2001
108th	Maj-11th	3	2	Jan. 15, 2003
109th	Maj-9th	5	4	Jan. 6, 2005

2nd FOREIGN RELATIONS
Dates: Jan. 25, 2001-Jan. 3, 2007
Departure: Left the Senate; lost re-election

Cong.	Ranking	Years in: Senate	Comm.	Date of Assignment
107th	Maj-8th	1	1	Jan. 25, 2001
+107th	Min-8th	1	1	June 6, 2001
108th	Maj-4th	3	2	Jan. 15, 2003
109th	Maj-4th	5	4	Jan. 6, 2005

3rd SMALL BUSINESS renamed June 29, 2001
SMALL BUSINESS AND ENTREPRENEURSHIP
Dates: Jan. 25, 2001-Jan. 3, 2007
Departure: Left the Senate; lost re-election

Cong.	Ranking	Years in: Senate	Comm.	Date of Assignment
107th	Maj-8th	1	1	Jan. 25, 2001
+107th	Min-8th	1	1	June 6, 2001
108th	Maj-8th	3	2	Jan. 15, 2003
109th	Maj-4th	5	4	Jan. 6, 2005

4th ENERGY AND NATURAL RESOURCES
Dates: Jan. 6, 2005-Jan. 3, 2007
Departure: Left the Senate; lost re-election

Cong.	Ranking	Years in: Senate	Comm.	Date of Assignment
109th	Maj-10th	5	1	Jan. 6, 2005

Thomas H. Allen (D-Me.)

Dates: April 16, 1945
House: Jan. 3, 1997-Jan. 3, 2009
Left the House: Lost U.S. Senate election in 2008

HOUSE STANDING COMMITTEES:

1st NATIONAL SECURITY, 105
ARMED SERVICES, 106-107

Dates: Jan. 7, 1997-Jan. 3, 2003
Departure: Moved to Energy and Commerce

Cong.	Ranking	Terms in: House	Comm.	Date of Assignment
105th	Min-18th	1	1	Jan. 7, 1997
106th	Min-14th	2	2	Jan. 6, 1999
107th	Min-12th	3	3	Jan. 31, 2001

2nd GOVERNMENT REFORM AND OVERSIGHT
Dates: Feb. 5, 1997-Jan. 3, 2003
Departure: Moved to Energy and Commerce

Cong.	Ranking	Terms in: House	Comm.	Date of Assignment
105th	Min-19th	1	1	Feb. 5, 1997
106th	Min-18th	2	2	Jan. 6, 1999
107th	Min-16th	3	3	Jan. 31, 2001

3rd ENERGY AND COMMERCE
Dates: Jan. 28, 2003-Jan. 3, 2009
Departure: Left the House; lost Senate election

Cong.	Ranking	Terms in: House	Comm.	Date of Assignment
108th	Min-23rd	4	1	Jan. 28, 2003
109th	Min-19th	5	2	Jan. 26, 2005
110th	Maj-18th	6	3	Jan. 4, 2007

4th BUDGET
Dates: Jan. 26, 2005-Jan. 3, 2009
Departure: Left the House; lost Senate election

Cong.	Ranking	Terms in: House	Comm.	Date of Assignment
109th	Min-12th	5	1	Jan. 26, 2005
110th	Maj-6th	6	2	Jan. 18, 2007

Jason Altmire (D-Penn.)

Dates: March 7, 1968
House: Jan. 3, 2007-date
Serving in the 111th Congress

HOUSE STANDING COMMITTEES:

1st EDUCATION AND LABOR
Dates: Jan. 10, 2007-date
Departure: Still serving in the 111th Congress

Cong.	Ranking	Terms in: House	Comm.	Date of Assignment
110th	Maj-22nd	1	1	Jan. 10, 2007
111th	Maj-19th	2	2	Jan. 21, 2009

2nd TRANSPORTATION AND INFRASTRUCTURE
Dates: Jan. 10, 2007-date
Departure: Still serving in the 111th Congress

Cong.	Ranking	Terms in: House	Comm.	Date of Assignment
110th	Maj-32nd	1	1	Jan. 10, 2007
111th	Maj-24th	2	2	Jan. 7, 2009

3rd SMALL BUSINESS
Dates: Jan. 23, 2007-date
Departure: Still serving in the 111th Congress

Cong.	Ranking	Terms in: House	Comm.	Date of Assignment
110th	Maj-13th	1	1	Jan. 23, 2007
111th	Maj-11th	2	2	Jan. 21, 2009

Michael A. Andrews (D-Tex.)

Dates: Feb. 7, 1944
House: Jan. 3, 1983-Jan. 3, 1995
Left the House: Lost U.S. Senate nomination in 1994

HOUSE STANDING COMMITTEES:

1st PUBLIC WORKS AND TRANSPORTATION
Dates: Jan. 6, 1983-July 29, 1986
Departure: Moved to Ways and Means

2nd SCIENCE AND TECHNOLOGY
Dates: Jan. 6, 1983-July 29, 1986
Departure: Moved to Ways and Means

3rd WAYS AND MEANS
Dates: July 29, 1986-Jan. 3, 1995
Departure: Left the House; lost Senate nomination

Cong.	Ranking	Terms in: House	Comm.	Date of Assignment
103rd	Maj-11th	6	5	Jan. 5, 1993

4th BUDGET
Dates: Jan. 5, 1993-Jan. 3, 1995
Departure: Left the House; lost Senate nomination

Cong.	Ranking	Terms in: House	Comm.	Date of Assignment
103rd	Maj-17th	6	1	Jan. 5, 1993

JOINT COMMITTEES:

1st JOINT ECONOMIC
House Dates: Jan. 27, 1993-Jan. 3, 1995
Departure: Left the House; lost Senate nomination

Cong.	Ranking	Terms in: House	Comm.	Date of Assignment
103rd	Maj-6th	6	1	Jan. 27, 1993

Robert E. Andrews (D-N.J.)

Dates: Aug. 4, 1957
House: Nov. 6, 1990-date
Serving in the 111th Congress

H: Andrews was elected to the 101st Congress by special election, Nov. 6, 1990, to fill the vacancy caused by the resignation of U.S. Representative James J. Florio (D-N.J.) who had been elected Governor. Andrews was not seated nor assigned to committees because the 101st Congress was not in session.

HOUSE STANDING COMMITTEES:

1st EDUCATION AND LABOR, 102-103
ECONOMIC AND EDUCATIONAL OPPORTUNITIES, 104
EDUCATION AND THE WORKFORCE, 105-109
EDUCATION AND LABOR, 110-111
Dates: Jan. 24, 1991-date
Departure: Still serving in the 111th Congress

Cong.	Ranking	Terms in: House	Comm.	Date of Assignment
103rd	Maj-13th	3	2	Jan. 5, 1993

104th	Min-10th	4	3	Jan. 4, 1995
105th	Min-8th	5	4	Jan. 7, 1997
106th	Min-8th	6	5	Jan. 6, 1999
107th	Min-6th	7	6	Jan. 31, 2001
108th	Min-5th	8	7	Jan. 28, 2003
109th	Min-5th	9	8	Jan. 26, 2005
110th	Maj-4th	10	9	Jan. 10, 2007
111th	Maj-4th	11	10	Jan. 21, 2009

2nd SMALL BUSINESS
Dates: Jan. 24, 1991-Jan. 3, 1993
Departure: Moved to Foreign Affairs

3rd FOREIGN AFFAIRS, 103
INTERNATIONAL RELATIONS, 104-106
Dates: Jan. 5, 1993-Jan. 3, 1999
Departure: Moved to Armed Services

Cong.	Ranking	Terms in: House	Comm.	Date of Assignment
103rd	Maj-15th	3	1	Jan. 5, 1993
104th	Min-12th	4	2	Jan. 4, 1995
105th	Min-9th	5	3	Jan. 7, 1997

4th ARMED SERVICES
1st Dates: Jan. 6, 1999-Feb. 12, 2003
1st Departure: Moved to Select Homeland Security
2nd Dates: Jan. 26, 2005-date
Departure: Still serving in the 111th Congress

Cong.	Ranking	Terms in: House	Comm.	Date of Assignment
106th	Min-25th	6 *1	1	Jan. 6, 1999
107th	Min-23rd	7 *1	2	Jan. 6, 2001
108th	Min-17th	8 *1	3	Jan. 28, 2003
109th	Min-15th	9 *2	1	Jan. 26, 2005
110th	Maj-14th	10 *2	2	Jan. 10, 2007
111th	Maj-13th	11 *2	3	Jan. 7, 2009

5th BUDGET
Dates: Jan. 18, 2007-date
Departure: Still serving in the 111th Congress

Cong.	Ranking	Terms in: House	Comm.	Date of Assignment
110th	Maj-16th	10	1	Jan. 18, 2007
111th	Maj-15th	11	2	Jan. 21, 2009

HOUSE SELECT AND SPECIAL COMMITTEES:

1st SELECT NARCOTICS ABUSE AND CONTROL (Temporary)
Dates: Feb. 21, 1991-Jan. 3, 1993
Termination: Committee not renewed in 1993

2nd SELECT HOMELAND SECURITY
Dates: Feb. 12, 2003-Jan. 3, 2005
Departure: Did not continue on reorganized standing committee

Cong.	Ranking	Terms in: House	Comm.	Date of Assignment
108th	Min-12th	8	1	Feb. 12, 2003

Thomas H. Andrews (D-Me.)

Dates: March 27, 1953
House: Jan. 3, 1991-Jan. 3, 1995
Left the House: Lost U.S. Senate election in 1994

HOUSE STANDING COMMITTEES:

1st ARMED SERVICES
Dates: Jan. 24, 1991-Jan. 3, 1995
Departure: Left the House; lost Senate election

Cong.	Ranking	Terms in: House	Comm.	Date of Assignment
103rd	Maj-22nd	2	2	Jan. 5, 1993

2nd SMALL BUSINESS
Dates: Jan. 24, 1991-Jan. 3, 1995
Departure: Left the House; lost Senate election

Cong.	Ranking	Terms in: House	Comm.	Date of Assignment
103rd	Maj-14th	2	2	Jan. 5, 1993

3rd MERCHANT MARINE AND FISHERIES
Dates: Jan. 21, 1993-Jan. 3, 1995
Departure: Left the House; lost Senate election

Cong.	Ranking	Terms in: House	Comm.	Date of Assignment
103rd	Maj-16th	2	1	Jan. 21, 1993

Douglas Applegate (D-Ohio)

Dates: March 27, 1928
House: Jan. 3, 1977-Jan 3, 1995
Left the House: Retired in 1994

HOUSE STANDING COMMITTEES:

1st PUBLIC WORKS AND TRANSPORTATION
Dates: Jan. 19, 1977-Jan. 3, 1995
Departure: Left the House; retired

Cong.	Ranking	Terms in: House	Comm.	Date of Assignment
103rd	Maj-4th	9	9	Jan. 5, 1993

2nd VETERANS' AFFAIRS
Dates: Jan. 19, 1977-Jan. 3, 1995
Departure: Left the House; retired

Cong.	Ranking	Terms in: House	Comm.	Date of Assignment
103rd	Maj-3rd	9	9	Jan. 5, 1993

3rd DISTRICT OF COLUMBIA
Temporary Dates: Jan. 27, 1977-Jan. 3, 1979
Departure: Temporary term expired

William R. Archer (R-Tex.)

Dates: March 22, 1928
House: Jan. 3, 1971-Jan. 3, 2001
Left the House: Retired in 2000

HOUSE STANDING COMMITTEES:

1st BANKING AND CURRENCY
Dates: Feb. 4, 1971-Jan. 3, 1973
Departure: Moved to Ways and Means

2nd WAYS AND MEANS
Dates: Jan. 24, 1973-Jan. 3, 2001
RM2: Archer succeeded John J. Duncan (R-Tenn.), who had died, as Ranking Minority Member on June 2, 1988.
Departure: Left the House; retired

Cong.	Ranking	Terms in: House	Comm.	Date of Assignment
103rd	Min-RM	12	11	Jan. 5, 1993
104th	Maj-Chr	13	12	Jan. 4, 1995
105th	Maj-Chr	14	13	Jan. 7, 1997
106th	Maj-Chr	15	14	Jan. 6, 1999

HOUSE SELECT AND SPECIAL COMMITTEES:

1st SELECT ENERGY (Ad Hoc)
Dates: Apr. 21, 1977-Dec. 29, 1978
Termination: House Report 1820 (95-2) filed

JOINT COMMITTEES:

1st JOINT TAXATION
House Dates: Feb. 19, 1985-Jan. 3, 2001
Departure: Left the House; retired

Cong.	Ranking	Terms in: House	Comm.	Date of Assignment
103rd	Min-1st	12	5	Mar. 18, 1993
104th	Maj-CVc	13	6	Jan. 10, 1995
105th	Maj-CVc	14	7	Jan. 10, 1997
106th	Maj-CVc	15	8	Jan. 19, 1999

Michael Arcuri (D-N.Y.)

Dates: June 11, 1959
House: Jan. 3, 2007-date
Serving in the 111th Congress

HOUSE STANDING COMMITTEES:

1st TRANSPORTATION AND INFRASTRUCTURE
Dates: Jan. 10, 2007-date
Departure: Still serving in the 111th Congress

Cong.	Ranking	Terms in: House	Comm.	Date of Assignment
110th	Maj-35th	1	1	Jan. 10, 2007
111th	Maj-27th	2	2	Jan. 7, 2009

2nd RULES
Dates: Jan. 12, 2007-date
Departure: Still serving in the 111th Congress

Cong.	Ranking	Terms in: House	Comm.	Date of Assignment
110th	Maj-8th	1	1	Jan. 12, 2007
111th	Maj-6th	2	2	Jan. 6, 2009

Richard K. Armey (R-Tex.)

Dates: July 7, 1940
House: Jan. 3, 1985-Jan. 3, 2003
Left the House: Retired in 2002

HOUSE STANDING COMMITTEES:

1st EDUCATION AND LABOR
1st Dates: Jan. 30, 1985-Aug. 3, 1989
1st Departure: Moved to Government Operations.
2nd Dates: Jan. 24, 1991-Jan. 3, 1995; returned to committee with seniority intact.
2nd Departure: Left committee; elected Majority Leader

Cong.	Ranking	Terms in: House	Comm.	Date of Assignment
103rd	Min-5th	5	5	Jan. 5, 1993

2nd GOVERNMENT OPERATIONS
1st Dates: Jan. 30, 1985-Jan. 3, 1987
1st Departure: Moved to Budget
2nd Dates: Aug. 3, 1989-Jan. 3, 1991
2nd Departure: Moved to Banking, Finance and Urban Affairs

3rd BUDGET
Dates: Jan. 21, 1987-June 30, 1991
Departure: Left committee; no new assignment

4th BANKING, FINANCE AND URBAN AFFAIRS
Dates: Feb. 6, 1991-Jan. 3, 1993
Departure: Left committee; no new assignment

HOUSE SELECT AND SPECIAL COMMITTEES:

1st SELECT HOMELAND SECURITY
House Dates: June 19, 2002-Jan. 3, 2003
Departure: Left the House; retired

Cong.	Ranking	Terms in: House	Comm.	Date of Assignment
107th	Maj-Chr	9	1	June 19, 2002

JOINT COMMITTEES:

1st JOINT DEFICIT REDUCTION (Temporary)
House Dates: Feb. 23, 1987-Sep. 29, 1987
Departure: Public Law 100-119 adjusted Gramm-Rudman-Hollings Act

2nd JOINT ECONOMIC
House Dates: Mar. 7, 1991-Jan. 3, 1995
Departure: Left committee; elected Majority Leader

Cong.	Ranking	Terms in: House	Comm.	Date of Assignment
103rd	Min-1st	5	2	Feb. 16, 1993

HOUSE LEADERSHIP POSTS

Dates: Jan. 3, 1995-Jan. 3, 2003
Departure: Left the House; retired

1st HOUSE MAJORITY FLOOR LEADER
Dates: Jan. 3, 1995-Jan. 3, 2003
Note: For the 104th Congress, Armey was elected without opposition as Majority Floor Leader and was unopposed for the 105th and 107th Congresses. He was the ultimate winner in a three ballot contest in the 106th Congress over Steve Largent (R-Okla.) 127-95 on the 3rd ballot on Nov. 18, 1998.
Departure: Left post; retired

Cong.	Ranking	Terms in: House	Post	Date of Selection
104th	Maj-2nd	6	1	Dec. 5, 1994
105th	Maj-2nd	7	2	Nov. 20, 1996
106th	Maj-2nd	8	3	Nov. 18, 1998
107th	Maj-2nd	9	4	Nov. 14, 2000

John D. Ashcroft (R-Mo.)

Dates: May 9, 1942
Senate: Jan. 3, 1995-Jan. 3, 2001
Left Senate: Defeated for re-election in 2000; appointed Attorney General in 2001

SENATE STANDING COMMITTEES:

1st COMMERCE, SCIENCE AND TRANSPORTATION
Dates: Jan. 4, 1995-Jan. 3, 2001
Departure: Left the Senate; lost re-election

Cong.	Ranking	Years in: Senate	Comm.	Date of Assignment
104th	Maj-10th	1	1	Jan. 4, 1995
105th	Maj-8th	3	3	Jan. 9, 1997
106th	Maj-8th	5	5	Jan. 7, 1999

2nd FOREIGN RELATIONS
Dates: Jan. 4, 1995-Jan. 3, 2001
Departure: Left the Senate; lost re-election

Cong.	Ranking	Years in: Senate	Comm.	Date of Assignment
104th	Maj-10th	1	1	Jan. 5, 1995
105th	Maj-7th	3	3	Jan. 9, 1997
106th	Maj-9th	5	5	Jan. 7, 1999

3rd LABOR AND HUMAN RESOURCES
Dates: Jan. 4, 1995-Jan. 9, 1997
Departure: Moved to Judiciary

Cong.	Ranking	Years in: Senate	Comm.	Date of Assignment
104th	Maj-7th	1	1	Jan. 4, 1995

4th JUDICIARY
Dates: Jan. 9, 1995-Jan. 3, 2001
Departure: Left the Senate; lost re-election

Cong.	Ranking	Years in: Senate	Comm.	Date of Assignment
105th	Maj-8th	3	1	Jan. 9, 1997
106th	Maj-7th	5	2	Jan. 7, 1999

Les Aspin (D-Wisc.)

Dates: July 21, 1938-May 21, 1995
House: Jan. 3, 1971-Jan. 20, 1993
Left the House: Resigned; appointed Secretary of Defense in 1993. Pending Senate confirmation as Secretary of Defense, Aspin was unassigned to committees in the 103rd Congress.

HOUSE STANDING COMMITTEES:

1st ARMED SERVICES
Dates: Feb. 4, 1971-Jan. 20, 1993
Chair: 99th-102nd, 1985-93
Departure: Resigned the House; appointed to Cabinet

Cong.	Ranking	Terms in: House	Comm.	Date of Assignment
103th	Maj-Chr	12	12	Jan. 5, 1993

2nd DISTRICT OF COLUMBIA
Dates: Jan. 24, 1973-Mar. 5, 1975
Departure: Moved to Government Operations

3rd GOVERNMENT OPERATIONS
Dates: Feb. 19, 1975-Jan. 3, 1981
Departure: Moved to Budget

4th BUDGET
Dates: Jan. 28, 1981-Jan. 3, 1985
Departure: Left committee to chair Armed Services

HOUSE SELECT AND SPECIAL COMMITTEES:

1st SELECT INTELLIGENCE (Pike)
Dates: July 17, 1975-Feb. 11, 1976
Termination: House Report 833 (94-2) filed

2nd PERMANENT SELECT INTELLIGENCE
Dates: July 27, 1977-Jan. 3, 1981
Departure: Moved to Budget.

3rd SELECT COMMITTEE TO INVESTIGATE COVERT
ARMS TRANSACTIONS WITH IRAN
Dates: Jan. 7, 1987-Dec. 15, 1987
Termination: House Report 433 (100-1) filed

Steve Austria (R-Ohio)

Dates: Oct. 12, 1958
House: Jan. 3, 2009-date
Serving in the 111th Congress

HOUSE STANDING COMMITTEES:

1st BUDGET
Dates: Jan. 9, 2009-date
Departure: Still serving in the 111th Congress

Cong.	Ranking	Terms in: House	Comm.	Date of Assignment
111th	Min-15th	1	1	Jan. 9, 2009

2nd HOMELAND SECURITY
Dates: Jan. 9, 2009-date
Departure: Still serving in the 111th Congress

Cong.	Ranking	Terms in: House	Comm.	Date of Assignment
111th	Min-13th	1	1	Jan. 9, 2009

B

Joe Baca (D-Cal.)

Dates: Jan. 23, 1947
House: Nov. 16, 1999-date
Serving in the 111th Congress

H: Baca was elected to the 106th Congress by special election, Nov. 16, 1999, to fill the vacancy caused by the death of U.S. Representative George E. Brown (D-Cal.). Baca was seated Nov. 18, 1999, and assigned to committees.

HOUSE STANDING COMMITTEES:

1st AGRICULTURE
Dates: Nov. 18, 1999-date
Departure: Still serving in the 111th Congress

Cong.	Ranking	Terms in: House	Comm.	Date of Assignment
106th	MnR-1st	1	1	Nov. 18, 1999
107th	Min-19th	2	2	Jan. 31, 2001
108th	Min-11th	3	3	Jan. 28, 2003
109th	Min-6th	4	4	Jan. 26, 2005
110th	Maj-6th	5	5	Jan. 12, 2007
111th	Maj-5th	6	6	Jan. 21, 2009

2nd SCIENCE
Dates: Nov. 18, 1999-Jan. 3, 2003
Departure: Moved to Financial Services

Cong.	Ranking	Terms in: House	Comm.	Date of Assignment
106th	MnR-4th	1	1	Nov. 18, 1999
107th	Min-21st	2	2	Jan. 31, 2001

3rd FINANCIAL SERVICES
Dates: Jan. 28, 2003-date
Departure: Still serving in the 111th Congress

Cong.	Ranking	Terms in: House	Comm.	Date of Assignment
108th	Min-27th	3	1	Jan. 28, 2003
109th	Min-23rd	4	2	Jan. 26, 2005
110th	Maj-17th	5	3	Jan. 12, 2007
111th	Maj-16th	6	4	Jan. 7, 2009

4th RESOURCES, 108
NATURAL RESOURCES, 110-111
1st Dates: Mar. 5, 2003-Jan. 3, 2005
1st Departure: Left committee; no new assignment
2nd Dates: Jan. 18, 2007-date
2nd Departure: Still serving in the 111th Congress

Cong.	Ranking	Terms in: House	Comm.	Date of Assignment
108th	MnR-1st	3 *1	1	Mar. 5, 2003
110th	Maj-24th	5 *2	1	Jan. 18, 2007
111th	Maj-23rd	6 *2	2	Jan. 21, 2009

James Bacchus (D-Fla.)

Dates: June 21, 1949
House: Jan. 3, 1991-Jan. 3, 1995
Left the House: Retired; later appointed Judge of World Trade Organization

HOUSE STANDING COMMITTEES:

1st BANKING, FINANCE AND URBAN AFFAIRS
Dates: Jan. 24, 1991-Jan. 3, 1995
Departure: Left the House; retired

Cong.	Ranking	Terms in: House	Comm.	Date of Assignment
103rd	Maj-14th	2	2	Jan. 5, 1993

2nd SCIENCE, SPACE AND TECHNOLOGY
Dates: Jan. 24, 1991-Jan. 3, 1995
Departure: Left the House; retired

Cong.	Ranking	Terms in: House	Comm.	Date of Assignment
103rd	Maj-15th	2	2	Jan. 5, 1993

HOUSE SELECT AND SPECIAL COMMITTEES:

1st SELECT CHILDREN, YOUTH AND FAMILIES (Temporary)
Dates: Feb. 21, 1991-Jan. 3, 1993
Termination: Committee not renewed in 1993

Michele Bachmann (R-Minn.)

Dates: April 6, 1956
House: Jan. 3, 2007-date
Serving in the 111th Congress

HOUSE STANDING COMMITTEES:

1st FINANCIAL SERVICES
Dates: Jan. 16, 2007-date
Departure: Still serving in the 111th Congress

Cong.	Ranking	Terms in: House	Comm.	Date of Assignment
110th	Min-32nd	1	1	Jan. 16, 2007
111th	Min-21st	2	2	Jan. 9, 2009

Spencer T. Bachus (R-Ala.)

Dates: Dec. 28, 1947
House: Jan. 3, 1993-date
Serving in the 111th Congress

HOUSE STANDING COMMITTEES:

1st BANKING, FINANCE AND URBAN AFFAIRS, 103
BANKING AND FINANCIAL SERVICES, 104-106
FINANCIAL SERVICES, 107-111
Dates: Jan. 5, 1993-date
Departure: Still serving in the 111th Congress

Cong.	Ranking	Terms in: House	Comm.	Date of Assignment
103rd	Min-17th	1	1	Jan. 5, 1993
104th	Maj-8th	2	2	Jan. 4, 1995
105th	Maj-7th	3	3	Jan. 7, 1997
106th	Maj-7th	4	4	Jan. 6, 1999
107th	Maj-6th	5	5	Jan. 6, 2001
108th	Maj-5th	6	6	Jan. 28, 2003
109th	Maj-5th	7	7	Jan. 26, 2005
110th	Min-RM	8	8	Jan. 4, 2007
111th	Min-RM	9	9	Jan. 6, 2009

2nd VETERANS' AFFAIRS
Dates: Jan. 5, 1993-Mar. 10, 1999
Departure: Resigned committee; had moved to Judiciary

Cong.	Ranking	Terms in: House	Comm.	Date of Assignment
103rd	Min-11th	1	1	Jan. 5, 1993
104th	Maj-9th	2	2	Jan. 4, 1995
105th	Maj-8th	3	3	Jan. 21, 1997
106th	Maj-8th	4	4	Jan. 6, 1999

3rd TRANSPORTATION AND INFRASTRUCTURE
Dates: Jan. 4, 1995-Jan. 3, 2007
Departure: Left committee; became Ranking Member on Financial Services

Cong.	Ranking	Terms in: House	Comm.	Date of Assignment
104th	Maj-24th	2	1	Jan. 4, 1995
105th	Maj-18th	3	2	Jan. 7, 1997
106th	Maj-16th	4	3	Jan. 6, 1999
107th	Maj-12th	5	4	Jan. 6, 2001
108th	Maj-11th	6	5	Jan. 28, 2003
109th	Maj-10th	7	6	Jan. 26, 2005

4th JUDICIARY
Dates: Feb. 2, 1999-Jan. 3, 2007
Departure: Left committee; became Ranking Member on Financial Services

Cong.	Ranking	Terms in: House	Comm.	Date of Assignment
106th	Maj-21st	4	1	Feb. 2, 1999
107th	Maj-14th	5	2	Jan. 6, 2001
108th	Maj-10th	6	3	Jan. 28, 2003
109th	Maj-11th	7	4	Jan. 26, 2005

H. Scott (Scotty) Baesler (D-Ky.)

Dates: July 9, 1941
House: Jan. 3, 1993-Jan. 3.1999
Left the House: Lost U.S. Senate election in 1998

HOUSE STANDING COMMITTEES:

1st AGRICULTURE
Dates: Jan. 5, 1993-Jan. 3, 1999
Departure: Left the House; lost Senate election

Cong.	Ranking	Terms in: House	Comm.	Date of Assignment
103rd	Maj-25th	1	1	Jan. 5, 1993
104th	Min-16th	2	2	Jan. 4, 1995
105th	Min-11th	3	3	Jan. 7, 1997

2nd EDUCATION AND LABOR
Dates: Jan. 21, 1993-Jan. 3, 1995
Departure: Left committee; no new assignment

Cong.	Ranking	Terms in: House	Comm.	Date of Assignment
103rd	Maj-27th	1	1	Jan. 21, 1993

3rd VETERANS' AFFAIRS
Dates: Jan. 5, 1993-Jan. 3, 1997
Departure: Moved to Budget

Cong.	Ranking	Terms in: House	Comm.	Date of Assignment
103rd	Maj-17th	1	1	Jan. 5, 1993
104th	Min-10th	2	2	Jan. 4, 1995

4th BUDGET
Dates: Jan. 7, 1997-Jan. 3, 1999
Departure: Left the House; lost Senate election

Cong.	Ranking	Terms in: House	Comm.	Date of Assignment
105th	Min-13th	3	1	Jan. 7, 1997

Brian Baird (D-Wash.)

Dates: March 7, 1956
House: Jan. 3, 1999-date
Serving in the 111th Congress

HOUSE STANDING COMMITTEES:

1st TRANSPORTATION AND INFRASTRUCTURE
Dates: Jan. 6, 1999-date
Departure: Still serving in the 111th Congress

Cong.	Ranking	Terms in: House	Comm.	Date of Assignment
106th	Min-33rd	1	1	Jan. 6, 1999
107th	Min-29th	2	2	Jan. 31, 2001
108th	Min-21st	3	3	Jan. 28, 2003
109th	Min-19th	4	4	Jan. 26, 2005
110th	Maj-16th	5	5	Jan. 10, 2007
111th	Maj-15th	6	6	Jan. 7, 2009

2nd SMALL BUSINESS
Dates: Jan. 19, 1999-Jan. 3, 2003
Departure: Moved to Budget

Cong.	Ranking	Terms in: House	Comm.	Date of Assignment
106th	Min-16th	1	1	Jan. 19, 1999
107th	Min-15th	2	2	Jan. 31, 2001

3rd SCIENCE, 106-109
SCIENCE AND TECHNOLOGY, 110
1st Dates: June 9, 1999-Feb. 5, 2003
1st Departure: Leave of absence; moved to Budget; returned on Feb. 13, 2003; seniority not credited
2nd Dates: Feb. 13, 2003-date
2nd Departure: Still serving in the 111th Congress

Cong.	Ranking	Terms in: House	Comm.	Date of Assignment
106th	MnR-1st	1 *1	1	June 9, 1999
107th	Min-18th	2 *1	2	Jan. 31, 2001
108th	Min-13th	3 *1	3	Jan. 28, 2003
108th	Min-17th	3 *2	1	Feb. 13, 2003
109th	Min-16th	4 *2	2	Feb. 2, 2005
110th	Maj-7th	5 *2	3	Jan. 18, 2007
111th	Maj-6th	6 *2	4	Jan. 21, 2009

4th BUDGET
Dates: Jan. 28, 2003-Jan. 3, 2009
Departure: Left committee; no new assignment

Cong.	Ranking	Terms in: House	Comm.	Date of Assignment
108th	Min-14th	3	1	Jan. 28, 2003
109th	Min-8th	4	2	Jan. 26, 2005
110th	Maj-20th	5	3	Jan. 18, 2007

Richard H. Baker (R-La.)

Dates: May 22, 1948
House: Jan. 3, 1987-Feb. 2, 2008
Left the House: Resigned in 2008; retired

HOUSE STANDING COMMITTEES:

1st INTERIOR AND INSULAR AFFAIRS, 100, 102
NATURAL RESOURCES, 103
1st Dates: Jan. 21, 1987-Jan. 3, 1989
1st Departure: Moved to Banking, Finance and Urban Affairs
2nd Dates: July 11, 1991-Jan. 3, 1995
2nd Departure: Moved to Agriculture

Cong.	Ranking	Terms in: House	Comm.	Date of Assignment
103rd	Min-11th	4	*2 2	Jan. 5, 1993

2nd SMALL BUSINESS
Dates: Jan. 21, 1987-Jan. 3, 1995
Departure: Moved to Agriculture

Cong.	Ranking	Terms in: House	Comm.	Date of Assignment
103rd	Min-3rd	4	4	Jan. 5, 1993

3rd BANKING, FINANCE AND URBAN AFFAIRS, 101-103
BANKING AND FINANCIAL SERVICES, 104-106
FINANCIAL SERVICES, 107-110
Dates: Jan. 20, 1989-Feb. 2, 2008
Departure: Resigned the House; retired

Cong.	Ranking	Terms in: House	Comm.	Date of Assignment
103rd	Min-8th	4	3	Jan. 5, 1993
104th	Maj-6th	5	4	Jan. 4, 1995
105th	Maj-5th	6	5	Jan. 7, 1997
106th	Maj-5th	7	6	Jan. 6, 1999
107th	Maj-5th	8	7	Jan. 6, 2001
108th	Maj-4th	9	8	Jan. 28, 2003
109th	Maj-3rd	10	9	Jan. 26, 2005
110th	Min-2nd	11	10	Jan. 10, 2007

4th AGRICULTURE
Dates: Jan. 4, 1995-Jan. 3, 1997
Departure: Left committee; no new assignment

Cong.	Ranking	Terms in: House	Comm.	Date of Assignment
104th	Maj-17th	5	1	Jan. 4, 1995

5th TRANSPORTATION AND INFRASTRUCTURE
Dates: June 6, 1996-Feb. 2, 2008
Departure: Resigned the House; retired

Cong.	Ranking	Terms in: House	Comm.	Date of Assignment
104th	MjA-35th	5	1	June 26, 1996
105th	Maj-22nd	6	2	Jan. 7, 1997
106th	Maj-20th	7	3	Jan. 6, 1999
107th	Maj-15th	8	4	Jan. 6, 2001
108th	Maj-14th	9	5	Jan. 28, 2003
109th	Maj-13th	10	6	Jan. 26, 2005
110th	Min-9th	11	7	Jan. 10, 2007

6th VETERANS' AFFAIRS
Dates: Mar. 11, 1999-Feb. 2, 2008
Departure: Resigned the House; retired

Cong.	Ranking	Terms in: House	Comm.	Date of Assignment
106th	MjR-1st	7	1	Mar. 11, 1999

Cong.	Ranking	Terms in: House	Comm.	Date of Assignment
107th	Maj-14th	8	2	Jan. 6, 2001
108th	Maj-9th	9	3	Jan. 28, 2003
109th	Maj-6th	10	4	Jan. 26, 2005
110th	Min-5th	11	5	Jan. 10, 2007

Cong.	Ranking	Terms in: House	Comm.	Date of Assignment
105th	MnR-1st	2	1	Mar. 27, 1998
106th	Min-30th	3	2	Jan. 6, 1999
107th	Min-27th	4	3	Jan. 31, 2001

William P. Baker (R-Cal.)

Dates: June 14, 1940
House: Jan. 3, 1993-Jan. 3, 1997
Left the House: Defeated for re-election in 1996

HOUSE STANDING COMMITTEES:

1st PUBLIC WORKS AND TRANSPORTATION, 103
TRANSPORTATION AND INFRASTRUCTURE, 104
Dates: Jan. 5, 1993-Jan. 3, 1997
Departure: Left the House; lost re-election

Cong.	Ranking	Terms in: House	Comm.	Date of Assignment
103rd	Min-14th	1	1	Jan. 5, 1993
104th	Maj-15th	2	2	Jan. 4, 1995

2nd SCIENCE, SPACE AND TECHNOLOGY, 103
SCIENCE, 104
Dates: Jan. 5, 1993-Jan. 3, 1997
Departure: Left the House; lost re-election

Cong.	Ranking	Terms in: House	Comm.	Date of Assignment
103rd	Min-21st	1	1	Jan. 5, 1993
104th	Maj-11th	2	2	Jan. 4, 1995

John E. Baldacci (D-Me.)

Dates: Jan. 30, 1955
House: Jan. 3, 1995-Jan. 3, 2003
Left the House: Elected Governor in 2002

HOUSE STANDING COMMITTEES:

1st AGRICULTURE
Dates: Jan. 4, 1995-Jan. 3, 2003
Departure: Left the House; elected Governor

Cong.	Ranking	Terms in: House	Comm.	Date of Assignment
104th	Min-22nd	1	1	Jan. 4, 1995
105th	Min-15th	2	2	Jan. 7, 1997
106th	Min-13th	3	3	Jan. 6, 1999
107th	Min-10th	4	4	Jan. 31, 2001

2nd SMALL BUSINESS
Dates: June 13, 1995-Mar. 27, 1998
Departure: Resigned committee; moved to Transportation and Infrastructure

Cong.	Ranking	Terms in: House	Comm.	Date of Assignment
104th	MnA-20th	1	1	June 13, 1995
105th	Min-8th	2	2	Feb. 5, 1997

3rd TRANSPORTATION AND INFRASTRUCTURE
Dates: Mar. 27, 1998-Jan. 3, 2003
Departure: Left the House; elected Governor

Tammy Baldwin (D-Wisc.)

Dates: Feb. 11, 1962
House: Jan. 3, 1999-date
Serving in the 111th Congress

HOUSE STANDING COMMITTEES:

1st BUDGET
Dates: Jan. 6, 1999-Jan. 3, 2005
Departure: Moved to Energy and Commerce

Cong.	Ranking	Terms in: House	Comm.	Date of Assignment
106th	Min-19th	1	1	Jan. 6, 1999
107th	Min-15th	2	2	Jan. 31, 2001
108th	Min-4th	3	3	Jan. 28, 2003

2nd JUDICIARY
1st Dates: Jan. 6, 1999-Jan. 3, 2005
1st Departure: Moved to Energy and Commerce
2nd Dates: Apr. 17, 2007-date
2nd Departure: Still serving in the 111th Congress

Cong.	Ranking	Terms in: House	Comm.	Date of Assignment
106th	Min-15th	1 *1	1	Jan. 6, 1999
107th	Min-15th	2 *1	2	Jan. 31, 2001
108th	Min-13th	3 *1	3	Jan. 28, 2003
110th	MjA-23rd	5 *2	1	Apr. 17, 2007
111th	Maj-18th	6 *2	2	Jan. 21, 2009

3rd ENERGY AND COMMERCE
Dates: Jan. 26, 2005-date
Departure: Still serving in the 111th Congress

Cong.	Ranking	Terms in: House	Comm.	Date of Assignment
109th	Min-25th	4	1	Jan. 26, 2005
110th	Maj-23rd	5	2	Jan. 4, 2007
111th	Maj-19th	6	3	Jan. 7, 2009

Frank W. Ballance (D-N.C.)

Dates: Feb. 15, 1942
House: Jan. 3, 2003-June 11, 2004
Left the House: Resigned and retired in 2004

HOUSE STANDING COMMITTEES:

1st AGRICULTURE
Dates: Feb. 5, 2003-June 11, 2004
Departure: Resigned the House; retired

Cong.	Ranking	Terms in: House	Comm.	Date of Assignment
108th	Min-17th	1	1	Feb. 5, 2003

2nd SMALL BUSINESS
Dates: Feb. 5, 2003-June 11, 2004
Departure: Resigned the House; retired

Cong.	Ranking	Terms in: House	Comm.	Date of Assignment
108th	Min-10th	1	1	Feb. 5, 2003

Cass Ballenger (R-N.C.)

Dates: Dec. 6, 1926
House: Nov. 4, 1986-Jan. 3, 2005
Left the House: Retired in 2004

H: Ballenger was elected to the 99th Congress by special election, Nov. 4, 1986, to fill the vacancy caused by the resignation of U.S. Representative James T. Broyhill (R-N.C.). Ballenger was not seated nor assigned to committees because the 99th Congress was not in session.

HOUSE STANDING COMMITTEES:

1st EDUCATION AND LABOR, 100-103
ECONOMIC AND EDUCATIONAL OPPORTUNITIES, 104
EDUCATION AND THE WORKFORCE, 105-108
Dates: Jan. 21, 1987-Jan. 3, 2005
Departure: Left the House; retired

Cong.	Ranking	Terms in: House	Comm.	Date of Assignment
103rd	Min-8th	5	4	Jan. 5, 1993
104th	Maj-6th	6	5	Jan. 4, 1995
105th	Maj-5th	7	6	Jan. 7, 1997
106th	Maj-4th	8	7	Jan. 6, 1999
107th	Maj-4th	9	8	Jan. 6, 2001
108th	Maj-3rd	10	9	Jan. 28, 2003

2nd PUBLIC WORKS AND TRANSPORTATION
Dates: Jan. 21, 1987-Jan. 3, 1993
Departure: Moved to Foreign Affairs and District of Columbia

3rd DISTRICT OF COLUMBIA
Dates: Feb. 4, 1993-Jan. 3, 1995
Departure: Committee abolished in 1995; no new assignment

Cong.	Ranking	Terms in: House	Comm.	Date of Assignment
103rd	Min-4th	5	1	Feb. 4, 1993

4th FOREIGN AFFAIRS, 103
INTERNATIONAL RELATIONS, 104-108
Dates: Jan. 5, 1993-Jan. 3, 2005
Departure: Left the House; retired

Cong.	Ranking	Terms in: House	Comm.	Date of Assignment
103rd	Min-13th	5	1	Jan. 5, 1993
104th	Maj-12th	6	2	Jan. 4, 1995
105th	Maj-10th	7	3	Jan. 7, 1997
106th	Maj-10th	8	4	Jan. 6, 1999
107th	Maj-9th	9	5	Jan. 6, 2001
108th	Maj-8th	10	6	Jan. 28, 2003

Peter W. Barca (D-Wisc.)

Dates: Aug. 7, 1955
House: May 14, 1993-Jan.3, 1995
Left the House: Defeated for re-election in 1994

H: Barca was elected to the 103rd Congress by special election May 14, 1993, to fill the vacancy caused by the resignation of U.S. Representative Les Aspin (D-Wisc.), who had been appointed Secretary of Defense. Barca was seated June 8, 1993, and assigned to committees.

HOUSE STANDING COMMITTEES:

1st PUBLIC WORKS AND TRANSPORTATION
Dates: June 23, 1993-Jan. 3, 1995
Departure: Left the House; lost re-election

Cong.	Ranking	Terms in: House	Comm.	Date of Assignment
103rd	MjA-40th	1	1	June 23, 1993

2nd SPACE, SCIENCE AND TECHNOLOGY
Dates: June 23, 1993-Jan. 3, 1995
Departure: Left the House; lost re-election

Cong.	Ranking	Terms in: House	Comm.	Date of Assignment
103rd	Maj-34th	1	1	June 23, 1993

James A. Barcia (D-Mich.)

Dates: Feb. 25, 1952
House: Jan 3.1993-Jan. 3, 2003
Left the House: Elected State Senator in 2002

HOUSE STANDING COMMITTEES:

1st PUBLIC WORKS AND TRANSPORTATION, 103
TRANSPORTATION AND INFRASTRUCTURE, 104-107
Dates: Jan. 5, 1993-Jan. 3, 2003
Departure: Left the House; elected state senator

Cong.	Ranking	Terms in: House	Comm.	Date of Assignment
103rd	Maj-35th	1	1	Jan. 5, 1993
104th	Min-24th	2	2	Jan. 4, 1995
105th	Min-18th	3	3	Jan. 7, 1997
106th	Min-15th	4	4	Jan. 6, 1999
107th	Min-12th	5	5	Jan. 31, 2001

2nd SPACE, SCIENCE AND TECHNOLOGY, 103
SCIENCE, 104-107
Dates: Jan. 5, 1993-Jan. 3, 2003
Departure: Left the House; elected state senator

Cong.	Ranking	Terms in: House	Comm.	Date of Assignment
103rd	Maj-19th	1	1	Jan. 5, 1993
104th	Min-9th	2	2	Jan. 4, 1995
105th	Min-7th	3	3	Feb. 13, 1997
106th	Min-7th	4	4	Jan. 6, 1999
107th	Min-4th	5	5	Jan. 31, 2001

Dean Barkley (Independence-Minn.)

Dates: Aug. 31, 1950
Senate: Nov. 4, 2002-Jan. 3, 2003
Left Senate: Left chamber; retired in 2002

S: Barkley was appointed to the 107th Congress, Nov. 4, 2002, to fill the vacancy caused by the death of U.S. Senator Paul D. Wellstone (DFL-Minn.).

Barkley was not a candidate for the vacancy. He was seated Nov. 12, 2002, but was not assigned to committees.

Thomas J. Barlow (D-Ky.)

Dates: Aug. 7, 1940
House: Jan. 3, 1993-Jan. 3, 1995
Left the House: Defeated for re-election in 1994

HOUSE STANDING COMMITTEES:

1st AGRICULTURE
Dates: Jan. 5, 1993-Jan. 3, 1995
Departure: Left the House; lost re-election

Cong.	Ranking	Terms in: House	Comm.	Date of Assignment
103rd	Maj-21st	1	1	Jan. 5, 1993

2nd MERCHANT MARINE AND FISHERIES
Dates: Jan. 5, 1993-Jan. 3, 1995
Departure: Left the House; lost re-election

Cong.	Ranking	Terms in: House	Comm.	Date of Assignment
103rd	Maj-23rd	1	1	Jan. 5, 1993

3rd NATURAL RESOURCES
Dates: Jan. 21, 1993-Jan. 3, 1995
Departure: Left the House; lost re-election

Cong.	Ranking	Terms in: House	Comm.	Date of Assignment
103rd	Maj-27th	1	1	Jan. 21, 1993

Bob Barr (R-Ga.)

Dates: Nov. 5, 1948
House: Jan. 3, 1995-Jan. 3, 2003
Left the House: Defeated for re-nomination in 2002

HOUSE STANDING COMMITTEES:

1st BANKING AND FINANCIAL SERVICES, 104-106
FINANCIAL SERVICES, 107
Dates: Jan. 4, 1995-Jan. 3, 2003
Departure: Left the House; lost re-nomination

Cong.	Ranking	Terms in: House	Comm.	Date of Assignment
104th	Maj-19th	1	1	Jan. 4, 1995
105th	Maj-16th	2	2	Jan. 7, 1997
106th	Maj-15th	3	3	Jan. 6, 1999
107th	Maj-12th	4	4	Jan. 6, 2001

2nd JUDICIARY
Dates: Jan. 4, 1995-Jan. 3, 2003
Departure: Left the House; lost re-nomination

Cong.	Ranking	Terms in: House	Comm.	Date of Assignment
104th	Maj-20th	1	1	Jan. 4, 1995
105th	Maj-16th	2	2	Jan. 7, 1997
106th	Maj-13th	3	3	Jan. 6, 1999
107th	Maj-9th	4	4	Jan. 6, 2001

3rd VETERANS' AFFAIRS
Dates: Jan. 4, 1995-Jan. 3, 1997
Departure: Moved to Government Reform and Oversight

Cong.	Ranking	Terms in: House	Comm.	Date of Assignment
104th	Maj-14th	1	1	Jan. 4, 1995

4th GOVERNMENT REFORM AND OVERSIGHT, 105
GOVERNMENT REFORM, 106-107
Dates: Jan. 21, 1997-Jan. 3, 2003
Departure: Left the House; lost re-nomination

Cong.	Ranking	Terms in: House	Comm.	Date of Assignment
105th	MjR-1st	2	1	Jan. 21, 1997
106th	Maj-16th	3	2	Jan. 6, 1999
107th	Maj-13th	4	3	Jan. 6, 2001

John A. Barrasso (R-Wyo.)

Dates: July 21, 1952
Senate: June 25, 2007-date
Serving in the 111th Congress

S: Barrasso was appointed to the 110th Congress, June 25, 2007, to fill the vacancy caused by the death of U.S. Senator Craig Thomas (R-Wyo.). Barrasso was seated June 25, 2007, and assigned to committees.

SENATE STANDING COMMITTEES:

1st ENERGY AND NATURAL RESOURCES
Dates: July 10, 2007-date
Departure: Still serving in the 111th Congress

Cong.	Ranking	Years in: Senate	Comm.	Date of Assignment
110th	MnR-1st	1	1	July 10, 2007
111th	Min-3rd	2	2	Jan. 21, 2009

2nd ENVIRONMENT AND PUBLIC WORKS
Dates: July 10, 2007-date
Departure: Still serving in the 111th Congress

Cong.	Ranking	Years in: Senate	Comm.	Date of Assignment
110th	MnR-1st	1	1	July 10, 2007
111th	Min-4th	2	2	Jan. 21, 2009

3rd FOREIGN AFFAIRS
Dates: Jan. 21, 2009-date
Departure: Still serving in the 111th Congress

Cong.	Ranking	Years in: Senate	Comm.	Date of Assignment
111th	Min-6th	2	1	Jan. 21, 2009

SENATE SELECT AND SPECIAL COMMITTEES:

1st INDIAN AFFAIRS (Permanent)
Dates: July 10, 2007-date
Departure: Still serving in the 111th Congress

Cong.	Ranking	Years in: Senate	Comm.	Date of Assignment
110th	MnR-1st	1	1	July 10, 2007
111th	Min-RM	2	2	Jan. 21, 2009

J. Gresham Barrett (R-S.C.)

Dates: Feb. 14, 1961
House: Jan. 3, 2003-date
Serving in the 111th Congress

HOUSE STANDING COMMITTEES:

1st BUDGET
Dates: Jan. 28, 2003-Jan. 3, 2009
Departure: Left committee; no new assignment

Cong.	Ranking	Terms in: House	Comm.	Date of Assignment
108th	Maj-20th	1	1	Jan. 28, 2003
109th	Maj-10th	2	2	Jan. 26, 2005
110th	Min-4th	3	3	Jan. 18, 2007

2nd FINANCIAL SERVICES
Dates: Jan. 28, 2003-date
Departure: Still serving in the 111th Congress

Cong.	Ranking	Terms in: House	Comm.	Date of Assignment
108th	Maj-35th	1	1	Jan. 28, 2003
109th	Maj-28th	2	2	Jan. 26, 2005
110th	Min-21st	3	3	Jan. 10, 2007
111th	Min-14th	4	4	Jan. 9, 2009

3rd INTERNATIONAL RELATIONS, 109
FOREIGN AFFAIRS, 110-111
Dates: Feb. 2, 2005-date
Departure: Still serving in the 111th Congress

Cong.	Ranking	Terms in: House	Comm.	Date of Assignment
109th	MjR-1st	2	1	Feb. 2, 2005
110th	Min-17th	3	2	Jan. 10, 2007
111th	Min-13th	4	3	Jan. 9, 2009

4th ENERGY AND COMMERCE
Dates: Oct. 26, 2005-Feb. 7, 2006
Departure: Resigned committee to open seat for Blunt

Cong.	Ranking	Terms in: House	Comm.	Date of Assignment
110th	MnR-1st	2	1	Oct. 26, 2005

5th STANDARDS OF OFFICIAL CONDUCT
Dates: Feb. 12, 2007-Sept. 24, 2009
Departure: Resigned committee; no new assignment

Cong.	Ranking	Terms in: House	Comm.	Date of Assignment
110th	Min-3rd	3	1	Feb. 12, 2007
111th	Min-2nd	4	2	Jan. 9, 2009

Thomas M. Barrett (D-Wisc.)

Dates: Dec. 8, 1953
House: Jan. 3, 1993-Jan. 3, 2003
Left the House: Lost nomination for Governor in 2002

HOUSE STANDING COMMITTEES:

1st BANKING, FINANCE AND URBAN AFFAIRS, 103
BANKING AND FINANCIAL SERVICES, 104-105
Dates: Jan. 5, 1993-Jan. 3, 1999
Departure: Moved to Commerce

Cong.	Ranking	Terms in: House	Comm.	Date of Assignment
103rd	Maj-21st	1	1	Jan. 5, 1993
104th	Min-15th	2	2	Jan. 4, 1995
105th	Min-13th	3	3	Jan. 7, 1997

2nd GOVERNMENT OPERATIONS, 103
GOVERNMENT REFORM AND OVERSIGHT, 104-105
Dates: Jan. 5, 1993-Jan. 3, 1999
Departure: Moved to Commerce

Cong.	Ranking	Terms in: House	Comm.	Date of Assignment
103rd	Maj-17th	1	1	Jan. 5, 1993
104th	Min-14th	2	2	Jan. 9, 1995
105th	Min-10th	3	3	Jan. 7, 1997

3rd NATURAL RESOURCES
Dates: Jan. 21, 1993-Jan. 3, 1995
Departure: Left committee; no new assignment

Cong.	Ranking	Terms in: House	Comm.	Date of Assignment
103rd	Maj-28th	1	1	Jan. 21, 1993

4th JUDICIARY
Dates: Sep. 11, 1998-Jan. 3, 1999
Departure: Moved to Commerce

Cong.	Ranking	Terms in: House	Comm.	Date of Assignment
105th	MnA-16th	3	1	Sep. 11, 1998

5th COMMERCE, 106
ENERGY AND COMMERCE, 107
Dates: Jan. 6, 1999-Jan. 3, 2003
Departure: Left the House; lost nomination for governor

Cong.	Ranking	Terms in: House	Comm.	Date of Assignment
106th	Min-22nd	4	1	Jan. 6, 1999
107th	Min-21st	5	2	Jan. 31, 2001

William E. Barrett (R-Neb.)

Dates: Feb. 9, 1929
House: Jan. 3, 1991-Jan. 3, 2001
Left the House: Retired in 2000

HOUSE STANDING COMMITTEES:

1st AGRICULTURE
Dates: Jan. 24, 1991-Jan. 3, 2001
Departure: Left the House; retired

Cong.	Ranking	Terms in: House	Comm.	Date of Assignment
103rd	Min-9th	2	2	Jan. 5, 1993
104th	Maj-6th	3	3	Jan. 4, 1995
105th	Maj-3rd	4	4	Jan. 7, 1997
106th	Maj-2nd	5	5	Jan. 6, 1999

2nd EDUCATION AND LABOR, 102-103
ECONOMIC AND EDUCATIONAL OPPORTUNITIES, 104
EDUCATION AND THE WORKFORCE, 105-106
Dates: Jan. 24, 1991-Jan. 3, 2001
Departure: Left the House; retired

Cong.	Ranking	Terms in: House	Comm.	Date of Assignment
103rd	Min-10th	2	2	Jan. 5, 1993
104th	Maj-7th	3	3	Jan. 4, 1995
105th	Maj-6th	4	4	Jan. 7, 1997
106th	Maj-5th	5	5	Jan. 6, 1999

3rd HOUSE ADMINISTRATION
Dates: Feb. 6, 1991-Jan. 3, 1995
Departure: Left committee; no new assignment

Cong.	Ranking	Terms in: House	Comm.	Date of Assignment
103rd	Min-5th	2	2	Jan. 5, 1993

HOUSE SELECT AND SPECIAL COMMITTEES:

1st SELECT CHILDREN, YOUTH AND FAMILIES (Temporary)
Dates: Feb. 21, 1991-Jan. 3, 1993
Termination: Committee not renewed in 1993

JOINT COMMITTEES:

1st JOINT LIBRARY
House Dates: Feb. 21, 1991-Jan. 3, 1995
Departure: Left committee; no new assignment

Cong.	Ranking	Terms in: House	Comm.	Date of Assignment
103rd	Min-1st	2	2	May 1, 1993 Provisional

John Barrow (D-Ga.)

Dates: Oct. 31, 1955
House: Jan. 3, 2005-date
Serving in the 111th Congress

HOUSE STANDING COMMITTEES:

1st AGRICULTURE
Dates: Jan. 26, 2005-Jan. 3, 2009
Departure: Left committee; no new assignment

Cong.	Ranking	Terms in: House	Comm.	Date of Assignment
109th	Min-17th	1	1	Jan. 26, 2005
110th	Maj-22nd	2	2	Jan. 12, 2007

2nd EDUCATION AND THE WORKPLACE
Dates: Jan. 26, 2005-Feb.15, 2006
Departure: Resigned committee; moved to Transportation and Infrastructure

Cong.	Ranking	Terms in: House	Comm.	Date of Assignment
109th	Min-22nd	1	1	Jan. 26, 2005

3rd SMALL BUSINESS
Dates: Feb. 2, 2005-Jan.3, 2007
Departure: Moved to Energy and Commerce

Cong.	Ranking	Terms in: House	Comm.	Date of Assignment
109th	Min-13th	1	1	Feb. 2, 2005

4th TRANSPORTATION AND INFRASTRUCTURE
Dates: Feb. 15, 2006-Jan. 3, 2007
Departure: Moved to Energy and Commerce

Cong.	Ranking	Terms in: House	Comm.	Date of Assignment
109th	MnR-1st	1	1	Feb. 15, 2006

5th ENERGY AND COMMERCE
Dates: Jan. 4, 2007-date
Departure: Still serving in the 111th Congress

Cong.	Ranking	Terms in: House	Comm.	Date of Assignment
110th	Maj-30th	2	1	Jan. 4, 2007
111th	Maj-25th	3	2	Jan. 7, 2009

Roscoe G. Bartlett (R-Md.)

Dates: June 3, 1926
House: Jan. 3, 1993-date
Serving in the 111th Congress

HOUSE STANDING COMMITTEES:

1st ARMED SERVICES, 103
NATIONAL SECURITY, 104-105
ARMED SERVICES, 106-111
Dates: Jan. 5, 1993-date
Departure: Still serving in the 111th Congress

Cong.	Ranking	Terms in: House	Comm.	Date of Assignment
103rd	Min-22nd	1	1	Jan. 5, 1993
104th	Maj-18th	2	2	Jan. 4, 1995
105th	Maj-15th	3	3	Jan. 7, 1997
106th	Maj-15th	4	4	Jan. 6, 1999
107th	Maj-10th	5	5	Jan. 6, 2001
108th	Maj-7th	6	6	Jan. 28, 2003
109th	Maj-7th	7	7	Jan. 26, 2005
110th	Min-5th	8	8	Jan. 10, 2007
111th	Min-2nd	9	9	Jan. 9, 2009

2nd SCIENCE, SPACE, AND TECHNOLOGY, 103
SCIENCE, 104-109
SCIENCE AND TECHNOLOGY, 110-111
Dates: Jan. 5, 1993-date
Departure: Still serving in the 111th Congress

Cong.	Ranking	Terms in: House	Comm.	Date of Assignment
103rd	Min-22nd	1	1	Jan. 5, 1993
104th	Maj-12th	2	2	Jan. 4, 1995
105th	Maj-10th	3	3	Jan. 21, 1997
106th	Maj-10th	4	4	Jan. 6, 1999
107th	Maj-10th	5	5	Jan. 6, 2001
108th	Maj-9th	6	6	Jan. 28, 2003
109th	Maj-7th	7	7	Jan. 26, 2005
110th	Min-6th	8	8	Jan. 10, 2007
111th	Min-5th	9	9	Jan. 9, 2009

3rd SMALL BUSINESS
Dates: Jan. 4, 1995-date
Departure: Still serving in the 111th Congress

Cong.	Ranking	Terms in: House	Comm.	Date of Assignment
104th	Maj-7th	2	1	Jan. 4, 1995
105th	Maj-5th	3	2	Jan. 21, 1997
106th	Maj-5th	4	3	Jan. 6, 1999
107th	Maj-4th	5	4	Jan. 6, 2001

108th	Maj-3rd	6	5	Jan. 28, 2003
109th	Maj-2nd	7	6	Jan. 26, 2005
110th	Min-2nd	8	7	Jan. 10, 2007
111th	Min-2nd	9	8	Jan. 9, 2009

Joe L. Barton (R-Tex.)

Dates: Sept. 15, 1949
House: Jan. 3, 1985-date
Serving in the 111th Congress

HOUSE STANDING COMMITTEES:

1st INTERIOR AND INSULAR AFFAIRS
Dates: Jan. 30, 1985-Jan. 3, 1987
Departure: Moved to Energy and Commerce

2nd SCIENCE AND TECHNOLOGY, 99
1st Dates: Jan. 30, 1985-Jan. 3, 1987
1st Departure: Moved to Energy and Commerce
SCIENCE, SPACE AND TECHNOLOGY, 102-103
SCIENCE, 104-108
2nd Dates: Jan. 24, 1991-Feb. 25, 2004
2nd Departure: Resigned committee; became Chair of Energy and Commerce

		Terms in:		Date of
Cong.	Ranking	House	Comm.	Assignment
103rd	Min-10th	5 *2	2	Jan. 5, 1993
104th	Maj-9th	6 *2	3	Jan. 4, 1995
105th	Maj-8th	7 *2	4	Jan. 21, 1997
106th	Maj-7th	8 *2	5	Jan. 6, 1999
107th	Maj-7th	9 *2	6	Jan. 6, 2001
108th	Maj-6th	10 *2	7	Jan. 28, 2003

3rd ENERGY AND COMMERCE, 100-103
COMMERCE, 104-106
ENERGY AND COMMERCE, 107-111
Dates: Jan. 21, 1987-date
Ch2: Replaced W. J. (Billy) Tauzin (R-La.) as Chair on Feb. 26, 2004
Departure: Still serving in the 111th Congress

		Terms in:		Date of
Cong.	Ranking	House	Comm.	Assignment
103rd	Min-7th	5	4	Jan. 5, 1993
104th	Maj-7th	6	5	Jan. 4, 1995
105th	Maj-6th	7	6	Jan. 7, 1997
106th	Maj-5th	8	7	Jan. 6, 1999
107th	Maj-3rd	9	8	Jan. 6, 2001
108th	Maj-3rd	10	9	Jan. 28, 2003
=108th	Maj-Ch2	10	9	Feb. 26, 2004
109th	Maj-Chr	11	10	Jan. 6, 2005
110th	Min-RM	12	11	Jan. 4, 2007
111th	Min-RM	13	12	Jan. 6, 2009

HOUSE SELECT AND SPECIAL COMMITTEES:

1st SELECT HOMELAND SECURITY
Dates: Apr. 27, 2004-Jan. 3, 2005
Departure: Did not continue on reorganized standing committee

		Terms in:		Date of
Cong.	Ranking	House	Comm.	Assignment
108th	MjR-1st	10	1	Apr. 27, 2004

Charles F. Bass (R-N.H.)

Dates: Jan. 8, 1952
House: Jan. 3, 1995-Jan. 3, 2007
Left the House: Defeated for re-election in 2006

HOUSE STANDING COMMITTEES:

1st BUDGET
Dates: Jan. 4, 1995-Jan. 3, 2003
Departure: Left committee; no new assignment

		Terms in:		Date of
Cong.	Ranking	House	Comm.	Assignment
104th	Maj-24th	1	1	Jan. 4, 1995
105th	Maj-16th	2	2	Jan. 7, 1997
106th	Maj-11th	3	3	Jan. 6, 1999
107th	Maj-4th	4	4	Jan. 6, 2001

2nd GOVERNMENT REFORM AND OVERSIGHT
Dates: Jan. 4, 1995-Jan. 3, 1997
Departure: Moved to Transportation and Infrastructure and Permanent Select Intelligence

		Terms in:		Date of
Cong.	Ranking	House	Comm.	Assignment
104th	Maj-24th	1	1	Jan. 4, 1995

3rd TRANSPORTATION AND INFRASTRUCTURE
Dates: Jan. 7, 1997-Feb. 7, 2001
Departure: Resigned committee; moved to Energy and Commerce

		Terms in:		Date of
Cong.	Ranking	House	Comm.	Assignment
105th	Maj-24th	2	1	Jan. 7, 1997
106th	Maj-21st	3	2	Jan. 6, 1999
107th	Maj-16th	4	3	Jan. 6, 2001

4th ENERGY AND COMMERCE
Dates: Feb. 8, 2001-Jan. 6, 2007
Departure: Left the House; lost re-election

		Terms in:		Date of
Cong.	Ranking	House	Comm.	Assignment
107th	Maj-27th	4	1	Feb. 8, 2001
108th	Maj-22nd	5	2	Jan. 28, 2003
109th	Maj-19th	6	3	Jan. 6, 2005

HOUSE SELECT AND SPECIAL COMMITTEES:

1st PERMANENT SELECT INTELLIGENCE
Dates: Feb. 10, 1997-Feb. 7, 2001
Departure: Resigned committee; moved to Energy and Commerce

		Terms in:		Date of
Cong.	Ranking	House	Comm.	Assignment
105th	Maj-8th	2	1	Feb. 10, 1997
106th	Maj-6th	3	2	Jan. 19, 1999
107th	Maj-5th	4	3	Jan. 30, 2001

Herbert H. Bateman (R-Va.)

Dates: Aug. 7, 1928-Sept. 11, 2000
House: Jan. 3, 1983-Sept. 11, 2000
Left the House: Died in office

HOUSE STANDING COMMITTEES:

1st MERCHANT MARINE AND FISHERIES
Dates: Jan. 6, 1983-Jan. 3, 1995
Departure: Committee abolished in 1995; moved to Transportation and Infrastructure

Cong.	Ranking	Terms in: House	Comm.	Date of Assignment
103rd	Min-3rd	6	6	Jan. 5, 1993

2nd SCIENCE AND TECHNOLOGY
Dates: Jan. 6, 1983-Jan. 3, 1985
Departure: Moved to Armed Services

3rd ARMED SERVICES, 99-103
NATIONAL SECURITY, 104-105
Dates: Jan. 30, 1985-Sept. 11, 2000
Departure: Died in office

Cong.	Ranking	Terms in: House	Comm.	Date of Assignment
103rd	Min-5th	6	5	Jan. 5, 1993
104th	Maj-5th	7	6	Jan. 4, 1995
105th	Maj-5th	8	7	Jan. 7, 1997
106th	Maj-5th	9	8	Jan. 6, 1999

4th TRANSPORTATION AND INFRASTRUCTURE
Dates: Jan. 7, 1995-Sept. 11, 2000
Departure: Died in office

Cong.	Ranking	Terms in: House	Comm.	Date of Assignment
104th	Maj-6th	7	1	Jan. 4, 1995
105th	Maj-5th	8	2	Jan. 7, 1997
106th	Maj-5th	9	3	Jan. 6, 1999

Max S. Baucus (D-Mont.)

Dates: Dec. 11, 1941
House: Jan. 3, 1975-Dec. 14, 1978
Left the House: Elected to the U.S. Senate in 1978
Senate: Dec. 15, 1978-date
Serving in the 111th Congress

S: Baucus was appointed to the 95th Congress, Dec. 15, 1978, to fill the vacancy caused by the death of U.S. Senator Lee Metcalf (D-Mont.). Metcalf had been initially replaced by Paul G. Hatfield (D-Mont.), an appointee, who was defeated for nomination to the 96th Congress by Baucus. Baucus was not seated nor assigned to committees because the 95th Congress was not in session.

HOUSE STANDING COMMITTEES:

1st APPROPRIATIONS
Dates: Jan. 20, 1975-Dec. 14, 1978
Departure: Resigned the House; elected to the Senate

SENATE STANDING COMMITTEES:

1st JUDICIARY
Dates: Jan. 23, 1979-Feb. 21, 1985
Departure: Left committee, no new assignment

2nd FINANCE
Dates: Jan. 23, 1979-date

Ch2: Replaced Charles E. Grassley (R-Iowa) as Chair on June 6, 2001, following Senate party control shift
Departure: Still serving in the 111th Congress

Cong.	Ranking	Years in: Senate	Comm.	Date of Assignment
103rd	Maj-3rd	15	14	Jan. 7, 1993
104th	Min-2nd	17	16	Jan. 4, 1995
105th	Min-2nd	19	18	Jan. 9, 1997
106th	Min-2nd	21	20	Jan. 7, 1999
=107th	Maj-ChT	23	22	Jan. 3, 2001
107th	Min-RM1	23	23	Jan. 25, 2001
+107th	Maj-Ch2	23	23	June 6, 2001
108th	Min-RM	25	24	Jan. 15, 2003
109th	Min-RM	27	26	Jan. 6, 2005
110th	Maj-Chr	29	28	Jan. 12, 2007
111th	Maj-Chr	31	30	Jan. 21, 2009

3rd ENVIRONMENT AND PUBLIC WORKS
Dates: Jan 5, 1981-date
Ch2: Replaced Daniel Patrick Moynihan (D-N.Y.) on Jan. 21, 1993; Moynihan became Chair of Finance
Departure: Still serving in the 111th Congress

Cong.	Ranking	Years in: Senate	Comm.	Date of Assignment
103rd	Maj-3rd	15	13	Jan. 7, 1993
=103rd	Maj-Ch2	15	13	Jan. 21, 1993
104th	Min-RM	17	14	Jan. 5, 1995
105th	Min-RM	19	17	Jan. 9, 1997
106th	Min-RM	21	19	Jan. 7, 1999
107th	Min-2nd	23	21	Jan. 25, 2001
+107th	Maj-3rd	23	21	July 10, 2001
108th	Min-2nd	25	23	Jan. 15, 2003
109th	Min-2nd	27	25	Jan. 6, 2005
110th	Maj-2nd	29	27	Jan. 12, 2007
111th	Maj-2nd	31	29	Jan. 21, 2009

4th SMALL BUSINESS
Dates: Mar. 25, 1981-Jan 21, 1993
Departure: Moved to chair Environment and Public Works

5th AGRICULTURE, NUTRITION AND FORESTRY
Dates: Feb. 2, 1989-date
Departure: Still serving in the 111th Congress

Cong.	Ranking	Years in: Senate	Comm.	Date of Assignment
103rd	Maj-8th	15	4	Jan. 7, 1993
104th	Min-7th	17	6	Jan. 4, 1995
105th	Min-5th	19	8	Jan. 9, 1997
106th	Min-5th	21	10	Jan. 7, 1999
107th	Min-5th	23	12	Jan. 25, 2001
+107th	Maj-5th	23	13	June 6, 2001
108th	Min-5th	25	14	Jan. 15, 2003
109th	Min-4th	27	16	Jan. 6, 2005
110th	Maj-4th	29	18	Jan. 12, 2007
111th	Maj-4th	31	20	Jan. 21, 2009

SENATE SELECT AND SPECIAL COMMITTEES:

1st SELECT SMALL BUSINESS
Dates: Jan. 23, 1979-Mar. 25, 1981
Departure: Continued on reorganized standing committee

2nd FOREIGN GOVERNMENT REPRESENTATION
Dates: July 25, 1980-Oct. 2, 1980
Departure: Senate Report 1015 (96-2) filed

3rd SELECT INTELLIGENCE (Permanent)
Dates: Jan. 27, 1993-Jan. 20, 2001
Departure: Left committee; no new assignment

Cong.	Ranking	Years in: Senate	Comm.	Date of Assignment
103rd	Maj-8th	15	1	Jan. 27, 1993
104th	Min-6th	17	2	Jan. 6, 1995
105th	Min-6th	19	4	Jan. 9, 1997
106th	Min-5th	21	6	Jan. 7, 1999

JOINT COMMITTEES:

1st JOINT TAXATION
Senate Dates: Feb. 28, 1991-date
VC2: Named as Vice Chair on June 6, 2001, replacing Charles E. Grassley (R-Iowa) as Senate party control shifted
Departure: Still serving in the 111th Congress

Cong.	Ranking	Years in: Senate	Comm.	Date of Assignment
103rd	Maj-2nd	15	2	Continued
104th	Min-2nd	17	4	Feb. 2, 1995
105th	Min-2nd	19	6	Continued
106th	Min-2nd	21	8	Continued
107th	Min-1st	23	10	Feb. 28, 2001
+107th	Maj-VC2	23	11	June 6, 2001
108th	Min-1st	25	12	Feb. 24, 2003
109th	Min-1st	27	14	Jan. 25, 2005
110th	Maj-VcC	29	16	Jan. 18, 2007
111th	Maj-VcC	31	18	Feb. 25, 2009

B. Evans Bayh (D-Ind.)

Dates: Dec. 26, 1955
Senate: Jan. 3, 1999-date
Serving in the 111th Congress

SENATE STANDING COMMITTEES:

1st BANKING, HOUSING AND URBAN AFFAIRS
Dates: Jan. 7, 1999-date
Departure: Still serving in the 111th Congress

Cong.	Ranking	Years in: Senate	Comm.	Date of Assignment
106th	Min-8th	1	1	Jan. 7, 1999
107th	Min-6th	3	3	Jan. 25, 2001
+107th	Maj-6th	3	3	June 6, 2001
108th	Min-6th	5	5	Jan. 15, 2003
109th	Min-6th	7	6	Jan. 6, 2005
110th	Maj-5th	9	9	Jan. 12, 2007
111th	Maj-5th	11	11	Jan. 21, 2009

2nd ENERGY AND NATURAL RESOURCES
1st Dates: Jan. 7, 1999-Jan. 6, 2005
1st Departure: Left committee; no new assignment
2nd Dates: Jan. 21, 2009-date
2nd Departure: Still serving in the 111th Congress

Cong.	Ranking	Years in: Senate	Comm.	Date of Assignment
106th	Min-8th	1 *1	1	Jan. 7, 1999
107th	Min-8th	3 *1	3	Jan. 25, 2001
+107th	Maj-8th	3 *1	3	June 6, 2001
108th	Min-8th	5 *1	5	Jan. 15, 2003
111th	Maj-10th	11 *2	1	Jan. 21, 2009

3rd SMALL BUSINESS AND ENTREPRENEURSHIP
Dates: Jan. 13, 2003-date
Departure: Still serving in the 111th Congress

4th ARMED SERVICES
Dates: Jan. 15, 2003-date
Departure: Still serving in the 111th Congress

Cong.	Ranking	Years in: Senate	Comm.	Date of Assignment
108th	Min-8th	5	1	Jan. 15, 2003
109th	Min-7th	7	2	Jan. 6, 2005
110th	Maj-7th	9	4	Jan. 12, 2007
111th	Maj-7th	11	7	Jan. 21, 2009

Cong.	Ranking	Years in: Senate	Comm.	Date of Assignment
108th	Min-10th	5	1	Jan. 15, 2003
109th	Min-10th	7	2	Jan. 6, 2005
110th	Maj-9th	9	4	Jan. 12, 2007
111th	Maj-9th	11	7	Jan. 21, 2009

SENATE SELECT AND SPECIAL COMMITTEES:

1st SPECIAL AGING (Permanent)
Dates: Jan. 7, 1999-date
Departure: Still serving in the 111th Congress

Cong.	Ranking	Years in: Senate	Comm.	Date of Assignment
106th	Min-7th	1	1	Jan. 7, 1999
107th	Min-6th	3	3	Jan. 25, 2001
+107th	Maj-7th	3	3	July 10, 2001
108th	Min-8th	5	5	Jan. 15, 2003
109th	Min-6th	7	6	Jan. 6, 2005
110th	Maj-4th	9	9	Jan. 12, 2007
111th	Maj-4th	11	11	Jan. 21, 2009

2nd SELECT INTELLIGENCE (Permanent)
Dates: Jan. 25, 2001-date
Departure: Still serving in the 111th Congress

Cong.	Ranking	Years in: Senate	Comm.	Date of Assignment
107th	Min-7th	3	1	Jan. 25, 2001
+107th	Maj-7th	3	1	June 6, 2001
108th	Min-6th	5	2	Jan. 15, 2003
109th	Min-5th	7	4	Jan. 6, 2005
110th	Maj-4th	9	6	Jan. 12, 2007
111th	Maj-4th	11	8	Jan. 21, 2009

Melissa L. Bean (D-Ill.)

Dates: Jan. 22, 1962
House: Jan. 3, 2005-date
Serving in the 111th Congress

HOUSE STANDING COMMITTEES:

1st FINANCIAL SERVICES
Dates: Jan. 26, 2005-date
Departure: Serving in the 111th Congress

Cong.	Ranking	Terms in: House	Comm.	Date of Assignment
109th	Min-31st	1	1	Jan. 26, 2005
110th	Maj-23rd	2	2	Jan. 12, 2007
111th	Maj-22nd	3	3	Jan. 7, 2009

2nd SMALL BUSINESS
Dates: Feb. 2, 2005-date
Departure: Serving in the 111th Congress

Cong.	Ranking	Terms in: House	Terms in: Comm.	Date of Assignment
109th	Min-14th	1	1	Feb. 2, 2005
110th	Maj-9th	2	2	Jan. 23, 2007
111th	Maj-9th	3	3	Jan. 21, 2009

Bob Beauprez (R-Colo.)

Dates: Sept. 22, 1948
House: Jan. 3, 2003-Jan. 3, 2007
Left the House: Lost election for Governor in 2006

HOUSE STANDING COMMITTEES:

1st SMALL BUSINESS
Dates: Jan. 28, 2003-Jan. 3, 2005
Departure: Moved to Ways and Means

Cong.	Ranking	Terms in: House	Terms in: Comm.	Date of Assignment
108th	Maj-17th	1	1	Jan. 28, 2003

2nd TRANSPORTATION AND INFRASTRUCTURE
Dates: Jan. 28, 2003-Jan. 3, 2005
Departure: Moved to Ways and Means

Cong.	Ranking	Terms in: House	Terms in: Comm.	Date of Assignment
108th	Maj-35th	1	1	Jan. 28, 2003

3rd VETERANS' AFFAIRS
Dates: Jan. 28, 2003-Jan. 3, 2005
Departure: Moved to Ways and Means

Cong.	Ranking	Terms in: House	Terms in: Comm.	Date of Assignment
108th	Maj-15th	1	1	Jan. 28, 2003

4th WAYS AND MEANS
Dates: Jan. 6, 2005-Jan. 3, 2007
Departure: Left the House; lost election for Governor

Cong.	Ranking	Terms in: House	Terms in: Comm.	Date of Assignment
109th	Maj-23rd	2	1	Jan. 6, 2005

Xavier Becerra (D-Cal.)

Dates: Jan. 26, 1958
House: Jan. 3, 1993-date
Serving in the 111th Congress

HOUSE STANDING COMMITTEES:

1st EDUCATION AND LABOR, 103
ECONOMIC AND EDUCATIONAL OPPORTUNITIES, 104
Dates: Jan. 5, 1993-Jan. 3, 1997
Departure: Moved to Ways and Means

Cong.	Ranking	Terms in: House	Terms in: Comm.	Date of Assignment
103rd	Maj-17th	1	1	Jan. 5, 1993
104th	Min-14th	2	2	Jan. 4, 1995

2nd SCIENCE, SPACE AND TECHNOLOGY
Dates: Jan. 5, 1993-Jan. 3, 1995
Departure: Left committee; no new assignment

Cong.	Ranking	Terms in: House	Terms in: Comm.	Date of Assignment
103rd	Maj-33rd	1	1	Jan. 5, 1993

3rd JUDICIARY
Dates: Jan. 21, 1993-Jan. 3, 1997
Departure: Moved to Ways and Means

Cong.	Ranking	Terms in: House	Terms in: Comm.	Date of Assignment
103rd	Maj-21st	1	1	Jan. 21, 1993
104th	Min-12th	2	2	Jan. 4, 1995

4th SMALL BUSINESS
Dates: Sep. 17, 1996-Jan. 3, 1997
Departure: Moved to Ways and Means

Cong.	Ranking	Terms in: House	Terms in: Comm.	Date of Assignment
104th	MnR-5th	2	1	Sep. 17, 1996

5th WAYS AND MEANS
Dates: Jan. 7, 1997-date
Departure: Still serving in the 111th Congress

Cong.	Ranking	Terms in: House	Terms in: Comm.	Date of Assignment
105th	Min-15th	3	1	Jan. 7, 1997
106th	Min-14th	4	2	Jan. 6, 1999
107th	Min-14th	5	3	Jan. 31, 2001
108th	Min-13th	6	4	Jan. 28, 2003
109th	Min-11th	7	5	Jan. 26, 2005
110th	Maj-9th	8	6	Jan. 4, 2007
111th	Maj-8th	9	7	Jan. 7, 2009

6th BUDGET
Dates: Jan. 18, 2007-date
Departure: Still serving in the 111th Congress

Cong.	Ranking	Terms in: House	Terms in: Comm.	Date of Assignment
110th	Maj-9th	8	1	Jan. 18, 2007
111th	Maj-4th	9	2	Jan. 21, 2009

Mark Begich (D-Alas.)

Dates: March 30, 1962
Senate: Jan. 3, 2009-date
Serving in the 111th Congress

SENATE STANDING COMMITTEES:

1st ARMED SERVICES
Dates: Jan. 21, 2009-date
Departure: Still serving in the 111th Congress

Cong.	Ranking	Years in: Senate	Years in: Comm.	Date of Assignment
111th	Maj-14th	1	1	Jan. 21, 2009

2nd COMMERCE, SCIENCE AND TRANSPORTATION
Dates: Jan. 21, 2009-date
Departure: Still serving in the 111th Congress

Cong.	Ranking	Years in: Senate	Years in: Comm.	Date of Assignment
111th	Maj-14th	1	1	Jan. 21, 2009

3rd VETERANS' AFFAIRS
Dates: Jan. 21, 2009-date
Departure: Still serving in the 111th Congress

Cong.	Ranking	Years in: Senate	Comm.	Date of Assignment
111th	Maj-8th	1	1	Jan. 21, 2009

Anthony C. Beilenson (D-Cal.)

Dates: Oct. 26, 1932
House: Jan. 3, 1977-date
Left the House: Retired in 1996

HOUSE STANDING COMMITTEES:

1st INTERNATIONAL RELATIONS
Dates: Jan. 19, 1977-Jan. 3, 1979
Departure: Moved to Rules

2nd SCIENCE AND TECHNOLOGY
Dates: Jan. 19, 1977-Jan. 3, 1979
Departure: Moved to Rules

3rd JUDICIARY
Temporary Dates: Jan. 27, 1977-Jan. 3, 1979
Departure: Temporary term expired; moved to Rules

4th RULES
Dates: Jan. 24, 1979-Jan. 3, 1997
Departure: Left the House; retired

Cong.	Ranking	Terms in: House	Comm.	Date of Assignment
103rd	Maj-3rd	9	8	Jan. 5, 1993
104th	Min-2nd	10	9	Jan. 4, 1995

5th BUDGET
Dates: Jan. 19, 1989-Jan. 5, 1995
Departure: Left committee; no new assignment

Cong.	Ranking	Terms in: House	Comm.	Date of Assignment
103rd	Maj-4th	9	3	Jan. 5, 1993

HOUSE SELECT AND SPECIAL COMMITTEES:

1st SELECT POPULATION
Dates: Oct. 14, 1977-Dec. 29, 1978
Termination: House Report 1842 (95-2) filed

2nd PERMANENT SELECT INTELLIGENCE
Dates: Jan. 30, 1984-Jan. 3, 1991
Departure: Left committee; no new assignment

Chris Bell (D-Tex.)

Dates: Nov. 23, 1959
House: Jan. 3, 2003-Jan. 3, 2005
Left the House: Defeated for re-nomination in 2004

HOUSE STANDING COMMITTEES:

1st INTERNATIONAL RELATIONS
Dates: Feb. 5, 2003-Mar. 26, 2004
Departure: Resigned committee; no new assignment

Cong.	Ranking	Terms in: House	Comm.	Date of Assignment
108th	Min-23rd	1	1	Feb. 5, 2003

2nd SCIENCE
Dates: Feb. 5, 2003-Jan. 28, 2004
Departure: Resigned committee; moved to Financial Services

Cong.	Ranking	Terms in: House	Comm.	Date of Assignment
108th	Min-16th	1	1	Feb. 5, 2003

3rd GOVERNMENT REFORM
Dates: Feb. 13, 2003-Jan. 28, 2004
Departure: Resigned committee; moved to Financial Services

Cong.	Ranking	Terms in: House	Comm.	Date of Assignment
108th	MnR-1st	1	1	Feb. 13, 2003

4th FINANCIAL SERVICES
Dates: Jan. 28, 2004-Jan 3, 2005
Departure: Left the House; lost re-nomination

Cong.	Ranking	Terms in: House	Comm.	Date of Assignment
108th	MnR-2nd	1	1	Jan. 28, 2004

Michael F. Bennet (D-Colo.)

Dates: Nov. 28, 1964
Senate: Jan. 21, 2009-date
Serving in the 111th Congress

S: Bennet was appointed to the 111th Congress, Jan. 21, 2009, to fill the vacancy caused by the resignation of U.S. Senator Kenneth L. Salazar (D-Colo.) who had been appointed Secretary of the Interior. Bennet was seated Jan. 22, 2009, and was assigned to committees

SENATE STANDING COMMITTEES:

1st AGRICULTURE, NUTRITION AND FORESTRY
Dates: Jan. 27, 2009-date
Departure: Still serving in the 111th Congress

Cong.	Ranking	Years in: Senate	Comm.	Date of Assignment
111th	Maj-11th	1	1	Jan. 27, 2009

2nd BANKING, HOUSING, AND URBAN AFFAIRS
Dates: Jan. 27, 2009-date
Departure: Still serving in the 111th Congress

Cong.	Ranking	Years in: Senate	Comm.	Date of Assignment
111th	Maj-13th	1	1	Jan. 27, 2009

3rd HOMELAND SECURITY AND GOVERNMENTAL AFFAIRS
Dates: Jan. 27, 2009-Sep. 29, 2009
Departure: Left committee; moved to Health, Education, Labor and Pensions

Cong.	Ranking	Years in: Senate	Comm.	Date of Assignment
111th	Maj-10th	1	1	Jan. 27, 2009

4th HEALTH, EDUCATION, LABOR, AND PENSIONS
Dates: Sep. 29, 2009-date
Departure: Still serving in the 111th Congress

Cong.	Ranking	Years in: Senate	Comm.	Date of Assignment
111th	MjR-2nd	1	1	Sep. 29, 2009

SENATE SELECT AND SPECIAL COMMITTEES:

1st SPECIAL AGING (Permanent)
Dates: Jan. 27, 2009-date
Departure: Still serving in the 111th Congress

Cong.	Ranking	Years in: Senate	Comm.	Date of Assignment
111th	Maj-10th	1	1	Jan. 27, 2009

Robert F. Bennett (R-Utah)

Dates: Sept. 18, 1933
Senate: Jan. 3, 1993-date
Serving in the 111th Congress

SENATE STANDING COMMITTEES:

1st BANKING, HOUSING AND URBAN AFFAIRS
Dates: Jan. 7, 1993-date
Departure: Still serving in the 111th Congress

Cong.	Ranking	Years in: Senate	Comm.	Date of Assignment
103rd	Min-6th	1	1	Jan. 7, 1993
104th	Maj-7th	3	2	Jan. 4, 1995
105th	Maj-6th	5	5	Jan. 9, 1997
106th	Maj-4th	7	7	Jan. 7, 1999
107th	Maj-3rd	9	9	Jan. 25, 2001
+107th	Min-3rd	9	9	June 6, 2001
108th	Maj-2nd	11	11	Jan. 15, 2003
109th	Maj-2nd	13	12	Jan. 6, 2005
110th	Min-2nd	15	15	Jan. 12, 2007
111th	Min-2nd	17	17	Jan. 21, 2009

2nd ENERGY AND NATURAL RESOURCES
Dates: Jan. 7, 1993-Jan. 4, 1995
Departure: Moved to Appropriations

Cong.	Ranking	Years in: Senate	Comm.	Date of Assignment
103rd	Min-7th	1	1	Jan. 7, 1993

3rd GOVERNMENTAL AFFAIRS renamed Oct. 9, 2004
HOMELAND SECURITY AND GOVERNMENTAL AFFAIRS
1st Dates: Sep. 30, 1993-Jan. 4, 1995
1st Departure: Moved to Appropriations
2nd Dates: May 21, 1997-Mar. 4, 1998
2nd Departure: Temporary assignment ended
3rd Dates: Jan. 25, 2001-Jan. 12, 2007
3rd Departure: Moved to Joint Committees on Library and Printing

4th Dates: July 21, 2009-date
4th Departure: Still serving in the 111th Congress

Cong.	Ranking	Years in: Senate	Comm.	Date of Assignment
103rd	Min-6th	1 *1	1	Sep. 30, 1993
105th	Maj-Tmp	5 *2	1	May 21, 1997
107th	Maj-8th	9 *3	1	Jan. 25, 2001
+107th	Min-8th	9 *3	1	June 6, 2001
108th	Maj-6th	11 *3	3	Jan. 15, 2003
109th	Maj-7th	13 *3	5	Jan. 6, 2005
111th	Min-7th	17 *4	1	July 21, 2009

4th SMALL BUSINESS renamed June 29, 2001
SMALL BUSINESS AND ENTREPRENEURSHIP

Dates: Jan. 21, 1993-Jan. 6, 2005
Departure: Moved to Rules and Administration

Cong.	Ranking	Years in: Senate	Comm.	Date of Assignment
103rd	Min-8th	1	1	Jan. 21, 1993
104th	Maj-7th	3	2	Jan. 6, 1995
105th	Maj-5th	5	4	Jan. 9, 1997
106th	Maj-4th	7	6	Jan. 7, 1999
107th	Maj-3rd	9	9	Jan. 25, 2001
+107th	Min-3rd	9	9	June 6, 2001
108th	Maj-4th	11	10	Jan. 15, 2003

5th APPROPRIATIONS
Dates: Jan. 4, 1995-date
Departure: Still serving in the 111th Congress

Cong.	Ranking	Years in: Senate	Comm.	Date of Assignment
104th	Maj-15th	3	1	Jan. 4, 1995
105th	Maj-11th	5	3	Jan. 9, 1997
106th	Maj-11th	7	5	Jan. 7, 1999
107th	Maj-10th	9	7	Jan. 25, 2001
+107th	Min-10th	9	7	June 6, 2001
108th	Maj-10th	11	9	Jan. 15, 2003
109th	Maj-10th	13	11	Jan. 6, 2005
110th	Min-9th	15	13	Jan. 12, 2007
111th	Min-7th	17	15	Jan. 21, 2009

6th ENVIRONMENT AND PUBLIC WORKS
1st Dates: Mar. 29, 1996-Jan. 9, 1997
1st Departure: Left committee; no new assignment
2nd Dates: Jan. 7, 1999-Jan. 25, 2001
2nd Departure: Returned to Governmental Affairs

Cong.	Ranking	Years in: Senate	Comm.	Date of Assignment
104th	MjA-10th	3	*1 1	Mar. 29, 1996
106th	Maj-9th	7	*2 1	Jan. 7, 1999

7th RULES AND ADMINISTRATION
Dates: Jan. 6, 2005-date
Departure: Still serving in the 111th Congress

Cong.	Ranking	Years in: Senate	Comm.	Date of Assignment
109th	Maj-9th	13	1	Jan. 6, 2005
110th	Min-RM	15	3	Jan. 12, 2007
111th	Min-RM	17	5	Jan. 21, 2009

SENATE SELECT AND SPECIAL COMMITTEES:

1st SPECIAL COMMITTEE TO INVESTIGATE WHITEWATER DEVELOPMENT CORPORATION AND RELATED MATTERS
Dates: July 20, 1995-June 17, 1996
Termination: Senate Report 104-280 filed

Cong.	Ranking	Years in: Senate	Comm.	Date of Assignment
104th	Maj-6th	3	1	July 20, 1995

2nd SPECIAL YEAR 2000 TECHNOLOGY PROBLEM
Dates: Apr. 3, 1998-Feb. 29, 2000
Termination: Senate Print 106-42 issued

Cong.	Ranking	Years in: Senate	Comm.	Date of Assignment
105th	Maj-Chr	6	1	Apr. 3, 1998
106th	Maj-Chr	7	1	Continued

JOINT COMMITTEES:

1st JOINT ECONOMIC
Senate Dates: Jan. 21, 1993-date
Departure: Still serving in the 111th Congress

Cong.	Ranking	Years in: Senate	Comm.	Date of Assignment
103rd	Min-4th	1	1	Jan. 21, 1993
104th	Maj-4th	3	2	Jan. 9, 1995
105th	Maj-3rd	5	4	Jan. 9, 1997
106th	Maj-3rd	7	6	Jan. 7, 1999
107th	Maj-VC1	9	9	Jan. 25, 2001
+107th	Min-1st	9	9	June 6, 2001
108th	Maj-Chr	11	10	Jan. 15, 2003
109th	Maj-VCh	13	12	Jan. 6, 2005
110th	Min-4th	15	14	Jan. 12, 2007
111th	Min-4th	17	17	Jan. 21, 2009

2nd JOINT LIBRARY
Senate Dates: Mar. 6, 2007-date
Departure: Still serving in the 111th Congress

Cong.	Ranking	Years in: Senate	Comm.	Date of Assignment
110th	Min-1st	15	1	Mar. 6, 2007
111th	Min-1st	17	3	Apr. 3, 2009

3rd JOINT PRINTING
Senate Dates: Mar. 6, 2007-date
Departure: Still serving in the 111th Congress

Cong.	Ranking	Years in: Senate	Comm.	Date of Assignment
110th	Min-1st	15	1	Mar. 6, 2007
111th	Min-1st	17	3	Apr. 3, 2009

Helen Delich Bentley (R-Md.)

Dates: Nov. 28, 1923
House: Jan. 3, 1985-Jan. 3, 1995
Left the House: Lost nomination for Governor in 1994

HOUSE STANDING COMMITTEES:

1st MERCHANT MARINE AND FISHERIES
1st Dates: Jan. 30, 1985-Jan. 3, 1993
1st Departure: Moved to Appropriations
2nd Dates: May 27, 1993-Jan. 3, 1995
2nd Departure: Left the House; lost nomination for Governor

Cong.	Ranking	Terms in: House	Comm.	Date of Assignment
103rd	Min-17th	5 *2	1	May 27, 1993

2nd PUBLIC WORKS AND TRANSPORTATION
1st Dates: Jan. 30, 1985-Jan. 3, 1989
1st Departure: Ceased active membership to serve on Budget; later returned with continuous seniority credited
2nd Dates: Jan. 24, 1991-Jan. 3, 1993
2nd Departure: Moved to Appropriations

3rd BUDGET
Dates: Jan. 20, 1989-Jan. 3, 1993
Departure: Moved to Appropriations

4th APPROPRIATIONS
Dates: Jan. 5, 1993-Jan. 3, 1995
Departure: Left the House; lost nomination for Governor

Cong.	Ranking	Terms in: House	Comm.	Date of Assignment
103rd	Min-18th	5	1	Jan. 5, 1993

HOUSE SELECT AND SPECIAL COMMITTEES:

1st SELECT AGING (Permanent)
Dates: Feb. 21, 1985-Jan. 3, 1993
Termination: Committee not renewed in 1993

Kenneth E. Bentsen Jr. (D-Tex.)

Dates: June 3, 1959
House: Jan. 3, 1995-Jan. 3, 2003
Left the House: Lost U.S. Senate nomination in 2002

HOUSE STANDING COMMITTEES:

1st BANKING AND FINANCIAL SERVICES
Dates: Jan. 4, 1995-Jan. 3, 2003
Departure: Left the House; lost Senate nomination

Cong.	Ranking	Terms in: House	Comm.	Date of Assignment
104th	Min-22nd	1	1	Jan. 4, 1995
105th	Min-18th	2	2	Jan. 7, 1997
106th	Min-11th	3	3	Jan. 6, 1999
107th	Min-10th	4	4	Jan. 31, 2001

2nd SMALL BUSINESS
Dates: Jan. 4, 1995-Jan. 3, 1997
Departure: Moved to Budget

Cong.	Ranking	Terms in: House	Comm.	Date of Assignment
104th	Min-16th	1	1	Jan. 4, 1995

3rd BUDGET
Dates: Jan. 7, 1997-Jan. 3, 2003
Departure: Left the House; lost Senate nomination

Cong.	Ranking	Terms in: House	Comm.	Date of Assignment
105th	Min-15th	2	1	Jan. 7, 1997
106th	Min-6th	3	2	Jan. 6, 1999
107th	Min-4th	4	3	Jan. 31, 2001

Lloyd M. Bentsen Jr. (D-Tex.)

Dates: Feb. 11, 1921-May 23, 2006
House: Dec. 4, 1948-Jan. 3, 1955
Left the House: Retired in 1954
Senate: Jan. 3, 1971-Jan. 20, 1993
Left the Senate: Resigned; appointed Secretary of the Treasury in 1993

H: Bentsen was elected to the 80th Congress by special election, Dec. 4, 1948, to fill the vacancy caused by the death of U.S. Representative Milton H. West (D-Tex.). Bentsen was seated Dec. 31, 1948, but was not assigned to committees.

S: Bentsen was assigned to committees in the 103rd Congress while he awaited Senate confirmation of his appointment as Secretary of the Treasury.

HOUSE STANDING COMMITTEES:

1st PUBLIC LANDS
Dates: Jan. 18, 1949-Feb. 2, 1951
INTERIOR AND INSULAR AFFAIRS

Dates: Feb. 2, 1951-Jan. 3, 1955
Departure: Left the House; retired

SENATE STANDING COMMITTEES:

1st ARMED SERVICES
Dates: Jan. 28, 1971-Jan. 4, 1973
Departure: Moved to Finance

2nd PUBLIC WORKS
Dates: Jan. 28, 1971-Feb. 11, 1977
ENVIRONMENT AND PUBLIC WORKS
Dates: Feb. 11, 1977-Jan. 6, 1987
Departure: Moved to Commerce, Science and Transportation

3rd FINANCE
Dates: Jan. 4, 1973-Jan. 21, 1993
Ch1: Succeeded by Daniel Patrick Moynihan (D-N.Y.) on Jan. 21, 1993
Departure: Resigned the Senate; appointed Secretary of the Treasury

Cong.	Ranking	Years in: Senate	Comm.	Date of Assignment
103rd	Maj-Ch1	23	21	Jan. 7, 1993

4th COMMERCE, SCIENCE AND TRANSPORTATION
Dates: Jan. 6, 1987-Jan. 21, 1993
Departure: Resigned the Senate; appointed Secretary of the Treasury

Cong.	Ranking	Years in: Senate	Comm.	Date of Assignment
103rd	Maj-6th	23	7	Jan. 7, 1993

SENATE SELECT AND SPECIAL COMMITTEES:

1st SENATE COMMITTEE SYSTEM I (Stevenson)
Dates: Apr. 6, 1976-May 17, 1977
Departure: Terminated, last reports filed

2nd SELECT INTELLIGENCE (Permanent)
Dates: Jan. 22, 1981-Jan. 3, 1989
Departure: Left committee; no new assignment

JOINT COMMITTEES:

1st JOINT ECONOMIC
Senate Dates: Jan. 28, 1971-Jan. 20, 1993
Departure: Resigned the Senate; appointed to Cabinet

Douglas K. Bereuter (R-Neb.)

Dates: Oct. 6, 1939
House: Jan. 3, 1979-Aug. 31, 2004
Left the House: Resigned and retired in 2004

HOUSE STANDING COMMITTEES:

1st INTERIOR AND INSULAR AFFAIRS
Dates: Jan. 24, 1979-Jan. 3, 1983
Departure: Moved to Foreign Affairs

2nd SMALL BUSINESS
Dates: Jan. 24, 1979-Apr. 29, 1981
Departure: Moved to Banking, Finance and Urban Affairs

3rd BANKING, FINANCE AND URBAN AFFAIRS, 97-103
BANKING AND FINANCIAL SERVICES, 104-106
FINANCIAL SERVICES, 107-108
Dates: Apr. 29, 1981-Aug. 31, 2004
Departure: Resigned the House; retired

Cong.	Ranking	Terms in: House	Comm.	Date of Assignment
103rd	Min-4th	8	7	Jan. 5, 1993
104th	Maj-4th	9	8	Jan. 4, 1995
105th	Maj-4th	10	9	Jan. 7, 1997
106th	Maj-4th	11	10	Jan. 6, 1999
107th	Maj-4th	12	11	Jan. 6, 2001
108th	Maj-3rd	13	12	Jan. 28, 2003

4th FOREIGN AFFAIRS, 98-103
INTERNATIONAL RELATIONS, 104-108
Dates: Jan. 6, 1983-Aug. 31, 2004
Departure: Resigned the House; retired

Cong.	Ranking	Terms in: House	Comm.	Date of Assignment
103rd	Min-7th	8	6	Jan. 5, 1993
104th	Maj-6th	9	7	Jan. 4, 1995
105th	Maj-5th	10	8	Jan. 7, 1997
106th	Maj-5th	11	9	Jan. 6, 1999
107th	Maj-4th	12	10	Jan. 6, 2001
108th	Maj-3rd	13	11	Jan. 28, 2003

5th TRANSPORTATION AND INFRASTRUCTURE
Dates: Feb. 2, 1999-Aug. 31, 2004
Departure: Resigned the House; retired

Cong.	Ranking	Terms in: House	Comm.	Date of Assignment
106th	Maj-38th	11	1	Feb. 2, 1999
107th	Maj-25th	12	2	Jan. 6, 2001
108th	Maj-20th	13	3	Jan. 28, 2003

HOUSE SELECT AND SPECIAL COMMITTEES:

1st SELECT AGING (Permanent)
Dates: Feb. 5, 1981-Apr. 29, 1981
Departure: Moved to Banking, Finance and Urban Affairs

2nd SELECT HUNGER (Temporary)
Dates: Mar. 20, 1985-Jan. 3, 1993
Termination: Committee not renewed in 1993

3rd PERMANENT SELECT INTELLIGENCE
1st Dates: Jan. 24, 1989-Jan. 3, 1995
1st Departure: Left committee; no new assignment
2nd Dates: Jan. 30, 2001-Aug. 31, 2004
2nd Departure: Resigned the House; retired

Cong.	Ranking	Terms in: House	Comm.	Date of Assignment
103rd	Min-2nd	8	*1 3	Feb. 3, 1993
107th	Maj-2nd	12	*2 1	Jan. 30, 2001
108th	Maj-2nd	13	*2 2	Jan. 8, 2003

4th SELECT NATIONAL SECURITY CONCERNS WITH CHINA
Dates: June 22, 1998-Apr. 30, 1999
Termination: House Report 851 (105-2) filed, Jan. 3, 1999

Cong.	Ranking	Terms in: House	Comm.	Date of Assignment
105th	Maj-3rd	10	1	June 22, 1998
106th	Maj-3rd	11	2	Jan. 19, 1999

Shelley Berkley (D-Nev.)

Dates: Jan. 20, 1951
House: Jan. 3, 1999-date
Serving in the 111th Congress

HOUSE STANDING COMMITTEES:

1st TRANSPORTATION AND INFRASTRUCTURE
Dates: Jan. 6, 1999-Jan. 3, 2007
Departure: Moved to Ways and Means

Cong.	Ranking	Terms in: House	Comm.	Date of Assignment
106th	Min-34th	1	1	Jan. 6, 1999
107th	Min-30th	2	2	Jan. 31, 2001
108th	Min-22nd	3	3	Jan. 28, 2003
109th	Min-20th	4	4	Jan. 26, 2005

2nd VETERANS' AFFAIRS
Dates: Feb. 2, 1999-Jan. 3, 2009
Departure: Returned to Foreign Affairs

Cong.	Ranking	Terms in: House	Comm.	Date of Assignment
106th	Min-12th	1	1	Feb. 2, 1999
107th	Min-12th	2	2	Jan. 31, 2001
108th	Min-11th	3	3	Feb. 13, 2003
109th	Min-11th	4	4	Feb. 2, 2005
110th	Maj-10th	5	5	Jan. 18, 2007

3rd SMALL BUSINESS
Dates: May 25, 1999-Feb. 7, 2001
Departure: Resigned committee; moved to International Relations

Cong.	Ranking	Terms in: House	Comm.	Date of Assignment
106th	MnR-1st	1	1	May 25, 1999
107th	Min-16th	2	2	Jan. 31, 2001

4th INTERNATIONAL RELATIONS, 107-109
FOREIGN AFFAIRS, 111
1st Dates: Feb. 8, 2001-Jan. 3, 2007
1st Departure: Moved to Ways and Means
2nd Dates: Jan. 21, 2009-date
2nd Departure: Still serving in the 111th Congress

Cong.	Ranking	Terms in: House	Comm.	Date of Assignment
107th	Min-21st	2 *1	1	Feb. 8, 2001
108th	Min-17th	3 *1	2	Jan. 28, 2003
109th	Min-16th	4 *1	3	Jan. 26, 2005
111th	Maj-20th	6 *2	1	Jan. 21, 2009

5th WAYS AND MEANS
Dates: Jan. 4, 2007-date
Departure: Still serving in the 111th Congress

Cong.	Ranking	Terms in: House	Comm.	Date of Assignment
110th	Maj-19th	5	1	Jan. 4, 2007
111th	Maj-16th	6	2	Jan. 7, 2009

HOUSE STANDING COMMITTEES:

1st FOREIGN AFFAIRS, 98-103
INTERNATIONAL RELATIONS, 104-109
FOREIGN AFFAIRS, 110-111
Dates: Jan. 6, 1983-date
Ch2: Succeeded Thomas P. Lantos as Chair (D-Cal.) on Mar. 11, 2008
Departure: Still serving in the 111th Congress

Cong.	Ranking	Terms in: House	Comm.	Date of Assignment
103rd	Maj-5th	6	6	Jan. 5, 1993
104th	Min-5th	7	7	Jan. 4, 1995
105th	Min-4th	8	8	Jan. 7, 1997
106th	Min-3rd	9	9	Jan. 6, 1999
107th	Min-2nd	10	10	Jan. 31, 2001
108th	Min-2nd	11	11	Jan. 28, 2003
109th	Min-2nd	12	12	Jan. 26, 2005
110th	Maj-2nd	13	13	Jan. 12, 2007
=110th	Maj-Ch2	13	13	Mar. 11, 2008
111th	Maj-Chr	14	14	Jan. 6, 2009

2nd JUDICIARY
Dates: Jan. 6, 1983-date
Departure: Still serving in the 111th Congress

Cong.	Ranking	Terms in: House	Comm.	Date of Assignment
103rd	Maj-11th	6	6	Jan. 5, 1993
104th	Min-5th	7	7	Jan. 4, 1995
105th	Min-4th	8	8	Jan. 7, 1997
106th	Min-3rd	9	9	Jan. 6, 1999
107th	Min-3rd	10	10	Jan. 31, 2001
108th	Min-2nd	11	11	Jan. 28, 2003
109th	Min-2nd	12	12	Jan. 26, 2005
110th	Maj-2nd	13	13	Jan. 18, 2007
111th	Maj-2nd	14	14	Jan. 21, 2009

3rd BUDGET
Dates: Jan. 19, 1989-Jan. 3, 1995
Departure: Left committee; no new assignment

Cong.	Ranking	Terms in: House	Comm.	Date of Assignment
103rd	Maj-6th	6	3	Jan. 5, 1993

4th RESOURCES
Dates: Jan. 21, 1993-June 18, 1993
Departure: Resigned committee; no new assignment

Cong.	Ranking	Terms in: House	Comm.	Date of Assignment
103rd	MjR-1st	6	1	Jan. 21, 1993

5th STANDARDS OF OFFICIAL CONDUCT
Dates: Feb. 10, 1997-Feb. 25, 2003
RM1: Replaced as Ranking Member by Alan B. Mollohan (D-W.Va.) on Feb. 25, 2003
Departure: Resigned committee; no new assignment

Cong.	Ranking	Terms in: House	Comm.	Date of Assignment
105th	Min-RM	8	1	Feb. 10, 1997
106th	Min-RM	9	2	Jan. 6, 1999
107th	Min-RM	10	3	Jan. 20, 2001
108th	Min-RM1	11	4	Jan. 8, 2003

Howard L. Berman (D-Cal.)

Dates: April 15, 1941
House: Jan. 3, 1983-date
Serving in the 111th Congress

R. Marion Berry (D-Ark.)

Dates: Aug. 27, 1942
House: Jan. 3, 1997-date
Serving in the 111th Congress

HOUSE STANDING COMMITTEES:

1st AGRICULTURE
Dates: Jan. 7, 1997-Jan. 3, 2003
Departure: Moved to Appropriations

Cong.	Ranking	Terms in: House	Comm.	Date of Assignment
105th	Min-16th	1	1	Jan. 7, 1997
106th	Min-14th	2	2	Jan. 6, 1999
107th	Min-11th	3	3	Jan. 31, 2001

2nd SMALL BUSINESS
Dates: May 14, 1997-Mar. 30, 1998
Departure: Resigned committee; moved to Transportation and Infrastructure

Cong.	Ranking	Terms in: House	Comm.	Date of Assignment
105th	MnR-2nd	1	1	May 14, 1997

3rd TRANSPORTATION AND INFRASTRUCTURE
Dates: Mar. 27, 1998-Jan. 3, 2003
Departure: Moved to Appropriations

Cong.	Ranking	Terms in: House	Comm.	Date of Assignment
105th	MnA-34th	1	1	Mar. 27, 1998
106th	Min-31st	2	2	Jan. 6, 1999
107th	Min-28th	3	3	Jan. 31, 2001

4th APPROPRIATIONS
Dates: Jan. 28, 2003-date
Departure: Still serving in the 111th Congress

Cong.	Ranking	Terms in: House	Comm.	Date of Assignment
108th	Min-29th	4	1	Jan. 28, 2003
109th	Min-29th	5	2	Jan. 26, 2005
110th	Maj-26th	6	3	Jan. 4, 2007
111th	Maj-25th	7	4	Jan. 7, 2009

5th BUDGET
Dates: Jan. 18, 2007-date
Departure: Still serving in the 111th Congress

Cong.	Ranking	Terms in: House	Comm.	Date of Assignment
110th	Maj-12th	6	1	Jan. 18, 2007
111th	Maj-7th	7	2	Jan. 21, 2009

Tom Bevill (D-Ala.)

Dates: March 27, 1921-March 28, 2005
House: Jan. 3, 1967-Jan. 3, 1997
Left the House: Retired in 1996

HOUSE STANDING COMMITTEES:

1st BANKING AND CURRENCY
Dates: Jan. 23, 1967-Jan. 27, 1972
Departure: Moved to Appropriations

2nd POST OFFICE AND CIVIL SERVICE
Dates: Feb. 4, 1971-Jan. 27, 1972
Departure: Moved to Appropriations

3rd APPROPRIATIONS
Dates: Jan. 27, 1972-Jan. 3, 1997
Departure: Left the House; retired

Cong.	Ranking	Terms in: House	Comm.	Date of Assignment
103rd	Maj-7th	14	12	Jan. 5, 1993
104th	Min-4th	15	13	Jan. 4, 1995

Joseph R. Biden Jr. (D-Del.)

Dates: Nov. 20, 1942
Senate: Jan. 3, 1973-Jan. 15, 2009
Left the Senate: Resigned; elected Vice President in 2008

S: Senator Biden was not assigned to committees in the 111th Congress pending his swearing-in as Vice President on Jan. 20, 2009.

SENATE STANDING COMMITTEES:

1st BANKING, HOUSING AND URBAN AFFAIRS
Dates: Jan. 4, 1973-Feb. 11, 1977
Departure: Moved to Judiciary

2nd PUBLIC WORKS
Dates: Jan. 4, 1973-Jan. 17, 1975
Departure: Moved to Foreign Relations

3rd BUDGET
Dates: July 25, 1974-Mar. 5, 1985
Departure: Left committee; no new assignment

4th FOREIGN RELATIONS
Dates: Jan. 17, 1975-Jan. 3, 2009
Ch2: Replaced Jesse A. Helms (R-N.C.) as Chair on June 6, 2001, following Senate party control shift
Departure: Resigned the Senate; elected Vice President

Cong.	Ranking	Years in: Senate	Comm.	Date of Assignment
103rd	Maj-2nd	21	18	Jan. 7, 1993
104th	Min-2nd	23	20	Jan. 4, 1995
105th	Min-RM	25	22	Jan. 9, 1997
106th	Min-RM	27	24	Jan. 7, 1999
=107th	Maj-ChT	29	26	Jan. 3, 2001
107th	Min-RM1	29	27	Jan. 25, 2001
+107th	Maj-Ch2	29	27	June 6, 2001
108th	Min-RM	31	28	Jan. 15, 2003
109th	Min-RM	33	30	Jan. 6, 2005
110th	Maj-Chr	35	32	Jan. 12, 2007

5th JUDICIARY
Dates: Feb. 11, 1977-Jan. 3, 2009
Departure: Resigned the Senate; elected Vice President

Cong.	Ranking	Years in: Senate	Comm.	Date of Assignment
103rd	Maj-Chr	21	16	Jan. 7, 1993
104th	Min-RM	23	18	Jan. 4, 1995
105th	Min-3rd	25	20	Jan. 9, 1997
106th	Min-3rd	27	22	Jan. 7, 1999
107th	Min-3rd	29	24	Jan. 25, 2001
+107th	Maj-3rd	29	25	June 6, 2001
108th	Min-3rd	31	26	Jan. 15, 2003
109th	Min-3rd	33	28	Jan. 6, 2005
110th	Maj-3rd	35	30	Jan. 12, 2007

SENATE SELECT AND SPECIAL COMMITTEES:

1st SELECT INTELLIGENCE (Permanent)
Dates: May 20, 1976-Jan. 3, 1985
Departure: Left committee; no new assignment

Judith B. Biggert (R-Ill.)

Dates: Aug. 15, 1937
House: Jan. 3, 1999-date
Serving in the 111th Congress

HOUSE STANDING COMMITTEES:

1st BANKING AND FINANCIAL SERVICES, 106
FINANCIAL SERVICES, 107-111
Dates: Jan. 6, 1999-date
Departure: Still serving in the 111th Congress

Cong.	Ranking	Terms in: House	Comm.	Date of Assignment
106th	Maj-29th	1	1	Jan. 6, 1999
107th	Maj-24th	2	2	Jan. 6, 2001
108th	Maj-19th	3	3	Jan. 28, 2003
109th	Maj-18th	4	4	Jan. 26, 2005
110th	Min-13th	5	5	Jan. 10, 2007
111th	Min-9th	6	6	Jan. 9, 2009

2nd GOVERNMENT REFORM
Dates: Jan. 6, 1999-Jan. 3, 2001
Departure: Moved to Education and the Workforce and Standards of Official Conduct

Cong.	Ranking	Terms in: House	Comm.	Date of Assignment
106th	Maj-20th	1	1	Jan. 6, 1999

3rd SCIENCE, 106-109
SCIENCE AND TECHNOLOGY, 110-111
Dates: Jan. 6, 1999-date
Departure: Still serving in the 111th Congress

Cong.	Ranking	Terms in: House	Comm.	Date of Assignment
106th	Maj-23rd	1	1	Jan. 6, 1999
107th	Maj-18th	2	2	Jan. 6, 2001
108th	Maj-14th	3	3	Jan. 28, 2003
109th	Maj-11th	4	4	Jan. 26, 2005
110th	Min-9th	5	5	Jan. 10, 2007
111th	Min-8th	6	6	Jan. 9, 2009

4th EDUCATION AND THE WORKFORCE, 107-109
EDUCATION AND LABOR, 110-111
Dates: Jan. 6, 2001-date
Departure: Still serving in the 111th Congress

Cong.	Ranking	Terms in: House	Comm.	Date of Assignment
107th	Maj-21st	2	1	Jan. 6, 2001
108th	Maj-15th	3	2	Jan. 28, 2003
109th	Maj-9th	4	3	Jan. 26, 2005
110th	Min-7th	5	4	Jan. 10, 2007
111th	Min-7th	6	5	Jan. 9, 2009

5th STANDARDS OF OFFICIAL CONDUCT
Dates: Mar. 6, 2001-Jan. 3, 2007
Departure: Left committee; no new assignment

Cong.	Ranking	Terms in: House	Comm.	Date of Assignment
107th	Maj-5th	2	1	Mar. 6, 2001
108th	Maj-3rd	3	2	Feb. 11, 2003
109th	Maj-2nd	4	3	Feb. 2, 2005

Brian P. Bilbray (R-Cal.)

Dates: Jan. 28, 1951
House 1: Jan. 3, 1995-Jan. 3, 2001

Left House 1: Defeated for re-election in 2000
House 2: June 6, 2006-date
Serving in the 111th Congress

H2: Bilbray was elected to the 109th Congress by special election, June 6, 2006 to fill the vacancy caused by the resignation of U.S. Representative Randall (Duke) Cunningham (R-Cal.). Bilbray was seated June 13, 2006, and assigned to committees.

HOUSE STANDING COMMITTEES:

1st COMMERCE
Dates: Jan. 4, 1995-Jan. 3, 2001
Departure: Left the House; lost re-election

Cong.	Ranking	Terms in: House	Comm.	Date of Assignment
104th	Maj-19th	1	1	Jan. 4, 1995
105th	Maj-19th	2	2	Jan. 7, 1997
106th	Maj-14th	3	3	Jan. 6, 1999

2nd ARMED SERVICES
Dates: June 29, 2006-Jan. 3, 2007
Departure: Moved to Science and Technology

Cong.	Ranking	Terms in: House	Comm.	Date of Assignment
109th	MjR-1st	4	1	June 29, 2006

3rd GOVERNMENT REFORM, 109
OVERSIGHT AND GOVERNMENT REFORM, 110-111
Dates: June 29, 2006-date
Departure: Still serving in the 111th Congress

Cong.	Ranking	Terms in: House	Comm.	Date of Assignment
109th	MjR-2nd	4	1	June 29, 2006
110th	Min-16th	5	2	Jan. 10, 2007
111th	Min-12th	6	3	Jan. 9, 2009

4th VETERANS' AFFAIRS
Dates: June 29, 2006-date
Departure: Still serving in the 111th Congress

Cong.	Ranking	Terms in: House	Comm.	Date of Assignment
109th	MjR-3rd	4	1	June 29, 2006
110th	Min-11th	5	2	Jan. 10, 2007
111th	Min-8th	6	3	Jan. 9, 2009

5th SCIENCE AND TECHNOLOGY
Dates: Jan. 10, 2007-date
Departure: Still serving in the 111th Congress

Cong.	Ranking	Terms in: House	Comm.	Date of Assignment
110th	Min-19th	5	1	Jan. 10, 2007
111th	Min-14th	6	2	Jan. 9, 2009

James H. Bilbray (D-Nev.)

Dates: May 19, 1938
House: Jan. 3, 1987-Jan. 3, 1995
Left the House: Defeated for re-election in 1994

HOUSE STANDING COMMITTEES:

1st FOREIGN AFFAIRS
Dates: Jan. 6, 1987-Jan. 3, 1989
Departure: Moved to Armed Services

2nd SMALL BUSINESS
Dates: Jan. 22, 1987-Jan. 3, 1995
Departure: Left the House; lost re-election

Cong.	Ranking	Terms in: House	Comm.	Date of Assignment
103rd	Maj-8th	4	4	Jan. 5, 1993

3rd ARMED SERVICES
Dates: Jan. 19, 1989-Jan. 3, 1995
Departure: Left the House; lost re-election

Cong.	Ranking	Terms in: House	Comm.	Date of Assignment
103rd	Maj-17th	4	3	Jan. 5, 1993

HOUSE SELECT AND SPECIAL COMMITTEES:

1st SELECT HUNGER (Temporary)
Dates: Jan. 22, 1987-Nov. 16, 1987
Departure: Moved earlier to Select Aging

2nd SELECT AGING (Permanent)
Dates: Oct. 20, 1987-Jan. 3, 1993
Termination: Committee not renewed in 1993

3rd PERMANENT SELECT INTELLIGENCE
Dates: Feb. 3, 1993-Jan. 3, 1995
Departure: Left the House; lost re-election

Cong.	Ranking	Terms in: House	Comm.	Date of Assignment
103rd	Maj-8th	4	1	Feb. 3, 1993

Gus Bilirakis (R-Fla.)

Dates: Feb. 8, 1963
House: Jan. 3, 2007-date
Serving in the 111th Congress

HOUSE STANDING COMMITTEES:

1st HOMELAND SECURITY
Dates: Jan. 10, 2007-date
Departure: Still serving in the 111th Congress

Cong.	Ranking	Terms in: House	Comm.	Date of Assignment
110th	Min-14th	1	1	Jan. 10, 2007
111th	Min-8th	2	2	Jan. 9, 2009

2nd VETERANS' AFFAIRS
Dates: Jan. 10, 2007-date
Departure: Still serving in the 111th Congress

Cong.	Ranking	Terms in: House	Comm.	Date of Assignment
110th	Min-13th	1	1	Jan. 10, 2007
111th	Min-9th	2	2	Jan. 9, 2009

3rd FOREIGN AFFAIRS
Dates: May 10, 2007-date
Departure: Still serving in the 111th Congress

Cong.	Ranking	Terms in: House	Comm.	Date of Assignment
110th	MnR-1st	1	1	May 10, 2007
111th	Min-19th	2	2	Jan. 9, 2009

Michael Bilirakis (R-Fla.)

Dates: July 16, 1930
House: Jan. 3, 1983-Jan. 3, 2007
Left the House: Retired in 2006

HOUSE STANDING COMMITTEES:

1st SMALL BUSINESS
Dates: Jan. 6, 1983-Jan. 3, 1985
Departure: Moved to Energy and Commerce

2nd VETERANS' AFFAIRS
Dates: Jan. 6, 1983-date
Departure: Left the House; retired

Cong.	Ranking	Terms in: House	Comm.	Date of Assignment
103rd	Min-4th	6	6	Jan. 5, 1993
104th	Maj-3rd	7	7	Jan. 4, 1995
105th	Maj-3rd	8	8	Jan. 21, 1997
106th	Maj-3rd	9	9	Jan. 6, 1999
107th	Maj-3rd	10	10	Jan. 6, 2001
108th	Maj-2nd	11	11	Jan. 28, 2003
109th	Maj-2nd	12	12	Jan. 26, 2005

3rd ENERGY AND COMMERCE, 99-103
COMMERCE, 104-106
ENERGY AND COMMERCE, 107-109
Dates: Jan. 30, 1985-Jan. 3, 2007
Departure: Left the House; retired

Cong.	Ranking	Terms in: House	Comm.	Date of Assignment
103rd	Min-5th	6	5	Jan. 5, 1993
104th	Maj-5th	7	6	Jan. 4, 1995
105th	Maj-4th	8	7	Jan. 7, 1997
106th	Maj-4th	9	8	Jan. 6, 1999
107th	Maj-2nd	10	9	Jan. 6, 2001
108th	Maj-2nd	11	10	Jan. 28, 2003
109th	Maj-3rd	12	11	Jan. 6, 2005

HOUSE SELECT AND SPECIAL COMMITTEES:

1st SELECT AGING (Permanent)
Dates: Feb. 8, 1983-Jan. 3, 1985
Departure: Moved to Energy and Commerce

2nd SELECT CHILDREN, YOUTH AND FAMILIES (Temporary)
Dates: Feb. 21, 1991-Jan. 3, 1993
Termination: Committee not renewed in 1993

J.F. (Jeff) Bingaman Jr. (D-N.M.)

Dates: Oct. 3, 1943
Senate: Jan. 3, 1983-date
Serving in the 111th Congress

SENATE STANDING COMMITTEES:

1st ARMED SERVICES
1st Dates: Jan. 3, 1983-Jan. 5, 2001
1st Departure: Moved to Finance
2nd Dates: July 10, 2001-Jan. 15, 2003
2nd Departure: Left committee; no new assignment

		Years in:		Date of
Cong.	Ranking	Senate	Comm.	Assignment
103rd	Maj-5th	11 *1	11	Jan. 7, 1993
104th	Min-5th	13 *1	13	Jan. 4, 1995
105th	Min-3rd	15 *1	15	Jan. 9, 1997
106th	Min-3rd	17 *1	17	Jan. 7, 1999
+107th	MjA-13th	19 *2	1	July 10, 2001

2nd GOVERNMENTAL AFFAIRS
1st Dates: Jan. 3, 1983-Feb. 21, 1985
1st Departure: Moved to Energy and Natural Resources
2nd Dates: Jan. 6, 1987-May 16, 1990
2nd Departure: Moved to Labor and Human Resources

3rd ENERGY AND NATURAL RESOURCES
Dates: Feb. 21, 1985-date
Ch2: Replaced Frank H. Murkowski (R-Alas.) as Chair on June 6, 2001, following Senate party control shift
Departure: Still serving in the 111th Congress

		Years in:		Date of
Cong.	Ranking	Senate	Comm.	Assignment
103rd	Maj-5th	11	8	Jan. 7, 1993
104th	Min-5th	13	10	Jan. 4, 1995
105th	Min-3rd	15	12	Jan. 9, 1997
106th	Min-RM	17	14	Jan. 7, 1999
=107th	Maj-ChT	19	16	Jan. 3, 2001
107th	Min-RM1	19	16	Jan. 25, 2001
+107th	Maj-Ch2	19	17	June 6, 2001
108th	Min-RM	21	18	Jan. 15, 2003
109th	Min-RM	23	20	Jan. 6, 2005
110th	Maj-Chr	25	22	Jan. 12, 2007
111th	Maj-Chr	27	24	Jan. 21, 2009

4th LABOR AND HUMAN RESOURCES renamed
HEALTH, EDUCATION, LABOR AND PENSIONS
1st Dates: May 16, 1990-Jan. 4, 1995
1st Departure: Left committee; no new assignment
2nd Dates: Jan. 9, 1997-date
2nd Departure: Still serving in the 111th Congress

		Years in:		Date of
Cong.	Ranking	Senate	Comm.	Assignment
103rd	Maj-8th	11 *1	3	Jan. 7, 1993
105th	Min-5th	15 *2	1	Jan. 9, 1997
106th	Min-5th	17 *2	2	Jan. 7, 1999
107th	Min-5th	19 *2	5	Jan. 25, 2001
+107th	Maj-6th	19 *2	5	July 10, 2001
108th	Min-6th	21 *2	7	Jan. 15, 2003
109th	Min-6th	23 *2	8	Jan. 6, 2005
110th	Maj-5th	25 *2	11	Jan. 12, 2007
111th	Maj-5th	27 *2	13	Jan. 21, 2009

5th FINANCE
Dates: Jan. 25, 2001-date
Departure: Still serving in the 111th Congress

		Years in:		Date of
Cong.	Ranking	Senate	Comm.	Assignment
107th	Min-7th	19	1	Jan. 25, 2001
+107th	Maj-8th	19	1	July 6, 2001
108th	Min-8th	21	2	Jan. 15, 2003
109th	Min-5th	23	4	Jan. 6, 2005
110th	Maj-4th	25	6	Jan. 12, 2007
111th	Maj-4th	27	8	Jan. 21, 2009

SENATE SELECT AND SPECIAL COMMITTEES:

1st SPECIAL AGING (Permanent)
Dates: Feb. 9, 1984-Jan. 6, 1987
Departure: Moved to Governmental Affairs

2nd JUDGE HARRY E. CLAIBORNE IMPEACHMENT
Dates: Aug. 14, 1986-Oct. 1, 1986
Departure: Senate Report 99-511 filed

3rd JUDGE ALCEE L. HASTINGS IMPEACHMENT
Dates: Mar. 16, 1989-Aug. 3, 1989
Departure: Senate Hearing 101-194, Parts 1-2A

4th SELECT ETHICS (Permanent)
Dates: May 22, 1991-Jan. 26, 1993
Departure: Left committee; no new assignment. Service on the committee was confined to matters unrelated to the Keating Five Investigation.

5th SPECIAL YEAR 2000 TECHNOLOGY PROBLEM
Dates: Apr. 23, 1998-Feb. 29, 2000
Departure: Senate Print 106-42 issued

		Years in:		Date of
Cong.	Ranking	Senate	Comm.	Assignment
105th	Min- 3rd	16	1	Apr. 23, 1998
106th	Min-3rd	17	1	Continued

JOINT COMMITTEES:

1st JOINT ECONOMIC
1st Senate Dates: Jan. 12, 1987-Jan. 25, 2001
1st Departure: Moved to Finance
2nd Senate Dates: July 10, 1987-date
2nd Departure: Still serving in the 111th Congress

		Years in:		Date of
Cong.	Ranking	Senate	Comm.	Assignment
103rd	Maj-3rd	11 *1	6	Jan. 21, 1993
104th	Min-1st	13 *1	8	Jan. 9, 1995
105th	Min-1st	15 *1	10	Jan. 9, 1997
106th	Min-4th	17 *1	12	Jan. 7, 1999
+107th	MjA-4th	19 *2	1	July 10, 2001
108th	Min-4th	21 *2	2	Jan. 15, 2003
109th	Min-4th	23 *2	4	Jan. 6, 2005
110th	Maj-3rd	25 *2	6	Jan. 12, 2007
111th	Maj-3rd	27 *2	8	Jan. 21, 2009

Robert Bishop (R-Utah)

Dates: July 13, 1951
House: Jan. 3, 2003-date
Serving in the 111th Congress

HOUSE STANDING COMMITTEES:

1st ARMED SERVICES
1st Dates: Jan. 28, 2003-Jan. 3, 2005
1st Departure: Moved to Rules
2nd Dates: Jan. 10, 2007-date
2nd Departure: Still serving in the 111th Congress

		Terms in:		Date of
Cong.	Ranking	House	Comm.	Assignment
108th	Maj-27th	1 *1	1	Jan. 28, 2003
110th	Min-18th	3 *2	1	Jan. 10, 2007
111th	Min-11th	4 *2	2	Jan. 9, 2009

2nd RESOURCES, 108
NATURAL RESOURCES, 110-111
1st Dates: Jan. 28, 2003-date

1st Departure: Moved to Rules
2nd Dates: Jan. 10, 2007-date
2nd Departure: Still serving in the 111th Congress

Cong.	Ranking	Terms in: House	Comm.	Date of Assignment
108th	Maj-27th	1 *1	1	Jan. 28, 2003
110th	Min-18th	3 *2	1	Jan. 10, 2007
111th	Min-9th	4 *2	2	Jan. 9, 2009

3rd SCIENCE
Dates: Jan. 28, 2003-Jan. 3, 2005
Departure: Moved to Rules

Cong.	Ranking	Terms in: House	Comm.	Date of Assignment
108th	Maj-22nd	1	1	Jan. 28, 2003

4th RULES
Dates: Jan. 4, 2005-Jan. 3, 2007
Departure: Returned to Armed Services and Natural Resources; and moved to Education and Labor

Cong.	Ranking	Terms in: House	Comm.	Date of Assignment
109th	Maj-8th	2	1	Jan. 4, 2005

5th EDUCATION AND LABOR
Dates: Jan. 10, 2007-date
Departure: Still serving in the 111th Congress

Cong.	Ranking	Terms in: House	Comm.	Date of Assignment
110th	Min-20th	3	1	Jan. 10, 2007
111th	Min-14th	4	2	Jan. 9, 2009

Sanford D. Bishop Jr. (D-Ga.)

Dates: Feb. 4, 1947
House: Jan. 3, 1993-date
Serving in the 111th Congress

HOUSE STANDING COMMITTEES:

1st AGRICULTURE
Dates: Jan. 5, 1993-Jan. 3, 2003
Departure: Moved to Appropriations

Cong.	Ranking	Terms in: House	Comm.	Date of Assignment
103rd	Maj-27th	1	1	Jan. 5, 1993
104th	Min-18th	2	2	Jan. 4, 1995
105th	Min-12th	3	3	Jan. 7, 1997
106th	Min-11th	4	4	Jan. 6, 1999
107th	Min-8th	5	5	Jan. 31, 2001

2nd POST OFFICE AND CIVIL SERVICE
Dates: Jan. 27, 1993-Jan. 3, 1995
Departure: Committee abolished in 1995; no new assignment

Cong.	Ranking	Terms in: House	Comm.	Date of Assignment
103rd	Maj-13th	1	1	Jan. 27, 1993

3rd VETERANS' AFFAIRS
Dates: Jan. 5, 1993-Mar. 6, 1997
Departure: Resigned committee; moved to Permanent Select Intelligence

Cong.	Ranking	Terms in: House	Comm.	Date of Assignment
103rd	Maj-18th	1	1	Jan. 5, 1993

Cong.	Ranking	Terms in: House	Comm.	Date of Assignment
104th	Min-11th	2	2	Jan. 4, 1995
105th	Min-5th	3	3	Feb. 6, 1997

4th APPROPRIATIONS
Dates: Jan. 28, 2003-date
Departure: Still serving in the 111th Congress

Cong.	Ranking	Terms in: House	Comm.	Date of Assignment
108th	Min-28th	6	1	Jan. 28, 2003
109th	Min-28th	7	2	Jan. 26, 2005
110th	Maj-25th	8	3	Jan. 4, 2007
111th	Maj-24th	9	4	Jan. 7, 2009

HOUSE SELECT AND SPECIAL COMMITTEES:

1st PERMANENT SELECT INTELLIGENCE
Dates: Mar. 6, 1997-Jan. 3, 2003
Departure: Moved to Appropriations

Cong.	Ranking	Terms in: House	Comm.	Date of Assignment
105th	Min-7th	3	1	Mar. 6, 1997
106th	Min-3rd	4	2	Feb. 12, 1999
107th	Min-2nd	5	3	Mar. 1, 2001

Timothy H. Bishop (D-N.Y.)

Dates: June 1, 1950
House: Jan. 3, 2003-date
Serving in the 111th Congress

HOUSE STANDING COMMITTEES:

1st TRANSPORTATION AND INFRASTRUCTURE
Dates: Jan. 28, 2003-date
Departure: Still serving in the 111th Congress

Cong.	Ranking	Terms in: House	Comm.	Date of Assignment
108th	Min-32nd	1	1	Jan. 28, 2003
109th	Min-27th	2	2	Jan. 26, 2005
110th	Maj-20th	3	3	Jan. 10, 2007
111th	Maj-18th	4	4	Jan. 7, 2009

2nd SCIENCE
Dates: Feb. 5, 2003-Feb. 27, 2003
Departure: Moved to Education and the Workforce

Cong.	Ranking	Terms in: House	Comm.	Date of Assignment
108th	Min-17th	1	1	Feb. 5, 2003

3rd EDUCATION AND THE WORKFORCE, 108-109
EDUCATION AND LABOR, 110-111
Dates: Mar. 5. 2003-date
Departure: Still serving in the 111th Congress

Cong.	Ranking	Terms in: House	Comm.	Date of Assignment
108th	Min-23rd	1	1	Mar. 5, 2003
109th	Min-21st	2	2	Jan. 26, 2005
110th	Maj-16th	3	3	Jan. 10, 2007
111th	Maj-15th	4	4	Jan. 21, 2009

4th BUDGET
Dates: Jan. 18, 2007-date
Departure: Still serving in the 111th Congress

Cong.	Ranking	Terms in: House	Comm.	Date of Assignment
110th	Maj-22nd	3	1	Jan. 18, 2007
111th	Maj-21st	4	2	Jan. 21, 2009

Marsha Blackburn (R-Tenn.)

Dates: June 6, 1952
House: Jan. 3, 2003-date
Serving in the 111th Congress

HOUSE STANDING COMMITTEES:

1st EDUCATION AND THE WORKFORCE
Dates: Jan. 28, 2003-Jan. 3, 2005
Departure: Moved to Energy and Commerce

Cong.	Ranking	Terms in: House	Comm.	Date of Assignment
108th	Maj-26th	1	1	Jan. 28, 2003

2nd GOVERNMENT REFORM
Dates: Jan. 28, 2003-Jan. 3, 2005
Departure: Moved to Energy and Commerce

Cong.	Ranking	Terms in: House	Comm.	Date of Assignment
108th	Maj-24th	1	1	Jan. 28, 2003

3rd JUDICIARY
Dates: Jan. 28, 2003-Jan. 3, 2005
Departure: Moved to Energy and Commerce

Cong.	Ranking	Terms in: House	Comm.	Date of Assignment
108th	Maj-21st	1	1	Jan. 28, 2003

4th ENERGY AND COMMERCE
1st Dates: Jan. 6, 2005-Jan. 3, 2007
1st Departure: Moved to Financial Services and Homeland Security; returned as a replacement
2nd Dates: Mar. 12, 2007-date
2nd Departure: Still serving in the 111th Congress

Cong.	Ranking	Terms in: House	Comm.	Date of Assignment
109th	Maj-31st	2 *1	1	Jan. 6, 2005
110th	MnR-1st	3 *2	1	Mar. 12, 2007
111th	Min-21st	4 *2	2	Jan. 9, 2009

5th FINANCIAL SERVICES
Dates: Jan. 10, 2007-Mar. 9, 2007
Departure: Resigned committee; returned to Energy and Commerce

Cong.	Ranking	Terms in: House	Comm.	Date of Assignment
110th	Min-31st	3	1	Jan. 10, 2007

6th HOMELAND SECURITY
Dates: Jan. 10, 2007-Mar. 9, 2007
Departure: Resigned committee; returned to Energy and Commerce

Cong.	Ranking	Terms in: House	Comm.	Date of Assignment
110th	Min-13th	3	1	Jan. 10, 2007

HOUSE SELECT AND SPECIAL COMMITTEES:

1st SELECT ENERGY INDEPENDENCE AND GLOBAL WARMING
Dates: Mar. 9, 2007-date
Departure: Still serving in the 111th Congress

Cong.	Ranking	Terms in: House	Comm.	Date of Assignment
110th	Min-5th	3	1	Mar. 9, 2007
111th	Min-4th	4	2	Feb. 3, 2009

Lucien E. Blackwell (D-Penn.)

Dates: Aug. 1, 1931-Jan. 24, 2003
House: Nov. 5, 1991-Jan. 3, 1995
Left the House: Defeated for re-nomination in 1994

H: Blackwell was elected to the 102nd Congress by special election, Nov. 5, 1991, to fill the vacancy caused by the resignation of U.S. Representative William H. Gray III (D-Penn.). Blackwell was seated Nov. 13, 1991, and assigned to committees.

HOUSE STANDING COMMITTEES:

1st PUBLIC WORKS AND TRANSPORTATION
Dates: Nov. 26, 1991-Jan. 3, 1995
Departure: Left the House; lost re-nomination

Cong.	Ranking	Terms in: House	Comm.	Date of Assignment
103rd	Maj-24th	2	2	Jan. 5, 1993

2nd MERCHANT MARINE AND FISHERIES
Dates: Feb. 5, 1992-Jan. 3, 1993
Departure: Moved to Budget

3rd BUDGET
Dates: Jan. 5, 1993-Jan. 3, 1995
Departure: Left the House; lost re-nomination

Cong.	Ranking	Terms in: House	Comm.	Date of Assignment
103rd	Maj-25th	2	1	Jan. 5, 1993

Rod R. Blagojevich (D-Ill.)

Dates: Dec. 10, 1956
House: Jan. 3, 1997-Jan. 3, 2003
Left the House: Elected Governor in 2002

HOUSE STANDING COMMITTEES:

1st GOVERNMENT REFORM AND OVERSIGHT, 105
GOVERNMENT REFORM, 106-107
Dates: Jan. 7, 1997-Jan. 3, 2003
Departure: Left the House; elected Governor

Cong.	Ranking	Terms in: House	Comm.	Date of Assignment
105th	Min-16th	1	1	Jan. 7, 1997
106th	Min-14th	2	2	Jan. 6, 1999
107th	Min-12th	3	3	Jan. 31, 2001

2nd NATIONAL SECURITY, 105
ARMED SERVICES, 106-107
Dates: Jan. 7, 1997-Jan. 3, 2003
Departure: Left the House; elected Governor

Cong.	Ranking	Terms in: House	Comm.	Date of Assignment
105th	Min-16th	1	1	Jan. 7, 1997

| 106th | Min-12th | 2 | 2 | Jan. 6, 1999 |
| 107th | Min-10th | 3 | 3 | Jan. 31, 2001 |

Thomas J. Bliley Jr. (R-Va.)

Dates: Jan. 28, 1932
House: Jan. 3, 1981-Jan. 3, 2001
Left the House: Retired in 2000

HOUSE STANDING COMMITTEES:

1st DISTRICT OF COLUMBIA
Dates: Jan. 28, 1981-Jan. 3, 1995
Departure: Committee abolished in 1995; no new assignment

Cong.	Ranking	Terms in: House	Comm.	Date of Assignment
103rd	Min-RM	7	7	Jan. 5, 1993

2nd ENERGY AND COMMERCE, 97-103
COMMERCE, 104-106
Dates: Jan. 28, 1981-Jan. 3, 2001
Departure: Left the House; retired

Cong.	Ranking	Terms in: House	Comm.	Date of Assignment
103rd	Min-2nd	7	7	Jan. 5, 1993
104th	Maj-Chr	8	8	Jan. 4, 1995
105th	Maj-Chr	9	9	Jan. 7, 1997
106th	Maj-Chr	10	10	Jan. 6, 1999

3rd STANDARDS OF OFFICIAL CONDUCT
Dates: May 9, 1984-Jan. 3, 1985
Departure: Left committee; no new assignment.

HOUSE SELECT AND SPECIAL COMMITTEES:

1st SELECT CHILDREN, YOUTH AND FAMILIES (Temporary)
Dates: Feb. 2, 1983-Jan. 3, 1991
Departure: Left committee; became Ranking Minority Member on District of Columbia

Earl Blumenauer (D-Ore.)

Dates: Aug. 16, 1948
House: May 21, 1996-date
Serving in the 111th Congress

H: Blumenauer was elected to the 104th Congress by special election, May 21, 1996, to fill the vacancy caused by the resignation of U.S. Representative Ronald L. Wyden (D-Ore.) who was elected to the U.S. Senate. Blumenauer was seated May 30, 1996, and assigned to committees.

HOUSE STANDING COMMITTEES:

1st ECONOMIC AND EDUCATIONAL OPPORTUNITIES
Dates: June 5, 1996-Mar. 5, 1997
Departure: Resigned committee; moved to Transportation and Infrastructure

Cong.	Ranking	Terms in: House	Comm.	Date of Assignment
104th	MnR-2nd	1	1	June 5, 1996
105th	Min-14th	2	2	Jan. 7, 1997

2nd SMALL BUSINESS
Dates: June 5, 1996-Jan. 3, 1997
Departure: Left committee; no new assignment

Cong.	Ranking	Terms in: House	Comm.	Date of Assignment
104th	MnR-4th	1	1	June 5, 1996

3rd TRANSPORTATION AND INFRASTRUCTURE
Dates: Mar. 6, 1997-Jan. 3, 2007
Departure: Moved to Ways and Means and Budget

Cong.	Ranking	Terms in: House	Comm.	Date of Assignment
105th	Min-31st	2	1	Mar. 6, 1997
106th	Min-22nd	3	2	Jan. 6, 1999
107th	Min-19th	4	3	Jan. 31, 2001
108th	Min-15th	5	4	Jan. 28, 2003
109th	Min-14th	6	5	Jan. 26, 2005

4th INTERNATIONAL RELATIONS
Dates: Feb. 8, 2001-Jan. 3, 2007
Departure: Moved to Ways and Means and Budget

Cong.	Ranking	Terms in: House	Comm.	Date of Assignment
107th	Min-20th	4	1	Feb. 8, 2001
108th	Min-16th	5	2	Jan. 28, 2003
109th	Min-15th	6	3	Jan. 26, 2005

5th WAYS AND MEANS
Dates: Jan. 4, 2007-date
Departure: Still serving in the 111th Congress

Cong.	Ranking	Terms in: House	Comm.	Date of Assignment
110th	Maj-16th	7	1	Jan. 4, 2007
111th	Maj-13th	8	2	Jan. 7, 2009

6th BUDGET
Dates: Jan. 18, 2007-date
Departure: Still serving in the 111th Congress

Cong.	Ranking	Terms in: House	Comm.	Date of Assignment
110th	Maj-11th	7	1	Jan. 18, 2007
111th	Maj-6th	8	2	Jan. 21, 2009

HOUSE SELECT AND SPECIAL COMMITTEES:

1st SELECT ENERGY INDEPENDENCE AND GLOBAL WARMING
Dates: Mar. 9, 2007-date
Departure: Still serving in the 111th Congress

Cong.	Ranking	Terms in: House	Comm.	Date of Assignment
110th	Maj-2nd	7	1	Mar. 9, 2007
111th	Maj-2nd	8	2	Feb. 3, 2009

Roy Blunt (R-Mo.)

Dates: Jan. 10, 1950
House: Jan. 3, 1997-date
Serving in the 111th Congress

HOUSE STANDING COMMITTEES:

1st AGRICULTURE
Dates: Jan. 7, 1997-Jan. 3, 1999
Departure: Moved to Commerce

Cong.	Ranking	Terms in: House	Comm.	Date of Assignment
105th	Maj-22nd	1	1	Jan. 7, 1997

2nd INTERNATIONAL RELATIONS, 105, 108
FOREIGN AFFAIRS, 110-111
1st Dates: Jan. 7, 1997-Jan. 3, 1999
1st Departure: Moved to Commerce
2nd Dates: Jan. 28, 2004-Jan. 3, 2005
2nd Departure: Left committee; no new assignment
Temporary Dates: Oct 10, 2007-Dec. 18, 2007
Temporary Departure: Resigned committee to open seat for Wittman; returned to Energy and Commerce

Cong.	Ranking	Terms in: House	Comm.	Date of Assignment
105th	Maj-24th	1 *1	1	Jan. 7, 1997
108th	MjR-1st	4 *2	1	Jan. 28, 2004
110th	Min-18th	6 *T	1	Oct. 10, 2007

3rd TRANSPORTATION AND INFRASTRUCTURE
Dates: Jan. 7, 1997-Jan. 3, 1999
Departure: Moved to Commerce

Cong.	Ranking	Terms in: House	Comm.	Date of Assignment
105th	Maj-29th	1	1	Jan. 7, 1997

4th COMMERCE, 106
ENERGY AND COMMERCE, 107-111
1st Dates: Jan. 6, 1999-Jan. 28, 2004
1st Departure: Resigned committee, moved to International Relations; returned with seniority intact
2nd Dates: Jan. 6, 2005-Jan. 3, 2007
Note: Temporarily stepped aside to serve as Interim Majority Leader from Sep. 29, 2005-Feb. 2, 2006; returned on Feb. 8, 2006
2nd Departure: Elected Republican Whip
3rd Dates: Dec. 18, 2007-date
3rd Departure: Still serving in the 111th Congress

Cong.	Ranking	Terms in: House	Comm.	Date of Assignment
106th	Maj-27th	2 *1	1	Jan. 6, 1999
107th	Maj-21st	3 *1	2	Jan. 6, 2001
108th	Maj-19th	4 *1	3	Jan. 28, 2003
109th	Maj-16th	5 *2	1	Jan. 6, 2005
110th	MnR-3rd	6 *3	1	Dec. 18, 2007
111th	Min-9th	7 *3	2	Jan. 9, 2009

5th APPROPRIATIONS
Dates: July 19, 1999-Feb. 1, 2000
Departure: Resigned committee to open seat for Goode; no new assignment

Cong.	Ranking	Terms in: House	Comm.	Date of Assignment
106th	MjR-1st	2	1	July 19, 1999

HOUSE SELECT AND SPECIAL COMMITTEES:

1st PERMANENT SELECT INTELLIGENCE
1st Dates: Sep. 29, 2004-Nov. 16, 2004
1st Departure: Resigned committee; no new assignment
2nd Dates: Feb. 4, 2009-date
2nd Departure: Still serving in the 111th Congress

Cong.	Ranking	Terms in: House	Comm.	Date of Assignment
108th	MjR-1st	4 *1	1	Sep. 29, 2004
111th	Min-6th	7 *2	1	Feb. 4, 2009

HOUSE LEADERSHIP POSTS

Dates: Jan. 3, 2003-Jan. 3, 2009
Departure: Left post; resumed committee service

1st HOUSE MAJORITY WHIP
Dates: Jan. 3, 2003-Jan. 3, 2007
Note: For the 108th Congress, Blunt was elected on Nov. 13, 2002, to succeed Majority Whip Thomas DeLay (R-Tex.) without opposition. He was re-elected unopposed for the 109th Congress.
Departure: Republican Party lost majority in 2006

Cong.	Ranking	Terms in: House	Post	Date of Selection
108th	Maj-3rd	4	1	Nov. 13, 2002
109th	Maj-3rd	5	2	Nov 16, 2004

2nd HOUSE MAJORITY FLOOR LEADER (Interim)
Dates: Sep. 29, 2005-Feb. 2, 2006
Note: In the 109th Congress, Blunt replaced DeLay as Majority Floor Leader *ad interim* on Sep. 29, 2005, but was defeated by John Boehner (R-Ohio) on the second ballot of the Majority Leader contest, 109-122, on Feb. 2, 2002.
Departure: Lost post; defeated in Republican Conference

Cong.	Ranking	Terms in: House	Post	Date of Selection
109th	Maj-2nd	5	1	Sep. 29, 2005

3rd HOUSE MINORITY WHIP
Dates: Jan. 3, 2007-Jan. 3, 2009
Note: For the 110th Congress, Blunt defeated John Shadegg (R-Ariz.), 137 to 57 on the first ballot on Nov. 17, 2006
Departure: Left post; no new assignment

Cong.	Ranking	Terms in: House	Post	Date of Selection
110th	Min-2nd	6	1	Nov. 17, 2006

Peter I. Blute (R-Mass.)

Dates: Jan. 28, 1956
House: Jan. 3, 1993-Jan. 3, 1997
Left the House: Defeated for re-election in 1996

HOUSE STANDING COMMITTEES:

1st PUBLIC WORKS AND TRANSPORTATION, 103
TRANSPORTATION AND INFRASTRUCTURE, 104
Dates: Jan. 5, 1993-Jan. 3, 1997
Departure: Left the House; lost re-election

Cong.	Ranking	Terms in: House	Comm.	Date of Assignment
103rd	Min-20th	1	1	Jan. 5, 1993
104th	Maj-19th	2	2	Jan. 4, 1995

2nd SCIENCE, SPACE AND TECHNOLOGY
Dates: Jan. 5, 1993-Jan. 3, 1995
Departure: Moved to Government Reform and Oversight

Cong.	Ranking	Terms in: House	Comm.	Date of Assignment
103rd	Min-19th	1	1	Jan. 5, 1993

3rd GOVERNMENT REFORM AND OVERSIGHT
Dates: Jan. 4, 1995-Jan. 3, 1997
Departure: Left the House; lost re-election

Cong.	Ranking	Terms in: House	Comm.	Date of Assignment
104th	Maj-12th	2	1	Jan. 4, 1995

John A. Boccieri (D-Ohio)

Dates: Oct. 5, 1969
House: Jan. 3, 2009-date
Serving in the 111th Congress

HOUSE STANDING COMMITTEES:

1st TRANSPORTATION AND INFRASTRUCTURE
Dates: Jan. 7, 2009-date
Departure: Still serving in the 111th Congress

Cong.	Ranking	Terms in: House	Comm.	Date of Assignment
111th	Maj-38th	1	1	Jan. 7, 2009

2nd AGRICULTURE
Dates: Jan. 21, 2009-date
Departure: Still serving in the 111th Congress

Cong.	Ranking	Terms in: House	Comm.	Date of Assignment
111th	Maj-25th	1	1	Jan. 21, 2009

Sherwood L. Boehlert (R-N.Y.)

Dates: June 28, 1936
House: Jan. 3, 1983-Jan. 3, 2007
Left the House: Retired in 2006

HOUSE STANDING COMMITTEES:

1st SCIENCE AND TECHNOLOGY, 98-99
SCIENCE, SPACE AND TECHNOLOGY, 100-103
SCIENCE, 104-109
Dates: Jan. 6, 1983-Jan. 3, 2007
Departure: Left the House; retired

Cong.	Ranking	Terms in: House	Comm.	Date of Assignment
103rd	Min-3rd	6	6	Jan. 5, 1993
104th	Maj-3rd	7	7	Jan. 4, 1995
105th	Maj-2nd	8	8	Jan. 21, 1997
106th	Maj-2nd	9	9	Jan. 6, 1999
107th	Maj-Chr	10	10	Jan. 6, 2001
108th	Maj-Chr	11	11	Jan. 8, 2003
109th	Maj-Chr	12	12	Jan. 6, 2005

2nd SMALL BUSINESS
Dates: Jan. 6, 1983-Jan. 3, 1985
Departure: Moved to Public Works and Transportation

3rd PUBLIC WORKS AND TRANSPORTATION, 99-103
TRANSPORTATION AND INFRASTRUCTURE, 104-109
Dates: Jan. 30, 1985-Jan. 3, 2007
Departure: Left the House; retired

Cong.	Ranking	Terms in: House	Comm.	Date of Assignment
103rd	Min-4th	6	5	Jan. 5, 1993
104th	Maj-5th	7	6	Jan. 4, 1995
105th	Maj-4th	8	7	Jan. 7, 1997
106th	Maj-4th	9	8	Jan. 6, 1999
107th	Maj-4th	10	9	Jan. 6, 2001
108th	Maj-3rd	11	10	Jan. 28, 2003
109th	Maj-3rd	12	11	Jan. 26, 2005

4th POST OFFICE AND CIVIL SERVICE
Dates: Feb. 18, 1993-Jan. 3, 1995
Departure: Committee abolished; no new assignment

Cong.	Ranking	Terms in: House	Comm.	Date of Assignment
103rd	Min-8th	6	1	Feb. 18, 1993

HOUSE SELECT AND SPECIAL COMMITTEES:

1st SELECT AGING (Permanent)
Dates: Feb. 21, 1985-Jan. 3, 1993
Termination: Committee not renewed in 1993

2nd FIRE SAFETY IN THE HOUSE
Dates: June 16, 1988-Jan. 3, 1989
Termination: Committee terminated in 1989

3rd HOUSE RECORDING STUDIO
Dates: Feb. 23, 1989-Jan. 3, 1993
Departure: Committee terminated.

Cong.	Ranking	Terms in: House	Comm.	Date of Assignment
102nd	Min-RM	5	2	Feb. 18,1992

4th PERMANENT SELECT INTELLIGENCE
Dates: Feb. 10, 1997-Jan. 3, 2005
Note: Temporarily removed by Speaker on Sep. 29, 2004; returned to committee on Nov. 16, 2004
Departure: Left committee; no new assignment

Cong.	Ranking	Terms in: House	Comm.	Date of Assignment
105th	Maj-7th	8	1	Feb. 10, 1997
106th	Maj-5th	9	2	Jan. 19, 1999
107th	Maj-4th	10	3	Jan. 30, 2001
108th	Maj-3rd	11	4	Jan. 8, 2003

5th SELECT HOMELAND SECURITY
Dates: Feb. 12, 2003-Jan. 3, 2005
Departure: Did not continue on reorganized standing committee

Cong.	Ranking	Terms in: House	Comm.	Date of Assignment
108th	Maj-10th	11	1	Feb. 12, 2003

John A. Boehner (R-Ohio)

Dates: Nov. 17, 1948
House: Jan. 3, 1991-date
Serving in the 111th Congress

HOUSE STANDING COMMITTEES:

1st AGRICULTURE
Dates: Jan. 24, 1991-Feb. 6, 2006
Departure: Resigned committee; elected Majority Leader

Cong.	Ranking	Terms in: House	Comm.	Date of Assignment
103rd	Min-11th	2	2	Jan. 5, 1993
104th	Maj-7th	3	3	Jan. 4, 1995
105th	Maj-4th	4	4	Jan. 7, 1997
106th	Maj-3rd	5	5	Jan. 6, 1999
107th	Maj-2nd	6	6	Jan. 6, 2001
108th	Maj-3rd	7	7	Jan. 28, 2003
109th	Maj-2nd	8	8	Jan. 26, 2005

2nd EDUCATION AND LABOR, 102-103
EDUCATION AND THE WORKFORCE, 106-109
1st Dates: Jan. 24, 1991-Jan. 3, 1995
1st Departure: Left committee; became Chair of Republican Conference
2nd Dates: Jan. 6, 1999-Feb. 6, 2006
Ch1: Replaced by Howard P. (Buck) McKeon (R-Cal.) on Feb. 15, 2006
2nd Departure: Resigned committee; elected Majority Leader

Cong.	Ranking	Terms in: House	Comm.	Date of Assignment
103rd	Min-11th	2 *1	2	Jan. 5, 1993
106th	Maj-6th	5 *2	1	Jan. 6, 1999
107th	Maj-Chr	6 *2	2	Jan. 6, 2001
108th	Maj-Chr	7 *2	3	Jan. 8, 2003
109th	Maj-Ch1	8 *2	4	Jan. 6, 2005

3rd SMALL BUSINESS
Dates: Jan. 24, 1991-Jan. 3, 1993
Departure: Moved to House Administration

4th HOUSE ADMINISTRATION, 103, 106
HOUSE OVERSIGHT, 104-105
Dates: Jan. 5, 1993-Jan. 3, 2001
Departure: Left committee; became Chair of Education and the Workforce

Cong.	Ranking	Terms in: House	Comm.	Date of Assignment
103rd	Min-6th	2	1	Jan. 5, 1993
104th	Maj-4th	3	2	Jan. 4, 1995
105th	Maj-2nd	4	3	Jan. 7, 1997
106th	Maj-2nd	5	4	Jan. 6, 1999

JOINT COMMITTEES:

1st JOINT LIBRARY
House Dates: Mar. 2, 1990-Jan. 3, 2001
Departure: Left committee; became Chair of Education and the Workforce

Cong.	Ranking	Terms in: House	Comm.	Date of Assignment
106th	Maj-2nd	5	1	Mar. 2, 1999

2nd JOINT PRINTING
House Dates: Mar. 2, 1999-Jan. 3, 2001
Departure: Left committee; became Chair of Education and the Workforce

Cong.	Ranking	Terms in: House	Comm.	Date of Assignment
106th	Maj-2nd	5	1	Mar. 2, 1999

HOUSE LEADERSHIP POSTS

Dates: Feb. 2, 2006-date
Departure: Still serving in the 111th Congress

1st HOUSE MAJORITY FLOOR LEADER
Dates: Feb. 2, 2006-Jan. 3, 2007
Note: In the 109th Congress, Boehner defeated Interim Floor Leader Roy Blunt (R-Mo.) on the second ballot, 122-109, Feb. 2, 2006
Departure: Republican Party lost House majority in 2006

Cong.	Ranking	Terms in: House	Post	Date of Selection
109th	Maj-2nd	8	1	Feb. 2, 2006

2nd HOUSE MINORITY FLOOR LEADER
Dates: Jan. 3, 2007-date
Note: For the 110th Congress, Boehner defeated Mike Pence (R-Ind.) and Joe Barton (R-Tex.), 168-27-1 on Nov. 17, 2006. He defeated Dan Lungren (R-Cal) for the 111th Congress.
Departure: Still serving in the 111th Congress

Cong.	Ranking	Terms in: House	Post	Date of Selection
110th	Min-1st	9	1	Nov. 17, 2006
111th	Min-1st	10	2	Nov. 18, 2008

Christopher S. (Kit) Bond (R-Mo.)

Dates: March 6, 1939
Senate: Jan. 3, 1987-date
Serving in the 111th Congress

SENATE STANDING COMMITTEES:

1st AGRICULTURE, NUTRITION AND FORESTRY
Dates: Jan. 6, 1987-Feb. 5, 1991
Departure: Moved to Appropriations

2nd BANKING, HOUSING AND URBAN AFFAIRS
Dates: Jan. 6, 1987-Jan. 3, 1997
Departure: Left committee; no new assignment

Cong.	Ranking	Years in: Senate	Comm.	Date of Assignment
103rd	Min-3rd	7	7	Jan. 7, 1993
104th	Maj-4th	9	8	Jan. 4, 1995

3rd SMALL BUSINESS renamed June 29, 2001
SMALL BUSINESS AND ENTREPRENEURSHIP
Dates: Jan. 6, 1987-date
Ch1: Replaced by John F. Kerry (D-Mass.) following party control shift on June 6, 2001, and became RM2
Departure: Still serving in the 111th Congress

Cong.	Ranking	Years in: Senate	Comm.	Date of Assignment
103rd	Min-3rd	7	7	Jan. 21, 1993
104th	Maj-Chr	9	9	Jan. 6, 1995
105th	Maj-Chr	11	11	Jan. 9, 1997
106th	Maj-Chr	13	13	Jan. 7, 1999
107th	Maj-Ch1	15	15	Jan. 25, 2001
+107th	Min-RM2	15	15	June 6, 2001
108th	Maj-2nd	17	17	Jan. 15, 2003
109th	Maj-2nd	19	19	Jan. 6, 2005
110th	Min-2nd	21	21	Jan. 12, 2007
111th	Min-2nd	23	23	Jan. 21, 2009

4th BUDGET
Dates: Feb. 2, 1989-Jan. 15, 2003
Departure: Moved to Select Intelligence

Cong.	Ranking	Years in: Senate	Comm.	Date of Assignment
103rd	Min-5th	7	4	Jan. 21, 1993
104th	Maj-5th	9	6	Jan. 6, 1995
105th	Maj-5th	11	8	Jan. 9, 1997
106th	Maj-5th	13	10	Jan. 7, 1999
107th	Maj-5th	15	12	Jan. 25, 2001
+107th	Min-5th	15	13	June 6, 2001

5th APPROPRIATIONS
Dates: Feb. 5, 1991-date
Departure: Still serving in the 111th Congress

Cong.	Ranking	Years in: Senate	Comm.	Date of Assignment
103rd	Min-9th	7	2	Jan. 7, 1993
104th	Maj-7th	9	4	Jan. 4, 1995
105th	Maj-5th	11	6	Jan. 9, 1997
106th	Maj-5th	13	8	Jan. 7, 1999
107th	Maj-5th	15	10	Jan. 25, 2001
+107th	Min-5th	15	11	June 6, 2001
108th	Maj-5th	17	12	Jan. 15, 2003

Cong.	Ranking	Senate	Comm.	Date of Assignment
109th	Maj-5th	19	14	Jan. 6, 2005
110th	Min-5th	21	16	Jan. 12, 2007
111th	Min-3rd	23	18	Jan. 21, 2009

6th ENVIRONMENT AND PUBLIC WORKS
Dates: Jan. 5, 1995-date
Departure: Still serving in the 111th Congress

		Years in:		Date of
Cong.	Ranking	Senate	Comm.	Assignment
104th	Maj-9th	9	1	Jan. 5, 1995
105th	Maj-7th	11	3	Jan. 9, 1997
106th	Maj-6th	13	5	Jan. 7, 1999
107th	Maj-4th	15	7	Jan. 25, 2001
+107th	Min-4th	15	7	June 6, 2001
108th	Maj-3rd	17	9	Jan. 15, 2003
109th	Maj-3rd	19	11	Jan. 6, 2005
110th	Min-9th	21	13	Jan. 12, 2007
111th	Maj-7th	23	15	Jan. 21, 2009

7th HEALTH, EDUCATION, LABOR AND PENSIONS
Dates: Jan. 25, 2001-Jan. 6, 2005
Departure: Left committee; no new assignment

		Years in:		Date of
Cong.	Ranking	Senate	Comm.	Assignment
107th	Maj-7th	15	1	Jan. 25, 2001
+107th	Min-6th	15	1	July 10, 2001
108th	Maj-5th	17	2	Jan. 15, 2003

SENATE SELECT AND SPECIAL COMMITTEES:

1st JUDGE ALCEE L. HASTINGS IMPEACHMENT
Dates: Mar. 16, 1989-Aug. 3, 1989
Termination: Senate Hearing 101-194, Parts 1-2A

2nd SPECIAL COMMITTEE TO INVESTIGATE WHITEWATER DEVELOPMENT CORPORATION AND RELATED MATTERS
Dates: July 20, 1995-June 17, 1996
Termination: Senate Report 104-280 filed

		Years in:		Date of
Cong.	Ranking	Senate	Comm.	Assignment
104th	Maj-3rd	9	1	July 20, 1995

3rd SELECT INTELLIGENCE (Permanent)
Dates: Jan. 15, 2003-date
Departure: Still serving in the 111th Congress.

		Years in:		Date of
Cong.	Ranking	Senate	Comm.	Assignment
108th	Maj-4th	17	1	Jan. 15, 2003
109th	Maj-4th	19	2	Jan. 6, 2005
110th	Min-VCh	21	4	Jan. 12, 2007
111th	Min-VCh	23	7	Jan. 21, 2009

Henry Bonilla (R-Tex.)

Dates: Jan. 2, 1954
House: Jan. 3, 1993-Jan. 3, 2007
Left the House: Defeated for re-election in 2006

HOUSE STANDING COMMITTEES:

1st APPROPRIATIONS
Dates: Jan. 5, 1993-Jan. 3, 2007
Departure: Left the House; lost re-election

		Terms in:		Date of
Cong.	Ranking	House	Comm.	Assignment
103rd	Min-23rd	1	1	Jan. 5, 1993
104th	Maj-21st	2	2	Jan. 4, 1995
105th	Maj-18th	3	3	Jan. 7, 1997
106th	Maj-16th	4	4	Jan. 6, 1999
107th	Maj-14th	5	5	Jan. 6, 2001
108th	Maj-11th	6	6	Jan. 28, 2003
109th	Maj-11th	7	7	Jan. 6, 2005

HOUSE SELECT AND SPECIAL COMMITTEES:

1st SELECT BIPARTISAN COMMITTEE TO INVESTIGATE THE PREPARATION FOR AND RESPONSE TO HURRICANE KATRINA
Dates: Sep. 21, 2005-Feb. 15, 2006
Departure: House Report 377 (109-2) filed

		Terms in:		Date of
Cong.	Ranking	House	Comm.	Assignment
109th	Maj-5th	7	1	Sep. 21, 2005

David E. Bonior (D-Mich.)

Dates: June 6, 1945
House: Jan. 3, 1977-Jan. 3, 2003
Left the House: Lost nomination for Governor in 2002

HOUSE STANDING COMMITTEES:

1st MERCHANT MARINE AND FISHERIES
Dates: Jan. 19, 1977-Jan. 3, 1981
Departure: Moved to Rules

2nd PUBLIC WORKS AND TRANSPORTATION
Dates: Jan. 19, 1977-Jan. 3, 1981
Departure: Moved to Rules

3rd RULES
Dates: Jan. 28, 1981-Jan. 3, 1995
Departure: Left committee; elected Minority Whip

		Terms in:		Date of
Cong.	Ranking	House	Comm.	Assignment
103rd	Maj-5th	9	7	Jan. 5, 1993

HOUSE SELECT AND SPECIAL COMMITTEES:

1st OUTER CONTINENTAL SHELF
Dates: Apr. 9, 1979-July 31, 1980
Termination: House Report 1214 (96-2) filed

2nd PERMANENT SELECT INTELLIGENCE
Dates: Feb. 5, 1991-Jan. 3, 1993
Departure: Left committee; no new assignment

HOUSE LEADERSHIP POSTS

Dates: July 11, 1991-Jan. 15, 2002
Departure: Resigned post to seek Democratic nomination for Governor

1st HOUSE MAJORITY WHIP
Dates: July 11, 1991-Jan. 3, 1995
Note: For the 102nd Congress, Bonior succeeded Majority Whip William H. Gray III (D-Penn.), who had resigned. Bonior defeated Steny H. Hoyer (D-Md.), 160 to 109 on the first ballot on July 11, 1991. Bonior's service began Sep. 11, 1991, following Gray's resignation. Bonior was unopposed for the 103rd Congress.
Departure: Democratic Party lost House majority in 1994

Cong.	Ranking	Terms in: House	Post	Date of Selection
103rd	Maj-3rd	9	2	Dec. 11, 1992

2nd HOUSE MINORITY WHIP
Dates: Jan. 3, 1995-Jan. 15, 2002
Note: For the 104th Congress, Bonior defeated Charles Stenholm (D-Tex.), 145-85 on Nov. 30, 1994. Bonior was unopposed for the 105th-107th Congresses.
Departure: Left post to seek Democratic nomination for Governor

Cong.	Ranking	Terms in: House	Post	Date of Selection
104th	Min-2nd	10	1	Nov. 30, 1994
105th	Min-2nd	11	2	Nov. 18, 1996
106th	Min-2nd	12	3	Nov. 16, 1998
107th	Min-2nd	13	4	Nov. 14, 2000

Josiah R. (Jo) Bonner Jr. (R-Ala.)

Dates: Nov. 19, 1959
House: Jan. 3, 2003-date
Serving in the 111th Congress

HOUSE STANDING COMMITTEES:

1st AGRICULTURE
Dates: Jan. 28, 2003-Feb. 25, 2008
Departure: Resigned committee; moved to Appropriations

Cong.	Ranking	Terms in: House	Comm.	Date of Assignment
108th	Maj-22nd	1	1	Jan. 28, 2003
109th	Maj-14th	2	2	Jan. 26, 2005
110th	Min-8th	3	3	Jan. 10, 2007

2nd BUDGET
Dates: Jan. 28, 2003-Jan. 3, 2009
Departure: Left committee; became Ranking Member on Standards of Official Conduct

Cong.	Ranking	Terms in: House	Comm.	Date of Assignment
108th	Maj-17th	1	1	Jan. 28, 2003
109th	Maj-8th	2	2	Jan. 26, 2005
110th	Min-2nd	3	3	Jan. 18, 2007

3rd SCIENCE
Dates: Jan. 28, 2003-Feb. 25, 2008
Departure: Resigned committee; moved to Appropriations

Cong.	Ranking	Terms in: House	Comm.	Date of Assignment
108th	Maj-24th	1	1	Jan. 28, 2003
109th	Maj-16th	2	2	Jan. 26, 2005
110th	Min-11th	3	3	Jan. 10, 2007

4th STANDARDS OF OFFICIAL CONDUCT
Dates: Feb. 12, 2007-date
Departure: Still serving in the 111th Congress

Cong.	Ranking	Terms in: House	Comm.	Date of Assignment
110th	Min-2nd	3	1	Feb. 12, 2007
111th	Min-RM	4	2	Jan. 9, 2009

5th APPROPRIATIONS
Dates: Feb. 26, 2008-date
Departure: Still serving in the 111th Congress

Cong.	Ranking	Terms in: House	Comm.	Date of Assignment
110th	MnR-2nd	3	1	Feb. 26, 2008
111th	Min-21st	4	2	Jan. 9, 2009

Mary Mack Bono (R-Cal.)

Dates: Oct. 24, 1961
House: April 7, 1998-date
Serving in the 111th Congress

H: Mary Bono was elected to the 105th Congress by special election, April 7, 1998, to fill the vacancy caused by the death of her husband, U.S. Representative Sonny Bono (R-Cal.). Mrs. Bono was seated April 21, 1998, and assigned to committees. Served as Mary Bono from the 105th through 110th Congresses

HOUSE STANDING COMMITTEES:

1st JUDICIARY
Dates: May 13, 1998-Jan. 3, 2001
Departure: Moved to Energy and Commerce

Cong.	Ranking	Terms in: House	Comm.	Date of Assignment
105th	MjR-2nd	1	1	May 13, 1998
106th	Maj-20th	2	2	Jan. 6, 1999

2nd NATIONAL SECURITY, 105
ARMED SERVICES, 106
Dates: May 13, 1998-Jan. 3, 2001
Departure: Moved to Energy and Commerce

Cong.	Ranking	Terms in: House	Comm.	Date of Assignment
105th	MjA-32nd	1	1	May 13, 1998
106th	Maj-28th	2	2	Jan. 6, 1999

3rd SMALL BUSINESS
Dates: Feb 2, 1999-Jan. 3, 2001
Departure: Moved to Energy and Commerce

Cong.	Ranking	Terms in: House	Comm.	Date of Assignment
106th	Maj-19th	2	1	Feb. 2, 1999

4th ENERGY AND COMMERCE
Dates: Jan. 6, 2001-date
Departure: Still serving in the 111th Congress

Cong.	Ranking	Terms in: House	Comm.	Date of Assignment
107th	Maj-29th	3	1	Jan. 6, 2001
108th	Maj-24th	4	2	Jan. 28, 2003
109th	Maj-21st	5	3	Jan. 6, 2005
110th	Min-18th	6	4	Jan. 10, 2007
111th	Min-13th	7	5	Jan. 9, 2009

Sonny Bono (R-Cal.)

Dates: Feb. 16, 1935-Jan. 5, 1998
House: Jan. 3, 1995-Jan. 5, 1998
Left the House: Died in office

HOUSE STANDING COMMITTEES:

1st BANKING AND FINANCIAL SERVICES
Dates: Jan. 4, 1995-Jan. 3, 1997
Departure: Moved to National Security

Cong.	Ranking	Terms in: House	Comm.	Date of Assignment
104th	Maj-16th	1	1	Jan. 4, 1995

2nd JUDICIARY
Dates: Jan. 4, 1995-Jan. 5, 1998
Departure: Died in office

Cong.	Ranking	Terms in: House	Comm.	Date of Assignment
104th	Maj-15th	1	1	Jan. 4, 1995
105th	Maj-13th	2	2	Jan. 7, 1997

3rd NATIONAL SECURITY
Dates: Jan. 7, 1997-Jan. 5, 1998
Departure: Died in office

Cong.	Ranking	Terms in: House	Comm.	Date of Assignment
105th	Maj-26th	2	1	Jan. 7, 1997

John Boozman (R-Ark.)

Dates: Dec. 10, 1950
House: Nov. 20, 2001-date
Serving in the 111th Congress

H: Boozman was elected to the 107th Congress by special election, Nov. 20, 2001, to fill the vacancy caused by the resignation of U.S. Representative Asa Hutchinson (R-Ark.). Boozman was seated Nov. 29, 2001 and assigned to committees.

HOUSE STANDING COMMITTEES:

1st TRANSPORTATION AND INFRASTRUCTURE
Dates: Dec. 4, 2001-date
Departure: Still serving in the 111th Congress

Cong.	Ranking	Terms in: House	Comm.	Date of Assignment
107th	MjR-4th	1	1	Dec. 4, 2001
108th	Maj-32nd	2	2	Jan. 28, 2003
109th	Maj-26th	3	3	Jan. 26, 2005
110th	Min-19th	4	4	Jan. 10, 2007
111th	Min-15th	5	5	Jan. 9, 2009

2nd VETERANS' AFFAIRS
Dates: Dec. 4, 2001-date
Departure: Still serving in the 111th Congress

Cong.	Ranking	Terms in: House	Comm.	Date of Assignment
107th	MjR-2nd	1	1	Dec. 4, 2001
108th	Maj-13th	2	2	Jan. 28, 2003
109th	Maj-10th	3	3	Jan. 26, 2005
110th	Min-8th	4	4	Jan. 10, 2007
111th	Min-6th	5	5	Jan. 9, 2009

3rd INTERNATIONAL RELATIONS, 109
FOREIGN AFFAIRS, 110-111
Dates: Jan. 26, 2005-date
Departure: Still serving in the 111th Congress

Cong.	Ranking	Terms in: House	Comm.	Date of Assignment
109th	Maj-23rd	3	1	Jan. 26, 2005
110th	Min-16th	4	2	Jan. 10, 2007
111th	Min-12th	5	3	Jan. 9, 2009

Madeleine Z. Bordallo (D-Guam)

Dates: May 31, 1933
House: Jan. 3, 2003-date
Serving in the 111th Congress

HOUSE STANDING COMMITTEES:

1st ARMED SERVICES
Dates: Feb. 5, 2003-date
Departure: Still serving in the 111th Congress

Cong.	Ranking	Terms in: House	Comm.	Date of Assignment
108th	Min-27th	1	1	Feb. 5, 2003
109th	Min-23rd	2	2	Jan. 26, 2005
110th	Maj-20th	3	3	Jan. 10, 2007
111th	Maj-19th	4	4	Jan. 7, 2009

2nd RESOURCES, 108-109
NATURAL RESOURCES, 110-111
Dates: Feb. 5, 2003-date
Departure: Still serving in the 111th Congress

Cong.	Ranking	Terms in: House	Comm.	Date of Assignment
108th	Min-22nd	1	1	Feb. 5, 2003
109th	Min-12th	2	2	Jan. 26, 2005
110th	Maj-11th	3	3	Jan. 18, 2007
111th	Maj-9th	4	4	Jan. 21, 2009

3rd SMALL BUSINESS
Dates: Feb. 13, 2003-Jan. 3, 2007
Departure: Left committee; no new assignment

Cong.	Ranking	Terms in: House	Comm.	Date of Assignment
108th	Min-15th	1	1	Feb. 13, 2003
109th	Min-9th	2	2	Feb. 2, 2005

Daniel D. Boren (D-Okla.)

Dates: Aug. 2, 1973
House: Jan. 3, 2005-date
Serving in the 111th Congress

HOUSE STANDING COMMITTEES:

1st ARMED SERVICES
1st Dates: Jan. 26, 2005-Feb. 5, 2009
1st Departure: Leave of absence; moved to Select Intelligence
2nd Dates: Apr. 30, 2009-date; returned without seniority
2nd Departure: Still serving in the 111th Congress

Cong.	Ranking	Terms in: House	Comm.	Date of Assignment
109th	Min-28th	1 *1	1	Jan. 26, 2005
110th	Maj-22nd	2 *1	2	Jan. 10, 2007
111th	Maj-20th	3 *1	3	Jan. 7, 2009
111th	MjR-1st	3 *2	1	Apr. 30, 2009

2nd RESOURCES, 109
NATURAL RESOURCES, 110-111
Dates: Jan. 26, 2005-date
Departure: Still serving in the 111th Congress

Cong.	Ranking	Terms in: House	Comm.	Date of Assignment
109th	Min-15th	1	1	Jan. 26, 2005
110th	Maj-13th	2	2	Jan. 18, 2007
111th	Maj-11th	3	3	Jan. 21, 2009

3rd FINANCIAL SERVICES
Dates: Jan. 18, 2007–June 6, 2008
Departure: Left committee; party ratio exceeded

Cong.	Ranking	Terms in: House	Comm.	Date of Assignment
110th	Maj-36th	2	1	Jan. 18, 2007

HOUSE SELECT AND SPECIAL COMMITTEES:

1st PERMANENT SELECT INTELLIGENCE
Dates: Feb. 4, 2009-date
Departure: Still serving in the 111th Congress

Cong.	Ranking	Terms in: House	Comm.	Date of Assignment
111th	Maj-13th	5	1	Feb. 4, 2009

David L. Boren (D-Okla.)

Dates: April 21, 1941
Senate: Jan. 3, 1979-Nov. 15, 1994
Left the Senate: Resigned the Senate, named President of the University of Oklahoma

SENATE STANDING COMMITTEES:

1st AGRICULTURE, NUTRITION AND FORESTRY
Dates: Jan. 23, 1979-Nov. 15, 1994
Departure: Resigned the Senate; retired

Cong.	Ranking	Years in: Senate	Comm.	Date of Assignment
103rd	Maj-3rd	15	14	Jan. 7, 1993

2nd FINANCE
Dates: Jan. 23, 1979-Nov. 15, 1994
Departure: Resigned the Senate; retired

Cong.	Ranking	Years in: Senate	Comm.	Date of Assignment
103rd	Maj-4th	15	14	Jan. 7, 1993

3rd SMALL BUSINESS
Dates: Jan. 3, 1983-Mar. 19, 1991
Departure: Left committee; no new assignment

SENATE SELECT AND SPECIAL COMMITTEES:

1st SELECT INTELLIGENCE (Permanent)
Dates: Jan. 3, 1985-Jan. 27, 1993
Departure: Moved to co-chair Joint Organization of Congress

2nd SECRET MILITARY ASSISTANCE TO IRAN AND THE NICARAGUAN OPPOSITION (Iran-Contra Affair)
Dates: Jan. 12, 1987-Nov. 17, 1987
Termination: Senate Report 100-216 filed

JOINT COMMITTEES:

1st JOINT ORGANIZATION OF CONGRESS (Ad Hoc)
Senate Dates: Oct. 8, 1992-Dec. 9, 1993
Termination: Senate Report 103-215 filed

Cong.	Ranking	Years in: Senate	Comm.	Date of Assignment
103rd	Maj-CoC	15	1	Continued

2nd JOINT TAXATION
Senate Dates: Jan. 20, 1993-Nov. 14, 1994
Departure: Resigned the Senate; retired

Cong.	Ranking	Years in: Senate	Comm.	Date of Assignment
103rd	Maj-3rd	15	1	Jan. 20, 1993

Robert A. Borski (D-Penn.)

Dates: Oct. 20, 1948
House: Jan. 3, 1983-Jan. 3, 2003
Left the House: Retired in 2002

HOUSE STANDING COMMITTEES:

1st MERCHANT MARINE AND FISHERIES
Dates: Jan. 6, 1983-Jan. 3, 1993
Departure: Moved to Foreign Affairs and Standards of Official Conduct.

2nd PUBLIC WORKS AND TRANSPORTATION, 98-103
TRANSPORTATION AND INFRASTRUCTURE, 104-107
Dates: Jan. 6, 1983-Jan. 3, 2003
Departure: Left the House; retired

Cong.	Ranking	Terms in: House	Comm.	Date of Assignment
103rd	Maj-6th	6	6	Jan. 5, 1993
104th	Min-4th	7	7	Jan. 4, 1995
105th	Min-3rd	8	8	Jan. 7, 1997
106th	Min-3rd	9	9	Jan. 6, 1999
107th	Min-3rd	10	10	Jan. 31, 2001

3rd FOREIGN AFFAIRS
Dates: Jan. 5, 1993-Jan. 3, 1995
Departure: Left committee; no new assignment

Cong.	Ranking	Terms in: House	Comm.	Date of Assignment
103rd	Maj-13th	6	1	Jan. 5, 1993

4th STANDARDS OF OFFICIAL CONDUCT
Dates: Feb. 4, 1993-Jan. 3, 1997
Departure: Left committee; no new assignment

Cong.	Ranking	Terms in: House	Comm.	Date of Assignment
103rd	Maj-6th	6	1	Feb. 4, 1993
104th	Min-4th	7	2	Jan. 20, 1995

HOUSE SELECT AND SPECIAL COMMITTEES:

1st SELECT AGING (Permanent)
Dates: Feb. 8, 1983-Jan. 3, 1993
Termination: Committee not renewed in 1993

2nd SELECT ETHICS
Dates: Jan. 7, 1997-Jan. 21, 1997
Termination: House Report 105-1 filed, Jan. 17, 1997

Cong.	Ranking	Terms in: House	Comm.	Date of Assignment
105th	Min-3rd	8	1	Jan. 7, 1997

Leonard L. Boswell (D-Iowa)

Dates: Jan. 10, 1934
House: Jan. 3, 1997-date
Serving in the 111th Congress

HOUSE STANDING COMMITTEES:

1st AGRICULTURE
1st Dates: Feb. 5, 1997-Feb. 5, 2003
1st Departure: Resigned committee; returned on Feb. 13, 2003
2nd Dates: Feb. 13, 2003-date
2nd Departure: Still serving in the 111th Congress

		Terms in:		Date of
Cong.	Ranking	House	Comm.	Assignment
105th	Min-23rd	1 *1	1	Feb. 5, 1997
106th	Min-20th	2 *1	2	Jan. 6, 1999
107th	Min-15th	3 *1	3	Jan. 31, 2001
108th	Min-8th	4 *1	4	Jan. 28, 2003
108th	Min-20th	4 *2	1	Feb. 13, 2003
109th	Min-19th	5 *2	2	Feb. 2, 2005
110th	Maj-5th	6 *2	3	Jan. 12, 2007
111th	Maj-4th	7 *2	4	Jan. 21, 2009

2nd TRANSPORTATION AND INFRASTRUCTURE
Dates: Jan. 7, 1997-date
Departure: Still serving in the 111th Congress

		Terms in:		Date of
Cong.	Ranking	House	Comm.	Assignment
105th	Min-29th	1	1	Jan. 7, 1997
106th	Min-26th	2	2	Jan. 6, 1999
107th	Min-23rd	3	3	Jan. 31, 2001
108th	Min-18th	4	4	Jan. 28, 2003
109th	Min-17th	5	5	Jan. 26, 2005
110th	Maj-14th	6	6	Jan. 10, 2007
111th	Maj-13th	7	7	Jan. 7, 2009

3rd ARMED SERVICES
Dates: May 6, 2010-date
Departure: Still serving in the 111th Congress

		Terms in:		Date of
Cong.	Ranking	House	Comm.	Assignment
111th	MjR-4th	7	1	May 6, 2010

HOUSE SELECT AND SPECIAL COMMITTEES:

1st PERMANENT SELECT INTELLIGENCE
Dates: Mar. 14, 2001-Jan. 3, 2009
Departure: Left committee; no new assignment

		Terms in:		Date of
Cong.	Ranking	House	Comm.	Assignment
107th	Min-9th	3	1	Mar. 14, 2001
108th	Min-4th	4	2	Jan. 8, 2003
109th	Min-4th	5	3	Jan. 26, 2005
110th	Maj-3rd	6	4	Jan. 17, 2007

Frederick C. Boucher (D-Va.)

Dates: Aug. 1, 1946
House: Jan. 3, 1983-date
Serving in the 111th Congress

HOUSE STANDING COMMITTEES:

1st EDUCATION AND LABOR
Dates: Jan. 6, 1983-Jan. 3, 1987
Departure: Moved to Energy and Commerce

2nd SCIENCE AND TECHNOLOGY, 98-99
SCIENCE, SPACE AND TECHNOLOGY, 100-103
Dates: Jan. 6, 1983-Jan. 3, 1995
Departure: Left committee; no new assignment

		Terms in:		Date of
Cong.	Ranking	House	Comm.	Assignment
103rd	Maj-9th	6	6	Jan. 5, 1993

3rd JUDICIARY
Temporary Dates: May 24, 1983-Nov. 18, 1983

Departure: Temporary term expired; filled own vacancy
2nd Dates: Feb. 29, 1984-date
2nd Departure: Still serving in the 111th Congress

		Terms in:		Date of
Cong.	Ranking	House	Comm.	Assignment
103rd	Maj-12th	6	6	Jan. 5, 1993
104th	Min-6th	7	7	Jan. 4, 1995
105th	Min-5th	8	8	Jan. 7, 1997
106th	Min-4th	9	9	Jan. 6, 1999
107th	Min-4th	10	10	Jan. 31, 2001
108th	Min-3rd	11	11	Jan. 28, 2003
109th	Min-3rd	12	12	Jan. 26, 2005
110th	Maj-3rd	13	13	Jan. 18, 2007
111th	Maj-3rd	14	14	Jan. 21, 2009

4th ENERGY AND COMMERCE, 100-103
COMMERCE, 104-106
ENERGY AND COMMERCE, 107-111
Dates: Jan. 22, 1987-date
Departure: Still serving in the 111th Congress

		Terms in:		Date of
Cong.	Ranking	House	Comm.	Assignment
103rd	Maj-14th	6	4	Jan. 5, 1993
104th	Min-8th	7	5	Jan. 4, 1995
105th	Min-6th	8	6	Jan. 7, 1997
106th	Min-5th	9	7	Jan. 6, 1999
107th	Min-5th	10	8	Jan. 31, 2001
108th	Min-5th	11	9	Jan. 28, 2003
109th	Min-4th	12	10	Jan. 26, 2005
110th	Maj-4th	13	11	Jan. 4, 2007
111th	Maj-4th	14	12	Jan. 7, 2009

HOUSE SELECT AND SPECIAL COMMITTEES:

1st SELECT AGING (Permanent)
Dates: Feb. 8, 1983-Jan. 3, 1989
Departure: Left committee; no new assignment

Charles W. Boustany Jr. (R-La.)

Dates: Feb. 21, 1956
House: Jan. 3, 2005-date
Serving in the 111th Congress

HOUSE STANDING COMMITTEES:

1ST AGRICULTURE
Dates: Jan. 26, 2005-Jan. 3, 2009
Departure: Moved to Ways and Means

		Terms in:		Date of
Cong.	Ranking	House	Comm.	Assignment
109th	Maj-20th	1	1	Jan. 26, 2005
110th	Min-13th	2	2	Jan. 10, 2007

2nd EDUCATION AND THE WORKFORCE, 109
EDUCATION AND LABOR, 110
Dates: Jan. 26, 2005-Jan. 3, 2009
Departure: Moved to Ways and Means

		Terms in:		Date of
Cong.	Ranking	House	Comm.	Assignment
109th	Maj-24th	1	1	Jan. 26, 2005
110th	Min-17th	2	2	Jan. 10, 2007

3rd TRANSPORTATION AND INFRASTRUCTURE
Dates: Jan. 26, 2005-Jan. 3, 2009
Departure: Moved to Ways and Means

Cong.	Ranking	Terms in: House	Comm.	Date of Assignment
109th	Maj-41st	1	1	Jan. 26, 2005
110th	Min-29th	2	2	Jan. 10, 2007

4th WAYS AND MEANS
Dates: Jan. 9, 2009-date
Departure: Still serving in the 111th Congress

Cong.	Ranking	Terms in: House	Comm.	Date of Assignment
111th	Min-13th	3	1	Jan. 9, 2009

Barbara Boxer (D-Cal.)

Dates: Nov. 11, 1940
House: Jan. 3, 1983-Jan. 3, 1993
Left the House: Elected to the U.S. Senate in 1992
Senate: Jan. 3, 1993-date
Serving in the 111th Congress

HOUSE STANDING COMMITTEES:

1st GOVERNMENT OPERATIONS
1st Dates: Jan. 6, 1983-Jan. 3, 1987
1st Departure: Ceased active service to move to Budget; later returned with continuous seniority credited
2nd Dates: Jan. 19, 1989-Jan. 3, 1993
2nd Departure: Left the House for the Senate

2nd MERCHANT MARINE AND FISHERIES
Dates: Jan. 6, 1983-Jan. 3, 1985
Departure: Moved to Budget

3rd INTERIOR AND INSULAR AFFAIRS
Dates: May 24, 1983-July 12,1983
Departure: Left committee; no new assignment

4th BUDGET
Dates: Jan. 30, 1985-Jan. 3, 1991
Departure: Returned to Armed Services

5th ARMED SERVICES
1st Dates: Jan. 22, 1987-Jan. 3, 1989
1st Departure: Ceased active membership to move to Budget; later returned with continuous seniority credited
2nd Dates: Jan. 24, 1991-Jan. 3, 1993
2nd Departure: Left the House for the Senate

HOUSE SELECT AND SPECIAL COMMITTEES:

1st SELECT CHILDREN, YOUTH AND FAMILIES (Temporary)
Dates: Feb. 2, 1983-Jan. 3, 1993
Departure: Left the House for the Senate

SENATE STANDING COMMITTEES:

1st BANKING, HOUSING AND URBAN AFFAIRS
Dates: Jan. 7, 1993-Jan. 7, 1999
Departure: Moved to Foreign Relations

Cong.	Ranking	Years in: Senate	Comm.	Date of Assignment
103rd	Maj-8th	1	1	Jan. 7, 1993
104th	Min-4th	3	2	Jan. 4, 1995
105th	Min-5th	5	5	Jan. 9, 1997

2nd BUDGET
Dates: Jan. 21, 1993-Jan. 25, 2001
Departure: Moved to Commerce, Science and Transportation

Cong.	Ranking	Years in: Senate	Comm.	Date of Assignment
103rd	Maj-11th	1	1	Jan. 21, 1993
104th	Min-9th	3	2	Jan. 6, 1995
105th	Min-5th	5	4	Jan. 9, 1997
106th	Min-5th	7	6	Jan. 7, 1999

3rd ENVIRONMENT AND PUBLIC WORKS
Dates: Jan. 7, 1993-date
Departure: Still serving in the 111th Congress

Cong.	Ranking	Years in: Senate	Comm.	Date of Assignment
103rd	Maj-10th	1	1	Jan. 7, 1993
104th	Min-7th	3	2	Jan. 4, 1995
105th	Min-7th	5	5	Jan. 9, 1997
106th	Min-7th	7	7	Jan. 7, 1999
107th	Min-5th	9	9	Jan. 25, 2001
+107th	Maj-6th	9	9	July 10, 2001
108th	Min-6th	11	11	Jan. 15, 2003
109th	Min-4th	13	12	Jan. 6, 2005
110th	Maj-Chr	15	15	Jan. 12, 2007
111th	Maj-Chr	17	17	Jan. 21, 2009

4th APPROPRIATIONS
Dates: Jan. 9, 1997-Jan. 7, 1999
Departure: Moved to Foreign Relations

Cong.	Ranking	Years in: Senate	Comm.	Date of Assignment
105th	Min-13th	5	1	Jan. 9, 1997

5th FOREIGN RELATIONS
Dates: Jan. 7, 1999-date
Departure: Still serving in the 111th Congress

Cong.	Ranking	Years in: Senate	Comm.	Date of Assignment
106th	Min-7th	7	1	Jan. 7, 1999
107th	Min-7th	9	3	Jan. 25, 2001
+107th	Maj-7th	9	3	June 6, 2001
108th	Min-6th	11	5	Jan. 15, 2003
109th	Min-6th	13	6	Jan. 6, 2005
110th	Maj-5th	15	9	Jan. 12, 2007
111th	Maj-4th	17	11	Jan. 12, 2007

6th COMMERCE, SCIENCE AND TRANSPORTATION
Dates: Jan. 25, 2001-date
Departure: Still serving in the 111th Congress

Cong.	Ranking	Years in: Senate	Comm.	Date of Assignment
107th	Min-9th	9	1	Jan. 25, 2001
+107th	Maj-9th	9	1	June 6, 2001
108th	Min-8th	11	2	Jan. 15, 2003
109th	Min-5th	13	4	Jan. 6, 2005
110th	Maj-5th	15	6	Jan. 12, 2007
111th	Maj-5th	17	8	Jan. 21, 2009

SENATE SELECT AND SPECIAL COMMITTEES:

1st SPECIAL COMMITTEE TO INVESTIGATE WHITEWATER DEVELOPMENT CORPORATION AND RELATED MATTERS
Dates: July 20, 1995-June 17, 1996
Termination: Senate Report 104-280 filed

Cong.	Ranking	Years in: Senate	Comm.	Date of Assignment
104th	Min-5th	3	1	July 20, 1995

2nd SELECT ETHICS
Dates: Jan. 12, 2007-date
ChA: Replaced Timothy Johnson (D-S.D.) as Acting Chair on Jan. 12, 2007
Departure: Still serving in the 111th Congress

Cong.	Ranking	Years in: Senate	Comm.	Date of Assignment
110th	Maj-ChA	15	1	Jan. 12, 2007
111th	Maj-Chr	17	3	Jan. 21, 2009

JOINT COMMITTEES:

1st JOINT DEFICIT REDUCTION (Temporary)
House Dates: Feb. 23, 1987-Sep. 29, 1987
Termination: Public Law 100-119 adjusted Gramm-Rudman-Hollings Act

2nd JOINT ECONOMIC
Senate Dates: May 6, 1993-Jan. 9, 1995
Departure: Left committee; no new assignment

Cong.	Ranking	Years in: Senatee	Comm.	Date of Assignment
103rd	MjR-1st	1	1	May 6, 1993

F. Allen Boyd Jr. (D-Fla.)

Dates: June 6, 1945
House: Jan. 3, 1997-date
Serving in the 111th Congress

HOUSE STANDING COMMITTEES:

1st NATIONAL SECURITY
Dates: Jan. 7, 1997-Jan. 3, 1999
Departure: Moved to Appropriations

Cong.	Ranking	Terms in: House	Comm.	Date of Assignment
105th	Min-21st	1	1	Jan. 7, 1997

2nd SMALL BUSINESS
Dates: Feb. 5, 1997-Jan. 3, 1999
Departure: Moved to Appropriations

Cong.	Ranking	Terms in: House	Comm.	Date of Assignment
105th	Min-13th	1	1	Feb. 5, 1997

3rd APPROPRIATIONS
Dates: Jan. 6, 1999-date
Departure: Still serving in the 111th Congress

Cong.	Ranking	Terms in: House	Comm.	Date of Assignment
106th	Min-27th	2	1	Jan. 6, 1999
107th	Min-27th	3	2	Jan. 31, 2001
108th	Min-25th	4	3	Jan. 28, 2003
109th	Min-25th	5	4	Jan. 26, 2005
110th	Maj-22nd	6	5	Jan. 4, 2007
111th	Maj-21st	7	6	Jan. 7, 2009

4th BUDGET
Dates: Jan. 18, 2007-date
Departure: Still serving in the 111th Congress

Cong.	Ranking	Terms in: House	Comm.	Date of Assignment
110th	Maj-13th	6	1	Jan. 18, 2007
111th	Maj-8th	7	2	Jan. 21, 2009

Nancy Boyda (D-Kans.)

Dates: Aug. 2, 1955
House: Jan. 3, 2007-Jan. 3, 2009
Left the House: Defeated for re-election in 2008

HOUSE STANDING COMMITTEES:

1st ARMED SERVICES
Dates: Jan. 10, 2007-Jan. 3, 2009
Departure: Left the House; lost re-election

Cong.	Ranking	Terms in: House	Comm.	Date of Assignment
110th	Maj-24th	1	1	Jan. 10, 2007

2nd AGRICULTURE
Dates: Jan. 12, 2007-Jan. 3, 2009
Departure: Left the House; lost re-election

Cong.	Ranking	Terms in: House	Comm.	Date of Assignment
110th	Maj-15th	1	1	Jan. 12, 2007

Jeb Bradley (R-N.H.)

Dates: Oct. 20, 1952
House: Jan. 3, 2003-Jan. 3, 2007
Left the House: Defeated for re-election in 2006

HOUSE STANDING COMMITTEES:

1st ARMED SERVICES
Dates: Jan. 28, 2003-Jan. 3, 2007
Departure: Left the House; lost re-election

Cong.	Ranking	Terms in: House	Comm.	Date of Assignment
108th	Maj-26th	1	1	Jan. 28, 2003
109th	Maj-23rd	2	2	Jan. 26, 2005

2nd SMALL BUSINESS
Dates: Jan. 28, 2003-Jan. 3, 2007
Departure: Left the House; lost re-election

Cong.	Ranking	Terms in: House	Comm.	Date of Assignment
108th	Maj-16th	1	1	Jan. 28, 2003
109th	Maj-9th	2	2	Feb. 2, 2005

3rd VETERANS' AFFAIRS
Dates: Jan. 28, 2003-Jan. 3, 2007
Departure: Left the House; lost re-election

Cong.	Ranking	Terms in: House	Comm.	Date of Assignment
108th	Maj-14th	1	1	Jan. 28, 2003
109th	Maj-11th	2	2	Jan. 26, 2005

4th BUDGET
Dates: Jan. 26, 2005-Jan. 3, 2007
Departure: Left the House; lost re-election

Cong.	Ranking	Terms in: House	Comm.	Date of Assignment
109th	Maj-19th	2	1	Jan. 26, 2005

William W. Bradley (D-N.J.)

Dates: July 28, 1943
Senate: Jan. 3, 1979-Jan. 3, 1997
Left Senate: Retired; later lost presidential nomination in 2000

SENATE STANDING COMMITTEES:

1st ENERGY AND NATURAL RESOURCES
Dates: Jan. 23, 1979-Jan. 3, 1997
Departure: Left the Senate; retired

Cong.	Ranking	Years in: Senate	Comm.	Date of Assignment
103rd	Maj-4th	15	14	Jan. 7, 1993
104th	Min-4th	17	16	Jan. 4, 1995

2nd FINANCE
Dates: Jan. 23, 1979-Jan. 3, 1997
Departure: Left the Senate; retired

Cong.	Ranking	Years in: Senate	Comm.	Date of Assignment
103rd	Maj-5th	15	14	Jan. 7, 1993
104th	Min-3rd	17	16	Jan. 4, 1995

SENATE SELECT AND SPECIAL COMMITTEES:

1st SPECIAL AGING (Permanent)
Dates: Jan. 23, 1979-Jan. 3, 1997
Departure: Left the Senate; retired

Cong.	Ranking	Years in: Senate	Comm.	Date of Assignment
103rd	Maj-3rd	15	14	Jan. 21, 1993
104th	Min-3rd	17	16	Jan. 6, 1995

2nd SELECT INTELLIGENCE (Permanent)
Dates: Jan. 3, 1985-Jan. 27, 1993
Departure: Left committee; no new assignment

Kevin P. Brady (R-Tex.)

Dates: April 11, 1955
House: Jan. 3, 1997-date
Serving in the 111th Congress

HOUSE STANDING COMMITTEES:

1st GOVERNMENT REFORM AND OVERSIGHT
Dates: Jan. 7, 1997-Feb. 5, 1997
Departure: Resigned committee; had moved to International Relations

Cong.	Ranking	Terms in: House	Comm.	Date of Assignment
105th	Maj-23rd	1	1	Jan. 7, 1997

2nd RESOURCES
Dates: Jan. 7, 1997-Feb. 8, 2001
Departure: Resigned committee; had moved to Ways and Means

Cong.	Ranking	Terms in: House	Comm.	Date of Assignment
105th	Maj-22nd	1	1	Jan. 7, 1997
106th	Maj-18th	2	2	Jan. 6, 1999
107th	Maj-17th	3	3	Jan. 6, 2001

3rd SCIENCE
Dates: Jan. 7, 1997-Jan. 3, 2001
Departure: Moved to Ways and Means

Cong.	Ranking	Terms in: House	Comm.	Date of Assignment
105th	Maj-20th	1	1	Jan. 7, 1997
106th	Maj-16th	2	2	Jan. 6, 1999

4th INTERNATIONAL RELATIONS
Dates: Jan. 21, 1997-Jan. 3, 2001
Departure: Moved to Ways and Means

Cong.	Ranking	Terms in: House	Comm.	Date of Assignment
105th	Maj-26th	1	1	Jan. 21, 1997
106th	Maj-21st	2	2	Jan. 6, 1999

5th WAYS AND MEANS
Dates: Jan. 6, 2001-date
Departure: Still serving in the 111th Congress

Cong.	Ranking	Terms in: House	Comm.	Date of Assignment
107th	Maj-23rd	3	1	Jan. 6, 2001
108th	Maj-22nd	4	2	Jan. 28, 2003
109th	Maj-17th	5	3	Jan. 26, 2005
110th	Min-10th	6	4	Jan. 4, 2007
111th	Min-4th	7	5	Jan. 9, 2009

JOINT COMMITTEES:

1st JOINT ECONOMIC
House Dates: Mar. 3, 2005-date
Departure: Still serving in the 111th Congress

Cong.	Ranking	Terms in: House	Comm.	Date of Assignment
109th	Maj-5th	5	1	Mar. 3, 2005
110th	Min-2nd	6	2	Mar. 27, 2007
111th	Min-1st	7	3	Jan. 22, 2009

Robert A. Brady (D-Penn.)

Dates: April 7, 1945
House: May 19, 1998-date
Serving in the 111th Congress

H: Brady was elected to the 105th Congress by special election, May 19, 1998, to fill the vacancy caused by the resignation of U.S. Representative Thomas Foglietta (D-Penn.) who had been appointed U.S. Ambassador to Italy. Brady was seated May 21, 1998, and assigned to committees.

HOUSE STANDING COMMITTEES:

1st ARMED SERVICES
Dates: June 24, 1998-date
Departure: Still serving in the 111th Congress

Cong.	Ranking	Terms in: House	Comm.	Date of Assignment
105th	MnR-2nd	1	1	June 24, 1998
106th	Min-24th	2	2	Jan. 6, 1999
107th	Min-22nd	3	3	Jan. 31, 2001
108th	Min-16th	4	4	Jan. 28, 2003
109th	Min-14th	5	5	Jan. 26, 2005
110th	Maj-13th	6	6	Jan. 10, 2007
111th	Maj-12th	7	7	Jan. 7, 2009

2nd SMALL BUSINESS
Dates: June 24, 1998-Feb. 27, 2003
Departure: Leave of absence; moved to House Administration;
never returned

Cong.	Ranking	Terms in: House	Comm.	Date of Assignment
105th	MnR-4th	1	1	June 24, 1998
106th	Min-9th	2	2	Jan. 6, 1999
107th	Min-8th	3	3	Jan. 31, 2001
108th	Min-6th	4	4	Jan. 28, 2003

3rd HOUSE ADMINISTRATION
Dates: Feb. 5, 2003-date
Ch2: Succeeded Juanita Millender-McDonald (D-Cal.) as Chair on May 24, 2007
Departure: Still serving in the 111th Congress

Cong.	Ranking	Terms in: House	Comm.	Date of Assignment
108th	Min-3rd	4	1	Feb. 5, 2003
109th	Min-2nd	5	2	Jan. 26, 2005
110th	Maj-2nd	6	3	Feb. 8, 2007
=110th	Maj-Ch2	6	3	May 24, 2007
111th	Maj-Chr	7	4	Jan. 6, 2009

JOINT COMMITTEES:

1st JOINT PRINTING
House Dates: Mar. 25, 2003-date
Ch2: Succeeded Juanita Millender-McDonald (D-Cal.) as Chair on May 24, 2007
Departure: Still serving in the 111th Congress

Cong.	Ranking	Terms in: House	Comm.	Date of Assignment
108th	Min-2nd	4	1	Mar. 25, 2003
109th	Min-2nd	5	2	Mar. 16, 2005
110th	Maj-2nd	6	3	Mar. 14, 2007
=110th	Maj-Ch2	6	3	May 24, 2007
111th	Maj-VCh	7	4	Mar. 31, 2009

2nd JOINT LIBRARY
House Dates: May 24, 2007-date
VC2: Succeeded Juanita Millender-McDonald (D-Cal.) as Vice Chair on May 24, 2007
Departure: Still serving in the 111th Congress

Cong.	Ranking	Terms in: House	Comm.	Date of Assignment
=110th	MjR-VC2	6	1	May 24, 2007
111th	Maj-Chr	7	2	Mar. 31, 2009

Bruce Braley (D-Iowa)

Dates: Oct. 30, 1957
House: Jan. 3, 2007-date
Serving in the 111th Congress

HOUSE STANDING COMMITTEES:

1st TRANSPORTATION AND INFRASTRUCTURE
Dates: Jan. 10, 2007-Jan. 3, 2009
Departure: Moved to Energy and Commerce

Cong.	Ranking	Terms in: House	Comm.	Date of Assignment
110th	Maj-31st	1	1	Jan. 10, 2007

2nd OVERSIGHT AND GOVERNMENT REFORM
Dates: Jan. 12, 2007-Jan. 3, 2009
Departure: Moved to Energy and Commerce

Cong.	Ranking	Terms in: House	Comm.	Date of Assignment
110th	Maj-15th	1	1	Jan. 12, 2007

3rd SMALL BUSINESS
Dates: Jan. 23, 2007-Jan. 3, 2009
Departure: Moved to Energy and Commerce

Cong.	Ranking	Terms in: House	Comm.	Date of Assignment
110th	Maj-14th	1	1	Jan. 23, 2007

4th ENERGY AND COMMERCE
Dates: Jan. 7, 2009-date
Departure: Still serving in the 111th Congress

Cong.	Ranking	Terms in: House	Comm.	Date of Assignment
111th	Maj-35th	2	1	Jan. 7, 2009

John B. Breaux (D-La.)

Dates: March 1, 1944
House: Sept. 30, 1972-Jan. 3, 1987
Left the House: Elected to the U.S. Senate in 1986
Senate: Jan. 3, 1987-Jan. 3, 2005
Left the Senate: Left chamber; retired

H: Breaux was elected to the 92nd Congress by special election, Sept. 30, 1972, to fill the vacancy caused by the resignation of U.S. Representative Edwin W. Edwards (D-La.) who had been elected Governor. Breaux was seated Oct. 12, 1972 and assigned to committees.

HOUSE STANDING COMMITTEES:

1st MERCHANT MARINE AND FISHERIES
Dates: Oct. 12, 1972-Jan. 3, 1987
Departure: Left the House for the Senate.

2nd PUBLIC WORKS, 92-93
PUBLIC WORKS AND TRANSPORTATION, 94-99
Dates: Oct. 12, 1972-Jan. 3, 1975
Dates: Jan. 20, 1975-Jan. 3, 1987
Departure: Left the House for the Senate.

HOUSE SELECT AND SPECIAL COMMITTEES:

1st OUTER CONTINENTAL SHELF (Ad Hoc)
Became the Select Committee on the Outer Continental Shelf, Mar. 29, 1979
Dates: Apr. 22, 1975-July 31, 1980
Termination: House Report 1214 (96-2) filed

2nd SELECT COMMITTEES II (Patterson)
Dates: Mar. 28, 1979-Apr. 1, 1980
Termination: House Report 1214 (96-2) filed

SENATE STANDING COMMITTEES:

1st COMMERCE, SCIENCE AND TRANSPORTATION
Dates: Jan. 6, 1987-Jan. 3, 2005
Departure: Left the Senate; retired

Cong.	Ranking	Years in: Senate	Comm.	Date of Assignment
103rd	Maj-8th	7	7	Jan. 7, 1993
104th	Min-7th	9	8	Jan. 4, 1995
105th	Min-6th	11	11	Jan. 9, 1997
106th	Min-5th	13	13	Jan. 7, 1999
107th	Min-5th	15	15	Jan. 25, 2001
+107th	Maj-5th	15	15	June 6, 2001
108th	Min-5th	17	17	Jan. 15, 2003

2nd ENVIRONMENT AND PUBLIC WORKS
Dates: Jan. 6, 1987-May 16, 1990
Departure: Moved to Finance

3rd AGRICULTURE, NUTRITION AND FORESTRY
Dates: May 12, 1987-Feb. 2, 1989
Departure: Left committee; no new assignment.

4th FINANCE
Dates: May 16, 1990-Jan. 3, 2005
Departure: Left the Senate; retired

Cong.	Ranking	Years in: Senate	Comm.	Date of Assignment
103rd	Maj-11th	7	3	Jan. 7, 1993
104th	Min- 6th	9	5	Jan. 4, 1995
105th	Min-4th	11	7	Jan. 9, 1997
106th	Min-4th	13	9	Jan. 7, 1999
107th	Min-4th	15	11	Jan. 25, 2001
+107th	Maj-4th	15	12	June 6, 2001
108th	Min-4th	17	13	Jan. 15, 2003

5th RULES AND ADMINISTRATION
Dates: Jan. 25, 2001-Jan. 3, 2005
Departure: Left the Senate; retired

Cong.	Ranking	Years in: Senate	Comm.	Date of Assignment
107th	Min-7th	15	1	Jan. 25, 2001
+107th	Maj-7th	15	1	June 6, 2001
108th	Min-6th	17	2	Jan. 15, 2003

SENATE SELECT AND SPECIAL COMMITTEES:

1st SPECIAL AGING (Permanent)
Dates: Jan. 6, 1987-Jan. 3, 2005
Ch2: Replaced Larry E. Craig (R-Ida.) on June 6, 2001, following Senate party control shift
Departure: Left the Senate; retired

Cong.	Ranking	Years in: Senate	Comm.	Date of Assignment
103rd	Maj-5th	7	7	Jan. 21, 1993
104th	Min-5th	9	9	Jan. 6, 1995
105th	Min-RM	11	11	Jan. 9, 1997
106th	Min-RM	13	13	Jan. 7, 1999
107th	Min-RM1	15	15	Jan. 25, 2001
+107th	Maj-Ch2	15	15	July 10, 2001
108th	Min-RM	17	17	Jan. 15, 2003

William K. Brewster (D-Okla.)

Dates: Nov. 8, 1941
House: Jan. 3, 1991-Jan. 3, 1997
Left the House: Retired in 1996

HOUSE STANDING COMMITTEES:

1st PUBLIC WORKS AND TRANSPORTATION, 102
TRANSPORTATION AND INFRASTRUCTURE, 104

1st Dates: Jan. 24, 1991-Jan. 3, 1993
1st Departure: Moved to Ways and Means
2nd Dates: Jan. 4, 1995-Jan. 3, 1997
2nd Departure: Left the House; retired

Cong.	Ranking	Terms in: House	Comm.	Date of Assignment
104th	Min-28th	3 *2	1	Jan. 4, 1995

2nd VETERANS' AFFAIRS
Dates: Jan. 24, 1991-Jan. 3, 1993
Departure: Moved to Ways and Means

3rd WAYS AND MEANS
Dates: Jan. 5, 1993-Jan. 3, 1995
Departure: Returned to Transportation and Infrastructure

Cong.	Ranking	Terms in: House	Comm.	Date of Assignment
103rd	Maj-23rd	2	1	Jan. 5, 1993

4th GOVERNMENT REFORM AND OVERSIGHT
Dates: June 13, 1995-Jan. 3, 1997
Departure: Left the House; retired

Cong.	Ranking	Terms in: House	Comm.	Date of Assignment
104th	Min-23rd	3	1	June 13, 1995

Bobby Neal Bright Sr. (D-Ala.)

Dates: July 21, 1952
House: Jan. 3, 2009-date
Serving in the 111th Congress

HOUSE STANDING COMMITTEES:

1st ARMED SERVICES
Dates: Jan. 7, 2009-date
Departure: Still serving in the 111th Congress

Cong.	Ranking	Terms in: House	Comm.	Date of Assignment
111th	Maj-37th	1	1	Jan. 7, 2009

2nd AGRICULTURE
Dates: Jan. 21, 2009-date
Departure: Still serving in the 111th Congress

Cong.	Ranking	Terms in: House	Comm.	Date of Assignment
111th	Maj-20th	1	1	Jan. 21, 2009

3rd SMALL BUSINESS
Dates: Jan. 21, 2009-date
Departure: Still serving in the 111th Congress

Cong.	Ranking	Terms in: House	Comm.	Date of Assignment
111th	Maj-15th	1	1	Jan. 21, 2009

Jack B. Brooks (D-Tex.)

Dates: Dec. 18, 1922
House: Jan. 3, 1953-Jan. 3, 1995
Left the House: Defeated for re-election in 1994

HOUSE STANDING COMMITTEES:

1st GOVERNMENT OPERATIONS
Dates: Jan. 19, 1953-Jan. 3, 1989
Departure: Left committee; became Chair of Judiciary

2nd JUDICIARY
Dates: Jan. 13, 1955-Jan. 3, 1995
Departure: Left the House; lost re-election

Cong.	Ranking	Terms in: House	Comm.	Date of Assignment
103rd	Maj-Chr	21	20	Jan. 5, 1993

HOUSE SELECT AND SPECIAL COMMITTEES:

1st STANDARDS AND CONDUCT
Dates: Oct. 20, 1966-Dec. 27, 1966
Termination: House Report 2338 (89-2) filed

2nd SELECT COMMITTEE ON CONGRESSIONAL OPERATIONS
Dates: Apr. 6, 1977-Jan. 2, 1979
Termination: House Report 1843 (95-2) filed

3rd SELECT SECRET MILITARY ASSISTANCE TO IRAN AND THE NICARAGUAN OPPOSITION (Iran-Contra Affair)
Dates: Jan. 12, 1987-Nov. 17, 1987
Termination: House Report 422 (100-1) filed

4th SELECT NARCOTICS ABUSE AND CONTROL (Temporary)
Dates: Mar. 8, 1989-Jan. 3, 1993
Termination: Committee not renewed in 1993

JOINT COMMITTEES:

1st JOINT ORGANIZATION OF CONGRESS
House Dates: Mar. 11, 1965-Dec. 31, 1967
Termination: Senate Con. Res. 32 (90-1)

2nd JOINT CONGRESSIONAL OPERATIONS
House Dates: Feb. 25, 1971-Feb. 4, 1977
Termination: Senate Res. 4 (95-1); remained on reorganized select committee

Paul C. Broun Jr. (R-Ga.)

Dates: Dec. 7, 1946
House: July 17, 2007-date
Serving in the 111th Congress

H: Broun was elected to the 110th Congress by special election, July 17, 2007, to fill the vacancy caused by the death of U.S. Representative Charles Norwood (R-Ga.). Broun was seated July 25, 2007, and assigned to committees.

HOUSE STANDING COMMITTEES:

1st HOMELAND SECURITY
Dates: July 25, 2007-date
Departure: Still serving in the 111th Congress

Cong.	Ranking	Terms in: House	Comm.	Date of Assignment
110th	MnR-2nd	1	1	July 25, 2007
111th	Min-9th	2	2	Jan. 9, 2009

2nd SCIENCE AND TECHNOLOGY
Dates: July 25, 2007-date
Departure: Still serving in the 111th Congress

Cong.	Ranking	Terms in: House	Comm.	Date of Assignment
110th	MnR-1st	1	1	July 25, 2007
111th	Min-16th	2	2	Jan. 9, 2009

3rd NATURAL RESOURCES
Dates: Jan. 9, 2009-date
Departure: Still serving in the 111th Congress

Cong.	Ranking	Terms in: House	Comm.	Date of Assignment
111th	Min-14th	2	1	Jan. 9, 2009

J. Glen Browder (D-Ala.)

Dates: Jan. 15, 1943
House: April 4, 1989-Jan. 3, 1997
Left the House: Lost U.S. Senate nomination in 1996

H: Browder was elected to the 101st Congress by special election, April 4, 1989, to fill the vacancy caused by the death of U.S. Representative Bill Nichols (D-Ala.). Browder was seated April 18, 1989, and assigned to committees.

HOUSE STANDING COMMITTEES:

1st PUBLIC WORKS AND TRANSPORTATION
Dates: Apr. 27, 1989-Nov. 8, 1989
Departure: Moved to Armed Services

2nd SCIENCE, SPACE AND TECHNOLOGY
Dates: Apr. 27, 1989-May 12, 1994
Departure: Temporarily resigned to retain service on Budget

Cong.	Ranking	Terms in: House	Comm.	Date of Assignment
103rd	Maj-13th	3	3	Jan. 5, 1993

3rd ARMED SERVICES, 101-103
NATIONAL SECURITY, 104
Dates: Nov. 8, 1989-Jan. 3, 1997
Departure: Left the House; lost Senate nomination

Cong.	Ranking	Terms in: House	Comm.	Date of Assignment
103rd	Maj-19th	3	3	Jan. 5, 1993
104th	Min-11th	4	4	Jan. 4, 1995

4th BUDGET
Dates: Mar. 3, 1993-Jan. 3, 1997
Departure: Left the House; lost Senate nomination

Cong.	Ranking	Terms in: House	Comm.	Date of Assignment
103rd	MjR-1st	3	1	Mar. 3, 1993
104th	Min-12th	4	2	Jan. 4, 1995

Corrine Brown (D-Fla.)

Dates: Nov. 11, 1946
House: Jan. 3, 1993-date
Serving in the 111th Congress

HOUSE STANDING COMMITTEES:

1st GOVERNMENT OPERATIONS
Dates: Feb. 4, 1993-Jan. 3, 1995
Departure: Left committee; no new assignment

Cong.	Ranking	Terms in: House	Comm.	Date of Assignment
103rd	Maj-22nd	1	1	Feb. 4, 1993

2nd PUBLIC WORKS AND TRANSPORTATION, 103
TRANSPORTATION AND INFRASTRUCTURE, 104-111
Dates: Jan. 5, 1993-date
Departure: Still serving in the 111th Congress

Cong.	Ranking	Terms in: House	Comm.	Date of Assignment
103rd	Maj-33rd	1	1	Jan. 5, 1993
104th	Min-22nd	2	2	Jan. 4, 1995
105th	Min-17th	3	3	Jan. 7, 1997
106th	Min-14th	4	4	Jan. 6, 1999
107th	Min-11th	5	5	Jan. 31, 2001
108th	Min-9th	6	6	Jan. 28, 2003
109th	Min-8th	7	7	Jan. 26, 2005
110th	Maj-7th	8	8	Jan. 10, 2007
111th	Maj-7th	9	9	Jan. 7, 2009

3rd VETERANS' AFFAIRS
Dates: Jan. 5, 1993-date
Departure: Still serving in the 111th Congress

Cong.	Ranking	Terms in: House	Comm.	Date of Assignment
103rd	Maj-21st	1	1	Jan. 5, 1993
104th	Min-13th	2	2	Jan. 4, 1995
105th	Min-7th	3	3	Feb. 6, 1997
106th	Min-4th	4	4	Jan. 6, 1999
107th	Min-4th	5	5	Jan. 31, 2001
108th	Min-4th	6	6	Jan. 28, 2003
109th	Min-4th	7	7	Jan. 26, 2005
110th	Maj-2nd	8	8	Jan. 12, 2007
111th	Maj-2nd	9	9	Jan. 21, 2009

George E. Brown Jr. (D-Cal.)

Dates: March 6, 1920-July 15, 1999
House 1: Jan. 3, 1963-Jan. 3, 1971
Left the House 1: Lost U.S. Senate nomination in 1970
House 2: Jan. 3, 1973-July 15, 1999
Left the House 2: Died in office

HOUSE STANDING COMMITTEES:

1st VETERANS' AFFAIRS
Dates: Jan. 17, 1963-Jan. 3, 1971
Departure: Left the House; lost Senate nomination

2nd EDUCATION AND LABOR
Dates: Jan. 31, 1963-Jan. 3, 1965
Departure: Moved to Science and Astronautics

3rd SCIENCE AND ASTRONAUTICS, 89-91, 93
SCIENCE AND TECHNOLOGY, 94-99
SCIENCE, SPACE AND TECHNOLOGY, 100-103
SCIENCE, 104-106
1st Dates: Jan. 18, 1965-Jan. 3, 1971
1st Departure: Left the House; lost Senate nomination

2nd Dates: Jan. 24, 1973-July 15, 1999
RM1: Replaced as Ranking Member by Ralph M. Hall (D-Tex.) on July 15, 1999
2nd Departure: Died in office

Cong.	Ranking	Terms in: House	Comm.	Date of Assignment
103rd	Maj-Chr	15 *2	11	Jan. 5, 1993
104th	Min-RM	16 *2	12	Jan. 4, 1995
105th	Min-RM	17 *2	13	Feb. 6, 1997
106th	Min-RM1	18 *2	14	Jan. 6, 1999

4th AGRICULTURE
Dates: Jan. 24, 1973-July 15, 1999
Departure: Died in office

Cong.	Ranking	Terms in: House	Comm.	Date of Assignment
103rd	Maj-2nd	15	11	Jan. 5, 1993
104th	Min-2nd	16	12	Jan. 4, 1995
105th	Min-2nd	17	13	Jan. 7, 1997
106th	Min-2nd	18	14	Jan. 6, 1999

HOUSE SELECT AND SPECIAL COMMITTEES:

1st PERMANENT SELECT INTELLIGENCE
Dates: Jan. 30, 1985-Nov. 18, 1987
Departure: Left committee; no new assignment

JOINT COMMITTEES:

1st JOINT ATOMIC ENERGY
House Dates: May 3, 1976-Sep. 20, 1977
Termination: Public Law 95-110

G. Hanks (Hank) Brown (R-Colo.)

Dates: Feb. 12, 1940
House: Jan. 3, 1981-Jan. 3, 1991
Left the House: Elected to the U.S. Senate in 1990
Senate: Jan. 3, 1991-Jan. 3, 1997
Left the Senate: Retired in 2002

HOUSE STANDING COMMITTEES:

1st INTERIOR AND INSULAR AFFAIRS
Dates: Jan. 28, 1981-Jan. 3, 1985
Departure: Moved to Budget

2nd STANDARDS OF OFFICIAL CONDUCT
1st Dates: Jan. 28, 1981-Jan 3, 1985
1st Departure: Moved to Budget and Judiciary
2nd Dates: Jan. 2, 1988-July 18, 1989
2nd Departure: Left committee; no new assignment

3rd BUDGET
Dates: Jan. 30, 1985-Jan. 3, 1987
Departure: Moved to Ways and Means

4th JUDICIARY
Dates: Jan. 30, 1985-Jan. 3, 1987
Departure: Moved to Ways and Means

5th WAYS AND MEANS
Dates: Jan. 21, 1987-Jan. 3, 1991
Departure: Left the House for the Senate

HOUSE SELECT AND SPECIAL COMMITTEES:

1st SELECT HUNGER (Temporary)
Dates: Apr. 9, 1987-Jan. 3, 1989
Departure: Left committee; no new assignment

SENATE STANDING COMMITTEES:

1st FOREIGN RELATIONS
Dates: Feb. 5, 1991-Jan. 3, 1997
Departure: Left the Senate; retired

Cong.	Ranking	Senate	Comm.	Date of Assignment
103rd	Min-6th	3	2	Jan. 7, 1993
104th	Maj-4th	5	4	Jan. 5, 1995

2nd JUDICIARY
Dates: Feb. 5, 1991-Jan. 3, 1997
Departure: Left the Senate; retired

Cong.	Ranking	Senate	Comm.	Date of Assignment
103rd	Min-6th	3	2	Jan. 7, 1993
104th	Maj-6th	5	4	Jan. 4, 1995

3rd BUDGET
Dates: Mar. 19, 1991-Jan. 3, 1997
Departure: Left the Senate; retired

Cong.	Ranking	Senate	Comm.	Date of Assignment
103rd	Min-7th	3	2	Jan. 21, 1993
104th	Maj-7th	5	4	Jan. 6, 1995

4th VETERANS' AFFAIRS
Dates: Jan. 6, 1995-Mar. 24, 1995
Departure: Left committee; no new assignment

Cong.	Ranking	Senate	Comm.	Date of Assignment
104th	Maj-7th	5	1	Jan. 6, 1995

5th GOVERNMENTAL AFFAIRS
Dates: Oct. 12, 1995-June 20, 1996
Departure: Resigned committee; no new assignment

Cong.	Ranking	Senate	Comm.	Date of Assignment
104th	MjR-1st	5	1	Oct. 12, 1995

SENATE SELECT AND SPECIAL COMMITTEES:

1st SELECT POW-MIA AFFAIRS
Dates: Aug. 2, 1991-Feb. 3, 1993
Termination: Senate Report 1 (103-1) filed

Henry E. Brown Jr. (R-S.C.)

Dates: Dec. 20, 1935
House: Jan. 3, 2001-date
Serving in the 111th Congress

HOUSE STANDING COMMITTEES:

1st BUDGET
Dates: Jan. 6, 2001-Jan. 3, 2005
Departure: Moved to Resources

Cong.	Ranking	House	Comm.	Date of Assignment
107th	Maj-20th	1	1	Jan. 6, 2001
108th	Maj-10th	2	2	Jan. 28, 2003

2nd TRANSPORTATION AND INFRASTRUCTURE
Dates: Jan. 6, 2001-date
Departure: Still serving in the 111th Congress

Cong.	Ranking	House	Comm.	Date of Assignment
107th	Maj-32nd	1	1	Jan. 6, 2001
108th	Maj-25th	2	2	Jan. 28, 2003
109th	Maj-20th	3	3	Jan. 26, 2005
110th	Min-14th	4	4	Jan. 10, 2007
111th	Min-10th	5	5	Jan. 9, 2009

3rd VETERANS' AFFAIRS
Dates: Feb. 8, 2001-date
Departure: Still serving in the 111th Congress

Cong.	Ranking	House	Comm.	Date of Assignment
107th	Maj-17th	1	1	Feb. 8, 2001
108th	Maj-11th	2	2	Jan. 28, 2003
109th	Maj-8th	3	3	Jan. 26, 2005
110th	Min-6th	4	4	Jan. 10, 2007
111th	Min-4th	5	5	Jan. 9, 2009

4th RESOURCES, 109
NATURAL RESOURCES, 110-111
Dates: Jan. 26, 2005-date
Departure: Still serving in the 111th Congress

Cong.	Ranking	House	Comm.	Date of Assignment
109th	Maj-22nd	3	1	Jan. 26, 2005
110th	Min-12th	4	2	Jan. 10, 2007
111th	Min-6th	5	3	Jan. 9, 2009

Scott P. Brown (R-Mass.)

Dates: Sep. 12, 1959-
Senate: Jan. 19, 2010-date
Serving in the 111th Congress

S: Brown was elected to the 111th Congress, Jan. 19, 2010, to fill the vacancy caused by the death of U.S. Senator Edward M. Kennedy (D-Mass.). Brown was seated on Feb. 4, 2010, and was assigned to committees.

SENATE STANDING COMMITTEES:

1st ARMED SERVICES
Dates: Mar. 2, 2010-date
Departure: Still serving in the 111th Congress

Cong.	Ranking	Senate	Comm.	Date of Assignment
111th	MnA-12th	1	1	Mar. 2, 2010

2nd HOMELAND SECURITY AND GOVERNMENTAL AFFAIRS
Dates: Mar. 2, 2010-date
Departure: Still serving in the 111th Congress

Cong.	Ranking	Senate	Comm.	Date of Assignment
111th	MnA-8th	1	1	Mar. 2, 2010

3rd VETERANS' AFFAIRS
Dates: Mar. 2, 2010-date
Departure: Still serving in the 111th Congress

Cong.	Ranking	Years in: Senate	Comm.	Date of Assignment
111th	MnR-1st	1	1	Mar. 2, 2010

Sherrod Brown (D-Ohio)

Dates: Nov. 9, 1952
House: Jan. 3, 1993-Jan. 3, 2007
Left the House: Elected to the U.S. Senate in 2006
Senate: Jan. 3, 2007-date
Serving in the 111th Congress

HOUSE STANDING COMMITTEES:

1st ENERGY AND COMMERCE, 103
COMMERCE, 104-106
ENERGY AND COMMERCE, 107-109
Dates: Jan. 5, 1993-Jan. 3, 2007
Departure: Left House for the Senate

Cong.	Ranking	Terms in: House	Comm.	Date of Assignment
103rd	Maj-24th	1	1	Jan. 5, 1993
104th	Min-13th	2	2	Jan. 4, 1995
105th	Min-9th	3	3	Jan. 7, 1997
106th	Min-8th	4	4	Jan. 6, 1999
107th	Min-8th	5	5	Jan. 31, 2001
108th	Min-8th	6	6	Jan. 28, 2003
109th	Min-7th	7	7	Jan. 26, 2005

2nd FOREIGN AFFAIRS, 103
INTERNATIONAL RELATIONS, 104-109
Dates: Jan. 5, 1993-Jan. 3, 2007
Departure: Left House for the Senate

Cong.	Ranking	Terms in: House	Comm.	Date of Assignment
103rd	Maj-17th	1	1	Jan. 5, 1993
104th	Min-14th	2	2	Jan. 4, 1995
105th	Min-11th	3	3	Jan. 7, 1997
106th	Min-9th	4	4	Jan. 6, 1999
107th	Min-7th	5	5	Jan. 31, 2001
108th	Min-7th	6	6	Jan. 28, 2003
109th	Min-7th	7	7	Jan. 26, 2005

3rd POST OFFICE AND CIVIL SERVICE
Dates: Jan. 27, 1993-Jan. 3, 1995
Departure: Committee abolished; no new assignment

Cong.	Ranking	Terms in: House	Comm.	Date of Assignment
103rd	Maj-14th	1	1	Jan. 27, 1993

SENATE STANDING COMMITTEES:

1st AGRICULTURE, NUTRITION, AND FORESTRY
Dates: Jan. 12, 2007-date
Departure: Still serving in the 111th Congress

Cong.	Ranking	Years in: Senate	Comm.	Date of Assignment
110th	Maj-9th	1	1	Jan. 12, 2007
111th	Maj-8th	3	3	Jan. 21, 2009

2nd BANKING, HOUSING, AND URBAN AFFAIRS
Dates: Jan. 12, 2007-date
Departure: Still serving in the 111th Congress

Cong.	Ranking	Years in: Senate	Comm.	Date of Assignment
110th	Maj-9th	1	1	Jan. 12, 2007
111th	Maj-8th	3	3	Jan. 21, 2009

3rd HEALTH, EDUCATION, LABOR AND PENSIONS
Dates: Jan. 12, 2007-date
Departure: Still serving in the 111th Congress

Cong.	Ranking	Years in: Senate	Comm.	Date of Assignment
110th	Maj-11th	1	1	Jan. 12, 2007
111th	Maj-9th	3	3	Jan. 21, 2009

4th VETERANS' AFFAIRS
Dates: Jan. 12, 2007-date
Departure: Still serving in the 111th Congress

Cong.	Ranking	Years in: Senate	Comm.	Date of Assignment
110th	Maj-6th	1	1	Jan. 12, 2007
111th	Maj-5th	3	3	Jan. 21, 2009

SENATE SELECT AND SPECIAL COMMITTEES:

1st SELECT ETHICS (Permanent)
Dates: Jan. 21, 2009-date
Departure: Still serving in the 111th Congress

Cong.	Ranking	Years in: Senate	Comm.	Date of Assignment
111th	Maj-3rd	3	1	Jan. 21, 2009

Virginia Brown-Waite (R-Fla.)

Dates: Oct. 5, 1943
House: Jan. 3, 2003-date
Serving in the 111th Congress

HOUSE STANDING COMMITTEES:

1st FINANCIAL SERVICES
Dates: Jan. 28, 2003-Jan. 3, 2009
Departure: Moved to Ways and Means

Cong.	Ranking	Terms in: House	Comm.	Date of Assignment
108th	Maj-34th	1	1	Jan. 28, 2003
109th	Maj-27th	2	2	Jan. 26, 2005
110th	Min-20th	3	3	Jan. 10, 2007

2nd VETERANS' AFFAIRS
Dates: Jan. 28, 2003-Jan. 3, 2009
Departure: Moved to Ways and Means

Cong.	Ranking	Terms in: House	Comm.	Date of Assignment
108th	Maj-16th	1	1	Jan. 28, 2003
109th	Maj-12th	2	2	Jan. 26, 2005
110th	Min-9th	3	3	Jan. 10, 2007

3rd BUDGET
Dates: Feb. 11, 2003-Jan. 3, 2005
Departure: Moved to Government Reform

Cong.	Ranking	Terms in: House	Comm.	Date of Assignment
108th	Maj-24th	1	1	Feb. 11, 2003

4th GOVERNMENT REFORM
Dates: Jan. 26, 2005-Sep. 30, 2005
Departure: Resigned committee; had moved to Homeland Security

Cong.	Ranking	Terms in: House	Comm.	Date of Assignment
109th	Maj-17th	2	1	Jan. 26, 2005

5th HOMELAND SECURITY
Dates: Sep.15, 2005-Jan. 3, 2009
Departure: Moved to Ways and Means

Cong.	Ranking	Terms in: House	Comm.	Date of Assignment
109th	MjR-1st	2	1	Sep. 15, 2005
110th	Min-12th	3	2	Jan. 10, 2007

6th WAYS AND MEANS
Dates: Jan. 9, 2009-date
Departure: Still serving in the 111th Congress

Cong.	Ranking	Terms in: House	Comm.	Date of Assignment
111th	Min-10th	4	1	Jan. 9, 2009

Sam D. Brownback (R-Kans.)

Dates: Sept. 12, 1956
House: Jan. 3, 1995-Nov. 7, 1996
Left the House: Resigned chamber; elected to the U.S. Senate
Senate: Nov. 6, 1996-date
Serving in the 111th Congress

S: Brownback was elected to the 104th Congress by special election, Nov. 5, 1996, to fill the vacancy caused by the resignation of U.S. Senator Robert J. Dole (R-Kans.) who lost the 1996 election for President. Dole was initially replaced by Sheila Frahm (R-Kans.), an appointee, who lost the primary to Brownback. Brownback was not seated nor assigned to committees because the 104th Congress was not in session. Brownback resigned the House on Nov. 27, 1996, retroactive to Nov. 7, 1996.

HOUSE STANDING COMMITTEES:

1st BUDGET
Dates: Jan. 4, 1995-Nov. 7, 1996
Departure: Resigned the House; elected to the Senate

Cong.	Ranking	Terms in: House	Comm.	Date of Assignment
104th	Maj-21st	1	1	Jan. 4, 1995

2nd INTERNATIONAL RELATIONS
Dates: Jan. 4, 1995-Nov. 7, 1996
Departure: Resigned the House; elected to the Senate

Cong.	Ranking	Terms in: House	Comm.	Date of Assignment
104th	Maj-18th	1	1	Jan. 4, 1995

3rd SMALL BUSINESS
Dates: Jan. 4, 1995-Nov. 7, 1996
Departure: Resigned the House; elected to the Senate

Cong.	Ranking	Terms in: House	Comm.	Date of Assignment
104th	Maj-18th	1	1	Jan. 4, 1995

SENATE STANDING COMMITTEES:

1st COMMERCE, SCIENCE AND TRANSPORTATION
1st Dates: Jan. 9, 1997-Jan. 6, 2005
1st Departure: Returned to Judiciary

2nd Dates: Jan. 21, 2009-date
2nd Departure: Still serving in the 111th Congress

Cong.	Ranking	Years in: Senate	Comm.	Date of Assignment
105th	Maj-11th	1 *1	1	Jan. 9, 1997
106th	Maj-11th	3 *1	2	Jan. 7, 1999
107th	Maj-7th	5 *1	5	Jan. 25, 2001
+107th	Min-7th	5 *1	5	June 6, 2001
108th	Maj-7th	7 *1	7	Jan. 15, 2003
111th	Min-9th	13 *2	1	Jan. 21, 2009

2nd FOREIGN RELATIONS
Dates: Jan. 9, 1997-Jan. 6, 2005
Departure: Returned to Judiciary

Cong.	Ranking	Years in: Senate	Comm.	Date of Assignment
105th	Maj-10th	1	1	Jan. 9, 1997
106th	Maj-7th	3	3	Jan. 7, 1999
107th	Maj-9th	5	5	Jan. 25, 2001
+107th	Min-9th	5	5	June 6, 2001
108th	Maj-5th	7	7	Jan. 15, 2003

3rd GOVERNMENTAL AFFAIRS
Dates: Jan. 9, 1997-Jan. 7, 1999
Departure: Moved to Labor and Human Resources

Cong.	Ranking	Years in: Senate	Comm.	Date of Assignment
105th	Maj-5th	1	1	Jan. 9, 1997

4th LABOR AND HUMAN RESOURCES renamed Jan. 21, 1999
as HEALTH, EDUCATION, LABOR AND PENSIONS
Dates: Jan. 7, 1999-Jan. 25, 2001
Departure: Moved to Judiciary

Cong.	Ranking	Years in: Senate	Comm.	Date of Assignment
106th	Maj-8th	3	1	Jan. 7, 1999

5th JUDICIARY
1st Dates: Jan. 25, 2001-Jan. 15, 2003
1st Departure: Moved to Appropriations
2nd Dates: Jan. 6, 2005-Jan. 21, 2009
2nd Departure: Returned to Commerce, Science and Transportation and moved to Energy and Natural Resources and Special Aging

Cong.	Ranking	Years in: Senate	Comm.	Date of Assignment
107th	Maj-8th	5 *1	1	Jan. 25, 2001
+107th	Min-8th	5 *1	1	June 6, 2001
109th	Maj-9th	9 *2	1	Jan. 6, 2005
110th	Min-8th	11 *2	3	Jan. 12, 2007

6th APPROPRIATIONS
Dates: Jan. 15, 2003-date
Departure: Still serving in the 111th Congress

Cong.	Ranking	Years in: Senate	Comm.	Date of Assignment
108th	Maj-15th	7	1	Jan. 15, 2003
109th	Maj-14th	9	2	Jan. 6, 2005
110th	Min-12th	11	4	Jan. 12, 2007
111th	Min-9th	13	7	Jan. 21, 2009

7th ENERGY AND NATURAL RESOURCES
Dates: Jan. 21, 2009-date
Departure: Still serving in the 111th Congress

Cong.	Ranking	Years in: Senate	Comm.	Date of Assignment
111th	Min-4th	13	1	Jan. 21, 2009

SENATE SELECT AND SPECIAL COMMITTEES:

1st SPECIAL AGING (Permanent)
Dates: Jan. 21, 2009-date
Departure: Still serving in the 111th Congress

		Years in:		Date of
Cong.	Ranking	Senate	Comm.	Assignment
111th	Min-7th	13	1	Jan. 21, 2009

JOINT COMMITTEES:

1st JOINT ECONOMIC
Senate Dates: Jan. 9, 1997-date
Departure: Still serving in the 111th Congress

		Years in:		Date of
Cong.	Ranking	Senate	Comm.	Assignment
105th	Maj-5th	1	1	Jan. 9, 1997
106th	Maj-5th	3	2	Jan. 7, 1999
107th	Maj-2nd	5	5	Jan. 25, 2001
+107th	Min-2nd	5	5	June 6, 2001
108th	Maj-2nd	7	7	Jan. 15, 2003
109th	Maj-2nd	9	8	Jan. 6, 2005
110th	Min-1st	11	11	Jan. 12, 2007
111th	Min-1st	13	13	Jan. 21, 2009

Richard H. Bryan (D-Nev.)

Dates: July 16, 1937
Senate: Jan. 3, 1989-Jan. 3, 2001
Left the Senate: Left chamber; retired

SENATE STANDING COMMITTEES:

1st BANKING, HOUSING AND URBAN AFFAIRS
Dates: Feb. 2, 1989-Jan. 3, 2001
Departure: Left the Senate; retired

		Years in:		Date of
Cong.	Ranking	Senate	Comm.	Assignment
103rd	Maj-7th	5	4	Jan. 7, 1993
104th	Min-4th	7	6	Jan. 4, 1995
105th	Min-4th	9	8	Jan. 9, 1997
106th	Min-4th	11	10	Jan. 7, 1999

2nd COMMERCE, SCIENCE AND TRANSPORTATION
Dates: Feb. 2, 1989-Jan. 3, 2001
Departure: Left the Senate; retired

		Years in:		Date of
Cong.	Ranking	Senate	Comm.	Assignment
103rd	Maj-9th	5	4	Jan. 7, 1993
104th	Min-8th	7	6	Jan. 4, 1995
105th	Min-7th	9	8	Jan. 9, 1997
106th	Min-6th	11	10	Jan. 7, 1999

3rd ARMED SERVICES
Dates: July 8, 1993-Jan. 9, 1997
Departure: Moved to Finance

		Years in:		Date of
Cong.	Ranking	Senate	Comm.	Assignment
103rd	MjA-13th	5	1	July 8 1993
104th	Min-10th	7	2	Jan. 4, 1995

4th FINANCE
Dates: Jan. 9, 1997-Jan. 3, 2001
Departure: Left the Senate; retired

		Years in:		Date of
Cong.	Ranking	Senate	Comm.	Assignment
105th	Min-8th	9	1	Jan. 9, 1997
106th	Min-7th	11	2	Jan. 7, 1999

SENATE SELECT AND SPECIAL COMMITTEES:

1st JUDGE ALCEE L. HASTINGS IMPEACHMENT
Dates: Mar. 16, 1989-Aug. 3, 1989
Termination: Senate Hearing 101-194, Parts 1-2A

2nd SELECT ETHICS (Permanent)
Dates: Aug. 2, 1991-Jan. 23, 1996
VC1: Replaced by Byron L. Dorgan (D-N.D.) on Jan. 23, 1996
Departure: Resigned committee; no new assignment

		Years in:		Date of
Cong.	Ranking	Senate	Comm.	Assignment
103rd	Maj-Chr	5	2	Jan. 26, 1993
104th	Min-VC1	7	4	Jan. 11, 1995

3rd SELECT INTELLIGENCE (Permanent)
Dates: Jan. 27, 1993-Jan. 3, 2001
VC2: Replaced J. Robert Kerrey (D-Neb.) as Vice Chair on Nov. 10, 1999
Departure: Left the Senate; retired

		Years in:		Date of
Cong.	Ranking	Senate	Comm.	Assignment
103rd	Maj-5th	5	1	Jan. 27, 1993
104th	Min-3rd	7	2	Jan. 6, 1995
105th	Min-3rd	9	4	Jan. 9, 1997
106th	Min-2nd	11	6	Jan. 7, 1999
=106th	Min-VC2	11	7	Nov. 10, 1999

4th SPECIAL COMMITTEE TO INVESTIGATE WHITEWATER DEVELOPMENT CORPORATION AND RELATED MATTERS
Dates: July 20, 1995 -June 17, 1996
Termination: Senate Report 104-280 filed

		Years in:		Date of
Cong.	Ranking	Senate	Comm.	Assignment
104th	Min-4th	7	1	July 20, 1995

5th SPECIAL AGING (Permanent)
Dates: Mar. 2, 1999-Jan. 3, 2001
Departure: Left the Senate; retired

		Years in:		Date of
Cong.	Ranking	Senate	Comm.	Assignment
106th	MnA-9th	11	1	Mar. 2, 1999

JOINT COMMITTEES:

1st JOINT ECONOMIC
Senate Dates: Feb. 2, 1989-May 6, 1993
Departure: Resigned committee; had become Chair of Select Ethics

		Years in:		Date of
Cong.	Ranking	Senate	Comm.	Assignment
103rd	Maj-4th	5	4	Jan. 5, 1993

Ed Bryant (R-Tex.)

Dates: Sept. 7, 1948
House: Jan. 3, 1995-Jan. 3, 2003
Left the House: Lost U.S. Senate nomination in 2002

HOUSE STANDING COMMITTEES:

1st AGRICULTURE
Dates: Jan. 4, 1995-Jan. 3, 1999
Departure: Moved to Commerce

Cong.	Ranking	Terms in: House	Comm.	Date of Assignment
104th	Maj-22nd	1	1	Jan. 4, 1995
105th	Maj-16th	2	2	Jan. 7, 1997

2nd JUDICIARY
1st Dates: Jan. 4, 1995-Jan. 24, 1999
1st Departure: Resigned committee to open seat for Vitter; no new assignment
2nd Dates: Oct. 2, 2001-May 16, 2002
2nd Departure: Left committee; no new assignment

Cong.	Ranking	Terms in: House	Comm.	Date of Assignment
104th	Maj-17th	1 *1	1	Jan. 4, 1995
105th	Maj-14th	2 *1	2	Jan. 7, 1997
106th	Maj-11th	3 *1	3	Jan. 6, 1999
107th	MjR-1st	4 *2	1	Oct. 2, 2001

3rd COMMERCE, 106
ENERGY AND COMMERCE, 107
Dates: Jan. 6, 2001-Jan. 3, 2003
Departure: Left the House; lost Senate nomination

Cong.	Ranking	Terms in: House	Comm.	Date of Assignment
106th	Maj-28th	3	1	Jan. 6, 1999
107th	Maj-23rd	4	2	Jan. 6, 2001

John W. Bryant (D-Tex.)

Dates: Feb. 22, 1947
House: Jan. 3, 1983-Jan. 3, 1997
Left the House: Lost U.S. Senate nomination in 1996

HOUSE STANDING COMMITTEES:

1st ENERGY AND COMMERCE, 98-103
COMMERCE, 104
Dates: Jan. 6, 1983-Jan. 3, 1997
Departure: Left the House; lost Senate nomination

Cong.	Ranking	Terms in: House	Comm.	Date of Assignment
103rd	Maj-13th	6	6	Jan. 5, 1993
104th	Min-7th	7	7	Jan. 4, 1995

2nd VETERANS' AFFAIRS
Dates: Jan. 6, 1983-Jan. 3, 1989
Departure: Moved to Budget

3rd JUDICIARY
Dates: June 5, 1985-Jan. 3, 1997
Departure: Left the House; lost Senate nomination

Cong.	Ranking	Terms in: House	Comm.	Date of Assignment
103rd	Maj-13th	6	5	Jan. 5, 1993
104th	Min-7th	7	6	Jan. 4, 1995

4th BUDGET
Dates: Jan. 19, 1989-Jan. 3, 1995
Departure: Left committee; no new assignment

Cong.	Ranking	Terms in: House	Comm.	Date of Assignment
103rd	Maj-8th	6	3	Jan. 5, 1993

Vernon G. Buchanan (R-Fla.)

Dates: May 8, 1951
House: Jan. 3, 2007-date
Serving in the 111th Congress

HOUSE STANDING COMMITTEES:

1st SMALL BUSINESS
Dates: Jan. 10, 2007-date
Departure: Still serving in the 111th Congress

Cong.	Ranking	Terms in: House	Comm.	Date of Assignment
110th	Min-14th	1	1	Jan. 10, 2007
111th	Min-8th	2	2	Jan. 9, 2009

2nd TRANSPORTATION AND INFRASTRUCTURE
Dates: Jan. 10, 2007-date
Departure: Still serving in the 111th Congress

Cong.	Ranking	Terms in: House	Comm.	Date of Assignment
110th	Min-34th	1	1	Jan. 10, 2007
111th	Min-25th	2	2	Jan. 9, 2009

3rd VETERANS' AFFAIRS
Dates: Mar. 12, 2007-date
Departure: Still serving in the 111th Congress

Cong.	Ranking	Terms in: House	Comm.	Date of Assignment
110th	MnR-1st	1	1	Mar. 12, 2007
111th	Min-10th	2	2	Jan. 9, 2009

Dale Bumpers (D-Ark.)

Dates: Aug. 12, 1925
Senate: Jan. 3, 1975-Jan 3, 1999
Left the Senate: Left chamber; retired in 1998

SENATE STANDING COMMITTEES:

1st AERONAUTICAL AND SPACE SCIENCES
Dates: Jan. 17, 1975-Feb. 11, 1977
Departure: Committee reorganized; moved to Armed Services

2nd INTERIOR AND INSULAR AFFAIRS renamed
ENERGY AND NATURAL RESOURCES
Dates: Jan. 17, 1975-Jan. 3, 1999
Departure: Left the Senate; retired

Cong.	Ranking	Years in: Senate	Comm.	Date of Assignment
103rd	Maj-2nd	19	19	Jan. 7, 1993
104th	Min-2nd	21	21	Jan. 4, 1995
105th	Min-RM	23	23	Jan. 3, 1997

3rd ARMED SERVICES
Dates: Feb. 11, 1977-Jan. 27, 1978
Departure: Moved to Appropriations

4th APPROPRIATIONS

Dates: Jan. 27, 1978-Jan. 3, 1999
Departure: Left the Senate; retired

Cong.	Ranking	Years in: Senate	Comm.	Date of Assignment
103rd	Maj-8th	19	15	Jan. 7, 1993
104th	Min-6th	21	17	Jan. 4, 1995
105th	Min-5th	23	19	Jan. 3, 1997

5th SMALL BUSINESS

Dates: Mar. 25, 1981-Jan. 3, 1999
Departure: Left the Senate; retired

Cong.	Ranking	Years in: Senate	Comm.	Date of Assignment
103rd	Maj-Chr	19	15	Jan. 21, 1993
104th	Min-RM	21	17	Jan. 6, 1995
105th	Min-2nd	23	19	Jan. 3, 1997

SENATE SELECT AND SPECIAL COMMITTEES:

1st SELECT SMALL BUSINESS

Dates: Jan. 23, 1979-Mar. 25, 1981
Departure: Continued on reorganized standing committee

Jim Bunn (R-Ore.)

Dates: Dec. 12, 1956
House: Jan. 3, 1995-Jan. 3, 1997
Left the House: Defeated for re-election in 1996

HOUSE STANDING COMMITTEES:

1st APPROPRIATIONS

Dates: Jan. 4, 1995-Jan. 3, 1997
Departure: Left the House; lost re-election

Cong.	Ranking	Terms in: House	Comm.	Date of Assignment
104th	Maj-31st	1	1	Jan. 4, 1995

James P.D. Bunning (R-Ky.)

Dates: Aug. 23, 1931
House: Jan. 3, 1987-Jan. 3, 1999
Left the House: Elected to the U.S. Senate in 1998
Senate: Jan. 3, 1999-date
Serving in the 111th Congress

HOUSE STANDING COMMITTEES:

1st BANKING, FINANCE AND URBAN AFFAIRS

Dates: Jan. 21, 1987-Jan. 3, 1991
Departure: Moved to Ways and Means and Standards of Official Conduct

2nd MERCHANT MARINE AND FISHERIES

Dates: Jan. 21, 1987-Jan. 3, 1991
Departure: Moved to Ways and Means and Standards of Official Conduct

3rd WAYS AND MEANS

Dates: Jan. 3, 1991-Jan. 3, 1999
Departure: Left the House for the Senate

Cong.	Ranking	Terms in: House	Comm.	Date of Assignment
103rd	Min-8th	4	2	Jan. 5, 1993
104th	Maj-6th	5	3	Jan. 4, 1995
105th	Maj-6th	6	4	Jan. 7, 1997

4th STANDARDS OF OFFICIAL CONDUCT

Dates: Feb. 6, 1991-Jan. 3, 1997
Departure: Left committee; no new assignment

Cong.	Ranking	Terms in: House	Comm.	Date of Assignment
103rd	Min-3rd	4	2	Jan. 5, 1993
104th	Maj-2nd	5	3	Jan. 20, 1995

5th BUDGET

Dates: Jan. 26, 1993-Jan. 3, 1999
Departure: Left the House for the Senate

Cong.	Ranking	Terms in: House	Comm.	Date of Assignment
103rd	Min-7th	4	1	Jan. 26, 1993
104th	Maj-7th	5	2	Jan. 4, 1995
105th	Maj-5th	6	3	Jan. 7, 1997

HOUSE SELECT AND SPECIAL COMMITTEES:

1st SELECT ETHICS

Dates: Jan. 7, 1997-Jan. 9, 1997
Termination: Resigned committee; no new assignment

Cong.	Ranking	Terms in: House	Comm.	Date of Assignment
105th	Maj-4th	6	1	Jan. 7, 1997

SENATE STANDING COMMITTEES:

1st BANKING, HOUSING AND URBAN AFFAIRS

Dates: Jan. 7, 1999-date
Departure: Still serving in the 111th Congress

Cong.	Ranking	Years in: Senate	Comm.	Date of Assignment
106th	Maj-10th	1	1	Jan. 7, 1999
107th	Maj-8th	3	3	Jan. 25, 2001
+107th	Min-8th	3	3	June 6, 2001
108th	Maj-7th	5	5	Jan. 15, 2003
109th	Maj-7th	7	6	Jan. 6, 2005
110th	Min-6th	9	9	Jan. 12, 2007
111th	Min-3rd	11	11	Jan. 21, 2009

2nd ENERGY AND NATURAL RESOURCES

1st Dates: Jan. 7, 1999-Jan. 25, 2001
1st Departure: Moved to Armed Services
2nd Dates: Jan. 15, 2003-date
2nd Departure: Still serving in the 111th Congress

Cong.	Ranking	Years in: Senate	Comm.	Date of Assignment
106th	Maj-8th	1 *1	1	Jan. 7, 1999
108th	Maj-11th	5 *2	1	Jan. 15, 2003
109th	Maj-12th	7 *2	2	Jan. 6, 2005
110th	Min-10th	9 *2	4	Jan. 12, 2007
111th	Min-8th	11 *2	7	Jan. 21, 2009

3rd ARMED SERVICES

Dates: Jan. 25, 2001-Jan. 15, 2003
Departure: Returned to Energy and Natural Resources and moved to Budget, Finance, and Veterans' Affairs

Cong.	Ranking	Years in: Senate	Comm.	Date of Assignment
107th	Maj-12th	3	1	Jan. 25, 2001
+107th	Min-12th	3	1	June 6, 2001

4th BUDGET

Dates: Jan. 15, 2003-date
Departure: Still serving in the 111th Congress

Cong.	Ranking	Years in: Senate	Comm.	Date of Assignment
108th	Maj-9th	5	1	Jan. 15, 2003
109th	Maj-7th	7	2	Jan. 6, 2005
110th	Min-7th	9	4	Jan. 12, 2007
111th	Min-5th	11	7	Jan. 21, 2009

5th FINANCE

Dates: Jan. 15, 2003-date
Departure: Still serving in the 111th Congress

Cong.	Ranking	Years in: Senate	Comm.	Date of Assignment
108th	Maj-11th	5	1	Jan. 15, 2003
109th	Maj-10th	7	2	Jan. 6, 2005
110th	Min-8th	9	4	Jan. 12, 2007
111th	Min-5th	11	7	Jan. 21, 2009

6th VETERANS' AFFAIRS

Dates: Jan. 15, 2003-Jan. 6, 2005
Departure: Left committee; no new assignment

Cong.	Ranking	Years in: Senate	Comm.	Date of Assignment
108th	Maj-5th	5	1	Jan. 15, 2003

SENATE SELECT AND SPECIAL COMMITTEES:

1st SPECIAL AGING (Permanent)

Dates: Jan.7, 1999-Jan. 25, 2001
Departure: Moved to Armed Services

Cong.	Ranking	Years in: Senate	Comm.	Date of Assignment
106th	Maj-10th	1	1	Jan. 7, 1999

Michael C. Burgess (R-Tex.)

Dates: Dec. 23, 1950
House: Jan. 3, 2003-date
Serving in the 111th Congress

HOUSE STANDING COMMITTEES:

1st SCIENCE

Dates: Jan. 28, 2003-Jan. 3, 2005
Departure: Moved to Energy and Commerce

Cong.	Ranking	Terms in: House	Comm.	Date of Assignment
108th	Maj-23rd	1	1	Jan. 28, 2003

2nd TRANSPORTATION AND INFRASTRUCTURE

Dates: Jan. 28, 2003-Jan. 3, 2005
Departure: Moved to Energy and Commerce

Cong.	Ranking	Terms in: House	Comm.	Date of Assignment
108th	Maj-36th	1	1	Jan. 28, 2003

3rd GOVERNMENT REFORM

Dates: Sep. 23, 2004-Jan. 3, 2005
Departure: Moved to Energy and Commerce

Cong.	Ranking	Terms in: House	Comm.	Date of Assignment
108th	MjR-3rd	1	1	Sep. 23, 2004

4th ENERGY AND COMMERCE

Dates: Jan. 26, 2005-date
Departure: Still serving in the 111th Congress

Cong.	Ranking	Terms in: House	Comm.	Date of Assignment
109th	Maj-30th	2	1	Jan. 6, 2005
110th	Min-26th	3	2	Jan. 10, 2007
111th	Min-20th	4	3	Jan. 9, 2009

JOINT COMMITTEES:

1st JOINT ECONOMIC

House Dates: Feb. 3, 2009-date
Departure: Still serving in the 111th Congress

Cong.	Ranking	Terms in: House	Comm.	Date of Assignment
111th	Min-3rd	4	1	Feb. 3, 2009

Conrad Burns (R-Mont.)

Dates: Jan. 25, 1935
Senate: Jan. 3, 1989-Jan. 3, 2007
Left the Senate: Defeated for re-election in 2006

SENATE STANDING COMMITTEES:

1st COMMERCE, SCIENCE AND TRANSPORTATION

Dates: Feb. 2, 1989-Jan. 3, 2007
Departure: Left the Senate; lost re-election

Cong.	Ranking	Years in: Senate	Comm.	Date of Assignment
103rd	Min-6th	5	4	Jan. 7, 1993
104th	Maj-5th	7	6	Jan. 4, 1995
105th	Maj-3rd	9	8	Jan. 9, 1997
106th	Maj-3rd	11	10	Jan. 7, 1999
107th	Maj-3rd	13	12	Jan. 25, 2001
+107th	Min-3rd	13	13	June 6, 2001
108th	Maj-3rd	15	14	Jan. 15, 2003
109th	Maj-3rd	17	16	Jan. 6, 2005

2nd ENERGY AND NATURAL RESOURCES

1st Dates: Feb. 2, 1989-Jan. 7, 1993
1st Departure: Moved to Appropriations
2nd Dates: Jan. 5, 1995-Jan. 3, 2007
2nd Departure: Left the Senate; lost re-election

Cong.	Ranking	Years in: Senate	Comm.	Date of Assignment
104th	Maj-10th	7 *2	1	Jan. 5, 1995
105th	Maj-11th	9 *2	3	Jan. 9, 1997
106th	Maj-11th	11 *2	5	Jan. 7, 1999
107th	Maj-8th	13 *2	7	Jan. 25, 2001
+107th	Min-8th	13 *2	7	June 6, 2001
108th	Maj-9th	15 *2	9	Jan. 15, 2003
109th	Maj-9th	17 *2	11	Jan. 6, 2005

3rd SMALL BUSINESS renamed June 29, 2001
SMALL BUSINESS AND ENTREPRENEURSHIP

Dates: Feb. 2, 1989-Jan. 3, 2007
Departure: Left the Senate; lost re-election

Cong.	Ranking	Years in: Senate	Comm.	Date of Assignment
103rd	Min-4th	5	4	Jan. 21, 1993
104th	Maj-3rd	7	6	Jan. 6, 1995
105th	Maj-2nd	9	8	Jan. 9, 1997
106th	Maj-2nd	11	10	Jan. 7, 1999
107th	Maj-2nd	13	12	Jan. 25, 2001
+107th	Min-2nd	13	13	June 6, 2001

Cong.	Ranking				Date of Assignment
108th	Maj-3rd	15	14		Jan. 15, 2003
109th	Maj-3rd	17	16		Jan. 6, 2005

4th APPROPRIATIONS
Dates: Jan. 7, 1993-Jan. 3, 2007
Departure: Left the Senate; lost re-election

		Years in:		Date of
Cong.	Ranking	Senate	Comm.	Assignment
103rd	Min-13th	5	1	Jan. 7, 1993
104th	Maj-11th	7	2	Jan. 4, 1995
105th	Maj-8th	9	5	Jan. 9, 1997
106th	Maj-8th	11	7	Jan. 7, 1999
107th	Maj-7th	13	9	Jan. 25, 2001
+107th	Min-7th	13	9	June 6, 2001
108th	Maj-7th	15	11	Jan. 15, 2003
109th	Maj-7th	17	12	Jan. 6, 2005

5th BUDGET
Dates: Jan. 15, 2003-Jan. 6, 2005
Departure: Returned to Special Aging

		Years in:		Date of
Cong.	Ranking	Senate	Comm.	Assignment
108th	Maj-6th	15	1	Jan. 15, 2003

SENATE SELECT AND SPECIAL COMMITTEES:

1st JUDGE ALCEE L. HASTINGS IMPEACHMENT
Dates: Mar. 16, 1989-Aug. 3, 1989
Termination: Senate Hearing 101-194, Parts 1-2A
Senate floor vote on impeachment, Oct. 20, 1989

2nd SPECIAL AGING (Permanent)
1st Dates: Mar. 19, 1991-Jan. 15, 2003
1st Departure: Moved to Budget
2nd Dates: Jan. 6, 2005-Jan. 3, 2007
2nd Departure: Left the Senate; lost re-election

		Years in:		Date of
Cong.	Ranking	Senate	Comm.	Assignment
103rd	Min-9th	5 *1	2	Jan. 21, 1993
104th	Maj-7th	7 *1	4	Jan. 11, 1995
105th	Maj-4th	9 *1	6	Jan. 9, 1997
106th	Maj-4th	11 *1	8	Jan. 7, 1999
107th	Maj-3rd	13 *1	10	Jan. 25, 2001
+107th	Min-2nd	13 *1	11	July 24, 2001
109th	Maj-9th	17 *2	1	Jan. 6, 2005

Max Burns (R-Ga.)

Dates: Nov. 8, 1948
House: Jan. 3, 2003-Jan. 3, 2005
Left the House: Defeated for re-election in 2004

HOUSE STANDING COMMITTEES:

1st AGRICULTURE
Dates: Jan. 28, 2003-Jan. 3, 2005
Departure: Left the House; lost re-election

		Terms in:		Date of
Cong.	Ranking	House	Comm.	Assignment
108th	Maj-21st	1	1	Jan. 28, 2003

2nd TRANSPORTATION AND INFRASTRUCTURE
Dates: Jan. 28, 2003-Jan. 3, 2005
Departure: Left the House; lost re-election

		Terms in:		Date of
Cong.	Ranking	House	Comm.	Assignment
108th	Maj-37th	1	1	Jan. 28, 2003

3rd EDUCATION AND THE WORKFORCE
Dates: Feb. 12, 2003-Jan. 3, 2005
Departure: Left the House; lost re-election

		Terms in:		Date of
Cong.	Ranking	House	Comm.	Assignment
108th	MjR-1st	1	1	Feb. 12, 2003

Richard M. Burr (R-N.C.)

Dates: Nov. 30, 1955
House: Jan. 3, 1995-Jan. 3, 2005
Left the House: Elected to the U.S. Senate in 2004
Senate: Jan. 3, 2005-date
Serving in the 111th Congress

HOUSE STANDING COMMITTEES:

1st COMMERCE 104-106
ENERGY AND COMMERCE, 107-108
Dates: Jan. 4, 1995-Jan. 3, 2005
Departure: Left the House for the Senate

		Terms in:		Date of
Cong.	Ranking	House	Comm.	Assignment
104th	Maj-18th	1	1	Jan. 4, 1995
105th	Maj-18th	2	2	Jan. 7, 1997
106th	Maj-13th	3	3	Jan. 6, 1999
107th	Maj-11th	4	4	Jan. 6, 2001
108th	Maj-10th	5	5	Jan. 28, 2003

2nd INTERNATIONAL RELATIONS
Dates: May 13, 1998-Feb. 19, 2002
Departure: Resigned committee; no new assignment

		Terms in:		Date of
Cong.	Ranking	House	Comm.	Assignment
105th	MjR-1st	2	1	May 13, 1998
106th	Maj-22nd	3	2	Jan. 6, 1999
107th	Maj-16th	4	3	Jan. 6, 2001

HOUSE SELECT AND SPECIAL COMMITTEES:

1st PERMANENT SELECT INTELLIGENCE
Dates: Jan. 30, 2001-Jan. 3, 2005
Departure: Left the House for the Senate

		Terms in:		Date of
Cong.	Ranking	House	Comm.	Assignment
107th	Maj-10th	4	1	Jan. 30, 2001
108th	Maj-8th	5	2	Jan. 8, 2003

SENATE STANDING COMMITTEES:

1st ENERGY AND NATURAL RESOURCES
Dates: Jan. 6, 2005-date
Departure: Still serving in the 111th Congress

		Years in:		Date of
Cong.	Ranking	Senate	Comm.	Assignment
109th	Maj-6th	1	1	Jan. 6, 2005
110th	Min-5th	3	3	Jan. 12, 2007
111th	Min-2nd	5	5	Jan. 21, 2009

2nd HEALTH, EDUCATION, LABOR, AND PENSIONS
Dates: Jan. 6, 2005-date
Departure: Still serving in the 111th Congress

		Years in:		Date of
Cong.	Ranking	Senate	Comm.	Assignment
109th	Maj-5th	1	1	Jan. 6, 2005

Cong.	Ranking	Senate	Comm.	Date of Assignment
110th	Min-4th	3	3	Jan. 12, 2007
111th	Min-4th	5	5	Jan. 21, 2009

3rd VETERANS' AFFAIRS
Dates: Jan. 6, 2005-date
Departure: Still serving in the 111th Congress

Cong.	Ranking	Senate	Comm.	Date of Assignment
109th	Maj-5th	1	1	Jan. 6, 2005
110th	Min-3rd	3	3	Jan. 12, 2007
111th	Min-RM	5	5	Jan. 21, 2009

SENATE SELECT AND SPECIAL COMMITTEES:

1st Indian AFFAIRS (Permanent)
Dates: Jan. 6, 2005-Jan. 21, 2009
Departure: Left committee; became Ranking Member on Veterans' Affairs

Cong.	Ranking	Senate	Comm.	Date of Assignment
109th	Maj-8th	1	1	Jan. 6, 2005
110th	Min-7th	3	3	Jan. 12, 2007

2nd SELECT INTELLIGENCE (Permanent)
Dates: Jan. 12, 2007-date
Departure: Still serving in the 111th Congress

Cong.	Ranking	Senate	Comm.	Date of Assignment
110th	Min-7th	3	1	Jan. 12, 2007
111th	Min-5th	5	3	Jan. 21, 2009

Roland W. Burris (D-Ill.)

Dates: Aug. 3, 1937
Senate: Dec. 31, 2008-date
Serving in the 111th Congress

S: Burris was appointed to the 110th Congress, Dec. 31, 2008, to fill the vacancy caused by the resignation of U.S. Senator Barack Obama (D-Ill.) who had been elected President in 2008. Burris was not seated in the 110th Congress but was seated on Jan. 15, 2009, in the 111th Congress and was assigned to committees.

1st ARMED SERVICES
Dates: Jan. 21, 2009-date
Departure: Still serving in the 111th Congress

Cong.	Ranking	Senate	Comm.	Date of Assignment
111th	Maj-15th	1	1	Jan. 21, 2009

2nd HOMELAND SECURITY AND GOVERNMENT AFFAIRS
Dates: Jan. 21, 2009-date
Departure: Still serving in the 111th Congress

Cong.	Ranking	Senate	Comm.	Date of Assignment
111th	Maj-9th	1	1	Jan. 21, 2009

3rd VETERANS' AFFAIRS
Dates: Jan. 21, 2009-date
Departure: Still serving in the 111th Congress

Cong.	Ranking	Senate	Comm.	Date of Assignment
111th	Maj-9th	1	1	Jan. 21, 2009

Danny L. Burton (R-Ind.)

Dates: June 21, 1938
House: Jan. 3, 1983-date
Serving in the 111th Congress

HOUSE STANDING COMMITTEES:

1st GOVERNMENT OPERATIONS, 98
GOVERNMENT REFORM AND OVERSIGHT, 104-105
GOVERNMENT REFORM, 106-109
OVERSIGHT AND GOVERNMENT REFORM, 110-111
1st Dates: Jan. 6, 1983-Jan. 3, 1985
1st Departure: Moved to Foreign Affairs and Post Office and Civil Service
2nd Dates: Jan. 4, 1995-date
2nd Departure: Still serving in the 111th Congress

Cong.	Ranking	House	Comm.	Date of Assignment
104th	Maj-3rd	7 *2	1	Jan. 4, 1995
105th	Maj-Chr	8 *2	2	Jan. 7, 1997
106th	Maj-Chr	9 *2	3	Jan. 6, 1999
107th	Maj-Chr	10 *2	4	Jan. 6, 2001
108th	Maj-2nd	11 *2	5	Jan. 28, 2003
109th	Maj-2nd	12 *2	6	Jan. 26, 2005
110th	Min-2nd	13 *2	7	Jan. 10, 2007
111th	Min-2nd	14 *2	8	Jan. 9, 2009

2nd VETERANS' AFFAIRS,
Dates: Jan. 6, 1983-Jan. 3, 1995
Departure: Returned to Government Reform and Oversight
Dates: Mar. 8, 2005-Mar. 12, 2007
Departure: Removed by Speaker

Cong.	Ranking	House	Comm.	Date of Assignment
103rd	Min-3rd	6 *1	6	Jan. 5, 1993
109th	MjR-1st	12 *2	1	Mar. 8, 2005
110th	Min-3rd	13 *2	2	Jan. 10, 2007

3rd FOREIGN AFFAIRS, 99-103
INTERNATIONAL RELATIONS, 104-109
FOREIGN AFFAIRS, 110-111
Dates: Jan. 30, 1985-date
Departure: Still serving in the 111th Congress

Cong.	Ranking	House	Comm.	Date of Assignment
103rd	Min-9th	6	5	Jan. 5, 1993
104th	Maj-8th	7	6	Jan. 4, 1995
105th	Maj-7th	8	7	Jan. 7, 1997
106th	Maj-7th	9	8	Jan. 6, 1999
107th	Maj-6th	10	9	Jan. 6, 2001
108th	Maj-5th	11	10	Jan. 28, 2003
109th	Maj-4th	12	11	Jan. 26, 2005
110th	Min-3rd	13	12	Jan. 10, 2007
111th	Min-3rd	14	13	Jan. 9, 2009

4th POST OFFICE AND CIVIL SERVICE
Dates: Jan. 30, 1985-Jan. 3, 1995
Departure: Committee abolished; reorganized into Government Reform and Oversight

Cong.	Ranking	House	Comm.	Date of Assignment
103rd	Min-4th	6	5	Jan. 5, 1993

HOUSE SELECT AND SPECIAL COMMITTEES:

1st SELECT CHILDREN, YOUTH AND FAMILIES (Temporary)
Dates: Feb. 2, 1983-Apr. 22, 1986
Departure: Left committee; no new assignment

George K. Butterfield Jr. (D-N.C.)

Dates: April 27, 1947
House: July 20, 2004-date
Serving in the 111th Congress

H: Butterfield was elected to the 108th Congress by special election, July 20, 2004, to fill the vacancy caused by the resignation of U.S. Representative Frank Ballance (D-N.C.). Butterfield was seated July 21, 2004, and assigned to committees.

HOUSE STANDING COMMITTEES:

1st AGRICULTURE
Dates: July 22, 2004-Jan. 3, 2007
Departure: Moved to Energy and Commerce

Cong.	Ranking	Terms in: House	Comm.	Date of Assignment
108th	MnR-3rd	1	1	July 22, 2004
109th	Min-12th	2	2	Jan. 26, 2005

2nd SMALL BUSINESS
Dates: July 22, 2004-Jan. 3, 2005
Departure: Moved to Armed Services

Cong.	Ranking	Terms in: House	Comm.	Date of Assignment
108th	MnR-5th	1	1	July 22, 2004

3rd ARMED SERVICES
Dates: Jan. 26, 2005-Jan. 3, 2007
Departure: Moved to Energy and Commerce

Cong.	Ranking	Terms in: House	Comm.	Date of Assignment
109th	Min-26th	2	1	Jan. 26, 2005

4th ENERGY AND COMMERCE
Dates: Jan. 4, 2007-date
Departure: Still serving in the 111th Congress

Cong.	Ranking	Terms in: House	Comm.	Date of Assignment
110th	Maj-28th	3	1	Jan. 4, 2007
111th	Maj-23rd	4	2	Jan. 7, 2009

5th STANDARDS OF OFFICIAL CONDUCT
Dates: Jan. 22, 2009-date
Departure: Still serving in the 111th Congress

Cong.	Ranking	Terms in: House	Comm.	Date of Assignment
111th	Maj-3rd	4	1	Jan. 22, 2009

Stephen E. Buyer (R-Ind.)

Dates: Nov. 26, 1958
House: Jan. 3, 1993-date
Serving in the 111th Congress

HOUSE STANDING COMMITTEES:

1st ARMED SERVICES, 103
NATIONAL SECURITY, 104-105
ARMED SERVICES, 106
Dates: Jan. 5, 1993-Jan. 3, 2001
Departure: Moved to Energy and Commerce

Cong.	Ranking	Terms in: House	Comm.	Date of Assignment
103rd	Min-16th	1	1	Jan. 5, 1993
104th	Maj-12th	2	2	Jan. 4, 1995
105th	Maj-10th	3	3	Jan. 7, 1997
106th	Maj-10th	4	4	Jan. 6, 1999

2nd VETERANS' AFFAIRS
Dates: Jan. 5, 1993-date
Departure: Still serving in the 111th Congress

Cong.	Ranking	Terms in: House	Comm.	Date of Assignment
103rd	Min-9th	1	1	Jan. 5, 1993
104th	Maj-7th	2	2	Jan. 4, 1995
105th	Maj-6th	3	3	Jan. 21, 1997
106th	Maj-6th	4	4	Jan. 6, 1999
107th	Maj-6th	5	5	Jan. 6, 2001
108th	Maj-4th	6	6	Jan. 28, 2003
109th	Maj-Chr	7	7	Jan. 6, 2005
110th	Min-RM	8	8	Jan. 4, 2007
111th	Min-RM	9	9	Jan. 6, 2009

3rd JUDICIARY
Dates: Jan. 4, 1995-Feb. 25, 1999
Departure: Resigned committee and requested rescission of waiver to serve on three standing committees

Cong.	Ranking	Terms in: House	Comm.	Date of Assignment
104th	Maj-13th	2	1	Jan. 4, 1995
105th	Maj-12th	3	2	Jan. 7, 1997
106th	Maj-10th	4	3	Jan. 6, 1999

4th ENERGY AND COMMERCE
Dates: Jan. 6, 2001-date
Departure: Still serving in the 111th Congress

Cong.	Ranking	Terms in: House	Comm.	Date of Assignment
107th	Maj-25th	5	1	Jan. 6, 2001
108th	Maj-20th	6	2	Jan. 28, 2003
109th	Maj-17th	7	3	Jan. 26, 2005
110th	Min-15th	8	4	Jan. 10, 2007
111th	Min-10th	9	5	Jan. 9, 2009

HOUSE SELECT AND SPECIAL COMMITTEES:

1st SELECT BIPARTISAN COMMITTEE TO INVESTIGATE THE PREPARATION FOR AND RESPONSE TO HURRICANE KATRINA
Dates: Sep. 21, 2005-Feb. 15, 2006
Departure: House Report 377 (109-2) filed

Cong.	Ranking	Terms in: House	Comm.	Date of Assignment
109th	Maj-6th	7	1	Sep. 21, 2005

Robert C. Byrd (D-W.Va.)

Dates: Jan. 15, 1918-June 28, 2010
House: Jan. 3, 1953-Jan. 3, 1959
Left the House: Elected to the U.S. Senate in 1958
Senate: Jan. 3, 1959-June 28, 2010
Left the Senate: Died in office

HOUSE STANDING COMMITTEES:

1st HOUSE ADMINISTRATION
Dates: Jan. 19, 1953-Jan. 3, 1959
Departure: Left the House for the Senate

2nd FOREIGN AFFAIRS
Dates: Jan. 13, 1955-Jan. 3, 1959
Departure: Left the House for the Senate

SENATE STANDING COMMITTEES:

1st APPROPRIATIONS
Dates: Jan. 14, 1959-June 28, 2010
Ch2: Replaced Theodore F. Stevens (R-Alas.) on June 6, 2001, following Senate Party control shift
Departure: Died in office

Cong.	Ranking	Years in: Senate	Comm.	Date of Assignment
103rd	Maj-Chr	35	34	Jan. 7, 1993
104th	Min-RM	37	36	Jan. 4, 1995
105th	Min-RM	39	38	Jan. 9, 1997
106th	Min-RM	41	40	Jan. 7, 1999
=107th	Maj-ChT	43	42	Jan. 3, 2001
107th	Min-RM1	43	43	Jan. 25, 2001
+107th	Maj-Ch2	43	43	June 6, 2001
108th	Min-RM	45	45	Jan. 15, 2003
109th	Min-RM	47	46	Jan. 6, 2005
110th	Maj-Chr	49	48	Jan. 12, 2007
111th	Maj-2nd	51	51	Jan. 21, 2009

2nd BANKING AND CURRENCY
Dates: Jan. 14, 1959-Jan. 10, 1961
Departure: Moved to Armed Services

3rd ARMED SERVICES
1st Dates: Jan. 10, 1961-Jan. 14, 1969
1st Departure: Moved to Judiciary
2nd Dates: Feb. 2, 1989-June 28, 2010
2nd Departure: Died in office

Cong.	Ranking	Years in: Senate	Comm.	Date of Assignment
103rd	Maj-8th	35 *2	4	Jan. 7, 1993
104th	Min-7th	37 *2	6	Jan. 4, 1995
105th	Min-5th	39 *2	8	Jan. 9, 1997
106th	Min-4th	41 *2	10	Jan. 7, 1999
107th	Min-3rd	43 *2	12	Jan. 25, 2001
+107th	Maj-3rd	43 *2	13	June 6, 2001
108th	Min-3rd	45 *2	14	Jan. 15, 2003
109th	Min-3rd	47 *2	16	Jan. 6, 2005
110th	Maj-3rd	49 *2	18	Jan. 12, 2007
111th	Maj-3rd	51 *2	20	Jan. 21, 2009

4th RULES AND ADMINISTRATION
Dates: Feb. 25, 1963-June 28, 2010
Departure: Died in office

Cong.	Ranking	Years in: Senate	Comm.	Date of Assignment
103rd	Maj-3rd	35	30	Jan. 21, 1993
104th	Min-3rd	37	32	Jan. 6, 1995
105th	Min-2nd	39	34	Jan. 9, 1997
106th	Min-2nd	41	36	Jan. 7, 1999
107th	Min-2nd	43	38	Jan. 25, 2001
+107th	Maj-2nd	43	39	June 6, 2001
108th	Min-2nd	45	40	Jan. 15, 2003
109th	Min-2nd	47	42	Jan. 6, 2005
110th	Maj-3rd	49	44	Jan. 12, 2007
111th	Maj-4th	51	46	Jan. 21, 2009

5th JUDICIARY
Dates: Jan. 14, 1969-Feb. 2, 1989
Departure: Returned to Armed Services

6th BUDGET
Dates: Jan. 25, 2001-June 28, 2010
Departure: Died in office

Cong.	Ranking	Years in: Senate	Comm.	Date of Assignment
107th	Min-8th	43	1	Jan. 25, 2001
+107th	Maj-8th	43	1	June 6, 2001
108th	Min-8th	45	2	Jan. 15, 2003
109th	Min-7th	47	4	Jan. 6, 2005
110th	Maj-5th	49	6	Jan. 12, 2007
111th	Maj-5th	51	8	Jan. 21, 2009

SENATE SELECT AND SPECIAL COMMITTEES:

1st SPECIAL YEAR 2000 TECHNOLOGY PROBLEM
Dates: Apr. 28, 1998-Feb. 29, 2000
Departure: Senate Print 106-42 issued

Cong.	Ranking	Years in: Senate	Comm.	Date of Assignment
105th	Min-ExO	40	1	Apr. 28, 1998
106th	Min-ExO	41	1	Continued

SENATE LEADERSHIP POSTS

Leader Dates: Jan. 21, 1971-Jan. 3, 1989
Leader Departure: Left post to chair Appropriations

1st SENATE MAJORITY WHIP
Dates: Jan. 3, 1971-Jan. 3, 1977
Note: For the 92nd Congress, Byrd defeated Majority Whip Edward M. Kennedy (D-Mass.). Byrd was unopposed for the 93rd and 94th Congresses.
Departure: Elected Majority Floor Leader

2nd SENATE MAJORITY FLOOR LEADER
1st Dates: Jan. 4, 1977-Jan. 3, 1981
Note: For the 96th Congress, Byrd succeeded Majority Floor Leader Michael J. Mansfield (D-Mont.) on Jan. 4, 1977, Byrd was unopposed for the 95th, 96th and 100th Congresses.
1st Departure: Democratic Party lost Senate majority in 1980
2nd Dates: Jan. 3, 1987-Jan. 3, 1989
2nd Departure: Left post to chair Appropriations

3rd SENATE MINORITY FLOOR LEADER
Dates: Jan. 3, 1981-Jan. 3, 1987
Note: Byrd was unopposed in the 97th-99th Congresses
Departure: Democratic Party gained Senate majority in 1986

4th SENATE PRESIDENT PRO TEMPORE
1st Dates: Jan. 3, 1989-Jan. 3, 1995
1st Departure: Democratic Party lost Senate majority in 1994
2nd Dates: June 6, 2001-Jan. 3, 2003
Note: Byrd succeeded J. Strom Thurmond (R-S.C.) as Senate President *pro tempore* following the switch of Senator James Jeffords of Vermont from Republican to Independent giving majority control to the Democrats.
2nd Departure: Democratic Party lost Senate majority in 2002
3rd Dates: Jan. 3, 2007-June 28, 2010
3rd Departure: Died in office

Cong.	Ranking	Years in: Senate	Post	Date of Service
103rd	Maj-Ppt	35	*1 5	Jan. 5, 1993
+107th	Maj-Ppt	43	*2 1	June 6, 2001
110th	Maj-Ppt	49	*3 1	Jan. 4, 2007
111th	Maj-Ppt	51	*3 3	Jan. 6, 2009

Leslie L. Byrne (D-Va.)

Dates: Oct. 27, 1946
House: Jan. 3, 1993-Jan. 3, 1995
Left the House: Defeated for re-election in 1994

HOUSE STANDING COMMITTEES:

1st PUBLIC WORKS AND TRANSPORTATION
Dates: Jan. 5, 1993-Jan. 3, 1995
Departure: Left the House; lost re-election

Cong.	Ranking	Terms in: House	Comm.	Date of Assignment
103rd	Maj-27th	1	1	Jan. 5, 1993

2nd POST OFFICE AND CIVIL SERVICE
Dates: Jan. 21, 1993-Jan. 3, 1995
Departure: Left the House; lost re-election

Cong.	Ranking	Terms in: House	Comm.	Date of Assignment
103rd	Maj-9th	1	1	Jan. 21, 1993

C

H.L. (Sonny) Callahan (R-Ala.)

Dates: Sept. 11, 1932
House: Jan. 3, 1985-Jan. 3, 2003
Left the House: Retired in 2002

HOUSE STANDING COMMITTEES:

1st MERCHANT MARINE AND FISHERIES
1st Dates: Jan. 30, 1985-Jan. 3, 1987
1st Departure: Moved to Energy and Commerce
2nd Dates: Jan. 24, 1991-Jan. 3, 1993
2nd Departure: Moved to Appropriations.

2nd PUBLIC WORKS AND TRANSPORTATION
Dates: Jan. 30, 1985-Jan. 21, 1987
Departure: Moved to Energy and Commerce

3rd ENERGY AND COMMERCE
Dates: Jan. 21, 1987-Jan. 3, 1993
Departure: Moved to Appropriations

4th APPROPRIATIONS
Dates: Jan. 5, 1993-Jan. 3, 2003
Departure: Left the House; retired

Cong.	Ranking	Terms in: House	Comm.	Date of Assignment
103rd	Min-17th	5	1	Jan. 5, 1993
104th	Maj-16th	6	2	Jan. 4, 1995
105th	Maj-13th	7	3	Jan. 7, 1997
106th	Maj-11th	8	4	Jan. 6, 1999
107th	Maj-9th	9	5	Jan. 6, 2001

Ken Calvert (R-Cal.)

Dates: June 8, 1953
House: Jan. 3, 1993-date
Serving in the 111th Congress

HOUSE STANDING COMMITTEES:

1st NATURAL RESOURCES, 103
RESOURCES, 104-109
NATURAL RESOURCES, 110
Dates: Jan. 5, 1993-May 14, 2007
Departure: Resigned committee; moved to Appropriations

Cong.	Ranking	Terms in: House	Comm.	Date of Assignment
103rd	Min-12th	1	1	Jan. 5, 1993
104th	Maj-10th	2	2	Jan. 5, 1995
105th	Maj-10th	3	3	Jan. 7, 1997
106th	Maj-10th	4	4	Jan. 6, 1999
107th	Maj-9th	5	5	Jan. 6, 2001
108th	Maj-9th	6	6	Jan. 28, 2003

Cong.	Ranking	Terms in: House	Comm.	Date of Assignment
109th	Maj-7th	7	7	Jan. 26, 2005
110th	Min-6th	8	8	Jan. 10, 2007

2nd SCIENCE, SPACE AND TECHNOLOGY, 103
SCIENCE, 104-109
SCIENCE AND TECHNOLOGY, 110
Dates: Jan. 5, 1993-May 14, 2007
Departure: Resigned committee; moved to Appropriations

Cong.	Ranking	Terms in: House	Comm.	Date of Assignment
103rd	Min-13th	1	1	Jan. 5, 1993
104th	Maj-10th	2	2	Jan. 4, 1995
105th	Maj-9th	3	3	Jan. 21, 1997
106th	Maj-8th	4	4	Jan. 6, 1999
107th	Maj-8th	5	5	Jan. 6, 2001
108th	Maj-7th	6	6	Jan. 28, 2003
109th	Maj-6th	7	7	Jan. 26, 2005
110th	Min-5th	8	8	Jan. 10, 2007

3rd AGRICULTURE
1st Dates: Jan. 4, 1995-Jan. 3, 1997
1st Departure: Left committee; no new assignment
2nd Dates: Jan. 4, 1999-Jan. 3, 2001
2nd Departure: Moved to Armed Services

Cong.	Ranking	Terms in: House	Comm.	Date of Assignment
104th	Maj-19th	2 *1	1	Jan. 4, 1995
106th	Maj-20th	4 *2	1	Jan. 6, 1999

4th ARMED SERVICES
Dates: Jan. 6, 2001-May 14, 2007
Departure: Resigned committee; moved to Appropriations

Cong.	Ranking	Terms in: House	Comm.	Date of Assignment
107th	Maj-26th	5	1	Jan. 6, 2001
108th	Maj-16th	6	2	Jan. 28, 2003
109th	Maj-15th	7	3	Jan. 26, 2005
110th	Min-10th	8	4	Jan. 10, 2007

5th APPROPRIATIONS
Dates: May 10, 2007-date
Departure: Still serving in the 111th Congress

Cong.	Ranking	Terms in: House	Comm.	Date of Assignment
110th	MnR-1st	8	1	May 10, 2007
111th	Min-20th	9	2	Jan. 9, 2009

David L. Camp (R-Mich.)

Dates: July 9, 1953
House: Jan. 3, 1991-date
Serving in the 111th Congress

HOUSE STANDING COMMITTEES:

1st AGRICULTURE
Dates: Jan. 24, 1991-Feb. 4, 1993
Departure: Resigned committee; moved to Ways and Means

Cong.	Ranking	Terms in: House	Comm.	Date of Assignment
103rd	Min-7th	2	2	Jan. 5, 1993

2nd SMALL BUSINESS
Dates: Jan. 24, 1991-Feb. 4, 1993
Departure: Resigned committee; moved to Ways and Means

Cong.	Ranking	Terms in: House	Comm.	Date of Assignment
103rd	Min-7th	2	2	Jan. 5, 1993

3rd WAYS AND MEANS
Dates: Feb. 4, 1993-date
Departure: Still serving in the 111th Congress

Cong.	Ranking	Terms in: House	Comm.	Date of Assignment
103rd	MnR-1st	2	1	Feb. 4, 1993
104th	Maj-11th	3	2	Jan. 4, 1995
105th	Maj-10th	4	3	Jan. 7, 1997
106th	Maj-9th	5	4	Jan. 6, 1999
107th	Maj-8th	6	5	Jan. 6, 2001
108th	Maj-8th	7	6	Jan. 28, 2003
109th	Maj-6th	8	7	Jan. 6, 2005
110th	Min-3rd	9	8	Jan. 4, 2007
111th	Min-RM	10	9	Jan. 6, 2009

4th STANDARDS OF OFFICIAL CONDUCT
Dates: Jan. 19, 1999-Jan. 3, 2001
Departure: Left committee; no new assignment

Cong.	Ranking	Terms in: House	Comm.	Date of Assignment
106th	Maj-4th	5	1	Jan. 19, 1999

HOUSE SELECT AND SPECIAL COMMITTEES:

1st SELECT CHILDREN, YOUTH AND FAMILIES (Temporary)
Dates: Feb. 21, 1991-Jan. 3, 1993
Termination: Committee not renewed in 1993

2nd SELECT HOMELAND SECURITY
Dates: Feb. 12, 2003-Jan. 3, 2005
Departure: Did not continue on reorganized standing committee

Cong.	Ranking	Terms in: House	Comm.	Date of Assignment
108th	Maj-15th	7	1	Feb. 12, 2003

JOINT COMMITTEES:

1st JOINT TAXATION
House Dates: Jan. 12, 2009-date
Departure: Still serving in the 111th Congress

Cong.	Ranking	Terms in: House	Comm.	Date of Assignment
111th	Min-1st	10	1	Jan. 12, 2009 Ltr

Ben Nighthorse Campbell (R-Colo.)

Dates: April 13, 1933
House: Jan. 3, 1987-Jan. 3, 1993

Left the House: Elected to the U.S. Senate in 1992
Senate: Jan. 3, 1993-Jan. 3, 2005
Left Senate: Left chamber; retired
Served as a Democrat: Jan. 3, 1987-Mar. 3, 1995
Served as a Republican: Mar. 3, 1995-Jan. 3, 2005

HOUSE STANDING COMMITTEES:

1st AGRICULTURE
Dates: Jan. 22, 1987-Jan. 3, 1993
Departure: Left the House for the Senate

2nd INTERIOR AND INSULAR AFFAIRS
Dates: Jan. 22, 1987-Jan. 3, 1993
Departure: Left the House for the Senate

3rd SMALL BUSINESS
Dates: Jan. 22, 1987-Jan. 3, 1989
Departure: Left committee; no new assignment

SENATE STANDING COMMITTEES:

1st BANKING, HOUSING AND URBAN AFFAIRS
Dates: Jan. 7, 1993-Jan. 4, 1995
Note: Campbell was erroneously listed in the *Congressional Record* of Jan. 4, 1995, as the 5th Majority Member
Departure: Left committee; no new assignment

Cong.	Ranking	Years in: Senate	Comm.	Date of Assignment
103rd	Maj-9th	1	1	Jan. 7, 1993

2nd ENERGY AND NATURAL RESOURCES
1st Dates: Jan. 7, 1993-Mar. 3, 1995
1st Departure: Changed party; seat vacated as Democrat; returned as a Republican in 6th slot with seniority retained
2nd Dates: Mar. 24, 1995-Jan. 3, 2005
2nd Departure: Left the Senate; retired

Cong.	Ranking	Years in: Senate	Comm.	Date of Assignment
103rd	Maj-9th	1	*1 1	Jan. 7, 1993
104th	Min-8th	3	*1 2	Jan. 5, 1995
104th	MjA-6th	3	*2 1	Mar. 24, 1995
105th	Maj-5th	5	*2 2	Jan. 9, 1997
106th	Maj-5th	7	*2 4	Jan. 7, 1999
107th	Maj-5th	9	*2 6	Jan. 25, 2001
+107th	Min-5th	9	*2 7	June 6, 2001
108th	Maj-4th	11	*2 8	Jan. 15, 2003

3rd VETERANS' AFFAIRS
1st Dates: Jan. 21, 1993-Mar. 3, 1995
1st Departure: Changed party; seat vacated as Democrat; returned as a Republican with seniority retained
2nd Dates: Mar. 24, 1995-Jan. 3, 2005
2nd Departure: Left the Senate; retired

Cong.	Ranking	Years in: Senate	Comm.	Date of Assignment
103rd	Maj-7th	1	*1 1	Jan. 21, 1993
104th	Min-4th	3	*1 2	Jan. 6, 1995
104th	MjR-1st	3	*2 1	Mar. 24, 1995
105th	Maj-5th	5	*2 2	Jan. 9, 1997
106th	Maj-5th	7	*2 4	Jan. 7, 1999
107th	Maj-5th	9	*2 6	Jan. 25, 2001
+107th	Min-4th	9	*2 7	July 10, 2001
108th	Maj-2nd	11	*2 8	Jan. 15, 2003

4th AGRICULTURE, NUTRITION AND FORESTRY
Dates: Mar. 24, 1995-Oct. 12, 1995
Departure: Left committee; moved to Appropriations

Cong.	Ranking	Years in: Senate	Comm.	Date of Assignment
104th	MjA-10th	3	1	Mar. 24, 1995

5th APPROPRIATIONS
Dates: Oct. 12, 1995-Jan. 3, 2005
Departure: Left the Senate; retired

Cong.	Ranking	Years in: Senate	Comm.	Date of Assignment
104th	MjR-1st	3	1	Oct. 12, 1995
105th	Maj-12th	5	2	Jan. 9, 1997
106th	Maj-12th	7	4	Jan. 7, 1999
107th	Maj-11th	9	6	Jan. 25, 2001
+107th	Min-11th	9	6	June 6, 2001
108th	Maj-11th	11	8	Jan. 15, 2003

6th ENVIRONMENT AND PUBLIC WORKS
Dates: Jan. 25, 2001-Jan. 15, 2003
Departure: Left committee; no new assignment

Cong.	Ranking	Years in: Senate	Comm.	Date of Assignment
107th	Maj-9th	9	1	Jan. 25, 2001
+107th	Min-9th	9	1	June 6, 2001
108th	Maj-9th	11	2	Jan. 15, 2003

SENATE SELECT AND SPECIAL COMMITTEES:

1st INDIAN AFFAIRS (Permanent)
1st Dates: Jan. 21, 1993-Mar. 3 1995
1st Departure: Changed party; seat vacated as Minority Democrat; returned as a Majority Republican in 7th slot with seniority retained
2nd Dates: Mar. 24, 1995-Jan. 3, 2005
Ch1: Replaced by Daniel K. Inouye (D-Hai) on June 6, 2001, following party control shift and became RM2.
2nd Departure: Left the Senate; retired

Cong.	Ranking	Years in: Senate	Comm.	Date of Assignment
103rd	Maj-9th	1 *1	1	Jan. 21, 1993
104th	Min-8th	3 *1	2	Jan. 9, 1995
104th	MjR-1st	3 *2	1	Mar. 24, 1995
105th	Maj-Chr	5 *2	2	Jan. 9, 1997
106th	Maj-Chr	7 *2	4	Jan. 7, 1999
107th	Maj-Ch1	9 *2	6	Jan. 25, 2001
+107th	Min-RM2	9 *2	7	June 6, 2001
108th	Maj-Chr	11 *2	8	Jan. 15, 2003

John Campbell (R-Cal.)

Dates: July 19, 1955
House: Dec. 6, 2005-date
Serving in the 111th Congress

H: John Campbell was elected to the 109th Congress by special election, Dec. 6, 2005, to fill the vacancy of U.S. Representative Christopher Cox (R-Cal.) who was appointed Chair of the Securities and Exchanges Commission. John Campbell was seated Dec. 7, 2005, and assigned to committees.

HOUSE STANDING COMMITTEES:

1st BUDGET
Dates: Feb. 8, 2006-date
Departure: Still serving in the 111th Congress.

Cong.	Ranking	Terms in: House	Comm.	Date of Assignment
109th	MjR-2nd	1	1	Feb. 8, 2006
110th	Min-13th	2	2	Jan. 18, 2007
111th	Min-10th	3	3	Jan. 9, 2009

2nd FINANCIAL SERVICES
Dates: Feb. 8, 2006-date
Departure: Still serving in the 111th Congress

Cong.	Ranking	Terms in: House	Comm.	Date of Assignment
109th	MjR-1st	1	1	Feb. 8, 2006
110th	Min-29th	2	2	Jan. 10, 2007
111th	Min-19th	3	3	Jan. 9, 2009

3rd VETERANS' AFFAIRS
Dates: Feb. 8, 2006-Jan. 3, 2007
Departure: Left committee; no new assignment

Cong.	Ranking	Terms in: House	Comm.	Date of Assignment
109th	MjR-2nd	1	1	Feb. 8, 2006

JOINT COMMITTEES:

1st JOINT ECONOMIC
House Dates: Feb. 3, 2009-date
Departure: Still serving in the 111th Congress

Cong.	Ranking	Terms in: House	Comm.	Date of Assignment
111th	Min-4th	3	1	Feb. 3, 2009

Thomas J. Campbell (R-Cal.)

Dates: Aug. 14, 1952
House 1: Jan. 3, 1989-Jan. 3, 1993
Left the House 1: Lost U.S. Senate nomination in 1992
House 2: Dec. 12, 1995-Jan. 3, 2001
Left the House 2: Lost U.S. Senate election in 2000

H2: Thomas Campbell was elected to the 104th Congress by special election, Dec. 12, 1995, to fill the vacancy caused by the resignation of U.S. Representative Norman Y. Mineta (D-Cal.). Thomas Campbell was seated Dec. 15, 1995, and assigned to committees.

HOUSE STANDING COMMITTEES:

1st SCIENCE, SPACE AND TECHNOLOGY
Dates: Jan. 20, 1989-Jan. 3, 1993
Departure: Left the House; lost Senate nomination

2nd SMALL BUSINESS
Dates: Jan. 20, 1989-Mar. 28, 1990
Departure: Moved to Judiciary

3rd JUDICIARY
Dates: Nov. 21, 1989-Jan. 3, 1993
Departure: Left the House; lost Senate nomination

4th BANKING, FINANCE AND URBAN AFFAIRS, 102
BANKING AND FINANCIAL SERVICES, 104-106
1st Dates: Jan. 24, 1991-Jan. 3, 1993
1st Departure: Left the House; lost Senate nomination
2nd Dates: Dec. 27, 1995-Jan. 3, 2001
2nd Departure: Left the House; lost Senate election

Cong.	Ranking	Terms in: House	Comm.	Date of Assignment
104th	MjA-28th	3	*2 1	Dec. 27, 1995
105th	Maj-10th	4	*2 2	Jan. 7, 1997
106th	Maj-10th	5	*2 3	Jan. 6, 1999

5th INTERNATIONAL RELATIONS
Dates: Dec. 27, 1995-Jan. 3, 2001
Departure: Left the House; lost Senate election

Cong.	Ranking	Terms in: House	Comm.	Date of Assignment
104th	MjA-24th	3	1	Dec. 27, 1995
105th	Maj-20th	4	2	Jan. 7, 1997
106th	Maj-19th	5	3	Jan. 6, 1999

JOINT COMMITTEES:

1st JOINT ECONOMIC
House Dates: Mar. 18, 1999-Jan. 3, 2001
Departure: Left the House; lost Senate election

Cong.	Ranking	Terms in: House	Comm.	Date of Assignment
106th	Maj-4th	5	1	Mar. 18, 1999

Charles T. Canady (R-Fla.)

Dates: June 22, 1954
House: Jan. 3, 1993-Jan. 3, 2001
Left the House: Retired in 2000

HOUSE STANDING COMMITTEES:

1st AGRICULTURE
Dates: Jan. 5, 1993-Jan. 3, 2001
Departure: Left the House; retired

Cong.	Ranking	Terms in: House	Comm.	Date of Assignment
103rd	Min-18th	1	1	Jan. 5, 1993
104th	Maj-12th	2	2	Jan. 4, 1995
105th	Maj-9th	3	3	Jan. 7, 1997
106th	Maj-7th	4	4	Jan. 6, 1999

2nd JUDICIARY
Dates: Jan. 5, 1993-Jan. 3, 2001
Departure: Left the House; retired

Cong.	Ranking	Terms in: House	Comm.	Date of Assignment
103rd	Min-12th	1	1	Jan. 5, 1993
104th	Maj-10th	2	2	Jan. 4, 1995
105th	Maj-9th	3	3	Jan. 7, 1997
106th	Maj-8th	4	4	Jan. 6, 1999

Christopher B. Cannon (R-Utah)

Dates: Oct. 20, 1950
House: Jan. 3, 1997-Jan. 3, 2009
Left the House: Defeated for re-nomination in 2008

HOUSE STANDING COMMITTEES:

1st JUDICIARY
Dates: Jan. 7, 1997-Jan. 3, 2009
Departure: Left the House; lost re-nomination

Cong.	Ranking	Terms in: House	Comm.	Date of Assignment
105th	Maj-20th	1	1	Jan. 7, 1997
106th	Maj-17th	2	2	Jan. 6, 1999
107th	Maj-12th	3	3	Jan. 6, 2001
108th	Maj-9th	4	4	Jan. 28, 2003
109th	Maj-10th	5	5	Jan. 26, 2005
110th	Min-8th	6	6	Jan. 10, 2007

2nd RESOURCES, 105-109
NATURAL RESOURCES, 110
Dates: Jan. 7, 1997-Jan. 3, 2009
Departure: Left the House; lost re-nomination

Cong.	Ranking	Terms in: House	Comm.	Date of Assignment
105th	Maj-21st	1	1	Jan. 7, 1997
106th	Maj-17th	2	2	Jan. 6, 1999
107th	Maj-16th	3	3	Jan. 6, 2001
108th	Maj-14th	4	4	Jan. 28, 2003
109th	Maj-11th	5	5	Jan. 26, 2005
110th	Min-7th	6	6	Jan. 10, 2007

3rd SCIENCE
Dates: Jan. 21, 1997-Jan. 6, 2003
Departure: Left committee; no new assignment

Cong.	Ranking	Terms in: House	Comm.	Date of Assignment
105th	Maj-19th	1	1	Jan. 21, 1997
106th	Maj-15th	2	2	Jan. 6, 1999
107th	Maj-14th	3	3	Jan. 6, 2001

4th GOVERNMENT REFORM, 107-109
OVERSIGHT AND GOVERNMENT REFORM, 110
Dates: Feb. 8, 2001-Jan. 3, 2009
Departure: Left the House; lost re-nomination

Cong.	Ranking	Terms in: House	Comm.	Date of Assignment
107th	Maj-22nd	3	1	Feb. 8, 2001
108th	Maj-13th	4	2	Jan. 28, 2003
109th	Maj-11th	5	3	Jan. 26, 2005
110th	Min-8th	6	4	Jan. 10, 2007

Eric I. Cantor (R-Va.)

Dates: June 6, 1963
House: Jan. 3, 2001-date
Serving in the 111th Congress

HOUSE STANDING COMMITTEES:

1st FINANCIAL SERVICES
Dates: Jan. 6, 2001-Jan. 3, 2003
Departure: Moved to Ways and Means

Cong.	Ranking	Terms in: House	Comm.	Date of Assignment
107th	Maj-31st	1	1	Jan. 6, 2001

2nd INTERNATIONAL RELATIONS
Dates: Jan. 6, 2001-Jan. 3, 2003
Departure: Moved to Ways and Means

Cong.	Ranking	Terms in: House	Comm.	Date of Assignment
107th	Maj-23rd	1	1	Jan. 6, 2001

3rd WAYS AND MEANS
Dates: Jan. 28, 2003-date
Departure: Still serving in the 111th Congress

Cong.	Ranking	Terms in: House	Comm.	Date of Assignment
108th	Maj-24th	2	1	Jan. 28, 2003
109th	Maj-20th	3	2	Jan. 6, 2005
110th	Min-13th	4	3	Jan. 4, 2007
111th	Min-6th	5	4	Jan. 9, 2009

4th GOVERNMENT REFORM
Dates: Sep. 9, 2004-Oct. 6, 2004
Departure: Left committee; no new assignment

Cong.	Ranking	Terms in: House	Comm.	Date of Assignment
108th	MjR-4th	2	1	Sep. 9, 2004

HOUSE LEADERSHIP POSTS

1st HOUSE MINORITY WHIP
Dates: Jan. 3, 2009-date
Note: In the 111th Congress, Cantor was elected House Minority Whip without opposition on Nov. 18, 2008
Departure: Still serving in the 111th Congress

Cong.	Ranking	Terms in: House	Post	Date of Selection
111th	Min-2nd	5	1	Nov. 18, 2008

Maria E. Cantwell (D-Wash.)

Dates: Oct. 13, 1958
House: Jan. 3, 1993-Jan. 3, 1995
Left the House: Defeated for re-election in 1994
Senate: Jan. 3, 2001-date
Serving in the 111th Congress

HOUSE STANDING COMMITTEES:

1st FOREIGN AFFAIRS
Dates: Jan. 5, 1993-Jan. 3, 1995
Departure: Left the House; lost re-election

Cong.	Ranking	Terms in: House	Comm.	Date of Assignment
103rd	Maj-19th	1	1	Jan. 5, 1993

2nd MERCHANT MARINE AND FISHERIES
Dates: Jan. 5, 1993-Jan. 3, 1995
Departure: Left the House; lost re-election

Cong	Ranking	Terms in: House	Comm.	Date of Assignment
103rd	Maj-26th	1	1	Jan. 5, 1993

3rd PUBLIC WORKS AND TRANSPORTATION
Dates: Jan. 5, 1993-Jan. 3, 1995
Departure: Left the House; lost re-election

Cong.	Ranking	Terms in: House	Comm.	Date of Assignment
103rd	Maj-28th	1	1	Jan. 5, 1993

SENATE STANDING COMMITTEES:

1st ENERGY AND NATURAL RESOURCES
Dates: Jan. 25, 2001-date
Departure: Still serving in the 111th Congress

Cong.	Ranking	Years in: Senate	Comm.	Date of Assignment
107th	Min-11th	1	1	Jan. 25, 2001
+107th	Maj-11th	1	1	June 6, 2001
108th	Min-11th	3	2	Jan. 15, 2003
109th	Min-8th	5	4	Jan. 6, 2005
110th	Maj-7th	7	6	Jan. 12, 2007
111th	Maj-6th	9	8	Jan. 21, 2009

2nd JUDICIARY
Dates: Jan. 25, 2001-Jan. 15, 2003
Departure: Moved to Commerce, Science and Transportation

Cong.	Ranking	Years in: Senate	Comm.	Date of Assignment
107th	Min-9th	1	1	Jan. 25, 2001
+107th	Maj-9th	1	1	June 6, 2001

3rd SMALL BUSINESS renamed June 29, 2001
SMALL BUSINESS AND ENTREPRENEURSHIP
Dates: Jan. 25, 2001-date
Departure: Still serving in the 111th Congress

Cong.	Ranking	Years in: Senate	Comm.	Date of Assignment
107th	Min-9th	1	1	Jan. 25, 2001
+107th	Maj-9th	1	1	June 6, 2001
108th	Min-7th	3	2	Jan. 15, 2003
109th	Min-6th	5	4	Jan. 6, 2005
110th	Maj-6th	7	6	Jan. 12, 2007
111th	Maj-6th	9	8	Jan. 21, 2009

4th COMMERCE, SCIENCE AND TRANSPORTATION
Dates: Jan. 15, 2003-date
Departure: Still serving in the 111th Congress

Cong.	Ranking	Years in: Senate	Comm.	Date of Assignment
108th	Min-10th	3	1	Jan. 15, 2003
109th	Min-7th	5	2	Jan. 6, 2005
110th	Maj-7th	7	4	Jan. 12, 2007
111th	Maj-7th	9	7	Jan. 21, 2009

5th FINANCE
Dates: Jan. 12, 2007-date
Departure: Still serving in the 111th Congress

Cong.	Ranking	Years in: Senate	Comm.	Date of Assignment
110th	Maj-10th	7	1	Jan. 12, 2007
111th	Maj-10th	9	3	Jan. 21, 2009

SENATE SELECT AND SPECIAL COMMITTEES:

1st INDIAN AFFAIRS (Permanent)
Dates: July 10, 2001-date
Departure: Still serving in the 111th Congress

Cong.	Ranking	Years in: Senate	Comm.	Date of Assignment
+107th	MjA-8th	1	1	July 10, 2001
108th	Min-7th	3	2	Jan. 15, 2003
109th	Min-6th	5	4	Jan. 6, 2005
110th	Maj-6th	7	6	Jan. 12, 2007
111th	Maj-6th	9	8	Jan. 21, 2009

Anh (Joseph) Cao (R-La.)

Dates: Mar. 13, 1967
House: Jan. 3, 2009-date
Serving in the 111th Congress

HOUSE STANDING COMMITTEES:

1st HOMELAND SECURITY
Dates: Jan. 9, 2009-date
Departure: Still serving in the 111th Congress

Cong.	Ranking	Terms in: House	Comm.	Date of Assignment
111th	Min-12th	1	1	Jan. 9, 2009

2nd TRANSPORTATION AND INFRASTRUCTURE
Dates: Jan. 9, 2009-date
Departure: Still serving in the 111th Congress

Cong.	Ranking	Terms in: House	Comm.	Date of Assignment
111th	Min-28th	1	1	Jan. 9, 2009

3rd OVERSIGHT AND GOVERNMENT REFORM
Dates: Oct. 7, 2009-date
Departure: Still serving in the 111th Congress

Cong.	Ranking	Terms in: House	Comm.	Date of Assignment
111th	MnR-3rd	1	1	Jan. 9, 2009

Shelley Moore Capito (R-W.Va.)

Dates: Nov. 26, 1953
House: Jan. 3, 2001-date
Serving in the 111th Congress

HOUSE STANDING COMMITTEES:

1st FINANCIAL SERVICES
1st Dates: Jan. 6, 2001-Jan. 3, 2005
1st Departure: Moved to Rules
2nd Dates: Jan. 10, 2007-date
2nd Departure: Still serving in the 111th Congress

Cong.	Ranking	Terms in: House	Comm.	Date of Assignment
107th	Maj-34th	1 *1	1	Jan. 6, 2001
108th	Maj-27th	2 *1	2	Jan. 28, 2003
110th	Min-16th	4 *2	1	Jan. 10, 2007
111th	Min-11th	5 *2	2	Jan. 9, 2009

2nd TRANSPORTATION AND INFRASTRUCTURE
1st Dates: Jan. 6, 2001-Jan. 3, 2005
1st Departure: Moved to Rules
2nd Dates: Mar. 12, 2007-date
2nd Departure: Still serving in the 111th Congress

Cong.	Ranking	Terms in: House	Comm.	Date of Assignment
107th	Maj-30th	1	*1 1	Jan. 6, 2001
108th	Maj-24th	2	*1 2	Jan. 28, 2003
110th	MnR-1st	4	*2 1	Mar. 12, 2007
111th	Min-16th	5	*2 2	Jan. 9, 2009

3rd SMALL BUSINESS
Dates: Feb. 28, 2001-Jan. 3, 2005
Departure: Moved to Rules

Cong.	Ranking	Terms in: House	Comm.	Date of Assignment
107th	Maj-19th	1	1	Feb. 28, 2001
108th	Maj-11th	2	2	Jan. 28, 2003

4th RULES
Dates: Jan. 4, 2005-Jan. 3, 2007
Departure: Returned to Financial Services

Cong.	Ranking	Terms in: House	Comm.	Date of Assignment
109th	Maj-6th	3	1	Jan. 4, 2005

HOUSE SELECT AND SPECIAL COMMITTEES:

1st SELECT ENERGY INDEPENDENCE AND GLOBAL WARMING
Dates: Feb. 3, 2009-date
Departure: Still serving in the 111th Congress

Cong.	Ranking	Terms in: House	Comm.	Date of Assignment
111th	Min-6th	5	1	Feb. 3, 2009

Lois Capps (D-Cal.)

Dates: Jan. 10, 1938
House: March 10, 1998-date
Serving in the 111th Congress

H: Lois Capps was elected to the 105th Congress by special election, March 10, 1998, to fill the vacancy caused by the death of her husband, U.S. Representative Walter Capps (D-Cal.). Mrs. Capps was seated March 17, 1998, and assigned to committees.

HOUSE STANDING COMMITTEES:

1st INTERNATIONAL RELATIONS
Dates: Mar. 27, 1998-Jan. 3, 1999
Departure: Moved to Commerce

Cong.	Ranking	Terms in: House	Comm.	Date of Assignment
105th	MnR-2nd	1	1	Mar. 27, 1998

2nd SCIENCE
Dates: Mar. 27, 1998-Jan. 3, 1999
Departure: Moved to Commerce

Cong.	Ranking	Terms in: House	Comm.	Date of Assignment
105th	MnR-2nd	1	1	Mar. 27, 1998

3rd COMMERCE, 106
ENERGY AND COMMERCE, 107-111
Dates: Jan. 6, 1999-date
Departure: Still serving in the 111th Congress

Cong.	Ranking	Terms in: House	Comm.	Date of Assignment
106th	Min-24th	2	1	Jan. 6, 1999
107th	Min-23rd	3	2	Jan. 31, 2001
108th	Min-20th	4	3	Jan. 28, 2003
109th	Min-17th	5	4	Jan. 6, 2005
110th	Maj-15th	6	5	Jan. 4, 2007
111th	Maj-13th	7	6	Jan. 7, 2009

4th BUDGET
Dates: Jan. 28, 2003-Feb. 15, 2007
Departure: Resigned committee; no new assignment

Cong.	Ranking	Terms in: House	Comm.	Date of Assignment
108th	Min-12th	4	1	Jan. 28, 2003
109th	Min-7th	5	2	Jan. 26, 2005
110th	Maj-4th	6	3	Jan. 18, 2007

5th NATURAL RESOURCES
Dates: Jan. 18, 2007-date
Departure: Still serving in the 111th Congress

Cong.	Ranking	Terms in: House	Comm.	Date of Assignment
110th	Maj-21st	6	1	Jan. 18, 2007
111th	Maj-21st	7	2	Jan. 21, 2009

Walter H. Capps (D-Cal.)

Dates: May 5, 1934-Oct. 28, 1997
House: Jan. 3, 1997-Oct. 28, 1997
Left the House: Died in office

HOUSE STANDING COMMITTEES:

1st INTERNATIONAL RELATIONS
Dates: Jan. 7, 1997-Oct. 28, 1997
Departure: Died in office

Cong.	Ranking	Terms in: House	Comm.	Date of Assignment
105th	Min-16th	1	1	Jan. 7, 1997

2nd SCIENCE
Dates: Feb. 13, 1997-Oct. 28, 1997
Departure: Died in office

Cong.	Ranking	Terms in: House	Comm.	Date of Assignment
105th	Min-17th	1	1	Feb. 13, 1997

Michael E. Capuano (D-Mass.)

Dates: Jan. 9, 1952
House: Jan. 3, 1999-date
Serving in the 111th Congress

HOUSE STANDING COMMITTEES:

1st BANKING AND FINANCIAL SERVICES, 106
FINANCIAL SERVICES, 107-111
Dates: Jan. 6, 1999
Departure: Still serving in the 111th Congress

Cong.	Ranking	Terms in: House	Comm.	Date of Assignment
106th	Min-27th	1	1	Jan. 6, 1999
107th	Min-24th	2	2	Jan. 31, 2001
108th	Min-18th	3	3	Jan. 28, 2003
109th	Min-16th	4	4	Jan. 26, 2005
110th	Maj-13th	5	5	Jan. 12, 2007
111th	Maj-12th	6	6	Jan. 7, 2009

2nd SCIENCE
Dates: Jan. 19, 1999-Feb. 7, 2001
Departure: Resigned committee; moved to Budget

Cong.	Ranking	Terms in: House	Comm.	Date of Assignment
106th	Min-23rd	1	1	Jan. 19, 1999
107th	Min-17th	2	2	Jan. 31, 2001

3rd BUDGET
Dates: Feb. 8, 2001-July 8, 2002
Departure: Resigned committee; moved to Transportation and Infrastructure

Cong.	Ranking	Terms in: House	Comm.	Date of Assignment
107th	Min-18th	2	1	Feb. 8, 2001

4th TRANSPORTATION AND INFRASTRUCTURE
Dates: July 8, 2002-date
Departure: Still serving in the 111th Congress

Cong.	Ranking	Terms in: House	Comm.	Date of Assignment
107th	MnR-1st	2	1	July 8, 2002
108th	Min-27th	3	2	Jan. 28, 2003
109th	Min-24th	4	3	Jan. 26, 2005
110th	Maj-18th	5	4	Jan. 10, 2007
111th	Maj-17th	6	5	Jan. 7, 2009

5th HOUSE ADMINISTRATION
Dates: Feb. 8, 2007-date
Departure: Still serving in the 111th Congress

Cong.	Ranking	Terms in: House	Comm.	Date of Assignment
110th	Maj-4th	5	1	Feb. 8, 2007
111th	Maj-3rd	6	2	Jan. 13, 2009

JOINT COMMITTEES:

1st JOINT PRINTING
House Dates: Mar. 14, 2007-date
Departure: Still serving in the 111th Congress

Cong.	Ranking	Terms in: House	Comm.	Date of Assignment
110th	Maj-3rd	5	1	Mar. 14, 2007
111th	Maj-2nd	6	2	Mar. 31, 2009

Benjamin L. Cardin (D-Md.)

Dates: Oct. 5, 1943
House: Jan. 3, 1987-Jan. 3, 2007
Left the House: Elected to the U.S. Senate in 2006
Senate: Jan. 3, 2007-date
Serving in the 111th Congress

HOUSE STANDING COMMITTEES:

1st PUBLIC WORKS AND TRANSPORTATION
Dates: Jan. 6, 1987-Oct. 16, 1989
Departure: Moved to Ways and Means

2nd JUDICIARY
Dates: Jan. 22, 1987-Oct. 16, 1989
Departure: Moved to Ways and Means

3rd WAYS AND MEANS
Dates: Oct. 16, 1989-Jan. 3, 2007
Departure: Left the House for the Senate

Cong.	Ranking	Terms in: House	Comm.	Date of Assignment
103rd	Maj-13th	4	3	Jan. 5, 1993
104th	Min-10th	5	4	Jan. 4, 1995
105th	Min-7th	6	5	Jan. 7, 1997
106th	Min-6th	7	6	Jan. 6, 1999
107th	Min-6th	8	7	Jan. 31, 2001
108th	Min-5th	9	8	Jan. 28, 2003
109th	Min-4th	10	9	Jan. 26, 2005

4th STANDARDS OF OFFICIAL CONDUCT
Dates: Feb. 6, 1991-Jan. 3, 1997
Departure: Moved to Budget

Cong.	Ranking	Terms in: House	Comm.	Date of Assignment
103rd	Maj-3rd	4	2	Feb. 4, 1993
104th	Min-2nd	5	3	Jan. 20, 1995

5th HOUSE ADMINISTRATION
Dates: Jan. 21, 1993-Jan. 3, 1995
Departure: Left committee; no new assignment

Cong.	Ranking	Terms in: House	Comm.	Date of Assignment
103rd	Maj-12th	4	1	Jan. 21, 1993

6th BUDGET
Dates: Jan. 7, 1997-Jan. 3, 1999
Departure: Left committee; no new assignment

Cong.	Ranking	Terms in: House	Comm.	Date of Assignment
105th	Min-12th	6	1	Jan. 7, 1997

HOUSE SELECT AND SPECIAL COMMITTEES:

1st SELECT ETHICS
Dates: Jan. 7, 1997-Jan. 21, 1997
Termination: House Report 105-1 filed, Jan. 17, 1997

Cong.	Ranking	Terms in: House	Comm.	Date of Assignment
105th	Min-RM	6	1	Jan. 7, 1997

2nd SELECT HOMELAND SECURITY
Dates: Feb. 12, 2003-Jan. 3, 2005
Departure: Did not continue on reorganized standing committee

Cong.	Ranking	Terms in: House	Comm.	Date of Assignment
108th	Min-8th	9	1	Feb. 12, 2003

SENATE STANDING COMMITTEES:

1st BUDGET
Dates: Jan. 12, 2007-date
Departure: Still serving in the 111th Congress

Cong.	Ranking	Years in: Senate	Comm.	Date of Assignment
110th	Maj-9th	1	1	Jan. 12, 2007
111th	Maj-9th	3	3	Jan. 21, 2009

2nd ENVIRONMENT AND PUBLIC WORKS
Dates: Jan. 12, 2007-date
Departure: Still serving in the 111th Congress

Cong.	Ranking	Years in: Senate	Comm.	Date of Assignment
110th	Maj-7th	1	1	Jan. 12, 2007
111th	Maj-5th	3	3	Jan. 21, 2009

3rd FO]REIGN RELATIONS
Dates: Jan. 12, 2007-date
Departure: Still serving in the 111th Congress

Cong.	Ranking	Years in: Senate	Comm.	Date of Assignment
110th	Maj-9th	1	1	Jan. 12, 2007
111th	Maj-6th	3	3	Jan. 21, 2009

4th JUDICIARY
Dates: Jan. 12, 2007-date
Departure: Still serving in the 111th Congress

Cong.	Ranking	Years in: Senate	Comm.	Date of Assignment
110th	Maj-9th	1	1	Jan. 12, 2007
111th	Maj-7th	3	3	Jan. 21, 2009

5th SMALL BUSINESS AND ENTREPRENEURSHIP
Dates: Jan. 12, 2007-date
Departure: Still serving in the 111th Congress

Cong.	Ranking	Years in: Senate	Comm.	Date of Assignment
110th	Maj-9th	1	1	Jan. 12, 2007
111th	Maj-9th	3	3	Jan. 21, 2009

Dennis A. Cardoza (D-Cal.)

Dates: March 3, 1959
House: Jan. 3, 2003-date
Serving in the 111th Congress

HOUSE STANDING COMMITTEES:

1st AGRICULTURE
Dates: Feb. 5, 2003-date
Departure: Still serving in the 111th Congress

Cong.	Ranking	Terms in: House	Comm.	Date of Assignment
108th	Min-18th	1	1	Feb. 5, 2003
109th	Min-8th	2	2	Jan. 26, 2005
110th	Maj-7th	3	3	Jan. 12, 2007
111th	Maj-6th	4	4	Jan. 21, 2009

2nd RESOURCES
Dates: Feb. 5, 2003-Jan. 3, 2007
Departure: Moved to Rules

Cong.	Ranking	Terms in: House	Comm.	Date of Assignment
108th	Min-21st	1	1	Feb. 5, 2003
109th	Min-21st	2	2	Feb. 2, 2005

3rd SCIENCE
Dates: Mar. 5, 2003-Jan. 3, 2005
Departure: Moved to International Relations

Cong.	Ranking	Terms in: House	Comm.	Date of Assignment
108th	MnR-2nd	1	1	Mar. 5, 2003

4th INTERNATIONAL RELATIONS
Dates: Jan. 26, 2005-Jan. 3, 2007
Departure: Moved to Rules

Cong.	Ranking	Terms in: House	Comm.	Date of Assignment
109th	Min-23rd	2	1	Jan. 26, 2005

5th RULES
Dates: Jan. 12, 2007-date
Departure: Still serving in the 111th Congress

Cong.	Ranking	Terms in: House	Comm.	Date of Assignment
110th	Maj-5th	3	1	Jan. 12, 2007
111th	Maj-5th	4	2	Jan. 6, 2009

Jean Carnahan (D-Mo.)

Dates: Dec. 20, 1933
Senate: Jan. 3, 2001-Nov. 25, 2002
Left Senate: Resigned; defeated in special election in 2002

S: Jean Carnahan was appointed to the 107th Congress to fill the vacancy caused by the death of her husband, U.S. Senator-elect Mel Carnahan

(D-Mo.). Mrs. Carnahan was not seated nor assigned to committees because the 107th Congress was not in session.

SENATE STANDING COMMITTEES:

1st ARMED SERVICES
Dates: Jan. 25, 2001-Nov. 25, 2002
Departure: Resigned the Senate; lost special election

Cong.	Ranking	Years in: Senate	Comm.	Date of Assignment
107th	Min-11th	1	1	Jan. 25, 2001
+107th	Maj-11th	1	1	June 6, 2001

2nd COMMERCE, SCIENCE AND TRANSPORTATION
Dates: Jan. 25, 2001-Nov. 25, 2002
Departure: Resigned the Senate; lost special election

Cong.	Ranking	Years in: Senate	Comm.	Date of Assignment
107th	Min-11th	1	1	Jan. 25, 2001
+107th	Maj-11th	1	1	June 6, 2001

3rd GOVERNMENTAL AFFAIRS
Dates: Jan. 25, 2001-Nov. 25, 2002
Departure: Resigned the Senate; lost special election

Cong.	Ranking	Years in: Senate	Comm.	Date of Assignment
107th	Min-8th	1	1	Jan. 25, 2001
+107th	Maj-11th	1	1	June 6, 2001

4th SMALL BUSINESS AND ENTREPRENEURSHIP
Dates: July 10, 2001-Nov. 25, 2002
Departure: Resigned the Senate; lost special election

Cong.	Ranking	Years in: Senate	Comm.	Date of Assignment
107th	MjA-10th	1	1	July 10, 2001

SENATE SELECT AND SPECIAL COMMITTEES:

1st SPECIAL AGING
Dates: Jan. 25, 2001-Nov. 25, 2002
Departure: Resigned the Senate; lost special election

Cong.	Ranking	Years in: Senate	Comm.	Date of Assignment
107th	Min-10th	1	1	Jan. 25, 2001
+107th	Maj-11th	1	1	July 10, 2001

Russ Carnahan (D-Mo.)

Dates: July 10, 1958
House: Jan. 3, 2005-date
Serving in the 111th Congress

HOUSE STANDING COMMITTEES:

1st SCIENCE, 109
SCIENCE AND TECHNOLOGY, 110-111
Dates: Jan. 26, 2005-date
Departure: Still serving in the 111th Congress

Cong.	Ranking	Terms in: House	Comm.	Date of Assignment
109th	Min-11th	1	1	Jan. 26, 2005
110th	Maj-20th	2	2	Jan. 18, 2007
111th	Maj-19th	3	3	Jan. 21, 2009

2nd TRANSPORTATION AND INFRASTRUCTURE
Dates: Jan. 26, 2005-date
Departure: Still serving in the 111th Congress

Cong.	Ranking	Terms in: House	Comm.	Date of Assignment
109th	Min-32nd	1	1	Jan. 26, 2005
110th	Maj-23rd	2	2	Jan. 10, 2007
111th	Maj-20th	3	3	Jan. 7, 2009

3rd INTERNATIONAL RELATIONS, 109
FOREIGN AFFAIRS, 110-111
Dates: Feb. 15, 2005-date
Departure: Still serving in the 111th Congress

Cong.	Ranking	Terms in: House	Comm.	Date of Assignment
109th	MnR-1st	1	1	Feb. 15, 2005
110th	Maj-13th	2	2	Jan. 12, 2007
111th	Maj-12th	3	3	Jan. 21, 2009

Chris Carney (D-Penn.)

Dates: March 2, 1959
House: Jan. 3, 2007-date
Serving in the 111th Congress

HOUSE STANDING COMMITTEES:

1st HOMELAND SECURITY
Dates: Jan. 12, 2007-date
Departure: Still serving in the 111th Congress

Cong.	Ranking	Terms in: House	Comm.	Date of Assignment
110th	Maj-15th	1	1	Jan. 12, 2007
111th	Maj-9th	2	2	Jan. 28, 2009

2nd TRANSPORTATION AND INFRASTRUCTURE
Dates: Jan. 10, 2007-date
Departure: Still serving in the 111th Congress

Cong.	Ranking	Terms in: House	Comm.	Date of Assignment
110th	Maj-37th	1	1	Jan. 10, 2007
111th	Maj-29th	2	2	Jan. 7, 2009

Thomas R. Carper (D-Del.)

Dates: Jan. 23, 1947
House: Jan. 3, 1983-Jan 3, 1993
Left the House: Elected Governor in 1992
Senate: Jan. 3, 2001-date
Serving in the 111th Congress

HOUSE STANDING COMMITTEES:

1st BANKING, FINANCE AND URBAN AFFAIRS
Dates: Jan. 6, 1983-Jan. 3, 1993
Departure: Left the House; elected Governor

2nd MERCHANT MARINE AND FISHERIES
Dates: Jan. 6, 1983-Jan. 3, 1993
Departure: Left the House; elected Governor

SENATE STANDING COMMITTEES:

1st BANKING, HOUSING, AND URBAN AFFAIRS
Dates: Jan. 25, 2001-Jan. 21, 2009
Departure: Moved to Finance

Cong.	Ranking	Years in: Senate	Comm.	Date of Assignment
107th	Min-8th	1	1	Jan. 25, 2001
+107th	Maj-8th	1	1	June 6, 2001
108th	Min-8th	3	2	Jan. 15, 2003
109th	Min-7th	5	4	Jan. 6, 2005
110th	Maj-6th	7	6	Jan. 12, 2007

2nd ENVIRONMENT AND PUBLIC WORKS
Dates: Jan. 25, 2001-date
Departure: Still serving in the 111th Congress

Cong.	Ranking	Years in: Senate	Comm.	Date of Assignment
107th	Min-7th	1	1	Jan. 25, 2001
+107th	Maj-8th	1	1	July 10, 2001
108th	Min-8th	3	2	Jan. 15, 2003
109th	Min-5th	5	4	Jan. 6, 2005
110th	Maj-4th	7	6	Jan. 12, 2007
111th	Maj-3rd	9	8	Jan. 21, 2009

3rd GOVERNMENTAL AFFAIRS renamed Oct. 9, 2004
HOMELAND SECURITY AND GOVERNMENTAL AFFAIRS
Dates: Jan. 25, 2001-date
Departure: Still serving in the 111th Congress

Cong.	Ranking	Years in: Senate	Comm.	Date of Assignment
107th	Min-7th	1	1	Jan. 25, 2001
+107th	Maj-7th	1	1	June 6, 2001
108th	Min-5th	3	2	Jan. 15, 2003
109th	Min-4th	5	4	Jan. 6, 2005
110th	Maj-4th	7	6	Jan. 12, 2007
111th	Maj-4th	9	8	Jan. 21, 2009

4th ENERGY AND NATURAL RESOURCES
Dates: July 10, 2001-Jan. 15, 2003
Departure: Left committee; no new assignment

Cong.	Ranking	Years in: Senate	Comm.	Date of Assignment
+107th	MjA-12th	1	1	July 10, 2001

5th COMMERCE, SCIENCE, AND TRANSPORTATION
Dates: Jan. 12, 2007-Jan. 21, 2009
Departure: Moved to Finance

Cong.	Ranking	Years in: Senate	Comm.	Date of Assignment
110th	Maj-10th	7	1	Jan. 12, 2007

6th FINANCE
Dates: Jan. 21, 2009-date
Departure: Still serving in the 111th Congress

Cong.	Ranking	Years in: Senate	Comm.	Date of Assignment
111th	Maj-13th	9	1	Jan. 21, 2009

SENATE SELECT AND SPECIAL COMMITTEES:

1st SPECIAL AGING (Permanent)
Dates: Jan. 25, 2001-Jan. 21, 2009
Departure: Moved to Finance

Cong.	Ranking	Years in: Senate	Comm.	Date of Assignment
107th	Min-8th	1	1	Jan. 25, 2001
+107th	Maj-9th	1	1	July 10, 2001

108th	Min-9th	3	2	Jan. 15, 2003
109th	Min-7th	5	4	Jan. 6, 2005
110th	Maj-5th	7	6	Jan. 12, 2007

M. Robert Carr (D-Mich.)

Dates: March 27, 1943
House 1: Jan. 3, 1975-Jan. 3, 1981
Left the House 1: Defeated for re-election in 1980
House 2: Jan. 3, 1983-Jan. 3, 1995
Left the House 2: Lost U.S. Senate election in 1994

HOUSE STANDING COMMITTEES:

1st INTERIOR AND INSULAR AFFAIRS
Dates: Jan. 20, 1975-Jan. 3, 1981
Departure: Left the House; lost seat

2nd ARMED SERVICES
Dates: Jan. 23, 1975-Jan. 3, 1981
Departure: Left the House; lost seat

3rd JUDICIARY
Dates: Feb. 6, 1980-Jan. 3, 1981
Departure: Left the House; lost seat

4th APPROPRIATIONS
Dates: Jan. 6, 1983-Jan. 3, 1995
Departure: Left the House; lost Senate election

Cong.	Ranking	Terms in: House	Comm.	Date of Assignment
103rd	Maj-16th	9	6	Jan. 5, 1993

HOUSE SELECT AND SPECIAL COMMITTEES:

1st SELECT HUNGER (Temporary)
Dates: Jan. 21, 1987-Jan. 3, 1993
Termination: Committee not renewed in 1993

Andre Carson (D-Ind.)

Dates: Oct. 16, 1974
House: Mar. 11, 2008-date
Serving in the 111th Congress

H: Andre Carson was elected to the 110th Congress by special election, Mar. 11, 2008, to fill the vacancy caused by the death of his grandmother, U.S. Representative Julia Carson (D-Ind.). Andre Carson was seated Mar. 13, 2008, and assigned to committees.

HOUSE STANDING COMMITTEES:

1st FINANCIAL SERVICES
Dates: Apr. 1, 2008-date
Departure: Still serving in the 111th Congress

Cong.	Ranking	Terms in: House	Comm.	Date of Assignment
110th	MjR-2nd	1	1	Apr. 1, 2008
111th	Maj-31st	2	2	Jan. 7, 2009

2nd SCIENCE AND TECHNOLOGY
Dates: June 10, 2008-Jan. 3, 2009
Departure: Left committee; no new assignment

Cong.	Ranking	Terms in: House	Comm.	Date of Assignment
110th	MjR-2nd	1	1	June 10, 2008

Brad Carson (D-Okla.)

Dates: March 11, 1967
House: Jan. 3, 2001-Jan. 3, 2005
Left the House: Lost U.S. Senate election in 2004

HOUSE STANDING COMMITTEES:

1st TRANSPORTATION AND INFRASTRUCTURE
Dates: Jan. 31, 2001-Jan. 3, 2005
Departure: Left the House; lost Senate election

Cong.	Ranking	Terms in: House	Comm.	Date of Assignment
107th	Min-31st	1	1	Jan. 31, 2001
108th	Min-23rd	2	2	Jan. 28, 2003

2nd RESOURCES
Dates: Feb. 8, 2001-Jan. 3, 2005
Departure: Left the House; lost Senate election

Cong.	Ranking	Terms in: House	Comm.	Date of Assignment
107th	Min-23rd	1	1	Feb. 8, 2001
108th	Min-19th	2	2	Jan. 28, 2003

3rd SMALL BUSINESS
Dates: Feb. 28, 2001-Jan. 3, 2003
Departure: Left committee; no new assignment

Cong.	Ranking	Terms in: House	Comm.	Date of Assignment
107th	MnR-3rd	1	1	Feb. 28, 2001

Julia M. Carson (D-Ind.)

Dates: July 3, 1938-Dec. 15, 2007
House: Jan. 3, 1997-Dec. 15, 2007
Left the House: Died in office

HOUSE STANDING COMMITTEES:

1st BANKING AND FINANCIAL SERVICES, 105-106
FINANCIAL SERVICES, 107-110
Dates: Jan. 7, 1997-Dec. 15, 2007
Departure: Died in office

Cong.	Ranking	Terms in: House	Comm.	Date of Assignment
105th	Min-24th	1	1	Jan. 7, 1997
106th	Min-14th	2	2	Jan. 6, 1999
107th	Min-13th	3	3	Jan. 31, 2001
108th	Min-11th	4	4	Jan. 28, 2003
109th	Min-11th	5	5	Jan. 26, 2005
110th	Maj-9th	6	6	Jan. 12, 2007

2nd VETERANS' AFFAIRS
Dates: Feb. 6, 1997-Jan. 3, 2003
Departure: Moved to Transportation and Infrastructure

Cong.	Ranking	Terms in: House	Comm.	Date of Assignment
105th	Min-11th	1	1	Feb. 6, 1997
106th	Min-7th	2	2	Jan. 6, 1999
107th	Min-7th	3	3	Jan. 31, 2001

3rd TRANSPORTATION AND INFRASTRUCTURE
Dates: Jan. 28, 2003-Dec. 15, 2007
Departure: Died in office

Cong.	Ranking	Terms in: House	Comm.	Date of Assignment
108th	Min-29th	4	1	Jan. 28, 2003
109th	Min-26th	5	2	Jan. 26, 2005
110th	Maj-19th	6	3	Jan. 10, 2007

John R. Carter (R-Tex.)

Dates: Nov. 6, 1941
House: Jan. 3, 2003-date
Serving in the 111th Congress

HOUSE STANDING COMMITTEES:

1st EDUCATION AND THE WORKFORCE
Dates: Jan. 28, 2003-Jan. 3, 2005
Departure: Moved to Appropriations

Cong.	Ranking	Terms in: House	Comm.	Date of Assignment
108th	Maj-24th	1	1	Jan. 28, 2003

2nd GOVERNMENT REFORM
Dates: Jan. 28, 2003-Jan. 3, 2005
Departure: Moved to Appropriations

Cong.	Ranking	Terms in: House	Comm.	Date of Assignment
108th	Maj-22nd	1	1	Jan. 28, 2003

3rd JUDICIARY
Dates: Jan. 28, 2003-Jan. 3, 2005
Departure: Moved to Appropriations

Cong.	Ranking	Terms in: House	Comm.	Date of Assignment
108th	Maj-19th	1	1	Jan. 28, 2003

4th APPROPRIATIONS
Dates: Jan. 6, 2005-date
Departure: Still serving in the 111th Congress

Cong.	Ranking	Terms in: House	Comm.	Date of Assignment
109th	Maj-36th	2	1	Jan. 6, 2005
110th	Min-28th	3	2	Jan. 4, 2007
111th	Min-18th	4	3	Jan. 9, 2009

Ed Case (D-Hai.)

Dates: Sept. 27, 1952
House: Nov. 30, 2002-Jan. 3, 2007
Left the House: Lost U.S. Senate nomination in 2006

H: Case was elected to the 107th Congress by special election, Nov. 30, 2002, to fill the vacancy caused by the death of U.S. Representative Patsy T. Mink (D-Hai.). Case was not seated nor assigned to committees because the 107th Congress was not in session. Case was also elected to the 108th Congress by special election, Jan. 4, 2003, to fill Mrs. Mink's posthumous term in that Congress. Case was seated Jan. 7, 2003, and assigned to committees.

HOUSE STANDING COMMITTEES:

1st AGRICULTURE
Dates: Feb. 5, 2003-Jan. 3, 2007
Departure: Left the House; lost Senate nomination

Cong.	Ranking	Terms in: House	Comm.	Date of Assignment
108th	Min-15th	2	1	Feb. 5, 2003
109th	Min-7th	3	2	Jan. 26, 2005

2nd EDUCATION AND THE WORKFORCE
Dates: Feb. 5, 2003-Jan. 3, 2005
Departure: Moved to Budget

Cong.	Ranking	Terms in: House	Comm.	Date of Assignment
108th	Min-18th	1	1	Feb. 5, 2003

3rd SMALL BUSINESS
Dates: Feb. 13, 2003-Jan. 3, 2007
Departure: Left the House; lost Senate nomination

Cong.	Ranking	Terms in: House	Comm.	Date of Assignment
108th	Min-14th	1	1	Feb. 13, 2003
109th	Min-8th	2	2	Feb. 2, 2005

4th BUDGET
Dates: Jan. 26, 2005-Jan. 3, 2007
Departure: Left the House; lost Senate nomination

Cong.	Ranking	Terms in: House	Comm.	Date of Assignment
109th	Min-13th	2	1	Jan. 26, 2005

Cong.	Ranking	Years in: Senate	Comm.	Date of Assignment
110th	Maj-10th	1	1	Jan. 12, 2007
111th	Maj-7th	3	3	Jan. 21, 2009

4th HEALTH, EDUCATION, LABOR AND PENSIONS
Dates: Jan. 21, 2009-date
Departure: Still serving in the 111th Congress

Cong.	Ranking	Years in: Senate	Comm.	Date of Assignment
111th	Maj-10th	3	1	Jan. 21, 2009

SENATE SELECT AND SPECIAL COMMITTEES:

1st SPECIAL AGING (Permanent)
Dates: Jan. 12, 2007-date
Departure: Still serving in the 111th Congress

Cong.	Ranking	Years in: Senate	Comm.	Date of Assignment
110th	Maj-9th	1	1	Jan. 12, 2007
111th	Maj-6th	3	3	Jan. 21, 2009

JOINT COMMITTEES:

1st JOINT ECONOMIC
House Dates: Jan. 12, 2007-date
Departure: Still serving in the 111th Congress

Cong.	Ranking	Years in: Senate	Comm.	Date of Assignment
110th	Maj-5th	1	1	Jan. 12, 2007
111th	Maj-5th	3	3	Jan. 21, 2009

Robert P. Casey, Jr. (D-Penn.)

Dates: April 13, 1960
Senate: Jan. 3, 2007-date
Serving in the 111th Congress

SENATE STANDING COMMITTEES:

1st AGRICULTURE, NUTRITION AND FORESTRY
Dates: Jan. 12, 2007-date
Departure: Still serving in the 111th Congress

Cong.	Ranking	Years in: Senate	Comm.	Date of Assignment
110th	Maj-10th	1	1	Jan. 12, 2007
111th	Maj-9th	3	3	Jan. 21, 2009

2nd BANKING, HOUSING, AND URBAN AFFAIRS
Dates: Jan. 12, 2007-Jan. 21, 2009
Departure: Moved to Heath, Education, Labor and Pensions

Cong.	Ranking	Years in: Senate	Comm.	Date of Assignment
110th	Maj-10th	1	1	Jan. 12, 2007

3rd FOREIGN RELATIONS
Dates: Jan. 12, 2007-date
Departure: Still serving in the 111th Congress

Bill Cassidy (R-La.)

Dates: Sept. 28, 1957
House: Jan. 3, 2009-date
Serving in the 111th Congress

HOUSE STANDING COMMITTEES:

1st EDUCATION AND LABOR
Dates: Jan. 9, 2009-date
Departure: Still serving in the 111th Congress

Cong.	Ranking	Terms in: House	Comm.	Date of Assignment
111th	Min-16th	1	1	Jan. 9, 2009

2nd NATURAL RESOURCES
Dates: Jan. 9, 2009-date
Departure: Still serving in the 111th Congress

Cong.	Ranking	Terms in: House	Comm.	Date of Assignment
111th	Min-20th	1	1	Jan. 9, 2009

3rd AGRICULTURE
Dates: Jan. 22, 2009-date
Departure: Still serving in the 111th Congress

Cong.	Ranking	Terms in: House	Comm.	Date of Assignment
111th	MnR-1st	1	1	Jan. 22, 2009

Michael N. Castle (R-Del.)

Dates: July 2, 1938
House: Jan. 3, 1993-date
Serving in the 111th Congress

HOUSE STANDING COMMITTEES:

1st BANKING, FINANCE AND URBAN AFFAIRS, 103
BANKING AND FINANCIAL SERVICES, 104-106
FINANCIAL SERVICES, 107-111
Dates: Jan. 5, 1993-date
Departure: Still serving in the 111th Congress

Cong.	Ranking	Terms in: House	Comm.	Date of Assignment
103rd	Min-19th	1	1	Jan. 5, 1993
104th	Maj-9th	2	2	Jan. 4, 1995
105th	Maj-8th	3	3	Jan. 7, 1997
106th	Maj-8th	4	4	Jan. 6, 1999
107th	Maj-7th	5	5	Jan. 6, 2001
108th	Maj-6th	6	6	Jan. 28, 2003
109th	Maj-6th	7	7	Jan. 26, 2005
110th	Min-4th	8	8	Jan. 10, 2007
111th	Min-2nd	9	9	Jan. 9, 2009

2nd MERCHANT MARINE AND FISHERIES
Dates: Jan. 5, 1993-Jan. 3, 1995
Departure: Committee abolished; moved to Select Intelligence

Cong.	Ranking	Terms in: House	Comm.	Date of Assignment
103rd	Min-13th	1	1	Jan. 5, 1993

3rd EDUCATION AND LABOR, 103
ECONOMIC AND EDUCATIONAL OPPORTUNITIES, 104
EDUCATION AND THE WORKFORCE, 105-109
EDUCATION AND LABOR, 110-111
Dates: Oct. 4, 1995-date
Departure: Still serving in the 111th Congress

Cong.	Ranking	Terms in: House	Comm.	Date of Assignment
103rd	MnR-1st	1	1	Oct. 4, 1993
104th	Maj-11th	2	2	Jan. 4, 1995
105th	Maj-9th	3	3	Jan. 7, 1997
106th	Maj-9th	4	4	Jan. 6, 1999
107th	Maj-7th	5	5	Jan. 6, 2001
108th	Maj-6th	6	6	Jan. 28, 2003
109th	Maj-4th	7	7	Jan. 26, 2005
110th	Min-4th	8	8	Jan. 10, 2007
111th	Min-4th	9	9	Jan. 9, 2009

SELECT AND SPECIAL COMMITTEES

1st PERMANENT SELECT INTELLIGENCE
Dates: Jan. 4, 1995-Jan. 3, 2003
Departure: Left committee; no new assignment

Cong.	Ranking	Terms in: House	Comm.	Date of Assignment
104th	Maj-9th	2	1	Jan. 4, 1995
105th	Maj-6th	3	2	Feb. 10, 1997
106th	Maj-4th	4	3	Jan. 19, 1999
107th	Maj-3rd	5	4	Jan. 30, 2001

Kathy Castor (D-Fla.)

Dates: Aug. 20, 1966
House: Jan. 3, 2007-date
Serving in the 111th Congress

HOUSE STANDING COMMITTEES:

1st ARMED SERVICES
Dates: Jan. 10, 2007-Jan. 3, 2009
Departure: Moved to Energy and Commerce and Standards of Official Conduct

Cong.	Ranking	Terms in: House	Comm.	Date of Assignment
110th	Maj-33rd	1	1	Jan. 10, 2007

2nd RULES
Dates: Jan. 12, 2007-Jan. 14, 2009
Departure: Resigned committee; moved to Energy and Commerce

Cong.	Ranking	Terms in: House	Comm.	Date of Assignment
110th	Maj-7th	1	1	Jan. 12, 2007
111th	Maj-7th	2	2	Jan. 6, 2009

3rd ENERGY AND COMMERCE
Dates: Jan. 7, 2009-date
Departure: Still serving in the 111th Congress

Cong.	Ranking	Terms in: House	Comm.	Date of Assignment
111th	Maj-29th	2	1	Jan. 7, 2009

4th STANDARDS OF OFFICIAL CONDUCT
Dates: Jan. 22, 2009-date
Departure: Still serving in the 111th Congress

Cong.	Ranking	Terms in: House	Comm.	Date of Assignment
111th	Maj-4th	2	1	Jan. 22, 2009

Donald J. Cazayoux Jr. (D-La.)

Dates: Jan. 17, 1964
House: May 3, 2008-Jan. 3, 2009
Left the House: Defeated for re-election in 2008

H: Cazayoux was elected to the 110th Congress by special election, May 3, 2006, to fill the vacancy caused by the resignation of U.S. Representative Richard Baker (R-La.). Cazayoux was seated May 6, 2008, and assigned to committees.

HOUSE STANDING COMMITTEES:

1st FINANCIAL SERVICES
Dates: June 10, 2008-Jan. 3, 2009
Departure: Left the House; lost re-election

Cong.	Ranking	Terms in: House	Comm.	Date of Assignment
110th	MjR-4th	1	1	June 10, 2008

2nd VETERANS' AFFAIRS
Dates: June 10, 2008-Jan. 3, 2009
Departure: Left the House; lost re-election

Cong.	Ranking	Terms in: House	Comm.	Date of Assignment
110th	MjR-3rd	1	1	June 10, 2008

Steven J. Chabot (R-Ohio)

Dates: Jan. 22, 1953
House: Jan. 3, 1995-Jan. 3, 2009
Left the House: Defeated for re-election in 2008

HOUSE STANDING COMMITTEES:

1st INTERNATIONAL RELATIONS, 104-109
FOREIGN AFFAIRS, 110
Dates: Jan. 4, 1995-Jan. 3, 2009
Departure: Left the House; lost re-election

Cong.	Ranking	Terms in: House	Comm.	Date of Assignment
104th	Maj-20th	1	1	Jan. 4, 1995
105th	Maj-16th	2	2	Jan. 7, 1997
106th	Maj-15th	3	3	Jan. 6, 1999
107th	Maj-13th	4	4	Jan. 6, 2001
108th	Maj-12th	5	5	Jan. 28, 2003
109th	Maj-10th	6	6	Jan. 26, 2005
110th	Min-8th	7	7	Jan. 10, 2007

2nd JUDICIARY
Dates: Jan. 4, 1995-Jan. 3, 2009
Departure: Left the House; lost re-election

Cong.	Ranking	Terms in: House	Comm.	Date of Assignment
104th	Maj-18th	1	1	Jan. 4 1995
105th	Maj-15th	2	2	Jan. 7, 1997
106th	Maj-12th	3	3	Jan. 6, 1999
107th	Maj-8th	4	4	Jan. 6, 2001
108th	Maj-7th	5	5	Jan. 28, 2003
109th	Maj-7th	6	6	Jan. 26, 2005
110th	Min-6th	7	7	Jan. 10, 2007

3rd SMALL BUSINESS
Dates: Jan. 4, 1995-Jan. 3, 2009
Departure: Left the House; lost re-election

Cong.	Ranking	Terms in: House	Comm.	Date of Assignment
104th	Maj-19th	1	1	Jan. 4, 1995
105th	Maj-11th	2	2	Jan. 21, 1997
106th	Maj-8th	3	3	Jan. 6, 1999
107th	Maj-7th	4	4	Jan. 6, 2001
108th	Maj-5th	5	5	Jan. 28, 2003
109th	Maj-4th	6	6	Jan. 26, 2005
110th	Min-RM	7	7	Jan. 4, 2007

John H. Chafee (R-R.I.)

Dates: Oct. 22, 1922-Oct. 24, 1999
Senate: Dec. 29, 1976-Oct. 24, 1999
Left Senate: Died in office

S: John Chafee was appointed to the 94th Congress, Dec. 29, 1976, to fill the vacancy caused by the resignation of U.S. Senator John O. Pastore (D-R.I.). John Chafee was not seated nor was he assigned to committees because the 94th Congress was not in session.

SENATE STANDING COMMITTEES:

1st JUDICIARY
Dates: Jan. 10, 1977-Feb. 22, 1977
Departure: Moved to Human Resources and Environment and Public Works

2nd BUDGET
Dates: Jan. 10, 1977-Feb. 22, 1977
Departure: Moved to Human Resources and Environment and Public Works

3rd COMMERCE
Dates: Jan. 12, 1977-Feb. 22, 1977
Departure: Moved to Human Resources and Environment and Public Works

4th HUMAN RESOURCES
Dates: Feb. 22, 1977-Jan. 23, 1979
Departure: Moved to Finance

5th ENVIRONMENT AND PUBLIC WORKS
Dates: Feb. 22, 1977-Oct. 24, 1999
Ch1: Succeeded by Robert C. Smith (R-N.H.) on Nov. 9, 1999
Departure: Died in office

Cong.	Ranking	Years in: Senate	Comm.	Date of Assignment
103rd	Min-RM	17	16	Jan. 7, 1993
104th	Maj-Chr	19	18	Jan. 5, 1995
105th	Maj-Chr	21	20	Jan. 9, 1997
106th	Maj-Ch1	23	22	Jan. 7, 1999

6th FINANCE
Dates: Jan. 23, 1979-Oct. 24, 1999
Departure: Died in office

Cong.	Ranking	Years in: Senate	Comm.	Date of Assignment
103rd	Min-5th	17	14	Jan. 7, 1993
104th	Maj-4th	19	16	Jan. 4, 1995
105th	Maj-2nd	21	18	Jan. 9, 1997
106th	Maj-2nd	23	20	Jan. 7, 1999

7th BANKING, HOUSING AND URBAN AFFAIRS
1st Dates: Jan. 5, 1981-Jan. 3, 1983
1st Departure: Moved to Energy and Natural Resources
2nd Dates: Jan. 6, 1987-Feb. 2, 1989
2nd Departure: Left committee; no new assignment
3rd Dates: June 4, 1991-Jan. 3, 1992
3rd Departure: Left committee; no new assignment

8th ENERGY AND NATURAL RESOURCES
Dates: Jan. 3, 1983-Feb. 21, 1985
Departure: Left committee; no new assignment

9th SMALL BUSINESS
Dates: Jan. 21, 1993-Jan. 6, 1995
Departure: Left committee; became Chair of Environment and Public Works

Cong.	Ranking	Years in: Senate	Comm.	Date of Assignment
103rd	Min-9th	17	1	Jan. 21, 1993

SENATE SELECT AND SPECIAL COMMITTEES:

1st SPECIAL OFFICIAL CONDUCT
Dates: Jan. 19, 1977-Mar. 10, 1977
Departure: Senate Report 49 (95-1) filed

2nd SELECT INTELLIGENCE (Permanent)
1st Dates: Feb. 21, 1977-Jan. 3, 1985
1st Departure: Left committee; became Chair of Environment and Public Works
2nd Dates: Feb. 5, 1991-Jan. 6, 1995
2nd Departure: Left committee; no new assignment
3rd Dates: Jan. 9, 1997-Oct. 24, 1999
3rd Departure: Died in office

Cong.	Ranking	Years in: Senate	Comm.	Date of Assignment
103rd	Min-5th	17 *2	2	Jan. 27, 1993

Cong.	Ranking			Date of
105th	Maj-2nd	21 *3	1	Jan. 9, 1997
106th	Maj-2nd	23 *3	2	Jan. 7, 1999

3rd SPECIAL AGING (Permanent)
Dates: Jan. 6, 1987-Feb. 2, 1989
Departure: Left committee; no new assignment

4th JUDGE WALTER L. NIXON IMPEACHMENT
Dates: May 11, 1989-Nov. 3, 1989
Departure: Senate floor vote on impeachment

JOINT COMMITTEES:

1st JOINT TAXATION
Senate Dates: Nov. 2, 1995-Oct. 24, 1999
Departure: Died in office

		Years in:		Date of
Cong.	Ranking	Senate	Comm.	Assignment
104th	MjR-1st	19	1	Nov. 2, 1995
105th	Maj-2nd	21	2	Continued
106th	Maj-2nd	23	4	Continued

Lincoln D. Chafee (R-R.I.)

Dates: March 26, 1953
Senate: Nov. 2, 1999-Jan. 3, 2007
Left Senate: Defeated for re-election in 2006

S: Lincoln Chafee was appointed to the 106th Congress, Nov. 2, 1999, to fill the vacancy caused by the death of his father, U.S. Senator John H. Chafee (R-R.I.) and was subsequently elected. Lincoln Chafee was seated Nov. 4, 1999, and assigned to committees.

1st ENVIRONMENT AND PUBLIC WORKS
Dates: Nov. 9, 1999-Jan. 3. 2007
Departure: Left the Senate; lost re-election

		Years in:		Date of
Cong.	Ranking	Senate	Comm.	Assignment
106th	MjR-1st	1	1	Nov. 9, 1999
107th	Maj-7th	2	2	Jan. 25, 2001
+107th	Min-7th	2	2	June 6, 2001
108th	Maj-6th	4	4	Jan. 15, 2003
109th	Maj-5th	6	6	Jan. 6, 2005

2nd FOREIGN RELATIONS
Dates: Nov. 9, 1999-Jan. 3. 2007
Departure: Left the Senate; lost re-election

		Years in:		Date of
Cong.	Ranking	Senate	Comm.	Assignment
106th	MjR-1st	1	1	Nov. 9, 1999
107th	Maj-7th	2	2	Jan. 25, 2001
+107th	Min-7th	2	2	June 6, 2001
108th	Maj-3rd	4	4	Jan. 15, 2003
109th	Maj-3rd	6	6	Jan. 6, 2005

3rd BANKING, HOUSING, AND URBAN AFFAIRS
Dates: Jan. 15, 2003-Jan. 6, 2005
Departure: Moved to Homeland Security and Governmental Affairs

		Years in:		Date of
Cong.	Ranking	Senate	Comm.	Assignment
108th	Maj-11th	4	1	Jan. 15, 2003

4th HOMELAND SECURITY AND GOVERNMENTAL AFFAIRS
Dates: Jan. 6, 2005-Jan. 3, 2007
Departure: Left the Senate; lost re-election

		Years in:		Date of
Cong.	Ranking	Senate	Comm.	Assignment
109th	Maj-6th	6	1	Jan. 6, 2005

JOINT COMMITTEES:

1st JOINT ECONOMIC
Dates: Jan. 25, 2001-Jan. 15, 2003
Departure: Moved to Banking, Housing and Urban Affairs

		Years in:		Date of
Cong.	Ranking	Senate	Comm.	Assignment
107th	Maj-5th	2	1	Jan. 25, 2001
+107th	Min-5th	2	1	June 6, 2001

Jason Chaffetz (R-Utah)

Dates: Mar. 26, 1957
House: Jan. 3, 2009-date
Serving in the 111th Congress

HOUSE STANDING COMMITTEES:

1st JUDICIARY
Dates: Jan. 9, 2009-date
Departure: Still serving in the 111th Congress

		Terms in:		Date of
Cong.	Ranking	House	Comm.	Assignment
111th	Min-14th	1	1	Jan. 9, 2009

2nd NATURAL RESOURCES
Dates: Jan. 9, 2009-date
Departure: Still serving in the 111th Congress

		Terms in:		Date of
Cong.	Ranking	House	Comm.	Assignment
111th	Min-17th	1	1	Jan. 9, 2009

3rd OVERSIGHT AND GOVERNMENT REFORM
Dates: Jan. 9, 2009-date
Departure: Still serving in the 111th Congress

		Terms in:		Date of
Cong.	Ranking	House	Comm.	Assignment
111th	Min-16th	1	1	Jan. 9, 2009

Saxby Chambliss (R-Ga.)

Dates: Nov. 11, 1943
House: Jan. 3, 1995-Jan. 3, 2003
Left the House: Elected to the U.S. Senate in 2002
Senate: Jan. 3, 2003-date
Serving in the 111th Congress

HOUSE STANDING COMMITTEES:

1st AGRICULTURE
Dates: Jan. 4, 1995-Jan. 3, 2003
Departure: Left the House for the Senate

		Terms in:		Date of
Cong.	Ranking	House	Comm.	Assignment
104th	Maj-26th	1	1	Jan. 4, 1995

Cong.	Ranking	House	Comm.	Date of Assignment
105th	Maj-18th	2	2	Jan. 7, 1997
106th	Maj-13th	3	3	Jan. 6, 1999
107th	Maj-8th	4	4	Jan. 6, 2001

2nd NATIONAL SECURITY, 104-105
ARMED SERVICES, 106-107
Dates: Jan. 4, 1995-Jan. 3, 2003
Departure: Left the House for the Senate

Cong.	Ranking	Terms in: House	Comm.	Date of Assignment
104th	Maj-24th	1	1	Jan. 4, 1995
105th	Maj-21st	2	2	Jan. 7, 1997
106th	Maj-20th	3	3	Jan. 6, 1999
107th	Maj-15th	4	4	Jan. 6, 2001

3rd BUDGET
Dates: Jan. 6, 1999-Jan. 3, 2001
Departure: Moved to Permanent Select Intelligence

Cong.	Ranking	Terms in: House	Comm.	Date of Assignment
106th	Maj-2nd	3	1	Jan. 6, 1999

HOUSE SELECT AND SPECIAL COMMITTEES:

1st PERMANENT SELECT INTELLIGENCE
Dates: Feb. 8, 2001-Jan. 3, 2003
Departure: Left the House for the Senate

Cong.	Ranking	Terms in: House	Comm.	Date of Assignment
107th	MjR-1st	4	1	Feb. 8, 2001

SENATE STANDING COMMITTEES:

1st AGRICULTURE, NUTRITION AND FORESTRY
Dates: Jan. 15, 2003-date
Departure: Still serving in the 111th Congress

Cong.	Ranking	Years in: Senate	Comm.	Date of Assignment
108th	Maj-6th	1	1	Jan. 15, 2003
109th	Maj-Chr	3	2	Jan. 6, 2005
110th	Min-RM	5	4	Jan. 12, 2007
111th	Min-RM	7	7	Jan. 21, 2009

2nd ARMED SERVICES
Dates: Jan. 15, 2003-date
Departure: Still serving in the 111th Congress

Cong.	Ranking	Years in: Senate	Comm.	Date of Assignment
108th	Maj-10th	1	1	Jan. 15, 2003
109th	Maj-9th	3	2	Jan. 6, 2005
110th	Min-7th	5	4	Jan. 12, 2007
111th	Min-4th	7	7	Jan. 21, 2009

3rd JUDICIARY
Dates: Jan. 15, 2003-Jan. 6, 2005
Departure: Left committee; became Chair of Agriculture, Nutrition and Forestry

Cong.	Ranking	Years in: Senate	Comm.	Date of Assignment
108th	Maj-9th	1	1	Jan. 15, 2003

4th RULES AND ADMINISTRATION
Dates: Jan. 15, 2003-date
Departure: Still serving in the 111th Congress

Cong.	Ranking	Years in: Senate	Comm.	Date of Assignment
108th	Maj-10th	1	1	Jan. 15, 2003

Cong.	Ranking	Senate	Comm.	Date of Assignment
109th	Maj-7th	3	2	Jan. 6, 2005
110th	Min-6th	5	4	Jan. 12, 2007
111th	Min-4th	7	7	Jan. 21, 2009

SENATE SELECT AND SPECIAL COMMITTEES:

1st SELECT INTELLIGENCE (Permanent)
Dates: Jan. 15, 2003-date
Departure: Still serving in the 111th Congress

Cong.	Ranking	Years in: Senate	Comm.	Date of Assignment
108th	Maj-8th	1	1	Jan. 15, 2003
109th	Maj-8th	3	2	Jan. 6, 2005
110th	Min-4th	5	4	Jan. 12, 2007
111th	Min-4th	7	7	Jan. 21, 2009

2nd SPECIAL AGING (Permanent)
Dates: July 21, 2009-date
Departure: Still serving in the 111th Congress

Cong.	Ranking	Years in: Senate	Comm.	Date of Assignment
111th	Maj-9th	7	1	July 21, 2009

JOINT COMMITTEES:

1st JOINT PRINTING
Senate Dates: Mar. 13, 2003-date
Departure: Still serving in the 111th Congress

Cong.	Ranking	Years in: Senate	Comm.	Date of Assignment
108th	Maj-VCh	1	1	Mar. 13, 2003
109th	Maj-3rd	3	2	Mar. 4, 2005
110th	Min-2nd	5	5	Mar. 6, 2007
111th	Min-2nd	7	7	Apr. 3, 2009

A. B. (Ben) Chandler (D-Ky.)

Dates: Sept. 12, 1959
House: Feb. 17, 2004-date
Serving in the 111th Congress

H: Chandler was elected to the 108th Congress by special election, Feb. 17, 2004, to fill the vacancy caused by the resignation of U.S. Representative Ernest Fletcher (R-Ky.) who had been elected Governor. Chandler was seated Feb. 24, 2004, and assigned to committees.

HOUSE STANDING COMMITTEES:

1st AGRICULTURE
Dates: Mar. 31, 2004-Jan. 3, 2007
Departure: Moved to Appropriations and Science and Technology

Cong.	Ranking	Terms in: House	Comm.	Date of Assignment
108th	MnR-1st	1	1	Mar. 31, 2004
109th	MnR-1st	2	2	Feb. 2, 2005

2nd INTERNATIONAL RELATIONS
Dates: Mar. 31, 2004-Jan. 3, 2007
Departure: Moved to Appropriations and Science and Technology

Cong.	Ranking	Terms in: House	Comm.	Date of Assignment
108th	MnR-1st	1	1	Mar. 31, 2004
109th	Min-22nd	2	2	Jan. 26, 2005

3rd TRANSPORTATION AND INFRASTRUCTURE
Dates: Jan. 26, 2005-Jan. 3, 2007
Departure: Moved to Appropriations and Science and Technology

Cong.	Ranking	Terms in: House	Comm.	Date of Assignment
109th	Min-30th	2	1	Jan. 26, 2005

4th APPROPRIATIONS
Dates: Jan. 4, 2007-date
Departure: Still serving in the 111th Congress

Cong.	Ranking	Terms in: House	Comm.	Date of Assignment
110th	Maj-35th	3	1	Jan. 4, 2007
111th	Maj-33rd	4	2	Jan. 7, 2009

5th SCIENCE AND TECHNOLOGY
Dates: Jan. 18, 2007-date
Departure: Still serving in the 111th Congress

Cong.	Ranking	Terms in: House	Comm.	Date of Assignment
110th	Maj-19th	3	1	Jan. 18, 2007
111th	Maj-18th	4	2	Jan. 21, 2009

6th STANDARDS OF OFFICIAL CONDUCT
Dates: Jan. 22, 2009-date
Departure: Still serving in the 111th Congress

Cong.	Ranking	Terms in: House	Comm.	Date of Assignment
111th	Maj-2nd	4	1	Jan. 22, 2009

Jim Chapman (D-Tex.)

Dates: March 8, 1945
House: Aug. 3, 1985-Jan. 3, 1997
Left the House: Lost U.S. Senate nomination in 1996

H: Chapman was elected to the 99th Congress by special election, Aug. 3, 1985, to fill the vacancy caused by the resignation of U.S. Representative Sam B. Hall Jr. (D-Tex.). Chapman was seated Sept. 4, 1985, and assigned to committees.

HOUSE STANDING COMMITTEES:

1st PUBLIC WORKS AND TRANSPORTATION
Dates: Sep. 12, 1985-Jan. 3, 1989
Departure: Moved to Appropriations

2nd SMALL BUSINESS
Dates: Sep. 12, 1985-July 29, 1986
Departure: Moved to Science and Technology

3rd SCIENCE AND TECHNOLOGY, 99
SCIENCE, SPACE AND TECHNOLOGY, 100
Dates: July 29, 1986-Jan. 3, 1989
Departure: Moved to Appropriations

4th APPROPRIATIONS
Dates: Jan. 3, 1989-Jan. 3, 1997
Departure: Left the House; lost Senate nomination

Cong.	Ranking	Terms in: House	Comm.	Date of Assignment
103rd	Maj-20th	5	3	Jan. 5, 1993
104th	Min-16th	6	4	Jan. 4, 1995

Helen P. Chenoweth-Hage (R-Ida.)

Dates: Jan. 27, 1938-Oct. 2, 2006
House: Jan. 3, 1995-Jan. 3, 2001
Left the House: Retired in 2000
Served as Helen P. Chenoweth in the 104th and 105th Congresses

HOUSE STANDING COMMITTEES:

1st AGRICULTURE
Dates: Jan. 4, 1995-Jan. 3, 2001
Departure: Left the House; retired

Cong.	Ranking	Terms in: House	Comm.	Date of Assignment
104th	Maj-20th	1	1	Jan. 4, 1995
105th	Maj-14th	2	2	Jan. 7, 1997
106th	Maj-11th	3	3	Jan. 6, 1999

2nd RESOURCES
Dates: Jan. 4, 1995-Jan. 3, 2001
Departure: Left the House; retired

Cong.	Ranking	Terms in: House	Comm.	Date of Assignment
104th	Maj-17th	1	1	Jan. 4, 1995
105th	Maj-13th	2	2	Jan. 7, 1997
106th	Maj-13th	3	3	Jan. 6, 1999

3rd VETERANS' AFFAIRS
Dates: Jan. 21, 1997-Jan. 3, 2001
Departure: Left the House; retired

Cong.	Ranking	Terms in: House	Comm.	Date of Assignment
105th	Maj-16th	2	1	Jan. 21, 1997
106th	Maj-12th	3	2	Jan. 6, 1999

4th GOVERNMENT REFORM
Dates: Feb. 2, 1999-Jan. 3, 2001
Departure: Left the House; retired

Cong.	Ranking	Terms in: House	Comm.	Date of Assignment
106th	MjR-1st	3	1	Feb. 2, 1999

Travis W. Childers (D-Miss.)

Dates: Mar. 29, 1958
House: May 13, 2008-date
Serving in the 111th Congress

H: Childers was elected to the 110th Congress by special election, May 13, 2008, to fill the vacancy caused by the resignation of U.S. Representative Roger F. Wicker (R-Miss.) who had been appointed to the U.S. Senate. Childers was seated May 20, 2008, and assigned to committees.

HOUSE STANDING COMMITTEES:

1st AGRICULTURE
Dates: June 10, 2008-date
Departure: Still serving in the 111th Congress

Cong.	Ranking	Terms in: House	Comm.	Date of Assignment
110th	MjR-1st	1	1	June 10, 2008
111th	Maj-28th	2	2	Jan. 21, 2009

2nd FINANCIAL SERVICES
Dates: June 10, 2008-date
Departure: Still serving in the 111th Congress

Cong.	Ranking	Terms in: House	Comm.	Date of Assignment
110th	MjR-5th	1	1	June 10, 2008
111th	Maj-33rd	2	2	Jan. 7, 2009

Chris Chocola (R-Ind.)

Dates: Feb. 24, 1962
House: Jan. 3, 2003-Jan. 3, 2007
Left the House: Defeated for re-election in 2006

HOUSE STANDING COMMITTEES:

1st AGRICULTURE
Dates: Jan. 28, 2003-Jan. 3, 2005
Departure: Moved to Ways and Means

Cong.	Ranking	Terms in: House	Comm.	Date of Assignment
108th	Maj-25th	1	1	Jan. 28, 2003

2nd TRANSPORTATION AND INFRASTRUCTURE
Dates: Jan. 28, 2003-Jan. 3, 2005
Departure: Moved to Ways and Means

Cong.	Ranking	Terms in: House	Comm.	Date of Assignment
108th	Maj-34th	1	1	Jan. 28, 2003

3rd SMALL BUSINESS
Dates: Feb. 11, 2003-Jan. 3, 2005
Departure: Moved to Ways and Means

Cong.	Ranking	Terms in: House	Comm.	Date of Assignment
108th	Maj-18th	1	1	Feb. 11, 2003

4th WAYS AND MEANS
Dates: Jan. 6, 2005-Jan. 3, 2007
Departure: Left the House; lost re-election

Cong.	Ranking	Terms in: House	Comm.	Date of Assignment
109th	Maj-24th	2	1	Jan. 6, 2005

5th BUDGET
Dates: May 17, 2005-Jan. 3, 2007
Departure: Left the House; lost re-election

Cong.	Ranking	Terms in: House	Comm.	Date of Assignment
109th	MjR-1st	2	1	May 17, 2005

Donna M.C. Christensen (D-V.I.)

Dates: Sept. 19, 1945
House: Jan. 3, 1997-date
Serving in the 111th Congress
Served as Donna Christian-Green in the 105th Congress

HOUSE STANDING COMMITTEES:

1st RESOURCES, 105-109
NATURAL RESOURCES, 110-111

Dates: Jan. 7, 1997-date
Departure: Still serving in the 111th Congress

Cong.	Ranking	Terms in: House	Comm.	Date of Assignment
105th	Min-23rd	1	1	Jan. 7, 1997
106th	Min-18th	2	2	Jan. 6, 1999
107th	Min-13th	3	3	Feb. 8, 2001
108th	Min-12th	4	4	Jan. 28, 2003
109th	Min-7th	5	5	Jan. 26, 2005
110th	Maj-7th	6	6	Jan. 18, 2007
111th	Maj-18th	7	7	Jan. 21, 2009

2nd SMALL BUSINESS
1st Dates: May 14, 1998-Feb. 12, 2003
1st Departure: Leave of absence; moved to Select Homeland Security
2nd Dates: Feb. 26, 2003-Jan. 3, 2007
2nd Departure: Left committee; no new assignment

Cong.	Ranking	Terms in: House	Comm.	Date of Assignment
105th	MnR-3rd	1 *1	1	May 14, 1998
106th	Min-8th	2 *1	2	Jan. 6, 1999
107th	Min-7th	3 *1	3	Jan. 31, 2001
108th	Min-5th	4 *1	4	Jan. 28, 2003
108th	Min-7th	4 *2	1	Feb. 26, 2003
109th	Min-6th	5 *2	2	Feb. 2, 2005

3rd HOMELAND SECURITY
Dates: Feb. 9, 2005-Jan. 3, 2009
Departure: Moved to Energy and Commerce

Cong.	Ranking	Terms in: House	Comm.	Date of Assignment
109th	Min-12th	5	2	Feb. 9, 2005
110th	Maj-11th	6	3	Jan. 12, 2007

4th ENERGY AND COMMERCE
Dates: Jan. 7, 2009-date
Departure: Still serving in the 111th Congress

Cong.	Ranking	Terms in: House	Comm.	Date of Assignment
111th	Maj-28th	7	1	Jan. 7, 2009

HOUSE SELECT AND SPECIAL COMMITTEES:

1st SELECT HOMELAND SECURITY
Dates: Feb. 12, 2003-Jan. 3, 2005
Departure: Continued on reorganized standing committee

Cong.	Ranking	Terms in: House	Comm.	Date of Assignment
108th	Min-18th	4	1	Feb. 12, 2003

Donna M. Christian-Green; see
Donna M.C. Christensen, above.

Jon L. Christensen (R-Neb.)

Dates: Feb. 20, 1963
House: Jan. 3, 1995-Jan. 3, 1999
Left the House: Lost nomination for Governor in 1998

HOUSE STANDING COMMITTEES:

1st WAYS AND MEANS
Dates: Jan. 4, 1995-Jan. 3, 1999
Departure: Left the House; lost nomination for Governor

Cong.	Ranking	Terms in: House	Comm.	Date of Assignment
104th	Maj-21st	1	1	Jan. 4, 1995
105th	Maj-19th	2	2	Jan. 7, 1997

Dick Chrysler (R-Mich.)

Dates: April 29, 1942
House: Jan. 3, 1995-Jan. 3, 1997
Left the House: Defeated for re-election in 1996

HOUSE STANDING COMMITTEES:

1st BANKING AND FINANCIAL SERVICES
Dates: Jan. 4, 1995-Jan. 3, 1997
Departure: Left the House; lost re-election

Cong.	Ranking	Terms in: House	Comm.	Date of Assignment
104th	Maj-20th	1	1	Jan. 4, 1995

2nd GOVERNMENT REFORM AND OVERSIGHT
Dates: Jan. 4, 1995-Jan. 3, 1997
Departure: Left the House; lost re-election

Cong.	Ranking	Terms in: House	Comm.	Date of Assignment
104th	Maj-17th	1	1	Jan. 4, 1995

3rd SMALL BUSINESS
Dates: Jan. 4, 1995-Jan. 3, 1997
Departure: Left the House; lost re-election

Cong.	Ranking	Terms in: House	Comm.	Date of Assignment
104th	Maj-12th	1	1	Jan. 4, 1995

Judy Chu (D-Cal.)

Dates: July 7, 1953
House: July 14, 2009-date
Left the House: Still serving in the 111th Congress

H: Ms. Chu was elected to the 111th Congress by special election, July 14, 2009, to fill the vacancy caused by the resignation of U.S. Representative Hilda Solis (D-Cal.) who had been appointed Secretary of Labor. Ms. Chu was seated July 16, 2009, and assigned to committees.

HOUSE STANDING COMMITTEES:

1st EDUCATION AND LABOR
Dates: July 16, 2009-date
Departure: Still serving in the 111th Congress

Cong.	Ranking	Terms in: House	Comm.	Date of Assignment
111th	Maj-30th	1	1	July 16, 2009

2nd JUDICIARY
Dates: Oct. 15, 2009-date
Departure: Still serving in the 111th Congress

Cong.	Ranking	Terms in: House	Comm.	Date of Assignment
111th	MjR-1st	1	1	Oct. 15, 2009

3rd OVERSIGHT AND GOVERNMENT REFORM
Dates: Oct. 15, 2009-date
Departure: Still serving in the 111th Congress

Cong.	Ranking	Terms in: House	Comm.	Date of Assignment
111th	MjA-25th	1	1	Oct. 15, 2009

Yvette D. Clarke (D-N.Y.)

Dates: Nov. 21, 1964
House: Jan. 3, 2007-date
Serving in the 111th Congress

HOUSE STANDING COMMITTEES:

1st EDUCATION AND LABOR
Dates: Jan. 10, 2007-date
Departure: Still serving in the 111th Congress

Cong.	Ranking	Terms in: House	Comm.	Date of Assignment
110th	Maj-25th	1	1	Jan. 10, 2007
111th	Maj-21st	2	2	Jan. 21, 2009

2nd HOMELAND SECURITY
Dates: Jan. 12, 2007-date
Departure: Still serving in the 111th Congress

Cong.	Ranking	Terms in: House	Comm.	Date of Assignment
110th	Maj-16th	1	1	Jan. 12, 2007
111th	Maj-10th	2	2	Jan. 28, 2009

3rd SMALL BUSINESS
Dates: Jan. 23, 2007-date
Departure: Still serving in the 111th Congress

Cong.	Ranking	Terms in: House	Comm.	Date of Assignment
110th	Maj-15th	1	1	Jan. 23, 2007
111th	Maj-12th	2	2	Jan. 21, 2009

William L. Clay Jr. (D-Mo.)

Dates: July 27, 1956
House: Jan. 3, 2001-date
Serving in the 111th Congress

HOUSE STANDING COMMITTEES:

1st FINANCIAL SERVICES
Dates: Feb. 8, 2001-date
Departure: Still serving in the 111th Congress

Cong.	Ranking	Terms in: House	Comm.	Date of Assignment
107th	Min-30th	1	1	Feb. 8, 2001
108th	Min-23rd	2	2	Jan. 28, 2003

109th	Min-20th	3	3	Jan. 26, 2005
110th	Maj-15th	4	4	Jan. 12, 2007
111th	Maj-14th	5	5	Jan. 7, 2009

2nd GOVERNMENT REFORM, 107-109
OVERSIGHT AND GOVERNMENT REFORM, 110-111
Dates: Feb. 8, 2001-date
Departure: Still serving in the 111th Congress

| | | Terms in: | | Date of |
Cong.	Ranking	House	Comm.	Assignment
107th	Min-19th	1	1	Feb. 8, 2001
108th	Min-13th	2	2	Jan. 28, 2003
109th	Min-11th	3	3	Jan. 26, 2005
110th	Maj-10th	4	4	Jan. 12, 2007
111th	Maj-7th	5	5	Jan. 28, 2009

William L. Clay Sr. (D-Mo.)

Dates: April 30, 1931
House: Jan. 3, 1969-Jan. 3, 2001
Left the House: Retired in 2000

HOUSE STANDING COMMITTEES:

1st EDUCATION AND LABOR, 91-103
ECONOMIC AND EDUCATIONAL OPPORTUNITIES, 104
EDUCATION AND THE WORKFORCE, 105-106
Dates: Jan. 29, 1969-Jan. 3, 2001
Departure: Left the House; retired

| | | Terms in: | | Date of |
Cong.	Ranking	House	Comm.	Assignment
103rd	Maj-2nd	13	13	Jan. 5, 1993
104th	Min-RM	14	14	Jan. 4, 1995
105th	Min-RM	15	15	Jan. 7, 1997
106th	Min-RM	16	16	Jan. 6, 1999

2nd POST OFFICE AND CIVIL SERVICE
Dates: Jan. 24, 1973-Jan. 3, 1995
Departure: Committee abolished; became Ranking Member
on Economic and Educational Opportunities

| | | Terms in: | | Date of |
Cong.	Ranking	House	Comm.	Assignment
103rd	Maj-Chr	13	11	Jan. 21, 1993

3rd HOUSE ADMINISTRATION
Dates: Jan. 30, 1985-Jan. 3, 1995
Departure: Left committee; became Ranking Member on Economic
and Educational Opportunities

| | | Terms in: | | Date of |
Cong.	Ranking	House	Comm.	Assignment
103rd	Maj-3rd	13	5	Jan. 21, 1993

HOUSE SELECT AND SPECIAL COMMITTEES:

1st SELECT COMMITTEES II (Patterson)
Dates: Mar. 28, 1979-Apr. 1, 1980
Termination: House Report 866 (95-2) filed

JOINT COMMITTEES:

1st JOINT LIBRARY
House Dates: Mar. 15, 1989-Jan. 3, 1991
Departure: Left committee; became chair of Post Office and Civil Service

Eva M. Clayton (D-N.C.)

Dates: Sept. 16, 1934
House: Nov. 3, 1992-Jan. 3, 2003
Left the House: Retired in 2002

H: Clayton was elected to the 102nd Congress by special election, Nov. 3, 1992, to fill the vacancy caused by the death of U.S. Representative Walter B. Jones (D-N.C.). Clayton was not seated nor assigned to committees because the 102nd Congress was not in session.

HOUSE STANDING COMMITTEES:

1st AGRICULTURE
Dates: Jan. 5, 1993-Jan. 3, 2003
Departure: Left the House; retired

| | | Terms in: | | Date of |
Cong.	Ranking	House	Comm.	Assignment
103rd	Maj-17th	2	1	Jan. 5, 1993
104th	Min-10th	3	2	Jan. 4, 1995
105th	Min-6th	4	3	Jan. 7, 1997
106th	Min-6th	5	4	Jan. 6, 1999
107th	Min-5th	6	5	Jan. 31, 2001

2nd SMALL BUSINESS
Dates: Jan. 5, 1993-Jan. 3, 1997
Departure: Moved to Budget

| | | Terms in: | | Date of |
Cong.	Ranking	House	Comm.	Assignment
103rd	Maj-15th	2	1	Jan. 5, 1993
104th	Min-7th	3	2	Jan. 4, 1995

3rd BUDGET
Dates: Feb. 5, 1997-Jan. 3, 2003
Departure: Left the House; retired

| | | Terms in: | | Date of |
Cong.	Ranking	House	Comm.	Assignment
105th	MnR-1st	4	1	Feb. 5, 1997
106th	Min-9th	5	2	Jan. 6, 1999
107th	Min-6th	6	3	Jan. 31, 2001

Emanuel Cleaver II (D-Mo.)

Dates: Oct. 26, 1944
House: Jan. 3, 2005-date
Serving in the 111th Congress

HOUSE STANDING COMMITTEES:

1st FINANCIAL SERVICES
Dates: Jan. 26, 2005-date
Departure: Still serving in the 111th Congress

| | | Terms in: | | Date of |
Cong.	Ranking	House	Comm.	Assignment
109th	Min-30th	1	1	Jan. 26, 2005
110th	Maj-22nd	2	2	Jan. 12, 2007
111th	Maj-21st	3	3	Jan. 7, 2009

2nd HOMELAND SECURITY
Dates: Jan. 28, 2009-date
Departure: Still serving in the 111th Congress

| | | Terms in: | | Date of |
Cong.	Ranking	House	Comm.	Assignment
111th	Maj-15th	3	1	Jan. 28, 2009

HOUSE SELECT AND SPECIAL COMMITEES

1st SELECT ENERGY INDEPENDENCE AND GLOBAL WARMING
Dates: Mar. 9, 2007-date
Departure: Still serving in the 111th Congress

Cong.	Ranking	Terms in: House	Comm.	Date of Assignment
110th	Maj-7th	2	1	Mar. 9, 2007
111th	Maj-6th	3	2	Feb. 3, 2009

J. Maxwell (Max) Cleland (D-Ga.)

Dates: Aug. 24, 1942
Senate: Jan. 7, 1997-Jan. 3, 2003
Left Senate: Defeated for re-election in 2002

SENATE STANDING COMMITTEES:

1st ARMED SERVICES
Dates: Jan. 9, 1997-Jan. 3, 2003
Departure: Left the Senate; lost re-election

Cong.	Ranking	Years in: Senate	Comm.	Date of Assignment
105th	Min-8th	1	1	Jan. 9, 1997
106th	Min-7th	3	2	Jan. 7, 1999
107th	Min-5th	5	5	Jan. 25, 2001
+107th	Maj-5th	5	5	June 6, 2001

2nd GOVERNMENTAL AFFAIRS
Dates: Jan. 9, 1997-Jan. 3, 2003
Departure: Left the Senate; lost re-election

Cong.	Ranking	Years in: Senate	Comm.	Date of Assignment
105th	Min-7th	1	1	Jan. 9, 1997
106th	Min-6th	3	2	Jan. 7, 1999
107th	Min-6th	5	5	Jan. 25, 2001
+107th	Maj-6th	5	5	June 6, 2001

3rd SMALL BUSINESS
Dates: Jan. 9, 1997-Jan. 3, 2003
Departure: Left the Senate; lost re-election

Cong.	Ranking	Years in: Senate	Comm.	Date of Assignment
105th	Min-7th	1	1	Jan. 9, 1997
106th	Min-6th	3	2	Jan. 7, 1999
107th	Min-6th	5	5	Jan. 25, 2001
+107th	Maj-6th	5	5	June 6, 2001

4th COMMERCE, SCIENCE AND TRANSPORTATION
Dates: Jan. 7, 1999-Jan. 3, 2003
Departure: Left the Senate; lost re-election

Cong.	Ranking	Years in: Senate	Comm.	Date of Assignment
106th	Min-9th	3	1	Jan. 7, 1999
107th	Min-8th	5	3	Jan. 25, 2001
+107th	Maj-8th	5	3	June 6, 2001

Robert N. Clement (D-Tenn.)

Dates: Sept. 23, 1943
House: Jan. 19, 1988-Jan. 3, 2003
Left the House: Lost U.S. Senate election in 2002

H: Clement was elected to the 100th Congress by special election, Jan. 19, 1988, to fill the vacancy caused by the resignation of U.S. Representative William H. Boner (D-Tenn.). Clement was seated Jan. 25, 1988, and assigned to committees.

HOUSE STANDING COMMITTEES:

1st MERCHANT MARINE AND FISHERIES
Dates: Mar. 2, 1988-Feb. 5, 1992
Departure: Moved to Veterans' Affairs.

2nd PUBLIC WORKS AND TRANSPORTATION, 100-103
TRANSPORTATION AND INFRASTRUCTURE, 104-107
Dates: Mar. 2, 1988-Jan. 3, 2003
Departure: Left the House; lost Senate election

Cong.	Ranking	Terms in: House	Comm.	Date of Assignment
103rd	Maj-13th	4	4	Jan 5, 1993
104th	Min-10th	5	5	Jan. 4, 1995
105th	Min-8th	6	6	Jan. 7, 1997
106th	Min-8th	7	7	Jan. 6, 1999
107th	Min-6th	8	8	Jan. 31, 2001

3rd VETERANS' AFFAIRS
Dates: Feb. 5, 1992-Jan. 3, 1997
Departure: Moved to International Relations

Cong.	Ranking	Terms in: House	Comm.	Date of Assignment
103rd	Maj-13th	4	2	Jan. 5, 1993
104th	Min-6th	5	3	Jan. 4, 1995

4th INTERNATIONAL RELATIONS
Dates: Feb. 5, 1997-Jan. 3, 1999
Departure: Moved to Budget

Cong.	Ranking	Terms in: House	Comm.	Date of Assignment
105th	Min-21st	6	1	Feb. 5, 1997

5th BUDGET
Dates: Jan. 6, 1999-Jan. 3, 2003
Departure: Left the House; lost Senate election

Cong.	Ranking	Terms in: House	Comm.	Date of Assignment
106th	Min-13th	7	1	Jan. 6, 1999
107th	Min-10th	8	2	Jan. 31, 2001

William F. Clinger Jr. (R-Penn.)

Dates: April 4, 1929
House: Jan. 3, 1979-Jan. 3, 1997
Left the House: Retired in 1996

HOUSE STANDING COMMITTEES:

1st PUBLIC WORKS AND TRANSPORTATION, 96-103
TRANSPORTATION AND INFRASTRUCTURE, 104
Dates: Jan. 24, 1979-Jan. 3, 1997
Departure: Left the House; retired

Cong.	Ranking	Terms in: House	Comm.	Date of Assignment
103rd	Maj-2nd	8	8	Jan. 5, 1993
104th	Min-3rd	9	9	Jan. 4, 1995

2nd GOVERNMENT OPERATIONS, 97-103
GOVERNMENT REFORM AND OVERSIGHT, 104
Dates: Jan. 28, 1981-Jan. 3, 1997
Departure: Left the House; retired

Cong.	Ranking	Terms in: House	Comm.	Date of Assignment
103rd	Min-RM	8	7	Jan. 5, 1993
104th	Maj-Chr	9	8	Jan. 4, 1995

HOUSE SELECT AND SPECIAL COMMITTEES:

1st SELECT AGING (Permanent)
Dates: Feb. 2, 1987-Jan. 3, 1991
Departure: Moved to Select Narcotics Abuse and Control.

2nd SELECT NARCOTICS ABUSE AND CONTROL (Temporary)
Dates: Feb. 21, 1991-Jan. 3, 1993
Termination: Committee not renewed in 1993

Hillary Rodham Clinton (D-N.Y.)

Dates: Oct. 26, 1947
Senate: Jan. 3, 2001-Jan. 21, 2009
Left Senate: Resigned chamber; appointed Secretary of State

S: Senator Clinton served in the 111th Congress but was unassigned to committees during her Senate confirmation hearings as Secretary of State

SENATE STANDING COMMITTEES:

1st BUDGET
Dates: Jan. 25, 2001-Jan. 6, 2003
Departure: Moved to Armed Services

Cong.	Ranking	Years in: Senate	Comm.	Date of Assignment
107th	Min-11th	1	1	Jan. 25, 2001
+107th	Maj-11th	1	1	June 6, 2001

2nd ENVIRONMENT AND PUBLIC WORKS
Dates: Jan. 25, 2001-Jan. 21, 2009
Departure: Resigned the Senate; named to Cabinet

Cong.	Ranking	Years in: Senate	Comm.	Date of Assignment
107th	Min-8th	1	1	Jan. 25, 2001
+107th	Maj-9th	1	1	July 10, 2001
108th	Min-9th	3	2	Jan. 15, 2003
109th	Min-6th	5	5	Jan. 6, 2005
110th	Maj-5th	7	6	Jan. 12, 2007

3rd HEALTH, EDUCATION, LABOR, AND PENSIONS
Dates: Jan. 25, 2001-Jan. 21, 2009
Departure: Resigned the Senate; named to Cabinet

Cong.	Ranking	Years in: Senate	Comm.	Date of Assignment
107th	Min-10th	1	1	Jan. 25, 2001
+107th	Maj-11th	1	1	July 10, 2001
108th	Min-10th	3	2	Jan. 15, 2003
109th	Min-9th	5	4	Jan. 6, 2005
110th	Maj-8th	7	6	Jan. 12, 2007

4th ARMED SERVICES
Dates: Jan. 15, 2003-Jan. 21, 2009
Departure: Resigned the Senate; named to Cabinet

Cong.	Ranking	Years in: Senate	Comm.	Date of Assignment
108th	Min-11th	3	1	Jan. 15, 2003
109th	Min-11th	5	2	Jan. 6, 2005
110th	Maj-10th	7	4	Jan. 12, 2007

SENATE SELECT AND SPECIAL COMMITTEES:

1st SPECIAL AGING (Permanent)
Dates: Jan. 6, 2005-Jan. 21, 2009
Departure: Resigned the Senate; named to Cabinet

Cong.	Ranking	Years in: Senate	Comm.	Date of Assignment
109th	Min-9th	5	1	Jan. 6, 2005
110th	Maj-7th	7	3	Jan. 12, 2007

James E. Clyburn (D-S.C.)

Dates: July 21, 1940
House: Jan. 3, 1993-date
Serving in the 111th Congress

HOUSE STANDING COMMITTEES:

1st PUBLIC WORKS AND TRANSPORTATION, 103
TRANSPORTATION AND INFRASTRUCTURE, 104-105
Dates: Jan. 5, 1993-Jan. 3, 1999
Departure: Moved to Appropriations

Cong.	Ranking	Terms in: House	Comm.	Date of Assignment
103rd	Maj-32nd	1	1	Jan. 5, 1993
104th	Min-21st	2	2	Jan. 4, 1995
105th	Min-16th	3	3	Jan. 7, 1997

2nd VETERANS' AFFAIRS
Dates: Jan. 5, 1993-Jan. 3, 1999
Departure: Moved to Appropriations

Cong.	Ranking	Terms in: House	Comm.	Date of Assignment
103rd	Maj-19th	1	1	Jan. 5, 1993
104th	Min-12th	2	2	Jan. 4, 1995
105th	Min-6th	3	3	Feb. 6, 1997

3rd SMALL BUSINESS
Dates: Sep. 17, 1996-Jan. 3, 1997
Departure: Left committee; no new assignment

Cong.	Ranking	Terms in: House	Comm.	Date of Assignment
104th	MnR-6th	2	1	Sep. 17, 1996

4th APPROPRIATIONS
1st Dates: Jan. 6, 1999-Aug. 5, 1999
1st Departure: Resigned committee to open seat for Michael Forbes
2nd Dates: Jan. 31, 2001-Jan. 3, 2007
2nd Departure: Left committee; elected Majority Whip

Cong.	Ranking	Terms in: House	Comm.	Date of Assignment
106th	Min-21st	4 *1	1	Jan. 6, 1999
107th	Min-21st	5 *2	1	Jan. 31, 2001
108th	Min-19th	6 *2	2	Jan. 28, 2003
109th	Min-19th	7 *2	3	Jan. 26, 2005

HOUSE LEADERSHIP POSTS

Dates: Jan. 3, 2007-date
Departure: Still serving in the 111th Congress

1st HOUSE MAJORITY WHIP
Dates: Jan. 4, 2007-date
Note: For the 110th Congress, Clyburn was elected unopposed to be the House Majority Whip on Nov. 16, 2006. He was re-elected without opposition for the 111th Congress.
Departure: Still serving in the 111th Congress

Cong.	Ranking	Terms in: House	Post	Date of Selection
110th	Maj-3rd	8	1	Nov. 16, 2006
111th	Maj-3rd	9	2	Nov. 17, 2008

Daniel R. Coats (R-Ind.)

Dates: May 16, 1943
House: Jan. 3, 1981-Dec. 12, 1988
Left the House: Resigned chamber; appointed to the U.S. Senate in 1988
Senate: Dec. 12, 1988-Jan. 3, 1999
Left the Senate: Retired in 1998

S: Coats was appointed to the 100th Congress, Dec. 12, 1988, to fill the vacancy of U.S. Senator J. Danforth Quayle (R-Ind.) who had been elected Vice President. Coats was not seated nor was assigned to committees because the 100th Congress was not in session. He was subsequently elected.

HOUSE STANDING COMMITTEES:

1st ENERGY AND COMMERCE
Dates: Jan. 28, 1981-Dec. 12, 1988
Departure: Resigned the House; appointed U.S. Senator.

HOUSE SELECT AND SPECIAL COMMITTEES:

1st SELECT AGING (Permanent)
Dates: Feb. 5, 1981-Jan. 3, 1983
Departure: Moved to Select Children, Youth and Families.

2nd SELECT CHILDREN, YOUTH AND FAMILIES (Temporary)
Dates: Feb. 2, 1983-Dec. 12, 1988
Departure: Resigned the House; appointed U.S. Senator

SENATE STANDING COMMITTEES:

1st ARMED SERVICES
Dates: Feb. 2, 1989-Jan. 3, 1999
Departure: Left the Senate; retired

Cong.	Ranking	Years in: Senate	Comm.	Date of Assignment
103rd	Min-6th	5	4	Jan. 7, 1993
104th	Maj-6th	7	6	Jan. 4, 1995
105th	Maj-4th	9	8	Jan. 9, 1997

2nd LABOR AND HUMAN RESOURCES
Dates: Feb. 2, 1989-Jan. 3, 1999
Departure: Left the Senate; retired

Cong.	Ranking	Years in: Senate	Comm.	Date of Assignment
103rd	Min-3rd	5	4	Jan. 7, 1993
104th	Maj-3rd	7	6	Jan. 4, 1995
105th	Maj-2nd	9	8	Jan. 9, 1997

SENATE SELECT AND SPECIAL COMMITTEES:

1st SELECT INTELLIGENCE (Permanent)
Dates: Jan. 9, 1997-Jan. 3, 1999
Departure: Left the Senate; retired

Cong.	Ranking	Years in: Senate	Comm.	Date of Assignment
105th	Maj-10th	9	1	Jan. 9, 1997

Howard Coble (R-N.C.)

Dates: March 18, 1931
House: Jan. 3, 1985-date
Serving in the 111th Congress

HOUSE STANDING COMMITTEES:

1st JUDICIARY
Dates: Jan. 30, 1985-date
Departure: Still serving in the 111th Congress

Cong.	Ranking	Terms in: House	Comm.	Date of Assignment
103rd	Min-7th	5	5	Jan. 5, 1993
104th	Maj-6th	6	6	Jan. 4, 1995
105th	Maj-5th	7	7	Jan. 7, 1997
106th	Maj-5th	8	8	Jan. 6, 1999
107th	Maj-4th	9	9	Jan. 6, 2001
108th	Maj-3rd	10	10	Jan. 28, 2003
109th	Maj-3rd	11	11	Jan. 26, 2005
110th	Min-3rd	12	12	Jan. 10, 2007
111th	Min-3rd	13	13	Jan. 9, 2009

2nd SMALL BUSINESS
Dates: Jan. 30, 1985-Jan. 3, 1987
Departure: Moved to Merchant Marine and Fisheries

3rd MERCHANT MARINE AND FISHERIES
Dates: Jan. 21, 1987-Jan. 3, 1995
Departure: Committee abolished; moved to Transportation and Infrastructure

Cong.	Ranking	Terms in: House	Comm.	Date of Assignment
103rd	Min-5th	5	4	Jan. 5, 1993

4th TRANSPORTATION AND INFRASTRUCTURE
Dates: Jan. 4, 1995-date
Departure: Still serving in the 111th Congress

Cong.	Ranking	Terms in: House	Comm.	Date of Assignment
104th	Maj-8th	6	1	Jan. 4, 1995
105th	Maj-6th	7	2	Jan. 7, 1997
106th	Maj-6th	8	3	Jan. 6, 1999
107th	Maj-5th	9	4	Jan. 6, 2001
108th	Maj-4th	10	5	Jan. 28, 2003
109th	Maj-4th	11	6	Jan. 26, 2005
110th	Min-4th	12	7	Jan. 10, 2007
111th	Min-4th	13	8	Jan. 9, 2009

HOUSE SELECT AND SPECIAL COMMITTEES:

1st SELECT NARCOTICS ABUSE AND CONTROL (Temporary)
Dates: Feb. 21, 1991-Jan. 3, 1993
Termination: Committee not renewed in 1993

Thomas A. Coburn (R-Okla.)

Dates: March 14, 1948
House: Jan. 3, 1995-Jan. 3, 2001
Left the House: Left chamber; retired, later elected to Senate
Senate: Jan. 3, 2005-date
Serving in the 111th Congress

HOUSE STANDING COMMITTEES:

1st COMMERCE
Dates: Jan. 4, 1995-Jan. 3, 2001
Departure: Left the House; retired

Cong.	Ranking	Terms in: House	Comm.	Date of Assignment
104th	Maj-25th	1	1	Jan. 4, 1995
105th	Maj-24th	2	2	Jan. 7, 1997
106th	Maj-18th	3	3	Jan. 6, 1999

2nd SCIENCE
Dates: Mar. 5, 1997-Jan. 3, 1999
Departure: Left committee; no new assignment

Cong.	Ranking	Terms in: House	Comm.	Date of Assignment
105th	Maj-24th	2	1	Mar. 5, 1997

SENATE STANDING COMMITTEES:

1st HOMELAND SECURITY AND GOVERNMENTAL AFFAIRS
Dates: Jan. 6, 2005-date
Departure: Still serving in the 111th Congress

Cong.	Ranking	Years in: Senate	Comm.	Date of Assignment
109th	Maj-5th	1	1	Jan. 6, 2005
110th	Min-5th	3	3	Jan. 12, 2007
111th	Min-2nd	5	5	Jan. 21, 2009

2nd JUDICIARY
Dates: Jan. 6, 2005-date
Departure: Still serving in the 111th Congress

Cong.	Ranking	Years in: Senate	Comm.	Date of Assignment
109th	Maj-10th	1	1	Jan. 6, 2005
110th	Min-9th	3	3	Jan. 12, 2007
111th	Min-8th	5	5	Jan. 21, 2009

3rd HEALTH, EDUCATION, LABOR AND PENSIONS
Dates: Jan 12, 2007-date
Departure: Still serving in the 111th Congress

Cong.	Ranking	Years in: Senate	Comm.	Date of Assignment
110th	Min-10th	3	1	Jan. 12, 2007
111th	Min-9th	5	3	Jan. 21, 2009

SENATE SELECT AND SPECIAL COMMITTEES:

1st INDIAN AFFAIRS (Permanent)
Dates: Jan. 6, 2005-date
Departure: Still serving in the 111th Congress

Cong.	Ranking	Years in: Senate	Comm.	Date of Assignment
109th	Maj-4th	1	1	Jan. 6, 2005
110th	Min-4th	3	3	Jan. 12, 2007
111th	Min-4th	5	5	Jan. 21, 2009

W. Thad Cochran (R-Miss.)

Dates: Dec. 7, 1937
House: Jan. 3, 1973-Dec. 26, 1978
Left the House: Elected to the U.S. Senate in 1978
Senate: Dec. 27, 1978-date
Serving in the 111th Congress

S: Cochran was appointed to the 95th Congress, Dec, 27.1978, to fill the vacancy caused by the resignation of U.S. Senator James O. Eastland (D-Miss.). Cochran was not seated nor assigned to committees because the 95th Congress was not in session. Cochran had been elected to succeed Eastland in the 96th Congress.

HOUSE STANDING COMMITTEES:

1st PUBLIC WORKS
Dates: Jan. 24, 1973-Jan. 3, 1975
PUBLIC WORKS AND TRANSPORTATION
Dates: Jan. 28, 1975-Dec. 26, 1978
Departure: Resigned the House; elected U.S. Senator.

2nd STANDARDS OF OFFICIAL CONDUCT
Dates: Jan. 28, 1975-Dec. 26, 1978
Departure: Resigned the House; elected U.S. Senator.

HOUSE SELECT AND SPECIAL COMMITTEES:

1st SELECT AGING (Permanent)
Dates: Jan. 31, 1977-Dec. 26, 1978
Departure: Resigned the House; elected U.S. Senator.

2nd SELECT ETHICS
Dates: Mar. 10, 1977-Dec. 26, 1978
Departure: Resigned the House; elected U.S. Senator.

SENATE STANDING COMMITTEES:

1st AGRICULTURE, NUTRITION AND FORESTRY
Dates: Jan. 23, 1979-date
Departure: Still serving in the 111th Congress

Cong.	Ranking	Years in: Senate	Comm.	Date of Assignment
103rd	Min-4th	15	14	Jan. 7, 1993
104th	Maj-4th	17	16	Jan. 4, 1995
105th	Maj-3rd	19	18	Jan. 9, 1997
106th	Maj-3rd	21	20	Jan. 7, 1999
107th	Maj-3rd	23	23	Jan. 25, 2001
+107th	Min-3rd	23	23	June 6, 2001
108th	Maj-Chr	25	24	Jan. 15, 2003
109th	Maj-3rd	27	26	Jan. 6, 2005
110th	Min-3rd	29	28	Jan. 12, 2007
111th	Min-3rd	31	30	Jan. 21, 2009

2nd JUDICIARY
Dates: Jan. 23, 1979-Jan. 5, 1981
Departure: Moved to Appropriations

3rd APPROPRIATIONS
Dates: Jan. 5, 1981-date
Departure: Still serving in the 111th Congress

Cong.	Ranking	Years in: Senate	Comm.	Date of Assignment
103rd	Min-3rd	15	13	Jan. 7, 1993

Cong.				Date of
104th	Maj-3rd	17	14	Jan. 4, 1995
105th	Maj-2nd	19	17	Jan. 9, 1997
106th	Maj-2nd	21	19	Jan. 7, 1999
107th	Maj-2nd	23	21	Jan. 25, 2001
+107th	Min-2nd	23	21	June 6, 2001
108th	Maj-2nd	25	23	Jan. 15, 2003
109th	Maj-Chr	27	25	Jan. 6, 2005
110th	Min-RM	29	27	Jan. 12, 2007
111th	Min-RM	31	29	Jan. 21, 2009

4th GOVERNMENTAL AFFAIRS
1st Dates: Jan. 3, 1983-Jan. 6, 1987
1st Departure: Moved to Labor and Human Resources
2nd Dates: Jan. 7, 1993-Jan. 15, 2003
2nd Departure: Left committee; became Chair of Agriculture, Nutrition and Forestry

		Years in:		Date of
Cong.	Ranking	Senate	Comm.	Assignment
103rd	Min-4th	15	*2 1	Jan. 7, 1993
104th	Maj-5th	17	*2 2	Jan. 5, 1995
105th	Maj-7th	19	*2 5	Jan. 9, 1997
106th	Maj-7th	21	*2 7	Jan. 7, 1999
107th	Maj-6th	23	*2 9	Jan. 25, 2001
+107th	Min-6th	23	*2 9	June 6, 2001

5th LABOR AND HUMAN RESOURCES
Dates: Jan. 6, 1987-Jan. 7, 1993
Departure: Returned to Governmental Affairs; moved to Rules and Administration

6th RULES AND ADMINISTRATION
Dates: Jan. 21, 1993-date
Departure: Still serving in the 111th Congress

		Years in:		
Cong.	Ranking	Senate	Comm.	Assignment
103rd	Min-7th	15	1	Jan. 21, 1993
104th	Maj-7th	17	2	Jan. 6, 1995
105th	Maj-5th	19	4	Jan. 9, 1997
106th	Maj-5th	21	6	Jan. 7, 1999
107th	Maj-5th	23	9	Jan. 25, 2001
+107th	Min-5th	23	9	June 6, 2001
108th	Maj-4th	25	10	Jan. 15, 2003
109th	Maj-4th	27	12	Jan. 6, 2005
110th	Min-4th	29	14	Jan. 12, 2007
111th	Min-3rd	31	17	Jan. 21, 2009

SENATE SELECT AND SPECIAL COMMITTEES:

1st SELECT ETHICS (Permanent)
Dates: Jan. 28, 1980-Jan. 21, 1981
Departure: Left committee; no new assignment

SELECT INDIAN AFFAIRS (Permanent), 101-102
2nd INDIAN AFFAIRS (Permanent), 103
Dates: Feb. 2, 1989-Jan. 11, 1995
Departure: Moved to Joint Library and Joint Printing

		Years in:		Date of
Cong.	Ranking	Senate	Comm.	Assignment
103rd	Min-3rd	15	4	Jan. 5, 1993

JOINT COMMITTEES:

1st JOINT LIBRARY
1st Senate Dates: Jan. 17, 1995-Nov. 5, 1995
1st Departure: Removed by S. Res. 192
2nd Senate Dates: Jan. 30, 1997-Mar. 26, 2007
2nd Departure: Left committee; no new assignment

		Years in:		Date of
Cong.	Ranking	Senate	Comm.	Assignment
104th	Maj-3rd	17	*1 1	Jan. 17, 1995
105th	Maj-3rd	19	*2 1	Jan. 28, 1997
106th	Maj-3rd	21	*2 3	Mar. 2, 1999
+107th	Min-2nd	23	*2 5	Sep. 19, 2001
108th	Maj-3rd	25	*2 7	Mar. 13, 2003
109th	Maj-2nd	27	*2 9	Mar. 4, 2005

2nd JOINT PRINTING
Senate Dates: Jan. 17, 1995-Mar. 26, 2007
Departure: Left committee; no new assignment

		Years in:		Date of
Cong.	Ranking	Senate	Comm.	Assignment
104th	Maj-3rd	17	1	Jan. 17, 1995
105th	Maj-2nd	19	3	Jan. 28, 1997
106th	Maj-2nd	21	5	Mar. 2, 1999
+107th	Min-1st	23	7	Sep. 19, 2001
108th	Maj-2nd	25	9	Mar. 13, 2003
109th	Maj-2nd	27	11	Mar. 4, 2005

Michael Coffman (R-Colo.)

Dates: March 19, 1955
House: Jan. 3, 2009-date
Serving in the 111th Congress

HOUSE STANDING COMMITTEES:

1st ARMED SERVICES
Dates: Jan. 9, 2009-date
Departure: Still serving in the 111th Congress

		Terms in:		Date of
Cong.	Ranking	House	Comm.	Assignment
111th	Min-24th	1	1	Jan. 9, 2009

2nd NATURAL RESOURCES
Dates: Jan. 9, 2009-date
Departure: Still serving in the 111th Congress

		Terms in:		Date of
Cong.	Ranking	House	Comm.	Assignment
111th	Min-16th	1	*1	Jan. 9, 2009

3rd SMALL BUSINESS
Dates: Feb. 8, 2009-date
Departure: Still serving in the 111th Congress

		Terms in:		Date of
Cong.	Ranking	House	Comm.	Assignment
111th	Min-12th	1	1	Feb. 4, 2009

Stephen L. Cohen (D-Tenn.)

Dates: May 24, 1949
House: Jan. 3, 2007-date
Serving in the 111th Congress

HOUSE STANDING COMMITTEES:

1st TRANSPORTATION AND INFRASTRUCTURE
Dates: Jan. 10, 2007-date
Departure: Still serving in the 111th Congress

| | | Terms in: | | Date of |
Cong.	Ranking	House	Comm.	Assignment
110th	Maj-40th	1	1	Jan. 10, 2007
111th	Maj-32nd	2	2	Jan. 7, 2009

2nd JUDICIARY
Dates: Jan. 18, 2007-date
Departure: Still serving in the 111th Congress

| | | Terms in: | | Date of |
Cong.	Ranking	House	Comm.	Assignment
110th	Maj-14th	1	1	Jan. 18, 2007
111th	Maj-12th	2	2	Jan. 21, 2009

William S. Cohen (R-Me.)

Dates: Aug. 28, 1940
House: Jan. 3, 1973-Jan. 3, 1979
Left the House: Elected to the U.S. Senate in 1978
Senate: Jan. 3, 1979-Jan. 3, 1997
Left the Senate: Left chamber; retired, then appointed Secretary of Defense in 1997

HOUSE STANDING COMMITTEES:

1st JUDICIARY
Dates: Jan. 24, 1973-Jan. 3, 1979
Departure: Left the House for the Senate

2nd MERCHANT MARINE AND FISHERIES
Dates: Jan. 24, 1973-Jan. 3, 1975
Departure: Moved to Small Business

3rd SMALL BUSINESS
Dates: Jan. 28, 1975-Jan. 3, 1979
Departure: Left the House for the Senate

HOUSE SELECT AND SPECIAL COMMITTEES:

1st SELECT AGING (Permanent)
Dates: Feb. 6, 1975-Jan. 3, 1979
Departure: Left the House for the Senate

SENATE STANDING COMMITTEES:

1st ARMED SERVICES
Dates: Jan. 23, 1979-Jan. 3, 1997
Departure: Left the Senate; retired, then appointed to Cabinet

| | | Years in: | | Date of |
Cong.	Ranking	Senate	Comm.	Assignment
103rd	Min-3rd	15	14	Jan. 7, 1993
104th	Maj-3rd	17	16	Jan. 4, 1995

2nd GOVERNMENTAL AFFAIRS
Dates: Jan. 23, 1979-Jan. 3, 1997
Departure: Left the Senate; retired, then appointed to Cabinet

| | | Years in: | | Date of |
Cong.	Ranking	Senate	Comm.	Assignment
103rd	Min-3rd	15	14	Jan. 7, 1993
104th	Maj-3rd	17	16	Jan. 5, 1995

3rd JUDICIARY
Dates: Jan. 7, 1993-Jan. 5, 1995
Departure: Returned to Select Intelligence; became Chair of Special Aging

| | | Years in: | | Date of |
Cong.	Ranking	Senate	Comm.	Assignment
103rd	Min-7th	15	1	Jan. 7, 1993

SENATE SELECT AND SPECIAL COMMITTEES:

1st SPECIAL AGING (Permanent)
Dates: Jan. 23. 1979-Jan 3, 1997
Departure: Left the Senate; retired, then appointed to Cabinet

| | | Years in: | | Date of |
Cong.	Ranking	Senate	Comm.	Assignment
103rd	Min-RM	15	14	Jan. 21, 1993
104th	Maj-Chr	17	16	Jan. 11, 1995

2nd SELECT INDIAN AFFAIRS (Permanent)
Dates: Feb. 6, 1979-Jan. 3, 1983
Departure: Moved to Select Intelligence

3rd SELECT INTELLIGENCE (Permanent)
1st Dates: Jan 3, 1983-Feb. 5, 1991
1st Departure: Left committee; no new assignment
2nd Dates: Jan. 4, 1995-Jan 3, 1997
2nd Departure: Left the Senate; retired, then appointed to Cabinet

| | | Years in: | | Date of |
Cong.	Ranking	Senate	Comm.	Assignment
104th	Maj-9th	17 *2	1	Jan. 4, 1995

4th SELECT SECRET MILITARY ASSISTANCE TO IRAN AND THE NICARAGUAN OPPOSITION (Iran-Contra Affair)
Dates: Jan. 12, 1987-Nov. 17, 1987
Termination: Senate Report 100-216 filed

JOINT COMMITTEES:

1st JOINT ORGANIZATION OF CONGRESS (Ad Hoc)
Senate Dates: Sep. 25. 1992-Dec. 9, 1993
Departure: Senate Report 103-215 filed

| | | Years in: | | Date of |
Cong.	Ranking	Senate	Comm.	Assignment
103rd	Min-6th	15	1	Continued

Tom Cole (R-Okla.)

Dates: April 28, 1949
House: Jan. 3, 2003-date
Serving in the 111th Congress

HOUSE STANDING COMMITTEES:

1st ARMED SERVICES
1st Dates: Jan. 28, 2003-Jan. 3, 2005
1st Departure: Moved to Rules and Standards of Official Conduct
2nd Dates: Jan. 10, 2007-Jan. 3, 2009
2nd Departure: Moved to Appropriations

| | | Terms in: | | Date of |
Cong.	Ranking	House	Comm.	Assignment
108th	Maj-25th	1 *1	1	Jan. 28, 2003
110th	Min-17th	3 *2	1	Jan. 10, 2007

2nd EDUCATION AND THE WORKFORCE
Dates: Jan. 28, 2003-Jan. 3, 2005
Departure: Moved to Rules and Standards of Official Conduct

		Terms in:		Date of
Cong.	Ranking	House	Comm.	Assignment
108th	Maj-21st	1	1	Jan. 28, 2003

3rd RESOURCES, 108
NATURAL RESOURCES, 110
1st Dates: Jan. 28, 2003-Jan. 3, 2005
1st Departure: Moved to Rules and Standards of Official Conduct
2nd Dates: Jan. 10, 2007-Jan. 3, 2009
2nd Departure: Moved to Appropriations

		Terms in:		Date of
Cong.	Ranking	House	Comm.	Assignment
108th	Maj-25th	1 *1	1	Jan. 28, 2003
110th	Min-17th	3 *2	1	Jan. 10, 2007

4th RULES
Dates: Jan. 4, 2005-Jan. 3, 2007
Departure: Returned to Armed Services and Natural Resources

		Terms in:		Date of
Cong.	Ranking	House	Comm.	Assignment
109th	Maj-7th	2	1	Jan. 4, 2005

5th STANDARDS OF OFFICIAL CONDUCT
Dates: Feb. 2, 2005-Jan. 3, 2007
Departure: Returned to Armed Services and Natural Resources

		Terms in:		Date of
Cong.	Ranking	House	Comm.	Assignment
109th	Maj-5th	2	1	Feb. 2, 2005

6th APPROPRIATIONS
Dates: Jan. 9, 2009-date
Departure: Still serving in the 111th Congress

		Terms in:		Date of
Cong.	Ranking	House	Comm.	Assignment
111th	Min-23rd	4	1	Jan. 9, 2009

Norman Coleman (R-Minn.)

Dates: Aug. 17, 1949
Senate: Jan. 3, 2003-Jan. 3, 2009
Left Senate: Defeated for re-election in 2008

1st AGRICULTURE, NUTRITION AND FORESTRY
Dates: Jan. 15, 2003-Jan 3, 2009
Departure: Left the Senate; lost re-election

		Years in:		Date of
Cong.	Ranking	Senate	Comm.	Assignment
108th	Maj-7th	1	1	Jan. 15, 2003
109th	Maj-9th	3	2	Jan. 6, 2005
110th	Min-7th	5	4	Jan. 12, 2007

2nd FOREIGN RELATIONS
Dates: Jan. 15, 2003-Jan 3, 2009
Departure: Left the Senate; lost re-election

		Years in:		Date of
Cong.	Ranking	Senate	Comm.	Assignment
108th	Maj-9th	1	1	Jan. 15, 2003
109th	Maj-5th	3	2	Jan. 6, 2005
110th	Min-3rd	5	4	Jan. 12, 2007

3rd GOVERNMENTAL AFFAIRS renamed Oct. 9, 2004
HOMELAND SECURITY AND GOVERNMENTAL AFFAIRS
Dates: Jan. 15, 2003-Jan 3, 2009
Departure: Left the Senate; lost re-election

		Years in:		Date of
Cong.	Ranking	Senate	Comm.	Assignment
108th	Maj-4th	1	1	Jan. 15, 2003
109th	Maj-4th	3	2	Jan. 6, 2005
110th	Min-4th	5	4	Jan. 12, 2007

4th SMALL BUSINESS AND ENTREPRENEURSHIP
Dates: Jan. 15, 2003-Jan 3, 2009
Departure: Left the Senate; lost re-election

		Years in:		Date of
Cong.	Ranking	Senate	Comm.	Assignment
108th	Maj-10th	1	1	Jan. 15, 2003
109th	Maj-5th	3	2	Jan. 6, 2005
110th	Min-3rd	5	4	Jan. 12, 2007

SENATE SELECT AND SPECIAL COMMITTEES:

1st SPECIAL AGING (Permanent)
Dates: Jan. 12, 2007-Jan 3, 2009
Departure: Left the Senate; lost re-election

		Years in:		Date of
Cong.	Ranking	Senate	Comm.	Assignment
110th	Min-7th	5	1	Jan. 12, 2007

Ronald D. Coleman (D-Tex.)

Dates: Nov. 29, 1941
House: Jan. 3, 1983-Jan. 3, 1997
Left the House: Retired in 1996

HOUSE STANDING COMMITTEES:

1st ARMED SERVICES
Dates: Jan. 6, 1983-Jan. 3, 1985
Departure: Moved to Appropriations

2nd GOVERNMENT OPERATIONS
Dates: Jan. 6, 1983-Jan. 3, 1985
Departure: Moved to Appropriations

3rd APPROPRIATIONS
Dates: Jan. 30, 1985-Jan. 3, 1997
Departure: Left the House; retired

		Terms in:		Date of
Cong.	Ranking	House	Comm.	Assignment
103rd	Maj-18th	6	5	Jan. 5, 1993
104th	Min-14th	7	6	Jan. 4, 1995

HOUSE SELECT AND SPECIAL COMMITTEES:

1st PERMANENT SELECT INTELLIGENCE
Dates: Feb. 3, 1993-Jan. 3, 1997
Departure: Left the House; retired

		Terms in:		Date of
Cong.	Ranking	House	Comm.	Assignment
103rd	Maj-6th	6	1	Feb. 3, 1993
104th	Min-5th	7	2	Jan. 4, 1995

Barbara-Rose Collins (D-Mich.)

Dates: April 13, 1939
House: Jan. 3, 1991-Jan. 3, 1997
Left the House: Defeated for re-nomination in 1996

HOUSE STANDING COMMITTEES:

1st PUBLIC WORKS AND TRANSPORTATION, 102-103
TRANSPORTATION AND INFRASTRUCTURE, 104
Dates: Jan. 24, 1991-Jan. 3, 1997
Departure: Left the House; lost re-nomination

Cong.	Ranking	Terms in: House	Comm.	Date of Assignment
103rd	Maj-22nd	2	2	Jan. 5, 1993
104th	Min-16th	3	3	Jan. 4, 1995

2nd SCIENCE, SPACE AND TECHNOLOGY
Dates: Jan. 24, 1991-May 20, 1991
Departure: Moved to Post Office and Civil Service

3rd POST OFFICE AND CIVIL SERVICE
Dates: May 9, 1991-Jan. 3, 1995
Departure: Committee abolished; no new assignment

Cong.	Ranking	Terms in: House	Comm.	Date of Assignment
103rd	Maj-8th	2	2	Jan. 21, 1993

4th GOVERNMENT OPERATIONS, 103
GOVERNMENT REFORM AND OVERSIGHT, 104
Dates: Feb. 4, 1993-Jan. 3, 1997
Departure: Left the House; lost re-nomination

Cong.	Ranking	Terms in: House	Comm.	Date of Assignment
103rd	Maj-21st	2	1	Feb. 4, 1993
104th	Min-16th	3	2	Jan. 9, 1995

HOUSE SELECT AND SPECIAL COMMITTEES:

1st SELECT CHILDREN, YOUTH AND FAMILIES (Temporary)
Dates: Feb. 21, 1991-Jan. 3, 1993
Termination: Committee not renewed in 1993

Cardiss Collins (D-Ill.)

Dates: Sept. 24, 1931
House: June 5, 1973-Jan. 3, 1997
Left the House: Retired in 1996

H: Cardiss Collins was elected to the 93rd Congress by special election, June 5, 1973, to fill the vacancy caused by the death of her husband, U.S. Representative George W. Collins (D-Ill.). Mrs. Collins was seated June 7, 1973, and assigned to committees.

HOUSE STANDING COMMITTEES:

1st GOVERNMENT OPERATIONS, 93-103
GOVERNMENT REFORM AND OVERSIGHT, 104
Dates: June 19, 1973-Jan. 3, 1997
Departure: Left the House; retired

Cong.	Ranking	Terms in: House	Comm.	Date of Assignment
103rd	Maj-2nd	11	11	Jan. 5, 1993
104th	Min-RM	12	12	Jan. 9, 1995

2nd PUBLIC WORKS
Dates: July 29, 1974-Jan. 3, 1975
Departure: Moved to International Relations

3rd INTERNATIONAL RELATIONS, 94-95
FOREIGN AFFAIRS, 96
Dates: Jan. 20, 1975-Jan. 3, 1981
Departure: Moved to Energy and Commerce

4th DISTRICT OF COLUMBIA
Temporary Dates: Feb. 9, 1977-Jan. 3, 1979
Departure: Temporary term expired

5th ENERGY AND COMMERCE
1st Dates: Jan. 28, 1981-Jan. 3, 1995
1st Departure: Left committee; became Ranking Member on Government Reform and Oversight
2nd Dates: Sep. 27, 1995-Jan. 3, 1997
2nd Departure: Left the House; retired

Cong.	Ranking	Terms in: House	Comm.	Date of Assignment
103rd	Maj-6th	11 *1	7	Jan. 5, 1993
104th	MjR-1st	12 *2	1	Sep. 27, 1995

HOUSE SELECT AND SPECIAL COMMITTEES:

1st SELECT POPULATION
Dates: Oct. 14, 1977-Dec. 29, 1978
Termination: House Report 1842 (95-2) filed

2nd SELECT NARCOTICS ABUSE AND CONTROL (Temporary)
Dates: Feb. 20, 1980-Jan. 3, 1993
Termination: Committee not renewed in 1993

Michael A. (Mac) Collins (R-Ga.)

Dates: Oct. 15, 1944
House: Jan. 3, 1993-Jan. 3, 2005
Left the House: Lost U.S. Senate nomination in 2004

HOUSE STANDING COMMITTEES:

1st PUBLIC WORKS AND TRANSPORTATION
Dates: Jan. 5, 1993-Jan. 3, 1995
Departure: Moved to Ways and Means

Cong.	Ranking	Terms in: House	Comm.	Date of Assignment
103rd	Min-15th	1	1	Jan. 5, 1993

2nd SMALL BUSINESS
Dates: Jan. 5, 1993-Jan. 3, 1995
Departure: Moved to Ways and Means

Cong.	Ranking	Terms in: House	Comm.	Date of Assignment
103rd	Min-10th	1	1	Jan. 5, 1993

3rd WAYS AND MEANS
Dates: Jan. 4, 1995-Jan. 3, 2005
Departure: Left the House; lost Senate nomination

Cong.	Ranking	Terms in: House	Comm.	Date of Assignment
104th	Maj-17th	2	1	Jan. 4, 1995
105th	Maj-15th	3	2	Jan. 7, 1997
106th	Maj-14th	4	3	Jan. 6, 1999
107th	Maj-13th	5	4	Jan. 6, 2001
108th	Maj-13th	6	5	Jan. 28, 2003

4th BUDGET
Dates: Jan. 19, 1999-Jan. 3, 2003
Departure: Moved to Permanent Select Intelligence

Cong.	Ranking	Terms in: House	Comm.	Date of Assignment
106th	MjR-1st	4	1	Jan. 19, 1999
107th	Maj-10th	5	2	Jan. 6, 2001

HOUSE SELECT AND SPECIAL COMMITTEES:

1st PERMANENT SELECT INTELLIGENCE
Dates: Feb. 11, 2003-Jan. 3, 2005
Departure: Left the House; lost Senate nomination

Cong.	Ranking	Terms in: House	Comm.	Date of Assignment
108th	Maj-11th	6	1	Feb. 11, 2003

Susan M. Collins (R-Me.)

Dates: Dec. 7, 1952
Senate: Jan. 3, 1997-date
Serving in the 111th Congress

SENATE STANDING COMMITTEES:

1st GOVERNMENTAL AFFAIRS renamed Oct. 9, 2004
HOMELAND SECURITY AND GOVERNMENTAL AFFAIRS
Dates: Jan. 9, 1997-date
Departure: Still serving in the 111th Congress

Cong.	Ranking	Years in: Senate	Comm.	Date of Assignment
105th	Maj-4th	1	1	Jan. 9, 1997
106th	Maj-4th	3	2	Jan. 7, 1999
107th	Maj-3rd	5	5	Jan. 25, 2001
+107th	Min-3rd	5	5	June 6, 2001
108th	Maj-Chr	7	7	Jan. 15, 2003
109th	Maj-Chr	9	8	Jan. 6, 2005
110th	Min-RM	11	11	Jan. 12, 2007
111th	Min-RM	13	13	Jan. 21, 2009

2nd LABOR AND HUMAN RESOURCES renamed Jan. 21, 1999
HEALTH, EDUCATION, LABOR AND PENSIONS
Dates: Jan. 9, 1997-Jan. 15, 2003
Departure: Left committee; became Chair of Governmental Affairs and moved to Joint Economic

Cong.	Ranking	Years in: Senate	Comm.	Date of Assignment
105th	Maj-8th	1	1	Jan. 9, 1997
106th	Maj-7th	3	2	Jan. 7, 1999
107th	Maj-9th	5	5	Jan. 25, 2001
+107th	Min-8th	5	5	July 10, 2001

3rd ARMED SERVICES
Dates: Jan. 25, 2001-date
Departure: Still serving in the 111th Congress

Cong.	Ranking	Years in: Senate	Comm.	Date of Assignment
107th	Maj-11th	5	1	Jan. 25, 2001
+107th	Min-11th	5	1	June 6, 2001
108th	Maj-7th	7	2	Jan. 15, 2003
109th	Maj-6th	9	4	Jan. 6, 2005
110th	Min-5th	11	6	Jan. 12, 2007
111th	Min-11th	13	8	Jan. 21, 2009

4th APPROPRIATIONS
Dates: Jan. 21, 2009-date
Departure: Still serving in the 111th Congress

Cong.	Ranking	Years in: Senate	Comm.	Date of Assignment
111th	Min-11th	13	1	Jan. 21, 2009

SENATE SELECT AND SPECIAL COMMITTEES:

1st SPECIAL AGING (Permanent)
Dates: Jan. 9, 1997-date
Departure: Still serving in the 111th Congress

Cong.	Ranking	Years in: Senate	Comm.	Date of Assignment
105th	Maj-9th	1	1	Jan. 9, 1997
106th	Maj-8th	3	2	Jan. 7, 1999
107th	Maj-6th	5	5	Jan. 25, 2001
+107th	Min-5th	6	5	July 24, 2001
108th	Maj-3rd	7	7	Jan. 15, 2003
109th	Maj-3rd	9	8	Jan. 6, 2005
110th	Min-3rd	11	11	Jan. 12, 2007
111th	Min-3rd	13	13	Jan. 21, 2009

2nd SPECIAL YEAR 2000 TECHNOLOGY PROBLEM
Dates: Apr. 28, 1998-June 30, 1999
Departure: Resigned committee; no new assignment

Cong.	Ranking	Years in: Senate	Comm.	Date of Assignment
105th	Maj-4th	2	1	Apr. 28, 1998
106th	Maj-4th	3	1	Continued

JOINT COMMITTEES:

1st JOINT ECONOMIC
Senate Dates: Jan. 15, 2003-Jan. 6, 2005
Departure: Left committee; no new assignment

Cong.	Ranking	Years in: Senate	Comm.	Date of Assignment
108th	Maj-6th	7	1	Jan. 15, 2003

Larry E. Combest (R-Tex.)

Dates: March 20, 1945
House: Jan. 3, 1985-May 31, 2003
Left the House: Resigned and retired in 2003

HOUSE STANDING COMMITTEES:

1st AGRICULTURE
Dates: Jan. 30, 1985-May 31, 2003
Departure: Resigned the House; retired

Cong.	Ranking	Terms in: House	Comm.	Date of Assignment
103rd	Min-6th	5	5	Jan. 5, 1993
104th	Maj-4th	6	6	Jan. 4, 1995
105th	Maj-2nd	7	7	Jan. 7, 1997
106th	Maj-Chr	8	8	Jan. 6, 1999
107th	Maj-Chr	9	9	Jan. 6, 2001
108th	Maj-2nd	10	10	Jan. 28, 2003

2nd DISTRICT OF COLUMBIA
Dates: Oct. 1, 1985-Jan. 3, 1993
Departure: Left committee; no new assignment

3rd SMALL BUSINESS
1st Dates: Oct. 10, 1985-Jan. 3, 1995
1st Departure: Left committee; became chair of Permanent Select Intelligence
2nd Dates: Jan. 21, 1997-May 31, 2003
2nd Departure: Resigned the House; retired

Cong.	Ranking	Terms in: House	Comm.	Date of Assignment
103rd	Min-2nd	5 *1	5	Jan. 5, 1993
105th	Maj-2nd	7 *2	1	Jan. 21, 1997
106th	Maj-2nd	8 *2	2	Jan. 6, 1999
107th	Maj-2nd	9 *2	3	Jan. 6, 2001
108th	Maj-2nd	10 *2	4	Jan. 28, 2003

HOUSE SELECT AND SPECIAL COMMITTEES:

1st PERMANENT SELECT INTELLIGENCE
Dates: Jan. 24, 1989-Jan. 3, 1997
Departure: Left committee; became chair of Agriculture and returned to Small Business

Cong.	Ranking	Terms in: House	Comm.	Date of Assignment
103rd	Min-RM	5	3	Feb. 3, 1993
104th	Maj-Chr	6	4	Jan. 4, 1995

K. Michael Conaway (R-Tex.)

Dates: June 11, 1948
House: Jan. 3, 2005-date
Serving in the 111th Congress

HOUSE STANDING COMMITTEES:

1st AGRICULTURE
Dates: Jan. 26, 2005-date
Departure: Still serving in the 111th Congress

Cong.	Ranking	Terms in: House	Comm.	Date of Assignment
109th	Maj-24th	1	1	Jan. 26, 2005
110th	Min-16th	2	2	Jan. 10, 2007
111th	Min-10th	3	3	Jan. 9, 2009

2nd ARMED SERVICES
Dates: Jan. 26, 2005-date
Departure: Still serving in the 111th Congress

Cong.	Ranking	Terms in: House	Comm.	Date of Assignment
109th	Maj-33rd	1	1	Jan. 26, 2005
110th	Min-27th	2	2	Jan. 10, 2007
111th	Min-18th	3	3	Jan. 9, 2009

3rd BUDGET
Dates: Jan. 26, 2005-Jan. 26, 2009
Departure: Resigned committee; moved to Permanent Select Intelligence

Cong.	Ranking	Terms in: House	Comm.	Date of Assignment
109th	Maj-22nd	1	1	Jan. 26, 2005
110th	Min-12th	2	2	Jan. 18, 2007
111th	Min-9th	3	3	Jan. 9, 2009

4th STANDARDS OF OFFICIAL CONDUCT
Dates: Jan. 9, 2009-date
Departure: Still serving in the 111th Congress

Cong.	Ranking	Terms in: House	Comm.	Date of Assignment
111th	Min-4th	3	1	Jan. 9, 2009

HOUSE SELECT AND SPECIAL COMMITTEES:

1st PERMANENT SELECT INTELLIGENCE
Dates: Feb. 4, 2009-date
Departure: Still serving in the 111th Congress

Cong.	Ranking	Terms in: House	Comm.	Date of Assignment
111th	Min-9th	3	1	Feb. 4, 2009

Gary A. Condit (D-Cal.)

Dates: April 21, 1948
House: Sept. 12, 1989-Jan. 3, 2003
Left the House: Defeated for re-nomination in 2002

H: Condit was elected to the 101st Congress by special election, Sept. 12, 1989, to fill the vacancy caused by the resignation of U.S. Representative Anthony L. Coelho (D-Cal.). Condit was seated Sept. 20, 1989, and assigned to committees.

HOUSE STANDING COMMITTEES:

1st AGRICULTURE
Dates: Oct. 16, 1989-Jan. 3, 2003
Departure: Left the House; lost re-nomination

Cong.	Ranking	Terms in: House	Comm.	Date of Assignment
103rd	Maj-14th	3	3	Jan. 5, 1993
104th	Min-7th	4	4	Jan. 4, 1995
105th	Min-3rd	5	5	Jan. 7, 1997
106th	Min-3rd	6	6	Jan. 6, 1999
107th	Min-2nd	7	7	Jan. 31, 2001

2nd GOVERNMENT OPERATIONS, 101-103
GOVERNMENT REFORM AND OVERSIGHT, 104-105
Dates: Oct. 16, 1989-Mar. 4, 1999
Departure: Leave of absence; had moved to Permanent Select Intelligence

Cong.	Ranking	Terms in: House	Comm.	Date of Assignment
103rd	Maj-10th	3	3	Jan. 5, 1993
104th	Min-10th	4	4	Jan. 9, 1995
105th	Min-7th	5	5	Jan. 7, 1997
106th	Min-7th	6	6	Jan. 6, 1999

HOUSE SELECT AND SPECIAL COMMITTEES:

1st PERMANENT SELECT INTELLIGENCE
Dates: Feb. 12, 1999-Jan. 3, 2003
Departure: Left the House; lost re-nomination

Cong.	Ranking	Terms in: House	Comm.	Date of Assignment
106th	Min-5th	6	1	Feb. 12, 1999
107th	Min-5th	7	2	Mar. 1, 2001

Gerald E. Connolly (D-Va.)

Dates: Mar. 30, 1950
House: Jan. 3, 2009-date
Serving in the 111th Congress

HOUSE STANDING COMMITTEES:

1st BUDGET
Dates: Jan. 21, 2009-date
Departure: Still serving in the 111th Congress

		Terms in:		Date of
Cong.	Ranking	House	Comm.	Assignment
111th	Maj-23rd	1	1	Jan. 21, 2009

2nd FOREIGN AFFAIRS
Dates: Jan. 21, 2009-date
Departure: Still serving in the 111th Congress

		Terms in:		Date of
Cong.	Ranking	House	Comm.	Assignment
111th	Maj-14th	1	1	Jan. 21, 2009

3rd OVERSIGHT AND GOVERNMENT REFORM
Dates: Jan. 28, 2009-date
Departure: Still serving in the 111th Congress

		Terms in:		Date of
Cong.	Ranking	House	Comm.	Assignment
111th	Maj-11th	1	1	Jan. 28, 2009

Kent Conrad (D-N.D.)

Dates: March 12, 1948
Senate 1: Jan. 3, 1987-Jan. 3, 1993
Left Senate 1: Retired and returned in other seat in 1992
Senate 2: Dec. 4, 1992-date
Serving in the 111th Congress

S: Conrad was first elected in 1986 to the 100th Congress and intended to resign at the end of the 102nd Congress. His seat was filled for the 103rd Congress by U.S. Representative Byron L. Dorgan (D-N.D.). However, North Dakota's other Senate seat fell vacant Sept. 8, 1992, following the death of U.S. Senator Quentin L. Burdick (D-N.D.). Burdick was initially replaced by his wife, Jocelyn B. Burdick (D-N.D.), an appointee, who was not a candidate for election. Conrad won the 1992 special election to fill the Burdick vacancy, thus his Senate service was uninterrupted.

SENATE STANDING COMMITTEES:

1st AGRICULTURE, NUTRITION AND FORESTRY
Dates: Jan. 6, 1987-date
Departure: Still serving in the 111th Congress

		Years in:		Date of
Cong.	Ranking	Senate	Comm.	Assignment
103rd	Maj-6th	7	7	Jan. 7, 1993
104th	Min-5th	9	8	Jan. 4, 1995
105th	Min-3rd	11	11	Jan. 9, 1997
106th	Min-3rd	13	13	Jan. 7, 1999
107th	Min-3rd	15	15	Jan. 25, 2001
+107th	Maj-3rd	15	15	June 6, 2001
108th	Min-3rd	17	17	Jan. 15, 2003
109th	Min-3rd	19	19	Jan. 6, 2005
110th	Maj-3rd	21	21	Jan. 12, 2007
111th	Maj-3rd	23	23	Jan. 21, 2009

2nd BUDGET
Dates: Jan. 6, 1987-date
Ch2: Replaced Pete V. Domenici (R-N.M.) on June 6, 2001, following Senate Party control shift
Departure: Still serving in the 111th Congress

		Years in:		Date of
Cong.	Ranking	Senate	Comm.	Assignment
103rd	Maj-8th	7	7	Jan. 21, 1993

104th	Min-6th	9	9	Jan. 6, 1995
105th	Min-3rd	11	11	Jan. 9, 1997
106th	Min-3rd	13	13	Jan. 7, 1999
=107th	Maj-ChT	15	14	Jan. 3, 2001
107th	Min-RM1	15	15	Jan. 25, 2001
+107th	Maj-Ch2	15	15	June 6, 2001
108th	Min-RM	17	17	Jan. 15, 2003
109th	Min-RM	19	19	Jan. 6, 2005
110th	Maj-Chr	21	21	Jan. 12, 2007
111th	Maj-Chr	23	23	Jan. 21, 2009

3rd ENERGY AND NATURAL RESOURCES
Dates: Jan. 6, 1987-Jan. 21, 1993
Departure: Moved to Finance

		Years in:		Date of
Cong.	Ranking	Senate	Comm.	Assignment
103rd	Maj-6th	7	7	Jan. 7, 1993

4th FINANCE
Dates: Jan. 21, 1993-date
Departure: Still serving in the 111th Congress

		Years in:		Date of
Cong.	Ranking	Senate	Comm.	Assignment
103rd	MjR-1st	7	1	Jan. 21, 1993
104th	Min-7th	9	2	Jan. 4, 1995
105th	Min-5th	11	4	Jan. 9, 1997
106th	Min-5th	13	6	Jan. 7, 1999
107th	Min-5th	15	9	Jan. 25, 2001
+107th	Maj-5th	15	9	June 6, 2001
108th	Min-5th	17	10	Jan. 15, 2003
109th	Min-3rd	19	12	Jan. 6, 2005
110th	Maj-3rd	21	14	Jan. 12, 2007
111th	Maj-3rd	23	17	Jan. 21, 2009

SENATE SELECT AND SPECIAL COMMITTEES:

1st SELECT INDIAN AFFAIRS (Permanent), 101-102
INDIAN AFFAIRS (Permanent), 104-111
1st Dates: Feb. 2, 1989-Jan. 21, 1993
1st Departure: Moved to Finance
2nd Dates: Jan. 9, 1995-date
2nd Departure: Still serving in the 111th Congress

		Years in:		Date of
Cong.	Ranking	Senate	Comm.	Assignment
104th	Min-2nd	9 *2	1	Jan. 9, 1995
105th	Min-2nd	11 *2	3	Jan. 9, 1997
106th	Min-2nd	13 *2	4	Jan. 7, 1999
107th	Min-2nd	15 *2	7	Jan. 25, 2001
+107th	Maj-2nd	15 *2	7	June 6, 2001
108th	Min-2nd	17 *2	9	Jan. 15, 2003
109th	Min-3rd	19 *2	10	Jan. 6, 2005
110th	Maj-3rd	21 *2	13	Jan. 12, 2007
111th	Maj-3rd	23 *2	15	Jan. 21, 2009

2nd SELECT ETHICS (Permanent)
Dates: Jan. 9, 1997-Jan. 25, 2001
Departure: Left committee; became Ranking Member on Budget

		Years in:		Date of
Cong.	Ranking	Senate	Comm.	Assignment
105th	Min-3rd	11	1	Jan. 9, 1997
106th	Min-2nd	13	2	Jan. 7, 1999

JOINT COMMITTEES:

1st JOINT DEFICIT REDUCTION (Temporary)
Senate Dates: Jan. 6, 1987-Sep. 29, 1987
Departure: Public Law 100-119 adjusted Gramm-Rudman-Hollings Act

2nd JOINT TAXATION
Senate Dates: Jan. 17, 2007-date
Departure: Still serving in the 111th Congress

Cong.	Ranking	Years in: Senate	Comm.	Date of Assignment
110th	Maj-3rd	21	1	Jan. 17, 2007
111th	Maj-3rd	23	3	Feb. 25, 2009

John Conyers Jr. (D-Mich.)

Dates: May 16, 1929
House: Jan. 3, 1965-date
Serving in the 111th Congress

HOUSE STANDING COMMITTEES:

1st JUDICIARY
Dates: Jan. 18, 1965-date
Departure: Still serving in the 111th Congress

Cong.	Ranking	Terms in: House	Comm.	Date of Assignment
103rd	Maj-3rd	15	15	Jan. 5, 1993
104th	Min-RM	16	16	Jan. 4, 1995
105th	Min-RM	17	17	Jan. 7, 1997
106th	Min-RM	18	18	Jan. 6, 1999
107th	Min-RM	19	19	Jan. 31, 2001
108th	Min-RM	20	20	Jan. 8, 2003
109th	Min-RM	21	21	Jan. 6, 2005
110th	Maj-Chr	22	22	Jan. 4, 2007
111th	Maj-Chr	23	23	Jan. 6, 2009

2nd GOVERNMENT OPERATIONS
Dates: Feb. 4, 1971-Jan. 3, 1995
Departure: Left committee; became Ranking Member on Judiciary

Cong.	Ranking	Terms in: House	Comm.	Date of Assignment
103rd	Maj-Chr	15	12	Jan. 5, 1993

3rd SMALL BUSINESS
Dates: Jan. 22, 1987-Jan. 3, 1995
Departure: Left committee; became Ranking Member on Judiciary

Cong.	Ranking	Terms in: House	Comm.	Date of Assignment
103rd	Maj-7th	15	4	Jan. 5, 1993

HOUSE SELECT AND SPECIAL COMMITTEES:

1st SELECT COMMITTEE ON THE SEATING OF ADAM CLAYTON POWELL
Dates: Jan. 19, 1967-Feb. 23, 1967
Termination: House Report 27 (90-1) filed

Merrill Cook (R-Utah)

Dates: May 6, 1946
House: Jan. 3, 1997-Jan. 3, 2001
Left the House: Defeated for re-nomination in 2000

HOUSE STANDING COMMITTEES:

1st BANKING AND FINANCIAL SERVICES
Dates: Jan. 7, 1997-Jan. 3, 2001
Departure: Left the House; lost re-nomination

Cong.	Ranking	Terms in: House	Comm.	Date of Assignment
105th	Maj-24th	1	1	Jan. 7, 1997
106th	Maj-20th	2	2	Jan. 6, 1999

2nd TRANSPORTATION AND INFRASTRUCTURE
Dates: Jan. 7, 1997-Jan. 3, 2001
Departure: Left the House; lost re-nomination

Cong.	Ranking	Terms in: House	Comm.	Date of Assignment
105th	Maj-32nd	1	1	Jan. 7, 1997
106th	Maj-26th	2	2	Jan. 6, 1999

3rd SCIENCE
Dates: Jan. 21, 1997-Jan. 3, 2001
Departure: Left the House; lost re-nomination

Cong.	Ranking	Terms in: House	Comm.	Date of Assignment
105th	Maj-21st	1	1	Jan. 21, 1997
106th	Maj-17th	2	2	Jan. 6, 1999

John Cooksey (R-La.)

Dates: Aug. 20, 1941
House: Jan. 3, 1997-Jan. 3, 2003
Left the House: Lost U.S. Senate nomination in 2002

HOUSE STANDING COMMITTEES:

1st AGRICULTURE
Dates: Jan. 7, 1997-Jan. 3, 2003
Departure: Left the House; lost Senate nomination

Cong.	Ranking	Terms in: House	Comm.	Date of Assignment
105th	Maj-27th	1	1	Jan. 7, 1997
106th	Maj-19th	2	2	Jan. 6, 1999
107th	Maj-13th	3	3	Jan. 6, 2001

2nd TRANSPORTATION AND INFRASTRUCTURE
Dates: Jan. 7, 1997-Apr. 17, 2002
Departure: Resigned committee; no new assignment

Cong.	Ranking	Terms in: House	Comm.	Date of Assignment
105th	Maj-33rd	1	1	Jan. 7, 1997
106th	Maj-27th	2	2	Jan. 6, 1999
107th	Maj-19th	3	3	Jan. 6, 2001

3rd VETERANS' AFFAIRS
Dates: Jan. 21, 1997-Jan. 3, 1999
Departure: Moved to International Relations

Cong.	Ranking	Terms in: House	Comm.	Date of Assignment
105th	Maj-12th	1	1	Jan. 21, 1997

4th INTERNATIONAL RELATIONS
Dates: Jan. 6, 1999-Jan. 3, 2003
Departure: Left the House; lost Senate nomination

Cong.	Ranking	Terms in: House	Comm.	Date of Assignment
106th	Maj-25th	2	1	Jan. 6, 1999
107th	Maj-17th	3	2	Jan. 6, 2001

Wes Cooley (R-Ore.)

Dates: March 28, 1932
House: Jan. 3, 1995-Jan. 3, 1997
Left the House: Retired in 1996

HOUSE STANDING COMMITTEES:

1st AGRICULTURE
Dates: Jan. 4, 1995-Jan. 3, 1997
Departure: Left the House; retired

Cong.	Ranking	Terms in: House	Comm.	Date of Assignment
104th	Maj-24th	1	1	Jan. 4, 1995

2nd RESOURCES
Dates: Jan. 4, 1995-Jan. 3, 1997
Departure: Left the House; retired

Cong.	Ranking	Terms in: House	Comm.	Date of Assignment
104th	Maj-16th	1	1	Jan. 4, 1995

3rd VETERANS' AFFAIRS
Dates: Jan. 4, 1995-Jan. 3, 1997
Departure: Left the House; retired

Cong.	Ranking	Terms in: House	Comm.	Date of Assignment
104th	Maj-18th	1	1	Jan. 4, 1995

James H.S. Cooper (D-Tenn.)

Dates: June 8, 1954
House 1: Jan. 3, 1983-Jan. 3, 1995
Left the House 1: Lost U.S. Senate election in 1994
House 2: Jan. 3, 2003-date
Serving in the 111th Congress

HOUSE STANDING COMMITTEES:

1st BANKING, FINANCE AND URBAN AFFAIRS
Dates: Jan. 6, 1983-Jan. 3, 1987
Departure: Moved to Energy and Commerce

2nd SMALL BUSINESS
Dates: Jan. 6, 1983-Jan. 3, 1991
Departure: Moved to Budget

3rd ENERGY AND COMMERCE
Dates: Jan. 22, 1987-Jan. 3, 1995
Departure: Left the House; lost Senate election

Cong.	Ranking	Terms in: House	Comm.	Date of Assignment
103rd	Maj-15th	6	4	Jan. 5, 1993

4th BUDGET
1st Dates: Jan. 24, 1991-Jan. 3, 1995
1st Departure: Left the House; lost Senate election
2nd Dates: Jan. 28, 2003-Jan. 3, 2009
2nd Departure: Left committee; no new assignment

Cong.	Ranking	Terms in: House	Comm.	Date of Assignment
103rd	Maj-12th	6	*1 2	Jan. 5, 1993

Cong.	Ranking	Terms in: House	Comm.	Date of Assignment
108th	Min-15th	7	*2 1	Jan. 28, 2003
109th	Min-9th	8	*2 2	Jan. 26, 2005
110th	Maj-5th	9	*2 3	Jan. 18, 2007

5th ARMED SERVICES
Dates: Feb. 5, 2003-date
Departure: Still serving in the 111th Congress

Cong.	Ranking	Terms in: House	Comm.	Date of Assignment
108th	Min-24th	7	1	Feb. 5, 2003
109th	Min-20th	8	2	Jan. 26, 2005
110th	Maj-18th	9	3	Jan. 10, 2007
111th	Maj-17th	10	4	Jan. 7, 2009

6th GOVERNMENT REFORM, 108
OVERSIGHT AND GOVERNMENT REFORM, 110-111
1st Dates: Feb. 13, 2003-Jan. 3, 2005
1st Departure: Left committee; no new assignment
2nd Dates: Jan. 12, 2007-date
2nd Departure: Still serving in the 111th Congress

Cong.	Ranking	Terms in: House	Comm.	Date of Assignment
108th	Min-19th	7 *1	1	Feb. 13, 2003
110th	Maj-18th	9 *2	1	Jan. 12, 2007
111th	Maj-10th	10 *2	2	Jan. 28, 2009

Samuel G. Coppersmith (D-Ariz.)

Dates: May 22, 1955
House: Jan. 3, 1993-Jan. 3, 1995
Left the House: Lost U.S. Senate election in 1994

HOUSE STANDING COMMITTEES:

1st PUBLIC WORKS AND TRANSPORTATION
Dates: Jan. 5, 1993-Jan. 3, 1995
Departure: Left the House; lost Senate election

Cong.	Ranking	Terms in: House	Comm.	Date of Assignment
103rd	Maj-26th	1	1	Jan. 5, 1993

2nd SCIENCE, SPACE AND TECHNOLOGY
Dates: Jan. 5, 1993-Jan. 3, 1995
Departure: Left the House; lost Senate election

Cong.	Ranking	Terms in: House	Comm.	Date of Assignment
103rd	Maj-25th	1	1	Jan. 5, 1993

Robert Corker (R-Tenn.)

Dates: Aug. 24, 1952
Senate: Jan. 3, 2007-date
Serving in the 111th Congress

SENATE STANDING COMMITTEES:

1st ENERGY AND NATURAL RESOURCES
Dates: Jan. 12, 2007-date
Departure: Still serving in the 111th Congress

Cong.	Ranking	Years in: Senate	Comm.	Date of Assignment
110th	Min-7th	1	1	Jan 12, 2007
111th	Min-10th	3	3	Jan. 21, 2009

2nd FOREIGN RELATIONS
Dates: Jan. 12, 2007-date
Departure: Still serving in the 111th Congress

Cong.	Ranking	Years in: Senate	Comm.	Date of Assignment
110th	Min-4th	1	1	Jan. 12, 2007
111th	Min-2nd	3	3	Jan. 21, 2009

3rd SMALL BUSINESS AND ENTREPRENEURSHIP
Dates: Jan. 12, 2007-Jan. 21, 2009
Departure: Left committee; no new assignment

Cong.	Ranking	Years in: Senate	Comm.	Date of Assignment
110th	Min-7th	1	1	Jan. 12, 2007

4th ARMED SERVICES
Dates: July 17, 2007-Jan. 24, 2008
Departure: Left committee; moved to Banking, Housing and Urban Affairs

Cong.	Ranking	Years in: Senate	Comm.	Date of Assignment
110th	MnR-1st	1	1	July 17, 2007

5th BANKING, HOUSING AND URBAN AFFAIRS
Dates: Jan. 24, 2008-date
Departure: Still serving in the 111th Congress

Cong.	Ranking	Years in: Senate	Comm.	Date of Assignment
110th	MnR-1st	2	1	Jan. 24, 2008
111th	Maj-6th	3	1	Jan. 21, 2009

SENATE SELECT AND SPECIAL COMMITTEES:

1st SPECIAL AGING (Permanent)
Dates: Jan. 12, 2007-date
Departure: Still serving in the 111th Congress
RM2: Succeeded Melquaides R. (Mel) Martinez (R-Fla.) as Ranking Member on Sep. 22, 2009.

Cong.	Ranking	Years in: Senate	Comm.	Date of Assignment
110th	Min-9th	1	1	Jan. 12, 2007
111th	Min-5th	3	3	Jan. 21, 2009
=111th	Min-RM2	3	3	Sep. 22, 2009

John Cornyn (R-Tex.)

Dates: Feb. 2, 1952-
Senate: Dec. 1, 2002-date
Serving in the 111th Congress

S: Cornyn was appointed to the 107th Congress, Dec. 1, 2002, to fill the vacancy caused by the resignation of U.S. Senator W. Phil Gramm (R-Tex.). Cornyn was not seated nor assigned to committees because the 107th Congress was not in session. Cornyn was elected to succeed Gramm in the 108th Congress.

SENATE STANDING COMMITTEES:

1st ARMED SERVICES
Dates: Jan. 15, 2003-Jan. 21, 2009
Departure: Moved to Finance

Cong.	Ranking	Years in: Senate	Comm.	Date of Assignment
108th	Maj-13th	1	1	Jan. 15, 2003
109th	Maj-12th	3	2	Jan. 6, 2005
110th	Min-10th	5	4	Jan. 12, 2007

2nd BUDGET
Dates: Jan. 15, 2003-date
Departure: Still serving in 111th Congress

Cong.	Ranking	Years in: Senate	Comm.	Date of Assignment
108th	Maj-12th	1	1	Jan. 15, 2003
109th	Maj-10th	3	2	Jan. 6, 2005
110th	Min-10th	5	4	Jan. 12, 2007
111th	Min-8th	7	7	Jan. 21, 2009

3rd ENVIRONMENT AND PUBLIC WORKS
Dates: Jan. 15, 2003-Jan. 6, 2005
Departure: Moved to Small Business and Entrepreneurship and Joint Economic

Cong.	Ranking	Years in: Senate	Comm.	Date of Assignment
108th	Maj-7th	1	1	Jan. 15, 2003

4th JUDICIARY
Dates: Jan. 15, 2003-date
Departure: Still serving in the 111th Congress

Cong.	Ranking	Years in: Senate	Comm.	Date of Assignment
108th	Maj-10th	1	1	Jan. 15, 2003
109th	Maj-8th	3	2	Jan. 6, 2005
110th	Min-7th	5	4	Jan. 12, 2007
111th	Min-7th	7	7	Jan. 21, 2009

5th SMALL BUSINESS AND ENTREPENEURSHIP
Dates: Jan. 6, 2005-Jan. 12, 2007
Departure: Moved to Select Ethics as Ranking Member

Cong.	Ranking	Years in: Senate	Comm.	Date of Assignment
109th	Maj-10th	3	1	Jan. 6, 2005

6th FINANCE
Dates: Jan. 21, 2009-date
Departure: Still serving in the 111th Congress

Cong.	Ranking	Years in: Senate	Comm.	Date of Assignment
111th	Min-10th	7	1	Jan. 21, 2009

7th AGRICULTURE, NUTRITION AND FORESTRY
Dates: Jan. 21, 2009-date
Departure: Still serving in the 111th Congress

Cong.	Ranking	Years in: Senate	Comm.	Date of Assignment
111th	Min-9th	7	1	Jan. 21, 2009

SENATE SELECT AND SPECIAL COMMITTEES:

1st SELECT ETHICS (Permanent)
Dates: Jan. 12, 2007-Jan. 21, 2009
Departure: Moved to Finance

Cong.	Ranking	Years in: Senate	Comm.	Date of Assignment
110th	Min-VCh	5	1	Jan. 12, 2007

JOINT COMMITTEES:

1st JOINT ECONOMIC
Senate Dates: Jan. 6, 2005-Jan. 12, 2007
Departure: Moved to Select Ethics as Ranking Member

Cong.	Ranking	Years in: Senate	Comm.	Date of Assignment
109th	Maj-6th	3	1	Jan. 6, 2005

Jon S. Corzine (D-N.J.)

Dates: Jan. 1, 1947
Senate: Jan. 3, 2001-Jan. 17, 2006
Left Senate: Resigned chamber; elected Governor in 2005

SENATE STANDING COMMITTEES:

1st BANKING, HOUSING AND URBAN AFFAIRS
Dates: Jan. 25, 2001-Jan. 17, 2006
Departure: Resigned the Senate; elected Governor

Cong.	Ranking	Years in: Senate	Comm.	Date of Assignment
107th	Min-10th	1	1	Jan. 25, 2001
+107th	Maj-10th	1	1	June 6, 2001
108th	Min-10th	3	2	Jan. 15, 2003
109th	Min-9th	5	4	Jan. 6, 2005

2nd ENVIRONMENT AND PUBLIC WORKS
Dates: Jan. 25, 2001-Jan. 15, 2003
Departure: Moved to Foreign Relations

Cong.	Ranking	Years in: Senate	Comm.	Date of Assignment
107th	Min-9th	1	1	Jan. 25, 2001
+107th	Maj-10th	1	1	July 10, 2001

3rd BUDGET
Dates: July 10, 2001-Jan. 17, 2006
Departure: Resigned the Senate; elected Governor

Cong.	Ranking	Years in: Senate	Comm.	Date of Assignment
+107th	MjA-12th	1	1	July 10, 2001
108th	Min-11th	3	2	Jan. 15, 2003
109th	Min-10th	5	4	Jan. 6, 2005

4th FOREIGN RELATIONS
Dates: Jan. 15, 2003-Jan. 6, 2005
Departure: Moved to Energy and Natural Resources and Select Intelligence

Cong.	Ranking	Years in: Senate	Comm.	Date of Assignment
108th	Min-9th	3	1	Jan. 15, 2003

5th ENERGY AND NATURAL RESOURCES
Dates: Jan. 6, 2005-Jan. 17, 2006
Departure: Resigned the Senate; elected Governor

Cong.	Ranking	Years in: Senate	Comm.	Date of Assignment
109th	Min-9th	5	1	Jan. 6, 2005

SENATE SELECT AND SPECIAL COMMITTEES:

1st SELECT INTELLIGENCE (Permanent)
Dates: Jan. 6, 2005-Jan. 17, 2006
Departure: Resigned the Senate; elected Governor

Cong.	Ranking	Years in: Senate	Comm.	Date of Assignment
109th	Min-7th	5	1	Jan. 6, 2005

JOINT COMMITTEES:

1st JOINT ECONOMIC
Senate Dates: Jan. 25, 2001-Jan. 15, 2003
Departure: Moved to Foreign Relations

Cong.	Ranking	Years in: Senate	Comm.	Date of Assignment
107th	Min-4th	1	1	Jan. 25, 2001
+107th	Maj-4th	1	1	June 6, 2001

Jim Costa (D-Cal.)

Dates: April 13, 1952
House: Jan. 3, 2005-date
Serving in the 111th Congress

HOUSE STANDING COMMITTEES:

1st AGRICULTURE
Dates: Jan. 26, 2005-date
Departure: Still serving in the 111th Congress

Cong.	Ranking	Terms in: House	Comm.	Date of Assignment
109th	Min-15th	1	1	Jan. 26, 2005
110th	Maj-12th	2	2	Jan. 12, 2007
111th	Maj-11th	3	3	Jan. 21, 2009

2nd RESOURCES, 109
NATURAL RESOURCES, 110-111
Dates: Jan. 26, 2005-date
Departure: Still serving in the 111th Congress

Cong.	Ranking	Terms in: House	Comm.	Date of Assignment
109th	Min-13th	1	1	Jan. 26, 2005
110th	Maj-12th	2	2	Jan. 18, 2007
111th	Maj-10th	3	3	Jan. 21, 2009

3rd SCIENCE
Dates: Feb. 2, 2005-Jan. 3, 2007
Departure: Moved to Foreign Affairs

Cong.	Ranking	Terms in: House	Comm.	Date of Assignment
109th	Min-18th	1	1	Feb. 2, 2005

4th FOREIGN AFFAIRS
Dates: Jan. 12, 2007-date
Departure: Still serving in the 111th Congress

Cong.	Ranking	Terms in: House	Comm.	Date of Assignment
110th	Maj-24th	2	1	Jan. 12, 2007
111th	Maj-25th	3	2	Jan. 21, 2009

Jerry F. Costello (D-Ill.)

Dates: Sept. 25, 1949
House: Aug. 9, 1988-date
Serving in the 111th Congress

H: Costello was elected to the 100th Congress by special election, Aug. 9,1988, to fill the vacancy caused by the death of U.S. Representative C. Melvin Price (D-Ill.). Costello was seated Aug. 11, 1988, and assigned to committees.

HOUSE STANDING COMMITTEES:

1st PUBLIC WORKS AND TRANSPORTATION, 100-103
TRANSPORTATION AND INFRASTRUCTURE, 104-111
Dates: Oct. 6, 1988-date
Departure: Still serving in the 111th Congress

Cong.	Ranking	Terms in: House	Comm.	Date of Assignment
103rd	Maj-14th	4	4	Jan. 5, 1993
104th	Min-11th	5	5	Jan. 4, 1995
105th	Min-9th	6	6	Jan. 7, 1997
106th	Min-9th	7	7	Jan. 6, 1999
107th	Min-7th	8	8	Jan. 31, 2001
108th	Min-5th	9	9	Jan. 28, 2003
109th	Min-4th	10	10	Jan. 26, 2005
110th	Maj-4th	11	11	Jan. 10, 2007
111th	Maj-4th	12	12	Jan. 7, 2009

2nd SCIENCE, SPACE AND TECHNOLOGY, 101-102
SCIENCE, 106-109
SCIENCE AND TECHNOLOGY, 110-111
1st Dates: Jan. 19, 1989-Jan. 3, 1993
1st Departure: Moved to Budget
2nd Dates: Jan. 6, 1999-date
2nd Departure: Still serving in the 111th Congress

Cong.	Ranking	Terms in: House	Comm.	Date of Assignment
106th	Min-5th	7	*2 1	Jan. 6, 1999
107th	Min-3rd	8	*2 2	Jan. 31, 2001
108th	Min-3rd	9	*2 3	Jan. 28, 2003
109th	Min-2nd	10	*2 4	Jan. 26, 2005
110th	Maj-2nd	11	*2 5	Jan. 18, 2007
111th	Maj-2nd	12	*2 6	Jan. 21, 2009

3rd BUDGET
Dates: Jan. 5, 1993-Jan. 3, 1999
Departure: Returned to Science

Cong.	Ranking	Terms in: House	Comm.	Date of Assignment
103rd	Maj-21st	4	1	Jan. 5, 1993
104th	Min-7th	5	2	Jan. 4, 1995
105th	Min-4th	6	3	Jan. 7, 1997

HOUSE SELECT AND SPECIAL COMMITTEES:

1st SELECT AGING (Permanent)
Dates: Oct. 3, 1988-Jan. 3, 1993
Termination: Committee not renewed in 1993

Joe Courtney (D-Conn.)

Dates: April 6, 1953
House: Jan. 3, 2007-date
Serving in the 111th Congress

HOUSE STANDING COMMITTEES:

1st ARMED SERVICES
Dates: Jan. 10, 2007-date
Departure: Still serving in the 111th Congress

Cong.	Ranking	Terms in: House	Comm.	Date of Assignment
110th	Maj-28th	1	1	Jan. 10, 2007
111th	Maj-25th	2	2	Jan. 7, 2009

2nd EDUCATION AND LABOR
Dates: Jan. 10, 2007-date
Departure: Still serving in the 111th Congress

Cong.	Ranking	Terms in: House	Comm.	Date of Assignment
110th	Maj-26th	1	1	Jan. 10, 2007
111th	Maj-22nd	2	2	Jan. 21, 2009

Paul Coverdell (R-Ga.)

Dates: Jan. 20, 1939-July 18, 2000
Senate: Jan. 3, 1993-July 18, 2000
Left Senate: Died in office

SENATE STANDING COMMITTEES:

1st AGRICULTURE, NUTRITION AND FORESTRY
Dates: Jan. 7, 1993-July 18, 2000
Departure: Died in office

Cong.	Ranking	Years in: Senate	Comm.	Date of Assignment
103rd	Min-7th	1	1	Jan. 7, 1993
104th	Maj-7th	3	2	Jan. 4, 1995
105th	Maj-5th	5	5	Jan. 9, 1997
106th	Maj-5th	7	7	Jan. 7, 1999

2nd FOREIGN RELATIONS
Dates: Jan. 7, 1993-Nov. 9, 1999
Departure: Left committee; moved to Finance

Cong.	Ranking	Years in: Senate	Comm.	Date of Assignment
103rd	Min-8th	1	1	Jan. 7, 1993
104th	Maj-5th	3	2	Jan. 5, 1995
105th	Maj-3rd	5	5	Jan. 9, 1997
106th	Maj-3rd	7	7	Jan. 7, 1999

3rd SMALL BUSINESS
Dates: Jan. 7, 1993-July 18, 2000
Departure: Died in office

Cong.	Ranking	Years in: Senate	Comm.	Date of Assignment
103rd	Min-6th	1	1	Jan. 21, 1993
104th	Maj-5th	3	2	Jan. 6, 1995
105th	Maj-3rd	5	5	Jan. 9, 1997
106th	Maj-3rd	7	6	Jan. 7, 1999

4th FINANCE
Dates: Nov. 9, 1999-July 18, 2000
Departure: Died in office

Cong.	Ranking	Years in: Senate	Comm.	Date of Assignment
106th	MjR-1st	7	1	Nov. 9, 1999

SENATE SELECT AND SPECIAL COMMITTEES:

1st INDIAN AFFAIRS (Permanent)
Dates: Jan. 11, 1995-Mar. 24, 1995
Departure: Resigned committee to open seat for Campbell

Cong.	Ranking	Years in: Senate	Comm.	Date of Assignment
104th	Maj-9th	3	1	Jan. 11, 1995

C. Christopher Cox (R-Cal.)

Dates: Oct. 16, 1952
House: Jan. 3, 1989-Aug. 2, 2005
Left the House: Resigned chamber; appointed Chair of the Securities and Exchange Commission in 2005

HOUSE STANDING COMMITTEES:

1st GOVERNMENT OPERATIONS, 101-103
GOVERNMENT REFORM AND OVERSIGHT, 105
GOVERNMENT REFORM, 106
1st Dates: Jan. 20, 1989-Jan. 3, 1995
1st Departure: Moved to Commerce
2nd Dates: Jan. 7, 1997-Jan. 19, 1999
2nd Departure: Resigned committee; became Chair of Select National Security Concerns with China

Cong.	Ranking	Terms in: House	Comm.	Date of Assignment
103rd	Min-7th	3	*1 3	Jan. 5, 1993
105th	Maj-7th	5	*2 1	Jan. 7, 1997
106th	Maj-5th	6	*2 2	Jan. 6, 1999

2nd PUBLIC WORKS AND TRANSPORTATION
Dates: Jan. 20, 1989-Jan. 3, 1993
Departure: Moved to Budget

3rd BUDGET
Dates: Jan. 5, 1993-Jan. 3, 1995
Departure: Moved to Commerce

Cong.	Ranking	Terms in: House	Comm.	Date of Assignment
103rd	Min-9th	3	1	Jan. 5, 1993

4th COMMERCE, 104-106
ENERGY AND COMMERCE, 107-108
Dates: Jan. 4, 1995-Jan. 3, 2005
Departure: Left committee; no new assignment

Cong.	Ranking	Terms in: House	Comm.	Date of Assignment
104th	Maj-17th	4	1	Jan. 4, 1995
105th	Maj-15th	5	2	Jan. 7, 1997
106th	Maj-10th	6	3	Jan. 6, 1999
107th	Maj-8th	7	4	Jan. 6, 2001
108th	Maj-8th	8	5	Jan. 28, 2003

5th FINANCIAL SERVICES
Dates: Jan. 6, 2001-Jan. 3, 2003
Departure: Moved to Select Homeland Security as Chair

Cong.	Ranking	Terms in: House	Comm.	Date of Assignment
107th	Maj-16th	7	1	Jan. 6, 2001

6th HOMELAND SECURITY
Dates: Jan. 6, 2005-Aug. 2, 2005
Ch1: Replaced by Peter T. King (R-N.Y.) on Sep. 15, 2005
Departure: Resigned the House; became Chair of the Securities and Exchange Commission

Cong.	Ranking	Terms in: House	Comm.	Date of Assignment
109th	Maj-Ch1	9	2	Jan. 6, 2005

HOUSE SELECT AND SPECIAL COMMITTEES:

1st SELECT NATIONAL SECURITY CONCERNS WITH CHINA
Dates: June 22, 1998-Apr. 30, 1999
Termination: House Report 851 (105-2) filed Jan. 3, 1999

Cong.	Ranking	Terms in: House	Comm.	Date of Assignment
105th	Maj-Chr	5	1	June 22, 1998
106th	Maj-Chr	6	2	Jan. 19, 1999

2nd SELECT HOMELAND SECURITY
Dates: Feb. 12, 2003-Jan. 3, 2005
Departure: Remained on reorganized standing committee

Cong.	Ranking	Terms in: House	Comm.	Date of Assignment
108th	Maj-Chr	8	1	Feb. 12, 2003

JOINT COMMITTEES:

1st JOINT ECONOMIC
House Dates: Feb. 16, 1993-Jan. 3, 1995
Departure: Moved to Commerce

Cong.	Ranking	Terms in: House	Comm.	Date of Assignment
103rd	Min-3rd	3	1	Feb. 16, 1993

William J. Coyne (D-Penn.)

Dates: Aug. 24, 1936
House: Jan. 3, 1981-Jan. 3, 2003
Left the House: Retired in 2002

HOUSE STANDING COMMITTEES:

1st BANKING, FINANCE AND URBAN AFFAIRS
Dates: Jan. 28, 1981-Jan. 3, 1985
Departure: Moved to Ways and Means

2nd HOUSE ADMINISTRATION
Dates: Jan. 28, 1981-Jan. 3, 1985
Departure: Moved to Ways and Means

3rd STANDARDS OF OFFICIAL CONDUCT
Dates: Jan. 6, 1983-Jan. 3, 1987
Departure: Left committee; no new assignment

4th WAYS AND MEANS
Dates: Jan. 30, 1985-Jan. 3, 2003
Departure: Left the House; retired

Cong.	Ranking	Terms in: House	Comm.	Date of Assignment
103rd	Maj-10th	7	5	Jan. 5, 1993
104th	Min-8th	8	6	Jan. 4, 1995
105th	Min-5th	9	7	Jan. 7, 1997
106th	Min-4th	10	8	Jan. 6, 1999
107th	Min-4th	11	9	Jan. 31, 2001

5th BUDGET
Dates: Jan. 5, 1993-Jan. 3, 1997
Departure: Left committee; no new assignment

Cong.	Ranking	Terms in: House	Comm.	Date of Assignment
103rd	Maj-15th	7	1	Jan. 5, 1993
104th	Min-5th	8	2	Jan. 4, 1995

JOINT COMMITTEES:

1st JOINT LIBRARY
House Dates: Feb. 5, 1981-Jan. 3, 1985
Departure: Left committee when departed House Administration

Larry E. Craig (R-Ida.)

Dates: July 20, 1945
House: Jan. 3, 1981-Jan. 3, 1991
Left the House: Elected to the U.S. Senate in 1990
Senate: Jan. 3, 1991-Jan. 3, 2009
Left Senate: Left chamber; retired in 2008

HOUSE STANDING COMMITTEES:

1st EDUCATION AND LABOR
Dates: Jan. 28, 1981-Mar. 2, 1983
Departure: Moved to Government Operations

2nd INTERIOR AND INSULAR AFFAIRS
Dates: Jan. 28, 1981-Jan. 3, 1991
Departure: Left the House for the Senate

3rd GOVERNMENT OPERATIONS
Dates: Mar. 1, 1983-Jan. 3, 1989
Departure: Moved to Public Works and Transportation

4th STANDARDS OF OFFICIAL CONDUCT
Dates: Jan. 21, 1987-Jan. 3, 1991
Departure: Left the House for the Senate

5th PUBLIC WORKS AND TRANSPORTATION
Dates: Jan. 20, 1989-Jan. 3, 1991
Departure: Left the House for the Senate

HOUSE SELECT AND SPECIAL COMMITTEES:

1st SELECT AGING (Permanent)
Dates: Feb. 5, 1981-Jan. 3, 1985
Departure: Left committee; no new assignment

SENATE STANDING COMMITTEES:

1st AGRICULTURE, NUTRITION AND FORESTRY
Dates: Feb. 5, 1991-Jan. 3, 2001
Departure: Left committee; became Chair of Special Aging

Cong.	Ranking	Years in: Senate	Comm.	Date of Assignment
103rd	Min-6th	3	2	Jan. 7, 1993
104th	Maj-6th	5	4	Jan. 9, 1995
105th	Maj-10th	7	6	Jan. 9, 1997
106th	Maj-9th	9	8	Jan. 7, 1999

2nd ENERGY AND NATURAL RESOURCES
Dates: Feb. 5, 1991-Jan. 3, 2009
Departure: Left the Senate; retired

Cong.	Ranking	Years in: Senate	Comm.	Date of Assignment
103rd	Min-6th	3	2	Jan. 7, 1993
104th	Maj-5th	5	4	Jan. 5, 1995
105th	Maj-4th	7	6	Jan. 9, 1997
106th	Maj-4th	9	8	Jan. 7, 1999
107th	Maj-4th	11	10	Jan. 25, 2001
+107th	Min-4th	11	11	June 6, 2001
108th	Maj-3rd	13	12	Jan. 15, 2003
109th	Maj-2nd	15	14	Jan. 6, 2005
110th	Min-2nd	17	16	Jan. 12, 2007

3rd VETERANS' AFFAIRS
Dates: Jan. 6, 1995-Jan. 3, 2009
Departure: Left the Senate; retired

Cong.	Ranking	Years in: Senate	Comm.	Date of Assignment
104th	Maj-6th	5	1	Jan. 6, 1995
105th	Maj-6th	7	3	Jan. 9, 1997
106th	Maj-6th	9	5	Jan. 7, 1999
107th	Maj-6th	11	7	Jan. 25, 2001
+107th	Min-5th	11	7	July 10, 2001
108th	Maj-3rd	13	9	Jan. 15, 2003
109th	Maj-Chr	15	11	Jan. 6, 2005
110th	Min-RM	17	13	Jan. 12, 2007

4th APPROPRIATIONS
Dates: Jan. 9, 1997-Jan. 3, 2009
Departure: Left the Senate; retired

Cong.	Ranking	Years in: Senate	Comm.	Date of Assignment
105th	Maj-13th	7	1	Jan. 9, 1997
106th	Maj-13th	9	2	Jan. 7, 1999
107th	Maj-12th	11	5	Jan. 25, 2001
+107th	Min-12th	11	5	June 6, 2001
108th	Maj-12th	13	7	Jan. 15, 2003
109th	Maj-11th	15	8	Jan. 6, 2005
110th	Min-10th	17	11	Jan. 12, 2007

5th FINANCE
Dates: Sep. 12, 2000-Jan. 25, 2001
Departure: Left committee; became Chair of Special Aging

Cong.	Ranking	Years in: Senate	Comm.	Date of Assignment
106th	MjR-2nd	10	1	Sep. 12, 2000

6th JUDICIARY
Dates: Jan. 15, 2003-Jan. 6, 2005
Departure: Left committee; became Chair of Veterans' Affairs

Cong.	Ranking	Years in: Senate	Comm.	Date of Assignment
108th	Maj-8th	13	1	Jan. 15, 2003

7th ENVIRONMENT AND PUBLIC WORKS
Dates: Jan. 12, 2007-Jan. 3, 2009
Departure: Left Senate; retired

Cong.	Ranking	Years in: Senate	Comm.	Date of Assignment
110th	Min-6th	17	1	Jan. 12, 2007

SENATE SELECT AND SPECIAL COMMITTEES:

1st SPECIAL AGING (Permanent)
Dates: Mar. 19, 1991-Jan. 3, 2009
Ch1: Replaced by John B. Breaux (D-La.) on June 6, 2001, following Senate party control shift and became RM2
Departure: Left Senate; retired.

Cong.	Ranking	Years in: Senate	Comm.	Date of Assignment
103rd	Min-8th	3	2	Jan. 21, 1993
104th	Maj-6th	5	4	Jan. 11, 1995
105th	Maj-3rd	7	6	Jan. 9, 1997
106th	Maj-3rd	9	8	Jan. 7, 1999
107th	Maj-Ch1	11	11	Jan. 25, 2001
+107th	Min-RM2	12	12	July 24, 2001
108th	Maj-Chr	13	12	Jan. 15, 2003

Cong.	Ranking			Date of
109th	Maj-7th	15	14	Jan. 6, 2005
110th	Min-5th	17	16	Jan. 12, 2007

2nd SELECT ETHICS (Permanent)
Dates: May 19, 1993-Jan. 9, 1997
Departure: Moved to Appropriations

		Years in:		Date of
Cong.	Ranking	Senate	Comm.	Assignment
103rd	MnR-1st	3	1	May 19, 1993
104th	Maj-3rd	5	2	Jan. 11, 1995

JOINT COMMITTEES:

1st JOINT ECONOMIC
Senate Dates: Jan. 21, 1993-Jan. 9, 1997
Departure: Moved to Appropriations

		Years in:		Date of
Cong.	Ranking	Senate	Comm.	Assignment
103rd	Min-3rd	3	1	Jan. 21, 1993
104th	Maj-3rd	5	2	Jan. 9, 1995

Robert E. (Bud) Cramer Jr. (D-Ala.)

Dates: Aug. 22, 1947
House: Jan. 3, 1991-Jan. 3, 2009
Left the House: Retired in 2008

HOUSE STANDING COMMITTEES:

1st PUBLIC WORKS AND TRANSPORTATION, 102-103
TRANSPORTATION AND INFRASTRUCTURE, 104-105
Dates: Jan. 24, 1991-Nov. 7, 1997
Departure: Resigned committee; moved to Appropriations

		Terms in:		Date of
Cong.	Ranking	House	Comm.	Assignment
103rd	Maj-21st	2	2	Jan. 5, 1993
104th	Min-15th	3	3	Jan. 4, 1995
105th	Min-11th	4	4	Jan. 7, 1997

2nd SCIENCE, SPACE AND TECHNOLOGY, 102-103
SCIENCE, 104-105
Dates: Jan. 24, 1991-Nov. 7, 1997
Departure: Resigned committee; moved to Appropriations

		Terms in:		Date of
Cong.	Ranking	House	Comm.	Assignment
103rd	Maj-17th	2	2	Jan. 5, 1993
104th	Min-8th	3	3	Jan. 4, 1995
105th	Min-6th	4	4	Feb. 13, 1997

3rd APPROPRIATIONS
Dates: Nov. 13, 1997-Jan. 3, 2009
Departure: Left the House; retired

		Terms in:		Date of
Cong.	Ranking	House	Comm.	Assignment
105th	MnR-1st	4	1	Nov. 13, 1997
106th	Min-20th	5	2	Jan. 6, 1999
107th	Min-19th	6	3	Jan. 31, 2001
108th	Min-17th	7	4	Jan. 28, 2003
109th	Min-17th	8	5	Jan. 26, 2005
110th	Maj-15th	9	6	Jan. 4, 2007

HOUSE SELECT AND SPECIAL COMMITTEES:

1st SELECT CHILDREN, YOUTH AND FAMILIES (Temporary)
Dates: Feb. 21, 1991-Jan. 3, 1993
Termination: Committee not renewed in 1993

2nd PERMANENT SELECT INTELLIGENCE
1st Dates: Feb. 3, 1993-Jan. 3, 1995
1st Departure: Left committee; no new assignment
2nd Dates: Apr. 11, 2002-Jan. 3, 2009
2nd Departure: Left the House; retired

		Terms in:		Date of
Cong.	Ranking	House	Comm.	Assignment
103rd	Maj-11th	2 *1	1	Feb. 3, 1993
107th	MnR-2nd	6 *2	1	Apr. 11, 2002
108th	Min-6th	7 *2	2	Jan. 8, 2003
109th	Min-5th	8 *2	3	Jan. 26, 2005
110th	Maj-4th	9 *2	4	Jan. 17, 2007

Philip M. Crane (R-Ill.)

Dates: Nov. 3, 1930
House: Nov. 25, 1969-Jan. 3, 2005
Left the House: Defeated for re-election in 2004

H: Crane was elected to the 91st Congress by special election, Nov. 25, 1969, to fill the vacancy caused by the resignation of U.S. Representative Donald Rumsfeld (R-Ill.). Crane was seated Dec. 1, 1969, and assigned to committees.

HOUSE STANDING COMMITTEES:

1st BANKING AND CURRENCY
Dates: Dec. 23, 1969-Jan. 3, 1975
Departure: Moved to Ways and Means

2nd HOUSE ADMINISTRATION
Dates: Dec. 23, 1969-Jan. 3, 1975
Departure: Moved to Ways and Means

3rd WAYS AND MEANS
Dates: Jan. 23, 1975-Jan. 3, 2005
Departure: Left the House; lost re-election

		Terms in:		Date of
Cong.	Ranking	House	Comm.	Assignment
103rd	Min-2nd	13	10	Jan. 5, 1993
104th	Maj-2nd	14	11	Jan. 4, 1995
105th	Maj-2nd	15	12	Jan. 7, 1997
106th	Maj-2nd	16	13	Jan. 6, 1999
107th	Maj-2nd	17	14	Jan. 6, 2001
108th	Maj-2nd	18	15	Jan. 28, 2003

HOUSE SELECT AND SPECIAL COMMITTEES:

1st HOUSE RECORDING STUDIO
Dates: Feb. 1, 1971-Jan. 3, 1979
Departure: Left committee; no new assignment

JOINT COMMITTEES:

1st JOINT TAXATION
House Dates: Mar. 18, 1993-Jan. 3, 2005
Departure: Left the House; lost re-election

		Terms in:		Date of
Cong.	Ranking	House	Comm.	Assignment
103rd	Min-2nd	13	1	Jan. 5, 1993 Ltr
104th	Maj-2nd	14	2	Jan. 10, 1995 Ltr
105th	Maj-2nd	15	3	Feb. 5, 1997 Ltr
106th	Maj-2nd	16	4	Jan. 6, 1999 Ltr
107th	Maj-2nd	17	5	Feb. 7, 2001 Ltr
108th	Maj-2nd	18	6	Jan. 29, 2003 Ltr

Michael D. Crapo (R-Ida.)

Dates: May 20, 1951
House: Jan. 3, 1993-Jan. 3, 1999
Left the House: Elected to the U.S. Senate in 1998
Senate: Jan. 3, 1999-date
Serving in the 111th Congress

HOUSE STANDING COMMITTEES:

1st ENERGY AND COMMERCE, 103
COMMERCE, 104-105
Dates: Jan. 5, 1993-Jan. 3, 1999
Departure: Left the House for the Senate

		Terms in:		Date of
Cong.	Ranking	House	Comm.	Assignment
103rd	Min-17th	1	1	Jan. 5, 1993
104th	Maj-16th	2	2	Jan. 4, 1995
105th	Maj-14th	3	3	Jan. 7, 1997

2nd AGRICULTURE
Dates: Jan. 4, 1995-Jan. 3, 1997
Departure: Moved to Resources

		Terms in:		Date of
Cong.	Ranking	House	Comm.	Assignment
104th	Maj-18th	2	1	Jan. 4, 1995

3rd RESOURCES
Dates: Jan. 21, 1997-Jan. 3, 1999
Departure: Left the House for the Senate

		Terms in:		Date of
Cong.	Ranking	House	Comm.	Assignment
105th	Maj-27th	3	1	Jan. 21, 1997

SENATE STANDING COMMITTEES:

1st BANKING, HOUSING AND URBAN AFFAIRS
Dates: Jan. 7, 1999-date
Departure: Still serving in the 111th Congress

		Years in:		Date of
Cong.	Ranking	Senate	Comm.	Assignment
106th	Maj-11th	1	1	Jan. 7, 1999
107th	Maj-9th	3	3	Jan. 25, 2001
+107th	Min-9th	3	3	June 6, 2001
108th	Maj-8th	5	5	Jan. 15, 2003
109th	Maj-8th	7	6	Jan. 6, 2005
110th	Min-7th	9	9	Jan. 12, 2007
111th	Min-4th	11	11	Jan. 21, 2009

2nd ENVIRONMENT AND PUBLIC WORKS
1st Dates: Jan. 7, 1999-Jan. 6, 2005
1st Departure: Moved to Finance and Indian Affairs
2nd Dates: Jan. 21, 2009-date
2nd Departure: Still serving in the 111th Congress

		Years in:		Date of
Cong.	Ranking	Senate	Comm.	Assignment
106th	Maj-8th	1 *1	1	Jan. 7, 1999
107th	Maj-6th	3 *1	3	Jan. 25, 2001
+107th	Min-6th	3 *1	3	June 6, 2001
108th	Maj-5th	5 *1	5	Jan. 15, 2003
111th	Min-6th	11 *2	1	Jan. 21, 2009

3rd SMALL BUSINESS renamed June 29, 2001
SMALL BUSINESS AND ENTREPRENEURSHIP
Dates: Jan. 7, 1999-Jan. 6, 2005
Departure: Moved to Finance and Indian Affairs

		Years in:		Date of
Cong.	Ranking	Senate	Comm.	Assignment
106th	Maj-8th	1	1	Jan. 7, 1999
107th	Maj-7th	3	3	Jan. 25, 2001
+107th	Min-7th	3	3	June 6, 2001
108th	Maj-7th	5	5	Jan. 15, 2003

4th AGRICULTURE, NUTRITION AND FORESTRY
Dates: Jan. 25, 2001-Jan. 21, 2009
Departure: Returned to Environment and Public Works

		Years in:		Date of
Cong.	Ranking	Senate	Comm.	Assignment
107th	Maj-10th	3	1	Jan. 25, 2001
+107th	Min-10th	3	1	June 6, 2001
108th	Maj-8th	5	2	Jan. 15, 2003
109th	Maj-10th	7	4	Jan. 6, 2005
110th	Min-8th	9	6	Jan. 12, 2007

5th BUDGET
Dates: Jan. 15, 2003-date
Departure: Still serving in the 111th Congress

		Years in:		Date of
Cong.	Ranking	Senate	Comm.	Assignment
108th	Maj-10th	5	1	Jan. 15, 2003
109th	Maj-8th	7	2	Jan. 6, 2005
110th	Min-8th	9	4	Jan. 12, 2007
111th	Min-6th	11	7	Jan. 21, 2009

6th FINANCE
Dates: Jan. 6, 2005-date
Departure: Still serving in the 111th Congress

		Years in:		Date of
Cong.	Ranking	Senate	Comm.	Assignment
109th	Maj-11th	7	1	Jan. 6, 2005
110th	Min-9th	9	3	Jan. 12, 2007
111th	Min-6th	11	5	Jan. 21, 2009

SENATE SELECT AND SPECIAL COMMITTEES:

1st INDIAN AFFAIRS (Permanent)
1st Dates: Jan. 6, 2005-Jan. 12, 2007
1st Departure: Left committee; no new assignment
2nd Dates: Jan. 21, 2009-date
2nd Departure: Still serving in the 111th Congress

		Years in:		Date of
Cong.	Ranking	Senate	Comm.	Assignment
109th	Maj-7th	7	*1 1	Jan. 6, 2005
111th	Min-5th	11	*2 1	Jan. 21, 2009

JOINT COMMITTEES:

1st JOINT ECONOMIC
Dates: Jan. 25, 2001-Jan. 15, 2003
Departure: Moved to Budget

		Years in:		Date of
Cong.	Ranking	Senate	Comm.	Assignment
107th	Maj-4th	3	1	Jan. 25, 2001
+107th	Min-4th	3	1	June 6, 2001

Frank A. Cremeans (R-Ohio)

Dates: April 5, 1943-Jan. 2, 2003
House: Jan. 3, 1995-Jan. 3, 1997
Left the House: Defeated for re-election in 1996

HOUSE STANDING COMMITTEES:

1st BANKING AND FINANCIAL SERVICES
Dates: Jan. 4, 1995-Jan. 3, 1997
Departure: Left the House; lost re-election

		Terms in:		Date of
Cong.	Ranking	House	Comm.	Assignment
104th	Maj-21st	1	1	Jan. 4, 1995

2nd RESOURCES
Dates: Jan. 4, 1995-Jan. 3, 1997
Departure: Left the House; lost re-election

Cong.	Ranking	Terms in: House	Comm.	Date of Assignment
104th	Maj-14th	1	1	Jan. 4, 1995

Ander Crenshaw (R-Fla.)

Dates: Sept. 1, 1944
House: Jan. 3, 2001-date
Serving in the 111th Congress

HOUSE STANDING COMMITTEES:

1st ARMED SERVICES
Dates: Jan. 6, 2001-Jan. 3, 2003
Departure: Moved to Appropriations

Cong.	Ranking	Terms in: House	Comm.	Date of Assignment
107th	Maj-28th	1	1	Jan. 6, 2001

2nd BUDGET
Dates: Jan. 6, 2001-Jan. 3, 2007
Departure: Left committee; no new assignment

Cong.	Ranking	Terms in: House	Comm.	Date of Assignment
107th	Maj-21st	1	1	Jan. 6, 2001
108th	Maj-11th	2	2	Jan. 31, 2003
109th	Maj-4th	3	3	Feb. 2, 2005

3rd VETERANS' AFFAIRS
Dates: Jan. 6, 2001-Jan. 3, 2003
Departure: Moved to Appropriations

Cong.	Ranking	Terms in: House	Comm.	Date of Assignment
107th	Maj-16th	1	1	Jan. 6, 2001

4th APPROPRIATIONS
Dates: Jan. 28, 2003-date
Departure: Still serving in the 111th Congress

Cong.	Ranking	Terms in: House	Comm.	Date of Assignment
108th	Maj-36th	2	1	Jan. 28, 2003
109th	Maj-34th	3	2	Jan. 6, 2005
110th	Min-26th	4	3	Jan. 4, 2007
111th	Min-16th	5	4	Jan. 9, 2009

Mark S. Critz (D-Penn.)

Dates: Jan. 5, 1962
House: May 18, 2010-date
Serving in the 111th Congress

H. Critz was elected to the 111th Congress by special election, May 18, 2010, to fill the vacancy caused by the death of U.S. Representative John P. Murtha, Jr. (D-Penn.). Critz was seated and assigned to committees.

Joseph Crowley (D-N.Y.)

Dates: March 16, 1962
House: Jan. 3, 1999-date
Serving in the 111th Congress

1st INTERNATIONAL RELATIONS, 106-109
FOREIGN AFFAIRS, 110-111
1st Dates: Jan. 6, 1999-Jan. 3, 2007
1st Departure: Moved to Ways and Means; returned on Apr. 19, 2007
2nd Dates: Apr. 19, 2007-date
2nd Departure: Still serving in the 111th Congress

Cong.	Ranking	Terms in: House	Comm.	Date of Assignment
106th	Min-18th	1 *1	1	Jan. 6, 1999
107th	Min-18th	2 *1	2	Jan. 31, 2001
108th	Min-14th	3 *1	3	Jan. 28, 2003
109th	Min-14th	4 *1	4	Jan. 26, 2005
110th	Maj-19th	5 *2	1	Apr. 19, 2007
111th	Maj-21st	6 *2	2	Jan. 21, 2009

2nd RESOURCES
Dates: Jan. 6, 1999-Jan. 3, 2001
Departure: Moved to Financial Services

Cong.	Ranking	Terms in: House	Comm.	Date of Assignment
106th	Min-24th	1	1	Jan. 6, 1999

3rd FINANCIAL SERVICES
Dates: Feb. 8, 2001-Jan. 3, 2007
Departure: Moved to Ways and Means

Cong.	Ranking	Terms in: House	Comm.	Date of Assignment
107th	Min-29th	2	1	Feb. 8, 2001
108th	Min-22nd	3	2	Jan. 28, 2003
109th	Min-19th	4	3	Jan. 26, 2005

4th WAYS AND MEANS
Dates: Jan. 4, 2007-date
Departure: Still serving in the 111th Congress

Cong.	Ranking	Terms in: House	Comm.	Date of Assignment
110th	Maj-20th	5	1	Jan. 4, 2007
111th	Maj-17th	6	2	Jan. 7, 2009

Barbara L. Cubin (R-Wyo.)

Dates: Nov. 30, 1946
House: Jan. 3, 1995-Jan. 3, 2009
Left the House: Retired in 2008

HOUSE STANDING COMMITTEES:

1st RESOURCES
Dates: Jan. 4, 1995-Jan. 3, 2007
Departure: Left committee; no new assignment

Cong.	Ranking	Terms in: House	Comm.	Date of Assignment
104th	Maj-15th	1	1	Jan. 4, 1995
105th	Maj-12th	2	2	Jan. 7, 1997
106th	Maj-12th	3	3	Jan. 6, 1999
107th	Maj-12th	4	4	Jan. 6, 2001
108th	Maj-11th	5	5	Jan. 28, 2003
109th	Maj-8th	6	6	Jan. 26, 2005

2nd SCIENCE
Dates: Jan. 4, 1995-Jan. 3, 1997
Departure: Moved to Commerce

Cong.	Ranking	Terms in: House	Comm.	Date of Assignment
104th	Maj-25th	1	1	Jan. 4, 1995

3rd COMMERCE, 105-106
ENERGY AND COMMERCE, 107-110
Dates: Jan. 7, 1997-Jan. 3, 2009
Departure: Left the House; retired

Cong.	Ranking	Terms in: House	Comm.	Date of Assignment
105th	Maj-26th	2	1	Jan. 7, 1997
106th	Maj-20th	3	2	Jan. 6, 1999
107th	Maj-15th	4	3	Jan. 6, 2001
108th	Maj-13th	5	4	Jan. 28, 2003
109th	Maj-10th	6	5	Jan. 6, 2005
110th	Min-9th	7	6	Jan. 10, 2007

Henry Cuellar (D-Tex.)

Dates: Sept. 19, 1955
House: Jan. 3, 2005-date
Serving in the 111th Congress

HOUSE STANDING COMMITTEES:

1st AGRICULTURE
Dates: Jan. 26, 2005-date
Departure: Still serving in the 111th Congress

Cong.	Ranking	Terms in: House	Comm.	Date of Assignment
109th	Min-13th	1	1	Jan. 26, 2005
110th	Maj-11th	2	2	Jan. 12, 2007
111th	Maj-10th	3	3	Jan. 21, 2009

2nd BUDGET
Dates: Jan. 26, 2005-Jan. 3, 2007
Departure: Moved to Homeland Security and Small Business

Cong.	Ranking	Terms in: House	Comm.	Date of Assignment
109th	Min-15th	1	1	Jan. 26, 2005

3rd HOMELAND SECURITY
Dates: Jan. 12, 2007-date
Departure: Still serving in the 111th Congress

Cong.	Ranking	Terms in: House	Comm.	Date of Assignment
110th	Maj-14th	2	1	Jan. 12, 2007
111th	Maj-8th	3	2	Jan. 28, 2009

4th SMALL BUSINESS
Dates: Jan. 23, 2007-Jan. 3, 2009
Departure: Moved to Oversight and Government Reform

Cong.	Ranking	Terms in: House	Comm.	Date of Assignment
110th	Maj-10th	2	1	Jan. 23, 2007

5th OVERSIGHT AND GOVERNMENT REFORM
Dates: Jan. 28, 2009-date
Departure: Still serving in the 111th Congress

Cong.	Ranking	Terms in: House	Comm.	Date of Assignment
111th	Maj-18th	3	1	Jan. 28, 2009

John Culberson (R-Tex.)

Dates: Aug. 24, 1956
House: Jan. 3, 2001-date
Serving in the 111th Congress

HOUSE STANDING COMMITTEES:

1st BUDGET
Dates: Jan. 6, 2001-Jan. 3, 2003
Departure: Moved to Appropriations

Cong.	Ranking	Terms in: House	Comm.	Date of Assignment
107th	Maj-19th	1	1	Jan. 6, 2001

2nd EDUCATION AND THE WORKFORCE
Dates: Jan. 6, 2001-Jan. 3, 2003
Departure: Moved to Appropriations

Cong.	Ranking	Terms in: House	Comm.	Date of Assignment
107th	Maj-26th	1	1	Jan. 6, 2001

3rd SCIENCE
Dates: Jan. 6, 2001-June 7, 2001
Departure: Resigned committee; moved to Transportation and Infrastructure

Cong.	Ranking	Terms in: House	Comm.	Date of Assignment
107th	Maj-19th	1	1	Jan. 6, 2001

4th TRANSPORTATION AND INFRASTRUCTURE
Dates: June 7, 2001-Jan. 3, 2003
Departure: Moved to Appropriations

Cong.	Ranking	Terms in: House	Comm.	Date of Assignment
107th	MjR-3rd	1	1	June 7, 2001

5th APPROPRIATIONS
Dates: Jan. 28, 2003-date
Departure: Still serving in the 111th Congress

Cong.	Ranking	Terms in: House	Comm.	Date of Assignment
108th	Maj-34th	2	1	Jan. 28, 2003
109th	Maj-32nd	3	2	Jan. 6, 2005
110th	Min-24th	4	3	Jan. 4, 2007
111th	Min-14th	5	4	Jan. 9, 2009

Elijah E. Cummings (D-Md.)

Dates: Jan. 18, 1951
House: April 16, 1996-date
Serving in the 111th Congress

H: Cummings was elected to the 104th Congress by special election, April 16, 1996, to fill the vacancy caused by the resignation of U.S. Representative Kweisi Mfume (D-Md.). Cummings was seated April 25, 1996, and assigned to committees.

HOUSE STANDING COMMITTEES:

1st GOVERNMENT REFORM AND OVERSIGHT, 104-105
GOVERNMENT REFORM, 106-109
OVERSIGHT AND GOVERNMENT REFORM, 110-111
Dates: Apr. 25, 1996-date
Departure: Still serving in the 111th Congress

Cong.	Ranking	Terms in: House	Comm.	Date of Assignment
104th	MnR-2nd	1	1	Apr. 25, 1996
105th	Min-14th	2	2	Jan. 7, 1997
106th	Min-12th	3	3	Jan. 6, 1999
107th	Min-10th	4	4	Jan. 31, 2001
108th	Min-8th	5	5	Jan. 28, 2003
109th	Min-7th	6	6	Jan. 26, 2005
110th	Maj-6th	7	7	Jan. 12, 2007
111th	Maj-4th	8	8	Jan. 28, 2009

2nd TRANSPORTATION AND INFRASTRUCTURE
Dates: Apr. 25, 1996-date
Departure: Still serving in the 111th Congress

Cong.	Ranking	Terms in: House	Comm.	Date of Assignment
104th	MnA-29th	1	1	Apr. 25, 1996
105th	Min-24th	2	2	Jan. 7, 1997

Cong.	Ranking	House	Comm.	Date of Assignment
106th	Min-21st	3	3	Jan. 6, 1999
107th	Min-18th	4	4	Jan. 31, 2001
108th	Min-14th	5	5	Jan. 28, 2003
109th	Min-13th	6	6	Jan. 26, 2005
110th	Maj-12th	7	7	Jan. 10, 2007
111th	Maj-11th	8	8	Jan. 7, 2009

3rd ARMED SERVICES
Dates: Jan. 12, 2007-Jan. 3, 2009
Departure: Left committee; no new assignment

Cong.	Ranking	Terms in: House	Comm.	Date of Assignment
110th	Maj-34th	7	1	Jan. 12, 2007

JOINT COMMITTEES:

1st JOINT ECONOMIC
House Dates: Mar. 3, 2005-date
Departure: Still serving in the 111th Congress

Cong.	Ranking	Terms in: House	Comm.	Date of Assignment
109th	Min-4th	6	1	Mar. 3, 2005
110th	Maj-5th	7	2	Mar. 27, 2007
111th	Maj-5th	8	3	Feb. 3, 2009

Randall (Duke) Cunningham
(R-Cal.)

Dates: Dec. 8, 1941
House: Jan. 3, 1991-Dec. 1, 2005
Left the House: Resigned and retired in 2005

HOUSE STANDING COMMITTEES:

1st ARMED SERVICES. 102-103
NATIONAL SECURITY, 104
Dates: Jan. 24, 1991-Jan. 3, 1997
Departure: Moved to Appropriations

Cong.	Ranking	Terms in: House	Comm.	Date of Assignment
103rd	Min-14th	2	2	Jan. 5, 1993
104th	Maj-11th	3	3	Jan. 4, 1995

2nd MERCHANT MARINE AND FISHERIES
Dates: Jan. 24, 1991-Jan. 3, 1995
Departure: Committee abolished; no new assignment

Cong.	Ranking	Terms in: House	Comm.	Date of Assignment
103rd	Min-10th	2	2	Jan. 5, 1993

3rd EDUCATION AND LABOR, 102-103
ECONOMIC AND EDUCATIONAL OPPORTUNITIES, 104
Dates: Oct. 23, 1991-Jan. 3, 1997
Departure: Moved to Appropriations

Cong.	Ranking	Terms in: House	Comm.	Date of Assignment
103rd	Min-12th	2	2	Jan. 5, 1993
104th	Maj-8th	3	3	Jan. 4, 1995

4th APPROPRIATIONS
Dates: Jan. 7, 1997-Dec. 1, 2005
Departure: Resigned the House; retired

Cong.	Ranking	Terms in: House	Comm.	Date of Assignment
105th	Maj-29th	4	1	Jan. 7, 1997
106th	Maj-25th	5	2	Jan. 6, 1999
107th	Maj-21st	6	3	Jan. 6, 2001
108th	Maj-17th	7	4	Jan. 28, 2003
109th	Maj-16th	8	5	Jan. 6, 2005

HOUSE SELECT AND SPECIAL COMMITTEES:

1st PERMANENT SELECT INTELLIGENCE
Dates: Jan. 30, 2001-Dec. 1, 2005
Departure: Resigned the House; retired

Cong.	Ranking	Terms in: House	Comm.	Date of Assignment
107th	Maj-8th	6	1	Jan. 30, 2001
108th	Maj-6th	7	2	Jan. 8, 2003
109th	Maj-3rd	8	3	Jan. 26, 2005

D

Kathleen A. Dahlkemper (D-Penn.)

Dates: Dec. 10, 1957
House: Jan. 3, 2009-date
Serving in the 111th Congress

HOUSE STANDING COMMITTEES:

1st AGRICULTURE
Dates: Jan. 21, 2009-date
Departure: Still serving in the 111th Congress

Cong.	Ranking	Years in: Senate	Comm.	Date of Assignment
111th	Maj-18th	1	1	Jan. 21, 2009

2nd SCIENCE AND TECHNOLOGY
Dates: Jan. 21, 2009-date
Departure: Still serving in the 111th Congress

Cong.	Ranking	Years in: Senate	Comm.	Date of Assignment
111th	Maj-23rd	1	1	Jan. 21, 2009

3rd SMALL BUSINESS
Dates: Jan. 21, 2009-date
Departure: Still serving in the 111th Congress

Cong.	Ranking	Years in: Senate	Comm.	Date of Assignment
111th	Maj-4th	1	1	Jan. 21, 2009

Alfonse M. D'Amato (R-N.Y.)

Dates: Aug. 1, 1937
Senate: Jan. 3, 1981-Jan. 3, 1999
Left the Senate: Defeated for re-election in 1998.

SENATE STANDING COMMITTEES:

1st APPROPRIATIONS
Dates: Jan. 5, 1981-Jan. 4, 1995
Departure: Moved to Finance

Cong.	Ranking	Years in: Senate	Comm.	Date of Assignment
103rd	Min-4th	13	13	Jan. 7, 1993

2nd BANKING, HOUSING AND URBAN AFFAIRS
Dates: Jan. 5, 1981-Jan. 3, 1999
Departure: Left the Senate; lost re-election

Cong.	Ranking	Years in: Senate	Comm.	Date of Assignment
103rd	Min-RM	13	13	Jan. 7, 1993
104th	Maj-Chr	15	14	Jan. 4, 1995
105th	Maj-Chr	17	17	Jan. 9, 1997

3rd SMALL BUSINESS
Dates: Mar. 25, 1981-Feb. 2, 1989
Departure: Moved to Select Intelligence

4th LABOR AND HUMAN RESOURCES
Dates: Jan. 3, 1983-Feb. 3, 1983
Departure: Moved to Joint Economic

5th FINANCE
Dates: Jan. 4, 1995-Jan. 3, 1999
Departure: Left the Senate; lost re-election

Cong.	Ranking	Years in: Senate	Comm.	Date of Assignment
104th	Maj-9th	15	1	Jan. 4, 1995
105th	Maj-5th	17	3	Jan. 9, 1997

SENATE SELECT AND SPECIAL COMMITTEES:

1st SELECT SMALL BUSINESS
Dates: Jan. 5, 1981-Mar. 25, 1981
Departure: Continued on reorganized standing committee

2nd SECURITY AND COOPERATION IN EUROPE
Dates: Nov. 18, 1983-Mar. 27, 1985
Termination: Public Law 99-7 signed

3rd SELECT INTELLIGENCE (Permanent)
Dates: Feb. 2, 1989-Jan. 4, 1995
Departure: Moved to Finance

Cong.	Ranking	Years in: Senate	Comm.	Date of Assignment
103rd	Min-2nd	13	4	Jan. 27, 1993

4th SPECIAL COMMITTEE TO INVESTIGATE WHITEWATER DEVELOPMENT CORPORATION AND RELATED MATTERS
Dates: July 20, 1995-June 17, 1996
Termination: Senate Report 104-280 filed

Cong.	Ranking	Years in: Senate	Comm.	Date of Assignment
104th	Maj-Chr	15	1	July 20, 1995

JOINT COMMITTEES:

1st JOINT ECONOMIC
Senate Dates: Feb. 3, 1983-Feb. 2, 1989
Departure: Moved to Select Intelligence.

John C. Danforth (R-Mo.)

Dates: Sept. 5, 1936
Senate: Dec. 27, 1976-Jan. 3, 1995
Left the Senate: Retired in 1994

S: Danforth was appointed to the 94th Congress, Dec. 27, 1976, to fill the vacancy caused by the resignation of U.S. Senator W. Stuart Symington (D-Mo.). Danforth was not seated nor assigned to committees because the 94th Congress was not in session. He had been elected to succeed Symington in the 95th Congress.

SENATE STANDING COMMITTEES:

1st FOREIGN RELATIONS
Dates: Jan. 10, 1977-Feb. 22, 1977
Departure: Moved to Governmental Affairs, Finance, and Commerce, Science and Transportation

2nd LABOR AND PUBLIC WELFARE
Dates: Jan. 10, 1977-Feb. 22, 1977
Departure: Moved to Governmental Affairs, Finance, and Commerce, Science and Transportation

3rd COMMERCE, SCIENCE AND TRANSPORTATION
Dates: Feb. 22, 1977-Jan. 3, 1995
Departure: Left the Senate; retired

Cong.	Ranking	Years in: Senate	Comm.	Date of Assignment
103rd	Min-RM	17	16	Jan. 7, 1993

4th FINANCE
Dates: Feb. 22, 1977-Jan. 3, 1995
Departure: Left the Senate; retired

Cong.	Ranking	Years in: Senate	Comm.	Date of Assignment
103rd	Min-4th	17	16	Jan. 7, 1993

5th GOVERNMENTAL AFFAIRS
Dates: Feb. 22, 1977-Feb. 21, 1985
Departure: Moved to Budget; became chair of Commerce, Science and Transportation

6th BUDGET
Dates: Feb. 21, 1985-Feb. 2, 1989
Departure: Moved to Select Intelligence

SENATE SELECT AND SPECIAL COMMITTEES:

1st SELECT INTELLIGENCE (Permanent)
Dates: Feb. 2, 1989-Jan. 3, 1995
Departure: Left the Senate; retired

Cong.	Ranking	Years in: Senate	Comm.	Date of Assignment
103rd	Min-3rd	17	4	Jan. 27, 1993

2nd JUDGE WALTER L. NIXON IMPEACHMENT
Dates: May 11, 1989-Sep. 13, 1989
Termination: Hearings concluded

JOINT COMMITTEES:

1st JOINT DEFICIT REDUCTION (Temporary)
Senate Dates: Jan. 6, 1987-Sep. 29, 1987
Departure: Public Law 100-119 adjusted Gramm-Rudman-Hollings Act

---

Patsy A. Danner (D-Mo.)

Dates: Jan. 13, 1934
House: Jan. 3, 1993-Jan. 3, 2001
Left the House: Retired in 2000

HOUSE STANDING COMMITTEES:

1st PUBLIC WORKS AND TRANSPORTATION, 103
TRANSPORTATION AND INFRASTRUCTURE, 104-106
Dates: Jan. 5, 1993-Jan. 3, 2001
Departure: Left the House; retired

Cong.	Ranking	Terms in: House	Terms in: Comm.	Date of Assignment
103rd	Maj-29th	1	1	Jan. 5, 1993
104th	Min-19th	2	2	Jan. 4, 1995
105th	Min-14th	3	3	Jan. 7, 1997
106th	Min-12th	4	4	Jan. 6, 1999

2nd SMALL BUSINESS
Dates: Jan. 5, 1993-Jan. 3, 1995
Departure: Left committee; no new assignment

Cong.	Ranking	Terms in: House	Terms in: Comm.	Date of Assignment
103rd	Maj-16th	1	1	Jan. 5, 1993

3rd INTERNATIONAL RELATIONS
Dates: Feb. 28, 1996-Jan. 3, 2001
Departure: Left the House; retired

Cong.	Ranking	Terms in: House	Terms in: Comm.	Date of Assignment
104th	MnA-20th	2	1	Feb. 28, 1996
105th	Min-14th	3	2	Jan. 7, 1997
106th	Min-12th	4	3	Jan. 6, 1999

George W. (Buddy) Darden (D-Ga.)

Dates: Nov. 22, 1943
House: Nov. 8, 1983-Jan. 3, 1995
Left the House: Defeated for re-election in 1994

H: Darden was elected to the 98th Congress by special election, Nov. 8, 1983, to fill the vacancy caused by the death of U.S. Representative Larry McDonald (D-Ga.). Darden was seated Nov. 10, 1983, and assigned to committees.

HOUSE STANDING COMMITTEES:

1st ARMED SERVICES
Dates: Nov. 17, 1983-Jan. 3, 1993
Departure: Moved to Appropriations

2nd GOVERNMENT OPERATIONS
Dates: Sep. 13, 1984-Jan. 3, 1985
Departure: Moved to Interior and Insular Affairs

3rd INTERIOR AND INSULAR AFFAIRS
Dates: Jan. 30, 1985-Jan. 3, 1993
Departure: Moved to Appropriations

4th STANDARDS OF OFFICIAL CONDUCT
Dates: Feb. 6, 1991-Jan. 3, 1995
Departure: Left the House; lost re-election

Cong.	Ranking	Terms in: House	Terms in: Comm.	Date of Assignment
103rd	Maj-2nd	6	2	Feb. 4, 1993

5th APPROPRIATIONS
Dates: Jan. 5, 1993-Jan. 3, 1995
Departure: Left the House; lost re-election

Cong.	Ranking	Terms in: House	Terms in: Comm.	Date of Assignment
103rd	Maj-28th	6	1	Jan. 5, 1993

Thomas A. Daschle (D-S.D.)

Dates: Dec. 9, 1947
House: Jan. 3, 1979-Jan. 3, 1987
Left the House: Elected to U.S. Senate in 1986
Senate: Jan. 3, 1987-Jan. 3, 2005
Left the Senate: Defeated for re-election in 2004

HOUSE STANDING COMMITTEES:

1st AGRICULTURE
Dates: Jan. 24, 1979-Jan. 3, 1987
Departure: Left the House for the Senate

2nd VETERANS' AFFAIRS
Dates: Jan. 24, 1979-Jan. 3, 1987
Departure: Left the House for the Senate

3rd POST OFFICE AND CIVIL SERVICE
Dates: Mar. 31, 1982-Nov. 18, 1983
Departure: Left committee; no new assignment

HOUSE SELECT AND SPECIAL COMMITTEES:

1st SELECT HUNGER (Temporary)
Dates: Mar. 13, 1984-Jan. 3, 1987
Departure: Left the House for the Senate

SENATE STANDING COMMITTEES:

1st AGRICULTURE, NUTRITION AND FORESTRY
Dates: Jan. 6, 1987-Jan. 3, 2005
Departure: Left the Senate; lost re-election

Cong.	Ranking	Years in: Senate	Years in: Comm.	Date of Assignment
103rd	Maj-7th	7	7	Jan. 7, 1993
104th	Min-6th	9	8	Jan. 4, 1995
105th	Min-4th	11	11	Jan. 9, 1997
106th	Min-4th	13	13	Jan. 7, 1999
107th	Min-4th	15	15	Jan. 25, 2001
+107th	Maj-4th	15	15	June 6, 2001
108th	Min-4th	17	17	Jan. 15, 2003

2nd FINANCE
1st Dates: Jan. 6, 1987-Jan. 4, 1995
1st Departure: Left committee; elected Minority Leader
2nd Dates: Jan. 25, 2001-Jan. 3, 2005
2nd Departure: Left the Senate; lost re-election

Cong.	Ranking	Years in: Senate	Years in: Comm.	Date of Assignment
103rd	Maj-10th	7	*1 7	Jan. 7, 1993
107th	Min-3rd	15	*2 1	Jan. 25, 2001
+107th	Maj-3rd	15	*2 1	June 6, 2001
108th	Min-3rd	17	*2 2	Jan. 15, 2003

3rd VETERANS' AFFAIRS
Dates: Mar. 19, 1991-Jan. 6, 1995
Departure: Left committee; elected Minority Leader

Cong.	Ranking	Years in: Senate	Comm.	Date of Assignment
103rd	Maj-6th	7	2	Jan. 21, 1993

4th RULES AND ADMINISTRATION
Dates: Jan. 4, 1995-Jan. 3, 2005
Departure: Left the Senate; lost re-election

Cong.	Ranking	Years in: Senate	Comm.	Date of Assignment
107th	Min-8th	15	1	Jan. 25, 2001
+107th	Maj-8th	15	1	June 6, 2001
108th	Min-7th	17	2	Jan. 15, 2003

SENATE SELECT AND SPECIAL COMMITTEES:

1st SELECT INDIAN AFFAIRS (Permanent), 100-102
INDIAN AFFAIRS (Permanent), 103
Dates: Jan. 6, 1987-Jan. 3, 1995
Departure: Left committee; elected Minority Leader

Cong.	Ranking	Years in: Senate	Comm.	Date of Assignment
103rd	Maj-3rd	7	6	Jan. 5, 1993

2nd SELECT POW-MIA AFFAIRS
Dates: Aug. 2, 1991-Feb. 3, 1993
Termination: Senate Report 1 (103-1) filed

3rd SELECT ETHICS (Permanent)
Dates: Jan. 26, 1993-Jan. 11, 1995
Departure: Left committee; elected Minority Leader

Cong.	Ranking	Years in: Senate	Comm.	Date of Assignment
103rd	Maj-3rd	7	1	Jan. 26, 1993

JOINT COMMITTEES:

1st JOINT TAXATION
Senate Dates: July 17, 2001-Feb. 24, 2003
Departure: Left committee; no new assignment

Cong.	Ranking	Years in: Senate	Comm.	Date of Assignment
+107th	MjA-3rd	15	1	July 17, 2001

SENATE LEADERSHIP POSTS

Dates: Jan. 4, 1995-Jan. 3, 2005
Departure: Left the Senate; lost re-election

1st SENATE MINORITY FLOOR LEADER
1st Dates: Jan. 4, 1995-June 6, 2001
Note: For the 104th Congress, Daschle succeeded Democratic Floor Leader George J. Mitchell (D-Me.) and was elected Minority Floor Leader over Christopher J. Dodd (D-Conn.), by a vote of 24 to 23 on Dec. 2, 1994. Daschle was re-elected without opposition as Minority Leader for the 105th-107th Congresses.
1st Departure: After Senator James Jeffords' switch from Republican to Independent, Democrats became the Senate majority and Daschle became Majority Floor Leader on June 6, 2001.
2nd Dates: Jan. 15, 2003-Jan. 3, 2005
Note: In the 108th Congress, Republicans regained control of the Senate and Daschle was re-elected as Minority Leader without opposition.
2nd Departure: Left the Senate; lost re-election

Cong.	Ranking	Years in: Senate	Post	Date of Selection
104th	Min-1st	9	1	Dec. 2, 1994
105th	Min-1st	11	3	Dec. 3, 1996
106th	Min-1st	13	5	Dec. 1, 1998
107th	Min-1st	15	7	Dec. 5, 2000
108th	Min-1st	17	9	Nov. 13, 2002

2nd SENATE MAJORITY FLOOR LEADER
Dates: June 6, 2001-Jan. 3, 2003
Note: After Senator James Jeffords' switch from Republican to Independent, Democrats became the Senate majority on June 6, 2001, and Daschle became Majority Floor Leader without a new election.
Departure: Democratic Party lost Senate majority in 2002

Cong.	Ranking	Years in: Senate	Post	Date of Service
+107th	Maj-1st	15	1	June 6, 2001

Artur Davis (D-Ala.)

Dates: Oct. 9, 1967
House: Jan. 3, 2003-date
Serving in the 111th Congress

HOUSE STANDING COMMITTEES:

1st BUDGET
Dates: Jan. 28, 2003-Jan. 3, 2007
Departure: Moved to Ways and Means and Judiciary

Cong.	Ranking	Terms in: House	Comm.	Date of Assignment
108th	Min-18th	1	1	Jan. 28, 2003
109th	Min-10th	2	2	Jan. 26, 2005

2nd FINANCIAL SERVICES
Dates: Feb. 5, 2003-Jan. 3, 2007
Departure: Moved to Ways and Means and Judiciary

Cong.	Ranking	Terms in: House	Comm.	Date of Assignment
108th	MnR-1st	1	1	Feb. 5, 2003
109th	Min-28th	2	2	Jan. 26, 2005

3rd WAYS AND MEANS
Dates: Dec. 12, 2006-date
Departure: Still serving in the 111th Congress

Cong.	Ranking	Terms in: House	Comm.	Date of Assignment
109th	MnR-1st	2	1	Dec. 12, 2006
110th	Maj-24th	3	2	Jan. 4, 2007
111th	Maj-21st	4	3	Jan. 7, 2009

4th JUDICIARY
Dates: Jan. 18, 2007-Jan. 3, 2009
Departure: Left committee; no new assignment

Cong.	Ranking	Terms in: House	Comm.	Date of Assignment
110th	Maj-21st	3	1	Jan. 18, 2007

5th HOUSE ADMINISTRATION
Dates: May 3, 2007-date
Departure: Still serving in the 111th Congress

Cong.	Ranking	Terms in: House	Comm.	Date of Assignment
110th	MjR-1st	3	1	May 3, 2007
111th	Maj-6th	4	2	Jan. 13, 2009

HOUSE SELECT AND SPECIAL COMMITTEES:

1st SELECT COMMITTEE TO INVESTIGATE THE VOTING IRREGULARITIES OF AUGUST 2, 2007

Dates: Sep. 5, 2007-Sep. 25, 2008
Termination: House Report 885 (110-2) filed

Cong.	Ranking	Terms in: House	Comm.	Date of Assignment
110th	Maj-2nd	3	1	Sep. 5, 2007

Danny K. Davis (D-Ill.)

Dates: Sept. 6, 1941
House: Jan. 3, 1997-date
Serving in the 111th Congress

HOUSE STANDING COMMITTEES:

1st GOVERNMENT REFORM AND OVERSIGHT, 105
GOVERNMENT REFORM, 106-109
OVERSIGHT AND GOVERNMENT REFORM, 110-111
Dates: Feb. 5, 1997-date
Departure: Still serving in the 111th Congress

Cong.	Ranking	Terms in: House	Comm.	Date of Assignment
105th	MnR-1st	1	1	Feb. 5, 1997
106th	Min-15th	2	2	Jan. 6, 1999
107th	Min-13th	3	3	Jan. 31, 2001
108th	Min-10th	4	4	Jan. 28, 2003
109th	Min-9th	5	5	Jan. 26, 2005
110th	Maj-8th	6	6	Jan. 12, 2007
111th	Maj-16th	7	7	Jan. 28, 2009

2nd SMALL BUSINESS
1st Dates: Feb. 5, 1997-Feb. 12, 2003
1st Departure: Resigned committee; had moved to Education and the Workforce
2nd Dates: Returned Feb. 26, 2003-Jan. 3, 2007
2nd Departure: Left committee; no new assignment

Cong.	Ranking	Terms in: House	Comm.	Date of Assignment
105th	Min-12th	1 *1	1	Feb. 5, 1997
106th	Min-4th	2 *1	2	Jan. 6, 1999
107th	Min-3rd	3 *1	3	Jan. 31, 2001
108th	Min-3rd	4 *1	4	Jan. 28, 2003
108th	Min-8th	4 *2	1	Feb. 26, 2003
109th	Min-7th	5 *2	2	Feb. 2, 2005

3rd EDUCATION AND THE WORKFORCE, 108-109
EDUCATION AND LABOR, 110
Dates: Jan. 28, 2003-Jan. 3, 2009
Departure: Moved to Ways and Means

Cong.	Ranking	Terms in: House	Comm.	Date of Assignment
108th	Min-17th	4	1	Jan. 28, 2003
109th	Min-17th	5	2	Jan. 26, 2005
110th	Maj-14th	6	3	Jan. 10, 2007

4th WAYS AND MEANS
Dates: Jan. 7, 2009-date
Departure: Still serving in the 111th Congress

Cong.	Ranking	Terms in: House	Comm.	Date of Assignment
111th	Maj-22nd	7	1	Jan. 7, 2009

David Davis (R-Tenn.)

Dates: Nov. 6, 1959
House: Jan. 3, 2007-Jan. 3, 2009
Left the House: Defeated for re-nomination in 2008

1st EDUCATION AND LABOR
Dates: Jan. 10, 2007-Jan. 3, 2009
Departure: Left the House; lost re-nomination

Cong.	Ranking	Terms in: House	Comm.	Date of Assignment
110th	Min-21st	1	1	Jan. 10, 2007

2nd HOMELAND SECURITY
Dates: Jan. 10, 2007-Jan. 3, 2009
Departure: Left the House; lost re-nomination

Cong.	Ranking	Terms in: House	Comm.	Date of Assignment
110th	Min-15th	1	1	Jan. 10, 2007

3rd SMALL BUSINESS
Dates: Jan. 10, 2007-Jan. 3, 2009
Departure: Left the House; lost re-nomination

Cong.	Ranking	Terms in: House	Comm.	Date of Assignment
110th	Min-12th	1	1	Jan. 10, 2007

Geoffrey C. Davis (R-Ky.)

Dates: Oct. 26, 1958
House: Jan. 3, 2005-date
Serving in the 111th Congress

HOUSE STANDING COMMITTEES:

1st ARMED SERVICES
Dates: Jan. 26, 2005-Jan. 3, 2009
Departure: Moved to Ways and Means

Cong.	Ranking	Terms in: House	Comm.	Date of Assignment
109th	Maj-34th	1	1	Jan. 26, 2005
110th	Min-28th	2	2	Jan. 10, 2007

2nd FINANCIAL SERVICES
Dates: Jan. 26, 2005-Jan. 3, 2009
Departure: Moved to Ways and Means

Cong.	Ranking	Terms in: House	Comm.	Date of Assignment
109th	Maj-36th	1	1	Jan. 26, 2005
110th	Min-27th	2	2	Jan. 10, 2007

3rd WAYS AND MEANS
Dates: Jan. 9, 2009-date
Departure: Still serving in the 111th Congress

Cong.	Ranking	Terms in: House	Comm.	Date of Assignment
111th	Min-11th	3	1	Jan. 9, 2009

Jim Davis (D-Fla.)

Dates: Oct. 11, 1957
House: Jan. 3, 1997-Jan. 3, 2007
Left the House: Lost election for Governor in 2006

HOUSE STANDING COMMITTEES:

1st BUDGET
Dates: Jan. 7, 1997-Jan. 3, 2003
Departure: Moved to Energy and Commerce

Cong.	Ranking	Terms in: House	Comm.	Date of Assignment
105th	Min-16th	1	1	Jan. 7, 1997
106th	Min-7th	2	2	Jan. 6, 1999
107th	Min-5th	3	3	Jan. 31, 2001

2nd INTERNATIONAL RELATIONS
Dates: Apr. 17, 1997-Jan. 3, 2003
Departure: Moved to Energy and Commerce

Cong.	Ranking	Terms in: House	Comm.	Date of Assignment
105th	MnA-22nd	1	1	Apr. 17, 1997
106th	Min-17th	2	2	Jan. 6, 1999
107th	Min-14th	3	3	Jan. 31, 2001

3rd HOUSE ADMINISTRATION
Dates: Feb. 10, 1999-Jan. 3, 2003
Departure: Moved to Energy and Commerce

Cong.	Ranking	Terms in: House	Comm.	Date of Assignment
106th	Min-3rd	2	1	Feb. 10, 1999
107th	Min-3rd	3	2	Jan. 31, 2001

4th ENERGY AND COMMERCE
Dates: Jan. 28, 2003-Jan. 3, 2007
Departure: Left the House; lost election for Governor

Cong.	Ranking	Terms in: House	Comm.	Date of Assignment
108th	Min-24th	4	1	Jan. 28, 2003
109th	Min-20th	5	2	Jan. 26, 2005

JOINT COMMITTEES:

1st JOINT LIBRARY
House Dates: Mar. 2, 1999-Jan. 3, 2003
Departure: Moved to Energy and Commerce

Cong.	Ranking	Terms in: House	Comm.	Date of Assignment
106th	Min-2nd	2	1	Mar. 2, 1999
107th	Min-2nd	3	2	June 5, 2001

Jo Ann Davis (R-Va.)

Dates: June 29, 1950-Oct. 6, 2007
House: Jan. 3, 2001-Oct. 6, 2007
Left the House: Died in office

HOUSE STANDING COMMITTEES:

1st ARMED SERVICES
Dates: Jan. 6, 2001-Oct. 6 2007
Departure: Died in office

Cong.	Ranking	Terms in: House	Comm.	Date of Assignment
107th	Maj-30th	1	1	Jan. 6, 2001
108th	Maj-18th	2	2	Jan. 28, 2003
109th	Maj-17th	3	3	Jan. 26, 2005
110th	Min-11th	4	4	Jan. 10, 2007

2nd GOVERNMENT REFORM
Dates: Jan. 6, 2001-Aug. 10, 2004
Departure: Resigned committee; moved to Permanent Select Intelligence

Cong.	Ranking	Terms in: House	Comm.	Date of Assignment
107th	Maj-19th	1	1	Jan. 6, 2001
108th	Maj-11th	2	2	Jan. 28, 2003

3rd INTERNATIONAL RELATIONS, 107-109
FOREIGN AFFAIRS, 110
Dates: Jan. 6, 2001-Oct. 6. 2007
Departure: Died in office

Cong.	Ranking	Terms in: House	Comm.	Date of Assignment
107th	Maj-26th	1	1	Jan. 6, 2001
108th	Maj-20th	2	2	Jan. 28, 2003
109th	Maj-16th	3	3	Jan. 26, 2005
110th	Min-12th	4	4	Jan. 10, 2007

HOUSE SELECT AND SPECIAL COMMITTEES:

1st PERMANENT SELECT INTELLIGENCE
Dates: Sep. 8, 2004-Jan. 3, 2007
Departure: Left committee; no new assignment

Cong.	Ranking	Terms in: House	Comm.	Date of Assignment
108th	MjR-1st	2	1	Sept. 8, 2004
109th	Maj-7th	3	2	Jan. 26, 2005

Lincoln Davis (D-Tenn.)

Dates: Sept. 13, 1943
House: Jan. 3, 2003-date
Serving in the 111th Congress

HOUSE STANDING COMMITTEES:

1st AGRICULTURE
Dates: Feb. 13, 2003-June 5, 2008
Departure: Resigned committee; no new assignment

Cong.	Ranking	Terms in: House	Comm.	Date of Assignment
108th	Min-24th	1	1	Feb. 13, 2003
109th	Min-21st	2	2	Feb. 2, 2005
110th	Maj-21st	3	3	Jan. 12, 2007

2nd SCIENCE, 108-109
SCIENCE AND TECHNOLOGY, 111
1st Dates: Feb. 5, 2003-Jan. 3, 2007
1st Departure: Moved to Financial Services
2nd Dates: Jan. 21, 2009-date
2nd Departure: Still serving in the 111th Congress

Cong.	Ranking	Terms in: House	Comm.	Date of Assignment
108th	Min-19th	1 *1	1	Feb. 5, 2003
109th	Min-9th	2 *1	2	Jan. 26, 2005
111th	Maj-17th	4 *2	1	Jan. 21, 2009

3rd TRANSPORTATION AND INFRASTRUCTURE
Dates: Jan. 28, 2003-Jan. 3, 2007
Departure: Moved to Financial Services

Cong.	Ranking	Terms in: House	Comm.	Date of Assignment
108th	Min-34th	1	1	Jan. 28, 2003
109th	Min-29th	2	2	Jan. 26, 2005

4th FINANCIAL SERVICES
1st Dates: Jan. 28, 2003-Feb. 5, 2003
1st Departure: Clerical error in resolution; replaced by Artur Davis
2nd Dates: Jan. 12, 2007-Jan. 3, 2009
2nd Departure: Returned to Science and Technology; moved to Appropriations

Cong.	Ranking	Terms in: House	Comm.	Date of Assignment
108th	Min-30th	1 *1	1	Jan. 28, 2003
110th	Maj-25th	3 *2	1	Jan. 12, 2007

5th APPROPRIATIONS
Dates: Jan. 7, 2009-date
Departure: Still serving in the 111th Congress

Cong.	Ranking	Terms in: House	Comm.	Date of Assignment
111th	Maj-36th	4	1	Jan. 7, 2009

Susan A. Davis (D-Cal.)

Dates: April 13, 1944
House: Jan. 3, 2001-date
Serving in the 111th Congress

HOUSE STANDING COMMITTEES:

1st ARMED SERVICES
Dates: Jan. 31, 2001-date
Departure: Still serving in the 111th Congress

Cong.	Ranking	Terms in: House	Comm.	Date of Assignment
107th	Min-27th	1	1	Jan. 31, 2001
108th	Min-20th	2	2	Jan. 28, 2003
109th	Min-16th	3	3	Jan. 26, 2005
110th	Maj-15th	4	4	Jan. 10, 2007
111th	Maj-14th	5	5	Jan. 7, 2009

2nd EDUCATION AND THE WORKFORCE, 107-109
EDUCATION AND LABOR, 110-111
Dates: Feb. 8, 2001-date
Departure: Still serving in the 111th Congress

Cong.	Ranking	Terms in: House	Comm.	Date of Assignment
107th	MnR-1st	1	1	Feb. 8, 2001
108th	Min-15th	2	2	Jan. 28, 2003
109th	Min-15th	3	3	Jan. 26, 2005
110th	Maj-13th	4	4	Jan. 10, 2007
111th	Maj-13th	5	5	Jan. 21, 2009

3rd VETERANS' AFFAIRS
Dates: Nov. 7, 2001-Jan. 3, 2005
Departure: Left committee; no new assignment

Cong.	Ranking	Terms in: House	Comm.	Date of Assignment
107th	MnR-2nd	1	1	Nov. 7, 2001
108th	Min-13th	2	2	Feb. 13, 2003

4th HOUSE ADMINISTRATION
Dates: Feb. 8, 2007-date
Departure: Still serving in the 111th Congress

Cong.	Ranking	Terms in: House	Comm.	Date of Assignment
110th	Maj-6th	4	1	Feb. 8, 2007
111th	Maj-5th	5	2	Jan. 13, 2009

JOINT COMMITTEES:

1st JOINT PRINTING
House Dates: June 12, 2007-date
Departure: Still serving in the 111th Congress

Cong.	Ranking	Terms in: House	Comm.	Date of Assignment
110th	MjR-1st	4	1	June 12, 2007
111th	Maj-3rd	5	2	Mar. 31, 2009

Thomas M. Davis III (R-Va.)

Dates: Jan. 5, 1949
House: Jan. 3, 1995-Nov. 24, 2008
Left the House: Resigned and retired in 2008

HOUSE STANDING COMMITTEES:

1st GOVERNMENT REFORM AND OVERSIGHT, 104-105
GOVERNMENT REFORM, 106-109
OVERSIGHT AND GOVERNMENT REFORM, 110
Dates: Jan. 4, 1995-Nov. 24, 2008
Departure: Resigned the House; retired

Cong.	Ranking	Terms in: House	Comm.	Date of Assignment
104th	Maj-13th	1	1	Jan. 4, 1995
105th	Maj-12th	2	2	Jan. 7, 1997
106th	Maj-10th	3	3	Jan. 6, 1999
107th	Maj-9th	4	4	Jan. 6, 2001
108th	Maj-Chr	5	5	Jan. 8, 2003
109th	Maj-Chr	6	6	Jan. 6, 2005
110th	Min-RM	7	7	Jan. 4, 2007

2nd SCIENCE
Dates: Jan. 4, 1995-Jan. 3, 1999
Departure: Left committee; no new assignment

Cong.	Ranking	Terms in: House	Comm.	Date of Assignment
104th	Maj-18th	1	1	Jan. 4, 1995
105th	Maj-14th	2	2	Jan. 21, 1997

3rd TRANSPORTATION AND INFRASTRUCTURE
Dates: Feb. 26, 1997-Jan. 3, 1999
Departure: Left committee; no new assignment

Cong.	Ranking	Terms in: House	Comm.	Date of Assignment
105th	Maj-38th	2	1	Feb. 26, 1997

4th ENERGY AND COMMERCE
Dates: Jan. 6, 2001-Jan. 3, 2003
Departure: Left committee; became Chair of Government Reform

Cong.	Ranking	Terms in: House	Comm.	Date of Assignment
107th	Maj-22nd	4	1	Jan. 6, 2001

5th HOMELAND SECURITY
Dates: Feb. 9, 2005-Nov. 24, 2008
Departure: Resigned the House; retired

Cong.	Ranking	Terms in: House	Comm.	Date of Assignment
109th	Maj-9th	6	1	Feb. 9, 2005
110th	Min-5th	7	2	Jan. 10, 2007

HOUSE SELECT AND SPECIAL COMMITTEES:

1st SELECT BIPARTISAN COMMITTEE TO INVESTIGATE THE PREPARATION FOR AND RESPONSE TO HURRICANE KATRINA
Dates: Sep. 21, 2005-Feb. 15, 2006
Departure: House Report 377 (109-2) filed

Cong.	Ranking	Terms in: House	Comm.	Date of Assignment
109th	Maj-Chr	6	1	Sep. 21, 2005

Mark Dayton (DFL-Minn.)

Dates: Jan. 26, 1947
Senate: Jan. 3, 2001-Jan. 3, 2007
Left the Senate: Retired in 2006

SENATE STANDING COMMITTEES:

1st AGRICULTURE, NUTRITION AND FORESTRY
Dates: Jan. 25, 2001-Jan. 3, 2007
Departure: Left the Senate; retired

Cong.	Ranking	Years in: Senate	Comm.	Date of Assignment
107th	Min-10th	1	1	Jan. 25, 2001
+107th	Maj-10th	1	1	June 6, 2001
108th	Min-10th	3	2	Jan. 15, 2003
109th	Min-8th	5	4	Jan. 6, 2005

2nd ARMED SERVICES
Dates: Jan. 25, 2001-Jan. 3, 2007
Departure: Left the Senate; retired

Cong.	Ranking	Years in: Senate	Comm.	Date of Assignment
107th	Min-12th	1	1	Jan. 25, 2001
+107th	Maj-12th	1	1	June 6, 2001
108th	Min-9th	3	2	Jan. 15, 2003
109th	Min-9th	5	4	Jan. 6, 2005

3rd RULES AND ADMINISTRATION
Dates: Jan.25, 2001-Jan. 3, 2007
Departure: Left the Senate; retired

Cong.	Ranking	Years in: Senate	Comm.	Date of Assignment
107th	Min-9th	1	1	Jan. 25, 2001
+107th	Maj-9th	1	1	June 6, 2001
108th	Min-8th	3	2	Jan. 15, 2003
109th	Min-6th	5	4	Jan. 6, 2005

4th GOVERNMENTAL AFFAIRS renamed Oct. 9, 2004
HOMELAND SECURITY AND GOVERNMENTAL AFFAIRS
Dates: July 10, 2001-Jan. 3, 2007
Departure: Left the Senate; retired

Cong.	Ranking	Years in: Senate	Comm.	Date of Assignment
+107th	MjA-9th	1	1	July 10, 2001
108th	Min-6th	3	2	Jan. 15, 2003
109th	Min-5th	5	4	Jan. 6, 2005

JOINT COMMITTEES:

1st JOINT LIBRARY
Senate Dates: Sep. 19, 2001-Mar. 13, 2003
Departure: Left committee; no new assignment

Cong.	Ranking	Years in: Senate	Comm.	Date of Assignment
+107th	Maj-3rd	1	1	Sep. 19, 2001

2nd JOINT PRINTING
Senate Dates: Sep. 19, 2001-Jan. 3, 2007
Departure: Left the Senate; retired

Cong.	Ranking	Years in: Senate	Comm.	Date of Assignment
+107th	Maj-Chr	1	1	Sep. 19, 2001
108th	Min-2nd	3	2	Mar. 13, 2003
109th	Min-2nd	5	4	Mar. 4, 2005

J. Nathan Deal (R-Ga.)

Dates: Aug. 25, 1942
House: Jan. 3, 1993-Mar. 21, 2010
Left the House: Resigned to seek governorship
Served as a Democrat: Jan. 3, 1993-April 10, 1995
Served as a Republican: April 10, 1995-date
Note: The *Biographical Directory* lists April 10, 1995, as the date that Deal departed the Democratic Party but his committee assignments were officially vacated on May 10, 1995.

HOUSE STANDING COMMITTEES:

1st NATURAL RESOURCES, 103
RESOURCES, 104
Dates: Jan. 5, 1993-May 10, 1995
Departure: Seat vacated as a Democrat; moved to Commerce as a Republican on May 25, 1995

Cong.	Ranking	Terms in: House	Comm.	Date of Assignment
103rd	Maj-22nd	1	1	Jan. 5, 1993
104th	Min-17th	2	2	Jan. 9, 1995

2nd PUBLIC WORKS AND TRANSPORTATION, 103
TRANSPORTATION AND INFRASTRUCTURE, 104
Dates: Jan. 5, 1993-May 10, 1995
Departure: Seat vacated as a Democrat; moved to Commerce as a Republican on May 25, 1995

Cong.	Ranking	Terms in: House	Comm.	Date of Assignment
103rd	Maj-34th	1	1	Jan. 5, 1993
104th	Min-23rd	2	2	Jan. 4, 1995

3rd SCIENCE, SPACE AND TECHNOLOGY
Dates: Jan. 21, 1993-Jan. 3, 1995
Departure: Left committee; no new assignment

Cong.	Ranking	Terms in: House	Comm.	Date of Assignment
103rd	Maj-31st	1	1	Jan. 21, 1993

4th COMMERCE, 104-106
ENERGY AND COMMERCE, 107-111
Dates: May 25, 1995-Mar. 21, 2010
Departure: Resigned the House to run for Governor

Cong.	Ranking	Terms in: House	Comm.	Date of Assignment
104th	MjA-26th	2	1	May 25, 1995
105th	Maj-16th	3	2	Jan. 7, 1997
106th	Maj-11th	4	3	Jan. 6, 1999
107th	Maj-9th	5	4	Jan. 6, 2001
108th	Maj-9th	6	5	Jan. 28, 2003
109th	Maj-7th	7	6	Jan. 6, 2005

| 110th | Min-6th | 8 | 7 | Jan. 10, 2007 |
| 111th | Min-5th | 9 | 8 | Jan. 9, 2009 |

5th EDUCATION AND THE WORKFORCE
Dates: Jan. 7, 1997-Jan. 3, 2001
Departure: Left committee; no new assignment

		Terms in:		Date of
Cong.	**Ranking**	**House**	**Comm.**	**Assignment**
105th	Maj-23rd	3	1	Jan. 7, 1997
106th	Maj-20th	4	2	Jan. 6, 1999

6th GOVERNMENT REFORM
Dates: Jan. 28, 2003-Jan. 3, 2005
Departure: Left committee; no new assignment

		Terms in:		Date of
Cong.	**Ranking**	**House**	**Comm.**	**Assignment**
108th	Maj-18th	6	1	Jan. 28, 2003

Dennis W. DeConcini (D-Ariz.)

Dates: May 8, 1937
Senate: Jan. 3, 1977-Jan. 3, 1995
Left the Senate: Retired in 1994

SENATE STANDING COMMITTEES:

1st PUBLIC WORKS
Dates: Jan. 10, 1977-Feb. 11, 1977
Departure: Moved to Judiciary

2nd APPROPRIATIONS
Temporary Dates: Jan. 10, 1977-Feb. 11, 1977
Began permanent service on committee
Dates: Feb. 11, 1977-Jan. 3, 1995
Departure: Left the Senate; retired

		Years in:		Date of
Cong.	**Ranking**	**Senate**	**Comm.**	**Assignment**
103rd	Maj-7th	17	16	Jan. 7, 1993

3rd JUDICIARY
Dates: Feb. 11, 1977-Jan. 3, 1995
Departure: Left the Senate; retired

		Years in:		Date of
Cong.	**Ranking**	**Senate**	**Comm.**	**Assignment**
103rd	Maj-4th	17	16	Jan. 7, 1993

4th RULES AND ADMINISTRATION
1st Dates: Jan. 23, 1979-Jan. 5, 1981
1st Departure: Left committee; no new assignment
2nd Dates: Jan. 3, 1983-Jan. 3, 1995
2nd Departure: Left the Senate; retired

		Years in:		Date of
Cong.	**Ranking**	**Senate**	**Comm.**	**Assignment**
103rd	Maj-5th	17 *2	11	Jan. 21, 1993

5th VETERANS' AFFAIRS
Dates: Jan. 5, 1981-Jan. 3, 1995
Departure: Left the Senate; retired

		Years in:		Date of
Cong.	**Ranking**	**Senate**	**Comm.**	**Assignment**
103rd	Maj-2nd	17	13	Jan. 21, 1993

SENATE SELECT AND SPECIAL COMMITTEES:

1st SPECIAL AGING (Permanent)
Dates: Feb. 11, 1977-Jan. 23, 1979
Departure: Moved to Indian Affairs

2nd SELECT INDIAN AFFAIRS (Permanent), 96-102
INDIAN AFFAIRS (Permanent), 103
Dates: Jan. 23, 1979-Jan. 3, 1995
Departure: Left the Senate; retired

		Years in:		Date of
Cong.	**Ranking**	**Senate**	**Comm.**	**Assignment**
103rd	Maj-2nd	17	14	Jan. 5, 1993

3rd FOREIGN GOVERNMENT REPRESENTATION
Dates: July 25, 1980-Oct. 2, 1980
Termination: Senate Report 1015 (96-2) filed

4th UNDERCOVER ACTIVITIES OF COMPONENTS OF THE DEPARTMENT OF JUSTICE
Dates: Mar. 29, 1982-Dec. 15, 1982
Termination: Senate Report 682 (97-2) filed

5th SECURITY AND COOPERATION IN EUROPE
Dates: Jan. 31, 1984-Mar. 27, 1985
Termination: Public Law 99-7

6th JUDGE HARRY E. CLAIBORNE IMPEACHMENT
Dates: Aug. 14, 1986-Oct. 1, 1986
Termination: Senate Report 99-511 filed

7th SELECT INTELLIGENCE (Permanent)
Dates: Jan. 12, 1987-Jan. 3, 1995
Departure: Left the Senate; retired

		Years in:		Date of
Cong.	**Ranking**	**Senate**	**Comm.**	**Assignment**
103rd	Maj-Chr	17	6	Jan. 27, 1993

8th SELECT POW-MIA AFFAIRS
Dates: Aug. 2, 1991-Oct. 30, 1991
Departure: Left committee; no new assignment

JOINT COMMITTEES:

1st JOINT LIBRARY
1st Senate Dates: Feb. 16, 1983-Apr. 17, 1985
1st Departure: Moved to Joint Printing
2nd Senate Dates: Jan. 29, 1987-Jan. 3, 1995
2nd Departure: Left the Senate; retired

		Years in:		Date of
Cong.	**Ranking**	**Senate**	**Comm.**	**Assignment**
103rd	Maj-2nd	17	*2 6	Jan. 28, 1993

2nd JOINT PRINTING
Senate Dates: Apr. 17, 1985-Jan. 3, 1995
Departure: Left the Senate; retired

		Years in:		Date of
Cong.	**Ranking**	**Senate**	**Comm.**	**Assignment**
103rd	Maj-2nd	17	8	Jan. 28, 1993

Peter A. DeFazio (D-Ore.)

Dates: May 27, 1947
House: Jan. 3, 1987-date
Serving in the 111th Congress

HOUSE STANDING COMMITTEES:

1st PUBLIC WORKS AND TRANSPORTATION, 100-103
TRANSPORTATION AND INFRASTRUCTURE, 104-111

Dates: Jan. 6, 1987-date
Departure: Still serving in the 111th Congress

Cong.	Ranking	Terms in: House	Comm.	Date of Assignment
103rd	Maj-11th	4	4	Jan. 5, 1993
104th	Min-8th	5	5	Jan. 4, 1995
105th	Min-7th	6	6	Jan. 7, 1997
106th	Min-7th	7	7	Jan. 6, 1999
107th	Min-5th	8	8	Jan. 31, 2001
108th	Min-4th	9	9	Jan. 28, 2003
109th	Min-3rd	10	10	Jan. 26, 2005
110th	Maj-3rd	11	11	Jan. 10, 2007
111th	Maj-3rd	12	12	Jan. 7, 2009

2nd INTERIOR AND INSULAR AFFAIRS, 100-102
NATURAL RESOURCES, 103
RESOURCES, 104-109
NATURAL RESOURCES, 110-111
1st Dates: Jan. 22, 1987-Feb. 12, 2003
1st Departure: Leave of absence; moved to Select Homeland Security; returned in the 109th Congress
2nd Dates: Feb. 2, 2005-date
2nd Departure: Still serving in the 111th Congress

Cong.	Ranking	Terms in: House	Comm.	Date of Assignment
103rd	Maj-12th	4 *1	4	Jan. 5, 1993
104th	Min-8th	5 *1	5	Jan. 9, 1995
105th	Min-8th	6 *1	6	Jan. 7, 1997
106th	Min-5th	7 *1	7	Jan. 6, 1999
107th	Min-5th	8 *1	8	Feb. 8, 2001
108th	Min-5th	9 *1	9	Jan. 28, 2003
109th	Min-18th	10 *2	1	Feb. 2, 2005
110th	Maj-17th	11 *2	2	Jan. 18, 2007
111th	Maj-16th	12 *2	3	Jan. 21, 2009

3rd SMALL BUSINESS
Dates: Jan. 22, 1987-Jan. 3, 1989
Departure: Left committee; no new assignment
4th HOMELAND SECURITY
Dates: Feb. 9, 2005-date
Departure: Still serving in the 111th Congress

Cong.	Ranking	Terms in: House	Comm.	Date of Assignment
109th	Min-6th	10	2	Feb. 9, 2005
110th	Maj-6th	11	3	Jan. 12, 2007
111th	Maj-4th	12	4	Jan. 28, 2009

HOUSE SELECT AND SPECIAL COMMITTEES:

1st SELECT AGING (Permanent)
Dates: Aug. 4, 1989-Jan. 3, 1993
Termination: Committee not renewed in 1993

2nd SELECT HOMELAND SECURITY
Dates: Feb. 12, 2003-Jan. 3, 2005
Departure: Continued on reorganized standing committee

Cong.	Ranking	Terms in: House	Comm.	Date of Assignment
108th	Min-10th	9	1	Feb. 12, 2003

HOUSE STANDING COMMITTEES:

1st COMMERCE, 105-106
ENERGY AND COMMERCE, 107-111
Dates: Jan. 7, 1997-date
Departure: Still serving in the 111th Congress

Cong.	Ranking	Terms in: House	Comm.	Date of Assignment
105th	Min-23rd	1	1	Jan. 7, 1997
106th	Min-21st	2	2	Jan. 6, 1999
107th	Min-20th	3	3	Jan. 31, 2001
108th	Min-19th	4	4	Jan. 28, 2003
109th	Min-16th	5	5	Jan. 26, 2005
110th	Maj-14th	6	6	Jan. 4, 2007
111th	Maj-12th	7	7	Jan. 7, 2009

2nd NATURAL RESOURCES
Dates: Jan. 21, 2009-date
Departure: Still serving in the 111th Congress

Cong.	Ranking	Terms in: House	Comm.	Date of Assignment
111th	Maj-19th	7	1	Jan. 21, 2009

E. (Kika) de la Garza (D-Tex.)

Dates: Sept. 22, 1927
House: Jan. 3, 1965-Jan. 3, 1997
Left the House: Retired in 1996

HOUSE STANDING COMMITTEES:

1st AGRICULTURE
Dates: Jan. 18, 1965-Jan. 3, 1997
Departure: Left the House; retired

Cong.	Ranking	Terms in: House	Comm.	Date of Assignment
103rd	Maj-Chr	15	15	Jan. 5, 1993
104th	Min-RM	16	16	Jan. 4, 1995

2nd MERCHANT MARINE AND FISHERIES
Dates: Feb. 4, 1971-Jan. 3, 1981
Departure: Left committee to chair Agriculture

3rd INTERNATIONAL RELATIONS
Temporary Dates: Jan. 27, 1977-Jan. 3, 1979
Departure: Temporary term expired

HOUSE SELECT AND SPECIAL COMMITTEES:

1st OUTER CONTINENTAL SHELF (Ad Hoc)
Dates: May 6, 1975-Jan. 3, 1977
Departure: Moved to International Relations

2nd SELECT NARCOTICS ABUSE AND CONTROL (Temporary)
Dates: Aug. 3, 1976-Jan. 3, 1981
Departure: Left committee to chair Agriculture

Diana DeGette (D-Colo.)

Dates: July 29, 1957
House: Jan. 3, 1997-date
Serving in the 111th Congress

William D. Delahunt (D-Mass.)

Dates: July 18, 1941
House: Jan. 3, 1997-date
Serving in the 111th Congress

HOUSE STANDING COMMITTEES:

1st JUDICIARY
Dates: Jan. 7, 1997-date
Departure: Still serving in the 111th Congress

Cong.	Ranking	Terms in: House	Comm.	Date of Assignment
105th	Min-13th	1	1	Jan. 7, 1997
106th	Min-12th	2	2	Jan. 6, 1999
107th	Min-12th	3	3	Jan. 31, 2001
108th	Min-11th	4	4	Jan. 28, 2003
109th	Min-11th	5	5	Jan. 26, 2005
110th	Maj-11th	6	6	Jan. 18, 2007
111th	Maj-10th	7	7	Jan. 21, 2009

2nd RESOURCES
Dates: Jan. 7, 1997-Feb. 24, 1999
Departure: Resigned committee; no new assignment

Cong.	Ranking	Terms in: House	Comm.	Date of Assignment
105th	Min-21st	1	1	Jan. 7, 1997
106th	Min-16th	2	2	Jan. 7, 1997

3rd INTERNATIONAL RELATIONS, 106-109
FOREIGN AFFAIRS, 110-111
Dates: Jan. 19, 1999-date
Departure: Still serving in the 111th Congress

Cong.	Ranking	Terms in: House	Comm.	Date of Assignment
106th	Min-19th	2	1	Jan. 19, 1999
107th	Min-15th	3	2	Jan. 31, 2001
108th	Min-11th	4	3	Jan. 28, 2003
109th	Min-11th	5	4	Jan. 26, 2005
110th	Maj-9th	6	5	Jan. 12, 2007
111th	Maj-8th	7	6	Jan. 21, 2009

4th STANDARDS OF OFFICIAL CONDUCT
Dates: Feb. 8, 2007-Jan. 3, 2009
Departure: Left committee; no new assignment

Cong.	Ranking	Terms in: House	Comm.	Date of Assignment
110th	Min-5th	6	1	Feb. 8, 2007

HOUSE SELECT AND SPECIAL COMMITTEES:

1st SELECT COMMITTEE TO INVESTIGATE THE VOTING IRREGULARITIES OF AUGUST 2, 2007
Dates: Sep. 5, 2007-Sep. 25, 2008
Termination: House Report 885 (110-2) filed

Cong.	Ranking	Terms in: House	Comm.	Date of Assignment
110th	Maj-Chr	6	1	Sep. 5, 2007

Rosa L. DeLauro (D-Conn.)

Dates: March 2, 1943
House: Jan. 3, 1991-date
Serving in the 111th Congress

HOUSE STANDING COMMITTEES:

1st GOVERNMENT OPERATIONS
Dates: Jan. 24, 1991-Jan. 3, 1993
Departure: Moved to Appropriations

2nd PUBLIC WORKS AND TRANSPORTATION
Dates: Jan. 24, 1991-Jan. 3, 1993
Departure: Moved to Appropriations

3rd APPROPRIATIONS
1st Dates: Jan. 5, 1993-Jan. 3, 1995
1st Departure: Moved to National Security
2nd Dates: Jan. 7, 1997-date
2nd Departure: Still serving in the 111th Congress

Cong.	Ranking	Terms in: House	Comm.	Date of Assignment
103rd	Maj-32nd	2 *1	1	Jan. 5, 1993
105th	Min-20th	4 *2	1	Jan. 7, 1997
106th	Min-13th	5 *2	2	Jan. 6, 1999
107th	Min-12th	6 *2	3	Jan. 31, 2001
108th	Min-11th	7 *2	4	Jan. 28, 2003
109th	Min-11th	8 *2	5	Jan. 26, 2005
110th	Maj-9th	9 *2	6	Jan. 4, 2007
111th	Maj-9th	10 *2	7	Jan. 7, 2009

4th NATIONAL SECURITY
Dates: Jan. 4, 1995-Jan. 3, 1997
Departure: Returned to Appropriations

Cong.	Ranking	Terms in: House	Comm.	Date of Assignment
104th	Min-23rd	2	1	Jan. 4, 1995

5th BUDGET
Dates: Jan. 28, 2003-date
Departure: Still serving in the 111th Congress

Cong.	Ranking	Terms in: House	Comm.	Date of Assignment
108th	Min-8th	7	1	Jan. 28, 2003
109th	Min-4th	8	2	Jan. 26, 2005
110th	Maj-2nd	9	3	Jan. 18, 2007
111th	Maj-16th	10	4	Jan. 21, 2009

HOUSE SELECT AND SPECIAL COMMITTEES:

1st SELECT AGING (Permanent)
Dates: Feb. 21, 1991-Jan. 3, 1993
Termination: Committee not renewed in 1993

2nd SELECT HOMELAND SECURITY
House Dates: June 19, 2002-Jan. 3, 2003
Departure: Moved to Budget

Cong.	Ranking	Terms in: House	Comm.	Date of Assignment
107th	Min-4th	6	1	June 19, 2002

Thomas D. DeLay (R-Tex.)

Dates: April 8, 1947
House: Jan. 3, 1985-June 9, 2006
Left the House: Resigned and retired in 2006

HOUSE STANDING COMMITTEES:

1st GOVERNMENT OPERATIONS
Dates: Jan. 30, 1985-Jan. 3, 1987
Departure: Moved to Appropriations

2nd PUBLIC WORKS AND TRANSPORTATION
Dates: Jan. 30, 1985-Jan. 21, 1987
Departure: Moved to Appropriations

3rd APPROPRIATIONS
1st Dates: Jan. 21, 1987-Jan. 3, 2003

1st Departure: Left committee; elected Majority Leader
2nd Dates: Feb. 8, 2006-June 9, 2006
2nd Departure: Resigned the House; retired

Cong.	Ranking	Terms in: House	Comm.	Date of Assignment
103rd	Min-11th	5 *1	4	Jan. 5, 1993
104th	Maj-11th	6 *1	5	Jan. 4, 1995
105th	Maj-10th	7 *1	6	Jan. 7, 1997
106th	Maj-8th	8 *1	7	Jan. 6, 1999
107th	Maj-7th	9 *1	8	Jan. 6, 2001
109th	MjR-1st	11 *2	1	Feb. 8, 2006

HOUSE SELECT AND SPECIAL COMMITTEES:

1st SELECT HOMELAND SECURITY
House Dates: June 19, 2002-Jan. 3, 2003
Departure: Elected Majority Leader

Cong.	Ranking	Terms in: House	Comm.	Date of Assignment
107th	Maj-2nd	9	1	June 19, 2002

HOUSE LEADERSHIP POSTS

Dates: Jan. 3, 1995-Sep. 28, 2005
Departure: Stepped aside due to caucus rules concerning legal issues

1st HOUSE MAJORITY WHIP
Dates: Jan. 3, 1995-Jan. 3, 2003
Note: For the 104th Congress, DeLay was elected Republican Whip on Dec. 5, 1994, to succeed Newton L. Gingrich (R-Ga.) who had become Speaker of the House. DeLay was elected on the first ballot with 119 votes over Robert Walker (R-Penn.) with 80 votes and Bill McCollum (R-Fla.) with 28 votes. DeLay was re-elected without opposition for the 105th-107th Congresses.
Departure: Elected Majority Floor Leader

Cong.	Ranking	Terms in: House	Post	Date of Selection
104th	Maj-3rd	6	1	Dec. 5, 1994
105th	Maj-3rd	7	2	Nov. 20, 1996
106th	Maj-3rd	8	3	Nov. 18, 1998
107th	Maj-3rd	9	4	Nov. 14, 2000

2nd HOUSE MAJORITY FLOOR LEADER
Dates: Jan. 3, 2003-Sep. 28, 2006
Notes: For the 108th Congress, DeLay was elected on Nov. 13, 2002, to succeed Majority Leader Richard A. Armey (R-Tex.) who had retired. DeLay was re-elected for the 109th Congress without opposition.
Departure: Legal issues led DeLay to step aside on Sep. 28, 2005, and on Jan. 7, 2006, he chose not to reclaim his post

Cong.	Ranking	Terms in: House	Post	Date of Selection
108th	Maj-2nd	10	1	Nov. 13, 2002
109th	Maj-2nd	11	2	Nov. 16, 2004

Ronald V. Dellums (D-Cal.)

Dates: Nov. 24, 1935
House: Jan. 3, 1971-Feb. 6, 1998
Left the House: Resigned and retired in 1998

HOUSE STANDING COMMITTEES:

1st DISTRICT OF COLUMBIA
1st Dates: Feb. 4, 1971-Jan. 3, 1993

1st Departure: Left committee to chair Armed Services
2nd Dates: Apr. 22, 1993-Jan. 3, 1995
2nd Departure: Committee abolished; no new assignment

Cong.	Ranking	Terms in: House	Comm.	Date of Assignment
103rd	MjR-1st	12 *2	1	Apr. 22, 1993

2nd FOREIGN AFFAIRS
Dates: Feb. 4, 1971-Jan. 3, 1973
Departure: Moved to Armed Services

3rd ARMED SERVICES, 93-103
NATIONAL SECURITY, 104-105
Dates: Jan. 24, 1973-Feb. 6, 1998
Chair2: Replaced Aspin as Chair on Jan. 27, 1993
Departure: Resigned the House; retired

Cong.	Ranking	Terms in: House	Comm.	Date of Assignment
103rd	Maj-3rd	12	11	Jan. 5, 1993
=103rd	Maj-Ch2	12	11	Jan. 27, 1993
104th	Min-RM	13	12	Jan. 4, 1995
105th	Min-RM	14	13	Jan. 7, 1997

4th POST OFFICE AND CIVIL SERVICE
1st Dates: Jan. 28, 1981-Jan. 3, 1983
1st Departure: Remained on committee on temporary assignment
Temporary Dates: Jan. 6, 1983-Feb. 3, 1983
Departure: Temporary term expired

HOUSE SELECT AND SPECIAL COMMITTEES:

1st SELECT INTELLIGENCE (Nedzi)
Dates: Feb. 19, 1975-July 17, 1975
Termination: Reorganized with new chair
SELECT INTELLIGENCE (Pike)
Dates: July 17, 1975-Feb. 11, 1976
Termination: House Report 833 (94-2) filed

2nd PERMANENT SELECT INTELLIGENCE
Dates: Feb. 5, 1991-Jan. 3, 1993
Departure: Left committee to chair Armed Services

Ron de Lugo (D-V.I.)

Dates: Aug. 2, 1930
House 1: Jan. 3, 1973-Jan. 3, 1979
Left the House 1: Lost election for Governor in 1978
House 2: Jan. 3, 1981-Jan. 3, 1995
Left the House 2: Retired in 1994

H: de Lugo was elected as a Democrat to be the first Territorial Delegate from the Virgin Islands in the 93rd Congress. He was first seated Jan. 3, 1973, and was assigned to committees and allowed to accrue seniority.

HOUSE STANDING COMMITTEES:

1st INTERIOR AND INSULAR AFFAIRS, 93-95, 97-102
NATURAL RESOURCES, 103
1st Dates: Jan. 24, 1973-Jan. 3, 1979
1st Departure: Left the House; lost election for Governor
2nd Dates: Jan. 28, 1981-Jan. 3, 1995
2nd Departure: Left the House; retired

Cong.	Ranking	Terms in: House	Comm.	Date of Assignment
103rd	Maj-8th	10	*2 7	Jan. 5, 1993

2nd MERCHANT MARINE AND FISHERIES
Dates: Jan. 20, 1975-Jan. 3, 1979
Departure: Left the House; lost election for Governor

3rd POST OFFICE AND CIVIL SERVICE
1st Dates: Jan. 28, 1981-Jan. 3, 1983
1st Departure: Left committee as a regular member, and was then temporarily assigned to the committee four times
Temporary 1: Jan. 6, 1983-Nov. 18, 1983
Temporary 2: Feb. 29, 1984-Jan. 3, 1985
Temporary 3: Jan. 30, 1985-Dec. 30, 1985
Temporary 4: Jan. 29, 1986-Jan. 3, 1987
2nd Dates: Jan. 22, 1987-Jan. 3, 1991
2nd Departure: Moved to Education and Labor

4th PUBLIC WORKS AND TRANSPORTATION
Dates: Jan. 28, 1981-Jan. 3, 1995
Departure: Left the House; retired

Cong.	Ranking	Terms in: House	Comm.	Date of Assignment
103rd	Maj-5th	9	7	Jan. 5, 1993

5th EDUCATION AND LABOR
Dates: Jan. 24, 1991-Jan. 3, 1995
Departure: Left the House; retired

Cong.	Ranking	Terms in: House	Comm.	Date of Assignment
103rd	Maj-25th	10	2	Jan. 21, 1993

HOUSE SELECT AND SPECIAL COMMITTEES:

1st SELECT NARCOTICS ABUSE AND CONTROL (Temporary)
Dates: Feb. 21, 1991-Jan. 3, 1993
Termination: Committee not renewed in 1993

James W. DeMint (R-S.C.)

Dates: Sept. 2, 1951
House: Jan. 3, 1999-Jan. 3, 2005
Left the House: Elected to U.S. Senate in 2004
Senate: Jan. 3, 2005-date
Serving in the 111th Congress

HOUSE STANDING COMMITTEES:

1st EDUCATION AND THE WORKFORCE
Dates: Jan. 6, 1999-Jan. 3, 2005
Departure: Left the House for the Senate

Cong.	Ranking	Terms in: House	Comm.	Date of Assignment
106th	Maj-26th	1	1	Jan. 6, 1999
107th	Maj-19th	2	2	Jan. 6, 2001
108th	Maj-13th	3	3	Jan. 28, 2003

2nd SMALL BUSINESS
Dates: Jan. 6, 1999-Jan. 3, 2005
Departure: Left the House for the Senate

Cong.	Ranking	Terms in: House	Comm.	Date of Assignment
106th	Maj-16th	1	1	Jan. 6, 1999
107th	Maj-10th	2	2	Jan. 6, 2001
108th	Maj-7th	3	3	Jan. 28, 2003

3rd TRANSPORTATION AND INFRASTRUCTURE
Dates: Jan. 6, 1999-Jan. 3, 2005
Departure: Left the House for the Senate

Cong.	Ranking	Terms in: House	Comm.	Date of Assignment
106th	Maj-37th	1	1	Jan. 6, 1999
107th	Maj-24th	2	2	Jan. 6, 2001
108th	Maj-19th	3	3	Jan. 28, 2003

SENATE STANDING COMMITTEES:

1st COMMERCE, SCIENCE AND TRANSPORTATION
Dates: Jan. 6, 2005-date
Departure: Still serving in the 111th Congress

Cong.	Ranking	Years in: Senate	Comm.	Date of Assignment
109th	Maj-11th	1	1	Jan. 6, 2005
110th	Min-9th	3	3	Jan. 12, 2007
111th	Min-4th	5	5	Jan. 21, 2009

2nd ENVIRONMENT AND PUBLIC WORKS
Dates: Jan. 6, 2005-Jan. 12, 2007
Departure: Moved to Foreign Relations and Energy and Natural Resources

Cong.	Ranking	Years in: Senate	Comm.	Date of Assignment
109th	Maj-8th	1	1	Jan. 6, 2005

3rd FOREIGN RELATIONS
Dates: Jan. 12, 2007-date
Departure: Still serving in the 111th Congress

Cong.	Ranking	Years in: Senate	Comm.	Date of Assignment
110th	Min-8th	3	1	Jan. 12, 2007
111th	Min-5th	5	3	Jan. 21, 2009

4th ENERGY AND NATURAL RESOURCES
Dates: Jan. 12, 2007-Jan. 21, 2009
Departure: Moved to Banking, Housing and Urban Affairs

Cong.	Ranking	Years in: Senate	Comm.	Date of Assignment
110th	Min-6th	3	1	Jan. 12, 2007

5th BANKING, HOUSING AND URBAN AFFAIRS
Dates: Jan. 21, 2009-date
Departure: Still serving in the 111th Congress

Cong.	Ranking	Years in: Senate	Comm.	Date of Assignment
111th	Min-7th	5	1	Jan. 21, 2009

SENATE SELECT AND SPECIAL COMMITTEES:

1st SPECIAL AGING (Permanent)
Dates: Jan. 6, 2005-Jan. 12, 2007
Departure: Moved to Foreign Relations

Cong.	Ranking	Years in: Senate	Comm.	Date of Assignment
109th	Maj-11th	1	1	Jan. 6, 2005

JOINT COMMITTEES:

1st JOINT ECONOMIC
Senate Dates: Jan. 6, 2005-date
Departure: Still serving in the 111th Congress

Cong.	Ranking	Years in: Senate	Comm.	Date of Assignment
109th	Maj-4th	1	1	Jan. 6, 2005
110th	Min-3rd	3	3	Jan. 12, 2007
111th	Min-2nd	5	5	Jan. 21, 2009

Charles W. Dent (R-Penn.)

Dates: May 24, 1960
House: Jan. 3, 2005-date
Serving in the 111th Congress

HOUSE STANDING COMMITTEES:

1st GOVERNMENT REFORM
Dates: Jan. 26, 2005-Jan. 3, 2007
Departure: Left committee; no new assignment

Cong.	Ranking	Terms in: House	Comm.	Date of Assignment
109th	Maj-22nd	1	1	Jan. 26, 2005

2nd TRANSPORTATION AND INFRASTRUCTURE
Dates: Jan. 26, 2005-date
Departure: Still serving in the 111th Congress

Cong.	Ranking	Terms in: House	Comm.	Date of Assignment
109th	Maj-34th	1	1	Jan. 26, 2005
110th	Min-23rd	2	2	Jan. 10, 2007
111th	Min-19th	3	3	Jan. 9, 2009

3rd HOMELAND SECURITY
Dates: Jan. 26, 2005-date
Departure: Still serving in the 111th Congress

Cong.	Ranking	Terms in: House	Comm.	Date of Assignment
109th	—	1	1	Jan. 26, 2005 provisional
109th	Maj-19th	1	1	Feb. 9, 2005 formal
110th	Min-11th	2	2	Jan. 10, 2007
111th	Min-7th	3	3	Jan. 9, 2009

4th STANDARDS OF OFFICIAL CONDUCT
Dates: Jan. 9, 2009-date
Departure: Still serving in the 111th Congress

Cong.	Ranking	Terms in: House	Comm.	Date of Assignment
111th	Min-5th	3	1	Jan. 9, 2009

Butler C. Derrick Jr. (D-S.C.)

Dates: Dec. 30, 1936
House: Jan. 3, 1975-Jan. 3, 1995
Left the House: Retired in 1994

HOUSE STANDING COMMITTEES:

1st SMALL BUSINESS
Dates: Jan. 20, 1975-Feb. 6, 1975
Departure: Moved to Budget

2nd BANKING, CURRENCY AND HOUSING, 94
BANKING, FINANCE AND URBAN AFFAIRS, 95
Dates: Jan. 23, 1975-Jan. 3, 1979
Departure: Moved to Rules

3rd BUDGET
1st Dates: Feb. 5, 1975-Jan. 3, 1979
1st Departure: Moved to Rules
2nd Dates: Jan. 6, 1983-Jan. 3, 1989
2nd Departure: Left committee; no new assignment

4th RULES
Dates: Jan. 24, 1979-Jan. 3, 1995
Departure: Left the House; retired

Cong.	Ranking	Terms in: House	Comm.	Date of Assignment
103rd	Maj-2nd	10	8	Jan. 5, 1993

5th HOUSE ADMINISTRATION
Dates: Jan. 21, 1993-Jan. 3, 1995
Departure: Left the House; retired

Cong.	Ranking	Terms in: House	Comm.	Date of Assignment
103rd	Maj-10th	10	1	Jan. 21, 1993

HOUSE SELECT AND SPECIAL COMMITTEES:

1st SELECT COMMITTEES II (Patterson)
Dates: Mar. 28, 1979-Apr. 1, 1980
Termination: House Report 866 (95-2) filed

2nd SELECT AGING (Permanent)
Dates: Feb. 5, 1981-Jan. 3, 1993
Termination: Committee not renewed in 1993

JOINT COMMITTEES:

1st DEFICIT REDUCTION (Temporary)
House Dates: Feb. 23, 1987-Sep. 29, 1987
Termination: Public Law 100-119 adjusted Gramm-Rudman-Hollings Act

Peter R. Deutsch (D-Fla.)

Dates: April 1, 1957
House: Jan. 3, 1994-Jan. 3, 2005
Left the House: Lost U.S. Senate nomination in 2004

HOUSE STANDING COMMITTEES:

1st BANKING, FINANCE AND URBAN AFFAIRS
Dates: Jan. 5, 1993-Jan. 3, 1995
Departure: Moved to Commerce

Cong.	Ranking	Terms in: House	Comm.	Date of Assignment
103rd	Maj-17th	1	1	Jan. 5, 1993

2nd FOREIGN AFFAIRS
Dates: Jan. 5, 1993-Jan. 3, 1995
Departure: Moved to Commerce

Cong.	Ranking	Terms in: House	Comm.	Date of Assignment
103rd	Maj-22nd	1	1	Jan. 5, 1993

3rd MERCHANT MARINE AND FISHERIES
Dates: Jan. 21, 1993-Jan. 3, 1995
Departure: Committee abolished; moved to Commerce

Cong.	Ranking	Terms in: House	Comm.	Date of Assignment
103rd	Maj-27th	1	1	Jan. 21, 1993

4th COMMERCE, 104-106
ENERGY AND COMMERCE, 107-108
Dates: Jan. 5, 1995-Jan. 3, 2005
Departure: Left the House; lost Senate nomination

Cong.	Ranking	Terms in: House	Comm.	Date of Assignment
104th	Min-17th	2	1	Jan. 5, 1995
105th	Min-12th	3	2	Jan. 7, 1997

106th	Min-10th	4	3	Jan. 6, 1999
107th	Min-10th	5	4	Jan. 31, 2001
108th	Min-10th	6	5	Jan. 28, 2003

Theodore E. Deutch (D-Fla.)

Dates: May 7, 1966
House: Apr. 13, 2010-date
Serving in the 111th Congress

H: Deutch was elected to the 111th Congress by special election, Apr. 13, 2010 to fill the vacancy caused by the resignation of U.S. Representative Robert Wexler (D-Fla.). Deutch was seated Apr. 15, 2010 and assigned to committees.

HOUSE STANDING COMMITTEES

1st FOREIGN AFFAIRS
Dates: May 6. 2010-date
Departure: Still serving in the 111th Congress

		Terms in:		Date of
Cong.	Ranking	House	Comm.	Assignment
111th	MjR-2nd	1	1	May 6, 2010

2nd JUDICIARY
Dates: May 6. 2010-date
Departure: Still serving in the 111th Congress

		Terms in:		Date of
Cong.	Ranking	House	Comm.	Assignment
111th	MjR-2nd	1	1	May 6, 2010

Michael DeWine (R-Ohio)

Dates: Jan. 5, 1947
House: Jan. 3, 1983-Jan. 3, 1991
Left the House: Elected Lt. Governor in 1990
Senate: Jan. 3, 1995-Jan. 3, 2007
Left the Senate: Defeated for re-election in 2006

HOUSE STANDING COMMITTEES:

1st JUDICIARY
Dates: Jan. 6, 1983-Jan. 3, 1991
Departure: Left the House; elected Lt. Governor

2nd FOREIGN AFFAIRS
Dates: Jan. 30, 1985-Jan. 3, 1991
Departure: Left the House; elected Lt. Governor

HOUSE SELECT AND SPECIAL COMMITTEES:

1st SELECT AGING (Permanent)
Dates: July 14, 1983-Jan. 3, 1985
Departure: Left committee; no new assignment

2nd SELECT COMMITTEE TO INVESTIGATE COVERT ARMS TRANSACTIONS WITH IRAN
Dates: Jan. 7, 1987-Nov. 17, 1987
Departure: House Report 433 (100-1) filed

SENATE STANDING COMMITTEES:

1st JUDICIARY
Dates: Jan. 4, 1995-Jan. 3, 2007
Departure: Left the Senate; lost re-election

		Years in:		Date of
Cong.	Ranking	Senate	Comm.	Assignment
104th	Maj-9th	1	1	Jan. 4, 1995
105th	Maj-7th	3	3	Jan. 9, 1997
106th	Maj-6th	5	5	Jan. 7, 1999
107th	Maj-6th	7	7	Jan. 25, 2001
+107th	Min-6th	7	7	June 6, 2001
108th	Maj-5th	9	9	Jan. 15, 2003
109th	Maj-5th	11	11	Jan. 6, 2005

2nd LABOR AND HUMAN RESOURCES renamed Jan. 21, 1999 HEALTH, EDUCATION, LABOR AND PENSIONS
1st Dates: Jan. 4, 1995-Jan. 25, 2001
1st Departure: Moved to Appropriations; returned
2nd Dates: July 10, 2001-Jan. 3, 2007
2nd Departure: Left the Senate; lost re-election

		Years in:		Date of
Cong.	Ranking	Senate	Comm.	Assignment
104th	Maj-6th	1	*1 1	Jan. 4, 1995
105th	Maj-5th	3	*1 3	Jan. 9, 1997
106th	Maj-4th	5	*1 5	Jan. 7, 1999
+107th	MnR-1st	7	*2 1	July 10, 2001
108th	Maj-6th	9	*2 2	Jan. 15, 2003
109th	Maj-7th	11	*2 4	Jan. 6, 2005

3rd APPROPRIATIONS
Dates: Jan. 25, 2001-Jan. 3, 2007
Departure: Left the Senate; lost re-election

		Years in:		Date of
Cong.	Ranking	Senate	Comm.	Assignment
107th	Maj-14th	7	1	Jan. 25, 2001
+107th	Min-14th	7	1	June 6, 2001
108th	Maj-14th	9	2	Jan. 15, 2003
109th	Maj-13th	11	4	Jan. 6, 2005

SENATE SELECT AND SPECIAL COMMITTEES:

1st SELECT INTELLIGENCE (Permanent)
1st Dates: Jan. 6, 1995-Nov. 10, 1999, effective Jan. 6, 2000
1st Departure: Removed by S. Res. 232
2nd Dates: Jan. 25, 2001-Jan. 3, 2007
2nd Departure: Left the Senate; lost re-election

		Years in:		Date of
Cong.	Ranking	Senate	Comm.	Assignment
104th	Maj-4th	1 *1	1	Jan. 6, 1995
105th	Maj-4th	3 *1	3	Jan. 9, 1997
106th	Maj-4th	5 *1	5	Jan. 7, 1999
107th	Maj-6th	7 *2	1	Jan. 25, 2001
+107th	Min-6th	7 *2	1	June 6, 2001
108th	Maj-3rd	9 *2	2	Jan. 15, 2003
109th	Maj-3rd	11 *2	4	Jan. 6, 2005

Lincoln Diaz-Balart (R-Fla.)

Dates: Aug. 13, 1954
House: Jan. 3, 1993-date
Serving in the 111th Congress

HOUSE STANDING COMMITTEES:

1st FOREIGN AFFAIRS
Dates: Jan. 5, 1993-Jan. 3, 1995
Departure: Moved to Rules and House Oversight

		Terms in:		Date of
Cong.	Ranking	House	Comm.	Assignment
103rd	Min-17th	1	1	Jan. 5, 1993

2nd MERCHANT MARINE AND FISHERIES
Dates: Jan. 5, 1993-Jan. 3, 1995

Departure: Committee abolished; moved to Rules and House Oversight

Cong.	Ranking	Terms in: House	Comm.	Date of Assignment
103rd	Min-15th	1	1	Jan. 5, 1993

3rd HOUSE OVERSIGHT
Dates: Jan. 4, 1995-Jan. 3, 1997
Departure: Left committee; no new assignment

Cong.	Ranking	Terms in: House	Comm.	Date of Assignment
104th	Maj-6th	2	1	Jan. 4, 1995

4th RULES
Dates: Jan. 4, 1995-date
Departure: Still serving in the 111th Congress

Cong.	Ranking	Terms in: House	Comm.	Date of Assignment
104th	Maj-7th	2	1	Jan. 4, 1995
105th	Maj-6th	3	2	Jan. 7, 1997
106th	Maj-5th	4	3	Jan. 6, 1999
107th	Maj-5th	5	4	Jan. 3, 2001
108th	Maj-5th	6	5	Jan. 7, 2003
109th	Maj-2nd	7	6	Jan. 4, 2005
110th	Min-2nd	8	7	Jan. 4, 2007
111th	Min-2nd	9	8	Jan. 9, 2009

HOUSE SELECT AND SPECIAL COMMITTEES:

1st SELECT HOMELAND SECURITY
Dates: Feb. 12, 2003-Jan. 3, 2005
Departure: Did not continue on reorganized standing committee

Cong.	Ranking	Terms in: House	Comm.	Date of Assignment
108th	Maj-16th	6	1	Feb. 12, 2003

Mario Diaz-Balart (R-Fla.)

Dates: Sept. 15, 1961
House: Jan. 3, 2003-date
Serving in the 111th Congress

HOUSE STANDING COMMITTEES:

1st BUDGET
Dates: Jan. 28, 2003-date
Departure: Still serving in the 111th Congress

Cong.	Ranking	Terms in: House	Comm.	Date of Assignment
108th	Maj-22nd	1	1	Jan. 28, 2003
109th	Maj-12th	2	2	Jan. 26, 2005
110th	Min-6th	3	3	Jan. 18, 2007
111th	Min-3rd	4	4	Jan. 9, 2009

2nd TRANSPORTATION AND INFRASTRUCTURE
Dates: Jan. 28, 2003-date
Departure: Still serving in the 111th Congress

Cong.	Ranking	Terms in: House	Comm.	Date of Assignment
108th	Maj-40th	1	1	Jan. 28, 2003
109th	Maj-29th	2	2	Jan. 26, 2005
110th	Min-21st	3	3	Jan. 10, 2007
111th	Min-18th	4	4	Jan. 9, 2009

3rd SCIENCE, 109
SCIENCE AND TECHNOLOGY, 110-111

Dates: Apr. 4, 2006-date
Departure: Still serving in the 111th Congress

Cong.	Ranking	Terms in: House	Comm.	Date of Assignment
109th	MjA-24th	2	1	Apr. 4, 2006
110th	Min-17th	3	2	Jan. 10, 2007
111th	Min-13th	4	3	Jan. 9, 2009

Jay W. Dickey Jr. (R-Ark.)

Dates: Dec. 14, 1939
House: Jan. 3, 1993-Jan. 3, 2001
Left the House: Defeated for re-election in 2000

HOUSE STANDING COMMITTEES:

1st AGRICULTURE
Dates: Jan. 5, 1993-Jan. 3, 1995
Departure: Moved to Appropriations

Cong.	Ranking	Terms in: House	Comm.	Date of Assignment
103rd	Min-16th	1	1	Jan. 5, 1993

2nd NATURAL RESOURCES
Dates: Jan. 5, 1993-Jan. 3, 1995
Departure: Moved to Appropriations

Cong.	Ranking	Terms in: House	Comm.	Date of Assignment
103rd	Min-15th	1	1	Jan. 5, 1993

3rd SMALL BUSINESS
Dates: Jan. 5, 1993-Jan. 3, 1995
Departure: Moved to Appropriations

Cong.	Ranking	Terms in: House	Comm.	Date of Assignment
103rd	Min-15th	1	1	Jan. 5, 1993

4th APPROPRIATIONS
Dates: Jan. 4, 1995-Jan. 3, 2001
Departure: Left the House; lost re-election

Cong.	Ranking	Terms in: House	Comm.	Date of Assignment
104th	Maj-24th	2	1	Jan. 4, 1995
105th	Maj-21st	3	2	Jan. 7, 1997
106th	Maj-19th	4	3	Jan. 6, 1999

Norman D. Dicks (D-Wash.)

Dates: Dec. 16, 1940
House: Jan. 3, 1977-date
Serving in the 111th Congress

HOUSE STANDING COMMITTEES:

1st APPROPRIATIONS
Dates: Jan. 19, 1977-date
Departure: Still serving in the 111th Congress

Cong.	Ranking	Terms in: House	Comm.	Date of Assignment
103rd	Maj-10th	9	9	Jan. 5, 1993
104th	Min-7th	10	10	Jan. 4, 1995
105th	Min-5th	11	11	Jan. 7, 1997

106th	Min-3rd	12	12	Jan. 6, 1999
107th	Min-3rd	13	13	Jan. 31, 2001
108th	Min-3rd	14	14	Jan. 28, 2003
109th	Min-3rd	15	15	Jan. 26, 2005
110th	Maj-3rd	16	16	Jan. 4, 2007
111th	Maj-3rd	17	17	Jan. 7, 2009

2nd HOMELAND SECURITY
Dates: Feb. 9, 2005-Jan. 3, 2009
Departure: Left committee; no new assignment

| | | Terms in: | | Date of |
Cong.	Ranking	House	Comm.	Assignment
109th	Min-4th	15	2	Feb. 9, 2005
110th	Maj-4th	16	3	Jan. 12, 2007

HOUSE SELECT AND SPECIAL COMMITTEES:

1st PERMANENT SELECT INTELLIGENCE
Dates: Feb. 5, 1991-Jan. 3, 1999
Departure: Left committee; no new assignment

| | | Terms in: | | Date of |
Cong.	Ranking	House	Comm.	Assignment
103rd	Maj-3rd	9	2	Feb. 3, 1993
104th	Min-RM	10	3	Jan. 4, 1995
105th	Min-RM	11	4	Feb. 10, 1997

2nd SELECT NATIONAL SECURITY CONCERNS WITH CHINA
Dates: June 22, 1998-Apr. 30, 1999
Termination: House Report 851 (105-2) filed, Jan. 3, 1999

| | | Terms in: | | Date of |
Cong.	Ranking	House	Comm.	Assignment
105th	Min-RM	11	1	June 22, 1998
106th	Min-RM	12	2	Jan. 19, 1999

3rd SELECT HOMELAND SECURITY
Dates: Feb. 12, 2003-Jan. 3, 2005
Departure: Remained on reorganized standing committee

| | | Terms in: | | Date of |
Cong.	Ranking	House	Comm.	Assignment
108th	Min-5th	14	1	Feb. 12, 2003

John D. Dingell Jr. (D-Mich.)

Dates: July 8, 1926
House: Dec. 13, 1955-date
Serving in the 111th Congress

H: John Dingell Jr. was elected to the 84th Congress by special election, Dec. 13, 1955, to fill the vacancy caused by the death of his father, U.S. Representative John D. Dingell (D-Mich.). Dingell Jr. was seated Jan. 3, 1956, and assigned to committees.

HOUSE STANDING COMMITTEES:

1st MERCHANT MARINE AND FISHERIES
Dates: Jan. 19, 1956-Jan. 3, 1981
Departure: Left committee to chair Energy and Commerce

2nd PUBLIC WORKS
Dates: Jan. 19, 1956-Jan. 3, 1957
Departure: Moved to Interstate and Foreign Commerce

3rd INTERSTATE AND FOREIGN COMMERCE, 85-97
ENERGY AND COMMERCE, 97-103
COMMERCE, 104-106
ENERGY AND COMMERCE, 107-111
Dates: Jan. 10, 1957-date
Departure: Still serving in the 111th Congress

| | | Terms in: | | Date of |
Cong.	Ranking	House	Comm.	Assignment
103rd	Maj-Chr	20	19	Jan. 5, 1993
104th	Min-RM	21	20	Jan. 4, 1995
105th	Min-RM	22	21	Jan. 7, 1997
106th	Min-RM	23	22	Jan. 6, 1999
107th	Min-RM	24	23	Jan. 31, 2001
108th	Min-RM	25	24	Jan. 8, 2003
109th	Min-RM	26	25	Jan. 6, 2005
110th	Maj-Chr	27	26	Jan. 4, 2007
111th	Maj-2nd	28	27	Jan. 7, 2009

4th SMALL BUSINESS
Dates: Jan. 20, 1975-Jan. 3, 1981
Departure: Left committee to chair Energy and Commerce

HOUSE SELECT AND SPECIAL COMMITTEES:

1st SELECT SMALL BUSINESS
Dates: Jan. 31, 1963-Jan. 3, 1975
Departure: Continued on reorganized standing committee

2nd SELECT ENERGY (Ad Hoc)
Dates: Apr. 21, 1977-Dec. 29, 1978
Termination: House Report 1820 (95-2) filed

Julian C. Dixon (D-Cal.)

Dates: Aug. 8, 1934-Dec. 8, 2000
House: Jan. 3, 1979-Dec. 8, 2000
Left the House: Died in office

HOUSE STANDING COMMITTEES:

1st APPROPRIATIONS
Dates: Jan. 24, 1979-Dec. 8, 2000
Departure: Died in office

| | | Terms in: | | Date of |
Cong.	Ranking	House	Comm.	Assignment
103rd	Maj-12th	8	8	Jan. 5, 1993
104th	Min-9th	9	9	Jan. 4, 1995
105th	Min-7th	10	10	Jan. 7, 1997
106th	Min-5th	11	11	Jan. 6, 1999

2nd STANDARDS OF OFFICIAL CONDUCT
Dates: Jan. 6, 1983-Jan. 3, 1991
Departure: Left committee; no new assignment

HOUSE SELECT AND SPECIAL COMMITTEES:

1st PERMANENT SELECT INTELLIGENCE
Dates: Feb. 3, 1993-Dec. 8, 2000
Departure: Died in office

| | | Terms in: | | Date of |
Cong.	Ranking	House	Comm.	Assignment
103rd	Maj-4th	8	1	Feb. 3, 1993
104th	Min-3rd	9	2	Jan. 4, 1995
105th	Min-2nd	10	3	Feb. 10, 1997
106th	Min-RM	11	4	Feb. 12, 1999

Charles Djou (R-Hawaii)

Dates: Aug. 9, 1971
House: May 22, 2010-date
Serving in the 111th Congress

H: Djou was elected to the 111th Congress by special election, May 22, 2010, to fill the vacancy caused by the resignation of U.S. Representative Neal Abercrombie (D-Hawaii) to seek the governorship of Hawaii. Djou was seated and assigned to committees.

Christopher J. Dodd (D-Conn.)

Dates: May 27, 1944
House: Jan. 3, 1975-Jan. 3, 1981
Left the House: Elected to U.S. Senate in 1980
Senate: Jan. 3, 1981-date
Serving in the 111th Congress

HOUSE STANDING COMMITTEES:

1st JUDICIARY
Dates: Jan. 20, 1975-Jan. 3, 1977
Departure: Moved to Rules

2nd SCIENCE AND TECHNOLOGY
Dates: Jan. 20, 1975-Jan. 3, 1977
Departure: Moved to Rules

3rd RULES
Dates: Jan. 19, 1977-Jan. 3, 1981
Departure: Left the House for the Senate

HOUSE SELECT AND SPECIAL COMMITTEES:

1st OUTER CONTINENTAL SHELF (Ad Hoc)
Dates: Apr. 22, 1975-July 31, 1980
Termination: House Report 1214 (96-2) filed

2nd SELECT ASSASSINATIONS
Dates: Sep. 21, 1976-Jan. 2, 1979
Termination: House Report 1828 (95-2) filed

SENATE STANDING COMMITTEES:

1st BANKING, HOUSING AND URBAN AFFAIRS
Dates: Jan. 5, 1981-date
Departure: Still serving in the 111th Congress

Cong.	Ranking	Years in: Senate	Comm.	Date of Assignment
103rd	Maj-3rd	13	13	Jan. 7, 1993
104th	Min-2nd	15	14	Jan. 4, 1995
105th	Min-2nd	17	17	Jan. 9, 1997
106th	Min-2nd	19	19	Jan. 7, 1999
107th	Min-2nd	21	21	Jan. 25, 2001
+107th	Maj-2nd	21	21	June 6, 2001
108th	Min-2nd	23	23	Jan. 15, 2003
109th	Min-2nd	25	25	Jan. 6, 2005
110th	Maj-Chr	27	27	Jan. 12, 2007
111th	Maj-Chr	29	29	Jan. 21, 2009

2nd FOREIGN RELATIONS
Dates: Jan. 5, 1981-date
Departure: Still serving in the 111th Congress

Cong.	Ranking	Years in: Senate	Comm.	Date of Assignment
103rd	Maj-4th	13	13	Jan. 7, 1993
104th	Min-4th	15	14	Jan. 4, 1995
105th	Min-3rd	17	17	Jan. 9, 1997
106th	Min-3rd	19	19	Jan. 7, 1999
107th	Min-3rd	21	21	Jan. 25, 2001
+107th	Maj-3rd	21	21	June 6, 2001
108th	Min-3rd	23	23	Jan. 15, 2003
109th	Min-3rd	25	25	Jan. 6, 2005
110th	Maj-2nd	27	27	Jan. 12, 2007
111th	Maj-2nd	29	29	Jan. 21, 2009

3rd LABOR AND HUMAN RESOURCES renamed Jan. 21, 1999
HEALTH, EDUCATION, LABOR AND PENSIONS
Dates: Feb. 3, 1983-date
Departure: Still serving in the 111th Congress

Cong.	Ranking	Years in: Senate	Comm.	Date of Assignment
103rd	Maj-4th	13	10	Jan. 7, 1993
104th	Min-3rd	15	12	Jan. 4, 1995
105th	Min-2nd	17	14	Jan. 9, 1997
106th	Min-2nd	19	16	Jan. 7, 1999
107th	Min-2nd	21	18	Jan. 25, 2001
+107th	Maj-2nd	21	19	June 6, 2001
108th	Min-2nd	23	20	Jan. 15, 2003
109th	Min-2nd	25	22	Jan. 6, 2005
110th	Maj-2nd	27	24	Jan. 12, 2007
111th	Maj-2nd	29	26	Jan. 21, 2009

4th BUDGET
Dates: Jan. 6, 1987-Jan. 9, 1997
Departure: Left committee; no new assignment

Cong.	Ranking	Years in: Senate	Comm.	Date of Assignment
103rd	Maj-9th	13	7	Jan. 21, 1993
104th	Min-7th	15	9	Jan. 6, 1995

5th RULES AND ADMINISTRATION
Dates: Jan. 6, 1987-date
Ch2: Replaced A. Mitchell McConnell (R-Ky.) on June 6, 2001, following Senate Party control shift
Departure: Still serving in the 111th Congress

Cong.	Ranking	Years in: Senate	Comm.	Date of Assignment
103rd	Maj-7th	13	7	Jan. 21, 1993
104th	Min-6th	15	9	Jan. 6, 1995
105th	Min-5th	17	11	Jan. 9, 1997
106th	Min-RM	19	13	Jan. 7, 1999
=107th	Maj-ChT	21	14	Jan. 3, 2001
107th	Min-RM1	21	15	Jan. 25, 2001
+107th	Maj-Ch2	21	15	June 6, 2001
108th	Min-RM	23	17	Jan. 15, 2003
109th	Min-RM	25	19	Jan. 6, 2005
110th	Maj-2nd	27	21	Jan. 12, 2007
111th	Maj-3rd	29	23	Jan. 21, 2009

SENATE SELECT AND SPECIAL COMMITTEES:

1st SPECIAL AGING (Permanent)
Dates: Jan. 21, 1981-Jan. 6, 1987
Departure: Moved to Budget and Rules and Administration

2nd SPECIAL COMMITTEE TO INVESTIGATE WHITEWATER DEVELOPMENT CORPORATION AND RELATED MATTERS
Dates: July 20, 1995-June 17, 1996
Termination: Senate Report 104-280 filed

Cong.	Ranking	Years in: Senate	Comm.	Date of Assignment
104th	Min-2nd	15	1	July 20, 1995

3rd SPECIAL YEAR 2000 TECHNOLOGY PROBLEM
Dates: Apr. 23, 1998-Feb. 29, 2000
Termination: Senate Print 106-42 issued

Cong.	Ranking	Years in: Senate	Comm.	Date of Assignment
105th	Min-VCh	18	1	Apr. 23, 1998
106th	Min-VCh	19	1	Continued

JOINT COMMITTEES:

1st JOINT DEFICIT REDUCTION (Temporary)
Senate Dates: Jan. 6, 1987-Sep. 29, 1987
Departure: Public Law 100-119, Adjusted Gramm-Rudman-Hollings Act

2nd JOINT LIBRARY
Senate Dates: Feb. 25, 1999-date
Departure: Still serving in the 111th Congress

Cong.	Ranking	Years in: Senate	Comm.	Date of Assignment
106th	Min-1st	19	1	Feb. 25, 1999
+107th	Maj-VCh	21	3	Sep. 19, 2001
108th	Min-1st	23	5	Mar. 13, 2003
109th	Min-1st	25	7	Mar. 4, 2005
110th	Maj-2nd	27	9	Mar. 6, 2007
111th	Maj-2nd	29	11	Apr. 3, 2009

Lloyd A. Doggett II (D-Tex.)

Dates: Oct. 6, 1946
House: Jan. 3, 1995-date
Serving in the 111th Congress

HOUSE STANDING COMMITTEES:

1st BUDGET
1st Dates: Jan. 4, 1995-Jan. 3, 1999
1st Departure: Moved to Ways and Means
2nd Dates: Jan. 18, 2001-date
2nd Departure: Still serving in the 111th Congress

Cong.	Ranking	Terms in: House	Comm.	Date of Assignment
104th	Min-18th	1 *1	1	Jan. 4, 1995
105th	Min-10th	2 *1	2	Jan. 7, 1997
110th	Maj-10th	7 *2	1	Jan. 18, 2007
111th	Maj-5th	8 *2	2	Jan. 21, 2009

2nd SCIENCE
Dates: Jan. 4, 1995-Apr. 17, 1997
Departure: Resigned committee; moved to Resources

Cong.	Ranking	Terms in: House	Comm.	Date of Assignment
104th	Min-20th	1	1	Jan. 4, 1995
105th	Min-13th	2	2	Feb. 13, 1997

3rd RESOURCES
Dates: Apr. 17, 1997-Jan. 3, 1999
Departure: Moved to Ways and Means

Cong.	Ranking	Terms in: House	Comm.	Date of Assignment
105th	MnR-3rd	2	1	Apr. 17, 1997

4th WAYS AND MEANS
Dates: Jan. 6, 1999-date
Departure: Still serving in the 111th Congress

Cong.	Ranking	Terms in: House	Comm.	Date of Assignment
106th	Min-16th	3	1	Jan. 6, 1999
107th	Min-16th	4	2	Jan. 31, 2001
108th	Min-14th	5	3	Jan. 28, 2003
109th	Min-12th	6	4	Jan. 26, 2005
110th	Maj-10th	7	5	Jan. 4, 2007
111th	Maj-9th	8	6	Jan. 7, 2009

JOINT COMMITTEES:

1st JOINT ECONOMIC
House Dates: Mar. 27, 2007-Jan. 3, 2009
Departure: Left committee; no new assignment

Cong.	Ranking	Terms in: House	Comm.	Date of Assignment
110th	Maj-6th	7	1	Mar. 27, 2007

Elizabeth Hanford Dole (R-N.C.)

Dates: July 29, 1936
Senate: Jan. 3, 2003-Jan. 3, 2009
Left the Senate: Defeated for re-election in 2008

SENATE STANDING COMMITTEES:

1st AGRICULTURE, NUTRITION AND FORESTRY
Dates: Jan. 15, 2003-Jan. 6, 2005
Departure: Left committee; no new assignment

Cong.	Ranking	Years in: Senate	Comm.	Date of Assignment
108th	Maj-10th	1	1	Jan. 15, 2003

2nd ARMED SERVICES
Dates: Jan. 15, 2003-Jan. 3, 2009
Departure: Left the Senate; lost re-election

Cong.	Ranking	Years in: Senate	Comm.	Date of Assignment
108th	Maj-12th	1	1	Jan. 15, 2003
109th	Maj-11th	3	2	Jan. 6, 2005
110th	Min-9th	5	4	Jan. 12, 2007

3rd BANKING, HOUSING AND URBAN AFFAIRS
Dates: Jan. 15, 2003-Jan. 3, 2009
Departure: Left the Senate; lost re-election

Cong.	Ranking	Years in: Senate	Comm.	Date of Assignment
108th	Maj-10th	1	1	Jan. 15, 2003
109th	Maj-10th	3	2	Jan. 6, 2005
110th	Min-9th	5	4	Jan. 12, 2007

4th SMALL BUSINESS AND ENTREPRENEURSHIP
Dates: Jan. 12, 2007-Jan. 3, 2009
Departure: Left the Senate; lost re-election

Cong.	Ranking	Years in: Senate	Comm.	Date of Assignment
110th	Min-5th	5	1	Jan. 12, 2007

SENATE SELECT AND SPECIAL COMMITTEES:

1st SPECIAL AGING (Permanent)
Dates: Jan. 15, 2003-Jan. 3, 2009
Departure: Left the Senate; lost re-election

Cong.	Ranking	Years in: Senate	Comm.	Date of Assignment
108th	Maj-9th	1	1	Jan. 15, 2003
109th	Maj-5th	3	2	Jan. 6, 2005
110th	Min-6th	5	4	Jan. 12, 2007

Robert J. Dole (R-Kans.)

Dates: June 22, 1923
House: Jan. 3, 1961-Jan. 3, 1969
Left the House: Elected to U.S. Senate in 1968
Senate: Jan. 3, 1969-June 11, 1996
Left the Senate: Resigned chamber; lost election for President in 1996

HOUSE STANDING COMMITTEES:

1st AGRICULTURE
Dates: Feb. 13, 1961-Jan. 3, 1969
Departure: Left the House for the Senate

2nd GOVERNMENT OPERATIONS
Dates: Aug. 31, 1965-Jan. 30, 1968
Departure: Left committee; no new assignment

SENATE STANDING COMMITTEES:

1st AGRICULTURE AND FORESTRY reorganized Feb. 11, 1977
AGRICULTURE, NUTRITION AND FORESTRY
Dates: Jan. 14. 1969-June 11, 1996
Departure: Resigned the Senate; lost presidential election

Cong.	Ranking	Years in: Senate	Comm.	Date of Assignment
103rd	Min-2nd	25	24	Jan. 7, 1993
104th	Maj-2nd	27	26	Jan. 4, 1995

2nd PUBLIC WORKS
Dates: Jan. 14, 1969-Jan. 12, 1973
Departure: Moved to Finance

3rd FINANCE
Dates: Jan. 12, 1973-June 11, 1996
Departure: Resigned the Senate; lost presidential election

Cong.	Ranking	Years in: Senate	Comm.	Date of Assignment
103rd	Min-2nd	25	20	Jan. 7, 1993
104th	Maj-2nd	27	22	Jan. 4, 1995

4th POST OFFICE AND CIVIL SERVICE
Dates: Jan. 24, 1974-Sep. 19, 1975
Departure: Left committee; no new assignment

5th BUDGET
Dates: Aug. 7, 1974-Jan. 23, 1979
Departure: Moved to Judiciary

6th JUDICIARY
Dates: Jan. 23, 1979-Feb. 21, 1985
Departure: Left committee; became Majority Floor Leader

7th RULES AND ADMINISTRATION
Dates: Jan. 5, 1981-June 11, 1996
Departure: Resigned the Senate; lost presidential election

Cong.	Ranking	Years in: Senate	Comm.	Date of Assignment
103rd	Min-5th	25	13	Jan. 21, 1993
104th	Maj-5th	27	15	Jan. 6, 1995

SENATE SELECT AND SPECIAL COMMITTEES:

1st SELECT SMALL BUSINESS
Dates: Jan. 22, 1969-Jan. 24, 1974
Departure: Moved to Post Office and Civil Service

2nd SELECT NUTRITION AND HUMAN NEEDS
Dates: Jan. 22, 1969-Dec. 31, 1977
Termination: S. Res. 4 (95-1) transferred authority to Agriculture, Nutrition and Forestry

3rd FOREIGN GOVERNMENT REPRESENTATION
Dates: July 25, 1980-Oct. 2, 1980
Termination: Senate Report 1015 (96-2) filed

4th SPECIAL SECURITY AND COOPERATION IN EUROPE
Dates: Nov. 18, 1983-Mar. 27, 1985
Termination: Public Law 99-7

JOINT COMMITTEES:

1st JOINT TAXATION
Senate Dates: Feb. 8, 1979-Feb. 2, 1995
Departure: Left committee; no new assignment

Cong.	Ranking	Years in: Senate	Comm.	Date of Assignment
103rd	Min-2nd	25	14	Continued

SENATE LEADERSHIP POSTS

Dates: Nov. 28, 1984-June 11, 1996
Departure: Resigned the Senate; lost election for President

1st SENATE MAJORITY FLOOR LEADER
1st Dates: Nov. 28, 1984-Jan. 3, 1987
Note: For the 99th Congress, Dole succeeded Majority Leader Howard H. Baker (R-Tenn.) defeating Majority Whip Theodore Stevens (R-Alas.) on the 4th ballot by a vote of 28 to 25 on Nov. 28, 1994.
1st Change: Republican Party lost Senate majority in 1986
2nd Dates: Jan. 3, 1995-June 11, 1996
Note: In the 104th Congress, Dole was unopposed for Majority Floor Leader
2nd Change: Resigned post to run for President

Cong.	Ranking	Years in: Senate	Post	Date of Selection
104th	Maj-1st	27	*2 1	Dec. 2, 1994

2nd SENATE MINORITY FLOOR LEADER
Dates: Jan. 3, 1987-Jan. 3, 1995
Note: For the 100th Congress, Dole was elected Minority Leader without opposition. He was elected unopposed for the 101st-103rd Congresses.
Change: Republican Party gained Senate majority in 1994

Cong.	Ranking	Years in: Senate	Post	Date of Selection
103rd	Min-1st	25	9	Nov. 10, 1992

Pete V. Domenici (R-N.M.)

Dates: May 7, 1932
Senate: Jan. 3, 1973-Jan. 3, 2009
Left the Senate: Retired in 2008

SENATE STANDING COMMITTEES:

1st AERONAUTICAL AND SPACE SCIENCES
Dates: Jan. 12, 1973-Feb. 22, 1977

Departure: Committee reorganized; moved to Energy and Natural Resources

2nd DISTRICT OF COLUMBIA
Dates: Jan. 12, 1973-Jan. 23, 1975
Departure: Moved to Budget

3rd PUBLIC WORKS renamed
ENVIRONMENT AND PUBLIC WORKS
Dates: Jan. 12, 1973-Jan. 6, 1987
Departure: Moved to Special Aging

4th BUDGET
Dates: Jan. 23, 1975-Jan. 3, 2009
Ch1: Replaced by Kent Conrad (D-N.D.) on June 6, 2001, following party control shift and became RM2.
Departure: Left the Senate; retired

Cong.	Ranking	Years in: Senate	Comm.	Date of Assignment
103rd	Min-RM	21	18	Jan. 21, 1993
104th	Maj-Chr	23	20	Jan. 6, 1995
105th	Maj-Chr	25	22	Jan. 9, 1997
106th	Maj-Chr	27	24	Jan. 7, 1999
107th	Maj-Ch1	29	27	Jan. 25, 2001
+107th	Min-RM	29	27	June 6, 2001
108th	Maj-2nd	31	28	Jan. 15, 2003
109th	Maj-2nd	33	30	Jan. 6, 2005
110th	Min-2nd	35	32	Jan. 12, 2007

5th ENERGY AND NATURAL RESOURCES
Dates: Feb. 22, 1977-Jan. 3. 2009
Departure: Left the Senate; retired

Cong.	Ranking	Years in: Senate	Comm.	Date of Assignment
103rd	Min-3rd	21	16	Jan. 7, 1993
104th	Maj-3rd	23	18	Jan. 5, 1995
105th	Maj-2nd	25	20	Jan. 9, 1997
106th	Maj-2nd	27	22	Jan. 7, 1999
107th	Maj-2nd	29	24	Jan. 25, 2001
+107th	Min-2nd	29	25	June 6, 2001
108th	Maj-Chr	31	26	Jan. 15, 2003
109th	Maj-Chr	33	28	Jan. 6, 2005
110th	Min-RM	35	30	Jan. 12, 2007

6th APPROPRIATIONS
Dates: Jan. 3, 1983-Jan. 3, 2009
Departure: Left the Senate; retired

Cong.	Ranking	Years in: Senate	Comm.	Date of Assignment
103rd	Min-6th	21	11	Jan. 7, 1993
104th	Maj-5th	23	13	Jan. 4, 1995
105th	Maj-4th	25	15	Jan. 9, 1997
106th	Maj-4th	27	17	Jan. 7, 1999
107th	Maj-3rd	29	19	Jan. 25, 2001
+107th	Min-3rd	29	19	June 6, 2001
108th	Maj-4th	31	21	Jan. 15, 2003
109th	Maj-4th	33	23	Jan. 6, 2005
110th	Min-4th	35	25	Jan. 12, 2007

7th BANKING, HOUSING AND URBAN AFFAIRS
1st Dates: Feb. 5, 1991-Jan. 4, 1995
1st Departure: Left committee; no new assignment
2nd Dates: Oct. 12, 1995-June 20, 1996
2nd Departure: Left committee; moved to Governmental Affairs

Cong.	Ranking	Years in: Senate	Comm.	Date of Assignment
103rd	Min-8th	21	*1 2	Jan. 7, 1993
104th	MjR-1st	23	*2 1	Oct. 12, 1995

8th GOVERNMENTAL AFFAIRS renamed Oct. 9, 2004
HOMELAND SECURITY AND GOVERNMENTAL AFFAIRS
1st Dates: June 20, 1996-Jan. 6, 2003
1st Departure: Left committee; no new assignment
2nd Dates: Jan. 6, 2005-Jan. 3, 2009
2nd Departure: Left the Senate; retired

Cong.	Ranking	Years in: Senate	Comm.	Date of Assignment
104th	MjR-2nd	24 *1	1	June 20, 1996
105th	Maj-6th	25 *1	1	Jan. 9, 1997
106th	Maj-6th	27 *1	3	Jan. 7, 1999
107th	Maj-5th	29 *1	5	Jan. 25, 2001
+107th	Min-5th	29 *1	5	June 6, 2001
109th	Maj-8th	33 *2	1	Jan. 6, 2005
110th	Min-6th	35 *2	3	Jan. 12, 2007

SENATE SELECT AND SPECIAL COMMITTEES:

1st SPECIAL AGING (Permanent)
Became Permanent Special Committee on Aging, Feb. 4, 1977
1st Dates: Jan. 12, 1973-Mar. 5, 1985
1st Departure: Left committee; no new assignment
2nd Dates: Jan. 6, 1987-Mar. 19, 1991
2nd Departure: Moved to Banking, Housing and Urban Affairs

2nd SENATE COMMITTEE SYSTEM I (Stevenson)
Dates: Apr. 6, 1976-May 17, 1977
Termination: Last reports filed

3rd SELECT INDIAN AFFAIRS (Permanent), 102
INDIAN AFFAIRS (Permanent), 103-110
Dates: Feb. 5, 1991-Jan. 3, 2009
Departure: Left the Senate; retired

Cong.	Ranking	Years in: Senate	Comm.	Date of Assignment
103rd	Min-5th	21	2	Jan. 5, 1993
104th	Maj-4th	23	4	Jan. 11, 1995
105th	Maj-5th	25	6	Jan. 9, 1997
106th	Maj-5th	27	8	Jan. 7, 1999
107th	Maj-4th	29	10	Jan. 25, 2001
+107th	Min-4th	29	11	June 6, 2001
108th	Maj-3rd	31	12	Jan. 15, 2003
109th	Maj-5th	33	14	Jan. 6, 2005
110th	Min-5th	35	16	Jan. 12, 2007

4th SPECIAL COMMITTEE TO INVESTIGATE WHITEWATER DEVELOPMENT CORPORATION AND RELATED MATTERS
Dates: Oct. 12, 1995-June 17, 1996
Termination: Senate Report 104-280 filed

Cong.	Ranking	Years in: Senate	Comm.	Date of Assignment
104th	MjR-1st	23	1	Oct. 12, 1995

JOINT COMMITTEES:

1st JOINT CONGRESSIONAL OPERATIONS
Senate Dates: Jan. 29, 1975-Sep. 30, 1977
Termination: Senate Resolution 4 (95-1)

2nd JOINT ATOMIC ENERGY
Senate Dates: Nov. 30, 1976-Sep. 20, 1977
Termination: Public Law 95-10

3rd JOINT DEFICIT REDUCTION (Temporary)
Senate Dates: Jan. 6, 1987-Sep. 29, 1987
Termination: Public Law 100-119 adjusted Gramm-Rudman-Hollings Act

4th JOINT ORGANIZATION OF CONGRESS (Ad Hoc)
Senate Dates: Sep. 25, 1992-Dec. 9, 1993
Termination: Senate Report 103-215 filed

Cong.	Ranking	Years in: Senate	Comm.	Date of Assignment
103rd	Min-RM	21	1	Continued

Joe Donnelly (D-Ind.)

Dates: Sept. 28, 1955
House: Jan. 3, 2007-date
Serving in the 111th Congress

HOUSE STANDING COMMITTEES:

1st AGRICULTURE
Dates: Jan. 12, 2007-Jan. 3, 2009
Departure: Left committee; no new assignment

Cong.	Ranking	Terms in: House	Comm.	Date of Assignment
110th	Maj-24th	1	1	Jan. 12, 2007

2nd FINANCIAL SERVICES
Dates: Jan. 12, 2007-date
Departure: Still serving in the 111th Congress

Cong.	Ranking	Terms in: House	Comm.	Date of Assignment
110th	Maj-34th	1	1	Jan. 12, 2007
111th	Maj-29th	2	2	Jan. 7, 2009

3rd VETERANS' AFFAIRS
Dates: Jan. 12, 2007-date
Departure: Still serving in the 111th Congress

Cong.	Ranking	Terms in: House	Comm.	Date of Assignment
110th	Maj-12th	1	1	Jan. 12, 2007
111th	Maj-12th	2	2	Jan. 21, 2009

Calvin M. Dooley (D-Cal.)

Dates: Jan. 11, 1954
House: Jan. 3, 1991-Jan 3, 2005
Left the House: Retired in 2004

HOUSE STANDING COMMITTEES:

1st AGRICULTURE
Dates: Jan. 24, 1991-Jan. 3, 2005
Departure: Left the House; retired

Cong.	Ranking	Terms in: House	Comm.	Date of Assignment
103rd	Maj-16th	2	2	Jan. 5, 1993
104th	Min-9th	3	3	Jan. 4, 1995
105th	Min-5th	4	4	Jan. 7, 1997
106th	Min-5th	5	5	Jan. 6, 1999
107th	Min-4th	6	6	Jan. 31, 2001
108th	Min-3rd	7	7	Jan. 28, 2003

2nd SMALL BUSINESS
Dates: Jan. 24, 1991-Oct. 9, 1991
Departure: Moved to Interior and Insular Affairs

3rd INTERIOR AND INSULAR AFFAIRS, 102
NATURAL RESOURCES, 103
RESOURCES, 104-108
Dates: Oct. 9, 1991-Jan. 3, 2005
Departure: Left the House; retired

Cong.	Ranking	Terms in: House	Comm.	Date of Assignment
103rd	Maj-17th	2	2	Jan. 5, 1993
104th	Min-15th	3	3	Jan. 4, 1995
105th	Min-14th	4	4	Jan. 7, 1997
106th	Min-11th	5	5	Jan. 6, 1999
107th	Min-10th	6	6	Feb. 8, 2001
108th	Min-10th	7	7	Jan. 28, 2003

4th BANKING, FINANCE AND URBAN AFFAIRS
Dates: Jan. 21, 1993-Jan. 3, 1995
Departure: Left committee; no new assignment

Cong.	Ranking	Terms in: House	Comm.	Date of Assignment
103rd	Maj-28th	2	1	Jan. 21, 1993

John T. Doolittle (R-Cal.)

Dates: Oct. 30, 1950
House: Jan. 3, 1991-Jan. 3, 2009
Left the House: Retired in 2008

HOUSE STANDING COMMITTEES:

1st INTERIOR AND INSULAR AFFAIRS, 102
NATURAL RESOURCES, 103
RESOURCES, 104-106
Dates: Jan. 24, 1991-Jan. 3, 2001
Departure: Moved to Appropriations and House Administration

Cong.	Ranking	Terms in: House	Comm.	Date of Assignment
103rd	Min-9th	2	2	Jan. 5, 1993
104th	Maj-7th	3	3	Jan. 4, 1995
105th	Maj-8th	4	4	Jan. 7, 1997
106th	Maj-8th	5	5	Jan. 6, 1999

2nd MERCHANT MARINE AND FISHERIES
Dates: Jan. 24, 1991-Jan. 3, 1993
Departure: Moved to Agriculture

3rd AGRICULTURE
Dates: Jan. 5, 1993-Jan. 3, 1999
Departure: Moved to Government Reform and Transportation and Infrastructure

Cong.	Ranking	Terms in: House	Comm.	Date of Assignment
103rd	Min-13th	2	1	Jan. 5, 1993
104th	Maj-9th	3	2	Jan. 4, 1995
105th	Maj-6th	4	3	Jan. 7, 1997

4th TRANSPORTATION AND INFRASTRUCTURE
Dates: Jan. 6, 1999-Jan. 3, 2001
Departure: Moved to Appropriations and House Administration

Cong.	Ranking	Terms in: House	Comm.	Date of Assignment
106th	Maj-32nd	5	1	Jan. 6, 1999

5th GOVERNMENT REFORM
Dates: Feb. 2, 1999-June 25, 1999
Departure: Resigned committee; no new assignment

Cong.	Ranking	Terms in: House	Comm.	Date of Assignment
106th	Maj-24th	5	1	Feb. 2, 1999

6th APPROPRIATIONS
Dates: Jan. 6, 2001-Jan. 3, 2009
Departure: Left the House; retired

Cong.	Ranking	Terms in: House	Comm.	Date of Assignment
107th	Maj-31st	6	1	Jan. 6, 2001
108th	Maj-27th	7	2	Jan. 28, 2003
109th	Maj-26th	8	3	Jan. 6, 2005
110th	Min-20th	9	4	Jan. 4, 2007

7th HOUSE ADMINISTRATION
Dates: Jan. 31, 2001-Jan. 3, 2007
Departure: Left committee; no new assignment

Cong.	Ranking	Terms in: House	Comm.	Date of Assignment
107th	Maj-5th	6	1	Jan. 31, 2001
108th	Maj-5th	7	2	Jan. 28, 2003
109th	Maj-4th	8	3	Jan. 26, 2005

8th BUDGET
Dates: Mar. 7, 2001-Jan. 3, 2003
Departure: Left committee; no new assignment

Cong.	Ranking	Terms in: House	Comm.	Date of Assignment
107th	MjR-1st	6	1	Mar. 7, 2001

JOINT COMMITTEES:

1st JOINT ECONOMIC
House Dates: Feb. 27, 1997-Jan. 3, 2001
Departure: Moved to Appropriations

Cong.	Ranking	Terms in: House	Comm.	Date of Assignment
105th	Maj-5th	4	1	Feb. 27, 1997
106th	Maj-3rd	5	2	Mar. 18, 1999

2nd JOINT PRINTING
House Dates: June 5, 2001-Jan. 3, 2007
Departure: Left committee; no new assignment

Cong.	Ranking	Terms in: House	Comm.	Date of Assignment
107th	Maj-2nd	6	1	June 5, 2001
108th	Maj-2nd	7	2	Mar. 25, 2003
109th	Maj-2nd	8	3	Mar. 16, 2005

Byron L. Dorgan (D-N.D.)

Dates: May 14, 1942
House: Jan. 3, 1981-Dec. 14, 1992
Left the House: Resigned; appointed to U.S. Senate in 1992
Senate: Dec. 14, 1992-date
Serving in the 111th Congress

S: Dorgan was appointed to the 102nd Congress, Dec. 14, 1992, to fill the vacancy caused by the resignation of U.S. Senator Kent Conrad (D-N.D.) who had been elected to fill the vacant seat of the late U.S. Senator Quentin N. Burdick (D-N.D.). Dorgan was not seated nor assigned to committees because the 102nd Congress was not in session. Dorgan was elected to succeed Conrad in the 103rd Congress.

HOUSE STANDING COMMITTEES:

1st AGRICULTURE
Dates: Jan. 28, 1981-Jan. 3, 1983
Departure: Moved to Ways and Means

2nd SMALL BUSINESS
Dates: Jan. 28, 1981-Jan. 3, 1983
Departure: Moved to Ways and Means

3rd VETERANS' AFFAIRS
Dates: Feb. 25, 1981-Jan. 3, 1983
Departure: Moved to Ways and Means

4th WAYS AND MEANS
Dates: Jan. 6, 1983-Dec. 14, 1992
Departure: Resigned House; appointed to the Senate

HOUSE SELECT AND SPECIAL COMMITTEES:

1st SELECT HUNGER (Temporary)
Dates: Mar. 20, 1985-Dec. 14, 1992
Departure: Resigned House; appointed to the Senate

SENATE STANDING COMMITTEES:

1st COMMERCE, SCIENCE AND TRANSPORTATION
Dates: Jan. 7, 1993-date
Departure: Still serving in the 111th Congress

Cong.	Ranking	Years in: Senate	Comm.	Date of Assignment
103rd	Maj-11th	1	1	Jan. 7, 1993
104th	Min-9th	3	2	Jan. 4, 1995
105th	Min-8th	5	5	Jan. 9, 1997
106th	Min-7th	7	7	Jan. 7, 1999
107th	Min-6th	9	9	Jan. 25, 2001
+107th	Maj-6th	9	9	June 6, 2001
108th	Min-6th	11	11	Jan. 15, 2003
109th	Min-4th	13	12	Jan. 6, 2005
110th	Maj-4th	15	15	Jan. 12, 2007
111th	Maj-4th	17	17	Jan. 21, 2009

2nd GOVERNMENTAL AFFAIRS
Dates: Jan. 7, 1993-Jan. 9, 1997
Departure: Moved to Appropriations

Cong.	Ranking	Years in: Senate	Comm.	Date of Assignment
103rd	Maj-8th	1	1	Jan. 7, 1993
104th	Min-7th	3	2	Jan. 4, 1995

3rd ENERGY AND NATURAL RESOURCES
1st Dates: July 15, 1993-Jan. 4, 1995
1st Departure: Left committee; no new assignment
2nd Dates: Mar. 28, 1995-date
Departure: Still serving in the 111th Congress

Cong.	Ranking	Years in: Senate	Comm.	Date of Assignment
103rd	MjR-2nd	1	*1 1	July 15, 1993
104th	MnA-9th	3	*2 1	Mar. 28, 1995
105th	Min-5th	5	*2 2	Jan. 9, 1997
106th	Min-3rd	7	*2 4	Jan. 7, 1999
107th	Min-3rd	9	*2 6	Jan. 25, 2001
+107th	Maj-3rd	9	*2 7	June 6, 2001
108th	Min-3rd	11	*2 8	Jan. 15, 2003
109th	Min-3rd	13	*2 10	Jan. 6, 2005
110th	Maj-3rd	15	*2 12	Jan. 12, 2007
111th	Maj-2nd	17	*2 14	Jan. 21, 2009

4th VETERANS' AFFAIRS
Dates: Jan. 6, 1995-Dec. 29, 1995
Departure: Resigned committee; became Ranking Member on Select Ethics

Cong.	Ranking	Years in: Senate	Comm.	Date of Assignment
104th	Min-5th	3	1	Jan. 6, 1995

5th APPROPRIATIONS
Dates: Jan. 9, 1997-date
Departure: Still serving in the 111th Congress

Cong.	Ranking	Years in: Senate	Comm.	Date of Assignment
105th	Min-12th	5	1	Jan. 9, 1997
106th	Min-11th	7	2	Jan. 7, 1999
107th	Min-10th	9	5	Jan. 25, 2001
+107th	Maj-10th	9	5	June 6, 2001
108th	Min-10th	11	7	Jan. 15, 2003
109th	Min-9th	13	8	Jan. 6, 2005
110th	Maj-8th	15	11	Jan. 12, 2007
111th	Maj-8th	17	13	Jan. 21, 2009

SENATE SELECT AND SPECIAL COMMITTEES:

1st INDIAN AFFAIRS (Permanent)
Dates: Jan. 21, 1993-date
Departure: Still serving in the 111th Congress

Cong.	Ranking	Years in: Senate	Comm.	Date of Assignment
103rd	Maj-8th	1	1	Jan. 21, 1993
104th	Min-7th	3	2	Jan. 9, 1995
105th	Min-6th	5	4	Jan. 9, 1997
106th	Min-6th	7	6	Jan. 7, 1999
107th	Min-6th	9	9	Jan. 25, 2001
+107th	Maj-6th	9	9	June 6, 2001
108th	Min-5th	11	10	Jan. 15, 2003
109th	Min-RM	13	12	Jan. 6, 2005
110th	Maj-Chr	15	14	Jan. 12, 2007
111th	Maj-Chr	17	16	Jan. 21, 2009

2nd SELECT ETHICS (Permanent)
Dates: Jan. 4, 1995-Jan. 9, 1997
VC2: Replaced Richard Bryan (D-Nev.) as Vice Chair on Jan. 23, 1996
Departure: Moved to Appropriations

Cong.	Ranking	Years in: Senate	Comm.	Date of Assignment
104th	Min-3rd	3	1	Jan. 4, 1995
=104th	Min-VC2	4	2	Jan. 23, 1996

JOINT COMMITTEES:

1st JOINT ECONOMIC
Senate Dates: Jan. 21, 1993-Jan. 9, 1995
Departure: Moved to Energy and Natural Resources, Veterans' Affairs and Select Ethics

Cong.	Ranking	Years in: Senate	Comm.	Date of Assignment
103rd	Maj-6th	1	1	Jan. 21, 1993

House 2: Jan. 3, 1985-Jan. 3, 1997
Left the House 2: Defeated for re-election in 1996

HOUSE STANDING COMMITTEES:

1st MERCHANT MARINE AND FISHERIES
Dates: Jan. 19, 1977-Jan. 3, 1981
Departure: Moved to Foreign Affairs

2nd SCIENCE AND TECHNOLOGY
Dates: Jan. 19, 1977-Jan. 3, 1981
Departure: Moved to Foreign Affairs

3rd FOREIGN AFFAIRS
1st Dates: Jan. 28, 1981-Jan. 3, 1983
1st Departure: Left the House; lost Senate nomination
2nd Dates: Jan. 30, 1985-Jan. 3, 1989
2nd Departure: Moved to Armed Services

4th EDUCATION AND LABOR
Dates: Oct. 10, 1986-Jan. 3, 1987
Departure: Moved to Veterans' Affairs

5th VETERANS' AFFAIRS
Dates: Jan. 21, 1987-Jan. 3, 1989
Departure: Moved to Armed Services

6th ARMED SERVICES, 103
NATIONAL SECURITY, 104
Dates: Jan. 20, 1989-Jan. 3, 1997
Departure: Left the House; lost re-election

Cong.	Ranking	Terms in: House	Comm.	Date of Assignment
103rd	Min-10th	8	3	Jan. 5, 1993
104th	Maj-8th	9	4	Jan. 4, 1995

HOUSE SELECT AND SPECIAL COMMITTEES:

1st SELECT AGING (Permanent)
Dates: Jan. 25, 1979-Aug. 12, 1982
Departure: Left committee; no new assignment.

2nd SELECT NARCOTICS ABUSE AND CONTROL (Temporary)
1st Dates: Apr. 5, 1979-Jan. 3, 1983
1st Departure: Left the House; lost Senate nomination
2nd Dates: Jan. 28, 1987-Jan. 3, 1993
Termination: Committee not renewed in 1993

3rd HOUSE RECORDING STUDIO
Dates: May 2, 1979-Jan. 3, 1983
Departure: Left the House; lost Senate nomination

4th PERMANENT SELECT INTELLIGENCE
Dates: Apr. 10, 1989-Jan. 3, 1997
Departure: Left the House; lost re-election

Cong.	Ranking	Terms in: House	Comm.	Date of Assignment
103rd	Min-3rd	8	3	Feb. 3, 1993
104th	Maj-2nd	9	4	Jan. 4, 1995

Robert K. Dornan (R-Cal.)

Dates: April 3, 1933
House 1: Jan. 3, 1977-Jan. 3, 1983
Left the House 1: Lost U.S. Senate nomination in 1982

Michael F. Doyle (D-Penn.)

Dates: Aug. 5, 1953
House: Jan. 3, 1995-date
Serving in the 111th Congress

HOUSE STANDING COMMITTEES:

1st SCIENCE

Dates: Jan. 4, 1995-Feb. 7, 2001
Departure: Resigned committee; moved to Energy and Commerce

Cong.	Ranking	Terms in: House	Comm.	Date of Assignment
104th	Min-21st	1	1	Jan. 4, 1995
105th	Min-14th	2	2	Feb. 13, 1997
106th	Min-13th	3	3	Jan. 6, 1999
107th	Min-9th	4	4	Jan. 31, 2001

2nd VETERANS' AFFAIRS

1st Dates: Jan. 4, 1995-Feb. 7, 2001
1st Departure: Resigned committee; moved to Energy and Commerce
2nd Dates: Jan. 12, 2007-June 10, 2008
2nd Departure: Resigned committee to open seat for Cazayoux

Cong.	Ranking	Terms in: House	Comm.	Date of Assignment
104th	Min-14th	1 *1	1	Jan. 4, 1995
105th	Min-8th	2 *1	2	Feb. 6, 1997
106th	Min-5th	3 *1	3	Jan. 6, 1999
107th	Min-5th	4 *1	4	Jan. 31, 2001
110th	Maj-9th	7 *2	1	Jan. 12, 2007

3rd ENERGY AND COMMERCE

Dates: Feb. 8, 2001-date
Departure: Still serving in the 111th Congress

Cong.	Ranking	Terms in: House	Comm.	Date of Assignment
107th	Min-24th	4	1	Feb. 8, 2001
108th	Min-21st	5	2	Jan. 28, 2003
109th	Min-18th	6	3	Jan. 26, 2005
110th	Maj-16th	7	4	Jan. 4, 2007
111th	Maj-14th	8	5	Jan. 7, 2009

4th STANDARDS OF OFFICIAL CONDUCT

Dates: Mar. 6, 2003-Jan. 3, 2009
Departure: Left committee; no new assignment

Cong.	Ranking	Terms in: House	Comm.	Date of Assignment
108th	Min-5th	5	1	Mar. 6, 2003
109th	Min-5th	6	2	Feb. 9, 2005
110th	Maj-4th	7	3	Feb. 8 , 2007

Thelma D. Drake (R-Va.)

Dates: Nov. 20, 1949
House: Jan. 3, 2005-Jan. 3, 2009
Left the House: Defeated for re-election in 2008

HOUSE STANDING COMMITTEES:

1st ARMED SERVICES

Dates: Jan. 26, 2005-Jan. 3, 2009
Departure: Left the House; lost re-election

Cong.	Ranking	Terms in: House	Comm.	Date of Assignment
109th	Maj-30th	1	1	Jan. 26, 2005
110th	Min-25th	2	2	Jan. 10, 2007

2nd EDUCATION AND THE WORKFORCE

Dates: Jan. 26, 2005-Jan. 3, 2007
Departure: Moved to Transportation and Infrastructure

Cong.	Ranking	Terms in: House	Comm.	Date of Assignment
109th	Maj-26th	1	1	Jan. 26, 2005

3rd RESOURCES

Dates: Jan. 26, 2005-Jan. 3, 2007
Departure: Moved to Transportation and Infrastructure

Cong.	Ranking	Terms in: House	Comm.	Date of Assignment
109th	Maj-23rd	1	1	Jan. 26, 2005

4th TRANSPORTATION AND INFRASTRUCTURE

Dates: Jan. 10, 2007-Jan. 3, 2009
Departure: Left the House; lost re-election

Cong.	Ranking	Terms in: House	Comm.	Date of Assignment
110th	Min-32nd	2	1	Jan. 10, 2007

David T. Dreier (R-Cal.)

Dates: July 5, 1952
House: Jan. 3, 1981-date
Serving in the 111th Congress

HOUSE STANDING COMMITTEES:

1st GOVERNMENT OPERATIONS

Dates: Jan. 28, 1981-July 24, 1981
Departure: Moved to Banking, Finance and Urban Affairs

2nd SMALL BUSINESS

Dates: Jan. 28, 1981-Jan. 3, 1991
Departure: Moved to Rules

3rd BANKING, FINANCE AND URBAN AFFAIRS

Dates: July 24, 1981-Jan. 3, 1991
Departure: Moved to Rules

4th RULES

Dates: Jan. 3, 1991-date
Departure: Still serving in the 111th Congress

Cong.	Ranking	Terms in: House	Comm.	Date of Assignment
103rd	Min-3rd	7	2	Jan. 5, 1993
104th	Maj-3rd	8	3	Jan. 4, 1995
105th	Maj-2nd	9	4	Jan. 7, 1997
106th	Maj-Chr	10	5	Jan. 6, 1999
107th	Maj-Chr	11	6	Jan. 3, 2001
108th	Maj-Chr	12	7	Jan. 7, 2003
109th	Maj-Chr	13	8	Jan. 4, 2005
110th	Min-RM	14	9	Jan. 4, 2007
111th	Min-RM	15	10	Jan. 6, 2009

HOUSE SELECT AND SPECIAL COMMITTEES:

1st SELECT HOMELAND SECURITY

Dates: Feb. 12, 2003-Jan. 3, 2005
Departure: Did not continue on reorganized standing committee

Cong.	Ranking	Terms in: House	Comm.	Date of Assignment
108th	Maj-7th	12	1	Feb. 12, 2003

JOINT COMMITTEES:

1st JOINT ORGANIZATION OF CONGRESS (Ad Hoc)
House Dates: Aug. 10, 1992-Dec. 17, 1993
Vice Chair2: Replaced Gradison on Feb. 1, 1993
Termination: House Report 103-413 filed

Cong.	Ranking	Terms in: House	Comm.	Date of Assignment
103rd	Min-4th	7	2	Jan. 5, 1993
=103rd	Min-VC2	7	2	Feb. 1, 1993

Steve Driehaus (D-Ohio)

Dates: June 4, 1966
House: Jan. 3, 2009-date
Serving in the 111th Congress

HOUSE STANDING COMMITTEES:

1st FINANCIAL SERVICES
Dates: Jan. 7, 2009-date
Departure: Still serving in the 111th Congress

Cong.	Ranking	Terms in: House	Comm.	Date of Assignment
111th	Maj-37th	1	1	Jan. 7, 2009

2nd OVERSIGHT AND GOVERNMENT REFORM
Dates: Jan. 7, 2009-date
Departure: Still serving in the 111th Congress

Cong.	Ranking	Terms in: House	Comm.	Date of Assignment
111th	Maj-24th	1	1	Jan. 7, 2009

John J. (Jimmy) Duncan Jr.
(R-Tenn.)

Dates: July 21, 1947
House: Nov. 8, 1988-date
Serving in the 111th Congress

H: John Duncan Jr. was elected to the 100th Congress by special election, Nov. 8, 1988, to fill the vacancy caused by the death of his father, U.S. Representative John J. Duncan (R-Tenn.). Duncan was not seated nor assigned to committees because the 100th Congress was not in session.

HOUSE STANDING COMMITTEES:

1st PUBLIC WORKS AND TRANSPORTATION, 101-103
TRANSPORTATION AND INFRASTRUCTURE, 104-111
Dates: Jan. 20, 1989-date
Departure: Still serving in the 111th Congress

Cong.	Ranking	Terms in: House	Comm.	Date of Assignment
103rd	Min-7th	4	3	Jan. 5, 1993
104th	Maj-9th	5	4	Jan. 4, 1995
105th	Maj-7th	6	5	Jan. 7, 1997
106th	Maj-7th	7	6	Jan. 6, 1999
107th	Maj-6th	8	7	Jan. 6, 2001
108th	Maj-5th	9	8	Jan. 28, 2003
109th	Maj-5th	10	9	Jan. 26, 2005
110th	Min-5th	11	10	Jan. 10, 2007
111th	Min-5th	12	11	Jan. 9, 2009

2nd INTERIOR AND INSULAR AFFAIRS, 101-102
NATURAL RESOURCES, 103
RESOURCES, 104-109
NATURAL RESOURCES, 110-111
Dates: May 4, 1989-date
Departure: Still serving in the 111th Congress

Cong.	Ranking	Terms in: House	Comm.	Date of Assignment
103rd	Min-7th	4	3	Jan. 5, 1993
104th	Maj-5th	5	4	Jan. 4, 1995
105th	Maj-6th	6	5	Jan. 7, 1997
106th	Maj-6th	7	6	Jan. 6, 1999
107th	Maj-6th	8	7	Jan. 6, 2001
108th	Maj-6th	9	8	Jan. 28, 2003
109th	Maj-5th	10	9	Jan. 26, 2005
110th	Min-4th	11	10	Jan. 10, 2007
111th	Min-4th	12	11	Jan. 9, 2009

3rd BANKING, FINANCE AND URBAN AFFAIRS
Dates: Jan. 24, 1991-Jan. 3, 1993
Departure: Left committee; no new assignment

4th GOVERNMENT REFORM, 107-109
OVERSIGHT AND GOVERNMENT REFORM, 110-111
Dates: June 7, 2001-date
Departure: Still serving in the 111th Congress

Cong.	Ranking	Terms in: House	Comm.	Date of Assignment
107th	MjR-2nd	8	1	June 7, 2001
108th	Maj-16th	9	2	Jan. 28, 2003
109th	Maj-12th	10	3	Jan. 26, 2005
110th	Min-9th	11	4	Jan. 10, 2007
111th	Min-7th	12	5	Jan. 9, 2009

HOUSE SELECT AND SPECIAL COMMITTEES:

1st SELECT AGING (Permanent)
Dates: Apr. 10, 1989-Jan. 3, 1991
Departure: Left committee; no new assignment

Jennifer B. Dunn (R-Wash.)

Dates: July 29, 1941-Sept. 5, 2007
House: Jan. 3, 1993-Jan. 3, 2005
Left the House: Retired in 2004

HOUSE STANDING COMMITTEES:

1st HOUSE ADMINISTRATION, 103
HOUSE OVERSIGHT, 104
Dates: Feb. 4, 1993-Jan. 3, 1997
Departure: Left committee; no new assignment

Cong.	Ranking	Terms in: House	Comm.	Date of Assignment
103rd	Min-7th	1	1	Feb. 4, 1993
104th	Maj-5th	2	2	Jan. 4, 1995

2nd PUBLIC WORKS AND TRANSPORTATION
Dates: Jan. 5, 1993-Jan. 3, 1995
Departure: Moved to Ways and Means

Cong.	Ranking	Terms in: House	Comm.	Date of Assignment
103rd	Min-12th	1	1	Jan. 5 , 1993

3rd SCIENCE, SPACE AND TECHNOLOGY
Dates: Jan. 5, 1993-Jan. 3, 1995
Departure: Moved to Ways and Means

Cong.	Ranking	Terms in: House	Comm.	Date of Assignment
103rd	Min-20th	1	1	Jan. 5, 1993

4th WAYS AND MEANS
Dates: Jan. 4, 1995-Jan. 3, 2005
Departure: Left the House; retired

Cong.	Ranking	Terms in: House	Comm.	Date of Assignment
104th	Maj-16th	2	1	Jan. 4, 1995
105th	Maj-14th	3	2	Jan. 7, 1997
106th	Maj-13th	4	3	Jan. 6, 1999
107th	Maj-12th	5	4	Jan. 6, 2001
108th	Maj-12th	6	5	Jan. 28, 2003

HOUSE SELECT AND SPECIAL COMMITTEES:

1st SELECT HOMELAND SECURITY
Dates: Feb. 12, 2003-Jan. 3, 2005
Departure: Left the House; retired

Cong.	Ranking	Terms in: House	Comm.	Date of Assignment
108th	Maj-2nd	6	1	Feb. 12, 2003

JOINT COMMITTEES:

1st JOINT ORGANIZATION OF CONGRESS
House Dates: Feb. 1, 1993-Dec. 17, 1993
Termination: House Report 103-413 filed

Cong.	Ranking	Terms in: House	Comm.	Date of Assignment
103rd	MnR-1st	1	1	Feb. 1, 1993

2nd JOINT ECONOMIC
House Dates: May 1, 2001-Jan. 3, 2005
Departure: Left the House; retired

Cong.	Ranking	Terms in: House	Comm.	Date of Assignment
107th	Maj-4th	5	1	May 1, 2001
108th	Maj-3rd	6	2	Feb. 25, 2003

Richard J. Durbin (D-Ill.)

Dates: Nov. 21, 1944
House: Jan. 3, 1983-Jan. 3, 1997
Left the House: Elected to the U.S. Senate in 1996
Senate: Jan. 3, 1997-date
Serving in the 111th Congress

HOUSE STANDING COMMITTEES:

1st AGRICULTURE
Dates: Jan. 6, 1983-Jan. 3, 1985
Departure: Moved to Appropriations

2nd SCIENCE AND TECHNOLOGY
Dates: Jan. 6, 1983-Jan. 3, 1985
Departure: Moved to Appropriations

3rd APPROPRIATIONS
Dates: Jan. 30, 1985-Jan. 3, 1997
Departure: Left the House for the Senate

Cong.	Ranking	Terms in: House	Comm.	Date of Assignment
103rd	Maj-17th	6	5	Jan. 5, 1993
104th	Min-13th	7	6	Jan. 4, 1995

4th BUDGET
Dates: Jan. 6, 1987-Jan. 3, 1993
Departure: Left committee; no new assignment

HOUSE SELECT AND SPECIAL COMMITTEES:

1st SELECT CHILDREN, YOUTH AND FAMILIES (Temporary)
Dates: Jan. 21, 1987-Jan. 3, 1993
Termination: Committee not renewed in 1993

JOINT COMMITTEES:

1st JOINT REDUCTION (Temporary)
House Dates: Jan. 6, 1987-Sep. 29, 1987
Termination: Public Law 100-119 adjusted Gramm-Rudman-Hollings Act

SENATE STANDING COMMITTEES:

1st BUDGET
Dates: Jan. 9, 1997-Jan. 25, 2001
Departure: Returned to Judiciary and moved to Select Intelligence

Cong.	Ranking	Years in: Senate	Comm.	Date of Assignment
105th	Min-10th	1	1	Jan. 9, 1997
106th	Min-10th	3	2	Jan. 7, 1999

2nd GOVERNMENTAL AFFAIRS renamed Oct. 9, 2004
HOMELAND SECURITY AND GOVERNMENTAL AFFAIRS
Dates: Jan. 9, 1997-Jan. 6, 2005
Departure: Left committee; elected Minority Whip

Cong.	Ranking	Years in: Senate	Comm.	Date of Assignment
105th	Min-5th	1	1	Jan. 9, 1997
106th	Min-4th	3	2	Jan. 7, 1999
107th	Min-4th	5	5	Jan. 25, 2001
+107th	Maj-4th	5	5	June 6, 2001
108th	Min-4th	7	7	Jan. 15, 2003

3rd JUDICIARY
1st Dates: Jan. 9, 1997-Jan. 7, 1999
1st Departure: Moved to Appropriations and Select Ethics
2nd Dates: Jan. 25, 2001-date
2nd Departure: Still serving in the 111th Congress

Cong.	Ranking	Years in: Senate	Comm.	Date of Assignment
105th	Min-7th	1 *1	1	Jan. 9, 1997
107th	Min-8th	5 *2	1	Jan. 25, 2001
+107th	Maj-8th	5 *2	1	June 6, 2001
108th	Min-8th	7 *2	2	Jan. 15, 2003
109th	Min-8th	9 *2	4	Jan. 6, 2005
110th	Maj-8th	11 *2	6	Jan. 12, 2007
111th	Maj-6th	13 *2	8	Jan. 21, 2009

4th APPROPRIATIONS
Dates: Jan. 7, 1999-date
Departure: Still serving in the 111th Congress

Cong.	Ranking	Years in: Senate	Comm.	Date of Assignment
106th	Min-13th	3	1	Jan. 7, 1999
107th	Min-12th	5	3	Jan. 25, 2001
+107th	Maj-12th	5	3	June 6, 2001
108th	Min-12th	7	5	Jan. 15, 2003
109th	Min-11th	9	6	Jan. 6, 2005
110th	Maj-10th	11	9	Jan. 12, 2007
111th	Maj-10th	13	11	Jan. 21, 2009

5th RULES AND ADMINISTRATION
Dates: July 10, 2001-date
Departure: Still serving in the 111th Congress

Cong.	Ranking	Years in: Senate	Comm.	Date of Assignment
+107th	MjA-10th	5	1	July 10, 2001
108th	Min-9th	7	2	Jan. 15, 2003
109th	Min-7th	9	4	Jan. 6, 2005
110th	Maj-6th	11	6	Jan. 12, 2007
111th	Maj-6th	13	8	Jan. 21, 2009

SENATE SELECT AND SPECIAL COMMITTEES:

1st SELECT ETHICS (Permanent)
Dates: Jan. 7, 1999-Jan. 25, 2001
Departure: Returned to Judiciary; moved to Select Intelligence

Cong.	Ranking	Years in: Senate	Comm.	Date of Assignment
106th	Min-3rd	3	1	Jan. 7, 1999

2nd SELECT INTELLIGENCE (Permanent)
Dates: Jan. 25, 2001-Jan. 6, 2005
Departure: Left committee; elected Minority Whip

Cong.	Ranking	Years in: Senate	Comm.	Date of Assignment
107th	Min-6th	5	1	Jan. 25, 2001
+107th	Maj-6th	5	1	June 6, 2001
108th	Min-5th	7	2	Jan. 15, 2003

SENATE LEADERSHIP POSTS

Dates: Jan. 3, 2005-date
Departure: Still serving in the 111th Congress

1st SENATE MINORITY WHIP
Dates: Jan. 3, 2005-Jan. 3, 2007
Note: For the 109th Congress, Durbin was elected Minority Whip without opposition on Nov. 16, 2004
Departure: Democratic Party gained Senate majority in 2006

Cong.	Ranking	Years in: Senate	Post	Date of Selection
109th	Min-2nd	9	1	Nov. 16, 2004

2nd SENATE MAJORITY WHIP
Dates: Jan. 3, 2007-date
Note: For the 110th Congress, Durbin was elected Majority Whip without opposition on Nov. 14, 2006. He was re-elected unopposed for the 111th Congress.
Departure: Still serving in the 111th Congress

Cong.	Ranking	Years in: Senate	Post	Date of Selection
110th	Maj-2nd	11	1	Nov. 14, 2006
111th	Maj-2nd	13	3	Nov. 18, 2008

David F. Durenberger (R-Minn.)

Dates: Aug. 19, 1934
Senate: Nov. 8, 1978-Jan. 3, 1995
Left the Senate: Retired in 1994

S: Durenberger was appointed to the 95th Congress, Nov. 8, 1978, to fill the unexpired term caused by the death of U.S. Senator Hubert H. Humphrey (DFL-Minn.) and was subsequently elected. Humphrey had initially been replaced by his wife, Muriel B. Humphrey (DFL-Minn.), an appointee, who was not a candidate for election. Durenberger began service Nov. 8, 1978, following Mrs. Humphrey's resignation, but was not seated nor assigned to committees because the 95th Congress was not in session.

SENATE STANDING COMMITTEES:

1st FINANCE
Dates: Jan. 23, 1979-Jan. 3, 1995
Departure: Left the Senate; retired

Cong.	Ranking	Years in: Senate	Comm.	Date of Assignment
103rd	Min-6th	15	14	Jan. 7, 1993

2nd GOVERNMENTAL AFFAIRS
Dates: Jan. 23, 1979-Feb. 19, 1987
Departure: Left committee; no new assignment

3rd ENVIRONMENT AND PUBLIC WORKS
Dates: Jan. 3, 1983-Jan. 3, 1995
Departure: Left the Senate; retired

Cong.	Ranking	Years in: Senate	Comm.	Date of Assignment
103rd	Min-3rd	15	11	Jan. 7, 1993

4th LABOR AND HUMAN RESOURCES
Dates: Feb. 2, 1989-Jan. 3, 1995
Departure: Left the Senate; retired

Cong.	Ranking	Years in: Senate	Comm.	Date of Assignment
103rd	Min-7th	15	4	Jan. 7, 1993

SENATE SELECT AND SPECIAL COMMITTEES:

1st SELECT INTELLIGENCE (Permanent)
Dates: Jan. 23, 1979-Jan. 6, 1987
Departure: Returned to Special Aging

2nd SPECIAL AGING (Permanent)
1st Dates: Jan. 22, 1981-Jan. 3, 1983
2nd Departure: Moved to Environment and Public Works
2nd Dates: Jan. 6, 1987-Feb. 2, 1989
2nd Departure: Moved to Labor and Human Resources
3rd Dates: Mar. 19,1991-Jan. 3, 1995
3rd Departure: Left the Senate; retired

Cong.	Ranking	Years in: Senate	Comm.	Date of Assignment
103rd	Min-7th	15	*3 3	Jan. 21, 1993

3rd SELECT ETHICS (Permanent)
Dates: Jan. 3, 1983-Mar. 5, 1985
Departure: Left committee; became Chair of Select Intelligence

4th JUDGE ALCEE L. HASTINGS IMPEACHMENT
Dates: Mar. 16, 1989-Aug. 3, 1989
Termination: Senate Hearing 101-194, Parts 1-2A
Senate floor vote on impeachment, Oct. 20, 1989

E

Donna F. Edwards (D-Md.)

Dates: June 28, 1958
House: June 17, 2008-date
Serving in the 111th Congress

H: Edwards was elected by special election, June 17, 2008, to fill the unexpired term of U.S. Representative Albert Wynn (D-Md.) who resigned after he had been defeated for re-nomination by Ms. Edwards. Ms. Edwards was seated June 19, 2008, and assigned to committees.

HOUSE STANDING COMMITTEES:

1st SCIENCE AND TECHNOLOGY
Dates: July 15, 2008-date
Departure: Still serving in the 111th Congress

Cong.	Ranking	Terms in: House	Comm.	Date of Assignment
110th	MjR-3rd	1	1	July 15, 2008
111th	Maj-10th	2	2	Jan. 21, 2009

2nd TRANSPORTATION AND INFRASTRUCTURE
Dates: July 15, 2008-date
Departure: Still serving in the 111th Congress

Cong.	Ranking	Terms in: House	Comm.	Date of Assignment
110th	MjR-3rd	1	1	July 15, 2008
111th	Maj-35th	2	2	Jan. 7, 2009

John Edwards (D-N.C.)

Dates: June 10, 1953
Senate: Jan. 3, 1999-Jan. 3, 2005
Left the Senate: Retired; lost election for Vice President in 2004

SENATE STANDING COMMITTEES:

1st BANKING, HOUSING AND URBAN AFFAIRS
Dates: Jan. 7, 1999-Jan. 25, 2001
Departure: Moved to Commerce, Science and Transportation, Health, Education, Labor and Pensions,and Select Intelligence

Cong.	Ranking	Years in: Senate	Comm.	Date of Assignment
106th	Min-9th	1	1	Jan. 7, 1999

2nd GOVERNMENTAL AFFAIRS
Dates: Jan. 7, 1999-Jan. 25, 2001
Departure: Moved to Commerce, Science and Transportation, Health, Education, Labor and Pensions, and Select Intelligence

Cong.	Ranking	Years in: Senate	Comm.	Date of Assignment
106th	Min-7th	1	1	Jan. 7, 1999

3rd SMALL BUSINESS renamed June 29, 2001
SMALL BUSINESS AND ENTREPRENEURSHIP

Dates: Jan. 7, 1999-Jan. 3, 2005
Departure: Left the Senate; lost vice presidential election

Cong.	Ranking	Years in: Senate	Comm.	Date of Assignment
106th	Min-8th	1	1	Jan. 7, 1999
107th	Min-8th	3	3	Jan. 25, 2001
+107th	Maj-8th	3	3	June 6, 2001
108th	Min-6th	5	5	Jan. 15, 2003

4th COMMERCE, SCIENCE AND TRANSPORTATION
Dates: Jan. 25, 2001-Jan. 15, 2003
Departure: Left committee; no new assignment

Cong.	Ranking	Years in: Senate	Comm.	Date of Assignment
107th	Min-10th	3	1	Jan. 25, 2001
+107th	Maj-10th	3	1	June 6, 2001

5th HEALTH, EDUCATION, LABOR AND PENSIONS
Dates: Jan. 25, 2001-Jan. 3, 2005
Departure: Left the Senate; lost vice presidential election

Cong.	Ranking	Years in: Senate	Comm.	Date of Assignment
107th	Min-9th	3	1	Jan. 25, 2001
+107th	Maj-10th	3	1	July 10, 2001
108th	Min-9th	5	2	Jan. 15, 2003

6th JUDICIARY
Dates: July 10, 2001-Jan. 3, 2005
Departure: Left the Senate; lost vice presidential election

Cong.	Ranking	Years in: Senate	Comm.	Date of Assignment
+107th	MjA-10th	3	1	July 10, 2001
108th	Min-9th	5	2	Jan. 15, 2003

SENATE SELECT AND SPECIAL COMMITTEES:

1st SELECT INTELLIGENCE (Permanent)
Dates: Jan. 25, 2001-Jan. 3, 2005
Departure: Left the Senate; lost vice presidential election

Cong.	Ranking	Years in: Senate	Comm.	Date of Assignment
107th	Min-8th	3	1	Jan. 25, 2001
+107th	Maj-8th	3	1	June 6, 2001
108th	Min-7th	5	2	Jan. 15, 2003

T. Chester (Chet) Edwards (D-Tex.)

Dates: Nov. 25, 1951
House: Jan. 3, 1991-date
Serving in the 111th Congress

HOUSE STANDING COMMITTEES:

1st ARMED SERVICES, 102-103
NATIONAL SECURITY, 104
Dates: Jan. 24, 1991-Jan. 3, 1997
Departure: Moved to Appropriations

Cong.	Ranking	Terms in: House	Comm.	Date of Assignment
103rd	Maj-23rd	2	2	Jan. 5, 1993
104th	Min-14th	3	3	Jan. 4, 1995

2nd VETERANS' AFFAIRS
Dates: Jan. 24, 1991-Jan. 3, 1997
Departure: Moved to Appropriations

Cong.	Ranking	Terms in: House	Comm.	Date of Assignment
103rd	Maj-11th	2	2	Jan. 5, 1993
104th	Min-4th	3	3	Jan. 4, 1995

3rd APPROPRIATIONS
Dates: Jan. 7, 1997-date
Departure: Still serving in the 111th Congress

Cong.	Ranking	Terms in: House	Comm.	Date of Assignment
105th	Min-26th	4	1	Jan. 7, 1997
106th	Min-19th	5	2	Jan. 6, 1999
107th	Min-18th	6	3	Jan. 31, 2001
108th	Min-16th	7	4	Jan. 28, 2003
109th	Min-16th	8	5	Jan. 26, 2005
110th	Maj-14th	9	6	Jan. 4, 2007
111th	Maj-14th	10	7	Jan. 7, 2009

4th BUDGET
Dates: Jan. 28, 2003-date
Departure: Still serving in the 111th Congress

Cong.	Ranking	Terms in: House	Comm.	Date of Assignment
108th	Min-9th	7	1	Jan. 28, 2003
109th	Min-5th	8	2	Jan. 26, 2005
110th	Maj-3rd	9	3	Jan. 18, 2007
111th	Maj-17th	10	4	Jan. 21, 2009

William D. (Don) Edwards (D-Cal.)

Dates: Jan. 6, 1915
House: Jan. 3, 1963-Jan. 3, 1995
Left the House: Retired in 1994

HOUSE STANDING COMMITTEES:

1st POST OFFICE AND CIVIL SERVICE
Dates: Jan. 17, 1963-July 25, 1963
Departure: Moved to Judiciary

2nd VETERANS' AFFAIRS
1st Dates: Jan. 17, 1963-July 25, 1963
1st Departure: Moved to Judiciary
2nd Dates: Jan. 29, 1969-Jan. 3, 1995
2nd Departure: Left the House; retired

Cong.	Ranking	Terms in: House	Comm.	Date of Assignment
103rd	Maj-2nd	16	*2 13	Jan. 5, 1993

3rd JUDICIARY
Dates: July 25, 1963-Jan. 3, 1995
Departure: Left the House; retired

Cong.	Ranking	Terms in: House	Comm.	Date of Assignment
103rd	Maj-2nd	16	16	Jan. 5, 1993

4th FOREIGN AFFAIRS
Dates: Jan. 21, 1993-Jan. 3, 1995
Departure: Left the House; retired

Cong.	Ranking	Terms in: House	Comm.	Date of Assignment
103rd	Maj-24th	16	1	Jan. 21, 1993

HOUSE SELECT AND SPECIAL COMMITTEES:

1st SELECT INTELLIGENCE (Nedzi)
Dates: Feb. 19, 1975-July 17, 1975
Termination: Reorganized with new chair
SELECT INTELLIGENCE (Pike)
Dates: July 17, 1975-Feb. 11, 1976
Termination: House Report 833 (94-2) filed

Vernon J. Ehlers (R-Mich.)

Dates: Feb. 6, 1934
House: Dec. 7, 1993-date
Serving in the 111th Congress

H: Ehlers was elected to the 103rd Congress by special election Dec. 7, 1993, to fill the vacancy caused by the death of U.S. Representative Paul Henry (R-Mich.). Ehlers was seated Jan. 25, 1994, and assigned to committees.

HOUSE STANDING COMMITTEES:

1st PUBLIC WORKS AND TRANSPORTATION, 103
TRANSPORTATION AND INFRASTRUCTURE, 104-111
Dates: Feb. 2, 1994-date
Departure: Still serving in the 111th Congress

Cong.	Ranking	Terms in: House	Comm.	Date of Assignment
103rd	MnA-25th	1	1	Feb. 2, 1994
104th	Maj-23rd	2	2	Jan. 4, 1995
105th	Maj-17th	3	3	Jan. 7, 1997
106th	Maj-15th	4	4	Jan. 6, 1999
107th	Maj-11th	5	5	Jan. 6, 2001
108th	Maj-10th	6	6	Jan. 28, 2003
109th	Maj-9th	7	7	Jan. 26, 2005
110th	Min-7th	8	8	Jan. 10, 2007
111th	Min-6th	9	9	Jan. 9, 2009

2nd SCIENCE, SPACE, AND TECHNOLOGY, 103
SCIENCE, 104-109
SCIENCE AND TECHNOLOGY, 110-111
Dates: Feb. 2, 1994-date
Departure: Still serving in the 111th Congress

Cong.	Ranking	Terms in: House	Comm.	Date of Assignment
103rd	MnR-1st	1	1	Feb. 2, 1994
104th	Maj-13th	2	2	Jan. 4, 1995
105th	Maj-11th	3	3	Jan. 21, 1997
106th	Maj-11th	4	4	Jan. 6, 1999
107th	Maj-11th	5	5	Jan. 6, 2001
108th	Maj-10th	6	6	Jan. 28, 2003

Cong.	Ranking	House	Comm.	Date of Assignment
109th	Maj-8th	7	7	Jan. 26, 2005
110th	Min-7th	8	8	Jan. 10, 2007
111th	Min-6th	9	9	Jan. 9, 2009

3rd HOUSE OVERSIGHT, 104-105
HOUSE ADMINISTRATION, 106-110
Dates: Jan. 4, 1995-Jan. 3, 2009
Ch2: Replaced Robert W. Ney (R-Ohio) as Chair on Feb. 1, 2006
Departure: Left committee; no new assignment

Cong.	Ranking	House	Comm.	Date of Assignment
104th	Maj-2nd	2	1	Jan. 4, 1995
105th	Maj-3rd	3	2	Jan. 7, 1997
106th	Maj-3rd	4	3	Jan. 6, 1999
107th	Maj-2nd	5	4	Jan. 31, 2001
108th	Maj-2nd	6	5	Jan. 28, 2003
109th	Maj-2nd	7	6	Jan. 26, 2005
=109th	Maj-Ch2	7	6	Feb. 1, 2006
110th	Min-RM	8	7	Jan. 4, 2007

4th EDUCATION AND THE WORKFORCE, 106-109
EDUCATION AND LABOR, 110-111
Dates: Jan. 6, 1999-date
Departure: Still serving in the 111th Congress

Cong.	Ranking	House	Comm.	Date of Assignment
106th	Maj-22nd	4	1	Jan. 6, 1999
107th	Maj-16th	5	2	Jan. 6, 2001
108th	Maj-12th	6	3	Jan. 28, 2003
109th	Maj-8th	7	4	Jan. 26, 2005
110th	Min-6th	8	5	Jan. 10, 2007
111th	Min-6th	9	6	Jan. 9, 2009

JOINT COMMITTEES:

1st JOINT LIBRARY
House Dates: Mar. 6, 1997-Jan. 3, 2009
Departure: Left committee; no new assignment

Cong.	Ranking	House	Comm.	Date of Assignment
105th	Maj-3rd	3	1	Mar. 6, 1997
106th	Maj-3rd	4	2	Mar. 2, 1999
107th	Maj-Chr	5	3	June 5, 2001
108th	Maj-VCh	6	4	Mar. 25, 2003
109th	Maj-2nd	7	5	Mar. 16, 2005
110th	Min-1st	8	6	Mar. 14, 2007

2nd JOINT PRINTING
House Dates: Mar. 14, 2007-Jan. 3, 2009
Departure: Left committee; no new assignment

Cong.	Ranking	House	Comm.	Date of Assignment
110th	Min-1st	8	1	Mar. 14, 2007

Robert L. Ehrlich Jr. (R-Md.)

Dates: Nov. 25, 1957
House: Jan. 3, 1995-Jan. 3, 2003
Left the House: Elected Governor in 2002

HOUSE STANDING COMMITTEES:

1st BANKING AND FINANCIAL SERVICES
Dates: Jan. 4, 1995-Jan. 3, 1999
Departure: Moved to Commerce

Cong.	Ranking	House	Comm.	Date of Assignment
104th	Maj-18th	1	1	Jan. 4, 1995
105th	Maj-15th	2	2	Jan. 7, 1997

2nd GOVERNMENT REFORM AND OVERSIGHT
Dates: Jan. 4, 1995-Mar. 19, 1997
Departure: Leave of absence to serve on Budget; never returned

Cong.	Ranking	House	Comm.	Date of Assignment
104th	Maj-27th	1	1	Jan. 4, 1995
105th	Maj-19th	2	2	Jan. 7, 1997

3rd BUDGET
Dates: Jan. 7, 1997-Jan. 3, 1999
Departure: Moved to Commerce

Cong.	Ranking	House	Comm.	Date of Assignment
105th	Maj-19th	2	1	Jan. 7, 1997

4th COMMERCE, 106
ENERGY AND COMMERCE, 107
Dates: Jan. 6, 1999-Jan. 3, 2003
Departure: Left the House; elected Governor

Cong.	Ranking	House	Comm.	Date of Assignment
106th	Maj-29th	3	1	Jan. 6, 1999
107th	Maj-24th	4	2	Jan. 6, 2001

Keith Ellison (DFL-Minn.)

Dates: Aug. 4, 1963
House: Jan. 3, 2007-date
Serving in the 111th Congress

HOUSE STANDING COMMITTEES:

1st FINANCIAL SERVICES
Dates: Jan. 12, 2007-date
Departure: Still serving in the 111th Congress

Cong.	Ranking	House	Comm.	Date of Assignment
110th	Maj-28th	1	1	Jan. 12, 2007
111th	Maj-25th	2	2	Jan. 7, 2009

2nd JUDICIARY
Dates: Jan. 18, 2007-Jan. 3, 2009
Departure: Moved to Foreign Affairs

Cong.	Ranking	House	Comm.	Date of Assignment
110th	Maj-23rd	1	1	Jan. 18, 2007

3rd FOREIGN AFFAIRS
Dates: Jan. 7, 2009-date
Departure: Still serving in the 111th Congress

Cong.	Ranking	House	Comm.	Date of Assignment
111th	Maj-26th	2	1	Jan. 7, 2009

Brad Ellsworth (D-Ind.)

Dates: Sept. 11, 1956
House: Jan. 3, 2007-date
Serving in the 111th Congress

HOUSE STANDING COMMITTEES:

1st ARMED SERVICES
Dates: Jan. 10, 2007-date
Departure: Still serving in the 111th Congress

Cong.	Ranking	Terms in: House	Comm.	Date of Assignment
110th	Maj-23rd	1	1	Jan. 10, 2007
111th	Maj-21st	2	2	Jan. 7, 2009

2nd AGRICULTURE
Dates: Jan. 12, 2007-date
Departure: Still serving in the 111th Congress

Cong.	Ranking	Terms in: House	Comm.	Date of Assignment
110th	Maj-14th	1	1	Jan. 12, 2007
111th	Maj-12th	2	2	Jan. 21, 2009

3rd SMALL BUSINESS
Dates: Jan. 23, 2007-date
Departure: Still serving in the 111th Congress

Cong.	Ranking	Terms in: House	Comm.	Date of Assignment
110th	Maj-16th	1	1	Jan. 23, 2007
111th	Maj-13th	2	2	Jan. 21, 2009

Rahm Emanuel (D-Ill.)

Dates: Nov. 29, 1959
House: Jan. 3, 2003-Jan. 2, 2009
Left the House: Resigned; appointed White House Chief of Staff in 2008

HOUSE STANDING COMMITTEES:

1st BUDGET
Dates: Jan. 28, 2003-Jan. 3, 2005
Departure: Moved to Ways and Means

Cong.	Ranking	Terms in: House	Comm.	Date of Assignment
108th	Min-17th	1	1	Jan. 28, 2003

2nd FINANCIAL SERVICES
Dates: Jan. 28, 2003-Jan. 3, 2005
Departure: Moved to Ways and Means

Cong.	Ranking	Terms in: House	Comm.	Date of Assignment
108th	Min-30th	1	1	Jan. 28, 2003

3rd WAYS AND MEANS
Dates: Jan. 26, 2005-Jan. 2, 2009
Departure: Left the House; appointed White House Chief of Staff

Cong.	Ranking	Terms in: House	Comm.	Date of Assignment
109th	Min-17th	2	1	Jan. 26, 2005
110th	Maj-15th	3	2	Jan. 4, 2007

Jo Ann Emerson (R-Mo.)

Dates: Sept. 16, 1950
House: Nov. 5, 1996-date

Serving in the 111th Congress
Served as an Independent: Nov. 5, 1996-Jan. 8, 1997
Served as a Republican: Jan. 8, 1997-date

H: Jo Ann Emerson was elected to the 104th Congress by special election, Nov. 5, 1996, to fill the vacancy caused by the death of her husband, U.S. Representative N. William Emerson (R-Mo.). Mrs. Emerson was not seated in the 104th Congress but was seated on Jan. 8, 1997, in the 105th Congress to which she had also been elected.

HOUSE STANDING COMMITTEES:

1st AGRICULTURE
Dates: Jan. 7, 1997-Jan. 3, 1999
Departure: Moved to Appropriations

Cong.	Ranking	Terms in: House	Comm.	Date of Assignment
105th	Maj-20th	2	1	Jan. 7, 1997

2nd TRANSPORTATION AND INFRASTRUCTURE
Dates: Jan. 7, 1997-Jan. 3, 1999
Departure: Moved to Appropriations

Cong.	Ranking	Terms in: House	Comm.	Date of Assignment
105th	Maj-27th	2	1	Jan. 7, 1997

3rd SMALL BUSINESS
Dates: Jan. 21, 1997-Jan. 3, 1999
Departure: Moved to Appropriations

Cong.	Ranking	Terms in: House	Comm.	Date of Assignment
105th	Maj-17th	2	1	Jan. 21, 1997

4th APPROPRIATIONS,
Dates: Jan. 6, 1999-date
Departure: Still serving in the 111th Congress

Cong.	Ranking	Terms in: House	Comm.	Date of Assignment
106th	Maj-31st	3	1	Jan. 6, 1999
107th	Maj-27th	4	2	Jan. 6, 2001
108th	Maj-23rd	5	3	Jan. 28, 2003
109th	Maj-22nd	6	4	Jan. 6, 2005
110th	Min-16th	7	5	Jan. 4, 2007
111th	Min-11th	8	6	Jan. 9, 2009

N. William Emerson (R-Mo.)

Dates: Jan. 1, 1939-June 22, 1996
House: Jan. 3, 1981-June 22, 1996
Left the House: Died in office

HOUSE STANDING COMMITTEES:

1st AGRICULTURE
Dates: Jan. 28, 1981-June 22, 1996
Departure: Died in office

Cong.	Ranking	Terms in: House	Comm.	Date of Assignment
103rd	Min-2nd	7	7	Jan. 5, 1993
104th	Maj-2nd	8	8	Jan. 4, 1995

2nd INTERIOR AND INSULAR AFFAIRS
Dates: Dec. 10, 1981-Sep. 23, 1988
Departure: Moved to Public Works and Transportation

3rd PUBLIC WORKS AND TRANSPORTATION, 103
TRANSPORTATION AND INFRASTRUCTURE, 104
Dates: Sep. 23, 1988-June 22, 1996
Departure: Died in office

Cong.	Ranking	Terms in: House	Comm.	Date of Assignment
103rd	Min-6th	7	4	Jan. 5, 1993
104th	Maj-7th	8	5	Jan. 4, 1995

HOUSE SELECT AND SPECIAL COMMITTEES:

1st SELECT HUNGER (Temporary)
Dates: Mar. 13, 1984-Jan. 3, 1993
Termination: Committee not renewed in 1993

JOINT COMMITTEES:

1st JOINT ORGANIZATION OF CONGRESS (Ad Hoc)
House Dates: Aug. 10, 1992-Dec. 17, 1993
Termination: House Report 103-413 filed

Cong.	Ranking	Terms in: House	Comm.	Date of Assignment
103rd	Min-5th	7	2	Jan. 5, 1993

Eliot L. Engel (D-N.Y.)

Dates: Feb. 18, 1947
House: Jan. 3, 1989-date
Serving in the 111th Congress

HOUSE STANDING COMMITTEES:

1st FOREIGN AFFAIRS, 103
INTERNATIONAL RELATIONS, 104, 107-109
FOREIGN AFFAIRS, 110-111
1st Dates: Jan. 19, 1989-Apr. 22, 1996
1st Departure: Resigned committee; moved to Commerce
2nd Dates: Feb. 27, 2001-date
2nd Departure: Still serving in the 111th Congress

Cong.	Ranking	Terms in: House	Comm.	Date of Assignment
103rd	Maj-8th	3 *1	3	Jan. 5, 1993
104th	Min-8th	4 *1	4	Jan. 4, 1995
107th	MnR-1st	7 *2	1	Feb. 27, 2001
108th	Min-10th	8 *2	2	Jan. 28, 2003
109th	Min-10th	9 *2	3	Jan. 26, 2005
110th	Maj-8th	10 *2	4	Jan. 12, 2007
111th	Maj-7th	11 *2	5	Jan. 21, 2009

2nd SMALL BUSINESS
Dates: Jan. 27, 1989-July 9, 1991
Departure: Moved to Science, Space and Technology

3rd BANKING, FINANCE AND URBAN AFFAIRS
Dates: Apr. 4, 1990-Jan. 3, 1991
Departure: Left committee; no new assignment

4th SCIENCE, SPACE AND TECHNOLOGY
Dates: June 27, 1991-Jan. 3, 1993
Departure: Moved to Education and Labor

5th EDUCATION AND LABOR, 103
ECONOMIC AND EDUCATIONAL OPPORTUNITIES, 104

Dates: Jan. 5, 1993-Apr. 22, 1996
Departure: Resigned committee; moved to Commerce

Cong.	Ranking	Terms in: House	Comm.	Date of Assignment
103rd	Maj-16th	3	1	Jan. 5, 1993
104th	Min-13th	4	2	Jan. 4, 1995

6th COMMERCE, 104-106
ENERGY AND COMMERCE, 107-111
Dates: Apr. 22, 1996-date
Departure: Still serving in the 111th Congress

Cong.	Ranking	Terms in: House	Comm.	Date of Assignment
104th	MnR-2nd	4	1	Apr. 22, 1996
105th	Min-17th	5	2	Jan. 7, 1997
106th	Min-15th	6	3	Jan. 6, 1999
107th	Min-14th	7	4	Jan. 31, 2001
108th	Min-14th	8	5	Jan. 28, 2003
109th	Min-12th	9	6	Jan. 26, 2005
110th	Maj-11th	10	7	Jan. 4, 2007
111th	Maj-10th	11	8	Jan. 7, 2009

HOUSE SELECT AND SPECIAL COMMITTEES:

1st SELECT HUNGER (Temporary)
Dates: Apr. 27, 1989-Jan. 3, 1993
Termination: Committee not renewed in 1993

Glenn L. English Jr. (D-Okla.)

Dates: Nov. 30, 1940
House: Jan. 3, 1975-Jan. 7, 1994
Left the House: Resigned the House; named Vice President of the National Rural Electric Cooperative Association in 1994

HOUSE STANDING COMMITTEES:

1st GOVERNMENT OPERATIONS
Dates: Jan. 20, 1975-Jan. 7, 1994
Departure: Resigned the House; private sector

Cong.	Ranking	Terms in: House	Comm.	Date of Assignment
103rd	Maj-3rd	10	10	Jan. 5, 1993

2nd AGRICULTURE
Dates: Jan. 23, 1975-Jan. 7, 1994
Departure: Resigned the House; private sector

Cong.	Ranking	Terms in: House	Comm.	Date of Assignment
103rd	Maj-4th	10	10	Jan. 5, 1993

HOUSE SELECT AND SPECIAL COMMITTEES:

1st SELECT NARCOTICS ABUSE AND CONTROL (Temporary)
Dates: Aug. 3, 1976-Jan. 3, 1983
Departure: Left committee; no new assignment

Karan English (D-Ariz.)

Dates: March 23, 1949
House: Jan. 3, 1993-Jan. 3, 1995
Left the House: Defeated for re-election in 1994

HOUSE STANDING COMMITTEES:

1st EDUCATION AND LABOR
Dates: Jan. 5, 1993-Jan. 3, 1995
Departure: Left the House; lost re-election

Cong.	Ranking	Terms in: House	Comm.	Date of Assignment
103rd	Maj-23rd	1	1	Jan. 5, 1993

2nd NATURAL RESOURCES
Dates: Jan. 5, 1993-Jan. 3, 1995
Departure: Left the House; lost re-election

Cong.	Ranking	Terms in: House	Comm.	Date of Assignment
103rd	Maj-20th	1	1	Jan. 5, 1993

Philip S. English (R-Penn.)

Dates: June 20, 1956
House: Jan. 3, 1995-Jan. 3, 2009
Left the House: Defeated for re-election in 2008

HOUSE STANDING COMMITTEES:

1st WAYS AND MEANS
Dates: Jan. 4, 1995-Jan. 3, 2009
Departure: Left the House; lost re-election

Cong.	Ranking	Terms in: House	Comm.	Date of Assignment
104th	Maj-19th	1	1	Jan. 4, 1995
105th	Maj-17th	2	2	Jan. 7, 1997
106th	Maj-16th	3	3	Jan. 6, 1999
107th	Maj-15th	4	4	Jan. 6, 2001
108th	Maj-15th	5	5	Jan. 28, 2003
109th	Maj-11th	6	6	Jan. 6, 2005
110th	Min-6th	7	7	Jan. 4, 2007

2nd SMALL BUSINESS
Dates: Jan. 21, 1997-Apr. 2, 2001
Departure: Resigned committee; moved to Joint Economic

Cong.	Ranking	Terms in: House	Comm.	Date of Assignment
105th	Maj-15th	2	1	Jan. 21, 1997
106th	Maj-9th	3	2	Jan. 6, 1999
107th	Maj-8th	4	3	Jan. 6, 2001

3rd SCIENCE
Dates: Mar. 5, 1997-Jan. 3, 1999
Departure: Left committee; no new assignment

Cong.	Ranking	Terms in: House	Comm.	Date of Assignment
105th	Maj-22nd	2	1	Mar. 5, 1997

JOINT COMMITTEES:

1st JOINT ECONOMIC
House Dates: May 1, 2001-Jan. 3, 2009
Departure: Left the House; lost re-election

Cong.	Ranking	Terms in: House	Comm.	Date of Assignment
107th	Maj-5th	4	1	May 1, 2001
108th	Maj-4th	5	2	Feb. 25, 2003
109th	Maj-3rd	6	3	Mar. 3, 2005
110th	Min-3rd	7	4	Mar. 27, 2007

John E. Ensign (R-Nev.)

Dates: March 25, 1958
House: Jan. 3, 1995-Jan. 3, 1999
Left the House: Lost U.S. Senate election in 1998
Senate: Jan. 3, 2001-date
Serving in the 111th Congress

HOUSE STANDING COMMITTEES:

1st WAYS AND MEANS
Dates: Jan. 4, 1995-Jan. 3, 1999
Departure: Left the House; lost Senate election

Cong.	Ranking	Terms in: House	Comm.	Date of Assignment
104th	Maj-20th	1	1	Jan. 4, 1995
105th	Maj-18th	2	2	Jan. 7, 1997

2nd RESOURCES
Dates: May 25, 1995-Jan. 3, 1999
Departure: Left the House; lost Senate election

Cong.	Ranking	Terms in: House	Comm.	Date of Assignment
104th	Maj-26th	1	1	May 25, 1995
105th	Maj-19th	2	2	Jan. 7, 1997

SENATE STANDING COMMITTEES:

1st BANKING, HOUSING AND URBAN AFFAIRS
Dates: Jan. 25, 2001-Jan. 15, 2003
Departure: Moved to Armed Services, Budget, Health, Education, Labor and Pensions, and Veterans' Affairs

Cong.	Ranking	Years in: Senate	Comm.	Date of Assignment
107th	Maj-10th	1	1	Jan. 25, 2001
+107th	Min-10th	1	1	June 6, 2001

2nd COMMERCE, SCIENCE AND TRANSPORTATION
Dates: Jan. 25, 2001-date
Departure: Still serving in the 111th Congress

Cong.	Ranking	Years in: Senate	Comm.	Date of Assignment
107th	Maj-10th	1	1	Jan. 25, 2001
+107th	Min-10th	1	1	June 6, 2001
108th	Maj-10th	3	2	Jan. 15, 2003
109th	Maj-8th	5	4	Jan. 6, 2005
110th	Min-7th	7	6	Jan. 12, 2007
111th	Min-3rd	9	8	Jan. 21, 2009

3rd SMALL BUSINESS renamed June 29, 2001
SMALL BUSINESS AND ENTREPRENEURSHIP
Dates: Jan. 25, 2001-Jan. 6, 2005
Departure: Left committee; no new assignment

Cong.	Ranking	Years in: Senate	Comm.	Date of Assignment
107th	Maj-9th	1	1	Jan. 25, 2001
+107th	Min-9th	1	1	June 6, 2001
108th	Maj-9th	3	2	Jan. 15, 2003

4th ARMED SERVICES
Dates: Jan. 15, 2003-July 17, 2007
Departure: Left committee; moved to Finance

Cong.	Ranking	Years in: Senate	Comm.	Date of Assignment
108th	Maj-8th	3	1	Jan. 15, 2003

109th	Maj-7th	5	2	Jan. 6, 2005
110th	Min-6th	7	4	Jan. 12, 2007

5th BUDGET
Dates: Jan. 15, 2003-date
Departure: Still serving in the 111th Congress

		Years in:		Date of
Cong.	Ranking	Senate	Comm.	Assignment
108th	Maj-11th	3	1	Jan. 15, 2003
109th	Maj-9th	5	2	Jan. 6, 2005
110th	Min-9th	7	4	Jan. 12, 2007
111th	Min-7th	9	7	Jan. 21, 2009

6th HEALTH, EDUCATION, LABOR, AND PENSIONS
Dates: Jan. 15, 2003-Jan. 12, 2007
Departure: Left committee; no new assignment

		Years in:		Date of
Cong.	Ranking	Senate	Comm.	Assignment
108th	Maj-9th	3	1	Jan. 15, 2003
109th	Maj-8th	5	2	Jan. 6, 2005

7th VETERANS' AFFAIRS
Dates: Jan. 15, 2003-Jan. 24, 2008
Departure: Left committee; moved to Rules and Administration

		Years in:		Date of
Cong.	Ranking	Senate	Comm.	Assignment
108th	Maj-6th	3	1	Jan. 15, 2003
109th	Maj-6th	5	2	Jan. 6, 2005
110th	Min-7th	7	4	Jan. 12, 2007

8th FINANCE
Dates: July 10, 2007-date
Departure: Still serving in the 111th Congress

		Years in:		Date of
Cong.	Ranking	Senate	Comm.	Assignment
110th	MnR-1st	7	1	July 10, 2007
111th	Min-8th	9	2	Jan. 21, 2009

9th RULES AND ADMINISTRATION
Dates: Jan. 24, 2008-date
Departure: Still serving in the 111th Congress

		Years in:		Date of
Cong.	Ranking	Senate	Comm.	Assignment
110th	MnR-1st	8	1	Jan. 24, 2008
111th	Min-8th	9	1	Jan. 21, 2009

10th HOMELAND SECURITY AND GOVERNMENTAL AFFAIRS
Dates: Jan. 21, 2009-date
Departure: Still serving in the 111th Congress

		Years in:		Date of
Cong.	Ranking	Senate	Comm.	Assignment
111th	Min-5th	9	1	Jan. 21, 2009

SENATE SELECT AND SPECIAL COMMITTEES:

1st SPECIAL AGING (Permanent)
Dates: Jan. 25, 2001-Jan. 15, 2003
Departure: Moved to Armed Services, Budget, Health, Education, Labor and Pensions, and Veterans' Affairs

		Years in:		Date of
Cong.	Ranking	Senate	Comm.	Assignment
107th	Maj-10th	1	1	Jan. 25, 2001
+107th	Min-9th	1	1	July 24, 2001

Michael B. Enzi (R-Wyo.)

Dates: Feb. 1, 1944
Senate: Jan. 3, 1997-date
Serving in the 111th Congress

SENATE STANDING COMMITTEES:

1st BANKING, HOUSING AND URBAN AFFAIRS
Dates: Jan. 9, 1997-Jan. 21, 2009
Departure: Moved to Finance

		Years in:		Date of
Cong.	Ranking	Senate	Comm.	Assignment
105th	Maj-9th	1	1	Jan. 9, 1997
106th	Maj-7th	3	2	Jan. 7, 1999
107th	Maj-5th	5	5	Jan. 25, 2001
+107th	Min-5th	5	5	June 6, 2001
108th	Maj-4th	7	7	Jan. 15, 2003
109th	Maj-4th	9	8	Jan. 6, 2005
110th	Min-4th	11	11	Jan. 12, 2007

2nd LABOR AND HUMAN RESOURCES renamed Jan. 21, 1999
HEALTH, EDUCATION, LABOR AND PENSIONS
Dates: Jan. 9, 1997-date
Departure: Still serving in the 111th Congress

		Years in:		Date of
Cong.	Ranking	Senate	Comm.	Assignment
105th	Maj-6th	1	1	Jan. 9, 1997
106th	Maj-5th	3	2	Jan. 7, 1999
107th	Maj-4th	5	5	Jan. 25, 2001
+107th	Min-3rd	5	5	July 10, 2001
108th	Maj-3rd	7	7	Jan. 15, 2003
109th	Maj-Chr	9	8	Jan. 6, 2005
110th	Min-RM	11	11	Jan. 12, 2007
111th	Min-RM	13	13	Jan. 21, 2009

3rd SMALL BUSINESS renamed June 29, 2001
SMALL BUSINESS AND ENTREPRENEURSHIP
Dates: Jan. 21, 1999-date
Departure: Still serving in the 111th Congress

		Years in:		Date of
Cong.	Ranking	Senate	Comm.	Assignment
105th	Maj-10th	1	1	Jan. 9, 1997
106th	Maj-6th	3	2	Jan. 7, 1999
107th	Maj-5th	5	5	Jan. 25, 2001
+107th	Min-5th	5	5	June 6, 2001
108th	Maj-5th	7	7	Jan. 15, 2003
109th	Maj-9th	9	8	Jan. 6, 2005
110th	Min-8th	11	11	Jan. 12, 2007
111th	Min-5th	13	13	Jan. 21, 2009

4th FOREIGN RELATIONS
Dates: July 10, 2001-Jan. 6, 2005
Departure: Left committee; no new assignment

		Years in:		Date of
Cong.	Ranking	Senate	Comm.	Assignment
107th	MnR-1st	5	1	July 10, 2001
108th	Maj-6th	7	2	Jan. 15, 2003

5th BUDGET
Dates: Jan. 15, 2003-date
Departure: Still serving in the 111th Congress

		Years in:		Date of
Cong.	Ranking	Senate	Comm.	Assignment
108th	Maj-7th	7	1	Jan. 15, 2003

Cong.	Ranking	House	Comm.	Date
109th	Maj-5th	9	2	Jan. 6, 2005
110th	Min-5th	11	4	Jan. 12, 2007
111th	Min-3rd	13	7	Jan. 21, 2009

6th FINANCE
Dates: Jan. 21, 2009-date
Departure: Still serving in the 111th Congress

Cong.	Ranking	Years in: Senate	Comm.	Date of Assignment
111th	Min-9th	13	1	Jan. 21, 2009

SENATE SELECT AND SPECIAL COMMITTEES:

1st SPECIAL AGING (Permanent)
Dates: Jan. 9, 1997-Jan. 6, 2005
Departure: Left committee; no new assignment

Cong.	Ranking	Years in: Senate	Comm.	Date of Assignment
105th	Maj-10th	1	1	Jan. 9, 1997
106th	Maj-9th	3	2	Jan. 7, 1999
107th	Maj-7th	5	5	Jan. 25, 2001
+107th	Min-6th	5	5	July 24, 2001
108th	Maj-4th	7	7	Jan. 14, 2003

Anna G. Eshoo (D-Cal.)

Dates: Dec. 13, 1942
House: Jan. 3, 1993-date
Serving in the 111th Congress

HOUSE STANDING COMMITTEES:

1st MERCHANT MARINE AND FISHERIES
Dates: Jan. 5, 1993-Jan. 3, 1995
Departure: Committee abolished; moved to Commerce

Cong.	Ranking	Terms in: House	Comm.	Date of Assignment
103rd	Maj-22nd	1	1	Jan. 5, 1993

2nd SCIENCE, SPACE AND TECHNOLOGY
Dates: Jan. 5, 1993-Jan. 3, 1995
Departure: Moved to Commerce

Cong.	Ranking	Terms in: House	Comm.	Date of Assignment
103rd	Maj-26th	1	1	Jan. 5, 1993

3rd COMMERCE, 104-106
ENERGY AND COMMERCE, 107-111
Dates: Jan. 4, 1995-date
Departure: Still serving in the 111th Congress

Cong.	Ranking	Terms in: House	Comm.	Date of Assignment
104th	Min-19th	2	1	Jan. 4, 1995
105th	Min-14th	3	2	Jan. 7, 1997
106th	Min-12th	4	3	Jan. 6, 1999
107th	Min-12th	5	4	Jan. 31, 2001
108th	Min-12th	6	5	Jan. 28, 2003
109th	Min-10th	7	6	Jan. 26, 2005
110th	Maj-9th	8	7	Jan. 4, 2007
111th	Maj-8th	9	8	Jan. 7, 2009

HOUSE SELECT AND SPECIAL COMMITTEES:

1st PERMANENT SELECT INTELLIGENCE
Dates: Jan. 8, 2003-date
Departure: Still serving in the 111th Congress

Cong.	Ranking	Terms in: House	Comm.	Date of Assignment
108th	Min-7th	6	1	Jan. 8, 2003
109th	Min-6th	7	2	Jan. 26, 2005
110th	Maj-5th	8	3	Jan. 17, 2007
111th	Maj-3rd	9	4	Feb. 4, 2009

A. Michael Espy (D-Miss.)

Dates: Nov. 28, 1953
House: Jan. 3, 1987-Jan. 22, 1993
Left the House: Resigned; appointed Secretary of Agriculture in 1993

H: Representative Espy was assigned to one of his committees in the 103rd Congress during his Senate confirmation hearings

HOUSE STANDING COMMITTEES:

1st AGRICULTURE
Dates: Jan. 22, 1987-Jan. 22, 1993
Departure: Resigned the House; appointed to Cabinet.

Cong.	Ranking	Terms in: House	Comm.	Date of Assignment
103rd	Maj-11th	4	4	Jan. 5, 1993

2nd BUDGET
Dates: Jan. 6, 1987-Jan. 20, 1993
Departure: Resigned the House; appointed to Cabinet.

HOUSE SELECT AND SPECIAL COMMITTEES:

1st SELECT HUNGER (Temporary)
Dates: Jan. 21, 1987-Jan. 3, 1993
Termination: Committee not renewed in 1993

JOINT COMMITTEES:

1st DEFICIT REDUCTION (Temporary)
House Dates: Feb. 23, 1987-Sep. 29, 1987
Termination: Public Law 100-119 adjusted Gramm-Rudman-Hollings Act

Bobby R. Etheridge (D-N.C.)

Dates: Aug. 7, 1941
House: Jan. 3, 1997-date
Serving in the 111th Congress

HOUSE STANDING COMMITTEES:

1st AGRICULTURE
Dates: Jan. 7, 1997-Jan. 3, 2009
Departure: Moved to Ways and Means

Cong.	Ranking	Terms in: House	Comm.	Date of Assignment
105th	Min-20th	1	1	Jan. 7, 1997

Cong.	Ranking	Terms in: House	Comm.	Date of Assignment
106th	Min-18th	2	2	Jan. 6, 1999
107th	Min-13th	3	3	Jan. 31, 2001
108th	Min-7th	4	4	Jan. 28, 2003
109th	Min-5th	5	5	Jan. 26, 2005
110th	Maj-4th	6	6	Jan. 12, 2007

2nd SCIENCE, SPACE AND TECHNOLOGY
Dates: Feb. 13, 1997-Feb. 12, 2003
Departure: Leave of absence; moved to Select Homeland Security

Cong.	Ranking	Terms in: House	Comm.	Date of Assignment
105th	Min-19th	1	1	Feb. 13, 1997
106th	Min-16th	2	2	Jan. 6, 1999
107th	Min-11th	3	3	Jan. 31, 2001
108th	Min-8th	4	4	Jan. 28, 2003

3rd HOMELAND SECURITY
Dates: Feb. 9, 2005-Jan. 3, 2009
Departure: Moved to Ways and Means

Cong.	Ranking	Terms in: House	Comm.	Date of Assignment
109th	Min-13th	5	2	Feb. 9, 2005
110th	Maj-12th	6	3	Jan. 12, 2007

4th BUDGET
Dates: Jan. 18, 2007-date
Departure: Still serving in the 111th Congress

Cong.	Ranking	Terms in: House	Comm.	Date of Assignment
110th	Maj-18th	6	1	Jan. 18, 2007
111th	Maj-11th	7	2	Jan. 21, 2009

5th WAYS AND MEANS
Dates: Jan. 7, 2009-date
Departure: Still serving in the 111th Congress

Cong.	Ranking	Terms in: House	Comm.	Date of Assignment
111th	Maj-23rd	7	1	Jan. 7, 2009

HOUSE SELECT AND SPECIAL COMMITTEES:

1st SELECT HOMELAND SECURITY
Dates: Feb. 12, 2003-Jan. 3, 2005
Departure: Remained on reorganized standing committee

Cong.	Ranking	Terms in: House	Comm.	Date of Assignment
108th	Min-19th	4	1	Feb. 12, 2003

Lane A. Evans (D-Ill.)

Dates: Aug. 4, 1951
House: Jan. 3, 1983-Jan. 3, 2007
Left the House: Retired in 2006

HOUSE STANDING COMMITTEES:

1st AGRICULTURE
Dates: Jan. 6, 1983-June 8, 1988
Departure: Had moved earlier to Armed Services

2nd VETERANS' AFFAIRS
Dates: Jan. 6, 1983-Jan. 3, 2007
Departure: Left the House; retired

Cong.	Ranking	Terms in: House	Comm.	Date of Assignment
103rd	Maj-4th	6	6	Jan. 5, 1993
104th	Min-2nd	7	7	Jan. 4, 1995
105th	Min-RM	8	8	Feb. 6, 1997
106th	Min-RM	9	9	Jan. 6, 1999
107th	Min-RM	10	10	Jan. 31, 2001
108th	Min-RM	11	11	Jan. 8, 2003
109th	Min-RM	12	12	Jan. 6, 2005

3rd ARMED SERVICES, 100-103
NATIONAL SECURITY, 104-105
ARMED SERVICES, 106-109
Dates: May 18, 1988-Jan. 3, 2007
Departure: Left the House; retired

Cong.	Ranking	Terms in: House	Comm.	Date of Assignment
103rd	Maj-16th	6	4	Jan. 5, 1993
104th	Min-9th	7	5	Jan. 4, 1995
105th	Min-7th	8	6	Jan. 7, 1997
106th	Min-6th	9	7	Jan. 6, 1999
107th	Min-5th	10	8	Jan. 31, 2001
108th	Min-4th	11	9	Jan. 28, 2003
109th	Min-4th	12	10	Jan. 26, 2005

4th NATURAL RESOURCES
Dates: Jan. 21, 1993-Jan. 3, 1995
Departure: Left committee; no new assignment

Cong.	Ranking	Terms in: House	Comm.	Date of Assignment
103rd	Maj-25th	6	1	Jan. 21, 1993

HOUSE SELECT AND SPECIAL COMMITTEES:

1st SELECT CHILDREN, YOUTH AND FAMILIES (Temporary)
Dates: Mar. 20, 1985-Jan. 3, 1993
Termination: Committee not renewed in 1993

R. Terry Everett (R-Ala.)

Dates: Feb. 15, 1937
House: Jan. 3, 1993-Jan. 3, 2009
Left the House: Retired in 2008

HOUSE STANDING COMMITTEES:

1st ARMED SERVICES, 103
NATIONAL SECURITY, 104-105
ARMED SERVICES, 106-110
Dates: Jan. 5, 1993-Jan. 3, 2009
Departure: Left the House; retired

Cong.	Ranking	Terms in: House	Comm.	Date of Assignment
103rd	Min-21st	1	1	Jan. 5, 1993
104th	Maj-17th	2	2	Jan. 4, 1995
105th	Maj-14th	3	3	Jan. 7, 1997
106th	Maj-14th	4	4	Jan. 6, 1999
107th	Maj-9th	5	5	Jan. 6, 2001
108th	Maj-6th	6	6	Jan. 28, 2003
109th	Maj-6th	7	7	Jan. 26, 2005
110th	Min-4th	8	8	Jan. 10, 2007

2nd VETERANS' AFFAIRS
Dates: Jan. 5, 1993-Jan. 3, 2007
Departure: Left committee; no new assignment

Cong.	Ranking	Terms in: House	Comm.	Date of Assignment
103rd	Min-8th	1	1	Jan. 5, 1993
104th	Maj-6th	2	2	Jan. 4, 1995
105th	Maj-5th	3	3	Jan. 21, 1997
106th	Maj-5th	4	4	Jan. 6, 1999
107th	Maj-5th	5	5	Jan. 6, 2001
108th	Maj-3rd	6	6	Jan. 28, 2003
109th	Maj-3rd	7	7	Jan. 26, 2005

3rd AGRICULTURE
Dates: May 27, 1993-Jan. 3, 2009
Departure: Left the House; retired

Cong.	Ranking	Terms in: House	Comm.	Date of Assignment
103rd	MnA-19th	1	1	May 27, 1993
104th	Maj-14th	2	2	Jan. 4, 1995
105th	Maj-11th	3	3	Jan. 7, 1997
106th	Maj-9th	4	4	Jan. 6, 1999
107th	Maj-6th	5	5	Jan. 6, 2001
108th	Maj-6th	6	6	Jan. 28, 2003
109th	Maj-4th	7	7	Jan. 26, 2005
110th	Min-2nd	8	8	Jan. 10, 2007

HOUSE SELECT AND SPECIAL COMMITTEES:

1st PERMANENT SELECT INTELLIGENCE
Dates: Jan. 23, 2002-Jan. 3, 2009
Departure: Left the House; retired

Cong.	Ranking	Terms in: House	Comm.	Date of Assignment
107th	MjR-2nd	5	1	Jan. 23, 2002
108th	Maj-9th	6	2	Jan. 8, 2003
109th	Maj-4th	7	3	Jan. 26, 2005
110th	Min-2nd	8	4	Jan. 17, 2007

Thomas W. Ewing (R-Ill.)

Dates: Sept. 13, 1935
House: July 2, 1991-Jan. 3, 2001
Left the House: Retired in 2000

H: Ewing was elected to the 102nd Congress by special election, July 2, 1991, to fill the vacancy caused by the resignation of U.S. Representative Edward Madigan (R-Ill.) who had been appointed Secretary of Agriculture. Ewing was seated July 10, 1991, and was assigned to committees.

HOUSE STANDING COMMITTEES:

1st AGRICULTURE
Dates: July 11, 1991-Jan. 3, 2001
Departure: Left the House; retired

Cong.	Ranking	Terms in: House	Comm.	Date of Assignment
103rd	Min-12th	2	2	Jan. 5, 1993
104th	Maj-8th	3	3	Jan. 4, 1995
105th	Maj-5th	4	4	Jan. 7, 1997
106th	Maj-4th	5	5	Jan. 6, 1999

2nd PUBLIC WORKS AND TRANSPORTATION, 103 TRANSPORTATION AND INFRASTRUCTURE, 104-106
Dates: July 11, 1991-Jan. 3, 2001
Departure: Left the House; retired

Cong.	Ranking	Terms in: House	Comm.	Date of Assignment
103rd	Min-10th	2	2	Jan. 5, 1993

Cong.	Ranking	Terms in: House	Comm.	Date of Assignment
104th	Maj-12th	3	3	Jan. 4, 1995
105th	Maj-9th	4	4	Jan. 7, 1997
106th	Maj-8th	5	5	Jan. 6, 1999

3rd SCIENCE
Dates: Jan. 21, 1997-Jan. 3, 2001
Departure: Left the House; retired

Cong.	Ranking	Terms in: House	Comm.	Date of Assignment
105th	Maj-17th	4	1	Jan. 21, 1997
106th	Maj-14th	5	2	Jan. 6, 1999

4th HOUSE ADMINISTRATION
Dates: Jan. 6, 1999-July 27, 2000
Departure: Resigned committee; no new assignment

Cong.	Ranking	Terms in: House	Comm.	Date of Assignment
106th	Maj-6th	5	1	Jan. 6, 1999

JOINT COMMITTEES:

1st JOINT ECONOMIC
House Dates: Jan. 19, 1995-Jan. 3, 1997
Departure: Moved to Science

Cong.	Ranking	Terms in: House	Comm.	Date of Assignment
104th	Maj-2nd	3	1	Jan. 19, 1995

J. James Exon (D-Neb.)

Dates: Aug. 9, 1921-June 10, 2005
Senate: Jan. 3, 1979-Jan. 3, 1997
Left the Senate: Retired in 1996

SENATE STANDING COMMITTEES:

1st ARMED SERVICES
Dates: Jan. 23, 1979-Jan. 3, 1997
Departure: Left the Senate; retired

Cong.	Ranking	Years in: Senate	Comm.	Date of Assignment
103rd	Maj-2nd	15	14	Jan. 7, 1993
104th	Min-2nd	17	16	Jan. 4, 1995

2nd BUDGET
Dates: Jan. 23, 1979-Jan. 3, 1997
Departure: Left the Senate; retired

Cong.	Ranking	Years in: Senate	Comm.	Date of Assignment
103rd	Maj-5th	15	14	Jan. 21, 1993
104th	Min-RM	17	16	Jan. 6, 1995

3rd COMMERCE, SCIENCE AND TRANSPORTATION
Dates: Jan. 23, 1979-Jan. 3, 1997
Departure: Left the Senate; retired

Cong.	Ranking	Years in: Senate	Comm.	Date of Assignment
103rd	Maj-4th	15	14	Jan. 7, 1993
104th	Min-4th	17	16	Jan. 4, 1995

JOINT COMMITTEES:

1st JOINT DEFICIT REDUCTION (Temporary)
Senate Dates: Jan. 6, 1987-Sep. 29, 1987
Departure: Public Law 100-119 adjusted Gramm-Rudman-Hollings Act

F

D.M. (Lauch) Faircloth (R-N.C.)

Dates: Jan. 14, 1928
Senate: Jan. 3, 1993-Jan. 3, 1999
Left the Senate: Defeated for re-election in 1998

SENATE STANDING COMMITTEES:

1st ARMED SERVICES
Dates: Jan. 7, 1993-Jan. 4, 1995
Departure: Left committee; no new assignment

| | | Years in: | | Date of |
Cong.	Ranking	Senate	Comm.	Assignment
103rd	Min-9th	1	1	Jan. 7, 1993

2nd BANKING, HOUSING AND URBAN AFFAIRS
Dates: Jan. 7, 1993-Jan. 3, 1995
Departure: Left the Senate; lost re-election

| | | Years in: | | Date of |
Cong.	Ranking	Senate	Comm.	Assignment
103rd	Min-5th	1	1	Jan. 7, 1993
104th	Maj-6th	3	2	Jan. 4, 1995
105th	Maj-5th	5	5	Jan. 9, 1997

3rd ENVIRONMENT AND PUBLIC WORKS
Dates: Jan. 7, 1993-Jan. 9, 1997
Departure: Moved to Appropriations and Small Business

| | | Years in: | | Date of |
Cong.	Ranking	Senate	Comm.	Assignment
103rd	Min-6th	1	1	Jan. 7, 1993
104th	Maj-4th	3	2	Jan. 5, 1995

4th LABOR AND HUMAN RESOURCES
Dates: Apr. 16, 1996-Jan. 9, 1997
Departure: Moved to Appropriations and Small Business

| | | Years in: | | Date of |
Cong.	Ranking	Senate	Comm.	Assignment
104th	MjR-1st	4	1	Apr. 16, 1996

5th APPROPRIATIONS
Dates: Jan. 9, 1997-Jan. 3, 1999
Departure: Left the Senate; lost re-election

| | | Years in: | | Date of |
Cong.	Ranking	Senate	Comm.	Assignment
105th	Maj-14th	5	1	Jan. 9, 1997

6th SMALL BUSINESS
Dates: Jan. 9, 1997-Jan. 3, 1999
Departure: Left the Senate; lost re-election

| | | Years in: | | Date of |
Cong.	Ranking	Senate	Comm.	Assignment
105th	Maj-9th	5	1	Jan. 9, 1997

SENATE SELECT AND SPECIAL COMMITTEES:

1st SPECIAL COMMITTEE TO INVESTIGATE WHITEWATER
DEVELOPMENT CORPORATION AND RELATED MATTERS

Dates: July 20, 1995-June 17, 1996
Termination: Senate Report 104-280 filed

| | | Years in: | | Date of |
Cong.	Ranking	Senate	Comm.	Assignment
104th	Maj-5th	3	1	July 20, 1995

Eni F.H. Faleomavaega (D-A.S.)

Dates: Aug. 15, 1943
House: Jan. 3, 1989-date
Serving in the 111th Congress

H: Faleomavaega was elected as a Democrat to serve as a Territorial Delegate in the 102nd Congress and is still serving. He was assigned to committees and allowed to accrue seniority.

HOUSE STANDING COMMITTEES:

1st FOREIGN AFFAIRS, 101-103
INTERNATIONAL RELATIONS, 104-109
FOREIGN AFFAIRS, 110-111
Dates: Jan. 19, 1989-date
Departure: Still serving in the 111th Congress

| | | Terms in: | | Date of |
Cong.	Ranking	House	Comm.	Assignment
103rd	Maj-9th	3	3	Jan. 5, 1993
104th	Min-9th	4	4	Jan. 4, 1995
105th	Min-6th	5	5	Jan. 7, 1997
106th	Min-5th	6	6	Jan. 6, 1999
107th	Min-4th	7	7	Jan. 31, 2001
108th	Min-4th	8	8	Jan. 28, 2003
109th	Min-4th	9	9	Jan. 26, 2005
110th	Maj-4th	10	10	Jan. 12, 2007
111th	Maj-3rd	11	11	Jan. 21, 2009

2nd INTERIOR AND INSULAR AFFAIRS, 101-102
NATURAL RESOURCES, 103
RESOURCES, 104-109
NATURAL RESOURCES, 110-111
Dates: Jan. 19, 1989-date
Departure: Still serving in the 111th Congress

| | | Terms in: | | Date of |
Cong.	Ranking	House	Comm.	Assignment
103rd	Maj-13th	3	3	Jan. 5, 1993
104th	Min-9th	4	4	Jan. 9, 1995
105th	Min-9th	5	5	Jan. 7, 1997
106th	Min-6th	6	6	Jan. 6, 1999
107th	Min-6th	7	7	Feb. 8, 2001
108th	Min-6th	8	8	Jan. 28, 2003
109th	Min-3rd	9	9	Jan. 26, 2005
110th	Maj-3rd	10	10	Jan. 18, 2007
111th	Maj-3rd	11	11	Jan. 21, 2009

3rd MERCHANT MARINE AND FISHERIES
Dates: Jan. 24, 1991-Jan. 3, 1993
Departure: Moved to Education and Labor

4th EDUCATION AND LABOR
Dates: Jan. 21, 1993-Jan. 3, 1995
Departure: Left committee; no new assignment

Cong.	Ranking	Terms in: House	Comm.	Date of Assignment
103rd	Maj-26th	3	1	Jan. 21, 1993

5th SMALL BUSINESS
Dates: Mar. 5, 2003-Jan. 3, 2007
Departure: Left committee; no new assignment

Cong.	Ranking	Terms in: House	Comm.	Date of Assignment
108th	MnR-2nd	8	1	Mar. 5, 2003
109th	Min-5th	9	2	Feb. 2, 2005

HOUSE SELECT AND SPECIAL COMMITTEES:

1st SELECT HUNGER (Temporary)
Dates: Apr. 4, 1989-Jan. 3, 1993
Terminated: Committee not renewed in 1993

Mary Fallin (R-Okla.)

Dates: Dec. 9, 1954
House: Jan. 3, 2007-date
Serving in the 111th Congress

HOUSE STANDING COMMITTEES:

1st SMALL BUSINESS
Dates: Jan. 10, 2007-date
Departure: Still serving in the 111th Congress

Cong.	Ranking	Terms in: House	Comm.	Date of Assignment
110th	Min-13th	1	1	Jan. 10, 2007
111th	Min-7th	2	2	Jan. 9, 2009

2nd TRANSPORTATION AND INFRASTRUCTURE
Dates: Jan. 10, 2007-date
Departure: Still serving in the 111th Congress

Cong.	Ranking	Terms in: House	Comm.	Date of Assignment
110th	Min-33rd	1	1	Jan. 10, 2007
111th	Min-24th	2	2	Jan. 9, 2009

3rd NATURAL RESOURCES
Dates: May 10, 2007-Jan. 3, 2009
Departure: Moved to Armed Services

Cong.	Ranking	Terms in: House	Comm.	Date of Assignment
110th	MnR-1st	1	1	May 10, 2007

4th ARMED SERVICES
Dates: Jan. 9, 2009-date
Departure: Still serving in the 111th Congress

Cong.	Ranking	Terms in: House	Comm.	Date of Assignment
111th	Min-21st	2	1	Jan. 9, 2009

Sam Farr (D-Cal.)

Dates: July 4, 1941
House: June 8, 1993-date
Serving in the 111th Congress

H: Farr was elected to the 103rd Congress by special election, June 8, 1993, to fill the vacancy caused by the resignation of U.S. Representative Leon Panetta (D-Cal.) who was appointed Director of the Office of Management and Budget. Farr was seated June 16, 1993, and assigned to committees.

HOUSE STANDING COMMITTEES:

1st AGRICULTURE
Dates: June 23, 1993-Jan. 3, 1999
Departure: Moved to Appropriations

Cong.	Ranking	Terms in: House	Comm.	Date of Assignment
103rd	MjA-29th	1	1	June 23, 1993
104th	Min-20th	2	2	Jan. 4, 1995
105th	Min-14th	3	3	Jan. 7, 1997

2nd NATURAL RESOURCES, 103
RESOURCES, 104-105
Dates: June 23, 1993-Jan. 3, 1999
Departure: Moved to Appropriations

Cong.	Ranking	Terms in: House	Comm.	Date of Assignment
103rd	MjR-2nd	1	1	June 23, 1993
104th	Min-20th	2	2	Jan. 9, 1995
105th	Min-18th	3	3	Jan. 7, 1997

3rd ARMED SERVICES
Dates: July 21, 1993-Jan. 3, 1995
Departure: Left committee; no new assignment

Cong.	Ranking	Terms in: House	Comm.	Date of Assignment
103rd	Maj-34th	1	1	July 21, 1993

4th APPROPRIATIONS
Dates: Jan. 6, 1999-date
Departure: Still serving in the 111th Congress

Cong.	Ranking	Terms in: House	Comm.	Date of Assignment
106th	Min-24th	4	1	Jan. 6, 1999
107th	Min-24th	5	2	Jan. 31, 2001
108th	Min-22nd	6	3	Jan. 28, 2003
109th	Min-22nd	7	4	Jan. 26, 2005
110th	Maj-19th	8	5	Jan. 4, 2007
111th	Maj-18th	9	6	Jan. 7, 2009

Chaka Fattah (D-Penn.)

Dates: Nov. 21, 1956
House: Jan. 3, 1995-date
Serving in the 111th Congress

HOUSE STANDING COMMITTEES:

1st SMALL BUSINESS
Dates: Jan. 4, 1995-Mar. 5, 1996
Departure: Resigned committee; no new assignment

Cong.	Ranking	Terms in: House	Comm.	Date of Assignment
104th	Min-15th	1	1	Jan. 4, 1995

2nd GOVERNMENT REFORM AND OVERSIGHT, 104-105
GOVERNMENT REFORM, 106
Dates: Jan. 9, 1995-Feb. 7, 2001
Departure: Resigned committee; moved to Appropriations

Cong.	Ranking	Terms in: House	Comm.	Date of Assignment
104th	Min-22nd	1	1	Jan. 9, 1995
105th	Min-12th	2	2	Jan. 7, 1997
106th	Min-11th	3	3	Jan. 6, 1999
107th	Min-9th	4	4	Jan. 31, 2001

3rd ECONOMIC AND EDUCATIONAL OPPORTUNITIES, 104
EDUCATION AND THE WORKFORCE, 105-106
Dates: Oct. 11, 1995-Feb. 7, 2001
Departure: Resigned committee; moved to Appropriations

Cong.	Ranking	Terms in: House	Comm.	Date of Assignment
104th	MnR-1st	1	1	Oct. 11, 1995
105th	Min-13th	2	2	Jan. 7, 1997
106th	Min-13th	3	3	Jan. 6, 1999
107th	Min-11th	4	4	Jan. 31, 2001

4th STANDARDS OF OFFICIAL CONDUCT
Dates: Sep. 29, 1997-Jan. 3, 2001
Departure: Moved to Appropriations

Cong.	Ranking	Terms in: House	Comm.	Date of Assignment
105th	Min-4th	2	1	Sept. 29, 1997
106th	Min-4th	3	2	Jan. 6, 1999

5th HOUSE ADMINISTRATION
Dates: Feb. 10, 1999-Jan. 3, 2003
Departure: Left committee; no new assignment

Cong.	Ranking	Terms in: House	Comm.	Date of Assignment
106th	Min-2nd	3	1	Feb. 10, 1999
107th	Min-2nd	4	2	Jan. 31, 2001

6th APPROPRIATIONS
Dates: Feb. 8, 2001-date
Departure: Still serving in the 111th Congress

Cong.	Ranking	Terms in: House	Comm.	Date of Assignment
107th	Min-28th	4	1	Feb. 8, 2001
108th	Min-26th	5	2	Jan. 28, 2003
109th	Min-26th	6	3	Jan. 26, 2005
110th	Maj-23rd	7	4	Jan. 4, 2007
111th	Maj-22nd	8	5	Jan. 7, 2009

JOINT COMMITTEES:

1st JOINT PRINTING
House Dates: Mar. 2, 1999-Jan. 3, 2003
Departure: Left committee; no new assignment

Cong.	Ranking	Terms in: House	Comm.	Date of Assignment
106th	Min-2nd	3	1	Mar. 2, 1999
107th	Min-2nd	4	2	June 5, 2001

Harris W. Fawell (R-Ill.)

Dates: March 5, 1929
House: Jan. 3, 1985-Jan. 3, 1999
Left the House: Retired in 1998

HOUSE STANDING COMMITTEES:

1st EDUCATION AND LABOR, 99-103
ECONOMIC AND EDUCATIONAL OPPORTUNITIES, 104
EDUCATION AND THE WORKFORCE, 105
Dates: Jan. 30, 1985-Jan. 3, 1999
Departure: Left the House; retired

Cong.	Ranking	Terms in: House	Comm.	Date of Assignment
103rd	Min-6th	5	5	Jan. 5, 1993
104th	Maj-5th	6	6	Jan. 4, 1995
105th	Maj-4th	7	7	Jan. 7, 1997

2nd SCIENCE AND TECHNOLOGY, 99
SCIENCE, SPACE AND TECHNOLOGY, 100-103
SCIENCE, 104-105
Dates: Jan. 30, 1985-Jan. 3, 1999
Departure: Left the House; retired

Cong.	Ranking	Terms in: House	Comm.	Date of Assignment
103rd	Min-6th	5	5	Jan. 5, 1993
104th	Maj-4th	6	6	Jan. 4, 1995
105th	Maj-3rd	7	7	Jan. 21, 1997

HOUSE SELECT AND SPECIAL COMMITTEES:

1st SELECT AGING (Permanent)
Dates: Feb. 21, 1985-Jan. 3, 1993
Termination: Committee not renewed in 1993

2nd SELECT CHILDREN, YOUTH AND FAMILIES (Temporary)
Dates: June 16, 1992-Jan. 3, 1993
Termination: Committee not renewed in 1993

Victor H. Fazio (D-Cal.)

Dates: Oct. 11, 1942
House: Jan. 3, 1979-Jan. 3, 1999
Left the House: Retired in 1998

HOUSE STANDING COMMITTEES:

1st ARMED SERVICES
Dates: Jan. 24, 1979-Feb. 26, 1980
Departure: Moved to Appropriations

2nd HOUSE ADMINISTRATION
1st Dates: Jan. 24, 1979-Feb. 26, 1980
1st Departure: Moved to Appropriations
2nd Dates: Jan. 4, 1995-Jan. 3, 1997
2nd Departure: Left committee; no new assignment

Cong.	Ranking	Terms in: House	Comm.	Date of Assignment
104th	Min-RM	9 *2	1	Jan. 4, 1995

3rd APPROPRIATIONS
Dates: Feb. 26, 1980-Jan. 3, 1999
Departure: Left the House; retired

Cong.	Ranking	Terms in: House	Comm.	Date of Assignment
103rd	Maj-13th	8	8	Jan. 5, 1993
104th	Min-10th	9	9	Jan. 4, 1995
105th	Min-8th	10	10	Jan. 7, 1997

4th BUDGET
Dates: Jan. 6, 1983-Jan. 3, 1989
Departure: Left committee; no new assignment

5th STANDARDS OF OFFICIAL CONDUCT
Dates: Jan. 6, 1983-Jan. 3, 1991
Departure: Left committee; no new assignment

HOUSE SELECT AND SPECIAL COMMITTEES:

1st SELECT HUNGER (Temporary)
Dates: Mar. 13, 1984-Jan. 3, 1993
Termination: Committee not renewed in 1993

JOINT COMMITTEES:

1st DEFICIT REDUCTION (Temporary)
House Dates: Feb. 23, 1987-Sep. 29, 1987
Termination: Public Law 100-119 adjusted Gramm-Rudman-Hollings Act

2nd JOINT LIBRARY
House Dates: Feb. 23, 1995-Jan. 3, 1997
Departure: Left committee; no new assignment

Cong.	Ranking	Terms in: House	Comm.	Date of Assignment
104th	Min-1st	9	1	Feb. 23, 1995

Tom Feeney (R-Fla.)

Dates: May 21, 1958
House: Jan. 3, 2003-Jan. 3, 2009
Left the House: Defeated for re-election in 2008

HOUSE STANDING COMMITTEES:

1st FINANCIAL SERVICES
Dates: Jan. 28, 2003-Jan. 3, 2009
Departure: Left the House; lost re-election

Cong.	Ranking	Terms in: House	Comm.	Date of Assignment
108th	Maj-30th	1	1	Jan. 28, 2003
109th	Maj-24th	2	2	Jan. 26, 2005
110th	Min-17th	3	3	Jan. 10, 2007

2nd JUDICIARY
Dates: Jan. 28, 2003-Jan. 3, 2009
Departure: Left the House; lost re-election

Cong.	Ranking	Terms in: House	Comm.	Date of Assignment
108th	Maj-20th	1	1	Jan. 28, 2003
109th	Maj-21st	2	2	Jan. 26, 2005
110th	Min-14th	3	3	Jan. 10, 2007

3rd SCIENCE, 108-109
SCIENCE AND TECHNOLOGY, 110
Dates: Feb. 11, 2003-Jan. 3, 2009
Departure: Left the House; lost re-election

Cong.	Ranking	Terms in: House	Comm.	Date of Assignment
108th	Maj-25th	1	1	Feb. 11, 2003
109th	Maj-17th	2	2	Jan. 26, 2005
110th	Min-12th	3	3	Jan. 10, 2007

Russell D. Feingold (D-Wisc.)

Dates: March 2, 1953
Senate: Jan. 3, 1993-date
Serving in the 111th Congress

SENATE STANDING COMMITTEES:

1st AGRICULTURE, NUTRITION AND FORESTRY
Dates: Jan. 7, 1993-Jan. 4, 1995
Departure: Moved to Judiciary

Cong.	Ranking	Years in: Senate	Comm.	Date of Assignment
103rd	Maj-10th	1	1	Jan. 7, 1993

2nd FOREIGN RELATIONS
Dates: Jan. 7, 1993-date
Departure: Still serving in the 111th Congress

Cong.	Ranking	Years in: Senate	Comm.	Date of Assignment
103rd	Maj-10th	1	1	Jan. 7, 1993
104th	Min-7th	3	2	Jan. 4, 1995
105th	Min-6th	5	5	Jan. 9, 1997
106th	Min-5th	7	7	Jan. 7, 1999
107th	Min-5th	9	9	Jan. 25, 2001
+107th	Maj-5th	9	9	June 6, 2001
108th	Min-5th	11	11	Jan. 15, 2003
109th	Min-5th	13	12	Jan. 6, 2005
110th	Maj-4th	15	15	Jan. 12, 2007
111th	Maj-3rd	17	17	Jan. 21, 2009

3rd JUDICIARY
Dates: Jan. 4, 1995-date
Departure: Still serving in the 111th Congress

Cong.	Ranking	Years in: Senate	Comm.	Date of Assignment
104th	Min-8th	3	1	Jan. 4, 1995
105th	Min-6th	5	3	Jan. 9, 1997
106th	Min-6th	7	5	Jan. 7, 1999
107th	Min-6th	9	7	Jan. 25, 2001
+107th	Maj-6th	9	7	June 6, 2001
108th	Min-6th	11	9	Jan. 15, 2003
109th	Min-6th	13	11	Jan. 6, 2005
110th	Maj-6th	15	13	Jan. 12, 2007
111th	Maj-4th	17	15	Jan. 21, 2009

4th BUDGET
Dates: Jan. 9, 1997-date
Departure: Still serving in the 111th Congress

Cong.	Ranking	Years in: Senate	Comm.	Date of Assignment
105th	Min-8th	5	1	Jan. 9, 1997
106th	Min-8th	7	2	Jan. 7, 1999
107th	Min-6th	9	5	Jan. 25, 2001
+107th	Maj-6th	9	5	June 6, 2001
108th	Min-6th	11	7	Jan. 15, 2003
109th	Min-5th	13	8	Jan. 6, 2005
110th	Maj-4th	15	11	Jan. 12, 2007
111th	Maj-4th	17	13	Jan. 21, 2009

SENATE SELECT AND SPECIAL COMMITTEES:

1st SPECIAL AGING (Permanent)
Dates: Jan. 21, 1993-Jan. 18, 2006
Departure: Left committee; moved to Select Intelligence

Cong.	Ranking	Years in: Senate	Comm.	Date of Assignment
103rd	Maj-10th	1	1	Jan. 21, 1993
104th	Min-8th	3	2	Jan. 6, 1995
105th	Min-5th	5	4	Jan. 9, 1997
106th	Min-4th	7	6	Jan. 7, 1999
107th	Min-4th	9	9	Jan. 25, 2001
+107th	Maj-5th	9	9	July 10, 2001
108th	Min-5th	11	10	Jan. 15, 2003
109th	Min-3rd	13	12	Jan. 6, 2005

2nd SELECT INTELLIGENCE (Permanent)
Dates: Jan. 18, 2006-date
Departure: Still serving in the 111th Congress

Cong.	Ranking	Years in: Senate	Comm.	Date of Assignment
109th	MnR-1st	13	1	Jan. 18, 2006
110th	Maj-6th	15	1	Jan. 12, 2007
111th	Maj-6th	17	4	Jan. 21, 2009

Dianne Feinstein (D-Cal.)

Dates: June 2, 1933
Senate: Jan. 3, 1993-date
Serving in the 111th Congress

SENATE STANDING COMMITTEES:

1st APPROPRIATIONS
1st Dates: Jan. 7, 1993-Jan. 4, 1995
1st Departure: Moved to Foreign Relations
2nd Dates: Jan. 7, 1999-date
2nd Departure: Still serving in the 111th Congress

Cong.	Ranking	Years in: Senate	Comm.	Date of Assignment
103rd	Maj-16th	1	*1 1	Jan. 7, 1993
106th	Min-12th	7	*2 1	Jan. 7, 1999
107th	Min-11th	9	*2 3	Jan. 25, 2001
+107th	Maj-11th	9	*2 3	June 6, 2001
108th	Min-11th	11	*2 5	Jan. 15, 2003
109th	Min-10th	13	*2 6	Jan. 6, 2005
110th	Maj-9th	15	*2 9	Jan. 12, 2007
111th	Maj-9th	17	*2 11	Jan. 21, 2009

2nd JUDICIARY
Dates: Jan. 7, 1993-date
Departure: Still serving in the 111th Congress

Cong.	Ranking	Years in: Senate	Comm.	Date of Assignment
103rd	Maj-9th	1	1	Jan. 7, 1993
104th	Min-7th	3	2	Jan. 4, 1995
105th	Min-5th	5	5	Jan. 9, 1997
106th	Min-5th	7	7	Jan. 7, 1999
107th	Min-5th	9	9	Jan. 25, 2001
+107th	Maj-5th	9	9	June 6, 2001
108th	Min-5th	11	11	Jan. 15, 2003
109th	Min-5th	13	12	Jan. 6, 2005
110th	Maj-5th	15	15	Jan. 12, 2007
111th	Maj-3rd	17	17	Jan. 21, 2009

3rd RULES AND ADMINISTRATION
Dates: Jan. 21, 1993-date
Departure: Still serving in the 111th Congress

Cong.	Ranking	Years in: Senate	Comm.	Date of Assignment
103rd	Maj-8th	1	1	Jan. 21, 1993

Cong.	Ranking	Years in: Senate	Comm.	Date of Assignment
104th	Min-7th	3	2	Jan. 6, 1995
105th	Min-6th	5	4	Jan. 9, 1997
106th	Min-5th	7	6	Jan. 7, 1999
107th	Min-4th	9	9	Jan. 25, 2001
+107th	Maj-4th	9	9	June 6, 2001
108th	Min-4th	11	10	Jan. 15, 2003
109th	Min-4th	13	12	Jan. 6, 2005
110th	Maj-Chr	15	14	Jan. 12, 2007
111th	Maj-2nd	17	17	Jan. 21, 2009

4th FOREIGN RELATIONS
Dates: Jan. 4, 1995-Jan. 7, 1999
Departure: Returned to Appropriations

Cong.	Ranking	Years in: Senate	Comm.	Date of Assignment
104th	Min-8th	3	1	Jan. 4, 1995
105th	Min-7th	5	3	Jan. 9, 1997

5th ENERGY AND NATURAL RESOURCES
Dates: Jan. 25, 2001-Jan. 12, 2007
Departure: Left committee; became Chair of Rules and Administration and moved to Joint Library and Joint Printing

Cong.	Ranking	Years in: Senate	Comm.	Date of Assignment
107th	Min-9th	9	1	Jan. 25, 2001
+107th	Maj-9th	9	1	June 6, 2001
108th	Min-9th	11	2	Jan. 15, 2003
109th	Min-7th	13	4	Jan. 6, 2005

SENATE SELECT AND SPECIAL COMMITTEES:

1st SELECT INTELLIGENCE (Permanent)
Dates: Jan. 25, 2001-date
Departure: Still serving in the 111th Congress

Cong.	Ranking	Years in: Senate	Comm.	Date of Assignment
107th	Min-4th	9	1	Jan. 25, 2001
+107th	Maj-4th	9	1	June 6, 2001
108th	Min-3rd	11	2	Jan. 15, 2003
109th	Min-3rd	13	4	Jan. 6, 2005
110th	Maj-2nd	15	6	Jan. 12, 2007
111th	Maj-Chr	17	8	Jan. 21, 2009

JOINT COMMITTEES:

1st JOINT LIBRARY
1st Senate Dates: Jan. 30, 1997-Feb. 25, 1999
1st Departure: Moved to Joint Printing
2nd Senate Dates: Mar. 6, 2007-Apr. 3. 2009
2nd Departure: Left committee; became Chair of Select Intelligence

Cong.	Ranking	Years in: Senate	Comm.	Date of Assignment
105th	Min-2nd	4	*1 1	Jan. 30, 1997
110th	Maj-Chr	15	*2 1	Mar. 6, 2007

2nd JOINT PRINTING
1st Senate Dates: Feb. 25, 1999-Mar. 13, 2003
1st Departure: Left committee; no new assignment
2nd Senate Dates: Mar. 6, 2007-Apr. 3, 2009
2nd Departure: Left committee; became Chair of Select Intelligence

Cong.	Ranking	Years in: Senate	Comm.	Date of Assignment
106th	Min-1st	7	*1 1	Feb. 25, 1999
+107th	Maj-2nd	9	*1 3	Sep. 19, 2001
110th	Maj-VCh	15	*2 1	Mar. 6, 2007

Michael Ferguson (R-N.J.)

Dates: June 22, 1970
House: Jan. 3, 2001-Jan. 3, 2009
Left the House: Retired in 2008

HOUSE STANDING COMMITTEES:

1st FINANCIAL SERVICES
Dates: Jan. 6, 2001-Jan. 3, 2003
Departure: Moved to Energy and Commerce

Cong.	Ranking	Terms in: House	Comm.	Date of Assignment
107th	Maj-35th	1	1	Jan. 6, 2001

2nd SMALL BUSINESS
Dates: Jan. 6, 2001-Jan. 3, 2003
Departure: Moved to Energy and Commerce

Cong.	Ranking	Terms in: House	Comm.	Date of Assignment
107th	Maj-13th	1	1	Jan. 6, 2001

3rd TRANSPORTATION AND INFRASTRUCTURE
Dates: Jan. 6, 2001-Jan. 3, 2003
Departure: Moved to Energy and Commerce

Cong.	Ranking	Terms in: House	Comm.	Date of Assignment
107th	Maj-37th	1	1	Jan. 6, 2001

4th ENERGY AND COMMERCE
Dates: Jan. 28, 2003-Jan. 10, 2009
Departure: Left the House; retired

Cong.	Ranking	Terms in: House	Comm.	Date of Assignment
108th	Maj-28th	2	1	Jan. 28, 2003
109th	Maj-24th	3	2	Jan. 6, 2005
110th	Min-21st	4	3	Jan. 10, 2007

Cleo Fields (D-La.)

Dates: Nov. 22, 1962
House: Jan. 3, 1993-Jan. 3, 1997
Left the House: Retired in 1996

HOUSE STANDING COMMITTEES:

1st BANKING, FINANCE AND URBAN AFFAIRS, 103
BANKING AND FINANCIAL SERVICES, 104
Dates: Jan. 5, 1993-Jan. 3, 1997
Departure: Left the House; retired

Cong.	Ranking	Terms in: House	Comm.	Date of Assignment
103rd	Maj-25th	1	1	Jan. 5, 1993
104th	Min-18th	2	2	Jan. 4, 1995

2nd SMALL BUSINESS
Dates: Jan. 5, 1993-Jan. 3, 1997
Departure: Left the House; retired

Cong.	Ranking	Terms in: House	Comm.	Date of Assignment
103rd	Maj-20th	1	1	Jan. 5, 1993
104th	Min-10th	2	2	Jan. 4, 1995

Jack M. Fields Jr. (R-Tex.)

Dates: Feb. 3, 1952
House: Jan. 3, 1981-Jan. 3, 1997
Left the House: Retired in 1996

HOUSE STANDING COMMITTEES:

1st MERCHANT MARINE AND FISHERIES
Dates: Jan. 28, 1981-Jan. 3, 1995
Departure: Committee abolished; no new assignment

Cong.	Ranking	Terms in: House	Comm.	Date of Assignment
103rd	Min-RM	7	7	Jan. 5, 1993

2nd PUBLIC WORKS AND TRANSPORTATION
Dates: Jan. 28, 1981-Jan. 3, 1983
Departure: Moved to Energy and Commerce.

3rd ENERGY AND COMMERCE, 98-103
COMMERCE, 104
Dates: Jan. 6, 1983-Jan. 3, 1997
Departure: Left the House; retired

Cong.	Ranking	Terms in: House	Comm.	Date of Assignment
103rd	Min-3rd	7	6	Jan. 5, 1993
104th	Maj-3rd	8	7	Jan. 4, 1995

Robert Filner (D-Cal.)

Dates: Sept. 4, 1942
House: Jan. 3, 1993-date
Serving in the 111th Congress

HOUSE STANDING COMMITTEES:

1st PUBLIC WORKS AND TRANSPORTATION, 103
TRANSPORTATION AND INFRASTRUCTURE, 104-111
Dates: Jan. 5, 1993-date
Departure: Still serving in the 111th Congress

Cong.	Ranking	Terms in: House	Comm.	Date of Assignment
103rd	Maj-37th	1	1	Jan. 5, 1993
104th	Min-25th	2	2	Jan. 4, 1995
105th	Min-19th	3	3	Jan. 7, 1997
106th	Min-16th	4	4	Jan. 6, 1999
107th	Min-13th	5	5	Jan. 31, 2001
108th	Min-10th	6	6	Jan. 28, 2003
109th	Min-9th	7	7	Jan. 26, 2005
110th	Maj-8th	8	8	Jan. 10, 2007
111th	Maj-8th	9	9	Jan. 7, 2009

2nd VETERANS' AFFAIRS
Dates: Jan. 5, 1993
Departure: Still serving in the 111th Congress

Cong.	Ranking	Terms in: House	Comm.	Date of Assignment
103rd	Maj-14th	1	1	Jan. 5, 1993
104th	Min-7th	2	2	Jan. 4, 1995
105th	Min-3rd	3	3	Feb. 6, 1997
106th	Min-2nd	4	4	Jan. 6, 1999
107th	Min-2nd	5	5	Jan. 31, 2001

108th	Min-2nd	6	6	Jan. 28, 2003
109th	Min-2nd	7	7	Jan. 26, 2005
110th	Maj-Chr	8	8	Jan. 4, 2007
111th	Maj-Chr	9	9	Jan. 6, 2009

Eric D. Fingerhut (D-Ohio)

Dates: May 6, 1959
House: Jan. 3, 1993-Jan. 3, 1995
Left the House: Defeated for re-election in 1994

HOUSE STANDING COMMITTEES:

1st FOREIGN AFFAIRS
Dates: Jan. 5, 1993-Jan. 3, 1995
Departure: Left the House; lost re-election

| | | Terms in: | | Date of |
Cong.	Ranking	House	Comm.	Assignment
103rd	Maj-21st	1	1	Jan. 5, 1993

2nd SCIENCE, SPACE AND TECHNOLOGY
Dates: Jan. 5, 1993-Jan. 3, 1995
Departure: Left the House; lost re-election

| | | Terms in: | | Date of |
Cong.	Ranking	House	Comm.	Assignment
103rd	Maj-21st	1	1	Jan. 5, 1993

3rd BANKING, FINANCE AND URBAN AFFAIRS
Dates: Jan. 21, 1993-Jan. 3, 1995
Departure: Left the House; lost re-election

| | | Terms in: | | Date of |
Cong.	Ranking	House	Comm.	Assignment
103rd	Maj-30th	1	1	Jan. 21, 1993

Hamilton Fish Jr. (R-N.Y.)

Dates: June 3, 1926-July 23, 1996
House: Jan. 3, 1969-Jan. 3, 1995
Left the House: Retired in 1994

HOUSE STANDING COMMITTEES:

1st JUDICIARY
Dates: Jan. 29, 1969-Jan. 3, 1995
Departure: Left the House; retired

| | | Terms in: | | Date of |
Cong.	Ranking	House	Comm.	Assignment
103rd	Min-RM	13	13	Jan. 5, 1993

2nd SMALL BUSINESS
Dates: Jan. 28, 1975-Jan. 3, 1977
Departure: Moved to Science and Technology

3rd SCIENCE AND TECHNOLOGY
Dates: Jan. 19, 1977-Jan. 3, 1983
Departure: Left committee; became Ranking Minority Member on Judiciary and moved to Select Children, Youth and Families

HOUSE SELECT AND SPECIAL COMMITTEES:

1st OUTER CONTINENTAL SHELF (Ad Hoc)
Dates: Apr. 22, 1975-Jan. 3, 1979
Departure: Left committee; no new assignment

2nd SELECT CHILDREN, YOUTH AND FAMILIES (Temporary)
Dates: Feb. 2, 1983-Jan. 3, 1987
Departure: Left committee; no new assignment

JOINT COMMITTEES:

1st JOINT ECONOMIC
House Dates: Jan. 21, 1987-Jan. 3, 1993
Departure: Left committee; no new assignment

Peter G. Fitzgerald (R-Ill.)

Dates: Oct. 20, 1960
Senate: Jan. 3, 1999-Jan. 3, 2005
Left the Senate: Retired in 2004

SENATE STANDING COMMITTEES:

1st AGRICULTURE, NUTRITION AND FORESTRY
Dates: Jan. 7, 1999-Jan. 3, 2005
Departure: Left the Senate; retired

| | | Years in: | | Date of |
Cong.	Ranking	Senate	Comm.	Assignment
106th	Maj-7th	1	1	Jan. 7, 1999
107th	Maj-6th	3	3	Jan. 25, 2001
+107th	Min-6th	3	3	June 6, 2001
108th	Maj-5th	5	5	Jan. 15, 2003

2nd ENERGY AND NATURAL RESOURCES
Dates: Jan. 7, 1999-Jan. 25, 2001
Departure: Moved to Commerce, Science and Transportation

| | | Years in: | | Date of |
Cong.	Ranking	Senate	Comm.	Assignment
106th	Maj-9th	1	1	Jan. 7, 1999

3rd SMALL BUSINESS
Dates: Jan. 7, 1999-Jan. 3, 2005
Departure: Left the Senate; retired

| | | Years in: | | Date of |
Cong.	Ranking	Senate	Comm.	Assignment
106th	Maj-7th	1	1	Jan. 7, 1999
107th	Maj-6th	3	3	Jan. 25, 2001
+107th	Min-6th	3	3	June 6, 2001
108th	Maj-6th	5	5	Jan. 15, 2003

4th COMMERCE, SCIENCE AND TRANSPORTATION
Dates: Jan. 25, 1999-Jan. 3, 2005
Departure: Left the Senate; retired

| | | Years in: | | Date of |
Cong.	Ranking	Senate	Comm.	Assignment
107th	Maj-9th	3	1	Jan. 25, 2001
+107th	Min-9th	3	1	June 6, 2001
108th	Maj-9th	5	2	Jan. 15, 2003

5th GOVERNMENTAL AFFAIRS renamed Oct. 9, 2004
HOMELAND SECURITY AND GOVERNMENTAL AFFAIRS
Dates: July 10, 2001-Jan. 3, 2005
Departure: Left the Senate; retired

Cong.	Ranking	Years in: Senate	Comm.	Date of Assignment
+107th	MnR-1st	3	1	July 10, 2001
108th	Maj-7th	5	2	Jan. 14, 2003

SENATE SELECT AND SPECIAL COMMITTEES:

1st SPECIAL AGING (Permanent)
1st Dates: Jan. 25, 2001-Apr. 30, 2002
1st Departure: Left committee; no new assignment
2nd Dates: Jan. 15, 2005-Jan. 3, 2005
2nd Departure: Left the Senate; retired

Cong.	Ranking	Years in: Senate	Comm.	Date of Assignment
107th	Maj-9th	3 *1	1	Jan. 25, 2001
+107th	Min-8th	3 *1	1	July 24, 2001
108th	Maj-7th	5 *2	1	Jan. 14, 2003

Michael G. Fitzpatrick (R-Penn.)

Dates: June 28, 1963
House: Jan. 3, 2005-Jan. 3, 2007
Left the House: Defeated for re-election in 2006

HOUSE STANDING COMMITTEES:

1st FINANCIAL SERVICES
Dates: Jan. 26, 2005-Jan. 3, 2007
Departure: Left the House; lost re-election

Cong.	Ranking	Terms in: House	Comm.	Date of Assignment
109th	Maj-35th	1	1	Jan. 26, 2005

2nd SMALL BUSINESS
Dates: Jan. 26, 2005-Jan. 3, 2007
Departure: Left the House; lost re-election

Cong.	Ranking	Terms in: House	Comm.	Date of Assignment
109th	Maj-16th	1	1	Jan. 26, 2005

Floyd H. Flake (D-N.Y.)

Dates: Jan. 30, 1945
House: Jan. 3, 1987-Nov. 17, 1997
Left the House: Resigned and retired in 1997

HOUSE STANDING COMMITTEES:

1st BANKING, FINANCE AND URBAN AFFAIRS, 100-103
BANKING AND FINANCIAL SERVICES, 104-105
Dates: Jan. 22, 1987-Nov. 17, 1997
Departure: Resigned the House; retired

Cong.	Ranking	Terms in: House	Comm.	Date of Assignment
103rd	Maj-9th	4	4	Jan. 5, 1993
104th	Min-8th	5	5	Jan. 4, 1995
105th	Min-8th	6	6	Jan. 7, 1997

2nd SMALL BUSINESS
Dates: Jan. 22, 1987-Nov. 17, 1997
Departure: Resigned the House; retired

Cong.	Ranking	Terms in: House	Comm.	Date of Assignment
103rd	Maj-10th	4	4	Jan. 5, 1993
104th	Min-5th	5	5	Jan. 4, 1995
105th	Min-4th	6	6	Feb. 5, 1997

3rd GOVERNMENT OPERATIONS
Dates: Feb. 4, 1993-Jan. 3, 1995
Departure: Left committee; no new assignment

Cong.	Ranking	Terms in: House	Comm.	Date of Assignment
103rd	Maj-18th	4	1	Feb. 4, 1993

HOUSE SELECT AND SPECIAL COMMITTEES:

1st SELECT CHILDREN, YOUTH AND FAMILIES (Temporary)
Dates: Jan. 21, 1987-Jan. 21, 1987
Departure: Moved to Select Hunger

2nd SELECT HUNGER (Temporary)
Dates: Jan. 21, 1987-Jan. 3, 1993
Termination: Committee not renewed in 1993

Jeff Flake (R-Ariz.)

Dates: Dec. 31, 1962
House: Jan. 3, 2001-date
Serving in the 111th Congress

HOUSE STANDING COMMITTEES:

1st INTERNATIONAL RELATIONS, 107-109
FOREIGN AFFAIRS, 110-111
Dates: Jan. 6, 2001-date
Departure: Still serving in the 111th Congress

Cong.	Ranking	Terms in: House	Comm.	Date of Assignment
107th	Maj-24th	1	1	Jan. 6, 2001
108th	Maj-19th	2	2	Jan. 28, 2003
109th	Maj-15th	3	3	Jan. 26, 2005
110th	Min-11th	4	4	Jan. 10, 2007
111th	Min-9th	5	5	Jan. 9, 2009

2nd GOVERNMENT REFORM, 107
OVERSIGHT AND GOVERNMENT REFORM, 111
1st Dates: Jan. 6, 2001-Feb. 8, 2001
1st Departure: Resigned committee; moved to Resources
2nd Dates: Jan. 9, 2009-date
2nd Departure: Still serving in the 111th Congress

Cong.	Ranking	Terms in: House	Comm.	Date of Assignment
107th	Maj-18th	1 *1	1	Jan. 6, 2001
111th	Min-14th	5 *2	1	Jan. 9, 2009

3rd JUDICIARY
Dates: Jan. 6, 2001-Jan. 3, 2007
Departure: Left committee; no new assignment

Cong.	Ranking	Terms in: House	Comm.	Date of Assignment
107th	Maj-21st	1	1	Jan. 6, 2001
108th	Maj-15th	2	2	Jan. 28, 2003
109th	Maj-17th	3	3	Jan. 26, 2005

4th RESOURCES, 107-109
NATURAL RESOURCES, 110-111

Dates: Feb. 8, 2001-date
Departure: Still serving in the 111th Congress

Cong.	Ranking	Terms in: House	Comm.	Date of Assignment
107th	MjR-1st	1	1	Feb. 8, 2001
108th	Maj-22nd	2	2	Jan. 28, 2003
109th	Maj-18th	3	3	Jan. 26, 2005
110th	Min-9th	4	4	Jan. 10, 2007
111th	Min-5th	5	5	Jan. 9, 2009

Michael Patrick Flanagan (R-Ill.)

Dates: Nov. 9, 1962
House: Jan. 3, 1995-Jan. 3, 1997
Left the House: Defeated for re-election in 1996

HOUSE STANDING COMMITTEES:

1st GOVERNMENT REFORM AND OVERSIGHT
Dates: Jan. 4, 1995-Jan. 3, 1997
Departure: Left the House; lost re-election

Cong.	Ranking	Terms in: House	Comm.	Date of Assignment
104th	Maj-23rd	1	1	Jan. 4, 1995

2nd JUDICIARY
Dates: Jan. 4, 1995-Jan. 3, 1997
Departure: Left the House; lost re-election

Cong.	Ranking	Terms in: House	Comm.	Date of Assignment
104th	Maj-19th	1	1	Jan. 4, 1995

3rd VETERANS' AFFAIRS
Dates: Jan. 4, 1995-Jan. 3, 1997
Departure: Left the House; lost re-election

Cong.	Ranking	Terms in: House	Comm.	Date of Assignment
104th	Maj-13th	1	1	Jan. 4, 1995

John Fleming (R-La.)

Dates: July 5, 1951
House: Jan. 3, 2009-date
Serving in the 111th Congress

HOUSE STANDING COMMITTEES:

1st ARMED SERVICES
Dates: Jan. 9, 2009-date
Departure: Still serving in the 111th Congress

Cong.	Ranking	Terms in: House	Comm.	Date of Assignment
111th	Min-23rd	1	1	Jan. 9, 2009

2nd NATURAL RESOURCES
Dates: Jan. 9, 2009-date
Departure: Still serving in the 111th Congress

Cong.	Ranking	Terms in: House	Comm.	Date of Assignment
111th	Min-15th	1	1	Jan. 9, 2009

Ernest L. Fletcher (R-Ky.)

Dates: Nov. 12, 1952
House: Jan. 3, 1999-Dec. 8, 2003
Left the House: Resigned; elected Governor in 2003

HOUSE STANDING COMMITTEES:

1st AGRICULTURE
Dates: Jan. 6, 1999-Mar. 20, 2002
Departure: Resigned committee; moved to Energy and Commerce

Cong.	Ranking	Terms in: House	Comm.	Date of Assignment
106th	Maj-27th	1	1	Jan. 6, 1999
107th	Maj-19th	2	2	Jan. 6, 2001

2nd BUDGET
Dates: Jan. 6, 1999-Mar. 20, 2002
Departure: Resigned committee; moved to Energy and Commerce

Cong.	Ranking	Terms in: House	Comm.	Date of Assignment
106th	Maj-21st	1	1	Jan. 6, 1999
107th	Maj-12th	2	2	Jan. 6, 2001

3rd EDUCATION AND THE WORKFORCE
Dates: Jan. 6, 1999-Mar. 20, 2002
Departure: Resigned committee; moved to Energy and Commerce

Cong.	Ranking	Terms in: House	Comm.	Date of Assignment
106th	Maj-25th	1	1	Jan. 6, 1999
107th	Maj-18th	2	2	Jan. 6, 2001

4th ENERGY AND COMMERCE
Dates: Mar. 20, 2002-Dec. 8, 2003
Departure: Resigned the House; elected Governor

Cong.	Ranking	Terms in: House	Comm.	Date of Assignment
107th	MjR-1st	2	1	Mar. 20, 2002
108th	Maj-27th	3	2	Jan. 28, 2003

Thomas M. Foglietta (D-Penn.)

Dates: Dec. 3, 1928-Nov. 13, 2004
House: Jan. 3, 1981-Nov. 11, 1997
Left the House: Resigned; appointed Ambassador to Italy in 1997

HOUSE STANDING COMMITTEES:

1st ARMED SERVICES
Dates: Jan. 28, 1981-Jan. 3, 1993
Departure: Moved to Appropriations

2nd MERCHANT MARINE AND FISHERIES
Dates: Jan. 28, 1981-Jan. 3, 1993
Departure: Moved to Appropriations

3rd FOREIGN AFFAIRS
Temporary Dates: Jan. 24, 1991-Jan. 3, 1993
Departure: Temporary term expired; moved to Appropriations

4th APPROPRIATIONS
Dates: Jan. 5, 1993-Nov. 11, 1997
Departure: Resigned the House; named Ambassador

Cong.	Ranking	Terms in: House	Comm.	Date of Assignment
103rd	Maj-26th	7	1	Jan. 5, 1993
104th	Min-21st	8	2	Jan. 4, 1995
105th	Min-16th	9	3	Jan. 7, 1997

HOUSE SELECT AND SPECIAL COMMITTEES:

1st SELECT HUNGER (Temporary)
Dates: Mar. 8, 1989-Mar. 19, 1991
Departure: Left committee; no new assignment

Mark A. Foley (R-Fla.)

Dates: Sept. 8, 1954
House: Jan. 3, 1995-Sept. 29, 2006
Left the House: Resigned and retired in 2006

HOUSE STANDING COMMITTEES:

1st AGRICULTURE
Dates: Jan. 4, 1995-Jan. 3, 1999
Departure: Moved to Ways and Means

Cong.	Ranking	Terms in: House	Comm.	Date of Assignment
104th	Maj-25th	1	1	Jan. 4, 1995
105th	Maj-17th	2	2	Jan. 7, 1997

2nd SCIENCE
Dates: Jan. 4, 1995-Jan. 3, 1999
Departure: Moved to Ways and Means

Cong.	Ranking	Terms in: House	Comm.	Date of Assignment
104th	Maj-26th	1	1	Jan. 4, 1995
105th	Maj-16th	2	2	Jan. 21, 1997

3rd BANKING AND FINANCIAL SERVICES
Dates: Apr. 16, 1997-Jan. 3, 1999
Departure: Moved to Ways and Means

Cong.	Ranking	Terms in: House	Comm.	Date of Assignment
105th	MjR-2nd	2	1	Apr. 16, 1997

4th WAYS AND MEANS
Dates: Jan. 6, 1999-Sept. 29, 2006
Departure: Resigned the House; retired, ethics issue

Cong.	Ranking	Terms in: House	Comm.	Date of Assignment
106th	Maj-23rd	3	1	Jan. 6, 1999
107th	Maj-22nd	4	2	Jan. 6, 2001
108th	Maj-21st	5	3	Jan. 28, 2003
109th	Maj-16th	6	4	Jan. 6, 2005

Thomas S. Foley (D-Wash.)

Dates: March 6, 1929
House: Jan. 3, 1965-Jan. 3, 1995
Left the House: Defeated for re-election in 1994

HOUSE STANDING COMMITTEES:

1st AGRICULTURE
Dates: Jan. 18, 1965-Jan. 3, 1987
Chr: 94th-96th (1975-81). Foley stepped down as Chair, beginning in the 97th Congress, to serve as House Majority Whip.
Departure: Left committee to become Majority Floor Leader

2nd INTERIOR AND INSULAR AFFAIRS
Dates: Jan. 18, 1965-Feb. 4, 1975
Departure: Left committee; became Chair of Agriculture

3rd STANDARDS OF OFFICIAL CONDUCT
Dates: Jan. 24, 1973-Jan. 3, 1977
Departure: Left committee; no new assignment

4th HOUSE ADMINISTRATION
Dates: Jan. 6, 1983-Jan. 3, 1987
Departure: Left committee; became Majority Floor Leader

5th POST OFFICE AND CIVIL SERVICE
Dates: Jan. 30, 1985-Feb. 27, 1985
Departure: Left committee; no new assignment

6th BUDGET
Dates: Jan. 6, 1987-June 6, 1989
Departure: Left committee; became Speaker of the House. Democrats reserve the 2nd rank on Budget for the House Floor Leader

HOUSE SELECT AND SPECIAL COMMITTEES:

1st SELECT ENERGY (Ad Hoc)
Dates: Apr. 21, 1977-Dec. 29, 1978
Termination: House Report 1820 (95-2) filed

2nd SELECT COMMITTEE TO INVESTIGATE COVERT ARMS TRANSACTIONS WITH IRAN
Dates: Jan. 7, 1987-Nov. 17, 1987
Departure: House Report 433 (100-1) filed

JOINT COMMITTEES:

1st JOINT DEFICIT REDUCTION (Temporary)
House Dates: Feb. 23, 1987-Sep. 29, 1987
Departure: Public Law 100-119 adjusted Gramm-Rudman-Hollings Act

HOUSE LEADERSHIP POSTS

Dates: Dec. 8, 1980-Jan. 3, 1995
Departure: Left the House; lost re-election

1st HOUSE MAJORITY WHIP
Dates: Dec. 8, 1980-Jan. 3, 1989
Note: For the 97th Congress, Foley was appointed Majority Whip to replace John Brademas (D-Ind.) who was defeated for re-election. Foley was reappointed for the 98th and 99th Congresses.
Departure: Elected Majority Floor Leader

2nd HOUSE MAJORITY FLOOR LEADER
Dates: Dec. 8, 1986-June 6, 1989
Note: For the 100th Congress, Foley was elected without opposition to succeed House Majority Leader James C. Wright Jr. (D-Tex.) who had become Speaker. Foley was re-elected without opposition for the 101st Congress.
Departure: Elected Speaker of the House

3rd SPEAKER OF THE HOUSE
Dates: June 6, 1989-Jan. 3, 1995
Notes: In the 101st Congress, Foley was elected on June 6, 1989, to replace Speaker James C. Wright Jr. (D-Tex.) who had resigned. He defeated Minority Leader Robert H. Michel (R-Ill.) 231 to 164. In the 102nd Congress Foley defeated Michel 262 to 185 and in the 103rd Congress Foley defeated Michel 255 to 174.
Departure: Defeated for re-election in 1994

Cong.	Ranking	Terms in: House	Post	Date of Election
103rd	Maj-1st	15	3	Jan. 5, 1993

J. Randy Forbes (R-Va.)

Dates: Feb. 17, 1952
House: June 19, 2001-date
Serving in the 111th Congress

H: Forbes was elected to the 107th Congress by special election, June 19, 2001, to fill the vacancy caused by the death of U.S. Representative Norman Sisisky (D-Va.). Forbes was seated June 26, 2001 and assigned to committees.

HOUSE STANDING COMMITTEES:

1st ARMED SERVICES
Dates: June 28, 2001-date
Departure: Still serving in the 111th Congress

Cong.	Ranking	Terms in: House	Comm.	Date of Assignment
107th	MjR-1st	1	1	June 28, 2001
108th	Maj-21st	2	2	Jan. 28, 2003
109th	Maj-19th	3	3	Jan. 26, 2005
110th	Min-13th	4	4	Jan. 10, 2007
111th	Min-7th	5	5	Jan. 9, 2009

2nd SCIENCE
1st Dates: June 28, 2001-May 16, 2002
1st Departure: Temporary leave to move to Judiciary
2nd Dates: Returned Jan. 28, 2003-Jan. 3, 2007
2nd Departure: Left committee; no new assignment

Cong.	Ranking	Terms in: House	Comm.	Date of Assignment
107th	Maj-25th	1 *1	1	June 28, 2001
108th	Maj-20th	2 *2	1	Jan. 28, 2003
109th	Maj-15th	3 *2	2	Jan. 26, 2005

3rd JUDICIARY
Dates: May 16, 2002-date
Departure: Still serving in the 111th Congress

Cong.	Ranking	Terms in: House	Comm.	Date of Assignment
107th	MjR-3rd	1	1	May 16, 2002
108th	Maj-17th	2	2	Jan. 28, 2003
109th	Maj-19th	3	3	Jan. 26, 2005
110th	Min-12th	4	4	Jan. 10, 2007
111th	Min-8th	5	5	Jan. 9, 2009

Michael P. Forbes (D-N.Y.)

Dates: July 16, 1962
House: Jan. 3, 1995-Jan. 3, 2001

Left the House: Defeated for re-nomination in 2000
Served as a Republican: Jan. 3.1995-Aug. 5, 1999
Served as a Democrat: Aug. 5, 1999-Jan. 3, 2001

HOUSE STANDING COMMITTEES:

1st APPROPRIATIONS
1st Dates: Jan. 4, 1995-Aug. 5, 1999
1st Departure: Service on committee as Republican was vacated; returned to committee as a Democrat
2nd Dates: Aug. 5, 1999-Jan. 3, 2001
2nd Departure: Left the House; lost re-nomination

Cong.	Ranking	Terms in: House	Comm.	Date of Assignment
104th	Maj-29th	1 *1	1	Jan. 4, 1995
105th	Maj-26th	2 *1	2	Jan. 7, 1997
106th	Maj-23rd	3 *1	3	Jan.. 6, 1999
106th	MnR-1st	3 *2	1	Aug. 5, 1999

2nd SMALL BUSINESS
Dates: Jan. 6, 1999-Aug. 5, 1999
Departure: Service on committee as Republican was vacated; moved to Banking and Financial Services as a Democrat

Cong.	Ranking	Terms in: House	Comm.	Date of Assignment
106th	Maj-13th	3	1	Jan. 6, 1999

3rd BANKING AND FINANCIAL SERVICES
Dates: Aug 5, 1999-Jan. 3, 2001
Departure: Left the House; lost re-nomination

Cong.	Ranking	Terms in: House	Comm.	Date of Assignment
106th	MnR-1st	3	1	Aug. 5, 1999

Harold E. Ford (D-Tenn.)

Dates: May 20, 1945
House: Jan. 3, 1975-Jan. 3, 1997
Left the House: Retired in 1996

HOUSE STANDING COMMITTEES:

1st VETERANS' AFFAIRS
Dates: Jan. 20, 1975-Sep. 30, 1975
Departure: Moved to Ways and Means

2nd BANKING, CURRENCY AND HOUSING
Dates: Jan. 23, 1975-Sep. 30, 1975
Departure: Moved to Ways and Means

3rd WAYS AND MEANS
Dates: Sep. 30, 1975-Jan. 3, 1997
Departure: Left the House; retired

Cong.	Ranking	Terms in: House	Comm.	Date of Assignment
103rd	Maj-7th	10	10	Jan. 5, 1993
104th	Min-5th	11	11	Jan. 4, 1995

HOUSE SELECT AND SPECIAL COMMITTEES:

1st SELECT AGING (Permanent)
Dates: Feb. 6, 1975-Jan. 3, 1993
Termination: Not renewed in 1993

2nd SELECT ASSASSINATIONS
Dates: Sep. 21, 1976-Jan. 3, 1979
Termination: House Report 1828 (95-2) filed

Harold E. Ford Jr. (D-Tenn.)

Dates: May 11, 1970
House: Jan. 3, 1997-Jan. 3, 2007
Left the House: Lost U.S. Senate election in 2006

HOUSE STANDING COMMITTEES:

1st EDUCATION AND THE WORKFORCE
Dates: Jan. 7, 1997-Jan. 3, 1993
Departure: Moved to Budget

Cong.	Ranking	Terms in: House	Comm.	Date of Assignment
105th	Min-20th	1	1	Jan. 7, 1997
106th	Min-19th	2	2	Jan. 6, 1999
107th	Min-17th	3	3	Jan. 31, 2001

2nd GOVERNMENT REFORM AND OVERSIGHT
Dates: Apr. 17, 1997-Feb. 8, 2001
Departure: Resigned committee; moved to Financial Services

Cong.	Ranking	Terms in: House	Comm.	Date of Assignment
105th	MnR-2nd	1	1	Apr. 17, 1997
106th	Min-19th	2	2	Jan. 6, 1999
107th	Min-17th	3	3	Jan. 31, 2001

3rd FINANCIAL SERVICES
Dates: Feb. 8, 2001-Jan. 3, 2007
Departure: Left the House; lost Senate election

Cong.	Ranking	Terms in: House	Comm.	Date of Assignment
107th	Min-25th	3	1	Feb. 8, 2001
108th	Min-19th	4	2	Jan. 28, 2003
109th	Min-17th	5	3	Jan. 26, 2005

4th BUDGET
Dates: Jan. 28, 2003-Jan. 3, 2007
Departure: Left the House; lost Senate election

Cong.	Ranking	Terms in: House	Comm.	Date of Assignment
108th	Min-11th	4	1	Jan. 28, 2003
109th	Min-6th	5	2	Jan. 26, 2005

Wendell H. Ford (D-Ky.)

Dates: Sept. 8, 1924
Senate: Dec. 28, 1974-Jan. 3, 1999
Left the Senate: Retired in 1998

S: Ford was appointed to the 93rd Congress, Dec. 28, 1974, to fill the vacancy caused by the resignation of U.S. Senator Marlow W. Cook (R-Ky.). Ford was not seated nor assigned to committees because the 93rd Congress was not in session. Ford had defeated Cook for election to the 94th Congress.

SENATE STANDING COMMITTEES:

1st COMMERCE reorganized Feb. 17, 1977
COMMERCE, SCIENCE AND TRANSPORTATION

Dates: Jan. 17, 1975-Jan. 3, 1999
Departure: Left the Senate; retired

Cong.	Ranking	Years in: Senate	Comm.	Date of Assignment
103rd	Maj-3rd	19	18	Jan. 7, 1993
104th	Min-3rd	21	20	Jan. 4, 1995
105th	Min-3rd	23	22	Jan. 9, 1997

2nd AERONAUTICAL AND SPACE SCIENCES
Dates: Jan. 17, 1975-Feb. 11, 1977
Departure: Moved to Energy and Natural Resources

3rd ENERGY AND NATURAL RESOURCES
Dates: Feb. 11, 1977-Jan. 3, 1999
Departure: Left the Senate; retired

Cong.	Ranking	Years in: Senate	Comm.	Date of Assignment
103rd	Maj-3rd	19	16	Jan. 7, 1993
104th	Min-3rd	21	18	Jan. 4, 1995
105th	Min-2nd	23	20	Jan. 9, 1997

4th RULES AND ADMINISTRATION
Dates: July 11, 1978-Jan. 3, 1999
Departure: Left the Senate; retired

Cong.	Ranking	Years in: Senate	Comm.	Date of Assignment
103rd	Maj-Chr	19	15	Jan. 21, 1993
104th	Min-RM	21	17	Jan. 6, 1995
105th	Min-RM	23	19	Jan. 9, 1997

JOINT COMMITTEES:

1st JOINT PRINTING
Senate Dates: Feb. 24, 1981-Jan. 3, 1999
Departure: Left the Senate; retired

Cong.	Ranking	Years in: Senate	Comm.	Date of Assignment
103rd	Maj-Chr	19	12	Jan. 28, 1993
104th	Min-1st	21	14	Jan. 17, 1995
105th	Min-1st	23	16	Jan. 28, 1997

2nd JOINT ORGANIZATION OF CONGRESS (Ad Hoc)
Senate Dates: Oct. 8, 1992-Dec. 9, 1993
Departure: Senate Report 103-215 filed

Cong.	Ranking	Years in: Senate	Comm.	Date of Assignment
103rd	Maj-3rd	19	1	Continued

SENATE LEADERSHIP POSTS

Dates: Jan. 3, 1991-Jan. 3, 1999
Departure: Left the Senate; retired

1st SENATE MAJORITY WHIP
Dates: Jan. 3, 1991-Jan. 3, 1995
Note: For the 101st Congress, Ford was defeated by Majority Whip Alan Cranston (D-Cal.), 12 to 30 on Nov. 29, 1988. For the 102nd Congress, Ford was elected Majority Whip without opposition on Nov. 13, 1990. He was re-elected unopposed for the 103rd Congress.
Departure: Democratic Party lost Senate majority in 1994

Cong.	Ranking	Years in: Senate	Post	Date of Selection
103rd	Maj-2nd	19	3	Nov. 10, 1992

2nd SENATE MINORITY WHIP
Dates: Jan. 3, 1995-Jan. 3, 1999
Note: For the 104th Congress, Ford was elected Minority Whip without opposition on Dec. 2, 1994. He was re-elected unopposed for the 105th Congress.
Departure: Left the Senate; retired

Cong.	Ranking	Years in: Senate	Post	Date of Selection
104th	Min-2nd	21	1	Dec. 2, 1994
105th	Min-2nd	23	3	Dec. 3, 1996

William D. Ford (D-Mich.)

Dates: Aug. 6, 1927-Aug. 14, 2004
House: Jan. 3, 1965-Jan. 3, 1995
Left the House: Retired in 1994

HOUSE STANDING COMMITTEES:

1st EDUCATION AND LABOR
Dates: Jan. 18, 1965-Jan. 3, 1995
Departure: Left the House; retired

Cong.	Ranking	Terms in: House	Comm.	Date of Assignment
103rd	Maj-Chr	15	15	Jan. 5, 1993

2nd POST OFFICE AND CIVIL SERVICE
Dates: Jan. 23, 1967-Jan. 3, 1991
Departure: Left committee; became chair of Education and Labor

Jeff Fortenberry (R-Neb.)

Dates: Dec. 27, 1960
House: Jan. 3, 2005-date
Serving in the 111th Congress

HOUSE STANDING COMMITTEES:

1st AGRICULTURE
Dates: Jan. 26, 2005-date
Departure: Still serving in the 111th Congress

Cong.	Ranking	Terms in: House	Comm.	Date of Assignment
109th	Maj-25th	1	1	Jan. 26, 2005
110th	Min-17th	2	2	Jan. 10, 2007
111th	Min-11th	3	3	Jan. 9, 2009

2nd INTERNATIONAL RELATIONS, 109
FOREIGN AFFAIRS, 110-111
Dates: Jan. 26, 2005-date
Departure: Still serving in the 111th Congress

Cong.	Ranking	Terms in: House	Comm.	Date of Assignment
109th	Maj-25th	1	1	Jan. 26, 2005
110th	Min-19th	2	2	Jan. 10, 2007
111th	Min-15th	3	3	Jan. 9, 2009

3rd SMALL BUSINESS
Dates: Jan. 26, 2005-Jan. 3, 2009
Departure: Moved to Oversight and Government Reform

Cong.	Ranking	Terms in: House	Comm.	Date of Assignment
109th	Maj-15th	1	1	Jan. 26, 2005
110th	Min-8th	2	2	Jan. 10, 2007

4th OVERSIGHT AND GOVERNMENT REFORM
Dates: Jan. 9, 2009-date
Departure: Still serving in the 111th Congress

Cong.	Ranking	Terms in: House	Comm.	Date of Assignment
111th	Min-15th	3	1	Jan. 9, 2009

Luis G. Fortuño (R-P.R.)

Dates: Oct. 31, 1960
House: Jan. 3, 2005-Jan. 3, 2009
Left the House: Elected Governor in 2008

HOUSE STANDING COMMITTEES:

1st EDUCATION AND THE WORKFORCE, 109
EDUCATION AND LABOR, 110
Dates: Jan. 26, 2005-Jan. 3, 2009
Departure: Left the House; elected Governor

Cong.	Ranking	Terms in: House	Comm.	Date of Assignment
109th	Maj-22nd	1	1	Jan. 26, 2005
110th	Min-16th	2	2	Jan. 10, 2007

2nd RESOURCES, 109
NATURAL RESOURCES, 110
Dates: Jan. 26, 2005-Jan. 3, 2009
Departure: Left the House; elected Governor

Cong.	Ranking	Terms in: House	Comm.	Date of Assignment
109th	Maj-24th	1	1	Jan. 26, 2005
110th	Min-13th	2	2	Jan. 10, 2007

3rd TRANSPORTATION AND INFRASTRUCTURE
Dates: Jan. 26, 2005-Jan. 3, 2007
Departure: Moved to Foreign Affairs

Cong.	Ranking	Terms in: House	Comm.	Date of Assignment
109th	Maj-39th	1	1	Jan. 26, 2005

4th FOREIGN AFFAIRS
Dates: Jan. 10, 2007-Jan. 3, 2009
Departure: Left the House; elected Governor

Cong.	Ranking	Terms in: House	Comm.	Date of Assignment
110th	Min-23rd	2	1	Jan. 10, 2007

Vito J. Fossella (R-N.Y.)

Dates: March 9, 1965
House: Nov. 4, 1997-Jan. 3, 2009
Left the House: Retired in 2008

H: Fossella was elected to the 105th Congress by special election, Nov. 4, 1997, to fill the vacancy caused by the resignation of U.S. Representative Susan Molinari (R-N.Y.). Fossella was seated Nov. 5, 1997, and assigned to committees.

HOUSE STANDING COMMITTEES:

1st BANKING AND FINANCIAL SERVICES, 105
FINANCIAL SERVICES, 107-109
1st Dates: Nov. 12, 1997-Jan. 3, 1999

1st Departure: Moved to Commerce
2nd Dates: Jan. 6, 2001-Jan. 3, 2007
2nd Departure: Left committee; no new assignment

Cong.	Ranking	Terms in: House	Comm.	Date of Assignment
105th	MjA-32nd	1 *1	1	Nov. 12, 1997
107th	Maj-29th	3 *2	1	Jan. 6, 2001
108th	Maj-24th	4 *2	2	Jan. 28, 2003
109th	Maj-20th	5 *2	3	Jan. 26, 2005

2nd TRANSPORTATION AND INFRASTRUCTURE
Dates: Nov. 12, 1997-Jan. 3, 1999
Departure: Moved to Commerce

Cong.	Ranking	Terms in: House	Comm.	Date of Assignment
105th	MjR-1st	1	1	Nov. 12, 1997

3rd COMMERCE, 106
ENERGY AND COMMERCE, 107-110
Dates: Jan. 6, 1999-Jan. 3, 2009
Departure: Left the House; retired

Cong.	Ranking	Terms in: House	Comm.	Date of Assignment
106th	Maj-26th	2	1	Jan. 6, 1999
107th	Maj-20th	3	2	Jan. 6, 2001
108th	Maj-18th	4	3	Jan. 28, 2003
109th	Maj-14th	5	4	Jan. 6, 2005
110th	Min-14th	6	5	Jan. 10, 2007

Bill Foster (D-Ill.)

Dates: Oct. 7, 1955
House: Mar. 8, 2008-date
Serving in the 111th Congress

H: Foster was elected to the 110th Congress by special election, Mar. 8, 2008, to fill the vacancy caused by the resignation of U.S. Representative J. Dennis Hastert (R-Ill.). Foster was seated Mar. 11, 2008, and assigned to committees.

HOUSE STANDING COMMITTEES:

1st FINANCIAL SERVICES
Dates: Apr. 1, 2008-date
Departure: Still serving in the 111th Congress

Cong.	Ranking	Terms in: House	Comm.	Date of Assignment
110th	MjR-1st	1	1	Apr. 1, 2008
111th	Maj-30th	2	2	Jan. 7, 2009

2nd OVERSIGHT AND GOVERNMENT REFORM
Dates: Jan. 7, 2009-date
Departure: Still serving in the 111th Congress

Cong.	Ranking	Terms in: House	Comm.	Date of Assignment
111th	Maj-22nd	2	1	Jan. 7, 2009

Tillie K. Fowler (R-Fla.)

Dates: Dec. 23, 1942-March 2, 2005
House: Jan. 3, 1993-Jan. 3, 2001
Left the House: Retired in 2000

HOUSE STANDING COMMITTEES:

1st ARMED SERVICES, 103
NATIONAL SECURITY, 104-105
ARMED SERVICES, 106
Dates: Jan. 5, 1993-Jan. 3, 2001
Departure: Left the House; retired

Cong.	Ranking	Terms in: House	Comm.	Date of Assignment
103rd	Min-18th	1	1	Jan. 5, 1993
104th	Maj-14th	2	2	Jan. 4, 1995
105th	Maj-11th	3	3	Jan. 7, 1997
106th	Maj-11th	4	4	Jan. 6, 1999

2nd MERCHANT MARINE AND FISHERIES
Dates: Jan. 5, 1993-Jan. 3, 1995
Departure: Committee abolished; moved to Transportation and Infrastructure

Cong.	Ranking	Terms in: House	Comm.	Date of Assignment
103rd	Min-12th	1	1	Jan. 5, 1993

3rd TRANSPORTATION AND INFRASTRUCTURE
Dates: Jan. 4, 1995-Jan. 3, 2001
Departure: Left the House; retired

Cong.	Ranking	Terms in: House	Comm.	Date of Assignment
104th	Maj-22nd	2	1	Jan. 4, 1995
105th	Maj-16th	3	2	Jan. 7, 1997
106th	Maj-14th	4	3	Jan. 6, 1999

Jon D. Fox (R-Penn.)

Dates: April 22, 1947
House: Jan. 3, 1995-Jan. 3, 1999
Left the House: Defeated for re-election in 1998

HOUSE STANDING COMMITTEES:

1st BANKING AND FINANCIAL SERVICES
Dates: Jan. 4, 1995-Jan. 3, 1999
Departure: Left the House; lost re-election

Cong.	Ranking	Terms in: House	Comm.	Date of Assignment
104th	Maj-22nd	1	1	Jan. 4, 1995
105th	Maj-17th	2	2	Jan. 7, 1997

2nd GOVERNMENT REFORM AND OVERSIGHT
Dates: Jan. 4, 1995-June 25, 1996
Departure: Resigned committee; moved to International Relations

Cong.	Ranking	Terms in: House	Comm.	Date of Assignment
104th	Maj-15th	1	1	Jan. 4, 1995

3rd VETERANS' AFFAIRS
Dates: Jan. 4, 1995-Jan. 3, 1997
Departure: Moved to Transportation and Infrastructure

Cong.	Ranking	Terms in: House	Comm.	Date of Assignment
104th	Maj-12th	1	1	Jan. 4, 1995

4th INTERNATIONAL RELATIONS
Dates: June 25, 1996-Jan. 3, 1999
Departure: Left the House; lost re-election

Cong.	Ranking	Terms in: House	Comm.	Date of Assignment
104th	MjA-25th	1	1	June 25, 1996
105th	Maj-21st	2	2	Jan. 7, 1997

5th TRANSPORTATION AND INFRASTRUCTURE
Dates: Feb. 26, 1997-Jan. 3, 1999
Departure: Left the House; lost re-election

Cong.	Ranking	Terms in: House	Comm.	Date of Assignment
105th	MjA-37th	2	1	Feb. 26, 1997

Virginia A. Foxx (R-N.C.)

Dates: June 29, 1943
House: Jan. 3, 2005-date
Serving in the 111th Congress

HOUSE STANDING COMMITTEES:

1st AGRICULTURE
Dates: Jan. 26, 2005-Jan. 15, 2009
Departure: Resigned committee; moved to Rules

Cong.	Ranking	Terms in: House	Comm.	Date of Assignment
109th	Maj-23rd	1	1	Jan. 26, 2005
110th	Min-15th	2	2	Jan. 10, 2007
111th	Min-9th	3	3	Jan. 9, 2009

2nd EDUCATION AND THE WORKFORCE, 109
EDUCATION AND LABOR, 110-111
Dates: Jan. 26, 2005-Jan. 15, 2009
Departure: Resigned committee; moved to Rules

Cong.	Ranking	Terms in: House	Comm.	Date of Assignment
109th	Maj-25th	1	1	Jan. 26, 2005
110th	Min-18th	2	2	Jan. 10, 2007
111th	Min-13th	3	3	Jan. 9, 2009

3rd GOVERNMENT REFORM, 109
OVERSIGHT AND GOVERNMENT REFORM, 110-111
Dates: Jan. 26, 2005-Jan. 15, 2009
Departure: Resigned committee; moved to Rules

Cong.	Ranking	Terms in: House	Comm.	Date of Assignment
109th	Maj-23rd	1	1	Jan. 26, 2005
110th	Min-15th	2	2	Jan. 10, 2007
111th	Min-11th	3	3	Jan. 9, 2009

4th RULES
Dates: Jan. 14, 2009-date
Departure: Still serving in the 111th Congress

Cong.	Ranking	Terms in: House	Comm.	Date of Assignment
111th	Min-4th	3	1	Jan. 14, 2009

Sheila Frahm (R-Kans.)

Dates: March 22, 1945
Senate: June 11, 1996-Nov. 5, 1996
Left the Senate: Resigned; defeated in special primary in 1996

S: Frahm was appointed to the 104th Congress, June 11, 1996, to fill the vacancy of U.S. Senator Robert J. Dole (R-Kans.) who resigned and lost the 1996 election for President. Frahm was defeated in a special primary by U.S. Representative Sam Brownback (R-Kans.) who succeeded her in the Senate.

SENATE STANDING COMMITTEES:

1st ARMED SERVICES
Dates: June 20, 1996-Nov. 5, 1996
Departure: Resigned the Senate; lost special primary

Cong.	Ranking	Years in: Senate	Comm.	Date of Assignment
104th	MjR-1st	1	1	June 20, 1996

2nd BANKING, HOUSING AND URBAN AFFAIRS
Dates: June 20, 1996-Nov. 5, 1996
Departure: Resigned the Senate; lost special primary

Cong.	Ranking	Years in: Senate	Comm.	Date of Assignment
104th	MjR-1st	1	1	June 20, 1996

Barney Frank (D-Mass.)

Dates: March 31, 1940
House: Jan. 3, 1981-date
Serving in the 111th Congress

HOUSE STANDING COMMITTEES:

1st BANKING, FINANCE AND URBAN AFFAIRS, 97-103
BANKING AND FINANCIAL SERVICES, 104-106
FINANCIAL SERVICES, 107-111
Dates: Jan. 28, 1981-date
Departure: Still serving in the 111th Congress

Cong.	Ranking	Terms in: House	Comm.	Date of Assignment
103rd	Maj-6th	7	7	Jan. 5, 1993
104th	Min-5th	8	8	Jan. 4, 1995
105th	Min-5th	9	9	Jan. 7, 1997
106th	Min-3rd	10	10	Jan. 6, 1999
107th	Min-2nd	11	11	Jan. 31, 2001
108th	Min-RM	12	12	Jan. 8, 2003
109th	Min-RM	13	13	Jan. 6, 2005
110th	Maj-Chr.	14	14	Jan. 4, 2007
111th	Maj-Chr.	15	15	Jan. 7, 2009

2nd GOVERNMENT OPERATIONS
Dates: Jan. 28, 1981-Jan. 3, 1991
Departure: Moved to Budget

3rd JUDICIARY
Dates: Jan. 28, 1981-Jan. 3, 2003
Departure: Moved to Select Homeland Security; became Ranking Member on Financial Services

Cong.	Ranking	Terms in: House	Comm.	Date of Assignment
103rd	Maj-9th	7	7	Jan. 5, 1993
104th	Min-3rd	8	8	Jan. 4, 1995
105th	Min-2nd	9	9	Jan. 7, 1997
106th	Min-2nd	10	10	Jan. 6, 1999
107th	Min-2nd	11	11	Jan. 31, 2001

4th BUDGET
Dates: Jan. 24, 1991-Jan. 3, 1995
Departure: Left committee; no new assignment

Cong.	Ranking	Terms in: House	Comm.	Date of Assignment
103rd	Maj-11th	7	2	Jan. 5, 1993

HOUSE SELECT AND SPECIAL COMMITTEES:

1st SELECT AGING (Permanent)
Dates: Feb. 5, 1981-Jan. 3, 1993
Termination: Committee not renewed in 1993

2nd SELECT HOMELAND SECURITY
Dates: Feb. 12, 2003-Jan. 3, 2005
Departure: Did not continue on reorganized standing committee

Cong.	Ranking	Terms in: House	Comm.	Date of Assignment
108th	Min-6th	12	1	Feb. 12, 2003

Al Franken (DFL-Minn.)

Dates: May 21, 1951
Senate: July 7, 2009-date
Serving in the 111th Congress
S: Franken was elected to the 111th Congress after being declared the winner of the contested 2008 Senate election over U.S. Senator Norman Coleman (R-Minn.) by the Minnesota Supreme Court on June 30, 2009. He was seated on July 7, 2009, and assigned to committees.

SENATE STANDING COMMITTEES:

1st JUDICIARY
Dates: July 7, 2009-date
Departure: Still serving in the 111th Congress

Cong.	Ranking	Years in: Senate	Comm.	Date of Assignment
111th	MjR-1st	1	1	July 7, 2009

2nd HEALTH, EDUCATION, LABOR, AND PENSIONS
Dates: July 15, 2009-date
Departure: Still serving in the 111th Congress

Cong.	Ranking	Years in: Senate	Comm.	Date of Assignment
111th	MjR-1st	1	1	July 15, 2009

SENATE SELECT AND SPECIAL COMMITTEES:

1st INDIAN AFFAIRS (Permanent)
Dates: July 7, 2009-date
Departure: Still serving in the 111th Congress

Cong.	Ranking	Years in: Senate	Comm.	Date of Assignment
111th	Maj-9th	1	1	July 7, 2009

2nd SPECIAL AGING
Dates: July 7, 2009-date
Departure: Still serving in the 111th Congress

Cong.	Ranking	Years in: Senate	Comm.	Date of Assignment
111th	MjA-13th	1	1	July 7, 2009

Gary A. Franks (R-Conn.)

Dates: Feb. 9, 1953
House: Jan. 3, 1991-Jan. 3, 1997
Left the House: Defeated for re-election in 1996

HOUSE STANDING COMMITTEES:

1st ARMED SERVICES
Dates: Jan. 24, 1991-Jan. 3, 1993
Departure: Moved to Energy and Commerce

2nd SMALL BUSINESS
Dates: Jan. 24, 1991-Jan. 3, 1993
Departure: Moved to Energy and Commerce

3rd ENERGY AND COMMERCE, 103
COMMERCE, 104
Dates: Jan. 5, 1993-Jan. 3, 1997
Departure: Left the House; lost re-election

Cong.	Ranking	Terms in: House	Comm.	Date of Assignment
103rd	Min-15th	2	1	Jan. 5, 1993
104th	Maj-14th	3	2	Jan. 4, 1995

HOUSE SELECT AND SPECIAL COMMITTEES:

1st SELECT AGING (Permanent)
Dates: Feb. 21, 1991-Jan. 3, 1993
Termination: Committee not renewed in 1993

Robert D. Franks (R-N.J.)

Dates: Sept. 21, 1951
House: Jan. 3, 1993-Jan. 3, 2001
Left the House: Lost U.S. Senate nomination in 2000

HOUSE STANDING COMMITTEES:

1st BUDGET
Dates: Jan. 5, 1993-Jan. 3, 2001
Departure: Left the House; lost Senate nomination

Cong.	Ranking	Terms in: House	Comm.	Date of Assignment
103rd	Min-14th	1	1	Jan. 5, 1993
104th	Maj-12th	2	2	Jan. 4, 1995
105th	Maj-8th	3	3	Jan. 7, 1997
106th	Maj-6th	4	4	Jan. 6, 1999

2nd PUBLIC WORKS AND TRANSPORTATION, 103
TRANSPORTATION AND INFRASTRUCTURE, 104-106
Dates: Jan. 5, 1993-Jan. 3, 2001
Departure: Left the House; lost Senate nomination

Cong.	Ranking	Terms in: House	Comm.	Date of Assignment
103rd	Min-19th	1	1	Jan. 5, 1993
104th	Maj-18th	2	2	Jan. 4, 1995
105th	Maj-13th	3	3	Jan. 7, 1997
106th	Maj-11th	4	4	Jan. 6, 1999

Trent Franks (R-Ariz.)

Dates: June 19, 1957
House: Jan. 3, 2003-date
Serving in the 111th Congress

HOUSE STANDING COMMITTEES:

1st ARMED SERVICES
Dates: Jan. 28, 2003-date
Departure: Still serving in the 111th Congress

Cong.	Ranking	Terms in: House	Comm.	Date of Assignment
108th	Maj-33rd	1	1	Jan. 28, 2003
109th	Maj-28th	2	2	Jan. 26, 2005
110th	Min-24th	3	3	Jan. 10, 2007
111th	Min-15th	4	4	Jan. 9, 2009

2nd BUDGET
Dates: Jan. 28, 2003-Jan. 3, 2005
Departure: Moved to Judiciary

Cong.	Ranking	Terms in: House	Comm.	Date of Assignment
108th	Maj-18th	1	1	Jan. 28, 2003

3rd SMALL BUSINESS
Dates: Jan. 28, 2003-Jan. 3, 2005
Departure: Moved to Judiciary

Cong.	Ranking	Terms in: House	Comm.	Date of Assignment
108th	Maj-14th	1	1	Jan. 28, 2003

4th JUDICIARY
Dates: Jan. 26, 2005-date
Departure: Still serving in the 111th Congress

Cong.	Ranking	Terms in: House	Comm.	Date of Assignment
109th	Maj-22nd	2	1	Jan. 26, 2005
110th	Min-15th	3	2	Jan. 10, 2007
111th	Min-10th	4	3	Jan. 9, 2009

Victor O. Frazer (Independent-V.I.)

Dates: May 24, 1943
House: Jan. 3, 1995-Jan. 3, 1997
Left the House: Defeated for re-election in 1996

HOUSE STANDING COMMITTEES:

1st INTERNATIONAL RELATIONS
Dates: Jan. 27, 1995-Jan. 3, 1997
Departure: Left the House; lost re-election

Cong.	Ranking	Terms in: House	Comm.	Date of Assignment
104th	3rd-1st	1	1	Jan. 27, 1995

Rodney P. Frelinghuysen (R-N.J.)

Dates: April 29, 1946
House: Jan. 3, 1995-date
Serving in the 111th Congress

HOUSE STANDING COMMITTEES:

1st APPROPRIATIONS
Dates: Jan. 4, 1995-date
Departure: Still serving in the 111th Congress

Cong.	Ranking	Terms in: House	Comm.	Date of Assignment
104th	Maj-27th	1	1	Jan. 4, 1995
105th	Maj-24th	2	2	Jan. 7, 1997
106th	Maj-21st	3	3	Jan. 6, 1999
107th	Maj-18th	4	4	Jan. 6, 2001
108th	Maj-14th	5	5	Jan. 28, 2003
109th	Maj-14th	6	6	Jan. 6, 2005
110th	Min-10th	7	7	Jan. 4, 2007
111th	Min-6th	8	8	Jan. 9, 2009

Daniel Frisa (R-N.Y.)

Dates: April 29, 1955
House: Jan. 3, 1995-Jan. 3, 1997
Left the House: Defeated for re-election in 1996

HOUSE STANDING COMMITTEES:

1st COMMERCE
Dates: Jan. 4, 1995-Jan. 3, 1997
Departure: Left the House; lost re-election

Cong.	Ranking	Terms in: House	Comm.	Date of Assignment
104th	Maj-22nd	1	1	Jan. 4, 1995

2nd TRANSPORTATION AND INFRASTRUCTURE
Dates: June 25, 1996-Jan. 3, 1997
Departure: Left the House; lost re-election

Cong.	Ranking	Terms in: House	Comm.	Date of Assignment
104th	MjR-1st	1	1	June 25, 1996

William H. Frist (R-Tenn.)

Dates: Feb. 22, 1952
Senate: Jan. 3, 1995-Jan. 3, 2007
Left the Senate: Retired in 2006.

SENATE STANDING COMMITTEES:

1st BANKING, HOUSING, AND URBAN AFFAIRS
Dates: Jan. 4, 1995-Oct. 12, 1995
Departure: Left committee; moved to Commerce, Science and Transportation

Cong.	Ranking	Years in: Senate	Comm.	Date of Assignment
104th	Maj-9th	1	1	Jan. 4, 1995

2nd BUDGET
Dates: Jan. 6, 1997-Jan. 15, 2003
Departure: Moved to Finance and Rules and Administration

Cong.	Ranking	Years in: Senate	Comm.	Date of Assignment
104th	Maj-12th	1	1	Jan. 6, 1995

105th	Maj-10th	3	3	Jan. 9, 1997
106th	Maj-10th	5	5	Jan. 7, 1999
107th	Maj-8th	7	7	Jan. 25, 2001
+107th	Min-8th	7	7	June 6, 2001

3rd LABOR AND HUMAN RESOURCES renamed Jan. 21, 1999
HEALTH, EDUCATION, LABOR AND PENSIONS
Dates: Jan. 4, 1995-Jan. 3, 2007
Departure: Left the Senate; retired

		Years in:		Date of
Cong.	Ranking	Senate	Comm.	Assignment
104th	Maj-5th	1	1	Jan. 4, 1995
105th	Maj-4th	3	3	Jan. 9, 1997
106th	Maj-3rd	5	5	Jan. 7, 1999
107th	Maj-3rd	7	7	Jan. 25, 2001
+107th	Min-2nd	7	7	July 10, 2001
108th	Maj-2nd	9	9	Jan. 15, 2003
109th	Maj-3rd	11	11	Jan. 6, 2005

4th SMALL BUSINESS
Dates: Jan. 6, 1995-Jan. 7, 1999
Departure: Left committee; no new assignment

		Years in:		Date of
Cong.	Ranking	Senate	Comm.	Assignment
104th	Maj-10th	1	1	Jan. 6, 1995
105th	Maj-7th	3	3	Jan. 9, 1997

5th COMMERCE, SCIENCE AND TRANSPORTATION
Dates: Oct. 12, 1995-Jan. 25, 2001
Departure: Left committee; elected Majority Leader

		Years in:		Date of
Cong.	Ranking	Senate	Comm.	Assignment
104th	MjR-1st	1	1	Oct. 12, 1995
105th	Maj-9th	3	2	Jan. 9, 1997
106th	Maj-9th	5	4	Jan. 7, 1999

6th FOREIGN RELATIONS
Dates: Jan. 9, 1997-Jan. 15, 2003
Departure: Moved to Finance

		Years in:		Date of
Cong.	Ranking	Senate	Comm.	Assignment
105th	Maj-9th	3	1	Jan. 9, 1997
106th	Maj-10th	5	2	Jan. 7, 1999
107th	Maj-6th	7	5	Jan. 25, 2001
+107th	Min-6th	7	5	June 6, 2001

7th FINANCE
Dates: Jan. 15, 2003-Jan. 3, 2007
Departure: Left the Senate; retired

		Years in:		Date of
Cong.	Ranking	Senate	Comm.	Assignment
108th	Maj-9th	9	1	Jan. 15, 2003
109th	Maj-8th	11	2	Jan. 6, 2005

8th RULES AND ADMINISTRATION
Dates: Jan. 15, 2003-Jan. 3, 2007
Departure: Left the Senate; retired

		Years in:		Date of
Cong.	Ranking	Senate	Comm.	Assignment
108th	Maj-8th	9	1	Jan. 15, 2003
109th	Maj-6th	11	2	Jan. 6, 2005

SENATE SELECT AND SPECIAL COMMITTEES:

1st SPECIAL COMMITTEE TO INVESTIGATE WHITEWATER DEVELOPMENT CORPORATION AND RELATED MATTERS

Dates: July 20, 1995-Oct. 12, 1995
Departure: Left committee; moved to Commerce, Science and Transportation

		Years in:		Date of
Cong.	Ranking	Senate	Comm.	Assignment
104th	Maj-8th	1	1	July 20, 1995

SENATE LEADERSHIP POSTS

Dates: Jan. 6, 2003-Jan. 3, 2007
Departure: Left the Senate; retired

1st SENATE MAJORITY FLOOR LEADER
Dates: Jan. 6, 2003-Jan. 3, 2007
Note: For the 108th Congress, Frist was elected without opposition on December 23, 2002, to succeed Majority Leader C. Trent Lott (R-Miss.) who resigned the post effective Jan. 6, 2003. Frist was re-elected Majority Leader without opposition for the 109th Congress.
Departure: Left the Senate; retired

		Years in:		Date of
Cong.	Ranking	Senate	Post	Selection
108th	Maj-1st	9	1	Dec. 23, 2002
109th	Maj-1st	11	3	Nov. 17, 2004

J. Martin Frost III (D-Tex.)

Dates: Jan. 1, 1942
House: Jan. 3, 1979-Jan. 3, 2005
Left the House: Defeated for re-election in 2004

HOUSE STANDING COMMITTEES:

1st RULES
Dates: Jan. 24, 1979-Jan. 3, 2005
RM2: Replaced J. Joseph Moakley (D-Mass.)
as Ranking Member on May 28, 2001
Departure: Left the House; lost re-election

		Terms in:		Date of
Cong.	Ranking	House	Comm.	Assignment
103rd	Maj-4th	8	8	Jan. 5, 1993
104th	Min-3rd	9	9	Jan. 4, 1995
105th	Min-2nd	10	10	Jan. 7, 1997
106th	Min-2nd	11	11	Jan. 6, 1999
107th	Min-2nd	12	12	Jan. 3, 2001
=107th	Min-RM2	12	12	May 28, 2001
108th	Min-RM	13	13	Jan. 7, 2003

2nd BUDGET
Dates: Jan. 6, 1983-Jan. 3, 1989
Departure: Moved to House Administration

3rd HOUSE ADMINISTRATION
Dates: Jan. 19, 1989-Jan. 3, 1995
Departure: Left committee; no new assignment

		Terms in:		Date of
Cong.	Ranking	House	Comm.	Assignment
103rd	Maj-5th	8	3	Jan. 21, 1993

HOUSE SELECT AND SPECIAL COMMITTEES:

1st SELECT HOMELAND SECURITY
Dates: June 19, 2002-Jan. 3, 2003
Departure: Left committee; no new assignment

Cong.	Ranking	Terms in: House	Comm.	Date of Assignment
107th	Min-2nd	12	1	June 19, 2002

JOINT COMMITTEES:

1st JOINT DEFICIT REDUCTION (Temporary)
House Dates: Feb. 23, 1987-Sep. 29,1987
Departure: Public Law 100-119 adjusted Gramm-Rudman-Hollings Act

2nd JOINT LIBRARY
House Dates: May 1, 1993-Jan. 3, 1995
Departure: Left committee; no new assignment

Cong.	Ranking	Terms in: House	Comm.	Date of Assignment
103rd	Maj-2nd	8	1	May 1, 1993 Provisional

Marcia L. Fudge (D-Ohio)

Dates: Oct. 29, 1952
House: Nov. 18, 2008-date
Serving in the 111th Congress

H: Fudge was elected to the 110th Congress by special election, Nov. 18, 2008, to fill the vacancy caused by the death of U.S. Representative Stephanie Tubbs Jones (D-Ohio). Fudge was seated Nov. 19, 2008, but not assigned to committees.

HOUSE STANDING COMMITTEES:

1st EDUCATION AND LABOR
Dates: Jan. 21, 2009-date
Departure: Still serving in the 111th Congress

Cong.	Ranking	Terms in: House	Comm.	Date of Assignment
111th	Maj-24th	2	1	Jan. 21, 2009

2nd SCIENCE AND TECHNOLOGY
Dates: Jan. 21, 2009-date
Departure: Still serving in the 111th Congress

Cong.	Ranking	Terms in: House	Comm.	Date of Assignment
111th	Maj-11th	2	1	Jan. 21, 2009

David Funderburk (R-N.C.)

Dates: April 29, 1944
House: Jan. 3, 1995-Jan. 3, 1997
Left the House: Defeated for re-election in 1996

HOUSE STANDING COMMITTEES:

1st ECONOMIC AND EDUCATIONAL OPPORTUNITIES
Dates: Jan. 4, 1995-Jan. 3, 1997
Departure: Left the House; lost re-election

Cong.	Ranking	Terms in: House	Comm.	Date of Assignment
104th	Maj-21st	1	1	Jan. 4, 1995

2nd INTERNATIONAL RELATIONS
Dates: Jan. 4, 1995-Jan. 3, 1997
Departure: Left the House; lost re-election

Cong.	Ranking	Terms in: House	Comm.	Date of Assignment
104th	Maj-19th	1	1	Jan. 4, 1995

3rd SMALL BUSINESS
Dates: Jan. 4, 1995-Sep. 4, 1996
Departure: Resigned committee; had moved to Agriculture

Cong.	Ranking	Terms in: House	Comm.	Date of Assignment
104th	Maj-21st	1	1	Jan. 4, 1995

4th AGRICULTURE
Dates: Aug. 2, 1996-Jan. 3, 1997
Departure: Left the House; lost re-election

Cong.	Ranking	Terms in: House	Comm.	Date of Assignment
104th	MjR-1st	1	1	Aug. 2, 1996

Elizabeth Furse (D-Ore.)

Dates: Oct. 13, 1936
House: Jan. 3, 1993-Jan. 3, 1999
Left the House: Retired in 1998

HOUSE STANDING COMMITTEES:

1st BANKING, FINANCE AND URBAN AFFAIRS
Dates: Jan. 5, 1993-Jan. 3, 1995
Departure: Moved to Commerce

Cong.	Ranking	Terms in: House	Comm.	Date of Assignment
103rd	Maj-22nd	1	1	Jan. 5, 1993

2nd MERCHANT MARINE AND FISHERIES
Dates: Jan. 5, 1993-Jan. 3, 1995
Departure: Committee abolished; moved to Commerce

Cong.	Ranking	Terms in: House	Comm.	Date of Assignment
103rd	Maj-16th	1	1	Jan. 5, 1993

3rd ARMED SERVICES
Dates: Jan. 27, 1993-Jan. 3, 1995
Departure: Moved to Commerce

Cong.	Ranking	Terms in: House	Comm.	Date of Assignment
103rd	Maj-33rd	1	1	Jan. 27, 1993

4th COMMERCE
Dates: Jan. 4, 1995-Jan. 3, 1999
Departure: Left the House; retired

Cong.	Ranking	Terms in: House	Comm.	Date of Assignment
104th	Min-16th	2	1	Jan. 4, 1995
105th	Min-11th	3	2	Jan. 7, 1997

G

Elton W. Gallegly (R-Cal.)

Dates: March 7, 1944
House: Jan. 3, 1987-date
Serving in the 111th Congress

HOUSE STANDING COMMITTEES:

1st INTERIOR AND INSULAR AFFAIRS, 100-102
NATURAL RESOURCES, 103
RESOURCES, 104-109
NATURAL RESOURCES, 110-111
Dates: Jan. 21, 1987-date
Departure: Still serving in the 111th Congress

Cong.	Ranking	Terms in: House	Comm.	Date of Assignment
103rd	Min-4th	4	4	Jan. 5, 1993
104th	Maj-4th	5	5	Jan. 4, 1995
105th	Maj-5th	6	6	Jan. 7, 1997
106th	Maj-5th	7	7	Jan. 6, 1999
107th	Maj-5th	8	8	Jan. 6, 2001
108th	Maj-5th	9	9	Jan. 28, 2003
109th	Maj-4th	10	10	Jan. 26, 2005
110th	Min-3rd	11	11	Jan. 10, 2007
111th	Min-3rd	12	12	Jan. 9, 2009

2nd SMALL BUSINESS
Dates: Jan. 21, 1987-Jan. 3, 1989
Departure: Moved to Foreign Affairs

3rd FOREIGN AFFAIRS, 101-103
INTERNATIONAL RELATIONS, 104-109
FOREIGN AFFAIRS, 110-111
Dates: Jan. 20, 1989-date
Departure: Still serving in the 111th Congress

Cong.	Ranking	Terms in: House	Comm.	Date of Assignment
103rd	Min-11th	4	3	Jan. 5, 1993
104th	Maj-10th	5	4	Jan. 4, 1995
105th	Maj-8th	6	5	Jan. 7, 1997
106th	Maj-8th	7	6	Jan. 6, 1999
107th	Maj-7th	8	7	Jan. 6, 2001
108th	Maj-6th	9	8	Jan. 28, 2003
109th	Maj-5th	10	9	Jan. 26, 2005
110th	Min-4th	11	10	Jan. 10, 2007
111th	Min-4th	12	11	Jan. 9, 2009

4th JUDICIARY
Dates: Jan. 5, 1993-date
Departure: Still serving in the 111th Congress

Cong.	Ranking	Terms in: House	Comm.	Date of Assignment
103rd	Min-11th	4	1	Jan. 5, 1993
104th	Maj-9th	5	2	Jan. 4, 1995
105th	Maj-8th	6	3	Jan. 7, 1997
106th	Maj-7th	7	4	Jan. 6, 1999
107th	Maj-6th	8	5	Jan. 6, 2001
108th	Maj-5th	9	6	Jan. 28, 2003
109th	Maj-5th	10	7	Jan. 26, 2005
110th	Min-4th	11	8	Jan. 10, 2007
111th	Min-4th	12	9	Jan. 9, 2009

HOUSE SELECT AND SPECIAL COMMITTEES:

1st PERMANENT SELECT INTELLIGENCE
1st Dates: Feb. 11, 2005-Jan. 3, 2007
1st Departure: Left committee; no new assignment
2nd Dates: May 1, 2007-date
2nd Departure: Still serving in the 111th Congress

Cong.	Ranking	Terms in: House	Comm.	Date of Assignment
108th	Maj-10th	9 *1	1	Feb. 11, 2003
109th	Maj-5th	10 *1	2	Jan. 26, 2005
110th	MnR-1st	11 *2	1	May 1, 2007
111th	Min-2nd	12 *2	2	Feb. 4, 2009

Dean A. Gallo (R-N.J.)

Dates: Nov. 23, 1935-Nov. 6, 1994
House: Jan. 3, 1985-Nov. 6, 1994
Left the House: Died in office

HOUSE STANDING COMMITTEES:

1st PUBLIC WORKS AND TRANSPORTATION
Dates: Jan. 30, 1985-Jan. 3, 1989
Departure: Moved to Appropriations and Budget

2nd SMALL BUSINESS
Dates: Jan. 30, 1985-Jan. 3, 1989
Departure: Moved to Appropriations and Budget

3rd APPROPRIATIONS
Dates: Jan. 20, 1989-Nov. 6, 1994
Departure: Died in office

Cong.	Ranking	Terms in: House	Comm.	Date of Assignment
103rd	Min-13th	5	3	Jan. 5, 1993

4th BUDGET
Dates: Jan. 20, 1989-Jan. 30, 1991
Departure: Left committee; no new assignment

Greg Ganske (R-Iowa)

Dates: March 31, 1939
House: Jan. 3, 1995-Jan. 3, 2003
Left the House: Lost U.S. Senate election in 2002

HOUSE STANDING COMMITTEES:

1st COMMERCE, 104-106
ENERGY AND COMMERCE, 107
Dates: Jan. 4, 1995-Jan. 3, 2003
Departure: Left the House; lost Senate election

Cong.	Ranking	Terms in: House	Comm.	Date of Assignment
104th	Maj-21st	1	1	Jan. 4, 1995
105th	Maj-21st	2	2	Jan. 7, 1997
106th	Maj-16th	3	3	Jan. 6, 1999
107th	Maj-13th	4	4	Jan. 6, 2001

John Garamendi (D-Cal.)

Dates: Jan. 24, 1945
House: Nov. 3, 2009-date
Serving in the 111th Congress
H: Garamendi was elected to the 111th Congress by special election, Nov. 3, 2009, to fill the vacancy caused by the resignation of U.S. Representative Ellen Tauscher (D-Cal.) who was appointed to the U.S. Department of State. Garamendi was seated Nov. 5, 2009, and assigned to committees.

HOUSE STANDING COMMITTEES:

1st SCIENCE AND TECHNOLOGY
Dates: Nov. 19, 2009-date
Departure: Still serving in the 111th Congress

Cong.	Ranking	Terms in: House	Comm.	Date of Assignment
111th	MjA-15	1	1	Nov. 19, 2009

2nd TRANSPORTATION AND INFRASTRUCTURE
Dates: Nov. 19, 2009-date
Departure: Still serving in the 111th Congress

Cong.	Ranking	Terms in: House	Comm.	Date of Assignment
111th	MjR-1st	1	1	Nov. 19, 2009

3rd ARMED SERVICES
Dates: May 6, 2010-date
Termination: Still serving in the 111th Congress

Cong.	Ranking	Terms in: House	Comm.	Date of Assignment
111th	MjR-3rd	1	1	May 6, 2010

Scott Garrett (R-N.J.)

Dates: July 9, 1959
House: Jan. 3, 2003-date
Serving in the 111th Congress

HOUSE STANDING COMMITTEES:

1st BUDGET
Dates: Jan. 28, 2003-date
Departure: Still serving in the 111th Congress

Cong.	Ranking	Terms in: House	Comm.	Date of Assignment
108th	Maj-19th	1	1	Jan. 28, 2003
109th	Maj-9th	2	2	Jan. 26, 2005
110th	Min-3rd	3	3	Jan. 18, 2007
111th	Min-2nd	4	4	Jan. 9, 2009

2nd FINANCIAL SERVICES
Dates: Jan. 28, 2003-date
Departure: Still serving in the 111th Congress

Cong.	Ranking	Terms in: House	Comm.	Date of Assignment
108th	Maj-32nd	1	1	Jan. 28, 2003
109th	Maj-26th	2	2	Jan. 26, 2005
110th	Min-19th	3	3	Jan. 10, 2007
111th	Min-13th	4	4	Jan. 9, 2009

Samuel Gejdenson (D-Conn.)

Dates: May 20, 1948
House: Jan. 3, 1981-Jan. 3, 2001
Left the House: Defeated for re-election in 2000

HOUSE STANDING COMMITTEES:

1st FOREIGN AFFAIRS, 97-103
INTERNATIONAL RELATIONS, 104-106
Dates: Jan. 28, 1981-Jan. 3, 2001
Departure: Left the House; lost re-election

Cong.	Ranking	Terms in: House	Comm.	Date of Assignment
103rd	Maj-2nd	7	7	Jan. 5, 1993
104th	Min-2nd	8	8	Jan. 4, 1995
105th	Min-2nd	9	9	Jan. 7, 1997
106th	Min-RM	10	10	Jan. 6, 1999

2nd INTERIOR AND INSULAR AFFAIRS, 97-102
NATURAL RESOURCES, 103
RESOURCES, 104-105
Dates: Jan. 28, 1981-Feb. 5, 1997
Departure: Resigned committee; moved to Joint Library and Joint Printing

Cong.	Ranking	Terms in: House	Comm.	Date of Assignment
103rd	Maj-9th	7	7	Jan. 5, 1993
104th	Min-6th	8	8	Jan. 9, 1995
105th	Min-6th	9	9	Jan. 7, 1997

3rd HOUSE ADMINISTRATION, 99-103
HOUSE OVERSIGHT, 104-105
Dates: Jan. 30, 1985-Jan. 3, 1999
Departure: Left committee; became Ranking Member on International Relations

Cong.	Ranking	Terms in: House	Comm.	Date of Assignment
103rd	Maj-4th	7	5	Jan. 21, 1993
104th	Min-2nd	8	6	Jan. 4, 1995
105th	Min-RM	9	7	Feb. 5, 1997

HOUSE SELECT AND SPECIAL COMMITTEES:

1st SELECT HUNGER (Temporary)
Dates: Mar. 13, 1984-Oct. 20, 1987
Departure: Left committee; no new assignment

JOINT COMMITTEES:

1st JOINT PRINTING
1st House Dates: Feb. 21, 1991-Jan. 3, 1995
1st Departure: Left committee; no new assignment
2nd House Dates: Mar. 6, 1997-Jan. 3, 1999
2nd Departure: Left committee; became Ranking Member on International Relations

Cong.	Ranking	Terms in: House	Comm.	Date of Assignment
103rd	Maj-2nd	7	*1 2	May 1, 1993 Provisional
105th	Min-2nd	9	*2 1	Mar. 6, 1997

2nd JOINT ORGANIZATION OF CONGRESS (Ad Hoc)
House Dates: Oct. 9, 1992-Dec. 17, 1993
Termination: House Report 103-413 filed

Cong.	Ranking	Terms in: House	Comm.	Date of Assignment
103rd	Maj-4th	7	2	Jan. 5, 1993

3rd JOINT LIBRARY
House Dates: Mar. 6, 1997-Jan. 3, 1999
Departure: Left committee; became Ranking Member on International Relations

Cong.	Ranking	Terms in: House	Comm.	Date of Assignment
105th	Min-2nd	9	1	Mar. 6, 1997

George W. Gekas (R-Penn.)

Dates: April 14, 1930
House: Jan. 3, 1983-Jan. 3, 2003
Left the House: Defeated for re-election in 2002

HOUSE STANDING COMMITTEES:

1st JUDICIARY
Dates: Jan. 6, 1983-Jan. 3, 2003
Departure: Left the House; lost re-election

Cong.	Ranking	Terms in: House	Comm.	Date of Assignment
103rd	Min-6th	6	6	Jan. 5, 1993
104th	Maj-5th	7	7	Jan. 4, 1995
105th	Maj-4th	8	8	Jan. 7, 1997
106th	Maj-4th	9	9	Jan. 6, 1999
107th	Maj-3rd	10	10	Jan. 6, 2001

2nd AGRICULTURE
Dates: July 26, 2002-Jan. 3, 2003
Departure: Left the House; lost re-election

Cong.	Ranking	Terms in: House	Comm.	Date of Assignment
107th	MjR-1st	10	1	July 26, 2002

HOUSE SELECT AND SPECIAL COMMITTEES:

1st SELECT AGING (Permanent)
Dates: Mar. 3, 1983-Jan. 3, 1987
Departure: Left committee; no new assignment

2nd PERMANENT SELECT INTELLIGENCE
Dates: Feb. 5, 1991-Jan. 3, 1995
Departure: Left committee; no new assignment

Cong.	Ranking	Terms in: House	Comm.	Date of Assignment
103rd	Min-5th	6	2	Feb. 3, 1993

Richard A. Gephardt (D-Mo.)

Dates: Jan. 31, 1941
House: Jan. 3, 1977-Jan. 3, 2005
Left the House: Retired; lost Democratic nomination for President in 2004

HOUSE STANDING COMMITTEES:

1st WAYS AND MEANS
Dates: Jan. 19, 1977-Oct. 16, 1989
Departure: Left committee; became Majority Floor Leader

2nd BUDGET
1st Dates: Jan. 24, 1979-Jan. 3, 1985
1st Departure: Left committee; no new assignment
2nd Dates: Oct. 16, 1989-Jan. 3, 1995
2nd Departure: Elected Minority Leader
Democrats used to reserve the 2nd rank on Budget for the House Floor Leader

Cong.	Ranking	Terms in: House	Comm.	Date of Assignment
103rd	Maj-2nd	9 *2	3	Jan. 5, 1993

HOUSE SELECT AND SPECIAL COMMITTEES:

1st SELECT POPULATION
Dates: Oct. 14, 1977-Dec. 29, 1978
Termination: House Report 1842 (95-2) filed

JOINT COMMITTEES:

1st JOINT ORGANIZATION OF CONGRESS (Ad Hoc)
House Dates: Oct. 9, 1992-Dec. 17, 1993
Termination: House Report 103-413 filed

Cong.	Ranking	Terms in: House	Comm.	Date of Assignment
103rd	Maj-ExO	9	2	Jan. 5, 1993

HOUSE LEADERSHIP POSTS

Dates: June 14, 1989-Jan. 3, 2003
Departure: Left leadership; lost presidential nomination in 2004

1st HOUSE MAJORITY FLOOR LEADER
Dates: June 14, 1989-Jan. 3, 1995
Note: In the 101st Congress, Gephardt was elected on June 14, 1989, to succeed Majority Leader Thomas S. Foley (D-Wash.), who had been elected Speaker of the House. Gephardt defeated Ed Jenkins (D-Ga.) 181 to 76 on the first ballot. Gephardt was re-elected without opposition for the 102nd and 103rd Congresses.
Departure: Democratic Party lost House majority in 1994

Cong.	Ranking	Terms in: House	Post	Date of Selection
103rd	Maj-2nd	9	3	Dec. 11, 1992

2nd HOUSE MINORITY FLOOR LEADER
Dates: Jan. 3, 1995-Jan. 3, 2003
Note: For the 104th Congress, Gephardt was elected Minority Leader on Nov. 30, 1994, defeating Charles Rose (D-N.C.), 150 to 50 on the first ballot. Gephardt was re-elected without opposition for the 105th-107th Congresses.
Departure: Left post to seek 2004 presidential nomination

Cong.	Ranking	Terms in: House	Post	Date of Selection
104th	Min-1st	10	1	Nov. 30, 1994
105th	Min-1st	11	2	Nov. 18, 1996
106th	Min-1st	12	3	Nov. 16, 1998
107th	Min-1st	13	4	Nov. 14, 2000

Preston M. (Pete) Geren (D-Tex.)

Dates: Jan. 29, 1951
House: Sept. 12, 1989-Jan. 3, 1997
Left the House: Retired in 1996

H: Geren was elected to the 101st Congress by special election, Sept. 12, 1989, to fill the vacancy caused by the resignation of U.S. Representative James C. Wright, Jr. (D-Tex.). Geren was seated Sept. 20, 1989, and assigned to committees.

HOUSE STANDING COMMITTEES:

1st PUBLIC WORKS AND TRANSPORTATION
TRANSPORTATION AND INFRASTRUCTURE
1st Dates: Oct. 16, 1989-Jan. 3, 1995
1st Departure: Left committee; no new assignment
2nd Dates: Nov. 20, 1995-Jan. 3, 1997
2nd Departure: Left the House; retired

Cong.	Ranking	Terms in: House	Comm.	Date of Assignment
103rd	Maj-17th	3 *1	3	Jan. 5, 1993
104th	MnR-3rd	4 *2	1	Nov. 20, 1995

2nd VETERANS' AFFAIRS
Dates: Nov. 8, 1989-Jan. 3, 1993
Departure: Moved to Armed Services

3rd SCIENCE, SPACE AND TECHNOLOGY, 102-103
SCIENCE, 104
Dates: Jan. 24, 1991-Nov. 20, 1995
Departure: Resigned committee; returned to Transportation and Infrastructure

Cong.	Ranking	Terms in: House	Comm.	Date of Assignment
103rd	Maj-14th	3	2	Jan. 5, 1993
104th	Min-6th	4	3	Jan. 4, 1995

4th ARMED SERVICES, 103
NATIONAL SECURITY, 104
Dates: Jan. 27, 1993-Jan. 3, 1997
Departure: Left the House; retired

Cong.	Ranking	Terms in: House	Comm.	Date of Assignment
103rd	Maj-32nd	3	1	Jan. 27, 1993
104th	Min-20th	4	2	Jan. 4, 1995

Jim Gerlach (R-Penn.)

Dates: Feb. 25, 1955
House: Jan. 3, 2003-date
Serving in the 111th Congress

HOUSE STANDING COMMITTEES:

1st SMALL BUSINESS
Dates: Jan. 28, 2003-Jan. 3, 2005
Departure: Left committee; no new assignment

Cong.	Ranking	Terms in: House	Comm.	Date of Assignment
108th	Maj-15th	1	1	Jan. 28, 2003

2nd TRANSPORTATION AND INFRASTRUCTURE
Dates: Jan. 28, 2003-date
Departure: Still serving in the 111th Congress

Cong.	Ranking	Terms in: House	Comm.	Date of Assignment
108th	Maj-39th	1	1	Jan. 28, 2003

109th	Maj-28th	2	2	Jan. 26, 2005
110th	Min-20th	3	3	Jan. 10, 2007
111th	Min-17th	4	4	Jan. 9, 2009

3rd FINANCIAL SERVICES
Dates: Sep. 23, 2004-date
Departure: Still serving in the 111th Congress

Cong.	Ranking	Terms in: House	Comm.	Date of Assignment
108th	MjR-1st	1	1	Sept. 23, 2004
109th	Maj-31st	2	2	Jan. 26, 2005
110th	Min-23rd	3	3	Jan. 10, 2007
111th	Min-15th	4	4	Jan. 9, 2009

James A. Gibbons (R-Nev.)

Dates: Dec. 16, 1944
House: Jan. 3, 1997-Dec. 31, 2006
Left the House: Resigned; elected Governor in 2006

HOUSE STANDING COMMITTEES:

1st NATIONAL SECURITY, 105
ARMED SERVICES, 106-109
Dates: Jan. 7, 1997-Dec. 31, 2006
Departure: Resigned the House; elected Governor

Cong.	Ranking	Terms in: House	Comm.	Date of Assignment
105th	Maj-30th	1	1	Jan. 7, 1997
106th	Maj-27th	2	2	Jan. 6, 1999
107th	Maj-22nd	3	3	Jan. 6, 2001
108th	Maj-13th	4	4	Jan. 28, 2003
109th	Maj-13th	5	5	Jan. 26, 2005

2nd RESOURCES
Dates: Jan. 7, 1997-Dec. 31, 2006
Departure: Resigned the House; elected Governor

Cong.	Ranking	Terms in: House	Comm.	Date of Assignment
105th	Maj-26th	1	1	Jan. 7, 1997
106th	Maj-22nd	2	2	Jan. 6, 1999
107th	Maj-20th	3	3	Jan. 6, 2001
108th	Maj-16th	4	4	Jan. 28, 2003
109th	Maj-13th	5	5	Jan. 26, 2005

3rd VETERANS' AFFAIRS
Dates: Feb. 2, 1999-Feb. 12, 2003
Departure: Resigned committee; moved to Select Homeland Security

Cong.	Ranking	Terms in: House	Comm.	Date of Assignment
106th	Maj-16th	2	1	Feb. 2, 1999
107th	Maj-12th	3	2	Jan. 6, 2001
108th	Maj-8th	4	3	Jan. 28, 2003

4th HOMELAND SECURITY
Dates: Feb. 9, 2005-Dec. 31, 2006
Departure: Resigned the House; elected Governor

Cong.	Ranking	Terms in: House	Comm.	Date of Assignment
109th	Maj-11th	5	2	Feb. 9, 2005

HOUSE SELECT AND SPECIAL COMMITTEES:

1st PERMANENT SELECT INTELLIGENCE
Dates: Feb. 10, 1997-Jan. 3, 2005
Departure: Left committee; no new assignment

Cong.	Ranking	Terms in: House	Comm.	Date of Assignment
105th	Maj-9th	1	1	Feb. 10, 1997
106th	Maj-7th	2	2	Jan. 19, 1999
107th	Maj-6th	3	3	Jan. 30, 2001
108th	Maj-4th	4	4	Jan. 8, 2003

2nd SELECT HOMELAND SECURITY
Dates: Feb. 12, 2003-Jan. 3, 2005
Departure: Remained on reorganized standing committee

Cong.	Ranking	Terms in: House	Comm.	Date of Assignment
108th	Maj-24th	4	1	Feb. 12, 2003

Sam M. Gibbons (D-Fla.)

Dates: Jan. 20, 1920
House: Jan. 3, 1963-Jan. 3, 1997
Left the House: Retired in 1996

HOUSE STANDING COMMITTEES:

1st EDUCATION AND LABOR
Dates: Jan. 17, 1963-Jan. 3, 1969
Departure: Moved to Ways and Means

2nd HOUSE ADMINISTRATION
Dates: Jan. 17, 1963-Jan. 14, 1969
Departure: Moved to Ways and Means

3rd WAYS AND MEANS
Dates: Jan. 14, 1969-Jan. 3, 1997
ChA: Replaced Daniel D. Rostenkowski (D-Ill.) as Acting Chair on June 8, 1994
Departure: Left the House; retired

Cong.	Ranking	Terms in: House	Comm.	Date of Assignment
103rd	Maj-2nd	16	13	Jan. 5, 1993
=103rd	Maj-Ch2	16	13	June 8, 1994
104th	Min-RM	17	14	Jan. 4, 1995

4th BUDGET
Dates: Feb. 5, 1975-Jan. 3, 1977
Departure: Left committee; no new assignment

HOUSE SELECT AND SPECIAL COMMITTEES:

1st SELECT WELFARE OF CONGRESSIONAL PAGES
Dates: Oct. 2, 1964-Jan. 2, 1965
Termination: House Report 1945 (88-2) filed

JOINT COMMITTEES:

1st JOINT TAXATION
House Dates: May 18, 1981-Jan. 3, 1997
Acting Vice Chair: Replaced Rostenkowski on June 8, 1994
Departure: Left the House; retired

Cong.	Ranking	Terms in: House	Comm.	Date of Assignment
103rd	Maj-2nd	16	7	Jan. 5, 1993 Ltr
103rd	Maj-VCA	16	7	June 8, 1994
104th	Min-1st	17	8	Jan. 10, 1995 Ltr

Gabrielle Giffords (D-Ariz.)

Dates: June 8, 1970
House: Jan. 3, 2007-date
Serving in the 111th Congress

HOUSE STANDING COMMITTEES:

1st ARMED SERVICES
Dates: Jan. 10, 2007-date
Departure: Still serving in the 111th Congress

Cong.	Ranking	Terms in: House	Comm.	Date of Assignment
110th	Maj-32nd	1	1	Jan. 10, 2007
111th	Maj-29th	2	2	Jan. 7, 2009

2nd FOREIGN AFFAIRS
Dates: Jan. 12, 2007-date
Departure: Still serving in the 111th Congress

Cong.	Ranking	Terms in: House	Comm.	Date of Assignment
110th	Maj-26th	1	1	Jan. 12, 2007
111th	Maj-27th	2	2	Jan. 21, 2009

3rd SCIENCE AND TECHNOLOGY
Dates: Jan. 18, 2007
Departure: Still serving in the 111th Congress

Cong.	Ranking	Terms in: House	Comm.	Date of Assignment
110th	Maj-11th	1	1	Jan. 18, 2007
111th	Maj-9th	2	2	Jan. 21, 2009

Wayne T. Gilchrest (R-Md.)

Dates: April 15, 1946
House: Jan. 3, 1991-Jan. 3, 2009
Left the House: Defeated for re-nomination in 2008

HOUSE STANDING COMMITTEES:

1st MERCHANT MARINE AND FISHERIES
Dates: Jan. 24, 1991-Jan. 3, 1995
Departure: Committee abolished; moved to Resources

Cong.	Ranking	Terms in: House	Comm.	Date of Assignment
103rd	Min-9th	2	2	Jan. 5, 1993

2nd SCIENCE, SPACE AND TECHNOLOGY, 102 SCIENCE, 107-109
1st Dates: Jan. 24, 1991-Jan. 3, 1993
1st Departure: Moved to Public Works and Transportation
2nd Dates: June 7, 2001-Jan. 3, 2007
2nd Departure: Left committee; no new assignment

		Terms in:		Date of
Cong.	Ranking	House	Comm.	Assignment
107th	MjR-2nd	6 *2	1	June 7, 2001
108th	Maj-15th	7 *2	2	Feb. 11, 2003
109th	Maj-12th	8 *2	3	Jan. 26, 2005

3rd PUBLIC WORKS AND TRANSPORTATION, 103
TRANSPORTATION AND INFRASTRUCTURE, 104-110
Dates: Jan. 5, 1993-Jan. 3, 2009
Departure: Left the House; lost re-nomination

		Terms in:		Date of
Cong.	Ranking	House	Comm.	Assignment
103rd	Min-11th	2	1	Jan. 5, 1993
104th	Maj-13th	3	2	Jan. 4, 1995
105th	Maj-10th	4	3	Jan. 7, 1997
106th	Maj-9th	5	4	Jan. 6, 1999
107th	Maj-7th	6	5	Jan. 6, 2001
108th	Maj-6th	7	6	Jan. 28, 2003
109th	Maj-6th	8	7	Jan. 26, 2005
110th	Min-6th	9	8	Jan. 10, 2007

4th RESOURCES, 104-109
NATURAL RESOURCES, 110
Dates: Jan. 4, 1995-Jan. 3, 2009
Departure: Left the House; lost re-nomination

		Terms in:		Date of
Cong.	Ranking	House	Comm.	Assignment
104th	Maj-9th	3	1	Jan. 4, 1995
105th	Maj-9th	4	2	Jan. 7, 1997
106th	Maj-9th	5	3	Jan. 6, 1999
107th	Maj-8th	6	4	Jan. 6, 2001
108th	Maj-8th	7	5	Jan. 28, 2003
109th	Maj-6th	8	6	Jan. 26, 2005
110th	Min-5th	9	7	Jan. 10, 2007

HOUSE SELECT AND SPECIAL COMMITTEES:

1st SELECT AGING (Permanent)
Dates: Feb. 21, 1991-Jan. 3, 1993
Termination: Committee not renewed in 1993

2nd SELECT HUNGER (Temporary)
Dates: Feb. 21, 1991-Jan. 3, 1993
Termination: Committee not renewed in 1993

		Terms in:		Date of
Cong.	Ranking	House	Comm.	Assignment
110th	Maj-18th	1	1	Jan. 12, 2007
111th	Maj-14th	2	2	Jan. 21, 2009

2nd ARMED SERVICES
Dates: Jan. 10, 2007-Jan. 26, 2009
Departure: Resigned the House; appointed to the Senate

		Terms in:		Date of
Cong.	Ranking	House	Comm.	Assignment
110th	Maj-30th	1	1	Jan. 10, 2007
111th	Maj-27th	2	2	Jan. 7, 2009

SENATE STANDING COMMITTEES:

1st AGRICULTURE, NUTRITION AND FORESTRY
Dates: Jan. 27, 2009-date
Departure: Still serving in the 111th Congress

		Years in:		Date of
Cong.	Ranking	Senate	Comm.	Assignment
111th	Maj-12th	1	1	Jan. 27, 2009

2nd ENVIRONMENT AND PUBLIC WORKS
Dates: Jan. 27, 2009-date
Departure: Still serving in the 111th Congress

		Years in:		Date of
Cong.	Ranking	Senate	Comm.	Assignment
111th	Maj-11th	1	1	Jan. 27, 2009

3rd FOREIGN RELATIONS
Dates: Jan. 27, 2009-date
Departure: Still serving in the 111th Congress

		Years in:		Date of
Cong.	Ranking	Senate	Comm.	Assignment
111th	Maj-11th	1	1	Jan. 27, 2009

SENATE SELECT AND SPECIAL COMMITTEES:

1st SPECIAL AGING (Permanent)
Dates: Jan. 27, 2009-date
Departure: Still serving in the 111th Congress

		Years in:		Date of
Cong.	Ranking	Senate	Comm.	Assignment
111th	Maj-11th	1	1	Jan. 27, 2009

Kirsten E. Gillibrand (D-N.Y.)

Dates: Dec. 9, 1966
House: Jan. 3, 2007-Jan. 26, 2009
Left the House: Appointed to the Senate in 2009
Senate: Jan. 26, 2009-date
Serving in the 111th Congress

S: Gillibrand was appointed to the 111th Congress, Jan. 23, 2009, to fill the vacancy caused by the resignation of U.S. Senator Hillary Rodham Clinton (D-N.Y.) who had been appointed Secretary of State. Gillibrand's Senate service began on Jan. 26, 2009, with her House resignation. Gillibrand was seated on Jan. 27, 2009, and was assigned to committees.

HOUSE STANDING COMMITTEES:

1st AGRICULTURE
Dates: Jan. 12, 2007-Jan. 26, 2009
Departure: Resigned the House; appointed to the Senate

Paul E. Gillmor (R-Ohio)

Dates: Feb. 1, 1939-Sept. 5, 2007
House: Jan. 3, 1989-Sept. 5, 2007
Left the House: Died in office

HOUSE STANDING COMMITTEES:

1st BANKING, FINANCE AND URBAN AFFAIRS, 101-102
FINANCIAL SERVICES, 107-110
1st Dates: Jan. 20, 1989-Jan. 3, 1993
1st Departure: Moved to Energy and Commerce
2nd Dates: Jan. 6, 2001-Sept. 5, 2007
2nd Departure: Died in office

		Terms in:		Date of
Cong.	Ranking	House	Comm.	Assignment
107th	Maj-15th	7	1	Jan. 6, 2001
108th	Maj-13th	8	2	Jan. 28, 2003

Cong.	Ranking		Date of Assignment
109th	Maj-13th	9	3	Jan. 26, 2005
110th	Min-9th	10	4	Jan. 10, 2007

2nd HOUSE ADMINISTRATION
Dates: Jan. 20, 1989-Jan. 3, 1993
Departure: Moved to Energy and Commerce

3rd PUBLIC WORKS AND TRANSPORTATION
Dates: Oct. 17, 1991-Jan. 3, 1993
Departure: Moved to Energy and Commerce in the 103rd Congress

4th ENERGY AND COMMERCE, 103
COMMERCE, 104-106
ENERGY AND COMMERCE, 107-110
1st Dates: Jan. 5, 1993-Jan. 3, 2007
1st Departure: Left committee; no new assignment
Temporary Dates: June 19, 2007-June 28, 2007
Departure: Temporary vacancy filled

		Terms in:		Date of
Cong.	Ranking	House	Comm.	Assignment
103rd	Min-13th	3 *1	1	Jan. 5, 1993
104th	Maj-12th	4 *1	2	Jan. 4, 1995
105th	Maj-11th	5 *1	3	Jan. 7, 1997
106th	Maj-8th	6 *1	4	Jan. 6, 1999
107th	Maj-6th	7 *1	5	Jan. 6, 2001
108th	Maj-6th	8 *1	6	Jan. 28, 2003
109th	Maj-6th	9 *1	7	Jan. 6, 2005
110th	MnR-2nd	10 *T	1	June 19, 2007

5th INTERNATIONAL RELATIONS
Dates: Jan. 6, 1999-Jan. 3, 2001
Departure: Moved to Financial Services

		Terms in:		Date of
Cong.	Ranking	House	Comm.	Assignment
106th	Maj-23rd	6	1	Jan. 6, 1999

HOUSE SELECT AND SPECIAL COMMITTEES:

1st SELECT NARCOTICS ABUSE AND CONTROL (Temporary)
Dates: Feb. 21, 1991-Jan. 3, 1993
Termination: Committee not renewed in 1993

JOINT COMMITTEES:

1st JOINT LIBRARY
House Dates: Mar. 15, 1989-Jan. 3, 1991
Departure: Moved to Select Narcotics Abuse and Control

Benjamin A. Gilman (R-N.Y.)

Dates: Dec. 6, 1922
House: Jan. 3, 1973-Jan. 3, 2003
Left the House: Retired in 2002

HOUSE STANDING COMMITTEES:

1st FOREIGN AFFAIRS, 93
INTERNATIONAL RELATIONS, 94-95
FOREIGN AFFAIRS, 96-103
INTERNATIONAL RELATIONS 104-107
Dates: Jan. 24, 1973-Jan. 3, 2003
Departure: Left the House; retired

		Terms in:		Date of
Cong.	Ranking	House	Comm.	Assignment
103rd	Min-RM	11	11	Jan. 5, 1993
104th	Maj-Chr	12	12	Jan. 4, 1995
105th	Maj-Chr	13	13	Jan. 7, 1997
106th	Maj-Chr	14	14	Jan. 6, 1999
107th	Maj-2nd	15	15	Jan. 6, 2001

2nd POST OFFICE AND CIVIL SERVICE
Dates: Jan. 28, 1975-Jan. 3, 1995
Departure: Committee abolished; moved to Government Reform and Oversight with seniority credited

		Terms in:		Date of
Cong.	Ranking	House	Comm.	Assignment
103rd	Min-2nd	11	10	Jan. 5, 1993

3rd GOVERNMENT REFORM AND OVERSIGHT, 104-105
GOVERNMENT REFORM, 106-107
Dates: Jan. 4, 1995-Jan. 3, 2003
Departure: Left the House; retired

		Terms in:		Date of
Cong.	Ranking	House	Comm.	Assignment
104th	Maj-2nd	12	1	Jan. 4, 1995
105th	Maj-2nd	13	2	Jan. 7, 1997
106th	Maj-2nd	14	3	Jan. 6, 1999
107th	Maj-2nd	15	4	Jan. 6, 2001

HOUSE SELECT AND SPECIAL COMMITTEES:

1st SELECT SERVICEMEN MISSING IN SOUTHEAST ASIA
Dates: Sep. 15, 1975-Jan. 3, 1977
Termination: House Report 1754 (94-2) filed, Dec. 13, 1976

2nd SELECT NARCOTICS ABUSE AND CONTROL (Temporary)
Dates: Aug. 3, 1976-Jan. 3, 1993
Termination: Committee not renewed in 1993

3rd SELECT HUNGER (Temporary)
Dates: Mar. 13, 1984-Jan. 3, 1993
Termination: Committee not renewed in 1993

Phil Gingrey (R-Ga.)

Dates: July 10, 1942
House: Jan. 3, 2003-date
Serving in the 111th Congress

HOUSE STANDING COMMITTEES:

1st ARMED SERVICES
1st Dates: Jan. 28, 2003-Jan. 3, 2005
1st Departure: Moved to Rules
2nd Dates: Jan. 10, 2007-Jan. 3, 2009
2nd Departure: Moved to Energy and Commerce

		Terms in:		Date of
Cong.	Ranking	House	Comm.	Assignment
108th	Maj-31st	1 *1	1	Jan. 28, 2003
110th	Min-22nd	3 *2	1	Jan. 10, 2007

2nd EDUCATION AND THE WORKFORCE
Dates: Feb. 11, 2003-Jan. 3, 2005
Departure: Moved to Rules

Cong.	Ranking	Terms in: House	Comm.	Date of Assignment
108th	Maj-27th	1	1	Feb. 11, 2003

3rd SCIENCE, 108
SCIENCE AND TECHNOLOGY, 110
1st Dates: Jan. 28, 2003-Jan. 3, 2005
1st Departure: Moved to Rules
2nd Dates: Jan. 10, 2007-Jan. 3, 2009
2nd Departure: Moved to Energy and Commerce

Cong.	Ranking	Terms in: House	Comm.	Date of Assignment
108th	Maj-21st	1 *1	1	Jan. 28, 2003
110th	Min-18th	3 *2	1	Jan. 10, 2007

4th RULES
Dates: Jan. 4, 2005-Jan. 3, 2007
Departure: Returned to Armed Services and Science and Technology

Cong.	Ranking	Terms in: House	Comm.	Date of Assignment
109th	Maj-9th	2	1	Jan. 6, 2005

5th ENERGY AND COMMERCE
Dates: Jan. 9, 2009-date
Departure: Still serving in the 111th Congress

Cong.	Ranking	Terms in: House	Comm.	Date of Assignment
111th	Min-22nd	4	1	Jan. 9, 2009

Newton L. Gingrich (R-Ga.)

Dates: June 17, 1943
House: Jan. 3, 1979-Jan. 3, 1999
Left the House: Resigned and retired.

HOUSE STANDING COMMITTEES:

1st HOUSE ADMINISTRATION
Dates: Jan. 24, 1979-date
Departure: Left committee; elected Speaker of the House

Cong.	Ranking	Terms in: House	Comm.	Date of Assignment
103rd	Min-2nd	8	8	Jan. 5, 1993

2nd PUBLIC WORKS AND TRANSPORTATION
Dates: Jan. 24, 1979-Apr. 18, 1989
Departure: Left committee; became Minority Whip

JOINT COMMITTEES:

1st JOINT LIBRARY
House Dates: Feb. 28, 1980-Jan. 3, 1989
Departure: Moved to Joint Printing

2nd JOINT PRINTING
1st House Dates: Feb. 5, 1981-Jan. 3, 1983
1st Departure: Left committee; no new assignment
2nd House Dates: Apr. 18, 1989-Jan. 3, 1995
2nd Departure: Elected Speaker of the House

Cong.	Ranking	Terms in: House	Comm.	Date of Assignment
103rd	Min-2nd	8 *2	3	May 1, 1993 Provisional

HOUSE LEADERSHIP POSTS

Dates: Mar. 22, 1989-Jan. 3, 1999
Departure: Resigned the House; retired

1st HOUSE MINORITY WHIP
Dates: Mar. 22, 1989-Jan. 3, 1995
Note: In the 101st Congress, Gingrich succeeded Minority Whip Richard B. Cheney (R-Wyo.) who had been appointed Secretary of Defense. Gingrich was elected on Mar. 22, 1989, defeating Ed Madigan (R-Ill.) 87 to 85 on the first ballot. Gingrich was re-elected without opposition for the 102nd and 103rd Congresses.
Departure: Elected Speaker of the House

Cong.	Ranking	Terms in: House	Post	Date of Selection
103rd	Min-2nd	8	3	Dec. 11, 1992

2nd SPEAKER OF THE HOUSE
Dates: Jan. 3, 1995-Jan. 3, 1999
Note: In the 104th Congress, Gingrich succeeded Speaker of the House Thomas S. Foley (D-Wash.) who had been defeated for re-election. Gingrich was elected Speaker over Richard Gephardt (D-Mo.) 228 to 202 in the 104th Congress and by 216 to 205 over Gephardt in the 105th Congress.
Departure: Resigned the House; retired

Cong.	Ranking	Terms in: House	Post	Date of Election
104th	Maj-1st	9	1	Jan. 4, 1995
105th	Maj-1st	10	2	Jan. 7, 1997

John H. Glenn Jr. (D-Ohio)

Dates: July 18, 1921
Senate: Dec. 24, 1974-Jan. 3, 1999
Left the Senate: Retired in 1998

S: Glenn was appointed to the 93rd Congress, Dec. 24, 1974, to fill the unexpired term caused by the resignation of U.S. Senator William H. Saxbe (R-Ohio), who had been appointed Attorney General. Saxbe had initially been replaced by Howard Metzenbaum (D-Ohio), an appointee, who had resigned after being defeated to fill the vacancy by Glenn. Glenn was not seated nor assigned to committees because the 93rd Congress was not in session.

SENATE STANDING COMMITTEES:

1st GOVERNMENT OPERATIONS reorganized Feb. 11, 1977
GOVERNMENTAL AFFAIRS
Dates: Jan. 17, 1975-Jan. 3, 1999
Departure: Left the Senate; retired

Cong.	Ranking	Years in: Senate	Comm.	Date of Assignment
103rd	Maj-Chr	19	18	Jan. 7, 1993
104th	Min-RM	21	20	Jan. 4, 1995
105th	Min-RM	23	22	Jan. 9, 1997

2nd INTERIOR AND INSULAR AFFAIRS
Dates: Jan. 17, 1975-Feb. 11, 1977
Departure: Moved to Foreign Relations

3rd DISTRICT OF COLUMBIA
Dates: Jan. 17, 1975-Feb. 11, 1977
Departure: Reorganized into Governmental Affairs, upon which he was already serving

4th FOREIGN RELATIONS
Dates: Feb. 11, 1977-Feb. 21, 1985
Departure: Moved to Armed Services

5th ARMED SERVICES
Dates: Feb. 21, 1985-Jan. 3, 1999
Departure: Left the Senate; retired

Cong.	Ranking	Years in: Senate	Comm.	Date of Assignment
103rd	Maj-6th	19	8	Jan. 7, 1993
104th	Min-6th	21	10	Jan. 4, 1995
105th	Min-4th	23	12	Jan. 9, 1997

SENATE SELECT AND SPECIAL COMMITTEES:

1st SELECT OFFICIAL CONDUCT
Dates: Jan. 19, 1977-Mar. 10, 1977
Termination: Senate Report 49 (95-1) filed

2nd SPECIAL AGING (Permanent)
Dates: Feb. 11, 1977-Jan. 3, 1999
Departure: Left the Senate; retired

Cong.	Ranking	Years in: Senate	Comm.	Date of Assignment
103rd	Maj-2nd	19	16	Jan. 21, 1993
104th	Min-2nd	21	18	Jan. 6, 1995
105th	Min-2nd	23	20	Jan. 9, 1997

3rd SELECT INTELLIGENCE (Permanent)
Dates: Feb. 2, 1989-Jan. 3, 1999
Departure: Left the Senate; retired

Cong.	Ranking	Years in: Senate	Comm.	Date of Assignment
103rd	Maj-3rd	19	4	Jan. 27, 1993
104th	Min-2nd	21	6	Jan. 6, 1995
105th	Min-2nd	23	8	Jan. 9, 1997

Daniel R. Glickman (D-Kans.)

Dates: Nov. 24, 1944
House: Jan. 3, 1977-Jan. 3, 1995
Left the House: Defeated for re-election in 1994; appointed Secretary of Agriculture in 1995

HOUSE STANDING COMMITTEES:

1st AGRICULTURE
Dates: Jan. 19, 1977-Jan. 3, 1995
Departure: Left the House; lost re-election

Cong.	Ranking	Terms in: House	Comm.	Date of Assignment
103rd	Maj-6th	9	9	Jan. 5, 1993

2nd SCIENCE AND TECHNOLOGY, 95-99
SCIENCE, SPACE AND TECHNOLOGY, 100-103
Dates: Jan. 19, 1977-Jan. 3, 1995
Departure: Left the House; lost re-election

Cong.	Ranking	Terms in: House	Comm.	Date of Assignment
103rd	Maj-3rd	9	9	Jan. 5, 1993

3rd JUDICIARY
Dates: Jan. 23, 1980-Jan. 3, 1995
Departure: Left the House; lost re-election

Cong.	Ranking	Terms in: House	Comm.	Date of Assignment
103rd	Maj-8th	9	8	Jan. 5, 1993

HOUSE SELECT AND SPECIAL COMMITTEES:

1st PERMANENT SELECT INTELLIGENCE
Dates: Nov. 18, 1987-Jan. 3, 1995
Departure: Left the House; lost re-election

Cong.	Ranking	Terms in: House	Comm.	Date of Assignment
103rd	Maj-Chr	9	4	Feb. 3, 1993

Louie Gohmert (R-Tex.)

Dates: Aug. 18, 1953
House: Jan. 3, 2005-date
Serving in the 111th Congress

HOUSE STANDING COMMITTEES:

1st JUDICIARY
Dates: Jan. 26, 2005-date
Departure: Still serving in the 111th Congress

Cong.	Ranking	Terms in: House	Comm.	Date of Assignment
109th	Maj-23rd	1	1	Jan. 26, 2005
110th	Min-16th	2	2	Jan. 10, 2007
111th	Min-11th	3	3	Jan. 9, 2009

2nd RESOURCES, 109
NATURAL RESOURCES, 110-111
Dates: Jan. 26, 2005-date
Departure: Still serving in the 111th Congress

Cong.	Ranking	Terms in: House	Comm.	Date of Assignment
109th	Maj-27th	1	1	Jan. 26, 2005
110th	Min-16th	2	2	Jan. 10, 2007
111th	Min-8th	3	3	Jan. 9, 2009

3rd SMALL BUSINESS
Dates: Jan. 26, 2005-date
Departure: Still serving in the 111th Congress

Cong.	Ranking	Terms in: House	Comm.	Date of Assignment
109th	Maj-18th	1	1	Jan. 26, 2005
110th	Maj-10th	2	2	Jan. 10, 2007
111th	Min-6th	3	3	Jan. 9, 2009

Charles A. Gonzalez (D-Tex.)

Dates: May 5, 1945
House: Jan. 3, 1999-date
Serving in the 111th Congress

HOUSE STANDING COMMITTEES:

1st BANKING AND FINANCIAL SERVICES, 106
FINANCIAL SERVICES, 107-108
Dates: Jan. 6, 1999-Jan. 20, 2004
Departure: Resigned committee; moved to Energy and Commerce

Cong.	Ranking	Terms in: House	Comm.	Date of Assignment
106th	Min-25th	1	1	Jan. 6, 1999
107th	Min-22nd	2	2	Jan. 31, 2001
108th	Min-17th	3	3	Jan. 28, 2003

2nd SMALL BUSINESS
1st Dates: Jan. 6, 1999-Feb. 12, 2003
1st Departure: Leave of absence; moved to Select Homeland Security
2nd Dates: Returned Feb. 26, 2003-Jan. 20, 2004
2nd Departure: Resigned committee; moved to Energy and Commerce
3rd Dates: Jan. 23, 2007-Jan. 3, 2009
3rd Departure: Moved to Judiciary

Cong.	Ranking	Terms in: House	Comm.	Date of Assignment
106th	Min-13th	1 *1	1	Jan. 6, 1999
107th	Min-12th	2 *1	2	Jan. 31, 2001
108th	Min-8th	3 *1	3	Jan. 28, 2003
108th	Min-9th	3 *2	1	Feb. 26, 2003
110th	Maj-5th	5 *3	1	Jan. 23, 2007

3rd ENERGY AND COMMERCE
Dates: Jan. 21, 2004-date
Departure: Still serving in the 111th Congress

Cong.	Ranking	Terms in: House	Comm.	Date of Assignment
108th	MnR-1st	3	1	Jan. 21, 2004
109th	Min-23rd	4	2	Jan. 26, 2005
110th	Maj-21st	5	3	Jan. 4, 2007
111th	Maj-17th	6	4	Jan. 7, 2009

4th HOUSE ADMINISTRATION
Dates: Feb. 8, 2007-date
Departure: Still serving in the 111th Congress

Cong.	Ranking	Terms in: House	Comm.	Date of Assignment
110th	Maj-5th	5	1	Feb. 8, 2007
111th	Maj-4th	6	2	Jan. 13, 2009

5th JUDICIARY
Dates: Jan. 21, 2009-date
Departure: Still serving in the 111th Congress

Cong.	Ranking	Terms in: House	Comm.	Date of Assignment
111th	Maj-19th	6	1	Jan. 21, 2009

HOUSE SELECT AND SPECIAL COMMITTEES:

1st SELECT HOMELAND SECURITY
Dates: Feb. 12, 2003-Jan. 20, 2004
Departure: Resigned committee; moved to Energy and Commerce

Cong.	Ranking	Terms in: House	Comm.	Date of Assignment
108th	Min-20th	3	1	Feb. 12, 2003

Henry B. Gonzalez (D-Tex.)

Dates: May 3, 1916-Nov. 28, 2000
House: Nov. 4, 1961-Jan. 3, 1999
Left the House: Retired in 1998

H: Gonzalez was elected to the 87th Congress by special election, Nov. 4, 1961, to fill the vacancy caused by the resignation of U.S. Representative Paul J. Kilday (D-Tex.). Gonzalez was seated Jan. 10, 1962, and assigned to committees.

HOUSE STANDING COMMITTEES:

1st BANKING AND CURRENCY, 87-93
BANKING, CURRENCY AND HOUSING, 94
BANKING, FINANCE AND URBAN AFFAIRS, 95-103
BANKING AND FINANCIAL SERVICES, 104-105
Dates: Jan. 18, 1962-Jan. 3, 1999
RM1: Replaced by John LaFalce (D-N.Y.) on Feb. 25, 1998
Departure: Left the House; retired

Cong.	Ranking	Terms in: House	Comm.	Date of Assignment
103rd	Maj-Chr	17	17	Jan. 5, 1993
104th	Min-RM	18	18	Jan. 4, 1995
105th	Min-RM1	19	19	Jan. 7, 1997

2nd SMALL BUSINESS
Dates: Jan. 20, 1975-Jan. 3, 1989
Departure: Left committee; became Chair of Banking, Finance and Urban Affairs

HOUSE SELECT AND SPECIAL COMMITTEES:

1st SELECT SERVICEMEN MISSING IN SOUTHEAST ASIA
Dates: Sep. 15, 1975-Jan. 3, 1977
Termination: House Report 1764 (94-2) filed, Dec. 13, 1976

2nd SELECT ASSASSINATIONS
Dates: Sep. 21, 1976-Mar. 8, 1977
Departure: Left committee; no new assignment.
Ch1: Replaced by Louis Stokes (D-Ohio) on Mar. 8, 1977

Virgil H. Goode Jr. (R-Va.)

Dates: Oct. 17, 1946
House: Jan. 3, 1997-Jan. 3, 2009
Left the House: Defeated for re-election in 2008
Served as a Democrat: Jan. 3, 1997-Jan. 27, 2000
Served as an Independent: Jan. 27, 2000-Aug. 1, 2002
Served as a Republican: Aug. 1, 2002-Jan. 3, 2009

HOUSE STANDING COMMITTEES:

1st AGRICULTURE
Dates: Jan. 7, 1997-Feb. 1, 2000
Departure: Service on committee as a Democrat vacated; moved to Appropriations as an Independent Majority member

Cong.	Ranking	Terms in: House	Comm.	Date of Assignment
105th	Min-17th	1	1	Jan. 7, 1997
106th	Min-15th	2	2	Jan. 6, 1999

2nd SMALL BUSINESS
Dates: Feb. 5, 1997-June 24, 1998
Departure: Resigned committee; moved to Banking and Financial Services

Cong.	Ranking	Terms in: House	Comm.	Date of Assignment
105th	Min-16th	1	1	Feb. 5, 1997

3rd BANKING AND FINANCIAL SERVICES
Dates: June 24, 1998-Feb. 1, 2000
Departure: Service on committee as a Democrat vacated; moved to Appropriations as an Independent Majority member

Cong.	Ranking	Terms in: House	Comm.	Date of Assignment
105th	MnA-28th	1	1	June 24, 1998
106th	Min-20th	2	2	Jan. 6, 1999

4th APPROPRIATIONS
Dates: Feb. 1, 2000-Jan. 3, 2009
Departure: Left the House; lost re-election

Cong.	Ranking	Terms in: House	Comm.	Date of Assignment
106th	Ind-1st	2	1	Feb. 1, 2000
107th	Ind-1st	3	2	Jan. 31, 2001
108th	Maj-26th	4	3	Jan. 28, 2003
109th	Maj-25th	5	4	Jan. 6, 2005
110th	Min-19th	6	5	Jan. 4, 2007

4th EDUCATION AND THE WORKFORCE
Dates: Mar. 7, 2001-Jan. 3, 2003
Departure: Moved to Select Homeland Security

Cong.	Ranking	Terms in: House	Comm.	Date of Assignment
107th	Maj-27th	5	1	Mar. 7, 2001

HOUSE SELECT AND SPECIAL COMMITTEES:

1st SELECT HOMELAND SECURITY
Dates: Feb. 12, 2003-Jan. 3, 2005
Departure: Did not continue on reorganized standing committee

Cong.	Ranking	Terms in: House	Comm.	Date of Assignment
108th	Maj-17th	6	1	Feb. 12, 2003

Robert W. Goodlatte (R-Va.)

Dates: Sept. 26, 1952
House: Jan. 3, 1993-date
Serving in the 111th Congress

HOUSE STANDING COMMITTEES:

1st AGRICULTURE
Dates: Jan. 5, 1993-date
Departure: Still serving in the 111th Congress

Cong.	Ranking	Terms in: House	Comm.	Date of Assignment
103rd	Min-15th	1	1	Jan. 5, 1993
104th	Maj-10th	2	2	Jan. 4, 1995
105th	Maj-7th	3	3	Jan. 7, 1997
106th	Maj-5th	4	4	Jan. 6, 1999
107th	Maj-3rd	5	5	Jan. 6, 2001
108th	Maj-Chr	6	6	Jan. 8, 2003
109th	Maj-Chr	7	7	Jan. 6, 2005
110th	Min-RM	8	8	Jan. 4, 2007
111th	Min-2nd	9	9	Jan. 9, 2009

2nd JUDICIARY
Dates: Jan. 5, 1993-date
Departure: Still serving in the 111th Congress

Cong.	Ranking	Terms in: House	Comm.	Date of Assignment
103rd	Min-14th	1	1	Jan. 5, 1993
104th	Maj-12th	2	2	Jan. 4, 1995
105th	Maj-11th	3	3	Jan. 7, 1997
106th	Maj-9th	4	4	Jan. 6, 1999
107th	Maj-7th	5	5	Jan. 6, 2001
108th	Maj-6th	6	6	Jan. 28, 2003
109th	Maj-6th	7	7	Jan. 26, 2005
110th	Min-5th	8	8	Jan. 10, 2007
111th	Min-5th	9	9	Jan. 9, 2009

3rd STANDARDS OF OFFICIAL CONDUCT
Dates: Sep. 29, 1997-Jan. 3, 1999
Departure: Left committee; no new assignment

Cong.	Ranking	Terms in: House	Comm.	Date of Assignment
105th	Maj-4th	3	1	Sep. 29, 1997

William F. Goodling (R-Penn.)

Dates: Dec. 5, 1927
House: Jan. 3, 1975-Jan. 3, 2001
Left the House: Retired in 2000

HOUSE STANDING COMMITTEES:

1st EDUCATION AND LABOR, 94-103
ECONOMIC AND EDUCATIONAL OPPORTUNITIES, 104
EDUCATION AND THE WORKFORCE, 105-106
Dates: Jan. 28, 1975-Jan. 3, 2001
Departure: Left the House; retired

Cong.	Ranking	Terms in: House	Comm.	Date of Assignment
103rd	Min-RM	10	10	Jan. 5, 1993
104th	Maj-Chr	11	11	Jan. 4, 1995
105th	Maj-Chr	12	12	Jan. 7, 1997
106th	Maj-Chr	13	13	Jan. 6, 1999

2nd SMALL BUSINESS
Dates: Jan. 28, 1975-Jan. 3, 1977
Departure: Moved to International Relations

3rd INTERNATIONAL RELATIONS, 95
FOREIGN AFFAIRS, 96-103
INTERNATIONAL RELATIONS 104-106
1st Dates: Jan. 19, 1977-Jan. 3, 1983
1st Departure: Moved to Select Intelligence
2nd Dates: Sep. 19, 1984-Jan. 3, 1985
2nd Departure: Ceased active membership to move to Budget; later returned with continuous seniority credited
3rd Dates: Jan. 3, 1991-Jan. 3, 2001
3rd Departure: Left the House; retired

Cong.	Ranking	Terms in: House	Comm.	Date of Assignment
103rd	Min-2nd	10 *3	6	Jan. 5, 1993
104th	Maj-2nd	11 *3	7	Jan. 4, 1995
105th	Maj-2nd	12 *3	8	Jan. 7, 1997
106th	Maj-2nd	13 *3	9	Jan. 6, 1999

4th BUDGET
Dates: Jan. 30, 1985-Jan. 3, 1991
Departure: Returned to Foreign Affairs

HOUSE SELECT AND SPECIAL COMMITTEES:

1st PERMANENT SELECT INTELLIGENCE
Dates: Feb. 2, 1983-Sep. 18, 1984
Departure: Returned to Foreign Affairs

JOINT COMMITTEES:

1st JOINT DEFICIT REDUCTION (Temporary)
House Dates: Feb. 23, 1987-Sep. 29, 1987
Departure: Public Law 100-119 adjusted Gramm-Rudman-Hollings Act

Barton J. Gordon (D-Tenn.)

Dates: Jan. 24, 1949
House: Jan. 3, 1985-date
Serving in the 111th Congress

HOUSE STANDING COMMITTEES:

1st BANKING, FINANCE AND URBAN AFFAIRS
Dates: Jan. 30, 1985-Feb. 19, 1987
Departure: Moved to Rules

2nd SCIENCE AND TECHNOLOGY, 99
SCIENCE, SPACE AND TECHNOLOGY, 100
SCIENCE, 105-109
SCIENCE AND TECHNOLOGY, 110
1st Dates: Jan. 30, 1985-Feb. 19, 1987
1st Departure: Moved to Rules
2nd Dates: Feb. 28, 1996-date; seniority restored
2nd Departure: Still serving in the 111th Congress

		Terms in:		Date of
Cong.	Ranking	House	Comm.	Assignment
104th	MnR-2nd	6 *2	1	Feb. 28, 1996
105th	Min-3rd	7 *2	2	Feb. 13, 1997
106th	Min-3rd	8 *2	3	Jan. 6, 1999
107th	Min-2nd	9 *2	4	Jan. 31, 2001
108th	Min-2nd	10 *2	5	Jan. 28, 2003
109th	Min-RM	11 *2	6	Jan. 6, 2005
110th	Maj-Chr	12 *2	7	Jan. 4, 2007
111th	Maj-Chr	13 *2	8	Jan. 6, 2009

3rd RULES
Dates: Feb. 19, 1987-Jan. 3, 1995
Departure: Moved to Commerce

		Terms in:		Date of
Cong.	Ranking	House	Comm.	Assignment
103rd	Maj-8th	5	4	Jan. 5, 1993

4th BUDGET
Dates: Jan. 5, 1993-Jan. 3, 1995
Departure: Moved to Commerce

		Terms in:		Date of
Cong.	Ranking	House	Comm.	Assignment
103rd	Maj-19th	5	1	Jan. 5, 1993

5th COMMERCE, 104-106
ENERGY AND COMMERCE, 107-111
Dates: Jan. 4, 1995-date
Departure: Still serving in the 111th Congress

		Terms in:		Date of
Cong.	Ranking	House	Comm.	Assignment
104th	Min-15th	6	1	Jan. 4, 1995

105th	Min-10th	7	2	Jan. 7, 1997
106th	Min-9th	8	3	Jan. 6, 1999
107th	Min-9th	9	4	Jan. 31, 2001
108th	Min-9th	10	5	Jan. 28, 2003
109th	Min-8th	11	6	Jan. 26, 2005
110th	Maj-7th	12	7	Jan. 4, 2007
111th	Maj-6th	13	8	Jan. 7, 2009

HOUSE SELECT AND SPECIAL COMMITTEES:

1st SELECT AGING (Permanent)
Dates: Feb. 6, 1985-Jan. 3, 1993
Termination: Committee not renewed in 1993

T. Slade Gorton III (R-Wash.)

Dates: Jan. 8, 1928
Senate 1: Jan. 3, 1981-Jan. 3, 1987
Left the Senate 1: Defeated for re-election in 1986
Senate 2: Jan. 3, 1989-Jan. 3, 2001
Left the Senate 2: Defeated for re-election in 2000

SENATE STANDING COMMITTEES:

1st COMMERCE, SCIENCE AND TRANSPORTATION
1st Dates: Jan. 5, 1981-Jan. 3, 1987
1st Departure: Left the Senate; lost re-election
2nd Dates: Feb. 2, 1989-Jan. 3, 2001
2nd Departure: Left the Senate; lost re-election

		Years in:		Date of
Cong.	Ranking	Senate	Comm.	Assignment
103rd	Min-7th	11 *2	4	Jan. 7, 1993
104th	Maj-6th	13 *2	6	Jan. 4, 1995
105th	Maj-4th	15 *2	8	Jan. 9, 1997
106th	Maj-4th	17 *2	10	Jan. 7, 1999

2nd ENVIRONMENT AND PUBLIC WORKS
Dates: Jan. 5, 1981-Jan. 3, 1983
Departure: Moved to Banking, Housing and Urban Affairs

3rd BUDGET
1st Dates: Jan. 5, 1981-Jan. 3, 1987
1st Departure: Left the Senate; lost re-election
2nd Dates: Jan. 21, 1993-Jan. 3, 2001
2nd Departure: Left the Senate; lost re-election

		Years in:		Date of
Cong.	Ranking	Senate	Comm.	Assignment
103rd	Min-8th	11 *2	1	Jan. 21, 1993
104th	Maj-8th	13 *2	2	Jan. 6, 1995
105th	Maj-6th	15 *2	4	Jan. 9, 1997
106th	Maj-6th	17 *2	6	Jan. 7, 1999

4th SMALL BUSINESS
Dates: Jan. 5, 1981-Jan. 3, 1987
As select committee, Jan. 3, 1981-Mar. 25, 1981
As standing committee, Mar. 25, 1981-Jan. 3, 1987
Departure: Left the Senate; lost re-election

5th BANKING, HOUSING AND URBAN AFFAIRS
Dates: Jan. 3, 1983-Jan. 3, 1987
Departure: Left the Senate; lost re-election

6th AGRICULTURE, NUTRITION AND FORESTRY
Dates: Feb. 2, 1989-Feb. 5, 1991
Departure: Moved to Appropriations

7th ARMED SERVICES
Dates: Feb. 2, 1989-Feb. 5, 1991
Departure: Moved to Appropriations

8th APPROPRIATIONS
Dates: Feb. 5, 1991-Jan. 3, 2001
Departure: Left the Senate; lost re-election

Cong.	Ranking	Years in: Senate	Comm.	Date of Assignment
103rd	Min-10th	11	2	Jan. 7, 1993
104th	Maj-8th	13	4	Jan. 4, 1995
105th	Maj-6th	15	6	Jan. 9, 1997
106th	Maj-6th	17	8	Jan. 7, 1999

9th LABOR AND HUMAN RESOURCES
Dates: Jan. 4, 1995-Jan. 9, 1997
Departure: Moved to Energy and Natural Resources

Cong.	Ranking	Years in: Senate	Comm.	Date of Assignment
104th	Maj-9th	13	1	Jan. 4, 1995

10th ENERGY AND NATURAL RESOURCES
Dates: Jan. 9, 1997-Jan. 3, 2001
Departure: Left the Senate; lost re-election

Cong.	Ranking	Years in: Senate	Comm.	Date of Assignment
105th	Maj-10th	15	1	Jan. 9, 1997
106th	Maj-10th	17	2	Jan. 7, 1999

SENATE SELECT AND SPECIAL COMMITTEES:

1st SELECT SMALL BUSINESS
Dates: Jan. 5, 1981-Mar. 25, 1981
Departure: Continued on reorganized standing committee

2nd SELECT INDIAN AFFAIRS (Permanent), 97-99, 101-102
INDIAN AFFAIRS (Permanent), 103
Became Permanent Select Committee on Indian Affairs on June 6, 1984
1st Dates: Jan. 19, 1981-Jan. 3, 1987
1st Departure: Left the Senate; lost re-election
2nd Dates: Apr. 11, 1989-Jan. 3, 2001
2nd Departure: Left the Senate; lost re-election

Cong.	Ranking	Years in: Senate	Comm.	Date of Assignment
103rd	Min-4th	11	*2 4	Jan. 5, 1993
104th	Maj-3rd	13	*2 6	Jan. 11, 1995
105th	Maj-4th	15	*2 8	Jan. 9, 1997
106th	Maj-4th	17	*2 10	Jan. 7, 1999

3rd JUDGE ALCEE L. HASTINGS IMPEACHMENT
Dates: Mar. 16, 1989-Aug. 3, 1989
Termination: Senate Hearing 101-194, Parts 1-2A

4th SELECT INTELLIGENCE (Permanent)
Dates: Feb. 5, 1991-Jan. 6, 1995
Departure: Moved to Labor and Human Resources

Cong.	Ranking	Years in: Senate	Comm.	Date of Assignment
103rd	Min-4th	11	2	Jan. 27, 1993

5th SELECT ETHICS (Permanent)
Dates: Aug. 2, 1991-Jan. 26, 1993
Departure: Moved to Budget

Porter J. Goss (R-Fla.)

Dates: Nov. 26, 1938
House: Jan. 3, 1989-Sept. 23, 2004
Left the House: Resigned; appointed Director of Central Intelligence Agency in 2004

HOUSE STANDING COMMITTEES:

1st FOREIGN AFFAIRS
Dates: Jan. 20, 1989-Jan. 3, 1993
Departure: Moved to Rules

2nd MERCHANT MARINE AND FISHERIES
Dates: Jan. 20, 1989-Jan. 3, 1993
Departure: Moved to Rules

3rd STANDARDS OF OFFICIAL CONDUCT
Dates: Feb. 6, 1991-Jan. 3, 1997
Departure: Left committee; no new assignment

Cong.	Ranking	Terms in: House	Comm.	Date of Assignment
103rd	Min-5th	3	2	Jan. 5, 1993
104th	Maj-3rd	4	3	Jan. 20, 1995

4th RULES
Dates: Jan. 5, 1993-Sept. 23, 2004
Departure: Resigned the House; became CIA Director

Cong.	Ranking	Terms in: House	Comm.	Date of Assignment
103rd	Min-4th	4	1	Jan. 5, 1993
104th	Maj-4th	5	2	Jan. 4, 1995
105th	Maj-3rd	6	3	Jan. 7, 1997
106th	Maj-2nd	7	4	Jan. 6, 1999
107th	Maj-2nd	8	5	Jan. 3, 2001
108th	Maj-2nd	9	6	Jan. 7, 2003

HOUSE SELECT AND SPECIAL COMMITTEES:

1st PERMANENT SELECT INTELLIGENCE
Dates: Jan. 4, 1995-Sept. 23, 2004
Ch1: Resigned Chair on Aug. 10, 2004; replaced by Peter Hoekstra (R-Mich.) on Aug. 25, 2004
Departure: Resigned the House; became CIA Director

Cong.	Ranking	Terms in: House	Comm.	Date of Assignment
104th	Maj-6th	4	1	Jan. 4, 1995
105th	Maj-Chr	5	2	Jan. 27, 1997
106th	Maj-Chr	6	3	Jan. 6, 1999
107th	Maj-Chr	7	4	Jan. 6, 2001
108th	Maj-Ch1	8	5	Jan. 8, 2003

2nd SELECT ETHICS
Dates: Jan. 7, 1997-Jan. 21, 1997
Termination: House Report 105-1 filed, Jan. 17, 1997

Cong.	Ranking	Terms in: House	Comm.	Date of Assignment
105th	Maj-2nd	5	1	Jan. 7, 1997

3rd SELECT NATIONAL SECURITY CONCERNS WITH CHINA
Dates: June 22, 1998-Apr. 30, 1999
Termination: House Report 851 (105-2) filed, Jan. 3, 1999

Cong.	Ranking	Terms in: House	Comm.	Date of Assignment
105th	Maj-2nd	5	1	June 22, 1998
106th	Maj-2nd	6	2	Jan. 19, 1999

4th SELECT HOMELAND SECURITY
Dates: Feb. 12, 2003-Sept. 23, 2004
Departure: Resigned the House; became CIA Director

Cong.	Ranking	Terms in: House	Comm.	Date of Assignment
108th	Maj-14th	8	1	Feb. 12, 2003

Willis D. Gradison Jr. (R-Ohio)

Dates: Dec. 28, 1928
House: Jan. 3, 1975-Jan. 31, 1993
Left the House: Resigned; named President of the Health Insurance Association of America in 1993

HOUSE STANDING COMMITTEES:

1st BANKING, CURRENCY AND HOUSING
Dates: Jan. 28, 1975-Jan. 3, 1977
Departure: Moved to Ways and Means

2nd GOVERNMENT OPERATIONS
Dates: Jan. 28, 1975-Jan. 3, 1977
Departure: Moved to Ways and Means

3rd WAYS AND MEANS
Dates: Jan. 19, 1977-Jan. 31, 1993
Departure: Resigned the House; named President of HIAA

Cong.	Ranking	Terms in: House	Comm.	Date of Assignment
103rd	Min-3rd	10	9	Jan. 5, 1993

4th BUDGET
Dates: Jan. 6, 1983-Jan. 3, 1993
Departure: Left committee; no new assignment

JOINT COMMITTEES:

1st JOINT DEFICIT REDUCTION (Temporary)
House Dates: Feb. 23, 1987-Sep. 29, 1987
Termination: Public Law 100-119 adjusted Gramm-Rudman-Hollings Act

2nd JOINT ORGANIZATION OF CONGRESS (Ad Hoc)
House Dates: Aug. 10, 1992-Jan. 31, 1993
Departure: Resigned the House; named President of HIAA

Cong.	Ranking	Terms in: House	Comm.	Date of Assignment
103rd	Min-CoV1	10	2	Jan. 5, 1993

D. Robert Graham (D-Fla.)

Dates: Nov. 9, 1936
Senate: Jan. 6, 1987-Jan. 3, 2005
Left the Senate: Lost Democratic nomination for President in 2004; retired

SENATE STANDING COMMITTEES:

1st BANKING, HOUSING AND URBAN AFFAIRS
Dates: Jan. 6, 1987-Jan. 7, 1993
Departure: Moved to Armed Services

2nd ENVIRONMENT AND PUBLIC WORKS
Dates: Jan. 6, 1987-Jan. 3, 2005
Departure: Left the Senate; retired

Cong.	Ranking	Years in: Senate	Comm.	Date of Assignment
103rd	Maj-6th	7	7	Jan. 7, 1993
104th	Min-5th	9	8	Jan. 4, 1995
105th	Min-5th	11	11	Jan. 9, 1997
106th	Min-5th	13	13	Jan. 7, 1999
107th	Min-3rd	15	15	Jan. 25, 2001
+107th	Maj-4th	15	15	July 10, 2001
108th	Min-4th	17	17	Jan. 15, 2003

3rd VETERANS' AFFAIRS
Dates: Jan. 6, 1987-Jan. 3, 2005
Departure: Left the Senate; retired

Cong.	Ranking	Years in: Senate	Comm.	Date of Assignment
103rd	Maj-4th	7	7	Jan. 21, 1993
104th	Min-2nd	9	8	Jan. 6, 1995
105th	Min-2nd	11	11	Jan. 9, 1997
106th	Min-2nd	13	13	Jan. 7, 1999
107th	Min-2nd	15	15	Jan. 25, 2001
+107th	Maj-2nd	15	15	June 6, 2001
108th	Min-RM	17	17	Jan. 15, 2003

4th ARMED SERVICES
Dates: Jan. 7, 1993-Jan. 6, 1995
Departure: Moved to Finance

Cong.	Ranking	Years in: Senate	Comm.	Date of Assignment
103rd	Maj-9th	7	1	Jan. 7, 1993

5th FINANCE
Dates: Jan. 4, 1995-Jan. 3, 2005
Departure: Left the Senate; retired

Cong.	Ranking	Years in: Senate	Comm.	Date of Assignment
104th	Min-8th	9	1	Jan. 4, 1995
105th	Min-6th	11	3	Jan. 9, 1997
106th	Min-6th	13	5	Jan. 7, 1999
107th	Min-6th	15	7	Jan. 25, 2001
+107th	Maj-6th	15	7	June 6, 2001
108th	Min-6th	17	9	Jan. 15, 2003

6th ENERGY AND NATURAL RESOURCES
Dates: Jan. 9, 1997-Jan. 3, 2005
Departure: Left the Senate; retired

Cong.	Ranking	Years in: Senate	Comm.	Date of Assignment
105th	Min-6th	11	1	Jan. 9, 1997
106th	Min-4th	13	2	Jan. 7, 1999
107th	Min-4th	15	5	Jan. 25, 2001
+107th	Maj-4th	15	5	June 6, 2001
108th	Min-4th	17	7	Jan. 15, 2003

SENATE SELECT AND SPECIAL COMMITTEES:

1st SPECIAL AGING (Permanent)
Dates: Feb. 2, 1989-Jan. 6, 1995
Departure: Moved to Finance

Cong.	Ranking	Years in: Senate	Comm.	Date of Assignment
103rd	Maj-8th	7	4	Jan. 21, 1993

2nd SELECT INTELLIGENCE (Permanent)
Dates: Jan. 27, 1993-Jan. 14, 2003
Ch2: Replaced Richard C. Shelby (R-Ala.) on June 6, 2001, following Senate party control shift
Departure: Left committee; no new assignment

Cong.	Ranking	Years in: Senate	Comm.	Date of Assignment
103rd	Maj-6th	7	1	Jan. 27, 1993
104th	Min-4th	9	2	Jan. 6, 1995
105th	Min-4th	11	4	Jan. 9, 1997
106th	Min-3rd	13	6	Jan. 7, 1999

=107th	Maj-ChT	15	8	Jan. 3, 2001
107th	Min-VC1	15	8	Jan. 25, 2001
+107th	Maj-Ch2	15	9	June 6, 2001

Lindsey O. Graham (R-S.C.)

Dates: July 9, 1955
House: Jan. 3, 1995-Jan. 3, 2003
Left the House: Elected to U.S. Senate in 2002
Senate: Jan. 3, 2003-date
Serving in the 111th Congress

HOUSE STANDING COMMITTEES:

1st ECONOMIC AND EDUCATIONAL OPPORTUNITIES, 104
EDUCATION AND THE WORKFORCE, 105-107
Dates: Jan. 4, 1995-Jan. 3, 2003
Departure: Left the House for the Senate

		Terms in:		Date of
Cong.	**Ranking**	**House**	**Comm.**	**Assignment**
104th	Maj-19th	1	1	Jan. 4, 1995
105th	Maj-15th	2	2	Jan. 7, 1997
106th	Maj-13th	3	3	Jan. 6, 1999
107th	Maj-10th	4	4	Jan. 6, 2001

2nd SCIENCE
Dates: Jan. 4, 1995-Jan. 3, 1997
Departure: Moved to International Relations and National Security

		Terms in:		Date of
Cong.	**Ranking**	**House**	**Comm.**	**Assignment**
104th	Maj-16th	1	1	Jan. 4, 1995

3rd INTERNATIONAL RELATIONS
Dates: Jan. 7, 1997-Jan. 3, 1999
Departure: Left committee; no new assignment

		Terms in:		Date of
Cong.	**Ranking**	**House**	**Comm.**	**Assignment**
105th	Maj-23rd	2	1	Jan. 7, 1997

4th NATIONAL SECURITY, 105
ARMED SERVICES, 106-107
Dates: Jan. 7, 1997-Jan. 3, 2003
Departure: Left the House for the Senate

		Terms in:		Date of
Cong.	**Ranking**	**House**	**Comm.**	**Assignment**
105th	Maj-25th	2	1	Jan. 7, 1997
106th	Maj-24th	3	2	Jan. 6, 1999
107th	Maj-19th	4	3	Jan. 6, 2001

5th JUDICIARY
Dates: Feb. 26, 1998-Jan. 3, 2003
Departure: Left the House for the Senate

		Terms in:		Date of
Cong.	**Ranking**	**House**	**Comm.**	**Assignment**
105th	MjA-21st	2	1	Feb. 26, 1998
106th	Maj-19th	3	2	Jan. 6, 1999
107th	Maj-13th	4	3	Jan. 6, 2001

SENATE STANDING COMMITTEES:

1st ARMED SERVICES
Dates: Jan. 15, 2003-date
Departure: Still serving in the 111th Congress

		Years in:		Date of
Cong.	**Ranking**	**Senate**	**Comm.**	**Assignment**
108th	Maj-11th	1	1	Jan. 15, 2003
109th	Maj-10th	3	2	Jan. 6, 2005
110th	Min-8th	5	4	Jan. 12, 2007
111th	Min-5th	7	7	Jan. 21, 2009

2nd HEALTH, EDUCATION, LABOR AND PENSIONS
Dates: Jan. 15, 2003-Jan. 6, 2005
Departure: Moved to Budget

		Years in:		Date of
Cong.	**Ranking**	**Senate**	**Comm.**	**Assignment**
108th	Maj-10th	1	1	Jan. 15, 2003

3rd JUDICIARY
Dates: Jan. 15, 2003-date
Departure: Still serving in the 111th Congress
RM2: Replaced Arlen Specter as Ranking Member on May 5, 2009, following Specter's switch to the Democratic Party

		Years in:		Date of
Cong.	**Ranking**	**Senate**	**Comm.**	**Assignment**
108th	Maj-7th	1	1	Jan. 15, 2003
109th	Maj-7th	3	2	Jan. 6, 2005
110th	Min-6th	5	4	Jan. 12, 2007
111th	Min-6th	7	7	Jan. 21, 2009
=111th	RM2	7	7	May 5, 2009

4th VETERANS' AFFAIRS
Dates: Jan. 15, 2003-date
Departure: Still serving in the 111th Congress

		Years in:		Date of
Cong.	**Ranking**	**Senate**	**Comm.**	**Assignment**
108th	Maj-7th	1	1	Jan. 15, 2003
109th	Maj-4th	3	2	Jan. 6, 2005
110th	Min-5th	5	4	Jan. 12, 2007
111th	Min-6th	7	7	Jan. 21, 2009

5th BUDGET
Dates: Jan. 6, 2005-date
Departure: Still serving in the 111th Congress

		Years in:		Date of
Cong.	**Ranking**	**Senate**	**Comm.**	**Assignment**
109th	Maj-12th	3	1	Jan. 6, 2005
110th	Min-11th	5	3	Jan. 12, 2007
111th	Min-9th	7	5	Jan. 21, 2009

6th AGRICULTURE, NUTRITION AND FORESTRY
Dates: Jan. 12, 2007-Jan. 21, 2009
Departure: Moved to Homeland Security and Governmental Affairs and Special Aging

		Years in:		Date of
Cong.	**Ranking**	**Senate**	**Comm.**	**Assignment**
110th	Min-6th	5	1	Jan. 12, 2007

7th HOMELAND SECURITY AND GOVERNMENTAL AFFAIRS
Dates: Jan. 21, 2009-date
Departure: Still serving in the 111th Congress

		Years in:		Date of
Cong.	**Ranking**	**Senate**	**Comm.**	**Assignment**
111th	Min-6th	7	1	Jan. 21, 2009

SENATE SELECT AND SPECIAL COMMITTEES:

1st SPECIAL AGING (Permanent)
Dates: Jan. 21, 2009-date
Departure: Still serving in the 111th Congress

		Years in:		Date of
Cong.	**Ranking**	**Senate**	**Comm.**	**Assignment**
111th	Min-8th	7	1	Jan. 21, 2009

W. Phil Gramm (R-Tex.)

Dates: July 8, 1942
House 1: Jan. 3, 1979-Jan. 5, 1983
Left the House 1: Resigned chamber as a Democrat
House 2: Feb. 12, 1983-Jan. 3, 1985
Left the House 2: Elected to U.S. Senate in 1984
Senate: Jan. 3, 1985-Nov. 30, 2002
Left the Senate: Resigned in 2002
Served as a Democrat: Nov. 7, 1978-Jan. 5, 1983
Served as a Republican: Feb. 22, 1983-Nov. 30, 2002

H2: Gramm was elected to the 98th Congress by special election, Feb. 22, 1983, to fill the vacancy caused by his own resignation as a Democrat. He was seated as a Republican on Feb. 22, 1983, and reassigned to committees.

HOUSE STANDING COMMITTEES:

1st INTERSTATE AND FOREIGN COMMERCE, 96
ENERGY AND COMMERCE, 97
Dates: Jan. 24, 1979-Jan. 3, 1983
Departure: Left the House as Majority Democrat

2nd VETERANS' AFFAIRS
1st Dates: Jan. 24, 1979-Jan. 3, 1983
1st Departure: Left the House as a Majority Democrat; returned as a Minority Republican, with seniority credited
2nd Dates: Mar. 1, 1983-Jan. 3, 1985
2nd Departure: Left the House for the Senate

3rd BUDGET
1st Dates: Jan. 28, 1981-Jan. 3, 1983
1st Departure: Left the House as a Majority Democrat; returned as a Minority Republican, with seniority credited
2nd Dates: Mar. 1, 1983-Jan. 3, 1985
2nd Departure: Left the House for the Senate

SENATE STANDING COMMITTEES:

1st ARMED SERVICES
Dates: Feb. 21, 1985-Feb. 2, 1989
Departure: Moved to Appropriations and Budget

2nd BANKING, HOUSING AND URBAN AFFAIRS
Dates: Feb. 21, 1985-Nov. 30, 2002
Ch1: Replaced by Paul S. Sarbanes (D-Md.) on June 6, 2001, following party control shift and became RM2
Departure: Resigned the Senate and retired

Cong.	Ranking	Years in: Senate	Comm.	Date of Assignment
103rd	Min-2nd	9	8	Jan. 7, 1993
104th	Maj-2nd	11	10	Jan. 4, 1995
105th	Maj-2nd	13	12	Jan. 9, 1997
106th	Maj-Chr	15	14	Jan. 7, 1999
107th	Maj-Ch1	17	16	Jan. 25, 2001
+107th	Min-RM2	17	17	June 6, 2001

3rd APPROPRIATIONS
Dates: Feb. 2, 1989-Oct. 12, 1995
Departure: Left committee; moved to Finance

Cong.	Ranking	Years in: Senate	Comm.	Date of Assignment
103rd	Min-8th	9	4	Jan. 7, 1993
104th	Maj-6th	11	6	Jan. 4, 1995

4th BUDGET
Dates: Feb. 2, 1989-Nov. 30, 2002
Departure: Resigned the Senate and retired

Cong.	Ranking	Years in: Senate	Comm.	Date of Assignment
103rd	Min-4th	9	4	Jan. 21, 1993
104th	Maj-4th	11	6	Jan. 6, 1995
105th	Maj-4th	13	8	Jan. 9, 1997
106th	Maj-4th	15	10	Jan. 7, 1999
107th	Maj-4th	17	12	Jan. 25, 2001
+107th	Min-4th	17	13	June 6, 2001

5th FINANCE
Dates: Oct. 12, 1995-Nov. 30, 2002
Departure: Resigned the Senate and retired

Cong.	Ranking	Years in: Senate	Comm.	Date of Assignment
104th	MjR-1st	11	1	Oct. 12, 1995
105th	Maj-8th	13	2	Jan. 9, 1997
106th	Maj-7th	15	4	Jan. 7, 1999
107th	Maj-5th	17	6	Jan. 25, 2001
+107th	Min-5th	17	6	June 6, 2001

6th AGRICULTURE, NUTRITION AND FORESTRY
Dates: June 20, 1996-Jan. 7, 1999
Departure: Left committee; became Chair of Banking, Housing and Urban Affairs

Cong.	Ranking	Years in: Senate	Comm.	Date of Assignment
104th	MjR-2nd	12	1	June 20, 1996
105th	Maj-9th	13	1	Jan. 9, 1997

Rod Grams (R-Minn.)

Dates: Feb. 4, 1948
House: Jan. 3, 1993-Jan. 3, 1995
Left the House: Elected to U.S. Senate in 1994
Senate: Jan. 3, 1995-Jan. 3, 2001
Left the Senate: Defeated for re-election in 2000

HOUSE STANDING COMMITTEES:

1st BANKING, FINANCE AND URBAN AFFAIRS
Dates: Jan. 5, 1993-Jan. 3, 1995
Departure: Left the House for the Senate

Cong.	Ranking	Terms in: House	Comm.	Date of Assignment
103rd	Min-16th	1	1	Jan. 5, 1993

2nd SCIENCE, SPACE AND TECHNOLOGY
Dates: Jan. 5, 1993-Jan. 3, 1995
Departure: Left the House for the Senate

Cong.	Ranking	Terms in: House	Comm.	Date of Assignment
103rd	Min-17th	1	1	Jan. 5, 1993

SENATE STANDING COMMITTEES:

1st BANKING, HOUSING AND URBAN AFFAIRS
Dates: Jan. 4, 1995-Jan. 3, 2001
Departure: Left the Senate; lost re-election

Cong.	Ranking	Years in: Senate	Comm.	Date of Assignment
104th	Maj-8th	1	1	Jan. 4, 1995
105th	Maj-7th	3	3	Jan. 9, 1997
106th	Maj-5th	5	5	Jan. 7, 1999

2nd ENERGY AND NATURAL RESOURCES
Dates: Jan. 5, 1995-Jan. 7, 1999
Departure: Left committee; no new assignment

Cong.	Ranking	Years in: Senate	Comm.	Date of Assignment
104th	Maj-8th	1	1	Jan. 5, 1995
105th	Maj-8th	3	3	Jan. 9, 1997

3rd FOREIGN RELATIONS
Dates: Jan. 5, 1995-Jan. 3, 2001
Departure: Left the Senate; lost re-election

Cong.	Ranking	Years in: Senate	Comm.	Date of Assignment
104th	Maj-9th	1	1	Jan. 5, 1995
105th	Maj-8th	3	3	Jan. 9, 1997
106th	Maj-6th	5	5	Jan. 7, 1999

4th BUDGET
Dates: Mar. 29, 1996-Jan. 3, 2001
Departure: Left the Senate; lost re-election

Cong.	Ranking	Years in: Senate	Comm.	Date of Assignment
104th	MjA-13th	2	1	Mar. 29, 1996
105th	Maj-11th	3	1	Jan. 9, 1997
106th	Maj-11th	5	3	Jan. 7, 1999

SENATE SELECT AND SPECIAL COMMITTEES:

1st SPECIAL COMMITTEE TO INVESTIGATE WHITEWATER DEVELOPMENT CORPORATION AND RELATED MATTERS
Dates: July 20, 1995-June 17, 1996
Termination: Senate Report 104-280 filed

Cong.	Ranking	Years in: Senate	Comm.	Date of Assignment
104th	Maj-7th	1	1	July 20, 1995

JOINT COMMITTEES:

1st JOINT ECONOMIC
Senate Dates: Jan. 9, 1995-Jan. 3, 2001
Departure: Left the Senate; lost re-election

Cong.	Ranking	Years in: Senate	Comm.	Date of Assignment
104th	Maj-6th	1	1	Jan. 9, 1995
105th	Maj-4th	3	3	Jan. 9, 1997
106th	Maj-4th	5	4	Jan. 7, 1999

Frederick L. Grandy (R-Iowa)

Dates: June 29, 1948
House: Jan. 3, 1987-Jan. 3, 1995
Left the House: Lost nomination for Governor in 1994

HOUSE STANDING COMMITTEES:

1st AGRICULTURE
Dates: Jan. 21, 1987-Jan. 3, 1991
Departure: Moved to Ways and Means

2nd EDUCATION AND LABOR
Dates: Jan. 21, 1987-Jan. 3, 1991
Departure: Moved to Ways and Means

3rd STANDARDS OF OFFICIAL CONDUCT
Dates: July 18, 1989-Jan. 3, 1995
Departure: Lost nomination for Governor

Cong.	Ranking	Terms in: House	Comm.	Date of Assignment
103rd	Min-RM	4	3	Jan. 5, 1993

4th WAYS AND MEANS
Dates: Jan. 3, 1991-Jan. 3, 1995
Departure: Lost nomination for Governor

Cong.	Ranking	Terms in: House	Comm.	Date of Assignment
103rd	Min-9th	4	2	Jan. 5, 1993

HOUSE SELECT AND SPECIAL COMMITTEES:

1st SELECT CHILDREN, YOUTH AND FAMILIES (Temporary)
Dates: Feb. 2, 1987-Aug. 4, 1989
Departure: Moved to Standards of Official Conduct

Kay Granger (R-Tex.)

Dates: Jan. 18, 1943
House: Jan. 3, 1997-date
Serving in the 111th Congress

HOUSE STANDING COMMITTEES:

1st BUDGET
1st Dates: Jan. 7, 1997-Jan. 3, 1999
1st Departure: Moved to Appropriations
2nd Dates: Jan. 6, 2001-Jan. 3, 2003
2nd Departure: Moved to Select Homeland Security

Cong.	Ranking	Terms in: House	Comm.	Date of Assignment
105th	Maj-22nd	1 *1	1	Jan. 7, 1997
107th	Maj-24th	3 *2	1	Jan. 6, 2001

2nd HOUSE OVERSIGHT
Dates: Jan. 7, 1997-Jan. 3, 1999
Departure: Moved to Appropriations

Cong.	Ranking	Terms in: House	Comm.	Date of Assignment
105th	Maj-5th	1	1	Jan. 7, 1997

3rd TRANSPORTATION AND INFRASTRUCTURE
Dates: Jan. 7, 1997-Jan. 3, 1999
Departure: Moved to Appropriations

Cong.	Ranking	Terms in: House	Comm.	Date of Assignment
105th	Maj-36th	1	1	Jan. 7, 1997

4th NATIONAL SECURITY
Dates: Feb. 11, 1998-Jan. 3, 1999
Departure: Moved to Appropriations

Cong.	Ranking	Terms in: House	Comm.	Date of Assignment
105th	MjR-1st	1	1	Feb. 11, 1998

5th APPROPRIATIONS
Dates: Jan. 6, 1999-date
Departure: Still serving in the 111th Congress

Cong.	Ranking	Terms in: House	Comm.	Date of Assignment
106th	Maj-33rd	2	1	Jan. 6, 1999

Cong.	Ranking			Date
107th	Maj-29th	3	2	Jan. 6, 2001
108th	Maj-24th	4	3	Jan. 28, 2003
109th	Maj-23rd	5	4	Jan. 6, 2005
110th	Min-17th	6	5	Jan. 4, 2007
111th	Min-12th	7	6	Jan. 9, 2009

HOUSE SELECT AND SPECIAL COMMITTEES:

1st SELECT HOMELAND SECURITY
Dates: Feb. 12, 2003-Jan. 3, 2005
Departure: Did not continue on reorganized standing committee

		Terms in:		Date of
Cong.	Ranking	House	Comm.	Assignment
108th	Maj-25th	4	1	Feb. 12, 2003

2nd SELECT BIPARTISAN COMMITTEE TO INVESTIGATE THE PREPARATION FOR AND RESPONSE TO HURRICANE KATRINA
Dates: Sep. 21, 2005-Feb. 15, 2006
Departure: House Report 377 (109-2) filed

		Terms in:		Date of
Cong.	Ranking	House	Comm.	Assignment
109th	Maj-9th	5	1	Sep. 21, 2005

JOINT COMMITTEES:

1st JOINT PRINTING
House Dates: Mar. 6, 1997-Jan. 3, 1999
Departure: Moved to Appropriations

		Terms in:		Date of
Cong.	Ranking	House	Comm.	Assignment
105th	Maj-3rd	1	1	Mar. 6, 1997

Charles E. Grassley (R-Iowa)

Dates: Sep. 17, 1933
House: Jan. 3, 1975-Jan. 3, 1981
Left the House: Elected to U.S. Senate in 1980
Senate: Jan. 3, 1981-date
Serving in the 111th Congress

HOUSE STANDING COMMITTEES:

1st AGRICULTURE
Dates: Jan. 28, 1975-Jan. 3, 1981
Departure: Left the House for the Senate

2nd BANKING, CURRENCY AND HOUSING, 94
BANKING, FINANCE AND URBAN AFFAIRS, 95
Dates: Jan. 28, 1975-Jan. 3, 1979
Departure: Left committee; no new assignment

HOUSE SELECT AND SPECIAL COMMITTEES:

1st SELECT AGING (Permanent)
Dates: Feb. 6, 1975-Jan. 3, 1981
Departure: Left the House for the Senate

SENATE STANDING COMMITTEES:

1st FINANCE
1st Dates: Jan. 5, 1981-Jan. 6, 1987

1st Departure: Moved to Appropriations
2nd Dates: Feb. 5, 1991-date
Ch1: Replaced by Max S. Baucus (D-Mont.) on June 6, 2001, following party control shift and became RM2.
2nd Departure: Still serving in the 111th Congress

		Years in:		Date of
Cong.	Ranking	Senate	Comm.	Assignment
103rd	Min-7th	13	*2 2	Jan. 7, 1993
104th	Maj-5th	15	*2 4	Jan. 4, 1995
105th	Maj-3rd	17	*2 6	Jan. 9, 1997
106th	Maj-3rd	19	*2 8	Jan. 7, 1999
107th	Maj-Ch1	21	*2 10	Jan. 25, 2001
+107th	Min-RM2	21	*2 11	June 6, 2001
108th	Maj-Chr	23	*2 12	Jan. 15, 2003
109th	Maj-Chr	25	*2 14	Jan. 6, 2005
110th	Min-RM	27	*2 16	Jan. 12, 2007
111th	Min-RM	29	*2 18	Jan. 21, 2009

2nd JUDICIARY
Dates: Jan. 5, 1981-date
Departure: Still serving in the 111th Congress

		Years in:		Date of
Cong.	Ranking	Senate	Comm.	Assignment
103rd	Min-4th	13	13	Jan. 7, 1993
104th	Maj-4th	15	14	Jan. 4, 1995
105th	Maj-3rd	17	17	Jan. 9, 1997
106th	Maj-3rd	19	19	Jan. 7, 1999
107th	Maj-3rd	21	21	Jan. 25, 2001
+107th	Min-3rd	21	21	June 6, 2001
108th	Maj-2nd	23	23	Jan. 15, 2003
109th	Maj-3rd	25	25	Jan. 6, 2005
110th	Min-3rd	27	27	Jan. 12, 2007
111th	Min-3rd	29	29	Jan. 21, 2009

3rd BUDGET
Dates: Jan. 5, 1981-date
Departure: Still serving in the 111th Congress

		Years in:		Date of
Cong.	Ranking	Senate	Comm.	Assignment
103rd	Min-2nd	13	13	Jan. 21, 1993
104th	Maj-2nd	15	15	Jan. 6, 1995
105th	Maj-2nd	17	17	Jan. 9, 1997
106th	Maj-2nd	19	19	Jan. 7, 1999
107th	Maj-2nd	21	21	Jan. 25, 2001
+107th	Min-2nd	21	21	June 6, 2001
108th	Maj-3rd	23	23	Jan. 15, 2003
109th	Maj-3rd	25	25	Jan. 6, 2005
110th	Min-3rd	27	27	Jan. 12, 2007
111th	Min-2nd	29	29	Jan. 21, 2009

4th LABOR AND HUMAN RESOURCES
Dates: Jan. 3, 1983-Jan. 6, 1987
Departure: Moved to Appropriations

5th APPROPRIATIONS
Dates: Jan. 6, 1987-Feb. 5, 1991
Departure: Moved to Agriculture, Nutrition and Forestry and returned to Finance

6th SMALL BUSINESS
Dates: Feb. 2, 1989-Mar. 19, 1991
Departure: Moved to Agriculture, Nutrition and Forestry and returned to Finance

7th AGRICULTURE, NUTRITION AND FORESTRY
1st Dates: Feb. 5, 1991-Jan. 5, 1995

1st Departure: Moved to Governmental Affairs
2nd Dates: Oct. 12, 1995-Jan. 25, 2001
2nd Departure: Left committee; became Chair of Finance
3rd Dates: Jan. 14, 2003-date
3rd Departure: Still serving in the 111th Congress

		Years in:		Date of
Cong.	Ranking	Senate	Comm.	Assignment
103rd	Min-8th	13 *1	2	Jan. 7, 1993
104th	MjR-1st	15 *2	1	Oct. 12, 1995
105th	Maj-8th	17 *2	2	Jan. 9, 1997
106th	Maj-8th	19 *2	4	Jan. 7, 1999
108th	Maj-11th	23 *3	1	Jan. 14, 2003
109th	Maj-11th	25 *3	2	Jan. 6, 2005
110th	Min-10th	27 *3	4	Jan. 12, 2007
111th	Min-7th	29 *3	7	Jan. 21, 2009

8th GOVERNMENTAL AFFAIRS
Dates: Jan. 5, 1995-Oct. 12, 1995
Departure: Left committee; returned to Agriculture, Nutrition and Forestry

		Years in:		Date of
Cong.	Ranking	Senate	Comm.	Assignment
104th	Maj-6th	15	1	Jan. 5, 1995

SENATE SELECT AND SPECIAL COMMITTEES:

1st SPECIAL AGING (Permanent)
Dates: Jan. 5, 1981-Jan. 25, 2001
Departure: Left committee; became Chair of Finance

		Years in:		Date of
Cong.	Ranking	Senate	Comm.	Assignment
103rd	Min-3rd	13	13	Jan. 21, 1993
104th	Maj-3rd	15	14	Jan. 4, 1995
105th	Maj-Chr	17	17	Jan. 9, 1997
106th	Maj-Chr	19	19	Jan. 7, 1999

2nd SELECT POW-MIA AFFAIRS
Dates: Aug. 2, 1991-Feb. 3, 1993
Termination: Senate Report 1 (103-1) filed

JOINT COMMITTEES:

1st JOINT DEFICIT REDUCTION (Temporary)
Senate Dates: Jan. 6, 1987-Sep. 29, 1987
Termination: Public Law 100-119 adjusted Gramm-Rudman-Hollings Act

2nd JOINT TAXATION
Senate Dates: Jan. 28, 1997-date
Departure: Still serving in the 111th Congress

		Years in:		Date of
Cong.	Ranking	Senate	Comm.	Assignment
105th	Maj-3rd	17	1	Jan. 28, 1997
106th	Maj-3rd	19	3	Continued
107th	Maj-VC1	21	5	Feb. 28, 2001
+107th	Min-1st	21	5	June 6, 2001
108th	Maj-VcC	23	7	Feb. 24, 2003
109th	Maj-VcC	25	9	Jan. 25, 2005
110th	Min-1st	27	11	Jan. 18, 2007
111th	Min-1st	29	13	Feb. 25, 2009

Samuel B. Graves (R-Mo.)

Dates: Nov. 7, 1963
House: Jan. 3, 2001-date
Serving in the 111th Congress

HOUSE STANDING COMMITTEES:

1st AGRICULTURE
Dates: Jan. 6, 2001-date
Departure: Still serving in the 111th Congress

		Terms in:		Date of
Cong.	Ranking	House	Comm.	Assignment
107th	Maj-25th	1	1	Jan. 6, 2001
108th	Maj-18th	2	2	Jan. 28, 2003
109th	Maj-13th	3	3	Jan. 26, 2005
110th	Min-7th	4	4	Jan. 10, 2007
111th	Min-5th	5	5	Jan. 9, 2009

2nd SMALL BUSINESS
Dates: Jan. 6, 2001-date
Departure: Still serving in the 111th Congress

		Terms in:		Date of
Cong.	Ranking	House	Comm.	Assignment
107th	Maj-15th	1	1	Jan. 6, 2001
108th	Maj-8th	2	2	Jan. 28, 2003
109th	Maj-5th	3	3	Jan. 26, 2005
110th	Min-3rd	4	4	Jan. 10, 2007
111th	Min-RM	5	5	Jan. 6, 2009

3rd TRANSPORTATION AND INFRASTRUCTURE
Dates: Jan. 6, 2001-date
Departure: Still serving in the 111th Congress

		Terms in:		Date of
Cong.	Ranking	House	Comm.	Assignment
107th	Maj-38th	1	1	Jan. 6, 2001
108th	Maj-29th	2	2	Jan. 28, 2003
109th	Maj-23rd	3	3	Jan. 26, 2005
110th	Min-17th	4	4	Jan. 10 2007
111th	Min-13th	5	5	Jan. 9, 2009

Alan Grayson (D-Fla.)

Dates: March 13, 1958
House: Jan. 3, 2009-date
Serving in the 111th Congress

HOUSE STANDING COMMITTEES:

1st FINANCIAL SERVICES
Dates: Jan. 7, 2009-date
Departure: Still serving in the 111th Congress

		Terms in:		Date of
Cong.	Ranking	House	Comm.	Assignment
111th	Maj-39th	1	1	Jan. 7, 2009

2nd SCIENCE AND TECHNOLOGY
Dates: Jan. 21, 2009-date
Departure: Still serving in the 111th Congress

		Terms in:		Date of
Cong.	Ranking	House	Comm.	Assignment
111th	Maj-24th	1	1	Jan. 21, 2009

Al Green (D-Tex.)

Dates: Sept. 1, 1947
House: Jan 3, 2005-date
Serving in the 111th Congress

HOUSE STANDING COMMITTEES:

1st FINANCIAL SERVICES
Dates: Jan. 26, 2005-date
Departure: Still serving in the 111th Congress

Cong.	Ranking	Terms in: House	Comm.	Date of Assignment
109th	Min-29th	1	1	Jan. 26, 2005
110th	Maj-21st	2	2	Jan. 12, 2007
111th	Maj-20th	3	3	Jan. 7, 2009

2nd SCIENCE
Dates: Feb. 2, 2005-Jan. 3, 2007
Departure: Moved to Homeland Security

Cong.	Ranking	Terms in: House	Comm.	Date of Assignment
109th	Min-19th	1	1	Feb. 2, 2005

3rd HOMELAND SECURITY
Dates: Jan. 12, 2007-date
Departure: Still serving in the 111th Congress

Cong.	Ranking	Terms in: House	Comm.	Date of Assignment
110th	Maj-17th	2	1	Jan. 12, 2007
111th	Maj-16th	3	2	Jan. 28, 2009

107th	Min-17th	5	3	Jan. 31, 2001
108th	Min-16th	6	4	Jan. 28, 2003
109th	Min-14th	7	5	Jan. 26, 2005
110th	Maj-13th	8	6	Jan. 4, 2007
111th	Maj-11th	9	7	Jan. 7, 2009

5th STANDARDS OF OFFICIAL CONDUCT
Dates: Aug. 1, 2001-Jan. 3, 2009
Ch2: Replaced Stephanie Tubbs Jones (D-Ohio) on Sep. 9, 2008
Departure: Left committee; no new assignment

Cong.	Ranking	Terms in: House	Comm.	Date of Assignment
107th	MnR-1st	5	1	Aug. 1, 2001
108th	Min-3rd	6	2	Mar. 6, 2003
109th	Min-3rd	7	3	Feb. 9, 2005
110th	Maj-2nd	8	4	Feb. 8, 2007
=110th	Maj-Ch2	8	4	Sep. 9, 2008

6th FOREIGN AFFAIRS
Dates: Apr. 19, 2007-date
Departure: Still serving in the 111th Congress

Cong.	Ranking	Terms in: House	Comm.	Date of Assignment
110th	Maj-15th	8	1	Apr. 19, 2007
111th	Maj-17th	9	2	Jan. 21, 2009

R. Eugene (Gene) Green (D-Tex.)

Dates: Oct. 17, 1947
House: Jan. 3, 1993-date
Serving in the 111th Congress

HOUSE STANDING COMMITTEES:

1st EDUCATION AND LABOR
Dates: Jan. 5, 1993-Jan. 3, 1997
Departure: Moved to Commerce

Cong.	Ranking	Terms in: House	Comm.	Date of Assignment
103rd	Maj-19th	1	1	Jan. 5, 1993
104th	Min-16th	2	2	Jan. 4, 1995

2nd GOVERNMENT REFORM AND OVERSIGHT
Dates: Jan. 5, 1993-Jan. 3, 1997
Departure: Moved to Commerce

Cong.	Ranking	Terms in: House	Comm.	Date of Assignment
103rd	Maj-24th	1	1	Jan. 5, 1993
104th	Min-19th	2	2	Jan. 9, 1995

3rd MERCHANT MARINE AND FISHERIES
Dates: Jan. 5, 1993-Jan. 3, 1995
Departure: Committee abolished; no new assignment

Cong.	Ranking	Terms in: House	Comm.	Date of Assignment
103rd	Maj-18th	1	1	Jan. 5, 1993

4th COMMERCE, 105-106
ENERGY AND COMMERCE, 107-111
Dates: Jan. 7, 1997-date
Departure: Still serving in the 111th Congress

Cong.	Ranking	Terms in: House	Comm.	Date of Assignment
105th	Min-20th	3	1	Jan. 7, 1997
106th	Min-18th	4	2	Jan. 6, 1999

Mark Green (R-Wisc.)

Dates: June 1, 1960
House: Jan. 3, 1999-Jan. 3, 2007
Left the House: Lost election for Governor in 2006

HOUSE STANDING COMMITTEES:

1st BANKING AND FINANCIAL SERVICES
Dates: Jan. 6, 1999-Jan. 3, 2005
Departure: Left committee; no new assignment

Cong.	Ranking	Terms in: House	Comm.	Date of Assignment
106th	Maj-31st	1	1	Jan. 6, 1999
107th	Maj-25th	2	2	Jan. 6, 2001
108th	Maj-20th	3	3	Jan. 28, 2003

2nd BUDGET
Dates: Jan. 6, 1999-Jan. 3, 2001
Departure: Moved to Judiciary

Cong.	Ranking	Terms in: House	Comm.	Date of Assignment
106th	Maj-20th	1	1	Jan. 6, 1999

3rd SCIENCE
Dates: Jan. 6, 1999-Jan. 3, 2001
Departure: Moved to Judiciary

Cong.	Ranking	Terms in: House	Comm.	Date of Assignment
106th	Maj-20th	1	1	Jan. 6, 1999

4th JUDICIARY
Dates: Jan. 6, 2001-Jan. 3, 2007
Departure: Left the House; lost election for Governor

Cong.	Ranking	Terms in: House	Comm.	Date of Assignment
107th	Maj-17th	2	1	Jan. 6, 2001
108th	Maj-12th	3	2	Jan. 28, 2003
109th	Maj-14th	4	3	Jan. 26, 2005

5th INTERNATIONAL RELATIONS
Dates: Feb. 26, 2002-Jan. 3, 2007
Departure: Left the House; lost election for Governor

Cong.	Ranking	Terms in: House	Comm.	Date of Assignment
107th	MjR-1st	2	1	Feb. 26, 2002
108th	Maj-21st	3	2	Jan. 28, 2003
109th	Maj-17th	4	3	Jan. 26, 2005

Enid Greene (R-Utah)

Elected as Enid Greene Waldholtz to the 104th Congress
Dates: June 5, 1958
House: Jan. 3, 1995-Jan. 3, 1997
Left the House: Retired in 1996

HOUSE STANDING COMMITTEES:

1st RULES
Dates: Jan. 4, 1995-Jan. 3, 1997
Departure: Left the the House; retired

Cong.	Ranking	Terms in: House	Comm.	Date of Assignment
104th	Maj-9th	1	1	Jan. 4, 1995

James C. Greenwood (R-Penn.)

Dates: May 4, 1951
House: Jan. 3, 1993-Jan. 3, 2005
Left the House: Retired in 2004

HOUSE STANDING COMMITTEES:

1st ENERGY AND COMMERCE, 103
COMMERCE, 104-106
ENERGY AND COMMERCE, 107
Dates: Jan. 5, 1993-Jan. 3, 2005
Departure: Left the House; retired

Cong.	Ranking	Terms in: House	Comm.	Date of Assignment
103rd	Min-16th	1	1	Jan. 5, 1993
104th	Maj-15th	2	2	Jan. 4, 1995
105th	Maj-13th	3	3	Jan. 7, 1997
106th	Maj-9th	4	4	Jan. 6, 1999
107th	Maj-7th	5	5	Jan. 6, 2001
108th	Maj-7th	6	6	Jan. 28, 2003

2nd ECONOMIC AND EDUCATIONAL OPPORTUNITIES, 104
EDUCATION AND THE WORKFORCE, 105-108
Dates: Jan. 4, 1995-Jan. 3, 2005
Departure: Left the House; retired

Cong.	Ranking	Terms in: House	Comm.	Date of Assignment
104th	Maj-15th	2	1	Jan. 4, 1995
105th	Maj-12th	3	2	Jan. 7, 1997
106th	Maj-12th	4	3	Jan. 6, 1999
107th	Maj-9th	5	4	Jan. 6, 2001
108th	Maj-8th	6	5	Jan. 28, 2003

Judd A. Gregg (R-N.H.)

Dates: Feb. 14, 1947
House: Jan. 3, 1981-Jan. 3, 1989
Left the House: Elected Governor in 1988
Senate: Jan. 3, 1993-date
Serving in the 111th Congress

HOUSE STANDING COMMITTEES:

1st GOVERNMENT OPERATIONS
Dates: Jan. 28, 1981-Jan. 3, 1985
Departure: Moved to Ways and Means

2nd SCIENCE AND TECHNOLOGY
Dates: Jan. 28, 1981-Jan. 3, 1985
Departure: Moved to Ways and Means

3rd WAYS AND MEANS
Dates: Jan. 30, 1985-Jan. 3, 1989
Departure: Left the House; elected Governor

HOUSE SELECT AND SPECIAL COMMITTEES:

1st SELECT AGING (Permanent)
Dates: Feb. 5, 1981-Jan. 3, 1985
Departure: Moved to Ways and Means

SENATE STANDING COMMITTEES:

1st COMMERCE, SCIENCE AND TRANSPORTATION
Dates: Jan. 7, 1993-July 1, 1993
Departure: Left committee; moved to Foreign Relations

Cong.	Ranking	Years in: Senate	Comm.	Date of Assignment
103rd	Min-9th	1	1	Jan. 7, 1993

2nd LABOR AND HUMAN RESOURCES renamed Jan. 21, 1999
HEALTH, EDUCATION, LABOR AND PENSIONS
Dates: Jan. 7, 1993-date
RM2: Replaced James M. Jeffords (Ind-Vt.) as senior
Republican on July 10, 2001
Departure: Still serving in the 111th Congress

Cong.	Ranking	Years in: Senate	Comm.	Date of Assignment
103rd	Min-4th	1	1	Jan. 7, 1993
104th	Maj-4th	3	2	Jan. 4, 1995
105th	Maj-3rd	5	5	Jan. 9, 1997
106th	Maj-2nd	7	7	Jan. 7, 1999
107th	Maj-2nd	9	9	Jan. 25, 2001
+107th	Min-RM2	9	9	July 10, 2001
108th	Maj-Chr	11	11	Jan. 15, 2003
109th	Maj-2nd	13	12	Jan. 6, 2005
110th	Min-2nd	15	15	Jan. 12, 2007
111th	Min-2nd	17	17	Jan. 21, 2009

3rd BUDGET
Dates: Jan. 21, 1993-date
Departure: Still serving in the 111th Congress

Cong.	Ranking	Years in: Senate	Comm.	Date of Assignment
103rd	Min-9th	1	1	Jan. 21, 1993
104th	Maj-9th	3	2	Jan. 6, 1995
105th	Maj-7th	5	4	Jan. 9, 1997

Cong.	Ranking	Senate	Comm.	Date of Assignment
106th	Maj-7th	7	6	Jan. 14, 1999
107th	Maj-6th	9	9	Jan. 25, 2001
+107th	Min-6th	9	9	June 6, 2001
108th	Maj-4th	11	10	Jan. 15, 2003
109th	Maj-Chr	13	12	Jan. 6, 2005
110th	Min-RM	15	14	Jan. 12, 2007
111th	Min-RM	17	17	Jan. 21, 2009

4th FOREIGN RELATIONS

Dates: July 1, 1993-Jan. 6, 1995
Departure: Moved to Appropriations

Cong.	Ranking	Years in: Senate	Comm.	Date of Assignment
103rd	MnA-9th	1	1	July 1, 1993

5th APPROPRIATIONS

Dates: Jan. 4, 1995-date
Departure: Still serving in the 111th Congress

Cong.	Ranking	Years in: Senate	Comm.	Date of Assignment
104th	Maj-14th	3	1	Jan. 4, 1995
105th	Maj-10th	5	3	Jan. 9, 1997
106th	Maj-10th	7	5	Jan. 7, 1999
107th	Maj-9th	9	7	Jan. 25, 2001
+107th	Min-9th	9	7	June 6, 2001
108th	Maj-9th	11	9	Jan. 15, 2003
109th	Maj-9th	13	11	Jan. 6, 2005
110th	Min-8th	15	13	Jan. 12, 2007
111th	Min-6th	17	15	Jan. 21, 2009

6th GOVERNMENTAL AFFAIRS

Dates: Jan. 7, 1999-July 10, 2001
Departure: Left committee; became Ranking Member on Health, Education, Labor and Pensions

Cong.	Ranking	Years in: Senate	Comm.	Date of Assignment
106th	Maj-9th	7	1	Jan. 7, 1999
107th	Maj-7th	9	3	Jan. 25, 2001
+107th	Min-7th	9	3	June 6, 2001

7th BANKING, HOUSING AND URBAN AFFAIRS

Dates: Sept. 22, 2009-date
Departure: Still serving in the 111th Congress

Cong.	Ranking	Years in: Senate	Comm.	Date of Assignment
111th	MnR-1st	17	1	Sept. 22, 2009

Parker Griffith (R-Ala.)

Dates: Aug. 6, 1942
House: Jan. 3, 2009-date
Serving in the 111th Congress
Served as a Democrat: Jan. 3, 2009-Dec. 22, 2009
Served as a Republican: Dec. 22, 2009-date

HOUSE STANDING COMMITTEES:

1st TRANSPORTATION AND INFRASTRUCTURE

Dates: Jan. 7, 2009-Dec. 22, 2009
Departure: Service on committee as a majority Democrat vacated; moved to Energy and Commerce as a Minority replacement

Cong.	Ranking	Terms in: House	Comm.	Date of Assignment
111th	Maj-41st	1	1	Jan. 7, 2009

2nd SCIENCE AND TECHNOLOGY

Dates: Jan. 21, 2009-Dec. 22, 2009
Departure: Service on committee as a majority Democrat vacated; moved to Energy and Commerce as a Minority replacement

Cong.	Ranking	Terms in: House	Comm.	Date of Assignment
111th	Maj-14th	1	1	Jan. 21, 2009

3rd SMALL BUSINESS

Dates: Jan. 21, 2009-Dec. 22, 2009
Departure: Service on committee as a majority Democrat vacated; moved to Energy and Commerce as a Minority replacement

Cong.	Ranking	Terms in: House	Comm.	Date of Assignment
111th	Maj-16th	1	1	Jan. 21, 2009

4th ENERGY AND COMMERCE

Dates: Feb. 23, 2010-date
Departure: Still serving in the 111th Congress

Cong.	Ranking	Terms in: House	Comm.	Date of Assignment
111th	MnR-1st	1	1	Feb. 23, 2010

Raúl M. Grijalva (D-Ariz.)

Dates: Feb. 19, 1948
House: Jan. 3, 2003-date
Serving in the 111th Congress

HOUSE STANDING COMMITTEES:

1st EDUCATION AND THE WORKFORCE, 108-109
EDUCATION AND LABOR, 110-111

Dates: Feb. 5, 2003-date
Departure: Still serving in the 111th Congress

Cong.	Ranking	Terms in: House	Comm.	Date of Assignment
108th	Min-19th	1	1	Feb. 5, 2003
109th	Min-18th	2	2	Jan. 26, 2005
110th	Maj-15th	3	3	Jan. 10, 2007
111th	Maj-14th	4	4	Jan. 21, 2009

2nd RESOURCES, 108-109
NATURAL RESOURCES, 110-111

Dates: Feb. 5, 2003-date
Departure: Still serving in the 111th Congress

Cong.	Ranking	Terms in: House	Comm.	Date of Assignment
108th	Min-20th	1	1	Feb. 5, 2003
109th	Min-11th	2	2	Jan. 26, 2005
110th	Maj-10th	3	3	Jan. 18, 2007
111th	Maj-8th	4	4	Jan. 21, 2009

3rd SMALL BUSINESS

Dates: Feb. 2, 2005-Jan. 3, 2009
Departure: Left committee; no new assignment

Cong.	Ranking	Terms in: House	Comm.	Date of Assignment
109th	Min-10th	2	1	Feb. 2, 2005
110th	Maj-7th	3	2	Jan. 23, 2007

Felix J. Grucci Jr. (R-N.Y.)

Dates: Nov. 25, 1951
House: Jan. 3, 2001-Jan. 3, 2003
Left the House: Defeated for re-election in 2002

HOUSE STANDING COMMITTEES:

1st FINANCIAL SERVICES
Dates: Jan. 6, 2001-Jan. 3, 2003
Departure: Left the House; lost re-election

Cong.	Ranking	Terms in: House	Comm.	Date of Assignment
107th	Maj-32nd	1	1	Jan. 6, 2001

2nd SCIENCE
Dates: Jan. 6, 2001-Jan. 3, 2003
Departure: Left the House; lost re-election

Cong.	Ranking	Terms in: House	Comm.	Date of Assignment
107th	Maj-23rd	1	1	Jan. 6, 2001

3rd SMALL BUSINESS
Dates: Jan. 6, 2001-Jan. 3, 2003
Departure: Left the House; lost re-election

Cong.	Ranking	Terms in: House	Comm.	Date of Assignment
107th	Maj-17th	1	1	Jan. 6, 2001

Steven C. Gunderson (R-Wisc.)

Dates: May 10, 1951
House: Jan. 3, 1981-Jan. 3, 1997
Left the House: Retired in 1996

HOUSE STANDING COMMITTEES:

1st AGRICULTURE
Dates: Jan. 28, 1981-Jan. 3, 1997
Departure: Left the House; retired

Cong.	Ranking	Terms in: House	Comm.	Date of Assignment
103rd	Min-3rd	7	7	Jan. 5, 1993
104th	Maj-3rd	8	8	Jan. 4, 1995

2nd EDUCATION AND LABOR, 97-103
ECONOMIC AND EDUCATIONAL OPPORTUNITIES, 104
Dates: June 9, 1982-Jan. 3, 1997
Departure: Left the House; retired

Cong.	Ranking	Terms in: House	Comm.	Date of Assignment
103rd	Min-4th	7	7	Jan. 5, 1993
104th	Maj-4th	8	8	Jan. 4, 1995

Brett Guthrie (R-Ky.)

Dates: Feb. 18, 1964
House: Jan. 3, 2009-date
Serving in the 111th Congress

HOUSE STANDING COMMITTEES:

1st EDUCATION AND LABOR
Dates: Jan. 9, 2009-date
Departure: Still serving in the 111th Congress

Cong.	Ranking	Terms in: House	Comm.	Date of Assignment
111th	Min-15th	1	1	Jan. 9, 2009

2nd TRANSPORTATION AND INFRASTRUCTURE
Dates: Jan. 22, 2009-date
Departure: Still serving in the 111th Congress

Cong.	Ranking	Terms in: House	Comm.	Date of Assignment
111th	Min-29th	1	1	Jan. 22, 2009

Luis V. Gutierrez (D-Ill.)

Dates: Dec. 10, 1953
House: Jan. 3, 1993-date
Serving in the 111th Congress

HOUSE STANDING COMMITTEES:

1st BANKING, FINANCE AND URBAN AFFAIRS, 103
BANKING AND FINANCIAL SERVICES, 104-106
FINANCIAL SERVICES, 107-111
Dates: Jan. 5, 1993-date
Departure: Still serving in the 111th Congress

Cong.	Ranking	Terms in: House	Comm.	Date of Assignment
103rd	Maj-18th	1	1	Jan. 5, 1993
104th	Min-13th	2	2	Jan. 4, 1995
105th	Min-11th	3	3	Jan. 7, 1997
106th	Min-7th	4	4	Jan. 6, 1999
107th	Min-6th	5	5	Jan. 31, 2001
108th	Min-6th	6	6	Jan. 28, 2003
109th	Min-6th	7	7	Jan. 26, 2005
110th	Maj-5th	8	8	Jan. 12, 2007
111th	Maj-5th	9	9	Jan. 7, 2009

2nd VETERANS' AFFAIRS
Dates: Jan. 5, 1993-Jan. 3, 2007
Departure: Moved to Judiciary

Cong.	Ranking	Terms in: House	Comm.	Date of Assignment
103rd	Maj-16th	1	1	Jan. 5, 1993
104th	Min-9th	2	2	Jan. 4, 1995
105th	Min-4th	3	3	Feb. 6, 1997
106th	Min-3rd	4	4	Jan. 6, 1999
107th	Min-3rd	5	5	Jan. 31, 2001
108th	Min-3rd	6	6	Jan. 28, 2003
109th	Min-3rd	7	7	Jan. 26, 2005

3rd FOREIGN AFFAIRS
Dates: Nov. 10, 1993-Jan. 3, 1995
Departure: Left committee; no new assignment

Cong.	Ranking	Terms in: House	Comm.	Date of Assignment
103rd	Maj-27th	1	1	Nov. 10, 1993

4th JUDICIARY
Dates: Jan. 18, 2007-date
Departure: Still serving in the 111th Congress

Cong.	Ranking	Terms in: House	Comm.	Date of Assignment
110th	Maj-16th	8	1	Jan. 18, 2007
111th	Maj-16th	9	2	Jan. 7, 2009

Gilbert W. Gutknecht (R-Minn.)

Dates: March 20, 1951
House: Jan. 3, 1995-Jan. 3, 2007
Left the House: Defeated for re-election in 2006

HOUSE STANDING COMMITTEES:

1st GOVERNMENT REFORM AND OVERSIGHT, 104
GOVERNMENT REFORM, 109
1st Dates: Jan. 4, 1995-Jan. 3, 1997
1st Departure: Moved to Budget
2nd Dates: Jan. 26, 2005-Jan. 3, 2007
2nd Departure: Left the House; lost re-election

Cong.	Ranking	Terms in: House	Comm.	Date of Assignment
104th	Maj-18th	1 *1	1	Jan. 4, 1995
109th	Maj-7th	6 *2	1	Jan. 26, 2005

2nd SCIENCE
Dates: Jan. 4, 1995-Jan. 3, 2007
Departure: Left the House; lost re-election

Cong.	Ranking	Terms in: House	Comm.	Date of Assignment
104th	Maj-20th	1	1	Jan. 4, 1995
105th	Maj-15th	2	2	Jan. 21, 1997
106th	Maj-13th	3	3	Jan. 6, 1999
107th	Maj-13th	4	4	Jan. 6, 2001

108th	Maj-11th	5	5	Jan. 28, 2003
109th	Maj-9th	6	6	Jan. 26, 2005

3rd BUDGET
Dates: Jan. 7, 1997-Jan. 3, 2005
Departure: Returned to Government Reform

Cong.	Ranking	Terms in: House	Comm.	Date of Assignment
105th	Maj-20th	2	1	Jan. 7, 1997
106th	Maj-12th	3	2	Jan. 6, 1999
107th	Maj-5th	4	3	Jan. 6, 2001
108th	Maj-3rd	5	4	Jan. 28, 2003

4th AGRICULTURE
Dates: Jan. 6, 1999-Jan. 3, 2007
Departure: Left the House; lost re-election

Cong.	Ranking	Terms in: House	Comm.	Date of Assignment
106th	Maj-21st	3	1	Jan. 6, 1999
107th	Maj-14th	4	2	Jan. 6, 2001
108th	Maj-10th	5	3	Jan. 28, 2003
109th	Maj-8th	6	4	Jan. 26, 2005

H

Kay R. Hagan (D-N.C.)

Dates: May 26, 1953
Senate: Jan. 3, 2009-date
Serving in the 111th Congress

SENATE STANDING COMMITTEES:

1st ARMED SERVICES
Dates: Jan. 21, 2009-date
Departure: Still serving in the 111th Congress

Cong.	Ranking	Years in: Senate	Comm.	Date of Assignment
111th	Maj-13th	1	1	Jan. 21, 2009

2nd HEALTH, EDUCATION, LABOR AND PENSIONS
Dates: Jan. 21, 2009-date
Departure: Still serving in the 111th Congress

Cong.	Ranking	Years in: Senate	Comm.	Date of Assignment
111th	Maj-11th	1	1	Jan. 21, 2009

3rd SMALL BUSINESS AND ENTREPENEURSHIP
Dates: Jan. 21, 2009-date
Departure: Still serving in the 111th Congress

Cong.	Ranking	Years in: Senate	Comm.	Date of Assignment
111th	Maj-10th	1	1	Jan. 21, 2009

Charles T. (Chuck) Hagel (R-Neb.)

Dates: Oct. 4, 1946
Senate: Jan. 3, 1997-Jan. 3, 2009
Left the Senate: Retired in 2008

SENATE STANDING COMMITTEES:

1st BANKING, HOUSING AND URBAN AFFAIRS
Dates: Jan. 9, 1997-Jan. 3, 2009
Departure: Left the Senate; retired

Cong.	Ranking	Years in: Senate	Comm.	Date of Assignment
105th	Maj-10th	1	1	Jan. 9, 1997
106th	Maj-8th	3	2	Jan. 7, 1999
107th	Maj-6th	5	5	Jan. 25, 2001
+107th	Min-6th	5	5	June 6, 2001
108th	Maj-5th	7	7	Jan. 15, 2003
109th	Maj-5th	9	8	Jan. 6, 2005
110th	Min-5th	11	11	Jan. 12, 2007

2nd FOREIGN RELATIONS
Dates: Jan. 9, 1997-Jan. 3, 2009
Departure: Left the Senate; retired

Cong.	Ranking	Years in: Senate	Comm.	Date of Assignment
105th	Maj-4th	1	1	Jan. 9, 1997
106th	Maj-4th	3	2	Jan. 7, 1999
107th	Maj-3rd	5	5	Jan. 25, 2001

Cong.	Ranking			Date
+107th	Min-3rd	5	5	June 6, 2001
108th	Maj-2nd	7	7	Jan. 15, 2003
109th	Maj-2nd	9	8	Jan. 6, 2005
110th	Min-2nd	11	11	Jan. 12, 2007

3rd LABOR AND HUMAN RESOURCES renamed Jan. 21, 1999
HEALTH, EDUCATION, LABOR AND PENSIONS
Dates: Jan. 7, 1999-Jan. 25, 2001
Departure: Moved to Budget and Energy and Natural Resources

Cong.	Ranking	Years in: Senate	Comm.	Date of Assignment
106th	Maj-9th	3	1	Jan. 7, 1999

4th BUDGET
Dates: Jan. 25, 2001-Jan. 15, 2003
Departure: Moved to Select Intelligence

Cong.	Ranking	Years in: Senate	Comm.	Date of Assignment
107th	Maj-11th	5	1	Jan. 25, 2001
+107th	Min-11th	5	1	June 6, 2001

5th ENERGY AND NATURAL RESOURCES
Dates: Jan. 25, 2001-Jan. 15, 2003
Departure: Moved to Select Intelligence

Cong.	Ranking	Years in: Senate	Comm.	Date of Assignment
107th	Maj-10th	5	1	Jan. 25, 2001
+107th	Min-10th	5	1	June 6, 2001

6th RULES AND ADMINISTRATION
Dates: Jan. 6, 2005-Jan. 3, 2009
Departure: Left the Senate; retired

Cong.	Ranking	Years in: Senate	Comm.	Date of Assignment
109th	Maj-10th	9	1	Jan. 6, 2005
110th	Min-8th	11	3	Jan. 12, 2007

SENATE SELECT AND SPECIAL COMMITTEES:

1st SPECIAL AGING (Permanent)
1st Dates: Jan. 9, 1997-Jan. 25, 2001
1st Departure: Moved to Budget and Energy and Natural Resources
2nd Dates: July 24, 2001-Jan. 14, 2003
2nd Departure: Moved to Select Intelligence

Cong.	Ranking	Years in: Senate	Comm.	Date of Assignment
105th	Maj-8th	1 *1	1	Jan. 9, 1997
106th	Maj-7th	3 *1	2	Jan. 7, 1999
+107th	MnR-1st	5 *2	1	July 24, 2001

2nd SELECT INTELLIGENCE (Permanent)
Dates: Jan. 15, 2003-Jan. 3, 2009
Departure: Left the Senate; retired

Cong.	Ranking	Years in: Senate	Comm.	Date of Assignment
108th	Maj-7th	7	1	Jan. 15, 2003
109th	Maj-7th	9	2	Jan. 6, 2005
110th	Min-3rd	11	4	Jan. 12, 2007

John Hall (D-N.Y.)

Dates: July 23, 1948
House: Jan. 3, 2007-date
Serving in the 111th Congress

HOUSE STANDING COMMITTEES:

1st TRANSPORTATION AND INFRASTRUCTURE
Dates: Jan. 10, 2007-date
Departure: Still serving in the 111th Congress

Cong.	Ranking	Terms in: House	Comm.	Date of Assignment
110th	Maj-38th	1	1	Jan. 10, 2007
111th	Maj-30th	2	2	Jan. 7, 2009

2nd VETERANS' AFFAIRS
Dates: Jan. 12, 2007-date
Departure: Still serving in the 111th Congress

Cong.	Ranking	Terms in: House	Comm.	Date of Assignment
110th	Maj-7th	1	1	Jan. 12, 2007
111th	Maj-7th	2	2	Jan. 21, 2009

HOUSE SELECT AND SPECIAL COMMITTEES:

1st SELECT ENERGY INDEPENDENCE AND GLOBAL WARMING
Dates: Mar. 9, 2007-date
Departure: Still serving in the 111th Congress

Cong.	Ranking	Terms in: House	Comm.	Date of Assignment
110th	Maj-8th	1	1	Mar. 9, 2007
111th	Maj-7th	2	2	Feb. 3, 2009

Ralph M. Hall (R-Tex.)

Dates: May 3, 1923
House: Jan. 3, 1981-date
Serving in the 111th Congress
Served as a Democrat: Jan. 3, 1981-Jan. 5, 2004
Served as a Republican: Jan. 5, 2004-date

HOUSE STANDING COMMITTEES:

1st ENERGY AND COMMERCE, 97-103
COMMERCE, 104-106
ENERGY AND COMMERCE, 107-111
1st Dates: Jan. 28, 1981-Jan. 5, 2004 as a Democrat
2nd Dates: Jan. 28, 2004-date as a Republican
Departure: Still serving in the 111th Congress

Cong.	Ranking	Terms in: House	Comm.	Date of Assignment
103rd	Maj-10th	7 *1	7	Jan. 5, 1993
104th	Min-6th	8 *1	8	Jan. 4, 1995
105th	Min-4th	9 *1	9	Jan. 7, 1997
106th	Min-4th	10 *1	10	Jan. 6, 1999
107th	Min-4th	11 *1	11	Jan. 31, 2001
108th	Min-4th	12 *1	12	Jan. 28, 2003
108th	MjR-1st	12 *2	1	Jan. 28, 2004
109th	Maj-2nd	13 *2	2	Jan. 26, 2005
110th	Min-2nd	14 *2	3	Jan. 4, 2007
111th	Min-2nd	15 *2	4	Jan. 9, 2009

2nd SCIENCE AND TECHNOLOGY, 97-99
SCIENCE, SPACE AND TECHNOLOGY, 100-103
SCIENCE, 104-109
SCIENCE AND TECHNOLOGY, 110-111
1st Dates: Jan. 28, 1981-Jan. 5, 2004 as a Democrat
RM2: Succeeded George E. Brown Jr. as Ranking Member on July 15, 1999

2nd Dates: Jan. 28, 2004-date as a Republican
Departure: Still serving in the 111th Congress

Cong.	Ranking	Terms in: House	Comm.	Date of Assignment
103rd	Maj-5th	7 *1	7	Jan. 5, 1993
104th	Min-2nd	8 *1	8	Jan. 4, 1995
105th	Min-2nd	9 *1	9	Feb. 13, 1997
106th	Min-2nd	10 *1	10	Jan. 6, 1999
106th	Min-RM2	10 *1	10	July 15, 1999
107th	Min-RM	11 *1	11	Jan. 31, 2001
108th	Min-RM	12 *1	12	Jan. 8, 2003
108th	MjR-2nd	12 *2	1	Jan. 28, 2004
109th	Maj-2nd	13 *2	2	Jan. 26, 2005
110th	Min-RM	14 *2	3	Jan. 4, 2007
111th	Min-RM	15 *2	4	Jan. 6, 2009

Tony P. Hall (D-Ohio)

Dates: Jan. 16, 1942
House: Jan. 3, 1979-Sept. 9, 2002
Left the House: Resigned; named US Ambassador to the UN for Food and Agriculture Agencies in 2002

HOUSE STANDING COMMITTEES:

1st FOREIGN AFFAIRS
Dates: Jan. 24, 1979-Jan. 3, 1981
Departure: Moved to Rules

2nd VETERANS' AFFAIRS
Dates: Jan. 24, 1979-Jan. 31, 1979
Departure: Moved to Small Business

3rd SMALL BUSINESS
Dates: Jan. 31, 1979-Jan. 3, 1981
Departure: Moved to Rules

4th RULES
Dates: Jan. 28, 1981-May 7, 2002
Departure: Resigned committee; later resigned House to become U.S. Ambassador to UN for Food and Agriculture

Cong.	Ranking	Terms in: House	Comm.	Date of Assignment
103rd	Maj-6th	8	7	Jan. 5, 1993
104th	Min-4th	9	8	Jan. 4, 1995
105th	Min-3rd	10	9	Jan. 7, 1997
106th	Min-3rd	11	10	Jan. 6, 1999
107th	Min-3rd	12	11	Jan. 3, 2001

HOUSE SELECT AND SPECIAL COMMITTEES:

1st SELECT HUNGER (Temporary)
Dates: Mar. 13, 1984-Jan. 3, 1993
Termination: Committee not renewed in 1993
Ch2: Hall succeeded G.T. (Mickey) Leland (D-Tex.) who had died. Hall was elected Chair on Sep. 28, 1989.

Deborah L. Halvorson (D-Ill.)

Dates: March 1, 1958
House: Jan. 3, 2009-date
Serving in the 111th Congress

HOUSE STANDING COMMITTEES:

1st AGRICULTURE
Dates: Jan. 21, 2009-date
Departure: Still serving in the 111th Congress

Cong.	Ranking	Terms in: House	Comm.	Date of Assignment
111th	Maj-17th	1	1	Jan. 21, 2009

2nd SMALL BUSINESS
Dates: Jan. 21, 2009-date
Departure: Still serving in the 111th Congress

Cong.	Ranking	Terms in: House	Comm.	Date of Assignment
111th	Maj-17th	1	1	Jan. 21, 2009

3rd VETERANS' AFFAIRS
Dates: Jan. 21, 2009-date
Departure: Still serving in the 111th Congress

Cong.	Ranking	Terms in: House	Comm.	Date of Assignment
111th	Maj-8th	1	1	Jan. 21, 2009

Daniel Hamburg (D-Cal.)

Dates: Oct. 6, 1948
House: Jan. 3, 1993-Jan. 3, 1995
Left the House: Defeated for re-election in 1994

HOUSE STANDING COMMITTEES:

1st MERCHANT MARINE AND FISHERIES
Dates: Jan. 5, 1993-Jan. 3, 1995
Departure: Left the House; lost re-election

Cong.	Ranking	Terms in: House	Comm.	Date of Assignment
103rd	Maj-20th	1	1	Jan. 5, 1993

2nd PUBLIC WORKS AND TRANSPORTATION
Dates: Jan. 5, 1993-Jan. 3, 1995
Departure: Left the House; lost re-election

Cong.	Ranking	Terms in: House	Comm.	Date of Assignment
103rd	Maj-36th	1	1	Jan. 5, 1993

Lee H. Hamilton (D-Ind.)

Dates: April 20, 1931
House: Jan. 3, 1965-Jan. 3, 1999
Left the House: Retired in 1998

HOUSE STANDING COMMITTEES:

1st FOREIGN AFFAIRS, 89-93
INTERNATIONAL RELATIONS, 94-95
FOREIGN AFFAIRS, 96-103
INTERNATIONAL RELATIONS, 104-105
Dates: Jan. 18, 1965-Jan. 3, 1999
Departure: Left the House; retired

Cong.	Ranking	Terms in: House	Comm.	Date of Assignment
103rd	Maj-Chr	15	15	Jan. 5, 1993

| 104th | Min-RM | 16 | 16 | Jan. 4, 1995 |
| 105th | Min-RM | 17 | 17 | Jan. 7, 1997 |

2nd POST OFFICE AND CIVIL SERVICE
Dates: Jan. 23, 1967-Jan. 3, 1973
Departure: Left committee; no new assignment

3rd STANDARDS OF OFFICIAL CONDUCT
Dates: Jan. 19, 1977-Jan. 3, 1981
Departure: Moved to Select Intelligence

4th SCIENCE, SPACE AND TECHNOLOGY
Dates: Jan. 22, 1987-Jan. 3, 1991
Departure: Left committee; no new assignment

HOUSE SELECT AND SPECIAL COMMITTEES:

1st SELECT U.S. INVOLVEMENT IN SOUTHEAST ASIA
Dates: June 15, 1970-July 6, 1970
Termination: House Report 1276 (91-2) filed

2nd SELECT ETHICS
Dates: Mar. 10, 1977-Jan. 3, 1979
Termination: House Report 1837 (95-2) filed

3rd PERMANENT SELECT INTELLIGENCE
Dates: Feb. 18,1981-Jan. 3, 1987
Departure: Moved to Science, Space and Technology; became Chair of Select Committee to Investigate Cover Arms Transactions with Iran

4th SELECT COMMITTEE TO INVESTIGATE COVERT ARMS TRANSACTIONS WITH IRAN
Dates: Jan. 7, 1987-Nov. 17, 1987
Departure: House Report 433 (100-1) filed

JOINT COMMITTEES:

1st JOINT ECONOMIC
House Dates: Jan. 27, 1975-Jan. 3, 1999
Departure: Left the House; retired

Cong.	Ranking	Terms in: House	Comm.	Date of Assignment
103rd	Maj-2nd	15	10	Jan. 27, 1993
104th	Min-3rd	16	11	Jan. 19, 1995
105th	Min-2nd	17	12	Mar. 11, 1997

2nd JOINT ORGANIZATION OF CONGRESS (Ad Hoc)
House Dates: Oct. 9, 1992-Dec. 17, 1993
Termination: House Report 103-413 filed

Cong.	Ranking	Terms in: House	Comm.	Date of Assignment
103rd	Maj-CoCh	15	2	Jan. 5, 1993

Melton D. Hancock (R-Mo.)

Dates: Sept. 14, 1929
House: Jan. 3, 1989-Jan. 3, 1997
Left the House: Retired in 1996

HOUSE STANDING COMMITTEES:

1st PUBLIC WORKS AND TRANSPORTATION
Dates: Jan. 20,1989-Jan. 3, 1993
Departure: Moved to Ways and Means

2nd SMALL BUSINESS
Dates: Jan. 20, 1989-Jan. 3, 1993
Departure: Moved to Ways and Means

3rd BANKING, FINANCE AND URBAN AFFAIRS
Dates: Jan. 24, 1991-Jan. 3, 1993
Departure: Moved to Ways and Means

4th WAYS AND MEANS
Dates: Jan. 5, 1993-Jan. 3, 1997
Departure: Left the House; retired

Cong.	Ranking	Terms in: House	Comm.	Date of Assignment
103rd	Min-13th	3	1	Jan. 5, 1993
104th	Maj-10th	4	2	Jan. 4, 1995

James V. Hansen (R-Utah)

Dates: Aug. 14, 1932
House: Jan. 3, 1981-Jan. 3, 2003
Left the House: Retired in 2002

HOUSE STANDING COMMITTEES:

1st INTERIOR AND INSULAR AFFAIRS, 97-102
NATURAL RESOURCES, 103
RESOURCES, 104-107
Dates: Jan. 28, 1981-Jan. 3, 2003
Departure: Left the House; retired

Cong.	Ranking	Terms in: House	Comm.	Date of Assignment
103rd	Min-2nd	7	7	Jan. 5, 1993
104th	Maj-2nd	8	8	Jan. 4, 1995
105th	Maj-3rd	9	9	Jan. 7, 1997
106th	Maj-3rd	10	10	Jan. 6, 1999
107th	Maj-Chr	11	11	Jan. 6, 2001

2nd STANDARDS OF OFFICIAL CONDUCT
1st Dates: Jan. 28, 1981-Jan. 3, 1993
1st Departure: Moved to Select Intelligence
2nd Dates: Jan. 7, 1997-Jan. 3, 1999
2nd Departure: Moved to Veterans' Affairs

Cong.	Ranking	Terms in: House	Comm.	Date of Assignment
105th	Maj-Chr	9 *2	1	Jan. 7, 1997

3rd POST OFFICE AND CIVIL SERVICE
Dates: Jan. 30, 1985-Jan. 3, 1987
Departure: Left committee; no new assignment

4th ARMED SERVICES, 99-103
NATIONAL SECURITY, 104-105
ARMED SERVICES, 106-107
Dates: Sep. 26, 1986-Jan. 3, 2003
Departure: Left the House; retired

Cong.	Ranking	Terms in: House	Comm.	Date of Assignment
103rd	Min-6th	7	5	Jan. 5, 1993
104th	Maj-6th	8	6	Jan. 4, 1995
105th	Maj-6th	9	7	Jan. 7, 1997
106th	Maj-6th	10	8	Jan. 6, 1999
107th	Maj-4th	11	9	Jan. 6, 2001

5th VETERANS' AFFAIRS
Dates: Feb. 2, 1999-Jan. 3, 2001
Departure: Left committee; no new assignment

Cong.	Ranking	Terms in: House	Comm.	Date of Assignment
106th	Maj-14th	10	1	Feb. 2, 1999

HOUSE SELECT AND SPECIAL COMMITTEES:

1st PERMANENT SELECT INTELLIGENCE
Dates: Feb. 3, 1993-Jan. 3, 1997
Departure: Moved to Standards of Official Conduct

Cong.	Ranking	Terms in: House	Comm.	Date of Assignment
103rd	Min-6th	7	1	Feb. 3, 1993
104th	Maj-4th	8	2	Jan. 4, 1995

2nd SELECT NATIONAL SECURITY CONCERNS WITH CHINA
Dates: June 22, 1998-Apr. 30, 1999
Termination: House Report 851 (105-2) filed, Jan. 3, 1999

Cong.	Ranking	Terms in: House	Comm.	Date of Assignment
105th	Maj-4th	9	1	June 22, 1998
106th	Maj-4th	10	2	Jan. 19, 1999

Phil Hare (D-Ill.)

Dates: Feb. 21, 1949
House: Jan. 3, 2007-date
Serving in the 111th Congress

HOUSE STANDING COMMITTEES:

1st EDUCATION AND LABOR
Dates: Jan. 10, 2007-date
Departure: Still serving in the 111th Congress

Cong.	Ranking	Terms in: House	Comm.	Date of Assignment
110th	Maj-24th	1	1	Jan. 10, 2007
111th	Maj-20th	2	2	Jan. 21, 2009

2nd VETERANS' AFFAIRS
Dates: Jan. 12, 2007-Jan. 3, 2009
Departure: Moved to Transportation and Infrastructure

Cong.	Ranking	Terms in: House	Comm.	Date of Assignment
110th	Maj-8th	1	1	Jan. 12, 2007

3rd TRANSPORTATION AND INFRASTRUCTURE
Dates: Jan. 7, 2009-date
Departure: Still serving in the 111th Congress

Cong.	Ranking	Terms in: House	Comm.	Date of Assignment
111th	Maj-37th	2	1	Jan. 7, 2009

Thomas R. Harkin (D-Iowa)

Dates: Nov. 19, 1939
House: Jan. 3, 1975-Jan. 3, 1985
Left the House: Elected to U.S. Senate in 1984
Senate: Jan. 3, 1985-date
Serving in the 111th Congress

HOUSE STANDING COMMITTEES:

1st SCIENCE AND TECHNOLOGY
Dates: Jan. 20, 1975-Jan. 3, 1985
Departure: Left the House for the Senate

2nd AGRICULTURE
Dates: Jan. 23, 1975-Jan. 3, 1985
Departure: Left the House for the Senate

HOUSE SELECT AND SPECIAL COMMITTEES:

1st SELECT SERVICEMEN MISSING IN SOUTHEAST ASIA
Dates: Sep. 15, 1975-Jan. 3, 1977
Termination: House Report 1764 (94-2) filed, Dec. 13, 1976

SENATE STANDING COMMITTEES:

1st AGRICULTURE, NUTRITION AND FORESTRY
Dates: Feb. 21, 1985-date
Ch2: Replaced Richard G. Lugar (R-Ind.) on June 6, 2001, following Senate party control shift
Departure: Still serving in the 111th Congress

Cong.	Ranking	Years in: Senate	Comm.	Date of Assignment
103rd	Maj-5th	9	8	Jan. 7, 1993
104th	Min-4th	11	10	Jan. 4, 1995
105th	Min-RM	13	12	Jan. 9, 1997
106th	Min-RM	15	14	Jan. 7, 1999
=107th	Maj-ChT	17	16	Jan. 3, 2001
107th	Min-RM1	17	16	Jan. 25, 2001
+107th	Maj-Ch2	17	17	June 6, 2001
108th	Min-RM	19	18	Jan. 15, 2003
109th	Min-RM	21	20	Jan. 6, 2005
110th	Maj-Chr	23	22	Jan. 12, 2007
111th	Maj-Chr	25	24	Jan. 21, 2009

2nd APPROPRIATIONS
Dates: Feb. 21, 1985-date
Departure: Still serving in the 111th Congress

Cong.	Ranking	Years in: Senate	Comm.	Date of Assignment
103rd	Maj-10th	9	8	Jan. 7, 1993
104th	Min-8th	11	10	Jan. 4, 1995
105th	Min-7th	13	12	Jan. 9, 1997
106th	Min-6th	15	14	Jan. 7, 1999
107th	Min-5th	17	16	Jan. 25, 2001
+107th	Maj-5th	17	17	June 6, 2001
108th	Min-5th	19	18	Jan. 15, 2003
109th	Min-4th	21	20	Jan. 6, 2005
110th	Maj-4th	23	22	Jan. 12, 2007
111th	Maj-4th	25	24	Jan. 21, 2009

3rd SMALL BUSINESS renamed June 29, 2001
SMALL BUSINESS AND ENTREPRENEURSHIP
Dates: Mar. 5, 1985-date
Departure: Still serving in the 111th Congress

Cong.	Ranking	Years in: Senate	Comm.	Date of Assignment
103rd	Maj-4th	9	8	Jan. 21, 1993
104th	Min-4th	11	10	Jan. 6, 1995
105th	Min-4th	13	12	Jan. 9, 1997
106th	Min-3rd	15	14	Jan. 7, 1999
107th	Min-3rd	17	16	Jan. 25, 2001
+107th	Maj-3rd	17	17	June 6, 2001
108th	Min-3rd	19	18	Jan. 15, 2003
109th	Min-3rd	21	20	Jan. 6, 2005

| 110th | Maj-3rd | 23 | 22 | Jan. 12, 2007 |
| 111th | Maj-4th | 25 | 24 | Jan. 21, 2009 |

4th LABOR AND HUMAN RESOURCES renamed Jan. 21, 1999
HEALTH, EDUCATION, LABOR AND PENSIONS
Dates: Jan. 6, 1987-date
Departure: Still serving in the 111th Congress

| | | Years in: | | Date of |
Cong.	Ranking	Senate	Comm.	Assignment
103rd	Maj-6th	9	7	Jan. 7, 1993
104th	Min-5th	11	8	Jan. 4, 1995
105th	Min-3rd	13	11	Jan. 9, 1997
106th	Min-3rd	15	13	Jan. 7, 1999
107th	Min-3rd	17	15	Jan. 25, 2001
+107th	Maj-3rd	17	15	June 6, 2001
108th	Min-3rd	19	17	Jan. 15, 2003
109th	Min-3rd	21	19	Jan. 6, 2005
110th	Maj-3rd	23	21	Jan. 12, 2007
111th	Maj-3rd	25	23	Jan. 21, 2009

Jane L. Harman (D-Cal.)

Dates: June 28, 1945
House 1: Jan. 3, 1993-Jan. 3, 1999
Left House 1: Lost nomination for Governor in 1998
House 2: Jan. 3, 2001-date
Serving in the 111th Congress

HOUSE STANDING COMMITTEES:

1st ARMED SERVICES, 103
NATIONAL SECURITY, 104-105
Dates: Jan. 5, 1993-Jan. 3, 1999
Departure: Left the House; lost nomination for Governor

| | | Terms in: | | Date of |
Cong.	Ranking	House	Comm.	Assignment
103rd	Maj-30th	1	1	Jan. 5, 1993
104th	Min-18th	2	2	Jan. 4, 1995
105th	Min-13th	3	3	Jan. 7, 1997

2nd SCIENCE, SPACE AND TECHNOLOGY, 103
SCIENCE, 104
Dates: Jan. 5, 1993-Jan. 3, 1997
Departure: Left committee; no new assignment

| | | Terms in: | | Date of |
Cong.	Ranking	House	Comm.	Assignment
103rd	Maj-23rd	1	1	Jan. 5, 1993
104th	Min-11th	2	2	Jan. 4, 1995

3rd ENERGY AND COMMERCE
1st Dates: Feb. 8, 2001-Jan. 3, 2003
1st Departure: Became Ranking Member on Permanent Select Intelligence
2nd Dates: Jan. 4, 2007-date
2nd Departure: Still serving in the 111th Congress

| | | Terms in: | | Date of |
Cong.	Ranking	House	Comm.	Assignment
107th	Min-26th	4 *1	1	Feb. 8, 2001
110th	Maj-17th	7 *2	1	Jan. 4, 2007
111th	Maj-15th	8 *2	2	Jan. 7, 2009

4th HOMELAND SECURITY
Dates: Feb. 9, 2005-date
Departure: Still serving in the 111th Congress

| | | Terms in: | | Date of |
Cong.	Ranking	House	Comm.	Assignment
109th	Min-5th	6	2	Feb. 9, 2005

| 110th | Maj-5th | 7 | 3 | Jan. 12, 2007 |
| 111th | Maj-3rd | 8 | 4 | Jan. 28, 2009 |

HOUSE SELECT AND SPECIAL COMMITTEES:

1st PERMANENT SELECT INTELLIGENCE
1st Dates: Sep. 27, 1996-Jan. 3, 1999
1st Departure: Left the House; lost nomination for Governor
2nd Dates: Mar. 1, 2001-Jan. 3, 2007
2nd Departure: Returned to Energy and Commerce

| | | Terms in: | | Date of |
Cong.	Ranking	House	Comm.	Assignment
104th	MnR-2nd	2 *1	1	Sep. 27, 1996
105th	Min-5th	3 *1	2	Feb. 10, 1997
107th	Min-3rd	4 *2	1	Mar. 1, 2001
108th	Min-RM	5 *2	2	Jan. 8, 2003
109th	Min-RM	6 *2	3	Jan. 6, 2005

2nd SELECT HOMELAND SECURITY
Dates: Feb. 12, 2003-Jan. 3, 2005
Departure: Continued on reorganized standing committee

| | | Terms in: | | Date of |
Cong.	Ranking	House	Comm.	Assignment
108th	Min-7th	5	1	Feb. 12, 2003

Gregg Harper (R-Miss.)

Dates: June 1, 1956
House: Jan. 3, 2009-date
Serving in the 111th Congress

HOUSE STANDING COMMITTEES:

1st HOUSE ADMINISTRATION
Dates: Jan. 9, 2009-date
Departure: Still serving in the 111th Congress

| | | Terms in: | | Date of |
Cong.	Ranking	House	Comm.	Assignment
111th	Min-3rd	1	1	Jan. 9, 2009

2nd JUDICIARY
Dates: Jan. 9, 2009-date
Departure: Still serving in the 111th Congress

| | | Terms in: | | Date of |
Cong.	Ranking	House	Comm.	Assignment
111th	Min-16th	1	1	Jan. 9, 2009

3rd BUDGET
Dates: Jan. 22, 2009-date
Departure: Still serving in the 111th Congress

| | | Terms in: | | Date of |
Cong.	Ranking	House	Comm.	Assignment
111th	MnR-2nd	1	1	Jan. 22, 2009

4th STANDARDS OF OFFICIAL CONDUCT
Dates: July 14, 2009-date
Departure: Still serving in the 111th Congress

| | | Terms in: | | Date of |
Cong.	Ranking	House	Comm.	Assignment
111th	MnR-1st	1	1	July 14, 2009

JOINT COMMITTEES:

1st JOINT LIBRARY
House Dates: Mar. 31, 2009-date
Departure: Still serving in the 111th Congress

Cong.	Ranking	Terms in: House	Comm.	Date of Assignment
111th	Min-2nd	1	1	Mar. 31, 2009

Katherine Harris (R-Fla.)

Dates: April 5, 1957
House: Jan. 3, 2003-Jan. 3, 2007
Left the House: Lost U.S. Senate election in 2006

HOUSE STANDING COMMITTEES:

1st FINANCIAL SERVICES
Dates: Jan. 28, 2003-Jan. 3, 2007
Departure: Left the House; lost Senate election

Cong.	Ranking	Terms in: House	Comm.	Date of Assignment
108th	Min-36th	1	1	Jan. 28, 2003
109th	Min-29th	2	2	Jan. 26, 2005

2nd INTERNATIONAL RELATIONS
Dates: Jan. 28, 2003-Jan. 3, 2007
Departure: Left the House; lost Senate election

Cong.	Ranking	Terms in: House	Comm.	Date of Assignment
108th	Maj-26th	1	1	Jan. 28, 2003
109th	Maj-21st	2	2	Jan. 26, 2005

3rd GOVERNMENT REFORM
Dates: Mar. 10, 2004-Feb. 8, 2005
Departure: Resigned committee; moved to Homeland Security

Cong.	Ranking	Terms in: House	Comm.	Date of Assignment
108th	MjR-2nd	1	1	Mar. 10, 2004
109th	Maj-15th	2	2	Jan. 26, 2005

4th HOMELAND SECURITY
Dates: Feb. 9, 2005-Jan. 3, 2007
Departure: Left the House; lost Senate election

Cong.	Ranking	Terms in: House	Comm.	Date of Assignment
109th	Maj-15th	2	1	Feb. 9, 2005

Melissa A. Hart (R-Penn.)

Dates: April 4, 1962
House: Jan. 3, 2001-Jan. 3, 2007
Left the House: Defeated for re-election in 2006

HOUSE STANDING COMMITTEES:

1st FINANCIAL SERVICES
Dates: Jan. 6, 2001-Jan. 3, 2005
Departure: Moved to Ways and Means and Standards of Official Conduct

Cong.	Ranking	Terms in: House	Comm.	Date of Assignment
107th	Maj-33rd	1	1	Jan. 6, 2001
108th	Maj-26th	2	2	Jan. 28, 2003

2nd JUDICIARY
Dates: Jan. 6, 2001-Jan. 3, 2005
Departure: Moved to Ways and Means and Standards of Official Conduct

Cong.	Ranking	Terms in: House	Comm.	Date of Assignment
107th	Maj-20th	1	1	Jan. 6, 2001
108th	Maj-14th	2	2	Jan. 28, 2003

3rd SCIENCE
Dates: Jan. 6, 2001-Jan. 3, 2005
Departure: Moved to Ways and Means and Standards of Official Conduct

Cong.	Ranking	Terms in: House	Comm.	Date of Assignment
107th	Maj-24th	1	1	Jan. 6, 2001
108th	Maj-18th	2	2	Jan. 28, 2003

4th WAYS AND MEANS
Dates: Jan. 26, 2005-Jan. 3, 2007
Departure: Left the House; lost re-election

Cong.	Ranking	Terms in: House	Comm.	Date of Assignment
109th	Maj-22nd	3	1	Jan. 26, 2005

5th STANDARDS OF OFFICIAL CONDUCT
Dates: Feb. 2, 2005-Jan. 3, 2007
Departure: Left the House; lost re-election

Cong.	Ranking	Terms in: House	Comm.	Date of Assignment
109th	Maj-4th	3	1	Feb. 2, 2005

J. Dennis Hastert (R-Ill.)

Dates: Jan. 2, 1942
House: Jan. 3, 1987-Nov. 26, 2007
Left the House: Resigned and retired in 2007

HOUSE STANDING COMMITTEES:

1st GOVERNMENT OPERATIONS, 100-103
GOVERNMENT REFORM AND OVERSIGHT, 104-105
1st Dates: Jan. 21, 1987-Jan. 3, 1995
1st Departure: Left committee; no new assignment
1st Dates: May 25, 1995-Jan. 3, 1999
1st Departure: Left committee; elected Speaker

Cong.	Ranking	Terms in: House	Comm.	Date of Assignment
103rd	Min-3rd	4 *1	4	Jan. 5, 1993
104th	MjA-28th	5 *2	1	May 25, 1995
105th	Maj-3rd	6 *2	2	Jan. 7, 1997

2nd PUBLIC WORKS AND TRANSPORTATION
Dates: Jan. 21, 1987-Jan. 3, 1991
Departure: Moved to Energy and Commerce

3rd ENERGY AND COMMERCE, 102-103
COMMERCE, 104-105
ENERGY AND COMMERCE, 110
1st Dates: Jan. 24, 1991-Jan. 3, 1999
1st Departure: Left committee; elected Speaker
2nd Dates: Jan. 10, 2007-Nov. 26, 2007
2nd Departure: Left the House; retired

Cong.	Ranking	Terms in: House	Comm.	Date of Assignment
103rd	Min-9th	4 *1	2	Jan. 5, 1993

Cong.	Ranking	House	Comm.	Date of Assignment
104th	Maj-8th	5 *1	3	Jan. 4, 1995
105th	Maj-7th	6 *1	4	Jan. 7, 1997
110th	Min-3rd	11 *2	1	Jan. 10, 2007

HOUSE SELECT AND SPECIAL COMMITTEES:

1st SELECT CHILDREN, YOUTH AND FAMILIES (Temporary)
Dates: Feb. 2, 1987-Oct. 8, 1991
Departure: Left committee; had moved to Select Hunger

2nd SELECT HUNGER (Temporary)
Dates: Aug. 15, 1991-Jan. 3, 1993
Termination: Committee not renewed in 1993

3rd PERMANENT SELECT INTELLIGENCE
Dates: Jan. 8, 2003-Jan. 3, 2007
Departure: *Ex Officio* status ended with speakership

Cong.	Ranking	House	Comm.	Date of Assignment
108th	Maj-ExO	9	1	Jan. 8, 2003
109th	Maj-ExO	10	2	Jan. 26, 2005

HOUSE LEADERSHIP POSTS

Dates: Jan. 3, 1999-Jan. 3, 2007
Departure: Republican Party lost House majority in 2006 and Hastert left the leadership to resume committee service

1st SPEAKER OF THE HOUSE
Dates: Jan. 6, 1999-Jan. 3, 2007
Notes: For the 106th Congress, Hastert succeeded Speaker of the House Newton L. Gingrich (R-Ga.) who had resigned the House on Jan. 3, 1997. Appropriations Chair Robert Livingston (R-La.), the anticipated successor to Gingrich, withdrew from his speakership nomination and resigned the House on Mar. 1, 1999. Hastert was nominated by the Republican Conference and was elected Speaker over Minority Leader Richard Gephardt (D-Mo.) 220 to 205 in the 106th Congress and 222 to 206 in the 107th Congress. In the 108th Congress, Hastert defeated Minority Leader Nancy Pelosi (D-Cal.) 228 to 201 and in the 109th Congress, by a vote of 226 to 199.
Departure: Resigned speakership; resumed committee service

Cong.	Ranking	House	Post	Date of Election
106th	Maj-1st	7	1	Jan. 6, 1999
107th	Maj-1st	8	2	Jan. 3, 2001
108th	Maj-1st	9	3	Jan. 7, 2003
109th	Maj-1st	10	4	Jan. 4, 2005

Alcee L. Hastings (D-Fla.)

Dates: Sept. 5, 1936
House: Jan. 3, 1993-date
Serving in the 111th Congress

HOUSE STANDING COMMITTEES:

1st FOREIGN AFFAIRS, 103
INTERNATIONAL RELATIONS, 104-107
Dates: Jan. 5, 1993-June 19, 2001
Departure: Resigned committee; moved to Rules

Cong.	Ranking	House	Comm.	Date of Assignment
103rd	Maj-20th	1	1	Jan. 5, 1993
104th	Min-16th	2	2	Jan. 4, 1995
105th	Min-13th	3	3	Jan. 7, 1997

| 106th | Min-11th | 4 | 4 | Jan. 6, 1999 |
| 107th | Min-9th | 5 | 5 | Jan. 31, 2001 |

2nd MERCHANT MARINE AND FISHERIES
Dates: Jan. 5, 1993-Jan. 3, 1995
Departure: Committee abolished; moved to Science

Cong.	Ranking	House	Comm.	Date of Assignment
103rd	Maj-19th	1	1	Jan. 5, 1993

3rd POST OFFICE AND CIVIL SERVICE
Dates: Jan. 27, 1993-Jan. 3, 1995
Departure: Committee abolished; moved to Science

Cong.	Ranking	House	Comm.	Date of Assignment
103rd	Maj-15th	1	1	Jan. 27, 1993

4th SCIENCE
Dates: Jan. 4, 1995-May 19, 1999
Departure: Leave of absence; had moved to Permanent Select Intelligence

Cong.	Ranking	House	Comm.	Date of Assignment
104th	Min-15th	2	1	Jan. 4, 1995
105th	Min-10th	3	2	Feb. 13, 1997
106th	Min-10th	4	3	Jan. 6, 1999

5th RULES
Dates: June 19, 2001-date
Departure: Still serving in the 111th Congress

Cong.	Ranking	House	Comm.	Date of Assignment
107th	MnR-1st	5	1	June 19, 2001
108th	Min-4th	6	2	Jan. 7, 2003
109th	Min-3rd	7	3	Jan. 26, 2005
110th	Maj-3rd	8	4	Jan. 12, 2007
111th	Maj-3rd	9	5	Jan. 6, 2009

HOUSE SELECT AND SPECIAL COMMITTEES:

1st PERMANENT SELECT INTELLIGENCE
1st Dates: Feb. 12, 1999-Apr. 11, 2002
1st Departure: Resigned committee; no new assignment
2nd Dates: Jan. 8, 2003-Dec. 12, 2007
2nd Departure: Resigned committee; no new assignment
3rd Dates: Feb. 4, 2009-date
3rd Departure: Still serving in the 111th Congress

Cong.	Ranking	House	Comm.	Date of Assignment
106th	Min-7th	4 *1	1	Feb. 12, 1999
107th	Min-7th	5 *1	2	Mar. 1, 2001
108th	Min-2nd	6 *2	1	Jan. 8, 2003
109th	Min-2nd	7 *2	2	Jan. 26, 2005
110th	Maj-2nd	8 *2	3	Jan. 17, 2007
111th	Maj-2nd	9 *3	1	Feb. 4, 2009

Richard (Doc) Hastings (R-Wash.)

Dates: Feb. 7, 1941
House: Jan. 3, 1995-date
Serving in the 111th Congress

HOUSE STANDING COMMITTEES:

1st NATIONAL SECURITY
Dates: Jan. 4, 1995-Jan. 3, 1997
Departure: Moved to Rules

Cong.	Ranking	Terms in: House	Comm.	Date of Assignment
104th	Maj-30th	1	1	Jan. 4, 1995

2nd RESOURCES, 104
NATURAL RESOURCES, 111
1st Dates: Jan. 4, 1995-Jan. 3, 1997
1st Departure: Moved to Rules
2nd Dates: Jan. 6, 2009-date
2nd Departure: Still serving in the 111th Congress

Cong.	Ranking	Terms in: House	Comm.	Date of Assignment
104th	Maj-22nd	1 *1	1	Jan. 4, 1995
111th	Min-RM	8 *2	1	Jan. 6, 2009

3rd RULES
Dates: Jan. 7, 1997-Jan. 3, 2009
Departure: Returned to Natural Resources as RM

Cong.	Ranking	Terms in: House	Comm.	Date of Assignment
105th	Maj-8th	2	1	Jan. 7, 1997
106th	Maj-6th	3	2	Jan. 6, 1999
107th	Maj-6th	4	3	Jan. 3, 2001
108th	Maj-6th	5	4	Jan. 7, 2003
109th	Maj-3rd	6	5	Jan. 4, 2005
110th	Min-3rd	7	6	Jan. 4, 2007

4th BUDGET
Dates: Jan. 6, 2001-Jan. 3, 2005
Departure: Left committee; became Chair of Standards of Official Conduct

Cong.	Ranking	Terms in: House	Comm.	Date of Assignment
107th	Maj-16th	4	1	Jan. 6, 2001
108th	Maj-7th	5	2	Jan. 28, 2003

5th STANDARDS OF OFFICIAL CONDUCT
Dates: Mar. 6, 2001-Jan. 3, 2009
Departure: Returned to Natural Resources

Cong.	Ranking	Terms in: House	Comm.	Date of Assignment
107th	Maj-3rd	4	1	Mar. 6, 2001
108th	Maj-2nd	5	2	Feb. 11, 2003
109th	Maj-Chr	6	3	Feb. 2, 2005
110th	Min-RM	7	4	Jan. 4, 2007

Orrin G. Hatch (R-Utah)

Dates: March 22, 1934
Senate: Jan. 3, 1977-date
Serving in the 111th Congress

SENATE STANDING COMMITTEES:

1st GOVERNMENT OPERATIONS
Dates: Jan. 10, 1977-Feb. 22, 1977
Departure: Moved to Human Resources and Judiciary

2nd INTERIOR AND INSULAR AFFAIRS
Dates: Jan. 10, 1977-Feb. 22, 1977
Departure: Moved to Human Resources and Judiciary

3rd HUMAN RESOURCES reorganized Jan. 23, 1979
LABOR AND HUMAN RESOURCES renamed Jan. 21, 1999
HEALTH, EDUCATION, LABOR AND PENSIONS
1st Dates: Feb. 22, 1977-Jan. 3, 1995

1st Departure: Moved to Indian Affairs; became Chair of Judiciary
2nd Dates: Jan. 6, 2005-date
2nd Departure: Still serving in the 111th Congress

Cong.	Ranking	Years in: Senate	Comm.	Date of Assignment
103rd	Min-6th	17 *1	16	Jan. 7, 1993
109th	Maj-9th	29 *2	1	Jan. 6, 2005
110th	Min-7th	31 *2	3	Jan. 12, 2007
111th	Min-7th	33 *2	5	Jan. 21, 2009

4th JUDICIARY
Dates: Feb. 22, 1977-date
Ch1: Replaced by Patrick J. Leahy (D-Vt.) on June 6, 2001 following party control shift and became RM2
Departure: Still serving in the 111th Congress

Cong.	Ranking	Years in: Senate	Comm.	Date of Assignment
103rd	Min-RM	17	16	Jan. 7, 1993
104th	Maj-Chr	19	18	Jan. 4, 1995
105th	Maj-Chr	21	20	Jan. 9, 1997
106th	Maj-Chr	23	22	Jan. 7, 1999
107th	Maj-Ch1	25	24	Jan. 25, 2001
+107th	Min-RM2	25	25	June 6, 2001
108th	Maj-Chr	27	26	Jan. 15, 2003
109th	Maj-2nd	29	28	Jan. 6, 2005
110th	Min-2nd	31	30	Jan. 12, 2007
111th	Min-2nd	33	32	Jan. 21, 2009

5th BUDGET
Dates: Jan. 23, 1979-Jan. 6, 1987
Departure: Left committee; no new assignment

6th SMALL BUSINESS
Dates: Mar. 25, 1981-Mar. 5, 1985
Departure: Moved to Select Intelligence

7th AGRICULTURE, NUTRITION AND FORESTRY
Dates: Apr. 27, 1982-Feb. 21, 1985
Departure: Moved to Select Intelligence

8th FOREIGN RELATIONS
Dates: Feb. 5, 1991-June 25, 1991
Departure: Moved to Finance

9th FINANCE
Dates: June 25, 1991-date
Departure: Still serving in the 111th Congress

Cong.	Ranking	Years in: Senate	Comm.	Date of Assignment
103rd	Min-8th	17	2	Jan. 7, 1993
104th	Maj-6th	19	4	Jan. 4, 1995
105th	Maj-4th	21	6	Jan. 9, 1997
106th	Maj-4th	23	8	Jan. 7, 1999
107th	Maj-2nd	25	10	Jan. 25, 2001
+107th	Min-2nd	25	10	June 6, 2001
108th	Maj-2nd	27	12	Jan. 15, 2003
109th	Maj-2nd	29	14	Jan. 6, 2005
110th	Min-2nd	31	16	Jan. 12, 2007
111th	Min-2nd	33	18	Jan. 21, 2009

SENATE SELECT AND SPECIAL COMMITTEES:

1st SELECT SMALL BUSINESS
Dates: Jan. 23, 1979-Mar. 25, 1981
Departure: Continued on reorganized standing committee

2nd SECURITY AND COOPERATION IN EUROPE
Dates: Nov. 18, 1983-Mar. 27, 1985
Termination: Public Law 99-7

3rd SELECT INTELLIGENCE (Permanent)
1st Dates: Jan. 3, 1985-Feb. 5, 1991
1st Departure: Moved to Foreign Relations
2nf Dates: Jan. 9, 1997-date
2nd Departure: Still serving in the 111th Congress

Cong.	Ranking	Years in: Senate	Comm.	Date of Assignment
105th	Maj-7th	21 *2	1	Jan. 9, 1997
106th	Maj-7th	23 *2	2	Jan. 7, 1999
107th	Maj-4th	25 *2	5	Jan. 25, 2001
+107th	Min-4th	25 *2	5	June 6, 2001
108th	Maj-2nd	27 *2	7	Jan. 15, 2003
109th	Maj-2nd	29 *2	8	Jan. 6, 2005
110th	Min-5th	31 *2	11	Jan. 12, 2007
111th	Min-2nd	33 *2	13	Jan. 21, 2009

4th JUDGE HARRY E. CLAIBORNE IMPEACHMENT
Dates: Aug. 14, 1986-Oct. 9. 1986
Termination: Senate Report 99-511 filed

5th SECRET MILITARY ASSISTANCE TO IRAN AND THE NICARAGUAN OPPOSITION (Iran-Contra Affair)
Dates: Jan. 12, 1987-Nov. 17, 1987
Termination: Senate Report 100-216 filed

6th JUDGE WALTER L. NIXON IMPEACHMENT
Dates: May 11, 1989-Nov. 3, 1989
Termination: Impeachment hearings concluded

7th SELECT INDIAN AFFAIRS (Permanent)
Dates: Jan. 11, 1995-Jan. 6, 2005
Departure: Returned to Health, Education, Labor and Pensions

Cong.	Ranking	Years in: Senate	Comm.	Date of Assignment
104th	Maj-8th	19	1	Jan. 11, 1995
105th	Maj-7th	21	2	Jan. 9, 1997
106th	Maj-7th	23	4	Jan. 7, 1999
107th	Maj-6th	25	7	Jan. 25, 2001
+107th	Min-6th	25	7	June 6, 2001
108th	Maj-5th	27	9	Jan. 15, 2003

8th SPECIAL COMMITTEE TO INVESTIGATE WHITEWATER DEVELOPMENT CORPORATION AND RELATED MATTERS
Dates: July 20, 1995-June 17, 1996
Termination: Senate Report 104-280 filed

Cong.	Ranking	Years in: Senate	Comm.	Date of Assignment
104th	Maj-9th	19	1	July 20, 1995

9th SPECIAL AGING (Permanent)
1st Dates: Jan. 15, 2003-Jan. 6, 2005
1st Departure: Returned to Health, Education, Labor and Pensions
2nd Dates: Jan. 21, 2009-date
2nd Departure: Still serving in the 111th Congress

Cong.	Ranking	Years in: Senate	Comm.	Date of Assignment
108th	Maj-8th	27 *1	1	Jan. 15, 2003
111th	Min-6th	31 *2	1	Jan. 21, 2009

JOINT COMMITTEES:

1st JOINT ECONOMIC
Senate Dates: Feb. 24, 1977-Jan. 23, 1979
Departure: Moved to Budget and Select Small Business

2nd JOINT TAXATION
1st Senate Dates: Feb. 2, 1995-Jan. 3, 1997
1st Departure: "for the duration of the 104th Congress only"

2nd Senate Dates: Nov. 19, 1999-date
2nd Departure: Still serving in the 111th Congress

Cong.	Ranking	Years in: Senate	Comm.	Date of Assignment
104th	MjR-1st	19 *1	1	Feb. 2, 1995
106th	MjR-1st	23 *2	1	Nov. 19, 1999
107th	Maj-2nd	25 *2	2	Feb. 28, 2001
+107th	Min-2nd	25 *2	2	June 6, 2001
108th	Maj-2nd	27 *2	4	Feb. 24, 2003
109th	Maj-2nd	29 *2	6	Jan. 25, 2005
110th	Min-2nd	31 *2	8	Jan. 18, 2007
111th	Min-2nd	33 *2	10	Feb. 25, 2009

Mark O. Hatfield (R-Ore.)

Dates: July 12, 1922
Senate: Jan. 10, 1967-Jan. 3, 1997
Left the Senate: Retired in 1996

S: Hatfield was elected to the 90th Congress, but was not eligible to be seated until Jan. 8, 1967, when he resigned as Governor. He was seated Jan. 10, 1967, and was assigned to committees.

SENATE STANDING COMMITTEES:

1st AGRICULTURE AND FORESTRY
Dates: Jan. 16, 1967-Sep. 12, 1968
Departure: Moved to Aeronautical and Space Sciences

2nd INTERIOR AND INSULAR AFFAIRS reorganized Feb. 22, 1977 ENERGY AND NATURAL RESOURCES
Dates: Jan. 16, 1967-Jan. 3, 1997
Departure: Left the Senate; retired

Cong.	Ranking	Years in: Senate	Comm.	Date of Assignment
103rd	Min-2nd	27	26	Jan. 7, 1993
104th	Maj-2nd	29	28	Jan. 5, 1995

3rd AERONAUTICAL AND SPACE SCIENCES
Dates: Sep. 12, 1968-Jan. 29, 1971
Departure: Moved to Commerce

4th COMMERCE
Dates: Jan. 29, 1971-Feb. 23, 1972
Departure: Moved to Appropriations

5th APPROPRIATIONS
Dates: Feb. 23, 1972-Jan. 3, 1997
Departure: Left the Senate; retired

Cong.	Ranking	Years in: Senate	Comm.	Date of Assignment
103rd	Min-RM	27	21	Jan. 7, 1993
104th	Maj-Chr	29	23	Jan. 4, 1995

6th RULES AND ADMINISTRATION
Dates: Jan. 12, 1973-Jan. 3, 1997
Departure: Left the Senate; retired

Cong.	Ranking	Years in: Senate	Comm.	Date of Assignment
103rd	Min-2nd	27	21	Jan. 21, 1993
104th	Maj-2nd	29	22	Jan. 6, 1995

SENATE SELECT AND SPECIAL COMMITTEES:

1st SELECT SMALL BUSINESS
Dates: Jan. 18, 1967-Jan. 12, 1973
Departure: Moved to Rules and Administration

2nd NUTRITION AND HUMAN NEEDS
1st Dates: Aug. 2, 1968-Jan. 22, 1969
1st Departure: Left committee; no new assignment
2nd Dates: Feb. 3, 1975-Feb. 24, 1977
2nd Departure: Moved to Select Indian Affairs

3rd EQUAL EDUCATIONAL OPPORTUNITY
Dates: Mar. 4, 1970-Dec. 31, 1972
Termination: Floor announcement of completed hearings and expiration of committee

4th SECRET AND CONFIDENTIAL GOVERNMENT DOCUMENTS
1st Dates: Sep. 22, 1972-Jan. 2, 1973
SECRET AND CONFIDENTIAL DOCUMENTS
2nd Dates: Jan. 11, 1973-Oct. 23, 1973
Termination: Senate Report 466 (93-1) filed

5th SELECT INTELLIGENCE (Permanent)
Dates: May 20, 1976-Feb. 21, 1977
Departure: Moved to Select Indian Affairs

6th SELECT INDIAN AFFAIRS (Permanent), 95-96
INDIAN AFFAIRS (Permanent), 103
1st Dates: Feb. 24, 1977-Jan. 21, 1981
1st Departure: Left committee; became Chair of Appropriations
2nd Dates: Feb. 2, 1993-Jan. 3, 1995
2nd Departure: Left committee; became Chair of Appropriations again

Cong.	Ranking	Years in: Senate	Comm.	Date of Assignment
103rd	Min-8th	27 *2	1	Feb. 2, 1993

7th SELECT ETHICS (Permanent)
Dates: Apr. 10, 1979-Jan. 28, 1980
Departure: Left committee; no new assignment

JOINT COMMITTEES:

1st JOINT LIBRARY
1st Senate Dates: Jan. 26, 1973-Mar. 3, 1977
1st Departure: Moved to Joint Printing
2nd Senate Dates: Feb. 3, 1981-Jan. 3, 1997
2nd Departure: Left the Senate; retired

Cong.	Ranking	Years in: Senate	Comm.	Date of Assignment
103rd	Min-1st	27 *2	12	Jan. 28, 1993
104th	Maj-Chr	29 *2	14	Jan. 17, 1995

2nd JOINT PRINTING
1st Senate Dates: Mar. 3, 1977-Feb. 5, 1981
1st Departure: Left committee; no new assignment
2nd Senate Dates: Feb. 24, 1981-Jan. 3, 1997
2nd Departure: Left the Senate; retired

Cong.	Ranking	Years in: Senate	Comm.	Date of Assignment
103rd	Min-2nd	27 *2	12	Jan. 28, 1993
104th	Maj-2nd	29 *2	14	Jan. 17, 1995

James A. Hayes (R-La.)

Dates: Dec. 21, 1946
House: Jan. 3, 1987-Jan. 2, 1997
Left the House: Lost U.S. Senate nomination in 1996

Served as a Democrat: Jan. 3, 1987-Dec. 12, 1995 (letter)
Served as a Republican: Dec. 12, 1995-Jan. 3, 1997

HOUSE STANDING COMMITTEES:

1st PUBLIC WORKS AND TRANSPORTATION, 100-103
TRANSPORTATION AND INFRASTRUCTURE, 104
Dates: Jan. 6, 1987-Dec. 12, 1995
Departure: Assignment was vacated as a Democrat; moved to Ways and Means as a Republican on Jan. 25, 1996

Cong.	Ranking	Terms in: House	Comm.	Date of Assignment
103rd	Maj-12th	4	4	Jan. 5, 1993
104th	Min-9th	5	5	Jan. 4, 1995

2nd SCIENCE, SPACE AND TECHNOLOGY, 100-103
SCIENCE, 104
Dates: Jan. 22, 1987-Dec. 12, 1995
Departure: Vacated assignment as a Democrat; moved to Ways and Means as a Republican on Jan. 25, 1996

Cong.	Ranking	Terms in: House	Comm.	Date of Assignment
103rd	Maj-11th	4	4	Jan. 5, 1993
104th	Min-4th	5	5	Jan. 4, 1995

3rd GOVERNMENT OPERATIONS
Dates: Feb. 4, 1993-Jan. 3, 1995
Departure: Left committee; no new assignment

Cong.	Ranking	Terms in: House	Comm.	Date of Assignment
103rd	Maj-19th	4	1	Feb. 4, 1993

4th WAYS AND MEANS
Dates: Jan. 25, 1996-Jan. 2, 1997 as a Republican
Departure: Left the House; lost Senate nomination

Cong.	Ranking	Terms in: House	Comm.	Date of Assignment
104th	MjA-23rd	5	1	Jan. 25, 1996

Robert (Robin) Hayes (R-N.C.)

Dates: Aug. 14, 1945
House: Jan. 3, 1999-Jan. 3, 2009
Left the House: Defeated for re-election in 2008

HOUSE STANDING COMMITTEES:

1st AGRICULTURE
Dates: Jan. 6, 1999-Jan. 3, 2009
Departure: Left the House; lost re-election

Cong.	Ranking	Terms in: House	Comm.	Date of Assignment
106th	Maj-26th	1	1	Jan. 6, 1999
107th	Maj-18th	2	2	Jan. 6, 2001
108th	Maj-12th	3	3	Jan. 28, 2003
109th	Maj-9th	4	4	Jan. 26, 2005
110th	Min-5th	5	5	Jan. 10, 2007

2nd ARMED SERVICES
Dates: Jan. 6, 1999-Jan. 3, 2009
Departure: Left the House; lost re-election

Cong.	Ranking	Terms in: House	Comm.	Date of Assignment
106th	Maj-30th	1	1	Jan. 6, 1999

Cong.	Ranking	Terms in: House	Comm.	Date of Assignment
107th	Maj-23rd	2	2	Jan. 6, 2001
108th	Maj-14th	3	3	Jan. 28, 2003
109th	Maj-14th	4	4	Jan. 26, 2005
110th	Min-9th	5	5	Jan. 10, 2007

3rd RESOURCES
Dates: Jan. 6, 1999-Feb. 7, 2001
Departure: Resigned committee; moved to Transportation and Infrastructure

Cong.	Ranking	Terms in: House	Comm.	Date of Assignment
106th	Maj-26th	1	1	Jan. 6, 1999
107th	Maj-24th	2	2	Jan. 6, 2001

4th TRANSPORTATION AND INFRASTRUCTURE
Dates: Feb. 8, 2001-Jan. 3, 2009
Departure: Left the House; lost re-election

Cong.	Ranking	Terms in: House	Comm.	Date of Assignment
107th	MjR-2nd	2	1	Feb. 8, 2001
108th	Maj-22nd	3	2	Jan. 28, 2003
109th	Maj-18th	4	3	Jan. 26, 2005
110th	Min-13th	5	4	Jan. 10, 2007

John D. Hayworth Jr. (R-Ariz.)

Dates: July 12, 1958
House: Jan. 3, 1995-Jan. 3, 2007
Left the House: Defeated for re-election in 2006

HOUSE STANDING COMMITTEES:

1st BANKING AND FINANCIAL SERVICES
Dates: Jan. 4, 1995-Jan. 3, 1997
Departure: Moved to Ways and Means

Cong.	Ranking	Terms in: House	Comm.	Date of Assignment
104th	Maj-14th	1	1	Jan. 4, 1995

2nd RESOURCES
1st Dates: Jan. 4, 1995-Jan. 3, 1997
1st Departure: Moved to Ways and Means
2nd Dates: June 20, 2001-Jan. 3, 2007
2nd Departure: Left the House; lost re-election

Cong.	Ranking	Terms in: House	Comm.	Date of Assignment
104th	Maj-13th	1 *1	1	Jan. 4, 1995
107th	MjR-3rd	4 *2	1	June 20, 2001
108th	Maj-20th	5 *2	2	Jan. 28, 2003
109th	Maj-17th	6 *2	3	Jan. 26, 2005

3rd VETERANS' AFFAIRS
Dates: Jan. 4, 1995-June 20, 2001
Departure: Resigned committee; returned to Resources

Cong.	Ranking	Terms in: House	Comm.	Date of Assignment
104th	Maj-17th	1	1	Jan. 4, 1995
105th	Maj-15th	2	2	Jan. 21, 1997
106th	Maj-11th	3	3	Jan. 6, 1999
107th	Maj-10th	4	4	Jan. 6, 2001

4th WAYS AND MEANS
Dates: Jan. 21, 1997-Jan. 3, 2007
Departure: Left the House; lost re-election

Cong.	Ranking	Terms in: House	Comm.	Date of Assignment
105th	Maj-21st	2	1	Jan. 21, 1997

Cong.	Ranking	Terms in: House	Comm.	Date of Assignment
106th	Maj-18th	3	2	Jan. 6, 1999
107th	Maj-17th	4	3	Jan. 6, 2001
108th	Maj-16th	5	4	Jan. 28, 2003
109th	Maj-12th	6	5	Jan. 26, 2005

Joel M. Hefley (R-Colo.)

Dates: April 18, 1935
House: Jan. 3, 1987-Jan. 3, 2007
Left the House: Retired in 2006

HOUSE STANDING COMMITTEES:

1st SCIENCE, SPACE AND TECHNOLOGY
Dates: Jan. 21, 1987-Jan. 3, 1989
Departure: Moved to Armed Services

2nd SMALL BUSINESS
Dates: Jan. 21, 1987-Jan. 3, 2003
Departure: Left committee; no new assignment

Cong.	Ranking	Terms in: House	Comm.	Date of Assignment
103rd	Min-4th	4	4	Jan. 5, 1993
104th	Maj-2nd	5	5	Jan. 4, 1995
105th	Maj-3rd	6	6	Jan. 21, 1997
106th	Maj-3rd	7	7	Jan. 6, 1999
107th	Maj-3rd	8	8	Jan. 6, 2001

3rd ARMED SERVICES, 101-103
NATIONAL SECURITY, 104-105
ARMED SERVICES, 106-109
Dates: Jan. 20, 1989-Jan. 3, 2007
Departure: Left the House; retired

Cong.	Ranking	Terms in: House	Comm.	Date of Assignment
103rd	Min-11th	4	3	Jan. 5, 1993
104th	Maj-9th	5	4	Jan. 4, 1995
105th	Maj-8th	6	5	Jan. 7, 1997
106th	Maj-8th	7	6	Jan. 6, 1999
107th	Maj-6th	8	7	Jan. 6, 2001
108th	Maj-3rd	9	8	Jan. 28, 2003
109th	Maj-3rd	10	9	Jan. 26, 2005

4th INTERIOR AND INSULAR AFFAIRS, 102
NATURAL RESOURCES, 103
RESOURCES, 104-108
Dates: Jan. 24, 1991-Jan. 30, 2003
Departure: Resigned committee; no new assignment

Cong.	Ranking	Terms in: House	Comm.	Date of Assignment
103rd	Min-8th	4	2	Jan. 5, 1993
104th	Maj-6th	5	3	Jan. 4, 1995
105th	Maj-7th	6	4	Jan. 7, 1997
106th	Maj-7th	7	5	Jan. 6, 1999
107th	Maj-7th	8	6	Jan. 6, 2001
108th	Maj-7th	9	7	Jan. 28, 2003

5th STANDARDS OF OFFICIAL CONDUCT
Dates: Sep. 29, 1997-Jan. 3, 2005
Departure: Left committee; no new assignment

Cong.	Ranking	Terms in: House	Comm.	Date of Assignment
105th	Maj-3rd	6	1	Sep. 29, 1997
106th	Maj-2nd	7	2	Jan. 19, 1999
107th	Maj-Chr	8	3	Jan. 20, 2001
108th	Maj-Chr	9	4	Jan. 8, 2003

Howell T. Heflin (D-Ala.)

Dates: June 19, 1921-March 29, 2005
Senate: Jan. 3, 1979-Jan. 3, 1997
Left the Senate: Retired in 1996

SENATE STANDING COMMITTEES:

1st COMMERCE, SCIENCE AND TRANSPORTATION
Dates: Jan. 23, 1979-Feb. 21, 1985
Departure: Left committee; no new assignment

2nd JUDICIARY
Dates: Jan. 23, 1979-Jan. 3, 1997
Departure: Left the Senate; retired

Cong.	Ranking	Years in: Senate	Comm.	Date of Assignment
103rd	Maj-6th	15	14	Jan. 7, 1993
104th	Min-4th	17	16	Jan. 4, 1995

3rd AGRICULTURE, NUTRITION AND FORESTRY
Dates: Jan. 5, 1981-Jan. 3, 1997
Departure: Left the Senate; retired

Cong.	Ranking	Years in: Senate	Comm.	Date of Assignment
103rd	Maj-4th	15	13	Jan. 7, 1993
104th	Min-3rd	17	14	Jan. 4, 1995

4th ENERGY AND NATURAL RESOURCES
1st Dates: Feb. 2, 1989-Feb. 5, 1991
1st Departure: Left committee; no new assignment
2nd Dates: Mar. 28, 1995-Jan. 3, 1997
2nd Departure: Left the Senate; retired

Cong.	Ranking	Years in: Senate	Comm.	Date of Assignment
104th	MnR-1st	17 *2	1	Mar. 28, 1995

5th SMALL BUSINESS
Dates: Jan. 21, 1993-Jan. 3, 1997
Departure: Left the Senate; retired

Cong.	Ranking	Years in: Senate	Comm.	Date of Assignment
103rd	Maj-9th	15	1	Jan. 21, 1993
104th	Min-8th	17	2	Jan. 6, 1995

SENATE SELECT AND SPECIAL COMMITTEES:

1st SELECT ETHICS (Permanent)
Dates: Oct. 31, 1979-Nov. 20, 1991
Departure: Left committee; no new assignment

2nd JUDGE HARRY E. CLAIBORNE IMPEACHMENT
Dates: Aug. 14, 1986-Oct. 9, 1986
Termination: Senate Report 99-511 filed

3rd SECRET MILITARY ASSISTANCE TO IRAN AND
THE NICARAGUAN OPPOSITION (Iran-Contra Affair)
Dates: Jan. 12, 1987-Nov. 17, 1987
Termination: Senate Report 100-216 filed

4th JUDGE WALTER L. NIXON IMPEACHMENT
Dates: May 11, 1989-Sep. 13, 1989
Termination: Impeachment hearings concluded

W.G. (Bill) Hefner (D-N.C.)

Dates: April 11, 1930
House: Jan. 3, 1975-Jan. 3, 1999
Left the House: Retired in 1998

HOUSE STANDING COMMITTEES:

1st INTERSTATE AND FOREIGN COMMERCE
Dates: Jan. 20, 1975-Apr. 8, 1976
Departure: Resigned committee; moved to Public Works and Transportation

2nd VETERANS' AFFAIRS
Dates: Jan. 20, 1975-Jan. 3, 1981
Departure: Moved to Budget

3rd PUBLIC WORKS AND TRANSPORTATION
Dates: Apr. 8, 1976-July 2, 1980
Departure: Resigned committee; moved to Appropriations

4th APPROPRIATIONS
Dates: July 2, 1980-Jan. 3, 1999
Departure: Left the House; retired

Cong.	Ranking	Terms in: House	Comm.	Date of Assignment
103rd	Maj-14th	10	8	Jan. 5, 1993
104th	Min-11th	11	9	Jan. 4, 1995
105th	Min-9th	12	10	Jan. 7, 1997

5th BUDGET
Dates: Jan. 28, 1981-Jan. 3, 1987
Departure: Left committee; no new assignment

Fred Heineman (R-N.C.)

Dates: Dec. 28, 1928
House: Jan. 3, 1995-Jan. 3, 1997
Left the House: Defeated for re-election in 1996

HOUSE STANDING COMMITTEES:

1st BANKING AND FINANCIAL SERVICES
Dates: Jan. 4, 1995-Jan. 3, 1997
Departure: Left the House; lost re-election

Cong.	Ranking	Terms in: House	Comm.	Date of Assignment
104th	Maj-23rd	1	1	Jan. 4, 1995

2nd JUDICIARY
Dates: Jan. 4, 1995-Jan. 3, 1997
Departure: Left the House; lost re-election

Cong.	Ranking	Terms in: House	Comm.	Date of Assignment
104th	Maj-16th	1	1	Jan. 4, 1995

Martin Heinrich (D-N.M.)

Dates: Oct. 17, 1971
House: Jan. 3, 2009-date
Serving in the 111th Congress

HOUSE STANDING COMMITTEES:

1st ARMED SERVICES
Dates: Jan. 7, 2009-date
Departure: Still serving in the 111th Congress

Cong.	Ranking	Terms in: House	Comm.	Date of Assignment
111th	Maj-34th	1	1	Jan. 7, 2009

2nd NATURAL RESOURCES
Dates: Jan. 21, 2009-date
Departure: Still serving in the 111th Congress

Cong.	Ranking	Terms in: House	Comm.	Date of Assignment
111th	Maj-13th	1	1	Jan. 21, 2009

Dean Heller (R-Nev.)

Dates: May 10, 1960
House: Jan. 3, 2007-date
Serving in the 111th Congress

HOUSE STANDING COMMITTEES:

1st NATURAL RESOURCES
Dates: Jan. 10, 2007-Feb. 25, 2008
Departure: Resigned committee; moved to Financial Services

Cong.	Ranking	Terms in: House	Comm.	Date of Assignment
110th	Min-20th	1	1	Jan. 10, 2007

2nd SMALL BUSINESS
Dates: Jan. 10, 2007-Feb. 25, 2008
Departure: Resigned committee; moved to Financial Services

Cong.	Ranking	Terms in: House	Comm.	Date of Assignment
110th	Min-11th	1	1	Jan. 10, 2007

3rd EDUCATION AND LABOR
Dates: Mar. 12, 2007-Feb. 25, 2008
Departure: Resigned committee; moved to Financial Services

Cong.	Ranking	Terms in: House	Comm.	Date of Assignment
110th	MnR-1st	1	1	Mar. 12, 2007

4th FINANCIAL SERVICES
Dates: Feb. 26, 2008-Jan. 3, 2009
Departure: Moved to Ways and Means

Cong.	Ranking	Terms in: House	Comm.	Date of Assignment
110th	MnR-4th	1	1	Feb. 26, 2008

5th WAYS AND MEANS
Dates: Jan. 9, 2009-date
Departure: Still serving in the 111th Congress

Cong.	Ranking	Terms in: House	Comm.	Date of Assignment
111th	Min-14th	2	1	Jan. 9, 2009

Jesse A. Helms (R-N.C.)

Dates: Oct. 18, 1921-July 4, 2008
Senate: Jan. 3, 1973-Jan. 3, 2003
Left the Senate: Retired in 2002

SENATE STANDING COMMITTEES:

1st AERONAUTICAL AND SPACE SCIENCES
Dates: Jan. 12, 1973-Jan. 23, 1975
Departure: Moved to Banking, Housing and Urban Affairs.

2nd AGRICULTURE AND FORESTRY reorganized Feb. 22, 1977
AGRICULTURE, NUTRITION AND FORESTRY
Dates: Jan. 12, 1973-Jan. 3, 2003
Departure: Left the Senate; retired

Cong.	Ranking	Years in: Senate	Comm.	Date of Assignment
103rd	Min-3rd	21	20	Jan. 7, 1993
104th	Maj-3rd	23	22	Jan. 4, 1995
105th	Maj-2nd	25	24	Jan. 9, 1997
106th	Maj-2nd	27	26	Jan. 7, 1999
107th	Maj-2nd	29	29	Jan. 25, 2001
+107th	Min-2nd	29	29	June 6, 2001

3rd BANKING, HOUSING AND URBAN AFFAIRS
Dates: Jan. 23, 1975-Feb. 22, 1977
Departure: Moved to Armed Services

4th ARMED SERVICES
Dates: Feb. 22, 1977-Jan. 23, 1979
Departure: Moved to Foreign Relations

5th FOREIGN RELATIONS
Dates: Jan. 23, 1979-Jan. 3, 2003
Ch1: Replaced by Joseph R. Biden (D-Del.) on June 6, 2001 following party control shift and became RM2
Departure: Left the Senate; retired

Cong.	Ranking	Years in: Senate	Comm.	Date of Assignment
103rd	Min-RM	21	14	Jan. 7, 1993
104th	Maj-Chr	23	16	Jan. 5, 1995
105th	Maj-Chr	25	18	Jan. 9, 1997
106th	Maj-Chr	27	20	Jan. 7, 1999
107th	Maj-Ch1	29	23	Jan. 25, 2001
+107th	Min-RM2	29	23	June 6, 2001

6th RULES AND ADMINISTRATION
Dates: Jan. 5, 1981-Jan. 3, 2003
Departure: Left the Senate; retired

Cong.	Ranking	Years in: Senate	Comm.	Date of Assignment
103rd	Min-3rd	21	13	Jan. 21, 1993
104th	Maj-3rd	23	15	Jan. 6, 1995
105th	Maj-2nd	25	17	Jan. 9, 1997
106th	Maj-2nd	27	19	Jan. 7, 1999
107th	Maj-3rd	29	21	Jan. 25, 2001
+107th	Min-3rd	29	21	June 6, 2001

SENATE SELECT AND SPECIAL COMMITTEES:

1st SENATE COMMITTEE SYSTEM I (Stevenson)
Dates: Apr. 6, 1976-May 17, 1977
Termination: Date last reports filed

2nd SELECT ETHICS (Permanent)
1st Dates: Apr. 10,1979-Jan. 6, 1981
1st Departure: Moved to Rules and Administration
2nd Dates: Jan. 21, 1981-Nov. 20, 1991
2nd Departure: Left committee; no new assignment

3rd SELECT POW-MIA AFFAIRS
Dates: Aug. 2, 1991-Feb. 3, 1993
Termination: Senate Report 1 (103-1) filed

JOINT COMMITTEES:

1st JOINT CONGRESSIONAL OPERATIONS
Senate Dates: Mar. 26, 1973-Sep. 30, 1977
Termination: Senate Res. 4 (95-1)

Paul B. Henry (R-Mich.)

Dates: July 9, 1942-July 31, 1993
House: Jan. 3, 1985-July 31, 1993
Left the House: Died in office

HOUSE STANDING COMMITTEES:

1st EDUCATION AND LABOR
Dates: Jan. 30, 1985-July 31, 1993
Departure: Died in office

Cong.	Ranking	Terms in: House	Comm.	Date of Assignment
103rd	Min-7th	5	5	Jan. 5, 1993

2nd SCIENCE AND TECHNOLOGY, 99
SCIENCE, SPACE AND TECHNOLOGY, 100-103
Dates: Jan. 30, 1985-July 31, 1993
Departure: Died in office

Cong.	Ranking	Terms in: House	Comm.	Date of Assignment
103rd	Min-5th	5	5	Jan. 5, 1993

HOUSE SELECT AND SPECIAL COMMITTEES:

1st SELECT AGING (Permanent)
Dates: Feb. 21, 1985-Jan. 3, 1993
Termination: Committee not renewed in 1993

Jeb Hensarling (R-Tex.)

Dates: May 29, 1957
House: Jan. 3, 2003-date
Serving in the 111th Congress

HOUSE STANDING COMMITTEES:

1st BUDGET
Dates: Jan. 28, 2003-date
Departure: Still serving in the 111th Congress

Cong.	Ranking	Terms in: House	Comm.	Date of Assignment
108th	Maj-23rd	1	1	Jan. 28, 2003
109th	Maj-13th	2	2	Jan. 26, 2005
110th	Min-7th	3	3	Jan. 18, 2007
111th	Min-4th	4	4	Jan. 9, 2009

2nd FINANCIAL SERVICES
Dates: Jan. 28, 2003-date
Departure: Still serving in the 111th Congress

Cong.	Ranking	Terms in: House	Comm.	Date of Assignment
108th	Min-31st	1	1	Jan. 28, 2003

109th	Min-25th	2	2	Jan. 26, 2005
110th	Maj-18th	3	3	Jan. 12, 2007
111th	Min-12th	4	4	Jan. 9, 2009

Walter W. Herger (R-Cal.)

Dates: May 20, 1945
House: Jan. 3, 1987-date
Serving in the 111th Congress

HOUSE STANDING COMMITTEES:

1st AGRICULTURE
Dates: Jan. 21, 1987-Jan. 3, 1993
Departure: Moved to Ways and Means and Budget

2nd MERCHANT MARINE AND FISHERIES
Dates: Jan. 21, 1987-Jan. 3, 1993
Departure: Moved to Ways and Means and Budget

3rd WAYS AND MEANS
Dates: Jan. 5, 1993-date
Departure: Still serving in the 111th Congress

Cong.	Ranking	Terms in: House	Comm.	Date of Assignment
103rd	Min-11th	4	1	Jan. 5, 1993
104th	Maj-8th	5	2	Jan. 4, 1995
105th	Maj-8th	6	3	Jan. 21, 1997
106th	Maj-7th	7	4	Jan. 6, 1999
107th	Maj-6th	8	5	Jan. 6, 2001
108th	Maj-6th	9	6	Jan. 28, 2003
109th	Maj-4th	10	7	Jan. 26, 2005
110th	Min-2nd	11	8	Jan. 10, 2007
111th	Min-2nd	12	9	Jan. 9, 2009

4th BUDGET
Dates: Jan. 26, 1993-Jan. 3, 2001
Departure: Left committee; no new assignment

Cong.	Ranking	Terms in: House	Comm.	Date of Assignment
103rd	Min-6th	4	1	Jan. 26, 1993
104th	Maj-6th	5	2	Jan. 4, 1995
105th	Maj-4th	6	3	Jan. 7, 1997
106th	Maj-4th	7	4	Jan. 6, 1999

HOUSE SELECT AND SPECIAL COMMITTEES:

1st SELECT HUNGER (Temporary)
Dates: Mar. 9, 1988-Jan. 3, 1991
Departure: Left committee; no new assignment

2nd SELECT NARCOTICS ABUSE AND CONTROL (Temporary)
Dates: Apr. 10, 1989-Jan. 3, 1993
Termination: Committee not renewed in 1993

JOINT COMMITTEES:

1st JOINT TAXATION
House Dates: Jan. 17, 2007-date
Departure: Still serving in the 111th Congress

Cong.	Ranking	Terms in: House	Comm.	Date of Assignment
110th	Min-2nd	11	1	Jan. 17, 2007
111th	Min-2nd	12	2	Jan. 12, 2009

Stephanie Herseth, see, Stephanie Herseth Sandlin p. 369.

Brian Higgins (D-N.Y.)

Dates: Oct. 6, 1959
House: Jan. 3, 2005-date
Serving in the 111th Congress

HOUSE STANDING COMMITTEES:

1st GOVERNMENT REFORM, 109
OVERSIGHT AND GOVERNMENT REFORM, 110
Dates: Jan. 26, 2005-Jan. 3, 2009
Departure: Moved to Ways and Means

Cong.	Ranking	Terms in: House	Comm.	Date of Assignment
109th	Min-17th	1	1	Jan. 26, 2005
110th	Maj-13th	2	2	Jan. 12, 2007

2nd TRANSPORTATION AND INFRASTRUCTURE
Dates: Jan. 26, 2005-Jan. 3, 2009
Departure: Moved to Ways and Means

Cong.	Ranking	Terms in: House	Comm.	Date of Assignment
109th	Min-31st	1	1	Jan. 26, 2005
110th	Maj-22nd	2	2	Jan. 10, 2007

3rd SMALL BUSINESS
Dates: Sep. 20, 2007-Jan. 3, 2009
Departure: Moved to Ways and Means

Cong.	Ranking	Terms in: House	Comm.	Date of Assignment
110th	MjR-1st	2	1	Sep. 20, 2007

4th WAYS AND MEANS
Dates: Jan. 7, 2009-date
Departure: Still serving in the 111th Congress

Cong.	Ranking	Terms in: House	Comm.	Date of Assignment
111th	Maj-25th	2	1	Jan. 7, 2009

Cong.	Ranking	Terms in: House	Comm.	Date of Assignment
106th	Min-24th	1	1	Jan. 6, 1999
107th	Min-18th	2	2	Jan. 31, 2001
108th	Min-10th	3	3	Jan. 28, 2003

2nd ARMED SERVICES
Dates: Jan. 6, 1999-Jan. 3, 2005
Departure: Left the House; lost re-election

Cong.	Ranking	Terms in: House	Comm.	Date of Assignment
106th	Min-26th	1	1	Jan. 6, 1999
107th	Min-24th	2	2	Jan. 31, 2001
108th	Min-18th	3	3	Jan. 28, 2003

3rd VETERANS' AFFAIRS
Dates: June 9, 1999-Jan. 3, 2003
Departure: Left committee; no new assignment

Cong.	Ranking	Terms in: House	Comm.	Date of Assignment
106th	Min-13th	1	1	June 9, 1999
107th	Min-13th	2	2	Jan. 31, 2001

4th ENERGY AND COMMERCE
Dates: Jan. 4, 2007-date
Departure: Still serving in the 111th Congress

Cong.	Ranking	Terms in: House	Comm.	Date of Assignment
110th	Maj-31st	4	1	Jan. 4, 2007
111th	Maj-26th	5	2	Jan. 7, 2009

5th SCIENCE AND TECHNOLOGY
Dates: Jan. 18, 2007-date
Departure: Still serving in the 111th Congress

Cong.	Ranking	Terms in: House	Comm.	Date of Assignment
110th	Maj-22nd	4	1	Jan. 18, 2007
111th	Maj-20th	5	2	Jan. 21, 2009

JOINT COMMITTEES:

1st JOINT ECONOMIC
1st House Dates: Apr. 18, 2002-Jan. 3, 2005
1st Departure: Left the House; lost re-election
2nd House Dates: Mar. 27, 2007-date
2nd Departure: Still serving in the 111th Congress

Cong.	Ranking	Terms in: House	Comm.	Date of Assignment
107th	Min-4th	2 *1	1	Apr. 18, 2002
108th	Min-4th	3 *1	2	Mar. 12, 2003
110th	Maj-3rd	4 *2	1	Mar. 27, 2007
111th	Maj-3rd	5 *2	2	Feb. 3, 2009

Baron P. Hill (D-Ind.)

Dates: June 22, 1953
House 1: Jan. 3, 1999-Jan. 3, 2005
Left the House 1: Defeated for re-election in 2004
House 2: Jan. 3, 2007-date
Serving in the 111th Congress

HOUSE STANDING COMMITTEES:

1st AGRICULTURE
Dates: Jan. 6, 1999-Jan. 3, 2005
Departure: Left the House; lost re-election

Rick Hill (R-Mont.)

Dates: Dec. 30, 1946
House: Jan. 3, 1997-Jan. 3, 2001
Left the House: Retired in 2000

HOUSE STANDING COMMITTEES:

1st BANKING AND FINANCIAL SERVICES
Dates: Jan. 7, 1997-Jan. 3, 2001
Departure: Left the House; retired

Cong.	Ranking	Terms in: House	Comm.	Date of Assignment
105th	Maj-27th	1	1	Jan. 7, 1997
106th	Maj-22nd	2	2	Jan. 6, 1999

2nd RESOURCES
Dates: Jan. 7, 1997-Jan. 3, 2001
Departure: Left the House; retired

Cong.	Ranking	Terms in: House	Comm.	Date of Assignment
105th	Maj-24th	1	1	Jan. 7, 1997
106th	Maj-20th	2	2	Jan. 6, 1999

3rd SMALL BUSINESS
Dates: Feb. 12, 1997-Jan. 3, 2001
Departure: Left the House; retired

Cong.	Ranking	Terms in: House	Comm.	Date of Assignment
105th	Maj-18th	1	1	Feb. 12, 1997
106th	Maj-11th	2	2	Jan. 6, 1999

Van Hilleary (R-Tenn.)

Dates: June 20, 1959
House: Jan. 3, 1995-Jan. 3, 2003
Left the House: Lost election for Governor in 2002

HOUSE STANDING COMMITTEES:

1st NATIONAL SECURITY, 104-105
ARMED SERVICES, 106-107
Dates: Jan. 4, 1995-Jan. 3, 2003
Departure: Left the House; lost election for Governor

Cong.	Ranking	Terms in: House	Comm.	Date of Assignment
104th	Maj-25th	1	1	Jan. 4, 1995
105th	Maj-22nd	2	2	Jan. 7, 1997
106th	Maj-21st	3	3	Jan. 6, 1999
107th	Maj-16th	4	4	Jan. 6, 2001

2nd SCIENCE
Dates: Jan. 4, 1995-Jan. 3, 1997
Departure: Moved to Budget and Education and the Workforce

Cong.	Ranking	Terms in: House	Comm.	Date of Assignment
104th	Maj-24th	1	1	Jan. 4, 1995

3rd SMALL BUSINESS
Dates: Jan. 4, 1995-Jan. 3, 1997
Departure: Moved to Budget and Education and the Workforce

Cong.	Ranking	Terms in: House	Comm.	Date of Assignment
104th	Maj-16th	1	1	Jan. 4, 1995

4th BUDGET
Dates: Jan. 7, 1997-Jan. 3, 2003
Departure: Left the House; lost election for Governor

Cong.	Ranking	Terms in: House	Comm.	Date of Assignment
105th	Maj-21st	2	1	Jan. 7, 1997
106th	Maj-13th	3	2	Jan. 6, 1999
107th	Maj-6th	4	3	Jan. 6, 2001

5th EDUCATION AND THE WORKFORCE
Dates: Jan. 21, 1997-Jan. 3, 2003
Departure: Left the House; lost election for Governor

Cong.	Ranking	Terms in: House	Comm.	Date of Assignment
105th	Maj-24th	2	1	Jan. 21, 1997
106th	Maj-21st	3	2	Jan. 6, 1999
107th	Maj-15th	4	3	Jan. 6, 2001

Earl F. Hilliard (D-Ala.)

Dates: April 9, 1942
House: Jan. 3, 1993-Jan. 3, 2003
Left the House: Defeated for re-nomination in 2002

HOUSE STANDING COMMITTEES:

1st AGRICULTURE
Dates: Jan. 5, 1993-Jan. 3, 2003
Departure: Left the House; lost re-nomination

Cong.	Ranking	Terms in: House	Comm.	Date of Assignment
103rd	Maj-19th	1	1	Jan. 5, 1993
104th	Min-12th	2	2	Jan. 4, 1995
105th	Min-8th	3	3	Jan. 7, 1997
106th	Min-8th	4	4	Jan. 6, 1999
107th	Min-6th	5	5	Jan. 31, 2001

2nd SMALL BUSINESS
Dates: Jan. 5, 1993-June 4, 1996
Departure: Resigned committee; moved to International Relations

Cong.	Ranking	Terms in: House	Comm.	Date of Assignment
103rd	Maj-25th	1	1	Jan. 5, 1993
104th	Min-12th	2	2	Jan. 4, 1995

3rd INTERNATIONAL RELATIONS
Dates: June 5, 1995-Jan. 3, 2003
Departure: Left the House; lost re-nomination

Cong.	Ranking	Terms in: House	Comm.	Date of Assignment
104th	MnR-2nd	2	1	June 5, 1995
105th	Min-15th	3	2	Jan. 7, 1997
106th	Min-13th	4	3	Jan. 6, 1999
107th	Min-10th	5	4	Jan. 31, 2001

James A. Himes (D-Conn.)

Dates: July 5, 1966
House: Jan. 3, 2009-date
Serving in the 111th Congress

HOUSE STANDING COMMITTEES:

1st FINANCIAL SERVICES
Dates: Jan. 7, 2009-date
Departure: Still serving in the 111th Congress

Cong.	Ranking	Terms in: House	Comm.	Date of Assignment
111th	Maj-40th	1	1	Jan. 7, 2009

2nd HOMELAND SECURITY
Dates: Jan. 28, 2009-date
Departure: Still serving in the 111th Congress

Cong.	Ranking	Terms in: House	Comm.	Date of Assignment
111th	Maj-17th	1	1	Jan. 28, 2009

Maurice D. Hinchey (D-N.Y.)

Dates: Oct. 27, 1938
House: Jan. 3, 1993-date
Serving in the 111th Congress

HOUSE STANDING COMMITTEES:

1st BANKING, FINANCE AND URBAN AFFAIRS, 103
BANKING AND FINANCIAL SERVICES, 104-105
Dates: Jan. 5, 1993-Jan. 3, 1999
Departure: Moved to Appropriations

Cong.	Ranking	Terms in: House	Comm.	Date of Assignment
103rd	Maj-27th	1	1	Jan. 5, 1993
104th	Min-20th	2	2	Jan. 4, 1995
105th	Min-16th	3	3	Jan. 7, 1997

2nd NATURAL RESOURCES, 103
RESOURCES, 104-105
NATURAL RESOURCES, 110-111
1st Dates: Jan. 5, 1993-Jan. 3, 1999
1st Departure: Moved to Appropriations
2nd Dates: Jan. 7, 2007-date
2nd Departure: Still serving in the 111th Congress

Cong.	Ranking	Terms in: House	Comm.	Date of Assignment
103rd	Maj-23rd	1 *1	1	Jan. 5, 1993
104th	Min-18th	2 *1	2	Jan. 9, 1995
105th	Min-16th	3 *1	3	Jan. 7, 1997
110th	Maj-18th	8 *2	1	Jan. 18, 2007
111th	Maj-17th	9 *2	2	Jan. 21, 2009

3rd APPROPRIATIONS
Dates: Jan. 6, 1999-date
Departure: Still serving in the 111th Congress

Cong.	Ranking	Terms in: House	Comm.	Date of Assignment
106th	Min-22nd	4	1	Jan. 6, 1999
107th	Min-22nd	5	2	Jan. 31, 2001
108th	Min-20th	6	3	Jan. 28, 2003
109th	Min-20th	7	4	Jan. 26, 2005
110th	Maj-17th	8	5	Jan. 4, 2007
111th	Maj-16th	9	6	Jan. 7, 2009

JOINT COMMITTEES:

1st JOINT ECONOMIC
1st House Dates: Mar. 7, 1996-Jan. 3, 1999
1st Departure: Moved to Appropriations
2nd House Dates: Mar. 3, 2005-date
2nd Departure: Still serving in the 111th Congress

Cong.	Ranking	Terms in: House	Comm.	Date of Assignment
104th	MnR-1st	3 *1	1	Mar. 7, 1996
105th	Min-3rd	4 *1	2	Mar. 11, 1997
109th	Min-2nd	7 *2	1	Mar. 3, 2005
110th	Maj-2nd	8 *2	2	Mar. 27, 2007
111th	Maj-2nd	9 *2	3	Feb. 3, 2009

Rubén Hinojosa (D-Tex.)

Dates: Aug. 20, 1940
House: Jan. 3, 1997-date
Serving in the 111th Congress

HOUSE STANDING COMMITTEES:

1st EDUCATION AND THE WORKFORCE, 105-109
EDUCATION AND LABOR, 110-111
Dates: Jan. 7, 1997-date
Departure: Still serving in the 111th Congress

Cong.	Ranking	Terms in: House	Comm.	Date of Assignment
105th	Min-15th	1	1	Jan. 7, 1997
106th	Min-14th	2	2	Jan. 6, 1999
107th	Min-12th	3	3	Jan. 31, 2001
108th	Min-7th	4	4	Jan. 28, 2003
109th	Min-8th	5	5	Jan. 26, 2005
110th	Maj-7th	6	6	Jan. 10, 2007
111th	Maj-7th	7	7	Jan. 21, 2009

2nd SMALL BUSINESS
Dates: Mar. 14, 1997-Feb. 28, 2001
Departure: Resigned committee; moved to Financial Services

Cong.	Ranking	Terms in: House	Comm.	Date of Assignment
105th	MnR-1'st	1	1	Mar. 14, 1997
106th	Min-7th	2	2	Jan. 6, 1999
107th	Min-6th	3	3	Jan. 31, 2001

3rd FINANCIAL SERVICES
Dates: Feb. 8, 2001-date
Departure: Still serving in the 111th Congress

Cong.	Ranking	Terms in: House	Comm.	Date of Assignment
107th	Min-26th	3	1	Feb. 8, 2001
108th	Min-20th	4	2	Jan. 28, 2003
109th	Min-18th	5	3	Jan. 26, 2005
110th	Maj-14th	6	4	Jan. 12, 2007
111th	Maj-13th	7	5	Jan. 7, 2009

4th RESOURCES
Dates: Mar. 5, 2003-Jan. 3, 2005
Departure: Left committee; no new assignment

Cong.	Ranking	Terms in: House	Comm.	Date of Assignment
108th	Min-23rd	4	1	Mar. 5, 2003

5th FOREIGN AFFAIRS
Dates: Jan. 12, 2007-Jan. 3, 2009
Departure: Left committee; no new assignment

Cong.	Ranking	Terms in: House	Comm.	Date of Assignment
110th	Maj-18th	6	1	Jan. 12, 2007

Mazie K. Hirono (D-Hai.)

Dates: Nov. 3, 1947
House: Jan. 3, 2007-date
Serving in the 111th Congress

HOUSE STANDING COMMITTEES:

1st EDUCATION AND LABOR
Dates: Jan. 10, 2007-date
Departure: Still serving in the 111th Congress

Cong.	Ranking	Terms in: House	Comm.	Date of Assignment
110th	Maj-21st	1	1	Jan. 10, 2007
111th	Maj-18th	2	2	Jan. 21, 2009

2nd TRANSPORTATION AND INFRASTRUCTURE
Dates: Jan. 10, 2007-date
Departure: Still serving in the 111th Congress

Cong.	Ranking	Terms in: House	Comm.	Date of Assignment
110th	Maj-30th	1	1	Jan. 10, 2007
111th	Maj-23rd	2	2	Jan. 7, 2009

3rd SMALL BUSINESS
Dates: Sep. 20, 2007-Jan. 3, 2009
Departure: Left committee; no new assignment

Cong.	Ranking	Terms in: House	Comm.	Date of Assignment
110th	MjR-2nd	1	1	Sep. 20, 2007

Peter D. Hoagland (D-Neb.)

Dates: Nov. 17, 1941
House: Jan. 3, 1989-Jan. 3, 1995
Left the House: Defeated for re-election in 1994

HOUSE STANDING COMMITTEES:

1st BANKING, FINANCE AND URBAN AFFAIRS
Dates: Jan. 19, 1989-Jan. 3, 1993
Departure: Moved to Ways and Means

2nd SMALL BUSINESS
Dates: Jan. 19, 1989-Jan. 3, 1991
Departure: Moved to Interior and Insular Affairs and Judiciary

3rd INTERIOR AND INSULAR AFFAIRS
Dates: Jan. 24, 1991-Jan. 3, 1993
Departure: Moved to Ways and Means

4th JUDICIARY
Dates: Jan. 24, 1991-Jan. 3, 1993
Departure: Moved to Ways and Means

5th WAYS AND MEANS
Dates: Jan. 5, 1993-Jan. 3, 1995
Departure: Left the House; lost re-election

Cong.	Ranking	Terms in: House	Comm.	Date of Assignment
103rd	Maj-19th	3	1	Jan. 5, 1993

David L. Hobson (R-Ohio)

Dates: Oct. 17, 1936
House: Jan. 3, 1991-Jan. 3, 2009
Left the House: Retired in 2008

HOUSE STANDING COMMITTEES:

1st GOVERNMENT OPERATIONS
Dates: Jan. 24, 1991-Jan. 3, 1993
Departure: Moved to Appropriations and Budget

2nd PUBLIC WORKS AND TRANSPORTATION
Dates: Jan. 24, 1991-Jan. 3, 1993
Departure: Moved to Appropriations and Budget

3rd STANDARDS OF OFFICIAL CONDUCT
Dates: Feb. 6, 1991-Jan. 3, 1997
Departure: Left committee; no new assignment

Cong.	Ranking	Terms in: House	Comm.	Date of Assignment
103rd	Min-6th	2	2	Jan. 5, 1993
104th	Maj-4th	3	3	Jan. 20, 1995

4th APPROPRIATIONS
Dates: Jan. 5, 1993-Jan. 3, 2009
Departure: Left the House; retired

Cong.	Ranking	Terms in: House	Comm.	Date of Assignment
103rd	Min-21st	2	1	Jan. 5, 1993
104th	Maj-19th	3	2	Jan. 4, 1995
105th	Maj-16th	4	3	Jan. 7, 1997
106th	Maj-14th	5	4	Jan. 6, 1999
107th	Maj-12th	6	5	Jan. 6, 2001
108th	Maj-9th	7	6	Jan. 28, 2003
109th	Maj-9th	8	7	Jan. 6, 2005
110th	Min-7th	9	8	Jan. 4, 2007

5th BUDGET
Dates: Jan. 26, 1993-Jan. 3, 1999
Departure: Left committee; no new assignment

Cong.	Ranking	Terms in: House	Comm.	Date of Assignment
103rd	Min-11th	2	1	Jan. 26, 1993
104th	Maj-2nd	3	2	Jan. 4, 1995
105th	Maj-2nd	4	3	Jan. 7, 1997

HOUSE SELECT AND SPECIAL COMMITTEES:

1st SELECT AGING (Permanent)
Dates: Feb. 21, 1991-Jan. 3, 1993
Termination: Committee not renewed in 1993

George J. Hochbrueckner (D-N.Y.)

Dates: Sept. 20, 1938
House: Jan. 3, 1987-Jan. 3, 1995
Left the House: Defeated for re-election in 1994

HOUSE STANDING COMMITTEES:

1st ARMED SERVICES
Dates: Jan. 22, 1987-Jan. 3, 1995
Departure: Left the House; lost re-election

Cong.	Ranking	Terms in: House	Comm.	Date of Assignment
103rd	Maj-13th	4	4	Jan. 5, 1993

2nd MERCHANT MARINE AND FISHERIES
Dates: Jan. 22, 1987-Jan. 3, 1995
Departure: Left the House; lost re-election

Cong.	Ranking	Terms in: House	Comm.	Date of Assignment
103rd	Maj-9th	4	4	Jan. 5, 1993

3rd SCIENCE, SPACE AND TECHNOLOGY
Dates: Dec. 15, 1987-Jan. 3, 1989
Departure: Left committee; no new assignment

4th VETERANS' AFFAIRS
Dates: Feb. 27, 1990-Jan. 3, 1991
Departure: Left committee; no new assignment

HOUSE SELECT AND SPECIAL COMMITTEES:

1st SELECT NARCOTICS ABUSE AND CONTROL (Temporary)
Dates: Feb. 21, 1991-Jan. 3, 1993
Termination: Committee not renewed in 1993

Paul W. Hodes (D-N.H.)

Dates: March 21, 1951
House: Jan. 3, 2007-date
Serving in the 111th Congress

HOUSE STANDING COMMITTEES:

1st FINANCIAL SERVICES
Dates: Jan. 12, 2007-date
Departure: Still serving in the 111th Congress

Cong.	Ranking	Terms in: House	Comm.	Date of Assignment
110th	Maj-27th	1	1	Jan. 12, 2007
111th	Maj-24th	2	2	Jan. 7, 2009

2nd OVERSIGHT AND GOVERNMENT REFORM
Dates: Jan. 12, 2007-date
Departure: Still serving in the 111th Congress

Cong.	Ranking	Terms in: House	Comm.	Date of Assignment
110th	Maj-20th	1	1	Jan. 12, 2007
111th	Maj-19th	2	2	Jan. 28, 2009

Joseph M. Hoeffel (D-Penn.)

Dates: Sept. 3, 1950
House: Jan. 3, 1999-Jan. 3, 2005
Left the House: Lost U.S. Senate election in 2004

HOUSE STANDING COMMITTEES:

1st BUDGET
Dates: Jan. 6, 1999-Jan. 3, 2003
Departure: Moved to Transportation and Infrastructure

Cong.	Ranking	Terms in: House	Comm.	Date of Assignment
106th	Min-18th	1	1	Jan. 6, 1999
107th	Min-14th	2	2	Jan. 31, 2001

2nd INTERNATIONAL RELATIONS
Dates: Jan. 6, 1999-Jan. 3, 2005
Departure: Left the House; lost Senate election

Cong.	Ranking	Terms in: House	Comm.	Date of Assignment
106th	Min-19th	1	1	Jan. 19, 1999
107th	Min-19th	2	2	Jan. 31, 2001
108th	Min-15th	3	3	Jan. 28, 2003

3rd SCIENCE
Dates: June 9, 1999-Jan. 3, 2003
Departure: Moved to Transportation and Infrastructure

Cong.	Ranking	Terms in: House	Comm.	Date of Assignment
106th	MnR-2nd	1	1	June 9, 1999
107th	Min-19th	2	2	Jan. 31, 2001

4th TRANSPORTATION AND INFRASTRUCTURE
Dates: Jan. 28, 2003-Jan. 3, 2005
Departure: Left the House; lost Senate election

Cong.	Ranking	Terms in: House	Comm.	Date of Assignment
108th	Min-30th	3	1	Jan. 28, 2003

Peter Hoekstra (R-Mich.)

Dates: Oct. 30, 1953
House: Jan. 3, 1993-date
Serving in the 111th Congress

HOUSE STANDING COMMITTEES:

1st EDUCATION AND LABOR, 103
ECONOMIC AND EDUCATIONAL OPPORTUNITIES, 104
EDUCATION AND THE WORKFORCE, 105-108
EDUCATION AND LABOR, 110-111
1st Dates: Jan. 5, 1993-Jan. 3, 2005
1st Departure: Left committee; became chair of Select Intelligence
2nd Dates: Jan. 10, 2007-date
2nd Departure: Still serving in the 111th Congress

Cong.	Ranking	Terms in: House	Comm.	Date of Assignment
103rd	Min-13th	1 *1	1	Jan. 5, 1993
104th	Maj-9th	2 *1	2	Jan. 4, 1995
105th	Maj-7th	3 *1	3	Jan. 7, 1997
106th	Maj-7th	4 *1	4	Jan. 6, 1999
107th	Maj-5th	5 *1	5	Jan. 6, 2001
108th	Maj-4th	6 *1	6	Jan. 28, 2003
110th	Min-3rd	8 *2	1	Jan. 10, 2007
111th	Min-3rd	9 *2	2	Jan. 21, 2009

2nd PUBLIC WORKS AND TRANSPORTATION, 103
TRANSPORTATION AND INFRASTRUCTURE, 108-109
1st Dates: Jan. 5, 1993-Jan. 3, 1995
1st Departure: Moved to Budget
2nd Dates: Jan. 28, 2003-Jan. 26, 2007
2nd Departure: Returned to Education and Labor

Cong.	Ranking	Terms in: House	Comm.	Date of Assignment
103rd	Min-23rd	1 *1	1	Jan. 5, 1993
108th	Maj-8th	6 *2	1	Jan. 28, 2003
109th	Maj-8th	7 *2	2	Jan. 26, 2005

3rd BUDGET
1st Dates: Jan. 4, 1995-Feb. 1, 1996
1st Departure: Resigned committee; no new assignment
2nd Dates: Jan. 7, 1997-Jan. 3, 2003
2nd Departure: Returned to Transportation and Infrastructure

Cong.	Ranking	Terms in: House	Comm.	Date of Assignment
104th	Maj-18th	2 *1	1	Jan. 4, 1995
105th	Maj-13th	3 *2	1	Jan. 7, 1997
106th	Maj-9th	4 *2	2	Jan. 6, 1999
107th	Maj-3rd	5 *2	3	Jan. 6, 2001

HOUSE SELECT AND SPECIAL COMMITTEES:

1st PERMANENT SELECT INTELLIGENCE
Dates: Jan. 30, 2001-date
Ch2: Replaced Porter Goss (R-Fla.) as Chair on Aug. 25, 2004
Departure: Still serving in the 111th Congress

Cong.	Ranking	Terms in: House	Comm.	Date of Assignment
107th	Maj-9th	5	1	Jan. 30, 2001
108th	Maj-7th	6	2	Jan. 8, 2003
=108th	Maj-Ch2	6	2	Aug. 25, 2004
109th	Maj-Chr	7	3	Jan. 4, 2005
110th	Min-RM	8	4	Jan. 5, 2007
111th	Min-RM	9	5	Jan. 6, 2009

Martin R. Hoke (R-Ohio)

Dates: May 18, 1952
House: Jan. 3, 1993-Jan. 3, 1997
Left the House: Defeated for re-election in 1996

HOUSE STANDING COMMITTEES:

1st BUDGET
Dates: Jan. 5, 1993-Jan. 3, 1997
Departure: Left the House; lost re-election

Cong.	Ranking	Terms in: House	Comm.	Date of Assignment
103rd	Min-17th	1	1	Jan. 5, 1993
104th	Maj-15th	2	2	Jan. 4, 1995

2nd SCIENCE, SPACE AND TECHNOLOGY
Dates: Jan. 5, 1993-Jan. 3, 1995
Departure: Moved to Judiciary

Cong.	Ranking	Terms in: House	Comm.	Date of Assignment
103rd	Min-14th	1	1	Jan. 5, 1993

3rd JUDICIARY
Dates: Jan. 4, 1995-Jan. 3, 1997
Departure: Left the House; lost re-election

Cong.	Ranking	Terms in: House	Comm.	Date of Assignment
104th	Maj-14th	2	1	Jan. 4, 1995

T. Timothy Holden (D-Penn.)

Dates: March 5, 1957
House: Jan. 3, 1993-date
Serving in the 111th Congress

HOUSE STANDING COMMITTEES:

1st AGRICULTURE
Dates: Jan. 5, 1993-date
Departure: Still serving in the 111th Congress

Cong.	Ranking	Terms in: House	Comm.	Date of Assignment
103rd	Maj-23rd	1	1	Jan. 5, 1993
104th	Min-14th	2	2	Jan. 4, 1995
105th	Min-10th	3	3	Jan. 7, 1997
106th	Min-10th	4	4	Jan. 6, 1999
107th	Min-7th	5	5	Jan. 31, 2001
108th	Min-4th	6	6	Jan. 28, 2003
109th	Min-2nd	7	7	Jan. 26, 2005
110th	Maj-2nd	8	8	Jan. 12, 2007
111th	Maj-2nd	9	9	Jan. 21, 2009

2nd ARMED SERVICES
Dates: Jan. 21, 1993-Jan. 3, 1995
Departure: Left committee; no new assignment

Cong.	Ranking	Terms in: House	Comm.	Date of Assignment
103rd	MjR-1st	1	1	Jan. 21, 1993

3rd GOVERNMENT REFORM AND OVERSIGHT
Dates: July 12, 1995-Apr. 17, 1997
Departure: Resigned committee; moved to Transportation and Infrastructure

Cong.	Ranking	Terms in: House	Comm.	Date of Assignment
104th	MnR-1st	2	1	July 12, 1995
105th	Min-13th	3	2	Jan. 7, 1997

4th TRANSPORTATION AND INFRASTRUCTURE
Dates: Apr. 17, 1997-date
Departure: Still serving in the 111th Congress

Cong.	Ranking	Terms in: House	Comm.	Date of Assignment
105th	Min-32nd	3	1	Apr. 17, 1997
106th	Min-28th	4	2	Jan. 6, 1999
107th	Min-25th	5	3	Jan. 31, 2001
108th	Min-19th	6	4	Jan. 28, 2003
109th	Min-18th	7	5	Jan. 26, 2005
110th	Maj-15th	8	6	Jan. 10, 2007
111th	Maj-14th	9	7	Jan. 7, 2009

5th RESOURCES
Dates: July 8, 2002-Jan. 3, 2003
Departure: Left committee; no new assignment

Cong.	Ranking	Terms in: House	Comm.	Date of Assignment
107th	MnR-1st	4	1	July 8, 2002

Ernest F. Hollings (D-S.C.)

Dates: Jan. 1, 1922
Senate: Nov. 9, 1966-Jan. 3, 2005
Left the Senate: Retired in 2004

S: Hollings was elected to the 89th Congress by special election, Nov. 9, 1966, to fill the unexpired term caused by the death of U.S. Senator Olin D. Johnston (D-S.C.). Johnston was initially replaced by Donald S. Russell (D-S.C.), an appointee who was defeated for the nomination by Hollings. Hollings was not seated nor assigned to committees because the 89th Congress was not in session.

SENATE STANDING COMMITTEES:

1st COMMERCE reorganized Feb. 11, 1977
COMMERCE, SCIENCE AND TRANSPORTATION

Dates: Jan. 11, 1967-Jan. 3, 2005
Ch2: Replaced John S. McCain III (R-Ariz.) on June 6, 2001, following Senate party control shift
Departure: Left the Senate; retired

Cong.	Ranking	Years in: Senate	Comm.	Date of Assignment
103rd	Maj-Chr	27	26	Jan. 7, 1993
104th	Min-RM	29	28	Jan. 4, 1995
105th	Min-RM	31	30	Jan. 9, 1997
106th	Min-RM	33	32	Jan. 7, 1999
=107th	Maj-ChT	35	34	Jan. 3, 2001
107th	Min-RM1	35	35	Jan. 25, 2001
107th	Maj-Ch2	35	35	June 6, 2001
108th	Min-RM	37	37	Jan. 15, 2003

2nd POST OFFICE AND CIVIL SERVICE
Dates: Jan. 11, 1967-Feb. 11, 1977
Departure: Did not continue on reorganized Governmental Affairs

3rd AGRICULTURE AND FORESTRY
Dates: Jan. 11, 1967-Jan. 14, 1969
Departure: Moved to Banking and Currency

4th BANKING AND CURRENCY
Dates: Jan. 14, 1969-Jan. 28, 1971
Departure: Moved to Appropriations

5th APPROPRIATIONS
Dates: Jan. 28, 1971-Jan. 3, 2005
Departure: Left the Senate; retired

Cong.	Ranking	Years in: Senate	Comm.	Date of Assignment
103rd	Maj-3rd	27	22	Jan. 7, 1993
104th	Min-3rd	29	24	Jan. 4, 1995
105th	Min-3rd	31	26	Jan. 9, 1997
106th	Min-3rd	33	28	Jan. 7, 1999
107th	Min-3rd	35	30	Jan. 25, 2001
+107th	Maj-3rd	35	31	June 6, 2001
108th	Min-3rd	37	32	Jan. 15, 2003

6th BUDGET
Dates: July 25, 1974-Jan. 3, 2005
Departure: Left the Senate; retired

Cong.	Ranking	Years in: Senate	Comm.	Date of Assignment
103rd	Maj-2nd	27	19	Jan. 21, 1993
104th	Min-2nd	29	21	Jan. 6, 1995
105th	Min-2nd	31	23	Jan. 9, 1997
106th	Min-2nd	33	25	Jan. 7, 1999
107th	Min-2nd	35	27	Jan. 25, 2001
+107th	Maj-2nd	35	27	June 6, 2001
108th	Min-2nd	37	29	Jan. 15, 2003

SENATE SELECT AND SPECIAL COMMITTEES:

1st SELECT INTELLIGENCE (Permanent)
Dates: Jan. 3, 1985-Jan. 27, 1993
Departure: Left committee; no new assignment

JOINT COMMITTEES:

1st JOINT DEFICIT REDUCTION (Temporary)
Senate Dates: Jan. 6, 1987-Sep. 29, 1987
Termination: Public Law 100-119 adjusted Gramm-Rudman-Hollings Act

Rush D. Holt (D-N.J.)

Dates: Oct. 15, 1948
House: Jan. 3, 1999-date
Serving in the 111th Congress

HOUSE STANDING COMMITTEES:

1st BUDGET
Dates: Jan. 6, 1999-Jan. 3, 2003
Departure: Moved to Permanent Select Intelligence

Cong.	Ranking	Terms in: House	Comm.	Date of Assignment
106th	Min-17th	1	1	Jan. 6, 1999
107th	Min-13th	2	2	Jan. 31, 2001

2nd EDUCATION AND THE WORKFORCE, 106-109
EDUCATION AND LABOR, 110-111
Dates: Jan. 6, 1999-date
Departure: Still serving in the 111th Congress

Cong.	Ranking	Terms in: House	Comm.	Date of Assignment
106th	Min-22nd	1	1	Jan. 6, 1999
107th	Min-20th	2	2	Jan. 31, 2001
108th	Min-14th	3	3	Jan. 28, 2003
109th	Min-14th	4	4	Jan. 26, 2005
110th	Maj-12th	5	5	Jan. 10, 2007
111th	Maj-12th	6	6	Jan. 21, 2009

3rd RESOURCES, 106-107
NATURAL RESOURCES, 110-111
1st Dates: June 9, 1999-Jan. 3, 2003
1st Departure: Moved to Permanent Select Intelligence
2nd Dates: Jan. 18, 2007-date
2nd Departure: Still serving in the 111th Congress

Cong.	Ranking	Terms in: House	Comm.	Date of Assignment
106th	MnR-1st	1	*11	June 9, 1999
107th	Min-19th	2	*12	Feb. 8, 2001
110th	Maj-9th	5	*21	Jan. 18, 2007
111th	Maj-7th	6	*22	Jan. 21, 2009

HOUSE SELECT AND SPECIAL COMMITTEES:

1st PERMANENT SELECT INTELLIGENCE
Dates: Jan. 8, 2003-date
Departure: Still serving in the 111th Congress

Cong.	Ranking	Terms in: House	Comm.	Date of Assignment
108th	Min-8th	3	1	Jan. 8, 2003
109th	Min-7th	4	2	Jan. 26, 2005
110th	Maj-6th	5	3	Jan. 17, 2007
111th	Maj-4th	6	4	Feb. 4, 2009

Michael M. Honda (D-Cal.)

Dates: June 27, 1941
House: Jan. 3, 2001-date
Serving in the 111th Congress

HOUSE STANDING COMMITTEES:

1st TRANSPORTATION AND INFRASTRUCTURE
Dates: Jan. 31, 2001-Jan. 3, 2007
Departure: Moved to Appropriations

Cong.	Ranking	Terms in: House	Comm.	Date of Assignment
107th	Min-33rd	1	1	Jan. 31, 2001
108th	Min-25th	2	2	Jan. 28, 2003
109th	Min-22nd	3	3	Jan. 26, 2005

2nd BUDGET
Dates: Feb. 8, 2001-Jan. 3, 2003
Departure: Left committee; no new assignment

Cong.	Ranking	Terms in: House	Comm.	Date of Assignment
107th	Min-19th	1	1	Feb. 8, 2001

3rd SCIENCE, 107-109
SCIENCE AND TECHNOLOGY, 110
Dates: May 2, 2001-Sep. 20, 2007
Departure: Resigned committee; no new assignment

Cong.	Ranking	Terms in: House	Comm.	Date of Assignment
107th	Min-22nd	1	1	May 2, 2001
108th	Min-15th	2	2	Jan. 28, 2003
109th	Min-8th	3	3	Jan. 26, 2005
110th	Maj-16th	4	4	Jan. 18, 2007

4th APPROPRIATIONS
Dates: Jan. 4, 2007-date
Departure: Still serving in the 111th Congress

Cong.	Ranking	Terms in: House	Comm.	Date of Assignment
110th	Maj-30th	4	1	Jan. 4, 2007
111th	Maj-28th	5	2	Jan. 7, 2009

Darlene Hooley (D-Ore.)

Dates: April 4, 1939
House: Jan. 3, 1997-Jan. 3, 2009
Left the House: Retired in 2008

HOUSE STANDING COMMITTEES:

1st BANKING AND FINANCIAL SERVICES, 105-106
FINANCIAL SERVICES, 107-109
Dates: Jan. 7, 1997-Jan. 3, 2007
Departure: Returned to Budget and moved to Energy and Commerce

Cong.	Ranking	Terms in: House	Comm.	Date of Assignment
105th	Min-23rd	1	1	Jan. 7, 1997
106th	Min-13th	2	2	Jan. 6, 1999
107th	Min-12th	3	3	Jan. 31, 2001
108th	Min-10th	4	4	Jan. 28, 2003
109th	Min-10th	5	5	Jan. 26, 2005

2nd SCIENCE, 105, 109
SCIENCE AND TECHNOLOGY, 110
1st Dates: Feb. 13, 1997-Jan. 3, 1999
1st Departure: Moved to Budget
2nd Dates: Feb. 13, 1997-June 10, 2008
2nd Departure: Resigned committee; no new assignment

Cong.	Ranking	Terms in: House	Comm.	Date of Assignment
105th	Min-21st	1 *1	1	Feb. 13, 1997

Cong.	Ranking	Terms in: House	Comm.	Date of Assignment
109th	Min-5th	5 *2	1	Feb. 2, 2005
110th	Maj-14th	6 *2	2	Jan. 23, 2007

3rd BUDGET, 106-108, 110
1st Dates: Jan. 6, 1999-Jan. 3, 2005
1st Departure: Returned to Science
2nd Dates: Jan. 18, 2007-Jan. 3, 2009
2nd Departure: Left the House; retired

Cong.	Ranking	Terms in: House	Comm.	Date of Assignment
106th	Min-15th	2 *1	1	Jan. 6, 1999
107th	Min-12th	3 *1	2	Jan. 31, 2001
108th	Min-3rd	4 *1	3	Jan. 28, 2003
110th	Maj-19th	6 *2	1	Jan. 18, 2007

4th VETERANS' AFFAIRS
Dates: Feb. 13, 2003-Jan. 3, 2007
Departure: Returned to Budget and moved to Energy and Commerce

Cong.	Ranking	Terms in: House	Comm.	Date of Assignment
108th	Min-8th	4	1	Feb. 13, 2003
109th	Min-9th	5	2	Feb. 2, 2005

5th ENERGY AND COMMERCE
Dates: Jan. 4, 2007-Jan. 3, 2009
Departure: Left the House; retired

Cong.	Ranking	Terms in: House	Comm.	Date of Assignment
110th	Maj-25th	6	1	Jan. 4, 2007

J. Stephen Horn (R-Cal.)

Dates: May 31, 1931
House: Jan. 3, 1993-Jan. 3, 2003
Left the House: Retired in 2002

HOUSE STANDING COMMITTEES:

1st GOVERNMENT OPERATIONS, 103
GOVERNMENT REFORM AND OVERSIGHT, 104-105
GOVERNMENT REFORM, 106-107
Dates: Jan. 5, 1993-Jan. 3, 2003
Departure: Left the House; retired

Cong.	Ranking	Terms in: House	Comm.	Date of Assignment
103rd	Min-14th	1	1	Jan. 5, 1993
104th	Maj-10th	2	2	Jan. 4, 1995
105th	Maj-10th	3	3	Jan. 7, 1997
106th	Maj-8th	4	4	Jan. 6, 1999
107th	Maj-7th	5	5	Jan. 6, 2001

2nd PUBLIC WORKS AND TRANSPORTATION, 103
TRANSPORTATION AND INFRASTRUCTURE, 104-107
Dates: Jan. 5, 1993-Jan. 3, 2003
Departure: Left the House; retired

Cong.	Ranking	Terms in: House	Comm.	Date of Assignment
103rd	Min-18th	1	1	Jan. 5, 1993
104th	Maj-17th	2	2	Jan. 4, 1995
105th	Maj-12th	3	3	Jan. 7, 1997
106th	Maj-10th	4	4	Jan. 6, 1999
107th	Maj-8th	5	5	Jan. 6, 2001

John N. Hostettler (R-Ind.)

Dates: June 19, 1961
House: Jan. 3, 1995-Jan. 3, 2007
Left the House: Defeated for re-election in 2006

HOUSE STANDING COMMITTEES:

1st AGRICULTURE
Dates: Jan. 4, 1995-Jan. 3, 2001
Departure: Moved to Judiciary

Cong.	Ranking	Terms in: House	Comm.	Date of Assignment
104th	Maj-21st	1	1	Jan. 4, 1995
105th	Maj-15th	2	2	Jan. 7, 1997
106th	Maj-12th	3	3	Jan. 6, 1999

2nd NATIONAL SECURITY, 104-105
ARMED SERVICES, 106-109
Dates: Jan. 4, 1995-Jan. 3, 2007
Departure: Left the House; lost re-election

Cong.	Ranking	Terms in: House	Comm.	Date of Assignment
104th	Maj-23rd	1	1	Jan. 4, 1995
105th	Maj-20th	2	2	Jan. 7, 1997
106th	Maj-19th	3	3	Jan. 6, 1999
107th	Maj-14th	4	4	Jan. 6, 2001
108th	Maj-10th	5	5	Jan. 28, 2003
109th	Maj-10th	6	6	Jan. 26, 2005

3rd JUDICIARY
Dates: Jan. 6, 2001-Jan. 3, 2007
Departure: Left the House; lost re-election

Cong.	Ranking	Terms in: House	Comm.	Date of Assignment
107th	Maj-16th	4	1	Jan. 6, 2001
108th	Maj-11th	5	2	Jan. 28, 2003
109th	Maj-13th	6	3	Jan. 26, 2005

Amory Houghton Jr. (R-N.Y.)

Dates: Aug. 7, 1926
House: Jan. 3, 1987-Jan. 3, 2005
Left the House: Retired in 2004

HOUSE STANDING COMMITTEES:

1st BUDGET
Dates: Jan. 21, 1987-Jan. 3, 1993
Departure: Moved to Ways and Means

2nd GOVERNMENT OPERATIONS
Dates: Jan. 21, 1987-Jan. 3, 1989
Departure: Moved to Foreign Affairs

3rd FOREIGN AFFAIRS, 101-102
INTERNATIONAL RELATIONS, 104-108
1st Dates: Jan. 20, 1989-Jan. 3, 1993
1st Departure: Moved to Ways and Means
2nd Dates: Jan. 27, 1995-Jan. 3, 2005
2nd Departure: Left the House; retired

Cong.	Ranking	Terms in: House	Comm.	Date of Assignment
104th	Maj-23rd	5 *2	1	Jan. 27, 1995
105th	Maj-19th	6 *2	2	Jan. 7, 1997
106th	Maj-18th	7 *2	3	Jan. 6, 1999
107th	Maj-14th	8 *2	4	Jan. 6, 2001
108th	Maj-13th	9 *2	5	Jan. 28, 2003

4th WAYS AND MEANS
Dates: Jan. 5, 1993-Jan. 3, 2005
Departure: Left the House; retired

Cong.	Ranking	Terms in: House	Comm.	Date of Assignment
103rd	Min-10th	4	1	Jan. 5, 1993
104th	Maj-7th	5	2	Jan. 4, 1995
105th	Maj-7th	6	3	Jan. 21, 1997
106th	Maj-6th	7	4	Jan. 6, 1999
107th	Maj-5th	8	5	Jan. 6, 2001
108th	Maj-5th	9	6	Jan. 28, 2003

HOUSE SELECT AND SPECIAL COMMITTEES:

1st SELECT AGING (Permanent)
Dates: Feb. 21, 1991-Jan. 3, 1993
Termination: Committee not renewed in 1993

JOINT COMMITTEES:

1st DEFICIT REDUCTION (Temporary)
House Dates: Feb. 23, 1987-Sep. 29,1987
Termination: Public Law 100-119 adjusted Gramm-Rudman-Hollings Act

Steny H. Hoyer (D-Md.)

Dates: June 14, 1949
House: June 3, 1981-date
Serving in the 111th Congress

H: Hoyer was elected to the 97th Congress by special election, May 19, 1981, to fill the vacancy caused by the resignation of U.S. Representative Gladys Noon Spellman (D-Md.). Hoyer was seated June 3, 1981 and assigned to committees.

HOUSE STANDING COMMITTEES:

1st BANKING, FINANCE AND URBAN AFFAIRS
Dates: June 8, 1981-Jan. 3, 1983
Departure: Moved to Appropriations

2nd POST OFFICE AND CIVIL SERVICE
Dates: June 8, 1981-Jan. 3, 1983
Departure: Moved to Appropriations

3rd APPROPRIATIONS
Dates: Jan. 6, 1983-Jan. 3, 2007
Departure: Left committee; elected Majority Leader

Cong.	Ranking	Terms in: House	Comm.	Date of Assignment
103rd	Maj-15th	7	7	Jan. 5, 1993
104th	Min-12th	8	8	Jan. 4, 1995
105th	Min-10th	9	9	Jan. 7, 1997
106th	Min-6th	10	10	Jan. 6, 1999
107th	Min-5th	11	11	Jan. 31, 2001

| 108th | Min-5th | 12 | 12 | Jan. 28, 2003 |
| 109th | Min-5th | 13 | 13 | Jan. 26, 2005 |

4th HOUSE ADMINISTRATION, 102-103
HOUSE OVERSIGHT, 104-105
HOUSE ADMINISTRATION 106-107
Dates: Jan. 24, 1991-Jan. 3, 2003
Departure: Left committee; elected Minority Whip

Cong.	Ranking	Terms in: House	Comm.	Date of Assignment
103rd	Maj-7th	7	2	Jan. 21, 1993
104th	Min-3rd	8	3	Jan. 4, 1995
105th	Min-2nd	9	4	Feb. 5, 1997
106th	Min-RM	10	5	Feb. 10, 1999
107th	Min-RM	11	6	Jan. 31, 2001

JOINT COMMITTEES:

1st JOINT PRINTING
House Dates: Feb. 23, 1995-Jan. 3, 2003
Departure: Left committee; elected Minority Whip

Cong.	Ranking	Terms in: House	Comm.	Date of Assignment
104th	Min-1st	8	1	Feb. 23, 1995
105th	Min-1st	9	2	Mar. 6, 1997
106th	Min-1st	10	3	Mar. 2, 1999
107th	Min-1st	11	4	June 5, 2001

2nd JOINT LIBRARY
House Dates: Mar. 2, 1999-Jan. 3, 2003
Departure: Left committee; elected Minority Whip

Cong.	Ranking	Terms in: House	Comm.	Date of Assignment
106th	Min-1st	10	1	Mar. 2, 1999
107th	Min-1st	11	2	June 5, 2001

HOUSE LEADERSHIP POSTS

Dates: Jan. 3, 2003-date
Departure: Still serving in the 111th Congress

1st HOUSE MINORITY WHIP
Dates: Jan. 3, 2003-Jan. 3, 2007
Note: For the 102nd Congress, Hoyer was defeated by David Bonior (D-Mich.) to succeed Majority Whip William Gray (D-Penn.) who had resigned the House. Hoyer was defeated by Bonior 109 to 160 on the first ballot. He was also defeated for the 107th Congress to succeed Bonior as Minority Whip on Oct. 10, 2001, by Nancy Pelosi (D-Cal.) by a vote of 93 to 118 for Pelosi. For the 108th and 109th Congresses, Hoyer was elected Minority Whip without opposition.
Departure: Elected Majority Floor Leader

Cong.	Ranking	Terms in: House	Post	Date of Selection
108th	Min-2nd	12	1	Nov. 14, 2002
109th	Min-2nd	13	2	Nov. 17, 2004

2nd HOUSE MAJORITY FLOOR LEADER
Dates: Jan. 3, 2007-date
Note: For the 110th Congress, Hoyer was elected on Nov. 16, 2006, to succeed Democratic Floor Leader Nancy J. Pelosi (D-Cal.) who had been elected Speaker of the House. Hoyer defeated John P. Murtha (D-Penn.) on the first ballot 149 to 86. He was re-elected for the 111th Congress without opposition.
Departure: Still serving in the 111th Congress

Cong.	Ranking	Terms in: House	Post	Date of Selection
110th	Maj-2nd	14	1	Nov. 16, 2006
111th	Maj-2nd	15	2	Nov. 17, 2008

Michael Huffington (R-Cal.)

Dates: Sept. 3, 1947
House: Jan. 3, 1993-Jan. 3, 1995
Left the House: Lost U.S. Senate election in 1994

HOUSE STANDING COMMITTEES:

1st BANKING, FINANCE AND URBAN AFFAIRS
Dates: Jan. 5, 1993-Jan. 3, 1995
Departure: Left the House; lost Senate election

Cong.	Ranking	Terms in: House	Comm.	Date of Assignment
103rd	Min-18th	1	1	Jan. 5, 1993

2nd SMALL BUSINESS
Dates: Jan. 5, 1993-Jan. 3, 1995
Departure: Left the House; lost Senate election

Cong.	Ranking	Terms in: House	Comm.	Date of Assignment
103rd	Min-12th	1	1	Jan. 5, 1993

William J. Hughes (D-N.J.)

Dates: Oct. 17, 1932
House: Jan. 3, 1975-Jan. 3, 1995
Left the House: Retired; appointed Ambassador to Panama in 1995

HOUSE STANDING COMMITTEES:

1st JUDICIARY
Dates: Jan. 20, 1975-Jan. 3, 1995
Departure: Left the House; retired

Cong.	Ranking	Terms in: House	Comm.	Date of Assignment
103rd	Maj-5th	10	10	Jan. 5, 1993

2nd MERCHANT MARINE AND FISHERIES
Dates: Jan. 19, 1977-Jan. 3, 1995
Departure: Left the House; retired

Cong.	Ranking	Terms in: House	Comm.	Date of Assignment
103rd	Maj-2nd	10	9	Jan. 5, 1993

HOUSE SELECT AND SPECIAL COMMITTEES:

1st SELECT AGING (Permanent)
Dates: Feb. 6, 1975-Jan. 3, 1993
Termination: Committee not renewed in 1993

2nd OUTER CONTINENTAL SHELF (Ad Hoc)
Became the Select Committee on the Outer Continental Shelf, Mar. 29, 1979.
Dates: Apr. 22, 1975-July 31, 1980
Termination: House Report 1214 (96-2) filed

3rd SELECT NARCOTICS ABUSE AND CONTROL (Temporary)
Dates: Feb. 22, 1983-Jan. 3, 1993
Termination: Committee not renewed in 1993

Kenny Hulshof (R-Mo.)

Dates: May 22, 1958
House: Jan. 3, 1997-Jan. 3, 2009
Left the House: Lost election for Governor in 2008

HOUSE STANDING COMMITTEES:

1st WAYS AND MEANS
Dates: Jan. 21, 1997-Jan. 3, 2009
Departure: Left the House; lost election for Governor

Cong.	Ranking	Terms in: House	Comm.	Date of Assignment
105th	Maj-23rd	1	1	Jan. 21, 1997
106th	Maj-20th	2	2	Jan. 6, 1999
107th	Maj-19th	3	3	Jan. 6, 2001
108th	Maj-18th	4	4	Jan. 28, 2003
109th	Maj-14th	5	5	Jan. 26, 2005
110th	Min-8th	6	6	Jan. 10, 2007

2nd STANDARDS OF OFFICIAL CONDUCT
Dates: July 11, 2001-Jan. 3, 2005
Departure: Left committee; no new assignment

Cong.	Ranking	Terms in: House	Comm.	Date of Assignment
107th	MjR-1st	3	1	July 11, 2001
108th	Maj-4th	4	2	Feb. 11, 2003

3rd BUDGET
Dates: Jan. 31, 2003-Jan. 3, 2007
Departure: Left committee; no new assignment

Cong.	Ranking	Terms in: House	Comm.	Date of Assignment
108th	Maj-15th	4	1	Jan. 31, 2003
109th	Maj-7th	5	2	Jan. 26, 2005

HOUSE SELECT AND SPECIAL COMMITTEES:

1st SELECT COMMITTEE TO INVESTIGATE THE VOTING IRREGULARITIES OF AUGUST 2, 2007
Dates: Sep. 5, 2007-Sep. 25, 2008
Termination: House Report 885 (110-2) filed

Cong.	Ranking	Terms in: House	Comm.	Date of Assignment
110th	Min-3rd	6	1	Sep. 5, 2007

Duncan D. Hunter (R-Cal.)

Dates: Dec. 7, 1976
House: Jan. 3, 2009-date
Serving in the 111th Congress

HOUSE STANDING COMMITTEES:

1st ARMED SERVICES
Dates: Jan. 9, 2009-date
Departure: Still serving in the 111th Congress

Cong.	Ranking	Terms in: House	Comm.	Date of Assignment
111th	Min-22nd	1	1	Jan. 9, 2009

2nd EDUCATION AND LABOR
Dates: Jan. 9, 2009-date
Departure: Still serving in the 111th Congress

Cong.	Ranking	Terms in: House	Comm.	Date of Assignment
111th	Min-18th	1	1	Jan. 9, 2009

Duncan L. Hunter (R-Cal.)

Dates: May 31, 1948
House: Jan. 3, 1981-Jan. 3, 2009
Left the House: Retired; lost Republican presidential nomination

HOUSE STANDING COMMITTEES:

1st ARMED SERVICES, 97-103
NATIONAL SECURITY, 104-105
ARMED SERVICES, 106-110
Dates: Jan. 28, 1981-Jan. 3, 2009
Departure: Left the House; lost presidential nomination

Cong.	Ranking	Terms in: House	Comm.	Date of Assignment
103rd	Min-3rd	7	7	Jan. 5, 1993
104th	Maj-3rd	8	8	Jan. 4, 1995
105th	Maj-3rd	9	9	Jan. 7, 1997
106th	Maj-3rd	10	10	Jan. 6, 1999
107th	Maj-3rd	11	11	Jan. 6, 2001
108th	Maj-Chr	12	12	Jan. 8, 2003
109th	Maj-Chr	13	13	Jan. 6, 2005
110th	Min-RM	14	14	Jan. 4, 2007

2nd VETERANS' AFFAIRS
Dates: Jan. 21, 1997-Feb. 10, 1997
Departure: Resigned committee; no new assignment

Cong.	Ranking	Terms in: House	Comm.	Date of Assignment
105th	Maj-14th	9	1	Jan. 21, 1997

HOUSE SELECT AND SPECIAL COMMITTEES:

1st SELECT NARCOTICS ABUSE AND CONTROL (Temporary)
Dates: Feb. 22, 1983-Oct. 6, 1988
Departure: Left committee; no new assignment

2nd SELECT HUNGER (Temporary)
Dates: Apr. 4, 1989-Jan. 3, 1993
Termination: Committee not renewed in 1993

3rd SELECT HOMELAND SECURITY
Dates: Feb. 12, 2003-Jan. 3, 2005
Departure: Did not continue on reorganized standing committee

Cong.	Ranking	Terms in: House	Comm.	Date of Assignment
108th	Maj-8th	12	1	Feb. 12, 2003

Asa Hutchinson (R-Ark.)

Dates: Dec. 3, 1950
House: Jan. 3, 1997-Aug. 6, 2001
Left the House: Resigned; appointed Director of Drug Enforcement Administration

HOUSE STANDING COMMITTEES:

1st JUDICIARY
Dates: Jan. 7, 1997-Aug. 6, 2001
Departure: Resigned the House; named Director of DEA

		Terms in:		Date of
Cong.	Ranking	House	Comm.	Assignment
105th	Maj-18th	1	1	Jan. 7, 1997
106th	Maj-15th	2	2	Jan. 6, 1999
107th	Maj-11th	3	3	Jan. 6, 2001

2nd TRANSPORTATION AND INFRASTRUCTURE
Dates: Jan. 7, 1997-Aug. 6, 2001
Departure: Resigned the House; named Director of DEA

		Terms in:		Date of
Cong.	Ranking	House	Comm.	Assignment
105th	Maj-31st	1	1	Jan. 7, 1997
106th	Maj-25th	2	2	Jan. 6, 1999
107th	Maj-18th	3	3	Jan. 6, 2001

3rd VETERANS' AFFAIRS
Dates: Jan. 21, 1997-Jan. 3, 1999
Departure: Moved to Government Reform

		Terms in:		Date of
Cong.	Ranking	House	Comm.	Assignment
105th	Maj-13th	1	1	Jan. 21, 1997

4th GOVERNMENT REFORM
Dates: Jan. 6, 1999-Aug. 6, 2001
Departure: Resigned the House; named Director of DEA

		Terms in:		Date of
Cong.	Ranking	House	Comm.	Assignment
106th	Maj-18th	2	1	Jan. 6, 1999
107th	Maj-15th	3	2	Jan. 6, 2001

5th STANDARDS OF OFFICIAL CONDUCT
Dates: Mar. 6, 2001-Aug. 6, 2001
Departure: Resigned the House; named Director of DEA

		Terms in:		Date of
Cong.	Ranking	House	Comm.	Assignment
107th	Maj-4th	3	1	Mar. 6, 2001

HOUSE SELECT AND SPECIAL COMMITTEES:

1st PERMANENT SELECT INTELLIGENCE
Dates: Jan. 30, 2001-Aug. 6, 2001
Departure: Resigned the House; named Director of DEA

		Terms in:		Date of
Cong.	Ranking	House	Comm.	Assignment
107th	Maj-11th	3	1	Jan. 30, 2001

Y. Timothy Hutchinson (R-Ark.)

Dates: Aug. 11, 1949
House: Jan. 3, 1993-Jan. 3, 1997
Left the House: Elected to U.S. Senate in 1996
Senate: Jan. 3, 1997-Jan. 3, 2003
Left the Senate: Defeated for re-election in 2002

HOUSE STANDING COMMITTEES:

1st PUBLIC WORKS AND TRANSPORTATION, 103
TRANSPORTATION AND INFRASTRUCTURE, 104
Dates: Jan. 5, 1993-Jan. 3, 1997
Departure: Left the House for the Senate

		Terms in:		Date of
Cong.	Ranking	House	Comm.	Assignment
103rd	Min-13th	1	1	Jan. 5, 1993
104th	Maj-14th	2	2	Jan. 4, 1995

2nd VETERANS' AFFAIRS
Dates: Jan. 5, 1993-Jan. 3, 1997
Departure: Left the House for the Senate

		Terms in:		Date of
Cong.	Ranking	House	Comm.	Assignment
103rd	Min-7th	1	1	Jan. 5, 1993
104th	Maj-5th	2	2	Jan. 4, 1995

3rd ECONOMIC AND EDUCATIONAL OPPORTUNITIES
Dates: Jan. 4, 1995-Jan. 3, 1997
Departure: Left the House for the Senate

		Terms in:		Date of
Cong.	Ranking	House	Comm.	Assignment
104th	Maj-16th	2	1	Jan. 4, 1995

SENATE STANDING COMMITTEES:

1st ENVIRONMENT AND PUBLIC WORKS
Dates: Jan. 9, 1997-Jan. 7, 1999
Departure: Moved to Armed Services and Special Aging

		Years in:		Date of
Cong.	Ranking	Senate	Comm.	Assignment
105th	Maj-8th	1	1	Jan. 9, 1997

2nd LABOR AND HUMAN RESOURCES renamed Jan. 21, 1999
HEALTH, EDUCATION, LABOR AND PENSIONS
Dates: Jan. 9, 1997-Jan. 3, 2003
Departure: Left the Senate; lost re-election

		Years in:		Date of
Cong.	Ranking	Senate	Comm.	Assignment
105th	Maj-7th	1	1	Jan. 9, 1997
106th	Maj-6th	3	2	Jan. 7, 1999
107th	Maj-5th	5	5	Jan. 25, 2001
+107th	Min-4th	5	5	July 10, 2001

3rd VETERANS' AFFAIRS
Dates: Jan. 9, 1997-Jan. 3, 2003
Departure: Left the Senate; lost re-election

		Years in:		Date of
Cong.	Ranking	Senate	Comm.	Assignment
105th	Maj-7th	1	1	Jan. 9, 1997
106th	Maj-7th	3	2	Jan. 7, 1999
107th	Maj-7th	5	5	Jan. 25, 2001
+107th	Min-6th	5	5	July 10, 2001

4th ARMED SERVICES
Dates: Jan. 7, 1999-Jan. 3, 2003
Departure: Left the Senate; lost re-election

		Years in:		Date of
Cong.	Ranking	Senate	Comm.	Assignment
106th	Maj-10th	3	1	Jan. 7, 1999
107th	Maj-9th	5	3	Jan. 25, 2001
+107th	Min-9th	5	3	June 6, 2001

5th AGRICULTURE, NUTRITION AND FORESTRY
Dates: Jan. 25, 2001-Jan. 3, 2003
Departure: Left the Senate; lost re-election

		Years in:		Date of
Cong.	Ranking	Senate	Comm.	Assignment
107th	Maj-9th	5	1	Jan. 25, 2001
+107th	Min-9th	5	1	June 6, 2001

SENATE SELECT AND SPECIAL COMMITTEES:

1st SPECIAL AGING (Permanent)
Dates: Jan. 14, 1999-Jan. 3, 2003
Departure: Left the Senate; lost re-election

Cong.	Ranking	Years in: Senate	Comm.	Date of Assignment
106th	MjA-11th	3	1	Jan. 14, 1999
107th	Maj-8th	5	3	Jan. 25, 2001
+107th	Min-7th	6	3	July 24, 2001

Kay Bailey Hutchison (R-Tex.)

Dates: July 22, 1943
Senate: June 5, 1993-date
Serving in the 111th Congress

S: Hutchison was elected to the 103rd Congress by special election, June 5, 1993, to fill the vacancy caused by the resignation of U.S. Senator Lloyd Bentsen (D-Tex.) who had been named Secretary of the Treasury. Bentsen had been initially replaced by Robert Krueger (D-Tex.), an appointee, who lost the special election to Hutchison. Hutchison was seated June 14, 1993, and assigned to committees.

SENATE STANDING COMMITTEES:

1st ARMED SERVICES
Dates: July 1, 1993-Jan. 7, 1997
Departure: Moved to Appropriations and Rules and Administration

Cong.	Ranking	Years in: Senate	Comm.	Date of Assignment
103rd	MnA-10th	1	1	July 1, 1993
104th	Maj-9th	2	2	Jan. 4, 1995

2nd COMMERCE, SCIENCE AND TRANSPORTATION
Dates: July 1, 1993-date
Departure: Still serving in the 111th Congress

Cong.	Ranking	Years in: Senate	Comm.	Date of Assignment
103rd	MnR-1st	1	1	July 1, 1993
104th	Maj-8th	2	2	Jan. 4, 1995
105th	Maj-6th	4	4	Jan. 9, 1997
106th	Maj-6th	6	6	Jan. 7, 1999
107th	Maj-5th	8	8	Jan. 25, 2001
+107th	Min-5th	9	8	June 6, 2001
108th	Maj-5th	10	10	Jan. 15, 2003
109th	Maj-5th	12	12	Jan. 6, 2005
110th	Min-4th	14	14	Jan. 12, 2007
111th	Min-RM	16	16	Jan. 21, 2009

3rd SMALL BUSINESS
Dates: July 1, 1993-Jan. 9, 1997
Departure: Moved to Appropriations and Rules and Administration

Cong.	Ranking	Years in: Senate	Comm.	Date of Assignment
103rd	MnA-10th	1	1	July 1, 1993
104th	Maj-8th	2	2	Jan. 6, 1995

4th APPROPRIATIONS
Dates: Jan. 9, 1997-date
Departure: Still serving in the 111th Congress

Cong.	Ranking	Years in: Senate	Comm.	Date of Assignment
105th	Maj-15th	4	1	Jan. 9, 1997
106th	Maj-14th	6	2	Jan. 7, 1999
107th	Maj-13th	8	5	Jan. 25, 2001
+107th	Min-13th	9	5	June 6, 2001
108th	Maj-13th	10	7	Jan. 15, 2003
109th	Maj-12th	12	8	Jan. 6, 2005
110th	Min-11th	14	11	Jan. 12, 2007
111th	Min-8th	16	13	Jan. 21, 2009

5th RULES AND ADMINISTRATION
Dates: Jan. 9, 1997-date
Departure: Still serving in the 111th Congress

Cong.	Ranking	Years in: Senate	Comm.	Date of Assignment
105th	Maj-9th	4	1	Jan. 9, 1997
106th	Maj-9th	6	2	Jan. 7, 1999
107th	Maj-9th	8	5	Jan. 25, 2001
+107th	Min-9th	9	5	June 6, 2001
108th	Maj-7th	10	7	Jan. 15, 2003
109th	Maj-8th	12	8	Jan. 6, 2005
110th	Min-7th	14	11	Jan. 12, 2007
111th	Min-5th	16	13	Jan. 21, 2009

6th ENVIONMENT AND PUBLIC WORKS
Dates: Jan. 7, 1999-Jan. 25, 2001
Departure: Left committee; no new assignment

Cong.	Ranking	Years in: Senate	Comm.	Date of Assignment
106th	Maj-10th	6	1	Jan. 7, 1999

7th VETERANS' AFFAIRS
Dates: July 25, 2001-Jan. 21, 2009
Departure: Moved to Banking, Housing and Urban Affairs

Cong.	Ranking	Years in: Senate	Comm.	Date of Assignment
+107th	MnR-1st	9	1	July 25, 2001
108th	Maj-4th	10	2	Jan. 15, 2003
109th	Maj-3rd	12	4	Jan. 6, 2005
110th	Min-6th	14	6	Jan. 12, 2007

8th BANKING, HOUSING AND URBAN AFFAIRS
Dates: Jan. 21, 2009-date
Departure: Still serving in the 111th Congress

Cong.	Ranking	Years in: Senate	Comm.	Date of Assignment
111th	Min-10th	16	1	Jan. 21, 2009

SELECT AND SPECIAL COMMITTEES:

1st SELECT INTELLIGENCE (Permanent)
Dates: Jan. 6, 1995-Jan. 9, 1997
Departure: Moved to Appropriations and Rules and Administration

Cong.	Ranking	Years in: Senate	Comm.	Date of Assignment
104th	Maj-7th	2	1	Jan. 6, 1995

Earl D. Hutto (D-Fla.)

Dates: May 12, 1926
House: Jan. 3, 1979-Jan. 3, 1995
Left the House: Retired in 1994

HOUSE STANDING COMMITTEES:

1st MERCHANT MARINE AND FISHERIES
Dates: Jan. 24, 1979-Jan. 3, 1995
Departure: Left the House; retired

Cong.	Ranking	Terms in: House	Comm.	Date of Assignment
103rd	Maj-3rd	8	8	Jan. 5, 1993

2nd PUBLIC WORKS AND TRANSPORTATION
Dates: Jan. 24, 1979-Mar. 19, 1980
Departure: Moved to Armed Services

3rd ARMED SERVICES
Dates: Mar. 19, 1980-Jan. 3, 1995
Departure: Left the House; retired

Cong.	Ranking	Terms in: House	Comm.	Date of Assignment
103rd	Maj-5th	8	8	Jan. 5, 1993

Henry J. Hyde (R-Ill.)

Dates: April 18, 1924-Nov. 29, 2007
House: Jan. 3, 1975-Jan. 3, 2007
Left the House: Retired in 2006

HOUSE STANDING COMMITTEES:

1st BANKING, CURRENCY AND HOUSING, 94
BANKING, FINANCE AND URBAN AFFAIRS, 95-97
Dates: Jan. 28, 1975-Jan. 3, 1977
Departure: Moved to Foreign Affairs

2nd JUDICIARY
Dates: Jan. 28, 1975-Jan. 3, 2007
Departure: Left the House; retired

Cong.	Ranking	Terms in: House	Comm.	Date of Assignment
103rd	Min-3rd	10	10	Jan. 5, 1993
104th	Maj-Chr	11	11	Jan. 4, 1995
105th	Maj-Chr	12	12	Jan. 7, 1997
106th	Maj-Chr	13	13	Jan. 6, 1999
107th	Maj-2nd	14	14	Jan. 6, 2001
108th	Maj-2nd	15	15	Jan. 28, 2003
109th	Maj-2nd	16	16	Jan. 26, 2005

3rd FOREIGN AFFAIRS, 97-103
INTERNATIONAL RELATIONS, 104-109
Dates: June 24, 1981-Jan. 3, 2007
Departure: Left the House; retired

Cong.	Ranking	Terms in: House	Comm.	Date of Assignment
103rd	Min-6th	10	7	Jan. 5, 1993
104th	Maj-5th	11	8	Jan. 4, 1995
105th	Maj-4th	12	9	Jan. 7, 1997
106th	Maj-4th	13	10	Jan. 6, 1999
107th	Maj-Chr	14	11	Jan. 6, 2001
108th	Maj-Chr	15	12	Jan. 8, 2003
109th	Maj-Chr	16	13	Jan. 6, 2005

HOUSE SELECT AND SPECIAL COMMITTEES:

1st PERMANENT SELECT INTELLIGENCE
Dates: Feb. 7, 1985-Jan. 3, 1991
Departure: Left committee; no new assignment

2nd SELECT COMMITTEE TO INVESTIGATE COVERT ARMS TRANSACTIONS WITH IRAN
Dates: Jan. 7, 1987-Nov. 17, 1987
Departure: House Report 433 (100-1) filed

I

Robert D. Inglis (R-S.C.)

Dates: Oct. 11, 1959
House 1: Jan. 3, 1993-Jan. 3, 1999
Left the House 1: Lost U.S. Senate election in 1998
House 2: Jan. 3, 2005-date
Serving in the 111th Congress

HOUSE STANDING COMMITTEES:

1st BUDGET
Dates: Jan. 5, 1993-Jan. 3, 1999
Departure: Left the House; lost Senate election

Cong.	Ranking	Terms in: House	Comm.	Date of Assignment
103rd	Min-16th	1	1	Jan. 5, 1993
104th	Maj-14th	2	2	Jan. 4, 1995
105th	Maj-10th	3	3	Jan. 7, 1997

2nd JUDICIARY
1st Dates: Jan. 5, 1993-Jan. 3, 1999

1st Departure: Left the House; lost Senate election
2nd Dates: Jan. 26, 2005-Jan. 3, 2007
2nd Departure: Moved to Foreign Affairs

Cong.	Ranking	Terms in: House	Comm.	Date of Assignment
103rd	Min-13th	1 *1	1	Jan. 5, 1993
104th	Maj-11th	2 *1	2	Jan. 4, 1995
105th	Maj-10th	3 *1	3	Jan. 7, 1997
109th	Maj-12th	4 *2	1	Jan. 26, 2005

3rd EDUCATION AND THE WORKFORCE, 109
EDUCATION AND LABOR, 110
Dates: Jan. 26, 2005-Mar. 9, 2007
Departure: Resigned committee; no new assignment

Cong.	Ranking	Terms in: House	Comm.	Date of Assignment
109th	Maj-18th	4	1	Jan. 26, 2005
110th	Min-12th	5	2	Jan. 10, 2007

4th SCIENCE, 109
SCIENCE AND TECHNOLOGY, 110-111
Dates: Jan. 26, 2005-date
Departure: Still serving in the 111th Congress

Cong.	Ranking	Terms in: House	Comm.	Date of Assignment
109th	Maj-19th	4	1	Jan. 26, 2005
110th	Min-14th	5	2	Jan. 4, 2007
111th	Min-11th	6	3	Jan. 9, 2009

5th FOREIGN AFFAIRS
Dates: Jan. 10, 2007-date
Departure: Still serving in the 111th Congress

Cong.	Ranking	Terms in: House	Comm.	Date of Assignment
110th	Min-22nd	5	1	Jan. 10, 2007
111th	Min-18th	6	2	Jan. 9, 2009

James M. Inhofe (R-Okla.)

Dates: Nov. 17, 1934
House: Jan. 3, 1987-Nov. 15, 1994
Left the House: Resigned; elected to U.S. Senate in 1994
Senate: Nov. 8, 1994-date
Serving in the 111th Congress

S: Inhofe was elected to the Senate of the 103rd Congress by special election, Nov. 8, 1994, to fill the vacancy caused by the resignation of U.S. Senator David L. Boren (D-Okla.). Inhofe resigned the House on Nov. 15, 1994, and was seated in the Senate, Nov. 17, 1994, but was not assigned to committees.

HOUSE STANDING COMMITTEES:

1st GOVERNMENT OPERATIONS
Dates: Jan. 21, 1987-Jan. 3, 1989
Departure: Moved to Merchant Marine and Fisheries

2nd PUBLIC WORKS AND TRANSPORTATION
Dates: Jan. 21, 1987-Nov. 15, 1994
Departure: Resigned the House; left for the Senate

Cong.	Ranking	Terms in: House	Comm.	Date of Assignment
103rd	Min-5th	4	4	Jan. 5, 1993

3rd MERCHANT MARINE AND FISHERIES
Dates: Jan. 20, 1989-Nov. 15, 1994
Departure: Resigned the House; left for the Senate

Cong.	Ranking	Terms in: Senate	Comm.	Date of Assignment
103rd	Min-7th	4	3	Jan. 5, 1993

4th ARMED SERVICES
Dates: Jan. 5, 1993-Nov. 15, 1994
Departure: Resigned the House; left for the Senate

Cong.	Ranking	Terms in: House	Comm.	Date of Assignment
103rd	Min-15th	4	1	Jan. 5, 1993

HOUSE SELECT AND SPECIAL COMMITTEES:

1st SELECT NARCOTICS ABUSE AND CONTROL (Temporary)
Dates: Oct. 6, 1988-Jan. 3, 1993
Termination: Committee not renewed in 1993

SENATE STANDING COMMITTEES:

1st ARMED SERVICES
Dates: Jan. 4, 1995-date
Departure: Still serving in the 111th Congress

Cong.	Ranking	Years in: Senate	Comm.	Date of Assignment
104th	Maj-10th	1	1	Jan. 4, 1995
105th	Maj-7th	3	3	Jan. 9, 1997
106th	Maj-5th	5	5	Jan. 7, 1999
107th	Maj-5th	7	7	Jan. 25, 2001
+107th	Min-5th	7	7	June 6, 2001
108th	Maj-3rd	9	9	Jan. 15, 2003
109th	Maj-3rd	11	11	Jan. 6, 2005
110th	Min-3rd	13	13	Jan. 12, 2007
111th	Min-2nd	15	15	Jan. 21, 2009

2nd ENVIRONMENT AND PUBLIC WORKS
Dates: Jan. 4, 1995-date
Departure: Still serving in the 111th Congress

Cong.	Ranking	Years in: Senate	Comm.	Date of Assignment
104th	Maj-6th	1	1	Jan. 4, 1995
105th	Maj-5th	3	3	Jan. 9, 1997
106th	Maj-4th	5	5	Jan. 7, 1999
107th	Maj-3rd	7	7	Jan. 25, 2001
+107th	Min-3rd	7	7	June 6, 2001
108th	Maj-Chr	9	9	Jan. 15, 2003
109th	Maj-Chr	11	11	Jan. 6, 2005
110th	Min-RM	13	13	Jan. 12, 2007
111th	Min-RM	15	15	Jan. 21, 2009

3rd FOREIGN RELATIONS
Dates: July 21, 2009-date
Departure: Still serving in the 111th Congress

Cong.	Ranking	Years in: Senate	Comm.	Date of Assignment
111th	Min-8th	15	1	July 21, 2009

SENATE SELECT AND SPECIAL COMMITTEES:

1st SELECT INTELLIGENCE (Permanent)
Dates: Jan. 6, 1995-Jan. 15, 2003
Departure: Left committee; became Chair of Environment and Public Works

Cong.	Ranking	Years in: Senate	Comm.	Date of Assignment
104th	Maj-6th	1	1	Jan. 6, 1995
105th	Maj-6th	3	3	Jan. 9, 1997
106th	Maj-6th	5	5	Jan. 7, 1999
107th	Maj-3rd	7	7	Jan. 25, 2001
+107th	Min-3rd	7	7	June 6, 2001

2nd INDIAN AFFAIRS (Permanent)
Dates: Jan. 9, 1997-Jan. 6, 2005
Departure: Left committee; no new assignment

Cong.	Ranking	Years in: Senate	Comm.	Date of Assignment
105th	Maj-8th	3	1	Jan. 9, 1997
106th	Maj-8th	5	3	Jan. 7, 1999
107th	Maj-7th	7	5	Jan. 25, 2001
+107th	Min-7th	7	5	June 6, 2001
108th	Maj-6th	9	7	Jan. 15, 2003

Daniel K. Inouye (D-Hai.)

Dates: Sept. 7, 1924
House: Aug. 21, 1959-Jan. 2, 1963
Left the House: Elected to U.S. Senate in 1962
Senate: Jan. 3, 1963-date
Serving in the 111th Congress

H: Inouye was elected to the 86th Congress, Aug. 21, 1959 as Hawaii's first Representative, following its elevation to statehood. Inouye was seated Aug. 21, 1959 and assigned to committees.

HOUSE STANDING COMMITTEES:

1st BANKING AND CURRENCY
Dates: Aug. 27, 1959-Jan. 3, 1961
Departure: Moved to Agriculture

2nd AGRICULTURE
Dates: Feb. 6, 1961-Jan. 3, 1963
Departure: Left the House for the Senate

SENATE STANDING COMMITTEES:

1st ARMED SERVICES
Dates: Feb. 25, 1963-Jan. 28, 1971
Departure: Moved to District of Columbia and Appropriations.

2nd PUBLIC WORKS
Dates: Feb. 25, 1963-Jan. 14, 1969
Departure: Moved to Commerce

3rd COMMERCE reorganized Feb. 11, 1977
COMMERCE, SCIENCE AND TRANSPORTATION
Dates: Jan. 14, 1969-date
Departure: Still serving in the 111th Congress

Cong.	Ranking	Years in: Senate	Comm.	Date of Assignment
103rd	Maj-2nd	31	24	Jan. 7, 1993
104th	Min-2nd	33	26	Jan. 4, 1995
105th	Min-2nd	35	28	Jan. 9, 1997
106th	Min-2nd	37	30	Jan. 7, 1999
107th	Min-2nd	39	33	Jan. 25, 2001
+107th	Maj-2nd	39	33	June 6, 2001
108th	Min-2nd	41	35	Jan. 15, 2003
109th	Min-RM	43	36	Jan. 6, 2005
110th	Maj-Chr	45	38	Jan. 12, 2007
111th	Maj-2nd	47	41	Jan. 21, 2009

4th DISTRICT OF COLUMBIA
Dates: Jan. 28, 1971-Feb. 11, 1977
Departure: Did not continue on reorganized Governmental Affairs

5th APPROPRIATIONS
Dates: Jan. 28, 1971-date
Departure: Still serving in the 111th Congress

Cong.	Ranking	Years in: Senate	Comm.	Date of Assignment
103rd	Maj-2nd	31	22	Jan. 7, 1993
104th	Min-2nd	33	24	Jan. 4, 1995
105th	Min-2nd	35	26	Jan. 9, 1997
106th	Min-2nd	37	28	Jan. 7, 1999
107th	Min-2nd	39	30	Jan. 25, 2001
+107th	Maj-2nd	39	31	June 6, 2001
108th	Min-2nd	41	32	Jan. 15, 2003
109th	Min-2nd	43	34	Jan. 6, 2005
110th	Maj-2nd	45	36	Jan. 12, 2007
111th	Maj-Chr	47	38	Jan. 21, 2009

6th RULES AND ADMINISTRATION
Dates: Apr. 20, 1982-date
Departure: Still serving in the 111th Congress

Cong.	Ranking	Years in: Senate	Comm.	Date of Assignment
103rd	Maj-4th	31	11	Jan. 21, 1993
104th	Min-4th	33	13	Jan. 6, 1995
105th	Min-3rd	35	15	Jan. 9, 1997
106th	Min-3rd	37	17	Jan. 7, 1999
107th	Min-3rd	39	19	Jan. 25, 2001
+107th	Maj-3rd	39	20	June 6, 2001
108th	Min-3rd	41	21	Jan. 15, 2003
109th	Min-3rd	43	23	Jan. 6, 2005
110th	Maj-4th	45	25	Jan. 12, 2007
111th	Maj-5th	47	27	Jan. 21, 2009

SENATE SELECT AND SPECIAL COMMITTEES:

1st EQUAL EDUCATIONAL OPPORTUNITY
Dates: Feb. 25, 1970-Dec. 31, 1972
Termination: Date of final report

2nd PRESIDENTIAL CAMPAIGN ACTIVITIES (Watergate)
Dates: Feb. 8, 1973-June 27, 1974
Termination: Senate Report 981 (93-2) filed

3rd SELECT INTELLIGENCE (Permanent)
Dates: May 20, 1976-Jan. 3, 1985
Departure: Left committee; no new assignment
Chair: 94th-95th, May 20, 1976-Jan. 27, 1978

4th SELECT OFFICIAL CONDUCT
Dates: Jan. 19, 1977-Mar. 10, 1977
Termination: Senate Report 49 (95-1)

5th SELECT INDIAN AFFAIRS (Permanent), 96-102
INDIAN AFFAIRS (Permanent), 103-111
Became Permanent Select Committee on Indian Affairs, June 6, 1984.
Dates: Jan. 23, 1979-date
Ch2: Replaced Ben Nighthorse Campbell (R-Colo.) on June 6, 2001, following Senate party control shift
Departure: Still serving in the 111th Congress

Cong.	Ranking	Years in: Senate	Comm.	Date of Assignment
103rd	Maj-Chr	31	14	Jan. 5, 1993
104th	Min-RM	33	16	Jan. 9, 1995
105th	Min-RM	35	18	Jan. 9, 1997
106th	Min-RM	37	20	Jan. 7, 1999
=107th	Maj-ChT	39	22	Jan. 3, 2001
107th	Min-RM1	39	23	Jan. 25, 2001
+107th	Maj-Ch2	39	23	June 6, 2001
108th	Min-RM	41	24	Jan. 15, 2003
109th	Min-2nd	43	26	Jan. 6, 2005
110th	Maj-2nd	45	28	Jan. 12, 2007
111th	Maj-2nd	47	30	Jan. 21, 2009

6th UNDERCOVER ACTIVITIES OF COMPONENTS OF THE DEPARTMENT OF JUSTICE
Dates: Mar. 29, 1982-Dec. 15, 1982
Termination: Senate Report 682 (97-2) filed

7th SECRET MILITARY ASSISTANCE TO IRAN AND THE NICARAGUAN OPPOSITION (Iran-Contra Affair)
Dates: Jan. 12, 1987-Nov. 17, 1987
Termination: Senate Report 100-216 filed

JOINT COMMITTEES:

1st JOINT LIBRARY
Senate Dates: July 27, 1982-Jan. 29, 1987
Departure: Left committee; became Chair of Secret Military Assistance to Iran and the Nicaraguan Opposition

2nd JOINT PRINTING
Senate Dates: Jan. 10, 1995-Apr. 3, 2009
Departure: Left committee; became Chair of Appropriations

Cong.	Ranking	Years in: Senate	Comm.	Date of Assignment
104th	Min-2nd	33	1	Jan. 17, 1995
105th	Min-2nd	35	3	Jan. 28, 1997
106th	Min-2nd	37	5	Feb. 25, 1999
+107th	Maj-3rd	39	7	Sep. 19, 2001
108th	Min-1st	41	9	Mar. 13, 2003
109th	Min-1st	43	11	Mar. 4, 2005
110th	Maj-2nd	45	13	Mar. 26, 2007

HOUSE SELECT AND SPECIAL COMMITTEES:

1st SELECT ENERGY INDEPENDENCE AND GLOBAL WARMING
Dates: Mar. 9, 2007-date
Departure: Still serving in the 111th Congress

Cong.	Ranking	Terms in: House	Comm.	Date of Assignment
110th	Maj-3rd	6	1	Mar. 9, 2007
111th	Maj-3rd	7	2	Feb. 3, 2009

Jay R. Inslee (D-Wash.)

Dates: Feb. 9, 1951
House 1: Jan. 3, 1993-Jan. 3, 1995
Left the House 1: Defeated for re-election in 1994
House 2: Jan. 3, 1999-date
Serving in the 111th Congress

HOUSE STANDING COMMITTEES:

1st AGRICULTURE
Dates: Jan. 5, 1993-Jan. 3, 1995
Departure: Left the House; lost re-election

Cong.	Ranking	Terms in: House	Comm.	Date of Assignment
103rd	Maj-20th	1	1	Jan. 5, 1993

2nd SCIENCE, SPACE AND TECHNOLOGY
Dates: Jan. 5, 1993-Jan. 3, 1995
Departure: Left the House; lost re-election

Cong.	Ranking	Terms in: House	Comm.	Date of Assignment
103rd	Maj-27th	1	1	Jan. 5, 1993

3rd BANKING AND FINANCIAL SERVICES, 106
FINANCIAL SERVICES, 107-108
Dates: Jan. 6, 1999-Jan. 3, 2005
Departure: Moved to Energy and Commerce

Cong.	Ranking	Terms in: House	Comm.	Date of Assignment
106th	Min-22nd	2	1	Jan. 6, 1999
107th	Min-19th	3	2	Jan. 31, 2001
108th	Min-15th	4	3	Jan. 28, 2003

4th RESOURCES, 106-109
NATURAL RESOURCES, 110-111
Dates: Jan. 6, 1999-date
Departure: Still serving in the 111th Congress

Cong.	Ranking	Terms in: House	Comm.	Date of Assignment
106th	Min-20th	2	1	Jan. 6, 1999
107th	Min-15th	3	2	Feb. 8, 2001
108th	Min-14th	4	3	Jan. 28, 2003
109th	Min-19th	5	4	Feb. 2, 2005
110th	Maj-22nd	6	5	Jan. 18, 2007
111th	Maj-22nd	7	6	Jan. 21, 2009

5th ENERGY AND COMMERCE
Dates: Jan. 26, 2005-date
Departure: Still serving in the 111th Congress

Cong.	Ranking	Terms in: House	Comm.	Date of Assignment
109th	Min-24th	5	1	Jan. 26, 2005
110th	Maj-22nd	6	2	Jan. 4, 2007
111th	Maj-18th	7	3	Jan. 7, 2009

Johnny Isakson (R-Ga.)

Dates: Dec. 28, 1944
House: Feb. 23, 1999-Jan. 3, 2005
Left the House: Elected to U.S. Senate in 2004
Senate: Jan. 3, 2005-date
Serving in the 111th Congress

H: Isakson was elected to the 106th Congress by special election Feb. 23, 1999, to fill the vacancy caused by the resignation of U.S. Representative Newton L. Gingrich (R-Ga.) who chose not to be seated in the 106th Congress. Isakson was seated Feb. 25, 1999, and assigned to committees.

HOUSE STANDING COMMITTEES:

1st EDUCATION AND THE WORKFORCE
Dates: Mar. 2, 1999-Jan. 3, 2005
Departure: Left the House for the Senate

Cong.	Ranking	Terms in: House	Comm.	Date of Assignment
106th	Maj-27th	1	1	Mar. 2, 1999
107th	Maj-20th	2	2	Jan. 6, 2001
108th	Maj-14th	3	3	Jan. 28, 2003

2nd TRANSPORTATION AND INFRASTRUCTURE
Dates: Mar. 2, 1999-Jan. 3, 2005
Departure: Left the House for the Senate

Cong.	Ranking	Terms in: House	Comm.	Date of Assignment
106th	Maj-41st	1	1	Mar. 2, 1999
107th	Maj-27th	2	2	Jan. 6, 2001
108th	Maj-21st	3	3	Jan. 28, 2003

SENATE STANDING COMMITTEES:

1st ENVIRONMENT AND PUBLIC WORKS
Dates: Jan. 6, 2005-Jan. 21, 2009
Departure: Moved to Commerce, Science and Transportation

Cong.	Ranking	Years in: Senate	Comm.	Date of Assignment
109th	Maj-9th	1	1	Jan. 6, 2005
110th	Min-4th	3	3	Jan. 12, 2007

2nd HEALTH, EDUCATION, LABOR AND PENSIONS
Dates: Jan. 6, 2005-date
Departure: Still serving in the 111th Congress

Cong.	Ranking	Years in: Senate	Comm.	Date of Assignment
109th	Maj-6th	1	1	Jan. 6, 2005
110th	Min-5th	3	3	Jan. 12, 2007
111th	Min-5th	5	5	Jan. 21, 2009

3rd SMALL BUSINESS AND ENTREPRENEURSHIP
Dates: Jan. 6, 2005-date
Departure: Still serving in the 111th Congress

Cong.	Ranking	Years in: Senate	Comm.	Date of Assignment
109th	Maj-7th	1	1	Jan. 6, 2005
110th	Min-9th	3	3	Jan. 12, 2007
111th	Min-6th	5	5	Jan. 21, 2009

4th VETERANS' AFFAIRS
Dates: Jan. 6, 2005-date
Departure: Still serving in the 111th Congress

Cong.	Ranking	Years in: Senate	Comm.	Date of Assignment
109th	Maj-8th	1	1	Jan. 6, 2005
110th	Min-4th	3	3	Jan. 12, 2007
111th	Min-3rd	5	5	Jan. 21, 2009

5th FOREIGN RELATIONS
Dates: Jan. 12, 2007-date
Departure: Still serving in the 111th Congress

Cong.	Ranking	Years in: Senate	Comm.	Date of Assignment
110th	Min-9th	3	1	Jan. 12, 2007
111th	Min-3rd	5	3	Jan. 21, 2009

6th COMMERCE, SCIENCE AND TRANSPORTATION
Dates: Jan. 21, 2009-date
Departure: Still serving in the 111th Congress

Cong.	Ranking	Years in: Senate	Comm.	Date of Assignment
111th	Min-7th	5	1	Jan. 21, 2009

SENATE SELECT AND SPECIAL COMMITTEES:

1st SELECT ETHICS (Permanent)
Dates: June 13, 2007-date
Departure: Still serving in the 111th Congress

Cong.	Ranking	Years in: Senate	Comm.	Date of Assignment
110th	MnR-1st	3	1	June 13, 2007
111th	Min-VCh	5	2	Jan. 21, 2009

Steve Israel (D-N.Y.)

Dates: May 30, 1958
House: Jan. 3, 2001-date
Serving in the 111th Congress

HOUSE STANDING COMMITTEES:

1st FINANCIAL SERVICES
Dates: Feb. 8, 2001-Jan. 3, 2007
Departure: Moved to Appropriations

Cong.	Ranking	Terms in: House	Comm.	Date of Assignment
107th	Min-31st	1	1	Feb. 8, 2001
108th	Min-24th	2	2	Jan. 28, 2003
109th	Min-21st	3	3	Jan. 26, 2005

2nd SCIENCE
Dates: Feb. 8, 2001-Feb. 5, 2003
Departure: Resigned committee; moved to Armed Services

Cong.	Ranking	Terms in: House	Comm.	Date of Assignment
107th	MnR-2nd	1	1	Feb. 8, 2001
108th	Min-14th	2	2	Jan. 28, 2003

3rd ARMED SERVICES
Dates: Feb. 5, 2003-Jan. 3, 2007
Departure: Moved to Appropriations

Cong.	Ranking	Terms in: House	Comm.	Date of Assignment
108th	Min-22nd	2	1	Feb. 5, 2003
109th	Min-18th	3	2	Jan. 26, 2005

4th APPROPRIATIONS
Dates: Jan. 4, 2007-date
Departure: Still serving in the 111th Congress

Cong.	Ranking	Terms in: House	Comm.	Date of Assignment
110th	Maj-32nd	4	1	Jan. 4, 2007
111th	Maj-30th	5	2	Jan. 7, 2009

Darrell E. Issa (R-Cal.)

Dates: Jan. 1, 1954
House: Jan. 3, 2001-date
Serving in the 111th Congress

HOUSE STANDING COMMITTEES:

1st INTERNATIONAL RELATIONS
1st Dates: Jan. 6, 2001-Jan. 3, 2003
1st Departure: Moved to Energy and Commerce
2nd Dates: Jan. 26, 2005-Jan. 3, 2007
2nd Departure: Moved to Permanent Select Intelligence

Cong.	Ranking	Terms in: House	Comm.	Date of Assignment
107th	Maj-22nd	1 *1	1	Jan. 6, 2001
109th	Maj-14th	3 *2	1	Jan. 26, 2005

2nd JUDICIARY
1st Dates: Jan. 6, 2001-Jan. 3, 2003
1st Departure: Moved to Energy and Commerce
2nd Dates: Jan. 26, 2005-date
2nd Departure: Still serving in the 111th Congress

Cong.	Ranking	Terms in: House	Comm.	Date of Assignment
107th	Maj-19th	1 *1	1	Jan. 6, 2001
109th	Maj-16th	3 *2	1	Jan. 26, 2005
110th	Min-10th	4 *2	2	Jan. 10, 2007
111th	Min-7th	5 *2	3	Jan. 9, 2009

3rd SMALL BUSINESS
Dates: Jan. 6, 2001-Jan. 3, 2003
Departure: Moved to Energy and Commerce

Cong.	Ranking	Terms in: House	Comm.	Date of Assignment
107th	Maj-14th	1	1	Jan. 6, 2001

4th ENERGY AND COMMERCE
Dates: Jan. 28, 2003-Jan. 3, 2005
Departure: Returned to International Relations and Judiciary; moved to Government Reform

Cong.	Ranking	Terms in: House	Comm.	Date of Assignment
108th	Maj-30th	2	1	Jan. 28, 2003

5th GOVERNMENT REFORM, 109
OVERSIGHT AND GOVERNMENT REFORM, 110-111
Dates: Jan. 26, 2005-date
Departure: Still serving in the 111th Congress

Cong.	Ranking	Terms in: House	Comm.	Date of Assignment
109th	Maj-16th	3	1	Jan. 26, 2005
110th	Min-11th	4	2	Jan. 10, 2007
111th	Min-RM	5	3	Jan. 6, 2009

HOUSE SELECT AND SPECIAL COMMITTEES:

1st PERMANENT SELECT INTELLIGENCE
Dates: Jan. 17, 2007-Jan. 3, 2009
Departure: Left committee; became Ranking Member on Oversight and Government Reform

Cong.	Ranking	Terms in: House	Comm.	Date of Assignment
110th	Min-9th	4	1	Jan. 17, 2007

Ernest Jim Istook Jr. (R-Okla.)

Dates: Feb. 11, 1950
House: Jan. 3, 1993-Jan. 3, 2007
Left the House: Lost nomination for Governor in 2006

HOUSE STANDING COMMITTEES:

1st APPROPRIATIONS
Dates: Jan. 5, 1993-Jan. 3, 2007
Departure: Left the House; lost nomination for Governor

Cong.	Ranking	Terms in: House	Comm.	Date of Assignment
103rd	Min-22nd	1	1	Jan. 5, 1993
104th	Maj-20th	2	2	Jan. 4, 1995
105th	Maj-17th	3	3	Jan. 7, 1997
106th	Maj-15th	4	4	Jan. 6, 1999
107th	Maj-13th	5	5	Jan. 6, 2001
108th	Maj-10th	6	6	Jan. 28, 2003
109th	Maj-10th	7	7	Jan. 6, 2005

HOUSE SELECT AND SPECIAL COMMITTEES:

1st SELECT HOMELAND SECURITY
Dates: Feb. 12, 2003-Jan. 3, 2005
Departure: Did not continue on reorganized standing committee

Cong.	Ranking	Terms in: House	Comm.	Date of Assignment
108th	Maj-18th	6	1	Feb. 12, 2003

J

Jesse L. Jackson Jr. (D-Ill.)

Dates: March 11, 1965
House: Dec. 12, 1995-date
Serving in the 111th Congress

H: Jackson was elected to the 104th Congress by special election, Dec. 12, 1995, to fill the vacancy caused by the resignation of U.S. Representative Mel Reynolds (D-Ill.). Jackson was seated Dec. 14, 1995, and assigned to committees.

HOUSE STANDING COMMITTEES:

1st BANKING AND FINANCIAL SERVICES
Dates: Jan. 5, 1996-Jan. 3, 1999
Departure: Moved to Appropriations

Cong.	Ranking	Terms in: House	Comm.	Date of Assignment
104th	MnA-23rd	1	1	Jan. 5, 1996
105th	Min-19th	2	2	Jan. 7, 1997

2nd SMALL BUSINESS
Dates: Apr. 22, 1996-Jan. 3, 1999
Departure: Moved to Appropriations

Cong.	Ranking	Terms in: House	Comm.	Date of Assignment
104th	MnR-2nd	1	1	Apr. 22, 1996
105th	Min-9th	2	2	Feb. 5, 1997

3rd APPROPRIATIONS
Dates: Jan. 6, 1999-date
Departure: Still serving in the 111th Congress

Cong.	Ranking	Terms in: House	Comm.	Date of Assignment
106th	Min-25th	3	1	Jan. 6, 1999
107th	Min-25th	4	2	Jan. 31, 2001
108th	Min-23rd	5	3	Jan. 28, 2003
109th	Min-23rd	6	4	Jan. 26, 2005
110th	Maj-20th	7	5	Jan. 4, 2007
111th	Maj-19th	8	6	Jan. 7, 2009

Sheila Jackson-Lee (D-Tex.)

Dates: Jan. 12, 1950
House: Jan. 3, 1995-date
Serving in the 111th Congress

HOUSE STANDING COMMITTEES:

1st JUDICIARY
Dates: Jan. 4, 1995-date
Departure: Still serving in the 111th Congress

Cong.	Ranking	Terms in: House	Comm.	Date of Assignment
104th	Min-15th	1	1	Jan. 4, 1995
105th	Min-10th	2	2	Jan. 7, 1997
106th	Min-9th	3	3	Jan. 6, 1999
107th	Min-9th	4	4	Jan. 31, 2001
108th	Min-8th	5	5	Jan. 28, 2003
109th	Min-8th	6	6	Jan. 26, 2005

| 110th | Maj-8th | 7 | 7 | Jan. 18, 2007 |
| 111th | Maj-8th | 8 | 8 | Jan. 21, 2009 |

2nd SCIENCE
1st Dates: Jan. 4, 1995-Feb. 13, 2003
1st Departure: Leave of absence; moved to Select
Homeland Security; returned on Mar. 5, 2003
2nd Dates: Mar. 5, 2003-Jan. 3, 2007
2nd Departure: Moved to Foreign Affairs

Cong.	Ranking	Terms in: House	Comm.	Date of Assignment
104th	Min-22nd	1 *1	1	Jan. 4, 1995
105th	Min-15th	2 *1	2	Feb. 13, 1997
106th	Min-14th	3 *1	3	Jan. 6, 1999
107th	Min-10th	4 *1	4	Jan. 31, 2001
108th	Min-7th	5 *1	5	Jan. 28, 2003
108th	Min-13th	5 *2	1	Mar. 5, 2003
109th	Min-13th	6 *2	2	Feb. 2, 2005

3rd HOMELAND SECURITY
Dates: Feb. 9, 2005-date
Departure: Still serving in the 111th Congress

Cong.	Ranking	Terms in: House	Comm.	Date of Assignment
109th	Min-10th	6	2	Feb. 9, 2005
110th	Maj-10th	7	3	Jan. 12, 2007
111th	Maj-7th	8	4	Jan. 28, 2009

4th FOREIGN AFFAIRS
Dates: Jan. 12, 2007-date
Departure: Still serving in the 111th Congress

Cong.	Ranking	Terms in: House	Comm.	Date of Assignment
110th	Maj-17th	7	1	Jan. 12, 2007
111th	Maj-18th	8	2	Jan. 21, 2009

HOUSE SELECT AND SPECIAL COMMITTEES:

1st SELECT HOMELAND SECURITY
Dates: Feb. 12, 2003-Jan. 3, 2005
Departure: Continued on reorganized standing committee

Cong.	Ranking	Terms in: House	Comm.	Date of Assignment
108th	Min-16th	5	1	Feb. 12, 2003

Andrew Jacobs Jr. (D-Ind.)

Dates: Feb. 24, 1932
House 1: Jan. 3, 1965-Jan. 3, 1973
Left the House 1: Defeated for re-election in 1972
House 2: Jan. 3, 1975-Jan. 3, 1997
Left the House 2: Retired in 1996

HOUSE STANDING COMMITTEES:

1st JUDICIARY
Dates: Jan. 18, 1965-Jan. 3, 1973
Departure: Left the House; lost re-election

2nd DISTRICT OF COLUMBIA
Dates: Jan. 23, 1967-Jan. 3, 1973
Departure: Left the House; lost re-election

3rd WAYS AND MEANS
Dates: Jan. 20, 1975-Jan. 3, 1997
Departure: Left the House; retired

Cong.	Ranking	Terms in: House	Comm.	Date of Assignment
103rd	Maj-6th	14	10	Jan. 5, 1993
104th	Min-4th	15	11	Jan. 4, 1995

HOUSE SELECT AND SPECIAL COMMITTEES:

1st SELECT COMMITTEE ON THE SEATING OF ADAM CLAYTON POWELL
Dates: Jan. 19, 1967-Feb. 23, 1967
Termination: House Report 27 (90-1) filed

William J. Janklow (R-S.D.)

Dates: Sept. 13, 1939
House: Jan. 3, 2003-Jan. 20, 2004
Left the House: Resigned and retired in 2004

HOUSE STANDING COMMITTEES:

1st AGRICULTURE
Dates: Jan. 28, 2003-Jan. 20, 2004
Departure: Resigned the House; retired

Cong.	Ranking	Terms in: House	Comm.	Date of Assignment
108th	Maj-20th	1	1	Jan. 28, 2003

2nd GOVERNMENT REFORM
Dates: Jan. 28, 2003-Jan. 20, 2004
Departure: Resigned the House; retired

Cong.	Ranking	Terms in: House	Comm.	Date of Assignment
108th	Maj-23rd	1	1	Jan. 28, 2003

3rd INTERNATIONAL RELATIONS
Dates: Jan. 28, 2003-Jan. 20, 2004
Departure: Resigned the House; retired

Cong.	Ranking	Terms in: House	Comm.	Date of Assignment
108th	Maj-25th	1	1	Jan. 28, 2003

William J. Jefferson (D-La.)

Dates: March 14, 1947
House: Jan. 3, 1991-Jan. 3, 2009
Left the House: Defeated for re-election in 2008

HOUSE STANDING COMMITTEES:

1st EDUCATION AND LABOR
Dates: Jan. 24, 1991-Jan. 3, 1993
Departure: Moved to District of Columbia and Ways and Means

2nd MERCHANT MARINE AND FISHERIES
Dates: Jan. 24, 1991-Jan. 3, 1993
Departure: Moved to District of Columbia and Ways and Means

3rd DISTRICT OF COLUMBIA
Dates: Feb. 18, 1993-Jan. 3, 1995
Departure: Committee abolished; moved to House Oversight and National Security

Cong.	Ranking	House	Comm.	Assignment
		Terms in:		
103rd	Maj-7th	2	1	Feb. 18, 1993

4th WAYS AND MEANS
1st Dates: Jan. 5, 1993-Jan. 3, 1995
1st Departure: Moved to House Oversight and National Security
2nd Dates: Feb. 6, 1997-June 16, 2006
2nd Departure: Voted removal from committee due to ethics issue

Cong.	Ranking	House	Comm.	Date of Assignment
		Terms in:		
103rd	Maj-22nd	2 *1	1	Jan. 5, 1993
105th	Min-13th	4 *2	1	Jan. 7, 1997
106th	Min-12th	5 *2	2	Jan. 6, 1999
107th	Min-12th	6 *2	3	Jan. 31, 2001
108th	Min-11th	7 *2	4	Jan. 28, 2003
109th	Min-9th	8 *2	5	Jan. 26, 2005

5th HOUSE OVERSIGHT
Dates: Jan. 4, 1995-Jan. 3, 1997
Departure: Returned to Ways and Means

Cong.	Ranking	House	Comm.	Date of Assignment
		Terms in:		
104th	Min-4th	3	1	Jan. 4, 1995

6th NATIONAL SECURITY
Dates: Jan. 4, 1995-Jan. 3, 1997
Departure: Returned to Ways and Means

Cong.	Ranking	House	Comm.	Date of Assignment
		Terms in:		
104th	Min-22nd	3	1	Jan. 4, 1995

7th BUDGET
Dates: Jan. 26, 2005-Jan. 3, 2007
Departure: Moved to Small Business

Cong.	Ranking	House	Comm.	Date of Assignment
		Terms in:		
109th	Min-11th	8	1	Jan. 26, 2005

8th SMALL BUSINESS
Dates: Jan. 23, 2007-June 5, 2007
Departure: Leave of absence to address legal issues

Cong.	Ranking	House	Comm.	Date of Assignment
		Terms in:		
110th	Maj-3rd	9	1	Jan. 23, 2007

JOINT COMMITTEES:

1st JOINT PRINTING
House Dates: Feb. 23, 1995-Jan. 3, 1997
Departure: Returned to Ways and Means

Cong.	Ranking	House	Comm.	Date of Assignment
		Terms in:		
104th	Min-2nd	2	1	Feb. 23, 1995

James M. Jeffords (I-Vt.)

Dates: May 11, 1934
House: Jan. 3, 1975-Jan. 3, 1989
Left the House: Elected to U.S. Senate in 1988

Senate: Jan. 3, 1989-Jan. 3, 2007
Left the Senate: Retired in 2006
Served as a Republican: Jan. 3, 1975-June 6, 2001
Served as an Independent: June 6, 2001-Jan. 3, 2007

HOUSE STANDING COMMITTEES:

1st AGRICULTURE
Dates: Jan. 28, 1975-Jan. 3, 1989
Departure: Left the House for the Senate

2nd EDUCATION AND LABOR
Dates: Jan. 28, 1975-Jan. 3, 1989
Departure: Left the House for the Senate

HOUSE SELECT AND SPECIAL COMMITTEES:

1st SELECT AGING (Permanent)
Dates: Feb. 5, 1981-Jan. 3, 1989
Departure: Left the House for the Senate

SENATE STANDING COMMITTEES:

1st ENVIRONMENT AND PUBLIC WORKS
1st Dates: Feb. 2, 1989-Jan. 7, 1993
1st Departure: Left committee; no new assignment
2nd Dates: July 10, 2001-Jan. 12, 2007
Ch3: Replaced Harry M. Reid (D-Nev.) on July 10, 2001, in the Senate party shift arrangement
2nd Departure: Left the Senate; retired

Cong.	Ranking	Senate	Comm.	Date of Assignment
		Years in:		
+107th	MjA-Ch3	13 *2	1	July 10, 2001
108th	Min-RM	15 *2	2	Jan. 15, 2003
109th	Min-RM	17 *2	4	Jan. 6, 2005

2nd LABOR AND HUMAN RESOURCES renamed Jan. 21, 1999
HEALTH, EDUCATION, LABOR AND PENSIONS
1st Dates: Feb. 2, 1989-June 6, 2001
1st Departure: Majority assignment vacated when he left the Republican Party; returned as an Independent in 5th majority slot
2nd Dates: July 10, 2001-Jan. 3, 2007
Ch1: Replaced by Edward M. Kennedy (D-Mass.) following party control shift on June 6, 2001 and became Chair of Environment and Public Works on July 10, 2001
2nd Departure: Left the Senate; retired

Cong.	Ranking	Senate	Comm.	Date of Assignment
		Years in:		
103rd	Min-2nd	5 *1	4	Jan. 7, 1993
104th	Maj-2nd	7 *1	6	Jan. 4, 1995
105th	Maj-Chr	9 *1	8	Jan. 9, 1997
106th	Maj-Chr	11 *1	10	Jan. 7, 1999
107th	Maj-Ch1	13 *1	12	Jan. 25, 2001
+107th	MjA-5th	13 *2	1	July 10, 2001
108th	Min-5th	15 *2	2	Jan. 15, 2003
109th	Min-5th	17 *2	4	Jan. 6, 2005

3rd VETERANS' AFFAIRS
1st Dates: Feb. 2, 1989-June 6, 2001
1st Departure: Majority assignment vacated when he left the Republican Party; returned as an Independent in 3rd majority slot
2nd Dates: July 10, 2001-Jan. 3, 2007
2nd Departure: Left the Senate; retired

Cong.	Ranking	Senate	Comm.	Date of Assignment
		Years in:		
103rd	Min-5th	5 *1	4	Jan. 21, 1993

104th	Maj-5th	7 *1	6	Jan. 6, 1995
105th	Maj-4th	9 *1	8	Jan. 9, 1997
106th	Maj-4th	11 *1	10	Jan. 7, 1999
107th	Maj-4th	13 *1	12	Jan. 25, 2001
+107th	MjA-3rd	13 *2	1	July 10, 2001
108th	Min-3rd	15 *2	2	Jan. 15, 2003
109th	Min-3rd	17 *2	4	Jan. 6, 2005

4th FOREIGN RELATIONS
Dates: July 9, 1991-Jan. 3, 1995
Departure: Moved to Appropriations and Energy and Natural Resources

| | | Years in: | | Date of |
Cong.	Ranking	Senate	Comm.	Assignment
103rd	Min-7th	5	3	Jan. 7, 1993

5th APPROPRIATIONS
Dates: Jan. 4, 1995-Jan. 3, 1997
Departure: Moved to Finance

| | | Years in: | | Date of |
Cong.	Ranking	Senate	Comm.	Assignment
104th	Maj-13th	7	1	Jan. 4, 1995

6th ENERGY AND NATURAL RESOURCES
Dates: Jan. 5, 1995-Jan. 3, 1997
Departure: Moved to Finance

| | | Years in: | | Date of |
Cong.	Ranking	Senate	Comm.	Assignment
104th	Maj-9th	7	1	Jan. 5, 1995

7th FINANCE
1st Dates: Jan. 9, 1997-June 6, 2001
1st Departure: Majority assignment vacated when he left the Republican Party; returned as an additional Independent in 7th majority slot
2nd Dates: July 10, 2001-Jan. 3, 2007
2nd Departure: Left the Senate; retired

| | | Years in: | | Date of |
Cong.	Ranking	Senate	Comm.	Assignment
105th	Maj-10th	9 *1	1	Jan. 9, 1997
106th	Maj-9th	11 *1	2	Jan. 7, 1999
107th	Maj-7th	13 *1	5	Jan. 25, 2001
+107th	MjA-7th	13 *2	1	July 10, 2001
108th	Min-7th	15 *2	2	Jan. 15, 2003
109th	Min-4th	17 *2	4	Jan. 6, 2005

SENATE SELECT AND SPECIAL COMMITTEES:

1st JUDGE WALTER L. NIXON IMPEACHMENT
Dates: May 11, 1989-Sep. 13, 1989
Termination: Impeachment hearings concluded

2nd SPECIAL AGING (Permanent)
1st Dates: Jan. 21, 1993-June 6, 2001
1st Departure: Majority assignment vacated when he left the Republican Party; returned as an additional Independent in 4th majority slot
2nd Dates: Mar. 19, 1991-Jan. 3, 2007
2nd Departure: Left the Senate; retired

| | | Years in: | | Date of |
Cong.	Ranking	Senate	Comm.	Assignment
103rd	Min-5th	5 *1	3	Jan. 21, 1993
104th	Maj-5th	7 *1	4	Jan. 11, 1995
105th	Maj-2nd	9 *1	6	Jan. 9, 1997
106th	Maj-2nd	11 *1	8	Jan. 7, 1999
107th	Maj-2nd	13 *1	11	Jan. 25, 2001
+107th	MjA-4th	13 *2	1	July 10, 2001
108th	Min-4th	15 *2	2	Jan. 15, 2003
109th	Min-2nd	17 *2	4	Jan. 6, 2005

Lynn Jenkins (R-Kans.)

Dates: June 10, 1963
House: Jan. 3, 2009-date
Serving in the 111th Congress

HOUSE STANDING COMMITTEES:

1st FINANCIAL SERVICES
Dates: Jan. 9, 2009-date
Departure: Still serving in the 111th Congress

| | | Terms in: | | Date of |
Cong.	Ranking	House	Comm.	Assignment
111th	Min-26th	1	1	Jan. 9, 2009

William L. Jenkins (R-Tenn.)

Dates: Nov. 29, 1936
House: Jan. 3, 1997-Jan. 3, 2007
Left the House: Retired in 2006

HOUSE STANDING COMMITTEES:

1st AGRICULTURE
Dates: Jan. 7, 1997-Jan. 3, 2007
Departure: Left the House; retired

| | | Terms in: | | Date of |
Cong.	Ranking	House	Comm.	Assignment
105th	Maj-26th	1	1	Jan. 7, 1997
106th	Maj-18th	2	2	Jan. 6, 1999
107th	Maj-12th	3	3	Jan. 6, 2001
108th	Maj-9th	4	4	Jan. 28, 2003
109th	Maj-7th	5	5	Jan. 26, 2005

2nd JUDICIARY
Dates: Jan. 7, 1997-Jan. 3, 2007
Departure: Left the House; retired

| | | Terms in: | | Date of |
Cong.	Ranking	House	Comm.	Assignment
105th	Maj-17th	1	1	Jan. 7, 1997
106th	Maj-14th	2	2	Jan. 6, 1999
107th	Maj-10th	3	3	Jan. 6, 2001
108th	Maj-8th	4	4	Jan. 28, 2003
109th	Maj-9th	5	5	Jan. 26, 2005

Bobb Jindal (R-La.)

Dates: June 10, 1971
House: Jan. 3, 2005-Jan. 14, 2008
Left the House: Resigned; elected Governor in 2007

HOUSE STANDING COMMITTEES:

1st EDUCATION AND THE WORKFORCE
Dates: Jan. 26, 2005-Jan. 3, 2007
Departure: Left committee; no new assignment

Cong.	Ranking	Terms in: House	Comm.	Date of Assignment
109th	Maj-23rd	1	1	Jan. 26, 2005

2nd HOMELAND SECURITY
Dates: Jan. 26, 2005-Jan. 14, 2008
Departure: Resigned the House; elected Governor

Cong.	Ranking	Terms in: House	Comm.	Date of Assignment
109th	Maj-16th	1	1	Jan. 26, 2005
110th	Min-8th	2	2	Jan. 10, 2007

3rd RESOURCES
Dates: Jan. 26, 2005-Jan. 14, 2008
Departure: Resigned the House; elected Governor

Cong.	Ranking	Terms in: House	Comm.	Date of Assignment
109th	Maj-26th	1	1	Jan. 26, 2005
110th	Min-15th	2	2	Jan. 10, 2007

Mike Johanns (R-Neb.)

Dates: June 18, 1950
Senate: Jan. 3, 2009-date
Serving in the 111th Congress

SENATE STANDING COMMITTEES:

1st AGRICULTURE, NUTRITION AND FORESTRY
Dates: Jan. 21, 2009-date
Departure: Still serving in the 111th Congress

Cong.	Ranking	Years in: Senate	Comm.	Date of Assignment
111th	Min-6th	1	1	Jan. 21, 2009

2nd BANKING, HOUSING AND URBAN AFFAIRS
Dates: Jan. 21, 2009-date
Departure: Still serving in the 111th Congress

Cong.	Ranking	Years in: Senate	Comm.	Date of Assignment
111th	Min-9th	1	1	Jan. 21, 2009

3rd COMMERCE, SCIENCE AND TRANSPORTATION
Dates: Jan. 21, 2009-date
Departure: Still serving in the 111th Congress

Cong.	Ranking	Years in: Senate	Comm.	Date of Assignment
111th	Min-11th	1	1	Jan. 21, 2009

4th VETERANS' AFFAIRS
Dates: Jan. 21, 2009-date
Departure: Still serving in the 111th Congress

Cong.	Ranking	Years in: Senate	Comm.	Date of Assignment
111th	Min-5th	1	1	Jan. 21, 2009

SENATE SELECT AND SPECIAL COMMITTEES:

1st INDIAN AFFAIRS (Permanent)
Dates: Jan. 21, 2009-date
Departure: Still serving in the 111th Congress

Cong.	Ranking	Years in: Senate	Comm.	Date of Assignment
111th	Min-6th	1	1	Jan. 21, 2009

Christopher John (D-La.)

Dates: Jan. 5, 1960
House: Jan. 3, 1997-Jan. 3, 2005
Left the House: Lost U.S. Senate election in 2004

HOUSE STANDING COMMITTEES:

1st AGRICULTURE
Dates: Jan. 7, 1997-Feb. 8, 2001
Departure: Resigned committee; moved to Energy and Commerce

Cong.	Ranking	Terms in: House	Comm.	Date of Assignment
105th	Min-21st	1	1	Jan. 7, 1997
106th	Min-19th	2	2	Jan. 6, 1999
107th	Min-14th	3	3	Feb. 8, 2001

2nd RESOURCES
Dates: Jan. 7, 1997-Jan. 3, 2001
Departure: Moved to Energy and Commerce

Cong.	Ranking	Terms in: House	Comm.	Date of Assignment
105th	Min-22nd	1	1	Jan. 7, 1997
106th	Min-17th	2	2	Jan. 6, 1999

3rd ENERGY AND COMMERCE
Dates: Feb. 8, 2001-Jan. 3, 2005
Departure: Left the House; lost Senate election

Cong.	Ranking	Terms in: House	Comm.	Date of Assignment
107th	Min-25th	3	1	Feb. 8, 2001
108th	Min-22nd	4	2	Jan. 28, 2003

C. Donald Johnson Jr. (D-Ga.)

Dates: Jan. 30, 1948
House: Jan. 3, 1993-Jan. 3, 1995
Left the House: Defeated for re-election in 1994

HOUSE STANDING COMMITTEES:

1st ARMED SERVICES
Dates: Jan. 5, 1993-Jan. 3, 1995
Departure: Left the House; lost re-election

Cong.	Ranking	Terms in: House	Comm.	Date of Assignment
103rd	Maj-24th	1	1	Jan. 5, 1993

2nd SCIENCE, SPACE AND TECHNOLOGY
Dates: Jan. 5, 1993-Jan. 3, 1995
Departure: Left the House; lost re-election

Cong.	Ranking	Terms in: House	Comm.	Date of Assignment
103rd	Maj-24th	1	1	Jan. 5, 1993

Eddie Bernice Johnson (D-Tex.)

Dates: Dec. 3, 1935
House: Jan. 3, 1993-date
Serving in the 111th Congress

HOUSE STANDING COMMITTEES:

1st PUBLIC WORKS AND TRANSPORTATION, 103
TRANSPORTATION AND INFRASTRUCTURE, 104-111

Dates: Jan. 5, 1993-date
Departure: Still serving in the 111th Congress

Cong.	Ranking	Terms in: House	Comm.	Date of Assignment
103rd	Maj-39th	1	1	Jan. 5, 1993
104th	Min-27th	2	2	Jan. 4, 1995
105th	Min-20th	3	3	Jan. 7, 1997
106th	Min-17th	4	4	Jan. 6, 1999
107th	Min-14th	5	5	Jan. 31, 2001
108th	Min-11th	6	6	Jan. 28, 2003
109th	Min-10th	7	7	Jan. 26, 2005
110th	Maj-9th	8	8	Jan. 10, 2007
111th	Maj-9th	9	9	Jan. 7, 2009

2nd SCIENCE, SPACE AND TECHNOLOGY, 103
SCIENCE, 104-109
SCIENCE AND TECHNOLOGY, 110-111
Dates: Jan. 5, 1993-date
Departure: Still serving in the 111th Congress

Cong.	Ranking	Terms in: House	Comm.	Date of Assignment
103rd	Maj-28th	1	1	Jan. 5, 1993
104th	Min-12th	2	2	Jan. 4, 1995
105th	Min-9th	3	3	Feb. 13, 1997
106th	Min-8th	4	4	Jan. 6, 1999
107th	Min-5th	5	5	Jan. 31, 2001
108th	Min-4th	6	6	Jan. 28, 2003
109th	Min-3rd	7	7	Jan. 26, 2005
110th	Maj-3rd	8	8	Jan. 18, 2007
111th	Maj-3rd	9	9	Jan. 21, 2009

Hank Johnson (D-Ga.)

Dates: Oct. 2, 1954
House: Jan. 3, 2007-date
Serving in the 111th Congress

HOUSE STANDING COMMITTEES:

1st ARMED SERVICES
Dates: Jan. 10, 2007-date
Departure: Still serving in the 111th Congress

Cong.	Ranking	Terms in: House	Comm.	Date of Assignment
110th	Maj-26th	1	1	Jan. 10, 2007
111th	Maj-23rd	2	2	Jan. 7, 2009

2nd JUDICIARY
Dates: Jan. 18, 2007-date
Departure: Still serving in the 111th Congress

Cong.	Ranking	Terms in: House	Comm.	Date of Assignment
110th	Maj-15th	1	1	Jan. 18, 2007
111th	Maj-13th	2	2	Jan. 21, 2009

3rd SMALL BUSINESS
Dates: Jan. 23, 2007-Jan. 3, 2009
Departure: Left committee; no new assignment

Cong.	Ranking	Terms in: House	Comm.	Date of Assignment
110th	Maj-17th	1	1	Jan. 23, 2007

4th TRANSPORTATION AND INFRASTRUCTURE
Dates: May 6, 2010-date
Departure: Still serving in the 111th Congress

Cong.	Ranking	Terms in: House	Comm.	Date of Assignment
111th	Maj-2nd	2	1	May 6, 2010

Jay W. Johnson (D-Wisc.)

Dates: Sept. 30, 1943
House: Jan. 3, 1997-Jan. 3, 1999
Left the House: Defeated for re-election in 1998

HOUSE STANDING COMMITTEES:

1st TRANSPORTATION AND INFRASTRUCTURE
Dates: Jan. 7, 1997-Jan. 3, 1999
Departure: Left the House; lost re-election

Cong.	Ranking	Terms in: House	Comm.	Date of Assignment
105th	Min-28th	1	1	Jan. 7, 1997

2nd AGRICULTURE
Dates: Feb. 5, 1997-Jan. 3, 1999
Departure: Left the House; lost re-election

Cong.	Ranking	Terms in: House	Comm.	Date of Assignment
105th	Min-22nd	1	1	Feb. 5, 1997

Nancy L. Johnson (R-Conn.)

Dates: Jan. 5, 1935
House: Jan. 3, 1983-Jan. 3, 2007
Left the House: Defeated for re-election in 2006

HOUSE STANDING COMMITTEES:

1st PUBLIC WORKS AND TRANSPORTATION
Dates: Jan. 6, 1983-Jan. 3, 1989
Departure: Moved to Ways and Means

2nd VETERANS' AFFAIRS
Dates: Jan. 6, 1983-Jan. 3, 1987
Departure: Moved to Budget

3rd BUDGET
Dates: Jan. 21, 1987-Jan. 3, 1989
Departure: Moved to Ways and Means

4th WAYS AND MEANS
Dates: Jan. 20, 1989-Jan. 3, 2007
Departure: Left the House; lost re-election

Cong.	Ranking	Terms in: House	Comm.	Date of Assignment
103rd	Min-7th	6	3	Jan. 5, 1993
104th	Maj-5th	7	4	Jan. 4, 1995
105th	Maj-5th	8	5	Jan. 7, 1997
106th	Maj-5th	9	6	Jan. 6, 1999
107th	Maj-4th	10	7	Jan. 6, 2001
108th	Maj-4th	11	8	Jan. 28, 2003
109th	Maj-3rd	12	9	Jan. 6, 2005

5th STANDARDS OF OFFICIAL CONDUCT
Dates: Feb. 6, 1991-Jan. 3, 1997
Departure: Left committee; no new assignment

Cong.	Ranking	Terms in: House	Comm.	Date of Assignment
103rd	Min-2nd	6	2	Jan. 5, 1993
104th	Maj-Chr	7	3	Jan. 20, 1995

HOUSE SELECT AND SPECIAL COMMITTEES:

1st SELECT CHILDREN, YOUTH AND FAMILIES (Temporary)
Dates: Feb. 2, 1983-Jan. 3, 1989
Departure: Moved to Ways and Means

2nd SELECT ETHICS
Dates: Jan. 7, 1997-Jan. 21, 1997
Termination: House Report 105-1 filed, Jan. 17, 1997

		Terms in:		Date of
Cong.	Ranking	House	Comm.	Assignment
105th	Maj-Chr	8	1	Jan. 7, 1997

JOINT COMMITTEES:

1st JOINT DEFICIT REDUCTION (Temporary)
House Dates: Feb. 23,1987-Sep. 29,1987
Termination: Public Law 100-119 adjusted Gramm-Rudman-Hollings Act

2nd JOINT TAXATION
House Dates: Feb. 7, 2005-Jan. 3, 2007
Departure: Left the House; lost re-election

		Terms in:		Date of
Cong.	Ranking	House	Comm.	Assignment
109th	Maj-3rd	12	1	Feb. 7, 2005

Sam Johnson (R-Tex.)

Dates: Oct. 11, 1930
House: May 8, 1991-date
Serving in the 111th Congress

H: Johnson was elected to the 102nd Congress by special election, May 8, 1991, to fill the vacancy caused by the resignation of U.S. Representative Steve Bartlett (R-Tex.) who had been elected Mayor of Dallas. Johnson was seated May 22, 1991, and assigned to committees.

HOUSE STANDING COMMITTEES:

1st BANKING, FINANCE AND URBAN AFFAIRS
Dates: June 7, 1991-Jan. 3, 1995
Departure: Moved to Economic and Educational Opportunities and Ways and Means

		Terms in:		Date of
Cong.	Ranking	House	Comm.	Assignment
103rd	Min-11th	2	2	Jan. 5, 1993

2nd SMALL BUSINESS
Dates: June 7, 1991-Jan. 3, 1995
Departure: Moved to Economic and Educational Opportunities and Ways and Means

		Terms in:		Date of
Cong.	Ranking	House	Comm.	Assignment
103rd	Min-8th	2	2	Jan. 5, 1993

3rd SCIENCE, SPACE AND TECHNOLOGY
Dates: Sep. 19, 1991-Jan. 3, 1995
Departure: Moved to Economic and Educational Opportunities and Ways and Means

		Terms in:		Date of
Cong.	Ranking	House	Comm.	Assignment
103rd	Min-12th	2	2	Jan. 5, 1993

4th ECONOMIC AND EDUCATIONAL OPPORTUNITIES, 104
EDUCATION AND THE WORKFORCE, 105-109
Dates: Jan. 4, 1995-Jan. 3, 2007
Departure: Left committee; no new assignment

		Terms in:		Date of
Cong.	Ranking	House	Comm.	Assignment
104th	Maj-13th	3	1	Jan. 4, 1995
105th	Maj-10th	4	2	Jan. 7, 1997
106th	Maj-10th	5	3	Jan. 6, 1999
107th	Maj-8th	6	4	Jan. 6, 2001
108th	Maj-7th	7	5	Jan. 28, 2003
109th	Maj-5th	8	6	Jan. 26, 2005

5th WAYS AND MEANS
Dates: Jan. 4, 1995-date
Departure: Still serving in the 111th Congress

		Terms in:		Date of
Cong.	Ranking	House	Comm.	Assignment
104th	Maj-15th	3	1	Jan. 4, 1995
105th	Maj-13th	4	2	Jan. 7, 1997
106th	Maj-12th	5	3	Jan. 6, 1999
107th	Maj-11th	6	4	Jan. 6, 2001
108th	Maj-11th	7	5	Jan. 28, 2003
109th	Maj-9th	8	6	Jan. 6, 2005
110th	Min-5th	9	7	Jan. 10, 2007
111th	Min-3rd	10	8	Jan. 9, 2009

Timothy P. Johnson (D-S.D.)

Dates: Dec. 28, 1946
House: Jan. 3, 1987-Jan. 3, 1997
Left the House: Elected to U.S. Senate in 1996
Senate: Jan. 3, 1997-date
Serving in the 111th Congress

HOUSE STANDING COMMITTEES:

1st AGRICULTURE
Dates: Jan. 22, 1987-Jan. 3, 1997
Departure: Left the House for the Senate

		Terms in:		Date of
Cong.	Ranking	House	Comm.	Assignment
103rd	Maj-10th	4	4	Jan. 5, 1993
104th	Min-6th	5	5	Jan. 4, 1995

2nd VETERANS' AFFAIRS
Dates: Jan. 22, 1987-Oct. 17, 1989
Departure: Moved to Interior and Insular Affairs

3rd INTERIOR AND INSULAR AFFAIRS, 101-102
NATURAL RESOURCES, 103
RESOURCES, 104
Dates: Oct. 16, 1989-Jan. 3, 1997
Departure: Left the House for the Senate

		Terms in:		Date of
Cong.	Ranking	House	Comm.	Assignment
103rd	Maj-14th	4	3	Jan. 5, 1993
104th	Min-10th	5	4	Jan. 4, 1995

HOUSE SELECT AND SPECIAL COMMITTEES:

1st SELECT CHILDREN, YOUTH AND FAMILIES (Temporary)
Dates: Feb. 21, 1991-Jan. 3, 1993
Termination: Committee not renewed in 1993

SENATE STANDING COMMITTEES:

1st AGRICULTURE, NUTRITION AND FORESTRY
Dates: Jan. 9, 1997-Jan. 25, 2001
Departure: Moved to Appropriations and Indian Affairs

		Years in:		Date of
Cong.	Ranking	Senate	Comm.	Assignment
105th	Min-8th	1	1	Jan. 9, 1997
106th	Min-7th	3	2	Jan. 7, 1999

2nd BANKING, HOUSING AND URBAN AFFAIRS
Dates: Jan. 9, 1997-date
Departure: Still serving in the 111th Congress

Cong.	Ranking	Years in: Senate	Comm.	Date of Assignment
105th	Min-7th	1	1	Jan. 9, 1997
106th	Min-5th	3	2	Jan. 7, 1999
107th	Min-3rd	5	5	Jan. 25, 2001
+107th	Maj-3rd	5	5	June 6, 2001
108th	Min-3rd	7	7	Jan. 15, 2003
109th	Min-3rd	9	8	Jan. 6, 2005
110th	Maj-2nd	11	11	Jan. 12, 2007
111th	Maj-2nd	13	13	Jan. 21, 2009

3rd BUDGET
Dates: Jan. 9, 1997-Jan. 12, 2007
Departure: Left committee; no new assignment

Cong.	Ranking	Years in: Senate	Comm.	Date of Assignment
105th	Min-9th	1	1	Jan. 9, 1997
106th	Min-9th	3	2	Jan. 7, 1999
107th	Min-7th	5	5	Jan. 25, 2001
+107th	Maj-7th	5	5	June 6, 2001
108th	Min-7th	7	7	Jan. 15, 2003
109th	Min-6th	9	8	Jan. 6, 2005

4th ENERGY AND NATURAL RESOURCES
Dates: Jan. 9, 1997-date
Departure: Still serving in the 111th Congress

Cong.	Ranking	Years in: Senate	Comm.	Date of Assignment
105th	Min-8th	1	1	Jan. 9, 1997
106th	Min-6th	3	2	Jan. 7, 1999
107th	Min-6th	5	5	Jan. 25, 2001
+107th	Maj-6th	5	5	June 6, 2001
108th	Min-6th	7	7	Jan. 15, 2003
109th	Min-5th	9	8	Jan. 6, 2005
110th	Maj-5th	11	11	Jan. 12, 2007
111th	Maj-4th	13	13	Jan. 21, 2009

5th APPROPRIATIONS
Dates: Jan. 25, 2001-date
Departure: Still serving in the 111th Congress

Cong.	Ranking	Years in: Senate	Comm.	Date of Assignment
107th	Min-13th	5	1	Jan. 25, 2001
+107th	Maj-13th	5	1	June 6, 2001
108th	Min-13th	7	2	Jan. 15, 2003
109th	Min-12th	9	4	Jan. 6, 2005
110th	Maj-11th	11	6	Jan. 12, 2007
111th	Maj-11th	13	8	Jan. 21, 2009

SENATE SELECT AND SPECIAL COMMITTEES:

1st INDIAN AFFAIRS (Permanent)
Dates: Jan. 25, 2001-date
Departure: Still serving in the 111th Congress

Cong.	Ranking	Years in: Senate	Comm.	Date of Assignment
107th	Min-7th	5	1	Jan. 25, 2001
+107th	Maj-7th	5	1	June 6, 2001
108th	Min-6th	7	2	Jan. 15, 2003
109th	Min-5th	9	4	Jan. 6, 2005
110th	Maj-5th	11	6	Jan. 12, 2007
111th	Maj-5th	13	8	Jan. 21, 2009

2nd SELECT ETHICS (Permanent)
Dates: Jan. 6, 2005-Mar. 31, 2008
Ch1: Replaced by Barbara Boxer (D-Cal.) as Acting Chair on Jan. 12, 2007
Departure: Left committee due to health issues

Cong.	Ranking	Years in: Senate	Comm.	Date of Assignment
109th	Min-VCh	9	1	Jan. 6, 2005
110th	Maj-Ch1	11	3	Jan. 12, 2007

Timothy V. Johnson (R-Ill.)

Dates: July 23, 1946
House: Jan. 3, 2001-date
Serving in the 111th Congress

HOUSE STANDING COMMITTEES:

1st AGRICULTURE
Dates: Jan. 6, 2001-date
Departure: Still serving in the 111th Congress

Cong.	Ranking	Terms in: House	Comm.	Date of Assignment
107th	Maj-21st	1	1	Jan. 6, 2001
108th	Maj-14th	2	2	Jan. 28, 2003
109th	Maj-10th	3	3	Jan. 26, 2005
110th	Min-6th	4	4	Jan. 10, 2007
111th	Min-4th	5	5	Jan. 9, 2009

2nd SCIENCE
Dates: Jan. 6, 2001-Jan. 3, 2007
Departure: Left committee; no new assignment

Cong.	Ranking	Terms in: House	Comm.	Date of Assignment
107th	Maj-21st	1	1	Jan. 6, 2001
108th	Maj-17th	2	2	Jan. 28, 2003
109th	Maj-14th	3	3	Jan. 26, 2005

3rd TRANSPORTATION AND INFRASTRUCTURE
Dates: Jan. 6, 2001-date
Departure: Still serving in the 111th Congress

Cong.	Ranking	Terms in: House	Comm.	Date of Assignment
107th	Maj-33rd	1	1	Jan. 6, 2001
108th	Maj-26th	2	2	Jan. 28, 2003
109th	Maj-21st	3	3	Jan. 26, 2005
110th	Min-15th	4	4	Jan. 10, 2007
111th	Min-11th	5	5	Jan. 9, 2009

Harry A. Johnston II (D-Fla.)

Dates: Dec. 2, 1931
House: Jan. 3, 1989-Jan. 3, 1997
Left the House: Retired in 1996

HOUSE STANDING COMMITTEES:

1st FOREIGN AFFAIRS, 101-103
INTERNATIONAL RELATIONS, 104
Dates: Jan. 19, 1989-Jan. 3, 1997
Departure: Left the House; retired

Cong.	Ranking	Terms in: House	Comm.	Date of Assignment
103rd	Maj-7th	3	3	Jan. 5, 1993
104th	Min-7th	4	4	Jan. 4, 1995

2nd SCIENCE, SPACE AND TECHNOLOGY
Dates: Jan. 19, 1989-Jan. 3, 1991
Departure: Moved to Interior and Insular Affairs

3rd INTERIOR AND INSULAR AFFAIRS
Dates: Jan. 24, 1991-Jan. 3, 1993
Departure: Moved to Budget

4th BUDGET
Dates: Jan. 5, 1993-Apr. 25, 1996
Departure: Resigned committee; no new assignment

Cong.	Ranking	Terms in: House	Comm.	Date of Assignment
103rd	Maj-22nd	3	1	Jan. 5, 1993
104th	Min-8th	4	2	Jan. 4, 1995

J. Bennett Johnston Jr. (D-La.)

Dates: June 10, 1932
Senate: Nov. 14, 1972-Jan. 3, 1997
Left the Senate: Retired in 1996

S: Johnston was appointed to the 92nd Congress, Nov. 14, 1972, to fill the unexpired term caused by the death of U.S. Senator Allen J. Ellender (D-La.). Ellender had initially been replaced by Elaine S. Edwards (D-La.), an appointee who had resigned. Johnston was not seated nor assigned to committees because the 92nd Congress was not in session. Johnston had been elected to the 93rd Congress.

SENATE STANDING COMMITTEES:

1st BANKING, HOUSING AND URBAN AFFAIRS
Dates: Jan. 4, 1973-Jan. 17, 1975
Departure: Moved to Appropriations

2nd INTERIOR AND INSULAR AFFAIRS reorganized Feb. 11, 1977
ENERGY AND NATURAL RESOURCES
Dates: Jan. 4, 1973-Jan. 3, 1997
Departure: Left the Senate; retired

Cong.	Ranking	Years in: Senate	Comm.	Date of Assignment
103rd	Maj-Chr	21	21	Jan. 7, 1993
104th	Min-RM	23	23	Jan. 4, 1995

3rd APPROPRIATIONS
Dates: Jan. 17, 1975-Jan. 3, 1997
Departure: Left the Senate; retired

Cong.	Ranking	Years in: Senate	Comm.	Date of Assignment
103rd	Maj-4th	21	18	Jan. 7, 1993
104th	Min-4th	23	20	Jan. 4, 1995

4th BUDGET
Dates: Feb. 11, 1977-Jan. 3, 1997
Departure: Left the Senate; retired

Cong.	Ranking	Years in: Senate	Comm.	Date of Assignment
103rd	Maj-3rd	21	16	Jan. 21, 1993
104th	Min-3rd	23	18	Jan. 6, 1995

SENATE SELECT AND SPECIAL COMMITTEES:

1st SELECT SMALL BUSINESS
Dates: Jan. 4, 1973-Feb. 11, 1977
Departure: Moved to Budget

2nd SENATE COMMITTEE SYSTEM II (Quayle)
Dates: June 13, 1984-Dec. 14, 1984
Termination: Senate Print 98-254 issued

3rd SPECIAL AGING (Permanent)
Dates: Feb. 9, 1984-Jan. 3, 1997
Departure: Left the Senate; retired

Cong.	Ranking	Years in: Senate	Comm.	Date of Assignment
103rd	Maj-4th	21	9	Jan. 21, 1993
104th	Min-4th	23	11	Jan. 6, 1995

4th SELECT INTELLIGENCE (Permanent)
Dates: Jan. 27, 1993-Jan. 3, 1997
Departure: Left the Senate; retired

Cong.	Ranking	Years in: Senate	Comm.	Date of Assignment
103rd	Maj-9th	21	1	Jan. 27, 1993
104th	Min-7th	23	2	Jan. 6, 1995

JOINT COMMITTEES:

1st JOINT DEFICIT REDUCTION (Temporary)
Senate Dates: Jan. 6, 1987-Sep. 29, 1987
Termination: Public Law 100-119 adjusted Gramm-Rudman-Hollings Act

Stephanie Tubbs Jones (D-Ohio)

Dates: Sept. 10, 1949-Aug. 20, 2008
House: Jan. 3, 1999-Aug. 20, 2008
Left the House: Died in office

HOUSE STANDING COMMITTEES:

1st BANKING AND FINANCIAL SERVICES, 106
FINANCIAL SERVICES, 107
Dates: Jan. 6, 1999-Jan. 3, 2003
Departure: Moved to Ways and Means

Cong.	Ranking	Terms in: House	Comm.	Date of Assignment
106th	Min-26th	1	1	Jan. 6, 1999
107th	Min-23rd	2	2	Jan. 31, 2001

2nd SMALL BUSINESS
Dates: Jan. 6, 1999-Jan. 3, 2003
Departure: Moved to Ways and Means

Cong.	Ranking	Terms in: House	Comm.	Date of Assignment
106th	Min-12th	1	1	Jan. 6, 1999
107th	Min-11th	2	2	Jan. 31, 2001

3rd STANDARDS OF OFFICIAL CONDUCT
1st Dates: Mar. 14, 2001-Jan. 3, 2003
1st Departure: Moved to Ways and Means
2nd Dates: Mar. 6, 2003-Aug. 20, 2008
Ch1: Succeeded by R. Eugene (Gene) Green (D-Tex.) on Sep. 9, 2008
Succeeded by Robert C. Scott (D-Va.) on Sep. 11, 2008
2nd Departure: Died in office

Cong.	Ranking	Terms in: House	Comm.	Date of Assignment
107th	Min-5th	2 *1	1	Mar. 14, 2001
108th	MnR-1st	3 *2	1	Mar. 6, 2003
109th	Min-2nd	4 *2	2	Jan. 26, 2005
110th	Maj-Ch1	5 *2	3	Jan. 4, 2007

4th WAYS AND MEANS
Dates: Jan. 28, 2003-Aug. 20, 2008
Departure: Died in office

Cong.	Ranking	Terms in: House	Comm.	Date of Assignment
108th	Min-17th	3	1	Jan. 28, 2003
109th	Min-14th	4	2	Jan. 26, 2005
110th	Maj-12th	5	3	Jan. 12, 2007

Walter B. Jones Jr. (R-N.C.)

Dates: Feb. 10, 1943
House: Jan. 3, 1995-date
Serving in the 111th Congress

HOUSE STANDING COMMITTEES:

1st NATIONAL SECURITY, 104-105
ARMED SERVICES, 106-111
Dates: Jan. 4, 1995-date
Departure: Still serving in the 111th Congress

Cong.	Ranking	Terms in: House	Comm.	Date of Assignment
104th	Maj-27th	1	1	Jan. 4, 1995
105th	Maj-24th	2	2	Jan. 7, 1997
106th	Maj-23rd	3	3	Jan. 6, 1999
107th	Maj-18th	4	4	Jan. 6, 2001
108th	Maj-11th	5	5	Jan. 28, 2003
109th	Maj-11th	6	6	Jan. 26, 2005
110th	Min-8th	7	7	Jan. 10, 2007
111th	Min-5th	8	8	Jan. 9, 2009

2nd RESOURCES
Dates: Jan. 4, 1995-Jan. 3, 2007
Departure: Left committee; no new assignment

Cong.	Ranking	Terms in: House	Comm.	Date of Assignment
104th	Maj-20th	1	1	Jan. 4, 1995
105th	Maj-16th	2	2	Jan. 7, 1997
106th	Maj-15th	3	3	Jan. 6, 1999
107th	Maj-14th	4	4	Jan. 6, 2001
108th	Maj-13th	5	5	Jan. 28, 2003
109th	Maj-10th	6	6	Jan. 26, 2005

3rd SMALL BUSINESS
Dates: Jan. 4, 1995-Apr. 14, 1997
Departure: Resigned committee; moved to Banking and Financial Services

Cong.	Ranking	Terms in: House	Comm.	Date of Assignment
104th	Maj-14th	1	1	Jan. 4, 1995
105th	Maj-9th	2	2	Jan. 21, 1997

4th BANKING AND FINANCIAL SERVICES, 105-107
FINANCIAL SERVICES, 108-111
Dates: Apr. 16, 1997-date
Departure: Still serving in the 111th Congress

Cong.	Ranking	Terms in: House	Comm.	Date of Assignment
105th	Maj-30th	2	1	Apr. 16, 1997
106th	Maj-25th	3	2	Jan. 6, 1999
107th	Maj-22nd	4	3	Jan. 6, 2001
108th	Maj-17th	5	4	Jan. 28, 2003
109th	Maj-17th	6	5	Jan. 26, 2005
110th	Min-12th	7	6	Jan. 10, 2007
111th	Maj-8th	8	7	Jan. 9, 2009

Jim Jordan (R-Ohio)

Dates: Feb. 17, 1964
House: Jan. 3, 2007-date
Serving in the 111th Congress

HOUSE STANDING COMMITTEES:

1st JUDICIARY
Dates: Jan. 10, 2007-date
Departure: Still serving in the 111th Congress

Cong.	Ranking	Terms in: House	Comm.	Date of Assignment
110th	Min-17th	1	1	Jan. 10, 2007
111th	Min-12th	2	2	Jan. 9, 2009

2nd SMALL BUSINESS
Dates: Jan. 10, 2007-Feb. 25, 2008
Departure: Resigned committee; moved to Budget

Cong.	Ranking	Terms in: House	Comm.	Date of Assignment
110th	Min-15th	1	1	Jan. 10, 2007

3rd OVERSIGHT AND GOVERNMENT REFORM
Dates: May 10, 2007-date
Departure: Still serving in the 111th Congress

Cong.	Ranking	Terms in: House	Comm.	Date of Assignment
110th	Min-18th	1	1	May 10, 2007
111th	Min-13th	2	2	Jan. 9, 2009

4th BUDGET
Dates: Feb. 26, 2008-date
Departure: Still serving in the 111th Congress

Cong.	Ranking	Terms in: House	Comm.	Date of Assignment
110th	MnR-1st	1	1	Feb. 26, 2008
111th	Min-12th	2	2	Jan. 9, 2009

K

Steven L. Kagen (D-Wisc.)

Dates: Dec. 12, 1949
House: Jan. 3, 2007-date
Serving in the 111th Congress

HOUSE STANDING COMMITTEES:

1st AGRICULTURE
Dates: Jan. 12, 2007-date
Departure: Still serving in the 111th Congress

Cong.	Ranking	Terms in: House	Comm.	Date of Assignment
110th	Maj-19th	1	1	Jan. 12, 2007
111th	Maj-15th	2	2	Jan. 21, 2009

2nd TRANSPORTATION AND INFRASTRUCTURE
Dates: Jan. 10, 2007-date
Departure: Still serving in the 111th Congress

Cong.	Ranking	Terms in: House	Comm.	Date of Assignment
110th	Maj-39th	1	1	Jan. 10, 2007
111th	Maj-31st	2	2	Jan. 7, 2009

Paul E. Kanjorski (D-Penn.)

Dates: April 2, 1937
House: Jan. 3, 1985-date
Serving in the 111th Congress

HOUSE STANDING COMMITTEES:

1st BANKING, FINANCE AND URBAN AFFAIRS, 99-103
BANKING AND FINANCIAL SERVICES, 104-106
FINANCIAL SERVICES, 107-111
Dates: Jan. 30, 1985-date
Departure: Still serving in the 111th Congress

Cong.	Ranking	Terms in: House	Comm.	Date of Assignment
103rd	Maj-7th	5	5	Jan. 5, 1993
104th	Min-6th	6	6	Jan. 4, 1995
105th	Min-6th	7	7	Jan. 7, 1997
106th	Min-4th	8	8	Jan. 6, 1999
107th	Min-3rd	9	9	Jan. 31, 2001
108th	Min-2nd	10	10	Jan. 28, 2003
109th	Min-2nd	11	11	Jan. 26, 2005
110th	Maj-2nd	12	12	Jan. 12, 2007
111th	Maj-2nd	13	13	Jan. 7, 2009

2nd VETERANS' AFFAIRS
Dates: Jan. 30, 1985-Mar. 1, 1989
Departure: Moved to Post Office and Civil Service

3rd SCIENCE, SPACE AND TECHNOLOGY, 100
SCIENCE AND TECHNOLOGY, 110
1st Dates: Dec. 15, 1987-Jan. 3, 1989
1st Departure: Left committee; later moved to Post Office and Civil Service
2nd Dates: Jan. 23, 2007-July 14, 2008
2nd Departure: Resigned committee; no new assignment

Cong.	Ranking	Terms in: House	Comm.	Date of Assignment
110th	Maj-13th	12 *2	1	Jan. 23, 2007

4th POST OFFICE AND CIVIL SERVICE
Dates: Mar. 1, 1989-Jan. 3, 1995
Departure: Committee abolished; moved to Government Reform and Oversight

Cong.	Ranking	Terms in: House	Comm.	Date of Assignment
103rd	Maj-6th	5	3	Jan. 21, 1993

5th GOVERNMENT REFORM AND OVERSIGHT, 104-106
GOVERNMENT REFORM, 107-109
OVERSIGHT AND GOVERNMENT REFORM, 110-111
Dates: Jan. 9, 1995-date
Departure: Still serving in the 111th Congress

Cong.	Ranking	Terms in: House	Comm.	Date of Assignment
104th	Min-9th	6	1	Jan. 9, 1995
105th	Min-6th	7	2	Jan. 7, 1997
106th	Min-6th	8	3	Jan. 6, 1999
107th	Min-5th	9	4	Jan. 31, 2001
108th	Min-5th	10	5	Jan. 28, 2003
109th	Min-5th	11	6	Jan. 26, 2005
110th	Maj-4th	12	7	Jan. 12, 2007
111th	Maj-2nd	13	8	Jan. 28, 2009

Marcia C. (Marcy) Kaptur (D-Ohio)

Dates: June 17, 1946
House: Jan. 3, 1983-date
Serving in the 111th Congress

HOUSE STANDING COMMITTEES:

1st BANKING, FINANCE AND URBAN AFFAIRS
Dates: Jan. 6, 1983-May 24, 1990
Departure: Resigned committee; moved to Appropriations

2nd VETERANS' AFFAIRS
Dates: Jan. 6, 1983-Jan. 3, 1989
Departure: Moved to Budget.

3rd BUDGET
1st Dates: Jan. 19, 1989-May 24, 1990
1st Departure: Resigned committee; moved to Appropriations
2nd Dates: Jan. 18, 2007-date
2nd Departure: Still serving in the 111th Congress

Cong.	Ranking	Terms in: House	Comm.	Date of Assignment
110th	Maj-8th	13 *2	1	Jan. 18, 2007
111th	Maj-3rd	14 *2	2	Jan. 21, 2009

4th APPROPRIATIONS
Dates: May 24, 1990-date
Departure: Still serving in the 111th Congress

Cong.	Ranking	Terms in: House	Comm.	Date of Assignment
103rd	Maj-21st	6	3	Jan. 5, 1993
104th	Min-17th	7	4	Jan. 4, 1995
105th	Min-12th	8	5	Jan. 7, 1997
106th	Min-8th	9	6	Jan. 6, 1999
107th	Min-7th	10	7	Jan. 31, 2001
108th	Min-7th	11	8	Jan. 28, 2003
109th	Min-7th	12	9	Jan. 26, 2005
110th	Maj-5th	13	10	Jan. 4, 2007
111th	Maj-5th	14	11	Jan. 7, 2009

5th OVERSIGHT AND GOVERNMENT REFORM
Dates: Apr. 30, 2009-date
Departure: Still serving in the 111th Congress

Cong.	Ranking	Terms in: House	Comm.	Date of Assignment
111th	MjA-13th	14	1	Apr. 30, 2009

John R. Kasich (R-Ohio)

Dates: May 13, 1952
House: Jan. 3, 1983-Jan. 3, 2001
Left the House: Retired; lost Republican presidential nomination in 2000

HOUSE STANDING COMMITTEES:

1st ARMED SERVICES, 98-103, 106
NATIONAL SECURITY, 104-105
Dates: Jan. 6, 1983-Jan. 3, 2001
Departure: Left House; lost Republican presidential nomination

Cong.	Ranking	Terms in: House	Comm.	Date of Assignment
103rd	Min-4th	6	6	Jan. 5, 1993
104th	Maj-4th	7	7	Jan. 4, 1995
105th	Maj-4th	8	8	Jan. 7, 1997
106th	Maj-4th	9	9	Jan. 6, 1999

2nd BUDGET
Dates: Jan. 20, 1989-Jan. 3, 2001
Departure: Left House; lost Republican presidential nomination

Cong.	Ranking	Terms in: House	Comm.	Date of Assignment
103rd	Min-RM	6	3	Jan. 5, 1993
104th	Maj-Chr	7	4	Jan. 4, 1995
105th	Maj-Chr	8	5	Jan. 7, 1997
106th	Maj-Chr	9	6	Jan. 6, 1999

Nancy Landon Kassebaum

(R-Kans.)

Dates: July 29, 1932
Senate: Dec. 23, 1978-Jan. 3, 1997
Left the Senate: Retired in 1996

S: Kassebaum was appointed to the 95th Congress, Dec. 23, 1978, to fill the vacancy caused by the resignation of U.S. Senator James B. Pearson (R-Kans.). She had been elected to succeed Pearson in the 96th Congress. Kassebaum was not seated nor assigned to committees because the 95th Congress was not in session.

SENATE STANDING COMMITTEES:

1st BUDGET
Dates: Jan. 23, 1979-Feb. 2, 1989
Departure: Left committee; moved to Labor and Human Resources and returned to Banking, Housing and Urban Affairs

2nd COMMERCE, SCIENCE AND TRANSPORTATION
Dates: Jan. 23, 1979-Feb. 2, 1989
Departure: Left committee; moved to Labor and Human Resources and returned to Banking, Housing and Urban Affairs

3rd BANKING, HOUSING AND URBAN AFFAIRS
1st Dates: Jan. 23, 1979-Jan. 5, 1981
1st Departure: Moved to Foreign Relations
2nd Dates: Feb. 2, 1989-Jan. 7, 1993
2nd Departure: Left committee; became Ranking Member on Labor and Human Resources in the 103rd Congress

4th FOREIGN RELATIONS
Dates: Jan. 5, 1981-Jan. 3, 1997
Departure: Left the Senate; retired

Cong.	Ranking	Years in: Senate	Comm.	Date of Assignment
103rd	Min-3rd	15	13	Jan. 7, 1993
104th	Maj-3rd	17	15	Jan. 5, 1995

5th LABOR AND HUMAN RESOURCES
Dates: Feb. 2, 1989-Jan. 3, 1997
Departure: Left the Senate; retired

Cong.	Ranking	Years in: Senate	Comm.	Date of Assignment
103rd	Min-RM	15	4	Jan. 7, 1993
104th	Maj-Chr	17	6	Jan. 4, 1995

SENATE SELECT AND SPECIAL COMMITTEES:

1st SPECIAL AGING (Permanent)
1st Dates: Jan. 23, 1979-Mar. 5, 1985
1st Departure: Moved to Select Ethics
2nd Dates: Feb. 2, 1989-Mar. 19, 1991
2nd Departure: Moved to Select Indian Affairs

2nd SELECT ETHICS (Permanent)
Dates: March 5, 1985-Feb. 2, 1989
Departure: Moved to Labor and Human Resources and returned to Banking, Housing and Urban Affairs

3rd SELECT INDIAN AFFAIRS (Permanent), 102
INDIAN AFFAIRS (Permanent), 103-104
Dates: Feb. 5, 1991-Jan. 3, 1997
Departure: Left the Senate; retired.

Cong.	Ranking	Years in: Senate	Comm.	Date of Assignment
103rd	Min-6th	15	2	Jan. 5, 1993
104th	Maj-5th	17	4	Jan. 11, 1995

4th SELECT POW-MIA AFFAIRS
Dates: Aug. 2, 1991-Feb. 3, 1993
Termination: Senate Report 1 (103-1) filed.

JOINT COMMITTEES:

1st JOINT DEFICIT REDUCTION (Temporary)
Senate Dates: Jan. 6, 1987-Sep. 29, 1987
Termination: Public Law 100-119 adjusted Gramm-Rudman-Hollings Act

2nd JOINT ORGANIZATION OF CONGRESS (Ad Hoc)
Senate Dates: Sep. 25, 1992-Dec. 9, 1993
Termination: Senate Report 103-215 filed

Cong.	Ranking	Years in: Senate	Comm.	Date of Assignment
103rd	Min-2nd	15	1	Continued

Edward E. Kaufman (D-Del.)

Dates: March 15, 1939
Senate: Jan. 15, 2009-date
Serving in the 111th Congress

S: Kaufman was appointed to the 111th Congress, Jan. 15, 2009, to fill the vacancy caused by the resignation of U.S. Senator Joseph R. Biden (D-Del.) who had been elected Vice President in 2008. Kaufman was seated on Jan. 16, 2009, and was assigned to committees.

SENATE STANDING COMMITTEES:

1st FOREIGN RELATIONS
Dates: Jan. 21, 2009-date
Departure: Still serving in the 111th Congress

Cong.	Ranking	Years in: Senate	Comm.	Date of Assignment
111th	Maj-10th	1	1	Jan. 21, 2009

2nd JUDICIARY
Dates: Jan. 21, 2009-date
Departure: Still serving in the 111th Congress

Cong.	Ranking	Years in: Senate	Comm.	Date of Assignment
111th	Maj-11th	1	1	Jan. 21, 2009

Richard (Ric) Keller (R-Fla.)

Dates: Sept. 5, 1964
House: Jan. 3, 2001-Jan. 3, 2009
Left the House: Defeated for re-election in 2008

HOUSE STANDING COMMITTEES:

1st EDUCATION AND THE WORKFORCE, 107-109
EDUCATION AND LABOR, 110
Dates: Jan. 6, 2001-Jan. 3, 2009
Departure: Left the House; lost re-election

Cong.	Ranking	Terms in: House	Comm.	Date of Assignment
107th	Maj-24th	1	1	Jan. 6, 2001
108th	Maj-18th	2	2	Jan. 28, 2003
109th	Maj-12th	3	3	Jan. 26, 2005
110th	Min-9th	4	4	Jan. 10, 2007

2nd JUDICIARY
Dates: Jan. 6, 2001-Jan. 3, 2009
Departure: Left the House; lost re-election

Cong.	Ranking	Terms in: House	Comm.	Date of Assignment
107th	Maj-18th	1	1	Jan. 6, 2001
108th	Maj-13th	2	2	Jan. 28, 2003
109th	Maj-15th	3	3	Jan. 26, 2005
110th	Min-9th	4	4	Jan. 10, 2007

3rd SMALL BUSINESS
Dates: Feb. 2, 2005-Jan. 3, 2007
Departure: Left committee; no new assignment

Cong.	Ranking	Terms in: House	Comm.	Date of Assignment
109th	Maj-12th	3	1	Feb. 2, 2005

Sue W. Kelly (R-N.Y.)

Dates: Sept. 26, 1936
House: Jan. 3, 1995-Jan. 3, 2007
Left the House: Defeated for re-election in 2006

HOUSE STANDING COMMITTEES:

1st BANKING AND FINANCIAL SERVICES, 104-106
FINANCIAL SERVICES, 107-109
Dates: Jan. 4, 1995-Jan. 3, 2007
Departure: Left the House; lost re-election

Cong.	Ranking	Terms in: House	Comm.	Date of Assignment
104th	Maj-27th	1	1	Jan. 4, 1995
105th	Maj-20th	2	2	Jan. 7, 1997
106th	Maj-16th	3	3	Jan. 6, 1999
107th	Maj-13th	4	4	Jan. 6, 2001
108th	Maj-11th	5	5	Jan. 28, 2003
109th	Maj-11th	6	6	Jan. 26, 2005

2nd SMALL BUSINESS
Dates: Jan. 4, 1995-Jan. 3, 2007
Departure: Left the House; lost re-election

Cong.	Ranking	Terms in: House	Comm.	Date of Assignment
104th	Maj-11th	1	1	Jan. 4, 1995

105th	Maj-8th	2	2	Jan. 21, 1997
106th	Maj-7th	3	3	Jan. 6, 1999
107th	Maj-6th	4	4	Jan. 6, 2001
108th	Maj-4th	5	5	Jan. 28, 2003
109th	Maj-3rd	6	6	Jan. 26, 2005

3rd TRANSPORTATION AND INFRASTRUCTURE
Dates: Jan. 4, 1995-Jan. 3, 2007
Departure: Left the House; lost re-election

Cong.	Ranking	Terms in: House	Comm.	Date of Assignment
104th	Maj-31st	1	1	Jan. 4, 1995
105th	Maj-20th	2	2	Jan. 7, 1997
106th	Maj-18th	3	3	Jan. 6, 1999
107th	Maj-14th	4	4	Jan. 6, 2001
108th	Maj-13th	5	5	Jan. 28, 2003
109th	Maj-12th	6	6	Jan. 26, 2005

Dirk Kempthorne (R-Ida.)

Dates: Oct. 29, 1951-
Senate: Jan. 3, 1993-Jan. 3, 1999
Left the Senate: Elected Governor in 1998

SENATE STANDING COMMITTEES:

1st ARMED SERVICES
Dates: Jan. 7, 1993-Jan. 3, 1999
Departure: Left the Senate; elected Governor

Cong.	Ranking	Years in: Senate	Comm.	Date of Assignment
103rd	Min-8th	1	1	Jan. 7, 1993
104th	Maj-8th	3	2	Jan. 4, 1995
105th	Maj-6th	5	5	Jan. 9, 1997

2nd ENVIRONMENT AND PUBLIC WORKS
Dates: Jan. 7, 1993-Jan. 3, 1999
Departure: Left the Senate; elected Governor

Cong.	Ranking	Years in: Senate	Comm.	Date of Assignment
103rd	Min-7th	1	1	Jan. 7, 1993
104th	Maj-5th	3	2	Jan. 5, 1995
105th	Maj-4th	5	5	Jan. 9, 1997

3rd SMALL BUSINESS
Dates: Jan. 7, 1993-Jan. 3, 1999
Departure: Left the Senate; elected Governor

Cong.	Ranking	Years in: Senate	Comm.	Date of Assignment
103rd	Min-7th	1	1	Jan. 21, 1993
104th	Maj-6th	3	2	Jan. 6, 1995
105th	Maj-4th	5	5	Jan. 9, 1997

Edward M. Kennedy (D-Mass.)

Dates: Feb. 22, 1932-Aug, 25, 2009
Senate: Nov. 7, 1962-Aug. 25, 2009
Left the Senate: Died in office

S: Kennedy was elected to the 87th Congress by special election, Nov. 6, 1962, to fill the unexpired term caused by the resignation of his brother, John

F. Kennedy (D-Mass.) who had been elected President. John Kennedy was initially replaced by Benjamin A. Smith II (D-Mass.), an appointee, who was not a candidate for election. Edward Kennedy was not seated nor assigned to committees because the 87th Congress was not in session.

SENATE STANDING COMMITTEES:

1st JUDICIARY
Dates: Feb. 25, 1963-Jan. 21, 2009
Departure: Left committee; no new assignment

Cong.	Ranking	Years in: Senate	Comm.	Date of Assignment
103rd	Maj-2nd	31	30	Jan. 7, 1993
104th	Min-2nd	33	32	Jan. 4, 1995
105th	Min-2nd	35	34	Jan. 9, 1997
106th	Min-2nd	37	36	Jan. 7, 1999
107th	Min-2nd	39	38	Jan. 25, 2001
+107th	Maj-2nd	39	39	June 6, 2001
108th	Min-2nd	41	40	Jan. 15, 2003
109th	Min-2nd	43	42	Jan. 6, 2005
110th	Maj-2nd	45	44	Jan. 12, 2007

2nd LABOR AND PUBLIC WELFARE reorganized as
HUMAN RESOURCES on Feb. 11, 1977; renamed Jan. 23, 1979
LABOR AND HUMAN RESOURCES renamed Jan. 21, 1999
HEALTH, EDUCATION, LABOR AND PENSIONS
Dates: Feb. 25, 1963-Aug. 25, 2009
Ch2: Replaced James M. Jeffords (Ind-Vt..) on June 6, 2001, following Senate party control shift
Departure: Died in office

Cong.	Ranking	Years in: Senate	Comm.	Date of Assignment
103rd	Maj-Chr	31	30	Jan. 7, 1993
104th	Min-RM	33	32	Jan. 4, 1995
105th	Min-RM	35	34	Jan. 9, 1997
106th	Min-RM	37	36	Jan. 7, 1999
=107th	Maj-ChT	39	38	Jan. 3, 2001
107th	Min-RM1	39	38	Jan. 25, 2001
+107th	Maj-Ch2	39	39	June 6, 2001
108th	Min-RM	41	40	Jan. 15, 2003
109th	Min-RM	43	42	Jan. 6, 2005
110th	Maj-Chr	45	44	Jan. 12, 2007
111th	Maj-Chr	47	46	Jan. 21, 2009

3rd ARMED SERVICES
Dates: Jan. 3, 1983-Aug. 25, 2009
Departure: Died in office

Cong.	Ranking	Years in: Senate	Comm.	Date of Assignment
103rd	Maj-4th	31	11	Jan. 7, 1993
104th	Min-4th	33	13	Jan. 4, 1995
105th	Min-2nd	35	15	Jan. 9, 1997
106th	Min-2nd	37	17	Jan. 7, 1999
107th	Min-2nd	39	19	Jan. 25, 2001
+107th	Maj-2nd	39	19	June 6, 2001
108th	Min-2nd	41	21	Jan. 15, 2003
109th	Min-2nd	43	23	Jan. 6, 2005
110th	Maj-2nd	45	25	Jan. 12, 2007
111th	Maj-2nd	47	27	Jan. 21, 2009

SENATE SELECT AND SPECIAL COMMITTEES:

1st SPECIAL AGING (Permanent)
Became Permanent Special Committee on Aging, Feb. 4, 1977
Dates: Mar. 1, 1963-Feb. 11, 1977
Departure: Left committee; no new assignment

2nd NUTRITION AND HUMAN NEEDS
Dates: Jan. 14, 1969-Dec. 31, 1977
Termination: S. Res 4 (95-1) transferred authority to Agriculture, Nutrition and Forestry

JOINT COMMITTEES:

1st JOINT ECONOMIC
Senate Dates: Jan. 17, 1975-Aug. 25, 2009
Departure: Died in office

Cong.	Ranking	Years in: Senate	Comm.	Date of Assignment
103rd	Maj-2nd	31	18	Jan. 21, 1993
104th	Min-3rd	33	20	Jan. 9, 1995
105th	Min-3rd	35	22	Jan. 9, 1997
106th	Min-2nd	37	24	Jan. 7, 1999
107th	Min-2nd	39	27	Jan. 25, 2001
+107th	Maj-2nd	39	27	June 6, 2001
108th	Min-2nd	41	28	Jan. 15, 2003
109th	Min-2nd	43	30	Jan. 6, 2005
110th	Maj-2nd	45	32	Jan. 12, 2007
111th	Maj-2nd	47	35	Jan. 21, 2009

SENATE LEADERSHIP POSTS

1st SENATE MAJORITY WHIP
Dates: Jan. 3, 1969-Jan. 3, 1971
Note: For the 91st Congress, Kennedy defeated Majority Whip Russell B. Long (D-La.). He was defeated for re-election as Whip for the 92nd Congress by Robert C. Byrd (D-W.Va.).
Departure: Lost post in Democratic Caucus

Joseph P. Kennedy II (D-Mass.)

Dates: Sept. 24, 1952
House: Jan. 3, 1987-Jan. 3, 1999
Left the House: Retired; chose not to run for Governor

HOUSE STANDING COMMITTEES:

1st BANKING, FINANCE AND URBAN AFFAIRS, 100-103
BANKING AND FINANCIAL SERVICES, 104-105
Dates: Jan. 22, 1987-Jan. 3, 1999
Departure: Left the House; retired

Cong.	Ranking	Terms in: House	Comm.	Date of Assignment
103rd	Maj-8th	4	4	Jan. 5, 1993
104th	Min-7th	5	5	Jan. 4, 1995
105th	Min-7th	6	6	Jan. 7, 1997

2nd VETERANS' AFFAIRS
Dates: Jan. 22, 1987-Jan. 3, 1999
Departure: Left the House; retired

Cong.	Ranking	Terms in: House	Comm.	Date of Assignment
103rd	Maj-8th	4	4	Jan. 5, 1993
104th	Min-3rd	5	5	Jan. 4, 1995
105th	Min-2nd	6	6	Feb. 6, 1997

HOUSE SELECT AND SPECIAL COMMITTEES:

1st SELECT AGING (Permanent)
Dates: Jan. 21, 1987-Jan. 3, 1993
Termination: Committee not renewed in 1993

Mark Kennedy (R-Minn.)

Dates: April 11, 1957
House: Jan. 3, 2001-Jan. 3, 2007
Left the House: Lost U.S. Senate election in 2006

HOUSE STANDING COMMITTEES:

1st AGRICULTURE
Dates: Jan. 6, 2001-Jan. 3, 2003
Departure: Moved to Financial Services

Cong.	Ranking	Terms in: House	Comm.	Date of Assignment
107th	Maj-27th	1	1	Jan. 6, 2001

2nd TRANSPORTATION AND INFRASTRUCTURE
Dates: Jan. 6, 2001-Jan. 3, 2007
Departure: Left the House; lost Senate election

Cong.	Ranking	Terms in: House	Comm.	Date of Assignment
107th	Maj-40th	1	1	Jan. 6, 2001
108th	Maj-30th	2	2	Jan. 28, 2003
109th	Maj-24th	3	3	Jan. 26, 2005

3rd FINANCIAL SERVICES
Dates: Jan. 28, 2003-Jan. 3, 2007
Departure: Left the House; lost Senate election

Cong.	Ranking	Terms in: House	Comm.	Date of Assignment
108th	Min-29th	2	1	Jan. 28, 2003
109th	Min-23rd	3	2	Jan. 26, 2005

Patrick J. Kennedy (D-R.I.)

Dates: July 14, 1967
House: Jan. 3, 1995-date
Serving in the 111th Congress

HOUSE STANDING COMMITTEES:

1st NATIONAL SECURITY, 104-105
ARMED SERVICES, 106
Dates: Jan. 4, 1995-Jan. 3, 2001
Departure: Moved to Appropriations

Cong.	Ranking	Terms in: House	Comm.	Date of Assignment
104th	Min-25th	1	1	Jan. 4, 1995
105th	Min-15th	2	2	Jan. 7, 1997
106th	Min-11th	3	3	Jan. 6, 1999

2nd SMALL BUSINESS
Dates: Jan. 4, 1995-Nov. 20, 1995
Departure: Resigned committee; moved to Resources

Cong.	Ranking	Terms in: House	Comm.	Date of Assignment
104th	Min-19th	1	1	Jan. 4, 1995

3rd RESOURCES, 104-106
NATURAL RESOURCES, 110
1st Dates: Nov. 20, 1995-Jan. 3, 2001
1st Departure: Moved to Appropriations
2nd Dates: Jan. 18, 2007-Jan. 3, 2009
2nd Departure: Moved to Oversight and Government Reform

Cong.	Ranking	Terms in: House	Comm.	Date of Assignment
104th	MnA-22nd	1 *1	1	Nov. 20, 1995
105th	Min-19th	2 *1	2	Jan. 7, 1997
106th	Min-14th	3 *1	3	Jan. 6, 1999
110th	Maj-19th	7 *2	1	Jan. 18, 2007

4th APPROPRIATIONS
Dates: Jan. 31, 2001-date
Departure: Still serving in the 111th Congress

Cong.	Ranking	Terms in: House	Comm.	Date of Assignment
107th	Min-20th	4	1	Jan. 31, 2001
108th	Min-18th	5	2	Jan. 28, 2003
109th	Min-18th	6	3	Jan. 26, 2005
110th	Maj-16th	7	4	Jan. 4, 2007
111th	Maj-15th	8	5	Jan. 7, 2009

5th OVERSIGHT AND GOVERNMENT REFORM
Dates: Jan. 28, 2009-date
Departure: Still serving in the 111th Congress

Cong.	Ranking	Terms in: House	Comm.	Date of Assignment
111th	Maj-13th	8	1	Jan. 28, 2009

Barbara B. Kennelly (D-Conn.)

Dates: July 10, 1936
House: Jan. 12, 1982-Jan. 3, 1999
Left the House: Lost election for Governor in 1998

H: Kennelly was elected to the 97th Congress by special election, Jan. 12, 1982, to fill the vacancy caused by the death of U.S. Representative William H. Cotter (D-Conn.). Kennelly was seated Jan. 25, 1982, and assigned to committees.

HOUSE STANDING COMMITTEES:

1st PUBLIC WORKS AND TRANSPORTATION
Dates: Feb. 24, 1982-Jan. 3, 1983
Departure: Moved to Ways and Means

2nd GOVERNMENT OPERATIONS
Dates: Feb. 24, 1982-Jan. 3, 1983
Departure: Moved to Ways and Means

3rd WAYS AND MEANS
Dates: Jan. 6, 1983-Jan. 3, 1999
Departure: Left the House; lost for Governor

Cong.	Ranking	Terms in: House	Comm.	Date of Assignment
103rd	Maj-9th	7	6	Jan. 5, 1993
104th	Min-7th	8	7	Jan. 4, 1995
105th	Min-4th	9	8	Jan. 7, 1997

4th BUDGET
Dates: Jan. 5, 1993-Jan. 3, 1995
Departure: Left committee; no new assignment

Cong.	Ranking	Terms in: House	Comm.	Date of Assignment
103rd	Maj-16th	7	1	Jan. 5, 1993

5th HOUSE ADMINISTRATION
Dates: Jan. 21, 1993-Jan. 3, 1995
Departure: Left committee; no new assignment

Cong.	Ranking	Terms in: House	Comm.	Date of Assignment
103rd	Maj-11th	7	1	Jan. 21, 1993

HOUSE SELECT AND SPECIAL COMMITTEES:

1st PERMANENT SELECT INTELLIGENCE
Dates: Jan. 21, 1987-Jan. 3, 1993
Departure: Left committee; no new assignment

Brian D. Kerns (R-Ind.)

Dates: May 22, 1957
House: Jan. 3, 2001-Jan 3, 2003
Left the House: Defeated for re-nomination in 2002

HOUSE STANDING COMMITTEES:

1st INTERNATIONAL RELATIONS
Dates: Jan. 6, 2001-Jan. 3, 2003
Departure: Left the House; lost re-nomination

Cong.	Ranking	Terms in: House	Comm.	Date of Assignment
107th	Maj-25th	1	1	Jan. 6, 2001

2nd TRANSPORTATION AND INFRASTRUCTURE
Dates: Jan. 6, 2001-Jan. 3, 2003
Departure: Left the House; lost re-nomination

Cong.	Ranking	Terms in: House	Comm.	Date of Assignment
107th	Maj-34th	1	1	Jan. 6, 2001

J. Robert Kerrey (D-Neb.)

Dates: Aug. 27, 1943
Senate: Jan. 3, 1989-Jan. 3, 2001
Left the Senate: Retired in 2000; named President of New School University

SENATE STANDING COMMITTEES:

1st AGRICULTURE, NUTRITION AND FORESTRY
Dates: Feb. 2, 1989-Jan. 3, 2001
Departure: Left the Senate; retired

Cong.	Ranking	Years in: Senate	Comm.	Date of Assignment
103rd	Maj-9th	5	4	Jan. 7, 1993
104th	Min-8th	7	6	Jan. 4, 1995
105th	Min-6th	9	8	Jan. 9, 1997
106th	Min-6th	11	10	Jan. 7, 1999

2nd APPROPRIATIONS
Dates: Feb. 2, 1989-Jan. 9, 1997
Departure: Moved to Finance

Cong.	Ranking	Years in: Senate	Comm.	Date of Assignment
103rd	Maj-13th	5	4	Jan. 7, 1993
104th	Min-11th	7	6	Jan. 4, 1995

3rd FINANCE
Dates: Jan. 9, 1997-Jan. 3, 2001
Departure: Left the Senate; retired

Cong.	Ranking	Years in: Senate	Comm.	Date of Assignment
105th	Min-9th	9	1	Jan. 9, 1997
106th	Min-8th	11	2	Jan. 7, 1999

SENATE SELECT AND SPECIAL COMMITTEES:

1st JUDGE ALCEE L. HASTINGS IMPEACHMENT
Dates: Mar. 16, 1989-Aug. 3, 1989
Termination: Senate Hearing 101-194, Parts 1-2A

2nd SELECT POW-MIA AFFAIRS
Dates: Aug. 2, 1991-Feb. 3, 1993
Termination: Senate Report 1 (103-1) filed

3rd SELECT INTELLIGENCE (Permanent)
Dates: Jan. 23, 1992-Jan. 6, 2000 effective
VC1: Replaced by Richard H. Bryan (D-Nev.) on Nov. 10, 1999
Departure: Removed by S. Res. 232, Nov. 10, 1999

Cong.	Ranking	Years in: Senate	Comm.	Date of Assignment
103rd	Maj-4th	5	2	Jan. 27, 1993
104th	Min-VCh	7	3	Jan. 4, 1995
105th	Min-VCh	9	5	Jan. 9, 1997
106th	Min-VC1	11	7	Jan. 7, 1999

John F. Kerry (D-Mass.)

Dates: Dec. 22, 1943
Senate: Jan. 3, 1985-date
Serving in the 111th Congress

S: Kerry was appointed to the 98th Congress, Jan. 2, 1985, to fill the vacancy caused by the resignation of U.S. Senator Paul E. Tsongas (D-Mass.). Kerry had been elected to succeed Tsongas for the 99th Congress. Kerry was not seated nor assigned to committees because the 98th Congress was not in session.

SENATE STANDING COMMITTEES:

1st FOREIGN RELATIONS
Dates: Feb. 21, 1985-date
Departure: Still serving in the 111th Congress

Cong.	Ranking	Years in: Senate	Comm.	Date of Assignment
103rd	Maj-5th	9	8	Jan. 7, 1993
104th	Min-5th	11	10	Jan. 4, 1995
105th	Min-4th	13	12	Jan. 9, 1997
106th	Min-4th	15	14	Jan. 7, 1999
107th	Min-4th	17	16	Jan. 25, 2001
+107th	Maj-4th	17	17	June 6, 2001
108th	Min-4th	19	18	Jan. 15, 2003
109th	Min-4th	21	20	Jan. 6, 2005
110th	Maj-3rd	23	22	Jan. 12, 2007
111th	Maj-Chr	25	24	Jan. 21, 2009

2nd LABOR AND HUMAN RESOURCES
Dates: Feb. 21, 1985-Jan. 6, 1987
Departure: Moved to Commerce, Science and Transportation

3rd SMALL BUSINESS renamed June 29, 2001
SMALL BUSINESS AND ENTREPRENEURSHIP
Dates: Mar. 5, 1985-date

Ch2: Replaced Christopher S. (Kit) Bond (R-Mo.) on June 6, 2001 following Senate party control shift
Departure: Still serving in the 111th Congress

		Years in:		Date of
Cong.	Ranking	Senate	Comm.	Assignment
103rd	Maj-5th	9	8	Jan. 21, 1993
104th	Min-5th	11	10	Jan. 6, 1995
105th	Min-RM	13	12	Jan. 9, 1997
106th	Min-RM	15	14	Jan. 7, 1999
=107th	Maj-ChT	17	16	Jan. 3, 2001
107th	Min-RM1	17	16	Jan. 25, 2001
+107th	Maj-Ch2	17	17	June 6, 2001
108th	Min-RM	19	18	Jan. 15, 2003
109th	Min-RM	21	20	Jan. 6, 2005
110th	Maj-Chr	23	22	Jan. 12, 2007
111th	Maj-2nd	25	24	Jan. 21, 2009

4th COMMERCE, SCIENCE AND TRANSPORTATION
Dates: Jan. 6, 1987-date
Departure: Still serving in the 111th Congress

		Years in:		Date of
Cong.	Ranking	Senate	Comm.	Assignment
103rd	Maj-7th	9	7	Jan. 7, 1993
104th	Min-6th	11	8	Jan. 4, 1995
105th	Min-5th	13	11	Jan. 9, 1997
106th	Min-4th	15	13	Jan. 7, 1999
107th	Min-4th	17	15	Jan. 25, 2001
+107th	Maj-4th	17	15	June 6, 2001
108th	Min-4th	19	17	Jan. 15, 2003
109th	Min-3rd	21	19	Jan. 6, 2005
110th	Maj-3rd	23	21	Jan. 12, 2007
111th	Maj-3rd	25	23	Jan. 21, 2009

5th BANKING, HOUSING AND URBAN AFFAIRS
Dates: Feb. 2, 1989-Jan. 25, 2001
Departure: Moved to Finance

		Years in:		Date of
Cong.	Ranking	Senate	Comm.	Assignment
103rd	Maj-6th	9	4	Jan. 7, 1993
104th	Min-3rd	11	6	Jan. 4, 1995
105th	Min-3rd	13	8	Jan. 9, 1997
106th	Min-3rd	15	10	Jan. 7, 1999

6th FINANCE
Dates: Jan. 25, 2001-date
Departure: Still serving in the 111th Congress

		Years in:		Date of
Cong.	Ranking	Senate	Comm.	Assignment
107th	Min-8th	17	1	Jan. 25, 2001
+107th	Maj-9th	17	1	July 10, 2001
108th	Min-9th	19	2	Jan. 15, 2003
109th	Min-6th	21	4	Jan. 6, 2005
110th	Maj-5th	23	6	Jan. 12, 2007
111th	Maj-5th	25	8	Jan. 21, 2009

SENATE SELECT AND SPECIAL COMMITTEES:

1st SELECT POW-MIA AFFAIRS
Dates: Aug. 2, 1991-Feb. 3, 1993
Termination: Senate Report 1 (103-1) filed

2nd SELECT INTELLIGENCE (Permanent)
Dates: Jan. 27, 1993-Jan. 25, 2001
Departure: Moved to Finance

		Years in:		Date of
Cong.	Ranking	Senate	Comm.	Assignment
103rd	Maj-7th	9	1	Jan. 27, 1993
104th	Min-5th	11	2	Jan. 6, 1995

| 105th | Min-5th | 13 | 4 | Jan. 9, 1997 |
| 106th | Min-4th | 15 | 6 | Jan. 7, 1999 |

3rd SPECIAL COMMITTEE TO INVESTIGATE WHITEWATER DEVELOPMENT CORPORATION AND RELATED MATTERS
Dates: July 20, 1995 -June 17, 1996
Termination: Senate Report 104-280 filed

		Years in:		Date of
Cong.	Ranking	Senate	Comm.	Assignment
104th	Min-3rd	11	1	July 20, 1995

Dale E. Kildee (D-Mich.)

Dates: Sept. 16, 1929
House: Jan. 3, 1977-date
Serving in the 111th Congress

HOUSE STANDING COMMITTEES:

1st EDUCATION AND LABOR, 95-103
ECONOMIC AND EDUCATIONAL OPPORTUNITIES, 104
EDUCATION AND THE WORKFORCE, 105-109
EDUCATION AND LABOR, 110-111
Dates: Jan. 19, 1977-date
Departure: Still serving in the 111th Congress

		Terms in:		Date of
Cong.	Ranking	House	Comm.	Assignment
103rd	Maj-5th	9	9	Jan. 5, 1993
104th	Min-3rd	10	10	Jan. 4, 1995
105th	Min-3rd	11	11	Jan. 7, 1997
106th	Min-3rd	12	12	Jan. 6, 1999
107th	Min-2nd	13	13	Jan. 31, 2001
108th	Min-2nd	14	14	Jan. 28, 2003
109th	Min-2nd	15	15	Jan. 26, 2005
110th	Maj-2nd	16	16	Jan. 10, 2007
111th	Maj-2nd	17	17	Jan. 21, 2009

2nd SMALL BUSINESS
Dates: Jan. 19, 1977-Jan. 3, 1981
Departure: Moved to Interior and Insular Affairs

3rd INTERIOR AND INSULAR AFFAIRS, 97-100
RESOURCES, 104-109
NATURAL RESOURCES, 110-111
1st Dates: Jan. 28, 1981-Jan. 3, 1989
1st Departure: Moved to Budget
2nd Dates: Jan. 9, 1995-date
2nd Departure: Still serving in the 111th Congress

		Terms in:		Date of
Cong.	Ranking	House	Comm.	Assignment
104th	Min-4th	10 *2	1	Jan. 9, 1995
105th	Min-5th	11 *2	2	Jan. 7, 1997
106th	Min-4th	12 *2	3	Jan. 6, 1999
107th	Min-4th	13 *2	4	Feb. 8, 2001
108th	Min-4th	14 *2	5	Jan. 28, 2003
109th	Min-2nd	15 *2	6	Jan. 26, 2005
110th	Maj-2nd	16 *2	7	Jan. 18, 2007
111th	Maj-2nd	17 *2	8	Jan. 21, 2009

4th BUDGET
Dates: Jan. 19, 1989-Jan. 3, 1995
Departure: Returned to Resources

		Terms in:		Date of
Cong.	Ranking	House	Comm.	Assignment
103rd	Maj-3rd	9	3	Jan. 5, 1993

5th HOUSE ADMINISTRATION
Dates: Oct. 30, 1991-Jan. 3, 1995
Departure: Returned to Resources

Cong.	Ranking	Terms in: House	Comm.	Date of Assignment
103rd	Maj-9th	9	2	Jan. 21, 1993

HOUSE SELECT AND SPECIAL COMMITTEES:

1st SELECT POPULATION
Dates: Oct. 14, 1977-Dec. 29, 1978
Termination: House Report 1842 (85-2) filed

Carolyn C. Kilpatrick (D-Mich.)

Dates: June 25, 1945
House: Jan. 3, 1997-date
Serving in the 111th Congress

HOUSE STANDING COMMITTEES:

1st BANKING AND FINANCIAL SERVICES
Dates: Jan. 7, 1997-Jan. 3, 1999
Departure: Moved to Appropriations

Cong.	Ranking	Terms in: House	Comm.	Date of Assignment
105th	Min-21st	1	1	Jan. 7, 1997

2nd HOUSE OVERSIGHT
Dates: Feb. 5, 1997-Jan. 3, 1999
Departure: Moved to Appropriations

Cong.	Ranking	Terms in: House	Comm.	Date of Assignment
105th	Min-3rd	1	1	Feb. 5, 1997

3rd APPROPRIATIONS
Dates: Jan. 6, 1999-date
Departure: Still serving in the 111th Congress

Cong.	Ranking	Terms in: House	Comm.	Date of Assignment
106th	Min-26th	2	1	Jan. 6, 1999
107th	Min-26th	3	2	Jan. 31, 2001
108th	Min-24th	4	3	Jan. 28, 2003
109th	Min-24th	5	4	Jan. 26, 2005
110th	Maj-21st	6	5	Jan. 4, 2007
111th	Maj-20th	7	6	Jan. 7, 2009

JOINT COMMITTEES:

1st JOINT LIBRARY
House Dates: Mar. 6, 1997-Jan. 3, 1999
Departure: Moved to Appropriations

Cong.	Ranking	Terms in: House	Comm.	Date of Assignment
105th	Min-1st	1	1	Mar. 6, 1997

Mary Jo Kilroy (D-Ohio)

Dates: April 30, 1949
House: Jan. 3, 2009-date
Serving in the 111th Congress

HOUSE STANDING COMMITTEES:

1st FINANCIAL SERVICES
Dates: Jan. 7, 2009-date
Departure: Still serving in the 111th Congress

Cong.	Ranking	Terms in: House	Comm.	Date of Assignment
111th	Maj-36th	1	1	Jan. 7, 2009

2nd HOMELAND SECURITY
Dates: Jan. 28, 2009-date
Departure: Still serving in the 111th Congress

Cong.	Ranking	Terms in: House	Comm.	Date of Assignment
111th	Maj-18th	1	1	Jan. 28, 2009

Jay C. Kim (R-Cal.)

Dates: March 27, 1939
House: Jan. 3, 1993-Jan. 3, 1999
Left the House: Defeated for re-nomination in 1998

HOUSE STANDING COMMITTEES:

1st PUBLIC WORKS AND TRANSPORTATION, 103
TRANSPORTATION AND INFRASTRUCTURE, 104-105
Dates: Jan. 5, 1993-Jan. 3, 1999
Departure: Left the House; lost re-nomination

Cong.	Ranking	Terms in: House	Comm.	Date of Assignment
103rd	Min-16th	1	1	Jan. 5, 1993
104th	Maj-16th	2	2	Jan. 4, 1995
105th	Maj-11th	3	3	Jan. 7, 1997

2nd SMALL BUSINESS
Dates: Jan. 5, 1993-Jan. 3, 1997
Departure: Moved to International Relations

Cong.	Ranking	Terms in: House	Comm.	Date of Assignment
103rd	Min-16th	1	1	Jan. 5, 1993

3rd INTERNATIONAL RELATIONS
Dates: Jan. 4, 1995-Jan. 3, 1999
Departure: Left the House; lost re-nomination

Cong.	Ranking	Terms in: House	Comm.	Date of Assignment
104th	Maj-17th	2	1	Jan. 4, 1995
105th	Maj-15th	3	2	Jan. 7, 1997

Ron Kind (D-Wisc.)

Dates: March 16, 1963
House: Jan. 3, 1997-date
Serving in the 111th Congress

HOUSE STANDING COMMITTEES:

1st EDUCATION AND THE WORKFORCE
Dates: Jan. 7, 1997-Jan. 3, 2007
Departure: Moved to Ways and Means

Cong.	Ranking	Terms in: House	Comm.	Date of Assignment
105th	Min-18th	1	1	Jan. 7, 1997
106th	Min-17th	2	2	Jan. 6, 1999
107th	Min-15th	3	3	Jan. 31, 2001
108th	Min-10th	4	4	Jan. 28, 2003
109th	Min-11th	5	5	Jan. 26, 2005

2nd RESOURCES, 105-109
NATURAL RESOURCES, 110-111
Dates: Feb. 13, 1997-date
Departure: Still serving in the 111th Congress

Cong.	Ranking	Terms in: House	Comm.	Date of Assignment
105th	MnR-2nd	1	1	Feb. 13, 1997
106th	Min-19th	2	2	Jan. 6, 1999
107th	Min-14th	3	3	Feb. 8, 2001
108th	Min-13th	4	4	Jan. 28, 2003
109th	Min-8th	5	5	Jan. 26, 2005
110th	Maj-20th	6	6	Jan. 18, 2007
111th	Maj-20th	7	7	Jan. 21, 2009

3rd AGRICULTURE
Dates: Mar. 14, 2001-Jan. 3, 2003
Departure: Moved to Budget

Cong.	Ranking	Terms in: House	Comm.	Date of Assignment
107th	Min-23rd	3	1	Mar. 14, 2001

4th BUDGET
Dates: Feb. 26, 2003-Jan. 3, 2007
Departure: Moved to Ways and Means

Cong.	Ranking	Terms in: House	Comm.	Date of Assignment
108th	MnR-1st	4	1	Feb. 26, 2003
109th	Min-16th	5	2	Feb. 2, 2005

5th WAYS AND MEANS
Dates: Jan. 12, 2007-date
Departure: Still serving in the 111th Congress

Cong.	Ranking	Terms in: House	Comm.	Date of Assignment
110th	Maj-17th	6	1	Jan. 12, 2007
111th	Maj-14th	7	2	Jan. 7, 2009

Peter T. King (R-N.Y.)

Dates: April 5, 1944
House: Jan. 3, 1993-date
Serving in the 111th Congress

HOUSE STANDING COMMITTEES:

1st BANKING, FINANCE AND URBAN AFFAIRS, 103
BANKING AND FINANCIAL SERVICES, 104-106
FINANCIAL SERVICES, 107-111
1st Dates: Jan. 5, 1993-Feb. 8, 2006
1st Departure: Resigned committee; had became Chair of Homeland Security; returned with seniority intact
2nd Dates: Jan. 10, 2007-date
2nd Departure: Still serving in the 111th Congress

Cong.	Ranking	Terms in: House	Comm.	Date of Assignment
103rd	Min-20th	1 *1	1	Jan. 5, 1993
104th	Maj-10th	2 *1	2	Jan. 4, 1995
105th	Maj-9th	3 *1	3	Jan. 7, 1997
106th	Maj-9th	4 *1	4	Jan. 6, 1999
107th	Maj-8th	5 *1	5	Jan. 6, 2001
108th	Maj-7th	6 *1	6	Jan. 28, 2003
109th	Maj-7th	7 *1	7	Jan. 26, 2005
110th	Min-5th	8 *2	1	Jan. 10, 2007
111th	Min-3rd	9 *2	2	Jan. 9, 2009

2nd MERCHANT MARINE AND FISHERIES
Dates: Jan. 5, 1993-Jan. 3, 1995
Departure: Committee abolished; moved to International Relations

Cong.	Ranking	Terms in: House	Comm.	Date of Assignment
103rd	Min-14th	1	1	Jan. 5, 1993

3rd VETERANS' AFFAIRS
Dates: May 27, 1993-Jan. 3, 1995
Departure: Moved to International Relations

Cong.	Ranking	Terms in: House	Comm.	Date of Assignment
103rd	Min-14th	1	1	May 27, 1993

4th INTERNATIONAL RELATIONS
Dates: Jan. 4, 1995-Jan. 3, 2007
Departure: Returned to Financial Services

Cong.	Ranking	Terms in: House	Comm.	Date of Assignment
104th	Maj-16th	2	1	Jan. 4, 1995
105th	Maj-14th	3	2	Jan. 7, 1997
106th	Maj-14th	4	3	Jan. 6, 1999
107th	Maj-12th	5	4	Jan. 6, 2001
108th	Maj-11th	6	5	Jan. 28, 2003
109th	Maj-9th	7	6	Jan. 26, 2005

5th HOMELAND SECURITY
Dates: Feb. 9, 2005-date
Ch1: Replaced C. Christopher Cox (R-Cal.) as Chair on Aug. 15, 2005
Departure: Still serving in the 111th Congress

Cong.	Ranking	Terms in: House	Comm.	Date of Assignment
109th	Maj-6th	7	2	Feb. 9, 2005
=109th	Maj-Ch2	7	2	Aug. 15, 2005
110th	Min-RM	8	3	Jan. 4, 2007
111th	Min-RM	9	4	Jan. 6, 2009

HOUSE SELECT AND SPECIAL COMMITTEES:

1st SELECT HOMELAND SECURITY
Dates: Feb. 12, 2003-Jan. 3, 2005
Departure: Remained on reorganized standing committee

Cong.	Ranking	Terms in: House	Comm.	Date of Assignment
108th	Maj-19th	6	1	Feb. 12, 2003

2nd PERMANENT SELECT INTELLIGENCE
Dates: June 25, 2009-date
Departure: Still serving in the 111th Congress

Cong.	Ranking	Terms in: House	Comm.	Date of Assignment
111th	MnR-1st	9	1	June 25, 2009

Steve King (R-Iowa)

Dates: May 28, 1949
House: Jan. 3, 2003-date
Serving in the 111th Congress

HOUSE STANDING COMMITTEES:

1st AGRICULTURE
Dates: Jan. 28, 2003-date
Departure: Still serving in the 111th Congress

Cong.	Ranking	Terms in: House	Comm.	Date of Assignment
108th	Maj-24th	1	1	Jan. 28, 2003
109th	Maj-16th	2	2	Jan. 26, 2005
110th	Min-10th	3	3	Jan. 10, 2007
111th	Min-7th	4	4	Jan. 9, 2009

2nd JUDICIARY
Dates: Jan. 28, 2003-date
Departure: Still serving in the 111th Congress

Cong.	Ranking	Terms in: House	Comm.	Date of Assignment
108th	Maj-18th	1	1	Jan. 28, 2003
109th	Maj-20th	2	2	Jan. 26, 2005
110th	Min-13th	3	3	Jan. 10, 2007
111th	Min-9th	4	4	Jan. 9, 2009

3rd SMALL BUSINESS
Dates: Feb. 25, 2003-date
Departure: Still serving in the 111th Congress

Cong.	Ranking	Terms in: House	Comm.	Date of Assignment
108th	Maj-19th	1	1	Feb. 25, 2003
109th	Maj-10th	2	2	Jan. 26, 2005
110th	Min-7th	3	3	Jan. 10, 2007
111th	Min-4th	4	4	Jan. 9, 2009

Jack Kingston (R-Ga.)

Dates: April 24, 1955
House: Jan. 3, 1993-date
Serving in the 111th Congress

HOUSE STANDING COMMITTEES:

1st AGRICULTURE
Dates: Jan. 5, 1993-Jan. 3, 1995
Departure: Moved to Appropriations

Cong.	Ranking	Terms in: House	Comm.	Date of Assignment
103rd	Min-14th	1	1	Jan. 5, 1993

2nd MERCHANT MARINE AND FISHERIES
Dates: Jan. 5, 1993-Jan. 3, 1995
Departure: Committee abolished; moved to Appropriations

Cong.	Ranking	Terms in: House	Comm.	Date of Assignment
103rd	Min-11th	1	1	Jan. 5, 1993

3rd APPROPRIATIONS
Dates: Jan. 4, 1995-date
Departure: Still serving in the 111th Congress

Cong.	Ranking	Terms in: House	Comm.	Date of Assignment
104th	Maj-25th	2	1	Jan. 4, 1995
105th	Maj-22nd	3	2	Jan. 7, 1997
106th	Maj-20th	4	3	Jan. 6, 1999
107th	Maj-17th	5	4	Jan. 6, 2001
108th	Maj-13th	6	5	Jan. 28, 2003
109th	Maj-13th	7	6	Jan. 6, 2005
110th	Min-9th	8	7	Jan. 4, 2007
111th	Min-5th	9	8	Jan. 9, 2009

JOINT COMMITTEES:

1st JOINT LIBRARY
House Dates: Mar. 25, 2003-Jan. 3, 2005
Departure: Left committee; no new assignment

Cong.	Ranking	Terms in: House	Comm.	Date of Assignment
108th	Maj-3rd	6	1	Mar. 25, 2003

Mark S. Kirk (R-Ill.)

Dates: Sept. 15, 1959
House: Jan. 3, 2001-date
Serving in the 111th Congress

HOUSE STANDING COMMITTEES:

1st ARMED SERVICES
Dates: Jan. 6, 2001-Jan. 3, 2003
Departure: Moved to Appropriations

Cong.	Ranking	Terms in: House	Comm.	Date of Assignment
107th	Maj-29th	1	1	Jan. 6, 2001

2nd TRANSPORTATION AND INFRASTRUCTURE
Dates: Jan. 6, 2001-Jan. 3, 2003
Departure: Moved to Appropriations

Cong.	Ranking	Terms in: House	Comm.	Date of Assignment
107th	Maj-31st	1	1	Jan. 6, 2001

3rd BUDGET
Dates: Feb. 8, 2001-Jan. 3, 2003
Departure: Moved to Appropriations

Cong.	Ranking	Terms in: House	Comm.	Date of Assignment
107th	Maj-23rd	1	1	Feb. 8, 2001

4th APPROPRIATIONS
Dates: Jan. 28, 2003-date
Departure: Still serving in the 111th Congress

Cong.	Ranking	Terms in: House	Comm.	Date of Assignment
108th	Maj-35th	2	1	Jan. 28, 2003
109th	Maj-33rd	3	2	Jan. 6, 2005
110th	Min-25th	4	3	Jan. 4, 2007
111th	Min-15th	5	4	Jan. 9, 2009

Paul G. Kirk Jr. (D-Mass.)

Dates: Jan. 18, 1938
Senate: Sept. 25, 2009-Feb. 4, 2010
Left the Senate: Resigned; temporary appointment expired; successor elected
S: Kirk was appointed to the 111th Congress, Sept. 24, 2009, to fill the vacancy caused by the death of U.S. Senator Edward M. Kennedy (D-Mass.). He was seated on Sept. 25, 2009, and appointed to committees.

SENATE STANDING COMMITTEES:

1st ARMED SERVICES
Dates: Sept. 29, 2009-Feb. 4, 2010
Departure: Appointment expired; successor sworn

Cong.	Ranking	Terms in: House	Comm.	Date of Assignment
111th	MnR-1st	1	1	Sept. 29, 2009

2nd HOMELAND SECURITY AND GOVERNMENTAL AFFAIRS
Dates: Sept. 29, 2009-Feb. 4, 2010
Departure: Appointment expired; successor sworn

Cong.	Ranking	Terms in: House	Comm.	Date of Assignment
111th	MnR-1st	1	1	Sept. 29, 2009

Ann Kirkpatrick (D-Ariz.)

Dates: March 14, 1950
House: Jan. 3, 2009-date
Serving in the 111th Congress

HOUSE STANDING COMMITTEES:

1st SMALL BUSINESS
Dates: Jan. 21, 2009-date
Departure: Still serving in the 111th Congress

Cong.	Ranking	Terms in: House	Comm.	Date of Assignment
111th	Maj-6th	1	1	Jan. 21, 2009

2nd VETERANS' AFFAIRS
Dates: Jan. 21, 2009-date
Departure: Still serving in the 111th Congress

Cong.	Ranking	Terms in: House	Comm.	Date of Assignment
111th	Maj-17th	1	1	Jan. 21, 2009

3rd HOMELAND SECURITY
Dates: Jan. 28, 2009-date
Departure: Still serving in the 111th Congress

Cong.	Ranking	Terms in: House	Comm.	Date of Assignment
111th	Maj-12th	1	1	Jan. 28, 2009

Larry Kissell (D-N.C.)

Dates: Jan. 31, 1951
House: Jan. 3, 2009-date
Serving in the 111th Congress

HOUSE STANDING COMMITTEES:

1st ARMED SERVICES
Dates: Jan. 7, 2009-date
Departure: Still serving in the 111th Congress

Cong.	Ranking	Terms in: House	Comm.	Date of Assignment
111th	Maj-33rd	1	1	Jan. 7, 2009

2nd AGRICULTURE
Dates: Jan. 21, 2009-date
Departure: Still serving in the 111th Congress

Cong.	Ranking	Terms in: House	Comm.	Date of Assignment
111th	Maj-24th	1	1	Jan. 21, 2009

Gerald D. Kleczka (D-Wisc.)

Dates: Nov. 26, 1943
House: April 3, 1984-Jan. 3, 2005
Left the House: Retired in 2004
H. Kleczka was elected to the 98th Congress by special election, April 3, 1984, to fill the vacancy caused by the death of U.S. Representative Clement J. Zablocki (D-Wisc.). Kleczka was seated April 10, 1984, and assigned to committees.

HOUSE STANDING COMMITTEES:

1st BANKING, FINANCE AND URBAN AFFAIRS
Dates: May 16, 1984-Jan. 3, 1993
Departure: Moved to Ways and Means

2nd GOVERNMENT OPERATIONS
Dates: May 16, 1984-Jan. 3, 1993
Departure: Moved to Ways and Means

3rd HOUSE ADMINISTRATION
Dates: Jan. 24, 1991-Jan. 3, 1995
Departure: Left committee; no new assignment

Cong.	Ranking	Terms in: House	Comm.	Date of Assignment
103rd	Maj-8th	6	2	Jan. 21, 1993

4th WAYS AND MEANS
Dates: Jan. 5, 1993-Jan. 3, 2005
Departure: Left the House; retired

Cong.	Ranking	Terms in: House	Comm.	Date of Assignment
103rd	Maj-15th	6	1	Jan. 5, 1993
104th	Min-12th	7	2	Jan. 4, 1995
105th	Min-9th	8	3	Jan. 7, 1997
106th	Min-8th	9	4	Jan. 6, 1999
107th	Min-8th	10	5	Jan. 31, 2001
108th	Min-7th	11	6	Jan. 28, 2003

5th BUDGET
Dates: Jan. 6, 1999-Jan. 3, 2003
Departure: Left committee; no new assignment

Cong.	Ranking	Terms in: House	Comm.	Date of Assignment
106th	Min-12th	9	1	Jan. 6, 1999
107th	Min-9th	10	2	Jan. 31, 2001

JOINT COMMITTEES:

1st JOINT PRINTING
House Dates: Feb. 21, 1991-Jan. 3, 1995
Departure: Left committee; no new assignment

Cong.	Ranking	Terms in: House	Comm.	Date of Assignment
103rd	Maj-3rd	6	2	May 1, 1993 Provisional

Herbert C. Klein (D-N.J.)

Dates: June 24, 1930
House: Jan. 3, 1993-Jan. 3, 1995
Left the House: Defeated for re-election in 1994

HOUSE STANDING COMMITTEES:

1st BANKING, FINANCE AND URBAN AFFAIRS
Dates: Jan. 5, 1993-Jan. 3, 1995
Departure: Left the House; lost re-election

Cong.	Ranking	Terms in: House	Comm.	Date of Assignment
103rd	Maj-15th	1	1	Jan. 5, 1993

2nd SCIENCE, SPACE AND TECHNOLOGY
Dates: Jan. 5, 1993-Jan. 3, 1995
Departure: Left the House; lost re-election

Cong.	Ranking	Terms in: House	Comm.	Date of Assignment
103rd	Maj-20th	1	1	Jan. 5, 1993

Ron Klein (D-Fla.)

Dates: July 10, 1957
House: Jan. 3, 2007-date
Serving in the 111th Congress

HOUSE STANDING COMMITTEES:

1st FINANCIAL SERVICES
Dates: Jan. 12, 2007-date
Departure: Still serving in the 111th Congress

Cong.	Ranking	Terms in: House	Comm.	Date of Assignment
110th	Maj-29th	1	1	Jan. 12, 2007
111th	Maj-26th	2	2	Jan. 7, 2009

2nd FOREIGN AFFAIRS
Dates: Jan. 12, 2007-date
Departure: Still serving in the 111th Congress

Cong.	Ranking	Terms in: House	Comm.	Date of Assignment
110th	Maj-27th	1	1	Jan. 12, 2007
111th	Maj-28th	2	2	Jan. 21, 2009

John H. Kline (R-Minn.)

Dates: Sept. 6, 1947
House: Jan. 3, 2003-date
Serving in the 111th Congress

HOUSE STANDING COMMITTEES:

1st ARMED SERVICES
Dates: Jan. 28, 2003-date
Departure: Still serving in the 111th Congress

Cong.	Ranking	Terms in: House	Comm.	Date of Assignment
108th	Maj-29th	1	1	Jan. 28, 2003
109th	Maj-25th	2	2	Jan. 26, 2005
110th	Min-20th	3	3	Jan. 10, 2007
111th	Min-13th	4	4	Jan. 9, 2009

2nd EDUCATION AND THE WORKFORCE, 108-109
EDUCATION AND LABOR, 110-111
Dates: Jan. 28, 2003-date
RM2: Replaced Howard P. (Buck) McKeon (R-Cal.) as Ranking Member on June 25, 2009
Departure: Still serving in the 111th Congress

Cong.	Ranking	Terms in: House	Comm.	Date of Assignment
108th	Maj-23rd	1	1	Jan. 28, 2003
109th	Maj-16th	2	2	Jan. 26, 2005
110th	Min-11th	3	3	Jan. 10, 2007
111th	Min-10th	4	4	Jan. 9, 2009
=111th	Min-RM2	4	4	June 25, 2009

3rd STANDARDS OF OFFICIAL CONDUCT
Dates: Feb. 12, 2007-July 14, 2009
Departure: Resigned committee; had become Ranking Member on Education and Labor

Cong.	Ranking	Terms in: House	Comm.	Date of Assignment
110th	Min-4th	3	1	Feb. 12, 2007
111th	Min-3rd	4	2	Jan. 9, 2009

HOUSE SELECT AND SPECIAL COMMITTEES:

1st PERMANENT SELECT INTELLIGENCE
Dates: Feb. 4, 2009-June 23, 2009
Departure: Resigned committee; had become Ranking Member on Education and Labor

Cong.	Ranking	Terms in: House	Comm.	Date of Assignment
111th	Min-8th	4	1	Feb. 4, 2009

Ronald Klink (D-Penn.)

Dates: Sept. 23, 1951
House: Jan. 3, 1993-Jan. 3, 2001
Left the House: Lost U.S. Senate election in 2000

HOUSE STANDING COMMITTEES:

1st EDUCATION AND LABOR
Dates: Jan. 5, 1993-Jan. 3, 1995
Departure: Moved to Commerce

Cong.	Ranking	Terms in: House	Comm.	Date of Assignment
103rd	Maj-22nd	1	1	Jan. 5, 1993

2nd SMALL BUSINESS
Dates: Jan. 5, 1993-Jan. 3, 1995
Departure: Moved to Commerce

Cong.	Ranking	Terms in: House	Comm.	Date of Assignment
103rd	Maj-23rd	1	1	Jan. 5, 1993

3rd BANKING, FINANCE AND URBAN AFFAIRS
Dates: Jan. 21, 1993-Jan. 3, 1995
Departure: Moved to Commerce

		Terms in:		Date of
Cong.	**Ranking**	**House**	**Comm.**	**Assignment**
103rd	Maj-29th	1	1	Jan. 21, 1993

4th COMMERCE
Dates: Jan. 4, 1995-Jan. 3, 2001
Departure: Left the House; lost Senate election

		Terms in:		Date of
Cong.	**Ranking**	**House**	**Comm.**	**Assignment**
104th	Min-20th	2	1	Jan. 4, 1995
105th	Min-15th	3	2	Jan. 7, 1997
106th	Min-13th	4	3	Jan. 6, 1999

Amy Klobuchar (DFL-Minn.)

Dates: May 25, 1960
Senate: Jan. 3, 2007-date
Serving in the 111th Congress

SENATE STANDING COMMITTEES:

1st AGRICULTURE, NUTRITION AND FORESTRY
Dates: Jan. 12, 2007-date
Departure: Still serving in the 111th Congress

		Years in:		Date of
Cong.	**Ranking**	**Senate**	**Comm.**	**Assignment**
110th	Maj-11th	1	1	Jan. 12, 2007
111th	Maj-10th	3	3	Jan. 21, 2009

2nd COMMERCE, SCIENCE AND TRANSPORTATION
Dates: Jan. 12, 2007-date
Departure: Still serving in the 111th Congress

		Years in:		Date of
Cong.	**Ranking**	**Senate**	**Comm.**	**Assignment**
110th	Maj-12th	1	1	Jan. 12, 2007
111th	Maj-11th	3	3	Jan. 21, 2009

3rd ENVIRONMENT AND PUBLIC WORKS
Dates: Jan. 12, 2007-date
Departure: Still serving in the 111th Congress

		Years in:		Date of
Cong.	**Ranking**	**Senate**	**Comm.**	**Assignment**
110th	Maj-9th	1	1	Jan. 12, 2007
111th	Maj-7th	3	3	Jan. 21, 2009

4th JUDICIARY
Dates: Jan. 21, 2009-date
Departure: Still serving in the 111th Congress

		Years in:		Date of
Cong.	**Ranking**	**Senate**	**Comm.**	**Assignment**
111th	Maj-10th	3	1	Jan. 21, 2009

JOINT COMMITTEES:

1st JOINT ECONOMIC
Senate Dates: Jan. 12, 2007-date
Departure: Still serving in the 111th Congress

		Years in:		Date of
Cong.	**Ranking**	**Senate**	**Comm.**	**Assignment**
110th	Maj-4th	1	1	Jan. 12, 2007
111th	Maj-4th	3	3	Jan. 21, 2009

Scott L. Klug (R-Wisc.)

Dates: Jan. 16, 1953
House: Jan. 3, 1991-Jan. 3, 1999
Left the House: Retired in 1998

HOUSE STANDING COMMITTEES:

1st EDUCATION AND LABOR
Dates: Jan. 24, 1991-Jan. 3, 1993
Departure: Moved to Energy and Commerce

2nd GOVERNMENT OPERATIONS, 103
GOVERNMENT REFORM AND OVERSIGHT, 104
1st Dates: Jan. 24, 1991-Jan. 3, 1993
1st Departure: Moved to Energy and Commerce
2nd Dates: July 22, 1996-Jan. 3, 1997
2nd Departure: Left committee; no new assignment

		Terms in:		Date of
Cong.	**Ranking**	**House**	**Comm.**	**Assignment**
104th	MjR-1st	3 *2	1	July 22, 1996

3rd ENERGY AND COMMERCE, 103
COMMERCE, 104-105
Dates: Jan. 5, 1993-Jan. 3, 1999
Departure: Left the House; retired

		Terms in:		Date of
Cong.	**Ranking**	**House**	**Comm.**	**Assignment**
103rd	Min-14th	2	1	Jan. 5, 1993
104th	Maj-13th	3	2	Jan. 4, 1995
105th	Maj-12th	4	3	Jan. 7, 1997

HOUSE SELECT AND SPECIAL COMMITTEES:

1st SELECT CHILDREN, YOUTH AND FAMILIES (Temporary)
Dates: Feb. 21, 1991-Jan. 3, 1993
Termination: Committee not renewed in 1993

Joseph Knollenberg (R-Mich.)

Dates: Nov. 28, 1933
House: Jan. 3, 1993-Jan. 3, 2009
Left the House: Defeated for re-election in 2008

HOUSE STANDING COMMITTEES:

1st BANKING, FINANCE AND URBAN AFFAIRS
Dates: Jan. 5, 1993-Jan. 3, 1995
Departure: Moved to Appropriations and Economic and Educational
Opportunities

		Terms in:		Date of
Cong.	**Ranking**	**House**	**Comm.**	**Assignment**
103rd	Min-14th	1	1	Jan. 5, 1993

2nd SMALL BUSINESS
Dates: Jan. 5, 1993-Jan. 3, 1995
Departure: Moved to Appropriations and Economic and Educational
Opportunities

		Terms in:		Date of
Cong.	**Ranking**	**House**	**Comm.**	**Assignment**
103rd	Min-14th	1	1	Jan. 5, 1993

3rd APPROPRIATIONS
Dates: Jan. 4, 1995-Jan. 3, 2009
Departure: Left the House; lost re-election

Cong.	Ranking	Terms in: House	Comm.	Date of Assignment
104th	Maj-22nd	2	1	Jan. 4, 1995
105th	Maj-19th	3	2	Jan. 7, 1997
106th	Maj-17th	4	3	Jan. 6, 1999
107th	Maj-15th	5	4	Jan. 6, 2001
108th	Maj-12th	6	5	Jan. 28, 2003
109th	Maj-12th	7	6	Jan. 6, 2005
110th	Min-8th	8	7	Jan. 4, 2007

4th ECONOMIC AND EDUCATIONAL OPPORTUNITIES, 104
EDUCATION AND THE WORKFORCE, 105
Dates: Jan. 4, 1995-Jan. 3, 1999
Departure: Moved to Budget

Cong.	Ranking	Terms in: House	Comm.	Date of Assignment
104th	Maj-17th	2	1	Jan. 4, 1995
105th	Maj-13th	3	2	Jan. 7, 1997

5th BUDGET
Dates: Jan. 6, 1999-Mar. 7, 2001
Departure: Left committee; no new assignment

Cong.	Ranking	Terms in: House	Comm.	Date of Assignment
106th	Maj-16th	4	1	Jan. 6, 1999
107th	Maj-7th	5	2	Jan. 6, 2001

6th STANDARDS OF OFFICIAL CONDUCT
Dates: Sep. 29, 1997-Jan. 3, 2001
Departure: Left committee; no new assignment

Cong.	Ranking	Terms in: House	Comm.	Date of Assignment
105th	Min-5th	3	1	Sep. 29, 1997
106th	Min-3rd	4	2	Jan. 19, 1999

Herbert H. Kohl (D-Wisc.)

Dates: Feb. 7, 1935
Senate: Jan. 3, 1989-date
Serving in the 111th Congress

SENATE STANDING COMMITTEES:

1st GOVERNMENTAL AFFAIRS
Dates: Feb. 2, 1989-Jan. 7, 1993
Departure: Moved to Appropriations and Small Business

2nd JUDICIARY
Dates: Feb. 2, 1989-date
Departure: Still serving in the 111th Congress

Cong.	Ranking	Years in: Senate	Comm.	Date of Assignment
103rd	Maj-8th	5	4	Jan. 7, 1993
104th	Min-6th	7	6	Jan. 4, 1995
105th	Min-4th	9	8	Jan. 9, 1997
106th	Min-4th	11	10	Jan. 7, 1999
107th	Min-4th	13	12	Jan. 25, 2001
+107th	Maj-4th	13	13	June 6, 2001
108th	Min-4th	15	14	Jan. 15, 2003
109th	Min-4th	17	16	Jan. 6, 2005
110th	Maj-4th	19	18	Jan. 12, 2007
111th	Maj-2nd	21	20	Jan. 21, 2009

3rd APPROPRIATIONS
Dates: Jan. 7, 1993-date
Departure: Still serving in the 111th Congress

Cong.	Ranking	Years in: Senate	Comm.	Date of Assignment
103rd	Maj-14th	5	1	Jan. 7, 1993
104th	Min-12th	7	2	Jan. 4, 1995
105th	Min-10th	9	5	Jan. 9, 1997
106th	Min-9th	11	7	Jan. 7, 1999
107th	Min-8th	13	9	Jan. 25, 2001
+107th	Maj-8th	13	9	June 6, 2001
108th	Min-8th	15	11	Jan. 15, 2003
109th	Min-7th	17	12	Jan. 6, 2005
110th	Maj-6th	19	15	Jan. 12, 2007
111th	Maj-6th	21	17	Jan. 21, 2009

4th SMALL BUSINESS
Dates: Jan. 21, 1993-Jan. 4, 1995
Departure: Left committee; no new assignment.

Cong.	Ranking	Years in: Senate	Comm.	Date of Assignment
103rd	Maj-11th	5	1	Jan. 21, 1993

SENATE SELECT AND SPECIAL COMMITTEES:

1st SPECIAL AGING (Permanent)
Dates: Feb. 2, 1989-date
Departure: Still serving in the 111th Congress

Cong.	Ranking	Years in: Senate	Comm.	Date of Assignment
103rd	Maj-9th	5	4	Jan. 21, 1993
104th	Min-7th	7	6	Jan. 6, 1995
105th	Min-4th	9	8	Jan. 9, 1997
106th	Min-3rd	11	10	Jan. 7, 1999
107th	Min-3rd	13	12	Jan. 25, 2001
+107th	Maj-3rd	13	13	June 6, 2001
108th	Min-3rd	15	14	Jan. 15, 2003
109th	Min-RM	17	16	Jan. 6, 2005
110th	Maj-Chr	19	18	Jan. 12, 2007
111th	Maj-Chr	21	20	Jan. 21, 2009

2nd JUDGE WALTER L. NIXON IMPEACHMENT
Dates: May 11, 1989-Sep. 13, 1989
Termination: Committee hearings concluded

3rd SELECT POW-MIA AFFAIRS
Dates: Oct. 30, 1991-Feb. 3, 1993
Termination: Senate Report 1 (103-1) filed

James T. Kolbe (R-Ariz.)

Dates: June 28, 1942
House: Jan. 3, 1985-Jan. 3, 2007
Left the House: Retired in 2006

HOUSE STANDING COMMITTEES:

1st BANKING, FINANCE AND URBAN AFFAIRS
Dates: Jan. 30, 1985-Jan. 3, 1987
Departure: Moved to Appropriations

2nd SMALL BUSINESS
Dates: Jan. 30, 1985-Jan. 3, 1987
Departure: Moved to Appropriations

3rd APPROPRIATIONS
Dates: Jan. 21, 1987-Jan. 3, 2007
Departure: Left the House; retired

Cong.	Ranking	Terms in: House	Comm.	Date of Assignment
103rd	Min-12th	5	4	Jan. 5, 1993
104th	Maj-12th	6	5	Jan. 4, 1995
105th	Maj-11th	7	6	Jan. 7, 1997
106th	Maj-9th	8	7	Jan. 6, 1999
107th	Maj-8th	9	8	Jan. 6, 2001
108th	Maj-6th	10	9	Jan. 28, 2003
109th	Maj-6th	11	10	Jan. 6, 2005

4th BUDGET
Dates: Jan. 30, 1991-Jan. 3, 1997
Departure: Left committee; no new assignment

Cong.	Ranking	Terms in: House	Comm.	Date of Assignment
103rd	Min-3rd	5	2	Jan. 5, 1993
104th	Maj-4th	6	3	Jan. 4, 1995

HOUSE SELECT AND SPECIAL COMMITTEES:

1st SELECT AGING (Permanent)
Dates: Feb. 21, 1985-Jan. 3, 1987
Departure: Moved to Appropriations

Michael J. Kopetski (D-Ore.)

Dates: Oct. 27, 1949
House: Jan. 3, 1991-Jan. 3, 1995
Left the House: Retired in 1994

HOUSE STANDING COMMITTEES:

1st AGRICULTURE
Dates: Jan. 24, 1991-Jan. 3, 1993
Departure: Moved to Ways and Means

2nd JUDICIARY
Dates: Jan. 24, 1991-Jan. 3, 1993
Departure: Moved to Ways and Means

3rd SCIENCE, SPACE AND TECHNOLOGY
Dates: Jan. 24, 1991-Jan. 3, 1993
Departure: Moved to Ways and Means

4th WAYS AND MEANS
Dates: Jan. 5, 1993-Jan. 3, 1995
Departure: Left the House; retired

Cong.	Ranking	Terms in: House	Comm.	Date of Assignment
103rd	Maj-21st	2	1	Jan. 5, 1993

Suzanne M. Kosmas (D-Fla.)

Dates: Feb. 25, 1944
House: Jan. 3, 2009-date
Serving in the 111th Congress

HOUSE STANDING COMMITTEES:

1st FINANCIAL SERVICES
Dates: Jan. 7, 2009-date
Departure: Still serving in the 111th Congress

Cong.	Ranking	Terms in: House	Comm.	Date of Assignment
111th	Maj-38th	1	1	Jan. 7, 2009

2nd SCIENCE AND TECHNOLOGY
Dates: Jan. 21, 2009-date
Departure: Still serving in the 111th Congress

Cong.	Ranking	Terms in: House	Comm.	Date of Assignment
111th	Maj-25th	1	1	Jan. 21, 2009

Frank M. Kratovil (D-Md.)

Dates: May 29, 1968
House: Jan. 3, 2009-date
Serving in the 111th Congress

HOUSE STANDING COMMITTEES:

1st ARMED SERVICES
Dates: Jan. 7, 2009-date
Departure: Still serving in the 111th Congress

Cong.	Ranking	Terms in: House	Comm.	Date of Assignment
111th	Maj-35th	1	1	Jan. 7, 2009

2nd AGRICULTURE
Dates: Jan. 21, 2009-date
Departure: Still serving in the 111th Congress

Cong.	Ranking	Terms in: House	Comm.	Date of Assignment
111th	Maj-22nd	1	1	Jan. 21, 2009

3rd NATURAL RESOURCES
Dates: Jan. 21, 2009-date
Departure: Still serving in the 111th Congress

Cong.	Ranking	Terms in: House	Comm.	Date of Assignment
111th	Maj-28th	1	1	Jan. 21, 2009

Myron B. (Mike) Kreidler
(D-Wash.)

Dates: Sept. 28, 1943
House: Jan. 3, 1993-Jan. 3, 1995
Left the House: Defeated for re-election in 1994

HOUSE STANDING COMMITTEES:

1st ENERGY AND COMMERCE
Dates: Jan. 5, 1993-Jan. 3, 1995
Departure: Left the House; lost re-election

Cong.	Ranking	Terms in: House	Comm.	Date of Assignment
103rd	Maj-25th	1	1	Jan. 5, 1993

2nd VETERANS' AFFAIRS
Dates: Jan. 5, 1993-Jan. 3, 1995
Departure: Left the House; lost re-election

Cong.	Ranking	Terms in: House	Comm.	Date of Assignment
103rd	Maj-20th	1	1	Jan. 5, 1993

Robert C. Krueger (D-Tex.)

Dates: Sept. 19, 1935
House: Jan. 3, 1975-Jan. 3, 1979
Left the House: Lost U.S. Senate election in 1978
Senate: Jan. 21, 1993-June 14, 1993
Left the Senate: Lost special election in 1993

S: Krueger was appointed to the U.S. Senate, Jan. 21, 1993, to fill the vacancy of U.S. Senator Lloyd M. Bentsen (D-Tex.) who had been appointed Secretary of the Treasury. Krueger lost the special election to fill the unexpired term.

HOUSE STANDING COMMITTEES:

1st INTERSTATE AND FOREIGN COMMERCE
Dates: Jan. 20, 1975-Jan. 3, 1979
Departure: Left the House; lost Senate election

2nd SCIENCE AND TECHNOLOGY
Dates: Jan. 20, 1975-Jan. 3, 1979
Departure: Left the House; lost Senate election

SENATE STANDING COMMITTEES:

1st COMMERCE, SCIENCE AND TRANSPORTATION
Dates: Jan. 21, 1993-June 14, 1993
Departure: Left the Senate; lost special election

Cong.	Ranking	Years in: Senate	Comm.	Date of Assignment
103rd	MjR-1st	1	1	Jan. 21, 1993

2nd ENERGY AND NATURAL RESOURCES
Dates: Jan. 21, 1993-June 14, 1993
Departure: Left the Senate; lost special election

Cong.	Ranking	Years in: Senate	Comm.	Date of Assignment
103rd	Maj-11th	1	1	Jan. 21, 1993

SENATE SELECT AND SPECIAL COMMITTEES:

1st SPECIAL AGING (Permanent)
Dates: Jan. 21, 1993-June 14, 1993
Departure: Left the Senate; lost special election

Cong.	Ranking	Years in: Senate	Comm.	Date of Assignment
103rd	Maj-11th	1	1	Jan. 21, 1993

Dennis Kucinich (D-Ohio)

Dates: Oct. 8, 1946
House: Jan. 3, 1997-date
Serving in the 111th Congress

HOUSE STANDING COMMITTEES:

1st GOVERNMENT REFORM AND OVERSIGHT, 105
GOVERNMENT REFORM, 106-109
OVERSIGHT AND GOVERNMENT REFORM, 110-111
Dates: Jan. 7, 1997-date
Departure: Still serving in the 111th Congress

Cong.	Ranking	Terms in: House	Comm.	Date of Assignment
105th	Min-15th	1	1	Jan. 7, 1997
106th	Min-13th	2	2	Jan. 6, 1999
107th	Min-11th	3	3	Jan. 31, 2001
108th	Min-9th	4	4	Jan. 28, 2003
109th	Min-8th	5	5	Jan. 26, 2005
110th	Maj-7th	6	6	Jan. 12, 2007
111th	Maj-5th	7	7	Jan. 28, 2009

2nd INTERNATIONAL RELATIONS
Dates: Jan. 7, 1997-Mar. 6, 1997
Departure: Resigned committee; moved to Education and the Workforce

Cong.	Ranking	Terms in: House	Comm.	Date of Assignment
105th	Min-19th	1	1	Jan. 7, 1997

3rd EDUCATION AND THE WORKFORCE, 105-109
EDUCATION AND LABOR, 110-111
Dates: Mar. 6, 1997-date
Departure: Still serving in the 111th Congress

Cong.	Ranking	Terms in: House	Comm.	Date of Assignment
105th	MnR-1st	1	1	Mar. 6, 1997
106th	Min-20th	2	2	Jan. 6, 1999
107th	Min-18th	3	3	Jan. 31, 2001
108th	Min-12th	4	4	Jan. 28, 2003
109th	Min-12th	5	5	Jan. 26, 2005
110th	Maj-10th	6	6	Jan. 10, 2007
111th	Maj-10th	7	7	Jan. 21, 2009

John R. (Randy) Kuhl Jr. (R-N.Y.)

Dates: April 19, 1943
House: Jan. 3, 2005-Jan. 3, 2009
Left the House: Defeated for re-election in 2008

HOUSE STANDING COMMITTEES:

1st AGRICULTURE
Dates: Jan. 26, 2005-Jan. 3, 2009
Departure: Left the House; lost re-election

Cong.	Ranking	Terms in: House	Comm.	Date of Assignment
109th	Maj-22nd	1	1	Jan. 26, 2005
110th	Min-14th	2	2	Jan. 10, 2007

2nd EDUCATION AND THE WORKFORCE, 109
EDUCATION AND LABOR, 110
Dates: Jan. 26, 2005-Jan. 3, 2009
Departure: Left the House; lost re-election

Cong.	Ranking	Terms in: House	Comm.	Date of Assignment
109th	Maj-27th	1	1	Jan. 26, 2005
110th	Min-19th	2	2	Jan. 10, 2007

3rd TRANSPORTATION AND INFRASTRUCTURE
Dates: Jan. 26, 2005-Jan. 3, 2009
Departure: Left the House; lost re-election

Cong.	Ranking	Terms in: House	Comm.	Date of Assignment
109th	Maj-38th	1	1	Jan. 26, 2005
110th	Min-27th	2	2	Jan. 10, 2007

Cong.	Ranking	Terms in: House	Comm.	Date of Assignment
103rd	Min-4th	4	2	Jan. 5, 1993

Steven T. Kuykendall (R-Cal.)

Dates: Jan. 27, 1947
House: Jan. 3, 1999-Jan. 3, 2001
Left the House: Defeated for re-election in 2000

HOUSE STANDING COMMITTEES:

1st ARMED SERVICES
Dates: Jan. 6, 1999-Jan. 3, 2001
Departure: Left the House; lost re-election

Cong.	Ranking	Terms in: House	Comm.	Date of Assignment
106th	Maj-31st	1	1	Jan. 6, 1999

2nd SCIENCE
Dates: Jan. 6, 1999-Jan. 3, 2001
Departure: Left the House; lost re-election

Cong.	Ranking	Terms in: House	Comm.	Date of Assignment
106th	Maj-21st	1	1	Jan. 6, 1999

3rd TRANSPORTATION AND INFRASTRUCTURE
Dates: Feb. 2, 1999-Jan. 3, 2001
Departure: Left the House; lost re-election

Cong.	Ranking	Terms in: House	Comm.	Date of Assignment
106th	Maj-39th	1	1	Feb. 2, 1999

Jon L. Kyl (R-Ariz.)

Dates: April 25, 1942
House: Jan. 3, 1987-Jan. 3, 1995
Left the House: Elected to U.S. Senate in 1994
Senate: Jan. 3, 1995-date
Serving in the 111th Congress

HOUSE STANDING COMMITTEES:

1st ARMED SERVICES
Dates: Jan. 21, 1987-Jan. 3, 1995
Departure: Left the House for the Senate

Cong.	Ranking	Terms in: House	Comm.	Date of Assignment
103rd	Min-8th	4	4	Jan. 5, 1993

2nd GOVERNMENT OPERATIONS
Dates: Jan. 21, 1987-Jan. 3, 1995
Departure: Left the House for the Senate

Cong.	Ranking	Terms in: House	Comm.	Date of Assignment
103rd	Min-4th	4	4	Jan. 5, 1993

3rd STANDARDS OF OFFICIAL CONDUCT
Dates: Feb. 6, 1991-Jan. 3, 1995
Departure: Left the House for the Senate

SENATE STANDING COMMITTEES:

1st ENERGY AND NATURAL RESOURCES
1st Dates: Jan. 5, 1995-Jan. 7, 1999
1st Departure: Moved to Appropriations
2nd Dates: Jan. 25, 2001-Jan. 6, 2005
2nd Departure: Left committee; no new assignment.

Cong.	Ranking	Years in: Senate	Comm.	Date of Assignment
104th	Maj-7th	1 *1	1	Jan. 5, 1995
105th	Maj-7th	3 *1	3	Jan. 9, 1997
107th	Maj-9th	7 *2	1	Jan. 25, 2001
+107th	Min-9th	7 *2	1	June 6, 2001
108th	Maj-12th	9 *2	2	Jan. 15, 2003

2nd JUDICIARY
Dates: Jan. 4, 1995-date
Departure: Still serving in the 111th Congress

Cong.	Ranking	Years in: Senate	Comm.	Date of Assignment
104th	Maj-8th	1	1	Jan. 4, 1995
105th	Maj-6th	3	3	Jan. 9, 1997
106th	Maj-5th	5	5	Jan. 7, 1999
107th	Maj-5th	7	7	Jan. 25, 2001
+107th	Min-5th	7	7	June 6, 2001
108th	Maj-4th	9	9	Jan. 15, 2003
109th	Maj-4th	11	11	Jan. 6, 2005
110th	Min-4th	13	13	Jan. 12, 2007
111th	Min-4th	15	15	Jan. 21, 2009

3rd APPROPRIATIONS
Dates: Jan. 7, 1999-Jan. 25, 2001
Departure: Moved to Finance and returned to Energy and Natural Resources

Cong.	Ranking	Years in: Senate	Comm.	Date of Assignment
106th	Maj-15th	5	1	Jan. 7, 1999

4th FINANCE
Dates: Jan. 25, 2001-date
Departure: Still serving in the 111th Congress

Cong.	Ranking	Years in: Senate	Comm.	Date of Assignment
107th	Maj-10th	7	1	Jan. 25, 2001
+107th	Min-9th	7	1	July 10, 2001
108th	Maj-6th	9	2	Jan. 15, 2003
109th	Maj-5th	11	4	Jan. 6, 2005
110th	Min-5th	13	6	Jan. 12, 2007
111th	Min-4th	15	8	Jan. 21, 2009

SENATE SELECT AND SPECIAL COMMITTEES:

1st SELECT INTELLIGENCE (Permanent)
Dates: Jan. 6, 1995-Jan. 15, 2003
Departure: Left committee; no new assignment

Cong.	Ranking	Years in: Senate	Comm.	Date of Assignment
104th	Maj-5th	1	1	Jan. 6, 1995
105th	Maj-5th	3	3	Jan. 9, 1997
106th	Maj-5th	5	5	Jan. 7, 1999
107th	Maj-2nd	7	7	Jan. 25, 2001
+107th	Min-2nd	7	7	June 6, 2001

2nd SPECIAL YEAR 2000 TECHNOLOGY PROBLEM
Dates: Apr. 28, 1998-Feb. 29, 2000
Termination: Senate Print 106-42 issued

Cong.	Ranking	Years in: Senate	Comm.	Date of Assignment
105th	Maj-2nd	4	1	Apr. 28, 1998
106th	Maj-2nd	5	1	Continued

SENATE LEADERSHIP POSTS

Dates: Dec. 6, 2007-date
Departure: Still serving in the 111th Congress

1st SENATE MINORITY WHIP
Dates: Dec. 6, 2007-date
Note: In the 110th Congress, Kyl was elected on Dec. 6, 2007, to succeed Minority Whip C. Trent Lott (R-Miss.) who had resigned his post. Kyl was elected without opposition and was re-elected for the 111th Congress without opposition.
Departure: Still serving in the 111th Congress

Cong.	Ranking	Years in: Senate	Post	Date of Service
110th	Min-2nd	11	1	Dec. 6, 2007
111th	Min-2nd	12	2	Nov. 18, 2008

L

John J. LaFalce (D-N.Y.)

Dates: Oct. 6, 1939
House: Jan. 3, 1975-Jan. 3, 2003
Left the House: Retired in 2002

HOUSE STANDING COMMITTEES:

1st SMALL BUSINESS
Dates: Jan. 20, 1975-Jan. 3, 1999
RM1: Became Ranking Member on Banking and Financial Services; replaced as Ranking Member by Nydia M. Velazquez (D-N.Y.) on Feb. 26, 1998
Departure: Left committee; no new assignment

Cong.	Ranking	Terms in: House	Comm.	Date of Assignment
103rd	Maj-Chr	10	10	Jan. 5, 1993
104th	Min-RM	11	11	Jan. 4, 1995
105th	Min-RM1	12	12	Feb. 5, 1997

2nd BANKING AND CURRENCY, 94
BANKING, FINANCE AND URBAN AFFAIRS, 95-103
BANKING AND FINANCIAL SERVICES, 104-106
FINANCIAL SERVICES, 107
Dates: Jan. 23, 1975-Jan. 3, 2003
RM2: Replaced Henry Gonzalez (D-Tex.) on Feb. 25, 1998
Departure: Left the House; retired

Cong.	Ranking	Terms in: House	Comm.	Date of Assignment
103rd	Maj-3rd	10	10	Jan. 5, 1993
104th	Min-2nd	11	11	Jan. 4, 1995
105th	Min-2nd	12	12	Jan. 7, 1997
=105th	Min-RM2	12	12	Feb. 25, 1998
106th	Min-RM	13	13	Jan. 6, 1999
107th	Min-RM	14	14	Jan. 6, 2001

Ray H. LaHood (R-Ill.)

Dates: Dec. 6, 1945
House: Jan. 3, 1995-Jan. 3, 2009
Left the House: Retired; later appointed Secretary of Transportation

HOUSE STANDING COMMITTEES:

1st AGRICULTURE
Dates: Jan. 4, 1995-Jan. 3, 2001
Departure: Moved to Appropriations

Cong.	Ranking	Terms in: House	Comm.	Date of Assignment
104th	Maj-27th	1	1	Jan. 4, 1995
105th	Maj-19th	2	2	Jan. 7, 1997
106th	Maj-14th	3	3	Jan. 6, 1999

2nd TRANSPORTATION AND INFRASTRUCTURE
Dates: Jan. 4, 1995-Jan. 3, 2001
Departure: Moved to Appropriations

Cong.	Ranking	Terms in: House	Comm.	Date of Assignment
104th	Maj-32nd	1	1	Jan. 4, 1995
105th	Maj-21st	2	2	Jan. 7, 1997
106th	Maj-19th	3	3	Jan. 6, 1999

3rd VETERANS' AFFAIRS
Dates: Feb. 6, 1997-Jan. 3, 2001
Departure: Moved to Appropriations

Cong.	Ranking	Terms in: House	Comm.	Date of Assignment
105th	Maj-17th	2	1	Feb. 6, 1997
106th	Maj-13th	3	2	Jan. 6, 1999

4th APPROPRIATIONS
Dates: Jan. 6, 2001-Jan. 3, 2009
Departure: Left the House; appointed to Cabinet

Cong.	Ranking	Terms in: House	Comm.	Date of Assignment
107th	Maj-32nd	4	1	Jan. 6, 2001
108th	Maj-28th	5	2	Jan. 28, 2003
109th	Maj-27th	6	3	Jan. 6, 2005
110th	Min-21st	7	4	Jan. 4, 2007

5th BUDGET
Dates: Mar. 7, 2001-Jan. 3, 2003
Departure: Left committee; no new assignment

Cong.	Ranking	Terms in: House	Comm.	Date of Assignment
107th	MjR-1st	4	1	Mar. 7, 2001

HOUSE SELECT AND SPECIAL COMMITTEES:

1st PERMANENT SELECT INTELLIGENCE
Dates: Jan. 19, 1999-Jan. 3, 2007
Departure: Left committee; no new assignment

Cong.	Ranking	Terms in: House	Comm.	Date of Assignment
106th	Maj-8th	3	1	Jan. 19, 1999
107th	Maj-7th	4	2	Jan. 30, 2001
108th	Maj-5th	5	3	Jan. 8, 2003
109th	Maj-2nd	6	4	Jan. 26, 2005

Doug Lamborn (R-Colo.)

Dates: May 24, 1954
House: Jan. 3, 2007-date
Serving in the 111th Congress

HOUSE STANDING COMMITTEES:

1st NATURAL RESOURCES
Dates: Jan. 10, 2007-date
Departure: Still serving in the 111th Congress

Cong.	Ranking	Terms in: House	Comm.	Date of Assignment
110th	Min-22nd	1	1	Jan. 10, 2007
111th	Min-11th	2	2	Jan. 9, 2009

2nd VETERANS' AFFAIRS
1st Dates: Jan. 10, 2007-Jan. 3, 2009
1st Departure: Left committee; no new assignment
2nd Dates: Returned Jan. 22, 2009-date
2nd Departure: Still serving in the 111th Congress

Cong.	Ranking	Terms in: House	Comm.	Date of Assignment
110th	Min-12th	1 *1	1	Jan. 10, 2007
111th	MnR-1st	2 *2	1	Jan. 22, 2009

3rd ARMED SERVICES
Dates: Oct. 10, 2007-date
Departure: Still serving in the 111th Congress

Cong.	Ranking	Terms in: House	Comm.	Date of Assignment
110th	MnR-1st	1	1	Oct. 10, 2007
111th	Min-19th	2	2	Jan. 9, 2009

Nicholas V. Lampson (D-Texas)

Dates: Feb. 14, 1945
House 1: Jan. 3, 1997-Jan. 3, 2005
Left the House 1: Defeated for re-election in 2004
House 2: Jan. 3, 2007-Jan. 3, 2009
Left the House 2: Defeated for re-election in 2008

HOUSE STANDING COMMITTEES:

1st SCIENCE, 105-108
SCIENCE AND TECHNOLOGY, 110
1st Dates: Feb. 13, 1997-Jan. 3, 2005
1st Departure: Left the House; lost re-election

2nd Dates: Jan. 18, 2007-Jan. 3, 2009
2nd Departure: Left the House; lost re-election

Cong.	Ranking	Terms in: House	Comm.	Date of Assignment
105th	Min-20th	1 *1	1	Feb. 13, 1997
106th	Min-17th	2 *1	2	Jan. 6, 1999
107th	Min-12th	3 *1	3	Jan. 31, 2001
108th	Min-10th	4 *1	4	Jan. 28, 2003
110th	Maj-7th	5 *2	1	Jan. 18, 2007

2nd RESOURCES
Dates: Feb. 5, 1997-Apr. 17, 1997
Departure: Resigned committee; moved to Transportation and Infrastructure

Cong.	Ranking	Terms in: House	Comm.	Date of Assignment
105th	MnR-1st	1	1	Feb. 5, 1997

3rd TRANSPORTATION AND INFRASTRUCTURE
Dates: Apr. 17, 1997-Jan. 3. 2005
1st Departure: Left the House; lost re-election
2nd Dates: Jan. 10, 2007-Jan. 3, 2009
2nd Departure: Left the House; lost re-election

Cong.	Ranking	Terms in: House	Comm.	Date of Assignment
105th	Min-33rd	1 *1	1	Apr. 17, 1997
106th	Min-29th	2 *1	2	Jan. 6, 1999
107th	Min-26th	3 *1	3	Jan. 31, 2001
108th	Min-20th	4 *1	4	Jan. 28, 2003
110th	Maj-28th	5 *2	1	Jan. 10, 2007

4th AGRICULTURE
Dates: Jan. 12, 2007-Jan. 3, 2009
Departure: Left the House; lost re-election

Cong.	Ranking	Terms in: House	Comm.	Date of Assignment
110th	Maj-23rd	5	1	Jan. 12, 2007

H. Martin Lancaster (D-N.C.)

Dates: March 24, 1943
House: Jan. 3, 1987-Jan. 3, 1995
Left the House: Defeated for re-election in 1994

HOUSE STANDING COMMITTEES:

1st PUBLIC WORKS AND TRANSPORTATION
Dates: Jan. 8, 1987-Mar. 9, 1988
Departure: Moved to Armed Services

2nd SMALL BUSINESS
Dates: Jan. 22, 1987-Jan. 3, 1995
Departure: Left the House; lost re-election

Cong.	Ranking	Terms in: House	Comm.	Date of Assignment
103rd	Maj-13th	4	4	Jan. 21, 1993

3rd AGRICULTURE
1st Dates: Dec. 15, 1987-Jan. 3, 1989
1st Departure: Remained on committee as a temporary member
Temporary Dates: Jan. 27, 1989-Jan. 3, 1991
Temporary Departure: Temporary term expired

4th ARMED SERVICES
Dates: Mar. 2, 1988-Jan. 3, 1995
Departure: Left the House; lost re-election

Cong.	Ranking	Terms in: House	Comm.	Date of Assignment
103rd	Maj-15th	4	4	Jan. 5, 1993

5th MERCHANT MARINE AND FISHERIES
Dates: Oct. 30, 1991-Jan. 3, 1995
Departure: Left the House; lost re-election

Cong.	Ranking	Terms in: House	Comm.	Date of Assignment
103rd	Maj-15th	4	2	Jan. 5, 1993

Leonard Lance (R-N.J.)

Dates: June 25, 1952
House: Jan. 3, 2009-date
Serving in the 111th Congress

HOUSE STANDING COMMITTEES:

1st FINANCIAL SERVICES
Dates: Jan. 9, 2009-date
Departure: Still serving in the 111th Congress

Cong.	Ranking	Terms in: House	Comm.	Date of Assignment
111th	Min-29th	1	1	Jan. 9, 2009

Mary L. Landrieu (D-La.)

Dates: Nov. 23, 1955
Senate: Jan. 3, 1997-date
Serving in the 111th Congress

SENATE STANDING COMMITTEES:

1st AGRICULTURE, NUTRITION AND FORESTRY
Dates: Jan. 9, 1997-Jan. 7, 1999
Departure: Moved to Armed Services

Cong.	Ranking	Years in: Senate	Comm.	Date of Assignment
105th	Min-7th	1	1	Jan. 9, 1997

2nd ENERGY AND NATURAL RESOURCES
Dates: Jan. 9, 1997-date
Departure: Still serving in the 111th Congress

Cong.	Ranking	Years in: Senate	Comm.	Date of Assignment
105th	Min-9th	1	1	Jan. 9, 1997
106th	Min-7th	3	2	Jan. 7, 1999
107th	Min-7th	5	5	Jan. 25, 2001
+107th	Maj-7th	5	5	June 6, 2001
108th	Min-7th	7	7	Jan. 15, 2003
109th	Min-6th	9	8	Jan. 6, 2005
110th	Maj-6th	11	11	Jan. 12, 2007
111th	Maj-5th	13	13	Jan. 21, 2009

3rd SMALL BUSINESS renamed June 29, 2001
SMALL BUSINESS AND ENTREPRENEURSHIP
Dates: Jan. 9, 1997-date
Departure: Still serving in the 111th Congress

Cong.	Ranking	Years in: Senate	Comm.	Date of Assignment
105th	Min-8th	1	1	Jan. 9, 1997
106th	Min-7th	3	2	Jan. 7, 1999
107th	Min-7th	5	5	Jan. 25, 2001
+107th	Maj-7th	5	5	June 6, 2001
108th	Min-5th	7	7	Jan. 15, 2003
109th	Min-5th	9	8	Jan. 6, 2005
110th	Maj-5th	11	11	Jan. 12, 2007
111th	Maj-Chr	13	13	Jan. 21, 2009

4th ARMED SERVICES
Dates: Jan. 7, 1999-Jan. 15, 2003
Departure: Left committee; no new assignment

Cong.	Ranking	Years in: Senate	Comm.	Date of Assignment
106th	Min-8th	3	1	Jan. 7, 1999
107th	Min-6th	5	3	Jan. 25, 2001
+107th	Maj-6th	5	3	June 6, 2001

5th APPROPRIATIONS
Dates: Jan. 25, 2001-date
Departure: Still serving in the 111th Congress

Cong.	Ranking	Years in: Senate	Comm.	Date of Assignment
107th	Min-14th	5	1	Jan. 25, 2001
+107th	Maj-14th	5	1	June 6, 2001
108th	Min-14th	7	2	Jan. 15, 2003
109th	Min-13th	9	4	Jan. 6, 2005
110th	Maj-12th	11	6	Jan. 12, 2007
111th	Maj-12th	13	8	Jan. 21, 2009

6th HOMELAND SECURITY AND GOVERNMENTAL AFFAIRS
Dates: Jan. 12, 2007-date
Departure: Still serving in the 111th Congress

Cong.	Ranking	Years in: Senate	Comm.	Date of Assignment
110th	Maj-6th	11	1	Jan. 12, 2007
111th	Maj-6th	13	3	Jan. 21, 2009

James R. Langevin (D-R.I.)

Dates: April 22, 1964
House: Jan. 3, 2001-date
Serving in the 111th Congress

HOUSE STANDING COMMITTEES:

1st ARMED SERVICES
1st Dates: Jan. 28, 2003-Jan. 18, 2007
1st Departure: Leave of absence; moved to Permanent Select Intelligence
2nd Dates: Sep. 30, 2007-Oct. 31, 2007
2nd Departure: Resigned committee; remained on Permanent Select Intelligence
3rd Dates: Jan. 7, 2009-date
3rd Departure: Still serving in the 111th Congress

Cong.	Ranking	Terms in: House	Comm.	Date of Assignment
107th	Min-28th	1 *1	1	Jan. 31, 2001
108th	Min-21st	2 *1	2	Jan. 28, 2003
109th	Min-17th	3 *1	3	Jan. 26, 2005
110th	Maj-16th	4 *1	4	Jan. 10, 2007
110th	MjR-2nd	4 *2	1	Sep. 20, 2007
111th	Maj-15th	5 *3	1	Jan. 7, 2009

2nd SMALL BUSINESS
Dates: Feb. 8, 2001-Feb. 12, 2003
Departure: Leave of absence; moved to Select Homeland Security; never returned

Cong.	Ranking	Terms in: House	Comm.	Date of Assignment
107th	MnR-1st	1	1	Feb. 8, 2001
108th	Min-9th	2	2	Jan. 28, 2003

3rd HOMELAND SECURITY
Dates: Feb. 9, 2005-Jan. 3, 2009
Departure: Moved to Budget and returned to Armed Services

Cong.	Ranking	Terms in: House	Comm.	Date of Assignment
109th	Min-14th	3	2	Feb. 9, 2005
110th	Maj-13th	4	3	Jan. 12, 2007

4th BUDGET
Dates: Jan. 21, 2009-date
Departure: Still serving in the 111th Congress

Cong.	Ranking	Terms in: House	Comm.	Date of Assignment
111th	Maj-19th	5	1	Jan. 21, 2009

HOUSE SELECT AND SPECIAL COMMITTEES:

1st SELECT HOMELAND SECURITY
Dates: Feb. 12, 2003-Jan. 3, 2005
Departure: Continued on reorganized standing committee

Cong.	Ranking	Terms in: House	Comm.	Date of Assignment
108th	Min-22nd	2	1	Feb. 12, 2003

2nd PERMANENT SELECT INTELLIGENCE
Dates: Jan. 17, 2007-date
Departure: Still serving in the 111th Congress

Cong.	Ranking	Terms in: House	Comm.	Date of Assignment
110th	Maj-11th	4	1	Jan. 17, 2007
111th	Maj-9th	5	2	Feb. 4, 2009

Thomas P. Lantos (D-Cal.)

Dates: Feb. 1, 1928-Feb. 11, 2008
House: Jan. 3, 1981-Feb. 11, 2008
Left the House: Died in office.

HOUSE STANDING COMMITTEES:

1st FOREIGN AFFAIRS, 97-103
INTERNATIONAL RELATIONS, 104-109
FOREIGN AFFAIRS, 110
Dates: Jan. 28, 1981-Feb. 11, 2008
Ch1: Succeeded by Howard J. Berman (D-Cal.) on Mar. 11, 2008
Departure: Died in office

Cong.	Ranking	Terms in: House	Comm.	Date of Assignment
103rd	Maj-3rd	7	7	Jan. 5, 1993
104th	Min-3rd	8	8	Jan. 4, 1995
105th	Min-3rd	9	9	Jan. 7, 1997
106th	Min-2nd	10	10	Jan. 6, 1999
107th	Min-RM	11	11	Jan. 31, 2001
108th	Min-RM	12	12	Jan. 8, 2003
109th	Min-RM	13	13	Jan. 6, 2005
110th	Maj-Ch1	14	14	Jan. 4, 2007

2nd GOVERNMENT OPERATIONS, 97-103
GOVERNMENT REFORM AND OVERSIGHT, 104-105
GOVERNMENT OPERATIONS, 106-109
OVERSIGHT AND GOVERNMENT REFORM, 110
Dates: Jan. 28, 1981-Feb. 11, 2008
Departure: Died in office

Cong.	Ranking	Terms in: House	Comm.	Date of Assignment
103rd	Maj-7th	7	7	Jan. 5, 1993
104th	Min-3rd	8	8	Jan. 9, 1995
105th	Min-2nd	9	9	Jan. 7, 1997
106th	Min-2nd	10	10	Jan. 6, 1999
107th	Min-2nd	11	11	Jan. 31, 2001
108th	Min-2nd	12	12	Jan. 28, 2003
109th	Min-2nd	13	13	Jan. 26, 2005
110th	Maj-2nd	14	14	Jan. 12, 2007

3rd BANKING, FINANCE AND URBAN AFFAIRS
Dates: July 12, 1990-Jan. 3, 1991
Departure: Left committee; no new assignment

HOUSE SELECT AND SPECIAL COMMITTEES:

1st SELECT AGING (Permanent)
Dates: Feb. 5, 1981-Jan. 3, 1993
Termination: Committee not renewed in the 103rd Congress

Steve Largent (R-Okla.)

Dates: Sept. 28, 1954
House: Nov. 29, 1994-Feb. 15, 2002
Left the House: Resigned; later lost election for Governor in 2002.

H: Largent was elected to the 104th Congress by special election, Nov. 8, 1994, to fill the impending vacancy of U.S. Representative James Inhofe (R-Okla.) who had been elected to the U.S. Senate and was appointed to the 103rd Congress by the Governor of Oklahoma on Nov. 29, 1994, pursuant to the provisions of Oklahoma Statute 26-12-101 (B) and accepted by H. Res. 585, 103rd Congress. Largent was seated Nov. 29, 1994, and was not assigned to committees.

HOUSE STANDING COMMITTEES:

1st BUDGET
Dates: Jan. 4, 1995-Jan. 3, 1997
Departure: Moved to Commerce

Cong.	Ranking	Terms in: House	Comm.	Date of Assignment
104th	Maj-19th	2	1	Jan. 4, 1995

2nd SCIENCE
Dates: Jan. 4, 1995-Jan. 3, 1997
Departure: Moved to Commerce

Cong.	Ranking	Terms in: House	Comm.	Date of Assignment
104th	Maj-23rd	2	1	Jan. 4, 1995

3rd COMMERCE, 105-106
ENERGY AND COMMERCE, 107
Dates: Jan. 7, 1997-Feb. 15, 2002
Departure: Resigned the House; lost election for Governor

Cong.	Ranking	Terms in: House	Comm.	Date of Assignment
105th	Maj-17th	3	1	Jan. 7, 1997

106th	Maj-12th	4	2	Jan. 6, 1999
107th	Maj-10th	5	3	Jan. 6, 2001

Larry LaRocco (D-Ida.)

Dates: Aug. 25, 1946
House: Jan. 3, 1991-Jan. 3, 1995
Left the House: Defeated for re-election in 1994

HOUSE STANDING COMMITTEES:

1st BANKING, FINANCE AND URBAN AFFAIRS
Dates: Jan. 24, 1991-Jan. 3, 1995
Departure: Left the House; lost re-election

		Terms in:		Date of
Cong.	Ranking	House	Comm.	Assignment
103rd	Maj-12th	2	2	Jan. 5, 1993

2nd INTERIOR AND INSULAR AFFAIRS, 102
NATURAL RESOURCES, 103
Dates: Jan. 24, 1991-Jan. 3, 1995
Departure: Left the House; lost re-election

		Terms in:		Date of
Cong.	Ranking	House	Comm.	Assignment
103rd	Maj-15th	2	2	Jan. 5, 1993

Richard R. (Rick) Larsen (D-Wash.)

Dates: June 15, 1965
House: Jan. 3, 2003-date
Serving in the 111th Congress

HOUSE STANDING COMMITTEES:

1st TRANSPORTATION AND INFRASTRUCTURE
Dates: Jan. 31, 2001-date
Departure: Still serving in the 111th Congress

		Terms in:		Date of
Cong.	Ranking	House	Comm.	Assignment
107th	Min-34th	1	1	Jan. 31, 2001
108th	Min-26th	2	2	Jan. 28, 2003
109th	Min-23rd	3	3	Jan. 26, 2005
110th	Maj-17th	4	4	Jan. 10, 2007
111th	Maj-16th	5	5	Jan. 7, 2009

2nd AGRICULTURE
1st Dates: Feb. 8, 2001-Feb. 5, 2003
1st Departure: Resigned committee due to permanent appointment on Armed Services; returned
2nd Dates: Feb. 13, 2003-Jan. 3, 2007
2nd Departure: Moved to Small Business

		Terms in:		Date of
Cong.	Ranking	House	Comm.	Assignment
107th	MnR-1st	1 *1	1	Feb. 8, 2001
108th	Min-12th	2 *1	2	Jan. 28, 2003
108th	Min-12th	2 *2	1	Feb. 13, 2003
109th	Min-20th	3 *2	2	Feb. 2, 2005

3rd ARMED SERVICES
Dates: July 25, 2001-date
Departure: Still serving in the 111th Congress

		Terms in:		Date of
Cong.	Ranking	House	Comm.	Assignment
107th	MnR-1st	1	1	July 25, 2001
108th	Min-23rd	2	2	Feb. 5, 2003
109th	Min-19th	3	3	Jan. 26, 2005
110th	Maj-17th	4	4	Jan. 10, 2007
111th	Maj-16th	5	5	Jan. 7, 2009

4th SMALL BUSINESS
Dates: Jan. 23, 2007-Jan. 3, 2009
Departure: Moved to Budget

		Terms in:		Date of
Cong.	Ranking	House	Comm.	Assignment
110th	Maj-6th	4	1	Jan. 23, 2007

5th BUDGET
Dates: Jan. 21, 2009-date
Departure: Still serving in the 111th Congress

		Terms in:		Date of
Cong.	Ranking	House	Comm.	Assignment
111th	Maj-20th	5	1	Jan. 21, 2009

John B. Larson (D-Conn.)

Dates: July 22, 1948
House: Jan. 3, 1999-date
Serving in the 111th Congress

HOUSE STANDING COMMITTEES:

1st SCIENCE
Dates: Jan. 6, 1999-Jan. 3, 2005
Departure: Moved to Ways and Means

		Terms in:		Date of
Cong.	Ranking	House	Comm.	Assignment
106th	Min-19th	1	1	Jan. 6, 1999
107th	Min-13th	2	2	Jan. 31, 2001
108th	Min-10th	3	3	Jan. 28, 2003

2nd ARMED SERVICES
Dates: Jan. 19, 1999-Jan. 3, 2005
Departure: Moved to Ways and Means

		Terms in:		Date of
Cong.	Ranking	House	Comm.	Assignment
106th	Min-28th	1	1	Jan. 19, 1999
107th	Min-26th	2	2	Jan. 31, 2001
108th	Min-19th	3	3	Jan. 28, 2003

3rd HOUSE ADMINISTRATION
Dates: Feb. 5, 2003-Jan. 3, 2005
Departure: Moved to Ways and Means

		Terms in:		Date of
Cong.	Ranking	House	Comm.	Assignment
108th	Min-RM	3	1	Feb. 5, 2003

4th WAYS AND MEANS
Dates: Jan. 26, 2005-date
Departure: Still serving in the 111th Congress

		Terms in:		Date of
Cong.	Ranking	House	Comm.	Assignment
109th	Min-16th	4	1	Jan. 26, 2005

| 110th | Maj-14th | 5 | 2 | Jan. 4, 2007 |
| 111th | Maj-12th | 6 | 3 | Jan. 7, 2009 |

HOUSE SELECT AND SPECIAL COMMITTEES:

1st SELECT ENERGY INDEPENDENCE AND GLOBAL WARMING
Dates: Mar. 9, 2007-date
Departure: Still serving in the 111th Congress

| | | Terms in: | | Date of |
Cong.	Ranking	House	Comm.	Assignment
110th	Maj-4th	5	1	Mar. 9, 2007
111th	Maj-4th	6	2	Feb. 3, 2009

JOINT COMMITTEES:

1st JOINT LIBRARY
House Dates: Mar. 25, 2003-Jan. 3, 2005
Departure: Moved to Ways and Means

| | | Terms in: | | Date of |
Cong.	Ranking	House	Comm.	Assignment
108th	Min-1st	3	1	Mar. 25, 2003

2nd JOINT PRINTING,
House Dates: Mar. 25, 2003-Jan. 3, 2005
Departure: Moved to Ways and Means

| | | Terms in: | | Date of |
Cong.	Ranking	House	Comm.	Assignment
108th	Min-1st	3	1	Mar. 25, 2003

Thomas Latham (R-Iowa)

Dates: July 14, 1948
House: Jan. 3, 1995-date
Serving in the 111th Congress

HOUSE STANDING COMMITTEES:

1st AGRICULTURE
Dates: Jan. 4, 1995-Jan. 3, 1997
Departure: Moved to Appropriations

| | | Terms in: | | Date of |
Cong.	Ranking	House	Comm.	Assignment
104th	Maj-23rd	1	1	Jan. 4, 1995

2nd TRANSPORTATION AND INFRASTRUCTURE
Dates: Jan. 4, 1995-Jan. 3, 1997
Departure: Moved to Appropriations

| | | Terms in: | | Date of |
Cong.	Ranking	House	Comm.	Assignment
104th	Maj-27th	1	1	Jan. 4, 1995

3rd APPROPRIATIONS
Dates: Jan. 7, 1997-date
Departure: Still serving in the 111th Congress

| | | Terms in: | | Date of |
Cong.	Ranking	House	Comm.	Assignment
105th	Maj-32nd	2	1	Jan. 7, 1997
106th	Maj-28th	3	2	Jan. 6, 1999
107th	Maj-24th	4	3	Jan. 6, 2001
108th	Maj-20th	5	4	Jan. 28, 2003
109th	Maj-19th	6	5	Jan. 6, 2005
110th	Min-14th	7	6	Jan. 4, 2007
111th	Min-9th	8	7	Jan. 9, 2009

Steven C. LaTourette (R-Ohio)

Dates: July 22, 1954
House: Jan. 4, 1995-date
Serving in the 111th Congress

HOUSE STANDING COMMITTEES:

1st GOVERNMENT REFORM AND OVERSIGHT, 104-105
GOVERNMENT REFORM, 106-109
Dates: Jan. 4, 1995-Jan. 3, 2007
Departure: Left committee; no new assignment

| | | Terms in: | | Date of |
Cong.	Ranking	House	Comm.	Assignment
104th	Maj-25th	1	1	Jan. 4, 1995
105th	Maj-17th	2	2	Jan. 7, 1997
106th	Maj-14th	3	3	Jan. 6, 1999
107th	Maj-12th	4	4	Jan. 6, 2001
108th	Maj-8th	5	5	Jan. 28, 2003
109th	Maj-9th	6	6	Jan. 26, 2005

2nd TRANSPORTATION AND INFRASTRUCTURE
Dates: Jan. 4, 1995-Jan. 3, 2009
Departure: Moved to Appropriations

| | | Terms in: | | Date of |
Cong.	Ranking	House	Comm.	Assignment
104th	Maj-28th	1	1	Jan. 4, 1995
105th	Maj-19th	2	2	Jan. 7, 1997
106th	Maj-17th	3	3	Jan. 6, 1999
107th	Maj-13th	4	4	Jan. 6, 2001
108th	Maj-12th	5	5	Jan. 28, 2003
109th	Maj-11th	6	6	Jan. 26, 2005
110th	Min-8th	7	7	Jan. 10, 2007

3rd SMALL BUSINESS
Dates: May 25, 1995-Jan. 3, 1997
Departure: Moved to Banking and Financial Services

| | | Terms in: | | Date of |
Cong.	Ranking	House	Comm.	Assignment
104th	MjA-23rd	1	1	May 25, 1995

4th BANKING AND FINANCIAL SERVICES, 105-106
FINANCIAL SERVICES, 107-110
Dates: Jan. 21, 1997-Jan. 3, 2009
Departure: Moved to Appropriations

| | | Terms in: | | Date of |
Cong.	Ranking	House	Comm.	Assignment
105th	Maj-29th	2	1	Jan. 21, 1997
106th	Maj-23rd	3	2	Jan. 6, 1999
107th	Maj-20th	4	3	Jan. 6, 2001
108th	Maj-15th	5	4	Jan. 28, 2003
109th	Maj-15th	6	5	Jan. 26, 2005
110th	Min-10th	7	6	Jan. 10, 2007

5th STANDARDS OF OFFICIAL CONDUCT
Dates: Oct. 10, 2001-Jan. 3, 2005
Departure: Left committee; no new assignment

| | | Terms in: | | Date of |
Cong.	Ranking	House	Comm.	Assignment
107th	MjR-2nd	4	1	Oct. 10, 2001
108th	Maj-5th	5	2	Feb. 11, 2003

6th APPROPRIATIONS
Dates: Jan. 9, 2009-date
Departure: Still serving in the 111th Congress

| | | Terms in: | | Date of |
Cong.	Ranking	House	Comm.	Assignment
111th	Min-22nd	8	1	Jan. 9, 2009

HOUSE SELECT AND SPECIAL COMMITTEES:

1st SELECT COMMITTEE TO INVESTIGATE THE VOTING
IRREGULARITIES OF AUGUST 2, 2007
Dates: Sep. 5, 2007- Sep. 25, 2008
Termination: House Report 885 (110-2) filed

Cong.	Ranking	Terms in: House	Comm.	Date of Assignment
110th	Min-2nd	7	1	Sep. 5, 2007

Robert E. Latta (R-Ohio)

Dates: Apr. 18, 1956
House: Dec. 11, 2007-date
Serving in the 111th Congress

H: Latta was elected to the 110th Congress by special election, Dec. 11, 2007, to fill the vacancy caused by the death of U.S. Representative Paul Gillmor (R-Ohio). Latta was seated Dec. 13, 2007, and assigned to committees.

HOUSE STANDING COMMITTEES:

1st AGRICULTURE
Dates: Dec. 18, 2007-Mar. 24, 2010
Departure: Resigned committee; moved to Energy and Commerce

Cong.	Ranking	Terms in: House	Comm.	Date of Assignment
110th	MnR-1st	1	1	Dec. 18, 2007
111th	Min-14th	2	2	Jan. 9, 2009

2nd SCIENCE AND TECHNOLOGY
Dates: Dec. 18, 2007-Dec. 18, 2007
Departure: Resigned committee; exceeded party ratio

Cong.	Ranking	Terms in: House	Comm.	Date of Assignment
110th	MnA-21st	1	1	Dec. 18, 2007

3rd TRANSPORTATION AND INFRASTRUCTURE
Dates: Feb. 26, 2008-Mar. 24, 2010
Departure: Resigned committee; moved to Energy and Commerce

Cong.	Ranking	Terms in: House	Comm.	Date of Assignment
110th	MnR-2nd	1	1	Feb. 26, 2008
111th	Min-26th	2	2	Jan. 9. 2009

4th BUDGET
Dates: Mar. 24, 2009-date
Departure: Still serving in the 111th Congress

Cong.	Ranking	Terms in: House	Comm.	Date of Assignment
111th	MnR-3rd	1	1	Mar. 24, 2009

5th ENERGY AND COMMERCE
Dates: Mar. 25, 2010-date
Departure: Still serving in the 111th Congress

Cong.	Ranking	Terms in: House	Comm.	Date of Assignment
111th	MnR-2nd	1	1	Mar. 25, 2010

Gregory H. Laughlin (R-Tex.)

Dates: Jan. 21, 1942
House: Jan. 3, 1989-Jan. 3, 1997
Left the House: Defeated for Republican re-nomination in 1996
Served as a Democrat: Jan. 3, 1989-June 26, 1995
Served as a Republican: June 26, 1995-Jan. 3, 1997

HOUSE STANDING COMMITTEES:

1st MERCHANT MARINE AND FISHERIES
Dates: Jan. 19, 1989-Jan. 3, 1995
Departure: Committee abolished; no new assignment

Cong.	Ranking	Terms in: House	Comm.	Date of Assignment
103rd	Maj-11th	3	3	Jan. 5, 1993

2nd PUBLIC WORKS AND TRANSPORTATION, 101-103
TRANSPORTATION AND INFRASTRUCTURE, 104
Dates: Jan. 19,1989-June 30, 1995
Departure: Assignment was vacated as Democrat and moved to Ways and Means as a Republican on July 10, 1995

Cong.	Ranking	Terms in: House	Comm.	Date of Assignment
103rd	Maj-16th	3	3	Jan. 5, 1993
104th	Min-13th	4	4	Jan. 4, 1995

3rd POST OFFICE AND CIVIL SERVICE
Dates: Jan. 27, 1993-Jan. 3, 1995
Departure: Committee abolished; no new assignment

Cong.	Ranking	Terms in: House	Comm.	Date of Assignment
103rd	Maj-12th	3	1	Jan. 27, 1993

4th WAYS AND MEANS
Dates: July 10, 1995-Jan. 3, 1997 as a Republican
Departure: Left the House; lost re-nomination

Cong.	Ranking	Terms in: House	Comm.	Date of Assignment
104th	MjA-22nd	4	1	July 10, 1995

HOUSE SELECT AND SPECIAL COMMITTEES:

1st PERMANENT SELECT INTELLIGENCE
Dates: Feb. 3, 1993-June 30, 1995
Departure: Seat vacated as a Democrat; moved to Ways and Means as a Republican

Cong.	Ranking	Terms in: House	Comm.	Date of Assignment
103rd	Maj-10th	3	1	Feb. 3, 1993
104th	Min-7th	4	2	Jan. 4, 1995

Frank R. Lautenberg (D-N.J.)

Dates: Jan. 23, 1924
Senate 1: Dec. 27, 1982-Jan. 3, 2001
Left the Senate 1: Retired in 2000 and returned
Senate 2: Jan. 3, 2003-date
Serving in the 111th Congress

S1: Lautenberg was appointed to the 97th Congress, Dec. 27, 1982, to fill the unexpired term caused by the resignation of U.S. Senator Harrison A. Williams (D-N.J.). Williams was initially replaced by Nicholas F. Brady (R-N.J.), an appointee who was not a candidate for election, and who had resigned. Lautenberg was not seated nor assigned to committees because the 97th Congress was not in session. Lautenberg had been elected to the 98th Congress.

SENATE STANDING COMMITTEES:

1st BANKING, HOUSING AND URBAN AFFAIRS
Dates: Jan. 3, 1983-Feb. 21, 1985
Departure: Moved to Appropriations and Budget

2nd COMMERCE, SCIENCE AND TRANSPORTATION
1st Dates: Jan. 3, 1983-Feb. 21, 1985
1st Departure: Moved to Appropriations and Budget
2nd Dates: Jan. 15, 2003-date
2nd Departure: Still serving in the 111th Congress

Cong.	Ranking	Years in: Senate	Comm.	Date of Assignment
108th	Min-11th	19 *2	1	Jan. 15, 2003
109th	Min-8th	21 *2	2	Jan. 6, 2005
110th	Maj-8th	23 *2	4	Jan. 12, 2007
111th	Maj-8th	25 *2	7	Jan. 21, 2009

3rd ENVIRONMENT AND PUBLIC WORKS
1st Dates: Feb. 9, 1984-Jan. 3, 2001
1st Departure: Left the Senate; retired
2nd Dates: Jan. 6, 2005-date
2nd Departure: Still serving in the 111th Congress

Cong.	Ranking	Years in: Senate	Comm.	Date of Assignment
103rd	Maj-4th	11 *1	9	Jan. 7, 1993
104th	Min-3rd	13 *1	10	Jan. 4, 1995
105th	Min-3rd	15 *1	13	Jan. 9, 1997
106th	Min-3rd	17 *1	15	Jan. 7, 1999
109th	Min-7th	21 *2	1	Jan. 6, 2005
110th	Maj-6th	23 *2	3	Jan. 12, 2007
111th	Maj-4th	25 *2	5	Jan. 21, 2009

4th APPROPRIATIONS
1st Dates: Feb. 21, 1985-Jan. 3, 2001
1st Departure: Left the Senate; retired
2nd Dates: Jan. 12, 2007-date
2nd Departure: Still serving in the 111th Congress

Cong.	Ranking	Years in: Senate	Comm.	Date of Assignment
103rd	Maj-9th	11 *1	8	Jan. 7, 1993
104th	Min-7th	13 *1	10	Jan. 4, 1995
105th	Min-6th	15 *1	12	Jan. 9, 1997
106th	Min-5th	17 *1	14	Jan. 7, 1999
110th	Maj-14th	23 *2	1	Jan. 12, 2007
111th	Maj-14th	25 *2	3	Jan. 21, 2009

5th BUDGET
1st Dates: Mar. 5, 1985-Jan. 3, 2001
1st Departure: Left the Senate; retired
2nd Dates: Jan. 12, 2007-Jan. 21, 2009
2nd Departure: Left committee; no new assignment

Cong.	Ranking	Years in: Senate	Comm.	Date of Assignment
103rd	Maj-6th	11 *1	9	Jan. 21, 1993
104th	Min-4th	13 *1	10	Jan. 6, 1995
105th	Min-RM	15 *1	12	Jan. 9, 1997
106th	Min-RM	17 *1	14	Jan. 7, 1999
110th	Maj-10th	23 *2	1	Jan. 12, 2007

6th SMALL BUSINESS
Dates: Jan. 21, 1993-Jan. 9, 1997
Departure: Moved to Select Intelligence

Cong.	Ranking	Years in: Senate	Comm.	Date of Assignment
103rd	Maj-10th	11	1	Jan. 21, 1993
104th	Min-9th	13	2	Jan. 6, 1995

7th GOVERNMENTAL AFFAIRS renamed Oct. 9, 2004
HOMELAND SECURITY AND GOVERNMENTAL AFFAIRS
Dates: Jan. 15, 2003-Jan. 12, 2007
Departure: Returned to Appropriations and Budget

Cong.	Ranking	Years in: Senate	Comm.	Date of Assignment
108th	Min-7th	19	1	Jan. 15, 2003
109th	Min-6th	21	2	Jan. 6, 2005

SENATE SELECT AND SPECIAL COMMITTEES:

1st SELECT INTELLIGENCE (Permanent)
Dates: Jan. 9, 1997-Jan. 3, 2001
Departure: Left the Senate; retired

Cong.	Ranking	Years in: Senate	Comm.	Date of Assignment
105th	Min-8th	15	1	Jan. 9, 1997
106th	Min-7th	17	2	Jan. 7, 1999

JOINT COMMITTEES:

1st JOINT DEFICIT REDUCTION (Temporary)
Senate Dates: Jan. 6, 1987-Sep. 29, 1987
Termination: Public Law 100-119 adjusted Gramm-Rudman-Hollings Act

---

Enrico A. (Rick) Lazio (R-N.Y.)

Dates: March 13, 1958
House: Jan. 3, 1993-Jan. 3, 2001
Left the House: Lost U.S. Senate election in 2000

HOUSE STANDING COMMITTEES:

1st BANKING, FINANCE AND URBAN AFFAIRS, 103
BANKING AND FINANCIAL SERVICES, 104-106
Dates: Jan. 5, 1993-Jan. 3, 2001
Departure: Left the House; lost Senate election

Cong.	Ranking	Terms in: House	Comm.	Date of Assignment
103rd	Min-15th	1	1	Jan. 5, 1993
104th	Maj-7th	2	2	Jan. 4, 1995
105th	Maj-6th	3	3	Jan. 7, 1997
106th	Maj-6th	4	4	Jan. 6, 1999

2nd BUDGET
Dates: Jan. 5, 1993-Jan. 3, 1997
Departure: Moved to Commerce

Cong.	Ranking	Terms in: House	Comm.	Date of Assignment
103rd	Min-13th	1	1	Jan. 5, 1993
104th	Maj-11th	2	2	Jan. 4, 1995

3rd COMMERCE
Dates: Jan. 7, 1997-Jan. 3, 2001
Departure: Left the House; lost Senate election

Cong.	Ranking	Terms in: House	Comm.	Date of Assignment
105th	Maj-25th	3	1	Jan. 7, 1997
106th	Maj-19th	4	2	Jan. 6, 1999

James A.S. Leach (R-Iowa)

Dates: Oct. 15, 1942
House: Jan. 3, 1977-Jan. 3, 2007
Left the House: Defeated for re-election in 2006

HOUSE STANDING COMMITTEES:

1st BANKING, FINANCE AND URBAN AFFAIRS, 95-103
BANKING AND FINANCIAL SERVICES, 104-106
FINANCIAL SERVICES, 107-109

Dates: Jan. 19, 1977-Jan. 3, 2007
Departure: Left the House; lost re-election

		Terms in:		Date of
Cong.	Ranking	House	Comm.	Assignment
103rd	Min-RM	9	9	Jan. 5, 1993
104th	Maj-Chr	10	10	Jan. 4, 1995
105th	Maj-Chr	11	11	Jan. 7, 1997
106th	Maj-Chr	12	12	Jan. 6, 1999
107th	Maj-2nd	13	13	Jan. 6, 2001
108th	Maj-2nd	14	14	Jan. 28, 2003
109th	Maj-2nd	15	15	Jan. 26, 2005

2nd POST OFFICE AND CIVIL SERVICE
Dates: Jan. 19, 1977-Jan. 3, 1981
Departure: Moved to Foreign Affairs

2nd FOREIGN AFFAIRS, 97-103
INTERNATIONAL RELATIONS, 104-109
Dates: Jan. 28, 1981-Jan. 3, 2007
Departure: Left the House; lost re-election

		Terms in:		Date of
Cong.	Ranking	House	Comm.	Assignment
103rd	Min-3rd	9	7	Jan. 5, 1993
104th	Maj-3rd	10	8	Jan. 4, 1995
105th	Maj-3rd	11	9	Jan. 7, 1997
106th	Maj-3rd	12	10	Jan. 6, 1999
107th	Maj-3rd	13	11	Jan. 6, 2001
108th	Maj-2nd	14	12	Jan. 28, 2003
109th	Maj-2nd	15	13	Jan. 26, 2005

HOUSE SELECT AND SPECIAL COMMITTEES:

1st SELECT COMMITTEES II (Patterson)
Dates: Mar. 28, 1979-Apr. 1, 1980
Departure: House Report 866 (96-2) filed

Patrick J. Leahy (D-Vt.)

Dates: March 31, 1940-
Senate: Jan. 3, 1975-date
Serving in the 111th Congress

SENATE STANDING COMMITTEES:

1st AGRICULTURE AND FORESTRY reorganized Feb. 11, 1977
AGRICULTURE, NUTRITION AND FORESTRY
Dates: Jan. 17, 1975-date
Departure: Still serving in the 111th Congress

		Years in:		Date of
Cong.	Ranking	Senate	Comm.	Assignment
103rd	Maj-Chr	19	18	Jan. 7, 1993
104th	Min-RM	21	20	Jan. 4, 1995
105th	Min-2nd	23	22	Jan. 9, 1997
106th	Min-2nd	25	24	Jan. 7, 1999
107th	Min-2nd	27	27	Jan. 25, 2001
+107th	Maj-2nd	27	27	June 6, 2001
108th	Min-2nd	29	28	Jan. 15, 2003
109th	Min-2nd	31	30	Jan. 6, 2005
110th	Maj-2nd	33	32	Jan. 12, 2007
111th	Maj-2nd	35	34	Jan. 21, 2009

2nd ARMED SERVICES
Dates: Jan. 17, 1975-Feb. 11, 1977
Departure: Moved to Appropriations

3rd POST OFFICE AND CIVIL SERVICE
Dates: Sep. 19, 1975-Feb. 11, 1977
Departure: Moved to Appropriations

4th APPROPRIATIONS
Dates: Feb. 11, 1977-date
Departure: Still serving in the 111th Congress

		Years in:		Date of
Cong.	Ranking	Senate	Comm.	Assignment
103rd	Maj-5th	19	16	Jan. 7, 1993
104th	Min-5th	21	18	Jan. 4, 1995
105th	Min-4th	23	20	Jan. 9, 1997
106th	Min-4th	25	22	Jan. 7, 1999
107th	Min-4th	27	24	Jan. 25, 2001
+107th	Maj-4th	27	25	June 6, 2001
108th	Min-4th	29	26	Jan. 15, 2003
109th	Min-3rd	31	28	Jan. 6, 2005
110th	Maj-3rd	33	30	Jan. 12, 2007
111th	Maj-3rd	35	32	Jan. 21, 2009

5th JUDICIARY
Dates: Jan. 23, 1979-date
Ch2: Replaced Orrin Hatch (R-Utah) on June 6, 2001, following Senate party control shift
Departure: Still serving in 111th Congress

		Years in:		Date of
Cong.	Ranking	Senate	Comm.	Assignment
103rd	Maj-5th	19	14	Jan. 7, 1993
104th	Min-3rd	21	16	Jan. 4, 1995
105th	Min-RM	23	18	Jan. 9, 1997
106th	Min-RM	25	20	Jan. 7, 1999
=107th	Maj-ChT	27	22	Jan. 3, 2001
107th	Min-RM1	27	23	Jan. 25, 2001
+107th	Maj-Ch2	27	23	June 6, 2001
108th	Min-RM	29	24	Jan. 15, 2003
109th	Min-RM	31	26	Jan. 6, 2005
110th	Maj-Chr	33	28	Jan. 12, 2007
111th	Maj-Chr	35	30	Jan. 21, 2009

SENATE SELECT AND SPECIAL COMMITTEES:

1st NUTRITION AND HUMAN NEEDS
Dates: Feb. 11, 1977-Dec. 31, 1977
Termination: S. Res. 4 (95-1) transferred authority to Agriculture, Nutrition and Forestry

2nd SELECT INTELLIGENCE (Permanent)
Dates: June 6, 1979-Feb. 17, 1987
Departure: Left committee; no new assignment

3rd FOREIGN GOVERNMENT REPRESENTATION
Dates: July 25, 1980-Oct. 2, 1980
Termination: Senate Report 1015 (96-2) filed

4th UNDERCOVER ACTIVITIES OF COMPONENTS OF THE DEPARTMENT OF JUSTICE
Dates: Mar. 29, 1982-Dec. 15, 1982
Termination: Senate Report 682 (97-2) filed

5th SECURITY AND COOPERATION IN EUROPE
Dates: Jan. 31, 1984-Mar. 27, 1985
Termination: Public Law 99-7

6th JUDGE ALCEE L. HASTINGS IMPEACHMENT
Dates: Mar. 16, 1989-Aug. 3, 1989
Termination: Senate Hearing 101-194, Parts 1-2A

Barbara Lee (D-Cal.)

Dates: July 16, 1946
House: April 7, 1998-date
Serving in the 111th Congress

H: Lee was elected by special election April 7, 1998, to fill the vacancy caused by the resignation of U.S. Representative Ronald Dellums (D-Cal.). Lee was seated April 21, 1998, and assigned to committees.

HOUSE STANDING COMMITTEES:

1st BANKING AND FINANCIAL SERVICES, 106
FINANCIAL SERVICES, 107-110
1st Dates: Apr. 29, 1998-Nov. 1, 1999
1st Departure: Left committee; returned on Feb. 1, 2000
2nd Dates: Feb. 1, 2000-Jan. 3, 2007
2nd Departure: Moved to Appropriations

Cong.	Ranking	Terms in: House	Comm.	Date of Assignment
105th	MnR-3rd	1 *1	1	Apr. 29, 1998
106th	Min-19th	2 *1	2	Jan. 6, 1999
106th	MnR-3rd	2 *2	1	Feb. 1, 2000
107th	Min-17th	3 *2	2	Jan. 31, 2001
108th	Min-14th	4 *2	3	Jan. 28, 2003
109th	Min-14th	5 *2	4	Jan. 26, 2005

2nd SCIENCE
Dates: Apr. 29, 1998-Feb. 3, 1999
Departure: Resigned committee; moved to International Relations

Cong.	Ranking	Terms in: House	Comm.	Date of Assignment
105th	MnR-3rd	1	1	Apr. 29, 1998
106th	Min-18th	2	2	Jan. 6, 1999

3rd INTERNATIONAL RELATIONS, 106-109
FOREIGN AFFAIRS, 110-111
1st Dates: Jan. 19, 1999-Jan. 3, 2007
1st Departure: Moved to Appropriations
2nd Dates: Feb. 26, 2008-date
2nd Departure: Still serving in the 111th Congress

Cong.	Ranking	Terms in: House	Comm.	Date of Assignment
106th	Min-21st	2 *1	1	Jan. 19, 1999
107th	Min-17th	3 *1	2	Jan. 31, 2001
108th	Min-13th	4 *1	3	Jan. 28, 2003
109th	Min-13th	5 *1	4	Jan. 26, 2005
110th	MjR-1st	6 *2	1	Feb. 26, 2008
111th	Maj-19th	7 *2	2	Jan. 7, 2009

4th APPROPRIATIONS
Dates: Jan. 4, 2007-date
Departure: Still serving in the 111th Congress

Cong.	Ranking	Terms in: House	Comm.	Date of Assignment
110th	Maj-27th	6	1	Jan. 4, 2007
111th	Maj-26th	7	2	Jan. 7, 2009

Christopher J. Lee (R-N.Y.)

Dates: April 1, 1964
House: Jan. 3, 2009-date
Serving in the 111th Congress

HOUSE STANDING COMMITTEES:

1st FINANCIAL SERVICES
Dates: Jan. 9, 2009-date
Departure: Still serving in the 111th Congress

Cong.	Ranking	Terms in: House	Comm.	Date of Assignment
111th	Min-27th	1	1	Jan. 9, 2009

Richard H. Lehman (D-Cal.)

Dates: July 20, 1948
House: Jan. 3, 1983-Jan. 3, 1995
Left the House: Defeated for re-election in 1994

HOUSE STANDING COMMITTEES:

1st BANKING, FINANCE AND URBAN AFFAIRS
Dates: Jan. 6, 1983-Jan. 3, 1991
Departure: Moved to Energy and Commerce

2nd INTERIOR AND INSULAR AFFAIRS, 98-102
NATURAL RESOURCES, 103
Dates: Jan. 6, 1983-Jan. 3, 1995
Departure: Left the House; lost re-election

Cong.	Ranking	Terms in: House	Comm.	Date of Assignment
103rd	Maj-10th	6	6	Jan. 5, 1993

3rd ENERGY AND COMMERCE
Dates: Jan. 24, 1991-Jan. 3, 1995
Departure: Left the House; lost re-election

Cong.	Ranking	Terms in: House	Comm.	Date of Assignment
103rd	Maj-20th	6	2	Jan. 5, 1993

George S. LeMieux (R-Fla.)

Dates: May 21, 1969
House: Sept. 10, 2009-date
Still serving in the 111th Congress

SENATE STANDING COMMITTEES:

1st ARMED SERVICES
Dates: Sept. 22, 2009-date
Departure: Still serving in the 111th Congress

Cong.	Ranking	Years in: Senate	Comm.	Date of Assignment
111th	MnR-1st	1	1	Sept. 22, 2009

2nd COMMERCE, SCIENCE AND TRANSPORTATION
Dates: Sept. 22, 2009-date
Departure: Still serving in the 111th Congress

Cong.	Ranking	Years in: Senate	Comm.	Date of Assignment
111th	MnR-1st	1	1	Sept. 22, 2009

SENATE SELECT AND SPECIAL COMMITTEES:

1st SPECIAL AGING
Dates: Sept. 22, 2009-date
Departure: Still serving in the 111th Congress

Cong.	Ranking	Years in: Senate	Comm.	Date of Assignment
111th	MnR-1st	1	1	Sept. 22, 2009

Carl M. Levin (D-Mich.)

Dates: June 28, 1934
Senate: Jan. 3, 1979-date
Serving in the 111th Congress

SENATE STANDING COMMITTEES:

1st ARMED SERVICES
Dates: Jan. 23, 1979-date
Ch2: Replaced John W. Warner (R-Va.) on June 6, 2001, following Senate party control shift
Departure: Still serving in the 111th Congress

Cong.	Ranking	Years in: Senate	Comm.	Date of Assignment
103rd	Maj-3rd	15	14	Jan. 7, 1993
104th	Min-3rd	17	16	Jan. 4, 1995
105th	Min-RM	19	18	Jan. 9, 1997
106th	Min-RM	21	20	Jan. 7, 1999
=107th	Maj-ChT	23	22	Jan. 3, 2001
107th	Min-RM1	23	23	Jan. 25, 2001
+107th	Maj-Ch2	23	23	June 6, 2001
108th	Min-RM	25	24	Jan. 15, 2003
109th	Min-RM	27	26	Jan. 6, 2005
110th	Maj-Chr	29	28	Jan. 12, 2007
111th	Maj-Chr	31	30	Jan. 21, 2009

2nd GOVERNMENTAL AFFAIRS renamed Oct. 9, 2004
HOMELAND SECURITY AND GOVERNMENTAL AFFAIRS
Dates: Jan. 23, 1979-date
Departure: Still serving in the 111th Congress

Cong.	Ranking	Years in: Senate	Comm.	Date of Assignment
103rd	Maj-3rd	15	14	Jan. 7, 1993
104th	Min-3rd	17	16	Jan. 4, 1995
105th	Min-2nd	19	18	Jan. 9, 1997
106th	Min-2nd	21	20	Jan. 7, 1999
107th	Min-2nd	23	23	Jan. 25, 2001
+107th	Maj-2nd	23	23	June 6, 2001
108th	Min-2nd	25	24	Jan. 15, 2003
109th	Min-2nd	27	26	Jan. 6, 2005
110th	Maj-2nd	29	28	Jan. 12, 2007
111th	Maj-2nd	31	30	Jan. 21, 2009

3rd SMALL BUSINESS renamed June 29, 2001
SMALL BUSINESS AND ENTREPRENEURSHIP
Dates: Mar. 25, 1981-date
Departure: Still serving in the 111th Congress

Cong.	Ranking	Years in: Senate	Comm.	Date of Assignment
103rd	Maj-3rd	15	14	Jan. 21, 1993
104th	Min-3rd	17	16	Jan. 6, 1995
105th	Min-3rd	19	18	Jan. 9, 1997
106th	Min-2nd	21	20	Jan. 7, 1999
107th	Min-2nd	23	23	Jan. 25, 2001
+107th	Maj-2nd	23	23	June 6, 2001
108th	Min-2nd	25	24	Jan. 15, 2003
109th	Min-2nd	27	26	Jan. 6, 2005
110th	Maj-2nd	29	28	Jan. 12, 2007
111th	Maj-3rd	31	30	Jan. 21, 2009

4th ENERGY AND NATURAL RESOURCES
Dates: Feb. 9, 1984-Feb. 21, 1985
Departure: Left committee; no new assignment

SENATE SELECT AND SPECIAL COMMITTEES:

1st SELECT SMALL BUSINESS
Dates: Jan. 23, 1979-Mar. 25, 1981
Departure: Continued on reorganized standing committee

2nd SELECT INTELLIGENCE (Permanent)
Dates: Jan. 9, 1997-Jan. 21, 2007
Departure: *Ex officio* as Chair of Armed Services

Cong.	Ranking	Years in: Senate	Comm.	Date of Assignment
105th	Min-9th	19	1	Jan. 9, 1997
106th	Min-8th	21	2	Jan. 7, 1999
107th	Min-2nd	23	5	Jan. 25, 2001
+107th	Maj-2nd	23	5	June 6, 2001
108th	Min-2nd	25	7	Jan. 15, 2003
109th	Min-2nd	27	8	Jan. 6, 2005
110th	Maj-ExO	29	11	Jan. 12, 2007
111th	Maj-ExO	31	13	Jan. 21, 2009

Sander M. Levin (D-Mich.)

Dates: Sept. 6, 1931
House: Jan. 3, 1983-date
Serving in the 111th Congress

HOUSE STANDING COMMITTEES:

1st BANKING FINANCE AND URBAN AFFAIRS
Dates: Jan. 6, 1983-Jan. 3, 1987
Departure: Moved to Ways and Means

2nd GOVERNMENT OPERATIONS
Dates: Jan. 6, 1983-Jan. 3, 1987
Departure: Moved to Ways and Means

3rd WAYS AND MEANS
Dates: Jan. 6, 1987-date
Departure: Still serving in the 111th Congress
ChA: Named Acting Chair to replace Charles Rangel (D-N.Y.) Mar. 4, 2010

Cong.	Ranking	Terms in: House	Comm.	Date of Assignment
103rd	Maj-12th	6	4	Jan. 5, 1993
104th	Min-9th	7	5	Jan. 4, 1995
105th	Min-6th	8	6	Jan. 7, 1997
106th	Min-5th	9	7	Jan. 6, 1999
107th	Min-5th	10	8	Jan. 31, 2001
108th	Min-4th	11	9	Jan. 28, 2003
109th	Min-3rd	12	10	Jan. 26, 2005
110th	Maj-3rd	13	11	Jan. 4, 2007
111th	Maj-3rd	14	12	Jan. 7, 2009
=111th	Maj-ChA	14	12	Mar. 4, 2010

4th DISTRICT OF COLUMBIA
Dates: Apr. 24, 1991-Feb. 22, 1993
Departure: Resigned committee; no new assignment

		Terms in:		Date of
Cong.	Ranking	House	Comm.	Assignment
103rd	Maj-5th	6	2	Feb. 18, 1993

5th BUDGET
Dates: Apr. 22, 1996-Jan. 3, 1997
Departure: Left committee; no new assignment

		Terms in:		Date of
Cong.	Ranking	House	Comm.	Assignment
104th	MnR-1st	7	1	Apr. 22, 1996

HOUSE SELECT AND SPECIAL COMMITTEES:

1st SELECT CHILDREN, YOUTH AND FAMILIES (Temporary)
Dates: Feb. 2, 1989-Jan. 3, 1993
Termination: Committee not renewed in 1993

JOINT COMMITTEES:

1st JOINT TAXATION
House Dates: Jan. 17, 2007-date
Departure: Still serving in the 111th Congress

		Terms in:		Date of
Cong.	Ranking	House	Comm.	Assignment
110th	Maj-3rd	13	1	Jan. 17, 2007
111th	Maj-3rd	14	2	Jan. 12, 2009

David A. Levy (R-N.Y.)

Dates: Dec. 18, 1953
House: Jan. 3, 1993-Jan. 3, 1995
Left the House: Defeated for re-nomination in 1994

HOUSE STANDING COMMITTEES:

1st FOREIGN AFFAIRS
Dates: Jan. 5, 1993-Jan. 3, 1995
Departure: Left the House; lost re-nomination

		Terms in:		Date of
Cong.	Ranking	House	Comm.	Assignment
103rd	Min-15th	1	1	Jan. 5, 1993

2nd PUBLIC WORKS AND TRANSPORTATION
Dates: Jan. 5, 1993-Jan. 3, 1995
Departure: Left the House; lost re-nomination

		Terms in:		Date of
Cong.	Ranking	House	Comm.	Assignment
103rd	Min-17th	1	1	Jan. 5, 1993

Charles J. (Jerry) Lewis (R-Cal.)

Dates: Oct. 21, 1934
House: Jan. 3, 1979-date
Serving in the 111th Congress

HOUSE STANDING COMMITTEES:

1st HOUSE ADMINISTRATION
Dates: Jan. 24, 1979-Jan. 3, 1981
Departure: Moved to Appropriations

2nd PUBLIC WORKS AND TRANSPORTATION
Dates: Jan. 24, 1979-Jan. 3, 1981
Departure: Moved to Appropriations

3rd APPROPRIATIONS
Dates: Jan. 28, 1981-date
Departure: Still serving in the 111th Congress

		Terms in:		Date of
Cong.	Ranking	House	Comm.	Assignment
103rd	Min-6th	8	7	Jan. 5, 1993
104th	Maj-6th	9	8	Jan. 4, 1995
105th	Maj-5th	10	9	Jan. 7, 1997
106th	Maj-3rd	11	10	Jan. 6, 1999
107th	Maj-3rd	12	11	Jan. 6, 2001
108th	Maj-3rd	13	12	Jan. 28, 2003
109th	Maj-Chr	14	13	Jan. 6, 2005
110th	Min-RM	15	14	Jan. 4, 2007
111th	Min-RM	16	15	Jan. 6, 2009

HOUSE SELECT AND SPECIAL COMMITTEES:

1st OUTER CONTINENTAL SHELF
Dates: Apr. 9, 1979-July 31, 1980
Termination: House Report 1214 (96-2) filed

2nd PERMANENT SELECT INTELLIGENCE
Dates: Feb. 3, 1993-Jan. 3, 2001
Departure: Left committee; no new assignment

		Terms in:		Date of
Cong.	Ranking	House	Comm.	Assignment
103rd	Min-7th	8	1	Feb. 3, 1993
104th	Maj-5th	9	2	Jan. 4, 1995
105th	Maj-3rd	10	3	Feb. 10, 1997
106th	Maj-2nd	11	4	Jan. 19, 1999

John R. Lewis (D-Ga.)

Dates: Feb. 21, 1940
House: Jan. 3, 1987-date
Serving in the 111th Congress

HOUSE STANDING COMMITTEES:

1st PUBLIC WORKS AND TRANSPORTATION
Dates: Jan. 6, 1987-Jan. 3, 1993
Departure: Moved to Ways and Means and District of Columbia

2nd PUBLIC WORKS AND TRANSPORTATION
Dates: Jan. 22, 1987-Jan. 3, 1993
Departure: Moved to Ways and Means and District of Columbia

3rd DISTRICT OF COLUMBIA
Dates: Feb. 18, 1993-Jan. 3, 1995
Departure: Committee abolished; no new assignment

		Terms in:		Date of
Cong.	Ranking	House	Comm.	Assignment
103rd	Maj-6th	4	1	Feb. 18, 1993

4th WAYS AND MEANS
Dates: Jan. 5, 1993-date
Departure: Still serving in the 111th Congress

		Terms in:		Date of
Cong.	Ranking	House	Comm.	Assignment
103rd	Maj-16th	4	1	Jan. 5, 1993

Cong.	Ranking	House	Comm.	Date of Assignment
104th	Min-13th	5	2	Jan. 4, 1995
105th	Min-10th	6	3	Jan. 7, 1997
106th	Min-9th	7	4	Jan. 6, 1999
107th	Min-9th	8	5	Jan. 31, 2001
108th	Min-8th	9	6	Jan. 28, 2003
109th	Min-6th	10	7	Jan. 26, 2005
110th	Maj-5th	11	8	Jan. 4, 2007
111th	Maj-5th	12	9	Jan. 7, 2009

5th BUDGET
Dates: Jan. 28, 2003-Jan. 3, 2005
Departure: Left committee; no new assignment

		Terms in:		Date of
Cong.	Ranking	House	Comm.	Assignment
108th	Min-6th	9	1	Jan. 28, 2003

HOUSE SELECT AND SPECIAL COMMITTEES:

1st SELECT AGING (Permanent)
Dates: Aug. 4, 1989-Jan. 3, 1993
Termination: Committee not renewed in 1993

Ron Lewis (R-Ky.)

Dates: Sept. 14, 1946
House: May 26, 1994-Jan. 3, 2009
Left the House: Retired in 2008

H: Lewis was elected to the 103rd Congress by special election May 26, 1994, to fill the vacancy caused by the death of U.S. Representative William Natcher (D-Ky.). Lewis was seated May 26, 1994, and assigned to committees.

HOUSE STANDING COMMITTEES:

1st AGRICULTURE
Dates: June 15, 1994-Jan. 3, 1999
Departure: Moved to Ways and Means

		Terms in:		Date of
Cong.	Ranking	House	Comm.	Assignment
103rd	MnA-21st	1	1	June 15, 1994
104th	Maj-16th	2	2	Jan. 4, 1995
105th	Maj-13th	3	3	Jan. 7, 1997

2nd VETERANS' AFFAIRS
Dates: June 15, 1994-Jan. 3, 1995
Departure: Moved to National Security

		Terms in:		Date of
Cong.	Ranking	House	Comm.	Assignment
103rd	MnA-15th	1	1	June 15, 1994

3rd NATIONAL SECURITY
Dates: Jan. 4, 1995-Jan. 3, 1999
Departure: Moved to Ways and Means

		Terms in:		Date of
Cong.	Ranking	House	Comm.	Assignment
104th	Maj-20th	2	1	Jan. 4, 1995
105th	Maj-17th	3	2	Jan. 7, 1997

4th GOVERNMENT REFORM
1st Dates: May 13, 1998-Jan. 3, 1999
1st Departure: Moved to Ways and Means
2nd Dates: Jan. 6, 2001-Jan. 3, 2005
2nd Departure: Left committee; no new assignment

		Terms in:		Date of
Cong.	Ranking	House	Comm.	Assignment
105th	MjR-4th	3 *1	1	May 13, 1998
107th	Maj-17th	5 *2	1	Jan. 6, 2001
108th	Maj-10th	6 *2	2	Jan. 28, 2003

5th WAYS AND MEANS
Dates: Jan. 6, 1999-Jan. 3, 2009
Departure: Left the House; retired

		Terms in:		Date of
Cong.	Ranking	House	Comm.	Assignment
106th	Maj-22nd	4	1	Jan. 6, 1999
107th	Maj-21st	5	2	Jan. 6, 2001
108th	Maj-20th	6	3	Jan. 28, 2003
109th	Maj-15th	7	4	Jan. 6, 2005
110th	Min-9th	8	5	Jan. 4, 2007

Thomas F. Lewis (R-Fla.)

Dates: Oct. 26, 1924
House: Jan. 3, 1983-Jan. 3, 1995
Left the House: Retired in 1994

HOUSE STANDING COMMITTEES:

1st GOVERNMENT OPERATIONS
Dates: Jan. 6, 1983-Jan. 3, 1985
Departure: Moved to Agriculture

2nd SCIENCE AND TECHNOLOGY, 98-99
SCIENCE, SPACE AND TECHNOLOGY, 100-103
Dates: Jan. 6, 1983-Jan. 3, 1995
Departure: Left the House; retired

		Terms in:		Date of
Cong.	Ranking	House	Comm.	Assignment
103rd	Min-4th	6	6	Jan. 5, 1993

3rd AGRICULTURE
Dates: Jan. 30, 1985-Jan. 3, 1995
Departure: Left the House; retired

		Terms in:		Date of
Cong.	Ranking	House	Comm.	Assignment
103rd	Min-4th	6	5	Jan. 5, 1993

HOUSE SELECT AND SPECIAL COMMITTEES:

1st SELECT NARCOTICS ABUSE AND CONTROL (Temporary)
1st Dates: Feb. 22, 1983-Jan. 3, 1985
1st Departure: Moved to Agriculture
2nd Dates: June 25, 1987-Jan. 3, 1993
Termination: Committee not renewed in 1993

Joseph I. Lieberman (D-Conn.)

Dates: Feb. 24, 1942
Senate: Jan. 3, 1989-date
Left: Serving in the 111th Congress
Served as a Democrat: 1989-2007
Served as an Independent Democrat: 2007-date

SENATE STANDING COMMITTEES:

1st ENVIRONMENT AND PUBLIC WORKS
Dates: Feb. 2, 1989-Jan. 21, 2009
Departure: Left committee; no new assignment

Cong.	Ranking	Years in: Senate	Comm.	Date of Assignment
103rd	Maj-7th	5	4	Jan. 7, 1993
104th	Min-6th	7	6	Jan. 4, 1995
105th	Min-6th	9	8	Jan. 9, 1997
106th	Min-6th	11	10	Jan. 7, 1999
107th	Min-4th	13	12	Jan. 25, 2001
+107th	Maj-5th	13	13	July 10, 2001
108th	Min-5th	15	14	Jan. 15, 2003
109th	Min-3rd	17	16	Jan. 6, 2005
110th	Maj-3rd	19	18	Jan. 12, 2007

2nd GOVERNMENTAL AFFAIRS renamed Oct. 9, 2004
HOMELAND SECURITY AND GOVERNMENTAL AFFAIRS
Dates: Feb. 2, 1989-date
Ch2: Replaced Craig L. Thomas (R-Wyo.) on June 6, 2001, following Senate party control shift
Departure: Still serving in the 111th Congress

Cong.	Ranking	Years in: Senate	Comm.	Date of Assignment
103rd	Maj-6th	5	4	Jan. 7, 1993
104th	Min-5th	7	6	Jan. 4, 1995
105th	Min-3rd	9	8	Jan. 9, 1997
106th	Min-RM	11	10	Jan. 7, 1999
=107th	Maj-ChT	13	12	Jan. 3, 2001
107th	Min-RM1	13	12	Jan. 25, 2001
+107th	Maj-Ch2	13	13	June 6, 2001
108th	Min-RM	15	14	Jan. 15, 2003
109th	Min-RM	17	16	Jan. 6, 2005
110th	Maj-Chr	19	18	Jan. 12, 2007
111th	Maj-Chr	21	20	Jan. 21, 2009

3rd SMALL BUSINESS renamed Jan. 29, 2001
SMALL BUSINESS AND ENTREPRENEURSHIP
Dates: Feb. 2, 1989-date
Departure: Still serving in the 111th Congress

Cong.	Ranking	Years in: Senate	Comm.	Date of Assignment
103rd	Maj-6th	5	4	Jan. 21, 1993
104th	Min-6th	7	6	Jan. 6, 1995
105th	Min-5th	9	8	Jan. 9, 1997
106th	Min-4th	11	10	Jan. 7, 1999
107th	Min-4th	13	12	Jan. 25, 2001
+107th	Maj-4th	13	13	June 6, 2001
108th	Min-4th	15	14	Jan. 15, 2003
109th	Min-4th	17	16	Jan. 6, 2005
110th	Maj-4th	19	18	Jan. 12, 2007
111th	Maj-5th	21	20	Jan. 21, 2009

4th ARMED SERVICES
Dates: Jan. 7, 1993-date
Departure: Still serving in the 111th Congress

Cong.	Ranking	Years in: Senate	Comm.	Date of Assignment
103rd	Maj-11th	5	1	Jan. 7, 1993
104th	Min-9th	7	2	Jan. 4, 1995
105th	Min-7th	9	5	Jan. 9, 1997
106th	Min-6th	11	7	Jan. 7, 1999
107th	Min-4th	13	9	Jan. 25, 2001
+107th	Maj-4th	13	9	June 6, 2001
108th	Min-4th	15	11	Jan. 15, 2003
109th	Min-4th	17	12	Jan. 6, 2005
110th	Maj-4th	19	15	Jan. 12, 2007
111th	Maj-4th	21	17	Jan. 21, 2009

SENATE SELECT AND SPECIAL COMMITTEES:

1st JUDGE ALCEE L. HASTINGS IMPEACHMENT
Dates: Mar. 16, 1989-Aug. 3, 1989
Termination: Senate Hearing 101-194, Parts 1-2A

Jim Ross Lightfoot (R-Iowa)

Dates: Sept. 27, 1938
House: Jan. 3, 1985-Jan. 3, 1997
Left the House: Lost U.S. Senate election in 1996

HOUSE STANDING COMMITTEES:

1st GOVERNMENT OPERATIONS
Dates: Jan. 30, 1985-Jan. 3, 1989
Departure: Moved to Interior and Insular Affairs

2nd PUBLIC WORKS AND TRANSPORTATION
Dates: Jan. 30, 1985-Feb. 28, 1991
Departure: Resigned committee; moved to Appropriations

3rd INTERIOR AND INSULAR AFFAIRS
Dates: Jan. 20, 1989-Feb. 28, 1991
Departure: Resigned committee; moved to Appropriations

4th APPROPRIATIONS
Dates: Feb. 28, 1991-Jan. 3, 1997
Departure: Left the House; lost Senate election

Cong.	Ranking	Terms in: House	Comm.	Date of Assignment
103rd	Min-15th	5	2	Jan. 5, 1993
104th	Maj-14th	6	3	Jan. 4, 1995

HOUSE SELECT AND SPECIAL COMMITTEES:

1st SELECT AGING (Permanent)
Dates: Feb. 21, 1985-Jan. 3, 1993
Termination: Committee not renewed in 1993

Blanche Lambert Lincoln

(D-Ark.)

Dates: Sept. 30, 1960
House: Jan. 3, 1993-Jan. 3, 1997
Left the House: Elected to U.S. Senate in 1998
Senate: Jan. 3, 1999-date
Serving in the 111th Congress
Served as Blanche Lambert in the 103rd Congress

HOUSE STANDING COMMITTEES:

1st ENERGY AND COMMERCE, 103
COMMERCE, 104
Dates: Jan. 5, 1993-Jan. 3, 1997
Departure: Left the House for a later Senate contest

Cong.	Ranking	Terms in: House	Terms in: Comm.	Date of Assignment
103rd	Maj-27th	1	1	Jan. 5, 1993
104th	Min-14th	2	2	Jan. 4, 1995

2nd MERCHANT MARINE AND FISHERIES
Dates: Jan. 5, 1993-Jan. 3, 1995
Departure: Committee abolished; no new assignment

Cong.	Ranking	Terms in: House	Terms in: Comm.	Date of Assignment
103rd	Maj-21st	1	1	Jan. 5, 1993

3rd AGRICULTURE
Dates: Feb. 4, 1993-Jan. 3, 1995
Departure: Left committee; no new assignment

Cong.	Ranking	Terms in: House	Terms in: Comm.	Date of Assignment
103rd	MjR-2nd	1	1	Feb. 4, 1993

SENATE STANDING COMMITTEES:

1st AGRICULTURE, NUTRITION AND FORESTRY
Dates: Jan. 7, 1999-date
Departure: Still serving in the 111th Congress

Cong.	Ranking	Years in: Senate	Years in: Comm.	Date of Assignment
106th	Min-8th	1	1	Jan. 7, 1999
107th	Min-6th	3	3	Jan. 25, 2001
+107th	Maj-6th	3	3	June 6, 2001
108th	Min-6th	5	5	Jan. 15, 2003
109th	Min-5th	7	6	Jan. 6, 2005
110th	Maj-5th	9	9	Jan. 12, 2007
111th	Maj-5th	11	11	Jan. 21, 2009

2nd ENERGY AND NATURAL RESOURCES
1st Dates: Jan. 7, 1999-Jan. 25, 2001
1st Departure: Moved to Finance and Select Ethics
2nd Dates: Jan. 12, 2007-date
2nd Departure: Still serving in the 111th Congress

Cong.	Ranking	Years in: Senate	Years in: Comm.	Date of Assignment
106th	Min-9th	1 *1	1	Jan. 7, 1999
110th	Maj-10th	9 *2	1	Jan. 12, 2007
111th	Maj-8th	11 *2	3	Jan. 21, 2009

3rd FINANCE
Dates: Jan. 25, 2001-date
Departure: Still serving in the 111th Congress

Cong.	Ranking	Years in: Senate	Years in: Comm.	Date of Assignment
107th	Min-10th	3	1	Jan. 25, 2001
+107th	Maj-11th	3	1	July 10, 2001
108th	Min-10th	5	2	Jan. 15, 2003
109th	Min-7th	7	4	Jan. 6, 2005
110th	Maj-6th	9	6	Jan. 12, 2007
111th	Maj-6th	11	8	Jan. 21, 2009

SENATE SELECT AND SPECIAL COMMITTEES:

1st SPECIAL AGING (Permanent)
Dates: Jan. 7, 1999-date
Departure: Still serving in the 111th Congress

Cong.	Ranking	Years in: Senate	Years in: Comm.	Date of Assignment
106th	Min-8th	1	1	Jan. 7, 1999
107th	Min-7th	3	3	Jan. 25, 2001
+107th	Maj-8th	3	3	July 10, 2001
108th	Min-7th	5	5	Jan. 15, 2003
109th	Min-5th	7	6	Jan. 6, 2005
110th	Maj-3rd	9	9	Jan. 12, 2007
111th	Maj-3rd	11	11	Jan. 21, 2009

2nd SELECT ETHICS (Permanent)
Dates: Jan. 25, 2001-Jan. 6, 2005
Departure: Left committee; no new assignment

Cong.	Ranking	Years in: Senate	Years in: Comm.	Date of Assignment
107th	Min-3rd	3	1	Jan. 25, 2001
+107th	Maj-3rd	3	1	June 6, 2001
108th	Min-3rd	5	2	Jan. 15, 2003

John E. Linder (R-Ga.)

Dates: Sept. 9, 1942
House: Jan. 3, 1997-date
Serving in the 111th Congress

HOUSE STANDING COMMITTEES:

1st BANKING, FINANCE AND URBAN AFFAIRS
Dates: Jan. 5, 1993-Jan. 3, 1995
Departure: Moved to Rules

Cong.	Ranking	Terms in: House	Terms in: Comm.	Date of Assignment
103rd	Min-13th	1	1	Jan. 5, 1993

2nd SCIENCE, SPACE AND TECHNOLOGY
Dates: Jan. 5, 1993-Jan. 3, 1995
Departure: Moved to Rules

Cong.	Ranking	Terms in: House	Terms in: Comm.	Date of Assignment
103rd	Min-18th	1	1	Jan. 5, 1993

3rd VETERANS' AFFAIRS
Dates: Jan. 5, 1993-Jan. 3, 1995
Departure: Moved to Rules

Cong.	Ranking	Terms in: House	Terms in: Comm.	Date of Assignment
103rd	Min-12th	1	1	Jan. 5, 1993

4th RULES
Dates: Jan. 4, 1995-Jan. 3, 2005
Departure: Moved to Ways and Means

Cong.	Ranking	Terms in: House	Terms in: Comm.	Date of Assignment
104th	Maj-5th	2	1	Jan. 4, 1995
105th	Maj-4th	3	2	Jan. 7, 1997
106th	Maj-3rd	4	3	Jan. 6, 1999
107th	Maj-3rd	5	4	Jan. 3, 2001
108th	Maj-3rd	6	5	Jan. 7, 2003

5th HOUSE ADMINISTRATION
Dates: July 27, 2000-Jan. 3, 2005
Departure: Moved to Ways and Means

Cong.	Ranking	Terms in: House	Terms in: Comm.	Date of Assignment
106th	MjR-1st	4	1	July 27, 2000
107th	Maj-4th	5	2	Jan. 31, 2001
108th	Maj-4th	6	3	Jan. 28, 2003

6th WAYS AND MEANS
Dates: Jan. 6, 2005-date
Departure: Still serving in the 111th Congress

Cong.	Ranking	Terms in: House	Comm.	Date of Assignment
109th	Maj-21st	7	1	Jan. 6, 2005
110th	Min-14th	8	2	Jan. 4, 2007
111th	Min-7th	9	3	Jan. 9, 2009

7th HOMELAND SECURITY
Dates: Feb. 9, 2005-Jan. 3, 2007
Departure: Left committee; no new assignment

Cong.	Ranking	Terms in: House	Comm.	Date of Assignment
109th	Maj-7th	7	2	Feb. 9, 2005

HOUSE SELECT AND SPECIAL COMMITTEES:

1st SELECT HOMELAND SECURITY
Dates: Feb. 12, 2003-Jan. 3, 2005
Departure: Continued on reorganized standing committee

Cong.	Ranking	Terms in: House	Comm.	Date of Assignment
108th	Maj-20th	6	1	Feb. 12, 2003

JOINT COMMITTEES:

1st JOINT PRINTING
House Dates: June 5, 2001-Jan. 3, 2005
Departure: Moved to Ways and Means

Cong.	Ranking	Terms in: House	Comm.	Date of Assignment
107th	Maj-3rd	5	1	June 5, 2001
108th	Maj-3rd	6	2	Mar. 25, 2003

Daniel Lipinski (D-Ill.)

Dates: July 15, 1966
House: Jan. 3, 2005-date
Serving in the 111th Congress

HOUSE STANDING COMMITTEES:

1st SCIENCE, 109
SCIENCE AND TECHNOLOGY, 110-111
Dates: Jan. 26, 2005-date
Departure: Still serving in the 111th Congress

Cong.	Ranking	Terms in: House	Comm.	Date of Assignment
109th	Min-12th	1	1	Jan. 26, 2005
110th	Maj-9th	2	2	Jan. 18, 2007
111th	Maj-8th	3	3	Jan. 21, 2009

2nd SMALL BUSINESS
Dates: Jan. 26, 2005-date
Departure: Still serving in the 111th Congress

Cong.	Ranking	Terms in: House	Comm.	Date of Assignment
109th	Min-4th	1	1	Jan. 26, 2005
110th	Maj-11th	2	2	Jan. 10, 2007
111th	Maj-10th	3	3	Jan. 21, 2009

3rd TRANSPORTATION AND INFRASTRUCTURE
Dates: Jan. 10, 2007-date
Departure: Still serving in the 111th Congress

Cong.	Ranking	Terms in: House	Comm.	Date of Assignment
110th	Maj-26th	2	1	Jan. 10, 2007
111th	Maj-22nd	3	2	Jan. 7, 2009

William O. Lipinski (D-Ill.)

Dates: Dec. 22, 1937
House: Jan. 3, 1983-Jan. 3, 2005
Left the House: Retired in 2004

HOUSE STANDING COMMITTEES:

1st MERCHANT MARINE AND FISHERIES
Dates: Jan. 6, 1983-Jan. 3, 1996
Departure: Committee abolished; no new assignment

Cong.	Ranking	Terms in: House	Comm.	Date of Assignment
103rd	Maj-5th	6	6	Jan. 5, 1993

2nd PUBLIC WORKS AND TRANSPORTATION, 103
TRANSPORTATION AND INFRASTRUCTURE, 104-108
Dates: Jan. 6, 1983-Jan. 3, 2005
Departure: Left the House; retired

Cong.	Ranking	Terms in: House	Comm.	Date of Assignment
103rd	Maj-8th	6	6	Jan. 5, 1993
104th	Min-5th	7	7	Jan. 4, 1995
105th	Min-4th	8	8	Jan. 7, 1997
106th	Min-4th	9	9	Jan. 6, 1999
107th	Min-4th	10	10	Jan. 31, 2001
108th	Min-3rd	11	11	Jan. 28, 2003

Robert L. Livingston Jr. (R-La.)

Dates: April 30, 1943
House: Aug. 27, 1977-Feb. 28, 1999
Left the House: Resigned and retired.

H: Livingston was elected to the 95th Congress by special election, Aug. 27, 1977, to fill the vacancy caused by the resignation of U.S. Representative Richard A. Tonry (D-La.). Livingston was seated Sept. 7, 1977, and assigned to committees.

1st PUBLIC WORKS AND TRANSPORTATION
Dates: Sep. 28, 1977-Jan. 3, 1981
Departure: Moved to Appropriations

2nd STANDARDS OF OFFICIAL CONDUCT
Dates: Sep. 24, 1979-Jan. 3, 1981
Departure: Moved to Appropriations

3rd MERCHANT MARINE AND FISHERIES
Dates: Mar. 10, 1980-Jan. 3, 1981
Departure: Moved to Appropriations

4th APPROPRIATIONS
Dates: Jan. 28, 1981-Jan. 3, 1999
Departure: Left committee; no new assignment

Cong.	Ranking	Terms in: House	Comm.	Date of Assignment
103rd	Min-5th	9	7	Jan. 5, 1993

| 104th | Maj-Chr | 10 | 8 | Jan. 4, 1995 |
| 105th | Maj-Chr | 11 | 9 | Jan. 7, 1997 |

5th HOUSE ADMINISTRATION
Dates: Feb. 6, 1991-Jan. 3, 1995
Departure: Left committee; became Chair of Appropriations

Cong.	Ranking	Terms in: House	Comm.	Date of Assignment
103rd	Min-4th	9	2	Jan. 5, 1993

HOUSE SELECT AND SPECIAL COMMITTEES:

1st OUTER CONTINENTAL SHELF
Dates: Apr. 9, 1979-July 31, 1980
Termination: House Report 1214 (96-2) filed

2nd SELECT INTELLIGENCE
Dates: Feb. 7, 1985-Jan. 3, 1991
Departure: Moved to House Administration

Marilyn L. Lloyd (D-Tenn.)

Dates: Jan. 9, 1929
House: Jan. 3, 1975-Jan. 3, 1995
Left the House: Retired in 1994

HOUSE STANDING COMMITTEES:

1st PUBLIC WORKS AND TRANSPORTATION
Dates: Jan. 20, 1975-Jan. 3, 1983
Departure: Left committee; no new assignment

2nd SCIENCE AND TECHNOLOGY, 94-199
SCIENCE, SPACE AND TECHNOLOGY, 100-103
Dates: Jan. 20, 1975-Jan. 3, 1995
Departure: Left the House; retired

Cong.	Ranking	Terms in: House	Comm.	Date of Assignment
103rd	Maj-2nd	10	10	Jan. 5, 1993

3rd ARMED SERVICES
Dates: Sep. 22, 1982-Jan. 3, 1995
Departure: Left the House; retired

Cong.	Ranking	Terms in: House	Comm.	Date of Assignment
103rd	Maj-8th	10	7	Jan. 5, 1993

HOUSE SELECT AND SPECIAL COMMITTEES:

1st SELECT AGING (Permanent)
Dates: Feb. 6, 1975-Jan. 3, 1993
Termination: Committee not renewed in 1993

Frank A. LoBiondo (R-N.J.)

Dates: May 12, 1946
House: Jan. 3, 1995-date
Serving in the 111th Congress

HOUSE STANDING COMMITTEES:

1st BANKING AND FINANCIAL SERVICES
Dates: Jan. 4, 1995-Feb. 25, 1997
Departure: Resigned committee; moved to Transportation and Infrastructure

Cong.	Ranking	Terms in: House	Comm.	Date of Assignment
104th	Maj-25th	1	1	Jan. 4, 1995
105th	Maj-18th	2	2	Jan. 7, 1997

2nd SMALL BUSINESS
Dates: Jan. 4, 1995-Jan. 3, 2003
Departure: Moved to Armed Services

Cong.	Ranking	Terms in: House	Comm.	Date of Assignment
104th	Maj-9th	1	1	Jan. 4, 1995
105th	Maj-7th	2	2	Jan. 21, 1997
106th	Maj-6th	3	3	Jan. 6, 1999
107th	Maj-5th	4	4	Jan. 6, 2001

3rd TRANSPORTATION AND INFRASTRUCTURE
Dates: Feb. 26, 1997-date
Departure: Still serving in the 111th Congress

Cong.	Ranking	Terms in: House	Comm.	Date of Assignment
105th	Maj-39th	2	1	Feb. 26, 1997
106th	Maj-29th	3	2	Jan. 6, 1999
107th	Maj-21st	4	3	Jan. 6, 2001
108th	Maj-16th	5	4	Jan. 28, 2003
109th	Maj-15th	6	5	Jan. 26, 2005
110th	Min-10th	7	6	Jan. 10, 2007
111th	Min-7th	8	7	Jan. 9, 2009

4th ARMED SERVICES
Dates: Jan. 28, 2003-date
Departure: Still serving in the 111th Congress

Cong.	Ranking	Terms in: House	Comm.	Date of Assignment
108th	Maj-24th	5	1	Jan. 28, 2003
109th	Maj-22nd	6	2	Jan. 26, 2005
110th	Min-16th	7	3	Jan. 10, 2007
111th	Min-10th	8	4	Jan. 9, 2009

Dave Loebsack (D-Iowa)

Dates: Dec. 23, 1952
House: Jan. 3, 2007-date
Serving in the 111th Congress

HOUSE STANDING COMMITTEES:

1st ARMED SERVICES
Dates: Jan. 10, 2007-date
Departure: Still serving in the 111th Congress

Cong.	Ranking	Terms in: House	Comm.	Date of Assignment
110th	Maj-29th	1	1	Jan. 10, 2007
111th	Maj-26th	2	2	Jan. 7, 2009

2nd EDUCATION AND LABOR
Dates: Jan. 10, 2007-date
Departure: Still serving in the 111th Congress

Cong.	Ranking	Terms in: House	Comm.	Date of Assignment
110th	Maj-20th	1	1	Jan. 10, 2007
111th	Maj-17th	2	2	Jan. 21, 2009

Zoe Lofgren (D-Cal.)

Dates: Dec. 21, 1947
House: Jan. 3, 1995-date
Serving in the 111th Congress

HOUSE STANDING COMMITTEES:

1st JUDICIARY
Dates: Jan. 4, 1995-date
Departure: Still serving in the 111th Congress

Cong.	Ranking	Terms in: House	Comm.	Date of Assignment
104th	Min-14th	1	1	Jan. 4, 1995
105th	Min-9th	2	2	Jan. 7, 1997
106th	Min-8th	3	3	Jan. 6, 1999
107th	Min-8th	4	4	Jan. 31, 2001
108th	Min-7th	5	5	Jan. 28, 2003
109th	Min-7th	6	6	Jan. 26, 2005
110th	Maj-7th	7	7	Jan. 18, 2007
111th	Maj-7th	8	8	Jan. 21, 2009

2nd SCIENCE
1st Dates: Jan. 4, 1995-Feb. 12, 2003
1st Departure: Leave of absence; moved to Select Homeland Security; returned on Mar. 5, 2003
2nd Dates: Mar. 5, 2003-Feb. 16, 2005
2nd Departure: Resigned committee; moved to House Administration

Cong.	Ranking	Terms in: House	Comm.	Date of Assignment
104th	Min-19th	1 *1	1	Jan. 4, 1995
105th	Min-12th	2 *1	2	Feb. 13, 1997
106th	Min-12th	3 *1	3	Jan. 6, 1999
107th	Min-8th	4 *1	4	Jan. 31, 2001
108th	Min-6th	5 *1	5	Jan. 28, 2003
108th	Min-14th	5 *2	1	Mar. 5, 2003
109th	Min-14th	6 *2	2	Feb. 2, 2005

3rd STANDARDS OF OFFICIAL CONDUCT
Dates: Sep. 29, 1997-Jan. 3, 2003
Departure: Moved to Select Homeland Security

Cong.	Ranking	Terms in: House	Comm.	Date of Assignment
105th	Min-5th	2	1	Sep. 29, 1997
106th	Min-5th	3	2	Jan. 6, 1999
107th	Min-4th	4	3	Mar. 6, 2001

4th HOMELAND SECURITY
Dates: Feb. 9, 2005-date
Departure: Still serving in the 111th Congress

Cong.	Ranking	Terms in: House	Comm.	Date of Assignment
109th	Min-9th	6	2	Feb. 9, 2005
110th	Maj-9th	7	3	Jan. 12, 2007
111th	Maj-6th	8	4	Jan. 28, 2009

5th HOUSE ADMINISTRATION
Dates: Feb. 16, 2005-date
Departure: Still serving in the 111th Congress

Cong.	Ranking	Terms in: House	Comm.	Date of Assignment
109th	Min-3rd	6	1	Feb. 16, 2005
110th	Maj-3rd	7	2	Feb. 8, 2007
111th	Maj-2nd	8	3	Jan. 13, 2009

HOUSE SELECT AND SPECIAL COMMITTEES:

1st SELECT HOMELAND SECURITY
Dates: Feb. 12, 2003-Jan. 3, 2005
Departure: Continued on reorganized standing committee

Cong.	Ranking	Terms in: House	Comm.	Date of Assignment
108th	Min-14th	5	1	Feb. 12, 2003

JOINT COMMITTEES:

1st JOINT LIBRARY
House Dates: Mar. 16, 2005-date
Departure: Still serving in the 111th Congress

Cong.	Ranking	Terms in: House	Comm.	Date of Assignment
109th	Min-2nd	6	1	Mar. 16, 2005
110th	Maj-2nd	7	2	Mar. 14, 2007
111th	Maj-2nd	8	3	Mar. 31, 2009

Jill L. Long (D-Ind.)

Dates: July 15, 1952
House: March 28, 1989-Jan. 3, 1995
Left the House: Defeated for re-election in 1994

H: Long was elected to the 101st Congress by special election, March 28, 1989, to fill the vacancy caused by the resignation of U.S. Representative Daniel R. Coats (R-Ind.) who had been appointed to the U.S. Senate. Long was seated April 5, 1989, and assigned to committees.

HOUSE STANDING COMMITTEES:

1st AGRICULTURE
Dates: Apr. 27, 1989-Jan. 3, 1995
Departure: Left the House; lost re-election

Cong.	Ranking	Terms in: House	Comm.	Date of Assignment
103rd	Maj-13th	3	3	Jan. 5, 1993

2nd VETERANS' AFFAIRS
Dates: Apr. 27, 1989-Jan. 3, 1995
Departure: Left the House; lost re-election

Cong.	Ranking	Terms in: House	Comm.	Date of Assignment
103rd	Maj-10th	3	3	Jan. 5, 1993

HOUSE SELECT AND SPECIAL COMMITTEES:

1st SELECT HUNGER (Temporary)
Dates: Feb. 8, 1990-Jan. 3, 1993
Termination: Committee not renewed in 1993

James B. Longley Jr. (R-Me.)

Dates: July 7, 1951
House: Jan. 3, 1995-Jan. 3, 1997
Left the House: Defeated for re-election in 1996

HOUSE STANDING COMMITTEES:

1st NATIONAL SECURITY
Dates: Jan. 4, 1995-Jan. 3, 1997
Departure: Left the House; lost re-election

Cong.	Ranking	Terms in: House	Comm.	Date of Assignment
104th	Maj-28th	1	1	Jan. 4, 1995

2nd RESOURCES
Dates: Jan. 4, 1995-Jan. 3, 1997
Departure: Left the House; lost re-election

Cong.	Ranking	Terms in: House	Comm.	Date of Assignment
104th	Maj-24th	1	1	Jan. 4, 1995

3rd SMALL BUSINESS
Dates: Jan. 4, 1995-Jan. 3, 1997
Departure: Left the House; lost re-election

Cong.	Ranking	Terms in: House	Comm.	Date of Assignment
104th	Maj-13th	1	1	Jan. 4, 1995

C. Trent Lott (R-Miss.)

Dates: Oct. 9, 1941
House: Jan. 3, 1973-Jan. 3, 1989
Left the House: Elected to U.S. Senate in 1988
Senate: Jan. 3, 1989-Dec. 18, 2007
Left the Senate: Resigned in 2007

HOUSE STANDING COMMITTEES:

1st JUDICIARY
Dates: Jan. 24, 1973-Jan. 3, 1975
Departure: Moved to Post Office and Civil Service and Rules

2nd MERCHANT MARINE AND FISHERIES
Dates: Jan. 24, 1973-Jan. 3, 1975
Departure: Moved to Post Office and Civil Service and Rules

3rd POST OFFICE AND CIVIL SERVICE
Dates: Jan. 28, 1975-Jan. 3, 1979
Departure: Left committee; no new assignment

4th RULES
Dates: Jan. 28, 1975-Jan. 3, 1989
Departure: Left the House for the Senate

5th ENERGY AND COMMERCE
Dates: July 23, 1986-Jan. 3, 1987
Departure: Left committee; no new assignment

HOUSE SELECT AND SPECIAL COMMITTEES:

1st OUTER CONTINENTAL SHELF
Dates: Apr. 9, 1979-July 31, 1980
Termination: House Report 1214 (96-2) filed

HOUSE LEADERSHIP POSTS

Dates: Dec. 8, 1980-Jan. 3, 1989
Departure: Left the House for the Senate

1st HOUSE MINORITY WHIP
Dates: Dec. 8, 1980-Jan. 3, 1989

Note: In the 97th Congress, Lott succeeded Minority Whip Robert H. Michel (R-III.) following Michel's election as Minority Leader. Lott was elected by a vote of 96 to 90 over Bud Shuster (R-Penn.) on Dec. 8, 1980. He was re-elected Minority Whip unopposed for the 98th-100th Congresses.
Departure: Left the House for the Senate

SENATE STANDING COMMITTEES:

1st ARMED SERVICES
Dates: Feb. 2, 1989-June 20, 1996
Departure: Moved to Finance and Rules and Administration; elected Majority Leader

Cong.	Ranking	Years in: Senate	Comm.	Date of Assignment
103rd	Min-5th	5	4	Jan. 7, 1993
104th	Maj-5th	7	6	Jan. 4, 1995

2nd COMMERCE, SCIENCE AND TRANSPORTATION
Dates: Feb. 2, 1989-Dec. 18, 2007
Departure: Resigned the Senate and retired

Cong.	Ranking	Years in: Senate	Comm.	Date of Assignment
103rd	Min-8th	5	4	Jan. 7, 1993
104th	Maj-7th	7	6	Jan. 4, 1995
105th	Maj-5th	9	8	Jan. 9, 1997
106th	Maj-5th	11	10	Jan. 7, 1999
107th	Maj-4th	13	12	Jan. 25, 2001
+107th	Min-4th	13	13	June 6, 2001
108th	Maj-4th	15	14	Jan. 15, 2003
109th	Maj-4th	17	16	Jan. 6, 2005
110th	Min-3rd	19	18	Jan. 12, 2007

3rd SMALL BUSINESS
Dates: Feb. 2, 1989-Mar. 19, 1991
Departure: Left committee; moved to Budget

4th BUDGET
Dates: Mar. 19, 1991-June 20, 1996
Departure: Moved to Finance and Rules and Administration; elected Majority Leader

Cong.	Ranking	Years in: Senate	Comm.	Date of Assignment
103rd	Min-6th	5	2	Jan. 21, 1993
104th	Maj-6th	7	4	Jan. 6, 1995

5th ENERGY AND NATURAL RESOURCES
Dates: Jan. 7, 1993-Jan. 4, 1995
Departure: Left committee; elected Majority Whip

Cong.	Ranking	Years in: Senate	Comm.	Date of Assignment
103rd	Min-9th	5	1	Jan. 7, 1993

6th FINANCE
Dates: June 20, 1996-Dec. 18, 2007
Departure: Resigned the Senate and retired

Cong.	Ranking	Years in: Senate	Comm.	Date of Assignment
104th	MjR-2nd	8	1	June 20, 1996
105th	Maj-9th	9	1	Jan. 9, 1997
106th	Maj-8th	11	2	Jan. 7, 1999
107th	Maj-6th	13	5	Jan. 25, 2001
+107th	Min-6th	13	5	June 6, 2001
108th	Maj-4th	15	7	Jan. 15, 2003
109th	Maj-3rd	17	9	Jan. 6, 2005
110th	Min-3rd	19	11	Jan. 12, 2007

7th RULES AND ADMINISTRATION
Dates: June 20, 1996-Dec. 18, 2007
Departure: Resigned the Senate and retired

Cong.	Ranking	Years in: Senate	Comm.	Date of Assignment
104th	MjR-1st	8	1	June 20, 1996
105th	Maj-8th	9	1	Jan. 9, 1997
106th	Maj-8th	11	2	Jan. 7, 1999
107th	Maj-8th	13	5	Jan. 25, 2001
+107th	Min-8th	13	5	June 6, 2001
108th	Maj-Chr	15	7	Jan. 15, 2003
109th	Maj-Chr	17	9	Jan. 6, 2005
110th	Min-5th	19	11	Jan. 12, 2007

SENATE SELECT AND SPECIAL COMMITTEES:

1st SELECT ETHICS (Permanent)
Dates: Feb. 2, 1989-Jan. 26, 1993
Departure: Moved to Energy and Natural Resources

2nd SELECT INTELLIGENCE (Permanent)
Dates: Jan. 15, 2003-Jan. 12, 2007
Departure: Left committee; elected Minority Whip

Cong.	Ranking	Years in: Senate	Comm.	Date of Assignment
108th	Maj-5th	15	1	Jan. 15, 2003
109th	Maj-5th	17	2	Jan. 6, 2005

JOINT COMMITTEES:

1st JOINT ORGANIZATION OF CONGRESS (Ad Hoc)
Senate Dates: Sep. 25, 1992-Dec. 9, 1993
Termination: Senate Report 103-215 filed

Cong.	Ranking	Years in: Senate	Comm.	Date of Assignment
103rd	Min-3rd	5	1	Continued

2nd JOINT LIBRARY
Senate Dates: Mar. 13, 2003-Jan. 12, 2007
Departure: Left committee; no new assignment

Cong.	Ranking	Years in: Senate	Comm.	Date of Assignment
108th	Maj-2nd	15	1	Mar. 13, 2003
109th	Maj-3rd	17	2	Mar. 4, 2005

3rd JOINT PRINTING
Senate Dates: Mar. 4, 2005-Jan. 12, 2007
Departure: Left committee; no new assignment

Cong.	Ranking	Years in: Senate	Comm.	Date of Assignment
109th	Maj-Chr	17	1	Mar. 4, 2005

4th JOINT TAXATION
Senate Dates: Mar. 4, 2005-Jan. 17, 2007
Departure: Left committee; no new assignment

Cong.	Ranking	Years in: Senate	Comm.	Date of Assignment
109th	Maj-3rd	17	1	Jan. 25, 2005

SENATE LEADERSHIP POSTS

1st Dates: Jan. 3, 1995-Jan. 6, 2003
1st Departure: Stepped aside as Majority Leader
2nd Dates: Jan. 3. 2009-Dec. 18, 2007
2nd Departure: Resigned the Senate and retired

1st SENATE MAJORITY WHIP
Dates: Jan. 3, 1995-June 12, 1996
Note: For the 104th Congress. Lott defeated Republican Whip Alan Simpson (R-Wyo.) by a vote of 27 to 26 on Dec. 2, 1994
Departure: Elected Majority Floor leader

Cong.	Ranking	Years in: Senate	Post	Date of Selection
104th	Maj-2nd	7	1	Dec. 2, 1994

2nd SENATE MAJORITY FLOOR LEADER
1st Dates: June 12, 1996-June 6, 2001
Note: In the 104th Congress, Lott succeeded Majority Leader Robert J. Dole (R-Kans.), who resigned to seek the presidency. Lott was elected Majority Leader on June 12, 1996, defeating Thad Cochran (R-Miss.) 44 to 8. He was re-elected without opposition for the 105th-107th Congresses.
1st Departure: Republicans lost their Senate majority when James Jeffords of Vermont left the Republican Party to become an Independent on June 6, 2001
2nd Dates: Jan. 3, 2003-Jan. 6, 2005
Note: For the 108th Congress, Lott was elected Majority Leader without opposition
2nd Departure: Resigned post; resumed committee service

Cong.	Ranking	Years in: Senate	Post	Date of Selection
104th	Maj-1st	8 *1	1	June 12, 1996
105th	Maj-1st	9 *1	1	Dec. 3, 1996
106th	Maj-1st	11 *1	3	Dec. 1, 1998
107th	Maj-1st	13 *1	5	Dec. 5, 2000
108th	Maj-1st	15 *2	1	Nov. 13, 2002

3rd SENATE MINORITY FLOOR LEADER
Dates: June 6, 2001-Jan. 3, 2003
Note: Lott became Minority Leader as a result of the Jeffords' shift. There was no new vote for Minority Leader.
Departure: Republican Party regained Senate majority in 2002

Cong.	Ranking	Years in: Senate	Post	Date of Service
107th	Min-1st	13	1	June 6, 2001

4th SENATE MINORITY WHIP
Dates: Jan. 3, 2007-Dec. 18, 2007
Note: For the 110th Congress, Lott succeeded Republican Whip Mitch McConnell (R-Ky.) who had been elected Minority Leader. Lott was elected on Nov. 15, 2006, defeating Lamar Alexander (R-Tenn.) by a vote of 25 to 24.
Departure: Resigned the Senate; retired

Cong.	Ranking	Years in: Senate	Post	Date of Selection
110th	Min-2nd	19	1	Nov. 14, 2006

Nita M. Lowey (D-N.Y.)

Dates: July 5, 1937
House: Jan. 3, 1989-date
Serving in the 111th Congress

HOUSE STANDING COMMITTEES:

1st EDUCATION AND LABOR
Dates: Jan. 19, 1989-Jan. 3, 1993
Departure: Moved to Appropriations

2nd MERCHANT MARINE AND FISHERIES
Dates: Jan. 19, 1989-Jan. 3, 1993
Departure: Moved to Appropriations

3rd APPROPRIATIONS
Dates: Jan. 5, 1993-date
Departure: Still serving in the 111th Congress

Cong.	Ranking	Terms in: House	Comm.	Date of Assignment
103rd	Maj-29th	3	1	Jan. 5, 1993

104th	Min-23rd	4	2	Jan. 4, 1995
105th	Min-18th	5	3	Jan. 7, 1997
106th	Min-11th	6	4	Jan. 6, 1999
107th	Min-10th	7	5	Jan. 31, 2001
108th	Min-9th	8	6	Jan. 28, 2003
109th	Min-9th	9	7	Jan. 26, 2005
110th	Maj-7th	10	8	Jan. 4, 2007
111th	Maj-7th	11	9	Jan. 7, 2009

4th HOMELAND SECURITY
Dates: Feb. 9, 2005-Jan. 3, 2009
Departure: Left committee; no new assignment

| | | Terms in: | | Date of |
Cong.	Ranking	House	Comm.	Assignment
109th	Min-7th	9	2	Feb. 9, 2005
110th	Maj-7th	10	3	Jan. 12, 2007

HOUSE SELECT AND SPECIAL COMMITTEES:

1st SELECT NARCOTICS ABUSE AND CONTROL (Temporary)
Dates: Mar. 8, 1989-Jan. 3, 1993
Departure: Committee not renewed in 1993

2nd SELECT HOMELAND SECURITY
Dates: Feb. 12, 2003-Jan. 3, 2005
Departure: Continued on reorganized standing committee

| | | Terms in: | | Date of |
Cong.	Ranking	House	Comm.	Assignment
108th	Min-11th	8	1	Feb. 12, 2003

Frank D. Lucas (R-Okla.)

Dates: Jan. 6, 1960
House: May 10, 1994-date
Serving in the 111th Congress

H: Lucas was elected to the 103rd election by special election, May 10, 1994, to fill the vacancy caused by the resignation of U.S. Representative Glenn English (R-Okla.). Lucas was seated May 17, 1994, and assigned to committees.

HOUSE STANDING COMMITTEES:

1st AGRICULTURE
Dates: May 24, 1994-date
Departure: Still serving in the 111th Congress

| | | Terms in: | | Date of |
Cong.	Ranking	House	Comm.	Assignment
103rd	MnA-20th	1	1	May 24, 1994
104th	Maj-15th	2	2	Jan. 4, 1995
105th	Maj-12th	3	3	Jan. 7, 1997
106th	Maj-10th	4	4	Jan. 6, 1999
107th	Maj-7th	5	5	Jan. 6, 2001
108th	Maj-7th	6	6	Jan. 28, 2003
109th	Maj-5th	7	7	Jan. 26, 2005
110th	Min-3rd	8	8	Jan. 10, 2007
111th	Min-RM	9	9	Jan. 6, 2009

2nd GOVERNMENT OPERATIONS
Dates: May 25, 1994-Jan. 3, 1995
Departure: Moved to Banking and Financial Services

| | | Terms in: | | Date of |
Cong.	Ranking	House	Comm.	Assignment
103rd	MnR-1st	1	1	May 25, 1994

3rd BANKING AND FINANCIAL SERVICES, 104-106
FINANCIAL SERVICES, 107-111
Dates: Jan. 4, 1995-date
Departure: Still serving in the 111th Congress

| | | Terms in: | | Date of |
Cong.	Ranking	House	Comm.	Assignment
104th	Maj-12th	2	1	Jan. 4, 1995
105th	Maj-12th	3	2	Jan. 7, 1997
106th	Maj-12th	4	3	Jan. 6, 1999
107th	Maj-10th	5	4	Jan. 6, 2001
108th	Maj-9th	6	5	Jan. 28, 2003
109th	Maj-9th	7	6	Jan. 26, 2005
110th	Min-7th	8	7	Jan. 10, 2007
111th	Min-5th	9	8	Jan. 9, 2009

4th SCIENCE, 106-109
SCIENCE AND TECHNOLOGY, 110-111
Dates: Jan. 6, 1999-date
Departure: Still serving in the 111th Congress

| | | Terms in: | | Date of |
Cong.	Ranking	House	Comm.	Assignment
106th	Maj-19th	4	1	Jan. 6, 1999
107th	Maj-16th	5	2	Jan. 6, 2001
108th	Maj-13th	6	3	Jan. 28, 2003
109th	Maj-10th	7	4	Jan. 26, 2005
110th	Min-8th	8	5	Jan. 10, 2007
111th	Min-7th	9	6	Jan. 9, 2009

Ken Lucas (D-Ky.)

Dates: Aug. 22, 1933
House: Jan. 3, 1999-Jan. 3, 2005
Left the House: Retired in 2004

HOUSE STANDING COMMITTEES:

1st AGRICULTURE
1st Dates: Jan. 6, 1999-Feb. 12, 2003
1st Departure: Resigned committee; moved to Select Homeland Security; returned on Feb. 26, 2003
2nd Dates: Feb. 26, 2003-Mar. 30, 2004
2nd Departure: Resigned committee; no new assignment

| | | Terms in: | | Date of |
Cong.	Ranking	House	Comm.	Assignment
106th	Min-22nd	1 *1	1	Jan. 6, 1999
107th	Min-22nd	2 *1	2	Mar. 14, 2001
108th	Min-9th	3 *1	3	Jan. 28, 2003
108th	MnR-1st	3 *2	1	Feb. 26, 2003

2nd BUDGET
Dates: Jan. 6, 1999-Jan. 3, 2001
Departure: Moved to Financial Services

| | | Terms in: | | Date of |
Cong.	Ranking	House	Comm.	Assignment
106th	Min-16th	1	1	Jan. 6, 1999

3rd FINANCIAL SERVICES
Dates: Feb. 8, 2001-Jan. 3, 2005
Departure: Left the House; retired

| | | Terms in: | | Date of |
Cong.	Ranking	House	Comm.	Assignment
107th	Min-27th	2	1	Feb. 8, 2001
108th	Min-21st	3	2	Jan. 28, 2003

HOUSE SELECT AND SPECIAL COMMITTEES:

1st SELECT HOMELAND SECURITY
Dates: Feb. 12, 2003-Jan. 3, 2005
Departure: Left the House; retired

Cong.	Ranking	Terms in: House	Comm.	Date of Assignment
108th	Min-21st	3	1	Feb. 12, 2003

Blaine Luetkemeyer (R-Mo.)

Dates: May 7, 1952
House: Jan. 3, 2009-date
Serving in the 111th Congress

HOUSE STANDING COMMITTEES:

1st AGRICULTURE
Dates: Jan. 9, 2009-date
Departure: Still serving in the 111th Congress

Cong.	Ranking	Terms in: House	Comm.	Date of Assignment
111th	Min-16th	1	1	Jan. 9, 2009

2nd SMALL BUSINESS
Dates: Jan. 9, 2009-date
Departure: Still serving in the 111th Congress

Cong.	Ranking	Terms in: House	Comm.	Date of Assignment
111th	Min-9th	1	1	Jan. 9, 2009

3rd OVERSIGHT AND GOVERNMENT REFORM
Dates: Sept. 9, 2009-date
Departure: Still serving in the 111th Congress

Cong.	Ranking	Terms in: House	Comm.	Date of Assignment
111th	MnR-2nd	1	1	Sept. 9, 2009

Richard G. Lugar (R-Ind.)

Dates: April 4, 1932
Senate: Jan. 3, 1977-date
Serving in the 111th Congress

SENATE STANDING COMMITTEES:

1st BUDGET
Dates: Jan. 10, 1977-Feb. 22, 1977
Departure: Left committee; moved to Agriculture, Nutrition and Forestry, and Banking, Housing and Urban Affairs

2nd GOVERNMENT OPERATIONS
Dates: Jan. 10, 1977-Feb. 22, 1977
Departure: Left committee; moved to Agriculture, Nutrition and Forestry, and Banking, Housing and Urban Affairs

3rd LABOR AND PUBLIC WELFARE
Dates: Jan. 12, 1977-Feb. 22, 1977
Departure: Left committee; moved to Agriculture, Nutrition and Forestry, and Banking, Housing and Urban Affairs

4th AGRICULTURE, NUTRITION AND FORESTRY
Dates: Feb. 22, 1977-date
Ch1: Replaced by Thomas R. Harkin (D-Iowa) following party control shift on June 6, 2001 and became RM2.
Departure: Still serving in the 111th Congress

Cong.	Ranking	Years in: Senate	Comm.	Date of Assignment
103rd	Min-RM	17	16	Jan. 7, 1993
104th	Maj-Chr	19	18	Jan. 4, 1995
105th	Maj-Chr	21	20	Jan. 9, 1997
106th	Maj-Chr	23	22	Jan. 7, 1999
107th	Maj-Ch1	25	24	Jan. 25, 2001
+107th	Min-RM2	25	25	June 6, 2001
108th	Maj-2nd	27	26	Jan. 15, 2003
109th	Maj-2nd	29	28	Jan. 6, 2005
110th	Min-2nd	31	30	Jan. 12, 2007
111th	Min-2nd	33	32	Jan. 21, 2009

5th BANKING, HOUSING AND URBAN AFFAIRS
Dates: Feb. 22, 1977-Jan. 3, 1983
Departure: Left committee; no new assignment

6th FOREIGN RELATIONS
Dates: Jan. 23, 1979-date
Departure: Still serving in the 111th Congress

Cong.	Ranking	Years in: Senate	Comm.	Date of Assignment
103rd	Min-2nd	17	14	Jan. 7, 1993
104th	Maj-2nd	19	16	Jan. 5, 1995
105th	Maj-2nd	21	18	Jan. 9, 1997
106th	Maj-2nd	23	20	Jan. 7, 1999
107th	Maj-2nd	25	23	Jan. 25, 2001
+107th	Min-2nd	25	23	June 6, 2001
108th	Maj-Chr	27	24	Jan. 15, 2003
109th	Maj-Chr	29	26	Jan. 6, 2005
110th	Min-RM	31	28	Jan. 12, 2007
111th	Min-RM	33	30	Jan. 21, 2009

SENATE SELECT AND SPECIAL COMMITTEES:

1st SELECT INTELLIGENCE (Permanent)
1st Dates: Feb. 21, 1977-Jan. 3, 1985
1st Departure: Left committee; no new assignment
2nd Dates: Jan. 27, 1993-Jan. 15, 2003
2nd Departure: Left committee; became Chair of Foreign Relations

Cong.	Ranking	Years in: Senate	Comm.	Date of Assignment
103rd	Min-7th	17 *2	1	Jan. 27, 1993
104th	Maj-2nd	19 *2	2	Jan. 6, 1995
105th	Maj-3rd	21 *2	4	Jan. 9, 1997
106th	Maj-3rd	23 *2	6	Jan. 7, 1999
107th	Maj-8th	25 *2	8	Jan. 25, 2001
+107th	Min-8th	25 *2	9	June 6, 2001

2nd FOREIGN GOVERNMENT REPRESENTATION
Dates: July 29, 1980-Oct. 2, 1980
Termination: Senate Report 1015 (96-2) filed

3rd SPECIAL YEAR 2000 TECHNOLOGY PROBLEM
Dates: June 30, 1999-Feb. 29, 2000
Departure: Senate Print 106-42 issued

Cong.	Ranking	Years in: Senate	Comm.	Date of Assignment
106th	MjR-1st	23	1	Continued

JOINT COMMITTEES:

1st JOINT ORGANIZATION OF CONGRESS (Ad Hoc)
Senate Dates: Sep. 25, 1992-Dec. 9, 1993
Termination: Senate Report 103-215 filed

Cong.	Ranking	Years in: Senate	Comm.	Date of Assignment
103rd	Min-6th	17	1	Continued

Ben Ray Luján (D-N.M.)

Dates: June 7, 1972
House: Jan. 3, 2009-date
Serving in the 111th Congress

HOUSE STANDING COMMITTEES:

1st SCIENCE AND TECHNOLOGY
Dates: Jan. 21, 2009-May 5, 2010
Departure: Resigned committee; moved to Natural Resources

Cong.	Ranking	Terms in: House	Comm.	Date of Assignment
111th	Maj-12th	1	1	Jan. 21, 2009

2nd HOMELAND SECURITY
Dates: Jan. 28, 2009-date
Departure: Still serving in the 111th Congress

Cong.	Ranking	Terms in: House	Comm.	Date of Assignment
111th	Maj-13th	1	1	Jan. 28, 2009

3rd NATURAL RESOURCES
Dates: May 6, 2010-date
Departure: Still serving in the 111th Congress

Cong.	Ranking	Terms in: House	Comm.	Date of Assignment
111th	MjR-1st	1	1	May 6, 2010

Cynthia M. Lummis (R-Wyo.)

Dates: Sept. 10, 1954-
House: Jan. 3, 2009-date
Serving in the 111th Congress

HOUSE STANDING COMMITTEES:

1st BUDGET
Dates: Jan. 9, 2009-date
Departure: Still serving in the 111th Congress

Cong.	Ranking	Terms in: House	Comm.	Date of Assignment
111th	Min-14th	1	1	Jan. 9, 2009

2nd NATURAL RESOURCES
Dates: Jan. 9, 2009-date
Departure: Still serving in the 111th Congress

Cong.	Ranking	Terms in: House	Comm.	Date of Assignment
111th	Min-18th	1	1	Jan. 9, 2009

3rd AGRICULTURE
Dates: Feb. 4, 2009-date
Departure: Still serving in the 111th Congress

Cong.	Ranking	Terms in: House	Comm.	Date of Assignment
111th	MnA-18th	1	1	Feb. 4, 2009

Daniel E. Lungren (R-Cal.)

Dates: Sept. 22, 1946
House 1: Jan. 3, 1979-Jan. 3, 1989
Left the House 1: Elected California Attorney General in 1990
House 2: Jan. 3, 2005-date
Serving in the 111th Congress

HOUSE STANDING COMMITTEES:

1st JUDICIARY
1st Dates: Jan. 24, 1979-Jan. 3, 1989
1st Departure: Left the House; elected state Attorney General
2nd Dates: Jan. 26, 2005-date
2nd Departure: Still serving in the 111th Congress

Cong.	Ranking	Terms in: House	Comm.	Date of Assignment
109th	Maj-8th	6 *2	1	Jan. 26, 2005
110th	Min-7th	7 *2	2	Jan. 10, 2007
111th	Min-6th	8 *2	3	Jan. 9, 2009

2nd BUDGET
Dates: Jan. 26, 2005-Jan. 16, 2009
Departure: Resigned committee; became Ranking Member on House Administration

Cong.	Ranking	Terms in: House	Comm.	Date of Assignment
109th	Maj-15th	6	1	Jan. 26, 2005
110th	Min-8th	7	2	Jan. 10, 2007
111th	Min-5th	8	3	Jan. 9, 2009

3rd HOMELAND SECURITY
Dates: Feb. 9, 2005-date
Departure: Still serving in the 111th Congress

Cong.	Ranking	Terms in: House	Comm.	Date of Assignment
109th	Maj-10th	6	1	Feb. 9, 2005
110th	Min-6th	7	2	Jan. 10, 2007
111th	Min-4th	8	3	Jan. 9, 2009

4th HOUSE ADMINISTRATION
Dates: Jan. 4, 2007-date
Departure: Still serving in the 111th Congress

Cong.	Ranking	Terms in: House	Comm.	Date of Assignment
110th	Min-2nd	7	1	Jan. 4, 2007
111th	Min-RM	8	2	Jan. 9, 2009

HOUSE SELECT AND SPECIAL COMMITTEES:

1st SELECT AGING (Permanent)
Dates: Jan. 25, 1979-Mar. 3, 1983
Departure: Moved to Joint Economic

2nd PERMANENT SELECT INTELLIGENCE
Dates: Jan. 28, 1987-Jan. 3, 1989
Departure: Left the House; elected state Attorney General

JOINT COMMITTEES:

1st JOINT ECONOMIC
House Dates: Jan. 25, 1983-Jan. 3, 1987
Departure: Moved to Permanent Select Intelligence

2nd JOINT LIBRARY
House Dates: Mar. 14, 2007-date
Departure: Still serving in the 111th Congress

Cong.	Ranking	Terms in: House	Comm.	Date of Assignment
110th	Min-2nd	7	1	Mar. 14, 2007
111th	Min-1st	8	2	Mar. 31, 2009

3rd JOINT PRINTING
House Dates: Mar. 31, 2009-date
Departure: Still serving in the 111th Congress

Cong.	Ranking	Terms in: House	Comm.	Date of Assignment
111th	Min-1st	8	1	Mar. 31, 2009

William P. Luther (DFL-Minn.)

Dates: June 27, 1945
House: Jan. 3, 1995-Jan. 3, 2003
Left the House: Defeated for re-election in 2002

HOUSE STANDING COMMITTEES:

1st SCIENCE
Dates: Jan. 4, 1995-Jan. 3. 1999
Departure: Moved to Commerce

Cong.	Ranking	Terms in: House	Comm.	Date of Assignment
104th	Min-23rd	1	1	Jan. 4, 1995
105th	Min-16th	2	2	Feb. 13, 1997

2nd SMALL BUSINESS
Dates: Jan. 4, 1995-Mar. 13, 1997
Departure: Resigned committee; moved to International Relations

Cong.	Ranking	Terms in: House	Comm.	Date of Assignment
104th	Min-18th	1	1	Jan. 4, 1995
105th	Min-7th	2	2	Feb. 5, 1997

3rd INTERNATIONAL RELATIONS
Dates: Mar. 21, 1997-Jan. 3, 1999
Departure: Moved to Commerce

Cong.	Ranking	Terms in: House	Comm.	Date of Assignment
105th	MnR-1st	2	1	Mar. 21, 1997

4th COMMERCE, 106
ENERGY AND COMMERCE, 107

Dates: Jan. 6, 1999-Jan. 3, 2003
Departure: Left the House; lost re-election

Cong.	Ranking	Terms in: House	Comm.	Date of Assignment
106th	Min-23rd	3	1	Jan. 6, 1999
107th	Min-22nd	4	2	Jan. 31, 2001

Stephen F. Lynch (D-Mass.)

Dates: March 31, 1955
House: Oct. 16, 2001-date
Serving in the 111th Congress

H: Lynch was elected to the 107th Congress by special election, Oct. 16, 2001, to fill the vacancy caused by the death of U.S. Representative John Joseph Moakley (D-Mass.). Lynch was seated Oct. 23, 2001, and assigned to committees.

HOUSE STANDING COMMITTEES:

1st VETERANS' AFFAIRS
Dates: Nov. 7, 2001-Jan. 3, 2003
Departure: Moved to Financial Services

Cong.	Ranking	Terms in: House	Comm.	Date of Assignment
107th	MnR-1st	1	1	Nov. 7, 2001

2nd GOVERNMENT REFORM, 107-109
OVERSIGHT AND GOVERNMENT REFORM, 110-111
Dates: Nov. 7, 2001-date
Departure: Still serving in the 111th Congress

Cong.	Ranking	Terms in: House	Comm.	Date of Assignment
107th	MnR-2nd	1	1	Nov. 7, 2001
108th	Min-15th	2	2	Jan. 28, 2003
109th	Min-13th	3	3	Jan. 26, 2005
110th	Maj-12th	4	4	Jan. 12, 2007
111th	Maj-9th	5	5	Jan. 28, 2009

3rd FINANCIAL SERVICES
Dates: Jan. 28, 2003-date
Departure: Still serving in the 111th Congress

Cong.	Ranking	Terms in: House	Comm.	Date of Assignment
108th	Min-29th	2	1	Jan. 28, 2003
109th	Min-25th	3	2	Jan. 26, 2005
110th	Maj-18th	4	3	Jan. 12, 2007
111th	Maj-17th	5	4	Jan. 7, 2009

M

Ronald K. Machtley (R-R.I.)

Dates: July 13, 1948
House: Jan. 3, 1989-Jan. 3, 1995
Left the House: Lost nomination for Governor in 1994

HOUSE STANDING COMMITTEES:

1st ARMED SERVICES
Dates: Jan. 20, 1989-Jan. 3, 1995
Departure: Left the House; lost nomination for Governor

Cong.	Ranking	Terms in: House	Comm.	Date of Assignment
103rd	Min-12th	3	3	Jan. 5, 1993

2nd SMALL BUSINESS
Dates: May 4, 1989-Jan. 3, 1995
Departure: Left the House; lost nomination for Governor

Cong.	Ranking	Terms in: House	Comm.	Date of Assignment
103rd	Min-5th	3	3	Jan. 5, 1993

3rd GOVERNMENT OPERATIONS
Dates: Jan. 24, 1991-Sep. 13, 1993
Departure: Resigned committee; no new assignment

Cong.	Ranking	Terms in: House	Comm.	Date of Assignment
103rd	Min-10th	3	2	Jan. 5, 1993

HOUSE SELECT AND SPECIAL COMMITTEES:

1st SELECT CHILDREN, YOUTH AND FAMILIES (Temporary)
Dates: Apr. 4, 1989-Jan. 3, 1993
Termination: Committee not renewed in 1993

Connie Mack III (R-Fla.)

Dates: Oct. 29, 1940
House: Jan. 3, 1983-Jan. 3, 1989
Left the House: Elected to U.S. Senate in 1988
Senate: Jan. 3, 1989-Jan. 3, 2001
Left the Senate: Retired in 2000

HOUSE STANDING COMMITTEES:

1st BUDGET
Dates: Jan. 6, 1983-Jan. 3, 1989
Departure: Left the House for the Senate

2nd POST OFFICE AND CIVIL SERVICE
Dates: Jan. 6, 1983-Jan. 3, 1985
Departure: Moved to Foreign Affairs

3rd FOREIGN AFFAIRS
Dates: Jan. 30, 1985-Jan. 3, 1989
Departure: Left the House for the Senate

SENATE STANDING COMMITTEES:

1st BANKING, HOUSING AND URBAN AFFAIRS
Dates: Feb. 2, 1989-Jan. 3, 2001
Departure: Left the Senate; retired

Cong.	Ranking	Years in: Senate	Comm.	Date of Assignment
103rd	Min-4th	5	4	Jan. 7, 1993
104th	Maj-5th	7	6	Jan. 4, 1995
105th	Maj-4th	9	8	Jan. 9, 1997
106th	Maj-3rd	11	10	Jan. 7, 1999

2nd FOREIGN RELATIONS
Dates: Feb. 2, 1989-Feb. 5, 1991
Departure: Moved to Armed Services and Small Business

3rd ARMED SERVICES
Dates: Feb. 5, 1991-Jan. 7, 1993
Departure: Moved to Appropriations

4th SMALL BUSINESS
Dates: Mar. 19, 1991-Jan. 9, 1997
Departure: Moved to Finance

Cong.	Ranking	Years in: Senate	Comm.	Date of Assignment
103rd	Min-5th	5	2	Jan. 21, 1993
104th	Maj-4th	7	4	Jan. 6, 1995

5th APPROPRIATIONS
Dates: Jan. 7, 1993-Jan. 9, 1997
Departure: Moved to Finance

Cong.	Ranking	Years in: Senate	Comm.	Date of Assignment
103rd	Min-12th	5	1	Jan. 7, 1993
104th	Maj-10th	7	2	Jan. 4, 1995

6th BUDGET
Dates: June 20, 1996-Jan. 9, 1997
Departure: Moved to Finance

Cong.	Ranking	Years in: Senate	Comm.	Date of Assignment
104th	MjR-1st	8	1	June 20, 1996

7th FINANCE
Dates: Jan. 9, 1997-Jan. 3, 2001
Departure: Left the Senate; retired

Cong.	Ranking	Years in: Senate	Comm.	Date of Assignment
105th	Maj-11th	9	1	Jan. 9, 1997
106th	Maj-10th	11	2	Jan. 7, 1999

SENATE SELECT AND SPECIAL COMMITTEES:

1st JUDGE WALTER L. NIXON IMPEACHMENT
Dates: May 11, 1989-Sep. 13, 1989
Termination: Hearings concluded

2nd SPECIAL COMMITTEE TO INVESTIGATE WHITEWATER DEVELOPMENT CORPORATION AND RELATED MATTERS
Dates: July 20, 1995-June 17, 1996
Termination: Senate Report 104-280 filed

Cong.	Ranking	Years in: Senate	Comm.	Date of Assignment
104th	Maj-4th	7	1	July 20, 1995

JOINT COMMITTEES:

1st JOINT DEFICIT REDUCTION (Temporary)
House Dates: Feb. 23, 1987-Sep. 29, 1987
Termination: Public Law 100-119 adjusted Gramm-Rudman-Hollings Act

2nd JOINT ECONOMIC
Senate Dates: Feb. 2, 1989-Jan. 3, 2001
Chair2: Replaced Roth on Feb. 2, 1995
Departure: Left the Senate; retired

Cong.	Ranking	Years in: Senate	Comm.	Date of Assignment
103rd	Min-2nd	5	4	Jan. 21, 1993
104th	Maj-2nd	7	6	Jan. 9, 1995
=104th	Maj-Ch2	7	6	Feb. 2, 1995
105th	Maj-VCh	9	8	Jan. 9, 1997
106th	Maj-Chr	11	10	Jan. 7, 1999

Connie Mack IV (R-Fla.)

Dates: Aug. 12, 1967
House: Jan. 3, 2005-date
Serving in the 111th Congress

HOUSE STANDING COMMITTEES:

1st BUDGET
Dates: Jan. 26, 2005-date
Departure: Still serving in the 111th Congress

Cong.	Ranking	Terms in: House	Terms in: Comm.	Date of Assignment
109th	Maj-21st	1	1	Jan. 26, 2005
110th	Min-11th	2	2	Jan. 10, 2007
111th	Min-8th	3	3	Jan. 9, 2009

2nd INTERNATIONAL RELATIONS, 109
FOREIGN AFFAIRS, 110-111
Dates: Jan. 26, 2005-date
Departure: Still serving in the 111th Congress

Cong.	Ranking	Terms in: House	Terms in: Comm.	Date of Assignment
109th	Maj-24th	1	1	Jan. 26, 2005
110th	Min-18th	2	2	Jan. 10, 2007
111th	Min-14th	3	3	Jan. 9, 2009

3rd TRANSPORTATION AND INFRASTRUCTURE
Dates: Jan. 26, 2005-date
Departure: Still serving in the 111th Congress

Cong.	Ranking	Terms in: House	Terms in: Comm.	Date of Assignment
109th	Maj-37th	1	1	Jan. 26, 2005
110th	Min-26th	2	2	Jan. 10, 2007
111th	Min-20th	3	3	Jan. 9, 2009

Mary Bono Mack; see Mary Mack Bono, p. 39

Daniel B. Maffei (D-N.Y.)

Dates: July 4, 1968
House: Jan. 3, 2009-date
Serving in the 111th Congress

HOUSE STANDING COMMITTEES:

1st FINANCIAL SERVICES
Dates: Jan. 7, 2009-date
Departure: Still serving in the 111th Congress

Cong.	Ranking	Terms in: House	Terms in: Comm.	Date of Assignment
111th	Maj-42nd	1	1	Jan. 7, 2009

2nd JUDICIARY
Dates: Jan. 21, 2009-date
Departure: Still serving in the 111th Congress

Cong.	Ranking	Terms in: House	Terms in: Comm.	Date of Assignment
111th	Maj-24th	1	1	Jan. 21, 2009

Tim Mahoney (D-Fla.)

Dates: Aug. 15, 1956
House: Jan. 3, 2007-Jan. 3, 2009
Left the House: Defeated for re-election in 2008

HOUSE STANDING COMMITTEES:

1st AGRICULTURE
Dates: Jan. 12, 2007-Jan. 3, 2009
Departure: Left the House; lost re-election

Cong.	Ranking	Terms in: House	Terms in: Comm.	Date of Assignment
110th	Maj-25th	1	1	Jan. 12, 2007

2nd FINANCIAL SERVICES
Dates: Jan. 12, 2007-Jan. 3, 2009
Departure: Left the House; lost re-election

Cong.	Ranking	Terms in: House	Terms in: Comm.	Date of Assignment
110th	Maj-30th	1	1	Jan. 12, 2007

Denise L. Majette (D-Ga.)

Dates: May 18, 1955
House: Jan. 3, 2003-Jan. 3, 2005
Left the House: Lost U.S. Senate election in 2004

HOUSE STANDING COMMITTEES:

1st BUDGET
Dates: Feb. 5, 2003-Jan. 3, 2005
Departure: Left the House; lost Senate election

Cong.	Ranking	Terms in: House	Terms in: Comm.	Date of Assignment
108th	Min-19th	1	1	Feb. 5, 2003

2nd EDUCATION AND THE WORKFORCE
Dates: Feb. 5, 2003-Jan. 3, 2005
Departure: Left the House; lost Senate election

Cong.	Ranking	Terms in: House	Terms in: Comm.	Date of Assignment
108th	Min-20th	1	1	Feb. 5, 2003

3rd SMALL BUSINESS
Dates: Feb. 26, 2003-Jan. 3, 2005
Departure: Left the House; lost Senate election

Cong.	Ranking	Terms in: House	Terms in: Comm.	Date of Assignment
108th	MnR-1st	1	1	Feb. 26, 2003

Carolyn B. Maloney (D-N.Y.)

Dates: Feb. 19, 1948
House: Jan. 3, 1993-date
Serving in the 111th Congress

HOUSE STANDING COMMITTEES:

1st BANKING, FINANCE AND URBAN AFFAIRS, 103
BANKING AND FINANCIAL SERVICES, 104-106
FINANCIAL SERVICES, 107-111

Dates: Jan. 5, 1993-date
Departure: Still serving in the 111th Congress

Cong.	Ranking	Terms in: House	Comm.	Date of Assignment
103rd	Maj-16th	1	1	Jan. 5, 1993
104th	Min-12th	2	2	Jan. 4, 1995
105th	Min-10th	3	3	Jan. 7, 1997
106th	Min-6th	4	4	Jan. 6, 1999
107th	Min-5th	5	5	Jan. 31, 2001
108th	Min-5th	6	6	Jan. 28, 2003
109th	Min-5th	7	7	Jan. 26, 2005
110th	Maj-4th	8	8	Jan. 12, 2007
111th	Maj-4th	9	9	Jan. 7, 2009

2nd GOVERNMENT OPERATIONS, 103
GOVERNMENT REFORM AND OVERSIGHT, 104-105
GOVERNMENT REFORM, 106-109
OVERSIGHT AND GOVERNMENT REFORM, 110-111
Dates: Jan. 5, 1993-date
Departure: Still serving in the 111th Congress

Cong.	Ranking	Terms in: House	Comm.	Date of Assignment
103rd	Maj-16th	1	1	Jan. 5, 1993
104th	Min-13th	2	2	Jan. 9, 1995
105th	Min-9th	3	3	Jan. 7, 1997
106th	Min-9th	4	4	Jan. 6, 1999
107th	Min-7th	5	5	Jan. 31, 2001
108th	Min-6th	6	6	Jan. 28, 2003
109th	Min-6th	7	7	Jan. 26, 2005
110th	Maj-5th	8	8	Jan. 12, 2007
111th	Maj-3rd	9	9	Jan. 28, 2009

JOINT COMMITTEES:

1st JOINT ECONOMIC
House Dates: Mar. 7, 1996-date
Departure: Still serving in the 111th Congress

Cong.	Ranking	Terms in: House	Comm.	Date of Assignment
104th	MnR-2nd	2	1	Mar. 7, 1996
105th	Min-4th	3	2	Mar. 11, 1997
106th	Min-2nd	4	3	Mar. 18, 1999
107th	Min-1st	5	4	May 1, 2001
108th	Min-2nd	6	5	Mar. 12, 2003
109th	Min-1st	7	6	Mar. 3, 2005
110th	Maj-VCh	8	7	Jan. 18, 2007
111th	Maj-Chr	9	8	Jan. 22, 2009

James H. Maloney (D-Conn.)

Dates: Sept. 17, 1948
House: Jan. 3, 1997-Jan. 3, 2003
Left the House: Defeated for re-election in 2002

HOUSE STANDING COMMITTEES:

1st BANKING AND FINANCIAL SERVICES, 105-106
FINANCIAL SERVICES, 107
Dates: Jan. 7, 1997-Jan. 3, 2003
Departure: Left the House; lost re-election

Cong.	Ranking	Terms in: House	Comm.	Date of Assignment
105th	Min-22nd	1	1	Jan. 7, 1997
106th	Min-12th	2	2	Jan. 6, 1999
107th	Min-11th	3	3	Jan. 31, 2001

2nd NATIONAL SECURITY, 105
ARMED SERVICES, 106-107
Dates: Feb. 5, 1997-Jan. 3, 2003
Departure: Left the House; lost re-election

Cong.	Ranking	Terms in: House	Comm.	Date of Assignment
105th	Min-24th	1	1	Feb. 5, 1997
106th	Min-19th	2	2	Jan. 6, 1999
107th	Min-17th	3	3	Jan. 31, 2001

David S. Mann (D-Ohio)

Dates: Sept. 25, 1939
House: Jan. 3, 1993-Jan. 3, 1995
Left the House: Defeated for re-election in 1994

HOUSE STANDING COMMITTEES:

1st ARMED SERVICES
Dates: Jan. 5, 1993-Jan. 3, 1995
Departure: Left the House; lost re-election

Cong.	Ranking	Terms in: House	Comm.	Date of Assignment
103rd	Maj-26th	1	1	Jan. 5, 1993

2nd JUDICIARY
Dates: Jan. 5, 1993-Jan. 3, 1995
Departure: Left the House; lost re-election

Cong.	Ranking	Terms in: House	Comm.	Date of Assignment
103rd	Maj-19th	1	1	Jan. 5, 1993

Thomas J. Manton (D-N.Y.)

Dates: Nov. 3, 1932
House: Jan. 3, 1985-Jan. 3, 1999
Left the House: Retired in 1998

HOUSE STANDING COMMITTEES:

1st BANKING, FINANCE AND URBAN AFFAIRS
Dates: Jan. 30, 1985-Jan. 3, 1989
Departure: Moved to Energy and Commerce

2nd MERCHANT MARINE AND FISHERIES
Dates: Jan. 30, 1985-Jan. 3, 1995
Departure: Committee abolished; no new assignment

Cong.	Ranking	Terms in: House	Comm.	Date of Assignment
103rd	Maj-7th	5	5	Jan. 5, 1993

3rd ENERGY AND COMMERCE, 101-103
COMMERCE, 104-105
Dates: Jan. 19, 1989-Jan. 3, 1999
Departure: Left the House; retired

Cong.	Ranking	Terms in: House	Comm.	Date of Assignment
103rd	Maj-17th	5	3	Jan. 5, 1993
104th	Min-9th	6	4	Jan. 4, 1995
105th	Min-7th	7	5	Jan. 7, 1997

4th HOUSE ADMINISTRATION
Dates: Oct. 16, 1989-Jan. 3, 1995
Departure: Left committee; no new assignment

Cong.	Ranking	Terms in: House	Comm.	Date of Assignment
103rd	Maj-6th	5	3	Jan. 21, 1993

HOUSE SELECT AND SPECIAL COMMITTEES:

1st SELECT AGING (Permanent)
Dates: Feb. 6, 1985-Jan. 3, 1993
Termination: Committee not renewed in 1993

2nd SELECT FIRE SAFETY IN THE HOUSE
Dates: June 16, 1988-Jan. 3, 1989
Termination: Committee not renewed in 1989

JOINT COMMITTEES:

1st JOINT LIBRARY
Dates: Feb. 21, 1991-Jan. 3, 1995
Departure: Left committee; no new assignment

Cong.	Ranking	Terms in: House	Comm.	Date of Assignment
103rd	Maj-3rd	5	2	May 1, 1993 Provisional

Donald A. Manzullo (R-Ill.)

Dates: March 24, 1944
House: Jan. 3, 1993-date
Serving in the 111th Congress

HOUSE STANDING COMMITTEES:

1st FOREIGN AFFAIRS, 103
INTERNATIONAL RELATIONS, 104-107
FOREIGN AFFAIRS, 110-111
1st Dates: Jan. 5, 1993-Jan. 3, 2001
1st Departure: Left committee; became Chair of Small Business
2nd Dates: Jan. 10, 2007-date
2nd Departure: Still serving in the 111th Congress

Cong.	Ranking	Terms in: House	Comm.	Date of Assignment
103rd	Min-16th	1 *1	1	Jan. 5, 1993
104th	Maj-14th	2 *1	2	Jan. 4, 1995
105th	Maj-12th	3 *1	3	Jan. 7, 1997
106th	Maj-12th	4 *1	4	Jan. 6, 1999
110th	Min-6th	8 *2	1	Jan. 10, 2007
111th	Min-6th	9 *2	2	Jan. 9, 2009

2nd SMALL BUSINESS
Dates: Jan. 5, 1993-Jan. 3, 2007
Departure: Returned to Foreign Affairs

Cong.	Ranking	Terms in: House	Comm.	Date of Assignment
103rd	Min-17th	1	1	Jan. 5, 1993
104th	Maj-5th	2	2	Jan. 4, 1995
105th	Maj-4th	3	3	Jan. 21, 1997
106th	Maj-4th	4	4	Jan. 6, 1999
107th	Maj-Chr	5	5	Jan. 6, 2001
108th	Maj-Chr	6	6	Jan. 8, 2003
109th	Maj-Chr	7	7	Jan. 6, 2005

3rd BANKING AND FINANCIAL SERVICES, 105-106
FINANCIAL SERVICES, 107-111
Dates: Apr. 16, 1997-date
Departure: Still serving in the 111th Congress

Cong.	Ranking	Terms in: House	Comm.	Date of Assignment
105th	MjR-1st	3	1	Apr. 16, 1997
106th	Maj-24th	4	2	Jan. 6, 1999
107th	Maj-21st	5	3	Jan. 6, 2001
108th	Maj-16th	6	4	Jan. 28, 2003
109th	Maj-16th	7	5	Jan. 26, 2005
110th	Min-11th	8	6	Jan. 10, 2007
111th	Min-7th	9	7	Jan. 9, 2009

JOINT COMMITTEES:

1st JOINT ECONOMIC
House Dates: Jan. 19, 1995-May 22, 1997
Departure: Resigned committee; moved to Financial Services

Cong.	Ranking	Terms in: House	Comm.	Date of Assignment
104th	Maj-5th	2	1	Jan. 19, 1995
105th	Maj-2nd	3	2	Feb. 27, 1997

Kenny Marchant (R-Tex.)

Dates: Feb. 23, 1951
House: Jan. 3, 2005-date
Serving in the 111th Congress

HOUSE STANDING COMMITTEES:

1st EDUCATION AND THE WORKFORCE, 109
EDUCATION AND LABOR, 110
Dates: Jan. 26, 2005-Jan. 3, 2009
Departure: Left committee; no new assignment

Cong.	Ranking	Terms in: House	Comm.	Date of Assignment
109th	Maj-20th	1	1	Jan. 26, 2005
110th	Min-14th	2	2	Jan. 10, 2007

2nd GOVERNMENT REFORM, 109
OVERSIGHT AND GOVERNMENT REFORM, 110
Dates: Jan. 26, 2005-Jan. 3, 2009
Departure: Left committee; no new assignment

Cong.	Ranking	Terms in: House	Comm.	Date of Assignment
109th	Maj-19th	1	1	Jan. 26, 2005
110th	Min-12th	2	2	Jan. 10, 2007

3rd TRANSPORTATION AND INFRASTRUCTURE
Dates: Jan. 26, 2005-Mar. 9, 2007
Departure: Resigned committee; moved to Financial Services

Cong.	Ranking	Terms in: House	Comm.	Date of Assignment
109th	Maj-32nd	1	1	Jan. 26, 2005
110th	Min-22nd	2	2	Jan. 10, 2007

4th FINANCIAL SERVICES
Dates: Mar. 12, 2007-date
Departure: Still serving in the 111th Congress

Cong.	Ranking	Terms in: House	Comm.	Date of Assignment
110th	MnR-1st	2	1	Mar. 12, 2007
111th	Min-22nd	3	2	Jan. 9, 2009

Marjorie Margolies-Mezvinsky

(D-Penn.)

Dates: June 21, 1942
House: Jan. 3, 1993-Jan. 3, 1995
Left the House: Defeated for re-election in 1994

HOUSE STANDING COMMITTEES:

1st ENERGY AND COMMERCE
Dates: Jan. 5, 1993-Jan. 3, 1995
Departure: Left the House; lost re-election

Cong.	Ranking	Terms in: House	Comm.	Date of Assignment
103rd	Maj-26th	1	1	Jan. 5, 1993

2nd SMALL BUSINESS
Dates: Jan. 5, 1993-Jan. 3, 1995
Departure: Left the House; lost re-election

Cong.	Ranking	Terms in: House	Comm.	Date of Assignment
103rd	Maj-21st	1	1	Jan. 5, 1993

3rd GOVERNMENT OPERATIONS
Dates: Feb. 4, 1993-Jan. 3, 1995
Departure: Left the House; lost re-election

Cong.	Ranking	Terms in: House	Comm.	Date of Assignment
103rd	Maj-23rd	1	1	Feb. 4, 1993

Betsy Markey (D-Colo.)

Dates: April 27, 1946
House: Jan. 3, 2009-date
Serving in the 111th Congress

HOUSE STANDING COMMITTEES:

1st TRANSPORTATION AND INFRASTRUCTURE
Dates: Jan. 7, 2009-date
Departure: Still serving in the 111th Congress

Cong.	Ranking	Terms in: House	Comm.	Date of Assignment
111th	Maj-40th	1	1	Jan. 7, 2009

2nd AGRICULTURE
Dates: Jan. 21, 2009-date
Departure: Still serving in the 111th Congress

Cong.	Ranking	Terms in: House	Comm.	Date of Assignment
111th	Maj-21st	1	1	Jan. 21, 2009

Edward J. Markey (D-Mass.)

Dates: July 11, 1946
House: Nov. 2, 1976-date
Serving in the 111th Congress

H: Markey was elected to the 94th Congress by special election, Nov. 2, 1976 to fill the vacancy caused by the death of U.S. Representative Torbert H. Macdonald (D-Mass.). Markey was not seated nor assigned to committees because the 94th Congress was not in session.

HOUSE STANDING COMMITTEES:

1st INTERIOR AND INSULAR AFFAIRS, 95-102
NATURAL RESOURCES, 103
RESOURCES, 104-105, 107-109
NATURAL RESOURCES, 110-111
1st Dates: Jan. 19, 1977-Jan. 3, 1995
1st Departure: Left committee; no new assignment
2nd Dates: Nov. 20, 1995-Jan. 3, 1999
2nd Departure: Moved to Budget
3rd Dates: Feb. 8, 2001-Feb. 12, 2003
Leave of absence from committee; moved to Select Homeland Security; returned on March 5, 2003
4th Dates: Mar. 5, 2003-date
Departure: Still serving in the 111th Congress

Cong.	Ranking	Terms in: House	Comm.	Date of Assignment
103rd	Maj-3rd	10 *1	9	Jan. 5, 1993
104th	MnR-2nd	11 *2	1	Nov. 20, 1995
105th	Min-2nd	12 *2	2	Jan. 7, 1997
107th	Min-3rd	14 *3	1	Feb. 8, 2001
108th	Min-3rd	15 *3	2	Jan. 28, 2003
108th	MnR-4th	15 *4	1	Mar. 5, 2003
109th	Min-17th	16 *4	2	Feb. 2, 2005
110th	Maj-16th	17 *4	3	Jan. 18, 2007
111th	Maj-15th	18 *4	4	Jan. 21, 2009

2nd INTERSTATE AND FOREIGN COMMERCE, 95-96
ENERGY AND COMMERCE, 97-103
COMMERCE, 104-106
ENERGY AND COMMERCE 107-111
Dates: Jan. 19, 1977-date
Departure: Still serving in the 111th Congress

Cong.	Ranking	Terms in: House	Comm.	Date of Assignment
103rd	Maj-4th	10	9	Jan. 5, 1993
104th	Min-3rd	11	10	Jan. 4, 1995
105th	Min-3rd	12	11	Jan. 7, 1997
106th	Min-3rd	13	12	Jan. 6, 1999
107th	Min-3rd	14	13	Jan. 31, 2001
108th	Min-3rd	15	14	Jan. 28, 2003
109th	Min-3rd	16	15	Jan. 26, 2005
110th	Maj-3rd	17	16	Jan. 4, 2007
111th	Maj-3rd	18	17	Jan. 7, 2009

3rd BUDGET
Dates: Jan. 6, 1999-Jan. 3, 2003
Departure: Moved to Select Homeland Security

Cong.	Ranking	Terms in: House	Comm.	Date of Assignment
106th	Min-11th	13	1	Jan. 6, 1999
107th	Min-8th	14	2	Jan. 31, 2001

4th HOMELAND SECURITY
Dates: Feb. 9, 2005-Jan. 3, 2009
Departure: Left committee; no new assignment

Cong.	Ranking	Terms in: House	Comm.	Date of Assignment
109th	Min-3rd	16	2	Feb. 9, 2005
110th	Maj-3rd	17	3	Jan. 12, 2007

HOUSE SELECT AND SPECIAL COMMITTEES:

1st SELECT HOMELAND SECURITY
Dates: Feb. 12, 2003-Jan. 3, 2005
Departure: Continued on reorganized standing committee

Cong.	Ranking	Terms in: House	Comm.	Date of Assignment
108th	Min-4th	15	1	Feb. 12, 2003

2nd SELECT ENERGY INDEPENDENCE AND GLOBAL WARMING
Dates: Mar. 9, 2007-date
Departure: Still serving in the 111th Congress

Cong.	Ranking	Terms in: House	Comm.	Date of Assignment
110th	Maj-Chr	17	1	Mar. 9, 2007
111th	Maj-Chr	18	2	Jan. 14, 2009

Jim Marshall (D-Ga.)

Dates: March 31, 1948
House: Jan. 3, 2003-date
Serving in the 111th Congress

HOUSE STANDING COMMITTEES:

1st AGRICULTURE
Dates: Feb. 5, 2003-date
Departure: Still serving in the 111th Congress

Cong.	Ranking	Terms in: House	Comm.	Date of Assignment
108th	Min-20th	1	1	Feb. 5, 2003
109th	Min-10th	2	2	Jan. 26, 2005
110th	Maj-9th	3	3	Jan. 12, 2007
111th	Maj-8th	4	4	Jan. 21, 2009

2nd ARMED SERVICES
Dates: Feb. 5, 2003-date
Departure: Still serving in the 111th Congress

Cong.	Ranking	Terms in: House	Comm.	Date of Assignment
108th	Min-25th	1	1	Feb. 5, 2003
109th	Min-21st	2	2	Jan. 26, 2005
110th	Maj-19th	3	3	Jan. 10, 2007
111th	Maj-18th	4	4	Jan. 7, 2009

3rd SMALL BUSINESS
Dates: Feb. 13, 2003-Jan. 3, 2005
Departure: Left committee; no new assignment

Cong.	Ranking	Terms in: House	Comm.	Date of Assignment
108th	Min-16th	1	1	Feb. 13, 2003

4th FINANCIAL SERVICES
Dates: Jan. 12, 2007-June 10, 2008
Departure: Resigned committee; no new assignment

Cong.	Ranking	Terms in: House	Comm.	Date of Assignment
110th	Maj-35th	3	1	Jan. 12, 2007

Matthew G. Martinez (R-Cal.)

Dates: Feb. 14, 1929
House: July 13, 1982-Jan. 3, 2001
Left the House: Defeated for re-nomination in 2002 as a Democrat;
Served as a Democrat: July 13, 1982-July 26, 2000
Democratic Caucus confirmation letter Sep. 13, 2000
Served as a Republican: July 27, 2000-Jan. 3, 2001

H: Martinez was elected to the 97th Congress by special election, July 13, 1982, to fill the vacancy caused by the resignation of U.S. Representative George E. Danielson (D-Cal.). Martinez was seated July 15, 1982, and assigned to committees.

HOUSE STANDING COMMITTEES:

1st VETERANS AFFAIRS
Dates: Aug. 19, 1982-Jan. 3, 1985
Departure: Moved to Small Business and Government Operations

2nd EDUCATION AND LABOR, 97-103
ECONOMIC AND EDUCATIONAL OPPORTUNITIES, 104
EDUCATION AND THE WORKFORCE, 105-106
Dates: Aug. 19, 1982-July 26, 2000
Departure: Lost re-nomination; service on committee as a Democrat was vacated; moved to Transportation and Infrastructure as a Republican.

Cong.	Ranking	Terms in: House	Comm.	Date of Assignment
103rd	Maj-7th	7	7	Jan. 5, 1993
104th	Min-5th	8	8	Jan. 4, 1995
105th	Min-4th	9	9	Jan. 7, 1997
106th	Min-4th	10	10	Jan. 6, 1999

3rd SMALL BUSINESS
1st Dates: Jan. 30, 1985-Feb. 27, 1985
1st Departure: Moved to Government Operations
2nd Dates: Jan. 22, 1987-Jan. 3, 1989
2nd Departure: Left committee; no new assignment

4th GOVERNMENT OPERATIONS
Dates: Feb. 27, 1985-Jan. 3, 1993
Departure: Moved to Foreign Affairs

5th FOREIGN AFFAIRS, 103
INTERNATIONAL RELATIONS, 104-106
Dates: Jan. 5, 1993-July 26, 2000
Departure: Lost re-nomination; service on committee as a Democrat was vacated; moved to Transportation and Infrastructure as a Republican

Cong.	Ranking	Terms in: House	Comm.	Date of Assignment
103rd	Maj-12th	7	1	Jan. 5, 1993
104th	Min-10th	8	2	Jan. 4, 1995
105th	Min-7th	9	3	Jan. 7, 1997
106th	Min-6th	10	4	Jan. 6, 1999

6th TRANSPORTATION AND INFRASTRUCTURE
Dates: Oct. 3, 2000-Jan. 3, 2001
Departure: Left the House; did not run as a Republican

Cong.	Ranking	Terms in: House	Comm.	Date of Assignment
106th	MjR-2nd	10	1	Oct. 3, 2000

HOUSE SELECT AND SPECIAL COMMITTEES:

1st SELECT CHILDREN, YOUTH AND FAMILIES (Temporary)
Dates: Mar. 13, 1984-Jan. 3, 1993
Termination: Committee not renewed in 1993; moved to Foreign Affairs

---

Melquiades R. (Mel) Martinez (R-Fla.)

Dates: Oct. 23, 1946-
Senate: Jan. 3, 2005-Sept. 9, 2009
Left the Senate: Resigned and retired in 2009

SENATE STANDING COMMITTEES:

1st BANKING, HOUSING, AND URBAN AFFAIRS
Dates: Jan. 6, 2005- Sept. 9, 2009
Departure: Resigned the Senate and retired

Cong.	Ranking	Years in: House	Comm.	Date of Assignment
109th	Maj-11th	1	1	Jan. 6, 2005
110th	Min-10th	3	3	Jan. 12, 2007
111th	Min-5th	5	5	Jan. 21, 2009

2nd ENERGY AND NATURAL RESOURCES
Dates: Jan. 6, 2005-Jan. 21, 2009
Departure: Moved to Commerce, Science and Transportation

Cong.	Ranking	Years in: Senate	Comm.	Date of Assignment
109th	Maj-7th	1	1	Jan. 6, 2005
110th	Min-11th	3	3	Jan. 12, 2007

3rd FOREIGN RELATIONS
Dates: Jan. 6, 2005-Jan. 12, 2007
Departure: Moved to Armed Services

Cong.	Ranking	Years in: Senate	Comm.	Date of Assignment
109th	Maj-10th	1	1	Jan. 6, 2005

4th ARMED SERVICES
Dates: Jan. 12, 2007- Sept. 9, 2009
Departure: Resigned the Senate and retired

Cong.	Ranking	Years in: Senate	Comm.	Date of Assignment
110th	Min-12th	3	1	Jan. 12, 2007
111th	Min-7th	5	3	Jan. 21, 2009

5th COMMERCE, SCIENCE, AND TRANSPORTATION
Dates: Jan. 21, 2009- Sept. 9, 2009
Departure: Resigned the Senate and retired

Cong.	Ranking	Years in: Senate	Comm.	Date of Assignment
111th	Min-10th	5	1	Jan. 21, 2009

SENATE SELECT AND SPECIAL COMMITTEES:

1st SPECIAL AGING (Permanent)
Dates: Jan. 6, 2005-Sept. 9, 2009
Departure: Resigned the Senate and retired

Cong.	Ranking	Years in: Senate	Comm.	Date of Assignment
109th	Maj-6th	1	1	Jan. 6, 2005
110th	Min-4th	3	3	Jan. 12, 2007
111th	Min-RM	5	5	Jan. 21, 2009

William J. Martini (R-N.J.)

Dates: Jan. 10, 1947
House: Jan. 3, 1995-Jan. 3, 1997
Left the House: Defeated for re-election in 1996.

HOUSE STANDING COMMITTEES:

1st GOVERNMENT REFORM AND OVERSIGHT
Dates: Jan. 4, 1995-Jan. 3, 1997
Departure: Left the House; lost re-election

Cong.	Ranking	Terms in: House	Comm.	Date of Assignment
104th	Maj-20th	1	1	Jan. 4, 1995

2nd TRANSPORTATION AND INFRASTRUCTURE
Dates: Jan. 4, 1995-Jan. 3, 1997
Departure: Left the House; lost re-election

Cong.	Ranking	Terms in: House	Comm.	Date of Assignment
104th	Maj-33rd	1	1	Jan. 4, 1995

Frank R. Mascara (D-Penn.)

Dates: Jan. 19, 1930
House: Jan. 3, 1995-Jan. 3, 2003
Left the House: Defeated for re-nomination in 2002

HOUSE STANDING COMMITTEES:

1st GOVERNMENT REFORM AND OVERSIGHT
Dates: Jan. 9, 1995-July 11, 1995
Departure: Resigned committee; moved to Transportation and Infrastructure

Cong.	Ranking	Terms in: House	Comm.	Date of Assignment
104th	Min-21st	1	1	Jan. 9, 1995

2nd VETERANS' AFFAIRS
Dates: Jan. 4. 1995-Jan. 3, 1999
Departure: Moved to Banking and Financial Services

Cong.	Ranking	Terms in: House	Comm.	Date of Assignment
104th	Min-15th	1	1	Jan. 4, 1995
105th	Min-9th	2	2	Feb. 6, 1997

3rd TRANSPORTATION AND INFRASTRUCTURE
Dates: July 12, 1995-Jan. 3, 2003
Departure: Left the House; lost re-nomination

Cong.	Ranking	Terms in: House	Comm.	Date of Assignment
104th	MnR-2nd	1	1	July 12, 1995
105th	Min-21st	2	2	Jan. 7, 1997
106th	Min-18th	3	3	Jan. 6, 1999
107th	Min-15th	4	4	Jan. 31, 2001

4th BANKING AND FINANCIAL SERVICES, 106 FINANCIAL SERVICES, 107
Dates: Jan. 6, 1999-Jan. 3, 2003
Departure: Left the House; lost re-nomination

Cong.	Ranking	Terms in: House	Comm.	Date of Assignment
106th	Min-21st	3	1	Jan. 6, 1999
107th	Min-18th	4	2	Jan. 31, 2001

Eric J. J. Massa (D-N.Y.)

Dates: Sept. 16, 1959
House: Jan. 3, 2009-Mar. 8, 2010
Left the House: Resigned; health and ethical issues

HOUSE STANDING COMMITTEES:

1st ARMED SERVICES
Dates: Jan. 7, 2009-Mar. 8, 2010
Departure: Resigned the House

Cong.	Ranking	Terms in: House	Comm.	Date of Assignment
111th	Maj-36th	1	1	Jan. 7, 2009

2nd AGRICULTURE
Dates: Jan. 21, 2009-Mar. 8, 2010
Departure: Resigned the House

Cong.	Ranking	Terms in: House	Comm.	Date of Assignment
111th	Maj-19th	1	1	Jan. 21, 2009

3rd HOMELAND SECURITY
Dates: Jan. 28, 2009-Mar. 8, 2010
Departure: Resigned the House

Cong.	Ranking	Terms in: House	Comm.	Date of Assignment
111th	Maj-19th	1	1	Jan. 28, 2009

James D. Matheson (D-Utah)

Dates: March 21, 1960
House: Jan. 3, 2001-date
Serving in the 111th Congress

HOUSE STANDING COMMITTEES:

1st TRANSPORTATION AND INFRASTRUCTURE
Dates: Jan. 31, 2001- Jan. 3, 2007
Departure: Moved to Energy and Commerce

Cong.	Ranking	Terms in: House	Comm.	Date of Assignment
107th	Min-32nd	1	1	Jan. 31, 2001
108th	Min-24th	2	2	Jan. 28, 2003
109th	Min-21st	3	3	Jan. 26, 2005

2nd SCIENCE, 107-109
SCIENCE AND TECHNOLOGY, 110-111
1st Dates: Feb. 8, 2001-Jan. 3, 2003
1st Departure: Moved to Financial Services
2nd Dates: Feb. 13, 2003-date
2nd Departure: Still serving in the 111th Congress

Cong.	Ranking	Terms in: House	Comm.	Date of Assignment
107th	MnR-1st	1 *1	1	Feb. 8, 2001
108th	MnR-1st	2 *2	1	Feb. 13, 2003
109th	Min-17th	3 *2	2	Feb. 2, 2005
110th	Maj-17th	4 *2	3	Jan. 18, 2007
111th	Maj-16th	5 *2	4	Jan. 21, 2009

3rd BUDGET
Dates: Mar. 14, 2001-Jan. 3, 2003
Departure: Moved to Financial Services

Cong.	Ranking	Terms in: House	Comm.	Date of Assignment
107th	MnR-1st	1	1	Mar. 14, 2001

4th FINANCIAL SERVICES
Dates: Jan. 28, 2003-Jan. 3, 2007
Departure: Moved to Energy and Commerce

Cong.	Ranking	Terms in: House	Comm.	Date of Assignment
108th	Min-28th	2	1	Jan. 28, 2003
109th	Min-24th	3	2	Jan. 26, 2005

5th ENERGY AND COMMERCE
Dates: Jan. 4, 2007-date
Departure: Still serving in the 111th Congress.

Cong.	Ranking	Terms in: House	Comm.	Date of Assignment
110th	Maj-27th	4	1	Jan. 4, 2007
111th	Maj-22nd	5	2	Jan. 7, 2009

Harlan Mathews (D-Tenn.)

Dates: Jan. 17, 1927
Senate: Jan. 2, 1993-Dec. 1, 1994
Left Senate: Resigned and retired in 1994

S: Mathews was appointed to the 102nd Congress, Jan. 2, 1993, to fill the vacancy caused by the resignation of U.S. Senator Albert A. Gore Jr. (D-Tenn.) who had been elected Vice President in 1992. Mathews was not a candidate in 1994 to fill the unexpired term.

SENATE STANDING COMMITTEES:

1st ENERGY AND NATURAL RESOURCES
Dates: Jan. 7, 1993-Dec. 1, 1994
Departure: Resigned the Senate and retired

Cong.	Ranking	Years in: Senate	Comm.	Date of Assignment
103rd	Maj-10th	1	1	Jan. 7, 1993

2nd FOREIGN RELATIONS
Dates: Jan. 7, 1993-Dec. 1, 1994
Departure: Resigned the Senate and retired

Cong.	Ranking	Years in: Senate	Comm.	Date of Assignment
103rd	Maj-11th	1	1	Jan. 7, 1993

3rd RULES AND ADMINISTRATION
Dates: Jan. 21, 1993-Dec. 1, 1994
Departure: Resigned the Senate and retired

Cong.	Ranking	Years in: Senate	Comm.	Date of Assignment
103rd	Maj-9th	1	1	Jan. 21, 1993

4th COMMERCE, SCIENCE AND TRANSPORTATION
Dates: July 15, 1993-Dec. 1, 1994
Departure: Resigned the Senate and retired

Cong.	Ranking	Years in: Senate	Comm.	Date of Assignment
103rd	MjR-2nd	1	1	July 15, 1993

JOINT COMMITTEES:

1st JOINT PRINTING
Senate Dates: Jan. 28, 1993-Dec. 1, 1994
Departure: Resigned the Senate and retired

Cong.	Ranking	Years in: Senate	Comm.	Date of Assignment
103rd	Maj-3rd	1	1	Jan. 28, 1993

Doris O. Matsui (D-Cal.)

Dates: Sept. 25, 1944-date
House: March 8, 2005-date
Serving in the 111th Congress

H: Doris Matsui was elected to the 109th Congress by special election, March 8, 2005, to fill the vacancy caused by the death of her husband, U.S. Representative Robert T. Matsui (D-Cal.) who died before the opening of the 109th Congress. Mrs. Matsui was seated March 10, 2005, and assigned to committees.

HOUSE STANDING COMMITTEES:

1st RULES
Dates: Mar. 16, 2005-date
Departure: Still serving in the 111th Congress

Cong.	Ranking	Terms in: House	Comm.	Date of Assignment
109th	Min-4th	1	1	Mar. 16, 2005
110th	Maj-4th	2	2	Jan. 12, 2007
111th	Maj-4th	3	3	Jan. 6, 2009

2nd SCIENCE
Dates: May 4, 2006-Jan. 3, 2007
Departure: Moved to Transportation and Infrastructure

Cong.	Ranking	Terms in: House	Comm.	Date of Assignment
109th	MnA-21st	1	1	May 4, 2006

3rd TRANSPORTATION AND INFRASTRUCTURE
Dates: Jan. 10, 2007-June 10, 2008
Departure: Resigned committee; moved to Energy and Commerce

Cong.	Ranking	Terms in: House	Comm.	Date of Assignment
110th	Maj-27th	2	1	Jan. 10, 2007

4th ENERGY AND COMMERCE
Dates: June 10, 2008-date
Departure: Still serving in the 111th Congress

Cong.	Ranking	Terms in: House	Comm.	Date of Assignment
110th	MjR-1st	2	1	June 10, 2008
111th	Maj-28th	3	2	Jan. 7, 2009

Robert T. Matsui (D-Cal.)

Dates: Sept. 17, 1941-Jan. 1, 2005
House: Jan. 3, 1979-Jan. 1, 2005
Left the House: Died in office

HOUSE STANDING COMMITTEES:

1st GOVERNMENT OPERATIONS
Dates: Jan. 24, 1979-Jan. 3, 1981
Departure: Moved to Ways and Means

2nd JUDICIARY
Dates: Jan. 24, 1979-Nov. 7, 1979
Departure: Moved to Interstate and Foreign Commerce

3rd INTERSTATE AND FOREIGN COMMERCE
Dates: Nov. 7, 1979-Jan. 3, 1981
Departure: Moved to Ways and Means

4th WAYS AND MEANS
Dates: Jan. 28, 1981-Jan. 1, 2005
Departure: Died in office

Cong.	Ranking	Terms in: House	Comm.	Date of Assignment
103rd	Maj-8th	8	7	Jan. 5, 1993
104th	Min-6th	9	8	Jan. 4, 1995
105th	Min-3rd	10	9	Jan. 7, 1997
106th	Min-3rd	11	10	Jan. 6, 1999
107th	Min-3rd	12	11	Jan. 31, 2001
108th	Min-3rd	13	12	Jan. 28, 2003

5th BUDGET
Dates: Jan. 24, 1991-Jan. 3, 1993
Departure: Left committee; no new assignment

HOUSE SELECT AND SPECIAL COMMITTEES:

1st SELECT NARCOTICS ABUSE AND CONTROL (Temporary)
Dates: Mar. 18, 1981-June 17, 1987
Departure: Left committee; no new assignment

Romano L. Mazzoli (D-Ky.)

Dates: Nov. 2, 1932
House: Jan. 3, 1971-Jan. 3, 1995
Left the House: Retired in 1994

HOUSE STANDING COMMITTEES:

1st EDUCATION AND LABOR
Dates: Feb. 4, 1971-Jan. 3, 1975
Departure: Moved to Judiciary

2nd DISTRICT OF COLUMBIA
Dates: Jan. 24, 1973-Jan. 3, 1989
Departure: Left committee; no new assignment

3rd JUDICIARY
Dates: Jan. 20, 1975-Jan. 3, 1995
Departure: Left the House; retired

Cong.	Ranking	Terms in: House	Comm.	Date of Assignment
103rd	Maj-4th	12	10	Jan. 5, 1993

4th SMALL BUSINESS
Dates: Jan. 28, 1981-Jan. 3, 1995
Departure: Left the House; retired

Cong.	Ranking	Terms in: House	Comm.	Date of Assignment
103rd	Maj-4th	12	7	Jan. 5, 1993

HOUSE SELECT AND SPECIAL COMMITTEES:

1st SELECT ETHICS
Dates: Mar. 10, 1977-Jan. 3, 1979
Termination: House Report 1837 (95-2) filed

2nd PERMANENT SELECT INTELLIGENCE
Dates: July 27, 1977-Jan. 3, 1985
Departure: Left committee; no new assignment

3rd SELECT NARCOTICS ABUSE AND CONTROL (Temporary)
Dates: Feb. 21, 1991-Jan. 3, 1993
Termination: Committee not renewed in 1993

John S. McCain III (R-Ariz.)

Dates: Aug. 29, 1936
House: Jan. 3, 1983-Jan. 3, 1987
Left the House: Elected to U.S. Senate in 1986

Senate: Jan. 3, 1987-date
Serving in the 111th Congress

HOUSE STANDING COMMITTEES:

1st INTERIOR AND INSULAR AFFAIRS
Dates: Jan. 6, 1983-Jan. 3, 1987
Departure: Left the House for the Senate

2nd EDUCATION AND LABOR
Dates: Jan. 26, 1984-Jan. 3, 1985
Departure: Moved to Foreign Affairs

3rd FOREIGN AFFAIRS
Dates: Jan. 30, 1985-Jan. 3, 1987
Departure: Left the House for the Senate

HOUSE SELECT AND SPECIAL COMMITTEES:

1st SELECT AGING (Permanent)
Dates: Feb. 8, 1983-Jan. 3, 1987
Departure: Left the House for the Senate

SENATE STANDING COMMITTEES:

1st ARMED SERVICES
Dates: Jan. 6, 1987-date
Departure: Still serving in the 111th Congress

Cong.	Ranking	Years in: Senate	Comm.	Date of Assignment
103rd	Min-4th	7	7	Jan. 7, 1993
104th	Maj-4th	9	8	Jan. 4, 1995
105th	Maj-3rd	11	11	Jan. 9, 1997
106th	Maj-3rd	13	13	Jan. 7, 1999
107th	Maj-3rd	15	15	Jan. 25, 2001
+107th	Min-3rd	15	15	June 6, 2001
108th	Maj-2nd	17	17	Jan. 15, 2003
109th	Maj-2nd	19	19	Jan. 6, 2005
110th	Min-RM	21	21	Jan. 12, 2007
111th	Min-RM	23	23	Jan. 21, 2009

2nd COMMERCE, SCIENCE AND TRANSPORTATION
Dates: Jan. 6, 1987-Jan. 21, 2009
Ch1: Replaced by Ernest F. Hollings (Dem-S.C.) following pary control shift on June 6, 2001, and became RM2.
Departure: Returned to Homeland Security and Governmental Affairs; moved to Energy and Natural Resources

Cong.	Ranking	Years in: Senate	Comm.	Date of Assignment
103rd	Min-5th	7	7	Jan. 7, 1993
104th	Maj-4th	9	8	Jan. 4, 1995
105th	Maj-Chr	11	11	Jan. 9, 1997
106th	Maj-Chr	13	13	Jan. 7, 1999
107th	Maj-Ch1	15	15	Jan. 25, 2001
+107th	Min-RM2	15	15	June 6, 2001
108th	Maj-Chr	17	17	Jan. 15, 2003
109th	Maj-2nd	19	19	Jan. 6, 2005
110th	Min-2nd	21	21	Jan. 12, 2007

3rd GOVERNMENTAL AFFAIRS, 103-104
HOMELAND SECURITY AND GOVERNMENTAL AFFAIRS, 111
1st Dates: Jan. 7, 1993-Jan. 3, 1997
1st Departure: Left committee; became Chair of Commerce, Science and Transportation
2nd Dates: Jan. 21, 2009-date
2nd Departure: Still serving in the 111th Congress

Cong.	Ranking	Years in: Senate	Comm.	Date of Assignment
103rd	Min-5th	7 *1	1	Jan. 7, 1993
104th	Maj-7th	9 *1	2	Jan. 5, 1995
111th	Min-3rd	23 *2	1	Jan. 21, 2009

4th ENERGY AND NATURAL RESOURCES
Dates: Jan. 21, 2009-date
Departure: Still serving in the 111th Congress

Cong.	Ranking	Years in: Senate	Comm.	Date of Assignment
111th	Min-6th	23	1	Jan. 21, 2009

SENATE SELECT AND SPECIAL COMMITTEES:

1st SELECT INDIAN AFFAIRS (Permanent), 100-102
INDIAN AFFAIRS (Permanent), 103-111
Dates: Jan. 6, 1987-date
Departure: Still serving in the 111th Congress.

Cong.	Ranking	Years in: Senate	Comm.	Date of Assignment
103rd	Min-RM	7	6	Jan. 5, 1993
104th	Maj-Chr	9	9	Jan. 11, 1995
105th	Maj-3rd	11	11	Jan. 9, 1997
106th	Maj-3rd	13	13	Jan. 7, 1999
107th	Maj-3rd	15	15	Jan. 25, 2001
+107th	Min-3rd	15	15	June 6, 2001
108th	Maj-2nd	17	17	Jan. 15, 2003
109th	Maj-Chr	19	19	Jan. 6, 2005
110th	Min-2nd	21	21	Jan. 12, 2007
111th	Min-2nd	23	23	Jan. 21, 2009

2nd SPECIAL AGING (Permanent)
Dates: Mar. 19, 1991-Jan. 11, 1995
Departure: Left committee; became Chair of Indian Affairs

Cong.	Ranking	Years in: Senate	Comm.	Date of Assignment
103rd	Min-6th	7	2	Jan. 21, 1993

3rd SELECT POW-MIA AFFAIRS
Dates: Sep. 17, 1991-Feb. 3, 1993
Termination: Senate Report 1 (103-1) filed

Alfred A. McCandless (R-Cal.)

Dates: July 23, 1927
House: Jan. 3, 1983-Jan. 3, 1995
Left the House: Retired in 1994

HOUSE STANDING COMMITTEES:

1st GOVERNMENT OPERATIONS
Dates: Jan. 6, 1983-Jan. 3, 1995
Departure: Left the House; retired

Cong.	Ranking	Terms in: House	Comm.	Date of Assignment
103rd	Min-2nd	6	6	Jan. 5, 1993

2nd SCIENCE AND TECHNOLOGY
Dates: Jan. 6, 1983-Jan. 3, 1985
Departure: Moved to Banking, Finance and Urban Affairs

3rd BANKING, FINANCE AND URBAN AFFAIRS
Dates: Jan. 30, 1985-Jan. 3, 1995
Departure: Left the House; retired

Cong.	Ranking	Terms in: House	Comm.	Date of Assignment
103rd	Min-7th	6	5	Jan. 5, 1993

Carolyn McCarthy (D-N.Y.)

Dates: Jan. 5, 1944
House: Jan. 3, 1997-date
Serving in the 111th Congress

HOUSE STANDING COMMITTEES:

1st EDUCATION AND THE WORKFORCE, 105-109
EDUCATION AND LABOR, 110-111
Dates: Jan. 7, 1997-date
Departure: Still serving in the 111th Congress

Cong.	Ranking	Terms in: House	Comm.	Date of Assignment
105th	Min-16th	1	1	Jan. 7, 1997
106th	Min-15th	2	2	Jan. 6, 1999
107th	Min-13th	3	3	Jan. 31, 2001
108th	Min-8th	4	4	Jan. 28, 2003
109th	Min-9th	5	5	Jan. 26, 2005
110th	Maj-8th	6	6	Jan. 10, 2007
111th	Maj-8th	7	7	Jan. 21, 2009

2nd SMALL BUSINESS
Dates: Feb. 5, 1997-Feb. 12, 2001
Departure: Leave of absence; moved to Budget; never returned

Cong.	Ranking	Terms in: House	Comm.	Date of Assignment
105th	Min-14th	1	1	Feb. 5, 1997
106th	Min-5th	2	2	Jan. 6, 1999
107th	Min-4th	3	3	Jan. 31, 2001

3rd BUDGET
Dates: Feb. 8, 2001-Jan. 3, 2003
Departure: Moved to Financial Services

Cong.	Ranking	Terms in: House	Comm.	Date of Assignment
107th	Min-16th	3	1	Feb. 8, 2001

4th FINANCIAL SERVICES
Dates: Jan. 28, 2003-date
Departure: Still serving in the 111th Congress.

Cong.	Ranking	Terms in: House	Comm.	Date of Assignment
108th	Min-26th	4	1	Jan. 28, 2003
109th	Min-22nd	5	2	Jan. 26, 2005
110th	Maj-16th	6	3	Jan. 12, 2007
111th	Maj-15th	7	4	Jan. 7, 2009

Karen McCarthy (D-Mo.)

Dates: March 18, 1947
House: Jan. 3, 1995-Jan. 3, 2005
Left the House: Retired in 2004

HOUSE STANDING COMMITTEES:

1st SCIENCE
Dates: Jan. 4, 1995-Jan. 3, 1997
Departure: Moved to Commerce

Cong.	Ranking	Terms in: House	Comm.	Date of Assignment
104th	Min-17th	1	1	Jan. 4, 1995

2nd SMALL BUSINESS
Dates: Jan. 5, 1995-June 13, 1995
Departure: Resigned committee; moved to Transportation and Infrastructure

Cong.	Ranking	Terms in: House	Comm.	Date of Assignment
104th	Min-17th	1	1	Jan. 5, 1995

3rd TRANSPORTATION AND INFRASTRUCTURE
Dates: June 13, 1995-Jan. 3, 1997
Departure: Moved to Commerce

Cong.	Ranking	Terms in: House	Comm.	Date of Assignment
104th	MnR-1st	1	1	June 13, 1995

4th COMMERCE, 105-106
ENERGY AND COMMERCE, 107-108
Dates: Jan. 7, 1997-Jan. 3, 2005
Departure: Left the House; retired

Cong.	Ranking	Terms in: House	Comm.	Date of Assignment
105th	Min-20th	2	1	Jan. 7, 1997
106th	Min-19th	3	2	Jan. 6, 1999
107th	Min-18th	4	3	Jan. 31, 2001
108th	Min-17th	5	4	Jan. 28, 2003

HOUSE SELECT AND SPECIAL COMMITTEES:

1st SELECT HOMELAND SECURITY
Dates: Feb. 12, 2003-Jan. 3, 2005
Departure: Left the House; retired

Cong.	Ranking	Terms in: House	Comm.	Date of Assignment
108th	Min-15th	5	1	Feb. 12, 2003

Kevin McCarthy (R-Cal.)

Dates: Jan. 16, 1965
House: Jan. 3, 2007-date
Serving in the 111th Congress

HOUSE STANDING COMMITTEES:

1st HOUSE ADMINISTRATION
Dates: Jan. 4, 2007-date
Departure: Still serving in the 111th Congress.

Cong.	Ranking	Terms in: House	Comm.	Date of Assignment
110th	Min-3rd	1	1	Jan. 4, 2007
111th	Min-2nd	2	2	Jan. 9, 2007

2nd AGRICULTURE
Dates: Jan. 10, 2007-Oct. 2, 2007
Departure: Resigned committee; moved to Financial Services

Cong.	Ranking	Terms in: House	Comm.	Date of Assignment
110th	Min-20th	1	1	Jan. 10, 2007

3rd HOMELAND SECURITY
Dates: Mar. 12, 2007-May 10, 2007
Departure: Resigned committee; moved to Natural Resources

Cong.	Ranking	Terms in: House	Comm.	Date of Assignment
110th	MnR-1st	1	1	Mar. 12, 2007

4th NATURAL RESOURCES
Dates: May 10, 2007-Oct 2, 2007
Departure: Resigned committee; moved to Financial Services

Cong.	Ranking	Terms in: House	Comm.	Date of Assignment
110th	MnR-2nd	1	1	May 10, 2007

5th FINANCIAL SERVICES
Dates: Oct. 2, 2007-date
Departure: Still serving in the 111th Congress.

Cong.	Ranking	Terms in: House	Comm.	Date of Assignment
110th	MnR-3rd	1	1	Oct. 2, 2007
111th	Min-24th	2	2	Jan. 9, 2009

JOINT COMMITTEES:

1st JOINT PRINTING
House Dates: Mar. 14, 2007-date
Departure: Still serving in the 111th Congress

Cong.	Ranking	Terms in: House	Comm.	Date of Assignment
110th	Min-2nd	1	1	Mar. 14, 2007
111th	Min-2nd	2	2	Mar. 31, 2009

Claire McCaskill (D-Mo.)

Dates: July 24, 1953
Senate: Jan. 3, 2007-date
Serving in the 111th Congress

SENATE STANDING COMMITTEES:

1st ARMED SERVICES
Dates: Jan. 12, 2007-date
Departure: Still serving in the 111th Congress

Cong.	Ranking	Years in: Senate	Comm.	Date of Assignment
110th	Maj-13th	1	1	Jan. 12, 2007
111th	Maj-11th	3	3	Jan. 21, 2009

2nd COMMERCE, SCIENCE AND TRANSPORTATION
Dates: Jan. 12, 2007-date
Departure: Still serving in the 111th Congress.

Cong.	Ranking	Years in: Senate	Comm.	Date of Assignment
110th	Maj-11th	1	1	Jan. 12, 2007
111th	Maj-10th	3	3	Jan. 21, 2009

3rd HOMELAND SECURITY AND GOVERNMENTAL AFFAIRS
Dates: Jan. 12, 2007-date
Departure: Still serving in the 111th Congress

Cong.	Ranking	Years in: Senate	Comm.	Date of Assignment
110th	Maj-8th	1	1	Jan. 12, 2007
111th	Maj-7th	3	3	Jan. 21, 2009

SENATE SELECT AND SPECIAL COMMITTEES:

1st SPECIAL AGING (Permanent)
Dates: Jan. 12, 2007-date
Departure: Still serving in the 111th Congress.

Cong.	Ranking	Years in: Senate	Comm.	Date of Assignment
110th	Maj-10th	1	1	Jan. 12, 2007
111th	Maj-7th	3	3	Jan. 21, 2009

2nd INDIAN AFFAIRS (Permanent)
Dates: Jan. 12, 2007-Jan. 21, 2009
Departure: Left committee; no new assignment

Cong.	Ranking	Years in: Senate	Comm.	Date of Assignment
110th	Maj-7th	1	1	Jan. 12, 2007

Michael T. McCaul (R-Tex.)

Dates: Jan. 14, 1962-date
House: Jan. 3, 2005-date
Serving in the 111th Congress

HOUSE STANDING COMMITTEES:

1st INTERNATIONAL RELATIONS, 109
FOREIGN AFFAIRS, 110-111
Dates: Jan. 26, 2005-date
Departure: Still serving in the 111th Congress

Cong.	Ranking	Terms in: House	Comm.	Date of Assignment
109th	Maj-26th	1	1	Jan. 26, 2005
110th	Min-20th	2	2	Jan. 10, 2007
111th	Min-16th	3	3	Jan. 9, 2009

2nd SCIENCE, 109
SCIENCE AND TECHNOLOGY, 110-111
Dates: Jan. 26, 2005-date
Departure: Still serving in the 111th Congress

Cong.	Ranking	Terms in: House	Comm.	Date of Assignment
109th	Maj-23rd	1	1	Jan. 26, 2005
110th	Min-16th	2	2	Jan. 10, 2007
111th	Min-12th	3	3	Jan. 9, 2009

3rd HOMELAND SECURITY
Dates: Feb. 9, 2005-date
Departure: Still serving in the 111th Congress

Cong.	Ranking	Terms in: House	Comm.	Date of Assignment
109th	Maj-18th	1	1	Feb. 9, 2005
110th	Min-10th	2	2	Jan. 10, 2007
111th	Min-6th	3	3	Jan. 9, 2009

4th STANDARDS OF OFFICIAL CONDUCT
1st Dates: Feb. 12, 2007-Jan. 3, 2009
1st Departure: Left committee; no new assignment
2nd Dates: Sept. 24, 2009-date
2nd Departure: Still serving in the 111th Congress

Cong.	Ranking	Terms in: House	Comm.	Date of Assignment
110th	Min-5th	2 *1	1	Feb. 12, 2007
111th	MnR-2nd	3 *2	1	Sept. 24, 2009

Thomas McClintock (R-Cal.)

Dates: July 10, 1956
House: Jan. 3, 2009-date
Serving in the 111th Congress

HOUSE STANDING COMMITTEES:

1st EDUCATION AND LABOR
Dates: Jan. 9, 2009-date
Departure: Still serving in the 111th Congress

Cong.	Ranking	Terms in: House	Comm.	Date of Assignment
111th	Min-17th	1	1	Jan. 9, 2009

2nd NATURAL RESOURCES
Dates: Jan. 9, 2009-date
Departure: Still serving in the 111th Congress

Cong.	Ranking	Terms in: House	Comm.	Date of Assignment
111th	Min-19th	1	1	Jan. 9, 2009

Francis X. McCloskey (D-Ind.)

Dates: June 12, 1939-Nov. 2, 2003
House 1: Jan. 3, 1983-Jan. 3, 1985
Left the House 1: Re-election decided by House; seniority was continued
House 2: May 1, 1985-Jan. 3, 1995
Left the House 2: Defeated for re-election in 1994

H: McCloskey was seated in the 99th Congress following a closely contested election by vote of the House, 236-190, May 1, 1985.

HOUSE STANDING COMMITTEES:

1st ARMED SERVICES
Dates: Jan. 6, 1983-Jan. 3, 1995
Departure: Left the House; lost re-election

Cong.	Ranking	Terms in: House	Comm.	Date of Assignment
103rd	Maj-11th	6	6	Jan. 5, 1993

2nd SMALL BUSINESS
Dates: Jan. 6, 1983-Nov. 17, 1983
Departure: Moved to Post Office and Civil Service

3rd POST OFFICE AND CIVIL SERVICE
Dates: Nov. 17, 1983-Jan. 3, 1995
Departure: Left the House; lost re-election

Cong.	Ranking	Terms in: House	Comm.	Date of Assignment
103rd	Maj-3rd	6	6	Jan. 21, 1993

4th VETERANS AFFAIRS
Dates: May 1, 1986-Jan. 3, 1987
Departure: Left committee; no new assignment

5th FOREIGN AFFAIRS
Dates: Jan. 27, 1989-Jan. 3, 1995
Departure: Left the House; lost re-election

Cong.	Ranking	Terms in: House	Comm.	Date of Assignment
103rd	Maj-25th	6	3	Jan. 21, 1993

Betty McCollum (DFL-Minn.)

Dates: July 12, 1954
House: Jan. 3, 2001-date
Serving in the 111th Congress

HOUSE STANDING COMMITTEES:

1st EDUCATION AND THE WORKFORCE
Dates: Jan. 31, 2001-Jan. 3, 2007
Departure: Moved to Appropriations and returned to Oversight and Government Reform

Cong.	Ranking	Terms in: House	Comm.	Date of Assignment
107th	Min-21st	1	1	Jan. 31, 2001
108th	Min-16th	2	2	Jan. 28, 2003
109th	Min-16th	3	3	Jan. 26, 2005

2nd RESOURCES
1st Dates: Feb. 8, 2001-Jan. 3, 2003
1st Departure: Moved to International Relations
2nd Dates: Mar. 5, 2003-June 14, 2004
2nd Departure: Resigned committee; moved to Government Reform

Cong.	Ranking	Terms in: House	Comm.	Date of Assignment
107th	Min-23rd	1 *1	1	Feb. 8, 2001
108th	MnR-2nd	2 *2	1	Mar. 5, 2003

3rd INTERNATIONAL RELATIONS
Dates: Feb. 5, 2003-Jan. 3, 2007
Departure: Moved to Appropriations and returned to Oversight and Government Reform

Cong.	Ranking	Terms in: House	Comm.	Date of Assignment
108th	Min-22nd	2	1	Feb. 5, 2003
109th	Min-21st	3	2	Jan. 26, 2005

4th GOVERNMENT REFORM, 108
OVERSIGHT AND GOVERNMENT REFORM, 110
1st Dates: June 14, 2004-Jan. 3, 2005
1st Departure: Left committee; no new assignment
2nd Dates: Jan. 12, 2007-Jan. 3, 2009
2nd Departure: Moved to Budget

Cong.	Ranking	Terms in: House	Comm.	Date of Assignment
108th	MnR-2nd	2 *1	1	June 14, 2004
110th	Maj-17th	4 *2	1	Jan. 12, 2007

5th APPROPRIATIONS
Dates: Jan. 4, 2007-date
Departure: Still serving in the 111th Congress

Cong.	Ranking	Terms in: House	Comm.	Date of Assignment
110th	Maj-31st	4	1	Jan. 4, 2007
111th	Maj-29th	5	2	Jan. 7, 2009

6th BUDGET
Dates: Jan. 21, 2009-date
Departure: Still serving in the 111th Congress

Cong.	Ranking	Terms in: House	Comm.	Date of Assignment
111th	Maj-12th	5	1	Jan. 21, 2009

Ira W. (Bill) McCollum Jr. (R-Fla.)

Dates: July 12, 1944
House: Jan. 3, 1981-Jan. 3, 2001
Left the House: Lost U.S. Senate election in 2000

HOUSE STANDING COMMITTEES:

1st BANKING, FINANCE AND URBAN AFFAIRS, 97-103
BANKING AND FINANCIAL SERVICES, 104-106
Dates: Jan. 28, 1981-Jan. 3, 2001
Departure: Left the House; lost Senate election

Cong.	Ranking	Terms in: House	Comm.	Date of Assignment
103rd	Min-2nd	7	7	Jan. 5, 1993
104th	Maj-2nd	8	8	Jan. 4, 1995
105th	Maj-2nd	9	9	Jan. 7, 1997
106th	Maj-2nd	10	10	Jan. 6, 1999

2nd JUDICIARY
Dates: Jan. 28, 1981-Jan. 3, 2001
Departure: Left the House; lost Senate election

Cong.	Ranking	Terms in: House	Comm.	Date of Assignment
103rd	Min-5th	7	7	Jan. 5, 1993
104th	Maj-4th	8	8	Jan. 4, 1995
105th	Maj-3rd	9	9	Jan. 7, 1997
106th	Maj-3rd	10	10	Jan. 6, 1999

HOUSE SELECT AND SPECIAL COMMITTEES:

1st SELECT COMMITTEE TO INVESTIGATE COVERT ARMS TRANSACTIONS WITH IRAN
Dates: Jan. 7, 1987-Nov. 17, 1987
Departure: House Report 433 (100-1) filed

2nd PERMANENT SELECT INTELLIGENCE
Dates: Jan. 4, 1995-Jan. 3, 2001
Departure: Left the House; lost Senate election

Cong.	Ranking	Terms in: House	Comm.	Date of Assignment
104th	Maj-8th	8	1	Jan. 4, 1995
105th	Maj-5th	9	2	Feb. 10, 1997
106th	Maj-3rd	10	3	Jan. 19, 1999

A. Mitchell (Mitch) McConnell (R-Ky.)

Dates: Feb. 20, 1942
Senate: Jan. 3, 1985-date
Serving in the 111th Congress

SENATE STANDING COMMITTEES:

1st AGRICULTURE, NUTRITION AND FORESTRY
Dates: Feb. 21, 1985-date
Departure: Still serving in the 111th Congress

Cong.	Ranking	Years in: Senate	Comm.	Date of Assignment
103rd	Min-5th	9	8	Jan. 7, 1993
104th	Maj-5th	11	10	Jan. 4, 1995
105th	Maj-4th	13	12	Jan. 9, 1997
106th	Maj-4th	15	14	Jan. 7, 1999
107th	Maj-4th	17	16	Jan. 25, 2001
+107th	Min-4th	17	17	June 6, 2001
108th	Maj-3rd	19	18	Jan. 15, 2003
109th	Maj-4th	21	20	Jan. 6, 2005
110th	Min-4th	23	22	Jan. 12, 2007
111th	Min-4th	25	24	Jan. 21, 2009

2nd JUDICIARY
1st Dates: Feb. 21, 1985-Jan. 6, 1987
1st Departure: Moved to Foreign Relations
2nd Dates: Jan. 25, 2001-Jan. 15, 2003
2nd Departure: Left committee; elected Majority Whip

Cong.	Ranking	Years in: Senate	Comm.	Date of Assignment
107th	Maj-9th	17 *2	1	Jan. 25, 2001
+107th	Min-9th	17 *2	1	June 6, 2001

3rd FOREIGN RELATIONS
Dates: Jan. 6, 1987-Jan. 7, 1993
Departure: Moved to Appropriations

4th ENERGY AND NATURAL RESOURCES
Dates: Feb. 2, 1989-Feb. 5, 1991
Departure: Left committee; no new assignment

5th RULES AND ADMINISTRATION
Dates: Feb. 2, 1989-date
Ch1: Replaced by Christopher J. Dodd (D-Conn.) following party control shift on June 6, 2001 and became RM2.
Departure: Still serving in the 111th Congress

Cong.	Ranking	Years in: Senate	Comm.	Date of Assignment
103rd	Min-6th	9	4	Jan. 21, 1993
104th	Maj-6th	11	6	Jan. 6, 1995
105th	Maj-4th	13	8	Jan. 9, 1997
106th	Maj-Chr	15	10	Jan. 7, 1999
107th	Maj-Ch1	17	12	Jan. 25, 2001
+107th	Min-RM2	17	13	June 6, 2001
108th	Maj-3rd	19	14	Jan. 15, 2003
109th	Maj-3rd	21	16	Jan. 6, 2005
110th	Min-3rd	23	18	Jan. 12, 2007
111th	Min-2nd	25	20	Jan. 21, 2009

6th APPROPRIATIONS
Dates: Jan. 7, 1993-date
Departure: Still serving in the 111th Congress

Cong.	Ranking	Years in: Senate	Comm.	Date of Assignment
103rd	Min-11th	9	1	Jan. 7, 1993
104th	Maj-9th	11	2	Jan. 4, 1995
105th	Maj-7th	13	5	Jan. 9, 1997
106th	Maj-7th	15	7	Jan. 7, 1999
107th	Maj-6th	17	9	Jan. 25, 2001
+107th	Min-6th	17	9	June 6, 2001
108th	Maj-6th	19	11	Jan. 15, 2003
109th	Maj-6th	21	12	Jan. 6, 2005
110th	Min-6th	23	15	Jan. 12, 2007
111th	Min-4th	25	17	Jan. 21, 2009

7th ENVIRONMENT AND PUBLIC WORKS
Dates: Jan. 5, 1995-Jan. 9, 1997
Departure: Moved to Labor and Human Resources and Joint Printing

Cong.	Ranking	Years in: Senate	Comm.	Date of Assignment
104th	Maj-8th	11	1	Jan. 5, 1995

8th LABOR AND HUMAN RESOURCES
Dates: Jan. 9, 1997-Jan. 7, 1999
Departure: Left committee; became Chair of Rules and Administration; moved to Joint Library

Cong.	Ranking	Years in: Senate	Comm.	Date of Assignment
105th	Maj-10th	13	1	Jan. 9, 1997

SENATE SELECT AND SPECIAL COMMITTEES:

1st SELECT INTELLIGENCE (Permanent)
Dates: Jan. 3, 1985-Jan. 6, 1987
Departure: Moved to Foreign Relations

2nd JUDGE HARRY E. CLAIBORNE IMPEACHMENT
Dates: Aug. 14, 1986-Oct. 1, 1986
Termination: Senate Report 99-511 filed

3rd SELECT ETHICS (Permanent)
Dates: Jan. 26, 1993-Jan. 30, 1997
Departure: Moved to Labor and Human Resources and Joint Printing

		Years in:		Date of
Cong.	Ranking	Senate	Comm.	Assignment
103rd	Min-VCh	9	1	Jan. 26, 1993
104th	Maj-Chr	11	2	Jan. 11, 1995

JOINT COMMITTEES:

1st JOINT PRINTING
Senate Dates: Jan. 28, 1997-Jan. 25, 2001
Departure: Moved to Judiciary

		Years in:		Date of
Cong.	Ranking	Senate	Comm.	Assignment
105th	Maj-3rd	13	1	Jan. 28, 1997
106th	Maj-VCh	15	3	Feb. 25, 1999

2nd JOINT LIBRARY
Senate Dates: Feb. 25, 1999-Jan. 25, 2001
Departure: Moved to Judiciary

		Years in:		Date of
Cong.	Ranking	Senate	Comm.	Assignment
106th	Maj-2nd	15	1	Feb. 25, 1999

SENATE LEADERSHIP POSTS

Dates: Jan. 3, 2003-date
Departure: Still serving in the 111th Congress

1st SENATE MAJORITY WHIP
Dates: Jan. 3, 2003-Jan. 3, 2007
Note: For the 108th Congress, McConnell succeeded Majority Whip Don Nickles (R-Okla.) who had served three terms. McConnell was elected on Nov. 13, 2002, without opposition. He was re-elected without opposition for the 109th Congress.
Departure: Elected Minority Floor Leader

		Years in:		Date of
Cong.	Ranking	Senate	Post	Selection
108th	Maj-2nd	19	1	Nov. 13, 2002
109th	Maj-2nd	21	3	Nov. 17, 2004

2nd SENATE MINORITY LEADER
Dates: Jan. 3, 2007-date
Note: For the 110th Congress, McConnell succeeded Republican Floor Leader William Frist (R-Tenn.), who had retired. McConnell was elected without opposition on Nov. 15, 2006. He was re-elected Minority Leader for the 111th Congress without opposition.
Departure: Still serving in the 111th Congress

		Years in:		Date of
Cong.	Ranking	Senate	Post	Selection
110th	Min-1st	23	1	Nov. 15, 2006
111th	Min-1st	25	3	Nov. 18, 2008

Thaddeus McCotter (R-Mich.)

Dates: Aug. 22, 1965
House: Jan. 3, 2003-date
Serving in the 111th Congress

HOUSE STANDING COMMITTEES:

1st BUDGET
Dates: Jan. 28, 2003-May 15, 2007
Departure: Resigned committee; moved to Financial Services

		Terms in:		Date of
Cong.	Ranking	House	Comm.	Assignment
108th	Maj-21st	1	1	Jan. 28, 2003
109th	Maj-11th	2	2	Jan. 26, 2005
110th	Min-5th	3	3	Jan. 18, 2007

2nd INTERNATIONAL RELATIONS, 108-109
FOREIGN AFFAIRS, 110
Dates: Jan. 28, 2003-May 15, 2007
Departure: Resigned committee; moved to Financial Services

		Terms in:		Date of
Cong.	Ranking	House	Comm.	Assignment
108th	Maj-24th	1	1	Jan. 28, 2003
109th	Maj-20th	2	2	Jan. 26, 2005
110th	Min-14th	3	3	Jan. 10, 2007

3rd SMALL BUSINESS
Dates: June 19, 2003-Jan. 3, 2007
Departure: Left committee; no new assignment

		Terms in:		Date of
Cong.	Ranking	House	Comm.	Assignment
108th	MjR-1st	1	1	June 19, 2003
109th	Maj-11th	2	2	Jan. 26, 2005

4th FINANCIAL SERVICES
Dates: May 10, 2007-date
Departure: Still serving in the 111th Congress.

		Terms in:		Date of
Cong.	Ranking	House	Comm.	Assignment
110th	MnR-2nd	3	1	May 10, 2007
111th	Min-23rd	4	2	Jan. 9, 2009

JOINT COMMITTEES:

1st JOINT ECONOMIC
House Dates: Mar. 3, 2005-Jan. 3, 2007
Departure: Left committee; no new assignment

		Terms in:		Date of
Cong.	Ranking	House	Comm.	Assignment
109th	Maj-6th	2	1	Mar. 3, 2005

James O. McCrery III (R-La.)

Dates: Sept. 18, 1949
House: April 16, 1988-Jan. 3, 2009
Left the House: Retired in 2008

H: McCrery was elected to the 100th Congress by special election, April 16, 1988, to fill the vacancy caused by the resignation of U.S. Representative Charles (Buddy) Roemer (D-La.) who had been elected Governor. McCrery was seated April 26, 1988, and assigned to committees.

HOUSE STANDING COMMITTEES:

1st BUDGET
Dates: May 18, 1988-Jan. 3, 1993
Departure: Moved to Ways and Means

2nd ARMED SERVICES
Dates: Jan. 20, 1989-Jan. 3, 1993
Departure: Moved to Ways and Means

3rd WAYS AND MEANS
Dates: Jan. 5, 1993-Jan. 3, 2009
Departure: Left the House; retired

Cong.	Ranking	Terms in: House	Comm.	Date of Assignment
103rd	Min-12th	4	1	Jan. 5, 1993
104th	Maj-9th	5	2	Jan. 4, 1995
105th	Maj-9th	6	3	Jan. 7, 1997
106th	Maj-8th	7	4	Jan. 6, 1999
107th	Maj-7th	8	5	Jan. 6, 2001
108th	Maj-7th	9	6	Jan. 28, 2003
109th	Maj-5th	10	7	Jan. 6, 2005
110th	Min-RM	11	8	Jan. 4, 2007

JOINT COMMITTEES:

1st JOINT ECONOMIC
House Dates: Feb. 27, 1997-Jan. 3, 1999
Departure: Left committee; no new assignment

Cong.	Ranking	Terms in: House	Comm.	Date of Assignment
105th	Maj-6th	6	1	Feb. 27, 1997

2nd JOINT TAXATION
House Dates: Jan. 12, 2007-Jan. 3, 2009
Departure: Left the House; retired

Cong.	Ranking	Terms in: House	Comm.	Date of Assignment
110th	Min-1st	11	1	Jan. 17, 2007

David K. McCurdy (D-Okla.)

Dates: March 30, 1950
House: Jan. 3, 1981-Jan. 3, 1995
Left the House: Lost U.S. Senate election in 1994

HOUSE STANDING COMMITTEES:

1st ARMED SERVICES
Dates: Jan. 28, 1981-Jan. 3, 1995
Departure: Left the House; lost Senate election

Cong.	Ranking	Terms in: House	Comm.	Date of Assignment
103rd	Maj-7th	7	7	Jan. 5, 1993

2nd SCIENCE AND TECHNOLOGY, 97-99
SCIENCE, SPACE AND TECHNOLOGY, 100-103
Dates: Jan. 28, 1981-Jan. 3, 1995
Departure: Left the House; lost Senate election

Cong.	Ranking	Terms in: House	Comm.	Date of Assignment
103rd	Maj-6th	7	7	Jan. 5, 1993

HOUSE SELECT AND SPECIAL COMMITTEES:

1st PERMANENT SELECT INTELLIGENCE
1st Dates: Feb. 2, 1983-Dec. 18, 1987
1st Departure: Left committee; no new assignment
2nd Dates: Jan. 19,1989-Jan. 3, 1993
2nd Departure: Left committee; no new assignment

Joseph M. McDade (R-Penn.)

Dates: Sept. 29, 1931
House: Jan. 3, 1963-Jan. 3, 1999
Left the House: Retired in 1998

HOUSE STANDING COMMITTEES:

1st BANKING AND CURRENCY
Dates: Jan. 24, 1963-Jan. 3, 1965
Departure: Moved to Appropriations

2nd APPROPRIATIONS
Dates: Jan. 21, 1965-Jan. 3, 1999
Departure: Left the House; retired

Cong.	Ranking	Terms in: House	Comm.	Date of Assignment
103rd	Min-RM	16	15	Jan. 5, 1993
104th	Maj-2nd	17	16	Jan. 4, 1995
105th	Maj-2nd	18	17	Jan. 7, 1997

3rd SMALL BUSINESS
Dates: Jan. 28, 1975-Jan. 3, 1993
Departure: Left committee; became Ranking Minority Member on Appropriations

HOUSE SELECT AND SPECIAL COMMITTEES:

1st SELECT SMALL BUSINESS
Dates: Mar. 3, 1971-Jan. 3, 1975
Departure: Continued on reorganized standing committee

JOINT COMMITTEES:

1st JOINT BICENTENNIAL ARRANGEMENTS
House Dates: June 23, 1976-Dec. 31, 1976
Termination: Committee completed at end of 1976

James A. McDermott (D-Wash.)

Dates: Dec. 28, 1936
House: Jan. 3, 1989-date
Serving in the 111th Congress

HOUSE STANDING COMMITTEES:

1st BANKING, FINANCE AND URBAN AFFAIRS
Dates: Jan. 19, 1989-Jan. 3, 1991
Departure: Moved to Ways and Means and Standards of Official Conduct

2nd INTERIOR AND INSULAR AFFAIRS
Dates: Jan. 19, 1989-Jan. 3, 1991
Departure: Moved to Ways and Means and Standards of Official Conduct

3rd DISTRICT OF COLUMBIA
Dates: Nov. 8, 1989-Jan. 3, 1995
Departure: Committee abolished; no new assignment

Cong.	Ranking	Terms in: House	Comm.	Date of Assignment
103rd	Maj-3rd	3	3	Feb. 18, 1993

4th WAYS AND MEANS
Dates: Jan. 3, 1991-date
Departure: Still serving in the 111th Congress

Cong.	Ranking	Terms in: House	Comm.	Date of Assignment
103rd	Maj-14th	3	2	Jan. 5, 1993
104th	Min-11th	4	3	Jan. 4, 1995
105th	Min-8th	5	4	Jan. 7, 1997
106th	Min-7th	6	5	Jan. 6, 1999
107th	Min-7th	7	6	Jan. 31, 2001
108th	Min-6th	8	7	Jan. 28, 2003
109th	Min-5th	9	8	Jan. 26, 2005
110th	Maj-4th	10	9	Jan. 4, 2007
111th	Maj-4th	11	10	Jan. 7, 2009

5th STANDARDS OF OFFICIAL CONDUCT
Dates: Feb 6, 1991-Jan. 3, 1997
Departure: Moved to Budget

Cong.	Ranking	Terms in: House	Comm.	Date of Assignment
103rd	Maj-Chr	3	2	Feb. 4, 1993
104th	Min-RM	4	3	Jan. 20, 1995

6th BUDGET
Dates: Mar. 6, 1997-Jan. 3, 2003
Departure: Left committee; no new assignment

Cong.	Ranking	Terms in: House	Comm.	Date of Assignment
105th	Min-19th	5	1	Mar. 6, 1997
106th	Min-2nd	6	2	Jan. 6, 1999
107th	Min-2nd	7	3	Jan. 31, 2001

James P. McGovern (D-Mass.)

Dates: Nov. 20, 1959
House: Jan. 3, 1997-date
Serving in the 111th Congress

HOUSE STANDING COMMITTEES:

1st TRANSPORTATION AND INFRASTRUCTURE
Dates: Jan. 7, 1997-May 7, 2002
Departure: Resigned committee; moved to Rules

Cong.	Ranking	Terms in: House	Comm.	Date of Assignment
105th	Min-30th	1	1	Jan. 7, 1997
106th	Min-27th	2	2	Jan. 6, 1999
107th	Min-24th	3	3	Jan. 31, 2001

2nd RESOURCES
Dates: Feb. 8, 2001-May 7, 2002
Departure: Resigned committee; moved to Rules

Cong.	Ranking	Terms in: House	Comm.	Date of Assignment
107th	Min-20th	1	1	Feb. 8, 2001

3rd RULES
Dates: May 7, 2002-date
Departure: Still serving in the 111th Congress.

Cong.	Ranking	Terms in: House	Comm.	Date of Assignment
107th	MnR-2nd	3	1	May 7, 2002
108th	Min-3rd	4	2	Jan. 7, 2003
109th	Min-2nd	5	3	Jan. 26, 2005
110th	Maj-2nd	6	4	Jan. 12, 2007
111th	Maj-2nd	7	5	Jan. 6, 2009

4th BUDGET
Dates: Jan. 10, 2007-date
Departure: Still serving in the 111th Congress.

Cong.	Ranking	Terms in: House	Comm.	Date of Assignment
110th	Maj-14th	6	1	Jan. 10, 2007
111th	Maj-9th	7	2	Jan. 21, 2009

Paul F. McHale Jr. (D-Penn.)

Dates: July 26, 1950
House: Jan. 3, 1993-Jan. 3, 1999
Left the House: Retired in 1998

HOUSE STANDING COMMITTEES:

1st ARMED SERVICES, 103
NATIONAL SECURITY, 104-105
Dates: Jan. 5, 1993-Jan. 3, 1999
Departure: Left the House; retired

Cong.	Ranking	Terms in: House	Comm.	Date of Assignment
103rd	Maj-31st	1	1	Jan. 5, 1993
104th	Min-19th	2	2	Jan. 4, 1995
105th	Min-14th	3	3	Jan. 7, 1997

2nd SCIENCE, SPACE AND TECHNOLOGY, 103
SCIENCE, 104-105
Dates: Jan. 5, 1993-Apr. 30, 1998
Departure: Resigned committee; no new assignment

Cong.	Ranking	Terms in: House	Comm.	Date of Assignment
103rd	Maj-22nd	1	1	Jan. 5, 1993
104th	Min-10th	2	2	Jan. 4, 1995
105th	Min-8th	3	3	Feb. 13, 1997

Patrick T. McHenry (R-N.C.)

Dates: Oct. 22, 1975
House: Jan. 3, 2005-date
Serving in the 111th Congress

HOUSE STANDING COMMITTEES:

1st BUDGET
Dates: Jan. 26, 2005-date
Departure: Still serving in the 111th Congress

Cong.	Ranking	Terms in: House	Comm.	Date of Assignment
109th	Maj-20th	1	1	Jan. 26, 2005
110th	Min-10th	2	2	Jan. 10, 2007
111th	Min-7th	3	3	Jan. 9, 2009

2nd FINANCIAL SERVICES
Dates: Jan. 26, 2005-date
Departure: Still serving in the 111th Congress

Cong.	Ranking	Terms in: House	Comm.	Date of Assignment
109th	Maj-37th	1	1	Jan. 26, 2005
110th	Min-28th	2	2	Jan. 10, 2007
111th	Min-18th	3	3	Jan. 9, 2009

3rd GOVERNMENT REFORM, 109
OVERSIGHT AND GOVERNMENT REFORM, 110-111
Dates: Jan. 26, 2005-date
Departure: Still serving in the 111th Congress

Cong.	Ranking	Terms in: House	Comm.	Date of Assignment
109th	Maj-21st	1	1	Jan. 26, 2005
110th	Min-14th	2	2	Jan. 10, 2007
111th	Min-10th	3	3	Jan. 9, 2009

John M. McHugh (R-N.Y.)

Dates: Sept. 29, 1948
House: Jan. 3, 1993-Sept. 21, 2009
Left the House: Resigned; appointed Secretary of the Army

HOUSE STANDING COMMITTEES:

1st ARMED SERVICES, 103
NATIONAL SECURITY, 104-105
ARMED SERVICES, 106-111
Dates: Jan. 5, 1993-June 3, 2009
Departure: Resigned committee; nominated as Secretary of the Army; replaced by Howard P. (Buck) McKeon as Ranking Member on June 16, 2009

Cong.	Ranking	Terms in: House	Comm.	Date of Assignment
103rd	Min-19th	1	1	Jan. 5, 1993
104th	Maj-15th	2	2	Jan. 4, 1995
105th	Maj-12th	3	3	Jan. 7, 1997
106th	Maj-12th	4	4	Jan. 6, 1999
107th	Maj-8th	5	5	Jan. 6, 2001
108th	Maj-5th	6	6	Jan. 28, 2003
109th	Maj-5th	7	7	Jan. 26, 2005
110th	Min-3rd	8	8	Jan. 10, 2007
111th	Min-RM1	9	9	Jan. 6, 2009

2nd GOVERNMENT OPERATIONS, 103
GOVERNMENT REFORM AND OVERSIGHT, 104-105
GOVERNMENT REFORM, 106-109
OVERSIGHT AND GOVERNMENT REFORM, 110-111
Dates: Jan. 5, 1993-Sept. 21, 2009
Departure: Resigned the House; appointed Secretary of the Army

Cong.	Ranking	Terms in: House	Comm.	Date of Assignment
103rd	Min-13th	1	1	Jan. 5, 1993
104th	Maj-9th	2	2	Jan. 4, 1995
105th	Maj-9th	3	3	Jan. 7, 1997
106th	Maj-7th	4	4	Jan. 6, 1999
107th	Maj-6th	5	5	Jan. 6, 2001
108th	Maj-5th	6	6	Jan. 28, 2003
109th	Maj-5th	7	7	Jan. 26, 2005
110th	Min-4th	8	8	Jan. 10, 2007
111th	Min-3rd	9	9	Jan. 9, 2009

3rd INTERNATIONAL RELATIONS
Dates: Jan. 7, 1997-Jan. 26, 2005
Departure: Resigned committee; moved to Permanent Select Intelligence

Cong.	Ranking	Terms in: House	Comm.	Date of Assignment
105th	Maj-22nd	3	1	Jan. 7, 1997
106th	Maj-20th	4	2	Jan. 6, 1999
107th	Maj-15th	5	3	Jan. 6, 2001
108th	Maj-14th	6	4	Jan. 28, 2003
109th	Maj-11th	7	5	Jan. 26, 2005

HOUSE SELECT AND SPECIAL COMMITTEES:

1st PERMANENT SELECT INTELLIGENCE
Dates: Jan. 26, 2005-Jan. 3, 2009
Departure: Left committee; became Ranking Member on Armed Services

Cong.	Ranking	Terms in: House	Comm.	Date of Assignment
109th	Maj-9th	7	1	Jan. 26, 2005
110th	Min-5th	8	2	Jan. 17, 2007

Scott McInnis (R-Colo.)

Dates: May 9, 1953
House: Jan. 3, 1993-Jan. 3, 2005
Left the House: Retired in 2004

HOUSE STANDING COMMITTEES:

1st NATURAL RESOURCES, 103
RESOURCES, 107-108
1st Dates: Jan. 5, 1993-Jan. 3, 1995
1st Departure: Moved to Rules
2nd Dates: Jan. 6, 2001-Jan. 3, 2005
2nd Departure: Left the House; retired

Cong.	Ranking	Terms in: House	Comm.	Date of Assignment
103rd	Min-13th	1 *1	1	Jan. 5, 1993
107th	Maj-10th	5 *2	1	Jan. 6, 2001
108th	Maj-10th	6 *2	2	Jan. 28, 2003

2nd SMALL BUSINESS
Dates: Jan. 5, 1993-Jan. 3, 1995
Departure: Moved to Rules

Cong.	Ranking	Terms in: House	Comm.	Date of Assignment
103rd	Min-11th	1	1	Jan. 5, 1993

3rd RULES
Dates: Jan. 4, 1995-Jan. 3, 1999
Departure: Moved to Ways and Means

Cong.	Ranking	Terms in: House	Comm.	Date of Assignment
104th	Maj-8th	2	1	Jan. 4, 1995
105th	Maj-7th	3	2	Jan. 7, 1997

4th WAYS AND MEANS
Dates: Jan. 6, 1999-Jan. 3, 2005
Departure: Left the House; retired

Cong.	Ranking	Terms in: House	Comm.	Date of Assignment
106th	Maj-21st	4	1	Jan. 6, 1999
107th	Maj-20th	5	2	Jan. 6, 2001
108th	Maj-19th	6	3	Jan. 28, 2003

David M. McIntosh (R-Ind.)

Dates: June 8, 1958
House: Jan. 3, 1995-Jan. 3, 2001
Left the House: Lost election for Governor in 2000

HOUSE STANDING COMMITTEES:

1st ECONOMIC AND EDUCATIONAL OPPORTUNITIES, 104
EDUCATION AND THE WORKFORCE, 105-106
Dates: Jan. 4, 1995-Jan. 3, 2001
Departure: Left the House; lost election for Governor

Cong.	Ranking	Terms in: House	Comm.	Date of Assignment
104th	Maj-23rd	1	1	Jan. 4, 1995
105th	Maj-17th	2	2	Jan. 7, 1997
106th	Maj-15th	3	3	Jan. 6, 1999

2nd GOVERNMENT REFORM AND OVERSIGHT, 104-105
GOVERNMENT REFORM, 106
Dates: Jan. 4, 1995-Jan. 3, 2001
Departure: Left the House; lost election for Governor

Cong.	Ranking	Terms in: House	Comm.	Date of Assignment
104th	Maj-14th	1	1	Jan. 4, 1995
105th	Maj-13th	2	2	Jan. 7, 1997
106th	Maj-11th	3	3	Jan. 6, 1999

3rd SMALL BUSINESS
Dates: Jan. 21, 1997-Jan. 3, 2001
Departure: Left the House; lost election for Governor

Cong.	Ranking	Terms in: House	Comm.	Date of Assignment
105th	Maj-16th	2	1	Jan. 21, 1997
106th	Maj-10th	3	2	Jan. 6, 1999

Mike McIntyre (D-N.C.)

Dates: Aug. 6, 1956
House: Jan. 3, 1997-date
Serving in the 111th Congress

HOUSE STANDING COMMITTEES:

1st NATIONAL SECURITY, 105
ARMED SERVICES, 106-111
Dates: Jan. 7, 1997-date
Departure: Still serving in the 111th Congress

Cong.	Ranking	Terms in: House	Comm.	Date of Assignment
105th	Min-25th	1	1	Jan. 7, 1997
106th	Min-20th	2	2	Jan. 6, 1999
107th	Min-18th	3	3	Jan. 31, 2001
108th	Min-13th	4	4	Jan. 28, 2003
109th	Min-12th	5	5	Jan. 26, 2005
110th	Maj-11th	6	6	Jan. 10, 2007
111th	Maj-10th	7	7	Jan. 7, 2009

2nd AGRICULTURE
Dates: Feb. 5, 1997-date
Departure: Still serving in the 111th Congress

Cong.	Ranking	Terms in: House	Comm.	Date of Assignment
105th	Min-18th	1	1	Feb. 5, 1997
106th	Min-16th	2	2	Jan. 6, 1999
107th	Min-12th	3	3	Jan. 31, 2001
108th	Min-6th	4	4	Jan. 28, 2003
109th	Min-4th	5	5	Jan. 26, 2005
110th	Maj-3rd	6	6	Jan. 12, 2007
111th	Maj-3rd	7	7	Jan. 21, 2009

Howard P. (Buck) McKeon
(R-Cal.)

Dates: Sept. 9, 1939
House: Jan. 3, 1993-date
Serving in the 111th Congress

HOUSE STANDING COMMITTEES:

1st EDUCATION AND LABOR, 103
ECONOMIC AND EDUCATIONAL OPPORTUNITIES, 104
EDUCATION AND THE WORKFORCE, 105-109
EDUCATION AND LABOR, 110-111
Dates: Jan. 5, 1993-date
Ch2: Replaced John Boehner (R-Ohio) as Chair on Feb. 15, 2006
RM1: Became Ranking Member on Armed Services; replaced by John Kline (R-Minn.) as Ranking Member on June 25, 2009
Departure: Still serving in the 111th Congress

Cong.	Ranking	Terms in: House	Comm.	Date of Assignment
103rd	Min-14th	1	1	Jan. 5, 1993
104th	Maj-10th	2	2	Jan. 4, 1995
105th	Maj-8th	3	3	Jan. 7, 1997
106th	Maj-8th	4	4	Jan. 6, 1999
107th	Maj-6th	5	5	Jan. 6, 2001
108th	Maj-5th	6	6	Jan. 28, 2003
109th	Maj-3rd	7	7	Jan. 26, 2005
=109th	Maj-Ch2	7	7	Feb. 15, 2006
110th	Min-RM	8	8	Jan. 4, 2007
111th	Min-RM1	9	9	Jan. 6, 2009

2nd PUBLIC WORKS AND TRANSPORTATION
Dates: Jan. 5, 1993-Jan. 3, 1995
Departure: Moved to National Security

Cong.	Ranking	Terms in: House	Comm.	Date of Assignment
103rd	Min-21st	1	1	Jan. 5, 1993

3rd NATIONAL SECURITY, 104-105
ARMED SERVICES, 106-111
1sr Dates: Jan. 4, 1995-June 29, 2006
1st Departure: Resigned committee; became Chair of Education and the Workforce; returned
2nd Dates: Jan. 10, 2007-date
RM2: Replaced John M. McHugh (R-N.Y.) as Ranking Member on June 16, 2009
2nd Departure: Still serving in the 111th Congress

Cong.	Ranking	Terms in: House	Comm.	Date of Assignment
104th	Maj-19th	2 *1	1	Jan. 4, 1995
105th	Maj-16th	3 *1	2	Jan. 7, 1997
106th	Maj-16th	4 *1	3	Jan. 6, 1999
107th	Maj-11th	5 *1	4	Jan. 6, 2001
108th	Maj-8th	6 *1	5	Jan. 28, 2003
109th	Maj-8th	7 *1	6	Jan. 26, 2005
110th	Min-6th	8 *2	1	Jan. 10, 2007
111th	Min-3rd	9 *2	2	Jan. 9, 2009
=111th	Min-RM2	9 *2	2	June 16, 2009

4th VETERANS' AFFAIRS
Dates: Feb. 2, 1999-Jan. 3, 2003
Departure: Left committee; no new assignment

Cong.	Ranking	Terms in: House	Comm.	Date of Assignment
106th	Maj-15th	4	1	Feb. 2, 1999
107th	Maj-11th	5	2	Jan. 6, 2001

Cynthia A. McKinney (D-Ga.)

Dates: March 17, 1955
House 1: Jan. 3, 1993-Jan. 3, 2003
Left the House 1: Defeated for re-nomination in 2002
House 2: Jan. 3, 2005-Jan. 3, 2007
Left the House 2: Defeated for re-nomination in 2006

HOUSE STANDING COMMITTEES:

1st AGRICULTURE
Dates: Jan. 5, 1993-Feb. 28, 1996
Departure: Resigned committee; moved to Banking and Financial Services

Cong.	Ranking	Terms in: House	Comm.	Date of Assignment
103rd	Maj-24th	1	1	Jan. 5, 1993
104th	Min-15th	2	2	Jan. 4, 1995

2nd FOREIGN AFFAIRS, 103
INTERNATIONAL RELATIONS, 104-107
Dates: Jan. 5, 1993-Jan. 3, 2003
Departure: Left the House; lost re-nomination

Cong.	Ranking	Terms in: House	Comm.	Date of Assignment
103rd	Maj-18th	1	1	Jan. 5, 1993
104th	Min-15th	2	2	Jan. 4, 1995
105th	Min-12th	3	3	Jan. 7, 1997
106th	Min-10th	4	4	Jan. 6, 1999
107th	Min-8th	5	5	Jan. 31, 2001

3rd BANKING AND FINANCIAL SERVICES
Dates: Feb. 28, 1996-July 31, 1997
Departure: Resigned committee; moved to National Security

Cong.	Ranking	Terms in: House	Comm.	Date of Assignment
104th	MnR-1st	2	1	Jan. 4, 1995
105th	Min-20th	3	2	Jan. 7, 1997

4th NATIONAL SECURITY, 105
ARMED SERVICES, 106-107, 109
1st Dates: July 31, 1997-Jan. 3, 2003
1st Departure: Left the House; lost re-nomination
2nd Dates: Jan. 26, 2005-Jan. 3, 2007
2nd Departure: Left the House; lost re-nomination

Cong.	Ranking	Terms in: House	Comm.	Date of Assignment
105th	MnA-26th	3 *1	1	July 31, 1997
106th	Min-22nd	4 *1	2	Jan. 6, 1999
107th	Min-20th	5 *1	3	Jan. 31, 2001
109th	Min-27th	6 *2	1	Jan. 26, 2005

5th BUDGET
Dates: Jan. 26, 2005-Jan. 3, 2007
Departure: Left the House; lost re-nomination

Cong.	Ranking	Terms in: House	Comm.	Date of Assignment
109th	Min-14th	6	1	Jan. 26, 2005

Michael E. McMahon (D-N.Y.)

Dates: Sept. 12, 1957
House: Jan. 3, 2009-date
Still serving in the 111th Congress

HOUSE STANDING COMMITTEES:

1st TRANSPORTATION AND INFRASTRUCTURE
Dates: Jan. 7, 2009-date
Departure: Still serving in the 111th Congress

Cong.	Ranking	Terms in: House	Comm.	Date of Assignment
111th	Maj-42nd	1	1	Jan. 7, 2009

2nd FOREIGN AFFAIRS
Dates: Jan. 21, 2009-date
Departure: Still serving in the 111th Congress

Cong.	Ranking	Terms in: House	Comm.	Date of Assignment
111th	Maj-15th	1	1	Jan. 21, 2009

J. Alex McMillan (R-N.C.)

Dates: May 9, 1932
House: Jan. 3, 1985-Jan. 3, 1995
Left the House: Retired in 1994

HOUSE STANDING COMMITTEES:

1st BANKING, FINANCE AND URBAN AFFAIRS
Dates: Jan. 30, 1985-Jan. 3, 1989
Departure: Moved to Energy and Commerce

2nd SMALL BUSINESS
Dates: Jan. 30, 1985-Jan. 3, 1989
Departure: Moved to Energy and Commerce

3rd ENERGY AND COMMERCE
Dates: Jan. 20, 1989-Jan. 3, 1995
Departure: Left the House; retired

Cong.	Ranking	Terms in: House	Comm.	Date of Assignment
103rd	Min-8th	5	3	Jan. 5, 1993

4th BUDGET
Dates: Jan. 24, 1991-Jan. 3, 1995
Departure: Left the House; retired

Cong.	Ranking	Terms in: House	Comm.	Date of Assignment
103rd	Min-2nd	5	2	Jan. 5, 1993

JOINT COMMITTEES:

1st JOINT ECONOMIC
House Dates: Jan. 21, 1987-Jan. 3, 1989
Departure: Left committee; no new assignment

Cathy McMorris; see Cathy
McMorris Rodgers, p. 354.

Jerry McNerney (D-Cal.)

Dates: June 18, 1951
House: Jan. 3, 2007-date
Serving in the 111th Congress

HOUSE STANDING COMMITTEES:

1st TRANSPORTATION AND INFRASTRUCTURE
Dates: Jan. 10, 2007-Jan. 3, 2009
Departure: Moved to Energy and Commerce

Cong.	Ranking	Terms in: House	Comm.	Date of Assignment
110th	Maj-41st	1	1	Jan. 10, 2007

2nd VETERANS' AFFAIRS
Dates: Jan. 12, 2007-date
Departure: Still serving in the 111th Congress

Cong.	Ranking	Terms in: House	Comm.	Date of Assignment
110th	Maj-14th	1	1	Jan. 12, 2007
111th	Maj-13th	2	2	Jan. 21, 2009

3rd SCIENCE AND TECHNOLOGY
Dates: Jan. 18, 2007-Jan. 3, 2009
Departure: Moved to Energy and Commerce

Cong.	Ranking	Terms in: House	Comm.	Date of Assignment
110th	Maj-12th	1	1	Jan. 18, 2007

4th ENERGY AND COMMERCE
Dares: Jan. 7, 2009-date
Departure: Still serving in the 111th Congress

Cong.	Ranking	Terms in: House	Comm.	Date of Assignment
111th	Maj-33rd	2	1	Jan. 7, 2009

HOUSE SELECT AND SPECIAL COMMITTEES:

1st SELECT ENERGY INDEPENDENCE AND GLOBAL WARMING
Dates: Mar. 9, 2007-Jan. 3, 2009
Departure: Moved to Energy and Commerce

Cong.	Ranking	Terms in: House	Comm.	Date of Assignment
110th	Maj-9th	1	1	Mar. 9, 2007

Michael R. McNulty (D-N.Y.)

Dates: Sept. 16, 1947
House: Jan. 3, 1989-Jan. 3, 2009
Left the House: Retired in 2008

HOUSE STANDING COMMITTEES:

1st ARMED SERVICES
Dates: Jan. 19, 1989-Jan. 3, 1993
Departure: Moved to Ways and Means

2nd SMALL BUSINESS
Dates: Jan. 19, 1989-Feb. 27, 1990
Departure: Moved to Post Office and Civil Service

3rd POST OFFICE AND CIVIL SERVICE
Dates: Feb. 27, 1990-Jan. 3, 1993
Departure: Moved to Ways and Means

4th WAYS AND MEANS
1st Dates: Jan. 5, 1993-Jan. 3, 1995
1st Departure: Moved to International Relations
2nd Dates: Jan. 25, 1996-Jan. 3, 2009
2nd Departure: Left the House; retired

Cong.	Ranking	Terms in: House	Comm.	Date of Assignment
103rd	Maj-20th	3 *1	1	Jan. 5, 1993
104th	MnA-16th	4 *2	1	Jan. 25, 1996
105th	Min-12th	5 *2	2	Jan. 7, 1997
106th	Min-11th	6 *2	3	Jan. 6, 1999
107th	Min-11th	7 *2	4	Jan. 31, 2001
108th	Min-10th	8 *2	5	Jan. 28, 2003
109th	Min-8th	9 *2	6	Jan. 26, 2005
110th	Maj-7th	10 *2	7	Jan. 4, 2007

5th INTERNATIONAL RELATIONS
Dates: Jan. 4, 1995-Jan. 24, 1996
Departure: Resigned committee; returned to Ways and Means

Cong.	Ranking	Terms in: House	Comm.	Date of Assignment
104th	Min-18th	4	1	Jan. 4, 1995

SELECT AND SPECIAL COMMITTEES:

1st SELECT HUNGER (Temporary)
Dates: Mar. 8, 1989-Jan. 3, 1993
Termination: Committee not renewed; moved to Ways and Means

Martin T. Meehan (D-Mass.)

Dates: Dec. 30, 1956
House: Jan. 3, 1993-July 1, 2007
Left the House: Resigned; named Chancellor of University of Massachusetts-Lowell

HOUSE STANDING COMMITTEES:

1st ARMED SERVICES, 103
NATIONAL SECURITY, 104-105
ARMED SERVICES, 106-110
Dates: Jan. 5, 1993-July 1, 2007
Departure: Resigned the House; retired

Cong.	Ranking	Terms in: House	Comm.	Date of Assignment
103rd	Maj-28th	1	1	Jan. 5, 1993
104th	Min-16th	2	2	Jan. 4, 1995
105th	Min-11th	3	3	Jan. 7, 1997
106th	Min-9th	4	4	Jan. 6, 1999
107th	Min-8th	5	5	Jan. 31, 2001
108th	Min-7th	6	6	Jan. 28, 2003
109th	Min-7th	7	7	Jan. 26, 2005
110th	Maj-6th	8	8	Jan. 10, 2007

2nd SMALL BUSINESS
Dates: Jan. 5, 1993-Jan. 3, 1997
Departure: Moved to Judiciary

Cong.	Ranking	Terms in: House	Comm.	Date of Assignment
103rd	Maj-16th	1	1	Jan. 5, 1993
104th	Min-8th	2	2	Jan. 4, 1995

3rd JUDICIARY
Dates: Jan. 7, 1997-July 1, 2007
Departure: Resigned the House; retired

Cong.	Ranking	Terms in: House	Comm.	Date of Assignment
105th	Min-12th	3	1	Jan. 7, 1997
106th	Min-11th	4	2	Jan. 6, 1999
107th	Min-11th	5	3	Jan. 31, 2001
108th	Min-10th	6	4	Jan. 28, 2003
109th	Min-10th	7	5	Jan. 26, 2005
110th	Maj-10th	8	6	Jan. 18, 2007

Carrie P. Meek (D-Fla.)

Dates: April 29, 1926
House: Jan. 3, 1993-Jan. 3, 2003
Left the House: Retired in 2002

HOUSE STANDING COMMITTEES:

1st APPROPRIATIONS
1st Dates: Jan. 5, 1993-Jan. 3, 1995
1st Departure: Moved to Budget and Government Reform and Oversight
2nd Dates: Jan. 7, 1997-Jan. 3, 2003
2nd Departure: Left the House; retired

Cong.	Ranking	Terms in: House	Comm.	Date of Assignment
103rd	Maj-37th	1 *1	1	Jan. 5, 1993
105th	Min-24th	3 *2	1	Jan. 7, 1997
106th	Min-17th	4 *2	2	Jan. 6, 1999
107th	Min-16th	5 *2	3	Jan. 31, 2001

2nd BUDGET
Dates: Jan. 4, 1995-Jan. 3, 1997
Departure: Returned to Appropriations

Cong.	Ranking	Terms in: House	Comm.	Date of Assignment
104th	Min-16th	2	1	Jan. 4, 1995

3rd GOVERNMENT REFORM AND OVERSIGHT
Dates: Jan. 9, 1995-Jan. 3, 1997
Departure: Returned to Appropriations

Cong.	Ranking	Terms in: House	Comm.	Date of Assignment
104th	Min-20th	2	1	Jan. 9, 1995

Kendrick B. Meek (D-Fla.)

Dates: Sept. 6, 1966
House: Jan. 3, 2003-date
Serving in the 111th Congress

HOUSE STANDING COMMITTEES:

1st ARMED SERVICES
1st Dates: Feb. 5, 2003-Jan. 3, 2007
1st Departure: Moved to Ways and Means
2nd Dates: Jan. 18, 2007-Jan. 3, 2009
2nd Departure: Left committee; no new assignment

Cong.	Ranking	Terms in: House	Comm.	Date of Assignment
108th	Min-26th	1 *1	1	Feb. 5, 2003

Cong.	Ranking	Terms in: House	Comm.	Date of Assignment
109th	Min-22nd	2 *1	2	Jan. 26, 2005
110th	MjR-1st	3 *2	1	Jan. 18, 2007

2nd BUDGET
Dates: Feb. 5, 2003-Feb. 12, 2003
Departure: Leave of absence; moved to Select Homeland Security

Cong.	Ranking	Terms in: House	Comm.	Date of Assignment
108th	Min-16th	1	1	Feb. 5, 2003

3rd HOMELAND SECURITY
Dates: Feb. 9, 2005-Jan. 3, 2007
Departure: Moved to Ways and Means

Cong.	Ranking	Terms in: House	Comm.	Date of Assignment
109th	Min-15th	2	2	Feb. 9, 2005

4th WAYS AND MEANS
Dates: Jan. 4, 2007-date
Departure: Still serving in the 111th Congress

Cong.	Ranking	Terms in: House	Comm.	Date of Assignment
110th	Maj-22nd	3	1	Jan. 4, 2007
111th	Maj-19th	4	2	Jan. 7, 2009

HOUSE SELECT AND SPECIAL COMMITTEES:

1st SELECT HOMELAND SECURITY
Dates: Feb. 12, 2003-Jan. 3, 2005
Departure: Continued on reorganized standing committee

Cong.	Ranking	Terms in: House	Comm.	Date of Assignment
108th	Min-23rd	1	1	Feb. 12, 2003

Gregory W. Meeks (D-N.Y.)

Dates: Sept. 25, 1953
House: Feb. 3, 1998-date
Serving in the 111th Congress

H: Meeks was elected to the 105th Congress by special election, Feb. 3, 1998, to fill the vacancy caused by the resignation of U.S. Representative Floyd H. Flake (D-N.Y.). Meeks was seated Feb. 5, 1998, and assigned to committees.

HOUSE STANDING COMMITTEES:

1st BANKING AND FINANCIAL SERVICES, 105-106
FINANCIAL SERVICES, 107-111
Dates: Feb. 5, 1998-date
Departure: Still serving in the 111th Congress

Cong.	Ranking	Terms in: House	Comm.	Date of Assignment
105th	MnA-27th	1	1	Feb. 5, 1998
106th	Min-18th	2	2	Jan. 6, 1999
107th	Min-16th	3	3	Jan. 31, 2001
108th	Min-13th	4	4	Jan. 28, 2003
109th	Min-13th	5	5	Jan. 26, 2005
110th	Maj-11th	6	6	Jan. 12, 2007
111th	Maj-10th	7	7	Jan. 7, 2009

2nd INTERNATIONAL RELATIONS, 106-109
FOREIGN AFFAIRS, 110-111
Dates: Jan. 19, 1999-date
Departure: Still serving in the 111th Congress

Cong.	Ranking	Terms in: House	Comm.	Date of Assignment
106th	Min-20th	2	1	Jan. 19, 1999
107th	Min-16th	3	2	Jan. 31, 2001
108th	Min-12th	4	3	Jan. 28, 2003
109th	Min-12th	5	4	Jan. 26, 2005
110th	Maj-10th	6	5	Jan. 12, 2007
111th	Maj-9th	7	6	Jan. 21, 2009

Charles J. Melancon (D-La.)

Dates: Oct. 3, 1947
House: Jan. 3, 2005-date
Serving in the 111th Congress

HOUSE STANDING COMMITTEES:

1st AGRICULTURE
Dates: Jan. 26, 2005-Jan. 3, 2007
Departure: Moved to Energy and Commerce

Cong.	Ranking	Terms in: House	Comm.	Date of Assignment
109th	Min-14th	1	1	Jan. 26, 2005

2nd RESOURCES
Dates: Jan. 26, 2005-Jan. 3, 2007
Departure: Moved to Energy and Commerce

Cong.	Ranking	Terms in: House	Comm.	Date of Assignment
109th	Min-14th	1	1	Jan. 26, 2005

3rd SCIENCE, 109
SCIENCE AND TECHNOLOGY, 110
Dates: Feb. 2, 2005-Jan. 3. 2009
Departure: Moved to Budget

Cong.	Ranking	Terms in: House	Comm.	Date of Assignment
109th	MnA-20th	1	1	Feb. 2, 2005
110th	Maj-21st	2	2	Jan. 18, 2007

4th ENERGY AND COMMERCE
Dates: Jan. 4, 2007-date
Departure: Still serving in the 111th Congress

Cong.	Ranking	Terms in: House	Comm.	Date of Assignment
110th	Maj-29th	2	1	Jan. 4, 2007
111th	Maj-24th	3	2	Jan. 7, 2009

5th BUDGET
Dates: Jan. 21, 2009-Mar. 3, 2010
Departure: Resigned committee; no new assignment

Cong.	Ranking	Terms in: House	Comm.	Date of Assignment
111th	Maj-13th	3	1	Jan. 21, 2009

Robert Menendez (D-N.J.)

Dates: Jan. 1, 1954
House: Jan. 3, 1993-Jan. 16, 2006
Left the House: Resigned; appointed to the U.S. Senate. In 2006
Senate: January 16, 2006-date
Serving in the 111th Congress

S: Menendez was appointed to the U.S. Senate on January 16, 2006, to fill the vacancy caused by the election of U.S. Senator Jon S. Corzine (D-N.J.) as Governor of New Jersey. He was sworn on January 18, 2006, and assigned to committees.

HOUSE STANDING COMMITTEES:

1st FOREIGN AFFAIRS, 103
INTERNATIONAL RELATIONS, 104-109
Dates: Jan. 5, 1993-Jan. 16, 2006
Departure: Resigned the House for Senate appointment

Cong.	Ranking	Terms in: House	Comm.	Date of Assignment
103rd	Maj-16th	1	1	Jan. 5, 1993
104th	Min-13th	2	2	Jan. 4, 1995
105th	Min-10th	3	3	Jan. 7, 1997
106th	Min-8th	4	4	Jan. 6, 1999
107th	Min-6th	5	5	Jan. 31, 2001
108th	Min-6th	6	6	Jan. 28, 2003
109th	Min-6th	7	7	Jan. 26, 2005

2nd PUBLIC WORKS AND TRANSPORTATION, 103
TRANSPORTATION AND INFRASTRUCTURE, 104-109
Dates: Jan. 5, 1993-Jan. 16, 2006
Departure: Resigned the House for Senate appointment

Cong.	Ranking	Terms in: House	Comm.	Date of Assignment
103rd	Maj-31st	1	1	Jan. 5, 1993
104th	Min-20th	2	2	Jan. 4, 1995
105th	Min-15th	3	3	Jan. 7, 1997
106th	Min-13th	4	4	Jan. 6, 1999
107th	Min-10th	5	5	Jan. 31, 2001
108th	Min-8th	6	6	Jan. 28, 2003
109th	Min-7th	7	7	Jan. 26, 2005

HOUSE SELECT AND SPECIAL COMMITTEES:

1st SELECT HOMELAND SECURITY
Dates: June 19, 2002-Jan. 3, 2003
Departure: Left committee; no new assignment

Cong.	Ranking	Terms in: House	Comm.	Date of Assignment
107th	Min-3rd	5	1	June 19, 2002

SENATE STANDING COMMITTEES:

1st BANKING, HOUSING, AND URBAN AFFAIRS
Dates: Jan. 18, 2006-date
Departure: Still serving in the 111th Congress

Cong.	Ranking	Years in: Senate	Comm.	Date of Assignment
109th	MnR-1st	1	1	Jan. 18, 2006
110th	Maj-7th	1	1	Jan. 12, 2007
111th	Maj-6th	4	4	Jan. 21, 2009

2nd BUDGET
Dates: Jan. 18, 2006-date
Departure: Still serving in the 111th Congress

Cong.	Ranking	Years in: Senate	Comm.	Date of Assignment
109th	MnR-1st	1	1	Jan. 18, 2006
110th	Maj-8th	1	1	Jan. 12, 2007
111th	Maj-8th	4	4	Jan. 21, 2009

3rd ENERGY AND NATURAL RESOURCES
Dates: Jan. 18, 2006-date
Departure: Still serving in the 111th Congress

Cong.	Ranking	Years in: Senate	Comm.	Date of Assignment
109th	MnR-1st	1	1	Jan. 18, 2006
110th	Maj-9th	1	1	Jan. 12, 2007
111th	Maj-7th	4	4	Jan. 21, 2009

4th FOREIGN RELATIONS
Dates: Jan. 12, 2007-date
Departure: Still serving in 111th Congress

Cong.	Ranking	Years in: Senate	Comm.	Date of Assignment
110th	Maj-8th	1	1	Jan. 12, 2007
111th	Maj-5th	4	3	Jan. 21, 2009

5th FINANCE
Dates: Jan. 21, 2009-date
Departure: Still serving in the 111th Congress

Cong.	Ranking	Years in: Senate	Comm.	Date of Assignment
111th	Maj-12th	4	1	Jan. 21, 2009

Jeff Merkley (D-Ore.)

Dates: Oct. 24, 1956
Senate: Jan. 3. 2009-date
Serving in the 111th Congress

SENATE STANDING COMMITTEES:

1st BANKING, HOUSING AND URBAN AFFAIRS
Dates: Jan. 21, 2009-date
Departure: Still serving in the 111th Congress

Cong.	Ranking	Years in: Senate	Comm.	Date of Assignment
111th	Maj-12th	1	1	Jan. 21, 2009

2nd BUDGET
Dates: Jan. 21, 2009-date
Departure: Still serving in the 111th Congress

Cong.	Ranking	Years in: Senate	Comm.	Date of Assignment
111th	Maj-13th	1	1	Jan. 21, 2009

3rd ENVIRONMENT AND PUBLIC WORKS
Dates: Jan. 21, 2009-date
Departure: Still serving in the 111th Congress

Cong.	Ranking	Years in: Senate	Comm.	Date of Assignment
111th	Maj-10th	1	1	Jan. 21, 2009

4th HEALTH, EDUCATION, LABOR AND PENSIONS
Dates: Jan. 21, 2009-date
Departure: Still serving in the 111th Congress

Cong.	Ranking	Years in: Senate	Comm.	Date of Assignment
111th	Maj-12th	1	1	Jan. 21, 2009

Jack Metcalf (R-Wash.)

Dates: Nov. 30, 1927-March 15, 2007
House: Jan. 3, 1995-Jan. 3, 2001
Left the House: Retired in 2000

HOUSE STANDING COMMITTEES:

1st BANKING AND FINANCIAL SERVICES
Dates: Jan. 4, 1995-Jan. 3, 2001
Departure: Left the House; retired

Cong.	Ranking	Terms in: House	Comm.	Date of Assignment
104th	Maj-15th	1	1	Jan. 4, 1995
105th	Maj-13th	2	2	Jan. 7, 1997
106th	Maj-13th	3	3	Jan. 6, 1999

2nd RESOURCES
Dates: Jan. 4, 1995-Jan. 3, 1997
Departure: Moved to Transportation and Infrastructure

Cong.	Ranking	Terms in: House	Comm.	Date of Assignment
104th	Maj-23rd	1	1	Jan. 4, 1995

3rd SMALL BUSINESS
Dates: Jan. 4, 1995-Jan. 3, 1997
Departure: Moved to Transportation and Infrastructure

Cong.	Ranking	Terms in: House	Comm.	Date of Assignment
104th	Maj-22nd	1	1	Jan. 4, 1995

4th TRANSPORTATION AND INFRASTRUCTURE
Dates: Jan. 7, 1997-Jan. 3, 2001
Departure: Left the House; retired

Cong.	Ranking	Terms in: House	Comm.	Date of Assignment
105th	Maj-26th	2	1	Jan. 7, 1997
106th	Maj-23rd	3	2	Jan. 6, 1999

5th SCIENCE
Dates: Feb. 2, 1999-Jan. 3, 2001
Departure: Left the House; retired

Cong.	Ranking	Terms in: House	Comm.	Date of Assignment
106th	Maj-25th	3	1	Feb. 2, 1999

Howard M. Metzenbaum (D-Ohio)

Dates: June 4, 1917-March 12, 2008
Senate 1: Jan. 4, 1974-Dec. 23, 1974
Left the Senate 1: Appointed; defeated for nomination in 1974; resigned
Senate 2: Dec. 29, 1976-Jan. 3, 1995
Left the Senate 2: Retired; named Chair of Consumer Federation of America

S1: Metzenbaum was appointed to the 93rd Congress, Jan. 4, 1974, to fill the vacancy caused by the resignation of U.S. Senator William B. Saxbe (R-Ohio) who had been named Attorney General. Metzenbaum was seated Jan. 21, 1974, and assigned to committees. He lost the special election for the unexpired term and resigned Dec. 23, 1974.

S2: Metzenbaum was appointed to the 94th Congress, Dec. 29, 1976, to fill the vacancy caused by the resignation of U.S. Senator Robert Taft Jr. (R-Ohio). He was not seated nor assigned to committees because the 94th Congress was not in session. Metzenbaum had defeated Taft for election to the 95th Congress.

SENATE STANDING COMMITTEES:

1st AERONAUTICAL AND SPACE SCIENCES
Dates: Jan. 23, 1974-Dec. 23, 1974
Departure: Resigned the Senate; lost election

2nd INTERIOR AND INSULAR AFFAIRS
1st Dates: Jan. 23, 1974-Dec. 23, 1974
1st Departure: Resigned the Senate; lost election
ENERGY AND NATURAL RESOURCES
2nd Dates: Feb. 22, 1977-May 16, 1990
2nd Departure: Moved to Environment and Public Works

3rd ARMED SERVICES
Dates: Jan. 10, 1977-Feb. 11, 1977
Departure: Moved to Judiciary and returned to Energy and Natural Resources

4th BANKING, HOUSING AND URBAN AFFAIRS
Dates: Jan. 10, 1977-Feb. 11, 1977
Departure: Moved to Judiciary and returned to Energy and Natural Resources

5th JUDICIARY
Dates: Feb. 11, 1977-Jan. 3, 1995
Departure: Left the Senate; retired

Cong.	Ranking	Years in: Senate	Comm.	Date of Assignment
103rd	Maj-3rd	19	16	Jan. 7, 1993

6th LABOR AND HUMAN RESOURCES
Dates: Jan. 23, 1979-Jan. 3, 1995
Departure: Left the Senate; retired

Cong.	Ranking	Years in: Senate	Comm.	Date of Assignment
103rd	Maj-3rd	19	14	Jan. 7, 1993

7th BUDGET
Dates: Jan. 23, 1979-Jan. 6, 1987
Departure: Left committee; no new assignment

8th ENVIRONMENT AND PUBLIC WORKS
Dates: May 16, 1990-Jan. 3, 1995
Departure: Left the Senate; retired

Cong.	Ranking	Years in: Senate	Comm.	Date of Assignment
103rd	Maj-8th	19	3	Jan. 7, 1993

SENATE SELECT AND SPECIAL COMMITTEES:

1st SELECT INDIAN AFFAIRS
Dates: Feb. 11, 1977-Jan. 23, 1979
Departure: Moved to Labor and Human Resources and Budget

2nd SELECT INTELLIGENCE (Permanent)
Dates: Feb. 17, 1987-Jan. 3, 1995
Departure: Left the Senate; retired

Cong.	Ranking	Years in: Senate	Comm.	Date of Assignment
103rd	Maj-2nd	19	6	Jan. 27, 1993

Jan Meyers (R-Kans.)

Dates: July 20, 1928
House: Jan. 3, 1985-Jan. 3, 1997
Left the House: Retired in 1996

HOUSE STANDING COMMITTEES:

1st SCIENCE AND TECHNOLOGY
Dates: Jan. 30, 1985-Jan. 3, 1987
Departure: Moved to Foreign Affairs

2nd SMALL BUSINESS
Dates: Jan. 30, 1985-Jan. 3, 1997
Departure: Left the House; retired

Cong.	Ranking	Terms in: House	Comm.	Date of Assignment
103rd	Min-RM	5	5	Jan. 5, 1993
104th	Maj- Chr	6	6	Jan. 4, 1995

3rd FOREIGN AFFAIRS, 100-103
INTERNATIONAL RELATIONS, 104
Dates: Jan. 21, 1987-Jan. 3, 1997
Departure: Left the House; retired

Cong.	Ranking	Terms in: House	Comm.	Date of Assignment
103rd	Min-10th	5	4	Jan. 5, 1993
104th	Maj-9th	6	5	Jan. 4, 1995

4th ECONOMIC AND EDUCATIONAL OPPORTUNITIES
Dates: Jan. 4, 1995-Jan. 3, 1997
Departure: Left the House; retired

Cong.	Ranking	Terms in: House	Comm.	Date of Assignment
104th	Maj-12th	6	1	Jan. 4, 1995

HOUSE SELECT AND SPECIAL COMMITTEES:

1st SELECT AGING (Permanent)
Dates: Feb. 21, 1985-Jan. 3, 1995
Departure: Committee not renewed; moved to Economic and Educational Opportunities

Kweisi Mfume (D-Md.)

Dates: Oct. 24, 1948
House: Jan. 3, 1987-Feb. 15, 1996
Resignation letter effective Feb. 18, 1996
Left the House: Resigned; named Chief Executive Officer of the National Association for the Advancement of Colored People.

HOUSE STANDING COMMITTEES:

1st BANKING, FINANCE AND URBAN AFFAIRS, 100-103
BANKING AND FINANCIAL SERVICES, 104
Dates: Jan. 22, 1987-Feb. 15, 1996
Departure: Resigned the House; private sector

Cong.	Ranking	Terms in: House	Comm.	Date of Assignment
103rd	Maj-10th	4	4	Jan. 5, 1993
104th	Min-9th	5	5	Jan. 4, 1995

2nd SMALL BUSINESS
Dates: Jan. 22, 1987-Feb. 15, 1996
Departure: Resigned the House; private sector

Cong.	Ranking	Terms in: House	Comm.	Date of Assignment
103rd	Maj-9th	4	4	Jan. 5, 1993
104th	Min-4th	5	5	Jan. 4, 1995

3rd EDUCATION AND LABOR
Temporary Dates: Jan. 27, 1989-Feb. 27, 1990
Departure: Temporary term expired
2nd Dates: June 14, 1990-Jan. 3, 1991
2nd Departure: Moved to Joint Economic

4th STANDARDS OF OFFICIAL CONDUCT
Dates: Feb. 4, 1993-Jan. 3, 1995
Departure: Left committee; no new assignment

Cong.	Ranking	Terms in: House	Comm.	Date of Assignment
103rd	Maj-5th	4	2	Feb. 4, 1993

HOUSE SELECT AND SPECIAL COMMITTEES:

1st SELECT HUNGER (Temporary)
Dates: Jan. 22, 1987-Jan. 3, 1989
Departure: Moved to Select Narcotics Abuse and Control

2nd SELECT NARCOTICS ABUSE AND CONTROL (Temporary)
Dates: Mar. 8, 1989-Jan. 3, 1993
Termination: Committee not renewed in 1993

JOINT COMMITTEES:

1st JOINT ECONOMIC
House Dates: Mar. 7, 1991-Feb. 15, 1996
Departure: Resigned the House; private sector

Cong.	Ranking	Terms in: House	Comm.	Date of Assignment
103rd	Maj-4th	4	2	Jan. 27, 1993
104th	Min-4th	5	3	Jan. 19, 1995

John L. Mica (R-Fla.)

Dates: Jan. 27, 1943
House: Jan. 3, 1993-date
Serving in the 111th Congress

HOUSE STANDING COMMITTEES:

1st GOVERNMENT OPERATIONS, 103
GOVERNMENT REFORM AND OVERSIGHT, 104-105
GOVERNMENT REFORM, 106-109
OVERSIGHT AND GOVERNMENT REFORM, 110-111
Dates: Jan. 5. 1993-date
Departure: Still serving in the 111th Congress

Cong.	Ranking	Terms in: House	Comm.	Date of Assignment
103rd	Min-16th	1	1	Jan. 5, 1993
104th	Maj-11th	2	2	Jan. 4, 1995
105th	Maj-11th	3	3	Jan. 7, 1997
106th	Maj-9th	4	4	Jan. 6, 1999
107th	Maj-8th	5	5	Jan. 6, 2001
108th	Maj-6th	6	6	Jan. 28, 2003
109th	Maj-6th	7	7	Jan. 26, 2005
110th	Min-5th	8	8	Jan. 10, 2007
111th	Min-4th	9	9	Jan. 9, 2009

2nd PUBLIC WORKS AND TRANSPORTATION, 103
TRANSPORTATION AND INFRASTRUCTURE, 104-111
Dates: Jan. 5. 1993-date
Departure: Still serving in the 111th Congress

Cong.	Ranking	Terms in: House	Comm.	Date of Assignment
103rd	Min-22nd	1	1	Jan. 5, 1993
104th	Maj-20th	2	2	Jan. 4, 1995
105th	Maj-14th	3	3	Jan. 7, 1997
106th	Maj-12th	4	4	Jan. 6, 1999

Cong.	Ranking	Terms in: House	Comm.	Date of Assignment
107th	Maj-9th	5	5	Jan. 6, 2001
108th	Maj-7th	6	6	Jan. 28, 2003
109th	Maj-7th	7	7	Jan. 26, 2005
110th	Min-RM	8	8	Jan. 4, 2007
111th	Min-RM	9	9	Jan. 6, 2009

3rd HOUSE OVERSIGHT, 105
HOUSE ADMINISTRATION, 106-109
Dates: Apr. 30, 1997-Jan. 3, 2007
Departure: Left committee; became Ranking Member on Transportation and Infrastructure

Cong.	Ranking	Terms in: House	Comm.	Date of Assignment
105th	Maj-6th	3	1	Apr. 30, 1997
106th	Maj-5th	4	2	Jan. 6, 1999
107th	Maj-3rd	5	3	Jan. 31, 2001
108th	Maj-3rd	6	4	Jan. 28, 2003
109th	Maj-3rd	7	5	Jan. 26, 2005

Michael H. Michaud (D-Me.)

Dates: Jan. 18, 1955
House: Jan. 3, 2003-date
Serving in the 111th Congress

HOUSE STANDING COMMITTEES:

1st TRANSPORTATION AND INFRASTRUCTURE
Dates: Jan. 28, 2003-date
Departure: Still serving in the 111th Congress

Cong.	Ranking	Terms in: House	Comm.	Date of Assignment
108th	Min-33rd	1	1	Jan. 28, 2003
109th	Min-28th	2	2	Jan. 26, 2005
110th	Maj-21st	3	3	Jan. 10, 2007
111th	Maj-19th	4	4	Jan. 7, 2009

2nd VETERANS' AFFAIRS
Dates: Feb. 5, 2003-date
Departure: Still serving in the 111th Congress

Cong.	Ranking	Terms in: House	Comm.	Date of Assignment
108th	Min-7th	1	1	Feb. 5, 2003
109th	Min-6th	2	2	Jan. 26, 2005
110th	Maj-4th	3	3	Jan. 12, 2007
111th	Maj-4th	4	4	Jan. 21, 2009

3rd SMALL BUSINESS
Dates: Feb. 13, 2003-date
Departure: Still serving in the 111th Congress

Cong.	Ranking	Terms in: House	Comm.	Date of Assignment
108th	Min-17th	1	1	Feb. 13, 2003
109th	Min-11th	2	2	Feb. 2, 2005
110th	Maj-8th	3	3	Jan. 23, 2007
111th	Maj-8th	4	4	Jan. 21, 2009

Robert H. Michel (R-Ill.)

Dates: March 2, 1923
House: Jan. 3, 1957-Jan 3, 1995
Left the House: Retired in 1994

HOUSE STANDING COMMITTEES:

1st GOVERNMENT OPERATIONS
Dates: Jan. 16, 1957-Jan. 3, 1959
Departure: Moved to Appropriations

2nd APPROPRIATIONS
1st Dates: Jan. 19, 1959-Jan. 3, 1981
1st Departure: Left committee; elected Minority Floor Leader
2nd Dates: Jan. 23, 1986-Jan. 3, 1987
2nd Departure: Left committee; no new assignment

3rd BUDGET
Dates: Aug. 14, 1974-Jan. 3, 1975
Departure: Left committee; became Minority Whip

HOUSE SELECT AND SPECIAL COMMITTEES:

1st SELECT STANDARDS AND CONDUCT
Dates: Oct. 20, 1966-Dec. 27, 1966
Departure: Committee terminated.

JOINT COMMITTEES:

1st JOINT ORGANIZATION OF CONGRESS (Ad Hoc)
House Dates: Oct. 9, 1992-Dec. 17, 1993
Termination: House Report 103-413 filed

		Terms in:		Date of
Cong.	Ranking	House	Comm.	Assignment
103rd	Min-ExO	19	2	Jan. 5, 1993

HOUSE LEADERSHIP POSTS

Dates: Dec. 2, 1974-Jan. 3, 1995
Departure: Left chamber; retired

1st HOUSE MINORITY WHIP
Dates: Dec. 2, 1974-Jan. 3, 1981
Note: For the 94th Congress, Michel succeeded Minority Whip Leslie M. Arends (R-Ill.) on Dec. 2, 1974. He received 75 first ballot votes defeating Jerry Pettis (R-Cal.) with 38 votes and John Erlenborn (R-Ill.) with 22 votes. He was re-elected without opposition for the 95th and 96th Congresses.
Departure: Elected Minority Leader

2nd HOUSE MINORITY FLOOR LEADER
Dates: Dec. 8, 1980-Jan. 3, 1995
Note: For the 97th Congress, Michel succeeded Minority Leader John Rhodes (R-Ariz.) on Dec. 8, 1980. He defeated Guy Vander Jagt (R-Mich.) on the first ballot 103 to 87. Michel was re-elected without opposition for the 98th-103rd Congresses.
Departure: Left the House; retired

		Terms in:		Date of
Cong.	Ranking	House	Post	Selection
103rd	Min-1st	19	7	Dec. 11, 1992

Barbara A. Mikulski (D-Md.)

Dates: July 20, 1936
House: Jan. 3, 1977-Jan. 3, 1987
Left the House: Elected to U.S. Senate in 1986
Senate: Jan. 6, 1987-date
Serving in the 111th Congress

HOUSE STANDING COMMITTEES:

1st INTERSTATE AND FOREIGN COMMERCE
Dates: Jan. 19, 1977-Jan. 3, 1981

2nd ENERGY AND COMMERCE
Dates: Jan. 28, 1981-Jan. 3, 1987
Departure: Left the House for the Senate

3rd MERCHANT MARINE AND FISHERIES
Dates: Jan. 19, 1977-Jan. 3, 1987
Departure: Left the House for the Senate

HOUSE SELECT AND SPECIAL COMMITTEES:

1st SELECT ENERGY (Ad Hoc)
Dates: Apr. 21, 1977-Dec. 29, 1978
Termination: House Report 1820 (95-2) filed

2nd SELECT CHILDREN, YOUTH AND FAMILIES (Temporary)
Dates: Feb. 2, 1983-Jan. 3, 1985
Departure: Left committee; no new assignment

SENATE STANDING COMMITTEES:

1st APPROPRIATIONS
Dates: Jan. 6, 1987-date
Departure: Still serving in the 111th Congress.

		Years in:		Date of
Cong.	Ranking	Senate	Comm.	Assignment
103rd	Maj-11th	7	7	Jan. 7, 1993
104th	Min-9th	9	8	Jan. 4, 1995
105th	Min-8th	11	11	Jan. 9, 1997
106th	Min-7th	13	13	Jan. 7, 1999
107th	Min-6th	15	15	Jan. 25, 2001
+107th	Maj-6th	15	15	June 6, 2001
108th	Min-6th	17	17	Jan. 15, 2003
109th	Min-5th	19	19	Jan. 6, 2005
110th	Maj-5th	21	21	Jan. 12, 2007
111th	Maj-5th	23	23	Jan. 21, 2009

2nd ENVIRONMENT AND PUBLIC WORKS
Dates: Jan. 6, 1987-Feb. 2, 1989
Departure: Left committee; no new assignment

3rd LABOR AND HUMAN RESOURCES renamed Jan. 21, 1999
HEALTH, EDUCATION, LABOR AND PENSIONS
Dates: Jan. 6, 1987-date
Departure: Still serving in the 111th Congress

		Years in:		Date of
Cong.	Ranking	Senate	Comm.	Assignment
103rd	Maj-7th	7	7	Jan. 7, 1993
104th	Min-6th	9	8	Jan. 4, 1995
105th	Min-4th	11	11	Jan. 9, 1997
106th	Min-4th	13	13	Jan. 7, 1999
107th	Min-4th	15	15	Jan. 25, 2001
+107th	Maj-4th	15	15	June 6, 2001
108th	Min-4th	17	17	Jan. 15, 2003
109th	Min-4th	19	19	Jan. 6, 2005
110th	Maj-4th	21	21	Jan. 12, 2007
111th	Maj-4th	23	23	Jan. 21, 2009

4th SMALL BUSINESS
Dates: Jan. 6, 1987-Jan. 21, 1993
Departure: Moved to Select Ethics

SENATE SELECT AND SPECIAL COMMITTEES:

1st SELECT ETHICS (Permanent)
Dates: Jan. 26, 1993-Jan. 23, 1996
Departure: Left committee; no new assignment

Cong.	Ranking	Years in: Senate	Comm.	Date of Assignment
103rd	Maj-2nd	7	1	Jan. 26, 1993
104th	Min-2nd	9	2	Jan. 11, 1995

2nd SELECT INTELLIGENCE (Permanent)
Dates: July 10, , 2001-date
Departure: Still serving in the 111th Congress

Cong.	Ranking	Years in: Senate	Comm.	Date of Assignment
+107th	MjA-9th	15	1	July 10, 2001
108th	Min-8th	17	2	Jan. 15, 2003
109th	Min-6th	19	4	Jan. 6, 2005
110th	Maj-5th	21	6	Jan. 12, 2007
111th	Maj-5th	23	8	Jan. 21, 2009

Juanita Millender-McDonald (D-Cal.)

Dates: Sept. 7, 1938-April 22, 2007
House: March 26, 1996-April 22, 2007
Left the House: Died in office

H: Millender-McDonald was elected to the 104th Congress by special election, March 26, 1996, to fill the vacancy caused by the resignation of U.S. Representative Walter R. Tucker III (D-Cal.). Millender-McDonald was seated April 16, 1996, and assigned to committees.

HOUSE STANDING COMMITTEES:

1st SMALL BUSINESS
Dates: Apr. 22, 1996-Apr. 22, 2007
Departure: Died in office

Cong.	Ranking	Terms in: House	Comm.	Date of Assignment
104th	MnR-3rd	1	1	Apr. 22, 1996
105th	Min-10th	2	2	Feb. 5, 1997
106th	Min-3rd	3	3	Jan. 6, 1999
107th	Min-2nd	4	4	Jan. 31, 2001
108th	Min-2nd	5	5	Jan. 28, 2003
109th	Min-2nd	6	6	Jan. 26, 2005
110th	Maj-2nd	7	7	Jan. 23, 2007

2nd TRANSPORTATION AND INFRASTRUCTURE
Dates: Apr. 22, 1996-Apr. 22, 2007
Departure: Died in office

Cong.	Ranking	Terms in: House	Comm.	Date of Assignment
104th	MnR-6th	1	1	Apr. 22, 1996
105th	Min-23rd	2	2	Jan. 7, 1997
106th	Min-20th	3	3	Jan. 6, 1999
107th	Min-17th	4	4	Jan. 31, 2001
108th	Min-13th	5	5	Jan. 28, 2003
109th	Min-12th	6	6	Jan. 26, 2005
110th	Maj-11th	7	7	Jan. 10, 2007

3rd HOUSE ADMINISTRATION
Dates: Feb. 5, 2003-Apr. 22, 2007
Ch1: Succeeded by Robert A. Brady (D-Penn.) as Chair on May 24, 2007
Departure: Died in office

Cong.	Ranking	Terms in: House	Comm.	Date of Assignment
108th	Min-2nd	5	1	Feb. 5, 2003

Cong.	Ranking	Years in: Senate	Comm.	Date of Assignment
109th	Min-RM	6	2	Jan. 26, 2005
110th	Maj-Ch1	7	3	Jan. 4, 2007

JOINT COMMITTEES:

1st JOINT LIBRARY
House Dates: Mar. 25, 2003-Apr. 22, 2007
VC1: Millender-McDonald was succeeded by Robert A. Brady (D-Penn) as Vice Chair on May 24, 2007
Departure: Died in office

Cong.	Ranking	Terms in: House	Comm.	Date of Assignment
108th	Min-2nd	5	1	Mar. 25, 2003
109th	Min-1st	6	2	Mar. 16, 2005
110th	Maj-VC1	7	3	Mar. 14, 2007

2nd JOINT PRINTING
House Dates: Mar. 16, 2005-Apr. 22, 2007
Ch1: Millender-McDonald was succeeded by Robert A. Brady (D-Penn) as Chair on May 24, 2007
Departure: Died in office

Cong.	Ranking	Terms in: House	Comm.	Date of Assignment
109th	Min-1st	6	1	Mar. 16, 2005
110th	Maj-Ch1	7	2	Mar. 14, 2007

Brad Miller (D-N.C.)

Dates: May 19, 1953
House: Jan. 3, 2003-date
Serving in the 111th Congress

HOUSE STANDING COMMITTEES:

1st FINANCIAL SERVICES
Dates: Jan. 28, 2003-date
Departure: Still serving in the 111th Congress

Cong.	Ranking	Terms in: House	Comm.	Date of Assignment
108th	Min-31st	1	1	Jan. 28, 2003
109th	Min-26th	2	2	Jan. 26, 2005
110th	Maj-19th	3	3	Jan. 12, 2007
111th	Maj-18th	4	4	Jan. 7, 2009

2nd SCIENCE, 108-109
SCIENCE AND TECHNOLOGY, 110-111
Dates: Feb. 5, 2003-date
Departure: Still serving in the 111th Congress

Cong.	Ranking	Terms in: House	Comm.	Date of Assignment
108th	Min-18th	1	1	Feb. 5, 2003
109th	Min-9th	2	2	Jan. 26, 2005
110th	Maj-8th	3	3	Jan. 18, 2007
111th	Maj-7th	4	4	Jan. 21, 2009

3rd SMALL BUSINESS
Dates: Apr. 30, 2003-Jan. 3, 2005
Departure: Left committee; no new assignment

Cong.	Ranking	Terms in: House	Comm.	Date of Assignment
108th	MnR-4th	1	1	Apr. 30, 2003

4th FOREIGN AFFAIRS
Dates: Jan. 12, 2007-date
Departure: Still serving in the 111th Congress

Cong.	Ranking	Terms in: House	Comm.	Date of Assignment
110th	Maj-21st	3	1	Jan. 12, 2007
111th	Maj-23rd	4	2	Jan. 21, 2009

Candice S. Miller (R-Mich.)

Dates: May 7, 1954
House: Jan. 3, 2003-date
Serving in the 111th Congress

HOUSE STANDING COMMITTEES:

1st ARMED SERVICES
Dates: Jan. 28, 2003-Mar. 10, 2008
Departure: Resigned committee; moved to Homeland Security

Cong.	Ranking	Terms in: House	Comm.	Date of Assignment
108th	Maj-30th	1	1	Jan. 28, 2003
109th	Maj-26th	2	2	Jan. 26, 2005
110th	Min-21st	3	3	Jan. 10, 2007

2nd GOVERNMENT REFORM
Dates: Jan. 28, 2003-Jan. 3, 2007
Departure: Moved to Transportation and Infrastructure and Select Energy Independence and Global Warming

Cong.	Ranking	Terms in: House	Comm.	Date of Assignment
108th	Maj-19th	1	1	Jan. 28, 2003
109th	Maj-13th	2	2	Jan. 26, 2005

3rd HOUSE ADMINISTRATION
Dates: Jan. 26, 2005-Jan. 3, 2007
Departure: Moved to Transportation and Infrastructure and Select Energy Independence and Global Warming

Cong.	Ranking	Terms in: House	Comm.	Date of Assignment
109th	Maj-6th	2	1	Jan. 26, 2005

4th TRANSPORTATION AND INFRASTRUCTURE
Dates: Jan. 10, 2007-date
Departure: Still serving in the 111th Congress

Cong.	Ranking	Terms in: House	Comm.	Date of Assignment
110th	Min-31st	3	1	Jan. 10, 2007
111th	Min-23rd	4	2	Jan. 9, 2009

5th HOMELAND SECURITY
Dates: Mar. 11, 2008-date
Departure: Still serving in the 111th Congress

Cong.	Ranking	Terms in: House	Comm.	Date of Assignment
110th	MnR-3rd	3	1	Mar. 11, 2008
111th	Min-10th	4	2	Jan. 9, 2009

HOUSE SELECT AND SPECIAL COMMITTEES:

1st SELECT ENERGY INDEPENDENCE AND GLOBAL WARMING
Dates: Mar. 9, 2007-date
Departure: Still serving in the 111th Congress

Cong.	Ranking	Terms in: House	Comm.	Date of Assignment
110th	Min-6th	3	1	Mar. 9, 2007
111th	Min-5th	4	2	Feb. 3, 2009

JOINT COMMITTEES:

1st JOINT LIBRARY
House Dates: Mar. 16, 2005-Jan. 3, 2007
Departure: Moved to Transportation and Infrastructure and Select Energy Independence and Global Warming

Cong.	Ranking	Terms in: House	Comm.	Date of Assignment
109th	Maj-3rd	2	1	Mar. 16, 2005

Daniel Miller (R-Fla.)

Dates: May 30, 1942
House: Jan. 3, 1993-Jan. 3, 2003
Left the House: Retired in 2002

HOUSE STANDING COMMITTEES:

1st BUDGET
Dates: Jan. 5, 1993-Jan. 19, 1999
Departure: Resigned committee; no new assignment

Cong.	Ranking	Terms in: House	Comm.	Date of Assignment
103rd	Min-12th	1	1	Jan. 5, 1993
104th	Maj-10th	2	2	Jan. 4, 1995
105th	Maj-7th	3	3	Jan. 7, 1997
106th	Maj-5th	4	4	Jan. 6, 1999

2nd EDUCATION AND LABOR
Dates: Jan. 5, 1993-Jan. 3, 1995
Departure: Moved to Appropriations

Cong.	Ranking	Terms in: House	Comm.	Date of Assignment
103rd	Min-15th	1	1	Jan. 5, 1993

3rd APPROPRIATIONS
Dates: Jan. 4, 1995-Jan. 3, 2003
Departure: Left the House; retired

Cong.	Ranking	Terms in: House	Comm.	Date of Assignment
104th	Maj-23rd	2	1	Jan. 4, 1995
105th	Maj-20th	3	2	Jan. 7, 1997
106th	Maj-18th	4	3	Jan. 6, 1999
107th	Maj-16th	5	4	Jan. 6, 2001

4th GOVERNMENT REFORM
Dates: Nov. 13, 1997-Jan. 3, 2003
Departure: Left the House; retired

Cong.	Ranking	Terms in: House	Comm.	Date of Assignment
105th	MjR-3rd	3	1	Nov. 13, 1997
106th	Maj-17th	4	2	Jan. 6, 1999
107th	Maj-14th	5	3	Jan. 6, 2001

Gary G. Miller (R-Cal.)

Dates: Oct. 16, 1948
House: Jan. 3, 1999-date
Serving in the 111th Congress

HOUSE STANDING COMMITTEES:

1st BUDGET
Dates: Jan. 6, 1999-Jan. 3, 2003
Departure: Returned to Transportation and Infrastructure

Cong.	Ranking	Terms in: House	Comm.	Date of Assignment
106th	Maj-22nd	1	1	Jan. 6, 1999
107th	Maj-13th	2	2	Jan. 6, 2001

2nd SCIENCE, 106-107
Dates: Jan. 6, 1999-Jan. 3, 2003
Departure: Returned to Transportation and Infrastructure

Cong.	Ranking	Terms in: House	Comm.	Date of Assignment
106th	Maj-22nd	1	1	Jan. 6, 1999
107th	Maj-17th	2	2	Jan. 6, 2001

3rd TRANSPORTATION AND INFRASTRUCTURE
1st Dates: Jan. 6, 1999-Jan. 3, 2001
1st Departure: Moved to Financial Services
2nd Dates: Jan. 28, 2003-date
2nd Departure: Still serving in the 111th Congress

Cong.	Ranking	Terms in: House	Comm.	Date of Assignment
106th	Maj-35th	1 *1	1	Jan. 6, 1999
108th	Maj-18th	3 *2	1	Jan. 28, 2003
109th	Maj-17th	4 *2	2	Jan. 26, 2005
110th	Min-12th	5 *2	3	Jan. 10, 2007
111th	Min-9th	6 *2	4	Jan. 9, 2009

4th FINANCIAL SERVICES
Dates: Jan. 6, 2001-date
Departure: Still serving in the 111th Congress

Cong.	Ranking	Terms in: House	Comm.	Date of Assignment
107th	Maj-30th	2	1	Jan. 6, 2001
108th	Maj-25th	3	2	Jan. 28, 2003
109th	Maj-21st	4	3	Jan. 26, 2005
110th	Min-15th	5	4	Jan. 10, 2007
111th	Min-10th	6	5	Jan. 9, 2009

George Miller (D-Cal.)

Dates: May 17, 1945
House: Jan. 3, 1975-date
Serving in the 111th Congress

HOUSE STANDING COMMITTEES:

1st EDUCATION AND LABOR, 94-103
ECONOMIC AND EDUCATIONAL OPPORTUNITIES, 104
EDUCATION AND THE WORKFORCE, 105-109
EDUCATION AND LABOR, 110-111
1st Dates: Jan. 20, 1975-Jan. 3, 1985
1st Departure: Ceased active service to move to Budget. Returned later with continuous seniority credited.
2nd Dates: Jan. 19, 1989-date
2nd Departure: Still serving in the 111th Congress

Cong.	Ranking	Terms in: House	Comm.	Date of Assignment
103rd	Maj-3rd	10 *2	3	Jan. 5, 1993
104th	Min-2nd	11 *2	4	Jan. 4, 1995
105th	Min-2nd	12 *2	5	Jan. 7, 1997
106th	Min-2nd	13 *2	6	Jan. 6, 1999
107th	Min-RM	14 *2	7	Jan. 31, 2001
108th	Min-RM	15 *2	8	Jan. 8, 2003
109th	Min-RM	16 *2	9	Jan. 6, 2005
110th	Maj-Chr	17 *2	10	Jan. 4, 2007
111th	Maj-Chr	18 *2	11	Jan. 6, 2009

2nd INTERIOR AND INSULAR AFFAIRS, 94-102
NATURAL RESOURCES, 103
RESOURCES, 104-109
NATURAL RESOURCES, 110
1st Dates: Jan. 20, 1975-Jan. 3, 2001
Ch2: Miller succeeded Morris K. Udall (D-Ariz.), who had retired. Miller was elected Chair on May 9, 1991
Departure: Still serving in the 111th Congress
1st Dates: Jan. 20, 1975-Jan. 3, 2001
1st Departure: Left committee; became Ranking Member on Education and the Workforce
2nd Dates: May 2, 2001-Feb. 2, 2003
2nd Departure: Left committee; no new assignment
3rd Dates: Mar. 5, 2003-date
3rd Departure: Still serving in the 111th Congress

Cong.	Ranking	Terms in: House	Comm.	Date of Assignment
103rd	Maj-Chr	10 *1	10	Jan. 5, 1993
104th	Min-RM	11 *1	11	Jan. 9, 1995
105th	Min-RM	12 *1	12	Jan. 7, 1997
106th	Min-RM	13 *1	13	Jan. 6, 1999
107th	Min-2nd	14 *2	1	May 2, 2001
108th	Min-2nd	15 *2	2	Jan. 28, 2003
108th	MnR-3rd	15 *3	1	Mar. 5, 2003
109th	Min-16th	16 *3	2	Feb. 2, 2005
110th	Maj-15th	17 *3	3	Jan. 18, 2007
111th	Maj-14th	18 *3	4	Jan. 21, 2009

3rd BUDGET
Dates: Jan. 6, 1983-Jan. 3, 1989
Departure: Returned to Education and Labor

HOUSE SELECT AND SPECIAL COMMITTEES:

1st OUTER CONTINENTAL SHELF (Ad Hoc)
Became Select Committee on the Outer Continental Shelf, Mar. 29, 1979.
Dates: May 6, 1975-June 30, 1980
Termination: House Report 1214 (96-2), July 31, 1980

2nd SELECT CHILDREN, YOUTH AND FAMILIES (Temporary)
Dates: Feb. 2, 1983-Jan. 3, 1993
Termination: Committee not renewed in 1993

JOINT COMMITTEES:

1st JOINT DEFICIT REDUCTION (Temporary)
House Dates: Feb. 23, 1987-Sep. 29, 1987
Termination: Public Law 100-119 adjusted Gramm-Rudman-Hollings Act.

Jefferson B. Miller (R-Fla.)

Dates: June 27, 1959
House: Oct. 16, 2001-date
Serving in the 111h Congress

H: Miller was elected to the 107th Congress by special election, Oct. 16, 2001, to fill the vacancy caused by the resignation of U.S. Representative Joseph Scarborough (R-Fla.). Miller was seated Oct. 23, 2001, and assigned to committees.

HOUSE STANDING COMMITTEES:

1st ARMED SERVICES
Dates: Nov. 8, 2001-date
Departure: Still serving in the 111th Congress

Cong.	Ranking	Terms in: House	Comm.	Date of Assignment
107th	MjR-2nd	1	1	Nov. 8, 2001
108th	Maj-22nd	2	2	Jan. 28, 2003
109th	Maj-20th	3	3	Jan. 26, 2005
110th	Min-14th	4	4	Jan. 10, 2007
111th	Min-8th	5	5	Jan. 9, 2009

2nd VETERANS' AFFAIRS
Dates: Nov. 8, 2001-date
Departure: Still serving in the 111th Congress

Cong.	Ranking	Terms in: House	Comm.	Date of Assignment
107th	MjR-1st	1	1	Nov. 8, 2001
108th	Maj-12th	2	2	Jan. 28, 2003
109th	Maj-9th	3	3	Jan. 26, 2005
110th	Min-7th	4	4	Jan. 10, 2007
111th	Min-5th	5	5	Jan. 9, 2009

HOUSE SELECT AND SPECIAL COMMITTEES:

1st SELECT BIPARTISAN COMMITTEE TO INVESTIGATE THE PREPARATION FOR AND RESPONSE TO HURRICANE KATRINA
Dates: Sep. 26, 2005-Feb. 15, 2006
Departure: House Report 377 (109-2) filed

Cong.	Ranking	Terms in: House	Comm.	Date of Assignment
109th	MjR-1st	3	1	Sep. 26, 2005

2nd PERMANENT SELECT INTELLIGENCE
Dates: Feb. 4, 2009-date
Departure: Still serving in the 111th Congress

Cong.	Ranking	Terms in: House	Comm.	Date of Assignment
111th	Min-7th	5	1	Feb. 4, 2009

Zell B. Miller (D-Ga.)

Dates: Feb. 24, 1932
Senate: July 24, 2000-Jan. 3, 2005
Left the Senate: Retired in 2004

S: Miller was appointed to the 106th Congress, July 24, 2000, to fill the vacancy caused by the death of U.S. Senator Paul Coverdell (R-Ga.) and was subsequently elected. Miller was seated July 27, 2000, and assigned to committees.

SENATE STANDING COMMITTEES:

1st AGRICULTURE, NUTRITION AND FORESTRY
Dates: Sep. 12, 2000-Jan. 3, 2005
Departure: Left the Senate; retired

Cong.	Ranking	Years in: Senate	Comm.	Date of Assignment
106th	MnA-9th	1	1	Sep. 12, 2000
107th	Min-7th	1	1	Jan. 25, 2001
+107th	Maj-7th	1	1	June 6, 2001
108th	Min-7th	3	3	Jan. 15, 2003

2nd BANKING, HOUSING AND URBAN AFFAIRS
Dates: Sep. 12, 2000-Jan. 3, 2005
Departure: Left the Senate; retired

Cong.	Ranking	Years in: Senate	Comm.	Date of Assignment
106th	MnA-10th	1	1	Sep. 12, 2000
107th	Min-7th	1	1	Jan. 25, 2001
+107th	Maj-7th	1	1	June 6, 2001
108th	Min-7th	3	3	Jan. 15, 2003

3rd VETERANS' AFFAIRS
Dates: Sep. 12, 2000-Jan. 3, 2005
Departure: Left the Senate; retired

Cong.	Ranking	Years in: Senate	Comm.	Date of Assignment
106th	MnA-6th	1	1	Sep. 12, 2000
107th	Min-6th	1	1	Jan. 25, 2001
+107th	Maj-7th	1	1	July 10, 2001
108th	Min-6th	3	3	Jan. 15, 2003

Norman Y. Mineta (D-Cal.)

Dates: Nov. 12, 1931
House: Jan. 3, 1975-Oct. 10, 1995
Left the House: Resigned; named Vice President of Lockheed Aircraft in 1995. Later named Secretary of Commerce.

HOUSE STANDING COMMITTEES:

1st POST OFFICE AND CIVIL SERVICE
Dates: Jan. 20, 1975-Jan. 3, 1977
Departure: Moved to Budget

2nd PUBLIC WORKS AND TRANSPORTATION
Dates: Jan. 20, 1975-Oct. 10, 1995
RM1: Replaced by James L. Oberstar (DFL-Minn.) as Ranking Member on Oct. 10, 1995
Departure: Resigned the House; private sector

Cong.	Ranking	Terms in: House	Comm.	Date of Assignment
103rd	Maj-Chr	10	10	Jan. 5, 1993
104th	Min-RM1	11	11	Jan. 4, 1995

3rd BUDGET
Dates: Jan. 11, 1977-Jan. 3, 1983
Departure: Moved to Science and Technology

4th SCIENCE AND TECHNOLOGY, 98-99
SCIENCE, SPACE AND TECHNOLOGY, 100-102
Dates: Jan. 6, 1983-Jan. 3, 1993
Departure: Left committee; became Chair of Public Works and Transportation

HOUSE SELECT AND SPECIAL COMMITTEES:

1st PERMANENT SELECT INTELLIGENCE
Dates: July 27, 1977-Jan. 3, 1985
Departure: Left committee; no new assignment

David B. Minge (DFL-Minn.)

Dates: March 19, 1942
House: Jan. 3, 1993-Jan. 3, 2001
Left the House: Defeated for re-election in 2000

HOUSE STANDING COMMITTEES:

1st AGRICULTURE
Dates: Jan. 5, 1993-Jan. 3, 2001
Departure: Left the House; lost re-election

Cong.	Ranking	Terms in: House	Comm.	Date of Assignment
103rd	Maj-18th	1	1	Jan. 5, 1993
104th	Min-11th	2	2	Jan. 4, 1995
105th	Min-7th	3	3	Jan. 7, 1997
106th	Min-7th	4	4	Jan. 6, 1999

2nd SCIENCE, SPACE AND TECHNOLOGY, 103
SCIENCE, 104
Dates: Jan. 5, 1993-Jan. 3, 1997
Departure: Moved to Budget

Cong.	Ranking	Terms in: House	Comm.	Date of Assignment
103rd	Maj-29th	1	1	Jan. 5, 1993
104th	Min-13th	2	2	Jan. 4, 1995

3rd BUDGET
Dates: Jan. 7, 1997-Jan. 3, 2001
Departure: Left the House; lost re-election

Cong.	Ranking	Terms in: House	Comm.	Date of Assignment
105th	Min-14th	3	1	Jan. 7, 1997
106th	Min-5th	4	2	Jan. 6, 1999

JOINT COMMITTEES:

1st JOINT ECONOMIC
House Dates: Mar. 18, 1999-Jan. 3, 2001
Departure: Left the House; lost re-election

Cong.	Ranking	Terms in: House	Comm.	Date of Assignment
106th	Min-3rd	4	1	Mar. 18, 1999

Patsy T. Mink (D-Hai.)

Dates: Dec. 6, 1927-Sept. 28, 2002
House 1: Jan. 3, 1965-Jan. 3, 1977
Left the House 1: Lost U.S. Senate nomination in 1976
House 2: Sept. 22, 1990-Sept. 28, 2002
Left the House 2: Died in office

H2: Mink was elected to the 101st Congress by special election, Sept. 22, 1990, to fill the vacancy caused by the resignation of U.S. Representative Daniel K. Akaka (D-Hai.) who had been elected to the U.S. Senate. Mink was seated Sept. 27, 1990, and assigned to committees. She was posthumously reelected to the 108th Congress in 2002.

HOUSE STANDING COMMITTEES:

1st EDUCATION AND LABOR, 89-94, 101-103
ECONOMIC AND EDUCATIONAL OPPORTUNITIES, 104
EDUCATION AND THE WORKFORCE, 105-107
1st Dates: Jan. 18, 1965-Jan. 3, 1977
1st Departure: Left the House; lost Senate nomination
2nd Dates: Oct. 10, 1990-Sept. 28, 2002
2nd Departure: Died in office

Cong.	Ranking	Terms in: House	Comm.	Date of Assignment
103rd	Maj-12th	9 *2	3	Jan. 5, 1993

Cong.	Ranking	Terms in: House	Comm.	Date of Assignment
104th	Min-9th	10 *2	4	Jan. 4, 1995
105th	Min-7th	11 *2	5	Jan. 7, 1997
106th	Min-7th	12 *2	6	Jan. 6, 1999
107th	Min-5th	13 *2	7	Jan. 31, 2001

2nd INTERIOR AND INSULAR AFFAIRS, 90-94
NATURAL RESOURCES, 103
1st Dates: Jan. 23, 1967-Jan. 3, 1977
1st Departure: Left the House; lost Senate nomination
2nd Dates: Jan. 21, 1993
2nd Departure: Left committee; no new assignment

Cong.	Ranking	Terms in: House	Comm.	Date of Assignment
103rd	Maj-26th	9 *2	1	Jan. 21, 1993

3rd BUDGET
1st Dates: Feb. 5, 1975-Jan. 3, 1977
1st Departure: Left the House; lost Senate nomination
2nd Dates: Jan. 5, 1993-Jan. 3, 1999
2nd Departure: Returned to Government Reform

Cong.	Ranking	Terms in: House	Comm.	Date of Assignment
103rd	Maj-23rd	9 *2	1	Jan. 5, 1993
104th	Min-9th	10 *2	2	Jan. 4, 1995
105th	Min-5th	11 *2	3	Jan. 5, 1997

4th GOVERNMENT OPERATIONS, 101-102
GOVERNMENT REFORM, 106-107
1st Dates: Oct. 10, 1990-Jan. 3, 1993
1st Departure: Returned to Budget and to renamed Natural Resources
2nd Dates: Jan. 6, 1999-Sept. 28, 2002
2nd Departure: Died in office

Cong.	Ranking	Terms in: House	Comm.	Date of Assignment
106th	Min-8th	12 *2	1	Jan. 6, 1999
107th	Min-6th	13 *2	2	Jan. 31, 2001

HOUSE SELECT AND SPECIAL COMMITTEES:

1st OUTER CONTINENTAL SHELF (Ad Hoc)
Dates: Apr. 22, 1975-Jan. 3, 1977
Departure: Left the House; lost Senate nomination

Walt Minnick (D-Ida.)

Dates: Sep. 20, 1942
House: Jan. 3, 2009-date
Still serving in the 111th Congress

HOUSE STANDING COMMITTEES:

1st FINANCIAL SERVICES
Dates: Jan. 7, 2009-date
Departure: Still serving in the 111th Congress

Cong.	Ranking	Terms in: House	Comm.	Date of Assignment
111th	Maj-34th	1	1	Jan. 7, 2009

2nd AGRICULTURE
Dates: Jan. 21, 2009-date
Departure: Still serving in the 111th Congress

Cong.	Ranking	Terms in: House	Comm.	Date of Assignment
111th	Maj-28th	1	1	Jan. 21, 2009

George J. Mitchell (D-Me.)

Dates: Aug. 20, 1933
Senate: May 19, 1980-Jan. 3, 1995
Left the Senate: Retired; named presidential adviser for Economic Initiatives in Ireland

S: Mitchell was appointed to the 96th Congress, May 17, 1980, to fill the vacancy caused by the resignation of U.S. Senator Edmund S. Muskie (D-Me.) who was appointed Secretary of State. Mitchell was subsequently elected. He was seated May 19, 1980, and assigned to committees.

SENATE STANDING COMMITTEES:

1st BANKING, HOUSING AND URBAN AFFAIRS
Dates: May 19, 1980-Jan. 5, 1981
Departure: Moved to Finance and Veterans' Affairs

2nd BUDGET
Dates: May 19, 1980-Jan. 5, 1981
Departure: Moved to Finance and Veterans' Affairs

3rd ENVIRONMENT AND PUBLIC WORKS
Dates: May 19, 1980-Jan. 3, 1995
Departure: Left the Senate; retired

Cong.	Ranking	Years in: Senate	Comm.	Date of Assignment
103rd	Maj-2nd	13	13	Jan. 7, 1993

4th FINANCE
Dates: Jan. 5, 1981-Jan. 3, 1995
Departure: Left the Senate; retired

Cong.	Ranking	Years in: Senate	Comm.	Date of Assignment
103rd	Maj-6th	13	13	Jan. 7, 1993

5th VETERANS' AFFAIRS
Dates: Jan. 5, 1981-Jan. 3, 1995
Departure: Left the Senate; retired

Cong.	Ranking	Years in: Senate	Comm.	Date of Assignment
103rd	Maj-3rd	13	13	Jan. 21, 1993

6th GOVERNMENTAL AFFAIRS
Dates: Jan. 6, 1987-Feb. 2, 1989
Departure: Left committee; elected Majority Floor Leader

SENATE SELECT AND SPECIAL COMMITTEES:

1st SECRET MILITARY ASSISTANCE TO IRAN AND THE NICARAGUAN OPPOSITION (Iran-Contra Affair)
Dates: Jan. 12, 1987-Nov. 17, 1987
Termination: Senate Report 100-216 filed

2nd SELECT INTELLIGENCE (Permanent)
Dates: Jan. 27, 1993-Jan. 3, 1995
Departure: Left the Senate; retired

Cong.	Ranking	Years in: Senate	Comm.	Date of Assignment
103rd	Maj-ExO	13	1	Jan. 27, 1993

SENATE LEADERSHIP POSTS

Dates: Jan. 3, 1989-Jan. 3, 1995
Departure: Left chamber; retired

1st SENATE MAJORITY FLOOR LEADER
Dates: Jan. 3, 1989-Jan. 3, 1995

Notes: For the 101st Congress, Mitchell succeeded Majority Leader Robert C. Byrd (D-W.Va.) who became Chair of Appropriations. Mitchell was elected with 27 votes on the first ballot on Jan. 7, 1989, after defeating Daniel K. Inouye (D-Hai.) and J. Bennett Johnston (D-La.), who received 14 votes each but withdrew in favor of acclamation for Mitchell. Mitchell was unopposed for the 102nd and 103rd Congresses.
Departure: Left the Senate; retired

Cong.	Ranking	Years in: Senate	Post	Date of Selection
103rd	Maj-1st	13	5	Nov. 10, 1992

Harry E. Mitchell (D-Ariz.)

Dates: July 18, 1940
House: Jan. 3, 2007-date
Serving in the 111th Congress

HOUSE STANDING COMMITTEES:

1st TRANSPORTATION AND INFRASTRUCTURE
Dates: Jan. 10, 2007-date
Departure: Still serving in the 111th Congress

Cong.	Ranking	Terms in: House	Comm.	Date of Assignment
110th	Maj-36th	1	1	Jan. 10, 2007
111th	Maj-28th	2	2	Jan. 7, 2009

2nd VETERANS' AFFAIRS
Dates: Jan. 12, 2007-date
Departure: Still serving in the 111th Congress

Cong.	Ranking	Terms in: House	Comm.	Date of Assignment
110th	Maj-6th	1	1	Jan. 12, 2007
111th	Maj-6th	2	2	Jan. 7, 2009

3rd SCIENCE AND TECHNOLOGY
Dates: Jan. 18, 2007-date
Departure: Still serving in the 111th Congress

Cong.	Ranking	Terms in: House	Comm.	Date of Assignment
110th	Maj-23rd	1	1	Jan. 18, 2007
111th	Maj-21st	2	2	Jan. 7, 2009

John Joseph Moakley (D-Mass.)

Dates: April 27, 1927-May 28, 2001
House: Jan. 3, 1973-May 28, 2001
Left the House: Died in office

HOUSE STANDING COMMITTEES:

1st BANKING AND CURRENCY
Dates: Jan. 24, 1973-Jan. 3, 1975
Departure: Moved to Rules

2nd POST OFFICE AND CIVIL SERVICE
Dates: Jan. 24, 1973-Jan. 3, 1975
Departure: Moved to Rules

3rd RULES
Dates: Jan. 20, 1975-May 28, 2001

RM1: Replaced by J. Martin Frost III as Ranking Member on May 28, 2001
Departure: Died in office

Cong.	Ranking	Terms in: House	Comm.	Date of Assignment
103rd	Maj-Chr	11	10	Jan. 5, 1993
104th	Min-RM	12	11	Jan. 4, 1995
105th	Min-RM	13	12	Jan. 7, 1997
106th	Min-RM	14	13	Jan. 6, 1999
107th	Min-RM1	15	14	Jan. 3, 2001

HOUSE SELECT AND SPECIAL COMMITTEES:

1st SELECT SERVICEMEN MISSING IN SOUTHEAST ASIA
Dates: Sep. 15, 1975-Jan. 3, 1977
Termination: House Report 1764 (94-2) filed, Dec. 13, 1976

Susan Molinari (R-N.Y.)

Dates: March 27, 1958
House: March 20, 1990-Aug. 1, 1997
Left the House: Resigned to work for CBS News

H: Susan Molinari was elected to the 101st Congress by special election, March 20, 1990, to fill the vacancy caused by the resignation of her father, U.S. Representative Guy V. Molinari (R-N.Y.). Susan Molinari was seated March 27, 1990, and assigned to committees.

HOUSE STANDING COMMITTEES:

1st PUBLIC WORKS AND TRANSPORTATION, 101-103
TRANSPORTATION AND INFRASTRUCTURE, 104-105
Dates: Mar. 28, 1990-Aug. 1, 1997
Departure: Resigned the House; private sector

Cong.	Ranking	Terms in: House	Comm.	Date of Assignment
103rd	Min-8th	3	3	Jan. 5, 1993
104th	Maj-10th	4	4	Jan. 4, 1995
105th	Maj-8th	5	5	Jan. 7, 1997

2nd SMALL BUSINESS
Dates: Mar. 28, 1990-Jan. 3, 1991
Departure: Moved to Education and Labor

3rd EDUCATION AND LABOR
Dates: Jan. 24, 1991-Jan. 3, 1995
Departure: Moved to Budget

Cong.	Ranking	Terms in: House	Comm.	Date of Assignment
103rd	Min-9th	3	2	Jan. 5, 1993

4th BUDGET
Dates: Jan. 4, 1995-Aug. 1, 1997
Departure: Resigned the House; private sector

Cong.	Ranking	Terms in: House	Comm.	Date of Assignment
104th	Maj-16th	4	1	Jan. 4, 1995
105th	Maj-11th	5	2	Jan. 7, 1997

Alan B. Mollohan (D-W.Va.)

Dates: May 14, 1943
House: Jan. 3, 1983-date
Serving in the 111th Congress

HOUSE STANDING COMMITTEES:

1st INTERIOR AND INSULAR AFFAIRS
Dates: Jan. 6, 1983-May 1, 1986
Departure: Moved to Appropriations

2nd VETERANS AFFAIRS
Dates: Jan. 6, 1983-May 1, 1986
Departure: Moved to Appropriations

3rd STANDARDS OF OFFICIAL CONDUCT
1st Dates: Jan. 30, 1985-Jan. 3, 1991
1st Departure: Left committee; no new assignment
2nd Dates: Feb. 5, 2003-Jan. 3, 2007
RM2: Replaced Howard Berman (D-Cal.) as Ranking Member on Feb. 25, 2003
2nd Departure: Left committee; no new assignment

Cong.	Ranking	Terms in: House	Comm.	Date of Assignment
108th	Min-2nd	11 *2	1	Feb. 5, 2003
=108th	Min-RM2	11 *2	1	Feb. 25, 2003
109th	Min-RM	12 *2	2	Jan. 26, 2005

4th APPROPRIATIONS
Dates: May 1, 1986-date
Departure: Still serving in the 111th Congress

Cong.	Ranking	Terms in: House	Comm.	Date of Assignment
103rd	Maj-19th	6	5	Jan. 5, 1993
104th	Min-15th	7	6	Jan. 4, 1995
105th	Min-11th	8	7	Jan. 7, 1997
106th	Min-7th	9	8	Jan. 6, 1999
107th	Min-6th	10	9	Jan. 31, 2001
108th	Min-6th	11	10	Jan. 28, 2003
109th	Min-6th	12	11	Jan. 26, 2005
110th	Maj-4th	13	12	Jan. 4, 2007
111th	Maj-4th	14	13	Jan. 7, 2009

5th BUDGET
Dates: Jan. 5, 1993-Jan. 3, 1999
Departure: Left committee; no new assignment

Cong.	Ranking	Terms in: House	Comm.	Date of Assignment
103rd	Maj-18th	6	1	Jan. 5, 1993
104th	Min-6th	7	2	Jan. 4, 1995
105th	Min-3rd	8	3	Jan. 7, 1997

G.V. (Sonny) Montgomery

(D-Miss.)

Dates: Aug. 5, 1920-May 12, 2006
House: Jan. 3, 1967-Jan. 3, 1997
Left the House: Retired in 1996

HOUSE STANDING COMMITTEES:

1st AGRICULTURE
Dates: Jan. 23, 1967-Jan. 3, 1971
Departure: Moved to Armed Services

2nd VETERANS AFFAIRS
Dates: Jan. 29, 1969-Jan. 3, 1997
Departure: Left the House; retired

Cong.	Ranking	Terms in: House	Comm.	Date of Assignment
103rd	Maj-Chr	14	13	Jan. 5, 1993
104th	Min-RM	15	14	Jan. 4, 1995

3rd ARMED SERVICES, 103
NATIONAL SECURITY, 104
Dates: Feb. 4, 1971-Jan. 3, 1997
Departure: Left the House; retired

Cong.	Ranking	Terms in: House	Comm.	Date of Assignment
103rd	Maj-2nd	14	12	Jan. 5, 1993
104th	Min-2nd	15	13	Jan. 4, 1995

HOUSE SELECT AND SPECIAL COMMITTEES:

1st SELECT U.S. INVOLVEMENT IN SOUTHEAST ASIA
Dates: June 15, 1970-July 6, 1970
Termination: House Report 1276 (91-2) filed

2nd SELECT SERVICEMEN MISSING IN SOUTHEAST ASIA
Dates: Sep. 15, 1975-Jan. 3, 1977
Termination: House Report 1764 (94-2) filed, Dec. 13, 1976

Dennis Moore (D-Kans.)

Dates: Nov. 8, 1945
House: Jan. 3, 1999-date
Serving in the 111th Congress

HOUSE STANDING COMMITTEES:

1st BANKING AND FINANCIAL SERVICES, 106
FINANCIAL SERVICES, 107-111
Dates: Jan. 6, 1999-date
Departure: Still serving in the 111th Congress

Cong.	Ranking	Terms in: House	Comm.	Date of Assignment
106th	Min-24th	1	1	Jan. 6, 1999
107th	Min-21st	2	2	Jan. 31, 2001
108th	Min-16th	3	3	Jan. 28, 2003
109th	Min-15th	4	4	Jan. 26, 2005
110th	Maj-12th	5	5	Jan. 12, 2007
111th	Maj-11th	6	6	Jan. 7, 2009

2nd SMALL BUSINESS
Dates: Jan. 6, 1999-Feb. 7, 2001
Departure: Resigned committee; moved to Budget

Cong.	Ranking	Terms in: House	Comm.	Date of Assignment
106th	Min-11th	1	1	Jan. 6, 1999
107th	Min-10th	2	2	Jan. 31, 2001

3rd SCIENCE
1st Dates: June 9, 1999-Jan. 3, 2005
1st Departure: Left committee; no new assignment
2nd Dates: June 8, 2005-Jan. 3, 2007
2nd Departure: Left committee; no new assignment

Cong.	Ranking	Terms in: House	Comm.	Date of Assignment
106th	MnR-3rd	1 *1	1	June 9, 1999
107th	Min-20th	2 *1	2	Jan. 31, 2001
108th	Min-21st	3 *1	3	Feb. 13, 2003
109th	MnR-1st	4 *2	1	June 8, 2005

4th BUDGET
1st Dates: Feb. 8, 2001-Jan. 3, 2009
1st Departure: Left committee; no new assignment
2nd Dates: Mar. 10, 2010-date
2nd Departure: Still serving in the 111th Congress

Cong.	Ranking	Terms in: House	Comm.	Date of Assignment
107th	Min-17th	2*1	1	Feb. 8, 2001
108th	Min-5th	3*1	2	Jan. 28, 2003
109th	Min-2nd	4*1	3	Jan. 26, 2005
110th	Maj-21st	5*1	4	Jan. 10, 2007
111th	MjR-1st	6*2	1	Mar. 10, 2010

Gwendolynne S. Moore (D-Wisc.)

Dates: April 18, 1951
House: Jan. 3, 2005-date
Serving in the 111th Congress

HOUSE STANDING COMMITTEES:

1st FINANCIAL SERVICES
Dates: Jan. 26, 2005-date
Departure: Still serving in the 111th Congress

Cong.	Ranking	Terms in: House	Comm.	Date of Assignment
109th	Min-33rd	1	1	Jan. 26, 2005
110th	Maj-24th	2	2	Jan. 12, 2007
111th	Maj-23rd	3	3	Jan. 7, 2009

2nd SMALL BUSINESS
Dates: Feb. 16, 2005-date
Departure: Still serving in the 111th Congress

Cong.	Ranking	Terms in: House	Comm.	Date of Assignment
109th	Min-15th	1	1	Feb. 16, 2005
110th	Maj-12th	2	2	Jan. 23, 2007
111th	Maj-2nd	3	3	Jan. 21, 2009

3rd BUDGET
Dates: Mar. 19, 2007-date
Departure: Still serving in the 111th Congress

Cong.	Ranking	Terms in: House	Comm.	Date of Assignment
110th	MjR-1st	2	1	Mar. 19, 2007
111th	Maj-22nd	3	2	Jan. 21, 2009

Carlos J. Moorhead (R-Cal.)

Dates: May 6, 1922
House: Jan. 3, 1973-Jan. 3, 1997
Left the House: Retired in 1996

HOUSE STANDING COMMITTEES:

1st JUDICIARY
Dates: Jan. 24, 1973-Jan. 3, 1997
Departure: Left the House; retired

Cong.	Ranking	Terms in: House	Comm.	Date of Assignment
103rd	Min-2nd	11	11	Jan. 5, 1993
104th	Maj-2nd	12	12	Jan. 4, 1995

2nd VETERANS AFFAIRS
Dates: Mar. 21, 1974-Jan. 3, 1975
Departure: Moved to Interstate and Foreign Commerce

3rd INTERSTATE AND FOREIGN COMMERCE, 94-96
ENERGY AND COMMERCE, 97-103
COMMERCE, 104
Dates: Jan. 28, 1975-Jan. 3, 1997
Departure: Left the House; retired

		Terms in:		Date of
Cong.	Ranking	House	Comm.	Assignment
103rd	Min-RM	11	10	Jan. 5, 1993
104th	Maj-2nd	12	11	Jan. 4, 1995

HOUSE SELECT AND SPECIAL COMMITTEES:

1st SELECT ENERGY (Ad Hoc)
Dates: Apr. 21, 1977-Dec. 29, 1978
Termination: House Report 1820 (95-2) filed

James P. Moran Jr. (D-Va.)

Dates: May 16, 1945
House: Jan. 3, 1991-date
Serving in the 111th Congress

HOUSE STANDING COMMITTEES:

1st BANKING, FINANCE AND URBAN AFFAIRS
Dates: Jan. 24, 1991-Jan. 3, 1993
Departure: Moved to Appropriations

2nd POST OFFICE AND CIVIL SERVICE
Dates: Jan. 24, 1991-Jan. 3, 1993
Departure: Moved to Appropriations

3rd APPROPRIATIONS, 103, 105-110
1st Dates: Jan. 5, 1993-Jan. 3, 1995
1st Departure: Moved to Government Reform and Oversight and to International Relations
2nd Dates: Jan. 7, 1997-date
2nd Departure: Still serving in the 111th Congress

		Terms in:		Date of
Cong.	Ranking	House	Comm.	Assignment
103rd	Maj-33rd	2 *1	1	Jan. 5, 1993
105th	Min-21st	4 *2	1	Jan. 7, 1997
106th	Min-14th	5 *2	2	Jan. 6, 1999
107th	Min-13th	6 *2	3	Jan. 31, 2001
108th	Min-12th	7 *2	4	Jan. 28, 2003
109th	Min-12th	8 *2	5	Jan. 26, 2005
110th	Maj-10th	9 *2	6	Jan. 4, 2007
111th	Maj-10th	10 *2	7	Jan. 7, 2009

4th INTERNATIONAL RELATIONS
Dates: Jan. 4, 1995-Jan. 3, 1997
Departure: Returned to Appropriations

		Terms in:		Date of
Cong.	Ranking	House	Comm.	Assignment
104th	Min-19th	3	1	Jan. 4, 1995

5th GOVERNMENT REFORM AND OVERSIGHT
Dates: Jan. 9, 1995-Jan. 3, 1997
Departure: Returned to Appropriations

		Terms in:		Date of
Cong.	Ranking	House	Comm.	Assignment
104th	Min-18th	3	1	Jan. 9, 1995

6th BUDGET
Dates: Jan. 6, 1999-Jan. 3, 2005
Departure: Left committee; no new assignment

		Terms in:		Date of
Cong.	Ranking	House	Comm.	Assignment
106th	Min-14th	5	1	Jan. 6, 1999
107th	Min-11th	6	2	Jan. 31, 2001
108th	Min-2nd	7	3	Jan. 28, 2003

HOUSE SELECT AND SPECIAL COMMITTEES:

1st SELECT HUNGER (Temporary)
Dates: May 14, 1992-Jan. 3, 1993
Termination: Committee not renewed in 1993

Jerry Moran (R-Kans.)

Dates: May 29, 1954
House: Jan. 3, 1997-date
Serving in the 111th Congress

HOUSE STANDING COMMITTEES:

1st AGRICULTURE
Dates: Jan. 7, 1997-date
Departure: Still serving in the 111th Congress

		Terms in:		Date of
Cong.	Ranking	House	Comm.	Assignment
105th	Maj-21st	1	1	Jan. 7, 1997
106th	Maj-15th	2	2	Jan. 6, 1999
107th	Maj-9th	3	3	Jan. 6, 2001
108th	Maj-8th	4	4	Jan. 28, 2003
109th	Maj-6th	5	5	Jan. 26, 2005
110th	Min-4th	6	6	Jan. 10, 2007
111th	Min-3rd	7	7	Jan. 9, 2009

2nd INTERNATIONAL RELATIONS
Dates: Jan. 7, 1997-July 31, 1997
Departure: Resigned committee; moved to Transportation and Infrastructure

		Terms in:		Date of
Cong.	Ranking	House	Comm.	Assignment
105th	Min-25th	1	1	Jan. 7, 1997

3rd VETERANS' AFFAIRS
Dates: Jan. 21, 1997-date
Departure: Still serving in the 111th Congress

		Terms in:		Date of
Cong.	Ranking	House	Comm.	Assignment
105th	Maj-11th	1	1	Jan. 21, 1997
106th	Maj-10th	2	2	Jan. 6, 1999
107th	Maj-9th	3	3	Jan. 6, 2001
108th	Maj-7th	4	4	Jan. 28, 2003
109th	Maj-5th	5	5	Jan. 26, 2005
110th	Min-4th	6	6	Jan. 10, 2007
111th	Min-3rd	7	7	Jan. 9, 2009

4th TRANSPORTATION AND INFRASTRUCTURE
Dates: Aug. 1, 1997-date
Departure: Still serving in the 111th Congress

Cong.	Ranking	Terms in: House	Comm.	Date of Assignment
105th	MjA-41st	1	1	Aug. 1, 1997
106th	Maj-31st	2	2	Jan. 6, 1999
107th	Maj-22nd	3	3	Jan. 6, 2001
108th	Maj-17th	4	4	Jan. 28, 2003
109th	Maj-16th	5	5	Jan. 26, 2005
110th	Min-11th	6	6	Jan. 10, 2007
111th	Min-8th	7	7	Jan. 9, 2009

Constance A. Morella (R-Md.)

Dates: Feb. 12, 1931
House: Jan. 3, 1987-Jan. 3, 2003
Left the House: Defeated for re-election in 2002

HOUSE STANDING COMMITTEES:

1st POST OFFICE AND CIVIL SERVICE
Dates: Jan. 21, 1987-Jan. 3, 1995
Departure: Committee abolished; moved to Government Reform and Oversight

Cong.	Ranking	Terms in: House	Comm.	Date of Assignment
103rd	Min-5th	4	4	Jan. 5, 1993

2nd SCIENCE, SPACE AND TECHNOLOGY, 100-103
SCIENCE, 104-107
Dates: Jan. 21, 1987-Jan. 3, 2003
Departure: Left the House; lost re-election

Cong.	Ranking	Terms in: House	Comm.	Date of Assignment
103rd	Min-7th	4	4	Jan. 5, 1993
104th	Maj-5th	5	5	Jan. 4, 1995
105th	Maj-4th	6	6	Jan. 21, 1997
106th	Maj-4th	7	7	Jan. 6, 1999
107th	Maj-4th	8	8	Jan. 6, 2001

3rd GOVERNMENT REFORM AND OVERSIGHT, 104-105
GOVERNMENT REFORM, 106-107
Dates: Jan. 4, 1995-Jan. 3, 2003
Departure: Left the House; lost re-election

Cong.	Ranking	Terms in: House	Comm.	Date of Assignment
104th	Maj-4th	5	1	Jan. 4, 1995
105th	Maj-4th	6	2	Jan. 7, 1997
106th	Maj-3rd	7	3	Jan. 6, 1999
107th	Maj-3rd	8	4	Jan. 6, 2001

HOUSE SELECT AND SPECIAL COMMITTEES:

1st SELECT AGING (Permanent)
Dates: Feb. 2, 1987-Jan. 3, 1993
Termination: Committee not renewed in 1993

Carol Moseley Braun (D-Ill.)

Dates: Aug. 16, 1947
Senate: Jan. 3, 1993-Jan. 3, 1999
Left the Senate: Defeated for re-election in 1998

SENATE STANDING COMMITTEES:

1st BANKING, HOUSING AND URBAN AFFAIRS
Dates: Jan. 7, 1993-Jan. 3, 1999
Departure: Left the Senate; lost re-election

Cong.	Ranking	Years in: Senate	Comm.	Date of Assignment
103rd	Maj-10th	1	1	Jan. 7, 1993
104th	Min-6th	3	2	Jan. 4, 1995
105th	Min-6th	5	5	Jan. 9, 1997

2nd JUDICIARY
Dates: Jan. 7, 1993-Jan. 4, 1995
Departure: Moved to Finance and Special Aging

Cong.	Ranking	Years in: Senate	Comm.	Date of Assignment
103rd	Maj-10th	1	1	Jan. 7, 1993

3rd SMALL BUSINESS
Dates: Jan. 21, 1993-Jan. 4, 1995
Departure: Moved to Finance and Special Aging

Cong.	Ranking	Years in: Senate	Comm.	Date of Assignment
103rd	Maj-12th	1	1	Jan. 21, 1993

4th FINANCE
Dates: Jan. 4, 1995-Jan. 3, 1999
Departure: Left the Senate; lost re-election

Cong.	Ranking	Years in: Senate	Comm.	Date of Assignment
104th	Min-9th	3	1	Jan. 4, 1995
105th	Min-7th	5	3	Jan. 9, 1997

SENATE SELECT AND SPECIAL COMMITTEES:

1st SPECIAL AGING (Permanent)
Dates: Jan. 6, 1995-Jan. 3, 1999
Departure: Left the Senate; lost re-election

Cong.	Ranking	Years in: Senate	Comm.	Date of Assignment
104th	Min-9th	3	1	Jan. 6, 1995
105th	Min-6th	5	3	Jan. 9, 1997

2nd SPECIAL COMMITTEE TO INVESTIGATE WHITEWATER DEVELOPMENT CORPORATION AND RELATED MATTERS
Dates: July 20, 1995-June 17, 1996
Termination: Senate Report 104-280 filed

Cong.	Ranking	Years in: Senate	Comm.	Date of Assignment
104th	Min-6th	3	1	July 20, 1995

Daniel Patrick Moynihan (D-N.Y.)

Dates: March 16, 1927-March 26, 2003
Senate: Jan. 3, 1977-Jan. 3, 2001
Left the Senate: Retired in 2000

SENATE STANDING COMMITTEES:

1st COMMERCE
Dates: Jan. 10, 1977-Feb. 11, 1977
Departure: Moved to Environment and Public Works and Finance.

2nd INTERIOR AND INSULAR AFFAIRS
Dates: Jan. 10, 1977-Feb. 11, 1977
Departure: Moved to Environment and Public Works and Finance

3rd BUDGET
1st Dates: Jan. 11, 1977-Feb. 11, 1977
1st Departure: Moved to Environment and Public Works and Finance
2nd Dates: Jan. 23, 1979-Jan. 6, 1987
2nd Departure: Moved to Foreign Relations and Rules and Administration

4th ENVIRONMENT AND PUBLIC WORKS
Dates: Feb. 11, 1977-Jan. 3, 2001
Ch1: Became Chair of Finance; replaced by Max S. Baucus (D-Mont.) on Jan. 21, 1993
Departure: Left the Senate; retired in 2000

Cong.	Ranking	Years in: Senate	Comm.	Date of Assignment
103rd	Maj-Ch1	17	16	Jan. 7, 1993
104th	Min-2nd	19	18	Jan. 4, 1995
105th	Min-2nd	21	20	Jan. 9, 1997
106th	Min-2nd	23	22	Jan. 7, 1999

5th FINANCE
Dates: Feb. 11, 1977-Jan. 3, 2001
Ch2: Succeeded Lloyd M. Bentsen (D-Tex.) on Jan, 21, 1993. Bentsen resigned to join the Cabinet.
Departure: Left the Senate; retired

Cong.	Ranking	Years in: Senate	Comm.	Date of Assignment
103rd	Maj-2nd	17	16	Jan. 7, 1993
=103rd	Maj-Ch2	17	16	Jan. 21, 1993
104th	Min-RM	19	18	Jan. 4, 1995
105th	Min-RM	21	20	Jan. 9, 1997
106th	Min-RM	23	22	Jan. 7, 1999

6th FOREIGN RELATIONS
Dates: Jan. 6, 1987-Jan. 4, 1995
Departure: Left committee; no new assignment

Cong.	Ranking	Years in: Senate	Comm.	Date of Assignment
103rd	Maj-7th	17	7	Jan. 7, 1993

7th RULES AND ADMINISTRATION
Dates: Jan. 6, 1987-Jan. 3, 2001
Departure: Left the Senate; retired

Cong.	Ranking	Years in: Senate	Comm.	Date of Assignment
103rd	Maj-6th	17	7	Jan. 21, 1993
104th	Min-5th	19	9	Jan. 6, 1995
105th	Min-4th	21	11	Jan. 9, 1997
106th	Min-4th	23	13	Jan. 7, 1999

SENATE SELECT AND SPECIAL COMMITTEES:

1st SELECT INTELLIGENCE (Permanent)
Dates: Feb. 11, 1977-Jan. 3, 1995
Departure: Left committee; no new assignment

2nd SPECIAL YEAR 2000 TECHNOLOGY PROBLEM
Dates: Apr. 23, 1998-Feb. 29, 2000
Termination: Senate Print 106-42 issued

Cong.	Ranking	Years in: Senate	Comm.	Date of Assignment
105th	Min-2nd	22	1	Apr. 23, 1998
106th	Min-2nd	23	2	Continued

JOINT COMMITTEES:

1st JOINT TAXATION
Senate Dates: Jan. 12, 1987-Jan. 3, 2001
Departure: Left the Senate; retired

Cong.	Ranking	Years in: Senate	Comm.	Date of Assignment
103rd	Maj-VcC	17	7	Continued
104th	Min-1st	19	9	Feb. 2, 1995
105th	Min-1st	21	11	Continued
106th	Min-1st	23	13	Continued

2nd JOINT LIBRARY
Senate Dates: Jan. 29, 1987-Jan. 3, 2001
Departure: Left the Senate; retired

Cong.	Ranking	Years in: Senate	Comm.	Date of Assignment
103rd	Maj-3rd	17	6	Jan. 28, 1993
104th	Min-2nd	19	8	Jan. 17, 1995
105th	Min-1st	21	10	Jan. 28, 1997
106th	Min-2nd	23	13	Feb. 25, 1999

Frank H. Murkowski (R-Alas.)

Dates: March 28, 1933
Senate: Jan. 3, 1981-Dec. 2, 2002
Left the Senate: Resigned; elected Governor in 2002

SENATE STANDING COMMITTEES:

1st ENERGY AND NATURAL RESOURCES
Dates: Jan. 5, 1981-Dec. 2, 2002
Ch1: Replaced by J.F. (Jeff) Bingaman (D-N.M.) following party control shift on June 6, 2001 and became RM2.
Departure: Resigned the Senate; elected Governor

Cong.	Ranking	Years in: Senate	Comm.	Date of Assignment
103rd	Min-4th	13	13	Jan. 7, 1993
104th	Maj-Chr	15	15	Jan. 5, 1995
105th	Maj-Chr	17	17	Jan. 9, 1997
106th	Maj-Chr	19	19	Jan. 7, 1999
107th	Maj-Ch1	21	21	Jan. 25, 2001
+107th	Min-RM2	21	21	June 6, 2001

2nd ENVIRONMENT AND PUBLIC WORKS
Dates: Jan. 5, 1981-Jan. 3, 1983
Departure: Moved to Foreign Relations

3rd VETERANS' AFFAIRS
Dates: Mar. 19, 1981-Dec. 2, 2002
Departure: Resigned the Senate; elected Governor

Cong.	Ranking	Years in: Senate	Comm.	Date of Assignment
103rd	Min-RM`	13	12	Jan. 21, 1993
104th	Maj-2nd	15	14	Jan. 6, 1995
105th	Maj-2nd	17	16	Jan. 9, 1997
106th	Maj-2nd	19	18	Jan. 7, 1999
107th	Maj-2nd	21	20	Jan. 25, 2001
+107th	Min-2nd	21	21	June 6, 2001

4th FOREIGN RELATIONS
Dates: Jan. 3, 1983-Jan. 4, 1995
Departure: Moved to Finance

Cong.	Ranking	Years in: Senate	Comm.	Date of Assignment
103rd	Min-5th	13	11	Jan. 7, 1993

5th FINANCE
Dates: Jan. 4, 1995-Dec. 2, 2002
Departure: Resigned the Senate; elected Governor

Cong.	Ranking	Years in: Senate	Comm.	Date of Assignment
104th	Maj-10th	15	1	Jan. 4, 1995
105th	Maj-6th	17	2	Jan. 3, 1997
106th	Maj-5th	19	5	Jan. 7, 1999
107th	Maj-3rd	21	7	Jan. 25, 2001
+107th	Min-3rd	21	7	June 6, 2001

SENATE SELECT AND SPECIAL COMMITTEES:

1st SELECT INDIAN AFFAIRS (Permanent), 98-102
INDIAN AFFAIRS (Permanent), 103-107
Dates: Jan. 3, 1983-Dec. 2, 2002
Departure: Resigned the Senate; elected Governor

Cong.	Ranking	Years in: Senate	Comm.	Date of Assignment
103rd	Min-2nd	13	11	Jan. 5, 1993
104th	Maj-2nd	15	13	Jan. 11, 1995
105th	Maj-2nd	17	15	Jan. 9, 1997
106th	Maj-2nd	19	17	Jan. 7, 1999
107th	Maj-2nd	21	19	Jan. 25, 2001
+107th	Min-2nd	21	19	June 6, 2001

2nd SELECT INTELLIGENCE (Permanent)
Dates: Jan. 3, 1985-Jan. 27, 1993
Departure: Left committee; returned to Veterans Affairs as Ranking Member

3rd JUDGE WALTER L. NIXON IMPEACHMENT
Dates: May 11, 1989-Sep. 13, 1989
Termination: Committee terminated; hearings concluded

4th SPECIAL COMMITTEE TO INVESTIGATE WHITEWATER DEVELOPMENT CORPORATION AND RELATED MATTERS
Dates: July 20, 1995-June 17, 1996
Termination: Senate Report 104-280 filed

Cong.	Ranking	Years in: Senate	Comm.	Date of Assignment
104th	Maj-10th	15	1	July 20, 1995

JOINT COMMITTEES:

1st JOINT TAXATION
Senate Dates: Feb. 28, 2001-June 6, 2001
Departure: Lost seat due to Senate ratio change; no new assignment

Cong.	Ranking	Years in: Senate	Comm.	Date of Assignment
107th	Maj-3rd	21	1	Feb. 28, 2001

Lisa Murkowski (R-Alas.)

Dates: May 22, 1957
Senate: Dec. 20, 2002-date
Serving in the 111th Congress

S: Lisa Murkowski was appointed to the 107th Congress, Dec. 20, 2002, to fill the vacancy of her father, U.S. Senator Frank H. Murkowski (R-Alas.) who had been elected Governor. Lisa Murkowski was subsequently elected. She was seated Jan. 7, 2003, in the 108th Congress. She was not seated nor assigned to committees in the 107th Congress.

SENATE STANDING COMMITTEES:

1st ENERGY AND NATURAL RESOURCES
Dates: Jan. 15, 2003-date
Departure: Still serving in the 111th Congress

Cong.	Ranking	Years in: Senate	Comm.	Date of Assignment
108th	Maj-7th	1	1	Jan. 15, 2003
109th	Maj-5th	3	2	Jan. 6, 2005
110th	Min-4th	5	4	Jan. 12, 2007
111th	Min-RM	7	7	Jan. 21, 2009

2nd VETERANS' AFFAIRS
Dates: Jan. 15, 2003-Jan.6, 2005
Departure: Moved to Foreign Relations

Cong.	Ranking	Years in: Senate	Comm.	Date of Assignment
108th	Maj-8th	1	1	Jan. 15, 2003

3rd ENVIRONMENT AND PUBLIC WORKS
Dates: Jan. 15, 2003-Jan. 12, 2007
Departure: Moved to Health, Education, Labor and Pensions

Cong.	Ranking	Years in: Senate	Comm.	Date of Assignment
108th	Maj-8th	1	1	Jan. 15, 2003
109th	Maj-6th	3	2	Jan. 6, 2005

4th FOREIGN RELATIONS
Dates: Jan. 6, 2005-date
Departure: Moved to Appropriations

Cong.	Ranking	Years in: Senate	Comm.	Date of Assignment
109th	Maj-9th	3	1	Jan. 6, 2005
110th	Min-7th	5	3	Jan. 12, 2007

5th HEALTH, EDUCATION, LABOR AND PENSIONS
Dates: Jan. 12, 2007-date
Departure: Still serving in the 111th Congress

Cong.	Ranking	Years in: Senate	Comm.	Date of Assignment
110th	Min-6th	5	1	Jan. 12, 2007
111th	Min-8th	7	3	Jan. 21, 2009

6th APPROPRIATIONS
Dates: Jan. 21, 2009-date
Departure: Still serving in the 111th Congress

Cong.	Ranking	Years in: Senate	Comm.	Date of Assignment
111th	Min-13th	7	1	Jan. 21, 2009

SENATE SELECT AND SPECIAL COMMITTEES:

1st INDIAN AFFAIRS (Permanent)
Dates: Jan. 15, 2003-date
RM2: Replaced Craig L. Thomas (R-Wyo.) as Ranking Member on July 10, 2007
Departure: Still serving in the 111th Congress

Cong.	Ranking	Years in: Senate	Comm.	Date of Assignment
108th	Maj-8th	1	1	Jan. 15, 2003
109th	Maj-3rd	3	2	Jan. 6, 2005
110th	Min-3rd	5	4	Jan. 12, 2007
=110th	Min-RM2	5	5	July 10, 2007
111th	Min-3rd	7	7	Jan. 21, 2009

Austin J. Murphy (D-Penn.)

Dates: June 17, 1927
House: Jan. 3, 1977-Jan. 3, 1995
Left the House: Retired in 1994

HOUSE STANDING COMMITTEES:

1st EDUCATION AND LABOR
Dates: Jan. 19, 1977-Jan. 3, 1995
Departure: Left the House; retired

Cong.	Ranking	Terms in: House	Comm.	Date of Assignment
103rd	Maj-4th	9	9	Jan. 5, 1993

2nd INTERIOR AND INSULAR AFFAIRS, 95-102
NATURAL RESOURCES, 103
Dates: Jan. 19, 1977-Jan. 3, 1995
Departure: Left the House; retired

Cong.	Ranking	Terms in: House	Comm.	Date of Assignment
103rd	Maj-4th	9	9	Jan. 5, 1993

3rd VETERANS AFFAIRS
Dates: Feb. 25, 1981-Jan. 3, 1983
Departure: Left committee; no new assignment

4th FOREIGN AFFAIRS
Temporary Dates: Jan. 24, 1991-Jan. 3, 1993
Departure: Temporary term expired

HOUSE SELECT AND SPECIAL COMMITTEES:

1st SELECT ENERGY (Ad Hoc)
Dates: Apr. 21, 1977-Dec. 29, 1978
Termination: House Report 1820 (95-2) filed

Christopher S. Murphy (D-Conn.)

Dates: Aug. 3, 1973
House: Jan. 3, 2007-date
Serving in the 111th Congress

HOUSE STANDING COMMITTEES:

1st FINANCIAL SERVICES
Dates: Jan. 12, 2007-Jan. 3, 2009
Departure: Moved to Energy and Commerce

Cong.	Ranking	Terms in: House	Comm.	Date of Assignment
110th	Maj-33rd	1	1	Jan. 12, 2007

2nd OVERSIGHT AND GOVERNMENT REFORM
Dates: Jan. 12, 2007-date
Departure: Still serving in the 111th Congress

Cong.	Ranking	Terms in: House	Comm.	Date of Assignment
110th	Maj-21st	1	1	Jan. 12, 2007
111th	Maj-18th	2	2	Jan. 28, 2009

3rd ENERGY AND COMMERCE
Dates: Jan. 7, 2009-date
Departure: Still serving in the 111th Congress

Cong.	Ranking	Terms in: House	Comm.	Date of Assignment
111th	Maj-31st	2	1	Jan. 7, 2009

Patrick J. Murphy (D-Pa.)

Dates: Oct. 19, 1973
House: Jan. 3, 2007-date
Serving in the 111th Congress

HOUSE STANDING COMMITTEES:

1st ARMED SERVICES
Dates: Jan. 10, 2007-May 5, 2010
Departure: Resigned Committee; moved to Appropriations

Cong.	Ranking	Terms in: House	Comm.	Date of Assignment
110th	Maj-25th	1	1	Jan. 10, 2007
111th	Maj-22nd	2	2	Jan. 7, 2009

2nd APPROPRIATIONS
Dates: May 6, 2010-date
Departure: Still serving in the 111th Congress

Cong.	Ranking	Terms in: House	Comm.	Date of Assignment
111th	MjR-1st	2	1	May 6, 2010

HOUSE SELECT AND SPECIAL COMMITTEES:

1st PERMANENT SELECT INTELLIGENCE
Dates: Jan. 17, 2007-date
Departure: Still serving in the 111th Congress

Cong.	Ranking	Terms in: House	Comm.	Date of Assignment
110th	Maj-12th	1	1	Jan. 17, 2007
111th	Maj-10th	2	2	Feb. 4, 2009

Scott Murphy (D-N.Y.)

Dates: Jan. 26, 1970
House: Mar. 31, 2009-date
Serving in the 111th Congress

H: Scott Murphy was elected to the 111th Congress by special election, Mar. 31, 2009, to fill the vacancy caused by the resignation of U.S. Representative Kirsten E. Gillibrand (D-N.Y.), who had been appointed to the U.S. Senate. Scott Murphy was seated April 29, 2009, and assigned to committees.

HOUSE STANDING COMMITTEES:

1st AGRICULTURE
Dates: Apr. 30, 2009-date
Departure: Still serving in the 111th Congress

Cong.	Ranking	Terms in: House	Comm.	Date of Assignment
111th	MjR-1st	1	1	Apr. 30, 2009

2nd ARMED SERVICES
Dates: Apr. 30, 2009-date
Departure: Still serving in the 111th Congress

Cong.	Ranking	Terms in: House	Comm.	Date of Assignment
111th	MjR-1st	1	1	Apr. 30, 2009

Timothy Murphy (R-Pa.)

Dates: Sept. 11, 1952
House: Jan. 3, 2003-date
Serving in the 111th Congress

HOUSE STANDING COMMITTEES:

1st FINANCIAL SERVICES
Dates: Jan. 28, 2003-Jan. 3, 2005
Departure: Moved to Energy and Commerce

Cong.	Ranking	Terms in: House	Comm.	Date of Assignment
108th	Maj-33rd	1	1	Jan. 28, 2003

2nd GOVERNMENT REFORM
Dates: Jan. 28, 2003-Jan. 3, 2005
Departure: Moved to Energy and Commerce

Cong.	Ranking	Terms in: House	Comm.	Date of Assignment
108th	Maj-20th	1	1	Jan. 28, 2003

3rd VETERANS' AFFAIRS
Dates: Feb. 25, 2003- Jan. 3, 2005
Departure: Moved to Energy and Commerce

Cong.	Ranking	Terms in: House	Comm.	Date of Assignment
108th	MjR-1st	1	1	Feb. 25, 2003

4th ENERGY AND COMMERCE
Dates: Jan. 6, 2005-date
Departure: Still serving in the 111th Congress

Cong.	Ranking	Terms in: House	Comm.	Date of Assignment
109th	Maj-29th	2	1	Jan. 6, 2005
110th	Min-25th	3	2	Jan. 10, 2007
111th	Min-19th	4	3	Jan. 9, 2009

Patty D. Murray (D-Wash.)

Dates: Oct. 11, 1950
Senate: Jan. 3, 1993-date
Serving in the 111th Congress

SENATE STANDING COMMITTEES:

1st APPROPRIATIONS
Dates: Jan. 7, 1993-date
Departure: Still serving in the 111th Congress

Cong.	Ranking	Years in: Senate	Comm.	Date of Assignment
103rd	Maj-15th	1	1	Jan. 7, 1993
104th	Min-13th	3	2	Jan. 4, 1995
105th	Min-11th	5	5	Jan. 9, 1997
106th	Min-10th	7	7	Jan. 7, 1999
107th	Min-9th	9	9	Jan. 25, 2001
+107th	Maj-9th	9	9	June 6, 2001
108th	Min-9th	11	11	Jan. 15, 2003
109th	Min-8th	13	12	Jan. 6, 2005
110th	Maj-7th	15	15	Jan. 12, 2007
111th	Maj-7th	17	17	Jan. 21, 2009

2nd BANKING, HOUSING AND URBAN AFFAIRS
Dates: Jan. 7, 1993-Jan. 9, 1997
Departure: Moved to Labor and Human Resources and Select Ethics

Cong.	Ranking	Years in: Senate	Comm.	Date of Assignment
103rd	Maj-11th	1	1	Jan. 7, 1993
104th	Min-7th	3	2	Jan. 4, 1995

3rd BUDGET
Dates: Jan. 21, 1993-date
Departure: Still serving in the 111th Congress

Cong.	Ranking	Years in: Senate	Comm.	Date of Assignment
103rd	Maj-12th	1	1	Jan. 21, 1993
104th	Min-10th	3	2	Jan. 6, 1995
105th	Min-6th	5	4	Jan. 9, 1997
106th	Min-6th	7	6	Jan. 7, 1999
107th	Min-4th	9	9	Jan. 25, 2001
+107th	Maj-4th	9	9	June 6 2001
108th	Min-4th	11	10	Jan. 15, 2003
109th	Min-3rd	13	12	Jan. 6, 2005
110th	Maj-2nd	15	14	Jan. 12, 2007
111th	Maj-2nd	17	17	Jan. 21, 2009

4th VETERANS AFFAIRS
Dates: Dec. 29, 1995-date
Departure: Still serving in the 111th Congress

Cong.	Ranking	Years in: Senate	Comm.	Date of Assignment
104th	MnR-2nd	3	1	Dec. 29, 1995
105th	Min-5th	5	2	Jan. 9, 1997
106th	Min-5th	7	4	Jan. 3, 1999
107th	Min-5th	9	6	Jan. 25, 2001
+107th	Maj-6th	9	6	July 10, 2001
108th	Min-5th	11	8	Jan. 15, 2003
109th	Min-4th	13	10	Jan. 6, 2005
110th	Maj-3rd	15	12	Jan. 12, 2007
111th	Maj-3rd	17	14	Jan. 21, 2009

5th LABOR AND HUMAN RESOURCES renamed Jan. 21, 1999
HEALTH, EDUCATION, LABOR AND PENSIONS
Dates: Jan. 9, 1997-date
Departure: Still serving in the 111th Congress

Cong.	Ranking	Years in: Senate	Comm.	Date of Assignment
105th	Min-7th	5	1	Jan. 9, 1997
106th	Min-7th	7	2	Jan. 7, 1999
107th	Min-7th	9	5	Jan. 25, 2001
+107th	Maj-8th	9	5	July 10, 2001
108th	Min-7th	11	7	Jan. 15, 2003
109th	Min-7th	13	8	Jan. 6, 2005
110th	Maj-6th	15	11	Jan. 12, 2007
111th	Maj-6th	17	13	Jan. 21, 2009

6th RULES AND ADMINISTRATION
Dates: Jan. 12, 2007-date
Departure: Still serving in the 111th Congress

Cong.	Ranking	Years in: Senate	Comm.	Date of Assignment
110th	Maj-9th	15	1	Jan. 12, 2007
111th	Maj-8th	17	3	Jan. 21, 2009

SENATE SELECT AND SPECIAL COMMITTEES:

1st SPECIAL COMMITTEE TO INVESTIGATE WHITEWATER DEVELOPMENT CORPORATION AND RELATED MATTERS
Dates: July 20, 1995-June 17, 1996
Termination: Senate Report 104-280 filed

Cong.	Ranking	Years in: Senate	Comm.	Date of Assignment
104th	Min-7th	3	1	July 20, 1995

2nd SELECT ETHICS (Permanent)
Dates: Jan. 9, 1997-Jan. 7, 1999
Departure: Left committee; no new assignment

Cong.	Ranking	Years in: Senate	Comm.	Date of Assignment
105th	Min-2nd	5	1	Jan. 9, 1997

JOINT COMMITTEES:

1st JOINT PRINTING
Senate Dates: Mar. 6, 2007-date
Departure: Still serving in the 111th Congress

Cong.	Ranking	Years in: Senate	Comm.	Date of Assignment
110th	Maj-3rd	15	1	Mar. 6, 2007
111th	Maj-2nd	17	3	Apr. 3, 2009

John P. Murtha Jr. (D-Penn.)

Dates: June 17, 1932-Feb. 8, 2010
House: Feb. 5, 1974-Feb. 8, 2010
Left House: Died in office

H: Murtha was elected to the 93rd Congress by special election, Feb. 5, 1974, to fill the vacancy caused by the death of U.S. Representative John P. Saylor (R-Penn.). Murtha was seated Feb. 20, 1974, and assigned to committees.

HOUSE STANDING COMMITTEES:

1st ARMED SERVICES
Dates: Mar. 13, 1974-Jan. 3, 1975
Departure: Moved to Appropriations

2nd APPROPRIATIONS
Dates: Jan. 20, 1975-Feb. 8, 2010
Departure: Died in office

Cong.	Ranking	Terms in: House	Comm.	Date of Assignment
103rd	Maj-8th	11	10	Jan. 5, 1993
104th	Min-5th	12	11	Jan. 4, 1995
105th	Min-4th	13	12	Jan. 7, 1997
106th	Min-2nd	14	13	Jan. 6, 1999
107th	Min-2nd	15	14	Jan. 31, 2001
108th	Min-2nd	16	15	Jan. 28, 2003
109th	Min-2nd	17	16	Jan. 26, 2005
110th	Maj-2nd	18	17	Jan. 4, 2007
111th	Maj-2nd	19	18	Jan. 7, 2009

3rd STANDARDS OF OFFICIAL CONDUCT
Dates: Jan. 31, 1979-Jan. 3, 1981
Departure: Left committee; no new assignment

Marilyn N. Musgrave (R-Colo.)

Dates: Jan. 27, 1949
House: Jan. 3, 2003-Jan. 3, 2009
Left the House: Defeated for re-election in 2008

HOUSE STANDING COMMITTEES:

1st AGRICULTURE
Dates: Jan. 28, 2003-Jan. 3, 2009
Departure: Left the House; lost re-election

Cong.	Ranking	Terms in: House	Comm.	Date of Assignment
108th	Maj-26th	1	1	Jan. 28, 2003

Cong.	Ranking	House	Comm.	Date of Assignment
109th	Maj-17th	2	2	Jan. 26, 2005
110th	Min-11th	3	3	Jan. 10, 2007

2nd EDUCATION AND THE WORKFORCE
Dates: Jan. 28, 2003-Jan. 3, 2007
Departure: Left committee; no new assignment

Cong.	Ranking	Terms in: House	Comm.	Date of Assignment
108th	Maj-25th	1	1	Jan. 28, 2003
109th	Maj-17th	2	2	Jan. 26, 2005

3rd SMALL BUSINESS
Dates: Jan. 28, 2003-Jan. 3, 2009
Departure: Left the House; lost re-election

Cong.	Ranking	Terms in: House	Comm.	Date of Assignment
108th	Maj-13th	1	1	Jan. 28, 2003
109th	Maj-8th	2	2	Jan. 26, 2005
110th	Min-6th	3	3	Jan. 10, 2007

4th RESOURCES
Dates: Feb. 16, 2005-Jan. 3, 2007
Departure: Left committee; no new assignment

Cong.	Ranking	Terms in: House	Comm.	Date of Assignment
109th	MjR-1st	1	1	Feb. 16, 2005

John T. Myers (R-Ind.)

Dates: Feb. 8, 1927
House: Jan. 3, 1967-Jan. 3, 1997
Left the House: Retired in 1996

HOUSE STANDING COMMITTEES:

1st AGRICULTURE
Dates: Jan. 26, 1967-Jan. 3, 1971
Departure: Moved to Appropriations

2nd GOVERNMENT OPERATIONS
Dates: Jan. 26, 1967-Jan. 3, 1971
Departure: Moved to Appropriations

3rd APPROPRIATIONS
Dates: Feb. 4, 1971-Jan. 3, 1997
Departure: Left the House; retired

Cong.	Ranking	Terms in: House	Comm.	Date of Assignment
103rd	Min-2nd	14	12	Jan. 5, 1993
104th	Maj-3rd	15	13	Jan. 4, 1995

4th STANDARDS OF OFFICIAL CONDUCT
Dates: Jan. 28, 1981-Jan. 3, 1991
RM2: Myers succeeded Floyd D. Spence (R-S.C.) as Ranking Minority Member on June 1, 1988
Departure: Left committee; no new assignment

5th POST OFFICE AND CIVIL SERVICE
Dates: Jan. 30, 1985-Jan. 3, 1995
Departure: Committee abolished; no new assignment

Cong.	Ranking	Terms in: House	Comm.	Date of Assignment
103rd	Min-RM	14	5	Jan. 5, 1993

Sue Myrick (R-N.C.)

Dates: Aug. 1, 1941
House: Jan. 3, 1995-date
Serving in the 111th Congress

HOUSE STANDING COMMITTEES:

1st BUDGET
Dates: Jan. 4, 1995-Jan. 3, 1997
Departure: Moved to Rules

Cong.	Ranking	Terms in: House	Comm.	Date of Assignment
104th	Maj-20th	1	1	Jan. 4, 1995

2nd SCIENCE
Dates: Jan. 4, 1995-Jan. 3, 1997
Departure: Moved to Rules

Cong.	Ranking	Terms in: House	Comm.	Date of Assignment
104th	Maj-27th	1	1	Jan. 4, 1995

3rd SMALL BUSINESS
Dates: Jan. 4, 1995-Jan. 3, 1997
Departure: Moved to Rules

Cong.	Ranking	Terms in: House	Comm.	Date of Assignment
104th	Maj-20th	1	1	Jan. 4, 1995

4th RULES
Dates: Jan. 7, 1997-Jan. 3, 2005
Departure: Moved to Energy and Commerce

Cong.	Ranking	Terms in: House	Comm.	Date of Assignment
105th	Maj-9th	2	1	Jan. 7, 1997
106th	Maj-7th	3	2	Jan. 6, 1999
107th	Maj-7th	4	3	Jan. 3, 2001
108th	Maj-7th	5	4	Jan. 7, 2003

5th ENERGY AND COMMERCE
Dates: Jan. 6, 2005-date
Departure: Still serving in the 111th Congress

Cong.	Ranking	Terms in: House	Comm.	Date of Assignment
109th	Maj-27th	6	1	Jan. 6, 2005
110th	Min-23rd	7	2	Jan. 10, 2007
111th	Min-17th	8	3	Jan. 9, 2009

HOUSE SELECT AND SPECIAL COMMITTEES:

1st SELECT BIPARTISAN COMMITTEE TO INVESTIGATE THE PREPARATION FOR AND RESPONSE TO HURRICANE KATRINA
Dates: Sep. 21, 2005-Feb. 15, 2006
Departure: House Report 377 (109-2) filed

Cong.	Ranking	Terms in: House	Comm.	Date of Assignment
109th	Maj-7th	6	1	Sep. 21, 2005

2nd PERMANENT SELECT INTELLIGENCE
Dates: Feb. 4, 2009-date
Departure: Still serving in the 111th Congress

Cong.	Ranking	Terms in: House	Comm.	Date of Assignment
111th	Min-5th	8	1	Feb. 4, 2009

N

Jerrold L. Nadler (D-N.Y.)

Dates: June 13, 1947
House: Nov. 3, 1992-date
Serving in the 111th Congress

H: Nadler was elected to the 102nd Congress by special election, Nov. 3, 1992, to fill the vacancy caused by the death of U.S. Representative Theodore Weiss (D-N.Y.). Nadler was not seated nor assigned to committees because the 102nd Congress was not in session.

HOUSE STANDING COMMITTEES:

1st JUDICIARY
Dates: Jan. 5, 1993-date
Departure: Still serving in the 111th Congress

Cong.	Ranking	Terms in: House	Comm.	Date of Assignment
103rd	Maj-17th	2	1	Jan. 5, 1993
104th	Min-9th	3	2	Jan. 4, 1995
105th	Min-6th	4	3	Jan. 7, 1997
106th	Min-5th	5	4	Jan. 6, 1999
107th	Min-5th	6	5	Jan. 31, 2001
108th	Min-4th	7	6	Jan. 28, 2003
109th	Min-4th	8	7	Jan. 26, 2005
110th	Maj-4th	9	8	Jan. 18, 2007
111th	Maj-4th	10	9	Jan. 7, 2009

2nd PUBLIC WORKS AND TRANSPORTATION, 103 TRANSPORTATION AND INFRASTRUCTURE, 104-111
Dates: Jan. 5, 1993-date
Departure: Still serving in the 111th Congress

Cong.	Ranking	Terms in: House	Comm.	Date of Assignment
103rd	Maj-25th	2	1	Jan. 5, 1993
104th	Min-18th	3	2	Jan. 4, 1995
105th	Min-13th	4	3	Jan. 7, 1997
106th	Min-11th	5	4	Jan. 6, 1999
107th	Min-9th	6	5	Jan. 31, 2001
108th	Min-7th	7	6	Jan. 28, 2003
109th	Min-6th	8	7	Jan. 26, 2005
110th	Maj-6th	9	8	Jan. 10, 2007
111th	Maj-6th	10	9	Jan. 7, 2009

Grace F. Napolitano (D-Cal.)

Dates: Dec. 4, 1936
House: Jan. 3, 1999-date
Serving in the 111th Congress

HOUSE STANDING COMMITTEES:

1st RESOURCES, 106-109
NATURAL RESOURCES, 110-111
Dates: Jan. 6, 1999-date
Departure: Still serving in the 111th Congress

Cong.	Ranking	Terms in: House	Comm.	Date of Assignment
106th	Min-21st	1	1	Jan. 6, 1999
107th	Min-16th	2	2	Feb. 8, 2001
108th	Min-15th	3	3	Jan. 28, 2003
109th	Min-9th	4	4	Jan. 26, 2005
110th	Maj-8th	5	5	Jan. 18, 2007
111th	Maj-6th	6	6	Jan. 21, 2009

2nd SMALL BUSINESS
Dates: Jan. 6, 1999-Jan. 3, 2005
Departure: Left committee; no new assignment

Cong.	Ranking	Terms in: House	Comm.	Date of Assignment
106th	Min-15th	1	1	Jan. 6, 1999
107th	Min-14th	2	2	Jan. 31, 2001
108th	Min-12th	3	3	Feb. 13, 2003

3rd INTERNATIONAL RELATIONS
Dates: Feb. 8, 2001-Jan. 3, 2007
Departure: Moved to Transportation and Infrastructure

Cong.	Ranking	Terms in: House	Comm.	Date of Assignment
107th	Min-22nd	2	1	Feb. 8, 2001
108th	Min-18th	3	2	Jan. 28, 2003
109th	Min-17th	4	3	Jan. 26, 2005

4th TRANSPORTATION AND INFRASTRUCTURE
Dates: Jan. 10, 2007-date
Departure: Still serving in the 111th Congress

Cong.	Ranking	Terms in: House	Comm.	Date of Assignment
110th	Maj-25th	5	1	Jan. 10, 2007
111th	Maj-21st	6	2	Jan. 7, 2009

William H. Natcher (D-Ky.)

Dates: Sept. 11, 1909-March 29, 1994
House: Jan. 3, 1953-March 29, 1994
Left the House: Died in office

H: Natcher was elected to the 83rd Congress by special election, Aug. 1, 1953, to fill the vacancy caused by the death of U.S. Representative Garrett L. Withers (D-Ky.). Natcher was seated Jan. 6, 1954, and assigned to committees.

HOUSE STANDING COMMITTEES:

1st VETERANS AFFAIRS
Dates: Jan. 25, 1954-Jan. 3, 1955
Departure: Moved to Appropriations

2nd APPROPRIATIONS
Dates: Jan. 13, 1955-Mar. 29,1994
Ch1: Succeeded by David R. Obey (D-Wisc.) as Chair on Apr. 12, 1994
Departure: Died in office

Cong.	Ranking	Terms in: House	Comm.	Date of Assignment
103rd	Maj-Ch1	21	20	Jan. 5, 1993

HOUSE SELECT AND SPECIAL COMMITTEES:

1st SELECT ASTRONAUTICS AND SPACE EXPLORATION
Dates: Mar. 5, 1958-Jan. 7, 1959
Departure: Did not continue on reorganized standing committee

Richard E. Neal (D-Mass.)

Dates: Feb. 14, 1949
House: Jan. 3, 1989-date
Serving in the 111th Congress

HOUSE STANDING COMMITTEES:

1st BANKING, FINANCE AND URBAN AFFAIRS
Dates: Jan. 19, 1989-Jan. 3, 1993
Departure: Moved to Ways and Means

2nd SMALL BUSINESS
Dates: Jan. 19, 1989-Jan. 3, 1993
Departure: Moved to Ways and Means

3rd WAYS AND MEANS
Dates: Jan. 5, 1993-date
Departure: Still serving in the 111th Congress

Cong.	Ranking	Terms in: House	Comm.	Date of Assignment
103rd	Maj-18th	3	1	Jan. 5, 1993
104th	Min-15th	4	2	Jan. 4, 1995
105th	Min-11th	5	3	Jan. 7, 1997
106th	Min-10th	6	4	Jan. 6, 1999
107th	Min-10th	7	5	Jan. 31, 2001
108th	Min-9th	8	6	Jan. 28, 2003
109th	Min-7th	9	7	Jan. 26, 2005
110th	Maj-6th	10	8	Jan. 4, 2007
111th	Maj-6th	11	9	Jan. 7, 2009

4th BUDGET
Dates: Jan. 28, 2003-Jan. 3, 2007
Departure: Left committee; no new assignment

Cong.	Ranking	Terms in: House	Comm.	Date of Assignment
108th	Min-7th	8	1	Jan. 28, 2003
109th	Min-3rd	9	2	Jan. 26, 2005

Stephen L. Neal (D-N.C.)

Dates: Nov. 7, 1934
House: Jan. 3, 1975-Jan. 3, 1995
Left the House: Retired in 1994

HOUSE STANDING COMMITTEES:

1st POST OFFICE AND CIVIL SERVICE
Dates: Jan. 20, 1975-Jan. 3, 1977
Departure: Moved to Science and Technology

2nd BANKING, CURRENCY AND HOUSING, 94
BANKING, FINANCE AND URBAN AFFAIRS, 95-103
Dates: Jan. 23, 1975-Jan. 3, 1995
Departure: Left the House; retired

Cong.	Ranking	Terms in: House	Comm.	Date of Assignment
103rd	Maj-2nd	10	10	Jan. 5, 1993

3rd SCIENCE AND TECHNOLOGY
Dates: Jan. 19, 1977-Jan. 31, 1979
Departure: Left committee; no new assignment

4th GOVERNMENT OPERATIONS
Dates: Jan. 28, 1981-Jan. 3, 1995
Departure: Left the House; retired

Cong.	Ranking	Terms in: House	Comm.	Date of Assignment
103rd	Maj-6th	10	7	Jan. 5, 1993

HOUSE SELECT AND SPECIAL COMMITTEES:

1st SELECT POPULATION
Dates: Oct. 14, 1977-Dec. 29, 1978
Termination: House Report 1842 (95-2) filed

2nd SELECT NARCOTICS ABUSE AND CONTROL (Temporary)
Dates: Apr. 5, 1979-Mar. 18, 1981
Departure: Left committee; no new assignment

C. William (Bill) Nelson (D-Fla.)

Dates: Sep. 9, 1942
House: Jan. 3, 1979-Jan. 3, 1991
Left the House: Lost nomination for Governor in 1990
Senate: Jan. 3, 2001-date
Serving in the 111th Congress

HOUSE STANDING COMMITTEES:

1st BUDGET
Dates: Jan. 24, 1979-Jan. 3, 1985
Departure: Moved to Banking, Finance and Urban Affairs

2nd SCIENCE AND TECHNOLOGY, 96-99
SCIENCE, SPACE AND TECHNOLOGY, 100-101
Dates: Jan. 24, 1979-Jan. 3, 1991
Departure: Left the House; lost nomination for Governor

3rd BANKING, FINANCE AND URBAN AFFAIRS
Dates: Jan. 30, 1985-Jan. 3, 1991
Departure: Left the House; lost nomination for Governor

SENATE STANDING COMMITTEES:

1st ARMED SERVICES
Dates: Jan. 25, 2001-date
Departure: Still serving in the 111th Congress

Cong.	Ranking	Years in: Senate	Comm.	Date of Assignment
107th	Min-9th	1	1	Jan. 25, 2001
+107th	Maj-9th	1	1	June 6, 2001
108th	Min-7th	3	2	Jan. 15, 2003
109th	Min-7th	5	4	Jan. 6, 2005
110th	Maj-7th	7	6	Jan. 12, 2007
111th	Maj-7th	9	8	Jan. 21, 2009

2nd BUDGET
Dates: Jan. 25, 2001-date
Departure: Still serving in the 111th Congress

Cong.	Ranking	Years in: Senate	Comm.	Date of Assignment
107th	Min-9th	1	1	Jan. 25, 2001
+107th	Maj-9th	1	1	June 6, 2001
108th	Min-9th	3	2	Jan. 15, 2003
109th	Min-8th	5	4	Jan. 6, 2005
110th	Maj-6th	7	6	Jan. 12, 2007
111th	Maj-6th	9	8	Jan. 21, 2009

3rd FOREIGN RELATIONS
Dates: Jan. 25, 2001-Jan. 21, 2009
Departure: Moved to Finance

Cong.	Ranking	Years in: Senate	Comm.	Date of Assignment
107th	Min-9th	1	1	Jan. 25, 2001
+107th	Maj-9th	1	1	June 6 2001
108th	Min-7th	3	2	Jan. 15, 2003
109th	Min-7th	5	4	Jan. 6, 2005
110th	Maj-6th	7	6	Jan. 12, 2007

4th COMMERCE, SCIENCE AND TRANSPORTATION
Dates: July 10, 2001-date
Departure: Still serving in the 111th Congress

Cong.	Ranking	Years in: Senate	Comm.	Date of Assignment
+107th	MjA-12th	1	1	July 10, 2001
108th	Min-9th	3	2	Jan. 15, 2003
109th	Min-6th	5	4	Jan. 6, 2005
110th	Maj-6th	7	6	Jan. 12, 2007
111th	Maj-6th	9	8	Jan. 21, 2009

5th FINANCE
Dates: Jan. 21, 2009-date
Departure: Still serving in the 111th Congress

Cong.	Ranking	Years in: Senate	Comm.	Date of Assignment
111th	Maj-11th	9	1	Jan. 21, 2009

SENATE SELECT AND SPECIAL COMMITTEES:

1st SPECIAL AGING (Permanent)
Dates: Jan. 6, 2005-date
Departure: Still serving in the 111th Congress

Cong.	Ranking	Years in: Senate	Comm.	Date of Assignment
109th	Min-8th	5	1	Jan. 6, 2005
110th	Maj-6th	7	3	Jan. 12, 2007
111th	Maj-5th	9	5	Jan. 21, 2009

2nd SELECT INTELLIGENCE (Permanent)
Dates: Jan. 12, 2007-date
Departure: Still serving in the 111th Congress

Cong.	Ranking	Years in: Senate	Comm.	Date of Assignment
110th	Maj-7th	7	1	Jan. 12, 2007
111th	Maj-7th	9	3	Jan. 21, 2009

E. Benjamin Nelson (D-Neb.)

Dates: May 17, 1941
Senate: Jan. 3, 2001-date
Serving in the 111th Congress

SENATE STANDING COMMITTEES:

1st AGRICULTURE, NUTRITION AND FORESTRY
Dates: Jan. 25, 2001-date
Departure: Still serving in the 111th Congress

Cong.	Ranking	Years in: Senate	Comm.	Date of Assignment
107th	Min-9th	1	1	Jan. 25, 2001
+107th	Maj-9th	1	1	June 6, 2001
108th	Min-9th	3	2	Jan. 15, 2003
109th	Min-7th	5	4	Jan. 6, 2005
110th	Maj-7th	7	6	Jan. 12, 2007
111th	Maj-7th	9	8	Jan. 21, 2009

2nd ARMED SERVICES
Dates: Jan. 25, 2001-date
Departure: Still serving in the 111th Congress

Cong.	Ranking	Years in: Senate	Comm.	Date of Assignment
107th	Min-10th	1	1	Jan. 25, 2001
+107th	Maj-10th	1	1	June 6, 2001
108th	Min-8th	3	2	Jan. 15, 2003
109th	Min-8th	5	4	Jan. 6, 2005
110th	Maj-8th	7	6	Jan. 12, 2007
111th	Maj-8th	9	8	Jan. 21, 2009

3rd VETERANS' AFFAIRS
Dates: Jan. 25, 2001-Jan. 6, 2005
Departure: Moved to Commerce, Science and Transportation and Rules and Administration

Cong.	Ranking	Years in: Senate	Comm.	Date of Assignment
107th	Min-7th	1	1	Jan. 25, 2001
+107th	Maj-8th	1	1	July 10, 2001
108th	Min-7th	3	2	Jan. 15, 2003

4th COMMERCE, SCIENCE AND TRANSPORTATION
Dates: Jan. 6, 2005-Jan. 12, 2007
Departure: Moved to Appropriations

Cong.	Ranking	Years in: Senate	Comm.	Date of Assignment
109th	Min-9th	5	1	Jan. 6, 2005

5th RULES AND ADMINISTRATION
Dates: Jan. 6, 2005-date
Departure: Still serving in the 111th Congress

Cong.	Ranking	Years in: Senate	Comm.	Date of Assignment
109th	Min-8th	5	1	Jan. 6, 2005
110th	Maj-7th	7	3	Jan. 12, 2007
111th	Maj-7th	9	5	Jan. 21, 2009

6th APPROPRIATIONS
Dates: Jan. 12, 2007-date
Departure: Still serving in the 111th Congress

Cong.	Ranking	Years in: Senate	Comm.	Date of Assignment
110th	Maj-15th	7	1	Jan. 12, 2007
111th	Maj-15th	9	3	Jan. 21, 2009

George R. Nethercutt Jr.
(R-Wash.)

Dates: Oct. 7, 1944
House: Jan. 3, 1995-Jan. 3, 2005
Left the House: Lost U.S. Senate election in 2004

HOUSE STANDING COMMITTEES:

1st APPROPRIATIONS
Dates: Jan. 4, 1995-Jan. 3, 2005
Departure: Left the House; lost Senate election

Cong.	Ranking	Terms in: House	Comm.	Date of Assignment
104th	Maj-30th	1	1	Jan. 4, 1995
105th	Maj-27th	2	2	Jan. 7, 1997
106th	Maj-24th	3	3	Jan. 6, 1999
107th	Maj-20th	4	4	Jan. 6, 2001
108th	Maj-16th	5	5	Jan. 28, 2003

2nd SCIENCE
Dates: Mar. 5, 1997-Jan. 3, 2005
Departure: Left the House; lost Senate election

Cong.	Ranking	Terms in: House	Comm.	Date of Assignment
105th	Maj-23rd	2	1	Mar. 5, 1997
106th	Maj-18th	3	2	Jan. 6, 1999
107th	Maj-15th	4	3	Jan. 6, 2001
108th	Maj-12th	5	4	Jan. 28, 2003

Randy Neugebauer (R-Tex.)

Dates: Dec. 24, 1949
House: June 3, 2003-date
Serving in the 111th Congress

H: Neugebauer was elected to the 108th Congress by special election, June 3, 2003, to fill the vacancy caused by the resignation of U.S. Representative Larry E. Combest (R-Tex.). Neugebauer was seated June 5, 2003, and assigned to committees.

HOUSE STANDING COMMITTEES:

1st AGRICULTURE
Dates: June 19, 2003-date
Departure: Still serving in the 111th Congress

Cong.	Ranking	Terms in: House	Comm.	Date of Assignment
108th	MjR-1st	1	1	June 19, 2003
109th	Maj-19th	2	2	Jan. 26, 2005
110th	Min-12th	3	3	Jan. 10, 2007
111th	Min-8th	4	4	Jan. 9, 2009

2nd RESOURCES
Dates: June 19, 2003-Jan. 3, 2005
Departure: Moved to Financial Services

Cong.	Ranking	Terms in: House	Comm.	Date of Assignment
108th	MjR-2nd	1	1	June 19, 2003

3rd SCIENCE, 108-109
SCIENCE AND TECHNOLOGY, 110-111

1st Dates: June 19, 2003-Jan. 3, 2005
1st Departure: Moved to Financial Services
2nd Dates: Apr. 4, 2006-date
2nd Departure: Still serving in the 111th Congress

Cong.	Ranking	Terms in: House	Comm.	Date of Assignment
108th	MjR-1st	1 *1	1	June 19, 2003
109th	MjA-23rd	2 *2	1	Apr. 4, 2006
110th	Min-13th	3 *2	2	Jan. 10, 2007
111th	Min-10th	4 *2	3	Jan. 9, 2009

4th FINANCIAL SERVICES
Dates: Jan. 26, 2005-date
Departure: Still serving in the 111th Congress

Cong.	Ranking	Terms in: House	Comm.	Date of Assignment
109th	Maj-33rd	2	1	Jan. 26, 2005
110th	Min-25th	3	2	Jan. 10, 2007
111th	Min-16th	4	3	Jan. 9, 2009

Mark W. Neumann (R-Wisc.)

Dates: Feb. 27, 1954
House: Jan. 3, 1995-Jan. 3, 1999
Left the House: Lost U.S Senate election in 1998

HOUSE STANDING COMMITTEES:

1st APPROPRIATIONS
Dates: Jan. 4, 1995-Jan. 3, 1999
Departure: Left the House; lost Senate election

Cong.	Ranking	Terms in: House	Comm.	Date of Assignment
104th	Maj-32rd	1	1	Jan. 4, 1995
105th	Maj-28th	2	2	Jan. 7, 1997

2nd BUDGET
Dates: Feb. 1, 1996-Jan. 3, 1999
Departure: Left the House; lost Senate election

Cong.	Ranking	Terms in: House	Comm.	Date of Assignment
104th	MjR-1st	1	1	Feb. 1, 1996
105th	Maj-17th	2	2	Jan. 7, 1997

Robert W. Ney (R-Ohio)

Dates: July 5, 1954
House: Jan. 3, 1995-Nov. 3, 2006
Left the House: Resigned the House; ethics issues

HOUSE STANDING COMMITTEES:

1st BANKING AND FINANCIAL SERVICES, 104-106
FINANCIAL SERVICES, 107-109
Dates: Jan. 4, 1995-Nov. 3, 2006
Departure: Resigned the House; ethics issues

Cong.	Ranking	Terms in: House	Comm.	Date of Assignment
104th	Maj-17th	1	1	Jan. 4, 1995
105th	Maj-14th	2	2	Jan. 7, 1997
106th	Maj-14th	3	3	Jan. 6, 1999
107th	Maj-11th	4	4	Jan. 6, 2001
108th	Maj-10th	5	5	Jan. 28, 2003
109th	Maj-10th	6	6	Jan. 26, 2005

2nd HOUSE OVERSIGHT, 104-105
HOUSE ADMINISTRATION, 106-109
Dates: Jan. 4, 1995-Nov. 3, 2006
Ch1: Resigned chairmanship on Jan. 17, 2006; replaced by Vernon J. Ehlers (R-Mich.) on Feb. 1, 2006
Departure: Resigned the House; ethics issues

Cong.	Ranking	Terms in: House	Comm.	Date of Assignment
104th	Maj-7th	1	1	Jan. 4, 1995
105th	Maj-4th	2	2	Jan. 7, 1997
106th	Maj-4th	3	3	Jan. 6, 1999
107th	Maj-Chr	4	4	Jan. 31, 2001
108th	Maj-Chr	5	5	Jan. 8, 2003
109th	Maj-Ch1	6	6	Jan. 6, 2005

3rd VETERANS' AFFAIRS
Dates: Jan. 4, 1995-Jan. 3, 1997
Departure: Moved to Transportation and Infrastructure

Cong.	Ranking	Terms in: House	Comm.	Date of Assignment
104th	Maj-11th	1	1	Jan. 4, 1995

4th TRANSPORTATION AND INFRASTRUCTURE
1st Dates: Jan. 7, 1997-Feb. 7, 2001
1st Departure: Resigned committee; became Chair of House Administration; returned with seniority intact
2nd Dates: June 7, 2001-Nov. 3, 2006
2nd Departure: Resigned the House; ethics issues

Cong.	Ranking	Terms in: House	Comm.	Date of Assignment
105th	Maj-25th	2 *1	1	Jan. 7, 1997
106th	Maj-22nd	3 *1	2	Jan. 6, 1999
107th	Maj-17th	4 *1	3	Jan. 6, 2001
107th	MjR-3rd	4 *2	1	June 7, 2001
108th	Maj-15th	5 *2	2	Jan. 28, 2003
109th	Maj-14th	6 *2	3	Jan. 26, 2005

JOINT COMMITTEES:

1st JOINT LIBRARY
1st House Dates: Jan. 17, 1995-Jan. 3, 1999
1st Departure: Left committee; no new assignment
2nd House Dates: June 5, 2001-Nov. 3, 2006
Ch1: Stepped down as Chair on Jan. 17, 2006
2nd Departure: Resigned the House; ethics issues

Cong.	Ranking	Terms in: House	Comm.	Date of Assignment
104th	Maj-3rd	1 *1	1	Feb. 23, 1995
105th	Maj-2nd	2 *1	2	Mar. 6, 1997
107th	Maj-2nd	4 *2	1	June 5, 2001
108th	Maj-2nd	5 *2	2	Mar. 25, 2003
109th	Maj-Ch1	6 *2	3	Mar. 16, 2005

2nd JOINT PRINTING
House Dates: Feb. 23, 1995-Nov. 3, 2006
ViC1: Stepped down as Vice Chair on Jan. 17, 2006
Departure: Resigned the House; ethics issues

Cong.	Ranking	Terms in: House	Comm.	Date of Assignment
104th	Maj-3rd	1	1	Feb. 23, 1995
105th	Maj-2nd	2	2	Mar. 6, 1997
106th	Maj-3rd	3	3	Mar. 2, 1999

107th	Maj-VCh	4	4	June 5, 2001
108th	Maj-Chr	5	5	Mar. 25, 2003
109th	Maj-VC1	6	6	Mar. 16, 2005

Donald L. Nickles (R-Okla.)

Dates: Dec. 6, 1948
Senate: Jan. 3, 1981-Jan. 3, 2005
Left the Senate: Retired in 2004

SENATE STANDING COMMITTEES:

1st ENERGY AND NATURAL RESOURCES
Dates: Jan. 5, 1981-Jan. 3, 2005
Departure: Left the Senate; retired

Cong.	Ranking	Years in: Senate	Comm.	Date of Assignment
103rd	Min-5th	13	13	Jan. 7, 1993
104th	Maj-4th	15	15	Jan. 5, 1995
105th	Maj-3rd	17	17	Jan. 9, 1997
106th	Maj-3rd	19	19	Jan. 7, 1999
107th	Maj-3rd	21	21	Jan. 25, 2001
+107th	Min-3rd	21	21	June 6, 2001
108th	Maj-2nd	23	23	Jan. 15, 2003

2nd LABOR AND HUMAN RESOURCES
Dates: Jan. 5, 1981-Jan. 6, 1987
Departure: Moved to Appropriations and Budget

3rd SMALL BUSINESS
Dates: Mar. 25, 1981-Jan. 6, 1987
Departure: Moved to Appropriations and Budget

4th APPROPRIATIONS
Dates: Jan. 6, 1987-Jan. 4, 1995
Departure: Moved to Finance and Rules and Administration

Cong.	Ranking	Years in: Senate	Comm.	Date of Assignment
103rd	Min-7th	13	7	Jan. 7, 1993

5th BUDGET
Dates: Jan. 6, 1987-Jan. 3, 2005
Departure: Left the Senate; retired

Cong.	Ranking	Years in: Senate	Comm.	Date of Assignment
103rd	Min-3rd	13	7	Jan. 21, 1993
104th	Maj-3rd	15	9	Jan. 6, 1995
105th	Maj-3rd	17	11	Jan. 9, 1997
106th	Maj-3rd	19	13	Jan. 7, 1999
107th	Maj-3rd	21	15	Jan. 25, 2001
+107th	Min-3rd	21	15	June 6, 2001
108th	Maj-Chr	23	17	Jan. 15, 2003

6th FINANCE
Dates: Jan. 4, 1995-Jan. 3, 2005
Departure: Left the Senate; retired

Cong.	Ranking	Years in: Senate	Comm.	Date of Assignment
104th	Maj-11th	15	1	Jan. 4, 1995
105th	Maj-7th	17	3	Jan. 9, 1997
106th	Maj-6th	19	5	Jan. 7, 1999
107th	Maj-4th	21	7	Jan. 25, 2001
+107th	Min-4th	21	7	June 6, 2001
108th	Maj-3rd	23	9	Jan. 15, 2003

7th RULES AND ADMINISTRATION
Dates: Jan. 6, 1995-Jan. 3, 2005
Departure: Left the Senate; retired

Cong.	Ranking	Years in: Senate	Comm.	Date of Assignment
104th	Maj-9th	15	1	Jan. 6, 1995
105th	Maj-7th	17	2	Jan. 3, 1997
106th	Maj-7th	19	5	Jan. 7, 1999
107th	Maj-7th	21	7	Jan. 25, 2001
+107th	Min-7th	21	7	June 6, 2001
108th	Maj-6th	23	9	Jan. 15, 2003

8th GOVERNMENTAL AFFAIRS
Dates: Jan. 9, 1997-Jan. 7, 1999
Departure: Moved to Joint Printing

Cong.	Ranking	Years in: Senate	Comm.	Date of Assignment
105th	Maj-8th	17	1	Jan. 9, 1997

9th BANKING, HOUSING AND URBAN AFFAIRS
Dates: Dec. 6, 2000-Jan. 25, 2001
Departure: Left committee; no new assignment

Cong.	Ranking	Years in: Senate	Comm.	Date of Assignment
106th	MjA-12th	20	1	Dec. 6, 2000

SENATE SELECT AND SPECIAL COMMITTEES:

1st SELECT SMALL BUSINESS
Dates: Jan. 5, 1981-Mar. 25, 1981
Departure: Continued on reorganized standing committee

2nd SPECIAL AGING (Permanent)
Dates: Mar. 5, 1985-Jan. 6, 1987
Departure: Moved to Appropriations and Budget

3rd SELECT INDIAN AFFAIRS (Permanent), 102
INDIAN AFFAIRS (Permanent), 103-104
Dates: Feb. 5, 1991-Jan. 9, 1997
Departure: Moved to Governmental Affairs

Cong.	Ranking	Years in: Senate	Comm.	Date of Assignment
103rd	Min-7th	13	2	Jan. 5, 1993
104th	Maj-6th	15	4	Jan. 11, 1995

JOINT COMMITTEES:

1st JOINT DEFICIT REDUCTION (Temporary)
Senate Dates: Jan. 6, 1987-Sep. 29, 1987
Termination: Public Law 100-119 adjusted Gramm-Rudman-Hollings Act

2nd JOINT PRINTING
Senate Dates: Mar. 2, 1999-Sep. 19, 2001
Departure: Left committee; no new assignment.

Cong.	Ranking	Years in: Senate	Comm.	Date of Assignment
106th	Maj-3rd	19	1	Mar. 2, 1999

3rd JOINT TAXATION
Senate Dates: Feb. 24, 2003-Jan. 3, 2005
Departure: Left the Senate; retired.

Cong.	Ranking	Years in: Senate	Comm.	Date of Assignment
108th	Maj-2nd	23	1	Feb. 24, 2003

SENATE LEADERSHIP POSTS

1st SENATE MAJORITY WHIP
Dates: June 12, 1996-June 6, 2001

Notes: For the 104th Congress, Nickles succeeded Majority Whip C. Trent Lott (R-Miss.) who had been elected Majority Leader on June 12, 1996. Nickles was elected without opposition and was re-elected unopposed for the 105-107th Congresses.

Departure: Nickles became Minority Whip as a result of the Jeffords' shift from Republican to Independent ion June 6, 2001

Cong.	Ranking	Years in: Senate	Post	Date of Service
104th	Maj-2nd	16	1	June 12, 1996
105th	Maj-2nd	17	1	Dec. 3, 1996
106th	Maj-2nd	19	3	Dec. 1, 1998
107th	Maj-2nd	21	5	Dec. 5, 2000

2nd SENATE MINORITY WHIP
Dates: June 6, 2001-Jan. 3, 2003
Note: There was no new vote for Minority Whip
Departure: Left post; became Chair of Budget

Cong.	Ranking	Years in: Senate	Post	Date of Service
107th	Min-2nd	2	1	June 6, 2001

Anne M. Northup (R-Ky.)

Dates: Jan. 22, 1948
House: Jan. 3, 1997-Jan. 3, 2007
Left the House: Defeated for re-election in 2006

HOUSE STANDING COMMITTEES:

1st APPROPRIATIONS
Dates: Jan. 7, 1997-Jan. 3, 2007
Departure: Left the House; lost re-election

Cong.	Ranking	Terms in: House	Comm.	Date of Assignment
105th	Maj-33rd	1	1	Jan. 7, 1997
106th	Maj-29th	2	2	Jan. 6, 1999
107th	Maj-25th	3	3	Jan. 6, 2001
108th	Maj-21st	4	4	Jan. 28, 2003
109th	Maj-20th	5	5	Jan. 6, 2005

Eleanor Holmes Norton (D-D.C.)

Dates: June 13, 1937
House: Jan. 3, 1991-date
Serving in the 111th Congress

H: Ms. Norton was elected as a Democrat to serve as a Delegate in the 102nd Congress and is still serving. She was assigned to committees and allowed to accrue seniority.

HOUSE STANDING COMMITTEES:

1st DISTRICT OF COLUMBIA
Dates: Jan. 24, 1991-Jan. 3, 1995
Departure: Committee abolished; moved to Government Reform and Oversight

Cong.	Ranking	Terms in: House	Comm.	Date of Assignment
103rd	Maj-4th	2	2	Feb. 18, 1993

2nd POST OFFICE AND CIVIL SERVICE
Dates: Jan. 24, 1991-Jan. 3, 1995
Departure: Committee abolished, moved to Government Reform and Oversight

Cong.	Ranking	Terms in: House	Comm.	Date of Assignment
103rd	Maj-7th	2	2	Jan. 21, 1993

3rd PUBLIC WORKS AND TRANSPORTATION, 102-103
TRANSPORTATION AND INFRASTRUCTURE, 104-111
Dates: Jan. 24, 1991-date
Departure: Still serving in the 111th Congress

Cong.	Ranking	Terms in: House	Comm.	Date of Assignment
103rd	Maj-23rd	2	2	Jan. 5, 1993
104th	Min-17th	3	3	Jan. 4, 1995
105th	Min-12th	4	4	Jan. 7, 1997
106th	Min-10th	5	5	Jan. 6, 1999
107th	Min-8th	6	6	Jan. 31, 2001
108th	Min-6th	7	7	Jan. 28, 2003
109th	Min-5th	8	8	Jan. 26, 2005
110th	Maj-5th	9	9	Jan. 10, 2007
111th	Maj-5th	10	10	Jan. 7, 2009

4th GOVERNMENT REFORM AND OVERSIGHT, 104-105
GOVERNMENT REFORM, 106-109
OVERSIGHT AND GOVERNMENT REFORM, 110-111
1st Dates: Jan. 9, 1995-Feb. 12, 2003
1st Departure: Leave of absence for Select Homeland Security
2nd Dates: Feb. 26, 2003-Jan. 3, 2005
2nd Departure: Left committee; no new assignment
3rd Dates: Feb. 2, 2005-date
3rd Departure: Still serving in the 111th Congress

Cong.	Ranking	Terms in: House	Comm.	Date of Assignment
104th	Min-17th	3 *1	1	Jan. 9, 1995
105th	Min-11th	4 *1	2	Jan. 7, 1997
106th	Min-10th	5 *1	3	Jan. 6, 1999
107th	Min-8th	6 *1	4	Jan. 31, 2001
108th	Min-7th	7 *1	5	Jan. 28, 2003
108th	Min-17th	7 *2	1	Feb. 26, 2003
109th	MnR-1st	8 *3	1	Feb. 2, 2005
110th	Maj-16th	9 *3	2	Jan. 12, 2007
111th	Maj-11th	10 *3	3	Jan. 28, 2009

5th SMALL BUSINESS
Dates: Sep. 17, 1996-Jan. 3, 1997
Departure: Left committee; no new assignment

Cong.	Ranking	Terms in: House	Comm.	Date of Assignment
104th	MnR-7th	3	1	Sep. 17, 1996

6th HOMELAND SECURITY
Dates: Feb. 9, 2005-date
Departure: Still serving in the 111th Congress

Cong.	Ranking	Terms in: House	Comm.	Date of Assignment
109th	Min-8th	8	2	Feb. 9, 2005
110th	Maj-8th	9	3	Jan. 12, 2007
111th	Maj-5th	10	4	Jan. 28, 2009

HOUSE SELECT AND SPECIAL COMMITTEES:

1st SELECT HOMELAND SECURITY
Dates: Feb. 12, 2003-Jan. 3, 2005
Departure: Continued on reorganized standing committee

Cong.	Ranking	Terms in: House	Comm.	Date of Assignment
108th	Min-13th	7	1	Feb. 12, 2003

JOINT COMMITTEES:

1st JOINT ORGANIZATION OF CONGRESS (Ad Hoc)
House Dates: Oct. 9, 1992-Dec. 17, 1993
Termination: House Report 103-413 filed

Cong.	Ranking	Terms in: House	Comm.	Date of Assignment
103rd	Maj-6th	2	2	Jan. 5, 1993

Charles W. Norwood Jr. (R-Ga.)

Dates: July 27, 1941-Feb. 13, 2007
House: Jan. 3, 1995-Feb. 13, 2007
Left the House: Died in office

HOUSE STANDING COMMITTEES:

1st COMMERCE, 104-106
ENERGY AND COMMERCE, 107-110
Dates: Jan. 4, 1995-Feb. 13, 2007
Departure: Died in office

Cong.	Ranking	Terms in: House	Comm.	Date of Assignment
104th	Maj-23rd	1	1	Jan. 4, 1995
105th	Maj-22nd	2	2	Jan. 7, 1997
106th	Maj-17th	3	3	Jan. 6, 1999
107th	Maj-14th	4	4	Jan. 6, 2001
108th	Maj-12th	5	5	Jan. 28, 2003
109th	Maj-9th	6	6	Jan. 6, 2005
110th	Min-8th	7	7	Jan. 10, 2007

2nd ECONOMIC AND EDUCATIONAL OPPORTUNITIES, 104
EDUCATION AND THE WORKFORCE, 105-109
Dates: Jan. 4, 1995-Jan. 3, 2007
Departure: Left committee; no new assignment

Cong.	Ranking	Terms in: House	Comm.	Date of Assignment
104th	Maj-24th	1	1	Jan. 4, 1995
105th	Maj-18th	2	2	Jan. 7, 1997
106th	Maj-16th	3	3	Jan. 6, 1999
107th	Maj-12th	4	4	Jan. 6, 2001
108th	Maj-10th	5	5	Jan. 28, 2003
109th	Maj-7th	6	6	Jan. 26, 2005

Devin Nunes (R-Cal.)

Dates: Oct. 1, 1973
House: Jan. 3, 2003-date
Serving in the 111th Congress

HOUSE STANDING COMMITTEES:

1st AGRICULTURE
Dates: Jan. 28, 2003-May 5, 2005
Departure: Resigned committee; moved to Ways and Means

Cong.	Ranking	Terms in: House	Comm.	Date of Assignment
108th	Maj-27th	1	1	Jan. 28, 2003
109th	Maj-18th	2	2	Jan. 26, 2005

2nd RESOURCES
Dates: Jan. 28, 2003-May 5, 2005
Departure: Resigned committee; moved to Ways and Means

Cong.	Ranking	Terms in: House	Comm.	Date of Assignment
108th	Maj-28th	1	1	Jan. 28, 2003
109th	Maj-21st	2	2	Jan. 26, 2005

3rd VETERANS' AFFAIRS
Dates: Feb. 2, 2005-May 5, 2005
Departure: Resigned committee; moved to Ways and Means

Cong.	Ranking	Terms in: House	Comm.	Date of Assignment
109th	Maj-14th	2	1	Feb. 2, 2005

4th WAYS AND MEANS
Dates: May 5, 2005-date
Departure: Still serving in the 111th Congress

Cong.	Ranking	Terms in: House	Comm.	Date of Assignment
109th	MjR-1st	2	1	May 5, 2005
110th	Min-15th	3	2	Jan. 4, 2007
111th	Min-8th	4	3	Jan. 9, 2009

5th BUDGET
Dates: Jan. 9, 2009-date
Departure: Still serving in the 111th Congress

Cong.	Ranking	Terms in: House	Comm.	Date of Assignment
111th	Min-13th	4	1	Jan. 9, 2009

Samuel A. Nunn (D-Ga.)

Dates: Sept. 8, 1938
Senate: Nov. 8, 1972-Jan. 3, 1997
Left the Senate: Retired in 1996

S: Nunn was appointed to the 92nd Congress, Nov. 7, 1972, to fill the vacancy caused by the death of U.S. Senator Richard B. Russell (D-Ga.). Russell was initially replaced by David H. Gambrell (D-Ga.), an appointee, who was defeated for the nomination by Nunn. Nunn began service Nov. 8, 1972, following the resignation of Gambrell, but was not seated nor assigned to committees as the 92nd Congress was not in session. Nunn had been elected to the 93rd Congress.

SENATE STANDING COMMITTEES:

1st GOVERNMENT OPERATIONS reorganized Feb. 11, 1977
GOVERNMENTAL AFFAIRS
Dates: Jan. 4, 1973-Jan. 3, 1997
Departure: Left the Senate; retired

Cong.	Ranking	Years in: Senate	Comm.	Date of Assignment
103rd	Maj-2nd	21	21	Jan. 7, 1993
104th	Min-2nd	23	23	Jan. 4, 1995

2nd ARMED SERVICES
Dates: Jan. 4, 1973-Jan. 3, 1997
Departure: Left the Senate; retired
Chair: 100th-102nd, 1987-1993
Ranking Member: 98th 2nd-99th, 1983-87

Cong.	Ranking	Years in: Senate	Comm.	Date of Assignment
103rd	Maj-Chr	21	21	Jan. 7, 1993
104th	Min-RM	23	23	Jan. 4, 1995

3rd BUDGET
Dates: Jan. 17, 1975-Feb. 11, 1977
Departure: Left committee; no new assignment

4th SMALL BUSINESS
Dates: Jan. 4, 1973-Mar. 25, 1981 as Select
Dates: Mar. 25, 1981-Jan. 3, 1997 as Standing
Departure: Left the Senate; retired
RM: gave up in 99th

Cong.	Ranking	Years in: Senate	Comm.	Date of Assignment
103rd	Maj-2nd	21	21	Jan. 21, 1993
104th	Min-2nd	23	23	Jan. 6, 1995

SENATE SELECT AND SPECIAL COMMITTEES:

1st SELECT SMALL BUSINESS
Dates: Jan. 4, 1973-Mar. 25, 1981
Departure: Continued on reorganized standing committee

2nd SELECT SENATE COMMITTEE SYSTEM I (Stevenson)
Dates: Apr. 1, 1976-Apr. 12, 1976
Departure: Left committee; no new assignment

3rd SELECT OFFICIAL CONDUCT
Dates: Jan. 19, 1977-Mar. 10, 1977
Termination: Senate Report 49 (95-1) filed

4th SELECT INTELLIGENCE (Permanent)
Dates: Sep. 12, 1983-Jan. 23, 1992
Departure: Left committee; no new assignment

5th SECRET MILITARY ASSISTANCE TO IRAN AND THE NICARAGUAN OPPOSITION (Iran-Contra Affair)
Dates: Jan. 12, 1987-Nov. 17, 1987
Termination: Senate Report 100-216 filed

James A. Nussle (R-Iowa)

Dates: June 27, 1960
House: Jan. 3, 1991-Jan. 3, 2007
Left the House: Lost election for Governor in 2006

HOUSE STANDING COMMITTEES:

1st AGRICULTURE
Dates: Jan. 24, 1991-Jan. 3, 1995
Departure: Moved to Budget and Ways and Means

Cong.	Ranking	Terms in: House	Comm.	Date of Assignment
103rd	Min-10th	2	2	Jan. 5, 1993

2nd BANKING, FINANCE AND URBAN AFFAIRS
Dates: Jan. 24, 1991-Jan. 3, 1995
Departure: Moved to Budget and Ways and Means

Cong.	Ranking	Terms in: House	Comm.	Date of Assignment
103rd	Min-9th	2	2	Jan. 5, 1993

3rd BUDGET
Dates: Jan. 4, 1995-Jan. 3, 2007
Departure: Left the House; lost election for Governor

Cong.	Ranking	Terms in: House	Comm.	Date of Assignment
104th	Maj-17th	3	1	Jan. 4, 1995
105th	Maj-12th	4	2	Jan. 7, 1997
106th	Maj-8th	5	3	Jan. 6, 1999
107th	Maj-Chr	6	4	Jan. 6, 2001
108th	Maj-Chr	7	5	Jan. 28, 2003
109th	Maj-Chr	8	6	Jan. 26, 2005

4th WAYS AND MEANS
Dates: Jan. 4, 1995-Jan. 3, 2007
Departure: Left the House; lost election for Governor

Cong.	Ranking	Terms in: House	Comm.	Date of Assignment
104th	Maj-14th	3	1	Jan. 4, 1995
105th	Maj-12th	4	2	Jan. 7, 1997
106th	Maj-11th	5	3	Jan. 6, 1999
107th	Maj-10th	6	4	Jan. 6, 2001
108th	Maj-10th	7	5	Jan. 28, 2003
109th	Maj-8th	8	6	Jan. 6, 2005

HOUSE SELECT AND SPECIAL COMMITTEES:

1st SELECT AGING (Permanent)
Dates: Feb. 21, 1991-Jan. 3, 1993
Termination: Committee not renewed in 1993

Glenn C. Nye III (D-Va.)

Dates: September 9, 1974
House: Jan. 3, 2009-date
Still serving in the 111th Congress

HOUSE STANDING COMMITTEES:

1st ARMED SERVICES
Dates: Jan. 7, 2009-date
Departure: Still serving in the 111th Congress

Cong.	Ranking	Terms in: House	Comm.	Date of Assignment
111th	Maj-31st	1	1	Jan. 7, 2009

2nd SMALL BUSINESS
Dates: Jan. 21, 2009-date
Departure: Still serving in the 111th Congress

Cong.	Ranking	Terms in: House	Comm.	Date of Assignment
111th	Maj-7th	1	1	Jan. 21, 2009

3rd VETERANS' AFFAIRS
Dates: Jan. 21, 2009-date
Departure: Still serving in the 111th Congress

Cong.	Ranking	Terms in: House	Comm.	Date of Assignment
111th	Maj-18th	1	1	Jan. 21, 2009

O

Barack Obama (D-Ill.)

Dates: Aug. 4, 1961
Senate: Jan. 3, 2005-Nov. 16, 2008
Left the Senate: Elected President in 2008

SENATE STANDING COMMITTEES:

1st ENVIRONMENT AND PUBLIC WORKS
Dates: Jan. 6, 2005-Jan. 12, 2007
Departure: Moved to Health, Education, Labor and Pensions and Homeland Security and Governmental Affairs

Cong.	Ranking	Years in: Senate	Comm.	Date of Assignment
109th	Min-8th	1	1	Jan. 6, 2005

2nd FOREIGN RELATIONS
Dates: Jan. 6, 2005-Nov. 16, 2008
Departure: Resigned the Senate; elected President

Cong.	Ranking	Years in: Senate	Comm.	Date of Assignment
109th	Min-8th	1	1	Jan. 6, 2005
110th	Maj-7th	3	3	Jan. 12, 2007

3rd VETERANS' AFFAIRS
Dates: Jan. 6, 2005-Nov. 16, 2008
Departure: Resigned the Senate; elected President

Cong.	Ranking	Years in: Senate	Comm.	Date of Assignment
109th	Min-5th	1	1	Jan. 6, 2005
110th	Maj-4th	3	3	Jan. 12, 2007

4th HEALTH, EDUCATION, LABOR, AND PENSIONS
Dates: Jan. 12, 2007-Nov. 16, 2008
Departure: Resigned the Senate; elected President

Cong.	Ranking	Years in: Senate	Comm.	Date of Assignment
110th	Maj-9th	3	1	Jan. 12, 2007

5th HOMELAND SECURITY AND GOVERNMENTAL AFFAIRS
Dates: Jan. 12, 2007-Nov. 16, 2008
Departure: Resigned the Senate; elected President

Cong.	Ranking	Years in: Senate	Comm.	Date of Assignment
110th	Maj-7th	3	1	Jan. 12, 2007

HOUSE STANDING COMMITTEES:

1st MERCHANT MARINE AND FISHERIES
Dates: Jan. 20, 1975-Jan. 3, 1987
Departure: Moved to Budget

2nd PUBLIC WORKS AND TRANSPORTATION, 94-103
TRANSPORTATION AND INFRASTRUCTURE, 104-111
Dates: Jan. 20, 1975-date
RM2: Replaced Norman Y. Mineta (D-Cal.) as Ranking Member on Oct. 10, 1995
Departure: Still serving in the 111th Congress

Cong.	Ranking	Terms in: House	Comm.	Date of Assignment
103rd	Maj-2nd	10	10	Jan. 5, 1993
104th	Min-2nd	11	11	Jan. 4, 1995
=104th	Min-RM2	11	11	Oct. 10, 1995
105th	Min-RM	12	12	Jan. 7, 1997
106th	Min-RM	13	13	Jan. 6, 1999
107th	Min-RM	14	14	Jan. 31, 2001
108th	Min-RM	15	15	Jan. 8, 2003
109th	Min-RM	16	16	Jan. 6, 2005
110th	Maj-Chr	17	17	Jan. 4, 2007
111th	Maj-Chr	18	18	Jan. 6, 2009

3rd BUDGET
Dates: Jan. 6, 1987-Jan. 3, 1993
Departure: Moved to Foreign Affairs

4th FOREIGN AFFAIRS
Dates: Jan. 5, 1993-Jan 3, 1995
Departure: Left committee; no new assignment

Cong.	Ranking	Terms in: House	Comm.	Date of Assignment
103rd	Maj-10th	10	1	Jan. 5, 1993

HOUSE SELECT AND SPECIAL COMMITTEES:

1st SELECT COMMITTEE ON CONGRESSIONAL OPERATIONS
Dates: Apr. 6, 1977-Jan. 2, 1979
Termination: House Report 1843 (95-2) filed

JOINT COMMITTEES:

1st JOINT CONGRESSIONAL OPERATIONS
House Dates: Jan. 17, 1977-Jan. 3, 1979
Departure: Committee terminated

2nd JOINT DEFICIT REDUCTION (Temporary)
House Dates: Feb. 23, 1987-Sep. 29, 1987
Termination: Public Law 100-119 adjusted Gramm-Rudman-Hollings Act.

James L. Oberstar (DFL-Minn.)

Dates: Sept. 10, 1934
House: Jan. 3, 1975-date
Serving in the 111th Congress

David F. Obey (D-Wisc.)

Dates: Oct. 3, 1938
House: April 1, 1969-date
Serving in the 111th Congress

H: Obey was elected to the 91st Congress by special election, April 1, 1969, to fill the vacancy caused by the resignation of U. S. Representative Melvin R. Laird (R-Wisc.) who had been appointed Secretary of Defense. Obey was seated April 3, 1969, and assigned to committees.

HOUSE STANDING COMMITTEES:

1st PUBLIC WORKS
Dates: Apr. 15, 1969-Nov. 12, 1969
Departure: Resigned committee; moved to Appropriations

2nd APPROPRIATIONS
Dates: Nov. 12, 1969-date
Ch2: Replaced William H. Natcher (D-Ky.) as Chair on April 12, 1994
Departure: Still serving in the 111th Congress

| | | Terms in: | | Date of |
Cong.	Ranking	House	Comm.	Assignment
103rd	Maj-5th	13	13	Jan. 5, 1993
=103rd	Maj-Ch2	13	13	Apr. 12, 1994
104th	Min-RM	14	14	Jan. 4, 1995
105th	Min-RM	15	15	Jan. 7, 1997
106th	Min-RM	16	16	Jan. 6, 1999
107th	Min-RM	17	17	Jan. 31, 2001
108th	Min-RM	18	18	Jan. 8, 2003
109th	Min-RM	19	19	Jan. 6, 2005
110th	Maj-Chr	20	20	Jan. 4, 2007
111th	Maj-Chr	21	21	Jan. 6, 2009

3rd BUDGET
Dates: Jan. 11, 1977-Jan. 3, 1983
Departure: Moved to Joint Economic.

HOUSE SELECT AND SPECIAL COMMITTEES:

1st SELECT ETHICS
Dates: Mar. 10, 1977-Jan. 3, 1979
Termination: House Report 1837 (95-2) filed

JOINT COMMITTEES:

1st JOINT ECONOMIC
House Dates: Jan. 6, 1983-Mar. 7, 1996
Departure: Resigned committee; no new assignment

| | | Terms in: | | Date of |
Cong.	Ranking	House	Comm.	Assignment
103rd	Maj-Chr	13	6	Jan. 27, 1993
104th	Min-2nd	14	7	Jan. 19, 1995

2nd JOINT ORGANIZATION OF CONGRESS (Ad Hoc)
House Dates: Oct. 9, 1992-Dec. 17, 1993
Termination: House Report 103-413 filed

| | | Terms in: | | Date of |
Cong.	Ranking	House	Comm.	Assignment
103rd	Maj-2nd	13	2	Jan. 5, 1993

Pete Olson (R-Tex.)

Dates: December 9, 1962
House: Jan. 3, 2009-date
Serving in the 111th Congress

HOUSE STANDING COMMITTEES:

1st HOMELAND SECURITY
Dates: Jan. 9, 2009-date
Departure: Serving in the 111th Congress

| | | Terms in: | | Date of |
Cong.	Ranking	House	Comm.	Assignment
111th	Min-11th	1	1	Jan. 9, 2009

2nd SCIENCE AND TECHNOLOGY
Dates: Jan. 9, 2009-date
Departure: Serving in the 111th Congress

| | | Terms in: | | Date of |
Cong.	Ranking	House	Comm.	Assignment
111th	Min-17th	1	1	Jan. 9, 2009

3rd TRANSPORTATION AND INFRASTRUCTURE
Dates: Jan. 22, 2009-date
Departure: Serving in the 111th Congress

| | | Terms in: | | Date of |
Cong.	Ranking	House	Comm.	Assignment
111th	MnR-1st	1	1	Jan. 22, 2009

John W. Olver (D-Mass.)

Dates: Sept. 3, 1936
House: June 4, 1991-date
Serving in the 111th Congress

H: Olver was elected to the 102nd Congress by special election, June 4, 1991, to fill the vacancy caused by the death of U.S. Representative Silvio O. Conte (R-Mass.). Olver was seated June 18, 1991, and assigned to committees.

HOUSE STANDING COMMITTEES:

1st EDUCATION AND LABOR
Dates: June 27, 1991-Jan. 3, 1993
Departure: Moved to Appropriations

2nd SCIENCE, SPACE AND TECHNOLOGY, 102
SCIENCE, 104
1st Dates: June 27, 1991-Jan. 3, 1993
1st Departure: Moved to Appropriations
2nd Dates: Jan. 4, 1995-Jan. 3, 1997
2nd Departure: Returned to Appropriations

| | | Terms in: | | Date of |
Cong.	Ranking	House	Comm.	Assignment
104th	Min-14th	3 *2	1	Jan. 4, 1995

3rd APPROPRIATIONS, 103, 105-110
1st Dates: Jan. 5, 1993-Jan. 3, 1995
1st Departure: Moved to Budget and returned to Science
2nd Dates: Jan. 7, 1997-date
2nd Departure: Still serving in the 111th Congress

Cong.	Ranking	Terms in: House	Comm.	Date of Assignment
103rd	Maj-35th	2 *1	1	Jan. 5, 1993
105th	Min-22nd	4 *2	1	Jan. 7, 1997
106th	Min-15th	5 *2	2	Jan. 6, 1999
107th	Min-14th	6 *2	3	Jan. 31, 2001
108th	Min-13th	7 *2	4	Jan. 28, 2003
109th	Min-13th	8 *2	5	Jan. 26, 2005
110th	Maj-11th	9 *2	6	Jan. 4, 2007
111th	Maj-11th	10 *2	7	Jan. 7, 2009

4th BUDGET
Dates: Jan. 4, 1995-Jan. 3, 1997
Departure: Returned to Appropriations

Cong.	Ranking	Terms in: House	Comm.	Date of Assignment
104th	Min-14th	3	1	Jan. 4, 1995

Solomon P. Ortiz (D-Tex.)

Dates: June 3, 1937
House: Jan. 3, 1983-date
Serving in the 111th Congress

HOUSE STANDING COMMITTEES:

1st ARMED SERVICES, 98-103
NATIONAL SECURITY, 104-105
ARMED SERVICES, 106-111
Dates: Jan. 6, 1983-date
Departure: Still serving in the 111th Congress

Cong.	Ranking	Terms in: House	Comm.	Date of Assignment
103rd	Maj-12th	6	6	Jan. 5, 1993
104th	Min-7th	7	7	Jan. 4, 1995
105th	Min-5th	8	8	Jan. 7, 1997
106th	Min-4th	9	9	Jan. 6, 1999
107th	Min-4th	10	10	Jan. 31, 2001
108th	Min-3rd	11	11	Jan. 28, 2003
109th	Min-3rd	12	12	Jan. 26, 2005
110th	Maj-3rd	13	13	Jan. 10, 2007
111th	Maj-3rd	14	14	Jan. 7, 2009

2nd MERCHANT MARINE AND FISHERIES
Dates: Jan. 6, 1983-Jan. 3, 1995
Departure: Committee abolished; moved to Resources

Cong.	Ranking	Terms in: House	Comm.	Date of Assignment
103rd	Maj-6th	6	6	Jan. 5, 1993

3rd RESOURCES, 104-109
NATURAL RESOURCES, 110
Dates: Jan. 9, 1995-Jan. 3, 2009
Departure: Moved to Transportation and Infrastructure

Cong.	Ranking	Terms in: House	Comm.	Date of Assignment
104th	Min-14th	7	1	Jan. 9, 1995
105th	Min-11th	8	2	Jan. 7, 1997
106th	Min-8th	9	3	Jan. 6, 1999
107th	Min-8th	10	4	Feb. 8, 2001
108th	Min-8th	11	5	Jan. 28, 2003
109th	Min-6th	12	6	Jan. 26, 2005
110th	Maj-5th	13	7	Jan. 18, 2007

4th TRANSPORTATION AND INFRASTRUCTURE
Dates: Jan. 7, 2009-date
Departure: Still serving in the 111th Congress

Cong.	Ranking	Terms in: House	Comm.	Date of Assignment
111th	Maj-36th	14	1	Jan. 7, 2009

HOUSE SELECT AND SPECIAL COMMITTEES:

1st SELECT NARCOTICS ABUSE AND CONTROL (Temporary)
Dates: Feb. 22, 1983-Jan. 3, 1993
Termination: Committee not renewed in 1993

William Orton (D-Utah)

Dates: Sept. 22, 1949
House: Jan. 3, 1991-Jan. 3, 1997
Left the House: Defeated for re-election in 1996

HOUSE STANDING COMMITTEES:

1st BANKING, FINANCE AND URBAN AFFAIRS, 102-103
BANKING AND FINANCIAL SERVICES, 104
Dates: Jan. 24, 1991-Jan. 3, 1997
Departure: Left the House; lost re-election

Cong.	Ranking	Terms in: House	Comm.	Date of Assignment
103rd	Maj-13th	2	2	Jan. 5, 1993
104th	Min-11th	3	3	Jan. 4, 1995

2nd FOREIGN AFFAIRS
Temporary Dates: Jan. 24, 1991-Jan. 3, 1993
Departure: Temporary term expired; moved to Budget

3rd SMALL BUSINESS
Dates: Jan. 24, 1991-Jan. 3, 1993
Departure: Moved to Budget

4th BUDGET
Dates: Jan. 5, 1993-Jan. 3, 1997
Departure: Left the House; lost re-election

Cong.	Ranking	Terms in: House	Comm.	Date of Assignment
103rd	Maj-24th	2	1	Jan. 5, 1993
104th	Min-10th	3	2	Jan. 4, 1995

Thomas Osborne (R-Neb.)

Dates: Feb. 23, 1937
House: Jan. 3, 2001-Jan. 3, 2007
Left the House: Lost nomination for Governor in 2006

HOUSE STANDING COMMITTEES:

1st AGRICULTURE
Dates: Jan. 6, 2001-Jan. 3, 2007
Departure: Left the House; lost nomination for Governor

Cong.	Ranking	Terms in: House	Comm.	Date of Assignment
107th	Maj-22nd	1	1	Jan. 6, 2001
108th	Maj-15th	2	2	Jan. 28, 2003
109th	Maj-11th	3	3	Jan. 26, 2005

2nd EDUCATION AND THE WORKFORCE
Dates: Jan. 6, 2001-Jan. 3, 2007
Departure: Left the House; lost nomination for Governor

Cong.	Ranking	Terms in: House	Comm.	Date of Assignment
107th	Maj-25th	1	1	Jan. 6, 2001
108th	Maj-19th	2	2	Jan. 28, 2003
109th	Maj-13th	3	3	Jan. 26, 2005

3rd RESOURCES
Dates: Jan. 6, 2001-Jan. 3, 2005
Departure: Moved to Transportation and Infrastructure

Cong.	Ranking	Terms in: House	Comm.	Date of Assignment
107th	Maj-28th	1	1	Jan. 6, 2001
108th	Maj-21st	2	2	Jan. 28, 2003

4th TRANSPORTATION AND INFRASTRUCTURE
Dates: Jan. 26, 2005-Jan. 3, 2007
Departure: Left the House; lost nomination for Governor

Cong.	Ranking	Terms in: House	Comm.	Date of Assignment
109th	Maj-31st	3	1	Jan. 26, 2005

Doug Ose (R-Cal.)

Dates: June 27, 1955
House: Jan. 3, 1999-Jan. 3, 2005
Left the House: Retired in 2004

HOUSE STANDING COMMITTEES:

1st AGRICULTURE
Dates: Jan. 6, 1999-Jan. 3, 2005
Departure: Left the House; retired

Cong.	Ranking	Terms in: House	Comm.	Date of Assignment
106th	Maj-25th	1	1	Jan. 6, 1999
107th	Maj-17th	2	2	Jan. 6, 2001
108th	Maj-11th	3	3	Jan. 28, 2003

2nd BANKING AND FINANCIAL SERVICES, 106
FINANCIAL SERVICES, 107-108
Dates: Jan. 6, 1999-Jan. 3, 2005
Departure: Left the House; retired

Cong.	Ranking	Terms in: House	Comm.	Date of Assignment
106th	Maj-27th	1	1	Jan. 6, 1999
107th	Maj-23rd	2	2	Jan. 6, 2001
108th	Maj-18th	3	3	Jan. 28, 2003

3rd GOVERNMENT REFORM
Dates: Jan. 6, 1999-Jan. 3, 2005
Departure: Left the House; retired

Cong.	Ranking	Terms in: House	Comm.	Date of Assignment
106th	Maj-22nd	1	1	Jan. 6, 1999
107th	Maj-16th	2	2	Jan. 6, 2001
108th	Maj-9th	3	3	Jan. 28, 2003

C.L. (Butch) Otter (R-Ida.)

Dates: May 3, 1942
House: Jan. 3, 2001-Jan. 3, 2007
Left the House: Elected Governor in 2006

HOUSE STANDING COMMITTEES:

1st RESOURCES
Dates: Jan. 6, 2001-Jan. 3, 2003
Departure: Moved to Energy and Commerce

Cong.	Ranking	Terms in: House	Comm.	Date of Assignment
107th	Maj-27th	1	1	Jan. 6, 2001

2nd TRANSPORTATION AND INFRASTRUCTURE
Dates: Jan. 6, 2001-Jan. 3, 2003
Departure: Moved to Energy and Commerce

Cong.	Ranking	Terms in: House	Comm.	Date of Assignment
107th	Maj-39th	1	1	Jan. 6, 2001

3rd GOVERNMENT REFORM
Dates: Feb. 8, 2001-Jan. 3, 2003
Departure: Moved to Energy and Commerce

Cong.	Ranking	Terms in: House	Comm.	Date of Assignment
107th	Maj-24th	1	1	Feb. 8, 2001

4th ENERGY AND COMMERCE
Dates: Jan. 28, 2003-Jan. 3, 2007
Departure: Left the House; elected Governor

Cong.	Ranking	Terms in: House	Comm.	Date of Assignment
108th	Maj-31st	2	1	Jan. 28, 2003
109th	Maj-26th	3	2	Jan. 6, 2005

Major R. Owens (D-N.Y.)

Dates: June 28, 1936
House: Jan. 3, 1983-Jan. 3, 2007
Left the House: Retired in 2006

HOUSE STANDING COMMITTEES:

1st EDUCATION AND LABOR, 103
ECONOMIC AND EDUCATIONAL OPPORTUNITIES, 104
EDUCATION AND THE WORKFORCE, 105-109
Dates: Jan. 6, 1983-Jan. 3, 2007
Departure: Left the House; retired

Cong.	Ranking	Terms in: House	Comm.	Date of Assignment
103rd	Maj-8th	6	6	Jan. 5, 1993
104th	Min-6th	7	7	Jan. 4, 1995
105th	Min-5th	8	8	Jan. 7, 1997
106th	Min-5th	9	9	Jan. 6, 1999
107th	Min-3rd	10	10	Jan. 31, 2001
108th	Min-3rd	11	11	Jan. 28, 2003
109th	Min-3rd	12	12	Jan. 26, 2005

2nd GOVERNMENT OPERATIONS, 98-103
GOVERNMENT REFORM AND OVERSIGHT, 104-105
GOVERNMENT REFORM, 106-109
Dates: Jan. 6, 1983-Jan. 3, 2007
Departure: Left the House; retired

Cong.	Ranking	Terms in: House	Comm.	Date of Assignment
103rd	Maj-8th	6	6	Jan. 5, 1993
104th	Min-5th	7	7	Jan. 9, 1995
105th	Min-4th	8	8	Jan. 7, 1997
106th	Min-4th	9	9	Jan. 6, 1999
107th	Min-3rd	10	10	Jan. 31, 2001
108th	Min-3rd	11	11	Jan. 28, 2003
109th	Min-3rd	12	12	Jan. 26, 2005

William L. Owens (D-N.Y.)

Dates: Jan. 20, 1949-date
House: Nov. 3, 2009-date
Serving in the 111th Congress

H: Owens was elected to the 111th Congress by special election, Nov. 3, 2009, to fill the vacancy caused by the resignation of U.S. Representative John McHugh (R-N.Y.) who was appointed Secretary of the Army. Owens was seated Nov. 6, 2009, and assigned to committees.

HOUSE STANDING COMMITTEES

1st ARMED SERVICES
Dates: Nov. 19,2009-date
Departure: Still serving in the 111th Congress

Cong.	Ranking	Terms in: House	Comm.	Date of Assignment
111th	MjR-2nd	1	1	Nov. 19, 2009

2nd HOMELAND SECURITY
Dates: Nov. 19,2009-date
Departure: Still serving in the 111th Congress

Cong.	Ranking	Terms in: House	Comm.	Date of Assignment
111th	MjA-21st	1	1	Nov. 19, 2009

3rd AGRICULTURE
Dates: May 6. 2010-date
Departure: Still serving in the 111th Congress

Cong.	Ranking	Terms in: House	Comm.	Date of Assignment
111th	MjR-2nd	1	1	May 6. 2010

Michael G. Oxley (R-Ohio)

Dates: Feb. 11, 1944
House: June 25, 1981-Jan. 3, 2007
Left the House: Retired in 2006

H: Oxley was elected to the 97th Congress by special election, June 25, 1981, to fill the vacancy caused by the death of U.S. Representative Tennyson Guyer (R-Ohio). Oxley was seated July 21, 1981, and assigned to committees.

HOUSE STANDING COMMITTEES:

1st GOVERNMENT OPERATIONS
Dates: Sep. 16, 1981-Jan. 3, 1983
Departure: Moved to Energy and Commerce

2nd ENERGY AND COMMERCE, 98-103
COMMERCE, 104-106
Dates: Jan. 6, 1983-Jan. 3, 2003
Departure: Moved to Financial Services

Cong.	Ranking	Terms in: House	Comm.	Date of Assignment
103rd	Min-4th	7	6	Jan. 5, 1993
104th	Maj-4th	8	7	Jan. 4, 1995
105th	Maj-3rd	9	8	Jan. 7, 1997
106th	Maj-3rd	10	9	Jan. 6, 1999

2nd FINANCIAL SERVICES
Dates: Jan. 6, 2001-Jan. 3, 2007
Departure: Left the House; retired

Cong.	Ranking	Terms in: House	Comm.	Date of Assignment
107th	Maj-Chr	11	1	Jan. 6, 2001
108th	Maj-Chr	12	2	Jan. 8, 2003
109th	Maj-Chr	13	3	Jan. 6, 2005

HOUSE SELECT AND SPECIAL COMMITTEES:

1st SELECT NARCOTICS ABUSE AND CONTROL (Temporary)
Dates: Sep. 16, 1981-Jan. 3, 1993
Termination: Committee not renewed in 1993

P

Ronald C. Packard (R-Cal.)

Dates: Jan. 19, 1931
House: Jan. 3, 1983-Jan. 3, 2001
Left the House: Retired in 2000

HOUSE STANDING COMMITTEES:

1st EDUCATION AND LABOR
Dates: Jan. 6, 1983-Jan. 3, 1985
Departure: Moved to Science and Technology

2nd PUBLIC WORKS AND TRANSPORTATION
Dates: Jan. 6, 1983-Jan. 3, 1993
Departure: Moved to Appropriations

3rd SCIENCE AND TECHNOLOGY, 99
SCIENCE, SPACE AND TECHNOLOGY, 100-102
Dates: Jan. 30, 1985-Jan. 3, 1993
Departure: Moved to Appropriations

4th APPROPRIATIONS
Dates: Jan. 5, 1993-Jan. 3, 2001
Departure: Left the House; retired

Cong.	Ranking	Terms in: House	Comm.	Date of Assignment
103rd	Min-16th	6	1	Jan. 5, 1993
104th	Maj-15th	7	2	Jan. 4, 1995
105th	Maj-12th	8	3	Jan. 7, 1997
106th	Maj-10th	9	4	Jan. 6, 1999

HOUSE SELECT AND SPECIAL COMMITTEES:

1st SELECT CHILDREN, YOUTH AND FAMILIES (Temporary)
Dates: Feb. 2, 1987-Jan. 3, 1991
Departure: Left committee; no new assignment

Robert W. Packwood (R-Ore.)

Dates: Sept. 11, 1932
Senate: Jan. 3, 1969-Oct. 1, 1995
Left the Senate: Resigned and retired in 1995

SENATE STANDING COMMITTEES:

1st BANKING AND CURRENCY renamed Jan 29, 1971as
BANKING, HOUSING AND URBAN AFFAIRS
Dates: Jan. 14, 1969-Feb. 22, 1977
Departure: Moved to Commerce, Science and Transportation.

2nd PUBLIC WORKS
Dates: Jan. 14, 1969-Jan. 29, 1971
Departure: Moved to Labor and Public Welfare.

3rd LABOR AND PUBLIC WELFARE
Dates: Jan. 29, 1971-Jan. 12, 1973
Departure: Moved to Finance

4th FINANCE
Dates: Jan. 12, 1973-Sep. 8, 1995
Ch1: Succeeded as Chair by William V. Roth (R-Del.) on Sep. 12, 1995
Departure: Resigned the Senate; retired

Cong.	Ranking	Years in: Senate	Comm.	Date of Assignment
103rd	Min-RM	25	20	Jan. 7, 1993
104th	Maj-Ch1	27	22	Jan. 4, 1995

5th COMMERCE, SCIENCE AND TRANSPORTATION
Dates: Feb. 22, 1977-Oct. 1, 1995
Departure: Resigned the Senate; retired

Cong.	Ranking	Years in: Senate	Comm.	Date of Assignment
103rd	Min-2nd	25	16	Jan. 7, 1993
104th	Maj-2nd	27	18	Jan. 4, 1995

6th BUDGET
Dates: Jan. 23, 1979-Jan. 5, 1981
Departure: Left committee; became Chair of Commerce, Science and Transportation

7th SMALL BUSINESS
Dates: Mar. 25, 1981-Feb. 21, 1985
Departure: Left committee; became Chair of Finance

SENATE SELECT AND SPECIAL COMMITTEES:

1st SELECT SMALL BUSINESS
Dates: June 13, 1975-Mar. 25, 1981
Departure: Continued on reorganized standing committee.

2nd SELECT SENATE COMMITTEE SYSTEM I (Stevenson)
Dates: Apr. 6, 1976-May 17, 1977
Termination: Last reports filed.

3rd SELECT OFFICIAL CONDUCT
Dates: Jan. 19, 1977-Mar. 10, 1977
Termination: Senate Report 49 (95-1) filed

JOINT COMMITTEES:

1st JOINT TAXATION
Senate Dates: Feb. 8, 1979-Oct. 1, 1995
Vice Chair/Chair: 98th, 1983-85
Departure: Resigned the Senate; retired

Cong.	Ranking	Years in: Senate	Comm.	Date of Assignment
103rd	Min-1st	25	14	Continued
104th	Maj-VC1	27	16	Feb. 2, 1995

Frank Pallone Jr. (D-N.J.)

Dates: Oct. 30, 1951
House: Nov. 8, 1988-date
Serving in the 111th Congress

H: Pallone was elected to the 100th Congress by special election, Nov. 8, 1988, to fill the vacancy caused by the death of U.S. Representative James J. Howard (D-N.J.). Pallone was not seated nor assigned to committees because the 100th Congress was not in session.

HOUSE STANDING COMMITTEES:

1st MERCHANT MARINE AND FISHERIES
Dates: Jan. 19, 1989-Jan. 3, 1995
Departure: Committee abolished; no new assignment

Cong.	Ranking	Terms in: House	Comm.	Date of Assignment
103rd	Maj-10th	4	3	Jan. 5, 1993

2nd PUBLIC WORKS AND TRANSPORTATION
Dates: Jan. 19, 1989-Jan. 3, 1993
Departure: Moved to Energy and Commerce

3rd ENERGY AND COMMERCE, 103
COMMERCE, 104-106
ENERGY AND COMMERCE, 107-111
1st Dates: Jan. 5, 1993-Jan. 3, 1997
1st Departure: Left committee; no new assignment
2nd Dates: Returned Feb. 13. 1997-date
2nd Departure: Still serving in the 111th Congress

Cong.	Ranking	Terms in: House	Comm.	Date of Assignment
103rd	Maj-21st	4 *1	1	Jan. 5, 1993
104th	Min-12th	5 *1	2	Jan. 4, 1995
105th	MnR-1st	6 *2	1	Feb. 13, 1997
106th	Min-7th	7 *2	2	Jan. 6, 1999
107th	Min-7th	8 *2	3	Jan. 31, 2001
108th	Min-7th	9 *2	4	Jan. 28, 2003
109th	Min-6th	10 *2	5	Jan. 26, 2005
110th	Maj-6th	11 *2	6	Jan. 4, 2007
111th	Maj-5th	12 *2	7	Jan. 7, 2009

3rd RESOURCES, 104-109
NATURAL RESOURCES, 110-111
Dates: June 13, 1995-date
Departure: Still serving in the 111th Congress

Cong.	Ranking	Terms in: House	Comm.	Date of Assignment
104th	MnA-21st	5	1	June 13, 1995
105th	Min-13th	6	2	Jan. 7, 1997
106th	Min-10th	7	3	Jan. 6, 1999
107th	Min-9th	8	4	Feb. 8, 2001
108th	Min-9th	9	5	Jan. 28, 2003
109th	Min-6th	10	6	Jan. 26, 2005
110th	Maj-6th	11	7	Jan. 18, 2007
111th	Maj-5th	12	8	Jan. 21, 2009

HOUSE SELECT AND SPECIAL COMMITTEES:

1st SELECT AGING (Permanent)
Dates: Mar. 8, 1989-Jan. 3, 1993
Termination: Committee not renewed in 1993

Leon E. Panetta (D-Cal.)

Dates: June 28, 1938
House: Jan. 3, 1977-Jan. 21, 1993
Left the House: Resigned; appointed Director of the Office of Management and Budget

HOUSE STANDING COMMITTEES:

1st AGRICULTURE
Dates: Jan. 19, 1977-Jan. 21, 1993
Departure: Left the House; appointed to federal post

Cong.	Ranking	Terms in: House	Comm.	Date of Assignment
103rd	Maj-5th	9	9	Jan. 5, 1993

2nd HOUSE ADMINISTRATION
1st Dates: Jan. 19, 1977-Jan. 3, 1979
1st Departure: Ceased active service to move to Budget; later returned with continuous seniority credited
2nd Dates: Jan. 30, 1985-Jan. 3, 1993
2nd Departure: Left committee; no new assignment

3rd BUDGET
1st Dates: Jan. 24, 1979-Jan. 3, 1985
1st Departure: Returned to House Administration
2nd Dates: Jan. 3, 1989-Jan. 21, 1993
Ch1: Replaced by Martin Olav Sabo (DFL-Minn.) on Jan. 25, 1993
2nd Departure: Left the House; appointed to federal post

Cong.	Ranking	Terms in: House	Comm.	Date of Assignment
103rd	Maj-Ch1	9	3	Jan. 5, 1993

HOUSE SELECT AND SPECIAL COMMITTEES:

1st SELECT HUNGER (Temporary)
Dates: Mar. 13, 1984-Jan. 3, 1993
Termination: Committee not renewed in 1993

JOINT COMMITTEES:

1st JOINT PRINTING
House Dates: Feb. 10, 1987-Jan. 3, 1989
Departure: Returned to Budget as Chair

Michael J. Pappas (R-N.J.)

Dates: Dec. 29, 1960
House: Jan. 3, 1997-Jan. 3, 1999
Left the House: Defeated for re-election in 1998

HOUSE STANDING COMMITTEES:

1st GOVERNMENT REFORM AND OVERSIGHT
Dates: Jan. 7, 1997-Jan. 3, 1999
Departure: Left the House; lost re-election

Cong.	Ranking	Terms in: House	Comm.	Date of Assignment
105th	Maj-22nd	1	1	Jan. 7, 1997

2nd NATIONAL SECURITY
Dates: Jan. 7, 1997-Jan. 3, 1999
Departure: Left the House; lost re-election

Cong.	Ranking	Terms in: House	Comm.	Date of Assignment
105th	Maj-28th	1	1	Jan. 7, 1997

3rd SMALL BUSINESS
Dates: Jan. 21, 1997-Jan. 3, 1999
Departure: Left the House; lost re-election

Cong.	Ranking	Terms in: House	Comm.	Date of Assignment
105th	Maj-14th	1	1	Jan. 21, 1997

Michael Parker (R-Miss.)

Dates: Oct. 31, 1949
House: Jan. 3, 1989-Jan. 3, 1999
Left the House: Retired in 1998; lost for Governor in 2000
Served as a Democrat: Jan. 3, 1989-Nov. 10, 1995
Served as a Republican: Nov. 10, 1995-Jan. 3, 1999

HOUSE STANDING COMMITTEES:

1st PUBLIC WORKS AND TRANSPORTATION, 103
TRANSPORTATION AND INFRASTRUCTURE, 104
Dates: Jan. 19, 1989-Nov. 13, 1995 as a Democrat
Departure: Assignment was vacated as a Democrat; moved to Appropriations as a Republican on Mar. 14, 1996

Cong.	Ranking	Terms in: House	Comm.	Date of Assignment
103rd	Maj-15th	3	3	Jan. 5, 1993
104th	Min-12th	4	4	Jan. 4, 1995

2nd VETERANS AFFAIRS
Dates: Jan. 19, 1989-Jan. 3, 1991
Departure: Moved to Budget

3rd BUDGET
1st Dates: Jan. 24, 1991-Nov. 13, 1995 as a Democrat
1st Departure: Assignment was vacated by Democratic Caucus; later moved to Appropriations
2nd Dates: Jan. 7, 1997-Jan. 3, 1999 as a Republican
2nd Departure: Left the House; later lost election for Governor

Cong.	Ranking	Terms in: House	Comm.	Date of Assignment
103rd	Maj-14th	3 *1	2	Jan. 5, 1993
104th	Min-4th	4 *1	3	Jan. 4, 1995
105th	Maj-18th	5 *2	1	Jan. 7, 1997

4th APPROPRIATIONS
Dates: Mar. 14, 1996-Jan. 3, 1999 as a Republican
Departure: Left the House; later lost election for Governor

Cong.	Ranking	Terms in: House	Comm.	Assignment
104th	MjA-33rd	4	1	Mar. 14, 1996
105th	Maj-23rd	5	2	Jan. 7, 1997

5th EDUCATION AND THE WORKFORCE
Dates: May 13, 1998-Jan. 3, 1999
Departure: Left the House; later lost election for Governor

Cong.	Ranking	Terms in: House	Comm.	Date of Assignment
105th	MjR-1st	5	1	May 13, 1998

William J. Pascrell Jr. (D-N.J.)

Dates: Jan. 27, 1937
House: Jan. 3, 1997-date
Serving in the 111th Congress

HOUSE STANDING COMMITTEES:

1st SMALL BUSINESS
Dates: Feb. 5, 1997-Feb. 12, 2003
Departure: Resigned committee; moved to Select Homeland Security

Cong.	Ranking	Terms in: House	Comm.	Date of Assignment
105th	Min-15th	1	1	Feb. 5, 1997
106th	Min-6th	2	2	Jan. 6, 1999
107th	Min-5th	3	3	Jan. 31, 2001
108th	Min-4th	4	4	Jan. 28, 2003

2nd TRANSPORTATION AND INFRASTRUCTURE
Dates: Jan. 7, 1997-Jan. 3, 2007
Departure: Moved to Ways and Means

Cong.	Ranking	Terms in: House	Comm.	Date of Assignment
105th	Min-27th	1	1	Jan. 7, 1997
106th	Min-25th	2	2	Jan. 6, 1999
107th	Min-22nd	3	3	Jan. 31, 2001
108th	Min-17th	4	4	Jan. 28, 2003
109th	Min-16th	5	5	Jan. 26, 2005

3rd HOMELAND SECURITY
1st Dates: Feb. 9, 2005-Jan. 3, 2007
1st Departure: Moved to Ways and Means
2nd Dates: Sep. 20, 2007-date
2nd Departure: Still serving in the 111th Congress

Cong.	Ranking	Terms in: House	Comm.	Date of Assignment
109th	Min-11th	5 *1	2	Feb. 9, 2005
110th	Maj-19th	6 *2	1	Sep. 20, 2007
111th	Maj-14th	7 *2	2	Jan. 28, 2009

4th WAYS AND MEANS
Dates: Jan. 4, 2007-date
Departure: Still serving in the 111th Congress

Cong.	Ranking	Terms in: House	Comm.	Date of Assignment
110th	Maj-18th	6	1	Jan. 4, 2007
111th	Maj-15th	7	2	Jan. 7, 2009

HOUSE SELECT AND SPECIAL COMMITTEES:

1st SELECT HOMELAND SECURITY
Dates: Feb. 12, 2003-Jan. 3, 2005
Departure: Continued on reorganized standing committee

Cong.	Ranking	Terms in: House	Comm.	Date of Assignment
108th	Min-17th	4	1	Feb. 12, 2003

Edward L. Pastor (D-Ariz.)

Dates: June 28, 1943
House: Sept. 24, 1991-date
Serving in the 111th Congress

H: Pastor was elected to the 102nd Congress by special election, Sept. 24, 1991, to fill the vacancy caused by the resignation of U.S. Representative Morris K. Udall (D-Ariz.). Pastor was seated Oct. 3, 1991, and assigned to committees.

HOUSE STANDING COMMITTEES:

1st EDUCATION AND LABOR
Dates: Oct. 9, 1991-Jan. 3, 1993
Departure: Moved to Appropriations

2nd SMALL BUSINESS
Dates: Oct. 9, 1991-Jan. 3, 1993
Departure: Moved to Appropriations

3rd APPROPRIATIONS
1st Dates: Jan. 5, 1993-Jan. 3, 1995
1st Departure: Moved to Agriculture and House Oversight
2nd Dates: Jan. 7, 1997-date
2nd Departure: Still serving in the 111th Congress

Cong.	Ranking	Terms in: House	Comm.	Date of Assignment
103rd	Maj-36th	2 *1	1	Jan. 5, 1993
105th	Min-23rd	4 *2	1	Jan. 7, 1997
106th	Min-16th	5 *2	2	Jan. 6, 1999
107th	Min-15th	6 *2	3	Jan. 31, 2001
108th	Min-14th	7 *2	4	Jan. 28, 2003
109th	Min-14th	8 *2	5	Jan. 26, 2005
110th	Maj-12th	9 *2	6	Jan. 4, 2007
111th	Maj-12th	10 *2	7	Jan. 7, 2009

4th AGRICULTURE
Dates: Jan. 4, 1995-Jan. 3, 1997
Departure: Returned to Appropriations

Cong.	Ranking	Terms in: House	Comm.	Date of Assignment
104th	Min-21st	3	1	Jan. 4, 1995

5th HOUSE OVERSIGHT
Dates: Jan. 4, 1995-Jan. 3, 1997
Departure: Returned to Appropriations

Cong.	Ranking	Terms in: House	Comm.	Date of Assignment
104th	Min-5th	3	1	Jan. 4, 1995

6th STANDARDS OF OFFICIAL CONDUCT
Dates: Sep. 29, 1997-Jan. 3, 2003
Departure: Left committee; no new assignment

Cong.	Ranking	Terms in: House	Comm.	Date of Assignment
105th	Min-3rd	4	1	Sep. 29, 1997
106th	Min-3rd	5	2	Jan. 6, 1999
107th	Min-3rd	6	3	Mar. 6, 2001

HOUSE SELECT AND SPECIAL COMMITTEES:

1st SELECT AGING (Permanent)
Dates: Mar. 4, 1992-Jan. 3, 1993
Termination: Committee not renewed in 1993

JOINT COMMITTEES:

1st JOINT LIBRARY
House Dates: Feb. 23, 1995-Jan. 3, 1997
Departure: Returned to Appropriations

Cong.	Ranking	Terms in: House	Comm.	Date of Assignment
104th	Min-2nd	3	1	Feb. 23, 1995

Ronald E. Paul (R-Tex.)

Dates: Aug. 20, 1935
House 1: April 3, 1976-Jan. 3, 1977
Left the House 1: Defeated for re-election in 1976
House 2: Jan. 3, 1979-Jan. 3, 1985
Left the House 2: Lost U.S. Senate nomination in 1984
House 3: Jan. 3, 1997-date
Serving in the 111th Congress

H1: Paul was elected to the 94th Congress by special election, April 3, 1976, to fill the vacancy caused by the resignation of U.S. Representative Bob Casey (D-Tex.). Paul was seated April 7, 1976, and assigned to committees.

HOUSE STANDING COMMITTEES:

1st BANKING, CURRENCY AND HOUSING, 94
BANKING, FINANCE AND URBAN AFFAIRS, 96-98
BANKING AND FINANCIAL SERVICES, 105-106
FINANCIAL SERVICES, 107-110
1st Dates: Apr. 14, 1976-Jan. 3, 1977
1st Departure: Left the House; lost re-election
2nd Dates: Jan. 24, 1979-Jan. 3, 1985
2nd Departure: Left the House; lost Senate nomination
3rd Dates: Jan. 7, 1997-date
3rd Departure: Still serving in the 111th Congress

Cong.	Ranking	Terms in: House	Comm.	Date of Assignment
105th	Maj-21st	5 *3	1	Jan. 7, 1997
106th	Maj-17th	6 *3	2	Jan. 6, 1999
107th	Maj-14th	7 *3	3	Jan. 6, 2001
108th	Maj-12th	8 *3	4	Jan. 28, 2003
109th	Maj-12th	9 *3	5	Jan. 26, 2005
110th	Min-8th	10 *3	6	Jan. 10, 2007
111th	Min-6th	11 *3	7	Jan. 9, 2009

2nd HOUSE ADMINISTRATION
Dates: Apr. 14, 1976-Jan. 3, 1977
Departure: Left the House; lost re-election

3rd EDUCATION AND THE WORKFORCE
Dates: Jan. 7, 1997-Jan. 3, 2001
Departure: Moved to International Relations

Cong.	Ranking	Terms in: House	Comm.	Date of Assignment
105th	Maj-19th	5	1	Jan. 7, 1997
106th	Maj-17th	6	2	Jan. 6, 1999

4th INTERNATIONAL RELATIONS, 107-109
FOREIGN AFFAIRS, 110-111
Dates: Jan. 6, 2001-date
Departure: Still serving in the 111th Congress

Cong.	Ranking	Terms in: House	Comm.	Date of Assignment
107th	Maj-19th	7	1	Jan. 6, 2001
108th	Maj-16th	8	2	Jan. 28, 2003

109th	Maj-13th	9	3	Jan. 26, 2005
110th	Min-10th	10	4	Jan. 10, 2007
111th	Min-8th	11	5	Jan. 9, 2009

JOINT COMMITTEES:

1st JOINT ECONOMIC
House Dates: Feb. 25, 2003-date
Departure: Still serving in the 111th Congress

Cong.	Ranking	Terms in: House	Comm.	Date of Assignment
108th	Maj-6th	8	1	Feb. 25, 2003
109th	Maj-4th	9	2	Mar. 3, 2005
110th	Min-4th	10	3	Mar. 27, 2007
111th	Min-2nd	11	4	Feb. 3, 2009

Erik Paulsen (R-Minn.)

Dates: May 14, 1965
House: Jan. 3, 2009-date
Serving in the 111th Congress

HOUSE STANDING COMMITTEES:

1st FINANCIAL SERVICES
Dates: Jan. 9, 2009-date
Departure: Still serving in the 111th Congress

Cong.	Ranking	Terms in: House	Comm.	Date of Assignment
111th	Min-28th	1	1	Jan. 9, 2009

L. William Paxon (R-N.Y.)

Dates: April 29, 1954
House: Jan. 3, 1989-Jan. 3, 1999
Left the House: Retired in 1998

HOUSE STANDING COMMITTEES:

1st BANKING, FINANCE AND URBAN AFFAIRS
Dates: Jan. 20, 1989-Jan. 3, 1993
Departure: Moved to Energy and Commerce

2nd VETERANS AFFAIRS
Dates: May 4, 1989-Jan. 3, 1993
Departure: Moved to Energy and Commerce

3rd BUDGET
Dates: July 9, 1991-Jan. 3, 1993
Departure: Moved to Energy and Commerce

4th ENERGY AND COMMERCE, 103
COMMERCE, 104-105
Dates: Jan. 5, 1993-Jan. 3, 1999
Departure: Left the House; retired

Cong.	Ranking	Terms in: House	Comm.	Date of Assignment
103rd	Min-12th	3	1	Jan. 5, 1993
104th	Maj-11th	4	2	Jan. 4, 1995
105th	Maj-10th	5	3	Jan. 7, 1997

HOUSE SELECT AND SPECIAL COMMITTEES:

1st SELECT NARCOTICS ABUSE AND CONTROL (Temporary)
Dates: Apr. 10, 1989-Jan. 3, 1993
Termination: Committee not renewed in 1993

Donald M. Payne (D-N.J.)

Dates: July 16, 1934
House: Jan. 3, 1989-date
Left the House: Serving in the 111th Congress

HOUSE STANDING COMMITTEES:

1st EDUCATION AND LABOR, 101-103
ECONOMIC AND EDUCATIONAL OPPORTUNITIES, 104
EDUCATION AND THE WORKFORCE, 105-109
EDUCATION AND LABOR, 110-111
Dates: Jan. 19, 1989-date
Departure: Still serving in the 111th Congress

Cong.	Ranking	Terms in: House	Comm.	Date of Assignment
103rd	Maj-10th	3	3	Jan. 5, 1993
104th	Min-8th	4	4	Jan. 4, 1995
105th	Min-6th	5	5	Jan. 7, 1997
106th	Min-6th	6	6	Jan. 6, 1999
107th	Min-4th	7	7	Jan. 31, 2001
108th	Min-4th	8	8	Jan. 28, 2003
109th	Min-4th	9	9	Jan. 26, 2005
110th	Maj-3rd	10	10	Jan. 10, 2007
111th	Maj-3rd	11	11	Jan. 21, 2009

2nd GOVERNMENT OPERATIONS
1st Dates: Jan. 19, 1989-Jan. 3, 1993
1st Departure: Left committee; no new assignment
2nd Dates: Returned as a replacement, Jan. 21, 1993-Jan. 3, 1995
2nd Departure: Left committee; no new assignment

Cong.	Ranking	Terms in: House	Comm.	Date of Assignment
103rd	MjR-1st	3 *2	1	Jan. 21, 1993

3rd FOREIGN AFFAIRS, 101-103
INTERNATIONAL RELATIONS, 104-109
FOREIGN AFFAIRS, 110-111
Temporary Dates: Jan. 27, 1989-Jan. 3, 1991
Departure: Became a permanent member
Dates: Jan. 24, 1991-date
Departure: Still serving in the 111th Congress

Cong.	Ranking	Terms in: House	Comm.	Date of Assignment
103rd	Maj-14th	3	3	Jan. 5, 1993
104th	Min-11th	4	4	Jan. 4, 1995
105th	Min-8th	5	5	Jan. 7, 1997
106th	Min-7th	6	6	Jan. 6, 1999
107th	Min-5th	7	7	Jan. 31, 2001
108th	Min-5th	8	8	Jan. 28, 2003
109th	Min-5th	9	9	Jan. 26, 2005
110th	Maj-5th	10	10	Jan. 12, 2007
111th	Maj-4th	11	11	Jan. 21, 2009

HOUSE SELECT AND SPECIAL COMMITTEES:

1st SELECT NARCOTICS ABUSE AND CONTROL (Temporary)
Dates: July 19, 1990-Jan. 3, 1993
Termination: Committee not renewed in 1993

Lewis F. Payne Jr. (D-Va.)

Dates: July 9, 1945
House: June 14, 1988-Jan. 3, 1997
Left the House: Retired in 1996

H: Lewis Payne was elected to the 100th Congress by special election, June 14, 1988, to fill the vacancy caused by the death of U.S. Representative Dan Daniel (D-Va.). He was seated June 21, 1988, and was assigned to committees.

HOUSE STANDING COMMITTEES:

1st PUBLIC WORKS AND TRANSPORTATION
Dates: July 13, 1988-Jan. 3, 1993
Departure: Moved to Ways and Means

2nd VETERANS AFFAIRS
Dates: Oct. 6, 1988-Jan. 3, 1991
Departure: Moved to Budget

3rd BUDGET
Dates: Jan. 24, 1991-Jan. 3, 1993
Departure: Moved to Ways and Means

4th WAYS AND MEANS
Dates: Jan. 5, 1993-Jan. 3, 1997
Departure: Left the House; retired

Cong.	Ranking	Terms in: House	Comm.	Date of Assignment
103rd	Maj-17th	4	1	Jan. 5, 1993
104th	Min-14th	5	2	Jan. 4, 1995

Stevan Pearce (R-N.M.)

Dates: Aug. 14, 1947
House: Jan. 3, 2003-Jan. 3, 2009
Left the House: Lost Senate election in 2008

HOUSE STANDING COMMITTEES:

1st RESOURCES, 108-109
NATURAL RESOURCES, 110
Dates: Jan. 28, 2003-Jan. 3, 2009
Departure: Left the House; lost Senate election

Cong.	Ranking	Terms in: House	Comm.	Date of Assignment
108th	Maj-26th	1	1	Jan. 28, 2003
109th	Maj-20th	2	2	Jan. 26, 2005
110th	Min-11th	3	3	Jan. 10, 2007

2nd TRANSPORTATION AND INFRASTRUCTURE
Dates: Jan. 28, 2003-Feb. 9, 2005
Departure: Resigned committee; moved to Financial Services and Homeland Security

Cong.	Ranking	Terms in: House	Comm.	Date of Assignment
108th	Maj-38th	1	1	Jan. 28, 2003
109th	Maj-27th	2	2	Jan. 26, 2005

3rd FINANCIAL SERVICES
Dates: Feb. 2, 2005-Jan. 3, 2009
Departure: Left the House; lost Senate election

Cong.	Ranking	Terms in: House	Comm.	Date of Assignment
109th	Maj-32nd	2	1	Feb. 2, 2005
110th	Min-24th	3	2	Jan. 10, 2007

4th HOMELAND SECURITY
Dates: Feb. 9, 2005-Jan. 3, 2007
Departure: Left committee; no new assignment

Cong.	Ranking	Terms in: House	Comm.	Date of Assignment
109th	Maj-14th	2	1	Feb. 9, 2005

Edward A. Pease (R-Ind.)

Dates: May 22, 1951
House: Jan. 3, 1997-Jan. 3, 2001
Left the House: Retired in 2000

HOUSE STANDING COMMITTEES:

1st JUDICIARY
Dates: Jan. 7, 1997-Jan. 3, 2001
Departure: Left the House, retired

Cong.	Ranking	Terms in: House	Comm.	Date of Assignment
105th	Maj-19th	1	1	Jan. 7, 1997
106th	Maj-16th	2	2	Jan. 6, 1999

2nd TRANSPORTATION AND INFRASTRUCTURE
Dates: Jan. 7, 1997-Jan. 3, 2001
Departure: Left the House, retired

Cong.	Ranking	Terms in: House	Comm.	Date of Assignment
105th	Maj-28th	1	1	Jan. 7, 1997
106th	Maj-24th	2	2	Jan. 6, 1999

3rd SMALL BUSINESS
Dates: Feb. 2, 1999-Jan. 3, 2001
Departure: Left the House; retired

Cong.	Ranking	Terms in: House	Comm.	Date of Assignment
106th	Maj-17th	2	1	Feb. 2, 1999

Claiborne D. Pell (D-R.I.)

Dates: Nov. 22, 1918-Jan. 1, 2009
Senate: Jan. 3, 1961-Jan. 3, 1997
Left the Senate: Retired in 1996

SENATE STANDING COMMITTEES:

1st LABOR AND PUBLIC WELFARE reorganized Feb. 11, 1977
HUMAN RESOURCES renamed Jan. 23, 1979
LABOR AND HUMAN RESOURCES
Dates: Jan. 10, 1961-Jan. 3, 1997
Departure: Left the Senate; retired

Cong.	Ranking	Years in: Senate	Comm.	Date of Assignment
103rd	Maj-2nd	33	32	Jan. 7, 1993
104th	Min-2nd	35	34	Jan. 4, 1995

2nd RULES AND ADMINISTRATION
Dates: Jan. 10, 1961-Jan. 3, 1997
Departure: Left the Senate; retired.

Cong.	Ranking	Years in: Senate	Comm.	Date of Assignment
103rd	Maj-2nd	33	33	Jan. 21, 1993
104th	Min-2nd	35	34	Jan. 6, 1995

3rd GOVERNMENT OPERATIONS
Dates: Feb. 25, 1963-Jan. 8, 1965
Departure: Moved to Foreign Relations

4th FOREIGN RELATIONS
Dates: Jan. 8, 1965-Jan. 3, 1997
Departure: Left the Senate; retired

Cong.	Ranking	Years in: Senate	Comm.	Date of Assignment
103rd	Maj-Chr	33	28	Jan. 7, 1993
104th	Min-RM	35	30	Jan. 4, 1995

SENATE SELECT AND SPECIAL COMMITTEES:

1st SELECT NUTRITION AND HUMAN NEEDS
Dates: Jan. 23, 1969-Jan. 28, 1971
Departure: Moved to Special Aging

2nd SPECIAL AGING (Permanent)
Became Permanent Special Committee on Aging, Feb. 4, 1977
1st Dates: Jan. 28, 1971-Jan. 4, 1973
1st Departure: Left committee; later returned
2nd Dates: Jan. 18, 1973-Feb. 11, 1977
2nd Departure: Left committee; no new assignment

3rd SELECT SMALL BUSINESS
Dates: Jan. 4, 1973-Jan. 18, 1973
Departure: Left committee; no new assignment.

4th SELECT TERMINATION OF NATIONAL EMERGENCY
Dates: Sep. 18, 1972-Mar. 1, 1974 renamed
SELECT NATIONAL EMERGENCIES AND DELEGATED POWERS
Dates: Mar. 1, 1974-May 28, 1976
Termination: Senate Report 922 (94-2) filed

5th FOREIGN GOVERNMENT REPRESENTATION
Dates: July 25, 1980-Oct. 2, 1980
Termination: Senate Report 1015 (96-2) filed

6th SPECIAL SECURITY AND COOPERATION IN EUROPE
Dates: Jan. 31, 1984-Mar. 27, 1985
Termination: Public Law 99-7

JOINT COMMITTEES:

1st JOINT ECONOMIC
Senate Dates: Jan. 26, 1961-Jan. 12, 1965
Departure: Left committee; no new assignment

2nd JOINT LIBRARY
1st Senate Dates: Jan. 31, 1961-Feb. 16, 1983
1st Departure: Moved to Joint Printing
2nd Senate Dates: Apr. 17, 1985-Jan. 3, 1997
2nd Departure: Left the Senate; retired

Cong.	Ranking	Years in: Senate	Comm.	Date of Assignment
103rd	Maj-VCh	33 *2	8	Jan. 28, 1993
104th	Min-1st	35 *2	10	Jan. 17, 1995

3rd JOINT PRINTING
1st Senate Dates: Jan. 27, 1978-Feb. 5, 1981
1st Departure: Left committee; no new assignment
2nd Senate Dates: Feb. 16, 1983-Apr. 17, 1985
2nd Departure: Returned to Joint Library

Nancy Pelosi (D-Cal.)

Dates: March 26, 1940
House: June 9, 1987-date
Serving in the 111th Congress

H: Pelosi was elected to the 100th Congress by special election, June 2, 1987, to fill the vacancy caused by the death of U.S. Representative Sala Burton (D-Cal.). She was seated June 9, 1987, and was assigned to committees.

HOUSE STANDING COMMITTEES:

1st BANKING, FINANCE AND URBAN AFFAIRS
Dates: June 18, 1987-Jan. 3, 1991
Departure: Moved to Appropriations and Standards of Official Conduct

2nd GOVERNMENT OPERATIONS
Dates: June 18, 1987-Jan. 3, 1991
Departure: Moved to Appropriations and Standards of Official Conduct

3rd APPROPRIATIONS
Dates: Jan. 3, 1991-Jan. 3, 2003
Departure: Elected House Minority Leader

Cong.	Ranking	Terms in: House	Comm.	Date of Assignment
103rd	Maj-24th	4	2	Jan. 5, 1993
104th	Min-19th	5	3	Jan. 4, 1995
105th	Min-14th	6	4	Jan. 7, 1997
106th	Min-9th	7	5	Jan. 6, 1999
107th	Min-8th	8	6	Jan. 31, 2001

4th STANDARDS OF OFFICIAL CONDUCT
Dates: Feb. 6, 1991-Jan. 3, 1997
Departure: Left committee; no new assignment

Cong.	Ranking	Terms in: House	Comm.	Date of Assignment
103rd	Maj-4th	4	2	Feb. 4, 1993
104th	Min-3rd	5	3	Jan. 20, 1995

HOUSE SELECT AND SPECIAL COMMITTEES:

1st PERMANENT SELECT INTELLIGENCE, 103-111
Dates: Feb. 3, 1993-date
Departure: Still serving un the 111th Congress

Cong.	Ranking	Terms in: House	Comm.	Date of Assignment
103rd	Maj-9th	4	1	Feb. 3, 1993
104th	Min-6th	5	2	Jan. 4, 1995
105th	Min-4th	6	3	Feb. 10, 1997
106th	Min-2nd	7	4	Feb. 12, 1999
107th	Min-RM	8	5	Jan. 6, 2001
108th	Min-ExO	9	6	Jan. 8, 2003
109th	Min-ExO	10	7	Jan. 26, 2005
110th	Maj-ExO	11	8	Jan. 5, 2007
111th	Maj-ExO	12	9	Jan. 7, 2009

2nd SELECT ETHICS
Dates: Jan. 7, 1997-Jan. 21, 1997
Termination: House Report 105-1 filed, Jan. 17, 1997

Cong.	Ranking	Terms in: House	Comm.	Date of Assignment
105th	Min-2nd	6	1	Jan. 7, 1997

3rd SELECT HOMELAND SECURITY
Dates: June 19, 2002-Jan. 3, 2003
Departure: Elected Minority Floor Leader

Cong.	Ranking	Terms in: House	Comm.	Date of Assignment
107th	Min-RM	8	1	June 19, 2002

HOUSE LEADERSHIP POSTS

Dates: Jan. 15, 2002-date
Departure: Still serving in the 111th Congress

1st HOUSE MINORITY WHIP
Dates: Jan. 15, 2002-Jan. 3, 2003
Note: In the 107th Congress, Pelosi succeeded Minority Whip David Bonior (D-Mich.) who resigned to seek the Democratic nomination for Governor of Michigan. Pelosi was elected Oct. 10, 2001, on the first ballot over Steny H. Hoyer (D-Md.) 118 to 95. She became Whip on Jan. 15, 2002.
Departure: Elected Minority Floor Leader

Cong.	Ranking	Terms in: House	Post	Date of Selection
107th	Min-2nd	8	1	Jan. 15, 2002

2nd HOUSE MINORITY FLOOR LEADER
Dates: Jan. 3, 2003-Jan. 3, 2007
Note: For the 108th Congress, Pelosi succeeded Minority Leader Richard A. Gephardt (D-Mo.) who resigned to seek the Democratic nomination for president. Pelosi was elected on Nov. 14, 2002 with a first ballot victory over Harold Ford Jr. (D-Tenn.), 177 to 29.
Departure: Elected Speaker of the House

Cong.	Ranking	Terms in: House	Post	Date of Selection
108th	Min-1st	9	1	Nov. 14, 2002
109th	Min-1st	10	2	Nov. 17, 2004

3rd SPEAKER OF THE HOUSE
Dates: Jan. 4, 2007-date
Note: In the 110th Congress, Pelosi was nominated unopposed for Speaker and was elected Speaker over John A. Boehner (R-Ohio), 233 to 202. She was re-elected Speaker over Boehner in the 111th Congress by a vote of 255-174
Departure: Still serving in the 111th Congress

Cong.	Ranking	Terms in: House	Post	Date of Election
110th	Maj-1st	11	1	Jan. 4, 2007
111th	Maj-1st	12	2	Jan. 6, 2009

Mike Pence (R-Ind.)

Dates: June 7, 1959
House: Jan. 3, 2001-date
Serving in the 111th Congress

HOUSE STANDING COMMITTEES:

1st AGRICULTURE
Dates: Jan. 6, 2001-Jan. 3, 2007
Departure: Left committee; no new assignment

Cong.	Ranking	Terms in: House	Comm.	Date of Assignment
107th	Maj-23rd	1	1	Jan. 6, 2001
108th	Maj-16th	2	2	Jan. 28, 2003
109th	Maj-12th	3	3	Jan. 26, 2005

2nd SCIENCE
Dates: Jan. 6, 2001-May 16, 2002
Departure: Resigned committee; later moved to Judiciary

Cong.	Ranking	Terms in: House	Comm.	Date of Assignment
107th	Maj-22nd	1	1	Jan. 6, 2001

3rd SMALL BUSINESS
Dates: Jan. 6, 2001-Jan. 3, 2003
Departure: Moved to International Relations

Cong.	Ranking	Terms in: House	Comm.	Date of Assignment
107th	Maj-12th	1	1	Jan. 6, 2001

4th JUDICIARY
Dates: Oct. 2, 2001-Jan. 3, 2009
Departure: Left committee; became Chair of Republican Conference

Cong.	Ranking	Terms in: House	Comm.	Date of Assignment
107th	MjR-2nd	1	1	Oct. 2, 2001
108th	Maj-16th	2	2	Jan. 28, 2003
109th	Maj-18th	3	3	Jan. 26, 2005
110th	Min-11th	4	4	Jan. 10, 2007

5th INTERNATIONAL RELATIONS, 108-109
FOREIGN AFFAIRS, 110-111
Dates: Jan. 28, 2003-date
Departure: Still serving in the 111th Congress

Cong.	Ranking	Terms in: House	Comm.	Date of Assignment
108th	Maj-23rd	2	1	Jan. 28, 2003
109th	Maj-19th	3	2	Jan. 26, 2005
110th	Min-13th	4	3	Jan. 10, 2007
111th	Min-10th	5	4	Jan. 9, 2009

HOUSE SELECT AND SPECIAL COMMITTEES:

1st SELECT COMMITTEE TO INVESTIGATE THE VOTING IRREGULARITIES OF AUGUST 2, 2007
Dates: Sep. 5, 2007-Sep. 25, 2008
Termination: House Report 885 (110-2) filed

Cong.	Ranking	Terms in: House	Comm.	Date of Assignment
110th	Min-RM	4	1	Sep. 5, 2007

Timothy J. Penny (DFL-Minn.)

Dates: Nov. 19, 1951
House: Jan. 3, 1983-Jan. 3, 1995
Left the House: Retired in 1994

HOUSE STANDING COMMITTEES:

1st AGRICULTURE
Dates: Jan. 6, 1983-Jan. 3, 1995
Departure: Left the House; retired

Cong.	Ranking	Terms in: House	Comm.	Date of Assignment
103rd	Maj-9th	6	6	Jan. 5, 1993

2nd VETERANS AFFAIRS
Dates: Jan. 6, 1983-Jan. 3, 1995
Departure: Left the House; retired

Cong.	Ranking	Terms in: House	Comm.	Date of Assignment
103rd	Maj-5th	6	6	Jan. 5, 1993

3rd EDUCATION AND LABOR
Dates *T1: May 4, 1983-Nov. 18, 1983
*T2: Feb. 9, 1984-Jan. 3, 1985
*T3: Feb. 6, 1985-Dec. 20, 1985
Departures: Temporary terms expired; filled own vacancies
4th Dates: Jan. 29, 1986-Jan. 3, 1989
4th Departure: Left committee; no new assignment

HOUSE SELECT AND SPECIAL COMMITTEES:

1st SELECT HUNGER (Temporary)
Dates: Jan. 21, 1987-Jan. 3, 1993
Termination: Committee not renewed in 1993

Ed Perlmutter (D-Colo.)

Dates: May 1, 1953
House: Jan. 3, 2007-date
Serving in the 111th Congress

HOUSE STANDING COMMITTEES:

1st FINANCIAL SERVICES
Dates: Jan. 12, 2007-date
Departure: Still serving in the 111th Congress

Cong.	Ranking	Terms in: House	Comm.	Date of Assignment
110th	Maj-32nd	1	1	Jan. 12, 2007
111th	Maj-28th	2	2	Jan. 7, 2009

2nd HOMELAND SECURITY
Dates: Jan. 12, 2007-Jan. 3, 2009
Departure: Moved to Rules

Cong.	Ranking	Terms in: House	Comm.	Date of Assignment
110th	Maj-18th	1	1	Jan. 12, 2007

3rd RULES
Dates: Jan. 13, 2009-date
Departure: Still serving in the 111th Congress

Cong.	Ranking	Terms in: House	Comm.	Date of Assignment
111th	MjR-1st	2	1	Jan. 13, 2009

Tom Perriello (D-Va.)

Dates: Oct. 9, 1974
House: Jan. 3, 2009-date
Serving in the 111th Congress

HOUSE STANDING COMMITTEES:

1st TRANSPORTATION AND INFRASTRUCTURE
Dates: Jan. 7, 2009-date
Departure: Still serving in the 111th Congress

Cong.	Ranking	Terms in: House	Comm.	Date of Assignment
111th	Maj-43rd	1	1	Jan. 7, 2009

2nd VETERANS' AFFAIRS
Dates: Jan. 21, 2009-date
Departure: Still serving in the 111th Congress

Cong.	Ranking	Terms in: House	Comm.	Date of Assignment
111th	Maj-9th	1	1	Jan. 21, 2009

Gary Peters (D-Mich.)

Dates: Dec. 1, 1958
House: Jan. 3, 2009-date
Serving in the 111th Congress

HOUSE STANDING COMMITTEES:

1st FINANCIAL SERVICES
Dates: Jan. 7, 2009-date
Departure: Still serving in the 111th Congress

Cong.	Ranking	Terms in: House	Comm.	Date of Assignment
111th	Maj-41st	1	1	Jan. 7, 2009

2nd SCIENCE AND TECHNOLOGY
Dates: Jan. 21, 2009-date
Departure: Still serving in the 111th Congress

Cong.	Ranking	Terms in: House	Comm.	Date of Assignment
111th	Maj-26th	1	1	Jan. 21, 2009

Collin C. Peterson (DFL-Minn.)

Dates: June 29, 1944
House: Jan. 3, 1991-date
Serving in the 111th Congress

HOUSE STANDING COMMITTEES:

1st AGRICULTURE
Dates: Jan. 24, 1991-date
Departure: Still serving in the 111th Congress

Cong.	Ranking	Terms in: House	Comm.	Date of Assignment
103rd	Maj-15th	2	2	Jan. 5, 1993
104th	Min-8th	3	3	Jan. 4, 1995
105th	Min-4th	4	4	Jan. 7, 1997
106th	Min-4th	5	5	Jan. 6, 1999
107th	Min-3rd	6	6	Jan. 31, 2001
108th	Min-2nd	7	7	Jan. 28, 2003
109th	Min-RM	8	8	Jan. 6, 2005
110th	Maj-Chr	9	9	Jan. 4, 2007
111th	Maj-Chr	10	10	Jan. 6, 2009

2nd GOVERNMENT OPERATIONS, 102-103
GOVERNMENT REFORM AND OVERSIGHT, 104-105
Dates: Jan. 24, 1991-Feb. 4, 1997
Departure: Resigned committee; no new assignment

Cong.	Ranking	Terms in: House	Comm.	Date of Assignment
103rd	Maj-12th	2	2	Jan. 21, 1993
104th	Min-11th	3	3	Jan. 9, 1995
105th	Min-8th	4	4	Jan. 7, 1997

3rd NATURAL RESOURCES
Dates: Jan. 5, 1993-Jan. 21, 1993
Departure: Left committee; no new assignment

Cong.	Ranking	Terms in: House	Comm.	Date of Assignment
103rd	Maj-18th	2	1	Jan. 5, 1993

4th VETERANS' AFFAIRS
Dates: Sep. 17, 1996-Apr. 26, 2001
Departure: Resigned committee; moved to Permanent Select Intelligence

Cong.	Ranking	Terms in: House	Comm.	Date of Assignment
104th	MnR-1st	3	1	Sep. 17, 1996
105th	Min-10th	4	2	Feb. 6, 1997
106th	Min-6th	5	3	Jan. 6, 1999
107th	Min-6th	6	4	Jan. 31, 2001

HOUSE SELECT AND SPECIAL COMMITTEES:

1st PERMANENT SELECT INTELLIGENCE, 107-108
Dates: Apr. 4, 2001-Jan. 3, 2005
Departure: Left committee; became Ranking Member on Agriculture

Cong.	Ranking	Terms in: House	Comm.	Date of Assignment
107th	MnR-1st	6	1	Apr. 4, 2001
108th	Min-5th	7	2	Jan. 8, 2003

Douglas B. (Pete) Peterson (D-Fla.)

Dates: June 26, 1935
House: Jan. 3, 1991-Jan. 3, 1997
Left the House: Retired; named Ambassador to Vietnam

HOUSE STANDING COMMITTEES:

1st PUBLIC WORKS AND TRANSPORTATION
Dates: Jan. 24, 1991-Jan. 3, 1993
Departure: Moved to Appropriations

2nd VETERANS AFFAIRS
Dates: Jan. 24, 1991-Jan. 3, 1993
Departure: Moved to Appropriations

3rd APPROPRIATIONS
Dates: Jan. 5, 1993-Jan. 3, 1995
Departure: Moved to National Security and Small Business

Cong.	Ranking	Terms in: House	Comm.	Date of Assignment
103rd	Maj-34th	2	1	Jan. 5, 1993

4th NATIONAL SECURITY
Dates: Jan. 4, 1995-Jan. 3, 1997
Departure: Left the House; appointed ambassador

Cong.	Ranking	Terms in: House	Comm.	Date of Assignment
104th	Min-21st	3	1	Jan. 4, 1995

5th SMALL BUSINESS
Dates: Jan. 4, 1995-Jan. 3, 1997
Departure: Left the House; appointed ambassador

Cong.	Ranking	Terms in: House	Comm.	Date of Assignment
104th	Min-13th	3	1	Jan. 4, 1995

HOUSE SELECT AND SPECIAL COMMITTEES:

1st SELECT CHILDREN, YOUTH AND FAMILIES (Temporary)
Dates: Feb. 21, 1991-Jan. 3, 1993
Termination: Committee not renewed in 1993

John E. Peterson (R-Penn.)

Dates: Dec. 25, 1938
House: Jan. 3, 1997-Jan. 3, 2009
Left the House: Retired in 2008

HOUSE STANDING COMMITTEES:

1st EDUCATION AND THE WORKFORCE
Dates: Jan. 7, 1997-Jan. 3, 1999
Departure: Moved to Appropriations

Cong.	Ranking	Terms in: House	Comm.	Date of Assignment
105th	Maj-21st	1	1	Jan. 7, 1997

2nd RESOURCES
Dates: Jan. 7, 1997-Jan. 3, 2007
Departure: Left committee; no new assignment

Cong.	Ranking	Terms in: House	Comm.	Date of Assignment
105th	Maj-23rd	1	1	Jan. 7, 1997
106th	Maj-19th	2	2	Jan. 6, 1999
107th	Maj-18th	3	3	Jan. 6, 2001
108th	Maj-15th	4	4	Jan. 28, 2003
109th	Maj-12th	5	5	Jan. 26, 2005

3rd APPROPRIATIONS
Dates: Jan. 6, 1999-Jan. 3, 2009
Departure: Left the House; retired

Cong.	Ranking	Terms in: House	Comm.	Date of Assignment
106th	Maj-34th	2	1	Jan. 6, 1999
107th	Maj-30th	3	2	Jan. 6, 2001
108th	Maj-25th	4	3	Jan. 28, 2003
109th	Maj-24th	5	4	Jan. 6, 2005
110th	Min-18th	6	5	Jan. 4, 2007

Thomas E. Petri (R-Wisc.)

Dates: May 28, 1940
House: April 3, 1979-date
Serving in the 111th Congress

H: Petri was elected to the 96th Congress by special election, Apr. 3, 1979, to fill the vacancy caused by the death of U.S. Representative William A. Steiger (R-Wisc.). He was seated Apr. 9, 1979, and was assigned to committees.

HOUSE STANDING COMMITTEES:

1st EDUCATION AND LABOR, 96-103
ECONOMIC AND EDUCATIONAL OPPORTUNITIES, 104
EDUCATION AND THE WORKFORCE, 105-109
EDUCATION AND LABOR, 110-111
Dates: Apr. 9, 1979-date
Departure: Still serving in the 111th Congress

Cong.	Ranking	Terms in: House	Comm.	Date of Assignment
103rd	Min-2nd	8	8	Jan. 5, 1993
104th	Maj-2nd	9	9	Jan. 4, 1995
105th	Maj-2nd	10	10	Jan. 7, 1997
106th	Maj-2nd	11	11	Jan. 6, 1999
107th	Maj-2nd	12	12	Jan. 6, 2001
108th	Maj-2nd	13	13	Jan. 28, 2003
109th	Maj-2nd	14	14	Jan. 26, 2005
110th	Min-2nd	15	15	Jan. 10, 2007
111th	Min-2nd	16	16	Jan. 9, 2009

2nd PUBLIC WORKS AND TRANSPORTATION, 98-103
TRANSPORTATION AND INFRASTRUCTURE, 104-110
Dates: Jan. 6, 1983-date
Departure: Still serving in the 111th Congress

Cong.	Ranking	Terms in: House	Comm.	Date of Assignment
103rd	Min-3rd	8	6	Jan. 5, 1993
104th	Maj-4th	9	7	Jan. 4, 1995
105th	Maj-3rd	10	8	Jan. 7, 1997
106th	Maj-3rd	11	9	Jan. 6, 1999
107th	Maj-3rd	12	10	Jan. 6, 2001
108th	Maj-2nd	13	11	Jan. 28, 2003
109th	Maj-2nd	14	12	Jan. 26, 2005
110th	Min-3rd	15	13	Jan. 10, 2007
111th	Min-3rd	16	14	Jan. 9, 2009

3rd STANDARDS OF OFFICIAL CONDUCT
Dates: Jan. 21, 1987-Jan. 3, 1991
Departure: Left committee; no new assignment

4th POST OFFICE AND CIVIL SERVICE
Dates: Feb. 18, 1993-Jan. 3, 1995
Departure: Committee abolished; no new assignment

Cong.	Ranking	Terms in: House	Comm.	Date of Assignment
103rd	Min-7th	8	1	Feb. 18, 1993

HOUSE SELECT AND SPECIAL COMMITTEES:

1st SELECT AGING (Permanent)
Dates: Feb. 5, 1981-Jan. 3, 1983
Departure: Moved to Public Works and Transportation

David D. Phelps (D-Ill.)

Dates: Oct. 26, 1947
House: Jan. 3, 1999-Jan. 3, 2003
Left the House: Defeated for re-election in 2002

HOUSE STANDING COMMITTEES:

1st AGRICULTURE
Dates: Jan. 6, 1999-Jan. 3, 2003
Departure: Left the House; lost re-election

Cong.	Ranking	Terms in: House	Comm.	Date of Assignment
106th	Min-21st	1	1	Jan. 6, 1999
107th	Min-16th	2	2	Jan. 31, 2001

2nd SMALL BUSINESS
Dates: Jan. 6, 1999-Jan. 3, 2003
Departure: Left the House; lost re-election

Cong.	Ranking	Terms in: House	Comm.	Date of Assignment
106th	Min-14th	1	1	Jan. 6, 1999
107th	Min-13th	2	2	Jan. 31, 2001

Charles W. (Chip) Pickering Jr. (R-Miss.)

Dates: Aug. 10, 1963
House: Jan. 3, 1997-Jan. 3, 2009
Left the House: Retired in 2008

HOUSE STANDING COMMITTEES:

1st AGRICULTURE
1st Dates: Jan. 7, 1997-Jan. 3, 1999
1st Departure: Moved to Commerce
2nd Dates: Jan. 6, 2001-Jan. 3, 2005
2nd Departure: Left committee; no new assignment

Cong.	Ranking	Terms in: House	Comm.	Date of Assignment
105th	Maj-23rd	1 *1	1	Jan. 7, 1997
107th	Maj-20th	3 *2	1	Jan. 6, 2001
108th	Maj-13th	4 *2	2	Jan. 28, 2003

2nd TRANSPORTATION AND INFRASTRUCTURE
Dates: Jan. 7, 1997-Jan. 3, 1999
Departure: Moved to Commerce

Cong.	Ranking	Terms in: House	Comm.	Date of Assignment
105th	Maj-35th	1	1	Jan. 7, 1997

3rd SCIENCE
Dates: Jan. 21, 1997-Jan. 3, 1999
Departure: Moved to Commerce

Cong.	Ranking	Terms in: House	Comm.	Date of Assignment
105th	Maj-18th	1	1	Jan. 21, 1997

4th COMMERCE, 106
ENERGY AND COMMERCE, 107-110
Dates: Jan. 6, 1999-Jan. 3, 2009
Departure: Left the House; retired

Cong.	Ranking	Terms in: House	Comm.	Date of Assignment
106th	Maj-25th	2	1	Jan. 6, 1999
107th	Maj-19th	3	2	Jan. 6, 2001
108th	Maj-17th	4	3	Jan. 28, 2003
109th	Maj-14th	5	4	Jan. 6, 2005
110th	Min-13th	6	5	Jan. 10, 2007

HOUSE SELECT AND SPECIAL COMMITTEES:

1st SELECT BIPARTISAN COMMITTEE TO INVESTIGATE THE PREPARATION FOR AND RESPONSE TO HURRICANE KATRINA
Dates: Sep. 21, 2005-Feb. 15, 2006
Departure: House Report 377 (109-2) filed

Cong.	Ranking	Terms in: House	Comm.	Date of Assignment
109th	Maj-10th	5	1	Sep. 21, 2005

Owen B. Pickett (D-Va.)

Dates: Aug. 31, 1930
House: Jan. 3, 1987-Jan. 3, 2001
Left the House: Retired in 2000

HOUSE STANDING COMMITTEES:

1st ARMED SERVICES, 100-103
NATIONAL SECURITY, 104-105
ARMED SERVICES, 106
Dates: Jan. 22, 1987-Jan. 3, 2001
Departure: Left the House; retired

Cong.	Ranking	Terms in: House	Comm.	Date of Assignment
103rd	Maj-14th	4	4	Jan. 5, 1993
104th	Min-8th	5	5	Jan. 4, 1995
105th	Min-6th	6	6	Jan. 7, 1997
106th	Min-5th	7	7	Jan. 6, 1999

2nd MERCHANT MARINE AND FISHERIES
Dates: Jan. 22, 1987-Jan. 3, 1995
Departure: Committee abolished; no new assignment

Cong.	Ranking	Terms in: House	Comm.	Date of Assignment
103rd	Maj-8th	4	4	Jan. 5, 1993

3rd VETERANS AFFAIRS
Dates: Jan. 24, 1991-Jan. 3, 1993
Departure: Left committee; no new assignment

4th RESOURCES
Dates: June 13, 1995-Jan. 3, 2001
Departure: Left the House; retired

Cong.	Ranking	Terms in: House	Comm.	Date of Assignment
104th	MnR-1st	5	1	June 13, 1995
105th	Min-12th	6	2	Jan. 7, 1997
106th	Min-9th	7	3	Jan. 6, 1999

J. J. (Jake) Pickle (D-Tex.)

Dates: Oct. 11, 1913-June 18, 2005
House: Dec. 17, 1963-Jan. 3, 1995
Left the House: Retired in 1994

H: Pickle was elected to the 86th Congress by special election, Dec. 21, 1963, to fill the vacancy caused by the resignation of U.S. Representative Homer Thornberry (D-Tex.) who was appointed a U.S. District Judge. Pickle was seated Dec. 21, 1963, and assigned to committees.

HOUSE STANDING COMMITTEES:

1st INTERSTATE AND FOREIGN COMMERCE
Dates: Feb. 25, 1964-Jan. 3, 1975
Departure: Moved to Ways and Means

2nd SCIENCE AND ASTRONAUTICS
Dates: Jan. 24, 1973-Jan. 3, 1975
Departure: Moved to Ways and Means

3rd WAYS AND MEANS
Dates: Jan. 20, 1975-Jan. 3, 1995
Departure: Left the House; retired

Cong.	Ranking	Terms in: House	Comm.	Date of Assignment
103rd	Maj-3rd	16	10	Jan. 5, 1993

JOINT COMMITTEES:

1st JOINT BICENTENNIAL ARRANGEMENTS
House Dates: Sep. 5, 1975-Dec. 31, 1976
Termination: Committee closed at end of 1976

2nd JOINT TAXATION
House Dates: May 18, 1981-Jan. 3, 1995
Departure: Left the House; retired

Cong.	Ranking	Terms in: House	Comm.	Date of Assignment
103rd	Maj-3rd	16	7	Jan. 5, 1993 Ltr

Pedro R. Pierluisi (PNP-P.R.)

Dates: April 26, 1959
House: Jan. 3, 2009-date
Serving in the 111th Congress

1st EDUCATION AND LABOR
Dates: Jan. 21, 2009-date
Departure: Still serving in the 111th Congress

Cong.	Ranking	Terms in: House	Comm.	Date of Assignment
111th	Maj-27th	1	1	Jan. 21, 2009

2nd JUDICIARY
Dates: Jan. 21, 2009-date
Departure: Still serving in the 111th Congress

Cong.	Ranking	Terms in: House	Comm.	Date of Assignment
111th	Maj-14th	1	1	Jan. 21, 2009

3rd NATURAL RESOURCES
Dates: Jan. 21, 2009-date
Departure: Still serving in the 111th Congress

Cong.	Ranking	Terms in: House	Comm.	Date of Assignment
111th	Maj-29th	1	1	Jan. 21, 2009

Chellie Pingree (D-Me.)

Dates: Apr. 2, 1955
House: Jan. 3, 2009-date
Serving in the 111th Congress

HOUSE STANDING COMMITTEES:

1st ARMED SERVICES
Dates: Jan. 7, 2009-date
Departure: Still serving in the 111th Congress

Cong.	Ranking	Terms in: House	Comm.	Date of Assignment
111th	Maj-32nd	1	1	Jan. 7, 2009

2nd RULES
Dates: Jan. 13, 2009-date
Departure: Still serving in the 111th Congress

Cong.	Ranking	Terms in: House	Comm.	Date of Assignment
111th	MjR-2nd	1	1	Jan. 13, 2009

Joseph R. Pitts (R-Penn.)

Dates: Oct. 10, 1939
House: Jan. 3, 1997-date
Serving in the 111th Congress

HOUSE STANDING COMMITTEES:

1st BUDGET
Dates: Jan. 7, 1997-Jan. 3, 2001
Departure: Moved to Energy and Commerce and International Relations

Cong.	Ranking	Terms in: House	Comm.	Date of Assignment
105th	Maj-24th	1	1	Jan. 7, 1997
106th	Maj-15th	2	2	Jan. 6, 1999

2nd TRANSPORTATION AND INFRASTRUCTURE
Dates: Jan. 7, 1997-Jan. 3, 1999
Departure: Moved to Armed Services

Cong.	Ranking	Terms in: House	Comm.	Date of Assignment
105th	Maj-30th	1	1	Jan. 7, 1997

3rd SMALL BUSINESS
Dates: Jan. 21, 1997-Jan. 3, 2001
Departure: Moved to Energy and Commerce and International Relations

Cong.	Ranking	Terms in: House	Comm.	Date of Assignment
105th	MjR-1st	1	1	Jan. 21, 1997
106th	Maj-12th	2	2	Jan. 6, 1999

4th ARMED SERVICES
Dates: Jan. 6, 1999-Jan. 3, 2001
Departure: Moved to Energy and Commerce and International Relations

Cong.	Ranking	Terms in: House	Comm.	Date of Assignment
106th	Maj-29th	2	1	Jan. 6, 1999

5th ENERGY AND COMMERCE
Dates: Jan. 6, 2001-date
Departure: Still serving in the 111th Congress

Cong.	Ranking	Terms in: House	Comm.	Date of Assignment
107th	Maj-28th	3	1	Jan. 6, 2001
108th	Maj-23rd	4	2	Jan. 28, 2003
109th	Maj-20th	5	3	Jan. 6, 2005
110th	Min-17th	6	4	Jan. 10, 2007
111th	Min-12th	7	5	Jan. 9, 2009

6th INTERNATIONAL RELATIONS
Dates: Jan. 6, 2001-Jan. 3, 2005
Departure: Left committee; no new assignment

Cong.	Ranking	Terms in: House	Comm.	Date of Assignment
107th	Maj-21st	3	1	Jan. 6, 2001
108th	Maj-18th	4	2	Jan. 28, 2003

JOINT COMMITTEES:

1st JOINT ECONOMIC
House Dates: Mar. 18, 1999-Jan. 3, 2001
Departure: Move to Energy and Commerce

Cong.	Ranking	Terms in: House	Comm.	Date of Assignment
106th	Maj-5th	2	1	Mar. 18, 1999

Todd R. Platts (R-Penn.)

Dates: March 5, 1962
House: Jan. 3, 2001-date
Serving in the 111th Congress

HOUSE STANDING COMMITTEES:

1st EDUCATION AND THE WORKFORCE, 107-109
EDUCATION AND LABOR, 110-111
Dates: Jan. 6, 2001-date
Departure: Still serving in the 111th Congress

Cong.	Ranking	Terms in: House	Comm.	Date of Assignment
107th	Maj-22nd	1	1	Jan. 6, 2001
108th	Maj-16th	2	2	Jan. 28, 2003
109th	Maj-10th	3	3	Jan. 26, 2005
110th	Min-8th	4	4	Jan. 10, 2007
111th	Min-8th	5	5	Jan. 9, 2009

2nd GOVERNMENT REFORM, 107-109
OVERSIGHT AND GOVERNMENT REFORM, 110-111
Dates: Jan. 6, 2001-June 15, 2009
Departure: Resigned committee; moved to Armed Services

Cong.	Ranking	Terms in: House	Comm.	Date of Assignment
107th	Maj-20th	1	1	Jan. 6, 2001
108th	Maj-12th	2	2	Jan. 28, 2003
109th	Maj-10th	3	3	Jan. 26, 2005
110th	Min-7th	4	4	Jan. 10, 2007
111th	Min-6th	5	4	Jan. 9, 2009

3rd TRANSPORTATION AND INFRASTRUCTURE
Dates: Jan. 6, 2001-date
Departure: Still serving in the 111th Congress

Cong.	Ranking	Terms in: House	Comm.	Date of Assignment
107th	Maj-36th	1	1	Jan. 6, 2001
108th	Maj-28th	2	2	Jan. 28, 2003
109th	Maj-22nd	3	3	Jan. 26, 2005
110th	Min-16th	4	4	Jan. 10, 2007
111th	Min-12th	5	5	Jan. 9, 2009

4th ARMED SERVICES
Dates: June 16, 2009-date
Departure: Still serving in the 111th Congress

Cong.	Ranking	Terms in: House	Comm.	Date of Assignment
111th	MnR-1st	5	1	June 16, 2009

Ted Poe (R-Tex.)

Dates: Sept. 10, 1948
House: Jan. 3, 2005-date
Serving in the 111th Congress

HOUSE STANDING COMMITTEES:

1st INTERNATIONAL RELATIONS, 109
FOREIGN AFFAIRS, 110-111
Dates: Jan. 26, 2005-date
Departure: Still serving in the 111th Congress

Cong.	Ranking	Terms in: House	Comm.	Date of Assignment
109th	Maj-27th	1	1	Jan. 26, 2005
110th	Min-21st	2	2	Jan. 10, 2007
111th	Min-17th	3	3	Jan. 9, 2009

2nd SMALL BUSINESS
Dates: Jan. 26, 2005-Jan. 3, 2007
Departure: Left committee; no new assignment

Cong.	Ranking	Terms in: House	Comm.	Assignment
109th	Maj-13th	1	1	Jan. 26, 2005

3rd TRANSPORTATION AND INFRASTRUCTURE
Dates: Jan. 26, 2005-Jan. 3, 2009
Departure: Moved to Judiciary

Cong.	Ranking	Terms in: House	Comm.	Date of Assignment
109th	Maj-35th	1	1	Jan. 26, 2005
110th	Min-24th	2	2	Jan. 10, 2007

4th JUDICIARY
Dates: Jan. 9, 2009-date
Departure: Still serving in the 111th Congress

Cong.	Ranking	Terms in: House	Comm.	Date of Assignment
111th	Min-13th	3	1	Jan. 9, 2009

Jared Polis (D-Colo.)

Dates: May 12, 1975
House: Jan. 3, 2009-date
Serving in the 111th Congress

HOUSE STANDING COMMITTEES:

1st RULES
Dates: Jan. 13, 2009-date
Departure: Still serving in the 111th Congress

Cong.	Ranking	Terms in: House	Comm.	Date of Assignment
111th	MjR-3rd	1	1	Jan. 13, 2009

2nd EDUCATION AND LABOR
Dates: Jan. 21, 2009-date
Departure: Still serving in the 111th Congress

Cong.	Ranking	Terms in: House	Comm.	Date of Assignment
111th	Maj-25th	1	1	Jan. 21, 2009

3rd JUDICIARY
Dates: May 6, 2010-date
Departure: Still serving in the 111th Congress

Cong.	Ranking	Terms in: House	Comm.	Date of Assignment
111th	MjR-3rd	1	1	May 6, 2010

Richard W. Pombo (R-Cal.)

Dates: Jan. 8, 1961
House: Jan. 3, 1993-Jan. 3, 2007
Left the House: Defeated for re-election in 2006.

HOUSE STANDING COMMITTEES:

1st AGRICULTURE
Dates: Jan. 5, 1993-Jan. 3, 2007
Departure: Left the House; lost re-election

Cong.	Ranking	Terms in: House	Comm.	Date of Assignment
103rd	Min-17th	1	1	Jan. 5, 1993
104th	Maj-11th	2	2	Jan. 4, 1995
105th	Maj-8th	3	3	Jan. 7, 1997
106th	Maj-6th	4	4	Jan. 6, 1999
107th	Maj-4th	5	5	Jan. 6, 2001
108th	Maj-4th	6	6	Jan. 28, 2003
109th	Maj-3rd	7	7	Jan. 26, 2005

2nd MERCHANT MARINE AND FISHERIES
Dates: Feb. 4, 1993-Jan. 3, 1995
Departure: Committee abolished; no new assignment

Cong.	Ranking	Terms in: House	Comm.	Date of Assignment
103rd	Min-16th	1	1	Feb. 4, 1993

3rd NATURAL RESOURCES, 103
RESOURCES, 104-109
Dates: Jan. 5, 1993-Jan. 3, 2007
Departure: Left the House; lost re-election

Cong.	Ranking	Terms in: House	Comm.	Date of Assignment
103rd	Min-14th	1	1	Jan. 5, 1993
104th	Maj-11th	2	2	Jan. 4, 1995
105th	Maj-11th	3	3	Jan. 7, 1997
106th	Maj-11th	4	4	Jan. 6, 1999
107th	Maj-11th	5	5	Jan. 6, 2001
108th	Maj-Chr	6	6	Jan. 8, 2003
109th	Maj-Chr	7	7	Jan. 6, 2005

4th TRANSPORTATION AND INFRASTRUCTURE
Dates: Feb. 8, 2001-Jan. 3, 2003
Departure: Left committee; became Chair of Resources

Cong.	Ranking	Terms in: House	Comm.	Date of Assignment
107th	Maj-41st	5	1	Feb. 8, 2001

Earl R. Pomeroy III (D-N.D.)

Dates: Sept. 2, 1952
House: Jan. 3, 1993-date
Serving in the 111th Congress

HOUSE STANDING COMMITTEES:

1st AGRICULTURE
1st Dates: Jan. 5, 1993-Jan. 3, 2001
1st Departure: Moved to Ways and Means
2nd Dates: Feb. 13, 2003-date
2nd Departure: Still serving in the 111th Congress

Cong.	Ranking	Terms in: House	Comm.	Date of Assignment
103rd	Maj-22nd	1 *1	1	Jan. 5, 1993
104th	Min-13th	2 *1	2	Jan. 4, 1995
105th	Min-9th	3 *1	3	Jan. 7, 1997
106th	Min-9th	4 *1	4	Jan. 6, 1999
108th	Min-21st	6 *2	1	Feb. 13, 2003
109th	Min-18th	7 *2	2	Feb. 2, 2005
110th	Maj-20th	8 *2	3	Jan. 12, 2007
111th	Maj-26th	9 *2	4	Jan. 21, 2009

2nd BUDGET
Dates: Jan. 5, 1993-Jan. 3, 1999
Departure: Moved to International Relations

Cong.	Ranking	Terms in: House	Comm.	Date of Assignment
103rd	Maj-26th	1	1	Jan. 5, 1993
104th	Min-11th	2	2	Jan. 4, 1995
105th	Min-6th	3	3	Jan. 7, 1997

3rd INTERNATIONAL RELATIONS
Dates: Jan. 19, 1999-Jan. 3, 2001
Departure: Moved to Ways and Means

Cong.	Ranking	Terms in: House	Comm.	Date of Assignment
106th	Min-18th	4	1	Jan. 19, 1999

4th WAYS AND MEANS
Dates: Jan. 31, 2001-date
Departure: Still serving in the 111th Congress

Cong.	Ranking	Terms in: House	Comm.	Date of Assignment
107th	Min-17th	5	1	Jan. 31, 2001
108th	Min-15th	6	2	Jan. 28, 2003
109th	Min-13th	7	3	Jan. 26, 2005
110th	Maj-11th	8	4	Jan. 4, 2007
111th	Maj-10th	9	5	Jan. 7, 2009

John Edward Porter (R-Ill.)

Dates: June 1, 1935
House: Jan. 22, 1980-Jan. 3, 2001
Left the House: Retired in 2000

H: Porter was elected to the 96th Congress by special election, Jan. 22, 1980, to fill the vacancy caused by the resignation of U.S. Representative Abner J. Mikva (D-Ill.) who had been appointed a federal judge. Porter was seated Jan. 24, 1980, and assigned to committees.

HOUSE STANDING COMMITTEES:

1st BANKING, FINANCE AND URBAN AFFAIRS
Dates: Feb. 7, 1980-Jan. 3, 1981
Departure: Moved to Appropriations

2nd SMALL BUSINESS
Dates: Feb. 7, 1980-Jan. 3, 1981
Departure: Moved to Appropriations

3rd APPROPRIATIONS
Dates: Jan. 28, 1981-Jan. 3. 2001
Departure: Left the House; retired

Cong.	Ranking	Terms in: House	Comm.	Date of Assignment
103rd	Min-7th	8	7	Jan. 5, 1993
104th	Maj-7th	9	8	Jan. 4, 1995
105th	Maj-6th	10	9	Jan. 7, 1997
106th	Maj-4th	11	10	Jan. 6, 1999

HOUSE SELECT AND SPECIAL COMMITTEES:

1st SELECT AGING (Permanent)
Dates: Jan. 20, 1989-Jan. 3, 1993
Termination: Committee not renewed in 1993

Jon C. Porter (R-Nev.)

Dates: May 16, 1955
House: Jan. 3, 2003-Jan. 3, 2009
Left the House: Defeated for re-election in 2008

HOUSE STANDING COMMITTEES:

1st EDUCATION AND THE WORKFORCE
Dates: Jan. 28, 2003-Jan. 3, 2007
Departure: Moved to Ways and Means and Budget

Cong.	Ranking	Terms in: House	Comm.	Date of Assignment
108th	Maj-22nd	1	1	Jan. 28, 2003
109th	Maj-15th	2	2	Jan. 26, 2005

2nd TRANSPORTATION AND INFRASTRUCTURE
Dates: Jan. 28, 2003-Jan. 3, 2007
Departure: Moved to Ways and Means and Budget

Cong.	Ranking	Terms in: House	Comm.	Date of Assignment
108th	Maj-41st	1	1	Jan. 28, 2003
109th	Maj-30th	2	2	Jan. 26, 2005

3rd GOVERNMENT REFORM
Dates: Jan. 26, 2005-Jan. 3, 2007
Departure: Moved to Ways and Means and Budget

Cong.	Ranking	Terms in: House	Comm.	Date of Assignment
109th	Maj-18th	2	1	Jan. 26, 2005

4th WAYS AND MEANS
Dates: Jan. 4, 2007-Jan. 3, 2009
Departure: Left the House; lost re-election

Cong.	Ranking	Terms in: House	Comm.	Date of Assignment
110th	Min-17th	3	1	Jan. 4, 2007

5th BUDGET
Dates: Jan. 10, 2007-Jan. 3, 2009
Departure: Left the House; lost re-election

Cong.	Ranking	Terms in: House	Comm.	Date of Assignment
110th	Min-15th	3	1	Jan. 10, 2007

Robert J. Portman (R-Ohio)

Dates: Dec. 19, 1955
House: May 4, 1993-April 29, 2005
Left the House: Resigned; appointed U.S. Trade Representative

H: Portman was elected to the 103rd Congress by special election, May 4, 1993, to fill the vacancy caused by the resignation of U.S. Representative Willis D. Gradison (R-Ohio). Portman was seated May 5, 1993, and assigned to committees.

HOUSE STANDING COMMITTEES:

1st SMALL BUSINESS
Dates: May 26, 1993-Jan. 3, 1995
Departure: Moved to Ways and Means

Cong.	Ranking	Terms in: House	Comm.	Date of Assignment
103rd	MnR-1st	1	1	May 26, 1993

2nd GOVERNMENT OPERATIONS, 103
GOVERNMENT REFORM AND OVERSIGHT, 104
1st Dates: May 26, 1993-Jan. 3, 1995
1st Departure: Moved to Ways and Means
2nd Dates: Apr. 9, 1997-Nov. 14, 1997
2nd Departure: Moved to investigative subcommittee of Standards of Official Conduct

Cong.	Ranking	Terms in: House	Comm.	Date of Assignment
103rd	MnA-17th	1 *1	1	May 26, 1993
105th	MjR-2nd	3 *2	1	Apr. 9, 1997

3rd WAYS AND MEANS
Dates: Jan. 4, 1995-Apr. 29, 2005
Departure: Resigned the House; named to federal post

Cong.	Ranking	Terms in: House	Comm.	Date of Assignment
104th	Maj-18th	2	1	Jan. 4, 1995
105th	Maj-16th	3	2	Jan. 7, 1997
106th	Maj-15th	4	3	Jan. 6, 1999
107th	Maj-14th	5	4	Jan. 6, 2001
108th	Maj-14th	6	5	Jan. 28, 2003
109th	Maj-10th	7	6	Jan. 6, 2005

4th STANDARDS OF OFFICIAL CONDUCT
Dates: Jan. 19, 1999-June 29, 2001
Departure: Resigned committee; no new assignment

Cong.	Ranking	Terms in: House	Comm.	Date of Assignment
106th	Maj-5th	4	1	Jan. 19, 1999
107th	Maj-2nd	5	2	Mar. 6, 2001

5th BUDGET
Dates: Jan. 6, 2001-Apr. 29, 2005
Departure: Resigned the House; named to federal post

Cong.	Ranking	Terms in: House	Comm.	Date of Assignment
107th	Maj-17th	5	1	Jan. 6, 2001
108th	Maj-8th	6	2	Jan. 31, 2003
109th	Maj-2nd	7	3	Jan. 26, 2005

HOUSE SELECT AND SPECIAL COMMITTEES:

1st SELECT HOMELAND SECURITY
Dates: June 19, 2002-Jan. 3, 2003
Departure: Left committee; no new assignment

Cong.	Ranking	Terms in: House	Comm.	Date of Assignment
107th	Maj-5th	5	1	June 19, 2002

Bill Posey (R-Fla.)

Dates: Dec. 18, 1947
House: Jan. 3, 2009-date
Serving in the 111th Congress

HOUSE STANDING COMMITTEES:

1st FINANCIAL SERVICES
Dates: Jan. 9. 2009-date
Departure: Still serving in the 111th Congress

Cong.	Ranking	Terms in: House	Comm.	Date of Assignment
111th	Min-25th	1	1	Jan. 9, 2009

Glenn Poshard (D-Ill.)

Dates: Oct. 30, 1945
House: Jan. 3, 1989-Jan. 3, 1999
Left the House: Lost election for Governor in 1998

HOUSE STANDING COMMITTEES:

1st EDUCATION AND LABOR
Dates: Jan. 19, 1989-Jan. 3, 1991
Departure: Moved to Public Works and Transportation

2nd SMALL BUSINESS
Dates: Jan. 19, 1989-Jan. 3, 1999
Departure: Left the House; lost election for Governor

Cong.	Ranking	Terms in: House	Comm.	Date of Assignment
103rd	Maj-12th	3	3	Jan. 5, 1993
104th	Min-6th	4	4	Jan. 4, 1995
105th	Min-5th	5	5	Feb. 5, 1997

3rd PUBLIC WORKS AND TRANSPORTATION, 102-103
TRANSPORTATION AND INFRASTRUCTURE, 104-105
Dates: Jan. 24, 1991-Jan. 3, 1999
Departure: Left the House; lost election for Governor

Cong.	Ranking	Terms in: House	Comm.	Date of Assignment
103rd	Maj-19th	3	2	Jan. 5, 1993
104th	Min-14th	4	3	Jan. 4, 1995
105th	Min-10th	5	4	Jan. 7, 1997

Larry L. Pressler (R-S.D.)

Dates: March 29, 1942
House: Jan. 3, 1975-Jan. 3, 1979
Left the House: Elected to U.S. Senate in 1978
Senate: Jan. 3, 1979-Jan. 3, 1997
Left the Senate: Defeated for re-election in 1996

HOUSE STANDING COMMITTEES:

1st EDUCATION AND LABOR
Dates: Jan. 28, 1975-Jan. 3, 1979
Departure: Left the House for the Senate

2nd SCIENCE AND TECHNOLOGY
Dates: May 15, 1975-Jan. 3, 1977
Departure: Moved to Small Business

3rd SMALL BUSINESS
Dates: Jan. 19, 1977-Jan. 3, 1979
Departure: Left the House for the Senate

SENATE STANDING COMMITTEES:

1st BUDGET
Dates: Jan. 23, 1979-Jan. 5, 1981
Departure: Moved to Foreign Relations

2nd COMMERCE, SCIENCE AND TRANSPORTATION
Dates: Jan. 23, 1979-Jan. 3, 1997
Departure: Left the Senate; lost re-election

Cong.	Ranking	Years in: Senate	Comm.	Date of Assignment
103rd	Min-3rd	15	14	Jan. 7, 1993
104th	Maj-Chr	17	16	Jan. 4, 1995

3rd ENVIRONMENT AND PUBLIC WORKS
1st Dates: Jan. 23, 1979-Jan. 5, 1981
1st Departure: Moved to Foreign Relations
2nd Dates: Jan. 6, 1987-Feb. 2, 1989
2nd Departure: Moved to Banking, Housing and Urban Affairs

4th FOREIGN RELATIONS
Dates: Jan. 5, 1981-Jan. 5, 1995
Departure: Moved to Finance; became Chair of Commerce, Science and Transportation

Cong.	Ranking	Years in: Senate	Comm.	Date of Assignment
103rd	Min-4th	15	13	Jan. 7, 1993

5th SMALL BUSINESS
Dates: Jan. 3, 1983-Jan. 3, 1997
Departure: Left the Senate; lost re-election

Cong.	Ranking	Years in: Senate	Comm.	Date of Assignment
103rd	Min-RM	15	*2 11	Jan. 21, 1993
104th	Maj-2nd	17	*2 13	Jan. 6, 1995

6th BANKING, HOUSING AND URBAN AFFAIRS
Dates: Feb. 2, 1989-Feb. 5, 1991
Departure: Left committee; no new assignment

7th JUDICIARY
Dates: Jan. 7, 1993-Jan. 6, 1995
Departure: Moved to Finance; became Chair of Commerce, Science and Transportation

Cong.	Ranking	Years in: Senate	Comm.	Date of Assignment
103rd	Min-8th	15	1	Jan. 7, 1993

8th FINANCE
Dates: Jan. 4, 1995-Jan. 3, 1997
Departure: Left the Senate; lost re-election

Cong.	Ranking	Years in: Senate	Comm.	Date of Assignment
104th	Maj-8th	17	1	Jan. 4, 1995

SENATE SELECT AND SPECIAL COMMITTEES:

1st SELECT SMALL BUSINESS
Dates: Jan. 23, 1979-Jan. 5, 1981
Departure: Moved to Foreign Relations and Special Aging

2nd SPECIAL AGING (Permanent)
Dates: Jan. 5, 1981-Jan. 3, 1997
Departure: Left the Senate; lost re-election

Cong.	Ranking	Years in: Senate	Comm.	Date of Assignment
103rd	Min-2nd	15	13	Jan. 21, 1993
104th	Maj-2nd	17	15	Jan. 11, 1995

3rd JUDGE HARRY E. CLAIBORNE IMPEACHMENT
Dates: Aug. 14, 1986-Oct. 1, 1986
Termination: Senate Report 99-511 filed

David E. Price (D-N.C.)

Dates: Aug. 17, 1940
House 1: Jan. 3, 1987-Jan. 3, 1995
Left the House 1: Defeated for re-election in 1994
House 2: Jan. 3, 1997-date
Serving in the 111th Congress

HOUSE STANDING COMMITTEES:

1st BANKING, FINANCE AND URBAN AFFAIRS
Dates: Jan. 22, 1987-Jan. 3, 1991
Departure: Moved to Appropriations

2nd SCIENCE, SPACE AND TECHNOLOGY
Dates: Jan. 22, 1987-Jan. 3, 1991
Departure: Moved to Appropriations

3rd SMALL BUSINESS
Dates: Mar. 30, 1987-Jan. 3, 1989
Departure: Left committee; no new assignment

4th APPROPRIATIONS
1st Dates: Jan. 3, 1991-Jan. 3, 1995
1st Departure: Left the House; lost re-election
2nd Dates: Jan. 7, 1997-date
2nd Departure: Still serving in the 111th Congress

Cong.	Ranking	Terms in: House	Comm.	Date of Assignment
103rd	Maj-23rd	4 *1	2	Jan. 5, 1993
105th	Min-25th	5 *2	1	Jan. 7, 1997
106th	Min-18th	6 *2	2	Jan. 6, 1999
107th	Min-17th	7 *2	3	Jan. 31, 2001
108th	Min-15th	8 *2	4	Jan. 28, 2003
109th	Min-15th	9 *2	5	Jan. 26, 2005
110th	Maj-13th	10 *2	6	Jan. 4, 2007
111th	Maj-13th	11 *2	7	Jan. 7, 2009

5th BUDGET
1st Dates: Jan. 5, 1993-Jan. 3, 1995
1st Departure: Left the House; lost re-election
2nd Dates: Nov. 13, 1997-Jan. 3, 2003
Service postponed until Jan. 1998 to permit a full six years on the Budget Committee.
2nd Departure: Left committee; no new assignment

Cong.	Ranking	Terms in: House	Comm.	Date of Assignment
103rd	Maj-20th	4 *1	1	Jan. 5, 1993
105th	MnR-2nd	5 *2	1	Nov. 13, 1997
106th	Min-10th	6 *2	2	Jan. 6, 1999
107th	Min-7th	7 *2	3	Jan. 31, 2001

Tom Price (R-Ga.)

Dates: Oct. 8, 1954
House: Jan. 3, 2005-date
Serving in the 111th Congress

HOUSE STANDING COMMITTEES:

1st EDUCATION AND THE WORKFORCE, 109
EDUCATION AND LABOR, 110-111

Dates: Jan. 26, 2005-date
Departure: Still serving in the 111th Congress

Cong.	Ranking	Terms in: House	Comm.	Date of Assignment
109th	Maj-21st	1	1	Jan. 26, 2005
110th	Min-15th	2	2	Jan. 10, 2007
111th	Min-12th	3	3	Jan. 9, 2009

2nd FINANCIAL SERVICES
Dates: Jan. 26, 2005-date
Departure: Still serving in the 111th Congress

Cong.	Ranking	Terms in: House	Comm.	Date of Assignment
109th	Maj-34th	1	1	Jan. 26, 2005
110th	Min-26th	2	2	Jan. 10, 2007
111th	Min-17th	3	3	Jan. 9, 2009

Deborah D. Pryce (R-Ohio)

Dates: July 29, 1951
House: Jan. 3, 1993-Jan. 3, 2009
Left the House: Retired in 2008

HOUSE STANDING COMMITTEES:

1st BANKING, FINANCE AND URBAN AFFAIRS, 103
FINANCIAL SERVICES, 109-110
1st Dates: Jan. 5, 1993-Jan. 3, 1995
1st Departure: Moved to Rules
2nd Dates: Jan. 26, 2005-Jan. 3, 2009
2nd Departure: Left the House; retired

Cong.	Ranking	Terms in: House	Comm.	Date of Assignment
103rd	Min-12th	1 *1	1	Jan. 5, 1993
109th	Maj-4th	7 *2	1	Jan. 26, 2005
110th	Min-3rd	8 *2	2	Jan. 10, 2007

2nd GOVERNMENT OPERATIONS
Dates: Jan. 5, 1993-Jan. 3, 1995
Departure: Moved to Rules

Cong.	Ranking	Terms in: House	Comm.	Date of Assignment
103rd	Min-15th	1	1	Jan. 5, 1993

3rd RULES
Dates: Jan. 4, 1995-Jan. 3, 2005
Departure: Returned to Financial Services

Cong.	Ranking	Terms in: House	Comm.	Date of Assignment
104th	Maj-6th	2	1	Jan. 4, 1995
105th	Maj-5th	3	2	Jan. 7, 1997
106th	Maj-4th	4	3	Jan. 6, 1999
107th	Maj-4th	5	4	Jan. 3, 2001
108th	Maj-4th	6	5	Jan. 7, 2003

HOUSE SELECT AND SPECIAL COMMITTEES:

1st SELECT HOMELAND SECURITY
Dates: June 19, 2002-Jan. 3, 2003
Departure: Left committee; no new assignment

Cong.	Ranking	Terms in: House	Comm.	Date of Assignment
107th	Maj-4th	5	1	June 19, 2002

David H. Pryor (D-Ark.)

Dates: Aug. 29, 1934
House: Nov. 8, 1966-Jan. 3, 1973
Left the House: Lost U.S. Senate nomination in 1972
Senate: Jan. 3, 1979-Jan. 3, 1997
Left the Senate: Retired in 1996

H: Pryor was elected to the 89th Congress by special election, Nov. 8, 1966, to fill the vacancy caused by the resignation of U.S. Representative Oren Harris (D-Ark.) who was appointed a U.S. District Judge. Pryor was not seated nor assigned to committees because the 89th Congress was not in session.

HOUSE STANDING COMMITTEES:

1st APPROPRIATIONS
Dates: Jan. 16, 1967-Jan. 3, 1973
Departure: Left the House; lost Senate nomination

SENATE STANDING COMMITTEES:

1st AGRICULTURE, NUTRITION AND FORESTRY
Dates: Jan. 23, 1979-Jan. 3, 1997
Departure: Left the Senate; retired

Cong.	Ranking	Years in: Senate	Comm.	Date of Assignment
103rd	Maj-2nd	15	14	Jan. 7, 1993
104th	Min-2nd	17	16	Jan. 4, 1995

2nd GOVERNMENTAL AFFAIRS
1st Dates: Jan. 23, 1979-Jan. 3, 1983
1st Departure: Moved to Finance
2nd Dates: Feb. 9, 1984-Feb. 21, 1985
2nd Departure: Left committee; no new assignment
3rd Dates: Jan. 6, 1987-Jan. 3, 1997
3rd Departure: Left the Senate; retired

Cong.	Ranking	Years in: Senate	Comm.	Date of Assignment
103rd	Maj-5th	15 *3	7	Jan. 7, 1993
104th	Min-4th	17 *3	8	Jan. 4, 1995

3rd FINANCE
Dates: Jan. 3, 1983-Jan. 3, 1997
Departure: Left the Senate; retired

Cong.	Ranking	Years in: Senate	Comm.	Date of Assignment
103rd	Maj-7th	15	11	Jan. 7, 1993
104th	Min-4th	17	13	Jan. 4, 1995

SENATE SELECT AND SPECIAL COMMITTEES:

1st SPECIAL AGING (Permanent)
Dates: Jan. 23, 1979-Jan. 3, 1997
Departure: Left the Senate; retired

Cong.	Ranking	Years in: Senate	Comm.	Date of Assignment
103rd	Maj-Chr	15	14	Jan. 21, 1993
104th	Min-RM	17	16	Jan. 6, 1995

2nd SELECT ETHICS (Permanent)
1st Dates: Jan. 25, 1980-May 22, 1991
1st Departure: Left committee; no new assignment
2nd Dates: Sep. 10, 1991-Nov. 20, 1991
2nd Departure: "Keating Five" Committee terminated with submission of final report

3rd JUDGE HARRY E. CLAIBORNE IMPEACHMENT
Dates: Aug. 14, 1986-Oct. 1, 1986
Termination: Senate Report 99-511 filed

4th JUDGE ALCEE L. HASTINGS IMPEACHMENT
Dates: Mar. 16, 1989-Aug. 3, 1989
Termination: Senate Hearing 101-194, Parts 1-2A

JOINT COMMITTEES:

1st JOINT ORGANIZATION OF CONGRESS
Senate Dates: Oct. 8, 1992-Dec. 9, 1993
Termination: Senate Report 103-215 filed

Cong.	Ranking	Years in: Senate	Comm.	Date of Assignment
103rd	Maj-6th	15	1	Continued

Mark Pryor (D-Ark.)

Dates: Jan. 10, 1963
Senate: Jan. 3, 2003-date
Serving in the 111th Congress

SENATE STANDING COMMITTEES:

1st ARMED SERVICES
1st Dates: Jan. 15, 2003-Jan. 6, 2005
1st Departure: Moved to Commerce, Science and Transportation and Select Ethics
2nd Dates: Jan. 12, 2007-Jan. 21, 2009
2nd Departure: Moved to Appropriations

Cong.	Ranking	Years in: Senate	Comm.	Date of Assignment
108th	Min-12th	1 *1	1	Jan. 15, 2003
110th	Maj-11th	5 *2	1	Jan. 12, 2007

2nd GOVERNMENTAL AFFAIRS renamed Oct. 9, 2004
HOMELAND SECURITY AND GOVERNMENTAL AFFAIRS
Dates: Jan. 15, 2003-date
Departure: Still serving in the 111th Congress

Cong.	Ranking	Years in: Senate	Comm.	Date of Assignment
108th	Min-8th	1	1	Jan. 15, 2003
109th	Min-7th	3	2	Jan. 6, 2005
110th	Maj-5th	5	4	Jan. 12, 2007
111th	Maj-5th	7	7	Jan. 21, 2009

3rd SMALL BUSINESS AND ENTRERENURSHIP
Dates: Jan. 15, 2003-date
Departure: Still serving in the 111th Congress

Cong.	Ranking	Years in: Senate	Comm.	Date of Assignment
108th	Min-9th	1	1	Jan. 15, 2003
109th	Min-8th	3	2	Jan. 6, 2005
110th	Maj-8th	5	4	Jan. 12, 2007
111th	Maj-8th	7	7	Jan. 21, 2009

4th COMMERCE, SCIENCE, AND TRANSPORTATION
Dates: Jan. 6, 2005-date
Departure: Still serving in the 111th Congress

Cong.	Ranking	Years in: Senate	Comm.	Date of Assignment
109th	Min-10th	3	1	Jan. 6, 2005
110th	Maj-9th	5	3	Jan. 12, 2007
111th	Maj-9th	7	5	Jan. 21, 2009

5th RULES AND ADMINISTRATION
Dates: Jan. 12, 2007-date
Departure: Still serving in the 111th Congress

Cong.	Ranking	Years in: Senate	Comm.	Date of Assignment
110th	Maj-10th	5	1	Jan. 12, 2007
111th	Maj-9th	7	3	Jan. 21, 2009

6th APPROPRIATIONS
Dates: Jan. 21, 2009-date
Departure: Still serving in the 111th Congress

Cong.	Ranking	Years in: Senate	Comm.	Date of Assignment
111th	Maj-16th	7	1	Jan. 21, 2009

SENATE SELECT AND SPECIAL COMMITTEES:

1st SELECT ETHICS (Permanent)
Dates: Jan. 6, 2005-date
Departure: Still serving in the 111th Congress

Cong.	Ranking	Years in: Senate	Comm.	Date of Assignment
109th	Min-3rd	3	1	Jan. 6, 2005
110th	Maj-3rd	5	3	Jan. 12, 2007
111th	Maj-2nd	7	5	Jan. 21, 2009

Adam H. Putnam Jr. (R-Fla.)

Dates: July 31, 1974
House: Jan. 3, 2001-date
Serving in the 111th Congress

HOUSE STANDING COMMITTEES:

1st AGRICULTURE
Dates: Jan. 6, 2001-Sep. 28, 2004
Departure: Resigned committee; moved to Rules

Cong.	Ranking	Terms in: House	Comm.	Date of Assignment
107th	Maj-26th	1	1	Jan. 6, 2001
108th	Maj-19th	2	2	Jan. 28, 2003

2nd BUDGET
Dates: Jan. 6, 2001-Jan. 3, 2007
Note: *Congressional Record* lists Sep. 28, 2004, letter of resignation from Budget but Putnam remained on the committee in the 109th Congress
Departure: Moved to Financial Services

Cong.	Ranking	Terms in: House	Comm.	Date of Assignment
107th	Maj-22nd	1	1	Jan. 6, 2001
108th	Maj-12th	2	2	Jan. 28, 2003
109th	Maj-5th	3	3	Jan. 26, 2005

3rd GOVERNMENT REFORM
1st Dates: Feb. 8, 2001-Sep. 28, 2004
1st Departure: Resigned committee; moved to Rules
2nd Dates: Oct. 7, 2004-Jan. 3, 2005
2nd Departure: Left committee; no new assignment

Cong.	Ranking	Terms in: House	Comm.	Date of Assignment
107th	Maj-23rd	1 *1	1	Feb. 8, 2001
108th	Maj-14th	2 *1	2	Jan. 28, 2003
108th	MjR-5th	2 *2	1	Oct. 7, 2004

4th RESOURCES
Dates: Apr. 29, 2003-June 19, 2003
Departure: Resigned committee; no new assignment

Cong.	Ranking	Terms in: House	Comm.	Date of Assignment
108th	MjR-1st	2	1	Apr. 29, 2003

5th RULES
Dates: Sep. 29, 2004-Jan. 3, 2007
Departure: Moved to Financial Services

Cong.	Ranking	Terms in: House	Comm.	Date of Assignment
108th	MjR-1st	2	1	Sep. 29, 2004
109th	Maj-5th	3	2	Jan. 4, 2005

6th FINANCIAL SERVICES
Dates: Jan. 10, 2007-date
Departure: Still serving in the 111th Congress

Cong.	Ranking	Terms in: House	Comm.	Date of Assignment
110th	Min-30th	4	1	Jan. 10, 2007
111th	Min-20th	5	2	Jan. 9, 2009

JOINT COMMITTEES:

1st JOINT ECONOMIC
House Dates: May 1, 2001-Jan. 3, 2005
Departure: Left committee; no new assignment

Cong.	Ranking	Terms in: House	Comm.	Date of Assignment
107th	Maj-6th	1	1	May 1, 2001
108th	Maj-5th	2	2	Feb. 25, 2003

Q

Mike Quigley (D-Ill.)

Dates: Oct. 17, 1958
House: Apr. 7, 2009-date
Still serving in the 111th Congress

H: Quigley was elected to the 111th Congress by special election, Mar. 31, 2009, to fill the vacancy caused by the resignation of U.S. Representative Rahm Emanuel (D-Ill.). who had been appointed White House Chief of Staff. Quigley was seated April 21, 2009, and assigned to committees.

HOUSE STANDING COMMITTEES:

1st JUDICIARY
Dates: Apr. 30, 2009-date
Departure: Still serving in the 111th Congress

Cong.	Ranking	Terms in: House	Comm.	Date of Assignment
111th	MjA-15th	1	1	Apr. 30, 2009

2nd OVERSIGHT AND GOVERNMENT REFORM
Dates: Apr. 30, 2009-date
Departure: Still serving in the 111th Congress

Cong.	Ranking	Terms in: House	Comm.	Date of Assignment
111th	MjA-12th	1	1	Apr. 30, 2009

James H. Quillen (R-Tenn.)

Dates: Jan. 11, 1916-Nov. 2, 2003
House: Jan. 3, 1963-Jan. 3, 1997
Left the House: Retired in 1996

HOUSE STANDING COMMITTEES:

1st PUBLIC WORKS
Dates: Jan. 24, 1963-Jan. 3, 1965
Departure: Moved to Rules

2nd RULES
Dates: Jan. 21, 1965-Jan. 3, 1997
Departure: Left the House; retired
RM: In the 102nd Congress, Quillen waived his Min-1st rank in favor of Gerald B.H. Solomon (R-N.Y.). Quillen was designated Republican Chair Emeritus of the committee by the Republican Conference

Cong.	Ranking	Terms in: House	Comm.	Date of Assignment
103rd	Min-2nd	16	15	Jan. 5, 1993
104th	Maj-2nd	17	16	Jan. 4, 1995

3rd STANDARDS OF OFFICIAL CONDUCT
Dates: May 1, 1967-Jan. 3, 1979
Departure: Left committee; no new assignment
RM: Quillen waived his Min-1st rank on the committee, beginning in the 94th Congress, to become Ranking Minority Member on Rules

John F. (Jack) Quinn (R-N.Y.)

Dates: April 13, 1951
House: Jan. 3, 1993-Jan. 3, 2005
Left the House: Retired in 2004

HOUSE STANDING COMMITTEES:

1st PUBLIC WORKS AND TRANSPORTATION, 103
TRANSPORTATION AND INFRASTRUCTURE, 104-108
Dates: Jan. 5, 1993-Jan. 3, 2005
Departure: Left the House; retired

Cong.	Ranking	Terms in: House	Comm.	Date of Assignment
103rd	Min-24th	1	1	Jan. 5, 1993
104th	Maj-21st	2	2	Jan. 4, 1995
105th	Maj-15th	3	3	Jan. 7, 1997
106th	Maj-13th	4	4	Jan. 6, 1999
107th	Maj-10th	5	5	Jan. 6, 2001
108th	Maj-9th	6	6	Jan. 28, 2003

2nd VETERANS' AFFAIRS
Dates: Jan. 5, 1993-Jan. 3, 2005
Departure: Left the House; retired

Cong.	Ranking	Terms in: House	Comm.	Date of Assignment
103rd	Min-10th	1	1	Jan. 5, 1993
104th	Maj-8th	2	2	Jan. 4, 1995
105th	Maj-7th	3	3	Jan. 21, 1997
106th	Maj-7th	4	4	Jan. 6, 1999
107th	Maj-7th	5	5	Jan. 6, 2001
108th	Maj-5th	6	6	Jan. 28, 2003

JOINT COMMITTEES:

1st JOINT ECONOMIC
House Dates: Jan. 19, 1995-Jan. 3, 1997
Departure: Left committee; no new assignment

Cong.	Ranking	Terms in: House	Comm.	Date of Assignment
104th	Maj-3rd	2	1	Jan. 19, 1995

R

George P. Radanovich (R-Cal.)

Dates: June 20, 1955
House: Jan. 3, 1995-date
Serving in the 111th Congress

HOUSE STANDING COMMITTEES:

1st BUDGET
Dates: Jan. 4, 1995-Jan. 3, 2001
Departure: Moved to Energy and Commerce

Cong.	Ranking	Terms in: House	Comm.	Date of Assignment
104th	Maj-23rd	1	1	Jan. 4, 1995
105th	Maj-15th	2	2	Jan. 7, 1997
106th	Maj-10th	3	3	Jan. 6, 1999

2nd RESOURCES
Dates: Jan. 4, 1995-Jan. 3, 2007
Departure: Left committee; no new assignment

Cong.	Ranking	Terms in: House	Comm.	Date of Assignment
104th	Maj-19th	1	1	Jan. 4, 1995

Cong.	Ranking	House	Comm.	Date of Assignment
105th	Maj-15th	2	2	Jan. 7, 1997
106th	Maj-14th	3	3	Jan. 6, 1999
107th	Maj-13th	4	4	Jan. 6, 2001
108th	Maj-12th	5	5	Jan. 28, 2003
109th	Maj-9th	6	6	Jan. 26, 2005

3rd INTERNATIONAL RELATIONS
Dates: Jan. 6, 1999-Jan. 3, 2001
Departure: Moved to Energy and Commerce

Cong.	Ranking	Terms in: House	Comm.	Date of Assignment
106th	Maj-24th	3	1	Jan. 6, 1999

4th ENERGY AND COMMERCE
Dates: Jan. 6, 2001-date
Departure: Still serving in the 111th Congress

Cong.	Ranking	Terms in: House	Comm.	Date of Assignment
107th	Maj-26th	4	1	Jan. 6, 2001
108th	Maj-21st	5	2	Jan. 28, 2003
109th	Maj-18th	6	3	Jan. 6, 2005
110th	Min-16th	7	4	Jan. 10, 2007
111th	Min-11th	8	5	Jan. 9, 2009

Nick Joe Rahall II (D-W.Va.)

Dates: May 20, 1949
House: Jan. 3, 1977-date
Serving in the 111th Congress

HOUSE STANDING COMMITTEES:

1st INTERIOR AND INSULAR AFFAIRS, 95-102
NATURAL RESOURCES, 103
RESOURCES, 104-109
NATURAL RESOURCES, 110-111
Dates: Jan. 19, 1977-date
Departure: Still serving in the 111th Congress

Cong.	Ranking	Terms in: House	Comm.	Date of Assignment
103rd	Maj-5th	9	9	Jan. 5, 1993
104th	Min-2nd	10	10	Jan. 9, 1995
105th	Min-3rd	11	11	Jan. 7, 1997
106th	Min-2nd	12	12	Jan. 6, 1999
107th	Min-RM	13	13	Feb. 8, 2001
108th	Min-RM	14	14	Jan. 8, 2003
109th	Min-RM	15	15	Jan. 6, 2005
110th	Maj-Chr	16	16	Jan. 4, 2007
111th	Maj-Chr	17	17	Jan. 6, 2009

2nd PUBLIC WORKS AND TRANSPORTATION, 95-103
TRANSPORTATION AND INFRASTRUCTURE, 104-111
Dates: Jan. 19, 1977-date
Departure: Still serving in the 111th Congress

Cong.	Ranking	Terms in: House	Comm.	Date of Assignment
103rd	Maj-3rd	9	9	Jan. 5, 1993
104th	Min-3rd	10	10	Jan. 4, 1995
105th	Min-2nd	11	11	Jan. 7, 1997
106th	Min-2nd	12	12	Jan. 6, 1999
107th	Min-2nd	13	13	Jan. 31, 2001
108th	Min-2nd	14	14	Jan. 28, 2003
109th	Min-2nd	15	15	Jan. 26, 2005

Cong.	Ranking	House	Comm.	Date of Assignment
110th	Maj-2nd	16	16	Jan. 10, 2007
111th	Maj-2nd	17	17	Jan. 9, 2009

3rd STANDARDS OF OFFICIAL CONDUCT
Dates: Mar. 26, 1980-Jan. 3, 1985
Departure: Left committee; no new assignment

4th EDUCATION AND LABOR
Temporary Dates: Jan. 27, 1989-June 14, 1990
Departure: Temporary term expired

James Ramstad (R-Minn.)

Dates: May 6, 1946
House: Jan. 3, 1991-Jan. 3, 2009
Left the House: Retired in 2008

HOUSE STANDING COMMITTEES:

1st JUDICIARY
Dates: Jan. 24, 1991-Jan. 3, 1995
Departure: Moved to Ways and Means

Cong.	Ranking	Terms in: House	Comm.	Date of Assignment
103rd	Min-10th	2	2	Jan. 5, 1993

2nd SMALL BUSINESS
Dates: Jan. 24, 1991-Jan. 3, 1995
Departure: Moved to Ways and Means

Cong.	Ranking	Terms in: House	Comm.	Date of Assignment
103rd	Min-6th	2	2	Jan. 5, 1993

3rd WAYS AND MEANS
Dates: Jan. 4, 1995-Jan. 3, 2007
Departure: Left the House; retired

Cong.	Ranking	Terms in: House	Comm.	Date of Assignment
104th	Maj-12th	3	1	Jan. 4, 1995
105th	Maj-11th	4	2	Jan. 7, 1997
106th	Maj-10th	5	3	Jan. 6, 1999
107th	Maj-9th	6	4	Jan. 6, 2001
108th	Maj-9th	7	5	Jan. 28, 2003
109th	Maj-7th	8	6	Jan. 6, 2005
110th	Min-4th	9	7	Jan. 4, 2007

HOUSE SELECT AND SPECIAL COMMITTEES:

1st SELECT NARCOTICS ABUSE AND CONTROL (Temporary)
Dates: Feb. 21, 1991-Jan. 3, 1993
Termination: Committee not renewed in 1993

JOINT COMMITTEES:

1st JOINT ECONOMIC
House Dates: Feb. 16, 1993-Jan. 3, 1995
Departure: Moved to Ways and Means

Cong.	Ranking	Terms in: House	Comm.	Date of Assignment
103rd	Min-4th	2	1	Feb. 16, 1993

Charles B. Rangel (D-N.Y.)

Dates: June 11, 1930
House: Jan. 3, 1971-date
Serving in the 111th Congress

HOUSE STANDING COMMITTEES:

1st PUBLIC WORKS
Dates: Feb. 4, 1971-Oct. 12, 1972
Departure: Resigned committee; moved to Judiciary

2nd SCIENCE AND ASTRONAUTICS
Dates: Feb. 4, 1971-Jan. 3, 1973
Departure: Moved to District of Columbia

3rd JUDICIARY
Dates: Oct. 12, 1972-Jan. 3, 1975
Departure: Moved to Ways and Means

4th DISTRICT OF COLUMBIA
Dates: Jan. 24, 1973-Jan. 3, 1975
Departure: Moved to Ways and Means

5th WAYS AND MEANS
Dates: Jan. 20, 1975-date
Departure: Still serving in the 111th Congress
Ch1: Stepped aside as Chair on Mar. 3, 2010

Cong.	Ranking	Terms in: House	Comm.	Date of Assignment
103rd	Maj-4th	12	10	Jan. 5, 1993
104th	Min-2nd	13	11	Jan. 4, 1995
105th	Min-RM	14	12	Jan. 7, 1997
106th	Min-RM	15	13	Jan. 6, 1999
107th	Min-RM	16	14	Jan. 31, 2001
108th	Min-RM	17	15	Jan. 8, 2003
109th	Min-RM	18	16	Jan. 6, 2005
110th	Maj-Chr	19	17	Jan. 4, 2007
111th	Maj-Ch1	20	18	Jan. 6, 2009

HOUSE SELECT AND SPECIAL COMMITTEES:

1st SELECT CRIME
Dates: Mar. 15, 1971-June 29, 1973
Departure: Committee terminated

2nd SELECT NARCOTICS ABUSE AND CONTROL (Temporary)
Dates: Aug. 3, 1976-Jan. 3, 1993
Termination: Committee not renewed in 1993

3rd SELECT ENERGY (Ad Hoc)
Dates: Apr. 21, 1977-Dec. 29, 1978
Termination: House Report 1820 (95-2) filed

JOINT COMMITTEES:

1st JOINT TAXATION
House Dates: Jan. 10, 1995-date
Departure: Still serving in the 111th Congress

Cong.	Ranking	Terms in: House	Comm.	Date of Assignment
104th	Min-2nd	13	1	Jan. 10, 1995 Ltr
105th	Min-1st	14	2	Feb. 5, 1997 Ltr
106th	Min-1st	15	3	Jan. 6, 1999 Ltr
107th	Min-1st	16	4	Feb. 7, 2001 Ltr
108th	Min-1st	17	5	Jan. 29, 2003 Ltr
109th	Min-1st	18	6	Feb. 7, 2005 Ltr
110th	Maj-CVc	19	7	Jan. 17, 2007 Ltr
111th	Maj-CVc	20	8	Jan. 12, 2009 Ltr

Arthur A. Ravenel Jr. (R-S.C.)

Dates: March 29, 1927
House: Jan. 3, 1987-Jan. 3, 1995
Left the House: Lost nomination for Governor in 1994

HOUSE STANDING COMMITTEES:

1st ARMED SERVICES
Dates: Jan. 21,1987-Jan. 3, 1995
Departure: Left the House; lost nomination for Governor

Cong.	Ranking	Terms in: House	Comm.	Date of Assignment
103rd	Min-9th	4	4	Jan. 5, 1993

2nd MERCHANT MARINE AND FISHERIES
Dates: Nov. 9, 1989-Jan. 3, 1995
Departure: Left the House; lost nomination for Governor

Cong.	Ranking	Terms in: House	Comm.	Date of Assignment
103rd	Min-8th	4	3	Jan. 5, 1993

William T. Redmond (R-N.M.)

Born: Jan. 28, 1955
House: May 13, 1997-Jan. 3, 1999
Left the House: Defeated for re-election in 1998

H: Redmond was elected to the 105th Congress by special election, May 13, 1997, to fill the vacancy caused by the resignation of U.S. Representative William B. Richardson (D-N.M.). Redmond was seated May 20, 1997, and assigned to committees.

1st BANKING AND FINANCIAL SERVICES
Dates: July 23, 1997-Jan. 3, 1999
Departure: Left the House; lost re-election

Cong.	Ranking	Terms in: House	Comm.	Date of Assignment
105th	MjA-31st	1	1	July 23, 1997

2nd NATIONAL SECURITY
Dates: July 23, 1997-Jan. 3, 1999
Departure: Left the House; lost re-election

Cong.	Ranking	Terms in: House	Comm.	Date of Assignment
105th	MjA-31st	1	1	July 23, 1997

3rd VETERANS' AFFAIRS
Dates: July 23, 1997-Jan. 3, 1999
Departure: Left the House; lost re-election

Cong.	Ranking	Terms in: House	Comm.	Date of Assignment
105th	MjR-1st	1	1	July 23, 1997

John F. Reed (D-R.I.)

Dates: Nov. 12, 1949
House: Jan. 3, 1991-Jan. 3, 1997
Left the House: Elected to U.S. Senate in 1996
Senate: Jan. 3, 1997-date
Serving in the 111th Congress

HOUSE STANDING COMMITTEES:

1st EDUCATION AND LABOR, 102
ECONOMIC AND EDUCATIONAL OPPORTUNITIES, 103-104
Dates: Jan. 24, 1991-Jan. 3, 1997
Departure: Left the House for the Senate

Cong.	Ranking	Terms in: House	Comm.	Date of Assignment
103rd	Maj-14th	2	2	Jan. 5, 1993
104th	Min-11th	3	3	Jan. 4, 1995

2nd JUDICIARY
Dates: Jan. 24, 1991-Jan. 3, 1997
Departure: Left the House for the Senate

Cong.	Ranking	Terms in: House	Comm.	Date of Assignment
103rd	Maj-16th	2	2	Jan. 5, 1993
104th	Min-8th	3	3	Jan. 4, 1995

3rd MERCHANT MARINE AND FISHERIES
Dates: Jan. 24, 1991-Jan. 3, 1995
Departure: Committee abolished; no new assignment

Cong.	Ranking	Terms in: House	Comm.	Date of Assignment
103rd	Maj-14th	2	2	Jan. 5, 1993

HOUSE SELECT AND SPECIAL COMMITTEES:

1st SELECT INTELLIGENCE (Permanent)
Dates: Feb. 3, 1993-Jan. 5, 1995
Departure: Left committee; no new assignment

Cong.	Ranking	Terms in: House	Comm.	Date of Assignment
103rd	Maj-12th	2	1	Feb. 3, 1993

SENATE STANDING COMMITTEES:

1st BANKING, HOUSING AND URBAN AFFAIRS
Dates: Jan. 9, 1997-date
Departure: Still serving in the 111th Congress

Cong.	Ranking	Years in: Senate	Comm.	Date of Assignment
105th	Min-8th	1	1	Jan. 9, 1997
106th	Min-6th	3	2	Jan. 7, 1999
107th	Min-4th	5	5	Jan. 25, 2001
+107th	Maj-4th	5	5	June 6, 2001
108th	Min-4th	7	7	Jan. 15, 2003
109th	Min-4th	9	8	Jan. 6, 2005
110th	Maj-3rd	11	11	Jan. 12, 2007
111th	Maj-3rd	13	13	Jan. 21, 2009

2nd LABOR AND HUMAN RESOURCES renamed Jan. 21, 1999
HEALTH, EDUCATION, LABOR AND PENSIONS
Dates: Jan. 9, 1997-date
Departure: Still serving in the 111th Congress

Cong.	Ranking	Years in: Senate	Comm.	Date of Assignment
105th	Min-8th	1	1	Jan. 9, 1997
106th	Min-8th	3	2	Jan. 7, 1999
107th	Min-8th	5	5	Jan. 25, 2001
+107th	Maj-9th	5	5	July 10, 2001
108th	Min-8th	7	7	Jan. 15, 2003
109th	Min-8th	9	8	Jan. 6, 2005
110th	Maj-7th	11	11	Jan. 12, 2007
111th	Maj-7th	13	13	Jan. 21, 2009

3rd ARMED SERVICES
Dates: Jan. 7, 1999-date
Departure: Still serving in the 111th Congress

Cong.	Ranking	Years in: Senate	Comm.	Date of Assignment
106th	Min-9th	3	1	Jan. 7, 1999
107th	Min-7th	5	3	Jan. 25, 2001
+107th	Maj-7th	5	3	June 6, 2001
108th	Min-5th	7	5	Jan. 15, 2003
109th	Min-5th	9	6	Jan. 6, 2005
110th	Maj-5th	11	9	Jan. 12, 2007
111th	Maj-5th	13	11	Jan. 21, 2009

4th APPROPRIATIONS
1st Dates: July 10, 2001-Jan 15, 2003
1st Departure: Left committee; no new assignment
2nd Dates: Jan. 12, 2007-date
2nd Dates: Still serving in the 111th Congress

Cong.	Ranking	Years in: Senate	Comm.	Date of Assignment
+107th	MjA-15th	5 *1	1	July 10, 2001
110th	Maj-13th	11 *2	1	Jan. 12, 2007
111th	Maj-13th	13 *2	3	Jan. 21, 2009

SENATE SELECT AND SPECIAL COMMITTEES:

1st SPECIAL AGING (Permanent)
Dates: Jan. 9, 1997-Jan. 25, 2001
Departure: Moved to Joint Economic

Cong.	Ranking	Years in: Senate	Comm.	Assignment
105th	Min-8th	1	1	Jan. 9, 1997
106th	Min-6th	3	2	Jan. 7, 1999

JOINT COMMITTEES:

1st JOINT ECONOMIC
Senate Dates: Jan. 25, 2001-Jan. 12, 2007
Departure: Left committee; returned to Appropriations

Cong.	Ranking	Years in: Senate	Comm.	Date of Assignment
107th	Min-1st	5	1	Jan. 25, 2001
+107th	Maj-VC2	5	1	June 6, 2001
108th	Min-1st	7	2	Jan. 15, 2003
109th	Min-1st	9	4	Jan. 6, 2005

Ralph S. Regula (R-Ohio)

Dates: Dec. 3, 1924
House: Jan. 3, 1973-Jan. 3, 2009
Left the House: Retired in 2008

HOUSE STANDING COMMITTEES:

1st GOVERNMENT OPERATIONS
Dates: Jan. 24, 1973-Jan. 3, 1975
Departure: Moved to Appropriations

2nd INTERIOR AND INSULAR AFFAIRS
Dates: Jan. 24, 1973-Jan. 3, 1975
Departure: Moved to Appropriations

3rd APPROPRIATIONS
Dates: Jan. 28, 1975-Jan. 3, 2009
Departure: Left the House; retired

Cong.	Ranking	Terms in: House	Comm.	Date of Assignment
103rd	Min-4th	11	10	Jan. 5, 1993
104th	Maj-5th	12	11	Jan. 4, 1995
105th	Maj-4th	13	12	Jan. 7, 1997
106th	Maj-2nd	14	13	Jan. 6, 1999
107th	Maj-2nd	15	14	Jan. 6, 2001
108th	Maj-2nd	16	15	Jan. 28, 2003
109th	Maj-3rd	17	16	Jan. 6, 2005
110th	Min-3rd	18	17	Jan. 4, 2007

4th BUDGET
Dates: Jan. 11, 1977-Jan. 3, 1983
Departure: Left committee; no new assignment

HOUSE SELECT AND SPECIAL COMMITTEES:

1st SELECT AGING (Permanent)
Dates: Aug. 1, 1977-Jan. 3, 1993
Termination: Committee not renewed in 1993

Dennis Rehberg (R-Mont.)

Dates: Oct. 5, 1955
House: Jan. 3, 2001-date
Serving in the 111th Congress

HOUSE STANDING COMMITTEES:

1st AGRICULTURE
Dates: Jan. 6, 2001-Jan. 3, 2005
Departure: Moved to Appropriations

Cong.	Ranking	Terms in: House	Comm.	Date of Assignment
107th	Maj-24th	1	1	Jan. 6, 2001
108th	Maj-17th	2	2	Jan. 28, 2003

2nd TRANSPORTATION AND INFRASTRUCTURE
Dates: Jan. 6, 2001-Jan. 3, 2005
Departure: Moved to Appropriations

Cong.	Ranking	Terms in: House	Comm.	Date of Assignment
107th	Maj-35th	1	1	Jan. 6, 2001
108th	Maj-27th	2	2	Jan. 28, 2003

3rd RESOURCES
Dates: Feb. 8, 2001-Jan. 3, 2005
Departure: Moved to Appropriations

Cong.	Ranking	Terms in: House	Comm.	Date of Assignment
107th	MjR-2nd	1	1	Feb. 8, 2001
108th	Min-23rd	2	2	Jan. 28, 2003

4th APPROPRIATIONS
Dates: Jan. 6, 2005-date
Departure: Still serving in the 111th Congress

Cong.	Ranking	Terms in: House	Comm.	Date of Assignment
109th	Maj-35th	3	1	Jan. 6, 2005
110th	Min-27th	4	2	Jan. 4, 2007
111th	Min-17th	5	3	Jan. 9, 2009

David G. Reichert (R-Wash.)

Dates: Aug. 29, 1950
House: Jan. 3, 2005-date
Serving in the 111th Congress

HOUSE STANDING COMMITTEES:

1st SCIENCE, 109
SCIENCE AND TECHNOLOGY, 110
Dates: Jan. 26, 2005-Jan. 3, 2009
Departure: Moved to Ways and Means

Cong.	Ranking	Terms in: House	Comm.	Date of Assignment
109th	Maj-20th	1	1	Jan. 26, 2005
110th	Min-15th	2	2	Mar. 12, 2007

2nd TRANSPORTATION AND INFRASTRUCTURE
Dates: Jan. 26, 2005-Jan. 3, 2009
Departure: Moved to Ways and Means

Cong.	Ranking	Terms in: House	Comm.	Date of Assignment
109th	Maj-36th	1	1	Jan. 26, 2005
110th	Min-25th	2	2	Jan. 10, 2007

3rd HOMELAND SECURITY
Dates: Feb. 9, 2005-Jan. 3, 2009
Departure: Moved to Ways and Means

Cong.	Ranking	Terms in: House	Comm.	Date of Assignment
109th	Maj-17th	1	1	Feb. 9, 2005
110th	Min-9th	2	2	Jan. 10, 2007

4th WAYS AND MEANS
Dates: Jan. 9, 2009-date
Departure: Still serving in the 111th Congress

Cong.	Ranking	Terms in: House	Comm.	Date of Assignment
111th	Min-12th	3	1	Jan. 9, 2009

Harry M. Reid (D-Nev.)

Dates: Dec. 2, 1939
House: Jan. 3, 1983-Jan. 3, 1987
Left the House: Elected to U.S. Senate in 1986
Senate: Jan. 3, 1987-date
Serving in the 111th Congress

HOUSE STANDING COMMITTEES:

1st FOREIGN AFFAIRS
Dates: Jan. 6, 1983-Jan. 3, 1987
Departure: Left the House for the Senate

2nd SCIENCE AND TECHNOLOGY
Dates: Jan. 6, 1983-Jan. 3, 1987
Departure: Left the House for the Senate

HOUSE SELECT AND SPECIAL COMMITTEES:

1st SELECT AGING (Permanent)
Dates: Feb. 8, 1983-Jan. 3, 1987
Departure: Left the House for the Senate

SENATE STANDING COMMITTEES:

1st APPROPRIATIONS
Dates: Jan. 6, 1987-Jan. 12, 2007
Departure: Moved to Rules and Administration and elected Majority Leader

Cong.	Ranking	Years in: Senate	Comm.	Date of Assignment
103rd	Maj-12th	7	7	Jan. 7, 1993
104th	Min-10th	9	8	Jan. 4, 1995
105th	Min-9th	11	11	Jan. 9, 1997
106th	Min-8th	13	13	Jan. 7, 1999
107th	Min-7th	15	15	Jan. 25, 2001
+107th	Maj-7th	15	15	June 6, 2001
108th	Min-7th	17	17	Jan. 15, 2003
109th	Min-6th	19	19	Jan. 6, 2005

2nd ENVIRONMENT AND PUBLIC WORKS
Dates: Jan. 6, 1987-Jan. 3, 2005
Ch2: Became Chair when Democrats gained control on June 6, 2001, and relinquished the chairmanship to James M. Jeffords (Ind-Vt.) on July 10, 2001
Departure: Left committee; elected Minority Leader

Cong.	Ranking	Years in: Senate	Comm.	Date of Assignment
103rd	Maj-5th	7	7	Jan. 7, 1993
104th	Min-4th	9	8	Jan. 4, 1995
105th	Min-4th	11	11	Jan. 9, 1997
106th	Min-4th	13	13	Jan. 7, 1999
=107th	Maj-ChT	15	15	Jan. 3, 2001
107th	Min-RM1	15	15	Jan. 25, 2001
+107th	Maj-Ch2	15	15	June 6, 2001
107th	Maj-2nd	15	15	July 10, 2001
108th	Min-3rd	17	17	Jan. 15, 2003

3rd RULES AND ADMINISTRATION
Dates: Jan. 12, 2007-date
Departures: Left committee; no new assignment

Cong.	Ranking	Years in: Senate	Comm.	Date of Assignment
110th	Maj-8th	21	1	Jan. 12, 2007

SENATE SELECT AND SPECIAL COMMITTEES:

1st SPECIAL AGING (Permanent)
Dates: Jan. 6, 1987-Jan. 6, 2005
Departure: Left committee; elected Minority Leader

Cong.	Ranking	Years in: Senate	Comm.	Date of Assignment
103rd	Maj-7th	7	7	Jan. 21, 1993
104th	Min-6th	9	9	Jan. 6, 1995
105th	Min-3rd	11	11	Jan. 9, 1997
106th	Min-2nd	13	13	Jan. 7, 1999
107th	Min-2nd	15	15	Jan. 25, 2001
+107th	Maj-2nd	15	15	June 6, 2001
108th	Min-2nd	17	17	Jan. 15, 2003

2nd SELECT INDIAN AFFAIRS (Permanent), 101-102
INDIAN AFFAIRS (Permanent), 103-108
Dates: Apr. 11, 1989-Jan. 3, 2005
Departure: Left committee; elected Minority Leader.

Cong.	Ranking	Years in: Senate	Comm.	Date of Assignment
103rd	Maj-4th	7	4	Jan. 5, 1993
104th	Min-3rd	9	6	Jan. 9, 1995
105th	Min-3rd	11	8	Jan. 9, 1997
106th	Min-3rd	13	10	Jan. 7, 1999
107th	Min-3rd	15	12	Jan. 25, 2001
+107th	Maj-3rd	15	13	June 6, 2001
108th	Min-3rd	17	14	Jan. 15, 2003

3rd JUDGE WALTER L. NIXON IMPEACHMENT
Dates: May 11, 1989-Sep. 13, 1989
Termination: Hearings concluded

4th SELECT POW-MIA AFFAIRS
Dates: Aug. 2, 1991-Feb. 3, 1993
Termination: Senate Report 1 (103-1) filed

5th SELECT ETHICS (Permanent)
Dates: Jan. 9, 1997-Jan. 6, 2005
Ch2: Replaced C. Patrick Roberts (R-Kans.) on June 6, 2001, following Senate party control shift
Departure: Left committee; elected Minority Leader

Cong.	Ranking	Years in: Senate	Comm.	Date of Assignment
105th	Min-VCh	11	1	Jan. 9, 1997
106th	Min-VCh	13	2	Jan. 7, 1999
107th	Min-VC1	15	5	Jan. 25, 2001
+107th	Maj-Ch2	15	5	June 6, 2001
108th	Min-VCh	17	7	Jan. 15, 2003

JOINT COMMITTEES:

1st JOINT ORGANIZATION OF CONGRESS (Ad Hoc)
Senate Dates: Oct. 8, 1992-Dec. 9, 1993
Termination: Senate Report 103-215 filed

Cong.	Ranking	Years in: Senate	Comm.	Date of Assignment
103rd	Maj-4th	7	1	Continued

SENATE LEADERSHIP POSTS

Dates: Jan. 3, 1997-date
Departure: Still serving in the 111th Congress

1st SENATE MINORITY WHIP
1st Dates: Jan. 3, 1999-June 6, 2001
Note: For the 106th Congress, Reid was elected on Dec. 1, 1998, without opposition to succeed Minority Whip Wendell H. Ford (D-Ky.), who had retired. Reid was re-elected without opposition for the 107th Congress.
1st Departure: The Jeffords switch gave majority control of the Senate to the Democrats and Reid became Majority Whip
2nd Dates: Jan. 3, 2003-Jan. 3, 2005
Note: For the 108th Congress, Reid was elected Minority Whip without opposition
2nd Departure: Elected Minority Floor Leader

Cong.	Ranking	Years in: Senate	Post	Date of Selection
106th	Min-2nd	13 *1	1	Dec. 1, 1998
107th	Min-2nd	15 *1	3	Dec. 5, 2000
108th	Min-2nd	17 *2	5	Nov. 13, 2002

2nd SENATE MAJORITY WHIP
1st Dates: June 6, 2001-Jan. 3, 2003

Note: The Jeffords switch gave majority control of the Senate to the Democrats and Reid became Majority Whip without a new election
Departure: Democratic Party lost Senate majority in 2002

Cong.	Ranking	Years in: Senate	Post	Date of Service
+107th	Min-2nd	15	1	June 6, 2001

3rd SENATE MINORITY FLOOR LEADER
Dates: Jan. 3, 2005-Jan. 3, 2007
Note: For the 109th Congress, Reid was elected on Nov. 16, 2004, without opposition to succeed Minority Leader Thomas Daschle (D-S.D.) who had been defeated for re-election
Departure: Democratic Party gained Senate majority in 2006

Cong.	Ranking	Years in: Senate	Post	Date of Selection
109th	Min-1st	19	1	Nov. 16, 2004

4th SENATE MAJORITY FLOOR LEADER
Dates: Jan. 3, 2007-date
Note: For the 110th Congress, Reid was elected to be Majority Leader on Nov. 14, 2006, without opposition. He was re-elected for the 111th Congress without opposition.
Departure: Still serving in the 111th Congress

Cong.	Ranking	Years in: Senate	Post	Date of Selection
110th	Maj-1st	21	1	Nov. 14, 2006
111th	Maj-1st	23	3	Nov. 18, 2008

Rick Renzi (R-Ariz.)

Dates: June 11, 1958
House: Jan. 3, 2003-Jan. 3, 2009
Left the House: Retired in 2008

HOUSE STANDING COMMITTEES:

1st FINANCIAL SERVICES
Dates: Jan. 28, 2003-Apr. 24, 2007
Departure: Resigned committee due to ethics issues

Cong.	Ranking	Terms in: House	Comm.	Date of Assignment
108th	Maj-37th	1	1	Jan. 28, 2003
109th	Maj-30th	2	2	Jan. 26, 2005
110th	Min-22nd	3	3	Jan. 10, 2007

2nd RESOURCES, 108-109
NATURAL RESOURCES, 110
Dates: Jan. 28, 2003-Apr. 24, 2007
Departure: Resigned committee due to ethics issues

Cong.	Ranking	Terms in: House	Comm.	Date of Assignment
108th	Maj-24th	1	1	Jan. 28, 2003
109th	Maj-19th	2	2	Jan. 26, 2005
110th	Min-10th	3	3	Jan. 10, 2007

3rd VETERANS' AFFAIRS
Dates: Jan. 28, 2003-Jan. 26, 2005
Departure: Resigned committee; moved to Permanent Select Intelligence

Cong.	Ranking	Terms in: House	Comm.	Date of Assignment
108th	Maj-17th	1	1	Jan. 28, 2003
109th	Maj-13th	2	2	Jan. 26, 2005

HOUSE SELECT AND SPECIAL COMMITTEES:

1st PERMANENT SELECT INTELLIGENCE
Dates: Jan. 26, 2005-Apr. 20, 2007
Departure: Resigned committee due to ethics issues

Cong.	Ranking	Terms in: House	Comm.	Date of Assignment
109th	Maj-12th	2	1	Jan. 26, 2005
110th	Min-8th	3	2	Jan. 17, 2007

Silvestre Reyes (D-Tex.)

Dates: Nov. 10, 1944
House: Jan. 3, 1997-date
Serving in the 111th Congress

HOUSE STANDING COMMITTEES:

1st NATIONAL SECURITY, 105
ARMED SERVICES, 106-111
Dates: Jan. 7, 1997-date
Departure: Still serving in the 111th Congress

Cong.	Ranking	Terms in: House	Comm.	Date of Assignment
105th	Min-17th	1	1	Jan. 7, 1997
106th	Min-13th	2	2	Jan. 6, 1999
107th	Min-11th	3	3	Jan. 31, 2001
108th	Min-8th	4	4	Jan. 28, 2003
109th	Min-8th	5	5	Jan. 26, 2005
110th	Maj-7th	6	6	Jan. 10, 2007
111th	Maj-6th	7	7	Jan. 7, 2009

2nd VETERANS' AFFAIRS
1st Dates: Feb. 6, 1997-June 15, 2004
1st Departure: Resigned committee; no new assignment
2nd Dates: Feb. 2, 2005-Jan. 3, 2007
2nd Departure: Left committee; became Chair of Permanent Select Intelligence

Cong.	Ranking	Terms in: House	Comm.	Date of Assignment
105th	Min-12th	1 *1	1	Feb. 6, 1997
106th	Min-8th	2 *1	2	Jan. 6, 1999
107th	Min-8th	3 *1	3	Jan. 31, 2001
108th	Min-9th	4 *1	4	Feb. 13, 2003
109th	Min-10th	5 *2	1	Feb. 2, 2005

HOUSE SELECT AND SPECIAL COMMITTEES:

1st PERMANENT SELECT INTELLIGENCE
Dates: Mar. 1, 2001-date
Departure: Still serving in the 111th Congress

Cong.	Ranking	Terms in: House	Comm.	Date of Assignment
107th	Min-8th	3	1	Mar. 1, 2001
108th	Min-3rd	4	2	Jan. 8, 2003
109th	Min-3rd	5	3	Jan. 26, 2005
110th	Maj-Chr	6	4	Jan. 5, 2007
111th	Maj-Chr	7	5	Jan. 6, 2009

Mel Reynolds (D-Ill.)

Dates: Jan. 8, 1952
House: Jan. 3, 1993-Oct. 1, 1995
Left the House: Resigned and retired

HOUSE STANDING COMMITTEES:

1st WAYS AND MEANS
Dates: Jan. 5, 1993-Jan. 3, 1995
Departure: Moved to Economic and Educational Opportunities

Cong.	Ranking	Terms in: House	Comm.	Date of Assignment
103rd	Maj-24th	1	1	Jan. 5, 1993

2nd ECONOMIC AND EDUCATIONAL OPPORTUNITIES
Dates: Jan. 4, 1995-Oct. 1, 1995
Departure: Resigned the House and retired

Cong.	Ranking	Terms in: House	Comm.	Date of Assignment
104th	Min-19th	2	1	Jan. 4, 1995

Thomas M. Reynolds (R-N.Y.)

Dates: Sept. 3, 1950
House: Jan. 3, 1999-Jan. 3, 2009
Left the House: Retired in 2008

HOUSE STANDING COMMITTEES:

1st RULES
Dates: Jan. 6, 1999-Jan. 3, 2005
Departure: Moved to Ways and Means

Cong.	Ranking	Terms in: House	Comm.	Date of Assignment
106th	Maj-9th	1	1	Jan. 6, 1999
107th	Maj-9th	2	2	Jan. 3, 2001
108th	Maj-9th	3	3	Jan. 7, 2003

2nd HOUSE ADMINISTRATION
Dates: Jan. 31, 2001-Jan. 3, 2007
Departure: Left committee; no new assignment

Cong.	Ranking	Terms in: House	Comm.	Date of Assignment
107th	Maj-6th	2	1	Jan. 31, 2001
108th	Maj-6th	3	2	Jan. 28, 2003
109th	Maj-5th	4	3	Jan. 26, 2005

3rd WAYS AND MEANS
Dates: Jan. 6, 2005-Jan. 3, 2009
Departure: Left the House; retired

Cong.	Ranking	Terms in: House	Comm.	Date of Assignment
109th	Maj-18th	4	1	Jan. 6, 2005
110th	Min-11th	5	2	Jan. 4, 2007

JOINT COMMITTEES:

1st JOINT PRINTING
House Dates: Mar. 16, 2005-Jan. 3, 2007
Departure: Left committee; no new assignment

Cong.	Ranking	Terms in: House	Comm.	Date of Assignment
109th	Maj-3rd	4	1	Mar. 16, 2005

Laura Richardson (D-Cal.)

Dates: April 14, 1962
House: Aug. 21, 2007-date
Serving in the 111th Congress

H: Richardson was elected to the 110th Congress by special election, Aug. 21, 2007, to fill the vacancy caused by the death of U.S. Representative Juanita Millender-McDonald (D-Cal.). Richardson was sworn Sept. 4, 2007, and assigned to committees.

HOUSE STANDING COMMITTEES:

1st SCIENCE AND TECHNOLOGY
Dates: Sep. 20, 2007-Jan. 3, 2009
Departure: Moved to Homeland Security

Cong.	Ranking	Terms in: House	Comm.	Date of Assignment
110th	MjR-1st	1	1	Sep. 20, 2007

2nd TRANSPORTATION AND INFRASTRUCTURE
Dates: Sep. 20, 2007-date
Departure: Still serving in the 111th Congress

Cong.	Ranking	Terms in: House	Comm.	Date of Assignment
110th	MjR-1st	1	1	Sep. 20, 2007
111th	Maj-33rd	2	2	Jan. 7, 2009

3rd HOMELAND SECURITY
Dates: Jan. 28, 2009-date
Departure: Still serving in the 111th Congress

Cong.	Ranking	Terms in: House	Comm.	Date of Assignment
111th	Maj-11th	2	1	Jan. 28, 2009

William B. Richardson (D-N.M.)

Dates: Nov. 15, 1947
House: Jan. 3, 1983-Feb. 13, 1997
Left the House: Resigned; appointed U.S. Ambassador to United Nations

HOUSE STANDING COMMITTEES:

1st ENERGY AND COMMERCE
1st Dates: Jan. 6, 1983-Jan. 3, 1995
1st Departure: Left committee; no new assignment
2nd Dates: Sep. 27, 1995-Feb. 13, 1997
2nd Departure: Resigned the House; appointed Ambassador to the United Nations

Cong.	Ranking	Terms in: House	Comm.	Date of Assignment
103rd	Maj-11th	6 *1	6	Jan. 5, 1993
104th	Maj-22nd	7 *2	1	Sep. 27, 1995
105th	Maj-5th	8 *2	2	Jan. 7, 1997

2nd VETERANS AFFAIRS
Dates: Jan. 6, 1983-Feb. 29, 1984
Departure: Moved to Interior and Insular Affairs

3rd INTERIOR AND INSULAR AFFAIRS, 98-102
NATURAL RESOURCES, 103
RESOURCES, 104-105
Dates: Feb. 29, 1984-Feb. 13, 1997
Departure: Resigned the House; appointed Ambassador to the United Nations

Cong.	Ranking	Terms in: House	Comm.	Date of Assignment
103rd	Maj-11th	6	6	Jan. 5, 1993
104th	Min-7th	7	7	Jan. 9, 1995
105th	Min-7th	8	8	Jan. 7, 1997

4th EDUCATION AND LABOR
Dates: Jan. 22, 1987-Jan. 3, 1989
Departure: Left committee; no new assignment

HOUSE SELECT AND SPECIAL COMMITTEES:

1st SELECT CHILDREN, YOUTH AND FAMILIES (Temporary)
Dates: Feb. 2, 1983-Feb. 17, 1983
Departure: Moved to Select Aging

2nd SELECT AGING (Permanent)
Dates: Mar. 3, 1983-Jan. 3, 1993
Termination: Committee not renewed in 1993

3rd PERMANENT SELECT INTELLIGENCE
1st Dates: Feb. 1, 1988-Sep. 27, 1996
1st Departure: Resigned committee and returned with permission of the House
2nd Dates: Oct. 4, 1996-Jan. 3, 1997
2nd Departure: Left committee; no new assignment

Cong.	Ranking	Terms in: House	Comm.	Date of Assignment
103rd	Maj-2nd	6 *1	4	Feb. 3, 1993
104th	Min-2nd	7 *1	5	Jan. 4, 1995
104th	MnR-3rd	7 *2	1	Oct. 4, 1996

Thomas J. Ridge (R-Penn.)

Dates: Aug. 26, 1945
House: Jan. 3, 1983-Jan. 3, 1995
Left the House: Elected Governor in 1994

HOUSE STANDING COMMITTEES:

1st BANKING, FINANCE AND URBAN AFFAIRS
Dates: Jan. 6, 1983-Jan. 3, 1995
Departure: Left the House; elected Governor

Cong.	Ranking	Terms in: House	Comm.	Date of Assignment
103rd	Min-5th	6	6	Jan. 5, 1993

2nd VETERANS AFFAIRS
Dates: Jan. 30, 1985-Jan. 3, 1995
Departure: Left the House; elected Governor

Cong.	Ranking	Terms in: House	Comm.	Date of Assignment
103rd	Min-5th	6	5	Jan. 5, 1993

3rd POST OFFICE AND CIVIL SERVICE
Dates: Feb. 22, 1989-Jan. 3, 1995
Departure: Left the House; elected Governor

Cong.	Ranking	Terms in: House	Comm.	Date of Assignment
103rd	Min-6th	6	3	Jan. 5, 1993

HOUSE SELECT AND SPECIAL COMMITTEES:

1st SELECT AGING (Permanent)
Dates: Feb. 8, 1983-Jan. 3, 1991
Departure: Left committee; no new assignment

Donald W. Riegle Jr. (D-Mich.)

Dates: Feb. 4, 1938
House: Jan. 3, 1967-Dec. 30, 1976
Left the House: Resigned; appointed to U.S. Senate in 1976
Senate: Dec. 30, 1976-Jan. 3, 1995
Left the Senate: Retired in 1994
Served as a Republican: Jan. 3, 1967-Feb. 27, 1973
Served as a Democrat: Feb. 27, 1973-Jan. 3, 1995

S: Riegle was appointed to the 94th Congress, Dec. 30, 1976, to fill the vacancy caused by the death of U.S. Senator Philip A. Hart (D-Mich.). Riegle had been elected to succeed Hart in the 95th Congress. Riegle was not seated nor assigned to committees because the 94th Congress was not in session

HOUSE STANDING COMMITTEES:

1st APPROPRIATIONS
Dates: Jan. 26, 1967-Mar. 5, 1973
Departure: Left committee as a Minority Republican; moved to Foreign Affairs as a Majority Democrat

2nd FOREIGN AFFAIRS
Dates: Mar. 27, 1973-Jan. 3, 1975
INTERNATIONAL RELATIONS
Dates: Jan. 20, 1975-Dec. 30, 1976
Departure: Resigned the House; elected to the Senate

SENATE STANDING COMMITTEES:

1st JUDICIARY
Dates: Jan. 10, 1977-Feb. 11, 1977
Departure: Moved to Commerce, Science and Transportation, Human Resources, and Banking, Housing and Urban Affairs

2nd APPROPRIATIONS
Dates: Jan. 10, 1977-Feb. 11, 1977
Departure: Moved to Commerce, Science and Transportation, Human Resources, and Banking, Housing and Urban Affairs

3rd COMMERCE, SCIENCE AND TRANSPORTATION
Dates: Feb. 11, 1977-Feb. 2, 1989
Departure: Left committee; became Chair of Banking, Housing and Urban Affairs

4th HUMAN RESOURCES renamed Jan. 23, 1979
LABOR AND HUMAN RESOURCES
Dates: Feb. 11, 1977-Feb. 21, 1985
Departure: Left committee; no new assignment

5th BANKING, HOUSING AND URBAN AFFAIRS
Dates: Feb. 11, 1977-Jan. 3, 1995
Departure: Left the Senate; retired

Cong.	Ranking	Years in: Senate	Comm.	Date of Assignment
103rd	Maj-Chr	17	16	Jan. 7, 1993

6th BUDGET
Dates: Jan. 23, 1979-Jan. 3, 1995
Departure: Left the Senate; retired

Cong.	Ranking	Years in: Senate	Comm.	Date of Assignment
103rd	Maj-4th	17	14	Jan. 21, 1993

7th FINANCE
Dates: Jan. 6, 1987-Jan. 3, 1995
Departure: Left the Senate; retired

Cong.	Ranking	Years in: Senate	Comm.	Date of Assignment
103rd	Maj-8th	17	7	Jan. 7, 1993

JOINT COMMITTEES:

1st JOINT DEFICIT REDUCTION (Temporary)
Senate Dates: Jan. 6, 1987-Sep. 29, 1987
Termination: Public Law 100-119 adjusted Gramm-Rudman-Hollings Act

Frank D. Riggs (R-Cal.)

Dates: Sept. 5, 1950
House 1: Jan. 3, 1991-Jan. 3, 1993
Left the House 1: Defeated for re-election in 1992.
House 2: Jan. 3, 1995-Jan. 3, 1999
Left the House 2: Retired; withdrew from U.S. Senate primary in 1998.

HOUSE STANDING COMMITTEES:

1st BANKING, FINANCE AND URBAN AFFSIRS
Dates: Jan. 24, 1991-Jan. 3, 1993
Departure: Left the House; lost re-election

2nd PUBLIC WORKS AND TRANSPORTATION, 102
TRANSPORTATION AND INFRASTRUCTURE, 105
1st Dates: Jan. 24, 1991-Jan. 3, 1993
1st Departure: Left the House; lost re-election
2nd Dates: Jan. 7, 1997-Jan. 3, 1999
2nd Departure: Left the House; retired

Cong.	Ranking	Terms in: House	Comm.	Date of Assignment
105th	Maj-23rd	3 *2	1	Jan. 7, 1997

3rd APPROPRIATIONS
Dates: Jan. 4, 1995-Jan. 3, 1997
Departure: Returned to Transportation and Infrastructure

Cong.	Ranking	Terms in: House	Comm.	Date of Assignment
104th	Maj-26th	2	1	Jan. 4, 1995

4th ECONOMIC AND EDUCATIONAL OPPORTUNITIES, 104
EDUCATION AND THE WORKFORCE, 105
Dates: Jan. 4, 1995-Jan. 3, 1999
Departure: Left the House; retired

Cong.	Ranking	Terms in: House	Comm.	Date of Assignment
104th	Maj-18th	2	1	Jan. 4, 1995
105th	Maj-14th	3	2	Jan. 7, 1997

HOUSE SELECT AND SPECIAL COMMITTEES:

1st SELECT CHILDREN, YOUTH AND FAMILIES
Dates: Feb. 21, 1991-Jan. 3, 1993
Departure: Left the House; lost re-election

2nd SELECT HUNGER
Dates: Feb. 21, 1991-May 15, 1991
Departure: Resigned committee; no new assignment

Robert Riley (R-S.C.)

Dates: Oct. 3, 1944
House: Jan. 3, 1997-Jan. 3, 2003
Left the House: Elected Governor in 2002

HOUSE STANDING COMMITTEES:

1st BANKING AND FINANCIAL SERVICES, 105-106
FINANCIAL SERVICES, 107
Dates: Jan. 7, 1997-Jan. 3, 2003
Departure: Left the House; elected Governor

Cong.	Ranking	Terms in: House	Comm.	Date of Assignment
105th	Maj-26th	1	1	Jan. 7, 1997
106th	Maj-21st	2	2	Jan. 6, 1999
107th	Maj-19th	3	3	Jan. 6, 2001

2nd NATIONAL SECURITY, 105
ARMED SERVICES, 106-107
Dates: Jan. 7, 1997-Jan. 3, 2003
Departure: Left the House; elected Governor

Cong.	Ranking	Terms in: House	Comm.	Date of Assignment
105th	Maj-29th	1	1	Jan. 7, 1997
106th	Maj-26th	2	2	Jan. 6, 1999
107th	Maj-21st	3	3	Jan. 6, 2001

3rd AGRICULTURE
Dates: Jan. 6, 1999-Jan. 3, 2003
Departure: Left the House; elected Governor

Cong.	Ranking	Terms in: House	Comm.	Date of Assignment
106th	Maj-22nd	2	1	Jan. 6, 1999
107th	Maj-15th	3	2	Jan. 6, 2001

James Risch (R-Idaho)

Dates: May 3, 1943
Senate: Jan. 3, 2009-date
Serving in the 111th Congress

SENATE STANDING COMMITTEES:

1st ENERGY AND NATURAL RESOURCES
Dates: Jan. 21, 2009-date
Departure: Still serving in the 111th Congress

Cong.	Ranking	Years in: Senate	Comm.	Date of Assignment
111th	Min-5th	1	1	Jan. 21, 2009

2nd FOREIGN RELATIONS
Dates: Jan. 21, 2009-date
Departure: Still serving in the 111th Congress

Cong.	Ranking	Years in: Senate	Comm.	Date of Assignment
111th	Min-4th	1	1	Jan. 21, 2009

3rd SMALL BUSINESS AND ENTREPENEURSHIP
Dates: July 21, 2009-date
Departure: Still serving in the 111th Congress

Cong.	Ranking	Years in: Senate	Comm.	Date of Assignment
111th	Min-8th	1	1	July 21, 2009

SENATE SELECT AND SPECIAL COMMITTEES:

1st SELECT ETHICS (Permanent)
Dates: Jan. 21, 2009-date
Departure: Still serving in the 111th Congress

Cong.	Ranking	Years in: Senate	Comm.	Date of Assignment
111th	Min-3rd	1	1	Jan. 21, 2009

2nd SELECT INTELLIGENCE (Permanent)
Dates: Jan. 21, 2009-date
Departure: Still serving in the 111th Congress

Cong.	Ranking	Years in: Senate	Comm.	Date of Assignment
111th	Min-7th	1	1	Jan. 21, 2009

JOINT COMMITTEES:

1st JOINT ECONOMIC
Dates: Jan. 21, 2009-date
Departure: Still serving in the 111th Congress

Cong.	Ranking	Years in: Senate	Comm.	Date of Assignment
111th	Min-3rd	1	1	Jan. 21, 2009

Lynn N. Rivers (D-Mich.)

Dates: Dec. 19, 1956
House: Jan. 3, 1995-Jan. 3, 2003
Left the House: Defeated for re-nomination in 2002

HOUSE STANDING COMMITTEES:

1st BUDGET
Dates: Jan. 4, 1995-Jan. 3, 2001
Departure: Moved to Education and the Workforce

Cong.	Ranking	Terms in: House	Comm.	Date of Assignment
104th	Min-17th	1	1	Jan. 4, 1995
105th	Min-9th	2	2	Jan. 7, 1997
106th	Min-3rd	3	3	Jan. 6, 1999

2nd SCIENCE
Dates: Jan. 4, 1995-Jan. 3, 2003
Departure: Left the House; lost re-nomination

Cong.	Ranking	Terms in: House	Comm.	Date of Assignment
104th	Min-16th	1	1	Jan. 4, 1995
105th	Min-11th	2	2	Feb. 13, 1997
106th	Min-11th	3	3	Jan. 6, 1999
107th	Min-7th	4	4	Jan. 31, 2001

3rd EDUCATION AND THE WORKFORCE
Dates: Jan. 31, 2001-Jan. 3, 2003
Departure: Left the House; lost re-nomination

Cong.	Ranking	Terms in: House	Comm.	Date of Assignment
107th	Min-10th	4	1	Jan. 31, 2001

Charles S. Robb (D-Va.)

Dates: June 26, 1939
Senate: Jan. 3, 1989-Jan. 3, 2001
Left the Senate: Defeated for re-election in 2000

SENATE STANDING COMMITTEES:

1st COMMERCE, SCIENCE, AND TRANSPORTATION
Dates: Feb. 2, 1989-Jan. 3, 1995
Departure: Moved to Select Intelligence

Cong.	Ranking	Years in: Senate	Comm.	Date of Assignment
103rd	Maj-10th	5	4	Jan. 7, 1993

2nd FOREIGN RELATIONS
Dates: Feb. 2, 1989-Jan. 7, 1999
Departure: Moved to Finance.

Cong.	Ranking	Years in: Senate	Comm.	Date of Assignment
103rd	Maj-8th	5	4	Jan. 7, 1993
104th	Min-6th	7	6	Jan. 4, 1995
105th	Min-5th	9	8	Jan. 9, 1997

3rd BUDGET
Dates: Feb. 2, 1989-Mar. 19, 1991
Departure: Left committee; no new assignment

4th ARMED SERVICES
Dates: Jan. 7, 1993-Jan. 3, 2001
Departure: Left the Senate; lost re-election

Cong.	Ranking	Years in: Senate	Comm.	Date of Assignment
103rd	Maj-10th	5	1	Jan. 7, 1993
104th	Min-8th	7	2	Jan. 4, 1995
105th	Min-6th	9	5	Jan. 9, 1997
106th	Min-5th	11	7	Jan. 7, 1999

5th FINANCE
Dates: Jan. 7, 1999-Jan. 3, 2001
Departure: Left the Senate; lost re-election

Cong.	Ranking	Years in: Senate	Comm.	Date of Assignment
106th	Min-9th	11	1	Jan. 7, 1999

SENATE SELECT AND SPECIAL COMMITTEES:

1st JUDGE WALTER L. NIXON IMPEACHMENT
Dates: May 11, 1989-Sep. 13, 1989
Departure: Committee terminated; hearings concluded

2nd SELECT POW-MIA AFFAIRS
Dates: Aug. 2, 1991-Feb. 3, 1993
Termination: Senate Report 1 (103-1) filed

3rd SELECT INTELLIGENCE (Permanent)
Dates: Jan. 6, 1995-Jan. 3, 2001
Departure: Left the Senate; lost re-election

Cong.	Ranking	Years in: Senate	Comm.	Date of Assignment
104th	Min-8th	7	1	Jan. 6, 1995
105th	Min-7th	9	3	Jan. 9, 1997
106th	Min-6th	11	5	Jan. 7, 1999

JOINT COMMITTEES:

1st JOINT ECONOMIC
Senate Dates: Jan. 21, 1993-Jan. 3, 2001
Departure: Left the Senate; lost re-election

Cong.	Ranking	Years in: Senate	Comm.	Date of Assignment
103rd	Maj-5th	5	1	Jan. 21, 1993
104th	Min-4th	7	2	Jan. 9, 1995
105th	Min-4th	9	4	Jan. 9, 1997
106th	Min-1st	11	6	Jan. 7, 1999

C. Patrick Roberts (R-Kans.)

Dates: April 20, 1936
House: Jan. 3, 1981-Jan. 3, 1997
Left the House: Elected to U.S. Senate in 1996
Senate: Jan. 3, 1997-date
Serving in the 111th Congress

HOUSE STANDING COMMITTEES:

1st AGRICULTURE
Dates: Jan. 28, 1981-Jan. 3, 1997
Departure: Left the House for the Senate

Cong.	Ranking	Terms in: House	Comm.	Date of Assignment
103rd	Min-RM	7	7	Jan. 5, 1993
104th	Maj-Chr	8	8	Jan. 4, 1995

2nd HOUSE ADMINISTRATION, 103
HOUSE OVERSIGHT, 104
Dates: July 20, 1983-Jan. 3, 1997
Departure: Left the House for the Senate

Cong.	Ranking	Terms in: House	Comm.	Date of Assignment
103rd	Min-3rd	7	6	Jan. 5, 1993
104th	Maj-3rd	8	7	Jan. 4, 1995

HOUSE SELECT AND SPECIAL COMMITTEES:

1st SELECT AGING (Permanent)
Dates: Feb. 5, 1981-July 14, 1983
Departure: Resigned committee; moved to House Administration

JOINT COMMITTEES:

1st JOINT LIBRARY
1st House Dates: July 20, 1983-Jan. 3, 1989
1st Departure: Left committee; no new assignment
2nd House Dates: Feb. 21, 1991-Jan. 3, 1997
2nd Departure: Left the House for the Senate

Cong.	Ranking	Terms in: House	Comm.	Date of Assignment
103rd	Min-2nd	7 *2	2	May 1, 1993 Provisional
104th	Maj-2nd	8 *2	3	Feb. 23, 1995

2nd JOINT PRINTING
House Dates: July 20, 1983-Jan. 3, 1997
Departure: Left the House for the Senate

Cong.	Ranking	Terms in: House	Comm.	Date of Assignment
103rd	Min-1st	7	6	May 1, 1993 Provisional
104th	Maj-2nd	8	7	Feb. 23, 1995

SENATE STANDING COMMITTEES:

1st AGRICULTURE, NUTRITION AND FORESTRY
Dates: Jan. 9, 1997-date
Departure: Still serving in the 111th Congress

Cong.	Ranking	Years in: Senate	Comm.	Date of Assignment
105th	Maj-7th	1	1	Jan. 9, 1997
106th	Maj-6th	3	2	Jan. 3, 1999
107th	Maj-5th	5	5	Jan. 25, 2001
+107th	Min-5th	5	5	June 6, 2001
108th	Maj-4th	7	7	Jan. 15, 2003
109th	Maj-5th	9	8	Jan. 6, 2005
110th	Min-5th	11	11	Jan. 12, 2007
111th	Min-5th	13	13	Jan. 21, 2009

2nd ARMED SERVICES
Dates: Jan. 9, 1997-Jan. 12, 2007
Departure: Moved to Finance

Cong.	Ranking	Years in: Senate	Comm.	Date of Assignment
105th	Maj-10th	1	1	Jan. 9, 1997
106th	Maj-8th	3	2	Jan. 3, 1999
107th	Maj-7th	5	5	Jan. 25, 2001
+107th	Min-7th	5	5	June 6, 2001
108th	Maj-4th	7	7	Jan. 15, 2003
109th	Maj-4th	9	8	Jan. 6, 2005

3rd HEALTH, EDUCATION, LABOR AND PENSIONS
Dates: Jan. 25, 2001-date
Departure: Still serving in the 111th Congress

Cong.	Ranking	Years in: Senate	Comm.	Date of Assignment
107th	Maj-8th	5	1	Jan. 25, 2001
+107th	Min-7th	5	1	July 10, 2001
108th	Maj-7th	7	2	Jan. 15, 2003
109th	Maj-11th	9	4	Jan. 6, 2005
110th	Min-8th	11	6	Jan. 12, 2007
111th	Min-10th	13	8	Jan. 21, 2009

4th FINANCE
Dates: Jan. 12, 2007-date
Departure: Still serving in the 111th Congress

Cong.	Ranking	Years in: Senate	Comm.	Date of Assignment
110th	Min-10th	11	1	Jan. 12, 2007
111th	Min-7th	13	3	Jan. 21, 2009

5th RULES AND ADMINISTRATION
Dates: Jan. 21, 2009-date
Departure: Still serving in the 111th Congress

Cong.	Ranking	Years in: Senate	Comm.	Date of Assignment
111th	Min-7th	13	1	Jan. 21, 2009

SENATE SELECT AND SPECIAL COMMITTEES:

1st SELECT ETHICS (Permanent)
Dates: Jan. 9, 1997-date
Ch2: Replaced Robert C. Smith (R-N.H.) who had become Chair of Environment and Public Works on Nov. 9, 1999
Ch1: Replaced by Harry M. Reid (D-Nev.) on June 6, 2001, following party control shift and became RM2.
Departure: Still serving in the 111th Congress

Cong.	Ranking	Years in: Senate	Comm.	Date of Assignment
105th	Maj-2nd	1	1	Jan. 9, 1997
106th	Maj-2nd	3	2	Jan. 7, 1999

Cong.	Ranking	Senate	Comm.	Date of Assignment
=106th	Maj-Ch2	3	2	Nov. 9, 1999
107th	Maj-Ch1	5	5	Jan. 25, 2001
+107th	Min-RM2	5	5	June 6, 2001
108th	Maj-2nd	7	7	Jan. 15, 2003
109th	Maj-2nd	9	8	Jan. 6, 2005
110th	Min-2nd	11	11	Jan. 12, 2007
111th	Min-2nd	13	13	Jan. 21, 2009

2nd SELECT INTELLIGENCE (Permanent)
Dates: Jan. 9, 1997-Jan. 12, 2007
Departure: Moved to Finance

Cong.	Ranking	Years in: Senate	Comm.	Date of Assignment
105th	Maj-8th	1	1	Jan. 9, 1997
106th	Maj-8th	3	2	Jan. 7, 1999
107th	Maj-5th	5	5	Jan. 25, 2001
+107th	Min-5th	5	5	June 6, 2001
108th	Maj-Chr	7	7	Jan. 15, 2003
109th	Maj-Chr	9	8	Jan. 6, 2005

John D. Rockefeller IV (D-W.Va.)

Dates: June 18, 1937
Senate: Jan. 15, 1985-date
Serving in the 111th Congress

S: Rockefeller was elected to the 99th Congress but did not begin service until Jan. 15, 1995, following his resignation as Governor. Rockefeller was seated Jan. 15, 1985, and assigned to committees.

SENATE STANDING COMMITTEES:

1st COMMERCE, SCIENCE AND TRANSPORTATION
Dates: Feb. 21, 1985-date
Departure: Still serving in the 111th Congress

Cong.	Ranking	Years in: Senate	Comm.	Date of Assignment
103rd	Maj-5th	9	8	Jan. 7, 1993
104th	Min-5th	11	10	Jan. 4, 1995
105th	Min-4th	13	12	Jan. 9, 1997
106th	Min-3rd	15	14	Jan. 7, 1999
107th	Min-3rd	17	16	Jan. 25, 2001
+107th	Maj-3rd	17	17	June 6, 2001
108th	Min-3rd	19	18	Jan. 15, 2003
109th	Min-2nd	21	20	Jan. 6, 2005
110th	Maj-2nd	23	22	Jan. 12, 2007
111th	Maj-Chr	25	24	Jan. 21, 2009

2nd ENERGY AND NATURAL RESOURCES
1st Dates: Feb. 21, 1985-Jan. 6, 1987
1st Departure: Moved to Finance
2nd Dates: Feb. 2, 1989-Feb. 5, 1991
2nd Departure: Left committee; no new assignment

3rd VETERANS' AFFAIRS
Dates: Mar. 5, 1985-date
Ch2: Replaced Arlen Specter (R-Penn.) on June 6, 2001, following Senate party control shift
Departure: Still serving in the 111th Congress

Cong.	Ranking	Years in: Senate	Comm.	Date of Assignment
103rd	Maj-Chr	9	8	Jan. 21, 1993
104th	Min-RM	11	10	Jan. 6, 1995
105th	Min-RM	13	12	Jan. 9, 1997
106th	Min-RM	15	14	Jan. 7, 1999
=107th	Maj-ChT	17	16	Jan. 3, 2001
107th	Min-RM1	17	16	Jan. 25, 2001

+107th	Maj-Ch2	17	17	June 6, 2001
108th	Min-2nd	19	18	Jan. 15, 2003
109th	Min-2nd	21	20	Jan. 6, 2005
110th	Maj-2nd	23	22	Jan. 12, 2007
111th	Maj-2nd	25	24	Jan. 21, 2009

4th FINANCE
Dates: Jan. 6, 1987-date
Departure: Still serving in the 111th Congress

Cong.	Ranking	Years in: Senate	Comm.	Date of Assignment
103rd	Maj-9th	9	7	Jan. 7, 1993
104th	Min-5th	11	8	Jan. 4, 1995
105th	Min-3rd	13	11	Jan. 9, 1997
106th	Min-3rd	15	13	Jan. 7, 1999
107th	Min-2nd	17	15	Jan. 25, 2001
+107th	Maj-2nd	17	15	June 6, 2001
108th	Min-2nd	19	17	Jan. 15, 2003
109th	Min-2nd	21	19	Jan. 6, 2005
110th	Maj-2nd	23	21	Jan. 12, 2007
111th	Maj-2nd	25	23	Jan. 21, 2009

5th FOREIGN RELATIONS
Dates: July 10, 2001-Jan. 3, 2005
Departure: Left committee; no new assignment

Cong.	Ranking	Years in: Senate	Comm.	Date of Assignment
+107th	MjA-10th	17	1	July 10, 2001
108th	Min-8th	19	2	Jan. 15, 2003

SENATE SELECT AND SPECIAL COMMITTEES:

1st SELECT INTELLIGENCE (Permanent)
Dates: Jan. 25, 2001-date
Departure: Still serving in the 111th Congress

Cong.	Ranking	Years in: Senate	Comm.	Date of Assignment
107th	Min-3rd	17	1	Jan. 25, 2001
+107th	Maj-3rd	17	1	June 6, 2001
108th	Min-VCh	19	2	Jan. 15, 2003
109th	Min-VCh	21	4	Jan. 6, 2005
110th	Maj-Chr	23	6	Jan. 12, 2007
111th	Maj-2nd	25	8	Jan. 21, 2009

JOINT COMMITTEES:

1st JOINT TAXATION
Senate Dates: Feb. 28, 2001-date
Departure: Still serving in the 111th Congress

Cong.	Ranking	Years in: Senate	Comm.	Date of Assignment
107th	Min-2nd	17	1	Feb. 28, 2001
+107th	Maj-2nd	17	1	July 17, 2001
108th	Min-2nd	19	2	Feb. 24, 2003
109th	Min-2nd	21	4	Jan. 25, 2005
110th	Maj-2nd	23	6	Jan. 17, 2007
111th	Maj-2nd	25	8	Feb. 25, 2009

Cathy McMorris Rodgers
(R-Wash.)

Dates: May 22, 1969
House: Jan. 3, 2005-date
Serving in the 111th Congress

Served as Cathy McMorris in 109th Congress and as Cathy McMorris Rodgers in 110th-111th

HOUSE STANDING COMMITTEES:

1st ARMED SERVICES
Dates: Jan. 26, 2005-date
Departure: Still serving in the 111th Congress

Cong.	Ranking	Terms in: House	Comm.	Date of Assignment
109th	Maj-32nd	1	1	Jan. 26, 2005
110th	Min-26th	2	2	Jan. 10, 2007
111th	Min-17th	3	3	Jan. 9, 2009

2nd EDUCATION AND THE WORKFORCE, 109
EDUCATION AND LABOR, 110-111
Dates: Jan. 26, 2005-date
Departure: Still serving in the 111th Congress

Cong.	Ranking	Terms in: House	Comm.	Date of Assignment
109th	Maj-19th	1	1	Jan. 26, 2005
110th	Min-13th	2	2	Jan. 10, 2007
111th	Min-11th	3	3	Jan. 9, 2009

3rd RESOURCES, 109
NATURAL RESOURCES, 110-111
Dates: Jan. 26, 2005-date
Departure: Still serving in the 111th Congress

Cong.	Ranking	Terms in: House	Comm.	Date of Assignment
109th	Maj-25th	1	1	Jan. 26, 2005
110th	Min-14th	2	2	Jan. 10, 2007
111th	Min-7th	3	3	Jan. 9, 2009

Ciro D. Rodriguez (D-Tex.)

Dates: Dec. 9, 1946
House 1: April 12, 1997-Jan. 3, 2005
Left the House 1: Defeated for re-nomination in 2004
House 2: Jan. 3, 2007-date
Serving in the 111th Congress

H: Rodriguez was elected to the 105th Congress by special election, April 12, 1997, to fill the vacancy caused by the death of U.S. Representative Frank Tejeda (D-Tex.). Rodriguez was seated April 17, 1997, and assigned to committees.

HOUSE STANDING COMMITTEES:

1st NATIONAL SECURITY, 105
ARMED SERVICES, 106-108
Dates: Apr. 17, 1997-Jan. 3, 2005
Departure: Left the House; lost re-nomination

Cong.	Ranking	Terms in: House	Comm.	Date of Assignment
105th	MnR-1st	1	1	Apr. 17, 1997
106th	Min-21st	2	2	Jan. 6, 1999
107th	Min-19th	3	3	Jan. 31, 2001
108th	Min-14th	4	4	Jan. 28, 2003

2nd VETERANS' AFFAIRS
1st Dates: May 14, 1997-Jan. 3, 2005
1st Departure: Left the House; lost re-nomination

2nd Dates: Jan. 12, 2007-date
2nd Departure: Still serving in the 111th Congress

Cong.	Ranking	Terms in: House	Comm.	Date of Assignment
105th	MnR-1st	1 *1	1	May 14, 1997
106th	Min-10th	2 *1	2	Jan. 6, 1999
107th	Min-10th	3 *1	3	Jan. 31, 2001
108th	Min-6th	4 *1	4	Jan. 28, 2003
110th	Maj-12th	5 *2	1	Jan. 12, 2007
111th	Maj-11th	6 *2	2	Jan. 21, 2009

3rd RESOURCES
Dates: Mar. 5, 2003-Jan. 3, 2005
Departure: Left the House; lost re-nomination

Cong.	Ranking	Terms in: House	Comm.	Date of Assignment
108th	Min-24th	4	1	Mar. 5, 2003

4th APPROPRIATIONS
Dates: Jan. 4, 2007-date
Departure: Still serving in the 111th Congress

Cong.	Ranking	Terms in: House	Comm.	Date of Assignment
110th	Maj-37th	5	1	Jan. 4, 2007
111th	Maj-35th	6	2	Jan. 7, 2009

David P. (Phil) Roe (R-Tenn.)

Dates: July 21, 1945
House: Jan. 3, 2009-date
Serving in the 111th Congress

HOUSE STANDING COMMITTEES:

1st AGRICULTURE
Dates: Jan. 9, 2009-date
Departure: Still serving in the 111th Congress

Cong.	Ranking	Terms in: House	Comm.	Date of Assignment
111th	Min-15th	1	1	Jan. 9, 2009

2nd EDUCATION AND LABOR
Dates: Jan. 9, 2009-date
Departure: Still serving in the 111th Congress

Cong.	Ranking	Terms in: House	Comm.	Date of Assignment
111th	Min-19th	1	1	Jan. 9, 2009

3rd VETERANS' AFFAIRS
Dates: Jan. 22, 2009-date
Departure: Still serving in the 111th Congress

Cong.	Ranking	Terms in: House	Comm.	Date of Assignment
111th	MnR-2nd	1	1	Jan. 22, 2009

Timothy J. Roemer (D-Ind.)

Dates: Oct. 30, 1956
House: Jan. 3, 1991-Jan. 3, 2003
Left the House: Retired in 2002

HOUSE STANDING COMMITTEES:

1st EDUCATION AND LABOR, 102-103
ECONOMIC AND EDUCATIONAL OPPORTUNITIES, 104
EDUCATION AND THE WORKFORCE, 105-107
Dates: Jan. 24, 1991-Jan. 3, 2003
Departure: Left the House; retired

Cong.	Ranking	Terms in: House	Comm.	Date of Assignment
103rd	Maj-15th	2	2	Jan. 5, 1993
104th	Min-12th	3	3	Jan. 4, 1995
105th	Min-9th	4	4	Jan. 7, 1997
106th	Min-9th	5	5	Jan. 6, 1999
107th	Min-7th	6	6	Jan. 31, 2001

2nd SPACE, SCIENCE AND TECHNOLOGY, 102-103
SCIENCE, 104-106
Dates: Jan. 24, 1991-Feb. 23, 1999
Departure: Leave of absence; had moved to Permanent Select Intelligence

Cong.	Ranking	Terms in: House	Comm.	Date of Assignment
103rd	Maj-16th	2	2	Jan. 5, 1993
104th	Min-7th	3	3	Jan. 4, 1995
105th	Min-5th	4	4	Feb. 13, 1997
106th	Min-6th	5	5	Jan. 6, 1999

HOUSE SELECT AND SPECIAL COMMITTEES:

1st PERMANENT SELECT INTELLIGENCE
Dates: Feb. 12, 1999-Jan. 3, 2003
Departure: Left the House; retired

Cong.	Ranking	Terms in: House	Comm.	Date of Assignment
106th	Min-6th	5	1	Feb. 12, 1999
107th	Min-6th	6	2	Mar. 1, 2001

James E. Rogan (R-Cal.)

Dates: Aug. 21, 1957
House: Jan. 3, 1997-Jan. 3, 2001
Left the House: Defeated for re-election in 2000

HOUSE STANDING COMMITTEES:

1st COMMERCE
Dates: Jan. 7, 1997-Jan. 3, 2001
Departure: Left the House; lost re-election

Cong.	Ranking	Terms in: House	Comm.	Date of Assignment
105th	Maj-27th	1	1	Jan. 7, 1997
106th	Maj-21st	2	2	Jan. 6, 1999

2nd JUDICIARY
Dates: Feb. 11, 1998-Jan. 3, 2001
Departure: Left the House; lost re-election

Cong.	Ranking	Terms in: House	Comm.	Date of Assignment
105th	MjR-1st	1	1	Feb. 11, 1998
106th	Maj-18th	2	2	Jan. 6, 1999

Harold D. Rogers (R-Ky.)

Dates: Dec. 31, 1937
House: Jan. 3, 1981-date
Serving in the 111th Congress

HOUSE STANDING COMMITTEES:

1st ENERGY AND COMMERCE
Dates: Jan. 28, 1981-Jan. 3, 1983
Departure: Moved to Appropriations

2nd APPROPRIATIONS
Dates: Jan. 6, 1983-date
Departure: Still serving in the 111th Congress

Cong.	Ranking	Terms in: House	Comm.	Date of Assignment
103rd	Min-8th	7	6	Jan. 5, 1993
104th	Maj-8th	8	7	Jan. 4, 1995
105th	Maj-7th	9	8	Jan. 7, 1997
106th	Maj-5th	10	9	Jan. 6, 1999
107th	Maj-4th	11	10	Jan. 6, 2001
108th	Maj-4th	12	11	Jan. 28, 2003
109th	Maj-4th	13	12	Jan. 6, 2005
110th	Min-4th	14	13	Jan. 4, 2007
111th	Min-3rd	15	14	Jan. 9, 2009

3rd BUDGET
Dates: Jan. 21, 1987-Jan. 3, 1993
Departure: Left committee; no new assignment

HOUSE SELECT AND SPECIAL COMMITTEES:

1st SELECT HOMELAND SECURITY
Dates: Feb. 12, 2003-Jan. 3, 2005
Departure: Did not continue on reorganized standing committee

Cong.	Ranking	Terms in: House	Comm.	Date of Assignment
108th	Maj-9th	12	1	Feb. 12, 2003

2nd SELECT BIPARTISAN COMMITTEE TO INVESTIGATE THE PREPARATION FOR AND RESPONSE TO HURRICANE KATRINA
Dates: Sep. 21, 2005-Feb. 15, 2006
Departure: House Report 377 (109-2) filed

Cong.	Ranking	Terms in: House	Comm.	Date of Assignment
109th	Maj-3rd	13	1	Sep. 21, 2005

JOINT COMMITTEES:

1st JOINT DEFICIT REDUCTION (Temporary)
House Dates: Feb. 23, 1987-Sep. 29, 1987
Termination: Public Law 100-119 adjusted Gramm-Rudman-Hollings Act

---

Mike Rogers (R-Mich.)

Dates: June 2, 1963
House: Jan. 3, 2001-date
Serving in the 111th Congress

HOUSE STANDING COMMITTEES:

1st FINANCIAL SERVICES
Dates: Jan. 6, 2001-Jan. 3, 2003
Departure: Moved to Energy and Commerce

Cong.	Ranking	Terms in: House	Comm.	Date of Assignment
107th	Maj-36th	1	1	Jan. 6, 2001

2nd TRANSPORTATION AND INFRASTRUCTURE
Dates: Jan. 6, 2001-Jan. 3, 2003
Departure: Moved to Energy and Commerce

Cong.	Ranking	Terms in: House	Comm.	Date of Assignment
107th	Maj-29th	1	1	Jan. 6, 2001

3rd ENERGY AND COMMERCE
Dates: Jan. 28, 2003-date
Departure: Still serving in the 111th Congress

Cong.	Ranking	Terms in: House	Comm.	Date of Assignment
108th	Maj-29th	2	1	Jan. 28, 2003
109th	Maj-25th	3	2	Jan. 6, 2005
110th	Min-22nd	4	3	Jan. 10, 2007
111th	Min-16th	5	4	Jan. 9, 2009

HOUSE SELECT AND SPECIAL COMMITTEES:

1st PERMANENT SELECT INTELLIGENCE
Dates: Jan. 26, 2005-date
Departure: Still serving in the 111th Congress

Cong.	Ranking	Terms in: House	Comm.	Date of Assignment
109th	Maj-11th	3	1	Jan. 26, 2005
110th	Min-7th	4	2	Jan. 17, 2007
111th	Min-4th	5	3	Jan. 15, 2009

Mike D. Rogers (R-Ala.)

Dates: July 16, 1958
House: Jan. 3, 2003-date
Serving in the 111th Congress

HOUSE STANDING COMMITTEES:

1st AGRICULTURE
Dates: Jan. 28, 2003-date
Departure: Still serving in the 111th Congress

Cong.	Ranking	Terms in: House	Comm.	Date of Assignment
108th	Maj-23rd	1	1	Jan. 28, 2003
109th	Maj-15th	2	2	Jan. 26, 2005
110th	Min-9th	3	3	Jan. 10, 2007
111th	Min-6th	4	4	Jan. 9, 2009

2nd ARMED SERVICES
Dates: Jan. 28, 2003-date
Departure: Still serving in the 111th Congress

Cong.	Ranking	Terms in: House	Comm.	Date of Assignment
108th	Maj-32nd	1	1	Jan. 28, 2003
109th	Maj-27th	2	2	Jan. 26, 2005
110th	Min-23rd	3	3	Jan. 10, 2007
111th	Min-14th	4	4	Jan. 9, 2009

3rd HOMELAND SECURITY
Dates: Feb. 9, 2005-date
Departure: Still serving in the 111th Congress

Cong.	Ranking	Terms in: House	Comm.	Date of Assignment
109th	Maj-13th	2	1	Feb. 9, 2005
110th	Min-7th	3	2	Jan. 10, 2007
111th	Min-5th	4	3	Jan. 9, 2009

Dana Rohrabacher (R-Cal.)

Dates: June 21, 1947
House: Jan. 3, 1989-date
Serving in the 111th Congress

HOUSE STANDING COMMITTEES:

1st DISTRICT OF COLUMBIA
Dates: Jan. 20, 1989-Jan. 3, 1995
Departure: Committee abolished; no new assignment

Cong.	Ranking	Terms in: House	Comm.	Date of Assignment
103rd	Min-2nd	3	3	Jan. 5, 1993

2nd SPACE, SCIENCE AND TECHNOLOGY, 101-103
SCIENCE, 104-109
SCIENCE AND TECHNOLOGY, 110-111
Dates: Jan. 20, 1989-date
Departure: Still serving in the 111th Congress

Cong.	Ranking	Terms in: House	Comm.	Date of Assignment
103rd	Min-8th	3	3	Jan. 5, 1993
104th	Maj-7th	4	4	Jan. 4, 1995
105th	Maj-6th	5	5	Jan. 21, 1997
106th	Maj-6th	6	6	Jan. 6, 1999
107th	Maj-6th	7	7	Jan. 6, 2001
108th	Maj-5th	8	8	Jan. 28, 2003
109th	Maj-5th	9	9	Jan. 26, 2005
110th	Min-4th	10	10	Jan. 10, 2007
111th	Min-4th	11	11	Jan. 9, 2009

3rd FOREIGN AFFAIRS, 103
INTERNATIONAL RELATIONS, 104-109
FOREIGN AFFAIRS, 110-111
Dates: Jan. 5, 1993-date
Departure: Still serving in the 111th Congress

Cong.	Ranking	Terms in: House	Comm.	Date of Assignment
103rd	Min-14th	3	1	Jan. 5, 1993
104th	Maj-13th	4	2	Jan. 4, 1995
105th	Maj-11th	5	3	Jan. 7, 1997
106th	Maj-11th	6	4	Jan. 6, 1999
107th	Maj-10th	7	5	Jan. 6, 2001
108th	Maj-9th	8	6	Jan. 28, 2003
109th	Maj-7th	9	7	Jan. 26, 2005
110th	Min-5th	10	8	Jan. 10, 2007
111th	Min-5th	11	9	Jan. 9, 2009

Carlos A. Romero-Barceló (New Progressive-P.R.)

Dates: Sept. 4, 1932
House: Jan. 3, 1993-Jan. 3, 2001

Left the House: Defeated for re-election in 2000
Note: Romero-Barcelo's committees were assigned by the Democratic Caucus

HOUSE STANDING COMMITTEES:

1st EDUCATION AND LABOR, 103
ECONOMIC AND EDUCATIONAL OPPORTUNITIES, 104
EDUCATION AND THE WORKFORCE, 105-106
Dates: Jan. 5, 1993-Jan. 3, 2001
Departure: Left the House; lost re-election

Cong.	Ranking	Terms in: House	Comm.	Date of Assignment
103rd	Maj-21st	1	1	Jan. 5, 1993
104th	Min-18th	2	2	Jan. 4, 1995
105th	Min-12th	3	3	Jan. 7, 1997
106th	Min-12th	4	4	Jan. 6, 1999

2nd NATURAL RESOURCES, 103
RESOURCES, 104-106
Dates: Jan. 5, 1993-Jan. 3, 2001
Departure: Left the House; lost re-election

Cong.	Ranking	Terms in: House	Comm.	Date of Assignment
103rd	Maj-19th	1	1	Jan. 5, 1993
104th	Min-16th	2	2	Jan. 9, 1995
105th	Min-15th	3	3	Jan. 7, 1997
106th	Min-12th	4	4	Jan. 6, 1999

Thomas J. Rooney (R-Fla.)

Dates: Nov. 21, 1970
House: Jan. 3, 2009-date
Serving in the 111th Congress

HOUSE STANDING COMMITTEES:

1st ARMED SERVICES
Dates: Jan. 9, 2009-date
Departure: Still serving in the 111th Congress

Cong.	Ranking	Terms in: House	Comm.	Date of Assignment
111th	Min-25th	1	1	Jan. 9, 2009

2nd JUDICIARY
Dates: Jan. 9, 2009-date
Departure: Still serving in the 111th Congress

Cong.	Ranking	Terms in: House	Comm.	Date of Assignment
111th	Min-15th	1	1	Jan. 9, 2009

Ileana Ros-Lehtinen (R-Fla.)

Dates: July 15, 1952
House: Aug. 28, 1989-date
Serving in the 111th Congress

H: Ros-Lehtinen was elected to the 101st Congress by special election, Aug. 28, 1989, to fill the vacancy caused by the death of U.S. Representative Claude D. Pepper (D-Fla.). Ros-Lehtinen was seated Sept. 6, 1989, and assigned to committees.

HOUSE STANDING COMMITTEES:

1st FOREIGN AFFAIRS, 101-103
INTERNATIONAL RELATIONS, 104-109
FOREIGN AFFAIRS, 110 -111
Dates: Oct. 5, 1989-date
Departure: Still serving in the 111th Congress

Cong.	Ranking	Terms in: House	Comm.	Date of Assignment
103rd	Min-12th	3	3	Jan. 5, 1993
104th	Maj-11th	4	4	Jan. 4, 1995
105th	Maj-9th	5	5	Jan. 7, 1997
106th	Maj-9th	6	6	Jan. 6, 1999
107th	Maj-8th	7	7	Jan. 6, 2001
108th	Maj-7th	8	8	Jan. 28, 2003
109th	Maj-6th	9	9	Jan. 26, 2005
110th	Min-RM	10	10	Jan. 4, 2007
111th	Min-RM	11	11	Jan. 6, 2009

2nd GOVERNMENT OPERATIONS, 101-103
GOVERNMENT REFORM AND OVERSIGHT, 104-106
GOVERNMENT REFORM, 107-109
Dates: Nov. 3, 1989-Jan. 3, 2007
Departure: Left committee; became Ranking Member on Foreign Affairs

Cong.	Ranking	Terms in: House	Comm.	Date of Assignment
103rd	Min-9th	3	3	Jan. 5, 1993
104th	Maj-7th	4	4	Jan. 4, 1995
105th	Maj-8th	5	5	Jan. 7, 1997
106th	Maj-6th	6	6	Jan. 6, 1999
107th	Maj-5th	7	7	Jan. 6, 2001
108th	Maj-4th	8	8	Jan. 28, 2003
109th	Maj-4th	9	9	Jan. 26, 2005

3rd BUDGET
Dates: Feb. 2, 2005-Feb. 8, 2006
Departure: Resigned committee; no new assignment

Cong.	Ranking	Terms in: House	Comm.	Date of Assignment
109th	Maj-14th	9	1	Feb. 2, 2005

Charles G. Rose III (D-N.C.)

Dates: Aug. 10, 1939
House: Jan. 3, 1973-Jan. 3, 1997
Left the House: Retired in 1996

HOUSE STANDING COMMITTEES:

1st AGRICULTURE
Dates: Jan. 24, 1973-Jan. 3, 1997
Departure: Left the House; retired

Cong.	Ranking	Terms in: House	Comm.	Date of Assignment
103rd	Maj-3rd	11	11	Jan. 5, 1993
104th	Min-3rd	12	12	Jan. 4, 1995

2nd HOUSE ADMINISTRATION
Dates: Jan. 23, 1975-Jan. 3, 1995
Departure: Left committee; no new assignment

Cong.	Ranking	Terms in: House	Comm.	Date of Assignment
103rd	Maj-Chr	11	10	Jan. 21, 1993

3rd DISTRICT OF COLUMBIA
Temporary Dates: Jan. 27, 1977-Jan. 3, 1999
Departure: Temporary term expired

4th INTERNATIONAL RELATIONS
Dates: Feb. 28, 1996-Jan. 3, 1997
Departure: Left the House; retired

Cong.	Ranking	Terms in: House	Comm.	Date of Assignment
104th	MnR-1st	12	1	Feb. 28, 1996

HOUSE SELECT AND SPECIAL COMMITTEES:

1st HOUSE RECORDING STUDIO
Dates: Feb. 8, 1973-Jan. 3, 1993
Departure: Committee abolished

2nd PERMANENT SELECT INTELLIGENCE
Dates: July 27, 1977-Jan. 3, 1983
Departure: Left committee; no new assignment

JOINT COMMITTEES:

1st JOINT LIBRARY
House Dates: Feb. 21,1991-Jan. 3, 1995
Departure: Left committee; no new assignment

Cong.	Ranking	Terms in: House	Comm.	Date of Assignment
103rd	Maj-Chr	10	2	May 1, 1993 Provisional

2nd JOINT PRINTING
House Dates: Feb. 21, 1991-Jan. 3, 1995
Departure: Left committee; no new assignment

Cong.	Ranking	Terms in: House	Comm.	Assignment
103rd	Maj-VCh	10	2	May 1, 1993 Provisonal

Peter Roskam (R-Ill.)

Dates: Sept. 13, 1961
House: Jan. 3, 2007-date
Serving in the 111th Congress

HOUSE STANDING COMMITTEES:

1st FINANCIAL SERVICES
Dates: Jan. 10, 2007-Jan. 3, 2009
Departure: Moved to Ways and Means

Cong.	Ranking	Terms in: House	Comm.	Date of Assignment
110th	Min-33rd	1	1	Jan. 10, 2007

2nd WAYS AND MEANS
Dates: Jan. 9, 2009-date
Departure: Still serving in the 111th Congress

Cong.	Ranking	Terms in: House	Comm.	Date of Assignment
111th	Min-15th	2	1	Jan. 9, 2009

Michael A. Ross (D-Ark.)

Dates: Sept. 1, 1961
House: Jan. 3, 2001-date
Serving in the 111th Congress

HOUSE STANDING COMMITTEES:

1st AGRICULTURE
Dates: Feb. 8, 2001-Jan. 3, 2005
Departure: Moved to Energy and Commerce

Cong.	Ranking	Terms in: House	Comm.	Date of Assignment
107th	Min-20th	1	1	Feb. 8, 2001
108th	Min-13th	2	2	Jan. 28, 2003

2nd FINANCIAL SERVICES
Dates: Feb. 8, 2001-Jan. 3, 2005
Departure: Moved to Energy and Commerce

Cong.	Ranking	Terms in: House	Comm.	Date of Assignment
107th	Min-32nd	1	1	Feb. 8, 2001
108th	Min-25th	2	2	Jan. 28, 2003

3rd SMALL BUSINESS
Dates: Feb. 28, 2001-Jan. 3, 2003
Departure: Left committee; no new assignment

Cong.	Ranking	Terms in: House	Comm.	Date of Assignment
107th	MnR-2nd	1	1	Feb. 28, 2001

4th ENERGY AND COMMERCE
Dates: Jan. 26, 2005-date
Departure: Still serving in the 111th Congress

Cong.	Ranking	Terms in: House	Comm.	Date of Assignment
109th	Min-26th	3	1	Jan. 26, 2005
110th	Maj-24th	4	2	Jan. 4, 2007
111th	Maj-20th	5	3	Jan. 7, 2009

5th SCIENCE AND TECHNOLOGY
Dates: Jan. 18, 2007-Jan. 3, 2009
Departure: Moved to Foreign Affairs

Cong.	Ranking	Terms in: House	Comm.	Date of Assignment
110th	Maj-18th	4	1	Jan. 18, 2007

6th FOREIGN AFFAIRS
Dates: Jan. 21, 2009-date
Departure: Still serving in the 111th Congress

Cong.	Ranking	Terms in: House	Comm.	Date of Assignment
111th	Maj-22nd	5	1	Jan. 21, 2009

Daniel D. Rostenkowski (D-Ill.)

Dates: Jan. 2, 1928
House: Jan. 3, 1959-Jan. 3, 1995
Left the House: Defeated for re-election in 1994

HOUSE STANDING COMMITTEES:

1st INTERSTATE AND FOREIGN COMMERCE
Dates: Jan. 19, 1959-May 5, 1964
Departure: Resigned committee; moved to Ways and Means

2nd WAYS AND MEANS
Dates: May 5, 1964-Jan. 3, 1995
Ch1: Removed by Caucus rules, June 8, 1994; and replaced by
Sam M. Gibbons (D-Fla.) on June 8, 1994
Departure: Left the House; lost re-election

Cong.	Ranking	Terms in: House	Comm.	Date of Assignment
103rd	Maj-Ch1	18	16	Jan. 5, 1993

HOUSE SELECT AND SPECIAL COMMITTEES:

1st SELECT ENERGY (Ad Hoc)
Dates: Apr. 21, 1977-Dec. 29, 1978
Termination: House Report 1820 (95-2) filed

JOINT COMMITTEES:

1st JOINT STUDY BUDGET CONTROL
House Dates: Nov. 27, 1972-Apr. 18, 1973
Termination: House Report 147 (93-1) filed

2nd JOINT INTERNAL REVENUE TAXATION, 94
Renamed JOINT TAXATION, 95-103
House Dates: Jan. 28, 1975-Jan. 3, 1995
CVc1: Replaced by Sam M. Gibbons (D-Fla.) on June 8, 1994
Departure: Left the House; lost re-election

Cong.	Ranking	Terms in: House	Comm.	Date of Assignment
103rd	Maj-CVc1	18	10	Mar. 18, 1993

Tobias A. Roth (R-Wisc.)

Dates: Oct. 10, 1938
House: Jan. 3, 1979-Jan. 3, 1997
Left the House: Retired in 1996

HOUSE STANDING COMMITTEES:

1st SCIENCE AND TECHNOLOGY
Dates: Jan. 24, 1979-Jan. 3, 1981
Departure: Moved to Foreign Affairs

2nd SMALL BUSINESS
1st Dates: Jan. 24, 1979-Jan. 3, 1981
1st Departure: Moved to Foreign Affairs.
2nd Dates: Jan. 6, 1983-Jan. 3, 1985
2nd Departure: Moved to Banking, Housing and Urban Affairs.

3rd FOREIGN AFFAIRS, 97-103
INTERNATIONAL RELATIONS, 104
Dates: Jan. 28, 1981-Jan. 3, 1997
Departure: Left the House; retired

Cong.	Ranking	Terms in: House	Comm.	Date of Assignment
103rd	Min-4th	8	7	Jan. 5, 1993
104th	Maj-4th	9	8	Jan. 4, 1995

4th BANKING, FINANCE AND URBAN AFFAIRS, 99-103
BANKING AND FINANCIAL SERVICES, 104
Dates: Jan. 30, 1985-Jan. 3, 1997
Departure: Left the House; retired

Cong.	Ranking	Terms in: House	Comm.	Date of Assignment
103rd	Min-6th	8	5	Jan. 5, 1993
104th	Maj-5th	9	6	Jan. 4, 1995

William V. Roth Jr. (R-Del.)

Dates: July 22, 1921-Dec. 13, 2003
House: Jan. 3, 1967-Dec. 31, 1970
Left the House: Resigned; elected to U.S. Senate in 1970
Senate: Jan. 1, 1971-Jan. 3, 2001
Left the Senate: Defeated for re-election in 2000

S: Roth was appointed to the 91st Congress, Jan. 1, 1971, to fill the vacancy caused by the resignation of U.S. Senator John J. Williams (R-Del.). Roth had been elected to succeed Williams in the 92nd Congress. He was seated Jan. 2, 1971, but not assigned to committees in the 91st Congress.

HOUSE STANDING COMMITTEES:

1st JUDICIARY
Dates: Jan. 26, 1967-Jan. 3, 1969
Departure: Moved to Foreign Affairs

2nd MERCHANT MARINE AND FISHERIES
Dates: Jan. 26, 1967-Jan. 3, 1969
Departure: Moved to Foreign Affairs

3rd FOREIGN AFFAIRS
Dates: Jan. 29, 1969-Dec. 31, 1970
Departure: Resigned the House; elected to U.S. Senate

SENATE STANDING COMMITTEES:

1st GOVERNMENT OPERATIONS reorganized Feb. 22, 1977
GOVERNMENTAL AFFAIRS
1st Dates: Jan. 29, 1971-May 21, 1997
Ch1: Became Chair of Finance; replaced by Theodore F. Stevens
(R-Alas.) on Sep. 12, 1995
1st Departure: Temporary leave
2nd Dates: Mar. 4, 1998-Jan. 3, 2001, returned with rank
2nd Departure: Left the Senate; lost re-election

Cong.	Ranking	Years in: Senate	Comm.	Date of Assignment
103rd	Min-RM	23 *1	22	Jan. 7, 1993
104th	Maj-Ch1	25 *1	24	Jan. 5, 1995
105th	Maj-2nd	27 *1	26	Jan. 9, 1997
105th	Maj-2nd	28 *2	1	Mar. 4, 1998
106th	Maj-2nd	29 *2	2	Jan. 7, 1999

2nd BANKING HOUSING AND URBAN AFFAIRS
1st Dates: Jan. 29, 1971-Jan. 12, 1973
1st Departure: Moved to Finance
2nd Dates: Feb. 2, 1989-Jan. 3, 1995
2nd Departure: Moved to Joint Taxation

Cong.	Ranking	Years in: Senate	Comm.	Date of Assignment
103rd	Min-7th	23	*2 4	Jan. 7, 1993

3rd FINANCE
Dates: Jan. 12, 1973-Jan. 3, 2001
Ch2: Replaced Robert F. Packwood (R-Ore.) who relinquished chairmanship on Sep. 8, 1995
Departure: Left the Senate; lost re-election

Cong.	Ranking	Years in: Senate	Comm.	Date of Assignment
103rd	Min-3rd	23	20	Jan. 7, 1993
104th	Maj-3rd	25	22	Jan. 4, 1995
=104th	Maj-Ch2	25	23	Sep. 12, 1995
105th	Maj-Chr	27	24	Jan. 9, 1997
106th	Maj-Chr	29	26	Jan. 7, 1999

SENATE SELECT AND SPECIAL COMMITTEES:

1st SELECT SMALL BUSINESS
Dates: Feb. 6, 1974-Jan. 31, 1975
Departure: Left committee; no new assignment

2nd SELECT PERMANENT INTELLIGENCE
Dates: Jan. 6, 1981-Feb. 2, 1989
Departure: Returned to Banking, Housing and Urban Affairs

JOINT COMMITTEES:

1st JOINT STUDY BUDGET CONTROL
Senate Dates: Jan. 3, 1973-Apr. 18, 1973
Termination: House Report 147 (93-1) filed

2nd JOINT ECONOMIC
Senate Dates: Sep. 22, 1976-Jan. 3, 2001
Ch1: Re-ranked after Mack on Feb. 2, 1995
Departure: Left the Senate; lost re-election

Cong.	Ranking	Years in: Senate	Comm.	Date of Assignment
103rd	Min-1st	23	17	Jan. 21, 1993
104th	Maj-Ch1	25	19	Jan. 9, 1995
105th	Maj-2nd	27	21	Jan. 9, 1997
106th	Maj-2nd	29	23	Jan. 7, 1999

3rd JOINT TAXATION
1st Senate Dates: Jan. 5, 1981-Jan. 12, 1987
1st Departure: Left committee; party ratio shift
2nd Dates: Feb. 2, 1995-Jan. 3, 2001
VcC2/Ch2: Replaced Robert L. Packwood (R-Ore.) who had resigned on Sep. 12, 1995
2nd Departure: Left the Senate; lost re-election.

Cong.	Ranking	Years in: Senate	Comm.	Date of Assignment
104th	Maj-3rd	25 *2	1	Feb. 2, 1995
=104th	Maj-VcC2	25 *2	1	Sep. 12, 1995
105th	Maj-VcC	27 *2	2	Continued
106th	Maj-VcC	29 *2	5	Continued

Steven R. Rothman (D-N.J.)

Dates: Oct. 14, 1952
House: Jan. 3, 1997-date
Serving in the 111th Congress

HOUSE STANDING COMMITTEES:

1st INTERNATIONAL RELATIONS
Dates: Jan. 7, 1997-Feb. 7, 2001
Departure: Resigned committee; moved to Appropriations

Cong.	Ranking	Terms in: House	Comm.	Date of Assignment
105th	Min-20th	1	1	Jan. 7, 1997
106th	Min-16th	2	2	Jan. 6, 1999
107th	Min-13th	3	3	Jan. 31, 2001

2nd JUDICIARY
Dates: Jan. 7, 1997-Feb. 7, 2001
Departure: Resigned committee; moved to Appropriations

Cong.	Ranking	Terms in: House	Comm.	Date of Assignment
105th	Min-15th	1	1	Jan. 7, 1997
106th	Min-14th	2	2	Jan. 6, 1999
107th	Min-14th	3	3	Jan. 31, 2001

3rd APPROPRIATIONS
Dates: Feb. 8, 2001-date
Departure: Still serving in the 111th Congress

Cong.	Ranking	Terms in: House	Comm.	Date of Assignment
107th	Min-29th	3	1	Feb. 8, 2001
108th	Min-27th	4	2	Jan. 28, 2003
109th	Min-27th	5	3	Jan. 26, 2005
110th	Maj-24th	6	4	Jan. 4, 2007
111th	Maj-23rd	7	5	Jan. 7, 2009

4th SCIENCE AND TECHNOLOGY
Dates: Jan. 18, 2007-date
Departure: Still serving in the 111th Congress

Cong.	Ranking	Terms in: House	Comm.	Date of Assignment
110th	Maj-15th	6	1	Jan. 18, 2007
111th	Maj-15th	7	2	Jan. 21, 2009

Margaret S. Roukema (R-N.J.)

Dates: Sept. 19, 1929
House: Jan. 3, 1981-Jan. 3, 2003
Left the House: Retired in 2002

HOUSE STANDING COMMITTEES:

1st BANKING, FINANCE AND URBAN AFFAIRS, 97-103
BANKING AND FINANCIAL SERVICES, 104-106
FINANCIAL SERVICES, 107
Dates: Jan. 28, 1981-Jan. 3, 2003
Departure: Left the House; retired

Cong.	Ranking	Terms in: House	Comm.	Date of Assignment
103rd	Min-3rd	7	7	Jan. 5, 1993
104th	Maj-3rd	8	8	Jan. 4, 1995
105th	Maj-3rd	9	9	Jan. 7, 1997
106th	Maj-3rd	10	10	Jan. 6, 1999
107th	Maj-3rd	11	11	Jan. 6, 2001

2nd EDUCATION AND LABOR, 97-103
ECONOMIC AND EDUCATIONAL OPPORTUNITIES, 104
EDUCATION AND THE WORKFORCE, 105-107
Dates: Jan. 28, 1981-Jan. 3, 2003
Departure: Left the House; retired

Cong.	Ranking	Terms in: House	Comm.	Date of Assignment
103rd	Min-3rd	7	7	Jan. 5, 1993
104th	Maj-3rd	8	8	Jan. 4, 1995
105th	Maj-3rd	9	9	Jan. 7, 1997

| 106th | Maj-3rd | 10 | 10 | Jan. 6, 1999 |
| 107th | Maj-3rd | 11 | 11 | Jan. 6, 2001 |

HOUSE SELECT AND SPECIAL COMMITTEES:

1st SELECT HUNGER (Temporary)
Dates: Mar. 13, 1984-Jan. 3, 1993
VCh1: Roukema was succeeded as Vice Chair by Bill Emerson (R-Mo.) on July 13, 1987. Roukema remained on the committee.
Termination: Committee not renewed in 1993

J. Roy Rowland (D-Ga.)

Dates: Feb. 3, 1926
House: Jan. 3, 1983-Jan. 3, 1995
Left the House: Retired in 1994

HOUSE STANDING COMMITTEES:

1st PUBLIC WORKS AND TRANSPORTATION
Dates: Jan. 6, 1983-Jan. 3, 1989
Departure: Moved to Energy and Commerce

2nd VETERANS AFFAIRS
Dates: Jan. 6, 1983-Jan. 3, 1995
Departure: Left the House; retired

| | | Terms in: | | Date of |
Cong.	Ranking	House	Comm.	Assignment
103rd	Maj-6th	6	6	Jan. 5, 1993

3rd ENERGY AND COMMERCE
Dates: Jan. 19, 1989-Jan. 3, 1995
Departure: Left the House; retired

| | | Terms in: | | Date of |
Cong.	Ranking	House	Comm.	Assignment
103rd	Maj-16th	6	3	Jan. 5, 1993

HOUSE SELECT AND SPECIAL COMMITTEES:

1st SELECT CHILDREN, YOUTH AND FAMILIES (Temporary)
Dates: Feb. 2, 1983-Jan. 3, 1993
Termination: Committee not renewed in 1993

Lucille Roybal-Allard (D-Cal.)

Born: June 12, 1941
House: Jan. 3, 1993-date
Serving in the 111th Congress

HOUSE STANDING COMMITTEES:

1st BANKING, FINANCE AND URBAN AFFAIRS, 103
BANKING AND FINANCIAL SERVICES, 104-105
Dates: Jan. 5, 1993-Jan. 3, 1999
Departure: Moved to Appropriations

| | | Terms in: | | Date of |
Cong.	Ranking	House	Comm.	Assignment
103rd	Maj-20th	1	1	Jan. 5, 1993

| 104th | Min-14th | 2 | 2 | Jan. 4, 1995 |
| 105th | Min-12th | 3 | 3 | Jan. 7, 1997 |

2nd SMALL BUSINESS
Dates: Jan. 5, 1993-Jan. 3, 1995
Departure: Moved to Budget

| | | Terms in: | | Date of |
Cong.	Ranking	House	Comm.	Assignment
103rd	Maj-24th	1	1	Jan. 5, 1993

3rd BUDGET
Dates: Jan. 4, 1995-Jan. 3, 1999
Departure: Moved to Appropriations

| | | Terms in: | | Date of |
Cong.	Ranking	House	Comm.	Assignment
104th	Min-15th	2	1	Jan. 4, 1995
105th	Min-8th	3	2	Jan. 7, 1997

4th APPROPRIATIONS
Dates: Jan. 6, 1999-date
Departure: Still serving in the 111th Congress

| | | Terms in: | | Date of |
Cong.	Ranking	House	Comm.	Assignment
106th	Min-23rd	4	1	Jan. 6, 1999
107th	Min-23rd	5	2	Jan. 31, 2001
108th	Min-21st	6	3	Jan. 28, 2003
109th	Min-21st	7	4	Jan. 26, 2005
110th	Maj-18th	8	5	Jan. 4, 2007
111th	Maj-17th	9	6	Jan. 7, 2009

5th STANDARDS OF OFFICIAL CONDUCT
Dates: Mar. 6, 2003-Jan. 3, 2009
Departure: Left committee; no new assignment

| | | Terms in: | | Date of |
Cong.	Ranking	House	Comm.	Assignment
108th	Min-4th	6	1	Mar. 6, 2003
109th	Min-4th	7	2	Feb. 9, 2005
110th	Maj-3rd	8	3	Feb. 8, 2007

HOUSE SELECT AND SPECIAL COMMITTEES:

1st SELECT NATIONAL SECURITY CONCERNS WITH CHINA
Dates: June 22, 1998-Apr. 30, 1999
Termination: House Report 851 (105-2) filed, Jan. 3, 1999

| | | Terms in: | | Date of |
Cong.	Ranking	House	Comm.	Assignment
105th	Min-3rd	3	1	June 22, 1998
106th	Min-3rd	4	2	Jan. 19, 1999

Edward R. Royce (R-Cal.)

Dates: Oct. 12, 1951
House: Jan. 3, 1993-date
Serving in the 111th Congress

HOUSE STANDING COMMITTEES:

1st FOREIGN AFFAIRS, 103
INTERNATIONAL RELATIONS, 104-109
FOREIGN AFFAIRS, 110
Dates: Jan. 5, 1993-date
Departure: Still serving in the 111th Congress

Cong.	Ranking	Terms in: House	Comm.	Date of Assignment
103rd	Min-18th	1	1	Jan. 5, 1993
104th	Maj-15th	2	2	Jan. 4, 1995
105th	Maj-13th	3	3	Jan. 7, 1997
106th	Maj-13th	4	4	Jan. 6, 1999
107th	Maj-11th	5	5	Jan. 6, 2001
108th	Maj-10th	6	6	Jan. 28, 2003
109th	Maj-8th	7	7	Jan. 26, 2005
110th	Min-7th	8	8	Jan. 10, 2007
111th	Min-7th	9	9	Jan. 9, 2009

2nd SCIENCE, SPACE AND TECHNOLOGY
Dates: Jan. 5, 1993-Jan. 3, 1995
Departure: Moved to Banking and Financial Services

Cong.	Ranking	Terms in: House	Comm.	Date of Assignment
103rd	Min-16th	1	1	Jan. 5, 1993

3rd BANKING AND FINANCIAL SERVICES, 104-106
FINANCIAL SERVICES, 107-110
Dates: Jan. 4, 1995-date
Departure: Still serving in the 111th Congress

Cong.	Ranking	Terms in: House	Comm.	Date of Assignment
104th	Maj-11th	2	1	Jan. 4, 1995
105th	Maj-11th	3	2	Jan. 7, 1997
106th	Maj-11th	4	3	Jan. 6, 1999
107th	Maj-9th	5	4	Jan. 6, 2001
108th	Maj-8th	6	5	Jan. 28, 2003
109th	Maj-8th	7	6	Jan. 26, 2005
110th	Min-6th	8	7	Jan. 10, 2007
111th	Min-4th	9	8	Jan. 9, 2009

C.A. (Dutch) Ruppersberger

(D-Md.)

Dates: Jan. 31, 1946
House: Jan 3, 2003-date
Serving in the 111th Congress

HOUSE STANDING COMMITTEES:

1st GOVERNMENT REFORM
Dates: Feb. 5, 2003-Jan. 3, 2007
Departure: Moved to Appropriations

Cong.	Ranking	Terms in: House	Comm.	Date of Assignment
108th	Min-18th	1	1	Feb. 5, 2003
109th	Min-16th	2	2	Jan. 26, 2005

2nd ARMED SERVICES
Dates: Mar. 5, 2003-Jan. 3, 2005
Departure: Leave of absence on Mar. 5, 2003, for existing service on Government Reform and Permanent Select Intelligence; does not return

Cong.	Ranking	Terms in: House	Comm.	Date of Assignment
108th	MnR-1st	1	1	Mar. 5, 2003

3rd APPROPRIATIONS
Dates: Jan. 4, 2007-date
Departure: Still serving in the 111th Congress

Cong.	Ranking	Terms in: House	Comm.	Date of Assignment
110th	Maj-34th	3	1	Jan. 4, 2007
111th	Maj-32nd	4	2	Jan. 7, 2009

HOUSE SELECT AND SPECIAL COMMITTEES:

1st PERMANENT SELECT INTELLIGENCE
Dates: Jan. 8, 2003-date
Departure: Still serving in the 111th Congress

Cong.	Ranking	Terms in: House	Comm.	Date of Assignment
108th	Min-9th	1	1	Jan. 8, 2003
109th	Min-8th	2	2	Jan. 26, 2005
110th	Maj-7th	3	3	Jan. 17, 2007
111th	Maj-5th	4	4	Feb. 4, 2009

Bobby L. Rush (D-Ill.)

Dates: Nov. 23, 1946
House: Jan. 3, 1993-date
Serving in the 111th Congress

HOUSE STANDING COMMITTEES:

1st BANKING, FINANCE AND URBAN AFFAIRS
Dates: Jan. 5, 1993-Jan. 3, 1995
Departure: Moved to Commerce

Cong.	Ranking	Terms in: House	Comm.	Date of Assignment
103rd	Maj-19th	1	1	Jan. 5, 1993

2nd GOVERNMENT OPERATIONS
Dates: Jan. 5, 1993-Jan. 3, 1995
Departure: Moved to Commerce

Cong.	Ranking	Terms in: House	Comm.	Assignment
103rd	Maj-15th	1	1	Jan. 5, 1993

3rd SCIENCE, SPACE AND TECHNOLOGY
Dates: Nov. 10, 1993-Jan. 3, 1995
Departure: Moved to Commerce

Cong.	Ranking	Terms in: House	Comm.	Date of Assignment
103rd	MjA-34th	1	1	Nov. 10, 1993

4th COMMERCE, 104-106
ENERGY AND COMMERCE, 107-111
Dates: Jan. 4, 1995-date
Departure: Still serving in the 111th Congress

Cong.	Ranking	Terms in: House	Comm.	Date of Assignment
104th	Min-18th	2	1	Jan. 4, 1995
105th	Min-13th	3	2	Jan. 7, 1997
106th	Min-11th	4	3	Jan. 6, 1999
107th	Min-11th	5	4	Jan. 31, 2001
108th	Min-11th	6	5	Jan. 28, 2003
109th	Min-9th	7	6	Jan. 26, 2005
110th	Maj-8th	8	7	Jan. 4, 2007
111th	Maj-7th	9	8	Jan. 7, 2009

Paul D. Ryan (R-Wisc.)

Dates: Jan. 29, 1970
House: Jan. 3, 1999-date
Serving in the 111th Congress

HOUSE STANDING COMMITTEES:

1st BANKING AND FINANCIAL SERVICES
Dates: Jan. 6, 1999-Jan. 3, 2001
Departure: Moved to Ways and Means

Cong.	Ranking	Terms in: House	Comm.	Date of Assignment
106th	Maj-26th	1	1	Jan. 6, 1999

2nd BUDGET
1st Dates: Jan. 6, 1999-Jan. 3, 2001
1st Departure: Moved to Ways and Means
2nd Dates: Jan. 26, 2005-date
2nd Departure: Still serving in the 111th Congress

Cong.	Ranking	Terms in: House	Comm.	Date of Assignment
106th	Maj-23rd	1 *1	1	Jan. 6, 1999
109th	Maj-17th	4 *2	1	Jan. 26, 2005
110th	Min-RM	5 *2	2	Jan. 4, 2007
111th	Min-RM	6 *2	3	Jan. 6, 2009

3rd GOVERNMENT REFORM
Dates: Jan. 6, 1999-Jan. 3, 2001
Departure: Moved to Ways and Means

Cong.	Ranking	Terms in: House	Comm.	Date of Assignment
106th	Maj-23rd	1	1	Jan. 6, 1999

4th WAYS AND MEANS
Dates: Jan. 6, 2001-date
Departure: Serving in the 111th Congress

Cong.	Ranking	Terms in: House	Comm.	Date of Assignment
107th	Maj-24th	2	1	Jan. 6, 2001
108th	Maj-23rd	3	2	Jan. 28, 2003
109th	Maj-19th	4	3	Jan. 6, 2005
110th	Min-12th	5	4	Jan. 4, 2007
111th	Min-5th	6	5	Jan. 9, 2009

JOINT COMMITTEES:

1st JOINT ECONOMIC
House Dates: Mar. 18, 1999-Jan. 3, 2007
Departure: Left committee; no new assignment

Cong.	Ranking	Terms in: House	Comm.	Date of Assignment
106th	Maj-6th	1	1	Mar. 18, 1999
107th	Maj-2nd	2	2	May 1, 2001
108th	Maj-2nd	3	3	Feb. 25, 2003
109th	Maj-2nd	4	4	Mar. 3, 2005

Timothy J. Ryan (D-Ohio)

Dates: July 16, 1973
House: Jan. 3, 2003-date
Serving in the 111th Congress

HOUSE STANDING COMMITTEES:

1st EDUCATION AND THE WORKFORCE
Dates: Feb. 5, 2003-Jan. 3, 2005
Departure: Moved to Appropriations

Cong.	Ranking	Terms in: House	Comm.	Date of Assignment
108th	Min-22nd	1	1	Feb. 5, 2003
109th	Min-20th	2	2	Jan. 26, 2005

2nd SMALL BUSINESS
Dates: Feb. 5, 2003-Mar. 4, 2003
Departure: Resigned committee; moved to Armed Services

Cong.	Ranking	Terms in: House	Comm.	Date of Assignment
108th	Min-11th	1	1	Feb. 5, 2003

3rd VETERANS' AFFAIRS
Dates: Feb. 13, 2003-Jan. 3, 2005
Departure: Left committee; no new assignment

Cong.	Ranking	Terms in: House	Comm.	Assignment
108th	Min-14th	1	1	Feb. 13, 2003

4th ARMED SERVICES
Dates: Mar. 5, 2003-Jan. 3, 2007
Departure: Moved to Appropriations

Cong.	Ranking	Terms in: House	Comm.	Date of Assignment
108th	MnR-1st	1	1	Mar. 5, 2003
109th	Min-24th	2	2	Jan. 26, 2005

5th APPROPRIATIONS
Dates: Jan. 4, 2007-date
Departure: Still serving in the 111th Congress

Cong.	Ranking	Terms in: House	Comm.	Date of Assignment
110th	Maj-33rd	3	1	Jan. 4, 2007
111th	Maj-31st	4	2	Jan. 7, 2009

Jim Ryun (R-Kan.)

Dates: April 29, 1947
House: Nov. 27, 1996-Jan. 3, 2007
Left the House: Defeated for re-election in 2006

H: Ryun was elected to the 104th Congress by special election, Nov. 27, 1996, to fill the vacancy caused by the resignation of U.S. Representative Sam Brownback (R-Kan.) who had been elected to the Senate. Under Kansas law Ryun was a member of the Congress even though he was not sworn or assigned to committees because the 104th Congress was no longer in session.

HOUSE STANDING COMMITTEES:

1st BANKING AND FINANCIAL SERVICES, 105-106
FINANCIAL SERVICES, 107-109
Dates: Jan. 7, 1997-Jan. 3, 2007
Departure: Left the House; lost re-election

Cong.	Ranking	Terms in: House	Comm.	Date of Assignment
105th	Maj-23rd	2	1	Jan. 7, 1997
106th	Maj-19th	3	2	Jan. 6, 1999

107th	Maj-19th	4	3	Jan. 6, 2001
108th	Maj-14th	5	4	Jan. 28, 2003
109th	Maj-14th	6	5	Jan. 26, 2005

2nd NATIONAL SECURITY, 105
ARMED SERVICES, 106-109
Dates: Jan. 7, 1997-Jan. 3, 2007
Departure: Left the House; lost re-election

		Terms in:		Date of
Cong.	**Ranking**	**House**	**Comm.**	**Assignment**
105th	Maj-27th	2	1	Jan. 7, 1997
106th	Maj-25th	3	2	Jan. 6, 1999
107th	Maj-20th	4	3	Jan. 6, 2001
108th	Maj-12th	5	4	Jan. 28, 2003
109th	Maj-12th	6	5	Jan. 26, 2005

3rd SMALL BUSINESS
Dates: Jan. 21, 1997-Jan. 3, 1999
Departure: Moved to Budget

		Terms in:		Date of
Cong.	**Ranking**	**House**	**Comm.**	**Assignment**
105th	Maj-12th	2	1	Jan. 21, 1997

4th BUDGET
Dates: Jan. 6, 1999-Jan. 3, 2007
Departure: Left the House; lost re-election

		Terms in:		Date of
Cong.	**Ranking**	**House**	**Comm.**	**Assignment**
106th	Maj-18th	3	1	Jan. 6, 1999
107th	Maj-9th	4	2	Jan. 6, 2001
108th	Maj-5th	5	3	Jan. 28, 2003
109th	Maj-3rd	6	4	Jan. 26, 2005

S

Gregorio Kilili Sablan (Ind-No.Mar.)

Dates: Jan. 19, 1955
House: Jan. 3, 2009-date
Serving in 111th Congress
Note: Sablan's committees were assigned by the Democratic Caucus

HOUSE STANDING COMMITTEES:

1st EDUCATION AND LABOR
Dates: Jan. 21, 2009-date
Departure: Still serving in the 111th Congress

		Terms in:		Date of
Cong.	**Ranking**	**House**	**Comm.**	**Assignment**
111th	Maj-28th	1	1	Jan. 21, 2009

2nd NATURAL RESOURCES
Dates: Jan. 21, 2009-date
Departure: Still serving in the 111th Congress

		Terms in:		Date of
Cong.	**Ranking**	**House**	**Comm.**	**Assignment**
111th	Maj-12th	1	1	Jan. 21, 2009

Martin Olav Sabo (DFL-Minn.)

Dates: Feb. 28, 1938
House: Jan. 3, 1979-Jan. 3, 2007
Left the House: Retired in 2006

HOUSE STANDING COMMITTEES:

1st APPROPRIATIONS
Dates: Jan. 24,1979-Jan. 3, 2007
Departure: Left the House; retired

		Terms in:		Date of
Cong.	**Ranking**	**House**	**Comm.**	**Assignment**
103rd	Maj-11th	8	8	Jan. 5, 1993
104th	Min-8th	9	9	Jan. 4, 1995
105th	Min-6th	10	10	Jan. 7, 1997
106th	Min-4th	11	11	Jan. 6, 1999
107th	Min-4th	12	12	Jan. 31, 2001
108th	Min-4th	13	13	Jan. 28, 2003
109th	Min-4th	14	14	Jan. 26, 2005

2nd BUDGET
Dates: Jan. 19, 1989-Jan. 3, 1987
Ch2: Replaced Leon Panetta (D-Cal.) as Chair on Jan. 25, 1993
Departure: Left committee; no new assignment

		Terms in:		Date of
Cong.	**Ranking**	**House**	**Comm.**	**Assignment**
103rd	Maj-5th	8	3	Jan. 5, 1993
=103rd	Maj-Ch2	8	3	Jan. 25, 1993
104th	Min-RM	9	4	Jan. 4, 1995

3rd STANDARDS OF OFFICIAL CONDUCT
Dates: Sep. 29, 1997-July 31, 2001
Departure: Resigned committee; no new assignment

		Terms in:		Date of
Cong.	**Ranking**	**House**	**Comm.**	**Assignment**
105th	Min-2nd	10	1	Sep. 29, 1997
106th	Min-2nd	11	2	Jan. 6, 1999
107th	Min-2nd	12	3	Mar. 6, 2001

HOUSE SELECT AND SPECIAL COMMITTEES:

1st PERMANENT SELECT INTELLIGENCE
Dates: Feb. 5, 1991-Jan. 3, 1993
Departure: Left committee; became Chair of Budget

John T. Salazar (D-Colo.)

Dates: July 21, 1953
House: Jan. 3, 2005-date
Serving in the 111th Congress

HOUSE STANDING COMMITTEES:

1st AGRICULTURE
Dates: Jan. 26, 2005-Jan. 3, 2009
Departure: Moved to Appropriations and Select Energy Independence and Global Warming

Cong.	Ranking	Terms in: House	Comm.	Date of Assignment
109th	Min-16th	1	1	Jan. 26, 2005
110th	Maj-13th	2	2	Jan. 12, 2007

2nd TRANSPORTATION AND INFRASTRUCTURE
Dates: Jan. 26, 2005-Jan 3, 2009
Departure: Moved to Appropriations and Select Energy Independence and Global Warming

Cong.	Ranking	Terms in: House	Comm.	Date of Assignment
109th	Min-34th	1	1	Jan. 26, 2005
110th	Maj-24th	2	2	Jan. 10, 2007

3rd VETERANS' AFFAIRS
Dates: Feb. 15, 2006-Jan. 3, 2009
Departure: Moved to Appropriations and Select Energy Independence and Global Warming

Cong.	Ranking	Terms in: House	Comm.	Date of Assignment
109th	MnA-13th	1	1	Feb. 15, 2006
110th	Maj-11th	2	2	Jan. 12, 2007

4th APPROPRIATIONS
Dates: Jan. 7, 2009-date
Departure: Still serving in the 111th Congress

Cong.	Ranking	Terms in: House	Comm.	Date of Assignment
111th	Maj-37th	3	1	Jan. 7, 2009

HOUSE SELECT AND SPECIAL COMMITTEES:

1st SELECT ENERGY INDEPENDENCE AND GLOBAL WARMING
Dates: Feb. 3, 2009-date
Departure: Still serving in the 111th Congress

Cong.	Ranking	Terms in: House	Comm.	Date of Assignment
111th	Maj-8th	3	1	Feb. 3, 2009

Kenneth L. Salazar (D-Colo.)

Dates: March 2, 1955-
Senate: Jan. 3, 2005-Jan. 20, 2009
Left the Senate: Resigned; appointed Secretary of the Interior in 2009
Note: Kenneth Salazar was unassigned to committees in the 111th pending his Senate confirmation as Secretary of the Interior

SENATE STANDING COMMITTEES:

1st AGRICULTURE, NUTRITION AND FORESTRY
Dates: Jan. 6, 2005-Jan. 20, 2009
Departure: Resigned the Senate; named to Cabinet

Cong.	Ranking	Years in: Senate	Comm.	Date of Assignment
109th	Min-9th	1	1	Jan. 6, 2005
110th	Maj-8th	3	3	Jan. 12, 2007

2nd ENERGY AND NATURAL RESOURCES
Dates: Jan. 6, 2005-Jan. 20, 2009
Departure: Resigned the Senate; named to Cabinet

Cong.	Ranking	Years in: Senate	Comm.	Date of Assignment
109th	Min-10th	1	1	Jan. 6, 2005
110th	Maj-8th	3	3	Jan. 12, 2007

3rd VETERANS AFFAIRS
Dates: Jan 6, 2005-Jan. 12, 2007
Departure: Moved to Finance

Cong.	Ranking	Years in: Senate	Comm.	Date of Assignment
109th	Min-6th	1	1	Jan. 6, 2005

4th FINANCE
Dates: Jan. 12, 2007-Jan. 20, 2009
Departure: Resigned the Senate; named to Cabinet

Cong.	Ranking	Years in: Senate	Comm.	Date of Assignment
110th	Maj-11th	3	1	Jan. 12, 2007

SENATE SELECT AND SPECIAL COMMITTEES:

1st SELECT ETHICS (Permanent)
Dates: Jan. 18, 2006-Jan. 20, 2009
Departure: Resigned the Senate; named to Cabinet

Cong.	Ranking	Years in: Senate	Comm.	Date of Assignment
109th	MnR-1st	2	1	Jan. 18, 2006
110th	Maj-4th	3	1	Jan. 12, 2007

2nd SPECIAL AGING (Permanent)
Dates: Jan. 18, 2006-Jan. 20, 2009
Departure: Resigned the Senate; named to Cabinet

Cong.	Ranking	Years in: Senate	Comm.	Date of Assignment
109th	MnR-1st	2	1	Jan. 18, 2006
110th	Maj-8th	3	1	Jan. 12, 2007

Bill Sali (R-Ida.)

Dates: Feb. 17, 1954
House: Jan. 3, 2007-Jan. 3, 2009
Left the House: Defeated for re-election in 2008

HOUSE STANDING COMMITTEES:

1st NATURAL RESOURCES
Dates: Jan. 10, 2007-Jan. 3, 2009
Departure: Left the House; lost re-election

Cong.	Ranking	Terms in: House	Comm.	Date of Assignment
110th	Min-21st	1	1	Jan. 10, 2007

2nd OVERSIGHT AND GOVERNMENT REFORM
Dates: Jan. 10, 2007-Jan. 3, 2009
Departure: Left the House; lost re-election

Cong.	Ranking	Terms in: House	Comm.	Date of Assignment
110th	Min-17th	1	1	Jan. 10, 2007

Matthew J. Salmon (R-Ariz.)

Dates: Jan. 21, 1958
House: Jan. 3, 1995-Jan. 3, 2001
Left the House: Retired; lost for Governor in 2002

HOUSE STANDING COMMITTEES:

1st INTERNATIONAL RELATIONS
Dates: Jan. 4, 1995-Jan. 3, 2001
Departure: Left the House, retired

Cong.	Ranking	Terms in: House	Comm.	Date of Assignment
104th	Maj-22nd	1	1	Jan. 4, 1995
105th	Maj-18th	2	2	Jan. 7, 1997
106th	Maj-17th	3	3	Jan. 6, 1999

2nd SCIENCE
Dates: Jan. 4, 1995-Jan. 3, 1999
Departure: Moved to Education and the Workforce

Cong.	Ranking	Terms in: House	Comm.	Date of Assignment
104th	Maj-17th	1	1	Jan. 4, 1995
105th	Maj-13th	2	2	Jan. 21, 1997

3rd SMALL BUSINESS,
Dates: Jan. 4, 1995-Jan. 3, 1997
Departure: Left committee; no new assignment

Cong.	Ranking	Terms in: House	Comm.	Date of Assignment
104th	Maj-15th	1	1	Jan. 4, 1995

4th EDUCATION AND THE WORKFORCE
Dates: Jan. 6, 1999-Jan. 3, 2001
Departure: Left the House; retired

Cong.	Ranking	Terms in: House	Comm.	Date of Assignment
106th	Maj-23rd	3	1	Jan. 6, 1999

Linda T. Sanchez (D-Cal.)

Dates: Jan. 28, 1969
House: Jan. 3, 2003-date
Serving in the 111th Congress

HOUSE STANDING COMMITTEES:

1st JUDICIARY
Dates: Jan. 28, 2003-date
Departure: Still serving in the 111th Congress

Cong.	Ranking	Terms in: House	Comm.	Date of Assignment
108th	Min-16th	1	1	Jan. 28, 2003
109th	Min-15th	2	2	Jan. 26, 2005
110th	Maj-13th	3	3	Jan. 18, 2007
111th	Maj-22nd	4	4	Jan. 21, 2009

2nd GOVERNMENT REFORM
Dates: Feb. 5, 2003-Jan. 3, 2007
Departure: Moved to Education and Labor and Foreign Affairs

Cong.	Ranking	Terms in: House	Comm.	Date of Assignment
108th	Min-17th	1	1	Feb. 5, 2003
109th	Min-15th	2	2	Jan. 26, 2005

3rd SMALL BUSINESS
Dates: Mar. 5, 2003-Jan. 3, 2007
Departure: Moved to Education and Labor and Foreign Affairs

Cong.	Ranking	Terms in: House	Comm.	Date of Assignment
108th	MnR-3rd	1	1	Mar. 5, 2003
109th	Min-12th	2	2	Jan. 26, 2005

4th EDUCATION AND LABOR
Dates: Jan. 10, 2007-Jan. 3, 2009
Departure: Moved to Ways and Means

Cong.	Ranking	Terms in: House	Comm.	Date of Assignment
110th	Maj-17th	3	1	Jan. 10, 2007

5th FOREIGN AFFAIRS
Dates: Jan. 12, 2007-Jan. 3, 2009
Departure: Moved to Ways and Means

Cong.	Ranking	Terms in: House	Comm.	Date of Assignment
110th	Maj-22nd	3	1	Jan. 12, 2007

6th WAYS AND MEANS
Dates: Jan. 7, 2009-date
Departure: Still serving in the 111th Congress

Cong.	Ranking	Terms in: House	Comm.	Date of Assignment
111th	Maj-24th	4	1	Jan. 7, 2009

Loretta Sanchez (D-Cal.)

Dates: Jan. 7, 1960
House: Jan. 3, 1997-date
Serving in the 111th Congress

HOUSE STANDING COMMITTEES:

1st EDUCATION AND THE WORKFORCE
Dates: Jan. 7, 1997-Feb. 12, 2003
Departure: Leave of absence; moved to Select Homeland Security

Cong.	Ranking	Terms in: House	Comm.	Date of Assignment
105th	Min-19th	1	1	Jan. 7, 1997
106th	Min-18th	2	2	Jan. 6, 1999
107th	Min-16th	3	3	Jan. 31, 2001
108th	Min-11th	4	4	Jan. 28, 2003

2nd NATIONAL SECURITY, 105
ARMED SERVICES, 106-111
Dates: Feb. 5, 1997-date
Departure: Still serving in the 111th Congress

Cong.	Ranking	Terms in: House	Comm.	Date of Assignment
105th	Min-23rd	1	1	Feb. 5, 1997
106th	Min-18th	2	2	Jan. 6, 1999
107th	Min-16th	3	3	Jan. 31, 2001
108th	Min-12th	4	4	Jan. 28, 2003
109th	Min-11th	5	5	Jan. 26, 2005

Cong.	Ranking			Date
110th	Maj-10th	6	6	Jan. 10, 2007
111th	Maj-9th	7	7	Jan. 7, 2009

3rd HOMELAND SECURITY
Dates: Feb. 9, 2005-date
Departure: Still serving in the 111th Congress

		Terms in:		Date of
Cong.	Ranking	House	Comm.	Assignment
109th	Min-2nd	5	2	Feb. 9, 2005
110th	Maj-2nd	6	3	Jan. 12, 2007
111th	Maj-2nd	7	4	Jan. 28, 2009

HOUSE SELECT AND SPECIAL COMMITTEES:

1st SELECT HOMELAND SECURITY
Dates: Feb. 12, 2003-Jan. 3, 2005
Departure: Continued on reorganized standing committee

		Terms in:		Date of
Cong.	Ranking	House	Comm.	Assignment
108th	Min-3rd	4	1	Feb. 12, 2003

JOINT COMMITTEES:

1st JOINT ECONOMIC
House Dates: Mar. 3, 2005-date
Departure: Still serving in the 111th Congress

		Terms in:		Date of
Cong.	Ranking	House	Comm.	Assignment
109th	Min-3rd	5	1	Mar. 3, 2005
110th	Maj-4th	6	2	Mar. 27, 2007
111th	Maj-4th	7	3	Feb. 3, 2009

Bernard Sanders (Ind.-Vt.)

Dates: Sept. 8, 1941
House: Jan. 3, 1991-Jan. 3, 2007
Left the House: Elected to U.S. Senate in 2006
Senate: Jan. 3, 2007-date
Serving in the 111th Congress

H: Sanders was elected to the House and seated as an Independent. He was assigned to committees by the Democratic Caucus.

S: Sanders was elected to the Senate and seated as an Independent. He was assigned to committees by the Democrats.

HOUSE STANDING COMMITTEES:

1st BANKING, FINANCE AND URBAN AFFAIRS, 103
BANKING AND FINANCIAL SERVICES, 104-106
FINANCIAL SERVICES, 107-109
Dates: Jan. 24, 1991-Jan. 3, 2007
Departure: Left the House for the Senate

		Terms in:		Date of
Cong.	Ranking	House	Comm.	Assignment
103rd	3Pm-1st	2	2	Feb. 18, 1993
104th	3Pm-1st	3	3	Jan. 9, 1995
105th	3Pm-1st	4	4	Jan. 7, 1997
106th	3Pm-1st	5	5	Jan. 6, 1999
107th	3Pm-1st	6	6	Feb. 13, 2001
108th	Min-4th	7	7	Jan. 28, 2003
109th	Min-4th	8	8	Jan. 26, 2005

2nd GOVERNMENT OPERATIONS, 103
GOVERNMENT REFORM AND OVERSIGHT, 104-105

GOVERNMENT REFORM, 106-109
Dates: Jan. 24, 1991-Jan. 3, 2007
Departure: Left the House for the Senate

		Terms in:		Date of
Cong.	Ranking	House	Comm.	Assignment
103rd	3Pm-1st	2	2	Feb. 18, 1993
104th	3Pm-1st	3	3	Jan. 9, 1995
105th	3Pm-1st	4	4	Jan. 7, 1997
106th	3Pm-1st	5	5	Jan. 6, 1999
107th	3Pm-1st	6	6	Feb. 13, 2001
108th	Min-6th	7	7	Jan. 28, 2003
109th	Min-6th	8	8	Jan. 26, 2005

SENATE STANDING COMMITTEES:

1st BUDGET
Dates: Jan. 12, 2007-date
Departure: Still serving in the 111th Congress

		Years in:		Date of
Cong.	Ranking	Senate	Comm.	Assignment
110th	Maj-11th	1	1	Jan. 12, 2007
111th	Maj-10th	3	3	Jan. 21, 2009

2nd ENERGY AND NATURAL RESOURCES
Dates: Jan. 12, 2007-date
Departure: Still serving in the 111th Congress

		Years in:		Date of
Cong.	Ranking	Senate	Comm.	Assignment
110th	Maj-11th	1	1	Jan. 12, 2007
111th	Maj-9th	3	3	Jan. 21, 2009

3rd ENVIRONMENT AND PUBLIC WORKS
Dates: Jan. 12, 2007-date
Departure: Still serving in the 111th Congress

		Years in:		Date of
Cong.	Ranking	Senate	Comm.	Assignment
110th	Maj-8th	1	1	Jan. 12, 2007
111th	Maj-6th	3	3	Jan. 21, 2009

4th HEALTH, EDUCATION, LABOR AND PENSIONS
Dates: Jan. 12, 2007-date
Departure: Still serving in the 111th Congress

		Years in:		Date of
Cong.	Ranking	Senate	Comm.	Assignment
110th	Maj-10th	1	1	Jan. 12, 2007
111th	Maj-8th	3	3	Jan. 21, 2009

5th VETERANS AFFAIRS
Dates: Jan. 12, 2007-date
Departure: Still serving in the 111th Congress

		Years in:		Date of
Cong.	Ranking	Senate	Comm.	Assignment
110th	Maj-5th	1	1	Jan. 12, 2007
111th	Maj-4th	3	3	Jan. 21, 2009

Max A. Sandlin (D-Tex.)

Dates: Sept. 29, 1952
House: Jan. 3, 1997-Jan. 3, 2005
Left the House: Defeated for re-election in 2004

HOUSE STANDING COMMITTEES:

1st TRANSPORTATION AND INFRASTRUCTURE
Dates: Jan. 7, 1997-Jan. 3, 2003
Departure: Moved to Ways and Means

Cong.	Ranking	Terms in: House	Comm.	Date of Assignment
105th	Min-25th	1	1	Jan. 7, 1997
106th	Min-23rd	2	2	Jan. 6, 1999
107th	Min-20th	3	3	Jan. 31, 2001

2nd BANKING AND FINANCIAL SERVICES, 105-106
FINANCIAL SERVICES, 107
Dates: Feb. 5, 1998-Jan. 3, 2003
Departure: Moved to Ways and Means

Cong.	Ranking	Terms in: House	Comm.	Date of Assignment
105th	MnR-2nd	1	1	Feb. 5, 1998
106th	Min-17th	2	2	Jan. 6, 1999
107th	Min-15th	3	3	Jan. 31, 2001

3rd WAYS AND MEANS
Dates: Jan. 28, 2003-Jan. 3, 2005
Departure: Left the House; lost re-election

Cong.	Ranking	Terms in: House	Comm.	Date of Assignment
108th	Min-16th	4	1	Jan. 28, 2003

Stephanie Herseth Sandlin

(D-S.D.)

Dates: Dec. 3, 1970
House: June 1, 2004-date
Serving in the 111th Congress

H: Herseth was elected to the 108th Congress by special election, June 1, 2004, to fill the vacancy caused by the resignation of U.S. Representative William Janklow (R-S.D.). Herseth was seated June 3, 2004, and assigned to committees. Listed as Stephanie Herseth, 108th-110th Congresses and as Stephanie Herseth Sandlin, 111th Congress

HOUSE STANDING COMMITTEES:

1st AGRICULTURE
Dates: June 3, 2004-date
Departure: Still serving in the 111th Congress

Cong.	Ranking	Terms in: House	Comm.	Date of Assignment
108th	MnR-2nd	1	1	June 3, 2004
109th	Min-11th	2	2	Jan. 26, 2005
110th	Maj-10th	3	3	Jan. 12, 2007
111th	Maj-9th	4	4	Jan. 21, 2009

2nd RESOURCES, 108-109
NATURAL RESOURCES, 110-111
Dates: June 16, 2004-date
Departure: Still serving in the 111th Congress

Cong.	Ranking	Terms in: House	Comm.	Date of Assignment
108th	MnR-5th	1	1	June 16, 2004
109th	Min-22nd	2	2	Jan. 26, 2005
110th	Maj-26th	3	3	Jan. 18, 2007
111th	Maj-24th	4	4	Jan. 21, 2009

3rd VETERANS' AFFAIRS
Dates: June 16, 2004-date
Departure: Still serving in the 111th Congress

Cong.	Ranking	Terms in: House	Comm.	Date of Assignment
108th	MnR-1st	1	1	June 16, 2004
109th	Min-7th	2	2	Jan. 26, 2005
110th	Maj-5th	3	3	Jan. 12, 2007
111th	Maj-5th	4	4	Jan. 21, 2009

HOUSE SELECT AND SPECIAL COMMITTEES:

1st SELECT ENERGY INDEPENDENCE AND GLOBAL WARMING
Dates: Mar. 9, 2007-date
Departure: Still serving in the 111th Congress

Cong.	Ranking	Terms in: House	Comm.	Date of Assignment
110th	Maj-6th	3	1	Mar. 9, 2007
111th	Maj-5th	4	2	Feb. 3, 2009

2nd SELECT COMMITTEE TO INVESTIGATE THE VOTING IRREGULARITIES OF AUGUST 2, 2007
Dates: Sep. 5, 2007-Sep. 25, 2008
Termination: House Report 885 (110-2) filed

Cong.	Ranking	Terms in: House	Comm.	Date of Assignment
110th	Maj-3rd	3	1	Sep. 5, 2007

Marshall C. (Mark) Sanford Jr.

(R-S.C.)

Dates: May 28, 1960
House: Jan. 3, 1995-Jan. 3, 2001
Left the House: Retired in 2000; later elected Governor in 2002

HOUSE STANDING COMMITTEES:

1st GOVERNMENT REFORM AND OVERSIGHT, 104-105
GOVERNMENT REFORM, 106
Dates: Jan. 4, 1995-Jan. 3, 2001
Departure: Left the House; retired

Cong.	Ranking	Terms in: House	Comm.	Date of Assignment
104th	Maj-26th	1	1	Jan. 4, 1995
105th	Maj-18th	2	2	Jan. 7, 1997
106th	Maj-15th	3	3	Jan. 6, 1999

2nd INTERNATIONAL RELATIONS
Dates: Jan. 4, 1995-Jan. 3, 2001
Departure: Left the House; retired

Cong.	Ranking	Terms in: House	Comm.	Date of Assignment
104th	Maj-21st	1	1	Jan. 4, 1995
105th	Maj-17th	2	2	Jan. 7, 1997
106th	Maj-16th	3	3	Jan. 6, 1999

3rd SCIENCE
Dates: Feb. 2, 1999-Jan. 3, 2001
Departure: Left the House; retired

Cong.	Ranking	Terms in: House	Comm.	Date of Assignment
106th	Maj-24th	3	1	Feb. 2, 1999

JOINT COMMITTEES:

1st JOINT ECONOMIC
House Dates: Jan. 19, 1995-Jan. 3, 2001
Departure: Left the House; retired

Cong.	Ranking	Terms in: House	Comm.	Date of Assignment
104th	Maj-6th	1	1	Jan. 19, 1995
105th	Maj-3rd	2	2	Feb. 27, 1997
106th	Maj-2nd	3	3	Mar. 18, 1999

George E. Sangmeister (D-Ill.)

Dates: Feb. 16, 1931-Oct. 7, 2007
House: Jan. 3, 1989-Jan. 3, 1995
Left the House: Retired in 1994

HOUSE STANDING COMMITTEES:

1st JUDICIARY
Dates: Jan. 19, 1989-Jan. 3, 1995
Departure: Left the House; retired

Cong.	Ranking	Terms in: House	Comm.	Date of Assignment
103rd	Maj-14th	3	3	Jan. 5, 1993

2nd VETERANS AFFAIRS
Dates: Jan. 19, 1989-Jan. 3, 1995
Departure: Left the House; retired

Cong.	Ranking	Terms in: House	Comm.	Date of Assignment
103rd	Maj-9th	3	3	Jan. 5, 1993

3rd PUBLIC WORKS AND TRANSPORTATION
Dates: Nov. 8, 1989-Jan. 3, 1995
Departure: Left the House; retired

Cong.	Ranking	Terms in: House	Comm.	Date of Assignment
103rd	Maj-18th	3	3	Jan. 5, 1993

Richard J. (Rick) Santorum
(R-Penn.)

Dates: May 10, 1958
House: Jan. 3, 1991-Jan. 3, 1995
Left the House: Elected to U.S. Senate in 1994
Senate: Jan. 3, 1995-Jan. 3, 2007
Left the Senate: Defeated for re-election in 2006

HOUSE STANDING COMMITTEES:

1st BUDGET
Dates: Jan. 24, 1991-Jan. 3, 1993
Departure: Moved to Ways and Means

2nd VETERANS AFFAIRS
Dates: Jan. 24, 1991-Jan. 3, 1993
Departure: Moved to Ways and Means

3rd WAYS AND MEANS
Dates: Jan. 5, 1993-Jan. 3, 1995
Departure: Left the House for the Senate

Cong.	Ranking	Terms in: House	Comm.	Date of Assignment
103rd	Min-14th	2	1	Jan. 5, 1993

HOUSE SELECT AND SPECIAL COMMITTEES:

1st SELECT CHILDREN, YOUTH AND FAMILIES (Temporary)
Dates: Feb. 21, 1991-Jan. 3, 1993
Termination: Committee not renewed in 1993

SENATE STANDING COMMITTEES:

1st AGRICULTURE, NUTRITION AND FORESTRY
1st Dates: Jan. 4, 1995-Jan. 25, 2001
1st Departure: Moved to Joint Printing
2nd Dates: Jan. 6, 2005-Jan. 3, 2007
2nd Departure: Left the Senate; lost re-election

Cong.	Ranking	Years in: Senate	Comm.	Date of Assignment
104th	Maj-8th	1 *1	1	Jan. 4, 1995
105th	Maj-6th	3 *1	3	Jan. 9, 1997
106th	Maj-10th	5 *1	5	Jan. 7, 1999
109th	Maj-8th	11 *2	1	Jan. 6, 2005

2nd ARMED SERVICES
Dates: Jan. 4, 1995-Jan. 3, 2003
Departure: Moved to Finance

Cong.	Ranking	Years in: Senate	Comm.	Date of Assignment
104th	Maj-11th	1	1	Jan. 4, 1995
105th	Maj-8th	3	3	Jan. 9, 1997
106th	Maj-6th	5	5	Jan. 7, 1999
107th	Maj-6th	7	7	Jan. 25, 2001
+107th	Min-6th	7	7	June 6, 2001

3rd RULES AND ADMINISTRATION
Dates: Jan. 6, 1995-Jan. 3, 2007
Departure: Left the Senate; lost re-election

Cong.	Ranking	Years in: Senate	Comm.	Date of Assignment
104th	Maj-8th	1	1	Jan. 6, 1995
105th	Maj-6th	3	3	Jan. 9, 1997
106th	Maj-6th	5	5	Jan. 7, 1999
107th	Maj-6th	7	7	Jan. 25, 2001
+107th	Min-6th	7	7	June 6, 2001
108th	Maj-5th	9	9	Jan. 15, 2003
109th	Maj-5th	11	11	Jan. 6, 2005

4th BANKING, HOUSING AND URBAN AFFAIRS
Dates: Jan. 7, 1999-Jan. 3, 2007
Departure: Left the Senate; lost re-election

Cong.	Ranking	Years in: Senate	Comm.	Date of Assignment
106th	Maj-9th	5	1	Jan. 7, 1999
107th	Maj-7th	7	3	Jan. 25, 2001
+107th	Min-7th	7	3	June 6, 2001
108th	Maj-6th	9	5	Jan. 15, 2003
109th	Maj-6th	11	6	Jan. 6, 2005

5th FINANCE
Dates: Jan. 15, 2003-Jan. 3, 2007
Departure: Left the Senate; lost re-election

Cong.	Ranking	Years in: Senate	Comm.	Date of Assignment
108th	Maj-8th	9	1	Jan. 15, 2003
109th	Maj-7th	11	2	Jan. 6, 2005

SENATE SELECT AND SPECIAL COMMITTEES:

1st SPECIAL AGING (Permanent)
Dates: Jan. 11, 1995-Jan. 3, 2007
Departure: Left the Senate; lost re-election

Cong.	Ranking	Years in: Senate	Comm.	Date of Assignment
104th	Maj-9th	1	1	Jan. 11, 1995
105th	Maj-6th	3	2	Jan. 9, 1997
106th	Maj-6th	5	4	Jan. 7, 1999
107th	Maj-5th	7	7	Jan. 25, 2001
+107th	Min-4th	7	7	July 24, 2001
108th	Maj-11th	9	9	Jan. 15, 2003
109th	Maj-8th	11	10	Jan. 6, 2005

JOINT COMMITTEES:

1st JOINT ECONOMIC
Senate Dates: Jan. 9, 1995-Jan. 9, 1999
Departure: Left committee; no new assignment

Cong.	Ranking	Years in: Senate	Comm.	Date of Assignment
104th	Maj-5th	1	1	Jan. 9, 1995

2nd JOINT PRINTING
Senate Dates: Sep. 19, 2001-Jan. 15, 2003
Departure: Moved to Finance

Cong.	Ranking	Years in: Senate	Comm.	Date of Assignment
+107th	Min-2nd	7	1	Sep. 19, 2001

John Sarbanes (D-Md.)

Dates: May 22, 1962
House: Jan. 3, 2007-date
Serving in the 111th Congress

HOUSE STANDING COMMITTEES:

1st EDUCATION AND LABOR
Dates: Jan. 10, 2007-Jan. 3, 2009
Departure: Moved to Energy and Commerce

Cong.	Ranking	Terms in: House	Comm.	Date of Assignment
110th	Maj-18th	1	1	Jan. 10, 2007

2nd OVERSIGHT AND GOVERNMENT REFORM
Dates: Jan. 12, 2007-Jan. 3, 2009
Departure: Moved to Energy and Commerce

Cong.	Ranking	Terms in: House	Comm.	Date of Assignment
110th	Maj-22nd	1	1	Jan. 12, 2007

3rd NATURAL RESOURCES
Dates: Jan. 18, 2007-date
Departure: Still serving in the 111th Congress

Cong.	Ranking	Terms in: House	Comm.	Date of Assignment
110th	Maj-14th	1	1	Jan. 18, 2007
111th	Maj-25th	2	2	Jan. 7, 2009

4th ENERGY AND COMMERCE
Dates: Jan. 7, 2009-date
Departure: Still serving in the 111th Congress

Cong.	Ranking	Terms in: House	Comm.	Date of Assignment
111th	Maj-30th	2	1	Jan. 7, 2009

Paul S. Sarbanes (D-Md.)

Dates: Feb. 3, 1933
House: Jan. 3, 1971-Jan. 3, 1977
Left the House: Elected to U.S. Senate in 1976
Senate: Jan. 3, 1977-Jan. 3, 2007
Left the Senate: Retired in 2006

HOUSE STANDING COMMITTEES:

1st JUDICIARY
Dates: Feb. 4, 1971-Jan. 3, 1977
Departure: Left the House for the Senate

2nd MERCHANT MARINE AND FISHERIES
Dates: Jan. 24, 1973-Jan. 3, 1977
Departure: Left the House for the Senate

HOUSE SELECT AND SPECIAL COMMITTEES:

1st SELECT COMMITTEES I (Bolling)
Dates: Jan. 31, 1973-Dec. 20, 1974
Termination: House Resolution 132 (93-1)

SENATE STANDING COMMITTEES:

1st APPROPRIATIONS
Dates: Jan. 10, 1977-Feb. 11, 1977
Departure: Moved to Foreign Relations and Banking, Housing and Urban Affairs

2nd INTERIOR AND INSULAR AFFAIRS
Dates: Jan. 10, 1977-Feb. 11, 1977
Departure: Moved to Foreign Relations and Banking, Housing and Urban Affairs

3rd FOREIGN RELATIONS
Dates: Feb. 11, 1977-Jan. 3, 2007
Departure: Left the Senate; retired

Cong.	Ranking	Years in: Senate	Comm.	Date of Assignment
103rd	Maj-3rd	17	16	Jan. 7, 1993
104th	Min-3rd	19	18	Jan. 4, 1995
105th	Min-2nd	21	20	Jan. 9, 1997
106th	Min-2nd	23	22	Jan. 7, 1999
107th	Min-2nd	25	24	Jan. 25, 2001
+107th	Maj-2nd	25	25	June 6, 2001
108th	Min-2nd	27	26	Jan. 15, 2003
109th	Min-2nd	29	28	Jan. 6, 2005

4th BANKING, HOUSING AND URBAN AFFAIRS
Dates: Feb. 11, 1977-Jan. 3, 2007
Ch2: Replaced W. Phillip Gramm (R-Tex.) on June 6, 2001 following Senate party control shift
Departure: Left the Senate; retired

Cong.	Ranking	Years in: Senate	Comm.	Date of Assignment
103rd	Maj-2nd	17	16	Jan. 7, 1993

104th	Min-RM	19	18	Jan. 4, 1995
105th	Min-RM	21	20	Jan. 9, 1997
106th	Min-RM	23	22	Jan. 7, 1999
=107th	Maj-ChT	25	24	Jan. 3, 2001
107th	Min-RM1	25	24	Jan. 25, 2001
+107th	Maj-Ch2	25	25	June 6, 2001
108th	Min-RM	27	26	Jan. 15, 2003
109th	Min-RM	29	28	Jan. 6, 2005

5th BUDGET
Dates: Jan. 21, 1993-Jan. 3, 2007
Departure: Left the Senate; retired

Cong.	Ranking	Years in: Senate	Comm.	Date of Assignment
103rd	Maj-10th	17	1	Jan. 21, 1993
104th	Min-8th	19	2	Jan. 6, 1995
105th	Min-4th	21	4	Jan. 7, 1997
106th	Min-4th	23	6	Jan. 3, 1999
107th	Min-3rd	25	9	Jan. 25, 2001
+107th	Maj-3rd	25	9	June 6, 2001
108th	Min-3rd	27	10	Jan. 15, 2003
109th	Min-2nd	29	12	Jan. 6, 2005

SENATE SELECT AND SPECIAL COMMITTEES:

1st JUDGE HARRY E. CLAIBORNE IMPEACHMENT
Dates: Aug. 14, 1986-Oct. 1, 1986
Termination: Senate Report 99-511 filed

2nd SECRET MILITARY ASSISTANCE TO IRAN AND
THE NICARAGUAN OPPOSITION (Iran-Contra Affair)
Dates: Jan. 12, 1987-Nov. 17, 1987
Termination: Senate Report 100-216 filed

3rd SPECIAL COMMITTEE TO INVESTIGATE WHITEWATER
DEVELOPMENT CORPORATION AND RELATED MATTERS
Dates: July 20, 1995 -June 17, 1996
Termination: Senate Report 104-280 filed

Cong.	Ranking	Years in: Senate	Comm.	Date of Assignment
104th	Min-RM	19	1	July 20, 1995

JOINT COMMITTEES:

1st JOINT ECONOMIC
Senate Dates: Mar. 7, 1979-Jan. 3, 2007
Chair: 100th, 1987-89; 102nd, 1991-93
Vice Chair: 101st, 1989-91
Departure: Left the Senate; retired

Cong.	Ranking	Years in: Senate	Comm.	Date of Assignment
103rd	Maj-VCh	17	14	Jan. 21, 1993
104th	Min-2nd	19	16	Jan. 9, 1995
105th	Min-2nd	21	18	Jan. 9, 1997
106th	Min-3rd	23	20	Jan. 7, 1999
107th	Min-3rd	25	22	Jan. 25, 2001
+107th	Maj-3rd	25	23	June 6, 2001
108th	Min-3rd	27	24	Jan. 15, 2003
109th	Min-3rd	29	26	Jan. 6, 2005

2nd JOINT ORGANIZATION OF CONGRESS (Ad Hoc)
Senate Dates: Oct. 8, 1992-Dec. 9, 1993
Termination: Senate Report 103-215 filed

Cong.	Ranking	Years in: Senate	Comm.	Date of Assignment
103rd	Maj-5th	17	1	Continued

William Sarpalius (D-Tex.)

Dates: Jan. 10, 1948
House: Jan. 3, 1989-Jan. 3, 1995
Left the House: Defeated for re-election in 1994

HOUSE STANDING COMMITTEES:

1st AGRICULTURE
Dates: Jan. 19, 1989-Jan. 3, 1995
Departure: Left the House; lost re-election

Cong.	Ranking	Terms in: House	Comm.	Date of Assignment
103rd	Maj-12th	3	3	Jan. 5, 1993

2nd SMALL BUSINESS
Dates: Jan. 19, 1989-Jan. 3, 1995
Departure: Left the House; lost re-election

Cong.	Ranking	Terms in: House	Comm.	Date of Assignment
103rd	Maj-11th	3	3	Jan. 5, 1993

HOUSE SELECT AND SPECIAL COMMITTEES:

1st SELECT CHILDREN, YOUTH AND FAMILIES (Temporary)
Dates: Mar. 8, 1989-Jan. 3, 1993
Termination: Committee not renewed in 1993

James R. Sasser (D-Tenn.)

Dates: Sept. 30, 1931
Senate: Jan. 3, 1977-Jan. 3, 1995
Left the Senate: Defeated for re-election in 1994

SENATE STANDING COMMITTEES:

1st GOVERNMENT OPERATIONS reorganized Feb. 11, 1977
GOVERNMENTAL AFFAIRS
1st Dates: Jan. 10, 1977-Feb. 21, 1995
1st Departure: Left committee; no new assignment.
2nd Dates: Jan. 6, 1987-Jan. 3, 1995
2nd Departure: Left the Senate; lost re-election

Cong.	Ranking	Years in: Senate	Comm.	Date of Assignment
103rd	Maj-4th	17	*2 7	Jan. 7, 1993

2nd JUDICIARY
Dates: Jan. 10, 1977-Feb. 11, 1977
Departure: Moved to Budget and Appropriations

3rd BUDGET
Dates: Feb. 11, 1977-Jan. 3, 1995
Departure: Left the Senate; lost re-election

Cong.	Ranking	Years in: Senate	Comm.	Date of Assignment
103rd	Maj-Chr	17	16	Jan. 21, 1993

4th APPROPRIATIONS
Dates: Feb. 11, 1977-Jan. 3, 1995
Departure: Left the Senate; lost re-election

Cong.	Ranking	Years in: Senate	Comm.	Date of Assignment
103rd	Maj-6th	17	16	Jan. 7, 1993

5th SMALL BUSINESS
Dates: Mar. 25, 1981-Feb. 2, 1989
Departure: Left committee; became Chair of Budget

6th BANKING, HOUSING AND URBAN AFFAIRS
Dates: Apr. 20, 1982-Jan. 3, 1995
Departure: Left the Senate; lost re-election

Cong.	Ranking	Years in: Senate	Comm.	Date of Assignment
103rd	Maj-4th	17	11	Jan. 7, 1993

SENATE SELECT AND SPECIAL COMMITTEES:

1st SELECT SMALL BUSINESS
Dates: Jan. 23, 1979-Mar. 25, 1981
Departure: Continued on reorganized standing committee

JOINT COMMITTEES:

1st JOINT DEFICIT REDUCTION (Temporary)
Senate Dates: Jan. 6, 1987-Sep. 29, 1987
Termination: Public Law 100-119 adjusted Gramm-Rudman-Hollings Act

2nd JOINT ORGANIZATION OF CONGRESS (Ad Hoc)
Senate Dates: Oct. 8, 1992-Dec. 9, 1993
Termination: Senate Report 103-215 filed

Cong.	Ranking	Years in: Senate	Comm.	Date of Assignment
103rd	Maj-2nd	17	1	Continued

Thomas C. Sawyer (D-Ohio)

Dates: Aug. 15, 1945
House: Jan. 3, 1987-Jan. 3, 2003
Left the House: Defeated for re-nomination in 2002

HOUSE STANDING COMMITTEES:

1st EDUCATION AND LABOR, 100-103
ECONOMIC AND EDUCATIONAL OPPORTUNITIES, 104
Dates: Jan. 22, 1987-Jan. 3, 1997
Departure: Moved to Commerce

Cong.	Ranking	Terms in: House	Comm.	Date of Assignment
103rd	Maj-9th	4	4	Jan. 5, 1993
104th	Min-7th	5	5	Jan. 4, 1995

2nd GOVERNMENT OPERATIONS
Dates: Jan. 22, 1987-Jan. 3, 1989
Departure: Moved to Post Office and Civil Service

3rd POST OFFICE AND CIVIL SERVICE
Dates: Jan. 19, 1989-Jan. 3, 1995
Departure: Committee abolished; no new assignment

Cong.	Ranking	Terms in: House	Comm.	Date of Assignment
103rd	Maj-5th	4	3	Jan. 21, 1993

4th FOREIGN AFFAIRS
Dates: Jan. 24, 1991-Jan. 3, 1995
Temporary assignment of Jan. 24, 1991 was made permanent in the 103rd Congress.
Departure: Left committee; no new assignment

Cong.	Ranking	Terms in: House	Comm.	Date of Assignment
103rd	Maj-26th	4	2	Jan. 21, 1993

5th STANDARDS OF OFFICIAL CONDUCT
Dates: Feb. 4, 1993-Jan. 3, 1997
Departure: Moved to Commerce

Cong.	Ranking	Terms in: House	Comm.	Date of Assignment
103rd	Maj-7th	4	1	Feb. 4, 1993
104th	Min-5th	5	2	Jan. 20, 1995

6th TRANSPORTATION AND INFRASTRUCTURE
Dates: Feb. 28, 1996-Jan. 3, 1997
Departure: Moved to Commerce

Cong.	Ranking	Terms in: House	Comm.	Date of Assignment
104th	MnR-4th	5	1	Feb. 28, 1996

7th COMMERCE, 105-106
ENERGY AND COMMERCE, 107
Dates: Jan. 7, 1997-Jan. 3, 2003
Departure: Left the House; lost re-renomination

Cong.	Ranking	Terms in: House	Comm.	Date of Assignment
105th	Min-23rd	6	1	Jan. 7, 1997
	(Reranked Maj-18th on Jan. 21, 1997)			
106th	Min-16th	7	2	Jan. 6, 1999
107th	Min-15th	8	3	Jan. 31, 2001

HOUSE SELECT AND SPECIAL COMMITTEES:

1st SELECT CHILDREN, YOUTH AND FAMILIES (Temporary)
Dates: Jan. 21, 1987-Jan. 3, 1989
Departure: Moved to Post Office and Civil Service

2nd SELECT ETHICS
Dates: Jan. 7, 1997-Jan. 21, 1997
Termination: House Report 105-1 filed, Jan. 17, 1997

Cong.	Ranking	Terms in: House	Comm.	Date of Assignment
105th	Min-4th	6	1	Jan. 7, 1997

H. James Saxton (R-N.J.)

Dates: Jan. 22, 1943
House: Nov. 6, 1984-Jan. 3, 2009
Left the House: Retired in 2008

H: Saxton was elected to the 98th Congress by special election, Nov. 6, 1984, to fill the vacancy caused by the death of U.S. Representative Edwin B. Forsyth (R-N.J.). Saxton was not seated nor assigned to committees because the 98th Congress was not in session.

HOUSE STANDING COMMITTEES:

1st GOVERNMENT OPERATIONS
Dates: Jan. 30,1985-Jan. 3, 1987
Departure: Moved to Banking, Finance and Urban Affairs

2nd MERCHANT MARINE AND FISHERIES
Dates: Jan. 30, 1985-Jan. 3, 1995
Departure: Committee abolished; moved to Resources

Cong.	Ranking	Terms in: House	Comm.	Date of Assignment
103rd	Min-4th	6	5	Jan. 5, 1993

3rd BANKING, FINANCE AND URBAN AFFAIRS
Dates: Jan. 21, 1987-Jan. 3, 1991
Departure: Moved to Armed Services

4th ARMED SERVICES, 102-103
NATIONAL SECURITY, 104-105
ARMED SERVICES, 106-110
Dates: Jan. 24, 1991-Jan. 3, 2009
Departure: Left the House; retired

Cong.	Ranking	Terms in: House	Comm.	Date of Assignment
103rd	Min-13th	6	2	Jan. 5, 1993
104th	Maj-10th	7	3	Jan. 4, 1995
105th	Maj-9th	8	4	Jan. 7, 1997
106th	Maj-9th	9	5	Jan. 6, 1999
107th	Maj-7th	10	6	Jan. 6, 2001
108th	Maj-4th	11	7	Jan. 28, 2003
109th	Maj-4th	12	8	Jan. 26, 2005
110th	Min-2nd	13	9	Jan. 10, 2007

5th DISTRICT OF COLUMBIA
Dates: Jan. 5, 1993-Jan. 3, 1995
Departure: Committee abolished; moved to Resources

Cong.	Ranking	Terms in: House	Comm.	Date of Assignment
103rd	Min-3rd	6	1	Jan. 5, 1993

6th POST OFFICE AND CIVIL SERVICE
Dates: Feb. 18, 1993-Sep. 13, 1993
Departure: Resigned committee; no new assignment

Cong.	Ranking	Terms in: House	Comm.	Date of Assignment
103rd	Min-9th	6	1	Feb. 18, 1993

7th RESOURCES, 104-109
NATURAL RESOURCES, 110
Dates: Jan. 4, 1995-Jan. 3, 2009
Departure: Left the House; retired

Cong.	Ranking	Terms in: House	Comm.	Date of Assignment
104th	Maj-3rd	7	1	Jan. 4, 1995
105th	Maj-4th	8	2	Jan. 7, 1997
106th	Maj-4th	9	3	Jan. 6, 1999
107th	Maj-4th	10	4	Jan. 6, 2001
108th	Maj-4th	11	5	Jan. 28, 2003
109th	Maj-3rd	12	6	Jan. 26, 2005
110th	Min-2nd	13	7	Jan. 10, 2007

HOUSE SELECT AND SPECIAL COMMITTEES:

1st SELECT AGING (Permanent)
Dates: Feb. 21, 1985-Jan. 3, 1993
Termination: Committee not renewed in 1993

JOINT COMMITTEES:

1st JOINT ECONOMIC
House Dates: Feb. 16, 1993-Jan. 3, 2009
Departure: Left the House; retired

Cong.	Ranking	Terms in: House	Comm.	Date of Assignment
103rd	Min-2nd	6	1	Feb. 16, 1993
104th	Maj-VCh	7	2	Jan. 19, 1995
105th	Maj-Chr	8	3	Jan. 20, 1997
106th	Maj-VCh	9	4	Feb. 3, 1999
107th	Maj-Chr	10	5	Mar. 22, 2001
108th	Maj-VCh	11	6	Jan. 8, 2003

| 109th | Maj-Chr | 12 | 7 | Jan. 20, 2005 |
| 110th | Min-1st | 13 | 8 | Jan. 22, 2007 |

Steve Scalise (R-La.)

Dates: Oct. 6, 1965
House: May 3, 2008-date
Serving in the 111th Congress

H: Scalise was elected to the 110th Congress by special election, May 3, 2008, to fill the vacancy caused by the resignation of U.S. Representative Bobby Jindal (R-La.) who had been elected Governor. Scalise was sworn May 6, 2008, and assigned to committees.

HOUSE STANDING COMMITTEES:

1st NATURAL RESOURCES
Dates: May 14, 2008-Jan. 3, 2009
Departure: Moved to Energy and Commerce and Transportation and Infrastructure

Cong.	Ranking	Terms in: House	Comm.	Date of Assignment
110th	MnR-5th	1	1	May 14, 2008

2nd VETERANS' AFFAIRS
Dates: May 14, 2008- Jan. 16, 2009
Departure: Resigned committee; moved to Energy and Commerce

Cong.	Ranking	Terms in: House	Comm.	Date of Assignment
110th	MnR-2nd	1	1	May 14, 2008
111th	Min-11th	2	2	Jan. 9, 2009

3rd TRANSPORTATION AND INFRASTRUCTURE
Dates: Jan. 9, 2009-Jan. 16, 2009
Departure: Resigned committee; moved to Energy and Commerce

Cong.	Ranking	Terms in: House	Comm.	Date of Assignment
111th	Min-27th	2	1	Jan. 9, 2009

4th ENERGY AND COMMERCE
Dates: Jan. 22, 2009-date
Departure: Still serving in the 111th Congress

Cong.	Ranking	Terms in: House	Comm.	Date of Assignment
111th	Min-23rd	2	1	Jan. 22, 2009

C. Joseph Scarborough (R-Fla.)

Dates: April 9, 1963
House: Jan. 3, 1995-Sept. 6, 2001
Left the House: Resigned and retired in 2001

HOUSE STANDING COMMITTEES:

1st GOVERNMENT REFORM AND OVERSIGHT, 104-105
GOVERNMENT REFORM, 106-107
Dates: Jan. 4, 1995-June 5, 2001
Departure: Resigned committee; no new assignment

Cong.	Ranking	Terms in: House	Comm.	Date of Assignment
104th	Maj-21st	1	1	Jan. 4, 1995

Cong.	Ranking	House	Comm.	Date of Assignment
105th	Maj-15th	2	2	Jan. 7, 1997
106th	Maj-13th	3	3	Jan. 6, 1999
107th	Maj-11th	4	4	Jan. 6, 2001

2nd NATIONAL SECURITY, 104-105
ARMED SERVICES, 106-107
Dates: Jan. 4, 1995-Sep. 6, 2001
Departure: Resigned the House; retired

Cong.	Ranking	Terms in: House	Comm.	Date of Assignment
104th	Maj-26th	1	1	Jan. 4, 1995
105th	Maj-23rd	2	2	Jan. 7, 1997
106th	Maj-22nd	3	3	Jan. 6, 1999
107th	Maj-17th	4	4	Jan. 6, 2001

3rd EDUCATION AND THE WORKFORCE
Dates: Jan. 21, 1997-May 6, 1998
Departure: Leave of absence; no new assignment

Cong.	Ranking	Terms in: House	Comm.	Date of Assignment
105th	Maj-25th	2	1	Jan. 21, 1997

4th JUDICIARY
Dates: Mar. 11, 1999-Sept. 6, 2001
Departure: Resigned the House; retired

Cong.	Ranking	Terms in: House	Comm.	Date of Assignment
106th	MjR-1st	3	1	Mar. 11, 1999
107th	Maj-15th	4	2	Jan. 6, 2001

Daniel L. Schaefer (R-Colo.)

Dates: Jan. 25, 1936-April 16, 2006
House: March 29, 1983-Jan. 3, 1999
Left the House: Retired in 1998

H: Schaefer was elected to the 98th Congress by special election, March 29, 1983, to fill the vacancy caused by the death of U.S. Representative-elect John L. Swigert (R-Colo.). Schaefer was seated April 7, 1983, and assigned to committees.

HOUSE STANDING COMMITTEES:

1st GOVERNMENT OPERATIONS
Dates: Apr. 21, 1983-Jan. 3, 1985
Departure: Moved to Energy and Commerce

2nd SMALL BUSINESS
Dates: Apr. 21, 1983-Jan. 3, 1985
Departure: Moved to Energy and Commerce

3rd ENERGY AND COMMERCE, 99-103
COMMERCE, 104-105
Dates: Jan. 30, 1985-Jan. 3, 1999
Departure: Left the House; retired

Cong.	Ranking	Terms in: House	Comm.	Date of Assignment
103rd	Min-6th	6	5	Jan. 5, 1993
104th	Maj-6th	7	6	Jan. 4, 1995
105th	Maj-5th	8	7	Jan. 7, 1997

4th VETERANS' AFFAIRS
Dates: Jan. 4, 1995-Jan. 3, 1999
Departure: Left the House; retired

Cong.	Ranking	Terms in: House	Comm.	Date of Assignment
104th	MjR-1st	7	1	Jan. 4, 1995
105th	Maj-10th	8	2	Jan. 21, 1997

Robert W. Schaffer (R-Colo.)

Dates: July 24, 1962
House: Jan. 3, 1997-Jan. 3, 2003
Left the House: Retired in 2002

HOUSE STANDING COMMITTEES:

1st AGRICULTURE
Dates: Jan. 7, 1997-Jan. 3, 2003
Departure: Left the House; retired

Cong.	Ranking	Terms in: House	Comm.	Date of Assignment
105th	Maj-24th	1	1	Jan. 7, 1997
106th	Maj-16th	2	2	Jan. 6, 1999
107th	Maj-10th	3	3	Jan. 6, 2001

2ND EDUCATION AND THE WORKFORCE
Dates: Jan. 7, 1997-Jan. 3, 2003
Departure: Left the House; retired

Cong.	Ranking	Terms in: House	Comm.	Date of Assignment
105th	Maj-20th	1	1	Jan. 7, 1997
106th	Maj-18th	2	2	Jan. 6, 1999
107th	Maj-13th	3	3	Jan. 6, 2001

3rd RESOURCES
Dates: Jan. 7, 1997-Jan. 3, 2003
Departure: Left the House; retired

Cong.	Ranking	Terms in: House	Comm.	Date of Assignment
105th	Maj-25th	1	1	Jan. 7, 1997
106th	Maj-21st	2	2	Jan. 6, 1999
107th	Maj-19th	3	3	Jan. 6, 2001

Janice D. Schakowsky (D-Ill.)

Dates: May 26, 1944
House: Jan. 3, 1999-date
Serving in the 111th Congress

HOUSE STANDING COMMITTEES:

1st BANKING AND FINANCIAL SERVICES, 106
FINANCIAL SERVICES, 107
Dates: Jan. 6, 1999-Jan. 3, 2003
Departure: Moved to Energy and Commerce

Cong.	Ranking	Terms in: House	Comm.	Date of Assignment
106th	Min-23rd	1	1	Jan. 6, 1999
107th	Min-20th	2	2	Jan. 31, 2001

2nd SMALL BUSINESS
Dates: Jan. 19, 1999-Mar. 17, 1999
Departure: Resigned committee; moved to Government Reform

Cong.	Ranking	Terms in: House	Comm.	Date of Assignment
106th	Min-17th	1	1	Jan. 19, 1999

3rd GOVERNMENT REFORM
Dates: Mar. 17, 1999-Jan. 3, 2003
Departure: Moved to Energy and Commerce

Cong.	Ranking	Terms in: House	Comm.	Date of Assignment
106th	MnR-1st	1	1	Mar. 17, 1999
107th	Min-18th	2	2	Jan. 31, 2001

4th ENERGY AND COMMERCE
Dates: Jan. 28, 2003-date
Departure: Still serving in the 111th Congress

Cong.	Ranking	Terms in: House	Comm.	Date of Assignment
108th	Min-25th	3	1	Jan. 28, 2003
109th	Min-21st	4	2	Jan. 26, 2005
110th	Maj-19th	5	3	Jan. 4, 2007
111th	Maj-16th	6	4	Jan. 7, 2009

HOUSE SELECT AND SPECIAL COMMITTEES:

1st PERMANENT SELECT INTELLIGENCE
Dates: Jan. 17, 2007-date
Departure: Still serving in the 111th Congress

Cong.	Ranking	Terms in: House	Comm.	Date of Assignment
110th	Maj-10th	5	1	Jan. 17, 2007
111th	Maj-8th	6	2	Feb. 4, 2009

Mark H. Schauer (D-Mich.)

Dates: Oct. 2, 1961
House: Jan. 3, 2009-date
Serving in the 111th Congress

HOUSE STANDING COMMITTEES:

1st TRANSPORTATION AND INFRASTRUCTURE
Dates: Jan. 7, 2009-date
Departure: Still serving in the 111th Congress

Cong.	Ranking	Terms in: House	Comm.	Date of Assignment
111th	Maj-39th	1	1	Jan. 7, 2009

2nd AGRICULTURE
Dates: Jan. 21, 2009-date
Departure: Still serving in the 111th Congress

Cong.	Ranking	Terms in: House	Comm.	Date of Assignment
111th	Maj-23rd	1	1	Jan. 21, 2009

Lynn Schenk (D-Cal.)

Dates: Jan. 5, 1945
House: Jan. 3, 1993-Jan. 3, 1995
Left the House: Defeated for re-election in 1994

HOUSE STANDING COMMITTEES:

1st ENERGY AND COMMERCE
Dates: Jan. 5, 1993-Jan. 3, 1995
Departure: Left the House; lost re-election

Cong.	Ranking	Terms in: House	Comm.	Date of Assignment
103rd	Maj-23rd	1	1	Jan. 5, 1993

2nd MERCHANT MARINE AND FISHERIES
Dates: Jan. 5, 1993-Jan. 3, 1995
Departure: Left the House; lost re-election

Cong.	Ranking	Terms in: House	Comm.	Date of Assignment
103rd	Maj-17th	1	1	Jan. 5, 1993

Adam B. Schiff (D-Cal.)

Dates: June 20, 1960
House: Jan. 3, 2001-date
Serving in the 111th Congress

HOUSE STANDING COMMITTEES:

1st INTERNATIONAL RELATIONS
Dates: Feb. 8, 2001-Jan. 3, 2007
Departure: Moved to Appropriations

Cong.	Ranking	Terms in: House	Comm.	Date of Assignment
107th	Min-23rd	1	1	Feb. 8, 2001
108th	Min-19th	2	2	Jan. 28, 2003
109th	Min-18th	3	3	Jan. 26, 2005

2nd JUDICIARY
Dates: Feb. 8, 2001-date
Departure: Still serving in the 111th Congress

Cong.	Ranking	Terms in: House	Comm.	Date of Assignment
107th	MnR-1st	1	1	Feb. 8, 2001
108th	Min-15th	2	2	Jan. 28, 2003
109th	Min-14th	3	3	Jan. 26, 2005
110th	Maj-20th	4	4	Jan. 18, 2007
111th	Maj-21st	5	5	Jan. 21, 2009

3rd APPROPRIATIONS
Dates: Jan. 4, 2007-date
Departure: Still serving in the 111th Congress

Cong.	Ranking	Terms in: House	Comm.	Date of Assignment
110th	Maj-29th	4	1	Jan. 4, 2007
111th	Maj-27th	5	2	Jan. 7, 2009

HOUSE SELECT AND SPECIAL COMMITTEES:

1st PERMANENT SELECT INTELLIGENCE
Dates: Jan. 22, 2008-date
Departure: Still serving in the 111th Congress

Cong.	Ranking	Terms in: House	Comm.	Assignment
110th	MjR-1st	4	1	Jan. 22, 2008
111th	Maj-11th	5	2	Feb. 4, 2009

Steven H. Schiff (R-N.M.)

Dates: March 18, 1947-March 25, 1998
House: Jan. 3, 1989-March 25, 1998
Left the House: Died in office

HOUSE STANDING COMMITTEES:

1st GOVERNMENT OPERATIONS, 101-103
GOVERNMENT REFORM AND OVERSIGHT, 104-105
Dates: Jan. 20,1989-Mar. 25, 1998
Departure: Died in office

Cong.	Ranking	Terms in: House	Comm.	Date of Assignment
103rd	Min-6th	3	3	Jan. 5, 1993
104th	Maj-6th	4	4	Jan. 4, 1995
105th	Maj-6th	5	5	Jan. 7, 1997

2nd SCIENCE, SPACE AND TECHNOLOGY, 101-103
SCIENCE, 104-105
Dates: Jan. 20, 1989-Mar. 25, 1998
Departure: Died in office

Cong.	Ranking	Terms in: House	Comm.	Date of Assignment
103rd	Min-9th	3	3	Jan. 5, 1993
104th	Maj-8th	4	4	Jan. 4, 1995
105th	Maj-7th	5	5	Jan. 21, 1997

3rd JUDICIARY
Dates: Jan. 24, 1991-Mar. 25, 1998
Departure: Died in office

Cong.	Ranking	Terms in: House	Comm.	Date of Assignment
103rd	Min-9th	3	2	Jan. 5, 1993
104th	Maj-8th	4	3	Jan. 4, 1995
105th	Maj-7th	5	4	Jan. 7, 1997

4th STANDARDS OF OFFICIAL CONDUCT
Dates: Jan. 5, 1993-Jan. 3, 1997
Departure: Left committee; no new assignment

Cong.	Ranking	Terms in: House	Comm.	Date of Assignment
103rd	Min-7th	3	1	Jan. 5, 1993
104th	Maj-5th	4	2	Jan. 20, 1995

HOUSE SELECT AND SPECIAL COMMITTEES

1st SELECT ETHICS
Dates: Jan. 7, 1997-Jan. 21, 1997
Termination: House Report 105-1 filed, Jan. 17, 1997

Cong.	Ranking	Terms in: House	Comm.	Date of Assignment
105th	Maj-3rd	5	1	Jan. 7, 1997

Jean Schmidt (R-Ohio)

Dates: Nov. 29, 1951
House: Aug. 2, 2005-date
Serving in the 111th Congress

H: Schmidt was elected to the 109th Congress by special election, Aug. 2, 2005, to fill the vacancy caused by the resignation of U.S. Representative Robert Portman (R-Ohio). She was seated Sept. 6, 2005 and assigned to committees.

HOUSE STANDING COMMITTEES:

1st AGRICULTURE
Dates: Sep. 15, 2005-date
Departure: Still serving in the 111th Congress

Cong.	Ranking	Terms in: House	Comm.	Date of Assignment
109th	MjR-1st	1	1	Sep. 15, 2005
110th	Min-18th	2	2	Jan. 10, 2007
111th	Min-12th	3	3	Jan. 9, 2009

2nd GOVERNMENT REFORM
Dates: Sep. 15, 2005-Jan. 3, 2007
Departure: Left committee; no new assignment

Cong.	Ranking	Terms in: House	Comm.	Date of Assignment
109th	MjR-1st	1	1	Sep. 15, 2005

3rd TRANSPORTATION AND INFASTRUCTURE
Dates: Sep. 15, 2005-date
Departure: Still serving in the 111th Congress

Cong.	Ranking	Terms in: House	Comm.	Date of Assignment
109th	MjR-1st	1	1	Sep. 15, 2005
110th	Min-30th	2	2	Jan. 10, 2007
111th	Min-22nd	3	3	Jan. 9, 2009

Aaron Schock (R-Ill.)

Dates: May 28, 1981-
House: Jan. 3, 2009-date
Serving in the 111th Congress

HOUSE STANDING COMMITTEES:

1st SMALL BUSINESS
Dates: Jan. 9, 2009-date
Departure: Still serving in the 111th Congress

Cong.	Ranking	Terms in: House	Comm.	Date of Assignment
111th	Min-10th	1	1	Jan. 9, 2009

2nd OVERSIGHT AND GOVERNMENT REFORM
Dates: Jan. 22, 2009-date
Departure: Still serving in the 111th Congress

Cong.	Ranking	Terms in: House	Comm.	Date of Assignment
111th	MnR-1st	1	1	Jan. 22, 2009

3rd TRANSPORTATION AND INFRASTRUCTURE
Dates: Jan. 22, 2009-date
Departure: Still serving in the 111th Congress

Cong.	Ranking	Terms in: House	Comm.	Date of Assignment
111th	Min-30th	1	1	Jan. 22, 2009

Kurt Schrader (D-Ore.)

Dates: Oct. 19, 1951
House: Jan. 3, 2009-date
Serving in the 111th Congrfoess

HOUSE STANDING COMMITTEES:

1st AGRICULTURE
Dates: Jan. 21, 2009-date
Departure: Still serving in the 111th Congress

		Terms in:		Date of
Cong.	Ranking	House	Comm.	Assignment
111th	Maj-16th	1	1	Jan. 21, 2009

2nd BUDGET
Dates: Jan. 21, 2009-date
Departure: Still serving in the 111th Congress

		Terms in:		Date of
Cong.	Ranking	House	Comm.	Assignment
111th	Maj-24th	1	1	Jan. 21, 2009

3rd SMALL BUSINESS
Dates: Jan. 21, 2009-date
Departure: Still serving in the 111th Congress

		Terms in:		Date of
Cong.	Ranking	House	Comm.	Assignment
111th	Maj-5th	1	1	Jan. 21, 2009

Edward Schrock (R-Va.)

Dates: April 6, 1941
House: Jan. 3, 2001-Jan. 3, 2005
Left the House: Retired in 2004

HOUSE STANDING COMMITTEES:

1st ARMED SERVICES
Dates: Jan. 6, 2001-Jan. 3, 2005
Departure: Left the House; retired

		Terms in:		Date of
Cong.	Ranking	House	Comm.	Assignment
107th	Maj-31st	1	1	Jan. 6, 2001
108th	Maj-19th	2	2	Jan. 28, 2003

2nd BUDGET
Dates: Jan. 6, 2001-Jan. 3, 2005
Departure: Left the House; retired

		Terms in:		Date of
Cong.	Ranking	House	Comm.	Assignment
107th	Maj-18th	1	1	Jan. 6, 2001
108th	Maj-9th	2	2	Jan. 28, 2003

3rd SMALL BUSINESS
Dates: Jan. 6, 2001-Jan. 3, 2005
Departure: Left the House; retired

		Terms in:		Date of
Cong.	Ranking	House	Comm.	Assignment
107th	Maj-16th	1	1	Jan. 6, 2001
108th	Maj-9th	2	2	Jan. 28, 2003

4th GOVERNMENT REFORM
Dates: Feb. 8, 2001-Jan. 3, 2005
Departure: Left the House; retired

		Terms in:		Date of
Cong.	Ranking	House	Comm.	Assignment
107th	MjR-1st	1	1	Feb. 8, 2001
108th	Maj-15th	2	2	Jan. 28, 2003

Patricia S. Schroeder (D-Colo.)

Dates: July 30, 1940
House: Jan. 3, 1973-Jan. 3, 1997
Left the House: Retired in 1996

HOUSE STANDING COMMITTEES:

1st ARMED SERVICES, 93-103
NATIONAL SECURITY, 104
Dates: Jan. 24, 1973-Jan. 3, 1997
Departure: Left the House; retired

		Terms in:		Date of
Cong.	Ranking	House	Comm.	Assignment
103rd	Maj-4th	11	11	Jan. 5, 1993
104th	Min-3rd	12	12	Jan. 4, 1995

2nd POST OFFICE AND CIVIL SERVICE
Dates: Jan. 24, 1973-Jan. 3, 1995
Departure: Committee abolished; no new assignment

		Terms in:		Date of
Cong.	Ranking	House	Comm.	Assignment
103rd	Maj-2nd	11	11	Jan. 21, 1993

3rd JUDICIARY
Dates: Jan. 28, 1981-Jan. 3, 1997
Departure: Left the House; retired

		Terms in:		Date of
Cong.	Ranking	House	Comm.	Assignment
103rd	Maj-7th	11	7	Jan. 5, 1993
104th	Min-2nd	12	8	Jan. 4, 1995

HOUSE SELECT AND SPECIAL COMMITTEES:

1st SELECT SERVICEMEN MISSING IN SOUTHEAST ASIA
Dates: Sep. 15, 1975-Jan. 3, 1977
Termination: House Report 1764 (94-2) filed, Dec. 13, 1976

2nd SELECT COMMITTEES II (Patterson)
Dates: Mar. 28, 1979-Apr. 1, 1980
Termination: House Report 866 (95-2) filed

3rd SELECT CHILDREN, YOUTH AND FAMILIES (Temporary)
Dates: Feb. 2, 1983-Jan. 3, 1993
Termination: Committee not renewed in 1993

Charles E. Schumer (R-N.Y.)

Dates: Nov. 23, 1950
House: Jan. 3, 1981-Jan. 3, 1999
Left the House: Elected to the U.S. Senate in 1998
Senate: Jan. 3, 1999-date
Serving in the 111th Congress

HOUSE STANDING COMMITTEES:

1st BANKING, FINANCE AND URBAN AFFAIRS, 97-103
BANKING AND FINANCIAL SERVICES, 104-105
Dates: Jan. 28, 1981-Jan. 3, 1999
Departure: Left the House for the Senate

		Terms in:		Date of
Cong.	Ranking	House	Comm.	Assignment
103rd	Maj-5th	7	7	Jan. 5, 1993
104th	Min-4th	8	8	Jan. 4, 1995
105th	Min-4th	9	9	Jan. 7, 1997

2nd POST OFFICE AND CIVIL SERVICE
1st Dates: Apr. 30, 1981-Jan. 3, 1983
1st Departure: Remained on committee as a temporary member

2nd Dates: Jan. 6, 1983-Nov. 18, 1983
2nd Departure: Left committee; no new assignment

3rd JUDICIARY
Dates: Jan. 6, 1983-Jan. 3, 1999
Departure: Left the House for the Senate

Cong.	Ranking	Terms in: House	Comm.	Date of Assignment
103rd	Maj-10th	7	6	Jan. 5, 1993
104th	Min-4th	8	7	Jan. 4, 1995
105th	Min-3rd	9	8	Jan. 7, 1997

4th BUDGET
Dates: Jan. 30, 1985-Jan. 3, 1991
Departure: Moved to Interior and Insular Affairs

5th INTERIOR AND INSULAR AFFAIRS
Dates: Jan. 24, 1991-Jan. 3, 1993
Departure: Moved to Foreign Affairs

6th FOREIGN AFFAIRS
Dates: Jan. 5, 1993-Jan. 3, 1995
Departure: Left committee; no new assignment

Cong.	Ranking	Terms in: House	Comm.	Date of Assignment
103rd	Maj-11th	7	1	Jan. 5, 1993

SENATE STANDING COMMITTEES:

1st BANKING, HOUSING AND URBAN AFFAIRS
Dates: Jan. 7, 1999-date
Departure: Still serving in the 111th Congress

Cong.	Ranking	Years in: Senate	Comm.	Date of Assignment
106th	Min-7th	1	1	Jan. 7, 1999
107th	Min-5th	3	3	Jan. 25, 2001
+107th	Maj-5th	3	3	June 6, 2001
108th	Min-5th	5	5	Jan. 15, 2003
109th	Min-5th	7	6	Jan. 6, 2005
110th	Maj-4th	9	9	Jan. 12, 2007
111th	Maj-4th	11	11	Jan. 21, 2009

2nd JUDICIARY
Dates: Jan. 7, 1999-date
Departure: Still serving in the 111th Congress

Cong.	Ranking	Years in: Senate	Comm.	Date of Assignment
106th	Min-8th	1	1	Jan. 7, 1999
107th	Min-7th	3	3	Jan. 25, 2001
+107th	Maj-7th	3	3	June 6, 2001
108th	Min-7th	5	5	Jan. 15, 2003
109th	Min-7th	7	6	Jan. 6, 2005
110th	Maj-7th	9	9	Jan. 12, 2007
111th	Maj-5th	11	11	Jan. 21, 2009

3rd RULES AND ADMINISTRATION
Dates: Jan. 7, 1999-date
Departure: Still serving in the 111th Congress

Cong.	Ranking	Years in: Senate	Comm.	Date of Assignment
106th	Min-7th	1	1	Jan. 7, 1999
107th	Min-6th	3	3	Jan. 25, 2001
+107th	Maj-6th	3	3	June 6, 2001
108th	Min-5th	5	5	Jan. 15, 2003
109th	Min-5th	7	6	Jan. 6, 2005
110th	Maj-5th	9	9	Jan. 12, 2007
111th	Maj-Chr	11	11	Jan. 21, 2009

4th ENERGY AND NATURAL RESOURCES
Dates: Jan. 25, 2001-Jan. 6, 2005
Departure: Moved to Finance

Cong.	Ranking	Years in: Senate	Comm.	Date of Assignment
107th	Min-10th	3	1	Jan. 25, 2001
+107th	Maj-10th	3	1	June 6, 2001
108th	Min-10th	5	2	Jan. 3, 2003

5th FINANCE
Dates: Jan. 6, 2005-date
Departure: Still serving in the 111th Congress

Cong.	Ranking	Years in: Senate	Comm.	Date of Assignment
109th	Min-9th	7	1	Jan. 6, 2005
110th	Maj-8th	9	3	Jan. 12, 2007
111th	Maj-8th	11	5	Jan. 21, 2009

JOINT COMMITTEES:

1st JOINT DEFICIT REDUCTION (Temporary)
House Dates: Feb. 23, 1987-Sep. 29, 1987
Termination: Public Law 100-119 adjusted Gramm-Rudman-Hollings Act

2nd JOINT LIBRARY
Senate Dates: Sep. 19, 2001-date
Departure: Still serving in the 111th Congress

Cong.	Ranking	Years in: Senate	Comm.	Date of Assignment
+107th	Maj-2nd	3	1	Sep. 19, 2001
108th	Min-2nd	5	2	Mar. 13, 2003
109th	Min-2nd	7	4	Mar. 4, 2005
110th	Maj-3rd	9	6	Mar. 26, 2007
111th	Maj-VCh	11	8	Apr. 3, 2009

Allyson Y. Schwartz (D-Penn.)

Dates: Oct. 3, 1948
House: Jan. 3, 2005-date
Serving in the 111th Congress

HOUSE STANDING COMMITTEES:

1st BUDGET
Dates: Feb. 9, 2005-date
Departure: Still serving in the 111th Congress

Cong.	Ranking	Terms in: House	Comm.	Date of Assignment
109th	Min-17th	1	1	Feb. 9, 2005
110th	Maj-7th	2	2	Jan. 10, 2007
111th	Maj-2nd	3	3	Jan. 21, 2009

2nd TRANSPORTATION AND INFRASTRUCTURE
Dates: Jan. 26, 2005-Jan. 3, 2009
Departure: Moved to Ways and Means

Cong.	Ranking	Terms in: House	Comm.	Date of Assignment
109th	Min-33rd	1	1	Jan. 26, 2005

3rd WAYS AND MEANS
Dates: Jan. 4, 2007-date
Departure: Still serving in the 111th Congress

Cong.	Ranking	Terms in: House	Comm.	Date of Assignment
110th	Maj-23rd	2	1	Jan. 4, 2007
111th	Maj-20th	3	2	Jan. 7, 2009

John J.H. (Joe) Schwarz (R-Mich.)

Dates: Nov. 15, 1937
House: Jan. 3, 2005-Jan. 3, 2007
Left the House: Defeated for re-nomination in 2006

HOUSE STANDING COMMITTEES:

1st AGRICULTURE
Dates: Jan. 26, 2005-Jan. 3, 2007
Departure: Left the House; lost re-nomination

Cong.	Ranking	Terms in: House	Comm.	Date of Assignment
109th	Maj-21st	1	1	Jan. 26, 2005

2nd ARMED SERVICES
Dates: Jan. 26, 2005-Jan. 3, 2007
Departure: Left the House; lost re-nomination

Cong.	Ranking	Terms in: House	Comm.	Date of Assignment
109th	Maj-31st	1	1	Jan. 26, 2005

3rd SCIENCE
Dates: Jan. 26, 2005-Jan. 3, 2007
Departure: Left the House; lost re-nomination

Cong.	Ranking	Terms in: House	Comm.	Date of Assignment
109th	Maj-22nd	1	1	Jan. 26, 2005

David Scott (D-Ga.)

Dates: June 27, 1946
House: Jan. 3, 2003-date
Serving in the 111th Congress

HOUSE STANDING COMMITTEES:

1st FINANCIAL SERVICES
Dates: Jan. 28, 2003-date
Departure: Still serving in the 111th Congress

Cong.	Ranking	Terms in: House	Comm.	Date of Assignment
108th	Min-33rd	1	1	Jan. 28, 2003
109th	Min-27th	2	2	Jan. 26, 2005
110th	Maj-20th	3	3	Jan. 12, 2007
111th	Maj-19th	4	4	Jan. 7, 2009

2nd AGRICULTURE
Dates: Feb. 5, 2003-date
Departure: Still serving in the 111th Congress

Cong.	Ranking	Terms in: House	Comm.	Date of Assignment
108th	Min-19th	1	1	Feb. 5, 2003
109th	Min-9th	2	2	Jan. 26, 2005
110th	Maj-8th	3	3	Jan. 12, 2007
111th	Maj-7th	4	4	Jan. 21, 2009

3rd FOREIGN AFFAIRS
Dates: Jan. 12, 2007-date
Departure: Still serving in the 111th Congress

Cong.	Ranking	Terms in: House	Comm.	Date of Assignment
110th	Maj-23rd	3	1	Jan. 12, 2007
111th	Maj-24th	4	2	Jan. 21, 2009

Robert C. Scott (D-Va.)

Dates: April 30, 1947
House: Jan. 3, 1993-date
Serving in the 111th Congress

HOUSE STANDING COMMITTEES:

1st EDUCATION AND LABOR, 103
ECONOMIC AND EDUCATIONAL OPPORTUNITIES, 104
EDUCATION AND THE WORKFORCE, 105-107, 109
EDUCATION AND LABOR, 110-111
1st Dates: Jan. 5, 1993-Jan. 3, 2003
1st Departure: Moved to Budget
2nd Dates: Jan. 26, 2005-date
2nd Departure: Still serving in the 111th Congress

Cong.	Ranking	Terms in: House	Comm.	Date of Assignment
103rd	Maj-18th	1 *1	1	Jan. 5, 1993
104th	Min-15th	2 *1	2	Jan. 4, 1995
105th	Min-10th	3 *1	3	Jan. 7, 1997
106th	Min-10th	4 *1	4	Jan. 6, 1999
107th	Min-8th	5 *1	5	Jan. 31, 2001
109th	Min-6th	7 *2	1	Jan. 26, 2005
110th	Maj-5th	8 *2	2	Jan. 10, 2007
111th	Maj-5th	9 *2	3	Jan. 21, 2009

2nd JUDICIARY
Dates: Jan. 5, 1993-date
Departure: Still serving in the 111th Congress

Cong.	Ranking	Terms in: House	Comm.	Date of Assignment
103rd	Maj-18th	1	1	Jan. 5, 1993
104th	Min-10th	2	2	Jan. 4, 1995
105th	Min-7th	3	3	Jan. 7, 1997
106th	Min-6th	4	4	Jan. 6, 1999
107th	Min-6th	5	5	Jan. 31, 2001
108th	Min-5th	6	6	Jan. 28, 2003
109th	Min-5th	7	7	Jan. 26, 2005
110th	Maj-5th	8	8	Jan. 18, 2007
111th	Maj-5th	9	9	Jan. 21, 2009

3rd SCIENCE, SPACE AND TECHNOLOGY
Dates: Jan. 5, 1993-Jan. 3, 1995
Departure: Left committee; no new assignment

Cong.	Ranking	Terms in: House	Comm.	Date of Assignment
103rd	Maj-32nd	1	1	Jan. 5, 1993

4th BUDGET
1st Dates: Jan. 28, 2003-Jan. 3, 2005
1st Departure: Returned to Education and the Workforce
2nd Dates: Jan. 10, 2007-date
2nd Departure: Still serving in the 111th Congress

Cong.	Ranking	Terms in: House	Comm.	Date of Assignment
108th	Min-10th	6 *1	1	Jan. 28, 2003

Cong.	Ranking	House	Comm.	Date of Assignment
110th	Maj-17th	8 *2	1	Jan. 10, 2007
111th	Maj-18th	9 *2	2	Jan. 21, 2009

5th STANDARDS OF OFFICIAL CONDUCT

Dates: Sep. 11, 2008-Jan. 3, 2009
Departure: Left committee; no new assignment

Cong.	Ranking	Terms in: House	Comm.	Date of Assignment
110th	MjR-1st	8	1	Sep. 11, 2008

HOUSE SELECT AND SPECIAL COMMITTEES:

1st SELECT NATIONAL SECURITY CONCERNS WITH CHINA

Dates: June 22, 1998-Apr. 30, 1999
Termination: House Report 851 (105-2) filed, Jan. 3, 1999

Cong.	Ranking	Terms in: House	Comm.	Date of Assignment
105th	Min-4th	3	1	June 22, 1998
106th	Min-4th	4	2	Jan. 19, 1999

Andrea Seastrand (R-Cal.)

Dates: Aug. 5, 1941
House: Jan. 3, 1995-Jan. 3, 1997
Left the House: Defeated for re-election in 1996

HOUSE STANDING COMMITTEES:

1st SCIENCE

Dates: Jan. 4, 1995-Jan. 3, 1997
Departure: Left the House; lost re-election

Cong.	Ranking	Terms in: House	Comm.	Date of Assignment
104th	Maj-21st	1	1	Jan. 4, 1995

2nd TRANSPORTATION AND INFRASTRUCTURE

Dates: Jan. 4, 1995-Jan. 3, 1997
Departure: Left the House; lost re-election

Cong.	Ranking	Terms in: House	Comm.	Date of Assignment
104th	Maj-29th	1	1	Jan. 4, 1995

Shelley Sekula Gibbs (R-Texas)

Dates: June 22, 1953
House: Nov. 13, 2006-Jan. 3, 2007
Left the House: Defeated in 2006

H: Sekula Gibbs was elected to the 109th Congress, Nov. 7, 2006, to fill the vacancy caused by the resignation of U.S. Representative Tom DeLay (R-Texas). She was sworn Nov. 13, 2006, but was not assigned to committees. DeLay's name remained on the ballot and Sekula Gibbs was unable to obtain enough write-in votes to win.

F. James Sensenbrenner Jr.
(R-Wisc.)

Dates: June 14, 1943
House: Jan. 3, 1979-date
Serving in the 111th Congress

HOUSE STANDING COMMITTEES:

1st JUDICIARY

Dates: Jan. 24, 1979-date
Departure: Still serving in the 111th Congress

Cong.	Ranking	Terms in: House	Comm.	Date of Assignment
103rd	Min-4th	8	8	Jan. 5, 1993
104th	Maj-3rd	9	9	Jan. 4, 1995
105th	Maj-2nd	10	10	Jan. 7, 1997
106th	Maj-2nd	11	11	Jan. 6, 1999
107th	Maj-Chr	12	12	Jan. 6, 2001
108th	Maj-Chr	13	13	Jan. 8, 2003
109th	Maj-Chr	14	14	Jan. 6, 2005
110th	Min-2nd	15	15	Jan. 10, 2007
111th	Min-2nd	16	16	Jan. 9, 2009

2nd STANDARDS OF OFFICIAL CONDUCT

Dates: Jan. 24, 1979-Jan. 3, 1981
Departure: Moved to Science and Technology

3rd SCIENCE AND TECHNOLOGY, 97-99
SCIENCE, SPACE AND TECHNOLOGY, 100-103
SCIENCE, 104-106
SCIENCE AND TECHNOLOGY, 110-111

1st Dates: Jan. 28, 1981-Feb. 6, 2001
1st Departure: Resigned committee; had become Chair of Judiciary
2nd Dates: Jan. 10, 2007-date
2nd Departure: Still serving in the 111th Congress

Cong.	Ranking	Terms in: House	Comm.	Date of Assignment
103rd	Min-2nd	8 *1	7	Jan. 5, 1993
104th	Maj-2nd	9 *1	8	Jan. 4, 1995
105th	Maj-Chr	10 *1	9	Jan. 9, 1997
106th	Maj-Chr	11 *1	10	Jan. 6, 1999
107th	Maj-2nd	12 *1	11	Jan. 6, 2001
110th	Min-2nd	15 *2	1	Jan. 10, 2007
111th	Min-2nd	16 *2	2	Jan. 4, 2009

HOUSE SELECT AND SPECIAL COMMITTEES:

1st SELECT NARCOTICS ABUSE AND CONTROL (Temporary)

Dates: Jan. 28, 1987-Jan. 3, 1993
Termination: Committee not renewed in 1993

2nd SELECT HOMELAND SECURITY

Dates: Feb. 12, 2003-Jan. 3, 2005
Departure: Did not continue on reorganized standing committee

Cong.	Ranking	Terms in: House	Comm.	Date of Assignment
108th	Maj-5th	13	1	Feb. 12, 2003

3rd SELECT BIPARTISAN COMMITTEE TO INVESTIGATE THE PREPARATION FOR AND RESPONSE TO HURRICANE KATRINA

Dates: Sep. 21, 2005-Sep. 23, 2005
Departure: Resigned committee; no new assignment

Cong.	Ranking	Terms in: House	Comm.	Date of Assignment
109th	Maj-2nd	14	1	Sep. 21, 2005

4th SELECT ENERGY INDEPENDENCE AND GLOBAL WARMING

Dates: Mar. 9, 2007-date
Departure: Still serving in the 111th Congress

Cong.	Ranking	Terms in: House	Comm.	Date of Assignment
110th	Min-RM	15	1	Mar. 9, 2007
111th	Min-RM	16	2	Jan. 14, 2009

Jose E. Serrano (D-N.Y.)

Dates: Oct. 24, 1943
House: March 20, 1990-date
Serving in the 111th Congress

H: Serrano was elected to the 101st Congress by special election, March 20, 1990, to fill the vacancy caused by the resignation of U.S. Representative Robert Garcia (D-N.Y.). Serrano was sworn March 28, 1990 and assigned to committees.

HOUSE STANDING COMMITTEES:

1st EDUCATION AND LABOR
Dates: Apr. 4, 1990-Jan. 3, 1993
Departure: Moved to Appropriations in the 103rd Congress

2nd SMALL BUSINESS
Dates: Apr. 4, 1990-Jan. 3, 1993
Departure: Moved to Appropriations in the 103rd Congress

3rd APPROPRIATIONS
1st Dates: Jan. 5, 1993-Jan. 3, 1995
1st Departure: Moved to Judiciary
2nd Dates: Returned Mar. 14, 1996-date
2nd Departure: Still serving in the 111th Congress

Cong.	Ranking	Terms in: House	Comm.	Date of Assignment
103rd	Maj-31st	3 *1	1	Jan. 5, 1993
104th	MnA-25th	4 *2	1	Mar. 14, 1996
105th	Min-19th	5 *2	2	Jan. 7, 1997
106th	Min-12th	6 *2	3	Jan. 6, 1999
107th	Min-11th	7 *2	4	Jan. 31, 2001
108th	Min-10th	8 *2	5	Jan. 28, 2003
109th	Min-10th	9 *2	6	Jan. 26, 2005
110th	Maj-8th	10 *2	7	Jan. 4, 2007
111th	Maj-8th	11 *2	8	Jan. 7, 2009

4th JUDICIARY
Dates: Jan. 4, 1995-Mar. 14, 1996
Departure: Resigned committee; returned to Appropriations

Cong.	Ranking	Terms in: House	Comm.	Date of Assignment
104th	Min-13th	4	1	Jan. 4, 1995

Jefferson B. Sessions III (R-Ala.)

Dates: Dec. 24, 1946
Senate: Jan. 3, 1997-date
Serving in the 111th Congress

SENATE STANDING COMMITTEES:

1st ENVIRONMENT AND PUBLIC WORKS
Dates: Jan. 9, 1997-Jan. 7, 1999
Departure: Moved to Armed Services and Labor and Human Resources

Cong.	Ranking	Years in: Senate	Comm.	Date of Assignment
105th	Maj-10th	1	1	Jan. 9, 1997

2nd JUDICIARY
Dates: Jan. 9, 1997-date

RM2: Replaced Arlen Specter (D-Penn.) as Ranking Member on May 5, 2009
Departure: Still serving in the 111th Congress

Cong.	Ranking	Years in: Senate	Comm.	Date of Assignment
105th	Maj-10th	1	1	Jan. 9, 1997
106th	Maj-9th	3	2	Jan. 7, 1999
107th	Maj-7th	5	5	Jan. 25, 2001
+107th	Min-7th	5	5	June 6, 2001
108th	Maj-6th	7	7	Jan. 15, 2003
109th	Maj-6th	9	8	Jan. 6, 2005
110th	Min-5th	11	11	Jan. 12, 2007
111th	Min-5th	13	13	Jan. 21, 2009
=111th	Min-RM2	13	13	May 5, 2009

3rd ARMED SERVICES
Dates: Jan. 7, 1999-date
Departure: Still serving in the 111th Congress

Cong.	Ranking	Years in: Senate	Comm.	Date of Assignment
106th	Maj-11th	3	1	Jan. 7, 1999
107th	Maj-10th	5	3	Jan. 25, 2001
+107th	Min-10th	5	3	June 6, 2001
108th	Maj-6th	7	5	Jan. 15, 2003
109th	Maj-5th	9	6	Jan. 6, 2005
110th	Min-4th	11	9	Jan. 12, 2007
111th	Min-3rd	13	11	Jan. 21, 2009

4th LABOR AND HUMAN RESOURCES renamed Jan. 21, 1999 HEALTH, EDUCATION, LABOR AND PENSIONS
Dates: Jan. 7, 1999-Jan. 12, 2007
Departure: Moved to Energy and Natural Resources

Cong.	Ranking	Years in: Senate	Comm.	Date of Assignment
106th	Maj-10th	3	1	Jan. 7, 1999
107th	Maj-10th	5	3	Jan. 25, 2001
+107th	Min-9th	5	3	June 6, 2001
108th	Maj-8th	7	5	Jan. 15, 2003
109th	Maj-10th	9	6	Jan. 6, 2005

5th BUDGET
Dates: Jan. 15, 2003-date
Departure: Still serving in the 111th Congress

Cong.	Ranking	Years in: Senate	Comm.	Date of Assignment
108th	Maj-8th	7	1	Jan. 15, 2003
109th	Maj-6th	9	2	Jan. 6, 2005
110th	Min-6th	11	4	Jan. 12, 2007
111th	Min-4th	13	7	Jan. 21, 2009

6th ENERGY AND NATURAL RESOURCES
Dates: July 10, 2007-date
Departure: Still serving in the 111th Congress.

Cong.	Ranking	Years in: Senate	Comm.	Date of Assignment
110th	Min-8th	11	1	Jan. 12, 2007
111th	Min-9th	13	2	Jan. 21, 2009

SENATE SELECT AND SPECIAL COMMITTEES:

1st SELECT ETHICS (Permanent)
Dates: Jan. 9, 1997-Jan. 7, 1999
Departure: Moved to Armed Services and Labor and Human Resources

Cong.	Ranking	Years in: Senate	Comm.	Date of Assignment
105th	Maj-3rd	1	1	Jan. 9, 1997

JOINT COMMITTEES:

1st JOINT ECONOMIC
Senate Dates: Jan. 9, 1997-Jan. 12, 2007
Departure: Moved to Energy and Natural Resources

Cong.	Ranking	Years in: Senate	Comm.	Date of Assignment
105th	Maj-6th	1	1	Jan. 9, 1997
106th	Maj-6th	3	2	Jan. 7, 1999
107th	Maj-3rd	5	5	Jan. 25, 2001
+107th	Min-3rd	5	5	June 6, 2001
108th	Maj-3rd	7	7	Jan. 15, 2003
109th	Maj-5th	9	8	Jan. 6, 2005

Pete Sessions (R-Tex.)

Dates: March 22, 1955
House: Jan. 3, 1997-date
Serving in the 111th Congress

HOUSE STANDING COMMITTEES:

1st BANKING AND FINANCIAL SERVICES
Dates: Jan. 7, 1997-Jan. 3, 1999
Departure: Moved to Rules

Cong.	Ranking	Terms in: House	Comm.	Date of Assignment
105th	Maj-28th	1	1	Jan. 7, 1997

2nd GOVERNMENT REFORM AND OVERSIGHT
Dates: Jan. 7, 1997-Jan. 3, 1999
Departure: Moved to Rules

Cong.	Ranking	Terms in: House	Comm.	Date of Assignment
105th	Maj-21st	1	1	Jan. 7, 1997

3rd SCIENCE
Dates: Mar. 5, 1997-Jan. 3, 1999
Departure: Moved to Rules

Cong.	Ranking	Terms in: House	Comm.	Date of Assignment
105th	Maj-25th	1	1	Mar. 5, 1997

4th RULES
Dates: Jan. 6, 1999-date
Departure: Still serving in the 111th Congress

Cong.	Ranking	Terms in: House	Comm.	Date of Assignment
106th	Maj-8th	2	1	Jan. 6, 1999
107th	Maj-8th	3	2	Jan. 3, 2001
108th	Maj-8th	4	3	Jan. 7, 2003
109th	Maj-4th	5	4	Jan. 4, 2005
110th	Min-4th	6	5	Jan. 4, 2007
111th	Min-3rd	7	6	Jan. 9, 2009

5th BUDGET
Dates: Jan. 26, 2005-Jan. 3, 2007
Departure: Left committee; no new assignment

Cong.	Ranking	Terms in: House	Comm.	Date of Assignment
109th	Maj-16th	5	1	Jan. 26, 2005

HOUSE SELECT AND SPECIAL COMMITTEES:

1st SELECT HOMELAND SECURITY
Dates: Feb. 12, 2003-Jan. 3, 2005
Departure: Did not continue on reorganized standing committee

Cong.	Ranking	Terms in: House	Comm.	Date of Assignment
108th	Maj-26th	4	1	Feb. 12, 2003

Joe Sestak (D-Pa.)

Dates: Dec. 12, 1951
House: Jan. 3, 2007-date
Serving in the 111th Congress

HOUSE STANDING COMMITTEES:

1st ARMED SERVICES
Dates: Jan. 10, 2007-date
Departure: Still serving in the 111th Congress

Cong.	Ranking	Terms in: House	Comm.	Date of Assignment
110th	Maj-31st	1	1	Jan. 10, 2007
111th	Maj-28th	2	2	Jan. 7, 2009

2nd EDUCATION AND LABOR
Dates: Jan. 10, 2007-date
Departure: Still serving in the 111th Congress

Cong.	Ranking	Terms in: House	Comm.	Date of Assignment
110th	Maj-19th	1	1	Jan. 10, 2007
111th	Maj-16th	2	2	Jan. 21, 2009

3rd SMALL BUSINESS
Dates: Jan. 23, 2007-date
Departure: Still serving in the 111th Congress

Cong.	Ranking	Terms in: House	Comm.	Date of Assignment
110th	Maj-18th	1	1	Jan. 23, 2007
111th	Maj-14th	2	2	Jan. 21, 2009

John B. Shadegg (R-Ariz.)

Dates: Oct. 22, 1949-
House: Jan. 3, 1995-date
Serving in the 111th Congress

HOUSE STANDING COMMITTEES:

1st BUDGET
Dates: Jan. 4, 1995-Jan. 3, 1999
Departure: Moved to Commerce

Cong.	Ranking	Terms in: House	Comm.	Date of Assignment
104th	Maj-22nd	1	1	Jan. 4, 1995
105th	Maj-14th	2	2	Jan. 7, 1997

2nd GOVERNMENT REFORM AND OVERSIGHT
Dates: Jan. 4, 1995-Jan. 3, 1999
Departure: Moved to Commerce

Cong.	Ranking	Terms in: House	Comm.	Date of Assignment
104th	Maj-22nd	1	1	Jan. 4, 1995
105th	Maj-16th	2	2	Jan. 7, 1997

3rd RESOURCES
Dates: Jan. 4, 1995-Jan. 3, 1999
Departure: Moved to Commerce

Cong.	Ranking	Terms in: House	Comm.	Date of Assignment
104th	Maj-25th	1	1	Jan. 4, 1995
105th	Maj-18th	2	2	Jan. 7, 1997

4th COMMERCE, 106
ENERGY AND COMMERCE, 107-111
Dates: Jan. 6, 1999-date
Departure: Still serving in the 111th Congress

Cong.	Ranking	Terms in: House	Comm.	Date of Assignment
106th	Maj-24th	3	1	Jan. 6, 1999
107th	Maj-18th	4	2	Jan. 6, 2001
108th	Maj-16th	5	3	Jan. 28, 2003
109th	Maj-13th	6	4	Jan. 6, 2005
110th	Min-12th	7	5	Jan. 10, 2007
111th	Min-8th	8	6	Jan. 9, 2009

5th FINANCIAL SERVICES
Dates: Jan. 6, 2001-Jan. 3, 2005
Departure: Left committee; no new assignment

Cong.	Ranking	Terms in: House	Comm.	Date of Assignment
107th	Maj-28th	4	1	Jan. 6, 2001
108th	Maj-23rd	5	2	Jan. 28, 2003

HOUSE SELECT AND SPECIAL COMMITTEES:

1st SELECT HOMELAND SECURITY
Dates: Feb. 12, 2003-Jan. 3, 2005
Departure: Did not continue on reorganized standing committee

Cong.	Ranking	Terms in: House	Comm.	Date of Assignment
108th	Maj-21st	5	1	Feb. 12, 2003

2nd SELECT ENERGY INDEPENDENCE AND GLOBAL WARMING
Dates: Mar. 9, 2007-date
Departure: Still serving in the 111th Congress

Cong.	Ranking	Terms in: House	Comm.	Date of Assignment
110th	Min-2nd	7	1	Mar. 9, 2007
111th	Min-2nd	8	2	Feb. 3, 2009

Jeanne Shaheen (D-N.H.)

Dates: Jan. 28, 1947
Senate: Jan. 3, 2009-date
Serving in the 111th Congress

SENATE STANDING COMMITTEES:

1st ENERGY AND NATURAL RESOURCES
Dates: Jan. 21, 2009-date
Departure: Still serving in the 111th Congress

Cong.	Ranking	Years in: Senate	Comm.	Date of Assignment
111th	Maj-13th	1	1	Jan. 21, 2009

2nd FOREIGN RELATIONS
Dates: Jan. 21, 2009-date
Departure: Still serving in the 111th Congress

Cong.	Ranking	Years in: Senate	Comm.	Date of Assignment
111th	Maj-9th	1	1	Jan. 21, 2009

3rd SMALL BUSINESS AND ENTREPRENEURSHIP
Dates: Jan. 21, 2009-date
Departure: Still serving in the 111th Congress

Cong.	Ranking	Years in: Senate	Comm.	Date of Assignment
111th	Maj-11th	1	1	Jan. 21, 2009

Philip R. Sharp (D-Ind.)

Dates: July 15, 1942
House: Jan. 3, 1975-Jan. 3, 1995
Left the House: Retired in 1994

HOUSE STANDING COMMITTEES:

1st DISTRICT OF COLUMBIA
Dates: Jan. 20, 1975-Jan. 3, 1977
Departure: Moved to Interior and Insular Affairs

2nd INTERSTATE AND FOREIGN COMMERCE, 94-96
ENERGY AND COMMERCE, 97-103
Dates: Jan. 20, 1975-Jan. 3, 1995
Departure: Left the House; retired

Cong.	Ranking	Terms in: House	Comm.	Date of Assignment
103rd	Maj-3rd	10	10	Jan. 5, 1993

3rd INTERIOR AND INSULAR AFFAIRS, 95-102
NATURAL RESOURCES, 103
Dates: Jan. 19, 1977-Jan. 3, 1995
Departure: Left the House; retired

Cong.	Ranking	Terms in: House	Comm.	Date of Assignment
103rd	Maj-2nd	10	9	Jan. 5, 1993

HOUSE SELECT AND SPECIAL COMMITTEES:

1st SELECT ENERGY (Ad Hoc)
Dates: Apr. 21, 1977-Jan. 3, 1979
Termination: House Report 1820 (95-2) filed

E. Clay Shaw Jr. (R-Fla.)

Dates: April 19, 1939
House: Jan. 3, 1981-Jan. 3, 2007
Left the House: Defeated for re-election in 2006

HOUSE STANDING COMMITTEES:

1st MERCHANT MARINE AND FISHERIES
Dates: Jan. 28, 1981-Aug. 3, 1982
Departure: Resigned committee; had moved to Judiciary earlier

2nd PUBLIC WORKS AND TRANSPORTATION
Dates: Jan. 28, 1981-July 7, 1988
Departure: Moved to Ways and Means

3rd JUDICIARY
Dates: June 9, 1982-July 7, 1988
Departure: Resigned committee; moved to Ways and Means

4th WAYS AND MEANS
Dates: July 7, 1988-Jan. 3, 2007
Departure: Left the House; lost re-election

Cong.	Ranking	Terms in: House	Comm.	Date of Assignment
103rd	Min-5th	7	4	Jan. 5, 1993
104th	Maj-4th	8	5	Jan. 4, 1995
105th	Maj-4th	9	6	Jan. 7, 1997
106th	Maj-4th	10	7	Jan. 6, 1999
107th	Maj-3rd	11	8	Jan. 6, 2001
108th	Maj-3rd	12	9	Jan. 28, 2003
109th	Maj-2nd	13	10	Jan. 6, 2005

HOUSE SELECT AND SPECIAL COMMITTEES:

1st SELECT NARCOTICS ABUSE AND CONTROL (Temporary)
Dates: Feb. 25, 1981-July 7, 1988
Departure: Moved to Ways and Means

JOINT COMMITTEES:

1st JOINT TAXATION
House Dates: Feb. 7, 2001-Jan. 3, 2007
Departure: Left the House; lost re-election

Cong.	Ranking	Terms in: House	Comm.	Date of Assignment
107th	Maj-3rd	11	1	Feb. 7, 2001 Ltr
108th	Maj-3rd	12	2	Jan. 29, 2003 Ltr
109th	Maj-2nd	13	3	Feb. 7, 2005 Ltr

Christopher H. Shays (R-Conn.)

Dates: Oct. 18, 1945
House: Aug. 18, 1987-Jan. 3, 2009
Left the House: Defeated for re-election in 2008

H: Shays was elected to the 100th Congress by special election, Aug. 18, 1987, to fill the vacancy caused by the death of U.S. Representative Stewart B. McKinney (R-Conn.). Shays was seated Sept. 9, 1987, and assigned to committees.

HOUSE STANDING COMMITTEES:

1st GOVERNMENT OPERATIONS, 100-103
GOVERNMENT REFORM AND OVERSIGHT, 104-105
GOVERNMENT REFORM, 106-109
OVERSIGHT AND GOVERNMENT REFORM, 110
Dates: Nov. 4, 1987-Jan 3, 2009
Departure: Left the House; lost re-election

Cong.	Ranking	Terms in: House	Comm.	Date of Assignment
103rd	Min-5th	4	4	Jan. 5, 1993
104th	Maj-5th	5	5	Jan. 4, 1995
105th	Maj-5th	6	6	Jan. 7, 1997
106th	Maj-4th	7	7	Jan. 6, 1999
107th	Maj-4th	8	8	Jan. 6, 2001
108th	Maj-3rd	9	9	Jan. 28, 2003
109th	Maj-3rd	10	10	Jan. 26, 2005
110th	Min-3rd	11	11	Jan. 10, 2007

2nd SCIENCE, SPACE AND TECHNOLOGY, 100-101
SCIENCE, 107-108
1st Dates: Nov. 4, 1987-Jan. 3, 1991
1st Departure: Moved to Budget
2nd Dates: Feb. 8, 2001-Feb. 12, 2003
2nd Departure: Leave of absence; became Vice Chair of Budget

Cong.	Ranking	Terms in: House	Comm.	Date of Assignment
107th	MjR-1st	8 *2	1	Feb. 8, 2001
108th	Maj-3rd	9 *2	2	Jan. 28, 2003

3rd BUDGET
1st Dates: Jan. 24, 1991-Jan. 3, 2001
1st Departure: Moved to Financial Services; returned to Science
2nd Dates: Feb. 11, 2003-Jan. 3, 2005
2nd Departure: Left committee; no new assignment

Cong.	Ranking	Terms in: House	Comm.	Date of Assignment
103rd	Min-4th	4 *1	2	Jan. 5, 1993
104th	Maj-5th	5 *1	3	Jan. 4, 1995
105th	Maj-3rd	6 *1	4	Jan. 7, 1997
106th	Maj-3rd	7 *1	5	Jan. 6, 1999
108th	Maj-VCh	9 *2	1	Feb. 11, 2003

4th FINANCIAL SERVICES
Dates: Jan. 6, 2001-Jan. 3, 2009
Departure: Left the House; lost re-election

Cong.	Ranking	Terms in: House	Comm.	Date of Assignment
107th	Maj-27th	8	1	Jan. 6, 2001
108th	Maj-22nd	9	2	Jan. 28, 2003
109th	Maj-19th	10	3	Jan. 26, 2005
110th	Min-14th	11	4	Jan. 10, 2007

5th HOMELAND SECURITY
Dates: Feb. 9, 2005-Jan. 3, 2009
Departure: Left the House; lost re-election

Cong.	Ranking	Terms in: House	Comm.	Date of Assignment
109th	Maj-5th	10	2	Feb. 9, 2005
110th	Min-3rd	11	3	Jan. 10, 2007

HOUSE SELECT AND SPECIAL COMMITTEES:

1st SELECT NARCOTICS ABUSE AND CONTROL (Temporary)
Dates: Apr. 10, 1989-Jan. 3, 1993
Termination: Committee not renewed in 1993

2nd SELECT HOMELAND SECURITY
Dates: Feb. 12, 2003-Jan. 3, 2005
Departure: Continued on reorganized standing committee

Cong.	Ranking	Terms in: House	Comm.	Date of Assignment
108th	Maj-13th	9	1	Feb. 12, 2003

3rd SELECT BIPARTISAN COMMITTEE TO INVESTIGATE THE PREPARATION FOR AND RESPONSE TO HURRICANE KATRINA
Dates: Sep. 21, 2005-Feb. 15, 2006
Departure: House Report 377 (109-2) filed

Cong.	Ranking	Terms in: House	Comm.	Date of Assignment
109th	Maj-4th	10	1	Sep. 21, 2005

Carol Shea-Porter (D-N.H.)

Dates: Dec. 2, 1952
House: Jan. 3, 2007-date
Serving in the 111th Congress

HOUSE STANDING COMMITTEES:

1st ARMED SERVICES
Dates: Jan. 10, 2007-date
Departure: Still serving in the 111th Congress

Cong.	Ranking	Terms in: House	Comm.	Date of Assignment
110th	Maj-27th	1	1	Jan. 10, 2007
111th	Maj-24th	2	2	Jan. 7, 2009

2nd EDUCATION AND LABOR
Dates: Jan. 10, 2007-date
Departure: Still serving in the 111th Congress

Cong.	Ranking	Terms in: House	Comm.	Date of Assignment
110th	Maj-27th	1	1	Jan. 10, 2007
111th	Maj-23rd	2	2	Jan. 21, 2009

3rd NATURAL RESOURCES
Dates: Jan. 21, 2009-date
Departure: Still serving in the 111th Congress

Cong.	Ranking	Terms in: House	Comm.	Date of Assignment
111th	Maj-26th	2	1	Jan. 21, 2009

Richard C. Shelby (R-Ala.)

Dates: May 6, 1934
House: Jan. 3, 1979-Jan. 3, 1987
Left the House: Elected to U.S. Senate in 1986
Senate: Jan. 3, 1987-date
Serving in the 111th Congress
Served as a Democrat: Jan. 3, 1979-Nov. 9, 1994
Served as a Republican: Nov. 9, 1994-date

HOUSE STANDING COMMITTEES:

1st INTERSTATE AND FOREIGN COMMERCE
Dates: Jan. 24, 1979-Jan. 3, 1981
ENERGY AND COMMERCE
Dates: Jan. 28, 1981-Jan. 3, 1987
Departure: Left the House for the Senate

2nd VETERANS AFFAIRS
Dates: Jan. 24, 1979-Jan. 3, 1987
Departure: Left the House for the Senate

3rd JUDICIARY
Dates: Jan. 31, 1979-Mar. 3, 1980
Departure: Left committee; temporary term expired

SENATE STANDING COMMITTEES:

1st ARMED SERVICES
Dates: Jan. 6, 1987-Jan. 4, 1995
Departure: Moved to Appropriations and Select Intelligence

Cong.	Ranking	Years in: Senate	Comm.	Date of Assignment
103rd	Maj-7th	7	7	Jan. 7, 1993

2nd BANKING, HOUSING AND URBAN AFFAIRS
Dates: Jan. 6, 1987-date
Departure: Still serving in 111th Congress

Cong.	Ranking	Years in: Senate	Comm.	Date of Assignment
103rd	Maj-5th	7	7	Jan. 7, 1993
104th	Maj-3rd	9	8	Jan. 4, 1995
105th	Maj-3rd	11	11	Jan. 9, 1997
106th	Maj-2nd	13	13	Jan. 7, 1999
107th	Maj-2nd	15	15	Jan. 25, 2001
+107th	Min-2nd	15	15	June 6, 2001
108th	Maj-Chr	17	17	Jan. 15, 2003
109th	Maj-Chr	19	19	Jan. 6, 2005
110th	Min-RM	21	21	Jan. 12, 2007
111th	Min-RM	23	23	Jan. 21, 2009

3rd ENERGY AND NATURAL RESOURCES
1st Dates: Feb. 5, 1991-Jan. 4, 1995
1st Departure: Moved to Appropriations and Select Intelligence
2nd Dates: Jan. 25, 2001-Jan. 15, 2003
2nd Departure: Moved to Governmental Affairs

Cong.	Ranking	Years in: Senate	Comm.	Date of Assignment
103rd	Maj-7th	7	*1 2	Jan. 7, 1993
107th	Maj-7th	15	*2 1	Jan. 25, 2001
+107th	Min-7th	15	*2 1	June 6, 2001

4th APPROPRIATIONS
Dates: Jan. 4, 1995-date
Departure: Still serving in the 111th Congress

Cong.	Ranking	Years in: Senate	Comm.	Date of Assignment
104th	Maj-12th	9	1	Jan. 4, 1995
105th	Maj-9th	11	3	Jan. 9, 1997
106th	Maj-9th	13	5	Jan. 7, 1999
107th	Maj-8th	15	7	Jan. 25, 2001
+107th	Min-8th	15	7	June 6, 2001
108th	Maj-8th	17	9	Jan. 15, 2003
109th	Maj-8th	19	11	Jan. 6, 2005
110th	Min-7th	21	13	Jan. 12, 2007
111th	Min-5th	23	15	Jan. 21, 2009

5th GOVERNMENTAL AFFAIRS renamed Oct. 9, 2004
HOMELAND SECURITY AND GOVERNMENTAL AFFAIRS
Dates: Jan. 15, 2003-Jan. 6, 2005
Departure: Left committee; no new assignment

Cong.	Ranking	Years in: Senate	Comm.	Date of Assignment
108th	Maj-9th	17	1	Jan. 15, 2003

SENATE SELECT AND SPECIAL COMMITTEES:

1st SPECIAL AGING (Permanent)
Dates: Jan. 6, 1987-date
Departure: Still serving in 111th Congress

Cong.	Ranking	Years in: Senate	Comm.	Date of Assignment
103rd	Maj-6th	7	7	Jan. 21, 1993
104th	Maj-8th	9	9	Jan. 11, 1995
105th	Maj-5th	11	11	Jan. 9, 1997
106th	Maj-5th	13	13	Jan. 7, 1999
107th	Maj-4th	15	15	Jan. 25, 2001
+107th	Min-3rd	15	15	July 24, 2001
108th	Maj-2nd	17	17	Jan. 15, 2003
109th	Maj-2nd	19	19	Jan. 6, 2005
110th	Min-2nd	21	21	Jan. 12, 2007
111th	Min-2nd	23	23	Jan. 21, 2009

2nd SELECT INTELLIGENCE (Permanent)
Dates: Jan. 6, 1995-Jan. 15, 2003
Ch1: Replaced by D. Robert Graham (D-Fla.) following party control shift on June 6, 2001and became RM2
Departure: Left committee; became Chair of Banking, Housing and Urban Affairs; moved to Governmental Affairs

Cong.	Ranking	Years in: Senate	Comm.	Date of Assignment
104th	Maj-3rd	9	1	Jan. 6, 1995
105th	Maj-Chr	11	3	Jan. 9, 1997
106th	Maj-Chr	13	5	Jan. 7, 1999
107th	Maj-Ch1	15	7	Jan. 25, 2001
+107th	Min-RM2	15	7	June 6, 2001

3rd SPECIAL COMMITTEE TO INVESTIGATE WHITEWATER DEVELOPMENT CORPORATION AND RELATED MATTERS
Dates: July 20, 1995-June 17, 1996
Termination: Senate Report 104-280 filed

Cong.	Ranking	Years in: Senate	Comm.	Date of Assignment
104th	Maj-2nd	9	1	July 20, 1995

Karen Shepherd (D-Utah)

Dates: July 5, 1940
House: Jan. 3, 1993-Jan. 3, 1995
Left the House: Defeated for re-election in 1994

HOUSE STANDING COMMITTEES:

1st NATURAL RESOURCES
Dates: Jan. 5, 1993-Jan. 3, 1995
Departure: Left the House; lost re-election

Cong.	Ranking	Terms in: House	Comm.	Date of Assignment
103rd	Maj-21st	1	1	Jan. 5, 1993

2nd PUBLIC WORKS AND TRANSPORTATION
Dates: Jan. 5, 1993-Jan. 3, 1995
Departure: Left the House; lost re-election

Cong.	Ranking	Terms in: House	Comm.	Date of Assignment
103rd	Maj-30th	1	1	Jan. 5, 1993

Brad Sherman (D-Cal.)

Dates: Oct. 24, 1954
House: Jan. 3, 1997-date
Serving in the 111th Congress

HOUSE STANDING COMMITTEES:

1st BUDGET
Dates: Jan. 7, 1997-Sept. 5, 1997
Departure: Resigned committee; moved to Banking and Financial Services

Cong.	Ranking	Terms in: House	Comm.	Date of Assignment
105th	Min-17th	1	1	Jan. 7, 1997

2nd INTERNATIONAL RELATIONS, 105-109
FOREIGN AFFAIRS, 110-111
Dates: Jan. 7, 1997-date
Departure: Still serving in the 111th Congress

Cong.	Ranking	Terms in: House	Comm.	Date of Assignment
105th	Min-17th	1	1	Jan. 7, 1997
106th	Min-14th	2	2	Jan. 6, 1999
107th	Min-11th	3	3	Jan. 31, 2001
108th	Min-8th	4	4	Jan. 28, 2003
109th	Min-8th	5	5	Jan. 26, 2005
110th	Maj-6th	6	6	Jan. 12, 2007
111th	Maj-5th	7	7	Jan. 21, 2009

3rd BANKING AND FINANCIAL SERVICES, 105-106
FINANCIAL SERVICES, 107-111
Dates: Sept. 5, 1997-date
Departure: Still serving in the 111th Congress

Cong.	Ranking	Terms in: House	Comm.	Date of Assignment
105th	MnA-26th	1	1	Sep. 5, 1997
106th	Min-16th	2	2	Jan. 6, 1999
107th	Min-14th	3	3	Jan. 31, 2001
108th	Min-12th	4	4	Jan. 28, 2003
109th	Min-12th	5	5	Jan. 26, 2005
110th	Maj-10th	6	6	Jan. 12, 2007
111th	Maj-9th	7	7	Jan. 7, 2009

4th SCIENCE
Dates: Sept. 18, 1998-Jan. 3, 1999
Departure: Left committee; no new assignment
Dates: Feb. 13, 2003-Jan. 3, 2007
Departure: Moved to Judiciary

Cong.	Ranking	Terms in: House	Comm.	Date of Assignment
105th	MnR-4th	1 *1	1	Sept. 18, 1998
108th	Min-20th	4 *2	1	Feb. 13, 2003
109th	Min-15th	5 *2	2	Feb. 2, 2005

5th JUDICIARY
Dates: Jan. 18, 2007-Oct. 14, 2009
Departure: Left committee; no new assignment

Cong.	Ranking	Terms in: House	Comm.	Date of Assignment
110th	Maj-17th	6	1	Jan. 18, 2007
111th	Maj-17th	7	2	Jan. 21, 2009

Don Sherwood (R-Penn.)

Dates: March 5, 1941
House: Jan. 3, 1999-Jan. 3, 2007
Left the House: Defeated for re-election in 2006

HOUSE STANDING COMMITTEES:

1st ARMED SERVICES
Dates: Jan. 6, 1999-Mar. 7, 2001
Departure: Resigned committee; moved to Appropriations

Cong.	Ranking	Terms in: House	Comm.	Date of Assignment
106th	Maj-32nd	1	1	Jan. 6, 1999
107th	Maj-24th	2	2	Jan. 6, 2001

2nd RESOURCES
Dates: Jan. 6, 1999-Mar. 7, 2001
Departure: Resigned committee; moved to Appropriations

Cong.	Ranking	Terms in: House	Comm.	Date of Assignment
106th	Maj-25th	1	1	Jan. 6, 1999
106th	Maj-23rd	2	2	Jan. 6, 2001

3rd TRANSPORTATION AND INFRASTRUCTURE
Dates: Jan. 6, 1999-Mar. 7, 2001
Departure: Resigned committee; moved to Appropriations

Cong.	Ranking	Terms in: House	Comm.	Date of Assignment
106th	Maj-34th	1	1	Jan. 6, 1999
107th	Maj-23rd	2	2	Jan. 6, 2001

4th APPROPRIATIONS
Dates: Mar. 7, 2001-Jan. 3, 2007
Departure: Left the House; lost re-election

Cong.	Ranking	Terms in: House	Comm.	Date of Assignment
107th	MjA-36th	2	1	Mar. 7, 2001
108th	Maj-31st	3	2	Jan. 28, 2003
109th	Maj-29th	4	3	Jan. 6, 2005

John M. Shimkus (R-Ill.)

Dates: Feb. 21, 1958
House: Jan. 3, 1997-date
Serving in the 111th Congress

HOUSE STANDING COMMITTEES:

1st COMMERCE, 105-106
ENERGY AND COMMERCE, 107-111
Dates: Jan. 7, 1997-date
Departure: Still serving in the 111th Congress

Cong.	Ranking	Terms in: House	Comm.	Date of Assignment
105th	Maj-28th	1	1	Jan. 7, 1997
106th	Maj-22nd	2	2	Jan. 6, 1999
107th	Maj-16th	3	3	Jan. 6, 2001
108th	Maj-14th	4	4	Jan. 28, 2003
109th	Maj-11th	5	5	Jan. 6, 2005
110th	Min-10th	6	6	Jan. 10, 2007
111th	Min-8th	7	7	Jan. 9, 2009

C. Ronald Shows (D-Miss.)

Dates: Jan. 26, 1947
House: Jan. 3, 1999-Jan. 3, 2003
Left the House: Defeated for re-election in 2002

HOUSE STANDING COMMITTEES:

1st TRANSPORTATION AND INFRASTRUCTURE
Dates: Jan. 6, 1999-Jan. 3, 2001
Departure: Moved to Financial Services and Agriculture

Cong.	Ranking	Terms in: House	Comm.	Date of Assignment
106th	Min-32nd	1	1	Jan. 6, 1999

2nd VETERANS AFFAIRS
Dates: Jan. 6, 1999-Jan. 3, 2003
Departure: Left the House; lost re-election

Cong.	Ranking	Terms in: House	Comm.	Date of Assignment
106th	Min-11th	1	1	Jan. 6, 1999
107th	Min-11th	2	2	Jan. 31, 2001

3rd FINANCIAL SERVICES
Dates: Feb. 8, 2001-Jan. 3, 2003
Departure: Left the House; lost re-election

Cong.	Ranking	Terms in: House	Comm.	Date of Assignment
107th	Min-28th	2	1	Feb. 8, 2001

4th AGRICULTURE
Dates: Mar. 14, 2001-Jan. 3, 2003
Departure: Left the House; lost re-election

Cong.	Ranking	Terms in: House	Comm.	Date of Assignment
107th	Min-24th	2	1	Mar. 14, 2001

Heath Shuler (D-N.C.)

Dates: Dec. 31, 1971
House: Jan. 3, 2007-date
Serving in the 111th Congress

HOUSE STANDING COMMITTEES:

1st TRANSPORTATION AND INFRASTRUCTURE
Dates: Jan. 10, 2007-date
Departure: Still serving in the 111th Congress

Cong.	Ranking	Terms in: House	Comm.	Date of Assignment
110th	Maj-34th	1	1	Jan. 10, 2007
111th	Maj-26th	2	2	Jan. 7, 2009

2nd NATURAL RESOURCES
Dates: Jan. 18, 2007-Jan. 3, 2009
Departure: Left committee; no new assignment

Cong.	Ranking	Terms in: House	Comm.	Date of Assignment
110th	Maj-27th	1	1	Jan. 18, 2007

3rd SMALL BUSINESS
Dates: Jan. 23, 2007-date
Departure: Still serving in the 111th Congress

Cong.	Ranking	Terms in: House	Comm.	Date of Assignment
110th	Maj-4th	1	1	Jan. 23, 2007
111th	Maj-3rd	2	2	Jan. 21, 2009

E.G. (Bud) Shuster (R-Penn.)

Dates: Jan. 23, 1932
House: Jan. 3, 1973-Feb. 2, 2001
Left the House: Resigned and retired

HOUSE STANDING COMMITTEES:

1st PUBLIC WORKS, 93
PUBLIC WORKS AND TRANSPORTATION, 94-103

TRANSPORTATION AND INFRASTRUCTURE, 104-107
Dates: Jan. 24, 1973-Feb. 2, 2001
Departure: Resigned the House; retired

Cong.	Ranking	Terms in: House	Comm.	Date of Assignment
103rd	Min-RM	11	11	Jan. 5, 1993
104th	Maj-Chr	12	12	Jan. 4, 1995
105th	Maj-Chr	13	13	Jan. 7, 1997
106th	Maj-Chr	14	14	Jan. 6, 1999
107th	Maj-2nd	15	15	Jan. 6, 2001

2nd DISTRICT OF COLUMBIA
Dates: Feb. 20, 1973-Jan. 3, 1975
Departure: Left committee; no new assignment

3rd EDUCATION AND LABOR
Dates: Jan. 19, 1977-Jan. 3, 1979
Departure: Moved to Budget

4th BUDGET
Dates: Jan. 24, 1979-Jan. 3, 1985
Departure: Left committee; no new assignment

HOUSE SELECT AND SPECIAL COMMITTEES:

1st PERMANENT SELECT INTELLIGENCE
1st Dates: Jan. 28, 1987-Jan. 3, 1993
1st Departure: Left committee; had become Ranking Member on Public Works and Transportation
2nd Dates: Jan. 4, 1995-Jan. 3, 1999
2nd Departure: Left committee; no new assignment

Cong.	Ranking	Terms in: House	Comm.	Date of Assignment
104th	Maj-7th	12 *2	1	Jan. 4, 1995
105th	Maj-4th	13 *2	2	Feb. 10, 1997

108th	Maj-31st	2	2	Jan. 28, 2003
109th	Maj-25th	3	3	Jan. 26, 2005
110th	Min-18th	4	4	Jan. 10, 2007
111th	Min-14th	5	5	Jan. 9, 2009

3rd ARMED SERVICES
1st Dates: Jan. 26, 2005-Jan. 3, 2007
1st Departure: Moved to Natural Resources
2nd Dates: May 10, 2007-date
2nd Departure: Still serving in the 111th Congress

Cong.	Ranking	Terms in: House	Comm.	Date of Assignment
109th	Maj-29th	3 *1	1	Jan. 26, 2005
110th	MnR-1st	4 *2	1	May 10, 2007
111th	Min-16th	5 *2	2	Jan. 9, 2009

4th NATURAL RESOURCES
Dates: Jan. 10, 2007-date
Departure: Still serving in the 111th Congress

Cong.	Ranking	Terms in: House	Comm.	Date of Assignment
110th	Min-19th	4	1	Jan. 10, 2007
111th	Min-10th	5	2	Jan. 9, 2009

HOUSE SELECT AND SPECIAL COMMITTEES:

1st SELECT BIPARTISAN COMMITTEE TO INVESTIGATE THE PREPARATION FOR AND RESPONSE TO HURRICANE KATRINA
Dates: Sep. 21, 2005-Feb. 15, 2006
Departure: House Report 377 (109-2) filed

Cong.	Ranking	Terms in: House	Comm.	Date of Assignment
109th	Maj-11th	3	1	Sep. 21, 2005

William Shuster (R-Penn.)

Dates: Jan. 10, 1960
House: May 15, 2001-date
Serving in the 111th Congress

H: William Shuster was elected to the 107th Congress by special election, May 15, 2001, to fill the vacancy caused by the resignation of his father U.S. Representative E.G. (Bud) Shuster (R-Penn.). William Shuster was seated May 17, 2001, and assigned to committees.

HOUSE STANDING COMMITTEES:

1st SMALL BUSINESS
Dates: June 7, 2001-Jan. 3, 2009
Departure: Left committee; no new assignment

Cong.	Ranking	Terms in: House	Comm.	Date of Assignment
107th	MjR-1st	1	1	June 7, 2001
108th	Maj-12th	2	2	Jan. 28, 2003
109th	Maj-7th	3	3	Feb. 2, 2005
110th	Min-5th	4	4	Jan. 10, 2007

2nd TRANSPORTATION AND INFRASTRUCTURE
Dates: June 27, 2001-date
Departure: Still serving in the 111th Congress

Cong.	Ranking	Terms in: House	Comm.	Date of Assignment
107th	MjR-3rd	1	1	June 27, 2001

Robert Simmons (R-Conn.)

Dates: Feb. 11, 1943
House: Jan. 3, 2001-Jan. 3, 2007
Left the House: Defeated for re-election in 2006

HOUSE STANDING COMMITTEES:

1st ARMED SERVICES
Dates: Jan. 6, 2001-Jan. 3, 2007
Departure: Left the House; lost re-election

Cong.	Ranking	Terms in: House	Comm.	Date of Assignment
107th	Maj-27th	1	1	Jan. 6, 2001
108th	Maj-17th	2	2	Jan. 28, 2003
109th	Maj-16th	3	3	Jan. 26, 2005

2nd TRANSPORTATION AND INFRASTRUCTURE
Dates: Jan. 6, 2001-Jan. 3, 2007
Departure: Left the House; lost re-election

Cong.	Ranking	Terms in: House	Comm.	Date of Assignment
107th	Maj-28th	1	1	Jan. 6, 2001
108th	Maj-23rd	2	2	Jan. 28, 2003
109th	Maj-19th	3	3	Jan. 26, 2005

3rd VETERANS AFFAIRS
Dates: Jan. 6, 2001-Feb. 9, 2005
Departure: Resigned committee; moved to Homeland Security

Cong.	Ranking	Terms in: House	Comm.	Date of Assignment
107th	Maj-15th	1	1	Jan. 6, 2001
108th	Maj-10th	2	2	Jan. 28, 2003
109th	Maj-7th	3	3	Jan. 26, 2005

4th HOMELAND SECURITY
Dates: Feb. 9, 2005-Jan. 3, 2007
Departure: Left the House; lost re-election

Cong.	Ranking	Terms in: House	Comm.	Date of Assignment
109th	Maj-12th	3	1	Feb. 9, 2005

Paul M. Simon (D-Ill.)

Dates: Nov. 29, 1928-Dec. 9, 2003
House: Jan. 3, 1975-Jan. 2, 1985
Left the House: Elected to U.S. Senate in 1984
Senate: Jan. 3, 1985-Jan. 3, 1997
Left Senate: Retired in 1996

HOUSE STANDING COMMITTEES:

1st EDUCATION AND LABOR
Dates: Jan. 20, 1975-Jan. 3, 1985
Departure: Left the House for the Senate

2nd POST OFFICE AND CIVIL SERVICE
Dates: Jan. 20, 1975-Jan. 3, 1977
Departure: Moved to Budget

3rd BUDGET
Dates: Jan. 11, 1977-Jan. 3, 1983
Departure: Moved to Science and Technology

4th SCIENCE AND TECHNOLOGY
Dates: Jan. 6, 1983-Jan. 3, 1985
Departure: Left the House for the Senate

HOUSE SELECT AND SPECIAL COMMITTEES:

1st SELECT POPULATION
Dates: Oct. 14, 1977-Dec. 29, 1978
Departure: House Report 1842 (95-2) filed

SENATE STANDING COMMITTEES:

1st JUDICIARY
Dates: Feb. 21, 1985-Jan. 3, 1997
Departure: Left the Senate; retired

Cong.	Ranking	Years in: Senate	Comm.	Date of Assignment
103rd	Maj-7th	9	8	Jan. 7, 1993
104th	Min-5th	11	10	Jan. 4, 1995

2nd LABOR AND HUMAN RESOURCES
Dates: Feb. 21, 1985-Jan. 3, 1997
Departure: Left the Senate; retired

Cong.	Ranking	Years in: Senate	Comm.	Date of Assignment
103rd	Maj-5th	9	8	Jan. 7, 1993
104th	Min-4th	11	10	Jan. 4, 1995

3rd RULES AND ADMINISTRATION
Dates: Mar. 5, 1985-Jan. 6, 1987
Departure: Moved to Budget and Foreign Relations

4th BUDGET
Dates: Jan. 6, 1987-Jan. 3, 1997
Departure: Left the Senate; retired

Cong.	Ranking	Years in: Senate	Comm.	Date of Assignment
103rd	Maj-7th	9	7	Jan. 21, 1993
104th	Min-5th	11	9	Jan. 6, 1995

5th FOREIGN RELATIONS
Dates: Jan. 6, 1987-Jan. 3, 1995
Departure: Left committee; no new assignment

Cong.	Ranking	Years in: Senate	Comm.	Date of Assignment
103rd	Maj-6th	9	7	Jan. 7, 1993

SENATE SELECT AND SPECIAL COMMITTEES:

1st SELECT INDIAN AFFAIRS (Permanent), 102
INDIAN AFFAIRS (Permanent), 103-104
Dates: Feb. 5, 1991-Jan. 3, 1997
Departure: Left the Senate; retired

Cong.	Ranking	Years in: Senate	Comm.	Date of Assignment
103rd	Maj-5th	9	2	Jan. 5, 1993
104th	Min-4th	11	4	Jan. 9, 1995

2nd SPECIAL COMMITTEE TO INVESTIGATE WHITEWATER DEVELOPMENT CORPORATION AND RELATED MATTERS
Dates: July 20, 1995-June 17, 1996
Termination: Senate Report 104-280 filed

Cong.	Ranking	Years in: Senate	Comm.	Date of Assignment
104th	Min-8th	11	1	July 20, 1995

JOINT COMMITTEES:

1st JOINT DEFICIT REDUCTION (Temporary)
Senate Dates: Jan. 6, 1987-Sep. 29, 1987
Termination: Public Law 100-119 adjusted Gramm-Rudman-Hollings Act

---

Alan K. Simpson (R-Wyo.)

Dates: Sept. 2, 1931
Senate: Jan. 1, 1979-Jan. 3, 1997
Left the Senate: Retired in 1996

S: Simpson was appointed to the 95th Congress, Jan. 1, 1979, to fill the vacancy caused by the resignation of U.S. Senator Clifford P. Hansen (R-Wyo.). Simpson had been elected to succeed Hansen in the 96th Congress. Simpson was not seated nor assigned to committees because the 95th Congress was not in session.

SENATE STANDING COMMITTEES:

1st ENVIRONMENT AND PUBLIC WORKS
Dates: Jan. 23, 1979-Jan. 4, 1995
Departure: Moved to Finance

Cong.	Ranking	Years in: Senate	Comm.	Date of Assignment
103rd	Min-2nd	15	14	Jan. 7, 1993

2nd JUDICIARY
Dates: Jan. 23, 1979-Jan. 3, 1997
Departure: Left the Senate; retired

Cong.	Ranking	Years in: Senate	Comm.	Date of Assignment
103rd	Min-3rd	15	14	Jan. 7, 1993
104th	Maj-3rd	17	16	Jan. 5, 1995

3rd VETERANS' AFFAIRS
Dates: Jan. 23, 1979-Jan. 3, 1997
Departure: Left the Senate; retired

Cong.	Ranking	Years in: Senate	Comm.	Date of Assignment
103rd	Min-3rd	15	14	Jan. 21, 1993
104th	Maj-Chr	17	16	Jan. 6, 1995

4th FINANCE
Dates: Jan. 4, 1995-Jan. 3, 1997
Departure: Left the Senate; retired

Cong.	Ranking	Years in: Senate	Comm.	Date of Assignment
104th	Maj-7th	17	1	Jan. 4, 1995

SENATE SELECT AND SPECIAL COMMITTEES:

1st UNDERCOVER ACTIVITIES OF COMPONENTS OF THE DEPARTMENT OF JUSTICE
Dates: Mar. 29, 1982-Dec. 15, 1982
Termination: Senate Report 682 (97-2) filed

2nd SPECIAL AGING (Permanent)
Dates: Jan. 6, 1987-Jan. 3, 1997
Departure: Left the Senate; retired

Cong.	Ranking	Years in: Senate	Comm.	Date of Assignment
103rd	Min-4th	15	7	Jan. 21, 1993
104th	Maj-4th	17	9	Jan. 11, 1995

SENATE LEADERSHIP POSTS

Dates: Jan. 3, 1985-Jan. 3, 1995
Departure: Lost post in Republican Conference

1st SENATE MAJORITY WHIP
Dates: Jan. 3, 1985-Jan. 3, 1987
Notes: In the 99th Congress, Simpson succeeded Majority Whip Theodore Stevens (R-Alas.) who was defeated for Majority Leader. Simpson was elected on Nov. 28, 1984 as Majority Whip on the second ballot 31 to 22 over Slade Gorton (R-Wash.).
Departure: Republican Party lost majority in 1986

2nd SENATE MINORITY WHIP
Dates: Jan. 3, 1987-Jan. 3, 1995
Notes: Simpson was elected as Senate Republican Minority Whip unopposed for the 100th-102nd Congresses. Simpson defeated Slade Gorton again, 25 to 14 in the 103rd Congress on Nov. 10, 1992, but was defeated by Trent Lott (R-Miss.) 26 to 27 in the 104th Congress on Dec. 2, 1994.
Departure: Defeated for election as Majority Whip in Republican Conference

Cong.	Ranking	Years in: House	Post	Date of Selection
103rd	Min-2nd	15	9	Nov. 10, 1992

Michael K. Simpson (R-Ida.)

Dates: Sept. 8, 1950
House: Jan. 3, 1999-date
Serving in the 111th Congress

HOUSE STANDING COMMITTEES:

1st AGRICULTURE
Dates: Jan. 6, 1999-Jan. 3, 2003
Departure: Moved to Appropriations

Cong.	Ranking	Terms in: House	Comm.	Date of Assignment
106th	Maj-24th	1	1	Jan. 6, 1999
107th	Maj-16th	2	2	Jan. 6, 2001

2nd RESOURCES
Dates: Jan. 6, 1999-Jan. 3, 2003
Departure: Moved to Appropriations

Cong.	Ranking	Terms in: House	Comm.	Date of Assignment
106th	Maj-27th	1	1	Jan. 6, 1999
107th	Maj-25th	2	2	Jan. 6, 2001

3rd VETERANS AFFAIRS
Dates: Jan. 6, 1999-Jan. 3, 2003
Departure: Moved to Appropriations

Cong.	Ranking	Terms in: House	Comm.	Date of Assignment
106th	Maj-17th	1	1	Jan. 6, 1999
107th	Maj-13th	2	2	Jan. 6, 2001

4th TRANSPORTATION AND INFRASTRUCTURE
Dates: Feb. 2, 1999-Jan. 3, 2003
Departure: Moved to Appropriations

Cong.	Ranking	Terms in: House	Comm.	Date of Assignment
106th	Maj-40th	1	1	Feb. 2, 1999
107th	Maj-26th	2	2	Jan. 6, 2001

5th APPROPRIATIONS
Dates: Jan. 28, 2003-date
Departure: Still serving in the 111th Congress

Cong.	Ranking	Terms in: House	Comm.	Date of Assignment
108th	Maj-33rd	3	1	Jan. 28, 2003
109th	Maj-31st	4	2	Jan. 6, 2005
110th	Min-23rd	5	3	Jan. 4, 2007
111th	Min-13th	6	4	Jan. 9, 2009

6th BUDGET
Dates: Feb. 8, 2005-date
Departure: Still serving in the 111th Congress

Cong.	Ranking	Terms in: House	Comm.	Date of Assignment
109th	Maj-18th	4	1	Feb. 8, 2005
110th	Min-9th	5	2	Jan. 10, 2007
111th	Min-6th	6	3	Jan. 9, 2009

Albio Sires (D-N.J.)

Dates: Jan. 26, 1951
House: Jan. 3, 2007-date
Serving in the 111th Congress

HOUSE STANDING COMMITTEES:

1st FINANCIAL SERVICES
Dates: Jan. 12, 2007-Mar. 11, 2008
Departure: Resigned committee; moved to Transportation and Infrastructure

Cong.	Ranking	Terms in: House	Comm.	Date of Assignment
110th	Maj-26th	1	1	Jan. 12, 2007

2nd FOREIGN AFFAIRS
Dates: Jan. 12, 2007-date
Departure: Still serving in the 111th Congress

Cong.	Ranking	Terms in: House	Comm.	Date of Assignment
110th	Maj-25th	1	1	Jan. 12, 2007
111th	Maj-13th	2	2	Jan. 21, 2009

3rd TRANSPORTATION AND INFRASTRUCTURE
Dates: Mar. 11, 2008-date
Departure: Still serving in the 111th Congress

Cong.	Ranking	Terms in: House	Comm.	Date of Assignment
110th	MjR-2nd	1	1	Mar. 11, 2008
111th	Maj-34th	2	2	Jan. 7, 2009

Norman Sisisky (D-Va.)

Dates: June 9, 1927-Mar. 29, 2001
House: Jan. 3, 1983-Mar. 29, 2001
Left the House: Died in office

HOUSE STANDING COMMITTEES:

1st ARMED SERVICES, 98-103
NATIONAL SECURITY, 104-105
ARMED SERVICES, 106-107
Dates: Jan. 6, 1983-Mar. 29, 2001
Departure: Died in office

Cong.	Ranking	Terms in: House	Comm.	Date of Assignment
103rd	Maj-9th	6	6	Jan. 5, 1993
104th	Min-5th	7	7	Jan. 4, 1995
105th	Min-3rd	8	8	Jan. 7, 1997
106th	Min-2nd	9	9	Jan. 6, 1999
107th	Min-2nd	10	10	Jan. 31, 2001

2nd SMALL BUSINESS
Dates: Jan. 6, 1983-Feb. 23, 1999
Departure: Leave of absence; moved to Permanent Select Intelligence

Cong.	Ranking	Terms in: House	Comm.	Date of Assignment
103rd	Maj-6th	6	6	Jan. 5, 1993
104th	Min-3rd	7	7	Jan. 4, 1995
105th	Min-3rd	8	8	Feb. 5, 1997
106th	Min-2nd	9	9	Jan. 6, 1999

HOUSE SELECT AND SPECIAL COMMITTEES:

1st SELECT AGING (Permanent)
Dates: Feb. 8, 1983-Jan. 3, 1993
Termination: Committee not renewed in 1993

2nd PERMANENT SELECT INTELLIGENCE
Dates: Feb. 12, 1999-Mar. 29, 2001
Departure: Died in office

Cong.	Ranking	Terms in: House	Comm.	Date of Assignment
106th	Min-4th	9	1	Feb. 12, 1999
107th	Min-4th	10	2	Mar. 1, 2001

David E. Skaggs (D-Colo.)

Dates: Feb. 22, 1943
House: Jan. 3, 1987-Jan. 3, 1999
Left the House: Retired in 1998

HOUSE STANDING COMMITTEES:

1st PUBLIC WORKS AND TRANSPORTATION
Dates: Jan. 6, 1987-Jan. 3, 1991
Departure: Moved to Appropriations

2nd GOVERNMENT OPERATIONS
Dates: Jan. 22, 1987-Apr. 7, 1987
Departure: Left committee; had moved to Science, Space and Technology earlier

3rd SCIENCE, SPACE AND TECHNOLOGY
Dates: Mar. 30, 1987-Jan. 3, 1991
Departure: Moved to Appropriations

4th APPROPRIATIONS
Dates: Jan. 3, 1991-Jan. 3, 1999
Departure: Left the House; retired

Cong.	Ranking	Terms in: House	Comm.	Date of Assignment
103rd	Maj-22nd	4	2	Jan. 5, 1993
104th	Min-18th	5	3	Jan. 4, 1995
105th	Min-13th	6	4	Jan. 7, 1997

HOUSE SELECT AND SPECIAL COMMITTEES:

1st SELECT CHILDREN, YOUTH AND FAMILIES (Temporary)
Dates: Jan. 21, 1987-Jan. 3, 1993
Termination: Committee not renewed in 1993

2nd PERMANENT SELECT INTELLIGENCE
1st Dates: Feb. 3, 1993-Jan. 3, 1995
1st Departure: Left committee; no new assignment
2nd Dates: Returned July 12, 1995-Jan. 3, 1999
2nd Departure: Left the House; retired

Cong.	Ranking	Terms in: House	Comm.	Date of Assignment
103rd	Maj-7th	4 *1	1	Feb. 3, 1993
104th	MnR-1st	5 *2	1	July 12, 1995
105th	Min-3rd	6 *2	2	Feb. 10, 1997

Joseph R. Skeen (R-N.M.)

Dates: June 30, 1927
House: Jan. 3, 1981-Jan. 3, 2003
Left the House: Retired in 2002

HOUSE STANDING COMMITTEES:

1st AGRICULTURE
Dates: Jan. 28, 1981-Jan. 3, 1985
Departure: Moved to Appropriations

2nd SCIENCE AND TECHNOLOGY
Dates: Jan. 28, 1981-Jan. 3, 1985
Departure: Moved to Appropriations

3rd APPROPRIATIONS
Dates: Jan. 30, 1985-Jan. 3, 2003
Departure: Left the House; retired

Cong.	Ranking	Terms in: House	Comm.	Date of Assignment
103rd	Min-9th	7	5	Jan. 5, 1993
104th	Maj-9th	8	6	Jan. 4, 1995
105th	Maj-8th	9	7	Jan. 7, 1997
106th	Maj-6th	10	8	Jan. 6, 1999
107th	Maj-5th	11	9	Jan. 6, 2001

Isaac N. (Ike) Skelton (D-Mo.)

Dates: Dec. 20, 1931
House: Jan. 3, 1977-date
Serving in the 111th Congress

HOUSE STANDING COMMITTEES:

1st AGRICULTURE
Dates: Jan. 19, 1977-Jan. 3, 1981
Departure: Moved to Armed Services

2nd SMALL BUSINESS
1st Dates: Jan. 27, 1977-Jan. 3, 1995
1st Departure: Left committee; no new assignment
2nd Dates: June 13, 1995-Mar. 10, 1997
2nd Departure: Resigned committee; moved to Permanent Select Intelligence

Cong.	Ranking	Terms in: House	Comm.	Date of Assignment
103rd	Maj-3rd	9 *1	9	Jan. 5, 1993
104th	MnR-1st	10 *2	1	June 13, 1995
105th	Min-2nd	11 *2	2	Feb. 5, 1997

3rd ARMED SERVICES, 96-103
NATIONAL SECURITY, 104-105
ARMED SERVICES, 106-111
Dates: Sep. 17, 1980-date
RM2: Replaced Ronald V. Dellums (D-Cal.) as Ranking Member on Feb. 6, 1998
Departure: Still serving in the 111th Congress

Cong.	Ranking	Terms in: House	Comm.	Date of Assignment
103rd	Maj-6th	9	7	Jan. 5, 1993
104th	Min-4th	10	8	Jan. 4, 1995
105th	Min-2nd	11	9	Jan. 7, 1997
=105th	Min-RM2	11	9	Feb. 6, 1998
106th	Min-RM	12	10	Jan. 6, 1999
107th	Min-RM	13	11	Jan. 8, 2001
108th	Min-RM	14	12	Jan. 8, 2003
109th	Min-RM	15	13	Jan. 6, 2005
110th	Maj-Chr	16	14	Jan. 4, 2007
111th	Maj-Chr	17	15	Jan. 9, 2009

HOUSE SELECT AND SPECIAL COMMITTEES:

1st SELECT AGING (Permanent)
Dates: Feb. 8, 1983-Jan. 3, 1993
Termination: Committee not renewed in 1993

2nd PERMANENT SELECT INTELLIGENCE
Dates: Mar. 6, 1997-Jan. 3, 1999
Departure: Left committee; no new assignment

Cong.	Ranking	Terms in: House	Comm.	Date of Assignment
105th	Min-6th	11	1	Mar. 6, 1997

James C. Slattery (D-Kans.)

Dates: Aug. 4, 1948
House: Jan. 3, 1983-Jan. 3, 1995
Left the House: Lost election for Governor in 1994

HOUSE STANDING COMMITTEES:

1st ENERGY AND COMMERCE
Dates: Jan. 6, 1983-Jan. 3, 1995
Departure: Left the House; lost election for Governor

Cong.	Ranking	Terms in: House	Comm.	Date of Assignment
103rd	Maj-12th	6	6	Jan. 5, 1993

2nd VETERANS AFFAIRS
1st Dates: Jan. 6, 1983-Jan. 3, 1985
1st Departure: Ceased active service to move to Budget; returned later with continuous seniority credited
2nd Dates: Jan. 24, 1991-Jan. 3, 1995
2nd Departure: Left the House; lost election for Governor

Cong.	Ranking	Terms in: House	Comm.	Date of Assignment
103rd	Maj-7th	6 *2	2	Jan. 5, 1993

3rd BUDGET
Dates: Jan. 30, 1985-Jan. 3, 1991
Departure: Moved to Banking, Finance and Urban Affairs and returned to Veterans Affairs

4th BANKING, FINANCE AND URBAN AFFAIRS
Temporary Dates: Jan. 24, 1991-Jan. 3, 1993
Departure: Temporary term expired

JOINT COMMITTEES:

1st JOINT DEFICIT REDUCTION (Temporary)
House Dates: Feb. 23, 1987-Sep. 29, 1987
Termination: Public Law 100-119 adjusted Gramm-Rudman-Hollings Act

Louise Macintosh Slaughter (D-N.Y.)

Dates: Aug. 14, 1929
House: Jan. 3, 1987-date
Serving in the 111th Congress

HOUSE STANDING COMMITTEES:

1st PUBLIC WORKS AND TRANSPORTATION
Dates: Jan. 6, 1987-July 25, 1989
Departure: Resigned committee; moved to Rules

2nd GOVERNMENT OPERATIONS, 100-101
GOVERNMENT REFORM AND OVERSIGHT, 104
1st Dates: Jan. 22, 1987-July 25, 1989

1st Departure: Resigned committee; moved to Rules
2nd Dates: Jan. 9, 1995-Jan. 3, 1997
2nd Departure: Returned to Rules

| | | Terms in: | | Date of |
Cong.	Ranking	House	Comm.	Assignment
104th	Min-8th	5 *2	1	Jan. 9, 1995

3rd RULES
1st Dates: June 14, 1989-Jan. 3, 1995
1st Departure: Returned to Government Reform and Oversight
2nd Dates: Jan. 7, 1997-date
2nd Departure: Still serving in the 111th Congress

| | | Terms in: | | Date of |
Cong.	Ranking	House	Comm.	Assignment
103rd	Maj-9th	4 *1	3	Jan. 5, 1993
105th	Min-4th	6 *2	1	Jan. 7, 1997
106th	Min-4th	7 *2	2	Jan. 6, 1999
107th	Min-4th	8 *2	3	Jan. 3, 2001
108th	Min-2nd	9 *2	4	Jan. 7, 2003
109th	Min-RM	10 *2	5	Jan. 6, 2005
110th	Maj-Chr	11 *2	6	Jan. 4, 2007
111th	Maj-Chr	12 *2	7	Jan. 6, 2009

4th BUDGET
Dates: Jan. 24, 1991-Jan. 3, 1997
Departure: Returned to Rules

| | | Terms in: | | Date of |
Cong.	Ranking	House	Comm.	Assignment
103rd	Maj-13th	4	2	Jan. 5, 1993
104th	Min-3rd	5	3	Jan. 4, 1995
105th	Min-2nd	6	4	Jan. 4, 1997

HOUSE SELECT AND SPECIAL COMMITTEES:

1st SELECT AGING (Permanent)
Dates: Jan. 21, 1987-Jan. 3, 1993
Termination: Committee not renewed in 1993

2nd SELECT HOMELAND SECURITY
Dates: Feb. 12, 2003-Jan. 3, 2005
Departure: Did not continue on reorganized standing committee

| | | Terms in: | | Date of |
Cong.	Ranking	House	Comm.	Assignment
108th	Min-9th	9	1	Feb. 12, 2003

Adam Smith (D-Wash.)

Dates: June 15, 1965
House: Jan. 3, 1997-date
Serving in the 111th Congress

HOUSE STANDING COMMITTEES:

1st NATIONAL SECURITY, 105
ARMED SERVICES, 106-111
Dates: Jan. 7, 1997-date
Departure: Still serving in the 111th Congress

| | | Terms in: | | Date of |
Cong.	Ranking	House	Comm.	Assignment
105th	Min-22nd	1	1	Jan. 7, 1997
106th	Min-17th	2	2	Jan. 6, 1999
107th	Min-15th	3	3	Jan. 31, 2001
108th	Min-11th	4	4	Jan. 28, 2003
109th	Min-10th	5	5	Jan. 26, 2005

110th	Maj-9th	6	6	Jan. 10, 2007
111th	Maj-8th	7	7	Jan. 7, 2009

2nd RESOURCES
Dates: Jan. 7, 1997-Feb. 5, 2003
Departure: Resigned committee; moved to International Relations

| | | Terms in: | | Date of |
Cong.	Ranking	House	Comm.	Assignment
105th	Min-20th	1	1	Jan. 7, 1997
106th	Min-15th	2	2	Jan. 6, 1999
107th	Min-12th	3	3	Feb. 8, 2001
108th	Min-11th	4	4	Jan. 28, 2003

3rd INTERNATIONAL RELATIONS, 108-109
FOREIGN AFFAIRS, 110-111
Dates: Feb. 5, 2003-Feb. 9, 2009
Departure: Leave of absence; moved to Select Intelligence

| | | Terms in: | | Date of |
Cong.	Ranking	House	Comm.	Assignment
108th	Min-21st	4	1	Feb. 5, 2003
109th	Min-20th	5	2	Jan. 26, 2005
110th	Maj-12th	6	3	Jan. 12, 2007
111th	Maj-11th	7	4	Jan. 21, 2009

4th JUDICIARY
Dates: Feb. 9, 2005-June 8, 2005
Departure: Resigned committee; no new assignment

| | | Terms in: | | Date of |
Cong.	Ranking	House	Comm.	Assignment
109th	Min-16th	5	1	Feb. 9, 2005

HOUSE SELECT AND SPECIAL COMMITTEES:

1st PERMANENT SELECT INTELLIGENCE
Dates: Feb. 4, 2009-date
Departure: Still serving in the 111th Congress

| | | Terms in: | | Date of |
Cong.	Ranking	House	Comm.	Assignment
111th	Maj-12th	7	1	Feb. 4, 2009

Adrian Smith (R-Neb.)

Dates: Dec. 19, 1970
House: Jan. 3, 2007-date
Serving in the 111th Congress

HOUSE STANDING COMMITTEES:

1st AGRICULTURE
Dates: Jan. 10, 2007-date
Departure: Still serving in the 111th Congress

| | | Terms in: | | Date of |
Cong.	Ranking	House	Comm.	Assignment
110th	Min-19th	1	1	Jan. 10, 2007
111th	Min-13th	2	2	Jan. 9, 2009

2nd BUDGET
Dates: Jan. 10, 2007-Jan. 3, 2009
Departure: Left committee; no new assignment

| | | Terms in: | | Date of |
Cong.	Ranking	House	Comm.	Assignment
110th	Min-17th	1	1	Jan. 10, 2007

3rd SCIENCE AND TECHNOLOGY
Dates: Jan. 10, 2007-date
Departure: Still serving in the 111th Congress

Cong.	Ranking	Terms in: House	Comm.	Date of Assignment
110th	Min-20th	1	1	Jan. 10, 2007
111th	Min-15th	2	2	Jan. 22, 2009

4th NATURAL RESOURCES
Dates: Feb. 26, 2008-date
Departure: Still serving in the 111th Congress

Cong.	Ranking	Terms in: House	Comm.	Date of Assignment
110th	MnR-3rd	1	1	Feb. 26, 2008
111th	Min-12th	2	2	Jan. 9, 2009

Christopher H. Smith (R-N.J.)

Dates: March 4, 1953
House: Jan. 3, 1981-date
Serving in the 111th Congress

HOUSE STANDING COMMITTEES:

1st SMALL BUSINESS
Dates: Jan. 28, 1981-Jan. 3, 1985
Departure: Moved to Foreign Affairs

2nd VETERANS AFFAIRS
Dates: Jan. 28, 1981-Jan. 3, 2005
Departure: Left committee; no new assignment

Cong.	Ranking	Terms in: House	Comm.	Date of Assignment
103rd	Min-2nd	7	7	Jan. 5, 1993
104th	Maj-2nd	8	8	Jan. 4, 1995
105th	Maj-2nd	9	9	Jan. 21, 1997
106th	Maj-2nd	10	10	Jan. 6, 1999
107th	Maj-Chr	11	11	Jan. 6, 2001
108th	Maj-Chr	12	12	Jan. 28, 2003

3rd FOREIGN AFFAIRS, 99-103
INTERNATIONAL RELATIONS, 104-109
FOREIGN AFFAIRS, 110-111
Dates: Jan. 30, 1985-date
Departure: Still serving in the 111th Congress

Cong.	Ranking	Terms in: House	Comm.	Date of Assignment
103rd	Min-8th	7	5	Jan. 5, 1993
104th	Maj-7th	8	6	Jan. 4, 1995
105th	Maj-6th	9	7	Jan. 7, 1997
106th	Maj-6th	10	8	Jan. 6, 1999
107th	Maj-5th	11	9	Jan. 6, 2001
108th	Maj-4th	12	10	Jan. 28, 2003
109th	Maj-3rd	13	11	Jan. 26, 2005
110th	Min-2nd	14	12	Jan. 10, 2007
111th	Min-2nd	15	13	Jan. 9, 2009

HOUSE SELECT AND SPECIAL COMMITTEES:

1st SELECT AGING (Permanent)
Dates: Mar. 3, 1983-Jan. 3, 1993
Termination: Committee not renewed in 1993

2nd SELECT HUNGER (Temporary)
Dates: Apr. 25, 1989-Jan. 3, 1993
Termination: Committee not renewed in 1993

Gordon H. Smith (R-Ore.)

Dates: May 25, 1952
Senate: Jan. 3, 1997-Jan. 3, 2009
Left Senate: Defeated for re-election in 2008

SENATE STANDING COMMITTEES:

1st BUDGET
Dates: Jan. 9, 1997-Jan. 15, 2003
Departure: Moved to Finance, Rules and Administration, Indian Affairs, and Joint Printing

Cong.	Ranking	Years in: Senate	Comm.	Date of Assignment
105th	Maj-12th	1	1	Jan. 9, 1997
106th	Maj-12th	3	2	Jan. 7, 1999
107th	Maj-9th	5	5	Jan. 25, 2001
+107th	Min-9th	5	5	June 6, 2001

2nd ENERGY AND NATURAL RESOURCES
Dates: Jan. 9, 1997-Jan. 3, 2009
Departure: Left the Senate; lost re-election.

Cong.	Ranking	Years in: Senate	Comm.	Date of Assignment
105th	Maj-9th	1	1	Jan. 9, 1997
106th	Maj-7th	3	2	Jan. 7, 1999
107th	Maj-11th	5	5	Jan. 25, 2001
+107th	Min-11th	5	5	June 6, 2001
108th	Maj-10th	7	7	Jan. 15, 2003
109th	Maj-11th	9	8	Jan. 6, 2005
110th	Min-9th	11	11	Jan. 12, 2007

3rd FOREIGN RELATIONS
Dates: Jan. 9, 1997-Jan. 15, 2003
Departure: Moved to Finance, Rules and Administration, Indian Affairs, and Joint Printing

Cong.	Ranking	Years in: Senate	Comm.	Date of Assignment
105th	Maj-5th	1	1	Jan. 9, 1997
106th	Maj-5th	3	2	Jan. 7, 1999
107th	Maj-4th	5	5	Jan. 25, 2001
+107th	Min-4th	5	5	June 6, 2001

4th AGRICULTURE, NUTRITION AND FORESTRY
Dates: Sept. 12, 2000-Jan. 25, 2001
Departure: Moved to Commerce, Science, and Transportation

Cong.	Ranking	Years in: Senate	Comm.	Date of Assignment
106th	MjR-1st	4	1	Sept. 12, 2000

5th COMMERCE, SCIENCE AND TRANSPORTATION
Dates: Jan. 25, 2001-Jan. 3, 2009
Departure: Left the Senate; lost re-election

Cong.	Ranking	Years in: Senate	Comm.	Date of Assignment
107th	Maj-8th	5	1	Jan. 25, 2001
+107th	Min-8th	5	1	June 6, 2001
108th	Maj-8th	7	2	Jan. 15, 2003
109th	Maj-7th	9	4	Jan. 6, 2005
110th	Min-6th	11	6	Jan. 12, 2007

6th FINANCE
Dates: Jan. 15, 2003-Jan. 3, 2009
Departure: Left the Senate; lost re-election

Cong.	Ranking	Years in: Senate	Comm.	Date of Assignment
108th	Maj-10th	7	1	Jan. 15, 2003
109th	Maj-9th	9	2	Jan. 6, 2005
110th	Min-7th	11	4	Jan. 12, 2007

7th RULES AND ADMINISTRATION
Dates: Jan. 15, 2003-Jan. 6, 2005
Departure: Left committee; became Chair on Special Aging

Cong.	Ranking	Years in: Senate	Comm.	Date of Assignment
108th	Maj-9th	7	1	Jan. 15, 2003

SENATE SELECT AND SPECIAL COMMITTEES:

1st SPECIAL YEAR 2000 TECHNOLOGY PROBLEM
Dates: Apr. 28, 1998-Feb. 29, 2000
Termination: Senate Print 106-42 issued

Cong.	Ranking	Years in: Senate	Comm.	Date of Assignment
105th	Maj-3rd	2	1	Apr. 28, 1998
106th	Maj-3rd	3	1	Continued

2nd INDIAN AFFAIRS (Permanent)
Dates: Jan. 15, 2003-Jan. 3, 2009
Departure: Left the Senate; lost re-election

Cong.	Ranking	Years in: Senate	Comm.	Date of Assignment
108th	Maj-7th	7	1	Jan. 15, 2003
109th	Maj-6th	9	2	Jan. 6, 2005
110th	Min-6th	11	4	Jan. 12, 2007

3rd SPECIAL AGING (Permanent)
Dates: Apr. 30, 2002-Jan. 3, 2009
Departure: Left the Senate; lost re-election

Cong.	Ranking	Years in: Senate	Comm.	Date of Assignment
+107th	MnR-2nd	6	1	Apr. 30, 2002
108th	Maj-5th	7	1	Jan. 15, 2003
109th	Maj-Chr	9	3	Jan. 6, 2005
110th	Min-RM	11	5	Jan. 12, 2007

JOINT COMMITTEES:

1st JOINT PRINTING
Senate Dates: Mar. 13, 2003-Jan. 6, 2005
Departure: Left committee; no new assignment

Cong.	Ranking	Years in: Senate	Comm.	Date of Assignment
108th	Maj-3rd	7	1	Mar. 13, 2003

Lamar S. Smith (R-Tex.)

Dates: Nov. 19, 1947
House: Jan. 3, 1987-date
Serving in the 111th Congress

HOUSE STANDING COMMITTEES:

1st JUDICIARY
Dates: Jan. 21, 1987-date
Departure: Still serving in the 111th Congress

Cong.	Ranking	Terms in: House	Comm.	Date of Assignment
103rd	Min-8th	4	4	Jan. 5, 1993
104th	Maj-7th	5	5	Jan. 4, 1995
105th	Maj-6th	6	6	Jan. 7, 1997
106th	Maj-6th	7	7	Jan. 6, 1999
107th	Maj-5th	8	8	Jan. 6, 2001
108th	Maj-4th	9	9	Jan. 28, 2003
109th	Maj-4th	10	10	Jan. 26, 2005
110th	Min-RM	11	11	Jan. 4, 2007
111th	Min-RM	12	12	Jan. 6, 2009

**2nd SCIENCE, SPACE AND TECHNOLOGY, 100-102
SCIENCE, 106-111**
1st Dates: Jan. 21, 1987-Jan. 3, 1993
1st Departure: Moved to Budget
2nd Dates: Jan. 6, 1999-date
2nd Departure: Still serving in the 111th Congress

Cong.	Ranking	Terms in: House	Comm.	Date of Assignment
106th	Maj-3rd	7 *2	1	Jan. 6, 1999
107th	Maj-3rd	8 *2	2	Jan. 6, 2001
108th	Maj-2nd	9 *2	3	Jan. 28, 2003
109th	Maj-3rd	10 *2	4	Jan. 26, 2005
110th	Min-3rd	11 *2	5	Jan. 10, 2007
111th	Min-3rd	12 *2	6	Jan. 9, 2009

3rd BUDGET
Dates: Jan. 5, 1993-Jan. 3, 1999
Departure: Returned to Science

Cong.	Ranking	Terms in: House	Comm.	Date of Assignment
103rd	Min-8th	4	1	Jan. 5, 1993
104th	Maj-8th	5	2	Jan. 4, 1995
105th	Maj-6th	6	3	Jan. 7, 1997

4th STANDARDS OF OFFICIAL CONDUCT
1st Dates: Sep. 29, 1997-Jan. 3, 2001
1st Departure: Left committee; no new assignment
2nd Dates: Feb. 2, 2005-Jan. 3, 2007
2nd Departure: Left committee; became Ranking Member on Judiciary

Cong.	Ranking	Terms in: House	Comm.	Date of Assignment
105th	Maj-2nd	6 *1	1	Sep. 29, 1997
106th	Maj-Chr	7 *1	2	Jan. 6, 1999
109th	Maj-3rd	10 *2	1	Feb. 2, 2005

5th HOMELAND SECURITY
Dates: Feb. 9, 2005-date
Departure: Still serving in the 111th Congress

Cong.	Ranking	Terms in: House	Comm.	Date of Assignment
109th	Maj-3rd	10	2	Feb. 9, 2005
110th	Min-2nd	11	3	Jan. 10, 2007
111th	Min-2nd	12	4	Jan. 9, 2009

HOUSE SELECT AND SPECIAL COMMITTEES:

1st SELECT CHILDREN, YOUTH AND FAMILIES (Temporary)
Dates: Apr. 4, 1989-Jan. 3, 1993
Termination: Committee not renewed in 1993

2nd SELECT ETHICS
Dates: Jan. 7, 1997-Jan. 21, 1997
Termination: House Report 105-1 filed, Jan. 17, 1997

Cong.	Ranking	Terms in: House	Comm.	Date of Assignment
105th	MjR-1st	6	1	Jan. 7, 1997

3rd SELECT HOMELAND SECURITY
Dates: Feb. 12, 2003-Jan. 3, 2005
Departure: Continued on reorganized standing committee

Cong.	Ranking	Terms in: House	Comm.	Date of Assignment
108th	Maj-11th	9	1	Feb. 12, 2003

JOINT COMMITTEES:

1st JOINT ECONOMIC
House Dates: May 1, 2001-Jan. 3, 2003
Departure: Moved to Select Homeland Security

Cong.	Ranking	Terms in: House	Comm.	Date of Assignment
107th	Maj-3rd	8	1	May 1, 2001

Linda Smith (R-Wash.)

Dates: July 16, 1950
House: Jan. 3, 1995-Jan. 3, 1999
Left the House: Lost U.S. Senate election in 1998

HOUSE STANDING COMMITTEES:

1st RESOURCES
Dates: Jan. 4, 1995-Jan. 3, 1999
Departure: Left the House; lost Senate election

Cong.	Ranking	Terms in: House	Comm.	Date of Assignment
104th	Maj-18th	1	1	Jan. 4, 1995
105th	Maj-14th	2	2	Jan. 7, 1997

2nd SMALL BUSINESS
Dates: Jan. 4, 1995-Jan. 3, 1999
Departure: Left the House; lost Senate election

Cong.	Ranking	Terms in: House	Comm.	Date of Assignment
104th	Maj-8th	1	1	Jan. 4, 1995
105th	Maj-6th	2	2	Jan. 21, 1997

Neal E. Smith (D-Iowa)

Dates: Mar. 23, 1920
House: Jan. 3, 1959-Jan. 3, 1995
Left the House: Defeated for re-election in 1994

HOUSE STANDING COMMITTEES:

1st GOVERNMENT OPERATIONS
Dates: Jan. 19, 1959-Jan. 3, 1963
Departure: Left committee; had moved to Appropriations earlier

2nd EDUCATION AND LABOR
Dates: Feb. 6, 1961-Aug. 28, 1962
Departure: Resigned committee; moved to Appropriations

3rd APPROPRIATIONS
Dates: Aug. 28, 1962-Jan. 3, 1995
Departure: Left the House; lost re-election

Cong.	Ranking	Terms in: House	Comm.	Date of Assignment
103rd	Maj-3rd	18	17	Jan. 5, 1993

4th BUDGET
Dates: Aug. 14, 1974-Jan. 3, 1977
Departure: Left committee; became Chair of Small Business

5th SMALL BUSINESS
Dates: Jan. 20, 1975-Jan. 3, 1995
Departure: Left the House; lost re-election

Cong.	Ranking	Terms in: House	Comm.	Date of Assignment
103rd	Maj-2nd	18	15	Jan. 5, 1993

HOUSE SELECT AND SPEC]AL COMMITTEES:

1st SELECT SMALL BUSINESS
Dates: Feb. 16, 1965-Jan. 3, 1975
Departure: Continued on reorganized standing committee

2nd SELECT CAMPAIGN EXPENDITURES
Dates: From assignment to commencement of the new Congress, for the 1966 through 1974 elections
Departure: Committees terminated for those elections

3rd SELECT U.S. INVOLVEMENT IN SOUTHEAST ASIA
Dates: June 15, 1970-July 6, 1970
Termination: House Report 1276 (91-2) filed

Nick H. Smith (R-Mich.)

Dates: Nov. 5, 1934
House: Jan. 3, 1993-Jan. 3, 2005
Left the House: Retired in 2004

HOUSE STANDING COMMITTEES:

1st BUDGET
Dates: Jan. 5, 1993-Jan. 3, 2001
Departure: Moved to International Relations

Cong.	Ranking	Terms in: House	Comm.	Date of Assignment
103rd	Min-15th	1	1	Jan. 5, 1993
104th	Maj-13th	2	2	Jan. 4, 1995
105th	Maj-9th	3	3	Jan. 7, 1997
106th	Maj-7th	4	4	Jan. 6, 1999

2nd SCIENCE, SPACE AND TECHNOLOGY, 103
SCIENCE, 106-108
1st Dates: Jan. 5, 1993-Jan. 3, 1995
1st Departure: Left committee; no new assignment
2nd Dates: Jan. 6, 1999-Jan. 3, 2005
2nd Departure: Left the House; retired

Cong.	Ranking	Terms in: House	Comm.	Date of Assignment
103rd	Min-15th	1 *1	1	Jan. 5, 1993
106th	Maj-9th	4 *2	1	Jan. 6, 1999
107th	Maj-9th	5 *2	2	Jan. 6, 2001
108th	Maj-8th	6 *2	3	Jan. 28, 2003

3rd AGRICULTURE
Dates: May 27, 1993-Jan. 3, 2005
Departure: Left the House; retired

Cong.	Ranking	Terms in: House	Comm.	Date of Assignment
103rd	MnR-1st	1	1	May 27, 1993
104th	Maj-13th	2	2	Jan. 4, 1995
105th	Maj-10th	3	3	Jan. 7, 1997
106th	Maj-8th	4	4	Jan. 6, 1999

Cong.	Ranking	Terms in: House	Comm.	Date of Assignment
107th	Maj-5th	5	5	Jan. 6, 2001
108th	Maj-5th	6	6	Jan. 28, 2003

4th INTERNATIONAL RELATIONS
Dates: Jan. 6, 2001-Jan. 3, 2005
Departure: Left the House; retired

Cong.	Ranking	Terms in: House	Comm.	Date of Assignment
107th	Maj-20th	5	1	Jan. 6, 2001
108th	Maj-17th	6	2	Jan. 28, 2003

Robert C. Smith (R-N.H.)

Dates: Mar. 30, 1941
House: Jan. 3, 1985-Dec. 4, 1990
Left the House: Resigned; elected to U.S. Senate in 1990
Senate: Dec. 7, 1990-Jan. 3, 2003
Left the Senate: Defeated for re-nomination in 2002
Served as a Republican: Jan. 3, 1985-July 13, 1999
Served as an Independent: July 13, 1999-Nov. 1, 1999
Served as a Republican: Nov. 1, 1999-Jan. 3, 2003

S: Smith was appointed to the 101st Congress, Dec. 7, 1990, to fill the vacancy caused by the resignation of U.S. Senator Gordon Humphrey (R-N.H.). Smith had been elected to succeed Humphrey in the 102nd Congress. Smith was not seated nor assigned to committees because the 101st Congress was not in session.

HOUSE STANDING COMMITTEES:

1st SCIENCE AND TECHNOLOGY, 99
SCIENCE, SPACE AND TECHNOLOGY, 100-101
Dates: Jan. 30, 1985-Mar. 7, 1990
Departure: Left committee; had moved earlier to Armed Services

2nd SMALL BUSINESS
Dates: Jan. 30, 1985-Jan. 3, 1987
Departure: Moved to Veterans Affairs

3rd VETERANS AFFAIRS
Dates: Jan. 21, 1987-Dec. 4, 1990
Departure: Left the House for the Senate

4th ARMED SERVICES
Dates: Nov. 3, 1989-Dec. 4, 1990
Departure: Left the House for the Senate

HOUSE SELECT AND SPECIAL COMMITTEES:

1st SELECT CHILDREN, YOUTH AND FAMILIES (Temporary)
Dates: Mar. 25, 1985-Jan. 3, 1987
Departure: Moved to Veterans Affairs

SENATE STANDING COMMITTEES:

1st ARMED SERVICES
Dates: Feb. 5, 1991-Jan. 3, 2003
Departure: Left the Senate; lost re-nomination

Cong.	Ranking	Years in: Senate	Comm.	Date of Assignment
103rd	Min-7th	3	2	Jan. 7, 1993
104th	Maj-7th	5	4	Jan. 4, 1995
105th	Maj-5th	7	6	Jan. 9, 1997
106th	Maj-4th	9	8	Jan. 7, 1999
107th	Maj-4th	11	10	Jan. 25, 2001
+107th	Min-4th	11	11	June 6, 2001

2nd ENVIRONMENT AND PUBLIC WORKS
Dates: Feb. 5, 1991-Jan. 3, 2003
Ch2: Succeeded John F. Chafee (R-R.I.) as Chair on Nov. 9, 1999. Chafee had died.
Ch1: Replaced by James M. Jeffords (Ind.Vt.) following party control shift on June 6, 2001and became RM2.
Departure: Left the Senate; lost re-nomination.

Cong.	Ranking	Years in: Senate	Comm.	Date of Assignment
103rd	Min-5th	3	2	Jan. 7, 1993
104th	Maj-3rd	5	4	Jan. 5, 1995
105th	Maj-3rd	7	6	Jan. 9, 1997
106th	Maj-3rd	9	8	Jan. 7, 1999
=106th	Maj-Ch2	9	8	Nov. 9, 1999
107th	Maj-Ch1	11	10	Jan. 25, 2001
+107th	Min-RM2	11	11	June 6, 2001

3rd GOVERNMENTAL AFFAIRS
1st Dates: Jan. 5, 1995-Jan. 3, 1997
1st Departure: Left committee; became Chair of Select Ethics
2nd Dates: May 21, 1997-Mar. 4, 1998
2nd Departure: Temporary assignment ended

Cong.	Ranking	Years in: Senate	Comm.	Date of Assignment
104th	Maj-8th	5 *1	1	Jan. 5, 1995
105th	Maj-Tmp	7 *2	1	May 21, 1997

4th JUDICIARY
Dates: Jan. 7, 1999-Jan. 25, 2001
Departure: Left committee; no new assignment

Cong.	Ranking	Years in: Senate	Comm.	Date of Assignment
106th	Maj-10th	9	1	Jan. 7, 1999

SENATE SELECT AND SPECIAL COMMITTEES:

1st SELECT POW-MIA AFFAIRS
Dates: Aug. 2, 1991-Feb. 3, 1993
Termination: Senate Report 1 (103-1) filed

2nd SELECT ETHICS (Permanent)
Dates: Jan. 26, 1993-Jan. 25, 2001
Departure: Left committee; no new assignment

Cong.	Ranking	Years in: Senate	Comm.	Date of Assignment
103rd	Min-3rd	3	1	Jan. 26, 1993
104th	Maj-2nd	5	2	Jan. 11, 1995
105th	Maj-Chr	7	4	Jan. 9, 1997
106th	Maj-Ch1	9	6	Jan. 7, 1999

JOINT COMMITTEES:

1st JOINT ECONOMIC
Senate Dates: Apr. 16, 1991-Jan. 5, 1993
Departure: Moved to Select Ethics

Robert F. Smith (R-Ore.)

Dates: June 16, 1931
House 1: Jan. 3, 1983-Jan. 3, 1995

Left the House 1: Retired and returned
House 2: Jan. 3, 1997-Jan. 3, 1999
Left the House 2: Retired in 1998

HOUSE STANDING COMMITTEES:

1st PUBLIC WORKS AND TRANSPORTATION
Dates: Jan. 6, 1983-Jan. 3, 1985
Departure: Moved to Agriculture

2nd AGRICULTURE
1st Dates: Jan. 30, 1985-Jan. 3, 1995
1st Departure: Left the House; retired
2nd Dates: Jan. 7, 1997-Jan. 3, 1999
2nd Departure: Left the House; retired

Cong.	Ranking	Terms in: House	Comm.	Date of Assignment
103rd	Min-5th	6 *1	5	Jan. 5, 1993
105th	Maj-Chr	7 *2	1	Jan. 7, 1997

3rd INTERIOR AND INSULAR AFFAIRS, 101-102
NATURAL RESOURCES, 103
RESOURCES, 105
1st Dates: Jan. 20, 1989-Jan. 3, 1995
1st Departure: Left the House; retired
2nd Dates: Jan. 7, 1997-Jan. 3, 1999
2nd Departure: Left the House; retired

Cong.	Ranking	Terms in: House	Comm.	Date of Assignment
103rd	Min-5th	6 *1	3	Jan. 5, 1993
105th	Maj-20th	7 *2	1	Jan. 7, 1997

HOUSE SELECT AND SPECIAL COMMITTEES:

1st SELECT HUNGER (Temporary)
Dates: Mar. 13, 1984-Jan. 3, 1993
Termination: Committee not renewed in 1993

Vincent K. Snowbarger (R-Kan.)

Dates: Oct. 16, 1949
House: Jan. 3, 1997-Jan. 3, 1999
Left the House: Defeated for re-election in 1998

HOUSE STANDING COMMITTEES:

1st BANKING AND FINANCIAL SERVICES
Dates: Jan. 7, 1997-Jan. 3, 1999
Departure: Left the House; lost re-election

Cong.	Ranking	Terms in: House	Comm.	Date of Assignment
105th	Maj-25th	1	1	Jan. 7, 1997

2nd GOVERNMENT REFORM AND OVERSIGHT
Dates: Jan. 7, 1997-Jan. 3, 1999
Departure: Left the House; lost re-election

Cong.	Ranking	Terms in: House	Comm.	Date of Assignment
105th	Maj-24th	1	1	Jan. 7, 1997

3rd SMALL BUSINESS
Dates: Jan. 21, 1997-Jan. 3, 1999
Departure: Left the House; lost re-election

Cong.	Ranking	Terms in: House	Comm.	Date of Assignment
105th	Maj-13th	1	1	Jan. 21, 1997

Olympia J.B. Snowe (R-Me.)

Dates: Feb. 21, 1947
House: Jan. 3, 1979-Jan. 3, 1995
Left the House: Elected to U.S. Senate in 1994
Senate: Jan. 3, 1995-date
Serving in the 111th Congress

HOUSE STANDING COMMITTEES:

1st GOVERNMENT OPERATIONS
Dates: Jan. 24, 1979-Jan. 3, 1981
Departure: Moved to Foreign Affairs

2nd SMALL BUSINESS
Dates: Jan. 24, 1979-Jan. 3, 1983
Departure: Moved to Joint Economic

3rd FOREIGN AFFAIRS
Dates: Jan. 28, 1981-Jan. 3, 1995
Departure: Left the House for the Senate

Cong.	Ranking	Terms in: House	Comm.	Date of Assignment
103rd	Min-5th	8	7	Jan. 5, 1993

4th BUDGET
Dates: Jan. 5, 1993-Jan. 3, 1995
Departure: Left the House for the Senate

Cong.	Ranking	Terms in: House	Comm.	Date of Assignment
103rd	Min-5th	8	1	Jan. 5, 1993

HOUSE SELECT AND SPECIAL COMMITTEES:

1st SELECT AGING (Permanent)
Dates: Jan. 25, 1979-Jan. 3, 1993
Termination: Committee not renewed in 1993

SENATE STANDING COMMITTEES:

1st BUDGET
Dates: Jan. 6, 1995-Jan. 15, 2003
Departure: Moved to Select Intelligence

Cong.	Ranking	Years in: Senate	Comm.	Date of Assignment
104th	Maj-10th	1	1	Jan. 6, 1995
105th	Maj-8th	3	3	Jan. 9, 1997
106th	Maj-8th	5	5	Jan. 7, 1999
107th	Maj-7th	7	7	Jan. 25, 2001
+107th	Min-7th	7	7	June 6, 2001

2nd COMMERCE, SCIENCE AND TRANSPORTATION
Dates: Jan. 4, 1995-date
Departure: Still serving in the 11tth Congress

Cong.	Ranking	Years in: Senate	Comm.	Date of Assignment
104th	Maj-9th	1	1	Jan. 4, 1995
105th	Maj-7th	3	3	Jan. 9, 1997

106th	Maj-7th	5	5	Jan. 7, 1999
107th	Maj-6th	7	7	Jan. 25, 2001
+107th	Min-6th	7	7	June 6, 2001
108th	Maj-6th	9	9	Jan. 14, 2003
109th	Maj-6th	11	10	Jan. 3, 2005
110th	Min-5th	13	13	Jan. 12, 2007
111th	Min-2nd	15	15	Jan. 21, 2009

3rd FOREIGN RELATIONS
Dates: Jan. 5, 1995-Jan. 9, 1997
Departure: Moved to Armed Services

Cong.	Ranking	Years in: Senate	Comm.	Date of Assignment
104th	Maj-6th	1	1	Jan. 5, 1995

4th SMALL BUSINESS renamed June 29, 2001
SMALL BUSINESS AND ENTREPRENEURSHIP
Dates: Jan. 17, 1995-date
Departure: Still serving in the 111th Congress

Cong.	Ranking	Years in: Senate	Comm.	Date of Assignment
104th	Maj-11th	1	1	Jan. 17, 1995
105th	Maj-8th	3	2	Jan. 9, 1997
106th	Maj-5th	5	4	Jan. 7, 1999
107th	Maj-4th	7	7	Jan. 25, 2001
+107th	Min-4th	7	7	June 6, 2001
108th	Maj-Chr	9	8	Jan. 15, 2003
109th	Maj-Chr	11	10	Jan. 6, 2005
110th	Min-RM	13	12	Jan. 12, 2007
111th	Min-RM	15	15	Jan. 21, 2009

5th ARMED SERVICES
Dates: Jan. 9, 1997-Jan. 25, 2001
Departure: Moved to Finance

Cong.	Ranking	Years in: Senate	Comm.	Date of Assignment
105th	Maj-9th	3	1	Jan. 9, 1997
106th	Maj-7th	5	2	Jan. 7, 1999

6th FINANCE
Dates: Jan. 25, 2001-date
Departure: Still serving in 111th Congress

Cong.	Ranking	Years in: Senate	Comm.	Date of Assignment
107th	Maj-9th	7	1	Jan. 25, 2001
+107th	Min-8th	7	1	July 10, 2001
108th	Maj-5th	9	2	Jan. 15, 2003
109th	Maj-4th	11	4	Jan. 6, 2005
110th	Min-4th	13	6	Jan. 12, 2007
111th	Min-3rd	15	8	Jan. 21, 2009

SENATE SELECT AND SPECIAL COMMITTEES:

1st SELECT INTELLIGENCE (Permanent)
Dates: Jan. 15, 2003-date
Departure: Still serving in 111th Congress

Cong.	Ranking	Years in: Senate	Comm.	Date of Assignment
108th	Maj-6th	9	1	Jan. 15, 2003
109th	Maj-6th	11	2	Jan. 6, 2005
110th	Min-6th	13	4	Jan. 12, 2007
111th	Min-3rd	15	7	Jan. 21, 2009

JOINT COMMITTEES:

1st JOINT ECONOMIC
House Dates: Jan. 25, 1983-Jan. 3, 1993
Departure: Moved to House Budget

Victor F. Snyder (D-Ark.)

Dates: Sept. 27, 1947
House: Jan. 3, 1997-date
Serving in the 111th Congress

HOUSE STANDING COMMITTEES:

1st NATIONAL SECURITY, 105
ARMED SERVICES, 106-111
Dates: Jan. 7, 1997-date
Departure: Still serving in the 111th Congress

Cong.	Ranking	Terms in: House	Comm.	Date of Assignment
105th	Min-19th	1	1	Jan. 7, 1997
106th	Min-15th	2	2	Jan. 6, 1999
107th	Min-13th	3	3	Jan. 31, 2001
108th	Min-9th	4	4	Jan. 28, 2003
109th	Min-9th	5	5	Jan. 26, 2005
110th	Maj-8th	6	6	Jan. 10, 2007
111th	Maj-7th	7	7	Jan. 9, 2009

2nd VETERANS AFFAIRS
Dates: Feb. 6, 1997-date
Departure: Still serving in the 111th Congress

Cong.	Ranking	Terms in: House	Comm.	Date of Assignment
105th	Min-13th	1	1	Feb. 6, 1997
106th	Min-9th	2	2	Jan. 6, 1999
107th	Min-9th	3	3	Jan. 31, 2001
108th	Min-5th	4	4	Jan. 28, 2003
109th	Min-5th	5	5	Jan. 26, 2005
110th	Maj-3rd	6	6	Jan. 12, 2007
111th	Maj-3rd	7	7	Jan. 9, 2009

JOINT COMMITTEES:

1st JOINT ECONOMIC
House Dates: Feb. 3, 2009-date
Departure: Still serving in the 111th Congress

Cong.	Ranking	Terms in: House	Comm.	Date of Assignment
111th	Maj-6th	7	1	Feb. 3, 2009

Michael E. Sodrel (R-Ind.)

Dates: Dec. 17, 1945
House: Jan. 3, 2005-Jan. 3, 2007
Left the House: Defeated for re-election in 2006

HOUSE STANDING COMMITTEES:

1st SCIENCE
Dates: Jan. 26, 2005-Jan. 3, 2007
Departure: Left the House; lost re-election

Cong.	Ranking	Terms in: House	Comm.	Date of Assignment
109th	Maj-21st	1	1	Jan. 26, 2005

2nd SMALL BUSINESS
Dates: Jan. 26, 2005-Jan. 3, 2007
Departure: Left the House; lost re-election

		Terms in:		Date of
Cong.	Ranking	House	Comm.	Assignment
109th	Maj-14th	1	1	Jan. 26, 2005

3rd TRANSPORTATION AND INFRASTRUCTURE
Dates: Jan. 26, 2005-Jan. 3, 2007
Departure: Left the House; lost re-election

		Terms in:		Date of
Cong.	Ranking	House	Comm.	Assignment
109th	Maj-33rd	1	1	Jan. 26, 2005

4th AGRICULTURE
Dates: Mar. 9, 2006-Jan. 3, 2007
Departure: Left the House; lost re-election

		Terms in:		Date of
Cong.	Ranking	House	Comm.	Assignment
109th	MjR-2nd	1	1	Mar. 9, 2006

Hilda L. Solis (D-Cal.)

Dates: Oct. 20, 1957
House: Jan. 3, 2001-Feb. 24, 2009
Left the House: Resigned; appointed Secretary of Labor in 2009
Note: Ms. Solis served in the 111th Congress but was unassigned to committees pending her Senate confirmation as Secretary of Labor

HOUSE STANDING COMMITTEES:

1st EDUCATION AND THE WORKFORCE
Dates: Jan. 31, 2001-Jan. 3, 2003
Departure: Moved to Energy and Commerce

		Terms in:		Date of
Cong.	Ranking	House	Comm.	Assignment
107th	Min-22nd	1	1	Jan. 31, 2001

2nd RESOURCES, 107
NATURAL RESOURCES, 110
1st Dates: Feb. 8, 2001-Jan. 3, 2003
1st Departure: Moved to Energy and Commerce
2nd Dates: Jan. 18, 2007-Jan. 3, 2009
2nd Departure: Left the House; appointed to Cabinet

		Terms in:		Date of
Cong.	Ranking	House	Comm.	Assignment
107th	Min-22nd	1 *1	1	Feb. 8, 2001
110th	Maj-25th	4 *2	1	Jan. 18, 2007

3rd ENERGY AND COMMERCE
Dates: Jan. 28, 2003-Jan. 3, 2009
Departure: Left the House; appointed to Cabinet

		Terms in:		Date of
Cong.	Ranking	House	Comm.	Assignment
108th	Min-26th	2	1	Jan. 28, 2003
109th	Min-22nd	3	2	Jan. 26, 2005
110th	Maj-20th	4	3	Jan. 4, 2007

HOUSE SELECT AND SPECIAL COMMITTEES:

1st SELECT ENERGY INDEPENDENCE AND GLOBAL WARMING
Dates: Mar. 9, 2007-Jan. 3, 2009
Departure: Left the House; appointed to Cabinet

		Terms in:		Date of
Cong.	Ranking	House	Comm.	Assignment
110th	Maj-5th	4	1	Mar. 9, 2007

Gerald B.H. Solomon (R-N.Y.)

Dates: Aug. 14, 1930-Oct. 26, 2001
House: Jan. 3, 1979-Jan. 3, 1999
Left the House: Retired in 2000

HOUSE STANDING COMMITTEES:

1st PUBLIC WORKS AND TRANSPORTATION
Dates: Jan. 24, 1979-Jan. 3, 1983
Departure: Moved to Foreign Affairs

2nd VETERANS AFFAIRS
Dates: Oct. 1, 1980-Jan. 3, 1989
Departure: Moved to Rules

3rd FOREIGN AFFAIRS
Dates: Jan. 6, 1983-Jan. 3, 1989
Departure: Moved to Rules

4th RULES
Dates: Jan. 20, 1989-Jan. 3, 1999
Departure: Left the House; retired

		Terms in:		Date of
Cong.	Ranking	House	Comm.	Assignment
103rd	Min-RM	8	3	Jan. 5, 1993
104th	Maj-Chr	9	4	Jan. 4, 1995
105th	Maj-Chr	10	5	Jan. 7, 1997

HOUSE SELECT AND SPECIAL COMMITTEES:

1st SELECT COMMITTEES II (Patterson)
Dates: July 10, 1979-Apr. 1, 1980
Termination: House Report 866 (95-2) filed

JOINT COMMITTEES:

1st JOINT ORGANIZATION OF CONGRESS (Ad Hoc)
House Dates: Aug. 10, 1992-Dec. 17, 1993
Termination: House Report 103-413 filed

		Terms in:		Date of
Cong.	Ranking	House	Comm.	Assignment
103rd	Min-3rd	8	2	Jan. 5, 1993

Mark E. Souder (R-Ind.)

Dates: July 18, 1950
House: Jan. 3, 1995-May 21, 2010
Left the House: Resigned and retired

HOUSE STANDING COMMITTEES:

1st ECONOMIC AND EDUCATIONAL OPPORTUNITIES, 104
EDUCATION AND THE WORKFORCE, 105-109
EDUCATION AND LABOR, 110-111
1st Dates: Jan. 4, 1995-Feb. 11, 2003
1st Departure: Resigned committee; moved to Select Homeland Security
2nd Dates: Feb. 2, 2005-May 21, 2010
2nd Departure: Resigned and retired

Cong.	Ranking	Terms in: House	Comm.	Date of Assignment
104th	Maj-22nd	1 *1	1	Jan. 4, 1995
105th	Maj-16th	2 *1	2	Jan. 7, 1997
106th	Maj-14th	3 *1	3	Jan. 6, 1999
107th	Maj-11th	4 *1	4	Jan. 6, 2001
108th	Maj-9th	5 *1	5	Jan. 28, 2003
109th	Maj-6th	6 *2	1	Feb. 2, 2005
110th	Min-5th	7 *2	2	Jan. 10, 2007
111th	Min-5th	8 *2	3	Jan. 9, 2009

2nd GOVERNMENT REFORM AND OVERSIGHT, 104-105
GOVERNMENT REFORM, 106-109
OVERSIGHT AND GOVERNMENT REFORM, 110-111
Dates: Jan. 4, 1995-May 21, 2010
Departure: Resigned and retired

Cong.	Ranking	Terms in: House	Comm.	Date of Assignment
104th	Maj-19th	1	1	Jan. 4, 1995
105th	Maj-14th	2	2	Jan. 7, 1997
106th	Maj-12th	3	3	Jan. 6, 1999
107th	Maj-10th	4	4	Jan. 6, 2001
108th	Maj-7th	5	5	Jan. 28, 2003
109th	Maj-8th	6	6	Jan. 26, 2005
110th	Min-6th	7	7	Jan. 10, 2007
111th	Min-5th	8	8	Jan. 9, 2009

3rd SMALL BUSINESS
Dates: Jan. 4, 1995-Jan. 3, 1999
Departure: Moved to Resources

Cong.	Ranking	Terms in: House	Comm.	Date of Assignment
104th	Maj-17th	1	1	Jan. 4, 1995
105th	Maj-10th	2	2	Jan. 21, 1997

4th RESOURCES
Dates: Jan. 6, 1999-Feb. 2, 2005
Departure: Resigned committee; returned to Education and the Workforce

Cong.	Ranking	Terms in: House	Comm.	Date of Assignment
106th	Maj-23rd	3	1	Jan. 6, 1999
107th	Maj-21st	4	2	Jan. 6, 2001
108th	Maj-17th	5	3	Jan. 28, 2003
109th	Maj-14th	6	4	Jan. 26, 2005

5th HOMELAND SECURITY
Dates: Feb. 9, 2005-May 21, 2010
Departure: Resigned and retired

Cong.	Ranking	Terms in: House	Comm.	Date of Assignment
109th	Maj-8th	6	2	Feb. 9, 2005
110th	Min-4th	7	3	Jan. 10, 2007
111th	Min-3rd	8	4	Jan. 9, 2009

HOUSE SELECT AND SPECIAL COMMITTEES:

1st SELECT HOMELAND SECURITY
Dates: Feb. 12, 2003-Jan. 3, 2005
Departure: Continued on reorganized standing committee

Cong.	Ranking	Terms in: House	Comm.	Date of Assignment
108th	Maj-22nd	5	1	Feb. 12, 2003

Zachary T. Space (D-Ohio)

Dates: Jan. 27, 1961
House: Jan. 3, 2007-date
Serving in the 111th Congress

HOUSE STANDING COMMITTEES:

1st TRANSPORTATION AND INFRASTRUCTURE
Dates: Jan. 10, 2007-Jan. 3, 2009
Departure: Moved to Energy and Commerce

Cong.	Ranking	Terms in: House	Comm.	Date of Assignment
110th	Maj-29th	1	1	Jan. 10, 2007

2nd AGRICULTURE
Dates: Jan. 12, 2007-Jan. 3, 2009
Departure: Moved to Energy and Commerce

Cong.	Ranking	Terms in: House	Comm.	Date of Assignment
110th	Maj-16th	1	1	Jan. 12, 2007

3rd VETERANS AFFAIRS
Dates: Jan. 12, 2007-date
Departure: Still serving in the 111th Congress

Cong.	Ranking	Terms in: House	Comm.	Date of Assignment
110th	Maj-15th	1	1	Jan. 12, 2007
111th	Maj-14th	2	2	Jan. 21, 2009

4th ENERGY AND COMMERCE
Dates: Jan. 12, 2009-date
Departure: Still serving in the 111th Congress

Cong.	Ranking	Terms in: House	Comm.	Date of Assignment
111th	Maj-32nd	2	1	Jan. 7, 2009

Arlen Specter (D-Penn.)

Dates: Feb. 12, 1930
Senate: Jan. 3, 1981-date
Serving in the 111th Congress
Served as a Republican: Jan. 3, 1981-May 5, 2009
Served as a Democrat: May 5, 2009-date

SENATE STANDING COMMITTEES:

1st APPROPRIATIONS
1st Dates: Jan. 5, 1981-May 5, 2009
1st Departure: Changed party; seat vacated as Republican; returned as a Democrat in 18th slot
2nd Dates: May 5, 2009-date
2nd Departure: Still serving in the 111th Congress

Cong.	Ranking	Years in: Senate	Comm.	Date of Assignment
103rd	Min-5th	13 *1	13	Jan. 7, 1993
104th	Maj-4th	15 *1	14	Jan. 4, 1995
105th	Maj-3rd	17 *1	17	Jan. 9, 1997
106th	Maj-3rd	19 *1	19	Jan. 7, 1999
107th	Maj-4th	21 *1	21	Jan. 25, 2001
+107th	Min-4th	21 *1	21	June 6, 2001
108th	Maj-3rd	23 *1	23	Jan. 15, 2003
109th	Maj-3rd	25 *1	25	Jan. 6, 2005
110th	Min-3rd	27 *1	27	Jan. 12, 2007
111th	Min-2nd	29 *1	29	Jan. 21, 2009
111th	MjA-18th	29 *2	1	May 5, 2009

2nd JUDICIARY
1st Dates: Jan. 5, 1981-May 5, 2009
1st Departure: Changed party; seat vacated as Republican; returned as a Democrat in 12th slot

RM1: Replaced by Jefferson B. Sessions III (R-Ala.) as Ranking Member on May 5, 2009
2nd Dates: May 5, 2009-date
2nd Departure: Still serving in the 111th Congress

Cong.	Ranking	Years in: Senate	Comm.	Date of Assignment
103rd	Min-5th	13 *1	13	Jan. 7, 1993
104th	Maj-5th	15 *1	14	Jan. 4, 1995
105th	Maj-4th	17 *1	17	Jan. 9, 1997
106th	Maj-4th	19 *1	19	Jan. 7, 1999
107th	Maj-4th	21 *1	21	Jan. 25, 2001
+107th	Min-4th	21 *1	21	June 6, 2001
108th	Maj-3rd	23 *1	23	Jan. 15, 2003
109th	Maj-Chr	25 *1	25	Jan. 6, 2005
110th	Min-RM	27 *1	27	Jan. 12, 2007
111th	Min-RM1	29 *1	29	Jan. 21, 2009
111th	MjA-12th	29 *2	1	May 5, 2009

3rd VETERANS AFFAIRS
1st Dates: Jan. 5, 1981-May 5, 2009
Ch1: Replaced by John D. Rockefeler IV (D-W.Va.) following party control shift on June 6, 2001and became RM2
1st Departure: Changed party; seat vacated as Republican; returned as a Democrat in 10th slot
2nd Dates: May 5, 2009-date
2nd Departure: Still serving in the 111th Congress

Cong.	Ranking	Years in: Senate	Comm.	Date of Assignment
103rd	Min-2nd	13 *1	13	Jan. 21, 1993
104th	Maj-3rd	15 *1	15	Jan. 6, 1995
105th	Maj-Chr	17 *1	17	Jan. 9, 1997
106th	Maj-Chr	19 *1	19	Jan. 7, 1999
107th	Maj-Ch1	21 *1	21	Jan. 25, 2001
+107th	Min-RM2	21 *1	21	June 6, 2001
108th	Maj-Chr	23 *1	23	Jan. 15, 2003
109th	Maj-2nd	25 *1	25	Jan. 6, 2005
110th	Min-2nd	27 *1	27	Jan. 12, 2007
111th	Min-2nd	29 *1	29	Jan. 21, 2009
111th	MjA-10th	29 *2	1	May 5, 2009

4th BANKING, HOUSING AND URBAN AFFAIRS
Dates: Jan. 23, 1992-Jan. 7, 1993
Departure: Moved to Energy and Natural Resources

5th ENERGY AND NATURAL RESOURCES
Dates: Jan. 7, 1993-Jan. 3, 1995
Departure: Moved to Select Intelligence

Cong.	Ranking	Years in: Senate	Comm.	Date of Assignment
103rd	Min-8th	13	1	Jan. 7, 1993

6th GOVERNMENTAL AFFAIRS renamed Oct. 9, 2004
HOMELAND SECURITY AND GOVERNMENTAL AFFAIRS
1st Dates: Jan. 9, 1997-Jan. 25, 2001
1st Departure: Moved to Environment and Public Works
2nd Dates: Jan. 15, 2003-Jan. 6, 2005
2nd Departure: Left committee; became Chair of Judiciary

Cong.	Ranking	Years in: Senate	Comm.	Date of Assignment
105th	Maj-9th	17 *1	1	Jan. 9, 1997
106th	Maj-8th	19 *1	2	Jan. 7, 1999
108th	Maj-5th	23 *2	1	Jan. 15, 2003

7th ENVIRONMENT AND PUBLIC WORKS
1st Dates: Jan. 25, 2001-Jan. 15, 2003
1st Departure: Returned to Governmental Affairs
2nd Dates: Jan. 21, 2009-May 5, 2009
2nd Departure: Changed party; seat vacated as Republican; returned as a Democrat in 12th slot

3rd Dates: May 5, 2009-date
3rd Departure: Still serving in the 111th Congress

Cong.	Ranking	Years in: Senate	Comm.	Date of Assignment
107th	Maj-8th	21 *1	1	Jan. 25, 2001
+107th	Min-8th	21 *1	1	June 6, 2001
111th	Min-5th	29 *2	1	Jan. 21, 2009
111th	MjA-12th	29 *3	1	May 5, 2009

SENATE SELECT AND SPECIAL COMMITTEES:

1st SELECT INTELLIGENCE (Permanent)
1st Dates: Jan. 3, 1985-Feb. 5, 1991
1st Departure: Left committee; became Ranking Member on Veterans Affairs
2nd Dates: Jan. 6, 1995-Jan. 9, 1997
2nd Departure: Moved to Governmental Affairs

Cong.	Ranking	Years in: Senate	Comm.	Date of Assignment
104th	Maj-Chr	15 *2	1	Jan. 6, 1995

2nd JUDGE ALCEE L. HASTINGS IMPEACHMENT
Dates: Mar. 16, 1989-Aug. 3, 1989
Termination: Senate Hearing 101-194, Parts 1-2A.

3rd SPECIAL AGING (Permanent)
1st Dates: June 6, 1991-Jan. 6, 1995
1st Departure: Returned to Select Intelligence as Chair
2nd Dates: Jan. 12, 2007-May 5, 2009
2nd Departure: Changed party; seat vacated as Republican; returned as a Democrat in 12th slot
3rd Dates: May 5, 2009-date
3rd Departure: Still serving in the 111th Congress

Cong.	Ranking	Years in: Senate	Comm.	Date of Assignment
103rd	Min-10th	13 *1	2	Jan. 21, 1993
110th	Min-10th	27 *2	1	Jan. 12, 2007
111th	Min-4th	29 *2	3	Jan. 21, 2009
111th	MjA-12th	29 *3	1	May 5, 2009

K. Jacqueline Speier (D-Cal.)

Dates: May 14, 1950
House: April 8, 2008-date
Serving in the 111th Congress

H: Speier was elected to the 110th Congress by special election, April 8, 2008, to fill the vacancy caused by the death of U.S. Representative Thomas P. Lantos (D-Cal.).

HOUSE STANDING COMMITTEES:

1st FINANCIAL SERVICES
Dates: June 10, 2008-date
Departure: Still serving in the 111th Congress

Cong.	Ranking	Terms in: House	Comm.	Date of Assignment
110th	MjR-3rd	1	1	June 10, 2008
111th	Maj-32nd	2	2	Jan. 7, 2009

2nd OVERSIGHT AND GOVERNMENT REFORM
Dates: July 15, 2008-date
Departure: Still serving in the 111th Congress

Cong.	Ranking	Terms in: House	Comm.	Date of Assignment
110th	MjR-1st	1	1	July 15, 2008
111th	Maj-21st	2	2	Jan. 28, 2009

HOUSE SELECT AND SPECIAL COMMITTEES:

1st SELECT ENERGY INDEPENDENCE AND GLOBAL WARMING
Dates: Feb. 3, 2009-date
Departure: Still serving in the 111th Congress

Cong.	Ranking	Terms in: House	Comm.	Date of Assignment
111th	Maj-9th	2	1	Feb. 3, 2009

Floyd D. Spence (R-S.C.)

Dates: April 9, 1928-Aug. 16, 2001
House: Jan. 3, 1971-Aug. 16, 2001
Left the House: Died in office

HOUSE STANDING COMMITTEES:

1st ARMED SERVICES, 92-103
NATIONAL SECURITY, 104-105
ARMED SERVICES, 106-107
Dates: Feb. 4, 1971-Aug. 16, 2001
Departure: Died in office

Cong.	Ranking	Terms in: House	Comm.	Date of Assignment
103rd	Min-RM	12	12	Jan. 5, 1993
104th	Maj-Chr	13	13	Jan. 4, 1995
105th	Maj-Chr	14	14	Jan. 7, 1997
106th	Maj-Chr	15	15	Jan. 6, 1999
107th	Maj-2nd	16	16	Jan. 6, 2001

2nd STANDARDS OF OFFICIAL CONDUCT
Dates: Oct. 27, 1971-June 1, 1988
RM1: Spence was succeeded as Ranking Minority Member by John T. Myers (R-Ind.) on June 1, 1988
Departure: Left committee; no new assignment

3rd VETERANS AFFAIRS
Dates: Jan. 24, 1991-Aug. 16, 2001
Departure: Died in office

Cong.	Ranking	Terms in: House	Comm.	Date of Assignment
103rd	Min-6th	12	2	Jan. 5, 1993
104th	Maj-4th	13	3	Jan. 4, 1995
105th	Maj-4th	14	4	Jan. 21, 1997
106th	Maj-4th	15	5	Jan. 6, 1999
107th	Maj-4th	16	6	Jan. 6, 2001

HOUSE SELECT AND SPECIAL COMMITTEES:

1st SELECT AGING (Permanent)
Dates: Feb. 2, 1987-Jan. 3, 1993
Termination: Committee not renewed in 1993

John M. Spratt Jr. (D-S.C.)

Dates: Nov. 1, 1942
House: Jan. 3, 1983-date
Serving in the 111th Congress

HOUSE STANDING COMMITTEES:

1st ARMED SERVICES, 98-103
NATIONAL SECURITY, 104-105
ARMED SERVICES, 106-111
Dates: Jan. 6, 1983-date
Departure: Still serving in the 111th Congress

Cong.	Ranking	Terms in: House	Comm.	Date of Assignment
103rd	Maj-10th	6	6	Jan. 5, 1993
104th	Min-6th	7	7	Jan. 4, 1995
105th	Min-4th	8	8	Jan. 7, 1997
106th	Min-3rd	9	9	Jan. 6, 1999
107th	Min-3rd	10	10	Jan. 31, 2001
108th	Min-2nd	11	11	Jan. 28, 2003
109th	Min-2nd	12	12	Jan. 26, 2005
110th	Maj-2nd	13	13	Jan. 10, 2007
111th	Maj-2nd	14	14	Jan. 7, 2009

2nd GOVERNMENT OPERATIONS, 98-103
GOVERNMENT REFORM AND OVERSIGHT, 104
1st Dates: Jan. 6, 1983-June 14, 1990
1st Departure: Moved to Budget
2nd Dates: Feb. 18, 1993-Jan. 3, 1997
2nd Departure: Returned to Budget

Cong.	Ranking	Terms in: House	Comm.	Date of Assignment
103rd	Maj-10th	6 *2	1	Feb. 18, 1993
104th	Min-7th	7 *2	2	Jan. 9, 1995

3rd BUDGET
1st Dates: June 14, 1990-Feb. 17, 1993
1st Departure: Resigned committee; returned to Government Operations
2nd Dates: Jan. 7, 1997-date
2nd Departure: Still serving in the 111th Congress

Cong.	Ranking	Terms in: House	Comm.	Date of Assignment
103rd	Maj-9th	6 *1	3	Jan. 5, 1993
105th	Min-RM	8 *2	1	Jan. 7, 1997
106th	Min-RM	9 *2	2	Jan. 6, 1999
107th	Min-RM	10 *2	3	Jan. 31, 2001
108th	Min-RM	11 *2	4	Jan. 8, 2003
109th	Min-RM	12 *2	5	Jan. 6, 2005
110th	Maj-Chr	13 *2	6	Jan. 4, 2007
111th	Maj-Chr	14 *2	7	Jan. 21, 2009

HOUSE SELECT AND SPECIAL COMMITTEES:

1st SELECT NATIONAL SECURITY CONCERNS WITH CHINA
Dates: June 22, 1998-Apr. 30, 1999
Termination: House Report 851 (105-2) filed, Jan. 3, 1999

Cong.	Ranking	Terms in: House	Comm.	Date of Assignment
105th	Min-2nd	8	1	June 22, 1998
106th	Min-2nd	9	2	Jan. 19, 1999

JOINT COMMITTEES:

1st JOINT ORGANIZATION OF CONGRESS (Ad Hoc)
House Dates: Oct. 9, 1992-Dec. 17, 1993
Termination: House Report 103-413 filed

Cong.	Ranking	Terms in: House	Comm.	Date of Assignment
103rd	Maj-5th	6	2	Jan. 5, 1993

Deborah Ann Stabenow (D-Mich.)

Dates: April 29, 1950
House: Jan. 3, 1997-Jan. 3, 2001
Left the House: Elected to U.S. Senate in 2000
Senate: Jan. 3, 2001-date
Serving in the 111th Congress

HOUSE STANDING COMMITTEES:

1st AGRICULTURE
Dates: Jan. 7, 1997-Jan. 3, 2001
Departure: Left the House for the Senate

Cong.	Ranking	Terms in: House	Comm.	Date of Assignment
105th	Min-19th	1	1	Jan. 7, 1997
106th	Min-17th	2	2	Jan. 6, 1999

2nd SCIENCE
Dates: Feb. 13, 1997-Jan. 3, 2001
Departure: Left the House for the Senate

Cong.	Ranking	Terms in: House	Comm.	Date of Assignment
105th	Min-18th	1	1	Feb. 13, 1997
106th	Min-15th	2	2	Jan. 6, 1999

SENATE STANDING COMMITTEES:

1st AGRICULTURE, NUTRITION AND FORESTRY
Dates: Jan. 25, 2001-date
Departure: Still serving in the 111th Congress

Cong.	Ranking	Years in: Senate	Comm.	Date of Assignment
107th	Min-8th	1	1	Jan. 25, 2001
+107th	Maj-8th	1	1	June 6, 2001
108th	Min-8th	3	2	Jan. 15, 2003
109th	Min-6th	5	4	Jan. 6, 2005
110th	Maj-6th	7	6	Jan. 12, 2007
111th	Maj-6th	9	8	Jan. 21, 2009

2nd BANKING, HOUSING AND URBAN AFFAIRS
Dates: Jan. 25, 2001-Jan. 12, 2007
Departure: Moved to Finance

Cong.	Ranking	Years in: Senate	Comm.	Date of Assignment
107th	Min-9th	1	1	Jan. 25, 2001
+107th	Maj-9th	1	1	June 6, 2001
108th	Min-9th	3	2	Jan. 15, 2003
109th	Min-8th	5	4	Jan. 6, 2005

3rd BUDGET
Dates: Jan. 25, 2001-date
Departure: Still serving in the 111th Congress

Cong.	Ranking	Years in: Senate	Comm.	Date of Assignment
107th	Min-10th	1	1	Jan. 25, 2001
+107th	Maj-10th	1	1	June 6, 2001
108th	Min-10th	3	2	Jan. 15, 2003
109th	Min-9th	5	4	Jan. 6, 2005
110th	Maj-7th	7	6	Jan. 12, 2007
111th	Maj-7th	9	8	Jan. 21, 2009

4th FINANCE
Dates: Jan. 12, 2007-date
Departure: Still serving in the 111th Congress

Cong.	Ranking	Years in: Senate	Comm.	Date of Assignment
110th	Maj-9th	7	1	Jan. 12, 2007
111th	Maj-9th	9	3	Jan. 21, 2009

4th ENERGY AND NATURAL RESOURCES
Dates: Jan. 21, 2009-date
Departure: Still serving in the 111th Congress

Cong.	Ranking	Years in: Senate	Comm.	Date of Assignment
111th	Maj-11th	9	1	Jan. 21, 2009

SENATE SELECT AND SPECIAL COMMITTEES:

1st SPECIAL AGING (Permanent)
Dates: Jan. 25, 2001-Jan. 6, 2005
Departure: Left committee; no new assignment

Cong.	Ranking	Years in: Senate	Comm.	Date of Assignment
107th	Min-9th	1	1	Jan. 25, 2001
+107th	Maj-10th	1	1	June 6, 2001
108th	Min-10th	3	2	Jan. 15, 2003

Fortney H. (Pete) Stark (D-Cal.)

Dates: Nov. 11, 1931
House: Jan. 3, 1973-date
Serving in the 111th Congress

HOUSE STANDING COMMITTEES:

1st BANKING AND CURRENCY
Dates: Jan. 24, 1973-Jan. 3, 1975
Departure: Moved to Ways and Means

2nd DISTRICT OF COLUMBIA
1st Dates: Jan. 24, 1973-Jan. 3, 1975
1st Departure: Moved to Ways and Means
2nd Dates: Jan. 27, 1977-Jan. 3, 1995
2nd Departure: Committee abolished; no new assignment

Cong.	Ranking	Terms in: House	Comm.	Date of Assignment
103rd	Maj-Chr	11 *2	9	Jan. 27, 1993

3rd WAYS AND MEANS
Dates: Jan. 20, 1975-date
Departure: Still serving in the 111th Congress
ChT: Temporary Chair replacing Charles Rangel (D-N.Y.), Mar. 3-Mar. 4, 2010

Cong.	Ranking	Terms in: House	Comm.	Date of Assignment
103rd	Maj-5th	11	10	Jan. 5, 1993
104th	Min-3rd	12	11	Jan. 4, 1995
105th	Min-2nd	13	12	Jan. 7, 1997
106th	Min-2nd	14	13	Jan. 6, 1999
107th	Min-2nd	15	14	Jan. 31, 2001
108th	Min-2nd	16	15	Jan. 28, 2003
109th	Min-2nd	17	16	Jan. 26, 2005
110th	Maj-2nd	18	17	Jan. 4, 2007
111th	Maj-2nd	19	18	Jan. 7, 2009
=111th	Maj-ChT	19	18	Mar. 3, 2010

HOUSE SELECT AND SPECIAL COMMITTEES:

1st SELECT NARCOTICS ABUSE AND CONTROL (Temporary)
Dates: Aug. 3, 1976-Jan. 3, 1993
Termination: Committee not renewed in 1993

JOINT COMMITTEES:

1st JOINT ECONOMIC
House Dates: Jan. 31, 1985-Jan. 3, 2005
Departure: Left committee, no new assignment

Cong.	Ranking	Terms in: House	Comm.	Date of Assignment
103rd	Maj-3rd	11	5	Jan. 27, 1993
104th	Min-1st	12	6	Jan. 19, 1995
105th	Min-1st	13	7	Mar. 11, 1997
106th	Min-1st	14	8	Mar. 25, 1999
107th	Min-1st	15	9	May 1, 2001
108th	Min-1st	16	10	Mar. 12, 2003

2nd JOINT TAXATION
Dates: Feb. 5, 1997-date
Departure: Still serving in the 111th Congress

Cong.	Ranking	Terms in: House	Comm.	Date of Assignment
105th	Min-2nd	13	1	Feb. 5, 1997 Ltr
106th	Min-2nd	14	2	Jan. 6, 1999 Ltr
107th	Min-2nd	15	3	Feb. 7, 2001 Ltr
108th	Min-2nd	16	4	Jan. 29, 2003 Ltr
109th	Min-2nd	17	5	Feb. 7, 2005 Ltr
110th	Maj-2nd	18	6	Jan. 17, 2007 Ltr
111th	Maj-2nd	19	7	Jan. 12, 2009 Ltr

Clifford B. Stearns (R-Fla.)

Dates: April 16, 1941
House: Jan. 3, 1989-date
Serving in the 111th Congress

HOUSE STANDING COMMITTEES:

1st BANKING, FINANCE AND URBAN AFFAIRS
Dates: Jan. 20, 1989-Jan. 3, 1993
Departure: Moved to Energy and Commerce

2nd VETERANS AFFAIRS
1st Dates: Jan. 20, 1989-Jan. 3, 1993
1st Departure: Moved to Energy and Commerce
2nd Dates: Returned May 27, 1993-date
2nd Departure: Still serving in the 111th Congress

Cong.	Ranking	Terms in: House	Comm.	Date of Assignment
103rd	Min-13th	3 *2	1	May 27, 1993
104th	Maj-10th	4 *2	2	Jan. 4, 1995
105th	Maj-9th	5 *2	3	Jan. 21, 1997
106th	Maj-9th	6 *2	4	Jan. 6, 1999
107th	Maj-8th	7 *2	5	Jan. 6, 2001
108th	Maj-6th	8 *2	6	Jan. 28, 2003
109th	Maj-4th	9 *2	7	Jan. 26, 2005
110th	Min-2nd	10 *2	8	Jan. 10, 2007
111th	Min-2nd	11 *2	9	Jan. 9, 2009

3rd ENERGY AND COMMERCE, 103
COMMERCE, 104-106
ENERGY AND COMMERCE
Dates: Jan. 5, 1993-date
Departure: Still serving in the 111th Congress

Cong.	Ranking	Terms in: House	Comm.	Date of Assignment
103rd	Min-11th	3	1	Jan. 5, 1993

Cong.	Ranking	Terms in: House	Comm.	Date of Assignment
104th	Maj-10th	4	2	Jan. 4, 1995
105th	Maj-9th	5	3	Jan. 7, 1997
106th	Maj-7th	6	4	Jan. 6, 1999
107th	Maj-5th	7	5	Jan. 6, 2001
108th	Maj-5th	8	6	Jan. 28, 2003
109th	Maj-5th	9	7	Jan. 6, 2005
110th	Min-5th	10	8	Jan. 10, 2007
111th	Min-4th	11	9	Jan. 9, 2009

HOUSE SELECT AND SPECIAL COMMITTEES:

1st SELECT AGING (Permanent)
Dates: Jan. 20, 1989-Jan. 3, 1993
Termination: Committee not renewed in 1993

Charles W. Stenholm (D-Tex.)

Dates: Oct. 26, 1938
House: Jan. 3, 1979-Jan. 3, 2005
Left the House: Defeated for re-election in 2004

HOUSE STANDING COMMITTEES:

1st AGRICULTURE
Dates: Jan. 24, 1979-Jan. 3, 2005
Departure: Left the House; lost re-election

Cong.	Ranking	Terms in: House	Comm.	Date of Assignment
103rd	Maj-7th	8	8	Jan. 5, 1993
104th	Min-4th	9	9	Jan. 4, 1995
105th	Min-RM	10	10	Jan. 7, 1997
106th	Min-RM	11	11	Jan. 6, 1999
107th	Min-RM	12	12	Jan. 31, 2001
108th	Min-RM	13	13	Jan. 8, 2003

2nd POST OFFICE AND CIVIL SERVICE
Dates: Jan. 24, 1979-Dec. 19, 1979
Departure: Resigned committee; moved to Small Business

3rd SMALL BUSINESS
Dates: Dec. 19, 1979-Jan. 3, 1987
Departure: Left committee; no new assignment

4th VETERANS AFFAIRS
Dates: Oct. 10, 1986-Jan. 3, 1991
Departure: Moved to Budget

5th BUDGET
Dates: Jan. 24, 1991-Jan. 3, 1997
Departure: Left committee; no new assignment

Cong.	Ranking	Terms in: House	Comm.	Date of Assignment
103rd	Maj-10th	8	2	Jan. 5, 1993
104th	Min-2nd	9	3	Jan. 4, 1995

6th ARMED SERVICES
Dates: Sep. 8, 2004-Jan. 3, 2005
Departure: Left the House; lost re-election

Cong.	Ranking	Terms in: House	Comm.	Date of Assignment
108th	MnR-3rd	13	1	Sep. 8, 2004

Theodore F. Stevens (R-Alas.)

Dates: Nov. 18, 1923
Senate: Dec. 23, 1968-Jan. 3, 2009
Left the Senate: Defeated for re-election in 2008

S: Stevens was appointed to the 90th Congress, Dec. 23, 1968, to fill the unexpired term caused by the death of U.S. Senator E.L. (Bob) Bartlett (D-Alas.) and was subsequently elected. Stevens was not seated nor assigned to committees because the 90th Congress was not in session.

SENATE STANDING COMMITTEES:

1st GOVERNMENT OPERATIONS
1st Dates: Jan. 14, 1969-Jan. 29, 1971
1st Departure: Moved to Commerce
GOVERNMENTAL AFFAIRS renamed Oct. 9, 2004
HOMELAND SECURITY AND GOVERNMENTAL AFFAIRS
2nd Dates: Feb. 22, 1977-May 21, 1997
2nd Departure: Temporary leave; campaign finance investigation
3rd Dates: Mar. 4, 1998-Jan. 3, 2009
Ch2: Replaced William V. Roth Jr. (R-Del.), who had become Chair of Finance, on Sep. 12, 1995
3rd Departure: Left the Senate; lost re-election

Cong.	Ranking	Years in: Senate	Comm.	Date of Assignment
103rd	Min-2nd	25 *2	16	Jan. 7, 1993
104th	Maj-2nd	27 *2	18	Jan. 5, 1995
=104th	Maj-Ch2	27 *2	19	Sep. 12, 1995
105th	Maj-3rd	29 *2	20	Jan. 9, 1997
105th	Maj-3rd	29 *3	1	Mar. 4, 1998
106th	Maj-3rd	31 *3	1	Jan. 7, 1999
107th	Maj-2nd	33 *3	3	Jan. 25, 2001
+107th	Min-2nd	33 *3	4	June 6, 2001
108th	Maj-2nd	35 *3	5	Jan. 15, 2003
109th	Maj-2nd	37 *3	7	Jan. 6, 2005
110th	Min-2nd	39 *3	9	Jan. 12, 2007

2nd INTERIOR AND INSULAR AFFAIRS
Dates: Jan. 14, 1969-Feb. 23, 1972
Departure: Moved to Appropriations

3rd POST OFFICE AND CIVIL SERVICE
Dates: Jan. 14, 1969-Feb. 22, 1977
Departure: Committee was reorganized into Governmental Affairs and seniority was continued.

4th COMMERCE reorganized Feb. 22, 1977
COMMERCE, SCIENCE AND TRANSPORTATION
1st Dates: Jan. 29, 1971-Jan. 23, 1979
1st Departure: Moved to Energy and Natural Resources
2nd Dates: Jan. 5, 1981-Jan. 3, 2009
2nd Departure: Left the Senate; lost re-election

Cong.	Ranking	Years in: Senate	Comm.	Date of Assignment
103rd	Min-4th	25 *2	13	Jan. 7, 1993
104th	Maj-3rd	27 *2	14	Jan. 4, 1995
105th	Maj-2nd	29 *2	17	Jan. 9, 1997
106th	Maj-2nd	31 *2	19	Jan. 7, 1999
107th	Maj-2nd	33 *2	21	Jan. 25, 2001
+107th	Min-2nd	33 *2	21	June 6, 2001
108th	Maj-2nd	35 *2	23	Jan. 15, 2003
109th	Maj-Chr	37 *2	25	Jan. 6, 2005
110th	Min-RM	39 *2	27	Jan. 12, 2007

5th VETERANS AFFAIRS
Dates: Jan. 29, 1971-Sep. 21, 1971
Departure: Moved to Rules and Administration

6th RULES AND ADMINISTRATION
1st Dates: Sep. 21, 1971-Feb. 23, 1972
1st Departure: Moved to Appropriations
2nd Dates: Feb. 21, 1985-Jan. 3, 2009
Ch1: Became Chair on Governmental Affairs; replaced as Chair by John W. Warner (R-Va.) on Sep. 12, 1995
2nd Departure: Left the Senate; lost re-election

Cong.	Ranking	Years in: Senate	Comm.	Date of Assignment
103rd	Min-RM	25 *2	8	Jan. 21, 1993
104th	Maj-Ch1	27 *2	10	Jan. 6, 1995
105th	Maj-3rd	29 *2	12	Jan. 9, 1997
106th	Maj-3rd	31 *2	14	Jan. 7, 1999
107th	Maj-4th	33 *2	16	Jan. 25, 2001
+107th	Min-4th	33 *2	17	June 6, 2001
108th	Maj-2nd	35 *2	18	Jan. 15, 2003
109th	Maj-2nd	37 *2	20	Jan. 6, 2005
110th	Min-2nd	39 *2	22	Jan. 12, 2007

7th APPROPRIATIONS
Dates: Feb. 23, 1972-Jan. 3, 2009
Ch1: Replaced by Robert C. Byrd (D-W.Va.) following party control shift on June 6, 2001, and became RM2
Departure: Left the Senate; lost re-election

Cong.	Ranking	Years in: Senate	Comm.	Date of Assignment
103rd	Min-2nd	25	21	Jan. 7, 1993
104th	Maj-2nd	27	23	Jan. 4, 1995
105th	Maj-Chr	29	25	Jan. 9, 1997
106th	Maj-Chr	31	27	Jan. 7, 1999
107th	Maj-Ch1	33	29	Jan. 25, 2001
+107th	Min-RM2	33	30	June 6, 2001
108th	Maj-Chr	35	31	Jan. 15, 2003
109th	Maj-2nd	37	33	Jan. 6, 2005
110th	Min-2nd	39	35	Jan. 12, 2007

8th ENERGY AND NATURAL RESOURCES
Dates: Jan. 23, 1979-Jan. 5, 1981
Departure: Returned to Commerce, Science and Transportation

9th SMALL BUSINESS
Dates: Feb. 2, 1989-Jan. 3, 1993
Dates: Left committee; no new assignment

SENATE SELECT AND SPECIAL COMMITTEES:

1st SELECT SMALL BUSINESS
Dates: Jan. 22, 1969-Feb. 23, 1971
Departure: Moved to Veterans Affairs, Commerce, and Appropriations; later returned to Small Business as a standing committee

2nd SELECT ETHICS (Permanent)
1st Dates: Jan. 3, 1983-Mar. 5, 1985
1st Departure: Returned to Rules and Administration
2nd Dates: Jan. 26, 1993-May 19, 1993
2nd Departure: Left committee; no new assignment

Cong.	Ranking	Years in: Senate	Comm.	Date of Assignment
103rd	Min-2nd	25 *2	1	Jan. 26, 1993

3rd SPECIAL YEAR 2000 TECHNOLOGY PROBLEM
Dates: Apr. 28, 1998-Feb. 29, 2000
Termination: Senate Print 106-42 issued

Cong.	Ranking	Years in: Senate	Comm.	Date of Assignment
105th	Min-ExO	40	1	Apr. 28, 1998
106th	Min-ExO	41	1	Continued

4th SELECT INTELLIGENCE (Permanent)
Dates: Jan. 27, 1993-Jan. 6, 1995
Departure: Left committee; became Chair of Rules and Administration

Cong.	Ranking	Years in: Senate	Comm.	Date of Assignment
103rd	Min-6th	25	1	Jan. 27, 1993

JOINT COMMITTEES:

1st JOINT PRINTING
Senate Dates: Apr. 17, 1985-Nov. 3, 1995
Departure: Removed from committee by S. Res. 192; became Chair of Governmental Affairs

Cong.	Ranking	Years in: Senate	Comm.	Date of Assignment
103rd	Min-1st	25	8	Jan. 28, 1993
104th	Maj-VCh	27	10	Jan. 17, 1995

2nd JOINT LIBRARY
Senate Dates: Jan. 29, 1987-Jan. 3, 2009
Departure: Left the Senate; lost re-election

Cong.	Ranking	Years in: Senate	Comm.	Date of Assignment
103rd	Min-2nd	25	6	Jan. 28, 1993
104th	Maj-2nd	27	8	Jan. 17, 1995
105th	Maj-VCh	29	10	Jan. 28, 1997
106th	Maj-Chr	31	13	Feb. 25, 1999
+107th	Min-1st	33	15	Sep. 19, 2001
108th	Maj-Chr	35	17	Mar. 13, 2003
109th	Maj-VCh	37	19	Mar. 4, 2005
110th	Min-2nd	39	21	Mar. 26, 2007

3rd JOINT ORGANIZATION OF CONGRESS (Ad Hoc)
Senate Dates: Sep. 25, 1992-Dec. 9, 1993
Termination: Senate Report 103-215 filed

Cong.	Ranking	Years in: Senate	Comm.	Date of Assignment
103rd	Min-4th	25	1	Continued

SENATE LEADERSHIP POSTS

1st SENATE MINORITY WHIP
Dates: Jan. 4, 1977-Jan. 3, 1981
Departure: Republican Party gained Senate majority in 1980

2nd SENATE MAJORITY WHIP
Dates: Dec. 2, 1980-Jan. 3, 1985
Departure: Lost contest for Majority Floor Leader to Robert J. Dole (R-Kans.)

3rd SENATE PRESIDENT *PRO TEMPORE*
Dates: Jan. 3, 2003-Jan. 3, 2007
Note: In the 108th Congress, Stevens replaced J. Strom Thurmond (R-S.C.) as Senate President *pro tempore* and held that post in the 109th Congress
Departure: Republican Party lost Senate majority in 2006

Cong.	Ranking	Years in: Senate	Post	Date of Service
108th	Maj-Ppt	36	1	Jan. 7, 2003
109th	Maj-Ppt	38	3	Jan. 4, 2005

Steve Stockman (R-Tex.)

Dates: Nov. 14, 1956
House: Jan. 3, 1995-Jan. 3, 1997
Left the House: Defeated for re-election in 1996

HOUSE STANDING COMMITTEES:

1st BANKING AND FINANCIAL SERVICES
Dates: Jan. 4, 1995-Jan. 3, 1997
Departure: Left the House; lost re-election

Cong.	Ranking	Terms in: House	Comm.	Date of Assignment
104th	Maj-24th	1	1	Jan. 4, 1995

2nd SCIENCE
Dates: Jan. 4, 1995-Jan. 3, 1997
Departure: Left the House; lost re-election

Cong.	Ranking	Terms in: House	Comm.	Date of Assignment
104th	Maj-19th	1	1	Jan. 4, 1995

3rd VETERANS AFFAIRS
Dates: Jan. 4, 1995-Feb. 15, 1995
Departure: Resigned committee; no new assignment

Cong.	Ranking	Terms in: House	Comm.	Date of Assignment
104th	Maj-15th	1	1	Jan. 4, 1995

Louis Stokes (D-Ohio)

Dates: Feb. 23, 1925
House: Jan. 3, 1969-Jan. 3, 1999
Left the House: Retired in 1998

HOUSE STANDING COMMITTEES:

1st EDUCATION AND LABOR
Dates: Jan. 29, 1969-Jan. 3, 1971
Departure: Moved to Appropriations

2nd INTERNAL SECURITY
Dates: Jan. 29, 1969-Jan. 3, 1971
Departure: Moved to Appropriations

3rd APPROPRIATIONS
Dates: Feb. 4, 1971-Jan. 3, 1999
Departure: Left the House; retired

Cong.	Ranking	Terms in: House	Comm.	Date of Assignment
103rd	Maj-6th	13	12	Jan. 5, 1993
104th	Min-3rd	14	13	Jan. 4, 1995
105th	Min-3rd	15	14	Jan. 7, 1997

4th BUDGET
Dates: Feb. 5, 1975-Jan. 3, 1981
Departure: Left committee; no new assignment

5th STANDARDS OF OFFICIAL CONDUCT
1st Dates: Feb. 6, 1980-Jan. 3, 1985
1st Departure: Left committee; no new assignment
2nd Dates: Feb. 6, 1991-Jan. 3, 1993
2nd Departure: Left committee; no new assignment

HOUSE SELECT AND SPECIAL COMMITTEES:

1st SELECT ASSASSINATIONS
Dates: Sep. 21, 1976-Jan. 2, 1979
Termination: House Report 1828 (95-2) filed
Ch2: Stokes succeeded Henry B. Gonzalez (D-Tex.), who had resigned the committee. Stokes was elected Chair on Mar. 8, 1977.

2nd PERMANENT SELECT INTELLIGENCE
Dates: Feb. 2, 1983-Jan. 3, 1989
Departure: Left committee; no new assignment

3rd SELECT COMMITTEE TO INVESTIGATE COVERT ARMS TRANSACTIONS WITH IRAN
Dates: Jan. 7, 1987-Dec. 15, 1987
Termination: House Report 433 (100-1) filed

Ted Strickland (D-Ohio)

Dates: Aug. 4, 1941
House 1: Jan. 3, 1993-Jan. 3, 1995
Left the House 1: Defeated for re-election in 1994
House 2: Jan. 3, 1997-Jan. 3, 2007
Left the House 2: Elected Governor in 2006

HOUSE STANDING COMMITTEES:

1st EDUCATION AND LABOR
Dates: Jan. 5, 1993-Jan. 3, 1995
Departure: Left the House; lost re-election

Cong.	Ranking	Terms in: House	Comm.	Date of Assignment
103rd	Maj-24th	1	1	Jan. 5, 1993

2nd SMALL BUSINESS
Dates: Jan. 5, 1993-Jan. 3, 1995
Departure: Left the House; lost re-election

Cong.	Ranking	Terms in: House	Comm.	Date of Assignment
103rd	Maj-18th	1	1	Jan. 5, 1993

3rd COMMERCE, 105-106
ENERGY AND COMMERCE, 107-109
Dates: Jan. 7, 1997-Jan. 3, 2007
Departure: Left the House; elected Governor

Cong.	Ranking	Terms in: House	Comm.	Date of Assignment
105th	Min-21st	2	1	Jan. 7, 1997
106th	Min-20th	3	2	Jan. 6, 1999
107th	Min-19th	4	3	Jan. 31, 2001
108th	Min-18th	5	4	Jan. 28, 2003
109th	Min-15th	6	5	Jan. 26, 2005

4th VETERANS AFFAIRS
Dates: Feb. 13, 2003-Jan. 3, 2007
Departure: Left the House; elected Governor

Cong.	Ranking	Terms in: House	Comm.	Date of Assignment
108th	Min-10th	4	1	Feb. 13, 2003
109th	Min-8th	5	2	Feb. 2, 2005

Gerry E. Studds (D-Mass.)

Dates: May 12, 1937
House: Jan. 3, 1973-Jan. 3, 1997
Left the House: Retired in 1996

HOUSE STANDING COMMITTEES:

1st MERCHANT MARINE AND FISHERIES
Dates: Jan. 24, 1973-Jan. 3, 1995
Departure: Committee abolished; moved to Resources
ChA: Studds replaced Walter B. Jones (D-N.C.), who had died. Studds became Acting Chair on Sep. 15, 1992.

Cong.	Ranking	Terms in: House	Comm.	Date of Assignment
103rd	Maj-Chr	11	11	Jan. 5, 1993

2nd PUBLIC WORKS, 93
PUBLIC WORKS AND TRANSPORTATION, 94
Dates: Jan. 24, 1973-Feb. 18, 1976
Departure: Resigned committee; moved to International Relations

3rd INTERNATIONAL RELATIONS, 94-95
FOREIGN AFFAIRS, 96
1st Dates: Feb. 18, 1976-Jan. 3, 1991
1st Departure: Remained on committee as a temporary member; not ranked by previous seniority
Temporary Dates: Jan. 3, 1991-Jan. 3, 1993
Departure: Left committee; became Chair of Merchant Marine and Fisheries

4th ENERGY AND COMMERCE, 102-103
COMMERCE, 104
Dates: Jan. 24, 1991-Jan. 3, 1997
Departure: Left the House; retired

Cong.	Ranking	Terms in: House	Comm.	Date of Assignment
103rd	Maj-19th	11	2	Jan. 5, 1993
104th	Min-11th	12	3	Jan. 4, 1995

5th RESOURCES
Dates: Jan. 9, 1995-Jan. 3, 1997
Departure: Left the House; retired

Cong.	Ranking	Terms in: House	Comm.	Date of Assignment
104th	Min-12th	12	1	Jan. 9, 1995

HOUSE SELECT AND SPECIAL COMMITTEES:

1st OUTER CONTINENTAL SHELF (Ad Hoc)
Became Select Committee on the Outer Continental Shelf on Mar. 29, 1979
Dates: Apr. 22, 1975-July 31, 1980
Termination: House Report 1214 (96-2) filed

2nd SELECT AGING (Permanent)
Dates: Feb. 21, 1991-Jan. 3, 1993
Termination: Committee not renewed in 1993

Robert L. Stump (R-Ariz.)

Dates: April 4, 1927-June 20, 2003
House: Jan. 3, 1977-Jan. 3, 2003
Left the House: Retired in 2002

Served as a Democrat: Jan. 3, 1977-Jan. 3, 1983
Served as a Republican: Jan. 3, 1983-Jan. 3, 2003

HOUSE STANDING COMMITTEES:

1st PUBLIC WORKS AND TRANSPORTATION
Dates: Jan. 19, 1977-Jan. 3, 1979
Departure: Left committee; no new assignment

2nd ARMED SERVICES, 95-103
NATIONAL SECURITY, 104-105
ARMED SERVICES, 106-107
1st Dates: Feb. 22, 1978-Jan. 3, 1983
1st Departure: Left committee as a Majority Democrat; returned as a Minority Republican with previous seniority credited
2nd Dates: Jan. 6, 1983-Jan. 3, 2003
2nd Departure: Left the House; retired

Cong.	Ranking	Terms in: House	Comm.	Date of Assignment
103rd	Min-2nd	9 *2	9	Jan. 5, 1993
104th	Maj-2nd	10 *2	10	Jan. 4, 1995
105th	Maj-2nd	11 *2	11	Jan. 7, 1997
106th	Maj-2nd	12 *2	12	Jan. 6, 1999
107th	Maj-Chr	13 *2	13	Jan. 6, 2001

3rd VETERANS AFFAIRS
1st Dates: Jan. 28, 1981-Jan. 3, 1983
1st Departure: Left committee as a Majority Democrat; returned later as a Minority Republican
2nd Dates: Jan. 21, 1987-Jan. 3, 2003
2nd Departure: Left the House; retired

Cong.	Ranking	Terms in: House	Comm.	Date of Assignment
103rd	Min-RM	9 *2	4	Jan. 5, 1993
104th	Maj-Chr	10 *2	5	Jan. 4, 1995
105th	Maj-Chr	11 *2	6	Jan. 9, 1997
106th	Maj-Chr	12 *2	7	Jan. 6, 1999
107th	Maj-2nd	13 *2	8	Jan. 6, 2001

HOUSE SELECT AND SPECIAL COMMITTEES:

1st PERMANENT SELECT INTELLIGENCE
1st Dates: Feb. 3, 1981-Jan. 3, 1983
1st Departure: Left committee as a Majority Democrat; returned as a Minority Republican with previous seniority credited
2nd Dates: Feb. 2, 1983-Jan. 3, 1987
2nd Departure: Moved to Veterans Affairs

Bart T. Stupak (D-Mich.)

Dates: Feb. 29, 1952
House: Jan. 3, 1993-date
Serving in the 111th Congress

HOUSE STANDING COMMITTEES:

1st ARMED SERVICES
Dates: Jan. 5, 1993-Jan. 3, 1995
Departure: Moved to Commerce

Cong.	Ranking	Terms in: House	Comm.	Date of Assignment
103rd	Maj-27th	1	1	Jan. 5, 1993

2nd MERCHANT MARINE AND FISHERIES
Dates: Jan. 5, 1993-Jan. 3, 1995
Departure: Committee abolished; moved to Commerce

Cong.	Ranking	Terms in: House	Comm.	Date of Assignment
103rd	Maj-24th	1	1	Jan. 5, 1993

3rd GOVERNMENT OPERATIONS
Dates: July 14, 1993-Jan. 3, 1995
Departure: Moved to Commerce

Cong.	Ranking	Terms in: House	Comm.	Date of Assignment
103rd	Maj-25th	1	1	July 14, 1993

4th COMMERCE, 104-106
ENERGY AND COMMERCE, 107-110
Dates: Jan. 4, 1995-date
Departure: Still serving in the 111th Congress

Cong.	Ranking	Terms in: House	Comm.	Date of Assignment
104th	Min-21st	2	1	Jan. 4, 1995
105th	Min-16th	3	2	Jan. 7, 1997
106th	Min-14th	4	3	Jan. 6, 1999
107th	Min-13th	5	4	Jan. 31, 2001
108th	Min-13th	6	5	Jan. 28, 2003
109th	Min-11th	7	6	Jan. 26, 2005
110th	Maj-10th	8	7	Jan. 4, 2007
111th	Maj-9th	9	8	Jan. 7, 2009

John Sullivan (R-Okla.)

Dates: Jan. 1, 1965
House: Feb. 15, 2002-date
Serving in the 111th Congress

H: Sullivan was elected to the 107th Congress by special election, Jan. 8, 2002, to fill the impending vacancy of U.S. Representative Steve Largent (R-Okla.). Sullivan was seated Feb. 15, 2002, and assigned to committees.

HOUSE STANDING COMMITTEES:

1st TRANSPORTATION AND INFRASTRUCTURE
Dates: Apr. 18, 2002-Jan. 28, 2004
Departure: Resigned committee; moved to Energy and Commerce

Cong.	Ranking	Terms in: House	Comm.	Date of Assignment
107th	MjR-5th	1	1	Apr. 18, 2002
108th	Maj-33rd	2	2	Jan. 28, 2003

2nd GOVERNMENT REFORM
Dates: May 16, 2002-Jan. 28, 2004
Departure: Resigned committee; moved to Energy and Commerce

Cong.	Ranking	Terms in: House	Comm.	Date of Assignment
107th	MjR-3rd	1	1	May 16, 2002
108th	Maj-17th	2	2	Jan. 28, 2003

3rd SCIENCE
Dates: May 16, 2002-Jan. 28, 2004
Departure: Resigned committee; moved to Energy and Commerce

Cong.	Ranking	Terms in: House	Comm.	Date of Assignment
107th	MjR-3rd	1	1	May 16, 2002
108th	Maj-19th	2	2	Jan. 28, 2003

4th ENERGY AND COMMERCE
Dates: Jan. 28, 2004-date
Departure: Still serving in the 111th Congress

Cong.	Ranking	Terms in: House	Comm.	Date of Assignment
108th	MjR-1st	2	1	Jan. 28, 2004
109th	Maj-28th	3	2	Jan. 6, 2005
110th	Min-24th	4	3	Jan. 10, 2007
111th	Min-18th	5	4	Jan. 9, 2009

HOUSE SELECT AND SPECIAL COMMITTEES:

1st SELECT ENERGY INDEPENDENCE AND GLOBAL WARMING
Dates: Mar. 9, 2007-date
Departure: Still serving in the 111th Congress

Cong.	Ranking	Terms in: House	Comm.	Date of Assignment
110th	Min-4th	4	1	Mar. 9, 2007
111th	Min-3rd	5	2	Feb. 3, 2009

Donald K. Sundquist (R-Tenn.)

Dates: March 15, 1936
House: Jan. 3, 1983-Jan. 3, 1995
Left the House: Elected Governor in 1994

HOUSE STANDING COMMITTEES:

1st PUBLIC WORKS AND TRANSPORTATION
Dates: Jan. 6, 1983-Jan. 3, 1989
Departure: Moved to Ways and Means

2nd VETERANS AFFAIRS
Dates: Jan. 6, 1983-Jan. 3, 1987
Departure: Moved to Budget

3rd BUDGET
Dates: Jan. 21, 1987-Jan. 3, 1989
Departure: Moved to Ways and Means.

4th WAYS AND MEANS
Dates: Jan. 20, 1989-Jan. 3, 1995
Departure: Left the House; elected Governor

Cong.	Ranking	Terms in: House	Comm.	Date of Assignment
103rd	Min-6th	6	3	Jan. 5, 1993

JOINT COMMITTEES:

1st JOINT DEFICIT REDUCTION (Temporary)
House Dates: Feb. 23, 1987-Sep. 29, 1987
Termination: Public Law 100-119 adjusted Gramm-Rudman-Hollings Act

John E. Sununu (R-N.H.)

Dates: Sept. 10, 1964
House: Jan. 3, 1997-Jan. 3, 2003
Left the House: Elected to U.S. Senate in 2002
Senate: Jan. 3, 2003-Jan. 3, 2009
Left the Senate: Defeated for re-election in 2008

HOUSE STANDING COMMITTEES:

1st BUDGET
Dates: Jan. 7, 1997-Jan. 3, 2003
Departure: Left the House for the Senate

Cong.	Ranking	Terms in: House	Comm.	Date of Assignment
105th	Maj-23rd	1	1	Jan. 7, 1997
106th	Maj-14th	2	2	Jan. 6, 1999
107th	Maj-2nd	3	3	Jan. 6, 2001

2nd GOVERNMENT REFORM AND OVERSIGHT
Dates: Jan. 7, 1997-Jan. 3, 1999
Departure: Moved to Appropriations

Cong.	Ranking	Terms in: House	Comm.	Date of Assignment
105th	Maj-20th	1	1	Jan. 7, 1997

3rd SMALL BUSINESS
Dates: Jan. 21, 1997-Jan. 3, 1999
Departure: Moved to Appropriations

Cong.	Ranking	Terms in: House	Comm.	Date of Assignment
105th	Maj-19th	1	1	Jan. 21, 1997

4th APPROPRIATIONS
Dates: Jan. 6, 1999-Jan. 3, 2003
Departure: Left the House for the Senate

Cong.	Ranking	Terms in: House	Comm.	Date of Assignment
106th	Maj-32nd	2	1	Jan. 6, 1999
107th	Maj-28th	3	2	Jan. 6, 2001

SENATE STANDING COMMITTEES:

1st BANKING, HOUSING AND URBAN AFFAIRS
Dates: Jan. 15, 2003-Jan. 3, 2009
Departure: Left the Senate; lost re-election

Cong.	Ranking	Years in: Senate	Comm.	Date of Assignment
108th	Maj-9th	1	1	Jan. 15, 2003
109th	Maj-9th	3	2	Jan. 6, 2005
110th	Min-8th	5	4	Jan. 12, 2007

2nd COMMERCE, SCIENCE AND TRANSPORTATION
Dates: Jan. 15, 2003-Jan. 3, 2009
Departure: Left the Senate; lost re-election

Cong.	Ranking	Years in: Senate	Comm.	Date of Assignment
108th	Maj-12th	1	1	Jan. 15, 2003
109th	Maj-10th	3	2	Jan. 6, 2005
110th	Min-8th	5	4	Jan. 12, 2007

3rd FOREIGN RELATIONS
Dates: Jan. 15, 2003-Jan. 3, 2009
Departure: Left the Senate; lost re-election

Cong.	Ranking	Years in: Senate	Comm.	Date of Assignment
108th	Maj-10th	1	1	Jan. 15, 2003
109th	Maj-8th	3	2	Jan. 6, 2005
110th	Min-5th	5	4	Jan. 12, 2007

4th GOVERNMENTAL AFFAIRS renamed Oct. 9, 2004
HOMELAND SECURITY AND GOVERNMENTAL AFFAIRS
1st Dates: Jan. 15, 2003-Jan. 6, 2005
1st Departure: Left committee; no new assignment
2nd Dates: Jan. 12, 2007-Jan. 3, 2009
2nd Departure: Left the Senate; lost re-election

Cong.	Ranking	Years in: Senate	Comm.	Date of Assignment
108th	Maj-8th	1 *1	1	Jan. 15, 2003
110th	Min-8th	5 *2	1	Jan. 12, 2007

5th FINANCE
Dates: Jan. 24, 2008-Jan. 3, 2009
Departure: Left the Senate; lost re-election

Cong.	Ranking	Years in: Senate	Comm.	Date of Assignment
110th	MnR-2nd	5	1	Jan. 24, 2008

JOINT COMMITTEES:

1st JOINT ECONOMIC
Senate Dates: Jan. 15, 2003-Jan. 3, 2009
Departure: Left the Senate; lost re-election

Cong.	Ranking	Years in: Senate	Comm.	Date of Assignment
108th	Maj-4th	1	1	Jan. 15, 2003
109th	Maj-3rd	3	2	Jan. 6, 2005
110th	Min-2nd	5	4	Jan. 12, 2007

Betty Sutton (D-Ohio)

Dates: July 31, 1963
House: Jan. 3, 2007-date
Serving in the 111th Congress

HOUSE STANDING COMMITTEES:

1st BUDGET
Dates: Jan. 10, 2007-July 12, 2007
Departure: Resigned committee; moved to Judiciary

Cong.	Ranking	Terms in: House	Comm.	Date of Assignment
110th	Maj-15th	1	1	Jan. 10, 2007

2nd RULES
Dates: Jan. 12, 2007-Jan. 14, 2009
Departure: Resigned committee; moved to Energy and Commerce

Cong.	Ranking	Terms in: House	Comm.	Date of Assignment
110th	Maj-9th	1	1	Jan. 12, 2007
111th	Maj-9th	2	2	Jan. 6, 2009

3rd JUDICIARY
Dates: July 12, 2007-Jan. 3, 2009
Departure: Moved to Energy and Commerce

Cong.	Ranking	Terms in: House	Comm.	Date of Assignment
110th	MjR-1st	1	1	July 12, 2007

4th ENERGY AND COMMERCE
Dates: Jan. 7, 2009-date
Departure: Still serving in the 111th Congress

Cong.	Ranking	Terms in: House	Comm.	Date of Assignment
111th	Maj-34th	2	1	Jan. 7, 2009

John E. Sweeney (R-N.Y.)

Dates: Aug. 9, 1955
House: Jan. 3, 1999-Jan. 3, 2007
Left the House: Defeated for re-election in 2006

HOUSE STANDING COMMITTEES:

1st BANKING AND FINANCIAL SERVICES
Dates: Jan. 6, 1999-Jan. 3, 2001
Departure: Moved to Appropriations

Cong.	Ranking	Terms in: House	Comm.	Date of Assignment
106th	Maj-28th	1	1	Jan. 6, 1999

2nd SMALL BUSINESS
Dates: Jan. 6, 1999-Jan. 3, 2001
Departure: Moved to Appropriations

Cong.	Ranking	Terms in: House	Comm.	Date of Assignment
106th	Maj-14th	1	1	Jan. 6, 1999

3rd TRANSPORTATION AND INFRASTRUCTURE
Dates: Jan. 6, 1999-Jan. 3, 2001
Departure: Moved to Appropriations

Cong.	Ranking	Terms in: House	Comm.	Date of Assignment
106th	Maj-36th	1	1	Jan. 6, 1999

4th APPROPRIATIONS
Dates: Jan. 6, 2001-Jan. 3, 2007
Departure: Left the House; lost re-election

Cong.	Ranking	Terms in: House	Comm.	Date of Assignment
107th	Maj-33rd	2	1	Jan. 6, 2001
108th	Maj-29th	3	2	Jan. 28, 2003
109th	Maj-28th	4	3	Jan. 6, 2005

HOUSE SELECT AND SPECIAL COMMITTEES:

1st SELECT HOMELAND SECURITY
Dates: Feb. 12, 2003-Jan. 3, 2005
Departure: Did not continue on reorganized standing committee

Cong.	Ranking	Terms in: House	Comm.	Date of Assignment
108th	Maj-27th	3	1	Feb. 12, 2003

Richard Swett (D-N.H.)

Dates: May 1, 1957
House: Jan. 3, 1991-Jan. 3, 1995
Left the House: Defeated for re-election in 1994

HOUSE STANDING COMMITTEES:

1st PUBLIC WORKS AND TRANSPORTATION
Dates: Jan. 24, 1991-Jan. 3, 1995
Departure: Left the House; lost re-election

Cong.	Ranking	Terms in: House	Comm.	Date of Assignment
103rd	Maj-20th	2	2	Jan. 5, 1993

2nd SCIENCE, SPACE AND TECHNOLOGY
Dates: Jan. 24, 1991-Jan. 3, 1995
Departure: Left the House; lost re-election

Cong.	Ranking	Terms in: House	Comm.	Date of Assignment
103rd	Maj-18th	2	2	Jan. 5, 1993

HOUSE SELECT AND SPECIAL COMMITTEES:

1st SELECT AGING (Permanent)
Dates: Feb. 21, 1991-Jan. 3, 1993
Termination: Committee not renewed in 1993

Allan B. Swift (D-Wash.)

Dates: Sept. 12, 1935
House: Jan. 3, 1979-Jan. 3, 1995
Left the House: Retired in 1994

HOUSE STANDING COMMITTEES:

1st INTERSTATE AND FOREIGN COMMERCE, 96
ENERGY AND COMMERCE, 97-103
Dates: Jan. 24, 1979-Jan. 3, 1995
Departure: Left the House; retired

Cong.	Ranking	Terms in: House	Comm.	Date of Assignment
103rd	Maj-5th	8	8	Jan. 5, 1993

2nd HOUSE ADMINISTRATION
Dates: Mar. 19, 1980-Jan. 3, 1995
Departure: Left the House; retired

Cong.	Ranking	Terms in: House	Comm.	Date of Assignment
103rd	Maj-2nd	8	8	Jan. 21, 1993

HOUSE SELECT AND SPECIAL COMMITTEES:

1st SELECT HOUSE RECORDING STUDIO
Dates: Mar. 2, 1987-Jan. 3, 1993
Departure: Committee abolished

JOINT COMMITTEES:

1st JOINT LIBRARY
House Dates: Feb. 5, 1981-Jan. 3, 1987
Departure: Left committee; no new assignment

2nd JOINT ORGANIZATION OF CONGRESS (Ad Hoc)
House Dates: Oct. 9, 1992- Dec. 17, 1993
Termination: House Report 103-413 filed

Cong.	Ranking	Terms in: House	Comm.	Date of Assignment
103rd	Maj-3rd	9	2	Jan. 5, 1993

Michael L. Synar (D-Okla.)

Dates: Oct. 17, 1950-Jan. 9, 1996
House: Jan. 3, 1979-Jan. 3, 1995
Left the House: Defeated for re-nomination in 1994

HOUSE STANDING COMMITTEES:

1st GOVERNMENT OPERATIONS
Dates: Jan. 24, 1979-Jan. 3, 1995
Departure: Left the House; lost re-nomination

Cong.	Ranking	Terms in: House	Comm.	Date of Assignment
103rd	Maj-5th	8	8	Jan. 5, 1993

2nd JUDICIARY
Dates: Jan. 24, 1979-Jan. 3, 1995
Departure: Left the House; lost re-nomination

Cong.	Ranking	Terms in: House	Comm.	Date of Assignment
103rd	Maj-6th	8	8	Jan. 5, 1993

3rd ENERGY AND COMMERCE
Dates: Jan. 28, 1981-Jan. 3, 1995
Departure: Left the House; lost re-nomination

Cong.	Ranking	Terms in: House	Comm.	Date of Assignment
103rd	Maj-7th	8	7	Jan. 5, 1993

HOUSE SELECT AND SPECIAL COMMITTEES:

1st SELECT AGING (Permanent)
Dates: Feb. 21, 1979-Jan. 3, 1991
Departure: Moved to Select Hunger

2nd SELECT HUNGER (Temporary)
Dates: Feb. 21, 1991-Jan. 3, 1993
Termination: Committee not renewed in 1993

T

James M. Talent (R-Mo.)

Dates: Oct. 18, 1956-
House: Jan. 3, 1993-Jan. 3, 2001
Left the House: Lost election for Governor in 2000

Senate: Nov. 25, 2002-Jan. 3, 2007
Left the Senate: Defeated for re-election in 2006

S: Talent was elected to the 107th Congress by special election, Nov. 5, 2002, to fill the unexpired term of U.S. Senator-elect Mel Carnahan (D-Mo.).

Carnahan was initially replaced by his wife Jean Carnahan (D-Mo.), an appointee, who lost the special election to Talent. The official certification date of the election returns was Nov. 25, 2002. Talent was not sworn nor assigned to committees because the 107th Congress was not in session.

HOUSE STANDING COMMITTEES:

1st ARMED SERVICES, 103
NATIONAL SECURITY, 104-105
ARMED SERVICES, 106
Dates: Jan. 5, 1993-Jan. 3, 2001
Departure: Left the Senate; lost election for governor

Cong.	Ranking	Terms in: House	Comm.	Date of Assignment
103rd	Min-20th	1	1	Jan. 5, 1993
104th	Maj-16th	2	2	Jan. 4, 1995
105th	Maj-13th	3	3	Jan. 7, 1997
106th	Maj-13th	4	4	Jan. 6, 1999

2nd SMALL BUSINESS
Dates: Jan. 5, 1993-Jan. 3, 2001
Departure: Left the Senate; lost election for governor

Cong.	Ranking	Terms in: House	Comm.	Date of Assignment
103rd	Min-13th	1	1	Jan. 5, 1993
104th	Maj-4th	2	2	Jan. 4, 1995
105th	Maj-Chr	3	3	Jan. 7, 1997
106th	Maj-Chr	4	4	Jan. 6, 1999

3rd ECONOMIC AND EDUCATIONAL OPPORTUNITIES, 104
EDUCATION AND THE WORKFORCE, 105-106
Dates: Jan. 4, 1995-Jan. 3, 2001
Departure: Left the Senate; lost election for governor

Cong.	Ranking	Terms in: House	Comm.	Date of Assignment
104th	Maj-14th	2	1	Jan. 4, 1995
105th	Maj-11th	3	2	Jan. 7, 1997
106th	Maj-11th	4	3	Jan. 6, 1999

SENATE STANDING COMMITTEES:

1st AGRICULTURE, NUTRITION AND FORESTRY
Dates: Jan. 15, 2003-Jan. 3, 2007
Departure: Left the Senate; lost re-election

Cong.	Ranking	Years in: Senate	Comm.	Date of Assignment
108th	Maj-9th	1	1	Jan. 15, 2003
109th	Maj-6th	3	2	Jan. 6, 2005

2nd ARMED SERVICES
Dates: Jan. 15, 2003-Jan. 3, 2007
Departure: Left the Senate; lost re-election

Cong.	Ranking	Years in: Senate	Comm.	Date of Assignment
108th	Maj-9th	1	1	Jan. 15, 2003
109th	Maj-8th	3	2	Jan. 6, 2005

3rd ENERGY AND NATURAL RESOURCES
Dates: Jan. 15, 2003-Jan. 3, 2007
Departure: Left the Senate; lost re-election

Cong.	Ranking	Years in: Senate	Comm.	Date of Assignment
108th	Maj-8th	1	1	Jan. 15, 2003
109th	Maj-8th	3	2	Jan. 6, 2005

SENATE SELECT AND SPECIAL COMMITTEES:

1st SPECIAL AGING (Permanent)
Dates: Jan. 15, 2003-Jan. 3, 2007
Departure: Left the Senate; lost re-election

Cong.	Ranking	Years in: Senate	Comm.	Date of Assignment
108th	Maj-6th	1	1	Jan. 15, 2003
109th	Maj-4th	3	2	Jan. 6, 2005

Thomas G. Tancredo (R-Colo.)

Dates: Dec. 20, 1945
House: Jan. 3, 1999-Jan. 3, 2009
Left the House: Retired; lost Republican presidential nomination in 2008

HOUSE STANDING COMMITTEES:

1st EDUCATION AND THE WORKFORCE
Dates: Jan. 6, 1999-Jan. 3, 2001
Departure: Moved to Budget

Cong.	Ranking	Terms in: House	Comm.	Date of Assignment
106th	Maj-24th	1	1	Jan. 6, 1999
107th	Maj-17th	2	2	Jan. 6, 2001

2nd INTERNATIONAL RELATIONS, 106-109
FOREIGN AFFAIRS, 110
Dates: Jan. 6, 1999-Jan. 3, 2009
Departure: Left the House; lost presidential nomination

Cong.	Ranking	Terms in: House	Comm.	Date of Assignment
106th	Maj-26th	1	1	Jan. 6, 1999
107th	Maj-18th	2	2	Jan. 6, 2001
108th	Maj-15th	3	3	Jan. 28, 2003
109th	Maj-12th	4	4	Jan. 26, 2005
110th	Min-9th	5	5	Jan. 10, 2007

3rd RESOURCES, 106-109
NATURAL RESOURCES, 110
Dates: Jan. 6, 1999-Jan. 3, 2009
Departure: Left the House; lost presidential nomination

Cong.	Ranking	Terms in: House	Comm.	Date of Assignment
106th	Maj-28th	1	1	Jan. 6, 1999
107th	Maj-26th	2	2	Jan. 6, 2001
108th	Maj-19th	3	3	Jan. 28, 2003
109th	Maj-16th	4	4	Jan. 26, 2005
110th	Min-8th	5	5	Jan. 10, 2007

4th BUDGET
Dates: Jan. 28, 2003-Jan. 3, 2005
Departure: Left committee; no new assignment

Cong.	Ranking	Terms in: House	Comm.	Date of Assignment
108th	Maj-15th	3	1	Jan. 28, 2003

John S. Tanner (D-Tenn.)

Dates: Sept. 22, 1944
House: Jan. 3, 1989-date
Serving in the 111th Congress

HOUSE STANDING COMMITTEES:

1st ARMED SERVICES, 101-103
NATIONAL SECURITY, 104
Dates: Jan. 19, 1989-Jan. 3, 1997
Departure: Moved to Ways and Means

Cong.	Ranking	Terms in: House	Comm.	Date of Assignment
103rd	Maj-18th	3	3	Jan. 5, 1993
104th	Min-10th	4	4	Jan. 4, 1995

2nd SCIENCE, SPACE AND TECHNOLOGY, 101-103
SCIENCE, 104
Dates: Jan. 19, 1989-Jan. 3, 1997
Departure: Moved to Ways and Means

Cong.	Ranking	Terms in: House	Comm.	Date of Assignment
103rd	Maj-12th	3	3	Jan. 5, 1993
104th	Min-5th	4	4	Jan. 4, 1995

3rd WAYS AND MEANS
Dates: Jan. 7, 1997-date
Departure: Still serving in the 111th Congress

Cong.	Ranking	Terms in: House	Comm.	Date of Assignment
105th	Min-14th	5	1	Jan. 7, 1997
106th	Min-13th	6	2	Jan. 6, 1999
107th	Min-13th	7	3	Jan. 31, 2001
108th	Min-12th	8	4	Jan. 28, 2003
109th	Min-10th	9	5	Jan. 26, 2005
110th	Maj-8th	10	6	Jan. 4, 2007
111th	Maj-7th	11	7	Jan. 7, 2009

4th FOREIGN AFFAIRS
Dates: Jan. 12, 2007-date
Departure: Still serving in the 111th Congress

Cong.	Ranking	Terms in: House	Comm.	Date of Assignment
110th	Maj-14th	10	1	Jan. 12, 2007
111th	Maj-16th	11	2	Jan. 21, 2009

Randy J. Tate (R-Wash.)

Dates: Nov. 23, 1965
House: Jan. 3, 1995-Jan. 3, 1997
Left the House: Defeated for re-election in 1996

HOUSE STANDING COMMITTEES:

1st GOVERNMENT REFORM AND OVERSIGHT
Dates: Jan. 4, 1995-Jan. 3, 1997
Departure: Left the House; lost re-election

Cong.	Ranking	Terms in: House	Comm.	Date of Assignment
104th	Maj-16th	1	1	Jan. 4, 1995

2nd TRANSPORTATION AND INFRASTRUCTURE
Dates: Jan. 4, 1995-Jan. 3, 1997
Departure: Left the House; lost re-election

Cong.	Ranking	Terms in: House	Comm.	Date of Assignment
104th	Maj-30th	1	1	Jan. 4, 1995

Ellen O. Tauscher (D-Cal.)

Dates: Nov. 15, 1951
House: Jan. 3, 1997-June 26, 2009
Left the House: Resigned; appointed Undersecretary of State for Arms Control and International Security in 2009

HOUSE STANDING COMMITTEES:

1st TRANSPORTATION AND INFRASTRUCTURE
Dates: Jan. 7, 1997-June 26, 2009
Departure: Resigned the House; appointed to State Department

Cong.	Ranking	Terms in: House	Comm.	Date of Assignment
105th	Min-26th	1	1	Jan. 7, 1997
106th	Min-24th	2	2	Jan. 6, 1999
107th	Min-21st	3	3	Jan. 31, 2001
108th	Min-16th	4	4	Jan. 28, 2003
109th	Min-15th	5	5	Jan. 26, 2005
110th	Maj-13th	6	6	Jan. 10, 2007
111th	Maj-12th	7	7	Jan. 7, 2009

2nd SCIENCE
Dates: Apr. 17, 1997-June 24, 1998
Departure: Resigned committee; moved to National Security

Cong.	Ranking	Terms in: House	Comm.	Date of Assignment
105th	MnR-1st	1	1	Apr. 17, 1997

3rd NATIONAL SECURITY, 105
ARMED SERVICES, 106-111
Dates: June 24, 1998-June 26, 2009
Departure: Resigned the House; appointed to State Department

Cong.	Ranking	Terms in: House	Comm.	Date of Assignment
105th	MnA-27th	1	1	June 24, 1998
106th	Min-23rd	2	2	Jan. 6, 1999
107th	Min-21st	3	3	Jan. 31, 2001
108th	Min-15th	4	4	Jan. 28, 2003
109th	Min-13th	5	5	Jan. 26, 2005
110th	Maj-12th	6	6	Jan. 10, 2007
111th	Maj-11th	7	7	Jan. 7, 2009

W.J. (Billy) Tauzin (R-La.)

Dates: June 14, 1943
House: May 17, 1980-Jan. 3, 2005
Left the House: Retired in 2004
Served as a Democrat: May 17, 1980-Aug. 8, 1995
Served as a Republican: Aug. 8, 1995-Jan. 3, 2005

H: Tauzin was elected to the 96th Congress by special election, May 17, 1980, to fill the vacancy of U.S. Representative David C. Treen (R-La.) who had been elected Governor. Tauzin was seated May 22, 1980, and assigned to committees.

HOUSE STANDING COMMITTEES:

1st PUBLIC WORKS AND TRANSPORTATION
Dates: June 18, 1980-Jan. 3, 1981
Departure: Moved to Energy and Commerce

2nd ENERGY AND COMMERCE, 97-103 as a Democrat
COMMERCE, 104 as a Democrat
COMMERCE, 104-106 as a Republican
ENERGY AND COMMERCE, 107-108
1st Dates: Jan. 28, 1981-Sep. 6, 1995
1st Departure: Assignment vacated as a Democrat; returned as Republican
2nd Dates: Sep. 12, 1995-Jan. 3, 2005
Ch1: Resigned as Chair on Feb. 16, 2004; replaced by Joe L. Barton (Rep-Tex.) on Feb. 26, 2004
Departure: Left the House; retired

Cong.	Ranking	Terms in: House	Comm.	Date of Assignment
103rd	Maj-8th	8 *1	7	Jan. 5, 1993
104th	Min-4th	9 *1	8	Jan. 4, 1995
104th	MjA-3rd	9 *2	1	Sep. 12, 1995
105th	Maj-2nd	10 *2	2	Jan. 7, 1997
106th	Maj-2nd	11 *2	3	Jan. 6, 1999
107th	Maj-Chr	12 *2	4	Jan. 6, 2001
108th	Maj-Ch1	13 *2	5	Jan. 28, 2003

3rd MERCHANT MARINE AND FISHERIES
Dates: Jan. 28, 1981-Jan. 3, 1995
Departure: Committee abolished; moved to Resources

Cong.	Ranking	Terms in: House	Comm.	Date of Assignment
103rd	Maj-4th	8	7	Jan. 5, 1993

4th RESOURCES
1st Dates: Jan. 9, 1995-Sep. 6, 1995
1st Departure: Assignment vacated as a Democrat; returned as a Republican
2nd Dates: Sep. 12, 1995-Jan. 3, 2005
2nd Departure: Left the House; retired

Cong.	Ranking	Terms in: House	Comm.	Date of Assignment
104th	Min-13th	9 *1	1	Jan. 9, 1995
104th	MjA-2nd	9 *2	1	Sep. 12, 1995
105th	Maj-2nd	10 *2	2	Jan. 7, 1997
106th	Maj-2nd	11 *2	3	Jan. 6, 1999
107th	Maj-3rd	12 *2	4	Jan. 6, 2001
108th	Maj-3rd	13 *2	5	Jan. 28, 2003

HOUSE SELECT AND SPECIAL COMMITTEES:

1st SELECT HOMELAND SECURITY
Dates: Feb. 12, 2003-Apr. 3, 2004
Departure: Resigned committee; no new assignment

Cong.	Ranking	Terms in: House	Comm.	Date of Assignment
108th	Maj-6th	13	1	Feb. 12, 2003

Charles H. Taylor (R-N.C.)

Dates: Jan. 23, 1941
House: Jan. 3, 1991-Jan. 3, 2007
Left the House: Defeated for re-election in 2006

HOUSE STANDING COMMITTEES:

1st INTERIOR AND INSULAR AFFAIRS
Dates: Jan. 24, 1991-Jan. 3, 1993
Departure: Moved to Appropriations

2nd PUBLIC WORKS AND TRANSPORTATION
Dates: Jan. 24, 1991-Jan. 3, 1993
Departure: Moved to Appropriations

3rd APPROPRIATIONS
Dates: Jan. 5, 1993-Jan. 3, 2007
Departure: Left the House; lost re-election

Cong.	Ranking	Terms in: House	Comm.	Date of Assignment
103rd	Min-20th	2	1	Jan. 5, 1993
104th	Maj-18th	3	2	Jan. 4, 1995
105th	Maj-15th	4	3	Jan. 7, 1997
106th	Maj-13th	5	4	Jan. 6, 1999
107th	Maj-11th	6	5	Jan. 31, 2001
108th	Maj-8th	7	6	Jan. 28, 2003
109th	Maj-8th	8	7	Jan. 6, 2005

4th MERCHANT MARINE AND FISHERIES
Dates: May 27, 1993-Jan. 3, 1995
Departure: Committee abolished; no new assignment

Cong.	Ranking	Terms in: House	Comm.	Date of Assignment
103rd	Min-18th	1	1	May 27, 1993

HOUSE SELECT AND SPECIAL COMMITTEES:

1st SELECT AGING (Permanent)
Dates: Feb. 21, 1991-Jan. 3, 1993
Termination: Committee not renewed in 1993

JOINT COMMITTEES:

1st JOINT LIBRARY
Dates: June 5, 2001-Jan. 3, 2003
Departure: Left committee; no new assignment

Cong.	Ranking	Terms in: House	Comm.	Date of Assignment
107th	Maj-3rd	6	1	June 5, 2001

G. Eugene (Gene) Taylor

(D-Miss.)

Dates: Sept. 17, 1953
House: Oct. 17, 1989-date
Serving in the 111th Congress

H: Taylor was elected to the 101st Congress by special election, Oct. 17, 1989, to fill the vacancy caused by the death of U.S. Representative Larkin Smith (R-Miss.). Taylor was seated Oct. 24, 1989, and assigned to committees.

HOUSE STANDING COMMITTEES:

1st ARMED SERVICES, 101-103
NATIONAL SECURITY, 104-105
ARMED SERVICES, 106-111
Dates: Nov. 8, 1989-date
Departure: Still serving in the 111th Congress

Cong.	Ranking	Terms in: House	Comm.	Date of Assignment
103rd	Maj-20th	3	3	Jan. 5, 1993

104th	Min-12th	4	4	Jan. 4, 1995
105th	Min-8th	5	5	Jan. 7, 1997
106th	Min-7th	6	6	Jan. 6, 1999
107th	Min-6th	7	7	Jan. 6, 2001
108th	Min-5th	8	8	Jan. 28, 2003
109th	Min-5th	9	9	Jan. 26, 2005
110th	Maj-4th	10	10	Jan. 10, 2007
111th	Maj-4th	11	11	Jan. 7, 2009

2nd MERCHANT MARINE AND FISHERIES
Dates: Nov. 8, 1989-Jan. 3, 1995
Departure: Committee abolished; moved to Government Reform and Oversight

| | | Terms in: | | Date of |
Cong.	Ranking	House	Comm.	Assignment
103rd	Maj-13th	3	3	Jan. 5, 1993

3rd GOVERNMENT REFORM AND OVERSIGHT
Dates: Jan. 9, 1995-Feb. 28, 1996
Departure: Resigned committee; moved to Transportation and Infrastructure

| | | Terms in: | | Date of |
Cong.	Ranking	House	Comm.	Assignment
104th	Min-15th	4	1	Jan. 9, 1995

4th TRANSPORTATION AND INFRASTRUCTURE
Dates: Feb. 28, 1996-date
Departure: Still serving in the 111th Congress

| | | Terms in: | | Date of |
Cong.	Ranking	House	Comm.	Assignment
104th	MnR-5th	4	1	Feb. 28, 1996
105th	Min-22nd	5	2	Jan. 7, 1997
106th	Min-19th	6	3	Jan. 6, 1999
107th	Min-16th	7	4	Jan. 31, 2001
108th	Min-12th	8	5	Jan. 28, 2003
109th	Min-11th	9	6	Jan. 26, 2005
110th	Maj-10th	10	7	Jan. 10, 2007
111th	Maj-10th	11	8	Jan. 7, 2009

Harry Teague (D-N.M.)

Dates: June 29, 1949
House: Jan. 3, 2009-date
Serving in the 111th Congress

HOUSE STANDING COMMITTEES:

1st TRANSPORTATION AND INFRASTRUCTURE
Dates: Jan. 7, 2009-date
Departure: Still serving in the 111th Congress

| | | Terms in: | | Date of |
Cong.	Ranking	House	Comm.	Assignment
111th	Maj-45th	1	1	Jan. 7, 2009

2nd VETERANS AFFAIRS
Dates: Jan. 21, 2009-date
Departure: Still serving in the 111th Congress

| | | Terms in: | | Date of |
Cong.	Ranking	House	Comm.	Assignment
111th	Maj-10th	1	1	Jan. 21, 2009

Frank M. Tejeda (D-Tex.)

Dates: Oct. 2, 1945-Jan. 30, 1997
House: Jan. 3, 1993-Jan. 30, 1997
Left the House: Died in office

HOUSE STANDING COMMITTEES:

1st ARMED SERVICES, 103
NATIONAL SECURITY, 104-105
Dates: Jan. 5, 1993-Jan. 30, 1997
Departure: Died in office

| | | Terms in: | | Date of |
Cong.	Ranking	House	Comm.	Assignment
103rd	Maj-25th	1	1	Jan. 5, 1993
104th	Min-15th	2	2	Jan. 4, 1995
105th	Min-10th	3	3	Jan. 7, 1997

2nd VETERANS AFFAIRS
Dates: Jan. 5, 1993-Jan. 3, 1997
Departure: Left committee; no new assignment

| | | Terms in: | | Date of |
Cong.	Ranking	House	Comm.	Assignment
103rd	Maj-15th	1	1	Jan. 5, 1993
104th	Min-8th	2	2	Jan. 4, 1995

Lee R. Terry (R-Neb.)

Dates: Jan. 29, 1962
House: Jan. 3, 1999-date
Serving in the 111th Congress

HOUSE STANDING COMMITTEES:

1st BANKING AND FINANCIAL SERVICES
Dates: Jan. 6, 1999-Jan. 3, 2001
Departure: Moved to Energy and Commerce

| | | Terms in: | | Date of |
Cong.	Ranking	House	Comm.	Assignment
106th	Maj-30th	1	1	Jan. 6, 1999

2nd GOVERNMENT REFORM
Dates: Jan. 6, 1999-Jan. 3, 2001
Departure: Moved to Energy and Commerce

| | | Terms in: | | Date of |
Cong.	Ranking	House	Comm.	Assignment
106th	Maj-19th	1	1	Jan. 6, 1999

3rd TRANSPORTATION AND INFRASTRUCTURE
Dates: Jan. 6, 1999-Jan. 3, 2001
Departure: Moved to Energy and Commerce

| | | Terms in: | | Date of |
Cong.	Ranking	House	Comm.	Assignment
106th	Maj-33rd	1	1	Jan. 6, 1999

4th ENERGY AND COMMERCE
Dates: Jan. 6, 2001-date
Departure: Still serving in the 111th Congress

| | | Terms in: | | Date of |
Cong.	Ranking	House	Comm.	Assignment
107th	Maj-31st	2	1	Jan. 6, 2001
108th	Maj-26th	3	2	Jan. 28, 2003
109th	Maj-23rd	4	3	Jan. 6, 2005
110th	Min-20th	5	4	Jan. 10, 2007
111th	Min-15th	6	5	Jan. 9, 2009

Jon Tester (D-Mont.)

Dates: Aug. 21, 1956
Senate: Jan. 3, 2007-date
Serving in the 111th Congress

SENATE STANDING COMMITTEES:

1st BANKING, HOUSING AND URBAN AFFAIRS
Dates: Jan. 12, 2007-date
Departure: Still serving in the 111th Congress

Cong.	Ranking	Years in: Senate	Comm.	Date of Assignment
110th	Maj-11th	1	1	Jan. 12, 2007
111th	Maj-9th	3	3	Jan. 21, 2009

2nd ENERGY AND NATURAL RESOURCES
Dates: Jan. 12, 2007-Jan. 21, 2009
Departure: Moved to Appropriations

Cong.	Ranking	Years in: Senate	Comm.	Date of Assignment
110th	Maj-12th	1	1	Jan. 12, 2007

3rd HOMELAND SECURITY AND GOVERNMENTAL AFFAIRS
Dates: Jan. 12, 2007-date
Departure: Still serving in the 111th Congress.

Cong.	Ranking	Years in: Senate	Comm.	Date of Assignment
110th	Maj-9th	1	1	Jan. 12, 2007
111th	Maj-8th	3	3	Jan. 21, 2009

4th SMALL BUSINESS AND ENTREPRENEURSHIP
Dates: Jan. 12, 2007-Jan. 21, 2009
Departure: Moved to Appropriations

Cong.	Ranking	Years in: Senate	Comm.	Date of Assignment
110th	Maj-10th	1	1	Jan. 12, 2007

5th VETERANS AFFAIRS
Dates: Jan. 12, 2007-date
Departure: Still serving in the 111th Congress

Cong.	Ranking	Years in: Senate	Comm.	Date of Assignment
110th	Maj-8th	1	1	Jan. 12, 2007
111th	Maj-7th	3	3	Jan. 21, 2009

6th APPROPRIATIONS
Dates: Jan. 21, 2009-date
Departure: Still serving in the 111th Congress

Cong.	Ranking	Years in: Senate	Comm.	Date of Assignment
111th	Maj-17th	3	1	Jan. 21, 2009

SENATE SELECT AND SPECIAL COMMITTEES:

1st INDIAN AFFAIRS (Permanent)
Dates: Jan. 12, 2007-date
Departure: Still serving in the 111th Congress

Cong.	Ranking	Years in: Senate	Comm.	Date of Assignment
110th	Maj-8th	1	1	Jan. 12, 2007
111th	Maj-7th	3	3	Jan. 21, 2009

Craig L. Thomas (R-Wyo.)

Dates: Feb. 17, 1933-June 4, 2007
House: Apr. 26, 1989-Jan. 3, 1995
Left the House: Elected to U.S. Senate in 1994
Senate: Jan. 3, 1995-June 4, 2007
Left the Senate: Died in office

H: Thomas was elected to the 101st Congress by special election, April 26, 1989, to fill the vacancy caused by the resignation of U.S. Representative Richard B. Cheney (R-Wyo.) who was appointed Secretary of Defense. Thomas was seated May 2, 1989, and assigned to committees.

HOUSE STANDING COMMITTEES:

1st GOVERNMENT OPERATIONS
Dates: May 4, 1989-Jan. 3, 1995
Departure: Left the House for the Senate

Cong.	Ranking	Terms in: House	Comm.	Date of Assignment
103rd	Min-8th	3	3	Jan. 5, 1993

2nd INTERIOR AND INSULAR AFFAIRS, 101-102 NATURAL RESOURCES, 103
Dates: May 4, 1989-Jan. 3, 1995
Departure: Left the House for the Senate

Cong.	Ranking	Terms in: House	Comm.	Date of Assignment
103rd	Min-6th	3	3	Jan. 5, 1993

3rd BANKING, FINANCE AND URBAN AFFAIRS
Dates: Feb. 6, 1991-Jan. 3, 1995
Departure: Left the House for the Senate

Cong.	Ranking	Terms in: House	Comm.	Date of Assignment
103rd	Min-10th	3	2	Jan. 5, 1993

SENATE STANDING COMMITTEES:

1st ENERGY AND NATURAL RESOURCES
Dates: Jan. 5, 1995-June 4, 2007
Departure: Died in office

Cong.	Ranking	Years in: Senate	Comm.	Date of Assignment
104th	Maj-6th	1	1	Jan. 5, 1995
105th	Maj-6th	3	3	Jan. 9, 1997
106th	Maj-6th	5	5	Jan. 7, 1999
107th	Maj-6th	7	7	Jan. 25, 2001
+107th	Min-6th	7	7	June 6, 2001
108th	Maj-5th	9	9	Jan. 15, 2003
109th	Maj-3rd	11	11	Jan. 6, 2005
110th	Maj-3rd	13	13	Jan. 12, 2007

2nd ENVIRONMENT AND PUBLIC WORKS
1st Dates: Jan. 5, 1995-Jan. 25, 2001
1st Departure: Moved to Agriculture, Nutrition and Forestry and Select Ethics
2nd Dates: Jan. 15, 2003-Jan. 6, 2005
2nd Departure: Returned to Agriculture, Nutrition and Forestry
3rd Dates: Jan. 12, 2007-June 4, 2007
3rd Departure: Died in office

Cong.	Ranking	Years in: Senate	Comm.	Date of Assignment
104th	Maj-7th	1 *1	1	Jan. 5, 1995
105th	Maj-6th	3 *1	3	Jan. 9, 1997
106th	Maj-5th	5 *1	5	Jan. 7, 1999
108th	Maj-9th	9 *2	1	Jan. 15, 2003
110th	Maj-8th	13 *3	1	Jan. 12, 2007

3rd FOREIGN RELATIONS
Dates: Jan. 5, 1995-July 10, 2001
Departure: Left committee; moved to Finance

Cong.	Ranking	Years in: Senate	Comm.	Date of Assignment
104th	Maj-8th	1	1	Jan. 5, 1995

105th	Maj-6th	3	3	Jan. 9, 1997
106th	Maj-8th	5	5	Jan. 7, 1999
107th	Maj-5th	7	7	Jan. 25, 2001
+107th	Min-5th	7	7	June 6, 2001

4th AGRICULTURE, NUTRITION AND FORESTRY
1st Dates: Jan. 25, 2001-Jan. 15, 2003
1st Departure: Returned to Environment and Public Works
2nd Dates: Jan. 6, 2005-Jan. 12, 2007
2nd Departure: Returned to Environment and Public Works

		Years in:		Date of
Cong.	Ranking	Senate	Comm.	Assignment
107th	Maj-7th	7 *1	1	Jan. 25, 2001
+107th	Min-7th	7 *1	1	June 6, 2001
109th	Maj-8th	11 *2	1	Jan. 6, 2005

5th FINANCE
Dates: July 10, 2001-June 4, 2007
Departure: Died in office

		Years in:		Date of
Cong.	Ranking	Senate	Comm.	Assignment
+107th	MnR-1st	7	1	July 10, 2001
108th	Maj-7th	9	2	Jan. 15, 2003
109th	Maj-6th	11	4	Jan. 6, 2005
110th	Min-6th	13	6	Jan. 12, 2007

SENATE SELECT AND SPECIAL COMMITTEES:

1st INDIAN AFFAIRS (Permanent)
Dates: Jan. 11, 1995-June 4, 2007
RM1: Replaced by Lisa Murkowski (R-Alas.) as Ranking Member on July 10, 2007
Departure: Died in office

		Years in:		Date of
Cong.	Ranking	Senate	Comm.	Assignment
104th	Maj-7th	1	1	Jan. 11, 1995
105th	Maj-6th	3	2	Jan. 9, 1997
106th	Maj-6th	5	4	Jan. 7, 1999
107th	Maj-5th	7	7	Jan. 25, 2001
+107th	Min-5th	7	7	June 6, 2001
108th	Maj-4th	9	9	Jan. 15, 2003
109th	Maj-2nd	11	10	Jan. 6, 2005
110th	Maj-RM1	13	13	Jan. 12, 2007

2nd SELECT ETHICS (Permanent)
Dates: Jan. 25, 2001-June 4, 2007
Departure: Died in office.

		Years in:		Date of
Cong.	Ranking	Senate	Comm.	Assignment
107th	Maj-3rd	7	1	Jan. 25, 2001
+107th	Min-3rd	7	1	June 6, 2001
108th	Maj-3rd	9	2	Jan. 15, 2003
109th	Maj-3rd	11	4	Jan. 6, 2005
110th	Min-3rd	13	6	Jan. 12, 2007

William M. Thomas (R-Cal.)

Dates: Dec. 6, 1941
House: Jan. 3, 1979-Jan. 3, 2007
Left the House: Retired in 2006

HOUSE STANDING COMMITTEES:

1st AGRICULTURE
Dates: Jan. 24, 1979-Jan. 3, 1983
Departure: Moved to Ways and Means

2nd STANDARDS OF OFFICIAL CONDUCT
Dates: Jan. 24, 1979-Jan. 3, 1981
Departure: Moved to House Administration

3rd HOUSE ADMINISTRATION, 97-103
HOUSE OVERSIGHT, 104-105
HOUSE ADMINISTRATION, 106
Dates: Jan. 28, 1981-Jan. 3, 2001
Departure: Left committee; became Chair of Ways and Means

		Terms in:		Date of
Cong.	Ranking	House	Comm.	Assignment
103rd	Min-RM	8	7	Jan. 5, 1993
104th	Maj-Chr	9	8	Jan. 4, 1995
105th	Maj-Chr	10	9	Jan. 7, 1997
106th	Maj-Chr	11	10	Jan. 6, 1999

4th WAYS AND MEANS
Dates: Jan. 6, 1983-Jan. 3, 2007
Departure: Left the House; retired

		Terms in:		Date of
Cong.	Ranking	House	Comm.	Assignment
103rd	Min-4th	8	6	Jan. 5, 1993
104th	Maj-3rd	9	7	Jan. 4, 1995
105th	Maj-3rd	10	8	Jan. 7, 1997
106th	Maj-3rd	11	9	Jan. 6, 1999
107th	Maj-Chr	12	10	Jan. 6, 2001
108th	Maj-Chr	13	11	Jan. 8, 2003
109th	Maj-Chr	14	12	Jan. 6, 2005

5th BUDGET
Dates: Jan. 21, 1987-Jan. 3, 1993
Departure: Left committee; no new assignment

JOINT COMMITTEES:

1st JOINT DEFICIT REDUCTION (Temporary)
House Dates: Feb. 23, 1987-Sep. 29, 1987
Termination: Public Law 100-119 adjusted Gramm-Rudman-Hollings Act

2nd JOINT TAXATION
House Dates: Jan. 10, 1995-Jan. 3, 2007
Departure: Left the House; retired

		Terms in:		Date of
Cong.	Ranking	House	Comm.	Assignment
104th	Maj-3rd	9	1	Jan. 10, 1995 Ltr
105th	Maj-3rd	10	2	Feb. 5, 1997 Ltr
106th	Maj-3rd	11	3	Jan. 6, 1999 Ltr
107th	Maj-CVc	12	4	Feb. 7, 2001 Ltr
108th	Maj-CVc	13	5	Jan. 29, 2003 Ltr
109th	Maj-CVc	14	6	Feb. 7, 2005 Ltr

3rd JOINT LIBRARY
House Dates: Feb. 23, 1995-Jan. 3, 2001
Departure: Left committee; became Chair of Ways and Means

		Terms in:		Date of
Cong.	Ranking	House	Comm.	Assignment
104th	Maj-VCh	9	1	Feb. 23, 1995
105th	Maj-Chr	10	2	Mar. 6, 1997
106th	Maj-VCh	11	3	Mar. 2, 1999

4th JOINT PRINTING
House Dates: Feb. 23, 1995-Jan. 3, 2001
Departure: Left committee; became Chair of Ways and Means

		Terms in:		Date of
Cong.	Ranking	House	Comm.	Assignment
104th	Maj-Chr	9	1	Feb. 23, 1995
105th	Maj-VCh	10	2	Mar. 6, 1997
106th	Maj-Chr	11	3	Mar. 2, 1999

Bennie Thompson (D-Miss.)

Dates: Jan. 28, 1948
House: April 13, 1993-date
Serving in the 111th Congress

H: Thompson was elected to the 103rd Congress by special election, April 13, 1993, to fill the vacancy caused by the resignation of U.S. Representative Mike Espy (D-Miss.) who was appointed Secretary of Agriculture. Thompson was seated April 20, 1993, and assigned to committees.

HOUSE STANDING COMMITTEES:

1st AGRICULTURE
Dates: Apr. 29, 1993-Feb. 1, 2005
Departure: Resigned committee; became Ranking Member on Select Homeland Security

Cong.	Ranking	Terms in: House	Comm.	Date of Assignment
103rd	MjA-28th	1	1	Apr. 29, 1993
104th	Min-19th	2	2	Jan. 4, 1995
105th	Min-13th	3	3	Jan. 7, 1997
106th	Min-12th	4	4	Jan. 6, 1999
107th	Min-9th	5	5	Jan. 31, 2001
108th	Min-5th	6	6	Jan. 28, 2003
109th	Min-3rd	7	7	Jan. 26, 2005

2nd MERCHANT MARINE AND FISHERIES
Dates: Apr. 29, 1993-Jan. 3, 1995
Departure: Committee abolished; no new assignment

Cong.	Ranking	Terms in: House	Comm.	Date of Assignment
103rd	MjA-29th	1	1	Apr. 29, 1993

3rd SMALL BUSINESS
Dates: June 23, 1993-Apr. 22, 1996
Departure: Resigned committee; moved to Budget

Cong.	Ranking	Terms in: House	Comm.	Date of Assignment
103rd	Maj-27th	1	1	June 23, 1993
104th	Min-14th	2	2	Jan. 4, 1995

4th BUDGET
Dates: Apr. 22, 1996-Jan. 3, 2003
Departure: Moved to Select Homeland Security

Cong.	Ranking	Terms in: House	Comm.	Date of Assignment
104th	MnR-2nd	2	1	Apr. 22, 1996
105th	Min-11th	3	2	Jan. 7, 1997
106th	Min-4th	4	3	Jan. 6, 1999
107th	Min-3rd	5	4	Jan. 31, 2001

5th HOMELAND SECURITY
Dates: Jan. 6, 2005-date
Departure: Still serving in the 111th Congress

Cong.	Ranking	Terms in: House	Comm.	Date of Assignment
109th	Min-RM	7	2	Jan. 6, 2005
110th	Maj-Chr	8	3	Jan. 4, 2007
111th	Maj-Chr	9	4	Jan. 28, 2009

HOUSE SELECT AND SPECIAL COMMITTEES:

1st SELECT HOMELAND SECURITY
Dates: Feb. 12, 2003-Jan. 3, 2005
Departure: Continued on reorganized standing committee

Cong.	Ranking	Terms in: House	Comm.	Date of Assignment
108th	Min-2nd	6	1	Feb. 12, 2003

Fred D. Thompson (R-Tenn.)

Dates: Aug. 19, 1942
Senate: Nov. 8, 1994-Jan. 3, 2003
Left the Senate: Retired in 2002

S: Thompson was elected to the 103rd Congress by special election, Nov. 8, 1994, to fill the unexpired term of U.S. Senator Albert A. Gore, Jr. (D-Tenn.) who had been elected Vice President. Gore was initially replaced by Harlan Matthews (D-Tenn.), an appointee who chose not to run for election. Thompson was seated Dec. 9, 1994, and was not assigned to committees.

SENATE STANDING COMMITTEES:

1st FOREIGN RELATIONS
Dates: Jan. 5, 1995-Jan. 9, 1997
Departure: Left committee; became Chair of Governmental Affairs

Cong.	Ranking	Years in: Senate	Comm.	Date of Assignment
104th	Maj-7th	1	1	Jan. 5, 1995

2nd GOVERNMENTAL AFFAIRS
Dates: Jan. 5, 1995-Jan. 3, 2003
Ch1: Replaced by Joseph I. Lieberman (D-Conn.) following party control shift on June 6, 2001 and became RM2
Departure: Left the Senate; retired.

Cong.	Ranking	Years in: Senate	Comm.	Date of Assignment
104th	Maj-4th	1	1	Jan. 5, 1995
105th	Maj-Chr	3	3	Jan. 9, 1997
106th	Maj-Chr	5	5	Jan. 7, 1999
107th	Maj-Ch1	7	7	Jan. 25, 2001
+107th	Min-RM2	7	7	June 6, 2001

3rd JUDICIARY
Dates: Jan. 4, 1995-Jan. 7, 1999
Departure: Moved to Finance

Cong.	Ranking	Years in: Senate	Comm.	Date of Assignment
104th	Maj-7th	1	1	Jan. 4, 1995
105th	Maj-5th	3	3	Jan. 9, 1997

4th FINANCE
Dates: Jan. 7, 1999-Jan. 3, 2003
Departure: Left the Senate; retired

Cong.	Ranking	Years in: Senate	Comm.	Date of Assignment
106th	Maj-11th	5	1	Jan. 7, 1999
107th	Maj-8th	7	3	Jan. 25, 2001
+107th	Min-7th	7	3	July 10, 2001

SENATE SELECT AND SPECIAL COMMITTEES:

1st SPECIAL AGING (Permanent)
Dates: Jan. 11, 1995-Jan. 9, 1997
Departure: Left committee; became Chair of Governmental Affairs

Cong.	Ranking	Years in: Senate	Comm.	Date of Assignment
104th	Maj-10th	1	1	Jan. 11, 1995

2nd SELECT INTELLIGENCE (Permanent)
Dates: Jan. 25, 2001-Jan. 3, 2003
Dates: Left the Senate; retired

Cong.	Ranking	Years in: Senate	Comm.	Date of Assignment
107th	Maj-7th	7	1	Jan. 25, 2001
+107th	Min-7th	7	1	June 6, 2001

Glenn Thompson (R-Pa.)

Dates: June 27, 1959
House: Jan. 3, 2009-date
Serving in the 111th Congress

HOUSE STANDING COMMITTEES:

1st AGRICULTURE
Dates: Jan. 9, 2009-date
Departure: Still serving in the 111th Congress

Cong.	Ranking	Terms in: House	Comm.	Date of Assignment
111th	Min-17th	1	1	Jan. 9, 2009

2nd SMALL BUSINESS
Dates: Jan. 9, 2009-date
Departure: Still serving in the 111th Congress

Cong.	Ranking	Terms in: House	Comm.	Date of Assignment
111th	Min-11th	1	1	Jan. 9, 2009

3rd EDUCATION AND LABOR
Dates: Feb. 4, 2009-date
Departure: Still serving in the 111th Congress

Cong.	Ranking	Terms in: House	Comm.	Date of Assignment
111th	MnR-1st	1	1	Feb. 4, 2009

Michael Thompson (D-Cal.)

Dates: Jan. 24, 1951
House: Jan. 3, 1999-date
Serving in the 111th Congress

HOUSE STANDING COMMITTEES:

1st AGRICULTURE
Dates: Jan. 6, 1999-June 3, 2004
Departure: Resigned committee to open seat for Herseth (now known as Herseth Sandlin)

Cong.	Ranking	Terms in: House	Comm.	Date of Assignment
106th	Min-23rd	1	1	Jan. 6, 1999
107th	Min-17th	2	2	Jan. 31, 2001
108th	Min-22nd	3	3	Feb. 13, 2003

2nd ARMED SERVICES
Dates: Jan. 6, 1999-Jan. 3, 2003
Departure: Moved to Budget and Transportation and Infrastructure

Cong.	Ranking	Terms in: House	Comm.	Date of Assignment
106th	Min-27th	1	1	Jan. 6, 1999
107th	Min-25th	2	2	Jan. 31, 2001

3rd BUDGET
Dates: Jan. 28, 2003-Jan. 3, 2005
Departure: Moved to Ways and Means

Cong.	Ranking	Terms in: House	Comm.	Date of Assignment
108th	Min-13th	3	1	Jan. 28, 2003

4th TRANSPORTATION AND INFRASTRUCTURE
Dates: Jan. 28, 2003-Jan. 3, 2005
Departure: Moved to Ways and Means

Cong.	Ranking	Terms in: House	Comm.	Date of Assignment
108th	Min-31st	3	1	Jan. 28, 2003

5th WAYS AND MEANS
Dates: Jan. 26, 2005-date
Departure: Still serving in the 111th Congress

Cong.	Ranking	Terms in: House	Comm.	Date of Assignment
109th	Min-15th	4	1	Jan. 26, 2005
110th	Maj-13th	5	2	Jan. 4, 2007
111th	Maj-11th	6	3	Jan. 7, 2009

HOUSE SELECT AND SPECIAL COMMITTEES:

1st PERMANENT SELECT INTELLIGENCE
Dates: Jan. 17, 2007-date
Departure: Still serving in the 111th Congress

Cong.	Ranking	Terms in: House	Comm.	Date of Assignment
110th	Maj-9th	5	1	Jan. 17, 2007
111th	Maj-7th	6	2	Feb. 4, 2009

William M. (Mac) Thornberry (R-Tex.)

Dates: July 15, 1958
House: Jan. 3, 1995-date
Serving in the 111th Congress

HOUSE STANDING COMMITTEES:

1st NATIONAL SECURITY, 104-105
ARMED SERVICES, 106-111
Dates: Jan. 4, 1995-date
Departure: Still serving in the 111th Congress

Cong.	Ranking	Terms in: House	Comm.	Date of Assignment
104th	Maj-22nd	1	1	Jan. 4, 1995
105th	Maj-19th	2	2	Jan. 7, 1997
106th	Maj-18th	3	3	Jan. 6, 1999
107th	Maj-13th	4	4	Jan. 6, 2001
108th	Maj-9th	5	5	Jan. 28, 2003
109th	Maj-9th	6	6	Jan. 26, 2005
110th	Min-7th	7	7	Jan. 10, 2007
111th	Min-4th	8	8	Jan. 9, 2009

2nd RESOURCES
Dates: Jan. 4, 1995-Jan. 3, 2003
Departure: Moved to Select Homeland Security

Cong.	Ranking	Terms in: House	Comm.	Date of Assignment
104th	Maj-21st	1	1	Jan. 4, 1995
105th	Maj-17th	2	2	Jan. 7, 1997
106th	Maj-16th	3	3	Jan. 6, 1999
107th	Maj-15th	4	4	Jan. 6, 2001

3rd BUDGET
Dates: Jan. 6, 1999-Jan. 3, 2005
Departure: Moved to Permanent Select Intelligence

Cong.	Ranking	Terms in: House	Comm.	Date of Assignment
106th	Maj-17th	3	1	Jan. 6, 1999
107th	Maj-8th	4	2	Jan. 6, 2001
108th	Maj-4th	5	3	Jan. 28, 2003

HOUSE SELECT AND SPECIAL COMMITTEES:

1st SELECT HOMELAND SECURITY
Dates: Feb. 12, 2003-Jan. 3, 2005
Departure: Did not continue on reorganized standing committee

Cong.	Ranking	Terms in: House	Comm.	Date of Assignment
108th	Maj-23rd	5	1	Feb. 12, 2003

2nd PERMANENT SELECT INTELLIGENCE
Dates: Sep. 28, 2004-date
Departure: Still serving in the 111th Congress

Cong.	Ranking	Terms in: House	Comm.	Date of Assignment
108th	MjR-1st	5	1	Sep. 28, 2004
109th	Maj-8th	6	2	Jan. 26, 2005
110th	Min-4th	7	3	Jan. 17, 2007
111th	Min-3rd	8	4	Feb. 4, 2009

3rd SELECT BIPARTISAN COMMITTEE TO INVESTIGATE THE PREPARATION FOR AND RESPONSE TO HURRICANE KATRINA
Dates: Sep. 21, 2005-Feb. 15, 2006
Departure: House Report 377 (109-2) filed

Cong.	Ranking	Terms in: House	Comm.	Date of Assignment
109th	Maj-8th	6	1	Sep. 21, 2005

JOINT COMMITTEES:

1st JOINT ECONOMIC
House Dates: Jan. 19, 1995-Jan. 3, 1999
Departure: Moved to Budget

Cong.	Ranking	Terms in: House	Comm.	Date of Assignment
104th	Maj-4th	1	1	Jan. 19, 1995
105th	Maj-4th	2	2	Feb. 27, 1997

Raymond H. Thornton Jr. (D-Ark.)

Dates: July 16, 1928
House 1: Jan. 3, 1973-Jan. 2, 1979
Left the House 1: Lost U.S. Senate nomination in 1978
House 2: Jan. 3, 1991-Jan. 1, 1997
Left the House 2: Resigned; elected to Arkansas Supreme Court in 1996

HOUSE STANDING COMMITTEES:

1st JUDICIARY
Dates: Jan. 24, 1973-Dec. 17, 1975
Departure: Moved to Agriculture

2nd SCIENCE AND ASTRONAUTICS, 93
SCIENCE AND TECHNOLOGY, 94-95
SCIENCE, SPACE AND TECHNOLOGY, 102

1st Dates: Jan. 24, 1973-Jan. 3, 1979
1st Departure: Left the House; lost Senate nomination
2nd Dates: Jan. 24, 1991-Jan. 3, 1993
2nd Departure: Moved to Appropriations

3rd AGRICULTURE
Dates: Dec. 17, 1975-Jan. 3, 1979
Departure: Left the House; lost Senate nomination

4th GOVERNMENT OPERATIONS
Dates: Jan. 24, 1991-Jan. 3, 1993
Departure: Moved to Appropriations

5th APPROPRIATIONS
Dates: Jan. 5, 1993-Jan. 1, 1997
Departure: Resigned the House; elected state justice

Cong.	Ranking	Terms in: House	Comm.	Date of Assignment
103rd	Maj-30th	5	1	Jan. 5, 1993
104th	Min-24th	6	2	Jan. 6, 1995

John R. Thune (R-S.D.)

Dates: Jan. 7, 1961
House: Jan. 3, 1997-Jan. 3, 2003
Left the House: Lost U.S. Senate election in 2002
Senate: Jan. 3, 2005-date
Serving in the 111th Congress

HOUSE STANDING COMMITTEES:

1st AGRICULTURE
Dates: Jan. 7, 1997-Jan. 3, 2001
Departure: Left the House; lost Senate election

Cong.	Ranking	Terms in: House	Comm.	Date of Assignment
105th	Maj-25th	1	1	Jan. 7, 1997
106th	Maj-17th	2	2	Jan. 6, 1999
107th	Maj-11th	3	3	Jan. 6, 2001

2nd TRANSPORTATION AND INFRASTRUCTURE
Dates: Jan. 7, 1997-Jan. 3, 2001
Departure: Left the House; lost Senate election

Cong.	Ranking	Terms in: House	Comm.	Date of Assignment
105th	Maj-34th	1	1	Jan. 7, 1997
106th	Maj-28th	2	2	Jan. 6, 1999
107th	Maj-20th	3	3	Jan. 6, 2001

3rd SMALL BUSINESS
Dates: Jan. 6, 1999-Jan. 3, 2003
Departure: Left the House; lost Senate election

Cong.	Ranking	Terms in: House	Comm.	Date of Assignment
106th	Maj-18th	2	1	Jan. 6, 1999
107th	Maj-11th	3	2	Jan. 6, 2001

SENATE STANDING COMMITTEES:

1st ARMED SERVICES
Dates: Jan. 6, 2005-date
Departure: Still serving in the 111th Congress

Cong.	Ranking	Years in: Senate	Comm.	Date of Assignment
109th	Maj-13th	1	1	Jan. 6, 2005
110th	Min-11th	3	3	Jan. 12, 2007
111th	Min-6th	5	5	Jan. 21, 2009

2nd ENVIRONMENT AND PUBLIC WORKS
Dates: Jan. 6, 2005-Jan. 12, 2007
Departure: Moved to Agriculture, Nutrition and Forestry and Commerce, Science and Transportation

Cong.	Ranking	Years in: Senate	Comm.	Date of Assignment
109th	Maj-7th	1	1	Jan. 6, 2005

3rd SMALL BUSINESS AND ENTREPRENEURSHIP
Dates: Jan. 6, 2005-date
Departure: Still serving in the 111th Congress

Cong.	Ranking	Years in: Senate	Comm.	Date of Assignment
109th	Maj-6th	1	1	Jan. 6, 2005
110th	Min-6th	3	3	Jan. 12, 2007
111th	Min-4th	5	5	Jan. 21, 2009

4th VETERANS AFFAIRS
Dates: Jan. 6, 2005-Jan. 12, 2007
Departure: Moved to Agriculture, Nutrition and Forestry and Commerce, Science and Transportation

Cong.	Ranking	Years in: Senate	Comm.	Date of Assignment
109th	Maj-7th	1	1	Jan. 6, 2005

5th AGRICULTURE, NUTRITION AND FORESTRY
Dates: Jan. 12, 2007-date
Departure: Still serving in the 111th Congress

Cong.	Ranking	Years in: Senate	Comm.	Date of Assignment
110th	Min-9th	3	1	Jan. 12, 2007
111th	Min-8th	5	3	Jan. 21, 2009

6th COMMERCE, SCIENCE AND TRANSPORTATION
Dates: Jan. 12, 2007-date
Departure: Still serving in the 111th Congress

Cong.	Ranking	Years in: Senate	Comm.	Date of Assignment
110th	Min-11th	3	1	Jan. 12, 2007
111th	Min-5th	5	3	Jan. 21, 2009

Karen L. Thurman (D-Fla.)

Dates: Jan. 12, 1951
House: Jan. 3, 1993-Jan. 3, 2003
Left the House: Defeated for re-election in 2002

HOUSE STANDING COMMITTEES:

1st AGRICULTURE
Dates: Jan. 5, 1993-Jan. 3, 1997
Departure: Moved to Ways and Means

Cong.	Ranking	Terms in: House	Comm.	Date of Assignment
103rd	Maj-26th	1	1	Jan. 5, 1993
104th	Min-17th	2	2	Jan. 4, 1995

2nd GOVERNMENT OPERATIONS, 103
GOVERNMENT REFORM AND OVERSIGHT, 104

Dates: Jan. 5, 1993-Jan. 5, 1997
Departure: Moved to Ways and Means

Cong.	Ranking	Terms in: House	Comm.	Date of Assignment
103rd	Maj-13th	1	1	Jan. 5, 1993
104th	Min-12th	2	2	Jan. 9, 1995

3rd WAYS AND MEANS
Dates: Jan. 7, 1997-Jan. 3, 2003
Departure: Left the House; lost re-election

Cong.	Ranking	Terms in: House	Comm.	Date of Assignment
105th	Min-16th	3	1	Jan. 7, 1997
106th	Min-15th	4	2	Jan. 6, 1999
107th	Min-15th	5	3	Jan. 31, 2001

J. Strom Thurmond (R-S.C.)

Dates: Dec. 5, 1902-June 26, 2003
Senate 1: Dec. 24, 1954-April 4, 1956
Left the Senate 1: Resigned; filled own vacancy
Senate 2: Nov. 7, 1956-Jan. 3, 2003
Left the Senate 2: Retired in 2002
Served as a Democrat: Dec. 24, 1954-Sept. 16, 1964
Served as a Republican: Sept. 16, 1964-Jan. 3, 2003

S1: Thurmond was appointed to the 83rd Congress, Dec. 24, 1954, to fill the vacancy caused by the death of U.S. Senator Burnet R. Maybank (D-S.C.). He was not seated nor assigned to committees because the 83rd Congress was not in session. Thurmond was assigned to committees in the 84th Congress and served until his resignation.

S2: Thurmond was elected to the 84th Congress, Nov. 7, 1956, to fill the vacancy caused by his own resignation. He was seated Jan. 3, 1957, and assigned to committees in the 85th Congress.

SENATE STANDING COMMITTEES:

1st GOVERNMENT OPERATIONS
1st Dates: Jan. 11, 1955-Apr. 4, 1956
1st Departure: Left the Senate; resigned
2nd Dates: Jan. 9, 1957-Jan. 14, 1959
2nd Departure: Moved to Armed Services

2nd INTERSTATE AND FOREIGN COMMERCE
1st Dates: Jan. 11, 1955-Apr. 4, 1956
1st Departure: Left the Senate; resigned
2nd Dates: Jan. 9, 1957-Feb. 25, 1963
COMMERCE
2nd Dates: Feb. 25, 1963-Sep. 16, 1964
2nd Departure: Left committee as a Majority Democrat and returned as a Minority Republican
3rd Dates: Sep. 17, 1964-Jan. 15, 1965
3rd Departure: Moved to Banking and Currency

3rd PUBLIC WORKS
Dates: Jan. 11, 1955-Apr. 4, 1956
Departure: Left the Senate; resigned

4th LABOR AND PUBLIC WELFARE
1st Dates: Jan. 9, 1957-Jan. 14, 1959
1st Departure: Moved to Armed Services
LABOR AND HUMAN RESOURCES

2nd Dates: Feb. 9, 1984-Jan. 4, 1995
2nd Departure: Left committee; became Chair of Armed Services

Cong.	Ranking	Years in: Senate	Comm.	Date of Assignment
103rd	Min-5th	38 *2	9	Jan. 7, 1993

5th ARMED SERVICES
1st Dates: Jan. 14, 1959-Sep. 16, 1964
1st Departure: Left committee as a Majority Democrat; returned as a Minority Republican
2nd Dates: Sep. 17, 1964-Jan. 3, 2003
2nd Departure: Left the Senate; retired

Cong.	Ranking	Years in: Senate	Comm.	Date of Assignment
103rd	Min-RM	38 *2	29	Jan. 7, 1993
104th	Maj-Chr	40 *2	31	Jan. 4, 1995
105th	Maj-Chr	42 *2	33	Jan. 9, 1997
106th	Maj-2nd	44 *2	35	Jan. 7, 1999
107th	Maj-2nd	46 *2	37	Jan. 25, 2001
+107th	Min-2nd	46 *2	37	June 6, 2001

6th BANKING AND CURRENCY
Dates: Jan. 15, 1965-Jan. 16, 1967
Departure: Moved to Judiciary

7th JUDICIARY
Dates: Jan. 16, 1967-Jan. 3, 2003
Departure: Left the Senate; retired

Cong.	Ranking	Years in: Senate	Comm.	Date of Assignment
103rd	Min-2nd	38	26	Jan. 7, 1993
104th	Maj-2nd	40	28	Jan. 4, 1995
105th	Maj-2nd	42	30	Jan. 9, 1997
106th	Maj-2nd	44	32	Jan. 7, 1999
107th	Maj-2nd	46	35	Jan. 25, 2001
+107th	Min-2nd	46	35	June 6, 2001

8th RULES AND ADMINISTRATION
Dates: Jan. 14, 1969-Jan. 29, 1971
Departure: Moved to Veterans Affairs

9th VETERANS AFFAIRS
Dates: Jan. 29, 1971-Jan. 3, 2003
Departure: Left the Senate; retired

Cong.	Ranking	Years in: Senate	Comm.	Assignment
103rd	Min-4th	38	22	Jan. 21, 1993
104th	Maj-4th	40	24	Jan. 6, 1995
105th	Maj-3rd	42	26	Jan. 9, 1997
106th	Maj-3rd	44	28	Jan. 7, 1999
107th	Maj-3rd	46	30	Jan. 25, 2001
+107th	Min-3rd	46	31	June 6, 2001

SENATE SELECT AND SPECIAL COMMITTEES:

1st SELECT INTELLIGENCE (Permanent)
Dates: May 20, 1976-Jan. 14, 1977
Departure: Moved to Select Official Conduct

2nd SELECT OFFICIAL CONDUCT
Dates: Jan. 19, 1977-Mar. 10, 1977
Termination: Senate Report 49 (95-1) filed

3rd FOREIGN GOVERNMENT REPRESENTATION
Dates: July 25, 1980-Oct. 2, 1980
Termination: Senate Report 1015 (96-2) filed

JOINT COMMITTEES:

1st JOINT LIBRARY
Senate Dates: Jan. 31, 1969-Feb. 24, 1971
Departure: Moved to Veterans Affairs as Ranking Minority Member.

2nd JOINT IMMIGRATION AND NATIONALITY
Senate Dates: Mar. 6, 1970-Oct. 26, 1970
Termination: Legislative Reorganization Act of 1970 (Public Law 91-510)

SENATE LEADERSHIP POSTS

1st SENATE PRESIDENT *PRO TEMPORE*
1st Dates: Jan. 3, 1995-June 6, 2001
Note: In the 104th Congress, Thurmond succeeded President Robert C. Byrd (D-W.Va.) as Senate President *pro tempore* when the Republicans gained control of the Senate in 1994.
Departure: Jeffords switch made Republicans a minority

Cong.	Ranking	Years in: Senate	Post	Date of Service
104th	Maj-Ppt	40	1	Jan. 4, 1995
105th	Maj-Ppt	42	3	Jan. 7, 1997
106th	Maj-Ppt	44	5	Jan. 6, 1999
107th	Maj-Ppt	46	7	Jan. 3, 2001

Todd Tiahrt (R-Kans.)

Dates: June 15, 1951
House: Jan. 3, 1995-date
Serving in the 111th Congress

HOUSE STANDING COMMITTEES:

1st NATIONAL SECURITY
Dates: Jan. 4, 1995-Jan. 3, 1997
Departure: Moved to Appropriations

Cong.	Ranking	Terms in: House	Comm.	Date of Assignment
104th	Maj-29th	1	1	Jan. 4, 1995

2nd SCIENCE
Dates: Jan. 4, 1995-Jan. 3, 1997
Departure: Moved to Appropriations

Cong.	Ranking	Terms in: House	Comm.	Date of Assignment
104th	Maj-22nd	1	1	Jan. 4, 1995

3rd TRANSPORTATION AND INFRASTRUCTURE
Dates: June 25, 1996-Jan. 3, 1997
Departure: Moved to Appropriations

Cong.	Ranking	Terms in: House	Comm.	Date of Assignment
104th	MjA-34th	1	1	June 25, 1996

4th APPROPRIATIONS
Dates: Jan. 7, 1997-date
Departure: Still serving in the 111th Congress

Cong.	Ranking	Terms in: House	Comm.	Date of Assignment
105th	Maj-30th	2	1	Jan. 7, 1997
106th	Maj-26th	3	2	Jan. 6, 1999
107th	Maj-22nd	4	3	Jan. 6, 2001
108th	Maj-18th	5	4	Jan. 28, 2003
109th	Maj-17th	6	5	Jan. 6, 2005
110th	Min-12th	7	6	Jan. 4, 2007
111th	Min-7th	8	7	Jan. 9, 2009

HOUSE SELECT AND SPECIAL COMMITTEES:

1st PERMANENT SELECT INTELLIGENCE
Dates: Jan. 26, 2005-Jan. 3, 2009
Departure: Left committee; no new assignment

Cong.	Ranking	Terms in: House	Comm.	Date of Assignment
109th	Maj-10th	6	1	Jan. 26, 2005
110th	Min-6th	7	2	Jan. 17, 2007

Patrick Tiberi (R-Ohio)

Dates: Oct. 21, 1962
House: Jan. 3, 2001-date
Serving in the 111th Congress

HOUSE STANDING COMMITTEES:

1st EDUCATION AND THE WORKFORCE
Dates: Jan. 6, 2001-Jan. 3, 2007
Departure: Moved to Ways and Means and Budget

Cong.	Ranking	Terms in: House	Comm.	Date of Assignment
107th	Maj-23rd	1	1	Jan. 6, 2001
108th	Maj-17th	2	2	Jan. 28, 2003
109th	Maj-11th	3	3	Jan. 26, 2005

2nd FINANCIAL SERVICES
Dates: Jan. 6, 2001-Jan. 3, 2007
Departure: Moved to Ways and Means and Budget

Cong.	Ranking	Terms in: House	Comm.	Date of Assignment
107th	Maj-37th	1	1	Jan. 6, 2001
108th	Maj-28th	2	2	Jan. 28, 2003
109th	Maj-22nd	3	3	Jan. 26, 2005

3rd GOVERNMENT REFORM
Dates: Mar. 10, 2004-Jan. 3, 2005
Departure: Left committee; no new assignment

Cong.	Ranking	Terms in: House	Comm.	Date of Assignment
108th	MjR-1st	2	1	Mar. 10, 2004

4th WAYS AND MEANS
Dates: Jan. 4, 2007-date
Departure: Still serving in the 111th Congress

Cong.	Ranking	Terms in: House	Comm.	Date of Assignment
110th	Min-16th	4	1	Jan. 4, 2007
111th	Min-9th	5	2	Jan. 9, 2009

5th BUDGET
Dates: Jan. 10, 2007-Jan. 3, 2009
Departure: Left committee; no new assignment

Cong.	Ranking	Terms in: House	Comm.	Date of Assignment
110th	Min-14th	4	1	Jan. 10, 2007

John F. Tierney (D-Mass.)

Dates: Sept. 18, 1951
House: Jan. 3, 1997-date
Serving in the 111th Congress

HOUSE STANDING COMMITTEES:

1st EDUCATION AND THE WORKFORCE, 105-109
EDUCATION AND LABOR, 110-111
Dates: Jan. 7, 1997-date
Departure: Still serving in the 111th Congress

Cong.	Ranking	Terms in: House	Comm.	Date of Assignment
105th	Min-17th	1	1	Jan. 7, 1997
106th	Min-16th	2	2	Jan. 6, 1999
107th	Min-14th	3	3	Jan. 31, 2001
108th	Min-9th	4	4	Jan. 28, 2003
109th	Min-10th	5	5	Jan. 26, 2005
110th	Maj-9th	6	6	Jan. 10, 2007
111th	Maj-9th	7	7	Jan. 21, 2009

2nd GOVERNMENT REFORM AND OVERSIGHT, 105
GOVERNMENT REFORM, 106-108
OVERSIGHT AND GOVERNMENT REFORM, 110
1st Dates: Feb. 5, 1997-Feb. 1, 2005
1st Departure: Leave of absence; moved to Select Intelligence
2nd Dates: Jan. 12, 2007-date
2nd Departure: Still serving in the 111th Congress

Cong.	Ranking	Terms in: House	Comm.	Date of Assignment
105th	Min-17th	1 *1	1	Feb. 5, 1997
106th	Min-16th	2 *1	2	Jan. 6, 1999
107th	Min-14th	3 *1	3	Jan. 31, 2001
108th	Min-11th	4 *1	4	Jan. 28, 2003
109th	Min-10th	5 *1	5	Jan. 26, 2005
110th	Maj-9th	6 *2	1	Jan. 12, 2007
111th	Maj-6th	7 *2	2	Jan. 12, 2009

HOUSE SELECT AND SPECIAL COMMITTEES:

1st PERMANENT SELECT INTELLIGENCE
Dates: Jan. 26, 2005-date
Departure: Still serving in the 111th Congress

Cong.	Ranking	Terms in: House	Comm.	Date of Assignment
109th	Min-9th	5	1	Jan. 26, 2005
110th	Maj-8th	6	2	Jan. 17, 2007
111th	Maj-6th	7	3	Feb. 4, 2009

Alice (Dina) Titus (D-Nev.)

Dates: May 23, 1950
House: Jan. 3, 2009-date
Serving in the 111th Congress

HOUSE STANDING COMMITTEES:

1st TRANSPORTATION AND INFRASTRUCTURE
Dates: Jan. 7, 2009-date
Departure: Still serving in the 111th Congress

Cong.	Ranking	Terms in: House	Comm.	Date of Assignment
111th	Maj-44th	1	1	Jan. 7, 2009

2nd EDUCATION AND LABOR
Dates: Jan. 21, 2009-date
Departure: Still serving in the 111th Congress

Cong.	Ranking	Terms in: House	Comm.	Date of Assignment
111th	Maj-29th	1	1	Jan. 21, 2009

3rd HOMELAND SECURITY
Dates: Jan. 28, 2009-date
Departure: Still serving in the 111th Congress

Cong.	Ranking	Terms in: House	Comm.	Date of Assignment
111th	Maj-20th	1	1	Jan. 28, 2009

Paul Tonko (D-N.Y.)

Dates: June 18, 1949-
House: Jan. 3, 2009-date
Serving in the 111th Congress

HOUSE STANDING COMMITTEES:

1st EDUCATION AND LABOR
Dates: Jan. 21, 2009-date
Departure: Still serving in the 111th Congress

Cong.	Ranking	Terms in: House	Comm.	Date of Assignment
111th	Maj-26th	1	1	Jan. 21, 2009

2nd SCIENCE AND TECHNOLOGY
Dates: Jan. 21, 2009-date
Departure: Still serving in the 111th Congress

Cong.	Ranking	Terms in: House	Comm.	Date of Assignment
111th	Maj-13th	1	1	Jan. 21, 2009

Patrick J. Toomey (R-Penn.)

Dates: Nov. 17, 1961
House: Jan. 3, 1999-Jan. 3, 2005
Left the House: Lost U.S. Senate nomination in 2004

HOUSE STANDING COMMITTEES:

1st BANKING AND FINANCIAL SERVICES, 106
FINANCIAL SERVICES, 107-108
Dates: Jan. 6, 1999-Jan. 3, 2005
Departure: Left the House; lost Senate nomination

Cong.	Ranking	Terms in: House	Comm.	Date of Assignment
106th	Maj-32nd	1	1	Jan. 6, 1999
107th	Maj-26th	2	2	Jan. 6, 2001
108th	Maj-21st	3	3	Jan. 28, 2003

2nd BUDGET
Dates: Jan. 6, 1999-Jan. 3, 2005
Departure: Left the House; lost Senate nomination

Cong.	Ranking	Terms in: House	Comm.	Date of Assignment
106th	Maj-24th	1	1	Jan. 6, 1999
107th	Maj-14th	2	2	Jan. 6, 2001
108th	Maj-6th	3	3	Jan. 28, 2003

3rd SMALL BUSINESS
Dates: Jan. 6, 1999-Jan. 3, 2005
Departure: Left the House; lost Senate nomination

Cong.	Ranking	Terms in: House	Comm.	Date of Assignment
106th	Maj-15th	1	1	Jan. 6, 1999

107th	Maj-9th	2	2	Jan. 6, 2001
108th	Maj-6th	3	3	Jan. 28, 2003

Peter G. Torkildsen (R-Mass.)

Dates: Jan. 28, 1958
House: Jan. 3, 1993-Jan. 3, 1997
Left the House: Defeated for re-election in 1996

HOUSE STANDING COMMITTEES:

1st ARMED SERVICES, 103
NATIONAL SECURITY, 104
Dates: Jan. 5, 1993-Jan. 3, 1997
Departure: Left the House; lost re-election

Cong.	Ranking	Terms in: House	Comm.	Date of Assignment
103rd	Min-17th	1	1	Jan. 5, 1993
104th	Maj-13th	2	2	Jan. 4, 1995

2nd SMALL BUSINESS
Dates: Jan. 5, 1993-Jan. 3, 1997
Departure: Left the House; lost re-election

Cong.	Ranking	Terms in: House	Comm.	Date of Assignment
103rd	Min-18th	1	1	Jan. 5, 1993
104th	Maj-6th	2	2	Jan. 4, 1995

3rd MERCHANT MARINE AND FISHERIES
Dates: Feb. 4, 1993-Jan. 3, 1995
Departure: Committee abolished; moved to Resources

Cong.	Ranking	Terms in: House	Comm.	Date of Assignment
103rd	MnA-19th	1	1	Feb. 4, 1993

4th RESOURCES
Dates: Jan. 4, 1995-Jan. 3, 1997
Departure: Left the House; lost re-election

Cong.	Ranking	Terms in: House	Comm.	Date of Assignment
104th	Maj-12th	2	1	Jan. 4, 1995

Esteban Edward Torres (D-Cal.)

Dates: Jan. 27, 1930
House: Jan. 3, 1983-Jan. 3, 1999
Left the House: Retired in 1998

HOUSE STANDING COMMITTEES:

1st BANKING, FINANCE AND URBAN AFFAIRS, 98-102
BANKING AND FINANCIAL SERVICES, 105
1st Dates: Jan. 6, 1983-Jan. 3, 1993
1st Departure: Moved to Appropriations.
2nd Dates: Apr. 16, 1997-Apr. 29, 1998
2nd Departure: Resigned committee; no new assignment

Cong.	Ranking	Terms in: House	Comm.	Date of Assignment
105th	MnA-25th	8 *2	1	Apr. 16, 1997

2nd SMALL BUSINESS
Dates: Jan. 6, 1983-Jan. 3, 1993
Departure: Moved to Appropriations

3rd APPROPRIATIONS
Dates: Jan. 5, 1993-Jan. 3, 1999
Departure: Left the House; retired

Cong.	Ranking	Terms in: House	Comm.	Date of Assignment
103rd	Maj-27th	6	1	Jan. 5, 1993
104th	Min-22nd	7	2	Jan. 4, 1995
105th	Min-17th	8	3	Jan. 7, 1997

Robert G. Torricelli (D-N.J.)

Dates: Aug. 26, 1951
House: Jan. 3, 1983-Jan. 3, 1997
Left the House: Elected to U.S. Senate in 1996
Senate: Jan. 3, 1997-Jan. 3, 2003
Left the Senate: Retired after being re-nominated

HOUSE STANDING COMMITTEES:

1st FOREIGN AFFAIRS, 103
INTERNATIONAL RELATIONS, 104
Dates: Jan. 6, 1983-Jan. 3, 1997
Departure: Left the House for the Senate

Cong.	Ranking	Terms in: House	Comm.	Date of Assignment
103rd	Maj-4th	6	6	Jan. 5, 1993
104th	Min-4th	7	7	Jan. 4, 1995

2nd SCIENCE AND TECHNOLOGY, 98-99
SCIENCE, SPACE AND TECHNOLOGY, 100-103
Dates: Jan. 6, 1983-Jan. 3, 1995
Departure: Left committee; no new assignment

Cong.	Ranking	Terms in: House	Comm.	Date of Assignment
103rd	Maj-8th	6	6	Jan. 5, 1993

HOUSE SELECT AND SPECIAL COMMITTEES:

1st PERMANENT SELECT INTELLIGENCE
Dates: Feb. 3, 1993-Jan. 3, 1997
Departure: Left the House for the Senate

Cong.	Ranking	Terms in: House	Comm.	Date of Assignment
103rd	Maj-5th	6	1	Feb. 3, 1993
104th	Min-4th	7	2	Jan. 4, 1995

SENATE STANDING COMMITTEES:

1st GOVERNMENTAL AFFAIRS
Dates: Jan. 9, 1997-Jan. 3, 2003
Departure: Left the Senate; retired

Cong.	Ranking	Years in: Senate	Comm.	Date of Assignment
105th	Min-6th	1	1	Jan. 9, 1997
106th	Min-5th	3	2	Jan. 7, 1999
107th	Min-5th	5	5	Jan. 25, 2001
+107th	Maj-5th	5	5	June 6, 2001

2nd JUDICIARY
Dates: Jan. 9, 1997-Jan. 25, 2001
Departure: Moved to Finance

Cong.	Ranking	Years in: Senate	Comm.	Date of Assignment
105th	Min-8th	1	1	Jan. 9, 1997
106th	Min-7th	3	2	Jan. 7, 1999

3rd RULES AND ADMINISTRATION
Dates: Jan. 9, 1997-Jan. 3, 2003
Departure: Left the Senate; retired

Cong.	Ranking	Years in: Senate	Comm.	Date of Assignment
105th	Min-7th	1	1	Jan. 9, 1997
106th	Min-6th	3	2	Jan. 7, 1999
107th	Min-5th	5	5	Jan. 25, 2001
+107th	Maj-5th	5	5	June 6, 2001

4th FOREIGN RELATIONS
Dates: Jan. 7, 1999-Jan. 3, 2003
Departure: Left the Senate; retired

Cong.	Ranking	Years in: Senate	Comm.	Date of Assignment
106th	Min-8th	3	1	Jan. 7, 1999
107th	Min-8th	5	3	Jan. 25, 2001
+107th	Maj-8th	5	3	June 6, 2001

5th FINANCE
Dates: Jan. 25, 2001-Jan. 3, 2003
Departure: Left the Senate; retired

Cong.	Ranking	Years in: Senate	Comm.	Date of Assignment
107th	Min-9th	5	1	Jan. 25, 2001
+107th	Maj-10th	5	1	July 10, 2001

SENATE SELECT AND SPECIAL COMMITTEES:

1st JOINT ECONOMIC
Dates: July 10, 2001-Jan. 3, 2003
Departure: Left the Senate; retired

Cong.	Ranking	Years in: Senate	Comm.	Date of Assignment
+107th	MjA-6th	5	1	July 10, 2001

Edolphus Towns (D-N.Y.)

Dates: July 21, 1934
House: Jan. 3, 1983-date
Serving in the 111th Congress

HOUSE STANDING COMMITTEES:

1st GOVERNMENT OPERATIONS, 98-103
GOVERNMENT REFORM AND OVERSIGHT, 104-105
GOVERNMENT REFORM, 106-109
OVERSIGHT AND GOVERNMENT REFORM, 110-111
Dates: Jan. 6, 1983-date
Departure: Still serving in the 111th Congress

Cong.	Ranking	Terms in: House	Comm.	Date of Assignment
103rd	Maj-9th	6	6	Jan. 5, 1993
104th	Min-6th	7	7	Jan. 9, 1995
105th	Min-5th	8	8	Jan. 7, 1997
106th	Min-5th	9	9	Jan. 6, 1999

Cong.	Ranking	House	Comm.	Date of Assignment
107th	Min-4th	10	10	Jan. 31, 2001
108th	Min-4th	11	11	Jan. 28, 2003
109th	Min-4th	12	12	Jan. 26, 2005
110th	Maj-3rd	13	13	Jan. 12, 2007
111th	Maj-Chr	14	14	Jan. 6, 2009

2nd PUBLIC WORKS AND TRANSPORTATION
Dates: Jan. 6, 1983-Nov. 8, 1989
Departure: Moved to Energy and Commerce

3rd ENERGY AND COMMERCE, 101-103
COMMERCE, 104-106
ENERGY AND COMMERCE, 107-110
Dates: Nov. 8, 1989-Jan. 3, 2009
Departure: Left committee; became Chair of Oversight and Government Reform

Cong.	Ranking	Terms in: House	Comm.	Date of Assignment
103rd	Maj-18th	6	3	Jan. 5, 1993
104th	Min-10th	7	4	Jan. 4, 1995
105th	Min-8th	8	5	Jan. 7, 1997
106th	Min-6th	9	6	Jan. 6, 1999
107th	Min-6th	10	7	Jan. 31, 2001
108th	Min-6th	11	8	Jan. 28, 2003
109th	Min-5th	12	9	Jan. 26, 2005
110th	Maj-5th	13	10	Jan. 4, 2007

HOUSE SELECT AND SPECIAL COMMITTEES:

1st SELECT NARCOTICS ABUSE AND CONTROL (Temporary)
Dates: Feb. 22, 1983-Jan. 3, 1993
Termination: Committee not renewed in 1993

James A. Traficant Jr. (D-Ohio)

Dates: May 8, 1941
House: Jan. 3, 1985-July 24, 2002
Left the House: Expelled from the House by a vote of 420-1

HOUSE STANDING COMMITTEES:

1st PUBLIC WORKS AND TRANSPORTATION, 99-103
TRANSPORTATION AND INFRASTRUCTURE, 104-106
Dates: Jan. 30, 1985-Jan. 3, 2001
Departure: Left committee; unassigned in 107th Congress

Cong.	Ranking	Terms in: House	Comm.	Date of Assignment
103rd	Maj-10th	5	5	Jan. 5, 1993
104th	Min-7th	6	6	Jan. 4, 1995
105th	Min-6th	7	7	Jan. 7, 1997
106th	Min-6th	8	8	Jan. 6, 1999

2nd SCIENCE AND TECHNOLOGY, 99
SCIENCE, SPACE AND TECHNOLOGY, 100-103
SCIENCE, 104-106
Dates: Jan. 30, 1985-Feb. 17, 1999
Departure: Leave of absence; no new assignment. Left committee; unassigned in 107th Congress

Cong.	Ranking	Terms in: House	Comm.	Date of Assignment
103rd	Maj-10th	5	5	Jan. 5, 1993
104th	Min-3rd	6	6	Jan. 4, 1995
105th	Min-4th	7	7	Feb. 13, 1997
106th	Min-4th	8	8	Jan. 6, 1999

HOUSE SELECT AND SPECIAL COMMITTEES:

1st SELECT NARCOTICS ABUSE AND CONTROL (Temporary)
Dates: June 17, 1987-Jan. 3, 1993
Termination: Committee not renewed in 1993

Nicola (Niki) Tsongas (D-Mass.)

Dates: April 26, 1946
House: Oct. 16, 2007-date
Serving in the 111th Congress

H: Niki Tsongas was elected to the 110th Congress by special election, Oct. 16, 2007, to fill the vacancy caused by the resignation of U.S. Representative Martin Meehan (D-Mass.). She was seated Oct. 18, 2007, and assigned to committees.

HOUSE STANDING COMMITTEES:

1st ARMED SERVICES
Dates: Nov. 1, 2007-date
Departure: Still serving in the 111th Congress

Cong.	Ranking	Terms in: House	Comm.	Date of Assignment
110th	MjR-3rd	1	1	Nov. 1, 2007
111th	Maj-30th	2	2	Jan. 7, 2009

2nd BUDGET
Dates: Nov. 1, 2007-date
Departure: Still serving in the 111th Congress

Cong.	Ranking	Terms in: House	Comm.	Date of Assignment
110th	MjR-2nd	1	1	Nov. 1, 2007
111th	Maj-10th	2	2	Jan. 21, 2009

3rd NATURAL RESOURCES
Dates: Jan. 21, 2009-date
Departure: Still serving in the 111th Congress

Cong.	Ranking	Terms in: House	Comm.	Date of Assignment
111th	Maj-27th	2	1	Jan. 21, 2009

Walter R. Tucker (D-Cal.)

Dates: May 28, 1957
House: Jan. 3, 1993-Dec. 15, 1995
Left the House: Resigned and retired

HOUSE STANDING COMMITTEES:

1st PUBLIC WORKS AND TRANSPORTATION, 103
TRANSPORTATION AND INFRASTRUCTURE, 104
Dates: Jan. 5, 1993-Dec. 15, 1995
Departure: Resigned the House and retired

Cong.	Ranking	Terms in: House	Comm.	Date of Assignment
103rd	Maj-38th	1	1	Jan. 5, 1993
104th	Min-26th	2	2	Jan. 4, 1995

2nd SMALL BUSINESS
Dates: Jan. 5, 1993-Dec. 15, 1995
Departure: Resigned the House and retired

Cong.	Ranking	Terms in: House	Comm.	Date of Assignment
103rd	Maj-22nd	1	1	Jan. 5, 1993
104th	Min-11th	2	2	Jan. 4, 1995

Cong.	Ranking	Terms in: House	Comm.	Date of Assignment
108th	Min-RM	4	1	Feb. 12, 2003

Jim Turner (D-Tex.)

Dates: Feb. 6, 1946
House: Jan. 3, 1997-Jan. 3, 2005
Left the House: Retired in 2004

HOUSE STANDING COMMITTEES:

1st GOVERNMENT REFORM AND OVERSIGHT, 105
GOVERNMENT REFORM, 106-108
Dates: Feb. 5, 1997-Feb. 5, 2003
Departure: Resigned committee to become Ranking Member on Select Homeland Security

Cong.	Ranking	Terms in: House	Comm.	Date of Assignment
105th	Min-18th	1	1	Feb. 5, 1997
106th	Min-17th	2	2	Jan. 6, 1999
107th	Min-15th	3	3	Jan. 31, 2001
108th	Min-12th	4	4	Jan. 28, 2003

2nd NATIONAL SECURITY, 105
ARMED SERVICES, 106-108
Dates: Jan. 7, 1997-Jan. 3, 2005
Departure: Left the House; retired

Cong.	Ranking	Terms in: House	Comm.	Date of Assignment
105th	Min-20th	1	1	Jan. 7, 1997
106th	Min-16th	2	2	Jan. 6, 1999
107th	Min-14th	3	3	Jan. 31, 2001
108th	Min-10th	4	4	Jan. 28, 2003

HOUSE SELECT AND SPECIAL COMMITTEES:

1st SELECT HOMELAND SECURITY
Dates: Feb. 12, 2003-Jan. 3, 2005
Departure: Left the House; retired

Michael R. Turner (R-Ohio)

Dates: Jan. 11, 1960
House: Jan. 3, 2003-date
Serving in the 111th Congress

HOUSE STANDING COMMITTEES:

1st ARMED SERVICES
Dates: Jan. 28, 2003-date
Departure: Still serving in the 111th Congress

Cong.	Ranking	Terms in: House	Comm.	Date of Assignment
108th	Maj-28th	1	1	Jan. 28, 2003
109th	Maj-24th	2	2	Jan. 26, 2005
110th	Min-19th	3	3	Jan. 10, 2007
111th	Min-12th	4	4	Jan. 9, 2009

2nd GOVERNMENT REFORM, 108-109
OVERSIGHT AND GOVERNMENT REFORM, 110-111
Dates: Jan. 28, 2003-date
Departure: Still serving in the 111th Congress

Cong.	Ranking	Terms in: House	Comm.	Date of Assignment
108th	Maj-21st	1	1	Jan. 28, 2003
109th	Maj-14th	2	2	Jan. 26, 2005
110th	Min-10th	3	3	Jan. 10, 2007
111th	Min-8th	4	4	Jan. 9, 2009

3rd VETERANS AFFAIRS
Dates: Feb. 2, 2005-Jan. 13, 2009
Departure: Resigned committee; became Ranking Republican on the Strategic Forces Subcommittee of the House Armed Services Committee

Cong.	Ranking	Terms in: House	Comm.	Date of Assignment
109th	Maj-15th	2	1	Feb. 2, 2005
110th	Min-10th	3	2	Jan. 10, 2007
111th	Min-7th	4	3	Jan. 9, 2009

U

Mark Udall (D-Colo.)

Dates: July 18, 1950
House: Jan. 3, 1999-Jan. 3, 2009
Left the House: Elected to the Senate in 2008
Serving in the 111th Congress

HOUSE STANDING COMMITTEES:

1st RESOURCES, 106-109
NATURAL RESOURCES, 110

Dates: Jan. 6, 1999-Jan. 3, 2009
Departure: Left the House for the Senate

Cong.	Ranking	Terms in: House	Comm.	Date of Assignment
106th	Min-23rd	1	1	Jan. 6, 1999
107th	Min-18th	2	2	Feb. 8, 2001
108th	Min-17th	3	3	Jan. 28, 2003
109th	Min-20th	4	4	Feb. 2, 2005
110th	Maj-23rd	5	5	Jan. 18, 2007

2nd SCIENCE, 106-109
SCIENCE AND TECHNOLOGY, 110

Dates: Jan. 6, 1999-Jan. 3, 2009
Departure: Left the House for the Senate

Cong.	Ranking	Terms in: House	Comm.	Date of Assignment
106th	Min-20th	1	1	Jan. 6, 1999
107th	Min-14th	2	2	Jan. 31, 2001
108th	Min-11th	3	3	Jan. 28, 2003
109th	Min-6th	4	4	Jan. 26, 2005
110th	Maj-5th	5	5	Jan. 18, 2007

3rd SMALL BUSINESS
Dates: May 25, 1999-Jan. 3, 2003
Departure: Moved to Agriculture

Cong.	Ranking	Terms in: House	Comm.	Date of Assignment
106th	MnR-2nd	1	1	May 25, 1999
107th	Min-17th	2	2	Jan. 31, 2001

4th AGRICULTURE
Dates: Feb. 13, 2003-Jan. 3, 2005
Departure: Moved to Armed Services

Cong.	Ranking	Terms in: House	Comm.	Date of Assignment
108th	Min-23rd	3	1	Feb. 13, 2003

5th ARMED SERVICES, 109-110
Dates: Jan. 26, 2005-Jan. 3, 2009
Departure: Left the House for the Senate

Cong.	Ranking	Terms in: House	Comm.	Date of Assignment
109th	Min-25th	4	1	Jan. 26, 2005
110th	Maj-21st	5	2	Jan. 10, 2007

SENATE STANDING COMMITTEES:

1st ARMED SERVICES
Dates: Jan. 21, 2009-date
Departure: Still serving in the 111th Congress

Cong.	Ranking	Years in: Senate	Comm.	Date of Assignment
111th	Maj-12th	1	1	Jan. 21, 2009

2nd ENERGY AND NATURAL RESOURCES
Dates: Jan. 21, 2009-date
Departure: Still serving in the 111th Congress

Cong.	Ranking	Years in: Senate	Comm.	Date of Assignment
111th	Maj-12th	1	1	Jan. 21, 2009

SENATE SELECT AND SPECIAL COMMITTEES:

1st SPECIAL AGING
Dates: Jan. 21, 2009-date
Departure: Still serving in the 111th Congress

Cong.	Ranking	Years in: Senate	Comm.	Date of Assignment
111th	Maj-9th	1	1	Jan. 21, 2009

Thomas Udall (D-N.M.)

Dates: May 18, 1948
House: Jan. 3, 1999-Jan. 3, 2009
Left the House: Elected to the Senate in 2008
Serving in the 111th Congress

HOUSE STANDING COMMITTEES:

1st RESOURCES
Dates: Jan. 6, 1999-Jan. 3, 2007
Departure: Moved to Appropriations

Cong.	Ranking	Terms in: House	Comm.	Date of Assignment
106th	Min-22nd	1	1	Jan. 6, 1999
107th	Min-17th	2	2	Feb. 8, 2001
108th	Min-16th	3	3	Jan. 28, 2003
109th	Min-10th	4	4	Jan. 26, 2005

2nd SMALL BUSINESS
Dates: Jan. 6, 1999-Jan. 3, 2007
Departure: Moved to Appropriations

Cong.	Ranking	Terms in: House	Comm.	Date of Assignment
106th	Min-10th	1	1	Jan. 6, 1999
107th	Min-9th	2	2	Jan. 31, 2001
108th	Min-7th	3	3	Jan. 28, 2003
109th	Min-3rd	4	4	Jan. 26, 2005

3rd VETERANS AFFAIRS
Dates: June 9, 1999-Jan. 3, 2007
Departure: Moved to Appropriations

Cong.	Ranking	Terms in: House	Comm.	Date of Assignment
106th	Min-14th	1	1	June 9, 1999
107th	Min-14th	2	2	Jan. 31, 2001
108th	Min-12th	3	3	Feb. 13, 2003
109th	Min-12th	4	4	Feb. 2, 2005

4th APPROPRIATIONS
Dates: Jan. 4, 2007-Jan. 3, 2009
Departure: Left the House for the Senate

Cong.	Ranking	Terms in: House	Comm.	Date of Assignment
110th	Maj-28th	5	1	Jan. 4, 2007

SENATE STANDING COMMITTEES:

1st COMMERCE, SCIENCE AND TRANSPORTATION
Dates: Jan. 21, 2009-date
Departure: Still serving in the 111th Congress

Cong.	Ranking	Years in: Senate	Comm.	Date of Assignment
111th	Maj-12th	1	1	Jan. 21, 2009

2nd ENVIRONMENT AND PUBLIC WORKS
Dates: Jan. 21, 2009-date
Departure: Still serving in the 111th Congress

Cong.	Ranking	Years in: Senate	Comm.	Date of Assignment
111th	Maj-9th	1	1	Jan. 21, 2009

3rd RULES AND ADMINISTRATION
Dates: Jan. 21, 2009-date
Departure: Still serving in the 111th Congress

Cong.	Ranking	Years in: Senate	Comm.	Date of Assignment
111th	Maj-11th	1	1	Jan. 21, 2009

SENATE SELECT AND SPECIAL COMMITTEES:

1st INDIAN AFFAIRS (Permanent)
Dates: Jan. 21, 2009-date
Departure: Still serving in the 111th Congress

Cong.	Ranking	Years in: Senate	Comm.	Date of Assignment
111th	Maj-8th	1	1	Jan. 21, 2009

Robert A. Underwood (D-Guam)

Dates: July 13, 1948
House: Jan. 3, 1993-Jan. 3, 2003
Left the House: Lost election for Governor in 2002

HOUSE STANDING COMMITTEES:

1st ARMED SERVICES, 103
NATIONAL SECURITY, 104-105
ARMED SERVICES, 106-107
Dates: Jan. 5, 1993-Jan. 3, 2003
Departure: Left the House; lost election for Governor

Cong.	Ranking	Terms in: House	Comm.	Date of Assignment
103rd	Maj-29th	1	1	Jan. 5, 1993
104th	Min-17th	2	2	Jan. 4, 1995
105th	Min-12th	3	3	Jan. 7, 1997
106th	Min-10th	4	4	Jan. 6, 1999
107th	Min-9th	5	5	Jan. 31, 2001

2nd NATURAL RESOURCES, 103
RESOURCES, 104-107
Dates: Jan. 5, 1993-Jan. 3, 2003
Departure: Left the House; lost election for Governor

Cong.	Ranking	Terms in: House	Comm.	Date of Assignment
103rd	Maj-24th	1	1	Jan. 5, 1993
104th	Min-19th	2	2	Jan. 9, 1995
105th	Min-17th	3	3	Jan. 7, 1997
106th	Min-13th	4	4	Jan. 6, 1999
107th	Min-11th	5	5	Feb. 8, 2001

3rd EDUCATION AND LABOR
Dates: Apr. 22, 1993-Jan. 3, 1995
Departure: Left committee; no new assignment

Cong.	Ranking	Terms in: House	Comm.	Date of Assignment
103rd	Maj-28th	1	1	Apr. 22, 1993

Jolene Unsoeld (D-Wash.)

Dates: Dec. 3, 1931
House: Jan. 3, 1989-Jan. 3, 1995
Left the House: Defeated for re-election in 1994

HOUSE STANDING COMMITTEES:

1st EDUCATION AND LABOR
Dates: Jan. 19, 1989-Jan. 3, 1995
Departure: Left the House; lost re-election

Cong.	Ranking	Terms in: House	Comm.	Date of Assignment
103rd	Maj-11th	3	3	Jan. 5, 1993

2nd MERCHANT MARINE AND FISHERIES
Dates: Jan. 19, 1989-Jan. 3, 1995
Departure: Left the House; lost re-election

Cong.	Ranking	Terms in: House	Comm.	Date of Assignment
103rd	Maj-12th	3	3	Jan. 5, 1993

HOUSE SELECT AND SPECIAL COMMITTEES:

1st SELECT AGING (Permanent)
Dates: Mar. 8, 1989-Jan. 3, 1993
Termination: Committee not renewed in 1993

Frederick S. Upton (R-Mich.)

Dates: April 23, 1953
House: Jan. 3, 1987-date
Serving in the 111th Congress

HOUSE STANDING COMMITTEES:

1st PUBLIC WORKS AND TRANSPORTATION
Dates: Jan. 21, 1987-Oct. 17, 1991
Departure: Left committee; had moved to Energy and Commerce earlier

2nd SMALL BUSINESS
Dates: Jan. 21, 1987-July 11, 1991
Departure: Left committee; had moved to Energy and Commerce earlier

3rd ENERGY AND COMMERCE, 102-103
COMMERCE, 104-106
ENERGY AND COMMERCE, 107-111
Dates: Mar. 11, 1991-date
Departure: Still serving in the 111th Congress

Cong.	Ranking	Terms in: House	Comm.	Date of Assignment
103rd	Min-10th	4	2	Jan. 5, 1993
104th	Maj-9th	5	3	Jan. 4, 1995
105th	Maj-8th	6	4	Jan. 7, 1997
106th	Maj-6th	7	5	Jan. 6, 1999
107th	Maj-4th	8	6	Jan. 6, 2001
108th	Maj-4th	9	7	Jan. 28, 2003
109th	Maj-4th	10	8	Jan. 6, 2005
110th	Min-4th	11	9	Jan. 10, 2007
111th	Min-3rd	12	10	Jan. 9, 2009

4th EDUCATION AND THE WORKFORCE
Dates: Jan. 21, 1997-Jan. 3, 2005
Departure: Left committee; no new assignment

Cong.	Ranking	Terms in: House	Comm.	Date of Assignment
105th	Maj-22nd	6	1	Jan. 21, 1997
106th	Maj-19th	7	2	Jan. 6, 1999
107th	Maj-14th	8	3	Jan. 6, 2001
108th	Maj-11th	9	4	Jan. 28, 2003

HOUSE SELECT AND SPECIAL COMMITTEES:

1st SELECT HUNGER (Temporary)
Dates: Feb. 2, 1987-Jan. 3, 1993
Termination: Committee not renewed in 1993

V

I.T. (Tim) Valentine Jr. (D-N.C.)

Dates: March 15, 1926
House: Jan. 3, 1983-Jan. 3, 1995
Left the House: Retired in 1994

HOUSE STANDING COMMITTEES:

1st PUBLIC WORKS AND TRANSPORTATION
Dates: Jan. 6, 1983-Jan. 3, 1995
Departure: Left the House; retired

Cong.	Ranking	Terms in: House	Comm.	Date of Assignment
103rd	Maj-7th	6	6	Jan. 5, 1993

2nd SCIENCE AND TECHNOLOGY, 98-99
SCIENCE, SPACE AND TECHNOLOGY, 100-103
Dates: Jan. 6, 1983-Jan. 3, 1995
Departure: Left the House; retired

Cong.	Ranking	Terms in: House	Comm.	Date of Assignment
103rd	Maj-7th	6	6	Jan. 5, 1993

Christopher Van Hollen (D-Md.)

Dates: Jan. 10, 1959
House: Jan. 3, 2003-date
Serving in the 111th Congress

HOUSE STANDING COMMITTEES:

1st EDUCATION AND THE WORKFORCE
Dates: Feb. 5, 2003-Jan. 3, 2007
Departure: Moved to Ways and Means

Cong.	Ranking	Terms in: House	Comm.	Date of Assignment
108th	Min-21st	1	1	Feb. 5, 2003
109th	Min-19th	2	2	Jan. 26, 2005

2nd GOVERNMENT REFORM, 108-109
OVERSIGHT AND GOVERNMENT REFORM, 110-111
Dates: Feb. 5, 2003-date
Departure: Still serving in the 111th Congress

Cong.	Ranking	Terms in: House	Comm.	Date of Assignment
108th	Min-16th	1	1	Feb. 5, 2003
109th	Min-14th	2	2	Jan. 26, 2005
110th	Maj-19th	3	3	Jan. 12, 2007
111th	Maj-15th	4	4	Jan. 28, 2009

3rd JUDICIARY
Dates: Feb. 9, 2005-Jan. 3, 2007
Departure: Moved to Ways and Means

Cong.	Ranking	Terms in: House	Comm.	Date of Assignment
109th	Min-17th	2	1	Feb. 9, 2005

4th WAYS AND MEANS
Dates: Jan. 4, 2007-date
Departure: Still serving in the 111th Congress

Cong.	Ranking	Terms in: House	Comm.	Date of Assignment
110th	Maj-21st	3	1	Jan. 4, 2007
111th	Maj-18th	4	2	Jan. 7, 2009

Nydia M. Velázquez (D-N.Y.)

Dates: March 22, 1953
House: Jan. 3, 1993-date
Serving in the 111th Congress

HOUSE STANDING COMMITTEES:

1st BANKING, FINANCE AND URBAN AFFAIRS, 103
BANKING AND FINANCIAL SERVICES, 104-106
FINANCIAL SERVICES, 107-111
Dates: Jan. 5, 1993-date
Departure: Still serving in the 111th Congress

Cong.	Ranking	Terms in: House	Comm.	Date of Assignment
103rd	Maj-23rd	1	1	Jan. 5, 1993
104th	Min-16th	2	2	Jan. 4, 1995
105th	Min-14th	3	3	Jan. 7, 1997
106th	Min-8th	4	4	Jan. 6, 1999
107th	Min-7th	5	5	Jan. 31, 2001
108th	Min-7th	6	6	Jan. 28, 2003
109th	Min-7th	7	7	Jan. 26, 2005
110th	Maj-6th	8	8	Jan. 12, 2007
111th	Maj-6th	9	9	Jan. 7, 2009

2nd SMALL BUSINESS
Dates: Jan. 5, 1993-date
RM2: Replaced John LaFalce (D-N.Y.) who had become Ranking Member on Banking and Financial Services on Feb. 26, 1998
Departure: Still serving in the 111th Congress

Cong.	Ranking	Terms in: House	Comm.	Date of Assignment
103rd	Maj-19th	1	1	Jan. 5, 1993
104th	Min-9th	2	2	Jan. 4, 1995
105th	Min-6th	3	3	Feb. 5, 1997
=105th	Min-RM2	3	3	Feb. 26, 1998
106th	Min-RM	4	4	Jan. 6, 1999
107th	Min-RM	5	5	Jan. 31, 2001
108th	Min-RM	6	6	Jan. 8, 2003
109th	Min-RM	7	7	Jan. 6, 2005
110th	Maj-Chr	8	8	Jan. 4, 2007
111th	Maj-Chr	9	9	Jan. 6, 2009

Bruce F. Vento (DFL-Minn.)

Dates: Oct. 7, 1940-Oct. 10, 2000
House: Jan. 3, 1977-Oct. 10, 2000
Left the House: Died in office

HOUSE STANDING COMMITTEES:

1st BANKING, FINANCE AND URBAN AFFAIRS, 95-103
BANKING AND FINANCIAL SERVICES, 104-106
Dates: Jan. 19, 1977-Oct. 10, 2000
Departure: Died in office

Cong.	Ranking	Terms in: House	Comm.	Date of Assignment
103rd	Maj-4th	9	9	Jan. 5, 1993
104th	Min-3rd	10	10	Jan. 4, 1995
105th	Min-3rd	11	11	Jan. 7, 1997
106th	Min-2nd	12	12	Jan. 6, 1999

2nd INTERIOR AND INSULAR AFFAIRS, 95-102
NATURAL RESOURCES, 103
RESOURCES, 104-106
Dates: Jan. 19, 1977-Oct. 10, 2000
Departure: Died in office

Cong.	Ranking	Terms in: House	Comm.	Date of Assignment
103rd	Maj-6th	9	9	Jan. 5, 1993
104th	Min-3rd	10	10	Jan. 9, 1995
105th	Min-4th	11	11	Jan. 7, 1997
106th	Min-3rd	12	12	Jan. 6, 1999

HOUSE SELECT AND SPECIAL COMMITTEES:

1st SELECT AGING (Permanent)
Dates: Feb. 5, 1981-Jan. 3, 1993
Termination: Committee not renewed in 1993

Peter J. Visclosky (D-Ind.)

Dates: Aug. 13, 1949
House: Jan. 3, 1985-date
Serving in the 111th Congress

HOUSE STANDING COMMITTEES:

1st INTERIOR AND INSULAR AFFAIRS
Dates: Jan. 30, 1985-Oct. 9, 1991
Departure: Moved to Appropriations

2nd PUBLIC WORKS AND TRANSPORTATION
Dates: Jan. 30, 1985-Oct. 9, 1991
Departure: Moved to Appropriations

3rd EDUCATION AND LABOR
1st Dates: Jan. 22, 1987-Jan. 3, 1989
1st Departure: Returned to committee as temporary member
Temporary Dates: Served until terms expired
T1: Jan. 27, 1989-Apr. 4, 1990
T2: Jan. 24, 1991-June 27, 1991
T2 Departure: Left committee; no new assignment

4th APPROPRIATIONS
Dates: Oct. 9, 1991-date
Departure: Still serving in the 111th Congress

Cong.	Ranking	Terms in: House	Comm.	Date of Assignment
103rd	Maj-25th	5	2	Jan. 5, 1993
104th	Min-20th	6	3	Jan. 4, 1995
105th	Min-15th	7	4	Jan. 7, 1997
106th	Min-10th	8	5	Jan. 6, 1999
107th	Min-9th	9	6	Jan. 31, 2001
108th	Min-8th	10	7	Jan. 28, 2003
109th	Min-8th	11	8	Jan. 26, 2005
110th	Maj-6th	12	9	Jan. 4, 2007
111th	Maj-6th	13	10	Jan. 7, 2009

David Vitter (R-La.)

Dates: May 3, 1961
House: May 29, 1999-Jan. 3, 2005
Left the House: Elected to U.S. Senate in 2004
Senate: Jan. 3, 2005-date
Serving in the 111th Congress

H: Vitter was elected to the 106th Congress by special election, May 29, 1999, to fill the vacancy caused by the resignation of U.S. Representative Robert L. Livingston (R-La.). Vitter was seated June 8, 1999, and assigned to committees.

HOUSE STANDING COMMITTEES:

1st GOVERNMENT REFORM
Dates: June 25, 1999-Jan. 3, 2001
Departure: Moved to Appropriations

Cong.	Ranking	Terms in: House	Comm.	Date of Assignment
106th	MjR-2nd	1	1	June 25, 1999

2nd JUDICIARY
Dates: June 25, 1999-Jan. 3, 2001
Departure: Moved to Appropriations

Cong.	Ranking	Terms in: House	Comm.	Date of Assignment
106th	MjR-2nd	1	1	June 25, 1999

3rd TRANSPORTATION AND INFRASTRUCTURE
Dates: June 25, 1999-Jan. 3, 2001
Departure: Moved to Appropriations

Cong.	Ranking	Terms in: House	Comm.	Date of Assignment
106th	MjR-1st	1	1	June 25, 1999

4th APPROPRIATIONS
Dates: Jan. 6, 2001-Jan. 3, 2005
Departure: Left the House for the Senate

Cong.	Ranking	Terms in: House	Comm.	Date of Assignment
107th	Maj-34th	2	1	Jan. 6, 2001
108th	Maj-30th	3	2	Jan. 28, 2003

5th BUDGET
Dates: Jan. 31, 2003-Jan. 3, 2005
Departure: Left the House for the Senate

Cong.	Ranking	Terms in: House	Comm.	Date of Assignment
108th	Maj-16th	3	1	Jan. 31, 2003

SENATE STANDING COMMITTEES:

1st COMMERCE, SCIENCE AND TRANSPORTATION
Dates: Jan. 6, 2005-date
Departure: Still serving in the 111th Congress

Cong.	Ranking	Years in: Senate	Comm.	Date of Assignment
109th	Maj-12th	1	1	Jan. 6, 2005
110th	Min-10th	3	3	Jan. 12, 2007
111th	Min-8th	5	5	Jan. 21, 2009

2nd ENVIRONMENT AND PUBLIC WORKS
Dates: Jan. 6, 2005-date
Departure: Still serving in the 111th Congress

Cong.	Ranking	Years in: Senate	Comm.	Date of Assignment
109th	Maj-10th	1	1	Jan. 6, 2005
110th	Min-5th	3	3	Jan. 12, 2007
111th	Min-3rd	5	5	Jan. 21, 2009

3rd SMALL BUSINESS AND ENTREPRENEURSHIP
Dates: Jan. 6, 2005-date
Departure: Still serving in the 111th Congress

Cong.	Ranking	Years in: Senate	Comm.	Date of Assignment
109th	Maj-8th	1	1	Jan. 6, 2005
110th	Min-4th	3	3	Jan. 12, 2007
111th	Min-3rd	5	5	Jan. 21, 2009

4th FOREIGN RELATIONS
Dates: Jan. 12, 2007-Jan. 21, 2009
Departure: Moved to Armed Services and Banking, Housing and Urban Affairs

Cong.	Ranking	Years in: Senate	Comm.	Date of Assignment
110th	Min-10th	3	1	Jan. 12, 2007

5th ARMED SERVICES
Dates: Jan. 21, 2009-date
Departure: Still serving in 111th Congress

Cong.	Ranking	Years in: Senate	Comm.	Date of Assignment
111th	Min-10th	5	1	Jan. 21, 2009

6th BANKING, HOUSING AND URBAN AFFAIRS
Dates: Jan. 21, 2009-date
Departure: Still serving in 111th Congress

Cong.	Ranking	Years in: Senate	Comm.	Date of Assignment
111th	Min-8th	5	1	Jan. 21, 2009

SENATE SELECT AND SPECIAL COMMITTEES:

1st SPECIAL AGING (Permanent)
Dates: Jan. 12, 2007-Jan. 21, 2009
Departure: Moved to Armed Services and Banking, Housing and Urban Affairs

Cong.	Ranking	Years in: Senate	Comm.	Date of Assignment
110th	Min-8th	3	1	Jan. 12, 2007

George V. Voinovich (R-Ohio)

Dates: July 15, 1936
Senate: Jan. 3, 1999-date
Serving in the 111th Congress

SENATE STANDING COMMITTEES:

1st ENVIRONMENT AND PUBLIC WORKS
Dates: Jan. 7, 1999-date
Departure: Still serving in the 111th Congress

Cong.	Ranking	Years in: Senate	Comm.	Date of Assignment
106th	Maj-7th	1	1	Jan. 7, 1999
107th	Maj-5th	3	3	Jan. 25, 2001
+107th	Min-5th	3	3	June 6, 2001
108th	Maj-4th	5	5	Jan. 15, 2003
109th	Maj-4th	7	6	Jan. 6, 2005
110th	Min-3rd	9	9	Jan. 12, 2007
111th	Min-2nd	11	11	Jan. 21, 2009

2nd GOVERNMENTAL AFFAIRS renamed Oct. 9, 2004 HOMELAND SECURITY AND GOVERNMENTAL AFFAIRS
Dates: Jan. 7, 1999-date
Departure: Still serving in the 111th Congress

Cong.	Ranking	Years in: Senate	Comm.	Date of Assignment
106th	Maj-5th	1	1	Jan. 7, 1999
107th	Maj-4th	3	3	Jan. 25, 2001
+107th	Min-4th	3	3	June 6, 2001
108th	Maj-3rd	5	5	Jan. 15, 2003
109th	Maj-3rd	7	6	Jan. 6, 2005
110th	Min-3rd	9	9	Jan. 12, 2007
111th	Min-4th	11	11	Jan. 21, 2009

3rd SMALL BUSINESS
Dates: Jan. 7, 1999-Jan. 25, 2001
Departure: Left committee; no new assignment

Cong.	Ranking	Years in: Senate	Comm.	Date of Assignment
106th	Maj-9th	1	1	Jan. 7, 1999

4th AGRICULTURE, NUTRITION AND FORESTRY
Dates: Dec. 6, 2000-Jan. 25, 2001
Departure: Left committee; no new assignment

Cong.	Ranking	Years in: Senate	Comm.	Date of Assignment
106th	MjA-11th	2	1	Dec. 6, 2000

5th FOREIGN RELATIONS
Dates: Jan. 15, 2003-Jan. 21, 2009
Departure: Moved to Appropriations

Cong.	Ranking	Years in: Senate	Comm.	Date of Assignment
108th	Maj-7th	5	1	Jan. 15, 2003
109th	Maj-6th	7	2	Jan. 6, 2005
110th	Min-6th	9	4	Jan. 12, 2007

6th APPROPRIATIONS
Dates: Jan. 21, 2009-date
Departure: Still serving in the 111th Congress

Cong.	Ranking	Years in: Senate	Comm.	Date of Assignment
111th	Min-12th	11	1	Jan. 21, 2009

SENATE SELECT AND SPECIAL COMMITTEES:

1st SELECT ETHICS (Permanent)
Dates: Jan. 7, 1999-Jan. 12, 2007
Departure: Left committee; no new assignment

| Cong. | Ranking | Years in: | | Date of |
		Senate	Comm.	Assignment
106th	Maj-3rd	1	1	Jan. 7, 1999
107th	Maj-2nd	3	3	Jan. 25, 2001
+107th	Min-2nd	3	3	June 6, 2001
108th	Maj-Chr	5	5	Jan. 15, 2003
109th	Maj-Chr	7	6	Jan. 6, 2005

Harold L. Volkmer (D-Mo.)

Dates: April 4, 1931
House: Jan. 3, 1977-Jan. 3, 1997
Left the House: Defeated for re-election in 1996

HOUSE STANDING COMMITTEES:

1st JUDICIARY
Dates: Jan. 19, 1977-Jan. 3, 1981
Departure: Returned to Agriculture

2nd AGRICULTURE
1st Dates: Jan. 27, 1977-Jan. 3, 1979
1st Departure: Moved to Science and Technology
2nd Dates: Jan. 30, 1981-Jan. 3, 1997
2nd Departure: Left the House; lost re-election

| Cong. | Ranking | Terms in: | | Date of |
		House	Comm.	Assignment
103rd	Maj-8th	9 *2	7	Jan. 5, 1993
104th	Min-5th	10 *2	8	Jan. 4, 1995

3rd SCIENCE AND TECHNOLOGY, 96-99
SCIENCE, SPACE AND TECHNOLOGY, 100-103
SCIENCE, 104
1st Dates: Jan. 24, 1979-Jan. 3, 1995
1st Departure: Left committee; no new assignment
2nd Dates: Feb. 28, 1996-Jan. 3, 1997
2nd Departure: Left the House; lost re-election

| Cong. | Ranking | Terms in: | | Date of |
		House	Comm.	Assignment
103rd	Maj-4th	9 *1	8	Jan. 5, 1993
104th	MnR-1st	10 *2	1	Feb. 28, 1996

HOUSE SELECT AND SPECIAL COMMITTEES:

1st SELECT AGING (Permanent)
Dates: Feb. 6, 1985-Jan. 3, 1993
Termination: Committee not renewed in 1993

Barbara F. Vucanovich (R-Nev.)

Dates: June 22, 1921
House: Jan. 3, 1983-Jan. 3, 1997
Left the House: Retired in 1996

HOUSE STANDING COMMITTEES:

1st INTERIOR AND INSULAR AFFAIRS, 98-102
NATURAL RESOURCES. 103
Dates: Jan. 6, 1983-Jan. 3, 1995
Departure: Left committee; no new assignment

| Cong. | Ranking | Terms in: | | Date of |
		House	Comm.	Assignment
103rd	Min-3rd	6	6	Jan. 5, 1993

2nd HOUSE ADMINISTRATION
Dates: June 8, 1983-Jan. 3, 1991
Departure: Moved to Appropriations

3rd APPROPRIATIONS
Dates: Jan. 3, 1991-Jan. 3, 1997
Departure: Left the House; retired

| Cong. | Ranking | Terms in: | | Date of |
		House	Comm.	Assignment
103rd	Min-14th	6	2	Jan. 5, 1993
104th	Maj-13th	7	3	Jan. 4, 1995

HOUSE SELECT AND SPECIAL COMMITTEES:

1st SELECT CHILDREN, YOUTH AND FAMILIES (Temporary)
Dates: Feb. 2, 1983-Jan. 3, 1991
Departure: Moved to Appropriations

JOINT COMMITTEES:

1st JOINT PRINTING
House Dates: July 20, 1983-Jan. 3, 1985
Departure: Left committee; no new assignment

Tim Walberg (R-Mich.)

Dates: April 12, 1951
House: Jan. 3, 2007-Jan. 3, 2009
Left the House: Defeated for re-election in 2008

HOUSE STANDING COMMITTEES:

1st AGRICULTURE
Dates: Jan. 10, 2007-Jan. 3, 2009
Departure: Left the the House; lost re-election

| Cong. | Ranking | Terms in: | | Date of |
		House	Comm.	Assignment
110th	Min-21st	1	1	Jan. 10, 2007

2nd EDUCATION AND LABOR
Dates: Jan. 10, 2007-Jan. 3, 2009
Departure: Left the the House; lost re-election

| Cong. | Ranking | Terms in: | | Date of |
		House	Comm.	Assignment
110th	Min-22nd	1	1	Jan. 10, 2007

Greg Walden (R-Ore.)

Dates: Jan. 10, 1957
House: Jan. 3, 1999-date
Serving in the 111th Congress

HOUSE STANDING CMMITTEES:

1st AGRICULTURE
Dates: Jan. 6, 1999-Jan. 3, 2001
Departure: Moved to Energy and Commerce

Cong.	Ranking	Terms in: House	Comm.	Date of Assignment
106th	Maj-23rd	1	1	Jan. 6, 1999

2nd GOVERNMENT REFORM
Dates: Jan. 6, 1999-Jan. 3, 2001
Departure: Moved to Energy and Commerce

Cong.	Ranking	Terms in: House	Comm.	Date of Assignment
106th	Maj-21st	1	1	Jan. 6, 1999

3rd RESOURCES
Dates: Jan. 6, 1999-Jan. 3, 2007
Departure: Moved to Select Energy Independence and Global Warming

Cong.	Ranking	Terms in: House	Comm.	Date of Assignment
106th	Maj-24th	1	1	Jan. 6, 1999
107th	Maj-22nd	2	2	Jan. 6, 2001
108th	Maj-18th	3	3	Jan. 28, 2003
109th	Maj-15th	4	4	Jan. 26, 2005

4th ENERGY AND COMMERCE
Dates: Jan. 6, 2001-Feb. 23, 2010
Departure: Stepped aside for Parker Griffith (R-Ala.), Chair of Republican leadership

Cong.	Ranking	Terms in: House	Comm.	Date of Assignment
107th	Maj-30th	2	1	Jan. 6, 2001
108th	Maj-25th	3	2	Jan. 28, 2003
109th	Maj-22nd	4	3	Jan. 6, 2005
110th	Min-19th	5	4	Jan. 10, 2007
111th	Min-14th	6	5	Jan. 9, 2009

HOUSE SELECT AND SPECIAL COMMITTEES:

1st SELECT ENERGY INDEPENDENCE AND GLOBAL WARMING
Dates: Mar. 9, 2007-Jan. 3, 2009
Departure: Left committee; no new assignment

Cong.	Ranking	Terms in: House	Comm.	Date of Assignment
110th	Min-3rd	5	1	Mar. 9, 2007

Enid Greene Waldholtz; see, Enid Greene p. 179.

Robert S. Walker (R-Penn.)

Dates: Dec. 23, 1942
House: Jan. 3, 1977-Jan. 3, 1997
Left the House: Retired in 1996

HOUSE STANDING COMMITTEES:

1st GOVERNMENT OPERATIONS
Dates: Jan. 19, 1977-May 10, 1989
Departure: Resigned committee; no new assignment

2nd SCIENCE AND TECHNOLOGY, 95-99
SCIENCE, SPACE AND TECHNOLOGY, 100-103
SCIENCE, 104
Dates: Jan. 19, 1977-Jan. 3, 1997
Departure: Left the House; retired

Cong.	Ranking	Terms in: House	Comm.	Date of Assignment
103rd	Min-RM	9	9	Jan. 5, 1993
104th	Maj-Chr	10	10	Jan. 4, 1995

3rd BUDGET
Dates: Jan. 4, 1995-Jan. 3, 1997
Departure: Left the House; retired

Cong.	Ranking	Terms in: House	Comm.	Date of Assignment
104th	Maj-3rd	10	1	Jan. 4, 1995

JOINT COMMITTEES:

1st JOINT ORGANIZATION OF CONGRESS
House Dates: Aug. 10, 1992-Dec. 17, 1993
Termination: House Report 103-413 filed

Cong.	Ranking	Terms in: House	Comm.	Date of Assignment
103rd	Min-2nd	9	2	Jan. 5, 1993

Malcolm Wallop (R-Wyo.)

Dates: Feb. 27, 1933
Senate: Jan. 3, 1977-Jan. 3, 1995
Left the Senate: Retired in 1994

SENATE STANDING COMMITTEES:

1st ARMED SERVICES
1st Dates: Jan. 10, 1977-Feb. 22, 1977
1st Departure: Moved to Environment and Public Works and Judiciary
2nd Dates: Feb. 2, 1989-Jan. 7, 1993
2nd Departure: Returned to Finance

2nd BANKING, HOUSING AND URBAN AFFAIRS
Dates: Jan. 10, 1977-Feb. 22, 1977
Departure: Moved to Environment and Public Works and Judiciary

3rd ENVIRONMENT AND PUBLIC WORKS
Dates: Feb. 22, 1977-Jan. 23, 1979
Departure: Moved to Finance and Energy and Natural Resources

4th JUDICIARY
Dates: Feb. 22, 1977-Jan. 23, 1979
Departure: Moved to Finance and Energy and Natural Resources

5th FINANCE
1st Dates: Jan. 23, 1979-Feb. 2, 1989
1st Departure: Returned to Armed Services
2nd Dates: Jan. 7, 1993-Jan. 3, 1995
2nd Departure: Left the Senate; retired

Cong.	Ranking	Years in: Senate	Comm.	Date of Assignment
103rd	Min-9th	17 *2	1	Jan. 7, 1993

6th ENERGY AND NATURAL RESOURCES
Dates: Jan. 23, 1979-Jan. 3, 1995
Departure: Left the Senate; retired

Cong.	Ranking	Years in: Senate	Comm.	Date of Assignment
103rd	Min-RM	17	14	Jan. 7, 1993

7th LABOR AND HUMAN RESOURCES
Dates: Feb. 21, 1985-Jan. 6, 1987
Departure: Moved to Small Business

8th SMALL BUSINESS
Dates: Jan. 6, 1987-Jan. 3, 1995.
Departure: Left the Senate; retired

Cong.	Ranking	Years in: Senate	Comm.	Date of Assignment
103rd	Min-2nd	17	7	Jan. 21, 1993

SENATE SELECT AND SPECIAL COMMITTEES:

1st SELECT INTELLIGENCE (Permanent)
1st Dates: Feb. 24, 1977-Jan. 3, 1985
1st Departure: Moved to Labor and Human Resources
2nd Dates: Jan. 27, 1993-Jan. 3, 1995
2nd Departure: Left the Senate; retired

Cong.	Ranking	Years in: Senate	Comm.	Date of Assignment
103rd	Min-8th	17	*2 1	Jan. 27, 1993

2nd SELECT ETHICS (Permanent)
Dates: Oct. 31, 1979-Jan. 3, 1983
Chair: 97th, 1981-83
Departure: Left committee; no new assignment

3rd SENATE COMMITTEE SYSTEM II (Quayle)
Dates: June 13, 1984-Dec. 14, 1984
Termination: Senate Print 98-254 issued

James T. Walsh (R-N.Y.)

Dates: June 19, 1947
House: Jan. 3, 1989-date
Left the House: Retired in 2008

HOUSE STANDING COMMITTEES:

1st AGRICULTURE
Dates: Jan. 20, 1989-Jan. 3, 1993
Departure: Moved to Appropriations

2nd HOUSE ADMINISTRATION
Dates: Mar. 2, 1989-Jan. 3, 1993
Departure: Moved to Appropriations

3rd APPROPRIATIONS
Dates: Jan. 5, 1993-Jan. 3, 2009
Departure: Left the House; retired

Cong.	Ranking	Terms in: House	Comm.	Date of Assignment
103rd	Min-19th	3	1	Jan. 5, 1993
104th	Maj-17th	4	2	Jan. 4, 1995
105th	Maj-14th	5	3	Jan. 7, 1997
106th	Maj-12th	6	4	Jan. 6, 1999
107th	Maj-10th	7	5	Jan. 6, 2001
108th	Maj-7th	8	6	Jan. 28, 2003
109th	Maj-7th	9	7	Jan. 6, 2005
110th	Min-6th	10	8	Jan. 4, 2007

HOUSE SELECT AND SPECIAL COMMITTEES:

1st SELECT CHILDREN, YOUTH AND FAMILIES (Temporary)
Dates: Apr. 4, 1989-Jan. 3, 1993
Termination: Committee not renewed in 1993

JOINT COMMITTEES:

1st JOINT LIBRARY
House Dates: Mar. 15, 1989-Jan. 3, 1991
Departure: Left committee; no new assignment

2nd JOINT PRINTING
House Dates: Mar. 15, 1989-Apr. 18, 1989
Departure: Left committee; no new assignment

Timothy J. Walz (DFL-Minn.)

Dates: April 6, 1964
House: Jan. 3, 2007-date
Serving in the 111th Congress

HOUSE STANDING COMMITTEES:

1st TRANSPORTATION AND INFRASTRUCTURE
Dates: Jan. 10, 2007-date
Departure: Still serving in the 111th Congress

Cong.	Ranking	Terms in: House	Comm.	Date of Assignment
110th	Maj-33rd	1	1	Jan. 10, 2007
111th	Maj-25th	2	2	Jan. 7, 2009

2nd AGRICULTURE
Dates: Jan. 12, 2007-date
Departure: Still serving in the 111th Congress

Cong.	Ranking	Terms in: House	Comm.	Date of Assignment
110th	Maj-17th	1	1	Jan. 12, 2007
111th	Maj-13th	2	2	Jan. 7, 2009

3rd VETERANS AFFAIRS
Dates: Jan. 18, 2007-date
Departure: Still serving in the 111th Congress

Cong.	Ranking	Terms in: House	Comm.	Date of Assignment
110th	Maj-16th	1	1	Jan. 18, 2007
111th	Maj-15th	2	2	Jan. 7, 2009

Zachary P. Wamp (R-Tenn.)

Dates: Oct. 28, 1957
House: Jan. 3, 1995-date
Serving in the 111th Congress

HOUSE STANDING COMMITTEES:

1st SCIENCE
Dates: Jan. 4, 1995-Jan. 3, 1997
Departure: Moved to Appropriations

Cong.	Ranking	Terms in: House	Comm.	Date of Assignment
104th	Maj-14th	1	1	Jan. 4, 1995

2nd SMALL BUSINESS
Dates: Jan. 4, 1995-Jan. 3, 1997
Departure: Moved to Appropriations

Cong.	Ranking	Terms in: House	Comm.	Date of Assignment
104th	Maj-10th	1	1	Jan. 4, 1995

3rd TRANSPORTATION AND INFRASTRUCTURE
Dates: Jan. 4, 1995-Jan. 3, 1997
Departure: Moved to Appropriations

Cong.	Ranking	Terms in: House	Comm.	Date of Assignment
104th	Maj-26th	1	1	Jan. 4, 1995

4th APPROPRIATIONS
Dates: Jan. 7, 1997-date
Departure: Still serving in the 111th Congress

Cong.	Ranking	Terms in: House	Comm.	Date of Assignment
105th	Maj-31st	2	1	Jan. 7, 1997
106th	Maj-27th	3	2	Jan. 6, 1999
107th	Maj-23rd	4	3	Jan. 6, 2001
108th	Maj-19th	5	4	Jan. 28, 2003
109th	Maj-18th	6	5	Jan. 6, 2005
110th	Min-13th	7	6	Jan. 4, 2007
111th	Min-8th	8	7	Jan. 7, 2009

5th BUDGET
Dates: Jan. 19, 1999-Mar. 7, 2001
Departure: Resigned committee; no new assignment

Cong.	Ranking	Terms in: House	Comm.	Date of Assignment
106th	Maj-19th	3	1	Jan. 19, 1999
107th	Maj-11th	4	2	Jan. 6, 2001

Michael D. Ward (D-Ky.)

Dates: Jan. 7, 1951
House: Jan. 3, 1995-Jan. 3, 1997
Left the House: Defeated for re-election in 1996.

HOUSE STANDING COMMITTEES:

1st NATIONAL SECURITY
Dates: Jan. 4, 1995-Jan. 3, 1997
Departure: Left the House; lost re-election

Cong.	Ranking	Terms in: House	Comm.	Date of Assignment
104th	Min-24th	1	1	Jan. 4, 1995

2nd SCIENCE
Dates: Jan. 4, 1995-Jan. 3, 1997
Departure: Left the House; lost re-election

Cong.	Ranking	Terms in: House	Comm.	Date of Assignment
104th	Min-18th	1	1	Jan. 4, 1995

John W. Warner (R-Va.)

Dates: Feb. 18, 1927
Senate: Jan. 2, 1979-Jan. 3, 2009
Left the Senate: Retired in 2008

S: Warner was appointed to the 95th Congress, Jan. 2, 1979, to fill the vacancy caused by the resignation of U.S. Senator William Lloyd Scott (R-Va.). Warner had been elected to succeed Scott in the 96th Congress. Warner was not seated nor assigned to committees because the 95th Congress was not in session.

SENATE STANDING COMMITTEES:

1st ARMED SERVICES
Dates: Jan. 23, 1979-Jan. 3, 2009
Ch1: Replaced by Carl Levin (D-Mich) following party control shift on June 6, 2001, and became RM2
Departure: Left the Senate; retired

Cong.	Ranking	Years in: Senate	Comm.	Date of Assignment
103rd	Min-2nd	15	14	Jan. 7, 1993
104th	Maj-2nd	17	16	Jan. 4, 1995
105th	Maj-2nd	19	18	Jan. 9, 1997
106th	Maj-Chr	21	20	Jan. 7, 1999
107th	Maj-Ch1	23	23	Jan. 25, 2001
+107th	Min-RM2	23	23	June 6, 2001
108th	Maj-Chr	25	24	Jan. 15, 2003
109th	Maj-Chr	27	26	Jan. 6, 2005
110th	Min-2nd	29	28	Jan. 12, 2007

2nd COMMERCE, SCIENCE AND TRANSPORTATION
Dates: Jan. 23, 1979-Jan. 5, 1981
Departure: Moved to Energy and Natural Resources and Rules and Administration

3rd ENERGY AND NATURAL RESOURCES
Dates: Jan. 5, 1981-Jan. 6, 1987
Departure: Moved to Environment and Public Works and Select Intelligence

4th RULES AND ADMINISTRATION
1st Dates: Jan. 5, 1981-Feb. 2, 1989
1st Departure: Moved to Special Aging
2nd Dates: Mar. 19, 1991-Jan. 15, 2003
Ch2: Replaced Theodore F. Stevens (R-Alas.) as Chair on Sep. 12, 1995. Stevens became Chair of Governmental Affairs.
2nd Departure: Returned to Select Intelligence

Cong.	Ranking	Years in: Senate	Comm.	Date of Assignment
103rd	Min-4th	15 *2	2	Jan. 21, 1993
104th	Maj-4th	17 *2	4	Jan. 6, 1995
=104th	Maj-Ch2	17 *2	5	Sep. 12, 1995
105th	Maj-Chr	19 *2	6	Jan. 9, 1997
106th	Maj-4th	21 *2	8	Jan. 7, 1999
107th	Maj-2nd	23 *2	10	Jan. 25, 2001
+107th	Min-2nd	23 *2	11	June 6, 2001

5th ENVIRONMENT AND PUBLIC WORKS
Dates: Jan. 6, 1987-Jan. 3, 2009
Departure: Left the Senate; retired

Cong.	Ranking	Years in: Senate	Comm.	Date of Assignment
103rd	Min-4th	15	7	Jan. 7, 1993
104th	Maj-2nd	17	8	Jan. 5, 1995
105th	Maj-2nd	19	11	Jan. 9, 1997
106th	Maj-2nd	21	13	Jan. 7, 1999
107th	Maj-2nd	23	15	Jan. 25, 2001
+107th	Min-2nd	23	15	June 6, 2001
108th	Maj-2nd	25	17	Jan. 15, 2003
109th	Maj-2nd	27	19	Jan. 6, 2005
110th	Min-2nd	29	21	Jan. 12, 2007

6th AGRICULTURE, NUTRITION AND FORESTRY
Dates: Jan. 4, 1995-Jan. 9, 1997
Departure: Moved to Labor and Human Resources and returned to Special Aging

Cong.	Ranking	Years in: Senate	Comm.	Date of Assignment
104th	Maj-9th	17	1	Jan. 4, 1995

7th SMALL BUSINESS
Dates: Jan. 6, 1995-Jan. 7, 1999
Departure: Left committee; became Chair of Armed Services

Cong.	Ranking	Years in: Senate	Comm.	Date of Assignment
104th	Maj-9th	17	1	Jan. 6, 1995
105th	Maj-6th	19	3	Jan. 9, 1997

8th LABOR AND HUMAN RESOURCES, 105
HEALTH, EDUCATION, LABOR, AND PENSIONS, 107-108
1st Dates: Jan. 9, 1997-Jan. 7, 1999
1st Departure: Left committee; became Chair of Armed Services
2nd Dates: Jan. 25, 2001-Jan. 6, 2005
2nd Departure: Moved to Homeland Security and Governmental Affairs

Cong.	Ranking	Years in: Senate	Comm.	Date of Assignment
105th	Maj-9th	19 *1	1	Jan. 9, 1997
107th	Maj-6th	23 *2	1	Jan. 25, 2001
+107th	Min-5th	23 *2	1	June 6, 2001
108th	Maj-11th	25 *2	2	Jan. 15, 2003

9th HOMELAND SECURITY AND GOVERNMENTAL AFFAIRS
Dates: Jan. 6, 2005-Jan. 3, 2009
Departure: Left the Senate; retired

Cong.	Ranking	Years in: Senate	Comm.	Date of Assignment
109th	Maj-9th	27	1	Jan. 6, 2005
110th	Min-7th	29	3	Jan. 12, 2007

SENATE SELECT AND SPECIAL COMMITTEES:

1st SPECIAL AGING (Permanent)
1st Dates: Feb. 9, 1984-Jan. 6, 1987
1st Departure: Moved to Environment and Public Works

2nd Dates: Jan. 9, 1997-Jan. 7, 1999
2nd Departure: Left committee; became Chair of Armed Services

Cong.	Ranking	Years in: Senate	Comm.	Date of Assignment
105th	Maj-7th	19 *2	1	Jan. 9, 1997

2nd JUDGE HARRY E. CLAIBORNE IMPEACHMENT
Dates: Aug. 14, 1986-Oct. 1, 1986
Termination: Senate Report 99-511 filed

3rd SELECT INTELLIGENCE (Permanent)
1st Dates: Jan. 12, 1987-Jan. 6, 1995
1st Departure: Moved to Agriculture, Nutrition, and Forestry and Small Business
2nd Dates: Jan. 15, 2003-Jan. 3, 2009
2nd Departure: Left the Senate; retired

Cong.	Ranking	Years in: Senate	Comm.	Date of Assignment
103rd	Min-VCh	15 *1	6	Jan. 27, 1993
108th	Maj-9th	25 *2	1	Jan. 15, 2003
109th	Maj-9th	27 *2	2	Jan. 6, 2005
110th	Min-2nd	29 *2	4	Jan. 12, 2007

JOINT COMMITTEES:

1st JOINT PRINTING
1st Senate Dates: Feb. 3, 1981-Feb. 16, 1983
1st Departure: Moved to Joint Library
2nd Senate Dates: Nov. 3, 1995-Mar. 2, 1999
2nd Departure: Left committee; became Chair of Armed Services

Cong.	Ranking	Years in: Senate	Comm.	Date of Assignment
104th	MjR-1st	17 *2	1	Nov. 3, 1995
105th	Maj-Chr	19 *2	2	Jan. 28, 1997

2nd JOINT LIBRARY
1st Senate Dates: Feb. 16, 1983-Jan. 29, 1987
1st Departure: Moved to Environment and Public Works and Select Intelligence
2nd Senate Dates: Nov. 3, 1995-Mar. 2, 1999
2nd Departure: Left committee; became Chair of Armed Services

Cong.	Ranking	Years in: Senate	Comm.	Date of Assignment
104th	MjR-1st	17 *2	1	Nov. 3, 1995
105th	Maj-2nd	19 *2	2	Jan. 28, 1997

Mark Warner (D-Va.)

Dates: Dec. 15, 1954
Senate: Jan. 3. 2009-date
Serving in the 111th Congress

SENATE STANDING COMMITTEES:

1st BANKING, HOUSING AND URBAN AFFAIRS
Dates: Jan. 21, 2009-date
Departure: Still serving in the 111th Congress

Cong.	Ranking	Years in: Senate	Comm.	Date of Assignment
111th	Maj-11th	1	1	Jan. 21, 2009

2nd BUDGET
Dates: Jan. 21, 2009-date
Departure: Still serving in the 111th Congress

Cong.	Ranking	Years in: Senate	Comm.	Date of Assignment
111th	Maj-12th	1	1	Jan. 21, 2009

3rd COMMERCE, SCIENCE AND TRANSPORTATION
Dates: Jan. 21, 2009-date
Departure: Still serving in the 111th Congress

Cong.	Ranking	Years in: Senate	Comm.	Date of Assignment
111th	Maj-13th	1	1	Jan. 21, 2009

4th RULES AND ADMINISTRATION
Dates: Jan. 21, 2009-date
Departure: Still serving in the 111th Congress

Cong.	Ranking	Years in: Senate	Comm.	Date of Assignment
111th	Maj-10th	1	1	Jan. 21, 2009

JOINT COMMITTEES:

1st JOINT ECONOMIC
House Dates: Sept. 29, 2009-date
Departure: Still serving in the 111th Congress

Cong.	Ranking	Terms in: House	Comm.	Date of Assignment
111th	MjR-1st	1	1	Sept. 29, 2009

Craig A. Washington (D-Tex.)

Dates: Oct. 12, 1941
House: Dec. 8, 1989-Jan. 3, 1995
Left the House: Defeated for re-nomination in 1994

H: Washington was elected to the 101st Congress by special election, Dec. 8, 1989, to fill the vacancy caused by the death of U.S. Representative George T. (Mickey) Leland (D-Tex.). Washington was seated Jan. 23, 1990, and assigned to committees.

HOUSE STANDING COMMITTEES:

1st EDUCATION AND LABOR
Dates: Feb. 27, 1990-Jan. 3, 1993
Departure: Moved to Energy and Commerce and Government Operations

2nd JUDICIARY
Dates: Feb. 27, 1990-Jan. 3, 1995
Departure: Left the House; lost re-nomination

Cong.	Ranking	Terms in: House	Comm.	Date of Assignment
103rd	Maj-15th	3	3	Jan. 5, 1993

3rd ENERGY AND COMMERCE
Dates: Jan. 5, 1993-Jan. 3, 1995
Departure: Left the House; lost re-nomination

Cong.	Ranking	Terms in: House	Comm.	Date of Assignment
103rd	Maj-22nd	3	1	Jan. 5, 1993

4th GOVERNMENT OPERATIONS
Dates: Feb. 4, 1993-Jan. 3, 1995
Departure: Left the House; lost re-nomination

Cong.	Ranking	Terms in: House	Comm.	Date of Assignment
103rd	Maj-20th	3	1	Feb. 4, 1993

HOUSE SELECT AND SPECIAL COMMITTEES:

1st SELECT NARCOTICS ABUSE AND CONTROL (Temporary)
Dates: Feb. 21, 1991-Jan. 3, 1993
Termination: Committee not renewed in 1993

Debbie Wasserman Schultz (D-Fla.)

Dates: Sept. 27, 1966
House: Jan. 3, 2005-date
Serving in the 111th Congress

HOUSE STANDING COMMITTEES:

1st FINANCIAL SERVICES
Dates: Jan. 26, 2005-Jan. 3, 2007
Departure: Moved to Appropriations

Cong.	Ranking	Terms in: House	Comm.	Date of Assignment
109th	Min-32nd	1	1	Jan. 26, 2005

2nd JUDICIARY
Dates: June 8, 2005-May 5, 2010
Departure: Resigned committee; no new assignment

Cong.	Ranking	Terms in: House	Comm.	Date of Assignment
109th	MnR-1st	1	1	June 8, 2005
110th	Maj-22nd	2	2	Jan. 23, 2007
111th	Maj-23rd	3	3	Jan. 21, 2009

3rd APPROPRIATIONS
Dates: Jan. 4, 2007-date
Departure: Still serving in the 111th Congress

Cong.	Ranking	Terms in: House	Comm.	Date of Assignment
110th	Maj-36th	2	1	Jan. 4, 2007
111th	Maj-34th	3	2	Jan. 7, 2009

JOINT COMMITTEES:

1st JOINT LIBRARY
House Dates: Mar. 14, 2007-date
Departure: Still serving in the 111th Congress

Cong.	Ranking	Terms in: House	Comm.	Date of Assignment
110th	Maj-3rd	2	1	Mar. 14, 2007
111th	Maj-3rd	3	2	Mar. 31, 2009

Maxine Waters (D-Cal.)

Dates: Aug. 31, 1938
House: Jan. 3, 1991-date
Serving in the 111th Congress

HOUSE STANDING COMMITTEES:

1ST BANKING, FINANCE AND URBAN AFFAIRS, 102-103
BANKING AND FINANCIAL SERVICES, 104-106
FINANCIAL SERVICES, 107-111

Dates: Jan. 24,1991-date
Departure: Still serving in the 111th Congress

Cong.	Ranking	Terms in: House	Comm.	Date of Assignment
103rd	Maj-11th	2	2	Jan. 5, 1993
104th	Min-10th	3	3	Jan. 4, 1995
105th	Min-9th	4	4	Jan. 7, 1997
106th	Min-5th	5	5	Jan. 6, 1999
107th	Min-4th	6	6	Jan. 31, 2001
108th	Min-3rd	7	7	Jan. 28, 2003
109th	Min-3rd	8	8	Jan. 26, 2005
110th	Maj-3rd	9	9	Jan. 12, 2007
111th	Maj-3rd	10	10	Jan. 7, 2009

2nd VETERANS AFFAIRS
Dates: Jan. 24, 1991-Apr. 22, 1996
Departure: Resigned committee; moved to Judiciary

Cong.	Ranking	Terms in: House	Comm.	Date of Assignment
103rd	Maj-12th	2	2	Jan. 5, 1993
104th	Min-5th	3	3	Jan. 4, 1995

3rd SMALL BUSINESS
1st Dates: Feb. 4, 1993-Jan. 3, 1995
1st Departure: Left committee; no new assignment
2nd Dates: Sep. 17, 1996-Jan. 3, 1997
2nd Departure: Left committee; no new assignment

Cong.	Ranking	Terms in: House	Comm.	Date of Assignment
103rd	Maj-26th	2 *1	1	Feb. 4, 1993
104th	MnR-8th	3 *2	1	Sep. 17, 1996

4th JUDICIARY
Dates: Apr. 25, 1996-date
Departure: Still serving in the 111th Congress

Cong.	Ranking	Terms in: House	Comm.	Date of Assignment
104th	MnR-1st	3	1	Apr. 25, 1996
105th	Min-11th	4	2	Jan. 7, 1997
106th	Min-10th	5	3	Jan. 6, 1999
107th	Min-10th	6	4	Jan. 31, 2001
108th	Min-9th	7	5	Jan. 28, 2003
109th	Min-9th	8	6	Jan. 26, 2005
110th	Maj-9th	9	7	Jan. 18, 2007
111th	Maj-9th	10	8	Jan. 21, 2009

Wesley W. Watkins (R-Okla.)

Dates: Dec. 13, 1938
House 1: Jan. 3, 1977-Jan. 3, 1991
Left the House 1: Lost nomination for Governor in 1990
House 2: Jan. 3, 1997-Jan. 3, 2003
Left the House 2: Retired in 2002
Served as a Democrat: Jan. 3, 1977-Jan. 3, 1991
Served as a Republican: Jan. 3, 1997-Jan. 3, 2003

HOUSE STANDING COMMITTEES:

1st BANKING, FINANCE AND URBAN AFFAIRS
Dates: Jan. 19, 1977-Jan. 3, 1981 as a Democrat
Departure: Moved to Appropriations

2nd SCIENCE AND TECHNOLOGY
Dates: Jan. 19, 1977-Jan. 3, 1981 as a Democrat
Departure: Moved to Appropriations

3rd APPROPRIATIONS
Dates: Jan. 28, 1981-Jan. 3, 1991 as a Democrat
Departure: Left the House; lost nomination for Governor

4th WAYS AND MEANS
Dates: Jan. 7, 1997-Jan. 3, 2003 as a Republican
Departure: Left the House; retired

Cong.	Ranking	Terms in: House	Comm.	Date of Assignment
105th	Maj-20th	8	1	Jan. 7, 1997
106th	Maj-17th	9	2	Jan. 6, 1999
107th	Maj-16th	10	3	Jan. 6, 2001

5th BUDGET
Dates: Jan. 6, 2001-Jan. 3, 2003 as a Republican
Departure: Left the House; retired

Cong.	Ranking	Terms in: House	Comm.	Date of Assignment
107th	Maj-15th	10	1	Jan. 6, 2001

HOUSE SELECT AND SPECIAL COMMITTEES:

1st SELECT AGING (Permanent)
Dates: Jan. 25, 1979-Jan. 3, 1981 as a Democrat
Departure: Moved to Appropriations

Diane E. Watson (D-Cal.)

Dates: Nov. 12, 1933
House: June 5, 2001-date
Serving in the 111th Congress

H: Watson was elected to the 107th Congress by special election, June 5, 2001, to fill the vacancy caused by the death of U.S. Representative Julian Dixon (D-Cal.). Watson was seated June 7, 2001, and assigned to committees.

HOUSE STANDING COMMITTEES:

1st GOVERNMENT REFORM, 107-109
OVERSIGHT AND GOVERNMENT REFORM, 110-111
Dates: June 19, 2001-date
Departure: Still serving in the 111th Congress

Cong.	Ranking	Terms in: House	Comm.	Date of Assignment
107th	MnR-1st	1	1	June 19, 2001
108th	Min-14th	2	2	Jan. 28, 2003
109th	Min-12th	3	3	Jan. 26, 2005
110th	Maj-11th	4	4	Jan. 12, 2007
111th	Maj-8th	5	5	Jan. 28, 2009

2nd INTERNATIONAL RELATIONS, 107-109
FOREIGN AFFAIRS, 110-111
Dates: June 19, 2001-date
Departure: Still serving in the 111th Congress

Cong.	Ranking	Terms in: House	Comm.	Date of Assignment
107th	MnR-2nd	1	1	June 19, 2001
108th	Min-20th	2	2	Jan. 28, 2003
109th	Min-19th	3	3	Jan. 26, 2005
110th	Maj-11th	4	4	Jan. 12, 2007
111th	Maj-10th	5	5	Jan. 21, 2009

Melvin L. Watt (D-N.C.)

Dates: Aug. 26, 1945
House: Jan. 3, 1993-date
Serving in the 111th Congress

HOUSE STANDING COMMITTEES:

1st BANKING, FINANCE AND URBAN AFFAIRS, 103
BANKING AND FINANCIAL SERVICES, 104-106
FINANCIAL SERVICES, 107-111
Dates: Jan. 5, 1993-date
Departure: Still serving in the 111th Congress

Cong.	Ranking	Terms in: House	Comm.	Date of Assignment
103rd	Maj-26th	1	1	Jan. 5, 1993
104th	Min-19th	2	2	Jan. 4, 1995
105th	Min-15th	3	3	Jan. 7, 1997
106th	Min-9th	4	4	Jan. 6, 1999
107th	Min-8th	5	5	Jan. 31, 2001
108th	Min-8th	6	6	Jan. 28, 2003
109th	Min-8th	7	7	Jan. 26, 2005
110th	Maj-7th	8	8	Jan. 12, 2007
111th	Maj-7th	9	9	Jan. 7, 2009

2nd JUDICIARY
Dates: Jan. 5, 1993-date
Departure: Still serving in the 111th Congress

Cong.	Ranking	Terms in: House	Comm.	Date of Assignment
103rd	Maj-20th	1	1	Jan. 5, 1993
104th	Min-11th	2	2	Jan. 4, 1995
105th	Min-8th	3	3	Jan. 7, 1997
106th	Min-7th	4	4	Jan. 6, 1999
107th	Min-7th	5	5	Jan. 31, 2001
108th	Min-6th	6	6	Jan. 28, 2003
109th	Min-6th	7	7	Jan. 26, 2005
110th	Maj-6th	8	8	Jan. 18, 2007
111th	Maj-6th	9	9	Jan. 21, 2009

3rd POST OFFICE AND CIVIL SERVICE
Dates: Jan. 21, 1993-Jan. 3, 1995
Departure: Committee abolished; no new assignment

Cong.	Ranking	Terms in: House	Comm.	Date of Assignment
103rd	Maj-10th	1	1	Jan. 21, 1993

JOINT COMMITTEES:

1st JOINT ECONOMIC
House Dates: Mar. 18, 1999-Jan. 3, 2005
Departure: Left committee, no new assignment

Cong.	Ranking	Terms in: House	Comm.	Date of Assignment
106th	Min-4th	2	1	Mar. 25, 1999
107th	Min-3rd	3	2	May 1, 2001
108th	Min-3rd	4	3	Mar. 12, 2003

Julius C. Watts Jr. (R-Okla.)

Dates: Nov. 18, 1957
House: Jan. 3, 1995-Jan. 3, 2003
Left the House: Retired in 2002

HOUSE STANDING COMMITTEES:

1st BANKING AND FINANCIAL SERVICES
Dates: Jan. 4, 1995-Feb. 27, 1997
Departure: Resigned committee; moved to Transportation and Infrastructure

Cong.	Ranking	Terms in: House	Comm.	Date of Assignment
104th	Maj-26th	1	1	Jan. 4, 1995
105th	Maj-19th	2	2	Jan. 7, 1997

2nd NATIONAL SECURITY, 104-105
ARMED SERVICES, 106-107
Dates: Jan. 4, 1995-Jan. 3, 2003
Departure: Left the House; retired

Cong.	Ranking	Terms in: House	Comm.	Date of Assignment
104th	Maj-21st	1	1	Jan. 4, 1995
105th	Maj-18th	2	2	Jan. 7, 1997
106th	Maj-17th	3	3	Jan. 6, 1999
107th	Maj-12th	4	4	Jan. 6, 2001

3rd TRANSPORTATION AND INFRASTRUCTURE
Dates: Feb. 26, 1997-June 25, 1999
Departure: Resigned committee; no new assignment

Cong.	Ranking	Terms in: House	Comm.	Date of Assignment
105th	Maj-40th	2	1	Feb. 26, 1997
106th	Maj-30th	3	2	Jan. 6, 1999

HOUSE SELECT AND SPECIAL COMMITTEES

1st SELECT HOMELAND SECURITY
Dates: June 19, 2002-Jan. 3, 2003
Departure: Left the House; retired

Cong.	Ranking	Terms in: House	Comm.	Date of Assignment
107th	Maj-3rd	4	1	June 19, 2002

Henry A. Waxman (D-Cal.)

Dates: Sept. 12, 1939
House: Jan. 3, 1975-date
Serving in the 111th Congress

HOUSE STANDING COMMITTEES:

1st INTERSTATE AND FOREIGN COMMERCE, 94-96
ENERGY AND COMMERCE, 95-103
COMMERCE, 104-106
ENERGY AND COMMERCE, 107-111
Dates: Jan. 20, 1975-date
Departure: Still serving in the 111th Congress

Cong.	Ranking	Terms in: House	Comm.	Date of Assignment
103rd	Maj-2nd	10	10	Jan. 5, 1993
104th	Min-2nd	11	11	Jan. 4, 1995
105th	Min-2nd	12	12	Jan. 7, 1997
106th	Min-2nd	13	13	Jan. 6, 1999
107th	Min-2nd	14	14	Jan. 31, 2001
108th	Min-2nd	15	15	Jan. 28, 2003
109th	Min-2nd	16	16	Jan. 26, 2005
110th	Maj-2nd	17	17	Jan. 4, 2007
111th	Maj-Chr	18	18	Jan. 6, 2009

2nd SCIENCE AND TECHNOLOGY
Dates: Jan. 20, 1975-Jan. 3, 1977
Departure: Moved to Government Operations

3rd GOVERNMENT OPERATIONS, 95-103
GOVERNMENT REFORM AND OVERSIGHT, 104-105
GOVERNMENT REFORM, 106-109
OVERSIGHT AND GOVERNMENT REFORM, 110
Dates: Jan. 19, 1977-Jan. 3, 2009
Departure: Left committee; became Chair of Energy and Commerce

Cong.	Ranking	Terms in: House	Comm.	Date of Assignment
103rd	Maj-4th	10	9	Jan. 5, 1993
104th	Min-2nd	11	10	Jan. 9, 1995
105th	Min-RM	12	11	Jan. 7, 1997
106th	Min-RM	13	12	Jan. 6, 1999
107th	Min-RM	14	13	Jan. 31, 2001
108th	Min-RM	15	14	Jan. 8, 2003
109th	Min-RM	16	15	Jan. 6, 2005
110th	Maj-Chr	17	16	Jan. 4, 2007

HOUSE SELECT AND SPECIAL COMMITTEES:

1st SELECT NARCOTICS ABUSE AND CONTROL (Temporary)
Dates: Aug. 3, 1976-Apr. 4, 1977
Departure: Left committee; no new assignment

2nd SELECT AGING (Permanent)
Dates: Feb. 21, 1979-Jan. 3, 1993
Termination: Committee not renewed in 1993

James Webb (D-Va.)

Dates: Feb. 9, 1946
Senate: Jan. 3, 2007-date
Serving in the 111th Congress

SENATE STANDING COMMITTEES:

1st ARMED SERVICES
Dates: Jan. 12, 2007-date
Departure: Still serving in the 111th Congress

Cong.	Ranking	Years in: Senate	Comm.	Date of Assignment
110th	Maj-12th	1	1	Jan. 12, 2007
111th	Maj-10th	3	3	Jan. 21, 2009

2nd FOREIGN AFFAIRS
Dates: Jan. 12, 2007-date
Departure: Still serving in the 111th Congress

Cong.	Ranking	Years in: Senate	Comm.	Date of Assignment
110th	Maj-11th	1	1	Jan. 12, 2007
111th	Maj-8th	3	3	Jan. 21, 2009

3rd VETERANS AFFAIRS
Dates: Jan. 12, 2007-date
Departure: Still serving in the 111th Congress

Cong.	Ranking	Years in: Senate	Comm.	Date of Assignment
110th	Maj-7th	1	1	Jan. 12, 2007
111th	Maj-6th	3	3	Jan. 21, 2009

JOINT COMMITTEES:

1st JOINT ECONOMIC
Senate Dates: Jan. 12, 2007-date
Departure: Still serving in the 111th Congress.

Cong.	Ranking	Years in: Senate	Comm.	Date of Assignment
110th	Maj-6th	1	1	Jan. 12, 2007
111th	Maj-6th	3	3	Jan. 21, 2009

Anthony D. Weiner (D-N.Y.)

Dates: Sept. 4, 1964
House: Jan. 3, 1999-date
Serving in the 111th Congress

HOUSE STANDING COMMITTEES:

1st JUDICIARY
Dates: Jan. 6, 1999-date
Departure: Still serving in the 111th Congress

Cong.	Ranking	Terms in: House	Comm.	Date of Assignment
106th	Maj-16th	1	1	Jan. 6, 1999
107th	Maj-16th	2	2	Jan. 6, 2001
108th	Maj-14th	3	3	Jan. 28, 2003
109th	Maj-13th	4	4	Jan. 26, 2005
110th	Min-19th	5	5	Jan. 10, 2007
111th	Min-20th	6	6	Jan. 21, 2009

2ND SCIENCE
Dates: Jan. 19, 1999-Jan. 3, 2005
Departure: Left committee; no new assignment

Cong.	Ranking	Terms in: House	Comm.	Date of Assignment
106th	Min-22nd	1	1	Jan. 19, 1999
107th	Min-16th	2	2	Jan. 31, 2001
108th	Min-22nd	3	3	Feb. 13, 2003

3rd TRANSPORTATION AND INFRASTRUCTURE
Dates: Jan. 28, 2003-Jan. 3, 2007
Departure: Moved to Energy and Commerce

Cong.	Ranking	Terms in: House	Comm.	Date of Assignment
108th	Min-28th	3	1	Jan. 28, 2003
109th	Min-25th	4	2	Jan. 26, 2005

4th ENERGY AND COMMERCE
Dates: Jan. 4, 2007-date
Departure: Still serving in the 111th Congress

Cong.	Ranking	Terms in: House	Comm.	Date of Assignment
110th	Maj-26th	5	1	Jan. 4, 2007
111th	Maj-21st	6	2	Jan. 7, 2009

Peter Welch (D-Vt.)

Dates: May 2, 1947
House: Jan. 3, 2007-date
Serving in the 111th Congress

HOUSE STANDING COMMITTEES:

1st OVERSIGHT AND GOVERNMENT REFORM
Dates: Jan. 12, 2007-date
Departure: Still serving in the 111th Congress

Cong.	Ranking	Terms in: House	Comm.	Date of Assignment
110th	Maj-23rd	1	1	Jan. 12, 2007
111th	Maj-19th	2	2	Jan. 28, 2009

2nd RULES
Dates: Jan. 12, 2007-Jan. 14, 2009
Departure: Resigned committee; moved to Energy and Commerce

Cong.	Ranking	Terms in: House	Comm.	Date of Assignment
110th	Maj-6th	1	1	Jan. 12, 2007
111th	Maj-6th	2	2	Jan. 6, 2009

3rd ENERGY AND COMMERCE
Dates: Jan. 7, 2009-date
Departure: Still serving in the 111th Congress

Cong.	Ranking	Terms in: House	Comm.	Date of Assignment
111th	Maj-36th	2	1	Jan. 7, 2009

4th STANDARDS OF OFFICIAL CONDUCT
Dates: Jan. 22, 2009-date
Departure: Still serving in the 111th Congress

Cong.	Ranking	Terms in: House	Comm.	Date of Assignment
111th	Maj-5th	2	1	Jan. 22, 2009

Wayne C. (Curt) Weldon (R-Penn.)

Dates: July 22, 1947
House: Jan. 3, 1987-Jan. 3, 2007
Left the House: Defeated for re-election in 2006

HOUSE STANDING COMMITTEES:

1st ARMED SERVICES, 100-103
NATIONAL SECURITY, 104-105
ARMED SERVICES, 106-109
Dates: Jan. 21, 1987-Jan. 3, 2007
Departure: Left the House; lost re-election

Cong.	Ranking	Terms in: House	Comm.	Date of Assignment
103rd	Min-7th	4	4	Jan. 5, 1993
104th	Maj-7th	5	5	Jan. 4, 1995
105th	Maj-7th	6	6	Jan. 7, 1997
106th	Maj-7th	7	7	Jan. 6, 1999
107th	Maj-5th	8	8	Jan. 6, 2001
108th	Maj-2nd	9	9	Jan. 28, 2003
109th	Maj-2nd	10	10	Jan. 26, 2005

2nd MERCHANT MARINE AND FISHERIES
Dates: Jan. 21,1987-Jan. 3, 1995
Departure: Committee abolished; moved to Science

Cong.	Ranking	Terms in: House	Comm.	Date of Assignment
103rd	Min-6th	4	4	Jan. 5, 1993

3rd SCIENCE
Dates: Jan. 4, 1995-Jan. 3, 2007
Departure: Left the House; lost re-election

Cong.	Ranking	Terms in: House	Comm.	Date of Assignment
104th	Maj-6th	5	1	Jan. 4, 1995
105th	Maj-5th	6	2	Jan. 21, 1997
106th	Maj-5th	7	3	Jan. 6, 1999
107th	Maj-5th	8	4	Jan. 6, 2001
108th	Maj-4th	9	5	Jan. 28, 2003
109th	Maj-4th	10	6	Jan. 26, 2005

4th HOMELAND SECURITY
Dates: Feb. 9, 2005-Jan. 3, 2007
Departure: Left the House; lost re-election

Cong.	Ranking	Terms in: House	Comm.	Date of Assignment
109th	Maj-4th	10	2	Feb. 9, 2005

HOUSE SELECT AND SPECIAL COMMITTEES:

1st SELECT FIRE SAFETY IN THE HOUSE
Dates: June 16, 1988-Jan. 3, 1989
Termination: Committee recommendations submitted

2nd SELECT CHILDREN, YOUTH AND FAMILIES (Temporary)
Dates: Apr. 4, 1989-Jan. 3, 1993
Termination: Committee not renewed in 1993

3rd SELECT NATIONAL SECURITY CONCERNS WITH CHINA
Dates: June 22, 1998-Apr. 30, 1999
Termination: House Report 851 (105-2) filed, Jan. 3, 1999

Cong.	Ranking	Terms in: House	Comm.	Date of Assignment
105th	Maj-5th	6	1	June 22, 1998
106th	Maj-5th	7	2	Jan. 19, 1999

4th SELECT HOMELAND SECURITY
Dates: Feb. 12, 2003-Jan. 3, 2005
Departure: Continued on reorganized standing committee

Cong.	Ranking	Terms in: House	Comm.	Date of Assignment
108th	Maj-12th	9	1	Feb. 12, 2003

David J. Weldon (R-Fla.)

Dates: Aug. 31, 1953
House: Jan. 3, 1995-Jan. 3, 2009
Left the House: Retired in 2008

HOUSE STANDING COMMITTEES:

1st ECONOMIC AND EDUCATIONAL OPPORTUNITIES
Dates: Jan. 4, 1995-Jan. 3, 1997
Departure: Moved to Banking and Financial Services

Cong.	Ranking	Terms in: House	Comm.	Date of Assignment
104th	Maj-20th	1	1	Jan. 4, 1995

2nd SCIENCE
Dates: Jan. 4, 1995-Jan. 3, 2003
Departure: Moved to Appropriations

Cong.	Ranking	Terms in: House	Comm.	Date of Assignment
104th	Maj-15th	1	1	Jan. 4, 1995
105th	Maj-12th	2	2	Jan. 21, 1997

106th	Maj-12th	3	3	Jan. 6, 1999
107th	Maj-12th	4	4	Jan. 6, 2001

3rd BANKING AND FINANCIAL SERVICES, 105-106
FINANCIAL SERVICES, 107
Dates: Jan. 7, 1997-Jan. 3, 2003
Departure: Moved to Appropriations

Cong.	Ranking	Terms in: House	Comm.	Date of Assignment
105th	Maj-22nd	2	1	Jan. 7, 1997
106th	Maj-18th	3	2	Jan. 6, 1999
107th	Maj-17th	4	3	Jan. 6, 2001

4th GOVERNMENT REFORM
Dates: Feb. 8, 2001-Jan. 3, 2003
Departure: Moved to Appropriations

Cong.	Ranking	Terms in: House	Comm.	Date of Assignment
107th	Maj-21st	4	1	Feb. 8, 2001

5th APPROPRIATIONS
Dates: Jan. 28, 2003-Jan. 3, 2009
Departure: Left the House; retired

Cong.	Ranking	Terms in: House	Comm.	Date of Assignment
108th	Maj-32nd	5	1	Jan. 28, 2003
109th	Maj-30th	6	2	Jan. 6, 2005
110th	Min-22nd	7	3	Jan. 4, 2007

Gerald C. Weller (R-Ill.)

Dates: July 7, 1957
House: Jan. 3, 1995-date
Left the House: Retired in 2008

HOUSE STANDING COMMITTEES:

1st BANKING AND FINANCIAL SERVICES
Dates: Jan. 4, 1995-Jan. 3, 1997
Departure: Moved to Ways and Means

Cong.	Ranking	Terms in: House	Comm.	Date of Assignment
104th	Maj-13th	1	1	Jan. 4, 1995

2nd TRANSPORTATION AND INFRASTRUCTURE
Dates: Jan. 4, 1995-Jan. 3, 1997
Departure: Moved to Ways and Means

Cong.	Ranking	Terms in: House	Comm.	Date of Assignment
104th	Maj-25th	1	1	Jan. 4, 1995

3rd VETERANS AFFAIRS
Dates: Jan. 4, 1995-Jan. 3, 1997
Departure: Moved to Ways and Means

Cong.	Ranking	Terms in: House	Comm.	Date of Assignment
104th	Maj-16th	1	1	Jan. 4, 1995

4th WAYS AND MEANS
Dates: Jan. 7, 1997-Jan. 3, 2009
Departure: Left the House; retired

Cong.	Ranking	Terms in: House	Comm.	Date of Assignment
105th	Maj-22nd	2	1	Jan. 7, 1997

106th	Maj-19th	3	2	Jan. 6, 1999
107th	Maj-18th	4	3	Jan. 6, 2001
108th	Maj-17th	5	4	Jan. 28, 2003
109th	Maj-13th	6	5	Jan. 6, 2005
110th	Min-7th	7	6	Jan. 4, 2007

5th INTERNATIONAL RELATIONS
Dates: Jan. 28, 2003-Jan. 3, 2007
Departure: Left committee; no new assignment

Cong.	Ranking	Terms in: House	Comm.	Date of Assignment
108th	Maj-22nd	5	1	Jan. 28, 2003
109th	Maj-18th	6	2	Jan. 26, 2005

Paul D. Wellstone (DFL-Minn.)

Dates: July 21, 1944-Oct. 25, 2002
Senate: Jan. 3, 1991-Oct. 25, 2002
Left the Senate: Died in office

SENATE STANDING COMMITTEES:

1st ENERGY AND NATURAL RESOURCES
Dates: Feb. 5, 1991-Jan. 9, 1997
Departure: Moved to Foreign Relations and Veterans Affairs

Cong.	Ranking	Years in: Senate	Comm.	Date of Assignment
103rd	Maj-8th	3	2	Jan. 7, 1993
104th	Min-7th	5	4	Jan. 4, 1995

2nd LABOR AND HUMAN RESOURCES renamed Jan. 21, 1999
HEALTH, EDUCATION, LABOR AND PENSIONS
Dates: Feb. 5, 1991-Oct. 25, 2002
Departure: Died in office

Cong.	Ranking	Years in: Senate	Comm.	Date of Assignment
103rd	Maj-9th	3	2	Jan. 7, 1993
104th	Min-7th	5	4	Jan. 4, 1995
105th	Min-6th	7	6	Jan. 9, 1997
106th	Min-6th	9	8	Jan. 7, 1999
107th	Min-6th	11	10	Jan. 25, 2001
+107th	Maj-7th	11	11	July 10, 2001

3rd SMALL BUSINESS renamed June 29, 2001
SMALL BUSINESS AND ENTREPRENEURSHIP
Dates: Mar. 19, 1991-Oct. 25, 2002
Departure: Died in office

Cong.	Ranking	Years in: Senate	Comm.	Date of Assignment
103rd	Maj-7th	3	2	Jan. 21, 1993
104th	Min-7th	5	4	Jan. 6, 1995
105th	Min-6th	7	6	Jan. 9, 1997
106th	Min-5th	9	8	Jan. 7, 1999
107th	Min-5th	11	10	Jan. 25, 2001
+107th	Maj-5th	11	11	June 6, 2001

4th FOREIGN RELATIONS
Dates: Jan. 9, 1997-Oct. 25, 2002
Departure: Died in office

Cong.	Ranking	Years in: Senate	Comm.	Date of Assignment
105th	Min-8th	7	1	Jan. 9, 1997
106th	Min-6th	9	2	Jan. 7, 1999
107th	Min-6th	11	5	Jan. 25, 2001
+107th	Maj-6th	11	5	June 6, 2001

5th VETERANS AFFAIRS
Dates: Mar. 28, 1995-Oct. 25, 2002
Departure: Died in office

| Cong. | Ranking | Years in: | | Date of |
		Senate	Comm.	Assignment
104th	MnR-1st	5	1	Mar. 28, 1995
105th	Min-4th	7	2	Jan. 9, 1997
106th	Min-4th	9	4	Jan. 7, 1999
107th	Min-4th	11	6	Jan. 25, 2001
+107th	Maj-5th	11	7	July 10, 2001

6th AGRICULTURE, NUTRITION AND FORESTRY
Dates: July 10, 2001-Oct. 25, 2002
Departure: Died in office

| Cong. | Ranking | Years in: | | Date of |
		Senate	Comm.	Assignment
+107th	MjA-11th	11	1	July 10, 2001

SENATE SELECT AND SPECIAL COMMITTEES:

1st SELECT INDIAN AFFAIRS (Permanent), 102
INDIAN AFFAIRS (Permanent), 103-107
Dates: Feb. 5, 1991-Oct. 25, 2002
Departure: Died in office

| Cong. | Ranking | Years in: | | Date of |
		Senate	Comm.	Assignment
103rd	Maj-7th	3	2	Jan. 5, 1993
104th	Min-6th	5	4	Jan. 9, 1995
105th	Min-5th	7	6	Jan. 9, 1997
106th	Min-5th	9	8	Jan. 7, 1999
107th	Min-5th	11	10	Jan. 25, 2001
+107th	Maj-5th	11	11	June 6, 2001

Lynn A. Westmoreland (R-Ga.)

Dates: April 2, 1950
House: Jan. 2, 2005-date
Serving in the 111th Congress

HOUSE STANDING COMMITTEES:

1st GOVERNMENT REFORM, 109
OVERSIGHT AND GOVERNMENT REFORM, 110-111
Dates: Jan. 26, 2005-date
Departure: Still serving in the 111th Congress

| Cong. | Ranking | Terms in: | | Date of |
		House	Comm.	Assignment
109th	Maj-20th	1	1	Jan. 26, 2005
110th	Min-13th	2	2	Jan. 10, 2007
111th	Min-9th	3	3	Jan. 9, 2009

2nd SMALL BUSINESS
Dates: Jan. 26, 2005-date
Departure: Still serving in the 111th Congress

| Cong. | Ranking | Terms in: | | Date of |
		House	Comm.	Assignment
109th	Maj-17th	1	1	Jan. 26, 2005
110th	Min-9th	2	2	Jan. 10, 2007
111th	Min-5th	3	3	Jan. 9, 2009

3rd TRANSPORTATION AND INFRASTRUCTURE
Dates: Jan. 26, 2005-date
Departure: Still serving in the 111th Congress

| Cong. | Ranking | Terms in: | | Date of |
		House	Comm.	Assignment
109th	Maj-40th	1	1	Jan. 26, 2005
110th	Min-28th	2	2	Jan. 10, 2007
111th	Min-21st	3	3	Jan. 9, 2009

Robert Wexler (D-Fla.)

Dates: Jan. 2, 1961
House: Jan. 3, 1997-Jan. 3, 2010
Left House: Resigned; named President of Center for Middle East Peace and Economic Cooperation

HOUSE STANDING COMMITTEES:

1st INTERNATIONAL RELATIONS, 105-109
FOREIGN AFFAIRS, 110-111
Dates: Jan. 7, 1997-Jan. 3, 2010
Departure: Resigned; privarte sector

| Cong. | Ranking | Terms in: | | Date of |
		House	Comm.	Assignment
105th	Min-18th	1	1	Jan. 7, 1997
106th	Min-15th	2	2	Jan. 6, 1999
107th	Min-12th	3	3	Jan. 31, 2001
108th	Min-9th	4	4	Jan. 28, 2003
109th	Min-9th	5	5	Jan. 26, 2005
110th	Maj-7th	6	6	Jan. 12, 2007
111th	Maj-6th	7	7	Jan. 21, 2009

2nd JUDICIARY
Dates: Jan. 7, 1997-Jan. 3, 2010
Departure: Resigned; private sector

| Cong. | Ranking | Terms in: | | Date of |
		House	Comm.	Assignment
105th	Min-14th	1	1	Jan. 7, 1997
106th	Min-13th	2	2	Jan. 6, 1999
107th	Min-13th	3	3	Jan. 31, 2001
108th	Min-12th	4	4	Jan. 28, 2003
109th	Min-12th	5	5	Jan. 26, 2005
110th	Maj-12th	6	6	Jan. 18, 2007
111th	Maj-11th	7	7	Jan. 21, 2009

3rd FINANCIAL SERVICES
Dates: Jan. 23, 2007-June 6, 2008
Departure: Resigned committee; no new assignment

| Cong. | Ranking | Terms in: | | Date of |
		House	Comm.	Assignment
110th	Maj-35th	6	1	Jan. 23, 2007

Robert A. Weygand (D-R.I.)

Dates: May 10, 1948
House: Jan. 3, 1997-Jan. 3, 2001
Left the House: Lost U.S. Senate election in 2000

HOUSE STANDING COMMITTEES:

1st BUDGET
Dates: Jan. 7, 1997-Jan. 3, 2001
Departure: Left the House; lost Senate election

Cong.	Ranking	Terms in: House	Comm.	Date of Assignment
105th	Min-18th	1	1	Jan. 7, 1997
106th	Min-8th	2	2	Jan. 6, 1999

2nd SMALL BUSINESS
Dates: Feb. 5, 1997-July 30, 1997
Departure: Leave of absence; moved to Banking and Financial Services

Cong.	Ranking	Terms in: House	Comm.	Date of Assignment
105th	Min-11th	1	1	Feb. 5, 1997

3rd BANKING AND FINANCIAL SERVICES
Dates: July 31, 1997-Jan. 3, 2001
Departure: Left the House; lost Senate election

Cong.	Ranking	Terms in: House	Comm.	Date of Assignment
105th	MnR-1st	1	1	July 31, 1997
106th	Min-15th	2	2	Jan. 6, 1999

Alan D. Wheat (D-Mo.)

Dates: Oct. 16, 1951
House: Jan. 3, 1983-Jan. 3, 1995
Left the House: Lost U.S. Senate election in 1994

HOUSE STANDING COMMITTEES:

1st RULES
Dates: Jan. 6, 1983-Jan. 3, 1995
Departure: Left the House; lost Senate election

Cong.	Ranking	Terms in: House	Comm.	Date of Assignment
103rd	Maj-7th	6	6	Jan. 5, 1993

2nd DISTRICT OF COLUMBIA
Dates: Feb. 27, 1985-date
Departure: Left the House; lost Senate election

Cong.	Ranking	Terms in: House	Comm.	Date of Assignment
103rd	Maj-2nd	6	5	Feb. 18, 1993

HOUSE SELECT AND SPECIAL COMMITTEES:

1st SELECT CHILDREN, YOUTH AND FAMILIES (Temporary)
Dates: Feb. 2, 1983-Jan. 3, 1993
Termination: Committee not renewed in 1993

2nd SELECT HUNGER (Temporary)
Dates: Feb. 8, 1990-Jan. 3, 1993
Termination: Committee not renewed in 1993

Richard A. White (R-Wash.)

Dates: Nov. 6, 1953
House: Jan. 3, 1995-Jan. 3, 1999
Left the House: Defeated for re-election in 1998

HOUSE STANDING COMMITTEES:

1st COMMERCE
Dates: Jan. 4, 1995-Jan. 3, 1999
Departure: Left the House; lost re-election

Cong.	Ranking	Terms in: House	Comm.	Date of Assignment
104th	Maj-24th	1	1	Jan. 4, 1995
105th	Maj-23rd	2	2	Jan. 7, 1997

Sheldon Whitehouse (D-R.I.)

Dates: Oct. 20, 1955
Senate: Jan. 3, 2007-date
Serving in the 111th Congress

SENATE STANDING COMMITTEES:

1st BUDGET
Dates: Jan. 12, 2007-date
Departure: Still serving in the 111th Congress

Cong.	Ranking	Years in: Senate	Comm.	Date of Assignment
110th	Maj-12th	1	1	Jan. 12, 2007
111th	Maj-11th	3	3	Jan. 21, 2009

2nd ENVIRONMENT AND PUBLIC WORKS
Dates: Jan. 12, 2007-date
Departure: Still serving in the 111th Congress

Cong.	Ranking	Years in: Senate	Comm.	Date of Assignment
110th	Maj-10th	1	1	Jan. 12, 2007
111th	Maj-8th	3	3	Jan. 21, 2009

3rd JUDICIARY
Dates: Jan. 12, 2007-date
Departure: Still serving in the 111th Congress

Cong.	Ranking	Years in: Senate	Comm.	Date of Assignment
110th	Maj-10th	1	1	Jan. 12, 2007
111th	Maj-8th	3	3	Jan. 21, 2009

4th HEALTH, EDUCATION, LABOR AND PENSIONS
Temporary Dates: May 5, 2009-July 15, 2009
Temporary Departure: Resigned committee to open seat for Al Franken

Cong.	Ranking	Years in: Senate	Comm.	Date of Assignment
111th	Maj-13th	3 *T	1	May 5, 2009

SENATE SELECT AND SPECIAL COMMITTEES:

1st SELECT INTELLIGENCE (Permanent)
Dates: Jan. 12, 2007-date
Departure: Still serving in the 111th Congress

Cong.	Ranking	Years in: Senate	Comm.	Date of Assignment
110th	Maj-8th	1	1	Jan. 12, 2007
111th	Maj-8th	3	3	Jan. 21, 2009

2nd SPECIAL AGING (Permanent)
Dates: Jan. 12, 2007-date
Departure: Still serving in the 111th Congress

Cong.	Ranking	Years in: Senate	Comm.	Date of Assignment
110th	Maj-11th	1	1	Jan. 12, 2007
111th	Maj-8th	3	3	Jan. 21, 2009

W. Edward Whitfield (R-Ky.)

Dates: May 25, 1943
House: Jan. 3, 1995-date
Serving in the 111th Congress

HOUSE STANDING COMMITTEES:

1st COMMERCE, 104-106
ENERGY AND COMMERCE, 107-111
Dates: Jan. 4, 1995-date
Departure: Still serving in the 111th Congress

Cong.	Ranking	Terms in: House	Comm.	Date of Assignment
104th	Maj-20th	1	1	Jan. 4, 1995
105th	Maj-20th	2	2	Jan. 7, 1997
106th	Maj-15th	3	3	Jan. 6, 1999
107th	Maj-12th	4	4	Jan. 6, 2001
108th	Maj-11th	5	5	Jan. 28, 2003
109th	Maj-8th	6	6	Jan. 6, 2005
110th	Min-7th	7	7	Jan. 10, 2007
111th	Min-6th	8	8	Jan. 9, 2009

Jamie L. Whitten (D-Miss.)

Dates: April 18, 1910-Sept. 9, 1995
House: Nov. 4, 1941-Jan. 3, 1995
Left the House: Retired in 1994

H: Whitten was elected to the 77th Congress by special election, Nov. 4, 1941, to fill the vacancy caused by the death of U.S. Representative Wall Doxey (D-Miss.). Whitten was seated Nov. 14, 1941, and assigned to committees.

HOUSE STANDING COMMITTEES:

1st APPROPRIATIONS
Dates: Jan. 8, 1947-Jan. 3, 1995
Departure: Left the House; retired

Cong.	Ranking	Terms in: House	Comm.	Date of Assignment
103rd	Maj-2nd	27	26	Jan. 5, 1993

2nd BUDGET
Dates: Aug. 14, 1974-Jan. 3, 1975
Departure: Left committee; no new assignment

JOINT COMMITTEES:

1st JOINT REDUCTION OF FEDERAL EXPENDITURES
House Dates: Sep. 9, 1970-July 12, 1974
Termination: Congressional Budget and Impoundment Control Act of 1975, Public Law 93-344

2nd JOINT STUDY BUDGET CONTROL
House Dates: Nov. 27, 1972-Apr. 18, 1973
Termination: House Report 147 (93-1) filed

Roger F. Wicker (R-Miss.)

Dates: July 5, 1951
House: Jan. 3, 1995-Dec. 31, 2007
Left the House: Resigned; appointed to U.S. Senate in 2007
Senate: Dec. 31, 2007-date
Serving in the 111th Congress

S: Wicker was appointed to the U.S. Senate, Dec. 31, 2007, to fill the vacancy caused by the resignation of U.S. Senator Trent Lott (R-Miss.). Wicker was sworn on Dec. 31, 2007, the same day, and assigned to committees.

HOUSE STANDING COMMITTEES:

1st APPROPRIATIONS
Dates: Jan. 4, 1995-Dec. 31, 2007
Departure: Resigned the House; appointed to Senate

Cong.	Ranking	Terms in: House	Comm.	Date of Assignment
104th	Maj-28th	1	1	Jan. 4, 1995
105th	Maj-25th	2	2	Jan. 7, 1997
106th	Maj-22nd	3	3	Jan. 6, 1999
107th	Maj-19th	4	4	Jan. 6, 2001
108th	Maj-15th	5	5	Jan. 28, 2003
109th	Maj-15th	6	6	Jan. 6, 2005
110th	Min-11th	7	7	Jan. 4, 2007

2nd BUDGET
Dates: Jan. 31, 2003-Jan. 3, 2007
Departure: Left committee; no new assignment

Cong.	Ranking	Terms in: House	Comm.	Date of Assignment
108th	Maj-13th	5	1	Jan. 31, 2003
109th	Maj-6th	6	2	Jan. 26, 2005

SENATE STANDING COMMITTEES:

1st ARMED SERVICES
Dates: Jan. 24, 2008-date
Departure: Still serving in the 111th Congress

Cong.	Ranking	Years in: Senate	Comm.	Date of Assignment
110th	MnR-2nd	1	1	Jan. 24, 2008
111th	Min-8th	2	1	Jan. 21, 2009

2nd COMMERCE, SCIENCE AND TRANSPORTATION
Dates: Jan. 24, 2008-date
Departure: Still serving in the 111th Congress

Cong.	Ranking	Years in: Senate	Comm.	Date of Assignment
110th	MnR-1st	1	1	Jan. 24, 2008
111th	Min-6th	2	1	Jan. 21, 2009

3rd VETERANS AFFAIRS
Dates: Jan. 24, 2008-date
Departure: Still serving in the 111th Congress

Cong.	Ranking	Years in: Senate	Comm.	Date of Assignment
110th	MnR-1st	1	1	Jan. 24, 2008
111th	Min-4th	2	1	Jan. 21, 2009

4th FOREIGN RELATIONS
Dates: Jan. 21, 2009-date
Departure: Still serving in the 111th Congress

Cong.	Ranking	Years in: Senate	Comm.	Date of Assignment
111th	Min-7th	2	1	Jan. 21, 2009

5th SMALL BUSINESS AND ENTREPRENEURSHIP
Dates: Jan. 21, 2009-date
Departure: Still serving in the 111th Congress

Cong.	Ranking	Years in: Senate	Comm.	Date of Assignment
111th	Min-7th	2	1	Jan. 21, 2009

J. Patrick Williams (D-Mont.)

Dates: Oct. 30, 1937
House: Jan. 3, 1979-Jan. 3, 1997
Left the House: Retired in 1996

HOUSE STANDING COMMITTEES:

1st EDUCATION AND LABOR, 96-103
ECONOMIC AND EDUCATIONAL OPPORTUNITIES, 104
Dates: Jan. 24, 1979-Jan. 3, 1997
Departure: Left the House; retired

Cong.	Ranking	Terms in: House	Comm.	Date of Assignment
103rd	Maj-6th	8	8	Jan. 5, 1993
104th	Min-4th	9	9	Jan. 4, 1995

2nd INTERIOR AND INSULAR AFFAIRS, 86-97, 101-102
NATURAL RESOURCES, 103
RESOURCES, 104
1st Dates: Jan. 24, 1979-Jan. 3, 1983
1st Departure: Moved to Budget
2nd Dates: Jan. 19, 1989-Jan. 3, 1997
2nd Departure: Left the House; retired

Cong.	Ranking	Terms in: House	Comm.	Date of Assignment
103rd	Maj-7th	8 *2	3	Jan. 5, 1993
104th	Min-5th	9 *2	4	Jan. 9, 1995

3rd BUDGET
Dates: Jan. 6, 1983-Jan. 3, 1989
Departure: Returned to Interior and Insular Affairs with seniority intact

4th AGRICULTURE
Dates: Feb. 4, 1993-Jan. 3, 1995
Departure: Left committee; no new assignment

Cong.	Ranking	Terms in: House	Comm.	Date of Assignment
103rd	MjR-1st	8	1	Feb. 4, 1993

JOINT COMMITTEES:

1st JOINT DEFICIT REDUCTION (Temporary)
House Dates: Feb. 23, 1987-Sep. 29, 1987
Termination: Public Law 100-119 adjusted Gramm-Rudman-Hollings Act

Addison G. (Joe) Wilson (R-S.C.)

Dates: July 31, 1947
House: Dec. 18, 2001-date
Serving in the 111th Congress

H: Wilson was elected to the 107th Congress by special election, Dec. 18, 2001, to fill the vacancy caused by the death of U.S. Representative Floyd D. Spence (R-S.C.). Wilson was seated Dec. 19, 2001, and assigned to committees.

HOUSE STANDING COMMITTEES:

1st ARMED SERVICES
Dates: Jan. 19, 2002-date
Departure: Still serving in the 111th Congress

Cong.	Ranking	Terms in: House	Comm.	Date of Assignment
107th	MjR-2nd	1	1	Jan. 19, 2002
108th	Maj-23rd	2	2	Jan. 28, 2003
109th	Maj-21st	3	3	Jan. 26, 2005
110th	Min-15th	4	4	Jan. 10, 2007
111th	Min-9th	5	5	Jan. 9, 2009

2nd EDUCATION AND THE WORKFORCE, 108-109
EDUCATION AND LABOR, 110-111
Dates: Apr. 18, 2002-date
Departure: Still serving in the 111th Congress

Cong.	Ranking	Terms in: House	Comm.	Date of Assignment
107th	MjR-1st	1	1	Apr. 18, 2002
108th	Maj-20th	2	2	Jan. 28, 2003
109th	Maj-14th	3	3	Jan. 26, 2005
110th	Min-10th	4	4	Jan. 10, 2007
111th	Min-9th	5	5	Jan. 9, 2009

3rd INTERNATIONAL RELATIONS, 109
FOREIGN AFFAIRS, 110-111
Dates: Jan. 26, 2005-date
Departure: Still serving in the 111th Congress

Cong.	Ranking	Terms in: House	Comm.	Date of Assignment
109th	Maj-22nd	3	1	Jan. 26, 2005
110th	Min-15th	4	2	Jan. 10, 2007
111th	Min-11th	5	3	Jan. 9, 2009

Charles Wilson (D-Tex.)

Dates: June 1, 1933
House: Jan. 3, 1973-Oct. 8, 1996
Left the House: Resigned and retired

HOUSE STANDING COMMITTEES:

1st FOREIGN AFFAIRS, 93
INTERNATIONAL RELATIONS, 94
Dates: Jan. 24, 1973-Feb. 3, 1976
Departure: Moved to Appropriations

2nd VETERANS AFFAIRS
Dates: Jan. 24, 1973-Feb. 3, 1976
Departure: Moved to Appropriations

3rd APPROPRIATIONS
Dates: Feb. 3, 1976-Oct. 8, 1996
Departure: Resigned the House and retired

Cong.	Ranking	Terms in: House	Comm.	Date of Assignment
103rd	Maj-9th	11	10	Jan. 5, 1993
104th	Min-6th	12	11	Jan. 4, 1995

4th STANDARDS OF OFFICIAL CONDUCT
Dates: Jan. 28, 1981-Jan. 3, 1983
Departure: Left committee; no new assignment

HOUSE SELECT AND SPECIAL COMMITTEES:

1st SELECT ENERGY (Ad Hoc)
Dates: Apr. 21, 1977-Dec. 29, 1978
Termination: House Report 1820 (95-2) filed

2nd PERMANENT SELECT INTELLIGENCE
Dates: Jan. 21, 1987-Jan. 3, 1993
Departure: Left committee; no new assignment

Charles A. Wilson (D-Ohio)

Dates: Jan. 18, 1943
House: Jan. 3, 2007-date
Serving in the 111th Congress

HOUSE STANDING COMMITTEES:

1st FINANCIAL SERVICES
Dates: Jan. 12, 2007-date
Departure: Still serving in the 111th Congress

Cong.	Ranking	Terms in: House	Comm.	Date of Assignment
110th	Maj-31st	1	1	Jan. 12, 2007
111th	Maj-27th	2	2	Jan. 7, 2009

2nd SCIENCE AND TECHNOLOGY
Dates: Jan. 18, 2007-date
Departure: Still serving in the 111th Congress

Cong.	Ranking	Terms in: House	Comm.	Date of Assignment
110th	Maj-24th	1	1	Jan. 18, 2007
111th	Maj-22nd	2	2	Jan. 21, 2009

Heather A. Wilson (R-N.M.)

Dates: Dec. 30, 1960
House: June 23, 1998-Jan. 3, 2009
Left the House: Lost nomination for U.S. Senate in 2008

H: Wilson was elected to the 105th Congress by special election, June 23, 1998, to fill the vacancy caused by the death of U.S. Representative Steven H. Schiff (R-N.M.). Wilson was seated June 25, 1998, and assigned to committees.

HOUSE STANDING COMMITTEES:

1st COMMERCE, 105-106
ENERGY AND COMMERCE, 107-110
Dates: Aug. 3, 1998-Jan. 3, 2009
Departure: Left the House; lost Senate nomination

Cong.	Ranking	Terms in: House	Comm.	Date of Assignment
105th	MjA-29th	1	1	Aug. 3, 1998
106th	Maj-23rd	2	2	Jan. 6, 1999
107th	Maj-17th	3	3	Jan. 6, 2001
108th	Maj-15th	4	4	Jan. 28, 2003
109th	Maj-12th	5	5	Jan. 6, 2005
110th	Min-11th	6	6	Jan. 10, 2007

2nd ARMED SERVICES
Dates: Oct. 3, 2000-Jan. 3, 2005
Departure: Returned to Permanent Select Intelligence

Cong.	Ranking	Terms in: House	Comm.	Date of Assignment
106th	MjR-1st	2	1	Oct. 3, 2000
107th	Maj-25th	3	2	Jan. 6, 2001
108th	Maj-15th	4	3	Jan. 28, 2003

HOUSE SELECT AND SPECIAL COMMITTEES:

1st PERMANENT SELECT INTELLIGENCE
1st Dates: Jan. 19, 1999-Jan. 3, 2001
1st Departure: Left committee; no new assignment
2nd Dates: Jan. 26, 2005-Jan. 3, 2009
2nd Departure: Left the House; lost Senate nomination

Cong.	Ranking	Terms in: House	Comm.	Date of Assignment
106th	Maj-9th	2 *1	1	Jan. 19, 1999
109th	Maj-6th	5 *2	1	Jan. 26, 2005
110th	Min-3rd	6 *2	2	Jan. 17, 2007

Robert E. Wise Jr. (D-W.Va.)

Dates: Jan. 6, 1948
House: Jan. 3, 1983-Jan. 3, 2001
Left the House: Elected Governor in 2000

HOUSE STANDING COMMITTEES:

1st GOVERNMENT OPERATIONS, 98-102
GOVERNMENT REFORM AND OVERSIGHT, 104-105
GOVERNMENT REFORM, 106
1st Dates: Jan. 6, 1983-Jan. 3, 1993
1st Departure: Returned to Public Works and Transportation
2nd Dates: Jan. 9, 1995-Jan. 3, 2001
2nd Departure: Left the House; elected Governor

Cong.	Ranking	Terms in: House	Comm.	Date of Assignment
104th	Min-4th	7 *2	1	Jan. 9, 1995
105th	Min-3rd	8 *2	2	Jan. 7, 1997
106th	Min-3rd	9 *2	3	Jan. 6, 1999

2nd PUBLIC WORKS AND TRANSPORTATION, 98-100, 103
TRANSPORTATION AND INFRASTRUCTURE, 104-106
1st Dates: Jan. 6, 1983-Jan. 3, 1989
1st Departure: Moved to Budget
2nd Dates: Jan. 5, 1993-Jan. 3, 2001
2nd Departure: Left the House; elected Governor

Cong.	Ranking	Terms in: House	Comm.	Date of Assignment
103rd	Maj-9th	6 *2	1	Jan. 5, 1993
104th	Min-6th	7 *2	2	Jan. 4, 1995
105th	Min-5th	8 *2	3	Jan. 7, 1997
106th	Min-5th	9 *2	4	Jan. 6, 1999

3rd EDUCATION AND LABOR
Dates: Jan. 22, 1987-Jan. 3, 1989
Departure: Moved to Budget

4th BUDGET
Dates: Jan. 19,1989-Jan. 3, 1995
Departure: Left committee; returned to Government Reform and Oversight

Cong.	Ranking	Terms in: House	Comm.	Date of Assignment
103rd	Maj-7th	6	3	Jan. 5, 1993

HOUSE SELECT AND SPECIAL COMMITTEES:

1st SELECT AGING (Permanent)
Dates: Feb. 8, 1983-Jan. 3, 1993
Termination: Committee not renewed in 1993

Robert J. Wittman (R-Va.)

Dates: Feb. 3, 1959
House: Dec. 13, 2007-date
Serving in the 111th Congress

H: Wittman was elected to the 110th Congress by special election, Dec. 11, 2007, to fill the vacancy caused by the death of U.S. Representative Jo Ann Davis (R-Va.). Wittman was seated Dec. 13, 2007, and assigned to committees.

HOUSE STANDING COMMITTEES:

1st SCIENCE AND TECHNOLOGY
Dates: Dec. 18, 2007-Dec. 18, 2007
Departure: Resigned committee; exceeded party ratio; moved to Foreign Affairs

Cong.	Ranking	Terms in: House	Comm.	Date of Assignment
110th	MnA-22nd	1	1	Dec. 18, 2007

2nd FOREIGN AFFAIRS
Dates: Dec. 18, 2007-Mar. 11, 2008
Departure: Resigned committee; moved to Armed Services

Cong.	Ranking	Terms in: House	Comm.	Date of Assignment
110th	MnR-3rd	1	1	Dec. 18, 2007

3rd NATURAL RESOURCES
Dates: Feb. 26, 2008-date
Departure: Still serving in the 111th Congress

Cong.	Ranking	Terms in: House	Comm.	Date of Assignment
110th	MnR-4th	1	1	Feb. 26, 2008
111th	Min-13th	2	2	Jan. 9, 2009

4th ARMED SERVICES
Dates: Mar. 11, 2008-date
Departure: Still serving in the 111th Congress

Cong.	Ranking	Terms in: House	Comm.	Date of Assignment
110th	MnR-2nd	1	1	Mar. 11, 2008
111th	Min-20th	2	2	Jan. 9, 2009

Harris Wofford (D-Penn.)

Dates: April 9, 1926
Senate: May 8, 1991-Jan. 3, 1995
Left the Senate: Defeated for re-election in 1994

S: Wofford was appointed to the 102nd Congress, May 8, 1991, to fill the vacancy caused by the death of U.S. Senator H. John Heinz III (R-Penn.) and was subsequently elected. Wofford was seated May 9, 1991, and assigned to committees.

SENATE STANDING COMMITTEES:

1st ENVIRONMENT AND PUBLIC WORKS
Dates: June 4, 1991-Jan. 3, 1995
Departure: Left the Senate; lost re-election

Cong.	Ranking	Years in: Senate	Comm.	Date of Assignment
103rd	Maj-9th	2	2	Jan. 7, 1993

2nd FOREIGN RELATIONS
Dates: June 4, 1991-Jan. 3, 1995
Departure: Left the Senate; lost re-election

Cong.	Ranking	Years in: Senate	Comm.	Date of Assignment
103rd	Maj-9th	2	2	Jan. 7, 1993

3rd SMALL BUSINESS
Dates: June 4, 1991-Jan. 3, 1995
Departure: Left the Senate; lost re-election

Cong.	Ranking	Years in: Senate	Comm.	Date of Assignment
103rd	Maj-8th	2	2	Jan. 21, 1993

4th LABOR AND HUMAN RESOURCES
Dates: Jan 7, 1993-Jan. 3, 1995
Departure: Left the Senate; lost re-election

Cong.	Ranking	Years in: Senate	Comm.	Date of Assignment
103rd	Maj-10th	2	1	Jan. 7, 1993

Frank R. Wolf (R-Va.)

Dates: Jan. 30, 1939
House: Jan. 3, 1981-date
Serving in the 111th Congress

HOUSE STANDING COMMITTEES:

1st POST OFFICE AND CIVIL SERVICE
Dates: Jan. 28, 1981-Jan. 3, 1985
Departure: Moved to Appropriations

2nd PUBLIC WORKS AND TRANSPORTATION
Dates: Jan. 28, 1981-Jan. 3, 1985
Departure: Moved to Appropriations

3rd APPROPRIATIONS
Dates: Jan. 30, 1985-date
Departure: Still serving in the 111th Congress

Cong.	Ranking	Terms in: House	Comm.	Date of Assignment
103rd	Min-10th	7	5	Jan. 5, 1993
104th	Maj-10th	8	6	Jan. 4, 1995
105th	Maj-9th	9	7	Jan. 7, 1997
106th	Maj-7th	10	8	Jan. 6, 1999
107th	Maj-6th	11	9	Jan. 6, 2001
108th	Maj-5th	12	10	Jan. 28, 2003
109th	Maj-5th	13	11	Jan. 6, 2005
110th	Min-5th	14	12	Jan. 4, 2007
111th	Min-4th	15	13	Jan. 9, 2009

HOUSE SELECT AND SPECIAL COMMITTEES:

1st SELECT CHILDREN, YOUTH AND FAMILIES (Temporary)
Dates: Feb. 2, 1983-Jan. 3, 1993
Termination: Committee not renewed in 1993

2nd SELECT HUNGER (Temporary)
Dates: Apr. 4, 1989-Jan. 3, 1993
Termination: Committee not renewed in 1993

Lynn C. Woolsey (D-Cal.)

Dates: Nov. 3, 1937
House: Jan. 3, 1993-date
Serving in the 111th Congress

HOUSE STANDING COMMITTEES:

1st EDUCATION AND LABOR, 103
ECONOMIC AND EDUCATIONAL OPPORTUNITIES, 104
EDUCATION AND THE WORKFORCE, 105-109
EDUCATION AND LABOR, 110-111
Dates: Jan. 5, 1993-date
Departure: Still serving in the 111th Congress

Cong.	Ranking	Terms in: House	Comm.	Date of Assignment
103rd	Maj-20th	1	1	Jan. 5, 1993
104th	Min-17th	2	2	Jan. 4, 1995
105th	Min-11th	3	3	Jan. 7, 1997
106th	Min-11th	4	4	Jan. 6, 1999
107th	Min-9th	5	5	Jan. 31, 2001
108th	Min-6th	6	6	Jan. 28, 2003
109th	Min-7th	7	7	Jan. 26, 2005
110th	Maj-6th	8	8	Jan. 10, 2007
111th	Maj-6th	9	9	Jan. 21, 2009

2nd GOVERNMENT OPERATIONS
1st Dates: Jan. 5, 1993-Jan. 21, 1993
1st Departure: Resigned committee; moved to Science, Space and Technology; returned on Feb. 4, 1993
2nd Dates: Feb. 4, 1993-Jan. 3, 1995
2nd Departure: Left committee; no new assignment

Cong.	Ranking	Terms in: House	Comm.	Date of Assignment
103rd	Maj-14th	1 *1	1	Jan. 5, 1993
103rd	Maj-22nd	1 *2	1	Feb. 4, 1993

3rd SCIENCE, SPACE, AND TECHNOLOGY, 103
SCIENCE, 106-109

SCIENCE AND TECHNOLOGY, 110
1st Dates: Jan. 21, 1993-Feb. 10, 1994
1st Departure: Temporarily resigned to remain on Budget
2nd Dates: Jan. 6, 1999-date
2nd Departure: Still serving in the 111th Congress

Cong.	Ranking	Terms in: House	Comm.	Date of Assignment
103rd	Maj-30th	1 *1	1	Jan. 21, 1993
106th	Min-9th	4 *2	1	Jan. 6, 1999
107th	Min-6th	5 *2	2	Jan. 31, 2001
108th	Min-5th	6 *2	3	Jan. 28, 2003
109th	Min-4th	7 *2	4	Jan. 26, 2005
110th	Maj-4th	8 *2	5	Jan. 18, 2007
111th	Maj-4th	9 *2	6	Jan. 21, 2009

4th BUDGET
Dates: Mar. 3, 1993-Jan. 3, 1999
Departure: Returned to Science

Cong.	Ranking	Terms in: House	Comm.	Date of Assignment
103rd	MjR-2nd	1	1	Mar. 3, 1993
104th	Min-13th	2	2	Jan. 4, 1995
105th	Min-7th	3	3	Jan. 7, 1997

5th FOREIGN AFFAIRS
1st Dates: Jan. 12, 2007-Jan. 3, 2009
1st Departure: Left committee; no new assignment
2nd Dates: Mar. 12, 2009-date
2nd Departure: Still serving in the 111th Congress

Cong.	Ranking	Terms in: House	Comm.	Date of Assignment
110th	Maj-16th	8 *1	1	Jan. 12, 2007
111th	MjR-1st	9 *2	1	Mar. 12, 2009

David Wu (D-Ore.)

Dates: April 8, 1955
House: Jan. 3, 1999-date
Serving in the 111th Congress

HOUSE STANDING COMMITTEES:

1st EDUCATION AND THE WORKFORCE, 106-109
EDUCATION AND LABOR, 110-111
Dates: Jan. 6, 1999-date
Departure: Still serving in the 111th Congress

Cong.	Ranking	Terms in: House	Comm.	Date of Assignment
106th	Min-21st	1	1	Jan. 6, 1999
107th	Min-19th	2	2	Jan. 31, 2001
108th	Min-13th	3	3	Jan. 28, 2003
109th	Min-13th	4	4	Jan. 26, 2005
110th	Maj-11th	5	5	Jan. 10, 2007
111th	Maj-11th	6	6	Jan. 21, 2009

2nd SCIENCE, 106-109
SCIENCE AND TECHNOLOGY, 110-111
Dates: Jan. 6, 1999-date
Departure: Still serving in the 111th Congress

Cong.	Ranking	Terms in: House	Comm.	Date of Assignment
106th	Min-21st	1	1	Jan. 6, 1999
107th	Min-15th	2	2	Jan. 31, 2001
108th	Min-12th	3	3	Jan. 28, 2003
109th	Min-7th	4	4	Jan. 26, 2005

| 110th | Maj-6th | 5 | 5 | Jan. 18, 2007 |
| 111th | Maj-5th | 6 | 6 | Jan. 21, 2009 |

3rd FOREIGN AFFAIRS
Dates: Jan. 12, 2007-Jan. 3, 2009
Departure: Left committee; no new assignment

| | | Terms in: | | Date of |
Cong.	Ranking	House	Comm.	Assignment
110th	Maj-20th	5	1	Jan. 12, 2007

Ronald L. Wyden (D-Ore.)

Dates: May 3, 1949
House: Jan. 3, 1981-Feb. 5, 1996
Left the House: Resigned; elected to U.S. Senate in 1996
Senate: Feb. 6, 1996-date
Serving in the 111th Congress

S: Wyden was elected to the U.S. Senate by special election, Jan. 30, 1996, to fill the unexpired term caused by the resignation of U.S. Senator Robert Packwood (R-Ore.). Wyden was seated Feb. 6, 1996, and assigned to committees.

HOUSE STANDING COMMITTEES:

1st ENERGY AND COMMERCE, 103
COMMERCE, 104
Dates: Jan. 28, 1981-Feb. 5, 1996
Departure: Resigned the House; elected to Senate

| | | Terms in: | | Date of |
Cong.	Ranking	House	Comm.	Assignment
103rd	Maj-9th	7	7	Jan. 5, 1993
104th	Min-5th	8	8	Jan. 4, 1995

2nd SMALL BUSINESS
Dates: Jan. 28, 1981-Feb. 5, 1996
Departure: Resigned the House; elected to Senate

| | | Terms in: | | Date of |
Cong.	Ranking	House	Comm.	Assignment
103rd	Maj-5th	7	7	Jan. 5, 1993
104th	Min-2nd	8	8	Jan. 4, 1995

HOUSE SELECT AND SPECIAL COMMITTEES:

1st SELECT AGING (Permanent)
Dates: Feb. 5, 1981-Jan. 3, 1993
Termination: Committee not renewed in 1993

SENATE STANDING COMMITTEES:

1st BUDGET
Dates: Mar. 29, 1996-date
Departure: Still serving in the 111th Congress

| | | Years in: | | Date of |
Cong.	Ranking	Senate	Comm.	Assignment
104th	MnA-11th	1	1	Mar. 29, 1996
105th	Min-7th	2	1	Jan. 9, 1997
106th	Min-7th	4	3	Jan. 7, 1999
107th	Min-5th	6	5	Jan. 25, 2001
+107th	Maj-5th	6	6	June 6, 2001
108th	Min-5th	8	7	Jan. 15, 2003
109th	Min-4th	10	9	Jan. 6, 2005
110th	Maj-3rd	12	11	Jan. 12, 2007
111th	Maj-3rd	14	13	Jan. 21, 2009

2nd COMMERCE, SCIENCE AND TRANSPORTATION
Dates: Mar. 29, 1996-Jan. 6, 2005
Departure: Moved to Finance

| | | Years in: | | Date of |
Cong.	Ranking	Senate	Comm.	Assignment
104th	MnA-10th	1	1	Mar. 29, 1996
105th	Min-9th	2	1	Jan. 9, 1997
106th	Min-8th	4	3	Jan. 7, 1999
107th	Min-7th	6	5	Jan. 25, 2001
+107th	Maj-7th	6	6	June 6, 2001
108th	Min-7th	8	7	Jan. 15, 2003

3rd ENVIRONMENT AND PUBLIC WORKS
Dates: Mar. 29, 1996-Jan. 6, 2005
Departure: Moved to Finance

| | | Years in: | | Date of |
Cong.	Ranking	Senate	Comm.	Assignment
104th	MnA-8th	1	1	Mar. 29, 1996
105th	Min-8th	2	1	Jan. 9, 1997
106th	Min-8th	4	3	Jan. 3, 1999
107th	Min-6th	6	5	Jan. 25, 2001
+107th	Maj-7th	6	6	July 10, 2001
108th	Min-7th	8	7	Jan. 15, 2003

4th ENERGY AND NATURAL RESOURCES
Dates: Jan. 9, 1997-date
Departure: Still serving in the 111th Congress

| | | Years in: | | Date of |
Cong.	Ranking	Senate	Comm.	Assignment
105th	Min-7th	2	1	Jan. 9, 1997
106th	Min-5th	4	2	Jan. 7, 1999
107th	Min-5th	6	5	Jan. 25, 2001
+107th	Maj-5th	6	5	June 6, 2001
108th	Min-5th	8	7	Jan. 15, 2003
109th	Min-4th	10	8	Jan. 6, 2005
110th	Maj-4th	12	11	Jan. 12, 2007
111th	Maj-3rd	14	13	Jan. 21, 2009

5th FINANCE
Dates: Jan. 6, 2005-date
Departure: Still serving in the 111th Congress

| | | Years in: | | Date of |
Cong.	Ranking	Senate	Comm.	Assignment
109th	Min-8th	10	1	Jan. 6, 2005
110th	Maj-7th	12	3	Jan. 12, 2007
111th	Maj-7th	14	5	Jan. 21, 2009

6th JUDICIARY
Dates: Jan. 21, 2009-July 7, 2009
Departure: Left committee to open seat for Al Franken (DFL-Minn.)

| | | Years in: | | Date of |
Cong.	Ranking	Senate	Comm.	Assignment
111th	Maj-9th	14	1	Jan. 21, 2009

SENATE SELECT AND SPECIAL COMMITTEES:

1st SPECIAL AGING (Permanent)
Dates: Mar. 29, 1996-date
Departure: Still serving in the 111th Congress

| | | Years in: | | Date of |
Cong.	Ranking	Senate	Comm.	Assignment
104th	MnA-10th	1	1	Mar. 29, 1996
105th	Min-7th	2	1	Jan. 9, 1997
106th	Min-5th	4	3	Jan. 7, 1999
107th	Min-5th	6	5	Jan. 25, 2001
+107th	Maj-6th	6	6	July 10, 2005
108th	Min-6th	8	7	Jan. 15, 2003

Cong.	Ranking	10	9	Jan. 6, 2005
109th	Min-4th	10	9	Jan. 6, 2005
110th	Maj-2nd	12	11	Jan. 12, 2007
111th	Maj-2nd	14	13	Jan. 21, 2009

2nd SELECT INTELLIGENCE (Permanent)
Dates: Jan. 25, 2001-date
Departure: Still serving in the 11th Congress

Cong.	Ranking	Years in: Senate	Comm.	Date of Assignment
107th	Min-5th	6	1	Jan. 25, 2001
+107th	Maj-5th	6	1	June 6, 2001
108th	Min-4th	8	2	Jan. 15, 2003
109th	Min-4th	10	4	Jan. 6, 2005
110th	Maj-3rd	12	6	Jan. 12, 2007
111th	Maj-3rd	14	8	Jan. 21, 2009

JOINT COMMITTEES:

1st JOINT ECONOMIC
House Dates: Jan. 27, 1993-Jan. 3, 1995
Departure: Left committee; no new assignment

Cong.	Ranking	Terms in: House	Comm.	Date of Assignment
103rd	Maj-5th	7	1	Jan. 27, 1993

Albert R. Wynn (D-Md.)

Dates: Sept. 10, 1951
House: Jan. 3, 1993-May 31, 2008
Left the House: Defeated for re-nomination; resigned in 2008

HOUSE STANDING COMMITTEES:

1st BANKING, FINANCE AND URBAN AFFAIRS, 103
BANKING AND FINANCIAL SERVICES, 104

Dates: Jan. 5, 1993-Jan. 3, 1997
Departure: Moved to Commerce

Cong.	Ranking	Terms in: House	Comm.	Date of Assignment
103rd	Maj-24th	1	1	Jan. 5, 1993
104th	Min-17th	2	2	Jan. 4, 1995

2nd FOREIGN AFFAIRS, 103
INTERNATIONAL RELATIONS, 104
Dates: Jan. 5, 1993-Jan. 3, 1997
Departure: Moved to Commerce

Cong.	Ranking	Terms in: House	Comm.	Date of Assignment
103rd	Maj-23rd	1	1	Jan. 5, 1993
104th	Min-17th	2	2	Jan. 4, 1995

3rd POST OFFICE AND CIVIL SERVICE
Dates: Jan. 21, 1993-Jan. 3, 1995
Departure: Committee abolished; no new assignment

Cong.	Ranking	Terms in: House	Comm.	Date of Assignment
103rd	Maj-11th	1	1	Jan. 21, 1993

4th COMMERCE, 105-106
ENERGY AND COMMERCE, 107-110
Dates: Jan. 7, 1997-May 31, 2008
Departure: Resigned the House; lost re-nomination

Cong.	Ranking	Terms in: House	Comm.	Date of Assignment
105th	Min-18th	3	1	Jan. 7, 1997
106th	Min-17th	4	2	Jan. 6, 1999
107th	Min-16th	5	3	Jan. 31, 2001
108th	Min-15th	6	4	Jan. 28, 2003
109th	Min-13th	7	5	Jan. 26, 2005
110th	Maj-12th	8	6	Jan. 4, 2007

Y

John Yarmuth (D-Ky.)

Dates: Nov. 4, 1947
House: Jan. 3, 2007-date
Serving in the 111th Congress

HOUSE STANDING COMMITTEES:

1st EDUCATION AND LABOR
Dates: Jan. 10, 2007-Jan. 3, 2009
Departure: Moved to Ways and Means and Budget

Cong.	Ranking	Terms in: House	Comm.	Date of Assignment
110th	Maj-23rd	1	1	Jan. 10, 2007

2nd OVERSIGHT AND GOVERNMENT REFORM
Dates: Jan. 12, 2007-Jan. 3, 2009
Departure: Moved to Ways and Means and Budget

Cong.	Ranking	Terms in: House	Comm.	Date of Assignment
110th	Maj-14th	1	1	Jan. 12, 2007

3rd WAYS AND MEANS
Dates: Jan. 7, 2009-date
Departure: Still serving in the 111th Congress

Cong.	Ranking	Terms in: House	Comm.	Date of Assignment
111th	Maj-26th	2	1	Jan. 7, 2009

4th BUDGET
Dates: Jan. 21, 2009-date
Departure: Still serving in the 111th Congress

Cong.	Ranking	Terms in: House	Comm.	Date of Assignment
111th	Maj-14th	2	1	Jan. 21, 2009

Sidney R. Yates (D-Ill.)

Dates: Aug. 27, 1909-Oct. 5, 2000
House 1: Jan. 3, 1949-Jan. 2, 1963
Left the House 1: Lost U.S. Senate election in 1962
House 2: Jan. 3, 1965-Jan. 3, 1999
Left the House 2: Retired in 1998

HOUSE STANDING COMMITTEES:

1st APPROPRIATIONS
1st Dates: Jan. 18, 1949-Jan. 3, 1963
1st Departure: Left the House; lost Senate election
2nd Dates: Jan. 18, 1965-Jan. 3, 1999
2nd Departure: Left the House; retired

Cong.	Ranking	Terms in: House	Comm.	Date of Assignment
103rd	Maj-4th	22 *2	15	Jan. 5, 1993
104th	Min-2nd	23 *2	16	Jan. 4, 1995
105th	Min-2nd	24 *2	17	Jan. 7, 1997

HOUSE SELECT AND SPECIAL COMMITTEES:

1st SELECT SMALL BUSINESS
Dates: Feb. 3, 1953-Jan. 3, 1963
Departure: Left the House; lost Senate election

C.W. Bill Young (R-Fla.)

Dates: Dec. 16, 1930
House: Jan. 3, 1971-date
Serving in the 111th Congress

HOUSE STANDING COMMITTEES:

1st ARMED SERVICES
Dates: Feb. 4, 1971-Dec. 20, 1973
Departure: Moved to Appropriations

2nd POST OFFICE AND CIVIL SERVICE
Dates: Mar. 3, 1971-Feb. 3, 1972
Departure: Left committee; no new assignment

3rd APPROPRIATIONS
Dates: Dec. 20, 1973-date
Departure: Still serving in the 111th Congress

Cong.	Ranking	Terms in: House	Comm.	Date of Assignment
103rd	Min-3rd	12	11	Jan. 5, 1993
104th	Maj-4th	13	12	Jan. 4, 1995
105th	Maj-3rd	14	13	Jan. 7, 1997
106th	Maj-Chr	15	14	Jan. 6, 1999
107th	Maj-Chr	16	15	Jan. 6, 2001
108th	Maj-Chr	17	16	Jan. 8, 2003
109th	Maj-2nd	18	17	Jan. 6, 2005
110th	Min-2nd	19	18	Jan. 4, 2007
111th	Min-2nd	20	19	Jan. 9, 2009

HOUSE SELECT AND SPECIAL COMMITTEES:

1st SELECT COMMITTEES I (Bolling)
Dates: Jan. 31, 1973-Dec. 20, 1974
Termination: House Resolution 132 (93-1)

2nd PERMANENT SELECT INTELLIGENCE
1st Dates: Feb. 5, 1979-Jan. 3, 1985
1st Departure: Left committee; no new assignment.
2nd Dates: Feb. 5, 1991-Jan. 3, 1999
2nc Departure: Left committee; became Chair of Appropriations

Cong.	Ranking	Terms in: House	Comm.	Date of Assignment
103rd	Min-4th	12 *2	2	Feb. 3, 1993
104th	Maj-3rd	13 *2	3	Jan. 4, 1995
105th	Maj-2nd	14 *2	4	Feb. 10, 1997

3rd SELECT HOMELAND SECURITY
Dates: Feb. 12, 2003-Jan. 3, 2005
Departure: Did not continue on reorganized standing committee

Cong.	Ranking	Terms in: House	Comm.	Date of Assignment
108th	Maj-3rd	17	1	Feb. 12, 2003

Donald E. Young (R-Alas.)

Dates: June 9, 1933
House: March 6, 1973-date
Serving in the 111th Congress

H: Young was elected to the 93rd Congress by special election, Mar. 6, 1973, to fill the vacancy caused by the death of Rep-elect Nick Begich (D-Alas.). He was seated Mar. 14, 1973, and assigned to committees.

HOUSE STANDING COMMITTEES:

1st INTERIOR AND INSULAR AFFAIRS, 93-102
NATURAL RESOURCES, 103
RESOURCES, 104-109
NATURAL RESOURCES, 110-111
Dates: Mar. 14, 1973-date
Departure: Still serving in the 111th Congress

Cong.	Ranking	Terms in: House	Comm.	Date of Assignment
103rd	Min-RM	11	11	Jan. 5, 1993
104th	Maj-Chr	12	12	Jan. 4, 1995
105th	Maj-Chr	13	13	Jan. 7, 1997
106th	Maj-Chr	14	14	Jan. 6, 1999
107th	Maj-2nd	15	15	Jan. 6, 2001
108th	Maj-2nd	16	16	Jan. 28, 2003
109th	Maj-2nd	17	17	Jan. 26, 2005
110th	Min-RM	18	18	Jan. 4, 2007
111th	Min-2nd	19	19	Jan. 9, 2009

2nd MERCHANT MARINE AND FISHERIES
Dates: Mar. 14, 1973-Jan. 3, 1995
Departure: Committee abolished; moved to Transportation and Infrastructure

Cong.	Ranking	Terms in: House	Comm.	Date of Assignment
103rd	Min-2nd	11	11	Jan. 5, 1993

3rd POST OFFICE AND CIVIL SERVICE
Dates: Jan. 30, 1985-Jan. 3, 1995
Departure: Committee abolished; moved to Transportation and Infrastructure

Cong.	Ranking	Terms in: House	Comm.	Date of Assignment
103rd	Min-3rd	11	5	Jan. 5, 1993

4th TRANSPORTATION AND INFRASTRUCTURE
Dates: Jan. 4, 1995-date
Departure: Still serving in the 111th Congress

Cong.	Ranking	Terms in: House	Comm.	Date of Assignment
104th	Maj-2nd	12	1	Jan. 4, 1995
105th	Maj-2nd	13	2	Jan. 7, 1997
106th	Maj-2nd	14	3	Jan. 6, 1999
107th	Maj-Chr	15	4	Jan. 6, 2001
108th	Maj-Chr	16	5	Jan. 8, 2003
109th	Maj-Chr	17	6	Jan. 6, 2005
110th	Min-2nd	18	7	Jan. 10, 2007
111th	Min-2nd	19	8	Jan. 9, 2009

5th HOMELAND SECURITY
Dates: Feb. 9, 2005-Jan. 3, 2007
Departure: Left committee; became Ranking Member on Natural Resources

Cong.	Ranking	Terms in: House	Comm.	Date of Assignment
109th	Maj-2nd	17	2	Feb. 9, 2005

HOUSE SELECT AND SPECIAL COMMITTEES:

1st OUTER CONTINENTAL SHELF (Ad Hoc)
Became Select Committee on the Outer Continental Shelf, Mar. 29, 1979
Dates: Apr. 22, 1975-June 30,1980
Termination: House Report 1214 (96-2) filed

2nd SELECT HOMELAND SECURITY
Dates: Feb. 12, 2003-Jan. 3, 2005
Departure: Continued on reorganized standing committee

Cong.	Ranking	Terms in: House	Comm.	Date of Assignment
108th	Maj-4th	16	1	Feb. 12, 2003

Z

William H. Zeliff Jr. (R-N.H.)

Dates: June 12, 1936
House: Jan. 3, 1991-Jan. 3, 1997
Left the House: Lost nomination for Governor in 1996

HOUSE STANDING COMMITTEES:

1st GOVERNMENT OPERATIONS, 102-103
GOVERNMENT REFORM AND OVERSIGHT, 104
Dates: Jan. 24, 1991-Jan. 3, 1997
Departure: Left the House; lost nomination for Governor

Cong.	Ranking	Terms in: House	Comm.	Date of Assignment
103rd	Min-12th	2	2	Jan. 5, 1993
104th	Maj-8th	3	3	Jan. 4, 1995

2nd PUBLIC WORKS AND TRANSPORTATION, 102-103
TRANSPORTATION AND INFRASTRUCTURE, 104
Dates: Jan. 24, 1991-Jan. 3, 1997
Departure: Left the House; lost nomination for Governor

Cong.	Ranking	Terms in: House	Comm.	Date of Assignment
103rd	Min-9th	2	2	Jan. 5, 1993
104th	Maj-11th	3	3	Jan. 4, 1995

3rd SMALL BUSINESS
Dates: July 11, 1991-Jan. 3, 1997
Departure: Left the House; lost nomination for Governor

Cong.	Ranking	Terms in: House	Comm.	Date of Assignment
103rd	Min-9th	2	2	Jan. 5, 1993
104th	Maj-3rd	3	3	Jan. 4, 1995

Richard Zimmer (R-N.J.)

Dates: Aug. 16, 1944
House: Jan. 3, 1991-Jan. 3, 1997
Left the House: Lost U.S. Senate election in 1996

HOUSE STANDING COMMITTEES:

1st GOVERNMENT OPERATIONS
Dates: Jan. 24, 1991-Jan. 3, 1995
Departure: Moved to Ways and Means

Cong.	Ranking	Terms in: House	Comm.	Date of Assignment
103rd	Min-11th	2	2	Jan. 5, 1993

2nd SCIENCE, SPACE AND TECHNOLOGY
Dates: Jan. 24, 1991-Jan. 3, 1995
Departure: Moved to Ways and Means

Cong.	Ranking	Terms in: House	Comm.	Date of Assignment
103rd	Min-11th	2	2	Jan. 5, 1993

3rd WAYS AND MEANS
Dates: Jan. 4, 1995-Jan. 3, 1997
Departure: Left the House; lost Senate election

Cong.	Ranking	Terms in: House	Comm.	Date of Assignment
104th	Maj-13th	3	1	Jan. 4, 1995

HOUSE SELECT AND SPECIAL COMMITTEES:

1st SELECT AGING (Permanent)
Dates: Feb. 21, 1991-Jan. 3, 1993
Termination: Committee not renewed in 1993